Holt Mathematics COURSE 3
Features Quicklist

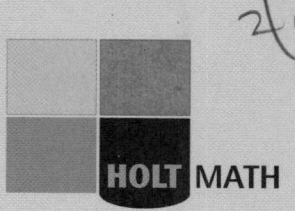

HOLT MATH

	SEE PAGE(S)
COMPREHENSIVE DIFFERENTIATED INSTRUCTION	
• Reaching All Learners includes strategies for adapting the material for all types of learners.	TE 65
• English Language Learners identifies strategies particularly effective with this group of students.	TE 81
• Hands-on Labs involve visual and kinesthetic learners in activities using manipulatives	96–97
• Reteach, Practice, Challenge, Reading Strategies, and Problem Solving reduced images make selecting worksheets quick and easy.	TE 78–79
• Teaching Tips provide suggestions for addressing various learning styles.	TE 77
• Additional Examples offer more classroom review for struggling students.	TE 77
• Assignment Guide recommends homework assignments based on student ability.	TE 78
• Power Presentations are editable PowerPoint® presentations for every lesson as well as extra examples and quizzes.	TE 79

	SEE PAGE(S)
BUILT-IN ASSESSMENT AND INTERVENTION	
• Are You Ready? at the beginning of each chapter assesses students' prerequisite skills.	61
• Ready to Go On? diagnoses students' skill development within the chapter.	90
• Ongoing Assessment and Intervention identifies specific resources to monitor student comprehension	TE 79
• Common Error Alert helps teachers anticipate potential pitfalls for students.	TE 81
• Lesson Quiz gives teachers a chance to check for understanding with every lesson.	TE 84
• Chapter Test assesses students' mastery of concepts and skills.	109

	SEE PAGE(S)
READING AND WRITING MATH FOR COMPREHENSION	
• Reading and Writing Math lessons help students develop strong communication skills as they master math concepts.	63
• Reading Math and Writing Math hints appear throughout each chapter to help students use the language of math.	65, 162
• Write About It exercises require students to explain a math concept or procedure.	75
• Journal suggestions encourage students to write about math.	TE 84
• Think and Discuss questions in every lesson extend and enrich student knowledge.	77
• Glossary contains definitions and illustrations of key mathematical terms in English and Spanish.	859–897

	SEE PAGE(S)
PROVEN INSTRUCTIONAL DESIGN	
• Consistent lesson format of **Example, Solution, Check It Out** provides a logical instructional approach.	80–81
• Step-by-step examples and color-coded explanations help students become independent learners.	92–93
• Exercises matched to examples mean no homework surprises!	94

	SEE PAGE(S)
ENGAGING CONNECTIONS AND APPLICATIONS	
• Links spark student interest by giving them the opportunity to apply math skills to other disciplines and the real world.	79, 86,88
• Focus on Problem Solving addresses a specific step in the problem-solving process.	31
• Game Time gives students a fun way to practice and apply skills	50
• It's in the Bag are creative, hands-on chapter review activities	51
• Problem Solving Project at the start of each chapter connects the chapter concepts to a career.	TE 60
• Problem Solving on Location	112–113

	SEE PAGE(S)
INTEGRATED TEST PREP	
• Countdown to Testing prepares students for state tests with daily practice questions.	C4–C27
• Test Prep and Spiral Review provide daily practice of new and previously taught skills in standardized test format.	25
• Test Prep Doctor addresses specific test-taking strategies related to the lesson.	TE 67
• Multi-Step Test Prep uses real-world scenarios to develop higher order thinking skills.	49
• Test Tackler targets specific test-taking strategies to help students become savvy test-takers.	56–57
• Standardized Test Prep provides cumulative assessment in standardized test format.	58–59

	SEE PAGE(S)
STUDENT SUPPORT	
• Study Guide: Preview prepares students for the concepts they will learn in the chapter and connects the concepts to the real world.	62
• Extra Practice directs students to additional, immediate practice of lesson concepts.	74,78,83
• Homework Help Online provides stepped-out solutions and additional practice for students as they work independently.	83
• Study Guide: Review highlights each lesson's vocabulary and key skills and offers additional examples and practice exercises.	52–54

HOLT
Mathematics
Course 3

Jennie M. Bennett

Edward B. Burger

David J. Chard

Audrey L. Jackson

Paul A. Kennedy

Freddie L. Renfro

Janet K. Scheer

Bert K. Waits

HOLT, RINEHART AND WINSTON

A Harcourt Education Company

Orlando • Austin • New York • San Diego • London

Course 3 Student Edition
Contents in Brief

CHAPTER 1 **Principles of Algebra** 2
CHAPTER 2 **Rational Numbers** 60
CHAPTER 3 **Graphs, Functions, and Sequences** 114
CHAPTER 4 **Exponents and Roots** 158
CHAPTER 5 **Ratios, Proportions, and Similarity** 212
CHAPTER 6 **Percents** 270
CHAPTER 7 **Foundations of Geometry** 320
CHAPTER 8 **Perimeter, Area, and Volume** 384
CHAPTER 9 **Data and Statistics** 458
CHAPTER 10 **Probability** 518
CHAPTER 11 **Multi-Step Equations and Inequalities** 580
CHAPTER 12 **Graphing Lines** 624
CHAPTER 13 **Sequences and Functions** 678
CHAPTER 14 **Polynomials** 730

Student Handbook

Extra Practice 782
Problem Solving Handbook 810
Skills Bank 820
Selected Answers 847
Glossary 859
Index 898
Symbols and Formulas . . . . **Inside Back Cover**

ISBN 0-03-038546-6

1 2 3 4 5 048 09 08 07 06

Cover photo: Getty Center, Los Angeles, CA. © Richard Cummins/ SuperStock

Course 3 Teacher's Edition
Contents in Brief

How to Prepare for Standardized Tests T2
Countdown to Testing T4
Program Highlights T28
Assessment and Intervention T30
Differentiated Instruction T32
Test Preparation T34
Integrated Technology T36
Program Research T38
Authors T39
Program Components T43

Chapter Teacher Material

Chapter 1   **Principles of Algebra** 2A–F, 6A–B, 32A–B
Chapter 2   **Rational Numbers** 60A–F, 64A–B, 92A–B
Chapter 3   **Graphs, Functions, and Sequences** 114A–F, 118A–B, 134A–B
Chapter 4   **Exponents and Roots** 158A–F, 162A–B, 182A–B
Chapter 5   **Ratios, Proportions, and Similarity** 212A–F, 216A–B, 236A–B
Chapter 6   **Percents** 270A–F, 274A–B, 294A–B
Chapter 7   **Foundations of Geometry** 320A–F, 324A–B, 354A–B
Chapter 8   **Perimeter, Area, and Volume** 384A–F, 388A–B, 406A–B
Chapter 9   **Data and Statistics** 458A–F, 462A–B, 484A–B
Chapter 10   **Probability** 518A–F, 522A–B, 540A–B
Chapter 11   **Multi-Step Equations and Inequalities** 580A–F, 584A–B, 600A–B
Chapter 12   **Graphing Lines** 624A–F, 628A–B, 650A–B
Chapter 13   **Sequences and Functions** 678A–F, 682A–B, 700A–B
Chapter 14   **Polynomials** 730A–F, 734A–B, 746A–B

Student Handbook

Extra Practice 782
Problem Solving Handbook 789
Skills Bank 799
Selected Answers 806
Additional Answers A1
Glossary A31
Index A70
Symbols and Formulas .... Inside Back Cover

Contributing Authors

Linda Antinone
Fort Worth, TX

Ms. Antinone teaches mathematics at R. L. Paschal High School in Fort Worth, Texas. She has received the Presidential Award for Excellence in Teaching Mathematics and the National Radio Shack Teacher award. She has coauthored several books for Texas Instruments on the use of technology in mathematics.

Carmen Whitman
Pflugerville, TX

Ms. Whitman travels nationally helping districts improve mathematics education. She has been a program coordinator on the mathematics team at the Charles A. Dana Center, and has served as a secondary math specialist for the Austin Independent School District.

Reviewers

Thomas J. Altonjy
Assistant Principal
Robert R. Lazar Middle School
Montville, NY

Jane Bash, M.A.
Math Education
Eisenhower Middle School
San Antonio, TX

Charlie Bialowas
District Math Coordinator
Anaheim Union High School District
Anaheim, CA

Lynn Bodet
Math Teacher
Eisenhower Middle School
San Antonio, TX

Sharon Butler
Adjunct Faculty
Montgomery College of The Woodlands
Spring, TX

Judy Cass
Mathematics Department Chair
Corpus Christi ISD
Corpus Christi, TX

Louis D' Angelo, Jr.
Math Teacher
Archmere Academy
Claymont, DE

Troy Deckebach
Math Teacher
Tredyffrin-Easttown Middle School
Berwyn, PA

Mary Gorman
Math Teacher
Sarasota, FL

Brian Griffith
Supervisor of Mathematics, K-12
Mechanicsburg Area School District
Mechanicsburg, PA

Ruth Harbin-Miles
District Math Coordinator
Instructional Resource Center
Olathe, KS

Kim Hayden
Math Teacher
Milford Jr. High School
Milford, OH

Susan Howe
Math Teacher
Lime Kiln Middle School
Fulton, MD

Sharron Ingram
Mathematics Teacher
Eanes ISD
Austin, TX

Paula Jenniges
Austin, TX

Lendy Jones
Mathematics Teacher
Killeen ISD
Killeen, TX

Ronald J. Labrocca
District Mathematics Coordinator
Manhasset Public Schools
Plainview, NY

Victor R. Lopez
Math Teacher
Washington School
Union City, NJ

Preparing for Standardized Tests

Holt Mathematics Course 3 provides many opportunities for you to prepare for standardized tests.

Test Prep Exercises

Use the Test Prep Exercises for daily practice of standardized test questions in various formats.

> **Multiple Choice**—choose your answer.
>
> **Gridded Response**—write your answer in a grid and fill in the corresponding bubbles.
>
> **Short Response**—write open-ended responses that are scored with a 2-point rubric.
>
> **Extended Response**—write open-ended responses that are scored with a 4-point rubric.

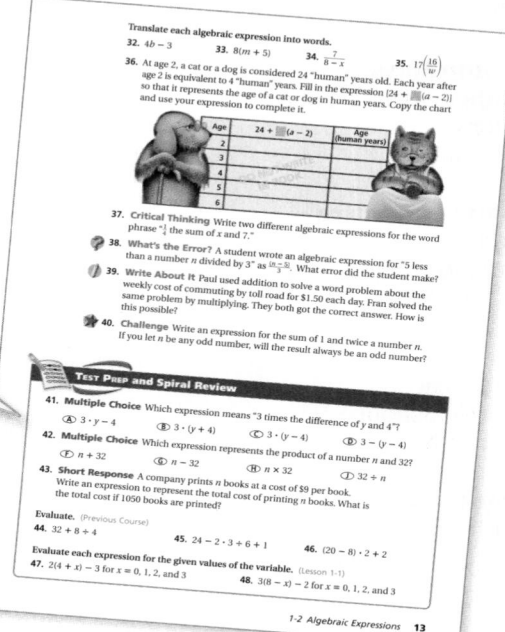

Test Tackler

Use the Test Tackler to become familiar with and practice test-taking strategies.

> The first page of this feature explains and shows an example of a test-taking strategy.

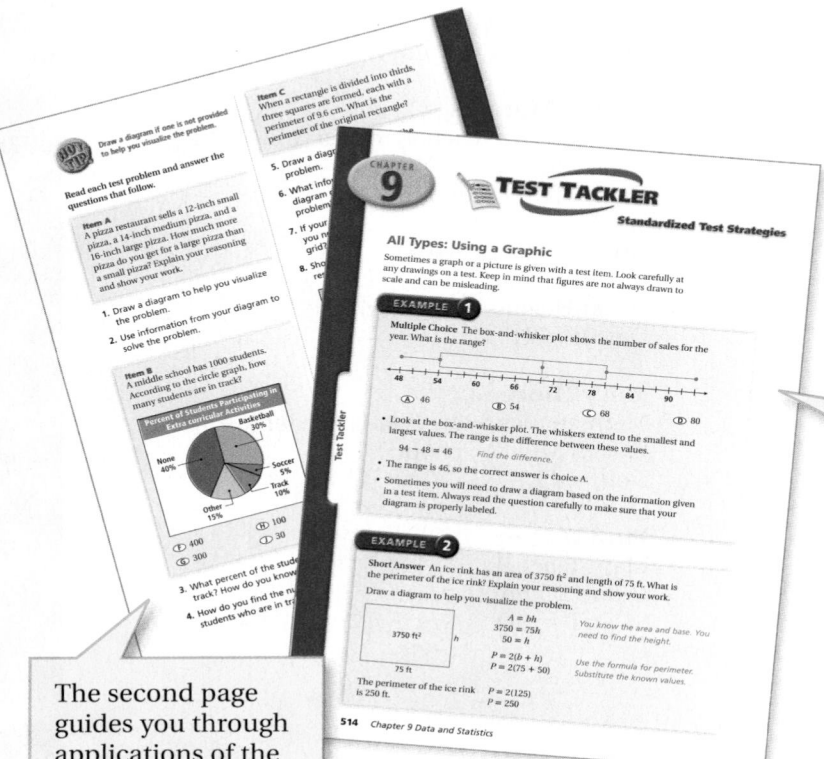

> The second page guides you through applications of the test-taking strategy.

Standardized Test Prep

Use the Standardized Test Prep to apply test-taking strategies.

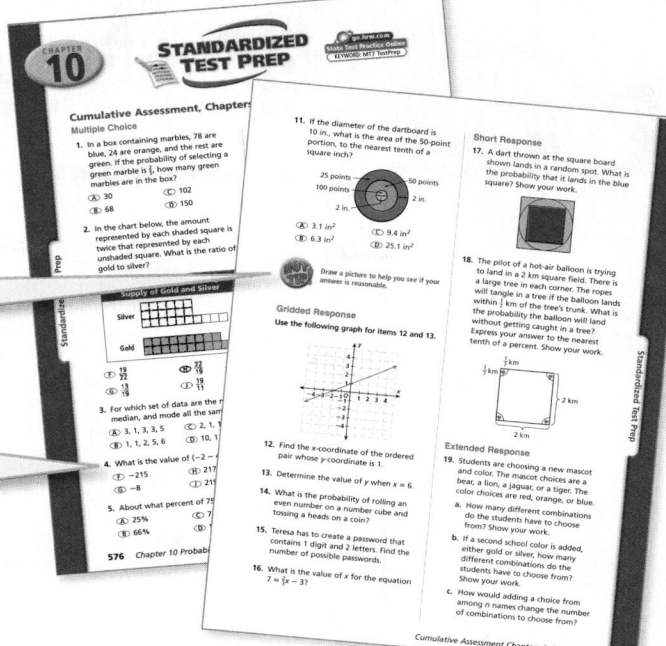

The Hot Tip provides test-taking tips to help you suceed on your tests.

These pages include practice with multiple choice, gridded response, short response, and extended response test items.

Countdown to Testing

Use the Countdown to Testing to practice for your state test every day.

There are 24 pages of practice for your state test. Each page is designed to be used in a week so that all practice will be completed before your state test is given.

Each week's page has five practice test items, one for each day of the week.

Test-Taking Tips

✓ Get plenty of sleep the night before the test. A rested mind thinks more clearly and you won't feel like falling asleep while taking the test.

✓ Draw a figure when one is not provided with the problem. If a figure is given, write any details from the problem on the figure.

✓ Read each problem carefully. As you finish each problem, read it again to make sure your answer is reasonable.

✓ Review the formula sheet that will be supplied with the test. Make sure you know when to use each formula.

✓ First answer problems that you know how to solve. If you do not know how to solve a problem, skip it and come back to it when you have finished the others.

✓ Use other test-taking strategies that can be found throughout this book, such as working backward and eliminating answer choices.

DAY 1

Six friends went to the movies. Admission cost $7.50. Two of them bought a bag of popcorn for $3.50. Which expression can be used to find the total amount they spent?

- (A) 6(7.50 + 3.50)
- (B) 6(7.50) + 2(3.50)
- (C) 6 · (7.50 + 3.50)
- (D) 6(7.50) + 2 + (3.50)

DAY 2

How many feet of wood molding would Jeremy need to trim all the walls of his bedroom?

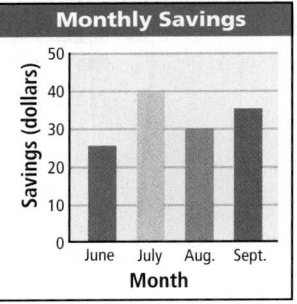

16 ft | **Bedroom**

20 ft

- (F) 4 feet
- (H) 72 feet
- (G) 32 feet
- (J) 320 feet

DAY 3

In which month were the savings greatest?

- (A) June
- (C) August
- (B) July
- (D) September

Monthly Savings

DAY 4

Ravi is studying fruit flies. What is the length of the smallest fly?

2.605 mm   2.456 mm   2.508 mm   2.6 mm

- (F) 2.605 mm
- (H) 2.6 mm
- (G) 2.501 mm
- (J) 2.456 mm

DAY 5

The science club is raising money for a trip. It needs to raise $240.50 so that the entire club can go. So far it has raised $169.75. How much more money does it need to raise?

- (A) $70.50
- (C) $70.85
- (B) $70.75
- (D) $71.75

DAY 1

Craig has 0.38 milliliters of a solution to pour into four equal parts. He determines that each part will contain 0.095 milliliters of the solution. Which of the following shows that Craig's solution is reasonable?

- (A) $4 \cdot 0.01 = 0.04$
- (B) $0.4 \cdot 4 = 1.6$
- (C) $0.1 \cdot 4 = 0.4$
- (D) $0.4 \cdot 0.01 = 0.004$

DAY 2

Missy's car can travel 30 miles per gallon. If Missy fills up her tank with 16 gallons of gas, which equation can be used to show how many gallons of gas are left in Missy's tank after she travels 90 miles?

- (F) $16(90 \div 30)$
- (G) $16 - \frac{90}{30}$
- (H) $30 + 30 + 30 - 16$
- (J) $90 \cdot 16 - 30$

DAY 3

What information does the circle graph not tell you about Chris?

- (A) Chris spends more time at soccer practice than at the library.
- (B) Chris spends the most amount of time doing his chores.
- (C) Chris spends less time at guitar practice than at soccer practice.
- (D) Chris spends more time doing chores than at the library.

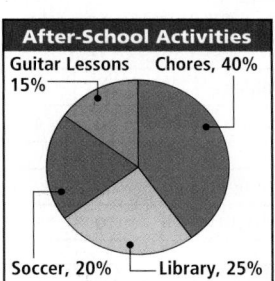

After-School Activities

Guitar Lessons 15% · Chores, 40% · Soccer, 20% · Library, 25%

DAY 4

Ivy's Fresh Eggs transports its eggs in crates. How many crates will 8 trucks carry?

Trucks	2	3	4	5
Crates	80	120	160	200

- (F) 220
- (G) 280
- (H) 320
- (J) 360

DAY 5

When Kit woke up, it was –15°C outside. By that afternoon, the temperature had risen 20 degrees. What was the afternoon temperature?

- (A) –5°C
- (B) 5°C
- (C) 20°C
- (D) 35°C

DAY 1

Annie makes gift baskets of mini muffins. If Annie needs 20 baskets with 25 muffins in each basket, which equation shows how many dozens of muffins she must make?

Ⓐ 12(20) − 25

Ⓑ 25(20) + 12

Ⓒ 20(25) ÷ 12

Ⓓ 12(25 + 20)

DAY 2

Beth saved $2,200. A laptop costs $2199.99, extra memory is $149.50, and an extra battery is $59.95. Beth also has a coupon for $300 off one purchase at the store. Which of the following shows that Beth has saved enough for all of these items?

Ⓕ 2200 − 300 + 150 − 60 = 1,890

Ⓖ 2200 − 150 − 60 − 300 = 1,690

Ⓗ 2200 + 150 + 60 = 2,410

Ⓙ 2200 + 150 + 60 − 300 = 2,110

DAY 3

At a restaurant, a rectangular table can seat 1 person on each end and 2 on each side. When 2 tables are pushed together end to end, 10 people can sit. Which table shows the number of people who can sit at 4 tables pushed together?

Ⓐ
Tables	1	2	3	4
People	6	10	14	18

Ⓒ
Tables	1	2	3	4
People	6	10	12	16

Ⓑ
Tables	1	2	3	4
People	6	10	18	24

Ⓓ
Tables	1	2	3	4
People	6	10	24	48

DAY 4

Rita is playing a board game. If she had 13 points before landing on the shown spot, how many points does she have now?

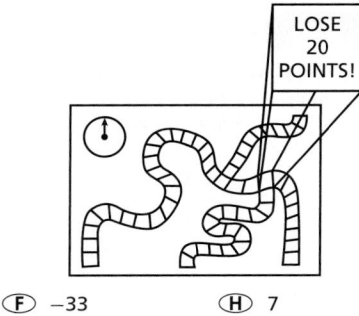

LOSE 20 POINTS!

Ⓕ −33

Ⓖ −7

Ⓗ 7

Ⓙ 33

DAY 5

Jorge recorded the following information while studying the effects of sunlight on plant growth. Which plant grew the most?

Plant	1	2	3	4
Change in Height (in.)	$\frac{1}{2}$	$-\frac{3}{8}$	$-\frac{1}{4}$	$\frac{7}{16}$

Ⓐ 1

Ⓒ 3

Ⓑ 2

Ⓓ 4

DAY 1

Juan deposits $200 at his bank. The first quarter, Juan withdraws $150. He deposits another $100 in each of the next two quarters. How much money does Juan have now?

(A) $50

(B) $250

(C) $350

(D) $450

DAY 2

Sandra uses 3.6 meters of ribbon to weave a small rug and 4.2 meters to weave a large rug. Which expression can be used to find the total length of ribbon used for 12 small rugs and 18 large rugs?

(F) 12(3.6) + 18(4.2)

(G) 18(3.6) + 12(4.2)

(H) 12 + 18(3.6 · 4.2)

(J) 12 + 18 + 3.6 + 4.2

DAY 3

To do his homework, Ethan estimates that he will need about 185 minutes, or 4 hours. What mistake did Ethan make?

(A) He rounded 185 minutes to 200.

(B) He multiplied 4 by 60.

(C) He underestimated the time needed.

(D) He divided 185 by 60 incorrectly.

DAY 4

Andre recorded the high temperature for each day this week. What was the temperature on the warmest day?

Day	M	T	W	Th	F
(°C)	5	−15	−10	−10	−20

(F) −20   (H) −10

(G) −15   (J) 5

DAY 5

At the factory, boxes of paper clips are packed into shipping cases. How many boxes come in 5 cases?

Cases	2	3	4	5
Boxes	192	288	384	?

(A) 384   (C) 500

(B) 480   (D) 672

DAY 1

Ari had 15.3 centimeters of metal pipe. He needed to make 3 equal-size pieces for a project. Should he add, subtract, multiply, or divide to find the length of each piece?

(A) Add 15.3 and 3

(B) Subtract 3 from 15.3

(C) Multiply 15.3 by 3

(D) Divide 15.3 by 3

DAY 2

Sue needed $3\frac{2}{7}$ yards of fringe to trim each drape. If she had 8 drapes to trim, how much fringe did she need?

(F) $4\frac{6}{7}$ yards

(G) $11\frac{2}{7}$ yards

(H) $24\frac{3}{7}$ yards

(J) $26\frac{2}{7}$ yards

DAY 3

Cara used the following table to predict the number of sit-ups she would do on Sunday. She predicted 40. Is her prediction reasonable?

Day	M	T	W	Th	F	S	Su
Number of Sit-ups	2	3	5	8	12		

(A) Yes, it is about right.

(B) No, it is too low.

(C) No, it is too high.

(D) No, there is no pattern in the table.

DAY 4

The table shows how much different numbers of tickets to a hockey game cost. How many dollars would 10 tickets cost?

Tickets	2	3	5	8
Cost ($)	4.80	7.20	12.00	19.20

(F) $21.60

(G) $24.00

(H) $29.20

(J) $32.00

DAY 5

Which is the greatest number in the list?

3.3, $3\frac{1}{4}$, 3.1, 3.13, 3.11, 3.31

(A) 3.13

(B) $3\frac{1}{4}$

(C) 3.3

(D) 3.31

DAY 1

Which point is located at (2, –3)?

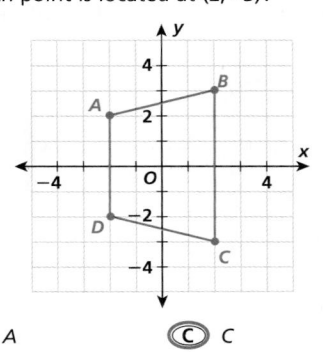

(A) A   (C) C
(B) B   (D) D

DAY 2

What are the coordinates of F?

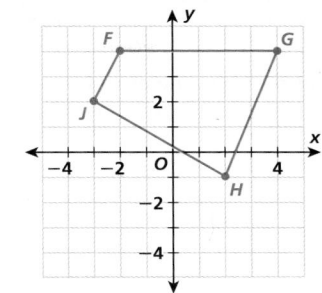

(F) (–3, 2)   (H) (4, 4)
(G) (–2, 4)   (J) (2, –1)

DAY 3

Carla is making a table based on the information in the graph. Complete the table for Monday.

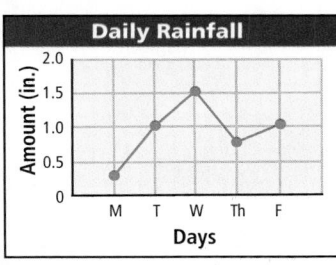

Day	M	T	W	Th	F
Inches		1	$1\frac{1}{2}$		1

(A) $\frac{1}{4}$ (B) $\frac{1}{2}$ (C) $\frac{3}{4}$ (D) 1

DAY 4

Blake works in a cheese store. The table shows how many cheese tidbits he has made at the end of each hour. If he continues at the same pace, how many tidbits will Blake have made in 6 hours?

Hours	2	3	4	5	6
Cheese Tidbits	234	351	468		

(F) 585   (H) 819
(G) 702   (J) 1404

DAY 5

Six samples of water (A, B, C, D, E, F) were collected from the lake.

A = 591.25 mL, B = 591.85 mL,
C = 591.5 mL, D = 591.75 mL,
E = 591.8 mL

If sample F measured between the greatest and least amounts, which of the following could be the amount of sample F?

(A) 591.15 mL   (C) 591.45 mL
(B) 591.2 mL   (D) 591.90 mL

DAY 1

Chandra gets paid 1.5 times her hourly wage of $12.50 per hour when she works overtime. This month she worked 20 hours of overtime.

Which of the following expressions shows how much extra money Chandra will earn this month?

(A) 1.5(12.50) + 20

(B) 12.50 ÷ 1.5 · 20

(C) 1.5(12.50) · 20

(D) 20 ÷ 12.50 · 1.5

DAY 2

Which of the following describes the distance of the E ring from the surface of Saturn?

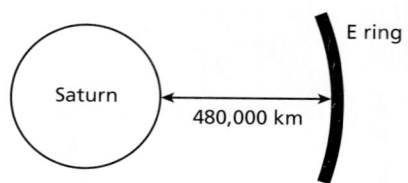

(F) $4.8 \cdot 10^5$

(G) $4.8 \cdot 10^6$

(H) $0.48 \cdot 10^4$

(J) $48 \cdot 10^5$

DAY 3

Which expression describes the following sequence?

10, 17, 31, 59, ...

(A) $x + 7$

(B) $2x - 3$

(C) $2(x - 2)$

(D) $3x - 13$

DAY 4

How many dots could be in the next figure in this sequence?

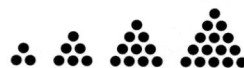

(F) 20

(G) 21

(H) 22

(J) 23

DAY 5

Every 2 hours, a hive of honeybees can produce 150 grams of honey. How many grams of honey does the hive produce in 5 hours?

(A) 300

(B) 375

(C) 450

(D) 750

DAY 1

Ronnie ties his dog to an 8-foot length of rope attached to a pole. What is the distance around the circle the dog can run? Use 3.14 for π.

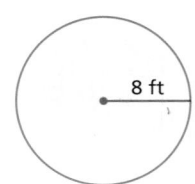

8 ft

A 25.12 feet   **C** 100.48 feet

B 50.24 feet   **D** 200.96 feet

DAY 2

Shawn uses a ramp to get in and out of his house. What is the height of the ramp? Round your answer to the nearest tenth.

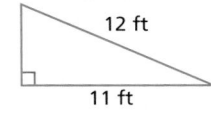

12 ft

11 ft

F 1.09 feet   **H** 3.6 feet

G 2.5 feet   **J** 4.8 feet

DAY 3

Carla receives a special offer from an online bookseller. For every $50 she spends, she'll receive $5 off her purchases. Carla spends $142.50 and estimates she'll pay about $133. Which of the following shows that Carla's estimate is reasonable?

A 142.50 − 50 = 92.50

B 142.50 + 50 − 50 = 197.50

C 142.50 − 2(5) = 132.50

D 142.50 − 3(5) = 127.50

DAY 4

Jerry is building two triangular tables from a piece of rectangular wood. If the wood measures 24 inches by 36 inches, how many inches will the third side of each table be? Round to the nearest tenth.

F 24.7 inches

G 36.3 inches

H 43.3 inches

J 60 inches

DAY 5

Carolyn is building a triangular headboard for her bed. What is its height? Round your answer to the nearest tenth.

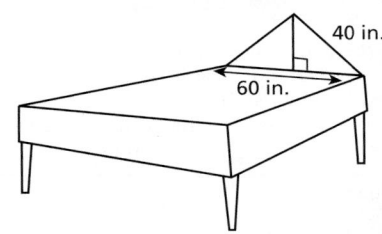

40 in.

60 in.

A 8.3 inches

B 10 inches

C 26.5 inches

D 100 inches

DAY 1

George gets paid an hourly rate to deliver pizza, in addition to a small nightly amount for using his own car. Which of the following shows how much George makes for 1 hour, 2 hours, 3 hours, and 4 hours of work?

(A) $3.00, $6.00, $12.00, $24.00

(B) $10.50, $16.00, $21.50, $27.00

(C) $2.00, $4.00, $6.00, $8.00

(D) $5.50, $11.00, $16.50, $22.00

DAY 2

Maria wants to enlarge a photo. If the photo is 5 inches by 7 inches and Maria wants to enlarge it 2.75 times, what is the best estimate of the size of the enlarged photo?

(F) 10 inches by 14 inches

(G) 12 inches by 14 inches

(H) 15 inches by 21 inches

(J) 16 inches by 22 inches

DAY 3

Identify which sequence does not have a proportional relationship?

(A) 10, 30, 90, 270, …

(B) 0.6, 0.12, 0.24, 0.48, …

(C) $\frac{1}{2}, \frac{4}{8}, \frac{16}{32}, \frac{64}{128}, …$

(D) $2.50, $3.00, $3.50, $4.00, …

DAY 4

Steve's wood-burning stove can heat his house 6°F an hour. He first lights the stove at 6:00 AM when it is 52°F. How many hours will it take for the temperature to reach 82°F?

Hour	0	1	2	3	4
Temperature (°F)	52	58	64		

(F) 3   (H) 5

(G) 4   (J) 6

DAY 5

If the pattern continues, how many white tiles will there be in the next set of tiles?

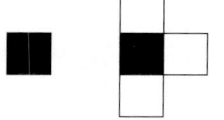

(A) 3   (C) 10

(B) 6   (D) 12

DAY 1

The table shows the typing rates of four applicants for a job. Based on typing rates, which applicant is the best choice to hire?

Applicant	Words	Minute
Ann	112	6
Theo	206	8
June	195	7
Andy	120	5

(A) June   (C) Andy

(B) Ann   (D) Theo

DAY 2

If figure *ABCD* is dilated by a scale factor of 3, which ordered pair describes the new location of *C*?

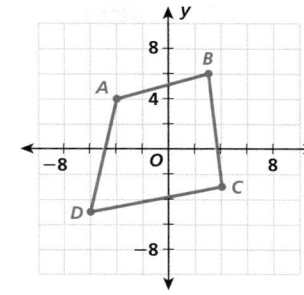

(F) (−12, 9)   (H) (4, −3)

(G) (9, 18)   (J) (12, −9)

DAY 3

Dylan is making a circular garden. Its diameter is 3.2 ft. What is its circumference? Use 3.14 for π. Round to the nearest tenth.

(A) 6.4 ft   (C) 20.1 ft

(B) 10 ft   (D) 32.2 ft

DAY 4

A chandelier uses three different sizes of bulbs. Each bulb is twice as large as the previous one. What is the diameter of the largest bulb?

C = 6.28 in.

 1x    2x    4x

(F) 2 inches

(G) 3.14 inches

(H) 8 inches

(J) 12.56 inches

DAY 5

Mr. Bryce bought a hybrid car that can travel 240 miles on 8 gallons of gas. How far can Mr. Bryce travel on 10 gallons of gas?

(A) 280 miles

(B) 300 miles

(C) 480 miles

(D) 2400 miles

DAY 1

Simon is shopping for a new mountain bike. He finds one that costs $179.95, but he has a coupon. By which number should Simon multiply the price of the bike to calculate how much money he'll save?

Metro Bikes

10% OFF

The purchase of any bike
offer good until 9/1

(A) 0.01   (C) 1.0

(B) 0.1   (D) 10.0

DAY 2

Christina wants to paint a circle with a radius of 4 feet on her bedroom wall. If 1 can of paint covers 26 square feet, how many cans of paint will Christina need to buy?

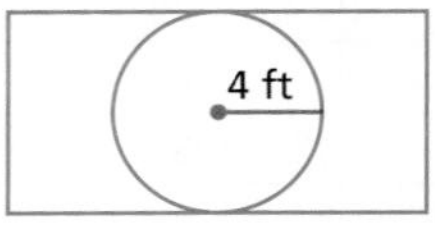

4 ft

(F) 1   (H) 3

(G) 2   (J) 4

DAY 3

Jake is a reporter for a local newspaper. He has rewritten 68% of an interview that lasted 87 minutes. Which is the best estimate of the number of minutes Jake has transcribed?

(A) 18 minutes   (C) 54 minutes

(B) 48 minutes   (D) 63 minutes

DAY 4

Four people are playing a trivia game. Their scores are shown in the table. Which player has the lowest score?

Player	1	2	3	4
Score	−30	10	−25	50

(F) 1   (H) 3

(G) 2   (J) 4

DAY 5

For every 3 scarves that Kendall knits, Rhonda can knit 4 hats. When Kendall has knit 15 scarves, how many hats will Rhonda have knit?

Kendall	3	6	9	12
Rhonda	4	8		

(A) 20   (C) 30

(B) 24   (D) 60

DAY 1

A manufacturer of doll clothes produces more white dresses than blue dresses by a factor of 3.5. Given b, the number of blue dresses produced, which equation shows w, the number of white dresses produced?

A $w = b \div 3.5$

B $w = \dfrac{3.5}{b}$

C $w = 3.5b$

D $w = 3.5 + b$

DAY 2

At dinner, Mr. and Mrs. Brandt decide to leave a 20% tip for their server. Which is the best estimate of their tip if their meals total $63.20?

F $1.20

G $12.00

H $14.00

J $120.00

DAY 3

Tom is working with his lab group on a chemistry project. Each group member recorded the weight of a sample after a chemical reaction. Which number, rounded to the nearest hundredth, should be used for the weight of solution B?

Solution	A	B	C	D
Weight (g)	42.28	$47\frac{12}{17}$	50.16	44.09

A 47.17 grams   C 47.71 grams

B 47.7 grams   D 48.42 grams

DAY 4

Ronald followed this recipe for fruit punch. How many cups did he make? Write your answer in simplest terms.

Fantastic Fruit Punch

$1\frac{3}{4}$ cups orange juice

$\frac{2}{3}$ cup cranberry juice

$1\frac{1}{3}$ cups white grape juice

$\frac{1}{4}$ cup lime juice

Combine ingredients. Chill until ready to serve.

F 3 cups   **H** 4 cups

G $3\frac{1}{2}$ cups   J $4\frac{2}{3}$ cups

DAY 5

Mark is researching the effects of diet on mice. The table below shows the percent change in weight of each mouse studied. If the mice weighed the same at the start of the experiment, which mouse lost the most weight?

Mouse	% Change in Weight
1	−9.2
2	3.25
3	−9.05
4	−9.095

A 1   C 3

B 2   D 4

COUNTDOWN TO TESTING

DAY 1

Which of the following correctly shows the length of the Earth's equator?

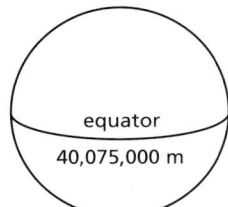

equator
40,075,000 m

- (A) 0.40075×10^7 meters
- (B) 4.0075×10^7 meters
- (C) 40.075×10^7 meters
- (D) $4,007.5 \times 10^7$ meters

DAY 2

Figure ABCD is dilated by a scale factor of $\frac{3}{2}$. What are the coordinates of C after the dilation?

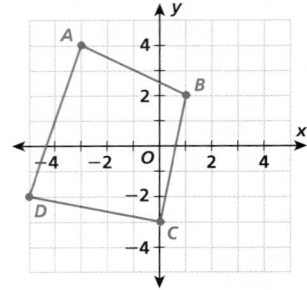

- (F) $(2, -4)$
- (G) $(0, -4\frac{1}{2})$
- (H) $(0, -1\frac{1}{2})$
- (J) $(0, -2)$

DAY 3

The Gordon family is driving to the Grand Canyon from Lubbock, Texas. If they drive an average of 55 miles per hour for h hours, which equation shows d, the distance they traveled?

- (A) $d = 55h$
- (B) $d = 55 \div h$
- (C) $d = \frac{h}{55}$
- (D) $d = 55 + h$

DAY 4

This rectangle is enlarged by a scale factor of 3. What is the new length in centimeters?

3 cm

7 cm

- (F) 9 centimeters
- (G) 10 centimeters
- (H) 20 centimeters
- (J) 21 centimeters

DAY 5

If these two figures are similar, what is the missing length of figure B?

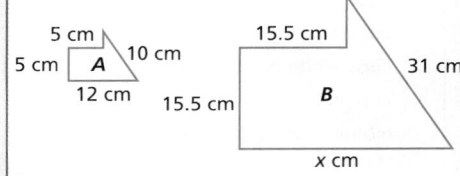

- (A) 3.1 centimeters
- (B) 22.5 centimeters
- (C) 25.2 centimeters
- (D) 37.2 centimeters

DAY 1

Television screen size is measured on the diagonal. What is the height of this screen? Round your answer to the nearest tenth.

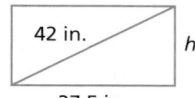

42 in.   h

37.5 in.

(A) 4.5 inches   (C) 18.9 inches

(B) 9.0 inches   (D) 20.3 inches

DAY 2

Which point is at $(-5, -1\frac{1}{2})$?

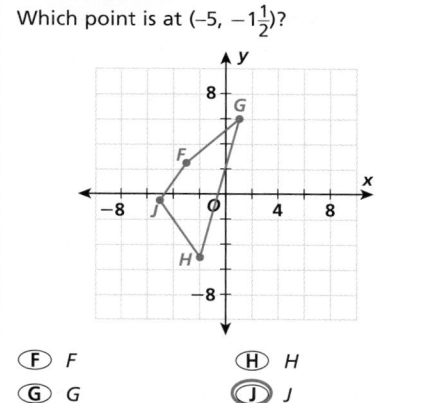

(F) F   (H) H

(G) G   (J) J

DAY 3

Martin can repair 7 watches in 1 hour when he begins work in the morning. The next hour, Martin repairs one less watch. If this pattern continues, which of the following shows how many watches Martin repairs in the third, fourth, fifth, and sixth hours?

(A) 5, 4, 3, 2   (C) 14, 21, 28, 35

(B) 6, 4, 2, 1   (D) 8, 9, 10, 11

DAY 4

If these two figures are similar, what is the missing measure in figure B?

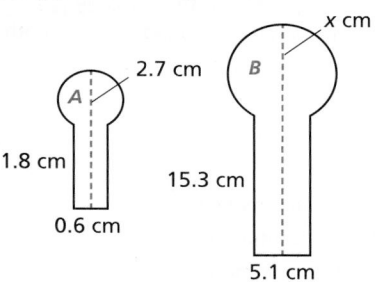

x cm

2.7 cm   B

A

1.8 cm   15.3 cm

0.6 cm

5.1 cm

(F) 18 centimeters

(G) 20.4 centimeters

(H) 22.95 centimeters

(J) 30.6 centimeters

DAY 5

Gina is drawing a scale model of a park. If the scale factor is 1 inch = 4 feet, what is the perimeter of the actual park?

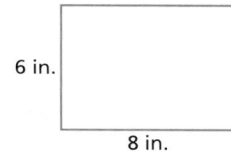

6 in.

8 in.

(A) 28 feet   (C) 112 feet

(B) 56 feet   (D) 768 feet

DAY 1

If figure *LMNO* is reflected across the x-axis, which point(s) will **not** change locations?

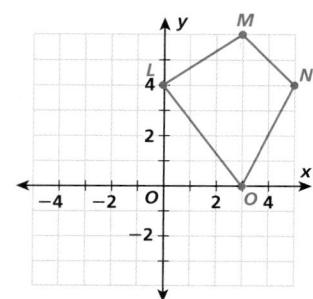

(A) L and O
(B) L
(C) O
(D) L and N

DAY 2

If figure *PQRS* is dilated by a scale factor of $\frac{1}{2}$, which point will be located at $(2, -1\frac{1}{2})$?

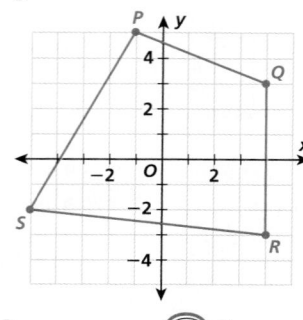

(F) P
(G) Q
(H) R
(J) S

DAY 3

The number 48 is 6% of which number?

(A) 28.8
(C) 288
(B) 80
(D) 800

DAY 4

Which figure does **not** form a tessellation?

Figure 1   **Figure 2**

Figure 3   **Figure 4**

(F) Figure 1
(H) Figure 3
(G) Figure 2
(J) Figure 4

DAY 5

What is the side length of this square? Round your answer to the nearest tenth.

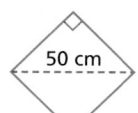

50 cm

(A) 5.0 centimeters
(B) 11.2 centimeters
(C) 25.0 centimeters
(D) 35.4 centimeters

DAY 1

A computer's hard drive spins at 5400 revolutions per minute. If the hard drive has been running for m minutes, which expression shows r, the number of revolutions?

(A) $r = m \div 5400$

(B) $r = 5400 \cdot m$

(C) $r = 5400 + m$

(D) $r = \frac{5400}{m}$

DAY 2

Which expression describes this sequence?

..., 23, 25, 27, 29, ...

(F) $3x - 3$

(G) $3 + 2x$

(H) $2x - 2$

(J) $x^2 + 1$

DAY 3

Figures A and B are similar. If the area of Figure A is 218.75 square centimeters, which expression could you use to determine the area of Figure B?

Figure A

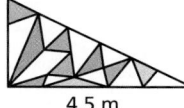

17.5 cm | 218.75 cm²

Figure B

? | 3.5 cm

(A) $17.5 \div 3.5$

(B) $218.75 \div 25$

(C) $5 \cdot 218.75$

(D) $3.5 \cdot 17.5$

DAY 4

Katie wants to frame this stained-glass window with wood. What length of wood does she need to buy? Round your answer to the nearest tenth.

2.25 m

4.5 m

(F) 5 meters

(G) 6.8 meters

(H) 11.8 meters

(J) 13.5 meters

DAY 5

What is the length of side c?

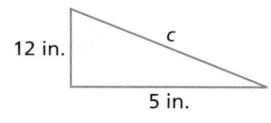

12 in.

c

5 in.

(A) 12 inches

(B) 13 inches

(C) 25 inches

(D) 169 inches

DAY 1

The Great Pyramid in Giza, Egypt, is a rectangular pyramid. Which formula could you use to determine the volume of the pyramid?

Ⓐ $V = \frac{1}{2}Bh$

Ⓑ $V = \frac{1}{3}Bh$

Ⓒ $V = Bh$

Ⓓ $V = \frac{4}{3}\pi r^3$

DAY 2

For which of the following shapes could you **not** use the formula $V = Bh$ to find the volume?

Ⓕ hexagonal prism

Ⓖ cylinder

Ⓗ rectangular prism

Ⓙ triangular pyramid

DAY 3

Nick buys a new fish tank for his living room. Which is the best estimate of the volume of water Nick needs to fill the tank?

Ⓐ 70 cubic inches

Ⓑ 147 cubic inches

Ⓒ 1080 cubic inches

Ⓓ 1470 cubic inches

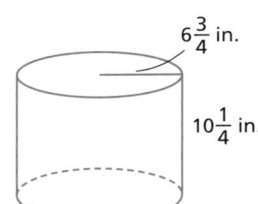

$6\frac{3}{4}$ in.

$10\frac{1}{4}$ in.

DAY 4

If △ACE is similar to △BCD, what is the length of AC?

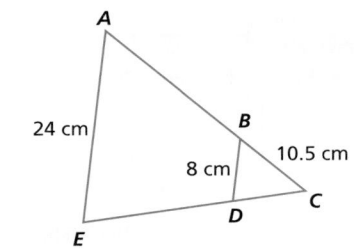

Ⓕ 5.5 centimeters

Ⓖ 13.5 centimeters

Ⓗ 21.5 centimeters

Ⓙ 31.5 centimeters

DAY 5

Candace is building a bookcase with shelves that are right triangles. What is the measure across the front of the bookcase? Round your answer to the nearest whole unit.

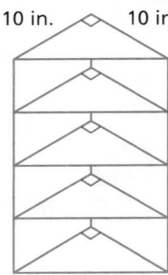

10 in.   10 in.

Ⓐ 4 inches   Ⓒ 50 inches

Ⓑ 14 inches   Ⓓ 72 inches

DAY 1

What is the surface area of this square pyramid?

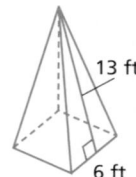

13 ft

6 ft

(A) 75 square feet

(B) 156 square feet

(C) 192 square feet

(D) 348 square feet

DAY 2

Sherman wants to paint the lateral surface area of the base for a sculpture he made. Which is the best estimate of the area Sherman wants to paint?

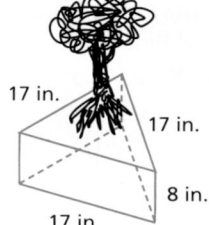

17 in.

17 in.

8 in.

17 in.

(F) 51 square inches

(G) 136 square inches

(H) 408 square inches

(J) 533 square inches

DAY 3

At a garage sale, Curtis buys a planter for his backyard. With base area B and height h, which formula should Curtis use to find the volume of soil he will need to fill the planter?

(A) $V = Bh$

(B) $V = \frac{1}{2}Bh$

(C) $V = \frac{4}{3}\pi r^3$

(D) $V = \frac{1}{3}Bh$

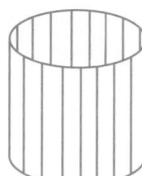

DAY 4

Nina is designing a pattern that is made up of equilateral triangles. If all the triangles are similar, what is the combined area of three shaded triangles?

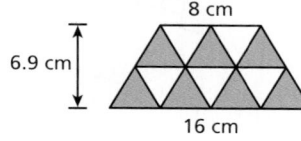

8 cm

6.9 cm

16 cm

(F) 6.9 square centimeters

(G) 20.7 square centimeters

(H) 27.6 square centimeters

(J) 82.8 square centimeters

DAY 5

What percent of the larger rectangle's area is the smaller rectangle's area?

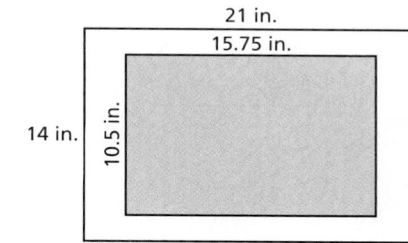

21 in.

15.75 in.

14 in.

10.5 in.

(A) 0.75%

(B) 5.25%

(C) 56.25%

(D) 103%

DAY 1

Which formula would you use to find the volume of this globe?

(A) $V = \frac{4}{3}\pi r^2$

(B) $V = Bh$

(C) $V = \frac{1}{3}Bh$

(D) $V = \frac{1}{2}Bh$

DAY 2

What is the best estimate of the lateral surface area of this vase if the radius is 6 inches and the slant height is 13 inches?

(F) 117 square inches

(G) 234 square inches

(H) 468 square inches

(J) 1404 square inches

DAY 3

Mia made this net of a triangular prism. What is the surface area of the prism?

(A) 615 square centimeters

(B) 840 square centimeters

(C) 877.5 square centimeters

(D) 915 square centimeters

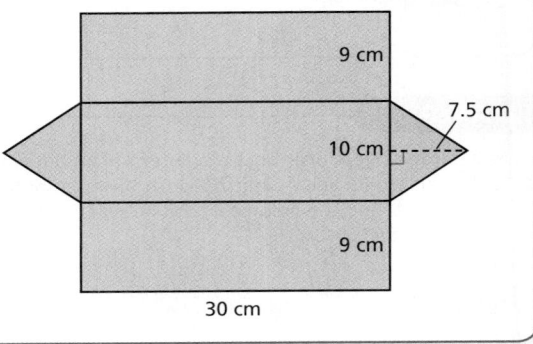

9 cm

7.5 cm

10 cm

9 cm

30 cm

DAY 4

Paola drew a circle with four congruent circles inside it. If the area of the large circle is 167.2 square meters, what is the area of one small circle?

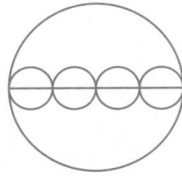

(F) 5.65 square meters

(G) 10.45 square meters

(H) 18.54 square meters

(J) 41.83 square meters

DAY 5

The roof of the greenhouse, which forms half a cylinder, is covered in glass. What is the surface area of the glass roof?

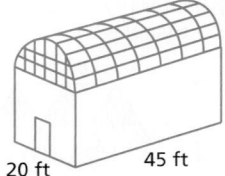

20 ft   45 ft

(A) 1,727 square feet

(B) 2,041 square feet

(C) 3,140 square feet

(D) 3,454 square feet

DAY 1

What is the best measure of the central tendency of these test scores?

$$92, 85, 89, 93, 74, 94$$

Ⓐ mean

Ⓑ median

Ⓒ mode

Ⓓ range

DAY 2

What is the lateral surface area of this pentagonal prism? Every side on the base has the same measurement.

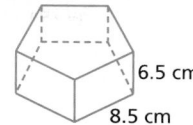

6.5 cm

8.5 cm

Ⓕ 120 square centimeters

Ⓖ 211.25 square centimeters

Ⓗ 212.5 square centimeters

Ⓙ 276.25 square centimeters

DAY 3

Philip created this table for the data in the graph. What mistake did he make?

Plant	A	B	C	D
Height (in.)	$1\frac{1}{2}$	3	1	$2\frac{1}{4}$

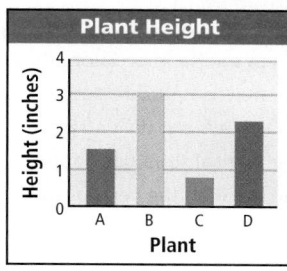

Plant Height

Ⓐ He confused the data for plants A and C.

Ⓑ He misread the data for plant C.

Ⓒ He rounded the data to the nearest $\frac{1}{4}$ inch.

Ⓓ He misread the data for plant D.

DAY 4

In this figure, each rectangle has $\frac{1}{4}$ less area than the rectangle directly enclosing it. What is the area of the smallest rectangle in this figure?

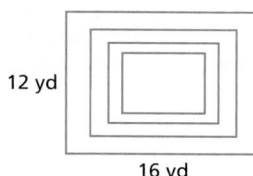

12 yd

16 yd

Ⓕ 81 square yards

Ⓖ 108 square yards

Ⓗ 144 square yards

Ⓙ 192 square yards

DAY 5

What is the possible next term in this pattern?

$$1, 8, 64, 512, \blacksquare$$

Ⓐ 576   Ⓒ 2,048

Ⓑ 582   Ⓓ 4,096

DAY 1

Liu is researching the speeds of some of the fastest animals on Earth. Which of the following is the most appropriate method for her to display the data she finds on animals and their top speeds?

(A) stem-and-leaf plot

(B) scatter plot

(C) line graph

(D) bar graph

DAY 2

Bruno surveys his classmates about their favorite pet. What is the best measure of central tendency of this data?

(F) mode

(G) range

(H) mean

(J) median

DAY 3

This graph shows a company's monthly profits, but it gives a false impression. Why?

(A) The horizontal scale does not start with 0.

(B) The scale is not divided into equal increments.

(C) The vertical scale does not start at 0.

(D) The break in the vertical scale exaggerates the data.

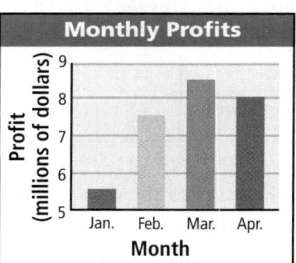

DAY 4

Keenan creates a sequence using blocks. The pattern of the sequence is shown in the table. How many blocks will he use for the fourteenth figure in the sequence?

Figure	1	2	3	4
Blocks	1	3	6	9

(F) 36

(G) 39

(H) 42

(J) 45

DAY 5

Jimmy buys 44 feet of wood to build a square frame for a sandbox. He decides to make the sandbox smaller and reduces its perimeter by 20%. How much wood will be left over?

(A) 8.8 feet   (C) 26.4 feet

(B) 17.6 feet   (D) 35.2 feet

DAY 1

Which conclusion can you draw about worker productivity based on the scatter plot?

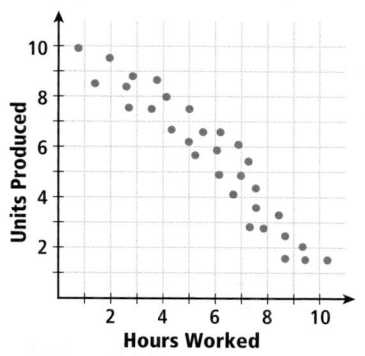

Ⓐ Productivity increases during the work day.

Ⓑ There is no trend for productivity in the scatter plot.

Ⓒ As the work day progresses, productivity declines.

Ⓓ Productivity remains constant during the work day.

DAY 2

Why is this bar graph misleading?

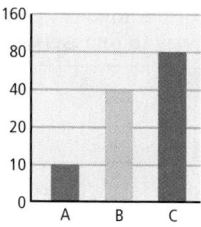

Ⓕ The scale is not divided into equal intervals, so the differences among the data seems less than they really are.

Ⓖ The horizontal scale does not start at 0, which skews the data.

Ⓗ The scale is not divided into equal intervals, so the differences among the data seems greater than they really are.

Ⓙ The bar graph is not misleading.

DAY 3

Kyle is studying the speed of cars as they drive by his house. Which of the following is the most appropriate way for Kyle to display his data?

Ⓐ circle graph   **Ⓒ** stem-and-leaf plot

Ⓑ bar graph   **Ⓓ** line graph

DAY 4

Ben is building a wall. What length of wood does Ben need to buy to create two cross beams for the frame? Round your answer to the nearest tenth.

Ⓕ 4.3 meters

Ⓖ 5.8 meters

Ⓗ 8.5 meters

Ⓙ 11.6 meters

2.1 m
3.7 m

DAY 5

If this pattern continues, how many circles will be in the eighth group in this sequence?

○ , ○△ , ○△□ ,
○△□○ , ○△□○△ , ...

Ⓐ 2   **Ⓒ** 4

Ⓑ 3   **Ⓓ** 5

COUNTDOWN TO TESTING

DAY 1

The frequency table shows the number of days of rain in each month for one year. Which of the following is the most appropriate way to represent this data?

Days of Rain	0–2	3–5	6–8	9–11
Frequency	4	6	2	0

(A) histogram

(B) bar graph

(C) circle graph

(D) line plot

DAY 2

Which conclusion can you draw based on the data in this scatter plot?

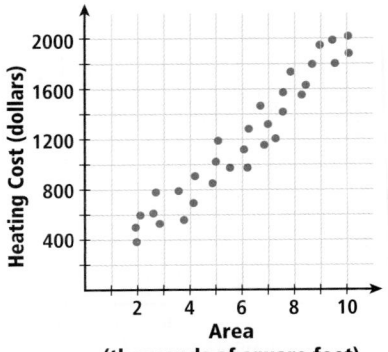

(F) The smaller the area, the more expensive the heating costs.

(G) Heating costs remain constant.

(H) The scatter plot does not show a trend.

(J) The larger the area, the greater the heating costs.

DAY 3

Tamara records the high temperature for each day this month. Which would be the most appropriate way for Tamara to display the data if she wants to see the change in temperature over time?

(A) circle graph

(B) line plot

(C) line graph

(D) scatter plot

DAY 4

If the two rectangles are similar, what is the length of the smaller rectangle?

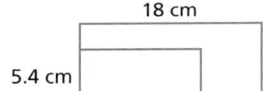

18 cm

5.4 cm   8.1 cm

(F) 6.7 centimeters   (H) 14.1 centimeters

(G) 12 centimeters   (J) 15 centimeters

DAY 5

If the side of this triangle is increased by a factor of 1.3, what is the perimeter of the new triangle?

(A) 7.3 meters

(B) 7.8 meters

(C) 21.9 meters

(D) 23.4 meters

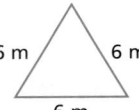

6 m   6 m

6 m

DAY 1

What kind of correlation would you expect to find in a scatter plot comparing people's ages and favorite colors?

Ⓐ negative

Ⓑ no correlation

Ⓒ positive

Ⓓ There is not enough information to answer the question.

DAY 2

Megan recorded the weight of each tomato in her garden this week. Which is the best measure of the central tendency for this data set?

220 grams, 225 grams,

213 grams, 140 grams,

210 grams, 209 grams

Ⓕ mean

Ⓖ range

Ⓗ mode

Ⓙ median

DAY 3

This graph shows a local politician's approval ratings for the last four months. What effect does the unequal scale interval have on the visual impression of the data?

Ⓐ It makes the drop in his approval ratings look more dramatic.

Ⓑ It makes the drop in his approval ratings look less dramatic.

Ⓒ It makes the politician appear less popular than he is.

Ⓓ It does not have any effect.

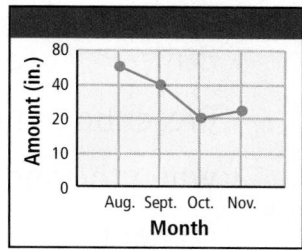

DAY 4

Mrs. Weyland is making 7 cups of juice for her children's friends. If she wants to serve each guest $\frac{3}{4}$ cup of juice, how many children will the juice serve?

Ⓕ 8   Ⓗ 10

Ⓖ 9   Ⓙ 11

DAY 5

Which number is missing from this sequence?

254, ▓, 22.86, 6.858, ...

Ⓐ 76.2

Ⓑ 99.06

Ⓒ 115.57

Ⓓ 138.43

HOLT MATH

You can count on Holt Mathematics for

1 Built-in Assessment and Intervention. Prescribe the resources your students need when they need them in order to lead your students to success.

2 Comprehensive Differentiated Instruction. Ensure all students have the opportunity to succeed with strategies designed to reach students of all learning styles and skill levels.

3 Success on High-Stakes Tests. Prepare students for success on test day with standards-based test preparation that's embedded into daily lessons.

4 Integrated Technology that Enhances Learning. Motivate your students to excel and manage your classroom with maximum effectiveness using Holt technology.

Student Success

ASSESSMENT AND INTERVENTION	DIFFERENTIATED INSTRUCTION	HIGH–STAKES TEST PREP	INTEGRATED TECHNOLOGY
1	2	3	4

GROUNDED IN RESEARCH · BUILT BY EXPERTS · PROVEN IN CLASSROOMS

Built for Student Success... from the Ground Up

Every student is unique with individual strengths and weaknesses. Starting with *Holt Mathematics* and *Pre-Algebra* for middle school through *Holt Algebra 1, Geometry,* and *Algebra 2,* Holt provides the instruction and resources you need to reach and teach every one of your students. Whether it's an alternative approach to a lesson, a modification for a visual learner, or extra practice with basic skills, Holt has what you need to help all of your students succeed.

> " *Deep and abstract ideas are challenging to all, but the* **challenge** *should be a pleasurable one that students want to conquer.* "
>
> — **Dr. Edward B. Burger, Holt author**

Count on **Holt Mathematics** for

Built-in assessment and intervention

1

Holt's at-a-glance system makes it easy to keep students on track.

You need to know how well your students understand the lesson BEFORE they take the test. With *Holt Mathematics*, informal and formal assessment options are given at every stage within the chapter. Intervention resources allow you to reteach or review material without merely sending students back to previous lessons in the book.

- **Assess Prior Knowledge** to make sure all students start the chapter on solid footing.

  Intervene with alternate teaching strategies and basic skills review in **Are You Ready? Intervention and Enrichment.**

- **Formative Assessment** diagnoses skill development within the chapter.

  Intervene with **Ready to Go On?, Lesson Tutorial Videos, Homework Help Online,** and more.

- **Summative Assessment** allows students to demonstrate their mastery of the concepts.

  Intervene with **Reteach** and **Lesson Tutorial Videos**.

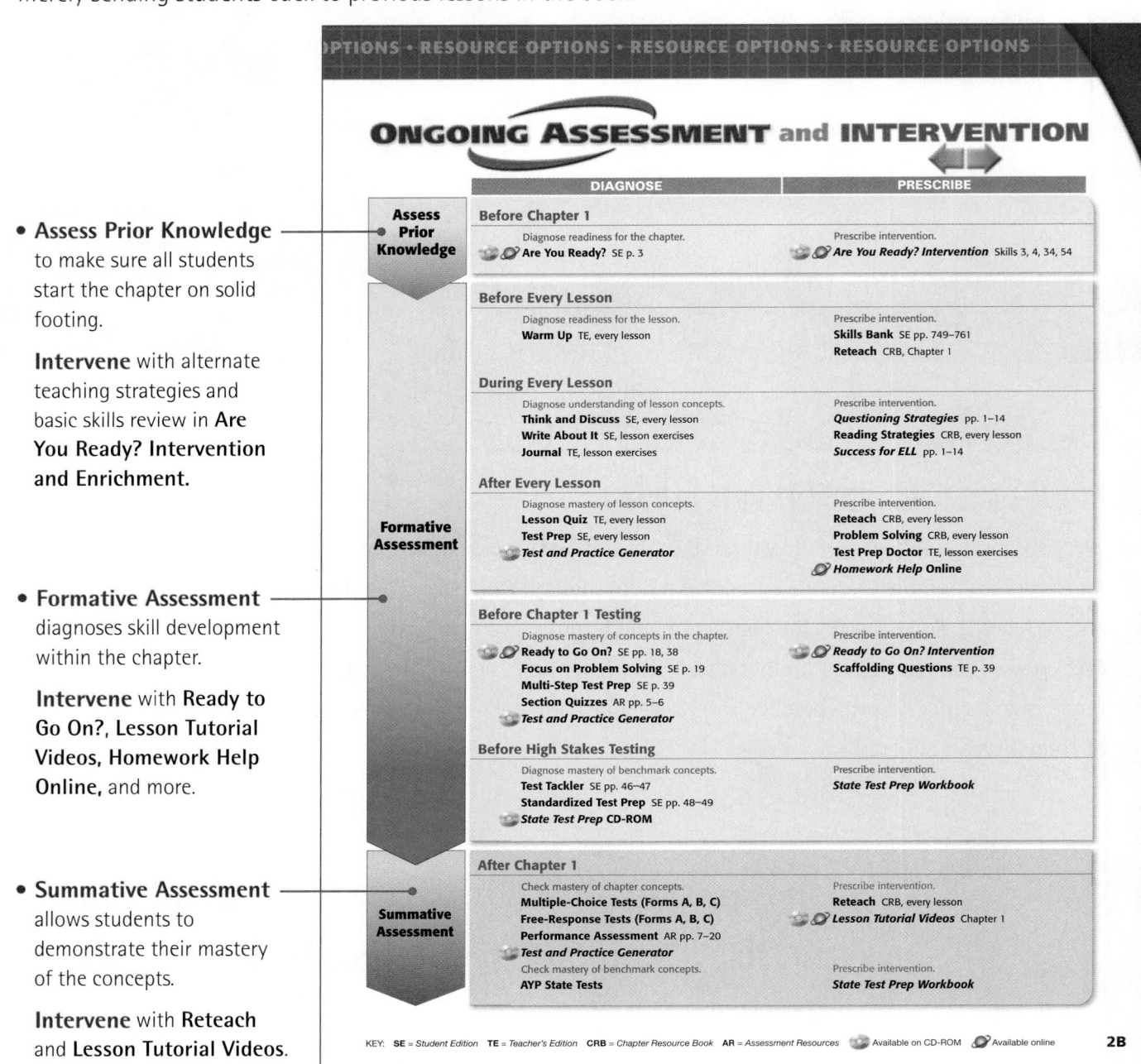

OPTIONS • RESOURCE OPTIONS • RESOURCE OPTIONS • RESOURCE OPTIONS

ONGOING ASSESSMENT and INTERVENTION

DIAGNOSE	PRESCRIBE

Assess Prior Knowledge

Before Chapter 1

Diagnose readiness for the chapter.
Are You Ready? SE p. 3

Prescribe intervention.
Are You Ready? Intervention Skills 3, 4, 34, 54

Before Every Lesson

Diagnose readiness for the lesson.
Warm Up TE, every lesson

Prescribe intervention.
Skills Bank SE pp. 749–761
Reteach CRB, Chapter 1

During Every Lesson

Diagnose understanding of lesson concepts.
Think and Discuss SE, every lesson
Write About It SE, lesson exercises
Journal TE, lesson exercises

Prescribe intervention.
Questioning Strategies pp. 1–14
Reading Strategies CRB, every lesson
Success for ELL pp. 1–14

Formative Assessment

After Every Lesson

Diagnose mastery of lesson concepts.
Lesson Quiz TE, every lesson
Test Prep SE, every lesson
Test and Practice Generator

Prescribe intervention.
Reteach CRB, every lesson
Problem Solving CRB, every lesson
Test Prep Doctor TE, lesson exercises
Homework Help Online

Before Chapter 1 Testing

Diagnose mastery of concepts in the chapter.
Ready to Go On? SE pp. 18, 38
Focus on Problem Solving SE p. 19
Multi-Step Test Prep SE p. 39
Section Quizzes AR pp. 5–6
Test and Practice Generator

Prescribe intervention.
Ready to Go On? Intervention
Scaffolding Questions TE p. 39

Before High Stakes Testing

Diagnose mastery of benchmark concepts.
Test Tackler SE pp. 46–47
Standardized Test Prep SE pp. 48–49
State Test Prep CD-ROM

Prescribe intervention.
State Test Prep Workbook

Summative Assessment

After Chapter 1

Check mastery of chapter concepts.
Multiple-Choice Tests (Forms A, B, C)
Free-Response Tests (Forms A, B, C)
Performance Assessment AR pp. 7–20
Test and Practice Generator

Prescribe intervention.
Reteach CRB, every lesson
Lesson Tutorial Videos Chapter 1

Check mastery of benchmark concepts.
AYP State Tests

Prescribe intervention.
State Test Prep Workbook

KEY: **SE** = *Student Edition* **TE** = *Teacher's Edition* **CRB** = *Chapter Resource Book* **AR** = *Assessment Resources* Available on CD-ROM Available online **2B**

ASSESSMENT AND INTERVENTION

When students are struggling they don't want to keep rereading the same lesson in the hope that eventually it will make sense. They need to try a new approach to the lesson. That's at the core of the assessment and intervention system in *Holt Mathematics*.

Are You Ready?
Intervention and Enrichment

- Diagnoses mastery of prerequisite skills
- Strengthens student weaknesses with direct instruction, conceptual models, and scaffolded practice
- Enriches every chapter with critical thinking activities
- Available in print, on CD-ROM, and online

Name _____ Skill _____

Practice on Your Own   Skill ①

Give the value of the digit 3.

BILLIONS			MILLIONS			THOUSANDS			ONES		
Hundreds	Tens	Ones ,	Hundreds	Tens	Ones ,	Hundreds	Tens	Ones ,	Hundreds	Tens	Ones
		2,		9	4	0,	6	3	5,	7	1	8

The 3 is in the thousands period.
The 3 is in the tens place.
The value of the digit 3 is 3 ten thousands or 30,000.

Give the period, the place, and the value of the digit in 2,940,635,718.

❶ Digit: 7   ❷ Digit: 0   ❸ Digit: 2

Period _____   Period _____   Period _____

Place _____   Place _____   Place _____

Value _____   Value _____   Value _____

Give the value of the underlined digit.

❹ 815,623,4**9**7 _____   ❺ 815,**6**23,497 _____   ❻ **8**15,623,497 _____

❼ 1,482,700,5**7**6 _____ ❾ 1,482,700,576 _____   1,482,7**0**0,576 _____

▶ **Check**

Give the value of the underlined digit.

❿ 3,175,2**6**4,358   ⑪ 3,**1**75,264,358   ⑫ 3,17**5**,264,358

_____   _____   _____

Name _____ Date _____ Class _____

**LESSON
1-2** **Ready to Go On? Skills Intervention**
Exponents

Numbers may be written as a **power**. The **exponent** tells how many times the **base** is multiplied by itself.

Vocabulary
power
exponent
base

Evaluating Powers
Find each value.

A. 7^3

$7^3 =$ _____   How many times is 7 multiplied by itself? ____
                        What is the base? ____ What is the exponent? ____
$=$ _____   Find the product.

B. 2^5

$2^5 =$ _____   How many times is 2 multiplied by itself? ____
                        What is the base? ____ What is the exponent? ____
$= __$ Find the product.

Expressing Whole Numbers as Powers
Write the number using an exponent and the given base.

64, base 4

$64 =$ _____   How many times must 4 be multiplied by itself to
                        equal 64? ____
$= 4^—$ What is the exponent? ____

Earth Science Application
A radar altimeter measures the distance from a space satellite to the surface of the earth by measuring the time delay between the emission of a short microwave pulse and the echo it produces when it bounces off the earth. The microwave region between 100 MHz and 10,000 MHz is used for this measurement. Find the microwave range as a power of ten.

What is the microwave range? _____
Write each value as a product of 10.

$100 =$ _____ $10,000 =$ _____
$= 10^—$ MHz $= 10^—$ MHz

The microwave region used by the radar altimeter is between ____ and ____ MHz.

Only from Holt!

Ready to Go On?
Intervention and Enrichment

- Diagnoses mastery of newly taught skills
- Addresses deficiencies with alternative instruction and practice
- Checks student progress with post tests
- Available in print, on CD-ROM, and online

" *Formative assessment and targeted intervention empower the teacher to build every student's math confidence.* "

— Audrey Jackson, Holt author

Comprehensive differentiated instruction 2

Reach all learners in your classroom—no matter what their skill levels or learning styles are.

Not all students "get it" at the same time or in the same way. *Holt Mathematics* accommodates the students in your classroom with different skill levels and those whose learning styles benefit from different approaches.

With leveled practice and tests, content presented in a variety of media, and teaching strategies built in at point-of-use, helping all of your students succeed has never been easier.

Think and Discuss

1. **Tell** what value of *n* makes $-n + 32$ equal to zero.
2. **Explain** why you would or would not multiply both sides of an equation by 0 to solve it.

Teaching Tip **Visual** Students might incorrectly divide 9 by -3 instead of multiplying in Example 2. Encourage students to write the step that shows multiplying each side by the same integer.

2 Teach

Guided Instruction

In this lesson, students learn to solve one-step equations with integers. Show students that the inverse operation with the same integer is applied to each side to isolate the variable, using the properties of equality. As students look at an equation, you may want to suggest that they begin solving by asking themselves, "What has been done to the variable?" and "What is the opposite of doing that?"

 Teaching Tip **Cooperative Learning** Have students work in pairs, with one student identifying the integer and the other student identifying the inverse operation needed to isolate the variable and solve the equation.

 Reaching All Learners
Through Visual Cues

Suggest that students use colored pencils to circle the integer that must be moved (or operated on) in order to isolate the variable. Then students can use a different color to write the step of performing the inverse operation on each side of the equation.

3 Close

Summarize

Ask students which operations undo, or are inverses of, each other. Discuss why it is necessary to perform the same operation on both sides of the equation when isolating the variable.

2-5 Solving Equations Containing Integers **101**

- **Reaching All Learners** recommends alternative approaches to the lesson at point-of-use.

- **Teaching Tips** make your teaching more adaptable to the range of learning styles in your classroom.

DIFFERENTIATED INSTRUCTION

Professor Edward Burger

KEY OBJECTIVE8

■ Learn to express large numbers in scientific notation.

LESSON TUTORIALS
HOLT, RINEHART AND WINSTON

HOLT MATHEMATICS COURSE 2

Chapter 1: Algebraic Reasoning
Lesson 1-4: Powers of Ten and Scientific Notation

Writing Numbers in Scientific Notation

Write 11,700,000 in scientific notation.

Move the decimal until the result is a number between 1 and 10.

Move 1 place	Move 2 places	Move 3 places	Move 4 places
1170000.0	117000.00	11700.000	1170.0000
> 10	> 10	> 10	> 10

Move 5 places	Move 6 places	Move 7 places	Move 8 places
117.00000	11.700000	1.1700000	0.11700000
> 10	> 10	< 10	< 1 too far!

$11,700,000 = 1.17 \times 10^7$

The exponent is equal to the number of places the decimal point is moved.

Scientific notation is a method of writing very large or very small numbers using powers of 10.

Hundreds of videos available!

Lesson Tutorial Videos

- Illustrate every example!
- Your students' personal take-home tutor
- Reach your visual and auditory learners
- Available online or on CD-ROM
- 276 videos for *Course 1*
- 294 videos for *Course 2*
- 333 videos for *Course 3*

Only from Holt!

IDEA Works!
Special Education CD-ROM

- Modified tests, quizzes, and worksheets
- Adapted format for students with special needs

LESSON **1-1**
Practice A
Variables and Expressions

Write each algebraic expression in words.

> **algebraic expression**
> a mathematical phrase that contains operations, numbers, and/or variables

1. $a + 3$

2. $2x$

_____

3. $5 - y$

4. $\frac{n}{4}$

_____

5. Clint runs c miles.
Brenda runs 2 miles more than Clint.
Write an expression for the number of miles Brenda runs. _____

Evaluate each expression for $a = 2$ and $b = 6$.
The first one has been started for you.

> **evaluate**
> replace the variable with a number

6. $a + b$

7. $b - a$

8. ab

_____ 2 + ___ = _____   _____   _____

Program Highlights

" *If they can hold it in their hand, they will hold it in their head.* " — Jan Scheer, Holt author

Success on High–Stakes Tests

3

Test prep that covers the basics AND develops higher order thinking

Integrated test prep means no surprises on test day. *Holt Mathematics* includes lesson and cumulative review in standardized test format throughout every lesson and chapter to develop student confidence in test-taking skills— without taking time away from core content.

Program Highlights

Multi–Step Test Prep uses real-world scenarios to develop higher order thinking skills.

Test Prep and Spiral Review provide daily practice of new and previously taught skills in standardized test format.

MULTI-STEP TEST PREP

CHAPTER 1

Go for the Gold The table shows the number of medals won by the United States at four Summer Olympic Games.

1. Find the total number of medals won by the United States at each Olympics. Then order the Olympic sites from the greatest number of medals won to the least.

2. Estimate the total number of gold medals won by the United States at these four Olympics. Explain how you found your estimate.

Olympic Medals Won by U.S. Athletes

Year	Site	Gold	Silver	Bronze
1992	Barcelona	37	34	37
1996	Atlanta	44	32	25
2000	Sydney	40	24	33
2004	Athens	35	39	29

3. To compare the performances of U.S. athletes at different Olympics, Jocelyn assigns 3 points to each gold medal, 2 points to each silver medal, and 1 point to each bronze medal. To find the total number of U.S. points for the Barcelona Olympics, she writes the expression $3 \times 37 + 2 \times 34 + 1 \times 37$. Explain how to evaluate this expression, and then find the point total.

4. In 1996, Romania won 2^2 gold medals, 7^1 silver medals, and 3^2 bronze medals. How many of each medal did Romania win? Find the difference in the number of medals won by the United States and the number of medals won by Romania in 1996.

5. The total number of medals won by the United States at each Summer Olympics since 1896 is $3^7 + 2$. About how many more medals do U.S. athletes need to win in order to have a total of 2,200?

Multi-Step Test Prep

HOLT MATH

STANDARDIZED TEST PREP

go.hrw.com
State Test Practice Online
KEYWORD: MS7 TestPrep

Standardized Test Prep
provides a cumulative
assessment in standardized
test format.

Cumulative Assessment, Chapter 1
Multiple Choice

1. Which expression has a value of 74
when $x = 10$, $y = 8$, and $z = 12$?

Ⓐ $4xyz$ Ⓒ $2xz - 3y$

Ⓑ $x + 5y + 2z$ Ⓓ $6xyz + 8$

2. What is the next number in the pattern?

$$3, 3^2, 27, 3^4, 3^5, \ldots$$

Ⓕ 729   Ⓗ 243

Ⓖ 3^7 Ⓙ 3^8

3. A contractor charges $22 to inst[all]
one miniblind. How much does [the]
contractor charge to install m
miniblinds?

Ⓐ $22m$ Ⓒ $22 + m$

Ⓑ $\frac{m}{22}$ Ⓓ $\frac{22}{m}$

4. Which of the following is an ex[ample]
of the Commutative Property?

Ⓕ $20 + 10 = 2(10 + 5)$

Ⓖ $20 + 10 = 10 + 20$

Ⓗ $5 + (20 + 10) = (5 + 20) + 1$[0]

Ⓙ $20 + 0 = 20$

5. Which expression simplifies to 9
when you combine like terms?

Ⓐ $10x^2 - x^2 - 3$

Ⓑ $3x + 7 - 4 + 3x$

Ⓒ $18 + 4x - 15 + 5x$

Ⓓ $7x^2 + 2x + 6 - 3$

6. What is the solution to the equ[ation]
$810 = x - 625$?

Ⓕ $x = 185$ Ⓗ $x = 845$

Ⓖ $x = 215$ Ⓙ $x = 1,43$[5]

7. Tia maps out her jogging route
as shown in the table. How many
kilometers does Tia plan to jog?

Tia's Jogging Route	
Street	**Meters**
1st to Park	428

TEST TACKLER

Standardized Test Strategies

Multiple Choice: Eliminate Answer Choices

With some multiple-choice test items, you can use mental math or
number sense to quickly eliminate some of the answer choices before
you begin solving the problem.

EXAMPLE 1

Which is the solution to the equation $x + 7 = 15$?

Ⓐ $x = 22$ Ⓑ $x = 15$ Ⓒ $x = 8$ Ⓓ $x = 7$

READ the question.
Then try to **eliminate** some of the answer choices.

Use number sense:

When you add, you get a greater number than what you started with. Since
$x + 7 = 15$, 15 must be greater than x, or x must be less than 15. Since 22
and 15 are not less than 15, you can eliminate answer choices A and B.

The correct answer choice is C.

EXAMPLE 2

Arnold measured 0.15 L of water and then poured the water into a
beaker labeled only in milliliters. What did the measurement read
on the beaker?

Ⓕ 0.015 mL   Ⓖ 0.15 mL   Ⓗ 15 mL   Ⓙ 150 mL

LOOK at the choices.
Then try to **eliminate** some of the answer choices.

Use mental math:

A milliliter is smaller than a liter, so the answer is greater than 0.15. You
can eliminate answer choices F and G.

The prefix *milli-* means "thousandth," so multiply 0.15 by 1,000 to get
150 mL, which is answer choice J.

Test Tackler targets
specific test-taking
strategies to help students
become savvy test-takers.

"*Rich problem solving experiences* help students
succeed both inside and outside of the math classroom."

— **Dr. Jennie Bennett**, Holt author

HOLT MATHEMATICS

Program Highlights

T35

Count on **Holt Mathematics** for

Integrated Technology that enhances learning

4

Resources help you manage your classroom and motivate students to take learning one step further.

Holt Mathematics empowers you with key management and presentation tools that help you meet the needs of a broad range of students.

Interactive Answers and Solutions CD-ROM allows teachers to create a screen of selected answers and access complete solutions.

One-Stop Planner® CD-ROM with Test and Practice Generator contains everything you need to plan and manage your lessons in one place.
- All print ancillaries
- Customizable lesson plans
- Holt Calendar Planner®
- Holt PuzzlePro®
- ExamView Test and Practice Generator

Transparencies CD-ROM enhances instruction with **Daily Warm-Ups, Teaching Transparencies, Additional Examples** and more! Available in print or on CD-ROM

Hundreds of transparencies per course!

Power Presentations CD-ROM contains colorful, animated, editable presentations for every lesson.

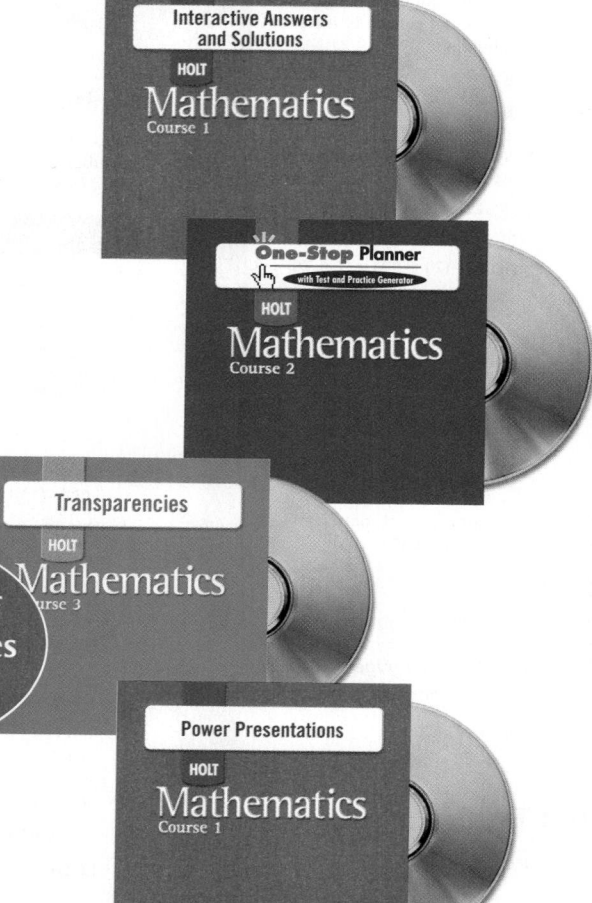

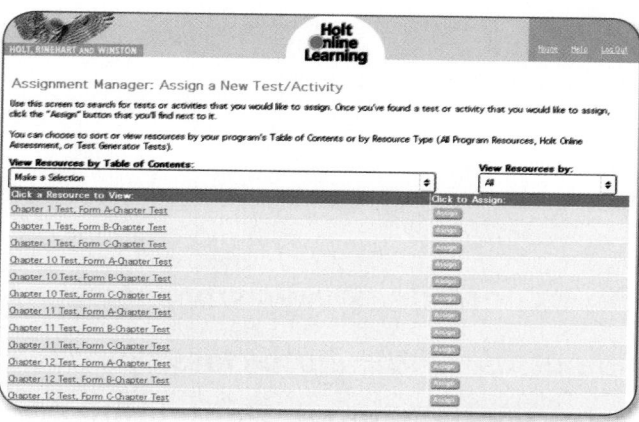

Holt Online Assessment
- Diagnoses individual student performance by standards and textbook objectives
- Automatically assigns resources to strengthen students' skills
- Tracks student progress in one easy-to-manage reporting system

INTEGRATED TECHNOLOGY

With *Holt Mathematics* technology, students get all the help they need, any time they need it. Interactive features and online tools make the math more meaningful to deepen student understanding.

Premier Online Edition makes math come alive!
- **Lesson Tutorial Videos**
- Interactive practice with feedback
- Online study tools

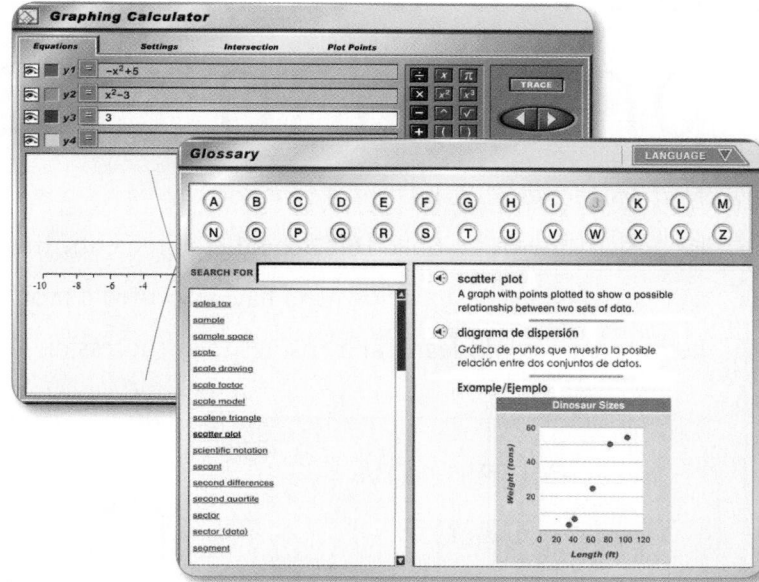

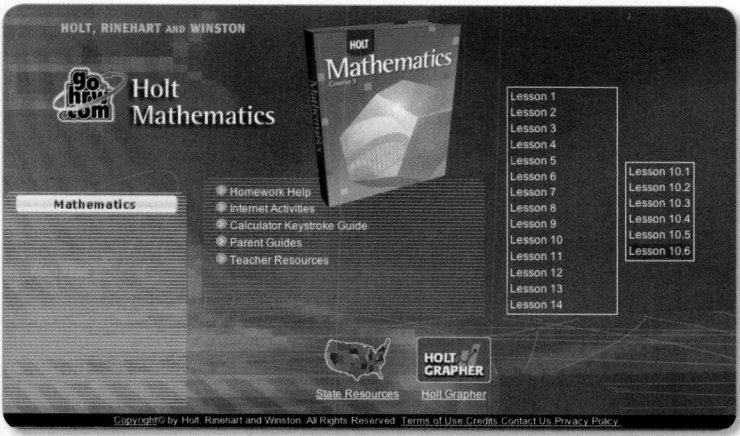

go.hrw.com gives students easy access to lesson resources.
- Homework Help Online
- **Intervention** and **Enrichment** exercises
- Online games and projects

Student One Stop CD-ROM solves the backpack problem.
- Entire *Student Edition*
- Workbooks
- **Intervention** and **Enrichment** exercises

> "*Technology, when used appropriately, can **improve students' mathematical understanding** and problem-solving skills.*"
>
> — Dr. Bert K. Waits, Holt author

Program Highlights

Count on **Holt Mathematics** to be

Grounded in research, built by experts, proven in classrooms

Holt Mathematics is built on a solid foundation of research, proven to work in the classroom, and is consistent with No Child Left Behind requirements. This research is backed by the expertise of a world-class team of authors who have executed a program that makes students *want* to learn, helps them *actually* learn, and ensures their success on high-stakes tests.

Students show major gains on national standardized tests!

Students using *Holt Middle School Math* consecutively for two years show a significant improvement in performance on the SAT 10, a national standardized test.

On average, *Holt Middle School Math* students score at least a full grade level ABOVE their peers!

* The national norms are established by the publisher of the SAT 10 TEST.

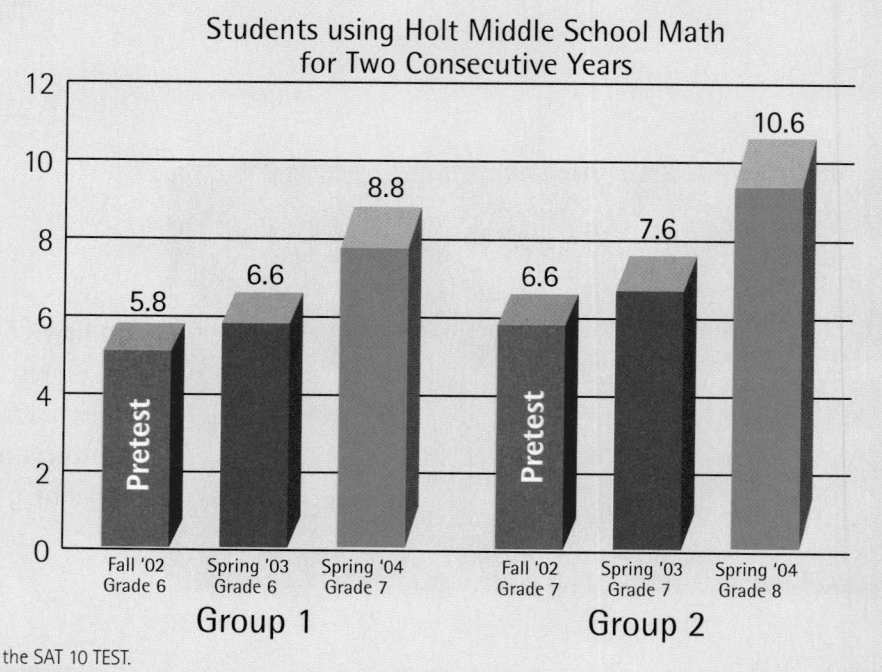

Students using Holt Middle School Math for Two Consecutive Years

	Group 1			Group 2	
Fall '02 Grade 6	Spring '03 Grade 6	Spring '04 Grade 7	Fall '02 Grade 7	Spring '03 Grade 7	Spring '04 Grade 8
5.8 (Pretest)	6.6	8.8	6.6 (Pretest)	7.6	10.6

The Research Underlying the Program

Holt established a pattern of interaction with the educational community throughout all stages of the program's development.

Needs Assessment
- Teacher Interviews
- University Faculty Interviews
- Federal, State, and Local Agencies
- Advisory Panels
- Task Forces
- Academic Conferences
- Surveys with Teachers, Sales, Administrators

Pedagogical Research
- Thorough
- Effective
- Scientifically-Based

Program Development
- Classroom Observation
- Field Testing of Prototypes
- Reviewed by Program and Field Consultants
- Reviewed by Teachers and Administrators

Program Validation
- User Surveys
- Student and Teacher Appraisals
- Field Consultant and Sales Reports

Program Effectiveness
- Post-Implementation Effectiveness Studies
- Valid and Reliable Tests

HOLT MATH

Jennie M. Bennett, Ed.D.
Mathematics Teacher, Hartman Middle School | Houston , TX

Strategic Problem-Solving

"Problem solving plays a pivotal role in mathematics learning and is an integral part of the *Holt Mathematics* program. Problem solving should strengthen and stretch students' thinking and build students' confidence in their ability to solve challenging problems.

Reading mathematics is a necessary skill for all students to master. Students who have English as a second language will face words that may be confusing to them. For example a table in mathematics can mean something different in a student's native language than in the context of mathematics. *Holt Mathematics* provides Reading and Writing Opportunities at the chapter level as well as at the lesson level. "

SUPPORTING RESEARCH
Artzt, Alice F., and Shirel Yaloz–Femia. (1999). *Mathematical reasoning during small-group problem solving. In Developing mathematical reasoning in grades K–12.* Reston, Va: National Council of Teachers of Mathematics.

Jensen, Eric. (1998). *Teaching with the brain in mind.* Alexandria, Va: Association for Supervision and Curriculum Development.

Edward B. Burger, Ph.D.
Professor of Mathematics and Chair | Williams College, MA

Student Engagement

"Learning should be fun. Deep and abstract ideas are challenging to all, but the challenge should be a pleasurable one that students want to conquer. Thus we offer levity through-out the *Holt Mathematics* series— jokes for the teachers to share with their students and entertaining antics on the accompanying videos, mixing mathematical insights with laughs. There is no better student than the student who wants to learn. In this program we worked hard to make learning fun so students enjoy the journey and, as a result, attain a deeper understanding of the mathematics they explore.

The mathematics is developed in a meaningful manner with student readers in mind. Questions such as "What would resonate with real middle school students today?" were asked at every stage of the writing. "

SUPPORTING RESEARCH
Ames, R., & Ames, C. (Eds.). (1984). *Research on motivation in education: Vol. 1. Student motivation.* New York: Academic Press.

Brewster, Cori, and Jennifer Fager. (2000). *Increasing Student Engagement and Motivation: From Time-on-Task to Homework.* Portland, Ore.: Northwest Regional Educational Laboratory.

Program Research

David J. Chard, Ph.D.
Assistant Professor and Director of Graduate Studies in Special Education| University of Oregon

Reaching All Learners

" *Holt Mathematics* is designed to assist teachers in helping all their students to learn conceptual knowledge, skills, and strategies essential to understanding sophisticated mathematics.

This program was designed with instructional features that represent a coherent pedagogical approach to mathematics instruction. Each lesson begins with carefully wrought examples of all of the skills, concepts, and strategies addressed. Key to any instructional program is sufficient scaffolding to support student learning. This ensures that all students are able to understand and solve increasingly complex problems. "

SUPPORTING RESEARCH

Bransford, J. D., Brown, A. L., & Cocking, R. R. (Eds.). (2000). *How people learn: Brain, mind, experience, and school.* Washington, DC: National Research Council.

Gersten, R., Chard, D. J., Baker, S., et al. (2005). *A meta-analysis of research on mathematics instruction for students with learning disabilities.* Signal Hill, CA: Instructional Research Group.

Audrey Jackson
Program Coordinator for Leadership Development | St. Louis, MO

Learning and the Classroom Environment

" The fundamental goal of *Holt Mathematics* is to provide teachers with the necessary tools and understanding of mathematics to ensure student success at all levels.

Highly qualified teachers of mathematics establish and create cultures for learning for all students within their classroom. *Holt Mathematics* promotes successful learning by supporting numerous teaching strategies, including direct instruction and cooperative learning. "

SUPPORTING RESEARCH

National Council of Teachers of Mathematics (2000). *Principles and Standards for School Mathematics.* Reston, VA: National Council of Teachers of Mathematics.

Tomlinson, C. (1995). *How to differentiate instruction in mixed ability classrooms.* Alexander, VA: Association for Supervision and Curriculum Development.

Wiggins, G. and J. McTighe (1998). *Understanding by design.* Alexander, VA: Association for Supervision and Curriculum Development.

Program Research

HOLT MATH

Paul A. Kennedy, Ph.D.
Professor, Department of Mathematics | Colorado State University

Algebraic Thinking

" When students enter the middle grades, they are beginning the preparation for the transition to more advanced mathematical topics such as algebra and geometry while enhancing their basic arithmetic knowledge. It is crucial that they develop abstract reasoning as well as symbolic manipulation skills.

In *Holt Mathematics,* content is carefully developed using methods aligned with standard best practices. The idea of "doing and undoing" is developed early in the program and carried thought the series. Additionally students need to see the relationships between the math they are learning and real-world scenarios. "

SUPPORTING RESEARCH

Vygotsky, L.S. (1978). *Mind and society: The development of higher mental processes.* Cambridge, MA: Harvard University Press.

Driscoll, Mark J. (1997). *Fostering algebraic thinking.* Portsmouth, NH.; Heinemann.

Freddie L. Renfro
Former Director of Mathematics Instruction K–12 | Texas City Independent School District

Differentiated Instruction

" Imagine a classroom where diversity in learning is the norm, and the teacher responds to the learners' needs with flexible strategies, open dialogue, and ongoing assessment.

Every child is unique. Finding ways to tailor instruction to meet individual student needs in the classroom can be a manageable task with the right support. In the *Holt Mathematics* series, we promote differentiated instruction by including activities that address a variety of learning styles: discovery learning, the use of concrete examples, and student interaction, to name a few.

The *Teacher's Edition* offers suggestions for differentiated assessment as well so that students have the opportunity to demonstrate their understanding in a manner that reflects their learning style. "

SUPPORTING RESEARCH

Tomlinson, C. (1999). *The differentiated classroom: Responding to the needs of all learners.* Alexandria, VA: Association for Supervision and Curriculum Development.

Willis, S. and Mann, Larry. (2000). *Differentiating instruction.* Alexandria, VA: Association for Supervision and Curriculum Development.

Program Research

Program Research

Jan Scheer, Ph.D.
Executive Director, Create-A-Vision

Concrete Understanding

" *Holt Mathematics* makes use of mathematical modeling and provides many options for the use of manipulatives to enhance student understanding of abstract concepts.

Educational research demonstrates the effectiveness of hands-on learning in supplementing understanding of mathematical ideas for students This is especially important in the middle grades, when students are exposed to increasingly abstract concepts. This program provides numerous Hands-On Labs where students use algebra tiles, pattern blocks, two-color counters, and other materials to provide opportunities for concrete methods for learning selected topics. "

SUPPORTING RESEARCH

Bohan, Harry J., and Peggy Bohan Shawaker (1994).
Using manipulatives effectively: A drive down rounding road.
Arithmetic Teacher 41 (5): 246-48

Stein, Mary Kay, and Jane W. Bovalino. (2001).
Manipulatives: One piece of the puzzle.
Mathematics Teaching in the Middle School, 6 (6): 356-59.

Bert K. Waits, Ph.D.
Professor Emeritus of Mathematics | The Ohio State University

Technology to Enhance Learning

" Research has demonstrated that technology, when used appropriately, can improve students' mathematical understanding and problem-solving skills. Similarly, technological tools can help teachers challenge students to use and understand mathematics in real-world scenarios.

The *Holt Mathematics* series presents a balanced approach to learning.
We stress that students must utilize all available tools, including mental and paper-and- pencil skills and technology, in the mathematics-learning process. This series uses technology not as an end in itself, but rather as a means for understanding and application. Current research supports this use of computer software including spreadsheets, dynamic geometry software, and graphing calculators. "

SUPPORTING RESEARCH

Graham, A.T., & J.O.J. Thomas. (2000). Building a versatile understanding of algebraic variables with a graphic calculator. *Educational Studies in Mathematics*, 41 (3), 265-282.

Hallar, Jeannie C., & Karen Norwood. (1999). The effects of a graphing-approach intermediate algebra curriculum on students' understanding of function. *Journal for Research in Mathematics Education*, 30 (2), 220-226.

Holt Mathematics
Program Components

Student Edition
Student One Stop CD-ROM
Premier Online Edition
Teacher's Edition

Assessment and Intervention

Are You Ready? Intervention and Enrichment
Assessment Resources
Questioning Strategies
Ready to Go On? Intervention and Enrichment

Differentiated Instruction

Alternate Openers: Explorations Transparencies
Family Involvement Activities
Hands-on Lab Activities
IDEA Works! Special Education CD-ROM
Lesson Tutorial Videos
Manipulatives Kit
Multilingual Glossary
Interdisciplinary Posters
Premier Online Edition
Student One Stop CD-ROM
Success for English Language Learners
Technology Lab Activities

Workbooks

Homework and Practice Workbook
Know-It Notebook
Problem Solving Workbook
State Test Prep Workbook

Spanish Resources

Student Edition
Are You Ready? Intervention and Enrichment
Assessment Resources
Homework and Practice Workbook
Lesson Tutorial Videos with Spanish closed captioning
Ready to Go On? Intervention and Assessment
Family Involvement Activities

High-Stakes Test Prep

Countdown to Testing Transparencies
Holt Mathematics State Test Prep for Middle School and High School CD-ROM
State Test Prep Workbook

Integrated Technology

Are You Ready? Intervention and Enrichment CD-ROM
Holt Mathematics State Test Prep for Middle School and High School CD-ROM
IDEA Works! Special Education CD-ROM
Interactive Answers and Solutions CD-ROM
Lesson Tutorial Videos CD-ROM
One-Stop Planner with Test and Practice Generator and State-Specific Resources CD-ROM
Power Presentations CD-ROM
Premier Online Edition
Ready to Go On? Intervention and Enrichment CD-ROM
Student One Stop CD-ROM
Technology Lab Activities
Transparencies CD-ROM

Teaching Resources

Chapter Resource Books
Interactive Answers and Solutions CD-ROM
Know-It Notebook Teacher's Guide with Transparencies
Lesson Plans
Lesson Transparencies
One-Stop Planner with Test and Practice Generator and State-Specific Resources CD-ROM
Power Presentations CD-ROM
Solutions Key
Transparencies CD-ROM

HOLT Professional Development

Anytime, Anyplace
Professional Development:
Building a Community of Learners

CHAPTER 1

Principles of Algebra

go.hrw.com
Online Resources
KEYWORD: MT7 TOC

ARE YOU READY?... **3**

Expressions and Integers
1-1 Variables and Expressions **6**
1-2 Algebraic Expressions **10**
1-3 Integers and Absolute Value **14**
1-4 Adding Integers **18**
1-5 Subtracting Integers **22**
1-6 Multiplying and Dividing Integers....................... **26**
    READY TO GO ON? QUIZ **30**
    Focus on Problem Solving: Solve....................... **31**

Equations and Inequalities
LAB Model Solving Equations................................ **32**
1-7 Solving Equations by Adding or Subtracting **34**
1-8 Solving Equations by Multiplying or Dividing **39**
1-9 Introduction to Inequalities............................ **44**
    READY TO GO ON? QUIZ **48**
    MULTI-STEP TEST PREP **49**

    Study Guide: Preview.. **4**
    Reading and Writing Math.................................... **5**
    Game Time: Math Magic..................................... **50**
    It's in the Bag!: Note-Taking Taking Shape **51**
    Study Guide: Review **52**
    Chapter Test **55**

Career: Firefighter

Tools for Success

Reading Math 5
Writing Math 9, 13, 17, 21, 25, 29, 38, 43, 47
Vocabulary 6, 14, 34, 44

Know-It Notebook Chapter 1
Homework Help Online 8, 12, 16, 20, 24, 28, 37, 41, 46
Study Skills 6, 14, 44, 45

Test Prep and Spiral Review 9, 13, 17, 21, 25, 29, 38, 43, 47
Multi-Step Test Prep 49
Test Tackler 56
Standardized Test Prep 58

Rational Numbers

ARE YOU READY? **61**

Rational Number Operations

2-1 Rational Numbers. **64**

2-2 Comparing and Ordering Rational Numbers. **68**

2-3 Adding and Subtracting Rational Numbers. **72**

2-4 Multiplying Rational Numbers **76**

2-5 Dividing Rational Numbers **80**

2-6 Adding and Subtracting with Unlike Denominators. **85**

LAB Add and Subtract Fractions **89**

READY TO GO ON? QUIZ. **90**

Focus on Problem Solving: Look Back **91**

Equations with Rational Numbers

2-7 Solving Equations with Rational Numbers **92**

LAB Model Two-Step Equations **96**

2-8 Solving Two-Step Equations **98**

READY TO GO ON? QUIZ **102**

MULTI-STEP TEST PREP **103**

Problem Solving on Location: New Jersey **112**

Study Guide: Preview. **62**

Reading and Writing Math **63**

Game Time: Egyptian Fractions **104**

It's in the Bag!: Canister Carry-All **105**

Study Guide: Review **106**

Chapter Test **109**

Table of Contents

Career: Nutritionist

Tools for Success

Writing Math 63, 65, 67, 71, 75, 79, 84, 88, 95, 101

Vocabulary 64, 68, 80

Know-It Notebook Chapter 2

Homework Help Online 66, 70, 74, 78, 83, 87, 94, 100

Student Help 64, 68, 73, 77, 92

Test Prep and Spiral Review 67, 71, 75, 79, 84, 88, 95, 101

Multi-Step Test Prep 103

Standardized Test Prep 110

CHAPTER 3

Graphs, Functions, and Sequences

Career: Pharmacist

ARE YOU READY? 115

Tables and Graphs
3-1 Ordered Pairs 118
3-2 Graphing on a Coordinate Plane 122
LAB Graph Points 126
3-3 Interpreting Graphs and Tables 127
     READY TO GO ON? QUIZ 132
     Focus on Problem Solving: Make a Plan 133

Functions and Sequences
3-4 Functions 134
3-5 Equations, Tables, and Graphs 138
3-6 Arithmetic Sequences 142
     READY TO GO ON? QUIZ 146
     MULTI-STEP TEST PREP 147

Study Guide: Preview 116
Reading and Writing Math 117
Game Time: Find the Phony! 148
It's in the Bag!: Clipboard Solutions for Graphs, Functions,
and Sequences 149
Study Guide: Review 150
Chapter Test 153

Tools for Success

Reading Math 117
Writing Math 121, 125, 131, 137, 141, 145
Vocabulary 118, 122, 134, 142

Know-It Notebook Chapter 3
Homework Help Online 120, 124, 129, 136, 140, 144

Test Prep and Spiral Review 121, 125, 131, 137, 141, 145
Multi-Step Test Prep 147
Test Tackler 154
Standardized Test Prep 156

Exponents and Roots

CHAPTER 4

ARE YOU READY? 159

Exponents

4-1   Exponents. 162
4-2   Look for a Pattern in Integer Exponents 166
4-3   Properties of Exponents 170
4-4   Scientific Notation 174
LAB Multiply and Divide Numbers in Scientific Notation 179
      READY TO GO ON? QUIZ 180
      Focus on Problem Solving: Solve. 181

Roots

4-5   Squares and Square Roots 182
4-6   Estimating Square Roots 186
LAB Evaluate Powers and Roots 190
4-7   The Real Numbers 191
LAB Explore Right Triangles 195
4-8   The Pythagorean Theorem. 196
      READY TO GO ON? QUIZ 200
      MULTI-STEP TEST PREP 201
      Problem Solving on Location: Ohio 210

      Study Guide: Preview. 160
      Reading and Writing Math. 161
      Game Time: Magic Squares. 202
      It's in the Bag!: It's a Wrap 203
      Study Guide: Review 204
      Chapter Test 207

go.hrw.com
Online Resources
KEYWORD: MT7 TOC

Career:
Nuclear Physicist

Tools for Success

Reading Math 162, 171

Writing Math 165, 169, 173, 178, 185, 189, 194, 199

Vocabulary 162, 174, 182, 191, 196

Know-It Notebook Chapter 4

Study Strategy 161

Homework Help Online 164, 168, 172, 176, 184, 188, 193, 198

Student Help 163, 167, 182, 183, 191

Test Prep and Spiral Review 165, 169, 173, 178, 185, 189, 194, 199

Multi-Step Test Prep 201

Standardized Test Prep 208

Ratios, Proportions, and Similarity

ARE YOU READY? 213

Ratios, Rates, and Proportions

5-1 Ratios and Proportions 216
5-2 Ratios, Rates, and Unit Rates. 220
5-3 Dimensional Analysis 224
5-4 Solving Proportions 229
     READY TO GO ON? QUIZ 234
     Focus on Problem Solving: Solve. 235

Similarity and Scale

LAB Explore Similarity 236
5-5 Similar Figures. 238
LAB Explore Dilations. 242
5-6 Dilations 244
5-7 Indirect Measurement 248
5-8 Scale Drawings and Scale Models 252
LAB Make a Scale Model 256
     READY TO GO ON? QUIZ 258
     MULTI-STEP TEST PREP. 259

     Study Guide: Preview. 214
     Reading and Writing Math. 215
     Game Time: Copy-Cat 260
     It's in the Bag!: A Worthwhile Wallet 261
     Study Guide: Review 262
     Chapter Test 265

go.hrw.com
Online Resources
KEYWORD: MT7 TOC

Career: Horticulturist

Tools for Success

Reading Math 216, 238, 252
Writing Math 215, 219, 223, 228, 233, 241, 247, 251, 255
Vocabulary 216, 220, 224, 229, 238, 244, 248, 252

Know-It Notebook Chapter 5
Homework Help Online 218, 222, 226, 231, 240, 246, 250, 254
Student Help 224

Test Prep and Spiral Review 219, 223, 228, 233, 241, 247, 251, 255
Multi-Step Test Prep 259
Test Tackler 266
Standardized Test Prep 268

Percents

go.hrw.com
Online Resources
KEYWORD: MT7 TOC

CHAPTER 6

ARE YOU READY? 271

Proportions and Percents

6-1 Relating Decimals, Fractions, and Percents 274
6-2 Estimate with Percents 278
6-3 Finding Percents 283
6-4 Finding a Number When the Percent is Known 288
     READY TO GO ON? QUIZ 292
     Focus on Problem Solving: Make a Plan 293

Applying Percents

6-5 Percent Increase and Decrease 294
6-6 Applications of Percents 298
6-7 Simple Interest 302
LAB Compute Compound Interest 306
     READY TO GO ON? QUIZ 308
     MULTI-STEP TEST PREP 309
     Problem Solving on Location: Pennsylvania 318

     Study Guide: Preview 272
     Reading and Writing Math 273
     Game Time: Percent Puzzlers 310
     It's in the Bag!: Origami Percents 311
     Study Guide: Review 312
     Chapter Test 315

**Career:
Sports Statistician**

Tools for Success

Reading Math 273, 274
Writing Math 277, 282, 287, 291, 297, 301, 305
Vocabulary 274, 278, 294, 298, 302

Know-It Notebook Chapter 6
Homework Help Online 276, 280, 285, 290, 296, 300, 304
Student Help 275

Test Prep and Spiral Review
277, 282, 287, 291, 297, 301, 305
Multi-Step Test Prep 309
Standardized Test Prep 316

CHAPTER
7

go.hrw.com
Online Resources
KEYWORD: MT7 TOC

Foundations of Geometry

ARE YOU READY? **321**

Two-Dimensional Geometry
7-1 Points, Lines, Planes, and Angles **324**
LAB Bisect Figures **329**
7-2 Parallel and Perpendicular Lines **330**
LAB Constructions **334**
7-3 Angles in Triangles **336**
7-4 Classifying Polygons **341**
LAB Exterior Angles of a Polygon **346**
7-5 Coordinate Geometry **347**
READY TO GO ON? QUIZ **352**
Focus on Problem Solving: Understand the Problem **353**

Patterns in Geometry
7-6 Congruence **354**
7-7 Transformations **358**
LAB Combine Transformations **362**
7-8 Symmetry **364**
7-9 Tessellations **368**
READY TO GO ON? QUIZ **372**
MULTI-STEP TEST PREP **373**

Study Guide: Preview **322**
Reading and Writing Math **323**
Game Time: Coloring Tessellations **374**
It's in the Bag!: Project CD Geometry **375**
Study Guide: Review **376**
Chapter Test **379**

Career: Playground
Equipment Designer

Tools for Success

Reading Math 325, 358, 364
Writing Math 323, 328, 331, 333, 340, 345, 351, 357, 361, 367, 371
Vocabulary 324, 330, 336, 341, 354, 358, 368

Know-It Notebook Chapter 7
Homework Help Online 326, 332, 338, 343, 349, 356, 360, 366, 369
Student Help 330, 347, 349

Test Prep and Spiral Review 328, 333, 340, 345, 351, 357, 361, 367, 371
Multi-Step Test Prep 373
Test Tackler 380
Standardized Test Prep 382

Perimeter, Area, and Volume

ARE YOU READY? 385

Perimeter and Area

8-1 Perimeter and Area of Rectangles & Parallelograms........ 388
LAB Explore the Effects of Changing Dimensions 393
8-2 Perimeter and Area of Triangles and Trapezoids 394
LAB Approximate *Pi* by Measuring 399
8-3 Circles 400
READY TO GO ON? QUIZ 404
Focus on Problem Solving: Look Back 405

Three-Dimensional Geometry

LAB Construct Nets 406
8-4 Drawing Three-Dimensional Figures..................... 408
LAB Find Volume of Prisms and Cylinders 412
8-5 Volume of Prisms and Cylinders...................... 413
LAB Find Volume of Pyramids and Cones................. 418
8-6 Volume of Pyramids and Cones 420
LAB Find Surface Area of Prisms and Cylinders 425
8-7 Surface Area of Prisms and Cylinders 427
LAB Find the Surface Area of Pyramids 431
8-8 Surface Area of Pyramids and Cones 432
8-9 Spheres 436
8-10 Scaling Three-Dimensional Figures 440
READY TO GO ON? QUIZ 444
MULTI-STEP TEST PREP 445
EXT Symmetry in Three Dimensions 446
Problem Solving on Location: Nevada 456

Study Guide: Preview.............................. 386
Reading and Writing Math........................... 387
Game Time: Planes in Space 448
It's in the Bag!: The Tube Journal 449
Study Guide: Review 450
Chapter Test 453

Career: Surgeon

Tools for Success

Reading Math 395

Writing Math 392, 398, 403, 411, 417, 424, 430, 435, 439, 443

Vocabulary 388, 400, 408, 413, 420, 427, 432, 436, 440, 446

Know-It Notebook Chapter 8

Study Strategy 387

Homework Help Online 391, 396, 402, 410, 416, 422, 429, 434, 438, 442

Student Help 388, 390, 400, 413

TEST PREP

Test Prep and Spiral Review 392, 398, 403, 411, 417, 424, 430, 435, 439, 443

Multi-Step Test Prep 445

Standardized Test Prep 454

Data and Statistics

go.hrw.com
Online Resources
KEYWORD: MT7 TOC

ARE YOU READY? **458**

Collecting and Describing Data

9-1   Samples and Surveys **462**

LAB   Explore Samples **466**

9-2   Organizing Data **467**

9-3   Measures of Central Tendency **472**

9-4   Variability **476**

LAB   Create Box-and-Whisker Plots **481**

READY TO GO ON? QUIZ **482**

Focus on Problem Solving: Make a Plan **483**

Displaying Data

LAB   Make a Circle Graph **484**

9-5   Displaying Data **485**

LAB   Create Histograms **489**

9-6   Misleading Graphs and Statistics **490**

9-7   Scatter Plots **494**

LAB   Create a Scatter Plot **498**

9-8   Choosing the Best Representation of Data **500**

LAB   Use a Spreadsheet to Create Graphs **504**

READY TO GO ON? QUIZ **506**

MULTI-STEP TEST PREP **507**

Study Guide: Preview **460**

Reading and Writing Math **461**

Game Time: Distribution of Primes **508**

It's in the Bag!: Data Pop-Ups **509**

Study Guide: Review **510**

Chapter Test **513**

Career: Quality Assurance Specialist

Tools for Success

Reading Math 461

Writing Math 465, 471, 475, 480, 488, 493, 497, 503

Vocabulary 462, 467, 472, 476, 485, 494

Know-It Notebook Chapter 9

Homework Help Online 464, 469, 474, 478, 487, 492, 496, 502

Test Prep and Spiral Review 465, 471, 475, 480, 488, 493, 497, 503

Multi-Step Test Prep 507

Test Tackler 514

Standardized Test Prep 516

Probability

ARE YOU READY? **519**

Experimental Probability

10-1 Probability **522**

10-2 Experimental Probability **527**

LAB Generate Random Numbers  **531**

10-3 Use a Simulation...................................... **532**

LAB Use Different Models for Simulations **536**

READY TO GO ON? QUIZ **538**

Focus on Problem Solving: Understand the Problem..... **539**

Theoretical Probability and Counting

10-4 Theoretical Probability **540**

10-5 Independent and Dependent Events..................... **545**

10-6 Making Decisions and Predictions **550**

10-7 Odds.. **554**

10-8 Counting Principles **558**

10-9 Permutations and Combinations **563**

READY TO GO ON? QUIZ **568**

MULTI-STEP TEST PREP **569**

Problem Solving on Location: South Carolina.......... **578**

Study Guide: Preview.................................. **520**

Reading and Writing Math.............................. **521**

Game Time: The Paper Chase........................... **570**

It's in the Bag!: Probability Post-Up.................... **571**

Study Guide: Review **572**

Chapter Test **575**

go.hrw.com
Online Resources
KEYWORD: MT7 TOC

Career: Cryptographer

Tools for Success

Reading and Writing Math

Reading Math 521, 563

Writing Math 526, 530, 535, 544, 549, 553, 557, 562, 567

Vocabulary 522, 527, 532, 540, 545, 554, 558, 563

Study Skills

Know-It Notebook Chapter 10

Homework Help Online 525, 529, 534, 543, 548, 552, 556, 560, 566

TEST PREP

Test Prep and Spiral Review 526, 530, 535, 544, 549, 553, 557, 562, 567

Multi-Step Test Prep 569

Standardized Test Prep 576

CHAPTER 11

go.hrw.com
Online Resources
KEYWORD: MT7 TOC

Multi-Step Equations and Inequalities

ARE YOU READY? **581**

Solving Linear Equations

11-1 Simplifying Algebraic Expressions **584**
11-2 Solving Multi-Step Equations **588**
LAB Model Equations with Variables on Both Sides **592**
11-3 Solving Equations with Variables on Both Sides **593**
READY TO GO ON? QUIZ **598**
Focus on Problem Solving: Make a Plan **599**

Solving Equations and Inequalities

11-4 Solving Inequalities by Multiplying or Dividing **600**
11-5 Solving Two-Step Inequalities **604**
11-6 Systems of Equations **608**
READY TO GO ON? QUIZ **612**
MULTI-STEP TEST PREP **613**

Study Guide: Preview **582**
Reading and Writing Math **583**
Game Time: Trans-Plants **614**
It's in the Bag!: Picture Envelopes **615**
Study Guide: Review **616**
Chapter Test **619**

Career: Hydrologist

Tools for Success

Writing Math 583, 587, 591, 597, 603, 607, 611
Vocabulary 584, 608

Know-It Notebook Chapter 11
Homework Help Online 586, 590, 596, 602, 606, 610
Student Help 585, 589, 600

Test Prep and Spiral Review 587, 591, 597, 603, 607, 611
Multi-Step Test Prep 613
Test Tackler 620
Standardized Test Prep 622

Graphing Lines

CHAPTER 12

ARE YOU READY? **625**

Linear Equations

12-1 Graphing Linear Equations **628**
12-2 Slope of a Line. **633**
12-3 Using Slopes and Intercepts **638**
LAB Graph Equations in Slope-Intercept Form **643**
12-4 Point-Slope Form **644**
READY TO GO ON? QUIZ **648**
Focus on Problem Solving: Understand the Problem. **649**

Linear Relationships

12-5 Direct Variation. **650**
12-6 Graphing Inequalities in Two Variables **655**
12-7 Lines of Best Fit. **660**
READY TO GO ON? QUIZ **664**
MULTI-STEP TEST PREP **665**
EXT Solving Systems of Equations by Graphing. **666**
Problem Solving on Location: Maryland. **676**

Study Guide: Preview. **626**
Reading and Writing Math. **627**
Game Time: Graphing in Space **668**
It's in the Bag!: Graphing Tri-Fold **669**
Study Guide: Review **670**
Chapter Test **673**

go.hrw.com
Online Resources
KEYWORD: MT7 TOC

Career: Wildlife Ecologist

Tools for Success

Reading Math 628
Writing Math 627, 632, 637, 642, 647, 654, 659, 663
Vocabulary 628, 638, 644, 650, 655

Know-It Notebook Chapter 12
Homework Help Online 631, 635, 641, 646, 653, 658, 662
Student Help 633, 660

Test Prep and Spiral Review 632, 637, 642, 647, 654, 659, 663
Multi-Step Test Prep 665
Standardized Test Prep 674

CHAPTER 13

go.hrw.com
Online Resources
KEYWORD: MT7 TOC

Sequences and Functions

ARE YOU READY? **679**

Sequences

13-1 Terms of Arithmetic Sequences **682**
13-2 Terms of Geometric Sequences **687**
LAB Explore the Fibonacci Sequence **692**
13-3 Other Sequences **693**
READY TO GO ON? QUIZ **698**
Focus on Problem Solving: Solve **699**

Functions

13-4 Linear Functions **700**
13-5 Exponential Functions **704**
13-6 Quadratic Functions **708**
LAB Explore Cubic Functions **712**
13-7 Inverse Variation **714**
READY TO GO ON? QUIZ **718**
MULTI-STEP TEST PREP **719**

Study Guide: Preview **680**
Reading and Writing Math **681**
Game Time: Squared Away **720**
It's in the Bag!: Springboard to Sequences **721**
Study Guide: Review **722**
Chapter Test **725**

Career: Bacteriologist

Tools for Success

Reading Math 700
Writing Math 683, 686, 691, 697, 703, 707, 711, 717
Vocabulary 687, 693, 700, 704, 708, 714

Know-It Notebook Chapter 13
Study Strategy 681
Homework Help Online 685, 689, 695, 702, 706, 710, 716

Test Prep and Spiral Review 686, 691, 697, 703, 707, 711, 717
Multi-Step Test Prep 719
Test Tackler 726
Standardized Test Prep 728

Polynomials

ARE YOU READY? 730

Introduction to Polynomials

14-1 Polynomials 734
LAB Model Polynomials 738
14-2 Simplifying Polynomials 740
READY TO GO ON? QUIZ 744
Focus on Problem Solving: Look Back 745

Polynomial Operations

LAB Model Polynomial Addition 746
14-3 Adding Polynomials 747
LAB Model Polynomial Subtraction 751
14-4 Subtracting Polynomials 752
14-5 Multiplying Polynomials and Monomials 756
LAB Multiply Binomials 760
14-6 Multiplying Binomials 762
READY TO GO ON? QUIZ 766
MULTI-STEP TEST PREP 767
EXT Dividing Polynomials by Monomials 768
Problem Solving on Location: Mississippi 778

Study Guide: Preview 732
Reading and Writing Math 733
Game Time: Short Cuts 770
It's in the Bag!: Polynomial Petals 771
Study Guide: Review 772
Chapter Test 775

go.hrw.com
Online Resources
KEYWORD: MT7 TOC

Career:
Financial Analyst

Tools for Success

Writing Math 737, 743, 750, 755, 759, 765

Vocabulary 734, 762

Know-It Notebook Chapter 14

Study Strategy 733

Homework Help Online 736, 742, 749, 754, 758, 764

Student Help 768

Test Prep and Spiral Review 737, 743, 750, 755, 759, 765

Multi-Step Test Prep 767

Standardized Test Prep 776

INTERDISCIPLINARY CONNECTIONS

Many fields of study require knowledge of the mathematical skills and concepts taught in *Holt Mathematics Course 3.* Examples and exercises throughout the book highlight the math you will need to understand in order to study other subjects, such as art or finance, or to pursue a career in fields such as medicine or architecture.

13. **Earth Science** When the Moon is between the Sun and Earth, it casts a conical shadow called the *umbra*. If the shadow is 2140 mi in diameter and 260,955 mi along the edge, what is the lateral surface area of the umbra?

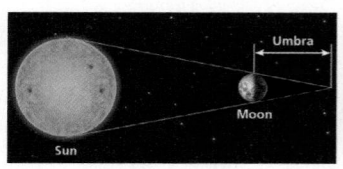

14. **Social Studies** The Pyramid Arena in Memphis, Tennessee, is 321 feet tall and has a square base with side length 200 yards. What is the lateral surface area of the pyramid in feet?

15. The table shows the dimensions of three square pyramids.
    a. Complete the table.

Dimensions of Giza Pyramids (ft)			
Pyramid	Height	Slant Height	Side of Base

Science

Anatomy 176
Animals 79
Astronomy 37, 172, 475, 709
Chemistry 17, 220
Computer 183
Earth Science 17, 23, 28, 29, 94, 297, 345, 435, 480, 557, 647, 659
Environment 217
Life Science 71, 165, 177, 227, 228, 252, 253, 284, 288, 290, 294-295, 417, 433, 535, 567, 647, 654, 691, 742
Meteorology 71
Physical Science 7, 38, 177, 226, 231, 232, 241, 275, 281, 288, 333, 401, 591, 597, 630, 631, 635, 652, 691, 701, 706, 711, 717
Physics 735
Technology 562

Language Arts

Language Arts 184, 287
Literature 297

Fine and Performing Arts

Art 241, 411, 428, 442, 567, 748
Crafts 610
Design 74
Entertainment 9, 218, 223, 403, 535, 606, 611, 632
Graphic Design 9
Music 125, 415, 715
Photography 247

Social Studies

Architecture 254, 424, 637
Geography 248, 254, 277, 285, 480
History 121
Social Studies 37, 69, 84, 178, 282, 286, 340, 367, 392, 417, 421, 435, 602, 657
Transportation 227, 228, 632, 737
Travel 140, 143, 589

Economics

Business 46, 136, 172, 218, 230, 281, 441, 465, 473, 557, 587, 595, 703, 711, 741, 750, 753, 755
Consumer Math 100, 119
Economics 21, 607, 691, 703
Finance 8, 281, 717
Home Economics 137
Money 40, 175, 305, 689

Health and Fitness

Cooking 567
Fitness 503, 686
Food 227, 403, 658
Games 185, 549
Health 19, 79, 759
Hobbies 185, 219, 586, 710
Medical 645
Nutrition 94
Recreation 42, 77, 86, 284, 443, 465, 686, 703
Safety 528, 637
Sports 14, 27, 47, 66, 70, 72, 74, 137, 145, 184, 227, 281, 403, 430, 503, 567, 587, 591, 607, 661, 690, 710

WHY LEARN MATHEMATICS?

Throughout the text, links to interesting application topics, such as entertainment, photography, and technology, will help you see how math is used in the real world. Some of these links have additional information and activities at go.hrw.com. For a complete list of all real-world problems in *Holt Mathematics Course 3,* see page 898 in the Index.

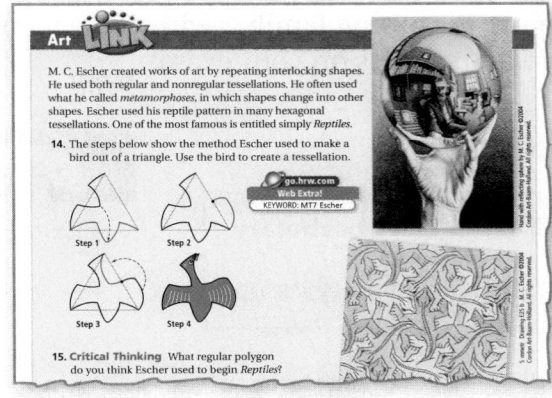

Art LINK

M. C. Escher created works of art by repeating interlocking shapes. He used both regular and nonregular tessellations. He often used what he called *metamorphoses*, in which shapes change into other shapes. Escher used his reptile pattern in many hexagonal tessellations. One of the most famous is entitled simply *Reptiles*.

14. The steps below show the method Escher used to make a bird out of a triangle. Use the bird to create a tessellation.

go.hrw.com
Web Extra!
KEYWORD: MT7 Escher

Step 1   Step 2
Step 3   Step 4

15. Critical Thinking What regular polygon do you think Escher used to begin *Reptiles?*

Real-World LINKS

Animals 79
Architecture 255
Art 241, 371, 567, 743
Business 465, 750
Career 424
Earth Science 17, 29, 88, 131, 345, 530, 647, 659
Economics 21, 301, 663
Entertainment 403, 611
Games 185, 549

Home Economics 137
Language Arts 471
Life Science 101, 165, 177, 289, 417, 433, 439, 497, 535, 544, 642, 654, 765
Literature 297
Meteorology 71
Money 305

Recreation 86, 703

Recreation LINK

The volume of a t pical hot air bal- loon is between 65,000 and 105,000 cubic feet. Most hot air balloons fl at altitudes of 1000 to 1500 feet.

Games LINK

In 1997, Deep Blue became the first computer to win a match against a chess grand master when it defeated world champion Garr Kasparov.

Health 233, 707
History 121

Money LINK

Man bank ATMs in Bangkok, Thailand, are located in sculp- tures to attract customers.

Music 125 , 697
Photography 247
Physical Science 328, 333, 398, 597, 691, 705

Science 169, 189
Social Studies 25, 291, 367, 735
Sports 47, 430, 503, 591
Technology 562
Transportation 632

USING YOUR BOOK FOR SUCCESS

This book has many features designed to help you learn and study math. Becoming familiar with these features will prepare you for greater success on your exams.

Learn

Preview new **vocabulary** terms listed at the beginning of every lesson.

Look for the **Student Help** for hints and reminders.

Study the **examples** to learn new math ideas and skills. The examples include step-by-step solutions.

Practice

Look back at examples from the lesson to solve the **Guided Practice** exercises.

If you get stuck, use the internet for **Homework Help Online**.

Review

Study and review **vocabulary** from the entire chapter.

Test yourself with **practice problems** from every lesson in the chapter.

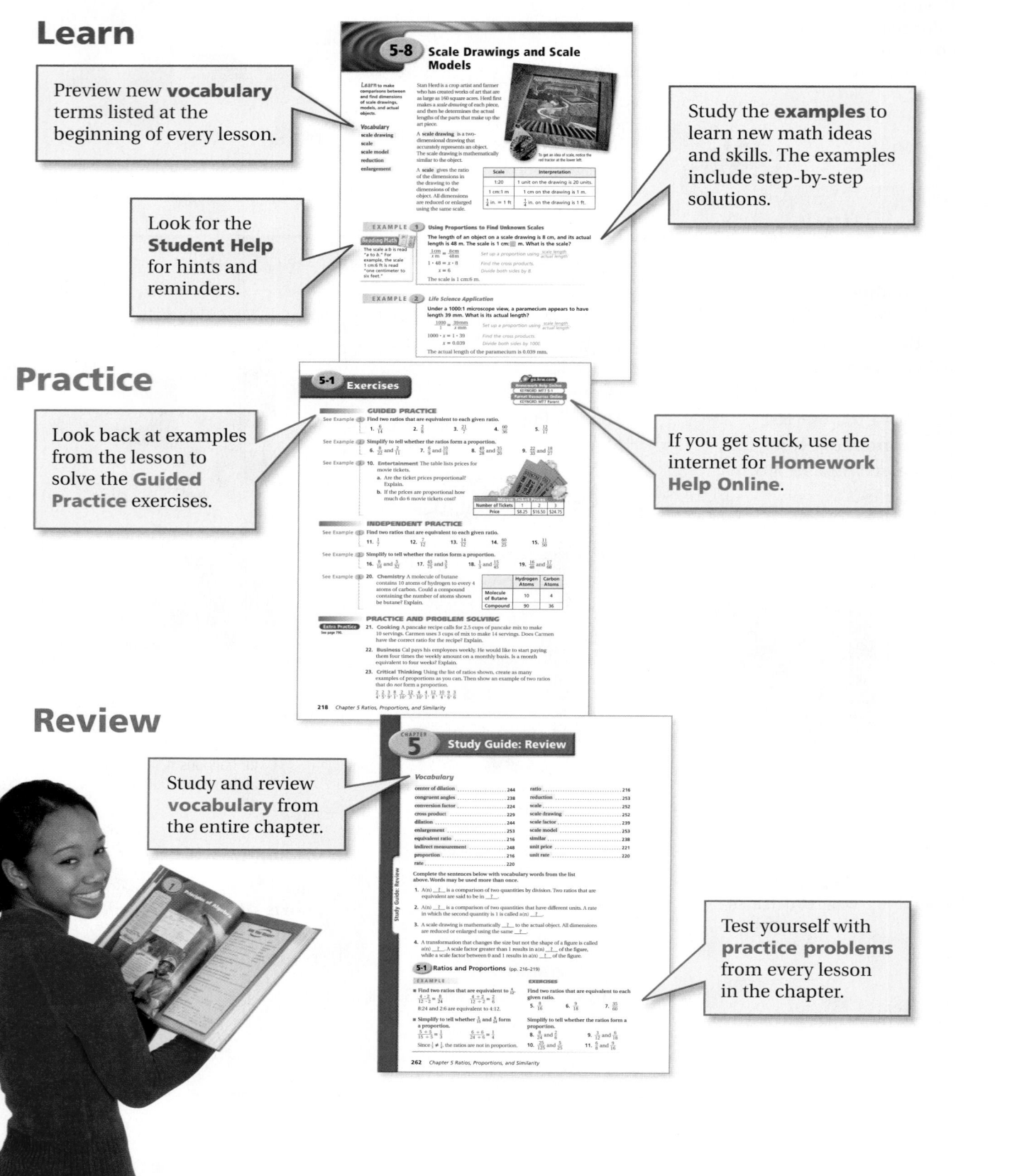

Focus on Problem Solving

The Problem Solving Plan

In order to be a good problem solver, you need to use a good problem-solving plan. The plan used in this book is detailed below. If you have another plan that you like to use, you can use it as well.

UNDERSTAND the Problem

■ **What are you asked to find?**	Restate the question in your own words.
■ **What information is given?**	Identify the important facts in the problem.
■ **What information do you need?**	Determine which facts are needed to answer the question.
■ **Is all the information given?**	Determine whether all the facts are given.
■ **Is there any information given**	Determine which facts, if any, are that you will not use? unnecessary to solve the problem.

Make a PLAN

■ **Have you ever solved a similar problem?**	Think about other problems like this that you successfully solved.
■ **What strategy or strategies can you use?**	Determine a strategy that you can use and how you will use it.

SOLVE

■ **Follow your plan.**	Show the steps in your solution. Write your answer as a complete sentence.

LOOK BACK

■ **Have you answered the question?**	Be sure that you answered the question that is being asked.
■ **Is your answer reasonable?**	Your answer should make sense in the context of the problem.
■ **Is there another strategy you could use?**	Solving the problem using another strategy is a good way to check your work.
■ **Did you learn anything that could help you solve similar problems in the future?**	Try to remember the problems you have solved and the strategies you used to solve them.

CHAPTER

1

Principles of Algebra

Section 1A	
Expressions and Integers	
1-1	Variables and Expressions
1-2	Algebraic Expressions
1-3	Integers and Absolute Value
1-4	Adding Integers
1-5	Subtracting Integers
1-6	Multiplying and Dividing Integers

Section 1B	
Equations and Inequalities	
1-7	Hands-On Lab Model Solving Equations
1-7	Solving Equations by Adding or Subtraction
1-8	Solving Equations by Multiplying or Dividing
1-9	Introduction to Inequalities

Pacing Guide for 45-Minute Classes

Chapter 1			Countdown to Testing Weeks ❶, ❷	
DAY 1	**DAY 2**	**DAY 3**	**DAY 4**	**DAY 5**
1-1 Lesson	1-2 Lesson	1-3 Lesson	1-4 Lesson	1-5 Lesson
DAY 6	**DAY 7**	**DAY 8**	**DAY 9**	**DAY 10**
1-6 Lesson	Ready to Go On? Focus on Problem Solving 1-7 Hands-On Lab	1-7 Hands-On Lab 1-7 Lesson	1-7 Lesson 1-8 Lesson	1-8 Lesson 1-9 Lesson
DAY 11	**DAY 12**	**DAY 13**		
1-9 Lesson Ready to Go On? Multi-Step Test Prep	Chapter 1 Review	Chapter 1 Test		

Pacing Guide for 90-Minute Classes

Chapter 1				
DAY 1	**DAY 2**	**DAY 3**	**DAY 4**	**DAY 5**
1-1 Lesson 1-2 Lesson	1-3 Lesson 1-4 Lesson	1-5 Lesson 1-6 Lesson	Ready to Go On? Focus on Problem Solving 1-7 Hands-On Lab 1-7 Lesson	1-7 Lesson 1-8 Lesson 1-9 Lesson
DAY 6	**DAY 7**			
1-9 Lesson Ready to Go On? Multi-Step Test Prep Chapter 1 Review	Chapter 1 Test			

ONGOING ASSESSMENT and INTERVENTION

DIAGNOSE	PRESCRIBE

Assess Prior Knowledge

Before Chapter 1

Diagnose readiness for the chapter.
Are You Ready? SE p. 3

Prescribe intervention.
Are You Ready? Intervention Skills 5, 34, 51, 54, 57

Formative Assessment

Before Every Lesson

Diagnose readiness for the lesson.
Warm Up TE, every lesson

Prescribe intervention.
Skills Bank SE pp. 820–834
Reteach CRB, Chapter 1

During Every Lesson

Diagnose understanding of lesson concepts.
Think and Discuss SE, every lesson
Write About It SE, lesson exercises
Journal TE, lesson exercises

Prescribe intervention.
Questioning Strategies Chapter 1
Reading Strategies CRB, every lesson
Success for ELL pp. 1–18

After Every Lesson

Diagnose mastery of lesson concepts.
Lesson Quiz TE, every lesson
Test Prep SE, every lesson
Test and Practice Generator

Prescribe intervention.
Reteach CRB, every lesson
Problem Solving CRB, every lesson
Test Prep Doctor TE, lesson exercises
Homework Help Online

Before Chapter 1 Testing

Diagnose mastery of concepts in the chapter.
Ready to Go On? SE pp. 30, 48
Focus on Problem Solving SE p. 31
Multi-Step Test Prep SE p. 49
Section Quizzes AR pp. 5–6
Test and Practice Generator

Prescribe intervention.
Ready to Go On? Intervention Chapter 1
Scaffolding Questions TE p. 49

Before High Stakes Testing

Diagnose mastery of benchmark concepts.
Test Tackler SE pp. 56–57
Standardized Test Prep SE pp. 58–59
State Test Prep CD-ROM

Prescribe intervention.
State Test Prep Workbook pp. 00–00

Summative Assessment

After Chapter 1

Check mastery of chapter concepts.
Multiple-Choice Tests (Forms A, B, C)
Free-Response Tests (Forms A, B, C)
Performance Assessment AR pp. 7–20
Test and Practice Generator
Check mastery of benchmark concepts.
AYP State Tests

Prescribe intervention.
Reteach CRB, every lesson
Lesson Tutorial Videos Chapter 1

Prescribe intervention.
State Test Prep Workbook

KEY: **SE** = *Student Edition* **TE** = *Teacher's Edition* **CRB** = *Chapter Resource Book* **AR** = *Assessment Resources* Available online Available on CD-ROM **2B**

CHAPTER
1

Supporting the Teacher

Chapter 1 Resource Book

Practice A, B, C
pp. 3–5, 11–13, 19–21, 27–29, 35–37, 43–45, 51–53, 59–61, 67–69

Reading Strategies ELL
pp. 9, 17, 25, 33, 41, 49, 57, 65, 73

Puzzles, Twisters, and Teasers
pp. 10, 18, 26, 34, 42, 50, 58, 66, 74

Reteach
pp. 6, 14, 22, 30, 38, 46, 54, 62, 70

Problem Solving
pp. 8, 16, 24, 32, 40, 48, 56, 64, 72

Challenge
pp. 7, 15, 23, 31, 39, 47, 55, 63, 71

Parent Letter pp. 1–2

Transparencies

Lesson Transparencies, Volume 1 .... Chapter 1
• Teaching Tools
• Warm Ups
• Problem of the Day
• Teaching Transparencies
• Lesson Quizzes

Know-It Notebook .... Chapter 1
• Additional Examples   • Chapter Review
• Vocabulary   • Big Ideas

Alternate Openers: Explorations .... pp. 1–9

Countdown to Testing .... pp. 1–4

Teacher Tools

Power Presentations®
Complete PowerPoint® presentations for Chapter 1 lessons

Lesson Tutorial Videos® SPANISH
Holt authors Ed Burger and Freddie Renfro present tutorials to support the Chapter 1 lessons.

One-Stop Planner® SPANISH
Easy access to all Chapter 1 resources and assessments, as well as software for lesson planning, test generation, and puzzle creation

IDEA Works!®
Key Chapter 1 resources and assessments modified to address special learning needs

Lesson Plans ....pp. 1–9

Questioning Strategies .... Chapter 1

Solutions Key .... Chapter 1

Interdisciplinary Posters and Worksheets .... Chapter 1

TechKeys    **Lab Resources**

Project Teacher Support   **Parent Resources**

Workbooks

Homework and Practice Workbook SPANISH
Teacher's Guide ....pp. 1–5

Know-It Notebook
Teacher's Guide.. Chapter 1

Problem Solving Workbook SPANISH
Teacher's Guide..pp. 1–5

State Test Prep
Teacher's Guide

Technology Highlights for the Teacher

Power Presentations
Dynamic presentations to engage students. Complete PowerPoint® presentations for every lesson in Chapter 1.

One-Stop Planner SPANISH
Easy access to Chapter 1 resources and assessments. Includes lesson-planning, test-generation, and puzzle-creation software.

Premier Online Edition SPANISH
Chapter 1 includes Tutorial Videos, Lesson Activities, Lesson Quizzes, Homework Help, and Chapter Project.

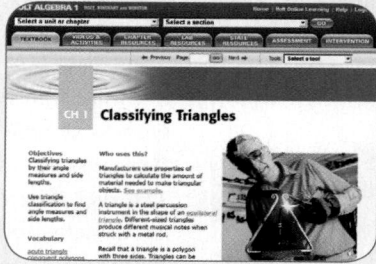

KEY: **SE** = Student Edition   **TE** = Teacher's Edition   English Language Learners   Spanish version available   Available on CD-ROM    Available online

2C   Chapter 1

Reaching All Learners

Resources for All Learners

Hands-On Lab Activities .... Chapter 1

Technology Lab Activities .... Chapter 1

Homework and Practice Workbook SPANISH ....pp. 1–9

Know-It Notebook .... Chapter 1

Problem Solving Workbook SPANISH ....pp. 1–9

DEVELOPING LEARNERS

Practice A .... CRB, every lesson

Reteach .... CRB, every lesson

Inclusion ....TE pp. 19, 40

Questioning Strategies .... Chapter 1

Modified Chapter 1 Resources .... *IDEA Works!*

Homework Help Online

ON-LEVEL LEARNERS

Practice B .... CRB, every lesson

Puzzles, Twisters, and Teasers .... CRB, every lesson

Cognitive Strategies ....TE p. 45

Cooperative Learning ....TE pp. 7, 35

ADVANCED LEARNERS

Practice C .... CRB, every lesson

Challenge .... CRB, every lesson

Extension ....TE pp. 5, 49, 50, 51

Critical Thinking ....TE pp. 23, 27

English Language Learners

Are You Ready? Vocabulary .... SE p. 3

Vocabulary Connections .... SE p. 4

Lesson Vocabulary ....SE, every lesson

Vocabulary Review .... SE p. 52

English Language Learners ....TE pp. 6, 10, 15

Reading Strategies ....CRB, every lesson

Success for English Language Learners....................pp. 1–18

Multilingual Glossary

Reaching All Learners Through...

Inclusion ....TE pp. 19, 40

Visual Cues ....TE p. 15

Kinesthetic Experience ....TE pp. 11, 45

Concrete Manipulatives ....TE p. 19

Cognitive Strategies ....TE p. 45

Cooperative Learning ....TE pp. 7, 35

Graphic Organizers ....TE p. 15

Critical Thinking ....TE pp. 23, 27

Test Prep Doctor.............TE pp. 9, 13, 17, 21, 25, 29, 38, 43, 47, 56, 58

Common Error Alerts ....TE pp. 15, 35, 40, 45

Scaffolding Questions ....TE pp. 49

Technology Highlights for Reaching All Learners

Lesson Tutorial Videos SPANISH

Starring Holt authors Ed Burger and Freddie Renfro! Live tutorials to support every lesson in Chapter 1.

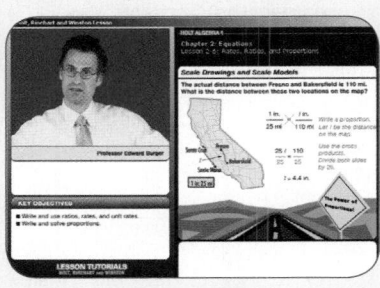

Multilingual Glossary

Searchable glossary includes definitions in English, Spanish, Vietnamese, Chinese, Hmong, Korean, and 4 other languages.

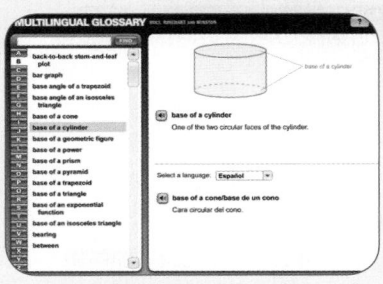

Online Interactivities

Interactive tutorials provide visually engaging alternative opportunities to learn concepts and master skills.

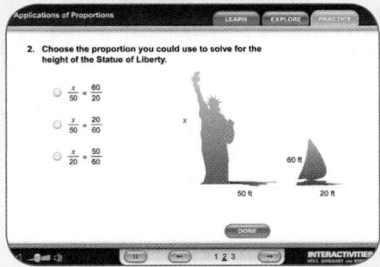

KEY: **SE** = *Student Edition*   **TE** = *Teacher's Edition*   **CRB** = *Chapter Resource Book*   SPANISH Spanish version available   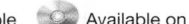 Available on CD-ROM    Available online

CHAPTER
1

Ongoing Assessment

Assessing Prior Knowledge

Determine whether students have the prerequisite concepts and skills for success in Chapter 1.

Are You Ready? SPANISH .... SE p. 3

Warm Up .... TE, every lesson

Test Preparation

Provide review and practice for Chapter 1 and standardized tests.

Multi-Step Test Prep .... SE p. 49

Study Guide: Review .... SE p. 52–54

Test Tackler .... SE p. 56–57

Standardized Test Prep .... SE p. 58–59

Countdown to Testing Transparencies .... pp. 1–4

State Test Prep Workbook

State Test Prep CD-ROM

IDEA Works!

Alternative Assessment

Assess students' understanding of Chapter 1 concepts and combined problem-solving skills.

Chapter 1 Project .... SE p. 2

Performance Assessment SPANISH .... AR pp. 19–20

Portfolio Assessment SPANISH .... AR p. xxxiv

Daily Assessment

Provide formative assessment for each day of Chapter 1.

Questioning Strategies .... Chapter 1

Think and Discuss .... SE, every lesson

Write About It .... SE, lesson exercises

Journal .... TE, lesson exercises

Lesson Quiz .... TE, every lesson

Modified Lesson Quizzes .... *IDEA Works!*

Weekly Assessment

Provide formative assessment for each week of Chapter 1.

Focus on Problem Solving .... SE p. 31

Multi-Step Test Prep .... SE p. 49

Ready to Go On? SPANISH .... SE pp. 30, 48

Cumulative Assessment .... SE pp. 58–59

Test and Practice Generator SPANISH .... *One-Stop Planner*

Formal Assessment

Provide summative assessment of Chapter 1 mastery.

Section Quizzes SPANISH .... AR pp. 5–6

Chapter 1 Test .... SE p. 55

Chapter Test (Levels A, B, C) SPANISH .... AR pp. 7–18
• Multiple-Choice • Free-Response

Cumulative Test SPANISH .... AR pp. 21–24

Test and Practice Generator SPANISH .... *One-Stop Planner*

Modified Chapter 1 Test .... *IDEA Works!*

Technology Highlights for the Teacher

Are You Ready? SPANISH
Automatically assess readiness and prescribe intervention for Chapter 1 prerequisite skills.

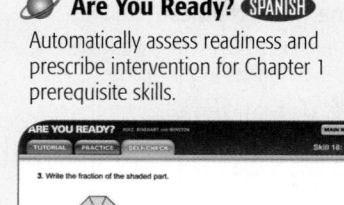
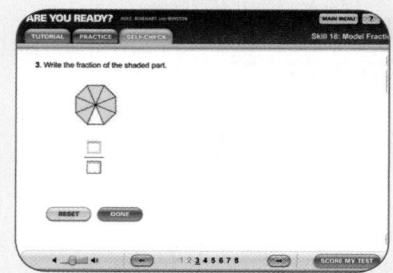

Ready to Go On? SPANISH
Automatically assess understanding of and prescribe intervention for Sections 1A and 1B.

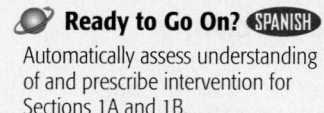
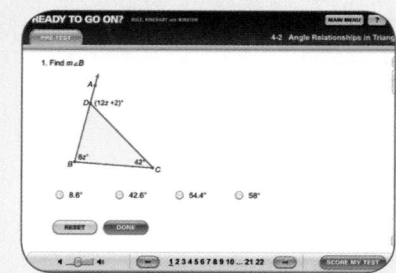

Test and Practice Generator SPANISH
Use Chapter 1 problem banks to create assessments and worksheets to print out or deliver online. Includes dynamic problems.

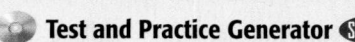
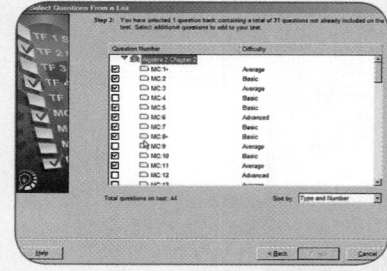

KEY: **SE** = *Student Edition* **TE** = *Teacher's Edition* **AR** = *Assessment Resources* SPANISH Spanish version available Available on CD-ROM 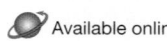 Available online

CHAPTER
1

Formal Assessment

Three levels (A, B, C) of multiple-choice and free-response chapter tests are available in the *Assessment Resources.*

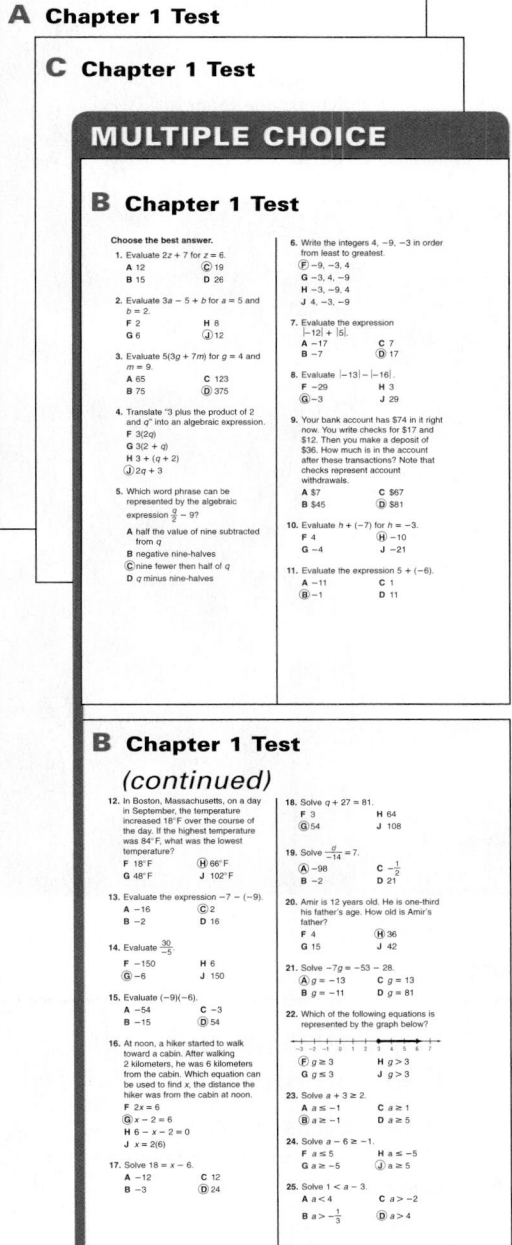

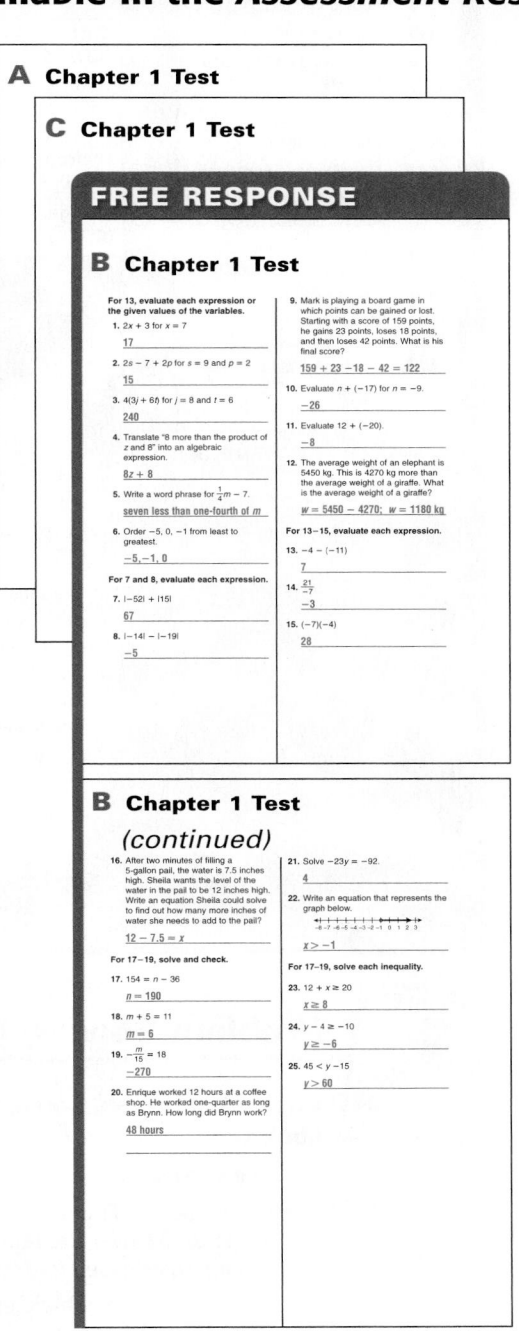

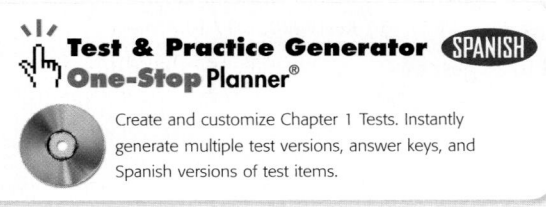

Test & Practice Generator SPANISH
One-Stop Planner®

Create and customize Chapter 1 Tests. Instantly generate multiple test versions, answer keys, and Spanish versions of test items.

CHAPTER 1 Principles of Algebra

Why Learn This?

Tell students that fire fighting is an example of a field in which different variables combine to create unique situations. A fire in which plastic is burning creates a different situation for the firefighter than one in which a refrigerant is burning. Firefighters, as well as those who make their equipment, must take into account many factors when determining the best method of extinguishing the fire and protecting the people around the fire.

Using Data

To begin the study of this chapter, have students:

- Identify whether hydrogen chloride is toxic at a concentration of 40 ppm. No, it is toxic at 50 ppm or more.

- Identify which two gases have the same danger level. Hydrogen chloride and hydrogen cyanide have the same danger level.

- Compare the danger level of HCl to that of $COCl_2$. The danger level of HCl is 25 times the danger level of $COCl_2$.

MULTI-STEP TEST PREP On page 49, students use addition, subtraction, multiplication, and division of integers to model scores in a basketball game.

1A Expressions and Integers
1-1 Variables and Expressions
1-2 Algebraic Expressions
1-3 Integers and Absolute Value
1-4 Adding Integers
1-5 Subtracting Integers
1-6 Multiplying and Dividing Integers

1B Equations and Inequalities
LAB Model Solving Equations
1-7 Solving Equations by Adding or Subtracting
1-8 Solving Equations by Multiplying or Dividing
1-9 Introduction to Inequalities

MULTI-STEP TEST PREP

go.hrw.com
Chapter Project Online
KEYWORD: MT7 Ch1

Toxic Gases Released by Fires		
Gas	Danger Level (ppm)	Source
Carbon monoxide (CO)	1200	Incomplete burning
Hydrogen chloride (HCl)	50	Plastics
Hydrogen cyanide (HCN)	50	Wool, nylon, polyurethane foam, rubber, paper
Phosgene ($COCl_2$)	2	Refrigerants

Career Firefighter

A firefighter approaching a fire should be aware of ventilation, space, what is burning, and what could be ignited. Oxygen, fuel, heat, and chemical reactions are at the core of a fire, but the amounts and materials differ.

The table above lists some of the toxic gases that firefighters frequently encounter.

Problem Solving Project

Understand, Plan, Solve, and Look Back

Have students:

- Complete the Firefighter worksheet to discover the relationships among toxic gases.

- Determine an algebraic expression that relates phosgene, carbon monoxide, hydrogen chloride, and hydrogen cyanide.

- Create a graph comparing the danger levels of the gases.

- Research the effects of toxic gases on the human body.

Physical Science Connection

Project Resources

All project resources for teachers and students are provided online.

Materials:

- Firefighter worksheet

go.hrw.com
Project Teacher Support
KEYWORD: MT7 PSProject1

Are You Ready?

✓ Vocabulary

Choose the best term from the list to complete each sentence.

addition

Associative Property

Commutative Property

division

multiplication

opposite operation

subtraction

1. __?__ is the __?__ of addition. subtraction; opposite operation
2. The expressions $3 \cdot 4$ and $4 \cdot 3$ are equal by the __?__. Commutative Property
3. The expressions $1 + (2 + 3)$ and $(1 + 2) + 3$ are equal by the __?__. Associative Property
4. Multiplication and __?__ are opposite operations. division
5. __?__ and __?__ are commutative. addition; multiplication

Complete these exercises to review skills you will need for this chapter.

✓ Whole Number Operations

Simplify each expression.

6. $8 + 116 + 43$ **167**
7. $2431 - 187$ **2244**
8. $204 \cdot 38$ **7752**
9. $6447 \div 21$ **307**

✓ Compare and Order Whole Numbers

Order each sequence of numbers from least to greatest.

10. 1050; 11,500; 105; 150
    105; 150; 1050; 11,500
11. 503; 53; 5300; 5030
    53; 503; 5030; 5300
12. 44,400; 40,040; 40,400; 44,040
    40,040; 40,400; 44,040; 44,400

✓ Inverse Operations

Rewrite each expression using the inverse operation.

13. $72 + 18 = 90$
    $90 - 18 = 72$
14. $12 \cdot 9 = 108$
    $108 \div 9 = 12$
15. $100 - 34 = 66$
    $66 + 34 = 100$
16. $56 \div 8 = 7$
    $7 \cdot 8 = 56$

✓ Order of Operations

Simplify each expression.

17. $2 + 3 \cdot 4$ **14**
18. $50 - 2 \cdot 5$ **40**
19. $6 \cdot 3 \cdot 3 - 3$ **51**
20. $(5 + 2)(5 - 2)$ **21**
21. $5 - 6 \div 2$ **2**
22. $16 \div 4 + 2 \cdot 3$ **10**
23. $(8 - 3)(8 + 3)$ **55**
24. $12 \div 3 \div 2 + 5$ **7**

✓ Evaluate Expressions

Determine whether the given expressions are equal.

25. $(4 \cdot 7) \cdot 2$ and $4 \cdot (7 \cdot 2)$ **yes**
26. $(2 \cdot 4) \div 2$ and $2 \cdot (4 \div 2)$ **yes**
27. $2 \cdot (3 - 3)$ and $(2 \cdot 3) - 3$ **no**
28. $5 \cdot (50 - 44)$ and $5 \cdot 50 - 44$ **no**
29. $9 - (4 \cdot 2)$ and $(9 - 4) \cdot 2$ **no**
30. $2 \cdot 3 + 2 \cdot 4$ and $2 \cdot (3 + 4)$ **yes**
31. $(16 \div 4) + 4$ and $16 \div (4 + 4)$ **no**
32. $5 + (2 \cdot 3)$ and $(5 + 2) \cdot 3$ **no**

Organizer

Objective: Help students organize the new concepts they will learn in Chapter 1.

 Online Edition
Multilingual Glossary

Resources

PuzzlePro®
One-Stop Planner®

 Multilingual Glossary Online
go.hrw.com
KEYWORD: MT7 Glossary

Possible answers to *Vocabulary Connections*

1. In math, a constant is a fixed—though sometimes unspecified—value.

2. The values of the expressions on either side of the equals sign are the same.

3. An inequality compares quantities that are not equal to each other.

4. A variable often represents an unknown quantity. Therefore, a variable's value can change from context to context.

Where You've Been

Previously, you

- simplified numerical expressions involving order of operations.

- compared and ordered integers and positive rational numbers.

- used concrete models to solve equations.

In This Chapter

You will study

- using an algebraic expression to find any term in a sequence.

- comparing and ordering rational numbers in various forms, including integers.

- estimating and finding solutions to application problems using algebraic equations.

- finding the absolute value of a number.

Where You're Going

You can use the skills learned in this chapter

- to find differences between extreme temperatures.

- to balance a checkbook.

- to solve a formula for a variable.

- to solve complex equations in later math courses.

Key Vocabulary/Vocabulario

absolute value	valor absoluto
constant	constante
equation	ecuación
inequality	desigualdad
integer	entero
inverse operation	operacione inversa
opposite	opuesto
variable	variable

Vocabulary Connections

To become familiar with some of the vocabulary terms in the chapter, consider the following. You may refer to the chapter, the glossary, or a dictionary if you like.

1. The word *constant* means "unchanging." What do you think a **constant** is in math?

2. The word **equation** looks like the word *equal*, which means "having the same value." How do you think this meaning applies to an equation?

3. The word **inequality** begins with the prefix *in-*, which means "not," and has the same root as the word *equation*. Together, what do you think the prefix and root mean?

4. The word *vary*, which is the root of **variable**, means "to change." How do you think this applies to math?

 **Reading and Writing Math**

Reading Strategy: Use Your Book for Success

Understanding how your textbook is organized will help you locate and use helpful information.

As you read through an example problem, pay attention to the **margin notes**, such as Helpful Hints, Reading Math notes, and Caution notes. These notes will help you understand concepts and avoid common mistakes.

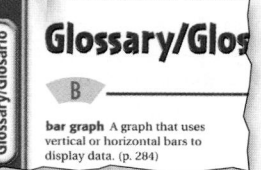 **Reading Math**
Read -4^3 as "-4 to the 3rd power or -4 cubed".

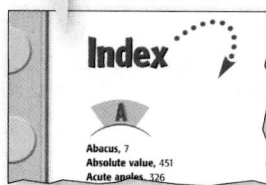 **Writing Math**
A repeating decimal can be written with a bar over the digits

 **Helpful Hint**
In Example 1A, parentheses are not needed because

Caution!
An open circle means that the corresponding value

The **glossary** is found in the back of your textbook. Use it to find definitions and examples of unfamiliar words or properties.

The **index** is located at the end of your textbook. Use it to find the page where a particular concept is taught.

The **Skills Bank** is found in the back of your textbook. These pages review concepts from previous math courses.

Glossary/Glos

B

bar graph A graph that uses vertical or horizontal bars to display data. (p. 284)

Index

A

Abacus, 7
Absolute value, 451
Acute angles, 326

Skills Bank

Place Value—H
Hundred-thousa

You can use a place-value ch

 **Try This**

Use your textbook for the following problems.

1. Use the glossary to find the definition of *supplementary angles*.
2. Where can you review factors and multiples?
3. Use the Problem Solving Handbook to list three different strategies for solving problems.
4. Use the index to find the page numbers where *algebraic expressions*, *mean*, and *volume of prisms* are explained.

Organizer

Objective: Help students apply strategies to understand and retain key concepts.

 Online Edition

Resources

 Chapter 1 Resource Book
Reading Strategies

Reading Strategy:
Use Your Book for Success

Discuss When students are aware of the various components of their book, and how to use them, they are able to become more independent learners.

Extend As students work through Chapter 1, have them answer their own questions by discussing where they might find the answer in their book. Have students find the answer and share with the class.

Have students discuss other resources they might use to find answers to math questions. Answers may include Internet sites and dictionaries.

Answers to *Try This*

1. Two angles whose measures have a sum of 180°
2. Skills Bank p. 822
3. Possible answer: draw a diagram, make a model, work backward
4. pp. 6, 472, and 413

Expressions and Integers

One-Minute Section Planner

Lesson	Materials	MiC and Lab Resources
Lesson 1-1 Variables and Expressions • Evaluate algebraic expressions. ☑ SAT-10 ☑ ITBS ☑ CTBS ☑ NAEP	Index cards	**MiC:** *Algebra Rules* pp. 25–29
Lesson 1-2 Algebraic Expressions • Translate between algebraic expressions and word phrases. ☑ SAT-10 ☑ ITBS ☑ CTBS ☑ NAEP	Index cards	**MiC:** *Patterns and Figures* pp. 1–7, 10–17 **MiC:** *Ups and Downs* pp. 17–19 **MiC:** *Algebra Rules* pp. 1–9
Lesson 1-3 Integers and Absolute Value • Compare and order integers and evaluate expressions containing absolute values. ☑ SAT-10 ☑ ITBS ☑ CTBS ☑ NAEP		**MiC:** *Revisiting Numbers* pp. 45–46
Lesson 1-4 Adding Integers • Add integers. ☑ SAT-10 ☑ ITBS ☑ CTBS ☑ NAEP	Integer chips (MK)	**MiC:** *Algebra Rules* pp. 3–8 *Hands-On Lab Activities* 1-4
Lesson 1-5 Subtracting Integers • Subtract integers. ☑ SAT-10 ☑ ITBS ☑ CTBS ☑ NAEP	Number line transparency	**MiC:** *Algebra Rules* pp. 3–8
Lesson 1-6 Multiplying and Dividing Integers • Multiply and divide integers. ☑ SAT-10 ☑ ITBS ☑ CTBS ☑ NAEP		**MiC:** *Algebra Rules* pp. 8–9 **MiC:** *Revisiting Numbers* pp. 37–39 *Technology Lab Activites* 1-6

MK = *Manipulatives Kit*

Mathematics in Context

The units *Algebra Rules, Patterns and Figures, Ups and Downs,* and *Revisiting Numbers* from the *Mathematics in Context* © 2006 series can be used with Section 1A. See Section Planner above for suggestions for integrating *MiC* with *Holt Mathematics.*

Section Overview

Writing and Evaluating Algebraic Expressions

Lessons 1-1, 1-2

Why? Formulas are written using algebraic expressions that show relationships between quantities. When you evaluate these algebraic expressions, you get a value for the formula.

> The **perimeter** of a rectangle is the **sum** of **twice the length** and **twice the width**
> $P = 2l + 2w$

Find the perimeter of a rectangle with length 3 inches and width 4 inches.

$P = 2l + 2w$

$\quad = 2(3) + 2(4)$

$\quad = 6 + 8$

$\quad = 14$

The perimeter is 14 inches.

> To **evaluate** an algebraic expression, **substitute** a given number for the variable, and find the value of the resulting numerical expression.

Integers and Absolute Value

Lesson 1-3

Why? Many real-world situations involve integers and absolute value.

> The **integers** are the set of whole numbers and their **opposites**

To order the integers -12, 14, -28, 77, 0, 51, and -79 from least to greatest, consider their relative positions on a number line.

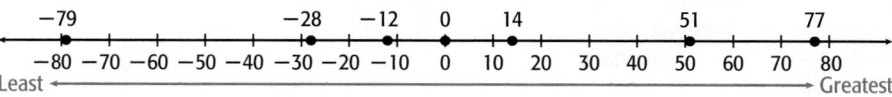

> The **absolute value** of an integer is the integer's distance from zero on a number line.

The numbers written from least to greatest are -79, -28, -12, 0, 14, 51, and 77.

Both 4 and -4 are 4 units from 0.

$|4| = 4$ and $|-4| = 4$

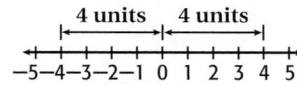

Integer Operations

Lessons 1-4, 1-5, 1-6

Why? To evaluate expressions, we need to be able to operate with integers.

Adding Integers		Subtracting Integers
If the signs are the same . . .	*If the signs are different . . .*	To subtract an integer, add its opposite.
Add the absolute values. The sign for the sum will be the same as the sign of the integers you are adding. $5 + 2 = 7$ $-5 + (-2) = -7$	Subtract the absolute values. The sign for the difference will be the same as that of the integer with the larger absolute value. $5 + (-2) = 3$ $-5 + 2 = -3$	$5 - 2 = 5 + (-2) = 3$ $5 - (-2) = 5 + 2 = 7$

Multiplying and Dividing Integers			
If the signs are the same . . .		*If the signs are different . . .*	
The sign of the product or quotient will be positive.		The sign of the product or quotient will be negative.	
$6(2) = 12$	$\frac{6}{2} = 3$	$6(-2) = -12$	$\frac{6}{-2} = -3$
$-6(-2) = 12$	$\frac{-6}{2} = 3$	$-6(2) = -12$	$\frac{-6}{2} = -3$

6B

Objective: Students evaluate algebraic expressions.

 Online Edition
Tutorial Videos, Interactivities

Countdown to Testing Week 1

Power Presentations
with PowerPoint®

Warm Up
Evaluate.

1. $21 - 2(3)$ 15

2. $4 + 3 \cdot 9$ 31

3. $2(9) + (3)$ 21

4. $6(1.4) + 12$ 20.4

5. $7(2.9) - 5$ 15.3

Problem of the Day
Miss Smith obtained the prices below from the landscape company. She plans to buy five birch, two elm, one dogwood, and two oak trees. The landscape company will charge her $15 to plant each tree. How much will it cost? **$337.90**

Trees	Price	Trees	Price
Maple	$22.99	Dogwood	$23.99
Elm	$16.99	Crab apple	$26.99
Oak	$19.99	Birch	$17.99

Also available on transparency

State Resources

go.hrw.com
State Resources Online
KEYWORD: MT7 Resources

Learn to evaluate algebraic expressions.

Vocabulary
variable
coefficient
algebraic expression
constant
evaluate
substitute

Adult giant pandas in the wild spend almost 12 hours each day feeding. On average, an adult panda eats about 30 pounds of food each day.

Let n be the number of adult pandas in the wild. You can approximate the total number of pounds of food they eat in one day using this expression:

Coefficient   Variable

There are about 1500 giant pandas that live in the wild.

A **variable** is a letter that represents a value that can change or vary. The **coefficient** is the number multiplied by the variable. An **algebraic expression** has one or more variables.

In the algebraic expression $x + 6$, the number 6 is a **constant** because it does not change. To **evaluate** an algebraic expression, **substitute** a given number for the variable, and find the value of the resulting numerical expression.

EXAMPLE 1 **Evaluating Algebraic Expressions with One Variable**

Evaluate each expression for the given value of the variable.

Remember!
Order of Operations
PEMDAS:
1. Parentheses
2. Exponents
3. Multiply and Divide from left to right.
4. Add and Subtract from left to right.

A $x + 5$ for $x = 11$

$11 + 5$ *Substitute 11 for x.*

16 *Add.*

B $2a + 3$ for $a = 4$

$2(4) + 3$ *Substitute 4 for a.*

$8 + 3$ *Multiply.*

11 *Add.*

C $4(3 + n) - 2$ for $n = 0, 1, 2$

n	Substitute	Parentheses	Multiply	Subtract
0	$4(3 + 0) - 2$	$4(3) - 2$	$12 - 2$	10
1	$4(3 + 1) - 2$	$4(4) - 2$	$16 - 2$	14
2	$4(3 + 2) - 2$	$4(5) - 2$	$20 - 2$	18

---

1 **Introduce**
Alternate Opener

EXPLORATION

1-1 **Variables and Expressions**

Catherine's dance team is planning a spring trip to the coast. Catherine is saving money in a bank account to pay for the trip. Her parents started her account with $100. She sells Christmas plants and adds $2.50 to her account for each plant she sells.

How much will be in her account if she sells 50 plants?

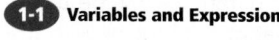
initial amount   Price × number of plants

$100 + 2.5n$

Evaluate the expression $100 + 2.5n$ by substituting 50 for n.

$100 + 2.5(50)$
$100 + 125$
225

There will be $225.00 in Catherine's account if she sells 50 plants.

Evaluate the expression $100 + 2.5n$ for each value of n.

1. $n = 10$ $100 + 2.5(10)$

2. $n = 25$ $100 + 2.5(\ \ )$

3. $n = 75$ $100 + 2.5(\ \ )$

Think and Discuss
4. Explain what n represents.
5. Describe how you evaluated the expression for different values of n.

Motivate

Ask students for the meanings of the words *variable* and *constant* in a context such as the following: "The air temperature in the desert was quite *variable* yesterday; it was cold overnight and warm during the day. The temperature at the equator was *constant* for 24 hours." Explain that the words have the same meaning in mathematics. A constant is a value that does not change, such as the number 5, and a variable is a symbol for a quantity that is not fixed, such as *x*.

ENGLISH LANGUAGE LEARNERS

Explorations and answers are provided in *Alternate Openers: Explorations Transparencies.*

EXAMPLE 2 Evaluating Algebraic Expressions with Two Variables

Evaluate each expression for the given values of the variables.

A $5x + 2y$ for $x = 13$ and $y = 11$

$5(13) + 2(11)$	*Substitute 13 for x and 11 for y.*
$65 + 22$	*Multiply.*
87	*Add.*

B $2.5p - 4q$ for $p = 12$ and $q = 6.5$

$2.5(12) - 4(6.5)$	*Substitute 12 for p and 6.5 for q.*
$30 - 26$	*Multiply.*
4	*Subtract.*

EXAMPLE 3 Physical Science Application

If c is a temperature in degrees Celsius, then $1.8c + 32$ can be used to find the temperature in degrees Fahrenheit. Convert each temperature from degrees Celsius to degrees Fahrenheit.

A freezing point of water: 0°C

$1.8c + 32$	
$1.8(0) + 32$	*Substitute 0 for c.*
$0 + 32$	*Multiply.*
32	*Add.*
$0°C = 32°F$	

Water freezes at 32°F.

B highest recorded temperature in the United States: 57°C

$1.8c + 32$	
$1.8(57) + 32$	*Substitute 57 for c.*
$102.6 + 32$	*Multiply.*
134.6	*Add.*
$57°C = 134.6°F$	

The highest recorded temperature in the United States is 134.6°F.

Think and Discuss

1. Give an example of an expression that is algebraic and of an expression that is not algebraic.

2. Tell how to evaluate an algebraic expression for a given value.

3. Explain why you cannot find a numerical value for the expression $4x - 5y$ for $x = 3$.

Possible answers to *Think and Discuss*:

1. algebraic: $x + 1$; not algebraic: $25 + 9$

2. Substitute the given value for the variable, and then find the value of the resulting numerical expression.

3. The *y*-value is not given.

2 Teach

Guided Instruction

In this lesson, students learn to evaluate algebraic expressions. Explain that to evaluate an algebraic expression, students must replace variables with given numbers and then evaluate the resulting expression by using the order of operations.

 **Reading Math** Remind students that when there is a coefficient in front of a variable, multiplication is indicated. Therefore, when they replace the variable with a value, they need to insert parentheses. For example, the expression $3x + 4$ should be written $3(5) + 4$ if x is replaced with 5.

Reaching All Learners
Through Cooperative Learning

Have students work in pairs. Each student should write an algebraic expression on a sheet of paper, such as $3x - 1$ or $x + 5$. The students should evaluate their partner's expression when the variable is equal to 0, 1, 2, 3, 4, and 5. Have them check each other's work and compare the values to determine whether the expressions have the same value for the given value of the variable.

3 Close

Summarize

Ask the students to decide which of the following is a constant and which is a variable: your age (variable); the year in which you were born (constant).

Have the students suggest additional examples of variables and constants.

Ask the students if an algebraic expression contains one or more variables (yes).

Ask the students if they would expect to see any variables in an expression after evaluating that expression. Why or why not?

Possible answer: No; because to evaluate an algebraic expression, you must replace the variables with numbers.

Assignment Guide

If you finished Example **1** assign:
Average 1–3, 10–12, 19–23 odd, 53–67
Advanced 10–12, 21–29 odd, 52–67

If you finished Example **2** assign:
Average 1–5, 10–14, 19–45 odd, 53–67
Advanced 10–14, 48–50, 52–67

If you finished Example **3** assign:
Average 1–18, 43–47 odd, 53–67
Advanced 11–17 odd, 19–67

Homework Quick Check

Quickly check key concepts.
Exercises: 12, 14, 18, 28, 46, 48

Math Background

In Lessons 3-2 and 12-1 through 12-4, students will learn to graph linear equations. An equation of a line that is not vertical is often written in the form $y = mx + b$. In this context, the letters x and y are variables, but the letters m and b are constants. For example, if m is the constant 2 and b is the constant 3, then the equation is $y = 2x + 3$. The graph of this equation is the set of all points (x, y) that make the equation true. The letters x and y are variables because their values vary.

1-1 Exercises

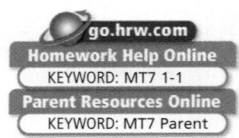
go.hrw.com
Homework Help Online
KEYWORD: MT7 1-1
Parent Resources Online
KEYWORD: MT7 Parent

GUIDED PRACTICE

See Example 1 Evaluate each expression for the given value of the variable.

1. $x + 4$ for $x = 11$ **15** **2.** $2a + 7$ for $a = 7$ **21** **3.** $2(4 + n) - 5$ for $n = 0$ **3**

See Example 2 Evaluate each expression for the given values of the variables.

4. $3x + 2y$ for $x = 8$ and $y = 10$ **44** **5.** $1.6p - 3q$ for $p = 4.5$ and $q = 1.4$ **3**

See Example 3 You can make papier-mâché paste by mixing $\frac{1}{4}$ as many cups of flour as water. How much flour do you need for each number of cups of water?

6. 12 cups **3 c** **7.** 8 cups **2 c** **8.** 7 cups $1\frac{3}{4}$ **c** **9.** 10 cups $2\frac{1}{2}$ **c**

INDEPENDENT PRACTICE

See Example 1 Evaluate each expression for the given value of the variable.

10. $x + 7$ for $x = 23$ **30** **11.** $7t + 2$ for $t = 5$ **37** **12.** $4(3 + k) - 7$ for $k = 0$ **5**

See Example 2 Evaluate each expression for the given values of the variables.

13. $4x + 7y$ for $x = 9$ and $y = 3$ **57** **14.** $4m - 2n$ for $m = 25$ and $n = 2.5$ **95**

See Example 3 If c is the number of cups, then $\frac{1}{2}c$ can be used to find the number of pints. Find the number of pints for each of the following.

15. 26 cups **13 pt** **16.** 12 cups **6 pt** **17.** 20 cups **10 pt** **18.** 34 cups **17 pt**

PRACTICE AND PROBLEM SOLVING

Extra Practice
See page 782.

Evaluate each expression for the given value of the variable.

19. $13d$ for $d = 1$ **13** **20.** $x + 4.3$ for $x = 6$ **10.3** **21.** $30 - n$ for $n = 8$ **22**

22. $5t + 5$ for $t = 1$ **10** **23.** $3a - 4$ for $a = 8$ **20** **24.** $2 + 4b$ for $b = 2.2$ **10.8**

25. $11 - 6m$ for $m = 0$ **11** **26.** $4g + 5$ for $g = 12$ **53** **27.** $x + 6.6$ for $x = 3.4$ **10**

28. $18 - 3y$ for $y = 6$ **0** **29.** $4y + 2$ for $y = 3.5$ **16** **30.** $3(z + 9)$ for $z = 6$ **45**

Evaluate each expression for $t = 0$, $x = 1.5$, $y = 6$, and $z = 23$.

31. $3z - 3y$ **51** **32.** yz **138** **33.** $4.2y - 3x$ **20.7** **34.** $1.4z - y$ **26.2**

35. $4(y - x)$ **18** **36.** $4(3 + y)$ **36** **37.** $4(2 + z) + 5$ **105** **38.** $3(y - 6) + 8$ **8**

39. $5(4 + t) - 6$ **14** **40.** $y(3 + t) - 7$ **11** **41.** $x + y + z$ **30.5** **42.** $10x + z - y$ **32**

43. $2y + 6(x + t)$ **21** **44.** $4(z - 5t) + 3$ **95** **45.** $8txz$ **0** **46.** $2z - 3xy$ **19**

47. Finance A bank charges interest on money it loans. Interest is sometimes a fixed amount of the loan. The expression $a(1 + i)$ gives the total amount due for a loan of a dollars with interest rate i. Find the amount due for a loan of $100 with an interest rate of 0.1. **$110**

RETEACH 1-1

LESSON 1-1 Reteach
Variables and Expressions

An **algebraic expression** uses at least one letter, or **variable**, which represents a value that can change.

A number that multiplies a variable is its **coefficient**. A **constant** is a specific number, whose value does not change.

To **evaluate** an algebraic expression, **substitute** a given number for a variable, and find the value of the resulting numerical expression.

Algebraic Expression
$$4x + 7$$
Coefficient   Variable   Constant

Follow the order of operations:
1. Parentheses
2. Multiply or Divide
3. Add or Subtract

Evaluate $5(m + 1) + 8n$ for $m = 10$ and $n = 2$.
$5(m + 1) + 8n$
$5(10 + 1) + 8(2)$ Substitute 10 for m and 2 for n.
$5(11) + 8(2)$ Parentheses, simplify inside.
$55 + 16$ Multiply, from left to right.
71 Add.

Complete to evaluate each expression.

1. $9 + 7z$ for $z = 3$
$9 + 7 \cdot \underline{3}$
$9 + \underline{21}$
$\underline{30}$

2. $5(q - 8)$ for $q = 17$
$5 \cdot (\underline{17} - 8)$
$5 \cdot (\underline{9})$
$\underline{45}$

3. $25 - 2x$ for $x = 8$
$25 - 2 \cdot (\underline{8})$
$25 - \underline{16}$
$\underline{9}$

4. $2(x + 6) + 4$ for $x = 9$
$2(\underline{9} + 6) + 4$
$2(\underline{15}) + 4$
$\underline{30} + 4$
$\underline{34}$

5. $42 - 3(x + 1)$ for $x = 3$
$42 - 3 \cdot (\underline{3} + 1)$
$42 - 3 \cdot (\underline{4})$
$42 - \underline{12}$
$\underline{30}$

6. $22 + 5(2z)$ for $z = 4$
$22 + 5 \cdot (2 \cdot \underline{4})$
$22 + 5 \cdot (\underline{8})$
$22 + \underline{40}$
$\underline{62}$

PRACTICE 1-1

LESSON 1-1 Practice B
Variables and Expressions

Evaluate each expression for the given value of the variable.

1. $6x + 2$ for $x = 3$ **20** **2.** $18 - a$ for $a = 13$ **5**

3. $\frac{1}{4}y$ for $y = 16$ **4** **4.** $9 - 2b$ for $b = 3$ **3**

5. $44 - 12n$ for $n = 3$ **8** **6.** $7.2 + 8k$ for $k = 2$ **23.2**

7. $20(b - 15)$ for $b = 19$ **80** **8.** $n(18 - 5)$ for $n = 4$ **52**

Evaluate each expression for the given value of the variables.

9. $2x + y$ for $x = 7$ and $y = 11$ **25** **10.** $4j - k$ for $j = 4$ and $k = 10$ **6**

11. $9a - 6b$ for $a = 6$ and $b = 2$ **42** **12.** $5s + 5t$ for $s = 15$ and $t = 12$ **135**

13. $7(n - m)$ for $m = 4$ and $n = 15$ **77** **14.** $w(14 - y)$ for $w = 8$ and $y = 5$ **72**

If q is the number of quarts of lemonade, then $\frac{1}{4}q$ can be used to find the number of cups of lemonade mix needed to make the lemonade. How much mix is needed to make each amount of lemonade?

15. 2 quarts $\frac{1}{2}$ **cup** **16.** 8 quarts **2 cups** **17.** 12 quarts **3 cups** **18.** 18 quarts $4\frac{1}{2}$ **cups**

19. If m is the number of minutes a taxi ride lasts, then $2 + 0.35m$ can be used to find the cost of a taxi ride with Bill's Taxi Company. How much will it cost for a 12-min taxi ride? **$6.20**

48. Graphic Design Rectangular shapes with a length-to-width ratio of approximately 5 to 3 are pleasing to the eye. This ratio is known as the golden ratio. A designer can use the expression $\frac{1}{3}(5w)$ to find the length of such a rectangle with a given width w. Find the length of such a rectangle with width 6 inches. **10 in.**

49. Entertainment There are 24 frames, or still shots, in one second of movie footage.

E.T. the Extra-Terrestrial (1982) has a running time of 115 minutes, or 6900 seconds.

   a. Write an expression to determine the number of frames in a movie.

   b. Using the running time of *E.T. the Extra-Terrestrial*, determine how many frames are in the movie. **165,600 frames**

50. Choose a Strategy A basketball league has 288 players and 24 teams, with an equal number of players per team. If the number of teams is reduced by 6 but the total number of players stays the same, there will be ___?___ players per team.

   (A) 6 more   (B) 4 more   (C) 4 fewer   (D) 6 fewer

51. Write About It A student says that the algebraic expression $5 + x \cdot 7$ can also be written as $5 + 7x$. Is the student correct? Explain.

52. Challenge Can the expressions $2x$ and $x + 2$ ever have the same value? If so, what must the value of x be?
Yes; when $x = 2$, both expressions have a value of 4.

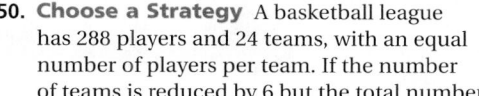

53. Multiple Choice What is the value of the expression $3x + 4$ for $x = 2$?

   (A) 4   (B) 6   (C) 9   (D) 10

54. Multiple Choice A bakery charges $7 for a dozen muffins and $2 for a loaf of bread. If a customer bought 2 dozen muffins and 4 loaves of bread, how much did she pay?

   (F) $22   (G) $38   (H) $80   (J) $98

55. Gridded Response What is the value of $7x + 9$ when $x = 2$? **23**

Identify the odd number(s) in each list of numbers. (Previous course)

56. 15, 18, 22, 34, 21, 61, 71, 100 **15, 21, 61, 71**
57. 101, 114, 122, 411, 117, 121 **101, 411, 117, 121**

58. 4, 6, 8, 16, 18, 20, 49, 81, 32 **49, 81**
59. 9, 15, 31, 47, 65, 93, 1, 3, 43 **All are odd.**

Find each sum, difference, product, or quotient. (Previous course)

60. $200 + 2$ **202**   **61.** $200 \div 2$ **100**   **62.** $200 \cdot 2$ **400**   **63.** $200 - 2$ **198**

64. $200 + 0.2$ **200.2**   **65.** $200 \div 0.2$ **1000**   **66.** $200 \cdot 0.2$ **40**   **67.** $200 - 0.2$ **199.8**

Answers

49. a. Possible answer: $24 \times 60 \times m$, where m is the run time in minutes.

51. Possible answer: The student is correct. In both expressions, x and 7 would be multiplied before adding 5.

TEST PREP DOCTOR For Exercise 53, remind students that a number and a variable written next to one another without an operation symbol imply the operation of *multiplication*. Students who answered **C** used addition; they added 3, 2, and 4, as opposed to multiplying 3 by 2, and then adding 4. Ask students to determine which terms are multiplied and which are added or subtracted in similar expressions, such as Exercise 55.

Journal

Have students write at least three examples of variables (quantities that change value) and constants (numbers that stay the same) from their everyday lives.

Power Presentations with PowerPoint®

1-1 Lesson Quiz

Evaluate each expression for the given values of the variables.

1. $6x + 9$ for $x = 3$ **27**

2. $x + 14$ for $x = 8$ **22**

3. $4x + 3y$ for $x = 2$, $y = 3$ **17**

4. $1.6x - 2.9y$ for $x = 19$, $y = 6$ **13**

5. If n is the amount of money in a savings account, then the expression $n + 0.03n$ can be used to find the amount in the account after it has earned interest for one year. Find the total in the account after one year if $500 is the initial amount. **$515**

Also available on transparency

TEST PREP and Spiral Review

CHALLENGE 1-1

LESSON 1-1 Challenge
Etaulave: Evaluate Backwards

Expression	Value for Variable	Substitution	Value of Expression
$2x + 5$	1	$2(1) + 5$	7
$2x + 5$	2	$2(2) + 5$	9
$2x + 5$	3	$2(3) + 5$	11

In the table above you use the values of the variable to evaluate the given expression. What if you are given the values of the expression and the values of the variable? How can you work backward to determine the expression?

Expression	Value for Variable	Substitution	Value of Expression
	1		5
	2		8
	3		11

Complete the following statements.

1. As the values of the variable increase by 1, the values of the expression increase ___**by 3**___.

2. Because the values of the expression depend on the values of the variables, your answer to Question 1 tells you the ___**coefficient**___ of the variable.

3. Using the coefficient and the variable x, you know that ___**3x**___ is part of the expression.

4. After each value of the variable is multiplied by ___**3**___, you still need to ___**add 2**___ to get the value of the expression.

Write the expression given the values of x and their corresponding values of the expression.

5. The values of the expression are 12, 14, 16, 18, 20 when $x = 10, 11, 12, 13$, and 14.
___**2x − 8**___

6. The values of the expression are 50, 45, 40, 35, 30 when $x = 2, 3, 4, 5$, and 6.
___**60 − 5x**___

PROBLEM SOLVING 1-1

LESSON 1-1 Problem Solving
Variables and Expressions

Write the correct answer.

1. If l is the length of a room and w is the width, then lw can be used to find the area of the room. Find the area of a room with $l = 10$ ft and $w = 15$ ft.
150 square feet

2. If l is the length of a room and w is the width, then $2l + 2w$ can be used to find the perimeter of the room. Find the perimeter of a room with $l = 12$ ft and $w = 16$ ft.
56 feet

3. Jaime earns 20% commission on her sales. If s is her total sales, then $0.2s$ can be used to find the amount she earns in commission. Find her commission if her sales are $1200.
$240

4. If p is the regular hourly rate of pay, then $1.5p$ can be used to find the overtime rate of pay. Find the overtime rate of pay if the regular hourly rate of pay is $6.00 per hour.
$9.00 per hour

Choose the letter for the best answer.

5. A plumber charges a fee of $75 per service call plus $15 per hour. If h is the number of hours the plumber works, then $75 + 15h$ can be used to find the total charges. Find the total charges if the plumber works 2.5 hours.
A $37.50
B $112.50
C $225
D $1127.50

6. Tickets to the movies cost $4 for students and $6 for adults. If s is the number of students and a is the number of adults, $4s + 6a$ can be used to find the cost of the tickets. Find the cost of the tickets for 3 students and 2 adults.
F $15
G $17
(H) $24
J $26

7. If c is the number of cricket chirps in a minute, then the expression $0.25c + 20$ can be used to estimate the temperature in degrees Farenheit. If there are 92 cricket chirps in a minute, find the temperature.
(A) 43 degrees
B 33 degrees
C 102 degrees
D 75 degrees

8. Flowers are sold in flats of 6 plants each. If f is the number of flats, then $6f$ can be used to find the number of flowers. Find the number of flowers in 18 flats.
F 3 flowers
(G) 108 flowers
H 24 flowers
J 12 flowers

Objective: Students write algebraic expressions.

 Online Edition
Tutorial Videos

 Countdown to Testing Week 1

 **Power Presentations**
with PowerPoint®

Warm Up

Evaluate each expression for the given values of the variables.

1. $9y - 13$ for $y = 4$ 23
2. $6n + 2p$ for $n = 2$ and $p = 3$ 18
3. $3x - y$ for $x = 1$ and $y = 2$ 1

Which operation symbol goes with each word?

4. Sum $+$ **5.** Product $\times$
6. Quotient $\div$ **7.** Difference $-$

Problem of the Day

Find a pair of numbers that fits the description. Their product is 221 and their sum is 30.   13, 17

Also available on transparency

Math Humor

It was impossible to know what sort of mood the equation was in; it had a variable expression.

State Resources

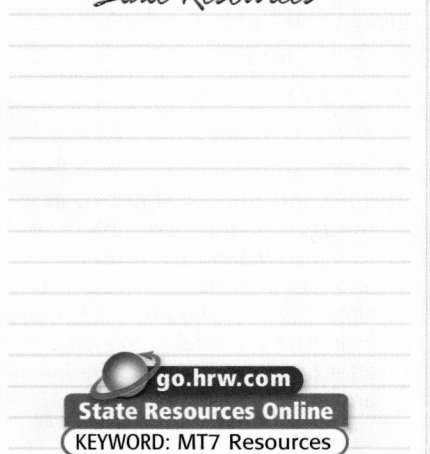

go.hrw.com
State Resources Online
KEYWORD: MT7 Resources

1-2 Algebraic Expressions

Learn to translate between algebraic expressions and word phrases.

Each 30-second block of commercial time during Super Bowl XXXIX cost an average of $2.4 million.

This information can be used to write an algebraic expression to determine how much a given number of 30-second blocks would have cost.

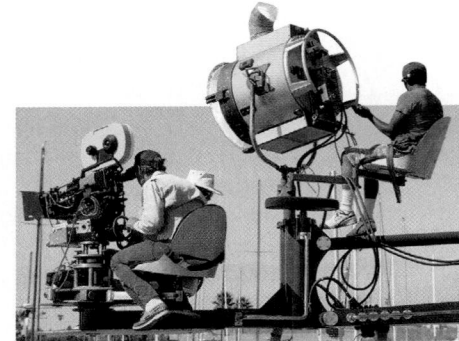

Sixty-eight different commercials aired during the 2005 Super Bowl.

	Word Phrases	Expression
+	• add 5 to a number • sum of a number and 5 • 5 more than a number	$n + 5$
−	• subtract 11 from a number • difference of a number and 11 • 11 less than a number	$x - 11$
×	• 3 multiplied by a number • product of 3 and a number	$3m$
÷	• 7 divided into a number • quotient of a number and 7	$\frac{a}{7}$ or $a \div 7$

EXAMPLE 1   **Translating Word Phrases into Math Expressions**

Write an algebraic expression for each word phrase.

A 1 more than the product of 12 and p

   1 **more than** the **product of** 12 and p

   1    $+$ $(12$ $\cdot$ $p)$

   $1 + 12p$

B 4 less than a number n divided by 2

   4 **less than** n **divided by** 2

   $(n$ $\div$ $2)$ $-$ 4   *4 is being subtracted from n ÷ 2*

   $\frac{n}{2} - 4$

Helpful Hint

In Example 1A, parentheses are not needed because multiplication is performed first by the order of operations.

---

1 Introduce

Alternate Opener

Motivate

Ask the students if any of them speak a language other than English. Ask volunteers to translate simple expressions, such as "hello" or "how are you?" into another language. Explain that in this lesson, they will learn how to "translate" words into algebraic expressions.

ENGLISH LANGUAGE LEARNERS

Explorations and answers are provided in *Alternate Openers: Explorations Transparencies.*

EXAMPLE 2 Translating Math Expressions into Word Phrases

Write a word phrase for the algebraic expression 4 − 7b.

4 − 7b

| 4 | − | 7 | · | b |

4 **minus** the **product of** 7 and b

4 minus the product of 7 and b

To solve a word problem, first interpret the action you need to perform and then choose the correct operation for that action.

EXAMPLE 3 Writing and Evaluating Expressions in Word Problems

Helpful Hint
When a word problem involves groups of equal size, use multiplication or division. Otherwise, use addition or subtraction.

A company aired its 30-second commercial n times during Super Bowl XXXIX at a cost of $2.4 million each time. Write an algebraic expression to evaluate what the cost would be if the commercial had aired 2, 3, and 4 times.

$2.4 million · n   *Combine n equal amounts of $2.4 million.*

2.4n   *In millions of dollars*

n	2.4n	Cost
2	2.4(2)	$4.8 million
3	2.4(3)	$7.2 million
4	2.4(4)	$9.6 million

Evaluate for n = 2, 3, and 4.

EXAMPLE 4 Writing a Word Problem from a Math Expression

Write a word problem that can be evaluated by the algebraic expression 14,917 + m, and evaluate the expression for m = 633.

At the beginning of the month, Benny's car had 14,917 miles on the odometer. If Benny drove m miles during the month, how many miles were on the odometer at the end of the month?

14,917 + m

14,917 + 633 = 15,550   *Substitute 633 for m.*

The car had 15,550 miles on the odometer at the end of the month.

Possible answers to *Think and Discuss*

1. plus, add; less than, minus; times, multiplied by; divided by; quotient of

2. the sum of 5 and 7 times n; 5 plus the product of 7 and n

Think and Discuss

1. **Give** two words or phrases that can be used to express each operation: addition, subtraction, multiplication, and division.

2. **Express** 5 + 7n in words in at least two different ways.

2 Teach

Guided Instruction

In this lesson, students learn to write algebraic expressions. Review the table of phrases and expressions with students (Teaching Transparency). Point out that there are several different words for each operation.

While reviewing the word problems in Examples 3 and 4, make sure students can identify the key words that determine the operation(s) that will be used to solve the problem. You may want to spend extra time to review the additional examples, as well.

Reaching All Learners
Through Kinesthetic Experience

Give each pair of students a few flash cards with a word phrase on one side and the corresponding algebraic expression on the other Lesson Transparencies. Have them place the cards, word phrase side up, between them. Students then take turns writing an algebraic expression for the word phrase. If the expression is correct, the student keeps the card. If not, the card is returned to the bottom of the deck. When the entire deck is gone, or when time is called, the student with the most cards wins.

3 Close

Summarize

Write the four operational symbols (+, −, ×, ÷) on the board, and ask students to think of as many words as they can to represent each one. Remind students that "translating" will help them solve many types of word problems.

Possible answers: addition: sum, added, more than, total, increased, plus; subtraction: difference, less than, minus, decrease, take away; multiplication: times, product, multiplied, each; division: divided, split, quotient, separated

1-2 Exercises

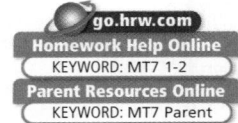
go.hrw.com
Homework Help Online
KEYWORD: MT7 1-2
Parent Resources Online
KEYWORD: MT7 Parent

Assignment Guide

If you finished Example **1** assign:
Average 1–4, 11–14, 23–31 odd, 38–48
Advanced 11–15, 22–31, 37–48

If you finished Example **2** assign:
Average 1–8, 11–19, 28–35, 38–48
Advanced 11–19, 28–35, 38–48

If you finished Example **3** assign:
Average 1–9, 11–20, 38–48
Advanced 11–20, 36–48

If you finished Example **4** assign:
Average 1–21, 38–48
Advanced 11–21, 36–48

Homework Quick Check
Quickly check key concepts.
Exercises: 12, 14, 18, 30, 34

Answers

5–8, 10, 16–21. See p. A1.

Math Background

The Egyptians had different symbols for addition and subtraction than those that are used today. The symbol for addition was two feet walking from right to left, which was the direction in which the Egyptians wrote. The symbol for subtraction was a pair of legs walking in the opposite direction, left to right.

State Resources

go.hrw.com
State Resources Online
KEYWORD: MT7 Resources

GUIDED PRACTICE

See Example **1** Write an algebraic expression for each word phrase.

1. 5 less than the product of 3 and p $\quad 3p - 5$
2. 77 more than the product of 2 and u $\quad 77 + 2u$
3. 16 more than the quotient of d and 7 $\quad 16 + \frac{d}{7}$
4. 6 minus the quotient of u and 2. $\quad 6 - \frac{u}{2}$

See Example **2** Write a word phrase for each algebraic expression.

5. $18 + 43s$ **6.** $\frac{22}{r} - 37$ **7.** $10 + \frac{y}{31}$ **8.** $29b - 93$

See Example **3** **9.** Mark is going to work for his father's pool cleaning business during the summer. Mark's father will pay him $5 for each pool he helps clean. Write an algebraic expression to evaluate how much Mark will earn if he cleans 15, 25, 35, or 45 pools. $5n$; $75, $125, $175, $225

See Example **4** **10.** Write a word problem that can be evaluated by the algebraic expression $x - 450$, and then evaluate the expression for $x = 1325$.

INDEPENDENT PRACTICE

See Example **1** Write an algebraic expression for each word phrase. $\quad 2 - 3p$

11. 1 more than the quotient of 5 and n $\quad 1 + \frac{5}{n}$
12. 2 minus the product of 3 and p.
13. 45 less than the product of 78 and j $\quad 78j - 45$
14. 4 plus the quotient of r and 5. $\quad 4 + \frac{r}{5}$
15. 14 more than the product of 59 and q $\quad 14 + 59q$

See Example **2** Write a word phrase for each algebraic expression.

16. $142 - 19t$ **17.** $16g + 12$ **18.** $14 + \frac{5}{d}$ **19.** $\frac{w}{182} - 51$

See Example **3** **20.** A community center is trying to raise $1680 to purchase exercise equipment. The center is hoping to receive equal contributions from members of the community. Write an algebraic expression to evaluate how much will be needed from each person if 10, 12, 14, or 16 people contribute.

See Example **4** **21.** Write a word problem that can be evaluated by the algebraic expression $372 + r$, and evaluate it for $r = 137$.

PRACTICE AND PROBLEM SOLVING

Extra Practice
See page 782.

Write an algebraic expression for each word phrase.

22. 6 times the sum of 4 and y $\quad 6(4 + y)$
23. half the sum of m and 5 $\quad \frac{1}{2}(m + 5)$
24. $\frac{1}{3}$ of the sum of 4 and p $\quad \frac{1}{3}(4 + p)$
25. 1 divided by the sum of 3 and g $\quad \frac{1}{3 + g}$
26. 9 more than the product of 6 and y $\quad 6y + 9$
27. 6 less than the product of 13 and y $\quad 13y - 6$
28. 2 less than m divided by 8 $\quad \frac{m}{8} - 2$
29. twice the quotient of m and 35 $\quad 2\left(\frac{m}{35}\right)$

30. $\frac{3}{4}(p - 7)$

31. $8\left(\frac{2}{3} + x\right)$
30. $\frac{3}{4}$ of the difference of p and 7
31. 8 times the sum of $\frac{2}{3}$ and x

---

32. 3 less than the product of 4 and b

33. 8 times the sum of m and 5

34. 7 divided by the difference of 8 and x

35. 17 times the quotient of 16 and w

Translate each algebraic expression into words.

32. $4b - 3$ **33.** $8(m + 5)$ **34.** $\dfrac{7}{8 - x}$ **35.** $17\left(\dfrac{16}{w}\right)$

36. At age 2, a cat or a dog is considered 24 "human" years old. Each year after age 2 is equivalent to 4 "human" years. Fill in the expression $[24 + \blacksquare(a - 2)]$ so that it represents the age of a cat or dog in human years. Copy the chart and use your expression to complete it. $24 + 4(a - 2)$; 24, 28, 32, 36, 40

Age	$24 + \blacksquare (a - 2)$	Age (human years)
2		
3		
4		
5		
6		

DO NOT WRITE IN BOOK

37. Critical Thinking Write two different algebraic expressions for the word phrase "$\frac{1}{4}$ the sum of x and 7." $\frac{1}{4}(x + 7)$ or $\frac{x + 7}{4}$

38. What's the Error? A student wrote an algebraic expression for "5 less than a number n divided by 3" as $\frac{(n - 5)}{3}$. What error did the student make?

39. Write About It Paul used addition to solve a word problem about the weekly cost of commuting by toll road for \$1.50 each day. Fran solved the same problem by multiplying. They both got the correct answer. How is this possible?

40. Challenge Write an expression for the sum of 1 and twice a number n. If you let n be any odd number, will the result always be an odd number?

TEST PREP and Spiral Review

41. Multiple Choice Which expression means "3 times the difference of y and 4"?

   (A) $3 \cdot y - 4$ (B) $3 \cdot (y + 4)$ (C) $3 \cdot (y - 4)$ (D) $3 - (y - 4)$

42. Multiple Choice Which expression represents the product of a number n and 32?

   (F) $n + 32$ (G) $n - 32$ (H) $n \times 32$ (J) $32 \div n$

43. Short Response A company prints n books at a cost of \$9 per book. Write an expression to represent the total cost of printing n books. What is the total cost if 1050 books are printed? $9n$; \$9,450

Evaluate. (Previous Course)

44. $32 + 8 \div 4$ **34**   **45.** $24 - 2 \cdot 3 \div 6 + 1$ **24**   **46.** $(20 - 8) \cdot 2 + 2$ **26**

Evaluate each expression for the given values of the variable. (Lesson 1-1)

47. $2(4 + x) - 3$ for $x = 0, 1, 2,$ and 3   **5; 7; 9; 11**   **48.** $3(8 - x) - 2$ for $x = 0, 1, 2,$ and 3
                                                          22; 19; 16; 13

CHALLENGE 1-2

Challenge
1-2 Amazing Math

Write an algebraic expression for each word phrase on the board. Evaluate each expression for $x = 2$.

Then find a path from the top row to the bottom row that gives a total of 22.

3 times x	1 less than twice x	6 more than x	x increased by 3	the quotient of twice x and 2
$3x = 6$	$2x - 1 = 3$	$x + 6 = 8$	$x + 3 = 5$	$\frac{2x}{2} = 2$
1 more than x	the product of 3 and x	x decreased by 1	half of x	twice x increased by 3
$x + 1 = 3$	$3x = 6$	$x - 1 = 1$	$\frac{x}{2} = 1$	$2x + 3 = 7$
1 less than 3 times x	the difference between 3 and x	the difference between 2 and x	the product of 4 and x	the sum of 6 and twice x
$3x - 1 = 5$	$3 - x = 1$	$2 - x = 0$	$4x = 8$	$6 + 2x = 10$
twice x	the difference between x and 1	the sum of x and 5	1 more than half of x	the product of 4 and 3 times x
$2x = 4$	$x - 1 = 1$	$x + 5 = 7$	$\frac{x}{2} + 1 = 2$	$4(3x) = 24$
x increased by 2	the quotient of x and 2	7 increased by x	the quotient of 6 and x	5 times x divided by 2
$x + 2 = 4$	$\frac{x}{2} = 1$	$7 + x = 9$	$\frac{6}{x} = 3$	$\frac{5x}{2} = 5$

PROBLEM SOLVING 1-2

Problem Solving
1-2 Algebraic Expressions

Write the correct answer.

1. Morton bought 15 new books to add to his collection of books b. Write an algebraic expression to evaluate the total number of books in Morton's collection if he had 20 books in his collection.

   $15b$; 300 books

2. Paul exercises m minutes per day 5 days a week. Write an algebraic expression to evaluate how many minutes Paul exercises each week if he exercises 45 minutes per day.

   $5m$; 225 m

3. Helen bought 3 shirts that each cost s dollars. Write an algebraic expression to evaluate how much Helen spent in all if each shirt cost \$22.

   $3s$; \$66

4. Claire makes b bracelets to divide evenly among four friends and herself. Write an algebraic expression to evaluate the number of bracelets each person will receive if Claire makes 15 bracelets.

   $\frac{b}{5}$; 3 bracelets

Choose the letter for the best answer.

5. Jonas collects baseball cards. He has 245 cards in his collection. For his birthday, he received r more cards, then he gave his brother g cards. Which algebraic expression represents the total number of cards he now has in his collection?

   A $245 + r + g$
   B $245 - r - g$
   C $245 + r - g$
   D $r + g - 245$

6. Monique is saving money for a computer. She has m dollars saved. For her birthday, her dad doubled her money, but then she spent s dollars on a shirt. Which algebraic expression represents the amount of money she has now saved for her computer?

   F $m + 2 - s$
   G $2m - s$
   H $2m + s$
   J $m + 2s$

7. Which algebraic expression represents the number of years in m months?

   A $12m$
   B $\frac{m}{12}$
   C $12 + m$
   D $12 - m$

8. Which algebraic expression represents how many minutes are in h hours?

   F $60h$
   G $\frac{h}{60}$
   H $h + 60$
   J $h - 60$

Answers

38. Possible answer: The student did not apply the Distributive Property correctly: $3(n - 5) = 3n - 15$.

39. Possible answer: Multiplication is repeated addition, so either operation can be used to solve the problem. Adding the cost 5 times or multiplying the cost by 5 will give the correct answer.

40. $1 + 2n$; yes; twice an odd number is always an even number, and adding 1 to an even number always results in an odd number.

TEST PREP DOCTOR + Students may misinterpret "per" in Exercise 43 and write the expression $9 \div n$. Explain that the total cost is the cost per book multiplied by the number of books.

Journal

Ask students to write why they think that mathematics is often called the universal language.

Power Presentations with PowerPoint®

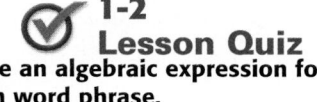

1-2 Lesson Quiz

Write an algebraic expression for each word phrase.

1. 5 less than a number k $k - 5$

2. a number x divided by 11 $\frac{x}{11}$

3. 4 times the sum of n and 5 $4(n + 5)$

Write an algebraic expression to evaluate the word problem.

4. Karen buys n raffle tickets for \$0.50 each. If she buys 13 of them, how much will they cost? $0.50n$; \$6.50

Also available on transparency

Objective: Students compare and order integers and evaluate expressions containing absolute values.

 Online Edition
Tutorial Videos

 Countdown to Testing Week 1

 **Power Presentations**
with PowerPoint®

Warm Up

Evaluate each expression for the given values of the variables.

1. $2x - 3y$ for $x = 17$ and $y = 6$ 16

2. $5(x + 3) + 4y$ for $x = 3$ and $y = 2$ 38

3. $6.9(x - 2.7) + 7.1$ for $x = 5.1$ 23.66

4. $5x - 4y$ for $x = 0.3$ and $y = 0.2$ 0.7

Problem of the Day

Janie's score is 3 times the sum of 1 and Maria's score on the final exam. Maria scored 12 points. Whose score is highest?   Janie

Also available on transparency

Math Humor

Teacher: Why are you looking at the back of your paper?

Student: I'm looking for the opposite side of the number line!

State Resources

 **go.hrw.com**
State Resources Online
KEYWORD: MT7 Resources

1-3 Integers and Absolute Value

Learn to compare and order integers and to evaluate expressions containing absolute values.

Vocabulary
integer
opposite
additive inverse
absolute value

In disc golf, a player tries to throw a disc to a target, or "hole," in as few throws as possible. The standard number of throws expected to complete a course is called "par." A player's score tells you how many throws he or she is above or below par.

Fred completes the course in 5 fewer throws than par. His score is 5 under par. Trevor completes the course in 3 more throws than par. His score is 3 over par. Monique is 4 over par, and Julie is 2 under par.

Patients of the Texas Scottish Rite Hospital for Children play disc golf as part of their orthopedic therapy.

These scores can be written as *integers*. **Integers** are the set of whole numbers and their *opposites*. **Opposites**, or **additive inverses**, are numbers that are the same distance from 0, but on opposite sides of 0 on a number line.

Expressed as integers, the scores relative to par are Fred −5, Trevor 3, Monique 4, and Julie −2.

EXAMPLE 1   *Sports Application*

Remember!
Numbers on a number line increase in value as you move from left to right.

A Use <, >, or = to compare Trevor's and Julie's scores.
Trevor's score is 3, and Julie's score is −2.

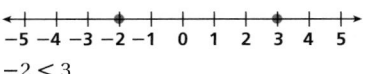

Place the scores on a number line.
$-2 < 3$
−2 is to the left of 3.

Julie's score is less then Trevor's.

B List the golfers in order from the lowest score to the highest.
The scores are −5, 3, 4, and −2.

Place the scores on a number line and read them from left to right.

In order from the lowest score to the highest, the golfers are Fred, Julie, Trevor, and Monique.

---

1 Introduce

Alternate Opener

Motivate

Ask students to identify situations that involve integers in everyday life. Possible answers: bank deposits/withdrawals; gained/lost yards in football; winter/summer temperatures Draw and label a number line from −5 to 5. To introduce opposites and absolute value, ask students to find the distance between −4 and 0 and between 0 and 4. 4; 4 Elicit that both integers are the same distance from 0 and that, therefore, distance is always positive.

Explorations and answers are provided in *Alternate Openers: Explorations Transparencies.*

EXAMPLE **2 Ordering Integers**

Write the integers 7, −4, and 3 in order from least to greatest.

$7 > -4$, $7 > 3$, and $-4 < 3$ *Compare each pair of integers.*

−4, 3, 7   *−4 is less than both 3 and 7.*

EXAMPLE 3 Finding Additive Inverses

Find the additive inverse of each integer.

A 8

−8   *−8 is the same distance from 0 as 8 is on the number line.*

B −15

15   *15 is the same distance from 0 as −15 is on the number line.*

C 0

0   *Zero is its own additive inverse.*

A number's **absolute value** is its distance from 0 on a number line. Absolute value is always positive because distance is always positive. "The absolute value of −4" is written as $|-4|$. Additive inverses have the same absolute value.

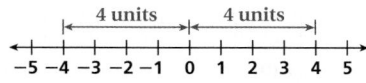

$|-4| = |4| = 4$ *Both 4 and −4 are 4 units from 0.*

EXAMPLE 4 Evaluating Absolute-Value Expressions

Possible answers to *Think and Discuss*
1. Negative numbers can be used to represent withdrawals from a bank account.

2. Additive inverses are 2 numbers that are opposites. So, even though −1 + (−4) = −5, the additive inverse of 5, −1 and −4 are not the additive inverse of 5.

Evaluate each expression.

A $|-9| + |7|$
$|-9| = 9$ *−9 is 9 units from 0.*
$|7| = 7$ *7 is 7 units from 0.*
$9 + 7 = 16$

B $|20 - 20|$
$|0|$ *20 − 20 = 0*
0 *0 is 0 units from 0.*

Think and Discuss

1. **Explain** how integers are used in real life to manage a bank account.

2. **Explain** whether −1, −4, and 5 are additive inverses.

COMMON ERROR ALERT

When ordering positive and negative integers from least to greatest, students sometimes write a greater negative integer as being less than a smaller negative integer, because they look at the number without its sign to order the integers.

Power Presentations with PowerPoint®

Additional Examples

Example 1

A. Use <, >, or = to compare the scores. Aaron's score is 4, and Felicity's score is −1. $-1 < 4$

B. List the golfers' scores in order from the lowest to the highest. The scores are −4, 2, 5, and −3.
−4, −3, 2, 5

Example 2

Write the integers 8, −5, and 4 in order from least to greatest.   −5, 4, 8

Example 3

Find the additive inverse of each integer.

A. 6   −6

B. −14   14

C. 0.5   −0.5

Example 4

Evaluate each expression.

A. $|-8| + |-5|$ 13

B. $|5 - 6|$ 1

Also available on transparency

---

2 Teach

ENGLISH LANGUAGE LEARNERS

Guided Instruction

First, show students how to use the number line (Teaching Transparency) to compare integers. Then show how to compare two integers at a time when ordering a set of integers. Use the number line to show the meanings of *absolute value* and *additive inverse*.

Teaching Tip

Visual Suggest that students think of the < and > symbols as arrows that point to the smaller number.

Reaching All Learners
Through Graphic Organizers

Have students work in groups of three. Students draw one number line from −50 to 50, with intervals of 10. Then, each student names an integer from −50 to 50. Students locate their integers on the number line and then compare and order the integers. They can repeat the activity if time permits.

3 Close

ENGLISH LANGUAGE LEARNERS

Summarize

Ask students which two vocabulary terms have the same meaning. additive inverse, opposite Then have students choose a positive and negative integer, compare them, and give their opposites and their absolute values.

Possible answer: −7, 3; −7 < 3; opposite of −7 is 7, opposite of 3 is −3; |−7| = 7, |3| = 3.

go.hrw.com
Homework Help Online
KEYWORD: MT7 1-3
Parent Resources Online
KEYWORD: MT7 Parent

Assignment Guide

If you finished Example **1** assign:
Average 1, 15, 29–36, 57–65
Advanced 15, 29–36, 52, 57–65

If you finished Example **2** assign:
Average 1–5, 15–19, 29–39
Advanced 15–19, 29–39, 52–53, 57–65

If you finished Example **3** assign:
Average 1–10, 29–39, 57–65
Advanced 15–24, 29–39, 48–53, 57–65

If you finished Example **4** assign:
Average 1–13 odd, 15–38, 29–51 odd, 57–65
Advanced 15–27 odd, 29–51 odd, 52–65

Homework Quick Check

Quickly check key concepts.
Exercises: 12, 16, 18, 30, 40

GUIDED PRACTICE

See Example **1**
1. After the first round of the 2005 Masters golf tournament, scores relative to par were Tiger Woods 2, Vijay Singh −4, Phil Mickelson −2, and Justin Leonard 5. Use <, >, or = to compare Vijay Singh's and Phil Mickelson's scores, and then list the golfers in order from the lowest score to the highest.
−4 < −2; Vijay Singh, Phil Mickelson, Tiger Woods, Justin Leonard

See Example **2** Write the integers in order from least to greatest.
2. −5, 2, −3   3. −17, 6, −8   4. −9, −21, −14   5. 3, −7, 0
  −5, −3, 2   **−17, −8, 6**   **−21, −14, −9**   **−7, 0, 3**

See Example **3** Find the additive inverse of each integer.
6. −7 **7**   7. 13 **−13**   8. −1 **1**   9. 25 **−25**   10. −13 **13**

See Example **4** Evaluate each expression.
11. |−3| + |11| **14**   12. |−12| + |−9| **21**   13. |22 − 7| **15**   14. |8 − 8| **0**

INDEPENDENT PRACTICE

See Example **1**
15. During a very cold week, the temperature in Philadelphia was −7°F on Monday, 4°F on Tuesday, 2°F on Wednesday, and −3°F on Thursday. Use <, >, or = to compare the temperatures on Wednesday and Thursday, and then list the days in order from the coldest to the warmest.
−3°F < 2°F; Monday, Thursday, Tuesday, Wednesday

See Example **2** Write the integers in order from least to greatest.
16. −6, 5, −2   17. 8, −11, −5   18. −25, −30, −27   19. 4, −2, −1
  −6, −2, 5   **−11, −5, 8**   **−30, −27, −25**   **−2, −1, 4**

See Example **3** Find the additive inverse of each integer.
20. 9 **−9**   21. −15 **15**   22. 0 **0**   23. −31 **31**   24. 8 **−8**

See Example **4** Evaluate each expression.
25. |7| + |−14| **21**   26. |−19| + |−13| **32**   27. |28 − 18| **10**   28. |6 + 3| **9**

PRACTICE AND PROBLEM SOLVING

Extra Practice
See page 782.

Compare. Write <, >, or =.
29. −9 ▨ 15 **<**   30. 13 ▨ −17 **>**   31. −23 ▨ −23 **=**   32. −14 ▨ 0 **<**

33. |−7| ▨ |6| **>**   34. |−3| ▨ |3| **=**   35. |−13| ▨ |2| **>**   36. |20| ▨ |−21| **<**

Write the integers in order from least to greatest.
37. 24, −16, −12   38. −46, −31, −52   39. −45, 35, −25
  −16, −12, 24   **−52, −46, −31**   **−45, −25, 35**

Evaluate each expression.
40. |17| + |−24| **41**   41. |−22| + |−28| **50**   42. |53 − 37| **16**   43. |21 − 20| **1**

44. |7 · |−9| **63**   45. |−6| · |−12| **72**   46. |72| ÷ |8| **9**   47. |3| + |−3| **6**

go.hrw.com
State Resources Online
KEYWORD: MT7 Resources

State Resources

RETEACH 1-3

LESSON 1-3 Reteach
Integers and Absolute Value

Use a number line to compare and order integers.
To compare 2 and −4, place each integer on a number line.

−5 −4 −3 −2 −1 0 1 2 3 4 5

Because −4 lies to the left of 2, −4 is less than 2: −4 < 2.
Because 2 lies to the right of −4, 2 is greater than −4: 2 > −4.
To order −1, 3, −2, and 0, place each integer on a number line.

−5 −4 −3 −2 −1 0 1 2 3 4 5

To order the integers from least to greatest, read the numbers as they appear in order from left to right on the number line.
From least to greatest: −2, −1, 0, 3.

Place the integers on the number line. Then use < or > to compare.
1. 3 and −1
−5 −4 −3 −2 −1 0 1 2 3 4 5
3 ▢>▢ −1

2. −1 and −4
−5 −4 −3 −2 −1 0 1 2 3 4 5
−1 ▢>▢ −4

3. −2 and 0
−5 −4 −3 −2 −1 0 1 2 3 4 5
−2 ▢<▢ 0

4. −5 and 2
−5 −4 −3 −2 −1 0 1 2 3 4 5
−5 ▢<▢ 2

Place the integers on the number line. List in order from least to greatest.
5. −3, 4, −5, 2
−5 −4 −3 −2 −1 0 1 2 3 4 5
−5, −3, 2, 4

6. 0, 1, −4, −1
−5 −4 −3 −2 −1 0 1 2 3 4 5
−4, −1, 0, 1

PRACTICE 1-3

LESSON 1-3 Practice B
Integers and Absolute Value

Write the integers in order from least to greatest.
1. 7, 3, −9   2. −6, 2, −5   3. −4, 1, −1
  −9, 3, 7   −6, −5, 2   −4, −1, 1

4. −8, 2, −11   5. −12, −15, 0   6. −24, −17, 30
  −11, −8, 2   −15, −12, 0   −24, −17, 30

7. 16, −14, −7   8. −9, −7, −16   9. −19, −23, −10
  −14, −7, 16   −16, −9, −7   −23, −19, −10

Find the additive inverse of each integer.
10. −8   11. 6   12. −14   13. 29
  8   −6   14   −29

Evaluate each expression.
14. |−8| + |−4| 15. |−12| + |12| 16. |19| + |−8|
  12   24   27

17. |29 − 16| 18. |35 − 9| 19. |14 − 14|
  13   24   0

20. |−15| + |10| 21. |−9| + |30| 22. |24| + |−8|
  25   39   32

23. Natalie keeps track of her bowling scores. The scores for the games she played this Saturday relative to her best score last Saturday are Game A, 6; Game B, −3; Game C, 8; and Game D, −5. Use <, >, or = to compare her first two games. Then list her games in order from the lowest score to the highest.

  6 > −3; Game D, Game B, Game A, Game C

Find the additive inverse of each integer and then perform the operation.

48. −48, −7; addition **55**

49. −8, −6; multiplication **48**

50. −60, −5; division **12**

51. −27, −25; subtraction **2**

52. Chemistry The boiling point of nitrogen is −196°C. The boiling point of oxygen is −183°C. Which element has the greater boiling point? Explain your answer. **oxygen**

53. Earth Science The table shows the lowest recorded temperatures for each continent. Write the continents in order from the lowest recorded temperature to the highest recorded temperature.

Lowest Recorded Temperatures	
Continent	**Temperature**
Africa	−11°F
Antarctica	−129°F
Asia	−90°F
Australia	−9°F
Europe	−67°F
North America	−81°F
South America	−27°F

54. Critical Thinking Write rules for using absolute value to compare two integers. Be sure to take all of the possible combinations into account.

 55. Write About It Explain why there is no number that can replace n to make the equation $|n| = -1$ true.

⭐ **56. Challenge** List the integers that can replace n to make the statement $-|8| < n \le -|-5|$ true. **−7, −6, −5**

53. Antarctica, Asia, North America, Europe, South America, Africa, Australia

55. The absolute value of a number is always positive.

TEST PREP and Spiral Review

57. Multiple Choice Which set of integers is in order from greatest to least?

Ⓐ −10, 8, −5   Ⓑ 8, −5, −10   Ⓒ −5, 8, −10   Ⓓ −10, −5, 8

58. Multiple Choice Which integer is between −4 and 2?

Ⓕ 0   Ⓖ 3   Ⓗ 4   Ⓙ −5

59. Short Answer After the final round of a golf tournament, the scores of the top 5 finishers were McKenna −3, Bernie −5, Shonda 0, Matt −1, and Kelly 1. Who won the tournament, and who came in fifth? **Possible answer: From least to greatest, the scores were −5, −3, −1, 0, and 1. Bernie won the tournament, and Kelly came in fifth.**

Evaluate each expression for $a = 3$, $b = 2.5$, and $c = 24$. (Lesson 1-1)

60. $c - 15$ **9**

61. $9a + 8$ **35**

62. $8(a + 2b)$ **64**

63. $bc - a$ **557**

Write an algebraic expression for each word phrase. (Lesson 1-2)

64. 8 more than the product of 7 and a number t **$7t + 8$**

65. A pizzeria delivered p pizzas on Thursday. On Friday, it delivered 3 more than twice the number of pizzas delivered on Thursday. Write an expression to show the number of pizzas delivered on Friday. **$2p + 3$**

CHALLENGE 1-3

Challenge
1-3 Opposite Opposites

You can think of a negative sign as signifying the opposite of an integer.

For example, you can write the opposite of 4 as −4. You can write the opposite of −4 as −(−4) or 4.

Simplify by writing an integer for each expression.

1. −(−8) _____ 8
2. −(27) _____ −27
3. −|36| _____ −36
4. |−45| _____ 45

5. −|−14| _____ −14
6. −|0| _____ 0
7. |−(−12)| _____ 12
8. −(−57) _____ 57

9. |−(−20)| _____ 20
10. −|51| _____ −51
11. −|−25| _____ −25
12. −|−(−16)| _____ −16

Complete.

13. Is there a least positive integer? Explain.

Yes. Possible answer: You can not find a

positive integer on the number line to the left of 1.

14. Is there a greatest positive integer? Explain.

No. Possible answer: You can always find an integer

on the number line to the right of any given positive integer.

15. Is there a least negative integer? Explain.

No. Possible answer: You can always find an

integer on the number line to the left of any given negative integer.

16. Is there a greatest negative integer? Explain.

Yes. Possible answer: You can not find a negative

integer on the number line to the right of −1.

PROBLEM SOLVING 1-3

Problem Solving
1-3 Integers and Absolute Value

Write the correct answer.

1. In Africa, Lake Asal reaches a depth of −153 meters. In Asia, the Dead Sea reaches a depth of −408 meters. Which reaches a greater depth, Lake Asal or the Dead Sea?

Dead Sea

2. Jeremy's scores for four golf games are: −1, 2, −3, and 1. Order his golf scores from least to greatest.

−3, −1, 1, 2

3. The lowest point in North America is Death Valley with an elevation of −282 feet. South America's lowest point is the Valdes Peninsula with an elevation of −131 feet. Which continent has the lowest point?

North America

4. Two undersea cameras are taking time lapse photos in a coral reef. The first camera is mounted at −45 feet. The second camera is mounted at −25. Which camera is closer to the surface?

the second camera

Use the table to answer Exercises 5–7. Choose the letter of the best answer.

5. Which state had the coldest temperature?
   A Alabama   C Massachusetts
   Ⓑ Indiana   D Texas

State Low Temperature Records	
State	**Temperature (°F)**
Alabama	−27
Indiana	−36
Massachusetts	−35
Texas	−23

6. Which is the greatest temperature listed?
   F −27°F   H −35°F
   G −36°F   Ⓙ −23°F

7. The lowest temperature recorded in Connecticut was between the lowest temperatures recorded in Alabama and Massachusetts. Which could be the lowest temperature recorded in Connecticut?
   A −40°F   Ⓒ −32°F
   B −37°F   D −40°F

Answers

54. Possible answer:
If a and b are both positive and $|a| > |b|$, then $a > b$.
If a and b are both positive and $|a| < |b|$, then $a < b$.
If a and b are both negative and $|a| > |b|$, then $a < b$.
If a and b are both negative and $|a| < |b|$, then $a > b$.
If a is positive and b is negative and $|a| > |b|$ or $|a| < |b|$, then $a > b$.
If a is negative and b is positive and $|a| > |b|$, or $|a| < |b|$, then $a < b$.

 Remind students that they must read the instructions carefully. For Exercise 57, the directions ask the student to list the integers from greatest to least. In previous exercises, the students listed integers from *least* to *greatest*. Students may answer this question incorrectly if they do not read directions carefully.

 **Journal**

Have students explain how absolute value helps to order integers. Ask them to use real world situations involving integers in their explanation.

Power Presentations
with PowerPoint®

1-3 Lesson Quiz

Write the integers in order from least to greatest.

1. −17, −26, 23 **−26, −17, 23**

2. 0, 5, −4, **−4, 0, 5**

Evaluate each expression.

3. the sum of 3 and the additive inverse of −8 **11**

4. $-|-4| + |-2|$ **−2**

5. At the end of the course, your golf score was −2. Your friend's score was 7. What is the difference between your scores? **9**

Also available on transparency

Objective: Students add integers.

 Hands-On Lab
In *Hands-On Lab Activities*

 Online Edition
Tutorial Videos, Interactivities

 Countdown to Testing Week 1

 **Power Presentations**
with PowerPoint®

Warm Up

Graph each number on a number line.

1. −5   **2.** 7
3. −4   **4.** 0

−5 −3 −1 0 1 2 3 4 5 6 7

Problem of the Day

Start at 0 on a number line. Walk 5 blocks west and 3 blocks east. Where are you on the number line?
−2

Also available on transparency

Math Humor

No wonder his company went bankrupt. He tried to make larger negative profits because they had a greater absolute value.

1-4 Adding Integers

Learn to add integers.

Melanie keeps a health journal. She knows that when she eats she adds calories, and when she exercises she burns calories. Melanie can add positive and negative integers to find the total number of calories she takes in.

You can model integer addition on a number line. Starting at zero, move to the first number in the addition expression. Then move the number of units represented by the second number.

EXAMPLE 1 **Using a Number Line to Add Integers**

Use a number line to find each sum.

A $3 + (-7)$

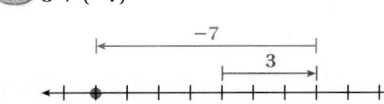
−5 −4 −3 −2 −1 0 1 2 3 4 5

Move right 3 units.
From 3, move left 7 units.

You finish at −4, so $3 + (-7) = -4$.

B $-2 + (-5)$

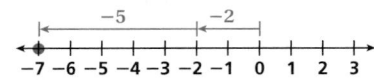
−7 −6 −5 −4 −3 −2 −1 0 1 2 3

Move left 2 units.
From −2, move left 5 units.

You finish at −7, so $-2 + (-5) = -7$.

Helpful Hint

To add a positive number, move to the right. To add a negative number, move to the left.

Another way to add integers is to use absolute value.

ADDING INTEGERS	
If the signs are the same...	**If the signs are different...**
find the sum of the absolute values. Use the same sign as the integers.	find the difference of the absolute values. Use the sign of the integer with the greater absolute value.

---

1 Introduce

Alternate Opener

EXPLORATION

1-4 Adding Integers

You can use a thermometer to model addition of integers.

1. Suppose the temperature starts at −50°F and increases 40° during the day. Complete the addition statement to show the new temperature.

    $-50° + 40° =$ ___

2. Suppose the temperature starts at 40°F and drops 70° overnight. Complete the addition statement to show the new temperature.

    $40° + (-70°) =$ ___

Complete the addition statement modeled by each number line.

3. $-4 +$ ___ $= 5$
  −6 −4 −2 0 2 4 6

4. $-1 + ($___$) = -8$
  −10 −8 −6 −4 −2 0 2

Think and Discuss

5. **Explain** how to add integers on a number line.

Motivate

To introduce students to adding integers, ask for examples of real-world situations that could be represented by integers (e.g., receiving $2 for allowance could be represented by +2; giving away three cookies could be represented by −3). Suggest a set of integers such as {−3, 1, −5, 2}. Ask students to order the integers from least to greatest.

Explorations and answers are provided in *Alternate Openers: Explorations Transparencies.*

State Resources

go.hrw.com
State Resources Online
KEYWORD: MT7 Resources

EXAMPLE 2 Using Absolute Value to Add Integers

Add.

A $-4 + (-6)$

$-4 + (-6)$	*Think: Find the sum of $|-4|$ and $|-6|$.*
-10	*Same sign; use the sign of the integers.*

B $8 + (-9)$

$8 + (-9)$	*Think: Find the difference of $|8|$ and $|-9|$.*
-1	*$9 > 8$; use the sign of 9.*

C $-5 + 11$

$-5 + 11$	*Think: Find the difference of $|-5|$ and $|11|$.*
6	*$11 > 5$; use the sign of 11.*

EXAMPLE 3 Evaluating Expressions with Integers

Evaluate $b + 11$ for $b = -6$.

$b + 11$	
$-6 + 11$	*Replace b with -6.*
	Think: Find the difference of $|11|$ and $|-6|$.
$-6 + 11 = 5$	*$11 > 6$; use the sign of 11.*

EXAMPLE 4 Health Application

Melanie wants to check her calorie count after breakfast and exercise. Use information from the journal entry to find her total.

Monday Morning
Calories

Oatmeal	145
Toast w/jam	62
8 fl oz juice	111

Calories burned

Walked six laps	110
Swam six laps	40

$145 + 62 + 111 + (-110) + (-40)$	*Use a positive sign for calories and a negative sign for calories burned.*
$(145 + 62 + 111) + (-110 + -40)$	*Group integers with same signs.*
$318 + (-150)$	*Add integers within each group.*
168	*$318 > 150$; use the sign of 318.*

Melanie's calorie count after breakfast and exercise is 168 calories.

Think and Discuss

1. Compare the sums $10 + (-22)$ and $-10 + 22$.

2. Explain whether an absolute value is ever negative.

3. Describe how to add the following addition expressions on a number line: $9 + (-13)$ and $-13 + 9$. Then compare the sums.

Possible answers to Think and Discuss

1. $10 + (-22) = -12$; $-10 + 22 = 12$; The sums are opposites.

2. No, an absolute value is a distance, and distance cannot be negative.

3. Start at 0 and draw an arrow to 9, then draw an arrow left 13 units; Start at 0 and draw an arrow left to -13, then draw an arrow right 9 units; Both arrows end at -4, so both sums are equal to -4.

2 Teach

Guided Instruction

In this lesson, students learn to add integers. Show students how to use a number line (Teaching Transparency) to add. Starting at zero, move to the first number in the addition expression. From there, move the number of spaces indicated by the second number, moving left for a negative number or right for a positive number. After students have mastered this method, show them that the same results are obtained by using the rules.

Teaching Tip **Inclusion** Suggest that students first determine the sign of the sum, which is always the sign of the number with the greatest absolute value.

Reaching All Learners
Through Concrete Manipulatives

Have students complete the following addition problems using integer chips (in Manipulatives Kit) to represent the numbers. Have students use yellow for positive numbers and red for negative numbers. (Pennies can also be used, with heads representing positive and tails representing negative.) Remind students that a positive chip and a negative chip are opposites and their sum is zero.

1. $-3 + 2$ -1

2. $5 + (-4)$ 1

3. $(-1) + (-5)$ -6

3 Close

Summarize

Have students write, in their own words, the rules for adding integers. Discuss how students can check their answers.

Possible answers: If the signs are the same, add the numbers and place the same sign in the answer. If the signs are different, determine which number is greater without the signs. The sign of the greater number (ignoring signs) will be the sign for the answer. Subtract the numbers. You can check your answer using a number line.

1-4 Exercises

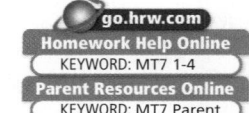
Assignment Guide

If you finished **Example 1** assign:
Average 1–4, 13–16, 29–38 odd, 49–56
Advanced 13–16, 29–38, 48–56

If you finished **Example 2** assign:
Average 1–8, 13–20, 31–38, 49–56
Advanced 13–20, 48–56

If you finished **Example 3** assign:
Average 1–11, 13–27, 39–44, 49–56
Advanced 13–27, 46, 48–56

If you finished **Example 4** assign:
Average 1–28, 29–44 odd, 49–56
Advanced 13–45 odd, 47–56

Homework Quick Check

Quickly check key concepts.
Exercises: 14, 18, 24, 26, 30, 36

Math Background

To find the sum of any two integers, exactly one of the following will apply:

Case 1 Add two numbers with the same sign. This requires two jumps in the same direction on the number line. Because both jumps are in the same direction, you add absolute values to get the final distance from zero.

Case 2 Add two numbers with different signs. This requires two jumps in opposite directions on the number line. Because the jumps are in opposite directions, you subtract absolute values to get the final distance from zero.

State Resources

go.hrw.com
State Resources Online
KEYWORD: MT7 Resources

GUIDED PRACTICE

See Example 1 **Use a number line to find each sum.**

1. $5 + 1$ 6
2. $6 + (-4)$ 2
3. $-7 + 9$ 2
4. $-4 + (-2)$ −6

See Example 2 **Add.**

5. $-12 + 5$ −7
6. $7 + (-3)$ 4
7. $-11 + 17$ 6
8. $-6 + (-8)$ −14

See Example 3 **Evaluate each expression for the given value of the variable.**

9. $t + 16$ for $t = -5$ 11
10. $m + 7$ for $m = -5$ 2
11. $p + (-5)$ for $p = -5$ −10

See Example 4 **12.** Lee opens a checking account. In the first month, he makes two deposits and writes three checks, as shown at right. Find what his balance is at the end of the month. (*Hint:* Checks count as negative amounts.) **$333**

Checks	Deposits
$134	$600
$56	$225
$302	

INDEPENDENT PRACTICE

See Example 1 **Use a number line to find each sum.**

13. $5 + (-7)$ −2
14. $-7 + 7$ 0
15. $4 + (-9)$ −5
16. $-4 + 7$ 3

See Example 2 **Add.**

17. $8 + 14$ 22
18. $-6 + (-7)$ −13
19. $-8 + (-8)$ −16
20. $19 + (-5)$ 14

21. $22 + (-15)$ 7
22. $17 + 9$ 26
23. $-20 + (-12)$ −32
24. $-18 + 7$ −11

See Example 3 **Evaluate each expression for the given value of the variable.**

25. $q + 13$ for $q = 10$ 23
26. $x + 21$ for $x = -7$ 14
27. $z + (-7)$ for $z = 16$ 9

See Example 4 **28.** On Monday morning, a mechanic has no cars in her shop. The table at right shows the number of cars dropped off and picked up each day. Find the total number of cars left in her shop on Friday. **12 cars**

	Cars Dropped Off	Cars Picked Up
Monday	8	4
Tuesday	11	6
Wednesday	9	12
Thursday	14	9
Friday	7	6

PRACTICE AND PROBLEM SOLVING

Extra Practice
See page 782.

Write an addition equation for each number line diagram.

$5 + (-9) = -4$

$-3 + (-4) = -7$

29.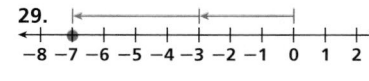

30.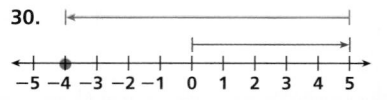

RETEACH 1-4

LESSON 1-4 Reteach
Adding Integers

You can model integer addition using two-color counters. Use the yellow side for 1 and the red side for −1. Remember that one yellow counter and one red counter are opposites, so their sum is zero.

$7 + 5 = $ ⓨⓨⓨⓨⓨⓨⓨ ⓨⓨⓨⓨⓨ = 12 yellow counters = 12

$7 + (-5) = $ ⓨⓨⓨⓨⓨⓨⓨ ⓡⓡⓡⓡⓡ = 2 yellow counters = 2

$-7 + (-5) = $ ⓡⓡⓡⓡⓡⓡⓡ ⓡⓡⓡⓡⓡ = 12 red counters = −12

$-7 + 5 = $ ⓡⓡⓡⓡⓡⓡⓡ ⓨⓨⓨⓨⓨ = 2 red counters = −2

If the given integers were added, state whether the result would be positive or negative.

1. $-4 + (-6)$ negative
2. $-3 + 8$ positive
3. $-5 + 2$ negative

Notice if the counters are the same color, you add the absolute values of the integers. The answer is the sign of the integers. If the counters are both colors, you subtract the absolute values of the integers. Use the sign of the integer with the greater absolute value.

To add the given integers, state whether you need to add or subtract absolute values.

4. $8 + 3$ add
5. $-4 + (-1)$ add
6. $3 + (-6)$ subtract

Complete to find each sum.
7. $5 + (-9) = ?$
8. $-6 + (-4) = ?$

Are the signs the same or different? different same
Which sign will you use for the sum? negative negative
Will you add or subtract absolute values? subtract add
Write the sum. −4 −10

PRACTICE 1-4

LESSON 1-4 Practice B
Adding Integers

Use a number line to find each sum.

1. $3 + 1$ 4

2. $-3 + 2$ −1

Add.
3. $-5 + 18$ 13
4. $-10 + 17$ 7
5. $-22 + (-9)$ −31
6. $24 + (-15)$ 9

Evaluate each expression for the given value of the variable.
7. $r + 7$ for $r = 3$ 10
8. $m + 5$ for $m = 9$ 14
9. $x + 9$ for $x = 4$ 13
10. $-6 + t$ for $t = -8$ −14
11. $-7 + y$ for $y = -4$ −11
12. $x + 9$ for $x = -8$ 1
13. $-5 + d$ for $d = -2$ −7
14. $x + (-4)$ for $x = -4$ −8
15. $k + (-3)$ for $k = -5$ −8
16. $-8 + b$ for $b = 13$ 5
17. $-10 + d$ for $d = -2$ −12
18. $t + (-3)$ for $t = 3$ 0

19. Joleen has 2560 trading cards in her collection. She buys 165 new cards for the collection. How many trading cards does she have now?

2725 trading cards

20. The running back for the Bears carries the ball twice in the first quarter. The first run he gained fifteen yards and the second run he lost eight yards. How many yards did the two runs total?

7 yards

Economics

The number one category of imported goods in the United States is industrial supplies, including petroleum and petroleum products. In 2004, this category accounted for over $412 million of imports.

Use a number line to find each sum.

31. $-9 + (-3)$ **−12**   **32.** $16 + (-22)$ **−6**   **33.** $-34 + 17$ **−17**   **34.** $44 + 39$ **83**

35. $45 + (-67)$ **−22**   **36.** $-14 + 85$ **71**   **37.** $52 + (-9)$ **43**   **38.** $-31 + (-31)$ **−62**

Evaluate each expression for the given value of the variable.

39. $c + 17$ for $c = -9$ **8**   **40.** $k + (-12)$ for $k = 4$ **−8**   **41.** $b + (-6)$ for $b = -24$ **−30**

42. $13 + r$ for $r = -19$ **−6**   **43.** $-9 + w$ for $w = -6$ **−15**   **44.** $3 + n + (-8)$ for $n = 5$ **0**

45. **Economics** Refer to the data at right about U.S. international trade for the year 2004. Consider values of exports as positive quantities and values of imports as negative quantities.

	Exports	Imports
Goods	$807,584,000,000	$1,473,768,000,000
Services	$338,553,000,000	$290,095,000,000

Source: U.S. Census Bureau

  a. What was the total of U.S. exports in 2004? **$1,146,137,000,000**

  b. What was the total of U.S. imports in 2004? **−$1,763,863,000,000**

  c. The sum of exports and imports is called the *balance of trade*. Approximate the 2004 U.S. balance of trade to the nearest billion dollars. **about −$618,000,000,000 or −$618 billion**

46. **What's the Error?** A student evaluated $-4 + d$ for $d = -6$ and gave an answer of 2. What might the student have done wrong?

47. **Write About It** Explain the different ways it is possible to add two integers and get a negative answer.

48. **Challenge** What is the sum of $3 + (-3) + 3 + (-3) + \dots$ when there are 10 terms? 19 terms? 24 terms? 25 terms? Explain any patterns that you find.

TEST PREP and Spiral Review

49. **Multiple Choice** Which of the following is the value of $-7 + 3h$ when $h = 5$?

  Ⓐ −22   Ⓑ −8   Ⓒ 8   Ⓓ 22

50. **Gridded Response** Evaluate the expression $12 - y$ for $y = -8$. **20**

Evaluate each expression for the given values of the variables. (Lesson 1-1)

51. $2x - 3y$ for $x = 8$ and $y = 4$ **4**   **52.** $6s - t$ for $s = 7$ and $t = 12$ **30**

Evaluate each expression. (Lesson 1-3)

53. $|-3| + |-9|$ **12**   **54.** $|-4 + (-7)|$ **11**   **55.** $|18| - |-5|$ **13**   **56.** $|-27| - |-5|$ **22**

CHALLENGE 1-4

Challenge
1-4 *Presto, Chango!*

A magic square has the same sum for every row, column, and diagonal.

4	−3	2
−1	1	3
0	5	−2

Magic Square A has a magic sum of __3__.

Magic Square A

Add 2 to each integer in Magic Square A to create Magic Square B.

6	−1	4
1	3	5
2	7	0

Magic Square B
magic sum is __9__

Add 5 to each integer in Magic Square A to create Magic Square C.

9	2	7
4	6	8
5	10	3

Magic Square C
magic sum is __18__

Add 23 to each integer in Magic Square A to create Magic Square D.

1	−6	−1
−4	−2	0
−3	2	−5

Magic Square D
magic sum is __−6__

Describe the relationship between the magic sum of Magic Square A and the magic sum of a new magic square created by adding any integer n to each integer in Magic Square A.

When *n* is added to each integer of Magic Square A, then 3*n* is added to its magic sum.

Use the relationship you just described to predict the magic sum of the magic square you would get if you added −6 to each integer in Magic Square A.

My prediction for the magic sum of magic square E is: $3 + (-18) = -15$

−2	−9	−4
−7	−5	−3
−6	−1	−8

Magic Square E

Verify your prediction by creating Magic Square E, and calculating its magic sum.

Magic Square E has a magic sum of __−15__.

PROBLEM SOLVING 1-4

Problem Solving
1-4 *Adding Integers*

Use the following information for Exercises 1–3. In golf, par 73 means that a golfer should take 73 strokes to finish 18 holes. A score of 68 is 5 under par, or −5. A score of 77 is 4 over par, or +4.

1. Use integers to write Tiger Woods's score for each round as over or under par.

  $-5, +1, +1, -8$

Tiger Woods's Scores Mercedes Championship January 6, 2002 Par 73 course	
Round	**Score**
1	68
2	74
3	74
4	65

2. Add the integers to find Tiger Woods's overall score.

  −11

3. Was Tiger Woods's overall score over or under par?

  11 under par

Choose the letter for the best answer.

4. At 9:00 A.M., the temperature was −15°. An hour later, the temperature had risen 7°. What is the temperature now?

  A −22°   Ⓒ −8°
  B 8°   D 22°

5. Sandra is reviewing her savings account statement. She withdrew amounts of $35, $20, and $15. She deposited $65. If her starting balance was $657, find the new balance.

  Ⓕ $652   H $662
  G $522   J $507

6. During a possession in a football game, the Vikings gained 22 yards, lost 15 yards, gained 3 yards, gained 20 yards and lost 5 yards. At the end of the possession, how many yards had they lost or gained?

  A gained 43 yards
  B lost 43 yards
  C lost 25 yards
  Ⓓ gained 25 yards

7. A submarine is cruising at 40 m below sea level. The submarine ascends 18 m. What is the submarine's new location?

  F 58 m below sea level
  Ⓖ 22 m below sea level
  H 18 m below sea level
  J 12 m below sea level

ONGOING ASSESSMENT and INTERVENTION

Diagnose Before the Lesson
1-4 Warm Up, TE p. 18

Monitor During the Lesson
1-4 Know-It Notebook
1-4 Questioning Strategies

Assess After the Lesson
1-4 Lesson Quiz, TE p. 21

Answers

46. Possible answer: The student may have substituted 6 instead of −6 into the equation.

47. Possible answer: If you add two negative integers, your answer will be negative. Also, if you add a negative integer and a positive integer and the negative integer has the greater absolute value, then your answer will be negative.

48. 0; 3; 0; 3; Possible answer: When there are an even number of terms, the sum is 0. When there are an odd number of terms, the sum is 3.

TEST PREP DOCTOR Encourage students to use parentheses when replacing a variable in an expression with a negative value. Students who answer 4 for Exercise 50 evaluated $12 - 8$ instead of $12 - (-8)$. The correct answer is 20.

Journal

Have students write a story involving one of these topics: a football team gaining and losing yards, a submarine diving and rising in the water, or the rising and falling value of a stock.

Power Presentations
with PowerPoint®

1-4 Lesson Quiz

Add.

1. $-7 + (-7)$ **−14**

2. $15 + (-9) + (-2)$ **4**

Evaluate each expression for the given value of the variable.

3. $13 + r$ for $r = -15$ **−2**

4. $2 + b + (-9)$ for $b = -6$ **−13**

5. On Monday, a local dog shelter had six dogs. By Friday, they had found homes for three, but took in two more. Then how many dogs were in the shelter?   **5 dogs**

Also available on transparency

Pacing: Traditional 1 day
Block $\frac{1}{2}$ day
Objective: Students subtract
integers.

 Online Edition
Tutorial Videos, Interactivities

Countdown to
Testing Week 1

 **Power Presentations**
with PowerPoint®

Warm Up

Add.
1. $-7 + 2$ -5
2. $-12 + (-9)$ -21
3. $32 + (-19)$ 13
4. $-6 + (-28)$ -34
5. $104 + (-87)$ 17
6. $-18 + (-24)$ -42

Problem of the Day

Copy and complete the magic
square. The magic sum is 0.

+5	−8	+3
−2	0	+2
−3	+8	−5

Also available on transparency

Math Fact

A number and its opposite are called
additive inverses of each other. The
sum of additive inverses is always zero.

Learn to subtract
integers.

Carlsbad Caverns in New Mexico
is one of the world's largest
underground caves. A tour of
the chambers in the cavern takes
explorers on many descents and
climbs.

Distances above or below the
entrance level of a cave can be
represented by integers. Negative
integers represent distances below,
and positive integers represent
distances above.

Subtracting a lesser number from
a greater number is the same as
finding how far apart the two
numbers are on a number line.
Subtracting an integer is the
same as adding its opposite.

SUBTRACTING INTEGERS		
Words	**Numbers**	**Algebra**
To subtract an integer, add its opposite.	$3 - 7 = 3 + (-7)$	$a - b = a + (-b)$
	$5 - (-8) = 5 + 8$	$a - (-b) = a + b$

EXAMPLE **1** **Subtracting Integers**

Subtract.

A $-7 - 7$
$-7 - 7 = -7 + (-7)$ *Add the opposite of 7.*
$\qquad\quad = -14$ *Same sign; use the sign of the integers.*

B $2 - (-4)$
$2 - (-4) = 2 + 4$ *Add the opposite of −4.*
$\qquad\quad = 6$ *Same sign; use the sign of the integers.*

C $-13 - (-5)$
$-13 - (-5) = -13 + 5$ *Add the opposite of −5.*
$\qquad\qquad\; = -8$ *13 > 5; use the sign of 13.*

1 Introduce

Alternate Opener

Motivate

To introduce students to subtraction of integers, review with them how to determine the
opposite of a number. You may want to use
a number line to demonstrate this (Teacher
Tools in Lesson Transparencies).

Review with students how to add integers.
Have them recite the rules and apply them
to several addition problems.

Explorations and answers are provided in
Alternate Openers: Explorations Transparencies.

EXAMPLE 2 · Evaluating Expressions with Integers

Evaluate each expression for the given value of the variable.

A $6 - t$ for $t = -4$

$6 - t$

$6 - (-4)$ *Substitute −4 for t.*

$6 + 4$ *Add the opposite of −4.*

10 *Same sign; use the sign of the integers.*

B $-4 - s$ for $s = -9$

$-4 - s$

$-4 - (-9)$ *Substitute −9 for s.*

$-4 + 9$ *Add the opposite of −9.*

5 *9 > 4; use the sign of 9.*

C $-3 - x$ for $x = 5$

$-3 - x$

$-3 - 5$ *Substitute 5 for x.*

$-3 + (-5)$ *Add the opposite of 5.*

-8 *Same sign; use the sign of the integers.*

EXAMPLE 3 · Earth Science Application

James enters a cave and climbs to a height 30 feet above the entrance level. Then he descends 210 feet. How far below the entrance level did James go?

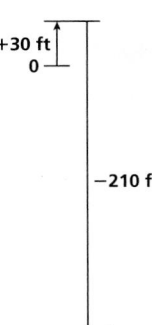

$30 - 210$ *Subtract the descent from the climb.*

$= 30 + (-210)$ *Add the opposite of 210.*

$= -180$ *210 > 30; use the sign of 210.*

James went 180 feet below the entrance level.

Possible answers to Think and Discuss

1. The differences are not the same because $10 - (-10)$ is positive and $-10 - 10$ is negative.

2. The answer is negative.

Think and Discuss

1. **Explain** why $10 - (-10)$ does not equal $-10 - 10$.

2. **Describe** the answer that you get when you subtract a greater number from a lesser number.

Power Presentations with PowerPoint®

Additional Examples

Example 1

Subtract.

A. $-7 - 4$ -11

B. $8 - (-5)$ 13

C. $-6 - (-3)$ -3

Example 2

Evaluate each expression for the given value of the variable.

A. $8 - j$ for $j = -6$ 14

B. $-9 - y$ for $y = -4$ -5

C. $n - 6$ for $n = -2$ -8

Example 3

The top of the Sears Tower, in Chicago, is 1454 feet above street level, while the lowest level is 43 feet below street level. How far is it from the lowest level to the top?

It is 1497 feet from bottom to top.

Also available on transparency

---

2 Teach

Guided Instruction

In this lesson, students learn to subtract integers. Explain to students that a subtraction sign can be read as "plus the opposite of." For example, $5 - 2$ can be read "5 minus 2" or "5 plus the opposite of 2." Stress that the answer is the same for either interpretation. You may want to use the Teaching Transparency.

 **Inclusion** Point out that subtraction is not commutative. In fact, if the order in a subtraction expression is reversed, the value of the new expression is the opposite of the original value. For example, $5 - 2 = 3$, and $2 - 5 = -3$.

Reaching All Learners

Through Critical Thinking

Have students compare the following expressions and determine which pairs have the same value.

$3 + 3$ $3 - 3$

$3 + (-3)$ $3 - (-3)$

Both $3 + 3$ and $3 - (-3)$ equal 6.

Both $3 - 3$ and $3 + (-3)$ equal 0.

3 Close

Summarize

Have the students describe how to express a subtraction as an addition. Then have them state the rules for addition. Emphasize the importance of the rules for adding and subtracting integers.

Possible answers: To write a subtraction as an addition, change the subtraction sign to addition and change the sign of the second number. To add two integers with the same sign, add the absolute values of the integers and use the same sign. To add two integers with different signs, subtract the absolute values of the integers and use the sign of the number with the greater absolute value.

Assignment Guide

If you finished Example ① assign:
Average 1–4, 9–12, 19–24, 36–42
Advanced 9–12, 17–24, 30–31, 36–42

If you finished Example ② assign:
Average 1–7, 9–15, 19–28, 36–42
Advanced 9–15, 17–28, 29–34, 36–42

If you finished Example ③ assign:
Average 1–29 odd, 30–42
Advanced 9–29 odd, 30–42

Homework Quick Check

Quickly check key concepts.
Exercises: 10, 14, 18, 22, 28

Math Background

The ancient Egyptians used the following symbols for the given numbers:

1,000   100   10   1

The number 118 would look like this:

The subtraction problem $118 - 95 = 23$, written with Egyptian symbols, might look like this:

If a subtraction required regrouping, the Egyptians replaced one symbol with ten symbols. The subtraction problem $118 - 95 = 23$, written with Egyptian symbols, might look like this:

State Resources

go.hrw.com
State Resources Online
KEYWORD: MT7 Resources

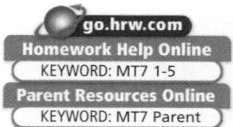
go.hrw.com
Homework Help Online
KEYWORD: MT7 1-5
Parent Resources Online
KEYWORD: MT7 Parent

1-5 Exercises

GUIDED PRACTICE

See Example ① **Subtract.**

1. $-5 - 9$ **−14**
2. $-8 - (-6)$ **−2**
3. $8 - (-4)$ **12**
4. $-11 - (-6)$ **−5**

See Example ② **Evaluate each expression for the given value of the variable.**

5. $9 - h$ for $h = -8$ **17**
6. $-7 - m$ for $m = -5$ **−2**
7. $-3 - k$ for $k = 12$ **−15**

See Example ③ **8.** The temperature rose from $-4°F$ to $45°F$ in Spearfish, South Dakota, on January 22, 1943, in only 2 minutes! By how many degrees did the temperature change? **49°**

INDEPENDENT PRACTICE

See Example ① **Subtract.**

9. $-3 - 7$ **−10**
10. $14 - (-9)$ **23**
11. $11 - (-6)$ **17**
12. $-8 - (-2)$ **−6**

See Example ② **Evaluate each expression for the given value of the variable.**

13. $14 - b$ for $b = -3$ **17**
14. $-7 - q$ for $q = -15$ **8**
15. $-5 - f$ for $f = 12$ **−17**

See Example ③ **16.** A submarine cruising at 27 m below sea level, or -27 m, descends 14 m. What is its new depth? **−41 m**

PRACTICE AND PROBLEM SOLVING

Extra Practice
See page 783.

Write a subtraction equation for each number line diagram.

17. 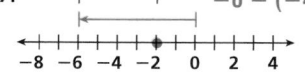 $-6 - (-4)$
18.  $6 - 11 = -5$

Perform the given operations.

19. $-8 - (-11)$ **3**
20. $24 - (-27)$ **51**
21. $-43 - 13$ **−56**
22. $-26 - 26$ **−52**
23. $-13 - 7 + (-6)$ **−26**
24. $-11 - (-4) + (-9)$ **−16**

Evaluate each expression for the given value of the variable.

25. $x - 16$ for $x = -4$ **−20**
26. $8 - t$ for $t = -5$ **13**
27. $-16 - y$ for $y = 8$ **−24**
28. $s - (-22)$ for $s = -18$ **4**

29. Estimation A roller coaster starts with a 160-foot climb and then plunges 228 feet down a canyon wall. It then climbs a gradual 72 feet before a steep climb of 189 feet. Approximately how far is the coaster above or below its starting point? **≈ 190 ft above the starting point**

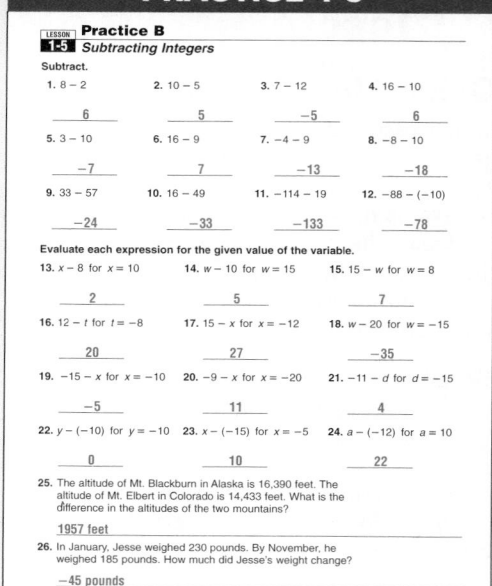

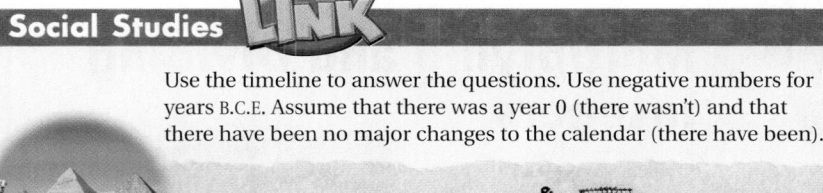
Use the timeline to answer the questions. Use negative numbers for years B.C.E. Assume that there was a year 0 (there wasn't) and that there have been no major changes to the calendar (there have been).

Great Pyramid built — Cleopatra takes throne — Turks rule Egypt — Napoleon invades Egypt

2600 B.C.E   **330 B.C.E**   **48 B.C.E**   **395 C.E.**   **1517 C.E.**   **1798 C.E.**

Greco-Roman Era

30. How long was the Greco-Roman era, when Greece and Rome ruled Egypt? **725 years**

31. Which was a longer period of time: from the Great Pyramid to Cleopatra, or from Cleopatra to the present? By how many years? **Great Pyramid to Cleopatra; about 500 years**

32. Queen Neferteri ruled Egypt about 2900 years before the Turks ruled. In what year did she rule? **1383 B.C.E.**

33. There are 1846 years between which two events on this timeline?

34. ✏️ **Write About It** What is it about years B.C.E. that make negative numbers a good choice for representing them?

35. ⭐ **Challenge** How would your calculations differ if you took into account the fact that there was no year 0?

🌐 **go.hrw.com**
Web Extra!
KEYWORD: MT7 Egypt

📱 **TEST PREP and Spiral Review**

36. **Multiple Choice** Which of the following is equivalent to $|7 - (-3)|$?

   Ⓐ $|7| - |-3|$ Ⓑ $|7| + |-3|$ Ⓒ -10 Ⓓ 4

37. **Gridded Response** Subtract: $-4 - (-12)$.   **8**

Write an algebraic expression to evaluate each word problem. (Lesson 1-2)

38. Tate bought a compact disc for $17.99. The sales tax on the disc was t dollars. What was the total cost including sales tax?   **$17.99 + t$**

Evaluate each expression for $m = -3$. (Lesson 1-4)

39. $m + 6$ **3**   40. $m + -5$ **−8**   41. $-9 + m$ **−12**   42. $m + 3$ **0**

Interdisciplinary

Social Studies

Exercises 39–44 involve reading a timeline. Reading and interpreting timelines is a prerequisite skill for middle school social studies courses, such as Holt, Rinehart & Winston's *People, Places, and Change.*

Answers

33–35. See p. A1.

TEST PREP DOCTOR + For Exercise 36, students should realize that they do not have to rewrite the given expression in order to correctly answer the problem. Students can eliminate **A, C,** and **D** as the correct answer choices by simplifying the choices and comparing them with the value of the given expression.

✏️ **Journal**

Have students write about a situation involving a vertical change, such as traveling on an elevator. Also have them write about another situation that might involve subtraction of integers.

CHALLENGE 1-5

LESSON 1-5 Challenge
Teeter Totter

Joel wants his math average for 6 tests to be at least 85. So far, his grades on the first 5 tests were 82, 91, 73, 83, and 88.

Complete the following table to figure out what grade he has to get on the 6th test in order to achieve his goal.

Grade	73	82	83	88	91
Grade − Average	73 − 85 =	82 − 85 =	83 − 85 =	88 − 85 =	91 − 85 =
	−12	−3	−2	3	6

After calculating the differences between the existing grades and the desired average of 85, notice that some of the differences are negative and some are positive. Add the positive and negative differences separately.

1. Sum of negative differences   2. Sum of positive differences

   $-12 + (-3) + (-2) = -17$ $3 + 6 = 9$

Joel thinks that since the average is the "middle" grade, the differences below the average should balance the differences above the average. If Joel's reasoning is correct:

3. Should the 6th grade be higher or lower than the average?   **higher**

4. By how many points?   **8 points**

5. What must the 6th grade be in order to achieve an average of at least 85?   **93**

6. Verify your answer by using it as the 6th grade. Find the average by your usual method: add the 6 grades and divide by 6.

   $\dfrac{73 + 82 + 83 + 88 + 91 + 93}{6} = 85$

Use Joel's method to find the necessary 6th grade for each set of grades if the given average is to be achieved.

7. 80, 93, 75, 82, 85; average to be 81

   6th grade should be ___ **71**

8. 85, 80, 90, 100, 80; average to be 88

   6th grade should be ___ **93**

PROBLEM SOLVING 1-5

LESSON 1-5 Problem Solving
Subtracting Integers

Write the correct answer.

1. In Fairbanks, Alaska, the average January temperature is −13°F, while the average April temperature is 30°F. What is the difference between the average temperatures?

   43°F

2. The highest point in North America is Mt. McKinley, Alaska, at 20,320 ft above sea level. The lowest point is Death Valley, California, at 282 ft below sea level. What is the difference in elevations?

   20,602 ft

3. The temperature fell from 44°F to −56°F in 24 hours in Browning, Montana, on January 23–24, 1916. By how many degrees did the temperature change?

   100°F

4. The boiling point of chlorine is −102°C, while the melting point is −34°C. What is the difference between the melting and boiling points of chlorine?

   68°C

Use the table below to answer Exercises 5–7. The table shows the first and fifth place finishers in a golf tournament. In golf, the winner has the lowest total for all five rounds. Choose the letter for the best answer.

5. By how many points did Mickelson beat Kelly in Round 2?
   Ⓐ 2   C 5
   B 3   D 8

6. By how many points did Kelly beat Mickelson in Round 3?
   F 2   Ⓗ 5
   G 3   J 9

Bob Hope Chrysler Classic January 20, 2002		
Round	J. Kelly	P. Mickelson
1	−8	−8
2	−3	−5
3	−7	−2
4	−4	−7
5	−5	−8

7. Who won the Bob Hope Chrysler Classic and how many points difference was there between first and fifth place?
   A Kelly; 4   C Kelly; 3
   B Mickelson; 4   Ⓓ Mickelson; 3

Power Presentations with PowerPoint®

✓ **1-5 Lesson Quiz**

Subtract.

1. $-6 - (-4)$ **−2**

2. $-3 - 3$ **−6**

3. $4 - (-5)$ **−1**

Evaluate each expression for the given value of the variable.

4. $9 - s$ for $s = -5$ **14**

5. $-4 - w + 5$ for $w = 21$ **−20**

6. Suretta is flying in an airplane, and rises an additional 20 feet. Then she descends 190 feet toward the ground. How far below her original height did Suretta go? **170 feet**

Also available on transparency

Technology Lab
In *Technology Lab Activities*

 Online Edition
Tutorial Videos

 Countdown to Testing Week 2

 **Power Presentations**
with PowerPoint®

Warm Up

Multiply or divide.

1. 5(8) 40   **2.** 6(12) 72

3. $\frac{36}{9}$ 4   **4.** $\frac{49}{7}$ 7

5. 18(7) 126   **6.** $\frac{192}{16}$ 12

Problem of the Day

Complete the pyramid by filling in the missing numbers. Each number is the sum of the numbers in the two boxes below it.

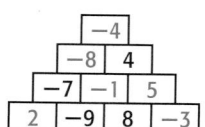

Also available on transparency

 **Math Humor**

Who invented algebra? a clever X-pert

State Resources

go.hrw.com
State Resources Online
KEYWORD: MT7 Resources

1-6 Multiplying and Dividing Integers

 **Learn** to multiply and divide integers.

When a football team has possession of the football, its goal is to move the ball toward its opponent's goal line. Each play run can result in a gain of yards, a loss of yards, or no change. If a team loses 10 yards in each of 3 successive plays, the net change in yards can be represented by 3(−10).

A positive number multiplied by an integer can be written as repeated addition.

$$3(-10) = -10 + (-10) + (-10) = -30$$

From what you know about adding integers, you can see that a positive integer times a negative integer is negative.

You know that multiplying two positive integers together gives you a positive answer. The pattern in the integer multiplication at right can help you understand the rules for multiplying two negative integers.

$3(-10) = -30$ ⎫ + 10
$2(-10) = -20$ ⎬ + 10
$1(-10) = -10$ ⎬ + 10
$0(-10) = 0$ ⎭ + 10

$-1(-10) = 10$ *The product of*
$-2(-10) = 20$ *two negative*
                   integers is a
$-3(-10) = 30$ *positive integer.*

MULTIPLYING AND DIVIDING TWO INTEGERS
If the signs are the same, the sign of the answer is **positive**.
If the signs are different, the sign of the answer is **negative**.

EXAMPLE 1 **Multiplying and Dividing Integers**

Multiply or divide.

Ⓐ 5(−8)   *Signs are different.*

    −40   *Answer is **negative**.*

Ⓑ $\frac{-45}{9}$ *Signs are different.*

    −5   *Answer is **negative**.*

Ⓒ −12(−3)   *Signs are the same.*

    36   *Answer is **positive**.*

Ⓓ $\frac{32}{-8}$ *Signs are different.*

    −4   *Answer is **negative**.*

---

1 Introduce

Alternate Opener

EXPLORATION

1-6 Multiplying and Dividing Integers

Imagine a person walking on a number line. If the person faced a **positive direction**, it would be **to the right**. If the person faced a **negative direction**, it would be **to the left**.

Suppose each step is 2 units long.

1. A person who is standing at 0 and facing a **positive direction** takes 3 steps backward. Complete the multiplication statement to find the person's location.

$$3 \cdot (-2) = \_\_\_$$

2. A person who is standing at 0 and facing a **negative direction** takes 4 steps forward. Complete the multiplication statement to find the person's location.

$$-4 \cdot 2 = \_\_\_$$

3. A person who is standing at 0 and facing a **negative direction** takes 5 steps backward. Complete the multiplication statement to find the person's location.

$$-5 \cdot (-2) = \_\_\_$$

Think and Discuss

4. Describe a situation for the multiplication statement $6 \cdot (-3) = -18$ by using a number line.

Motivate

To introduce students to multiplication and division of integers, point out that multiplication of whole numbers is repeated addition. Give examples of repeated addition, such as $6 + 6 + 6 = 3 \cdot 6$. Review the rules for adding integers.

Explorations and answers are provided in *Alternate Openers: Explorations Transparencies.*

EXAMPLE  **2** **Using the Order of Operations with Integers**

Simplify.

A $-3(2 - 8)$

$-3(2 - 8)$	*Subtract inside the parentheses.*
$= -3(-6)$	*Think: The signs are the same.*
$= 18$	*The answer is positive.*

B $4(-7 - 2)$

$4(-7 - 2)$	*Subtract inside the parentheses.*
$= 4(-9)$	*Think: The signs are different.*
$= -36$	*The answer is negative.*

C $-2(14 - 6)$

$-2(14 - 6)$	*Subtract inside the parentheses.*
$= -2(8)$	*Think: The signs are different.*
$= -16$	*The answer is negative.*

EXAMPLE **3** *Sports Application*

A football team runs 10 plays. On 6 plays, it has a gain of 4 yards each. On 4 plays, it has a loss of 5 yards each. Each gain in yards can be represented by a positive integer, and each loss can be represented by a negative integer. Find the total net change in yards.

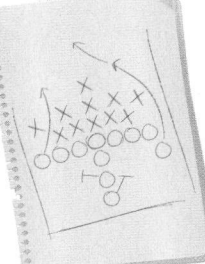

$6(4) + 4(-5)$	*Add the losses to the gains.*
$= 24 + (-20)$	*Multiply.*
$= 4$	*Add.*

The team gained 4 yards.

Possible answers to
Think and Discuss

1. $5 \cdot 6 = 30$,
$(-5) \cdot 6 = -30$,
$5 \cdot (-6) = -30$,
$(-5) \cdot (-6) = 30$,
$6 \cdot 5 = 30$,
$(-6) \cdot 5 = -30$,
$6 \cdot (-5) = 30$,
$(-6) \cdot (-5) = 30$,
$30 \div 5 = 6$,
$30 \div 6 = 5$,
$(-30) \div 5 = -6$,
$(-30) \div (-6) = 5$,
$30 \div (-5) = -6$,
$30 \div (-6) = -5$,
$(-30) \div (-5) = 6$,
$(-30) \div 6 = -5$

Think and Discuss

1. List all possible multiplication and division statements for the integers with absolute values of 5, 6, and 30. For example, $5 \cdot 6 = 30$.

2. Compare the sign of the product of two negative integers with the sign of the sum of two negative integers.

3. Suppose the product of two integers is positive. What do you know about the signs of the integers?

Power Presentations
with PowerPoint®

Additional Examples

Example **1**

Multiply or divide.

A. $-6(4)$	-24	**B.** $-8(-5)$	40
C. $\frac{-18}{2}$	-9	**D.** $\frac{-25}{-5}$	5

Example **2**

Simplify.

A. $3(-6 - 12)$	**B.** $-5(-5 + 2)$
-54	15
C. $-2(14 - 5)$	-18

Example **3**

A golfer plays 5 holes. On 3 holes, he has a gain of 4 strokes each. On 2 holes, he has a loss of 4 strokes each. Each gain in strokes can be represented by a positive integer, and each loss can be represented by a negative integer. Find the total net change in strokes.   4

Also available on transparency

Possible answers to
Think and Discuss

2. The product of two negative numbers is positive, while the sum of two negative numbers is negative.

3. The sign of the integers is the same; that is, either both are positive or both are negative.

---

2 Teach

Guided Instruction

In this lesson, students learn to multiply and divide integers. Review with students the pattern given in the lesson. They should be able to determine the sign rules for multiplication and division (Teaching Transparency). Point out that the sign rules are the same for both operations.

Teaching Tip **Communicating Math** Remind students of the order of operations. Ask students to explain each step in Example 2, referring to both the rules for multiplication and division of integers and the order of operations.

Reaching All Learners
Through Critical Thinking

Have students answer True or False to the following statements, and then provide an example and an explanation for each.

If a product is negative, then there must be an odd number of negative factors in the expression. True; $-3(-2)(-1) = -6$. Because every two negative factors make a positive, an odd number results in one extra negative.

If a quotient is negative, there must be an even number of positive factors in the numerator and denominator combined. False; $\frac{-3(6)(2)}{(4)} = -9$. The sign of the quotient is determined only by the number of negative factors.

---

3 Close

Summarize

Review the rules for the four operations. Discuss why the rules for multiplication and division are the same, while the rules for addition and subtraction are different.

Possible answers: The rules for multiplication and division are the same because one can rewrite division as multiplication without changing any of the signs. The rules for addition and subtraction are different because to change subtraction into addition, the sign of the second number must change.

1-6 **Exercises**

go.hrw.com
Homework Help Online
KEYWORD: MT7 1-6
Parent Resources Online
KEYWORD: MT7 Parent

Assignment Guide

If you finished Example ① assign:
Average 1–4, 11–14, 22–29, 41–49
Advanced 11–14, 22–35, 41–49

If you finished Example ② assign:
Average 1–8, 11–18, 23–35 odd, 41–49
Advanced 11–18, 22–36, 41–49

If you finished Example ③ assign:
Average 1–20, 23–35 odd, 38–49
Advanced 11–21, 30–49

Homework Quick Check

Quickly check key concepts.
Exercises: 12, 16, 20, 28, 34

Math Background

One situation that illustrates multiplication of integers is as follows:

Imagine a road that is laid out like a number line. Mile markers to the north are positive, and to the south negative. A car moving south at 30 mi/h can be represented by −30 mi/h. If the car starts at mile marker 0, its position after 2 hours would be at mile marker −60 (2 × −30 = −60). The car's position 2 hours before it reached mile marker 0 would have been at mile marker 60 (−2 × −30 = 60). Similar examples can be created using a northbound car traveling at +30 mi/h.

State Resources

go.hrw.com
State Resources Online
KEYWORD: MT7 Resources

GUIDED PRACTICE

See Example ① **Multiply or divide.**

1. $8(-4)$ **−32**
2. $\frac{-54}{9}$ **−6**
3. $-7(-4)$ **28**
4. $\frac{32}{-8}$ **−4**

See Example ② **Simplify.**

5. $-7(5 - 12)$ **49**
6. $4(-3 - 9)$ **−48**
7. $-6(-5 + 9)$ **−24**
8. $11(-7 + 3)$ **−44**

See Example ③ An investor buys shares of stock A and stock B. Stock A loses $8 per share, and stock B gains $5 per share. Given the number of shares, how much does the investor lose or gain?

9. stock A: 20 shares, stock B: 35 shares **gains $15**
10. stock A: 30 shares, stock B: 20 shares **loses $140**

INDEPENDENT PRACTICE

See Example ① **Multiply or divide.**

11. $-3(-7)$ **21**
12. $\frac{72}{-6}$ **−12**
13. $12(-7)$ **−84**
14. $\frac{-42}{6}$ **−7**

See Example ② **Simplify.**

15. $12(9 - 14)$ **−60**
16. $-13(-2 - 8)$ **130**
17. $13(8 - 11)$ **−39**
18. $10 + 4(5 - 8)$ **−2**

See Example ③ A student puts $50 in the bank each time he makes a deposit. He takes $20 each time he makes a withdrawal. Given the number of transactions, what is the net change in the student's account?

19. deposits: 4, withdrawals: 5 **+$100**
20. deposits: 3, withdrawals: 8 **−$10**

PRACTICE AND PROBLEM SOLVING

Extra Practice
See page 783.

21. $\frac{15}{3}$; 5
$\frac{-6}{3}$; −2
$\frac{9}{3}$; 3
$\frac{-15}{3}$; −5

21. **Earth Science** Ocean tides are the result of the gravitational force between the sun, the moon, and the earth. When ocean tides occur, the earth's crust also moves. This is called an earth tide. The formula for the height of an earth tide is $y = \frac{x}{3}$, where x is the height of the ocean tide. Fill in the table.

Ocean Tide Height (x)	$\frac{x}{3}$	Earth Tide Height (y)
15	▦	▦
−6	▦	▦
9	▦	▦
−15	▦	▦

Perform the given operations.

22. $-7(6)$ **−42**
23. $\frac{-144}{12}$ **−12**
24. $-7(-7)$ **49**
25. $\frac{160}{-40}$ **−4**
26. $2(-3)(-5)$ **30**
27. $\frac{-96}{-12}$ **8**
28. $12(3)(-2)$ **−72**
29. $\frac{-18(6)}{-3}$ **36**

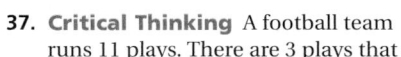

Earth Science

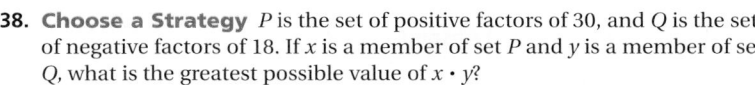

Anoplogaster cornuta, often called a fangtooth or ogrefish, is a predatory fish that reaches a maximum length of 15 cm. It can be found in tropical and temperate waters at −16,000 ft.

Evaluate the expressions for the given value of the variable.

30. $-4t - 5$ for $t = 3$ **−17** **31.** $-x + 2$ for $x = -9$ **11** **32.** $6(s + 9)$ for $s = -1$ **24**

33. $\dfrac{-r}{8}$ for $r = 64$ **−8** **34.** $\dfrac{-42}{t}$ for $t = -6$ **7** **35.** $\dfrac{y - 11}{-4}$ for $y = 35$ **−6**

36. Earth Science The ocean floor is extremely uneven. It includes underwater mountains, ridges, and extremely deep areas called *trenches*. To the nearest foot, find the average depth of the trenches shown. **−32,148 ft**

Depths of Ocean Trenches

(Sea level) 0
−20,000
−25,000
−30,000
−35,000
−40,000

Depth (ft)

Bonin −32,788   Kuril −31,988   Yap −27,976
Mariana −35,840

37. Critical Thinking A football team runs 11 plays. There are 3 plays that result in a loss of 2 yards each and 8 plays that result in a gain of 4 yards each. To find the total yards gained, Art evaluates the expression $3(-2) + 8(4)$. Bella first finds the total yards lost, 6, and the total yards gained, 32. Then she subtracts 6 from 32. Compare these two methods.

37. Possible answer: Both methods give the correct result. Art is adding negative yardage. Bella is subtracting total yards lost.

38. Choose a Strategy P is the set of positive factors of 30, and Q is the set of negative factors of 18. If x is a member of set P and y is a member of set Q, what is the greatest possible value of $x \cdot y$?

(A) 540   (B) 180   (C) 90   (D) −1

39. Write About It If you know that the product of two integers is negative, what can you say about the two integers? Give examples.

40. Challenge How many yards must be gained after a loss of 3 yards to have a total gain of 10 yards? **13 yd**

TEST PREP and Spiral Review

41. Multiple Choice What is the product of −7 and −10?

(A) −70   (B) −17   (C) −3   (D) 70

42. Short Response Brenda donates part of her salary to the local children's hospital each month by having $15 deducted from her monthly paycheck. Write an integer to represent the deduction recorded on each paycheck. Find an integer to represent the change in the amount of money in Brenda's paychecks after 1.5 years. **−$15, −$270**

Write an algebraic expression for each word phrase. (Lesson 1-2)

43. j decreased by 18 $j - 18$ **44.** twice b less 12 $2b - 12$ **45.** 22 less than y $y - 22$

Find each sum or difference. (Lessons 1-4 and 1-5)

46. $-7 + 3$ **−4**   **47.** $5 - (-4)$ **9**   **48.** $-3 + (-6)$ **−9**   **49.** $-513 - (-259)$ **−254**

CHALLENGE 1-6

Challenge
1-6 *Pearls of Wisdom*

For security, bead bracelets are strung with knots between beads.

Starting to the right of the equals-sign clasp and moving clockwise, write × or ÷ as the knots between numbered beads to make the expression around the bracelet true.

Example

③ ÷ 1 × 4 ÷ −2 − −2 × 8 × −1 ÷ −4 ÷ 2 = ③

1.

2.

3.

PROBLEM SOLVING 1-6

Problem Solving
1-6 *Multiplying and Dividing Integers*

Write the correct answer.

1. A submersible started at the surface of the water and was moving down at −12 meters per minute toward the ocean floor. The submersible traveled at this rate for 32 minutes before coming to rest on the ocean floor. What is the depth of the ocean floor?

___−384 m___

2. For the first week in January, the daily high temperatures in Bismarck, North Dakota, were 7°F, −10°F, −10°F, −7°F, 8°F, 12°F, and 14°F. What was the average daily high temperature for the week?

___2°F___

3. Sally went golfing and recorded her scores as −2 on the first hole, −2 on the second hole, and 1 on the third hole. What is her average for the first three holes?

___−1___

4. The ocean floor is at −96 m. Tom has reached −15 m. If he continues to move down at −3 m per minute, how far will he be from the ocean floor after 7 minutes?

___60 m___

Use the table below to answer Exercises 5–7. Choose the letter for the best answer.

5. What is the caloric impact of 2 hours of in-line skating?
   A −477 Cal   C −583 Cal
   B −479 Cal   D −954 Cal

6. What is the caloric impact of eating a hamburger and then playing Frisbee for 3 hours?
   F 220 Cal   H 190 Cal
   G −190 Cal   J −220 Cal

7. Tim plays basketball for 1 hour, skates for 5 hours, and plays Frisbee for 4 hours. What is the average amount of calories Tim burns per hour?
   A −375 Cal   C −545 Cal
   B −1250 Cal D −409 Cal

| Calories Consumed or Burned | |
Food or Exercise	Calories
Apple	125
Pepperoni pizza (slice)	181
Hamburger	425
Basketball (1hr)	−545
In-line skating (1 hr)	−477
Frisbee (1 hr)	−205

ONGOING ASSESSMENT and INTERVENTION

Diagnose Before the Lesson
1-6 Warm Up, TE p. 26

Monitor During the Lesson
1-6 Know-It Notebook
1-6 Questioning Strategies

Assess After the Lesson
1-6 Lesson Quiz, TE p. 19

Answers

39. Possible answer: If the product of two integers is negative, then the integers have opposite signs; for example, $2 \cdot (-3) = -6$ and $-2 \cdot 3 = -6$.

TEST PREP DOCTOR For Exercise 42, remind students that multiplication is also repeated addition. Encourage students to create a table of values to determine the change in the amount of money in Brenda's paychecks if they are struggling with calculating the change by using multiplication.

Journal

Have students write about a career or activity in which someone might want to find an average (mean) of negative integers. One possibility is meteorology; a meteorologist might need an average winter temperature.

Power Presentations with PowerPoint®

1-6 Lesson Quiz

Multiply or divide.

1. $-8(4)$ −32

2. $\dfrac{-12(5)}{-10}$ 6

Simplify.

3. $-2(13 - 4)$ 18

4. $6(-5 - 3)$ −48

5. Evin completes 11 transactions in his bank account. In 6 transactions, he withdraws $10. In 5 transactions, he deposits $20. Find the total net change in dollars. $40

Also available on transparency

Organizer

Objective: Assess students' mastery of concepts and skills in Lessons 1-1 through 1-6.

Resources

 Assessment Resources
Section 1A Quiz

 Test & Practice Generator
One-Stop Planner®

INTERVENTION ◄══►

Resources

 Ready to Go On?
Intervention and
Enrichment Worksheets

🔘 **Ready to Go On? CD-ROM**

🪐 **Ready to Go On? Online**

my.hrw.com

Ready to Go On? (sidebar)

Quiz for Lessons 1-1 Through 1-6

☑ **1-1** **Variables and Expressions**

Evaluate each expression for the given values of the variables.

1. $5x + 6y$ for $x = 8$ and $y = 4$ **64**   **2.** $6(r - 7t)$ for $r = 80$ and $t = 8$ **144**

☑ **1-2** **Algebraic Expressions**

5. 46 is less than the product of 7 and y
6. 2 times the sum of 18 and t

Write an algebraic expression for each word phrase.

$10 + 16m$

3. one-sixth the sum of r and 7 $\frac{1}{6}(r + 7)$ **4.** 10 plus the product of 16 and m

Write a word phrase for each algebraic expression.

5. $7y - 46$ **6.** $2(18 + t)$ **7.** $\frac{x - 10}{3}$ **8.** $15 + \frac{p}{32}$

☑ **1-3** **Integers and Absolute Value**

7. one-third the difference of x and 10
8. 15 more than the quotient of p and 32

Write the integers in order from least to greatest.

9. $-17, 25, 18, -2$ **$-17, -2, 18, 25$**   **10.** $0, -8, 9, 1$ **$-8, 0, 1, 9$**

Evaluate each expression.

11. $|14 - 7|$ **7**   **12.** $|-15| - |-12|$ **3**   **13.** $|26| + |-14|$ **40**

☑ **1-4** **Adding Integers**

Evaluate each expression for the given value of the variable.

14. $p + 14$ for $p = -8$ **6**   **15.** $w + (-9)$ for $w = -4$ **-13**

16. In Loma, Montana, on January 15, 1972, the temperature increased 103 degrees in a 24-hour period. If the lowest temperature on that day was $-54°F$, what was the highest temperature? **49°F**

☑ **1-5** **Subtracting Integers**

Subtract.

17. $12 - (-8)$ **20**   **18.** $-7 - (-5)$ **-2**   **19.** $-5 - (-16)$ **11**   **20.** $-22 - 5$ **-27**

21. The point of highest elevation in the United States is on Mount McKinley, Alaska, at 20,320 feet. The point of lowest elevation is in Death Valley, California, at -282 feet. What is the difference in the elevations? **20,602 ft**

☑ **1-6** **Multiplying and Dividing Integers**

Multiply or divide.

-60

22. $(-8)(-6)$ **48**   **23.** $\frac{-28}{7}$ **-4**   **24.** $\frac{39}{-3}$ **-13**   **25.** $(-2)(-5)(-6)$

READY TO GO ON?

Diagnose and Prescribe

 NO INTERVENE

 YES ENRICH

READY TO GO ON? Intervention, Section 1A			
Ready to Go On? Intervention	🗞 **Worksheets**	🔘 **CD-ROM**	🪐 **Online**
☑ Lesson 1-1	1-1 Intervention	Activity 1-1	
☑ Lesson 1-2	1-2 Intervention	Activity 1-2	
☑ Lesson 1-3	1-3 Intervention	Activity 1-3	Diagnose and Prescribe Online
☑ Lesson 1-4	1-4 Intervention	Activity 1-4	
☑ Lesson 1-5	1-5 Intervention	Activity 1-5	
☑ Lesson 1-6	1-6 Intervention	Activity 1-6	

READY TO GO ON?
Enrichment, **Section 1A**

🗞 **Worksheets**
🔘 **CD-ROM**
🪐 **Online**

Focus on Problem Solving

Solve
• Choose an operation: Addition or Subtraction

To decide whether to add or subtract, you need to determine what action is taking place in the problem. If you are combining numbers or putting numbers together, you need to add. If you are taking away or finding out how far apart two numbers are, you need to subtract.

Action	Operation	Illustration
Combining or putting together	Add	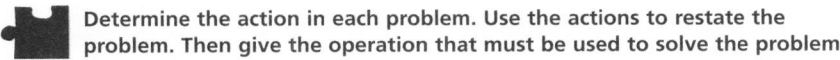
Removing or taking away	Subtract	
Finding the difference	Subtract	

Jan has 10 red marbles. Joe gives her 3 more. How many marbles does Jan have now? The action is combining marbles. Add 10 and 3.

Determine the action in each problem. Use the actions to restate the problem. Then give the operation that must be used to solve the problem.

❶ Lake Superior is the largest of the Great Lakes and contains approximately 3000 mi^3 of water. Lake Michigan is the second largest Great Lake by volume and contains approximately 1180 mi^3 of water. Estimate the difference in volumes of water.

❷ The average temperature in Homer, Alaska, is approximately 53°F in July and approximately 24°F in December. Find the difference between the average temperature in Homer in July and in December.

❸ Einar has $18 to spend on his friend's birthday presents. He buys one present that costs $12. How much does he have left to spend?

❹ Dinah got 87 points on her first test and 93 points on her second test. What is her combined point total for the first two tests?

Answers

1. 3000 − 1180 = 1820 mi^3

2. 53 − 24 = 29°F

3. 18 − 12 = $6

4. 87 + 93 = 180 points

Equations and Inequalities

One-Minute Section Planner

Lesson	Materials	MiC and Lab Resources
1-7 Hands-On Lab Model Solving Equations • Use algebra tiles to model solving equations. **Lesson 1-7** Solving Equations by Adding or Subtracting • Solve equations using addition and subtraction. ☑ SAT-10 ☑ ITBS ☑ CTBS ☑ NAEP	Algebra tiles (MK), balance scale	**MiC:** *Algebra Rules* pp. 33–36 *Hands-On Lab Activities* 1-7
Lesson 1-8 Solving Equations by Multiplying or Dividing • Solve equations using multiplication and division. ☑ SAT-10 ☑ ITBS ☑ CTBS ☑ NAEP	Square and circle cutouts	**MiC:** *Algebra Rules* pp. 33–36 *Hands-On Lab Activities* 1-8
Lesson 1-9 Introduction to Inequalities • Solve and graph inequalities. ☑ SAT-10 ☑ ITBS ☑ CTBS ☐ NAEP	Index cards	**MiC:** *Graphing Equations* pp. 6–7

MK = *Manipulatives Kit*

Mathematics in Context

The units *Algebra Rules* and *Graphing Equations* from the *Mathematics in Context* © 2006 series can be used with Section 1B. See Section Planner above for suggestions for integrating *MiC* with *Holt Mathematics*.

Section Overview

Solving Equations Containing Integers

Why? Many real-world problems may be solved by using equations.

To solve an equation, isolate the variable on one side of the equation alone.
To do this, *undo* the operation that is performed on the variable in the equation.

$$25 = r - 5$$
$$\underline{+\ 15 = \ \ +\ 15}$$
$$40 = r$$

To *undo the subtraction* and isolate the variable *r*, add 15 to both sides of the equation.

$$225 = -5r$$
$$\frac{225}{-5} = \frac{-5r}{-5}$$
$$-45 = r$$

To *undo the multiplication* and isolate the variable *r*, divide both sides by −5.

$$25 = r + 15$$
$$\underline{-\ 15 \quad \ -\ 15}$$
$$10 = r$$

To *undo the addition* and isolate the variable *r*, subtract 15 from both sides of the equation.

$$45 = \frac{r}{-5}$$
$$(-5)(45) = (-5)\left(\frac{r}{-5}\right)$$
$$-225 = r$$

To *undo the division* and isolate the variable *r*, multiply both sides by −5.

Inequalities

Why? Students must be able to recognize and interpret inequalities before they can solve them and understand how to apply them.

Inequality	Graph
$x > 1$	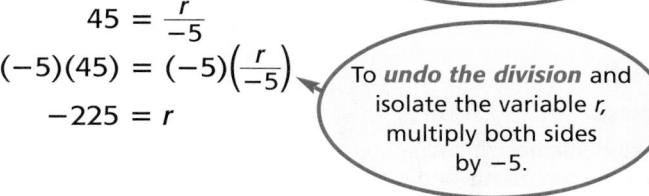
$x \leq 1$	

○ Use an open circle when the graph does not include the point.

● Use a closed circle when the graph includes the point.

Word Phrase	Inequality	Sample Solutions	Solution Set
x is less than 5	$x < 5$	$x = 4$ *4 < 5* $x = 2.1$ *2.1 < 5*	
a is greater than 0 *a* is more than 0	$a > 0$	$a = 7$ *7 > 0* $a = 25$ *25 > 0*	
y is less than or equal to 2 *y* is at most 2	$y \leq 2$	$y = 0$ *0 ≤ 2* $y = 1.5$ *1.5 ≤ 2*	
m is greater than or equal to 3 *m* is at least 3	$m \geq 3$	$m = 17$ *17 ≥ 3* $m = 3$ *3 ≥ 3*	

Organizer

Pacing:
Traditional 1 day
Block $\frac{1}{2}$ day

Objective: Use algebra tiles to model solving equations.

Materials: Algebra tiles

 Online Edition
Algebra Tiles

 Countdown to Testing Week 2

Resources

 Hands-On Lab Activities
Lab 1-7 Recording Sheet

Teach

Discuss

Have students describe what each algebra tile represents and how to represent each side of an equation using algebra tiles.

Close

Key Concept

You can use algebra tiles to solve equations.

Assessment

Use algebra tiles to model and solve each equation.

1. $x + 1 = 4$

2. $x + (-2) = -3$

State Resources

go.hrw.com
State Resources Online
KEYWORD: MT7 Resources

Hands-On
Model Solving Equations

Use with Lesson 1-7

go.hrw.com
Lab Resources Online
KEYWORD: MT7 Lab1

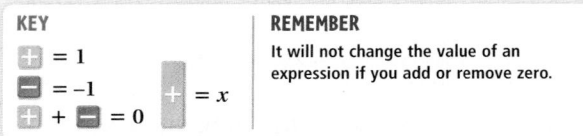

KEY
$\boxed{+} = 1$
$\boxed{-} = -1$
$\boxed{+} + \boxed{-} = 0$ $\boxed{+} = x$

REMEMBER
It will not change the value of an expression if you add or remove zero.

You can use algebra tiles to help you solve equations.

Activity

To solve the equation $x + 3 = 5$, you need to get x alone on one side of the equal sign. You can add or remove tiles as long as you add the same amount or remove the same amount on both sides.

$x + 3 = 5$ *Remove 3 from each side.* $x = 2$

❶ Use algebra tiles to model and solve each equation.

   a. $x + 2 = 6$ $x = 4$ **b.** $x + 2 = 7$ $x = 5$ **c.** $x + (-4) = -7$ $x = -3$ **d.** $x + 7 = 7$ $x = 0$

The equation $x + 4 = 2$ is more difficult to solve because there are not enough yellow tiles on the right side. You can use the fact that the sum of two opposites is equal to zero to help you solve the equation.

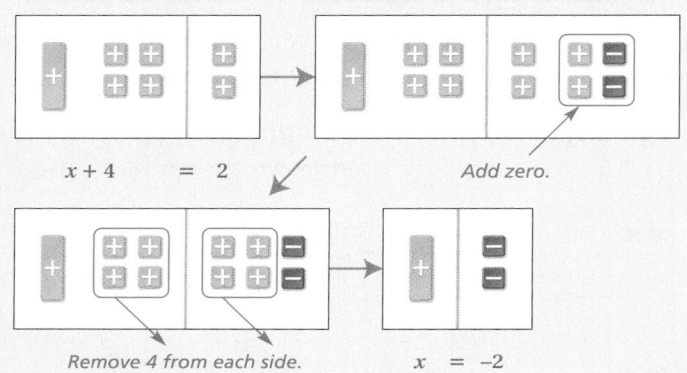

$x + 4 = 2$ *Add zero.*

$x = -2$

Remove 4 from each side. $x = -2$

State Resources

Karen Smith
Duxbury, Massachusetts

Teacher to Teacher

Instead of using algebra tiles, I use *cups and chips*. I provide each student with a few yellow and red disposable cups and several red and yellow chips.

To start the activity, I model an equation with cups representing variables and chips representing numbers (e.g., for the equation $x - 4 = 2$, I would place a yellow cup and four red chips on one side and two yellow chips on the other). I explain to the students that we want to find out how much the cup represents so we must get the cup alone.

I ask the students how we can do this, and then we solve the equation together by adding or removing the appropriate number of chips to both sides of the equation.

2 Use algebra tiles to model and solve each equation.

a. $x + 5 = 8$ $x = 3$ **b.** $x + 8 = 3$ $x = -5$ **c.** $x + (-5) = -2$ $x = 3$ **d.** $x + (-11) = -4$
$x = 7$

Modeling $x - 4 = 2$ is similar to modeling $x + 4 = 2$. Remember that you can add the same amount to both sides of an equation and the equation's value does not change.

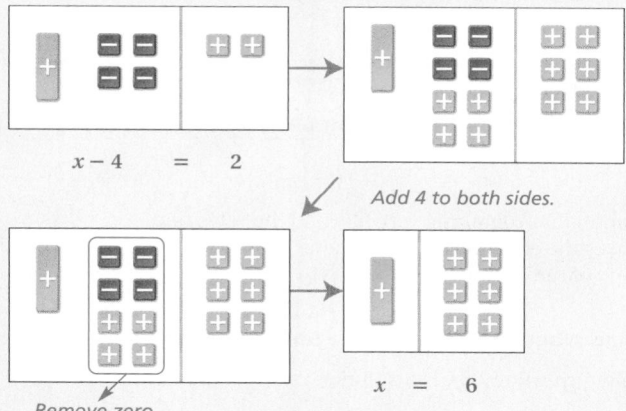

$x - 4 \quad = \quad 2$

Add 4 to both sides.

$x \quad = \quad 6$

Remove zero.

3 Use algebra tiles to model and solve each equation.

a. $x - 1 = 2$ $x = 3$ **b.** $x - 3 = 7$ $x = 10$ **c.** $x - 6 = -4$ $x = 2$ **d.** $x - 8 = 3$ $x = 11$

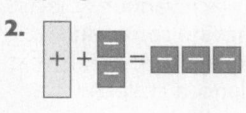 **Think and Discuss**

1. When you add zero to an equation, how do you know the numbers of yellow square tiles and red square tiles that you need to represent the addition?
1. Possible answer: Determine how many tiles you need to remove from each side. Add pairs of positive and negative tiles until you have enough tiles to remove the correct number.

2. When you remove tiles, what operation are you representing? When you add tiles, what operation are you representing?   subtraction; addition

3. How can you use the original model to check your solution?   To check, replace the x-tile with the number of unit tiles from the answer and see if the equation balances.

4. Give an example of an equation with a negative solution that would require your adding 2 red square tiles and 2 yellow square tiles to model and solve it. $x + 2 = -5$

5. Give an example of an equation with a positive solution that would require your adding 2 red square tiles and 2 yellow square tiles to model and solve it. $x + (-2) = 4$

Try This

Use algebra tiles to model and solve each equation.

1. $x - 8 = 12$
$x = 20$
2. $x + 3 = -9$
$x = -12$
3. $x + (-2) = -8$
$x = -6$
4. $x - 9 = -6$
$x = 3$

5. Kensho used a gift card to buy a $6 book. After the purchase, he had $14 left on his card. Model and solve an equation to find the original value of the gift card. $c - 6 = 14$; $c = \$20$

6. Sari ran a total of 15 miles on two days. On the first day, she ran 6 miles. Model and solve an equation to find how far she ran on the second day. $6 + m = 15$; $m = 9$ mi

Answers to Assessment

1.

$x = 3$

2.

$x = -1$

Answers to *Activity*

1. a.

b.

c.

d.

2. a.

b.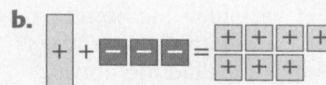

c.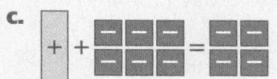

d.

3. a.

b.

c.

d.

Objective: Students solve equations using addition and subtraction.

 Hands-On Lab
In *Hands-On Lab Activities*

 Online Edition
Tutorial Videos, Interactivities

 Countdown to Testing Week 2

Power Presentations
with PowerPoint®

Warm Up

Add, subtract, multiply, or divide.

1. $24 + 17$ 41   **2.** $23 - 19$ 4

3. $12 \cdot 3$ 36   **4.** $6(-7)$ -42

5. $\frac{-64}{8}$ -8 **6.** $-250 + (-85)$ -335

Problem of the Day

Janie's horse refused to do 5 jumps today and cleared 14 jumps. Yesterday, the horse cleared 9 more jumps than today. How many jumps did the horse clear in the two-day jumping event?   37

Also available on transparency

Math Humor

After he put his algebra homework in a jar of hot water, the student explained, "I thought you told us to *dissolve* the equations!"

State Resources

 **go.hrw.com**
State Resources Online
KEYWORD: MT7 Resources

1-7 Solving Equations by Adding or Subtracting

Learn to solve equations using addition and subtraction.

Vocabulary
equation
inverse operation

An **equation** is a mathematical sentence that uses an equal sign to show that two expressions have the same value. All of these are equations.

$$3 + 8 = 11 \qquad r + 6 = 14 \qquad -24 = x - 7 \qquad \frac{-100}{2} = -50$$

To *solve* an equation that contains a variable, find the value of the variable that makes the equation true. This value of the variable is called the *solution* of the equation.

EXAMPLE 1   Determining Whether a Number Is a Solution of an Equation

Determine which value of *x* is a solution of the equation.

$x - 7 = 13; x = 12$ or 20

Substitute each value for *x* in the equation.

$x - 7 = 13$
$12 - 7 \stackrel{?}{=} 13$ *Substitute 12 for x.*
$5 \stackrel{?}{=} 13$ ✗

So 12 **is not** a solution.

$x - 7 = 13$
$20 - 7 \stackrel{?}{=} 13$ *Substitute 20 for x.*
$13 \stackrel{?}{=} 13$ ✔

So 20 **is** a solution.

Helpful Hint

The phrase "subtraction 'undoes' addition" can be understood with this example: If you start with 3 and add 4, you can get back to 3 by subtracting 4.

$$\begin{array}{r} 3 + 4 \\ -\ 4 \\ \hline 3 \end{array}$$

Addition and subtraction are **inverse operations**, which means they "undo" each other. To solve an equation, use inverse operations to isolate the variable. In other words, get the variable alone on one side of the equal sign.

To solve a subtraction equation, like $y - 15 = 7$, you would use the *Addition Property of Equality*.

ADDITION PROPERTY OF EQUALITY		
Words	**Numbers**	**Algebra**
You can add the same number to both sides of an equation, and the statement will still be true.	$\begin{array}{r} 2 + 3 = \ \ 5 \\ +\ 4 \ \ +4 \\ \hline 2 + 7 = \ \ 9 \end{array}$	$x = y$ $x + z = y + z$

---

1 Introduce

Alternate Opener

EXPLORATION

1-7 Solving Equations by Adding or Subtracting

Evaluate the expressions for each given value of *x*.

1.
x	$x+1$
0	
1	
2	
3	

2.
x	$x-2$
3	
4	
5	
6	

Each expression below has been evaluated. Find the value of *x*.

3.
x	$x+2$
	3
	4
	5
	6

4.
x	$x-5$
	0
	1
	2
	3

Think and Discuss

5. Explain how you evaluated the expressions in Problems 1 and 2.

6. Explain how you found the values of *x* in Problems 3 and 4.

Motivate

Ask students what makes a scale stay in balance. Have students place various objects on a two-pan scale, removing some, and observing the results. Explain to students that an equation is like a balanced scale, so they must add and subtract carefully.

Explorations and answers are provided in *Alternate Openers: Explorations Transparencies.*

There is a similar property for solving addition equations, like $x + 9 = 11$. It is called the *Subtraction Property of Equality*.

SUBTRACTION PROPERTY OF EQUALITY		
Words	**Numbers**	**Algebra**
You can subtract the same number from both sides of an equation, and the statement will still be true.	$\begin{array}{r} 4 + 7 = 11 \\ \underline{-3 -3} \\ 4 + 4 = 8 \end{array}$	$x = y$ $x - z = y - z$

Power Presentations
with PowerPoint®

EXAMPLE 2  **Solving Equations Using Addition and Subtraction Properties**

Solve.

A $6 + t = 28$

$6 + t = 28$
$\underline{-6 -6}$ $\qquad$ *Subtract 6 from both sides.*
$0 + t = 22$
$t = 22$ $\qquad$ *Identity Property of Zero: $0 + t = t$*

Check

$6 + t = 28$
$6 + 22 \overset{?}{=} 28$ $\qquad$ *Substitute 22 for t.*
$28 \overset{?}{=} 28$ ✔

B $m - 8 = -14$

$m - 8 = -14$
$\underline{ +8 +8}$ $\qquad$ *Add 8 to both sides.*
$m + 0 = -6$
$m = -6$

Check

$m - 8 = -14$
$-6 - 8 \overset{?}{=} -14$ $\qquad$ *Substitute −6 for m.*
$-14 \overset{?}{=} -14$ ✔

C $15 = w + (-14)$

$15 = w + (-14)$
$15 - (-14) = w + (-14) - (-14)$ $\qquad$ *Subtract −14 from both sides.*
$29 = w + 0$
$29 = w$
$w = 29$ $\qquad$ *Definition of Equality*

---

2 Teach

Guided Instruction

In this lesson, students learn to solve equations using addition and subtraction. Before actually solving an equation, review with students how to determine whether a given value is a solution of an equation. Stress the importance of writing all of the steps when solving equations. Share with students the reason for developing the habit—that they will solve equations later that require more steps.

 **Reaching All Learners**
Through Cooperative Learning

Have students work in pairs. Each student writes an addition or subtraction equation, such as $8 + x = 32$ and $x - 3 = 12$, on a sheet of paper. Each student solves the equation and then gives the paper to his or her partner to check the solution. If both solutions are correct, they exchange again to get their original papers and write and solve another equation. If a solution is not correct, the two students work together to find the correct solution.

Possible answers to *Think and Discuss*

1. The dog on the left is pulling with more force, so the rope would move to the left.

2. Add 5 to each side to isolate *y*. The numerical expression on the right side of the equation is the value of *y*. *y* = 21.
   Check the answer:
   21 − 5 = 16.

EXAMPLE 3 **PROBLEM SOLVING APPLICATION**

PROBLEM SOLVING

Net force is the sum of all forces acting on an object. Expressed in newtons (N), it tells you in which direction and how quickly the object will move. If two dogs are playing tug-of-war, and the dog on the right pulls with a force of 12 N, what force is the dog on the left exerting on the rope if the net force is 2 N?

Helpful Hint

Force is measured in newtons (N). The number of newtons tells the size of the force and the sign tells its direction. Positive is to the right, and negative is to the left.

1 Understand the Problem

The **answer** is the force that the left dog exerts on the rope.

List the **important information:**
- The dog on the right pulls with a force of 12 N.
- The net force is 2 N.

Show the **relationship** of the information:

| net force | = | left dog's force | + | right dog's force |

2 3 ~~ke~~ a Plan

Write an equation and solve it. Let *f* represent the left dog's force on the rope, and use the equation model.

$$2 = f + 12$$

3 Solve

$2 = f + 12$
$\underline{-12 \quad\quad -12}$ *Subtract 12 from both sides.*
$-10 = f$

The left dog is exerting a force of −10 newtons on the rope.

4 Look Back

The problem states that the net force is 2 N, which means that the dog on the right must be pulling with more force. The absolute value of the left dog's force is less than the absolute value of the right dog's force, $|-10| < |12|$, so the answer is reasonable.

Think and Discuss

1. **Explain** what the result would be in the tug-of-war match in Example 3 if the dog on the left pulled with a force of −7 N and the dog on the right pulled with a force of 6 N.

2. **Describe** the steps to solve $y - 5 = 16$.

---

3 Close

Summarize

Show students a group of several addition equations. For example:

$x + 4 = 9$ $12 + y = 15$
$10 = n + 3$ $16 = 4 + z$

Point out the plus sign in each of the equations. Ask students what operation they would use to solve each of those equations. subtraction Show the solutions and point out the subtraction step in each one. Repeat the procedure with a group of subtraction equations.

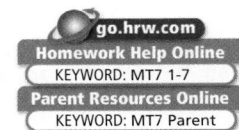

GUIDED PRACTICE

See Example 1 Determine which value of x is a solution of each equation.

1. $x + 6 = 18$; $x = 10, 12,$ or 25 **12** **2.** $x - 7 = 14$; $x = 2, 7,$ or 21 **21**

See Example 2 Solve.

3. $m - 9 = -23$ **−14** **4.** $8 + t = 13$ **5** **5.** $p - (-13) = -10$ **−23**

6. $q + (-25) = 81$ **106** **7.** $26 = t - 13$ **39** **8.** $52 = p + (-41)$ **93**

See Example 3 **9.** A team of mountain climbers descended 3600 feet to a camp that was at an altitude of 12,035 feet. At what altitude did they start? **15,635 ft**

INDEPENDENT PRACTICE

See Example 1 Determine which value of x is a solution for each equation.

10. $x - 14 = 8$; $x = 6, 22,$ or 32 **22** **11.** $x + 23 = 55$; $x = 15, 28,$ or 32 **32**

See Example 2 Solve.

12. $9 = w + (-8)$ **17** **13.** $m - 11 = 33$ **44** **14.** $4 + t = 16$ **12**

15. $z + (-22) = -96$ **−74** **16.** $102 = p - (-130)$ **−28** **17.** $27 = h + (-8)$ **35**

See Example 3 **18.** Olivia owns 43 CDs. This is 15 more CDs than Angela owns. How many CDs does Angela own? **28**

PRACTICE AND PROBLEM SOLVING

Extra Practice
See page 783.

Solve. Check your answer.

19. $7 + t = 12$ **5** **20.** $h - 21 = -52$ **−31** **21.** $15 = m + (-9)$ **24**

22. $m - 5 = -10$ **−5** **23.** $h + 8 = 11$ **3** **24.** $-6 + t = -14$ **−8**

25. $1785 = t - (-836)$ **949** **26.** $m + 35 = -172$ **−207** **27.** $x - 29 = 81$ **110**

28. $p + 8 = 23$ **15** **29.** $n + (-14) = -31$ **−17** **30.** $20 = -8 + w$ **28**

31. $8 + t = -130$ **−138** **32.** $57 = c - 28$ **85** **33.** $-987 = w + 797$
−1784

34. **Social Studies** In 1990, the population of Cheyenne, Wyoming, was 73,142. By 2000, the population had increased to 81,607. Write and solve an equation to find n, the increase in Cheyenne's population from 1990 to 2000. **73,142 + n = 81,607; 8465**

35. **Astronomy** Mercury's surface temperature has a range of 600°C. This range is the broadest of any planet in the solar system. Given that the lowest temperature on Mercury's surface is −173°C, write and solve an equation to find the highest temperature. $t - 600 = -173$; **427°C**

1-7 Exercises

Assignment Guide

If you finished Example **1** assign:
Average 1, 2, 10, 11, 36–41, 46–56
Advanced 10, 11, 36–41, 46–56

If you finished Example **2** assign:
Average 1–8, 10–17, 19–41 odd, 46–56
Advanced 10–17, 28–42, 45–56

If you finished Example **3** assign:
Average 1–17 odd, 42–56
Advanced 15–18, 42–56

Homework Quick Check

Quickly check key concepts.
Exercises: 10, 16, 24, 28, 40

Math Background

An equation with a variable is sometimes called an open sentence. To find a solution to an equation is to find a number that makes an open sentence a true sentence. For example, $x + 5 = 7$ is an open sentence. If you substitute the solution 2 for x, you get the true sentence $2 + 5 = 7$.

Two properties used in solving equations in this lesson are the Addition and Subtraction Properties of Equality. After discussing negative numbers in Chapter 2, the Addition Property of Equality alone can serve the purpose of both properties. To solve the equation $x + 5 = 7$, you can either subtract 5 from both sides or add −5 to both sides.

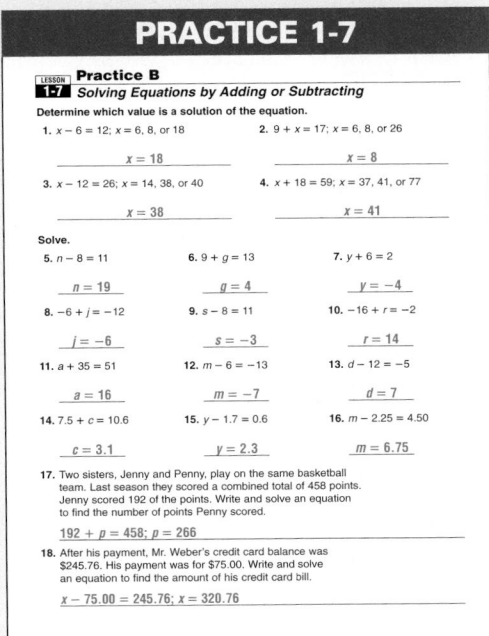

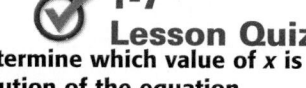

42.
$13 + c = 3$; -10
$9 + c = -1$; -10
$8 + c = -2$; -10
$11 + c = 1$; -10

43. Possible answer: The student either subtracted 3 from -7 or added -3 to -7; $-7 - (-3) = -4$.

44. Possible answer: Gaining negative yardage is the same as losing that many yards.

Determine which value of the variable is a solution of the equation.

36. $d + 4 = 24$; $d = 6, 20,$ or 28 **20**
37. $k + (-13) = 27$; $k = 40, 45,$ or 50 **40**
38. $d - 17 = -36$; $d = 19, 17,$ or -19 **−19**
39. $k + 3 = 4$; $k = 1, 7,$ or 17 **1**
40. $12 = -14 + s$; $s = 20, 26,$ or 32 **26**
41. $-32 = 27 + g$; $g = 58, -25, -59$ **−59**

42. **Physical Science** An ion is a charged particle. Each proton in an ion has a charge of $+1$ and each electron has a charge of -1. The ion charge is the electron charge plus the proton charge. Write and solve an equation to find the electron charge for each ion.

Hydrogen sulfate ion (HSO_4^-)

Name of Ion	Proton Charge	Electron Charge	Ion Charge
Aluminum ion (Al^{3+})	+13		+3
Hydroxide ion (OH^-)	+9		−1
Oxide ion (O^{2-})	+8		−2
Sodium ion (Na^+)	+11		+1

43. **What's the Error?** A student evaluated the expression $-7 - (-3)$ and came up with the answer -10. What did the student do wrong?

44. **Write About It** Explain what a gain of negative yardage means in football.

45. **Challenge** Explain how you could solve for *h* in the equation $14 - h = 8$ using algebra. Then find the value of *h*. **Possible answer: Subtract 14 from both sides, and then divide by −1; $h = 6$**

TEST PREP and Spiral Review

46. **Multiple Choice** Which value of *x* is the solution of the equation $x - 5 = 8$?
   Ⓐ 3   Ⓑ 11   Ⓒ 13   Ⓓ 15

47. **Multiple Choice** Len bought a pair of $12 flip-flops and a shirt. He paid $30 in all. Which equation can you use to find the price *p* he paid for the shirt?
   Ⓕ $12 - p = 30$ Ⓖ $12 + p = 30$ Ⓗ $30 + p = 12$ Ⓙ $p - 12 = 30$

48. **Gridded Response** What value of *x* is the solution of the equation $-4x - 3 = -19$?   **4**

Add. (Lesson 1-4)
49. $-5 + (-9)$ **−14**   50. $16 + (-22)$ **−6**   51. $-64 + 51$ **−13**   52. $82 + (-75)$ **7**

Multiply or divide. (Lesson 1-6)
53. $7(-8)$ **−56**   54. $-63 \div (-7)$ **9**   55. $\frac{38}{-19}$ **−2**   56. $-8(-13)$ **104**

CHALLENGE 1-7

LESSON 1-7 Challenge
What's Next?

Integers that differ by one, such as 7, 8, 9, are called *consecutive integers*.

Find three consecutive integers whose sum is −12.

Let $x =$ the 1st of the consecutive integers.
Let $x + 1 =$ the 2nd of the consecutive integers.
Let $x + 2 =$ the 3rd of the consecutive integers.

$(x) + (x + 1) + (x + 2) = -12$	Write an equation.
$3x + 3 = -12$	Combine like terms.
$\underline{-3} = \underline{-3}$	Add −3 to each side.
$3x = -15$	
$\frac{3x}{3} = \frac{-15}{3}$	Divide each side by 3.
$x = -5$	

$x + 1 = -5 + 1 = -4$
$x + 2 = -5 + 2 = -3$

So, $-5, -4, -3$ are the three consecutive integers whose sum is -12.

Write and solve an equation to find the three consecutive integers that satisfy the given condition.

1. Three consecutive integers whose sum is 33 are __10__, __11__, __12__.
   Equation $\underline{(x) + (x + 1) + (x + 2) = 33}$
   $x = \underline{10}$

2. Three consecutive integers whose sum is −60 are __−21__, __−20__, __−19__.
   Equation $\underline{(x) + (x + 1) + (x + 2) = -60}$
   $x = \underline{-21}$

3. Three consecutive integers whose sum is −96 are __−33__, __−32__, __−31__.
   Equation $\underline{(x) + (x + 1) + (x + 2) = -96}$
   $x = \underline{-33}$

PROBLEM SOLVING 1-7

LESSON 1-7 Problem Solving
Solving Equations by Adding or Subtracting

Write the correct answer.

1. The 1954 elevation of Mt. Everest was 29,028 ft. In 1999, that elevation was revised to be 29,035 ft. Write an equation to find the change *c* in elevation of Mt. Everest.
   $29,028 + c = 29,035$
   $c = 7$ ft

2. The difference between the boiling and melting points of fluorine is 32°C. If the boiling point of fluorine is −188°C, write an equation and solve to find the melting point *m* of fluorine.
   $-188 - m = 32$;
   $m = -220°C$

3. Lisa sold her old bike for $140 less than she paid for it. She sold the bike for $85. Write and solve an equation to find how much Lisa paid for her bike.
   $p - 140 = 85$;
   $p = $225

4. The average January temperature in Fairbanks, Alaska, is −13°F. The April average is 43°F higher than the January average. Write an equation to find the average April temperature.
   $a - (-13) = 43$;
   $a = 30°F$

Choose the letter for the best answer.

5. A survey found that female teens watched 3 hours of TV per week less than male teens. The female teens reported watching an average of 18 hours of TV. Find the number of hours *h* the male teens watched.
   A $h = 6$ C $h = 18$
   B $h = 15$ **D** $h = 21$

6. It costs about $125 more per year to feed a hamster than it does to feed a bird. If it costs $256 per year to feed a hamster, find the cost *c* to feed a bird.
   F $c = $131   H $c = $256
   G $c = $125   J $c = $381

7. Naples, Florida, is the second fastest growing U.S. metropolitan area. From 1990 to 2000, the population increased by 99,278. If the 2000 population was 251,377, find the population *p* in 1990.
   A $p = 253,377$ C $p = 249,377$
   B $p = 350,655$ **D** $p = 152,099$

8. In 1940, the life expectancy for a female was 65 years. In 1999, the life expectancy for a female was 79 years. Find the increase in the life expectancy for females.
   F 14 yrs   H −14 yrs
   G 1.2 yrs   J 144 yrs

Solving Equations by Multiplying or Dividing

Learn to solve equations using multiplication and division.

Helene plays baritone in her school's marching band. The band has been invited to compete in a national band festival, but they need to raise money in order to make the trip. So far, the band's fundraisers have brought in $720, but that's only one-third of what is needed.

You can write and solve a multiplication equation to figure out how much the band needs to raise in all.

You can solve a multiplication equation using the *Division Property of Equality*.

DIVISION PROPERTY OF EQUALITY		
Words	**Numbers**	**Algebra**
You can divide both sides of an equation by the same nonzero number, and the statement will still be true.	$4 \cdot 3 = 12$ $\dfrac{4 \cdot 3}{2} = \dfrac{12}{2}$ $\dfrac{12}{2} = 6$	$x = y$ $\dfrac{x}{z} = \dfrac{y}{z},$ $z \neq 0$

EXAMPLE 1 Solving Equations Using Division

Solve and check.

A $8x = 32$

$8x = 32$

$\dfrac{8x}{8} = \dfrac{32}{8}$ *Divide both sides by 8.*

$1x = 4$ *1 · x = x*

$x = 4$

Check

$8x = 32$

$8(4) \overset{?}{=} 32$ *Substitute 4 for x.*

$32 \overset{?}{=} 32$ ✔

B $-7y = -91$

$-7y = -91$

$\dfrac{-7y}{-7} = \dfrac{-91}{-7}$ *Divide both sides by −7.*

$1y = 13$ *1 · y = y*

$y = 13$

Check

$-7y = -91$

$-7(13) \overset{?}{=} -91$ *Substitute 13 for y.*

$-91 \overset{?}{=} -91$ ✔

---

1 Introduce

Alternate Opener

Explorations and answers are provided in *Alternate Openers: Explorations Transparencies.*

Motivate

In Lesson 1–7, students may have learned that an equation is like a balanced scale. As with addition and subtraction, remind students to be vigilant about multiplying and dividing by constants.

Warm Up

Write an algebraic expression for each word phrase.

1. a number *x* decreased by 9
$x - 9$

2. 5 times the sum of *p* and 6
$5(p + 6)$

3. 2 plus the product of 8 and *n*
$2 + 8n$

4. the quotient of 4 and a number *c*
$\dfrac{4}{c}$

Problem of the Day

How many pieces do you have if you cut a log into six pieces and then cut each piece into 4 pieces? 24

Also available on transparency

Math Fact

One of the first mathematical achievements was the equation. Equations can be found in written texts of the Babylonians as far back as 3000 B.C.

State Resources

Power Presentations
with PowerPoint®

Additional Examples

Example 1
Solve.
A. $6x = 48$ $x = 8$
B. $-9y = 45$ $y = -5$

Example 2
Solve.
$\frac{b}{-4} = 5$ $b = -20$

Example 3
To go on a school trip, Helene has raised $670, which is only one-fourth of what she needs. What is the total amount needed? **$2680**

Example 4
Solve.
$3x + 2 = 14$ $x = 4$

Also available on transparency

You can solve division equations using the *Multiplication Property of Equality*.

MULTIPLICATION PROPERTY OF EQUALITY		
Words	**Numbers**	**Algebra**
Multiply both sides of an equation by the same number, and the statement will still be true.	$2 \cdot 3 = 6$ $4 \cdot 2 \cdot 3 = 4 \cdot 6$ $8 \cdot 3 = 24$	$x = y$ $zx = zy$

EXAMPLE 2  **Solving Equations Using Multiplication**

Solve $\frac{h}{-3} = 6$.

$$\frac{h}{-3} = 6$$

$$-3 \cdot \frac{h}{-3} = -3 \cdot 6 \qquad \textit{Multiply both sides by } -3.$$

$$h = -18$$

Check

$$\frac{h}{-3} = 6$$

$$\frac{-18}{-3} \overset{?}{=} 6 \qquad \textit{Substitute } -18 \text{ for } h.$$

$$6 \overset{?}{=} 6 ✓$$

EXAMPLE 3 *Money Application*

Helene's band needs money to go to a national competition. So far, band members have raised $720, which is only one-third of what they need. What is the total amount needed?

fraction of total amount raised so far	·	total amount needed	=	amount raised so far
$\frac{1}{3}$	·	x	=	$720

$$\frac{1}{3}x = 720 \qquad \textit{Write the equation.}$$

$$3 \cdot \frac{1}{3}x = 3 \cdot 720 \qquad \textit{Multiply both sides by 3.}$$

$$x = 2160$$

The band needs to raise a total of $2160.

---

2 Teach

Guided Instruction

In this lesson, students learn to solve equations using multiplication and division. Point out that the process is similar to solving equations with addition or subtraction. Review the multiplication and division properties of equality before working through the examples.

 **Inclusion** Encourage students to check their work by substituting the solution into the original equation.

Reaching All Learners
Through Concrete Manipulatives

Use squares and circles to solve the equation $x + 2 = 5$. Have a square represent x and a circle represent 1. Draw or place a square and two circles on the left side of the equal sign and five circles on the right side. Take two circles away from each side to isolate the variable. Students should see that $x = 3$. Ask students to solve $4x = 12$ using squares and circles and explain how they solved this equation.

Students should draw four squares on the left side and twelve circles on the right. They should group the twelve circles into four groups of three each. $x = 3$

Sometimes it is necessary to solve equations by using two inverse operations. For instance, the equation $6x - 2 = 10$ has multiplication and subtraction.

Variable term

Multiplication ⟶ $\boxed{6x} - 2 = 10$

Subtraction

To solve this equation, add to isolate the term with the variable in it. Then divide to solve.

EXAMPLE 4 **Solving a Simple Two-Step Equation**

Solve $2x + 1 = -7$.

Step 1: $\begin{aligned} 2x + 1 &= -7 \\ -1 &= -1 \\ \hline 2x &= -8 \end{aligned}$ *Subtract 1 from both sides to isolate the term with x in it.*

Step 2: $\dfrac{2x}{2} = \dfrac{-8}{2}$ *Divide both sides by 2.*

$x = -4$

Think and Discuss

1. **Explain** what property you would use to solve $\frac{k}{2.5} = 6$.

2. **Give** the equation you would solve to figure out how much money the band would need to raise if their trip cost twice as much.

Possible answers to Think and Discuss

1. Use the Multiplication Property of Equality to multiply both sides of the equation by 2.5.

2. Multiply the cost of the trip by 2: $\frac{1}{3}(2x) = 720$ or $\frac{2}{3}x = 720$.

1-8 Exercises

1-8 Exercises

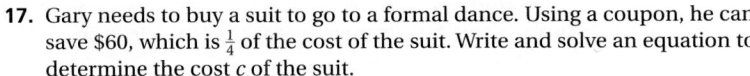

go.hrw.com
Homework Help Online
KEYWORD: MT7 1-8
Parent Resources Online
KEYWORD: MT7 Parent

GUIDED PRACTICE   17. $\frac{1}{4}c = 60$; $c = \$240$

See Example 1   Solve and check.

1. $-4x = 28$ -7 2. $7t = -49$ -7 3. $3y = 42$ 14 4. $2w = 26$ 13

5. $-12q = -24$ 2 6. $25m = -125$ -5 7. $13p = 39$ 3 8. $22y = -88$ -4

See Example 2   9. $\frac{l}{-15} = 4$ -60 10. $\frac{k}{8} = 9$ 72 11. $\frac{h}{19} = -3$ -57 12. $\frac{m}{-6} = 1$ -6

13. $\frac{t}{23} = -9$ -207 14. $\frac{t}{13} = 52$ 676 15. $\frac{w}{-12} = 7$ -84 16. $\frac{f}{45} = -3$ -135

See Example 3   17. Gary needs to buy a suit to go to a formal dance. Using a coupon, he can save \$60, which is $\frac{1}{4}$ of the cost of the suit. Write and solve an equation to determine the cost c of the suit.

Assignment Guide

If you finished Example **1** assign:
Average   1–8, 22–29, 68–77
Advanced 22–29, 43–46, 67–77

If you finished Example **2** assign:
Average   1–16, 22–37, 60, 68–77
Advanced 22–37, 43–50, 66–77

If you finished Example **3** assign:
Average   1–17, 23–37 odd, 60–63, 68–77
Advanced 22–38, 59–77

If you finished Example **4** assign:
Average   1–41 odd, 59–63, 68–77
Advanced 23–57 odd, 59–77

Homework Quick Check

Quickly check key concepts.
Exercises: 24, 30, 36, 40, 42

3 Close

Summarize

Review the properties used in solving equations. Have students state the rules for adding, subtracting, multiplying, and dividing integers. Stress the importance of working equations one step at a time, writing out each step, and checking each solution.

Possible answers: Addition: If the signs are the same, add the absolute values and keep the sign. If the signs are different, subtract the absolute values and use the sign of the larger absolute value. Subtraction: change to adding the opposite. Multiplication and division: If the signs are the same, the answer is positive; if the signs are different, the answer is negative.

State Resources

go.hrw.com
State Resources Online
KEYWORD: MT7 Resources

See Example 4   **Solve and check.**

18. $3x + 2 = 23$ 7   **19.** $\frac{k}{-5} - 1 = 7$ −40   **20.** $-3y - 8 = 1$ −3   **21.** $\frac{m}{6} + 4 = 10$ 36

INDEPENDENT PRACTICE

See Example 1   **Solve and check.**

22. $3d = 57$ 19   **23.** $-7x = 105$ −15   **24.** $-4g = -40$ 10   **25.** $16y = 112$ 7

26. $-8p = 88$ −11   **27.** $17n = 34$ 2   **28.** $-212b = -424$ 2   **29.** $41u = -164$ −4

See Example 2   **30.** $\frac{n}{9} = -63$ −567   **31.** $\frac{h}{-27} = -2$ 54   **32.** $\frac{a}{6} = 102$ 612   **33.** $\frac{j}{8} = 12$ 96

34. $\frac{y}{-9} = 11$ −99   **35.** $\frac{d}{7} = -23$ −161   **36.** $\frac{t}{5} = 60$ 300   **37.** $\frac{p}{-84} = 3$ −252

See Example 3   **38.** Fred gathered 150 eggs on his family's farm today. This is $\frac{1}{3}$ the number he usually gathers. Write and solve an equation to determine the number of eggs n that Fred usually gathers. $\frac{1}{3}n = 150$; $n = 450$

See Example 4   **Solve.**

39. $6x - 5 = 7$ 2   **40.** $\frac{n}{-3} - 4 = 1$ −15   **41.** $2y + 5 = -9$ −7   **42.** $\frac{h}{7} + 2 = 2$ 0

PRACTICE AND PROBLEM SOLVING

Extra Practice
See page 783.

Solve.

43. $-2x = 14$ −7   **44.** $4y = -80$ −20   **45.** $6y = 12$ 2   **46.** $-9m = -9$ 1

47. $\frac{k}{8} = 7$ 56   **48.** $\frac{1}{5}x = 121$ 605   **49.** $\frac{b}{6} = -12$ −72   **50.** $\frac{n}{15} = 1$ 15

51. $3x = 51$ 17   **52.** $15g = 75$ 5   **53.** $16y - 18 = -66$ −3   **54.** $3z - 14 = 58$ 24

55. $\frac{b}{-4} = 12$ −48   **56.** $\frac{m}{24} = -24$ −576   **57.** $\frac{n}{5} - 3 = 4$ 35   **58.** $\frac{a}{-2} + 8 = 14$ −12

59. Possible answer: The solution will be less than 11 because the solution must be negative. Both the divisor and the dividend must be negative because the quotient is positive.

59. **Critical Thinking** Will the solution of $\frac{x}{-5} = 11$ be greater than 11 or less than 11? Explain how you know.

60. **Multi-Step** Joy earns $8 per hour at an after-school job. Each month she earns $128. How many hours does she work each month? After six months, she gets a $2 per hour raise. How much money does she earn per month now?   16 hr; $160

61. Elvira estimates that meetings take up about $\frac{1}{4}$ of the time she spends at work. If Elvira spent 12 hours in meetings last week, how many hours did she work?   48 hr

62. **Recreation** While on vacation, Milo drove his car a total of 370 miles. This was 5 times as many miles as he drives in a normal week. How many miles does Milo drive in a normal week?   74 mi

63. **Multi-Step** Forty-two students and 6 faculty members at Byrd Middle School chose to retake their school pictures. These numbers represent $\frac{1}{12}$ of the students and $\frac{1}{6}$ of the faculty. What is the combined number of students and faculty members at Byrd Middle School?   540 students and faculty

---

RETEACH 1-8

Reteach
1-8 *Solving Equations by Multiplying or Dividing*

To solve a multiplication equation, use division.

Solve $3x = 24$.

$$3x = 24$$
$$\frac{3x}{3} = \frac{24}{3}$$
$$x = 8$$

To solve a division equation, use multiplication.

Solve $\frac{x}{4} = 20$.

$$\frac{x}{4} = 20$$
$$4 \cdot \frac{x}{4} = 20 \cdot 4$$
$$x = 80$$

When an equation has two operations, undo addition or subtraction first. Then undo multiplication or division.

Solve $2x + 11 = 35$.

$$2x + 11 = 35$$
$$\underline{-11 \quad -11} \text{ Undo the addition.}$$
$$2x = 24$$
$$\frac{2x}{2} = \frac{24}{2} \text{ Undo the multiplication.}$$
$$x = 12$$

Tell what number you would multiply or divide by to solve the equation.

1. $5a = 60$ Divide by 5.   **2.** $\frac{x}{6} = 12$ Multiply by 6.   **3.** $144 = 12f$ Divide by 12.

Solve.

4. $6x = 42$
$$\frac{6x}{6} = \frac{42}{6}$$
$$x = 7$$

5. $\frac{a}{3} = 9$
$$7 \cdot \frac{a}{3} = 9 \cdot 7$$
$$a = 27$$

6. $25 = \frac{k}{5}$
$$5 \cdot 25 = \frac{k}{5} \cdot 5$$
$$125 = k$$

7. $2x + 3 = 11$
$$\underline{-3 \quad -3}$$
$$\frac{2x}{2} = \frac{8}{2}$$
$$x = 4$$

8. $\frac{b}{4} + 5 = 6$
$$\underline{-5 \quad -5}$$
$$4 \cdot \frac{b}{4} = 1 \cdot 4$$
$$b = 4$$

9. $5t - 9 = 36$
$$\underline{+9 \quad +9}$$
$$\frac{5t}{5} = \frac{45}{5}$$
$$t = 9$$

PRACTICE 1-8

Practice B
1-8 *Solving Equations by Multiplying or Dividing*

Solve and check.

1. $4w = 48$ $w = 12$ **2.** $8y = 56$ $y = 7$ **3.** $-4b = 64$ $b = -16$

4. $\frac{x}{4} = -9$ $x = -36$ **5.** $\frac{v}{-6} = -14$ $v = 84$ **6.** $\frac{n}{21} = -3$ $n = -63$

7. $5a = -75$ $a = -15$ **8.** $54 = 3q$ $q = 18$ **9.** $23b = 161$ $b = 7$

10. $\frac{k}{21} = 15$ $k = 315$ **11.** $\frac{w}{-17} = 17$ $w = -289$ **12.** $11 = \frac{r}{34}$ $r = 374$

13. $672 = -24b$ $b = -28$ **14.** $\frac{u}{25} = 13$ $u = 325$ **15.** $42m = -966$ $m = -23$

16. $3x + 7 = 16$ $x = 3$ **17.** $\frac{t}{5} + 8 = 10$ $t = 10$ **18.** $5 = 2n - 3$ $n = 4$

19. Alex scored 13 points in the basketball game. This was $\frac{1}{5}$ of the total points the team scored. Write and solve an equation to determine the total points t the team scored. $\frac{t}{5} = 13$; $t = 65$

20. Jar candles at the Candle Co. cost $4. Nikki spent $92 buying jar candles for party favors. Write and solve an equation to determine how many jar candles c Nikki bought at the Candle Co. $4c = 92$; $c = 23$

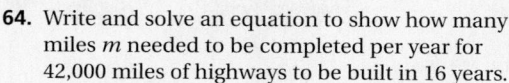
In 1956, during President Eisenhower's term, construction began on the United States interstate highway system. The original plan was for 42,000 miles of highways to be completed within 16 years. It actually took 37 years to complete. The last part, Interstate 105 in Los Angeles, was completed in 1993.

64. Write and solve an equation to show how many miles m needed to be completed per year for 42,000 miles of highways to be built in 16 years.

65. Interstate 35 runs north and south from Laredo, Texas, to Duluth, Minnesota, covering 1568 miles. There are 505 miles of I-35 in Texas and 262 miles in Minnesota. Write and solve an equation to find m, the number of miles of I-35 that are not in either state.
$m + (505 + 262) = 1568; m = 801$ miles

66. A portion of I-476 in Pennsylvania, known as the Blue Route, is about 22 miles long. The length of the Blue Route is about one-sixth the total length of I-476. Write and solve an equation to calculate the length of I-476 in miles m. $\frac{1}{6}m = 22; m = 132$ miles

67. ⭐ **Challenge** Interstate 80 extends from California to New Jersey. At right are the number of miles of Interstate 80 in each state the highway passes through.

    a. ___?___ has 134 more miles than ___?___. **Iowa; Indiana**

    b. ___?___ has 174 fewer miles than ___?___. **Ohio; Nevada**

Number of I-80 Miles	
State	Miles
California	195
Nevada	410
Utah	197
Wyoming	401
Nebraska	455
Iowa	301
Illinois	163
Indiana	167
Ohio	236
Pennsylvania	314
New Jersey	68

TEST PREP and Spiral Review

68. Multiple Choice Solve the equation $7x = -42$.

   Ⓐ $x = -49$ Ⓑ $x = -35$ Ⓒ $x = -6$ Ⓓ $x = 6$

69. Gridded Response On a game show, Paul missed q questions, each worth -100 points. Paul received a total of -900 points. How many questions did he miss? **9**

Subtract. (Lesson 1-5)

70. $-8 - 8$ **−16**   **71.** $-3 - (-7)$ **4**   **72.** $-10 - 2$ **−12**   **73.** $11 - (-9)$ **20**

Solve each equation. (Lesson 1-7)

74. $4 + x = 13$ **$x = 9$**   **75.** $x - 4 = -9$ **$x = -5$**   **76.** $-17 = x + 9$ **$x = -26$**   **77.** $19 = x + 11$ **$x = 8$**

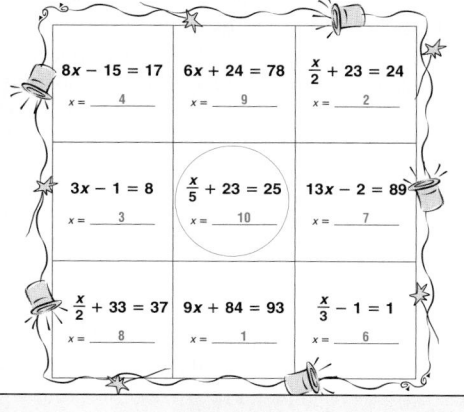

Answers

64. $16 \cdot m = 42,000$; 2625 miles per year

Pacing: Traditional 1 day
Block $\frac{1}{2}$ day

Objective: Students solve and graph inequalities.

 Online Edition
Tutorial Videos, Interactivities

Countdown to Testing Week 2

 **Power Presentations**
with PowerPoint®

Warm Up

Solve.

1. $x + 6 = 13$ $x = 7$

2. $8n = 48$ $n = 6$

3. $t - 2 = 56$ $t = 58$

4. $6 = \frac{z}{6}$ $z = 36$

Problem of the Day

Bill and Brad are taking Drivers Education class. Bill drives with his instructor for one and a half hours three times a week. He needs a total of 27 hours. Brad drives two times a week, two hours each time. He needs 26 hours. Who will finish his hours first?   Bill

Also available on transparency

Math Fact

To completely escape Earth's gravity, a rocket must travel at a speed equal to or greater than about 25,000 miles per hour. To go into orbit, the rocket can travel slower—at a speed greater than or equal to about 10,000 miles per hour.

State Resources

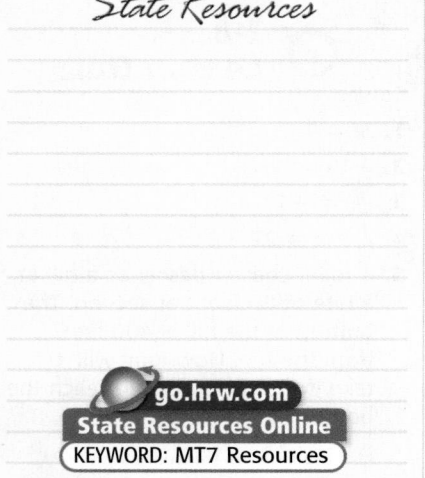
go.hrw.com
State Resources Online
KEYWORD: MT7 Resources

Learn to solve and graph inequalities.

Vocabulary
inequality
algebraic inequality
solution set

The aircraft carrier USS *Ronald Reagan* was commissioned on July 12, 2003, over five years after construction began. At 1092 feet long, the *Reagan* is longer than four commercial jumbo jets sitting nose to tail.

An **inequality** compares two quantities and typically uses one of these symbols:

$<$	$>$	$\leq$	$\geq$
is less than	*is greater than*	*is less than or equal to*	*is greater than or equal to*

Remember!
The inequality symbol opens to the side with the greater number.
$2 < 10$

EXAMPLE 1   **Completing an Inequality**

Compare. Write $<$ or $>$.

A $13 - 9$ ▢ 6
    4 ▢ 6
    $4 < 6$

B $2(8)$ ▢ 10
    16 ▢ 10
    $16 > 10$

An inequality that contains one or more variables is an **algebraic inequality**. A number that makes an inequality true is a *solution of the inequality*.

The set of all solutions is called the **solution set**. The solution set can be shown by graphing it on a number line.

Word Phrase	Inequality	Sample Solutions	Solution Set
x is less than 5	$x < 5$	$x = 4$ $4 < 5$ $x = 2.1$ $2.1 < 5$	⟵─┼─┼─┼─┼─○─┼─┼→ 0 1 2 3 4 5 6 7
a is greater than 0 a is more than 0	$a > 0$	$a = 7$ $7 > 0$ $a = 25$ $25 > 0$	⟵─┼─┼─┼─○─┼─┼─┼→ −3 −2 −1 0 1 2 3
y is less than or equal to 2 y is at most 2	$y \leq 2$	$y = 0$ $0 \leq 2$ $y = 1.5$ $1.5 \leq 2$	⟵─┼─┼─┼─┼─┼─●─┼─┼→ −3 −2 −1 0 1 2 3 4 5
m is greater than or equal to 3 m is at least 3	$m \geq 3$	$m = 17$ $17 \geq 3$ $m = 3$ $3 \geq 3$	⟵─┼─┼─┼─┼─●─┼─┼─┼→ −1 0 1 2 3 4 5 6

---

1 **Introduce**

Alternate Opener

Motivate

Make some statements like, "Tonight you will have fewer than 15 homework questions to answer" and "Tomorrow the temperature is going to be greater than 60 degrees." Ask students what the phrases "fewer than" and "greater than" mean. Have them give specific numbers that would make the statements true.

Explorations and answers are provided in *Alternate Openers: Explorations Transparencies.*

Most inequalities can be solved the same way equations are solved. Use inverse operations on both sides of the inequality to isolate the variable.

EXAMPLE 2 · Solving and Graphing Inequalities

Solve and graph each inequality.

A $x + 7 < -10$

$$x + 7 < -10$$
$$\underline{-7 \quad -7} \qquad \text{Subtract 7 from both sides.}$$
$$x < -17$$

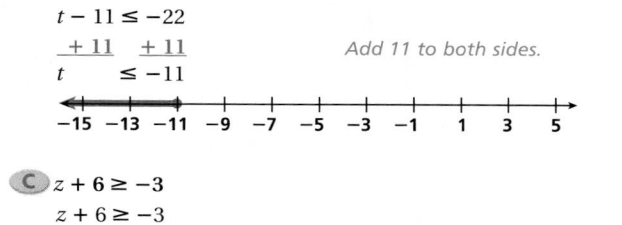

Caution!

An open circle means that the corresponding value is not a solution. A solid circle means that the value is part of the solution set.

Check

According to the graph, -20 should be a solution, since $-20 < -17$, and 3 should not be a solution because $3 > -17$.

$$x + 7 < -10$$
$$-20 + 7 \overset{?}{<} -10 \qquad \text{Substitute } -20 \text{ for } x.$$
$$-13 \overset{?}{<} -10 \checkmark$$

So -20 is a solution.

$$x + 7 < -10$$
$$3 + 7 \overset{?}{<} -10 \qquad \text{Substitute 3 for } x.$$
$$10 \overset{?}{<} -10 \; \text{✗}$$

And 3 is not a solution.

B $t - 11 \le -22$

$$t - 11 \le -22$$
$$\underline{+11 \quad +11} \qquad \text{Add 11 to both sides.}$$
$$t \le -11$$

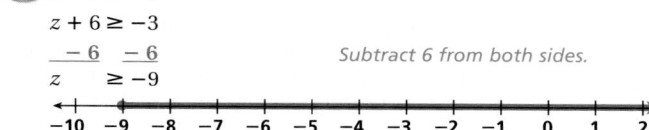

C $z + 6 \ge -3$

$$z + 6 \ge -3$$
$$\underline{-6 \quad -6} \qquad \text{Subtract 6 from both sides.}$$
$$z \ge -9$$

Think and Discuss

1. **Give** all the symbols that make $5 + 8 \;\blacksquare\; 13$ true. Explain.

2. **Compare** and contrast expressions, equations, and inequalities.

COMMON ERROR ALERT

Students sometimes shade in the wrong direction when they attempt to graph the solution set of an inequality, such as $3 < x$. Reading $3 < x$ as "x is greater than 3" serves as a reminder to shade to the right.

Power Presentations
with PowerPoint®

Additional Examples

Example 1

Compare. Write $<$ or $>$.

A. $23 - 14 \;\blacksquare\; 6 \qquad >$

B. $5(12) \;\blacksquare\; 70 \qquad <$

Example 2

Solve and graph each inequality.

A. $x + 2.5 \le 8$
   $x \le 5.5$

B. $w - 1 < 8$
   $w < 9$

Also available on transparency

Possible answers to *Think and Discuss*

1. $=, \le, \ge$; Since both sides are equal, it can be any symbol that includes equality.

2. An equation shows that two expressions are equal in value. An inequality compares the value of two expressions that are not equal.

---

2 Teach

Guided Instruction

In this lesson, students learn to solve and graph inequalities. Begin by reminding students that the symbols $<$, $>$, $\le$, and $\ge$ are used in inequalities. The $\ne$ symbol may also be considered an inequality. Explain why statements like $6 > 2$ and $4 \ge 4$ are true, while statements like $7 < 5$ and $4.1 \le 4$ are false. Review the table of examples (Teacher Tools in Lesson Transparencies).

Teaching Tip

Cognitive Stratgegies Show students that the processes previously used to solve equations are the same processes that are used to solve inequalities.

Reaching All Learners
Through Cooperative Learning

Have students work in pairs. Have each pair of students create two sets of index cards: one set with basic inequalities (e.g., $x \ge 2$ and $x < 5$) and another set with the corresponding graphs of the solution sets. Have the students shuffle each set and trade both sets with another pair of students. Students then can take turns matching each inequality with its graph.

3 Close

Summarize

Tell students that one way to remember the meaning of each of the symbols $<$ and $>$ is to imagine that the small end of each symbol "points" to the lesser number. Ask students for other suggestions for remembering the meanings of the symbols $<$ and $>$.

Possible answer: The "mouth" of the sign opens to eat the greater number.

1-9 Exercises

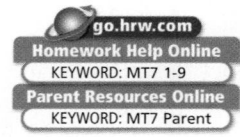
go.hrw.com
Homework Help Online
KEYWORD: MT7 1-9
Parent Resources Online
KEYWORD: MT7 Parent

Assignment Guide

If you finished Example ① assign:
Average   1–6, 15–20, 38, 56–65
Advanced 15–20, 54–65

If you finished Example ② assign:
Average   1–43 odd, 56–65
Advanced 15–28, 45–65

Homework Quick Check

Quickly check key concepts.
Exercises: 26, 30, 38, 48

Answers

7–14, 21–28. For graphs, see p. A1.

Math Background

In this lesson, the graphs of inequalities are placed on number lines. Graphs of the same inequalities may be placed on coordinate planes. For example, the graph of $x > 2$ below shows the solution set consisting of all ordered pairs (x, y) that have x-values that are greater than 2.

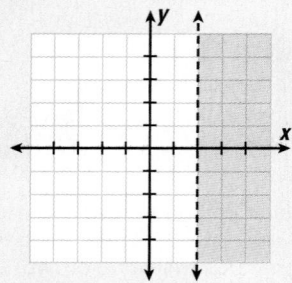

go.hrw.com
State Resources Online
KEYWORD: MT7 Resources

GUIDED PRACTICE

See Example ① **Compare. Write < or >.**

1. $5 + 9$ ▨ 13 >
2. $4(-2)$ ▨ 7 <
3. $27 - 13$ ▨ 11 >

4. $5(9)$ ▨ 42 >
5. $9 + (-2)$ ▨ 10 <
6. $3(8)$ ▨ -27 >

See Example ② **Solve and graph each inequality.**

7. $x + 3 < -4$
  $x < -7$
8. $4 + b \geq 20$
  $b \geq 16$
9. $m - 4 \leq 28$
  $m \leq 32$
10. $x + (-3) < 5$
  $x < 8$
11. $y + 8 \geq 25$
  $y \geq 17$
12. $-6 + f < -30$
  $f < -24$
13. $z - 8 > 13$
  $z > 21$
14. $x + 2 \geq -7$
  $x \geq -9$

INDEPENDENT PRACTICE

See Example ① **Compare. Write < or >.**

15. $4 + 7$ ▨ 12 <
16. $6(8)$ ▨ 25 >
17. $15 - 9$ ▨ 4 >

18. $7(-6)$ ▨ -40 <
19. $13 + 5$ ▨ 17 >
20. $5 + (-23)$ ▨ -12 <

See Example ② **Solve and graph each inequality.**

21. $b + 4 < 8$
  $b < 4$
22. $-7 + x \geq 49$
  $x \geq 56$
23. $h - 2 \geq 3$
  $h \geq 5$
24. $1 < t - 4$
  $5 < t$
25. $6 + a > 9$
  $a > 3$
26. $-3 + x \geq 12$
  $x \geq 15$
27. $f - 9 \leq 2$
  $f \leq 11$
28. $2 < a + (-5)$
  $7 < a$

PRACTICE AND PROBLEM SOLVING

Extra Practice
See page 783.

Write the inequality shown by each graph.

29.
```
←+++++++++○++++→
 -4 -2  0  2  4  6  8
```
$x < 6$

30.
```
←+++++++++++++++→
     0  2  4  6  8 10 12
```
$x \leq 9$

31.
```
←+++++○++++++++→
 -4 -2  0  2  4  6  8
```
$x > 4$

32.
```
←+++++++++++++→
 -4 -2  0  2  4  6  8
```
$x \geq 4$

33.
```
←+++++++○+++++→
 -6 -4 -2  0  2  4  6
```
$x < 1$

34.
```
←+++++++++++++→
 -4 -2  0  2  4  6  8
```
$x \leq 5$

35. Business The financial officers of Toshi Business Solutions are looking at the budget for the current fiscal year. They estimate that the company will have operating costs of at least $201,522 for the entire year. So far, the company has had sales of $98,200. At least how much money must Toshi earn in sales for the remainder of the year in order to show a profit?
  $s \geq \$103,322$

36. Suly earned an 87 on her first test. She needs a total of 140 points on her first two tests to pass the class. What score must Suly make on her second test to ensure that she passes the class? $x \geq 53$

37.
$60 + 246 \overset{?}{\geq} 300;$
$306 \overset{?}{\geq} 300;$ no

37. Reginald's cement truck can travel up to 300 miles on a single tank of gas. Reginald has driven 246 miles so far today, and now he has to make a delivery to a construction site that is 30 miles away. Write and solve an inequality to determine whether Reginald will be able to get to the construction site and back without having to fill his gas tank.

RETEACH 1-9

LESSON 1-9 Reteach
Introduction to Inequalities

A **solution of an inequality** is a number that makes the inequality true. An inequality usually has more than one solution. All the solutions are contained in the **solution set**.
As with equations, solve a simple inequality by using inverse operations to isolate the variable.

Solve and graph $x + 4 > 9$.

```
++++++++++○++
0 1 2 3 4 5 6 7 8
```
Draw an open circle at 5 to show that 5 is not included in the solution set.

$x + 4 > 9$
$\underline{-4 \quad -4}$ Subtract 4.
$x > 5$

```
++++++++++○++
0 1 2 3 4 5 6 7 8
```
Draw an arrow to the right of 5 to show that all numbers greater than 5 are included in the solutions.

According to the graph, 6 should be a solution and 4 should not be a solution.

Check:
$x + 4 > 9$ $x + 4 > 9$
$6 + 4 \overset{?}{>} 9$ $4 + 4 \overset{?}{>} 9$
$10 > 9$ $8 > 9$

So, 6 is in the solution set and 4 *is not* in the solution set. Thus, the solution set for the inequality $x + 4 > 9$ is $x > 5$.

Write true or false.
1. $7 < 4$ false
2. $0 \leq 9$ true
3. $-3 > 4$ false

Using the variable *n*, write the inequality shown by each graph.
4.
```
++++++++++
0 1 2 3 4 5 6 7 8
```
$n \geq 3$

5.
```
+++++++++○
-7-6-5-4-3-2-1 0 1
```
$n < -1$

Complete. Is the given value in the solution set? Answer *is* or *is not*.
6. 3 <u>is not</u> in the solution set of $x - 1 > 5$.
$x - 1 > 5$
$\underline{3} - 1 \overset{?}{>} 5$
$\underline{2} > 5$

7. 0 <u>is</u> in the solution set of $z + (-4) \geq -4$.
$z + (-4) \geq -4$
$\underline{0} + (-4) \geq -4$
$\underline{-4} \geq -4$

8. 14 <u>is</u> in the solution set of $w + 10 \leq 25$.
$w + 10 \leq 25$
$\underline{14} + 10 \leq 25$
$\underline{24} \leq 25$

PRACTICE 1-9

LESSON 1-9 Practice B
Introduction to Inequalities

Compare each inequality. Write < or >.
1. $7 + 10$ ⟩ 16
2. 21 ⟨ $4(5)$
3. $25 - 7$ ⟨ 19
4. 58 ⟩ $7(8)$
5. $-4(8)$ ⟨ -30
6. $3 - 8$ ⟨ -2
7. $7 + (-7)$ ⟩ -17
8. $9(-7)$ ⟩ -70
9. $-43 + (-18)$ ⟨ -23

Solve and graph each inequality.
10. $x + 4 > 9$
```
+++++++
0 1 2 3 4 5 6
```
$x > 5$

11. $c - 6 \leq 1$
```
+++++++
3 4 5 6 7 8 9
```
$c \leq 7$

12. $y + 3 \geq 8$
```
++++++++
-13-12-11-10-9 -8 -7
```
$y \geq -11$

13. $3 + v < -5$
```
+++++++
-11-10-9 -8 -7 -6 -5
```
$v < -8$

14. $7 + x \leq 10$
```
+++++++
0 1 2 3 4 5 6
```
$x \leq 3$

15. $s - 4 < -10$
```
+++++++
-9 -8 -7 -6 -5 -4 -3
```
$s < -6$

16. $b - 2 \leq 5$
```
+++++++
3 4 5 6 7 8 9
```
$b \leq 7$

17. $7 + n > -2$
```
+++++++
-11-10-9 -8 -7 -6 -5
```
$n > -9$

18. $r + 6 \geq -1$
```
+++++++
-9 -8 -7 -6 -5 -4 -3
```
$r \geq -7$

19. $-9 + w < -15$
```
+++++++
-9 -8 -7 -6 -5 -4 -3
```
$w < -6$

20. $14 + k > 25$
```
+++++++
8 9 10 11 12 13 14
```
$k > 11$

21. $a - 8 \geq -12$
```
+++++++
-6 -5 -4 -3 -2 -1 0
```
$a \geq -4$

22. $k + 3 \leq 0$
```
+++++++
-5 -4 -3 -2 -1 0 1
```
$k \leq -3$

23. $n + 7 \geq 2$
```
+++++++
-6 -5 -4 -3 -2 -1 0
```
$n \geq -4$

24. $-1 + b \leq -1$
```
+++++++
-3 -2 -1 0 1 2 3
```
$b \leq 0$

Sports

The Global Challenge 2004–2005 began on October 31, 2004, and ended July 2005.

Compare. Write < or >.

38. $52 - 37$ ▮ 14 $>$
39. $8(7)$ ▮ 54 $>$
40. $2 - 7$ ▮ -10 $>$
41. $-5(7)$ ▮ -30 $<$
42. $15 + (-7)$ ▮ -9 $>$
43. $-23 + (-15)$ ▮ -39 $>$

44. Sports After each leg of the Global Challenge 2004–2005 yacht race, the yachts are given points for that leg. Through the first four legs, the *BP Explorer* led the *Team Save the Children* by as many as 9 points in a leg. If the *Team Save the Children's* lowest score for a leg of the race was 4 points, at least how many points did the *BP Explorer* score in its best of the first 4 legs? $x \geq 13$ points

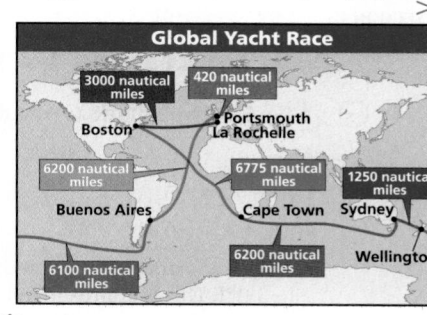

Global Yacht Race

3000 nautical miles · 420 nautical miles · Portsmouth · La Rochelle · Boston · 6200 nautical miles · 6775 nautical miles · 1250 nautical miles · Buenos Aires · Cape Town · Sydney · 6200 nautical miles · Wellington · 6100 nautical miles

Solve and graph each inequality.

45. $-21 + b \geq 13$
$b \geq 34$
46. $p - 54 < -21$
$p < 33$
47. $q + 13 \geq -22$
$q \geq -9$
48. $25 + y > -13$
$y > -38$
49. $p - 1 \leq -17$
$p \leq -16$
50. $10 + k > -22$
$k > -32$
51. $y - 2 \geq -6$
$y \geq -4$
52. $z + 4 < -5$
$z < -9$

53. Write a Problem The weight limit for an elevator is 2500 pounds. Passengers and cargo weighing a total of 2342 pounds are already on the elevator. Write and solve a problem to find the maximum additional weight the elevator can carry. $2342 + x \leq 2500; x \leq 158$

54. Write About It In mathematics, the conventional way to write an inequality is with the variable on the left, such as $x > 5$. Explain how to rewrite the inequality $4 \leq x$ in the conventional way.

55. Challenge The inequality $3 \leq x < 5$ means both $3 \leq x$ and $x < 5$ are true at the same time. Solve and graph $6 < x \leq 12$. $x > 6$ and $x \leq 12$.

54. Possible answer: Switch the variable and the constant, and then reverse the inequality sign. $4 \leq x$ becomes $x \geq 4$.

TEST PREP and Spiral Review

56. Short Answer Solve $x + 7 < 15$. $x < 8$

57. Multiple Choice Which number is NOT a solution of $n - 7 < 1$?

Ⓐ 2   Ⓑ 4   Ⓒ 6   Ⓓ 8

Write each set of integers in order from least to greatest. (Lesson 1-3)

58. $-22, -18, -35$
$-35, -22, -18$
59. $1, -2, 0, 3$
$-2, 0, 1, 3$
60. $-17, -22, -29$
$-29, -22, -17$
61. $-15, 0, -23$
$-23, -15, 0$

Solve each equation. (Lesson 1-8)

62. $7x = -45.5$
$x = -6.5$
63. $\frac{x}{6} = 11.2$
$x = 67.2$
64. $-1,032 = -129x$
$x = 8$
65. $14y = -42$
$y = -3$

Answers

45–52. For graphs, see p. A1.

TEST PREP DOCTOR For Exercise 57, students need to read the problem carefully and understand that they are looking for the number that makes the inequality *false*. Have students replace *n* in the inequality with each answer choice. The number that does not satisfy the inequality is the answer.

 Journal

At an amusement park there is a sign that reads, "You must be at least 4 feet tall to ride this roller coaster." Ask students to write about any other real-world situation in which an inequality is represented.

Power Presentations
with PowerPoint®

1-9 Lesson Quiz

Compare. Write < or >.

1. 13 ▮ $5(2)$ $>$
2. $14 - 2$ ▮ 11 $>$

Solve and graph each inequality.

3. $k + 9 < 12$ $k < 3$

4. $3 \leq \frac{m}{2}$ $6 \leq m$

5. A school bus can hold 64 passengers. Three classes would like to use the bus for a field trip. Each class has 21 students. Write and solve an inequality to determine whether all three classes will fit on the bus. $3(21) \overset{?}{\leq} 64; 63 \leq 64;$ yes

Also available on transparency

CHALLENGE 1-9

LESSON 1-9 Challenge
You Make the Call

Sometimes, an inequality is expressed with words like *no* or *not*. But, the algebraic inequality may be clearer if you avoid those words.

Example
The fire regulation says that this restaurant may seat no more than 350 people.
• the inequality as stated: no more than 350
• the equivalent without *no*: less than or equal to 350
• algebraic inequality: Let $x =$ the number of diners allowed. $x \leq 350$

Sometimes, two conditions of inequality can be expressed as a single inequality.

Example
$x > -9$ and $x < -3$ means that x is between -9 and -3, and can be written as $-9 < x < -3$.

Write an algebraic inequality, identifying what the variable represents.

1. The recipe calls for not less than 15 oz of butter.
   Let $x =$ oz of butter; $x \geq 15$

2. Mr. Valdez says he cannot contribute more than $500.
   Let $x =$ money contributed; $x \leq 500$

3. On his typing test, Philip can have no more than 4 errors to pass.
   Let $x =$ errors allowed; $x \leq 4$

4. The team will have to score no fewer than 20 points to win.
   Let $x =$ points needed; $x \geq 20$

5. This canister can hold at most 5 lb of rice.
   Let $x =$ number of lb; $x \leq 5$

6. The sleeping bag is useful for camping when temperatures are at least $-5°F$.
   Let $x =$ degrees farenheit; $x \geq -5$

If x is a whole number, write the solution of each inequality.

7. $7 \leq x < 11$
   7; 8; 9; 10

8. $15 > x \geq 9$
   14; 13; 12; 11; 10; 9

9. $-2 < x < 7$
   $-1, 0, 1, 2, 3, 4, 5, 6$

10. $-10 \leq x \leq -5$
    $-10, -9, -8, -7, -6$

PROBLEM SOLVING 1-9

LESSON 1-9 Problem Solving
Introduction to Inequalities

Use the table.

1. Write an inequality that compares the population p of Los Angeles to the population of New York.
   $p < 8,008,278$

2. Write an inequality that compares the population p of Los Angeles to the population of Chicago.
   $p > 2,896,016$

Top 3 U.S. Cities by Population 2000		
Rank	City	Population
1	New York	8,008,278
2	Los Angeles	p
3	Chicago	2,896,016

Write the correct answer.

3. Paul wants to ride his bike at least 30 miles this week to train for a race. He has already ridden 18 miles. How many more miles should Paul ride this week?
   $m \geq 12$ mi

4. To avoid a service charge, Jose must keep more than $500 in his account. His current balance is $536, but he plans to write a check for $157. Find the amount of the deposit d Jose must make to avoid a service charge.
   $d > 121$

Choose the letter for the best answer.

5. Mia wants to spend no more than $10 on an ad in the paper. The first 10 words cost $3. Find the amount of money m she has left to spend on the ad.
   A $m \geq 7$
   B $m \leq 13$
   C $m \leq 7$
   D $m \geq 13$

6. An auto shop estimates parts and labor for a repair will cost less than $200. Parts cost $59. Find the maximum cost c of the labor.
   F $c < $141
   G $c > $259
   H $c > $141
   J $c > $259

7. To advance to the next level of a competition, Rachel must earn at least 180 points. She has already earned 145 points. Find the number of points p she needs to advance to the next level of the competition.
   A $p \leq 35$
   B $p \leq 325$
   C $p \geq 35$
   D $p \geq 325$

8. The Conway's hiked more than 25 miles on their backpacking trip. If they hiked 8 miles on their last day, find how many miles m they hiked on the rest of the trip.
   F $m > 17$
   G $m > 33$
   H $m < 17$
   J $m < 33$

Organizer

Objective: Assess students' mastery of concepts and skills in Lessons 1-7 through 1-9.

Resources

 Assessment Resources
Section 1B Quiz

 Test & Practice Generator
One-Stop Planner®

INTERVENTION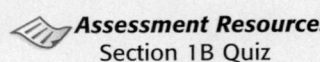

Resources

 Ready to Go On? Intervention and Enrichment Worksheets

● *Ready to Go On?* **CD-ROM**

🪐 *Ready to Go On?* **Online**

my.hrw.com

Answers

18–23. See p. A1.

 **READY TO GO ON?**
SECTION 1B

Quiz for Lessons 1-7 Through 1-9

☑ **1-7** **Solving Equations by Adding or Subtracting**

Solve.

1. $p - 12 = -5$ $p = 7$ **2.** $w + (-9) = 14$ $w = 23$ **3.** $t + (-14) = 8$ $t = 22$

4. $23 + k = -5$ $k = -28$ **5.** $-52 + p = 17$ $p = 69$ **6.** $y - (-6) = -74$
$y = -80$

7. The approximate surface temperature of Pluto, the coldest planet, is $-391°$F. This is approximately 1255 degrees cooler than the approximate surface temperature of Venus, the hottest planet. What is the approximate surface temperature of Venus? **864°F**

☑ **1-8** **Solving Equations by Multiplying or Dividing**

Solve.

8. $\frac{x}{6} = -48$ $x = -288$ **9.** $3x = 21$ $x = 7$ **10.** $14y = -84$ $y = -6$ **11.** $\frac{y}{12} = -72$ $y = -864$

12. $-5p = 75$ $p = -15$ **13.** $\frac{r}{-7} = 3$ $r = -21$ **14.** $\frac{d}{12} = -10$ $d = -120$ **15.** $8y = -96$ $y = -12$

16. Ahmed's baseball card collection consists of 228 cards. This is 4 times as many cards as Ming has. How many baseball cards are in Ming's collection?

17. The College of Liberal Arts at Middletown University has 342 students. This is $\frac{1}{8}$ the size of the entire student body. How many students attend Middletown University? **2736 students**

16. 57 baseball cards

☑ **1-9** **Introduction to Inequalities**

Solve and graph each inequality.

18. $t - 12 < -4$ $t < 8$ **19.** $x + 3 \geq 9$ $x \geq 6$ **20.** $x - 7 > -91$ $x > -84$

21. $u + 88 \geq -107$ $u \geq -195$ **22.** $p - 17 < 74$ $p < 91$ **23.** $76 + v \leq -18$ $v \leq -94$

24. Barbara is saving money so that she can buy a new CD player and a couple of CDs. She knows that she needs at least $60, and she has saved $22 so far. At least how much more money does Barbara need to save? **at least $38**

25. Montel is playing in a four-round golf tournament. He estimates that he needs to have a score of at most -3 after the second round in order to make the cut and play the third and fourth rounds. If Montel scored $+4$ in the first round of the tournament, how high can he score at most in the second round and still make the cut? **at most -7**

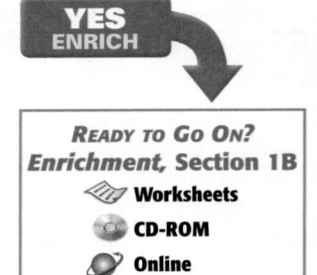

READY TO GO ON?
Diagnose and Prescribe

NO INTERVENE				**YES ENRICH**

READY TO GO ON? Intervention, Section 1B				
Ready to Go On? Intervention	🖊 **Worksheets**	💿 **CD-ROM**	🪐 **Online**	**READY TO GO ON?** Enrichment, Section 1B
☑ Lesson 1-7	1-7 Intervention	Activity 1-7		🖊 **Worksheets**
☑ Lesson 1-8	1-8 Intervention	Activity 1-8	Diagnose and Prescribe Online	💿 **CD-ROM**
☑ Lesson 1-9	1-9 Intervention	Activity 1-9		🪐 **Online**

Ready to Go On?

MULTI-STEP TEST PREP

Have a Ball A physical education class is playing a variation of basketball. When a team makes a basket from inside the three-point line, the team scores a "Climb" (C), or 2 points. When a team makes a basket from outside the three-point line, the other team scores a "Slide" (S), or −1 point.

1. During the first 20 minutes of the game, a team scores the following: C, C, S, S, C, S, C, C, and S. Evaluate the expression $2 + 2 + (-1) + (-1) + 2 + (-1) + 2 + 2 + (-1)$ to determine the team's score. **6**

2. The points scored by two teams during a game are shown in the table. Which team won the game? What was the difference in the teams' scores? **Team 1 won the game; 1 point**

3. Diego's team scores 3 Climbs and 2 Slides, but not necessarily in that order. Find his team's score by substituting $S = -1$ and $C = 2$ in the expression $3C + 2S$. **5**

4. After four consecutive baskets are made, Leann's team's score is −8. After the next basket is made, the team's score is −6. Write and solve an equation for the last made basket. $-8 + x = -5; x = 3$

5. Daryl's team finishes the game with a score of 12. If his team scored 9 times, how many Climbs did the team score? **6**

6. Is it possible to finish with a score of 2 after five baskets are made? Explain your reasoning.

Game Results	
Team 1	**Team 2**
C	C
S	C
S	C
S	S
S	S
C	S
C	S
C	S

Multi-Step Test Prep

INTERVENTION

Scaffolding Questions

1. As you add from left to right, is the sum of −2 and −2 positive or negative? Negative What is this sum? −4 How do you add −4 + 3? Find the difference of the absolute values (1) and use the sign of the larger absolute value (−)

2. How can you group the red spins to write the expression compactly? $3 + 4(-3)$ or $G + 4R$

3. What expression do you get by substituting the values of R and G? $3(3) + 2(-2)$ What is the order of operations in evaluating the expression? Multiply, then add

4. If x represents the value of the last spin, what equation can you write? $-8 + x = -5$ How do you solve this equation? Add 8 to both sides

5. Did Daryl spin mostly red or mostly green? Why? Mostly green, since he has a positive score

6. What strategies can you use to find all the possible final positions? Make a table, make an organized list, etc.

Extension

1. Suppose the players each take 7 turns. What would be the best and worst final positions in this case? 21 and −14

2. The players decide on a new rule: After the second turn, you multiply your current position by −3 and then continue the game as before. Mei spins R R G G R. What is her final position? 16 Daryl spins G R R R G. What is his final position? −4

Organizer

Objective: Assess students' ability to apply concepts and skills in Chapter 1 in a real-world format.

 Online Edition

Resources

Middle School Assessments
www.mathtekstoolkit.org

Problem	Text reference
1	Lesson 1-4
2	Lesson 1-5
3	Lesson 1-6
4	Lesson 1-7
5	Lesson 1-8
6	Lesson 1-9

Answers

6. The only possible final positions are −10, −5, 0, 5, 10, 15. It is not possible to finish at 2. The table shows all the possibilities.

Green	Red	Final Pos.
0(3)	5(−2)	−10
1(3)	4(−2)	−5
2(3)	3(−2)	0
3(3)	2(−2)	5
4(3)	1(−2)	10
5(3)	0(−2)	15

State Resources

go.hrw.com
State Resources Online
KEYWORD: MT7 Resources

Organizer

Objective: Participate in games to practice and apply skills learned in Chapter 1.

 Online Edition

Resources

Chapter 1 Resource Book
Puzzles, Twisters & Teasers

Math Magic

Purpose: To apply the problem-solving skill of translating words into math to perform a fun trick

Discuss Ask students to explain how the trick works. What does the variable *n* represent? How does this trick use combining like terms?
Possible answer: Operations are performed on the variable in such a way that the result is a constant. The variable *n* represents whatever number a person begins with. In the last step, when like terms are combined, the variable disappears because the like terms are opposites.

Extend Challenge students to create their own math magic tricks. Have them explain how their tricks work by using variables and combining like terms.
Possible answer: Think of a number. Multiply the number by 10. Divide the result by 5. Add 7. Subtract 2 times the original number. Your answer is 7. The algebraic representation is as follows: n, $10n$, $\frac{10n}{5}$, $2n + 7$, $2n + 7 - 2n = 7$.

Crazy Cubes

Purpose: To apply the problem-solving skill of guess and check to a classic brainteaser

Discuss Discuss some strategies that students can use to begin the game.
Possible answer: Set the first cube, and then try to place the other cubes, one at a time, so that no number is repeated along the front, back, top, and bottom.

Ask students why this game is a challenge. Possible answer: because you can't see all the sides at once and because the order of the cubes might change as you go along

Extend Have students explore the number of possible ways to position a cube. There are 24 possible ways to position the cube (6 faces to serve as base, with 4 options for the front).

Game Time

Math Magic

You can guess what your friends are thinking by learning to "operate" your way into their minds! For example, try this math magic trick.

Think of a number. Multiply the number by 8, divide by 2, add 5, and then subtract 4 times the original number.

No matter what number you choose, the answer will always be 5. Try another number and see. You can use what you know about variables to prove it. Here's how:

	What you say:	What the person thinks:	What the math is:
Step 1:	Pick any number.	6 (for example)	n
Step 2:	Multiply by **8**.	$8(6) = 48$	$8n$
Step 3:	Divide by **2**.	$48 \div 2 = 24$	$8n \div 2 = 4n$
Step 4:	Add **5**.	$24 + 5 = 29$	$4n + 5$
Step 5:	Subtract **4** times the original number.	$29 - 4(6) = 29 - 24 = 5$	$4n + 5 - 4n = 5$

Invent your own math magic trick that has at least five steps. Show an example using numbers and variables. Try it on a friend!

Crazy Cubes

This game, called The Great Tantalizer around 1900, was reintroduced in the 1960s as "Instant Insanity™." Make four cubes with paper and tape, numbering each side as shown.

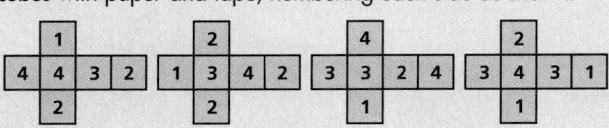

The goal is to line up the cubes so that 1, 2, 3, and 4 can be seen along the top, bottom, front, and back of the row of cubes. They can be in any order, and the numbers do not have to be right-side up.

A complete copy of the rules is available online.

go.hrw.com
Game Time Extra
KEYWORD: MT7 Games

Materials
- sheet of decorative paper ($8\frac{1}{2}$ by 11 in.)
- ruler
- pencil
- scissors
- glue
- markers

PROJECT ## Note-Taking Taking Shape

Make this notebook to help you organize examples of algebraic expressions.

Directions

1 Hold the sheet of paper horizontally. Make two vertical lines $3\frac{5}{8}$ in. from each end of the sheet.

2 Fold the sheet in half lengthwise. Then cut it in half by cutting along the fold. **Figure A**

3 On one half of the sheet, cut out rectangles A and B. On the other half, cut out rectangles C and D. **Figure B**

  Rectangle A: $\frac{3}{4}$ in. by $3\frac{5}{8}$ in.
  Rectangle B: $1\frac{1}{2}$ in. by $3\frac{5}{8}$ in.
  Rectangle C: $2\frac{1}{4}$ in. by $3\frac{5}{8}$ in.
  Rectangle D: 3 in. by $3\frac{5}{8}$ in.

4 Place the piece with the taller rectangular panels on top of the piece with the shorter rectangular panels. Glue the middle sections of the two pieces together. **Figure C**

5 Fold the four panels into the center, starting with the tallest panel and working your way down to the shortest.

Taking Note of the Math

Write "Addition," "Subtraction," "Multiplication," and "Division" on the tabs at the top of each panel. Use the space below the name of each operation to list examples of verbal, numerical, and algebraic expressions.

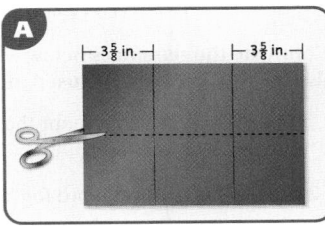

A | $3\frac{5}{8}$ in. | $3\frac{5}{8}$ in. |

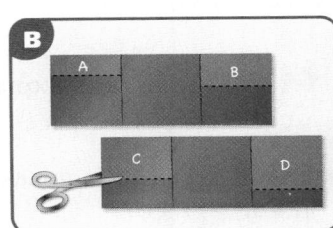

B

C

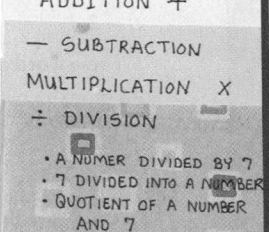

DIVISION EXPRESSION

$$\frac{a}{7} \text{ or } a \div 7$$

ADDITION +
— SUBTRACTION
MULTIPLICATION X
÷ DIVISION
• A NUMER DIVIDED BY 7
• 7 DIVIDED INTO A NUMBER
• QUOTIENT OF A NUMBER AND 7

Organizer

Objective: Make a notebook in which to record examples of algebraic expressions.

Materials: sheet of decorative paper ($8\frac{1}{2}$ by 11 in.), ruler, pencil, scissors, glue, markers

 **Online Edition**

Using the Page

Preparing the Materials
If class time is limited, you may wish to photocopy $8\frac{1}{2}$ by 11 in. sheets of paper that have preprinted lines for making the necessary cuts.

Making the Project
This project incorporates a hands-on review of measurement skills. Have students work in pairs to ensure accurate measurements.

Extending the Project
Challenge students to make similar notebooks that have six or eight panels. Students will need to plan carefully to calculate the appropriate dimensions for the panels.

Tips from the Bag Ladies!

We've found that the project works especially well when students begin with sheets of paper in different colors. Once students have cut their sheets in half, they can swap one of the halves with a partner. By doing so, each student's booklet will have panels in two different colors!

Organizer

Objective: Help students organize and review key concepts and skills presented in Chapter 1.

Online Edition
Multilingual Glossary

Resources

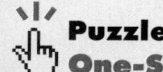
PuzzlePro®
One-Stop Planner®

***Multilingual Glossary* Online**

go.hrw.com
KEYWORD: MT7 Glossary

Lesson Tutorial Videos
CD-ROM

Test & Practice Generator
One-Stop Planner®

Answers

1. equation
2. opposite
3. absolute value
4. 147
5. 152
6. 278
7. $2(k + 4)$
8. $4t + 5$
9. 10 less than the product of 5 and b
10. 32 plus the product of 23 and s
11. 12 less than 10 divided by r
12. 16 more than y divided by 8

Study Guide: Review

Vocabulary

absolute value 15
additive inverse 14
algebraic expression 6
algebraic inequality 44
coefficient 6

constant 6
equation 34
evaluate 6
inequality 44
integer 14

inverse operation 34
opposite 14
solution set 44
substitute 6
variable 6

Complete the sentences below with vocabulary words from the list above. Words may be used more than once.

1. An ___?___ is a statement that two expressions have the same value.

2. ___?___ is another word for "additive inverse."

3. The ___?___ of 3 is 3.

 **Variables and Expressions** (pp. 6–9)

EXAMPLE

■ Evaluate $4x + 9y$ for $x = 2$ and $y = 5$.
$4x + 9y$
$4(2) + 9(5)$ *Substitute 2 for x and 5 for y.*
$8 + 45$ *Multiply.*
53 *Add.*

EXERCISES

Evaluate each expression.

4. $9a + 7b$ for $a = 7$ and $b = 12$
5. $17m - 3n$ for $m = 10$ and $n = 6$
6. $1.5r + 19s$ for $r = 8$ and $s = 14$

1-2 **Algebraic Expressions** (pp. 10–13)

EXAMPLE

■ Write an algebraic expression for the word phrase "2 less than a number n."
$n - 2$ *Write as subtraction.*

■ Write a word phrase for $25 + 13t$.
25 plus the product of 13 and t

EXERCISES

Write an algebraic expression for each phrase.

7. twice the sum of k and 4
8. 5 more than the product of 4 and t

Write a word phrase for each algebraic expression.

9. $5b - 10$
10. $32 + 23s$
11. $\frac{10}{r} - 12$
12. $16 + \frac{y}{8}$

1-3 Integers and Absolute Value (pp. 14–17)

EXAMPLE

■ Evaluate the expression. $|-9| - |3|$

$|-9| - |3|$
$9 - 3$ *$|9| = 9$ and $|3| = 3$*
6 *Subtract.*

EXERCISES

Evaluate each expression.

13. $|7 - 6|$ **14.** $|-8| + |-7|$
15. $|15| + |19|$ **16.** $|14 + 7|$
17. $|16 - 20|$ **18.** $|-7| - |-8|$

1-4 Adding Integers (pp. 18–21)

EXAMPLE

■ Add.

$-8 + 2$ *Find the difference of $|-8|$ and $|2|$.*
-6 *$8 > 2$; use the sign of the 8.*

■ Evaluate.

$-4 + a$ for $a = -7$
$-4 + (-7)$ *Substitute.*
-11 *Same sign*

EXERCISES

Add.

19. $-6 + 4$ **20.** $-3 + (-9)$
21. $4 + (-7)$ **22.** $4 + (-3)$
23. $-11 + (-5) + (-8)$

Evaluate.

24. $k + 11$ for $k = -3$
25. $-6 + m$ for $m = -2$

1-5 Subtracting Integers (pp. 22–25)

EXAMPLE

■ Subtract.

$-3 - (-5)$
$-3 + 5$ *Add the opposite of -5.*
2 *$5 > 3$; use the sign of the 5.*

■ Evaluate.

$-9 - d$ for $d = 2$
$-9 - 2$ *Substitute.*
$-9 + (-2)$ *Add the opposite of 2.*
-11 *Same sign*

EXERCISES

Subtract.

26. $-7 - 9$ **27.** $8 - (-9)$
28. $-2 - (-5)$ **29.** $13 - (-2)$
30. $-5 - 17$ **31.** $16 - 20$

Evaluate.

32. $9 - h$ for $h = -7$
33. $12 - z$ for $z = 17$

1-6 Multiplying and Dividing Integers (pp. 26–29)

EXAMPLE

Multiply or divide.

■ $4(-9)$ *The signs are **different**.*
-36 *The answer is **negative**.*

■ $\frac{-33}{-11}$ *The signs are the **same**.*
3 *The answer is **positive**.*

EXERCISES

Multiply or divide.

34. $7(-5)$ **35.** $\frac{72}{-4}$
36. $-4(-13)$ **37.** $\frac{-100}{-4}$
38. $8(-3)(-5)$ **39.** $\frac{10(-5)}{-25}$

Answers

40. $z = 23$
41. $t = 8$
42. $k = 15$
43. $x = -15$
44. 1300 lb
45. 3300 mi^2
46. $g = -8$
47. $k = 9$
48. $p = -80$
49. $w = -48$
50. $y = -40$
51. $z = 192$
52. 705 mi
53. 24 months
54. $h < 10$;

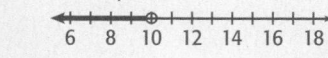
6 8 10 12 14 16 18

55. $y > 7$;

4 6 8 10 12 14 16

56. $x \geq 6$;

−2 0 2 4 6 8 10

57. $w \geq 2$;

0 2 4 6 8 10 12

58. $x \leq 4$;

−2 0 2 4 6 8 10

59. $q \leq -3$;

−6 −4 −2 0 2 4

60. $p < -2$;

−8 −6 −4 −2 0 2 4

61. $m \leq 48$;

38 40 42 44 46 48 50

62. $y > 0$;

−4 −2 0 2 4 6 8

63. $3 < x$;

−4 −2 0 2 4 6 8

64. $6 - 2 < y$;

−4 −2 0 2 4 6 8

65. $4 \geq x$;

−6 −4 −2 0 2 4 6

1-7 Solving Equations by Adding or Subtracting (pp. 34–38)

EXAMPLE

Solve.

■ $x + 7 = 12$
  $\underline{-7 \quad -7}$ Subtract 7 from both sides.
  $x + 0 = 5$
  $ x = 5$ Identity Property of Zero

■ $y - 3 = 1.5$
  $\underline{+3 \quad +3}$ Add 3 to both sides.
  $y + 0 = 4.5$
  $ y = 4.5$ Identity Property of Zero

EXERCISES

Solve and check.

40. $z - 9 = 14$ **41.** $t + 3 = 11$
42. $6 + k = 21$ **43.** $x + 2 = -13$

Write an equation and solve.

44. A polar bear weighs 715 lb, which is 585 lb less than a sea cow. How much does the sea cow weigh?

45. The Mojave Desert, at 15,000 mi^2, is 11,700 mi^2 larger than Death Valley. What is the area of Death Valley?

1-8 Solving Equations by Multiplying or Dividing (pp. 39–43)

EXAMPLE

Solve.

■ $4h = 24$
  $\dfrac{4h}{4} = \dfrac{24}{4}$ Divide both sides by 4.
  $1h = 6$ $4 \div 4 = 1$
  $h = 6$ $1 \cdot h = h$

■ $\dfrac{t}{4} = 16$
  $4 \cdot \dfrac{t}{4} = 4 \cdot 16$ Multiply both sides by 4.
  $1t = 64$ $4 \div 4 = 1$
  $t = 64$ $1 \cdot t = t$

EXERCISES

Solve and check.

46. $-7g = 56$ **47.** $108 = 12k$
48. $0.1p = -8$ **49.** $-\dfrac{w}{4} = 12$
50. $-20 = \dfrac{y}{2}$ **51.** $\dfrac{z}{24} = 8$

52. The Lewis family drove 235 mi toward their destination. This was $\frac{1}{3}$ of the total distance. What was the total distance?

53. Luz will pay a total of $9360 on her car loan. Her monthly payment is $390. For how many months is the loan?

1-9 Introduction to Inequalities (pp. 44–47)

EXAMPLE

Solve and graph.

■ $x + 5 \leq 8$
  $\underline{-5 \quad -5}$
  $x \leq 3$

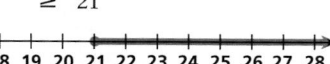
−6 −4 −2 0 2 4 6

■ $w - 3 \geq 18$
  $\underline{+3 \quad +3}$
  $w \geq 21$

18 19 20 21 22 23 24 25 26 27 28

EXERCISES

Solve and graph.

54. $h - 3 < 7$ **55.** $y - 2 > 5$
56. $2 + x \geq 8$ **57.** $w + 2 \geq 4$
58. $x - 3 \leq 1$ **59.** $3 + q \leq 0$
60. $4 + p < 2$ **61.** $m - 2 \leq 46$
62. $y + 4 > 4$ **63.** $4 < x + 1$
64. $2 < y - 4$ **65.** $8 \geq 4 + x$

Study Guide: Review

Evaluate each expression for the given value of the variable.

1. $16 - p$ for $p = -12$ **28**

2. $t - 7$ for $t = -14$ **−21**

3. $13 - x + (-2)$ for $x = 4$ **7**

4. $-8y + 27$ for $y = -9$ **99**

Write an algebraic expression for each word phrase.

5. 15 more than the product of 33 and y $15 + 33y$

6. 18 less than the quotient of x and 7 $\frac{x}{7} - 18$

7. 4 times the sum of -7 and h $4(-7 + h)$

8. 18 divided by the difference of t and 9 $\frac{18}{t - 9}$

Write each set of integers in order from least to greatest.

9. $-7, 7, 2, -3, 0, 1$ $-7, -3, 0, 1, 2, 7$

10. $-12, -45, 13, 100, 20$ $-45, -12, 13, 20, 100$

11. $120, -7, 54, 41, 7$ $-7, 7, 41, 54, 120$

12. $-41, -78, 5, 0, 2$ $-78, -41, 0, 2, 5$

13. $-25, -8, -70, -2, -13$ $-70, -25, -13, -8, -2$

14. $-100, 12, 9, 0, -23$ $-100, -23, 0, 9, 12$

Perform the given operations.

15. $-9 + (-12)$ **−21**

16. $11 - 17$ **−6**

17. $6(-22)$ **−132**

18. $(-20) \div (-4)$ **5**

19. $42 - (-5)$ **47**

20. $-18 \div 3$ **−6**

21. $-9 - (-13)$ **4**

22. $12 - (-6) + (-5)$ **13**

23. $-2(-21 - 17)$ **76**

24. $(-15 + 3) \div (-4)$ **3**

25. $(54 \div 6) - (-1)$ **10**

26. $-(16 + 4) - 20$ **−40**

27. The temperature on a winter day increased 37°F. If the beginning temperature was −9°F, what was the temperature after the increase? **28°F**

Solve.

28. $y + 19 = 9$ $y = -10$

29. $4z = -32$ $z = -8$

30. $52 = p - 3$ $p = 55$

31. $\frac{w}{3} = 9$ $w = 27$

32. $\frac{t}{7} = 12$ $t = 84$

33. $-9p = -27$ $p = 3$

34. $\frac{q}{-5} = 18$ $q = -90$

35. $\frac{g}{4} = -11$ $g = -44$

36. The O'Malley family is driving cross-country to see their cousins. So far, they have traveled 275 miles. This is $\frac{1}{5}$ of the way to their cousins' house. How far do the O'Malleys live from their cousins? **1375 mi**

Solve and graph each inequality.

37. $x + 7 > -4$ $x > -11$

38. $n - 14 \leq -3$ $n \leq 11$

39. $74 + p \geq -26$ $p \geq -100$

40. $-4 + t < 7$ $t < 11$

41. $z - 52 \leq -18$ $z \leq 34$

42. $p + 22 > 8$ $p > -14$

43. $-4 + u \leq -20$ $u \leq -16$

44. $8 + z > -6$ $z > -14$

45. The choir is selling tickets to the school's fall musical. The auditorium can hold at most 435 people. So far, 237 tickets have been sold. At most, how many more tickets can be sold? **at most 198 more tickets**

46. Anthony is working on a term paper for his literature class. The teacher wants the papers to be at least 1000 words long. So far, Anthony's paper is 698 words long. At least how many more words must Anthony's paper have? **at least 302 more words**

Chapter Test

Organizer

Objective: Assess students' mastery of concepts and skills in Chapter 1.

 Online Edition

Resources

 Assessment Resources

Chapter 1 Tests
• Free Response
  (Levels A, B, C)
• Multiple Choice
  (Levels A, B, C)
• Performance Assessment

 IDEA Works! CD-ROM
Modified Chapter 1 Test

Test & Practice Generator
One-Stop Planner®

State Resources

go.hrw.com
State Resources Online
KEYWORD: MT7 Resources

Organizer

Objective: Provide opportunities to learn and practice common test-taking strategies.

 Online Edition

Resources

 State Test Prep Workbook

 State Test Prep CD-ROM

 State Test Practice Online

 **go.hrw.com**
KEYWORD: MT7 TestPrep

TEST PREP DOCTOR When students are faced with a test item that they do not know how to solve, encourage them to eliminate some options and then make an educated guess. Help them identify which options are distracters. In Example 1, show students that Option B is a distracter; it is a common student error to subtract instead of add.

Test Tackler

Multiple Choice: Eliminate Answer Choices

With some multiple-choice test items, you can use logical reasoning or estimation to eliminate some of the answer choices. Test writers often create the incorrect choices, called distracters, using common student errors.

EXAMPLE 1

Which choice represents "4 times the sum of x and 8"?

- (A) $4 \cdot (x + 8)$
- (C) $4 \cdot x + 8$
- (B) $4 \cdot (x - 8)$
- (D) $4 \div (x + 8)$

Read the question. Then try to eliminate some of the answer choices.

Use logical reasoning.

Times means "to multiply," and *sum* means "to add." You can eliminate any option without a multiplication symbol and an addition symbol. You can eliminate B and D.

The sum of x and 8 is being multiplied by 4, so you need to add before you multiply. Because multiplication comes before addition in the order of operations, $x + 8$ should be in parentheses. The correct answer is A.

EXAMPLE 2

Which value for k is a solution to the equation $k - 3.5 = 12$?

- (F) $k = 8.5$
- (H) $k = 42$
- (G) $k = 15.5$
- (J) $k = 47$

Read the question. Then try to eliminate some of the answer choices.

Use estimation.

You can eliminate H and J immediately because they are too large. Estimate by rounding 3.5 to 4. If $x = 47$, then $47 - 4 = 43$. This is not even close to 12. Similarly, if $x = 42$, then $42 - 4 = 38$, which is also too large to be correct.

Choice F is called a *distracter* because it was created using a common student error, subtracting 3.5 from 12 instead of adding 3.5 to 12. Therefore, F is also incorrect. The correct answer is G.

Even if the answer you calculated is an answer choice, it may not be the correct answer. It could be a distracter. Always check your answers!

Read each test problem and answer the questions that follow.

Item A

The table shows average high temperatures for Nome, Alaska. Which answer choice lists the months in order from coolest to warmest?

Month	Temperature (°C)
Jan.	−11
Feb	−10
Mar	−8
Apr	−3
May	6
Jun	12
Jul	15
Aug	13
Sep	9
Oct	1
Nov	−5
Dec	−9

Ⓐ Jul, Aug, Jun, Sep, May, Oct, Apr, Nov, Mar, Dec, Feb, Jan

Ⓑ Jul, Jun, Aug, Jan, Feb, Sep, Dec, Mar, May, Nov, Apr, Oct

Ⓒ Jan, Apr, Jun, Jul, Sep, Nov, Feb, Mar, May, Jul, Sep, Nov

Ⓓ Jan, Feb, Dec, Mar, Nov, Apr, Oct, May, Sep, Jun, Aug, Jul

1. Which two choices can you eliminate by using logic? Explain your reasoning.

2. What common error does choice A represent?

Item B

Which value for *p* is a solution to the equation *p* + 5.2 = 15?

Ⓕ *p* = −30.2   Ⓗ *p* = 20.2

Ⓖ *p* = 9.8   Ⓙ *p* = 78

3. Which choices can you eliminate by using estimation? Explain your reasoning.

4. What common error does choice H represent?

Item C

Which inequality corresponds to the graph below?

Number line from −5 to 5.

Ⓐ *x* < 2   Ⓒ *x* > 2

Ⓑ *x* ≤ 2   Ⓓ *x* ≥ 2

5. Is *x* = 2 a solution to the inequality? How do you know?

6. Which two choices can you eliminate by using the answer in Problem 5?

Item D

Which word phrase can be translated into the algebraic expression 2*x* − 6?

Ⓕ six more than twice a number

Ⓖ the sum of twice a number and six

Ⓗ twice the difference of a number and six

Ⓙ six less than twice a number

7. Can you eliminate any of the choices immediately by using logic? Explain your reasoning.

8. Describe how you can determine the correct answer from the remaining choices.

Test Tackler

Answers

Possible Answers:

1. Both Option A and Option B can be eliminated because they are not reasonable. Both options begin with July, which is the warmest month, not the coolest month.

2. Distracter A was created by listing the months from warmest to coolest.

3. Both Option F and Option J can be eliminated using estimation. Round 5.2 to 5. If *p* = −30.2, estimate −30 + 5 = −25. If *p* = 78, estimate 80 + 5 = 85. Neither answer is close to 15.

4. Distracter H was created by adding 5.2 instead of subtracting it.

5. Yes, *x* = 2 is a solution because there is a solid circle on 2 on the number line.

6. Both Option A and Option C can be eliminated because they do not have the "or equal to" symbol, and the answer to Problem 7 says that 2 is a solution to the inequality.

7. Both Option F and Option G can be eliminated because they use the words *six more* and *sum*. Because there is a subtraction symbol, the addition concept cannot be included.

8. Option H is incorrect because "Twice the difference of a number and six" would correspond to the expression 2(*x* −6). The correct answer is Option D.

Answers

A. D

B. G

C. B

D. J

State Resources

go.hrw.com
State Resources Online
KEYWORD: MT7 Resources

Organizer

Objective: Provide review and practice for Chapters 1 and standardized tests.

 Online Edition

Resources

 Assessment Resources
Chapter 1 Cumulative Test

 State Test Prep Workbook

 State Test Prep CD-ROM

 State Test Practice Online

go.hrw.com
KEYWORD: MT7 TestPrep

CHAPTER
1

STANDARDIZED
TEST PREP

go.hrw.com
State Test Practice Online
KEYWORD: MT7 TestPrep

Standardized Test Prep

Cumulative Assessment, Chapter 1
Multiple Choice

1. Which expression has a value of 12 when $x = 2$, $y = 3$, and $z = 1$?

Ⓐ $3xyz$ Ⓒ $3xz + 2y$

Ⓑ $2x + 3y + z$ Ⓓ $4xyz + 2$

2. The word phrase "10 less than 4 times a number" can be represented by which expression?

Ⓕ $10 - 4x$ Ⓗ $10 + 4x$

Ⓖ $4x - 10$ Ⓙ $10x - 4$

3. A copy center prints c copies at a cost of $0.10 per copy. What is the total cost of the copies?

Ⓐ $0.10c$ Ⓒ $\frac{0.10}{c}$

Ⓑ $0.10 + c$ Ⓓ $\frac{c}{0.10}$

4. Which value of x makes the equation $x - 15 = 20$ true?

Ⓕ $x = 5$ Ⓗ $x = 35$

Ⓖ $x = 30$ Ⓙ $x = 300$

5. What is the solution of $s + 12 = 16$?

Ⓐ $s = 4$ Ⓒ $s = 28$

Ⓑ $s = 8$ Ⓓ $s = 192$

6. Carlos owes his mother money. His paycheck is $105. If he pays his mother the money he owes her, he will have $63 left. Which equation represents this situation?

Ⓕ $-x + 63 = 105$

Ⓖ $x - 63 = 105$

Ⓗ $105 - x = 63$

Ⓙ $x - 105 = 63$

7. To ride a roller coaster at the local amusement park, a person must be at least 48 inches tall. Which inequality represents this requirement?

Ⓐ $h < 48$ Ⓒ $h \le 48$

Ⓑ $h > 48$ Ⓓ $h \ge 48$

8. Which addition equation represents the number line diagram below?

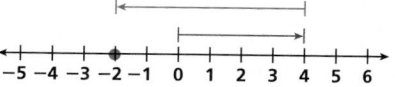

Ⓕ $4 + (-2) = 2$

Ⓖ $4 + (-6) = -2$

Ⓗ $4 + 6 = 10$

Ⓙ $-4 + (-6) = -10$

9. Which equation has the solution $x = 16$?

Ⓐ $x - 16 = 4$ Ⓒ $2x = 32$

Ⓑ $\frac{x}{2} = 32$ Ⓓ $x + 2 = 16$

10. Which inequality is represented by this graph?

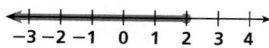

Ⓕ $x < 2$ Ⓗ $x \le 2$

Ⓖ $x > 2$ Ⓙ $x \ge 2$

11. A scuba diver swimming at a depth of 35 ft below sea level, or -35 ft, dives another 15 ft deeper to get a closer look at a fish. What is the diver's new depth?

Ⓐ -50 ft   Ⓒ 20 ft

Ⓑ -20 ft   Ⓓ 50 ft

State Resources

TEST PREP DOCTOR ✚

For item 4, students who answered **F** subtracted 15 from both sides instead of adding 15 to both sides.

For item 10, students who answered **G** or **J** do not understand that the greater than symbol is supposed to represent those numbers greater than 2.

Answers

20. b. $42; Substitute 6 for t in the expression $7t$.

    c. $18; Three $20 bills is $60, which is $18 more than the price of the tickets.

21. a. $C = 0.15w$

    b. 80; Substitute 12 for C and solve $C = 0.15w$ for w.

22. See 4-Point Response work sample.

go.hrw.com
State Resources Online
KEYWORD: MT7 Resources

HOT TIP! The incorrect answer choices in a multiple-choice test item are called distracters. They are the results of common mistakes. Be sure to check your work!

12. Which set of numbers is in order from least to greatest?

  Ⓕ −15, 13, −10   Ⓗ −10, −15, 13

  Ⓖ 13, −10, −15   Ⓙ −15, −10, 13

13. Which expression is equivalent to $|9 - (-5)|$?

  Ⓐ $|9| + |-5|$ Ⓒ −14

  Ⓑ $|9| - |-5|$ Ⓓ 4

Gridded Response

14. What is the value of the expression $2xy - y$ when $x = 3$ and $y = 5$? **25**

15. What is the solution to the equation $x - 27 = -16$? **11**

16. Evaluate the expression $m + 11 + (-3)$ for $m = -5$. **3**

17. Nora collects 15 magazines every week for 6 weeks. She plans to use the magazines for an art project. After 6 weeks, however, she still does not have enough magazines to complete the project. If Nora needs 20 more magazines to complete the project, how many total magazines does she need? **110**

18. Patricia works twice as many days as Laura works each month. Laura works 3 more days than Jaime. If Jaime works 10 days each month, how many days does Patricia work? **26**

19. On a trip, the Parker family stopped to rest after covering $\frac{3}{5}$ of the distance. They still had 750 miles to travel to complete their trip. How far did they travel? **1,875**

Short Response

20. The Hun family plans to visit the Sea Center. Tickets cost $7 each.

  a. Write an expression to represent the cost of admission for any number of tickets t. **7t**

  b. How much will it cost the Hun family if they buy 6 tickets? Explain your answer.

  c. Mrs. Hun pays with three $20 bills. How much change will she get back? Explain your answer.

21. It costs $0.15 per word to place an advertisement in the school newspaper. Let w represent the number of words in an advertisement and C represent the cost of the advertisement.

  a. Write an equation that relates the number of words to the cost of the advertisement.

  b. If Bernard has $12.00, how many words can he use in his advertisement? Explain your answer.

Extended Response

22. **Statement 1:** Currently there are 8 more students in the student council than there are officers. There are 18 students total in the student council.

  Statement 2: In addition, there have to be at least 4 officers in the council.

  a. Write an equation to represent Statement 1 and an inequality to represent Statement 2.

  b. Solve the equation, and plot the solution to the equation on a number line.

  c. Graph the solution set to the inequality.

  d. Explain what the solution sets have in common, and then explain how they are different.

Short Response Rubric

Items 20–21

2 Points = The student's answer is an accurate and complete execution of the task or tasks.

1 Point = The student's answer contains attributes of an appropriate response but is flawed.

0 Points = The student's answer contains no attributes of an appropriate response.

Extended Response Rubric

Item 22

4 points = The student demonstrates a thorough understanding of all concepts and shows all work correctly.

3 points = The student demonstrates a basic understanding of all concepts, but the work shows some flaws reflecting inattentive execution of mathematical procedures or some misunderstanding of the underlying mathematics.

2 points = The student demonstrates only a partial understanding of the concepts or procedures embodied in the tasks. The approach may be correct but the work shows a misunderstanding of one or more important concepts.

1 point = The student demonstrates a very limited understanding of the concepts or procedures embodied in the tasks. The response may show some understanding but exhibits many flaws or is incomplete.

0 points = The student provides no response at all or a completely incorrect or uninterpretable response.

Student Work Samples for Item 22

4-Point Response

a. Statement 1 : $x + 8 = 12$
   Statement 2 : $x \geq 4$

b. $x + 8 = 12$
   $\underline{-8 \quad -8}$
   $x = 4$

c. $x \geq 4$

d. They both are equal to 4 but the inequality means more than 4 students are also allowed to be officers.

The student demonstrated an understanding of setting up, solving, and graphing equations and inequalities, and found the correct answers.

3-Point Response

a. statement 1 : $x + 8 = 12$
   statement 2 : $x \geq 4$

b. $x + 8 = 12$
   $x = 4$

c. $x \geq 4$

d. They both are equal to 4 but the inequality means 4 or less students can be officers.

The student graphed the solution set incorrectly in part **c**. As a result, the answer and explanation for part **d** are wrong.

2-Point Response

a. $x - 8 = 12$, $x \geq 4$

b. $x - 8 = 12$
   $\underline{+8 \quad +8}$
   $x = 20$

c. $x \geq 4$

d. Both solution sets have $x = 20$ but the inequality also has $x \geq 4$ as well.

Based on the equations given in part **a**, the answers given in parts **b**, **c**, and **d** appear to be correct and sufficient. However, the student wrote the equation incorrectly in part **a**, so the answers to **a**, **b**, and **d** are incorrect.

2

Rational Numbers

Section 2A
Rational Number Operations

2-1 Rational Numbers
2-2 Comparing and Ordering Rational Numbers
2-3 Adding and Subtracting Rational Numbers
2-4 Multiplying Rational Numbers
2-5 Dividing Rational Numbers
2-6 Adding and Subtracting with Unlike Denominators
2-6 **Technology Lab** Add and Subtract Fractions

Section 2B
Equations with Rational Numbers

2-7 Solving Equations with Rational Numbers
2-8 **Hands-On Lab** Model Two-Step Equations
2-8 Solving Two-Step Equations

Pacing Guide for 45-Minute Classes

Chapter 2

Countdown to Testing Weeks ❸, ❹

DAY 1	DAY 2	DAY 3	DAY 4	DAY 5
2-1 Lesson	2-2 Lesson	2-3 Lesson	2-4 Lesson	2-5 Lesson

DAY 6	DAY 7	DAY 8	DAY 9	DAY 10
2-6 Lesson	2-6 Technology Lab Ready to Go On? Focus on Problem Solving	2-7 Lesson	2-8 Hands-On Lab 2-8 Lesson	2-8 Lesson Ready to Go On? Multi-Step Test Prep

DAY 11	DAY 12
Chapter 2 Review	Chapter 2 Test

Pacing Guide for 90-Minute Classes

Chapter 2

DAY 1	DAY 2	DAY 3	DAY 4	DAY 5
2-1 Lesson 2-2 Lesson	2-3 Lesson 2-4 Lesson	2-5 Lesson 2-6 Lesson	2-6 Technology Lab Ready to Go On? Focus on Problem Solving 2-7 Lesson	2-8 Hands-On Lab 2-8 Lesson Ready to Go On? Multi-Step Test Prep

DAY 6
Chapter 2 Review Chapter 2 Test

ONGOING ASSESSMENT and INTERVENTION

DIAGNOSE	PRESCRIBE

Assess Prior Knowledge

Before Chapter 2

Diagnose readiness for the chapter.
Are You Ready? SE p. 61

Prescribe intervention.
Are You Ready? Intervention Skills 18, 21, 22, 24

Formative Assessment

Before Every Lesson

Diagnose readiness for the lesson.
Warm Up TE, every lesson

Prescribe intervention.
Skills Bank SE pp. 820–834
Reteach CRB, Chapters 1–2

During Every Lesson

Diagnose understanding of lesson concepts.
Think and Discuss SE, every lesson
Write About It SE, lesson exercises
Journal TE, lesson exercises

Prescribe intervention.
Questioning Strategies Chapter 2
Reading Strategies CRB, every lesson
Success for ELL pp. 19–34

After Every Lesson

Diagnose mastery of lesson concepts.
Lesson Quiz TE, every lesson
Test Prep SE, every lesson
Test and Practice Generator

Prescribe intervention.
Reteach CRB, every lesson
Problem Solving CRB, every lesson
Test Prep Doctor TE, lesson exercises
Homework Help Online

Before Chapter 2 Testing

Diagnose mastery of concepts in the chapter.
Ready to Go On? SE pp. 90, 102
Focus on Problem Solving SE p. 91
Multi-Step Test Prep SE p. 103
Section Quizzes AR pp. 25–26
Test and Practice Generator

Prescribe intervention.
Ready to Go On? Intervention Chapter 2
Scaffolding Questions TE p. 103

Before High Stakes Testing

Diagnose mastery of benchmark concepts.
Standardized Test Prep SE pp. 110–111
State Test Prep CD-ROM

Prescribe intervention.
State Test Prep Workbook

Summative Assessment

After Chapter 2

Check mastery of chapter concepts.
Multiple-Choice Tests (Forms A, B, C)
Free-Response Tests (Forms A, B, C)
Performance Assessment AR pp. 27–40
Test and Practice Generator

Prescribe intervention.
Reteach CRB, every lesson
Lesson Tutorial Videos Chapter 2

Check mastery of benchmark concepts.
AYP State Tests

Prescribe intervention.
State Test Prep Workbook

CHAPTER
2

Supporting the Teacher

Chapter 2 Resource Book

Practice A, B, C
pp. 3–5, 12–14, 20–22, 28–30, 36–38, 44–46, 53–55, 61–63

Reading Strategies ELL
pp. 10, 18, 26, 34, 42, 51, 59, 68

Puzzles, Twisters, and Teasers
pp. 11, 19, 27, 35, 43, 52, 60, 69

Reteach
pp. 6–7, 15, 23, 31, 39, 47–48, 56, 64–65

Problem Solving
pp. 9, 17, 25, 33, 41, 50, 58, 67

Challenge
pp. 8, 16, 24, 32, 40, 49, 57, 66

Parent Letter pp. 1–2

Transparencies

Lesson Transparencies, Volume 1 .... Chapter 2
• Teaching Tools
• Warm Ups
• Problem of the Day
• Teaching Transparencies
• Lesson Quizzes

Know-It Notebook .... Chapter 2
• Additional Examples   • Chapter Review
• Vocabulary   • Big Ideas

Alternate Openers: Explorations .... pp. 10–17

Countdown to Testing .... pp. 5–8

Teacher Tools

Power Presentations®
Complete PowerPoint® presentations for Chapter 2 lessons

Lesson Tutorial Videos® SPANISH
Holt authors Ed Burger and Freddie Renfro present tutorials to support the Chapter 2 lessons.

One-Stop Planner® SPANISH
Easy access to all Chapter 2 resources and assessments, as well as software for lesson planning, test generation, and puzzle creation

IDEA Works!®
Key Chapter 2 resources and assessments modified to address special learning needs

Lesson Plans .... pp. 10–17

Questioning Strategies .... Chapter 2

Solutions Key .... Chapter 2

Interdisciplinary Posters and Worksheets .... Chapter 2

TechKeys   **Lab Resources**

Project Teacher Support   **Parent Resources**

Workbooks

Homework and Practice Workbook SPANISH
Teacher's Guide .... pp. 5–9

Know-It Notebook
Teacher's Guide .... Chapter 2

Problem Solving Workbook SPANISH
Teacher's Guide .... pp. 5–9

State Test Prep
Teacher's Guide

Technology Highlights for the Teacher

 Power Presentations
Dynamic presentations to engage students. Complete PowerPoint® presentations for every lesson in Chapter 2.

 One-Stop Planner SPANISH
Easy access to Chapter 2 resources and assessments. Includes lesson-planning, test-generation, and puzzle-creation software.

 Premier Online Edition SPANISH
Chapter 2 includes Tutorial Videos, Lesson Activities, Lesson Quizzes, Homework Help, and Chapter Project.

KEY: **SE** = *Student Edition*   **TE** = *Teacher's Edition*   English Language Learners   Spanish version available   Available on CD-ROM   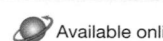 Available online

CHAPTER

2

Reaching All Learners

Resources for All Learners

Hands-On Lab Activities................................... Chapter 2

Technology Lab Activities............................... Chapter 2

Homework and Practice Workbook **SPANISH** ....pp. 10–17

Know-It Notebook... Chapter 2

Problem Solving Workbook **SPANISH** ....pp. 10–17

DEVELOPING LEARNERS

Practice A..CRB, every lesson

Reteach..CRB, every lesson

Inclusion..TE pp. 82, 99

Questioning Strategies................................ Chapter 2

Modified Chapter 2 Resources .... *IDEA Works!*

Homework Help **Online**

ON-LEVEL LEARNERS

Practice B...CRB, every lesson

Puzzles, Twisters, and Teasers..............CRB, every lesson

Multiple Representations..........................TE pp. 65, 77

Cognitive Strategies.....................................TE p. 81

ADVANCED LEARNERS

Practice C..CRB, every lesson

Challenge...CRB, every lesson

Extension..............................TE pp. 63, 103, 104, 105

Critical Thinking..TE pp. 65, 73

English Language Learners

ENGLISH LANGUAGE LEARNERS

Are You Ready? Vocabulary............................SE p. 61

Vocabulary Connections.................................SE p. 62

Lesson Vocabulary..............................SE, every lesson

Vocabulary Review..SE p. 106

English Language Learners.................TE p. 63, 65, 81

Reading Strategies...........................CRB, every lesson

Success for English Language Learners.................pp. 19–34

Multilingual Glossary

Reaching All Learners Through...

Inclusion..TE pp. 82, 99

Concrete Manipulatives.............................TE pp. 69, 86

Multiple Representations...........................TE pp. 65, 77

Cognitive Strategies......................................TE p. 81

Cooperative Learning................................TE pp. 93, 99

Critical Thinking..TE pp. 65, 73

Test Prep Doctor...TE pp. 67, 71, 75, 79, 84, 88, 95, 101, 110

Common Error Alerts...................TE pp. 65, 69, 77, 81

Scaffolding Questions.................................TE p. 103

Technology Highlights for Reaching All Learners

 Lesson Tutorial Videos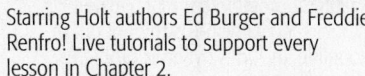

Starring Holt authors Ed Burger and Freddie Renfro! Live tutorials to support every lesson in Chapter 2.

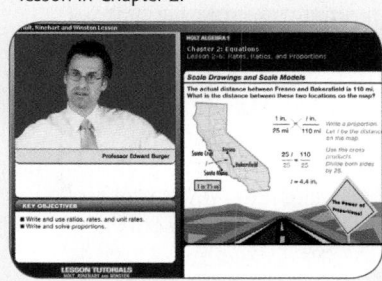

Multilingual Glossary

Searchable glossary includes definitions in English, Spanish, Vietnamese, Chinese, Hmong, Korean, and 4 other languages.

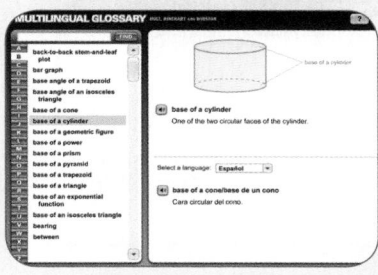

Online Interactivities

Interactive tutorials provide visually engaging alternative opportunities to learn concepts and master skills.

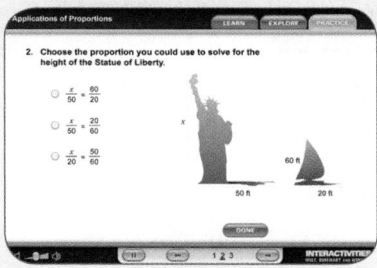

KEY: **SE** = *Student Edition* **TE** = *Teacher's Edition* **CRB** = *Chapter Resource Book* **SPANISH** Spanish version available ◉ Available on CD-ROM 🪐 Available online

60D

CHAPTER 2

Ongoing Assessment

Assessing Prior Knowledge

Determine whether students have the prerequisite concepts and skills for success in Chapter 2.

Are You Ready? SPANISH .... SE p. 61
Warm Up .... TE, every lesson

Test Preparation

Provide review and practice for Chapter 2 and standardized tests.

Multi-Step Test Prep .... SE p. 103
Study Guide: Review .... SE pp. 106–107
Standardized Test Prep .... SE pp. 110–111
Countdown to Testing Transparencies .... pp. 5–8
State Test Prep Workbook
State Test Prep CD-ROM
IDEA Works!

Alternative Assessment

Assess students' understanding of Chapter 2 concepts and combined problem-solving skills.

Chapter 2 Project .... SE p. 60
Performance Assessment SPANISH .... AR pp. 39–40
Portfolio Assessment SPANISH .... AR p. xxxiv

Daily Assessment

Provide formative assessment for each day of Chapter 2.

Questioning Strategies .... Chapter 2
Think and Discuss .... SE, every lesson
Write About It .... SE, lesson exercises
Journal .... TE, lesson exercises
Lesson Quiz .... TE, every lesson
Modified Lesson Quizzes .... IDEA Works!

Weekly Assessment

Provide formative assessment for each week of Chapter 2.

Focus on Problem Solving .... SE p. 91
Multi-Step Test Prep .... SE p. 103
Ready to Go On? SPANISH .... SE pp. 90, 102
Cumulative Assessment .... SE pp. 110–111
Test and Practice Generator SPANISH ...One-Stop Planner

Formal Assessment

Provide summative assessment of Chapter 2 mastery.

Section Quizzes SPANISH .... AR pp. 25–26
Chapter 2 Test .... SE p. 109
Chapter Test (Levels A, B, C) SPANISH ..... AR pp. 27–38
    • Multiple-Choice • Free-Response
Cumulative Test SPANISH .... AR pp. 41–44
Test and Practice Generator SPANISH ...One-Stop Planner
Modified Chapter 2 Test .... IDEA Works!

Technology Highlights for the Teacher

Are You Ready? SPANISH
Automatically assess readiness and prescribe intervention for Chapter 2 prerequisite skills.

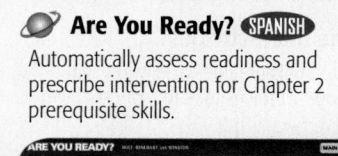
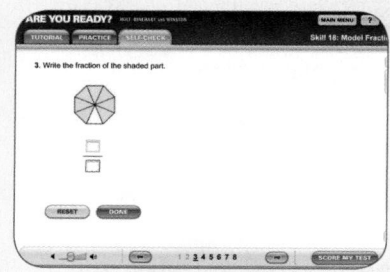

Ready to Go On? SPANISH
Automatically assess understanding of and prescribe intervention for Sections 2A and 2B.

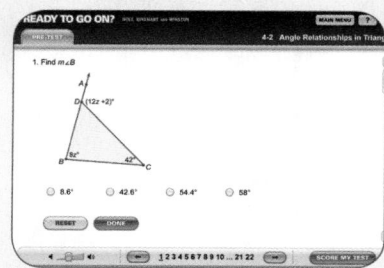

Test and Practice Generator SPANISH
Use Chapter 2 problem banks to create assessments and worksheets to print out or deliver online. Includes dynamic problems.

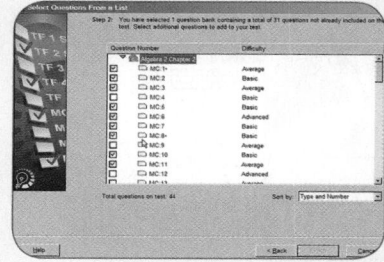

KEY: **SE** = *Student Edition*   **TE** = *Teacher's Edition*   **AR** = *Assessment Resources*   SPANISH Spanish version available   Available on CD-ROM   Available online

Formal Assessment

Three levels (A, B, C) of multiple-choice and free-response chapter tests are available in the *Assessment Resources.*

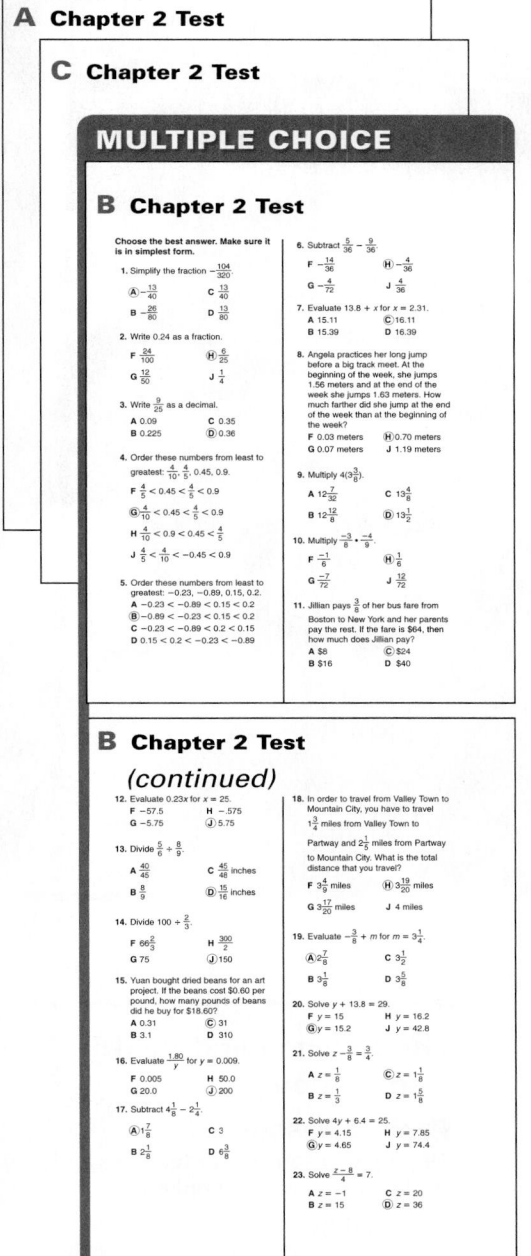

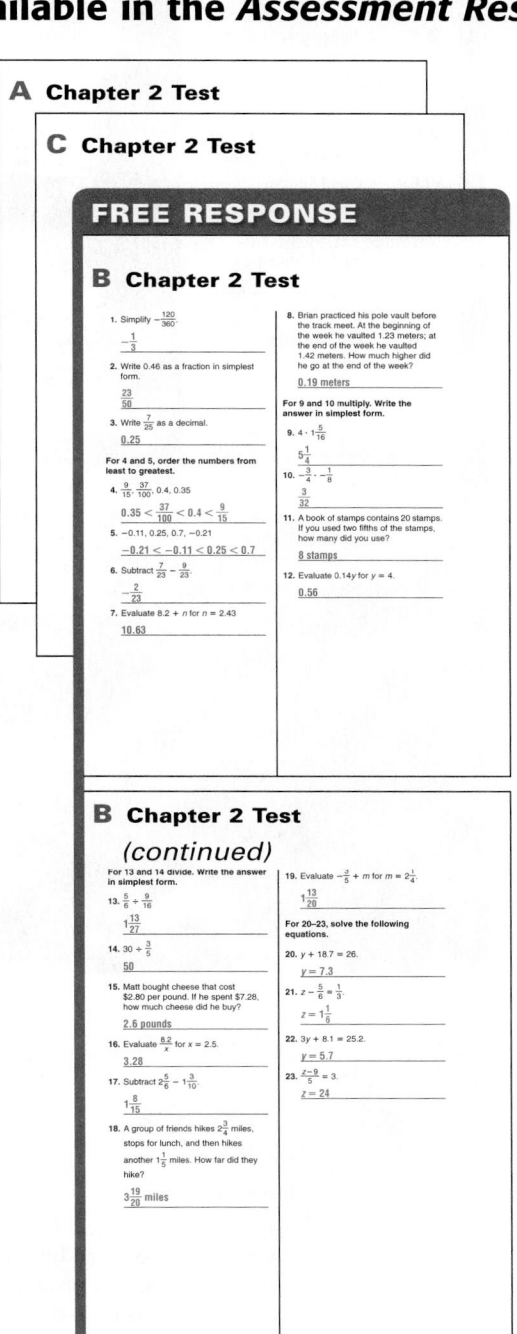

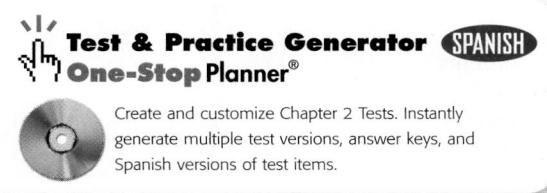

Test & Practice Generator SPANISH
One-Stop Planner®

Create and customize Chapter 2 Tests. Instantly
generate multiple test versions, answer keys, and
Spanish versions of test items.

Rational Numbers

Why Learn This?

Tell students that the set of real numbers includes all numbers they have studied so far—whole numbers, fractions, decimals, square roots, etc. Tell them that numbers that are not real are called *imaginary numbers* and that they will study them in a few years. *Fractions* will now be referred to as *rational numbers.* Point out to students that all the numbers in the table can be classified as real numbers and as rational numbers.

Using Data

To begin the study of this chapter, have students:

- Give the daily iron requirement for a 16-year-old boy. 11 mg

- Calculate how many more calories are needed by a 15-year-old boy than by a 15-year-old girl. 800

- Calculate how much more protein a boy needs when he is 17 than when he is 10. 20 g

MULTI-STEP TEST PREP On page 103, students use addition, subtraction, multiplication, and division of rational numbers to convert temperatures.

2A	Rational Number Operations
2-1	Rational Numbers
2-2	Comparing and Ordering Rational Numbers
2-3	Adding and Subtracting Rational Numbers
2-4	Multiplying Rational Numbers
2-5	Dividing Rational Numbers
2-6	Adding and Subtracting with Unlike Denominators
LAB	Add and Subtract Fractions
2B	Equations with Rational Numbers
2-7	Solving Equations with Rational Numbers
LAB	Model Two-Step Equations
2-8	Solving Two-Step Equations

MULTI-STEP TEST PREP

go.hrw.com
Chapter Project Online
KEYWORD: MT7 Ch2

Nutrient Requirements			
Nutrient	**Girls and Boys 9–13 Years**	**Girls 14–18 Years**	**Boys 14–18 Years**
Protein (g)	46	55	66
Iron (mg)	8	15	11
Calcium (mg)	1300	1300	1300
Calories	2200–2500	2200	3000

The table lists recommended nutrient requirements for boys and girls age 9–18.

Career *Nutritionist*

Nutritionists use their knowledge of the nutrient content of food to help promote healthful eating. Together with food scientists they develop guidelines for people who must follow medically necessary diets as well as for people who just want to improve their eating habits.

Problem Solving Project

Understand, Plan, Solve, and Look Back

Have students:

- Complete the Food for Thought worksheet to learn how foods can provide varying amounts of the daily-required nutrients.

- Research why the human body needs the nutrients in the table. What happens when a body is deficient in one of them?

- Bring in some labels from food products. Compare the nutrients on the labels with those in the tables and calculate the fraction of the daily requirements a serving of each food contains.

Life Science and Health Connection

Project Resources
All project resources for teachers and students are provided online.

Materials:
- Food for Thought worksheet

go.hrw.com
Project Teacher Support
KEYWORD: MT7 PSProject2

ARE YOU READY?

✓ Vocabulary

Choose the best term from the list to complete each sentence.

1. A number that consists of a whole number and a fraction is called a(n) __?__. **mixed number**

2. A(n) __?__ is a number that represents a part of a whole. **fraction**

3. A fraction whose absolute value is greater than 1 is called a(n) __?__, and a fraction whose absolute value is between 0 and 1 is called a(n) __?__. **improper fraction; proper fraction**

4. A(n) __?__ names the same value. **equivalent fraction**

equivalent fraction
fraction
improper fraction
mixed number
proper fraction

Complete these exercises to review skills you will need for this chapter.

✓ Model Fractions

Write a fraction to represent the shaded portion of each diagram.

5. 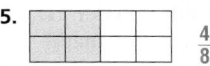 $\frac{4}{8}$

6. 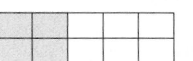 $\frac{4}{10}$

7.  $\frac{5}{4}$

8.  $\frac{4}{16}$

✓ Write a Fraction as a Mixed Number

Write each improper fraction as a mixed number.

9. $\frac{22}{7}$ $3\frac{1}{7}$ 10. $\frac{18}{5}$ $3\frac{3}{5}$ 11. $\frac{104}{25}$ $4\frac{4}{25}$ 12. $\frac{65}{9}$ $7\frac{2}{9}$ 13. $\frac{37}{3}$ $12\frac{1}{3}$

✓ Write a Mixed Number as a Fraction

Write each mixed number as an improper fraction.

14. $7\frac{1}{4}$ $\frac{29}{4}$ 15. $10\frac{3}{7}$ $\frac{73}{7}$ 16. $5\frac{3}{8}$ $\frac{43}{8}$ 17. $11\frac{1}{11}$ $\frac{122}{11}$ 18. $3\frac{5}{6}$ $\frac{23}{6}$

✓ Write Equivalent Fractions

Supply the missing information.

19. $\frac{3}{8} = \frac{\blacksquare}{24}$ 9   20. $\frac{5}{13} = \frac{\blacksquare}{52}$ 20   21. $\frac{7}{12} = \frac{\blacksquare}{36}$ 21   22. $\frac{8}{15} = \frac{\blacksquare}{45}$ 24   23. $\frac{3}{5} = \frac{\blacksquare}{75}$ 45

Organizer

Objective: Assess students' understanding of prerequisite skills.

Prerequisite Skills

Model Fractions
Write a Fraction as a Mixed Number
Write a Mixed Number as a Fraction
Write Equivalent Fractions

Assessing Prior Knowledge

INTERVENTION

Diagnose and Prescribe

Use this page to determine whether intervention is necessary or whether enrichment is appropriate.

Resources

 Are You Ready? Intervention and Enrichment Worksheets

 Are You Ready? CD-ROM

 Are You Ready? Online

my.hrw.com

ARE YOU READY?

Diagnose and Prescribe

NO INTERVENE

YES ENRICH

✓ Prerequisite Skill	🗞 Worksheets	💿 CD-ROM	🌐 Online
ARE YOU READY? Intervention, Chapter 2			
✓ Model Fractions	Skill 18	Activity 18	
✓ Write a Fraction as a Mixed Number	Skill 21	Activity 21	Diagnose and Prescribe Online
✓ Write a Mixed Number as a Fraction	Skill 22	Activity 22	
✓ Write Equivalent Fractions	Skill 24	Activity 24	

ARE YOU READY? Enrichment, Chapter 2

🗞 **Worksheets**
 💿 **CD-ROM**
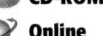 🌐 **Online**

Organizer

Objective: Help students organize the new concepts they will learn in Chapter 2.

 Online Edition
Multilingual Glossary

Resources

 **PuzzlePro®**
One-Stop Planner®

 Multilingual Glossary Online

go.hrw.com
KEYWORD: MT7 Glossary

Possible answers to *Vocabulary Connections*

1. A rational number is a number that can be written as a fraction.
2. The least common denominator is the smallest factor that is the same for every denominator.
3. They are numbers whose only common factor is 1.

Study Guide: Preview

Where You've Been

Previously, you

- compared and ordered positive rational numbers.
- added, subtracted, multiplied, and divided integers.
- used models to solve equations.

In This Chapter

You will study

- comparing and ordering positive and negative fractions and decimals.
- using appropriate operations to solve problems involving fractions and decimals.
- finding solutions to application problems using equations.
- solving two-step equations.

Where You're Going

You can use the skills learned in this chapter

- to compare and manipulate measurements.
- to find the size of a fraction of a group or an item.
- to solve more-complicated equations in future math courses.

Key Vocabulary/Vocabulario

least common denominator (LCD)	mínimo común denominador (mcd)
rational number	número racional
reciprocal	recíproco
relatively prime	primos relativos

Vocabulary Connections

To become familiar with some of the vocabulary terms in the chapter, consider the following. You may refer to the chapter, the glossary, or a dictionary if you like.

1. The word *rational* has as its root the word *ratio* and sounds somewhat like the word *fraction*. What do you think a **rational number** is in math?

2. The word *least* means "smallest," and the word *common* means "the same." What do you think these words mean in combination in **least common denominator**?

3. The word *relative* means "in relation to each other." What do you think **relatively prime** numbers are?

 **Reading and Writing Math**

Writing Strategy: Translate Between Words and Math

When reading a real-world math problem, look for key words to help you translate between the words and the math.

There are several different ways to indicate a mathematical operation in words.

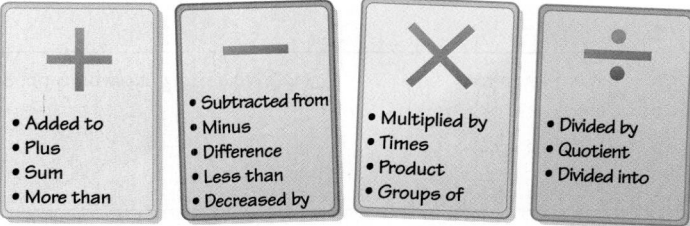

+	−	×	÷
• Added to • Plus • Sum • More than	• Subtracted from • Minus • Difference • Less than • Decreased by	• Multiplied by • Times • Product • Groups of	• Divided by • Quotient • Divided into

In the problem below, use the highlighted terms to translate the words into math.

The Montez family went to the state fair over the weekend. They spent $52.50 on rides, food, and drinks, in addition to the $5.50-per-person price of admission. How much did the Montez family spend at the fair?

They spent $52.50 **in addition to** $5.50 **per** **person** .

Let p represent the number of people.

$\quad$ $52.50 $\qquad$ **+** $\qquad$ $5.50 **×** $\quad$ p $\quad$ $= 52.5 + 5.5p$

 **Try This**

Identify the mathematical operation described by the key terms in each statement. Explain your choice.

1. The male calf weighs 0.55 pounds less than the female calf.
2. Bob has 9 more books than Kerri.
3. The number of treats is divided by the number of students.
4. The rate is $15 plus two times the cost of the paint.

Organizer

Objective: Help students apply strategies to understand and retain key concepts.

 Online Edition

Resources

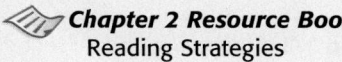 **Chapter 2 Resource Book**
Reading Strategies

ENGLISH
LANGUAGE
LEARNERS

Writing Strategy:
Translate Between
Words and Math

Discuss Students find it useful to be aware of key terms that will help them translate between words and math.

Extend As students work through Chapter 2, encourage them to make a list of key terms from each lesson to help them solve problems. Have them practice translating sentences using the terms.

Students can work in pairs to write sentences and translate them into mathematical statements.

Answers to *Try This*

1. subtraction; less than
2. addition; more than
3. division; divided by
4. addition; plus; multiplication; times

Rational Number Operations

One-Minute Section Planner

Lesson	Materials	MiC and Lab Resources
Lesson 2-1 Rational Numbers • Write rational numbers in equivalent forms. ☑ SAT-10 ☑ ITBS ☑ CTBS ☑ NAEP	Fraction bars (MK)	*Technology Lab Activities* 2-1
Lesson 2-2 Comparing and Ordering Rational Numbers • Compare and order positive and negative rational numbers written as fractions, decimals, and integers. ☑ SAT-10 ☑ ITBS ☑ CTBS ☑ NAEP	Fraction bars (MK)	**MiC:** *Revisiting Numbers* pp. 50–51
Lesson 2-3 Adding and Subtracting Rational Numbers • Add and subtract decimals and rational numbers with like denominators. ☑ SAT-10 ☑ ITBS ☑ CTBS ☑ NAEP		*Hands-On Lab Activities* 2-3
Lesson 2-4 Multiplying Rational Numbers • Multiply fractions, mixed numbers, and decimals. ☑ SAT-10 ☑ ITBS ☑ CTBS ☑ NAEP		**MiC:** *Revisiting Numbers* pp. 27–31, 36–39, 45–51
Lesson 2-5 Dividing Rational Numbers • Divide fractions and decimals. ☑ SAT-10 ☑ ITBS ☑ CTBS ☑ NAEP		**MiC:** *Revisiting Numbers* pp. 27–31, 36–39 *Hands-On Lab Activities* 2-5
Lesson 2-6 Adding and Subtracting with Unlike Denominators • Add and subtract fractions with unlike denominators. **2-6 Technology Lab** Add and Subtract Fractions • Use a graphing calculator to add and subtract fractions. ☑ SAT-10 ☑ ITBS ☑ CTBS ☑ NAEP	Graph paper, graphing calculator	*Technology Lab Activities* 2-6

MK = *Manipulatives Kit*

Mathematics in Context

The unit ***Revisiting Numbers*** from the *Mathematics in Context* © 2006 series can be used with Section 2A. See Section Planner above for suggestions for integrating *MiC* with *Holt Mathematics*.

Section Overview

Comparing and Ordering Rational Numbers   *Lessons 2-1, 2-2*

Why? Many quantities and measurements are expressed with rational numbers.

> A **rational number** is a number that can be expressed as a *ratio* (fraction) in the form $\frac{n}{d}$, where n and d are integers, and $d \neq 0$.
> **Examples:**
>
> $$5 = \frac{5}{1} \qquad \frac{3}{4} \qquad 1.59 = 1\frac{59}{100} = \frac{159}{100}$$

Comparing Two Fractions with Different Denominators

Compare $\frac{5}{8}$ and $\frac{2}{3}$.

$$\frac{5}{8} = \frac{5 \cdot 3}{8 \cdot 3} = \frac{15}{24} \qquad \frac{2}{3} = \frac{2 \cdot 8}{3 \cdot 8} = \frac{16}{24}$$

Write the fractions as **fractions with the same denominators.** Then compare the numerators.

$$\frac{15}{24} < \frac{16}{24}, \text{ so } \frac{5}{8} < \frac{2}{3}$$

Comparing Decimals

Compare 0.387 and 0.39.

0.387

0.390

So, 0.387 < 0.390

Write the **decimals with the same number of decimal places.** Compare each place from left to right.

Operations with Rational Numbers   *Lessons 2-3 through 2-6*

Why? To evaluate expressions, we need to be able to operate with rational numbers.

Addition

$$\frac{3}{8} + \frac{7}{8}$$
$$= \frac{3 + 7}{8}$$
$$= \frac{10}{8}$$
$$= \frac{5}{4}$$
$$= 1\frac{1}{4}$$

Add numerators and keep the common denominator.

Subtraction

$$\frac{3}{4} - \frac{1}{6}$$
$$= \frac{3}{4}\left(\frac{3}{3}\right) - \frac{1}{6}\left(\frac{2}{2}\right)$$
$$= \frac{9}{12} - \frac{2}{12}$$
$$= \frac{7}{12}$$

When necessary, multiply the fractions by **a form of 1** to obtain common denominators.

Multiplication

$$1\frac{3}{8}\left(-\frac{2}{3}\right)$$
$$= \frac{11}{8}\left(-\frac{2}{3}\right)$$
$$= \frac{(11)(-2)}{(8)(3)}$$
$$= \frac{-22}{24}$$
$$= -\frac{11}{12}$$

Write the mixed number $1\frac{3}{8}$ as an improper fraction, $\frac{11}{8}$.

Division

$$\frac{8}{9} \div \frac{2}{3}$$
$$= \frac{8}{9} \cdot \frac{3}{2}$$
$$= \frac{24}{18}$$
$$= \frac{4}{3}$$
$$= 1\frac{1}{3}$$

To divide by $\frac{2}{3}$, multiply by its reciprocal, $\frac{3}{2}$.

Objective: Students write rational numbers in equivalent forms.

Technology Lab
In *Technology Lab Activities*

Online Edition
Tutorial Videos

Countdown to Testing Week 3

Power Presentations
with PowerPoint®

Warm Up

Divide.

1. $36 \div 3$ **12**   **2.** $144 \div 6$ **24**

3. $68 \div 17$ **4**   **4.** $345 \div 115$ **3**

5. $1024 \div 64$ **16**

Problem of the Day

An ice cream parlor has 6 flavors of ice cream. A dish with two scoops can have any two flavors, including the same flavor twice. How many different double-scoop combinations are possible?   **21**

Also available on transparency

Math Humor

Numbers like $\frac{1}{6}$ and $\frac{2}{3}$ in decimal form are like people who make sense but say the same thing over and over. They're rational, but they repeat!

State Resources

go.hrw.com
State Resources Online
KEYWORD: MT7 Resources

2-1 Rational Numbers

Learn to write rational numbers in equivalent forms.

Vocabulary
rational number
relatively prime

In 2005, there were 325 NCAA Division I women's basketball teams. At the end of the season, 64 teams were selected for the women's NCAA basketball tournament. Only $\frac{64}{325}$ of the teams qualified for the tournament.

A **rational number** is any number that can be written as a fraction $\frac{n}{d}$, where n and d are integers and $d \neq 0$.

The goal of simplifying fractions is to make the numerator and the denominator *relatively prime*. **Relatively prime** numbers have no common factors other than 1.

The Baylor women's basketball team won its first national championship in 2005.

You can often simplify fractions by dividing both the numerator and denominator by the same nonzero integer. You can simplify the fraction $\frac{12}{15}$ to $\frac{4}{5}$ by dividing both the numerator and denominator by 3.

12 of the 15 boxes are shaded. 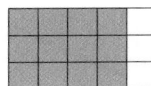 $\frac{12 \div 3}{15 \div 3} = \frac{4}{5}$  4 of the 5 boxes are shaded.

The same total area is shaded.

EXAMPLE 1 Simplifying Fractions

Remember!
$\frac{0}{a} = 0$ for $a \neq 0$
$\frac{a}{a} = 1$ for $a \neq 0$
$\frac{-7}{8} = \frac{7}{-8} = -\frac{7}{8}$

Simplify.

A $\frac{9}{55}$ $9 = 3 \cdot 3$
$55 = 5 \cdot 11$; there are no common factors.

$\frac{9}{55} = \frac{9}{55}$ *9 and 55 are relatively prime.*

B $\frac{-24}{32}$

$\frac{-24}{32} = \frac{-24 \div 8}{32 \div 8}$ $24 = \boxed{2 \cdot 2 \cdot 2} \cdot 3$ *8 is a common factor.*
$32 = \boxed{2 \cdot 2 \cdot 2} \cdot 2 \cdot 2$

$= \frac{-3}{4}$, or $-\frac{3}{4}$ *Divide the numerator and denominator by 8.*

---

1 Introduce
Alternate Opener

EXPLORATION

2-1 Rational Numbers

Comparing numbers with $\frac{1}{2}$ is useful in many situations.

Phil surveyed 317 voters and found that 156 supported his reelection. He reasoned the following way to determine whether he had a majority.
$156 \times 2 = 150 \times 2 + 6 \times 2$
$= 300 + 12$
$= 312$

Phil concluded that he did not have a majority. Look at how Phil checked his estimate with a calculator.

Double the numerator and compare it with the denominator of each fraction to determine whether the fraction is greater than or less than $\frac{1}{2}$. Check your work with a calculator.

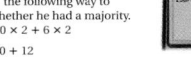

	Fraction	$> \frac{1}{2}$?	$< \frac{1}{2}$?
1.	$\frac{51}{101}$		
2.	$\frac{221}{425}$		
3.	$\frac{260}{513}$		
4.	$\frac{578}{1152}$		

Think and Discuss
5. Explain how you checked your work with a calculator.

Motivate

Show students this diagram:

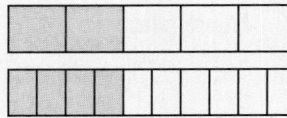

Ask students: "What fraction of each bar is shaded? Is there a way to write one of these fractions as a decimal?" The responses should illustrate that there are three equivalent forms of the same rational number: $\frac{2}{5}$, $\frac{4}{10}$, and 0.4.

Explorations and answers are provided in *Alternate Openers: Explorations Transparencies.*

A repeating decimal can be written with a bar over the digits that repeat. So $0.13333\ldots = 0.1\overline{3}$.

Decimals that terminate or repeat are rational numbers.

To write a terminating decimal as a fraction, identify the place value of the digit farthest to the right. Then write all of the digits after the decimal point as the numerator with the place value as the denominator.

Rational Number	Description	Written as a Fraction
−3.2	Terminating decimal	$-\frac{32}{10}$
$0.1\overline{3}$	Repeating decimal	$\frac{2}{15}$

EXAMPLE 2 Writing Decimals as Fractions

Write each decimal as a fraction in simplest form.

A −5.59

$-5.59 = -5\frac{59}{100}$ *9 is in the hundredths place.*

B 0.5714

$0.5714 = \frac{5714}{10,000}$ *4 is in the ten-thousandths place.*

$= \frac{2857}{5000}$ *Simplify by dividing by the common factor 2.*

To write a fraction as a decimal, divide the numerator by the denominator.

EXAMPLE 3 Writing Fractions as Decimals

Write each fraction as a decimal.

A $\frac{5}{4}$

$$
\begin{array}{r}
1.25 \\
4\overline{)5.00} \\
-4\downarrow \\
\hline
1\,0 \\
-8\downarrow \\
\hline
20 \\
-20 \\
\hline
0
\end{array}
$$

The remainder is 0. This is a terminating decimal.

The fraction $\frac{5}{4}$ is equivalent to the decimal 1.25.

B $-\frac{1}{6}$

$$
\begin{array}{r}
0.1\overline{6} \\
6\overline{)1.000} \\
-6\downarrow \\
\hline
40 \\
-36\downarrow \\
\hline
40
\end{array}
$$

Leave the negative sign off while dividing. The pattern repeats.

The fraction $-\frac{1}{6}$ is equivalent to the decimal $-0.1\overline{6}$.

Think and Discuss

1. **Explain** how you can be sure that a fraction is simplified.
2. **Give** the sign of a fraction in which the numerator is negative and the denominator is negative.

Power Presentations with PowerPoint®

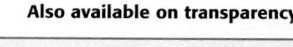

Additional Examples

Example 1

Simplify.

A. $\frac{16}{80}$ $\frac{1}{5}$

B. $\frac{-18}{29}$ $-\frac{18}{29}$

Example 2

Write each decimal as a fraction in simplest form.

A. 5.37 $5\frac{37}{100}$

B. 0.622 $\frac{311}{500}$

Example 3

Write each fraction as a decimal.

A. $\frac{11}{9}$ $1.\overline{2}$ **B.** $\frac{7}{20}$ 0.35

Also available on transparency

Answers to Think and Discuss:

1. Possible answer: When the numerator and denominator have no common factors other than 1, the fraction is in simplest form.

2. Positive; a negative number divided by a negative number gives a positive quotient.

2 Teach

ENGLISH LANGUAGE LEARNERS

Guided Instruction

In this lesson, students learn to write rational numbers in equivalent forms. Review the definition of *rational number*. Discuss how to simplify a fraction and the meaning of *relatively prime*. Review the place-value chart (Teaching Transparency) to prepare students for writing decimals as fractions. Explain that the fraction bar indicates division of the numerator by the denominator. Work Example 3B out a few extra places so that students can see the pattern developing. Point out that many fractions will have a repeating pattern of digits when written as decimals.

Reaching All Learners
Through Multiple Representations

Give each student a set of fractions (e.g., $\frac{1}{2}, \frac{2}{3}, \frac{3}{4}, \frac{4}{5}$) in random order. Have students write each fraction as a decimal and use the values to write the fractions in order from least to greatest. Have students analyze the pattern, and then see if they can put other fractions in a set in ascending order without writing them as decimals.

3 Close

Summarize

Remind students that a fraction, such as $\frac{3}{4}$, is another way of showing a division problem (3 divided by 4). To write a fraction as a decimal, solve the division problem. Point out that fractions and decimals are two ways to show numbers that are smaller than 1. Ask students to write the value of 0.20 in as many ways as they can, and write their responses on the chalkboard. Point out that all correct responses have the same value.

Possible answers:
0.2; 0.200; $\frac{20}{100}$; $\frac{2}{10}$; $\frac{1}{5}$; 20 ÷ 100; $100\overline{)20}$; twenty-hundredths; two-tenths

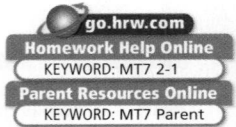

go.hrw.com
Homework Help Online
KEYWORD: MT7 2-1
Parent Resources Online
KEYWORD: MT7 Parent

Assignment Guide

If you finished Example **1** assign:
Average 1–10, 29–38, 67–79
Advanced 29–38, 57, 58, 63, 64, 66–79

If you finished Example **2** assign:
Average 1–18, 29–46, 59, 67–79
Advanced 29–46, 57–59, 63, 64, 66–79

If you finished Example **3** assign:
Average 1–60, 67–79
Advanced 34–38, 43–51, 57–79

Homework Quick Check

Quickly check key concepts.
Exercises: 36, 44, 48, 58

Math Background

A fraction can be written in simplest form as either a mixed number or an improper fraction. Students may prefer a mixed number because they will probably have a clearer concept of its value if it can be easily compared to integers. For example, students may understand that $5\frac{3}{7}$ is between 5 and 6, but they may have difficulty making the same conclusion about the equivalent improper fraction $\frac{38}{7}$. For this reason, the answers to the Exercises have been given as mixed numbers. In more advanced courses, however, improper fractions may prove more useful.

State Resources

go.hrw.com
State Resources Online
KEYWORD: MT7 Resources

GUIDED PRACTICE

See Example **1** Simplify.

1. $\frac{11}{22}$ $\frac{1}{2}$　　2. $\frac{6}{10}$ $\frac{3}{5}$　　3. $-\frac{16}{24}$ $-\frac{2}{3}$　　4. $\frac{14}{25}$ $\frac{14}{25}$　　5. $\frac{17}{51}$ $\frac{1}{3}$

6. $\frac{57}{69}$ $\frac{19}{23}$　　7. $-\frac{6}{8}$ $-\frac{3}{4}$　　8. $\frac{9}{28}$ $\frac{9}{28}$　　9. $\frac{49}{112}$ $\frac{7}{16}$　　10. $\frac{22}{44}$ $\frac{1}{2}$

See Example **2** Write each decimal as a fraction in simplest form.

11. 0.75 $\frac{3}{4}$　　12. 1.125 $1\frac{1}{8}$　　13. 0.4 $\frac{2}{5}$　　14. 0.35 $\frac{7}{20}$

15. -2.2 $-2\frac{1}{5}$　　16. 0.625 $\frac{5}{8}$　　17. 3.21 $3\frac{21}{100}$　　18. -0.3878 $-\frac{1939}{5000}$

See Example **3** Write each fraction as a decimal.

19. $\frac{5}{8}$ 0.625　　20. $-\frac{3}{5}$ -0.6　　21. $\frac{5}{12}$ $0.41\overline{6}$　　22. $\frac{1}{4}$ 0.25　　23. $\frac{1}{9}$ $0.\overline{1}$

24. $-\frac{18}{9}$ -2　　25. $\frac{3}{8}$ 0.375　　26. $-\frac{14}{5}$ -2.8　　27. $\frac{5}{4}$ 1.25　　28. $\frac{2}{3}$ $0.\overline{6}$

INDEPENDENT PRACTICE

See Example **1** Simplify.

29. $\frac{21}{28}$ $\frac{3}{4}$　　30. $\frac{25}{65}$ $\frac{5}{13}$　　31. $-\frac{17}{34}$ $-\frac{1}{2}$　　32. $-\frac{17}{21}$ $-\frac{17}{21}$　　33. $\frac{25}{30}$ $\frac{5}{6}$

34. $\frac{13}{17}$ $\frac{13}{17}$　　35. $\frac{22}{35}$ $\frac{22}{35}$　　36. $\frac{64}{76}$ $\frac{16}{19}$　　37. $-\frac{78}{126}$ $-\frac{13}{21}$　　38. $\frac{14}{22}$ $\frac{7}{11}$

See Example **2** Write each decimal as a fraction in simplest form.

39. 0.6 $\frac{3}{5}$　　40. 3.5 $3\frac{1}{2}$　　41. 0.72 $\frac{18}{25}$　　42. -0.183 $-\frac{183}{1000}$

43. 1.377 $1\frac{377}{1000}$　　44. 1.450 $1\frac{9}{20}$　　45. -1.4 $-1\frac{2}{5}$　　46. -2.9 $-2\frac{9}{10}$

See Example **3** Write each fraction as a decimal.

47. $-\frac{3}{8}$ -0.375　　48. $\frac{7}{12}$ $0.58\overline{3}$　　49. $-\frac{9}{5}$ -1.8　　50. $\frac{13}{20}$ 0.65　　51. $\frac{8}{5}$ 1.6

52. $\frac{18}{40}$ 0.45　　53. $-\frac{23}{5}$ -4.6　　54. $\frac{28}{25}$ 1.12　　55. $\frac{4}{3}$ $1.\overline{3}$　　56. $-\frac{7}{4}$ -1.75

PRACTICE AND PROBLEM SOLVING

Extra Practice
See page 784.

57. Make up a fraction that cannot be simplified and has 36 as its denominator. **Possible answer:** $\frac{11}{36}$

58. Make up a fraction that cannot be simplified and has 24 as its denominator. **Possible answer:** $\frac{5}{24}$

59. **Sports** The thickness of a surfboard is often matched to the weight of the rider. For example, a person weighing 170 pounds might need a surfboard that is 3.375 inches thick. Write 3.375 as a fraction in simplest form. $3\frac{3}{8}$

60. Bondi weighed his mobile phone and found it to be approximately $\frac{7}{25}$ pound. What is the weight of Bondi's phone written as a decimal? 0.28

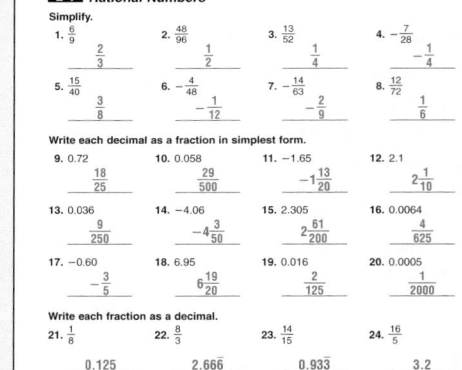

RETEACH 2-1

Reteach
2-1 *Rational Numbers (continued)*

To write a fraction as a decimal, divide numerator by denominator.

A decimal may terminate.　　A decimal may repeat.

$\frac{3}{4} = 4\overline{)3.00}$
$\quad\ \ 0.75$
$\quad -28\!\downarrow$
$\quad\ \ \ 20$
$\quad -20$
$\quad\ \ \ \ 0$

$\frac{1}{3} = 3\overline{)1.00}$
$\quad\ \ 0.\overline{3}$
$\quad -9\!\downarrow$
$\quad\ \ 10$
$\quad -9$
$\quad\ \ 1$

Complete to write each fraction as a decimal.

14. $\frac{15}{4} = 4\overline{)15.00}$ → 3.75

15. $\frac{5}{6} = 6\overline{)5.00}$ → $0.8\overline{3}$

16. $\frac{11}{3} = 3\overline{)11.00}$ → $3.6\overline{6}$

Write each fraction as a decimal.

18. $\frac{5}{2} = $ _____ 2.5

19. $\frac{15}{8} = $ _____ 1.875

20. $\frac{28}{6} = $ _____ $4.\overline{6}$

21. $\frac{22}{4} = $ _____ 5.5

22. $\frac{62}{12} = $ _____ $5.1\overline{6}$

23. $\frac{105}{10} = $ _____ 10.5

PRACTICE 2-1

Practice B
2-1 *Rational Numbers*

Simplify.

1. $\frac{6}{9}$ $\frac{2}{3}$　　2. $\frac{48}{96}$ $\frac{1}{2}$　　3. $\frac{13}{52}$ $\frac{1}{4}$　　4. $-\frac{7}{28}$ $-\frac{1}{4}$

5. $\frac{15}{40}$ $\frac{3}{8}$　　6. $-\frac{4}{48}$ $-\frac{1}{12}$　　7. $-\frac{14}{63}$ $-\frac{2}{9}$　　8. $\frac{12}{72}$ $\frac{1}{6}$

Write each decimal as a fraction in simplest form.

9. 0.72 $\frac{18}{25}$　　10. 0.058 $\frac{29}{500}$　　11. -1.65 $-1\frac{13}{20}$　　12. 2.1 $2\frac{1}{10}$

13. 0.036 $\frac{9}{250}$　　14. -4.06 $-4\frac{3}{50}$　　15. 2.305 $2\frac{61}{200}$　　16. 0.0064 $\frac{4}{625}$

17. -0.60 $-\frac{3}{5}$　　18. 6.95 $6\frac{19}{20}$　　19. 0.016 $\frac{2}{125}$　　20. 0.0005 $\frac{1}{2000}$

Write each fraction as a decimal.

21. $\frac{1}{8}$ 0.125　　22. $\frac{8}{3}$ $2.6\overline{6}$　　23. $\frac{14}{15}$ $0.9\overline{3}$　　24. $\frac{16}{5}$ 3.2

25. $\frac{11}{16}$ 0.6875　　26. $\frac{7}{9}$ $0.7\overline{7}$　　27. $\frac{4}{5}$ 0.8　　28. $\frac{31}{25}$ 1.24

29. Make up a fraction that cannot be simplified that has 24 as its denominator. **sample answer:** $\frac{5}{24}$

---

66 Chapter 2 Rational Numbers

61. a. Simplify each fraction.

$$\frac{8}{18} \quad \frac{4}{9} \quad \frac{8}{48} \quad \frac{1}{6} \quad \frac{5}{20} \quad \frac{1}{4} \quad \frac{21}{45} \quad \frac{7}{15} \quad \frac{18}{32} \quad \frac{9}{16} \quad \frac{24}{50} \quad \frac{12}{25} \quad \frac{45}{72} \quad \frac{5}{8} \quad \frac{36}{96} \quad \frac{3}{8}$$

b. Write the denominator of each simplified fraction as the product of prime factors.

c. Write each simplified fraction as a decimal. Label each as a terminating or repeating decimal.

63. GCF = 2; $\frac{21}{34}$; No, the fraction cannot be further simplified because the numerator and denominator are relatively prime.

62. The ruler is marked at every $\frac{1}{16}$ in. Do the labeled measurements convert to terminating or repeating decimals?   **terminating**

63. Critical Thinking The greatest common factor, GCF, is the largest common factor of two or more given numbers. Find and remove the GCF of 42 and 68 from the fraction $\frac{42}{68}$. Can the resulting fraction be further simplified? Explain.

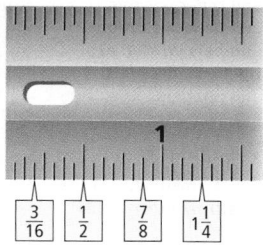

$$\frac{3}{16} \quad \frac{1}{2} \quad \frac{7}{8} \quad 1\frac{1}{4}$$

 64. What's the Error? A student simplified a fraction in this manner: $\frac{-25}{-30} = -\frac{5}{6}$. What error did the student make?

 65. Write About It Using your answers to Exercise 61, examine the prime factors in the denominators of the simplified fractions that are equivalent to terminating decimals. Then examine the prime factors in the denominators of the simplified fractions that are equivalent to repeating decimals. What pattern do you see?

 66. Challenge A student simplified a fraction to $-\frac{2}{9}$ by removing the common factors, which were 2 and 9. What was the original fraction? $-\frac{36}{162}$

TEST PREP and Spiral Review

67. Multiple Choice If $y = -\frac{3}{9}$, which is NOT equal to y?

Ⓐ $\frac{-1}{3}$ Ⓑ $-\frac{1}{3}$ Ⓒ $-\left(\frac{-1}{3}\right)$ Ⓓ $-\left(\frac{-1}{-3}\right)$

68. Multiple Choice Which shows the decimal 0.68 as a fraction in simplest form?

Ⓕ $\frac{17}{25}$ Ⓖ $\frac{34}{50}$ Ⓗ $\frac{3}{4}$ Ⓙ $\frac{6}{8}$

69. Gridded Response What is the decimal equivalent of the fraction $\frac{119}{8}$?   **14.875**

Evaluate each expression for the given values of the variable. (Lesson 1-1)

70. $3x + 5$ for $x = 2$ and $x = 3$ **11; 14**   **71.** $4(x + 1)$ for $x = 6$ and $x = 11$ **28; 48**

Simplify. (Lesson 1-6)

72. $-3(6 - 8)$ **6**   **73.** $4(-3 - 2)$ **−20**   **74.** $-5(3 + 2)$ **−25**   **75.** $-3(1 - 8)$ **21**

76. $-12(-4 - 9)$ **156**   **77.** $15(11 - (-1))$ **180**   **78.** $6(-5 - (-4))$ **−6**   **79.** $-7(1 - (-17))$ **−126**

Objective: Students compare and order positive and negative rational numbers written as fractions, decimals, and integers.

 Online Edition
Tutorial Videos

 Countdown to Testing Week 3

 **Power Presentations**
with PowerPoint®

Warm Up
Write each fraction as a decimal.

1. $\frac{1}{3}$ $0.\overline{3}$ 2. $\frac{4}{5}$ 0.8

3. $\frac{3}{4}$ 0.75 4. $\frac{2}{3}$ $0.\overline{6}$

Problem of the Day
How much pie do you have if you take 2 of 5 total pieces? **0.4**

Also available on transparency

Math Humor

Parent: Why are you stirring that paper with a spoon?

Student: It's my homework. I'm supposed to create some *mixed* fractions.

 *State Resources*

 **go.hrw.com**
State Resources Online
KEYWORD: MT7 Resources

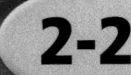

Learn to compare and order positive and negative rational numbers written as fractions, decimals, and integers.

Vocabulary
least common denominator (LCD)

The population within the United States is constantly changing. The table shows the percent change in populations from 2000 to 2003 for three states and the District of Columbia. A negative percent indicates that the population declined.

Population Change from 2000–2003			
Location	Change (%)	Location	Change (%)
Maine	$\frac{12}{5}$	Washington	4.0
North Dakota	-1.3	Washington, D.C.	$-1\frac{1}{2}$

To compare or order rational numbers, first write them in the same form. To compare fractions, find a common denominator. This could be the **least common denominator** (LCD), which is the least common multiple of the denominators.

EXAMPLE 1   **Comparing Fractions by Finding a Common Denominator**

Compare. Write <, >, or =.

A $\frac{5}{8}$ 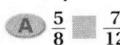 $\frac{7}{12}$

Method 1: Multiply to find a common denominator.

$8 \cdot 12 = 96$ *Multiply 8 and 12 to find a common denominator.*

$\frac{5}{8} \cdot \frac{12}{12} = \frac{5 \cdot 12}{8 \cdot 12} = \frac{60}{96}$ *Write the fractions with a common denominator.*
$\frac{7}{12} \cdot \frac{8}{8} = \frac{7 \cdot 8}{12 \cdot 8} = \frac{56}{96}$

$\frac{60}{96} > \frac{56}{96}$, so $\frac{5}{8} > \frac{7}{12}$ *Compare the fractions.*

Remember!
The least common multiple (LCM) of two numbers is the smallest number, other than 0, that is a multiple of both numbers.

B $\frac{3}{4}$ 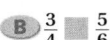 $\frac{5}{6}$

Method 2: Find the least common denominator.

$4: 4, 8, 12 \ldots$ $6: 6, 12 \ldots$ *List multiples of 4 and 6. The LCM is 12.*

$\frac{3}{4} \cdot \frac{3}{3} = \frac{3 \cdot 3}{4 \cdot 3} = \frac{9}{12}$ *Write the fractions with a*
$\frac{5}{6} \cdot \frac{2}{2} = \frac{5 \cdot 2}{6 \cdot 2} = \frac{10}{12}$ *common denominator.*

$\frac{9}{12} < \frac{10}{12}$, so $\frac{3}{4} < \frac{5}{6}$ *Compare the fractions.*

---

1 Introduce
Alternate Opener

EXPLORATION

2-2 Comparing and Ordering Rational Numbers

You can use a number line to compare rational numbers. For example, the number line shows that $\frac{1}{8} < \frac{1}{4}$ because $\frac{1}{8}$ is to the left of $\frac{1}{4}$.

Use the number line to compare each pair of fractions by writing < or >. Then convert the fractions to decimals and use < or > to compare the decimals.

1. $\frac{5}{8} \square \frac{2}{3}$

2. $\frac{3}{8} \square \frac{1}{3}$

3. $\frac{7}{8} \square \frac{3}{4}$

4. $\frac{3}{8} \square \frac{2}{3}$

5. $\frac{3}{4} \square \frac{2}{3}$

6. $\frac{1}{4} \square \frac{1}{3}$

Think and Discuss

7. **Explain** how you know that $\frac{3}{8} < \frac{5}{8}$ without using the number line.

8. **Describe** how you could use the number line to compare $5\frac{3}{8}$ and $5\frac{1}{2}$.

Motivate

Have students discuss how they have compared and ordered integers. Then discuss the different forms in which a rational number can be expressed (integer, fraction, mixed number, decimal). Have students represent the same rational number in different forms
(e.g., $2\frac{1}{2} = 2.5 = \frac{5}{2}$).

Explorations and answers are provided in *Alternate Openers: Explorations Transparencies.*

EXAMPLE 2 **Comparing by Using Decimals**

Compare. Write $<$, $>$, or $=$.

A $3\frac{3}{8}$ ▢ $3\frac{3}{5}$

$3\frac{3}{8} = 3.375$ and $3\frac{3}{5} = 3.6$ *Write the fractions as decimals.*

$3.375 < 3.6$, so $3\frac{3}{8} < 3\frac{3}{5}$ *Compare the decimals.*

B -0.53 ▢ $-\frac{6}{10}$

$-\frac{6}{10} = -0.6$ *Write $-\frac{6}{10}$ as a decimal.*

$-0.53 > -0.6$, so $-0.53 > -\frac{6}{10}$ *Compare the decimals.*

C $\frac{9}{11}$ ▢ 0.8

$\frac{9}{11} = 0.\overline{81}$ *Write $\frac{9}{11}$ as a decimal.*

$0.\overline{81} > 0.8$, so $\frac{9}{11} > 0.8$ *Compare the decimals.*

To order fractions and decimals, you can either write them all in the same form and then compare them, or place them on a number line.

EXAMPLE 3 *Social Studies Application*

From 2000 to 2003, the percent changes in populations for three states and the District of Columbia were as follows: $\frac{12}{5}$ for Maine, -1.3 for North Dakota, 4.0 for Washington, and $-1\frac{1}{2}$ for Washington, D.C. List these numbers in order from least to greatest.

Place the numbers on a number line and read them from left to right.

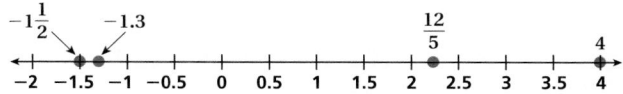

The percent changes in population from least to greatest are $-1\frac{1}{2}$, -1.3, $\frac{12}{5}$, and 4.0.

Answers to Think and Discuss

1. Yes; to compare two rational numbers, they need to be written in the same form.

2. Possible answer: Place both decimals on a number line. From least to greatest, they are 0.235 and 0.239.

Think and Discuss

1. **Explain** whether you need to find a common denominator to compare $\frac{2}{3}$ and $-\frac{1}{2}$.

2. **Describe** the steps you would use to compare 0.235 and 0.239.

COMMON ERROR ALERT

Students sometimes confuse the direction of the inequality. Rather than trying to memorize the meaning of the inequality symbols, point out to students that they can easily remember which symbol to use by always having the greater side of the symbol open towards the greater quantity in the expression. If the inequality symbol were the beak of a hungry bird, it would want to be open toward the larger quantity.

Power Presentations with PowerPoint®

Additional Examples

Example 1

Compare. Write $<$, $>$, or $=$.

A. $\frac{5}{6}$ ▢ $\frac{7}{10}$ $>$

B. $\frac{2}{3}$ ▢ $\frac{4}{5}$ $<$

Example 2

Compare. Write $<$, $>$, or $=$.

A. $5\frac{2}{9}$ ▢ $5\frac{2}{7}$ $<$

B. -0.44 ▢ $-\frac{2}{5}$ $<$

C. $\frac{1}{9}$ ▢ 0.1 $>$

Example 3

The numbers $\frac{14}{4}$, -3.4, 6.0, and -2.5 represent the percentage of change in populations for three states. List these numbers in order from least to greatest. $-3.4, -2.5, \frac{14}{4}, 6.0$

Also available on transparency

---

② Teach

Guided Instruction

In this lesson, students learn to compare rational numbers in fractional form by finding a common denominator or by converting the fractions to decimals. Students also learn to order rational numbers on a number line. First, introduce rewriting fractions by using an LCD and comparing the numerators. Next, demonstrate how to change a fraction and a mixed number to a decimal, and compare decimals. Then use a number line to order rational numbers.

Reaching All Learners
Through Concrete Manipulatives

Have students research the sizes in a customary-measure socket set. Socket sizes are given in sixteenths of an inch, reduced to simplest form. If students can obtain a socket set, have students put the sockets in order from least to greatest size. The students should then write the socket sizes in order from least to greatest.

③ Close

Summarize

Ask students to describe how to compare two fractions. Then ask them to describe how to compare a fraction and a decimal.

Possible answers: To compare two fractions, rewrite them with their LCD and compare numerators; to compare fraction and decimal, change fraction to decimal by dividing, line up the decimal points, find first decimal place where digits differ, compare those digits.

2-2 Exercises

go.hrw.com
Homework Help Online
KEYWORD: MT7 2-2
Parent Resources Online
KEYWORD: MT7 Parent

Assignment Guide

If you finished Example **1** assign:
Average 1–4, 10–17, 27, 42–53
Advanced 10–17, 27, 31, 42–53

If you finished Example **2** assign:
Average 1–8, 10–25, 27–30, 42–53
Advanced 10–25, 27–34, 39–53

If you finished Example **3** assign:
Average 1–30, 37, 38, 42–53
Advanced 10–24, 22–53

Homework Quick Check
Quickly check key concepts.
Exercises: 16, 22, 26, 34, 38

GUIDED PRACTICE

See Example **1** Compare. Write <, >, or =.

1. $\frac{3}{8}$ ▨ $\frac{3}{7}$ <
2. $\frac{9}{11}$ ▨ $\frac{9}{10}$ <
3. $\frac{6}{15}$ ▨ $\frac{2}{5}$ =
4. $-\frac{7}{10}$ ▨ $-\frac{5}{8}$ <

See Example **2**
5. $\frac{7}{8}$ ▨ $\frac{9}{11}$ >
6. 4.2 ▨ $4\frac{1}{5}$ =
7. $-\frac{3}{7}$ ▨ -0.375 <
8. $-1\frac{1}{2}$ ▨ $-1\frac{7}{9}$ >

See Example **3**
9. In Mr. Corsetti's shop class, students were instructed to measure and cut boards to a length of 8 inches. In checking four students' work, Mr. Corsetti found that one board was 8.25 inches, the second was $8\frac{1}{8}$ inches, the third was 7.5 inches, and the fourth was $7\frac{5}{16}$ inches. List these measurements in order from least to greatest. $7\frac{5}{16}$ in., 7.5 in., $8\frac{1}{8}$ in., 8.25 in.

INDEPENDENT PRACTICE

See Example **1** Compare. Write <, >, or =.

10. $\frac{5}{8}$ ▨ $\frac{16}{21}$ <
11. $\frac{13}{11}$ ▨ $\frac{8}{7}$ >
12. $-\frac{1}{3}$ ▨ $-\frac{1}{4}$ <
13. $-\frac{3}{4}$ ▨ $-\frac{9}{12}$ =

14. $-\frac{2}{3}$ ▨ $-\frac{5}{7}$ >
15. $-\frac{16}{9}$ ▨ $-\frac{8}{3}$ >
16. $\frac{17}{20}$ ▨ $\frac{5}{6}$ >
17. $-\frac{2}{9}$ ▨ $-\frac{1}{8}$ <

See Example **2**
18. $5\frac{8}{9}$ ▨ $5\frac{7}{8}$ >
19. $-\frac{1}{6}$ ▨ $-\frac{1}{5}$ >
20. $-\frac{4}{7}$ ▨ $-\frac{2}{5}$ <
21. $\frac{6}{7}$ ▨ 0.87 <

22. $-\frac{9}{7}$ ▨ $-\frac{10}{8}$ >
23. $1\frac{2}{3}$ ▨ $1\frac{8}{12}$ =
24. $\frac{15}{22}$ ▨ $0.6\overline{81}$ =
25. $\frac{13}{20}$ ▨ 0.65 =

See Example **3**
26. **Sports** During the qualifying for the first NASCAR event at Texas Motor Speedway in 2005, the fastest speed was 192.582 mi/h. The next four fastest speeds, relative to the fastest speed, were approximately $-\frac{17}{25}$ mi/h, -0.15 mi/h, -1.15 mi/h, and $-1\frac{1}{40}$ mi/h. List these relative speeds in order from least to greatest. -1.15, $1\frac{1}{40}$, $-\frac{17}{25}$, -0.15

PRACTICE AND PROBLEM SOLVING

Extra Practice
See page 784.

Compare. Write <, >, or =.

27. $-\frac{5}{7}$ ▨ $-\frac{6}{10}$ <
28. -5.00 ▨ $-\frac{20}{5}$ <
29. 7.2 ▨ $7\frac{2}{9}$ <
30. 14.7 ▨ 14.6885 >

Write a fraction or decimal that has a value between the given numbers.

31. $\frac{1}{4}$ and $\frac{1}{3}$ $\frac{3}{10}$
32. 0.89 and 0.9 0.899
33. $-\frac{2}{3}$ and 0.5 $-\frac{1}{3}$
34. 0.27 and $\frac{4}{5}$ 0.5

31–34. Possible answers given.

35. **Critical Thinking** On Tuesday, stock A's price fell -0.56 and stock B's price fell -0.50. Stock C's price did not fall as much as stock A's, but it fell more than stock B's. What is a reasonable answer for how much stock C's price fell? Explain.

35. Possible answer: A reasonable answer is -0.54 because $-0.56 <$ stock C < -0.50 and $-0.56 < -0.54 < -0.50$.

36. **Multi-Step** Alejandro, Becky, Marcus, and Kathy ate lunch at a restaurant. The total amount of the bill, including tax and tip, was $34.20. Alejandro paid $10.00, Becky paid $\frac{1}{4}$ of the bill, Marcus paid 0.2 of the bill, and Kathy paid the rest. Who paid the greatest part of the bill?

36. Alejandro

State Resources
go.hrw.com
State Resources Online
KEYWORD: MT7 Resources

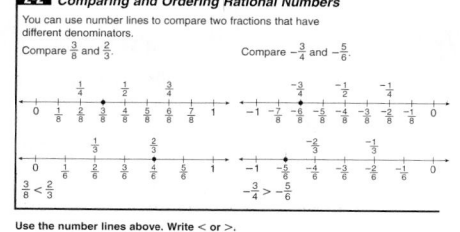

RETEACH 2-2

Reteach
2-2 Comparing and Ordering Rational Numbers

You can use number lines to compare two fractions that have different denominators.

Compare $\frac{3}{8}$ and $\frac{2}{3}$.

Compare $-\frac{3}{4}$ and $-\frac{5}{6}$.

$\frac{3}{8} < \frac{2}{3}$

$-\frac{3}{4} > -\frac{5}{6}$

Use the number lines above. Write < or >.
1. $\frac{1}{4}$ > $\frac{1}{6}$
2. $\frac{5}{6}$ > $\frac{1}{2}$
3. $-\frac{2}{3}$ < $-\frac{1}{4}$
4. $-\frac{5}{6}$ < $-\frac{5}{8}$

You can also use number lines to compare a fraction and a decimal.

Compare 0.2 and $\frac{1}{3}$.

Compare $-\frac{5}{8}$ and -0.9.

$0.2 < \frac{1}{3}$

$-\frac{5}{8} > -0.9$

Use the number lines above. Write < or >.
5. $\frac{5}{6}$ > 0.5
6. 0.6 < $\frac{2}{3}$
7. -0.4 < $-\frac{1}{4}$
8. $-\frac{7}{8}$ < -0.8

PRACTICE 2-2

Practice B
2-2 Comparing and Ordering Rational Numbers

Compare. Write <, >, or =.

1. $\frac{1}{8}$ > $\frac{1}{10}$
2. $\frac{3}{5}$ < $\frac{7}{10}$
3. $-\frac{1}{3}$ > $-\frac{3}{4}$

4. $\frac{5}{6}$ > $\frac{3}{4}$
5. $-\frac{2}{7}$ > $-\frac{1}{2}$
6. $1\frac{2}{9}$ < $1\frac{2}{3}$

7. $-\frac{8}{9}$ < $-\frac{3}{10}$
8. $-\frac{4}{5}$ = $-\frac{8}{10}$
9. 0.08 < $\frac{3}{10}$

10. $\frac{11}{15}$ = 0.73
11. $2\frac{4}{9}$ < $2\frac{3}{4}$
12. $-\frac{5}{6}$ < -0.58

13. $3\frac{1}{4}$ < 3.3
14. $-\frac{1}{8}$ > $-\frac{1}{9}$
15. 0.75 = $\frac{3}{4}$

16. $-2\frac{1}{8}$ < -2.1
17. $1\frac{1}{2}$ > 1.456
18. $-\frac{3}{5}$ = -0.6

19. On Monday, Gina ran 1 mile in 9.3 minutes. Her times for running 1 mile on each of the next four days, relative to her time on Monday, were $-1\frac{2}{3}$ minutes, -1.45 minutes, -1.8 minutes, and $-1\frac{3}{8}$ minutes. List these relative times in order from least to greatest.
-1.8 minutes, $-1\frac{2}{3}$ minutes, -1.45 minutes, $-1\frac{3}{8}$ minutes

20. Trail A is 3.1 miles long. Trail C is $3\frac{1}{4}$ miles long. Trail B is longer than Trail A but shorter than Trail C. What is a reasonable distance for the length of Trail B?
Possible answer: 3.2 miles

37. Life Science The lengths of some butterflies' wingspans are shown in the table.

a. List the butterflies in order from smallest to largest wingspan.

b. The pink-spotted swallowtail's wingspan can measure $3\frac{5}{16}$ inches. Between which two butterflies should the pink-spotted swallowtail be in your list from part **a**?

Butterfly	Wingspan (in.)
Great white	3.75
Large orange sulphur	$3\frac{3}{8}$
Apricot sulphur	2.625
White-angled sulphur	3.5

37a. apricot sulphur, large orange sulphur, white-angled sulphur, great white

37b. between the apricot sulphur and the large orange sulphur

38. Meteorology One measure of average global temperature shows how each year varies from a base measure. The table shows results for several years.

Year	1958	1964	1965	1978	2002
Difference from Base	0.10°C	−0.17°C	−0.10°C	$\frac{1}{50}$°C	0.54°C

a. Order the five years from coldest to warmest. **1964, 1965, 1978, 1958, 2002**

b. In 1946, the average temperature varied by −0.03°C from the base measure. Between which two years should 1946 fall when the years are ordered from coldest to warmest? **between 1965 and 1978**

39. What's the Error?  A student compared $-\frac{1}{4}$ and −0.3. He changed $-\frac{1}{4}$ to the decimal −0.25 and wrote, "Since 0.3 is greater than 0.25, −0.3 is greater than −0.25." What was the student's error?

40. Write About It  Describe two methods to compare $\frac{13}{17}$ and 0.82. Which do you think is easier? Why?

41. Challenge Write $\left|-\frac{2}{3}\right|$, $|-0.75|$, $|0.62|$, and $\left|\frac{5}{6}\right|$ in order from least to greatest. **$|0.62|, \left|\frac{2}{3}\right|, |-0.75|, \left|\frac{5}{6}\right|$**

TEST PREP and Spiral Review

42. Multiple Choice Which pair of numbers does $\frac{3}{7}$ NOT come between?

(A) 0.3 and 0.45 (B) $\frac{9}{25}$ and $\frac{1}{2}$ (C) 0.2 and $\frac{1}{3}$ (D) $\frac{2}{5}$ and 0.65

43. Multiple Choice Which list of numbers is in order from least to greatest?

(F) 0.3, $\frac{4}{5}$, $\frac{1}{4}$, 0 (G) $\frac{4}{5}$, 0.3, 0, $\frac{1}{4}$ (H) $\frac{1}{4}$, $\frac{4}{5}$, 0, 0.3 (J) 0, $\frac{1}{4}$, 0.3, $\frac{4}{5}$

Simplify. (Lesson 1-5)

44. −5 − (−4) **45.** 8 − (−2) **46.** −19 − 13 **47.** 72 − 119 **48.** 24 − 37
   −1   10   − 32   − 47   − 13

Write each fraction as a decimal. (Lesson 2-1)

49. $\frac{3}{4}$ 0.75 **50.** $\frac{1}{8}$ 0.125 **51.** $\frac{10}{4}$ 2.5 **52.** $\frac{9}{15}$ 0.6 **53.** $\frac{19}{20}$ 0.95

Answers

39. Possible answer: When ordering negative numbers, the number with the greater absolute value is *less than*, not greater than, the number with the smaller absolute value.

40. Possible answer: Method 1: Convert both numbers to decimals. Method 2: convert both numbers to fractions. To make and compare two fractions, the least common denominator is very large, so it is easier to convert $\frac{13}{17}$ to a decimal and compare the decimals on a number line.

TEST PREP DOCTOR Students may find it helpful to draw one or more number lines to help them determine the answer to Exercise 42. Have them plot the pairs of points given in the answer choices, and then decide whether $\frac{3}{7}$ comes between those values.

Journal

Have students explain how ordering rational numbers can be used in everyday life. Ask them to use an inequality in their explanation.

Power Presentations with PowerPoint®

2-2 Lesson Quiz

Compare. Write <, >, or =.

1. $\frac{1}{4}$ ☐ $\frac{1}{3}$ <

2. $-\frac{2}{9}$ ☐ −0.29   >

3. $-2\frac{6}{7}$ ☐ $-2\frac{7}{8}$ >

4. Sarah competed in a long-jump contest. Her first jump was 3.75 m, her second jump was $3\frac{8}{9}$ m, and her third jump was $3\frac{9}{11}$ m. Which jump was the longest?   **second**

Also available on transparency

Objective: Students add and subtract decimals and rational numbers with like denominators.

 Hands-On Lab
In *Hands-On Lab Activities*

 Online Edition
Tutorial Videos

 Countdown to Testing Week 3

Power Presentations
with PowerPoint®

Warm Up

Simplify.

1. $\frac{21}{14}$ $1\frac{1}{2}$ 2. $\frac{12}{30}$ $\frac{2}{5}$

3. $\frac{24}{56}$ $\frac{3}{7}$

Write each decimal as a fraction in simplest form.

4. 1.15 $1\frac{3}{20}$ 5. −0.22 $-\frac{11}{50}$

Problem of the Day

Four sprinters run a race. In how many different ways can they arrive at the finish line, assuming there are no ties? **24**

Also available on transparency

Math Humor

How do we know that the fractions $\frac{3}{c}, \frac{6}{c},$ and $\frac{8}{c}$ are not from the United States? Because their numerators are all over *c*'s!

State Resources

 **go.hrw.com**
State Resources Online
KEYWORD: MT7 Resources

2-3 Adding and Subtracting Rational Numbers

Learn to add and subtract decimals and rational numbers with like denominators.

Olympic swimming events are measured in hundredths of a second. In the Athens 2004 Summer Olympic Games, the difference in times between the gold and silver medal winners in the men's 100-meter backstroke was 0.29 second.

EXAMPLE 1 *Sports Application*

In the Athens 2004 Olympic Games, Aaron Piersol of the United States won the gold medal in the 100-meter backstroke with a time of 54.06 seconds. The eighth place finisher, Marco di Carli, completed the race in 55.27 seconds. What was the difference in times between the first- and eighth-place finishers?

$$\begin{array}{r} 55.27 \\ -54.06 \\ \hline 1.21 \end{array}$$ *Write the numbers so that the decimals line up.*

The difference between the first- and eighth-place finishers was 1.21 seconds.

EXAMPLE 2 **Using a Number Line to Add Rational Numbers**

Use a number line to find each sum.

Ⓐ −0.4 + 1.3

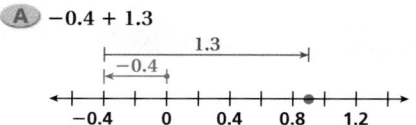

Move left 0.4 units. From −0.4, move right 1.3 units.

You finish at 0.9, so −0.4 + 1.3 = 0.9.

Ⓑ $-\frac{7}{8} + \left(-\frac{3}{8}\right)$

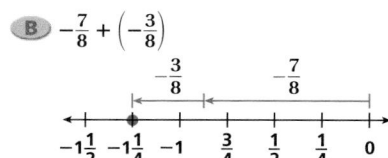

Move left $\frac{7}{8}$ units. From $-\frac{7}{8}$, move left $\frac{3}{8}$ units.

You finish at $-1\frac{1}{4}$, so $-\frac{7}{8} + \left(-\frac{3}{8}\right) = -1\frac{1}{4}$.

1 Introduce
Alternate Opener

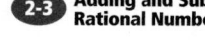

EXPLORATION

2-3 Adding and Subtracting Rational Numbers

Beckie has $454.96 in a checking account. She needs to pay bills in the amounts $25.95, $313.00, $45.76, and $87.95.

Beckie estimates the following:

Account: $454.96 ≈ $455.00

Bills: $25.95 ≈ $ 25.00
$313.00 ≈ $310.00
$45.76 ≈ $ 45.00
$87.95 ≈ $ 90.00
$470.00

Beckie determines that she does not have enough money in her account to pay her bills. She then checks her estimate with a calculator.

Estimate the solution to each expression in the table. Then use a calculator to solve.

		Estimate	Actual
1.	120 − 9.8		
2.	45 − 17.8 + 15.9 + 16.1 − 1.07		
3.	88.10 + 109.85		
4.	34.12 − 18.30 + 65.25		

Think and Discuss
5. **Describe** the estimation strategies you used.

Motivate

Use the following examples to review the rules for adding signed numbers (Lesson 1-4):

Same signs: 5 + 2 = 7, −5 + (−2) = −7

Opposite signs: 5 + (−2) = 3, −5 + 2 = −3

Review how to use a number line to perform these additions. Remind students that to subtract a number, you add its opposite (Lesson 1-5).

Explorations and answers are provided in *Alternate Openers: Explorations Transparencies.*

ADDING AND SUBTRACTING WITH LIKE DENOMINATORS		
Words	**Numbers**	**Algebra**
To add or subtract rational numbers with the same denominator, add or subtract the numerators and keep the denominator.	$\frac{1}{5} + \left(-\frac{4}{5}\right) = \frac{1 + (-4)}{5}$ $= \frac{-3}{5}, \text{ or } -\frac{3}{5}$	$\frac{a}{d} + \frac{b}{d} = \frac{a + b}{d}$

E X A M P L E 3 **Adding and Subtracting Fractions with Like Denominators**

Add or subtract. Write each answer in simplest form.

Ⓐ $\frac{7}{13} + \frac{11}{13}$

$\frac{7}{13} + \frac{11}{13} = \frac{7 + 11}{13}$ *Add numerators. Keep the denominator.*

$= \frac{18}{13}, \text{ or } 1\frac{5}{13}$

Ⓑ $-\frac{3}{8} - \frac{5}{8}$

$-\frac{3}{8} - \frac{5}{8} = \frac{-3}{8} + \frac{-5}{8}$ $-\frac{5}{8}$ *can be written as* $\frac{-5}{8}$.

$= \frac{-3 + (-5)}{8} = \frac{-8}{8} = -1$

E X A M P L E 4 **Evaluating Expressions with Rational Numbers**

Evaluate each expression for the given value of the variable.

Ⓐ $33.5 + x$ for $x = -48.2$

$33.5 + (-48.2)$ *Substitute −48.2 for x.*

-14.7 *Think: 48.2 > 33.5. Use sign of 48.2.*

Ⓑ $-\frac{3}{8} + c$ for $c = 1\frac{7}{8}$

$-\frac{3}{8} + 1\frac{7}{8}$ *Substitute* $1\frac{7}{8}$ *for c.*

$\frac{-3}{8} + \frac{15}{8}$ $1\frac{7}{8} = \frac{1(8) + 7}{8} = \frac{15}{8}$

$\frac{-3 + 15}{8} = \frac{12}{8}$ *Add numerators. Keep the denominator.*

$\frac{3}{2}, \text{ or } 1\frac{1}{2}$ *Simplify.*

Think and Discuss

1. Give an example of an addition problem that involves simplifying an improper fraction in the final step.

2. Explain why $\frac{7}{9} + \frac{7}{9}$ does not equal $\frac{14}{18}$.

Possible answers to
Think and Discuss:

1. $\frac{5}{8} + \frac{5}{8} = \frac{10}{8} = \frac{5}{4} = 1\frac{1}{4}$

2. To add fractions with like denominators, add the numerators, but keep the same denominator.

$\frac{7}{9} + \frac{7}{9} = \frac{14}{9} = 1\frac{5}{9}$

② Teach

Guided Instruction

In this lesson, students learn to add and subtract decimals and rational numbers with like denominators. Review with students how to align decimals for addition and subtraction. Explain that you can't add or subtract digits that are in different places because they don't share the same value. Review Example 2 to show students how to add and subtract fractions using a number line, and then point out that the same results are obtained by adding or subtracting the numerators and keeping the same denominator. Remind students to write their answers in simplest form.

 Reaching All Learners
Through Critical Thinking

Give each pair of students a set of related exercises, such as those shown below.

1. $2.51 + 4.2$ 6.71

2. $-2.51 + (-4.2)$ −6.71

3. $-2.51 + 4.2$ 1.69

4. $2.51 + (-4.2)$ −1.69

Have students compare the answers in each set, and make a generalization about the rules for adding positive and negative numbers. Have students compare generalizations until a consensus is reached.

③ Close

Summarize

Remind students that decimal points must be aligned when adding or subtracting decimals. Remind students that to add or subtract fractions with like denominators, they should add or subtract the numerators and keep the same denominator. Ask students if it's possible to add a decimal and a fraction, and ask them how they would do it.

Possible answer: Yes; you can write the fraction as a decimal and then add the decimals together, or you can write the decimal as a fraction and add the fractions together.

2-3 Exercises

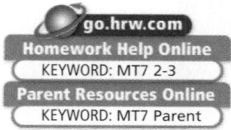
go.hrw.com
Homework Help Online
KEYWORD: MT7 2-3
Parent Resources Online
KEYWORD: MT7 Parent

Assignment Guide

If you finished Example **1** assign:
Average 1, 13, 43–53
Advanced 13, 38, 39, 43–53

If you finished Example **2** assign:
Average 1–5, 13–17, 43–53
Advanced 13–17, 32–34, 43–53

If you finished Example **3** assign:
Average 1–9, 13–21, 29, 30–33, 43–53
Advanced 13–21, 28, 29, 33–36, 38–41, 43–53

If you finished Example **4** assign:
Average 1–25, 29, 30–33, 43–53
Advanced 13–28, 29, 36–53

Homework Quick Check

Quickly check key concepts.
Exercises: 13, 16, 18, 24

Math Background

The Commutative Property of Addition states that $a + b = b + a$. It holds for all real numbers a and b (e.g., $0.21 + 3.4 = 3.4 + 0.21 = 3.61$). There is no commutative property for subtraction, because $a - b = b - a$ is *not* true for all real numbers a and b (e.g., $\frac{2}{3} - \frac{1}{3} = \frac{1}{3}$, but $\frac{1}{3} - \frac{2}{3} = -\frac{1}{3}$). The Associative Property of Addition states that $a + (b + c) = (a + b) + c$. It holds for all real numbers a, b, and c. However, there is no associative property for subtraction [(e.g., $1.2 - (0.8 - 0.3) = 0.7$, but $(1.2 - 0.8) - 0.3 = 0.1$)].

State Resources

go.hrw.com
State Resources Online
KEYWORD: MT7 Resources

GUIDED PRACTICE

See Example **1**
1. **Sports** In the Athens 2004 Olympic Games, Jodie Henry of Australia won the gold medal in the 100-meter freestyle swim with a time of 53.84 seconds. The bronze medal winner, Natalie Coughlin of the United States, completed the race in 54.4 seconds. What was the difference between the two times? **0.56 s**

See Example **2** Use a number line to find each sum.
2. $-0.9 + 3.2$ **2.3**
3. $-\frac{7}{3} + \left(-\frac{2}{3}\right)$ **−3**
4. $-2.7 + 0.5$ **−2.2**
5. $-\frac{1}{2} + \left(-\frac{4}{2}\right)$ **$-2\frac{1}{2}$**

See Example **3** Add or subtract. Write each answer in simplest form.
6. $\frac{1}{6} - \frac{5}{6}$ **$-\frac{2}{3}$**
7. $-\frac{3}{10} - \frac{9}{10}$ **$-1\frac{1}{5}$**
8. $\frac{3}{12} + \frac{7}{12}$ **$\frac{5}{6}$**
9. $\frac{9}{25} + \left(-\frac{4}{25}\right)$ **$\frac{1}{5}$**

See Example **4** Evaluate each expression for the given value of the variable.
10. $3.7 + x$ for $x = -9.3$ **−5.6**
11. $-\frac{4}{9} + x$ for $x = \frac{8}{9}$ **$\frac{4}{9}$**
12. $-\frac{14}{15} + x$ for $x = 1$ **$\frac{1}{15}$**

INDEPENDENT PRACTICE

See Example **1**
13. **Sports** Reaction time measures how quickly a runner reacts to the starter pistol. In the 100-meter dash at the 2004 Olympic Games, Lauryn Williams had a reaction time of 0.214 second. Her total race time, including reaction time, was 11.03 seconds. How long did it take her to run the actual distance? **10.816 s**

See Example **2** Use a number line to find each sum.
14. $-3.2 + 1.6$ **−1.6**
15. $-\frac{7}{8} + \left(-\frac{7}{8}\right)$ **$-1\frac{3}{4}$**
16. $-0.5 + 9.1$ **8.6**
17. $-\frac{5}{18} + \left(-\frac{1}{18}\right)$ **$-\frac{1}{3}$**

See Example **3** Add or subtract. Write each answer in simplest form.
18. $\frac{7}{13} - \frac{5}{13}$ **$\frac{2}{13}$**
19. $-\frac{1}{17} - \frac{13}{17}$ **$-\frac{14}{17}$**
20. $\frac{9}{17} + \frac{16}{17}$ **$1\frac{8}{17}$**
21. $\frac{11}{33} + \left(-\frac{19}{33}\right)$ **$-\frac{8}{33}$**

See Example **4** Evaluate each expression for the given value of the variable.
22. $47.3 + x$ for $x = -18.6$
23. $\frac{11}{12} + x$ for $x = -\frac{7}{12}$
24. $-\frac{23}{25} + x$ for $x = \frac{7}{25}$

PRACTICE AND PROBLEM SOLVING

Extra Practice
See page 784.

22. 28.7
23. $\frac{1}{3}$
24. $-\frac{16}{25}$
25. 7.9375 or $7\frac{15}{16}$
26. $\frac{5}{21}$
27. $4\frac{69}{200}$ or 4.345

Evaluate each expression for the given value of the variable.
25. $8.25 - x$ for $x = \frac{5}{16}$
26. $x + \left(-\frac{3}{7}\right)$ for $x = \frac{2}{3}$
27. $x + \left(-\frac{3}{8}\right)$ for $x = 4.72$

28. **Design** The distance from the floor of one level of a building to the floor of the level above it is 9 feet $\frac{3}{8}$ inches. If the distance from the floor to the ceiling is 8 feet $2\frac{1}{2}$ inches, how thick is the space between the ceiling of one floor and the floor of the level above it? **$9\frac{7}{8}$ in.**

29. **Sports** The circumference of a women's NCAA college softball must be between $11\frac{7}{8}$ inches and $12\frac{1}{8}$ inches. What is the greatest possible difference in circumference between two softballs that meet the standards? **$\frac{1}{4}$ in.**

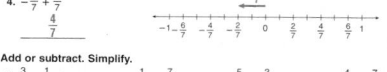
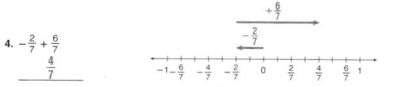

Add or subtract. Write each answer in simplest form.

30. $\frac{4}{9} - \frac{1}{9}$ $\frac{1}{3}$ **31.** $-\frac{7}{11} + \frac{3}{11} - \frac{2}{11}$ $-\frac{6}{11}$ **32.** $\frac{13}{5} + \frac{8}{5}$ $4\frac{1}{5}$ **33.** $-\frac{17}{18} - \frac{29}{18}$ $-2\frac{5}{9}$

34. $-1.7 + 3\frac{3}{5}$ 1.9 **35.** $-\frac{13}{21} + \left(-\frac{8}{21}\right)$ -1 **36.** $-8 + 6\frac{4}{5}$ -1.2 **37.** $-1\frac{15}{16} + \left(-\frac{9}{16}\right)$ $-1\frac{1}{2}$

Energy The circle graph shows the sources of renewable energy and their use in the United States in British thermal units (Btu).

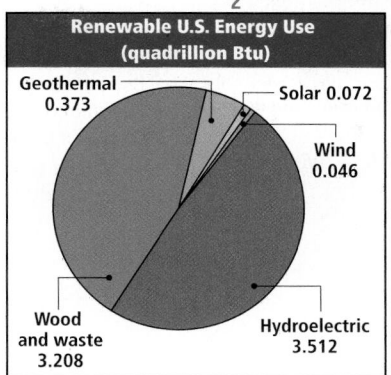

Renewable U.S. Energy Use (quadrillion Btu)

Geothermal 0.373 — Solar 0.072 — Wind 0.046 — Hydroelectric 3.512 — Wood and waste 3.208

38. How many quadrillion Btu's from geothermal, wood and waste, and hydroelectric sources combined were used?   **7.093 quadrillion Btu**

39. How many more Btu's from hydroelectric sources were used than those from wind, solar, and wood and waste sources combined?   **0.186 quadrillion Btu**

40. Write a Problem Write a problem that requires a decimal to be converted to a fraction and that also involves addition or subtraction of fractions.

41. Write About It Explain how to subtract fractions.

42. Challenge The gutter of a bowling lane measures $9\frac{5}{16}$ inches wide. This is $\frac{3}{16}$ inch less than the widest gutter permitted and $\frac{5}{16}$ inch greater than the narrowest gutter permitted. What is the greatest possible difference in the width of two gutters? $\frac{1}{2}$ in.

TEST PREP and Spiral Review

43. Multiple Choice Evaluate the expression $25.18 - x$ for $x = -18.7$.

   (A) 6.48   (B) 23.31   (C) 27.05   (D) 43.88

44. Multiple Choice Gregory filled a fish tank with $4\frac{5}{12}$ gallons of water. Linda added $3\frac{11}{12}$ more gallons of water. How many gallons of water were in the tank?

   (F) $7\frac{1}{2}$ gal   (G) $8\frac{1}{3}$ gal   (H) $8\frac{5}{12}$ gal   (J) $8\frac{2}{3}$ gal

45. Gridded Response Evaluate $\frac{7}{15} - x$ for $x = -\frac{4}{15}$. $\frac{11}{15}$

Solve. (Lesson 1-7)

46. $x + 13 = 22$ $x = 9$ **47.** $b + 5 = -2$ $b = -7$ **48.** $2y + 9 = 19$ $y = 5$ **49.** $4a + 2 = -18$ $a = -5$

Compare. Write <, >, or =. (Lesson 2-2)

50. 0.25 ▓ $\frac{1}{3}$ $<$ **51.** $-0.5\overline{3}$ ▓ -0.5 $<$ **52.** $\frac{4}{7}$ ▓ 0.57 $>$ **53.** $-\frac{9}{11}$ ▓ $-0.\overline{81}$ $=$

CHALLENGE 2-3

LESSON 2-3 Challenge
Number Code

Each sum is the code for a letter. As you find a sum, write its letter code in the message below. Write the sum in simplest form. Some letters appear more than once. An example is done for you.

$4.5 + (-6.5)$ $\underline{-2}$, T   1. $14.56 + (-10.09)$ $\underline{4.47}$, V

2. $\frac{7}{8} + \left(-1\frac{3}{8}\right)$ $\underline{-\frac{1}{2}}$, M   3. $\frac{6}{8} + \left(-\frac{3}{8}\right)$ $\underline{\frac{3}{8}}$, N

4. $-1.05 + 0.85$ $\underline{-0.2}$, I   5. $\frac{-2}{4} + \left(\frac{-3}{4}\right)$ $\underline{-1\frac{1}{4}}$, U

6. $-7.08 + (-12.02)$ $\underline{-19.1}$, S   7. $-9.5 + 3.1$ $\underline{-6.4}$, E

8. $\frac{-4}{5} + 1$ $\underline{\frac{1}{5}}$, E   9. $-1\frac{1}{2} + \left(-1\frac{1}{2}\right)$ $\underline{-3}$, H

10. $1\frac{2}{4} + \left(\frac{-3}{4}\right)$ $\underline{\frac{3}{4}}$, P   11. $5 + \left(-4\frac{1}{10}\right)$ $\underline{\frac{9}{10}}$, I

12. $8 + (-6.4)$ $\underline{1.6}$, Y   13. $-3\frac{1}{4} + 3\frac{1}{4}$ $\underline{0}$, S

14. $\frac{7}{8} + \left(-1\frac{7}{8}\right)$ $\underline{-1}$, L   15. $6.52 + (-5)$ $\underline{1.52}$, Z

16. $-62.3 + 23.9$ $\underline{-38.4}$, A   17. $9\frac{1}{8} + (-10)$ $\underline{-\frac{7}{8}}$, R

18. $-2.9 + 0.85$ $\underline{-2.05}$, O   19. $2.7 + (-0.9)$ $\underline{1.8}$, O

$\underline{S}\ \underline{U}\ \underline{R}\ \underline{E}$ $\underline{Y}\ \underline{O}\ \underline{U}$ $\underline{A}\ \underline{R}\ \underline{E}$
$-19.1\ -1\frac{1}{4}\ -\frac{7}{8}\ -6.4$ $1.6\ -2.05\ -1\frac{1}{4}$ $-38.4\ -\frac{7}{8}\ \frac{1}{5}$

$\underline{N}\ \underline{O}\ \underline{T}$ $\underline{L}\ \underline{E}\ \underline{S}\ \underline{S}$ $\underline{T}\ \underline{H}\ \underline{A}\ \underline{N}$
$\frac{3}{8}\ 1.8\ -2$ $-1\ \frac{1}{5}\ -19.1\ 0$ $-2\ -3\ -38.4\ \frac{3}{8}$

$\underline{Z}\ \underline{E}\ \underline{R}\ \underline{O}$?
$1.52\ -6.4\ -\frac{7}{8}\ -2.05$

$\underline{I}'\ \underline{M}$ $\underline{P}\ \underline{O}\ \underline{S}\ \underline{I}\ \underline{T}\ \underline{I}\ \underline{V}\ \underline{E}$!
$-0.2\ -\frac{1}{2}$ $\frac{3}{4}\ -2.05\ 0\ \frac{9}{10}\ -2\ -0.2\ 4.47\ \frac{1}{5}$

PROBLEM SOLVING 2-3

LESSON 2-3 Problem Solving
Adding and Subtracting Rational Numbers

Write the correct answer.

1. In 2004, Yuliya Nesterenko of Belarus won the Olympic Gold in the 100-m dash with a time of 10.93 seconds. In 2000, American Marion Jones won the 100-m dash with a time of 10.75 seconds. How many seconds faster did Marion Jones run the 100-m dash?   **0.18 s**

2. The snowfall in Rochester, NY in the winter of 1999–2000 was 91.5 inches. Normal snowfall is about 76 inches per winter. How much more snow fell in the winter of 1999–2000 than is normal?   **15.5 inches**

3. In a survey, $\frac{76}{100}$ people indicated that they check their e-mail daily, while $\frac{23}{100}$ check their e-mail weekly, and $\frac{1}{100}$ check their e-mail less than once a week. What fraction of people check their e-mail at least once a week? $\frac{99}{100}$

4. To make a small amount of play dough, you can mix the following ingredients: 1 cup of flour, $\frac{1}{2}$ cup of salt and $\frac{1}{2}$ cup of water. What is the total amount of ingredients added to make the play dough?   **2 cups**

Choose the letter for the best answer.

5. How much more expensive is it to buy a ticket in Boston than in Minnesota?
   A $20.95   C $5.40
   B $55.19   D $26.35

Baseball Ticket Prices	
Location	**Average Price**
Minnesota	$14.42
League Average	$19.82
Boston	$40.77

6. How much more expensive is it to buy a ticket in Boston than the league average?
   F $60.59
   G $20.95
   H $5.40
   J $26.35

7. What is the total cost of a ticket in Boston and a ticket in Minnesota?
   A $55.19
   B $34.24
   C $60.59
   D $54.19

2-3 Adding and Subtracting Rational Numbers   **75**

Objective: Students multiply fractions, mixed numbers, and decimals.

Online Edition
Tutorial Videos

Countdown to Testing Week 3

Power Presentations
with PowerPoint®

Warm Up

Write each number as an improper fraction.

1. $2\frac{1}{3}$ $\frac{7}{3}$ **2.** $1\frac{7}{8}$ $\frac{15}{8}$ **3.** $3\frac{2}{5}$ $\frac{17}{5}$

4. $6\frac{2}{3}$ $\frac{20}{3}$ **5.** $5\frac{3}{8}$ $\frac{43}{8}$

Problem of the Day

The sum of three consecutive integers is 168. What are the three integers?   55, 56, and 57

Also available on transparency

Math Humor

5 out of 4 people have trouble with fractions.

2-4 Multiplying Rational Numbers

Learn to multiply fractions, mixed numbers, and decimals.

Andrew walks his dog each day. His route is $\frac{1}{8}$ mile. What is the total distance that Andrew walks his dog in a 5-day week?

Recall that multiplication is repeated addition.

$$3\left(\frac{1}{4}\right) = \frac{1}{4} + \frac{1}{4} + \frac{1}{4}$$
$$= \frac{1+1+1}{4}$$
$$= \frac{3}{4}$$

Notice that multiplying a fraction by a whole number is the same as multiplying the whole number by just the numerator of the fraction and keeping the same denominator.

RULES FOR MULTIPLYING TWO RATIONAL NUMBERS

If the signs of the factors are the same, the product is positive.

$$(+) \cdot (+) = (+) \text{ or } (-) \cdot (-) = (+)$$

If the signs of the factors are different, the product is negative.

$$(+) \cdot (-) = (-) \text{ or } (-) \cdot (+) = (-)$$

EXAMPLE 1 **Multiplying a Fraction and an Integer**

Multiply. Write each answer in simplest form.

A $6\left(\frac{2}{3}\right)$

$6\left(\frac{2}{3}\right)$

$\frac{6 \cdot 2}{3}$

$\frac{12}{3}$ *Multiply*

4 *Simplify.*

B $-2\left(3\frac{1}{5}\right)$

$-2\left(3\frac{1}{5}\right)$

$-2\left(\frac{16}{5}\right)$ $3\frac{1}{5} = \frac{3(5)+1}{5} = \frac{16}{5}$

$-\frac{32}{5}$ *Multiply* $(-) \cdot (+) = (-)$.

$-6\frac{2}{5}$ *Simplify.*

Helpful Hint

To write $-\frac{32}{5}$ as a mixed number, divide:

$$-\frac{32}{5} = -6 \text{ R2}$$
$$= -6\frac{2}{5}$$

---

1 Introduce

Alternate Opener

EXPLORATION

2-4 Multiplying Rational Numbers

To find the product of $\frac{1}{2} \cdot \frac{1}{3}$, use one color to color in $\frac{1}{2}$ of a square vertically. Use a second color to color in $\frac{1}{3}$ of the square horizontally. The product is represented by the area where the two colors intersect.

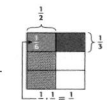

Use a similar model to find each product.

1. $\frac{1}{2} \cdot \frac{4}{6}$ **2.** $\frac{2}{3} \cdot \frac{3}{4}$

To multiply $2 \cdot 1\frac{1}{2}$, color in 2 squares across and $1\frac{1}{2}$ down.

$$2 \cdot 1\frac{1}{2} = 3$$

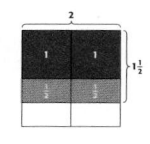

Use a similar model to find each product.

3. $3 \cdot 4\frac{1}{2}$ **4.** $8\frac{1}{4} \cdot 4$

Think and Discuss

5. Explain how the model shows that $2.5 \cdot 2.5 = 6.25$.

Motivate

Ask students if they have ever mixed ingredients for a recipe. Ask them if they have had to use fractions to measure the ingredients. Ask them if they would have known how much of each ingredient to use to make a double batch, a half batch, or a batch and a half. Tell the students that it is helpful to be able to multiply rational numbers for such purposes.

Explorations and answers are provided in *Alternate Openers: Explorations Transparencies.*

EXAMPLE **2** **Multiplying Fractions**

 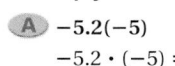
Multiply. Write each answer in simplest form.

A $-\frac{3}{5}\left(-\frac{1}{4}\right)$

$-\frac{3}{5}\left(-\frac{1}{4}\right) = \frac{-3}{5}\left(\frac{-1}{4}\right)$

$= \frac{(-3)(-1)}{5(4)}$ *Multiply numerators.*
Multiply denominators.

$= \frac{3}{20}$ *Simplify.*

B $\frac{5}{12}\left(-\frac{12}{5}\right)$

$\frac{5}{12}\left(-\frac{12}{5}\right) = \frac{5}{12}\left(\frac{-12}{5}\right)$

$= \frac{\overset{1}{5}(-\overset{1}{\cancel{12}})}{\underset{1}{\cancel{12}}(\underset{1}{5})}$ *Look for common factors: 12, 5.*

$= \frac{-1}{1} = -1$ *Simplify.*

EXAMPLE **3** **Multiplying Decimals**

Multiply.

A $-5.2(-5)$
$-5.2 \cdot (-5) = 26.0$ *Product is positive with 1 decimal place.*
$= 26$
You can drop the zero after the decimal point.

B $-0.07(4.6)$
$-0.07 \cdot 4.6 = -0.322$
Product is negative with 3 decimal places.

EXAMPLE **4** **Recreation Application**

Andrew walks his dog $\frac{1}{8}$ mile each day. What is the total distance that Andrew walks his dog in a 5-day week?

$\frac{1}{8}(5) = \frac{1 \cdot 5}{8}$

$= \frac{5}{8}$ *Multiply.*

Andrew walks his dog $\frac{5}{8}$ mile in a 5-day week.

Answers to *Think and Discuss*

1. 5 decimal places; the number of decimal places is the sum of the decimal places in the factors.

2. Possible answer: $\frac{3}{2} \cdot \frac{4}{3} = 2$

Think and Discuss

1. **Name** the number of decimal places in the product of 5.625 and 2.75.

2. **Give an example** of two fractions whose product is an integer due to common factors.

 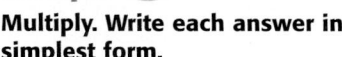

When multiplying a mixed number by a whole number, some students may multiply the whole numbers and leave the fraction unchanged. Remind students to write the mixed number as an improper fraction before multiplying.

Power Presentations with PowerPoint®

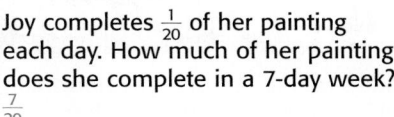
Additional Examples

Example 1

Multiply. Write each answer in simplest form.

A. $-8\left(\frac{6}{7}\right)$ $-6\frac{6}{7}$ **B.** $2\left(5\frac{1}{3}\right)$ $10\frac{2}{3}$

Example 2

Multiply. Write each answer in simplest form.

A. $\frac{1}{8}\left(\frac{6}{7}\right)$ $\frac{3}{28}$ **B.** $-\frac{2}{3}\left(\frac{9}{2}\right)$ -3

Example 3

Multiply.

A. $2(-0.51)$ -1.02

B. $(-0.4)(-3.75)$ 1.5

Example 4

Joy completes $\frac{1}{20}$ of her painting each day. How much of her painting does she complete in a 7-day week?
$\frac{7}{20}$

Also available on transparency

Teaching Tip   **Number Sense** Explain to students that multiplying two fractions or two decimals does not necessarily result in a product that is greater than the factors, as shown in Example 2.

---

2 **Teach**

Guided Instruction

In this lesson, students learn to multiply fractions and mixed numbers. Review the concept of multiplication as repeated addition and the rules for multiplying signed numbers (Teaching Transparency). Review Examples 1 and 2 and point out that students may "cancel out" common factors between numerators and denominators. For multiplying decimals, remind students that the number of decimal places in the product should be the total number of decimal places in the two factors.

 Reaching All Learners

Through Multiple Representations

Show students two ways to evaluate $\frac{1}{2}(0.7)$:

$\frac{1}{2}(0.7) = 0.5 \cdot 0.7 = 0.35$

$\frac{1}{2}(0.7) = \frac{1}{2} \cdot \frac{7}{10} = \frac{7}{20}$

Show that $\frac{7}{20} = 0.35$ by dividing:

$20)\overline{7.00}$ 0.35

Have students find each of the following products both ways and show that the results are equal in each case.

1. $\frac{1}{2}(0.3)$ $\frac{3}{20}$, 0.15   2. $\frac{1}{5}(0.4)$ $\frac{2}{25}$, 0.08

3. $\frac{3}{4}(0.1)$ $\frac{3}{40}$, 0.075   4. $1\frac{1}{2}(0.2)$ $\frac{3}{10}$, 0.3

---

3 **Close**

Summarize

Ask students to explain how to multiply each of the following:

1) a fraction and a mixed number
2) two decimals
3) a decimal and a fraction

Possible answers:

1. Change the mixed number to an improper fraction, multiply numerators, multiply denominators, and write in simplest form.

2. Multiply the numbers and count the total number of decimal places in the two factors.

3. Either write the decimal as a fraction or the fraction as a decimal, and then multiply.

2-4 Exercises

go.hrw.com
Homework Help Online
KEYWORD: MT7 2-4
Parent Resources Online
KEYWORD: MT7 Parent

Assignment Guide

If you finished Example **1** assign:
Average 1–4, 14–21, 42, 43, 57–67
Advanced 14–21, 40–43, 57–67

If you finished Example **2** assign:
Average 1–8, 14–29, 42, 43, 48, 49, 57–67
Advanced 14–29, 41, 42, 48–51, 54, 56–67

If you finished Example **3** assign:
Average 1–12, 14–37, 42, 43, 46–49, 57–67
Advanced 14–37 evens, 41–51 odds, 54, 56–67

If you finished Example **4** assign:
Average 1–39, 42–52, 57–67
Advanced 14–52 evens, 52–67

Homework Quick Check

Quickly check key concepts.
Exercises: 16, 26, 34, 38, 52

Math Background

Models can be useful for demonstrating multiplication of rational numbers and the Commutative Property. The expression $3 \cdot \frac{1}{2}$ is read "three times one-half," and it means $\frac{1}{2} + \frac{1}{2} + \frac{1}{2}$.

The expression $\frac{1}{2} \cdot 3$ is read "one-half times three," and it means "one-half of three."

By the Commutative Property,
$3 \cdot \frac{1}{2} = \frac{1}{2} \cdot 3$.

State Resources

go.hrw.com
State Resources Online
KEYWORD: MT7 Resources

GUIDED PRACTICE

See Example **1** Multiply. Write each answer in simplest form.

1. $5\left(\frac{1}{2}\right)$ $2\frac{1}{2}$ **2.** $-7\left(1\frac{3}{4}\right)$ $-12\frac{1}{4}$ **3.** $3\left(\frac{5}{8}\right)$ $1\frac{7}{8}$ **4.** $-4\left(5\frac{2}{3}\right)$ $-22\frac{2}{3}$

See Example **2** **5.** $-\frac{1}{4}\left(-\frac{5}{8}\right)$ $\frac{5}{32}$ **6.** $\frac{3}{8}\left(-\frac{7}{10}\right)$ $-\frac{21}{80}$ **7.** $6\frac{3}{7}\left(\frac{7}{8}\right)$ $5\frac{5}{8}$ **8.** $-\frac{3}{5}\left(-\frac{5}{9}\right)$ $\frac{1}{3}$

See Example **3** Multiply.

9. $-2.1(-7)$ **14.7**   **10.** $0.03(5.4)$ **0.162**   **11.** $-4.8(-2)$ **9.6**   **12.** $-0.15(2.8)$ **-0.42**

See Example **4** **13.** Tran jogs $\frac{3}{4}$ mile each day. What is the total distance Tran jogs in 6 days? $4\frac{1}{2}$ miles

INDEPENDENT PRACTICE

See Example **1** Multiply. Write each answer in simplest form.

14. $5\left(\frac{1}{7}\right)$ $\frac{5}{7}$ **15.** $-3\left(1\frac{5}{6}\right)$ $-5\frac{1}{2}$ **16.** $9\left(\frac{4}{21}\right)$ $1\frac{5}{7}$ **17.** $-7\left(1\frac{2}{3}\right)$ $-11\frac{2}{3}$

18. $9\left(\frac{14}{15}\right)$ $8\frac{2}{5}$ **19.** $-3\left(6\frac{7}{9}\right)$ $-20\frac{1}{3}$ **20.** $8\left(\frac{3}{4}\right)$ 6 **21.** $-7\left(3\frac{1}{5}\right)$ $-22\frac{2}{5}$

See Example **2** **22.** $-\frac{2}{3}\left(-\frac{5}{6}\right)$ $\frac{5}{9}$ **23.** $\frac{2}{9}\left(-\frac{7}{8}\right)$ $-\frac{7}{36}$ **24.** $5\frac{7}{8}\left(\frac{5}{11}\right)$ $2\frac{59}{88}$ **25.** $-\frac{1}{3}\left(-\frac{7}{8}\right)$ $\frac{7}{24}$

26. $\frac{3}{7}\left(-\frac{5}{6}\right)$ $-\frac{5}{14}$ **27.** $2\frac{1}{7}\left(\frac{7}{10}\right)$ $1\frac{1}{2}$ **28.** $-\frac{2}{3}\left(-\frac{1}{9}\right)$ $\frac{2}{27}$ **29.** $\frac{7}{8}\left(\frac{3}{5}\right)$ $\frac{21}{40}$

See Example **3** Multiply.

30. $-1.7(-4)$ **6.8**   **31.** $-0.05(4.7)$ **-0.235**   **32.** $-6.2(-7)$ **43.4**   **33.** $-0.75(5.5)$ **-4.125**

34. $-6.2(-9)$ **55.8**   **35.** $-0.08(6.2)$ **-0.496**   **36.** $-2.4(-9)$ **21.6**   **37.** $-0.04(9.2)$ **-0.368**

See Example **4** **38.** There was $\frac{3}{4}$ of a pizza left over from a family gathering. The next day, Tina ate $\frac{1}{2}$ of what was left. How much of the whole pizza did Tina eat? $\frac{3}{8}$

PRACTICE AND PROBLEM SOLVING

Extra Practice
See page 784.

39. Consumer Economics At a bookstore, the ticketed price of a book is $\frac{1}{4}$ off the original price. Kayla has a discount coupon for $\frac{1}{2}$ off the ticketed price. What fraction of the original price is the additional discount? $\frac{3}{8}$

Multiply.

40. $6\left(\frac{3}{7}\right)$ $2\frac{4}{7}$ **41.** $-5\left(1\frac{8}{11}\right)$ $-8\frac{7}{11}$ **42.** $7\left(\frac{4}{5}\right)$ $5\frac{3}{5}$ **43.** $5\left(3\frac{1}{9}\right)$ $15\frac{5}{9}$

44. $-5.9(-7)$ **41.3**   **45.** $0.7(2.6)$ **1.82**   **46.** $-3.6(-4)$ **14.4**   **47.** $-0.06(9.3)$ **-0.558**

48. $\frac{4}{11}\left(-\frac{4}{7}\right)$ $-\frac{16}{77}$ **49.** $3\frac{5}{6}\left(\frac{7}{9}\right)$ $2\frac{53}{54}$ **50.** $-\frac{8}{9}\left(-\frac{3}{5}\right)$ $\frac{8}{15}$ **51.** $\frac{5}{12}\left(-\frac{11}{16}\right)$ $-\frac{55}{192}$

RETEACH 2-4

LESSON 2-4 Reteach
Multiplying Rational Numbers

To model $\frac{1}{3} \times \frac{3}{4}$:

Divide a square into 4 equal parts. Lightly shade 3 of the 4.

Darken 1 of the 3 shaded parts.

Compare the 1 darkened part to the original 4.

$\frac{1}{3} \times \frac{3}{4} = \frac{1}{4}$

Model each multiplication. Write the result. Possible models are shown.

1. $\frac{1}{2} \times \frac{2}{4} = \frac{1}{4}$

2. $\frac{3}{4} \times \frac{4}{6} = \frac{1}{2}$

3. $\frac{2}{3} \times \frac{3}{9} = \frac{2}{9}$

To multiply fractions:
• Cancel common factors, one in a numerator and the other in a denominator.
• Multiply the remaining factors in the numerator and in the denominator.
• If the signs of the factors are the same, the product is positive. If the signs of the factors are different, the product is negative.

$\frac{1}{\cancel{4}} \times \frac{\cancel{8}}{3} = \frac{1 \times 2}{1 \times 3} = \frac{2}{3}$

Multiply. Answer in simplest form.

4. $\frac{1}{2} \times \frac{4}{9} = \frac{2}{9}$

5. $\frac{2}{3} \times \frac{6}{7} = \frac{4}{7}$

6. $\frac{3}{5} \times \frac{15}{17} = \frac{9}{17}$

7. $\frac{2}{3} \times \left(-\frac{9}{10}\right) = -\frac{3}{5}$

8. $\left(-\frac{2}{9}\right) \times \frac{27}{40} = -\frac{3}{20}$

9. $\left(-\frac{4}{7}\right) \times \left(-\frac{21}{8}\right) = 1\frac{1}{2}$

PRACTICE 2-4

LESSON 2-4 Practice B
Multiplying Rational Numbers

Multiply. Write each answer in simplest form.

1. $8\left(\frac{3}{4}\right)$ **6**

2. $-6\left(\frac{9}{18}\right)$ **-3**

3. $-9\left(\frac{5}{6}\right)$ **$-7\frac{1}{2}$**

4. $-6\left(-\frac{7}{12}\right)$ **$3\frac{1}{2}$**

5. $-\frac{5}{18}\left(\frac{8}{15}\right)$ **$-\frac{4}{27}$**

6. $\frac{7}{12}\left(\frac{14}{21}\right)$ **$\frac{7}{18}$**

7. $-\frac{1}{9}\left(\frac{27}{24}\right)$ **$-\frac{1}{8}$**

8. $-\frac{1}{11}\left(-\frac{3}{2}\right)$ **$\frac{3}{22}$**

9. $\frac{7}{20}\left(-\frac{15}{28}\right)$ **$-\frac{3}{16}$**

10. $\frac{16}{25}\left(-\frac{18}{32}\right)$ **$-\frac{9}{25}$**

11. $\frac{1}{9}\left(-\frac{18}{17}\right)$ **$-\frac{2}{17}$**

12. $\frac{17}{20}\left(-\frac{12}{34}\right)$ **$-\frac{3}{10}$**

13. $-4\left(2\frac{1}{6}\right)$ **$-8\frac{2}{3}$**

14. $\frac{3}{4}\left(1\frac{3}{8}\right)$ **$1\frac{1}{32}$**

15. $3\frac{1}{5}\left(\frac{2}{3}\right)$ **$2\frac{2}{15}$**

16. $-\frac{5}{6}\left(2\frac{1}{2}\right)$ **$-2\frac{1}{12}$**

Multiply.

17. $-2(-5.2)$ **10.4**

18. $0.53(0.04)$ **0.0212**

19. $(-7)(-3.9)$ **27.3**

20. $-2(8.13)$ **-16.26**

21. $0.02(-4.62)$ **-0.0924**

22. $0.5(-7.8)$ **-3.9**

23. $(-0.41)(-8.5)$ **3.485**

24. $-(8)(6.3)$ **-50.4**

25. $15(-0.05)$ **-0.75**

26. $(-3.04)(-1.7)$ **5.168**

27. $10(-0.09)$ **-0.9**

28. $(-0.8)(-0.15)$ **0.12**

29. Travis painted for $6\frac{2}{5}$ hours. He received $27 an hour for his work. How much was Travis paid for doing this painting job?   **$180**

52. **Health** The directions for a pain reliever recommend that children 96 pounds and over take 4 tablets every 4 hours as needed, and children who weigh between 60 and 71 pounds take only $2\frac{1}{2}$ tablets every 4 hours as needed. Each tablet is $\frac{4}{25}$ gram.

   a. If a 105-pound child takes 4 tablets, how many grams of pain reliever is he or she receiving? $\frac{16}{25}$ g

   b. How many grams of pain reliever is the recommended dose for a child weighing 65 pounds? $\frac{2}{5}$ g

53. **Animals** The label on a bottle of pet vitamins lists dosage guidelines. What dosage would you give to each of these animals?

   a. a 50 lb adult dog $1\frac{1}{4}$ tsp

   b. a 12 lb cat $1\frac{1}{2}$ tsp

   c. a 40 lb pregnant dog 2 tsp

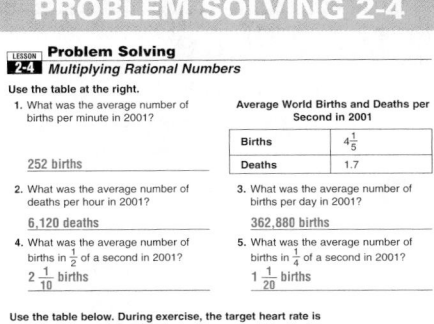

Do-Good Pet Vitamins
- **Adult dogs:**
  $\frac{1}{2}$ tsp per 20 lb body weight
- **Puppies, pregnant dogs, or nursing dogs:**
  $\frac{1}{2}$ tsp per 10 lb body weight
- **Cats:**
  $\frac{1}{4}$ tsp per 2 lb body weight

54. **What's the Error?** A student multiplied two mixed numbers in the following fashion: $2\frac{4}{7} \cdot 3\frac{1}{4} = 6\frac{1}{7}$. What's the error?

55. **Write About It** In the pattern $\frac{1}{3} + \frac{1}{4} + \frac{1}{5} + \ldots$, which fraction makes the sum greater than 1? Explain.

56. **Challenge** Of the 42 presidents who preceded George W. Bush, $\frac{1}{3}$ were elected to a second term. Of those elected to a second term, $\frac{1}{7}$ were former vice presidents of the United States. What fraction of the first 42 presidents were elected to a second term and were former vice presidents? $\frac{1}{3} \times \frac{1}{7} = \frac{1}{21}$

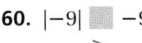

TEST PREP and Spiral Review

57. **Multiple Choice** Lindsay walked $\frac{3}{4}$ mile on Monday. She walked $1\frac{5}{8}$ that distance on Tuesday. How far did she walk on Tuesday?

   Ⓐ $1\frac{7}{32}$ miles   Ⓑ $1\frac{15}{32}$ miles   Ⓒ $2\frac{3}{8}$ miles   Ⓓ $2\frac{15}{32}$ miles

58. **Multiple Choice** What is the product of $-5\frac{1}{3}$ and $3\frac{3}{4}$?

   Ⓕ -20 Ⓖ $-15\frac{1}{4}$ Ⓗ $15\frac{1}{4}$ Ⓙ 20

59. **Multiple Choice** Multiply: -0.98×-8.4.

   Ⓐ -82.83 Ⓑ -8.232 Ⓒ 8.232 Ⓓ 82.83

Compare. Write $<$, $>$, or $=$. (Lesson 1-3)

60. $|-9|$ ▮ -9 61. -13 ▮ -22 62. $|5|$ ▮ $|-5|$ 63. $|-17|$ ▮ $|-13|$
    $>$ $>$ $=$ $>$

Find each sum. (Lesson 2-3)

64. $-1.7 + 2.3$ 0.6 65. $-\frac{2}{3} + \left(-\frac{1}{6}\right)$ $-\frac{5}{6}$ 66. $23.75 + (-25.15)$ -1.4 67. $-\frac{4}{9} + \frac{2}{9}$ $-\frac{2}{9}$

2-4 Lesson Quiz

Multiply.

1. $9\left(\frac{1}{7}\right)$ $1\frac{2}{7}$

2. $\frac{2}{3}\left(-\frac{5}{8}\right)$ $-\frac{5}{12}$

3. $-0.47(2.2)$ -1.034

4. Evaluate $2\frac{1}{2}(x)$ for $x = \frac{4}{5}$. 2

5. Edgar runs $\frac{8}{9}$ mile each day. What is the total distance that Edgar runs in a 7-day week? $6\frac{2}{9}$ miles

Also available on transparency

Pacing: Traditional 1 day
Block $\frac{1}{2}$ day
Objective: Students divide fractions and decimals.

Hands-On Lab
In *Hands-On Activities*

Online Edition
Tutorial Videos

Countdown to Testing Week 3

Power Presentations
with PowerPoint®

Warm Up

Multiply.

1. $-3\left(\frac{5}{6}\right)$ $-2\frac{1}{2}$

2. $-15\left(-\frac{2}{3}\right)$ 10

3. $0.05(2.8)$ 0.14

4. $-0.9(16.1)$ -14.49

Problem of the Day

Katie made a bookshelf that is 5 feet long. The first 6 books she put on it took up 8 inches of shelf space. About how many books should fit on the shelf?   45

Also available on transparency

Math Humor

Teacher: Do you know how many quarters go into a half?

Student: No, but I know how many go into a video game!

State Resources

go.hrw.com
State Resources Online
KEYWORD: MT7 Resources

Learn to divide fractions and decimals.

Vocabulary
reciprocal

A number and its **reciprocal** have a product of 1. To find the reciprocal of a fraction, exchange the numerator and the denominator. Remember that an integer can be written as a fraction with a denominator of 1.

Number	Reciprocal	Product
$\frac{3}{4}$	$\frac{4}{3}$	$\frac{3}{4}\left(\frac{4}{3}\right) = 1$
$-\frac{5}{12}$	$-\frac{12}{5}$	$-\frac{5}{12}\left(-\frac{12}{5}\right) = 1$
6	$\frac{1}{6}$	$6\left(\frac{1}{6}\right) = 1$

Multiplication and division are inverse operations. They undo each other.

$$\frac{1}{3}\left(\frac{2}{5}\right) = \frac{2}{15} \longrightarrow \frac{2}{15} \div \frac{2}{5} = \frac{1}{3}$$

Notice that multiplying by the reciprocal gives the same result as dividing.

$$\left(\frac{2}{15}\right)\left(\frac{5}{2}\right) = \frac{2 \cdot 5}{15 \cdot 2} = \frac{10}{30} = \frac{1}{3}$$

DIVIDING RATIONAL NUMBERS IN FRACTION FORM		
Words	**Numbers**	**Algebra**
To divide by a fraction, multiply by the reciprocal.	$\frac{1}{7} \div \frac{4}{5} = \frac{1}{7} \cdot \frac{5}{4} = \frac{5}{28}$	$\frac{a}{b} \div \frac{c}{d} = \frac{a}{b} \cdot \frac{d}{c} = \frac{ad}{bc}$

EXAMPLE **1** **Dividing Fractions**

Divide. Write each answer in simplest form.

Ⓐ $\frac{7}{15} \div \frac{4}{5}$

$\frac{7}{15} \div \frac{4}{5} = \frac{7}{15} \cdot \frac{5}{4}$ *Multiply by the reciprocal.*

$= \frac{7 \cdot \cancel{5}^{1}}{{}_{3}\cancel{15} \cdot 4}$ *Remove common factors.*

$= \frac{7}{12}$ *Simplest form*

---

1 **Introduce**
Alternate Opener

Motivate

Write the following problems on the board: $12 \div 3 = ?$ and $12 \cdot \frac{1}{3} = ?$. Ask for volunteers to solve both problems and to show the solutions on the board. Both equal 4. Point out that 3 can be expressed as $\frac{3}{1}$. Ask students to describe the relationship between $\frac{3}{1}$ and $\frac{1}{3}$. Explain that these numbers are called *reciprocals*. Tell students that in this lesson, they will see that division is the same as multiplication by the reciprocal.

Explorations and answers are provided in *Alternate Openers: Explorations Transparencies*.

Divide. Write each answer in simplest form.

B $5\frac{1}{3} \div (-7)$

$$5\frac{1}{3} \div (-7) = \frac{16}{3} \div \left(-\frac{7}{1}\right)$$ *Write as improper fractions.*

$$= \frac{16}{3}\left(-\frac{1}{7}\right)$$ *Multiply by the reciprocal.*

$$= \frac{16 \cdot (-1)}{3 \cdot 7}$$ *No common factors*

$$= -\frac{16}{21}$$ *Simplest form*

When dividing a decimal by a decimal, multiply both numbers by a power of 10 so you can divide by a whole number. To decide which power of 10 to multiply by, look at the denominator. The number of decimal places is the number of zeros to write after the 1.

$$\frac{1.32}{0.4} = \frac{1.32}{0.4}\left(\frac{10}{10}\right) = \frac{13.2}{4}$$

1 decimal place   1 zero

EXAMPLE 2   **Dividing Decimals**

Find $7.48 \div 0.4$.

$$7.48 \div 0.4 = \frac{7.48}{0.4}\left(\frac{10}{10}\right) = \frac{74.8}{4}$$ *0.4 has 1 decimal place, so use $\frac{10}{10}$.*

$$= 18.7$$ *Divide.*

EXAMPLE 3   **Evaluating Expressions with Fractions and Decimals**

Evaluate each expression for the given value of the variable.

A $\frac{7.2}{n}$ for $n = -0.24$

$$-\frac{7.2}{0.24} = -\frac{7.2}{0.24}\left(\frac{100}{100}\right)$$ *0.24 has 2 decimal places, so use $\frac{100}{100}$.*

$$= -\frac{720}{24}$$ *Divide.*

$$= -30$$

When $n = -0.24$, $\frac{7.2}{n} = -30$.

B $m \div \frac{5}{24}$ for $m = 3\frac{3}{4}$

$$3\frac{3}{4} \div \frac{5}{24} = \frac{15}{4} \cdot \frac{24}{5}$$ *Rewrite $3\frac{3}{4}$ as an improper fraction and multiply by the reciprocal.*

$$= \frac{\overset{3}{15} \cdot \overset{6}{24}}{\underset{1}{4} \cdot \underset{1}{5}}$$ *Remove common factors.*

$$= \frac{18}{1} = 18$$

When $m = 3\frac{3}{4}$, $m \div \frac{5}{24} = 18$.

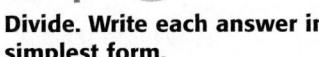

Power Presentations
with PowerPoint®

Additional Examples

Example 1

Divide. Write each answer in simplest form.

A. $\frac{5}{11} \div \frac{1}{2}$ $\frac{10}{11}$ **B.** $2\frac{3}{8} \div 2$ $1\frac{3}{16}$

Example 2

Find. $0.384 \div 0.24$ 1.6

Example 3

Evaluate each expression for the given value of the variable.

A. $\frac{5.25}{n}$ for $n = 0.15$ 35

B. $k \div \frac{4}{5}$ for $k = 5$ $6\frac{1}{4}$

Also available on transparency

---

2 Teach

Guided Instruction

ENGLISH LANGUAGE LEARNERS

In this lesson, students learn to divide fractions. Define and discuss *reciprocals* (Teaching Transparency). Show that dividing by a number and multiplying by the reciprocal of the number give the same result. Remind students that they may "cancel out" common factors once they have changed the division into multiplication by a reciprocal.

Teaching Tip   **Number Sense** For Example 2, show students how to choose which power of 10 to use to clear the decimal from the denominator. You may want to review place value.

Reaching All Learners
Through Cognitive Strategies

Explain to students that a quart contains 32 oz. Ask students to find out how many servings are in a quart if the serving size is 8 oz. 4 servings Ask students to describe how they found the answer. division Have students find out how many servings one quart contains for the following serving sizes.

1. 5 oz   6.4   **2.** 4 oz   8
3. 3 oz $10\frac{2}{3}$ **4.** 1 oz   32
5. $\frac{2}{3}$ oz   48   **6.** $\frac{1}{2}$ oz   64

Teaching Tip

Inclusion In Example 4, you may want to replace the fractions with whole numbers first to show how to set up the division. For example, "If you pour 8 cups into a container and the serving size is 2 cups, how many servings did you pour?"

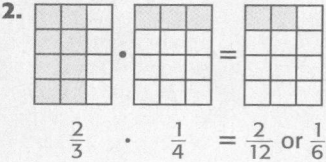

8	÷	2	=	4
amount poured	÷	serving size	=	number of servings

Possible answers to *Think and Discuss*

1. When you divide a fraction by itself, you multiply it by its reciprocal, and the answer is 1.

2.

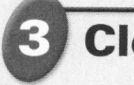

$$\frac{2}{3} \cdot \frac{1}{4} = \frac{2}{12} \text{ or } \frac{1}{6}$$

EXAMPLE 4 **PROBLEM SOLVING APPLICATION**

Ella ate $\frac{2}{3}$ cup of lowfat yogurt. The serving size listed on the container is 6 ounces, or $\frac{3}{4}$ cup. How many servings did Ella eat? How many calories did Ella eat?

1 **Understand the Problem**

The number of calories Ella ate is the number of calories in the fraction of a serving.

List the **important information:**
• Ella ate $\frac{2}{3}$ cup.
• A full serving is $\frac{3}{4}$ cup.
• There are 100 calories in one serving.

2 **Make a Plan**

Set up an equation to find the number of servings Ella ate.

amount Ella ate	÷	serving size	=	number of servings

Using the number of servings, find the number of calories Ella ate.

number of servings	·	calories per serving	=	total calories

3 **Solve**

Let n = number of servings. Let c = total calories.

Servings: $\frac{2}{3} \div \frac{3}{4} = n$ Calories: $\frac{8}{9} \cdot 100 = c$

$\qquad\quad \frac{2}{3} \cdot \frac{4}{3} = n$ $\qquad\qquad \frac{8 \cdot 100}{9} = c$

$\qquad\qquad \frac{8}{9} = n$ $\qquad\qquad \frac{800}{9} \approx 88.9$

Ella ate $\frac{8}{9}$ of a serving, which is about 88.9 calories.

4 **Look Back**

Ella did not eat a full serving, so $\frac{8}{9}$ of a serving is a reasonable answer. Since $\frac{8}{9}$ is less than 1 and 88.9 calories is less than 100, the calories in a full serving, 88.9 calories is a reasonable answer.

Think and Discuss

1. Tell what happens when you divide a fraction by itself. Show that you are correct using multiplication by the reciprocal.

2. Model the product of $\frac{2}{3}$ and $\frac{1}{4}$.

---

3 ## Close

Summarize

Ask students to explain how multiplication and division of fractions are the same and how they are different. Review the process for dividing decimals. Ask the students what power of 10 they would use to simplify the expression 22.5 ÷ 1.125.

Possible answer: Division of fractions is the same as multiplication, except that in division, you multiply by the reciprocal; 1000.

2-5 Exercises

go.hrw.com
Homework Help Online
KEYWORD: MT7 2-5
Parent Resources Online
KEYWORD: MT7 Parent

GUIDED PRACTICE

See Example 1 Divide. Write each answer in simplest form.

1. $\frac{1}{2} \div \frac{3}{4}$ $\frac{2}{3}$

2. $4\frac{1}{5} \div 5\frac{2}{3}$ $\frac{63}{85}$

3. $-\frac{6}{7} \div 3$ $-\frac{2}{7}$

4. $\frac{5}{6} \div \frac{3}{8}$ $2\frac{2}{9}$

5. $5\frac{1}{18} \div 4\frac{4}{9}$ $1\frac{11}{80}$

6. $-\frac{5}{8} \div 12$ $-\frac{5}{96}$

7. $\frac{14}{15} \div \frac{2}{3}$ $1\frac{2}{5}$

8. $4\frac{3}{10} \div \frac{3}{5}$ $7\frac{1}{6}$

See Example 2 Find each quotient.

9. $3.72 \div 0.3$ **12.4**

10. $2.1 \div 0.07$ **30**

11. $10.71 \div 0.7$ **15.3**

12. $1.72 \div 0.2$ **8.6**

13. $2.54 \div 0.6$ **4.23**

14. $11.04 \div 0.4$ **27.6**

15. $2.45 \div 0.005$ **490**

16. $4.41 \div 0.7$ **6.3**

See Example 3 Evaluate each expression for the given value of the variable.

17. $\frac{9.7}{x}$ for $x = -0.5$ **−19.4**

18. $\frac{6.2}{x}$ for $x = 0.2$ **31**

19. $\frac{40.5}{x}$ for $x = 0.9$ **45**

20. $\frac{9.2}{x}$ for $x = 2.3$ **4**

21. $\frac{32.4}{x}$ for $x = -1.8$ **−18**

22. $\frac{14.7}{x}$ for $x = 0.07$ **210**

See Example 4 23. You eat $\frac{1}{4}$ ounce of cheddar cheese. One serving of cheddar cheese is $1\frac{1}{2}$ ounces. How much of a serving did you eat? $\frac{1}{6}$ **serving**

INDEPENDENT PRACTICE

See Example 1 Divide. Write each answer in simplest form.

24. $\frac{1}{6} \div \frac{3}{4}$ $\frac{2}{9}$

25. $4\frac{2}{5} \div 3\frac{1}{2}$ $1\frac{9}{35}$

26. $-\frac{5}{12} \div \frac{2}{3}$ $-\frac{5}{8}$

27. $\frac{4}{5} \div \frac{1}{2}$ $1\frac{3}{5}$

28. $1\frac{2}{3} \div 2\frac{1}{6}$ $\frac{10}{13}$

29. $-\frac{2}{9} \div \frac{7}{12}$ $-\frac{8}{21}$

30. $\frac{2}{3} \div \frac{3}{10}$ $2\frac{2}{9}$

31. $2\frac{3}{8} \div 1\frac{1}{6}$ $2\frac{1}{28}$

See Example 2 Find each quotient.

32. $12.11 \div 0.7$ **17.3**

33. $2.49 \div 0.03$ **83**

34. $6.64 \div 0.4$ **16.6**

35. $4.85 \div 0.5$ **9.7**

36. $5.49 \div 0.003$ **1830**

37. $32.44 \div 0.8$ **40.55**

38. $9.36 \div 0.03$ **312**

39. $12.24 \div 0.9$ **13.6**

See Example 3 Evaluate each expression for the given value of the variable.

40. $\frac{7.2}{x}$ for $x = -0.4$ **−18**

41. $\frac{9.6}{x}$ for $x = 0.8$ **12**

42. $\frac{15}{x}$ for $x = -0.05$ **−300**

43. $\frac{15.4}{x}$ for $x = -1.4$ **−11**

44. $\frac{4.24}{x}$ for $x = 0.8$ **5.3**

45. $\frac{22.2}{x}$ for $x = 0.06$ **370**

See Example 4 46. The platform on the school stage is $8\frac{3}{4}$ feet wide. Each chair is $1\frac{5}{12}$ feet wide. How many chairs will fit across the platform? **6 chairs**

PRACTICE AND PROBLEM SOLVING

Extra Practice
See page 785.

47. Maya is drinking her favorite juice. There are $2\frac{3}{4}$ servings remaining in the bottle. Maya pours only $\frac{1}{4}$ of a serving into her glass at a time. How many glasses can Maya have before the bottle is empty? **11 glasses**

2-5 Exercises

Assignment Guide

If you finished Example **1** assign:
Average 1–8, 24–31, 54–63
Advanced 24–31, 52, 54–63

If you finished Example **2** assign:
Average 1–16, 24–39, 54–63
Advanced 24–39, 52, 54–63

If you finished Example **3** assign:
Average 1–22, 24–45, 54–63
Advanced 24–45, 52, 54–63

If you finished Example **4** assign:
Average 1–46, 47–49, 54–63
Advanced 24–46 evens, 47–63

Homework Quick Check

Quickly check key concepts.
Exercises: 28, 34, 44, 46

Math Background

A division expression containing fractions can be written as a *complex fraction*.

$\frac{1}{2} \div \frac{3}{4}$ can be written as $\dfrac{\frac{1}{2}}{\frac{3}{4}}$.

To find the quotient, multiply the numerator and denominator of the complex fraction by the reciprocal of the fraction in the denominator. The denominator then becomes one, and the numerator is a multiplication expression that can be simplified:

$$\frac{\frac{1}{2}}{\frac{3}{4}} = \frac{\frac{1}{2} \cdot \frac{4}{3}}{\frac{3}{4} \cdot \frac{4}{3}} = \frac{\frac{2}{3}}{1} = \frac{2}{3}.$$

RETEACH 2-5

LESSON 2-5 Reteach
Dividing Rational Numbers

To write the **reciprocal** of a fraction, interchange the numerator and denominator.

$\frac{2}{3} \longleftrightarrow \frac{3}{2}$
  Fraction Reciprocal

The product of a number and its reciprocal is 1.

$\frac{2}{3} \times \frac{3}{2} = 1$

Write the reciprocal of each rational number.

1. The reciprocal of $\frac{3}{5}$ is: $\frac{5}{3}$

2. The reciprocal of 6 is: $\frac{1}{6}$

3. The reciprocal of $2\frac{1}{3}$ is: $\frac{3}{7}$

To divide by a fraction, multiply by its reciprocal.

$\frac{2}{3} \div 6$ $\frac{3}{5} \div \frac{9}{10}$

$\frac{2}{3} \times \frac{1}{6}$ $\frac{3}{5} \times \frac{10}{9}$

$\frac{1 \times 1}{3 \times 3} = \frac{1}{9}$ $\frac{3 \times 10}{5 \times 9} = \frac{2}{3}$

Complete to divide and simplify.

4. $\frac{3}{8} \div 12 = \frac{3}{8} \times \frac{1}{12} = \frac{3}{96} = \frac{1}{32}$

5. $\frac{4}{3} \div 16 = \frac{4}{3} \times \frac{1}{16} = \frac{4}{48} = \frac{1}{12}$

6. $\frac{5}{7} \div \frac{20}{21} = \frac{5}{7} \times \frac{21}{20} = \frac{3}{4}$

7. $-\frac{3}{4} \div \left(\frac{9}{8}\right) = -\frac{3}{4} \times \left(\frac{8}{9}\right) = -\frac{2}{3}$

Change a decimal divisor to a whole number. Using the number of places in the divisor, move the decimal point to the right in both the divisor and the dividend.

$0.7\overline{)4.34} \rightarrow 0.7\overline{)4.3.4} \rightarrow 7\overline{)43.4}$ 6.2

Rewrite each division with a whole-number divisor. Then, do the division.

8. $0.6\overline{)1.14} \rightarrow 6\overline{)11.4} = 1.9$

9. $0.3\overline{)4.56} \rightarrow 3\overline{)45.6} = 15.2$

10. $0.02\overline{)7.12} \rightarrow 2\overline{)712} = 356$

11. $0.08\overline{)57.28} \rightarrow 8\overline{)5728} = 716$

PRACTICE 2-5

LESSON 2-5 Practice B
Dividing Rational Numbers

Divide. Write each answer in simplest form.

1. $\frac{1}{5} \div \frac{3}{10}$ $\frac{2}{3}$

2. $-\frac{5}{8} \div \frac{3}{4}$ $-\frac{5}{6}$

3. $\frac{1}{4} \div \frac{1}{8}$ 2

4. $-\frac{2}{3} \div \frac{4}{15}$ $-2\frac{1}{2}$

5. $1\frac{2}{9} \div 1\frac{2}{3}$ $\frac{11}{15}$

6. $-\frac{7}{10} \div \left(\frac{2}{5}\right)$ $-1\frac{3}{4}$

7. $\frac{6}{11} \div \frac{3}{22}$ 4

8. $\frac{4}{9} \div \left(-\frac{8}{15}\right)$ $-\frac{5}{6}$

9. $\frac{3}{8} \div -15$ $-\frac{1}{40}$

10. $-\frac{5}{6} \div 12$ $-\frac{5}{72}$

11. $6\frac{1}{2} \div 1\frac{5}{8}$ 4

12. $-\frac{9}{10} \div 6$ $-\frac{3}{20}$

Divide.

13. $24.35 \div 0.5$ **48.7**

14. $2.16 \div 0.04$ **54**

15. $3.16 \div 0.02$ **158**

16. $7.32 \div 0.3$ **24.4**

17. $87.36 \div 0.6$ **145.6**

18. $79.36 \div 0.8$ **99.2**

19. $4.27 \div 0.007$ **610**

20. $63.81 \div 0.9$ **70.9**

21. $1.23 \div 0.003$ **410**

22. $62.46 \div 0.09$ **694**

23. $21.12 \div 0.4$ **52.8**

24. $82.68 \div 0.06$ **1378**

Evaluate each expression for the given value of the variable.

25. $\frac{18}{x}$ for $x = 0.12$ **4.25**

26. $\frac{10.8}{x}$ for $x = 0.03$ **360**

27. $\frac{9.18}{x}$ for $x = -1.2$ **−7.65**

28. A can of fruit contains $3\frac{1}{2}$ cups of fruit. The suggested serving size is $\frac{1}{2}$ cup. How many servings are in the can of fruit? **7 servings**

State Resources

go.hrw.com
State Resources Online
KEYWORD: MT7 Resources

ONGOING ASSESSMENT
and INTERVENTION

Diagnose Before the Lesson
2-5 Warm Up, TE p. 80

Monitor During the Lesson
2-5 Know-It Notebook
2-5 Questioning Strategies

Assess After the Lesson
2-5 Lesson Quiz, TE p. 84

52. Possible answer: The quotient will have an even denominator. When the division is changed to multiplication by the reciprocal, the factor 5 will be in the numerator. This factor can be divided out with the 10 in the denominator, leaving the factor 2 in the denominator. Because the quotient will have a factor of 2, it must be even.

51.
Possible answer:
$20\frac{1}{4} \div 2 =$
$\frac{81}{4} \cdot \frac{1}{2} = \frac{81}{8} =$
$10\frac{1}{8}$; after the split, the price of the stock was $10\frac{1}{8}$.

48. The width of a DVD case is about $\frac{1}{3}$ inch. How many DVD cases are in a box set if the set is about $1\frac{2}{3}$ inches thick?   **5 cases**

49. Social Studies Nesting dolls called *matrushkas* are a well-known type of Russian folk art. Use the information in the picture to find the height of the largest doll.

$3\frac{31}{48}$ in. $\frac{6}{25}x = \frac{7}{8}$ in.

x in.

50. Estimation Leo's bowl contains 16 ounces of cereal. His spoon can hold $1\frac{1}{8}$ ounces. Approximately how many spoonfuls are in the bowl? **about 14 spoonfuls**

51. Choose a Strategy Before 2000, the prices of all stocks traded on the New York Stock Exchange were given in fractions. When a stock is split 2-for-1, the price of the stock is halved and the number of shares doubles. A stock trading at $20\frac{1}{4}$ was split 2-for-1. What was the price of the stock after the split?

52. Write About It A proper fraction with denominator 10 is divided by a proper fraction with denominator 5. Will the denominator of the quotient be odd or even? Explain.

53. Challenge In 2003, the U.S. Census Bureau estimated that about $\frac{1}{25}$ of the U.S. population resided in Los Angeles County. At that time, about $\frac{3}{25}$ of the U.S. population resided in California. Approximately what fraction of the California population resided in Los Angeles County? **about $\frac{1}{3}$**

TEST PREP and Spiral Review

54. Multiple Choice Evaluate the expression $\frac{7.92}{x}$ for $x = 3.3$.

  Ⓐ 2.4   Ⓑ 4.62   Ⓒ 11.22   Ⓓ 26.136

55. Multiple Choice A recipe calls for $2\frac{1}{2}$ cups of sugar to make a batch of cookies. To make one-third of a batch, Betty needs to divide the amount of each ingredient in the recipe by 3. How many cups of sugar will she use?

  Ⓕ $\frac{3}{4}$ cup   Ⓖ $\frac{5}{6}$ cup   Ⓗ $1\frac{1}{5}$ cups   Ⓙ $7\frac{1}{2}$ cups

56. Gridded Response Frank bought 12.6 gallons of gasoline for $26.96. How much, to the nearest cent, was the cost per gallon of gasoline? **$2.14**

Evaluate each expression for the given values of the variables. (Lesson 1-1)

57. $7x - 4y$ for $x = 5$ and $y = 6$ **11**   **58.** $6.5p - 9.1q$ for $p = 2.5$ and $q = 0$ **16.25**

Write each decimal as a fraction or mixed number in simplest form. (Lesson 2-1)

59. 0.65 $\frac{13}{20}$ **60.** −1.25 $-1\frac{1}{4}$ **61.** 0.723 $\frac{723}{1000}$ **62.** 11.17 $11\frac{17}{100}$ **63.** −0.8 $-\frac{4}{5}$

TEST PREP DOCTOR + Encourage students to read the problem carefully. For Exercise 55, Betty is dividing the amount of each ingredient in the recipe by 3. Be sure students realize that the answer should be less than the original amount of each ingredient. Students can eliminate **J** because the number of cups is greater than it is in the original recipe.

 Journal

Ask students to write about a situation from their everyday lives in which they might need to divide by a fraction.

Power Presentations
with PowerPoint®

 2-5
✓ **Lesson Quiz**

Divide.

1. $2\frac{5}{6} \div \left(-1\frac{1}{2}\right)$ $-1\frac{8}{9}$

2. $-14 \div 1.25$ -11.2

3. $3.9 \div 0.65$ 6

4. Evaluate $\frac{112}{x}$ for $x = 6.3$. $17.\overline{7}$

5. A penny weighs 2.5 grams. How many pennies would it take to equal one pound (453.6 grams)? **181**

Also available on transparency

CHALLENGE 2-5

LESSON 2-5 Challenge
A New License to Operate

You can invent new operations based on the familiar operations of addition, subtraction, multiplication, and division, and the familiar order of operations.

If $a \triangle b = \frac{a+b}{2}$ where a and b represent any rational numbers,

then $3 \triangle 5 = \frac{3+5}{2} = 4$.

Use the given definition of operation $\triangle$ to evaluate each expression.

1. $\frac{1}{2} \triangle (-10) = \underline{-4.75}$ **2.** $\frac{100 \triangle (-10)}{10} = \underline{4.5}$

3. $4 \triangle 6 \triangle 3 = \underline{4}$ **4.** $[5.5 \triangle (-6)] + [-6 \triangle 5.5] = \underline{-0.5}$

Use the operation shown to answer each question. $\frac{a}{c}\frac{b}{d} = ac - bd$

5. $\frac{1}{3}\frac{8}{4} = \underline{-29}$ **6.** $\frac{-2}{3}\frac{3}{-2} = \underline{0}$

7. If $\frac{1}{x}\frac{3}{2} = 18$, then $x = \underline{24}$ **8.** If $\frac{6}{x}\frac{2}{x} = 12$, then $x = \underline{3}$

Use the operation shown to answer each question. $a \diamond b = \frac{a^2}{b^2}$

9. $(3 \diamond 5) = \underline{\frac{9}{25}}$ **10.** $(1 \diamond 8) - (5 \diamond 8) = \underline{-\frac{3}{8}}$

11. $(1 \diamond 3) \times (3 \diamond 6) = \underline{\frac{1}{36}}$ **12.** $(1 \diamond 10)^2 = \underline{\frac{1}{10,000}}$

If $\lrcorner n \lrcorner$ means 1 less than the number of digits in the integer n, then, for example, $\lrcorner 77 \lrcorner = 1$ since 77 has 2 digits.

Use the definition of $\lrcorner n \lrcorner$ to answer each question.

13. If n is a positive integer less than 100, what is the greatest value for $\lrcorner n \lrcorner$? $\underline{1}$

14. If n is a positive integer less than 1001, what is the greatest value for $\lrcorner n \lrcorner$? $\underline{3}$

15. If n has 100 digits, what is the value of $\lrcorner \lrcorner n \lrcorner \lrcorner$? Explain.

By definition, $\lrcorner 100$-digit number$\lrcorner = 99$. Then, since 99 has 2 digits, $\lrcorner 99 \lrcorner = 1$.

PROBLEM SOLVING 2-5

LESSON 2-5 Problem Solving
Dividing Rational Numbers

Use the table at the right that shows the maximum speed over a quarter mile of different animals. Find the time is takes each animal to travel one-quarter mile at top speed. Round to the nearest thousandth.

1. Quarter horse

  0.005 hours

2. Greyhound

  0.006 hours

3. Human

  0.009 hours

4. Giant tortoise

  1.471 hours

5. Three-toed sloth

  1.667 hours

Maximum Speeds of Animals	
Animal	**Speed (mph)**
Quarter Horse	47.50
Greyhound	39.35
Human	27.89
Giant Tortoise	0.17
Three-toed sloth	0.15

Choose the letter for the best answer.

6. A piece of ribbon is $1\frac{7}{8}$ inches long. If the ribbon is going to be divided into 15 pieces, how long should each piece be?

  Ⓐ $\frac{1}{8}$ in.
  B $\frac{1}{15}$ in.
  C $\frac{2}{3}$ in.
  D $28\frac{1}{8}$ in.

7. The recorded rainfall for each day of a week was 0 in., $\frac{1}{4}$ in., $\frac{3}{4}$ in., 1 in., 0 in., $1\frac{1}{4}$ in., $1\frac{1}{4}$ in. What was the average rainfall per day?

  F $\frac{9}{10}$ in.
  Ⓖ $\frac{9}{14}$ in.
  H $\frac{7}{8}$ in.
  J $4\frac{1}{2}$ in.

8. A drill bit that is $\frac{7}{32}$ in. means that the hole the bit makes has a diameter of $\frac{7}{32}$ in. Since the radius is half of the diameter, what is the radius of a hole drilled by a $\frac{7}{32}$ in. bit?

  A $\frac{14}{32}$ in.
  B $\frac{7}{32}$ in.
  C $\frac{9}{16}$ in.
  Ⓓ $\frac{7}{64}$ in.

9. A serving of a certain kind of cereal is $\frac{2}{3}$ cup. There are 12 cups of cereal in the box. How many servings of cereal are in the box?

  Ⓕ 18
  G 15
  H 8
  J 6

Adding and Subtracting with Unlike Denominators

Learn to add and subtract fractions with unlike denominators.

North Dome trail in Yosemite National Park is $5\frac{3}{4}$ miles to the summit. Two hikers walk $2\frac{1}{8}$ miles before taking a break. They then hike another $1\frac{1}{2}$ miles before taking a second break. How many more miles do they have to hike before reaching the summit?

To solve this problem, add and subtract rational numbers with unlike denominators. First find a common denominator using one of these methods:

Method 1   Find a common denominator by multiplying one denominator by the other denominator.

Method 2   Find the least common denominator (LCD).

EXAMPLE 1   **Adding and Subtracting Fractions with Unlike Denominators**

Add or subtract.

A $\frac{4}{5} + \frac{1}{6}$

Method 1: $\frac{4}{5} + \frac{1}{6}$ *Find a common denominator: 5(6) = 30.*

$= \frac{4}{5}\left(\frac{6}{6}\right) + \frac{1}{6}\left(\frac{5}{5}\right)$ *Multiply by fractions equal to 1.*

$= \frac{24}{30} + \frac{5}{30}$ *Rewrite with a common denominator.*

$= \frac{29}{30}$ *Simplify.*

B $2\frac{1}{6} - 2\frac{2}{9}$

Method 2: $2\frac{1}{6} - 2\frac{2}{9}$

$= \frac{13}{6} - \frac{20}{9}$ *Write as improper fractions.*

Multiples of 6: 6, 12, ⑱ . . .   *List the multiples of each denominator and find the LCD.*
Multiples of 9: 9, ⑱ 27, . . .

$= \frac{13}{6}\left(\frac{3}{3}\right) - \frac{20}{9}\left(\frac{2}{2}\right)$ *Multiply by fractions equal to 1.*

$= \frac{39}{18} - \frac{40}{18}$ *Rewrite with the LCD.*

$= -\frac{1}{18}$ *Simplify.*

Organizer   2-6

Pacing: Traditional 1 day
Block $\frac{1}{2}$ day

Objective: Students add and subtract fractions with unlike denominators.

 Online Edition
Tutorial Videos

Countdown to Testing Week 4

Power Presentations
with PowerPoint®

Warm Up
Add or subtract.
1. $1\frac{3}{5} + \left(-\frac{2}{5}\right)$ $1\frac{1}{5}$
2. $3\frac{11}{12} - 2\frac{7}{12}$ $1\frac{1}{3}$
3. $6.5 + -1.2$ 5.3
4. $3.4 - 0.9$ 2.5

Problem of the Day
The least common multiple of 6 and a number is 24. What is the other number?   8 or 24

Also available on transparency

Math Humor

Clerk: That $2.50 pen is on sale for $2.00.

Customer: But the sign says, "Half off everything."

Clerk: That's right. It was $2\frac{1}{2}$ dollars, so I took off the $\frac{1}{2}$.

---

1 Introduce

Alternate Opener

EXPLORATION

2-6 Adding and Subtracting with Unlike Denominators

You can use models to show addition and subtraction of fractions with unlike denominators. Look at the models for $\frac{1}{2} + \frac{1}{3}$ and $\frac{1}{2} - \frac{1}{3}$.

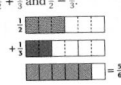 

1. Draw a picture to show that $\frac{1}{2} + \frac{4}{5} = 1\frac{3}{10} = 1.3$.
2. Draw a picture to show that $\frac{1}{2} + \frac{2}{3} = \frac{7}{6} = 1\frac{1}{6}$.
3. Complete each addition problem. Simplify your answers.
   a. $\frac{7}{10} + \frac{4}{5}$ b. $\frac{3}{5} + \frac{3}{4}$

Think and Discuss
4. **Explain** how to add and subtract fractions with unlike denominators.
5. **Discuss** why the fraction that results from adding or subtracting fractions with unlike denominators has a different denominator than the fractions.

Motivate
To introduce adding and subtracting with unlike denominators, ask students to list the multiples of 5 and the multiples of 2. Then ask the students to identify the *least common* multiple. Show them that although there are many common multiples (10, 20, 30, etc.), there is only one least common multiple (10).

5, ⑩, 15, <u>20</u>, 25, <u>30</u>, . . .

2, 4, 6, 8, ⑩, 12, 14, 16, 18, <u>20</u>, 22, 24, 26, 28, <u>30</u>, . . .

Explorations and answers are provided in *Alternate Openers: Explorations Transparencies.*

State Resources

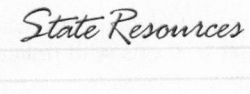

go.hrw.com
State Resources Online
KEYWORD: MT7 Resources

2-6   Adding and Subtracting with Unlike Denominators   **85**

Additional Examples

Example ①

Add or subtract.

A. $\frac{1}{8} + \frac{2}{7}$ $\frac{23}{56}$ **B.** $1\frac{1}{6} - 1\frac{5}{8}$ $-\frac{11}{24}$

Example ②

Evaluate $t - \frac{4}{5}$ for $t = \frac{5}{6}$. $\frac{1}{30}$

Example ③

Two dancers are making necklaces from ribbon for their costumes. They need pieces measuring $13\frac{3}{4}$ inches and $12\frac{7}{8}$ inches. How much ribbon will be left over after the pieces are cut from a 36-inch length?

There will be $9\frac{3}{8}$ inches left.

Also available on transparency

Possible answers to *Think and Discuss*

1. 3 and 7; 4 and 9; 27 and 16

2. Negative; $\left|-2\frac{1}{5}\right| = 2\frac{1}{5}$, and $\left|-2\frac{3}{16}\right| = 2\frac{3}{16}$; since $2\frac{3}{15} > 2\frac{3}{16}$, the answer takes the sign of $-2\frac{1}{5}$.

3. Using the Commutative Property, add the whole number portions, add the fractional portions by finding a common denominator, and combine the two results.
$2\frac{2}{5} + 9\frac{1}{3} = 2 + 9 + \frac{2}{5} + \frac{1}{3} = 11\frac{11}{15}$

EXAMPLE ②   **Evaluating Expressions with Rational Numbers**

Evaluate $n - \frac{11}{16}$ for $n = -\frac{1}{3}$.

$$n - \frac{11}{16} = \left(-\frac{1}{3}\right) - \frac{11}{16}$$ *Substitute $-\frac{1}{3}$ for n.*

$$= \left(-\frac{1}{3}\right)\left(\frac{16}{16}\right) - \frac{11}{16}\left(\frac{3}{3}\right)$$ *Multiply by fractions equal to 1.*

$$= -\frac{16}{48} - \frac{33}{48}$$ *Rewrite with a common denominator: 3(16) = 48.*

$$= -\frac{49}{48}, \text{ or } -1\frac{1}{48}$$ *Simplify.*

EXAMPLE ③   *Recreation Application*

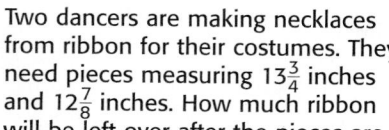

Abraham Lincoln established Yosemite National Park as a natural preserve in 1864.

Two hikers begin hiking the North Dome trail in Yosemite National Park, which is $5\frac{3}{4}$ miles to the summit. The hikers cover $2\frac{1}{8}$ miles before taking a break. They then hike another $1\frac{1}{2}$ miles before taking a second break. How many more miles do the hikers have to go before reaching the summit?

$$2\frac{1}{8} + 1\frac{1}{2}$$ *Add to find the distance hiked.*

$$= \frac{17}{8} + \frac{3}{2}$$ *Write as improper fractions.*

$$= \frac{17}{8} + \frac{12}{8}$$ *The LCD is 8.*

$$= \frac{29}{8}, \text{ or } 3\frac{5}{8}$$

The hikers have hiked $3\frac{5}{8}$ miles. Now find the number of miles remaining.

$$5\frac{3}{4} - 3\frac{5}{8}$$ *Subtract the distance hiked from the total distance.*

$$= \frac{23}{4} - \frac{29}{8}$$ *Write as improper fractions.*

$$= \frac{46}{8} - \frac{29}{8}$$ *The LCD is 8.*

$$= \frac{17}{8}, \text{ or } 2\frac{1}{8}$$ *Simplify.*

The hikers have $2\frac{1}{8}$ miles to go before reaching the summit.

Think and Discuss

1. **Give an example** of two denominators with no common factors.

2. **Tell** if $-2\frac{1}{5} - \left(-2\frac{3}{16}\right)$ is positive or negative. Explain.

3. **Explain** how to add $2\frac{2}{5} + 9\frac{1}{3}$ without first writing them as improper fractions.

---

② Teach

Guided Instruction

In this lesson, students learn to add and subtract fractions with unlike denominators. Discuss the two methods for finding a common denominator. To help students understand why fractions must have common denominators before adding across the numerators, you may want to compare the denominators of fractions with units of measure. For example, just as you cannot add 2 inches and 3 centimeters without first writing them in terms of the same unit, you cannot add $\frac{2}{5}$ and $\frac{3}{10}$ without first writing them in terms of the same denominator.

Reaching All Learners
Through Concrete Manipulatives

Give each student (or group of students) a set of manipulative cutouts that represent $\frac{1}{2}$, $\frac{1}{3}$, $\frac{1}{4}$, $\frac{1}{6}$, and $\frac{1}{12}$. (Teaching Tools).

Have students use the cutouts to complete the following exercises.

1. $\frac{1}{2} + \frac{1}{3}$ $\frac{5}{6}$ 2. $\frac{1}{4} + \frac{1}{3}$ $\frac{7}{12}$

3. $\frac{1}{4} + \frac{1}{6}$ $\frac{5}{12}$ 4. $\frac{1}{12} + \frac{1}{6}$ $\frac{1}{4}$

5. $\frac{1}{3} + \frac{1}{12}$ $\frac{5}{12}$ 6. $\frac{1}{4} + \frac{1}{12}$ $\frac{1}{3}$

7. $\frac{1}{2} + \frac{1}{6}$ $\frac{2}{3}$ 8. $\frac{1}{2} + \frac{1}{12}$ $\frac{7}{12}$

---

③ Close

Summarize

Review both methods of finding common denominators. Remind students that fractions can only be added or subtracted when the denominators are the same. Ask them if this is true for multiplication or division. no Ask the students to find the sum of $-1\frac{1}{4}$ and $\frac{5}{6}$ by both of the methods presented in the lesson. Remind students to give the answer in simplest form.

$$-1\frac{1}{4} + \frac{5}{6} = -\frac{5}{4} + \frac{5}{6} = -\frac{30}{24} + \frac{20}{24}$$
$$= -\frac{10}{24} = -\frac{5}{12}$$

$$-1\frac{1}{4} + \frac{5}{6} = -\frac{5}{4} + \frac{5}{6} = -\frac{15}{12} + \frac{10}{12} = -\frac{5}{12}$$

go.hrw.com
Homework Help Online
KEYWORD: MT7 2-6
Parent Resources Online
KEYWORD: MT7 Parent

2-6 **Exercises**

GUIDED PRACTICE

See Example 1 — **Add or subtract.**

1. $\frac{4}{7} + \frac{1}{3}$ $\frac{19}{21}$

2. $\frac{1}{2} - \frac{7}{8}$ $-\frac{3}{8}$

3. $3\frac{1}{2} + \left(-7\frac{4}{5}\right)$ $-4\frac{3}{10}$

4. $3\frac{7}{12} + \left(-2\frac{4}{5}\right)$ $\frac{47}{60}$

See Example 2 — **Evaluate each expression for the given value of the variable.**

5. $4\frac{3}{8} + x$ for $x = -3\frac{2}{9}$ $1\frac{11}{72}$

6. $n - \frac{3}{8}$ for $n = -\frac{4}{5}$ $-1\frac{7}{40}$

7. $\frac{3}{7} + y$ for $y = \frac{1}{2}$ $\frac{13}{14}$

See Example 3 — 8. Gavin needs $2\frac{5}{8}$ yards of fabric each to make two shirts. This amount is cut from a bolt containing $9\frac{1}{4}$ yards of fabric. How much fabric remains on the bolt? **4 yd**

INDEPENDENT PRACTICE

See Example 1 — **Add or subtract.**

9. $\frac{7}{13} + \frac{2}{7}$ $\frac{75}{91}$

10. $\frac{1}{3} + \frac{4}{7}$ $\frac{19}{21}$

11. $\frac{11}{12} - \frac{4}{5}$ $\frac{7}{60}$

12. $\frac{2}{5} + \frac{14}{15}$ $1\frac{1}{3}$

13. $5\frac{4}{5} + \left(-3\frac{2}{7}\right)$ $2\frac{18}{35}$

14. $\frac{5}{9} - \frac{11}{14}$ $-\frac{29}{126}$

15. $2\frac{1}{4} - 4\frac{3}{7}$ $-2\frac{5}{28}$

16. $\frac{1}{5} + \frac{8}{9}$ $1\frac{4}{45}$

See Example 2 — **Evaluate each expression for the given value of the variable.**

17. $2\frac{3}{4} + x$ for $x = -3\frac{2}{3}$ $-\frac{11}{12}$

18. $n - \frac{2}{3}$ for $n = \frac{3}{4}$ $\frac{1}{12}$

19. $r - \frac{4}{5}$ for $r = \frac{3}{4}$ $-\frac{1}{20}$

20. $3\frac{1}{6} + x$ for $x = -2\frac{5}{7}$ $\frac{19}{42}$

21. $n - \frac{11}{13}$ for $n = \frac{2}{3}$ $-\frac{7}{39}$

22. $\frac{12}{17} - n$ for $n = \frac{1}{2}$ $\frac{7}{34}$

See Example 3 — 23. An oxygen tank contained $212\frac{2}{3}$ liters of oxygen before $27\frac{1}{3}$ liters were used. If the tank can hold $240\frac{3}{8}$ liters, how much space in the tank is unused? $55\frac{1}{24}$

PRACTICE AND PROBLEM SOLVING

Extra Practice
See page 785.

24. **Multi-Step** The heights of the starting players for the Davis High School boy's basketball team are $78\frac{1}{8}$ in., 74 in., $71\frac{5}{8}$ in., $70\frac{3}{4}$ in., and $69\frac{1}{2}$ in. Find the average height of the starting players. $72\frac{4}{5}$ **in.**

25. **Measurement** A water pipe has an outside diameter of $1\frac{1}{4}$ inches and a wall thickness of $\frac{5}{16}$ inch. What is the inside diameter of the pipe? $\frac{5}{8}$ **in.**

26.
Possible answer: No; $7\frac{3}{8}$ is about $7\frac{1}{2}$, and $5\frac{1}{16}$ is about 5.
$7\frac{1}{2} + 7\frac{1}{2} + 5 + 5 = 25$ inches. She has only 24 inches of ribbon.

26. **Estimation** Georgia is making a rectangular gift box. She plans to glue ribbon along the bottom edge. The length of the box is $7\frac{3}{8}$ inches, and the width is $5\frac{1}{16}$ inches. She has 2 feet of ribbon. Does she have enough for the bottom edge? Explain your reasoning.

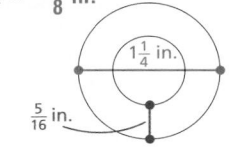

27. **Multi-Step** Karl rode his bike $16\frac{3}{8}$ miles. Neeka rode her bike m fewer miles.
   a. Write an expression to represent how many miles Neeka rode. $16\frac{3}{8} - m$
   b. How far did Neeka ride if she rode $5\frac{1}{4}$ fewer miles? $11\frac{1}{8}$ **mi**
   c. Elda rode as far as Karl and Neeka combined. How far did Elda ride? $27\frac{1}{2}$ **mi**

Assignment Guide

If you finished Example 1 assign:
Average 1–4, 9–16, 32–40
Advanced 9–16, 25, 32–40

If you finished Example 2 assign:
Average 1–7, 9–22, 32–40
Advanced 16–22, 25, 32–40

If you finished Example 3 assign:
Average 1–23, 25, 28, 29, 32–40
Advanced 13–20, 24–40

Homework Quick Check
Quickly check key concepts.
Exercises: 16, 20, 23, 28

Math Background

Another method for finding the least common multiple of a set of numbers involves prime factors. To find the LCM of 60 and 45, factor each number into its prime factors, using exponents: $60 = 2^2 \cdot 3 \cdot 5$ and $45 = 3^2 \cdot 5$. The LCM is the product of the greatest powers of all the prime factors: $LCM = 2^2 \cdot 3^2 \cdot 5 = 180$. This method is useful for rational expressions as well. To find the sum $\frac{1}{6ab^2} + \frac{1}{4a^2b}$, you would need the LCM of the denominators.
$6ab^2 = 2 \cdot 3 \cdot a \cdot b^2$
$4a^2b = 2^2 \cdot a^2 \cdot b$
$LCM = 2^2 \cdot 3 \cdot a^2 \cdot b^2 = 12\,a^2\,b^2$

RETEACH 2-6

Reteach
2-6 *Adding and Subtracting with Unlike Denominators*

To model $\frac{1}{2} + \frac{1}{3}$, use two rectangles of the same size and shape.

A. 1st rectangle: Shade $\frac{1}{2}$ vertically.

B. 2nd rectangle: Shade $\frac{1}{3}$ horizontally.

$\frac{1}{2}$ $\frac{1}{3}$

C. Separate the shaded portions into parts of equal size.

$\frac{1}{2} = \frac{3}{6}$ $\frac{1}{3} = \frac{2}{6}$

D. Use a new rectangle to show the sum.

$\frac{1}{2} + \frac{1}{3} = \frac{3}{6} + \frac{2}{6} = \frac{5}{6}$

Model $\frac{1}{2} + \frac{2}{5}$. **Write the result. Possible model.**

1.

$\frac{1}{2}$ $\frac{2}{5}$ $\frac{1}{2} + \frac{2}{5} = \frac{5}{10} + \frac{4}{10} = \frac{9}{10}$

Model $\frac{1}{3} + \frac{3}{5}$. **Write the result. Possible model.**

2.

$\frac{1}{3}$ $\frac{3}{5}$ $\frac{1}{3} + \frac{3}{5} = \frac{5}{15} + \frac{9}{15} = \frac{14}{15}$

PRACTICE 2-6

Practice B
2-6 *Adding and Subtracting with Unlike Denominators*

Add or subtract.

1. $\frac{2}{3} + \frac{1}{2}$ $1\frac{1}{6}$

2. $\frac{3}{5} + \frac{1}{3}$ $\frac{14}{15}$

3. $\frac{3}{4} - \frac{1}{3}$ $\frac{5}{12}$

4. $\frac{1}{2} - \frac{5}{9}$ $-\frac{1}{18}$

5. $\frac{5}{16} - \frac{5}{8}$ $-\frac{5}{16}$

6. $\frac{7}{9} + \frac{5}{6}$ $1\frac{11}{18}$

7. $\frac{7}{8} - \frac{1}{4}$ $\frac{5}{8}$

8. $\frac{5}{6} - \frac{3}{8}$ $\frac{11}{24}$

9. $2\frac{7}{8} + 3\frac{5}{12}$ $6\frac{17}{24}$

10. $\frac{2}{9} + 2\frac{1}{18}$ $3\frac{5}{18}$

11. $3\frac{2}{3} - 1\frac{3}{5}$ $2\frac{1}{15}$

12. $1\frac{5}{6} + \left(-2\frac{3}{4}\right)$ $-\frac{11}{12}$

13. $8\frac{1}{3} - 3\frac{5}{9}$ $4\frac{7}{9}$

14. $5\frac{1}{3} + 1\frac{11}{12}$ $7\frac{1}{4}$

15. $7\frac{1}{4} + \left(-2\frac{5}{6}\right)$ $4\frac{5}{6}$

16. $5\frac{2}{5} - 7\frac{3}{10}$ $-1\frac{9}{10}$

Evaluate each expression for the given value of the variable.

17. $2\frac{3}{8} + x$ for $x = 1\frac{5}{6}$ $4\frac{5}{24}$

18. $x - \frac{2}{5}$ for $x = \frac{1}{3}$ $-\frac{1}{15}$

19. $x - \frac{3}{10}$ for $x = \frac{3}{7}$ $\frac{9}{70}$

20. $1\frac{5}{8} + x$ for $x = -2\frac{1}{6}$ $-\frac{13}{24}$

21. $x - \frac{3}{4}$ for $x = \frac{1}{6}$ $-\frac{7}{12}$

22. $x - \frac{3}{10}$ for $x = \frac{1}{2}$ $\frac{1}{5}$

23. Ana worked $6\frac{1}{2}$ h on Monday, $5\frac{3}{4}$ h on Tuesday and $7\frac{1}{6}$ h on Friday. How many total hours did she work these three days? $19\frac{5}{12}$ h

State Resources

go.hrw.com
State Resources Online
KEYWORD: MT7 Resources

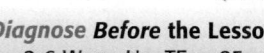
Interdisciplinary

Earth Science

Exercises 28–31 involve using facts about the erosion of Niagara Falls. Water flow and erosion are studied in middle school Earth science programs, such as *Holt Science & Technology*.

 **TEST PREP DOCTOR** Suggest that students estimate before looking at the answer choices. For Exercise 32, students can subtract 4 ft from 7 ft to get 3 ft. Students also need to subtract the fractional parts of the measurements. Since $\frac{5}{8}$ is slightly more than $\frac{1}{2}$, the final answer should be a little *less than* 3 ft, so they can eliminate **A** and **B** as possible answers.

 Journal

Ask students to consider the two methods for finding a common denominator, multiplying the denominators or finding the least common denominator. Ask them to describe situations in which it would be better to use one method over the other.

Power Presentations
with **PowerPoint®**

2-6 Lesson Quiz

Add or subtract.

1. $\frac{5}{14} + \frac{1}{7}$ $\frac{1}{2}$

2. $8\frac{2}{3} - 1\frac{1}{2}$ $7\frac{1}{6}$

3. $\frac{3}{5} + \left(-2\frac{2}{3}\right)$ $-2\frac{1}{15}$

4. Evaluate $1\frac{3}{8} - n$ for $n = \frac{9}{16}$. $\frac{13}{16}$

5. Robert is 5 feet $6\frac{1}{2}$ inches tall. Judy is 5 feet $3\frac{3}{4}$ inches tall. How much taller is Robert than Judy? $2\frac{3}{4}$ in.

Also available on transparency

Earth Science LINK

Niagara Falls, on the border of Canada and the United States, has two major falls, Horseshoe Falls on the Canadian side and American Falls on the U.S. side. Surveys of the erosion of the falls began in 1842. From 1842 to 1905, Horseshoe Falls eroded $239\frac{2}{5}$ feet.

28. In 1986, Thomas Martin noted that American Falls eroded $7\frac{1}{2}$ inches and Horseshoe Falls eroded $2\frac{4}{25}$ feet. What is the difference between the two measurements? $18\frac{21}{50}$ in.

29. From 1842 to 1875, the yearly erosion of Horseshoe Falls varied from a minimum of $\frac{61}{100}$ meter to a maximum of $1\frac{17}{50}$ meters. By how much did these rates of erosion differ? $\frac{73}{100}$ meter

30. In the 48 years between 1842 and 1890, the average rate of erosion at Horseshoe Falls was $\frac{33}{50}$ meter per year. In the 22 years between 1905 and 1927, the rate of erosion was $\frac{7}{10}$ meter per year. Approximately how much total erosion occurred during these two time periods? $47\frac{2}{25}$ meters

31. ⭐ **Challenge** Rates of erosion of American Falls have been recorded as $\frac{23}{100}$ meter per year for 33 years, $\frac{9}{40}$ meter per year for 48 years, and $\frac{1}{5}$ meter per year for 4 years. What is the total amount of erosion during these three time spans? $19\frac{19}{100}$ meters

TEST PREP and Spiral Review

32. **Multiple Choice** A $4\frac{5}{8}$ ft section of wood was cut from a $7\frac{1}{2}$ ft board. How much of the original board remained?

   (A) $3\frac{5}{8}$ ft   (B) $3\frac{9}{16}$ ft   (C) $2\frac{7}{8}$ ft   (D) $2\frac{3}{8}$ ft

33. **Extended Response** A rectangular swimming pool measured $75\frac{1}{2}$ feet by $25\frac{1}{4}$ feet. Schmidt Pool Supply computed the perimeter of the pool to be $200\frac{1}{3}$ feet. Explain what the company did incorrectly when computing the perimeter. What is the correct perimeter?   **The company did not find a common denominator when adding $\frac{1}{2}$ and $\frac{1}{4}$. The correct perimeter is $201\frac{1}{2}$ feet.**

Evaluate each expression for the given value of the variable. (Lesson 1-4)

34. $c + 4$ for $c = -8$ -4 35. $m - 2$ for $m = 13$ 11 36. $5 + d$ for $d = -10$ -5

Divide. Write each answer in simplest form. (Lesson 2-5)

37. $-\frac{4}{11} \div \frac{2}{7}$ $-1\frac{3}{11}$ 38. $\frac{4}{9} \div 8$ $\frac{1}{18}$ 39. $-\frac{7}{15} \div \frac{14}{25}$ $-\frac{5}{6}$ 40. $3\frac{1}{3} \div \frac{7}{9}$ $4\frac{2}{7}$

CHALLENGE 2-6

LESSON 2-6 Challenge
Please Repeat That.

A decimal that repeats one digit is equivalent to a fraction with denominator 9.

$0.\overline{1} = \frac{1}{9}$ $0.\overline{2} = \frac{2}{9}$ $0.\overline{5} = \frac{5}{9}$

A decimal that repeats two digits is equivalent to a fraction with denominator 99.

$0.\overline{43} = \frac{43}{99}$ $0.\overline{61} = \frac{61}{99}$ $0.\overline{38} = \frac{38}{99}$

The pattern continues so that $0.\overline{681} = \frac{681}{999}$ and $0.\overline{24793} = \frac{24,793}{99,999}$.

Use a calculator to write each decimal equivalent.

1. $\frac{1}{90} = \underline{0.0\overline{1}}$ 2. $\frac{21}{990} = \underline{0.0\overline{21}}$ 3. $\frac{358}{9990} = \underline{0.0\overline{358}}$

Predict the decimal equivalent of each fraction. Verify your results on a calculator.

4. $\frac{4}{90} = \underline{0.0\overline{4}}$ 5. $\frac{62}{990} = \underline{0.0\overline{62}}$ 6. $\frac{617}{9990} = \underline{0.0\overline{617}}$

Write each fractional equivalent and simplify.

7. $0.\overline{7} = \underline{\frac{7}{9}}$ 8. $0.\overline{08} = \underline{\frac{8}{90} = \frac{4}{45}}$ 9. $0.00\overline{24} = \underline{\frac{24}{9900} = \frac{2}{825}}$

When one digit repeats but does not begin in the first decimal place, and the digit in the first place is other than 0, you must add fractions.

$0.3\overline{7} = 0.3 + 0.0\overline{7}$
$= \frac{3}{10} + \frac{7}{90}$
$= \frac{27}{90} + \frac{7}{90} = \frac{34}{90} = \frac{17}{45}$

Write each repeating decimal as the sum of two fractions. Find the sum and simplify. Verify.

10. $0.2\overline{8} = $
$\frac{2}{10} + \frac{8}{90} = \frac{26}{90} = \frac{13}{45}$

11. $0.25\overline{32} = $
$\frac{25}{100} + \frac{32}{9900} = \frac{2507}{9900}$

12. $0.1\overline{27} = $
$\frac{1}{10} + \frac{27}{990} = \frac{126}{990} = \frac{7}{55}$

13. $0.75\overline{483} = $
$\frac{75}{100} + \frac{483}{99,900} = \frac{75,408}{99,900} = \frac{6284}{8325}$

PROBLEM SOLVING 2-6

LESSON 2-6 Problem Solving
Adding and Subtracting with Unlike Denominators

Write the correct answer.

1. Nick Hysong of the United States won the Olympic gold medal in the pole vault in 2000 with a jump of 19 ft $4\frac{1}{4}$ inches, or $232\frac{1}{4}$ inches. In 1900, Irving Baxter of the United States won the pole vault with a jump of 10 ft $9\frac{7}{8}$ inches, or $129\frac{7}{8}$ inches. How much higher did Hysong vault than Baxter?
$102\frac{3}{8}$ inches

2. In the 2000 Summer Olympics, Ivan Pedroso of Cuba won the Long jump with a jump of 28 ft $3\frac{7}{8}$ inches, or $336\frac{7}{8}$ inches. Alvin Kraenzlein of the Unites States won the long jump in 1900 with a jump of 23 ft $6\frac{7}{8}$ inches, or $282\frac{7}{8}$ inches. How much farther did Pedroso jump than Kraenzlein?
$53\frac{7}{8}$ inches

3. A recipe calls for $\frac{1}{8}$ cup of sugar and $\frac{3}{4}$ cup of brown sugar. How much total sugar is added to the recipe?
$\frac{7}{8}$ cup

4. The average snowfall in Norfolk, VA for January is $2\frac{3}{5}$ inches, February $2\frac{9}{10}$ inches, March 1 inch, and December $\frac{9}{10}$ inches. If these are the only months it typically snows, what is the average snowfall per year?
$7\frac{2}{5}$ inches

Use the table at the right that shows the average snowfall per month in Vail, Colorado.

5. What is the average annual snowfall in Vail, Colorado?

   A $15\frac{13}{20}$ in.   C $187\frac{7}{10}$ in.

   B 153 in.   (D) $187\frac{4}{5}$ in.

6. The peak of the skiing season is from December through March. What is the average snowfall for this period?

   F $30\frac{19}{10}$ in.   (H) $123\frac{4}{5}$ in.

   G $123\frac{3}{5}$ in.   J 127 in.

Average Snowfall in Vail, CO			
Month	**Snowfall (in.)**	**Month**	**Snowfall (in.)**
Jan	$36\frac{7}{10}$	July	0
Feb	$35\frac{7}{10}$	August	0
March	$25\frac{2}{5}$	Sept	1
April	$21\frac{1}{5}$	Oct	$7\frac{4}{5}$
May	4	Nov	$29\frac{7}{10}$
June	$\frac{3}{10}$	Dec	26

Technology LAB 2-6

Add and Subtract Fractions

Use with Lesson 2-6

go.hrw.com
Lab Resources Online
KEYWORD: MT7 Lab2

You can add and subtract fractions using your graphing calculator. To display decimals as fractions, use the **MATH** key.

Activity

1 Use a graphing calculator to add $\frac{7}{12} + \frac{3}{8}$. Write the sum as a fraction.

Type 7 **÷** 12 and press **ENTER**. You can see that the decimal equivalent is a repeating decimal, $0.58\overline{3}$.

Type **+** 3 **÷** 8 **ENTER**. The decimal form of the sum is displayed.

Press **MATH** **ENTER** **ENTER**.

The fraction form of the sum, $\frac{23}{24}$, is displayed as 23/24.

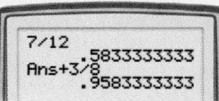
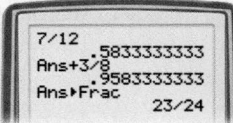
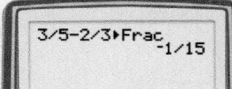

2 Use a graphing calculator to subtract $\frac{3}{5} - \frac{2}{3}$. Write the difference as a fraction.

Type 3 **÷** 5 **−** 2 **÷** 3 **MATH** **ENTER** **ENTER**.

The answer is $-\frac{1}{15}$.

Think and Discuss

1. Why is the difference in **2** negative?

2. Type 0.33333 . . . (pressing 3 at least twelve times). Press **MATH** **ENTER** **ENTER** to write $0.\overline{3}$ as a fraction. Now do the same for $0.\overline{9}$. What happens to $0.\overline{9}$? How does the fraction for $0.\overline{3}$ help to explain this result?

Try This

Use a calculator to add or subtract. Write each result as a fraction.

1. $\frac{1}{4} + \frac{2}{7}$ $\frac{15}{28}$
2. $\frac{7}{8} - \frac{2}{3}$ $\frac{5}{24}$
3. $\frac{7}{15} + \frac{3}{10}$ $\frac{23}{30}$
4. $\frac{1}{3} - \frac{5}{7}$ $\frac{-8}{21}$
5. $\frac{5}{32} + \frac{2}{11}$ $\frac{119}{352}$
6. $\frac{31}{101} - \frac{3}{5}$ $\frac{-148}{505}$
7. $\frac{4}{15} + \frac{7}{16}$ $\frac{169}{240}$
8. $\frac{3}{35} - \frac{3}{37}$ $\frac{6}{1295}$

Possible answers to *Think and Discuss*

1. The difference is negative because $\frac{2}{3}$ is greater than $\frac{3}{5}$.

2. $\frac{1}{3}$; 1; Since $3(0.0\overline{3}) = 0.0\overline{9}$, we have $3(0.\overline{3}) = 3(\frac{1}{3}) = 1$.

Technology LAB Organizer

Use with Lesson 2-6

Pacing:
Traditional $\frac{1}{2}$ day
Block $\frac{1}{4}$ day

Objective: Use a graphing calculator to add and subtract fractions.

Materials: Graphing calculator

Online Edition
Scientific Calculator, TechKeys

Resources
Technology Lab Activities
Lab 2-6 Recording Sheet

Teach
Discuss

Have students practice adding and subtracting fractions with like and unlike denominators. Ask them why it might be easier to use a calculator to add or subtract fractions with unlike denominators.

Close
Key Concept

When you add or subtract fractions with unlike denominators, it can save time to use your calculator. It is important to know how to change a decimal into a fraction using a calculator.

Assessment

Use a calculator to add or subtract. Write each result as a fraction.

1. $\frac{3}{8} + \frac{1}{5}$ $\frac{23}{40}$
2. $\frac{5}{12} - \frac{11}{18}$ $\frac{-7}{36}$

State Resources

go.hrw.com
State Resources Online
KEYWORD: MT7 Resources

Organizer

Objective: Assess students' mastery of concepts and skills in Lessons 2-1 through 2-6.

Resources

 Assessment Resources
Section 2A Quiz

 Test & Practice Generator
One-Stop Planner®

INTERVENTION

Resources

 Ready to Go On?
Intervention and
Enrichment Worksheets

💿 **Ready to Go On? CD-ROM**

🪐 **Ready to Go On? Online**

my.hrw.com

Quiz for Lessons 2-1 Through 2-6

✓ **2-1** Rational Numbers

Simplify.

1. $\frac{12}{36}$ $\frac{1}{3}$

2. $\frac{15}{48}$ $\frac{5}{16}$

3. $\frac{33}{88}$ $\frac{3}{8}$

4. $\frac{55}{122}$ $\frac{55}{122}$

✓ **2-2** Comparing and Ordering Rational Numbers

Write the numbers in order from least to greatest.

5. $-1.2, \frac{2}{3}, 0.5, -\frac{3}{4}$

6. $3\frac{5}{7}, 0.1, \frac{7}{8}, 0.275$

7. $2.3, -\frac{3}{2}, -3, -3\frac{8}{9}$

8. $2\frac{10}{13}, 1.3, \frac{33}{8}, 2.99$

Answer boxes (top right):

5. $-1.2, -\frac{3}{4}, 0.5, \frac{2}{3}$

6. $0.1, 0.275, \frac{7}{8}, 3\frac{5}{7}$

7. $-3\frac{8}{9}, -3, -\frac{3}{2}, 2.3$

8. $1.3, 2\frac{10}{13}, 2.99, \frac{33}{8}$

✓ **2-3** Adding and Subtracting Rational Numbers

Add or subtract. Write each answer in simplest form.

9. $65.8 - 24.24$ **41.56**

10. $-\frac{3}{7} + 2\frac{4}{7}$ $2\frac{1}{7}$

11. $\frac{5}{6} + \left(-2\frac{1}{6}\right)$ $-1\frac{1}{3}$

12. Darius and Jamal ride their bicycles home from school every day. Each day this week, they have timed themselves to see how long the ride takes. On Monday, they made it home in about 0.25 hour. Today, it took them $\frac{3}{10}$ hour. How much longer did it take today? $\frac{1}{20}$ hour or 0.05 hour

✓ **2-4** Multiplying Rational Numbers

Multiply. Write each answer in simplest form.

13. $2\left(4\frac{2}{3}\right)$ $9\frac{1}{3}$

14. $2\frac{2}{5}\left(\frac{7}{36}\right)$ $\frac{7}{15}$

15. $3.8(4)$ **15.2**

16. $\frac{-1}{7}\left(\frac{-3}{4}\right)$ $\frac{3}{28}$

17. Robert has a piece of twine that is $\frac{3}{4}$ yard long. He needs a piece of twine that is $\frac{2}{3}$ of this length. How long of a piece of twine does Robert need? $\frac{1}{2}$ yd

✓ **2-5** Dividing Rational Numbers

Divide. Write each answer in simplest form.

18. $\frac{3}{5} \div \frac{4}{15}$ $2\frac{1}{4}$

19. $2.7 \div 3$ **0.9**

20. $-\frac{2}{3} \div 1$ $-\frac{2}{3}$

21. $-4\frac{6}{7} \div 2\frac{5}{6}$ $-1\frac{5}{7}$

✓ **2-6** Adding and Subtracting with Unlike Denominators

Add or subtract. Write each answer in simplest form.

22. $\frac{2}{7} + \frac{1}{4}$ $\frac{15}{28}$

23. $1\frac{2}{3} + 3\frac{5}{9}$ $5\frac{2}{9}$

24. $6\frac{4}{7} - 3\frac{1}{5}$ $3\frac{13}{35}$

25. $3\frac{1}{6} - 1\frac{3}{4}$ $1\frac{5}{12}$

READY TO GO ON?
Diagnose and Prescribe

NO INTERVENE

YES ENRICH

READY TO GO ON? Intervention, Section 2A			
Ready to Go On? Intervention	📝 **Worksheets**	💿 **CD-ROM**	🪐 **Online**
✓ Lesson 2-1	2-1 Intervention	Activity 2-1	
✓ Lesson 2-2	2-2 Intervention	Activity 2-2	
✓ Lesson 2-3	2-3 Intervention	Activity 2-3	Diagnose and Prescribe Online
✓ Lesson 2-4	2-4 Intervention	Activity 2-4	
✓ Lesson 2-5	2-5 Intervention	Activity 2-5	
✓ Lesson 2-6	2-6 Intervention	Activity 2-6	

READY TO GO ON? Enrichment, Section 2A
📝 Worksheets
💿 CD-ROM
🪐 Online

Focus on Problem Solving

Focus on Problem Solving

Look Back

• **Is your answer reasonable?**

After you solve a word problem, ask yourself if your answer makes sense. You can round the numbers in the problem and estimate to find a reasonable answer. It may also help to write your answer in sentence form.

Read the problems below and tell which answer is most reasonable.

❶ Tonia calculates that she needs $47\frac{2}{3}$ pounds of compost to spread on her garden. There are 38.9 pounds of compost in her compost pile. How much compost does Tonia need to purchase?

Ⓐ about 9 pounds   Ⓒ about 6 pounds

Ⓑ about 87 pounds   Ⓓ about 15 pounds

❷ The Qin Dynasty in China began about 2170 years before the People's Republic of China was formed in 1949. When did the Qin Dynasty begin?

Ⓕ before 200 B.C.E.

Ⓖ between 200 B.C.E. and 200 C.E.

Ⓗ between 200 C.E. and 1949 C.E.

Ⓙ after 1949 C.E.

❸ On Mercury, the coldest temperature is about 600°C below the hottest temperature of 430°C. What is the coldest temperature on the planet?

Ⓐ about 1030°C

Ⓑ about −1030°C

Ⓒ about −170°C

Ⓓ about 170°C

❹ Julie is balancing her checkbook. Her beginning balance is $325.46, her deposits add up to $285.38, and her withdrawals add up to $683.27. What is her ending balance?

Ⓕ about −$70

Ⓖ about −$600

Ⓗ about $700

Ⓙ about $1300

SECTION 2B

Equations with Rational Numbers

One-Minute Section Planner

Lesson	Materials	MiC and Lab Resources
Lesson 2-7 Solving Equations with Rational Numbers • Solve equations with rational numbers. ☑ SAT-10 ☑ ITBS ☑ CTBS ☑ NAEP		
2-8 Hands-On Lab Model Two-Step Equations • Use algebra tiles to model and solve two-step equations. **Lesson 2-8** Solving Two-Step Equations • Solve two-step equations. ☑ SAT-10 ☑ ITBS ☑ CTBS ☑ NAEP	Algebra tiles (MK)	**MiC:** *Graphing Equations* pp. 28–35 **MiC:** *Algebra Rules* pp. 33–34 *Hands-On Lab Activities* 2-8

MK = *Manipulatives Kit*

Mathematics in Context

The units *Graphing Equations* and *Algebra Rules* from the *Mathematics in Context* © 2006 series can be used with Section 2B. See Section Planner above for suggestions for integrating *MiC* with *Holt Mathematics.*

Section Overview

Algebra with Rational Numbers

Why? Most real-world applications involve rational numbers.

Solving Equations with Rational Numbers

$$x - \frac{1}{3} = \frac{1}{2}$$
$$+ \frac{1}{3} = + \frac{1}{3}$$
$$x = \frac{1}{2} + \frac{1}{3}$$
$$x = \frac{3}{6} + \frac{2}{6}$$
$$x = \frac{5}{6}$$

$$1.25m = 40$$
$$\frac{1.25m}{1.25} = \frac{40}{1.25}$$
$$m = 32$$

$$\frac{2}{3}x = -\frac{1}{6}$$
$$\frac{2}{3}x \cdot \frac{3}{2} = -\frac{1}{6} \cdot \frac{3}{2}$$
$$x = -\frac{3}{12}$$
$$x = -\frac{1}{4}$$

Two-Step Equations

Why? You can solve some problems by using two-step equations.

Jill's auto repair bill was $225.
The parts cost $95 and the labor cost $52 per hour.
For how many hours of labor was Jill charged?

Solve
total bill = parts + labor

$$\begin{array}{rcl} 225 & = & 95 + 52h \\ -95 & = & -95 \\ \hline 130 & = & 52h \\ \frac{130}{52} & = & \frac{52h}{52} \\ 2.5 & = & h \end{array}$$

Check
$$225 = 95 + 52h$$
$$225 \overset{?}{=} 95 + 52(2.5)$$
$$225 \overset{?}{=} 95 + 130$$
$$225 \overset{?}{=} 225 ✔$$

Jill was charged for 2.5 hours of labor.

Objective: Students solve equations with rational numbers.

 Online Edition
Tutorial Videos, Interactivities

Countdown to Testing Week 4

Warm Up

Add or subtract.

1. $\frac{7}{10} + \frac{5}{10}$ $1\frac{1}{5}$

2. $2\frac{3}{8} - 1\frac{5}{16}$ $1\frac{1}{16}$

3. $4.8 + 3.6$ 8.4

4. $2.4 - 0.05$ 2.35

Problem of the Day

A computer word is made of strings of 0's and 1's. How many different words can be formed using 3 characters? (An example is 010.) **8**

Also available on transparency

Math teachers never die; they just reduce to lowest terms.

State Resources

2-7 Solving Equations with Rational Numbers

Learn to solve equations with rational numbers.

Painting a house can be a difficult task. In order to have a good surface for the new paint, the old paint must be cleaned, and sometimes even scraped off completely.

Sully runs his own house-painting business. When he plans a job, he estimates that he can paint $\frac{2}{5}$ of a house in one work day. You can write and solve an equation to find how long it would take Sully to paint 3 houses.

EXAMPLE 1 Solving Equations with Decimals

Solve.

A $y - 17.5 = 11$

$$y - 17.5 = 11$$
$$\underline{+\ 17.5 \quad\ +\ 17.5}$$ *Add 17.5 to both sides.*
$$y = 28.5$$

B $-4.2p = 12.6$

$$-4.2p = 12.6$$
$$\frac{-4.2p}{-4.2} = \frac{12.6}{-4.2}$$ *Divide both sides by −4.2.*
$$p = -3$$

C $\frac{t}{7.5} = 4$

$$\frac{t}{7.5} = 4$$
$$7.5 \cdot \frac{t}{7.5} = 7.5 \cdot 4$$ *Multiply both sides by 7.5.*
$$t = 30$$

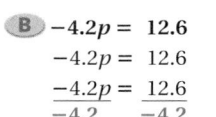 **Remember!**

Once you have solved an equation, it is a good idea to check your answer. To check your answer, substitute your answer for the variable in the original equation.

EXAMPLE 2 Solving Equations with Fractions

Solve.

A $x + \frac{1}{9} = -\frac{4}{9}$

$$x + \frac{1}{9} = -\frac{4}{9}$$
$$x + \frac{1}{9} - \frac{1}{9} = -\frac{4}{9} - \frac{1}{9}$$ *Subtract $\frac{1}{9}$ from both sides.*
$$x = -\frac{5}{9}$$

---

1 Introduce

Alternate Opener

EXPLORATION

2-7 Solving Equations with Rational Numbers

A box of cookies has 6 servings. Each serving contains 40.5 calories. How many calories are in the whole box?

40.5	40.5	= 81
40.5	40.5	= 81
40.5	40.5	= $\frac{81}{243}$

Equation
$40.5 \cdot 6 = c$
$243 = c$

Estimate the solution for each equation. Then use a calculator to solve.

	Equation	Estimate	Actual
1.	$124.75 - x = 50$		
2.	$x + 16.9 = 15.5$		
3.	$0.6x = 15$		
4.	$\frac{x}{1.25} = 8$		

Think and Discuss

5. **Describe** how you estimated the solutions for the equations in Problems 1−4.

6. **Discuss** whether it is easier to estimate the solutions of some equations than the solutions of others.

Motivate

Show the students equations such as $n + 4 = 9$, $3x = 12$, and $\frac{y}{5} = 4$.

Remind students that they learned how to solve these equations in Chapter 1. Have the students solve and check these equations. Tell the students that they will solve equations in the new lesson by the same methods.
$n = 5, x = 4, y = 20$

Explorations and answers are provided in *Alternate Openers: Explorations Transparencies.*

Solve.

B $x - \frac{1}{8} = \frac{9}{16}$

$$x - \frac{1}{8} = \frac{9}{16}$$

$$x - \frac{1}{8} + \frac{1}{8} = \frac{9}{16} + \frac{1}{8} \qquad \textit{Add } \frac{1}{8} \textit{ to both sides.}$$

$$x = \frac{9}{16} + \frac{2}{16} \qquad \textit{Find a common denominator, 16.}$$

$$x = \frac{11}{16}$$

C $\frac{3}{5}w = \frac{3}{16}$

$$\frac{3}{5}w = \frac{3}{16}$$

$$\frac{3}{5}w \div \frac{3}{5} = \frac{3}{16} \div \frac{3}{5} \qquad \textit{Divide both sides by } \frac{3}{5}.$$

$$\frac{\cancel{3}}{\cancel{5}}w \cdot \frac{\cancel{5}}{\cancel{3}} = \frac{3}{16} \cdot \frac{5}{\cancel{3}} \qquad \textit{Multiply by the reciprocal. Simplify.}$$

$$w = \frac{5}{16}$$

EXAMPLE **Solving Word Problems Using Equations**

Sully has agreed to paint 3 houses. If he knows that he can paint $\frac{2}{5}$ of a house in one day, how many days will it take him to paint all 3 houses?

Write an equation:

number of days	×	houses per day	=	number of houses
d	×	$\frac{2}{5}$	=	3

$$d \cdot \frac{2}{5} = 3$$

$$d \cdot \frac{2}{5} \div \frac{2}{5} = 3 \div \frac{2}{5} \qquad \textit{Divide both sides by } \frac{2}{5}.$$

$$d \cdot \frac{2}{5} \cdot \frac{5}{2} = 3 \cdot \frac{5}{2} \qquad \textit{Multiply by the reciprocal.}$$

$$d = \frac{15}{2}, \text{ or } 7\frac{1}{2} \qquad \textit{Simplify.}$$

Sully can paint 3 houses in $7\frac{1}{2}$ days.

Think and Discuss

1. Explain the first step in solving an addition equation with fractions having *like* denominators.

2. Explain the first step in solving an addition equation with fractions having *unlike* denominators.

Example 1

Solve.

A. $m + 4.6 = 9$ $m = 4.4$

B. $8.2p = -32.8$ $p = -4$

C. $\frac{x}{1.2} = 15$ $x = 18$

Example 2

Solve.

A. $n + \frac{2}{7} = -\frac{3}{7}$ $n = -\frac{5}{7}$

B. $y - \frac{1}{6} = \frac{2}{3}$ $y = \frac{5}{6}$

C. $\frac{5}{6}x = \frac{5}{8}$ $x = \frac{3}{4}$

Example 3

Mr. Rios wants to prepare a dessert, but only has $2\frac{2}{3}$ tablespoons of sugar. If each serving of the dessert has $\frac{2}{3}$ tablespoon of sugar, how many servings can he make for the party?   4

Also available on transparency

Possible answers to
Think and Discuss

1. Subtract the same fraction from both sides of the equation to isolate the variable on one side.

2. Find the least common denominator, or subtract the same fraction from both sides of the equation to isolate the variable on one side.

---

2 Teach

Guided Instruction

In this lesson, students learn to solve equations with rational numbers. To begin, remind students of the methods they used to solve equations with whole numbers and integers (Lessons 1-7 and 1-8). Demonstrate the similarity between solving those equations and solving equations in which the numbers are decimals and fractions. Emphasize that the algebra procedures are the same as those used to solve whole number and integer equations.

 Reaching All Learners
Through Cooperative Learning

Have students work in pairs. Each pair should have a sheet of paper with an incomplete equation such as $x + \underline{\quad} = \underline{\quad}$. Tell students to take turns replacing the blanks with rational numbers and then having their partner solve the equation. It may be helpful to provide students with a list of rational numbers to use, such as 3.4, 1.2, 4.2, 5.3, 0.3, -2.9, $\frac{1}{2}$, $\frac{2}{3}$, $-\frac{3}{5}$, $\frac{5}{8}$.

3 Close

Summarize

Remind students that one-step equations are solved the same way whether the constant numbers in the equations are whole numbers, integers, or rational numbers. Ask students what steps they would take to solve the equations that follow: $x + 8 = 12$, $x + 6 = -3$, $x + 2.4 = 1.5$, and $x + \frac{3}{4} = \frac{7}{8}$.

Possible answers: Subtract 8 from both sides; subtract 6 from both sides; subtract 2.4 from both sides; subtract $\frac{3}{4}$ from both sides.

Point out that these equations are all addition equations and that they all should be solved by subtraction.

2-7 Exercises

go.hrw.com
Homework Help Online
KEYWORD: MT7 2-7
Parent Resources Online
KEYWORD: MT7 Parent

Assignment Guide

If you finished Example **1** assign:
Average 1–6, 14–19, 34, 35, 54–61
Advanced 14–19, 47–49, 54–61

If you finished Example **2** assign:
Average 1–12, 14–27, 33–40, 54–61
Advanced 17–23, 37–46, 52, 54–61

If you finished Example **3** assign:
Average 1–40, 54–61
Advanced 17–23, 29–43, 50–61

Homework Quick Check

Quickly check key concepts.
Exercises: 14, 26, 28, 38, 44

Math Background

It is important for students to be able to solve equations that contain fractions and decimals as well as integers. They may find it helpful if they can begin to recognize equations by the included operation(s), rather than by the types of numbers they contain. For example, $x + \frac{3}{4} = -\frac{1}{2}$ should be recognized as an addition equation rather than a fraction problem. When teaching the Guided Practice exercises, you may want to have students first identify the type of equation before they solve it.

GUIDED PRACTICE

See Example **1** Solve.

1. $y + 17.3 = -65$
$y = -82.3$

2. $-5.2f = 36.4$ $f = -7$

3. $\frac{m}{3.2} = -6$ $m = -19.2$

4. $r - 15.8 = 24.6$
$r = 40.4$

5. $\frac{s}{15.42} = 6.3$ $s = 97.146$

6. $0.06g = 0.474$ $g = 7.9$

See Example **2**

7. $x + \frac{1}{9} = -\frac{4}{9}$ $x = -\frac{5}{9}$

8. $-\frac{3}{8} + k = -\frac{7}{8}$ $k = -\frac{1}{2}$

9. $\frac{5}{6}w = -\frac{7}{18}$ $w = -\frac{7}{15}$

10. $m - \frac{4}{3} = -\frac{4}{3}$ $m = 0$

11. $\frac{7}{17}y = -\frac{56}{17}$ $y = -8$

12. $t + \frac{4}{13} = \frac{12}{39}$ $t = 0$

See Example **3** 13. Alonso runs a company called Speedy House Painters. His workers can paint $\frac{3}{4}$ of a house in one day. How many days would it take them to paint 6 houses? **9 days**

INDEPENDENT PRACTICE

24. $x = \frac{1}{2}$ 25. $r = -\frac{5}{7}$

See Example **1** Solve.

14. $y + 16.7 = -49$
$y = -65.7$

15. $4.7m = -32.9$ $m = -7$

16. $-\frac{h}{7.8} = 2$ $h = -15.6$

17. $k - 3.2 = -6.8$
$k = -3.6$

18. $\frac{z}{11.4} = 6$ $z = 68.4$

19. $c + 5.98 = 9.1$
$c = 3.12$

See Example **2** 20. $j + \frac{1}{3} = \frac{3}{4}$ $j = \frac{5}{12}$ 21. $\frac{5}{6}d = \frac{3}{15}$ $d = \frac{6}{25}$ 22. $7h = \frac{14}{33}$ $h = \frac{2}{33}$ 23. $\frac{2}{3} + x = \frac{5}{8}$ $-\frac{1}{24}$

24. $x - \frac{1}{16} = \frac{7}{16}$
$x = \frac{1}{2}$

25. $r + \frac{4}{7} = -\frac{1}{7}$
$r = -\frac{5}{7}$

26. $\frac{5}{6}c = \frac{7}{24}$ $c = \frac{7}{20}$

27. $\frac{7}{8}d = \frac{11}{12}$ $1\frac{1}{21}$

See Example **3** 28. A professional lawn care service can mow $2\frac{3}{4}$ acres of lawn in one hour. How many hours would it take them to mow a lawn that is $6\frac{7}{8}$ acres? $5\frac{1}{2}$ **hours**

PRACTICE AND PROBLEM SOLVING

Extra Practice
See page 785.

Earth Science The largest of all known diamonds, the Cullinan diamond, weighed 3106 carats before it was cut into 105 gems. The largest cut, Cullinan I, or the Great Star of Africa, weighs $530\frac{1}{3}$ carats. Another cut, Cullinan II, weighs $317\frac{2}{5}$ carats. Cullinan III weighs $94\frac{2}{5}$ carats, and Cullinan IV weighs $63\frac{3}{5}$ carats.

29. How many carats of the original Cullinan diamond were left after the Great Star of Africa and Cullinan II were cut? $2258\frac{2}{5}$ **carats**

30. How much more does Cullinan II weigh than Cullinan IV? $253\frac{4}{5}$ **carats**

31. Which diamond weighs 223 carats less than Cullinan II? **Cullinan III**

32. **Nutrition** An entire can of chicken noodle soup has 6.25 grams of total fat. There are 2.5 servings per can. How many grams of total fat are in a single serving of chicken noodle soup? **2.5 g**

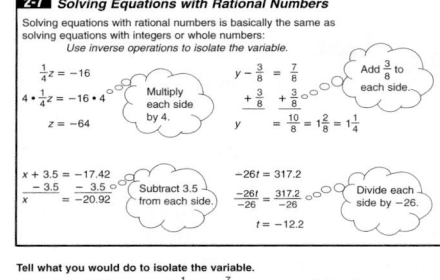

State Resources

go.hrw.com
State Resources Online
KEYWORD: MT7 Resources

Solve.

33. $z - \frac{2}{9} = \frac{1}{9}$ $z = \frac{1}{3}$ **34.** $-5f = -1.5$ $f = 0.3$ **35.** $\frac{j}{7.2} = -3$ $j = -21.6$ **36.** $\frac{2}{5} + x = 0.25$ $-\frac{3}{20}$

37. $t - \frac{3}{4} = 6\frac{1}{4}$ $t = 7$ **38.** $\frac{x}{0.5} = \frac{7}{8}$ $\frac{7}{16}$ **39.** $\frac{6}{7}d = -\frac{3}{7}$ $d = -\frac{1}{2}$ **40.** $-4.7g = -28.2$ $g = 6$

41. $\frac{v}{5.5} = -5.5$ $v = -30.25$ **42.** $r + \frac{5}{6} = -3\frac{1}{6}$ $r = -4$ **43.** $y + 2.8 = -1.4$ $y = -4.2$

44. $-\frac{1}{15} + r = \frac{3}{5}$ $r = \frac{2}{3}$ **45.** $-3c = \frac{3}{20}$ $c = -\frac{1}{20}$ **46.** $m - 2.34 = 8.2$ $m = 10.54$

47. $y - 57 = -2.8$ $y = 54.2$ **48.** $-18 = -9.6 + f$ $f = -8.4$ **49.** $\frac{4m}{0.8} = -7$ $m = -1.4$

50. Multi-Step Jack is tiling along the walls of the rectangular kitchen with the tile shown. The kitchen has a length of $243\frac{3}{4}$ inches and a width of $146\frac{1}{4}$ inches.

   a. How many tiles will fit along the length of the room?   **15 tiles**

   b. How many tiles will fit along its width? **9 tiles**

   c. If Jack needs 48 tiles to tile around all four walls of the kitchen, how many boxes of ten tiles must he buy? (*Hint:* He must buy whole boxes of tile.)   **5 boxes**

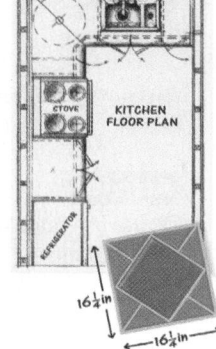

KITCHEN FLOOR PLAN

$16\frac{1}{4}$ in

$16\frac{1}{4}$ in

51.
Possible answer: The salesperson multiplied 60 by 1.8 instead of dividing by 1.8 to get about 33 seconds.

52. Possible answer: No, *a* is $\frac{1}{3}$ of *b* describes the equation $a = \frac{1}{3}b$, but $\frac{1}{3}a = b$ means that *b* is $\frac{1}{3}$ of *a*.

 51. What's the Error? Janice is thinking about buying a CD writer that burns 1.8 megabytes of data per second. A computer salesperson told her that if she had 60 megabytes of data to burn, she could burn it in about 2 minutes with this writer. What was his error?

52. Write About It If *a* is $\frac{1}{3}$ of *b*, is it correct to say $\frac{1}{3}a = b$? Explain.

53. Challenge A 200-carat diamond was cut into two equal pieces to form two diamonds. One of the diamonds was cut again, reducing it by $\frac{1}{5}$ its weight. In a final cut, it was reduced by $\frac{1}{4}$ its new weight. How many carats remained? **60 carats**

TEST PREP and Spiral Review

54. Multiple Choice If $\frac{12}{36} = 2w$, what is the value of w?

  Ⓐ $\frac{24}{36}$ Ⓑ $\frac{24}{72}$ Ⓒ $\frac{1}{3}$ Ⓓ $\frac{1}{6}$

55. Short Response The performance of a musical arrangement lasted $6\frac{1}{4}$ minutes. The song consisted of 3 verses that each lasted the same number of minutes. Write and solve an equation to find the length of each verse.

$$3v = 6\tfrac{1}{4};\ 2\tfrac{1}{12}\ \text{minutes}$$

Write an algebraic expression for each word phrase. (Lesson 1-2)

56. 15 less than a number p $p - 15$ **57.** half of the sum of m and 19 $\frac{1}{2}(m + 19)$

Add or subtract. Write each answer in simplest form. (Lesson 2-6)

58. $\frac{7}{8} + \frac{1}{6}$ $1\frac{1}{24}$ **59.** $4\frac{2}{3} + 5\frac{3}{4}$ $10\frac{5}{12}$ **60.** $6\frac{5}{8} - 2\frac{1}{20}$ $4\frac{23}{40}$ **61.** $2\frac{8}{9} - \frac{4}{5}$ $2\frac{4}{45}$

CHALLENGE 2-7

Challenge
2-7 *Location, Location, Location*

An equation that has a variable in the denominator of one or more of its terms is called a **fractional equation**.

One method of solution is to clear the equation of fractions by multiplying each side of the equation by the LCD.

$\frac{1}{2} + \frac{1}{x} = \frac{3}{5}$ The LCD of 2, x, and 5 is $10x$, with $x \neq 0$.

$10x\left(\frac{1}{2} + \frac{1}{x}\right) = 10x\left(\frac{3}{5}\right)$ Multiply each side by $10x$.

$10x \cdot \frac{1}{2} + 10x \cdot \frac{1}{x} = 10x \cdot \frac{3}{5}$ Distributive Property

$5x + 10 = 6x$ Simplify.

$5x - 5x + 10 = 6x - 5x$ Subtract $5x$ from each side.

$10 = x$

Check:
$\frac{1}{2} + \frac{1}{x} = \frac{3}{5}$

$\frac{1}{2} + \frac{1}{10} \stackrel{?}{=} \frac{3}{5}$ Substitute 10 for x in the original equation.

$\frac{5}{10} + \frac{1}{10} \stackrel{?}{=} \frac{3}{5}$ Do not repeat the method of solution.

$\frac{6}{10} \stackrel{?}{=} \frac{3}{5}$ Work each side separately.

$\frac{3}{5} = \frac{3}{5}$ ✔

Solve and check.

1. $\frac{4}{7} + \frac{2}{x} = \frac{2}{3}$ **2.** $\frac{10}{x} + \frac{8}{x} = 9$ **3.** $\frac{15}{x} = 7 + \frac{9}{2x}$

   $x = 21$ $x = 2$ $x = 1\frac{1}{2}$

PROBLEM SOLVING 2-7

Problem Solving
2-7 *Solving Equations with Rational Numbers*

Write the correct answer.

1. In the last 150 years, the average height of people in industrialized nations has increased by $\frac{1}{3}$ foot. Today, American men have an average height of $5\frac{7}{12}$ feet. What was the average height of American men 150 years ago?

$5\frac{1}{4}$ feet

2. Jaime has a length of ribbon that is $23\frac{1}{2}$ in. long. If she plans to cut the ribbon into pieces that are $\frac{3}{4}$ in. long, into how many pieces can she cut the ribbon? (She cannot use partial pieces.)

31 pieces

3. Todd's restaurant bill for dinner was $15.55. After he left a tip, he spent a total of $18.00 on dinner. How much money did Todd leave for a tip?

$2.45

4. The difference between the boiling point and melting point of Hydrogen is 6.47°C. The melting point of Hydrogen is −259.34°C. What is the boiling point of Hydrogen?

−252.87°C

Choose the letter for the best answer.

5. Justin Gatlin won the Olympic gold in the 100-m dash in 2004 with a time of 9.85 seconds. His time was 0.95 seconds faster than Francis Jarvis who won the 100-m dash in 1900. What was Jarvis' time in 1900?

A 8.95 seconds
B 10.65 seconds
Ⓒ 10.80 seconds
D 11.20 seconds

6. The balance in Susan's checking account was $245.35. After the bank deposited interest into the account, her balance went to $248.02. How much interest did the bank pay Susan?

F $1.01
Ⓖ $2.67
H $3.95
J $493.37

7. After a morning shower, there was $\frac{17}{100}$ in. of rain in the rain gauge. It rained again an hour later and the rain gauge showed $\frac{1}{4}$ in. of rain. How much did it rain the second time?

Ⓐ $\frac{2}{25}$ in.
B $\frac{1}{6}$ in.
C $\frac{21}{50}$ in.
D $\frac{3}{8}$ in.

8. Two-third of John's savings account is being saved for his college education. If $2500 of his savings is for his college education, how much money in total is in his savings account?

F $1666.67
Ⓖ $3750
H $4250.83
J $5000

ONGOING ASSESSMENT and INTERVENTION ⬅◆➡

Diagnose Before the Lesson
2-7 Warm Up, TE p. 92

Monitor During the Lesson
2-7 Know-It Notebook
2-7 Questioning Strategies

Assess After the Lesson
2-7 Lesson Quiz, TE p. 95

TEST PREP DOCTOR ➕ Students may not realize that they do not have to solve the equation in Exercise 54 by direct methods. Instead of solving the given equation for the value of *w*, suggest that students reduce the fraction on the left side of the equation, then substitute the values from all answer choices until they find the correct answer.

✍ **Journal**
Remind students that they solved one-step equations in Chapter 1. Have students write about how the equations are the same and how they are different.

Power Presentations with PowerPoint®

✓ **2-7 Lesson Quiz**

Solve.

1. $x - 23.3 = 17.8$ $x = 41.1$

2. $j + \frac{2}{3} = -14\frac{3}{4}$ $j = -15\frac{5}{12}$

3. $9y = \frac{3}{5}$ $y = \frac{1}{15}$

4. $\frac{d}{4} = 2\frac{3}{8}$ $d = 9\frac{1}{2}$

5. Tamara can mow $\frac{2}{5}$ acre in one hour. If her yard is 2 acres, how many hours will it take her to mow the entire yard? 5

Also available on transparency

Pacing:
Traditional $\frac{1}{2}$ day
Block $\frac{1}{4}$ day

Objective: Use algebra tiles to model and solve two-step equations.

Materials: Algebra tiles

 Online Edition
Algebra Tiles

 Countdown to Testing Week 4

Resources

 Hands-On Lab Activities
Lab 2-8 Recording Sheet

Teach
Discuss

Have students use guess-and-check to find the solution to the equation $3x + 4 = 10$. Then have them use algebra tiles to model and solve the equation.

Close
Key Concept

When you use algebra tiles to model and solve an equation, you can see how the numbers in the equation are grouped to calculate the final answer.

Assessment

Use algebra tiles to solve each equation.

1. $3x + 4 = 7$ $x = 1$
2. $2x - 9 = 3$ $x = 6$
3. $5x + 6 = 1$ $x = -1$

State Resources

go.hrw.com
State Resources Online
KEYWORD: MT7 Resources

Hands-On LAB 2-8

Model Two-Step Equations

Use with Lesson 2-8

go.hrw.com
Lab Resources Online
KEYWORD: MT7 Lab2

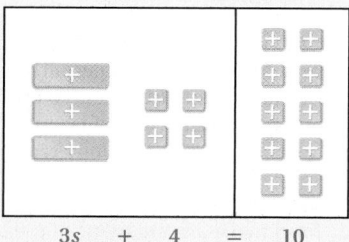

KEY
   = +1
   = −1
   = variable

REMEMBER
   +   = 0
• You can perform the same operation with the same numbers on both sides of an equation without changing the value of the equation.

You can use algebra tiles to model and solve two-step equations. To solve a two-step equation, you use two different operations.

Activity

1   Use algebra tiles to model and solve $3s + 4 = 10$.

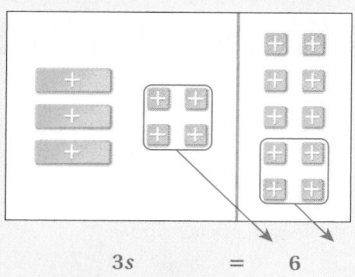

$3s \quad + \quad 4 \quad = \quad 10$

Two steps are needed to solve this equation.

Step 1: Remove 4 yellow tiles from each side.   **Step 2:** Divide each side into 3 equal groups.

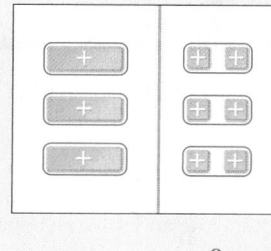

$3s \quad = \quad 6$ $s \quad = \quad 2$

Substitute to check:

$$3s + 4 \stackrel{?}{=} 10$$
$$3(2) + 4 \stackrel{?}{=} 10$$
$$6 + 4 \stackrel{?}{=} 10$$
$$10 \stackrel{?}{=} 10 \checkmark$$

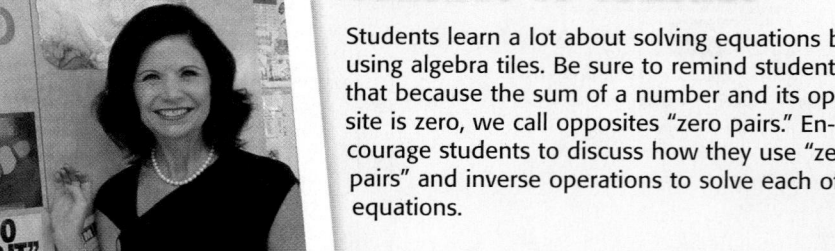

Debbie Brown
Austin, Texas

Teacher to Teacher

Students learn a lot about solving equations by using algebra tiles. Be sure to remind students that because the sum of a number and its opposite is zero, we call opposites "zero pairs." Encourage students to discuss how they use "zero pairs" and inverse operations to solve each of the equations.

② Use algebra tiles to model and solve $2r + 4 = -6$.

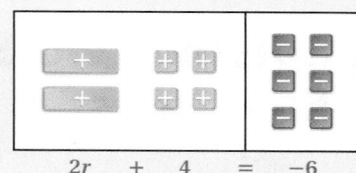

$$2r \quad + \quad 4 \quad = \quad -6$$

Step 1: Since 4 is being added to $2r$, add 4 red tiles to both sides and remove the zero pairs on the left side.

Step 2: Divide each side into 2 equal groups.

Add −4 to both sides.

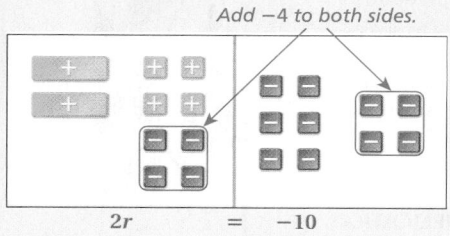

$$2r \quad = \quad -10$$

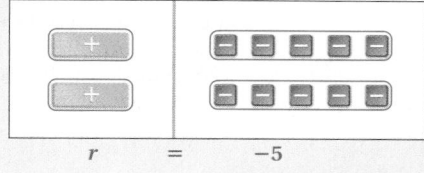

$$r \quad = \quad -5$$

Substitute to check:

$$2r + 4 \overset{?}{=} -6$$
$$2(-5) + 4 \overset{?}{=} -6$$
$$-10 + 4 \overset{?}{=} -6$$
$$-6 = -6 ✔$$

Think and Discuss

1. Why can you add zero pairs to one side of an equation without having to add them to the other side as well?

2. Show how you could have modeled to check your solution for each equation.

Try This

Use algebra tiles to model and solve each of the following equations.

1. $2x + 3 = 5$ $x = 1$ 2. $4p - 3 = 9$ $p = 3$ 3. $5r - 6 = -11$ $r = -1$ 4. $3n + 5 = -4$
$n = -3$
5. $6b + 8 = 2$ 6. $2a + 2 = 6$ $a = 2$ 7. $4m + 4 = 4$ $m = 0$ 8. $7h - 8 = 41$
$b = -1$ $h = 7$

9. Gerry walked dogs five times a week and got paid the same amount each day. One week his boss added on a $15 bonus. That week Gerry earned $90. What was his daily salary?   **$15**

1. Adding zero pairs in a model is equivalent to adding zero on one side of an algebraic equation. The equation remains balanced.

2.

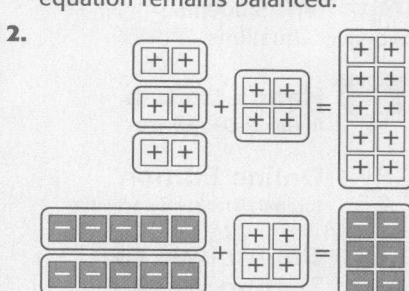

Answers to *Try This*

1.
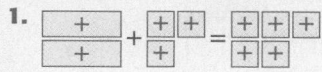

2.
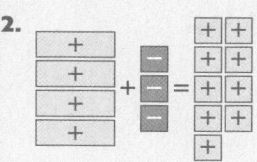

3.
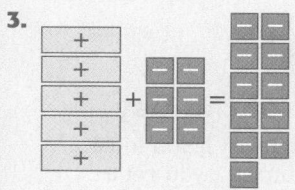

4.
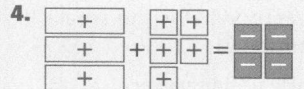

5.
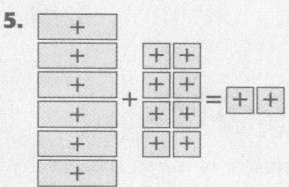

6.
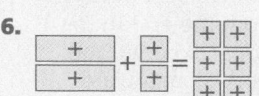

7.

8.
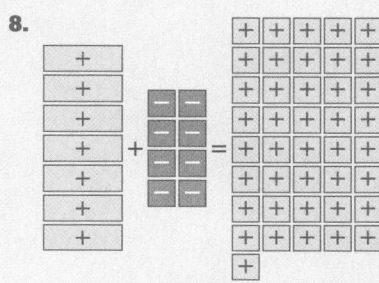

Objective: Students solve two-step equations.

 Hands-On Lab
In *Hands-On Activities*

 Online Edition
Tutorial Videos, Interactivities

 Countdown to Testing Week 4

 **Power Presentations**
with PowerPoint®

Warm Up

Solve.

1. $x + 12 = 35$ $x = 23$

2. $8x = 120$ $x = 15$

3. $\frac{y}{9} = 7$ $y = 63$

4. $-34 = y + 56$ $y = -90$

Problem of the Day

x is an odd integer. If you triple x and then subtract 7, you get a prime number. What is the smallest possible x? (*Hint:* What is the smallest prime number?) $x = 3$

Also available on transparency

Math Humor

Several surgeries only made the author's condition worse. So he wrote his new novel from the end to the beginning. He hoped to undo the operations by working backward.

State Resources

 **go.hrw.com**
State Resources Online
KEYWORD: MT7 Resources

Learn to solve two-step equations.

Sometimes more than one inverse operation is needed to solve an equation. Before solving, ask yourself, "What is being done to the variable and in what order?" One method to solve the equation is to then work backward to undo the operations.

The Kuhr family bought tickets to see a circus. The ticket service charged a service fee for the order. The number of tickets the Kuhrs bought can be found by solving a two-step equation.

EXAMPLE 1 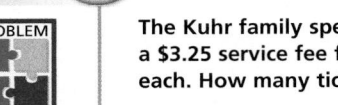 **PROBLEM SOLVING APPLICATION**

The Kuhr family spent $52.00 for circus tickets. This cost included a $3.25 service fee for the order, and the circus tickets cost $9.75 each. How many tickets did the Kuhrs buy? Justify your answer.

1 Understand the Problem

The **answer** is the number of tickets that the Kuhrs bought. List the **important information:** The service fee is $3.25 per order, the tickets cost $9.75 each, and the total cost is $52.

Let t represent the number of tickets bought.

Total cost	=	Tickets	+	Service Fee
52.00	=	9.75t	+	3.25

2 Make a Plan

Think: First the variable is multiplied by 9.75, and then 3.25 is added to the result. Work backward to solve the equation. Undo the operations in reverse order: First subtract 3.25 from both sides of the equation, and then divide both sides of the new equation by 9.75.

3 Solve

$$\begin{array}{rl} 52.00 &= 9.75t + 3.25 \\ -\,3.25 & \qquad -\,3.25 \quad \textit{Subtract 3.25 from both sides.} \\ \hline 48.75 &= 9.75t \end{array}$$

$$\frac{48.75}{9.75} = \frac{9.75t}{9.75} \qquad \textit{Divide both sides by 9.75.}$$

$$5 = t$$

The Kuhrs bought 5 tickets.

---

1 Introduce

Alternate Opener

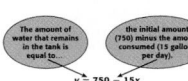
Motivate

Show the students a box wrapped in paper with a string or ribbon wrapped around it. You may want to wrap a small box in front of the class. Demonstrate that to open it, the ribbon is removed, then the wrapping paper is removed, and then the box is opened. Ask the students to think about the steps that were taken when the gift was wrapped. Point out that to unwrap the gift, the steps must be reversed.

Explorations and answers are provided in *Alternate Openers: Explorations Transparencies*.

 **Look Back**

You can use a table to decide whether your answer is reasonable.

Tickets	Cost of Tickets	Service Charge	Total Cost
1	$9.75	$3.25	$13.00
2	$19.50	$3.25	$22.75
3	$29.25	$3.25	$32.50
4	$39.00	$3.25	$42.25
5	$48.75	$3.25	$52.00

Five tickets is a reasonable answer.

Sometimes, a two-step equation contains a term or an expression with a denominator. In these cases, it is often easier to first multiply both sides of the equation by the denominator in order to remove it, and then work to isolate the variable.

EXAMPLE 2 **Solving Two-Step Equations**

Solve $\frac{r+7}{4} = 5$.

A Method 1: Work backward to isolate the variable.

$$\frac{r+7}{4} = 5$$
$$\frac{r}{4} + \frac{7}{4} = 5 \qquad \textit{Rewrite the expression as the sum of two fractions.}$$

Think: First the variable is **divided by 4**, and then $\frac{7}{4}$ **is added.**
To isolate the variable, **subtract $\frac{7}{4}$**, and then **multiply by 4.**

$$\frac{r}{4} + \frac{7}{4} - \frac{7}{4} = 5 - \frac{7}{4} \qquad \textit{Subtract } \frac{7}{4} \textit{ from both sides.}$$
$$(4)\frac{r}{4} = \frac{13}{4}(4) \qquad \textit{Multiply both sides by 4.}$$
$$r = 13$$

B Method 2: Multiply both sides of the equation by the denominator.

$$\frac{r+7}{4} = 5$$
$$(4)\frac{r+7}{4} = 5(4) \qquad \textit{Multiply both sides by 4.}$$
$$r + 7 = 20$$
$$\underline{-7 \quad -7} \qquad \textit{Subtract 7 from both sides.}$$
$$r = 13$$

Think and Discuss

1. Describe how you would solve $4(x - 2) = 16$.

2. Explain how to check your solution to an equation.

Power Presentations
with PowerPoint®

Additional Examples

Example 1
The mechanic's bill to repair Mr. Wong's car was $650. The mechanic charges $45 an hour for labor, and the parts that were used cost $443. How many hours did the mechanic work on the car? **4.6 hr**

Example 2
Solve.

A. $\frac{n}{3} + 7 = 22$ $\qquad n = 45$

B. $\frac{y - 4}{3} = 9$ $\qquad y = 31$

Also available on transparency

Possible answers to
Think and Discuss

1. Divide both sides by 4, and then add 2 to both sides.

2. Substitute the solution for the variable in the original equation to see if it makes the equation true.

 **Teach**

Guided Instruction

In this lesson, students learn to solve two-step equations. Remind students of the order of operations for evaluating expressions. Tell students that to solve an equation, the order of operations must be reversed. Point out that they should usually undo addition and subtraction first and then undo multiplication and division.

Teaching Tip **Inclusion** Remind students to check solutions by substituting the value into the original equation and evaluating to make sure both sides are equal.

 Reaching All Learners
Through Cooperative Learning

Give each student the following situations:

1. Car repair: $40 per hour labor, $430 parts, $690 total cost. How many hours of labor? **6.5**

2. T-shirt printing $120 set up fee, $3 per shirt, total cost $264. How many shirts were ordered? **48**

3. Salesman's salary $9 per hour, $250 in sales commissions, total weekly salary $565. How many hours of work this week? **35**

Have each student write an equation for the problem and pass it to the student on their left, who solves the equation. Then the next student checks the solution.

 Close

Summarize

Remind students to reverse the order of operations to solve equations. Point out that addition and subtraction are not always the operations that should be undone first. For an equation such as the one in Example 2B, division should be undone first.

2-8 Exercises

go.hrw.com
Homework Help Online
KEYWORD: MT7 2-8
Parent Resources Online
KEYWORD: MT7 Parent

Assignment Guide

If you finished **Example ①** assign:
Average 1, 10, 34–36, 38–41, 43–52
Advanced 10, 34–52

If you finished **Example ②** assign:
Average 1–18, 19–26, 34–36, 38–41, 43–52
Advanced 10, 25–52

Homework Quick Check
Quickly check key concepts.
Exercises: 10, 16, 26, 36, 38

Math Background

The method of reversing the order of operations suggested in the lesson is not the only possible method for solving equations. Some equations may be solved with different steps in different orders as long as algebraic properties are applied correctly. For example, the equation in the first Think and Discuss can be solved in at least two different ways:

$$4(x - 2) = 16$$
$$4x - 8 = 16$$
$$\underline{+8 \quad +8}$$
$$4x = 24$$
$$\frac{4x}{4} = \frac{24}{4}$$
$$x = 6$$

$$4(x - 2) = 16$$
$$\frac{4(x - 2)}{4} = \frac{16}{4}$$
$$x - 2 = 4$$
$$\underline{+2 \quad +2}$$
$$x = 6$$

State Resources

go.hrw.com
State Resources Online
KEYWORD: MT7 Resources

GUIDED PRACTICE

See Example ① **1.** Adele is paid a weekly salary of $685. She is paid an additional $23.50 for every hour of overtime he works. This week his total pay, including regular salary and overtime, was $849.50. How many hours of overtime did Adele work this week? **7 hours**

See Example ② Solve.

2. $\frac{t - 3}{2} = 75$ **153**   **3.** $\frac{t + 10}{6} = 11$ **56**   **4.** $\frac{r - 12}{7} = 6$ **54**   **5.** $\frac{x + 7}{11} = 11$ **114**

6. $\frac{b + 24}{2} = 13$ **2**   **7.** $\frac{q - 11}{5} = 23$ **126**   **8.** $\frac{a - 3}{28} = 3$ **87**   **9.** $\frac{y - 13}{8} = 14$ **125**

INDEPENDENT PRACTICE

See Example ① **10.** The cost of a family membership at a health club is $58 per month plus a one-time $129 start-up fee. If a family spent $651, how many months is their membership? **9 months**

See Example ② Solve.

11. $\frac{m + 6}{-3} = 4$ **−18** **12.** $\frac{c - 1}{2} = 12$ **25** **13.** $\frac{g - 2}{2} = -46$ **−90** **14.** $\frac{h + 20}{9} = 11$ **79**

15. $\frac{h + 19}{19} = 2$ **19** **16.** $\frac{y - 3}{4} = -27$ **−105** **17.** $\frac{z - 4}{10} = 9$ **94** **18.** $\frac{n - 31}{10} = 22$ **251**

PRACTICE AND PROBLEM SOLVING

Extra Practice
See page 785.

Solve.

19. $5w + 2.7 = 12.8$ **2.02** **20.** $15 - 3x = -6$ **7** **21.** $\frac{m}{5} + 6 = 9$ **15**

22. $\frac{z + 9}{4} = 2.1$ **−0.6** **23.** $2x + \frac{2}{3} = \frac{4}{5}$ **$\frac{2}{30}$** **24.** $9 = -5g - 23$ **−6.4 or −6$\frac{2}{5}$**

25. $6z - 3 = 0$ **0.5 or $\frac{1}{2}$** **26.** $\frac{5}{2}d - \frac{3}{2} = -\frac{1}{2}$ **$\frac{2}{5}$** **27.** $58k + 35 = 615$ **10**

28. $8 = 6 + \frac{p}{2}$ **4** **29.** $40 - 3n = -23$ **21** **30.** $\frac{17 + s}{15} = -4$ **−77**

31. $9y - 7.2 = 4.5$ **1.3** **32.** $\frac{2}{3} - 6h = -\frac{13}{6}$ **$\frac{17}{36}$** **33.** $-1 = \frac{5}{8}b + \frac{3}{8}$ **$-\frac{11}{5}$**

37.
Possible answer:
Method 1: Work backward to isolate the variable.
$$\frac{m}{2} - \frac{3}{2} = 37$$
$$\frac{m}{2} - \frac{3}{2} + \frac{3}{2} = 37 + \frac{3}{2}$$
$$(2)\frac{m}{2} = \frac{77}{2}(2)$$
$$m = 77$$

Method 2: Multiply both sides by the denominator.
$$(2)\frac{m - 3}{2} = 37(2)$$
$$m - 3 = 74$$
$$m = 77$$

Translate each sentence into an equation. Then solve the equation.

34. The quotient of a number and 2, minus 9, is 14. **$\frac{n}{2} - 9 = 14$; 46**

35. A number decreased by 7 and then divided by 5 is 13. **$\frac{n - 7}{5} = 13$; 72**

36. The sum of 15 and 7 times a number is 99. **$15 + 7n = 99$; 12**

37. Show two ways to solve the equation $\frac{m - 3}{2} = 37$. Check your answer.

38. Consumer Math A long distance phone company charges $19.95 per month plus $0.05 per minute for calls. If a family's monthly long distance bill is $23.74, how many minutes of long distance did they use? **75 minutes**

RETEACH 2-8

LESSON **2-8**
Reteach
Solving Two-Step Equations

To solve an equation, it is important to first note how it is formed. Then, work backward to undo each operation.

$4z + 3 = 15$ $\frac{z}{4} - 3 = 7$ $\frac{z + 3}{4} = 7$

| The variable is multiplied by 4 and then 3 is added. | The variable is divided by 4 and then 3 is subtracted. | 3 is added to the variable and then the result is divided by 4. |

| To solve, first subtract 3 and then divide by 4. | To solve, first add 3 and then multiply by 4. | To solve, multiply by 4 and then subtract 3. |

Describe how each equation is formed. Then, tell the steps needed to solve.

1. $3x - 5 = 7$
The variable is ___multiplied by 3___ and then ___5 is subtracted___.
To solve, first ___add 5___ and then ___divide by 3___.

2. $\frac{x}{3} + 5 = 7$
The variable is ___divided by 3___ and then ___5 is added___.
To solve, first ___subtract 5___ and then ___multiply by 3___.

3. $\frac{x + 5}{3} = 7$
___5 is added to the variable___ and then the result is ___divided by 3___.
To solve, first ___multiply by 3___ and then ___subtract 5___.

4. $10 = -3x - 2$
The variable is ___multiplied by −3___ and then ___2 is subtracted___.
To solve, first ___add 2___ and then ___divide by −3___.

5. $10 = \frac{x - 2}{5}$
___2 is subtracted from___ the variable and then the result is ___divided by 5___.
To solve, first ___multiply by 5___ and then ___add 2___.

PRACTICE 2-8

LESSON **2-8**
Practice B
Solving Two-Step Equations

Write and solve a two-step equation to answer the following questions.

1. The school purchased baseball equipment and uniforms for a total cost of $1762. The equipment costs $598 and the uniforms were $24.25 each. How many uniforms did the school purchase?

$x = $ # of uniforms
$1762 = 598 + 24.25x$
$1762 - 598$
$= 598 - 598 + 24.25x$
$1164 = 24.25x$
$\frac{1164}{24.25} = \frac{24.25x}{24.25}$
$48 = x$

2. Carla runs 4 miles every day. She jogs from home to the school track, which is $\frac{3}{4}$ mile away. She then runs laps around the $\frac{1}{4}$-mile track. Carla then jogs home. How many laps does she run at the school?

$x = $ # of laps
$4 = \frac{3}{4} + \frac{1}{4}x + \frac{3}{4}$
$4 - \frac{6}{4} = \frac{6}{4} - \frac{6}{4} + \frac{1}{4}x$
$\frac{5}{2} = \frac{1}{4}x$
$4(\frac{5}{2}) = (\frac{1}{4}x)4$
$10 = x$

Solve.

3. $\frac{a + 5}{3} = 12$ **4.** $\frac{x + 2}{4} = -2$ **5.** $\frac{y - 4}{6} = -3$ **6.** $\frac{k + 1}{8} = 7$
$a = 31$ $x = -10$ $y = -14$ $k = 55$

7. $0.5x - 6 = -4$ **8.** $\frac{x}{2} + 3 = -4$ **9.** $\frac{1}{5}n + 3 = 6$ **10.** $2a - 7 = -9$
$x = 4$ $x = -14$ $n = 15$ $a = -1$

11. $\frac{3x - 1}{4} = 2$ **12.** $-7.8 = 4.4 + 2r$ **13.** $\frac{-4w + 5}{-3} = -7$ **14.** $1.3 - 5r = 7.4$
$x = 3$ $r = -6.1$ $w = -4$ $r = -1.22$

15. A phone call costs $0.58 for the first 3 minutes and $0.15 for each additional minute. If the total charge for the call was $4.78, how many minutes was the call? ___31 minutes___

16. Seventeen less than four times a number is twenty-seven. Find the number. ___11___

Life Science LINK

About 20% of the more than 2500 species of snakes are venomous. The United States has 20 domestic venomous snake species.

39. The inland taipan of central Australia is the world's most toxic venomous snake. Just 1 mg of its venom can kill 1000 mice. One bite contains up to 110 mg of venom. About how many mice could be killed with just one inland taipan bite? **110,000**

40. A rattlesnake grows a new rattle segment each time it sheds its skin. Rattlesnakes shed their skin an average of three times per year. However, segments often break off. If a rattlesnake had 44 rattle segments break off in its lifetime and it had 10 rattles when it died, approximately how many years did the rattlesnake live? **18 yr**

41. All snakes shed their skin. The shed skin of a snake is an average of 10% longer than the actual snake. If the shed skin of a coral snake is 27.5 inches long, estimate the length of the coral snake. **25 in.**

42. ⭐ **Challenge** Black mambas feed mainly on small rodents and birds. Suppose a black mamba is 100 feet away from an animal that is running at 8 mi/h. About how long will it take for the mamba to catch the animal? (*Hint*: 1 mile = 5280 feet) **17 s**

go.hrw.com
Web Extra!
KEYWORD: MT7 Snakes

Venom is collected from snakes and injected into horses, which develop antibodies. The horses' blood is sterilized to make antivenom.

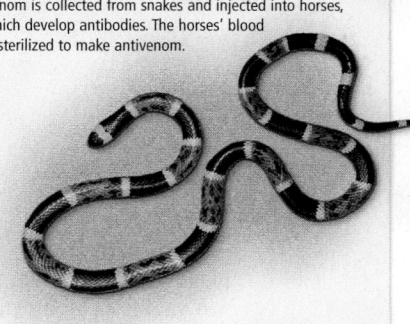

Records of World's Most Venomous Snakes

Category	Record	Type of Snake
Fastest	12 mi/h	Black mamba
Longest	18 ft 9 in.	King cobra
Heaviest	34 lb	Eastern diamondback rattlesnake
Longest fangs	2 in.	Gaboon viper

TEST PREP and Spiral Review

43. Multiple Choice A plumber charges $75 for a house call plus $45 per hour. How many hours did the plumber work if he charged $210?

Ⓐ 2 Ⓑ 3 Ⓒ 4 Ⓓ 6

44. Gridded Response What value of y makes the equation $4.4y + 1.75 = 43.99$ true? **9.6**

Solve and graph each inequality. (Lesson 1-9)

45. $3x < 15$ $x < 5$
46. $x + 2 \geq 4$ $x \geq 2$
47. $x + 1 \leq 3$ $x \leq 2$
48. $x - 4 < 4$ $x < 8$

Solve. (Lesson 2-7)

49. $y - 27.6 = -32$ $y = -4.4$
50. $-5.3f = 74.2$ $f = -14$
51. $\frac{m}{3.2} = -8$ $m = -25.6$
52. $x + \frac{1}{8} = -\frac{5}{8}$ $x = -\frac{3}{4}$

ONGOING ASSESSMENT and INTERVENTION ⬅️➡️

Diagnose Before the Lesson
2-8 Warm Up, TE p. 98

Monitor During the Lesson
2-8 Know-It Notebook
2-8 Questioning Strategies

Assess After the Lesson
2-8 Lesson Quiz, TE p. 101

Interdisciplinary LINK

Life Science

Exercises 39–42 involve using data about venomous snakes to solve two-step equations. Snakes and other reptiles are studied in middle school life science programs, such as *Holt Science & Technology*.

Answers

45–48. For graphs, see p. A1.

 **TEST PREP DOCTOR ➕** For Exercise 43, encourage students to work backwards. Instead of trying to guess the number of hours or writing an equation, students can find the answer by subtracting the cost for a house call from the total charge, and then dividing the result by the hourly cost. Encourage students to check their answer.

 Journal

Ask students to write about how they would explain the process of solving two-step equations to a friend who has not seen them yet.

Power Presentations with PowerPoint®

✓ 2-8 Lesson Quiz

Solve.

1. $\frac{x}{-9} - 3 = 10$ $x = -117$

2. $7y + 25 = -24$ $y = -7$

3. $-8.3 = -3.5x + 13.4$ $x = 6.2$

4. $\frac{y + 5}{11} = 3$ $y = 28$

5. The cost for a new cell phone plan is $39 per month plus a one-time start-up fee of $78. If you are charged $1014, how many months will the contract last? **24**

Also available on transparency

CHALLENGE 2-8

LESSON 2-8 Challenge
Work It Algebraically!

An equation may be used to solve a problem involving probability.

A bag contains marbles of four colors: red, white, blue, and yellow. There are 3 more blue marbles than red, and 48 marbles in all. How many blue marbles are there if, in one draw, the probability of getting a blue marble is $\frac{5}{12}$?

Let x = the number of blue marbles.

$P(\text{blue}) = \frac{\text{number of successes}}{\text{total number}}$

$\frac{5}{12} = \frac{x}{48}$

$\frac{5}{12} \cdot 48 = 48 \cdot \frac{x}{48}$ Multiply by 48.

$20 = x$

So, there are 20 blue marbles in the bag.

Write and solve an equation for each problem.

1. A box has four kinds of candies: lime, orange, cherry, and mint. There are 9 more lime than orange, and 36 candies in all. How many lime candies are there if, in one draw, the probability of getting a lime candy is $\frac{4}{9}$?

Let x = number of lime candies.

$\frac{x}{36} = \frac{4}{9}$

$36 \cdot \frac{x}{36} = \frac{4}{9} \cdot 36$

$x = 16$

There are __16__ lime candies.

2. A carton has four kinds of cookies: lemon, mint, vanilla, and chocolate. There are 7 fewer mint than lemon, and 64 cookies in all. How many mint cookies are there if, in one draw, the probability of getting a lemon cookie is $\frac{5}{8}$?

Let x = number of lemon cookies.

Then $x - 7$ = number of mint cookies.

$\frac{x}{64} = \frac{5}{8}$

$64 \cdot \frac{x}{64} = \frac{5}{8} \cdot 64$

$x = 24$ ← lemon cookies

There are __17__ mint cookies.

PROBLEM SOLVING 2-8

LESSON 2-8 Problem Solving
Solving Two-Step Equations

The chart below describes three different long distance calling plans. Jamie has budgeted $20 per month for long distance calls. Write the correct answer.

Plan	Monthly Access Fee	Charge per minute
A	$3.95	$0.08
B	$8.95	$0.06
C	$0	$0.10

1. How many minutes will Jamie be able to use per month with plan A? Round to the nearest minute.
201 min

2. How many minutes will Jamie be able to use per month with plan B? Round to the nearest minute.
184 min

3. How many minutes will Jamie be able to use per month with plan C? Round to the nearest minute.
200 min

4. Which plan is the best deal for Jamie's budget?
Plan A

5. Nolan has budgeted $50 per month for long distance. Which plan is the best deal for Nolan's budget?
Plan B

The table describes four different car loans that Susana can get to finance her new car. The total column gives the amount she will end up paying for the car including the down payment and the payments with interest. Choose the letter for the best answer.

Loan	Down Payment	Number of Months	Total
A	$2000	60	$19,821.20
B	$1000	48	$19,390.72
C	$0	60	$20,197.20

6. How much will Susana pay each month with loan A?
A $252.04   C $330.35
Ⓑ $297.02   D $353.68

7. How much will Susana pay each month with loan B?
F $300.85   H $323.17
G $306.50   Ⓙ $383.14

8. How much will Susana pay each month with loan C?
Ⓐ $336.62   C $369.95
B $352.28   D $420.78

9. Which loan will give Susana the smallest monthly payment?
Ⓕ Loan A   H Loan C
G Loan B   J They are equal

2-8 Solving Two-Step Equations **101**

Organizer

Objective: Assess students' mastery of concepts and skills in Lessons 2-7 through 2-8.

Resources

Assessment Resources
Section 2B Quiz

Test & Practice Generator
One-Stop Planner®

INTERVENTION

Resources

Ready to Go On?
Intervention and
Enrichment Worksheets

Ready to Go On? CD-ROM

Ready to Go On? Online

my.hrw.com

Quiz for Lessons 2-7 Through 2-8

 **2-7** Solving Equations with Rational Numbers

Solve.

1. $p - 1.2 = -5$ **6.2**

2. $-9w = 13.5$ **1.5**

3. $\frac{m}{3.7} = -8$ **29.6**

4. $x + \frac{1}{9} = -\frac{4}{7}$ **$-\frac{43}{63}$**

5. $m - \frac{3}{4} = -\frac{4}{3}$ **$-\frac{1}{3}$**

6. $\frac{7}{33}y = -\frac{56}{3}$ **-99**

7. $\frac{y}{-2.6} = 3.2$ **-8.32**

8. $s + 0.45 = 10.07$ **9.62**

9. $p + 2.7 = 4.5$ **1.8**

10. $\frac{h}{2.5} = 3.8$ **9.5**

11. $y - \frac{7}{8} = -\frac{25}{12}$ **$-1\frac{5}{24}$**

12. $\frac{8}{11}k = \frac{29}{44}$ **$\frac{29}{32}$**

13. The Montegro Flooring Company can replace 200 square feet of carpet with tile in one day. They accept a job replacing carpet with tile in an apartment that measures 977.5 square feet. How many days will it take the Montegro Flooring Company to complete this job? **4.25 days**

14. From start to finish, Ellen took $15\frac{2}{3}$ days to write a research paper for her literature class. This was $\frac{9}{10}$ the time it took Rebecca to write her paper. How long did it take Rebecca to write her research paper? **$17\frac{11}{27}$ days**

 **2-8** Solving Two-Step Equations

Solve.

15. $\frac{x+7}{6} = -48$ **-295**

16. $3x + 4.2 = 21$ **5.6**

17. $\frac{1}{4}y - \frac{2}{3} = \frac{5}{6}$ **6**

18. $\frac{y}{12} + 6 = -72$ **-7**

19. $-5p + 10 = 75$ **-13**

20. $\frac{r-2}{-7} = 3$ **-19**

21. $2w + 7.1 = 2.85$ **-2.125**

22. $-8.9y - 10.11 = 74.44$ **9.05**

23. $\frac{p+17}{25} = 4$ **83**

24. Marvin sold newspaper subscriptions during summer break. He earned $125.00 per week plus $5.75 for each subscription that he sold. During the last week of the summer, Marvin earned $228.50. How many subscriptions did he sell that week? **18**

25. A cell phone company charges $13.50 per month plus $3\frac{1}{2}$ cents for each minute used. If Angelina's cell phone bill was $17.70 last month, how many minutes did she use? **120**

NO
INTERVENE

READY TO GO ON?
Diagnose and Prescribe

YES
ENRICH

READY TO GO ON? Intervention			
Ready to Go On? Intervention	 **Worksheets**	**CD-ROM**	**Online**
✓ Lesson 2-7	2-7 Intervention	Activity 2-7	Diagnose and Prescribe Online
✓ Lesson 2-8	2-8 Intervention	Activity 2-8	

READY TO GO ON?
Enrichment, Section 2B

 **Worksheets**

 CD-ROM

Online

Some Like It Cold Scientists usually use the Celsius scale to measure temperatures. You can use the formula $C = \frac{5}{9}(F - 32)$ to convert a temperature in degrees Fahrenheit, °F, to a temperature in degrees Celsius, °C.

1. Water freezes at 32 degrees Fahrenheit (32°F) and boils at 212 degrees Fahrenheit (212°F). Use the formula to convert 32°F and 212°F to degrees Celsius. Why do you think scientists prefer the Celsius scale?

2. When temperatures are converted from Fahrenheit to Celsius, an interesting thing happens as the Fahrenheit temperature decreases. Convert −4°F, −22°F, and −40°F to degrees Celsius. What do you notice?

3. Use the above formula to write an equation to find the temperature in degrees Fahrenheit that corresponds to 40°C. Then solve the equation.

4. The formula $F = \frac{9}{5}C + 32$ converts a temperature in degrees Celsius to a temperature in degrees Fahrenheit. Use this formula to convert $-\frac{5}{18}$°C to degrees Fahrenheit.

5. The table shows the temperature in Nome, Alaska, recorded at several different times during a day in April. At which time was the lowest temperature recorded? Explain.

Temperature in Nome, Alaska	
Time	**Temperature**
1:00 P.M.	25.7°F
3:00 P.M.	$25\frac{2}{5}$°F
5:00 P.M.	−3.5°C
7:00 P.M.	$-3\frac{4}{5}$°C

Wisconsin high school students participate in the annual Polar Plunge for Special Olympics.

MULTI-STEP TEST PREP

CHAPTER
2

Organizer

Objective: Assess students' ability to apply concepts and skills in Chapter 2 in a real-world format.

 **Online Edition**

Resources

 Middle School Assessments
www.mathtekstoolkit.org

Problem	Text reference
1	Lesson 2-7
2	Lesson 2-7
3	Lesson 2-7
4	Lesson 2-7
5	Lesson 2-2

Answers

1. 0°C; 100°C; It is easy to work with numbers such as 0 and 100.

2. −20; −30; −40; They are all multiples of 10.

3. $40 = \frac{5}{9}(F - 32)$; 104°F

4. $31\frac{1}{2}$°F

5. 7:00 P.M.; since $-3.5 > -3\frac{4}{5}$.

INTERVENTION

Scaffolding Questions

1. What steps should you take to evaluate $\frac{5}{9}(F - 32)$ for a particular value of F? Subtract 32 first, then multiply by $\frac{5}{9}$

2. When you convert negative degrees Fahrenheit, will you always get negative degrees Celsius? Why? Yes, because you subtract 32 from the negative number, which gives a negative value, and then you multiply by the positive number $\frac{5}{9}$, which also gives a negative value

3. What value should you substitute into the formula to get the equation? $C = 40$ How can you solve the equation? Multiply both sides by $\frac{9}{5}$. Then add 32 to both sides.

4. What expression do you get when you substitute $C = \frac{5}{18}$? $\frac{9}{5}\left(\frac{-5}{18}\right) + 32$ How can you simplify the expression? First multiply the fractions, then add 32.

5. How can you compare the temperatures? Convert them all to degrees Celsius or degrees Fahrenheit. Then convert them all to decimals.

Extension

The Kelvin scale is a third way to measure temperatures. To convert degrees Celsius to degrees Kelvin, you add 273.16 to the Celsius temperature. Convert 36.5°F to degrees Celsius and then to degrees Kelvin. 2.5°C; 275.66 Kelvin

State Resources

 go.hrw.com
State Resources Online
KEYWORD: MT7 Resources

Organizer

Objective: Participate in games to practice and apply skills learned in Chapter 2.

 Online Edition

Resources

Chapter 2 Resource Book
Puzzles, Twisters & Teasers

Egyptian Fractions

Purpose: To apply operations with fractions to a historical activity

Discuss Ask students: What fraction would you subtract first in order to express the fraction $\frac{3}{8}$ as the Egyptians would have? Explain. You subtract $\frac{1}{3}$ from $\frac{3}{8}$ first, because it is the largest unit fraction that is less than $\frac{3}{8}$. How do you know when to stop? when the difference is a unit fraction

Extend Have students determine how many fractions can be written using the fractions $\frac{1}{2}, \frac{1}{3}, \frac{1}{4}$, and/or $\frac{1}{5}$ as addends a maximum of one time each. Have them write all the fractions.

11 fractions:
$$\frac{1}{2} + \frac{1}{3} = \frac{5}{6}$$
$$\frac{1}{2} + \frac{1}{4} = \frac{3}{4}$$
$$\frac{1}{2} + \frac{1}{5} = \frac{7}{10}$$
$$\frac{1}{3} + \frac{1}{4} = \frac{7}{12}$$
$$\frac{1}{3} + \frac{1}{5} = \frac{8}{15}$$
$$\frac{1}{4} + \frac{1}{5} = \frac{9}{20}$$
$$\frac{1}{2} + \frac{1}{3} + \frac{1}{4} = \frac{13}{12}$$
$$\frac{1}{2} + \frac{1}{3} + \frac{1}{5} = \frac{31}{30}$$
$$\frac{1}{2} + \frac{1}{4} + \frac{1}{5} = \frac{19}{20}$$
$$\frac{1}{3} + \frac{1}{4} + \frac{1}{5} = \frac{47}{60}$$
$$\frac{1}{2} + \frac{1}{3} + \frac{1}{4} + \frac{1}{5} = \frac{77}{60}$$

Egg Fractions

Purpose: To practice adding fractions in a game format

Discuss Have students give a combination of fractions with a sum of $\frac{2}{3}$.
Possible answer: $\frac{7}{12}$ and $\frac{1}{12}$

Game Time

Egyptian Fractions

If you were to divide 9 loaves of bread among 10 people, you would give each person $\frac{9}{10}$ of a loaf. The answer was different on the ancient Egyptian Ahmes papyrus, because ancient Egyptians used only *unit fractions*, which have a numerator of 1. All other fractions were written as sums of different unit fractions. So $\frac{5}{6}$ could be written as $\frac{1}{2} + \frac{1}{3}$, but not as $\frac{1}{6} + \frac{1}{6} + \frac{1}{6} + \frac{1}{6} + \frac{1}{6}$.

Method	Example
Suppose you want to write a fraction as a sum of different unit fractions.	$\frac{9}{10}$
Step 1. Choose the largest fraction of the form $\frac{1}{n}$ that is less than the fraction you want.	
Step 2. Subtract $\frac{1}{n}$ from the fraction you want.	$\frac{9}{10} - \frac{1}{2} = \frac{2}{5}$ remaining
Step 3. Repeat steps 1 and 2 using the difference of the fractions until the result is a unit fraction.	$\frac{2}{5} - \frac{1}{3} = \frac{1}{15}$ remaining
Step 4. Write the fraction you want as the sum of the unit fractions.	$\frac{9}{10} = \frac{1}{2} + \frac{1}{3} + \frac{1}{15}$

Write each fraction as a sum of different unit fractions. **Possible answers:**

1. $\frac{3}{4}$ $\frac{1}{2} + \frac{1}{4}$ **2.** $\frac{5}{8}$ $\frac{1}{2} + \frac{1}{8}$ **3.** $\frac{11}{12}$ $\frac{1}{2} + \frac{1}{4} + \frac{1}{6}$ **4.** $\frac{3}{7}$ $\frac{1}{4} + \frac{1}{7} + \frac{1}{28}$ **5.** $\frac{7}{5}$

                                                      $1 + \frac{1}{3} + \frac{1}{15}$

Egg Fractions

This game is played with an empty egg carton. Each compartment represents a fraction with a denominator of 12. The goal is to place tokens in compartments with a given sum.

A complete copy of the rules is available online.

go.hrw.com
Game Time Extra
KEYWORD: MT7 Games

Extend Have students play the game again, but this time they must make each sum using 3 tokens instead of 2. (Students should replace $\frac{1}{6}$ with $\frac{11}{12}$.)

Materials
- film canister with lid
- adding-machine tape
- ruler
- markers
- self-stick label

It's in the Bag!

PROJECT ## Canister Carry-All

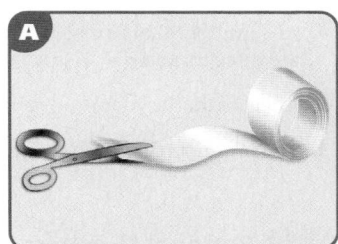

Turn a film canister into a handy carrying case for a number line and notes about rational numbers.

Directions

1 If necessary, cut off a strip along the bottom edge of the adding-machine tape so that the tape will fit into the film canister when it is rolled up. When you're done, the tape should be about $1\frac{3}{4}$ in. wide.
Figure A

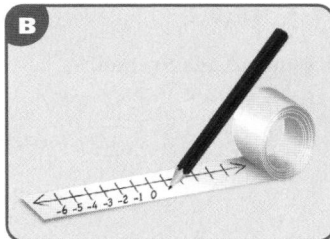

2 Use a ruler to make a long number line on one side of the adding-machine tape.
Figure B

3 Write the number and title of the chapter on a self-stick label. Then peel the backing off the label and place the label on the outside of the canister.

Taking Note of the Math

Place examples of rational numbers on the number line. Choose examples that will help you remember how to compare and order rational numbers. Then turn the adding-machine tape over, and use the other side to write notes and sample problems from the chapter.

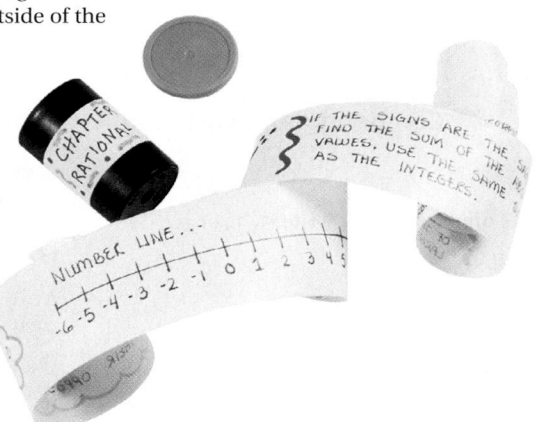

Organizer

Objective: Make a carrying case for a number line that serves as a study guide for the chapter.

Materials: empty film canister with lid, adding-machine tape, ruler, markers, self-stick label

PREMIER **Online Edition**

Using the Page

Preparing the Materials
Photo-developing centers may have empty 35 mm film canisters that they can donate to your class. Alternatively, you can do the project with any type of cylindrical containers, such as the containers used to package peanuts or other foods.

Making the Project
Have students make simple number lines at first, perhaps making marks only for integers. Later, students can add additional marks as they place rational numbers in the appropriate spots along the line.

Extending the Project
Students can save their number lines and add information to them throughout the course. For example, students might add examples of square roots (Chapter 4) and percents (Chapter 6).

Tips from the Bag Ladies!

To add a fun twist to the project, have students cut a slit in the side of the film canister. When the rolled-up adding-machine tape is placed inside the canister, students can pull it out through the slit to read their notes.

We've used film canisters to store all kinds of things. For instance, when we teach probability we have students keep coins and number cubes in the canisters. Students can even put an eye screw in the lid and attach a short plastic cord. This makes it easy to tie the canister to a spiral notebook for quick access.

Organizer

Objective: Help students organize and review key concepts and skills presented in Chapter 2.

Online Edition
Multilingual Glossary

Resources

PuzzlePro®
One-Stop Planner®

Multilingual Glossary Online

go.hrw.com
KEYWORD: MT7 Glossary

Lesson Tutorial Videos
CD-ROM

Test & Practice Generator
One-Stop Planner®

Answers

1. rational number
2. relatively prime
3. reciprocal
4. $\frac{3}{5}$
5. $\frac{1}{4}$
6. $\frac{21}{40}$
7. 1.75
8. $0.2\overline{6}$
9. $0.\overline{7}$
10. $\frac{2}{3}$
11. $\frac{2}{3}$
12. $\frac{3}{4}$
13. $<$
14. $=$
15. $-0.9, -\frac{2}{3}, 0.25, \frac{1}{2}$
16. $-0.11, 0, 0.67, \frac{9}{10}$

Study Guide: Review

Vocabulary

least common denominator (LCD) 68   reciprocal 80
rational number 64   relatively prime 64

Complete the sentences below with vocabulary words from the list above.

1. Any number that can be written as a fraction $\frac{n}{d}$ (where n and d are integers and $d \neq 0$) is called a ___?___.

2. Integers that have no common factors other than 1 are ___?___.

3. The product of a number and its ___?___ is 1.

2-1 Rational Numbers (pp. 64–67)

EXAMPLE

■ Write 0.8 as a fraction.

$0.8 = \frac{8}{10}$ *8 is in the tenths place.*

$= \frac{8 \div 2}{10 \div 2}$ *Divide numerator and denominator by 2.*

$= \frac{4}{5}$

EXERCISES

Write each decimal as a fraction.

4. 0.6   **5.** 0.25   **6.** 0.525

Write each fraction as a decimal.

7. $\frac{7}{4}$ **8.** $\frac{4}{15}$ **9.** $\frac{7}{9}$

Simplify.

10. $\frac{14}{21}$ **11.** $\frac{22}{33}$ **12.** $\frac{75}{100}$

2-2 Comparing and Ordering Rational Numbers (pp. 68–71)

EXAMPLE

■ Compare $\frac{2}{3}$ ▮ $\frac{5}{8}$. Write <, >, or =.

$\frac{2}{3}$ ▮ $\frac{5}{8}$

$\frac{2 \cdot 8}{3 \cdot 8} = \frac{16}{24}$ *24 is the LCD.*

$\frac{5 \cdot 3}{8 \cdot 3} = \frac{15}{24}$

$\frac{16}{24} > \frac{15}{24}$, so $\frac{2}{3} > \frac{5}{8}$

EXERCISES

Compare. Write <, >, or =.

13. $\frac{5}{7}$ ▮ $\frac{9}{10}$ **14.** $\frac{7}{8}$ ▮ $\frac{28}{32}$

Write the numbers in order from least to greatest.

15. $-\frac{2}{3}, 0.25, \frac{1}{2}, -0.9$

16. $0.67, \frac{9}{10}, 0, -0.11$

Study Guide: Review

2-3 Adding and Subtracting Rational Numbers (pp. 72–75)

EXAMPLE

Add or subtract.

- $\dfrac{3}{7} + \dfrac{4}{7}$

  $= \dfrac{3+4}{7} = \dfrac{7}{7} = 1$

- $\dfrac{8}{11} - \left(-\dfrac{2}{11}\right)$

  $= \dfrac{8-(-2)}{11} = \dfrac{8+2}{11} = \dfrac{10}{11}$

EXERCISES

Add or subtract.

17. $\dfrac{-8}{13} + \dfrac{2}{13}$

18. $\dfrac{3}{5} - \left(\dfrac{-4}{5}\right)$

19. $\dfrac{-2}{9} + \dfrac{7}{9}$

20. $\dfrac{-5}{12} - \left(\dfrac{-7}{12}\right)$

21. $\dfrac{-9}{11} + \dfrac{10}{11}$

22. $\dfrac{5}{13} - \dfrac{(-7)}{13}$

2-4 Multiplying Rational Numbers (pp. 76–79)

EXAMPLE

- Multiply. Write the answer in simplest form.

  $5\left(3\dfrac{1}{4}\right) = \left(\dfrac{5}{1}\right)\left(\dfrac{3(4)+1}{4}\right)$

  $= \left(\dfrac{5}{1}\right)\left(\dfrac{13}{4}\right)$ *Write as improper fractions.*

  $= \dfrac{65}{4} = 16\dfrac{1}{4}$ *Multiply and simplify.*

EXERCISES

Multiply. Write each answer in simplest form.

23. $3\left(-\dfrac{2}{5}\right)$

24. $2\left(3\dfrac{4}{5}\right)$

25. $\dfrac{-2}{3}\left(\dfrac{-4}{5}\right)$

26. $\dfrac{8}{11}\left(\dfrac{-22}{4}\right)$

27. $5\dfrac{1}{4}\left(\dfrac{3}{7}\right)$

28. $2\dfrac{1}{2}\left(1\dfrac{3}{10}\right)$

29. $4\dfrac{7}{8}\left(2\dfrac{2}{3}\right)$

30. $-\dfrac{8}{9}\left(\dfrac{7}{16}\right)$

2-5 Dividing Rational Numbers (pp. 80–84)

EXAMPLE

- Divide. Write the answer in simplest form.

  $\dfrac{7}{8} \div \dfrac{3}{4} = \dfrac{7}{8} \cdot \dfrac{4}{3}$ *Multiply by the reciprocal.*

  $= \dfrac{7 \cdot 4}{8 \cdot 3}$ *Write as one fraction.*

  $\dfrac{7 \cdot \overset{1}{4}}{\underset{2}{8} \cdot 3} = \dfrac{7 \cdot 1}{2 \cdot 3}$ *Remove common factors.*

  $\dfrac{7}{6} = 1\dfrac{1}{6}$

EXERCISES

Divide. Write each answer in simplest form.

31. $\dfrac{3}{4} \div \dfrac{1}{8}$

32. $\dfrac{3}{10} \div \dfrac{4}{5}$

33. $\dfrac{2}{3} \div 3$

34. $4 \div \dfrac{-1}{4}$

35. $3\dfrac{3}{4} \div 3$

36. $1\dfrac{1}{3} \div \dfrac{2}{3}$

2-6 Adding and Subtracting with Unlike Denominators (pp. 85–88)

EXAMPLE

- Add.

  $\dfrac{3}{4} + \dfrac{2}{5}$ *Multiply denominators, 4 · 5 = 20.*

  $\dfrac{3 \cdot 5}{4 \cdot 5} = \dfrac{15}{20}$ $\dfrac{2 \cdot 4}{5 \cdot 4} = \dfrac{8}{20}$

  $\dfrac{15}{20} + \dfrac{8}{20} = \dfrac{15+8}{20} = \dfrac{23}{20} = 1\dfrac{3}{20}$ *Add and simplify.*

EXERCISES

Add or subtract.

37. $\dfrac{5}{6} + \dfrac{1}{3}$

38. $\dfrac{5}{6} - \dfrac{5}{9}$

39. $3\dfrac{1}{2} + 7\dfrac{4}{5}$

40. $7\dfrac{1}{10} - 2\dfrac{3}{4}$

41. $\dfrac{19}{20} + \dfrac{7}{3}$

42. $-1\dfrac{5}{9} - 7\dfrac{3}{4}$

Answers

17. $-\dfrac{6}{13}$

18. $\dfrac{7}{5}$

19. $\dfrac{5}{9}$

20. $\dfrac{1}{11}$

21. $\dfrac{1}{11}$

22. $\dfrac{12}{13}$

23. $-1\dfrac{1}{5}$

24. $7\dfrac{3}{5}$

25. $\dfrac{8}{15}$

26. -4

27. $2\dfrac{1}{4}$

28. $3\dfrac{1}{4}$

29. 13

30. $-\dfrac{7}{18}$

31. 6

32. $\dfrac{3}{8}$

33. $\dfrac{2}{9}$

34. -16

35. $\dfrac{5}{4}$

36. 2

37. $1\dfrac{1}{6}$

38. $\dfrac{5}{18}$

39. $11\dfrac{3}{10}$

40. $4\dfrac{7}{20}$

41. $3\dfrac{17}{60}$

42. $-9\dfrac{11}{36}$

Study Guide: Review

2-7 Solving Equations with Rational Numbers (pp. 92–95)

EXAMPLE

Solve.

■ $x - 13.7 = -22$

$\underline{+13.7 = +13.7}$ *Add 13.7 to each side.*

$x = -8.3$

■ $\frac{7}{9}x = \frac{2}{5}$

$\frac{9}{7} \cdot \frac{7}{9}x = \frac{9}{7} \cdot \frac{2}{5}$ *Multiply both sides by $\frac{9}{7}$*

$x = \frac{18}{35}$

EXERCISES

Solve.

43. $y + 7.8 = -14$ **44.** $2.9z = -52.2$

45. $w + \frac{3}{4} = \frac{1}{8}$ **46.** $\frac{3}{8}p = \frac{3}{4}$

47. $x - \frac{7}{9} = \frac{2}{11}$ **48.** $7.2x = -14.4$

49. $y - 18.7 = 25.9$ **50.** $\frac{19}{21}t = -\frac{38}{7}$

51. Freda paid $126 for groceries for her family. This was $1\frac{1}{6}$ as much as she paid the previous time she shopped. How much did Freda pay on her previous shopping trip?

2-8 Solving Two-Step Equations (pp. 98–101)

EXAMPLE

Solve.

■ $7x + 12 = 33$

Think: First the variable is **multiplied by 7**, and then **12 is added**. To isolate the variable, **subtract 12**, and then **divide by 7**.

$7x + 12 = 33$

$\underline{\quad -12 \quad -12}$ *Subtract 12 from both sides.*

$7x = 21$

$\frac{7x}{7} = \frac{21}{7}$ *Divide both sides by 7.*

$x = 3$

■ $\frac{z}{3} - 8 = 5$

Think: First the variable is **divided by 3**, and then **8 is subtracted**. To isolate the variable, **add 8**, and then **multiply by 3**.

$\frac{z}{3} - 8 = 5$

$\underline{\quad +8 \quad +8}$ *Add 8 to both sides.*

$\frac{z}{3} = 13$

$3 \cdot \frac{z}{3} = 3 \cdot 13$ *Multiply both sides by 3.*

$z = 39$

EXERCISES

Solve.

52. $3m + 5 = 35$ **53.** $55 = 7 - 6y$

54. $2c + 1 = -31$ **55.** $5r + 15 = 0$

56. $\frac{t}{2} + 7 = 15$ **57.** $\frac{w}{4} - 5 = 11$

58. $-25 = \frac{r}{3} - 11$ **59.** $\frac{h}{5} - 9 = -19$

60. $\frac{x + 2}{3} = 18$ **61.** $\frac{d - 3}{4} = -9$

62. $21 = \frac{a - 4}{3}$ **63.** $14 = \frac{c + 8}{7}$

64. A music club charges an annual membership fee of $20.50 plus $12.99 for each CD purchased. If Naomi's total bill for the year was $163.39, how many CDs did she purchase?

Study Guide: Review

Simplify.

1. $\frac{36}{72}$ $\frac{1}{2}$

2. $\frac{21}{35}$ $\frac{3}{5}$

3. $-\frac{16}{88}$ $-\frac{2}{11}$

4. $\frac{18}{25}$ $\frac{18}{25}$

Write each decimal as a fraction in simplest form.

5. 0.225 $\frac{9}{40}$

6. 0.04 $\frac{1}{25}$

7. -0.101 $-\frac{101}{1000}$

8. 0.875 $\frac{7}{8}$

Write each fraction as a decimal.

9. $\frac{7}{8}$ 0.875

10. $-\frac{13}{25}$ -0.52

11. $\frac{5}{12}$ $0.41\overline{6}$

12. $\frac{4}{33}$ $0.\overline{12}$

Write the numbers in order from least to greatest.

13. $\frac{2}{3}$, -0.36, 0.2, $-\frac{1}{4}$ -0.36 $-\frac{1}{4}$, 0.2, $\frac{2}{3}$

14. 0.55, $-\frac{7}{8}$, -0.8, $\frac{5}{6}$ $-\frac{7}{8}$, -0.8, 0.55, $\frac{5}{6}$

15. $\frac{9}{10}$, 0.7, 1.6, $\frac{7}{5}$ 0.7, $\frac{9}{10}$, $\frac{7}{5}$, 1.6

Add or subtract. Write each answer in simplest form.

16. $\frac{-3}{11} - \left(\frac{-4}{11}\right)$ $\frac{1}{11}$

17. $7.25 - 2.75$ 4.5

18. $\frac{5}{6} + \frac{7}{18}$ $1\frac{2}{9}$

19. $\frac{5}{6} - \frac{8}{9}$ $-\frac{1}{18}$

20. $4.5 + 5.875$ 10.375

21. $8\frac{1}{5} - 1\frac{2}{3}$ $-6\frac{8}{15}$

22. Kory is making Thai food for several friends. She needs to triple her recipe. The recipe calls for $\frac{3}{4}$ teaspoon of curry. How much curry does she need? $2\frac{1}{4}$ tsp

Multiply or divide. Write each answer in simplest form.

23. $9(0.63)$ 5.67

24. $\frac{7}{8} \div \frac{5}{24}$ $4\frac{1}{5}$

25. $\frac{2}{3}\left(\frac{-9}{20}\right)$ $-\frac{3}{10}$

26. $3\frac{3}{7}\left(1\frac{5}{16}\right)$ $4\frac{1}{2}$

27. $34 \div 3.4$ 10

28. $-4\frac{2}{3} \div 1\frac{1}{6}$ -4

29. Lucie drank $\frac{3}{4}$ pint of bottled water. One serving of the water is $\frac{7}{8}$ pint. How much of a serving did Lucie drink? $\frac{6}{7}$

Solve.

30. $x - \frac{1}{4} = -\frac{3}{8}$ $-\frac{1}{8}$

31. $-3.14y = 53.38$ -17

32. $\frac{x+7}{12} = 11$ 125

33. $-2k = \frac{1}{4}$ $-\frac{1}{8}$

34. $2h - 3.24 = -1.1$ 1.07

35. $4m = -29$ $-7\frac{1}{4}$

36. $\frac{4}{7}y + 7 = 31$ 42

37. $\frac{x-18}{32} = -3$ -78

38. $s - \frac{2}{3} = \frac{7}{8}$ $1\frac{13}{24}$

39. Rachel walked to a friend's house, then to the store, and then back home. The distance from Rachel's house to her friend's house is $1\frac{5}{6}$ miles. This is twice the distance from Rachel's house to the store. How far does Rachel live from the store? $\frac{11}{12}$ mi

40. Tickets to an orchestra concert cost $25.50 apiece plus a $2.50 handling fee for each order. If Jamal spent $79, how many tickets did he purchase? **3 tickets**

Chapter Test

Organizer

Objective: Assess students' mastery of concepts and skills in Chapter 2.

 Online Edition

Resources

Assessment Resources

Chapter 2 Tests
- Free Response
  (Levels A, B, C)
- Multiple Choice
  (Levels A, B, C)
- Performance Assessment

 IDEA Works! CD-ROM
Modified Chapter 2 Test

Test & Practice Generator
One-Stop Planner®

go.hrw.com
State Resources Online
KEYWORD: MT7 Resources

State Resources

CHAPTER
2
STANDARDIZED
TEST PREP

CHAPTER
2
STANDARDIZED
TEST PREP

go.hrw.com
State Test Practice Online
KEYWORD: MT7 TestPrep

Organizer

Objective: Provide review and practice for Chapters 1–2 and standardized tests.

 Online Edition

Resources

 Assessment Resources
Chapter 2 Cumulative Test

 State Test Prep Workbook

 State Test Prep CD-ROM

 State Test Practice Online

go.hrw.com
KEYWORD: MT7 TestPrep

Standardized Test Prep

Cumulative Assessment, Chapters 1–2

Multiple Choice

1. What is the value of the expression $12 - k$ if $k = -3$?

Ⓐ -15 Ⓒ 9

Ⓑ -9 Ⓓ 15

2. Which expression is equivalent to $2x - 5$ if $x = -4$?

Ⓕ -13 Ⓗ 3

Ⓖ -3 Ⓙ 13

3. Which of the following is equivalent to $|10 - (-5)|$?

Ⓐ -15 Ⓒ 5

Ⓑ -5 Ⓓ 15

4. Which value of x is the solution of the equation $\frac{x}{3} = -12$?

Ⓕ $x = -36$ Ⓗ $x = -4$

Ⓖ $x = -15$ Ⓙ $x = 9$

5. If a pitcher contains $\frac{3}{4}$ gallon of juice and each glass will hold $\frac{1}{8}$ gallon of juice, how many glasses can be filled?

Ⓐ $\frac{3}{32}$ glass   Ⓒ 6 glasses

Ⓑ $\frac{3}{4}$ glass   Ⓓ 8 glasses

6. Skip drove 55.6 miles. Then he drove another $42\frac{1}{5}$ miles. How many miles did he drive in all?

Ⓕ 97.7 miles   Ⓗ 97.8 miles

Ⓖ 98.5 miles   Ⓙ 13.4 miles

7. Which number is greater than $\frac{3}{4}$?

Ⓐ $\frac{4}{5}$ Ⓒ $\frac{5}{8}$

Ⓑ 0.75   Ⓓ $0.\overline{6}$

8. Which model correctly represents the number $\frac{1}{4}$?

Ⓕ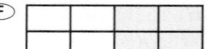

Ⓖ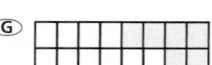

Ⓗ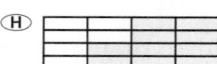

Ⓙ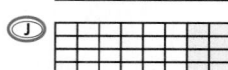

9. According to the graph, what fraction of games resulted in something other than a tie?

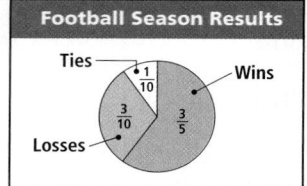

Football Season Results

Ties $\frac{1}{10}$ Wins $\frac{3}{10}$ $\frac{3}{5}$ Losses

Ⓐ $\frac{9}{10}$ Ⓒ $\frac{6}{15}$

Ⓑ $\frac{3}{10}$ Ⓓ $\frac{9}{50}$

10. Which value of x makes the equation $\frac{2}{3}x = -\frac{5}{6}$ true?

Ⓕ $x = -\frac{5}{9}$ Ⓗ $x = -1\frac{1}{4}$

Ⓖ $x = \frac{1}{6}$ Ⓙ $x = 1\frac{1}{4}$

11. If $\frac{3}{5} = 9s$, what is the value of s?

Ⓐ 15   Ⓒ $\frac{5}{3}$

Ⓑ $\frac{27}{5}$ Ⓓ $\frac{1}{15}$

State Resources

go.hrw.com
State Resources Online
KEYWORD: MT7 Resources

TEST PREP DOCTOR ✚

For Item 3, students who answered **A** may think that the absolute value of a number and the opposite of a number are the same. Students who answered **B** or **C** may need to review subtraction of negative numbers.

For Item 4, students who answered **H** divided both sides by 3 instead of multiplying both sides by 3. If they make a similar mistake on Item 10, review solving equations by multiplying and dividing.

Answers

18. a. $C = 39m + 99$

   b. 18

19. a. $7 + |x| = 12$

   b. Subtract 7 from both sides so that the equation is $|x| = 5$.

   c. Two numbers make the sentence true, 5 and -5. This is because both 5 and -5 are 5 units from zero on the number line.

20. $21\frac{1}{4} \div \frac{3}{4}$

   $\frac{85}{4} \cdot \frac{4}{3} = \frac{85}{3} = 28.\overline{3}$

   She can cut 28 pieces that are $\frac{3}{4}$ in. long.

21. See 4-Point Response work sample.

12. Jeremy has started drinking $\frac{1}{4}$ cup of grape juice every Wednesday at lunch. If he has had a total of 5 cups of juice so far, how many Wednesdays has Jeremy had grape juice?

Ⓕ 4 Ⓗ 20
Ⓖ 5 Ⓙ 80

HOT TIP! Make sure you look at all the answer choices before making your decision. Try substituting each answer choice into the problem if you are unsure of the answer.

13. Oscar bought a bag of almonds. He ate $\frac{3}{8}$ of the bag on Sunday. On Monday, he ate $\frac{2}{3}$ of the almonds left. What fraction of the entire bag did he eat on Monday?

Ⓐ $\frac{9}{16}$ Ⓒ $\frac{1}{4}$
Ⓑ $\frac{5}{11}$ Ⓓ $\frac{1}{12}$

Gridded Response

14. The diameter of a standard CD is $4\frac{3}{4}$ in. The diameter of the circular hole in the middle is $\frac{1}{2}$ in. Find the distance from the edge of the hole to the outer edge of the CD. **2 1/8**

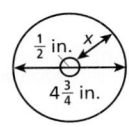

15. Evaluate the expression $|-3 - 8|$. **11**

16. Alana has three times as many pairs of shoes as Marie. If Alana has 18 pairs of shoes, how many pairs of shoes does Marie have? **6**

17. Fifteen students earned the National Merit Scholarship out of 600 students in the school. Write this value as a simplified fraction. **1/40**

Short Response

18. A health club charges a one-time fee of $99 and then $39 per month for membership. Let m represent the number of months, and let C represent the total amount of money spent on the health club membership.

a. Write an equation that relates m and C.

b. If Jillian has spent $801 on her membership, how many months has she been a member of the club?

19. The sum of 7 and the absolute value of a number is the same as 12.

a. Write an equation that can be used to solve for the number.

b. Describe the first step of solving the equation.

c. Determine how many numbers make the equation true. Explain your reasoning.

20. Brigid has a $21\frac{1}{4}$ in. long ribbon. For a project she is cutting it into $\frac{3}{4}$ in. pieces. Into how many $\frac{3}{4}$ in. pieces can she cut the ribbon? Show or explain how you found your answer.

Extended Response

21. Use a diagram to model the expression $\frac{4}{5} \div \frac{4}{3}$.

a. Draw a diagram to model the fraction $\frac{4}{5}$.

b. What fraction do you multiply by that is equivalent to dividing by $\frac{4}{3}$?

c. Use your answer from part b and shade that fraction of the $\frac{4}{5}$ that is already shaded. What does this shaded area represent?

d. Use your diagram to write the quotient in simplest form.

Student Work Samples for Item 21

4-Point Response

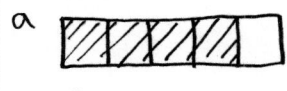

The student created correct diagrams, wrote fractions, and used the diagram to write the quotient.

3-Point Response

The calculations in part **d** are correct, but the student did not use the diagram to answer part **c** and the explanation is inadequate.

2-Point Response

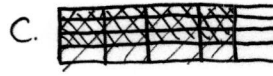

The student applied the correct formulas and explanations are sufficient. However, the student displays a misunderstanding in the miscalculation in part **b**.

Problem Solving on Location

Organizer

Objective: Choose appropriate problem-solving strategies and use them with skills from Chapters 1 and 2 to solve real-world problems.

 Online Edition

✪ Ice House

Reading Strategies

Encourage students to rewrite each problem in their own words. Have them identify all of the given information first. In Problem 1, the information is given in the problem. In Problems 2 and 3, some of the information is given in the table. Students should rewrite the problems using words and phrases that make sense to them.

Using Data Have students calculate the total cost of a day of skating at the Ice House for the number of people in their own families.

Problem Solving on Location

NEW JERSEY

→ Hackensack

→ Atlantic City

✪ Ice House

Ice House, located in Hackensack, New Jersey, is one of the nation's premier ice-skating facilities. With its four regulation-size rinks, Ice House is used as a training facility by National Hockey League teams and by Olympic figure skaters. For those just starting out, Ice House offers skating lessons and four-day skate camps.

Choose one or more strategies to solve each problem.

1. Ice House has year-round public skating. Admission costs $8.50 for adults and $6.50 for children. Skate rentals are available for $3.50 per person. A group of 4 visitors pays a total of $42, with everyone in the group renting skates. How many adults and how many children are in the group? **1 adult; 3 children**

For 2 and 3, use the table.

2. For figure skating, water is added to a rink and then frozen until it reaches a temperature of −2°C. Suppose water is added to a rink and cooled at the rate shown in the table. At what time will the water reach the proper temperature for figure skating? **3 P.M.**

Ice Rink Surface Temperatures	
Time	Temperature (°C)
9:00 A.M.	10
9:30 A.M.	9
10:00 A.M.	8
10:30 A.M.	7

3. Ice hockey requires colder, harder ice. To reach the appropriate temperature, water is added to a rink at 9:00 A.M. and cooled at the rate shown in the table for 7.5 hours. What is the temperature of the ice for ice hockey? **−5°C**

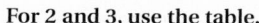

🔍 Problem Solving Focus

Encourage students to use the four-step problem-solving process for the problems. Focus on the first step: **(1) Understand the Problem.**

Discuss with students what information is given about each person in the group in Problem 1. Ask whether any information about one person is related to information about another person. The admission costs are different for the adults and the children in the group. The cost of skate rentals is related to all of the people in the group.

State Resources

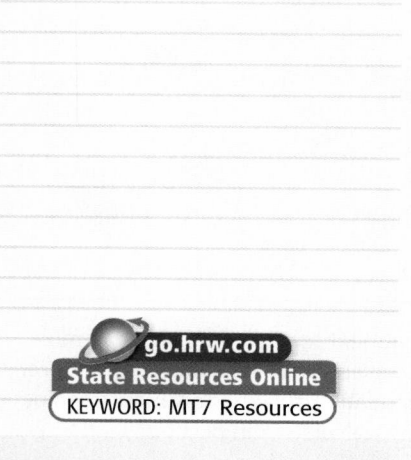

go.hrw.com
State Resources Online
KEYWORD: MT7 Resources

Problem Solving Strategies

Draw a Diagram
Make a Model
Guess and Test
Work Backward
Find a Pattern
Make a Table
Solve a Simpler Problem
Use Logical Reasoning
Act It Out
Make an Organized List

✪ The Atlantic City Boardwalk

Reading Strategies

Have students read the problems aloud. For Problem 2, ask students how many different areas of seating there are in Boardwalk Hall. In this case, there are three different areas of seating.

Using Data Discuss with students what information is presented in the table for Problem 3. information about the price per number of tickets

🔳 Problem Solving Focus

Ask students what strategies they used to solve each problem. Have them compare the different strategies they each used to solve Problem 3. One student might use trial and error to find the answer. This student might indicate that $50 \div 80$ is 0.625, and $5 \cdot 0.625$ is about $3.12, so the answer must be Plan B. Another student may find the cost per ticket, $\frac{3.12}{5} = 0.624$, and then find the average price per ticket for each plan, selecting the plan that has the average price per ticket that is closest to 0.624.

✪ The Atlantic City Boardwalk

The first section of the famous Atlantic City boardwalk opened in 1870. Today the boardwalk stretches for 4 miles along the beachfront, offering a dazzling mix of restaurants, arcades, art galleries, and thrill rides.

Choose one or more strategies to solve each problem.

1. The city's tourist bureau proposes placing an information booth at each end of the boardwalk. It also recommends placing a booth every 0.8 mi along the boardwalk. How many booths would be needed? **6**

2. Boardwalk Hall, located just off the boardwalk, hosts concerts and sporting events. Its total seating capacity is about 6.2 times the number of seats located on the arena floor. The number of seats on the arena floor is about 5.1 times the number of club seats. There are 432 club seats. What is the approximate seating capacity of Boardwalk Hall? **13,660**

For 3, use the table.

3. The boardwalk has several piers with games and thrill rides. Steel Pier has three different plans for purchasing ride tickets. With one of the plans, a 5-ticket ride costs about $3.12. Which plan is it? **plan B**

Steel Pier Tickets		
Plan	**Number of Tickets**	**Price**
A	35	$25
B	80	$50
C	200	$100

CHAPTER 3

Graphs, Functions, and Sequences

Section 3A	Section 3B
Tables and Graphs	**Functions and Sequences**
3-1 Ordered Pairs	3-4 Functions
3-2 Graphing on a Coordinate Plane	3-5 Equations, Tables, and Graphs
3-2 Technology Lab Graph Points	3-6 Arithmetic Sequences
3-3 Interpreting Graphs and Tables	

Pacing Guide for 45-Minute Classes

Chapter 3   Countdown to Testing Week ❺

DAY 1	DAY 2	DAY 3	DAY 4	DAY 5
3-1 Lesson	3-2 Lesson	3-2 Technology Lab 3-3 Lesson	3-3 Lesson	Ready to Go On? Focus on Problem Solving 3-4 Lesson

DAY 6	DAY 7	DAY 8	DAY 9	DAY 10
3-4 Lesson 3-5 Lesson	3-5 Lesson 3-6 Lesson	3-6 Lesson Ready to Go On? Multi-Step Test Prep	Chapter 3 Review	Chapter 3 Test

Pacing Guide for 90-Minute Classes

Chapter 3

DAY 1	DAY 2	DAY 3	DAY 4	DAY 5
3-1 Lesson 3-2 Lesson	3-2 Technology Lab 3-3 Lesson	3-3 Lesson Ready to Go On? Focus on Problem Solving 3-4 Lesson	3-4 Lesson 3-5 Lesson 3-6 Lesson	3-6 Lesson Ready to Go On? Multi-Step Test Prep

DAY 6
Chapter 3 Review Chapter 3 Test

ONGOING ASSESSMENT and INTERVENTION

DIAGNOSE	PRESCRIBE

Assess Prior Knowledge

Before Chapter 3

Diagnose readiness for the chapter.
Are You Ready? SE p. 115

Prescribe intervention.
Are You Ready? Intervention Skills 34, 40, 42, 47

Formative Assessment

Before Every Lesson

Diagnose readiness for the lesson.
Warm Up TE, every lesson

Prescribe intervention.
Skills Bank SE pp. 820–834
Reteach CRB, Chapters 1–3

During Every Lesson

Diagnose understanding of lesson concepts.
Think and Discuss SE, every lesson
Write About It SE, lesson exercises
Journal TE, lesson exercises

Prescribe intervention.
Questioning Strategies Chapter 3
Reading Strategies CRB, every lesson
Success for ELL pp. 35–46

After Every Lesson

Diagnose mastery of lesson concepts.
Lesson Quiz TE, every lesson
Test Prep SE, every lesson
Test and Practice Generator

Prescribe intervention.
Reteach CRB, every lesson
Problem Solving CRB, every lesson
Test Prep Doctor TE, lesson exercises
Homework Help Online

Before Chapter 3 Testing

Diagnose mastery of concepts in the chapter.
Ready to Go On? SE pp. 132, 146
Focus on Problem Solving SE p. 133
Multi-Step Test Prep SE p. 147
Section Quizzes AR pp. 45–46
Test and Practice Generator

Prescribe intervention.
Ready to Go On? Intervention Chapter 3
Scaffolding Questions TE pp. 147

Before High Stakes Testing

Diagnose mastery of benchmark concepts.
Test Tackler SE pp. 154–155
Standardized Test Prep SE pp. 156–157
State Test Prep CD-ROM

Prescribe intervention.
State Test Prep Workbook

Summative Assessment

After Chapter 3

Check mastery of chapter concepts.
Multiple-Choice Tests (Forms A, B, C)
Free-Response Tests (Forms A, B, C)
Performance Assessment AR pp. 47–60
Test and Practice Generator

Prescribe intervention.
Reteach CRB, every lesson
Lesson Tutorial Videos Chapter 3

Check mastery of benchmark concepts.
AYP State Tests

Prescribe intervention.
State Test Prep Workbook

KEY: **SE** = *Student Edition* **TE** = *Teacher's Edition* **CRB** = *Chapter Resource Book* **AR** = *Assessment Resources* Available on CD-ROM Available online **114B**

Supporting the Teacher

Chapter 3 Resource Book

Practice A, B, C
pp. 3–5, 11–13, 19–21, 28–30, 37–39, 45–47

Reading Strategies ELL
pp. 9, 17, 26, 35, 43, 51

Puzzles, Twisters, and Teasers
pp. 10, 18, 27, 36, 44, 52

Reteach
pp. 6, 14, 22–23, 31–32, 40, 48

Problem Solving
pp. 8, 16, 25, 34, 42, 50

Challenge
pp. 7, 15, 24, 33, 41, 49

Parent Letter pp. 1–2

Transparencies

Lesson Transparencies, Volume 1 .... Chapter 3
• Teaching Tools
• Warm Ups
• Problem of the Day
• Teaching Transparencies
• Lesson Quizzes

Know-It Notebook .... Chapter 3
• Additional Examples   • Chapter Review
• Vocabulary   • Big Ideas

Alternate Openers: Explorations .... pp. 18–23

Countdown to Testing .... pp. 9–10

Teacher Tools

Power Presentations®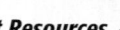
Complete PowerPoint® presentations for Chapter 3 lessons

Lesson Tutorial Videos® SPANISH
Holt authors Ed Burger and Freddie Renfro present tutorials to support the Chapter 3 lessons.

One-Stop Planner® SPANISH
Easy access to all Chapter 3 resources and assessments, as well as software for lesson planning, test generation, and puzzle creation

IDEA Works!®
Key Chapter 3 resources and assessments modified to address special learning needs

Lesson Plans .... pp. 18–23

Questioning Strategies .... Chapter 3

Solutions Key .... Chapter 3

Interdisciplinary Posters and Worksheets .... Chapter 3

TechKeys   **Lab Resources**

Project Teacher Support   **Parent Resources**

Workbooks

Homework and Practice Workbook SPANISH
Teacher's Guide .... pp. 9–12

Know-It Notebook
Teacher's Guide .... Chapter 3

Problem Solving Workbook SPANISH
Teacher's Guide .... pp. 9–12

State Test Prep
Teacher's Guide

Technology Highlights for the Teacher

 Power Presentations
Dynamic presentations to engage students. Complete PowerPoint® presentations for every lesson in Chapter 3.

 One-Stop Planner SPANISH
Easy access to Chapter 3 resources and assessments. Includes lesson-planning, test-generation, and puzzle-creation software.

 Premier Online Edition SPANISH
Chapter 3 includes Tutorial Videos, Lesson Activities, Lesson Quizzes, Homework Help, and Chapter Project.

KEY: **SE** = *Student Edition*   **TE** = *Teacher's Edition*   English Language Learners   Spanish version available   Available on CD-ROM    Available online

 # Reaching All Learners

Resources for All Learners

Hands-On Lab Activities .... Chapter 3

Technology Lab Activities .... Chapter 3

Homework and Practice Workbook **SPANISH** ....pp. 18–23

Know-It Notebook .... Chapter 3

Problem Solving Workbook **SPANISH** ....pp. 18–23

DEVELOPING LEARNERS

Practice A .... CRB, every lesson

Reteach .... CRB, every lesson

Inclusion .... TE p. 135

Questioning Strategies .... Chapter 3

Modified Chapter 3 Resources .... *IDEA Works!*

Homework Help Online

ON-LEVEL LEARNERS

Practice B .... CRB, every lesson

Puzzles, Twisters, and Teasers ....CRB, every lesson

Multiple Representations ....TE pp. 123, 143

Cooperative Learning .... TE p. 139

ADVANCED LEARNERS

Practice C .... CRB, every lesson

Challenge .... CRB, every lesson

Extension ....TE pp. 117, 147, 148, 149

Critical Thinking .... TE p. 135

English Language Learners

ENGLISH LANGUAGE LEARNERS

Are You Ready? Vocabulary .... SE p. 115

Vocabulary Connections .... SE p. 116

Lesson Vocabulary ....SE, every lesson

Vocabulary Review .... SE p. 150

English Language Learners ....TE p. 135

Reading Strategies .... CRB, every lesson

Success for English Language Learners ....pp. 35–46

Multilingual Glossary

Reaching All Learners Through...

Inclusion .... TE p. 135

Visual Cues ....TE p. 119

Multiple Representations ....TE pp. 123, 143

Cooperative Learning .... TE p. 139

Critical Thinking ....TE p. 135

Test Prep Doctor ....TE pp. 121, 125, 131, 137, 141,
145, 154, 156

Common Error Alerts ....TE pp. 139, 143

Scaffolding Questions ....TE p. 147

Technology Highlights for Reaching All Learners

 Lesson Tutorial Videos **SPANISH**

Starring Holt authors Ed Burger and Freddie Renfro! Live tutorials to support every lesson in Chapter 3.

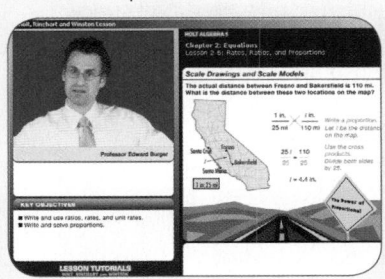

 Multilingual Glossary

Searchable glossary includes definitions in English, Spanish, Vietnamese, Chinese, Hmong, Korean, and 4 other languages.

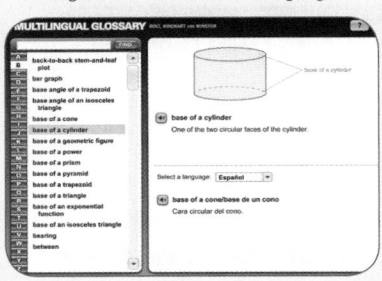

 Online Interactivities

Interactive tutorials provide visually engaging alternative opportunities to learn concepts and master skills.

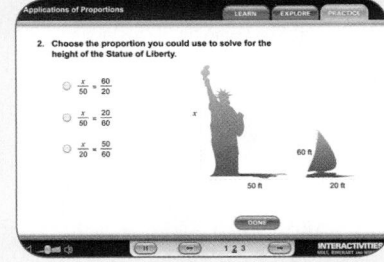

KEY: **SE** = *Student Edition* **TE** = *Teacher's Edition* **CRB** = *Chapter Resource Book* **SPANISH** Spanish version available   Available on CD-ROM  Available online

CHAPTER 3

Ongoing Assessment

Assessing Prior Knowledge

Determine whether students have the prerequisite concepts and skills for success in Chapter 3.

Are You Ready? SPANISH .... SE p. 115
Warm Up .... TE, every lesson

Test Preparation

Provide review and practice for Chapter 3 and standardized tests.

Multi-Step Test Prep .... SE p. 147
Study Guide: Review .... SE pp. 150–152
Test Tackler .... SE pp. 154–155
Standardized Test Prep .... SE pp. 156–157
Countdown to Testing Transparencies ......pp. 9–10
State Test Prep Workbook
State Test Prep CD-ROM
IDEA Works!

Alternative Assessment

Assess students' understanding of Chapter 3 concepts and combined problem-solving skills.

Chapter 3 Project .... SE p. 114
Performance Assessment SPANISH ....AR pp. 59–60
Portfolio Assessment SPANISH .... AR p. xxxiv

Daily Assessment

Provide formative assessment for each day of Chapter 3.

Questioning Strategies .... Chapter 3
Think and Discuss ....SE, every lesson
Write About It .... SE, lesson exercises
Journal .... TE, lesson exercises
Lesson Quiz .... TE, every lesson
Modified Lesson Quizzes .... *IDEA Works!*

Weekly Assessment

Provide formative assessment for each week of Chapter 3.

Focus on Problem Solving .... SE p. 133
Multi-Step Test Prep .... SE p. 147
Ready to Go On? SPANISH .... SE pp. 132, 146
Cumulative Assessment .... SE pp. 156–157
Test and Practice Generator SPANISH ...*One-Stop Planner*

Formal Assessment

Provide summative assessment of Chapter 3 mastery.

Section Quizzes SPANISH ....AR pp. 45–46
Chapter 3 Test .... SE p. 153
Chapter Test (Levels A, B, C) SPANISH ....AR pp. 47–58
  • Multiple-Choice • Free-Response
Cumulative Test SPANISH ....AR pp. 61–64
Test and Practice Generator SPANISH ...*One-Stop Planner*
Modified Chapter 3 Test .... *IDEA Works!*

Technology Highlights for Ongoing Assessment

Are You Ready? SPANISH
Automatically assess readiness and prescribe intervention for Chapter 3 prerequisite skills.

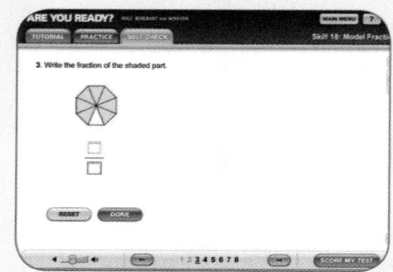

Ready to Go On? SPANISH
Automatically assess understanding of and prescribe intervention for Sections 3A and 3B.

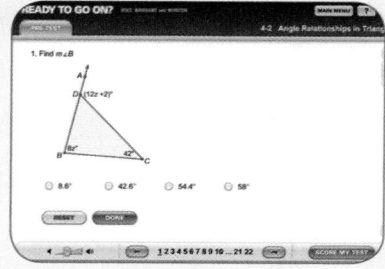

Test and Practice Generator SPANISH
Use Chapter 3 problem banks to create assessments and worksheets to print out or deliver online. Includes dynamic problems.

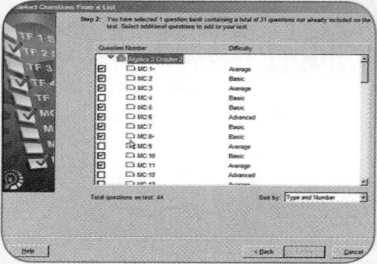

KEY: **SE** = *Student Edition* **TE** = *Teacher's Edition* **AR** = *Assessment Resources* SPANISH Spanish version available   Available on CD-ROM  Available online

CHAPTER
3

Three levels (A, B, C) of multiple-choice and free-response chapter tests are available in the *Assessment Resources.*

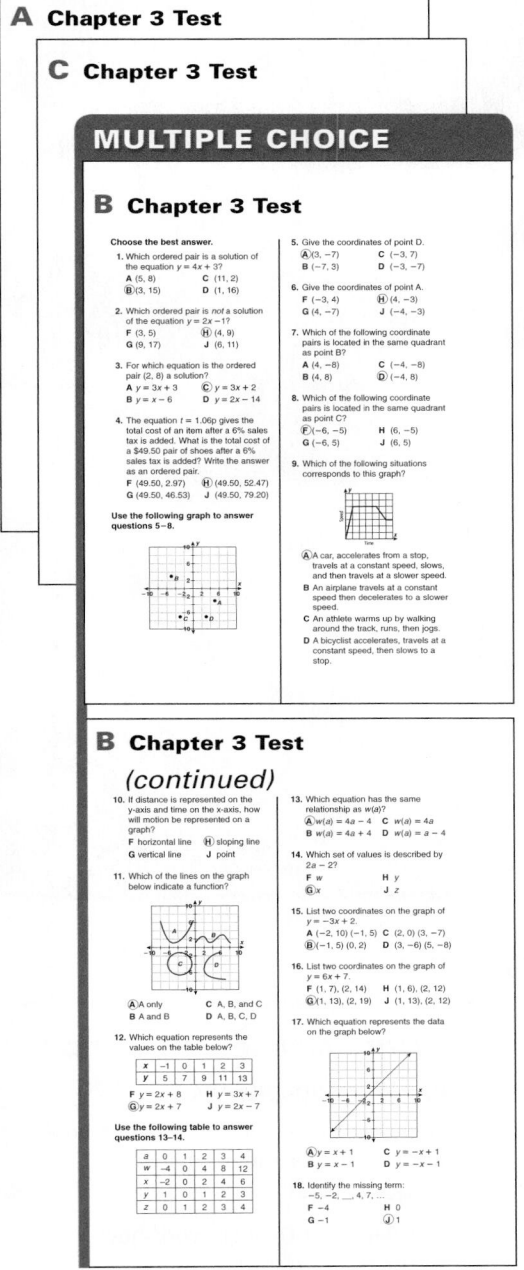

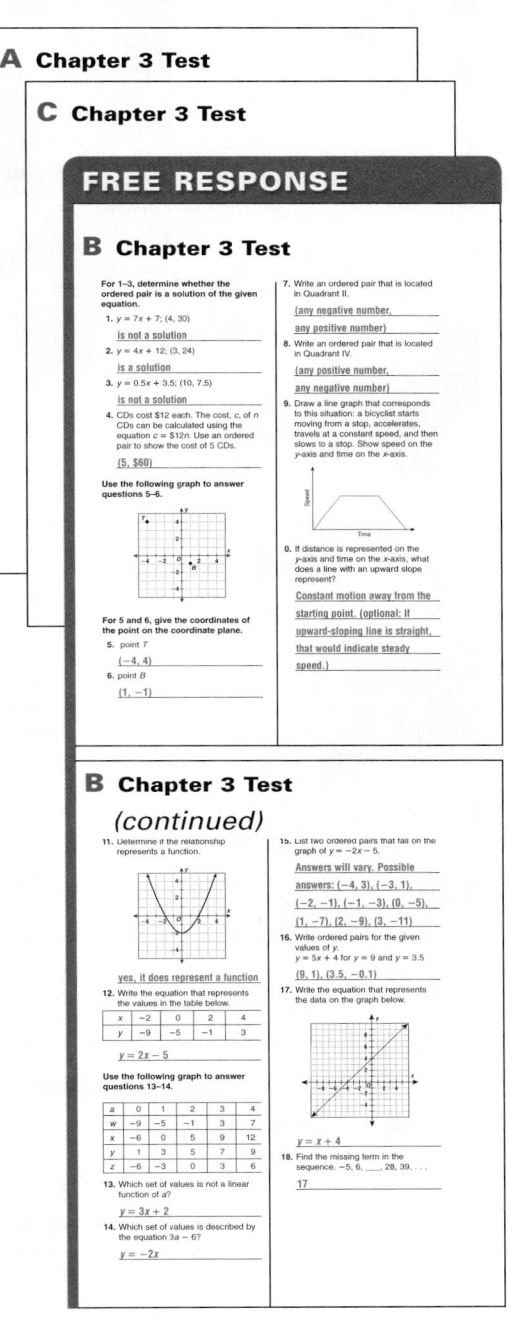

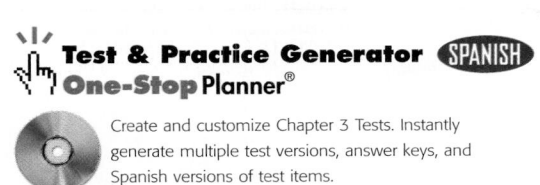

Graphs, Functions, and Sequences

Why Learn This?

Discuss with students that people in professions of all kinds rely on data to do their job. Have students look at the table. A pharmacist uses the table to provide patients with drug dosages. Tables, graphs, and equations help organize the information so that it is easier to use and interpret.

Using Data

To begin the study of this chapter, have students:

- Identify the weights of children based on information from the table.   25, 30, 35
- Calculate the recommended dosage of Paracetamol for a child that weighs 30 lbs.   162 mg
- Calculate the recommended dosage of Ibuprofen for a child that weighs 35 lbs.   77 mg

MULTI-STEP TEST PREP   On page 147, students create and interpret graphs that model the motion of remote-controlled cars.

3A	Tables and Graphs
3-1	Ordered Pairs
3-2	Graphing on a Coordinate Plane
LAB	Graph Points
3-3	Interpreting Graphs and Tables
3B	Functions and Sequences
3-4	Functions
3-5	Equations, Tables, and Graphs
3-6	Arithmetic Sequences

MULTI-STEP TEST PREP

go.hrw.com
Chapter Project Online
KEYWORD: MT7 Ch3

Recommended Doses for Children		
Weight of Child (lb)	Dose of Paracetamol (mg)	Dose of Ibuprofen (mg)
25	135	55
30	162	66
35	189	77

Career *Pharmacist*

In addition to dispensing medicine that has been prescribed by doctors, pharmacists advise patients about the uses and possible side effects of medications. Pharmacists may also make recommendations to help patients manage conditions such as diabetes and high blood pressure.

Although many pharmacists work in drugstores, others work closely with doctors and nurses in hospitals. Pharmacists in hospitals use tables like the one shown to help doctors provide correct doses of medicine to children.

Problem Solving Project

Understand, Plan, Solve, and Look Back

Have students:

- Complete the Painkiller Dosage worksheet to model the relationships between weight and dosages.
- Make a new dosage table using age instead of weight.
- Define interpolation and extrapolation and discuss how a pharmacist might use these.

Earth Science Connection

Project Resources

All project resources for teachers and students are provided online.

Materials:

- Painkiller Dosage worksheet
- graphing calculator

go.hrw.com
Project Teacher Support
KEYWORD: MT7 PSProject3

ARE YOU READY?

✓ Vocabulary

Choose the best term from the list to complete each sentence.

algebraic expression
equation
integer
rational number
variable

1. An __?__ states that two expressions have the same value.
2. Any number that can be written as a fraction is a __?__.
3. A __?__ serves as a placeholder for a number. **variable**
4. An __?__ can be a whole number or its opposite. **integer**

1. equation   2. rational number

Complete these exercises to review skills you will need for this chapter.

✓ Whole Number Operations

Evaluate each expression.

5. $5 + 12$ **17**   6. $18 - 9$ **9**   7. $25 \cdot 11$ **275**   8. $56 \div 4$ **14**
9. $8 \cdot 40$ **320**   10. $102 \div 3$ **34**   11. $250 - 173$ **77**   12. $107 + 298$ **405**

✓ Decimal Operations   13. 4.95   14. 39.8

Evaluate each expression.

13. $1.25 + 3.7$ 14. $52.7 - 12.9$ 15. $3.2 \cdot 1.2$ **3.84**   16. $5.7 \div 0.3$ **19**
17. $2.84 \div 1.3$ 18. $17.5 \cdot 12.1$ 19. $17.5 - 12.45$ 20. $2.75 + 13.254$
≈ 2.18 **211.75**   **5.05**   **16.004**

✓ Operations with Fractions

Evaluate each expression.

21. $\frac{2}{3} - \frac{1}{2}$ $\frac{1}{6}$ 22. $\frac{13}{18} + \frac{19}{24}$ $1\frac{37}{72}$ 23. $\frac{7}{8}\left(\frac{6}{11}\right)$ $\frac{21}{44}$ 24. $\frac{9}{10} \div \frac{9}{13}$ $1\frac{3}{10}$
25. $\frac{5}{6}\left(\frac{8}{15}\right)$ $\frac{4}{9}$ 26. $\frac{11}{12} \div \frac{121}{144}$ $1\frac{1}{11}$ 27. $\frac{1}{6} + \frac{5}{8}$ $\frac{19}{24}$ 28. $\frac{19}{20} - \frac{4}{5}$ $\frac{3}{20}$

✓ Integer Operations

Evaluate each expression.

29. $-15 + 7$ **−8** 30. $25 - (-23)$ **48** 31. $20(-13)$ **−260** 32. $\frac{-108}{9}$ **−12**
33. $\frac{161}{-7}$ **−23**   34. $-13 + (-28)$ 35. $-72 - 18$ **−90** 36. $-31(14)$ **−434**
                               −41

Organizer

Objective: Assess students' understanding of prerequisite skills.

Prerequisite Skills

Whole Number Operations
Decimal Operations
Operations with Fractions
Integer Operations

Assessing Prior Knowledge

Assessing Prior Knowledge

INTERVENTION

Diagnose and Prescribe

Use this page to determine whether intervention is necessary or whether enrichment is appropriate.

Resources

 Are You Ready? Intervention and Enrichment Worksheets

 Are You Ready? CD-ROM

Are You Ready? Online
my.hrw.com

ARE YOU READY?
Diagnose and Prescribe

 NO INTERVENE

 YES ENRICH

	ARE YOU READY? Intervention, Chapter 3		
✓ Prerequisite Skill	📖 Worksheets	💿 CD-ROM	🪐 Online
✓ Whole Number Operations	Skill 34	Activity 34	Diagnose and Prescribe Online
✓ Decimal Operations	Skill 40	Activity 40	
✓ Operations with Fractions	Skill 42	Activity 42	
✓ Integer Operations	Skill 47	Activity 47	

ARE YOU READY? Enrichment, Chapter 3
📖 **Worksheets**
💿 **CD-ROM**
🪐 **Online**

Organizer

Objective: Help students organize the new concepts they will learn in Chapter 3.

 Online Edition
Multilingual Glossary

Resources

 **PuzzlePro®**
One-Stop Planner®

 Multilingual Glossary Online

go.hrw.com
KEYWORD: MT7 Glossary

Possible answers to *Vocabulary Connections*

1. The origin is the first point of reference on a coordinate plane.
2. A quadrant is one of four sections of the graph.
3. Yes, the first number is related to the second number by a rule, which usually wouldn't be followed if the first and second number were switched.

Study Guide: Preview

Where You've Been

Previously, you

- located and named pairs of integers on a coordinate plane.
- graphed data to demonstrate familiar relationships.
- interpreted graphs, tables, and equations.

In This Chapter

You will study

- locating ordered pairs of rational numbers on a coordinate plane.
- generating different representations of data using tables, graphs, and equations.
- using an algebraic expression to determine any term in an arithmetic sequence.
- using function notation to describe relationships among data.

Where You're Going

You can use the skills learned in this chapter

- to use functions to analyze and describe relationships among data.
- to make predictions based on analysis of data.

Key Vocabulary/Vocabulario

coordinate plane	plano cartesiano
domain	dominio
function	functión
ordered pair	par ordenado
origin	origin
quadrant	cuadrante
range	recorrido o rango
sequence	successión
x-axis	eje de las *x*
y-axis	eje de las *y*

Vocabulary Connections

To become familiar with some of the vocabulary terms in the chapter, consider the following. You may refer to the chapter, the glossary, or a dictionary if you like.

1. The word **origin** means "beginning." How do you think this might apply to graphing?
2. The root of the word **quadrant** is *quad*, which means "four." What do you think a quadrant of a graph might be?
3. The word *ordered* means "arranged according to a rule." Do you think it matters which number comes first in an **ordered pair**? Explain.

 **Reading** and **Writing Math**

Reading Strategy: Read a Lesson for Understanding

You need to be actively involved as you work through each lesson in your textbook. To begin with, find the lesson's objective, which can be found at the top of the first page. As you progress through the lesson, keep the objective in mind while you work through examples and answer questions.

Lesson Features

Reading Tips

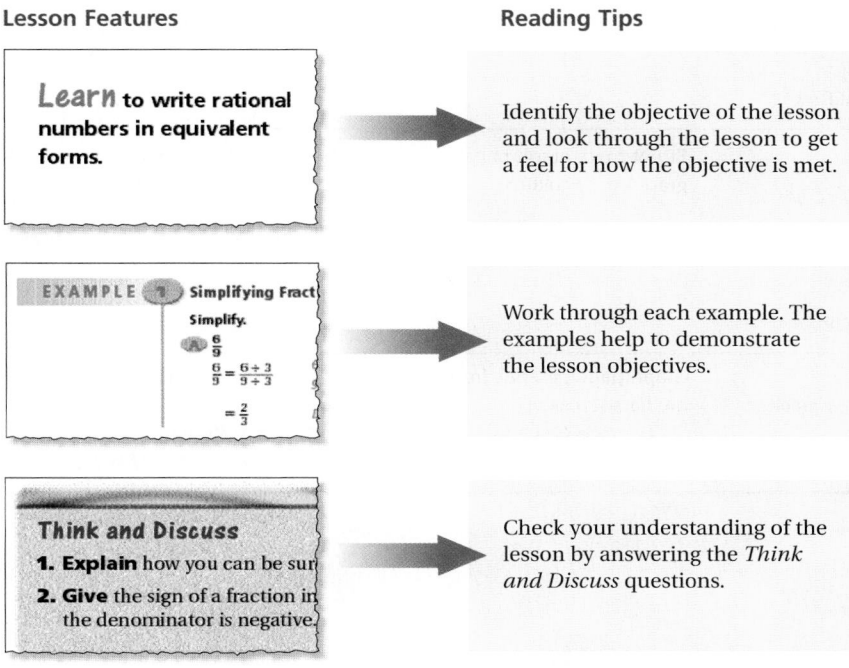

Learn to write rational numbers in equivalent forms.

→ Identify the objective of the lesson and look through the lesson to get a feel for how the objective is met.

EXAMPLE 1 Simplifying Fract
Simplify.
A $\frac{6}{9}$
$\frac{6}{9} = \frac{6 \div 3}{9 \div 3}$
$= \frac{2}{3}$

→ Work through each example. The examples help to demonstrate the lesson objectives.

Think and Discuss
1. **Explain** how you can be sur
2. **Give** the sign of a fraction i the denominator is negative.

→ Check your understanding of the lesson by answering the *Think and Discuss* questions.

Try This

Use Lesson 3-1 in your textbook to answer each question.

1. What is the objective of the lesson?
2. What questions or problems did you have when you read the lesson?
3. Write your own example problem similar to Example 2.
4. What skill is being practiced in the first *Think and Discuss* question?

Reading and Writing Math

Organizer

Objective: Help students apply strategies to understand and retain key concepts.

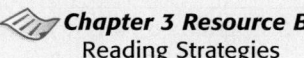 **Online Edition**

Resources

Chapter 3 Resource Book
Reading Strategies

Reading Strategy: Read a Lesson for Understanding

Discuss Students that do not understand why they are learning certain math skills will often become frustrated.

Remind students that paying attention to objectives will help them remember when and how to apply what they learn.

Extend Each time students complete a lesson in Chapter 3, ask whether they have met the lesson objective. Discuss how meeting the objective will help them in a real-life situation, pointing out word problems from the exercises or the examples.

Answers to *Try This*

1. Learn to write solutions of equations in two variables as ordered pairs
2. Students' answers will vary.
3. Check students' work.
4. Possible answer: Finding a solution of a two-variable equation.

Tables and Graphs

One-Minute Section Planner

Lesson	Materials	MiC and Lab Resources
Lesson 3-1 Ordered Pairs • Write solutions of equations in two variables as ordered pairs. ☐ SAT-10 ☑ ITBS ☑ CTBS ☑ NAEP		**MiC:** *Revisiting Numbers* pp. 45–46 *Technology Lab Activities* 3-1
Lesson 3-2 Graphing on a Coordinate Plane • Graph points and lines on the coordinate plane. **3-2 Technology Lab** Graph Points • Use a graphing calculator to plot points described by ordered pairs and adjust the viewing window. ☑ SAT-10 ☑ ITBS ☑ CTBS ☑ NAEP	Street map, graph paper, graphing calculator	**MiC:** *Revisiting Numbers* pp. 49–50 *Technology Lab Activities* 3-2
Lesson 3-3 Interpreting Graphs and Tables • Interpret information given in a graph or table and make a graph to solve problems. ☑ SAT-10 ☑ ITBS ☑ CTBS ☑ NAEP	Graph paper, graphs from media sources	**MiC:** *Ups and Downs* pp. 6–9, 17–19, 24–27, 36–39 **MiC:** *Algebra Rules* pp. 13–14 *Technology Lab Activities* 3-3

MK = *Manipulatives Kit*

Mathematics in Context

The units ***Revisiting Numbers, Ups and Downs,*** and ***Algebra Rules*** from the *Mathematics in Context* © 2006 series can be used with Section 3A. See Section Planner above for suggestions for integrating *MiC* with *Holt Mathematics*.

Section Overview

Ordered Pair Solutions of Equations in Two Variables

Lesson 3-1

 Why? Functional relationships between two quantities can be expressed using ordered pairs of numbers.

A solution of a two-variable equation is written as an **ordered pair.**

When the numbers in the ordered pair are substituted in the equation, they make it true.

Find solutions of $y = x + 3$.

$(1, 4)$ is a solution. → $4 = 1 + 3$

Make a table of solutions for $y = x + 3$.

x	$y = x + 3$	(x, y)
1	4	$(1, 4)$
2	5	$(2, 5)$
4	7	$(4, 7)$

Graphing an Equation

Lesson 3-2

Why? The graph of an equation displays relationships and patterns between two variables.

Graph the equation $y = x + 3$.

From the table above, $(1, 4)$, $(2, 5)$, and $(4, 7)$ are points of the equation.

Plot these points.

Draw the line through the points. The line represents all possible solutions.

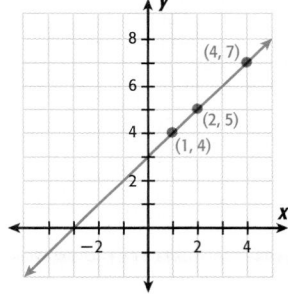

> The graph of an equation is the set of all ordered pairs that are solutions of the equation.

Interpreting Graphs and Tables

Lesson 3-3

Why? Real-world situations may be described by tables or graphs.

Sally walks to the end of the street and then quickly runs down a steep hill. At the bottom of the hill, Sally stops to tie her shoe. Then she walks over to Amy's house and stops.

Time	Speed (mi/h)
4:00	4
4:01	7
4:02	0
4:03	4
4:04	0

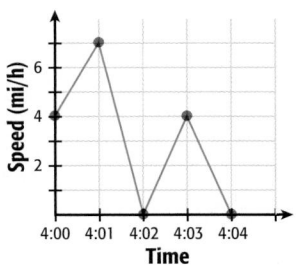

Pacing: Traditional 1 day
Block $\frac{1}{2}$ day

Objective: Students write solutions of equations in two variables as ordered pairs.

Technology Lab
In *Technology Lab Activities*

Online Edition
Tutorial Videos

Countdown to Testing Week 5

Power Presentations
with PowerPoint®

Warm Up

Solve.

1. $x - 8 = 19$ $x = 27$

2. $5 = a - 2$ $a = 7$

3. $7 + n = 24$ $n = 17$

4. $3c - 7 = 32$ $c = 13$

5. $17y + 7 = 58$ $y = 3$

Problem of the Day

A moving van travels 50 miles per hour. Use the equation $y = 50x$ where x represents the number of hours. How far will the van travel in 4.5 hours? 225 miles

Also available on transparency

Math Humor

Can you believe a student tried to cheat on his graphing test? Some people just don't know where to draw the line.

Learn to write solutions of equations in two variables as ordered pairs.

Vocabulary
ordered pair

The company that makes team uniforms for a soccer league charges a $20 fee for team artwork and $10 for each jersey. Dominic's team has 14 players, and Alyssa's team has 12 players. Find the cost for a set of jerseys for each team.

Let y be the total cost of a set of jerseys and x be the number of jerseys needed.

| total cost of jerseys | = | $20 | + | $10 | · | number of jerseys |

$$y = \$20 + \$10 \cdot x$$

Dominic's team: $y = \$20 + (\$10 \cdot 14)$ Alyssa's team: $y = \$20 + (\$10 \cdot 12)$
         $y = \$160$ $y = \$140$

An **ordered pair** (x, y) is a pair of numbers that can be used to locate a point on a coordinate plane. A solution of a two-variable equation can be written as an ordered pair.

The ordered pair $(14, 160)$ is a solution because $160 = \$20 + (\$10 \cdot 14)$.
The ordered pair $(12, 140)$ is a solution because $140 = \$20 + (\$10 \cdot 12)$.

EXAMPLE 1 **Deciding Whether an Ordered Pair Is a Solution of an Equation**

Determine whether each ordered pair is a solution of $y = 3x + 2$.

Helpful Hint

The order in which a solution is written is important. Always write x first, then y.

(A) $(2, 5)$ $y = 3x + 2$
                $5 \stackrel{?}{=} 3(2) + 2$ *Substitute 2 for x and 5 for y.*
                $5 \stackrel{?}{=} 8$ ✗   *Simplify.*
          $(2, 5)$ is *not* a solution.

(B) $(3, 11)$ $y = 3x + 2$
               $11 \stackrel{?}{=} 3(3) + 2$ *Substitute 3 for x and 11 for y.*
               $11 \stackrel{?}{=} 11$ ✔   *Simplify.*
          $(3, 11)$ is a solution.

---

1 Introduce

Alternate Opener

EXPLORATION

3-1 **Ordered Pairs**

At the GasCo station, gasoline costs $3 per gallon. Let x represent the number of gallons of gasoline that you buy and let y represent the total cost of the gasoline.

1. Complete the table.

Number of Gallons, x	Total cost, y
1	$3
2	
3	
4	
5	
6	

2. Each row of the table contains an *ordered pair*. An ordered pair lists an x-value and its corresponding y-value. For example, the first row of the table contains the ordered pair $(1, 3)$. Write the ordered pairs in the other rows of your table.

3. The equation $y = 3x$ gives the cost of x gallons of gasoline. Use the equation to find the cost of 12 gallons of gasoline.

4. Write the ordered pair from Problem 3.

Think and Discuss

5. Describe how you could find a new ordered pair for the above situation.

6. Explain whether you think the ordered pair $(1, 3)$ is the same as $(3, 1)$.

Motivate

Show the students a simple two-variable equation, such as $x + y = 10$. Ask students to supply pairs of numbers whose sum is 10. Organize their answers in a table using one value of each pair for x and the other in the same pair for y. Explain to students that because there are two variables, each solution is a pair of numbers.

Explorations and answers are provided in *Alternate Openers: Explorations Transparencies.*

EXAMPLE 2 Creating a Table of Ordered Pair Solutions

Use the given values to make a table of solutions.

A $y = 8x$ for $x = 1, 2, 3, 4$

Helpful Hint

A table of solutions can be set up vertically or horizontally.

x	8x	y	(x, y)
1	8(1)	8	(1, 8)
2	8(2)	16	(2, 16)
3	8(3)	24	(3, 24)
4	8(4)	32	(4, 32)

B $n = 4m - 3$ for $m = -4, -3, -2, -1$

m	−4	−3	−2	−1
4m − 3	4(−4) − 3	4(−3) − 3	4(−2) − 3	4(−1) − 3
n	−19	−15	−11	−7
(m, n)	(−4, −19)	(−3, −15)	(−2, −11)	(−1, −7)

EXAMPLE 3 *Consumer Math Application*

In most states, the price of each item is not the total cost. Sales tax must be added. If sales tax is 6%, the equation for total cost is $c = 1.06p$, where p is the price before tax.

A How much will Dominic's $160 set of jerseys cost after sales tax?

$c = 1.06(160)$ *The price of Dominic's set of jerseys before tax is $160.*

$c = 169.6$ *Multiply.*

After tax, Dominic's $160 set of jerseys will cost $169.60, so (160, 169.60) is a solution of the equation.

B How much will Alyssa's $140 set of jerseys cost after sales tax?

$c = 1.06(140)$ *The price of Alyssa's set of jerseys before tax is $140.*

$c = 148.4$ *Multiply.*

After tax, Alyssa's $140 set of jerseys will cost $148.40, so (140, 148.40) is a solution of the equation.

Possible answers to *Think and Discuss*

1. Substitute a value for one variable into the equation and solve to find the value of the other variable.

2. In general, there is no limit to the number of values you can substitute into the equation.

3. $y = x + 1$ and $y = 2x$

Think and Discuss

1. **Describe** how to find a solution of a two-variable equation.

2. **Explain** why an equation with two variables has an infinite number of solutions.

3. **Give** two equations using x and y that have (1, 2) as a solution.

Power Presentations with PowerPoint®

Additional Examples

Example 1

Determine whether each ordered pair is a solution of $y = 4x - 1$.

A. (3, 11)   yes   **B.** (10, 3)   no

Example 2

Use the given values to make a table of solutions.

A. $y = x + 3$ for $x = 1, 2, 3, 4$

x	x + 3	y	(x, y)
1	1 + 3	4	(1, 4)
2	2 + 3	5	(2, 5)
3	3 + 3	6	(3, 6)
4	4 + 3	7	(4, 7)

B. $n = 6m - 5$ for $m = 1, 2, 3$

m	1	2	3
6m − 5	6(1) − 5	6(2) − 5	6(3) − 5
n	1	7	13
(m, n)	(1, 1)	(2, 7)	(3, 13)

Example 3

A salesman marks up the price of everything he sells by 20%. The equation for the sales price p is $p = 1.2w$, where w is wholesale cost.

A. What will be the sales price of a sweater with a wholesale cost of $48? $57.60

B. What will be the sales price of a jacket with a wholesale cost of $85? $102

Also available on transparency

---

2 Teach

Guided Instruction

In this lesson, students learn to write solutions of equations in two variables as ordered pairs. To see if an ordered pair is a solution of a two-variable equation, substitute the first number in the ordered pair for x and the second number in the ordered pair for y. If the result is true, then the ordered pair is a solution of the equation. To find a solution of a two-variable equation, substitute any number for x in the equation, and then solve the equation for y.

Reaching All Learners
Through Visual Cues

Have students make a table of solutions for $y = 2x$ using $x = 1, 2, 3$, and 4. When they have the solutions (1, 2), (2, 4), (3, 6), and (4, 8), have them describe any patterns they notice. Help students see that the y-value is always twice the x-value. Have them find y when x is 1000 ($y = 2000$). Then have them find x when y is 1000 ($x = 500$).

3 Close

Summarize

Discuss the similarities and differences between one-variable equations and two-variable equations. Ask students to define an ordered pair. Make sure students understand that two-variable equations have an infinite number of solutions.

Possible answers: Both types of equations have variables, and solutions can be checked by substituting values and solving. One-variable equations usually have one solution that is a single number, but two-variable equations have many solutions that are ordered pairs of numbers.

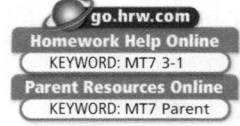

go.hrw.com
Homework Help Online
KEYWORD: MT7 3-1
Parent Resources Online
KEYWORD: MT7 Parent

Assignment Guide

If you finished Example **1** assign:
Average 1–4, 8–11, 23, 24, 36–44
Advanced 8–11, 17–24, 32, 36–44

If you finished Example **2** assign:
Average 1–6, 8–15, 23, 24, 27, 28, 36–44
Advanced 8–11, 17–24, 29, 30, 32–34, 36–44

If you finished Example **3** assign:
Average 1–16, 23, 24, 26–28, 31, 36–44
Advanced 8–26, 29–44

Homework Quick Check

Quickly check key concepts.
Exercises: 8, 14, 16, 18, 26

Answers

5, 6, 12–15. See pp. A1–A2.

Math Background

In Think and Discuss problem 2, it is noted that a two-variable equation generally has an infinite number of solutions. It is easy to see that some solutions of the equation $y = x + 2$ are (1, 3), (2, 4), (3, 5), (4, 6), (5, 7), etc. What may not be as obvious is that solutions can contain negative values and non-integer values. Some other solutions of the same equation are (−1, 1), (1.4, 3.4), and $\left(\frac{3}{8}, 2\frac{3}{8}\right)$.

GUIDED PRACTICE

See Example **1** Determine whether each ordered pair is a solution of $y = 2x - 4$.

1. (3, 2) **yes**   **2.** (−4, 5) **no**   **3.** (6, 8) **yes**   **4.** (2, 0) **yes**

See Example **2** Use the given values to make a table of solutions.

5. $y = 2x$ for $x = 1, 2, 3, 4$ **6.** $y = 4x - 1$ for $x = -4, -3, -2, -1$

See Example **3** **7.** The cost of a small frozen yogurt is $2.50 plus $0.15 per topping. The equation that gives the total cost c of a small frozen yogurt is $c = 0.15n + 2.50$, where n is the number of toppings. What is the cost of a small frozen yogurt with 3 toppings? **$2.95**

INDEPENDENT PRACTICE

See Example **1** Determine whether each ordered pair is a solution of $y = 4x + 3$.

8. (2, 9) **no**   **9.** (4, 20) **no**   **10.** (5, 23) **yes**   **11.** (6, 28) **no**

See Example **2** Use the given values to make a table of solutions.

12. $y = 2x - 1$ for $x = 1, 2, 3, 4$ **13.** $y = 3x + 9$ for $x = -4, -3, -2, -1$

14. $y = 4x - 5$ for $x = 2, 4, 6, 8$ **15.** $y = 3x - 4$ for $x = 2, 4, 6, 8$

See Example **3** **16.** The fine for speeding in one town is $90 plus $7 for every mile over the speed limit. The equation that gives the total cost c of a speeding ticket is $c = 90 + 7m$, where m is the number of miles over the posted speed limit. Rhonda was issued a ticket for going 63 mi/h in a 50 mi/h zone. What was the total cost of the ticket? **$181**

PRACTICE AND PROBLEM SOLVING

Extra Practice
See page 786.

Determine whether each ordered pair is a solution of $y = x + 3$.

17. (4, 7) **yes**   **18.** (−3, 0) **yes**   **19.** (5, 8) **yes**   **20.** (2, 6) **no**

Determine whether each ordered pair is a solution of $y = 3x - 5$.

21. (−2, 2) **no**   **22.** (4, 8) **no**   **23.** (3, 4) **yes**   **24.** (6, 12) **no**

25. Multi-Step A wireless phone company charges a monthly fee of $39.99 plus $0.49 per minute for usage that exceeds the included minutes. Write an equation for the monthly cost c in terms of the number of exceeded minutes m. Solve the equation to find the cost when the number of exceeded minutes is 29. Write your answer as an ordered pair. $c = 39.99 + 0.49m$; (29, 54.20)

26. Geometry The perimeter P of a square is four times the length of one side s, or $P = 4s$. Is (14, 55) a solution of this equation? If not, find a solution that uses one of the given values. **no; (14, 56) or (13.75, 55)**

State Resources

go.hrw.com
State Resources Online
KEYWORD: MT7 Resources

RETEACH 3-1

LESSON **3-1** Reteach
Ordered Pairs

An **ordered pair** can be used to write a solution for a two-variable equation. For the equation $y = x + 5$, a solution is (0, 5). When the x-value is 0, the y-value is 5.   (0, 5) *x-value y-value*

Which of the ordered pairs (5, 3) or (3, 5) is a solution of $y = 2x - 1$?

$y = 2x - 1$		$y = 2x - 1$	
$3 \stackrel{?}{=} 2(5) - 1$	Substitute 5 for x and 3 for y.	$5 \stackrel{?}{=} 2(3) - 1$	Substitute 3 for x and 5 for y.
$3 \stackrel{?}{=} 10 - 1$		$5 \stackrel{?}{=} 6 - 1$	
$3 \neq 9$		$5 = 5$	

So, (5, 3) *is not* a solution of $y = 2x - 1$.

So, (3, 5) *is a solution* of $y = 2x - 1$.

Determine whether each ordered pair is a solution of the given equation. Write *is* or *is not*.

1. $y = 4x + 3$; (1, 6)   **2.** $y = 4x + 3$; (0, 3)   **3.** $y = x + 3$; (3, 0)
    is not   is   is not

4. $y = 5x$; (3, 15)   **5.** $y = 3x - 4$; (5, 3)   **6.** $y = 6 - x$; (4, 2)
    is   is not   is

A two-variable equation has infinitely many solutions. Use a table to find and record some solutions to a given equation. Use $x = 1, 2,$ and 3, for example, to make a table of values for $y = 5x - 1$. Substitute each given value of x in the expression for x. Evaluate the expression to find the value of y that completes the ordered pair.

x	$5x - 9 = y$	(x, y)
1	$5(1) - 1 = 4$	(1, 4)
2	$5(2) - 1 = 9$	(2, 9)
3	$5(3) - 1 = 14$	(3, 14)

Complete each table.

7. $y = 4x$

x	$4x = y$	(x, y)
0	$4(0) = 0$	(0, 0)
1	$4(1) = 4$	(1, 4)
2	$4(2) = 8$	(2, 8)

8. $y = 5x - 3$

x	$5x - 3 = y$	(x, y)
1	$5(1) - 3 = 2$	(1, 2)
2	$5(2) - 3 = 7$	(2, 7)
3	$5(3) - 3 = 12$	(3, 12)

PRACTICE 3-1

LESSON **3-1** Practice B
Ordered Pairs

Determine whether each ordered pair is a solution of $y = 4 + 2x$.

1. (1, 1)   **2.** (2, 8)   **3.** (0, 4)   **4.** (8, 2)
    no   yes   yes   no

Determine whether each ordered pair is a solution of $y = 3x - 2$.

5. (1, 1)   **6.** (3, 7)   **7.** (5, 15)   **8.** (6, 16)
    yes   yes   no   yes

Use the given values to complete the table of solutions.

9. $y = x + 5$ for $x = 0, 1, 2, 3, 4$

x	$x + 5$	y	(x, y)
0	$0 + 5$	5	(0, 5)
1	$1 + 5$	6	(1, 6)
2	$2 + 5$	7	(2, 7)
3	$3 + 5$	8	(3, 8)
4	$4 + 5$	9	(4, 9)

10. $y = 3x + 1$ for $x = 1, 2, 3, 4, 5$

x	$3x + 1$	y	(x, y)
1	$3(1) + 1$	4	(1, 4)
2	$3(2) + 1$	7	(2, 7)
3	$3(3) + 1$	10	(3, 10)
4	$3(4) + 1$	13	(4, 13)
5	$3(5) + 1$	16	(5, 16)

11. $y = 2x + 6$ for $x = 0, 1, 2, 3, 4$

x	$2x + 6$	y	(x, y)
0	$2(0) + 6$	6	(0, 6)
1	$2(1) + 6$	8	(1, 8)
2	$2(2) + 6$	10	(2, 10)
3	$2(3) + 6$	12	(3, 12)
4	$2(4) + 6$	14	(4, 14)

12. $y = 4x - 2$ for $x = 2, 4, 6, 8, 10$

x	$4x - 2$	y	(x, y)
2	$4(2) - 2$	6	(2, 6)
4	$4(4) - 2$	14	(4, 14)
6	$4(6) - 2$	22	(6, 22)
8	$4(8) - 2$	30	(8, 30)
10	$4(10) - 2$	38	(10, 38)

13. Alexis opened a savings account with a $120 deposit. Each week she will put $20 into the account. The equation that gives the total amount t in her account is $t = 120 + 20w$, where w is the number of weeks since she opened the account. How much money will Alexis have in her account after 5 weeks?

$220

Use the given values to make a table of solutions.

27. $y = 2x - 2$ for $x = 1, 2, 3, 4$

28. $y = 3x - 1$ for $x = -4, -3, -2, -1$

29. $y = x + 7$ for $x = 1, 2, 3, 4, 5$

30. $y = 3x + 2$ for $x = 2, 4, 6, 8, 10$

31. **History** The life expectancy of Americans has been rising steadily since 1940. An ordered pair can be used to show the relationship between your birth year and life expectancy.

Life Expectancy in Years

a. Write an ordered pair that shows the approximate life expectancy of an American born in 1980. **(1980, 74)**

b. The data on the chart can be approximated by the equation $L = 0.2n - 323$, where L is the life expectancy and n is the year of birth. Use the equation to find an ordered pair that shows the approximate life expectancy for an American born in 2020. **(2020, 81)**

In 1513, Ponce de León went in search of the legendary Fountain of Youth, which people believed would give them eternal youth. While searching, he discovered Florida, which he named Pascua de Florida.

32. **Critical Thinking** Two solutions of an equation are (6, 5) and (8, 5). What could the equation be? Explain. $y = 5$; possible answer: for any value of x, y is 5.

33. **What's The Error?** A student thinks that (1, 2) is the solution to $y = 2x - 3$. While checking the solution, the student gets $1 = 2(2) - 3$. What is wrong with this calculation? Explain the error.
The student switched the values for x and y.

34. **Write About It** Write an equation that has (2, 6) as a solution. Explain how you found the equation.
Possible answer: $y = x + 4$ because 6 is 4 more than 2.

35. **Challenge** In the NBA, a shot made from beyond the arc is worth 3 points. A shot made on or in front of the arc is worth 2 points. If x equals the number of 3-point baskets scored and y equals the number of 2-point baskets scored, find the possible solutions of the equation $36 = 3x + 2y$.
(0, 18), (2, 15), (4, 12), (6, 9), (8, 6), (10, 3), (12, 0)

TEST PREP and Spiral Review

36. **Multiple Choice** Which ordered pair is a solution of $2y - 3x = 8$?

(A) (6, 13)   (B) (19, 4)   (C) (10, 4)   (D) (4, 0)

37. **Multiple Choice** Which ordered pair is NOT a solution of $y = 3x - 2$?

(F) (0, -2)   (G) (-2, -8)   (H) (2, 4)   (J) (2, 0)

Solve. (Lesson 2-7)

38. $y + 10.2 = -33$ -43.2

39. $-\frac{x}{3.2} = -4$ 12.8

40. $2.6m = -23.4$ -9

Multiply or divide. Write each answer in simplest form. (Lessons 2-4 and 2-5)

41. $\frac{2}{3} \cdot \frac{9}{10}$ $\frac{3}{5}$

42. $\frac{4}{5} \cdot \frac{3}{8}$ $\frac{3}{10}$

43. $\frac{1}{3} \div \frac{2}{3}$ $\frac{1}{2}$

44. $\frac{11}{15} \div \frac{5}{22}$ $3\frac{17}{75}$

3-1 Lesson Quiz

Determine whether each ordered pair is a solution of $y = 4x - 7$.

1. (2, 15)   no
2. (4, 9)   yes

3. Use the given values to make a table of solutions.
$y = 4x - 6$ for $x = 2, 4, 6, 8,$ and 10

x	$4x - 6$	y	(x, y)
2	$4(2) - 6$	2	(2, 2)
4	$4(4) - 6$	10	(4, 10)
6	$4(6) - 6$	18	(6, 18)
8	$4(8) - 6$	26	(8, 26)
10	$4(10) - 6$	34	(10, 34)

4. A plumbing company charges $50 for a service call and $15 per hour. They went on a 3-hour job. How much did the company earn?
$C = 15n + 50$; $95

Also available on transparency

CHALLENGE 3-1

LESSON 3-1 Challenge
1-2-3, x-y-z

The solution of a three-variable equation is written as an ordered triple. For example, (x, y, z) represents a solution of the equation $3x + 2y + 7z = 32$. You can verify that $(1, 4, 3)$ is a solution of $3x + 2y + 7z = 32$ by substituting $x = 1$, $y = 4$, and $z = 3$.

Arrange the numbers of the given ordered triple so that the result is a solution of the given equation.

1. (0, 0, 8)   2. (7, 3, 0)   3. (2, 3, 10)

$5x + 8y - 3z = 64$ $4x + 5y - z = 8$ $7x - y + 2z = 10$

(0, 8, 0)   (0, 3, 7)   (2, 10, 3)

4. $\left(\frac{1}{2}, \frac{1}{3}, \frac{1}{4}\right)$ 5. $\left(4, 0, \frac{1}{5}\right)$ 6. $\left(2, \frac{1}{3}, 1\right)$

$10x + 9y + 8z = 10$ $15x - 21y + z = 7$ $3x + 12y - 2z = 9$

$\left(\frac{1}{2}, \frac{1}{3}, \frac{1}{4}\right)$ $\left(\frac{1}{5}, 0, 4\right)$ $\left(\frac{1}{3}, 1, 2\right)$

Determine the value of the indicated variable(s) so that the resulting ordered triple is a solution of the given equation.

7. (x, 0, 5)   8. (2, y, 0)   9. (2, 3, z)

$2x - 6y + z = 13$ $5x - y + 3z = 9$ $3x + 5y + 8z = 37$

(4, 0, 5)   (2, 1, 0)   (2, 3, 2)

10. (x, y, 0)   11. (x, 8, z)   12. (0, y, z)

$7x + 5y - 4z = 25$ $x + 3y - 5z = 15$ $3x - 4y - z = 0$

(0, 5, 0)   (1, 8, 2)   (0, 0, 0)

Possible answers are shown for Exercises 10–12.

PROBLEM SOLVING 3-1

LESSON 3-1 Problem Solving
Ordered Pairs

Use the table at the right for Exercises 1–2.

1. Write the ordered pair that shows the average miles per gallon in 1990.
(1990, 20.2)

Average Miles per Gallon	
Year	Miles per Gallon
1970	13.5
1980	15.9
1990	20.2
1995	21.1
1996	21.2
1997	21.5

2. The data can be approximated by the equation $m = 0.30887x - 595$ where m is the average miles per gallon and x is the year. Use the equation to find an ordered pair (x, m) that shows the estimated miles per gallon in the year 2020.
(2020, 28.9)

For Exercises 3–4 use the equation $F = 1.8C + 32$, which relates Fahrenheit temperatures F to Celsius temperatures C.

3. Write ordered pair (C, F) that shows the Celsius equivalent of 86°F.
(30, 86)

4. Write ordered pair (C, F) that shows the Fahrenheit equivalent of 22°C.
(22, 71.6)

Choose the letter for the best answer.

5. A taxi charges a $2.50 flat fee plus $0.30 per mile. Use an equation for taxi fare t in terms of miles m. Which ordered pair (m, t) shows the taxi fare for a 23-mile cab ride?
A (23, 6.90)   C (23, 9.40)
B (23, 18.50)   D (23, 64.40)

6. The perimeter p of a square is four times the length of a side s, or $p = 4s$. Which ordered pair (C, F) shows the perimeter for a square that has sides that are 5 in.?
F (5, 1.25)   H (5, 9)
G (5, 20)   J (5, 25)

7. Maria pays a monthly fee of $3.95 plus $0.10 per minute for long distance calls. Use an equation for the phone bill p in terms of the number of minutes m. Which ordered pair (m, p) shows the phone bill for 120 minutes?
A (120, 15.95)   C (120, 28.30)
B (120, 474.10)   D (120, 486.00)

8. Tickets to a baseball game cost $12 each, plus $2 each for transportation. Use an equation for the cost c of going to the game in terms of the number of people p. Which ordered pair (p, c) shows the cost for 6 people?
F (6, 74)   H (6, 84)
G (6, 96)   J (6, 102)

Objective: Students graph points and lines on the coordinate plane.

 Online Edition
Tutorial Videos

Countdown to Testing Week 5

Power Presentations
with PowerPoint®

Warm Up
Find the values for _y_ by substituting 1, 3, 5, and 7 for _x_.

1. $y = 2x - 3$ −1, 3, 7, 11
2. $y = 4x + 1$ 5, 13, 21, 29
3. $y = 5x - 5$ 0, 10, 20, 30

Problem of the Day
What day is four days after the day before Saturday? Tuesday
Also available on transparency

Power Presentations
with PowerPoint®

Additional Example

Example 1

Give the coordinates and quadrant of each point.

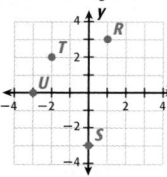

_R_ (1,3); Quadrant I
_S_ (0,−3); no quadrant
_T_ (−2,2); Quadrant II
_U_ (−3,0); no quadrant

Also available on transparency

State Resources

go.hrw.com
State Resources Online
KEYWORD: MT7 Resources

3-2 Graphing on a Coordinate Plane

Learn to graph points and lines on the coordinate plane.

Vocabulary
coordinate plane
_x_-axis
_y_-axis
quadrant
_x_-coordinate
_y_-coordinate
origin
graph of an equation

Helpful Hint

The sign of a number indicates which direction to move. Positive: up or right Negative: down or left

Mary left a message for Pedro that read, "Meet me at the corner of East Lincoln Street and North Third Street." On the map, you can identify a location by the intersection of two streets. Finding points on a coordinate plane is like finding a location on a map.

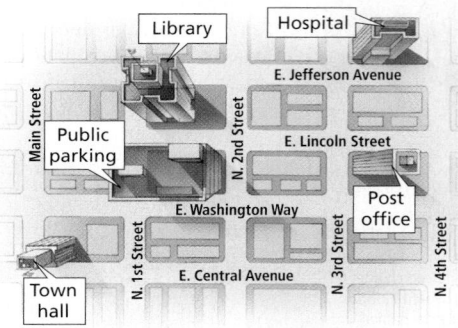

The **coordinate plane** is formed by two number lines, the **_x_-axis** and the **_y_-axis** . They intersect at right angles and divide the plane into four **quadrants** . The **_x_-coordinate** is the first number in an ordered pair. The **_y_-coordinate** is the second number of an ordered pair.

To plot an ordered pair, begin at the **origin**, the point (0, 0). It is the intersection of the _x_-axis and the _y_-axis. The _x_-coordinate tells how many units to move left or right; the _y_-coordinate tells how many units to move up or down.

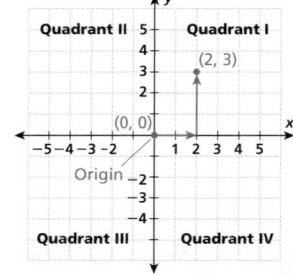

move right 2 units **(2, 3)** *move up 3 units*

EXAMPLE 1 **Finding the Coordinates and Quadrants of Points on a Plane**

Give the coordinates and quadrant of each point.

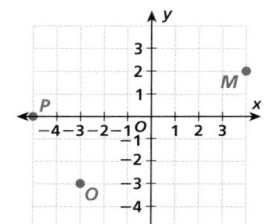

Point _M_ is (4, 2); in Quadrant I.
4 units right, 2 units up
Point _O_ is (−3, −3); in Quadrant III.
3 units left, 3 units down
Point _P_ is (−5, 0); it has no quadrant because _P_ is on the _x_-axis.
5 units left, 0 units up

---

1 Introduce
Alternate Opener

EXPLORATION

3-2 **Graphing on a Coordinate Plane**

You are about to give directions to the locations labeled on the grid. The only restrictions are the following:

• You can move only horizontally (sideways) or vertically (up and down).
• Your first move should be horizontal. Use the directions *left* or *right*.
• Your second move should be vertical. Use the directions *up* or *down*.

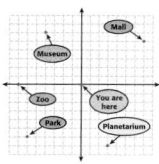

Give directions to go to each location.
1. the museum
2. the park
3. the mall
4. the zoo
5. the planetarium

Think and Discuss
6. **Explain** how to write the directions for the locations in Problems 1–5 using *ordered-pair* notation. (*Hint:* the museum is at (−4, 6).)

Motivate
Discuss some situations in which locations are determined by a grid. Examples may include street maps, latitude and longitude, or games like computer chess or Battleship®. Show the students a map with a grid. Demonstrate how to use the labels on the top, bottom, and sides to find a particular area on the map. Explain that a similar procedure will be used in the lesson.

Explorations and answers are provided in *Alternate Openers: Explorations Transparencies.*

EXAMPLE 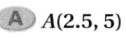 **2** **Graphing Points on a Coordinate Plane**

Graph each point on a coordinate plane.

A $A(2.5, 5)$ **B** $B\left(0, 4\frac{1}{2}\right)$

right 2.5, up 5   right 0, up $4\frac{1}{2}$

C $C\left(-1\frac{1}{5}, 2.7\right)$ **D** $D(2.3, -3)$

left $1\frac{1}{5}$, up 2.7   right 2.3, down 3

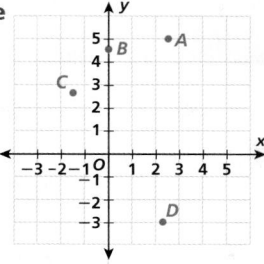

The **graph of an equation** is the set of all ordered pairs that are solutions of the equation.

EXAMPLE **3** **Graphing an Equation of a Line**

Complete each table of ordered pairs. Graph each ordered pair on a coordinate plane.

A $y = 2\frac{1}{2}x$

x	$2\frac{1}{2}x$	y	(x, y)
1	$2\frac{1}{2}(1)$	$2\frac{1}{2}$	$(1, 2\frac{1}{2})$
2	$2\frac{1}{2}(2)$	5	$(2, 5)$
3	$2\frac{1}{2}(3)$	$7\frac{1}{2}$	$(3, 7\frac{1}{2})$

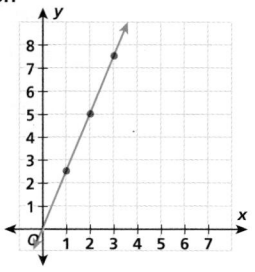

The points of each equation are on a straight line. Draw a line through the points to represent all possible solutions.

B $y = 3x - 2$

x	$3x - 2$	y	(x, y)
0	$3(0) - 2$	-2	$(0, -2)$
1	$3(1) - 2$	1	$(1, 1)$
2	$3(2) - 2$	4	$(2, 4)$

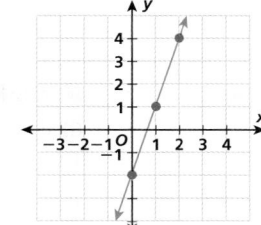

Possible answers to Think and Discuss

1. x-axis: $(3, 0)$; y-axis: $(0, 4)$

2. $y = 7$; $y = 17$; $y = 52$

Think and Discuss

1. Give the coordinates of a point on the x-axis and a point on the y-axis.

2. Give the missing y-coordinates for the solutions to $y = 5x + 2$: $(1, y)$, $(3, y)$, $(10, y)$.

Power Presentations with PowerPoint®

Additional Examples

Example **2**

Graph each point on a coordinate plane.

A. $A (3, 4)$ **B.** $B (4, 0)$

C. $C (-4, 4)$ **D.** $D (-1, -3)$

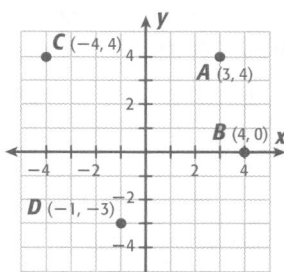

Example **3**

Complete the table for $y = 2x - 3$. Graph the ordered pairs on a coordinate plane.

x	$2x - 3$	y	(x, y)
0	$2(0) - 3$	-3	$(0, -3)$
1	$2(1) - 3$	-1	$(1, -1)$
2	$2(2) - 3$	1	$(2, 1)$
3	$2(3) - 3$	3	$(3, 3)$

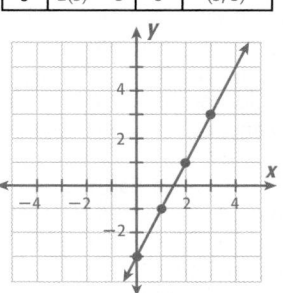

Also available on transparency

---

2 **Teach**

Guided Instruction

In this lesson, students learn to graph points and lines on a coordinate plane. To begin, show students how to create a coordinate plane by using graph paper. Explain that each axis is a number line, and show them how to label and number the axes. You may want to display the Teaching Transparency. Use your sample to define the vocabulary terms. Show students how to identify the location of a point by giving its coordinates, and then show them how to graph points and lines.

 Reaching All Learners
Through Critical Thinking

For each set of equations and ordered pairs below, have each student graph the four points and determine which point is not a solution to the equation (i.e., the point not in line with the other three). Have them check their work algebraically.

1. $y = x + 2$; $(0, 2)$, $(1, 5)$, $(2, 4)$, $(3, 5)$ $(1, 5)$

2. $y = 2x - 3$; $(5, 7)$, $(3, 3)$, $(1, -1)$, $(0, 0)$ $(0, 0)$

3. $y = 2x + 1$; $(0, 1)$, $(2, 5)$, $(3, 6)$, $(4, 9)$ $(3, 6)$

4. $y = 3x - 4$; $(0, -4)$, $(4, 4)$, $(3, 5)$, $(1, -1)$ $(4, 4)$

3 **Close**

Summarize

Draw an unlabeled coordinate plane on the board and plot a point with the coordinates labeled $(?, ?)$. Ask students to identify and label any important parts of the graph.

Possible answers: x-axis, y-axis, origin, point, $(3, 4)$

Remind students that when graphing points on a coordinate plane, order is important. Show them that the points that correspond to ordered pairs like $(2, 3)$ and $(3, 2)$ are in different locations on the coordinate plane.

3-2 **Exercises**

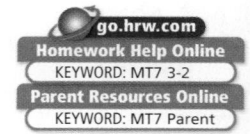

go.hrw.com
Homework Help Online
KEYWORD: MT7 3-2
Parent Resources Online
KEYWORD: MT7 Parent

Assignment Guide

If you finished Example **1** assign:
Average 1–6, 17–22, 38–47
Advanced 17–22, 36, 39–48

If you finished Example **2** assign:
Average 1–14, 17–30, 38–47
Advanced 17–30, 36, 38–47

If you finished Example **3** assign:
Average 1–32, 34, 38–47
Advanced 17–47

Homework Quick Check

Quickly check key concepts.
Exercises: 8, 26, 32, 34

Answers

7–16, 23–30. See p. A2.

Math Background

Knowing how coordinate graphs are used in real-world situations can make the topic more meaningful for students. Cartography, the science of map making, is an application of graphing on a coordinate plane. Cartographers map a region of the surface of Earth onto part of a plane. Because Earth is nearly spherical and the coordinate plane is flat, there are different methods for mapping Earth's surface onto a flat plane. The different methods are called *projections*.

State Resources

go.hrw.com
State Resources Online
KEYWORD: MT7 Resources

GUIDED PRACTICE

See Example **1** Give the coordinates and quadrant of each point.

1. *A* (−2, 3); Quadrant II 2. *B* (3, 5); Quadrant I

3. *C* (2, −3); Quadrant IV 4. *D* (5, −1); Quadrant IV

5. *E* (5, 5); Quadrant I 6. *F* (−3, −4); Quadrant III

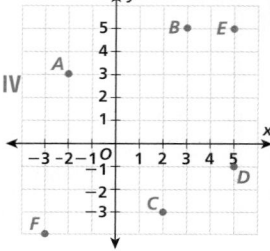

See Example **2** Graph each point on a coordinate plane.

7. $A(3.5, 4)$ 8. $B\left(6, 1\frac{1}{3}\right)$ 9. $C(-1, 6)$ 10. $D\left(2.7, -5\frac{1}{2}\right)$

11. $E(4.5, 7)$ 12. $F(6, -2)$ 13. $G\left(3, 7\frac{1}{2}\right)$ 14. $H(1.5, -4)$

See Example **3** Complete each table of ordered pairs. Graph each ordered pair on a coordinate plane.

15. $y = x + 0.5$

x	x + 0.5	y	(x, y)
0			
1			
2			

16. $y = \frac{1}{2}x - 1$

x	$\frac{1}{2}x - 1$	y	(x, y)
0			
1			
2			

INDEPENDENT PRACTICE

See Example **1** Give the coordinates and quadrant of each point.

17. *G* (0, 3); no quadrant 18. *H* (−1, 5); Quadrant II

19. *J* (2, −4); Quadrant IV 20. *K* (3, 2); Quadrant I

21. *L* (−2, 5); Quadrant II 22. *M* (−4, −3); Quadrant III

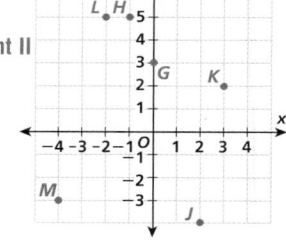

See Example **2** Graph each point on a coordinate plane.

23. $A\left(2\frac{1}{3}, 6.5\right)$ 24. $B(0.7, 4.2)$ 25. $C(-1, -7)$ 26. $D(-2.7, 0)$

27. $E\left(4\frac{1}{3}, 7\right)$ 28. $F(-2, 5)$ 29. $G(0, 3)$ 30. $H(6.5, 3)$

RETEACH 3-2

Reteach
3-2 *Graphing on a Coordinate Plane*

Point *A* is described by the ordered pair (3, −2). The first number, 3, is the **x-coordinate** and the second number, −2, is the **y-coordinate**.

Using a grid to represent a **coordinate plane**, graph point *A* by starting at the **origin**, where the **x-axis** and **y-axis** intersect. The x-coordinate, 3, tells you to go right 3. The y-coordinate, −2, tells you to go down 2.

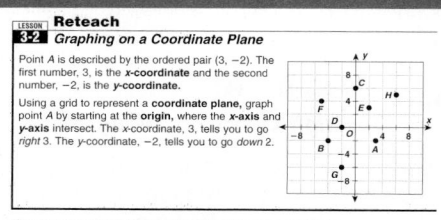

Write an ordered pair to describe each point on the coordinate plane above.

1. point *C* __(0, 6)__ 2. point *F* __(−5, 4)__ 3. point *G* __(−2, −6)__

Graph each ordered pair.

4. *J*(2, 1) 5. *K*(−3, 0)

6. *L*(5, −4) 7. *M*(−4, −4)

8. *N*(−2, 6) 9. *P*(3, −2)

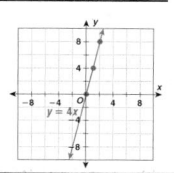

The graph of an equation is the set of all ordered pairs that are solutions of the equation.

Complete the table. Graph each ordered pair. Draw a line through the points.

10. $y = 4x$

x	4x = y	(x, y)
0	4(0) = 0	(0, 0)
1	4(1) = 4	(1, 4)
2	4(2) = 8	(2, 8)

PRACTICE 3-2

Practice B
3-2 *Graphing on a Coordinate Plane*

Give the coordinates of each point and quadrant.

1. *F* 2. *X*
   __(−2, −3); III__ __(−6, 3); II__

3. *T* 4. *B*
   __(8, −3); IV__ __(5, −4); IV__

5. *D* 6. *R*
   __(−4, 4); II__ __(1, −8); IV__

7. *H* 8. *Y*
   __(3, 8); I__ __(−5, −6); III__

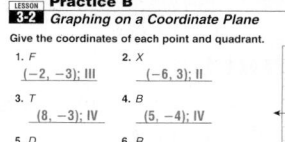

Graph each point on a coordinate plane.

9. *A*(2½, 1) 10. *B*(0, 4)

11. *C*(2, −1.5) 12. *D*(−2, 3.5)

13. $E(-2\frac{1}{3}, 0)$ 14. $F(-1\frac{1}{2}, -3)$

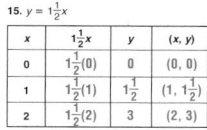

Complete the table of ordered pairs. Graph each ordered pair on a coordinate plane. Draw a line through the points.

15. $y = 1\frac{1}{2}x$

x	$1\frac{1}{2}x$	y	(x, y)
0	$1\frac{1}{2}(0)$	0	(0, 0)
1	$1\frac{1}{2}(1)$	$1\frac{1}{2}$	$(1, 1\frac{1}{2})$
2	$1\frac{1}{2}(2)$	3	(2, 3)

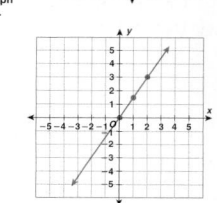

See Example **3** Complete each table of ordered pairs. Graph each ordered pair on a
coordinate plane.

31. $y = \frac{1}{3}x$

x	$\frac{1}{3}x$	y	(x, y)
0			
1			
2			

32. $y = 2x + 1.5$

x	2x + 1.5	y	(x, y)
0			
1			
2			

PRACTICE AND PROBLEM SOLVING

Extra Practice
See page 786.

33. Multi-Step A truck travels at 55 miles per hour. To find the distance
traveled in x hours, use the equation $y = 55x$. Make a table of ordered
pairs and graph the solution. How far will the truck travel in 7.5 hours?

34. Construction To build house walls, carpenters place a stud, or board,
every 16 inches. Use the equation $y = \frac{x}{16} + 1$ to determine the number of
studs in a wall of length x inches. Make a table of ordered pairs and graph
the solution. How many studs should be placed in a wall 8 feet long? **7 studs**

35. Write a Problem Write an equation whose solution is in Quadrant IV.
Possible answer: $y = -4x + 5$

36. Write About It The point (0, 0) on the coordinate plane is called the
origin. Explain why this is. **Possible answer: When graphing a point, you always
start at (0, 0) and count from there. Since (0, 0) is the starting point, it is the origin.**

37. Challenge Write a problem whose solution is a geometric shape on the
coordinate plane. **Possible answer: Graph the points (1, 3), (7, 3), (4, 0),
(4, 6). Connect the points and identify the figure. (square)**

TEST PREP and Spiral Review

38. Multiple Choice Which ordered pair lies on the line that is a graph of
the equation $y = 2x + 1$?

Ⓐ (0, 0) Ⓒ (0, 1)

Ⓑ (2, 6) Ⓓ (5, 13)

39. Multiple Choice Which ordered pair shows the
coordinates for point W on the grid?

Ⓕ (2, 3) Ⓗ (2, −3)

Ⓖ (−2, 3) Ⓙ (−2, −3)

Solve and graph each inequality. (Lesson 1-9)

40. $y + 4 > 1$ **41.** $4p \le 12$ **42.** $f - 3 \ge 2$ **43.** $4 < \frac{w}{3}$

Determine whether each ordered pair is a solution of $y = 4x - 3$. (Lesson 3-1)

44. (−3, −9) **45.** (0, −3) **46.** (−4, −19) **47.** (5, 23)

Answers

31–34. See p. A2.

40–43. For graphs, see p. A2.

ONGOING ASSESSMENT
and **INTERVENTION**

Diagnose Before the Lesson
3-2 Warm Up, TE p. 122

Monitor During the Lesson
3-2 Know-It Notebook
3-2 Questioning Strategies

Assess After the Lesson
3-2 Lesson Quiz, TE p. 125

TEST PREP DOCTOR + For Exercise 39, suggest
that students use their
knowledge of quadrants
to check the signs of their answer. In
this case, point W is in Quadrant II,
where x-values are always negative, and
y-values are always positive.

Journal

Ask students to draw a map of the
streets around the school, their houses,
or any other areas that interest them.
Have students describe the location of
one of the buildings in the area.

Power Presentations
with PowerPoint®

3-2
Lesson Quiz
Give the coordinates and quadrant
of each point.

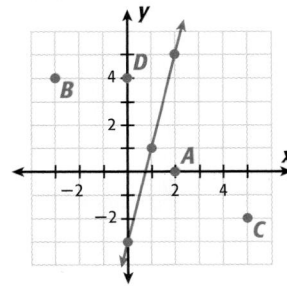

1. A (2, 0), none **2.** B (−3, 4) II

**Graph each point on a coordinate
plane. Label points C, D.**

3. C(5, −2) **4.** D(0, 4)

5. Complete the table for
$y = 4x - 3$. Graph each ordered
pair.

x	4x − 3	y	(x, y)
0	4(0) − 3	−3	(0, −3)
1	4(1) − 3	1	(1, 1)
2	4(2) − 3	5	(2, 5)

Answers on graph above

Also available on transparency

CHALLENGE 3-2

LESSON 3-2 Challenge
Dr. King's Point

Graph the following points. Read down the columns and, in the
order given, connect the points with line segments. Start a new
line after each stop. When you are done, you will read a well-
known statement made by Rev. Dr. Martin Luther King, Jr.

(−11, 9)	(−2, 7)	(11, 5)	(−5, −7)	(0, −5)
(−11, 5)	(0, 7)	(13, 9)	(−5, −3)	(1, −5)
STOP	STOP	(15, 5)	(−2, −3)	STOP
		STOP	(−1, −4)	
(−4, 9)	(1, 9)		(−1, −5)	(3, −7)
(−4, 7)	(3, 5)	(12, 7)	(−3, −5)	(5, −3)
(−7, 7)	(5, 9)	(14, 7)	(−1, −7)	(7, −7)
(−7, 9)	STOP	STOP	STOP	STOP
STOP				
	(8, 5)	(−10, −7)	(−3, −5)	(4, −5)
(−7, 7)	(6, 5)	(−10, −3)	(−5, −5)	(6, −5)
(−7, 5)	(6, 9)	(−7, −3)	STOP	STOP
	(8, 9)	(−6, −4)		
STOP	STOP	(−6, −6)	(2, −3)	(8, −7)
		(−7, −7)	(0, −3)	(8, −3)
(−4, 5)	(6, 7)	(−10, −7)	(0, −7)	(10, −6)
(−4, 7)	(7, 7)	STOP	(2, −7)	(12, −3)
STOP	STOP		STOP	(12, −7)
(−3, 5)				STOP
(−1, 9)				
(1, 5)				
STOP				

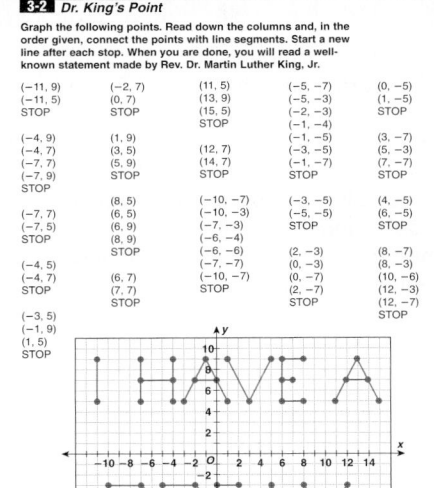

PROBLEM SOLVING 3-2

LESSON 3-2 Problem Solving
Graphing on the Coordinate Plane

Complete the table of ordered pairs. Graph each ordered pair.
Draw a line through the points. Answer the question.

1. John earns $150 per week plus 5% of
his computer software sales. John's
weekly pay y in terms of his sales x is
$y = 150 + 0.05x$. Complete the table.
How much does John get paid for
$200 in sales?

$160

x	y	(x, y)
0	150	0, 150
10	150.5	10, 150.5
25	151.25	25, 151.25
50	152.5	50, 152.5
100	155	100, 155

2. Margarite starts out with $100. Each
week, she spends $6 to go to the
movies. The amount of money y
Margarite has left each week x, is
$y = 100 − 6x$. How much money
does she have left after 11 weeks?

$34

x	y	(x, y)
0	100	0, 100
1	94	1, 94
2	88	2, 88
3	82	3, 82
4	76	4, 76

The graph at the right represents the miles traveled y in x
hours. Use the graph to choose the best letter.

3. Which of the ordered pairs below
represents a solution?
Ⓐ (1, 65) C (5, 120)
B (2, 70) D (7, 300)

4. The graph represents a car traveling
how fast?
F 60 mi/h H 70 mi/h
Ⓖ 65 mi/h J 75 mi/h

Organizer

Use with Lesson 3-2

Pacing:
Traditional $\frac{1}{2}$ day
Block $\frac{1}{4}$ day

Objective: Use a graphing calculator to plot points described by ordered pairs and to adjust the graphing window.

Materials: Graphing calculator

Online Edition
Graphing Calculator, TechKeys

Resources

Technology Lab Activities
Lab 3-2 Recording Sheet

Teach
Discuss

Have students plot points on their graphing calculators, and then ask them what window settings would be ideal to view the plotted points. Show students examples of window sizes that are too small or too large.

Close
Key Concept

You can view points by entering the ordered pairs into a graphing calculator and adjusting the graphing window when necessary.

Assessment

1. How could you set the calculator to show the *x*- and *y*-axes from −100 to +100 by tens?

Answers

For all answers, see p. A2.

State Resources

go.hrw.com
State Resources Online
KEYWORD: MT7 Resources

Graph Points

Use with Lesson 3-2

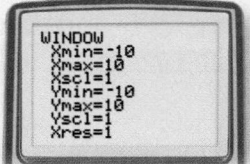
go.hrw.com
Lab Resources Online
KEYWORD: MT7 Lab3

On a graphing calculator, the [WINDOW] menu settings determine which points you see and the spacing between those points. In the standard viewing window, the *x*- and *y*-values each go from −10 to 10, and the tick marks are one unit apart. The boundaries are set by **Xmin, Xmax, Ymin,** and **Ymax. Xscl** and **Yscl** give the distance between the tick marks.

Activity

Plot the points (2, 5), (−2, 3), ($-\frac{3}{2}$, 4), and (1.75, −2) in the standard window. Then change the minimum and maximum *x*- and *y*-values of the window to −5 and 5.

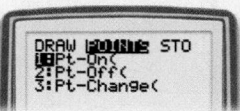

Press [WINDOW] to check that you have the standard window settings. To plot (2, 5), press [2nd] [PRGM] **POINTS** [ENTER].

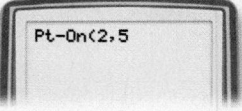

Then press 2 [,] 5 [ENTER]. After you see the grid with a point at (2, 5), press [2nd] [MODE] to quit. Repeat the steps above to graph (−2, 3), ($-\frac{3}{2}$, 4), and (1.75, −2).

This is the graph in the standard window.

Press [WINDOW]. Change the **Xmin, Xmax, Ymin,** and **Ymax** values as shown.

Repeat the steps above to graph the points in the new window.

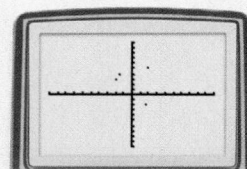 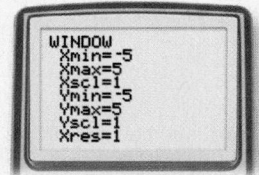 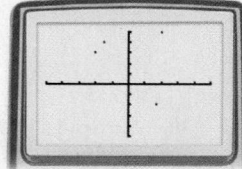

Think and Discuss

1. Compare the two graphs above. Describe and explain any differences you see.

Try This

Graph the points (−3, −8), (2, 3), (3.5, 6), (4, 9), and (−5.5, 11) in each window.

1. standard window
2. **Xmin = −10; Xmax = 10; Ymin = −15; Ymax = 15; Yscl = 3**

Lendy Jones
Killeen, Texas

Teacher to Teacher

I find that it's helpful for students to graph with graph paper first so that students get a solid understanding of how to use a coordinate plane and locate points using ordered pairs. Then students can graph by using technology, either a graphing calculator, a spreadsheet, or both. When students first have the solid understanding by using graph paper first, then they are able to compare and contrast the different methods better.

Interpreting Graphs and Tables

Learn to interpret information given in a graph or table and to make a graph to solve problems.

A commercial airliner climbs to an altitude of 30,000 feet to maintain cruising altitude. After a few hours it descends to the ground for a safe landing.

You can create a table of values to show the altitude of the airliner at different times during its flight. Plotting the values on a graph will give you a visual model of the airliner's flight.

EXAMPLE 1 Matching Situations to Tables

The table gives the speeds of three snowboarders in mi/h at given times during a race. Tell which snowboarder corresponds to each situation.

Time (s)	6.00	12.00	18.00	24.00	30.00
Snowboarder 1	15	18	22	19	24
Snowboarder 2	17	20	0	15	21
Snowboarder 3	16	19	22	25	26

A Jordan gets off to a good start and continues through the course, picking up speed.

Snowboarder 3—The racer's speed increases throughout the race.

B Ethan gets off to a good start and picks up speed. Toward the end of the race, he nearly falls. He rights himself and finishes the race, reaching his greatest speed.

Snowboarder 1—The racer's speed increases until the 24-second mark, when his speed decreases. The racer then picks up speed to finish the race.

C Xavier gets off to a good start but falls around the middle of the race. He gets up and finishes the race, gaining speed through the finish line.

Snowboarder 2—The racer's speed increases until the 18-second mark, when it is 0. After this, the racer's speed increases through the finish line.

Motivate

Find some simple line graphs and tables that were published in recent newspapers or magazines, and show them to the students. Explain that the graphs and tables can show important information if you know how to read them. Point out that tables and graphs are two ways to visually organize information.

Explorations and answers are provided in *Alternate Openers: Explorations Transparencies.*

Power Presentations
with PowerPoint®

Additional Examples

Example 1

The table gives the speeds in mi/h of two cars at given times. Tell which car corresponds to the situation described below.

Time	1:00	1:05	1:10	1:15	1:20
Car 1	50	50	30	25	0
Car 2	55	10	0	0	55

Mr. Lee is traveling on the highway. He pulls over, stops, and then gets back onto the highway. **car 2**

Example 2

Tell which graph corresponds to the situation described above.

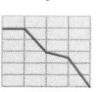 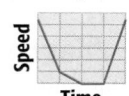

Graph 1   Graph 2

Graph 2

Example 3

Create a graph that illustrates the temperature (°F) inside the car.

Location	Arrival	Departure
Work	68° at 12:30	42° at 4:30
Cleaners	65° at 4:50	60° at 5:00
Market	65° at 5:10	49° at 5:40

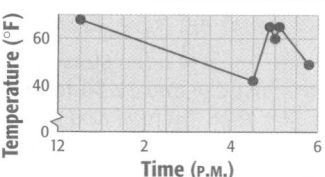

Also available on transparency

EXAMPLE 2 Matching Situations to Graphs

Tell which graph corresponds to each situation described in Example 1.

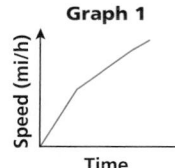 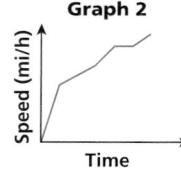 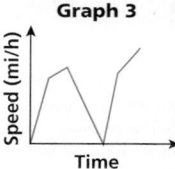

Graph 1   Graph 2   Graph 3

A Snowboarder 1

Graph 2—The racer's speed slows down near the end of the race and then increases.

B Snowboarder 2

Graph 3—The racer falls about halfway through the race.

C Snowboarder 3

Graph 1—The racer gains speed throughout the race.

EXAMPLE 3 Creating a Graph of a Situation

The flight of a commercial airliner can be modeled with a graph. Create a graph that models the flight of a commercial airliner.

Time (min)	Altitude (ft)
0	0
10	10,000
20	20,000
30	30,000
60	30,000
70	20,000
80	10,000
90	0

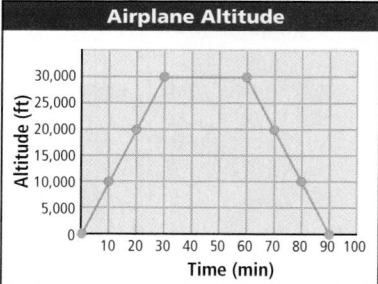

Possible answers to Think and Discuss

1. If a graph starts at (0, 0), then the object was not moving at the start.

2. Gina rides her bike to the park, stops and talks to a friend, and then rides home.

Think and Discuss

1. **Describe** what it means when a graph of speed starts at (0, 0).

2. **Give** a situation that, when graphed, would include a horizontal segment.

---

2 Teach

Guided Instruction

In this lesson, students learn to interpret information given in a graph or a table and to make a graph to help solve problems. Show students a simple table and explain how to read it. Emphasize the importance of headings for columns and rows. Illustrate how to find a particular piece of information in the table by finding the intersection of the appropriate row and column (similar to the coordinates of a point on a plane).

 Reaching All Learners

Through Kinesthetic Experience

Have students gather data on time and distance. Students can use stop watches to measure how long it takes different objects, such as a marble, a pencil, and a can, to roll down a sloped surface. Alternatively, students can measure how long it takes to walk or run known distances. Have them create a table with appropriate labels for their data; then, have students use their table to make a graph. Ask students questions about the results of their experiments and have them use the graphs to answer them.

3 Close

Summarize

Discuss different ways of presenting information, including written paragraphs, tables, and graphs. Ask students for the pros and cons of each. Ask if they have an opinion about which of these methods is the most efficient.

Possible answers: Paragraphs are clear but they take a long time to read. Tables are good for numbers and finding specific information quickly, but sometimes they leave out details. Graphs give you a visual idea of changes in data, but they are not as specific or detailed as the other ways.

3-3 Exercises

GUIDED PRACTICE

See Example 1

1. The table gives the speeds in mi/h of three people who are riding jet skis. Tell which rider corresponds to each situation.

Time	1:00	1:05	1:10	1:15	1:20
Rider 1	10	15	25	20	15
Rider 2	10	0	10	15	20
Rider 3	10	15	25	25	25

a. Rider 2

b. Rider 1

c. Rider 3

a. David begins his ride slowly but then stops to talk with some friends on jet skis. After a few minutes, he continues his ride, gradually increasing his speed.

b. Amber steadily increases her speed through most of her ride. After about 10 minutes, she slows down to turn around and returns to the boat dock.

c. Kai steadily increases his speed for the first part of his ride. He then keeps a constant speed as he continues his ride.

See Example 2

Graph 1: Kai

Graph 2: David

Graph 3: Amber

2. Tell which graph corresponds to each situation described in Exercise 1.

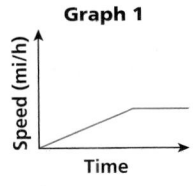

Graph 1

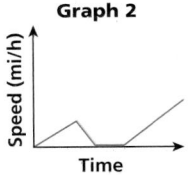

Graph 2

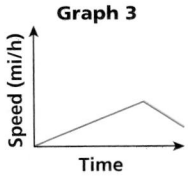

Graph 3

See Example 3

3. A ride at an amusement park can be modeled with a graph. Create a graph that illustrates the information in the table about the ride.

Time	3:20	3:21	3:22	3:23	3:24	3:25
Speed (mi/h)	0	14	41	62	8	0

4. You are watching a race at a local speedway. The lead car gets a flat tire 2 minutes into the race and has to stop. You collect the following data while watching the race. Construct a graph that models the information in the table.

Time (min)	0	0.5	1.0	1.5	2.0	2.5	3.0
Distance (mi)	0	1.0	1.75	3.0	4.25	4.25	4.25

Assignment Guide

If you finished Example **1** assign:
Average 1, 5, 12–21
Advanced 5, 12–21

If you finished Example **2** assign:
Average 1, 2, 5, 6, 10, 12–21
Advanced 5, 6, 10, 12–21

If you finished Example **3** assign:
Average 1–7, 10, 12–21
Advanced 5–21

Homework Quick Check

Quickly check key concepts.
Exercises: 5, 6, 7, 10

Answers

3.

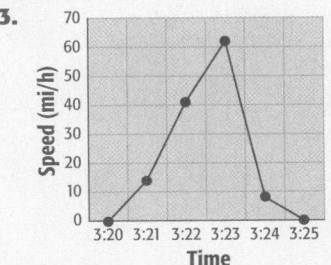

4.

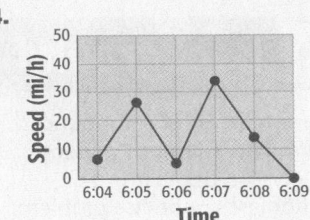

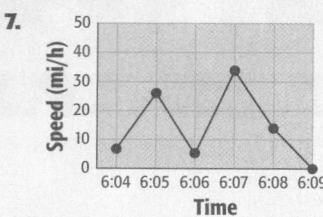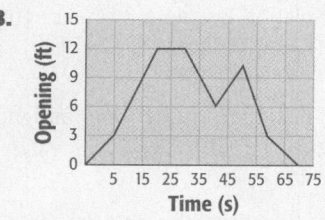
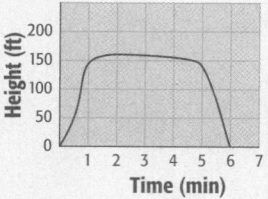
Math Background

In 1736, Leonhard Euler (pronounced "oiler") published a famous paper in which he solved a popular puzzle, called the Königsberg bridge problem. The problem was based on determining whether someone could cross each of the seven bridges of Königsberg, Prussia, once and only once. Euler's solution relied on a diagram that he called a *graph*. The graph was composed of points, called *vertices,* and segments joining the points, called *edges.* Euler's solution introduced a new branch of mathematics known as graph theory.

INDEPENDENT PRACTICE

See Example **1**

5. The table gives the speeds in mi/h of three dogs at given times during an obstacle course race. Tell which dog corresponds to each situation.

Time (s)	15.00	30.00	45.00	60.00
Dog 1	19	23	15	17
Dog 2	17	25	27	28
Dog 3	15	11	17	21

a. Dog 2
b. Dog 3
c. Dog 1

a. Brandy increases her speed throughout the race.

b. Bruno decreases his speed early in the race to run around cones on the course. After this, he steadily increases his speed.

c. Max gets off to a fast start and picks up speed for several seconds. He slows down to run through a tunnel but then increases his speed right afterward.

See Example **2**

Graph 1: Dog 3
Graph 2: Dog 1
Graph 3: Dog 2

6. Tell which graph corresponds to each situation described in Exercise 4.

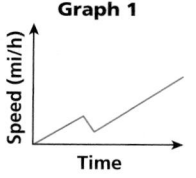
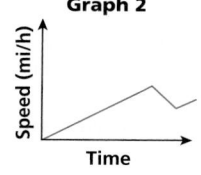
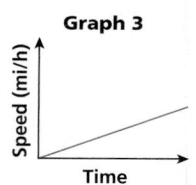

See Example **3**

7. Create a graph that illustrates the information in the table about Mrs. Parr's commute from work to home.

Time	Speed (mi/h)	Time	Speed (mi/h)
6:04	5	6:07	34
6:05	27	6:08	14
6:06	6	6:09	0

PRACTICE AND PROBLEM SOLVING

Extra Practice
See page 786.

8. Create a graph that illustrates the information in the table about the movement of an electronic security gate.

Time (s)	0	10	20	30	40	50	60	70
Gate Opening (ft)	0	6	12	12	6	10	3	0

9. Physical Science Explain what the data tells about the flight of a model rocket. Make a graph.

Height of Model Rocket								
Time	1:00	1:01	1:02	1:03	1:04	1:05	1:06	1:07
Average Height (ft)	0	147	153	155	152	148	0	0

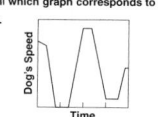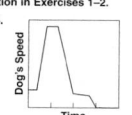

Earth Science LINK

Old Faithful is the most famous geyser at Yellowstone National Park.

10. Use the chart to choose the correct geyser name to label each graph.

Yellowstone National Park Geysers

Geyser Name	Old Faithful	Grand	Riverside
Duration (min)	1.5 to 5	10	20

a.

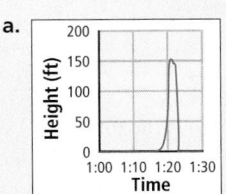

b.

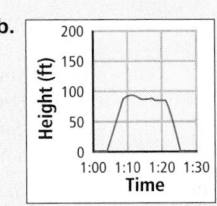

11. ⭐ **Challenge** Old Faithful erupts to heights between 105 ft and 184 ft. It erupted at 7:34 A.M. for 4.5 minutes. Later it erupted for 2.5 minutes. It then erupted a third time for 3 minutes. Use the table to determine how many minutes followed each of the three eruptions. Sketch a possible graph.

go.hrw.com
Web Extra!
KEYWORD: MT7 Geyser

Old Faithful Eruption Information

Duration	Time Until Next Eruption
2.5 min	70 min
3 min	72 min
3.5 min	74 min
4 min	82 min
4.5 min	93 min

TEST PREP and Spiral Review

12. **Multiple Choice** Which graph most likely represents a car approaching a stop sign?

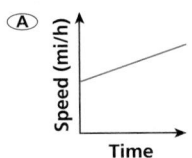 (A) 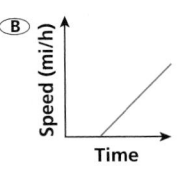 (B) 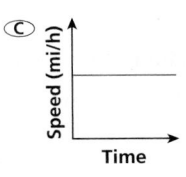 (C) 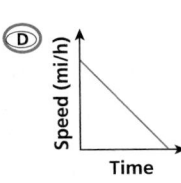 (D)

13. **Short Response** Lisa climbed up to the diving board, dove into the water, swam 10 meters, and returned to the surface of the water. Draw a graph to represent her distance from the surface of the water.

Check students' graphs.

Add or subtract. (Lesson 2-6)

14. $\frac{5}{7} + \frac{2}{3}$ $1\frac{8}{21}$

15. $\frac{4}{9} + \left(-1\frac{3}{4}\right)$ $-1\frac{11}{36}$

16. $\frac{3}{5} - \frac{7}{10}$ $-\frac{1}{10}$

17. $2\frac{7}{9} - 1\frac{8}{11}$ $1\frac{5}{99}$

Graph each point on a coordinate plane. (Lesson 3-2) **Possible answers are given.**

18. $(-3, 4)$
$(-3, 0), (-3, 1)$

19. $(2, -7)$
$(2, 5), (2, -1)$

20. $(-5, -1)$
$(-5, 4), (-5, 10)$

21. $(0, 1)$
$(0, 8), (0, -6)$

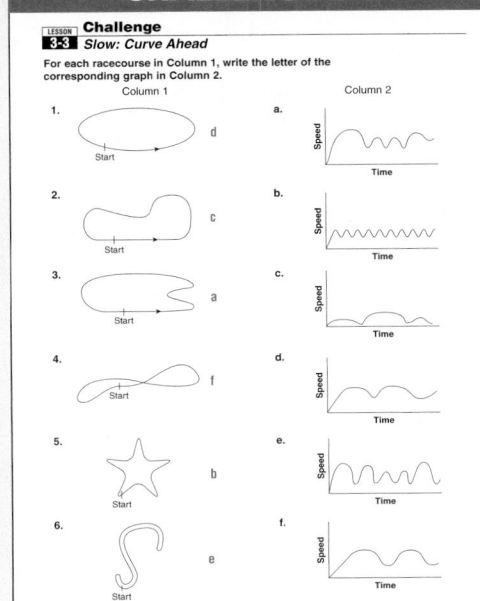
PROBLEM SOLVING 3-3

LESSON 3-3 Problem Solving

Interpreting Graphs and Table

Tell which table corresponds to each situation.

1. Ryan walks for several blocks, and then he begins to run. After running for 10 minutes, he walks for several blocks and then stops.

Table 2 ____

Table 1	
Time	Speed (mi/h)
8:00	0
8:10	3
8:20	7.5
8:30	0

2. Susanna starts running. After 10 minutes, she sees a friend and stops to talk. When she leaves her friend, she runs home and stops.

Table 3 ____

Table 2	
Time	Speed (mi/h)
8:00	3
8:10	7.5
8:20	3
8:30	0

3. Mark stands on the porch and talks to a friend. Then he starts walking home. Part way home he decides to run the rest of the way, and he doesn't stop until he gets home.

Table 1 ____

Table 3	
Time	Speed (mi/h)
8:00	7.5
8:10	0
8:20	7.5
8:30	0

The graph represents the height of water in a bathtub over time. Choose the correct letter.

4. Which part of the graph best represents the tub being filled with water?
A a   C c
B d   D g

5. Which part of the graph shows the tub being drained of water?
A c   C d
B e   D g

6. Which part of the graph shows someone soaking in the tub?
F b   H d
G e   J f

7. Which part of the graph shows when someone gets into the tub?
A a   C c
B e   D f

8. Which parts of the graph show when the water level is not changing in the tub?
F a, b, c   H b, d, g
G b, d, f   J c, e, f

ONGOING ASSESSMENT
and INTERVENTION

Diagnose Before the Lesson
3-3 Warm Up, TE p. 127

Monitor During the Lesson
3-3 Know-It Notebook
3-3 Questioning Strategies

Assess After the Lesson
3-3 Lesson Quiz, TE p. 131

Interdisciplinary LINK

Earth Science

Exercises 10–11 involve interpreting data about geysers from graphs and tables. Geysers are studied in middle school earth science programs, such as *Holt Science & Technology*.

Answers

10. **a.** Old Faithful
b. Riverside

11. See p. A2.

TEST PREP DOCTOR + For Exercise 12, remind students that the car has a speed of zero when it stops.

📝 Journal

Have students write about a table such as a bus schedule that they have used to obtain information.

Power Presentations
with PowerPoint®

✓ 3-3 Lesson Quiz

Tell which table corresponds to the situation.

A tour bus sits at the gas station while the mechanic inspects the tires. It then leaves and makes its first stop five miles down the road. The bus then continues on to its destination by getting on the expressway and driving for 40 miles. **Table 2**

Table 1		Table 2	
Time	Speed	Time	Speed
3:00	20 mi/h	3:00	0 mi/h
3:05	20 mi/h	3:05	20 mi/h
3:10	0 mi/h	3:10	0 mi/h
3:15	55 mi/h	3:15	55 mi/h

Also available on transparency

Organizer

Objective: Assess students' mastery of concepts and skills in Lessons 3-1 through 3-3.

Resources

 Assessment Resources
Section 3A Quiz

 Test & Practice Generator
One-Stop Planner®

INTERVENTION ⟸ ⟹

Resources

 Ready to Go On?
Intervention and
Enrichment Worksheets

💿 **Ready to Go On? CD-ROM**

🪐 **Ready to Go On? Online**

my.hrw.com

Answers

15–18. See pp. A2–A3.

Ready to Go On?

READY TO GO ON?

Quiz for Lessons 3-1 Through 3-3

☑ **3-1 Ordered Pairs**

Determine whether each ordered pair is a solution of $y = 2x - 7$.

1. $(14, 21)$ **yes**   **2.** $(3, 13)$ **no**   **3.** $(10, 13)$ **yes**   **4.** $(1.5, -4)$ **yes**

When dining out, it is customary to give a tip to the server. The amount of the tip is generally 15 to 20 percent of the total bill. The equation for the cost c of a meal, including a 15 percent tip, is $c = 1.15a$, where a is the total amount shown on the bill. Find the total cost of each meal to the nearest cent.

5. $a = \$35.20$ **6.** $a = \$40.00$ **7.** $a = \$22.35$ **8.** $a = \$15.50$
   $\$40.48$ $\$46.00$ $\$25.70$ $\$17.83$

☑ **3-2 Graphing on a Coordinate Plane**

Give the coordinates and quadrant of each point.

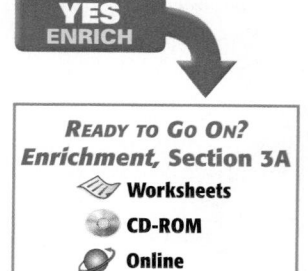

9. A **10.** B
11. C **12.** D
13. E **14.** F

9. $(3, 2)$; Quadrant I   **10.** $(0, -4)$; no quadrant
11. $(-4, -3)$; Quadrant III   **12.** $(-2, 3)$; Quadrant II
13. $(0, 0)$; no quadrant   **14.** $(6, -2)$; Quadrant IV

Make a table of ordered pairs for each equation and then graph the ordered pairs on a coordinate plane. Draw a line through the points.

15. $y = 7x + 3$ **16.** $y = -3x + 1$ **17.** $y = \frac{3}{4}x$ **18.** $y = 1.2x + 3$

☑ **3-3 Interpreting Graphs and Tables**

Tell which graph corresponds to each situation below.

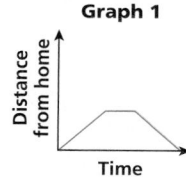

Graph 1

Distance from home / Time

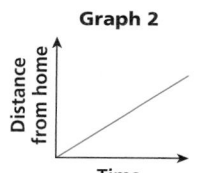

Graph 2

Distance from home / Time

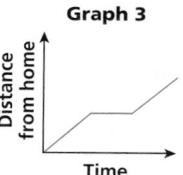

Graph 3

Distance from home / Time

19. Gwendolyn started from home and walked to a friend's house. She stayed with her friend for a while and then walked to another friend's house farther from home. **Graph 3**

20. Francisco started from home and walked to the store. After shopping, he walked back home. **Graph 1**

READY TO GO ON?

Diagnose and Prescribe

NO
INTERVENE

YES
ENRICH

READY TO GO ON? Intervention, Section 3A			
Ready to Go On? Intervention	📝 **Worksheets**	💿 **CD-ROM**	🪐 **Online**
☑ Lesson 3-1	3-1 Intervention	Activity 3-1	Diagnose and Prescribe Online
☑ Lesson 3-2	3-2 Intervention	Activity 3-2	
☑ Lesson 3-3	3-3 Intervention	Activity 3-3	

READY TO GO ON?
Enrichment, Section 3A
📝 **Worksheets**
💿 **CD-ROM**
🪐 **Online**

Focus on Problem Solving

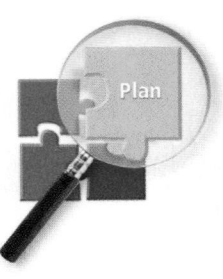

Make a Plan
- **Prioritize and sequence information**

Some problems contain a lot of information. Read the entire problem carefully to be sure you understand all of the facts. You may need to read it over several times—perhaps aloud so that you can hear yourself say the words.

Then decide which information is most important (prioritize). Is there any information that is absolutely necessary to solve the problem? This information is most important.

Finally, put the information in order (sequence). Use comparison words like *before, after, longer, shorter,* and so on to help you. Write down the sequence before you try to solve the problem.

Read each problem below, and then answer the questions that follow.

1. Five friends are standing in line for the opening of a movie. They are in line according to their arrival. Tiffany arrived 3 minutes after Cedric. Roy took his place in line at 8:01 P.M. He was 1 minute behind Celeste and 7 minutes ahead of Tiffany. The first person arrived at 8:00 P.M. Blanca showed up 6 minutes after the first person. List the time of each person's arrival.

   a. Whose arrival information helped you determine each arrival time?

   b. Can you determine the order without the time?

   c. List the friends' order from the earliest to arrive to the last to arrive.

2. There are four children in the Putman family. Isabelle is half the age of Maxwell. Joe is 2 years older than Isabelle. Maxwell is 14. Hazel is twice Joe's age and 4 years older than Maxwell. What are the ages of the children?

   a. Whose age must you figure out first before you can find Joe's age?

   b. What are two ways to figure out Hazel's age?

   c. List the Putman children from oldest to youngest.

Answers

1. a. Roy

   b. Yes

   c. Celeste, Roy, Cedric, Blanca, Tiffany

2. a. Isabelle

   b. Multiply Joe's age by 2 or add 4 years to Maxwell's age.

   c. Hazel, Maxwell, Joe, Isabelle

SECTION 3B

Functions and Sequences

One-Minute Section Planner

Lesson	Materials	MiC and Lab Resources
Lesson 3-4 Functions • Represent functions with tables, graphs, or equations. ☑ SAT-10 ☑ ITBS ☑ CTBS ☑ NAEP	Graph paper	**MiC: *Ups and Downs*** pp. 17–19, 24–27 **MiC: *Algebra Rules*** pp. 16–17
Lesson 3-5 Equations, Tables, and Graphs • Generate different representations of the same data. ☐ SAT-10 ☑ ITBS ☑ CTBS ☑ NAEP	Graph paper	**MiC: *Ups and Downs*** pp. 6–9, 24–27 ***Hands-On Lab Activities*** 3-5
Lesson 3-6 Arithmetic Sequences • Identify and evaluate arithmetic sequences. ☐ SAT-10 ☑ ITBS ☑ CTBS ☑ NAEP		**MiC: *Ups and Downs*** pp. 15–18 **MiC: *Patterns and Figures*** pp. 1–7, 10–11, 32–33 ***Hands-On Lab Activities*** 3-6

MK = *Manipulatives Kit*

Mathematics in Context

The units ***Ups and Downs, Algebra Rules,*** and ***Patterns and Figures*** from the *Mathematics in Context* © 2006 series can be used with Section 3B. See Section Planner above for suggestions for integrating *MiC* with *Holt Mathematics.*

Section Overview

Professional Development

Functions

 Why? Many topics in higher mathematics involve functions.

Functions can be represented in various ways, including equations, tables, and graphs.

> A **function** assigns exactly one output value to each input value.

$$f(x) = x^2 + 1$$

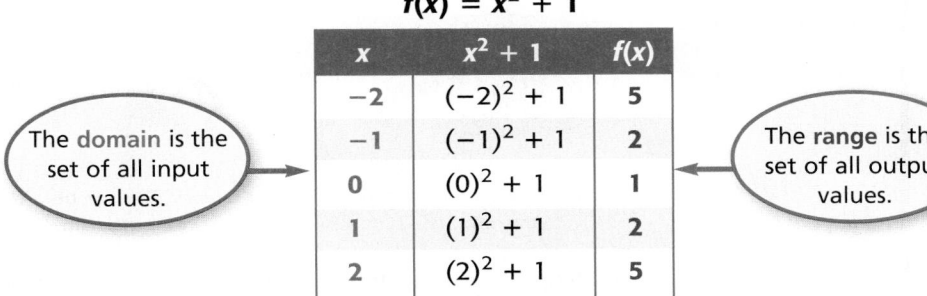

The **domain** is the set of all input values.

x	$x^2 + 1$	$f(x)$
-2	$(-2)^2 + 1$	5
-1	$(-1)^2 + 1$	2
0	$(0)^2 + 1$	1
1	$(1)^2 + 1$	2
2	$(2)^2 + 1$	5

The **range** is the set of all output values.

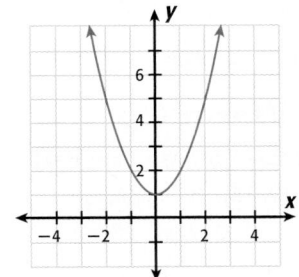

Equations, Tables, and Graphs

 Why? You can model many real-world relationships with multiple representations, such as equations, tables, and graphs.

A hotel charges a daily $4 for use of the in-room video system, plus $3 for each hour the game system is used.

You can use the equation $y = 4 + 3x$ to find y, the cost in dollars of using the game system of x hours.

x	$y = 4 + 3x$	y	Ordered Pairs
0	$y = 4 + 3(0)$	4	(0, 4)
1	$y = 4 + 3(1)$	7	(1, 7)
2	$y = 4 + 3(2)$	10	(2, 10)
3	$y = 4 + 3(3)$	13	(3, 13)
4	$y = 4 + 3(4)$	16	(4, 16)

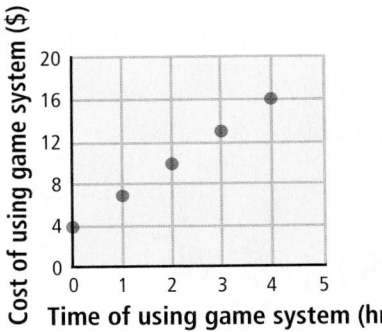

Arithmetic Sequences

 Why? You can use an arithmetic sequence to model many real-world linear relationships between variables.

The cost of a field trip will be the sum of a $100 transportation fee plus $17.75 per student.

Number of Students	1	2	3	4
Total cost	$117.25	$135.50	$153.25	$171.00

$17.75　　　$17.75　　　$17.75

This situation can be modeled with an **arithmetic sequence,** or an ordered list of numbers in which there is a **common difference** between consecutive terms. The common difference, $17.75, is added to each side to get the next term.

Pacing: Traditional 1 day
Block $\frac{1}{2}$ day

Objective: Students represent functions with tables, graphs, or equations.

 Online Edition
Tutorial Videos

 Countdown to Testing Week 5

Warm Up

What three terms come next?
1. 9, 12, 15, 18, 21, 24, 27
2. −8, −3, 2, 7, 12, 17, 22
3. 9, 10, 12, 15, 19, 24, 30, 37

Problem of the Day

Sandra, Greg, and Michael team up for a competitive eating contest. If Sandra can eat 3 hot dogs per minute, Greg can eat 4 hot dogs per minute, and Michael can eat $5\frac{1}{2}$ hot dogs per minute, how long will it take them to eat a combined total of 100 hot dogs? 8 minutes

Also available on transparency

 **Math Humor**

The brothers and sisters were always arguing about how many outputs there were for each input. They were truly a *dysfunctional* family.

 *State Resources*

go.hrw.com
State Resources Online
KEYWORD: MT7 Resources

3-4 Functions

Learn to represent functions with tables, graphs, or equations.

Vocabulary
function
input
output
domain
range
vertical line test

A **function** is a rule that relates two quantities so that each **input** value corresponds to exactly one **output** value.

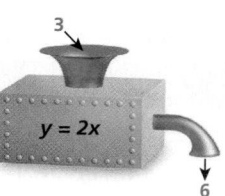

The **domain** is the set of all possible input values, and the **range** is the set of all possible output values.

Function
One input gives one output.

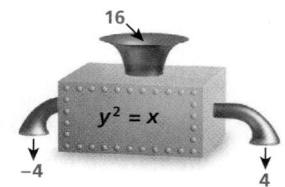

Example: The output is 2 times the input.

Not a Function
One input gives more than one output.

Example: The outputs are the square roots of the input.

Functions can be represented in many ways, including tables, graphs, and equations. If the domain of a function has infinitely many values, it is impossible to represent them all in a table, but a table can be used to show some of the values and to help in creating a graph.

EXAMPLE 1 Finding Different Representations of a Function

Make a table and a graph of $y = 2x + 1$.

Make a table of inputs and outputs. Use the table to make a graph.

x	$2x + 1$	y
−2	$2(-2) + 1$	−3
−1	$2(-1) + 1$	−1
0	$2(0) + 1$	1
1	$2(1) + 1$	3
2	$2(2) + 1$	5

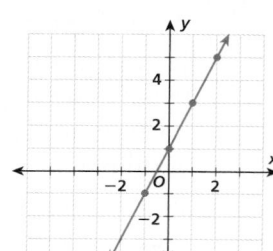

---

1 Introduce

Alternate Opener

Motivate

Use the formula for converting degrees Celsius to degrees Fahrenheit, $F = 1.8C + 32$, to show the students an example of a function. Show them that entering any value of C will determine the value of F, using values for C such as 0° or 100°. Ask the students if it's possible for a temperature in degrees Fahrenheit to be equivalent to two different temperatures in degrees Celsius. no Inform the students that temperature cannot get below −273°C and have them enter this value in the formula to determine the lowest value of degrees Fahrenheit. −459.4°F

Explorations and answers are provided in *Alternate Openers: Explorations Transparencies.*

If a relationship is a function, each input has exactly one output. When the relationship is graphed, use the **vertical line test**. Place a vertical line on the graph. If the line intersects the graph at only one point, then the relationship is a function. If the line intersects the graph at more than one point, then the relationship is not a function.

EXAMPLE 2 Identifying Functions

Determine if each relationship represents a function.

A

x	y
0	5
1	4
2	3
3	2

Each input x has only one output y. The relationship is a function.

B

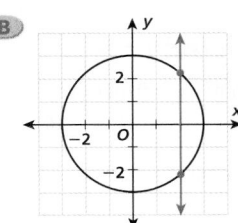

The vertical line intersects the graph at two points. The relationship is not a function.

C $y = x^2$

Make an input-output table and use it to graph $y = x^2$.

x	y
−2	$(-2)^2 = 4$
−1	$(-1)^2 = 1$
0	$(0)^2 = 0$
1	$(1)^2 = 1$
2	$(2)^2 = 4$

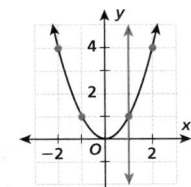

The vertical line intersects the graph at one point. The relationship is a function.

Possible answers to *Think and Discuss*

1. Domain: all numbers; range: 2

2. Verify that each input only has one output.

3. $y = 3x - 4$; {−1, 0, 1}; {−7, −4, −1}; −1; −7

Think and Discuss

1. **Describe** the domain and range for $y = 2$.

2. **Describe** how to tell if a relationship is a function.

3. **Identify** the function, the domain, the range, an input, and the output.

x	y = 3x − 4	y
−1	3(−1) − 4	−7
0	3(0) − 4	−4
1	3(1) − 4	−1

Example 1

Make a table and a graph of $y = 3 - x^2$.

x	3 − x²	y
−2	$3 - (-2)^2$	−1
−1	$3 - (-1)^2$	2
0	$3 - (0)^2$	3
1	$3 - (1)^2$	2
2	$3 - (2)^2$	−1

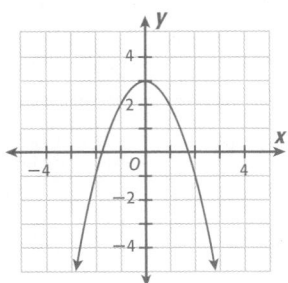

Example 2

Determine if each relationship represents a function.

A.

x	2	3	3	2
y	3	4	5	6

no

B.

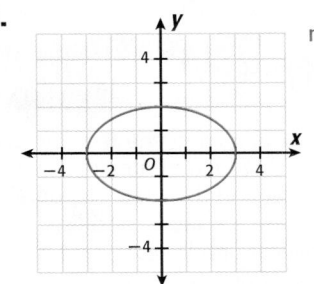

no

C. $y = x^3$ yes

Also available on transparency

---

2 Teach

Guided Instruction

In this lesson, students learn to represent functions with tables, graphs, or equations. Introduce the important vocabulary terms in the lesson. You may want to use the example in Motivate to give examples of *input, output, domain, range,* and *function.* Emphasize that a function assigns exactly one *output* to each *input.*

Teaching Tip **Inclusion** As you explain function notation to students, you may want to provide several examples, as this topic will be new for most students.

Reaching All Learners
Through Critical Thinking

Each function rule below is incomplete. Have students use the given input and output values in each table to complete the function rules.

1. $5x + 7$

Input	Rule	Output
1	5x + ?	12
2	5x + ?	17
3	5x + ?	22

2. $-x^2 + (-3)$

Input	Rule	Output
3	−x² + ?	−12
4	−x² + ?	−19
5	−x² + ?	−28

3. $2x - 3$

Input	Rule	Output
4	?x − 3	5
5	?x − 3	7
6	?x − 3	9

4. $\frac{1}{2}x + 4$

Input	Rule	Output
2	?x + 4	5
3	?x + 4	5.5
4	?x + 4	6

3 Close

Summarize

Review the vocabulary terms with students. Show students the following function table. Ask students to identify the function, the domain, the range, an input, and an output.

x	3x − 1	f(x)
3	3(3) − 1	8
4	3(4) − 1	11
5	3(5) − 1	14

$y = 3x - 1$; {3, 4, 5}; {8, 11, 14}; 3; 8

Assignment Guide

If you finished Example **1** assign:
Average 1–4, 8–11, 20, 25–35
Advanced 8–11, 15–18, 22, 24–35

If you finished Example **2** assign:
Average 1–14, 16–19, 20, 25–35
Advanced 8–16, 20–35

Homework Quick Check

Quickly check key concepts.
Exercises: 10, 12, 16, 20

Answers

1–4, 8–11, 19c. See p. A3.

15. $D = 1, 4, 8, 14$
$R = 27, 39, 50, 62$

16. $D = 100, 120, 150, 170$
$R = 5.4, 3.5, 2.7, 0.2$

17. $D = 30, 40, 50, 60$
$R = 60, 50, 40, 30$

18. $D = 20, 25, 35, 40$
$R = 12, 15, 21, 24$

Math Background

Over 4000 years ago, the Babylonians had a working idea of functions, which is represented in their tablets containing mathematical tables and lists of mathematical problems.

It was not until over 3600 years later that the term *function*, in its Latin equivalent, was used to denote a quantity and its relationship to a curve.

State Resources

go.hrw.com
State Resources Online
KEYWORD: MT7 Resources

3-4 Exercises

go.hrw.com
Homework Help Online
KEYWORD: MT7 3-4
Parent Resources Online
KEYWORD: MT7 Parent

GUIDED PRACTICE

See Example **1** Make a table and a graph of each function.

1. $y = 2x - 4$ **2.** $y = 3x + 4$ **3.** $y = 4x - 3$ **4.** $y = -x + 1$

See Example **2** Determine if each relationship represents a function.

5.

x	y
−1	−7
9	1
12	8
15	−7

The relationship is not a function.

6.

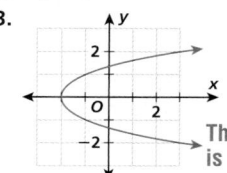

The relationship is a function.

7. $y = 1.5x - 0.5$
The relationship is a function.

INDEPENDENT PRACTICE

See Example **1** Make a table and a graph of each function.

8. $y = 2x + 5$ **9.** $y = 3(x + 1)$ **10.** $y = -(3 - x)$ **11.** $y = 2(1 - 2x)$

See Example **2** Determine if each relationship represents a function.

12.

x	y
2	4
5	5
8	6
2	7

The relationship is a function.

13.

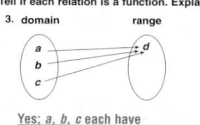

The relationship is not a function.

14. $y = -2x + 1$
The relationship is a function.

PRACTICE AND PROBLEM SOLVING

Extra Practice
See page 787.

Give the domain and the range of each function.

15.

x	y
1	27
4	39
8	50
14	62

16.

x	y
100	5.4
120	3.5
150	2.7
170	0.2

17.

x	y
30	60
40	50
50	40
60	30

18.

x	y
20	12
25	15
35	21
40	24

19. Sports A distance runner trains by running 750 meters at a time. Her coach records the distance covered by the runner every 20 seconds. The results of one run are presented in the table.

Time x (s)	0	20	40	60	80	100
Distance y (m)	0	150	300	450	600	750

a. Does the relationship represent a function? **yes**

b. What is the domain of the function? What is the range?

c. Graph the data to verify your answer for part **a**.

Domain: {0, 20, 40, 60, 80, 100};
Range: {0, 150, 300, 450, 600, 750}

RETEACH 3-4

LESSON
3-4 Reteach
Functions

A **relation** is a set of ordered pairs.   {(1, 2), (3, 4), (5, 6)}

The **domain** of a relation is the set of all <u>first components</u> of the ordered pairs.   {1, 3, 5}

The **range** of a relation is the set of all <u>second components</u> of the ordered pairs.   {2, 4, 6}

Write the domain and range for each relation.

1. relation: {(−1, 1), (−2, 3), (−3, 5)}

domain: {−1, _−2, −3}_

range: { 1, _3, 5}_

2. relation: {(a, 1), (b, 2), (c, 3)}

domain: { a, _b, c}_

range: {1, _2, 3}_

A **function** is a relation in which each element of the domain corresponds to *exactly one* element of the range.

The relation below is a function.

domain   range

a
b → d
c → e

The relation below is not a function.

domain   range

a
b → d
c → e

function: {(a, d), (b, d), (c, e)}
a has only one partner, d.
b has only one partner, d.
c has only one partner, e.

relation: {(a, d), (b, d), (c, d), (c, e)}
a has only one partner, d.
b has only one partner, d.
c has two partners, d and e.

Tell if each relation is a function. Explain.

3. domain   range

a
b → d
c

4. domain   range

a
b → d
c → e

Yes; a, b, c each have one partner, d.

No; a has two partners, d and e.

PRACTICE 3-4

LESSON
3-4 Practice B
Functions

Complete the table and graph each function.

1. $y = -2x + 5$

x	x − 2	y
−2	−2 − 2	−4
−1	−1 − 2	−3
0	0 − 2	−2
1	1 − 2	−1
2	2 − 2	0

2. $y = x - 2$

x	x − 2	y
−2	−2 − 2	−4
−1	−1 − 2	−3
0	0 − 2	−2
1	1 − 2	−1
2	2 − 2	0

Determine if each relationship represents a function.

3. $y = \frac{1}{3}x - \frac{2}{5}$

yes

4.

x	1	2	1	2
y	6	5	−6	−5

no

4.

x	y
0	0
1	−1
2	−8
3	−27
4	−64

yes

5.

no

Home Economics

In 1879, Thomas Edison used a carbonized piece of sewing thread to form a light bulb filament that lasted 13.5 hours before burning out.

20. Business The function $y = 50x - 750$ gives the daily profit of a company that manufactures x items. Make a table and a graph of the function to determine how many items the company must manufacture in order to break even. (*Hint:* When the company breaks even, $y = 0$.)

21. Home Economics The cost of using a 60-watt light bulb is given by the function $y = 0.0036x$. The cost is in dollars, and x represents the number of hours the bulb is lit.

   a. How much does it cost to use a 60-watt light bulb 8 hours a day for a week? **$0.20**

   b. What is the domain of the function? **any nonnegative number of hours ($x \geq 0$)**

   c. If the cost of using a 60-watt bulb was $1.98, for how many hours was it used? **550 hours**

22. What's the Question? The following set of points defines a function: {(3, 6), (−4, 1), (5, −5), (9, −6), (10, −2), (−2, 10)}. If the answer is 6, 1, −5, −6, −2, and 10, what is the question? **Possible answer: What is the range of the function?**

23. Write About It Can you tell if a relationship is a function by just looking at the range? Explain why or why not.

24. Challenge Create a table of values for $y = \frac{1}{x}$ using $x = -3, -2, -1, -0.5, -0.25, 0.5, 1, 2,$ and 3. Sketch the graph of the function. What happens when $x = 0$?

23. No; you must look at the domain and range. A relationship is not a function if a domain value corresponds to more than one range value.

 TEST PREP and Spiral Review

25. Multiple Choice Which relationship does NOT represent a function?

   Ⓐ (0, 8), (3, 8), (1, 6)

   Ⓒ
x	4	6	8
y	2	1	9

   Ⓑ $y = 3x + 17$

   Ⓓ (0, 3), (2, 3), (2, 0)

26. Gridded Response For the function $y = 1.3x - 5.4$, find y when $x = 9$. **6.3**

Evaluate each expression for the given value of the variable. (Lesson 1-5)

27. $7 - t$ for $t = -16$ **23**   **28.** $f - (-31)$ for $f = 76$ **107**   **29.** $-28 - g$ for $g = 32$ **−60**

30. $65 + b$ for $b = -101$ **−36**   **31.** $89 - d$ for $d = -15$ **104**   **32.** $62 - (-m)$ for $m = 71$ **133**

Solve. Check your answer. (Lesson 2-7)

33. $n + 10.7 = -23$ **−33.7**   **34.** $-6.8x = 47.6$ **−7**   **35.** $-\frac{2}{3}m = -\frac{1}{9}$ **$\frac{1}{6}$**

CHALLENGE 3-4

PROBLEM SOLVING 3-4

Answers
20, 24. See p. A3.

 **TEST PREP DOCTOR** For Exercise 25, students who answered **A** probably noticed that two different ordered pairs contained the same y-value, 8, and two different x-values, 0 and 3. Remind students that it is okay for a function to have multiple x-values with the same y-values. Similarly, make sure that students who answered **D** did so because of the ordered pairs (2, 3) and (2, 0) rather than (0, 3) and (2, 3).

Journal

Ask students to write about how they use a graph to determine whether or not a relationship is a function.

Power Presentations with PowerPoint®

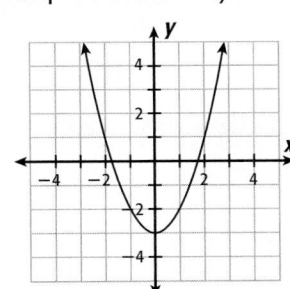

3-4 Lesson Quiz

1. Graph the function $y = x^2 - 3$.

Determine if each relationship represents a function.

2.
x	−2	−1	0	1	1
y	3	4	3	5	6

no

3. $y = 3x + 5$ **yes**

Also available on transparency

Objective: Students generate different representations of the same data.

 Hands-On Lab
In *Hands-On Lab Activities*

 Online Edition
Tutorial Videos

 Countdown to Testing Week 5

Power Presentations
with PowerPoint®

Warm Up

For each function, find the value of y for $x = 0$, $x = 4$, and $x = -5$.

1. $y = 6x - 3$ $-3, 21, -33$

2. $y = 3.8x - 12$ $-12, 3.2, -31$

3. $y = 1.6x + 5.9$ $5.9, 12.3, -2.1$

Problem of the Day

You buy two fruit baskets. Each basket contains three bunches of bananas. Each bunch contains five bananas. How many bananas do you have?   30

Also available on transparency

Math Humor

Boy: I failed all my math subjects except algebra.

Girl: How did you keep from failing?

Boy: I didn't take algebra!

State Resources

go.hrw.com
State Resources Online
KEYWORD: MT7 Resources

Learn to generate different representations of the same data.

Functions can be modeled as equations, tables, or graphs. Each representation shows the same data, but in a different way.

EXAMPLE 1 **Using Equations to Generate Different Representations of Data**

Make a table and sketch a graph of the path of a submarine diving at 50 ft per minute. The depth of the submarine is represented by the equation $d = -50m$, where d is the depth and m is the number of minutes.

Helpful Hint

The number of minutes m is the input value. The depth d is the output value.

Equation	Table			Graph
$d = -50m$ *An equation shows how the variables are related.*	m	$-50m$	d	
	0	$-50(0)$	0	
	1	$-50(1)$	-50	
	2	$-50(2)$	-100	
	3	$-50(3)$	-150	
	4	$-50(4)$	-200	
	A table identifies values that make the function true.			*A graph is a visual image of the values in the table.*

To write an equation from data in a table, you need to look for a pattern in the data. Look for the changes in the input values and the changes in the output values. Then see how the changes are related.

1 Introduce

Alternate Opener

EXPLORATION

3-5 Equations, Tables, and Graphs

Jerome is driving at a constant speed of 50 mi/h. You can use an equation, a table, and a graph to represent the distance d that Jerome travels in t hours.

1. Complete the table.

Time (hr), t	distance (mi), d
0.5	
1	50
1.5	
2	
2.5	
3	

2. Plot the points in your table and then connect the points to make a graph that shows Jerome's distance as a function of time.

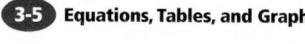

Think and Discuss

3. **Describe** the graph that you made.
4. **Explain** how distance is related to time. How can you use this to write an equation relating d and t?

Motivate

Ask students to imagine they buy a hot dog stand that sells 2000 hot dogs the first year, 3500 the second year, and 5000 the third year. How many will they sell in the fourth year?   6500   In the 10th year?   15,500 Solve by making a table and graph with the students and see if they can determine the equation. $y = 1500x + 500$ Explain that knowing different ways of organizing data yields insight about relationships. Of the graph, table, and equation, which did students find the most helpful?

Explorations and answers are provided in *Alternate Openers: Explorations Transparencies.*

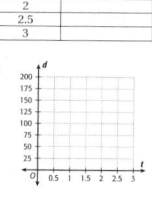

EXAMPLE 2 Using Tables to Generate Different Representations of Data

Use the table to make a graph and to write an equation.

x	0	1	2	3	4
y	0	6	12	18	24

Look for a pattern in the values:

$6 = 6 \times 1$ *Each value of y is six*
$12 = 6 \times 2$ *times the value of x*
$18 = 6 \times 3$

$y = 6 \times x$

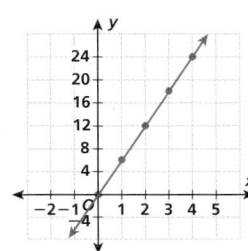

To find an equation from a graph, it might be easier to first create a table of values from the graph. Then you can look for a pattern in the values as in Example 2.

EXAMPLE 3 Using Graphs to Generate Different Representations of Data

Use the graph to make a table and to write an equation.

Look for a pattern in the values:

x	y
−3	−2
−2	−1
−1	0
0	1
2	3

$-2 = -3 + 1$
$-1 = -2 + 1$
$0 = -1 + 1$ *Each value of y is one*
$1 = 0 + 1$ *more than the value*
$3 = 2 + 1$ *of x.*

$y = x + 1$

Possible answers to *Think and Discuss*

1. An equation gives the most accurate information because it allows you to identify any point.

2. A graph shows the relationship most quickly because you can immediately see how changes in one variable affect the other.

Think and Discuss

1. **Which** representation of data do you think gives the most accurate information? Justify your answer.

2. **Which** representation of data do you think shows the relationship most quickly? Justify your answer.

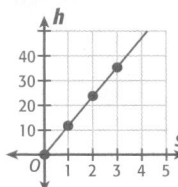
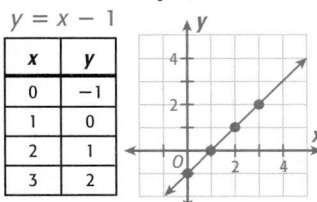
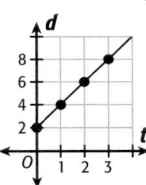
2 Teach

Guided Instruction

Briefly review interpreting graphs and tables, as students should be familiar with these concepts by now. Then discuss how to use tables, graphs, and equations together to interpret data. Be sure to point out when the equations are also functions. Also, emphasize finding equations from data points, since similar skills will be needed for sequences later on.

 Reaching All Learners
Through Cooperative Learning

Divide the class into groups of three. Have each student make up an equation and write it on a piece of paper. Students should then shift their papers to the next person in the group. Each student should create a table with eight ordered pairs using the equations handed to him or her. After they have completed the tables, have them shift their papers again. Each student should then create a graph using the table handed to him or her.

3 Close

Summarize

Review various word problems and ask students to discuss the advantages and disadvantages of representing data with equations, tables, or graphs.

3-5 Exercises

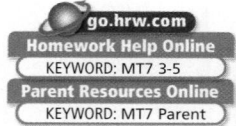
go.hrw.com
Homework Help Online
KEYWORD: MT7 3-5
Parent Resources Online
KEYWORD: MT7 Parent

Assignment Guide

If you finished **Example 1** assign:
Average 1, 4, 7, 8, 12–20
Advanced 4, 7, 8, 10–20

If you finished **Example 2** assign:
Average 1, 2, 4, 5, 7, 8, 12–20
Advanced 4, 5, 7–20

If you finished **Example 3** assign:
Average 1–8, 12–20
Advanced 4–20

Homework Quick Check

Quickly check key concepts.
Exercises: 4, 5, 6, 8

Answers

1. Possible answer:

m	0	1	2	3	4
g	0	15	30	45	60

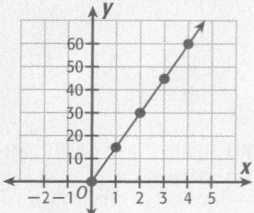

2, 4–5, 7. See p. A4.

State Resources

go.hrw.com
State Resources Online
KEYWORD: MT7 Resources

GUIDED PRACTICE

See Example 1 1. The amount of water in a pool being filled is represented by the equation $g = 15m$, where g is the number of gallons of water in the pool and m is the number of minutes since filling began. Make a table and sketch a graph of the equation.

See Example 2 2. Use the table to make a graph and to write an equation.

x	0	2	5	9	12
y	3	5	8	12	15

See Example 3 3. Use the graph to make a table and to write an equation.

x	−1	0	1
y	−3	0	3

$y = 3x$

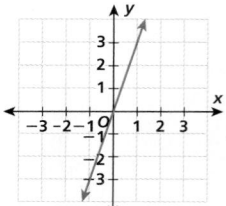

INDEPENDENT PRACTICE

See Example 1 4. The amount of sand in the top half of an hourglass is represented by the equation $h = -0.5s$, where h is the height of the sand in centimeters and s is the number of seconds since the top half began draining. Make a table and sketch a graph of the equation.

See Example 2 5. Use the table to make a graph and to write an equation.

x	0	2	4	6	8
y	12	10	8	6	4

See Example 3 6. Use the graph to make a table and to write an equation.

x	−3	−2	−1	0	1
y	0	1	2	3	4

$y = x + 3$

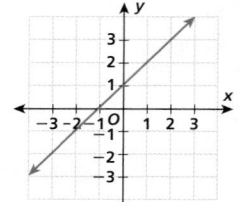

7. The graph does not show the same relationship; the graph shows $y = 4x - 1$.

PRACTICE AND PROBLEM SOLVING

Extra Practice
See page 787.

7. **Travel** The distance Jackson can drive on a tank of gas is represented by the function $d = 20g$, where d is the distance in miles and g is the number of gallons of gas in the tank. Make a table and sketch a graph of the data.

RETEACH 3-5

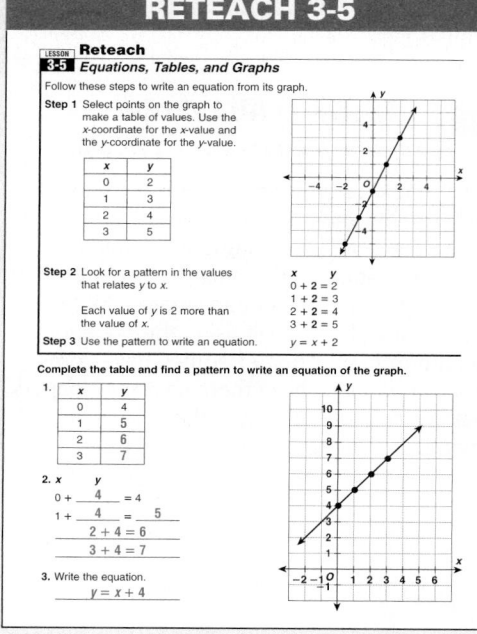

PRACTICE 3-5

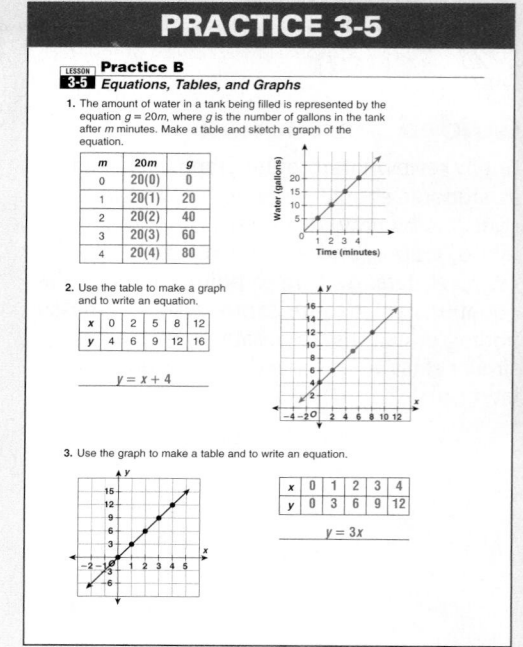

---

8. Choose the representation that does not show the same relationship as the other two.

$y = 4x + 1$

x	0	3	6	9	12
y	1	13	25	37	49

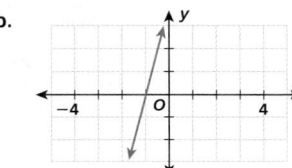

9. Conservation A faucet is leaking water at the rate of 2.5 gallons per hour. Let x be the number of hours the faucet leaks and y be the total number of gallons leaked. Write an equation and make a table.

 10. Write a Problem Write a situation for each relationship.

a. $y = 2x + 3$

b.

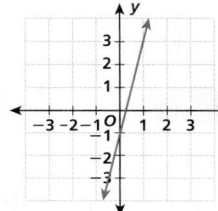

 11. Challenge Graph the function $y = |x|$. Be sure to include negative values of x. How does the graph differ from the others in this lesson?

TEST PREP and Spiral Review

12. Multiple Choice Jeff began the week with $30.00. He took a city bus to and from school, paying $0.75 for each trip. Let x be the number of trips he took and y be the amount of money he had left at the end of the week. Which equation represents the relationship in the situation?

Ⓐ $y = 0.75x + 30$ Ⓒ $x = 3 - 0.75y$

Ⓑ $y = 30 - 0.75x$ Ⓓ $y = 0.75x - 30$

13. Extended Response The equation $y = 2.5x - 2000$ represents the profit made by a manufacturer that sells a product for $2.50 each, where y is the profit and x is the number of units sold. Construct a table to find the number of units that must be sold for the manufacturer to break even. The break-even point is where profit is equal to 0. Explain the data in the table.

Simplify. (Lesson 1-6)

14. $-3(-9)$ **27**   **15.** $7(-3)$ -21 **16.** $\frac{2(-6)}{4}$ -3 **17.** $\frac{-8(-5)}{-10}$ -4

Solve. Check your answer. (Lesson 2-8)

18. $5p - 2 = 0$ $\frac{2}{5}$ **19.** $\frac{s}{4} + 8 = 12$ **16**   **20.** $12 - 3x = -6$ **6**

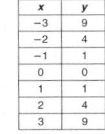
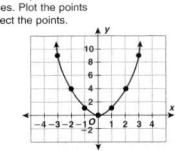
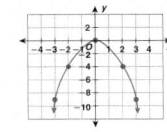
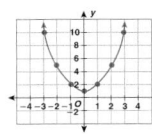
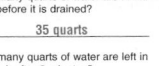
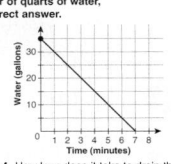

Answers

8–11, 13. See p. A4.

 **TEST PREP DOCTOR** ✛ If students have difficulty with Exercise 12, remind them that words such as "each" often imply multiplication. This should help them decide which number is being multiplied by x in the equation. Note that "each" is also used this way in Exercise 13.

 Journal

Have students think of a relationship in their life, such as number of weeks and allowance money. Have them create an equation, table, and graph that represent the relationship.

 Power Presentations
with PowerPoint®

3-5
Lesson Quiz

1. Make a table and sketch the graph of $w = -2x + 3$.

2. Use the table to sketch a graph and write an equation.

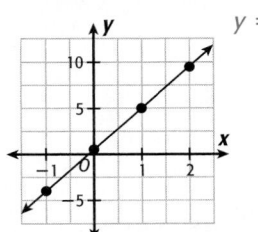

x	y
-1	1
0	0
1	-1
2	-2

$y = -x$

3. Use the graph to make a table and to write an equation.

$y = 4x + 1$

Answers 1–3. See p. A4.

Also available on transparency

Objective: Students identify and evaluate arithmetic sequences.

Hands-On Lab
In *Hands-On Lab Activities*

Online Edition
Tutorial Videos

Countdown to Testing Week 6

Power Presentations
with PowerPoint®

Warm Up

Use the table to write an equation.

1.

x	1	2	3	4
y	5	10	15	20

$y = 5x$

2.

x	1	2	3	4
y	−2.5	−5	−7.5	−10

$y = -2.5x$

3.

x	1	2	3	4
y	5	8	11	14

$y = 3x + 2$

Problem of the Day

A movie ticket at a certain theater costs $4.50 for a child and $8.75 for an adult. How much will it cost for a family of two adults and three children to see a movie? **$31**

Also available on transparency

State Resources

go.hrw.com
State Resources Online
KEYWORD: MT7 Resources

3-6 Arithmetic Sequences

Learn to identify and evaluate arithmetic sequences.

Vocabulary
sequence
term
arithmetic sequence
common difference

A school choir is planning a trip to a water park. The choir must pay a $100.00 transportation fee plus $17.75 for each student to enter the park. Under the plan, one student would cost a total of $117.75, two students $135.50, three students $153.25, and so on.

Number of Students	1	2	3	4
Total cost	$117.25	$135.50	$153.25	$171.00

$17.75 $17.75 $17.75

A **sequence** is an ordered list of numbers or objects, called **terms**. In an **arithmetic sequence**, the difference between one term and the next is always the same. This difference is called the **common difference**. The common difference is added to each term to get the next term.

EXAMPLE 1 **Finding the Common Difference in an Arithmetic Sequence**

Find the common difference in each arithmetic sequence.

A 7, 10, 13, 16, . . .

7, 10, 13, 16
+3 +3 +3   *The terms increase by 3.*

The common difference is 3

B 7.5, 6, 4.5, 3, . . .

7.5,   6,   4.5,   3
−1.5 −1.5 −1.5   *The terms decrease by 1.5.*

The common difference is −1.5

EXAMPLE 2 **Finding Missing Terms in an Arithmetic Sequence**

Find the next three terms in the arithmetic sequence
−12, −4, 4, 12, . . .

Each term is 8 more than the previous term.

$12 + 8 = 20$
$20 + 8 = 28$ *Use the common difference to find the next three terms.*
$28 + 8 = 36$

The next three terms are 20, 28, and 36.

---

1 Introduce
Alternate Opener

EXPLORATION

3-6 Arithmetic Sequences

Maya is a structural engineer. She is designing support structures for a bridge. As shown in the figures, the structures consist of regular beams (the horizontal and vertical beams) and cross beams (the diagonal beams).

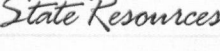

One section   Two sections   Three sections

1. Maya makes a table showing the number of cross beams needed for various numbers of sections. Complete the table.

Number of Sections	1	2	3	4	5
Number of Cross Beams	2	4			

2. She also makes a table showing the number of regular beams needed for various numbers of sections. Complete the table.

Number of Sections	1	2	3	4	5
Number of Regular Beams	4	7			

Think and Discuss

3. Describe any patterns you notice in the table for the number of cross beams.

4. Explain how you could find the number of regular beams needed to make 6 sections based on the patterns in your table.

Motivate

Explain to students that arithmetic sequences are closely related to many of the functions they have studied thus far. Write a table showing values 1 through 4 in the x-column, and write 3, 6, 9, and '?' in the y-column. Ask students what the value of the function is when x is 4. **12** Point out that in order to get the answer, students must use the arithmetic sequence in the y-column to infer the next number in the sequence.

Explorations and answers are provided in *Alternate Openers: Explorations Transparencies.*

You can use a function table to help identify the pattern in a sequence and to find missing terms. Each term's position in the sequence is the input, and the value of each term is the output.

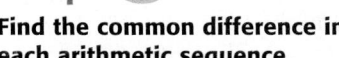
 EXAMPLE 3 Identifying Functions in Arithmetic Sequences

Find a function that describes each arithmetic sequence. Use y to identify each term in the sequence and n to identify each term's position.

A 2, 4, 6, 8, . . .

n	$n \cdot 2$	y
1	$1 \cdot 2$	2
2	$2 \cdot 2$	4
3	$3 \cdot 2$	6
4	$4 \cdot 2$	8
n	$n \cdot 2$	$2n$

Multiply n by 2.

$y = 2n$

B $-3, -6, -9, -12, \ldots$

n	$n \cdot (-3)$	y
1	$1 \cdot (-3)$	-3
2	$2 \cdot (-3)$	-6
3	$3 \cdot (-3)$	-9
4	$4 \cdot (-3)$	-12
n	$n \cdot (-3)$	$-3n$

Multiply n by -3.

$y = -3n$

 EXAMPLE 4 *Travel Application*

A school choir is taking a trip to a water park. The choir must pay a transportation fee of $100.00 plus $17.75 for each student to enter the park. Find a function that describes the arithmetic sequence. Then find the total cost for a group of 23 students to enter the park.

n	$100 + 17.75n$	y
1	$100 + 17.75(1)$	117.75
2	$100 + 17.75(2)$	135.50
3	$100 + 17.75(3)$	153.25
4	$100 + 17.75(4)$	171.00
n	$100 + 17.75(n)$	$17.75n + 100$

Multiply n by $17.75, and then add the $100 transportation fee.

$17.75n + 100$ *Write a function to find the 23rd term.*
$17.75(23) + 100$ *Substitute 23 for n.*
$408.25 + 100$ *Multiply.*
508.25 *Add.*

It will cost a group of 23 students $508.25 to go to the water park.

Possible answers to Think and Discuss

1. Sequences help you to see patterns.

2. Multiplying each term by a fraction or a decimal less than one will produce a sequence in which the values decrease.

Think and Discuss

1. **How** are sequences useful in every day situations?

2. **Explain** how multiplication can be used to make a sequence with terms that decrease in value.

2 Teach

Guided Instruction

Review how to find equations using tables before introducing students to arithmetic sequences. Discuss how to find common differences and how they can be used to find other terms in a sequence. Then show students how to describe sequences with functions and use this method to solve word problems.

 Reaching All Learners
Through Multiple Representations

Have students redo Example 3A. This time, have them use the values 0 through 3 instead of 1 through 4 in the n-column of the table. The resulting function will be $y = 2n + 2$ instead of $y = 2n$. Explain that both functions are correct, and that there are many different functions that can describe any sequence (in fact, infinitely many). Point out that in this case, adding 2 to the right side of the equation made up for the change in the values of n.

3 Close

Summarize

Discuss with students how sequences reveal the patterns that exist between numbers, and that these patterns are not usually as apparent in function form.

3-6 Exercises

3-6 Exercises

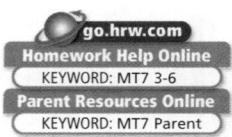
go.hrw.com
Homework Help Online
KEYWORD: MT7 3-6
Parent Resources Online
KEYWORD: MT7 Parent

Assignment Guide

If you finished Example **1** assign:
Average 1–6, 17–22, 48–55
Advanced 17–22, 48–55

If you finished Example **2** assign:
Average 1–12, 17–28, 33–35, 48–55
Advanced 17–28, 33–38, 45, 48–55

If you finished Example **3** assign:
Average 1–15, 17–31, 33–35, 41, 42, 48–55
Advanced 17–31, 33–42, 45–55

If you finished Example **4** assign:
Average 1–35, 41–44, 48–55
Advanced 17–32, 36–38, 41–55

Homework Quick Check

Quickly check key concepts.
Exercises: 18, 24, 30, 32, 34, 42

Answers

7. 25, 30, 35

8. 3.5, 4, 4.5

9. 12, 5, −2

23. 45, 54, 63

24. 12.5, 15, 17.5

25. −2, −11, −20

GUIDED PRACTICE

See Example **1** Find the common difference in each arithmetic sequence.

1. 4, 8, 12, 16, . . . **4**
2. 6, 13, 20, 27, . . . **7**
3. 25, 19, 13, 7, . . . **−6**
4. 3.4, 4, 4.6. 5.2, . . . **0.6**
5. 15, 12, 9, 6, 3, . . . **−3**
6. 10, 19, 28, 37, . . . **9**

See Example **2** Find the next three terms in each arithmetic sequence.

7. 5, 10, 15, 20, . . .
8. 1.5, 2, 2.5, 3, . . .
9. 40, 33, 26, 19, . . .
10. 6, 12, 18, 24, . . . **30, 36, 42**
11. −2, −4, −6, −8, . . . **−10, −12, −14**
12. $\frac{1}{2}$, 1, $1\frac{1}{2}$, 2, . . . **$2\frac{1}{2}$, 3, $3\frac{1}{2}$**

See Example **3** Find a function that describes each arithmetic sequence. Use y to identify each term in the sequence and n to identify each term's position.

13. 3, 6, 9, 12, . . . $y = 3n$
14. 1, 4, 7, 10, . . . $y = 3n − 2$
15. 2, 6, 10, 14, . . . $y = 4n − 2$

See Example **4** **16.** A long distance phone plan costs $19.95 per month, plus $0.03 per minute used. Find a function that describes the arithmetic sequence. Then find the total charges for a month in which 3 hours of long distance were used.
$c = 19.95 + 0.03m$; $25.35

INDEPENDENT PRACTICE

See Example **1** Find the common difference in each arithmetic sequence.

17. 7, 14, 21, 28, . . . **7**
18. −5, −1, 3, 7, . . . **4**
19. 32, 26, 20, 14, . . . **−6**
20. 4.9, 6, 7.1, 8.2, . . . **1.1**
21. 63, 56, 49, 42, . . . **−7**
22. 3, 15, 27, 39, . . . **12**

See Example **2** Find the next three terms in each arithmetic sequence.

23. 9, 18, 27, 36, . . .
24. 2.5, 5, 7.5, 10, . . .
25. 34, 25, 16, 7, . . .
26. 8, 16, 24, 32, . . . **40, 48, 56**
27. −3, −6, −9, −12, . . . **−15, −18, −21**
28. $\frac{1}{3}$, $\frac{2}{3}$, 1, $1\frac{1}{3}$, . . . **$1\frac{2}{3}$, 2, $2\frac{1}{3}$**

See Example **3** Find a function that describes each arithmetic sequence. Use y to identify each term in the sequence and n to identify each term's position.

29. 4, 8, 12, 16, . . . $y = 4n$
30. 1, 6, 11, 16, . . . $y = 5n − 4$
31. 3, 10, 17, 24, . . . $y = 7n − 4$

See Example **4** **32.** A book club charges $10.50 to join. Members of the club pay $4.50 each for books sold by the club. Find a function that describes the arithmetic sequence. Then find the total charges for a member who buys 27 books.
$c = 10.50 + 4.50b$; $132

PRACTICE AND PROBLEM SOLVING

Extra Practice
See page 787.

Find the missing term in each arithmetic sequence.

33. 13, 26, 39, 52, ▩, . . . **65**
34. −8, −5, −2, ▩, 4, . . . **1**
35. ▩, 24, 18, 12, 6, . . . **30**
36. 2.7, 4.2, 5.7, ▩, 8.7, . . . **7.2**
37. ▩, 37, 30, 23, 16, . . . **44**
38. $\frac{7}{8}$, $\frac{13}{16}$, $\frac{3}{4}$, $\frac{11}{16}$, ▩, . . . **$\frac{5}{8}$**

RETEACH 3-6

LESSON **3-6** *Reteach*
Arithmetic Sequences

In an **arithmetic sequence**, the difference between one term and the next term is always the same. That difference is called the **common difference**.

If the terms increase, the common difference is positive.
If the terms decrease, the common difference is negative.

2, 6, 10, 14, . . .
50, 47, 44, 41, . . .

Look at pairs of differences:
6 − 2 = 4
10 − 6 = 4
14 − 10 = 4
The common difference is 4.

Look at pairs of differences:
47 − 50 = −3
44 − 47 = −3
41 − 44 = −3
The common difference is −3.

To find next term in the sequence, add 4 to the last term.
14 + 4 = 18
So, the next term is 18.

To find next term in the sequence, add −3 to the last term.
41 + (−3) = 38
So, the next term is 38.

Complete to find the common difference of each arithmetic sequence. Then find the next term in the sequence.

1. 3, 9, 15, 21, . . .
9 − 3 = __6__
15 − 9 = __6__
21 − 15 = __6__
Common difference: __6__
Next term: 21 + __6__ = __27__

2. 44, 42, 40, 38, . . .
42 − 44 = __−2__
40 − 42 = −2
38 − 40 = −2
Common difference: __−2__
Next term: __36__

3. 4, 9, 14, 19, . . .
9 − 4 = 5
14 − 9 = 5
19 − 14 = 5
Common difference: __5__
Next term: __24__

PRACTICE 3-6

LESSON **3-6** *Practice B*
Arithmetic Sequences

Find the common difference in each arithmetic sequence.

1. 5, 9, 13, 17, . . . **4**
2. 3, 10, 17, 24, . . . **7**
3. 35, 32, 29, 26, . . . **−3**
4. 36, 15, 24, 33, . . . **9**
5. 92, 87, 82, 77, . . . **−5**
6. 60, 54, 48, 42, . . . **−6**
7. 108, 96, 84, 72, . . . **−12**
8. 3.8, 4, 4.2, 4.4, . . . **0.2**
9. 95, 88, 81, 74, . . . **−7**

Find the next three terms in each arithmetic sequence.

10. 12, 18, 24, 30, . . . **36, 42, 48**
11. $1\frac{1}{2}$, 2, $2\frac{1}{2}$, 3, . . . **$3\frac{1}{2}$, 4, $4\frac{1}{2}$**
12. −7, −14, −21, −28, . . . **−35, −42, −49**
13. 0.5, 1, 1.5, 2, . . . **2.5, 3, 3.5**
14. −8, −16, −24, −32, . . . **−40, −48, −56**
15. 72, 63, 54, 45, . . . **36, 27, 18**
16. 3.5, 7, 10.5, 14, . . . **17.5, 21, 24.5**
17. $\frac{1}{3}$, $\frac{2}{3}$, 1, $1\frac{1}{3}$, . . . **$1\frac{2}{3}$, 2, $2\frac{1}{3}$**
18. 10, 9.5, 9, 8.5, . . . **8, 7.5, 7**

Find a function that describes each arithmetic sequence. Use y to identify each term in the sequence and n to identify each term's position.

19. 6, 12, 18, 24, . . . $y = 6n$
20. −8, −16, −24, −32, . . . $y = −8n$
21. 12, 24, 36, 48, . . . $y = 12n$

22. It costs $12 to rent a mini-car to go around the track, plus $4 per lap. Find a function that describes the sequence. Then find the total cost of driving 5 laps around the track.
$y = 12 + 4n$; $32

State Resources

go.hrw.com
State Resources Online
KEYWORD: MT7 Resources

Find the given term in each arithmetic sequence. (*Hint:* To find a term n of an arithmetic sequence that has a common difference, add the 1st term of the sequence to the product of the common difference and $(n - 1)$.)

39. 11th term: 3, 9, 15, 21, . . . **63**

40. 15th term: 4, 11, 18, 25, . . . **102**

41. 18th term: 9, 13, 17, 21, . . . **77**

42. 20th term: 2, 5, 8, 11, . . . **59**

43. **Sports** Tyler ran 10 laps around the track on Monday. Each day after that, he ran 3 more laps than the day before. How many laps did Tyler run on the eighth day? **31**

44. A restaurant has square tables. Each table can seat 4 people. If 2 square tables are pushed together, 6 people can be seated around the new table. If 12 square tables are pushed together to form one long table, how many people can be seated around the table? **26**

45. Possible answer: 32 is the 11th term of the sequence. The rule for the sequence is $3n - 1$.

 45. **What's the Error?** A student said that the 10th term of the arithmetic sequence 2, 5, 8, 11, . . . is 32. What was the student's error?

 46. **Critical Thinking** Matthew is making a sequence in which -3 is added to each successive term. The 6th term in his sequence is -1. What is the 1st term in his sequence? **243**

 47. **Challenge** Tell whether the given term belongs to the sequence defined by the given rule if n is a whole number.

a. 62; $4n$ **no**   **b.** 87; $3n$ **yes**   **c.** 42; $-6n$ **no**

TEST PREP and Spiral Review

48. **Multiple Choice** What is the next term in the sequence 25, 18, 11, 4, . . . ?

Ⓐ -11 Ⓑ -7 Ⓒ -3 Ⓓ 0

49. **Short Response** What is the 10th term in the sequence $-10, -7, -4, -1, \dots$? **17**

Find each sum, difference, product, or quotient. Write the answer in simplest form.
(Lessons 2-4, 2-5, and 2-6)

50. $\frac{7}{12} - \frac{1}{4}$ $\frac{1}{3}$ **51.** $\frac{3}{8} \times \frac{4}{9}$ $\frac{1}{6}$ **52.** $\frac{3}{8} \div \frac{3}{4}$ $\frac{1}{2}$

Make a table and a graph of each function. (Lessons 3-4)

53. $y = 3x - 1$ **54.** $y = 2x + 2$ **55.** $y = -x$

ONGOING ASSESSMENT
and **INTERVENTION**

Diagnose Before the Lesson
3-6 Warm Up, TE p. 142

Monitor During the Lesson
3-6 Know-It Notebook
3-6 Questioning Strategies

Assess After the Lesson
3-6 Lesson Quiz, TE p. 145

Answers
53–55. See p. A4.

 **TEST PREP DOCTOR +** If students have difficulty with Exercise 49, they may be trying to find the 10th term by adding 3 over and over. Make sure students are making a function to which they can input 10 to find the answer.

 Journal

Have students explain how multiplication is related to addition when describing sequences using functions.

Power Presentations
with **PowerPoint®**

 3-6 Lesson Quiz

Find the common difference in each arithmetic sequence.

1. 4, 2, 0, -2, . . . -2

2. $\frac{4}{3}$, 2, $\frac{8}{3}$, $\frac{10}{3}$, . . . $\frac{2}{3}$

Find the next three terms in each arithmetic sequence.

3. 18, 13, 8, 3, . . . $-2, -7, -12$

4. 3.6, 5, 6.4, 7.8, . . . 9.2, 10.6, 12

Find a function that describes the arithmetic sequence.

5. $-5, -10, -15, -20, \dots$
Possible answer: $y = -5n$

6. $-1, 2, 5, 8, \dots$
Possible answer: $y = 3n - 4$

7. A runner finishes a lap in 55 seconds. Her goal is to decrease her time by two seconds every week. Find a function that describes the arithmetic sequence and find how many seconds her lap should be after 12 weeks of training.
Possible answer: $s = -2w + 55$; **31 seconds**

Also available on transparency

CHALLENGE 3-6

LESSON 3-6 Challenge
Coming to Terms

You can use the following rule to find the nth term of an arithmetic sequence:

$a_n = a_1 + (n - 1)d$

In this rule, a_n represents the nth term, a_1 represents the first term, n represents the number of the term, and d represents the common difference of the sequence.

Find the 20th term of the sequence: 2, 5, 8, 11, . . .

Step 1 Identify the number of the term and the first term, and find the common difference.

$n = 20$ $a_1 = 2$ $d = 3$

Step 2 Substitute the values for n, a_1, and d in the rule.

$a_n = a_1 + (n - 1)d$
$a_{20} = 2 + (20 - 1)(3)$
$= 2 + 19(3)$
$= 2 + 57$
$= 59$

The 20th term of the sequence is 59.

Find the given term in each arithmetic sequence.

1. 18th term: 8, 15, 22, 29, . . .
127

2. 25th term: 13, 26, 39, 52, . . .
325

3. 30th term: 6, 15, 24, 33, . . .
270

4. 24th term: 3, 11, 19, 27, . . .
192

5. 21st term: 3.5, 7, 10.5, 14, . . .
73.5

6. 35th term: 3.8, 4, 4.2, 4.4, . . .
10.6

7. 40th term: 1.3, 3.4, 5.5, 7.6, . . .
83.2

8. 52nd term: $-8, -16, -24, -32, \dots$
-416

PROBLEM SOLVING 3-6

LESSON 3-6 Problem Solving
Arithmetic Sequences

Write the correct answer.

1. An English teacher gives her class 6 vocabulary words on Monday. Each day for the rest of the week she adds 3 more vocabulary words to the list. How many words are on the list on Friday?
18 vocabulary words

2. A cab ride costs $1.50 plus $2.00 for each mile. What is the total cost of a 5-mile cab ride?
$11.50

3. Rosie ran 8 laps around the track. Each week after that she ran 3 more laps than the week before. How many laps will she run around the track in the sixth week?
23 laps

4. Lee has saved $85. Each week he uses his savings to buy a CD for $9. How much money will he have left after the fourth week?
$49

Use the table to answer Exercises 5–7. The table shows the number of seats in each row of a theater. Choose the letter of the best answer.

5. The number of seats is an arithmetic sequence. What is the common difference?

A 6   C 9
Ⓑ 8   D 35

Row	Number of Seats
1	35
2	43
3	51
4	59
5	67

6. If the sequence continues, how many seats will be in the next row?

F 68   Ⓗ 75
G 73   J 76

7. If the sequence continues, how many seats will be in the tenth row?

A 80   C 134
Ⓑ 107   D 147

8. A class is taking a field trip to the zoo. Admission for the class costs $50 plus $2 for each student to visit the special exhibits. Which function best describes the total cost for n students?

F $y = 50n - 2$
G $y = 50n + 2$
H $y = 50 - 2n$
Ⓙ $y = 50 + 2n$

Organizer

Objective: Assess students' mastery of concepts and skills in Lessons 3-4 through 3-6.

Resources

Assessment Resources
Section 3B Quiz

Test & Practice Generator
One-Stop Planner®

INTERVENTION ◀▶

Resources

Ready to Go On?
Intervention and
Enrichment Worksheets

Ready to Go On? CD-ROM

Ready to Go On? Online

my.hrw.com

Answers

1–4, 9–13. See pp. A4–A5.

READY TO GO ON?

Quiz for Lessons 3-4 Through 3-6

✓ 3-4 Functions

Make a table and a graph of each function.

1. $y = x + 7$ **2.** $y = 4x + 2$ **3.** $y = \frac{2}{3}x + \frac{1}{3}$ **4.** $y = 5.2x$

Determine if each relationship represents a function.

5.
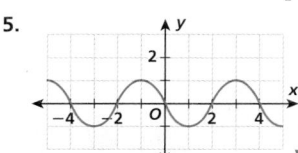
yes

6.

x	y
0	9
1	8
2	7
3	8

no

7. $y = 4x - 8$
yes

8. $y = x^2$
yes

✓ 3-5 Equations, Tables, and Graphs

Use each table to make a graph and to write an equation.

9.

x	2	4	6	8
y	13	19	25	31

10.

x	3	6	9	12
y	3.5	5	6.5	8

Use each graph to make a table and to write an equation.

11.
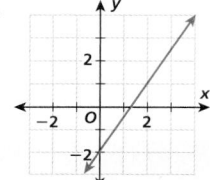

12.
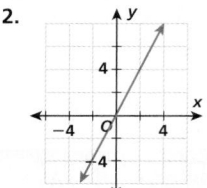

13. The number of tons of plankton that a blue whale eats during the summer is represented by the equation $p = 8d$, where d is the number of days. Make a table and sketch a graph of the equation.

✓ 3-6 Arithmetic Sequences

Find the missing term in each sequence.

14. 2, 5, 8, 11, ▓, . . . 14   **15.** ▓, 8, 16, 24, 32, . . . 0   **16.** 1.5, 3, ▓, 6, 7.5, . . . 4.5

17. −5, ▓, 5, 10, 15, . . . 0   **18.** 1, 3, 5, 7, ▓, . . . 9   **19.** ▓, 2.7, 4, 5.3, 6.6, . . . 1.4

20. Tickets to a dance cost $5 each. Decorations, food, and music cost $350. Find a function that describes the sequence. Then find the total profit if 93 tickets are sold. $p = 5t - 350$; $115

READY TO GO ON?

Diagnose and Prescribe

NO
INTERVENE

YES
ENRICH

Ready to Go On?	*READY TO GO ON? Intervention, Section 3B*		
Intervention	*Worksheets*	CD-ROM	Online
✓ Lesson 3-4	3-4 Intervention	Activity 3-4	Diagnose and Prescribe Online
✓ Lesson 3-5	3-5 Intervention	Activity 3-5	
✓ Lesson 3-6	3-6 Intervention	Activity 3-6	

READY TO GO ON?
Enrichment, Section 3B

Worksheets

CD-ROM

Online

Start Your Engines Ms. Naranja's class is conducting an experiment with remote-controlled cars. The cars move in a straight line away from a wall. Students record each car's distance from the wall at one-second intervals.

1. The motion of car A is given by the equation, $y = 2.5x + 1.5$, where x is the time in seconds and y is the car's distance from the wall in feet. Complete the table of data for car A.

2. Graph the data for car A on a coordinate plane.

3. How far is car A from the wall at the start of the experiment? How far is the car from the wall after 3 seconds? **1.5 ft; 9 ft**

Car A	
Time (s)	Distance (ft)
0	■ 2.5
1	■ 4
2	■ 6.5
3	■ 9

4. Find the value of y when $x = 6$ for the function $y = 2.5x + 1.5$. What does this value represent?

5. The data for car B is shown in the graph. Make a table of data for car B. Include times from 0 to 6 seconds.

6. Describe the motion of car B in words. What do you think happened to the car after 3 seconds? **The car starts 2 ft from the wall. It moves forward at 3 ft/sec for 3 seconds. At 3 seconds the car stops (it may have hit an obstacle or the battery may have run out of power).**

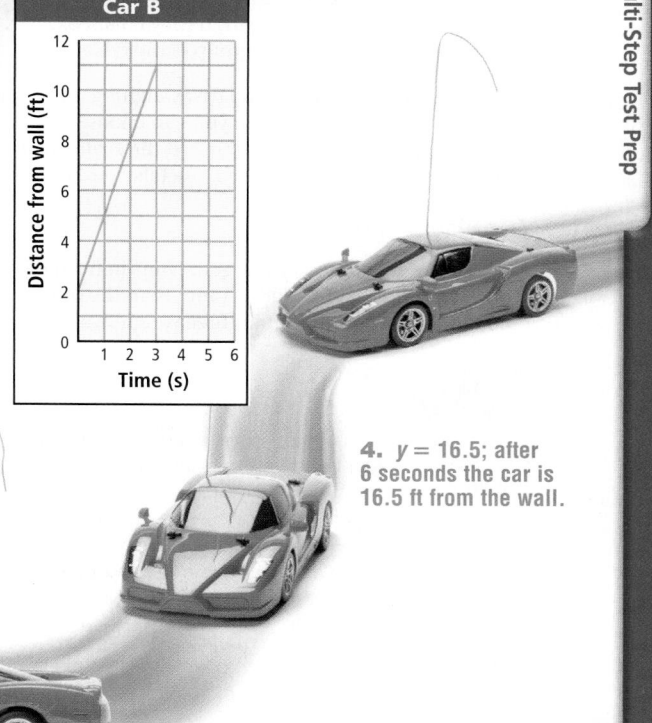

Car B

(graph: Distance from wall (ft) vs Time (s))

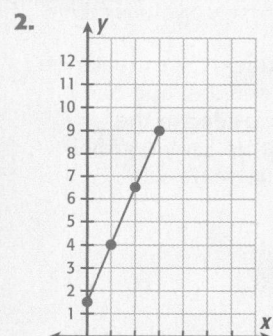

4. $y = 16.5$; after 6 seconds the car is 16.5 ft from the wall.

Organizer

Objective: Assess students' ability to apply concepts and skills in Chapter 3 in a real-world format.

 Online Edition

Resources

 Middle School Assessments
www.mathtekstoolkit.org

Problem	Text reference
1	Lesson 3-1
2	Lesson 3-2
3	Lesson 3-3
4	Lesson 3-4
5	Lesson 3-5
6	Lesson 3-6

Answers

2.

(graph showing points)

3. 1.5 ft; 9 ft

5. See p. A5.

Multi-Step Test Prep *(side tab)*

INTERVENTION

Scaffolding Questions

1. How do you complete the table of data? Substitute the values 0, 1, 2, and 3 for x in the equation.

2. What ordered pairs should you plot on a coordinate plane? (0, 2.5), (1, 4), (2, 6.5), (3, 9) What type of graph do you get when you connect these points? Straight line

3. What does the point (0, 1.5) tell you? At the start (0 seconds), the car was 1.5 ft from the wall. What point represents the data for the car at 3 seconds? (3, 9)

4. How do you find y when $x = 6$? Evaluate $f(x) = 2.5x + 1.5$ for $x = 6$ What time does $f(6)$ correspond to? 6 seconds What is the distance of the car from the wall after 6 seconds? 16.5 ft

5. What ordered pairs should you include in the table? (0, 2), (1, 5), (2, 8), (3, 11), (4, 11), (5, 11), (6, 11)

6. Where is the car at the start of the experiment? 2 ft from the wall For how many seconds does the car move forward? 3 seconds At what time does the car stop moving? At 3 seconds

Extensions

1. The motion of Car C is given by the equation $y = 10 - 2x$. Where does this car start? 10 ft from the wall

2. What happens once Car C starts moving? It moves closer to the wall

State Resources

go.hrw.com
State Resources Online
KEYWORD: MT7 Resources

Game Time

Organizer

Objective: Participate in games to practice and apply skills learned in Chapter 3.

 Online Edition

Resources

Chapter 3 Resource Book
Puzzles, Twisters & Teasers

Find the Phony!

Purpose: To apply logic to solving a brainteaser

Discuss Have students discuss why there were three groups of three pearls. Because the scale has two trays, dividing the pearls into groups of three ensures that you can compare two groups and evaluate the third by elimination. Because each group has three pearls, you can repeat the process and solve the problem with only two weighings.

Extend Have students use a balance scale, eight real pennies, and one play-money penny (provided in the Manipulatives Kit) to carry out their solution. Check students' work.

Sprouts

Purpose: To increase critical thinking and encourage students to think several steps ahead in their work

Discuss Ask students to describe a situation in which no more legal moves are possible. Possible answer: All of the dots have three paths connected, or those that have only two paths are surrounded by others that already have three paths connected.

Extend Challenge players to consider the shortest or longest games possible. Is it possible for the game to go on indefinitely? **no** What is the least number of moves possible before the game ends? **6** What is the greatest number of moves possible before the game ends? **8**

Game Time

Find the Phony!

Suppose you have nine identical-looking pearls. Eight are real, and one is fake. Using a balance scale that consists of two pans, you must find the bogus pearl. The real pearls weigh the same, and the fake weighs less. The scale can be used only twice. How can you find the phony?

First you must split the pearls into equal groups. Place any three pearls on one side of the scale and any other three on the other side. If one side weighs less than the other, then the fake pearl is on that side. But you are not done yet! You still need to find the imitation, and you can use the scale only once more. Take any of the two pearls from the lighter pan, and weigh them against each other. If one pan is lighter, then that pan contains the fake pearl. If they balance, then the leftover pearl of the group is the fake.

If the scale balances during the first weighing, then you know the fake is in the third group. Then you can choose two pearls from that group for the second weighing. If the scale balances, the fake is the one left. If it is unbalanced, the false pearl is the lighter one.

You Play Detective

Suppose you have 12 identical gold coins in front of you. One is counterfeit and weighs slightly more than the others. How can you identify the counterfeit in three weighings?

Sprouts

You and a partner play against each other to try to make the last move in the game. You start with three dots. Player one draws a path to join two dots or a path that starts and ends at the same dot. A new dot is then placed somewhere on that path. No dot can have more than three paths drawn from it, and no path can cross another.

A complete copy of the rules is available online.

go.hrw.com
Game Time Extra
KEYWORD: MT7 Games

Answer

You Play Detective Place any six coins on side of the scale and the other six coins on the other side. Take the group of six coins that weighs more and place three of the coins on one side of the scale and the other three coins on the other side. Take the group of six coins that weighs more and weigh any two of them against each other. If one pan is hevier, that pan contains the heavier coin. If the pans balance, the leftover coin is the heavier one.

Materials
- paper lunch bag
- hole punch
- lined paper
- 2 brass fasteners
- string, ribbon, or yarn
- golf pencil
- card stock

PROJECT **Clipboard Solutions for Graphs, Functions, and Sequences**

Make your own clipboard for taking notes on graphs, functions, and sequences.

Directions

1 Fold the bag flat and hold it with the flap at the top. Punch two holes at the bottom of the flap, about 3 inches apart. The holes should go through only the flap, not the entire bag. **Figure A**

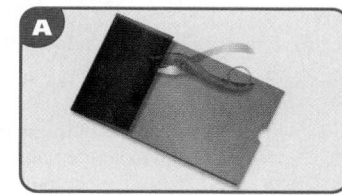

2 Slide about ten sheets of lined paper under the flap and mark where the holes should be punched. Then punch holes through the sheets.

3 Fasten the sheets under the flap using brass fasteners. **Figure B**

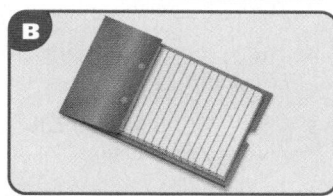

4 Punch holes in the upper left and upper right corners of the flap. Tie one end of the string to the left-hand hole. Thread the string through the right-hand hole and tie it there, leaving some slack at the top of the bag. Tie the golf pencil to the end of the string. **Figure C**

5 Slide a piece of card stock into the bag to make it more sturdy.

Taking Note of the Math

Summarize each lesson of the chapter on a separate page of the clipboard. Use any extra pages to write down sample problems.

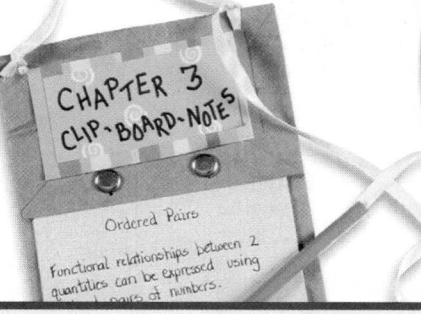

Organizer

Objective: Make a clipboard that can be used to take notes on graphs, functions, and sequences.

Materials: paper lunch bag; hole punch; about 10 sheets of lined paper ($7\frac{1}{2}$ in. by $4\frac{3}{4}$ in.); 2 brass fasteners; about 3 ft of string, ribbon, or yarn; golf pencil; card stock (approx. 7 in. by $4\frac{3}{4}$ in.)

 **Online Edition**

Using the Page
Preparing the Materials

Golf pencils can be purchased at office supply stores by the gross.

Making the Project

Before students punch holes at the bottom of the bag's flap, be sure to emphasize that the holes should go through only the flap and not through the entire bag.

Extending the Project

Students can include sheets of graph paper in their clipboards. They can use the graph paper to record examples of ordered pairs and graphs of functions.

Tips from the Bag Ladies!

We sometimes have students glue library pockets onto the backs of their clipboards. Students can use the pocket to house the pencil. The pocket also makes a handy holder for index cards.

If time permits, have students use decorative paper, markers, and glue sticks to personalize their clipboards. Some of our students have given their clipboards themes, such as favorite sports or movies.

Organizer

Objective: Help students organize and review key concepts and skills presented in Chapter 3.

Online Edition
Multilingual Glossary

Resources

PuzzlePro®
One-Stop Planner®

Multilingual Glossary Online
go.hrw.com
KEYWORD: MT7 Glossary

Lesson Tutorial Videos
CD-ROM

Test & Practice Generator
One-Stop Planner®

Answers

1. common difference
2. function
3. origin
4. sequence; arithmetic sequence
5. vertical line test
6. x-axis; y-axis
7. yes
8. no
9. yes
10. no

11.
x	0	1	2	3	4
y	2	5	8	11	14

12.
x	0	2	4	6
y	5	$\frac{27}{4}$	$\frac{17}{2}$	$\frac{41}{4}$

13.
x	−4	−3	−2	−1
y	−10.5	−8.3	−6.1	−3.9

Vocabulary

arithmetic sequence ...142
common difference 142
coordinate plane 122
domain 134
function 134
graph of an equation ...123
input 134
ordered pair 118
origin 122
output 134
quadrant 122
range 134
sequence 142
term 142
vertical line test 135
x-axis 122
x-coordinate 122
y-axis 122
y-coordinate 122

Complete the sentences below with vocabulary words from the list above.

1. In an arithmetic sequence, there is a(n) __?__ between each term.

2. A(n) __?__ is a mathematical relationship in which each input corresponds to exactly one output.

3. The __?__ is the point (0, 0) on a coordinate plane.

4. A(n) __?__ is an ordered list of numbers or objects, which are also called a(n) __?__.

5. The __?__ is a method for testing whether or not a graph represents a function.

6. The coordinate plane is formed by the intersection of two number lines called the __?__ and the __?__.

3-1 Ordered Pairs (pp. 118–121)

EXAMPLE

■ Determine whether (8, 3) is a solution of the equation $y = x − 6$.
$y = x − 6$
$3 \overset{?}{=} 8 − 6$ Substitute 8 for x
$3 \overset{?}{=} 2$ ✗   and 3 for y.
(8, 3) is not a solution.

■ Use the values to make a table of solutions.
$y = 5x − 1$ for $x = 1, 2, 3$.

x	5x − 1	y	(x, y)
1	5(1) − 1	4	(1, 4)
2	5(2) − 2	9	(2, 9)
3	5(3) − 1	14	(3, 14)

EXERCISES

Determine whether each ordered pair is a solution of the given equation.

7. (27, 0); $y = 81 − 3x$ 8. (4, 5); $y = 5x$
9. (−3, 7); $y = 2x + 13$ 10. (2, 4); $y = 3x$

Use the values to make a table of solutions.

11. $y = 3x + 2$ for $x = 0, 1, 2, 3, 4$
12. $y = \frac{7}{8}x + 5$ for $x = 0, 2, 4, 6$
13. $y = 2.2x − 1.7$ for $x = −4, −3, −2, −1$

3-2 Graphing on a Coordinate Plane (pp. 122–125)

EXAMPLE

■ Graph $A(3, -1)$, $B(0, 4)$, $C(-2, -3)$, and $D(1, 0)$ on a coordinate plane.

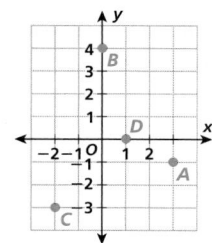

■ Give the missing coordinate for the solution of $y = -3x + 2$.

$(11, y)$

$y = -3(11) + 2$ *Substitute 11 for x.*

$y = -33 + 2$ *Multiply.*

$y = -31$ *Add.*

$(11, -31)$

EXERCISES

Graph each point on a coordinate plane.

14. $A(3, 2)$ **15.** $B(-1, 0)$ **16.** $C(0, -5)$

17. $D(1, -3)$ **18.** $E(0, 4)$ **19.** $F(-3, -5)$

20. $G(5, 0)$ **21.** $H(-2, 3)$ **22.** $J(0, 0)$

Give the missing coordinate for the solutions of $y = 3x + 5$.

23. $(0, y)$ **24.** $(1, y)$ **25.** $(5, y)$

26. $(7, y)$ **27.** $(1.7, y)$ **28.** $\left(\dfrac{7}{9}, y\right)$

Complete the table of ordered pairs. Graph each ordered pair on a coordinate plane. Draw a line through the points.

29. $y = x - 2$

x	x − 2	y	(x, y)
0			
1			
2			

3-3 Interpreting Graphs and Tables (pp. 127–131)

EXAMPLE

■ Explain which car has the faster acceleration?

Acceleration	Car A (s)	Car B (s)
0 to 30 mi/h	1.8	3.2
0 to 40 mi/h	2.8	4.7
0 to 50 mi/h	3.9	6.4
0 to 60 mi/h	5.1	8.8

Car A; Car A accelerates from 0 to each measured speed in fewer seconds than car B.

EXERCISES

30. Which oven had not been preheated? Explain.

Baking Time (min)	Oven D (°F)	Oven E (°F)
0	450°	70°
1	435°	220°
2	445°	440°
3	450°	440°

31. If there are 5 s between floors, which person rode an elevator? Explain.

Time (s)	Altitude of Person A (ft)	Altitude of Person B (ft)
0	0	0
5	5	10
10	10	20
15	15	30

Answers

14–22.

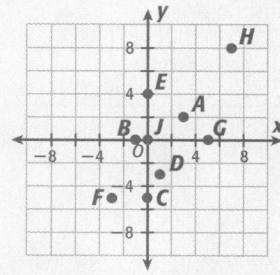

23. 5

24. 8

25. 20

26. 26

27. 10.1

28. $\dfrac{22}{3}$

29.

x	x − 2	y	(x, y)
0	−2	−2	(0, −2)
1	−1	−1	(1, −1)
2	0	0	(2, 0)

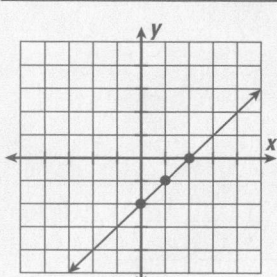

30. Oven E

31. Person B

Answers

32. Possible answer:

x	0	1	2	3
y	−4	3	10	17

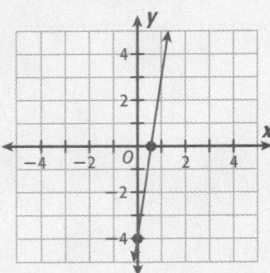

33. Possible answer:

x	0	1	2	3
y	1	7	13	19

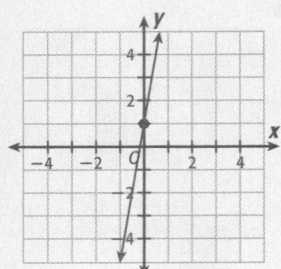

34. Possible answer:

x	0	1	2	3
y	3	1	−1	−3

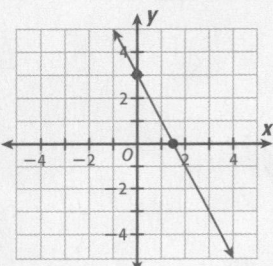

35. Possible answer:

x	0	1	2	3
y	4	1	−2	−5

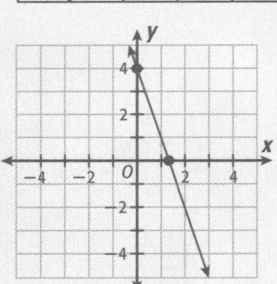

36. yes

37. no

Study Guide: Review

3-4 Functions (pp. 134–137)

EXAMPLE

■ Make a table and a graph of $y = x − 3$.

x	x − 3	y
0	0 − 3	−3
1	1 − 3	−2
2	2 − 3	−1
3	3 − 3	0

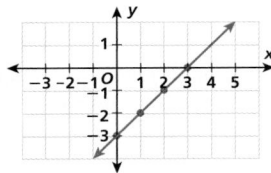

EXERCISES

Make a table and a graph of each function.

32. $y = 7x − 4$ **33.** $y = 6x + 1$

34. $y = −2x + 3$ **35.** $y = −3x + 4$

Determine if each relationship represents a function.

36.

x	1	2	3	4	5
y	17	19	21	23	25

37.

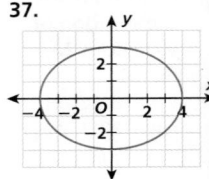

3-5 Equations, Tables, and Graphs (pp. 138–141)

EXAMPLE

■ Use the table to make a graph and to write an equation.

x	1	2	3	4	5
y	8	16	24	32	40

Each value of y is 8 times the corresponding value of x, so the equation is $y = 8x$.

EXERCISES

Use each table to make a graph and to write an equation.

38.

x	1	2	3	4	5
y	2.3	4.6	6.9	9.2	11.5

39.

x	1	2	3	4	5
y	$\frac{1}{2}$	1	$1\frac{1}{2}$	2	$2\frac{1}{2}$

40.

x	1	2	3	4	5
y	1	2	3	4	5

3-6 Arithmetic Sequences (pp. 142–145)

EXAMPLE

■ Find the next three terms in the sequence $−7, −3, 1, 5, \ldots$

Each term is 4 more than the previous term.

5 + 4 = 9
9 + 4 = 13   The next three terms
13 + 4 = 17   are 9, 13, and 17.

EXERCISES

Find the next three terms in each sequence.

41. 1, 8, 15, 22, . . .   **42.** 1.5, 4, 6.5, 9, . . .

43. $\frac{2}{3}, 1\frac{1}{3}, 2, 2\frac{2}{3}, \ldots$ **44.** 5, 7, 9, 11, . . .

45. −3, −6, −9, −12, . . .

38. $y = 2.3x$

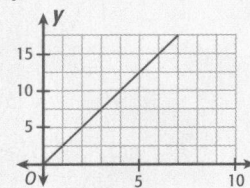

39. $y = \frac{1}{2}x$

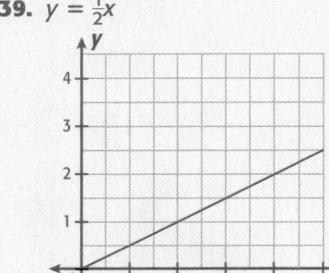

40. $y = x$

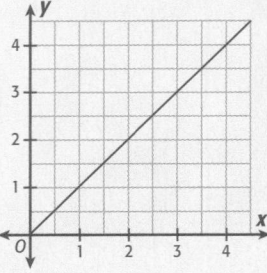

41. 29, 36, 43

42. 11.5, 14, 16.5

43. $3\frac{1}{3}, 4, 4\frac{2}{3}$

44. 13, 15, 17

45. −15, −18, −21

Determine whether the ordered pair is a solution of the given equation.

1. $(6, 5)$ for $y = 5x - 25$ **yes**
2. $(-3, 10)$ for $y = -3x - 1$ **no**
3. $(2, 4)$ for $y = 5x - 6$
   yes

Give the coordinates for each point.

4. A $(-2; -5)$
5. B $(3; 0)$

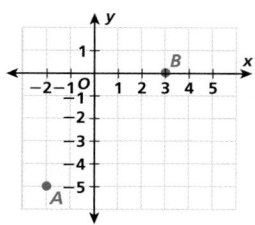

6. Suppose the cost of mailing a letter is $0.23 per ounce plus $0.14. The equation that gives the total cost c of mailing a letter is $c = 0.23w + 0.14$, where w is the weight in ounces. What is the cost of mailing a 6-ounce letter?   **$1.52**

7. The cost of renting a sailboat at a lake is $20 per hour plus $12 for lifejackets. The total cost is represented by the equation $c = 20h + 12$, where h is the number of hours and c is the total cost. How much does it cost to rent a sailboat for 3.5 hours?   **$82**

8. Use the table to graph the speed of the car over time.

Time (s)	0	5	10	15
Speed (mi/h)	0	20	30	35

Make a table and a graph of each function.

9. $y = 5x - 3$
10. $y = 9x + 2$
11. $y = -2x - 5$
12. $y = \frac{3}{5}x - \frac{2}{3}$

Use each table to make a graph and to write an equation.

13.

x	4	5	6	7
y	12	15	18	21

14.

x	$\frac{1}{2}$	1	$1\frac{1}{2}$	2
y	$3\frac{1}{2}$	7	$10\frac{1}{2}$	14

15. A pool contains 125 gallons of water. Every minute, an additional 55 gallons is added. Find a function to describe this sequence, and find the number of gallons of water in the pool after 1 hour.   **$w = 55m + 125$; 3425 gal**

16. An hourglass contains 10,235 beads in the top half. Every minute, 150 beads fall to the bottom half. Find a function to describe this sequence, and find the number of beads remaining in the top half of the hourglass after 35 minutes.   **$b = 10{,}235 - 150m$; 4985 beads**

17. The amount of water being emptied from a pool is represented by the equation $g = -12m$, where g is the number of gallons of water emptied and m is the number of minutes since emptying began. Make a table and sketch a graph of the equation.

Chapter Test

9. Possible answer:

x	0	1	2	3
y	-2	2	7	12

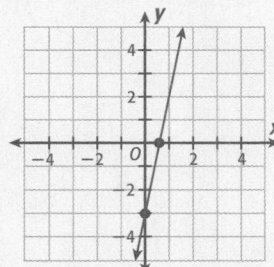

10. Possible answer:

x	0	1	2	3
y	2	11	20	29

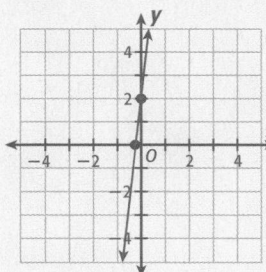

11–14, 17. See p. A5.

Organizer

Objective: Assess students' mastery of concepts and skills in Chapter 3.

 Online Edition

Resources

 Assessment Resources

Chapter 3 Tests
• Free Response
  (Levels A, B, C)
• Multiple Choice
  (Levels A, B, C)
• Performance Assessment

 IDEA Works! CD-ROM
Modified Chapter 3 Test

 **Test & Practice Generator**
One-Stop Planner®

Answers

8.

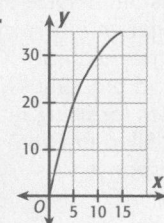

State Resources

Organizer

Objective: Provide opportunities to learn and practice common test-taking strategies.

 Online Edition

Resources

 State Test Prep **Workbook**

 State Test Prep **CD-ROM**

 State Test Practice **Online**

go.hrw.com
KEYWORD: MT7 TestPrep

TEST PREP DOCTOR ✚ This Test Tackler focuses on how to correctly fill in the answer to a gridded response item. Students often solve the test item correctly, but get an incorrect answer score because they did not complete the answer grid properly. This strategy reviews the rules for filling in a grid. Students examine filled-in grids and identify why the response was marked as incorrect.

Test Tackler

Gridded Response: Write Gridded Responses

When responding to a test item that requires you to place your answer in a grid, you must fill out the grid on your answer sheet correctly, or the item will be marked as incorrect.

EXAMPLE 1

Gridded Response: Divide. $3000 \div 7.5$

$3000 \div 7.5 = \dfrac{3000}{7.5}\left(\dfrac{10}{10}\right)$ *7.5 has 1 decimal place, so multiply by $\frac{10}{10}$.*

$\qquad\qquad = \dfrac{30{,}000}{75}$ *Divide.*

$\qquad\qquad = 400$ *Simplify.*

- Write your answer in the answer boxes at the top of the grid.
- Put only one digit in each box. Do not leave a blank box in the middle of an answer.
- Shade the bubble for each digit in the column beneath it.

EXAMPLE 2

Gridded Response: Solve. $x - \dfrac{1}{2} = \dfrac{2}{3}$

$x - \dfrac{1}{2} + \dfrac{1}{2} = \dfrac{2}{3} + \dfrac{1}{2}$ *Add $\frac{1}{2}$ to both sides of the equation.*

$\qquad x = \dfrac{4}{6} + \dfrac{3}{6}$ *Find a common denominator.*

$\qquad x = \dfrac{7}{6},\ 1\dfrac{1}{6};\ \text{or } 1.1\overline{6}$ *Add.*

- Mixed numbers and repeating decimals cannot be gridded, so you must grid the answer as $\frac{7}{6}$.
- Write your answer in the answer boxes at the top of the grid.
- Put only one digit or symbol in each box. On some grids, the fraction bar and the decimal point have a designated box. Do not leave a blank box in the middle of an answer.
- Shade the bubble for each digit or symbol in the column beneath it.

HOT TIP! You cannot grid a negative number in a gridded response item because the grid does not include the negative sign. If you get a negative answer to a test item, recalculate the problem because you probably made a math error.

Read each statement and then answer the questions that follow.

Item A
A student correctly evaluated an expression and got $\frac{9}{13}$ as a result. Then the student filled in the grid as shown.

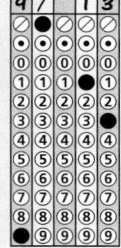

1. What error did the student make when filling in the grid?

2. Explain how to fill in the answer correctly.

Item B
A student added 0.21 and 0.49 and got an answer of 0.7. This answer is displayed in the grid.

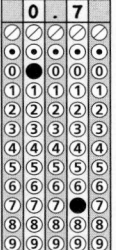

3. What errors did the student make when filling in the grid?

4. Explain how to fill in the answer correctly.

Item C
A student found -0.65 as the answer to $-5 \cdot (-0.13)$. Then the student filled in the grid as shown.

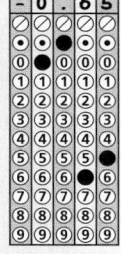

5. What error does the grid show?

6. Another student got an answer of -0.65. Explain why the student knew this answer was wrong.

Item D
A student found that $x = 5\frac{1}{2}$ was the solution to the equation $2x - 3 = 8$. Then the student filled in the grid as shown.

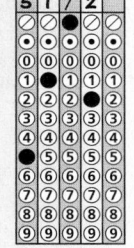

7. What answer does the grid show?

8. Explain why you cannot fill in a mixed number.

9. Write the answer $5\frac{1}{2}$ in two forms that could be entered in the grid correctly.

Test Tackler

TEST PREP DOCTOR Remind students that they can also write their answer in the grid by placing the last digit of the answer in the far right box. Reassure students that it is okay for the first box to be blank, as long as the last box is filled and there are no blanks between numbers. Use the grid above Problem 3 to show how the decimal 0.7 could be written by placing the 0 in the third column, the decimal point in the fourth column and the 7 in the last column.

Possible answers

1. The student placed a blank after the fraction bar. Blanks cannot be used in the middle of an answer.

2. The student could correctly fill in the grid in either of these two ways:
   a. 9 in first column, / in the second column, 1 in the third column, and a 3 in the fourth column
   b. 9 in second column, / in the third column, 1 in the fourth column, and a 3 in the fifth column

3. The student centered the answer in the grid, rather than placing the first digit in the far left box or placing the last digit in the far right box. The student also forgot to fill in the dot for the decimal point.

4. The student could correctly fill in the grid in either of these two ways:
   a. 0 in first column, dot in the second column, 7 in the third column
   b. 0 in third column, dot in the fourth column, 7 in the fifth column

5. There is not a negative sign in the grid.

6. You cannot have a negative answer to a gridded response test item.

7. The grid shows the answer $\frac{51}{2}$.

8. You cannot use a blank in the middle of an answer to represent the space between the whole number and the fraction. Without a blank, the answer is read as a fraction, not a mixed number.

9. 5.5; $\frac{11}{2}$

go.hrw.com
State Resources Online
KEYWORD: MT7 Resources

State Resources

CHAPTER 3 STANDARDIZED TEST PREP

Organizer

Objective: Provide review and practice for Chapters 1–3 and standardized tests.

PREMIER Online Edition

Resources

Assessment Resources
Chapter 3 Cumulative Test

State Test Prep **Workbook**

State Test Prep **CD-ROM**

State Test Practice **Online**

go.hrw.com
KEYWORD: MT7 TestPrep

CHAPTER 3

STANDARDIZED TEST PREP

go.hrw.com
State Test Practice Online
KEYWORD: MT7 TestPrep

Cumulative Assessment, Chapters 1–3

Multiple Choice

1. A cell phone company charges \$0.21 per minute for phone calls. Which expression represents the cost of a phone call of m minutes?

(A) $0.21m$ (C) $0.21 - m$
(B) $0.21 + m$ (D) $0.21 \div m$

2. Laurie had \$88 in her bank account on Sunday. The table below shows her account activity for the past 5 days. What is the balance in her account on Friday?

Day	Deposit	Withdraw
Monday	\$25	
Tuesday		\$58
Wednesday		\$45
Thursday	\$32	
Friday	\$91	

(F) \$91 (H) \$133
(G) \$103 (J) \$236

3. Which equation has a solution of $x = -5$?

(A) $2x + 8 = -2$ (C) $\frac{1}{5}x - 6 = -10$
(B) $\frac{1}{5}x + 10 = 5$ (D) $-2x + 10 = -5$

4. You volunteer to bring in 7 gallons of juice for a class party. There are 28 students in the class. You plan to give each student an equal amount of juice. Which equation can you use to determine the amount of juice per student?

(F) $7x = 28$ (H) $28 + x = 7$
(G) $\frac{x}{28} = 7$ (J) $28x = 7$

5. In order to apply for a driver's permit in Ohio, you have to be at least 16 years old. Which graph correctly represents the possible ages of Ohioans who can apply for a driver's permit?

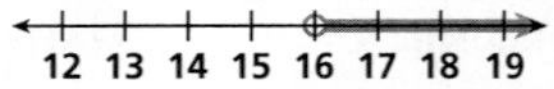

(A) 12 13 14 15 16 17 18 19

(B) 12 13 14 15 16 17 18 19

(C) 12 13 14 15 16 17 18 19

(D) 12 13 14 15 16 17 18 19

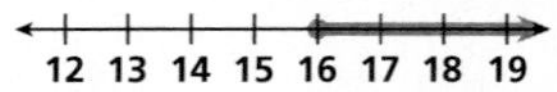

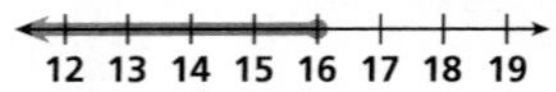

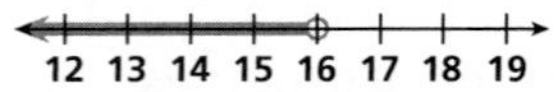

6. Which ordered pair is NOT a solution of $y = 2x - 6$?

(F) (6, 6) (H) (3, 0)
(G) (0, −6) (J) (−3, 0)

7. Which ordered pair is located on the x-axis?

(A) (0, −3) (C) (−3, 0)
(B) (3, −3) (D) (1, −3)

8. Which is the next term in this arithmetic sequence?
4, 8, 12, 16, . . .

(F) 22 (H) 18
(G) 20 (J) 17

9. A snack package has 4 ounces of mixed nuts, $1\frac{1}{2}$ ounces of wheat crackers, $5\frac{3}{4}$ ounces of pretzels, and $2\frac{1}{8}$ ounces of popcorn. What is the total weight of the snacks?

(A) $13\frac{3}{8}$ ounces (C) $12\frac{5}{8}$ ounces
(B) $13\frac{1}{8}$ ounces (D) $9\frac{3}{8}$ ounces

Standardized Test Prep

State Resources

go.hrw.com
State Resources Online
KEYWORD: MT7 Resources

TEST PREP DOCTOR

For items 1 and 4, students may have trouble choosing a correct operation. Remind students that words such as "each" and "per" usually indicate multiplication or division. Once the students rule out addition and subtraction, they can use basic logic to determine the correct operation. Dividing will usually make a smaller number, whereas multiplying will usually make a larger number.

Answers

15. a. The domain is {−1, 0, 1, 2, 3, 4, 5}. The range is {1, 2, 3, 4, 5, 6, 7}.

b. The set is a function because for each x in the domain there is only one y in the range.

16. Speed
20
15
10
5
0
7:15 7:16 7:17 7:18 7:19 7:20 7:21 7:22
Time

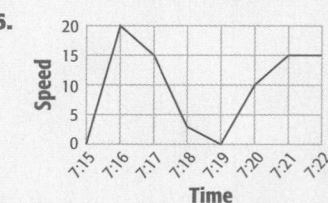

17. $c = 3.50m + 12.95$; \$54.95

18. See 4-Point Response work sample.

10. The graph of the line $y = 2x - 1$ is shown below.

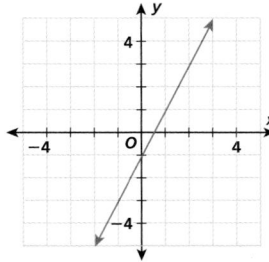

Which ordered pairs contains only points on this line?

F $(-1, -2), (0, 0), (1, 2), (2, 4)$

G $(-2, -3), (0, -1), (2, 1), (4, 3)$

H $(-4, 7), (-2, 3), (0, -1), (2, 3)$

J $(0, -1), (1, 1), (2, 3), (3, 5)$

Sometimes remembering the rules of integers can help you eliminate one or two of the answer choices.

Gridded Response

11. In 2004, the minimum wage for workers was $5.85 per hour. To find the amount of money someone can make in x hours, use the equation $y = 5.85x$. How much money does a person who works 5 hours earn? **$29.25**

12. Solve the equation $\frac{4}{9}x = \frac{1}{3}$ for x. $\frac{3}{4}$ **or 0.75**

13. The sum of two consecutive integers is 53. What is the smaller of the two numbers? **26**

14. The function $d = -16t^2 + 35$ represents the distance a stone falls after t seconds when dropped from a bridge 35 feet over a river. How many feet does the stone fall after 1 second? **19**

Short Response

15. Consider the set of coordinate points $\{(-1, 1), (0, 2), (1, 3), (2, 4), (3, 5), (4, 6), (5, 7), (x, x + 2)\}$.

  a. Determine the domain and the range of the set.

  b. Is the set a function? Explain why or why not.

  c. Write an equation that will relate x and y. $y = x + 2$

16. Pablo leaves for school on his bike at 7:15 and arrives at 7:20. The table shows his rate of speed at one-minute intervals. Represent the information in the table with a line graph.

Time (min)	7:15	7:16	7:17	7:18	7:19	7:20
Speed (mi/h)	0	20	15	3	0	10

17. A craft club charges $12.95 to join. Members of the club pay $3.50 each month for a craft kit. Find a function that describes the arithmetic sequence, and then find the total charges for a member who buys a year's worth of craft kits. Show your work.

Extended Response

18. A train travels at a rate of 50 miles per hour from Baton Rouge, Louisiana, to Orlando, Florida. To find the distance y traveled in x hours, use the equation $y = 50x$.

  a. Make a table of ordered pairs using the domain $x = 1, 2, 3, 4,$ and 5.

  b. Graph the solutions from the table of ordered pairs.

  c. Maria leaves Baton Rouge at 5:30 A.M. on a train. She needs to be in Orlando by 6:30 P.M. If Baton Rouge is 602 miles from Orlando, will Maria make it on time? Explain.

Standardized Test Prep

Short Response Rubric

Items 15–17

2 Points = The student's answer is an accurate and complete execution of the task or tasks.

1 Point = The student's answer contains attributes of an appropriate response but is flawed.

0 Points = The student's answer contains no attributes of an appropriate response.

Extended Response Rubric

Item 18

4 points = The student demonstrates a thorough understanding of all concepts and shows all work correctly.

3 points = The student demonstrates a basic understanding of all concepts, but the work shows some flaws reflecting inattentive execution of mathematical procedures or some misunderstanding of the underlying mathematics.

2 points = The student demonstrates only a partial understanding of the concepts or procedures embodied in the tasks. The approach may be correct, but the work shows a misunderstanding of one or more important concepts.

1 point = The student demonstrates a very limited understanding of the concepts or procedures embodied in the tasks. The response may show some understanding but exhibits many flaws or is incomplete.

0 points = The student provides no response at all or a completely incorrect or uninterpretable response.

Student Work Samples for Item 18

4-Point Response

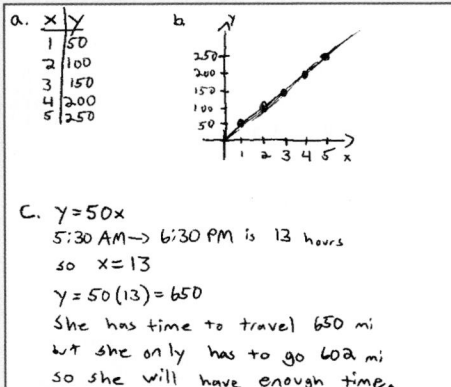

The student correctly constructed the table and graph, and the math and explanation are accurate.

3-Point Response

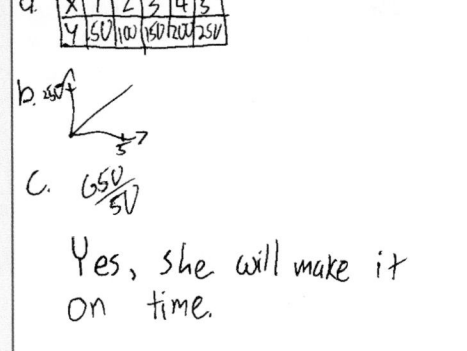

The table is correct but the graph is unclear. The math in part **c** is not very detailed and the explanation is inadequate.

2-Point Response

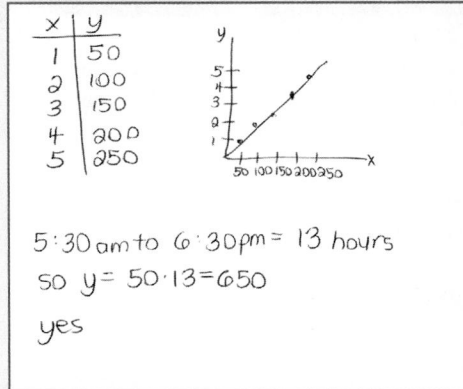

The student made a table and also answered part **c** correctly, but shows little understanding in part **b** of how to set up the x- and y-axes for a graph.

CHAPTER 4

Exponents and Roots

Section 4A	Section 4B
Exponents	**Roots**
4-1 Exponents	4-5 Squares and Square Roots
4-2 Look for a Pattern in Integer Exponents	4-6 Estimating Square Roots
4-3 Properties of Exponents	4-6 Technology Lab Evaluate Powers and Roots
4-4 Scientific Notation	4-7 The Real Numbers
4-4 Technology Lab Multiply and Divide Numbers in Scientific Notation	4-8 Hands-On Lab Explore Right Triangles
	4-8 The Pythagorean Theorem

Pacing Guide for 45-Minute Classes

Chapter 4

Countdown to Testing Weeks ⑥, ⑦

DAY 1	DAY 2	DAY 3	DAY 4	DAY 5
4-1 Lesson	4-2 Lesson	4-3 Lesson	4-4 Lesson	4-4 Technology Lab Ready to Go On? Focus on Problem Solving
DAY 6	**DAY 7**	**DAY 8**	**DAY 9**	**DAY 10**
4-5 Lesson	4-6 Lesson	4-6 Technology Lab	4-7 Lesson	4-8 Hands-On Lab 4-8 Lesson
DAY 11	**DAY 12**	**DAY 13**		
4-8 Lesson Ready to Go On? Multi-Step Test Prep	Chapter 4 Review	Chapter 4 Test		

Pacing Guide for 90-Minute Classes

Chapter 4

DAY 1	DAY 2	DAY 3	DAY 4	DAY 5
4-1 Lesson 4-2 Lesson	4-3 Lesson 4-4 Lesson	4-4 Technology Lab Ready to Go On? Focus on Problem Solving 4-5 Lesson	4-6 Lesson 4-6 Technology Lab	4-7 Lesson 4-8 Hands-On Lab 4-8 Lesson
DAY 6	**DAY 7**			
4-8 Lesson Ready to Go On? Multi-Step Test Prep Chapter 4 Review	Chapter 4 Test			

ONGOING ASSESSMENT and INTERVENTION

DIAGNOSE	PRESCRIBE

Assess Prior Knowledge

Before Chapter 4

Diagnose readiness for the chapter.
Are You Ready? SE p. 159

Prescribe intervention.
Are You Ready? Intervention Skills 35, 37, 51, 58

Formative Assessment

Before Every Lesson

Diagnose readiness for the lesson.
Warm Up TE, every lesson

Prescribe intervention.
Skills Bank SE pp. 820–834
Reteach CRB, Chapters 1–4

During Every Lesson

Diagnose understanding of lesson concepts.
Think and Discuss SE, every lesson
Write About It SE, lesson exercises
Journal TE, lesson exercises

Prescribe intervention.
Questioning Strategies Chapter 4
Reading Strategies CRB, every lesson
Success for ELL pp. 47–62

After Every Lesson

Diagnose mastery of lesson concepts.
Lesson Quiz TE, every lesson
Test Prep SE, every lesson
Test and Practice Generator

Prescribe intervention.
Reteach CRB, every lesson
Problem Solving CRB, every lesson
Test Prep Doctor TE, lesson exercises
Homework Help Online

Before Chapter 4 Testing

Diagnose mastery of concepts in the chapter.
Ready to Go On? SE pp. 180, 200
Focus on Problem Solving SE p. 181
Multi-Step Test Prep SE p. 201
Section Quizzes AR pp. 65–66
Test and Practice Generator

Prescribe intervention.
Ready to Go On? Intervention Chapter 4
Scaffolding Questions TE p. 201

Before High Stakes Testing

Diagnose mastery of benchmark concepts.
Standardized Test Prep SE pp. 208–209
State Test Prep CD-ROM

Prescribe intervention.
State Test Prep Workbook

Summative Assessment

After Chapter 4

Check mastery of chapter concepts.
Multiple-Choice Tests (Forms A, B, C)
Free-Response Tests (Forms A, B, C)
Performance Assessment AR pp. 67–80
Test and Practice Generator
Check mastery of benchmark concepts.
AYP State Tests

Prescribe intervention.
Reteach CRB, every lesson
Lesson Tutorial Videos Chapter 4

Prescribe intervention.
State Test Prep Workbook

KEY: **SE** = *Student Edition* **TE** = *Teacher's Edition* **CRB** = *Chapter Resource Book* **AR** = *Assessment Resources* ⊙ Available on CD-ROM ✐ Available online **158B**

CHAPTER
4

Supporting the Teacher

Chapter 4 Resource Book

Practice A, B, C
pp. 3–5, 11–13, 19–21, 27–29, 35–37, 43–45, 51–53, 59–61

Reading Strategies ELL
pp. 9, 17, 25, 33, 41, 49, 57, 66

Puzzles, Twisters, and Teasers
pp. 10, 18, 26, 34, 42, 50, 58, 67

Reteach
pp. 6, 14, 22, 30, 38, 46, 54, 62–63

Problem Solving
pp. 8, 16, 24, 32, 40, 48, 56, 65

Challenge
pp. 7, 15, 23, 31, 39, 47, 55, 64

Parent Letter   pp. 1–2

Transparencies

Lesson Transparencies, Volume 1 .... Chapter 4
• Teaching Tools
• Warm Ups
• Problem of the Day
• Teaching Transparencies
• Lesson Quizzes

Know-It Notebook .... Chapter 4
• Additional Examples   • Chapter Review
• Vocabulary   • Big Ideas

Alternate Openers: Explorations .... pp. 24–31

Countdown to Testing .... pp. 11–14

Teacher Tools

Power Presentations®
Complete PowerPoint® presentations for Chapter 4 lessons

Lesson Tutorial Videos® SPANISH
Holt authors Ed Burger and Freddie Renfro present tutorials to support the Chapter 4 lessons.

One-Stop Planner® SPANISH
Easy access to all Chapter 4 resources and assessments, as well as software for lesson planning, test generation, and puzzle creation

IDEA Works!®
Key Chapter 4 resources and assessments modified to address special learning needs

Lesson Plans ....pp. 24–31

Questioning Strategies .... Chapter 4

Solutions Key .... Chapter 4

Interdisciplinary Posters and Worksheets .... Chapter 4

TechKeys   **Lab Resources**

Project Teacher Support   **Parent Resources**

Workbooks

Homework and Practice Workbook SPANISH
Teacher's Guide .... pp. 12–16

Know-It Notebook
Teacher's Guide .... Chapter 4

Problem Solving Workbook SPANISH
Teacher's Guide .... pp. 12–16

State Test Prep
Teacher's Guide

Technology Highlights for the Teacher

 Power Presentations
Dynamic presentations to engage students. Complete PowerPoint® presentations for every lesson in Chapter 4.

 One-Stop Planner SPANISH
Easy access to Chapter 4 resources and assessments. Includes lesson-planning, test-generation, and puzzle-creation software.

 Premier Online Edition SPANISH
Chapter 4 includes Tutorial Videos, Lesson Activities, Lesson Quizzes, Homework Help, and Chapter Project.

KEY: **SE** = *Student Edition*   **TE** = *Teacher's Edition*   ELL English Language Learners   SPANISH Spanish version available   Available on CD-ROM    Available online

 # Reaching All Learners

Resources for All Learners

Hands-On Lab Activities... Chapter 4

Technology Lab Activities...................................... Chapter 4

Homework and Practice Workbook SPANISH ....pp. 24–31

Know-It Notebook .... Chapter 4

Problem Solving Workbook SPANISH ....pp. 24–31

DEVELOPING LEARNERS

Practice A ....CRB, every lesson

Reteach ....CRB, every lesson

Inclusion ....TE p. 167

Questioning Strategies............................ Chapter 4

Modified Chapter 4 Resources .... *IDEA Works!*

Homework Help Online

ON-LEVEL LEARNERS

Practice B ....CRB, every lesson

Puzzles, Twisters, and Teasers...............CRB, every lesson

Multiple Representations ....TE p. 167

Cognitive Strategies ....TE p. 163

ADVANCED LEARNERS

Practice C ....CRB, every lesson

Challenge ....CRB, every lesson

Extension ....TE pp. 161, 201, 202, 203

Critical Thinking ....TE p. 171

English Language Learners

ENGLISH
LANGUAGE
LEARNERS

Are You Ready? Vocabulary .... SE p. 159

Vocabulary Connections .... SE p. 160

Lesson Vocabulary ....SE, every lesson

Vocabulary Review..SE p. 204

English Language Learners...........TE pp. 163, 192, 197, 211

Reading Strategies ....CRB, every lesson

Success for English Language Learners.................pp. 47–62

Multilingual Glossary

Reaching All Learners Through...

Inclusion ....TE p. 167

Kinesthetic Experience ....TE p. 187

Concrete Manipulatives............................TE p. 163

Multiple Representations ....TE p. 167

Cognitive Strategies ....TE p. 163

Cooperative Learning ....TE p. 183

Modeling ....TE p. 197

Graphic Organizers ....TE p. 192

Critical Thinking ....TE p. 171

Test Prep Doctor..................TE pp. 165, 169, 173, 178, 185,
                                        189, 194, 199, 208

Common Error Alerts ....TE pp. 163, 171, 175, 183, 192

Scaffolding Questions..............................TE p. 201

Technology Highlights for Reaching All Learners

 **Lesson Tutorial Videos** SPANISH

Starring Holt authors Ed Burger and Freddie Renfro! Live tutorials to support every lesson in Chapter 4.

Multilingual Glossary

Searchable glossary includes definitions in English, Spanish, Vietnamese, Chinese, Hmong, Korean, and 4 other languages.

Online Interactivities

Interactive tutorials provide visually engaging alternative opportunities to learn concepts and master skills.

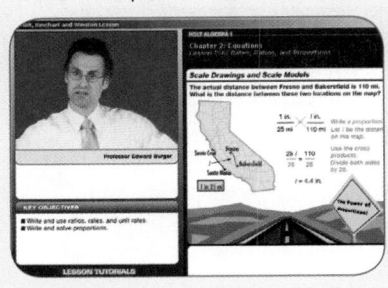

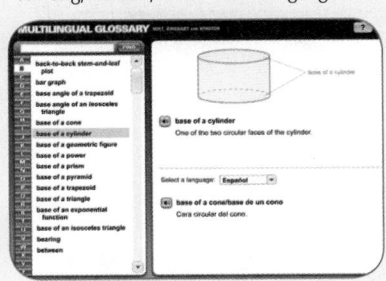

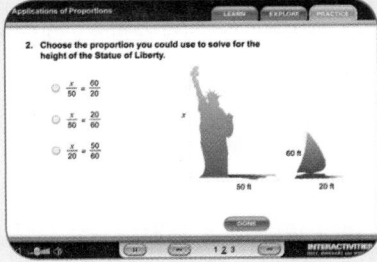

KEY: **SE** = *Student Edition*   **TE** = *Teacher's Edition*   **CRB** = *Chapter Resource Book*   SPANISH Spanish version available   Available on CD-ROM   Available online

158D

CHAPTER
4

Ongoing Assessment

Assessing Prior Knowledge

Determine whether students have the prerequisite concepts and skills for success in Chapter 4.

Are You Ready? SPANISH .... SE p. 159
Warm Up .... TE, every lesson

Test Preparation

Provide review and practice for Chapter 4 and standardized tests.

Multi-Step Test Prep .... SE p. 201
Study Guide: Review .... SE pp. 204–206
Standardized Test Prep .... SE pp. 208–209
Countdown to Testing Transparencies ....pp. 11–14
State Test Prep Workbook
State Test Prep CD-ROM
IDEA Works!

Alternative Assessment

Assess students' understanding of Chapter 4 concepts and combined problem-solving skills.

Chapter 4 Project .... SE p. 158
Performance Assessment SPANISH .... AR pp. 79–80
Portfolio Assessment SPANISH .... AR p. xxxiv

Daily Assessment

Provide formative assessment for each day of Chapter 4.

Questioning Strategies .... Chapter 4
Think and Discuss .... SE, every lesson
Write About It .... SE, lesson exercises
Journal .... TE, lesson exercises
Lesson Quiz .... TE, every lesson
Modified Lesson Quizzes .... *IDEA Works!*

Weekly Assessment

Provide formative assessment for each week of Chapter 4.

Focus on Problem Solving .... SE p. 181
Multi-Step Test Prep .... SE p. 201
Ready to Go On? SPANISH .... SE pp. 180, 200
Cumulative Assessment .... SE pp. 208–209
Test and Practice Generator SPANISH ...*One-Stop Planner*

Formal Assessment

Provide summative assessment of Chapter 4 mastery.

Section Quizzes SPANISH .... AR pp. 65–66
Chapter 4 Test .... SE p. 207
Chapter Test (Levels A, B, C) SPANISH .... AR pp. 67–68
   • Multiple-Choice   • Free-Response
Cumulative Test SPANISH .... AR pp. 81–84
Test and Practice Generator SPANISH ...*One-Stop Planner*
Modified Chapter 4 Test .... *IDEA Works!*

Technology Highlights for the Teacher

 Are You Ready? SPANISH
Automatically assess readiness and prescribe intervention for Chapter 4 prerequisite skills.

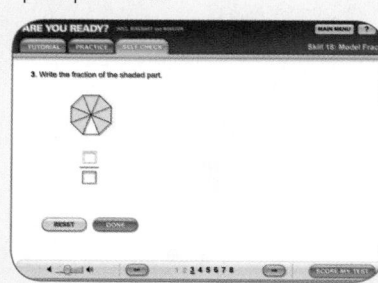

 Ready to Go On? SPANISH
Automatically assess understanding of and prescribe intervention for Sections 4A and 4B.

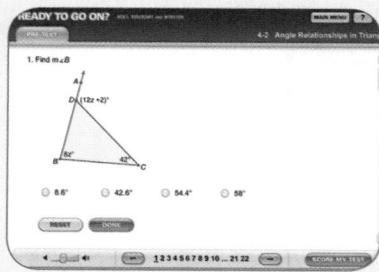

 Test and Practice Generator SPANISH
Use Chapter 4 problem banks to create assessments and worksheets to print out or deliver online. Includes dynamic problems.

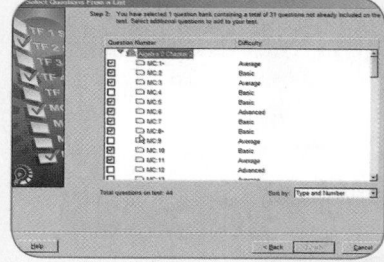

KEY: **SE** = *Student Edition*   **TE** = *Teacher's Edition*   **AR** = *Assessment Resources*   SPANISH Spanish version available   Available on CD-ROM   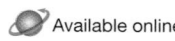 Available online

Formal Assessment

Three levels (A, B, C) of multiple-choice and free-response chapter tests are available in the *Assessment Resources.*

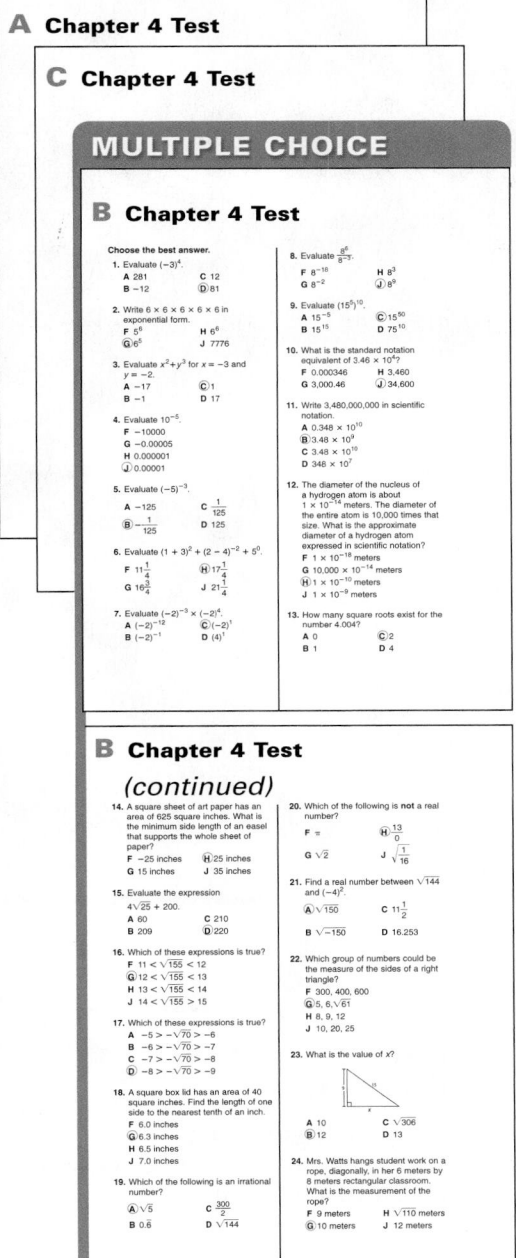

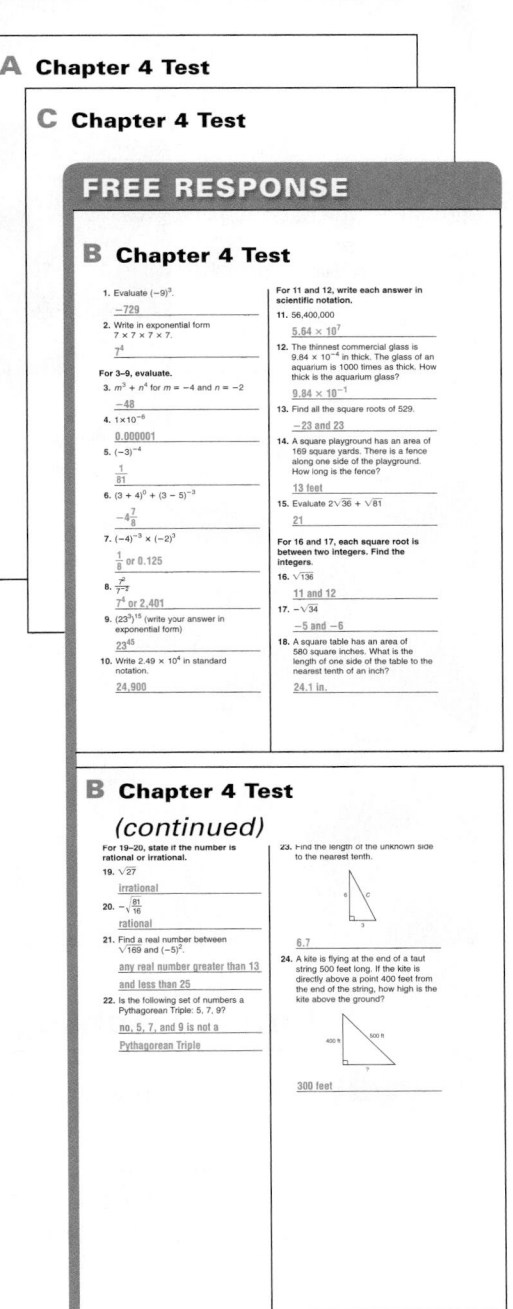

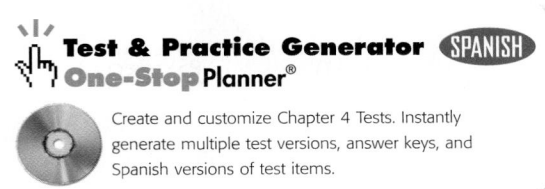

Test & Practice Generator SPANISH
One-Stop Planner®

Create and customize Chapter 4 Tests. Instantly generate multiple test versions, answer keys, and Spanish versions of test items.

Exponents and Roots

Why Learn This?

Tell students that equations are used in science to determine the value of unknown quantities. Also, exponents are used to help express very large or very small numbers. For example, the independent life span of a muon is expressed as 2.2×10^{-6} seconds instead of 0.0000022 seconds because it is easier to understand and use numbers written in scientific notation.

Using Data

To begin the study of this chapter, have students:

- Write a number sentence using $<$, $>$, or $=$ to compare the independent life span of a neutron to that of a muon. $920 > 2.2 \times 10^{-6}$

- Determine how long the independent life span of a neutron is in minutes. 15 minutes and 20 seconds Write 920 as 9.2 times a power of 10. 9.2×10^2

MULTI-STEP TEST PREP On page 201, students use exponents and roots to conclude facts about bacterial growth.

4A	Exponents
4-1	Exponents
4-2	Look for a Pattern in Integer Exponents
4-3	Properties of Exponents
4-4	Scientific Notation
LAB	Multiply and Divide Numbers in Scientific Notation
4B	Roots
4-5	Squares and Square Roots
4-6	Estimating Square Roots
LAB	Evaluate Powers and Roots
4-7	The Real Numbers
LAB	Explore Right Triangles
4-8	The Pythagorean Theorem

MULTI-STEP TEST PREP

Atomic Particle	Independent Life Span (s)
Electron	Indefinite
Proton	Indefinite
Neutron	920
Muon	2.2×10^{-6}

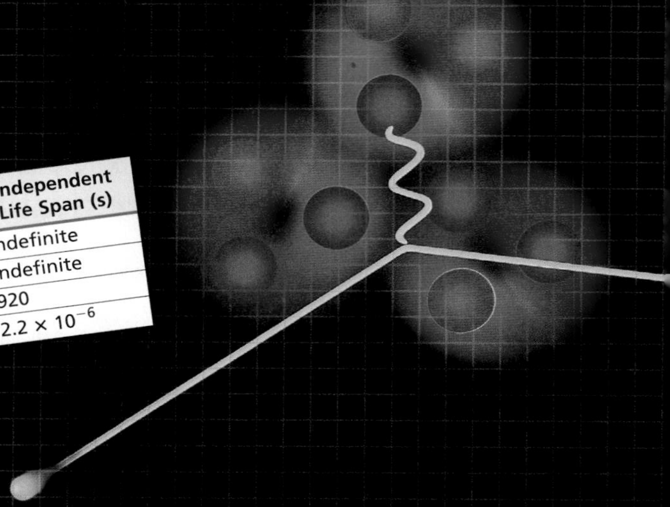

go.hrw.com
Chapter Project Online
KEYWORD: MT7 Ch4

career Nuclear Physicist

The atom was defined by the ancient Greeks as the smallest particle of matter. We now know that atoms are made up of many smaller particles.

Nuclear physicists study these particles using large machines—such as linear accelerators, synchrotrons, and cyclotrons—that can smash atoms to uncover their component parts.

Nuclear physicists use mathematics along with the data they discover to create models of the atom and the structure of matter.

Problem Solving Project

Understand, Plan, Solve, and Look Back

Have students:

- Complete The Lives of Particles worksheet to learn about the independent life spans of some atomic particles.

- Construct a drawing or model of the atom and its component particles.

Physical Science Connection

Project Resources

All project resources for teachers and students are provided online.

Materials:

- The Lives of Particles worksheet
- modeling materials

go.hrw.com
Project Teacher Support
KEYWORD: MT7 PSProject4

ARE YOU READY?

✓ Vocabulary

Choose the best term from the list to complete each sentence.

1. According to the __?__, you must multiply or divide before you add or subtract when simplifying a numerical __?__. **order of operations; expression**

2. An algebraic expression is a mathematical sentence that has at least one __?__. **variable**

3. In a(n) __?__, an equal sign is used to show that two quantities are the same. **equation**

4. You use a(n) __?__ to show that one quantity is greater than another quantity. **inequality**

equation

expression

inequality

order of operations

variable

Complete these exercises to review skills you will need for this chapter.

✓ Order of Operations

Simplify by using the order of operations.

5. $12 + 4(2)$ **20**
6. $12 + 8 \div 4$ **14**
7. $15(14 - 4)$ **150**
8. $(23 - 5) - 36 \div 2$ **0**
9. $12 \div 2 + 10 \div 5$ **8**
10. $40 \div 2 \cdot 4$ **80**

✓ Equations

Solve.

11. $x + 9 = 21$ $x = 12$
12. $3z = 42$ $z = 14$
13. $\frac{w}{4} = 16$ $w = 64$
14. $24 + t = 24$ $t = 0$
15. $p - 7 = 23$ $p = 30$
16. $12m = 0$ $m = 0$

✓ Use Repeated Multiplication

Find the product.

17. $7 \times 7 \times 7 \times 7 \times 7$
18. $12 \times 12 \times 12$
19. $3 \times 3 \times 3 \times 3$
20. $11 \times 11 \times 11 \times 11$
21. $8 \times 8 \times 8 \times 8 \times 8 \times 8$
22. $2 \times 2 \times 2$
23. $100 \times 100 \times 100 \times 100$
24. $9 \times 9 \times 9 \times 9 \times 9$
25. $1 \times 1 \times 1 \times 1$

✓ Multiply and Divide by Powers of Ten

Multiply or divide.

26. $358(10)$ **3580**
27. $358(1000)$ **358,000**
28. $358(100,000)$ **35,800,000**
29. $\frac{358}{10}$ **35.8**
30. $\frac{358}{1000}$ **0.358**
31. $\frac{358}{100,000}$ **0.00358**

Organizer

Objective: Assess students' understanding of prerequisite skills.

Prerequisite Skills

Order of Operations

Equations

Use Repeated Multiplication

Multiply and Divide by Powers of Ten

Assessing Prior Knowledge

INTERVENTION

Diagnose and Prescribe

Use this page to determine whether intervention is necessary or whether enrichment is appropriate.

Resources

 Are You Ready? Intervention and Enrichment Worksheets

 Are You Ready? CD-ROM

 Are You Ready? Online

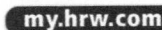 **my.hrw.com**

Answers

17–25. See p. A5.

ARE YOU READY?

Diagnose and Prescribe

NO INTERVENE

YES ENRICH

	ARE YOU READY? Intervention, Chapter 4		
✓ **Prerequisite Skill**	**Worksheets**	**CD-ROM**	**Online**
✓ Order of Operations	Skill 51	Activity 51	
✓ Equations	Skill 58	Activity 58	Diagnose and Prescribe Online
✓ Use Repeated Multiplication	Skill 35	Activity 35	
✓ Multiply and Divide by Powers of Ten	Skill 37	Activity 37	

ARE YOU READY? Enrichment, Chapter 4

Worksheets

CD-ROM

Online

Organizer

Objective: Help students organize the new concepts they will learn in Chapter 4.

 Online Edition
Multilingual Glossary

Resources

 PuzzlePro®
One-Stop Planner®

 Multilingual Glossary Online
go.hrw.com
KEYWORD: MT7 Glossary

Possible answers to *Vocabulary Connections*

1. Irrational numbers are numbers that cannot be expressed as a fraction with integers.

2. Real numbers are actual numbers with which we can perform calculations and do other mathematical operations. Numbers that are not real do not exist.

CHAPTER 4 Study Guide: Preview

Study Guide: Preview

Where You've Been

Previously, you

- simplified expressions involving order of operations and exponents.

- used models to represent squares and square roots.

In This Chapter

You will study

- expressing numbers in scientific notation, including negative exponents.

- approximating the values of irrational numbers.

- modeling the Pythagorean Theorem.

- using the Pythagorean Theorem to solve real-life problems.

Where You're Going

You can use the skills learned in this chapter

- to evaluate expressions containing exponents in future math courses.

- to express the magnitude of interstellar distances.

- to use right triangle geometry in future math courses.

Key Vocabulary/Vocabulario

exponent	exponente
hypotenuse	hipotenusa
irrational number	número irracional
perfect square	cuadrado perfecto
power	potencia
Pythagorean Theorem	teorema de Pitágoras
real number	número real
scientific notation	notación cientifica

Vocabulary Connections

To become familiar with some of the vocabulary terms in the chapter, consider the following. You may refer to the chapter, the glossary, or a dictionary if you like.

1. The word *irrational* contains the prefix *ir-*, which means "not." Knowing what you do about rational numbers, what do you think is true of **irrational numbers**?

2. The word *real* means "actual" or "genuine." How do you think this applies to math, and how do you think **real numbers** differ from numbers that are not real?

Study Strategy: Take Effective Notes

Good note taking is an important study strategy. The Cornell system of note taking is an effective way to organize and review main ideas. This method involves dividing your notebook paper into three main sections. You take notes in the note-taking column during the lecture. You write questions and key phrases in the cue column as you review your notes. You write a brief summary of the lecture in the summary area.

Step 2: Cues
After class, write down key phrases or questions in the left column.

Step 3: Summary
Use the cues to restate the main points in your own words.

Step 1: Notes
Draw a vertical line about 2.5 inches from the left side of your paper. During class, write your notes about the main points of the lecture in the right column.

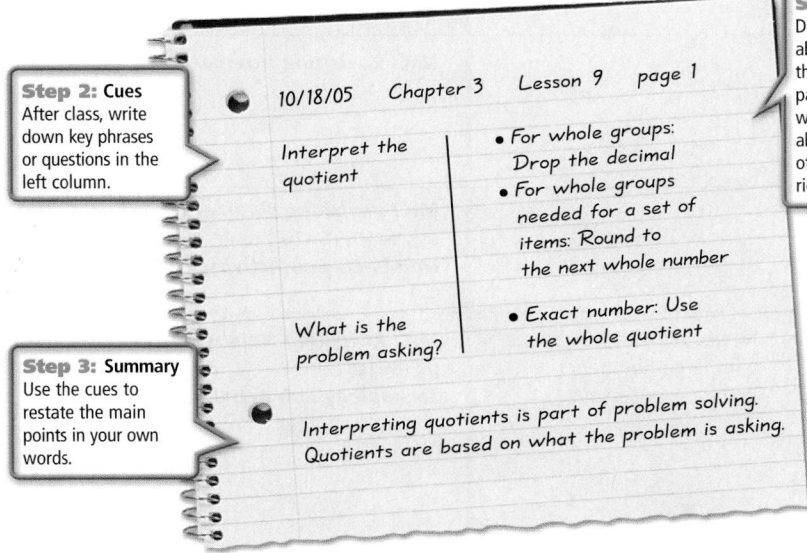

10/18/05   Chapter 3   Lesson 9   page 1

Interpret the quotient

- For whole groups: Drop the decimal
- For whole groups needed for a set of items: Round to the next whole number

What is the problem asking?

- Exact number: Use the whole quotient

Interpreting quotients is part of problem solving. Quotients are based on what the problem is asking.

Try This

1. Research and write a paragraph describing the Cornell system of note taking. Describe how you can benefit from using this type of system.

2. In your next class, use the Cornell system of note taking. Compare these notes to your notes from a previous lecture. Do you think your old notes or the notes using the Cornell system would better prepare you for tests and quizzes?

Organizer

Objective: Help students apply strategies to understand and retain key concepts.

 Online Edition

Resources

Chapter 4 Resource Book
Reading Strategies

Study Strategy: Take Effective Notes

Discuss Ask students what methods they use for taking notes. Explain how headings and dates will make their notes easier to reference, and suggest that being able to quickly reference notes will reduce the amount of time it takes them to study. Show them an example of good note-taking.

Extend Write the date and a heading on the board at the beginning of every lesson and remind students to write these down. As you progress through the chapter, ask students for definitions or formulas that were taught in previous lessons. Have them use their notes to find the answers instead of using the textbook.

Answers to *Try This*

1. Check students' work.
2. Check students' work.

Reading and Writing Math

Exponents

One-Minute Section Planner

Lesson	Materials	MiC and Lab Resources
Lesson 4-1 Exponents • Evaluate expressions with exponents. ☐ SAT-10 ☑ ITBS ☑ CTBS ☑ NAEP	Calculators, two-color counters (MK)	
Lesson 4-2 Problem Solving Skill: Look for a Pattern in Integer Exponents • Evaluate expressions with negative exponents and evaluate the zero exponent. ☐ SAT-10 ☑ ITBS ☑ CTBS ☑ NAEP		**MiC:** *Revisiting Numbers* pp. 9–10, 16–20
Lesson 4-3 Properties of Exponents • Apply the properties of exponents. ☐ SAT-10 ☑ ITBS ☑ CTBS ☑ NAEP		**MiC:** *Revisiting Numbers* pp. 9–10, 16–20 ***Hands-On Lab Activities*** 4-3
Lesson 4-4 Scientific Notation • Express large and small numbers in scientific notation and compare two numbers written in scientific notation. **4-4 Technology Lab** Multiply and Divide Numbers in Scientific Notation • Use a graphing calculator to perform operations with numbers written in scientific notation. ☐ SAT-10 ☑ ITBS ☑ CTBS ☑ NAEP	Newspapers or magazines with large numbers, graphing calculators	**MiC:** *Revisiting Numbers* pp. 8–10, 20–21 ***Technology Lab Activities*** 4-4

MK = *Manipulatives Kit*

Mathematics in Context

The unit ***Revisiting Numbers*** from the *Mathematics in Context* © 2006 series can be used with Section 4A. See Section Planner above for suggestions for integrating *MiC* with *Holt Mathematics.*

Section Overview

Exponents

 Exponents are used to write multiplication expressions that have repeated factors.

Simplify $3 \cdot (-10)^3$.

$3 \cdot (-10)^3$

$= 3 \cdot (-10) \cdot (-10) \cdot (-10)$

$= 3 \cdot (-1000)$

$= -3000$

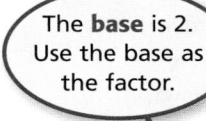

The **base** is 2. Use the base as the factor.

The **exponent** is 4. The exponent indicates how many times to use the base as a factor.

$2^4 = 2 \cdot 2 \cdot 2 \cdot 2 = 16$

2^4 is read "two to the fourth power."

Negative Exponents and Properties of Exponents

 Properties of exponents allow us to simplify expressions that have exponents.

Properties	Examples
$b^m \cdot b^n = b^{m+n}$	$3^5 \cdot 3^8 = 3^{5+8} = 3^{13}$
$\dfrac{b^m}{b^n} = b^{m-n}$, if $b \neq 0$	$\dfrac{6^9}{6^4} = 6^{9-4} = 6^5$
$\left(b^m\right)^n = b^{m \cdot n}$	$\left(9^4\right)^5 = 9^{4 \cdot 5} = 9^{20}$
$a^0 = 1$, if $a \neq 0$	$100^0 = 1$ or $(-7)^0 = 1$

If the values $m = 2$ and $n = 5$ are used in the property $\dfrac{b^m}{b^n} = b^{m-n}$, we have $\dfrac{b^2}{b^5} = b^{2-5} = b^{-3}$. Cases such as this suggest another reason to have a definition for negative exponents.

Negative Exponents

Definition	Examples
$b^{-n} = \dfrac{1}{b^n}$, if $b \neq 0$.	$3^{-2} = \dfrac{1}{3^2} = \dfrac{1}{3 \cdot 3} = \dfrac{1}{9}$
	$(-2)^{-4} = \dfrac{1}{(-2)^4} = \dfrac{1}{(-2) \cdot (-2) \cdot (-2) \cdot (-2) \cdot (-2)} = \dfrac{1}{16}$

Scientific Notation

 Scientific notation is a useful way to express very large or very small numbers. To express very small numbers in scientific notation, we need negative exponents.

Scientific Notation				**Standard Notation**
2.3×10^3	=	2.3×1000	=	2300
9.05×10^{-2}	=	9.05×0.01	=	0.0905

Use a number that is at least one but less than ten here.

Use a power of 10 here.

Pacing: Traditional 1 day
Block $\frac{1}{2}$ day

Objective: Students evaluate expressions with exponents.

 Online Edition
Tutorial Videos, Interactivities

Countdown to Testing Week 6

Learn to evaluate expressions with exponents.

Vocabulary
exponential form
exponent
base
power

Fold a piece of $8\frac{1}{2}$-by-11-inch paper in half. If you fold it in half again, the paper is 4 sheets thick. After the third fold in half, the paper is 8 sheets thick. How many sheets thick is the paper after 7 folds?

With each fold the number of sheets doubles.

$$2 \cdot 2 \cdot 2 \cdot 2 \cdot 2 \cdot 2 \cdot 2 = 128 \text{ sheets thick after 7 folds}$$

This multiplication problem can also be written in *exponential form*.

$$2 \cdot 2 \cdot 2 \cdot 2 \cdot 2 \cdot 2 \cdot 2 = 2^7 \quad \textit{The number 2 is a factor 7 times.}$$

If a number is in **exponential form**, the **exponent** represents how many times the **base** is to be used as a factor. A number produced by raising a base to an exponent is called a **power**. Both 27 and 3^3 represent the same power.

Base   Exponent

2^7

 **Power Presentations**
with PowerPoint®

Warm Up
Find the product.
1. $5 \cdot 5 \cdot 5 \cdot 5$ 625
2. $3 \cdot 3 \cdot 3$ 27
3. $(-7)(-7)(-7)$ -343
4. $9 \cdot 9$ 81

EXAMPLE 1 **Writing Exponents**

Write in exponential form.

A $5 \cdot 5 \cdot 5 \cdot 5 \cdot 5 \cdot 5 \cdot 5$
$5 \cdot 5 \cdot 5 \cdot 5 \cdot 5 \cdot 5 \cdot 5 = 5^7$ *Identify how many times 5 is a factor.*

B $(-4) \cdot (-4) \cdot (-4)$
$(-4) \cdot (-4) \cdot (-4) = (-4)^3$ *Identify how many times −4 is a factor.*

C $8 \cdot 8 \cdot 8 \cdot 8 \cdot p \cdot p \cdot p$
$8 \cdot 8 \cdot 8 \cdot 8 \cdot p \cdot p \cdot p = 8^4 p^3$ *Identify how many times 8 and p are each used as a factor.*

 **Reading Math**

Read (-4^3) as "−4 to the 3rd power or −4 cubed".

Problem of the Day
What two positive integers when multiplied together also equal the sum of the same two numbers?
2 and 2

Also available on transparency

EXAMPLE 2 **Evaluating Powers**

Evaluate.

A 3^4
$3^4 = 3 \cdot 3 \cdot 3 \cdot 3$ *Find the product of four 3's.*
$= 81$

B 12^2
$12^2 = 12 \cdot 12$ *Find the product of two 12's.*
$= 144$

Math Fact
The modern notation for exponents is believed to have originated with René Descartes around 1637.

 1 Introduce
Alternate Opener

Motivate

To introduce the concept of exponents, ask students if there is a simpler expression for the sum $5 + 5 + 5 + 5$. They might suggest the multiplication expression $4 \cdot 5$. Explain that just as repeated addition can be simplified by multiplication, repeated multiplication can be simplified by using exponents. For example, $5 \cdot 5 \cdot 5 \cdot 5 = 5^4$.

State Resources

EXPLORATION

 **4-1** **Exponents**

You can multiply $(-5) \cdot (-5) \cdot (-5) \cdot (-5) \cdot (-5) \cdot (-5)$ using exponents and a calculator.

The number −5 is a factor 6 times, so you can write it as $(-5)^6$.

The expressions are equivalent because they have the same value.

$(-5) \cdot (-5) \cdot (-5) \cdot (-5) \cdot (-5) \cdot (-5) =$ 15,625 and $(-5)^6 = 15,625$

Write each of the following using exponents. Then use a calculator to find the value of the expression.

1. $2 \cdot 2 \cdot 2 \cdot 2$
2. $8 \cdot 8 \cdot 8 \cdot 8 \cdot 8 \cdot 8$
3. $(-4) \cdot (-4) \cdot (-4)$
4. $(-5) \cdot (-5)$
5. $3 \cdot 3 \cdot 3 \cdot 3 \cdot 3 \cdot 3 \cdot 3 \cdot 3 \cdot 3$
6. $9 \cdot 9 \cdot 9$

Think and Discuss
7. **Discuss** whether 3^9 is the same as 9^3.
8. **Explain** why 4^6 is greater than 4^5.

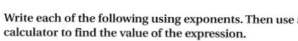 **go.hrw.com**
State Resources Online
KEYWORD: MT7 Resources

Explorations and answers are provided in *Alternate Openers: Explorations Transparencies.*

Evaluate.

C $(-8)^2$

$(-8)^2 = (-8) \cdot (-8)$ *Find the product of two −8's.*

$= 64$

D -2^3

$-2^3 = -(2 \cdot 2 \cdot 2)$ *Find the product of three 2's and then*

$= -8$ *make the answer negative.*

E X A M P L E  **3** **Using the Order of Operations**

Evaluate $x - y(z \cdot y^z)$ for $x = 20$, $y = 4$, and $z = 2$.

$x - y(z \cdot y^z)$

$20 - 4(2 \cdot 4^2)$ *Substitute 20 for x, 4 for y, and 2 for z.*

$= 20 - 4(2 \cdot 16)$ *Evaluate the exponent.*

$= 20 - 4(32)$ *Multiply inside the parentheses.*

$= 20 - 128$ *Multiply from left to right.*

$= -108$ *Subtract from left to right.*

E X A M P L E **4** *Geometry Application*

The number of diagonals of an n-sided figure is $\frac{1}{2}(n^2 - 3n)$. Use the formula to find the number of diagonals for a 6-sided figure.

$\frac{1}{2}(n^2 - 3n)$

$\frac{1}{2}(6^2 - 3 \cdot 6)$ *Substitute the number of sides for n.*

$\frac{1}{2}(36 - 18)$ *Simplify inside the parentheses.*

$\frac{1}{2}(18)$ *Subtract inside the parentheses.*

9 *Multiply.*

A 6-sided figure has 9 diagonals. You can verify your answer by sketching the diagonals.

Answers to *Think and Discuss*

1. $(-5)^2$ means to find the product of two -5's. -5^2 means to find the product of two 5's and then make the final answer negative.

2. $3 \cdot 2 = 6$; $3^2 = 3 \cdot 3 = 9$; $2^3 = 2 \cdot 2 \cdot 2 = 8$

3. $(4 - 11)^2 = (-7)^2$; $4^2 - 11^2 = 16 - 121 = -105$ $49 \neq -105$

Think and Discuss

1. Explain the difference between $(-5)^2$ and -5^2.

2. Compare $3 \cdot 2$, 3^2, and 2^3.

3. Show that $(4 - 11)^2$ is not equal to $4^2 - 11^2$.

Some students may multiply the exponent and the base (e.g., $3^4 = 12$). Encourage students to expand the power before multiplying (e.g., $3^4 = 3 \cdot 3 \cdot 3 \cdot 3 = 81$).

Power Presentations with **PowerPoint®**

Additional Examples

Example **1**

Write in exponential form.

A. $4 \cdot 4 \cdot 4 \cdot 4$ 4^4

B. $(-6) \cdot (-6) \cdot (-6)$ $(-6)^3$

C. $5 \cdot 5 \cdot d \cdot d \cdot d \cdot d$ $5^2 d^4$

Example

Evaluate. **2**

A. 3^5 243   **B.** $(-3)^5$ -243

C. $(-4)^4$ 256   **D.** 2^8 256

Example **3**

Evaluate $x(y^x - z^y) + x^y$ for $x = 4$, $y = 2$, and $z = 3$.   44

Example **4**

Use the formula $\frac{1}{2}(n^2 - 3n)$ to find the number of diagonals in a 7-sided figure.   14 diagonals

Also available on transparency

---

2 Teach

Guided Instruction

In this lesson, students learn to evaluate expressions with exponents. Show students an example, such as 3^4. Point out the *base*, the *exponent*, and the *power*. Show them how to evaluate the power ($3 \cdot 3 \cdot 3 \cdot 3 = 81$). You may want to show that the same result can be obtained by working the multiplications in any order.

Teaching Tip **Cognitive Strategies** Point out that the sign rules for multiplication still apply. Work the examples containing negative bases step-by-step so students will understand why the result is sometimes positive (when the exponent is even) and sometimes negative (when the exponent is odd).

Reaching All Learners
Through Concrete Manipulatives

Give each student or group of students a set of 16 counters (provided in the Manipulatives Kit). Ask students to divide the counters into 4 equal groups and to write an addition expression that represents the grouping ($4 + 4 + 4 + 4$). Then have them write a multiplication expression that represents the same grouping ($4 \cdot 4$) and then an expression with an exponent (4^2). After simplifying each expression to get 16, they should begin to see how addition, multiplication, and powers are related.

3 Close

ENGLISH LANGUAGE LEARNERS

Summarize

Review the vocabulary terms *power*, *base*, and *exponent*. Discuss how each term is related to multiplication. You may wish to have students identify the base, exponent, and power in the expression 2^3.

Possible answers: A power is an expression where a number is multiplied by itself a certain number of times. A base is the factor in a power. An exponent is the number of times the factor is used. In the expression 2^3, 2 is the base, 3 is the exponent, and 2^3 is the power.

4-1 Exercises

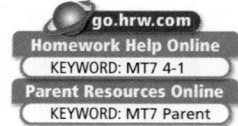

Assignment Guide

If you finished Example **1** assign:
Average 1–4, 15–20, 51–61
Advanced 15–20, 31–34, 51–61

If you finished Example **2** assign:
Average 1–9, 15–25, 51–61
Advanced 15–25, 31–38, 49, 51–61

If you finished Example **3** assign:
Average 1–13, 15–29, 39–44, 51–61
Advanced 15–29, 31, 32, 37–44, 46–61

If you finished Example **4** assign:
Average 1–30, 39–45, 51–61
Advanced 15–32, 37–61

Homework Quick Check

Quickly check key concepts.
Exercises: 16, 22, 28, 30, 42

Math Background

The second power of a number is commonly called the *square* of the number. This name comes from the fact that the area of a square is given by the formula $A = s^2$, where s is the length of a side of the square.

The third power of a number is called the *cube* of the number because the volume of a cube is given by the formula $V = s^3$, where s is the length of an edge of the cube.

State Resources

go.hrw.com
State Resources Online
KEYWORD: MT7 Resources

GUIDED PRACTICE

See Example **1** Write in exponential form.

1. 12 12^1 **2.** $18 \cdot 18$ 18^2 **3.** $2b \cdot 2b \cdot 2b \cdot 2b$ $(2b)^4$ **4.** $(-3) \cdot (-3)$ $(-3)^2$

See Example **2** Evaluate.

5. 2^6 64   **6.** $(-7)^2$ 49   **7.** $(-5)^3$ -125 **8.** -7^4 -2401 **9.** 8^4 4096

See Example **3** Evaluate each expression for the given values of the variables.

10. $a^5 + 4b$ for $a = 3$ and $b = 12$ 291

11. $2x^9 - (y + z)$ for $x = -1$, $y = 7$, and $z = -4$ -5

12. $s + (t^u - 1)$ for $s = 13$, $t = 5$, $u = 3$ 137

13. $100 - n(p^q - 4)$ for $n = 10$, $p = 3$, and $q = 8$ -710

See Example **4** **14.** The sum of the first n positive integers is $\frac{1}{2}(n^2 + n)$. Check the formula for the first 5 positive integers. Then use the formula to find the sum of the first 14 positive integers.   105

INDEPENDENT PRACTICE

See Example **1** Write in exponential form.

15. $5 \cdot 5 \cdot 5 \cdot 5 \cdot 5 \cdot 5$ 5^6 **16.** $(-9) \cdot (-9) \cdot (-9)$ $(-9)^3$ **17.** $3d \cdot 3d \cdot 3d$ $3^3 d^3$

18. -8 $(-8)^1$ **19.** $(-4) \cdot (-4) \cdot c \cdot c \cdot c$ $(-4)^2 c^3$ **20.** $x \cdot x \cdot y$ $x^2 y$

See Example **2** Evaluate.

21. 4^4 256   **22.** $(-3)^6$ 729   **23.** 8^5 32,768   **24.** -2^9 -512 **25.** $(-4)^2$ 16

See Example **3** Evaluate each expression for the given values of the variables.

26. b^2 for $b = -7$ 49

27. $2^c + 3d(g + 2)$ for $c = 7$, $d = 5$, and $g = 1$ 173

28. $m + n^p$ for $m = 12$, $n = 11$, and $p = 2$ 133

29. $x \div y^z$ for $x = 9$, $y = 3$, and $z = 2$ 1

See Example **4** **30.** A circle can be divided by n lines into a maximum of $\frac{1}{2}(n^2 + n) + 1$ regions. Use the formula to find the maximum number of regions for 7 lines.   29

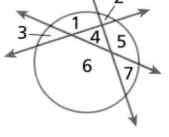

3 lines → 7 regions

PRACTICE AND PROBLEM SOLVING

Extra Practice
See page 788.

Write in exponential form.

31. $(-3) \cdot (-3) \cdot (-3) \cdot (-3)$ $(-3)^4$ **32.** $5h \cdot 5h \cdot 5h$ $(5h)^3$

33. $6 \cdot 6 \cdot 6 \cdot 6 \cdot 6 \cdot 6$ 6^6 **34.** $(4)(4)(4)(4)(4)$ 4^5

RETEACH 4-1

LESSON 4-1 Reteach
Exponents

The fifth power of 3   base→3^5←exponent $= 3 \cdot 3 \cdot 3 \cdot 3 \cdot 3$
3 used as a factor 5 times

Complete to write each expression using an exponent. State the power.

1. $5 \cdot 5 \cdot 5 \cdot 5 = 5^{\underline{4}}$ **2.** $(-7) \cdot (-7) \cdot (-7) = (-7)^{\underline{3}}$
the __fourth__ power of 5   the __third__ power of $\underline{-7}$

Complete to evaluate each expression.

3. $(-2)^3 = (-2)(-2)(-2) = \underline{-8}$

4. $10^4 = \underline{10} \cdot \underline{10} \cdot \underline{10} \cdot \underline{10} = \underline{10,000}$

5. $(-5)^4 = (\underline{-5})(\underline{-5})(\underline{-5})(\underline{-5}) = \underline{625}$

When an expression is a product that includes a power, you simplify the power first.
$3 \cdot 2^3 = 3 \cdot 2 \cdot 2 \cdot 2 = 3 \cdot 8 = 24$

Complete to simplify each expression.

6. $4 \cdot (-2)^3 = 4(\underline{-2})(\underline{-2})(\underline{-2}) = \underline{-32}$

7. $5 \cdot 3^3 = \underline{5} \cdot \underline{3} \cdot \underline{3} \cdot \underline{3} = \underline{135}$

8. $(3 \cdot 2)^3 = 6^3 = \underline{6} \cdot \underline{6} \cdot \underline{6} = \underline{216}$

9. $(-4(-2))^3 = (\underline{8})^3 = (\underline{8})(\underline{8})(\underline{8}) = \underline{512}$

10. $25 - 3(4 \cdot 3^2)$ **11.** $-100 - 2(3 \cdot 4)^2$ **12.** $15 - 4(3 + 3^2)$
$= 25 - 3(4 \cdot \underline{9})$ $= -100 - 2(\underline{12})^2$ $= 15 - 4(3 + \underline{9})$
$= 25 - 3(\underline{36})$ $= -100 - 2(\underline{144})$ $= 15 - 4(\underline{12})$
$= 25 - \underline{108}$ $= -100 - \underline{288}$ $= 15 - \underline{48}$
$= \underline{-83}$ $= \underline{-388}$ $= \underline{-33}$

PRACTICE 4-1

LESSON 4-1 Practice B
Exponents

Write in exponential form.

1. $6 \cdot 6 \cdot 6 \cdot 6 \cdot 6 \cdot 6$ **2.** $7 \cdot 7 \cdot 7 \cdot 7$
   6^6 7^4

3. $(-8) \cdot (-8) \cdot (-8) \cdot (-8)$ **4.** $5 \cdot 5 \cdot 5 \cdot b \cdot b \cdot b \cdot b$
   $(-8)^4$ $5^3 b^4$

Evaluate.

5. 10^2 **6.** $(-6)^2$ **7.** 8^2 **8.** $(-7)^2$
  100   36   64   49

9. $(-5)^3$ **10.** 12^2 **11.** $(-9)^2$ **12.** $(-4)^3$
  -125 144   81 -64

13. 2^5 **14.** 5^4 **15.** $(-3)^4$ **16.** 6^3
  32   625   81   216

Evaluate each expression for the given values of the variables.

17. $n^3 - 5$ for $n = 4$ **18.** $4x^2 + y^3$ for $x = 5$ and $y = -2$
  59   92

19. $m^p + q^2$ for $m = 5$, $p = 2$, and $q = 4$ **20.** $a^4 + 2(b - c^2)$ for $a = 2$, $b = 4$, and $c = -1$
  41   22

21. Write an expression for five times a number used as a factor three times.
  $5x^3$

22. Find the volume of a regular cube if the length of a side is 10 cm. (Hint: $V = l^3$.)
  1000 cm^3

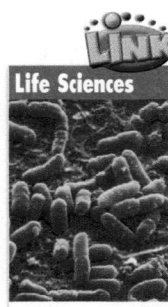

Life Sciences

Evaluate.

35. 5^3 **125**

36. 8^2 **64**

37. $(-14)^3$ **−2744**

38. -4^5 **−1024**

Simplify.

39. $44 - (5 \cdot 4^2)$ **−36**

40. $(4 + 4^4)$ **260**

41. $(6 - 7^1)$ **−1**

42. $84 - [8 - (-2)^3]$ **68**

Evaluate each expression for the given value of the variable.

43. $m(p - n^q)$ for $m = 2$, $n = 6$, $p = 3$, and $q = 3$ **−426**

44. $r + (t \cdot s^v)$ for $r = 42$, $s = 4$, $t = 3$, and $v = 2$ **90**

45. **Life Science** Bacteria can divide every 20 minutes, so 1 bacterium can multiply to 2 in 20 minutes, 4 in 40 minutes, and so on. How many bacteria will there be in 6 hours? Write your answer using exponents, and then evaluate. $2^{18} = 262{,}144$ **bacteria**

Most bacteria reproduce by a type of simple cell division known as binary fission. Each species reproduces best at a specific temperature and moisture level.

46. **Critical Thinking** For any whole number n, $5^n - 1$ is divisible by 4. Verify this for $n = 4$ and $n = 6$.

47. **Estimation** A gift shaped like a cube has sides that measure 12.3 cm long. What is the approximate volume of the gift? (*Hint:* $V = s^3$) ≈ 1728 cm^3

48. **Choose a Strategy** Place the numbers 1, 2, 3, 4, and 5 in the boxes to make a true statement: $\blacksquare \cdot \blacksquare^{\blacksquare} = \blacksquare^2 - \blacksquare^{\blacksquare}$. $3 \cdot 2^3 = 5^2 - 1^4$

49. **Write About It** Compare 10^2 and 2^{10}. For any two numbers, make a conjecture about which usually gives the greater number, using the greater number as the base or as the exponent? Give at least one exception.

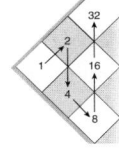 **50.** **Challenge** Write $(4^2)^3$ using a single exponent. 4^6

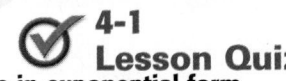

TEST PREP and Spiral Review

51. **Multiple Choice** Which expression has the greatest value?

Ⓐ 2^5 Ⓑ 3^4 Ⓒ 4^3 Ⓓ 5^2

52. **Multiple Choice** The volume of a cube is calculated by using the formula $V = s^3$, where s is the length of the sides of the cube. What is the volume of a cube that has sides 8 meters long?

Ⓕ 24 m^3 Ⓖ 512 m^3 Ⓗ 888 m^3 Ⓙ 6561 m^3

53. **Gridded Response** What is the value of 5^4? **625**

Find each sum. (Lessons 1-4 and 1-5)

54. $-18 + -65$ **−83**

55. $-123 + 95$ **−28**

56. $87 - (-32)$ **119**

57. $-74 - (-27)$ **−47**

Write each fraction as a decimal. (Lesson 2-1)

58. $\frac{7}{50}$ **0.14**

59. $\frac{4}{15}$ **0.2$\overline{6}$**

60. $\frac{3}{8}$ **0.375**

61. $\frac{5}{24}$ **0.2083$\overline{3}$**

Answers

46. $\dfrac{5^4 - 1}{4} = \dfrac{624}{4}$
$= 156;$
$\dfrac{5^6 - 1}{4} = \dfrac{15{,}624}{4}$
$= 3906$

49. Possible answer: using the larger number as the exponent; $10^2 = 100$ and $2^{10} = 1024$, so $10^2 < 2^{10}$

4-1 Lesson Quiz

Write in exponential form.

1. $n \cdot n \cdot n \cdot n$ n^4

2. $(-8)(-8)(-8)(h)$ $(-8)^3 h$

3. Evaluate $(-4)^4$. 256

4. Evaluate $xz - y^x$ for $x = 5$, $y = 3$, and $z = 6$. 213

5. A population of bacteria doubles in size every minute. The number of bacteria after 5 minutes is $15 \cdot 2^5$. How many are there after 5 minutes? 480

Also available on transparency

Objective: Students evaluate expressions with negative exponents and evaluate the zero exponent.

Online Edition
Tutorial Videos

Countdown to Testing Week 6

Power Presentations
with PowerPoint®

Warm Up
Evaluate.
1. 10^3 1000
2. 10^0 1
3. $10^2 \cdot 10^2$ 10,000
4. $\dfrac{10^7}{10^4}$ 1000
5. $\dfrac{10^6}{10^6}$ 1

Problem of the Day
Find two different numbers for the values of x and y that will make x^y and y^x equal. 2 and 4

Also available on transparency

Math Humor
Why did the integer get a bad evaluation at work? He had a negative attitude.

Look for a Pattern in Integer Exponents

 Problem Solving Skill

Learn to evaluate expressions with negative exponents and to evaluate the zero exponent.

The nanoguitar is the smallest guitar in the world. It is no larger than a single cell, at about 10^{-5} meters long.

Look for a pattern in the table to extend what you know about exponents to include negative exponents.

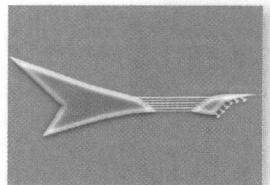

10^2	10^1	10^0	10^{-1}	10^{-2}	10^{-3}
$10 \cdot 10$	10	1	$\dfrac{1}{10}$	$\dfrac{1}{10 \cdot 10}$	$\dfrac{1}{10 \cdot 10 \cdot 10}$
100	10	1	$\dfrac{1}{10} = 0.1$	$\dfrac{1}{100} = 0.01$	$\dfrac{1}{1000} = 0.001$

$\div 10$ $\div 10$ $\div 10$ $\div 10$ $\div 10$

EXAMPLE 1 **Using a Pattern to Evaluate Negative Exponents**

Evaluate the powers of 10.

Ⓐ 10^{-4}

$10^{-4} = \dfrac{1}{10 \cdot 10 \cdot 10 \cdot 10}$ *Extend the pattern from the table.*

$= \dfrac{1}{10,000}$ *Multiply.*

$= 0.0001$ *Write as a decimal.*

Ⓑ 10^{-5}

$10^{-5} = \dfrac{1}{10 \cdot 10 \cdot 10 \cdot 10 \cdot 10}$ *Extend the pattern from Example 1A.*

$= \dfrac{1}{100,000}$ *Multiply.*

$= 0.00001$ *Write as a decimal.*

Remember!
The reciprocal of a number is 1 divided by that number.

NEGATIVE EXPONENTS		
Words	**Numbers**	**Algebra**
Any number except 0 with a negative exponent equals its reciprocal with the opposite exponent.	$5^{-3} = \left(\dfrac{1}{5}\right)^3 = \dfrac{1}{125}$	$b^{-n} = \left(\dfrac{1}{b}\right)^n, b \neq 0$

---

go.hrw.com
State Resources Online
KEYWORD: MT7 Resources

---

1 Introduce
Alternate Opener

EXPLORATION

4-2 **Look for a Pattern in Integer Exponents**

Suppose the height of a magic plant doubles every hour, beginning with a height of 1 inch at the "zero hour."

Use the bar graph to think about how tall the plant was 1 hour before (−1) and 2 hours before (−2) the zero hour.

1. Draw and label a bar on the bar graph to show the height at hour −1 and hour −2. (*Hint:* The height doubles each hour.)

2. Use the graph and the pattern in the table to find the value of each exponential expression.

Time, x	Plant Height, 2^x
−3	$2^{-3} = \dfrac{1}{2^3} = \dfrac{1}{8}$
−2	
−1	
0	
1	
2	
3	

Think and Discuss
3. **Describe** the pattern in the bar graph.
4. **Describe** the pattern in the table.

Motivate
Prior to beginning this lesson, ask students to evaluate the following expressions:
A. 4^5 1024
B. 5^0 1
C. 7^1 7

After they have evaluated them, ask them to describe, in their own words, how they got their answers.

Explorations and answers are provided in *Alternate Openers: Explorations Transparencies.*

EXAMPLE 2 Evaluating Negative Exponents

Evaluate.

A $(-2)^{-3}$

$$(-2)^{-3}$$

$$= \left(\frac{1}{-2}\right)^3 \qquad \text{Write the reciprocal; change the sign of the exponent.}$$

$$= \frac{1}{-2} \cdot \frac{1}{-2} \cdot \frac{1}{-2} \qquad \text{Find the product of three } \left(\frac{1}{-2}\right)\text{'s.}$$

$$= -\frac{1}{8} \qquad \text{Simplify.}$$

B 6^{-4}

$$6^{-4}$$

$$= \left(\frac{1}{6}\right)^4 \qquad \text{Write the reciprocal; change the sign of the exponent.}$$

$$= \frac{1}{6} \cdot \frac{1}{6} \cdot \frac{1}{6} \cdot \frac{1}{6} \qquad \text{Find the product of four } \frac{1}{6}\text{'s.}$$

$$= \frac{1}{1296} \qquad \text{Simplify.}$$

Notice from the table on the previous page that $10^0 = 1$. This is true for any number to the zero power.

THE ZERO POWER

Words	Numbers	Algebra
The zero power of any number except 0 equals 1.	$100^0 = 1$ $(-7)^0 = 1$	$a^0 = 1$, if $a \neq 0$

EXAMPLE 3 Using the Order of Operations

Evaluate $2 + (-7)^0 - (4 + 2)^{-2}$.

$$2 + (-7)^0 - (4 + 2)^{-2}$$

$$= 2 + (-7)^0 - 6^{-2} \qquad \text{Add inside the parentheses.}$$

$$= 2 + 1 - \frac{1}{36} \qquad \text{Evaluate the exponents.}$$

$$= 2\frac{35}{36} \qquad \text{Add and subtract from left to right.}$$

Think and Discuss

1. **Express** $\frac{1}{2}$ using a negative exponent.

2. **Tell** whether an integer raised to a negative exponent can ever be greater than 1. Justify your answer.

Teaching Tip **Inclusion** For Example 3, remind students that any nonzero number to the zero power is one.

Possible answers to *Think and Discuss*

1. 2^{-1}

2. No, but 1^{-1} is 1. An integer raised to a negative exponent results in the reciprocal of the integer, which is always less than 1.

 **Teach**

Guided Instruction

In this lesson, students learn to evaluate expressions with negative exponents. Begin by using the pattern shown in the table on the Teaching Transparency to provide a meaningful definition of an expression with a negative exponent. Then give students an opportunity to apply the meaning to evaluate powers and expressions containing negative exponents.

Teaching Tip **Inclusion** Remind students that a negative exponent does not indicate a negative value, but instead a fractional expression.

 Reaching All Learners

Through Multiple Representations

Have the class work in pairs. Show students a series of equivalent expressions, such as $\frac{5^2}{5^4} = 5^{-2} = \frac{1}{5^2} = \frac{1}{25}$. Explain that all of the expressions are equal. Have each student create two expressions involving exponents that can be simplified. Encourage students to use negative exponents. Then have the students in each pair exchange problems and solve each other's work.

Sample expressions:

Simplify. **1.** $(-4)^{-2}$ $\quad \frac{1}{16}$

2. $\frac{6^2}{6^5}$ $\quad \frac{1}{216}$

 Close

Summarize

Have students describe how to evaluate an expression with a positive exponent and then how to evaluate an expression with a negative exponent. Ask students to provide examples of each.

Possible answers: To evaluate an expression with a positive exponent, multiply, using the base as a factor the number of times indicated by the exponent. To evaluate an expression with a negative exponent, place the expression in the denominator of a fraction with 1 as the numerator and replace the negative exponent with its opposite. Then evaluate the new expression.

4-2 **Exercises**

go.hrw.com
Homework Help Online
KEYWORD: MT7 4-2
Parent Resources Online
KEYWORD: MT7 Parent

Assignment Guide

If you finished Example **1** assign:
Average 1–4, 13–16, 44, 49–58
Advanced 13–16, 44, 49–58

If you finished Example **2** assign:
Average 1–8, 13–20, 37–40, 44, 49–58
Advanced 13–20, 37–42, 44, 49–58

If you finished Example **3** assign:
Average 1–30, 34–40, 44–47, 49–58
Advanced 13–24, 31–34, 39–58

Homework Quick Check

Quickly check key concepts.
Exercises: 14, 20, 24, 34, 40

Answers

37–43. See p. A5.

Math Background

The pattern of powers of ten shown at the beginning of this lesson is an effective introduction to scientific notation, which will be investigated further in Lesson 4-4.

Because scientists must frequently work with very large and small numbers, they use powers of ten to keep the numbers simple. Positive exponents are used for very large numbers, such as those used in astronomy and physics. Negative exponents are used for very small numbers, such as those used in chemistry and biology.

State Resources

go.hrw.com
State Resources Online
KEYWORD: MT7 Resources

GUIDED PRACTICE

See Example **1** Evaluate the powers of 10.

1. 10^{-2} **0.01** 2. 10^{-7} **0.0000001** 3. 10^{-6} **0.000001** 4. 10^{-10} **0.0000000001**

See Example **2** Evaluate.

5. $(2)^{-6}$ $\frac{1}{64}$ 6. $(-3)^{-4}$ $-\frac{1}{81}$ 7. 3^{-3} $\frac{1}{27}$ 8. $(-2)^{-5}$ $-\frac{1}{32}$

See Example **3** 9. $4 + 3(4 - 9^0) + 5^{-3}$ $13\frac{1}{125}$ 10. $7 - 8(2)^{-3} + 13$ **19**

11. $(2 + 2)^{-2} + (1 + 1)^{-4}$ $\frac{1}{8}$ 12. $2 - (2^{-3})$ $1\frac{7}{8}$

INDEPENDENT PRACTICE

See Example **1** Evaluate the powers of 10.

13. 10^{-1} **0.1** 14. 10^{-9} **0.000000001** 15. 10^{-8} **0.00000001** 16. 10^{-12} **0.000000000001**

See Example **2** Evaluate.

17. $(-4)^{-1}$ $-\frac{1}{4}$ 18. 5^{-2} $\frac{1}{25}$ 19. $(-10)^{-4}$ $\frac{1}{10,000}$, or **0.0001** 20. $(-2)^{-6}$ $\frac{1}{64}$

See Example **3** 21. $128(2 + 6)^{-3} + (4^0 - 3)$ $-1\frac{3}{4}$ 22. $3 + (-3)^{-2} - (9 + 7)^0$ $2\frac{1}{9}$

23. $12 - (-5)^0 + (3^{-3} + 9^{-2})$ $11\frac{4}{81}$ 24. $5^0 + 49(1 + 6)^{-2}$ **2**

PRACTICE AND PROBLEM SOLVING

Extra Practice
See page 788.

Evaluate.

25. $(18 - 16)^{-5}$ $\frac{1}{32}$ 26. $25 + (6 \cdot 10^0)$ **31** 27. $(3 \cdot 3)^{-3}$ $\frac{1}{729}$ 28. $(1 - 2^{-2})$ $\frac{3}{4}$

29. $3^{-2} \cdot 2^2 \cdot 4^0$ $\frac{4}{9}$ 30. $10 + 4^3 \cdot 2^{-2}$ **26**

31. $6^2 - 3^2 + 1^{-1}$ **28** 32. $16 - [15 - (-2)^{-3}]$ $\frac{7}{8}$

Evaluate each expression for the given value of the variable.

33. $2(x^2 + x)$ for $x = 2.1$ **13.02** 34. $(4n)^{-2} + n$ for $n = 3$ $3\frac{1}{144}$

35. $c^2 + c$ for $c = \frac{1}{2}$ $\frac{3}{4}$ 36. $m^{-2} \cdot m^0 \cdot m^2$ for $m = 9$ **1**

Write each expression as repeated multiplication. Then evaluate the expression.

37. 11^{-4} 38. 1^{-10} 39. -6^{-3} 40. $(-6)^{-3}$

41. Make a table with the column headings n, n^{-2}, and $-2n$. Complete the table for $n = -5, -4, -3, -2, -1, 0, 1, 2, 3, 4,$ and 5.

42. **Pattern** Describe the following pattern: $(-1)^1 = \blacksquare$; $(-1)^{-2} = \blacksquare$; $(-1)^{-3} = \blacksquare$; $(-1)^{-4} = \blacksquare$. Determine what $(-1)^{-100}$ would be. Justify your thinking.

43. **Critical Thinking** Evaluate $n^1 \cdot n^{-1}$ for $n = 1, 2,$ and 3. Then make a conjecture what $n^1 \cdot n^{-1}$ is for any value of n. Explain your reasoning.

RETEACH 4-2

Reteach
4-2 *Look for a Pattern in Integer Exponents*

To rewrite a negative exponent, move the power to the denominator of a unit fraction. $5^{-2} = \frac{1}{5^2}$

Complete to rewrite each power with a positive exponent.

1. $7^{-3} = \frac{1}{7^3}$ 2. $9^{-5} = \frac{1}{9^5}$ 3. $13^{-4} = \frac{1}{13^4}$

Complete each pattern.

4. $10^{-1} = \frac{1}{10} = 0.1$

$10^{-2} = \frac{1}{10^2} = \frac{1}{100} = 0.01$

$10^{-3} = \frac{1}{10^3} = \frac{1}{1000} = 0.001$

5. $5^{-1} = \frac{1}{5}$

$5^{-2} = \frac{1}{5^2} = \frac{1}{5 \cdot 5} = \frac{1}{25}$

$5^{-3} = \frac{1}{5^3} = \frac{1}{5 \cdot 5 \cdot 5} = \frac{1}{125}$

6. $3^{-1} = \frac{1}{3}$

$3^{-2} = \frac{1}{3^2} = \frac{1}{3 \cdot 3} = \frac{1}{9}$

$3^{-3} = \frac{1}{3^3} = \frac{1}{3 \cdot 3 \cdot 3} = \frac{1}{27}$

7. $(-4)^{-1} = \frac{1}{-4}$

$(-4)^{-2} = \frac{1}{(-4)^2} = \frac{1}{(-4) \cdot (-4)} = \frac{1}{16}$

$(-4)^{-3} = \frac{1}{(-4)^3} = \frac{1}{(-4) \cdot (-4) \cdot (-4)} =$

Evaluate.

8. $2^{-3} = \frac{1}{2^3}; \frac{1}{8}$ 9. $(-6)^{-2} = \frac{1}{(-6)^2}; \frac{1}{36}$

10. $4^{-2} = \frac{1}{4^2}; \frac{1}{16}$ 11. $(-3)^{-3} = \frac{1}{(-3)^3}; \frac{1}{27}$

12. $6^{-2} = \frac{1}{36}$ 13. $(-2)^{-3} = -\frac{1}{8}$

14. $6^{-3} = \frac{1}{216}$ 15. $(-5)^{-2} = \frac{1}{25}$

16. $2^{-4} = \frac{1}{16}$ 17. $(-9)^{-1} = -\frac{1}{9}$

PRACTICE 4-2

Practice B
4-2 *Look for a Pattern in Integer Exponents*

Evaluate the powers of 10.

1. 10^{-3} $\frac{1}{10,000}$ 2. 10^3 **1000** 3. 10^{-5} **0.00001** 4. 10^{-2} **0.01**

5. 10^0 **1** 6. 10^4 **10,000** 7. 10^1 **10** 8. 10^5 **100,000**

Evaluate.

9. $(-6)^{-2}$ $\frac{1}{36}$ 10. $(-9)^{-3}$ $\frac{1}{729}$ 11. 2^{-5} $\frac{1}{32}$

12. $(-3)^{-4}$ $\frac{1}{81}$ 13. $(-12)^{-1}$ $\frac{1}{12}$ 14. 6^{-3} $\frac{1}{216}$

15. $10 - (3 + 2)^0 + 2^{-1}$ $9\frac{1}{2}$ 16. $15 + (-6)^0 - 3^{-2}$ $15\frac{8}{9}$

17. $6(8 - 2)^0 + 4^{-2}$ $6\frac{1}{16}$ 18. $2^{-2} + (-4)^{-1}$ **0**

19. $3(1 - 4)^{-2} + 9^{-1} + 12^0$ $1\frac{4}{9}$ 20. $9^0 + 64(3 + 5)^{-2}$ **2**

21. One milliliter equals 10^{-3} liter. Evaluate 10^{-3}. $\frac{1}{1000}$

22. The volume of a cube is 10^{-6} cubic feet. Evaluate 10^{-6}. $\frac{1}{1,000,000}$

44. The sperm whale is the deepest diving whale. It can dive to depths greater than 10^{12} nanometers. Evaluate 10^{12}.
1,000,000,000,000

45. Blubber makes up 27% of a blue whale's body weight. Davis found the average weight of blue whales and used it to calculate the average weight of their blubber. He wrote the amount as $2^2 \times 3^3 \times 5 \times 71$ pounds. Evaluate this amount. **38,340 lb**

46. Most baleen whales migrate an average of $2^5 \times 125$ km each way. The gray whale has the longest known migration of any mammal, a distance of $2^4 \times 3 \times 125$ km farther each way than the average baleen whale migration. How far does the gray whale migrate each way? **10,000 km**

47. A blue whale may eat between 6 and 7 tons of krill each day. Krill are approximately $2^{-5} \times 3^{-1} \times 5^{-1}$ of the length of a blue whale. Evaluate this amount. $\dfrac{1}{480}$

48. ⭐ **Challenge** A cubic centimeter is the same as 1 mL. If a humpback whale has more than 1 kL of blood, how many cubic centimeters of blood does the humpback whale have?
more than 10^6 or 1,000,000 cm^3

Krill are a food source for different species of baleen whales, such as the humpback whale, pictured above.

TEST PREP and Spiral Review

49. Multiple Choice Evaluate $(-5)^{-2}$.

    Ⓐ -25 Ⓑ $-\dfrac{1}{25}$ Ⓒ $\dfrac{1}{25}$ Ⓓ 25

50. Extended Response Evaluate $8^3, 8^2, 8^1, 8^0, 8^{-1},$ and 8^{-2}. Describe the pattern of the values. Use the pattern of the values to predict the value of 8^{-3}.

Give the coordinates and quadrant of each point. (Lesson 3-2)

51. A **52.** B **53.** C **54.** D
$(-1, 4)$; II $(2, 3)$; I $(-2, -3)$; III $(3, -1)$; IV

Evaluate. (Lesson 4-1)

55. $(-3)^4$ **56.** 5^2 **57.** $(10 - 15)^3$ **58.** $(-9)^3$
81   **25**   **−125**   **−729**

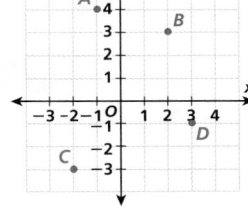

ONGOING ASSESSMENT
and INTERVENTION ⬅➡

Diagnose Before the Lesson
4-2 Warm Up, TE p. 166

Monitor During the Lesson
4-2 Know-It Notebook
4-2 Questioning Strategies

Assess After the Lesson
4-2 Lesson Quiz, TE p. 169

Interdisciplinary LINK

Science

Exercises 44–48 involve using integer exponents to describe characteristics of some sea creatures. Integer exponents are used throughout middle school science programs such as *Holt Science & Technology.*

Answers

50. See p. A5.

TEST PREP DOCTOR ✚ In Exercise 49, students who circled **B** probably have trouble remembering the sign rules for raising negative numbers to even powers. Review with students that an expression of the form $(-a)^2$ will have a positive answer, whereas $-a^2$ would have a negative answer. Show them this trend also applies to negative even exponents.

✏ Journal

Have students write about something that is very small, and have them describe the measurement using negative exponents. Examples do not need to be factual but should be realistic. For example: The flea was 2^{-4} inches long.

Power Presentations with PowerPoint®

4-2 Lesson Quiz
Evaluate the powers of 10.
1. 10^{-3} 0.001
2. 10^{-7} 0.0000001
Evaluate.
3. $(-6)^{-2}$ $\dfrac{1}{36}$
4. $4 \cdot 2^{-3} + 10^{-1}$ $\dfrac{3}{5}$
5. $8^0 - (11 - 2^4)^{-2}$ $\dfrac{24}{25}$
6. $(4w)^{-2} + w^{-1}$ for $w = 4$ $\dfrac{65}{256}$

Also available on transparency

CHALLENGE 4-2

LESSON 4-2 Challenge
Stuff It!

$9^{\frac{1}{2}}$ means $\sqrt[2]{9^1}$.

   To find the value, first evaluate the root: $\sqrt[2]{9} = 3$.
   Then, raise the result to the indicated power: $3^1 = 3$.
   So, $9^{\frac{1}{2}} = \sqrt[2]{9^1} = 3^1 = 3$.

In general, here's the way to rewrite a term with a fractional exponent:

$$x^{\frac{a}{b}} = \sqrt[b]{x^a}$$

Evaluate $8^{\frac{2}{3}}$.

$8^{\frac{2}{3}} = \sqrt[3]{8^2}$ Rewrite using radical form.
    $= 2^2$ Evaluate the root; $\sqrt[3]{8} = 2$ since $2 \cdot 2 \cdot 2 = 8$.
    $= 4$ Evaluate the power.

Rewrite each term using radical form. Evaluate the root. Evaluate the power.

1. $64^{\frac{1}{2}} = \sqrt[2]{64^1}$ **2.** $100^{\frac{1}{2}} = \sqrt[2]{100^1}$ **3.** $400^{\frac{1}{2}} = \sqrt[2]{400^1}$
    $= 8^1$ $= 10^1$ $= 20^1$
    $= 8$ $= 10$ $= 20$

4. $64^{\frac{2}{3}} = \sqrt[3]{64^2}$ **5.** $216^{\frac{2}{3}} = \sqrt[3]{216^2}$ **6.** $1000^{\frac{2}{3}} = \sqrt[3]{1000^2}$
    $= 4^2$ $= 6^2$ $= 10^2$
    $= 16$ $= 36$ $= 100$

7. $625^{\frac{3}{4}} = \sqrt[4]{625^3}$ **8.** $32^{\frac{2}{5}} = \sqrt[5]{32^2}$ **9.** $10,000^{\frac{5}{4}} = \sqrt[4]{10,000^5}$
    $= 5^3$ $= 2^2$ $= 10^5$
    $= 125$ $= 4$ $= 100,000$

PROBLEM SOLVING 4-2

LESSON 4-2 Problem Solving
Look for a Pattern in Integer Exponents

Write the correct answer.

1. The weight of 10^7 dust particles is 1 gram. Evaluate 10^7.
10,000,000

2. The weight of one dust particle is 10^{-7} gram. Evaluate 10^{-7}.
0.0000001

3. As of 2001, only 10^6 rural homes in the United States had broadband Internet access. Evaluate 10^6.
1,000,000

4. Atomic clocks measure time in microseconds. A microsecond is 10^{-6} second. Evaluate 10^{-6}.
0.000001

Choose the letter for the best answer.

5. The diameter of the nucleus of an atom is about 10^{-15} meter. Evaluate 10^{-15}.
   A 0.0000000000001
   B 0.00000000000001
   C 0.000000000000001
   Ⓓ 0.000000000000001

6. The diameter of the nucleus of an atom is 0.000001 nanometer. How many nanometers is the diameter of the nucleus of an atom?
   F $(-10)^5$
   G $(-10)^6$
   Ⓗ 10^{-6}
   J 10^{-5}

7. A ruby-throated hummingbird weighs about 3^{-2} ounce. Evaluate 3^{-2}.
   A -9
   B -6
   Ⓒ $\dfrac{1}{9}$
   D $\dfrac{1}{6}$

8. A ruby-throated hummingbird breathes 2×5^3 times per minute while at rest. Evaluate this amount.
   F 1,000
   Ⓖ 250
   H 125
   J 30

4-3 Properties of Exponents

Learn to apply the properties of exponents.

The factors of a power, such as 7^4, can be grouped in different ways. Notice the relationship of the exponents in each product.

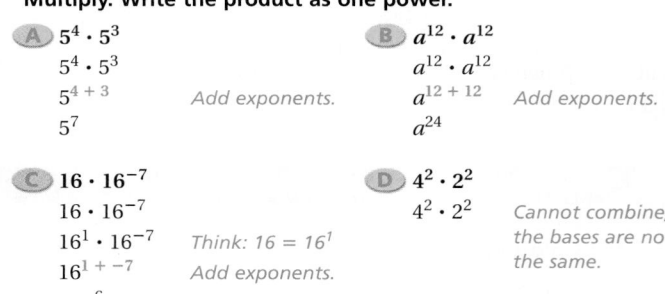

$7 \cdot 7 \cdot 7 \cdot 7 = 7^4$
$(7 \cdot 7 \cdot 7) \cdot 7 = 7^3 \cdot 7^1 = 7^4$
$(7 \cdot 7) \cdot (7 \cdot 7) = 7^2 \cdot 7^2 = 7^4$

MULTIPLYING POWERS WITH THE SAME BASE		
Words	**Numbers**	**Algebra**
To multiply powers with the same base, keep the base and add the exponents.	$3^5 \cdot 3^8 = 3^{5+8} = 3^{13}$	$b^m \cdot b^n = b^{m+n}$

EXAMPLE 1 Multiplying Powers with the Same Base

Multiply. Write the product as one power.

A $5^4 \cdot 5^3$
$5^4 \cdot 5^3$
5^{4+3} *Add exponents.*
5^7

B $a^{12} \cdot a^{12}$
$a^{12} \cdot a^{12}$
a^{12+12} *Add exponents.*
a^{24}

C $16 \cdot 16^{-7}$
$16 \cdot 16^{-7}$
$16^1 \cdot 16^{-7}$ *Think: $16 = 16^1$*
16^{1+-7} *Add exponents.*
16^{-6}

D $4^2 \cdot 2^2$
$4^2 \cdot 2^2$ *Cannot combine; the bases are not the same.*

Notice what occurs when you divide powers with the same base.

$$\frac{5^5}{5^3} = \frac{5 \cdot 5 \cdot 5 \cdot 5 \cdot 5}{5 \cdot 5 \cdot 5} = \frac{\cancel{5} \cdot \cancel{5} \cdot \cancel{5} \cdot 5 \cdot 5}{\cancel{5} \cdot \cancel{5} \cdot \cancel{5}} = 5 \cdot 5 = 5^2$$

DIVIDING POWERS WITH THE SAME BASE		
Words	**Numbers**	**Algebra**
To divide powers with the same base, keep the base and subtract the exponents.	$\frac{6^9}{6^4} = 6^{9-4} = 6^5$	$\frac{b^m}{b^n} = b^{m-n}$

1 Introduce

Alternate Opener

Motivate

Before introducing students to the properties of exponents, review what an exponent is. Write an expression such as 3^5 on the chalkboard. Have students identify the base and the exponent. Ask them for a step-by-step explanation of how to simplify the expression using multiplication. Encourage students to use the proper vocabulary.

base: 3; exponent: 5; $3 \cdot 3 \cdot 3 \cdot 3 \cdot 3 = 243$

Explorations and answers are provided in *Alternate Openers: Explorations Transparencies*.

EXAMPLE **2** **Dividing Powers with the Same Base**

Divide. Write the quotient as one power.

A $\dfrac{10^8}{10^5}$

$\dfrac{10^8}{10^5}$

10^{8-5} *Subtract exponents.*

10^3

B $\dfrac{x^9}{y^4}$

$\dfrac{x^9}{y^4}$ *Cannot combine; the bases are not the same.*

To see what happens when you raise a power to a power, use the order of operations.

$(4^3)^2 = (4 \cdot 4 \cdot 4)^2$ *Evaluate the power inside the parentheses.*

$= (4 \cdot 4 \cdot 4) \cdot (4 \cdot 4 \cdot 4)$ *Evaluate the power outside the parentheses.*

$= 4^6$

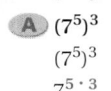 **Reading Math**

$(9^4)^5$ is read as "nine to the fourth, to the fifth."

RAISING A POWER TO A POWER		
Words	**Numbers**	**Algebra**
To raise a power to a power, keep the base and multiply the exponents.	$(9^4)^5 = 9^{4 \cdot 5} = 9^{20}$	$(b^m)^n = b^{m \cdot n}$

EXAMPLE **3** **Raising a Power to a Power**

Simplify.

A $(7^5)^3$

$(7^5)^3$ *Multiply exponents.*

$7^{5 \cdot 3}$

7^{15}

B $(8^9)^{11}$

$(8^9)^{11}$ *Multiply exponents.*

$8^{9 \cdot 11}$

8^{99}

C $(2^{-7})^{-2}$

$(2^{-7})^{-2}$

$2^{-7 \cdot (-2)}$ *Multiply exponents.*

2^{14}

D $(12^{10})^{-6}$

$(12^{10})^{-6}$ *Multiply exponents.*

$12^{10 \cdot (-6)}$

12^{-60}

Think and Discuss

1. Explain why the exponents cannot be added in the product $14^3 \cdot 18^3$.

2. List two ways to express 4^5 as a product of powers.

Power Presentations with PowerPoint®

Additional Examples

Example **1**

Multiply. Write the product as one power.

A. $6^6 \cdot 6^3$ 6^9 **B.** $n^5 \cdot n^7$ n^{12}

C. $2^5 \cdot 2$ 2^6 **D.** $24^4 \cdot 24^4$ 24^8

Example **2**

Divide. Write the quotient as one power.

A. $\dfrac{7^5}{7^3}$ 7^2 **B.** $\dfrac{x^{10}}{x^9}$ x^1 or x

Example **3**

Simplify.

A. $(5^4)^2$ 5^8 **B.** $(6^7)^9$ 6^{63}

C. $\left(\left(\frac{2}{3}\right)^{12}\right)^{-3}$ $\frac{2}{3}^{-36}$ **D.** $(17^2)^{-20}$ 17^{-40}

Also available on transparency

Possible answers to *Think and Discuss*

1. The exponents cannot be added because the bases are not the same. However, the bases could be multiplied together under the same exponent, for example, $(14 \cdot 18)^3$.

2. $4^5 \cdot 4^0$, $4^3 \cdot 4^2$, $2^5 \cdot 2^5$, $2^8 \cdot 2^2$

2 Teach

Guided Instruction

In this lesson, students learn to apply the properties of exponents and to evaluate the zero exponent. Help students discover the property $b^m \cdot b^n = b^{m+n}$ by having them write several expressions in expanded form, such as $2^3 \cdot 2^4 = (2 \cdot 2 \cdot 2)(2 \cdot 2 \cdot 2 \cdot 2) = 2^7$. Use a similar process for the property $\dfrac{b^m}{b^n} = b^{m-n}$. You may want to display the Teaching Transparency. To discover the property $a^0 = 1$ if $a \neq 0$, have students write several statements, such as $\dfrac{5^2}{5^2}$, and simplify them using both the expansion method and the properties of exponents.

Reaching All Learners
Through Critical Thinking

To reinforce the concepts that $x = x^1$ and $x^0 = 1$ for $x \neq 0$, ask students to simplify the following expressions using both the expansion method and the properties of exponents: $4 \cdot 4^2$ and $4^0 \cdot 4^2$. Have students compare the results.

Possible answers:
$4 \cdot 4^2 = (4)(4 \cdot 4) = 4^3$
$4 \cdot 4^2 = 4^1 \cdot 4^2 = 4^{1+2} = 4^3$
$4^0 \cdot 4^2 = 4^{0+2} = 4^2$
$4^0 \cdot 4^2 = (1)(4 \cdot 4) = 4^2$

3 Close

Summarize

Review the rules by showing an example for each and then showing the same example in expanded form. Remind students that if they have trouble remembering the rules, they can use the expansion method to relearn them. Ask students which method would be better for solving a problem with large exponents, such as $\dfrac{7^{23}}{7^{19}}$, and have them explain their answers.

Possible answer: The rules would be better because the expansion would take a lot of time and space to work out.

4-3 Exercises

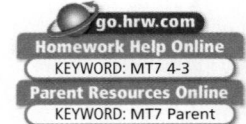

go.hrw.com
Homework Help Online
KEYWORD: MT7 4-3
Parent Resources Online
KEYWORD: MT7 Parent

Assignment Guide

If you finished Example **1** assign:
Average 1–4, 13–16, 26, 29, 30, 32, 36, 49–60
Advanced 13–16, 26, 29, 30, 32, 36, 41, 45, 49–60

If you finished Example **2** assign:
Average 1–8, 13–20, 25–30, 32–36, 38, 49–60
Advanced 13–20, 35–41, 43, 45–60

If you finished Example **3** assign:
Average 1–36, 38, 49–60
Advanced 13–24, 35–60

Homework Quick Check
Quickly check key concepts.
Exercises: 16, 18, 24, 28, 38

Math Background

Students may have trouble understanding the rule $a^0 = 1$, if $a \neq 0$. Recall that an exponent indicates the number of times the base is used as a factor. An exponent of 0 indicates that the base is not used as a factor at all; the only factor is 1. This approach can also be demonstrated in the following pattern:

$2^4 = 1 \cdot 2^4 = 1 \cdot 2 \cdot 2 \cdot 2 \cdot 2$
$2^3 = 1 \cdot 2^3 = 1 \cdot 2 \cdot 2 \cdot 2$
$2^2 = 1 \cdot 2^2 = 1 \cdot 2 \cdot 2$
$2^1 = 1 \cdot 2^1 = 1 \cdot 2$
$2^0 = 1 \cdot 2^0 = 1$

GUIDED PRACTICE

See Example **1** **Multiply. Write the product as one power.**

1. $5^6 \cdot 5^9$ 5^{15} **2.** $12^3 \cdot 12^{-2}$ 12 **3.** $m \cdot m^3$ m^4 **4.** $5^3 \cdot 7^3$ cannot combine

See Example **2** **Divide. Write the quotient as one power.**

5. $\frac{6^5}{6^3}$ 6^2 **6.** $\frac{a^8}{a^{-1}}$ a^9 **7.** $\frac{12^5}{12^5}$ $12^0 = 1$ **8.** $\frac{5^{16}}{5^4}$ 5^{12}

See Example **3** **Simplify.**

9. $(3^4)^5$ 3^{20} **10.** $(2^2)^0$ $2^0 = 1$ **11.** $(4^{-2})^3$ 4^{-6} or $\frac{1}{4^6}$ **12.** $(-y^2)^6$ $-y^{12}$

INDEPENDENT PRACTICE

See Example **1** **Multiply. Write the product as one power.**

13. $10^{10} \cdot 10^7$ 10^{17} **14.** $3^4 \cdot 3^4$ 3^8 **15.** $r^3 \cdot r^{-2}$ r **16.** $18 \cdot 18^5$ 18^6

See Example **2** **Divide. Write the quotient as one power.**

17. $\frac{5^{10}}{5^6}$ 5^4 **18.** $\frac{m^{10}}{d^3}$ cannot combine **19.** $\frac{t^9}{t^{-4}}$ t^{13} **20.** $\frac{12^5}{12^5}$ $12^0 = 1$

See Example **3** **Simplify.**

21. $(5^0)^8$ $5^0 = 1$ **22.** $(6^4)^{-1}$ 6^{-4} **23.** $(3^{-2})^2$ 3^{-4} **24.** $(x^5)^2$ x^{10}

PRACTICE AND PROBLEM SOLVING

Extra Practice
See page 788.

Simplify. Write the product or quotient as one power.

25. $\frac{4^7}{4^3}$ 4^4 **26.** $3^8 \cdot 3^{-1}$ 3^7 **27.** $\frac{a^4}{a^{-3}}$ a^7 **28.** $\frac{10^{18}}{10^9}$ 10^9

29. $x^3 \cdot x^7$ x^{10} **30.** $a^6 \cdot b^9$ cannot combine **31.** $(7^4)^3$ 7^{12} **32.** $2 \cdot 2^4$ 2^5

33. $\frac{10^4}{5^2}$ cannot combine **34.** $\frac{11^7}{11^6}$ 11^1 or 11 **35.** $\frac{y^8}{y^8}$ $y^0 = 1$ **36.** $y^8 \cdot y^{-8}$ 1

37. There are 26^3 ways to make a 3-letter "word" (from *aaa* to *zzz*) and 26^5 ways to make a 5-letter word. How many times more ways are there to make a 5-letter word than a 3-letter word? 26^2, or 676

38. Astronomy The mass of the sun is about 10^{27} metric tons, or 10^{30} kilograms. How many kilograms are in one metric ton? 10^3 kg, or 1000 kg

39. Business Using the manufacturing terms below, tell how many dozen are in a great gross. How many gross are in a great gross? 12^2; 12^1

1 dozen	= 12^1 items
1 gross	= 12^2 items
1 great gross	= 12^3 items

go.hrw.com
State Resources Online
KEYWORD: MT7 Resources

State Resources

RETEACH 4-3

Reteach
4-3 Properties of Exponents

To multiply powers with the same base, keep the base and add exponents.
$x^a \cdot x^b = x^{a+b}$
$4^5 \cdot 4^2 = 4^{5+2} = 4^7$
$8^3 \cdot 8 = 8^{3+1} = 8^4$

To divide powers with the same base, keep the base and subtract exponents.
$x^a \div x^b = x^{a-b}$
$4^5 \div 4^2 = 4^{5-2} = 4^3$
$8^3 \div 8 = 8^{3-1} = 8^2$

To raise a power to a power, keep the base and multiply exponents.
$(x^a)^b = x^{ab}$
$(4^5)^2 = 4^{5(2)} = 4^{10}$

Complete to see why the rules for exponents work.

1. $4^5 \cdot 4^2 = (\underline{4})(\underline{4})(\underline{4})(\underline{4})(\underline{4}) \cdot (\underline{4})(\underline{4}) = 4^{\underline{7}}$
2. $8^3 \cdot 8 = (\underline{8})(\underline{8})(\underline{8}) \cdot (\underline{8}) = 8^{\underline{4}}$
3. $4^5 \div 4^2 = \frac{4^5}{4^2} = \frac{4 \cdot 4 \cdot 4 \cdot 4 \cdot 4}{4 \cdot 4} = 4^{\underline{3}}$
4. $8^3 \div 8 = \frac{8^3}{8} = \frac{8 \cdot 8 \cdot 8}{8} = 8^{\underline{2}}$
5. $(4^2)^3 = 4^2 \cdot 4^2 \cdot 4^2 = 4^{2+2+2} = 4^{\underline{6}}$

Complete to write each product or quotient as one power.

6. $12^3 \cdot 12^2 = 12^{3+2} = 12^{\underline{5}}$
7. $9^4 \cdot 9^3 = 9^{4+3} = 9^{\underline{7}}$
8. $\frac{7^6}{7^2} = 7^{6-2} = 7^{\underline{4}}$
9. $\frac{12^6}{12^4} = 12^{6-4} = 12^{\underline{2}}$

Write each product or quotient as one power.

10. $10^4 \cdot 10^6 = \underline{10^{10}}$
11. $5^5 \cdot 5 = \underline{5^6}$
12. $4^5 \cdot 4 \cdot 4^3 = \underline{4^9}$
13. $\frac{15^6}{15^2} = \underline{15^4}$
14. $\frac{9^6}{9} = \underline{9^4}$
15. $\frac{2^{10}}{2^2} = \underline{2^8}$

Simplify.

16. $(5^3)^4 = 5^{3(4)} = \underline{5^{12}}$
17. $(6^2)^4 = 6^{2(4)} = \underline{6^8}$
18. $(2^5)^2 = \underline{2^{10}}$

PRACTICE 4-3

Practice B
4-3 Properties of Exponents

Multiply. Write the product as one power.

1. $10^5 \cdot 10^7$ $\underline{10^{12}}$
2. $x^9 \cdot x^8$ $\underline{x^{17}}$
3. $14^7 \cdot 14^9$ $\underline{14^{16}}$
4. $12^6 \cdot 12^8$ $\underline{12^{14}}$
5. $y^{12} \cdot y^{10}$ $\underline{y^{22}}$
6. $15^9 \cdot 15^{14}$ $\underline{15^{23}}$
7. $(-11)^{20} \cdot (-11)^{10}$ $\underline{(-11)^{30}}$
8. $(-a)^6 \cdot (-a)^7$ $\underline{(-a)^{13}}$

Divide. Write the quotient as one power.

9. $\frac{(-11)^{12}}{12^2}$ $\underline{12^7}$
10. $\frac{(-11)^{12}}{(-11)^8}$ $\underline{(-11)^4}$
11. $\frac{x^{10}}{x^5}$ $\underline{x^5}$
12. $\frac{16^{10}}{16^2}$ $\underline{16^8}$
13. $\frac{17^{19}}{17^2}$ $\underline{17^{17}}$
14. $\frac{14^{15}}{14^{13}}$ $\underline{14^2}$
15. $\frac{23^{17}}{23^9}$ $\underline{23^8}$
16. $\frac{(-a)^{12}}{(-a)^7}$ $\underline{(-a)^5}$

Simplify.

17. $(6^2)^4$ $\underline{6^8}$
18. $(2^4)^{-3}$ $\underline{2^{-12}}$
19. $(3^5)^{-1}$ $\underline{3^{-5}}$
20. $(y^5)^2$ $\underline{y^{10}}$
21. $(9^{-2})^3$ $\underline{9^{-6}}$
22. $(10^0)^3$ $\underline{10^0}$
23. $(x^4)^{-2}$ $\underline{x^{-8}}$
24. $(5^{-2})^0$ $\underline{5^0}$

Write the product or quotient as one power.

25. $\frac{w^{12}}{w^3}$ $\underline{w^9}$
26. $d^8 \cdot d^5$ $\underline{d^{13}}$
27. $(-15)^5 \cdot (-15)^{10}$ $\underline{(-15)^{15}}$

28. Jefferson High School has a student body of 6^4 students. Each class has approximately 6^2 students. How many classes does the school have? Write the answer as one power.
$\underline{6^2}$

29. Write the expression for a number used as a factor fifteen times multiplied by a number used as a factor ten times. Then, write the product as one power.
$\underline{x^{15} \cdot x^{10} = x^{25}}$

40. Estimation The distance from Earth to the moon is about 22^4 miles. The distance from Earth to Neptune is about 22^7 miles. Which distance is greater? About how much greater? **distance from Earth to Neptune; 22^3, or 2,494,123,632 mi greater**

Find the missing exponent.

41. $b^{\blacksquare} \cdot b^4 = b^8$ **4** **42.** $(v^2)^{\blacksquare} = v^{-6}$ **−3** **43.** $\dfrac{w^{\blacksquare}}{w^3} = w^{-3}$ **0** **44.** $(a^4)^{\blacksquare} = a^0$ **0**

45. A googol is the number 1 followed by 100 zeros.
   a. What is a googol written as a power? 10^{100}
   b. What is a googol times a googol written as a power? 10^{200}

46. What's the Error? A student said that $\dfrac{3^5}{9^5}$ is the same as $\dfrac{1}{3}$. What mistake has the student made? **Possible answer: The student did not consider the exponents.**

47. Write About It Why do you subtract exponents when dividing powers with the same base?

48. Challenge A number to the 11th power divided by the same number to the 8th power equals 64. What is the number? **4**

TEST PREP and Spiral Review

49. Multiple Choice In computer technology, a kilobyte is 2^{10} bytes in size. A gigabyte is 2^{30} bytes in size. The size of a terabyte is the product of the size of a kilobyte and the size of a gigabyte. What is the size of a terabyte?

Ⓐ 2^{20} bytes   Ⓑ 2^{40} bytes   Ⓒ 2^{300} bytes   Ⓓ 4^{300} bytes

50. Short Response A student claims that $10^3 \cdot 10^{-5}$ is greater than 1. Explain whether the student is correct. $10^3 \cdot 10^{-5} = 10^{3 + (-5)} = 10^{-2} = \dfrac{1}{10^2} = \dfrac{1}{100}$; $\dfrac{1}{100}$ **is less than 1.**

Evaluate each expression for the given value of the variable. (Lesson 2-3)

51. $19.4 - x$ for $x = -5.6$ **25** **52.** $11 - r$ for $r = 13.5$ **−2.5** **53.** $p + 65.1$ for $p = -42.3$ **22.8**

54. $-\dfrac{3}{7} - t$ for $t = 1\dfrac{5}{7}$ **$-2\dfrac{1}{7}$** **55.** $3\dfrac{5}{11} + y$ for $y = -2\dfrac{4}{11}$ **$1\dfrac{1}{11}$** **56.** $-\dfrac{1}{19} + g$ for $g = \dfrac{18}{19}$ **$\dfrac{17}{19}$**

Evaluate. (Lesson 4-2)

57. $(-3)^{-2}$ **$\dfrac{1}{9}$** **58.** $(-2)^{-3}$ **$-\dfrac{1}{8}$** **59.** 1^{-3} **1** **60.** $-(2)^{-4}$ **$-\dfrac{1}{16}$**

CHALLENGE 4-3

LESSON 4-3 Challenge
Square Dance

Study these patterns.

$1 = 1^2$

$1^2 + 1 + 2 = 4 = 2^2$

$2^2 + 2 + 3 = 9 = 3^2$

$3^2 + 3 + 4 = 16 = 4^2$

So, according to the pattern, 5^2 can be written as the sum of 4^2 and two consecutive integers.

1. Draw a diagram and write an equation to illustrate 5^2.

Equation: _____ $4^2 + 4 + 5 = 25 = 5^2$

2. Draw a diagram and write an equation to illustrate 8^2.

Equation: _____ $7^2 + 7 + 8 = 64 = 8^2$

3. Use the pattern to write an equation to indicate that, for any integer n, $(n + 1)^2$ can be written as the sum of n^2 and two consecutive integers.

Equation: _____ $n^2 + (n) + (n + 1) = (n + 1)^2$

4. If you know that $20^2 = 400$, use the pattern to calculate 21^2.

$21^2 = $ _____ $400 + 20 + 21 = 441$

PROBLEM SOLVING 4-3

LESSON 4-3 Problem Solving
Properties of Exponents

Write each answer as a power.

1. Cindy separated her fruit flies into equal groups. She estimates that there are 2^{10} fruit flies in each of 2^2 jars. How many fruit flies does Cindy have in all?

2^{12} fruit flies

2. Suppose a researcher tests a new method of pasteurization on a strain of bacteria in his laboratory. If the bacteria are killed at a rate of 8^9 per sec, how many bacteria would be killed after 8^2 sec?

8^{11} bacteria

3. A satellite orbits the earth at about 13^4 km per hour. How long would it take to complete 24 orbits, which is a distance of about 13^5 km?

13 hr

4. The side of a cube is 3^4 centimeters long. What is the volume of the cube? (Hint: $V = s^3$.)

3^{12} cm

Use the table to answer Exercises 5–6. The table describes the number of people involved at each level of a pyramid scheme. In a pyramid scheme each individual recruits so many others to participate who in turn recruit others, and so on. Choose the letter of the best answer.

5. Using exponents, how many people will be involved at level 6?
A 6^6 C 5^5
B 6^5 Ⓓ 5^6

6. How many more people will be involved at level 6 than at level 2?
Ⓕ 5^4 H 5^5
G 5^3 J 5^6

7. There are 10^3 ways to make a 3-digit combination, but there are 10^6 ways to make a 6-digit combination. How many times more ways are there to make a 6-digit combination than a 3-digit combination?
A 5^{10} C 2^5
B 2^{10} Ⓓ 10^3

8. After 3 hours, a bacteria colony has $(25^3)^3$ bacteria present. How many bacteria are in the colony?
F 25^1 Ⓗ 25^9
G 25^6 J 25^{33}

Pyramid Scheme
Each person recruits 5 others.

Level	Total Number of People
1	5
2	5^2
3	5^3
4	5^4

ONGOING ASSESSMENT and **INTERVENTION**

Diagnose Before the Lesson
4-3 Warm Up, TE p. 170

Monitor During the Lesson
4-3 Know-It Notebook
4-3 Questioning Strategies

Assess After the Lesson
4-3 Lesson Quiz, TE p. 173

Answers

47. Possible answer: Dividing is the same as multiplying by the reciprocal, so when dividing powers with the same base, you add the opposite of the exponent in the denominator. This is the same as subtracting the exponents.

TEST PREP DOCTOR Some students will see that the expression in Exercise 50 is positive and agree with the student's claim. Remind students that there are positive numbers that are less than one, and encourage them to write down all of their work.

Journal

Ask students to write about a topic in science or any other subject that seems likely to make use of large numbers.

Power Presentations with PowerPoint®

4-3 Lesson Quiz
Write the product or quotient as one power.

1. $n^3 \times n^4$ n^7

2. $8 \cdot 8^8$ 8^9

3. $\dfrac{10^9}{10^5}$ 10^4

4. $\dfrac{t^9}{t^7}$ t^2

5. $3^2 \cdot 3^3 \cdot 3^5$ 3^{10}

6. $(m^2)^{19}$ m^{38}

7. $(9^{-8})^9$ 9^{-72}

8. $(10^4)^0$ 1

Also available on transparency

Pacing: Traditional 1 day
Block $\frac{1}{2}$ day

Objective: Students express large and small numbers in scientific notation and compare two numbers written in scientific notation.

 Technology Lab
In *Technology Lab Activities*

 Online Edition
Tutorial Videos, Interactivities

Countdown to Testing Week 6

 **Power Presentations**
with PowerPoint®

Warm Up

Order each set of numbers from least to greatest.

1. $10^4, 10^{-2}, 10^0, 10^{-1}$
$10^{-2}, 10^{-1}, 10^0, 10^4$

2. $8^2, 8^{-2}, 8^3, 8^0$
$8^{-2}, 8^0, 8^2, 8^3$

3. $2^3, 2^{-6}, 2^{-4}, 2^1$
$2^{-6}, 2^{-4}, 2^1, 2^3$

4. $5.2^2, 5.2^9, 5.2^{-1}, 5.2^{-2}$
$5.2^{-2}, 5.2^{-1}, 5.2^2, 5.2^9$

Problem of the Day

Order the powers from least to greatest: $(3^3)^3, 3^{(3^3)}, \left((-3^3)^3\right)^3$
$\left((-3^3)^3\right)^3, (3^3)^3, 3^{(3^3)}$

Also available on transparency

State Resources

 **go.hrw.com**
State Resources Online
KEYWORD: MT7 Resources

Learn to express large and small numbers in scientific notation and to compare two numbers written in scientific notation.

Vocabulary
scientific notation

An ordinary quarter contains about 97,700,000,000,000,000,000,000 atoms. The average size of an atom is about 0.00000003 centimeter across.

The length of these numbers in standard notation makes them awkward to work with. **Scientific notation** is a shorthand way of writing such numbers.

To express any number in scientific notation, write it as the product of a power of ten and a number greater than or equal to 1 but less than 10.

In scientific notation, the number of atoms in a quarter is 9.77×10^{22}, and the size of each atom is 3.0×10^{-8} centimeters across.

$$9.77 \times 10^{22}$$

EXAMPLE 1 **Translating Scientific Notation to Standard Notation**

Write each number in standard notation.

A 3.12×10^9
3.12×10^9
$3.12 \times 1,000,000,000$ *$10^9 = 1,000,000,000$*
$3,120,000,000$ *Think: Move the decimal right 9 places.*

Helpful Hint

A positive exponent means move the decimal to the right. A negative exponent means move the decimal to the left.

B 1.35×10^{-4}
1.35×10^{-4}
$1.35 \times \frac{1}{10,000}$ *$10^{-4} = \frac{1}{10,000}$*
$1.35 \div 10,000$ *Divide by the reciprocal.*
0.000135 *Think: Move the decimal left 4 places.*

C -4.7×10^7
-4.7×10^7
$-4.7 \times 10,000,000$ *$10^7 = 10,000,000$*
$-47,000,000$ *Think: Move the decimal right 7 places.*

1 Introduce
Alternate Opener

EXPLORATION

 **4-4** **Scientific Notation**

1. Complete the table of values for the powers of ten.

Exponent	Power
−6	$10^{-6} =$
−5	$10^{-5} =$
−4	$10^{-4} =$
−3	$10^{-3} =$
−2	$10^{-2} = \frac{1}{10^2} = \frac{1}{10 \times 10} = 0.01$
−1	$10^{-1} = \frac{1}{10^1} = \frac{1}{10} = 0.1$
0	$10^0 = 1$
1	$10^1 = 10$
2	$10^2 = 10 \times 10 = 100$
3	$10^3 =$
4	$10^4 =$
5	$10^5 =$
6	$10^6 =$

Think and Discuss
2. Discuss the pattern you see in the table of values for powers of ten.
3. Explain how you know that $10^{-9} = 0.000000001$.

Motivate

Ask students how they would simplify the following expressions: 2×10^1, 3.5×10^4, and 3.5×10^{15}. Show them how to multiply by a power of ten by moving the decimal point to the right the number of spaces equal to the exponent and then adding zeros. Show some examples and explain that this lesson is about using powers of ten to simplify working with large and small numbers.

Explorations and answers are provided in *Alternate Openers: Explorations Transparencies.*

EXAMPLE 2 **Translating Standard Notation to Scientific Notation**

Write 0.0000003 in scientific notation.

0.0000003

3   *Think: The decimal needs to move 7 places to get a number between 1 and 10.*

$3 \times 10^{\blacksquare}$ *Set up scientific notation.*

Think: The decimal needs to move left to change 3 to 0.0000003, so the exponent will be negative.

So 0.0000003 written in scientific notation is 3×10^{-7}.

Check $3 \times 10^{-7} = 3 \times 0.0000001$
                $= 0.0000003$

EXAMPLE 3 *Money Application*

Suppose you have a million dollars in pennies. A penny is 1.55 mm thick. How tall would a stack of all your pennies be? Write the answer in scientific notation.

$1.00 = 100$ pennies
$1,000,000 = 100,000,000$ pennies   *Multiply each side by 1,000,000.*
1.55 mm $\times 100,000,000$ *Find the total height.*
$155,000,000$ mm   *Multiply.*

$1.55 \times 10^{\blacksquare}$ *Set up scientific notation.*

Think: The decimal needs to move 8 places.

Think: The decimal needs to move right to change 1.55 to 155,000,000, so the exponent will be positive.

In scientific notation the total height of one million dollars in stacked pennies is 1.55×10^8 mm. This is about 96 miles tall.

To compare two numbers written in scientific notation, first compare the powers of ten. The number with the greater power of ten is greater. If the powers of ten are the same, compare the values between one and ten.

$2.7 \times 10^{13} > 2.7 \times 10^9$ $10^{13} > 10^9$

$3.98 \times 10^{22} > 2.52 \times 10^{22}$ $3.98 > 2.52$

2 Teach

Guided Instruction

In this lesson, students learn to express large and small numbers in scientific notation. First, show students how to convert scientific notation to standard notation. Review how to multiply by a power of ten by moving the decimal point to the left or right. Move the decimal point to the right for a positive exponent and to the left for a negative exponent.

Next, discuss how to write numbers in standard notation in scientific notation. Show students how to move the decimal so there is only one digit in front of the decimal point. Then write the correct power of ten by counting the number of decimal spaces moved.

Reaching All Learners
Through Home Connection

Have students work with an adult to find some real-world examples of very large or very small numbers. They may find these examples in newspapers, books, or magazines, or they may use an example from the adult's workplace. Have students record five numbers and write them in both standard notation and scientific notation.

Check students' work.

Possible answers to *Think and Discuss*

1. It makes extremely large or extremely small numbers less awkward to use.

2. The exponent is 6 and the sign of the exponent is positive, so move the decimal six places to the right.

3. The speed of a car, because it is usually a 1-, 2-, or 3-digit number.

EXAMPLE 4 *Life Science Application*

The major components of human blood are red blood cells, white blood cells, platelets, and plasma. A typical red blood cell has a diameter of approximately 7×10^{-6} meter. A typical platelet has a diameter of approximately 2.33×10^{-6} meter. Which has a greater diameter, a red blood cell or a platelet?

$7 \times 10^{-6} \ \blacksquare \ 2.33 \times 10^{-6}$

$10^{-6} = 10^{-6}$ *Compare powers of 10.*

$7 > 2.33$ *Compare the values between 1 and 10.*

$7 \times 10^{-6} > 2.33 \times 10^{-6}$

A typical red blood cell has a greater diameter than a typical platelet.

Think and Discuss

1. **Explain** the benefit of writing numbers in scientific notation.

2. **Describe** how to write 2.977×10^{6} in standard notation.

3. **Determine** which measurement would be least likely to be written in scientific notation: size of bacteria, speed of a car, or number of stars in a galaxy.

4-4 Exercises

4-4 Exercises

go.hrw.com
Homework Help Online
KEYWORD: MT7 4-4
Parent Resources Online
KEYWORD: MT7 Parent

Assignment Guide

If you finished Example **1** assign:
Average   1–4, 11–14, 21–26, 34, 53–60
Advanced   11–14, 27–32, 34, 50, 53–60

If you finished Example **2** assign:
Average   1–8, 11–18, 21–26, 34, 36–42, 53–60
Advanced   11–18, 27–32, 34, 36, 43–48, 50, 53–60

If you finished Example **3** assign:
Average   1–9, 11–19, 21–26, 33, 34, 36–42, 53–60
Advanced   11–19, 29–42, 50, 53–60

If you finished Example **4** assign:
Average   1–26, 33, 34, 36–42, 49, 51, 53–60
Advanced   11–20, 29–36, 43–60

Homework Quick Check

Quickly check key concepts.
Exercises: 12, 16, 19, 20, 36

GUIDED PRACTICE

See Example **1**   Write each number in standard notation.

1. 4.17×10^{3} **4170**
2. 1.33×10^{-5} **0.0000133**
3. 6.2×10^{7} **62,000,000**
4. 3.9×10^{-4} **0.00039**

See Example **2**   Write each number in scientific notation.

5. 0.000057   **5.7×10^{-5}**
6. 0.0004   **4×10^{-4}**
7. 6,980,000   **6.98×10^{6}**
8. 0.000000025   **2.5×10^{-8}**

See Example **3**   9. The distance from Earth to the Moon is about 384,000 km. Suppose an astronaut travels this distance a total of 250 times. How many kilometers does the astronaut travel? Write the answer in scientific notation. **9.6×10^{7}**

See Example **4**   10. The maximum length of a particle that can fit through a surgical mask is 1×10^{-4} millimeters. The average length of a dust mite is approximately 1.25×10^{-1} millimeters. Which is longer, the largest particle that can fit through a surgical mask or a dust mite of average length? **dust mite**

---

3 Close

Summarize

Discuss with students the meaning and uses of scientific notation. Ask them how many zeros are in a million dollars. Then ask how they would write one million in scientific notation. Repeat the process with one billion dollars. Challenge the class to write one cent in dollars in scientific notation.

Possible answers: Scientific notation is a way to write very large or very small numbers without including a lot of zeros. Scientific notation can make it easier to compare numbers. One million has six zeros, so it can be written as 1×10^{6}. One billion has nine zeros, so it can be written as 1×10^{9}. One cent can be written as 1×10^{-2} dollars.

INDEPENDENT PRACTICE

See Example ① Write each number in standard notation.

11. 9.2×10^6 **12.** 6.7×10^{-4} **13.** 3.6×10^{-2} **14.** 5.24×10^8
    9,200,000   **0.00067**   **0.036**   **524,000,000**

See Example ② Write each number in scientific notation.

15. 0.00007   **16.** 6,500,000   **17.** 100,000,000   **18.** 0.00000003
    7×10^{-5} 6.5×10^6 1×10^8 3×10^{-8}

See Example ③ 19. Protons and neutrons are the most massive particles in the nucleus of an atom. If a nucleus were the size of an average grape, it would have a mass greater than 9 million metric tons. A metric ton is 1000 kg. What would the mass of a grape-size nucleus be in kilograms? Write your answer in scientific notation. 9×10^9 **kg**

Atom

Electron

Proton   Neutron

Nucleus

See Example ④ 20. The orbits of Neptune and Pluto cross each other. Neptune's average distance from the Sun is approximately 4.5×10^9 kilometers. Pluto's average distance from the Sun is approximately 5.87×10^9 kilometers. Which planet has the greater average distance from the Sun? **Pluto**

PRACTICE AND PROBLEM SOLVING

Extra Practice
See page 788.

Write each number in standard notation.
                                                                0.0000021

21. 1.4×10^5 **22.** 3.24×10^{-2} **23.** 7.8×10^1 **78**   **24.** 2.1×10^{-6}
    140,000   **0.0324**
25. 5.3×10^{-8} **26.** 8.456×10^{-4} **27.** 5.59×10^5 **28.** 7.1×10^3
   0.000000053   **0.0008456**   **559,000**   **7100**
29. 7.113×10^6 **30.** 4.5×10^{-1} **31.** 2.9×10^{-4} **32.** 5.6×10^2 **560**
   7,113,000   **0.045**   **0.00029**

Life Science

33. Life Science Duckweed plants live on the surface of calm ponds and are the smallest flowering plants in the world. They weigh about 0.00015 g.

   a. Write this number in scientific notation. 1.5×10^{-4} **g**

   b. If left unchecked, one duckweed plant, which reproduces every 30–36 hours, could produce 1×10^{30} (a nonillion) plants in four months. How much would one nonillion duckweed plants weigh?
                                          1.5×10^{26} **g**

This frog is covered with duckweed plants. Duckweed plants can grow both in sunlight and in shade and produce tiny white flowers.

34. Life Science The diameter of a human red blood cell ranges from approximately 6×10^{-6} to 8×10^{-6} meters. Write this range in standard notation.   **0.000006 m to 0.000008 m**

35. Physical Science The *atomic mass* of an element is the mass, in grams, of one *mole* (mol), or 6.02×10^{23} atoms.
                            $2.5(6.02 \times 10^{23}) =$

   a. How many atoms are there in 2.5 mol of helium? 1.505×10^{24} **atoms**

   b. If you know that 2.5 mol of helium weighs 10 grams, what is the atomic mass of helium? $10 \div 2.5 = 4$ **g**

   c. Using your answer from part **b**, find the approximate mass of one atom of helium. $4 \div (6.02 \times 10^{23}) \approx 6.64 \times 10^{-24}$

Math Background

Although people often think of zero as having no value, it can make a number much greater or much smaller when used as a placeholder. For instance, by writing 11 zeros to the right of the number 2, you get the approximate number of stars in the Andromeda Galaxy, 200,000,000,000,000.

Writing numbers with so many zeros can be very cumbersome. Scientific notation was developed to alleviate this problem. Scientific notation can be used with very large and very small numbers, and it makes computation easier and tables more readable.

State Resources

go.hrw.com
State Resources Online
KEYWORD: MT7 Resources

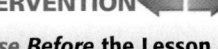
Answers

36. a. $\approx 2.21 \times 10^7$; $\approx 1.4 \times 10^4$ mi^2

b. $14{,}032 \div 22{,}113{,}250 \approx$ 0.000635; about 6.35×10^{-4} mi^2/person

51–53. See p. A5.

TEST PREP DOCTOR + Encourage students to read through the choices for Exercise 54 and eliminate answers that would be expressed with negative powers of 10. By doing so, students can eliminate choice **J.**

 Journal

Have students write a story about traveling from Earth to the Moon. Have them include estimates of the distance in scientific notation and the time it would take to get there.

Power Presentations
with PowerPoint®

4-4 Lesson Quiz

Write each number in standard notation.

1. 1.72×10^4 17,200

2. 6.9×10^{-3} 0.0069

Write each number in scientific notation.

3. 0.0053 5.3×10^{-3}

4. 57,000,000 5.7×10^7

5. Order the numbers from least to greatest.
2×10^{-4}, 9×10^{-5}, 7×10^{-5}
7×10^{-5}, 9×10^{-5}, 2×10^{-4}

6. A human body contains about 5.6×10^6 microliters of blood. Write this number in standard notation. 5,600,000

Also available on transparency

---

36. Social Studies

  a. Express the population and area of Taiwan in scientific notation.

  b. Divide the number of square miles by the population to find the number of square miles per person in Taiwan. Express your answer in scientific notation.

Taiwan	
Population:	22,113,250
Area:	14,032 mi^2
Capital:	Taipei
Number of televisions:	10,800,000
Languages:	Taiwanese (Min), Mandarin, Hakka dialects

Write each number in scientific notation.

37. 0.00858   **38.** 0.0000063   **39.** 5,900,000
8.58×10^{-3} 6.3×10^{-6} 5.9×10^6

40. 7,045,000,000 **41.** 0.0076   **42.** 400 4×10^2
7.045×10^9 7.6×10^{-3}

43. 4200   **44.** 0.0000000082 **45.** 0.0000000003 3×10^{-10}
4.2×10^3 8.2×10^{-9}

46. 0.000005   **47.** 7,000,000   **48.** 0.0095678
5×10^{-6} 7×10^6 9.5678×10^{-3}

49. Order the list of numbers below from least to greatest.
1.5×10^{-2}, 1.2×10^6, 5.85×10^{-3}, 2.3×10^{-2}, 5.5×10^6
5.85×10^{-3}, 1.5×10^{-2}, 2.3×10^{-2}, 1.2×10^6, 5.5×10^6

50. Write a Problem An electron has a mass of about 9.11×10^{-31} kg. Use this information to write a problem. **Possible answer: Write the mass of an electron in standard notation.**

51. Write About It Two numbers are written in scientific notation. How can you tell which number is greater?

52. Challenge Where on a number line does the value of a positive number in scientific notation with a negative exponent lie?

TEST PREP and Spiral Review

53. Short Response Explain how you can determine the sign of the exponent when 29,600,000,000,000 is written in scientific notation?

54. Multiple Choice The distance light can travel in one year is 9.46×10^{12} kilometers. What is this distance in standard form?

  (A) 94,600,000,000,000,000 km   (C) 9,460,000,000,000

  (B) 946,000,000,000 km   (D) 0.000000000946

Use each table to make a graph and to write an equation. (Lesson 3-5)

55.

x	0	5	6	4
y	−4	11	14	20

56.

x	0	1	3	6
y	6	7	9	12

Check students' graphs; $y = 3x - 4$.   Check students' graphs; $y = x + 6$.

Simplify. Write each product or quotient as one power. (Lesson 4-3)

57. $\dfrac{7^4}{7^2}$ 7^2 **58.** $5^3 \cdot 5^8$ 5^{11} **59.** $\dfrac{t^8}{t^5}$ t^3 **60.** $10^9 \cdot 10^{-3}$ 10^6

Technology LAB 4-4

Multiply and Divide Numbers in Scientific Notation

Use with Lesson 4-4

go.hrw.com
Lab Resources Online
KEYWORD: MT7 Lab4

You can use a graphing calculator to perform operations with numbers written in scientific notation. Use the key combination  to enter numbers in scientific notation. On a graphing calculator, 9.5×10^{16} is displayed as 9.5E16.

Activity

Use a calculator to find $(4.8 \times 10^{12})(9.4 \times 10^9)$.

Press 4.8 12 $\times$ 9.4  9 ENTER .

The calculator displays the answer 4.512 E22, which is the same as 4.512×10^{22}.

Think and Discuss

1. When you use the associative and communicative properties to multiply 4.8×10^{12} and 9.4×10^9, you get $(4.8 \cdot 9.4)(10^{12} \cdot 10^9) = 45.12 \times 10^{21}$. Explain why this answer is different from the answer you obtained in the activity.

Try This

Use a graphing calculator to evaluate each expression.

1. $(5.76 \times 10^{13})(6.23 \times 10^{-20})$

2. $\dfrac{9.7 \times 10^{10}}{2.9 \times 10^7}$

3. $(1.6 \times 10^5)(9.65 \times 10^9)$

4. $\dfrac{5.25 \times 10^{13}}{6.14 \times 10^8}$

5. $(1.1 \times 10^9)(2.2 \times 10^3)$

6. $\dfrac{8.56 \times 10^{97}}{2.34 \times 10^{80}}$

7. $(2.74 \times 10^{11})(3.2 \times 10^{-5})$
8.768×10^6

8. $\dfrac{5.82 \times 10^{-11}}{8.96 \times 10^{11}}$
$6.49553571 \times 10^{-23}$

9. $(4.5 \times 10^{12})(3.7 \times 10^8)$
1.665×10^{21}

10. The star Betelgeuse, in the constellation of Orion, is approximately 3.36×10^{15} miles from Earth. This is approximately 1.24×10^6 times as far as Pluto's minimum distance from Earth. What is Pluto's approximate minimum distance from Earth? Write your answer in scientific notation.
$\approx 2.71 \times 10^9$

11. If 446 billion telephone calls were placed by 135 million United States telephone subscribers, what was the average number of calls placed per subscriber?
3304 calls

Possible answers to *Think and Discuss*

1. Multiplying 4.8 and 9.4 produced an answer above ten, so it is not in scientific notation. In the Activity, the calculator automatically put the answer in scientific notation.

Answers to *Try This*

1. 3.5885×10^{-6}
2. ≈ 3344.83
3. 1.544×10^{15}
4. $\approx 85,504.89$
5. 2.42×10^{12}
6. $\approx 3.658 \times 10^{17}$

Organizer

Objective: Assess students' mastery of concepts and skills in Lessons 4-1 through 4-4.

Resources

 Assessment Resources
Section 4A Quiz

 Test & Practice Generator
One-Stop Planner®

INTERVENTION ⬅ ➡

Resources

 Ready to Go On?
Intervention and
Enrichment Worksheets

🔘 **Ready to Go On? CD-ROM**

🪐 **Ready to Go On? Online**

my.hrw.com

Ready to Go On?

Quiz for Lessons 4-1 Through 4-4

✅ 4-1 Exponents

Evaluate.

1. 10^1 **10**
2. 8^6 **262,144**
3. -3^4 **−81**
4. $(-5)^3$ **−125**
5. Write $5 \cdot 5 \cdot 5 \cdot 5$ in exponential form. 5^4
6. Evaluate $a^7 - 4b$ for $a = 3$ and $b = -1$. **2191**

✅ 4-2 Look for a Pattern in Integer Exponents

Evaluate.

7. 10^{-6} $\frac{1}{1,000,000}$
8. $(-3)^{-4}$ $\frac{1}{81}$
9. -6^{-2} $\frac{1}{36}$
10. 4^0 **1**
11. $8 + 10^0(-6)$ **2**
12. $5^{-1} + 3(5)^{-2}$ $\frac{8}{25}$
13. $-4^{-3} + 2^0$ $\frac{63}{64}$
14. $3^{-2} - (6^0 - 6^{-2})$ $-\frac{31}{36}$

✅ 4-3 Properties of Exponents

Simplify. Write the product or quotient as one power.

15. $9^3 \cdot 9^5$ 9^8
16. $\frac{5^{10}}{5^{10}}$ **1**
17. $q^9 \cdot q^6$ q^{15}
18. $3^3 \cdot 3^{-2}$ **3**

Simplify.

19. $(33)^{-2}$ 3^{-6}
20. $(4^2)^0$ **1**
21. $(-x^2)^4$ x^8
22. $(4^{-2})^5$ 4^{-10}

23. The mass of the known universe is about 10^{23} solar masses, which is 10^{50} metric tons. How many metric tons is one solar mass? 10^{27}

✅ 4-4 Scientific Notation

Write each number in scientific notation.

24. 0.00000015 1.5×10^{-7}
25. 99,980,000 9.998×10^7
26. 0.434 4.34×10^{-1}
27. 100 1×10^2

Write each number in standard notation.

28. 1.38×10^5 **138,000**
29. 4×10^6 **4,000,000**
30. 1.2×10^{-3} **0.0012**
31. 9.37×10^{-5} **0.0000937**

32. The average distance from Earth to the Sun is approximately 149,600,000 kilometers. Pluto is about 39.5 times as far from the Sun as Earth is. What is the approximate average distance from Pluto to the Sun? Write your answer in scientific notation. 5.9092×10^9 km

33. Picoplankton can be as small as 0.00002 centimeter. Microplankton are about 100 times as large as picoplankton. How large is a microplankton that is 100 times the size of the smallest picoplankton? Write your answer in scientific notation. 2×10^{-1}

READY TO GO ON?

Diagnose and Prescribe

 **NO INTERVENE**

 YES ENRICH

READY TO GO ON? Intervention, Section 4A		
Ready to Go On? Intervention	📝 **Worksheets**	💿 **CD-ROM**	🪐 **Online**
✅ Lesson 4-1	4-1 Intervention	Activity 4-1	
✅ Lesson 4-2	4-2 Intervention	Activity 4-2	Diagnose and Prescribe Online
✅ Lesson 4-3	4-3 Intervention	Activity 4-3	
✅ Lesson 4-4	4-4 Intervention	Activity 4-4	

READY TO GO ON? Enrichment, Section 4A

📝 **Worksheets**

💿 **CD-ROM**

🪐 **Online**

Focus on Problem Solving

Solve
- **Choose an operation**

To decide whether to add, subtract, multiply, or divide to solve a problem, you need to determine the action taking place in the problem.

Action	Operation
Combining numbers or putting numbers together	Addition
Taking away or finding out how far apart two numbers are	Subtraction
Combining equal groups	Multiplication
Splitting things into equal groups or finding how many equal groups you can make	Division

Determine the action for each problem. Write the problem using the actions. Then show what operation you used to get the answer.

❶ Mary is making a string of beads. If each bead is 7.0×10^{-1} cm wide, how many beads does she need to make a string that is 35 cm long?

❷ The total area of the United States is 9.63×10^6 square kilometers. The total area of Canada is 9.98×10^6 square kilometers. What is the total area of both the United States and Canada?

❸ Suppose $\frac{1}{3}$ of the fish in a lake are considered game fish. Of these, $\frac{2}{5}$ meet the legal minimum size requirement. What fraction of the fish in the lake are game fish that meet the legal minimum size requirement?

❹ Part of a checkbook register is shown below. Find the amount in the account after the transactions shown.

TRANSACTION	DATE	DESCRIPTION	AMOUNT	FEE	DEPOSITS	BALANCE	$287.34
		RECORD ALL CHARGES OR CREDITS THAT AFFECT YOUR ACCOUNT					$43.16
Withdrawal	11/16	autodebit for phone bill	$43.16				
							$27.56
Check 1256	11/18	groceries	$27.56				
							$74.23
Check 1257	11/23	new clothes	$74.23				
							$41.25
Withdrawal	11/27	ATM withdrawal	$40.00	$1.25			

Answers
1. 50
2. 19.61×10^6 km^2
3. $\frac{2}{15}$
4. $101.14

Objective: Focus on choosing an operation.

Online Edition

Resources

Chapter 4 Resource Book
Reading Strategies

Problem Solving Process
This page focuses on the third step of the problem-solving process: **Solve**

Discuss
Have students discuss which action is taking place in each problem, rewrite the problem using action words, and then indicate the operation used to get the answer.

Possible answers:

1. Finding how many equal groups you can make; how many equal lengths of 0.7 cm are there in 35 cm?; division.

2. Combining numbers; what is the total area of both countries?; addition.

3. Splitting things into equal groups (multiplying by a fraction is the same as dividing); what is $\frac{1}{3}$ of $\frac{2}{5}$?; multiplication.

4. Taking away; what remains of $287.34 after $43.16, $27.56, $74.23, and $41.25 have been taken away?; subtraction.

State Resources

go.hrw.com
State Resources Online
KEYWORD: MT7 Resources

Roots

One-Minute Section Planner

Lesson	Materials	MiC and Lab Resources
Lesson 4-5 Squares and Square Roots • Find square roots. ☐ SAT-10 ☑ ITBS ☑ CTBS ☑ NAEP	Calculators, index cards	**MiC:** *Revisiting Numbers* pp. 50–51 **MiC:** *Patterns and Figures* pp. 20–25
Lesson 4-6 Estimating Square Roots • Estimate square roots to a given number of decimal places and solve problems using square roots. **4-6 Technology Lab** Evaluate Powers and Roots • Use a graphing calculator to evaluate expressions with negative exponents. ☐ SAT-10 ☑ ITBS ☑ CTBS ☑ NAEP	Calculators, index cards, graphing calculators	**MiC:** *Revisiting Numbers* pp. 6–7, 50–51 **Technology Lab Activities** 4-6
Lesson 4-7 The Real Numbers • Determine if a number is rational or irrational. ☐ SAT-10 ☐ ITBS ☐ CTBS ☑ NAEP	Calculators	**MiC:** *Revisiting Numbers* pp. 50–52 **Hands-On Lab Activities** 4-7 **Technology Lab Activities** 4-7
4-8 Hands-On Lab Explore Right Triangles • Use scissors and paper to explore right triangles. **Lesson 4-8** The Pythagorean Theorem • Use the Pythagorean Theorem to solve problems. ☑ SAT-10 ☑ ITBS ☐ CTBS ☑ NAEP	Scissors, straightedges (MK), graph paper, string or cord or yarn	**MiC:** *It's All the Same* pp. 35–37, 39 **MiC:** *Looking At An Angle* pp. 47–50 **Hands-On Lab Activities** 4-8 **Technology Lab Activities** 4-8

MK = *Manipulatives Kit*

Mathematics in Context

The units *Revisiting Numbers, Patterns and Figures, It's All the Same,* and *Looking At An Angle* from the *Mathematics in Context* © 2006 series can be used with Section 4B. See Section Planner above for suggestions for integrating *MiC* with *Holt Mathematics.*

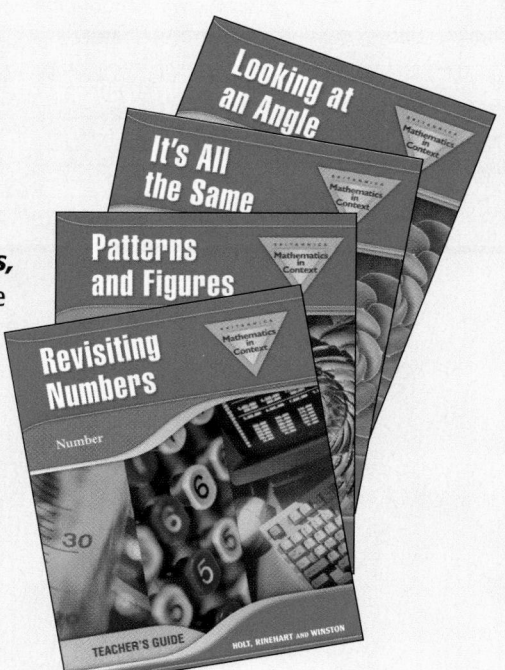

Section Overview

Squares and Square Roots

Lessons 4-5, 4-6

Why? Squares and square roots are important and necessary concepts in algebra, geometry, and higher levels of mathematics.

Squares

The **square** of both 6 and -6 is 36.

$6^2 = 36$ $(-6)^2 = 36$

A **perfect square** has an integer square root

Examples: 0, 1, 4, 9, 16, 25, . . .

Estimate $\sqrt{27}$ to the nearest tenth.

Step 1:

$\sqrt{25} = 5$ and $\sqrt{36} = 6$

So $\sqrt{27}$ is between 5 and 6, closer to 5.

Step 2:

$5.1^2 = 26.01$ (too low) and
$5.2^2 = 27.04$ (too high)

To the nearest tenth, $\sqrt{27} \approx 5.2$.

Square Roots

The positive square root of 36 is 6: $\sqrt{36} = 6$.

The negative square root of 36 is -6. $-\sqrt{36} = -6$.

The **principal square root** is the positive square root.

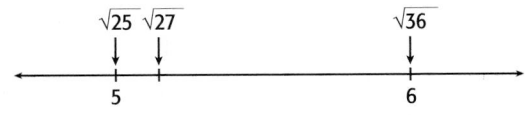

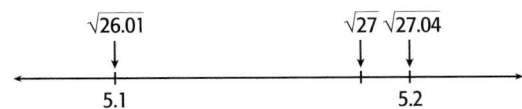

The Real Numbers

Lesson 4-7

Why? The set of real numbers includes rational and irrational numbers.

A **rational number** can be written as a quotient of two integers. Every rational number can be written as a decimal that either terminates or repeats.

$3\frac{4}{5} = 3.8$ $-3 = -3.0$ $\frac{2}{3} = 0.\overline{6}$

$\sqrt{1.44} = 1.2$ $\sqrt{\frac{4}{25}} = \frac{2}{5} = 0.4$ $\frac{0}{2} = 0$

An **irrational number** cannot be written as a quotient of two integers. There is no exact decimal representation for an irrational number.

$\sqrt{7} \approx 2.646$ $\sqrt{2.8} \approx 1.673$

$\sqrt{\frac{3}{8}} \approx 0.612$ $\pi \approx 3.14159 \approx \frac{22}{7}$

The Pythagorean Theorem

Lesson 4-8

Why? You can use the Pythagorean Theorem to find information about triangles, such as the area of a triangle whose height is unknown.

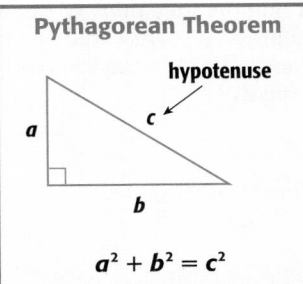

Pythagorean Theorem

hypotenuse

$a^2 + b^2 = c^2$

Find the area of the triangle.

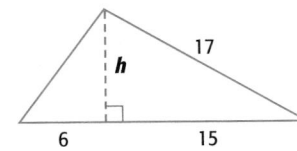

First, use the right triangle to find h.

$h^2 + 15^2 = 17^2$
$h^2 + 225 = 289$
$h^2 = 64$
$h = 8$

Then, use the area formula to find the area of the large triangle.

$A = \frac{1}{2}bh$

$A = \frac{1}{2}(21)(8)$

$A = 84$ units^2

Objective: Students find square roots.

 Online Edition
Tutorial Videos, Interactivities

 Countdown to Testing Week 7

Power Presentations
with PowerPoint®

Warm Up

Simplify.

1. 5^2 25   **2.** 8^2 64

3. 12^2 144   **4.** 15^2 225

5. 20^2 400

Problem of the Day

A Shakespearean sonnet is a poem made up of 3 quatrains (4 lines each) and a couplet (2 lines). Each line is in iambic pentameter (which means it has 5 iambic feet). So how many iambic feet long is a Shakespearean sonnet? 70

Also available on transparency

Math Humor

Why wouldn't the tree fit in the round pot? It had square roots!

State Resources

 **go.hrw.com**
State Resources Online
KEYWORD: MT7 Resources

Learn to find square roots.

Vocabulary
principal square root
perfect square

Think about the relationship between the area of a square and the length of one of its sides.

area = 36 square units
side length = $\sqrt{36}$ = 6 units

Quilts are often pieced together from small squares to form a large design.

Taking the square root of a number is the inverse of squaring the number.

$$6^2 = 36 \qquad \sqrt{36} = 6$$

Every positive number has two square roots, one positive and one negative. One square root of 16 is 4, since $4 \cdot 4 = 16$. The other square root of 16 is -4, since $(-4)(-4)$ is also 16. You can write the square roots of 16 as ± 4, meaning "**plus or minus**" 4.

Caution!

$\sqrt{-49}$ is not the same as $-\sqrt{49}$. A negative number has no real square roots.

When you press the $\sqrt{}$ key on a calculator, only the nonnegative square root appears. This is called the **principal square root** of the number.

$$+\sqrt{16} = 4 \qquad\qquad -\sqrt{16} = -4$$

The numbers 16, 36, and 49 are examples of perfect squares. A **perfect square** is a number that has integers as its square roots. Other perfect squares include 1, 4, 9, 25, 64, and 81.

EXAMPLE 1   **Finding the Positive and Negative Square Roots of a Number**

Find the two square roots of each number.

A 81
$$\sqrt{81} = 9 \qquad \text{9 is a square root, since } 9 \cdot 9 = 81.$$
$$-\sqrt{81} = -9 \qquad -9 \text{ is also a square root, since } -9 \cdot -9 = 81.$$

B 1
$$\sqrt{1} = 1 \qquad \text{1 is a square root, since } 1 \cdot 1 = 1.$$
$$-\sqrt{1} = -1 \qquad -1 \text{ is also a square root, since } -1 \cdot -1 = 1.$$

C 144
$$\sqrt{144} = 12 \qquad \text{12 is a square root, since } 12 \cdot 12 = 144.$$
$$-\sqrt{144} = -12 \qquad -12 \text{ is also a square root, since } -12 \cdot (-12) = 144.$$

---

1 Introduce

Alternate Opener

EXPLORATION

4-5 Squares and Square Roots

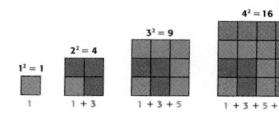

The sequence shows the square numbers 1, 4, 9, and 16.

$1^2 = 1$ $2^2 = 4$ $3^2 = 9$ $4^2 = 16$

1   1 + 3   1 + 3 + 5   1 + 3 + 5 + 7

1. Draw a picture to show that $5^2 = 1 + 3 + 5 + 7 + 9$.

2. Add the odd numbers $1 + 3 + 5 + 7 + 9 + \cdots + 17 + 19$. What square number do you get?

3. The table starts with $11^2 = 1 + 3 + 5 + 7 + 9 + 11 + 13 + 15 + 17 + 19 + 21 = 121$. Complete the table by adding the next odd number to this sum.

11^2	12^2	13^2	14^2	15^2	16^2	17^2	18^2	19^2	20^2
121									

Think and Discuss

4. **Explain** how you can determine square numbers using sums of odd numbers.

5. **Demonstrate** that the value of 22^2 can be determined by adding odd numbers.

Motivate

Use a calculator to demonstrate the use of the square-root button. Use the calculator to find $\sqrt{9}$, $\sqrt{16}$, and $\sqrt{25}$. Ask students what number they think will be the output if you press $\sqrt{36}$. Ask students to describe the function of the square-root key in their own words.

Explorations and answers are provided in *Alternate Openers: Explorations Transparencies.*

EXAMPLE 2 *Computer Application*

The square computer icon contains 676 pixels. How many pixels tall is the icon?

Find the square root of 676 to find the length of the side. Use the positive square root; a negative length has no meaning.

$$26^2 = 676$$

So $\sqrt{676} = 26$.

The icon is 26 pixels tall.

The square computer icon contains 676 colored dots that make up the picture. These dots are called *pixels*.

In the order of operations everything under the square root symbol is treated as if it were in parentheses. $\sqrt{5 - 3} = \sqrt{(5 - 3)}$

EXAMPLE 3 **Evaluating Expressions Involving Square Roots**

Evaluate each expression.

A $3\sqrt{25} + 4$

$$3\sqrt{25} + 4 = 3(5) + 4 \qquad \text{\textit{Evaluate the square root.}}$$
$$= 15 + 4 \qquad \text{\textit{Multiply.}}$$
$$= 19 \qquad \text{\textit{Add.}}$$

B $\sqrt{\dfrac{16}{4}} + \dfrac{1}{2}$

$$\sqrt{\dfrac{16}{4}} + \dfrac{1}{2} = \sqrt{4} + \dfrac{1}{2} \qquad \dfrac{16}{4} = 4.$$
$$= 4 + \dfrac{1}{2} \qquad \text{\textit{Evaluate the square roots.}}$$
$$= 4\dfrac{1}{2} \qquad \text{\textit{Add.}}$$

Possible answers to *Think and Discuss*

2. Each positive number has 2 square roots, one is positive and the other is its opposite.

3. 0 has one square root, 0. Square roots of negative numbers do not exist in the real number system.

Think and Discuss

1. Describe what is meant by a perfect square. Give an example.

2. Explain how many square roots a positive number can have. How are these square roots different?

3. Decide how many square roots 0 has. Tell what you know about square roots of negative numbers.

Possible answers to *Think and Discuss*

1. A perfect square is a number that has integers as its square roots. An example is 25.

2 Teach

Guided Instruction

In this lesson, students learn to find square roots. Remind students that they are familiar with inverse operations, such as addition and subtraction. Tell students that they will learn about another pair of inverse operations: squaring and finding a square root. Explain that 4 and −4 are the two square roots of 16 because $4^2 = 16$ and $(-4)^2 = 16$. Discuss the fact that the $\sqrt{}$ symbol indicates *principal square root,* which is always either positive or 0. Emphasize that the opposite of a square root is a real number, but that a negative number has no real square roots. For example, $-\sqrt{49} = -7$, but $\sqrt{-49}$ is not a real number.

Reaching All Learners
Through Cooperative Learning

Give each group of students several cards containing integers from −5 to 5 (Teacher Tools). Give the class problems involving square roots that have those integers as answers. For example, some questions could be as follows:

• Find $\sqrt{9} + 1$. 4

• Find $-\sqrt{25}$. −5

• Find a square root of 1. ±1

• What number has exactly one square root? 0

Have groups solve each problem and hold up the card with the correct answer.

3 Close

Summarize

Remind students that every positive number has two square roots, one positive and one negative. The statement that gives the positive, or principal, square root of 9 is $\sqrt{9} = 3$. The statement that gives the negative square root of 9 is $-\sqrt{9} = -3$. Remind students that the square root of a negative number is not a real number. Ask students to help you create a list of the first 15 perfect squares.

1, 4, 9, 16, 25, 36, 49, 64, 81, 100, 121, 144, 169, 196, and 225

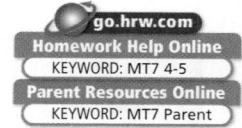

go.hrw.com
Homework Help Online
KEYWORD: MT7 4-5
Parent Resources Online
KEYWORD: MT7 Parent

Assignment Guide

If you finished Example 1 assign:
Average 1–8, 14–21, 27–30, 38–41, 52–61
Advanced 14–21, 31–34, 40–45, 49, 52–61

If you finished Example 2 assign:
Average 1–9, 14–22, 27–30, 36–41, 47, 52–61
Advanced 14–22, 31–49, 52–61

If you finished Example 3 assign:
Average 1–30, 36–41, 47, 50, 52–61
Advanced 14–26, 31–37, 40–61

Homework Quick Check

Quickly check key concepts.
Exercises: 20, 22, 26, 40

Answers

35. See p. A5.

Math **Background**

By agreement among mathematicians, the $\sqrt{\ }$ symbol means *principal* square root, which is nonnegative. Therefore, $\sqrt{36}$ represents just one number, 6. The expression $\pm\sqrt{36}$ represents both square roots of 36.

An important property of square roots is used in Practice and Problem Solving Exercises 38–45.

Property	Example
$\sqrt{\dfrac{a}{b}} = \dfrac{\sqrt{a}}{\sqrt{b}}, b \neq 0$	$\sqrt{\dfrac{1}{4}} = \dfrac{\sqrt{1}}{\sqrt{4}} = \dfrac{1}{2}$

In the property, *a* and *b* represent non-negative real numbers.

State Resources

go.hrw.com
State Resources Online
KEYWORD: MT7 Resources

GUIDED PRACTICE

See Example 1 Find the two square roots of each number.

1. 4 ± 2 **2.** 16 ± 4 **3.** 64 ± 8 **4.** 121 ± 11

5. 1 ± 1 **6.** 441 ± 21 **7.** 9 ± 3 **8.** 484 ± 22

See Example 2 **9.** A square court for playing the game four square has an area of 256 ft². How long is one side of the court? **16 ft**

See Example 3 Evaluate each expression.

10. $\sqrt{5 + 11}$ **4**   **11.** $\sqrt{\dfrac{81}{9}}$ **3**

12. $3\sqrt{400} - 125$ **−65**   **13.** $-\left(\sqrt{169} - \sqrt{144}\right)$ **−1**

Area = 256 ft²

INDEPENDENT PRACTICE

See Example 1 Find the two square roots of each number.

14. 25 ± 5 **15.** 144 ± 12 **16.** 81 ± 9 **17.** 169 ± 13

18. 196 ± 14 **19.** 400 ± 20 **20.** 361 ± 19 **21.** 225 ± 15

See Example 2 **22.** Elisa found a square digital image of a famous painting on a Web site. The image contained 360,000 pixels. How many pixels high is the image? **600 pixels**

See Example 3 Evaluate each expression.

23. $\sqrt{25} - 6$ **−1**   **24.** $\sqrt{\dfrac{64}{4}}$ **4**   **25.** $-\left(\sqrt{36}\sqrt{9}\right)$ **−18**   **26.** $5(\sqrt{225} - 10)$ **25**

PRACTICE AND PROBLEM SOLVING

Extra Practice
See page 789.

Find the two square roots of each number.

27. 36 ± 6 **28.** 100 ± 10 **29.** 49 ± 7 **30.** 900 ± 30

31. 529 ± 23 **32.** 289 ± 17 **33.** 576 ± 24 **34.** 324 ± 18

35. Estimation Mr. Barada bought a square rug. The area of the rug was about 68.06 ft². He estimated that the length of a side was about 7 ft. Is Mr. Barada's estimate reasonable? Explain.

36. Language Arts *Crelle's Journal* is the oldest mathematics periodical in existence. Zacharias Dase's incredible calculating skills were made famous by *Crelle's Journal* in 1844. Dase produced a table of factors of all numbers between 7,000,000 and 10,000,000. He listed 7,022,500 as a perfect square. What is the square root of 7,022,500? **2650**

37. Sports A karate match is held on a square mat that has an area of 676 ft². What is the length of the mat? **26 ft**

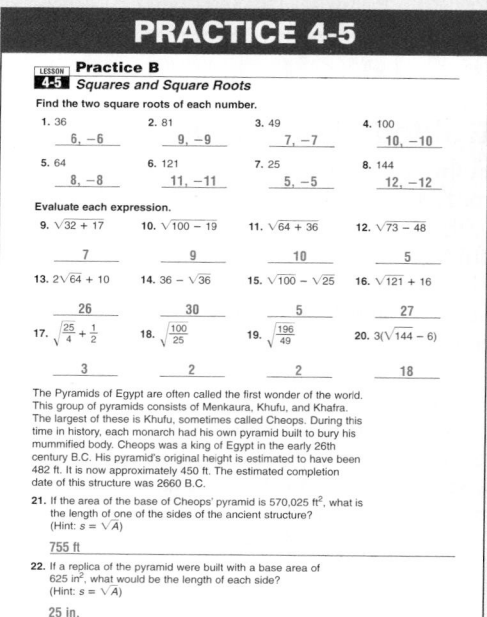

RETEACH 4-5

LESSON **Reteach**
4-5 *Squares and Square Roots*

A perfect square has two identical factors.
$25 = 5 \times 5 = 5^2$ or $25 = (-5) \times (-5) = (-5)^2$ then 25 is a perfect square.

Tell if the number is a perfect square.
If yes, write its identical factors.

1. 121 ___11^2 or $(-11)^2$___   **2.** 200 ___not a perfect square___

3. 400 ___20^2 or $(-20)^2$___

Since $5^2 = 25$ and also $(-5)^2 = 25$, $\sqrt{25} = 5$ and $-\sqrt{25} = -5$
both 5 and −5 are **square roots** of 25.
The **principal square root** of 25 is 5: $\sqrt{25} = 5$

Write the two square roots of each number.

4. $\sqrt{81} = $ ___9___   **5.** $\sqrt{625} = $ ___25___   **6.** $\sqrt{169} = $ ___13___

$-\sqrt{81} = $ ___−9___ $-\sqrt{625} = $ ___−25___ $-\sqrt{169} = $ ___−13___

Write the principal square root of each number.

7. $\sqrt{144} = $ ___12___   **8.** $\sqrt{6400} = $ ___80___   **9.** $\sqrt{10,000} = $ ___100___

Use the principal square root when $5\sqrt{100} - 3$
evaluating an expression. For the $5(10) - 3$
order of operations, do square root $50 - 3$
first, as you would an exponent. 47

Complete to evaluate each expression.

10. $3\sqrt{144} - 20$ **11.** $\sqrt{25 + 144} + 13$ **12.** $\sqrt{\dfrac{100}{25}} + \dfrac{1}{2}$

$3 \times$ ___12___ $- 20$ $\sqrt{169} + 13$ $\dfrac{\sqrt{100}}{\sqrt{25}} + \dfrac{1}{2}$

___36___ $- 20$ ___13___ $+ 13$ $\dfrac{10}{5} + \dfrac{1}{2}$

___16___   ___26___   ___2___ $+ \dfrac{1}{2}$

$2\dfrac{1}{2}$

PRACTICE 4-5

LESSON **Practice B**
4-5 *Squares and Square Roots*

Find the two square roots of each number.

1. 36   **2.** 81   **3.** 49   **4.** 100
___6, −6___   ___9, −9___   ___7, −7___   ___10, −10___

5. 64   **6.** 121   **7.** 25   **8.** 144
___8, −8___   ___11, −11___   ___5, −5___   ___12, −12___

Evaluate each expression.

9. $\sqrt{32 + 17}$ **10.** $\sqrt{100 - 19}$ **11.** $\sqrt{64 + 36}$ **12.** $\sqrt{73 - 48}$
___7___   ___9___   ___10___   ___5___

13. $2\sqrt{64} + 10$ **14.** $36 - \sqrt{36}$ **15.** $\sqrt{100} - \sqrt{25}$ **16.** $\sqrt{121} + 16$
___26___   ___30___   ___5___   ___27___

17. $\sqrt{\dfrac{25}{4}} + \dfrac{1}{2}$ **18.** $\sqrt{\dfrac{100}{25}}$ **19.** $\sqrt{\dfrac{196}{49}}$ **20.** $3(\sqrt{144} - 6)$
___3___   ___2___   ___2___   ___18___

The Pyramids of Egypt are often called the first wonder of the world. This group of pyramids consists of Menkaura, Khufu, and Khafra. The largest of these is Khufu, sometimes called Cheops. During this time in history, each monarch had his own pyramid built to bury his mummified body. Cheops was a king of Egypt in the early 26th century B.C. His pyramid's original height is estimated to have been 482 ft. It is now approximately 450 ft. The estimated completion date of this structure was 2660 B.C.

21. If the area of the base of Cheops' pyramid is 570,025 ft², what is the length of one of the sides of the ancient structure?
(Hint: $s = \sqrt{A}$)

___755 ft___

22. If a replica of the pyramid were built with a base area of 625 in², what would be the length of each side?
(Hint: $s = \sqrt{A}$)

___25 in.___

47. a. 64 small squares; 1 small square left

49. Possible answer: $\sqrt{40}$ is closer to 6 than to 7 because 40 is closer to 36 than it is to 49.

Find the two square roots of each number.

38. $\frac{1}{9}$ $\pm\frac{1}{3}$ **39.** $\frac{1}{121}$ $\pm\frac{1}{11}$ **40.** $\frac{16}{9}$ $\pm\frac{4}{3}$ **41.** $\frac{81}{16}$ $\pm\frac{9}{4}$

42. $\frac{9}{4}$ $\pm\frac{3}{2}$ **43.** $\frac{324}{81}$ ±2 **44.** $\frac{1000}{100,000}$ $\pm\frac{1}{10}$ **45.** $\frac{169}{676}$ $\pm\frac{1}{2}$

46. Multi-Step An office building has a square courtyard with an area of 289 ft². What is the distance around the edge of the courtyard? **68 ft**

47. Games A chessboard contains 32 black and 32 white squares. How many squares are along each side of the game board? **8**

48. Hobbies A quilter wants to use as many of his 65 small fabric squares as possible to make one large square quilt. **16 small squares**

 a. How many small squares can the quilter use? How many small squares would he have left?

 b. How many more small squares would the quilter need to make the next largest possible square quilt?

49. What's the Error? A student said that since the square roots of a certain number are 1.5 and −1.5, the number must be their product, −2.25. What error did the student make?

50. Write About It Explain the steps you would take to evaluate the expression $\sqrt{14 + 35} - 20$.

51. Challenge The square root of a number is four less than three times seven. What is the number? **289**

TEST PREP and Spiral Review

52. Multiple Choice Which number does NOT have a square root that is an integer?

  (A) 81   (B) 196   (C) 288   (D) 400

53. Short Response Deanna knows that the floor in her kitchen is a square with an area of 169 square feet. The perimeter of her kitchen floor is found by adding the lengths of all its sides. What is the perimeter of her kitchen floor? Explain your answer. **52 feet; the positive square root of 169 is 13, so each side is 13 feet. 13 feet × 4 = 52 feet.**

Write each decimal as a fraction in simplest form. (Lesson 2-1)

54. 0.35 $\frac{7}{20}$ **55.** 2.6 $2\frac{3}{5}$ **56.** −7.18 $-7\frac{9}{50}$ **57.** 0.125 $\frac{1}{8}$

Write each number in scientific notation. (Lesson 4-4)

58. 1,970,000,000 1.97×10^9 **59.** 2,500,000 2.5×10^6

60. 31,400,000,000 3.14×10^{10} **61.** 5,680,000,000,000,000 5.68×10^{15}

Answers

49. Possible answer: The student multiplied the two square roots together instead of squaring one of them. The number should be 1.5^2 or $(-1.5)^2$, which equal 2.25.

50. Possible answer: First, add the terms under the square root symbol to get 49. Next, find the principal square root of 49, which is 7. Finally, subtract 20 from 7 to get −13.

TEST PREP DOCTOR + Students who have trouble with Exercise 53 may benefit from a visual reference. Use a diagram to show students how to calculate area and perimeter. Remind them to discount negative answers since they do not make sense in this context.

Journal
Ask students to list as many perfect squares as they can remember from the lesson.

Power Presentations
 with PowerPoint®

✓ 4-5 Lesson Quiz
Find the two square roots of each number.

1. 81   ±9

2. 2500   ±50

Evaluate each expression.

3. $3\sqrt{16} + 1$ 13

4. $7\sqrt{9} - 2\sqrt{49}$ 7

5. Ms. Estefan wants to put a fence around 3 sides of a square garden that has an area of 225 ft². How much fencing does she need? **45 ft**

Also available on transparency

CHALLENGE 4-5

LESSON 4-5 Challenge
Dig It!
Find the digital root of a number by adding its digits, adding the digits of the result, and so on, until the result is a single digit.

358→3 + 5 + 8 = 16→1 + 6 = 7   The digital root of 358 is 7.

1. Complete the table to find the digital roots of the squares of 1–17.

Number	Square	Calculation		
1	1		=	1
2	4		=	4
3	9		=	9
4	16	1 + 6	=	7
5	25	2 + 5	=	7
6	36	3 + 6 = 9	=	9
7	49	4 + 9 = 13→1 + 3	=	4
8	64	6 + 4 = 10→1 + 0	=	1
9	81	8 + 1	=	9
10	100	1 + 0 + 0	=	1
11	121	1 + 2 + 1	=	4
12	144	1 + 4 + 4	=	9
13	169	1 + 6 + 9 = 16→1 + 6	=	7
14	196	1 + 9 + 6 = 16→1 + 6	=	7
15	225	2 + 2 + 5	=	9
16	256	2 + 5 + 6 = 13→1 + 3	=	4
17	289	2 + 8 + 9 = 19→1 + 9 = 10→1 + 0	=	1

2. Make an observation about the results. **Possible answers:**
The only results are 1, 4, 7, or 9.

3. Make a conjecture about the digital root of any whole-number perfect square. Verify your conjecture by using at least three more perfect squares.
The result is one of the numbers 1, 4, 7, or 9. Choices vary.

4. A palindrome is a number that is the same when read forward or backward, such as 14741. Find two palindromes in the table.
The digital roots of the squares of the numbers 1–8 and then 1–17.

PROBLEM SOLVING 4-5

LESSON 4-5 Problem Solving
Squares and Square Roots
Write the correct answer.

1. For college wrestling competitions, the NCAA requires that the wrestling mat be a square with an area of 1764 square feet. What is the length of each side of the mat?

42 feet

2. For high school wrestling competitions, the wrestling mat must be a square with an area of 1444 square feet. What is the length of each side of the wrestling mat?

38 feet

3. The Japanese art of origami requires folding square pieces of paper. Elena begins with a large sheet of square paper that is 169 square inches. How many squares can she cut out of the paper that are 4 inches on each side?

9 squares

4. When the James family moved into a new house they had a square area rug that was 132 square feet. In their new house, there are three bedrooms. Bedroom one is 11 feet by 11 feet. Bedroom two is 10 feet by 12 feet and bedroom three is 13 feet by 13 feet. In which bedroom will the rug fit?

Bedroom three

Choose the letter for the best answer.

5. A square picture frame measures 36 inches on each side. The actual wood trim in the frame is 2 inches wide. The photograph in the frame is surrounded by a bronze mat that measures 5 inches. What is the maximum area of the photograph?

A 841 sq. inches   B 900 sq. inches
C 1156 sq. inches (D) 484 sq. inches

6. To create a square patchwork quilt wall hanging, square pieces of material are sewn together to form a larger square. Which number of smaller squares can be used to create a square patchwork quilt wall hanging?

F 35 squares   (G) 64 squares
H 84 squares   J 125 squares

7. A can of paint claims that one can will cover 400 square feet. If you painted a square with the can of paint, how long would it be on each side?

A 200 feet   B 65 feet
C 25 feet   (D) 20 feet

8. A box of tile contains 12 tiles. If you tile a square area using whole tiles, how many tiles will you have left from the box?

F 9   G 6
(H) 3   J 0

Objective: Students estimate square roots to a given number of decimal places and solve problems using square roots.

 Technology Lab
In *Technology Lab Activities*

 Online Edition
Tutorial Videos

 Countdown to Testing Week 7

Power Presentations
with PowerPoint®

Warm Up
Find the two square roots of each number.
1. 144 ±12   2. 256 ±16
Evaluate each expression.
3. $8 + \sqrt{144}$ 20   4. $7\sqrt{289}$ 119

Problem of the Day
A pyramid of blocks is built in layers. The bottom layer has 6^2, or 36, blocks. The next layer has 5^2 blocks, and so on until the top layer has 1 block. How many blocks are there in all? 91 blocks

Also available on transparency

State Resources

go.hrw.com
State Resources Online
KEYWORD: MT7 Resources

4-6 Estimating Square Roots

Learn to estimate square roots to a given number of decimal places and solve problems using square roots.

A couple wants to install a square stained-glass window. The window has an area of 500 square inches with wood trim around it. You can calculate the length of the trim using your knowledge of squares and square roots.

EXAMPLE 1 Estimating Square Roots of Numbers

Each square root is between two integers. Name the integers. Explain your answer.

A $\sqrt{30}$ *Think: What are perfect squares close to 30?*
$5^2 = 25$ *$25 < 30$*
$6^2 = 36$ *$36 > 30$*
$\sqrt{30}$ is between 5 and 6 because 30 is between 25 and 36.

B $-\sqrt{150}$ *Think: What are perfect squares close to 150?*
$(-12)^2 = 144$ *$144 < 150$*
$(-13)^2 = 169$ *$169 > 150$*
$-\sqrt{150}$ is between -12 and -13 because 150 is between 144 and 169.

EXAMPLE 2 PROBLEM SOLVING APPLICATION

A couple wants to install a square stained-glass window that has an area of 500 square inches. Calculate the length of each side and the length of trim needed to the nearest tenth of an inch.

 Understand the Problem

First find the length of a side. Then you can use the length of a side to find the *perimeter*, the length of the trim around the window.

 Make a Plan

The length of a side, in inches, is the number that you multiply by itself to get 500. Find this number to the nearest tenth.

Use guess and check to find $\sqrt{500}$.

---

1 Introduce
Alternate Opener

EXPLORATION

4-6 Estimating Square Roots

Knowing the square numbers can help you estimate square roots.

1. Complete the table of squares.

1^2	2^2	3^2	4^2	5^2	6^2	7^2	8^2	9^2	10^2
1									

11^2	12^2	13^2	14^2	15^2	16^2	17^2	18^2	19^2	20^2
121									

Use the table of squares above to help you estimate each square root to the nearest tenth. Use a calculator to check your estimates. Round to two decimal places.

	Square Root	Estimate	Calculator
2.	$\sqrt{10}$		
3.	$\sqrt{20}$		
4.	$\sqrt{200}$		
5.	$\sqrt{300}$		
6.	$\sqrt{57}$		
7.	$\sqrt{130}$		

Think and Discuss
8. **Discuss** your strategy for estimating square roots.

Motivate
Ask students to find $\sqrt{4}$ and $\sqrt{9}$. Show the number line diagram:

$$\sqrt{4} \ \sqrt{5} \qquad\qquad \sqrt{8} \ \sqrt{9}$$
2 2.24   2.83 3

Ask students where they think $\sqrt{8}$ should be placed on the diagram. If they say "between 2 and 3," ask whether it should be closer to 2 or to 3. Then use a calculator to find the approximation $\sqrt{8} \approx 2.83$. Try the same process with $\sqrt{5}$ (≈ 2.24).

Explorations and answers are provided in *Alternate Openers: Explorations Transparencies.*

3 Solve

Because 500 is between 22^2 (484) and 23^2 (529), the square root of 500 is between 22 and 23.

Guess 22.5	Guess 22.2	Guess 22.4	Guess 22.3
$22.5^2 = 506.25$	$22.2^2 = 492.84$	$22.4^2 = 501.76$	$22.3^2 = 497.29$
Too high	Too low	Too high	Too low
Square root is between 22 and 22.5.	Square root is between 22.2 and 22.5.	Square root is between 22.2 and 22.4.	Square root is between 22.3 and 22.4.

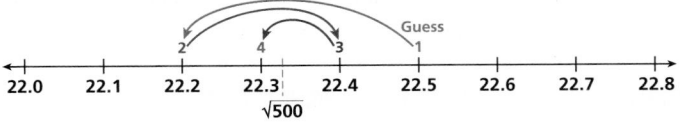

The square root is between 22.3 and 22.4. To round to the nearest tenth, consider 22.35.

$$22.35^2 = 499.5225 \qquad \textit{Too low}$$

The square root must be *greater than* 22.35, so you can round *up*. To the nearest tenth, $\sqrt{500}$ is about 22.4.

Now estimate the length around the window. The length of a side of the window to the nearest tenth of an inch is 22.4 inches.

$$4 \cdot 22.4 = 89.6 \qquad \textit{Perimeter} = 4 \cdot \textit{side}$$

The trim is about 89.6 inches long.

4 Look Back

The length 90 inches divided by 4 is 22.5 inches. A 22.5-inch square has an area of 506.25 square inches, which is close to 500, so the answers are reasonable.

EXAMPLE 3 **Using a Calculator to Estimate the Value of a Square Root**

Use a calculator to find $\sqrt{700}$. **Round to the nearest tenth.**

Using a calculator, $\sqrt{700} \approx 26.45751311\ldots$. Rounded, $\sqrt{700}$ is 26.5.

Think and Discuss

1. **Discuss** whether 9.5 is a good first guess for $\sqrt{75}$.

2. **Determine** which square root or roots would have 7.5 as a good first guess.

Additional Examples

Example 1

Each square root is between two integers. Name the integers. Explain your answer.

A. $\sqrt{55}$ 7 and 8 because 55 is between 49 and 64

B. $-\sqrt{90}$ −9 and −10 because 90 is between 81 and 100

Example 2

You want to sew a fringe on a square tablecloth with an area of 500 square inches. Calculate the length of each side of the tablecloth and the length of fringe you will need to the nearest tenth of an inch.

The length of each side of the table is about 22.4 in., and you will need about 89.6 in. of fringe.

Example 3

Use a calculator to find $\sqrt{600}$. Round to the nearest tenth. 24.5

Also available on transparency

Possible answers to Think and Discuss

1. No; $9^2 = 81$, so $\sqrt{75}$ must be less than 9; 8.5 is a better first guess.

2. Two good choices would be $\sqrt{56}$ and $\sqrt{57}$. $7^2 = 49$ and $8^2 = 64$, so a number that has a square root close to 7.5 is about halfway between 49 and 64. In fact, $7.5^2 = 56.25$.

---

2 Teach

Guided Instruction

In this lesson, students learn to estimate square roots to a given number of decimal places and solve problems using square roots. Tell students that all positive numbers have square roots, but most of those square roots are not integers. If students have calculators, you may want to ask them to enter $\sqrt{7}$ to see an example. Discuss with students how to identify the two integers that a given square root is between. Show students how to get an approximation of a square root to the nearest tenth by repeated use of the guess-and-check method.

Reaching All Learners
Through Kinesthetic Experience

Place papers showing the integers 1 to 10 (one per sheet) around the room in order. Give each student a card showing the square root of a positive number between 1 and 100, such as $\sqrt{28}$. Have each student place his or her card between the appropriate pair of integers. For example, $\sqrt{28}$ should be placed between 5 and 6. Continue until all the cards are placed. Then have the class determine if all the placements are correct.

3 Close

Summarize

Remind students that sometimes it is sufficient to approximate a square root by naming the two integers it is between. At other times, they may need to approximate a square root to a given number of decimal places. Emphasize the value of knowing at least the first ten perfect squares: 1, 4, 9, 16, 25, 36, 49, 64, 81, and 100.

Before students begin the Exercises, you may want to clarify the procedure for solving multi-step problems that involve rounding. Answers are given in the most accurate form with rounding as the final step.

4-6 Exercises

go.hrw.com
Homework Help Online
KEYWORD: MT7 4-6
Parent Resources Online
KEYWORD: MT7 Parent

Assignment Guide

If you finished Example **1** assign:
Average 1–5, 12–16, 23–28, 40–49
Advanced 12–16, 23–29, 40–49

If you finished Example **2** assign:
Average 1–6, 12–17, 23–28, 36, 37, 40–49
Advanced 12–17, 23–28, 35–37, 38–49

If you finished Example **3** assign:
Average 1–34, 36, 37, 40–49
Advanced 12–49

Homework Quick Check

Quickly check key concepts.
Exercises: 12, 17, 20, 24, 34

Answers

1–4, 12–15. See p. A5.

Math Background

In this lesson, students use guess-and-check to estimate square roots. A more reliable method for estimating square roots involves repeated division. For example, to find $\sqrt{28}$, choose the integer whose perfect square is closest to 28 ($5^2 = 25$).

Divide 28 by that integer: $5\overline{)28.0}$ = 5.6

Find the average of the quotient and the divisor: $(5 + 5.6) \div 2 = 5.3$.

Check the result: $5.3^2 = 28.09$.

You can then repeat the process with your new estimate and continue repeating the algorithm until your estimate has the desired accuracy.

State Resources

go.hrw.com
State Resources Online
KEYWORD: MT7 Resources

GUIDED PRACTICE

See Example **1** Each square root is between two integers. Name the integers. Explain your answer.

1. $\sqrt{40}$ **2.** $-\sqrt{90}$ **3.** $\sqrt{156}$ **4.** $-\sqrt{306}$ **5.** $\sqrt{250}$
5. 15 and 16; possible answer: 250 is between 225 and 256.

See Example **2** **6.** A square photo is placed behind a piece of glass that has an area of 20 square inches. To the nearest hundredth, what length of frame is needed to go around all edges of the glass? **4.47 in.**

See Example **3** Use a calculator to find each value. Round to the nearest tenth.

7. $\sqrt{74}$ **8.6** **8.** $\sqrt{34.1}$ **5.8** **9.** $\sqrt{3600}$ **60.0** **10.** $\sqrt{190}$ **13.8** **11.** $\sqrt{5120}$ **71.6**

INDEPENDENT PRACTICE

See Example **1** Each square root is between two integers. Name the integers. Explain your answer.

12. $-\sqrt{52}$ **13.** $\sqrt{3}$ **14.** $\sqrt{600}$ **15.** $-\sqrt{2000}$ **16.** $\sqrt{410}$
16. 20 and 21; possible answer: 410 is between 400 and 441.

See Example **2** **17.** Each square on Laura's chessboard is 13 square centimeters. A chessboard has 8 squares on each side. To the nearest hundredth, what is the width of Laura's chessboard? **≈28.84 cm**

See Example **3** Use a calculator to find each value. Round to the nearest tenth.

18. $\sqrt{58}$ **7.6** **19.** $\sqrt{91.5}$ **9.6** **20.** $\sqrt{550}$ **23.5** **21.** $\sqrt{150}$ **12.2** **22.** $\sqrt{330}$ **18.2**

PRACTICE AND PROBLEM SOLVING

Extra Practice
See page 789.

Write the letter that identifies the position of each square root.

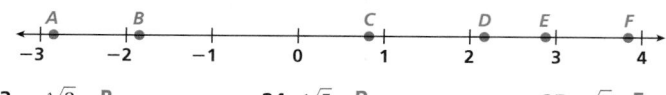

23. $-\sqrt{3}$ **B** **24.** $\sqrt{5}$ **D** **25.** $\sqrt{7}$ **E**
26. $-\sqrt{8}$ **A** **27.** $\sqrt{14}$ **F** **28.** $\sqrt{0.75}$ **C**

Find each product to the nearest hundredth.

29. $\sqrt{51} \cdot \sqrt{25}$ **35.71** **30.** $-\sqrt{70} \cdot \sqrt{16}$ **−33.47** **31.** $\sqrt{215} \cdot (-\sqrt{1})$ **−14.66**
32. $-\sqrt{113} \cdot \sqrt{9}$ **−31.89** **33.** $\sqrt{22} \cdot (-\sqrt{49})$ **−32.83** **34.** $\sqrt{210} \cdot \sqrt{169}$ **188.39**

35. Multi-Step On a baseball field, the infield area created by the baselines is a square. In a youth baseball league for 9- to 12-year-olds, this area is 3600 ft². The distance between each base in a league for 4-year-olds is 20 ft less than it is for 9- to 12-year-olds. What is the distance between each base for 4-year-olds? **40 ft**

RETEACH 4-6

LESSON 4-6 Reteach
Estimating Square Roots

To locate a square root between two integers, refer to the table.

Number	1	2	3	4	5	6	7	8	9	10
Square	1	4	9	16	25	36	49	64	81	100
Number	11	12	13	14	15	16	17	18	19	20
Square	121	144	169	196	225	256	289	324	361	400

Locate $\sqrt{260}$ between two integers.
260 is between the perfect squares 256 and 289: 256 < 260 < 289
So: $\sqrt{256} < \sqrt{260} < \sqrt{289}$
And: 16 < $\sqrt{260}$ < 17

Use the table to complete the statements.

1. $\underline{36}$ < 39 < $\underline{49}$
$\underline{\sqrt{36}}$ < $\sqrt{39}$ < $\underline{\sqrt{49}}$
$\underline{6}$ < $\sqrt{39}$ < $\underline{7}$

2. $\underline{121}$ < 130 < $\underline{144}$
$\underline{\sqrt{121}}$ < $\sqrt{130}$ < $\underline{\sqrt{144}}$
$\underline{11}$ < $\sqrt{130}$ < $\underline{12}$

After locating a square root between two integers, you can determine which of the two integers the square root is closer to.
27 is between the perfect squares 25 and 36: 25 < 27 < 36
So: $\sqrt{25} < \sqrt{27} < \sqrt{36}$
And: 5 < $\sqrt{27}$ < 6

The difference between 27 and 25 is 2; 25 < 27 < 36
the difference between 36 and 27 is 9. 2   9
So, $\sqrt{27}$, is closer to 5.

Complete the statements.

4. 100 < 106 < 121
$\underline{\sqrt{100}}$ < $\sqrt{106}$ < $\underline{\sqrt{121}}$
$\underline{10}$ < $\sqrt{106}$ < $\underline{11}$
106 − 100 = $\underline{6}$
121 − 106 = $\underline{15}$
$\sqrt{106}$ is closer to $\underline{10}$ than $\underline{11}$

5. $\underline{225}$ < 250 < $\underline{256}$
$\underline{\sqrt{225}}$ < $\sqrt{250}$ < $\underline{\sqrt{256}}$
$\underline{15}$ < $\sqrt{250}$ < $\underline{16}$
250 − $\underline{225}$ = $\underline{25}$
$\underline{256}$ − 250 = $\underline{6}$
$\sqrt{250}$ is closer to $\underline{16}$ than $\underline{15}$

PRACTICE 4-6

LESSON 4-6 Practice B
Estimating Square Roots

Each square root is between two integers. Name the integers. Explain your answer.

1. $\sqrt{6}$
   2 and 3; 6 is between 4 and 9
2. $\sqrt{20}$
   4 and 5; 20 is between 16 and 25
3. $\sqrt{28}$
   5 and 6; 28 is between 25 and 36
4. $\sqrt{44}$
   6 and 7; 44 is between 36 and 49
5. $\sqrt{31}$
   5 and 6; 31 is between 25 and 36
6. $\sqrt{52}$
   7 and 8; 52 is between 49 and 64

Use a calculator to find each value. Round to the nearest tenth.

7. $\sqrt{14}$ __3.7__ 8. $\sqrt{42}$ __6.5__ 9. $\sqrt{21}$ __4.6__ 10. $\sqrt{47}$ __6.9__
11. $\sqrt{58}$ __7.6__ 12. $\sqrt{60}$ __7.7__ 13. $\sqrt{35}$ __5.9__ 14. $\sqrt{75}$ __8.7__

Police use the formula $r = 2\sqrt{5L}$ to approximate the rate of speed in miles per hours of a vehicle from its skid marks, where L is the length of the skid marks in feet.

15. About how fast is a car going that leaves skid marks of 80 ft?
   __40 mi/h__
16. About how fast is a car going that leaves skid marks of 245 ft?
   __70 mi/h__
17. If the formula for finding the length of the skid marks is $L = \frac{r^2}{20}$, what would be the length of the skid marks from a vehicle traveling 80 mi/h?
   __320 ft__

Science LINK

Tsunamis, sometimes called tidal waves, move across deep oceans at high speeds with barely a ripple on the water surface. It is only when tsunamis hit shallow water that their energy moves them upward into a mammoth destructive force.

36. The rate of speed of a tsunami, in feet per second, can be found by the formula $r = \sqrt{32d}$, where d is the water depth in feet. Suppose the water depth is 20,000 ft. How fast is the tsunami moving?

37. The speed of a tsunami in miles per hour can be found using $r = \sqrt{14.88d}$, where d is the water depth in feet. Suppose the water depth is 25,000 ft.

   a. How fast is the tsunami moving in miles per hour?

   b. How long would it take a tsunami to travel 3000 miles if the water depth were a consistent 10,000 ft?

38. **What's the Error?** Ashley found the speed of a tsunami, in feet per second, by taking the square root of 32 and multiplying by the depth, in feet. What was her error?

39. **Challenge** Find the depth of the water if a tsunami's speed is 400 miles per hour.

Tsunamis can be caused by earthquakes, volcanoes, landslides, or meteorites.

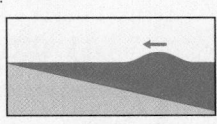

As the wave approaches the beach, it slows, builds in height, and crashes on shore.

go.hrw.com
Lab Resources Online
KEYWORD: MT7 Wave

TEST PREP and Spiral Review

40. Multiple Choice Which expression has a value between 15 and 14?

   Ⓐ $\sqrt{188}$ Ⓑ $\sqrt{200}$ Ⓒ $\sqrt{227}$ Ⓓ $\sqrt{324}$

41. Gridded Response Find the product $\sqrt{42} \cdot \sqrt{94}$ to the nearest hundredth. **62.83**

Evaluate each expression for the given values of the variables. (Lesson 1-1)

42. $4x + 5y$ for $x = 3$ and $y = 9$ **57**   **43.** $7m - 2n$ for $m = 5$ and $n = 7$ **21**

44. $8h + 9j$ for $h = 11$ and $j = 2$ **106**   **45.** $6s - 2t$ for $s = 7$ and $t = 12$ **18**

Find the two square roots of each number. (Lesson 4-5)

46. 100 **±10**   **47.** 64 **±8**   **48.** 484 **±22**   **49.** 1296 **±36**

ONGOING ASSESSMENT
and INTERVENTION ⬅➡

Diagnose Before the Lesson
4-6 Warm Up, TE p. 186

Monitor During the Lesson
4-6 Know-It Notebook
4-6 Questioning Strategies

Assess After the Lesson
4-6 Lesson Quiz, TE p. 189

Interdisciplinary LINK

Science

Exercises 36–39 involve using formulas with square roots to determine the speeds of tsunamis. Tsunamis are studied in middle school science programs such as *Holt Science & Technology*.

Answers

36–39. See p. A5.

TEST PREP DOCTOR + Make sure that students know to use their calculator for Exercise 41. Since neither 42 nor 94 have integer square roots, the students may struggle with rounding. Encourage them to type the whole expression into their calculator before multiplying to eliminate intermittent rounding.

Journal

Ask students to describe how they would estimate the square root of 1000.

Power Presentations
with PowerPoint®

 **4-6 Lesson Quiz**

Each square root is between two integers. Name the two integers.

1. $\sqrt{27}$ 5 and 6

2. $-\sqrt{456}$ −22 and −21

Use a calculator to find each value. Round to the nearest tenth.

3. $\sqrt{89}$ 9.4

4. $\sqrt{1223}$ 35.0

5. A square field has an area of 2000 square feet. To the nearest foot, how much fencing would be needed to enclose the field?

179 ft

Also available on transparency

CHALLENGE 4-6

LESSON 4-6 Challenge
Dig Deeper!

The **digital root** of a number is found by adding its digits, adding the digits of the result, and so on, until the result is a single digit. $918 \rightarrow 9 + 1 + 8 = 18 \rightarrow 1 + 8 = 9$ The digital root of 918 is 9.

1. Complete the table to display numbers and their digital roots and to determine if they are divisible by 3 (remainder = 0). Make an observation about the results.

A number is divisible by 3 if its digital root is divisible by 3.

Number	Divisible by 3?	Digital Root Calculation			Divisible by 3?
81	yes	$8 + 1$	=	9	yes
92	no	$9 + 2 = 11 \rightarrow 1 + 1$	=	2	no
226	no	$2 + 2 + 6 = 10 \rightarrow 1 + 0$	=	1	no
315	yes	$3 + 1 + 5$	=	9	yes
659	no	$6 + 5 + 9 = 20 \rightarrow 2 + 0$	=	2	no
704	no	$7 + 0 + 4 = 11 \rightarrow 1 + 1$	=	2	no
1064	no	$1 + 0 + 6 + 4 = 11 \rightarrow 1 + 1$	=	2	no

2. Complete the table to display the products of numbers and the products of their digital roots. Make an observation about the results.

The digital root of a product of whole numbers equals the product of their digital roots.

Product	Digital Root of Factor	Digital Root of Factor	Product of Digital Roots of Factors	Digital Root of Product
24 × 32 = 768	$2 + 4 = 6$	$3 + 2 = 5$	$6 \times 5 = 30 \rightarrow 3 + 0 = 3$	$7 + 6 + 8 = 21 \rightarrow 2 + 1 = 3$
11 × 17 = 187	$1 + 1 = 2$	$1 + 7 = 8$	$2 \times 8 = 16 \rightarrow 1 + 6 = 7$	$1 + 8 + 7 = 16 \rightarrow 1 + 6 = 7$
121 × 42 = 5082	$1 + 2 + 1 = 4$	$4 + 2 = 6$	$4 \times 6 = 24 \rightarrow 2 + 4 = 6$	$5 + 0 + 8 + 2 = 15 \rightarrow 1 + 5 = 6$
243 × 35 = 8505	$2 + 4 + 3 = 9$	$3 + 5 = 8$	$9 \times 8 = 72 \rightarrow 7 + 2 = 9$	$8 + 5 + 0 + 5 = 18 \rightarrow 1 + 8 = 9$
81 × 72 = 5832	$8 + 1 = 9$	$7 + 2 = 9$	$9 \times 9 = 81 \rightarrow 8 + 1 = 9$	$5 + 8 + 3 + 2 = 18 \rightarrow 1 + 8 = 9$
360 × 54 = 19,440	$3 + 6 + 0 = 9$	$5 + 4 = 9$	$9 \times 9 = 81 \rightarrow 8 + 1 = 9$	$1 + 9 + 4 + 4 + 0 = 18 \rightarrow 1 + 8 = 9$

PROBLEM SOLVING 4-6

LESSON 4-6 Problem Solving
Estimating Square Roots

The distance to the horizon can be found using the formula $d = 112.88\sqrt{h}$ where d is the distance in kilometers and h is the number of kilometers from the ground. Round your answer to the nearest kilometer.

1. How far is it to the horizon when you are standing on the top of Mt. Everest, a height of 8.85 km?

336 km

2. Find the distance to the horizon from the top of Mt. McKinley, Alaska, a height of 6.194 km.

281 km

3. How far is it to the horizon if you are standing on the ground and your eyes are 2 m above the ground?

5 km

4. Mauna Kea is an extinct volcano on Hawaii that is about 4 km tall. You should be able to see the top of Mauna Kea when you are how far away?

at most 226 km

You can find the approximate speed of a vehicle that leaves skid marks before it stops. The formulas $S = 5.5\sqrt{0.7L}$ and $S = 5.5\sqrt{0.8L}$, where S is the speed in miles per hour and L is the length of the skid marks in feet, will give the minimum and maximum speeds that the vehicle was traveling before the brakes were applied. Round to the nearest mile per hour.

5. A vehicle leaves a skid mark of 40 feet before stopping. What was the approximate speed of the vehicle before it stopped?

  A 25–35 mph   Ⓒ 29–31 mph
  B 28–32 mph   D 68–70 mph

6. A vehicle leaves a skid mark of 100 feet before stopping. What was the approximate speed of the vehicle before it stopped?

  Ⓕ 46–49 mph   H 62–64 mph
  G 50–55 mph   J 70–73 mph

7. A vehicle leaves a skid mark of 150 feet before stopping. What was the approximate speed of the vehicle before it stopped?

  A 50–55 mph   C 55–70 mph
  B 53–58 mph   Ⓓ 56–60 mph

8. A vehicle leaves a skid mark of 200 feet before stopping. What was the approximate speed of the vehicle before it stopped?

  F 60–63 mph   Ⓖ 65–70 mph
  H 72–78 mph   J 80–90 mph

Technology LAB

Organizer

Use with Lesson 4-6

Pacing:
Traditional 1 day
Block $\frac{1}{2}$ day

Objective: Use a graphing calculator to evaluate expressions that have negative exponents.

Materials: Graphing calculator

Online Edition
Scientific Calculator, TechKeys

Resources

  Technology Lab Activities
Lab 4-6 Recording Sheet

Teach
Discuss

Have students read the Try This problems before attempting to answer them. Ask if any of the answers will be negative. no For Exercises 2 and 3, ask what will happen to the expressions as the values of x increase? 2. The expression increases; 3. The expression decreases

Close
Key Concept

You can use graphing calculators to evaluate expressions involving powers and roots.

Assessment

1. How could you use the calculator to evaluate the expression x^{-3} for $x = $ 2, 3, and 4?

Answers

For all answers, see pp. A5–A6.

Technology LAB 4-6 Evaluate Powers and Roots

Use with Lesson 4-6

go.hrw.com
Lab Resources Online
KEYWORD: MT7 Lab4

A graphing calculator can be used to evaluate expressions that have negative exponents and square roots.

Activity

❶ Use the **STO▶** button to evaluate x^{-3} for $x = 2$. View the answer as a decimal and as a fraction.

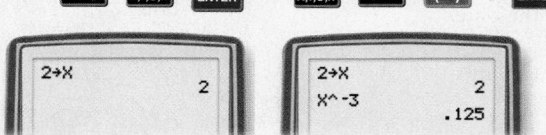

Notice that $2^{-3} = 0.125$, which is equivalent to $\frac{1}{2^3}$, or $\frac{1}{8}$.

❷ Use the **TABLE** feature to evaluate $-\sqrt{x}$ for several x-values. Match the settings shown.

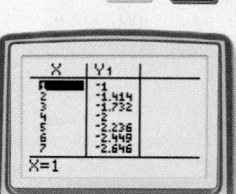

The **Y1** list shows the value of $-\sqrt{x}$ for several x-values.

Think and Discuss

1. When you evaluated 2^{-3} in Activity 1, the result was not a negative number. Is this surprising? Why or why not?

Try This

Evaluate each expression for the given x-value(s). Give your answers as fractions and as decimals rounded to the nearest hundredth.

1. $4^{-x}; x = 2$

2. $\sqrt{x}; x = 1, 2, 3, 4$

3. $x^{-2}; x = 1, 2, 5$

State Resources

go.hrw.com
State Resources Online
KEYWORD: MT7 Resources

Stacie Tarbet
Prince William County, Virginia

Teacher to Teacher

As an introduction to cubes and cube roots, I divided the class into pairs and gave each pair of students a random number of centimeter cubes. I asked my students if they could create a larger cube using all of their centimeter cubes. After a few minutes, we created a class table with two columns, one for the number of cubes and one indicating whether or not that number of cubes could create a larger cube with no small cubes left over. When a larger cube could be made, the class counted to see how many centimeter cubes made up the length, width, and height of the larger cube. The students immediately noticed that all of the measurements were the same.

The Real Numbers

Learn to determine if a number is rational or irrational.

Vocabulary
irrational number
real number
Density Property

Biologists classify animals based on shared characteristics. The horned lizard is an animal, a reptile, a lizard, and a gecko.

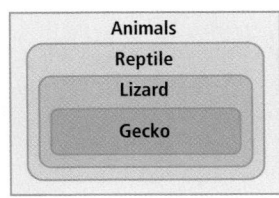

Animals
Reptile
Lizard
Gecko

Horned lizards are commonly called "horny toads" because of their flattened, toad-like bodies.

You already know that some numbers can also be classified as whole numbers, integers, or rational numbers. The number 2 is a whole number, an integer, and a rational number. It is also a *real* number.

Rational numbers can be written as fractions and as decimals that either terminate or repeat.

$$3\frac{4}{5} = 3.8 \qquad \frac{2}{3} = 0.\overline{6} \qquad \sqrt{1.44} = 1.2$$

Caution!

A repeating decimal may not appear to repeat on a calculator because calculators show a finite number of digits.

Irrational numbers can only be written as decimals that do *not* terminate or repeat. If a whole number is not a perfect square, then its square root is an irrational number.

$$\sqrt{2} \approx 1.41421356237309050488016\ldots$$

The set of **real numbers** consists of the set of rational numbers and the set of irrational numbers.

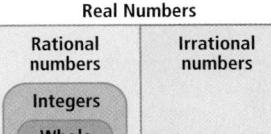

Real Numbers

Rational numbers	Irrational numbers
Integers	
Whole numbers	

EXAMPLE 1 **Classifying Real Numbers**

Write all names that apply to each number.

A $\sqrt{3}$ *3 is a whole number that is not a perfect square.*
irrational, real

B -52.28 *−52.28 is a terminating decimal.*
rational, real

C $\dfrac{\sqrt{16}}{4}$ $\dfrac{\sqrt{16}}{4} = \dfrac{4}{4} = 1$
whole, integer, rational, real

1 Introduce

Alternate Opener

EXPLORATION

4-7 The Real Numbers

The Set of Real Numbers

Rational numbers can be written as fractions or as decimals that terminate or repeat.	*Irrational numbers* are decimals that do not terminate or repeat.
Examples: $\frac{1}{4}$ $5 = \frac{5}{1}$ $\sqrt{1.69} = 1.3$ $\frac{1}{6} = 1.\overline{6}$	Examples: $\sqrt{7} = 2.645751311\ldots$ $\pi = 3.141592654\ldots$

Classify each number as rational or irrational.

		Rational	Irrational
1.	$2\frac{1}{2}$		
2.	$\sqrt{24}$		
3.	$\sqrt{16}$		
4.	$7.\overline{7}$		
5.	$\sqrt{\frac{4}{9}}$		

Think and Discuss

6. **Explain** how to classify numbers as rational.
7. **Explain** how to classify numbers as irrational.

Motivate

Show students that entering $\sqrt{2}$ on a calculator results in 1.414213562. Then show students that if 1.414213562² is entered into the calculator, the result is 1.999999999. Explain that because $\sqrt{2}$ is not a perfect square, there is no exact decimal representation for $\sqrt{2}$. The number $\sqrt{2}$ is an example of an *irrational number*.

Explorations and answers are provided in *Alternate Openers: Explorations Transparencies.*

Organizer 4-7

Pacing: Traditional 1 day
Block $\frac{1}{2}$ day
Objective: Students determine if a number is rational or irrational.

 Hands-On Lab
In *Hands-On Lab Activities*

 Technology Lab
In *Technology Lab Activities*

 Online Edition
Tutorial Videos, Interactivities

 Countdown to Testing Week 7

Power Presentations
with PowerPoint®

Warm Up

Each square root is between two integers. Name the two integers.
1. $\sqrt{119}$ 10 and 11
2. $-\sqrt{15}$ −4 and −3
Use a calculator to find each value. Round to the nearest tenth.
3. $\sqrt{2}$ 1.4
4. $-\sqrt{123}$ −11.1

Problem of the Day

The circumference of a circle is approximately 3.14 times its diameter. A circular path 1 meter wide has an inner diameter of 100 meters. How much farther is it around the outer edge of the path than the inner edge? 6.28 m

Also available on transparency

State Resources

go.hrw.com
State Resources Online
KEYWORD: MT7 Resources

Power Presentations with PowerPoint®

Additional Examples

Example 1

Write all names that apply to each number.

A. $\sqrt{5}$
irrational, real

B. -12.75
rational, real

C. $\frac{\sqrt{16}}{2}$ whole, integer, rational, real

Example 2

State if each number is rational, irrational, or not a real number.

A. $\sqrt{21}$
irrational

B. $\frac{0}{3}$
rational

C. $\sqrt{-4}$
not a real number

D. $\sqrt{\frac{4}{9}}$
rational

Example 3

Find a real number between $3\frac{2}{5}$ and $3\frac{3}{5}$. Possible answer: $3\frac{1}{2}$

Also available on transparency

Possible answers to *Think and Discuss*

1. Integers are rational numbers. Rational numbers can be expressed as quotients of two integers.

The square root of a negative number is not a real number. A fraction with a denominator of 0 is undefined because you cannot divide by zero. So it is not a number at all.

EXAMPLE **2 Determining the Classification of All Numbers**

State if each number is rational, irrational, or not a real number.

A $\sqrt{15}$ *15 is a whole number that is not a perfect square.*
irrational

B $\frac{3}{0}$
undefined, so not a real number

C $\sqrt{\frac{1}{9}}$ $\left(\frac{1}{3}\right)\left(\frac{1}{3}\right) = \frac{1}{9}$
rational

D $\sqrt{-13}$
not a real number

The **Density Property** of real numbers states that between any two real numbers is another real number. This property is not true for whole numbers or integers. For instance, there is no integer between -2 and -3.

EXAMPLE 3 Applying the Density Property of Real Numbers

Possible answers to *Think and Discuss*

2. A number cannot be irrational and whole because all whole numbers can be written as fractions.

3. The Density Property states that there is always another real number between any two real numbers. So, if you find a number x between 0 and 1, there is a number y between 0 and x and a number z between x and 1, and so on.

Find a real number between $1\frac{1}{3}$ and $1\frac{2}{3}$.

There are many solutions. One solution is halfway between the two numbers. To find it, add the numbers and divide by 2.

$\left(1\frac{1}{3} + 1\frac{2}{3}\right) \div 2$

$= \left(2\frac{3}{3}\right) \div 2$

$= 3 \div 2 = 1\frac{1}{2}$

A real number between $1\frac{1}{3}$ and $1\frac{2}{3}$ is $1\frac{1}{2}$.

Think and Discuss

1. **Explain** how rational numbers are related to integers.

2. **Tell** if a number can be irrational and whole. Explain.

3. **Use** the Density Property to explain why there are infinitely many real numbers between 0 and 1.

---

2 Teach

Guided Instruction

ENGLISH LANGUAGE LEARNERS

In this lesson, students learn to determine if a number is rational or irrational. Remind students that a rational number is a number that can be written as a ratio (fraction) of two integers with a nonzero denominator. Describe an *irrational* number as a number that *cannot* be written as a ratio of two integers. Tell students that the set of real numbers consists of the set of all rational numbers together with the set of all irrational numbers (Teaching Transparency).

Review the Density Property with students, and show them how to find a real number between two real numbers by finding the mean (average) of the numbers.

Reaching All Learners
Through Graphic Organizers

Give students a list of numbers (include terminating and repeating decimals, fractions, integers, and rational and irrational square roots) and a graphic organizer as shown below.

Real number		Not a real number
Rational	Irrational	
Integer		
Whole number		

Ask students to write each number in the list in the correct section of the organizer.

3 Close

Summarize

Remind students that a real number is rational if it can be written as a terminating or repeating decimal. A real number is irrational if it cannot be written as a terminating or repeating decimal.

go.hrw.com
Homework Help Online
KEYWORD: MT7 4-7
Parent Resources Online
KEYWORD: MT7 Parent

GUIDED PRACTICE

See Example **1** Write all names that apply to each number.

1. $\sqrt{10}$ irrational, real   **2.** $\sqrt{49}$ whole, integer, rational, real   **3.** 0.25 rational, real   **4.** $-\frac{\sqrt{16}}{3}$ rational, real

See Example **2** State if each number is rational, irrational, or not a real number.

5. $\sqrt{9}$ rational   **6.** $\sqrt{\frac{9}{16}}$ rational   **7.** $\sqrt{72}$ irrational   **8.** $-\sqrt{-3}$ not real

9. $-\sqrt{25}$ rational   **10.** $\sqrt{-9}$ not real   **11.** $\sqrt{\frac{25}{-36}}$ not real   **12.** $\frac{0}{0}$ not real

See Example **3** Find a real number between each pair of numbers.

13. $3\frac{1}{8}$ and $3\frac{2}{8}$ Possible answer: $3\frac{3}{16}$ **14.** 4.14 and $\frac{29}{7}$ Possible answer: $\frac{2899}{700}$ **15.** $\frac{1}{8}$ and $\frac{1}{4}$ $\frac{3}{16}$

INDEPENDENT PRACTICE

See Example **1** Write all names that apply to each number.

16. $\sqrt{35}$ irrational, real   **17.** $\frac{5}{8}$ rational, real   **18.** 3 whole, integer, rational, real   **19.** $\frac{\sqrt{81}}{-3}$ integer, rational, real

See Example **2** State if each number is rational, irrational, or not a real number.

20. $\frac{\sqrt{-16}}{-4}$ not real   **21.** $-\sqrt{\frac{0}{4}}$ rational   **22.** $\sqrt{-8(-2)}$ rational   **23.** $-\sqrt{3}$ irrational

24. $\frac{\sqrt{25}}{8}$ rational   **25.** $\sqrt{14}$ irrational   **26.** $\sqrt{-\frac{1}{4}}$ not real   **27.** $-\sqrt{\frac{4}{0}}$ not real

See Example **3** Find a real number between each pair of numbers.

28. $3\frac{2}{5}$ and $3\frac{3}{5}$ Possible answer: $3\frac{1}{2}$ **29.** $-\frac{1}{10}$ and 0 Possible answer: $-\frac{1}{20}$ **30.** 4 and $\sqrt{9}$ Possible answer: 3.5

PRACTICE AND PROBLEM SOLVING

Extra Practice
See page 789.

Write all names that apply to each number.

31. 6 whole, integer, rational, real   **32.** $-\sqrt{36}$ integer, rational, real   **33.** $\sqrt{10}$ irrational, real   **34.** $\frac{1}{3}$ rational, real

35. $\sqrt{2.56}$ rational, real   **36.** $\sqrt{36} + 6$ whole, integer, rational, real   **37.** $0.\overline{21}$ rational, real   **38.** $\frac{\sqrt{100}}{20}$ rational, real

39. -4.3134 rational, real   **40.** $\sqrt{4.5}$ irrational, real   **41.** -312 integer, rational, real   **42.** $\frac{0}{7}$ whole, integer, rational, real

43. Explain the difference between $-\sqrt{16}$ and $\sqrt{-16}$.

Give an example of each type of number.

44. an irrational number that is less than -3 Possible answer: $-\sqrt{30}$

45. a rational number that is less than 0.3   Possible answer: 0.2

46. a real number between $\frac{5}{9}$ and $\frac{6}{9}$ Possible answer: $\frac{11}{18}$

47. a real number between $-3\frac{2}{7}$ and $-3\frac{3}{7}$ Possible answer: $-3\frac{5}{14}$

43. $-\sqrt{16}$ is the negative of the square root of 16. $\sqrt{-16}$ is undefined and not real.

Assignment Guide

If you finished Example **1** assign:
Average 1–4, 16–19, 34–38, 63–73
Advanced 16–19, 31–38, 54–60, 63–73

If you finished Example **2** assign:
Average 1–12, 16–27, 34–38, 43, 63–73
Advanced 16–27, 39–45, 54–73

If you finished Example **3** assign:
Average 1–30, 35–38, 43–47, 63–73
Advanced 16–30, 39–45, 48–73

Homework Quick Check

Quickly check key concepts.
Exercises: 16, 26, 28, 38

Math Background

The only numbers that students at this level have encountered are real numbers. The use of the word *real* implies that there are numbers that are *not* real numbers.

In fact, there are *imaginary* numbers. Imaginary numbers are useful for specific purposes in science and engineering. The imaginary unit is $\sqrt{-1}$; it is represented by the letter *i*. An example of an imaginary number is $\sqrt{-9}$, which is simplified as follows:

$$\sqrt{-9} = \sqrt{9} \cdot \sqrt{-1} = 3i.$$

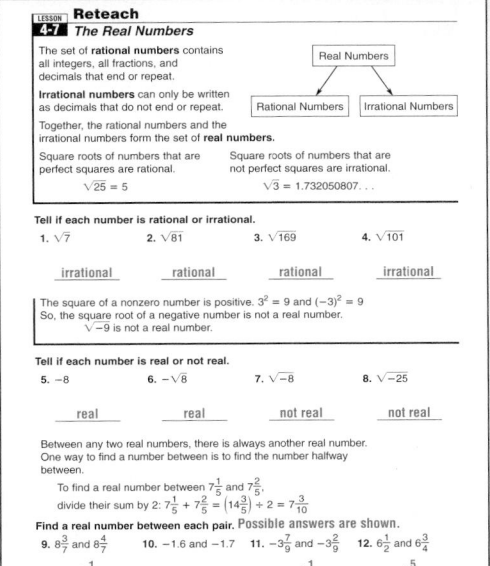

go.hrw.com
State Resources Online
KEYWORD: MT7 Resources

Answers

60. Possible answer: Negative integers are not whole numbers. Integers are the whole numbers and their opposites. All the whole numbers are integers.

61. Possible answer: If the calculator shows a terminating decimal, then the number is rational. If the decimal does not terminate, you cannot tell from the display on the calculator whether it repeats or not because you see only a limited number of digits.

TEST PREP DOCTOR Students who choose **F** in Exercise 64 may need reminding that repeating decimals are rational numbers. Show them that $0.\overline{7}$ is the same as $\frac{7}{9}$, which is rational.

Journal

Have students write about what they think it means when a number is called real. Have them write about what kinds of numbers might not be real.

Power Presentations with PowerPoint®

4-7 Lesson Quiz

Write all names that apply to each number.

1. $\sqrt{2}$ real, irrational

2. $-\dfrac{\sqrt{16}}{2}$ real, integer, rational

State if each number is rational, irrational, or not a real number.

3. $\dfrac{\sqrt{25}}{0}$ not a real number

4. $\sqrt{4} \cdot \sqrt{9}$ rational

5. Find a real number between $-2\frac{3}{4}$ and $-2\frac{3}{8}$. Possible answer: $-2\frac{5}{8}$

Also available on transparency

---

48. Find a rational number between $\sqrt{\frac{1}{9}}$ and $\sqrt{1}$. Possible answer: $\frac{2}{3}$

49. Find a real number between $\sqrt{6}$ and $\sqrt{7}$. **Possible answer: 2.5**

50. Find a real number between $\sqrt{5}$ and $\sqrt{11}$. **Possible answer: 3**

51. Find a real number between $\sqrt{50}$ and $\sqrt{55}$. **Possible answer: 7.2**

52. Find a real number between $-\sqrt{20}$ and $-\sqrt{17}$. **Possible answer: −4.25**

53. a. Find a real number between 1 and $\sqrt{3}$. Possible answer: 1.7
   b. Find a real number between 1 and your answer to part **a**. **Possible answer: 1.2**
   c. Find a real number between 1 and your answer to part **b**. **Possible answer: 1.1**

For what values of x is the value of each expression a real number?

54. $\sqrt{2x}$ $x \geq 0$

55. $3 - \sqrt{x}$ $x \geq 0$

56. $\sqrt{x+2}$ $x \geq -2$

57. $\sqrt{3x-6}$ $x \geq 2$

58. $\sqrt{5x+2}$ $x \geq -\frac{2}{5}$

59. $\sqrt{1 - \frac{x}{5}}$ $x \leq 5$

 60. What's the Error? A student said that all integers are whole numbers. What mistake did the student make? Explain.

61. Write About It Can you ever use a calculator to determine if a number is rational or irrational? Explain.

62. Challenge The circumference of a circle divided by its diameter is an irrational number, represented by the Greek letter π (pi). Could a circle with a diameter of 2 have a circumference of 6? Why or why not?
Possible answer: no, because the circumference divided by the diameter would be 3, which is rational

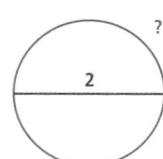

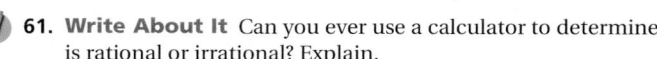

TEST PREP and Spiral Review

63. Multiple Choice Which value is between −8 and −10?

  Ⓐ -7.12 Ⓑ $-\sqrt{61}$ Ⓒ $-3 \cdot \pi$ Ⓓ $-\dfrac{123}{11}$

64. Multiple Choice Which value is NOT a rational number?

  Ⓕ $0.\overline{7}$ Ⓖ $\dfrac{11}{13}$ Ⓗ $\sqrt{19}$ Ⓙ $\sqrt{225}$

65. Multiple Choice For which values of x is $\sqrt{x-19}$ a real number?

  Ⓐ $x \geq -19$ Ⓑ $x \leq -19$ Ⓒ $x \geq 19$ Ⓓ $x \leq 19$

Evaluate the function $y = -5x + 2$ for each value of x. (Lesson 3-4)

66. $x = 0$ 2   **67.** $x = -3$ 17   **68.** $x = 7$ −33   **69.** $x = -1$ 7

Evaluate. (Lesson 4-1)

70. 8^5 32,768   **71.** $(-3)^3$ −27   **72.** $(-5)^4$ 625   **73.** 9^2 81

CHALLENGE 4-7

LESSON 4-7 Challenge
Searching for Perfection

Numbers that are equal to the sum of all their factors (not including the number itself) are called **perfect numbers**.

$$6 = 1 + 2 + 3 \qquad 6 \text{ is the smallest perfect number.}$$

1. Which of the numbers 24 or 28 is a perfect number? Explain.

24 is not perfect since $1 + 2 + 3 + 4 + 6 + 8 + 12 \neq 24$.

28 is perfect since $1 + 2 + 4 + 7 + 14 = 28$.

The ancient Greek mathematician Euclid devised a method for computing perfect numbers.
• Begin with the number 1 and keep adding powers of 2 until you get a sum that is a *prime number* (only factors are itself and 1).
• Multiply this sum by the last power of 2.

2. Complete the table to write the first three perfect numbers.

	Sum	Prime?	Euclid's Method	Perfect Number
$1 + 2$	= 3	yes	2×3	6
$1 + 2 + 4$	= 7	yes	4×7	28
$1 + 2 + 4 + 8$	= 15	no		
$1 + 2 + 4 + 8 + 16$	= 31	yes	16×31	496

So the first three perfect numbers are 6, 28, 496 .

The next perfect number is tedious to calculate in this manner. If, however, the calculations are written with exponents, a new pattern emerges.

3. Complete the table to write the sums using exponents.

Series	Sum
$1 + 2^1$	$= 2^2 - 1$
$1 + 2^1 + 2^2$	$= 2^3 - 1$
$1 + 2^1 + 2^2 + 2^3$	$= 2^4 - 1$
$1 + 2^1 + 2^2 + 2^3 + 2^4$	$= 2^5 - 1$

Incorporating this information, Euclid proved that whenever a prime number of the form $2^n - 1$ is found, a perfect number can be written.

If $2^n - 1$ is prime, then $2^{n-1}(2^n - 1)$ is a perfect number.

4. Find the fourth perfect number. $2^6(2^7 - 1) = 8128$

5. Find the fifth perfect number. $2^{12}(2^{13} - 1) = 33,550,336$

PROBLEM SOLVING 4-7

LESSON 4-7 Problem Solving
The Real Numbers

Write the correct answer.

1. Twin primes are prime numbers that differ by 2. Find an irrational number between twin primes 5 and 7.
Possible answer: $\sqrt{31}$

2. Rounded to the nearest ten-thousandth, $\pi = 3.1416$. Find a rational number between 3 and π.
Possible answer: $\frac{31}{10}$

3. One famous irrational number is e. Rounded to the nearest ten-thousandth $e \approx 2.7823$. Find a rational number that is between 2 and e.
Possible answer: $\frac{5}{2}$

4. Perfect numbers are those that the divisors of the number sum to the number itself. The number 6 is a perfect number because $1 + 2 + 3 = 6$. The number 28 is also a perfect number. Find an irrational number between 6 and 28.
Possible answer: $\sqrt{43}$

Choose the letter for the best answer.

5. Which is a rational number?
  A the length of a side of a square with area 2 cm²
  B the length of a side of a square with area 4 cm²
  C a non-terminating decimal
  D the square root of a prime number

6. Which is an irrational number?
  F a number that can be expressed as a fraction
  G the length of a side of a square with area 4 cm²
  H the length of a side of a square with area 2 cm²
  J the square root of a negative number

7. Which is an integer?
  A the number half-way between 6 and 7
  B the average rainfall for the week if it rained 0.5 in., 2.3 in., 0 in., 0 in., 0.2 in., 0.75 in. during the week
  C the money in an account if the balance was $213.00 and $21.87 was deposited
  D the net yardage after plays that resulted in a 15 yard loss, 10 yard gain, 6 yard gain and 5 yard loss

8. Which is a whole number?
  F the number half-way between 6 and 7
  G the total amount of sugar in a recipe that calls for $\frac{1}{4}$ cup of brown sugar and $\frac{3}{4}$ cup of granulated sugar
  H the money in an account if the balance was $213.00 and $21.87 was deposited
  J the net yardage after plays that resulted in a 15 yard loss, 10 yard gain, 6 yard gain and 5 yard loss

Explore Right Triangles

Use with Lesson 4-8

 **go.hrw.com**
Lab Resources Online
KEYWORD: MT7 Lab4

REMEMBER
Right triangles have 1 right angle and 2 acute angles. The side opposite the right angle is called the *hypotenuse*, and the other two sides are called *legs*.

Activity

1 The Pythagorean Theorem states that if a and b are the lengths of the legs of a right triangle, then c is the length of the hypotenuse, where $a^2 + b^2 = c^2$. Prove the Pythagorean Theorem using the following steps.

a. Draw two squares side by side. Label one with side a and one with side b.

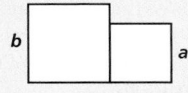

Notice that the area of this composite figure is $a^2 + b^2$.

b. Draw hypotenuses of length c, so that we have right triangles with sides a, b, and c. Use a protractor to make sure that the hypotenuses form a right angle.

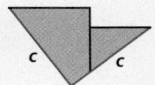

c. Cut out the triangles and the remaining piece.

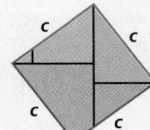

d. Fit the pieces together to make a square with sides c and area c^2. You have shown that the area $a^2 + b^2$ can be cut up and rearranged to form the area c^2, so $a^2 + b^2 = c^2$.

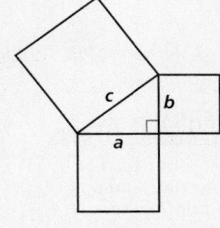

Possible answer: The area of the square on the hypotenuse of the right triangle is equal to the sum of the areas of the squares on the legs.

Think and Discuss

1. The diagram shows another way of understanding the Pythagorean Theorem. How are the areas of the squares shown in the diagram related.

Try This

1. If you know that the lengths of two legs of a right triangle are 8 and 15, can you find the length of the hypotenuse? Show your work.

2. Take a piece of paper and fold the right corner down so that the top edge of the paper matches the side edge. Crease the paper. Without measuring, find the diagonal's length.

1. Yes; $8^2 + 15^2 = 64 + 225 = 289 = c^2$; $c = \sqrt{289} = 17$

Organizer

Use with Lesson 4-8

Pacing:
Traditional $\frac{1}{2}$ day
Block $\frac{1}{4}$ day

Objective: Use scissors and paper to explore right triangles.

Materials: Scissors, paper

 Online Edition

Resources

 Hands-On Lab Activities
Lab 4-8 Recording Sheet

Teach
Discuss

Before doing the Activity, explain that the area of a square can be used to model square numbers. Draw a 12-inch line on the board, and create a square using the line as one of the sides. The area of the square is 12^2.

Close
Key Concept

You can use geometric shapes to observe visual proof of the Pythagorean Theorem.

Assessment

Find the length of the hypotenuse using the given lengths of the legs.

1. 3 and 4   5
2. 20.5 and 38.9 ≈ 43.97
3. $\frac{1}{20}$ and $\frac{3}{25}$ $\frac{13}{100}$ or 0.13

Answers to *Try This*

2. See p. A6.

Teacher to Teacher

I find that students have trouble drawing the hypotenuses of length c on regular paper, so I pass out large sheets of graph paper to each student. The students are then able to draw the squares and hypotenuses with ease. I have them find the areas of the squares with side lengths a and b as well as the square with side length c. Doing this helps them to see the Pythagorean Theorem more clearly. After the activity is finished, I display the students' work and use it as a teaching tool for later lessons.

Miguel Carrizales
San Antonio, Texas

State Resources

 **go.hrw.com**
State Resources Online
KEYWORD: MT7 Resources

Objective: Students use the Pythagorean Theorem to solve problems.

 Hands-On Lab
In *Hands-On Lab Activities*

 Technology Lab
In *Technology Lab Activities*

 Online Edition
Tutorial Videos, Interactivities

 Countdown to Testing Week 7

 **Power Presentations**
with PowerPoint®

Warm Up
Use a calculator to find each value. Round to the nearest hundredth.
1. $\sqrt{30}$ 5.48
2. $\sqrt{14}$ 3.74
3. $\sqrt{55}$ 7.42
4. $\sqrt{48}$ 6.93

Problem of the Day
A side of square *A* is 5 times the length of a side of square *B*. How many times as great is the area of *A* than the area of *B*? 25

Also available on transparency

Math Humor
The right triangle suffered from acute angles. So the mathematical doctor gave it a dose of the Pythagorean serum.

State Resources

go.hrw.com
State Resources Online
KEYWORD: MT7 Resources

4-8 The Pythagorean Theorem

Learn to use the Pythagorean Theorem to solve problems.

Vocabulary
Pythagorean Theorem
leg
hypotenuse

Pythagoras was born on the Aegean island of Samos sometime between 580 B.C. and 569 B.C. He is best known for the *Pythagorean Theorem*, which relates the side lengths of a right triangle.

A Babylonian tablet known as Plimpton 322 provides evidence that the relationship between the side lengths of right triangles was known as early as 1900 B.C. Many people, including U.S. president James Garfield, have written proofs of the Pythagorean Theorem. In 1940, E. S. Loomis presented 370 proofs of the theorem in *The Pythagorean Proposition*.

This statue of Pythagoras is located in the Pythagorion Harbor on the island of Samos.

THE PYTHAGOREAN THEOREM		
Words	**Numbers**	**Algebra**
In any right triangle, the sum of the squares of the lengths of the two **legs** is equal to the square of the length of the **hypotenuse**.	$6^2 + 8^2 = 10^2$ $36 + 64 = 100$	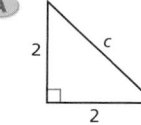 $a^2 + b^2 = c^2$

EXAMPLE 1 Finding the Length of a Hypotenuse

Find the length of each hypotenuse to the nearest hundredth.

Helpful Hint
Since length can only be positive, use only the principal square root.

A

$$a^2 + b^2 = c^2 \quad \text{Pythagorean Theorem}$$
$$2^2 + 2^2 = c^2 \quad \text{Substitute 2 for a and 2 for b.}$$
$$4 + 4 = c^2 \quad \text{Simplify powers.}$$
$$8 = c^2 \quad \text{Add.}$$
$$\sqrt{8} = \sqrt{c^2} \quad \text{Find the square roots.}$$
$$2.83 \approx c \quad \text{Round to the nearest hundredth.}$$

---

1 Introduce
Alternate Opener

EXPLORATION

4-8 The Pythagorean Theorem

The model shows a visual example of the Pythagorean Theorem.

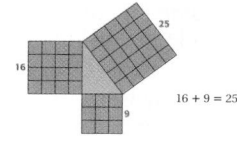

16 + 9 = 25

1. Find the lengths of the sides of the right triangle that is surrounded by the three squares.
2. What is the area of each square on each side of the triangle?
3. How does the length of each side of the triangle relate to the area of the corresponding square?
4. Can you form another example of the Pythagorean Theorem with the squares below?

Think and Discuss
5. **Explain** how you found the answer for Problem 4.

Motivate
With a 2 ft long piece of cord, tie one knot 6 in. from one end and another 10 in. from the other end. Hold the ends together. Have two students hold the knots. Pull the cord taut to form a right triangle. Tell students that builders from ancient times to modern times have created right angles this way, which uses the converse of the Pythagorean Theorem.

Explorations and answers are provided in *Alternate Openers: Explorations Transparencies.*

Find the length of each hypotenuse to the nearest hundredth.

B triangle with coordinates $(3, 1)$, $(0, 5)$, and $(0, 1)$

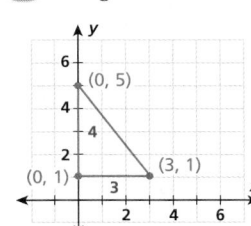

The points form a right triangle with $a = 4$ and $b = 3$.

$a^2 + b^2 = c^2$	*Pythagorean Theorem*
$4^2 + 3^2 = c^2$	*Substitute for a and b.*
$16 + 9 = c^2$	*Simplify powers.*
$25 = c^2$	*Add.*
$5 = c$	*Find the square roots.*

EXAMPLE 2 **Finding the Length of a Leg in a Right Triangle**

Solve for the unknown side in the right triangle to the nearest tenth.

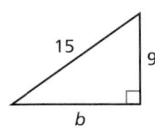

$a^2 + b^2 = c^2$	*Pythagorean Theorem*
$9^2 + b^2 = 15^2$	*Substitute for a and b.*
$81 + b^2 = 225$	*Simplify powers.*
$\underline{-81 \qquad = -81}$	*Subtract 81 from*
$b^2 = 144$	*each side.*
$b = 12$	*Find the square roots.*

EXAMPLE 3 **Using the Pythagorean Theorem for Measurement**

Mark and Sarah start walking at the same point, but Mark walks 50 feet north while Sarah walks 75 feet east. How far apart are Mark and Sarah when they stop?

Mark and Sarah's distance from each other when they stop walking is equal to the hypotenuse of a right triangle.

$a^2 + b^2 = c^2$	*Pythagorean Theorem*
$50^2 + 75^2 = c^2$	*Substitute for a and b.*
$2500 + 5625 = c^2$	*Simplify powers.*
$8125 = c^2$	*Add.*
$90.1 \approx c$	*Find the square roots.*

Mark and Sarah are approximately 90.1 feet apart.

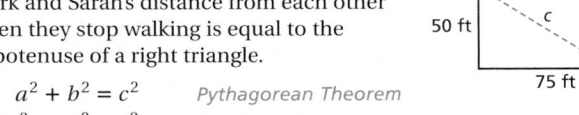

Think and Discuss

1. Tell which side of a right triangle is always the longest side.

2. Explain if 2, 3, and 4 cm could be side lengths of a right triangle.

Example 1

Find the length of each hypotenuse to the nearest hundredth.

A.

$c = \sqrt{41} \approx 6.40$

B. triangle with coordinates $(1, -2)$, $(1, 7)$, and $(13, -2)$

$c = 15$

Example 2

Solve for the unknown side in the right triangle to the nearest tenth.

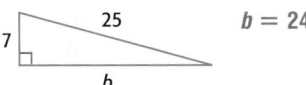

Example 3

Two airplanes leave the same airport at the same time. The first plane flies to a landing strip 350 miles south, while the other plane flies to an airport 725 miles west. How far apart are the two planes after they land?

$\sqrt{648,125} \approx 805$ miles

Also available on transparency

Possible answers to
Think and Discuss

1. hypotenuse

2. No, because if 2, 3, and 4 are put into the formula of the Pythagorean Theorem, it is not true; $4 + 9 \neq 16$.

---

2 Teach

ENGLISH LANGUAGE LEARNERS

Guided Instruction

In this lesson, students learn to use the Pythagorean Theorem and its converse to solve problems. Introduce the Pythagorean Theorem with the Teaching Transparency. Stress that in the equation $a^2 + b^2 = c^2$, c is always the longest side of the triangle, the *hypotenuse*. Explain that the hypotenuse is always the side opposite the right angle. Discuss examples that require finding the hypotenuse and examples that require finding one of the legs.

Reaching All Learners
Through Modeling

Give students a pair of scissors and a sheet that contains a right triangle and adjacent squares divided into numbered regions (Teacher Tools). Have them cut out the five numbered regions and arrange them to fit within the largest square to demonstrate that the sum of the squares of the legs equals the square of the hypotenuse.

3 Close

Summarize

Draw a right triangle on the board. Have students help you to apply the following labels: hypotenuse, leg, leg, a, b, and c. Then, label the hypotenuse 17 and the longer leg 15. Ask students to write the equation that must be solved to find the missing leg length. Ask students if the missing leg length could be 10, and why or why not.

Possible answers:
$a^2 + 15^2 = 17^2$; a could not be 10 because $10^2 + 15^2 \neq 17^2$. In fact, $a = 8$.

4-8 Exercises

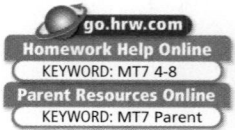
go.hrw.com
Homework Help Online
KEYWORD: MT7 4-8
Parent Resources Online
KEYWORD: MT7 Parent

Assignment Guide

If you finished Example **1** assign:
Average 1–4, 9–12, 17, 19, 23–25, 37–48
Advanced 9–12, 17, 19, 23–30, 35, 37–48

If you finished Example **2** assign:
Average 1–7, 9–15, 17–25, 37–48
Advanced 9–15, 20–30, 35–48

If you finished Example **3** assign:
Average 1–25, 31, 32, 37–48
Advanced 9–16, 20–48

Homework Quick Check

Quickly check key concepts.
Exercises: 10, 14, 16, 20, 24

GUIDED PRACTICE

See Example **1** Find the length of each hypotenuse to the nearest hundredth.

1. 15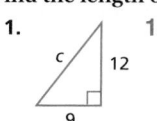

2. 10.6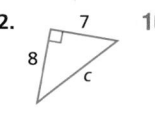

3. 8.5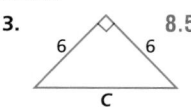

4. triangle with coordinates $(-4, 0)$, $(-4, 5)$, and $(0, 5)$ 6.4

See Example **2** Solve for the unknown side in each right triangle to the nearest tenth.

5. 8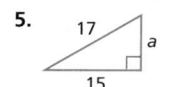

6. 5.3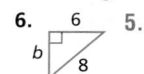

7. 16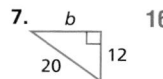

See Example **3** **8.** A traffic helicopter flies 10 miles due north and then 24 miles due east. Then the helicopter flies in a straight line back to its starting point. What was the distance of the helicopter's last leg back to its starting point?   26 mi

INDEPENDENT PRACTICE

See Example **1** Find the length of each hypotenuse to the nearest hundredth.

9. 5.4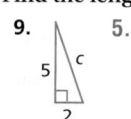

10. 13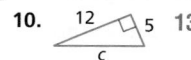

11. 26.9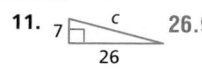

12. triangle with coordinates $(-5, 3)$, $(5, -3)$, and $(-5, -3)$ 11.7

See Example **2** Solve for the unknown side in each right triangle to the nearest tenth.

13. 12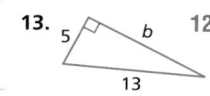

14. 12.4

15. 10.2

See Example **3** **16.** Mr. and Mrs. Flores commute to work each morning. Mr. Flores drives 8 miles east to his office. Mrs. Flores drives 15 miles south to her office. How many miles away do Mr. and Mrs. Flores work from each other?   17 mi

PRACTICE AND PROBLEM SOLVING

Extra Practice
See page 789.

Find the missing length for each right triangle to the nearest tenth.

17. $a = 4$, $b = 7$, $c = \blacksquare$ $\sqrt{65} \approx 8.1$

18. $a = \blacksquare$, $b = 40$, $c = 41$ 9

19. $a = 30$, $b = 72$, $c = \blacksquare$ 78

20. $a = 16$, $b = \blacksquare$, $c = 38$ $\sqrt{1188} \approx 34.5$

21. $a = \blacksquare$, $b = 47$, $c = 60$ $\sqrt{1391} \approx 37.3$

22. $a = 65$, $b = \blacksquare$, $c = 97$ 72

RETEACH 4-8

LESSON 4-8 Reteach
The Pythagorean Theorem

In a right triangle,
the sum of the areas of the squares on the legs is equal to
the area of the square on the hypotenuse.

$3^2 + 4^2 = 5^2$
$9 + 16 = 25$

Given the squares that are on the legs of a right triangle, draw the square for the hypotenuse.

1. leg   leg   hypotenuse

Without drawing the squares, you can find the length of a side.

a leg c hypotenuse
b leg

3 in.   4 in.

$a^2 + b^2 = c^2$
$3^2 + 4^2 = c^2$
$9 + 16 = c^2$
$25 = c^2$
$c = 5$ in.

Complete to find the length of each hypotenuse.

2. 5 ft, 12 ft
$a^2 + b^2 = c^2$
$\underline{5}^2 + \underline{12}^2 = c^2$
$\underline{25} + \underline{144} = c^2$
$\underline{169} = c^2$
$c = \underline{13}$ ft

3. 8 in., 15 in.
$a^2 + b^2 = c^2$
$\underline{8}^2 + \underline{15}^2 = c^2$
$\underline{64} + \underline{225} = c^2$
$\underline{289} = c^2$
$c = \underline{17}$ in.

PRACTICE 4-8

LESSON 4-8 Practice B
The Pythagorean Theorem

Find the length of the hypotenuse to the nearest tenth.

1. 13

2. 10.5

3. 51

Solve for the unknown side in each right triangle to the nearest tenth.

4. 14.1

5. 13.4

6. 20

7. 18.2

8. 17.7

9. 72

10. A glider flies 8 miles south from the airport and then 15 miles east. Then it flies in a straight line back to the airport. What was the distance of the glider's last leg back to the airport?   17 mi

The *converse* of the Pythagorean Theorem states that any three nonzero whole numbers that make the equation $a^2 + b^2 = c^2$ true are the side lengths of a right triangle. These numbers are called *Pythagorean triples.* Determine whether each set is a Pythagorean triple.

23. 3, 6, 9 **no**   **24.** 3, 4, 5 **yes**   **25.** 5, 12, 13 **yes**   **26.** 7, 24, 25 **yes**

27. 10, 24, 26 **yes**   **28.** 8, 14, 16 **no**   **29.** 10, 16, 19 **no**   **30.** 9, 40, 41 **yes**

31. For safety reasons, the base of a 24-foot ladder must be placed at least 8 feet from the wall. To the nearest tenth of a foot, how high can a 24-foot ladder safely reach? **22.6 ft**

32. How far is the sailboat from the lighthouse, to the nearest kilometer? **139 km**

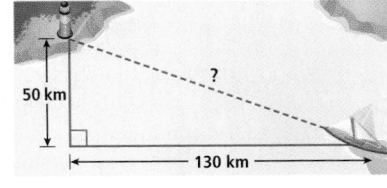

33. Critical Thinking A construction company is pouring a rectangular concrete foundation. The dimensions of the foundation are 24 ft by 48 ft. Describe a procedure to confirm that the sides of the foundation meet at a right angle.

34. Write a Problem Use a street map to write and solve a problem that requires the use of the Pythagorean Theorem. **Check students' work.**

35. Write About It Explain how to use the converse of the Pythagorean Theorem to show that a triangle is a right triangle. (See Exercises 23–30.)

36. Challenge A right triangle has legs of length $3x$ m and $4x$ m and hypotenuse of length 75 m. Find the lengths of the legs of the triangle. **45 m and 60 m**

TEST PREP and Spiral Review

37. Multiple Choice A flagpole is 40 feet tall. A rope is tied to the top of the flagpole and secured to the ground 9 feet from the base of the flagpole. What is the length of the rope to the nearest foot?

(A) 19 feet   (B) 39 feet   (C) 41 feet   (D) 1519 feet

38. Gridded Response Brad leans his 15-foot ladder against his house. The base of the ladder is placed 4 feet from the base of the house. How far up the house does the ladder reach? Round your answer to the nearest hundredth. **14.46 feet**

Find the next term in each sequence. (Lesson 3-6)

39. −3, 0, 3, 6, . . . **9**   **40.** 0.55, 0.65, 0.75, 0.85, . . . **0.95**   **41.** 9, 16, 23, 30, 37, 44, . . . **51**

42. 1, 1.5, 2, 2.5, . . . **3**   **43.** −1, 1, 3, 5, . . . **7**   **44.** 0, −2, −4, −6, . . . **−8**

Estimate each square root to two decimal places. (Lesson 4-6)

45. $\sqrt{30}$ **5.48**   **46.** $\sqrt{42}$ **6.48**   **47.** $\sqrt{55}$ **7.42**   **48.** $\sqrt{67}$ **8.19**

Answers

33. Possible answer: Use the Pythagorean Theorem to find the expected length of the diagonal. If the measured diagonal is $\sqrt{24^2 + 48^2} = \sqrt{2880} \approx 53.7$ ft, the sides form a right angle.

35. Possible answer: Find the sum of the squares of both legs and see if it equals the hypotenuse squared. If so, then the triangle is a right triangle.

TEST PREP DOCTOR For Exercise 37, students who chose **B** used the technique for finding a leg instead of a hypotenuse. Suggest that students draw a diagram for triangle problems. With a visual aid, it is more apparent that in this problem, the missing value is a hypotenuse.

Journal

Ask students to list some real-world examples of right triangles. Have them write about why it might be important to know the lengths of the sides of these triangles. Examples might include a set of stairs, a sail on a sailboat, or a triangular garden.

CHALLENGE 4-8

LESSON 4-8 Challenge
Triple Play

Three numbers connected by the Pythagorean relation are called **Pythagorean triples.**

Since $3^2 + 4^2 = 5^2$, the numbers 3-4-5 are a Pythagorean Triple.

Consider the Pythagorean triples shown in the table.

	Column A	Column B	Column C
row 1	3	4	5
row 2	5	12	13
row 3	7	24	25
row 4	9	40	41
row 5	11	60	61

1. Make an observation about the numbers in Column A.
   consecutive odd numbers

2. How are the numbers in Column C related to those in Column B?
   $C = B + 1$

3. Complete this table by carrying out the indicated calculation. Two calculations are done.
Compare the results to the Pythagorean triples in Columns A, B, and C of the original table.

	Column A	row × A + row
row 1	3	1 × 3 + 1 = 4
row 2	5	2 × 5 + 2 = 12
row 3	7	3 × 7 + 3 = 24
row 4	9	4 × 9 + 4 = 40
row 5	11	5 × 11 + 5 = 60

   results = Column B

4. In the original table, how do the squares of the numbers in Column A relate to the numbers in Columns B and C?
   $A^2 = B + C$

5. Using the relationships you have observed, calculate rows 6 and 10 of the table of Pythagorean triples. Verify your results by applying the Pythagorean Theorem.

	Column A	Column B	Column C	Verify $A^2 + B^2 = C^2$
row 6	13	84	85	$13^2 + 84^2 \stackrel{?}{=} 85^2$; $7225 = 7225$ ✓
row 10	21	220	221	$21^2 + 220^2 \stackrel{?}{=} 221^2$; $48,841 = 48,841$ ✓

PROBLEM SOLVING 4-8

LESSON 4-8 Problem Solving
The Pythagorean Theorem

Write the correct answer. Round to the nearest tenth.

1. A utility pole 10 m high is supported by two guy wires. Each guy wire is anchored 3 m from the base of the pole. How many meters of wire are needed for the guy wires?
   20.9 m

2. A 12 foot-ladder is resting against a wall. The base of the ladder is 2.5 feet from the base of the wall. How far up the wall will the ladder reach?
   11.7 ft

3. The base-path of a baseball diamond form a square. If it is 90 ft from home to first, how far does the catcher have to throw to catch someone stealing second base?
   127.3 ft

4. A football field is 100 yards with 10 yards at each end for the end zones. The field is 45 yards wide. Find the length of the diagonal of the entire field, including the end zones.
   128.2 yd

Choose the letter for the best answer.

5. The frame of a kite is made from two strips of wood, one 27 inches long, and one 18 inches long. What is the perimeter of the kite? Round to the nearest tenth.

   A 18.8 in.   (C) 65.7 in.
   B 32.8 in.   D 131.2 in.

6. The glass for a picture window is 8 feet wide. The door it must pass through is 3 feet wide. How tall must the door be for the glass to pass through the door? Round to the nearest tenth.
   F 3.3 ft   (H) 7.4 ft
   G 6.7ft   J 8.5 ft

7. A television screen measures approximately 15.5 in. high and 19.5 in. wide. A television is advertised by giving the approximate length of the diagonal of its screen. How should this television be advertised?
   (A) 25 in.   C 12 in.
   B 21 in.   D 6 in.

8. To meet federal guidelines, a wheelchair ramp that is constructed to rise 1 foot off the ground must extend 12 feet along the ground. How long will the ramp be? Round to the nearest tenth.
   F 11.9 ft   H 13.2 ft
   (G) 12.0 ft   J 15.0 ft

Power Presentations with PowerPoint®

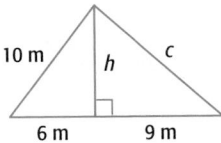

4-8 Lesson Quiz

Use the figure for Problems 1 and 2.

1. Find the height h of the triangle. **8 m**

2. Find the length of side c to the nearest meter. **12 m**

3. An escalator in a shopping mall is 40 ft long and 32 ft tall. What distance does the escalator carry shoppers? $\sqrt{2624} \approx 51$ ft

Also available on transparency

Organizer

Objective: Assess students' mastery of concepts and skills in Lessons 4-5 through 4-8.

Resources

 Assessment Resources
Section 4B Quiz

Test & Practice Generator
One-Stop Planner®

INTERVENTION ◄►

Resources

 Ready to Go On?
Intervention and
Enrichment Worksheets

💿 **Ready to Go On? CD-ROM**

🪐 **Ready to Go On? Online**

my.hrw.com

Answers

8. 14 and 15; 200 is between 196 and 225.

9. 18 and 19; 340 is between 324 and 361.

10. 24 and 25; 610 is between 576 and 625.

Ready to Go On? (sidebar, vertical)

READY TO GO ON?

Quiz for Lessons 4-5 Through 4-8

✓ 4-5 Squares and Square Roots

Find the two square roots of each number.
1. 16   ±4   **2.** 9801   ±99   **3.** 10,000   ±100   **4.** 529   ±23

5. The Merryweathers want a new square rug for their living room. If the living room is 20 ft × 16 ft, will a square rug with an area of 289 square feet fit? Explain your answer.

6. How many 2 in. × 2 in. square tiles will fit along the edge of a square mosaic that has an area of 196 square inches?   **7 tiles**

5. Possible answer: No; a square rug with an area of 289 ft² is 17 ft long on each side, so it is too long for the 16 ft side of the room.

✓ 4-6 Estimating Square Roots

Each square root is between two integers. Name the integers. Explain your answer.   **7.** −8 and −9; possible answer: $-8^2 = -64$ and $-9^2 = -81$

7. $-\sqrt{72}$ **8.** $\sqrt{200}$ **9.** $-\sqrt{340}$ **10.** $\sqrt{610}$

11. A square table has a top with an area of 11 square feet. To the nearest hundredth, what length of edging is needed to go around all edges of the tabletop?   **13.27 ft**

12. The area of a chess board is 110 square inches. Find the length of one side of the board to the nearest hundredth.   **10.49 in.**

✓ 4-7 The Real Numbers

Write all names that apply to each number.   **15.** whole number, integer, rational, real

13. $\sqrt{12}$ irrational, real   **14.** 0.15   rational, real   **15.** $\sqrt{1600}$ **16.** $-\dfrac{\sqrt{144}}{4}$ integer, rational, real

17. Give an example of an irrational number that is less than −5.   Possible answer: $-\sqrt{30}$

18. Find a real number between 5 and $\sqrt{36}$.
Possible answer: 5.2

✓ 4-8 The Pythagorean Theorem

Find the missing length for each right triangle. Round your answer to the nearest tenth.

19. $a = 3$, $b = 6$, $c = $ ▨   **6.7**   **20.** $a = $ ▨, $b = 24$, $c = 25$ **7**

21. $a = 20$, $b = $ ▨, $c = 46$ **41.4**   **22.** $a = $ ▨, $b = 53$, $c = 70$ **45.7**

23. $a = 14$, $b = 15$, $c = $ ▨   **20.5**   **24.** $a = 8$, $b = $ ▨, $c = 17$ **15**

25. A construction company is pouring a concrete foundation. The measures of two sides that meet in a corner are 33 ft and 56 ft. For the corner to be a right angle, what would the length of the diagonal have to be?   **65 ft**

READY TO GO ON?

Diagnose and Prescribe

NO INTERVENE ⬇

YES ENRICH ⬇

	READY TO GO ON? Intervention, Section 4B		
Ready to Go On? Intervention	📝 **Worksheets**	💿 **CD-ROM**	🪐 **Online**
✓ Lesson 4-5	4-5 Intervention	Activity 4-5	Diagnose and Prescribe Online
✓ Lesson 4-6	4-6 Intervention	Activity 4-6	
✓ Lesson 4-7	4-7 Intervention	Activity 4-7	
✓ Lesson 4-8	4-8 Intervention	Activity 4-8	

READY TO GO ON?
Enrichment, Section 4B
📝 **Worksheets**
💿 **CD-ROM**
🪐 **Online**

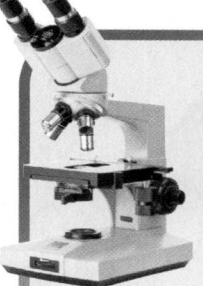

Divide and Conquer

A biologist is growing colonies of two bacteria. As shown in the table, the cells of bacterium A divide in two every hour. The cells of bacterium B divide in two every two hours.

Elapsed Time	Number of Cells	
	Bacterium A	Bacterium B
Start	1	1
1 hour	2^1	—
2 hours	2^2	2^1
3 hours	2^3	—
4 hours	2^4	2^2

1. After 8 hours, how many more cells are there of bacterium A than of bacterium B?

2. How many hours does it take until there are more than 1000 cells of bacterium A?

3. After 24 hours, how many times as many cells are there of bacterium A as bacterium B?

4. At the end of 24 hours, there are about 1.68×10^7 cells of bacterium A. The biologist divides this colony into 3 roughly equal portions. About how many cells are in each portion?

5. As a rule of thumb, if an experiment yields n colonies of bacteria, future experiments are likely to yield between $n - \sqrt{n}$ and $n + \sqrt{n}$ colonies. Suppose an experiment produces 170 colonies of bacterium A. Explain how you can estimate the range of the number of colonies that future experiments will produce.

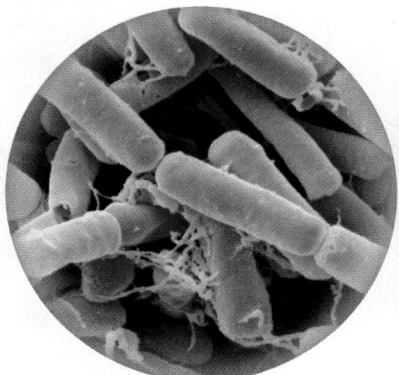
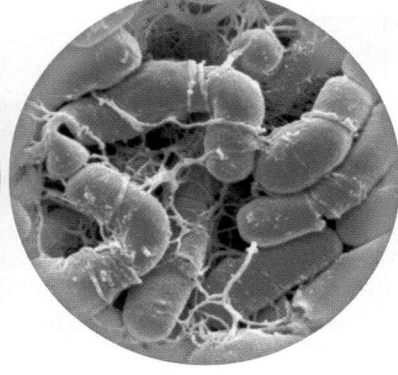

Multi-Step Test Prep

Organizer

Objective: Assess students' ability to apply concepts and skills in Chapter 4 in a real-world format.

 **Online Edition**

Resources

 Middle School Assessments
www.mathtekstoolkit.org

Problem	Text reference
1	Lesson 4-1
2	Lesson 4-2
3	Lesson 4-3
4	Lesson 4-4
5	Lesson 4-5

Answers

1. 240

2. 10 hours

3. $2^{12} = 4096$

4. 5.6×10^6

5. 157 to 183. $\sqrt{169} = 13$, so $\sqrt{170} \approx 13$ and the approximate range is $170 - 13$ to $170 + 13$.

INTERVENTION

Scaffolding Questions

1. How many cells of Bacterium A are there after n hours? 2^n of Bacterium B? $2^{\frac{n}{2}}$ How many cells of each bacterium are there after 8 hours? 2^8 and 2^4 How can you write these numbers without exponents? 256 and 16

2. What strategy can you use to solve this problem? Possible answer: extend the table How many cells of Bacterium A are there after 10 hours? 1024

3. How many cells of each bacterium are there after 24 hours? 2^{24} and 2^{12} What operation should you use to solve this problem? Division How do you divide 2^{24} by 2^{12}? Subtract the exponents

4. What is 1.68×10^7 in standard notation? 16,800,000 What is this number divided by 3? 5,600,000 How do you write this in scientific notation? 5.6×10^6

5. How can you estimate $\sqrt{170}$? 170 is close to 169 and $\sqrt{169} = 13$, so $\sqrt{170} \approx 13$

Extension

1. How many hours does it take until there are more than 1×10^6 cells of Bacterium B? 40 How many cells are there at this time? 1,048,580

State Resources

 **go.hrw.com**
State Resources Online
KEYWORD: MT7 Resources

Organizer

Objective: Participate in games to practice and apply skills learned in Chapter 4.

 Online Edition

Resources

📖 **Chapter 4 Resource Book**
Puzzles, Twisters & Teasers

Magic Squares

Purpose: To apply the skill of writing and solving equations to completing a magic square

Discuss Ask students to explain what a magic square is. How can writing and solving equations help you find the missing numbers in a magic square?

Possible answer: In a magic square, the sum of the numbers in any row, column, or diagonal is the same. To find the missing numbers, assign a variable to each. Then write equations and solve them to find the value of one variable. Use that value to find the sum of one row, column, or diagonal. Then use the sum to find the values of the other variables.

Extend Challenge students to create a magic square using the numbers 1–9.

Possible answer:

8	1	6
3	5	7
4	9	2

Equation Bingo

Purpose: To practice solving equations in a game format

Discuss When students get "Bingo," have them demonstrate for the class how the winning solution was obtained.

Extend Have students create new equation cards for each solution on their Bingo cards. Use the new equation cards to play again.

Game Time

Magic Squares

A *magic square* is a square with numbers arranged so that the sums of the numbers in each row, column, and diagonal are the same.

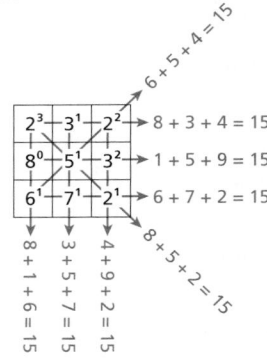

$6 + 5 + 4 = 15$

2^3	3^1	2^2	$8 + 3 + 4 = 15$
8^0	5^1	3^2	$1 + 5 + 9 = 15$
6^1	7^1	2^1	$6 + 7 + 2 = 15$

$8 + 1 + 6 = 15$ $3 + 5 + 7 = 15$ $4 + 9 + 2 = 15$ $8 + 5 + 2 = 15$

According to an ancient Chinese legend, a tortoise from the Lo river had the pattern of this magic square on its shell.

1 Complete each magic square below.

$\sqrt{36}$		2^2
8^0	$\sqrt{9}$	
	$3^2 - 2$	

	$-(\sqrt{4} + 4)$	$-(9^0)$
$-(\sqrt{16})$		0^3
$-(\sqrt{9})$	$2^0 + 1$	

2 Use the numbers $-4, -3, -2, -1, 0, 1, 2, 3,$ and 4 to make a magic square with row, column, and diagonal sums of 0.

Equation Bingo

Each bingo card has numbers on it. The caller has a collection of equations. The caller reads an equation, and then the players solve the equation for the variable. If players have the solution on their cards, they place a chip on it. The winner is the first player with a row of chips either down, across, or diagonally.

A complete copy of the rules and game boards are available online.

🪐 **go.hrw.com**
Game Time Extra
KEYWORD: MT7 Games

Answers

1. $-1, 1, 5, -2, 2, 0, -5$

2. Possible answer:

-1	-2	3
4	0	-4
-3	2	1

Materials
- strip of white paper (18 in. by 7 in.)
- piece of decorative paper (6 in. by 6 in.)
- tape
- scraps of decorative paper
- markers
- glue

It's in the Bag!

FOLDNOTES

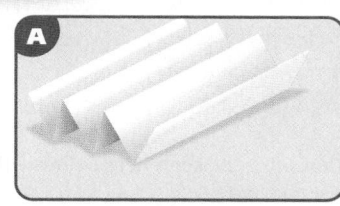

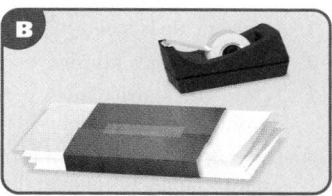

PROJECT It's a Wrap

Design your own energy-bar wrapper to hold your notes on exponents and roots.

Directions

❶ Make accordion folds on the strip of white paper so that there are six panels, each about 3 in. wide. **Figure A**

❷ Fold up the accordion strip.

❸ Wrap the decorative paper around the accordion strip. The accordion strip will stick out on either side. Tape the ends of the decorative paper together to make a wrapper. **Figure B**

❹ Write the number and title of the chapter on scraps of decorative paper, and glue these to the wrapper.

Taking Note of the Math

Use the panels of the accordion strip to take notes on the key concepts in this chapter. Include examples that will help you remember facts about exponents, roots, and the Pythagorean Theorem. Fold up the strip and slide it back into the wrapper.

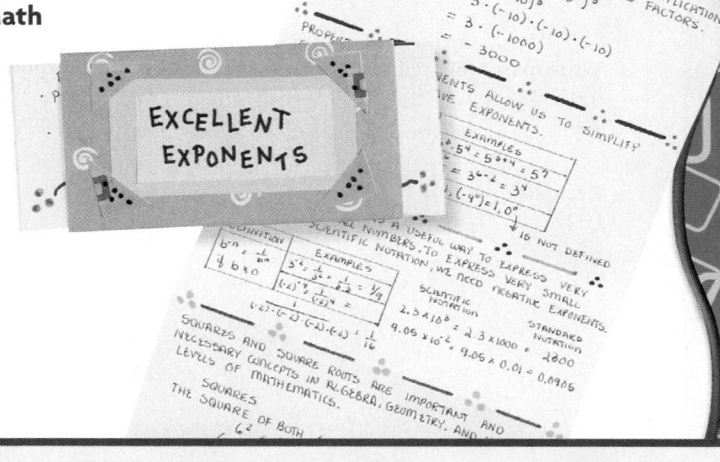

Organizer

Objective: Make a wrapper for an accordion strip that contains notes on exponents and roots.

Materials: strip of white paper (18 in. by 7 in.), piece of decorative paper (6 in. by 6 in.), tape, scraps of decorative paper, markers, glue

PREMIER **Online Edition**

Using the Page

Preparing the Materials
You can prepare the long strips of white paper by cutting strips from a roll of butcher paper. Alternatively, you might have students tape together shorter pieces of paper until they have a strip of the required length.

Making the Project
Encourage students to fold the accordion strip carefully so that each panel is about the same size. This will make it easier to create a wrapper that fits perfectly.

Extending the Project
Students can start with paper strips of different lengths. Have them calculate the appropriate dimensions of the decorative paper to produce a wrapper that fits snugly.

Tips from the Bag Ladies!

Sometimes we have students do this project using actual wrappers from energy bars and other favorite foods. In this case, students can decorate the accordion strip to match the colors of the wrapper.

Many types of paper work well for the wrapper: pieces of wallpaper, construction paper, gift-wrapping paper, and so on. Whatever type of paper students use, you might have them add an ingredients list that shows the contents of the accordion strip.

Organizer

Objective: Help students organize and review key concepts and skills presented in Chapter 4.

Online Edition
Multilingual Glossary

Resources

PuzzlePro®
One-Stop Planner®

Multilingual Glossary Online

go.hrw.com
KEYWORD: MT7 Glossary

Lesson Tutorial Videos
CD-ROM

Test & Practice Generator
One-Stop Planner®

Answers

1. base, exponent
2. irrational number
3. scientific notation
4. Pythagorean Theorem; legs; hypotenuse
5. real numbers
6. 7^3
7. $(-3)^2$
8. k^4
9. $(-9)^1$
10. $(-2)^2 d^2$
11. $(3n)^3$
12. $6x^2$
13. 10^4
14. 625
15. -32
16. -1
17. 256
18. -3
19. 64
20. -27
21. 25
22. 15
23. 1296
24. 100,000
25. -128

Study Guide: Review

Vocabulary

base 162
Density Property 192
exponent 162
exponential form 162
hypotenuse 196
irrational number 191
leg 196

perfect square 182
power 162
principal square root 182
Pythagorean Theorem 196
real number 191
scientific notation 174

Complete the sentences below with vocabulary words from the list above.

1. A power consists of a(n) ___?___ raised to a(n) ___?___.
2. A(n) ___?___ is a number that cannot be written as a fraction.
3. ___?___ is a short-hand way of writing extremely large or extremely small numbers.
4. The ___?___ states that the sum of the squares of the ___?___ of a right triangle is equal to the square of the ___?___.
5. The set of ___?___ is the set of all rational and irrational numbers.

4-1 Exponents (pp. 162–165)

EXAMPLE

■ Write in exponential form.
  $4 \cdot 4 \cdot 4$
  4^3 *Identify how many times 4 is used as a factor.*

■ Evaluate.
  $(-2)^3$
  $(-2) \cdot (-2) \cdot (-2)$ *Find the product of*
  -8 *three -2's.*

EXERCISES

Write in exponential form.

6. $7 \cdot 7 \cdot 7$ 7. $(-3) \cdot (-3)$
8. $k \cdot k \cdot k \cdot k$ 9. -9
10. $(-2) \cdot (-2) \cdot d \cdot d$ 11. $3n \cdot 3n \cdot 3n$
12. $6 \cdot x \cdot x$ 13. 10,000

Evaluate.

14. 5^4 15. $(-2)^5$ 16. $(-1)^9$
17. 2^8 18. $(-3)^1$ 19. 4^3
20. $(-3)^3$ 21. $(-5)^2$ 22. 15^1
23. 6^4 24. 10^5 25. $(-2)^7$

4-2 Look for a Pattern in Integer Exponents (pp. 166–169)

EXAMPLE

Evaluate.

- $(-3)^{-2}$

  $\dfrac{1}{(-3)^2}$ *Write the reciprocal; change the*

  $\dfrac{1}{9}$ *sign of the exponent.*

- 2^0

  1

EXERCISES

Evaluate.

26. 5^{-3} **27.** $(-4)^{-3}$ **28.** 11^{-1}

29. 10^{-4} **30.** 100^0 **31.** -6^{-2}

32. -3^{-4} **33.** $(-10)^{-2}$

34. $(9-7)^{-3}$ **35.** $(6-9)^{-3}$

36. $(8-5)^{-1}$ **37.** $(7-10)^0$

38. $4^{-1}+(5-7)^{-2}$ **39.** $3^{-2}\cdot 2^{-3}\cdot 9^0$

40. $10-9(3^{-2}+6^0)$

4-3 Properties of Exponents (pp. 170–173)

EXAMPLE

Write the product or quotient as one power.

- $2^5\cdot 2^3$

  2^{5+3} *Add exponents.*

  2^8

- $\dfrac{10^9}{10^2}$

  10^{9-2} *Subtract exponents.*

  10^7

EXERCISES

Write the product or quotient as one power.

41. $4^2\cdot 4^5$ **42.** $9^2\cdot 9^4$ **43.** $p\cdot p^3$

44. $15\cdot 15^2$ **45.** $6^2\cdot 3^2$ **46.** $x^4\cdot x^6$

47. $\dfrac{8^5}{8^2}$ **48.** $\dfrac{9^3}{9}$ **49.** $\dfrac{m^7}{m^2}$

50. $\dfrac{3^5}{3^{-2}}$ **51.** $\dfrac{4^{-5}}{4^{-5}}$ **52.** $\dfrac{y^6}{y^{-3}}$

53. $5^0\cdot 5^3$ **54.** $y^6\div y$ **55.** $k^4\div k^4$

4-4 Scientific Notation (pp. 174–178)

EXAMPLE

Write in standard notation.

- 3.58×10^4

  $3.58\times 10,000$

  $35,800$

- 3.58×10^{-4}

  $3.58\times \dfrac{1}{10,000}$

  $3.58\div 10,000$

  0.000358

Write in scientific notation.

- $0.000007=7\times 10^{-6}$ ■ $62,500=6.25\times 10^4$

EXERCISES

Write in standard notation.

56. 1.62×10^3 **57.** 1.62×10^{-3}

58. 9.1×10^5 **59.** 9.1×10^{-5}

Write in scientific notation.

60. 0.000000008 **61.** $73,000,000$

62. 0.0000096 **63.** $56,400,000,000$

Study Guide: Review

Answers

26. $\frac{1}{125}$

27. $-\frac{1}{64}$

28. $\frac{1}{11}$

29. $\frac{1}{10,000}$

30. 1

31. $-\frac{1}{36}$

32. $-\frac{1}{81}$

33. $\frac{1}{100}$

34. $\frac{1}{8}$

35. $-\frac{1}{27}$

36. $\frac{1}{3}$

37. 1

38. $\frac{1}{2}$

39. $\frac{1}{72}$

40. 0

41. 4^7

42. 9^6

43. p^4

44. 15^3

45. cannot combine

46. x^{10}

47. 8^3

48. 9^2

49. m^5

50. 3^7

51. 4^0, or 1

52. y^9

53. 5^3

54. y^5

55. k^0, or 1

56. 1620

57. 0.00162

58. $910,000$

59. 0.000091

60. 8×10^{-9}

61. 7.3×10^7

62. 9.6×10^{-6}

63. 5.64×10^{10}

Study Guide: Review

4-5 **Squares and Square Roots** (pp. 182–185)

EXAMPLE

■ Find the two square roots of 400.

$20 \cdot 20 = 400$

$(-20) \cdot (-20) = 400$

The square roots are 20 and −20.

EXERCISES

Find the two square roots of each number.

64. 16   **65.** 900   **66.** 676

Evaluate each expression.

67. $\sqrt{4 + 21}$ **68.** $\frac{\sqrt{100}}{20}$ **69.** $\sqrt{3^4}$

4-6 **Estimating Square Roots** (pp. 186–189)

EXAMPLE

■ Find the side length of a square with area 359 ft² to one decimal place. Then find the distance around the square to the nearest tenth.

Side = $\sqrt{359} \approx 18.9$

Distance around $\approx 4(18.9) \approx 75.6$ feet

EXERCISES

Find the distance around each square with the area given. Round to the nearest tenth.

70. Area of square *ABCD* is 500 in².

71. Area of square *MNOP* is 1750 cm².

72. Name the integers $\sqrt{82}$ is between.

4-7 **The Real Numbers** (pp. 191–194)

EXAMPLE

■ State if the number is rational, irrational, or not a real number.

$-\sqrt{2}$ irrational   *The decimal equivalent does not repeat or end.*

$\sqrt{-4}$ not real   *Square roots of negative numbers are not real.*

EXERCISES

State if the number is rational, irrational, or not a real number.

73. $\sqrt{81}$ **74.** $\sqrt{122}$ **75.** $\sqrt{-16}$

76. $-\sqrt{5}$ **77.** $\frac{0}{-4}$ **78.** $\frac{7}{0}$

79. Find a real number between $\sqrt{9}$ and $\sqrt{16}$.

4-8 **The Pythagorean Theorem** (pp. 196–199)

EXAMPLE

■ Find the length of side *b* in the right triangle where *a* = 8 and *c* = 17.

$a^2 + b^2 = c^2$

$8^2 + b^2 = 17^2$

$64 + b^2 = 289$

$b^2 = 225$

$b = \sqrt{225} = 15$

EXERCISES

Solve for the unknown side in each right triangle.

80. If *a* = 6 and *b* = 8, find *c*.

81. If *b* = 24 and *c* = 26, find *a*.

82. Find the length between opposite corners of a square with side lengths 10 inches to the nearest tenth.

 **CHAPTER TEST**  **CHAPTER 4**

Evaluate.

1. 10^9 **2.** 11^{-3} **3.** 2^7 **4.** 3^{-4}

Evaluate each expression. Write your answer as one power.

5. $\dfrac{3^3}{3^6}$ **6.** $7^9 \cdot 7^2$ **7.** $(5^{10})^6$ **8.** $\dfrac{11^{-7}}{11^7}$

9. $27^3 \cdot 27^{-18}$ **10.** $(52^{-7})^{-3}$ **11.** $13^0 \cdot 13^9$ **12.** $\dfrac{8^{12}}{8^7}$

Write each number in standard notation.

13. 2.7×10^{12} **2,700,000,000,000**

14. 3.53×10^{-2} **0.0353**

15. 4.257×10^5 **425,700**

16. 9.87×10^{10} **98,700,000,000**

17. -4.8×10^8 **−480,000,000**

18. 6.09×10^{-3} **0.00609**

19. -8.1×10^6 **−8,100,000**

20. -3.5×10^{-4} **−0.00035**

Write each number in scientific notation.

21. $19,000,000,000$ **21.** 1.9×10^{10}

22. 0.0000039 **22.** 3.9×10^{-6}

23. $1,980,000,000$ **1.9×10^9**

24. 0.00045 **4.5×10^{-4}**

25. A sack of cocoa beans weighs about 132 lb. How much would 1000 sacks of cocoa beans weigh? Write the answer in scientific notation.   **1.32×10^5 lb**

Find the two square roots of each number.

26. 196 **±14**   **27.** 1 **±1**   **28.** $10,000$ **±100**   **29.** 625 **±25**

30. The minimum area of a square, high school wrestling mat is 1444 square feet. What is the length of the mat?   **38 ft**

Each square root is between two integers. Name the integers. Explain your answer.

31. $\sqrt{230}$ **15 and 16**   **32.** $\sqrt{125}$ **11 and 12**   **33.** $\sqrt{89}$ **9 and 10**   **34.** $-\sqrt{60}$ **−7 and −8**

35. $-\sqrt{3}$ **−1 and −2**   **36.** $\sqrt{175}$ **13 and 14**   **37.** $-\sqrt{410}$ **−20 and −21**   **38.** $\sqrt{325}$ **18 and 19**

39. A square has an area of 13 ft². To the nearest tenth, what is its perimeter?   **14.4 ft**

Write all names that apply to each number.

40. $-\sqrt{121}$ **integer, rational, real**

41. $-1.\overline{7}$ **irrational, real**

42. $\sqrt{-9}$ **not a real number**

43. $\dfrac{\sqrt{225}}{3}$ **whole number, integer, rational, real**

Find the missing length for each right triangle.

44. $a = 10$, $b = 24$, $c = \blacksquare$ **26**

45. $a = \blacksquare$, $b = 15$, $c = 175$ **8**

46. $a = 12$, $b = \blacksquare$, $c = 20$ **16**

47. Lupe wants to use a fence to divide her square garden in half diagonally. If each side of the garden is 16 ft long, how long will the fence have to be? Round your answer to the nearest hundredth of a foot.   **22.63 ft**

48. A right triangle has a hypotenuse that is 123 in. long. If one of the legs is 75 in. long, how long is the other leg? Round your answer to the nearest tenth of an inch.   **97.5 in.**

Organizer

Objective: Provide review and practice for Chapters 1–4 and standardized tests.

Online Edition

Resources

Assessment Resources
Chapter 4 Cumulative Test

State Test Prep Workbook

State Test Prep CD-ROM

State Test Practice Online

go.hrw.com
KEYWORD: MT7 TestPrep

Standardized Test Prep

Cumulative Assessment, Chapters 1–4

Multiple Choice

1. Which expression is NOT equivalent to $3 \cdot 3 \cdot 3 \cdot 3 \cdot 3 \cdot 3$?
   - (A) 3^6
   - (B) 9^3
   - (C) 18
   - (D) 729

2. A number to the 8th power divided by the same number to the 4th power is 16. What is the number?
   - (F) 2
   - (G) 4
   - (H) 6
   - (J) 8

3. Which expression is equivalent to 81?
   - (A) 2^9
   - (B) 3^{-4}
   - (C) $\left(\frac{1}{3}\right)^{-4}$
   - (D) $\left(\frac{1}{3}\right)^4$

4. The airports in the United States serve more than 635,000,000 people each year. Which of the following is the same number written in scientific notation?
   - (F) 635×10^6
   - (G) 6.35×10^{-8}
   - (H) 6.35×10^8
   - (J) 6.35×10^9

5. For which equation is the ordered pair $(-3, 4)$ a solution?
   - (A) $2x - y = -6$
   - (B) $x - 2y = 5$
   - (C) $\frac{1}{2}x - y = 6$
   - (D) $x - \frac{1}{2}y = -5$

6. The population of India is close to 1.08×10^9. Which of the following represents this population written in standard notation?
   - (F) 1,080,000,000
   - (G) 180,000,000
   - (H) 1,080,000
   - (J) 108,000

7. Jenny finds that a baby lizard grows about 0.5 inch every week. Which equation best represents the number of weeks it will take for the lizard to grow to 1 foot long if it was 4 inches long when it hatched?
   - (A) $0.5w + 4 = 1$
   - (B) $0.5w + 4 = 12$
   - (C) $\frac{w + 4}{12} = 0.5$
   - (D) $\frac{w}{0.5 + 4} = 1$

8. A number k is decreased by 8, and the result is multiplied by 8. This product is then divided by 2. What is the final result?
   - (F) $8k - 4$
   - (G) $4k - 8$
   - (H) $4k - 32$
   - (J) $8k - 64$

9. Which ordered pair lies on the x-axis?
   - (A) $(-1, 2)$
   - (B) $(1, -2)$
   - (C) $(0, 2)$
   - (D) $(-1, 0)$

10. A quilt is made with 10 square pieces of fabric. If the area of each square piece is 169 square inches, what is the length of each square piece?
    - (F) 12 inches
    - (G) 13 inches
    - (H) 14 inches
    - (J) 15 inches

11. Which number is NOT between 1.5 and 1.75?
    - (A) $1\frac{1}{4}$
    - (B) 1.73
    - (C) 1.62
    - (D) $1\frac{13}{25}$

12. The $\sqrt{18}$ is between which pair of numbers?
    - (F) 8 and 9
    - (G) 7 and 8
    - (H) 4 and 5
    - (J) 3 and 4

(sidebar) Standardized Test Prep

TEST PREP DOCTOR

For item 3, students who answered **B** or **D** think that $\frac{1}{81}$ is the same as 81 or do not understand negative exponents.

For item 13, students who answered **F** did not subtract the total eaten pizza from the total amount of pizza, 5.

For item 22 part b, students may miss subtracting 2.5 ft from Marissa's height of 5.5 feet. Remind students to read each item closely.

Answers

20. a. 2,100,000 pounds
    b. 2.10×10^2, 1.0×10^4
    c. $(2.1 \times 10^2)(1.0 \times 10^4) = (2.1 \times 1.0)(10^2 \times 10^4) = 2.1 \times 10^6$. You can add the exponents in 10^2 and 10^4 because the bases are the same. This becomes 10^6. The product of 2.1 and 1.0 is 2.1. So the answer is 2.1×10^6.

21. a. between 29 feet and 30 feet
    b. Using an estimated length of 30 feet, Jack and his dad need 900 square feet, or 100 square yards of carpet to make sure that they have enough.

22. See 4-Point Response work sample.

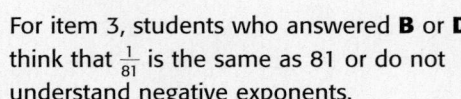
go.hrw.com
State Resources Online
KEYWORD: MT7 Resources

13. Mrs. Graham ordered five pizzas for her top-performing class. The students ate $\frac{7}{8}$ of the pepperoni pizza, $\frac{3}{4}$ of the cheese pizza, $\frac{4}{5}$ of the veggie pizza, $\frac{2}{3}$ of the Hawaiian pizza, and $\frac{1}{2}$ of the barbecue chicken pizza. How much total pizza was left over?

Ⓕ $3\frac{71}{120}$ Ⓗ $1\frac{49}{120}$

Ⓖ $2\frac{1}{8}$ Ⓙ $1\frac{7}{15}$

 Pay attention to the units given in a test question, especially if there are mixed units, such as inches and feet.

Gridded Response

14. What exponent makes the statement $3^? = 27^2$ true? **6**

15. Determine the value of x when y = 3 in the graph. **2**

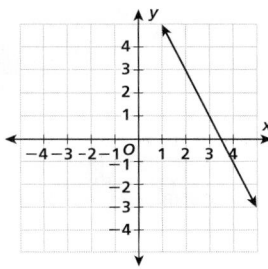

16. Chrissy is 25 years older than her dog. The sum of their ages is 37. How old is Chrissy's dog? **6**

17. Evaluate the expression, $\frac{4}{5} - \left|\frac{1}{2} - x\right|$ for $x = \frac{1}{5}$. **1/2**

18. The area of a square is 169 square feet. What is the length in feet of a side? **13**

19. From her house, Lea rode her bike 8 miles north and then 15 miles west to a friend's house. How far in miles was she from her house along a straight path? **17**

Short Response

20. A bag of pinto beans weighs 210 pounds.

   a. How much does 10,000 bags of pinto beans weigh? Write your answer in standard form.

   b. Write the numbers 210 and 10,000 in scientific notation.

   c. Explain how to use rules of exponents to write the weight of 10,000 bags of pinto beans in scientific notation.

21. Jack works part time with his dad installing carpet. They need to install carpet in a square room that has an area of about 876 square feet. Carpet can only be ordered in whole square yards.

   a. About how many feet long is the room?

   b. About how many square yards of carpet do Jack and his dad need in order to cover the floor of the room? Explain your reasoning.

Extended Response

22. Marissa's cat is stuck in a tree. The cat is on a branch 23 feet from the ground. Marissa is 5.5 feet tall, and she owns a 16-foot ladder.

   a. Create a table that shows how high up on the tree the top of the ladder will reach if Marissa places the base of the ladder 1 foot, 2 feet, 3 feet, 4 feet, and 5 feet from the tree.

   b. How high will Marissa be if she places the base of the ladder the distances from the tree in part **a** and stands on the rung 2.5-feet from the top of the ladder?

   c. Do you think Marissa can use this ladder to reach her cat? Explain your reasoning.

Standardized Test Prep

Student Work Samples for Item 22

4-Point Response

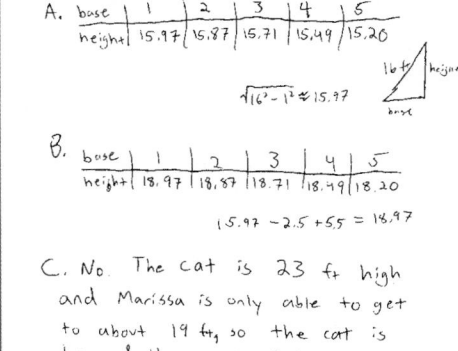

The student calculated both tables correctly and showed work for the first pair of elements in each table. The explanation in part **c** is also correct.

3-Point Response

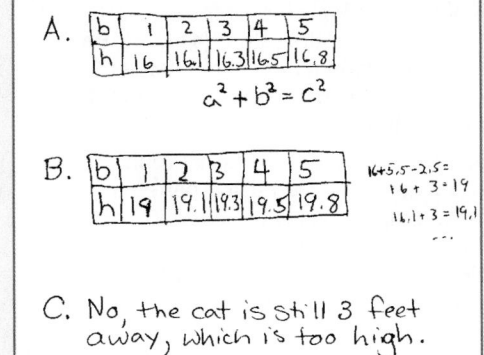

The student knew to use the Pythagorean Theorem, but solved for a hypotenuse instead of a leg.

2-Point Response

a.	base	height	b.	base	height
	1	16		1	13.5
	2	15.9		2	13.4
	3	15.7		3	13.2
	4	15.5		4	13
	5	15.2		5	12.7

$\sqrt{16^2 - b^2} = h$

c. No, even with the ladder 1 ft from the base of the tree, she will still be almost 10 ft away from her cat.

The student used the Pythagorean Theorem and completed part **a** correctly. However, the student did not account for Marissa's height in part **b**, so answers to parts **b** and **c** were therefore incorrect.

Cumulative Assessment, Chapters 1–4 **209**

Organizer

Objective: Choose appropriate problem-solving strategies and use them with skills from Chapters 3 and 4 to solve real-world problems.

 Online Edition

✪ The Ohio and Erie Canal

Reading Strategies

Make sure that students read Problem 1 carefully. It can be confusing since the boat's starting point is 14 miles south of Cleveland. Have students compare what they read to the graph to make sure it is consistent. They should notice that the distance is 14 miles when the time is zero hours on the graph.

Using Data Ask the students questions to familiarize them with the graph. How far has the boat gone in 1 hour? 18 mi How long does it take for the boat to travel 26 miles? 3 hours

Problem Solving on Location

O H I O

Cleveland

Portsmouth

✪ The Ohio and Erie Canal

In 1825, work began on the historic Ohio & Erie Canal, a waterway that connected the cities of Cleveland and Portsmouth. By 1832, traffic flowed along the entire 308-mile route. The Ohio & Erie is no longer a working canal, but its grassy towpath remains a popular destination for joggers and cyclists.

Choose one or more strategies to solve each problem. For Problems 1–3, use the graph.

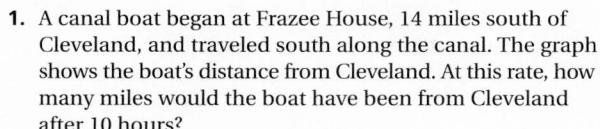
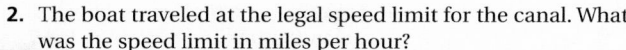
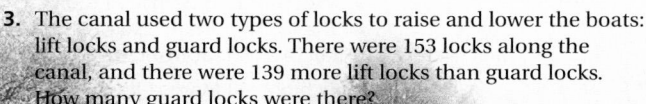

1. A canal boat began at Frazee House, 14 miles south of Cleveland, and traveled south along the canal. The graph shows the boat's distance from Cleveland. At this rate, how many miles would the boat have been from Cleveland after 10 hours?

2. The boat traveled at the legal speed limit for the canal. What was the speed limit in miles per hour?

3. The canal used two types of locks to raise and lower the boats: lift locks and guard locks. There were 153 locks along the canal, and there were 139 more lift locks than guard locks. How many guard locks were there?

Boat Travel on the Ohio & Erie Canal

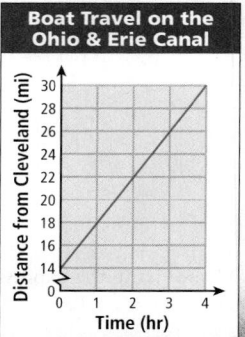

Problem Solving Focus

Encourage students to use the four-step problem-solving process for the problems. Focus on the fourth step: **(4) Look Back.** Have the students use their answer for Problem 3 to solve Problem 1 to make sure both are correct.

Discuss with students how Problems 1 and 2 can be solved using patterns to make graphs, tables or series. Then show them how they can save time by completing Problem 3 first and finding the answers with multiplication.

Answers

1. 54 miles
2. 4 mi/hr
3. 7

State Resources

go.hrw.com
State Resources Online
KEYWORD: MT7 Resources

☆ The Glenn Research Center

The Glenn Research Center, in northern Ohio, is one of NASA's key research facilities. The technologies developed at the Glenn Research Center have made it possible for humans to walk on the Moon, receive photographs from Mars, and explore the outer reaches of our solar system.

Problem Solving Strategies

Draw a Diagram
Make a Model
Guess and Test
Work Backward
Find a Pattern
Make a Table
Solve a Simpler Problem
Use Logical Reasoning
Act It Out
Make an Organized List

Choose one or more strategies to solve each problem.

1. The Flight Research Building is an enormous hangar that can hold several aircraft at the same time. The base of the hangar is a rectangle measuring 250 feet by 65 feet. To the nearest foot, what is the length of the longest pole that can be stored on the floor of the hangar?

2. The center's supersonic wind tunnel can produce wind speeds of up to 2280 mi/h. Here, scientists can test the effects of doubling wind speed. If scientists begin with a wind speed of 2^5 mi/h. How many times can they double the speed and still stay within the wind tunnel's capabilities?

For Problem 3, use the table.

3. The table shows some of the famous space missions that involved the Glenn Research Center. Use the following information to determine the destination of each mission.

   • One mission went to Saturn, and one went to Mars.

   • The shortest mission was a mission to the Moon.

   • Saturn is farther from Earth than Mars.

   What was the destination of the Pathfinder mission? the Apollo mission? the Cassini mission?

Glenn Research Center Missions	
Name	Distance to Destination (mi)
Pathfinder	4×10^7
Apollo	2.4×10^5
Cassini	2×10^9

☆ The Glenn Research Center

Reading Strategies

ENGLISH LANGUAGE LEARNERS

Encourage students to pick up on key words that suggest geometry. In Problem 1, words such as "base" and "length," as well as the phrase "250 feet by 65 feet" indicate that this problem can be visualized geometrically. Suggest that students draw a sketch of the information as they read.

Using Data Discuss how students can compare numbers in scientific notation with each other. Ask them to arrange the missions by least to greatest distances. Apollo, Pathfinder, Cassini

🔍 Problem Solving Focus

Encourage students to use the four-step problem-solving process for the problems. Focus on the second step: (2) **Make a Plan.** After reading through Problem 3, ask students to explain how they intend to use the three given pieces of information about the missions to solve the problem.

Possible answer: Use the second clue to find which mission went to the moon. This will leave only two missions left to solve for. The first clue tells us that the one mission went to Saturn and the other went to Mars. The third clue tells us that the larger of the two missions went to Saturn, and the smaller went to Mars.

1. 258 ft

2. 6

3. Pathfinder: Mars; Apollo: Moon; Cassini: Saturn

CHAPTER
5

Ratios, Proportions, and Similarity

Section 5A

Ratios, Rates, and Proportions

5-1   Ratios and Proportions

5-2   Ratios, Rates, and Unit Rates

5-3   Dimensional Analysis

5-4   Solving Proportions

Section 5B

Similarity and Scale

5-5   **Hands-On Lab**   Explore Similarity

5-5   Similar Figures

5-6   **Hands-On Lab**   Explore Dilations

5-6   Dilations

5-7   Indirect Measurement

5-8   Scale Drawings and Scale Models

5-8   **Hands-On Lab**   Make a Scale Model

Pacing Guide for 45-Minute Classes

Chapter 5			Countdown to Testing Weeks **8**, **9**	
DAY 1	**DAY 2**	**DAY 3**	**DAY 4**	**DAY 5**
5-1 Lesson	5-2 Lesson	5-3 Lesson	5-4 Lesson	Ready to Go On? Focus on Problem Solving 5-5 Hands-On Lab
DAY 6	**DAY 7**	**DAY 8**	**DAY 9**	**DAY 10**
5-5 Lesson	5-6 Hands-On Lab 5-6 Lesson	5-6 Lesson 5-7 Lesson	5-7 Lesson 5-8 Lesson	5-8 Lesson
DAY 11	**DAY 12**	**DAY 13**		
5-6 Hands-On Lab Ready to Go On? Multi-Step Test Prep	Chapter 5 Review	Chapter 5 Test		

Pacing Guide for 90-Minute Classes

Chapter 5				
DAY 1	**DAY 2**	**DAY 3**	**DAY 4**	**DAY 5**
5-1 Lesson 5-2 Lesson	5-3 Lesson 5-4 Lesson	Ready to Go On? Focus on Problem Solving 5-5 Hands-On Lab 5-5 Lesson	5-6 Hands-On Lab 5-6 Lesson 5-7 Lesson	5-7 Lesson 5-8 Lesson
DAY 6	**DAY 7**			
5-6 Hands-On Lab Ready to Go On? Multi-Step Test Prep Chapter 5 Review	Chapter 5 Test			

ONGOING ASSESSMENT and INTERVENTION

	DIAGNOSE	PRESCRIBE

Assess Prior Knowledge

Before Chapter 5

Diagnose readiness for the chapter.

Are You Ready? SE p. 213

Prescribe intervention.

Are You Ready? Intervention Skills 17, 19, 23, 59, 71

Formative Assessment

Before Every Lesson

Diagnose readiness for the lesson.

Warm Up TE, every lesson

Prescribe intervention.

Skills Bank SE pp. 820–834

Reteach CRB, Lessons 1–5

During Every Lesson

Diagnose understanding of lesson concepts.

Think and Discuss SE, every lesson
Write About It SE, lesson exercises
Journal TE, lesson exercises

Prescribe intervention.

Questioning Strategies Chapter 5
Reading Strategies CRB, every lesson
Success for ELL pp. 63–78

After Every Lesson

Diagnose mastery of lesson concepts.

Lesson Quiz TE, every lesson
Test Prep SE, every lesson
Test and Practice Generator

Prescribe intervention.

Reteach CRB, every lesson
Problem Solving CRB, every lesson
Test Prep Doctor TE, lesson exercises
Homework Help Online

Before Chapter 5 Testing

Diagnose mastery of concepts in the chapter.

Ready to Go On? SE pp. 234, 258
Focus on Problem Solving SE p. 235
Multi-Step Test Prep SE p. 259
Section Quizzes AR pp. 85–86
Test and Practice Generator

Prescribe intervention.

Ready to Go On? Intervention Chapter 5
Scaffolding Questions TE p. 259

Before High Stakes Testing

Diagnose mastery of benchmark concepts.

Test Tackler SE pp. 266–267
Standardized Test Prep SE pp. 268–269
State Test Prep CD-ROM

Prescribe intervention.

State Test Prep Workbook

Summative Assessment

After Chapter 5

Check mastery of chapter concepts.

Multiple-Choice Tests (Forms A, B, C)
Free-Response Tests (Forms A, B, C)
Performance Assessment AR pp. 87–100
Test and Practice Generator
Check mastery of benchmark concepts.

AYP State Tests

Prescribe intervention.

Reteach CRB, every lesson
Lesson Tutorial Videos Chapter 5

Prescribe intervention.

State Test Prep Workbook

KEY: **SE** = *Student Edition* **TE** = *Teacher's Edition* **CRB** = *Chapter Resource Book* **AR** = *Assessment Resources* — Available on CD-ROM — Available online **212B**

Supporting the Teacher

Chapter 5 Resource Book

Practice A, B, C
pp. 3–5, 11–13, 19–21, 28–30, 36–38, 45–47, 54–56, 62–64

Reading Strategies ELL
pp. 9, 17, 26, 34, 43, 52, 60, 68

Puzzles, Twisters, and Teasers
pp. 10, 18, 27, 35, 44, 53, 61, 69

Reteach
pp. 6, 14, 22–23, 31, 39–40, 48–49, 57, 65

Problem Solving
pp. 8, 16, 25, 33, 42, 51, 59, 67

Challenge
pp. 7, 15, 24, 32, 41, 50, 58, 66

Parent Letter pp. 1–2

Transparencies

Lesson Transparencies, Volume 1 .... Chapter 5
- Teaching Tools
- Warm Ups
- Problem of the Day
- Teaching Transparencies
- Lesson Quizzes

Know-It Notebook .... Chapter 5
- Additional Examples
- Vocabulary
- Chapter Review
- Big Ideas

Alternate Openers: Explorations ....pp. 32–39

Countdown to Testing ....pp. 15–18

Teacher Tools

Power Presentations®
Complete PowerPoint® presentations for Chapter 5 lessons

Lesson Tutorial Videos® SPANISH
Holt authors Ed Burger and Freddie Renfro present tutorials to support the Chapter 5 lessons.

One-Stop Planner® SPANISH
Easy access to all Chapter 5 resources and assessments, as well as software for lesson planning, test generation, and puzzle creation

IDEA Works!®
Key Chapter 5 resources and assessments modified to address special learning needs

Lesson Plans ....pp. 32–39

Questioning Strategies.................................... Chapter 5

Solutions Key .... Chapter 5

Interdisciplinary Posters and Worksheets.............. Chapter 5

TechKeys 🪐   **Lab Resources** 🪐

Project Teacher Support 🪐   **Parent Resources** 🪐

Workbooks

Homework and Practice Workbook SPANISH
Teacher's Guide...pp. 16–20

Know-It Notebook
Teacher's Guide.. Chapter 5

Problem Solving Workbook SPANISH
Teacher's Guide...pp. 16–20

State Test Prep Workbook
Teacher's Guide

Technology Highlights for the Teacher

 Power Presentations
Dynamic presentations to engage students. Complete PowerPoint® presentations for every lesson in Chapter 5.

 One-Stop Planner SPANISH
Easy access to Chapter 5 resources and assessments. Includes lesson-planning, test-generation, and puzzle-creation software.

 Premier Online Edition SPANISH
Chapter 5 includes Tutorial Videos, Lesson Activities, Lesson Quizzes, Homework Help, and Chapter Project.

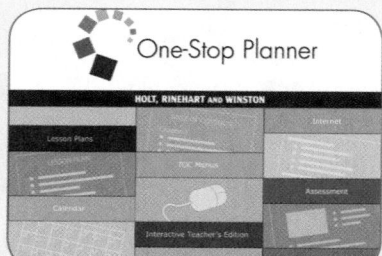

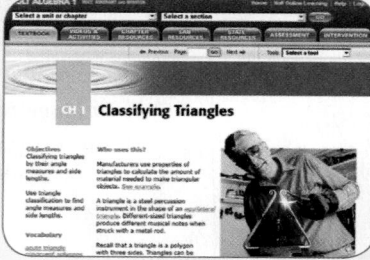

2-1 Solving One-Step Equations

Isolate a variable by using inverse operations which "undo" operations on the variable.

An equation is like a balanced scale. To keep the balance, perform the same operation on both sides.

Inverse Operations	
Operation	**Inverse Operation**
Addition	Subtraction
Subtraction	Addition

KEY: **SE** = *Student Edition*   **TE** = *Teacher's Edition*   English Language Learners   Spanish version available   Available on CD-ROM   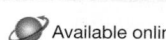 Available online

 # Reaching All Learners

ENGLISH
LANGUAGE
LEARNERS

Resources for All Learners

Hands-On Lab Activities.................................... Chapter 5

Technology Lab Activities................................... Chapter 5

Homework and Practice Workbook SPANISH ....pp. 32–39

Know-It Notebook .... Chapter 5

Problem Solving Workbook SPANISH ....pp. 32–39

English Language Learners

Are You Ready? Vocabulary .... SE p. 213

Vocabulary Connections .... SE p. 214

Lesson Vocabulary .... SE, every lesson

Vocabulary Review .... SE p. 262

English Language Learners ....TE pp. 215, 220, 238

Reading Strategies .... CRB, every lesson

Success for English Language Learners ....pp. 63–78

Multilingual Glossary

DEVELOPING LEARNERS

Practice A ....CRB, every lesson
Reteach ....CRB, every lesson
Inclusion ....TE p. 217
Questioning Strategies..........................Chapter 5
Modified Chapter 5 Resources ....*IDEA Works!*
Homework Help Online

ON-LEVEL LEARNERS

Practice B ....CRB, every lesson
Puzzles, Twisters, and Teasers ....CRB, every lesson
Cognitive Strategies ....TE p. 221
Cooperative Learning ....TE p. 217

ADVANCED LEARNERS

Practice C ....CRB, every lesson
Challenge ....CRB, every lesson
Extension ....TE pp. 215, 259, 260, 261
Critical Thinking ....TE p. 239

Reaching All Learners Through...

Inclusion ....TE p. 217

Diversity.......................................TE p. 230

Visual Cues.............................TE pp. 239, 249

Kinesthetic Experience ....TE p. 249

Multiple Representations ....TE p. 245

Cognitive Strategies ....TE p. 221

Cooperative Learning ....TE p. 217

Modeling ....TE p. 253

Critical Thinking ....TE p. 239

Test Prep Doctor...................TE pp. 219, 223, 228, 233, 241,
247, 251, 255, 266, 268

Common Error Alerts ....TE pp. 217, 225, 230, 249

Scaffolding Questions.........................TE p. 259

Technology Highlights for Reaching All Learners

 Lesson Tutorial Videos SPANISH

Starring Holt authors Ed Burger and Freddie Renfro! Live tutorials to support every lesson in Chapter 5.

Multilingual Glossary

Searchable glossary includes definitions in English, Spanish, Vietnamese, Chinese, Hmong, Korean, and 4 other languages.

Online Interactivities

Interactive tutorials provide visually engaging alternative opportunities to learn concepts and master skills.

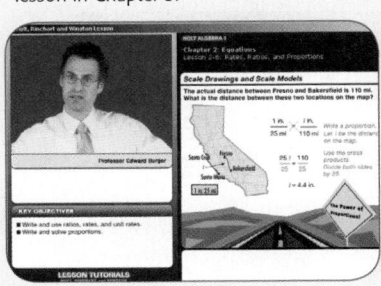

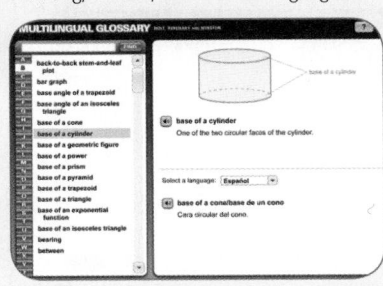

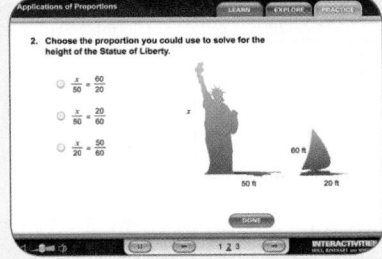

KEY: **SE** = *Student Edition* **TE** = *Teacher's Edition* **CRB** = *Chapter Resource Book*  SPANISH Spanish version available 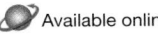 Available on CD-ROM Available online

CHAPTER 5

Ongoing Assessment

Assessing Prior Knowledge

Determine whether students have the prerequisite concepts and skills for success in Chapter 5.

Are You Ready? SPANISH .... SE p. 213
Warm Up .... TE, every lesson

Test Preparation

Provide review and practice for Chapter 5 and standardized tests.

Multi-Step Test Prep .... SE p. 259
Study Guide: Review .... SE pp. 262–264
Test Tackler .... SE pp. 266–267
Standardized Test Prep .... SE pp. 268–269
Countdown to Testing Transparencies ....pp. 15–18
State Test Prep Workbook
State Test Prep CD-ROM
IDEA Works!

Alternative Assessment

Assess students' understanding of Chapter 5 concepts and combined problem-solving skills.

Chapter 5 Project .... SE p. 212
Performance Assessment SPANISH .... AR pp. 99–100
Portfolio Assessment SPANISH .... AR p. xxxiv

Daily Assessment

Provide formative assessment for each day of Chapter 5.

Questioning Strategies .... Chapter 5
Think and Discuss .... SE, every lesson
Write About It .... SE, lesson exercises
Journal .... TE, lesson exercises
Lesson Quiz .... TE, every lesson
Modified Lesson Quizzes .... IDEA Works!

Weekly Assessment

Provide formative assessment for each week of Chapter 5.

Focus on Problem Solving .... SE p. 235
Multi-Step Test Prep .... SE p. 259
Ready to Go On? SPANISH .... SE pp. 234, 258
Cumulative Assessment .... SE pp. 268–269
Test and Practice Generator SPANISH ...One-Stop Planner

Formal Assessment

Provide summative assessment of Chapter 5 mastery.

Section Quizzes SPANISH .... AR pp. 85–86
Chapter 5 Test .... SE p. 265
Chapter Test (Levels A, B, C) SPANISH .... AR pp. 87–98
• Multiple-Choice • Free-Response
Cumulative Test SPANISH .... AR pp. 101–104
Test and Practice Generator SPANISH ...One-Stop Planner
Modified Chapter 5 Test .... IDEA Works!

Technology Highlights for the Teacher

Are You Ready? SPANISH
Automatically assess readiness and prescribe intervention for Chapter 5 prerequisite skills.

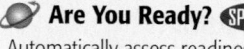
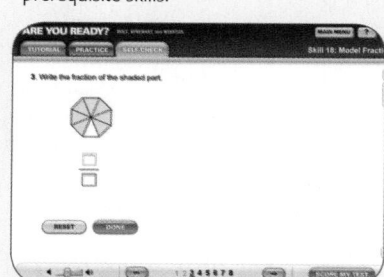

Ready to Go On? SPANISH
Automatically assess understanding of and prescribe intervention for Sections 5A and 5B.

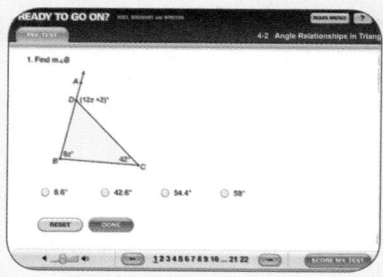

Test and Practice Generator SPANISH
Use Chapter 5 problem banks to create assessments and worksheets to print out or deliver online. Includes dynamic problems.

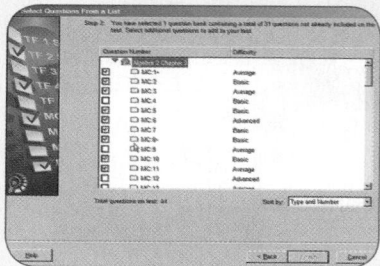

KEY: **SE** = *Student Edition*   **TE** = *Teacher's Edition*   **AR** = *Assessment Resources*   SPANISH Spanish version available   Available on CD-ROM   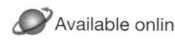 Available online

Formal Assessment

Three levels (A, B, C) of multiple-choice and free-response chapter tests are available in the *Assessment Resources.*

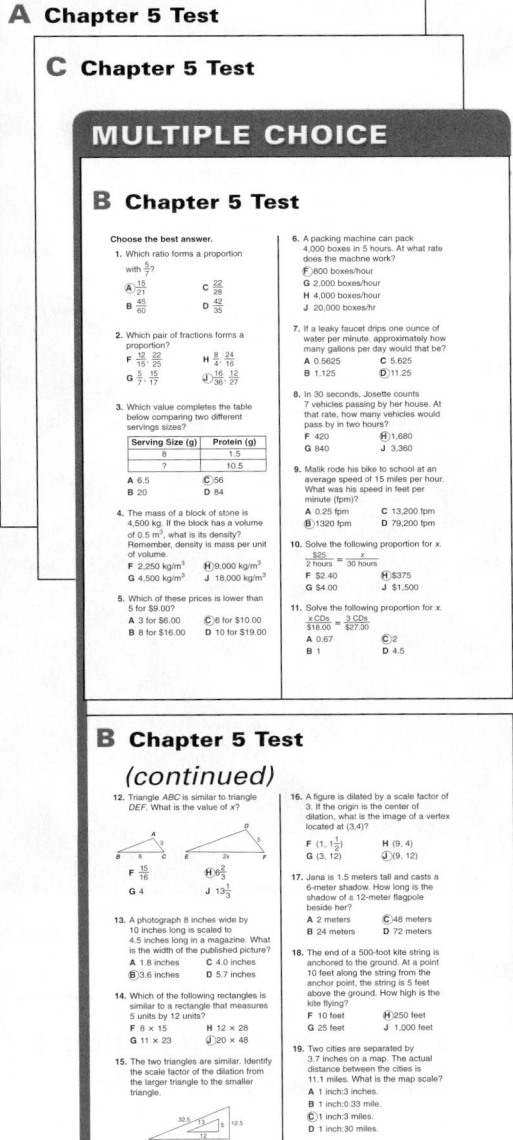

A Chapter 5 Test

C Chapter 5 Test

MULTIPLE CHOICE

B Chapter 5 Test

Choose the best answer.

1. Which ratio forms a proportion with $\frac{5}{7}$?
   - A $\frac{15}{21}$
   - B $\frac{45}{60}$
   - C $\frac{22}{28}$
   - D $\frac{42}{35}$

2. Which pair of fractions forms a proportion?
   - F $\frac{12}{15}, \frac{22}{25}$
   - G $\frac{5}{7}, \frac{15}{17}$
   - H $\frac{3}{4}, \frac{24}{19}$
   - J $\frac{16}{36}, \frac{12}{27}$

3. Which value completes the table below comparing two different servings sizes?

Serving Size (g)	Protein (g)
8	1.5
?	10.5

   - A 6.5
   - B 20
   - C 56
   - D 84

4. The mass of a block of stone is 4,500 kg. If the block has a volume of 0.5 m³, what is its density? Remember, density is mass per unit of volume.
   - F 2,250 kg/m³
   - G 4,500 kg/m³
   - H 9,000 kg/m³
   - J 18,000 kg/m³

5. Which of these prices is lower than 5 for $9.00?
   - A 3 for $6.00
   - B 8 for $16.00
   - C 6 for $10.00
   - D 10 for $19.00

6. A packing machine can pack 4,000 boxes in 5 hours. At what rate does the machine work?
   - F 800 boxes/hour
   - G 2,000 boxes/hour
   - H 4,000 boxes/hour
   - J 20,000 boxes/hr

7. If a leaky faucet drips one ounce of water per minute, approximately how many gallons per day would that be?
   - A 0.5625
   - B 1.125
   - C 5.625
   - D 11.25

8. In 30 seconds, Josette counts 7 vehicles passing by her house. At that rate, how many vehicles would pass by in two hours?
   - F 420
   - G 840
   - H 1,680
   - J 3,360

9. Malik rode his bike to school at an average speed of 15 miles per hour. What was his speed in feet per minute (fpm)?
   - A 0.25 fpm
   - B 1320 fpm
   - C 13,200 fpm
   - D 79,200 fpm

10. Solve the following proportion for x.
    $$\frac{\$25}{2 \text{ hours}} = \frac{x}{30 \text{ hours}}$$
    - F $2.40
    - G $4.00
    - H $375
    - J $1,500

11. Solve the following proportion for x.
    $$\frac{x \text{ CDs}}{\$18.00} = \frac{3 \text{ CDs}}{\$27.00}$$
    - A 0.67
    - B 1
    - C 2
    - D 4.5

B Chapter 5 Test
(continued)

12. Triangle *ABC* is similar to triangle *DEF*. What is the value of *x*?
    - F $\frac{15}{16}$
    - G 4
    - H $6\frac{2}{3}$
    - J $13\frac{1}{3}$

13. A photograph 8 inches wide by 10 inches long is scaled to 4.5 inches long in a magazine. What is the width of the published picture?
    - A 1.8 inches
    - B 3.6 inches
    - C 4.0 inches
    - D 5.7 inches

14. Which of the following rectangles is similar to a rectangle that measures 5 units by 12 units?
    - F 8 × 15
    - G 11 × 23
    - H 12 × 28
    - J 20 × 48

15. The two triangles are similar. Identify the scale factor of the dilation from the larger triangle to the smaller triangle.
    - A 0.40
    - B 0.60
    - C 2.5
    - D 250

16. A figure is dilated by a scale factor of 3. If the origin is the center of dilation, what is the image of a vertex located at (3,4)?
    - F $(1, 1\frac{1}{3})$
    - G (3, 12)
    - H (9, 4)
    - J (9, 12)

17. Jana is 1.5 meters tall and casts a 6-meter shadow. How long is the shadow of a 12-meter flagpole beside her?
    - A 2 meters
    - B 24 meters
    - C 48 meters
    - D 72 meters

18. The end of a 500-foot kite string is anchored to the ground. At a point 10 feet along the string from the anchor point, the string is 5 feet above the ground. How high is the kite flying?
    - F 10 feet
    - G 25 feet
    - H 250 feet
    - J 1,000 feet

19. Two cities are separated by 3.7 inches on a map. The actual distance between the cities is 11.1 miles. What is the map scale?
    - A 1 inch:3 inches.
    - B 1 inch:0.33 mile.
    - C 1 inch:3 miles.
    - D 1 inch:30 miles.

20. A model boat is 15 inches long. If it is built to a scale of 1:250, how long is the real boat?
    - F 16.7 feet
    - G 167 feet
    - H 312.5 feet
    - J 3,750 feet

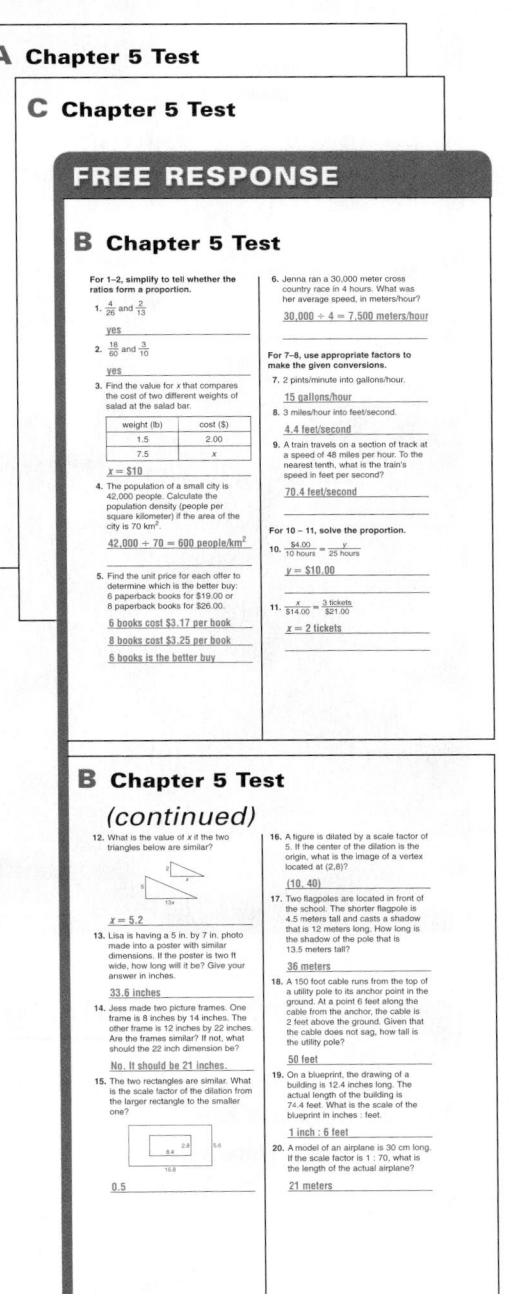

A Chapter 5 Test

C Chapter 5 Test

FREE RESPONSE

B Chapter 5 Test

For 1–2, simplify to tell whether the ratios form a proportion.

1. $\frac{4}{26}$ and $\frac{2}{13}$

   yes

2. $\frac{18}{60}$ and $\frac{3}{10}$

   yes

3. Find the value for *x* that compares the cost of two different weights of salad at the salad bar.

weight (lb)	cost ($)
1.5	2.00
7.5	x

   $x = \$10$

4. The population of a small city is 42,000 people. Calculate the population density (people per square kilometer) if the area of the city is 70 km².

   $42,000 \div 70 = 600 \text{ people/km}^2$

5. Find the unit price for each offer to determine which is the better buy: 6 paperback books for $19.00 or 8 paperback books for $26.00.

   6 books cost $3.17 per book

   8 books cost $3.25 per book

   6 books is the better buy

6. Jenna ran a 30,000 meter cross country race in 4 hours. What was her average speed, in meters/hour?

   $30,000 \div 4 = 7,500 \text{ meters/hour}$

For 7–8, use appropriate factors to make the given conversions.

7. 2 pints/minute into gallons/hour.

   15 gallons/hour

8. 3 miles/hour into feet/second.

   4.4 feet/second

9. A train travels on a section of track at a speed of 48 miles per hour. To the nearest tenth, what is the train's speed in feet per second?

   70.4 feet/second

For 10 – 11, solve the proportion.

10. $\frac{\$4.00}{10 \text{ hours}} = \frac{y}{25 \text{ hours}}$

    $y = \$10.00$

11. $\frac{x}{\$14.00} = \frac{3 \text{ tickets}}{\$21.00}$

    $x = 2 \text{ tickets}$

B Chapter 5 Test
(continued)

12. What is the value of *x* if the two triangles below are similar?

    $x = 5.2$

13. Lisa is having a 5 in. by 7 in. photo made into a poster with similar dimensions. If the poster is two ft wide, how long will it be? Give your answer in inches.

    33.6 inches

14. Jess made two picture frames. One frame is 8 inches by 14 inches. The other frame is 12 inches by 22 inches. Are the frames similar? If not, what should the 22 inch dimension be?

    No. It should be 21 inches.

15. The two rectangles are similar. What is the scale factor of the dilation from the larger rectangle to the smaller one?

    0.5

16. A figure is dilated by a scale factor of 5. If the center of the dilation is the origin, what is the image of a vertex located at (2,8)?

    (10, 40)

17. Two flagpoles are located in front of the school. The shorter flagpole is 4.5 meters tall and casts a shadow that is 12 meters long. How long is the shadow of the pole that is 13.5 meters tall?

    36 meters

18. A 150 foot cable runs from the top of a utility pole to its anchor point in the ground. At a point 6 feet along the cable from the anchor, the cable is 2 feet above the ground. Given that the cable does not sag, how tall is the utility pole?

    50 feet

19. On a blueprint, the drawing of a building is 12.4 inches long. The actual length of the building is 74.4 feet. What is the scale of the blueprint in inches : feet.

    1 inch : 6 feet

20. A model of an airplane is 30 cm long. If the scale factor is 1 : 70, what is the length of the actual airplane?

    21 meters

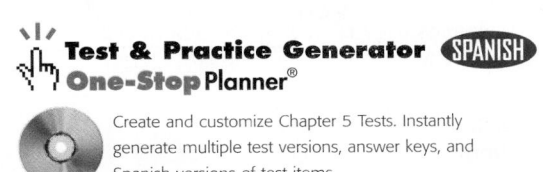

Test & Practice Generator ⟨SPANISH⟩
One-Stop Planner®

Create and customize Chapter 5 Tests. Instantly generate multiple test versions, answer keys, and Spanish versions of test items.

CHAPTER 5

Ratios, Proportions, and Similarity

Why Learn This?

Tell students that a horticulturist creating a bonsai plant may use ratios and proportions to determine the ideal height of the bonsai. For example, the height of the bonsai juniper tree is $\frac{6}{120}$, or $\frac{1}{20}$, of the height of the natural juniper tree. The horticulturist might use this ratio in a proportion to determine the seedling height, adult height, pruning guidelines, etc.

Using Data

To begin the study of this chapter, have students:

- Write the height of the bonsai pitch pine as a fraction of the height of the natural pitch pine. $\frac{14}{2000}$ Write the fraction in simplest form. $\frac{7}{1000}$

- Write an equation to determine how many times taller the natural brush cherry is than the bonsai brush cherry. $8t = 50(12);\ 8t = 600$ Have them solve the equation. $t = 75$

MULTI-STEP TEST PREP On page 259, students use scales to calculate the actual dimensions of a scale model.

5A	Ratios, Rates, and Proportions
5-1	Ratios and Proportions
5-2	Ratios, Rates, and Unit Rates
5-3	Dimensional Analysis
5-4	Solving Proportions
5B	**Similarity and Scale**
LAB	Explore Similarity
5-5	Similar Figures
LAB	Explore Dilations
5-6	Dilations
5-7	Indirect Measurement
5-8	Scale Drawings and Scale Models
LAB	Make a Scale Model

MULTI-STEP TEST PREP

go.hrw.com
Chapter Project Online
KEYWORD: MT7 Ch5

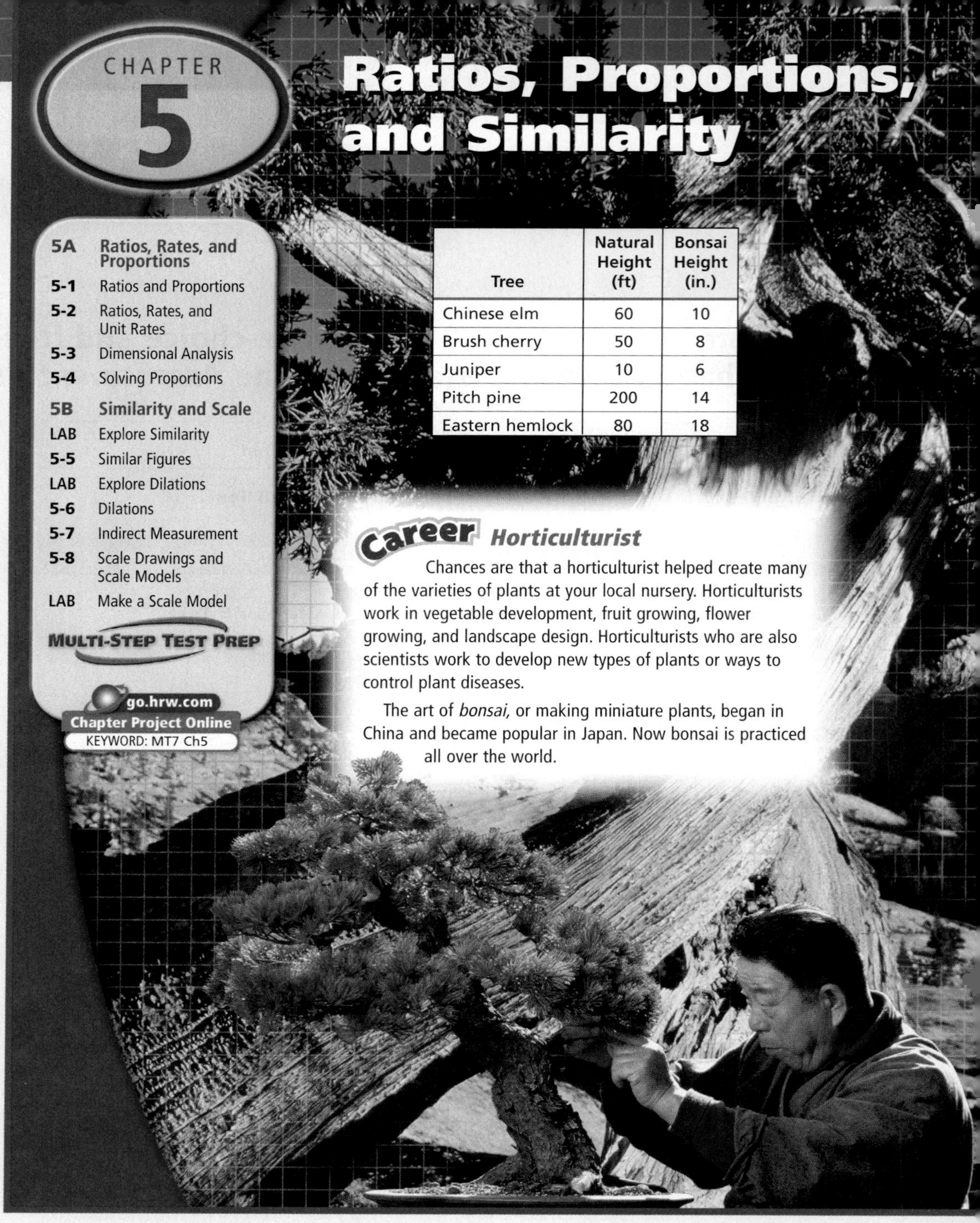

Tree	Natural Height (ft)	Bonsai Height (in.)
Chinese elm	60	10
Brush cherry	50	8
Juniper	10	6
Pitch pine	200	14
Eastern hemlock	80	18

Career *Horticulturist*

Chances are that a horticulturist helped create many of the varieties of plants at your local nursery. Horticulturists work in vegetable development, fruit growing, flower growing, and landscape design. Horticulturists who are also scientists work to develop new types of plants or ways to control plant diseases.

The art of *bonsai*, or making miniature plants, began in China and became popular in Japan. Now bonsai is practiced all over the world.

Problem Solving Project

Understand, Plan, Solve, and Look Back

Have students:

- Complete the Growing Tiny Trees worksheet to learn more about ratios, proportions, and scale.

- Create a full-size drawing of a small tree that they selected. Divide them into groups to create scale drawings of the tree using different scales that they select. Compare the scale drawings and note their similarities and differences, as well as with the full-size drawing.

- Research the history of bonsai. Invite a bonsai grower to bring some bonsai to class.

Life Science Connection

Project Resources

All project resources for teachers and students are provided online.

Materials:
- Growing Tiny Trees worksheet
- drawing and modeling materials

go.hrw.com
Project Teacher Support
KEYWORD: MT7 PSProject5

ARE YOU READY?

✓ Vocabulary

Choose the best term from the list to complete each sentence.

1. To solve an equation, you use __?__ to isolate the variable. So to solve the __?__ $3x = 18$, divide both sides by 3. **inverse operations; multiplication equation**

2. In the fractions $\frac{2}{3}$ and $\frac{1}{6}$, 18 is a(n) __?__, but 6 is the __?__.
common denominator; least common denominator

3. If two polygons are congruent, all of their __?__ sides and angles are congruent. **corresponding**

common denominator

corresponding

inverse operations

least common denominator

multiplication equation

Complete these exercises to review skills you will need for this chapter.

✓ Simplify Fractions

Write each fraction in simplest form.

4. $\frac{8}{24}$ $\frac{1}{3}$ 5. $\frac{15}{50}$ $\frac{3}{10}$ 6. $\frac{18}{72}$ $\frac{1}{4}$ 7. $\frac{25}{125}$ $\frac{1}{5}$

✓ Use a Least Common Denominator

Find the least common denominator for each set of fractions.

8. $\frac{2}{3}$ and $\frac{1}{5}$ 15   9. $\frac{3}{4}$ and $\frac{1}{8}$ 8   10. $\frac{5}{7}$, $\frac{3}{7}$, and $\frac{1}{14}$ 14   11. $\frac{1}{2}$, $\frac{2}{3}$, and $\frac{3}{5}$ 30

✓ Order Decimals

Write each set of decimals in order from least to greatest.

12. 4.2, 2.24, 2.4, 0.242   13. 1.1, 0.1, 0.01, 1.11   14. $1.\underline{4}$, 2.53, $1.\overline{3}$, $0.\overline{9}$
0.242, 2.24, 2.4, 4.2   0.01, 0.1, 1.1, 1.11   0.9, 1.3, 1.4, 2.53

✓ Solve Multiplication Equations

Solve.

15. $5x = 60$ 16. $0.2y = 14$ 17. $\frac{1}{2}t = 10$ 18. $\frac{2}{3}z = 9$
$x = 12$ $y = 70$ $t = 20$ $z = 13.5$

✓ Customary Units

19. 54

Change each to the given unit.
60   480   8
19. 18 yd = ▨ ft   20. 15 gal = ▨ qt   21. 30 lb = ▨ oz   22. 96 in. = ▨ ft

23. 46 c = ▨ pt   24. 160 oz = ▨ lb   25. 39 ft = ▨ yd   26. 108 qt = ▨ gal
23   10   13   27

Organizer

Objective: Assess students' understanding of prerequisite skills.

Prerequisite Skills

Simplify Fractions

Use a Least Common Denominator

Order Decimals

Solve Multiplication Equations

Customary Units

Assessing Prior Knowledge
INTERVENTION

Diagnose and Prescribe

Use this page to determine whether intervention is necessary or whether enrichment is appropriate.

Resources

 Are You Ready? Intervention and Enrichment Worksheets

 Are You Ready? CD-ROM

 Are You Ready? Online

my.hrw.com

ARE YOU READY?
Diagnose and Prescribe

 NO INTERVENE

 YES ENRICH

| | ARE YOU READY? Intervention, Chapter 5 | | |
✓ Prerequisite Skill	〰 Worksheets	💿 CD-ROM	🪐 Online
✓ Simplify Fractions	Skill 19	Activity 19	
✓ Use a Least Common Denominator	Skill 23	Activity 23	Diagnose and Prescribe Online
✓ Order Decimals	Skill 17	Activity 17	
✓ Solve Multiplication Equations	Skill 59	Activity 59	
✓ Customary Units	Skill 71	Activity 71	

ARE YOU READY? Enrichment, Chapter 5
〰 Worksheets
💿 CD-ROM
🪐 Online

Organizer

Objective: Help students organize the new concepts they will learn in Chapter 5.

Online Edition
Multilingual Glossary

Resources

PuzzlePro®
One-Stop Planner®

Multilingual Glossary Online
go.hrw.com
KEYWORD: MT7 Glossary

Possible answers to *Vocabulary Connections*

1. You multiply the values at opposite ends of the X formed by connecting the values.

2. Using indirect measurement, you use a method that is not direct, for instance, without using a ruler or tape measure.

3. A rational number is a number that can be expressed as a fraction, so you use division in a ratio.

Where You've Been

Previously, you

- used division to find ratios and unit rates.
- used critical attributes to define similarity.
- found solutions to application problems involving related measurement units.

In This Chapter

You will study

- using unit rates to represent proportional relationships.
- estimating and finding solutions to application problems involving proportional relationships.
- generating similar figures using dilations.
- using proportional relationships in similar figures to find missing measurements.

Where You're Going

You can use the skills learned in this chapter

- to compare prices to find bargains
- to convert units in science courses
- to create scale drawings and scale models.

Key Vocabulary/Vocabulario

cross product	producto cruzado
dilation	dilatación
indirect measurement	medición indirecta
proportion	proporción
rate	tasa
ratio	razón
scale drawing	dibujo a escala
scale model	modelo a escala
similar	semejante
unit rate	tasa unitaria

Vocabulary Connections

To become familiar with some of the vocabulary terms in the chapter, consider the following. You may refer to the chapter, the glossary, or a dictionary if you like.

1. The word *cross* can mean "to intersect," forming an "X" shape. Since a *product* is the result of multiplying, what do you suppose you multiply to find the **cross products** of two fractions?

2. The word *indirect* means "not direct." What do you think it means to find the length of something using **indirect measurement**?

3. A **ratio** compares two quantities using a particular operation. Knowing what you do about *rational numbers*, which operation do you think you use in a ratio?

Reading and Writing Math

Writing Strategy: Write a Convincing Argument

Your ability to write a convincing argument proves that you have a solid understanding of the concept. An effective argument should include the following four parts:

(1) A goal
(2) A response to the goal
(3) Evidence to support the response
(4) A summary statement

> **From Lesson 4-1**
>
> **49. Write About It**
> Compare 10^2 and 2^{10}. For any two numbers, which usually gives the greater number, using the greater number as the base or as the exponent? Give at least one exception.

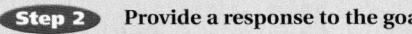

Step 1  **Identify the goal.**

For any two numbers, explain whether using the greater number as the base or as the exponent will generally result in a greater number. Find one exception.

Step 2 **Provide a response to the goal.**

Using the greater number as the exponent usually gives the greater number.

Step 3 **Provide evidence to support your response.**

> For the numbers 10 and 2, using the greater number, 10, as the exponent will result in a greater number.
>
> $10^2 = 100$
> $2^{10} = 1024$
> $100 < 1024$
> $10^2 < 2^{10}$

> Exception: For the numbers 2 and 3, using the greater number, 3, as the exponent will not result in a greater number.
>
> $3^2 = 9$
> $2^3 = 8$
> $9 > 8$
> $3^2 > 2^3$

Step 4 **Summarize your argument.**

Generally, for any two numbers, using the greater number as the exponent instead of as the base will result in a greater number.

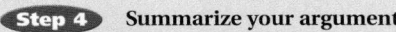

 **Try This**

Write a convincing argument or explanation.

1. A student said a number raised to a negative power is always negative. What is the student's error?

Reading and Writing Math

Organizer

Objective: Help students apply strategies to understand and retain key concepts.

 Online Edition

Resources

 Chapter 5 Resource Book
Reading Strategies

ENGLISH LANGUAGE LEARNERS

Writing Strategy: Write a Convincing Argument

Discuss Students benefit from explaining math concepts in their own words.

Writing a clear explanation helps them organize their thoughts and identify any misconceptions.

Extend As students work through the *Think and Discuss* exercises in Chapter 5, choose items for which they should write out their explanations, using the strategies presented on this page.

Have students exchange their writing samples to check if others can understand their explanations.

Possible answers to *Try This*

1. **Goal:** Find and explain the error.
   Response: A number raised to a negative power is 1 divided by that power with its opposite exponent. So a positive number raised to a negative exponent will always be positive. A negative number raised to a negative even exponent will be positive. A negative number raised to a negative odd exponent will be negative.

   Evidence:
   $2^{-3} = \frac{1}{2^3} = \frac{1}{8}$;
   $(-3)^{-2} = \frac{1}{(-3)^2} = \frac{1}{9}$;
   $(-2)^{-3} = \frac{1}{(-2)^3} = \frac{1}{-8}$

   Summarize: The sign of the number is affected by whether the base is positive or negative and whether the power is odd or even, not whether the power is negative.

Ratios, Rates, and Proportions

One-Minute Section Planner

Lesson	Materials	MiC and Lab Resources
Lesson 5-1 Ratios and Proportions • Find equivalent ratios to create proportions. ☑ SAT-10 ☑ ITBS ☑ CTBS ☑ NAEP		**MiC:** *Revisiting Numbers* pp. 1–8 **MiC:** *It's All the Same* pp. 9–10 **MiC:** *Looking at an Angle* pp. 34–41, 49–53 *Hands-On Lab Activities* 5-1 *Technology Lab Activities* 5-1
Lesson 5-2 Ratios, Rates, and Unit Rates • Work with rates and ratios. ☑ SAT-10 ☑ ITBS ☑ CTBS ☑ NAEP		**MiC:** *Revisiting Numbers* pp. 1–8 **MiC:** *Looking at an Angle* pp. 25–29, 34–41 *Technology Lab Activities* 5-2
Lesson 5-3 Dimensional Analysis • Use one or more conversions factors to solve rate problems. ☑ SAT-10 ☑ ITBS ☑ CTBS ☑ NAEP		*Hands-On Lab Activities* 5-3
Lesson 5-4 Solving Proportions • Solve proportions. ☑ SAT-10 ☑ ITBS ☑ CTBS ☑ NAEP		**MiC:** *Looking at an Angle* pp. 32–44

MK = *Manipulatives Kit*

Mathematics in Context

The units *Revisiting Numbers, It's All the Same,* and *Looking at an Angle* from the *Mathematics in Context* © 2006 series can be used with Section 5A. See Section Planner above for suggestions for integrating *MiC* with *Holt Mathematics.*

Section Overview

Ratios, Proportions, Rates, and Unit Rates
Lessons 5-1, 5-2

Why? Unit rates can be used to compare ratios, such as unit prices for a grocery item.

> A **rate** is a ratio of two quantities with different units.
> $$\frac{66 \text{ mi}}{3 \text{ gal}}$$

> A **unit rate** is a rate with a denominator of 1.
> $$\frac{22 \text{ mi}}{1 \text{ gal}}, \text{ or 22 miles per gallon}$$

Equivalent Ratios

$$\frac{10}{20} = \frac{10 \div \mathbf{10}}{20 \div \mathbf{10}} = \frac{1}{2} \qquad \frac{10}{20} = \frac{10 \cdot \mathbf{5}}{20 \cdot \mathbf{5}} = \frac{50}{100}$$

The ratios $\frac{10}{20}, \frac{1}{2}$, and $\frac{50}{100}$ are **equivalent ratios.**

Proportions

A **proportion** is a statement that two ratios are equivalent.

$$\frac{2}{8} = \frac{5}{20} \text{ is a \textbf{proportion}.}$$

$\frac{2}{8}$ and $\frac{5}{20}$ are **proportional** because $\frac{2}{8} = \frac{1}{4}$ and $\frac{5}{20} = \frac{1}{4}$.

Ordering Ratios

To order ratios, write them as fractions or decimals.

$$3{:}2 = \frac{3}{2} = 1.5 \qquad 20{:}13 = \frac{20}{13} \approx 1.54 \qquad 13{:}9 = \frac{13}{9} = 1.\overline{4}$$

Order from least to greatest: $1.\overline{4}$ 1.5 1.54

        ↓   ↓   ↓

      $13{:}9$ $3{:}2$ $20{:}13$

Dimensional Analysis
Lesson 5-3

Why? To convert rates to equivalent rates using different units, use dimensional analysis.

Using Conversion Factors

> A **conversion factor** is a ratio of equal quantities.
> $$\frac{1 \text{ ft}}{12 \text{ in.}}$$

If a car travels 1800 feet in one minute on a residential street, is it going too fast?

$$\frac{1800 \text{ ft}}{1 \text{ min.}} = \frac{1800 \text{ ft}}{1 \text{ min.}} \cdot \frac{1 \text{ mi}}{5280 \text{ ft}} \cdot \frac{60 \text{ min}}{1 \text{ h}} = \frac{1800 \cdot 60 \text{ mi}}{5280 \text{ h}} \approx 20 \text{ mi/h}$$

The car is traveling about 20 miles per hour, which is probably not too fast.

Solving Proportions
Lesson 5-4

Why? Proportions can be used to solve problems involving mixtures, such as mixing cement and sand in a given ratio.

> In a proportion, **cross products are equal.**

$$\frac{2}{8} \diagdown\hspace{-0.6em}\diagup \frac{5}{20} \qquad \begin{aligned} 2 \times 20 &= 8 \times 5 \\ 40 &= 40 \end{aligned}$$

Hands-On Lab
In *Hands-On Lab Activities*

 Technology Lab
In *Technology Lab Activities*

 Online Edition
Tutorial Videos

 Countdown to Testing Week 8

Power Presentations
with PowerPoint®

Warm Up

Write each fraction in lowest terms.

1. $\frac{14}{16}$ $\frac{7}{8}$ 2. $\frac{24}{64}$ $\frac{3}{8}$
3. $\frac{9}{72}$ $\frac{1}{8}$ 4. $\frac{45}{120}$ $\frac{3}{8}$

Problem of the Day

A magazine has page numbers from 1 to 80. What fraction of those page numbers include the digit 5? $\frac{17}{80}$

Also available on transparency

 **Math Humor**

Mathematics is made up of $\frac{1}{2}$ formulas, $\frac{1}{2}$ proofs, and $\frac{1}{2}$ imagination.

State Resources

 go.hrw.com
State Resources Online
KEYWORD: MT7 Resources

5-1 Ratios and Proportions

Learn to find equivalent ratios to create proportions.

Vocabulary
ratio
equivalent ratio
proportion

On average, each person in the United States produces about 4.5 pounds of trash per day. About $\frac{27}{25}$, or 1.08 pounds, of this trash is recycled.

Comparisons of the number of people to total trash produced per day are shown in the table. These comparisons are *ratios* that are all equivalent.

The United States leads the world in both producing and recycling trash.

Comparisons of Number of People to Total Trash Produced per Day				
Number of People	1	2	3	4
Total Trash (lb)	4.5	9	13.5	18

 **Reading Math**

Ratios can be written in several ways. 7 to 5, 7:5, and $\frac{7}{5}$ name the same ratio.

A **ratio** is a comparison of two quantities by division. Both rectangles have equivalent shaded areas. Ratios that make the same comparison are **equivalent ratios**.

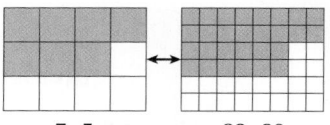

7 : 5   28 : 20

EXAMPLE 1 **Finding Equivalent Ratios**

Find two ratios that are equivalent to each given ratio.

A $\frac{6}{9}$

$\frac{6}{9} = \frac{6 \cdot 3}{9 \cdot 3} = \frac{18}{27}$ *Multiply or divide the numerator and denominator by the same nonzero number.*
$\frac{6}{9} = \frac{6 \div 3}{9 \div 3} = \frac{2}{3}$

Two ratios equivalent to $\frac{6}{9}$ are $\frac{18}{27}$ and $\frac{2}{3}$.

B $\frac{51}{36}$

$\frac{51}{36} = \frac{51 \cdot 2}{36 \cdot 2} = \frac{102}{72}$ *Multiply or divide the numerator and denominator by the same nonzero number.*
$\frac{51}{36} = \frac{51 \div 3}{36 \div 3} = \frac{17}{12}$

Two ratios equivalent to $\frac{51}{36}$ are $\frac{102}{72}$ and $\frac{17}{12}$.

Ratios that are equivalent are said to be *proportional*, or in **proportion**. Equivalent ratios are identical when they are written in simplest form.

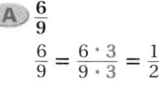 **1 Introduce**
Alternate Opener

EXPLORATION

5-1 Ratios and Proportions

Sam and Jill counted the number of foreign cars and the number of domestic cars that entered the parking lot of a movie theater between 5:30 P.M. and 5:45 P.M. for a week. Their results are listed in the table.

	Mon	Tue	Wed	Thu	Fri	Sat	Sun
Foreign	16	25	15	20	40	40	45
Domestic	8	25	10	25	20	50	45

They compared the number of foreign cars to the number of domestic cars by using ratios. For example, the ratio for Monday was $\frac{foreign}{domestic} = \frac{16}{8} = \frac{2}{1}$.

1. Write a ratio for each day.
2. Which ratios are greater than the Monday ratio?
3. Which ratios are less than the Monday ratio?
4. Which ratio is the same as the Monday ratio?

Think and Discuss

5. **Explain** what it means if two ratios are equal.
6. **Describe** how the ratios are different if you write them as $\frac{domestic}{foreign}$.

Motivate

Pose the following question to the students: "If there are 16 cookies for 8 children, how many cookies will each child receive?" 2 cookies Explain to students that the number of cookies can be compared with the number of students by using the ratio $\frac{16 \text{ cookies}}{8 \text{ children}}$. Show them that the ratio can be simplified to $\frac{2 \text{ cookies}}{1 \text{ child}}$. Explain that the ratios are equiv-alent because they express the same relation-ship between the two quantities.

Explorations and answers are provided in *Alternate Openers: Explorations Transparencies.*

EXAMPLE 2 **Determining Whether Two Ratios Are in Proportion**

Simplify to tell whether the ratios form a proportion.

A $\frac{9}{36}$ and $\frac{2}{8}$

$\frac{9}{36} = \frac{9 \div 9}{36 \div 9} = \frac{1}{4}$

$\frac{2}{8} = \frac{2 \div 2}{8 \div 2} = \frac{1}{4}$

Since $\frac{1}{4} = \frac{1}{4}$, the ratios are in proportion.

B $\frac{9}{12}$ and $\frac{16}{24}$

$\frac{9}{12} = \frac{9 \div 3}{12 \div 3} = \frac{3}{4}$

$\frac{16}{24} = \frac{16 \div 8}{24 \div 8} = \frac{2}{3}$

Since $\frac{3}{4} \neq \frac{2}{3}$, the ratios are *not* in proportion.

 EXAMPLE 3 *Environment Application*

On average, each American recycles about 1.08 pounds of trash per day. To see how his family compared, Ahmed weighed the family's recycling on Earth Day and recorded the results in a table. Is Ahmed's family's recycling in proportion with the U.S. average? Explain.

Recycling		
	Number of People	Trash Recycled (lb)
Average in the U.S.	1	1.08
Ahmed's Family	4	5.1

$\frac{1}{1.08} \overset{?}{=} \frac{4}{5.1}$

$\frac{1}{1.08} \overset{?}{=} \frac{4 \div 4}{5.1 \div 4}$ *Divide.*

$\frac{1}{1.08} \neq \frac{1}{1.275}$ *Simplify.*

Since $\frac{1}{1.08}$ is not equal to $\frac{1}{1.275}$, the amount recycled by Ahmed's family is not in proportion with the average person in the United States. Ahmed's family recycles more than the average.

Possible answers to *Think and Discuss*

1. Two ratios can be written to form a proportion if they are equivalent ratios.

2. 1:2, 4:8, 24:48

 **Think and Discuss**

1. **Describe** how two ratios can form a proportion.

2. **Give** three ratios equivalent to 12:24.

3. **Explain** why the ratios 2:4 and 6:10 do not form a proportion.

4. **Give an example** of two ratios that are proportional and have numerators with different signs.

Power Presentations with PowerPoint®

Additional Examples

Example 1

Find two ratios that are equivalent to each given ratio.

A. $\frac{9}{27}$ possible answer: $\frac{18}{54}, \frac{1}{3}$

B. $\frac{64}{24}$ possible answer: $\frac{128}{48}, \frac{8}{3}$

Example 2

Simplify to tell whether the ratios form a proportion.

A. $\frac{3}{27}$ and $\frac{2}{18}$ $\frac{1}{9} = \frac{1}{9}$; yes

B. $\frac{12}{15}$ and $\frac{27}{36}$ $\frac{4}{5} \neq \frac{3}{4}$; no

Example 3

At 4°C, four cubic feet of silver has the same mass as 42 cubic feet of water. At 4°C, would 210 cubic feet of water have the same mass as 20 cubic feet of silver? yes

Also available on transparency

Possible answers to *Think and Discuss*

3. 2:4 simplifies to 1:2, and 6:10 simplifies to 3:5. Their simplest forms are not equivalent, so they do not form a proportion.

4. $\frac{-2}{4} = \frac{5}{-10}$

---

2 Teach

Guided Instruction

In this lesson, students learn to find equivalent ratios to create proportions. Explain that ratios are comparisons between two numbers. Point out that ratios are similar to fractions but that ratios can have numbers other than integers in both the numerator and denominator. Teach students to find equivalent ratios by either multiplying or dividing the numerator and denominator by the same number. Discuss how two ratios that can be simplified to equivalent fractions are said to be *in proportion.*

 **Inclusion** You may want to use the shaded square diagram as an example of equivalent ratios (Teaching Transparency). Discuss how two ratios that can be simplified to equivalent fractions are said to be *in proportion.*

 Reaching All Learners
Through Cooperative Learning

Have pairs of students find the missing number to make each pair of ratios form a proportion.

1. $\frac{5}{8} = \frac{?}{40}$ 25

2. $\frac{?}{21} = \frac{3}{7}$ 9

3. $\frac{10}{?} = \frac{20}{40}$ 20

4. $\frac{6}{27} = \frac{18}{?}$ 81

Have students explain the strategies they used to find their answers.

---

3 Close

Summarize

Remind students that a ratio can be expressed with a colon, or as a fraction. Ask students to name two ways to find equivalent ratios. Ask them how many equivalent ratios can be found for the ratio 2:5. Recall that two equivalent ratios can be used to form a proportion.

Possible answers: Multiply the numerator and denominator by the same number or divide the numerator and denominator by the same number. Because you can multiply or divide the quantities in a ratio by any number, there are an infinite number of equivalent ratios for 2:5.

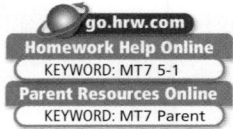

go.hrw.com
Homework Help Online
KEYWORD: MT7 5-1
Parent Resources Online
KEYWORD: MT7 Parent

Assignment Guide

If you finished Example **1** assign:
Average   1–5, 11–15, 37–47
Advanced   11–15, 37–47

If you finished Example **2** assign:
Average   1–9, 11–19, 24–29, 37–47
Advanced   11–19, 23, 26–32, 34–47

If you finished Example **3** assign:
Average   1–22, 24–29, 37–47
Advanced   11–23, 28–47

Homework Quick Check

Quickly check key concepts.
Exercises: 14, 18, 20, 26

Answers

6. $\frac{4}{11} \neq \frac{2}{11}$; no

7–9, 16–19, 22–23. See p. A6.

Math Background

The proportion $\frac{3}{4} = \frac{6}{8}$ can also be written 3:4 = 6:8. It is read "3 is to 4 as 6 is to 8." The four terms of the proportion are 3, 4, 6, and 8. The 3 and 8 are called the *extremes,* and the 4 and 6 are called the *means.* Notice that the extremes are the "outside" numbers and the means are the "inside" numbers in the statement 3:4 = 6:8. An important property of proportions is that the product of the means equals the product of the extremes (the cross-products are equal). For the proportion $\frac{a}{b} = \frac{c}{d}$, $bc = ad$.

State Resources

go.hrw.com
State Resources Online
KEYWORD: MT7 Resources

GUIDED PRACTICE

See Example **1**   Find two ratios that are equivalent to each given ratio. **Possible answers:**

1. $\frac{6}{14}$ $\frac{3}{7}, \frac{12}{28}$
2. $\frac{2}{8}$ $\frac{1}{4}, \frac{4}{16}$
3. $\frac{21}{7}$ $\frac{3}{1}, \frac{42}{14}$
4. $\frac{60}{36}$ $\frac{30}{18}, \frac{15}{9}$
5. $\frac{12}{17}$ $\frac{24}{34}, \frac{60}{85}$

See Example **2**   Simplify to tell whether the ratios form a proportion.

6. $\frac{8}{22}$ and $\frac{2}{11}$
7. $\frac{6}{9}$ and $\frac{10}{18}$
8. $\frac{49}{28}$ and $\frac{35}{20}$
9. $\frac{22}{33}$ and $\frac{18}{27}$

See Example **3**   10. **Entertainment** The table lists prices for movie tickets.

   a. Are the ticket prices proportional? Explain. **yes**

   b. If the prices are proportional how much do 6 movie tickets cost?
   $49.50

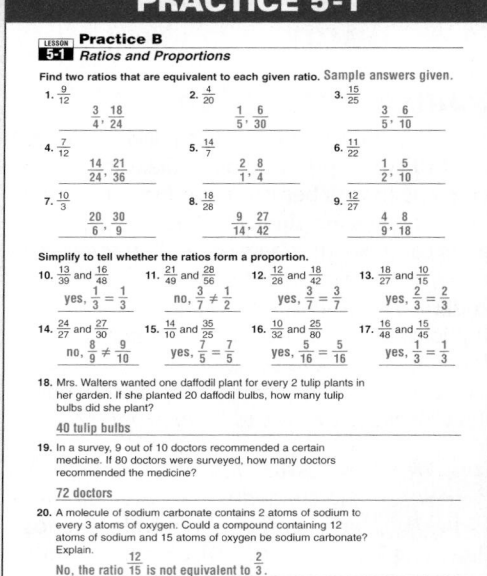

Movie Ticket Prices			
Number of Tickets	1	2	3
Price	$8.25	$16.50	$24.75

INDEPENDENT PRACTICE

See Example **1**   Find two ratios that are equivalent to each given ratio. **Possible answers:**

11. $\frac{1}{7}$ $\frac{2}{14}, \frac{3}{21}$
12. $\frac{7}{12}$ $\frac{14}{24}, \frac{21}{36}$
13. $\frac{14}{12}$ $\frac{7}{6}, \frac{28}{24}$
14. $\frac{60}{25}$ $\frac{12}{5}, \frac{24}{10}$
15. $\frac{11}{50}$ $\frac{22}{100}, \frac{44}{200}$

See Example **2**   Simplify to tell whether the ratios form a proportion.

16. $\frac{8}{16}$ and $\frac{5}{32}$
17. $\frac{45}{75}$ and $\frac{3}{5}$
18. $\frac{1}{3}$ and $\frac{15}{45}$
19. $\frac{16}{48}$ and $\frac{17}{68}$

See Example **3**   20. **Chemistry** A molecule of butane contains 10 atoms of hydrogen to every 4 atoms of carbon. Could a compound containing the number of atoms shown be butane? Explain.
Yes; the ratio $\frac{4}{10}$ is equivalent to $\frac{36}{90}$.

	Hydrogen Atoms	Carbon Atoms
Molecule of Butane	10	4
Compound	90	36

PRACTICE AND PROBLEM SOLVING

Extra Practice
See page 790.

21. **Cooking** A pancake recipe calls for 2.5 cups of pancake mix to make 10 servings. Carmen uses 3 cups of mix to make 14 servings. Does Carmen have the correct ratio for the recipe? Explain.

22. **Business** Cal pays his employees weekly. He would like to start paying them four times the weekly amount on a monthly basis. Is a month equivalent to four weeks? Explain.

23. **Critical Thinking** Using the list of ratios shown, create as many examples of proportions as you can. Then show an example of two ratios that do *not* form a proportion.

$\frac{2}{4}, \frac{2}{5}, \frac{3}{9}, \frac{8}{1}, \frac{2}{10}, \frac{12}{3}, \frac{4}{10}, \frac{4}{1}, \frac{12}{8}, \frac{10}{4}, \frac{9}{6}, \frac{3}{6}$

21. No; she needs $3\frac{1}{2}$ cups of pancake mix to make 14 servings.

RETEACH 5-1

LESSON 5-1 Reteach
Ratios and Proportions

A **ratio** compares two quantities by division. **Equivalent ratios** make the same comparison.

$\frac{8}{32} = \frac{2}{8} = \frac{1}{4}$

To find equivalent ratios:

Divide by a common factor.   Multiply by a common factor.

$\frac{10 \div 5}{15 \div 5} = \frac{2}{3}$ $\frac{10 \times 2}{15 \times 2} = \frac{20}{30}$

So, two ratios equivalent to $\frac{10}{15}$ are $\frac{2}{3}$ and $\frac{20}{30}$.

Complete to find two ratios equivalent to each given ratio.

1. $\frac{16 \div 4}{40 \div 4} = \frac{4}{10}$ $\frac{16 \times 3}{40 \times 3} = \frac{48}{120}$
2. $\frac{75 \div 25}{100 \div 25} = \frac{3}{4}$ $\frac{75 \times 2}{100 \times 2} = \frac{150}{200}$

Name two ratios equivalent to the given ratio. **Sample answers given.**

3. $\frac{6}{9}$ $\frac{2}{3}, \frac{18}{27}$
4. $\frac{1}{3}$ $\frac{3}{9}, \frac{9}{27}$
5. $\frac{2}{5}$ $\frac{12}{30}, \frac{8}{20}$
6. $\frac{16}{20}$ $\frac{8}{10}, \frac{4}{5}$

When two equivalent ratios are set equal to each other, they form a **proportion**.

To tell whether two ratios form a proportion, write each in simplest form.

Does $\frac{16}{32} = \frac{50}{100}$?   Does $\frac{8}{18} = \frac{10}{15}$?

$\frac{16 \div 16}{32 \div 16}$ $\frac{50 \div 50}{100 \div 50}$ $\frac{8 \div 2}{18 \div 2}$ $\frac{10 \div 5}{15 \div 5}$

$\frac{1}{2}$ $\frac{1}{2}$ $\frac{4}{9}$ $\frac{2}{3}$

The ratios form a proportion.   The ratios do not form a proportion.

Tell whether the ratios form a proportion.

7. $\frac{14}{21} = \frac{50}{75}$ yes
8. $\frac{27}{48} = \frac{54}{72}$ no

PRACTICE 5-1

LESSON 5-1 Practice B
Ratios and Proportions

Find two ratios that are equivalent to each given ratio. **Sample answers given.**

1. $\frac{9}{12}$ $\frac{3}{4}, \frac{18}{24}$
2. $\frac{4}{20}$ $\frac{1}{5}, \frac{6}{30}$
3. $\frac{15}{25}$ $\frac{3}{5}, \frac{6}{10}$
4. $\frac{7}{12}$ $\frac{14}{24}, \frac{21}{36}$
5. $\frac{14}{7}$ $\frac{2}{1}, \frac{8}{4}$
6. $\frac{11}{22}$ $\frac{1}{2}, \frac{5}{10}$
7. $\frac{10}{3}$ $\frac{20}{6}, \frac{30}{9}$
8. $\frac{18}{28}$ $\frac{9}{14}, \frac{27}{42}$
9. $\frac{12}{27}$ $\frac{4}{9}, \frac{8}{18}$

Simplify to tell whether the ratios form a proportion.

10. $\frac{13}{39}$ and $\frac{16}{48}$
yes, $\frac{1}{3} = \frac{1}{3}$
11. $\frac{21}{49}$ and $\frac{28}{56}$
no, $\frac{3}{7} \neq \frac{1}{2}$
12. $\frac{12}{28}$ and $\frac{18}{42}$
yes, $\frac{3}{7} = \frac{3}{7}$
13. $\frac{18}{27}$ and $\frac{10}{15}$
yes, $\frac{2}{3} = \frac{2}{3}$

14. $\frac{24}{27}$ and $\frac{27}{30}$
no, $\frac{8}{9} \neq \frac{9}{10}$
15. $\frac{14}{10}$ and $\frac{35}{25}$
yes, $\frac{7}{5} = \frac{7}{5}$
16. $\frac{32}{10}$ and $\frac{25}{80}$
yes, $\frac{5}{16} = \frac{5}{16}$
17. $\frac{16}{48}$ and $\frac{15}{45}$
yes, $\frac{1}{3} = \frac{1}{3}$

18. Mrs. Walters wanted one daffodil plant for every 2 tulip plants in her garden. If she planted 20 daffodil bulbs, how many tulip bulbs did she plant?

40 tulip bulbs

19. In a survey, 9 out of 10 doctors recommended a certain medicine. If 80 doctors were surveyed, how many doctors recommended the medicine?

72 doctors

20. A molecule of sodium carbonate contains 2 atoms of sodium to every 3 atoms of oxygen. Could a compound containing 12 atoms of sodium and 15 atoms of oxygen be sodium carbonate? Explain.

No, the ratio $\frac{12}{15}$ is not equivalent to $\frac{2}{3}$.

Tell whether the ratios form a proportion. If not, find a ratio that would form a proportion with the first ratio.   **Possible answers:**

24. $\frac{4}{12}$ and $\frac{10}{15}$ no; $\frac{1}{3}$ **25.** $\frac{5}{7}$ and $\frac{100}{140}$ yes   **26.** $\frac{4}{7}$ and $\frac{12}{49}$ no; $\frac{8}{14}$

27. $\frac{30}{36}$ and $\frac{15}{16}$ no; $\frac{5}{6}$ **28.** $\frac{15}{14}$ and $\frac{45}{42}$ yes   **29.** $\frac{12}{25}$ and $\frac{24}{50}$ yes

30. $\frac{18}{84}$ and $\frac{6}{56}$ no; $\frac{3}{14}$ **31.** $\frac{22}{12}$ and $\frac{42}{16}$ no; $\frac{11}{6}$ **32.** $\frac{22}{242}$ and $\frac{44}{484}$ yes

33. Hobbies A bicycle chain moves along two sprockets when you shift gears. The number of teeth on the front sprocket and the number of teeth on the rear sprocket form a ratio. Equivalent ratios provide equal pedaling power. Find a ratio equivalent to the ratio $\frac{52}{24}$. $\frac{39}{18}$

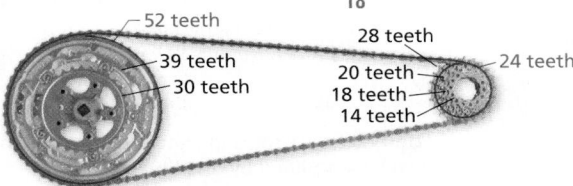

52 teeth
39 teeth
30 teeth
28 teeth
20 teeth
18 teeth
14 teeth
24 teeth

 34. What's the Error? A student said that the ratios $\frac{3}{4}$ and $\frac{9}{16}$ were proportional. What error did the student make?

 35. Write About It Describe at least two ways, given a ratio, to create a proportion.

 **36. Challenge** Using each of the numbers 3, 9, 27, and 81 once, write all possible proportions.

TEST PREP and Spiral Review

37. Multiple Choice Which of the following ratios is equivalent to the ratio 3:4?

Ⓐ 6:10   Ⓑ 8:6   Ⓒ 9:12   Ⓓ 10:40

38. Multiple Choice Which of the following does NOT form a proportion?

Ⓕ $\frac{5}{8} = \frac{10}{16}$ Ⓖ $\frac{15}{24} = \frac{10}{16}$ Ⓗ $\frac{5}{9} = \frac{10}{16}$ Ⓙ $\frac{25}{40} = \frac{10}{16}$

39. Short Response One ticket to the aquarium costs $10.50. Three tickets to the aquarium cost $31.50. Are ticket prices proportional? If so, how much would 4 tickets cost?   **Yes, 4 tickets would cost $42.00.**

Compare. Write < or >. (Lesson 1-9)

40. $2 + 5$ ▨ 8 **41.** $27 - 11$ ▨ 15 **42.** $2(7)$ ▨ 27 **43.** $17 + 18$ ▨ 27
　　　$<$　　　　　　$>$　　　　　　$<$　　　　　　$>$

Multiply. (Lesson 2-4)

44. $-2.4(-7)$ **16.8**   **45.** $3.2(-1.7)$ **-5.44**   **46.** $-0.03(8.6)$ **-0.258**   **47.** $-1.07(-0.6)$ **0.642**

Technology Lab
In *Technology Lab Activities*

Online Edition
Tutorial Videos

Countdown to Testing Week 8

Power Presentations
with PowerPoint®

Warm Up

Divide. Round answers to the nearest tenth.

1. $\frac{420}{18}$ 23.3
2. $\frac{73}{21}$ 3.5
3. $\frac{380}{16}$ 23.8
4. $\frac{430}{18}$ 23.9

Problem of the Day

There are 3 bags of flour for every 2 bags of sugar in a freight truck. A bag of flour weighs 60 pounds, and a bag of sugar weighs 80 pounds. Which part of the truck's cargo is heavier, the flour or the sugar? flour

Also available on transparency

Math Humor

Wow! 9 out of 10 cars this company has built in the past 20 years are still on the road.

Amazing. Except that the company just started manufacturing cars last year!

State Resources

go.hrw.com
State Resources Online
KEYWORD: MT7 Resources

5-2 Ratios, Rates, and Unit Rates

Learn to work with rates and ratios.

Vocabulary
rate
unit rate
unit price

Density is a ratio that compares mass and volume. Different substances have different densities. For example, gold has a density of $\frac{19,300 \text{ kg}}{1 \text{ m}^3}$, or 19,300 kilograms per cubic meter.

The Excentrique MP-400 MP3 player is made of 24-carat gold.

A **rate** is a comparison of two quantities that have different units.

ratio: $\frac{90}{3}$ rate: $\frac{90 \text{ miles}}{3 \text{ hours}}$ ← *Read as "90 miles per 3 hours."*

Unit rates are rates in which the second quantity is 1. The ratio $\frac{90}{3}$ can be simplified by dividing: $\frac{90}{3} = \frac{30}{1}$.

unit rate: $\frac{30 \text{ miles}}{1 \text{ hour}}$, or 30 mi/h

EXAMPLE 1 Finding Unit Rates

Miki can type 120 words in 3 minutes. How many words can she type per minute?

$\frac{120 \text{ words}}{3 \text{ minutes}}$ *Write the rate.*

$\frac{120 \text{ words} \div 3}{3 \text{ minutes} \div 3} = \frac{40 \text{ words}}{1 \text{ minute}}$ *Divide to find words per minute.*

Miki can type 40 words in one minute.

Since density is measured in units of mass per unit of volume, it is a unit rate.

EXAMPLE 2 Chemistry Application

A Four cubic meters of silver has a mass of 41,960 kilograms. What is the density of silver?

$\frac{41,960 \text{ kg}}{4 \text{ m}^3}$ *Write the rate.*

$\frac{41,960 \text{ kg} \div 4}{4 \text{ m}^3 \div 4}$ *Divide to find kilograms per 1 m³.*

$\frac{10,490 \text{ kg}}{1 \text{ m}^3}$

Silver has a density of 10,490 kg/m³.

B Aluminum weighing 1350 kilograms has a volume of 0.5 cubic meters. What is the density of aluminum?

$\frac{1350 \text{ kg}}{0.5 \text{ m}^3}$ *Write the rate.*

$\frac{1350 \text{ kg} \cdot 2}{0.5 \text{ m}^3 \cdot 2}$ *Multiply to find kilograms per 1 m³.*

$\frac{2700 \text{ kg}}{1 \text{ m}^3}$

Aluminum has a density of 2700 kg/m³.

---

1 Introduce

Alternate Opener

EXPLORATION

5-2 Ratios, Rates, and Unit Rates

The bar graph shows the number of acres of wilderness burned each year from 1991 to 2000. Each bar represents a *unit rate*, because it shows the number of acres burned in *one* year.

Acres of Wilderness Burned: 1991–2000

1. The National Interagency Fire Center reported that an average of 3,647,883 acres were burned per year from 1991 to 2000.
   a. Is the average also a unit rate?
   b. In what years were the number of acres burned above the average?
   c. In what years were the number of acres burned below the average?

Think and Discuss

2. **Explain** why a unit rate such as 40 miles per hour may be more useful than an equivalent rate such as 60 miles per

Motivate

Present the following problem: A package of 8 rolls costs $2.00. A package of 10 rolls costs $2.79. Which is the better buy?

The 8-roll package; unit prices are 25 cents and 27.9 cents, respectively.

Encourage students to give answers and explain how they got their answers. Explain that one way to compare prices is to use *unit prices*, such as the price per roll. A unit price is a type of *unit rate*, one of the lesson topics.

ENGLISH LANGUAGE LEARNERS

Explorations and answers are provided in *Alternate Openers: Explorations Transparencies.*

EXAMPLE **3** **Estimating Unit Rates**

Estimate each unit rate.

A 323 students to 11 teachers

$$\frac{323 \text{ students}}{11 \text{ teachers}} \approx \frac{319 \text{ students}}{11 \text{ teachers}}$$ *Choose a number close to 323 that is divisible by 11.*

$$\approx \frac{29 \text{ students}}{1 \text{ teacher}}$$ *Divide to find students per teacher.*

323 students to 11 teachers is approximately 29 students per teacher.

B 560 miles in 9 hours

$$\frac{560 \text{ miles}}{9 \text{ hours}} \approx \frac{560 \text{ miles}}{10 \text{ hours}}$$ *Choose a number close to 9 that is a factor of 560.*

$$\approx \frac{56 \text{ miles}}{1 \text{ hour}}$$ *Divide to find miles per hour.*

560 miles in 9 hours is approximately 56 miles per hour.

Unit price is a unit rate used to compare price per item.

EXAMPLE **4** **Finding Unit Prices to Compare Costs**

A Blank CD's can be purchased in packages of 3 for $1.99 or 20 for $10.99. Which is the better buy?

$$\frac{\text{price for package}}{\text{number of CD's}} = \frac{\$1.99}{3 \text{ CD's}} \approx \$0.66 \text{ per CD}$$ *Divide the price by the number of CD's.*

$$\frac{\text{price for package}}{\text{number of CD's}} = \frac{\$10.99}{20 \text{ CD's}} \approx \$0.55 \text{ per CD}$$

The better buy is the package of 20 for $10.99.

B Arnie can buy a 16 oz box of cereal for $5.49 or a 20 oz box for $5.99. Which is the better buy?

$$\frac{\text{price for box}}{\text{number of ounces}} = \frac{\$5.49}{16 \text{ oz}} \approx \$0.34/\text{oz}$$ *Divide the price by the number of ounces.*

$$\frac{\text{price for box}}{\text{number of ounces}} = \frac{\$5.99}{20 \text{ oz}} \approx \$0.30/\text{oz}$$

The better buy is the 20 oz box for $5.99.

Think and Discuss

1. Choose the quantity that has a lower unit price: 6 oz for $1.29 or 15 oz for $3.00. Explain your answer.

2. Determine two different units of measurement for speed.

Possible answers to
Think and Discuss

1. 15 oz has the lower unit price at $0.20 per ounce. The unit price for 6 oz is $0.22 per ounce.

2. miles per hour; feet per second

---

2 Teach

Guided Instruction

In this lesson, students learn to work with rates and ratios. Review simplifying fractions and writing fractions as decimals. Remind students how to order decimals. Discuss the concepts of *rate* and *unit rate,* and use Example 1 to explain how to convert from a rate to a unit rate. Point out that a *unit price* is a type of unit rate, and use Example 4 to find and compare unit prices.

Teaching Tip **Cognitive Strategies** To help students remember the distinction between rate and ratio, point out that a heart *rate* compares *beats* and *minutes,* two quantities that have different units.

 Reaching All Learners
Through Home Connection

Ask students to go to the grocery store with a family member and make a list of five products. For each product, students should record the brand and quantity they purchase (or would purchase) and its unit price. For each product, students should also record one other brand or quantity they decided not to purchase (or would not purchase) and its unit price. Ask students to give a reason for each decision. Suggest that not all decisions must be based only on cost, but that cost is one consideration along with preference, quality, and other considerations.

3 Close

Summarize

Have the students match each term below with its corresponding example. Ask them to be as specific as possible and to use each term only once. Ask them to explain their choices.

Ratio —————— 120 miles per 3 hours
Rate ——×—— 15 ft/s
Unit rate ——×—— $1.15 per pound
Unit price ———— 4:2

A ratio is a comparison of two quantities. A rate is a ratio that has two different units. A unit rate is a rate in which the second quantity is 1. A unit price is a unit rate involving the cost of an item.

5-2 Exercises

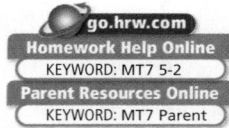
go.hrw.com
Homework Help Online
KEYWORD: MT7 5-2
Parent Resources Online
KEYWORD: MT7 Parent

Assignment Guide

If you finished Example **1** assign:
Average 1, 8, 16–19, 28, 32–41
Advanced 1, 8, 16–19, 28, 29, 31–41

If you finished Example **2** assign:
Average 1, 2, 8, 9, 16–19, 28, 32–41
Advanced 8, 9, 16–19, 26, 28, 29, 31–41

If you finished Example **3** assign:
Average 1–6, 8–13, 16–23, 27, 28, 32–41
Advanced 8–13, 16–23, 26–29, 31–41

If you finished Example **4** assign:
Average 1–25, 27, 28, 32–41
Advanced 8–41

Homework Quick Check

Quickly check key concepts.
Exercises: 8, 9, 10, 14

Math Background

The golden ratio has fascinated artists, architects, and mathematicians for centuries. If a line segment is divided into sections of lengths a and b so that the proportion $\frac{a}{b} = \frac{b}{a+b}$ is satisfied, then those lengths form the *golden ratio* $\frac{b}{a}$. The value of the golden ratio is $\frac{b}{a} = \frac{1+\sqrt{5}}{2} \approx 1.62$.

GUIDED PRACTICE

See Example **1**   1. Ana Maria walks 9 miles in 3 hours. How many miles does she walk per hour? **3 mi**

See Example **2**   2. A nickel has a mass of 5 g and a volume of approximately 0.689 cm³. What is the approximate density of a nickel? **≈ 7.26 g/cm³**

See Example **3**   Estimate each unit rate.

3. 121 students in 3 buses
about 40 students per bus

4. $31.50 for 4 hours
about $8 per hr

5. 4008 Calories for 8 servings of pot pie
about 500 Calories per serving

6. 10 laps in 22 minutes
about 2 min per lap

See Example **4**   7. A 16 oz box of crackers costs $3.99 and a 38 oz box of crackers costs $6.99. Which is the better buy? **38 oz box**

INDEPENDENT PRACTICE

See Example **1**   8. Kenji earns $32 in 4 hours. How much does he earn per hour? **$8**

See Example **2**   9. The mass of a diamond is 1.76 g. The volume is 0.5 cm³. What is the density of the diamond? **3.52 g/cm³**

See Example **3**   Estimate each unit rate.

10. 268 chairs in 9 rows
about 30 chairs per row

11. 9 cups of flour for 4 batches of muffins
about 2 cups per batch

12. $59.95 for 5 CDs
about $12 per CD

13. $2.19 for $\frac{1}{2}$ pound
about $4 per lb

See Example **4**   14. One yard of ribbon costs $0.49 and 3 yards of ribbon costs $1.49. Which is the better buy? **1 yard of ribbon**

15. A 16 oz package of brown rice costs $0.79 and a 32 oz package of brown rice costs $3.49. Which is the better buy? **16 oz package**

PRACTICE AND PROBLEM SOLVING

Extra Practice
See page 790.

Find each unit rate.

16. travel 804 miles in 16 hours
50.25 mi/h

17. score 84 points in 6 games
14 points per game

18. $7.05 for 3 tacos
$2.35 per taco

19. 64 beats in 4 measures of music
16 beats per measure

Estimate each unit rate.

20. $107 for 22 magazines
approximately $5 per magazine

21. 250 heartbeats in 6 minutes
approximately 50 beats per minute

22. 295 words in 6 minutes
approximately 50 words per minute

23. 17 apples weigh 4 pounds
approximately 4 apples per pound

Find each unit price and tell which is the better buy. **$0.16/fl oz; $0.08/fl oz; 90 fl oz**

24. $3.99 for 25 fl oz of detergent or $6.99 for 90 fl oz of detergent

25. $\frac{2}{3}$ pound of walnuts for $2.50 or $\frac{1}{2}$ pound of walnuts for $2.25   **$3.75/lb; $4.50/lb; $\frac{2}{3}$ lb**

RETEACH 5-2

LESSON 5-2 Reteach
Ratios, Rates, and Unit Rates

A **rate** is a ratio that compares two *different kinds* of quantities.

2 aides for 18 students	135 words in 3 minutes	7 ads per 4 pages of copy
$\frac{2\ aides}{18\ students}$	$\frac{135\ words}{3\ minutes}$	$\frac{7\ ads}{4\ pages\ of\ copy}$

Express each comparison as a rate in ratio form.

1. 275 students per 11 teachers $\frac{275\ students}{11\ teachers}$

2. 3 books in 2 months $\frac{3\ books}{2\ months}$

3. 15 strike-outs in 6 innings $\frac{15\ strike\text{-}outs}{6\ innings}$

In a **unit rate**, the second quantity is 1.

300 miles in 6 hours
$\frac{300\ miles}{6\ hours} = \frac{300 \div 6}{6 \div 6} = \frac{50\ miles}{1\ hour}$

81 entries in 4 minutes
$\frac{81\ entries}{4\ minutes} = \frac{81 \div 4}{4 \div 4} = \frac{20.25\ entries}{1\ minute}$

Express each comparison as a unit rate.

4. 28 patients for 2 nurses
$\frac{28\ patients}{2\ nurses} = \frac{28 \div 2}{2 \div 2} = \frac{14\ patients}{1\ nurse}$

5. 16 children in 7 families
$\frac{16\ children}{7\ families} = \frac{16 \div 7}{7 \div 7} = \frac{2.3\ children}{1\ family}$

A **unit price** tells the price per 1 unit.

$2.49 for 3 muffins
$\frac{\$2.49}{3\ muffins} = \frac{2.49 \div 3}{3 \div 3} = \frac{\$0.83}{1\ muffin}$
$0.83 for 1 muffin

$1.67 for 10 pencils
$\frac{\$1.67}{10\ pencils} = \frac{1.67 \div 10}{10 \div 10} = \frac{\$0.167}{1\ pencil}$
$0.17 for 1 pencil

Find each unit price.

6. $10.74 for 3 reams of paper
$\frac{\$10.74}{3\ reams} = \frac{10.74 \div 3}{3 \div 3}$
$\frac{\$3.58}{1\ ream}$

7. $9.99 for 6 blank jewel cased CDs
$\frac{\$9.99}{6\ CDs} = \frac{9.99 \div 6}{6 \div 6}$
$\frac{\$1.665}{1\ CD}$

8. $8.99 for a 12-pack of gel pens
$\frac{\$8.99}{12\ pens} = \frac{8.99 \div 12}{12 \div 12}$
$\frac{\$0.7492}{1\ pen}$

PRACTICE 5-2

LESSON 5-2 Practice B
Ratios, Rates, and Unit Rates

1. Copper weighing 4480 kilograms has a volume of 0.5 cubic meters. What is the density of copper?
$\frac{8960\ kg}{m^3}$

2. Yoshi's yogurt contains 15 calories per ounce. How many calories are in an 8-ounce container of Yoshi's yogurt?
120 calories

3. Emily earns $7.50 per hour. How much does she earn in 3 hours?
$22.50

Estimate the unit rate.

4. 43 apples in 5 bags
about 9 apples per bag

5. $71.00 for 8 hours
about $9 per hour

6. 146 students in 6 classes
about 25 students per class

7. $52.00 for 5 hours
about $10 per hour

8. 7 miles in 64 minutes
about 9 minutes per mile

9. $3.55 for 4 pounds
about $0.90 per pound

Determine the better buy.

10. 8.2 oz of toothpaste for $2.99 or 6.4 oz of toothpaste for $2.49
8.2 oz for $2.99

11. a 3 lb bag of apples for $2.99 or a 5 lb bag of apples for $4.99
3 lb bag for $2.99

12. 16 oz bottle of soda for $1.25 or 20 oz bottle of soda for $1.55
20 oz bottle for $1.55

13. Mavis rides the bus every day. She bought a bus pass good for the month of October for $38.75. How much was Mavis charged per day for the bus pass?
$1.25

go.hrw.com
State Resources Online
KEYWORD: MT7 Resources

State Resources

26. Multi-Step Before 1986, a gold bullion in the Federal Reserve Bank was rectangular and had a volume of approximately 727.7 cm³. The density of gold is 19.3 g/cm³. A pound is approximately 454 g. Find the weight of one gold bullion to the nearest tenth of a pound. **30.9 lb**

27. Estimation Maura received $790 for work she did for a catering company during one week. Find Maura's approximate daily rate.
approximately $110 per day

28. Entertainment Tom, Cherise, and Tina work as film animators. The circle graph shows the number of frames each rendered in an 8-hour day.

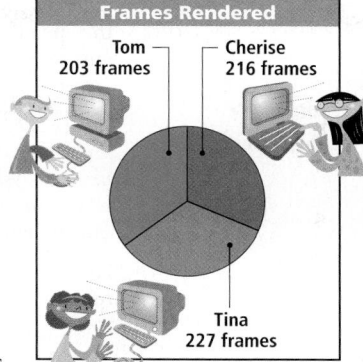

Frames Rendered
Tom 203 frames
Cherise 216 frames
Tina 227 frames

28a. Tom: $25\frac{3}{8}$ frames per hour; Cherise: 27 frames per hour; Tina $28\frac{3}{8}$ frames per hour

a. Find the hourly unit rendering rate for each employee.

b. Who was the most efficient? **Tina**

c. How many more frames per hour did Cherise render than Tom? $1\frac{5}{8}$

d. How many more frames per hour did Tom and Cherise together render than Tina? **24**

 29. What's the Error? A clothing store charges $25 for 4 T-shirts. A student says that the unit price is $0.16 per T-shirt. What is the error? What is the correct unit price?

 30. Write About It Explain how to find unit rates. Give an example, and explain how consumers can use unit rates to save money.

 31. Challenge The size of a television (13 in., 25 in., 32 in., and so on) represents the length of the diagonal of the television screen. An aspect ratio describes a screen by comparing its width to its height. A 25 in. television has an aspect ratio of 4:3. What is the width and height of the screen? **width: 20 in.; height: 15 in.**

TEST PREP and Spiral Review

32. Multiple Choice A 24 lb bag of dog food sells for $10.56. What is the unit price per pound?

(A) $0.44/lb   (B) $0.53/lb   (C) $13.44/lb   (D) $34.56/lb

33. Extended Response Flowers can be purchased in bunches of 4 for $2.48 or 6 for $3.96. Which is the better buy? Explain. **The unit price of the bunch of 4 is $0.62 per flower. The unit price of the bunch of 6 is $0.66. The better buy is the bunch of 4 for $2.48.**

Solve. (Lesson 1-7)

34. $p - 8 = 12$
$p = 20$

35. $y + 9 = 15$
$y = 6$

36. $w - 7 = 8$
$w = 15$

37. $k + 4 = 11$
$k = 7$

Find two ratios that are equivalent to each given ratio. (Lesson 5-1)

38. $\frac{3}{5}$ $\frac{6}{10}, \frac{9}{15}$

39. $\frac{13}{26}$ $\frac{1}{2}, \frac{2}{4}$

40. $\frac{4}{11}$ $\frac{8}{22}, \frac{12}{33}$

41. $\frac{10}{9}$ $\frac{20}{18}, \frac{30}{27}$

ONGOING ASSESSMENT
and INTERVENTION

Diagnose **Before** the Lesson
5-2 Warm Up, TE p. 220

Monitor **During** the Lesson
5-2 Know-It Notebook
5-2 Questioning Strategies

Assess **After** the Lesson
5-2 Lesson Quiz, TE p. 223

Answers

29. Possible answer: The student divided the number of shirts by the cost instead of the cost by the number of shirts; $6.25 per T-shirt

30. Possible answer; Simplify the ratio so that the second quantity is 1. An example is the cost per pound of fruit. Consumers can use the unit rate to find the better buy.

TEST PREP DOCTOR + For Exercise 32, encourage students to look over all answer choices before making any calculations. They can eliminate **C** and **D** by realizing that the unit price per pound of dog food will not be greater than the price of a 24 lb bag.

 Journal

Ask students to describe why they think it is or is not helpful for supermarkets to include unit prices on price labels.

Power Presentations with PowerPoint®

 **5-2 Lesson Quiz**

1. Meka can make 6 bracelets per half hour. How many bracelets can she make in 1 hour? 12

2. A penny has a mass of 2.5 g and a volume of approximately 0.360 cm³. What is the approximate density of a penny? ≈6.94 g/cm³

Estimate the unit rate.

3. $2.22 for 6 stamps
$0.37 per stamp

4. 8 heartbeats in 6 seconds
≈1.3 beats/s

Determine the better buy.

5. a half dozen carnations for $4.75 or a dozen for $9.24 a dozen

6. 4 pens for $5.16 or a ten-pack for $12.90 They cost the same.

Also available on transparency

Pacing: Traditional 1 day
Block $\frac{1}{2}$ day

Objective: Students use one or more conversion factors to solve rate problems.

Hands-On Lab
In *Hands-On Lab Activities*

Online Edition
Tutorial Videos, Interactivities

Countdown to Testing Week 8

Power Presentations
with PowerPoint®

Warm Up

Find each unit rate.

1. jump rope 192 times in 6 minutes **32 jumps/min**

2. four pounds of bananas for $2.36 **$0.59/lb**

3. 16 anchor bolts for $18.56 **$1.16/bolt**

4. 288 movies on 9 shelves **32 movies/shelf**

Problem of the Day

Replace each • with a digit from 0 to 6 to make equivalent ratios. Use each digit only once.

$\frac{\bullet\bullet}{\bullet\bullet} = \frac{\bullet}{\bullet\bullet}$ Possible answer: $\frac{13}{65} = \frac{4}{20}$

Also available on transparency

State Resources

go.hrw.com
State Resources Online
KEYWORD: MT7 Resources

5-3 Dimensional Analysis

 Problem Solving Skill

Learn to use one or more conversion factors to solve rate problems.

Vocabulary
conversion factor

Officials at tennis tournaments can determine the speed of a serve by using radar. A radar gun sends out radio waves to determine how far away the ball is at given intervals of time.

The process of converting from one unit to another is called *dimensional analysis*, or *unit analysis*. To convert units, multiply by one or more ratios of equal quantities called **conversion factors**.

For example, to convert inches to feet use the ratio $\frac{1\,\text{ft}}{12\,\text{in.}}$ as a conversion factor.

$$\frac{1\,\text{ft}}{12\,\text{in.}} = \frac{12\,\text{in.}}{12\,\text{in.}} = \frac{1\,\text{ft}}{1\,\text{ft}}, = 1$$

Multiplying by a conversion factor is like multiplying by 1.

EXAMPLE 1 Finding Conversion Factors

Find the appropriate factor for each conversion.

Caution!
Be sure to put the units you are converting to in the numerator and the units you are converting from in the denominator.

A ounces to pounds

There are 16 ounces in 1 pound. To convert ounces to pounds, multiply the number of **ounces** by $\frac{1\,\text{lb}}{16\,\text{oz}}$.

B kilometers to meters

There are 1000 meters in 1 kilometer. To convert kilometers to meters, multiply the number of **kilometers** by $\frac{1000\,\text{m}}{1\,\text{km}}$.

EXAMPLE 2 Using Conversion Factors to Solve Problems

In the United States in 2003, the average person drank approximately 22 gallons of milk. Find the number of quarts of milk the average person drank.

Convert the ratio 22 *gallons* per year to *quarts* per year.

$$\frac{22\,\text{gal}}{1\,\text{yr}} \cdot \frac{4\,\text{qt}}{1\,\text{gal}}$$ *Multiply the ratio by the conversion factor.*

$$= \frac{22 \cdot 4\,\text{qt}}{1\,\text{yr}}$$ *Divide out like units.* $\frac{\text{gal}}{\text{yr}} \cdot \frac{\text{qt}}{\text{gal}} = \frac{\text{qt}}{\text{yr}}$

$$= 88\,\text{qt per year}$$ *Multiply 22 by 4 qt.*

The average person drank 88 quarts of milk in 2003.

---

1 Introduce

Alternate Opener

EXPLORATION

5-3 Dimensional Analysis

The radius of a planet is called the *equatorial radius* and is the imaginary line between the center of the planet and a point on its equator.

The table shows the radius of each planet in our solar system measured in two different units. In the second column, each radius is measured using the radius of Earth. In the third column, each radius is measured in kilometers.

Calculate the equatorial radius of each planet.

	Planet	Equatorial Radius (number of Earth radii)	Equatorial Radius (km)
1.	Mercury	0.38	
2.	Venus	0.95	
3.	Earth	1	6378.14
4.	Mars	0.53	
5.	Jupiter	11	
6.	Saturn	9	
7.	Uranus	4	
8.	Neptune	4	
9.	Pluto	0.19	

Think and Discuss

10. **Explain** how you found the equatorial radius of each planet.

11. **Discuss** whether using Earth's radius or the kilometer

Motivate

Have students determine the missing values.

_?_ inches = 1 foot		12
_?_ centimeters = 1 meter		100
_?_ ounces = 1 pound		16
_?_ seconds = 1 minute		60
_?_ minutes = 1 hour		60

Explain that these facts allow people to convert from one measurement to another.

Explorations and answers are provided in *Alternate Openers: Explorations Transparencies.*

EXAMPLE

PROBLEM SOLVING APPLICATION

A car traveled 330 feet down a road in 5 seconds. How many miles per hour was the car traveling?

1 Understand the Problem

The problem is stated in units of **feet** and **seconds**. The question asks for the **answer** in units of **miles** and **hours**. You will need to use several conversion factors.

List the important information:

- Feet to miles $\longrightarrow \dfrac{1 \text{ mi}}{5280 \text{ ft}}$

- Seconds to minutes $\longrightarrow \dfrac{60 \text{ s}}{1 \text{ min}}$

- Minutes to hours $\longrightarrow \dfrac{60 \text{ min}}{1 \text{ h}}$

2 Make a Plan

Multiply by each conversion factor separately, or **simplify the problem** and multiply by several conversion factors at once.

3 Solve

$\dfrac{330 \text{ ft}}{5 \text{ s}} = \dfrac{(330 \div 5) \text{ ft}}{(5 \div 5) \text{ s}} = \dfrac{66 \text{ ft}}{1 \text{ s}}$
Convert 330 feet in 5 seconds into a unit rate.

$\dfrac{60 \text{ s}}{1 \text{ min}} \cdot \dfrac{60 \text{ min}}{1 \text{ h}} = \dfrac{3600 \text{ s}}{1 \text{ h}}$
Convert seconds directly to hours.

$\dfrac{66 \text{ ft}}{1 \text{ s}} \cdot \dfrac{1 \text{ mi}}{5280 \text{ ft}} \cdot \dfrac{3600 \text{ s}}{1 \text{ h}}$
Set up the conversion factors.

$\dfrac{66 \cancel{\text{ft}}}{1 \cancel{\text{s}}} \cdot \dfrac{1 \text{ mi}}{5280 \cancel{\text{ft}}} \cdot \dfrac{3600 \cancel{\text{s}}}{1 \text{ h}}$
Divide out like units.

$= \dfrac{66 \cdot 1 \text{ mi} \cdot 3600}{1 \cdot 5280 \cdot 1 \text{ h}} = \dfrac{237,600 \text{ mi}}{5280 \text{ h}}$
Multiply.

$= \dfrac{45 \text{ mi}}{1 \text{ h}}$
Divide.

The car was traveling 45 miles per hour.

4 Look Back

A rate of 45 mi/h is less than 1 mi/min. 5 seconds is $\frac{1}{12}$ min. A car traveling 45 mi/h would go less than $\frac{1}{12}$ of 5280 ft in 5 seconds. It goes 330 ft, so 45 mi/h is a reasonable speed.

2 Teach

Guided Instruction

In this lesson, students learn to use one or more conversion factors to solve rate problems. Show students how to write common rates in fractional form $\left(\text{e.g., 40 miles per hour} = \dfrac{40 \text{ mi}}{1 \text{ h}}\right)$. Then explain how to choose the correct conversion factors by setting up rates that cancel the appropriate units. In Examples 1 and 2, show students how the original units are canceled out by the units in the denominator of the conversion factor. Review Examples 3 and 4 with students. You may want to show the work at every step because these concepts may be new for many of them.

Reaching All Learners
Through Curriculum Integration

Physical Science The speed of sound in air is approximately 770 mi/h. Have students use the conversion factors given below to express the speed of sound in ft/s and m/s to the nearest whole unit. The speed of light is approximately 300,000 km/s. Have students express the speed of light in cm/s, mi/s, and mi/h in scientific notation.

conversion factors: 1 mi = 5280 ft, 1 m = 3.28 ft, 1 km = 10^5 cm, 1 km = 0.62 mi

speed of sound: 1129 ft/s; 344 m/s
speed of light: 3.0×10^{10} cm/s; 1.86×10^5 mi/s; 6.696×10^8 mi/h

Additional Example

Example 4

A strobe lamp can be used to measure the speed of an object. The lamp flashes every $\frac{1}{100}$ of a second. A camera records the object moving 52 cm between flashes. How fast is the object moving in m/s? **52 m/s**

Also available on transparency

Answers to Think and Discuss

1. $\frac{1 \text{ yr}}{12 \text{ mo}}$

2. Possible answer: Convert 10 mi/h to ft/s by multiplying by the conversion factors $\frac{1 \text{ h}}{3600 \text{ s}}$ and $\frac{5280 \text{ ft}}{1 \text{ mi}}$. (10 miles per hour ≈ 14.67 feet per second, so 10 miles per hour is slower than 15 feet per second.)

5-3 ## Exercises

Assignment Guide

If you finished Example **1** assign:
Average 1–3, 7–9, 31–45
Advanced 7–9, 31–45

If you finished Example **2** assign:
Average 1–4, 7–10, 13–18, 21, 31–45
Advanced 7–10, 13–18, 26, 27, 29, 31–45

If you finished Example **3** assign:
Average 1–5, 7–11, 13–21, 25, 31–45
Advanced 7–11, 13–21, 23–45

If you finished Example **4** assign:
Average 1–23, 25, 31–45
Advanced 7–45

Homework Quick Check

Quickly check key concepts.
Exercises: 8, 10, 11, 12

EXAMPLE 4 *Physical Science Application*

On June 11, 2004, tennis player Andy Roddick delivered the fastest tennis serve ever recorded by radar. If the radar gun being used that day sent out signals every $\frac{1}{10}$ s and recorded the ball moving 269.28 in. between flashes, how fast was Andy Roddick's serve in mi/h?

$$\frac{269.28 \text{ in.}}{\frac{1}{10} \text{ s}} \qquad \text{Use rate} = \frac{distance}{time}.$$

$$\frac{269.28 \text{ in.}}{\frac{1}{10} \text{ s}} = \frac{10 \cdot 269.28 \text{ in.}}{10 \cdot \frac{1}{10} \text{ s}} \qquad \text{Multiply top and bottom by 10 to eliminate the fraction in the denominator.}$$

$$= \frac{2692.8 \text{ in.}}{1 \text{ s}}$$

Now convert inches per second to miles per hour.

$$\frac{2692.8 \text{ in.}}{1 \text{ s}} \cdot \frac{1 \text{ mi}}{63,360 \text{ in.}} \cdot \frac{3600 \text{ s}}{1 \text{ h}} \qquad \text{Divide out like units.}$$

$$= \frac{2692.8 \cdot 1 \text{ mi} \cdot 3600}{1 \cdot 63,360 \cdot 1 \text{ h}} \qquad \text{Multiply.}$$

$$= 153 \text{ mi/h} \qquad \text{Divide.}$$

The serve traveled 153 mi/h.

Think and Discuss

1. **Give** the conversion factor for converting $\frac{\text{lb}}{\text{yr}}$ to $\frac{\text{lb}}{\text{mo}}$.
2. **Explain** how to find whether 10 mi/h is faster than 15 ft/s.

5-3 ## Exercises

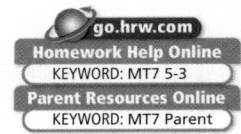

go.hrw.com
Homework Help Online
KEYWORD: MT7 5-3
Parent Resources Online
KEYWORD: MT7 Parent

GUIDED PRACTICE

See Example **1**   **Find the appropriate factor for each conversion.**

1. $\frac{60 \text{ s}}{1 \text{ min}}$ 1. minutes to seconds   2. quarts to gallons $\frac{1 \text{ gal}}{4 \text{ qt}}$ 3. grams to kilograms

3. $\frac{1 \text{ kg}}{1000 \text{ g}}$

See Example **2**   4. Ali uses 12 gallons of gas for his car each week. Find the total number of quarts Ali uses in a year. **2496 qt**

See Example **3**   5. A model airplane flies 22 feet in 2 seconds. What is the airplane's speed in miles per hour? **7.5 mi/h**

See Example **4**   6. If a bird flies 0.7 decimeter every tenth of a second, how fast in meters per second does it fly? **0.7 m/s**

3 Close

Summarize

Review the process for using conversion factors to convert rates from one set of units to another. Have students choose the correct conversion factor for each conversion:

1. $\frac{\text{mi}}{\text{h}}$ to $\frac{\text{ft}}{\text{h}}$ **A.** $\frac{1 \text{ yr}}{12 \text{ mo}}$ **E.** $\frac{1 \text{ kg}}{1000 \text{ g}}$

2. $\frac{\text{g}}{\text{yr}}$ to $\frac{\text{g}}{\text{mo}}$ **B.** $\frac{1 \text{ mi}}{5280 \text{ ft}}$ **F.** $\frac{1 \text{ h}}{3600 \text{ s}}$

3. $\frac{\text{ft}}{\text{h}}$ to $\frac{\text{ft}}{\text{s}}$ **C.** $\frac{1 \text{ h}}{3600 \text{ ft}}$ **G.** $\frac{5280 \text{ ft}}{1 \text{ mi}}$

4. $\frac{\text{g}}{\text{yr}}$ to $\frac{\text{kg}}{\text{yr}}$ **D.** $\frac{12 \text{ mo}}{1 \text{ yr}}$ **H.** $\frac{1000 \text{ g}}{1 \text{ kg}}$

1. G   2. A   3. F   4. E

INDEPENDENT PRACTICE

See Example ① **Find the appropriate factor for each conversion.**

7. meters to millimeters   8. feet to miles $\frac{1\ mi}{5280\ ft}$ 9. minutes to hours

7. $\frac{1000\ mm}{1m}$ $\frac{1\ hr}{60\ min}$

See Example ② 10. An Olympic athlete can run 110 yards in 10 seconds. How fast in miles per hour can the athlete run? **22.5 mi/h**

See Example ③ 11. A yellow jacket can fly 4.5 meters in 9 seconds. How fast in kilometers per hour can a yellow jacket fly? **1.8 km/h**

See Example ④ 12. Anolin, Inc., produces cans at a rate of 0.03 per hundredth of a second. How many cans can be produced in a 7 hour day? **75,600 cans**

PRACTICE AND PROBLEM SOLVING

Extra Practice
See page 790.

Use conversion factors to find each of the following.

13. cereal boxes assembled in 4 minutes at a rate of 2 boxes per second
480 cereal boxes

14. distance traveled in feet after 12 seconds at 87 miles per hour   **1531.2 ft**

15. fish caught in a day at a rate of 42 fish caught each week   **6 fish**

16. concert tickets sold in an hour at a rate of 6 tickets sold per minute   **360 tickets**

17. miles jogged in 1 hour at an average rate of 8.5 feet per second $\approx$ **5.8 mi**

18. calls made in a 3 day telephone fund-raiser at a rate of 10 calls per hour
720 calls

19. There are about 400 cocoa beans in a pound. There are 2.2 pounds in a kilogram. About how many grams does a cocoa bean weigh? $\approx$ **1.14 g**

20. **Estimation** Assume that one dollar is equal to 1.14 euros. If 500 g of an item is selling for 25 euros, what is its approximate price in dollars per kilogram?
$43.86/kg

21. **Food** The largest block of cheese on record weighed 920,136 oz. How many tons is this?   **28.75 tons**

22.
A $\approx$ 22.90 mi/h;

B $\approx$ 23.16 mi/h;

C $\approx$ 21.76 mi/h

22. **Sports** Use the graph to find each world-record speed in miles per hour. (*Hint:* 1 mi $\approx$ 1609 m.)

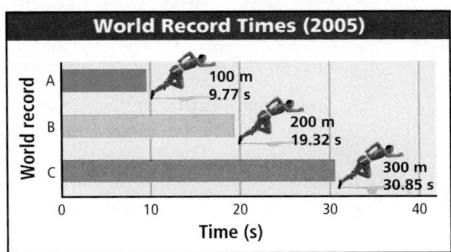

World Record Times (2005)

A 100 m 9.77 s
B 200 m 19.32 s
C 300 m 30.85 s

Time (s)

23. **Transportation** The rate of one knot equals one nautical mile per hour. One nautical mile is 1852 meters. What is the speed in meters per second of a ship traveling at 20 knots?   **10.3 m/s**

24. **Life Science** The Dolphin Bay exhibit at the Texas State Aquarium holds about 400,000 gallons of saltwater. How many days would it take to fill the exhibit at a rate of 1 gallon per second? $\approx$ **4.63 days**

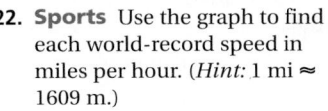
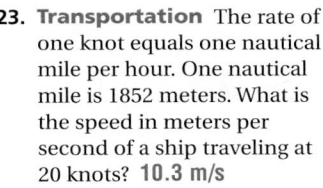

Answers

26. Possible answer: 2.76 miles is equal to 14,572.8 feet, so the runway at JFK is longer.

28. Possible answer: The student used 60 seconds per hour, but there are 3600 seconds in 1 hour. The correct answer is 25.2 km/h.

29. Possible answer: Conversion factors allow you to change from one rate to another. For example, to change mi/h into ft/s, multiply by $\frac{5280 \text{ ft}}{1 \text{ mi}} \cdot \frac{1 \text{ h}}{3600 \text{ s}}$

TEST PREP DOCTOR + Point out to students that Exercise 33 is a multi-step problem. To solve it, they should first convert 12 hours to minutes. Then, divide the total minutes by 45 to find the number of 45-minute intervals in 12 hours. Now, students should be able to calculate the number of cars built in 12 hours.

Journal

Have students write about a situation in which they might need to convert a rate to a different rate.

Power Presentations with PowerPoint®

5-3 Lesson Quiz

Find the appropriate factor for each conversion.

1. kilograms to grams $\frac{1000 \text{ g}}{\text{kg}}$

2. pints to gallons $\frac{1 \text{ gal}}{8 \text{ pt}}$

3. You drive 136 miles from your house to your aunt's house at the lake. You use 8 gallons of gas. How many yards does your car get to the gallon? $\frac{29,920 \text{ yd}}{\text{gal}}$

4. A cheetah was timed running 200 yards in 6 seconds. What was its average speed in miles per hour? $\approx$ 68 mi/h

Also available on transparency

---

25. Life Science A vampire bat consumes approximately 2 tablespoons of animal blood each day. Approximately how many gallons of blood does a vampire bat consume in a year? (*Hint:* 1 tablespoon = 0.5 ounce) $\approx$ 2.85 gal

26. Transportation The longest runway at Chicago's O'Hare International Airport is 13,001 ft long. The longest runway at New York's JFK International Airport is 2.76 miles long. Which runway is longer? Justify your answer.

 27. Choose a Strategy Sondra's recipe for barbecue sauce calls for 3 tablespoons of brown sugar. Sondra does not have a tablespoon. Which spoon can Sondra use to measure the sugar? (*Hint:* 1 tablespoon = $\frac{1}{2}$ ounce)

(A) 2.5 oz spoon   (C) 1.5 oz spoon
(B) 2 oz spoon   (D) None of these

 28. What's the Error? To convert 7 meters per second to kilometers per hour, a student wrote $\frac{7 \text{ m}}{1 \text{ s}} \cdot \frac{1 \text{ km}}{1000 \text{ m}} \cdot \frac{60 \text{ s}}{1 \text{ h}} = 0.42$ km/h. What error did the student make? What should the correct answer be?

29. Write About It Describe the important role that conversion factors play in solving rate problems. Give an example.

30. Challenge Convert each measure. (*Hint:* 1 oz = 28.35 g)
   a. 8 oz = ▢ g   226.8   **b.** 198.45 g = ▢ oz   7
   c. 538.65 g = ▢ lb   1.1875   **d.** 1.5625 lb = ▢ g   708.75

TEST PREP and Spiral Review

31. Multiple Choice A boat travels 110 feet in 5 seconds. What is the boat's speed in miles per hour?
(A) 11 mi/h   (B) 15 mi/h   (C) 20 mi/h   (D) 22.5 mi/h

32. Multiple Choice How long would it take to drain a 750-gallon hot tub at a rate of 112.5 gallons per minute?
(F) 45 minutes   (G) 55 minutes   (H) 60 minutes   (J) 80 minutes

33. Gridded Response How many cars are produced in 12 hours at a factory where 2 cars are built every 45 minutes? 32

Evaluate. (Lesson 4-3)

34. $\frac{3^9}{3^2}$ 2,187   **35.** $2^5 \cdot 2^{-7}$ 0.25   **36.** $\frac{w^5}{w^1}$ w^4 **37.** $\frac{10^2}{10^{-10}}$ 1,000,000,000,000

38. $\frac{8^3}{8^2}$ 8   **39.** $2^3 \cdot 2^4$ 128   **40.** $\frac{4^7}{4^5}$ 16   **41.** $m^5 \cdot m^8$ m^{13}

Find each unit price. (Lesson 5-2)

42. $11.98 for 2 yd of fencing $5.99 per yd
43. 20 oz of cereal for $3.49 $\approx$ $0.175 per oz
44. 4 tickets for $110 $27.50 per ticket
45. $747 for 3 computer monitors $249 per monitor

CHALLENGE 5-3

Challenge
5-3 *Water, Water, Everywhere*

Next time you are in a supermarket, pick up a gallon of water to verify what you will now determine.

How many pounds does a gallon of water weigh?

The amount of space between particles of a substance is what determines its **density**.

Lead is more dense than wood, which is more dense than foam rubber.

Density *d* is equal to the mass (weight) *m* of a substance divided by its volume *V*. $d = \frac{m}{V}$

Water was used as the basis for establishing the metric unit of mass.

The density of water is 1 gram per milliliter: $\frac{1 \text{ g}}{1 \text{ mL}}$.

1. Use the conversion relation 1 mL = 1 cm³ to write the density of water in terms of grams per cubic centimeter.

density of water = $\frac{1 \text{ g}}{1 \text{ mL}} \times \frac{1 \text{ mL}}{1 \text{ cm}^3} = \frac{1 \text{ g}}{1 \text{ cm}^3}$

2. Since 1 m = 100 cm, how many cubic centimeters are there in 1 cubic meter?

1 m³ = __1,000,000__ cm³

3. Use your results from Exercises 1 and 2, and the conversion relation 1 kg = 1000 g to write the density of water in terms of kilograms per cubic meters. Round your answer to the nearest hundredth.

density of water = $\frac{1 \text{ g}}{1 \text{ cm}^3} \times \frac{1 \text{ kg}}{1000 \text{ g}} \times \frac{1,000,000 \text{ cm}^3}{1 \text{ m}^3} = \frac{1000 \text{ kg}}{1 \text{ m}^3}$

4. Use your result from Exercise 3 and these conversion relations to write the density of water as a unit rate in terms of pounds per gallon:

1 kg = 2.205 lb and 1 m³ = 264.2 gal

density of water = $\frac{1000 \text{ kg}}{1 \text{ m}^3} \times \frac{2.205 \text{ lb}}{1 \text{ kg}} \times \frac{1 \text{ m}^3}{264.2 \text{ gal}} = \frac{8.35 \text{ lb}}{1 \text{ gal}}$

5. So, a gallon of water weighs about __8.35__ pounds.

PROBLEM SOLVING 5-3

Problem Solving
5-3 *Dimensional Analysis*

Use the following: 1 mile = 1.609 km; 1 kg = 2.2046 lb. Round to the nearest tenth.

1. Worker bees travel up to 14 km to find pollen and nectar. How far will a worker bee travel in miles?
__8.7 mi__

2. Worker bees can travel at 24 km/h. How fast can the worker bee travel in miles per hour?
__14.9 miles an hour__

3. The average hippopotamus weighs 1800 kg. How many pounds does the average hippopotamus weigh?
__3,968.3 lb__

4. At the age of 45, an elephant grows teeth, each weighing 4 kg. How many pounds do these teeth weigh?
__8.8 lb__

Paraceratherium was the biggest land mammal there has ever been. It lived about 35 million years ago and was 8 m tall and 11 m long. It looked like a gigantic rhinoceros but had a long neck like a giraffe. 1 foot = 0.3048 meters. Round to the nearest tenth.

5. How tall was the paraceratherium in feet?
__26.2 ft__

6. How long was the paraceratherium in feet?
__36.1 ft__

Round to the nearest tenth. Choose the letter for the best answer.

7. The fastest sporting animal is the racing pigeon that flies up to 110 mi an hour. How fast is the racing pigeon in feet each second?
A 75.0 ft/s   C 543.2 ft/s
(B) 161.3 ft/s   D 9,680 ft/s

8. The longest gloved fight between two Americans lasted for more than seven hours before being declared a draw. How many seconds did the fight last?
F 127 s   H 420 s
G 385 s   (J) 25,200 s

9. The average person falls asleep in seven minutes. How many seconds does it take the average person to fall asleep?
A 127 s   (C) 420 s
B 385 s   D 25,200 s

10. The brain of an average adult male weighs 55 oz. How many pounds does the average male brain weigh?
(F) 3.4 lb   H 13.8 lb
G 5.8 lb   J 880 lb

5-4 Solving Proportions

Learn to solve proportions.

Vocabulary
cross product

Unequal masses will not balance on a *fulcrum* if they are an equal distance from it; one side will go up and the other side will go down.

Unequal masses will balance when the following proportion is true:

$$\frac{\text{mass 1}}{\text{length 2}} = \frac{\text{mass 2}}{\text{length 1}}$$

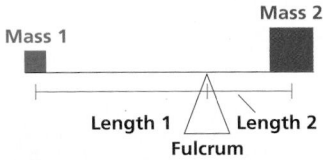

Alexander Calder's sculpture *Totem* stands in Paris. Calder is known as the father of the mobile.

One way to find whether ratios are equal is to find a common denominator. Since $\frac{6}{8} = \frac{72}{96}$ and $\frac{9}{12} = \frac{72}{96}$, $\frac{6}{8}$ is equal to $\frac{9}{12}$.

Helpful Hint

The cross product represents the numerator of the fraction when a common denominator is found by multiplying the denominators.

CROSS PRODUCTS

Cross products in proportions are equal. If the ratios are *not* in proportion, the cross products are not equal.

Proportions		*Not* Proportions	
$\frac{6}{8} \times \frac{9}{12}$	$\frac{5}{2} \times \frac{15}{6}$	$\frac{1}{6} \times \frac{2}{7}$	$\frac{5}{12} \times \frac{2}{5}$
$6 \cdot 12 = 8 \cdot 9$	$5 \cdot 6 = 2 \cdot 15$	$1 \cdot 7 \neq 6 \cdot 2$	$5 \cdot 5 \neq 12 \cdot 2$
$72 = 72$	$30 = 30$	$7 \neq 12$	$25 \neq 24$

E X A M P L E 1 Using Cross Products to Identify Proportions

A Tell whether the ratios $\frac{5}{6}$ and $\frac{15}{21}$ are proportional.

$$\frac{5}{6} \stackrel{?}{=} \frac{15}{21}$$

$$\frac{5}{6} \times \frac{15}{21} \begin{array}{l} \to 90 \\ \to 105 \end{array}$$ *Find the cross products.*

$$105 \neq 90$$

Since the cross products are not equal, the ratios are not proportional.

Organizer 5-4

Pacing: Traditional 1 day
Block $\frac{1}{2}$ day
Objective: Students solve proportions.

Online Edition
Tutorial Videos

Countdown to Testing Week 8

Power Presentations
with PowerPoint®

Warm Up

Find two ratios that are equivalent to each given ratio.
Possible answers:

1. $\frac{3}{5}$ $\frac{6}{10}, \frac{9}{15}$ **2.** $\frac{10}{12}$ $\frac{5}{6}, \frac{20}{24}$

3. $\frac{45}{30}$ $\frac{3}{2}, \frac{90}{60}$ **4.** $\frac{8}{9}$ $\frac{16}{18}, \frac{24}{27}$

Problem of the Day

Replace each ● with a digit from 1 to 7 to write a proportion. Use each digit once. The digits 2 and 3 are already shown.

$\frac{2^{3}}{\bullet\bullet} = \frac{\bullet}{\bullet}$ Possible answer: $\frac{2^{3}}{56} = \frac{1^{4}}{7}$

Also available on transparency

Math Humor

Teacher: Why are you using a first-aid kit to solve a proportion?

Student: The problem is printed in red, so I'm using a Red Cross product.

---

1 Introduce
Alternate Opener

State Resources

EXPLORATION

5-4 Solving Proportions

The grid shows three rectangles aligned by a diagonal line.

Complete the table. Use the grid to measure the length and width of each rectangle. Divide the length by the width and write this answer as a fraction in simplest form.

		Length	Width	Length Width
1.	Blue rectangle			
2.	Red rectangle			
3.	Green rectangle			

Think and Discuss

4. Compare the fractions you found in Problems 1–3.
5. Explain how you wrote each fraction in simplest form.

go.hrw.com
State Resources Online
KEYWORD: MT7 Resources

Motivate

Give students the following two statements: $\frac{2}{3} \stackrel{?}{=} \frac{6}{10}$ and $\frac{3}{4} \stackrel{?}{=} \frac{6}{8}$. Ask them to decide whether each statement is true or false. $\frac{2}{3} \neq \frac{6}{10}, \frac{3}{4} = \frac{6}{8}$ Ask students to explain how they decided whether the statements were true or false. Remind students that $\frac{3}{4} = \frac{6}{8}$ is a proportion because it is true. Tell them they will learn to solve proportions in this new lesson.

Explorations and answers are provided in *Alternate Openers: Explorations Transparencies.*

Power Presentations
with PowerPoint®

Additional Examples

Example 1

Tell whether the ratios are proportional.

A. $\frac{6}{15} \overset{?}{=} \frac{4}{10}$ yes

B. A mixture of fuel for a certain small engine should be 4 parts gasoline to 1 part oil. If you combine 5 quarts of oil with 15 quarts of gasoline, will the mixture be correct? no

Example 2

Solve the proportion

$\frac{\$x}{1 \text{ items}} = \frac{\$48}{3 \text{ items}}$. $16

Example 3

Solve the proportion $\frac{y}{21} = \frac{1}{3}$.   7

Example 4

J & A Department Store is selling 3 pairs of children's socks for $5. Mrs. Wagner wants to buy a dozen pairs of socks. How much will this cost? $20

Also available on transparency

B A shade of paint is made by mixing 5 parts red paint with 7 parts blue paint. If you mix 21 quarts of blue paint with 15 quarts of red paint, will you get the correct shade? Explain.

$\frac{5 \text{ parts red}}{7 \text{ parts blue}} \overset{?}{=} \frac{15 \text{ quarts red}}{21 \text{ quarts blue}}$ *Set up equal ratios.*

$5 \cdot 21 = 105 \quad 7 \cdot 15 = 105$ *Find the cross products.*

$105 = 105$

The cross products are equal. You will get the correct shade of paint.

To solve problems involving proportional relationships, you can use unit rates, equivalent fractions, factors of change, or cross products.

EXAMPLE 2 **Solving Proportions Using Unit Rates**

Solve the proportion $\frac{\$d}{12 \text{ items}} = \frac{\$96}{4 \text{ items}}$.

$\frac{\$d}{12 \text{ items}} = \frac{\$96}{4 \text{ items}}$

$\frac{\$(d \div 12)}{1 \text{ item}} = \frac{\$24}{1 \text{ item}}$ *Find the unit rates.*

$d \div 12 = 24$ *The numerators are equal because the denominators are equal.*

$12(d \div 12) = 12(24)$ *Multiply both sides by 12.*

$d = \$288$ *Simplify.*

EXAMPLE 3 **Solving Proportions Using Equivalent Fractions**

Solve the proportion $\frac{x}{6} = \frac{4}{8}$.

$\frac{x}{6} = \frac{4}{8}$

$\frac{(x \cdot 4)}{(6 \cdot 4)} = \frac{(4 \cdot 3)}{(8 \cdot 3)}$ *Multiply to write the fractions with the LCD.*

$\frac{4x}{24} = \frac{12}{24}$

$4x = 12$ *The numerators are equal because the denominators are equal.*

$\frac{4x}{4} = \frac{12}{4}$ *Divide both sides by 4.*

$x = 3$ *Simplify.*

EXAMPLE 4 *Business Application*

On "2 fer Tuesday", 2 bagels with cream cheese cost $2.50. Jimmy wants to buy 2 dozen. How much will this cost?

2 dozen bagels = 24 bagels

$\frac{2 \text{ bagels}}{\$2.50} = \frac{24 \text{ bagels}}{\$d}$ *Set up the proportion.*

$\frac{24 \text{ bagels}}{2 \text{ bagels}} = 12$ *Divide to find the factor of change.*

$\$2.50 \cdot 12 = \$30$ *Multiply by the factor of change to find cost.*

② Teach

Guided Instruction

In this lesson, students learn to solve proportions. Remind them that one way to determine whether ratios are equivalent is to simplify the ratios and see whether they are the same (Lesson 5-1). A second method is to find the *cross products*. If the cross products are equal, then the ratios are in proportion (Teaching Transparency). Show students that if they are given a proportion with one value missing, they can write an equation using cross products to find it.

Reaching All Learners
Through Diversity

Ask students to find a recipe at home for a particular number of servings. Ask them to use a proportion to find the amount of each ingredient needed for a different number of servings. Suggest that students use the following proportion:

original amount of ingredient	new amount of ingredient
original number of servings	new number of servings

EXAMPLE 5 *Physical Science Application*

Two children can be balanced on a seesaw when $\frac{\text{mass 1}}{\text{length 2}} = \frac{\text{mass 2}}{\text{length 1}}$. The child on the left and the child on the right are balanced. What is the mass of the child on the right?

24 lb   ?

14 ft   8 ft

$$\frac{24}{8} = \frac{m}{14}$$ *Set up the proportion.*

$24 \cdot 14 = 8m$ *Find the cross products.*

$$\frac{336}{8} = \frac{8m}{8}$$ *Divide both sides by 8.*

$42 = m$ *Simplify.*

The mass of the child on the right is 42 lb.

Think and Discuss

1. **Explain** what the cross products of two ratios represent.

2. **Tell** what it means if the cross products are not equal.

3. **Describe** how to solve a proportion when one of the four numbers is a variable.

Power Presentations
with PowerPoint®

Additional Examples

Example 5

Allyson weighs 55 pounds and sits on a seesaw 4 feet away from its center. If Marco sits on the seesaw 5 feet away from the center and the seesaw is balanced, how much does Marco weigh? **44 lb**

Also available on transparency

5-4 Exercises

Assignment Guide

If you finished Example ① assign:
Average 1–5, 18–22, 39–42, 53–58
Advanced 18–22, 42–47, 51, 53–58

If you finished Example ② assign:
Average 1–11, 18–28, 39–42, 53–58
Advanced 18–28, 42–47, 53–58

If you finished Example ③ assign:
Average 1–15, 18–36, 39–42, 53–58
Advanced 18–36, 42–47, 53–58

If you finished Example ④ assign:
Average 1–16, 18–37, 39–42, 53–58
Advanced 18–37, 42–47, 49, 51, 53–58

If you finished Example ⑤ assign:
Average 1–42, 48, 50, 51, 53–58
Advanced 18–38, 42–58

Homework Quick Check

Quickly check key concepts.
Exercises: 20, 26, 30, 37, 38

5-4 Exercises

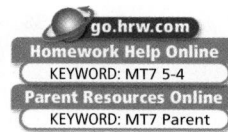
go.hrw.com
Homework Help Online
KEYWORD: MT7 5-4
Parent Resources Online
KEYWORD: MT7 Parent

GUIDED PRACTICE

See Example ① **Tell whether the ratios are proportional.**

1. $\frac{6}{12} \overset{?}{=} \frac{12}{24}$ **yes**   2. $\frac{2}{9} \overset{?}{=} \frac{6}{27}$ **yes**   3. $\frac{5}{7} \overset{?}{=} \frac{10}{15}$ **no**   4. $\frac{10}{25} \overset{?}{=} \frac{6}{15}$ **yes**

5. A bubble solution can be made with a ratio of 1 part detergent to 8 parts water. Would a mixture of 56 oz water and 8 oz detergent be proportional to this ratio? Explain. **no; $\frac{1}{8} \neq \frac{8}{56}$**

See Example ② **Solve each proportion.**

6. $\frac{\$d}{12 \text{ hours}} = \frac{\$96}{8 \text{ hours}}$ **$144**   7. $\frac{m \text{ miles}}{6 \text{ hours}} = \frac{110 \text{ mile}}{2 \text{ hours}}$ **330 mi**

8. $\frac{s \text{ students}}{6 \text{ teachers}} = \frac{209 \text{ students}}{11 \text{ teachers}}$ **114 students**   9. $\frac{\$d}{4 \text{ enchiladas}} = \frac{\$13.50}{6 \text{ enchiladas}}$ **$9**

10. $\frac{c \text{ Calories}}{3 \text{ servings}} = \frac{290 \text{ Calories}}{2 \text{ servings}}$ **435 Calories**   11. $\frac{p \text{ photos}}{13 \text{ orders}} = \frac{441 \text{ photos}}{21 \text{ orders}}$ **273 photos**

③ Close

Summarize

Remind students that they can use cross products to determine whether two ratios form a proportion. Ask students to determine whether each of the following is a proportion.

1. $\frac{1}{2} \overset{?}{=} \frac{50}{100}$ **yes**   2. $\frac{3}{8} \overset{?}{=} \frac{7}{20}$ **no**

3. $\frac{2}{8} \overset{?}{=} \frac{6}{24}$ **yes**   4. $\frac{8}{12} \overset{?}{=} \frac{2}{3}$ **yes**

Possible answers to *Think and Discuss*

1. the numerators of the fractions when you find a common denominator by multiplying the denominators

2. The ratios are not equal.

3. Cross multiply, isolate the variable, and solve the equation.

State Resources

go.hrw.com
State Resources Online
KEYWORD: MT7 Resources

Proportions are used to represent *direct* relationships and *inverse* relationships.

The dimensions of similar polygons (to be studied in Lesson 5-5) are directly proportional. The dimensions of two different rectangles that have the same area are *inversely proportional,* as shown below.

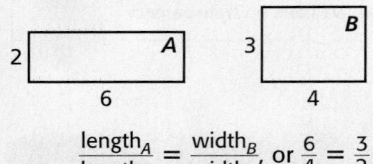

$$\frac{\text{length}_A}{\text{length}_B} = \frac{\text{width}_B}{\text{width}_A}, \text{ or } \frac{6}{4} = \frac{3}{2}$$

See Example 3   **12.** $\frac{x}{5} = \frac{3.78}{10}$ **1.89**   **13.** $\frac{w}{20} = \frac{210}{8}$ **525**   **14.** $\frac{s}{4} = \frac{15}{6}$ **10**   **15.** $\frac{g}{6} = \frac{25}{15}$ **10**

See Example 4   **16.** Mitchell bought 3 postcards for $3.14. At this rate, how much would 12 postcards cost? **$12.56**

See Example 5   **17.** A 12 lb weight is positioned 8 in. from a fulcrum. At what distance from the fulcrum must an 18 lb weight be positioned to keep the scale balanced? $5\frac{1}{3}$ in.

INDEPENDENT PRACTICE

See Example 1   **Tell whether the ratios are proportional.**

18. $\frac{22}{42} \overset{?}{=} \frac{3}{7}$ **no**   **19.** $\frac{17}{51} \overset{?}{=} \frac{2}{6}$ **yes**   **20.** $\frac{40}{36} \overset{?}{=} \frac{20}{16}$ **no**   **21.** $\frac{8}{9} \overset{?}{=} \frac{40}{45}$ **yes**

22. An after-school club had 10 girls and 12 boys. Then 5 more girls and 6 more boys signed up. Did the ratio of girls to boys stay the same? Explain.

yes; $\frac{10}{12} = \frac{15}{18}$

See Example 2   **Solve each proportion.**

23. $\frac{\$d}{8 \text{ CDs}} = \frac{\$38.97}{3 \text{ CDs}}$ **$103.92**

24. $\frac{c \text{ chairs}}{9 \text{ rows}} = \frac{27 \text{ chairs}}{3 \text{ rows}}$ **81 chairs**

25. $\frac{\$d}{4 \text{ tickets}} = \frac{\$72}{6 \text{ tickets}}$ **$48**

26. $\frac{m \text{ minutes}}{8 \text{ miles}} = \frac{24 \text{ minutes}}{3 \text{ miles}}$ **64 min**

27. $\frac{c}{\text{computers}} = \frac{20 \text{ computers}}{25 \text{ students}}$ **12 computers**

28. $\frac{t \text{ tissues}}{5 \text{ packages}} = \frac{1500 \text{ tissues}}{30 \text{ packages}}$ **250 tissues**

See Example 3   **29.** $\frac{b}{15} = \frac{6}{10}$ **9**   **30.** $\frac{c}{9} = \frac{4}{6}$ **6**   **31.** $\frac{h}{9} = \frac{16}{6}$ **24**   **32.** $\frac{c}{9} = \frac{8}{6}$ **12**

33. $\frac{q}{7} = \frac{19}{133}$ **1**   **34.** $\frac{j}{18} = \frac{10}{60}$ **3**   **35.** $\frac{d}{24} = \frac{15}{40}$ **9**   **36.** $\frac{s}{50} = \frac{3}{15}$ **10**

See Example 4   **37.** Zoe bought 4 book covers for $7.50. At this rate, how much would 12 book covers cost? **$22.50**

See Example 5   **38.** A 150 kg weight is positioned 3 m from a fulcrum. If a 200 kg weight is placed at the opposite end of the balance, how far from the fulcrum should it be positioned? **2.25 m**

PRACTICE AND PROBLEM SOLVING

Extra Practice
See page 790.

For each set of ratios, find the two that are proportional.

39. $\frac{8}{4}, \frac{24}{12}, \frac{55}{27}$ $\frac{8}{4}, \frac{24}{12}$

40. $\frac{1}{4}, \frac{4}{16}, \frac{110}{444}$ $\frac{1}{4} \text{ and } \frac{4}{16}$

41. $\frac{35}{26}, \frac{81}{39}, \frac{27}{13}$ $\frac{81}{39}, \frac{27}{13}$

42. $\frac{49}{182}, \frac{7}{26}, \frac{45}{160}$ $\frac{49}{182}, \frac{7}{26}$

43. $\frac{0.5}{6}, \frac{0.25}{9}, \frac{1}{12}$ $\frac{0.5}{6}, \frac{1}{12}$

44. $\frac{a}{c}, \frac{a}{b}, \frac{4a}{4b}$ $\frac{a}{b}, \frac{4a}{4b}$

45. $\frac{1.1}{11}, \frac{10}{110}, \frac{11}{121}$ $\frac{10}{110} \text{ and } \frac{11}{121}$

46. $\frac{13}{50}, \frac{91}{350}, \frac{26}{75}$ $\frac{13}{50} \text{ and } \frac{91}{350}$

47. $\frac{7}{15}, \frac{70}{165}, \frac{84}{180}$ $\frac{7}{15} \text{ and } \frac{84}{180}$

48. Physical Science One molecule of nitrogen reacting with 3 molecules of hydrogen makes 2 molecules of ammonia. How many molecules of nitrogen must react with 42 molecules of hydrogen to make 28 molecules of ammonia? **14 molecules**

49. Multi-Step Jacob is selling T-shirts at a music festival. Yesterday, he sold 51 shirts and earned $191.25. How many shirts must Jacob sell today and tomorrow to earn a total of $536.25 for all three days? **92**

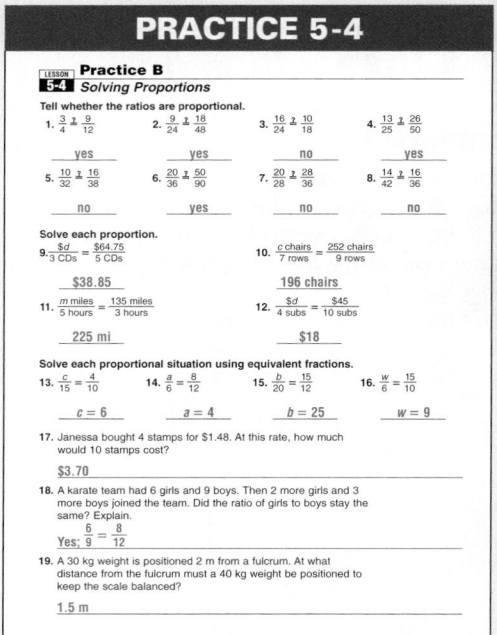

Health LINK

A doctor reports blood pressure in millimeters of mercury (mm Hg) as a ratio of *systolic* blood pressure to *diastolic* blood pressure (such as 140 over 80). Systolic pressure is measured when the heart beats, and diastolic pressure is measured when it rests. Refer to the table of blood pressure ranges for adults for Exercise 40.

Blood Pressure Ranges

	Normal	Prehypertension	Hypertension (very high)
Systolic	under 120 mm Hg	120–139 mm Hg	140 mm Hg and above
Diastolic	under 80 mm Hg	80–89 mm Hg	90 mm Hg and above

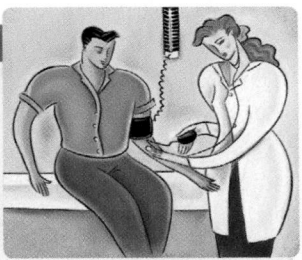

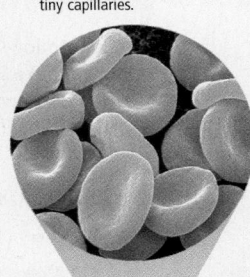

The disc-like shape of red blood cells allows them to pass through tiny capillaries.

50. Estimation Eduardo is a healthy 37-year-old man whose blood pressure is in the normal category.

a. Calculate an approximate ratio of systolic to diastolic blood pressure in the normal range. **about 3:2**

b. If Eduardo's systolic blood pressure is 102 mm Hg, use the ratio from part **a** to predict his diastolic blood pressure. **about 68 mm Hg**

51. Write About It A ratio related to heart health is LDL cholesterol to HDL cholesterol. The optimal ratio of LDL to HDL is below 3. A patient's total cholesterol is 168 and HDL is 44. Is the patient's ratio optimal? Explain. **Yes; the ratio is less than 2.82:1.**

52. Challenge The sum of Ken's LDL and HDL cholesterol is 210, and his LDL to HDL ratio is 2.75. What are his LDL and HDL? **154 and 56**

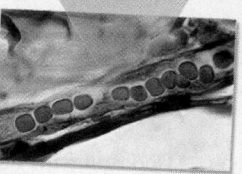

go.hrw.com
Web Extra!
KEYWORD: MT7 Health

Test Prep and Spiral Review

53. Multiple Choice A tree was 3.5 feet tall after 2 years and 8.75 feet tall after 5 years. If the tree grew at a constant rate, how tall was it after 3 years?

(A) 5 feet (B) 5.25 feet (C) 5.75 feet (D) 6.5 feet

54. Gridded Response What value of b makes the proportion $\frac{4}{5} = \frac{b}{20}$ true? **16**

Divide. Write each answer in simplest form. (Lesson 2-5)

55. $\frac{3}{4} \div \frac{1}{2}$ $\frac{3}{2}$

56. $3\frac{1}{7} \div \left(-\frac{2}{21}\right)$ -33

57. $-2\frac{1}{8} \div \left(-2\frac{1}{2}\right)$ $\frac{17}{20}$

58. A high speed train travels at 200 miles per hour. What is the train's speed in feet per second? (Lesson 5-3) **$293\frac{1}{3}$ feet per second**

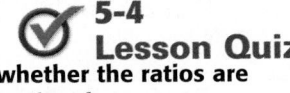

CHALLENGE 5-4

LESSON 5-4 **Challenge**
Meanwhile . . .

In a proportion, there are 4 terms.

The 1st and 4th are called **extremes.** The 2nd and 3rd are called **means.**

$$\frac{\text{1st (extreme)}}{\text{2nd (mean)}} = \frac{\text{3rd (mean)}}{\text{4th (extreme)}}$$

When the means of a proportion are equal, either is a **mean proportional.**

$$\frac{2}{6} = \frac{6}{18}$$

6 is the mean proportional between 2 and 18.

To find the mean proportional m between 4 and 25:

$\frac{4}{m} = \frac{m}{25}$

$m^2 = 100$

$m = \sqrt{100} = 10$

Check by showing equal ratios.

$\frac{4}{10} \stackrel{?}{=} \frac{10}{25}$

$\frac{4 \div 2}{10 \div 2} \mid \frac{10 \div 5}{25 \div 5}$

$\frac{2}{5} = \frac{2}{5}$

Find the mean proportional m between each pair of numbers. Check by showing equal ratios.

1. 4 and 9

$\frac{4}{m} = \frac{m}{9}$

$m^2 = 36$

$m = \sqrt{36} = 6$

Check: $\frac{4}{6} \stackrel{?}{=} \frac{6}{9}$

$\frac{4 \div 2}{6 \div 2} \mid \frac{6 \div 3}{9 \div 3}$

$\frac{2}{3} = \frac{2}{3}$

2. 0.3 and 1.2

$\frac{0.3}{m} = \frac{m}{1.2}$

$m^2 = 0.36$

$m = \sqrt{0.36} = 0.6$

Check: $\frac{0.3}{0.6} \stackrel{?}{=} \frac{0.6}{1.2}$

$\frac{0.3 \times 10}{0.6 \times 10} \mid \frac{0.6 \times 10}{1.2 \times 10}$

$\frac{3 \div 3}{6 \div 3}$ $\frac{6 \div 6}{12 \div 6}$

$\frac{1}{2} = \frac{1}{2}$

3. $\frac{1}{2}$ and $\frac{1}{8}$

$\frac{\frac{1}{2}}{m} = \frac{m}{\frac{1}{8}}$

$m^2 = \frac{1}{16}$

$m = \sqrt{\frac{1}{16}} = \frac{1}{4}$

Check: $\frac{\frac{1}{2}}{\frac{1}{4}} \stackrel{?}{=} \frac{\frac{1}{4}}{\frac{1}{8}}$

$\frac{1}{2} \times \frac{4}{1} \mid \frac{1}{4} \times \frac{8}{1}$

$2 = 2$

fractio

PROBLEM SOLVING 5-4

LESSON 5-4 **Problem Solving**
Solving Proportions

Scientists have researched the ratio of human body parts and height. Use the ratios in the table to answer each

Body Part	$\frac{\text{Body Part}}{\text{Height}}$
Femur	$\frac{1}{4}$
Tibia	$\frac{1}{5}$
Hand span	$\frac{2}{17}$
Arm span	$\frac{1}{1}$
Head circumference	$\frac{1}{3}$

1. Which body part is the same length as the person's height?
arm span

2. If a person's tibia is 13 inches, how tall would you expect the person to be?
65 inches

3. If a person's hand span is 8.5 inches, about how tall would you expect the person to be?
72.3 inches

4. If a femur is 18 inches long, how many feet tall would you expect the person to be?
6 feet

5. What would you expect the head circumference to be of a person who is 5.5 feet tall?
1.8 feet

6. What would you expect the hand span to be of a person who is 5 feet tall?
0.6 feet

Choose the letter for the best answer.

7. Five milliliters of a children's medicine contains 400 mg of the drug amoxicillin. How many mg of amoxicillin does 25 mL contain?
A 0.3 mg (C) 2000 mg
B 80 mg D 2500 mg

8. Vladimir Radmanovic of the Seattle Supersonics makes, on average, about 2 three-pointers for every 5 he shoots. If he attempts 10 three-pointers in a game, how many would you expect him to make?
(F) 4 H 8
G 5 J 25

9. In 2002, a 30-second commercial during the Super Bowl cost an average of $1,900,000. At this rate, how much would a 45-second commercial cost?
A $1,266,666 C $3,500,000
(B) $2,850,000 D $4,000,000

10. A medicine for dogs indicates that the medicine should be administered in the ratio 2 teaspoons per 5 lb, based on the weight of the dog. How much should be given to a 70 lb dog?
F 5 teaspoons H 14 teaspoons
G 12 teaspoons (J) 28 teaspoons

Ongoing Assessment and Intervention

***Diagnose Before* the Lesson**
5-4 Warm Up, TE p. 229

***Monitor During* the Lesson**
5-4 Know-It Notebook
5-4 Questioning Strategies

***Assess After* the Lesson**
5-4 Lesson Quiz, TE p. 233

Interdisciplinary LINK

Health

Exercises 50–52 involve using information about heart health. Students learn about blood pressure and cholesterol in middle school health programs such as Holt, Rinehart & Winston's Decisions for Health.

Test Prep Doctor For Exercise 53, point out to students that there are two proportions they can use to solve this problem. However, suggest that they choose the proportion with the smaller numbers, because it will make the calculations easier with less chance for error.

Journal

An *analogy* is a comparison of pairs of words or ideas that have a similar relationship. For example, in the analogy *"good* is to *bad* as *big* is to *small,"* both sets of words have opposite meanings. Have students write about how proportions are like analogies.

Power Presentations with PowerPoint®

5-4 Lesson Quiz

Tell whether the ratios are proportional.

1. $\frac{48}{42} \stackrel{?}{=} \frac{16}{14}$ yes **2.** $\frac{40}{15} \stackrel{?}{=} \frac{3}{4}$ no

Solve each proportion.

3. $\frac{n}{12} = \frac{45}{18}$ $n = 30$ **4.** $\frac{6}{9} = \frac{n}{24}$ $n = 16$

5. Two weights are balanced on a fulcrum. If a 6 lb weight is positioned 1.5 ft from the fulcrum, at what distance from the fulcrum must an 18 lb weight be placed to keep the weights balanced? **0.5 ft**

Also available on transparency

Organizer

Objective: Assess students' mastery of concepts and skills in Lessons 5-1 through 5-4.

Resources

 Assessment Resources
Section 5A Quiz

 Test & Practice Generator
One-Stop Planner®

INTERVENTION

Resources

 Ready to Go On?
Intervention and
Enrichment Worksheets

Ready to Go On? CD-ROM

Ready to Go On? Online

my.hrw.com

Ready to Go On? (side tab)

READY TO GO ON?

Quiz for Lessons 5-1 Through 5-4

5-1 Ratios and Proportions

Simplify to tell whether the ratios form a proportion.

1. $\frac{6}{7}$ and $\frac{18}{21}$ **yes**
2. $\frac{36}{48}$ and $\frac{12}{15}$ **no**
3. $\frac{12}{42}$ and $\frac{6}{21}$ **yes**
4. $\frac{4}{5}$ and $\frac{16}{25}$ **no**

5. Cody is following a recipe that calls for 1.5 cups of flour to make 2 dozen mini corn muffins. He uses the amounts shown in the table to make 3 dozen mini corn muffins. Has he followed the recipe? Explain.
   No; $\frac{1.5}{2} \neq \frac{2.5}{3}$ he should have used 2.25 cups.

Flour (c)	Mini Corn Muffins (dozen)
1.5	2
2.5	3

5-2 Ratios, Rates, and Unit Rates

6. The mass of a piece of iron pyrite, or "fools gold," is 57.2 g. The volume is 11 cm³. What is the density of the piece of iron pyrite?   **5.2 g/cm³**

7. Adela drinks 28 glasses of water per week. How many glasses does she drink per day?   **4 glasses**

Estimate each unit rate.

8. type 242 words in 6 minutes   **about 40 words per minute**
9. $7.98 for 2 pounds   **about $4/lb**

Determine the better buy.

10. a long distance phone charge of $1.40 for 10 min or $4.50 for 45 min   **$0.14 per min; $0.10 per min; 45 min**
11. a dozen eggs for $2.78 or a half dozen for $1.49   **$0.23 per egg; $0.25 per egg; a dozen eggs**

5-3 Dimensional Analysis

Find the appropriate factor for each conversion.

12. pounds to ounces $\frac{16 \text{ oz}}{1 \text{ lb}}$
13. feet to miles $\frac{1 \text{ mi}}{5280 \text{ ft}}$
14. minutes to days $\frac{1 \text{ day}}{1440 \text{ min}}$

Use conversion factors to find each unit to the nearest hundredth.

15. 10 quarts to gallons   **2.5 gal**
16. 90 km per min to km per s   **1.5 km/s**

17. Driving at a constant rate, Shawna covered 325 miles 6.5 in hours. Express her driving rate in feet per minute.   **4400 ft/min**

5-4 Solving Proportions

Solve each proportion.

18. $\frac{\$180}{12 \text{ hours}} = \frac{\$d}{20 \text{ hours}}$ **$300**
19. $\frac{360 \text{ miles}}{6 \text{ hours}} = \frac{m \text{ miles}}{4 \text{ hours}}$ **240 mi**

20. Tim can input 110 data items in 2.5 minutes. Typing at the same rate, how many data items can he input in 7 minutes?   **308 data items**

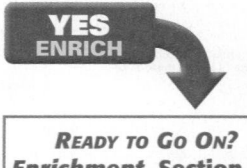

READY TO GO ON?
Diagnose and Prescribe

READY TO GO ON? Intervention, Section 5A			
Ready to Go On? Intervention	**Worksheets**	**CD-ROM**	**Online**
Lesson 5-1	5-1 Intervention	Activity 5-1	
Lesson 5-2	5-2 Intervention	Activity 5-2	Diagnose and Prescribe Online
Lesson 5-3	5-3 Intervention	Activity 5-3	
Lesson 5-4	5-4 Intervention	Activity 5-4	

NO INTERVENE

YES ENRICH

READY TO GO ON?
Enrichment, Section 5A
Worksheets
CD-ROM
Online

Focus on Problem Solving

Solve

• **Choose an operation: multiplication or division**

When you are converting units, think about whether the number in the answer will be greater or less than the number given in the question. This will help you to decide whether to multiply or divide to convert the units.

For example, if you are converting feet to inches, you know that the number of inches will be greater than the number of feet because each foot is 12 inches. So you know that you should multiply by 12 to get a greater number.

In general, if you are converting to smaller units, the number of units will have to be greater to represent the same quantity.

For each problem, determine whether the number in the answer will be greater or less than the number given in the question. Use your answer to decide whether to multiply or divide by the conversion factor. Then solve the problem.

1 The speed a boat travels is usually measured in nautical miles per hour, or knots. The Staten Island Ferry in New York, which provides service between Manhattan and Staten Island, can travel at 15.5 knots. Find the speed in miles per hour. (*Hint:* 1 knot = 1.15 miles per hour)

2 When it is finished, the Crazy Horse Memorial in the Black Hills of South Dakota will be the world's largest sculpture. The sculpture's height will be 563 feet. Find the height in meters. (*Hint:* 1 meter = 3.28 feet)
Answer: 171.65 m

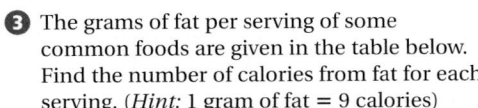

3 The grams of fat per serving of some common foods are given in the table below. Find the number of calories from fat for each serving. (*Hint:* 1 gram of fat = 9 calories)

Food	Fat per Serving (g)
Avocado (1 c, sliced)	22.3
Pretzels (1 oz)	1
Baked Potato (7 oz)	0.4
Plain Bagel (4 oz)	1.8

4 Nearly a quarter of the Texas Gulf Coast is national seashore or state park. At 372 miles long, it is undergoing a seaward advance at the rate of about 0.0095 miles per year. Find the length of the Texas shoreline in kilometers. (*Hint:* 1 mile = 1.61 kilometers)
Possible answer: Greater; a kilometer is less than a mile, so you should multiply.
Answer: about 599 km

Answers

1. 17.825 mi/h

3.

Food	Calories per Serving (cal)
Avocado (1 c, sliced)	200.7
Pretzels (1 oz)	9
Baked potato (7 oz)	3.6
Plain bagel (4 oz)	16.2

SECTION 5B

Similarity and Scale

One-Minute Section Planner

Lesson	Materials	MiC and Lab Resources
5-5 Hands-On Lab Explore Similarity • Use a number cube and graph paper to explore similarity. **Lesson 5-5** Similar Figures • Determine whether figures are similar, to use scale factors, and to find missing dimensions in similar figures. ☑ SAT-10 ☑ ITBS ☑ CTBS ☑ NAEP	Number cubes (MK), 2 different sizes of graph paper, metric rulers (MK), protractors (MK)	**MiC: *It's All the Same*** pp. 27–28, 31, 36–38 **MiC: *Looking at an Angle*** pp. 13–21, 32–36 ***Hands-On Lab Activities*** 5-5
5-6 Hands-On Lab Explore Dilations • Use graph paper and a ruler to explore dilations of geometric figures. **Lesson 5-6** Dilations • Identify and create dilations of plane figures. ☑ SAT-10 ☑ ITBS ☑ CTBS ☑ NAEP	Graph paper, metric rulers (MK)	**MiC: *It's All the Same*** pp. 9–13 ***Hands-On Lab Activities*** 5-6 ***Technology Lab Activities*** 5-6
Lesson 5-7 Indirect Measurement • Find measures indirectly by applying the properties of similar figures. ☑ SAT-10 ☑ ITBS ☑ CTBS ☑ NAEP		**MiC: *Looking at an Angle*** pp. 1–5, 13–21, 25–29, 32–36
Lesson 5-8 Scale Drawings and Scale Models • Make comparisons between and find dimensions of scale drawings, models, and actual objects. **5-8 Hands-On Lab** Make a Scale Model • Become familiar with the concept of scale by making scale models. ☑ SAT-10 ☐ ITBS ☑ CTBS ☑ NAEP	Tape measures (MK), card stock, scissors, tape, customary rulers (MK), calculators	**MiC: *Looking at an Angle*** pp. 1–5, 13–21, 25–29, 32–36 ***Hands-On Lab Activities*** 5-8

MK = *Manipulatives Kit*

Mathematics in Context

The units *It's All the Same* and *Looking at an Angle* from the *Mathematics in Context* © 2006 series can be used with Section 5B. See Section Planner above for suggestions for integrating *MiC* with *Holt Mathematics*.

Section Overview

Similar Figures, Dilations, and Indirect Measurement *Lessons 5-5, 5-6, 5-7*

 Similar figures, dilations, and scale drawings are used in blueprints for construction, photography, medical research, and many other applications.

Similar figures have congruent angles and proportional sides.	A **dilation** produces an image similar to the original figure. Scale factor > 1 → **Enlargement** Scale factor < 1 → **Reduction**	**Indirect Measurement** The triangle formed by the height of the man and his shadow and the similar triangle formed by the height of the building and its shadow are similar. Find the height of the building.

Similar Figures

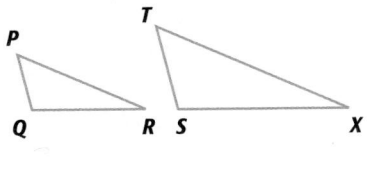

$$\angle Q \cong \angle S$$
$$\angle P \cong \angle T$$
$$\angle R \cong \angle X$$

$$\frac{PQ}{TS} = \frac{RP}{XT} = \frac{QR}{SX}$$

Dilations

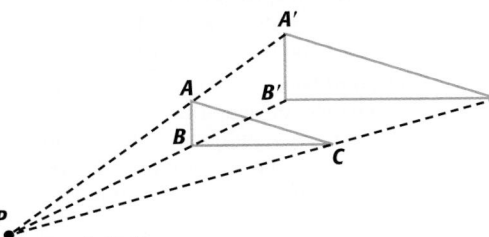

center of dilation

Scale factor = 1.5

$$\frac{PA'}{PA} = \frac{PB'}{PB} = \frac{PC'}{PC} = 1.5$$

$$\frac{A'B'}{AB} = \frac{A'C'}{AC} = \frac{B'C'}{BC} = 1.5$$

$$\frac{6}{2} = \frac{h}{40}$$
$$2 \cdot h = 6 \cdot 40$$
$$2 \cdot h = 240$$
$$h = 120$$

The height of the building is 120 ft.

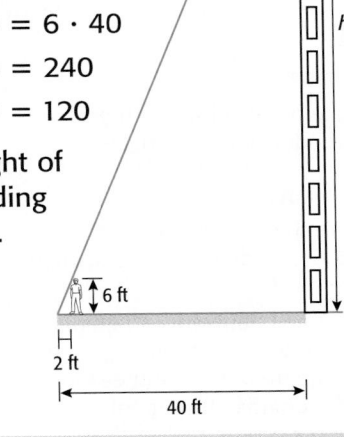

6 ft

2 ft

40 ft

Scale Drawings and Scale Models *Lesson 5-8*

 A scale drawing or model is an accurate and similar three-dimensional representation of an object.

Scale Drawings

A **scale** is a ratio between two sets of measurements.

The scale on a map is 1 in. = 50 mi.

If the map measurement between two points on a map is 4.5 in., what is the actual distance?

$$\frac{1}{50} = \frac{4.5}{d}$$
$$d = 50 \cdot 4.5$$
$$d = 225$$

The actual distance is 225 miles.

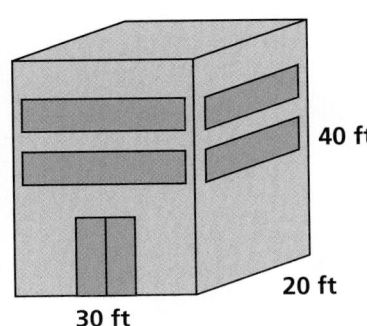

40 ft

20 ft

30 ft

Scale: 2 in. = 5 ft

Scale Models

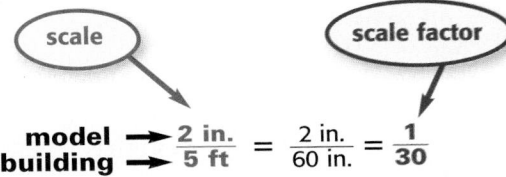

scale   scale factor

$$\text{model} \rightarrow \frac{2 \text{ in.}}{5 \text{ ft}} = \frac{2 \text{ in.}}{60 \text{ in.}} = \frac{1}{30}$$
$$\text{building} \rightarrow$$

The height of the building is 40 ft, or 480 inches. To find the height of the model, solve a proportion.

$$\frac{1}{30} = \frac{h \text{ in.}}{480 \text{ in.}}$$ ← height of the model
← height of the building

$$h = 16 \text{ in.}$$

Hands-On
Organizer
Use with Lesson 5-5

Pacing:
Traditional $\frac{1}{2}$ day
Block $\frac{1}{4}$ day

Objective: Use a number cube and graph paper to explore similarity.

Materials: Graph paper, number cube, metric ruler, protractor

Online Edition

Countdown to Testing Week 8

Resources

Hands-On Lab Activities
Lab 5-5 Recording Sheet

Teach
Discuss

Have students become familiar with translating points horizontally and vertically. Begin by plotting the point (1, −1).

Close
Key Concept

You can use points plotted on graph paper to model similar triangles.

Assessment

1. What are the coordinates of the point 5 units down and 3 units right from (1,−1)? (4, −6)

2. Draw a small pentagon on graph paper. Use a copier to enlarge the size. Compare the angle measures and side lengths of the pentagons. The angle measures are the same and the side lengths are proportional.

State Resources

go.hrw.com
State Resources Online
KEYWORD: MT7 Resources

Hands-On
LAB 5-5
Explore Similarity

Use with Lesson 5-5

go.hrw.com
Lab Resources Online
KEYWORD: MT7 Lab5

WHAT YOU NEED:
- Two pieces of graph paper with different-sized boxes, such as 1 cm graph paper and $\frac{1}{4}$ in. graph paper
- Number cube
- Metric ruler
- Protractor

Triangles that have the same shape have some interesting relationships.

Activity

1. Follow the steps below to draw two triangles.

   a. On a sheet of graph paper, plot a point below and to the left of the center of the paper. Label the point *A*. On the other sheet of paper, plot a point below and to the left of the center and label this point *D*.

   b. Roll a number cube twice. On each sheet of graph paper, move up the number on the first roll, move right the number on the second roll, and plot this location as point *B* on the first sheet and point *E* on the second sheet.

   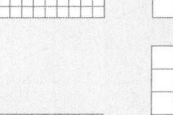

   c. Roll the number cube twice again. On each sheet of graph paper, move down the number on the first roll, move right the number on the second roll, and plot point *C* on the first sheet and point *F* on the second sheet.

   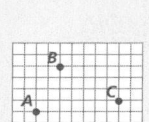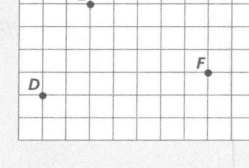

   d. Connect the three points on each sheet of graph paper to form triangles *ABC* and *DEF*.

   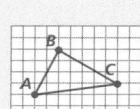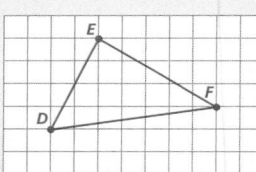

e. Measure the angles of each triangle. Measure the side lengths of each triangle to the nearest millimeter. Find the following:

m∠A	m∠D	m∠B	m∠E	m∠C	m∠F
AB	DE	$\frac{AB}{DE}$	BC	EF	$\frac{BC}{EF}$
AC	DF	$\frac{AC}{DF}$			

2 Follow the steps below to draw two triangles.

a. On one sheet of graph paper, plot a point below and to the left of the center of the paper. Label the point *A*.

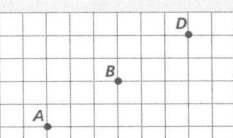

b. Roll a number cube twice. Move up the number on the first roll, move right the number on the second roll, and plot this location as point *B*. From *B*, move up the number on the first roll, move right the number on the second roll, and label this point *D*.

c. Roll a number cube twice. From *B*, move down the number on the first roll, move right the number on the second roll, and plot this location as point *C*.

d. From *D*, move down twice the number on the first roll, move right twice the number on the second roll, and label this point *E*.

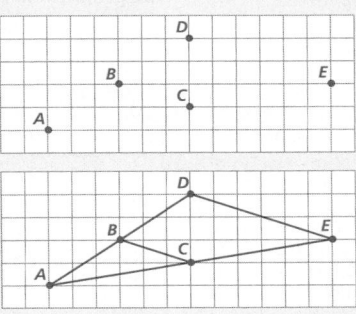

e. Connect points to form triangles *ABC* and *ADE*.

f. Measure the angles of each triangle. Measure the side lengths of each triangle to the nearest millimeter.

Think and Discuss

1. How do corresponding angles of triangles with the same shape compare?

2. How do corresponding side lengths of triangles with the same shape compare?

3. Suppose you enlarge a triangle on a copier machine. What measurements or values would be the same on the enlargement?

Try This

1. Make a small trapezoid on graph paper and triple the length of each side. Compare the angle measures and side lengths of the trapezoids.

2. Make a large polygon on graph paper. Use a copier to reduce the size of the polygon. Compare the angle measures and side lengths of the polygons.

Answers to *Think and Discuss*

1. They are equal.

2. They are proportional.

3. The angles will be the same.

Answers to *Try This*

1. Check students' work. The angles should be the same, and side lengths should be proportional.

2. Check students' work. The angles should be the same, and side lengths should be proportional.

Teacher to Teacher

Discuss with the class the usefulness of proportions in the real world. How are proportions useful for problem solving in real-life situations? Students' responses could include the following: enlarging or decreasing photographs, watching a news report on television requiring transmitting images by scaling proportions from the video camera to a satellite to the television screen, creating a scale model/plan of a house, converting cooking recipes from home-use quantities to class-size quantities, and using computer technology to enlarge and decrease font size. This discussion may also lead to individual student projects.

Sara Fox
New City, New York

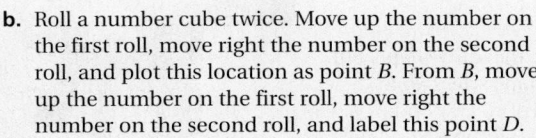

State Resources

go.hrw.com
State Resources Online
KEYWORD: MT7 Resources

Objective: Students determine whether figures are similar, use scale factors, and find missing dimensions in similar figures.

 Hands-On Lab
In *Hands-On Lab Activities*

 Online Edition
Tutorial Videos

 Countdown to Testing Week 9

Power Presentations
with PowerPoint®

Warm Up
Solve each proportion.

1. $\frac{3}{9} = \frac{b}{30}$ $b = 10$
2. $\frac{y}{5} = \frac{56}{35}$ $y = 8$
3. $\frac{p}{9} = \frac{4}{12}$ $p = 3$
4. $\frac{28}{26} = \frac{56}{m}$ $m = 52$

Problem of the Day
A rectangle that is 10 in. wide and 8 in. long is the same shape as one that is 8 in. wide and x in. long. What is the length of the smaller rectangle? 6.4 in.

Also available on transparency

 **Math Humor**

How many times can you subtract 7 from 22, and what is left afterwards?

I can subtract it as many times as I want, and it leaves 15 every time!

State Resources

 **go.hrw.com**
State Resources Online
KEYWORD: MT7 Resources

5-5 Similar Figures

Learn to determine whether figures are similar, to use scale factors, and to find missing dimensions in similar figures.

Vocabulary
similar
congruent angles
scale factor

Photos that have been resized are examples of similar figures. Erin takes an 8 in. × 8 in. photo to a print shop. The printer reduces the image to a $3\frac{1}{2}$-inch × $3\frac{1}{2}$-inch photo and prints it onto a cube.

Similar figures have the same shape, but not necessarily the same size. Two triangles are similar if the lengths of corresponding sides are proportional and the corresponding angles are *congruent*. **Congruent angles** have equal measures.

Reading Math
∠A is read as "angle A." △ABC is read as "triangle ABC." "△ABC ~ △EFG" is read as "triangle ABC is similar to triangle EFG."

SIMILAR POLYGONS		
Words	**Diagram**	**Corresponding Parts**
For two polygons to be similar, corresponding angles must be congruent, and corresponding sides must have lengths that form equivalent ratios.	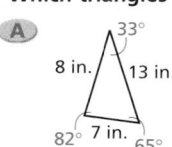 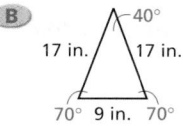 △ABC ~ △EFG	∠A and ∠E ∠B and ∠F ∠C and ∠G $\frac{AB}{EF} = \frac{BC}{FG} = \frac{AC}{EG} = \frac{2}{1}$

EXAMPLE 1 **Identifying Similar Figures**

Which triangles are similar?

Both triangles *A* and *C* have angle measures of 82°, 33°, and 65°, while triangle *B* has angle measures of 70°, 40°, and 70°, so triangle *B* cannot be similar to triangles *A* or *C*.

Compare the ratios of corresponding sides in triangles *A* and *C* to see if they are equal.

$$\frac{13}{26} = \frac{7}{14} = \frac{8}{16} \text{ or } \frac{1}{2} = \frac{1}{2} = \frac{1}{2}$$

The ratios are equal. So triangle *A* is similar to triangle *C*.

---

1 Introduce
Alternate Opener

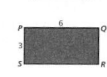

EXPLORATION

5-5 Similar Figures

Similar figures have the same shape, but not necessarily the same size. The two triangles shown below are similar.

1. What appears to be true about each pair of angles below?
   ∠A and ∠D   ∠B and ∠E   ∠C and ∠F

2. Calculate each of the ratios shown below. What do you notice?
   $\frac{\text{length of } \overline{AB}}{\text{length of } \overline{DE}}$ $\frac{\text{length of } \overline{BC}}{\text{length of } \overline{EF}}$ $\frac{\text{length of } \overline{BC}}{\text{length of } \overline{DF}}$

3. The two rectangles are similar to each other. What is true about the pairs of angles ∠J and ∠P, ∠K and ∠Q, ∠L and ∠R, and ∠M and ∠S?

4. What is true about all the ratios $\frac{\text{length of } \overline{JK}}{\text{length of } \overline{PQ}}$, $\frac{\text{length of } \overline{KL}}{\text{length of } \overline{QR}}$, $\frac{\text{length of } \overline{LM}}{\text{length of } \overline{RS}}$, and $\frac{\text{length of } \overline{MJ}}{\text{length of } \overline{SP}}$?

Think and Discuss
5. **Describe** what must be true when two polygons are similar to each other.

Motivate

ENGLISH LANGUAGE LEARNERS

Ask students what the word *similar* means in everyday use (showing likeness or resemblance). Show students three rectangles, of which only two are similar in the mathematical sense. Explain that someone might say the three figures are similar in the everyday meaning of the word, but only two of the rectangles are mathematically similar. You may want to review proportions (Lessons 5-1 and 5-4).

Explorations and answers are provided in *Alternate Openers: Explorations Transparencies.*

The ratio formed by the corresponding sides is the **scale factor**.

EXAMPLE 2 **Using Scale Factors to Find Missing Dimensions**

A A picture that is 8 in. tall and 10 in. wide is to be scaled to 3.5 in. tall to be displayed on a Web page. How wide should the picture be on the Web page for the two pictures to be similar?

$\frac{3.5}{8} = 0.4375$ *Divide the height of the scaled picture by the corresponding height of the original picture.*

$0.4375 \cdot 10$ *Multiply the width of the original picture by the scale factor.*

4.375 *Simplify.*

The picture should be 4.375 in. wide.

B In Jonathan Swift's *Gulliver's Travels*, the Lilliputians were only 6 inches tall. Suppose a Lilliputian's body is similar to a human's body. What is the length of a Lilliputian's femur, if a 5 ft tall person has a femur that is about 15 in. long?

$\frac{6 \text{ in.}}{60 \text{ in.}} = 0.1$ *Divide the Lilliputian height by the human height, in inches, to find the scale factor.*

$0.1 \cdot 15 \text{ in.}$ *Multiply the length of the human femur by the scale factor.*

1.5 in. *Simplify.*

The Lilliputian's femur is approximately 1.5 in. long.

EXAMPLE 3 *Architecture Application*

Helpful Hint

Draw a diagram to help you visualize the problem.

A souvenir model of the pyramid over the entrance of the Louvre in Paris has faces in the shape of a triangle. Two sides are each 4 in. long and the base is 5.1 in. long. On the actual pyramid, each triangular face has two sides that are each 27.8 m long. What is the length of the base of the actual pyramid?

$\frac{4 \text{ in.}}{27.8 \text{ m}} = \frac{5.1 \text{ in.}}{x \text{ m}}$ *Set up a proportion.*

$4 \text{ in.} \cdot x \text{ m} = 27.8 \text{ m} \cdot 5.1 \text{ in.}$ *Find the cross products.*

$4x = 27.8 \cdot 5.1$ *Divide out the units.*

$4x = 141.78$ *Multiply.*

$x = \frac{141.78}{4} = 35.445$ *Solve for x.*

The base of the actual pyramid is 35.445 m long.

Possible answers to
Think and Discuss

1. A scale factor greater than 1 means that the original figure was enlarged. A scale factor less than 1 means that the original factor was reduced.

Think and Discuss

1. **Compare** an image formed by a scale factor greater than 1 to an image formed by a scale factor less than 1.

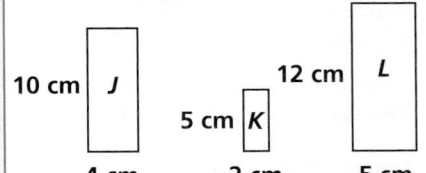

2 Teach

Guided Instruction

In this lesson, students learn to determine whether figures are similar, to use scale factors, and to find missing dimensions in similar figures. Explain that *similar* figures have the same shape but can be different sizes (Teaching Transparency). For polygons, this means corresponding angles are congruent and corresponding sides are proportional. Point out that the ratio of corresponding sides represents the scale factor.

Teaching Tip

Visual It will be helpful to draw diagrams when discussing Examples 1 and 2.

Reaching All Learners
Through Critical Thinking

Ask students to find the perimeters of the similar rectangles in Additional Example 1 and the ratio of the perimeters. 28 cm; 14 cm; $\frac{2}{1}$ Ask them to compare this ratio to the scale factor. They are the same Then have them find the scale factor for the triangles that were discussed in Example 1. $\frac{1}{2}$ Ask students to find the perimeters of the triangles and the ratio of the perimeters. 28 cm; 56 cm; $\frac{1}{2}$ Ask them to make a hypothesis about the relationship between the ratio of the perimeters and the scale factor. The ratio of perimeters is equal to the scale factor.

3 Close

Summarize

Show students the following sketch, and tell them the triangles are similar.

Ask students to find the measures of angles *D* and *F* and the lengths *x* and *y*.
m∠*D* = 60°; m∠*F* = 30°; *x* = 12; *y* = 10.35

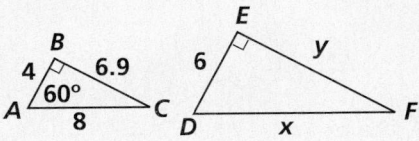

5-5 **Exercises**

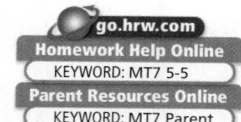

go.hrw.com
Homework Help Online
KEYWORD: MT7 5-5
Parent Resources Online
KEYWORD: MT7 Parent

Assignment Guide

If you finished Example **1** assign:
Average 1, 4, 7–9, 21–28
Advanced 4, 7–10, 19, 21–28

If you finished Example **2** assign:
Average 1, 2, 4, 5, 7–9, 12–16, 21–28
Advanced 4, 5, 7–16, 18, 19, 21–28

If you finished Example **3** assign:
Average 1–9, 12–17, 21–28
Advanced 4–28

Homework Quick Check

Quickly check key concepts.
Exercises: 4, 5, 6, 12

Math Background

The methods used in Examples 2 and 3 of the lesson may appear to be different, but they are essentially the same. The proportion method used in Example 3 allows you to solve for a missing dimension without first identifying the scale factor. The proportion method can be used on Example 2A as shown below.

$$\frac{x}{10} = \frac{3.5}{8}$$

$8x = 10 \cdot 3.5$

$8x = 35$

$x = 4.375$

State Resources

go.hrw.com
State Resources Online
KEYWORD: MT7 Resources

GUIDED PRACTICE

See Example **1**

1. Which triangles are similar? $\triangle ABC \sim \triangle FDE$

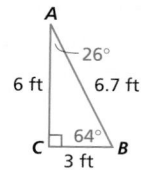
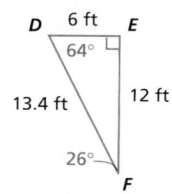
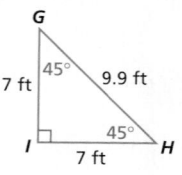

See Example **2**

2. Gwen scans a photo that is 4 in. wide by 6 in. tall into her computer. If she scales the length down to 5 in., how wide should the similar photo be? ≈ **3.3 in.**

See Example **3**

3. A triangle has a base of 11 cm and legs measuring 16 cm. How wide is the base of a similar triangle with legs measuring 24 cm? **16.5 cm**

INDEPENDENT PRACTICE

See Example **1**

4. Which triangles are similar? $\triangle JKL \sim \triangle PQR$

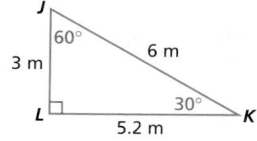
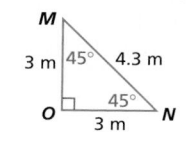
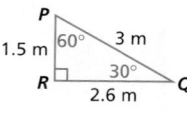

See Example **2**

5. A rectangular park measures 6.5 mi wide and 9.1 mi long. On a map, the width of the park is 2.13 in. How long is the park on the map? ≈ **2.98 in.**

See Example **3**

6. Vernon drew an 8 in. by 5 in. picture that will be turned into a 48 ft wide billboard. How tall will the billboard be? **30 ft**

PRACTICE AND PROBLEM SOLVING

Extra Practice
See page 791.

Tell whether the figures are similar. If they are not similar, explain.

7. similar

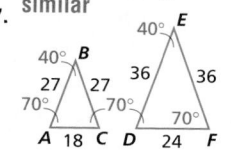

8. Not similar; corresponding sides are not in proportion.

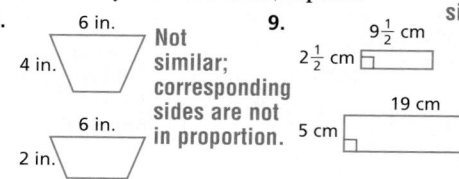

9. similar

10. Draw a right triangle with vertices (0, 0), (6, 0), and (6, 4) on a coordinate plane. Draw another triangle with vertices (9, 6), (0, 0) and (9, 0). Are the triangles similar? Explain. Yes; the sides are proportional. $\frac{6}{4} = \frac{9}{6}$

11. Sari's garden is 12 ft by 16 ft 6 in. Her sketch of the garden is 8 in. by 11 in. Is Sari's sketch a scale drawing? If so, what scale factor did she use? Yes; $\frac{1}{18}$ or $\frac{2 \text{ in.}}{3 \text{ ft}}$

RETEACH 5-5

LESSON
5-5 Reteach
Similar Figures (continued)

Use the scale factor to find a missing dimension.

scale factor = $\frac{6}{9} = \frac{2}{3}$
Since $\overline{EF}$ corresponds to $\overline{BC}$,
multiply EF by the scale factor to find BC.
$BC = \frac{2}{3}(15) = 10$ m

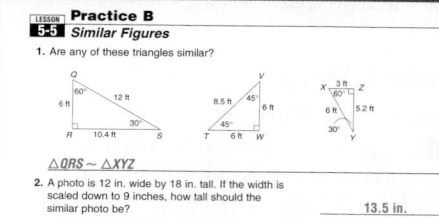

Complete to find each missing dimension.

2.

scale factor $\frac{PQ}{JK} = \frac{4}{10}$ or $\frac{2}{5}$

RQ = scale factor • (KL)

$RQ = \frac{2}{5} \times$ __12__ or __4.8__ cm

3.

scale factor $\frac{MA}{RO} = \frac{14}{8}$ or $\frac{7}{4}$

MH = scale factor • (RE)

$MH = \frac{7}{4} \times$ __6__ or __10.5__ in.

Use a proportion to find a missing dimension. Corresponding sides are in proportion.

$\frac{AB}{DE} = \frac{BC}{EF}$
$\frac{6}{9} = \frac{BC}{15}$
$9(BC) = 90$
$BC = 10$ m

Complete to find the missing dimension.

4. $\frac{MH}{RE} = \frac{MA}{RO}$

$\frac{MH}{6} = \frac{14}{8}$

__8__ • $(MH) = $ __84__

$MH = $ __10.5__ in.

PRACTICE 5-5

LESSON
5-5 Practice B
Similar Figures

1. Are any of these triangles similar?

$\triangle QRS \sim \triangle XYZ$

2. A photo is 12 in. wide by 18 in. tall. If the width is scaled down to 9 inches, how tall should the similar photo be?   **13.5 in.**

3. An isosceles triangle has a base of 20 cm and legs measuring 36 cm. How long are the legs of a similar triangle with base measuring 50 cm?   **90 cm**

4. A picture of a school's mascot is 18 in. wide and 24 in. long. It is enlarged proportionally to banner size. If the width is enlarged to 63 in., what is the length of the banner?   **84 in.**

5. Carol has a 24 cm × 36 cm photo that she reduces to $\frac{3}{4}$ of its size. What are the dimensions of the new photo?   **18 cm × 27 cm**

6. Erik is drawing a picture of his school's basketball court. The actual basketball court is 84 ft long and 50 ft wide. If Erik draws the court with a length of 21 in., what will be the width?   **12.5 in.**

7. IMAX theaters have the world's largest screens. There are numerous IMAX theaters around the world. The Henry Ford Museum in Dearborn, Michigan hosts an IMAX theater with a 60 ft × 84 ft screen. If a classroom projection screen were changed to be in direct proportion with the IMAX screen at the Henry Ford Museum, the dimensions would be 5 ft × ___ ft.   **7**

Art

Many reproductions of artwork have been enlarged to fit unusual surfaces.

The figures in each pair are similar. Use the scale factor to solve for x.

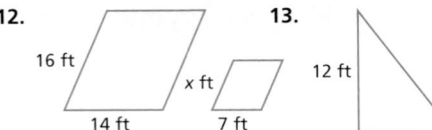

12. 16 ft, x ft, 14 ft, *x* = 8 ft

13. 12 ft, 8 ft, 7 ft, *x* = 6 ft 9 ft, x ft

14. 18 ft, *x* = 24 ft, 6 ft, x, 8 ft

15. Art Helen is copying a printed reproduction of the Mona Lisa. The print is 24 in. wide and 36 in. tall. If Helen's canvas is 12 in. wide, how tall should her canvas be? **18 in.**

16. A rectangle is 16 cm long and 7 cm wide. A similar rectangle is 3.5 cm wide and *x* cm long. Find *x*. **8 cm**

17. Physical Science Will is 5 ft tall. He casts a 3 ft shadow at the same time that a tree casts a 9 ft shadow. Use similar triangles to find the height of the tree. **15 ft**

18. Write a Problem A drawing on a sheet of graph paper shows a rectangle 9 cm wide and 12 cm long. The width of the rectangle is labeled 3 ft. Write and solve a problem about the rectangle.

19. Write About It Consider the statement "All similar figures are congruent." Is this statement true or false? Explain.

20. Challenge In right triangle *ABC*, $\angle B$ is the right angle, $AB = 36$ cm, and $BC = 28$ cm. Right triangle *ABC* is similar to right triangle *DEF*. If $DE = 9$ cm, what is the area of triangle *DEF*? **31.5 cm²**

TEST PREP and Spiral Review

21. Multiple Choice An isosceles triangle has two sides that are each 4.5 centimeters long and a base that is 3 centimeters long. A similar triangle has a base that is 1.5 centimeters long. How long are each of the other two sides of the similar triangle?

ⓐ 2.25 cm   Ⓑ 3.75 cm   Ⓒ 4.5 cm   Ⓓ 150 cm

22. Gridded Response A rectangle is 6 feet wide by 35 feet long. A similar rectangle has a width of 12 in. How many inches long is the similar rectangle? **70**

Use each table of values to make an equation of the data. (Lesson 3-5)

23.

x	0	1	2	3	4	5
y	1	3	5	7	9	11

$y = 2x + 1$

24.

x	0	1	2	3	4	5
y	0	3	6	9	12	15

$y = 3x$

Solve each proportion. (Lesson 5-4)

25. $\frac{6}{12} = \frac{9}{x}$ *x* = 18   **26.** $\frac{4}{9} = \frac{2.4}{y}$ *y* = 5.4   **27.** $\frac{44}{12} = \frac{w}{3}$ *w* = 11   **28.** $\frac{18}{6} = \frac{15}{k}$ *k* = 5

CHALLENGE 5-5

LESSON 5-5 Challenge
In Like Manner

The ratio of a pair of corresponding sides of similar polygons is known as the **scale factor** and is also called the **ratio of similitude**.

The symbol ~ means *is similar to.*
In the diagram, $\triangle ABC \sim \triangle DEF$.

(figure: triangles with C 3 cm, 5 cm, A 4 cm B; F 4.5 cm, 7.5 cm, D 6 cm E)

1. Find the ratio of similitude of $\triangle ABC$ to $\triangle DEF$. $\frac{AB}{DE} = \frac{4}{6}$ or $\frac{2}{3}$

2. a. Find the perimeter of $\triangle ABC$.   12 cm
   b. Find the perimeter of $\triangle DEF$.   18 cm
   c. Find the ratio $\frac{\text{perimeter of } \triangle ABC}{\text{perimeter of } \triangle DEF}$ in simplest form. $\frac{2}{3}$

3. Make an observation from the result of Exercises 2 and 3.

The ratio of the perimeters of two similar triangles is the same as the ratio of similitude.

The sides of $\triangle JKL$ measure 5 in., 7 in., and 9 in.
The shortest side of a similar triangle, $\triangle J'K'L'$, measures 10 in.

4. Find the ratio of similitude of $\triangle JKL$ to $\triangle J'K'L'$. $\frac{5}{10}$ or $\frac{1}{2}$

5. Find the ratio $\frac{\text{perimeter of } \triangle JKL}{\text{perimeter of } \triangle J'K'L'}$. $\frac{1}{2}$

6. Find the perimeter of $\triangle J'K'L'$.
$\frac{\text{perimeter } \triangle JKL}{\text{perimeter } \triangle J'K'L'} = \frac{1}{2} \longrightarrow \frac{21}{\text{perimeter } \triangle J'K'L'} = \frac{1}{2} \longrightarrow$ perimeter $\triangle J'K'L' = 42$ in.

PROBLEM SOLVING 5-5

LESSON 5-5 Problem Solving
Similar Figures

Write the correct answer.

1. Until 1929, United States currency measured 3.13 in. by 7.42 in. The current size is 2.61 in. by 6.14 in. Are the bills similar?
no

2. Owen has a 3 in. by 5 in. photograph. He wants to make it as large as he can to fit in a 10 in. by 12.5 in. ad. What scale factor will he use? What will be the new size?
$\frac{1}{2.5}$; 7.5 in. by 12.5 in.

3. A painting is 15 cm long and 8 cm wide. In a reproduction that is similar to the original painting, the length is 36 cm. How wide is the reproduction?
19.2 cm

4. The two shortest sides of a right triangle are 10 in. and 24 in. long. What is the length of the shortest side of a similar right triangle whose two longest sides are 36 in. and 39 in.?
15 in.

The scale on a map is 1 inch = 40 miles. Round to the nearest mile.

5. On the map, it is 5.75 inches from Orlando to Miami. How many miles is it from Orlando to Miami?
A 46 miles   Ⓒ 230 miles
B 175 miles   D 340 miles

6. On the map it is $18\frac{1}{8}$ inches from Norfolk, VA, to Indianapolis, IN. How many miles is it from Norfolk to Indianapolis?
F 58 miles   H 800 miles
Ⓖ 725 miles   J 1025 miles

7. It is 185 miles from Chicago to Indianapolis. On the map it is 2.5 inches from Indianapolis to Terra Haute, IN. How far is it from Chicago to Terra Haute going through Indianapolis?
A 100 miles   C 430 miles
Ⓑ 285 miles   D 7500 miles

8. On the map, it is 7.5 inches from Chicago to Cincinnati. Traveling at 65 mi/h, how long will it take to drive from Chicago to Cincinnati? Round to the nearest tenth of an hour.
Ⓕ 4.6 hours   H 8.7 hours
G 5.2 hours   J 12.0 hours

ONGOING ASSESSMENT and INTERVENTION

Diagnose Before the Lesson
5-5 Warm Up, TE p. 238

Monitor During the Lesson
5-5 Know-It Notebook
5-5 Questioning Strategies

Assess After the Lesson
5-5 Lesson Quiz, TE p. 241

Answers
18–19. See p. A6.

TEST PREP DOCTOR Students will need to read Exercise 22 carefully. The question asks for a number of inches. If students convert 12 inches to 1 foot, they may forget that they need to convert their numerical answer, 5.83, from feet to inches. Remind students to multiply by 12 to get the correct answer of $5.8\overline{3} \cdot 12 = 70$ inches.

Journal

In the lesson, situations involving similar figures included reducing a picture and enlarging a design for a billboard. Have students write about some other situations in which using similar figures would be useful.

Power Presentations
with PowerPoint®

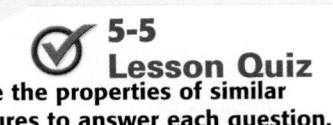

5-5 Lesson Quiz

Use the properties of similar figures to answer each question.

1. A rectangular house is 32 ft wide and 68 ft long. On a blueprint, the width is 8 in. Find the length on the blueprint. **17 in.**

2. Karen enlarged a 3 in. wide by 5 in. tall photo into a poster. If the poster is 2.25 ft wide, how tall is it? **3.75 ft**

3. Which rectangles are similar?

8 in. A 12 in.   C 16 in.   4 in. B 6 in.   10 in.

A and *B* are similar.

Also available on transparency

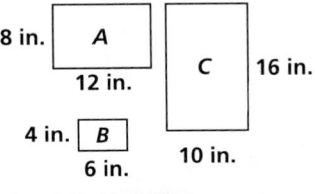

Hands-On

LAB 5-6   Explore Dilations

Use with Lesson 5-6

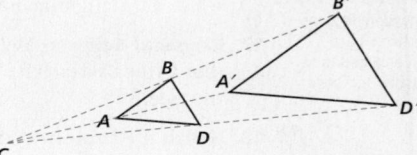 **go.hrw.com**
Lab Resources Online
KEYWORD: MT7 Lab5

Activity 1

Triangle *A'B'D'* is a dilation of triangle *ABD*. Point *C* is called the center of dilation.

1. Use a ruler to measure segments *CA'* and *CA* to the nearest millimeter.

2. Calculate the ratio $\frac{\text{length of } CA'}{\text{length of } CA}$.

3. Repeat 1 and 2 for segments *CB'*, *CB*, *CD'*, and *CD*. Copy the table below and record your measurements.

CA'	CA	$\frac{CA'}{CA}$	CB'	CB	$\frac{CB'}{CB}$	CD'	CD	$\frac{CD}{CD'}$
4 cm	2 cm	2	6.2 cm	3.1 cm	2	6.8 cm	3.4 cm	2

Think and Discuss

1. What seems to be true about the ratios you calculated? Write a conjecture about the ratios of the segments you measured. **The ratios are all equal to 2. The ratios are in proportion.**

2. Measure segment *AD* and segment *A'D'* to the nearest millimeter. What is the ratio of the length of *A'D'* to the length of *AD*? How does this compare to the ratios you recorded in the table above? **The ratio is 2. This is the same as the ratios in the table.**

3. If the corresponding angles of each triangle are congruent, can you conclude that triangles *ABD* and *A'B'D'* are similar? Explain. **Yes; the corresponding sides of the figures are in proportion, and the corresponding angles are congruent.**

Try This

The center of dilation can be a point on the figure itself. In the figure at right, the center of dilation is point *D*. **A point on a figure that is also the center of dilation does not move.**

1. What seems to be true of the dilation of a point on a figure if that point is also the center of dilation?

2. Measure the lengths of the corresponding sides of quadrilaterals *DEFG* and *D'E'F'G'*. Are the ratios of the corresponding sides in proportion? Can you conclude that the quadrilaterals are similar?

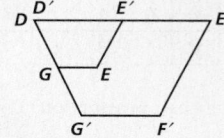

Activity 1

Answers to *Try This*

2. The ratios of the corresponding sides are in proportion. The quadrilaterals are similar.

You can also graph dilations in the coordinate plane. Quadrilateral $P'Q'R'S'$ is a dilation of $PQRS$. The origin is the center of dilation.

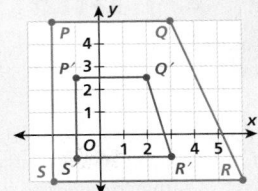

1. For each pair of corresponding vertices, record the x- and y-coordinates.

2. Calculate the ratio of the coordinates.

3. Copy and complete the table below. The first row of the table has been completed for you.

Vertex	x	y	Vertex	x	y	Ratio of x-coordinates (P'Q'R'S' ÷ PQRS)	Ratio of y-coordinates (P'Q'R'S' ÷ PQRS)
P'	−1	2.5	P	−2	5	$\frac{-1}{-2} = 0.5$	$\frac{2.5}{5} = 0.5$
Q'	1.5	2.5	Q	3	5	0.5	0.5
R'	3	−1	R	6	−2	0.5	0.5
S'	−2	−2	S	−1	−1	0.5	0.5

Think and Discuss

1. What seems to be true about the ratios you calculated? Write a conjecture about the ratios of the coordinates of a dilation image to the coordinates of the original.   **The ratios are all equal to 0.5. The ratios are in proportion.**

2. In Activity 1, triangle $A'B'D'$ was larger than triangle ABD. How is the relationship between quadrilateral $P'Q'R'S'$ and quadrilateral $PQRS$ different?   **$P'Q'R'S'$ is smaller than $PQRS$.**

Try This

Use what you learned from your observations above to create a dilation of each figure below. Use the origin as the center of dilation.

1.
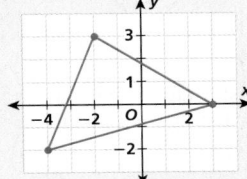

Check students' work.

2.
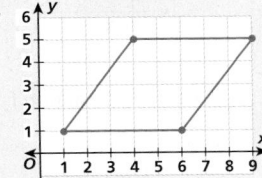

Check students' work.

Objective: Students identify and create dilations of plane figures.

 Hands-On Lab
In *Hands-On Lab Activities*

 Technology Lab
In *Technology Lab Activities*

 Online Edition
Tutorial Videos, Interactivities

 Countdown to Testing Week 9

Power Presentations
with PowerPoint®

Warm Up

Multiply.

1. $4 \cdot \frac{3}{4}$ 3   **2.** $12 \cdot \frac{3}{4}$ 9

3. $24 \cdot \frac{3}{4}$ 18   **4.** $-36 \cdot \frac{3}{4}$ −27

5. $4 \cdot 2.5$ 10   **6.** $12 \cdot 2.5$ 30

Problem of the Day

Every day, a plant grows to three times its size. Every night, it shrinks to half of its size. After three days and nights, it is 6.75 in. tall. How tall was the plant at the start? **2 in.**

Also available on transparency

 **Math Humor**

Why was the geometry teacher wearing dark glasses in class? Her pupils were dilating.

State Resources

go.hrw.com
State Resources Online
KEYWORD: MT7 Resources

5-6 Dilations

Learn to identify and create dilations of plane figures.

Vocabulary
dilation
center of dilation

Your pupils are the black areas in the center of your eyes. When you go to the eye doctor, the doctor may *dilate* your pupils, which makes them larger.

Some transformations of geometric figures do not change the size or shape of a figure. A **dilation** is a transformation that changes the size, but not the shape, of a figure. A dilation can enlarge or reduce a figure.

Every dilation has a fixed point that is the *center of dilation*. To find the center of dilation, draw a line that connects each pair of corresponding vertices. The lines intersect at one point. This point is the **center of dilation** .

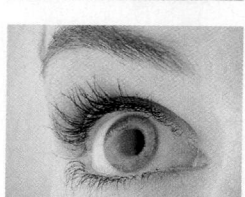
Your pupil works like a camera lens, dilating to let in more or less light.

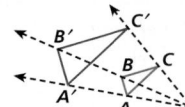

EXAMPLE 1 **Identifying Dilations**

Tell whether each transformation is a dilation.

Ⓐ
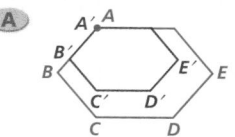
The transformation is a dilation.

Ⓑ
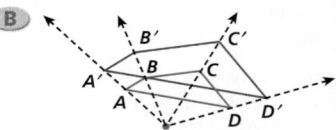
The transformation is a dilation.

Ⓒ
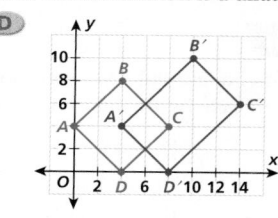
The transformation is a dilation.

Ⓓ

The transformation is *not* a dilation. The figure is distorted.

A scale factor describes how much a figure is enlarged or reduced. A scale factor can be expressed as a decimal, fraction, or percent. A 10% increase is a scale factor of 1.1, and a 10% decrease is a scale factor of 0.9.

---

1 Introduce

Alternate Opener

EXPLORATION

5-6 Dilations

A *dilation* is an enlargement or a reduction of a figure.

For each figure, draw a new figure that has the same shape but is twice as large as the original.

1.

2.

For each figure, draw a new figure that has the same shape but is half as large as the original.

3.

4.

Think and Discuss

5. Explain how you maintained the same shape when enlarging the figures in Problems 1 and 2.

6. Explain how you maintained the same shape when reducing the figures in Problems 3 and 4.

Motivate

Point out that transformations such as translations, rotations, and reflections maintain the shape and size of the original figure. Explain that a *dilation* is a transformation that preserves the shape but changes the size of the original figure.

Explorations and answers are provided in *Alternate Openers: Explorations Transparencies.*

EXAMPLE **Dilating a Figure**

Dilate the figure by a scale factor of 0.2 with *P* as the center of dilation.

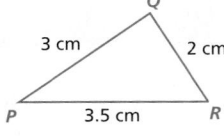

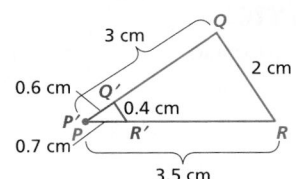

Multiply each side by 0.2.
P' and P are the same point.

EXAMPLE **Using the Origin as the Center of Dilation**

 A Dilate the figure by a scale factor of 2.5. What are the vertices of the image?

Helpful Hint

A scale factor between 0 and 1 reduces a figure. A scale factor greater than 1 enlarges it.

Multiply the coordinates by 2.5 to find the vertices of the image.

△ *ABC*   △ *A'B'C'*

$A(2, 2) \rightarrow A'(2 \cdot 2.5, 2 \cdot 2.5) \rightarrow A'(5, 5)$
$B(3, 4) \rightarrow B'(3 \cdot 2.5, 4 \cdot 2.5) \rightarrow B'(7.5, 10)$
$C(5, 2) \rightarrow C'(5 \cdot 2.5, 2 \cdot 2.5) \rightarrow C'(12.5, 5)$

The vertices of the image are
$A'(5, 5)$, $B'(7.5, 10)$, and $C'(12.5, 5)$.

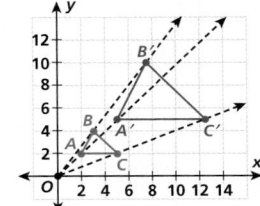

B Dilate the figure by a scale factor of $\frac{2}{3}$. What are the vertices of the image?

Multiply the coordinates by $\frac{2}{3}$ to find the vertices of the image.

△ *ABC*   △ *A'B'C'*

$A(3, 9) \rightarrow A'\left(3 \cdot \frac{2}{3}, 9 \cdot \frac{2}{3}\right) \rightarrow A'(2, 6)$
$B(9, 6) \rightarrow B'\left(9 \cdot \frac{2}{3}, 6 \cdot \frac{2}{3}\right) \rightarrow B'(6, 4)$
$C(6, 3) \rightarrow C'\left(6 \cdot \frac{2}{3}, 3 \cdot \frac{2}{3}\right) \rightarrow C'(4, 2)$

The vertices of the image are
$A'(2, 6)$, $B'(6, 4)$, and $C'(4, 2)$.

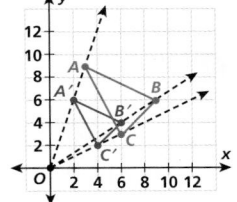

Think and Discuss

• **Describe** the image of a dilation with a scale factor of 1.

• **Compare** a dilation with the origin as the center of dilation to a dilation with a vertex of the figure as the center of dilation.

Possible Answers to *Think and Discuss*

1. The image is congruent to the original figure.

2. If a figure is dilated with a vertex as the center of dilation, then the new figure will share one vertex with the original figure and some sides of the image will be collinear. If a figure is dilated with the origin as the center of dilation, then there may be no shared vertices or collinear sides. However, if a side passes through the origin, then the side will be a shared side. If a vertex is at the origin, then it will be a shared vertex.

Example 1

Tell whether each transformation is a dilation.

A.   yes

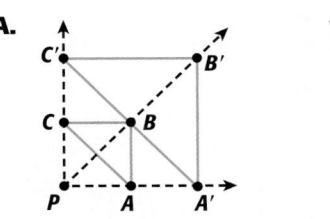

B.   no

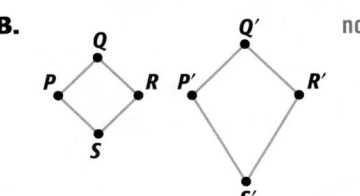

Example 2

Dilate the figure by a scale factor of 1.5 with *P* as the center of dilation.

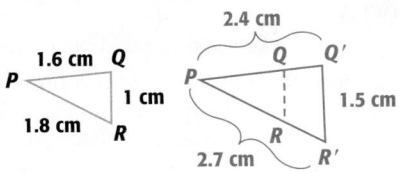

Example 3

A. Dilate the figure in Example 3A by a scale factor of 2. What are the vertices of the image?
$A'(4, 4)$, $B'(6, 8)$, $C'(10, 4)$

B. Dilate the figure in Example 3B by a scale factor of $\frac{1}{3}$. What are the vertices of the image?
$A'(1, 3)$, $B'(3, 2)$, $C'(2, 1)$

Also available on transparency

---

2 Teach

Guided Instruction

In this lesson, students learn to identify and create dilations of plane figures. Tell students that the scale factor in a dilation determines precisely how much the size changes. Explain that scale factors greater than 1 will enlarge the figure, and scale factors less than 1 will reduce the figure. Show students how to draw lines through corresponding vertices to determine whether a transformation is a dilation and, if so, to find the center of dilation (Teaching Transparency). Teach students to dilate a figure using one of its vertices as the center of dilation. Then show them how to dilate figures on a coordinate plane.

Reaching All Learners
Through Multiple Representations

Have students work in groups of three. Ask each student to graph the triangle *ABC* on a coordinate plane (Teacher Tools), using $A(2, 4)$, $B(2, -4)$, and $C(-2, 2)$. Give each group the three scale factors 0.5, 1.5, and 2.5 on folded scraps of paper. Instruct students to choose one of the scale factors but not to show it to the other group members. Then ask each student to use the scale factor to dilate the triangle. When the drawings are complete, have the other members of each group try to identify the scale factor used to create each drawing.

3 Close

Summarize

Remind students that dilations are transformations that change the size of a figure without changing its shape. If you have an overhead projector, you may want to use the projector to show students some examples of how to dilate figures. Ask them to describe what will happen to a figure that is dilated using the following scale factors: 1.2, 3, 0.5, and 1.

Possible answers: Each side will be 20% longer than the original. Each side will be triple the length of the original. Each side will be half as long as the original. The figures will be congruent.

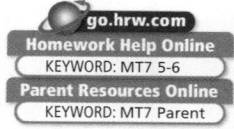
Assignment Guide

If you finished Example **1** assign:
Average 1, 2, 7, 8, 15, 18–23
Advanced 7, 8, 15, 16, 18–23

If you finished Example **2** assign:
Average 1–4, 7–10, 15, 18–23
Advanced 7–10, 14–16, 18–23

If you finished Example **3** assign:
Average 1–13, 15, 18–23
Advanced 7–23

Homework Quick Check

Quickly check key concepts.
Exercises: 8, 10, 12

Answers

3–4, 9–10. See p. A6.

Math Background

In any transformation, there is a pre-image (the original figure) and an image. For any translation, reflection, or rotation, the two are congruent. For a dilation, the preimage and image are similar. The table below summarizes properties of transformations addressed thus far.

Image Compared to Preimage			
	Orientation	**Size**	**Shape**
Translation	Same	Same	Same
Reflection	Changed	Same	Same
Rotation	Changed	Same	Same
Dilation	Same	Changed	Same

State Resources

GUIDED PRACTICE

See Example 1 Tell whether each transformation is a dilation.

1. no
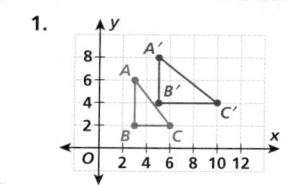

2. yes
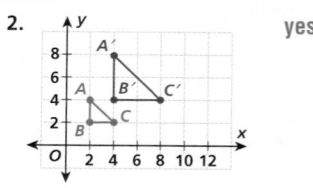

See Example 2 Dilate each figure by the given scale factor with *P* as the center of dilation.

3. Scale factor = 1.5
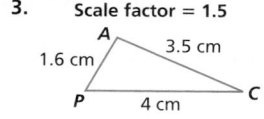

4. Scale factor = $\frac{1}{2}$
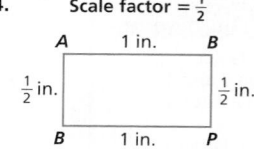

See Example 3 Dilate each figure by the given scale factor with the origin as the center of dilation. What are the vertices of the image?

5. Scale factor = $\frac{1}{3}$
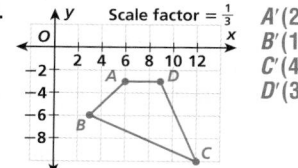 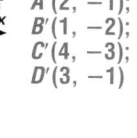
$A'(2, -1)$;
$B'(1, -2)$;
$C'(4, -3)$;
$D'(3, -1)$

6. Scale factor = 4
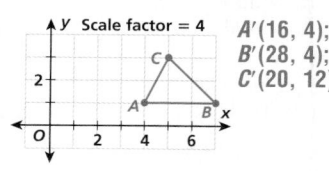
$A'(16, 4)$;
$B'(28, 4)$;
$C'(20, 12)$

INDEPENDENT PRACTICE

See Example 1 Tell whether each transformation is a dilation.

7. no
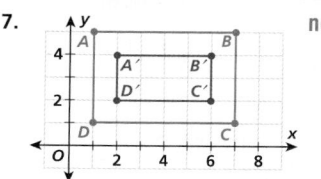

8. no
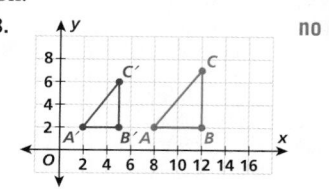

See Example 2 Dilate each figure by the given scale factor with *P* as the center of dilation.

9. Scale factor = 2
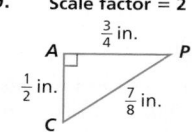

10. Scale factor = $\frac{1}{4}$
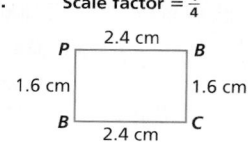

RETEACH 5-6

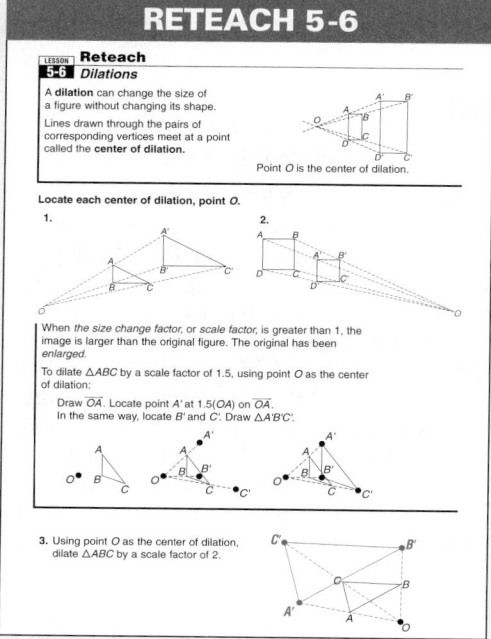

PRACTICE 5-6

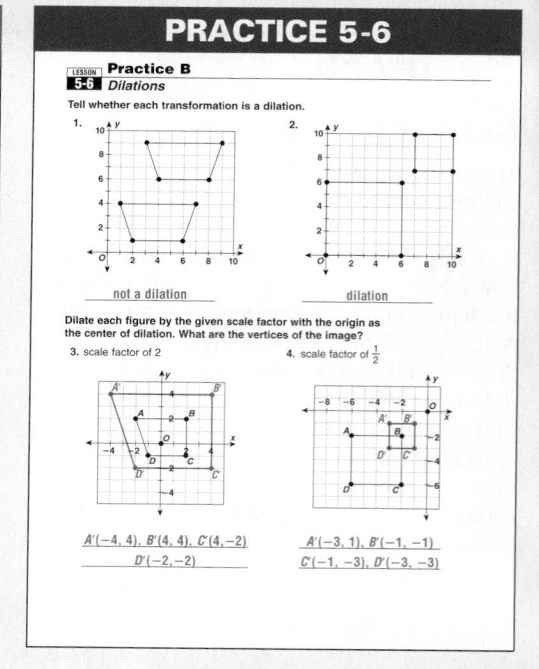

Dilate each figure by the given scale factor with the origin as the center of dilation. What are the vertices of the image?

11.
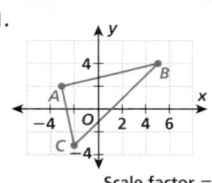

Scale factor = 3

$A'(-9, 6)$;
$B'(15, 12)$;
$C'(-6, -9)$

12.
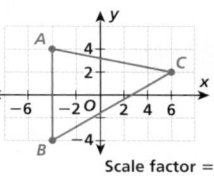

Scale factor = $\frac{1}{2}$

$A'(-2, 2)$;
$B'(-2, -2)$;
$C'(3, 1)$

PRACTICE AND PROBLEM SOLVING

$A'(3, 6)$; $B'(10.5, 6)$;
$C'(10.5, 0)$; $D'(3, 0)$

Extra Practice
See page 791.

13. A rectangle has vertices $A(2, 4)$, $B(7, 4)$, $C(7, 0)$, and $D(2, 0)$. Give the coordinates after dilating from the origin by a scale factor of 1.5.

14. Choose a Strategy The perimeter of an equilateral triangle is 36 cm. If the triangle is dilated by a scale factor of 0.75, what is the length of each side of the new triangle?

(A) 3 cm   (B) 4 cm   (C) 9 cm   (D) 12 cm

Photography

In a camera lens, a larger aperture lets in more light than a smaller one.

15. Photography The aperture is the polygonal opening in a camera lens when a picture is taken. The aperture can be small or large. Is an aperture a dilation? Why or why not? **Yes, the aperture is a dilation of the image as the light flows into the camera.**

16. Write About It Explain how you can check the drawing of a dilation for accuracy.

17. Challenge What scale factor was used in the dilation of a triangle with vertices $A(4, -8)$, $B(10, 4)$, and $C(-2, 12)$, to the triangle with vertices $A'(-3, 6)$, $B'\left(-7\frac{1}{2}, -3\right)$, and $C'\left(1\frac{1}{2}, -9\right)$? $-\frac{3}{4}$

TEST PREP and Spiral Review

18. Multiple Choice An equilateral triangle has a perimeter of 18 centimeters. If the triangle is dilated by a factor of 0.5, what is the length of each side of the new triangle?

(A) 36 cm   (B) 12 cm   (C) 9 cm   (D) 3 cm

19. Short Response A square has a side length of 4.8 feet. If the square is dilated by a factor of 4, what is the length of a side of the new square? What is its perimeter? What is its area? **19.2 ft; 76.8 ft; 368.64 ft²**

Find the missing term in each sequence. (Lesson 3-6)

20. 5, 15, 25, ▮, 45, . . . **35**   **21.** 9, 3, −3, −9, ▮, . . . **−15**   **22.** 3, 4.5, ▮, 7.5, 9, . . . **6**

Find the length of the indicated side. (Lesson 5-5)

23. A rectangle has a length of 20 yd and a width of 12 yd. A similar rectangle has a length of x yd and a width of 9 yd. Find the length of the similar rectangle. **15 yd**

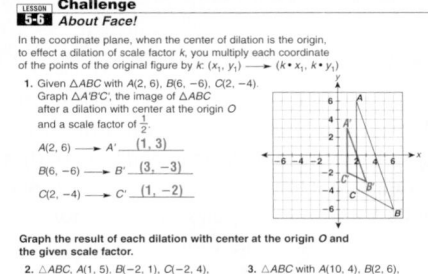
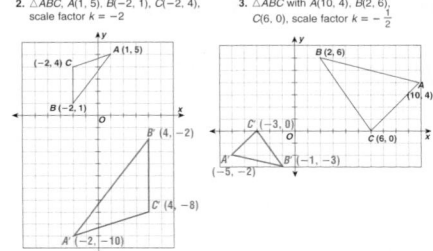
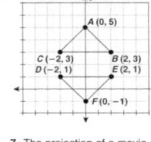

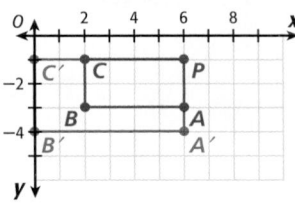

Pacing: Traditional 1 day
Block $\frac{1}{2}$ day

Objective: Students find measures indirectly by applying the properties of similar figures.

Online Edition
Tutorial Videos

Countdown to Testing Week 9

Power Presentations
with PowerPoint®

Warm Up
Solve each proportion.
1. $\frac{3}{5} = \frac{x}{75}$ 45 2. $\frac{6}{x} = \frac{2.4}{8}$ 20
3. $\frac{9}{27} = \frac{x}{6}$ 2 4. $\frac{x}{3.5} = \frac{8}{7}$ 4

Problem of the Day
A plane figure is dilated and gets 50% larger. What scale factor should you use to dilate the figure back to its original size? (*Hint:* The answer is not $\frac{1}{2}$.) $\frac{2}{3}$

Also available on transparency

Math Humor

Teacher: Why didn't you finish your math homework?

Student: I have a solar-powered calculator and it was cloudy.

Learn to find measures indirectly by applying the properties of similar figures.

Vocabulary
indirect measurement

A scout troop wants to make a temporary bridge across a river. To do this, they need to know how wide the river is.

Sometimes, distances cannot be measured directly. One way to find such a distance is to use **indirect measurement**, a way of using similar figures and proportions to find a measure.

The distance across the river can be found by using a pair of similar triangles.

EXAMPLE 1 *Geography Application*

A scout troop wants to make a temporary bridge across the river. The diagram shows the measurements the troop knows. The triangles in the diagram are similar. How wide is the river where the troop wants to make the bridge?

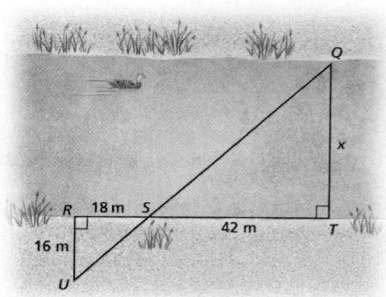

Triangles *RSU* and *TSQ* are similar.

$\frac{QT}{UR} = \frac{ST}{SR}$ *Set up a proportion.*

$\frac{x}{16} = \frac{42}{18}$ *Substitute 16 for UR, 42 for ST, and 18 for SR.*

$18x = 672$ *Find the cross products.*

$\frac{18x}{18} = \frac{672}{18}$ *Divide both sides by 18.*

$x \approx 37.\overline{3}$

The distance across the river is approximately 37.3 meters.

1 Introduce
Alternate Opener

EXPLORATION

5-7 Indirect Measurement

Mr. Kelly's science class is tracking the motion of the sun during the year. To do so, they measure the shadow cast by a 120-foot building on four different days of the year. To check the measurements, the students also measure the shadow cast by a 36-inch stick. The table shows their findings.

Day	Height of Building	Length of Building's Shadow	Height of Stick	Length of Stick's Shadow
1	120 ft	20 ft	36 in.	6 in.
2	120 ft	30 ft	36 in.	9 in.
3	120 ft	40 ft	36 in.	12 in.
4	120 ft	80 ft	36 in.	24 in.

1. a. On Day 1, what was the ratio of the height of the building to the length of the building's shadow?
   b. What was the ratio of the height of the stick to the length of the stick's shadow?
   c. What do you notice about these ratios?

2. Does your observation about the ratios also hold for Day 2, Day 3, and Day 4?

Think and Discuss
3. **Describe** how you could find the length of the stick's shadow if you know that the length of the building's shadow is 60 ft.
4. **Explain** what must be true about the building's shadow on a day when the stick's shadow is 36 in.

Motivate
Ask students to identify situations where they would need to know a measurement, but could not measure it directly, such as with a tape measure. Draw two similar figures. Ask students to name the pairs of corresponding sides. Remind students that corresponding sides of similar figures are proportional.

Explorations and answers are provided in *Alternate Openers: Explorations Transparencies.*

EXAMPLE 2 PROBLEM SOLVING APPLICATION

PROBLEM SOLVING

A flagpole casts a 32 ft shadow, while a 6 ft tall man standing nearby casts a 4.5 ft shadow. How tall is the pole?

 Understand the Problem

The **answer** is the height of the flagpole.

List the important information:
- The length of the flagpole's shadow is 32 ft.
- The height of the man is 6 ft.
- The length of the man's shadow is 4.5 ft.

2 Make a Plan

Use the information to *draw a diagram.*

 Solve

Draw a diagram. Then draw the dashed lines to form triangles. The flagpole and its shadow and the man and his shadow form similar right triangles.

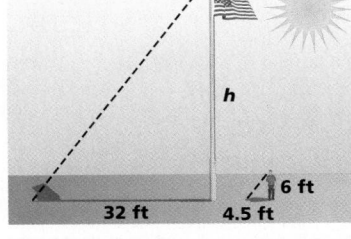

$\frac{6}{4.5} = \frac{h}{32}$ *Corresponding sides of similar figures are proportional.*

$4.5h = 192$ *Find the cross products.*

$\frac{4.5h}{4.5} = \frac{192}{4.5}$ *Divide both sides by 4.5.*

$h \approx 42.\overline{6}$

The height of the flagpole is approximately 42.7 ft.

4 Look Back

Since $\frac{4.5}{6} = \frac{3}{4}$, the man's shadow is $\frac{3}{4}$ of his height. So, the flagpole's shadow should also be $\frac{3}{4}$ of its height and $\frac{3}{4}$ of 42.7 is approximately 32.

Think and Discuss

1. **Explain** why it is easier to use triangles instead of other polygons for indirect measurement.

2. **Explain** how you can tell whether the terms of a proportion you have written are in the correct order.

Students sometimes set up proportions incorrectly. When setting up a proportion that uses corresponding sides of two similar figures, suggest that students point to the corresponding sides as they include them in a proportion.

Power Presentations
with PowerPoint®

Additional Examples

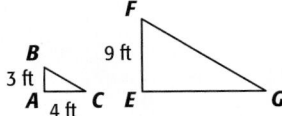

Example 1

Triangles *ABC* and *EFG* are similar. Find the length of side *EG*. 12 ft

Example 2

A 30-ft building casts a shadow that is 75 ft long. A nearby tree casts a shadow that is 35 ft long. How tall is the tree? 14 ft

Also available on transparency

Possible answers to
Think and Discuss

1. Since triangles have the fewest sides of any polygon, you need the least number of measurements.

2. Use number sense: check that both ratios are in the same order: smaller to larger or larger to smaller.

---

2 Teach

Guided Instruction

Before solving problems using indirect measurement, review how to solve proportions using the cross products. Then show students which sides of similar figures are proportional. Use the corresponding sides of two similar figures to write proportions.

 **Visual** Suggest that students draw and label the similar figures before writing the proportions.

 Reaching All Learners
Through Kinesthetic Experience

Present students with a problem similar to the one in Example 1. Have them build a bridge across an open expanse, such as between two desks. Give them three of the measurements and ask them to find the missing one through indirect measurement. Then have students make the bridge using the measurement they calculated to test whether or not it connects the two objects.

3 Close

Summarize

Ask students to explain why similar figures can be used to find a dimension through indirect measurement.

You can find the unknown length by solving a proportion because the side lengths of similar figures are proportional.

5-7 Exercises

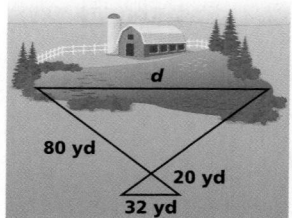

go.hrw.com
Homework Help Online
KEYWORD: MT7 5-7
Parent Resources Online
KEYWORD: MT7 Parent

Assignment Guide

If you finished Example **1** assign:
Average   1, 4, 7–9, 15–24
Advanced 4, 7–9, 12, 13, 15–24

If you finished Example **2** assign:
Average   1–11, 15–24
Advanced 4–24

Homework Quick Check

Quickly check key concepts.
Exercises: 4, 6, 8

GUIDED PRACTICE

See Example **1**
1. Walter wants to know the width of the pond on his farm. He drew the diagram and labeled it with measurements he made. The triangles in the diagram are similar. How wide is the pond? **128 yd**

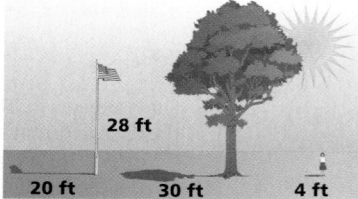

See Example **2**
Use the diagram for Exercises 2 and 3.

2. How tall is the tree? **42 ft**

3. How tall is the girl? **5.6 ft**

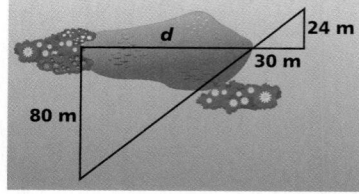

INDEPENDENT PRACTICE

See Example **1**
4. The town council has decided to build a footbridge over a pond in the park. An engineer drew a diagram of the pond and labeled it with measurements she made. The triangles in the diagram are similar. How long will the footbridge be? **100 m**

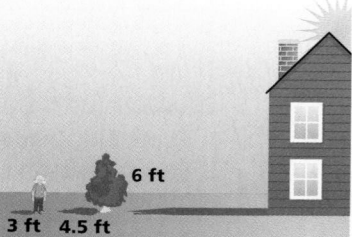

See Example **2**
Use the diagram for Exercises 5 and 6.

5. How tall is the child? **4 ft**

6. The house is 19 ft tall. How long is its shadow?
   14.25 ft

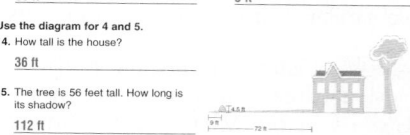

State Resources

go.hrw.com
State Resources Online
KEYWORD: MT7 Resources

RETEACH 5-7

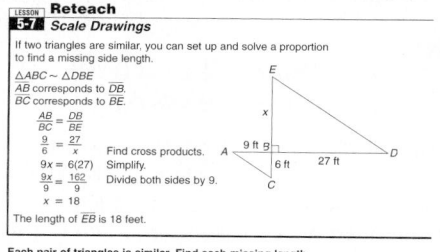

PRACTICE 5-7

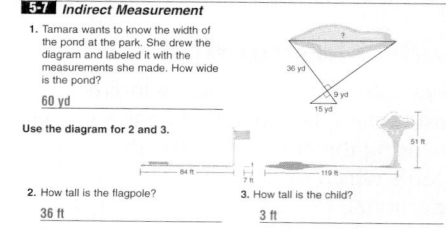

PRACTICE AND PROBLEM SOLVING

Extra Practice
See page 791.

7. There is a 3 m tall vertical ladder from the ground to a ramp. The bottom of the ladder is 10 m from the base of the ramp. The distance along the ramp from the top of the ladder to the loading platform is 24 m. How high above the ground is the loading platform? **7.2 m**

8. Brooke is 5 ft tall. She and her class are walking through a wooded area looking for a tree that is 50 ft tall. If the length of Brooke's shadow is 2 ft, how will the students know when they have found a 50 ft tree?

9. A ramp is built by putting a triangle on top of a trapezoid. How long is the ramp? **85 ft.**

10. Estimation An 11 m tall sign casts a 19 m shadow when the shadow of a boy standing next to it is 3 m long. To the nearest tenth of a meter, approximately how tall is the boy? **1.7 m**

11. A 40 ft tall monument casts a shadow that just reaches the base of a 4 ft tall parking meter. If the parking meter's shadow is 6.5 ft long, how far apart are the monument and the meter? **65 ft**

 12. Write a Problem Write a problem using indirect measurement to measure an object at home or school.

 13. Write About It Explain how you might use similar rectangles to measure indirectly.

 14. Challenge Stanley is 6 ft tall. He wants to stand in the shade of a tree that is 35 ft tall. If the tree casts a 10 ft shadow, what is the farthest Stanley can stand from the tree and be completely in its shadow? Round your answer to the nearest tenth of a foot. **8.3 ft**

8. The tree's shadow will be 20 ft long.

TEST PREP and Spiral Review

15. Multiple Choice Triangles *ABC* and *DEF* are similar right triangles. If you know the lengths of sides *AB*, *AC*, *BC*, and *DE*, which other length(s) can you find?

Ⓐ Only *DF*   Ⓑ Only *EF*   Ⓒ *DF* and *EF*   Ⓓ None of them

16. Short Answer At the same time that a tree casts a 44 ft shadow, a 3.5 ft girl standing next to the tree casts a 5 ft shadow. How much taller than the girl is the tree?

Multiply. Write each answer in simplest form. (Lesson 2-4)

17. $-\frac{1}{4}\left(\frac{4}{5}\right)$ $-\frac{1}{5}$ **18.** $\frac{4}{7}\left(\frac{3}{8}\right)$ $\frac{3}{14}$ **19.** $-\frac{2}{3}\left(-\frac{1}{4}\right)$ $\frac{1}{6}$ **20.** $\frac{3}{8}\left(-\frac{2}{3}\right)$ $-\frac{1}{4}$

Write in exponential form. (Lesson 4-1)

21. $3 \cdot 3 \cdot 3 \cdot 3$ 3^4 **22.** -8 8^{-1} **23.** $(-2) \cdot (-2) \cdot (-2)$ $(-2)^3$ **24.** $e \cdot e \cdot e \cdot e \cdot e$ e^4

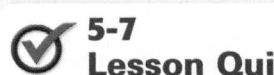

Answers

12. Possible answer: A fellow student is 4 ft tall and casts a 1.5 ft shadow. If a flag pole casts a 15 ft shadow, how tall is the flag pole? Answer: 40 ft

13. Possible answer: If you are given any vertical and horizontal measurement, you can then use the same process as you would with triangles.

TEST PREP DOCTOR For Exercise 15, suggest that students draw the two similar triangles and label the sides. This will help them identify the corresponding sides. By looking at the diagram, they should realize they can find the lengths of sides *DF* and *EF*.

 Journal

Have students give an example of how they use proportions in a real world situation. Ask them to use real measurements or quantities in their explanation.

Power Presentations
with **PowerPoint®**

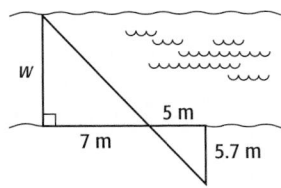

Objective: Students make comparisons between and find dimensions of scale drawings, models, and actual objects.

Online Edition
Tutorial Videos, Interactivities

Countdown to Testing Week 9

Power Presentations
with PowerPoint®

Warm Up

Evaluate the following for $x = 16$.

1. $3x$ 48   **2.** $\frac{3}{4}x$ 12

Evaluate the following for $x = \frac{2}{5}$.

3. $10x$ 4   **4.** $\frac{1}{4}x$ $\frac{1}{10}$

Problem of the Day

An isosceles triangle with a base length of 6 cm and side lengths of 5 cm is dilated by a scale factor of 3. What is the area of the image?
108 cm²

Also available on transparency

Math Humor

Teacher: Why did you turn in a picture of a snake?

Student: You said to make a *scale drawing*.

State Resources

go.hrw.com
State Resources Online
KEYWORD: MT7 Resources

5-8 Scale Drawings and Scale Models

Learn to make comparisons between and find dimensions of scale drawings, models, and actual objects.

Vocabulary
scale drawing
scale
scale model
reduction
enlargement

Stan Herd is a crop artist and farmer who has created works of art that are as large as 160 square acres. Herd first makes a *scale drawing* of each piece, and then he determines the actual lengths of the parts that make up the art piece.

A **scale drawing** is a two-dimensional drawing that accurately represents an object. The scale drawing is mathematically similar to the object.

A **scale** gives the ratio of the dimensions in the drawing to the dimensions of the object. All dimensions are reduced or enlarged using the same scale.

To get an idea of scale, notice the red tractor at the lower left.

Scale	Interpretation
1:20	1 unit on the drawing is 20 units.
1 cm:1 m	1 cm on the drawing is 1 m.
$\frac{1}{4}$ in. = 1 ft	$\frac{1}{4}$ in. on the drawing is 1 ft.

EXAMPLE 1 **Using Proportions to Find Unknown Scales**

Reading Math

The scale $a:b$ is read "a to b." For example, the scale 1 cm:6 ft is read "one centimeter to six feet."

The length of an object on a scale drawing is 8 cm, and its actual length is 48 m. The scale is 1 cm:☐ m. What is the scale?

$\dfrac{1 \text{ cm}}{x \text{ m}} = \dfrac{8 \text{ cm}}{48 \text{ m}}$ *Set up a proportion using $\frac{scale\ length}{actual\ length}$.*

$1 \cdot 48 = x \cdot 8$ *Find the cross products.*

$x = 6$ *Divide both sides by 8.*

The scale is 1 cm:6 m.

EXAMPLE 2 **Life Science Application**

Under a 1000:1 microscope view, a paramecium appears to have length 39 mm. What is its actual length?

$\dfrac{1000}{1} = \dfrac{39 \text{ mm}}{x \text{ mm}}$ *Set up a proportion using $\frac{scale\ length}{actual\ length}$.*

$1000 \cdot x = 1 \cdot 39$ *Find the cross products.*

$x = 0.039$ *Divide both sides by 1000.*

The actual length of the paramecium is 0.039 mm.

---

1 Introduce

Alternate Opener

EXPLORATION

5-8 Scale Drawings and Scale Models

A coffee house rents the floor space modeled by the figure below.

☐ = 1 ft²

[figure: Kitchen, Dining room, Restrooms]

Count the number of squares to answer each question.

1. What is the actual area of the dining room?
2. What is the actual area of the kitchen?
3. What is the actual area of the restrooms?

Think and Discuss

4. **Show** a possible arrangement of square tables in the dining area if the tabletops each measure 2 ft by 2 ft.
5. **Discuss** real-world situations in which scale drawings are used.

Motivate

On the chalkboard, sketch a rough scale drawing of the classroom floor. (You will need to measure the room ahead of time and decide on a scale; you may want to use a scale of 1:10 or 1:20.) Ask students how much larger they think the actual floor is than the drawing. Have students measure the drawing and the actual floor and determine the scale.

Explorations and answers are provided in *Alternate Openers: Explorations Transparencies.*

A **scale model** is a three-dimensional model that accurately represents a solid object. The scale model is mathematically similar to the solid object.

EXAMPLE 3 Finding Unknown Dimensions Given Scale Factors

A model of a 36 ft tall house was made using the scale 3 in:2 ft. What is the height of the model?

$$\frac{3 \text{ in.}}{2 \text{ ft}} = \frac{3 \text{ in.}}{24 \text{ in.}} = \frac{1 \text{ in.}}{8 \text{ in.}}$$ *Find the scale factor.*

The scale factor for the model is $\frac{1}{8}$. Now set up a proportion.

$$\frac{1}{8} = \frac{h \text{ in.}}{432 \text{ in.}}$$ *Convert: 36 ft = 432 in.*

$432 = 8h$ *Find the cross products.*

$h = 54$ *Divide both sides by 8.*

The height of the model is 54 in.

EXAMPLE 4 Life Science Application

A DNA model was built using the scale 2 cm:0.0000001 mm. If the model of the DNA chain is 17 cm long, what is the length of the actual chain?

$$\frac{2 \text{ cm}}{0.0000001 \text{ mm}} = \frac{20 \text{ mm}}{0.0000001 \text{ mm}} = 200{,}000{,}000$$ *Find the scale factor.*

The scale factor for the model is 200,000,000. This means the model is 200 million times larger than the actual chain.

$$\frac{200{,}000{,}000}{1} = \frac{17 \text{ cm}}{x \text{ cm}}$$ *Set up a proportion.*

$200{,}000{,}000x = 17(1)$ *Find the cross products.*

$x = 0.000000085$ *Divide both sides by 200,000,000.*

The length of the DNA chain is 8.5×10^{-8} cm.

A scale drawing or model that is smaller than the actual object is called a **reduction**. A scale drawing or model that is larger than the object is called an **enlargement**.

Think and Discuss

1. **Describe** which scale would produce the largest drawing of an object: 1:20, 1 in. = 1 ft, or $\frac{1}{4}$ in. = 1 ft.

2. **Explain** why comparing models with different scale factors, such as the paramecium in Example 2 and the house in Example 3, can be misleading.

Answers to Think and Discuss

1. The scale 1 in. = 1 ft would produce the largest drawing.

2. The different units make the model and the object seem a lot closer in size than they actually are.

---

2 Teach

Guided Instruction

In this lesson, students learn to make comparisons between and find dimensions of scale drawings, scale models, and actual objects. Explain that a scale drawing represents an actual object that is either larger or smaller than the drawing. Explain that a scale model is similar to a scale drawing except that it shows all three dimensions. Define *scale,* and use the chart on p. 252 (Teaching Transparency) to point out that a scale may contain different units or no units at all. Show students how to simplify scale factors by writing ratios with the same units. You may want to review the use of conversion factors (Lesson 5-3).

Reaching All Learners
Through Modeling

Have students use tape measures (Manipulatives Kit) and graph paper (Teacher Tools) to make a scale drawing of a room in their home. Students will need to measure important lines, walls, or objects, such as a bed or other large furniture, and decide on an appropriate scale. Then, students should work with an adult or family member to create a scale model of the room. Suggest that students design the scale model using materials of their choice (sugar cubes, balsa wood, cardstock, etc.). Each student should submit the scale factor and all calculations, along with the model and drawing.

3 Close

Summarize

Review the process of simplifying scale factors. For each scale below, ask students to write the scale factor. Ask them to also write whether the actual object would be larger or smaller than the scale model.

1. 1 in.:4 ft
   1/48; actual object is larger

2. 2 ft:6 in.
   4/1; actual object is smaller

3. 2 cm:1 km
   1/50,000; actual object is larger

5-8 Exercises

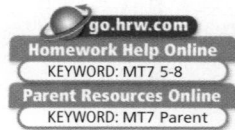

go.hrw.com
Homework Help Online
KEYWORD: MT7 5-8
Parent Resources Online
KEYWORD: MT7 Parent

Assignment Guide

If you finished Example **1** assign:
Average 1, 5, 9–14, 31–40
Advanced 5, 9–14, 31–40

If you finished Example **2** assign:
Average 1, 2, 5, 6, 9–14, 21, 31–40
Advanced 5, 6, 9–14, 21, 22, 31–40

If you finished Example **3** assign:
Average 1–3, 5–7, 9–21, 24–29, 31–40
Advanced 5–7, 12–17, 21–40

If you finished Example **4** assign:
Average 1–21, 24–29, 31–40
Advanced 5–8, 12–17, 21–40

Homework Quick Check

Quickly check key concepts.
Exercises: 5, 6, 7, 8, 14, 16

Math Background

The Museum of Science in Boston, Massachusetts, recently installed a full-scale version of *Tyrannosaurus rex*. The process used to create the full-scale version involved a reduction followed by an enlargement. First, a scale-model sculpture was created using a 1:12 scale. Then the model was sliced from snout to tail, like a banana. Next, images of each slice were projected using a 12:1 scale. The enlarged images were then traced and cut from foam. The foam pieces were glued together to create a dinosaur display 14 feet tall and 39 feet long.

State Resources

go.hrw.com
State Resources Online
KEYWORD: MT7 Resources

GUIDED PRACTICE

See Example **1** — 1. A 10 ft fence is 8 in. long on a scale drawing. What is the scale? **1in.:1.25 ft**

See Example **2** — 2. Under a 200:1 microscope, a microorganism appears to have a length of 0.75 in. How long is the microorganism? **0.00375 in.**

See Example **3** — 3. A model of a 42 ft tall shopping mall was built using the scale 1 in:3 ft. What is the height of the model? **14 in.**

See Example **4** — 4. A molecular model uses the scale 2.5 cm:0.00001 mm. If the model is 7 cm long, how long is the molecule? **0.000028 mm**

INDEPENDENT PRACTICE

See Example **1** — 5. What is the scale of a drawing where a 6 m wall is 4 cm long? **1 cm = 1.5 m**

See Example **2** — 6. Under a 750:1 magnification microscope, a paramecium has a length of 19 mm. What is the actual length of the paramecium? **0.0253 mm**

See Example **3** — 7. A model of a house was built using the scale 5 in:25 ft. If a window in the model is 1.5 in. wide, how wide is the actual window? **7.5 ft**

See Example **4** — 8. To create a model of an artery, a health teacher uses the scale 2.5 cm:0.75 mm. If the diameter of the artery is 2.7 mm, what is the diameter on the model? **9 cm**

PRACTICE AND PROBLEM SOLVING

Extra Practice
See page 791.

Tell whether each scale reduces, enlarges, or preserves the size of an actual object.

9. 10 ft:24 in. **enlarges**   10. 1 mi:5280 ft **preserves**   11. 20 cm:1000 mm **reduces**

12. 0.2 in:2 ft **reduces**   13. 50 ft:1 in. **enlarges**   14. 250 cm:1 km **reduces**

Change both measurements to the same unit of measure, and find the scale factor.

15. 1 ft model of a 1 in. fossil $\frac{12}{1}$ 16. 20 cm model of a 28 m rocket $\frac{1}{140}$

17. 2 ft model of a 30 yd sports field $\frac{1}{45}$ 18. 3 ft model of a 5 yd whale $\frac{1}{5}$

19. 30 cm model of a 6 m tree $\frac{1}{20}$ 20. 6 in. model of a 6 ft sofa $\frac{1}{12}$

21. **Architecture** Maurice is building a 2 ft tall model of the Gateway Arch in St. Louis, Missouri. If he is using a 3 in:78.75 ft scale, how tall is the actual arch? **630 ft**

22. **Geography** The straight-line distances between Houston and several cities on a map of Texas are shown in the table. The scale is 2 cm:50 mi. Find the actual distances in miles.

22. Abilene: 317.5 mi; Austin: 145 mi; Dallas: 225 mi; Galveston: 47.5 mi; San Antonio: 190 mi

23. 6.25 ft

23. On a scale drawing, a fence is $6\frac{1}{4}$ in. tall. The scale factor is $\frac{1}{12}$. Find the height of the actual fence in feet.

City	Distance from Houston (cm)
Abilene	12.7
Austin	5.8
Dallas	9.0
Galveston	1.9

RETEACH 5-8

LESSON
5-8 Reteach
Scale Drawings and Scale Models

In a **scale drawing** or a **scale model**, all the dimensions of the actual object are reduced or enlarged proportionally.

A map is a scale drawing in which actual distance is reduced.

The towns of Ardon and Bacton are on a map with scale 1 cm = 15 km.

If the map distance between Ardon and Bacton is 4.5 cm, what is the actual distance?

$$\frac{actual\ distance}{map\ distance} = \frac{actual\ distance}{map\ distance}$$

$$\frac{15\ km}{1\ cm} = \frac{x\ km}{4.5\ cm}$$

$$1(x) = 15(4.5)$$

$$x = 67.5\ km \leftarrow \text{actual distance between Ardon and Bacton}$$

● Bacton

Ardon ●

Complete to find each unknown measure.

1. A map scale is 1 in. = 75 mi. The map distance between two towns is 3.5 in. Find the actual distance *x* between the towns.

$$\frac{actual\ distance}{map\ distance} = \frac{actual\ distance}{map\ distance}$$

$$\frac{75\ mi}{1\ in.} = \frac{x\ mi}{3.5\ in.}$$

$$x = \underline{262.5}$$

actual distance = __262.5 mi__

2. The actual distance between two towns is 175 km. If the distance between them on a map is 7 cm, what is the map scale?

$$\frac{x\ km}{1\ cm} = \frac{175\ km}{7\ cm}$$

$$7x = 175$$

$$x = \underline{25}$$

map scale: 1 cm = __25 km__

3. An archway in a $\frac{1}{2}$ in. drawing is 4.5 in. tall. Find the actual height *x*.

$$\frac{actual\ height}{scale\ height} = \frac{actual\ height}{scale\ height}$$

$$\frac{1\ ft}{0.5\ in.} = \frac{x\ ft}{4.5\ in.}$$

$$0.5x = 4.5$$

$$x = 9$$

actual height = __9 ft__

4. Under a 7:1 magnification, this letter F appears to be 84 points high. Find the actual height *x*.

$$\frac{actual\ height}{scale\ height} = \frac{actual\ height}{scale\ height}$$

$$\frac{1}{7} = \frac{x\ points}{84\ points}$$

$$7x = 84$$

$$x = 12$$

actual height = __12 points__

PRACTICE 5-8

LESSON
5-8 Practice B
Scale Drawings and Scale Models

The scale of a drawing is $\frac{1}{4}$ in. = 15 ft. Find the actual measurement.

1. 9 in. __540 ft__   2. 12 in. __720 ft__   3. 14 in. __840 ft__   4. 15 in. __900 ft__

The scale is 2 cm = 25 m. Find the length each measurement would be on a scale drawing.

5. 150 m __12 cm__   6. 475 m __38 cm__   7. 350 m __28 cm__   8. 500 m __40 cm__

Tell whether each scale reduces, enlarges, or preserves the size of an actual object.

9. 1 m : 25 cm __enlarges__   10. 8 in. : 1 ft __reduces__   11. 12 in. : 1 ft __preserves__

12. On a map the distance between Atlanta, Georgia, and Nashville, Tennessee, is 12.5 in. The actual distance between these two cities is 250 miles. What is the scale?

__1 in. = 20 mi__

13. Blueprints of a house are drawn to the scale of $\frac{1}{4}$ in. = 1 ft. A kitchen measures 3.5 in. by 5 in. on the blueprints. What is the actual size of the kitchen?

__14 ft × 20 ft__

14. A scale model of a house is 1 ft long. The actual house is 50 ft long. In the model, the window is $1\frac{1}{5}$ in. high. How many feet high is the actual window?

__5 ft__

15. A model of a skyscraper is 1.6 in. long, 2.8 in. wide, and 11.2 in. high. The scale factor is 8 in. : 250 ft. What are the actual dimensions of the skyscraper?

__50 ft long, 87.5 ft wide, 350 ft high__

Architecture LINK

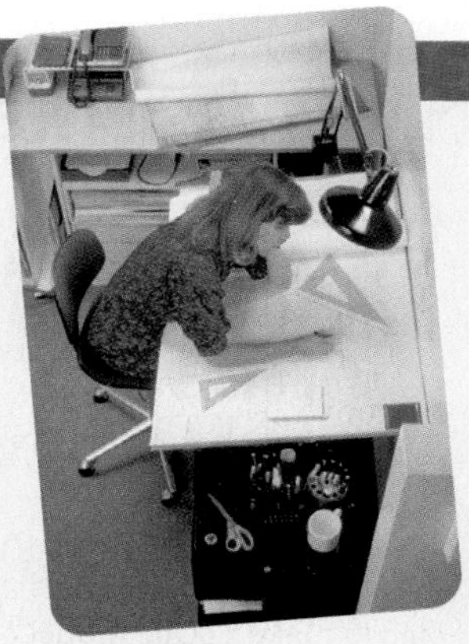

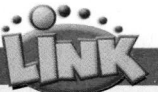

The blueprint shows the design for the Anderson's new family room. Use a metric ruler to measure the width of the 36-inch-wide door on the blueprint and determine the scale factor. **The scale is about 1.2 cm:36 in.**

For Exercises 24–30, indicate the scale that you used.

24. How wide are the pocket doors (shown by the red line)? **≈ 63 in.**
25. What is the distance *s* between two interior studs? **≈ 18 in.**
26. How long is the oak mantle? (The right side ends just above the *B* in the word *BRICK*.) **≈ 81 in.**
27. What is the area of the tiled hearth in square inches? in square feet? **$\approx 945\ in^2$; $\approx 6.6\ ft^2$**
28. What is the area of the entire family room in square feet? **$\approx 298\ ft^2$**

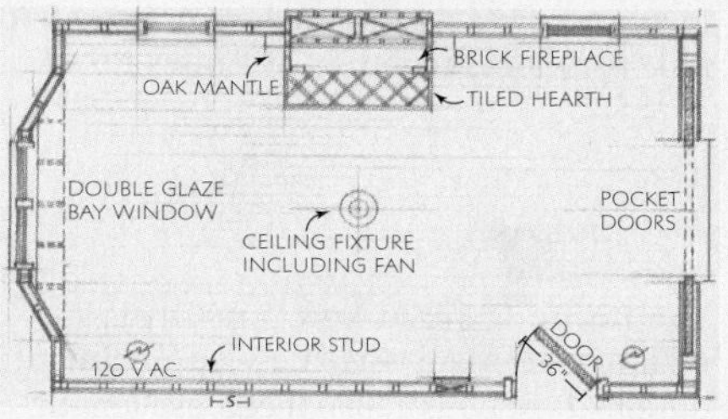

OAK MANTLE
BRICK FIREPLACE
TILED HEARTH
DOUBLE GLAZE BAY WINDOW
CEILING FIXTURE INCLUDING FAN
POCKET DOORS
INTERIOR STUD
120 V AC
DOOR
36"
s

29. **Write About It** Could a 4 ft wide bookcase fit along the right-hand wall without blocking the pocket doors? Explain.
30. **Challenge** Suppose the architect used a $\frac{1}{8}$ in. = 1 ft scale.
    a. What would the dimensions of the family room be? **28 ft by 16 ft**
    b. Use the result from part **a** to find the area of the family room. **$448\ ft^2$**
    c. If the carpet the Andersons want costs $4.99 per square foot, how much would it cost to carpet the family room? **$2235.52**

go.hrw.com
Web Extra!
KEYWORD: MT7 Scale

TEST PREP and Spiral Review

31. **Multiple Choice** What scale factor was used to create a 10-inch-tall model of a 15-foot-tall statue?

    Ⓐ 1:1.5 Ⓑ 1:3 Ⓒ 1:15 **Ⓓ 1:18**

32. **Short Response** The height of a building on a $\frac{1}{4}$-inch scale drawing is 5 inches tall. How tall is the actual building? Explain. **20 feet; 5 feet ÷ 0.25 = 20 feet**

State if the number is rational, irrational, or not a real number. (Lesson 4-7)

33. $\sqrt{9}$ **rational**
34. $\sqrt{-25}$ **not real**
35. $\sqrt{48}$ **irrational**
36. $\sqrt{36}$ **rational**
37. $\frac{1}{\sqrt{4}}$ **rational**

Find each unit rate. (Lesson 5-2)

38. $90 for 8 hours of work **$11.25 per hour**
39. 5 apples for $0.85 **$0.17 per apple**
40. 24 players on 2 teams **12 players per team**

CHALLENGE 5-8

LESSON 5-8 **Challenge**
Too Small, Too Big

A scientist invented a machine that shrinks an object to half its original size. The pictures below show Spot before he was shrunk and after he was shrunk 1, 2, and 3 times.

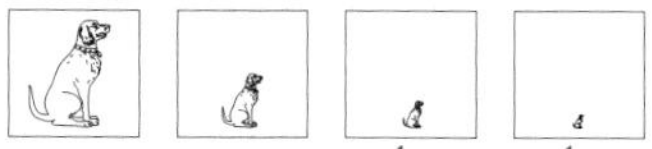

2 ft 1 ft $\frac{1}{2}$ ft $\frac{1}{4}$ ft

1. How tall would Spot be if he were shrunk 1 more time? 5 more times? **$\frac{1}{8}$ ft; $\frac{1}{128}$ ft**
2. If you were 6 ft tall and were shrunk 10 times, how tall would you be? **$\frac{3}{512}$ ft**
3. Write an expression for Spot's size after he has been shrunk *n* times. **$2 \times \left(\frac{1}{2}\right)^n$ ft**

The scientist then invented a machine to triple the size of an object. The pictures below show Spot before his size was tripled and after being tripled 1, 2, and 3 times.

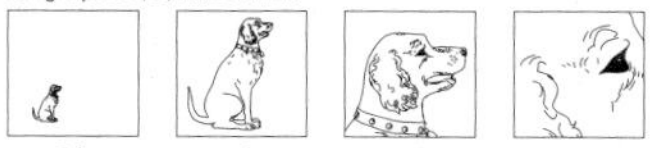

2 ft 6 ft 18 ft 54 ft

4. How tall would Spot be if he were tripled 1 more time? 5 more times? **162 ft; 13,122 ft**
5. If you were 6 ft tall and the machine tripled your size 10 times, how tall would you be? **354,294 ft**
6. Write an expression for Spot's size after he has been tripled *n* times. **2×3^n ft**
7. Could Spot be tripled in size in one machine and then returned to normal size in the shrinking machine? Explain. **Possible answer: 2 and 3 are relatively prime so there are no positive integers *n* and *m* such that $\frac{3^m}{2^n} = 1$.**

PROBLEM SOLVING 5-8

LESSON 5-8 **Problem Solving**
Scale Drawings and Scale Models

Round to the nearest tenth. Write the correct answer.

1. The Statue of Liberty is approximately 305 feet tall. A scale model of the Statue of Liberty is 5 inches tall. The scale of the model is 1 in. : ____ ft. **61**
2. The right arm of the Statue of Liberty is 42 feet long. How long is the right arm of the Statue of Liberty model given in Exercise 1? **0.7 inches**
3. The diameter of an atom is 10^{-9} cm. If a scale drawing of an atom has a diameter of 10 cm, the scale of the drawing is 1 cm : ____ cm. **10^{-10}**
4. The diameter of the nucleus of an atom is 10^{-13} cm. If a scale drawing of the nucleus of an atom has a diameter of 1 cm, the scale of the drawing is 1 cm : ____ cm. **10^{-13}**

The toy car in Exercises 5-6 has a scale of $\frac{1}{40.}$ Choose the letter for the best answer.

5. The diameter of the steering wheel of the actual car is 15 inches. What is the diameter of the toy car's steering wheel?
   Ⓐ $\frac{3}{8}$ in. C $1\frac{1}{2}$ in.
   B $\frac{1}{2}$ in. D $2\frac{2}{3}$ in.
6. The diameter of the toy car's tire is $\frac{5}{8}$ in. What is the diameter of the tire of the actual car?
   F $12\frac{1}{2}$ in. **Ⓗ 25 in.**
   G 16 in. J 64 in.
7. On a scale drawing, a 14 ft room is pictured as 3.5 inches. What is the scale of the drawing?
   Ⓐ $\frac{1}{4}$ in. C $\frac{1}{4}$:14
   B $\frac{1}{2}$ in. D 1:56
8. On a scale drawing, $\frac{1}{2}$ inch = 1 foot. A room is pictured as 7.5 inches by 6 inches. How many square yards of carpet are needed for the room?
   F $5\ yd^2$ H $45\ yd^2$
   Ⓖ $20\ yd^2$ J $90\ yd^2$
9. On a scale drawing of a computer component, $\frac{1}{4}$ in. = 4 in. On the drawing, a piece is $\frac{3}{8}$ in. long. How long is the actual piece?
   A 1.5 in. **Ⓒ 6 in.**
   B 3 in. D 7.5 in.
10. A scale drawing has a $\frac{1}{4}$ inch scale. The width of a 12 foot room is going to be increased by 4 feet. How much wider will the room be on the drawing?
    F $\frac{1}{4}$ in. **Ⓗ 1 in.**
    G $\frac{1}{2}$ in. J 4 in.

ONGOING ASSESSMENT and INTERVENTION

***Diagnose Before* the Lesson**
5-8 Warm Up, TE p. 252

***Monitor During* the Lesson**
5-8 Know-It Notebook
5-8 Questioning Strategies

***Assess After* the Lesson**
5-8 Lesson Quiz, TE p. 255

Interdisciplinary LINK

Architecture

Exercises 24–30 involve using a scale drawing, or an architectural blueprint, to find actual dimensions.

Answers

29. No; the bookcase is 48 in. wide, but each wall next to the doors is only about 45 in. wide.

TEST PREP DOCTOR For Exercise 31, students who answered **A** did not convert the feet to inches. Instead, they divided 15 feet by 10 inches. Students who answered **D** correctly converted the feet to inches before dividing.

Journal

Explain to students that one kind of common scale drawing is a highway map. Ask students to write about how the scale on a map could be helpful to them when they are taking a trip.

Power Presentations with PowerPoint®

5-8 Lesson Quiz

1. What is the scale of a drawing in which a 9 ft wall is 6 cm long? **1 cm = 1.5 ft**
2. Using a $\frac{1}{4}$ in. = 1 ft scale, how long would a drawing of a 22 ft car be? **5.5 in.**
3. The height of a person on a scale drawing is 4.5 in. The scale is 1:16. What is the actual height of the person? **72 in.**

Also available on transparency

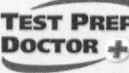

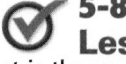

Make a Scale Model

> **REMEMBER**
> A scale such as 1 in. = 200 ft results in a smaller-scale model than a scale of 1 in. = 20 feet.

You can make a scale model of a solid object, such as a rectangular prism, in many ways; you can make a net and fold it, or you can cut card stock and tape the pieces together. The most important thing is to find a good scale.

Activity 1

The Trump Tower in New York City is a rectangular prism with these approximate dimensions: height, 880 feet; base length, 160 feet; base width, 80 feet.

❶ Make a scale model of the Trump Tower.

First determine the appropriate height for your model and find a good scale.

To use $8\frac{1}{2}$ in. by 11 in. card stock, divide the longest dimension by 11 to find a scale.

$$\frac{880\ \text{ft}}{11\ \text{in.}} = \frac{80\ \text{ft}}{1\ \text{in.}}$$

Let 1 in. = 80 ft.

The dimensions of the model using this scale are

$\frac{880}{80} = 11$ in., $\frac{160}{80} = 2$ in., and $\frac{80}{80} = 1$ in.

So you will need to cut the following:

Two 11 in. × 2 in. rectangles

Two 11 in. × 1 in. rectangles

Two 2 in. × 1 in. rectangles

Tape the pieces together to form the model.

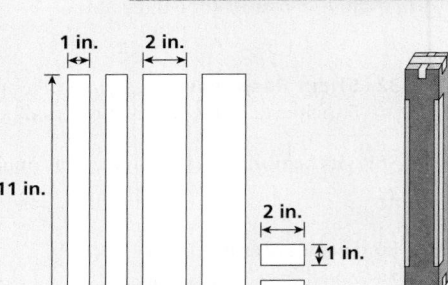

Close

Key Concept

When you make a scale model, it's important to choose the best scale to use. Use the largest dimension of the material you're using to determine the scale.

Assessment

1. What scale would you use to make a model of a building 850 ft tall with a rectangular base 300 ft by 150 ft out of the following:

a. 8.5 in. by 11 in. card stock
Possible answer: 1 in. = 100 ft

b. 11 in. by 17 in. card stock
Possible answer: 1 in. = 75 ft

c. 30 in. by 40 in. poster board
Possible answer: 1 in. = 28 ft

Think and Discuss

1. How tall would a model of a 500 ft tall building be if the same scale were used?

2. Why would a building stand more solidly than your model?

3. What could be another scale of the model if the numbers were without units?

Try This

1. Build a scale model of a four-wall handball court. The court is an open-topped rectangular prism 20 feet wide and 40 feet long. Three of the walls are 20 feet tall, and the back wall is 14 feet tall.

A scale model can also be used to make a model that is larger than the original object.

Activity 2

❶ A size-AA battery has a diameter of about 0.57 inches and a height of about 2 inches. Make a scale model of a AA battery.

You can roll up paper or card stock to create a cylinder. Find the circumference of the battery: $0.57\pi \approx 1.8$ in.

Note that the height is greater than the circumference, so use the height to find a scale.

$$\frac{\text{paper height}}{\text{battery height}} = \frac{11 \text{ in.}}{2 \text{ in.}} = 5.5$$

To use $8\frac{1}{2}$ in. by 11 in. paper or card stock, try multiplying the dimensions of the battery by 5.5.

$2(5.5) = 11$ in. $1.8(5.5) = 9.9$ in.

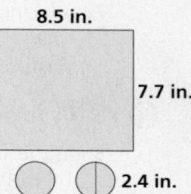

Note that 9.9 in. by 11 in. is larger than an 8.5 in. by 11 in. piece of paper. If you use the width of the paper as the height of the scale model, you can find a smaller scale factor: $\frac{8.5 \text{ in.}}{2 \text{ in.}} = 4.25$. Then use the smaller scale factor to find the corresponding circumference ($4.25 \cdot 1.8$ in. ≈ 7.7 in.) and diameter ($4.25 \cdot 0.57$ in. ≈ 2.4 in.). The pieces for the scale model are shown.

8.5 in.

7.7 in.

2.4 in.

Think and Discuss

1. A salt crystal is a cube $\frac{1}{16}$ inch long on each side. What would a good scale be for a model of the crystal?

Try This

1. Measure the diameter and height of a can of soup. Determine a scale needed to use a $8\frac{1}{2}$ in. by 11 in. paper or card stock and make a scale model of the can.

Check students' work.

Organizer

Objective: Assess students' mastery of concepts and skills in Lessons 5-5 through 5-8.

Resources

 Assessment Resources
Section 5B Quiz

 Test & Practice Generator
One-Stop Planner®

INTERVENTION

Resources

 Ready to Go On?
Intervention and
Enrichment Worksheets

● **Ready to Go On? CD-ROM**

🪐 **Ready to Go On? Online**

my.hrw.com

Ready to Go On?

READY TO GO ON?

Quiz for Lessons 5-5 Through 5-8

✓ **5-5** **Similar Figures**

Tell whether the triangles are similar.

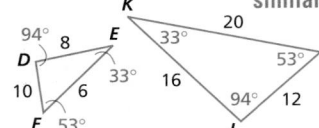

1. △DEF and △JKL   **not similar**

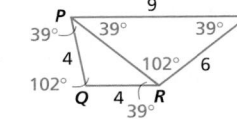

2. △PQR and △PRS   **similar**

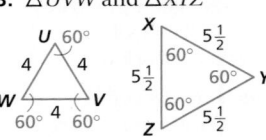

3. △UVW and △XYZ   **similar**

4. A picture 4 in. tall and 9 in. wide is to be scaled to 2.5 in. tall. How wide should the picture be for the two pictures to be similar?   **5.625 in.**

✓ **5-6** **Dilations**

Tell whether each transformation is a dilation.

5. 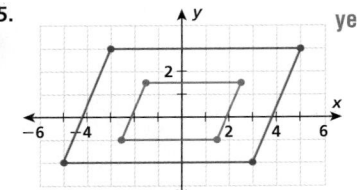   **yes**

6. 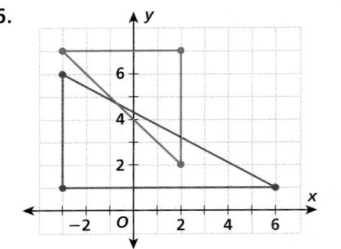   **no**

7. A triangle has vertices with coordinates $(2, 0)$, $(3, -1)$, and $(-2, -5)$. If the triangle is dilated by a scale factor of 3, what are the coordinates of the vertices of the image? $(6, 0)$, $(9, -\frac{1}{3})$, and $(-6, -15)$

✓ **5-7** **Indirect Measurement**

8. At the same time that a flagpole casts a 4.5 m shadow, a meter stick casts a 1.5 m shadow. How tall is the flagpole?   **3 m**

9. A tree casts a 30 foot shadow. Mi-Ling, standing next to the tree, casts a 13.5 foot shadow. If Mi-Ling is 5 ft tall, how tall is the tree?   **11.1 ft**

✓ **5-8** **Scale Drawings and Scale Models**

10. $\frac{4}{20} = \frac{x}{16}$ **3.2**   11. $\frac{10}{4} = \frac{15}{x}$ **6**   12. $\frac{x}{3} = \frac{3}{12}$ **0.75**   13. $\frac{65}{x} = \frac{5}{15}$ **195**

14. The model of a 27 ft tall house was made using the scale 2 in:3 ft. What is the height of the model?   **18 in.**

READY TO GO ON?
Diagnose and Prescribe

NO
INTERVENE

YES
ENRICH

READY TO GO ON? Intervention, Section 5B			
Ready to Go On? Intervention	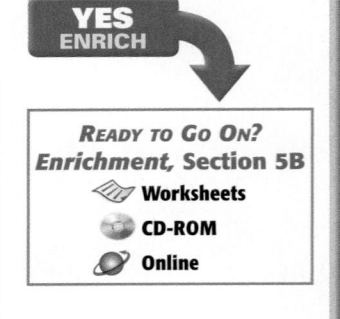 Worksheets	● CD-ROM	🪐 Online
✓ Lesson 5-5	5-5 Intervention	Activity 5-5	
✓ Lesson 5-6	5-6 Intervention	Activity 5-6	Diagnose and Prescribe Online
✓ Lesson 5-7	5-7 Intervention	Activity 5-7	
✓ Lesson 5-8	5-8 Intervention	Activity 5-8	

READY TO GO ON?
Enrichment, Section 5B

Worksheets

CD-ROM

Online

Javier Builds a Model Javier, an architect, builds a scale model of the new faculty center at the university. The diagram shows the scale model.

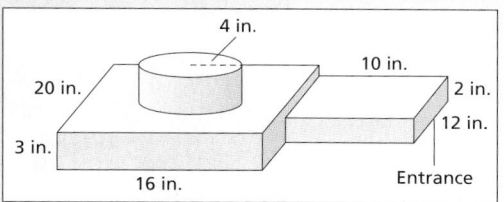

1. In the scale model, the entrance is 12 inches wide. If the entrance is actually 60 feet wide, what scale did Javier use to create the model? Explain your reasoning. $\frac{1}{60}$; the entrance in the model is 1 ft wide.

2. Find the actual dimensions of the new faculty center. Use the table to organize your work.

Model Dimensions	Actual Dimensions
2 in.	10 ft
3 in.	15 ft
4 in.	20 ft
10 in.	50 ft
12 in.	60 ft
16 in.	80 ft
20 in.	100 ft

3. Redraw the model and label its actual dimensions.

4. Javier makes a new model of the building using a scale of 1 in:10 ft. What is the width of the entrance in the new model? **6 in.**

5. How does the new model compare with the original one? Is it larger or smaller? Explain. **It is smaller because the scale is half that of the original model.**

Multi-Step Test Prep

INTERVENTION

Scaffolding Questions

1. What is the ratio of the model's entrance to the actual entrance? 12 in : 60 ft

2. Do you have to convert inches to feet in order to complete the table? no What is the scale used to create the model that you found in Problem 1? 1 in : 5 ft

3. What is the correct label for the actual width of the entrance? 60 ft Will your redrawn model be labeled in feet or inches? feet

4. What proportion could you use to find the entrance width in the new model? $\frac{1}{10} = \frac{x}{60}$

5. How many feet does 1 inch represent in the scale you found in Problem 1? 12 ft How many feet does 1 inch represent in the new scale? 10 ft

Extension

1. Javier wants to enlarge the model to twice the size shown in the diagram. What scale should he use? 1 in : 2.5 ft

---

MULTI-STEP TEST PREP · CHAPTER 5

Organizer

Objective: Assess students' ability to apply concepts and skills in Chapter 5 in a real-world format.

PREMIER **Online Edition**

Resources

 Middle School Assessments
www.mathtekstoolkit.org

Problem	Text reference
1	Lesson 5-3
2	Lesson 5-4
3	Lesson 5-5
4	Lesson 5-7
5	Lesson 5-8

Answers

3.

 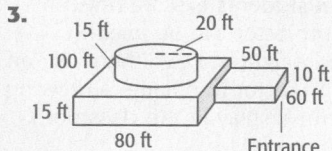

State Resources

 **go.hrw.com**
State Resources Online
KEYWORD: MT7 Resources

Organizer

Objective: Participate in games to practice and apply skills learned in Chapter 5.

 Online Edition

Resources

📖 **Chapter 5 Resource Book**
Puzzles, Twisters & Teasers

Copy-Cat

Purpose: To apply drawing skills to creating similar figures

Discuss What geometry word describes the relationship between the original and the copy? similar If 1-inch square gridlines are drawn on a 10 in. × 13 in. photo and the photo is copied so that its dimensions are 5 in. × $6\frac{1}{2}$ in., what size grid was used on the copy? $\frac{1}{2}$ in. × $\frac{1}{2}$ in. squares

Extend Let students explore how an overhead projector can be used to create similar figures. Have them use an overhead projector to enlarge a drawing or picture for display in the classroom. Check students' work.

Tic-Frac-Toe

Purpose: To practice forming proportions in a game format

Discuss What would a player have to spin in order to win a square containing the equation $\frac{2}{3} = \frac{8}{\blacksquare}$? 12 What would a player have to spin in order to block a square containing the equation $\frac{2}{3} = \frac{\blacksquare}{\blacksquare}$? Possible answer: The player could spin a 10 and place it in the missing denominator.

Extend Have students model each proportion formed in the game using fraction strips or other manipulatives.

Copy-Cat

You can use this method to copy a well-known work of art or any drawing. First, draw a grid over the work you want to copy, or draw a grid on tracing paper and tape it over the picture.

Next, on a separate sheet of paper draw a blank grid with the same number of squares. The squares do not have to be the same size. Copy each square from the original exactly onto the blank grid. Do not look at the overall picture as you copy. When you have copied all of the squares, the drawing on your finished grid should look just like the original work.

Suppose you are copying an image from a 12 in. by 18 in. print, and that you use 1-inch squares on the first grid.

❶ If you use 3-inch squares on the blank grid, what size will your finished copy be?

❷ If you want to make a copy that is 10 inches tall, what size should you make the squares on your blank grid? How wide will the copy be?

❸ Choose a painting, drawing, or cartoon, and copy it using the method above.

1. 36 in. by 54 in.   **2.** $\frac{5}{6}$ in.; 15 in.   **3.** Check students' work.

Tic-Frac-Toe

Draw a large tic-tac-toe board. In each square, draw a blank proportion, $\frac{\blacksquare}{\blacksquare} = \frac{\blacksquare}{\blacksquare}$. Players take turns using a spinner with 12 sections or a 12-sided die. A player's turn consists of placing a number anywhere in one of the proportions. The player who correctly completes the proportion can claim that square. A square may also be blocked by filling in three parts of a proportion that cannot be completed with a number from 1 to 12. The first player to claim three squares in a row wins.

🪐 **go.hrw.com**
Game Time Extra
KEYWORD: MT7 Games

A complete copy of the gameboard is available online.

Materials
- wide duct tape
- ruler
- scissors
- 6 index cards (3 in. by 5 in.)
- markers

It's in the Bag!

PROJECT ## A Worthwhile Wallet

Make a duct-tape wallet to carry index cards. The index cards will help you study ratios, proportions, and similarity.

Directions

❶ Cut three strips of duct tape at least 9 inches long. Lay the strips next to each other, sticky side up, so that they overlap slightly. The total width should be about $5\frac{1}{2}$ inches. **Figure A**

❷ Lay three more strips of duct tape on top of the first three, sticky side down. Trim the ends. This will make a sheet of duct-tape "fabric."

❸ Fold up the fabric about $3\frac{1}{2}$ inches from the bottom to form a pocket. Use duct tape to seal the sides shut. **Figure B**

❹ Fold the top down. Trim the corners of the flap. **Figure C**

Taking Note of the Math

Review the chapter to identify key concepts. Then write vocabulary, examples, and practice problems on the index cards. Store the cards in the duct-tape wallet.

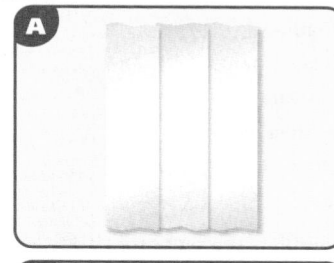

A

B

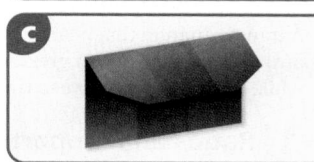

C

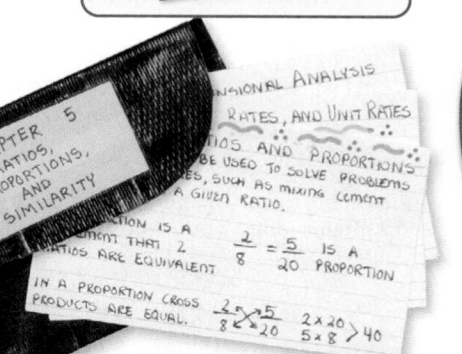

It's in the Bag!

Organizer

Objective: Make a duct-tape wallet to store cards that contain notes on ratios, proportions, and similarity.

Materials: wide duct tape, ruler, scissors, 6 index cards (3 in. by 5 in.), markers

 Online Edition

Using the Page

Preparing the Materials
Each student will need approximately 5 feet of duct tape.

Making the Project
Remind students to work carefully as they lay down the strips of duct tape. Students should check that the strips are parallel and that the total width of the side-by-side strips is about $5\frac{1}{2}$ inches.

Extending the Project
Challenge students to design a billfold-style wallet. If necessary, students can trim the index cards to fit inside.

Tips from the Bag Ladies!

After students have prepared the duct-tape "fabric," encourage them to use an index card as a sizing guide. This way students will be sure that the cards fit once the fabric has been folded to form a wallet.

It's fun to make these wallets using different colors of duct tape. Students can make wallets in various colors to hold notes for different chapters.

Organizer

Objective: Help students organize and review key concepts and skills presented in Chapter 5.

Online Edition
Multilingual Glossary

Resources

PuzzlePro®
One-Stop Planner®

Multilingual Glossary Online
go.hrw.com
KEYWORD: MT7 Glossary

Lesson Tutorial Videos
CD-ROM

Test & Practice Generator
One-Stop Planner®

Answers

1. ratio; proportion

2. rate; unit rate

3. similar; scale factor

4. dilation; enlargement; reduction

5. Possible answers: $\frac{1}{2}$, $\frac{2}{4}$

6. Possible answers: $\frac{3}{6}$, $\frac{4}{8}$

7. Possible answers: $\frac{7}{12}$, $\frac{14}{24}$

8. yes

9. no

10. yes

11. no

Study Guide: Review

Vocabulary

center of dilation 244
congruent angles 238
conversion factor 224
cross product 229
dilation 244
enlargement 253
equivalent ratio 216
indirect measurement 248
proportion 216
rate 220
ratio 216
reduction 253
scale 252
scale drawing 252
scale factor 239
scale model 253
similar 238
unit price 221
unit rate 220

Complete the sentences below with vocabulary words from the list above. Words may be used more than once.

1. A(n) __?__ is a comparison of two quantities by division. Two ratios that are equivalent are said to be in __?__.

2. A(n) __?__ is a comparison of two quantities that have different units. A rate in which the second quantity is 1 is called a(n) __?__.

3. A scale drawing is mathematically __?__ to the actual object. All dimensions are reduced or enlarged using the same __?__.

4. A transformation that changes the size but not the shape of a figure is called a(n) __?__. A scale factor greater than 1 results in a(n) __?__ of the figure, while a scale factor between 0 and 1 results in a(n) __?__ of the figure.

5-1 Ratios and Proportions (pp. 216–219)

EXAMPLE

■ Find two ratios that are equivalent to $\frac{4}{12}$.

$$\frac{4 \cdot 2}{12 \cdot 2} = \frac{8}{24} \qquad \frac{4 \div 2}{12 \div 2} = \frac{2}{6}$$

8:24 and 2:6 are equivalent to 4:12.

■ Simplify to tell whether $\frac{5}{15}$ and $\frac{6}{24}$ form a proportion.

$$\frac{5 \div 5}{15 \div 5} = \frac{1}{3} \qquad \frac{6 \div 6}{24 \div 6} = \frac{1}{4}$$

Since $\frac{1}{3} \neq \frac{1}{4}$, the ratios are not in proportion.

EXERCISES

Find two ratios that are equivalent to each given ratio.

5. $\frac{8}{16}$ 6. $\frac{9}{18}$ 7. $\frac{35}{60}$

Simplify to tell whether the ratios form a proportion.

8. $\frac{8}{24}$ and $\frac{2}{6}$ 9. $\frac{3}{12}$ and $\frac{6}{18}$

10. $\frac{25}{125}$ and $\frac{5}{25}$ 11. $\frac{6}{8}$ and $\frac{9}{16}$

5-2 Ratios, Rates, and Unit Rates (pp. 220–223)

EXAMPLE

■ Alex can buy a 4 pack of AA batteries for $2.99 or an 8 pack for $4.98. Which is the better buy?

$$\frac{\text{price per package}}{\text{number of batteries}} = \frac{\$2.99}{4} \approx \$0.75 \text{ per battery}$$

$$\frac{\text{price per package}}{\text{number of batteries}} = \frac{\$4.98}{8} \approx \$0.62 \text{ per battery}$$

The better buy is the 8 pack for $4.98.

EXERCISES

Determine the better buy.

12. 50 formatted computer disks for $14.99 or 75 disks for $21.50

13. 6 boxes of 3-inch incense sticks for $22.50 or 8 boxes for $30

14. a package of 8 binder dividers for $23.09 or a 25 pack for $99.99

5-3 Dimensional Analysis (pp. 224–228)

EXAMPLE

■ At a rate of 75 kilometers per hour, how many meters does a car travel in 1 minute?

km to m: $\frac{1000 \text{ m}}{1 \text{ km}}$ h to min: $\frac{1 \text{ h}}{60 \text{ min}}$

$$\frac{75 \text{ km}}{1 \text{ h}} \cdot \frac{1000 \text{ m}}{1 \text{ km}} \cdot \frac{1 \text{ h}}{60 \text{ min}} = \frac{75 \cdot 1000 \text{ m}}{60 \text{ min}}$$

$$= \frac{1250 \text{ m}}{1 \text{ min}}$$

The car travels 1250 meters in 1 minute.

EXERCISES

Use conversion factors to find each rate.

15. 90 km/h to m/h

16. 75 feet per second to feet per minute

17. 35 kilometers per hour to meters per minute

5-4 Solving Proportions (pp. 229–233)

EXAMPLE

■ Solve the proportion $\frac{18}{12} = \frac{x}{2}$.

$12x = 18 \cdot 2$ *Find the cross products.*

$\frac{12x}{12} = \frac{36}{12}$ *Divide both sides by 12.*

$x = 3$ *Simplify.*

EXERCISES

Solve each proportion.

18. $\frac{3}{5} = \frac{9}{x}$ 19. $\frac{24}{h} = \frac{16}{4}$

20. $\frac{w}{6} = \frac{7}{2}$ 21. $\frac{3}{8} = \frac{11}{y}$

5-5 Similar Figures (pp. 238–241)

EXAMPLE

■ A stamp 1.2 in. tall and 1.75 in. wide is to be scaled to 4.2 in. tall. How wide should the new stamp be?

$\frac{\text{scaled height}}{\text{original height}} = \frac{4.2}{1.2} = 3.5 = \text{scale factor}$

scaled width = original width · scale factor

$= 1.75(3.5) = 6.125$

The larger stamp should be 6.125 in. wide.

EXERCISES

22. A picture 3 in. wide by 5 in. tall is to be scaled to 7.5 in. wide to be put on a flyer. How tall should the flyer picture be?

23. A picture 8 in. wide by 10 in. tall is to be scaled to 2.5 in. wide to be put on an invitation. How tall should the invitation picture be?

Answers

12. $0.30 per disk; $0.29 per disk; 75 disks

13. $3.75 per box; $3.75 per box; unit prices are the same.

14. $2.89 per divider; $4.00 per divider; 8-pack

15. 90,000 m/h

16. 4500 ft/min

17. $583\frac{1}{3}$ m/min

18. $x = 15$

19. $h = 6$

20. $w = 21$

21. $y = 29\frac{1}{3}$

22. 12.5 in.

23. 3.125 in.

Answers

24.

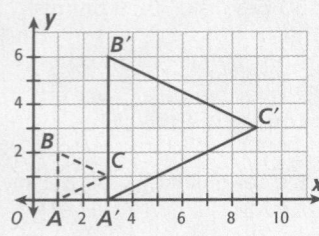

25.

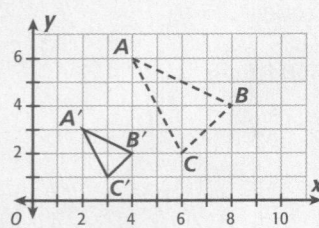

26.

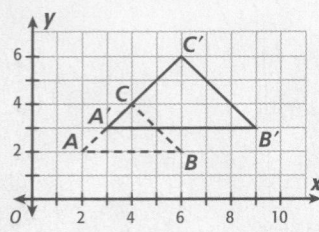

27. 18 ft

28. 6.2 ft

29. 64.8 m

30. 6.6 in.

31. 1 in:16 ft

32. 46 mi

33. 57.5 mi

34. 153 mi

35. 72.5 mi

5-6 Dilations (pp. 244–247)

EXAMPLE

■ Dilate triangle *ABC* by a scale factor of 2 with *O*(0, 0) as the center of dilation.

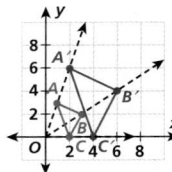

EXERCISES

Dilate each triangle *ABC* by the given scale factor with *O*(0, 0) as the center of dilation.

24. *A*(1, 0), *B*(1, 2), *C*(3, 1); scale factor = 3

25. *A*(4, 6), *B*(8, 4), *C*(6, 2); scale factor = 0.5

26. *A*(2, 2), *B*(6, 2), *C*(4, 4); scale factor = 1.5

5-7 Indirect Measurement (pp. 248–251)

EXAMPLE

■ A telephone pole casts a 5 ft shadow at the same time that a man standing next to it casts a 1.5 ft shadow. If the man is 6 ft tall, how tall is the telephone pole?

$\frac{1.5}{5} = \frac{6}{x}$ *Set up a proportion.*

$1.5x = 30$ *Find the cross products.*

$\frac{1.5x}{1.5} = \frac{30}{1.5}$ *Divide both sides by 1.5.*

$x = 20$ *Simplify.*

The telephone pole is 20 ft tall.

EXERCISES

27. A flagpole casts a 15 ft shadow at the same time Jon casts a 5 ft shadow. If Jon is 6 ft tall, how tall is the flagpole?

28. April casts a 16.5 ft shadow at the same time that Ron casts an 18.6 ft shadow. If April is 5.5 ft tall, how tall is Ron?

5-8 Scale Drawings and Scale Models (pp. 252–255)

EXAMPLE

■ A length on a map is 4.2 in. The scale is 1 in:100 mi. Find the actual distance.

$\frac{1 \text{ in.}}{100 \text{ mi}} = \frac{4.2 \text{ in.}}{x \text{ mi}}$ *Set up a proportion using* $\frac{scale\ length}{actual\ length}$

$1 \cdot x = 100 \cdot 4.2$ *Find the cross products.*

$x = 420 \text{ mi}$ *Simplify.*

The actual distance is 420 mi.

EXERCISES

29. A length on a scale drawing is 5.4 cm. The scale is 1 cm:12 m. Find the actual length.

30. A 79.2 ft length is to be scaled on a drawing with the scale 1 in:12 ft. Find the scaled length.

31. A locomotive of a model train is 5 inches long. If the actual locomotive is 80 feet long, what is the scale of the model?

The scale of a map is 1 in.:10 mi. How many actual miles does each measurement represent?

32. 4.6 in.   **33.** $5\frac{3}{4}$ in.

34. 15.3 in.   **35.** $7\frac{1}{4}$ in.

 **CHAPTER TEST**
CHAPTER 5

Simplify to tell whether the ratios form a proportion.

1. $\frac{4}{5}$ and $\frac{16}{20}$ **yes** **2.** $\frac{33}{60}$ and $\frac{11}{21}$ **no** **3.** $\frac{7}{9}$ and $\frac{35}{45}$ **yes** **4.** $\frac{8}{20}$ and $\frac{4}{25}$ **no**

Estimate each unit rate.

5. \$3.59 for $\frac{1}{2}$ pound **about \$7.20 per pound** **6.** 57 students in 3 classrooms **about 20 students per classroom**

7. \$46.50 for 5 hours **about \$9 per hour** **8.** 62 books on 5 shelves **about 12 books per shelf**

9. You can buy one 10 pack of AAA batteries for \$5.49 and get one free, or buy two 4 packs for \$2.98. Which is the better buy? **two 4 packs for \$2.98**

Find the appropriate factor for each conversion.

10. gallons to quarts $\frac{1 \text{ gal}}{4 \text{ qt}}$ **11.** millimeters to centimeters $\frac{1 \text{ cm}}{10 \text{ mm}}$ **12.** hours to days $\frac{1 \text{ day}}{24 \text{ hr}}$

Use conversion factors to find each unit to the nearest hundredth.

13. Change 60 ounces to pounds. **3.75 pounds** **14.** Change 35 pounds to ounces. **560 ounces**

15. Simon bought 5 cans of chili for \$10.95. At this rate, how much would 12 cans of chili cost? **\$26.28**

Solve each proportion.

16. $\frac{6}{9} = \frac{n}{72}$ **48** **17.** $\frac{18}{12} = \frac{3}{x}$ **2** **18.** $\frac{0.7}{1.4} = \frac{z}{28}$ **14** **19.** $\frac{12}{y} = \frac{32}{16}$ **6**

20. Fran scans a document that is 8.5 in. wide by 11 in. long into her computer. If she scales the length down to 7 in., how wide should the similar document be? **5.4 in.**

Tell whether each transformation is a dilation.

21. 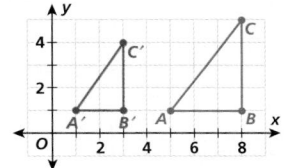 **no** **22.** 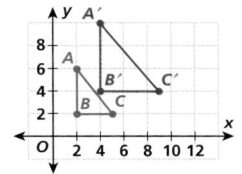 **yes**

23. Wally has an 18 in. model of a 42 ft. dinosaur, *Tyrannosaurus rex*. What scale factor does this represent? **3 in.:7 ft**

24. Margie's school building casts a 12.5 ft shadow at the same time that Margie casts a 2.875 ft shadow. If Margie is 5.75 ft tall, how tall is the school? **25 ft**

25. If a wall in a $\frac{1}{4}$ in. scale drawing is 3 in. tall, how tall is the actual wall? **12 in.**

Chapter Test

Organizer

Objective: Assess students' mastery of concepts and skills in Chapter 5.

PREMIER **Online Edition**

Resources

Assessment Resources

Chapter 5 Tests
• Free Response
  (Levels A, B, C)
• Multiple Choice
  (Levels A, B, C)
• Performance Assessment

IDEA Works! CD-ROM
Modified Chapter 5 Test

Test & Practice Generator
One-Stop Planner®

State Resources

go.hrw.com
State Resources Online
KEYWORD: MT7 Resources

Organizer

Objective: Provide opportunities to learn and practice common test-taking strategies.

 Online Edition

Resources

 State Test Prep **Workbook**

 State Test Prep **CD-ROM**

 State Test Practice **Online**

go.hrw.com
KEYWORD: MT7 TestPrep

 **TEST PREP DOCTOR** This Test Tackler focuses on how short response test items are scored and demonstrates how to write a response worth full credit. Explain that responses to these types of test items are scored and points are awarded based on the completeness and correctness of the response. The scoring guides, or rubrics, are designed so that all test scorers will arrive at the same result for a given student response.

Point out to students that many times, short response test items have several steps. Remind students to answer each part of the test item.

Test Tackler

Short Response: Write Short Responses

To answer a short response test item completely, you must show how you solved the problem and explain your answer. Short response test items are scored using a 2-point scoring rubric. A sample scoring rubric is shown below.

EXAMPLE 1

Short Response A carpenter is pouring a concrete foundation for a garden planter in the shape of a right triangle. The length of one leg of the planter is 18 feet, and the length of the diagonal is 22 feet. What is the length of the other leg of the planter? Round your answer to the nearest tenth. Show all of your work.

Here are examples of how different responses were scored using the scoring rubric shown.

2-point response:

Let s = the length of the other leg.

$18^2 + s^2 = 22^2$ Use the Pythagorean Theorem.

$s^2 = 160$

$\sqrt{s} = \sqrt{160}$ Find the square root.

$s = 12.64911$ Round to the nearest tenth.

$s = 12.6 \text{ ft.}$

The length of the other leg is 12.6 ft.

1-point response:

Let s = the length of the other leg.

$18^2 + s^2 = 22^2$

$324 + s^2 = 484$

$\sqrt{s} = \sqrt{160}$

$s = 13 \text{ ft}$

The length of the other leg is 13 ft.

The student showed all of the work, but there was a minor computation error, which resulted in an incorrect answer.

0-point response:

$s = 12$ *The student's answer is not rounded to the nearest tenth, and there is no explanation.*

Scoring Rubric

2 points: The student demonstrates a thorough understanding of the concept, correctly answers the question, and provides a complete explanation.

1 point: The student correctly answers the question but does not show all work or does not provide an explanation.

1 point: The student makes minor errors, resulting in an incorrect solution, but shows an understanding of the concept through explanation.

0 points: The student gives a response showing no work or giving no explanation, or the student gives no response.

Read each test item, and answer the questions that follow by using the scoring rubric on page 266.

Item A

Dilate the figure by a scale factor of $\frac{1}{4}$ with the origin as the center of dilation. What are the vertices of the image? Show all of your work.

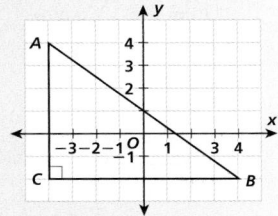

Student's Response

$A'(-1, 1), B'\left(1, -\frac{1}{2}\right), C'\left(-1, -\frac{1}{2}\right)$

1. What score should the student's response receive? Explain your reasoning.

2. What additional information, if any, should the student's answer include in order for the student to receive full credit?

Item B

The ratio of the length of a rectangular garden to its width is 12:5. If the width of the garden is 8 feet, find the area of the garden. Show all of your work.

Student's Response

$\frac{l}{w} = \frac{12}{5}$ The ratio of the length to the width is 12:5.

$\frac{12}{5} = \frac{8}{l}$; $12l = 40$; $l = 3.\overline{3}$ The length is 3.3 ft.

$A = lw$; $A = 3.3 \times 8 = 26.4$

The area is 26.4 ft^2.

3. What score should the student's response receive? Explain your reasoning.

4. What additional information, if any, should the student's answer include in order for the student to receive full credit?

Item C

An office supply store charges $24 for 72 file folders. A student says that the unit price is $3 per folder. What is the student's error? What is the correct unit price? Show all of your work.

Student's Response

The student divided wrong. The student should have divided 24 by 72, not 72 by 24.

5. What score should the student's response receive? Explain your reasoning.

6. What additional information, if any, should the student's answer include in order for the student to receive full credit?

Test Tackler

Possible answers:

1. The response is worth 1 point because the responding student correctly identified the error but did not give the correct unit price. The response is incomplete.

2. To receive full credit, the student should find the dilation of all three coordinate points and show all of the work. The original points of $\triangle ABC$ are $A(-4, 4)$, $B(4, -2)$, and $C(-4, -2)$. The new points are: $A'\left(-4\left(\frac{1}{4}\right), 4\left(\frac{1}{4}\right)\right)$, $B'\left(4\left(\frac{1}{4}\right), -2\left(\frac{1}{4}\right)\right)$, and $C'\left(-4\left(\frac{1}{4}\right), -2\left(\frac{1}{4}\right)\right)$. $A'(-12, 1)$, $B'\left(1, -\frac{1}{2}\right)$, and $C'\left(-1, -\frac{1}{2}\right)$.

3. The response is worth 1 point because the student set up the ratio incorrectly, which resulted in an incorrect measurement for the length. $\frac{12}{5} = \frac{l}{8}$; $5l = 96$; $l = 19.2$ ft

4. To receive full credit, the student would need to fix the error and find the correct solution.

5. The response is worth 0 points because the student gave a response showing no work or explanation.

6. To receive full credit, the student should include the correct unit price and show the solution. $\frac{\$24}{72 \text{ folders}} = \$0.33/\text{folder}$

State Resources

go.hrw.com
State Resources Online
KEYWORD: MT7 Resources

Organizer

Objective: Provide review and practice for Chapters 1–5 and standardized tests.

 Online Edition

Resources

 Assessment Resources
Chapter 5 Cumulative Test

 State Test Prep Workbook

 State Test Prep CD-ROM

 State Test Practice Online

go.hrw.com
KEYWORD: MT7 TestPrep

go.hrw.com
State Test Practice Online
KEYWORD: MT7 TestPrep

Cumulative Assessment, Chapters 1–5
Multiple Choice

Standardized Test Prep

1. Which inequality describes the graph?

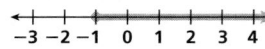

Ⓐ $x < -1$ Ⓒ $x \le -1$
Ⓑ $x > -1$ Ⓓ $x \ge -1$

2. Which value of x is the solution of the equation $-6x = 48$?

Ⓕ $x = -8$ Ⓗ $x = 42$
Ⓖ $x = -6$ Ⓙ $x = 54$

3. Which two numbers both have an absolute value of 6?

Ⓐ 0 and 6   Ⓒ -3 and 3
Ⓑ -6 and 6   Ⓓ 5 and -1

4. What is the next number in this sequence? $-1, -4, -7, -10,$ ▇ ...

Ⓕ 16   Ⓗ -12
Ⓖ 13   Ⓙ -13

5. If a drinking glass holds $\frac{1}{16}$ gallon of water, how many gallons of water are contained in 8 drinking glasses?

Ⓐ $\frac{1}{8}$ gallon   Ⓒ 2 gallons
Ⓑ $\frac{1}{2}$ gallon   Ⓓ 64 gallons

6. A turnstile counted 1040 people who entered a zoo in a 4-hour period. Which proportion can be used to find how many people p entered in an 8-hour period at the same hourly rate?

Ⓕ $\frac{4}{1040} = \frac{p}{8}$ Ⓗ $\frac{4}{p} = \frac{8}{1040}$
Ⓖ $\frac{1040}{4} = \frac{p}{8}$ Ⓙ $\frac{4}{1040} = \frac{12}{p}$

7. Which ratio pairs are NOT in proportion?

Ⓐ $\frac{3}{7}$ and $\frac{9}{21}$ Ⓒ $\frac{3}{8}$ and $\frac{4}{9}$
Ⓑ $\frac{9}{4}$ and $\frac{18}{8}$ Ⓓ $\frac{2}{3}$ and $\frac{10}{15}$

8. Which figure is similar to the figure below?

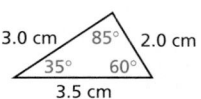

Ⓕ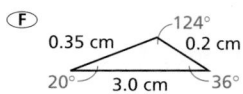

Ⓖ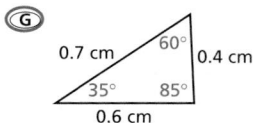

Ⓗ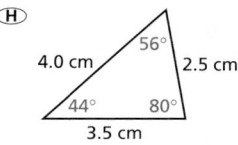

Ⓙ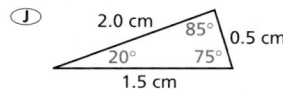

9. Which set of fractions are in order from least to greatest?

Ⓐ $\frac{3}{8}, \frac{1}{4}, \frac{2}{5}, \frac{1}{3}$ Ⓒ $\frac{1}{4}, \frac{1}{3}, \frac{2}{5}, \frac{3}{8}$
Ⓑ $\frac{1}{3}, \frac{1}{4}, \frac{2}{5}, \frac{3}{8}$ Ⓓ $\frac{1}{4}, \frac{1}{3}, \frac{3}{8}, \frac{2}{5}$

TEST PREP DOCTOR +

For Item 8, students may incorrectly choose answer **F** if they do not consider all three sides of the triangle. Remind students that all sides of similar figures must correspond.

For Item 15, remind students that they must do two conversions to solve this problem. They must change centimeters to meters and seconds to minutes.

Answers

17. a. 150; $\frac{5}{7} = \frac{n}{210}$; $\frac{5}{7}(210) = 150 = n$
b. 360; $150 + 210 = 360$

18. a. 12 for $1.25; The unit price, $0.10/pencil, is less than the unit price of the box of 8 pencils, which is $0.11/pencil.
b. $0.34; $\frac{1.25}{12} \times 48 = \$5.00$ and $\frac{0.89}{8} \times 48 = \$5.34$
$5.00 - \$5.34 = \$0.34$

19. See 4-point Response work sample.

State Resources

go.hrw.com
State Resources Online
KEYWORD: MT7 Resources

It is helpful to draw or redraw a figure. Answers to geometry problems may become clearer as you redraw the figure.

10. The area of a square is 85 square feet. Which measurement best approximates a side length?

Ⓕ 8.8 ft   Ⓗ 9.2 ft

Ⓖ 9 ft   Ⓙ 9.9 ft

Gridded Response

11. A football team earns a first down when the team has moved the ball 10 yards forward. If a team has moved the ball forward 15 feet, what is the least number of yards the team needs to earn a first down? **5**

12. A ballet class has a rule that all productions must have a ratio of 4 boys for every 5 girls. If there are 12 boys in a production, how many girls can be in the same production? **15**

13. What is the length, in feet, of the base of the sail, x?

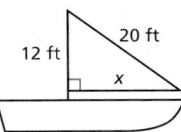

14. A 60-yard piece of string is divided into three pieces. The first piece is twice the length of the second piece, and the third piece is three times the length of the second piece. What is the length in yards of the longest piece? **16**

15. If a snail moves 5 centimeters in 10 seconds, how fast in meters per minute can a snail move? **1/12**

16. Three friends split the cost of a birthday present and a meal for another friend. The present cost $56.75, and the meal cost $23.65. Find the amount that each friend paid. **$26.80**

Short Response

17. At the student store, the ratio of notebooks sold to three-ring binders sold is 5 to 7.

a. At this rate, how many notebooks can you predict will be sold if 210 three-ring binders are sold? Show your work.

b. At the same rate, predict how many total notebooks and three-ring binders will be sold. Explain your reasoning.

18. While shopping for school supplies Sara finds boxes of pencils in two sizes. One box has 8 pencils for $0.89, and the other box has 12 pencils for $1.25.

a. Which box is the better bargain? Why? Round your answer to the nearest cent.

b. How much would it save to buy 48 pencils at the better rate? Show your work.

Extended Response

19. To build an accurate model of the solar system, choose a diameter for the model of the Sun. Then all distances and sizes of the planets can be calculated proportionally using the table below.

a. What is the diameter of Pluto in the model?

b. What is Pluto's distance from the Sun in the model?

c. What would Pluto's distance from the Sun be in the model if the Sun's diameter were changed to 2 ft?

	Sun	Mars	Jupiter	Pluto
Diameter (mi)	864,000	4200	88,640	1410
Distance from Sun (million mi)		141	483	3670

Standardized Test Prep

Short Response Rubric

Items 17–18

2 Points = The student's answer is an accurate and complete execution of the task or tasks.

1 Point = The student's answer contains attributes of an appropriate response but is flawed.

0 Points = The student's answer contains no attributes of an appropriate response.

Extended Response Rubric

Item 19

4 Points = The student demonstrates a thorough understanding of all concepts and shows all work correctly.

3 Points = The student demonstrates a basic understanding of all concepts, but the work shows some flaws reflecting inattentive execution of mathematical procedures or some misunderstanding of the underlying mathematics.

2 Points = The student demonstrates only a partial understanding of the concepts or procedures embodied in the tasks. The approach may be correct, but the work shows a misunderstanding of one or more important concepts.

1 Point = The student demonstrates a very limited understanding of the concepts or procedures embodied in the tasks. The response may show some understanding but exhibits many flaws or is incomplete.

0 Points = The student provides no response at all, or a completely incorrect or uninterpretable response.

Student Work Samples for Item 19

4-Point Response

a. $\frac{1}{864,000} = \frac{x}{1410}$

$864,000 x = 1410$

$x = 0.0016319 \approx 0.0016$ in.

b. $(0.0016)(3670) = 5.87 \approx 6$ in.

c. $\frac{2}{864,000} = \frac{x}{1410}$

$864,000 = 2820$

$x = 0.0032639 \approx 0.0032$

$(0.0032)(3670) = 11.744 \approx 12$ ft

In part **b,** the student correctly used the calculated answer from part **a** and the correct information in the table to calculate the answer.

3-Point Response

a. $\frac{1}{864,000} = \frac{x}{1410}$

$864,000 x = 1410$

$x = 0.0016319$

$x = 0.0016$ in.

b. $\frac{1}{864,000} = \frac{x}{3670}$

$864,000 x = 3670$

$x = 0.0042476$

$x = 0.0042$ in.

c. $\frac{2}{864,000} = \frac{x}{1410}$

$864,000 x = 2820$

$x = 0.0032639 = 0.0032$ in.

The student correctly set up and solved a proportion in part **a,** but incorrectly used a proportion to solve part **b.**

2-Point Response

a. $\frac{1}{864,000} = \frac{x}{1410}$

$864,000 x = 1410$

$x = 0.0016319 = 0.0016$ in

b.

c. $\frac{2}{864,000} = \frac{x}{1410}$

$864,000 x = 2820$

$x = 0.0032639 = 0.0032$

The student correctly set up and solved a proportion in part **a,** but did not use the given information to correctly answer part **b** and **c.**

CHAPTER
6

Percents

Section 6A		Section 6B	
Proportions and Percents		**Applying Percents**	
6-1	Relating Decimals, Fractions, and Percents	6-5	Percent Increase and Decrease
6-2	Estimate with Percents	6-6	Applications of Percents
6-3	Finding Percents	6-7	Simple Interest
6-4	Finding a Number When the Percent is Known	6-7	**Technology Lab** Compute Compound Interest

Pacing Guide for 45-Minute Classes

Chapter 6

Countdown to Testing Weeks ⑩, ⑪

DAY 1	DAY 2	DAY 3	DAY 4	DAY 5
6-1 Lesson	6-2 Lesson	6-3 Lesson	6-4 Lesson	Ready to Go On? Focus on Problem Solving 6-5 Lesson
DAY 6	**DAY 7**	**DAY 8**	**DAY 9**	**DAY 10**
6-5 Lesson 6-6 Lesson	6-6 Lesson	6-7 Lesson	6-7 Technology Lab Ready to Go On? Multi-Step Test Prep	Chapter 6 Review
DAY 11				
Chapter 6 Test				

Pacing Guide for 90-Minute Classes

Chapter 6

DAY 1	DAY 2	DAY 3	DAY 4	DAY 5
6-1 Lesson 6-2 Lesson	6-3 Lesson 6-4 Lesson	Ready to Go On? Focus on Problem Solving 6-5 Lesson 6-6 Lesson	6-6 Lesson 6-7 Lesson	6-7 Technology Lab Ready to Go On? Multi-Step Test Prep Chapter 6 Review
DAY 6				
Chapter 6 Test				

ONGOING ASSESSMENT and INTERVENTION

DIAGNOSE	PRESCRIBE

Assess Prior Knowledge

Before Chapter 6

Diagnose readiness for the chapter.

Are You Ready? SE p. 271

Prescribe intervention.

Are You Ready? Intervention Skills 26, 32, 45, 65

Formative Assessment

Before Every Lesson

Diagnose readiness for the lesson.

Warm Up TE, every lesson

Prescribe intervention.

Skills Bank SE pp. 820–834
Reteach CRB, Chapters 1–6

During Every Lesson

Diagnose understanding of lesson concepts.

Think and Discuss SE, every lesson
Write About It SE, lesson exercises
Journal TE, lesson exercises

Prescribe intervention.

Questioning Strategies Chapter 6
Reading Strategies CRB, every lesson
Success for ELL pp. 79–92

After Every Lesson

Diagnose mastery of lesson concepts.

Lesson Quiz TE, every lesson
Test Prep SE, every lesson
Test and Practice Generator

Prescribe intervention.

Reteach CRB, every lesson
Problem Solving CRB, every lesson
Test Prep Doctor TE, lesson exercises
Homework Help Online

Before Chapter 6 Testing

Diagnose mastery of concepts in the chapter.

Ready to Go On? SE pp. 292, 308
Focus on Problem Solving SE p. 293
Multi-Step Test Prep SE p. 309
Section Quizzes AR pp. 105–106
Test and Practice Generator

Prescribe intervention.

Ready to Go On? Intervention Chapter 6
Scaffolding Questions TE p. 309

Before High Stakes Testing

Diagnose mastery of benchmark concepts.

Standardized Test Prep SE pp. 316–317
State Test Prep CD-ROM

Prescribe intervention.

State Test Prep Workbook

Summative Assessment

After Chapter 6

Check mastery of chapter concepts.

Multiple-Choice Tests (Forms A, B, C)
Free-Response Tests (Forms A, B, C)
Performance Assessment AR pp. 107–120
Test and Practice Generator

Check mastery of benchmark concepts.

AYP State Tests

Prescribe intervention.

Reteach CRB, every lesson
Lesson Tutorial Videos Chapter 6

Prescribe intervention.

State Test Prep Workbook

KEY: **SE** = *Student Edition*   **TE** = *Teacher's Edition*   **CRB** = *Chapter Resource Book*   **AR** = *Assessment Resources*   Available on CD-ROM   Available online   **270B**

Supporting the Teacher

Chapter 6 Resource Book

Practice A, B, C
pp. 3–5, 11–13, 20–22, 29–31, 37–39, 46–48, 55–57

Reading Strategies ELL
pp. 9, 18, 27, 35, 44, 53, 62

Puzzles, Twisters, and Teasers
pp. 10, 19, 28, 36, 45, 54, 63

Reteach
pp. 6, 14–15, 23–24, 32, 40–41, 49–50, 58–59

Problem Solving
pp. 8, 17, 26, 34, 43, 52, 61

Challenge
pp. 7, 16, 25, 33, 42, 51, 60

Parent Letter pp. 1–2

Transparencies

Lesson Transparencies, Volume 1 .... Chapter 6
  • Teaching Tools
  • Warm Ups
  • Problem of the Day
  • Teaching Transparencies
  • Lesson Quizzes

Know-It Notebook .... Chapter 6
  • Additional Examples   • Chapter Review
  • Vocabulary   • Big Ideas

Alternate Openers: Explorations .... pp. 40–46

Countdown to Testing .... pp. 19–22

Teacher Tools

Power Presentations®
Complete PowerPoint® presentations for Chapter 6 lessons

Lesson Tutorial Videos® SPANISH
Holt authors Ed Burger and Freddie Renfro present tutorials to support the Chapter 6 lessons.

One-Stop Planner® SPANISH
Easy access to all Chapter 6 resources and assessments, as well as software for lesson planning, test generation, and puzzle creation

IDEA Works!®
Key Chapter 6 resources and assessments modified to address special learning needs

Lesson Plans .... pp. 40–46

Questioning Strategies .... Chapter 6

Solutions Key .... Chapter 6

Interdisciplinary Posters and Worksheets .... Chapter 6

TechKeys   **Lab Resources**

Project Teacher Support   **Parent Resources**

Workbooks

Homework and Practice Workbook SPANISH
  Teacher's Guide .... pp. 20–23

Know-It Notebook
  Teacher's Guide .... Chapter 6

Problem Solving Workbook SPANISH
  Teacher's Guide .... pp. 20–23

State Test Prep Workbook
  Teacher's Guide

Technology Highlights for the Teacher

Power Presentations
Dynamic presentations to engage students. Complete PowerPoint® presentations for every lesson in Chapter 6.

2-1 Solving One-Step Equations

Isolate a variable by using inverse operations which "undo" operations on the variable.

An equation is like a balanced scale. To keep the balance, perform the same operation on both sides.

Inverse Operations

Operation	Inverse Operation
Addition	Subtraction
Subtraction	Addition

One-Stop Planner SPANISH
Easy access to Chapter 6 resources and assessments. Includes lesson-planning, test-generation, and puzzle-creation software.

Premier Online Edition SPANISH
Chapter 6 includes Tutorial Videos, Lesson Activities, Lesson Quizzes, Homework Help, and Chapter Project.

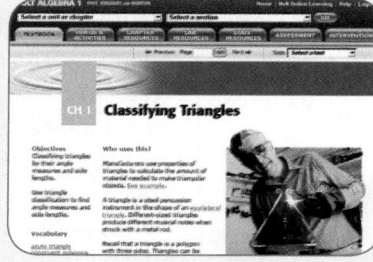

KEY: **SE** = *Student Edition*   **TE** = *Teacher's Edition*   ELL English Language Learners   SPANISH Spanish version available   Available on CD-ROM    Available online

Reaching All Learners

Resources for All Learners

Hands-On Lab Activities.................................Chapter 6

Technology Lab Activities.............................Chapter 6

Homework and Practice Workbook **SPANISH** ....pp. 40–46

Know-It Notebook......................................Chapter 6

Problem Solving Workbook **SPANISH** ....pp. 40–46

DEVELOPING LEARNERS

Practice A...................................CRB, every lesson

Reteach......................................CRB, every lesson

Inclusion.......................................TE pp. 279, 284

Questioning Strategies..........................Chapter 6

Modified Chapter 6 Resources ....*IDEA Works!*

Homework Help Online

ON-LEVEL LEARNERS

Practice B...................................CRB, every lesson

Puzzles, Twisters, and Teasers...............CRB, every lesson

Multiple Representations...........................TE p. 289

Cognitive Strategies................................TE p. 303

ADVANCED LEARNERS

Practice C...................................CRB, every lesson

Challenge....................................CRB, every lesson

Extension..........................TE pp. 273, 309, 310, 311

Critical Thinking...............................TE pp. 289, 299

English Language Learners

Are You Ready? Vocabulary.........................SE p. 271

Vocabulary Connections............................SE p. 272

Lesson Vocabulary............................SE, every lesson

Vocabulary Review.................................SE p. 312

English Language Learners..............TE pp. 273, 275, 284, 295, 319

Reading Strategies..........................CRB, every lesson

Success for English Language Learners.................pp. 79–92

Multilingual Glossary

Reaching All Learners Through...

Inclusion......................................TE pp. 279, 284

Kinesthetic Experience..............................TE p. 275

Multiple Representations...........................TE p. 289

Cooperative Learning...............................TE p. 303

Critical Thinking................................TE pp. 289, 299

Test Prep Doctor...............TE pp. 277, 282, 287, 291, 297, 301, 305, 316

Common Error Alerts..............TE pp. 279, 289, 299, 303

Scaffolding Questions...............................TE p. 309

Technology Highlights for Reaching All Learners

Lesson Tutorial Videos **SPANISH**

Starring Holt authors Ed Burger and Freddie Renfro! Live tutorials to support every lesson in Chapter 6.

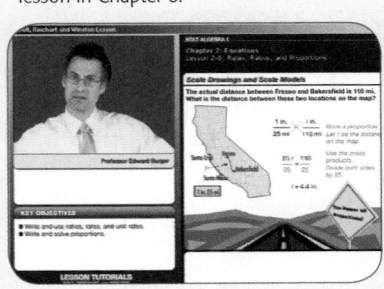

Multilingual Glossary

Searchable glossary includes definitions in English, Spanish, Vietnamese, Chinese, Hmong, Korean, and 4 other languages.

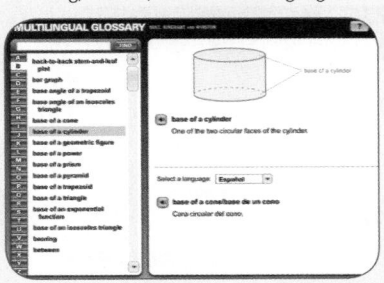

Online Interactivities

Interactive tutorials provide visually engaging alternative opportunities to learn concepts and master skills.

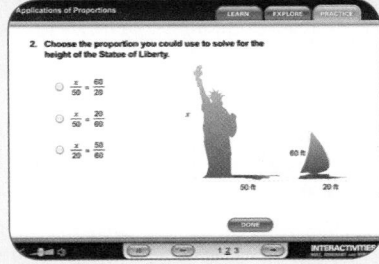

KEY: **SE** = *Student Edition* **TE** = *Teacher's Edition* **CRB** = *Chapter Resource Book* **SPANISH** Spanish version available  Available on CD-ROM   Available online

CHAPTER **6**

Ongoing Assessment

Assessing Prior Knowledge

Determine whether students have the prerequisite concepts and skills for success in Chapter 6.

Are You Ready? SPANISH .... SE p. 271
Warm Up .... TE, every lesson

Test Preparation

Provide review and practice for Chapter 6 and standardized tests.

Multi-Step Test Prep .... SE p. 309
Study Guide: Review .... SE pp. 312–314
Standardized Test Prep .... SE pp. 316–317
Countdown to Testing Transparencies ....pp. 19–22
State Test Prep Workbook
State Test Prep CD-ROM
IDEA Works!

Alternative Assessment

Assess students' understanding of Chapter 6 concepts and combined problem-solving skills.

Chapter 6 Project .... SE p. 270
Performance Assessment SPANISH .... AR pp. 119–120
Portfolio Assessment SPANISH .... AR p. xxxiv

Daily Assessment

Provide formative assessment for each day of Chapter 6.

Questioning Strategies .... Chapter 6
Think and Discuss .... SE, every lesson
Write About It .... SE, lesson exercises
Journal .... TE, lesson exercises
Lesson Quiz .... TE, every lesson
Modified Lesson Quizzes .... IDEA Works!

Weekly Assessment

Provide formative assessment for each week of Chapter 6.

Focus on Problem Solving .... SE p. 293
Multi-Step Test Prep .... SE p. 309
Ready to Go On? SPANISH .... SE pp. 292, 308
Cumulative Assessment .... SE pp. 316–317
Test and Practice Generator SPANISH ...One-Stop Planner

Formal Assessment

Provide summative assessment of Chapter 6 mastery.

Section Quizzes SPANISH .... AR pp. 105–106
Chapter 6 Test .... SE p. 315
Chapter Test (Levels A, B, C) SPANISH .... AR pp. 107–118
• Multiple-Choice • Free-Response
Cumulative Test SPANISH .... AR pp. 121–124
Test and Practice Generator SPANISH ...One-Stop Planner
Modified Chapter 6 Test .... IDEA Works!

Technology Highlights for the Teacher

Are You Ready? SPANISH
Automatically assess readiness and prescribe intervention for Chapter 6 prerequisite skills.

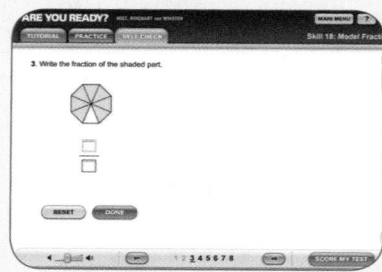

Ready to Go On? SPANISH
Automatically assess understanding of and prescribe intervention for Sections 6A and 6B.

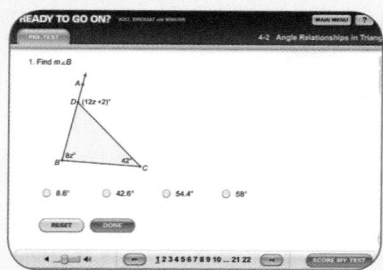

Test and Practice Generator SPANISH
Use Chapter 6 problem banks to create assessments and worksheets to print out or deliver online. Includes dynamic problems.

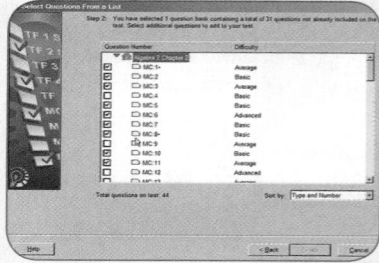

KEY: **SE** = Student Edition   **TE** = Teacher's Edition   **AR** = Assessment Resources   SPANISH Spanish version available   Available on CD-ROM   Available online

Formal Assessment

Three levels (A, B, C) of multiple-choice and free-response chapter tests are available in the *Assessment Resources.*

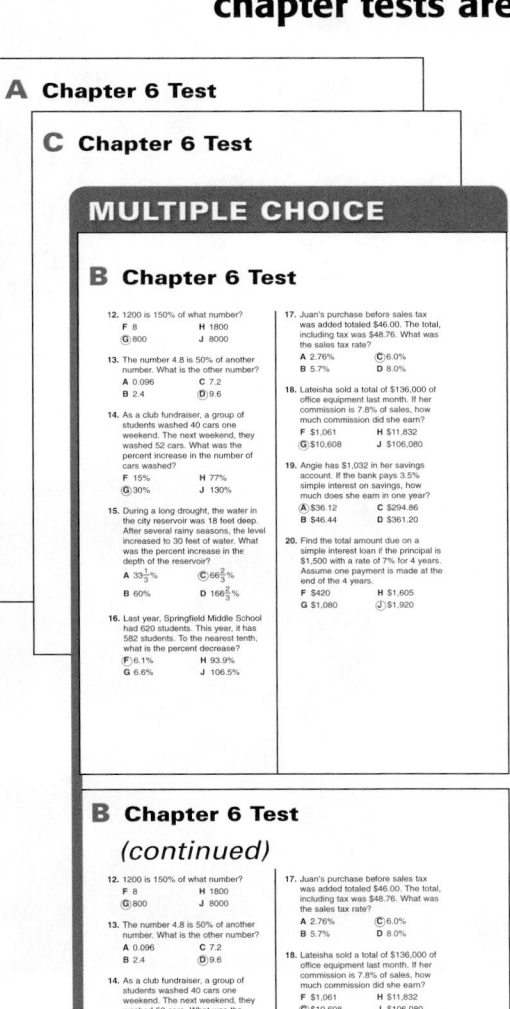

A Chapter 6 Test

C Chapter 6 Test

MULTIPLE CHOICE

B Chapter 6 Test

12. 1200 is 150% of what number?
F 8   H 1800
G 800   J 8000

13. The number 4.8 is 50% of another number. What is the other number?
A 0.096   C 7.2
B 2.4   D 9.6

14. As a club fundraiser, a group of students washed 40 cars one weekend. The next weekend, they washed 52 cars. What was the percent increase in the number of cars washed?
F 15%   H 77%
G 30%   J 130%

15. During a long drought, the water in the city reservoir was 18 feet deep. After several rainy seasons, the level increased to 30 feet of water. What was the percent increase in the depth of the reservoir?
A $33\frac{1}{3}$%   C $66\frac{2}{3}$%
B 60%   D $166\frac{2}{3}$%

16. Last year, Springfield Middle School had 620 students. This year, it has 582 students. To the nearest tenth, what is the percent decrease?
F 6.1%   H 93.9%
G 6.6%   J 106.5%

17. Juan's purchase before sales tax was added totaled $46.00. The total, including tax was $48.76. What was the sales tax rate?
A 2.76%   C 6.0%
B 5.7%   D 8.0%

18. Lateisha sold a total of $136,000 of office equipment last month. If her commission is 7.8% of sales, how much commission did she earn?
F $1,061   H $11,832
G $10,608   J $106,080

19. Angie has $1,032 in her savings account. If the bank pays 3.5% simple interest on savings, how much does she earn in one year?
A $36.12   C $294.86
B $46.44   D $361.20

20. Find the total amount due on a simple interest loan if the principal is $1,500 with a rate of 7% for 4 years. Assume one payment is made at the end of the 4 years.
F $420   H $1,605
G $1,080   J $1,920

B Chapter 6 Test
(continued)

12. 1200 is 150% of what number?
F 8   H 1800
G 800   J 8000

13. The number 4.8 is 50% of another number. What is the other number?
A 0.096   C 7.2
B 2.4   D 9.6

14. As a club fundraiser, a group of students washed 40 cars one weekend. The next weekend, they washed 52 cars. What was the percent increase in the number of cars washed?
F 15%   H 77%
G 30%   J 130%

15. During a long drought, the water in the city reservoir was 18 feet deep. After several rainy seasons, the level increased to 30 feet of water. What was the percent increase in the depth of the reservoir?
A $33\frac{1}{3}$%   C $66\frac{2}{3}$%
B 60%   D $166\frac{2}{3}$%

16. Last year, Springfield Middle School had 620 students. This year, it has 582 students. To the nearest tenth, what is the percent decrease?
F 6.1%   H 93.9%
G 6.6%   J 106.5%

17. Juan's purchase before sales tax was added totaled $46.00. The total, including tax was $48.76. What was the sales tax rate?
A 2.76%   C 6.0%
B 5.7%   D 8.0%

18. Lateisha sold a total of $136,000 of office equipment last month. If her commission is 7.8% of sales, how much commission did she earn?
F $1,061   H $11,832
G $10,608   J $106,080

19. Angie has $1,032 in her savings account. If the bank pays 3.5% simple interest on savings, how much does she earn in one year?
A $36.12   C $294.86
B $46.44   D $361.20

20. Find the total amount due on a simple interest loan if the principal is $1,500 with a rate of 7% for 4 years. Assume one payment is made at the end of the 4 years.
F $420   H $1,605
G $1,080   J $1,920

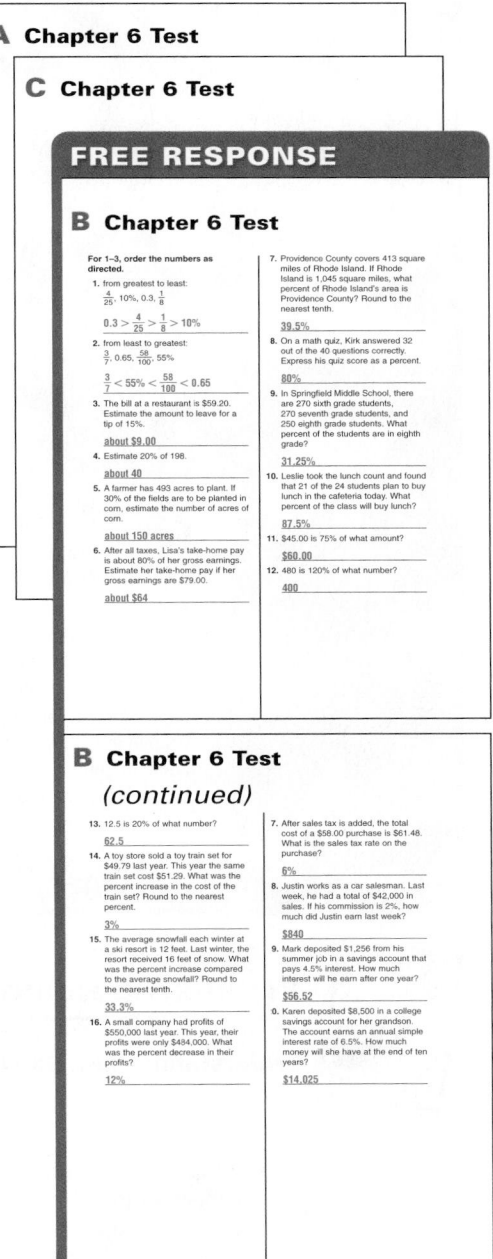

A Chapter 6 Test

C Chapter 6 Test

FREE RESPONSE

B Chapter 6 Test

For 1–3, order the numbers as directed.

1. from greatest to least:
$\frac{4}{25}$, 10%, 0.3, $\frac{1}{8}$
$0.3 > \frac{4}{25} > \frac{1}{8} > 10\%$

2. from least to greatest:
$\frac{3}{7}$, 0.65, $\frac{58}{100}$, 55%
$\frac{3}{7} < 55\% < \frac{58}{100} < 0.65$

3. The bill at a restaurant is $59.20. Estimate the amount to leave for a tip of 15%.
about $9.00

4. Estimate 20% of 198.
about 40

5. A farmer has 493 acres to plant. If 30% of the fields are to be planted in corn, estimate the number of acres of corn.
about 150 acres

6. After all taxes, Lisa's take-home pay is about 80% of her gross earnings. Estimate her take-home pay if her gross earnings are $79.00.
about $64

7. Providence County covers 413 square miles of Rhode Island. If Rhode Island is 1,045 square miles, what percent of Rhode Island's area is Providence County? Round to the nearest tenth.
39.5%

8. On a math quiz, Kirk answered 32 out of the 40 questions correctly. Express his quiz score as a percent.
80%

9. In Springfield Middle School, there are 270 sixth grade students, 270 seventh grade students, and 250 eighth grade students. What percent of the students are in eighth grade?
31.25%

10. Leslie took the lunch count and found that 21 of the 24 students plan to buy lunch in the cafeteria today. What percent of the class will buy lunch?
87.5%

11. $45.00 is 75% of what amount?
$60.00

12. 480 is 120% of what number?
400

B Chapter 6 Test
(continued)

13. 12.5 is 20% of what number?
62.5

14. A toy store sold a toy train set for $49.79 last year. This year the same train set cost $51.29. What was the percent increase in the cost of the train set? Round to the nearest percent.
3%

15. The average snowfall each winter at a ski resort is 12 feet. Last winter, the resort received 16 feet of snow. What was the percent increase compared to the average snowfall? Round to the nearest tenth.
33.3%

16. A small company had profits of $550,000 last year. This year, their profits were only $484,000. What was the percent decrease in their profits?
12%

7. After sales tax is added, the total cost of a $58.00 purchase is $61.48. What is the sales tax rate on the purchase?
6%

8. Justin works as a car salesman. Last week, he had a total of $42,000 in sales. If his commission is 2%, how much did Justin earn last week?
$840

9. Mark deposited $1,256 from his summer job in a savings account that pays 4.5% interest. How much interest will he earn after one year?
$56.52

0. Karen deposited $8,500 in a college savings account for her grandson. The account earns an annual simple interest rate of 6.5%. How much money will she have at the end of ten years?
$14,025

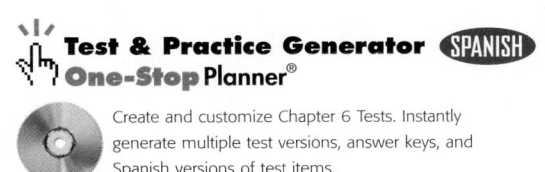

CHAPTER
6
Percents

Why Learn This?

Tell students that statistics are used to compare players. For example, in order to determine the hitter with the most frequent home runs, statisticians compare the at bats/home run statistic for each player. These statistics help statisticians find the percent of time that a player who comes up to bat will hit a home run. Point out to students that the player with the best at bats/home run statistic may not be the player with the most home runs.

Using Data

To begin the study of this chapter, using the table have students:

- Order the players from fewest to most home runs. Rodriguez, Griffey, Sosa, Bonds

- Predict the number of At Bats each player would need to hit 73 home runs.

  Bonds: 73(12.9) ≈ 942

  Sosa: 73(14.0) = 1022

  Griffey: 73(14.7) ≈ 1073

  Rodriguez: 73(14.7) ≈ 1073

MULTI-STEP TEST PREP On page 309, students use percents to calculate the cost of their purchases for a camping trip.

6A	Proportions and Percents
6-1	Relating Decimals, Fractions, and Percents
6-2	Estimate with Percents
6-3	Finding Percents
6-4	Finding a Number When the Percent Is Known
6B	Applying Percents
6-5	Percent Increase and Decrease
6-6	Applications of Percents
6-7	Simple Interest
LAB	Compute Compound Interest

MULTI-STEP TEST PREP

go.hrw.com
Chapter Project Online
KEYWORD: MT7 Ch6

Player	Age	At Bats	Home Runs	At Bats/Home Runs
Barry Bonds	40	9098	703	12.9
Sammy Sosa	36	8021	574	14.0
Ken Griffey Jr.	35	7376	501	14.7
Alex Rodriguez	29	5590	381	14.7

Career *Sports Statistician*

Statisticians are mathematicians who work with data, creating statistics, graphs, and tables that describe and explain the real world. Sports statisticians combine their love of sports with their ability to use mathematics.

Statistics not only explain what has happened, but can help you predict what may happen in the future. The table describes the home run hitting of some Major League baseball players as of the 2004 season.

Problem Solving Project

Understand, Plan, Solve, and Look Back

Have students:

- Complete the Home Run Derby worksheet to learn more about working with percents.

- Estimate the number of home runs each player would hit if they each had 500 at bats in a given season.

- Research the number of home runs hit by their favorite players. What percent of their favorite players' total hits were home runs? What other kinds of hits did they have? Create a circle graph to show the results.

Social Studies and Sports Connection

Project Resources

All project resources for teachers and students are provided online.

Materials:

- Home Run Derby worksheet

go.hrw.com
Project Teacher Support
KEYWORD: MT7 PSProject6

ARE YOU READY?

✓ Vocabulary

Choose the best term from the list to complete each sentence.

1. A(n) __?__ is a comparison of two quantities by division. ratio

2. Ratios that make the same comparison are __?__. equivalent ratios

3. Two ratios that are equivalent are in __?__. proportion

4. To solve a proportion, you can __?__. cross multiply

cross multiply

equivalent ratios

proportion

ratio

Complete these exercises to review skills you will need for this chapter.

✓ Write Fractions as Decimals

Write each fraction as a decimal.

5. $\frac{3}{4}$ **0.75** 6. $\frac{5}{8}$ **0.625** 7. $\frac{2}{5}$ **0.4** 8. $\frac{2}{3}$ **$0.\overline{6}$**

✓ Write Decimals as Fractions

Write each decimal as a fraction in simplest form.

9. 0.7 $\frac{7}{10}$ 10. 0.6 $\frac{3}{5}$ 11. 0.25 $\frac{1}{4}$ 12. 0.375 $\frac{3}{8}$

13. 0.2 $\frac{1}{5}$ 14. 0.9 $\frac{9}{10}$ 15. 0.86 $\frac{43}{50}$ 16. 0.99 $\frac{99}{100}$

✓ Solve Proportions

Solve each proportion.

17. $\frac{x}{3} = \frac{9}{27}$ $x = 1$ 18. $\frac{7}{8} = \frac{h}{4}$ $h = 3.5$ 19. $\frac{9}{n} = \frac{2}{3}$ $n = 13.5$

20. $\frac{3}{8} = \frac{12}{t}$ $t = 32$ 21. $\frac{4}{5} = \frac{28}{z}$ $z = 35$ 22. $\frac{100}{p} = \frac{90}{45}$ $p = 50$

✓ Multiply with Fractions and Decimals

Multiply.

23. $\frac{12}{13} \times 8$ $\frac{96}{13}$

24. $\begin{array}{r} 18 \\ \times\ 0.45 \end{array}$ **8.1**

25. $20 \times \frac{9}{10}$ **18**

26. $\begin{array}{r} 2.75 \\ \times\ \ 11 \end{array}$ **30.25**

27. $\frac{1}{5} \times 12$ $\frac{12}{5}$

28. $\begin{array}{r} 6 \\ \times\ 0.08 \end{array}$ **0.48**

29. $13 \times \frac{25}{26}$ $\frac{25}{2}$

30. $\begin{array}{r} 15.32 \\ \times\ \ \ 9 \end{array}$ **137.88**

31. $\frac{2}{9} \times 78$ $\frac{52}{3}$

ARE YOU READY?

Organizer

Objective: Assess students' understanding of prerequisite skills.

Prerequisite Skills

Write Fractions as Decimals

Write Decimals as Fractions

Solve Proportions

Multiply with Fractions and Decimals

Assessing Prior Knowledge

INTERVENTION

Diagnose and Prescribe

Use this page to determine whether intervention is necessary or whether enrichment is appropriate.

Resources

 Are You Ready? Intervention and Enrichment Worksheets

 Are You Ready? CD-ROM

🪐 **Are You Ready? Online**

 **my.hrw.com**

ARE YOU READY?
Diagnose and Prescribe

NO INTERVENE

YES ENRICH

✓ Prerequisite Skill	📜 Worksheets	💿 CD-ROM	🪐 Online
ARE YOU READY? Intervention, Chapter 6			
✓ Write Fractions as Decimals	Skill 26	Activity 26	Diagnose and Prescribe Online
✓ Write Decimals as Fractions	Skill 32	Activity 32	
✓ Solve Proportions	Skill 65	Activity 65	
✓ Multiply with Fractions and Decimals	Skill 45	Activity 45	

ARE YOU READY? Enrichment, Chapter 6
📜 Worksheets
💿 CD-ROM
🪐 Online

Organizer

Objective: Help students organize the new concepts they will learn in Chapter 6.

 Online Edition
Multilingual Glossary

Resources

PuzzlePro®
One-Stop Planner®

 Multilingual Glossary Online

go.hrw.com
KEYWORD: MT7 Glossary

Possible answers to Vocabulary Connections

1. The original amount of money from which interest is calculated

2. Money received with making a sale

3. One hundredth of a whole

Study Guide: Preview

Where You've Been

Previously, you

- compared and ordered integers and positive rational numbers.

- found solutions to application problems involving proportional relationships.

In This Chapter

You will study

- comparing and ordering rational numbers, including integers, percents, and positive and negative fractions and decimals.

- estimating and solving application problems involving percents.

Where You're Going

You can use the skills learned in this chapter

- to estimate tips.

- to find sales tax.

- to calculate discounts or markups.

- to find the amount of interest earned over a given time.

Key Vocabulary/Vocabulario

commission	comisión
compatible numbers	números compatibles
estimate	estimación
interest	interés
percent	por ciento
percent decrease	porcentaje de disminución
percent increase	porcentaje de aumento
principal	capital
sales tax	impuesto sobre la venta
simple interest	interés simple

Vocabulary Connections

To become familiar with some of the vocabulary terms in the chapter, consider the following. You may refer to the chapter, the glossary, or a dictionary if you like.

1. The word *principal* means "first." What do you suppose **principal** means when referring to interest?

2. The word **commission** has the Latin prefix *com-*, which means "with," and the Latin root *mis,* which means "send." What do you think these Latin parts mean together when referring to money?

3. The word *percent* contains the root word *cent,* which means "one hundred." What do you think a **percent** is?

 **Reading** and **Writing Math**

Reading Strategy: Read Problems for Understanding

When solving a word problem, first read the problem to identify exactly what the problems asks you to do. Then read the problem again, slowly and carefully, to break the problem into parts. Highlight or underline the key information. Then make a plan to solve the problem.

From Lesson 5-5

15. **Art** Helen is copying a printed reproduction of the *Mona Lisa*. The print is 24 in. wide and 36 in. tall. If Helen's canvas is 12 in. wide, how tall should her canvas be?

> Slowly read the exercise again.

Step 1	Identify exactly what the problem asks you to do.	• Find the height of the canvas Helen should use.
Step 2	Break the problem into parts. Highlight or underline the key information.	• The print is **24 in. wide** and **36 in. tall**. • The canvas is **12 in. wide** • The **height** of the canvas is **unknown**. • The print and the copy are **similar rectangles**.
Step 3	Make a plan to solve the problem.	• Set up a proportion using the corresponding sides of the similar rectangles. • Find the cross products, and solve for *x*. • Check the answer by making sure the cross products are equal.

 **Try This**

For the problem below,
   a. identify exactly what the problem asks you to do.
   b. break the problem into parts. Highlight or underline the key information.
   c. Make a plan to solve the problem.

1. An 8-pound weight is positioned 2 feet from a fulcrum. Another weight is placed 12 feet from the fulcrum on the opposite end. For the scale to balance, how much should this second weight weigh?

Organizer

Objective: Help students apply strategies to understand and retain key concepts.

 Online Edition

Resources

 Chapter 6 Resource Book
  Reading Strategies

ENGLISH
LANGUAGE
LEARNERS

Reading Strategy: Read Problems for Understanding

Discuss Sometimes word problems can be intimidating. Suggest that students take their time and read through a word problem more than once before trying to solve it.

Remind students to look for information other than numbers, such as words and phrases that can give them a clue about which math operations to use.

Extend As you go through examples that are word problems in the Chapter 6 lessons, ask students to use the strategies presented on this page.

Choose at least one word problem from each lesson. Ask students to highlight the key information, break the problem into parts, and explain their plan to solve it.

Answers to *Try This*

1. a. Find how much weight is needed to balance a scale.

   b. An 8-pound weight is 2 feet from a fulcrum. On the opposite side, an unknown weight is placed 12 feet from the fulcrum. Find the weight needed to balance the scale.

   c. For the scale to balance, $\frac{\text{mass 1}}{\text{length 2}} = \frac{\text{mass 2}}{\text{length 1}}$. Set up the proportion. Find the cross products, and solve for the unknown. Check the answer by making sure the cross products are equal.

Proportions and Percents

One-Minute Section Planner

Lesson	Materials	MiC and Lab Resources
Lesson 6-1 Relating Decimals, Fractions, and Percents • Relate decimals, fractions, and percents. ☑ SAT-10 ☑ ITBS ☑ CTBS ☑ NAEP	Media advertisements with percents, index cards	**MiC:** *It's All the Same* pp. 9–17 **MiC:** *Great Predictions* All sections *Hands-On Lab Activities* 6-1
Lesson 6-2 Problem Solving Skill: Estimate with Percents • Estimate with percents. ☐ SAT-10 ☑ ITBS ☑ CTBS ☑ NAEP	Calculators	
Lesson 6-3 Finding Percents • Find percents. ☐ SAT-10 ☑ ITBS ☑ CTBS ☑ NAEP	Calculators, index cards	**MiC:** *Great Predictions* pp. 4–10, 12–19 *Hands-On Lab Activities* 6-3 *Technology Lab Activities* 6-3
Lesson 6-4 Finding a Number When the Percent is Known • Find a number when the percent is known. ☐ SAT-10 ☑ ITBS ☑ CTBS ☑ NAEP		**MiC:** *Great Predictions* pp. 32–37

MK = *Manipulatives Kit*

Mathematics in Context

The units *It's All the Same* and *Great Predictions* from the *Mathematics in Context* © 2006 series can be used with Section 6A. See Section Planner above for suggestions for integrating *MiC* with *Holt Mathematics*.

Section Overview

Decimals, Fractions, and Percents

Lessons 6-1, 6-2

Why? Any rational number can be represented by a decimal, a fraction, or a percent.

A **percent** is a ratio that compares a number to 100.

> To write a fraction as a decimal, divide the numerator by the denominator.
> $$\frac{1}{8} = 1 \div 8 = 0.125$$

> To write a decimal as a percent, multiply by 100 and insert the percent symbol, which means "divided by 100."
> $$0.125 \cdot 100 = 12.5\%$$

> Common percents and their equivalent fractions:
> $$10\% = \frac{1}{10}$$
> $$12.5\% = \frac{1}{8}$$
> $$16\frac{2}{3}\% = \frac{1}{6}$$
> $$20\% = \frac{1}{5}$$
> $$25\% = \frac{1}{4}$$
> $$33\frac{1}{3}\% = \frac{1}{3}$$
> $$50\% = \frac{1}{2}$$
> $$66\frac{2}{3}\% = \frac{2}{3}$$
> $$75\% = \frac{3}{4}$$

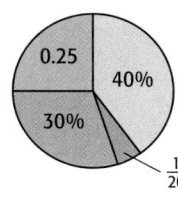

Fraction	Decimal	Percent
$\frac{25}{100} = \frac{1}{4}$	$\frac{1}{4} = 0.25$	25%
$\frac{40}{100} = \frac{2}{5}$	$\frac{2}{5} = 0.4$	40%
$\frac{5}{100} = \frac{1}{20}$	$\frac{1}{20} = 0.05$	5%
$\frac{30}{100} = \frac{3}{10}$	$\frac{3}{10} = 0.3$	30%

Methods of Estimating Percents

> ➤ Use compatible numbers.
> ➤ Round to common percents: e.g., 10%, 25%, 50%
> ➤ Break percents into smaller parts: e.g., 1% 5%, 10%

Percent Problems

Lessons 6-3, 6-4

Why? Using percents is a way of comparing numbers.

Finding a Percent of a Number

What number is 25% of 32?

Set up an equation.

What number is 25% of 32?

$n = 25\% \cdot 32$
$n = 0.25 \cdot 32$
$n = 8$

So **8** is 25% of 32.

Set up a proportion.

25 is to 100 as **what number** is to 32?

$$\frac{25}{100} = \frac{n}{32}$$
$100n = 25 \cdot 32$
$100n = 800$
$n = 8$

Finding the Percent One Number Is of Another

What percent of 120 is 90?

Set up an equation.

What percent of 120 is 90?

$p \cdot 120 = 90$
$$p = \frac{90}{120}$$
$p = 0.75$

So 90 is **75%** of 120.

Set up a proportion.

What number is to 100 as 90 is to 120?

$$\frac{n}{100} = \frac{90}{120}$$
$120n = 100 \cdot 90$
$120n = 9000$
$n = 75$

Finding a Number When the Percent Is Known

36 is 4% of what number?

Set up an equation.

36 is 4% of **what number**?

$36 = 4\% \cdot n$
$36 = 0.04n$
$$\frac{36}{0.04} = \frac{0.04}{0.04}n$$
$900 = n$

So 36 is 4% of **900**.

Set up a proportion.

4 is to 100 as 36 is to **what number**?

$$\frac{4}{100} = \frac{36}{n}$$
$4n = 100 \cdot 36$
$4n = 3600$
$n = 900$

Objective: Students compare and order decimals, fractions, and percents.

Hands-On Lab
In *Hands-On Lab Activities*

Online Edition
Tutorial Videos, Interactivities

Countdown to Testing Week 10

Power Presentations
with PowerPoint®

Warm Up

Evaluate.

1. $\frac{2}{15} + \frac{3}{15}$ $\frac{1}{3}$ **2.** $\frac{7}{12} - \frac{3}{12}$ $\frac{1}{3}$

3. $\frac{4}{5} \cdot \frac{7}{2}$ $\frac{14}{5}$ or $2\frac{4}{5}$ **4.** $3\frac{1}{2} \div \frac{1}{4}$ 14

Problem of the Day

A fast-growing flower grows to a height of 12 inches in 12 weeks by doubling its height every week. If you want your flower to be only 6 inches tall, after how many weeks should you pick it? 11 weeks

Also available on transparency

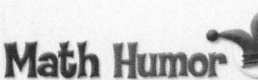
Math Humor

Which of these numbers is under the most stress, 30%, $\frac{1}{3}$, or 0.2? The last, because it's *too tense*.

State Resources

go.hrw.com
State Resources Online
KEYWORD: MT7 Resources

6-1 Relating Decimals, Fractions, and Percents

Learn to compare and order decimals, fractions, and percents.

Vocabulary
percent

In an average day, a typical newborn baby sleeps 16 out of 24 hours. The part of a day the baby sleeps can be shown in several ways.

$$\frac{16}{24} = 0.66\overline{6} = 66.\overline{6}\%$$

So newborns sleep over 60% of the time.

Percents are ratios that compare a number to 100.

Reading Math
Think of the % symbol as meaning per 100 or /100.
75% = 75/100 = 0.75

Ratio	Decimal	Percent
$\frac{3}{10} = \frac{30}{100}$	0.30	30%
$\frac{1}{2} = \frac{50}{100}$	0.50	50%
$\frac{3}{4} = \frac{75}{100}$	0.75	75%

To convert a fraction to a decimal, divide the numerator by the denominator.

$$\frac{1}{8} = 1 \div 8 = 0.125$$

To convert a decimal to a percent, multiply by 100 and insert the percent symbol.

$$0.125 \cdot 100 \rightarrow 12.5\%$$

$$\begin{array}{r} 0.125 \\ 8{\overline{)1.000}} \\ \underline{8} \\ 20 \\ \underline{16} \\ 40 \\ \underline{40} \\ 0 \end{array}$$

EXAMPLE 1 **Finding Equivalent Ratios and Percents**

Find the missing ratio or percent equivalent for each letter on the number line.

a: $0\% = \frac{0}{100} = 0$

b: $\frac{7}{40} = 0.175 = 17.5\% = 17\frac{1}{2}\%$

c: $25\% = \frac{25}{100} = \frac{5}{20} = \frac{1}{4}$

d: $37\frac{1}{2}\% = 0.375 = \frac{375}{1000} = \frac{3}{8}$

e: $\frac{1}{2} = 0.5 = 50\%$

f: $66\frac{2}{3}\% = 0.66\overline{6} = \frac{2}{3}$

g: $100\% = \frac{100}{100} = 1$

h: $1\frac{1}{5} = 1.2 = 120\%$

---

1 Introduce
Alternate Opener

EXPLORATION

6-1 Relating Decimals, Fractions, and Percents

A *percent* is a ratio that compares a number to 100. Percents can be modeled on circle graphs. The circle graph below shows the results of a survey in which 25 students were asked which type of music they preferred.

- 16% means 16 per 100.
- 16% as a decimal is 0.16.
- 16% as a fraction is $\frac{16}{100} = \frac{4}{25}$.

Music Preference
Hip Hop 16%
Rock 24%
R & B 12%
Electronic 48%

Use the percents in the circle graph to complete the table.

	Music Type	Percent	Decimal	Fraction
1.	Electronic	48%		
2.	Rock	24%		
3.	Hip Hop	16%		
4.	R & B	12%		

Think and Discuss

5. Explain how you wrote each percent as a decimal.
6. Explain how you wrote each decimal as a fraction.

Motivate

Show students magazines or newspapers that advertise sales using percents. Ask the students whether they can explain how much money would be saved and what the sale price would be as a result of the percent savings.

Explorations and answers are provided in *Alternate Openers: Explorations Transparencies*.

To compare and order fractions, decimals, and percents, write them in the same form first.

EXAMPLE 2 Comparing Fractions, Decimals, and Percents

Compare. Write <, >, or =.

Ⓐ $\frac{1}{2}$ ▨ 37%

$\frac{1}{2} = 0.50 = 50\%$ *Write as a percent.*

$50\% > 37\%$ *Compare.*

$\frac{1}{2} > 37\%$

Ⓑ 0.125 ▨ 19%

$0.125 = 12.5\%$ *Write as a percent.*

$12.5\% < 19\%$ *Compare.*

$0.125 < 19\%$

Remember!
When multiplying a decimal by 100, simply move the decimal point two spaces to the right.

EXAMPLE 3 Ordering Fractions, Decimals, and Percents

Write 0.25%, $\frac{13}{5}$, 0.57, and 300% in order from least to greatest.

$\frac{13}{5} = 2.6 = 260\%$ *Write as percents.*

$0.57 = 57\%$

$0.25\% < 57\% < 260\% < 300\%$ *Compare.*

$0.25\%,\ 0.57,\ \frac{13}{5},\ 300\%$

Possible answers to *Think and Discuss*
1. (1) money; (2) measurements in recipes; (3) sales tax
2. (1) $\frac{1}{4}$; (2) 25%; (3) 0.25; 0.25 is most common when writing it.

EXAMPLE 4 *Physical Science Application*

3. Possible answer: If the number is a decimal, you can find the equivalent percent by multiplying by 100, or the equivalent fraction by writing the value over the correct power of 10. If the number is a fraction, you can find the decimal by dividing the numerator by the denominator. If the number is a percent, you can find the decimal by dividing by 100.

The United States nickel was once made of 100% nickel. Today nickels are 3 parts copper and 1 part nickel. What percent of today's nickel is pure nickel?

$\frac{\text{parts pure nickel}}{\text{total parts}} \rightarrow \frac{1}{4}$ *Set up a ratio and simplify.*

$\frac{1}{4} = 1 \div 4 = 0.25 = 25\%$ *Find the percent.*

So today's nickel is 25% pure nickel.

Think and Discuss

1. **Give an example** of a real-world situation in which you would use (1) decimals, (2) fractions, and (3) percents.

2. **Show** 25 cents as a part of a dollar in terms of (1) a reduced fraction, (2) a percent, and (3) a decimal. Which is most common?

3. **Explain** how you can find a fraction, decimal, or percent when you have only one form of a number.

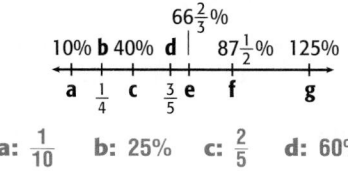

② Teach

Guided Instruction

In this lesson, students learn to relate decimals, fractions, and percents. Demonstrate to students that fractions, decimals, and percents are all ratios. Remind students how to convert between fractions and decimals. Explain that percents are ratios in the form of *parts per hundred*.

Teaching Tip **Reading Math** Ask students how many cents there are in a dollar. 100 Then ask what the word *per* means. "for each" or "divided by" Then explain that the word *percent* means "divided by one hundred" (e.g., 20% literally means "20 divided by 100" or "20 for each 100"). **ENGLISH LANGUAGE LEARNERS**

Reaching All Learners
Through Kinesthetic Experience

Prepare sets of number cards (Teacher Tools) that contain three equivalent numbers, such as $\frac{1}{4}$, 0.25, and 25%. Distribute the numbers randomly so that each student gets a decimal, a fraction, or a percent. Have each student find the two students in the class with the numbers equivalent to his or her number. Once students have formed their groups of three, have the class form a human number line (three deep) so that the numbers are in increasing order.

③ Close

Summarize

Remind students that fractions, terminating or repeating decimals, and percents are all ratios. In a fraction, the denominator can be any nonzero integer. A percent is equivalent to a ratio with a denominator of 100. A terminating decimal is equivalent to a ratio with a denominator of 10, 100, 1000, or some other power of 10. Any of the three forms can be changed to the other two forms.

6-1 Exercises

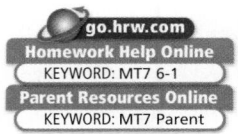

go.hrw.com
Homework Help Online
KEYWORD: MT7 6-1
Parent Resources Online
KEYWORD: MT7 Parent

Assignment Guide

If you finished Example **1** assign:
Average 1–4, 12–15, 23–25, 32–40
Advanced 12–15, 23–25, 27, 31–40

If you finished Example **2** assign:
Average 1–8, 12–19, 23–25, 32–40
Advanced 12–19, 23–25, 27, 31–40

If you finished Example **3** assign:
Average 1–10, 12–21, 23–25, 30, 32–40
Advanced 12–21, 23–27, 30–40

If you finished Example **4** assign:
Average 1–25, 28, 30, 32–40
Advanced 12–40

Homework Quick Check
Quickly check key concepts.
Exercises: 2, 6, 10, 11, 24

Math Background

Using 10-by-10 grids is an excellent way to reinforce the meaning of *percent*. On the grid, each square represents 1%, or $\frac{1}{100}$, of the grid's area. You can shade different percents on the grid and then divide the grid into equal areas to show fractional equivalents. The example below shows that 20% is equal to $\frac{1}{5}$.

State Resources

go.hrw.com
State Resources Online
KEYWORD: MT7 Resources

GUIDED PRACTICE

See Example **1** Find the missing ratio or percent equivalent for each letter on the number line.

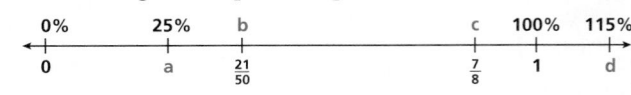

1. a $\frac{1}{4}$
2. b 42%
3. c 87.5%
4. d $\frac{23}{20}$

See Example **2** Compare. Write <, >, or =.

5. $\frac{3}{4}$ > 70%
6. 42% > $\frac{2}{5}$
7. 87.5% = 0.875
8. 0.99 < 100%

See Example **3** Order the numbers from least to greatest.

9. 36%, 0.3, $33\frac{1}{3}$%, $\frac{3}{8}$ 0.3, $33\frac{1}{3}$%, 36%, $\frac{3}{8}$
10. $\frac{4}{5}$, −0.5, 500%, $66\frac{2}{3}$% −0.5, $66\frac{2}{3}$%, $\frac{4}{5}$, 500%

See Example **4** 11. A molecule of water is made up of 2 atoms of hydrogen and 1 atom of oxygen. What percent of the atoms of a water molecule is oxygen? $33\frac{1}{3}$%

INDEPENDENT PRACTICE

See Example **1** Find the missing ratio or percent equivalent for each letter on the number line.

12. e 20%
13. f $\frac{39}{100}$
14. g $\frac{4}{5}$
15. h 125%

See Example **2** Compare. Write <, >, or =.

16. $\frac{2}{3}$ > 66%
17. 37% < $\frac{3}{8}$
18. 6% < 0.6
19. 0.09 = 9%

See Example **3** Order the numbers from least to greatest.

20. −6%, 0.6, $66\frac{1}{3}$%, $\frac{3}{6}$ −6%, $\frac{3}{6}$, 0.6, $66\frac{1}{3}$%
21. $\frac{2}{5}$, 0.04, 42%, 70% 0.04, $\frac{2}{5}$, 70% 42%,

See Example **4** 22. Sterling silver is an alloy combining 925 parts pure silver and 75 parts of another metal, such as copper. What percent of sterling silver is not pure silver? 7.5%

PRACTICE AND PROBLEM SOLVING

Extra Practice
See page 792.

Write the labels from each circle graph as percents.

23. 40%, 30%, 20%, 10%

24. 15%, 25%, 52%, 8%

25. 40%, 30%, 25%, 5%

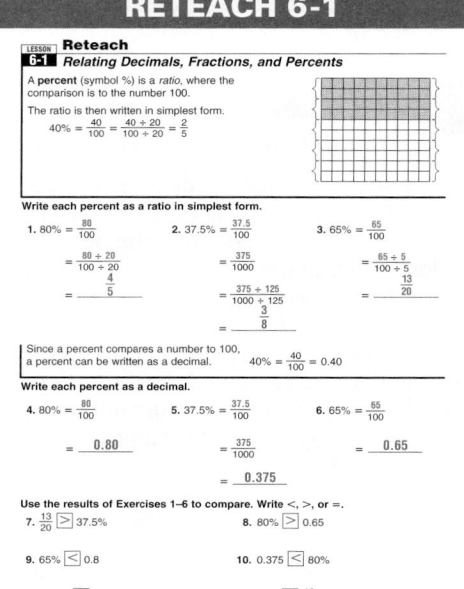

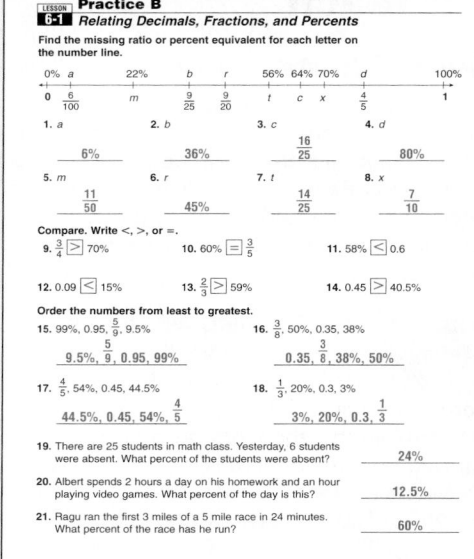

RETEACH 6-1

Reteach
6-1 *Relating Decimals, Fractions, and Percents*

A **percent** (symbol %) is a *ratio*, where the comparison is to the number 100.

The ratio is then written in simplest form.

$40\% = \frac{40}{100} = \frac{40 \div 20}{100 \div 20} = \frac{2}{5}$

Write each percent as a ratio in simplest form.

1. $80\% = \frac{80}{100}$
   $= \frac{80 \div 20}{100 \div 20}$
   $= \frac{4}{5}$

2. $37.5\% = \frac{37.5}{100}$
   $= \frac{375}{1000}$
   $= \frac{375 \div 125}{1000 \div 125}$
   $= \frac{3}{8}$

3. $65\% = \frac{65}{100}$
   $= \frac{65 \div 5}{100 \div 5}$
   $= \frac{13}{20}$

Since a percent compares a number to 100, a percent can be written as a decimal. $40\% = \frac{40}{100} = 0.40$

Write each percent as a decimal.

4. $80\% = \frac{80}{100}$
   $= 0.80$

5. $37.5\% = \frac{37.5}{100}$
   $= \frac{375}{1000}$
   $= 0.375$

6. $65\% = \frac{65}{100}$
   $= 0.65$

Use the results of Exercises 1–6 to compare. Write <, >, or =.

7. $\frac{13}{20}$ > 37.5%
8. 80% > 0.65
9. 65% < 0.8
10. 0.375 < 80%
11. 37.5% < 0.65
12. 65% = $\frac{13}{20}$

PRACTICE 6-1

Practice B
6-1 *Relating Decimals, Fractions, and Percents*

Find the missing ratio or percent equivalent for each letter on the number line.

1. a 6%
2. b 36%
3. c $\frac{16}{25}$
4. d 80%

5. m $\frac{11}{50}$
6. r 45%
7. t $\frac{14}{25}$
8. x $\frac{7}{10}$

Compare. Write <, >, or =.

9. $\frac{3}{4}$ > 70%
10. 60% = $\frac{3}{5}$
11. 58% < 0.6
12. 0.09 < 15%
13. $\frac{2}{3}$ > 59%
14. 0.45 > 40.5%

Order the numbers from least to greatest.

15. 99%, 0.95, $\frac{5}{9}$, 9.5%
    9.5%, $\frac{5}{9}$, 0.95, 99%

16. $\frac{3}{8}$, 50%, 0.35, 38%
    0.35, $\frac{3}{8}$, 38%, 50%

17. $\frac{4}{5}$, 54%, 0.45, 44.5%
    44.5%, 0.45, 54%, $\frac{4}{5}$

18. $\frac{1}{3}$, 20%, 0.3, 3%
    3%, 20%, 0.3, $\frac{1}{3}$

19. There are 25 students in math class. Yesterday, 6 students were absent. What percent of the students were absent? 24%

20. Albert spends 2 hours a day on his homework and an hour playing video games. What percent of the day is this? 12.5%

21. Ragu ran the first 3 miles of a 5 mile race in 24 minutes. What percent of the race has he run? 60%

26. Patterns Find the next three numbers in this pattern. Then describe the pattern.

$\frac{1}{8}$, 25%, 0.375, $\frac{1}{2}$, 62.5%, 0.75

27. Critical Thinking Describe a situation when changing a fraction to a percent would be helpful.

28a. $\frac{4}{25}$; 0.16

28b. 23%; Possible answer: Alaska and Texas make up nearly $\frac{1}{4}$ of the total land area in the United States.

28. Geography The graph shows the percents of the total U.S. land area taken up by the five largest states. The sixth section of the graph represents the area of the remaining 45 states.

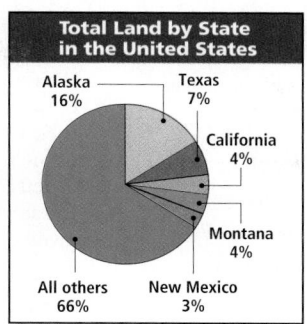

Total Land by State in the United States

Alaska 16%
Texas 7%
California 4%
Montana 4%
New Mexico 3%
All others 66%

  a. Alaska is the largest state in total land area. Write Alaska's portion of the total U.S. land area as a fraction and as a decimal.

  b. What percent of the total U.S. land area is taken up by Alaska and Texas? How might you describe this percent?

 29. What's the Error? An analysis showed that 0.06% of the T-shirts made by one company were defective. A student says this is 6 out of every 100. What is the student's error?

 30. Write About It Explain the steps you would take to order $\frac{1}{3}$, 0.33, and 30% from least to greatest.

 31. Challenge Wyatt and Allyson were asked to solve a percent problem using the numbers 13 and 38. Wyatt found 13% of 38, and Allyson found 38% of 13. Explain why they both got the same answer. Would this work for other numbers as well? Why or why not?

TEST PREP and Spiral Review

32. Multiple Choice Of the 32 students in Mr. Smith's class, 12 have jobs during the summer. What percent of the students have a summer job?

(A) 12%   (B) 20%   (C) 37.5%   (D) 62.5%

33. Multiple Choice Claudia has 40 CDs. Of these, 14 are country music CDs. What percent of Claudia's CD collection is country music?

(F) 40%   (G) 35%   (H) 14%   (J) 12%

Compare. Write <, >, =. (Lesson 2-2)

34. $\frac{4}{9}$ ▨ $\frac{21}{25}$ <   **35.** $\frac{3}{7}$ ▨ $\frac{8}{9}$ <   **36.** $-\frac{1}{3}$ ▨ $-\frac{2}{5}$ >   **37.** $-\frac{8}{14}$ ▨ $-\frac{4}{7}$ =

Find the common difference in each sequence. (Lesson 3-6)

38. 1.2, 2.4, 3.6, 4.8, . . . **1.2**   **39.** 27, 23, 19, 15, . . . **4**   **40.** 0, −8, −16, −24, . . . **8**

CHALLENGE 6-1

LESSON 6-1 Challenge
100% Filled

Materials needed: colored pencils or pens

For each exercise, select from the box a different combination of numbers whose sum is 100%. An item may be used only once in a combination, but may be used again in a different combination. Write your selection on the line below the grid. Shade the squares in the grid with a different color for each number you selected.

68%	$\frac{1}{2}$	60%	$\frac{1}{20}$	1%	0.9	0.04	$\frac{13}{20}$	$\frac{1}{7}$
$\frac{3}{25}$	16%	55%	0.02	$\frac{1}{9}$	0.15	$\frac{1}{8}$	24%	0.44
0.06	$\frac{1}{6}$	$\frac{1}{4}$	29%	0.037	$\frac{1}{3}$	19%	$\frac{17}{50}$	

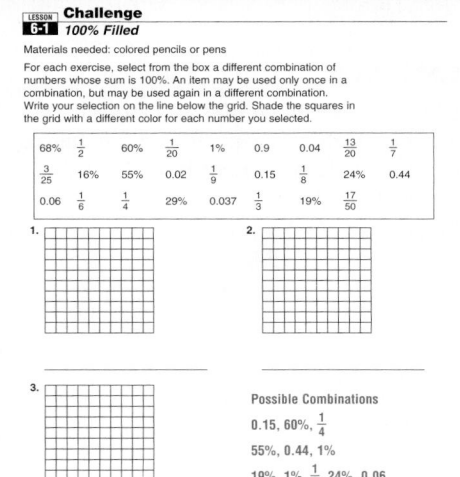

1.   **2.**   **3.**

Possible Combinations
0.15, 60%, $\frac{1}{4}$
55%, 0.44, 1%
19%, 1%, $\frac{1}{2}$, 24%, 0.06

PROBLEM SOLVING 6-1

LESSON 6-1 Problem Solving
Relating Decimals, Fractions, and Percents

The table shows the ratio of brain weight to body size in different animals. Use the table for Exercises 1–3. Write the correct answer.

1. Complete the table to show the percent of each animal's body weight that is brain weight. Round to the nearest hundredth.

Animal	Brain Weight / Body Weight	Percent
Mouse	$\frac{1}{40}$	2.5%
Cat	$\frac{1}{100}$	1%
Dog	$\frac{1}{125}$	0.8%
Horse	$\frac{1}{600}$	0.17%
Elephant	$\frac{1}{560}$	0.18%

2. Which animal has a greater brain weight to body size ratio, a dog or an elephant?

   dog

3. List the animals from least to greatest brain weight to body size ratio.

   horse, elephant, dog, cat, mouse

The table shows the number of wins and losses of the top teams in the National Football Conference from 2004. Choose the letter of the best answer. Round to the nearest tenth.

4. What percent of games did the Green Bay Packers win?

   A 10%   C 37.5%
   B 60%   **D** 62.5%

Team	Wins	Losses
Philadelphia Eagles	13	3
Green Bay Packers	10	6
Atlanta Falcons	11	5
Seattle Seahawks	9	7

5. Which decimal is equivalent to the percent of games the Seattle Seahawks won?

   F 0.05625   H 5.625
   G 0.5625   J 56.25

6. Which team listed had the highest percentage of wins?
   A Philadelphia Eagles
   B Green Bay Packers
   C Atlanta Falcons
   D Seattle Seahawks

6-1 Lesson Quiz

Find each equivalent value.

1. $\frac{3}{8}$ as a percent   37.5%

2. 20% as a fraction $\frac{1}{5}$

3. $\frac{5}{8}$ as a decimal   0.625

Compare. Write <, >, or =.

4. $\frac{7}{11}$ ▨ 30%   >

5. 0.650 ▨ 97%   <

6. Write 245%, $\frac{1}{5}$, 0.133, and 66.6% in order from least to greatest.
   0.133, $\frac{1}{5}$, 66.6%, 245%

7. About 342,000 km² of Greenland's total area (2,175,000 km²) is not covered with ice. To the nearest percent, what percent of Greenland's total area is not covered with ice?   16%

Also available on transparency

Pacing: Traditional 1 day
Block $\frac{1}{2}$ day

Objective: Students estimate percents.

 Online Edition
Tutorial Videos

Countdown to Testing Week 10

Power Presentations
with PowerPoint®

Warm Up
Write each percent as a fraction.

1. 33% $\frac{1}{3}$ **2.** 75% $\frac{3}{4}$

3. 20% $\frac{1}{5}$ **4.** 60% $\frac{3}{5}$

Problem of the Day
If you enlarge a picture by 25%, by what percent do you need to reduce it to return it to its original size? (*Hint:* Try using a simple number for the original area of the picture.)   **20%**

Also available on transparency

Math Fact
One thousand seconds pass in about 17 minutes. One million seconds pass in about 12 days. One billion seconds pass in about 32 years.

State Resources

 **go.hrw.com**
State Resources Online
KEYWORD: MT7 Resources

 6-2 # Estimate with Percents

Problem Solving Skill

Learn to estimate percents.

Vocabulary
estimate
compatible numbers
benchmark

Waiters, waitresses, and other restaurant employees depend upon tips for much of their income. Typically, a tip is 15% to 20% of the bill. Tips do not have to be calculated exactly, so estimation is often used. When the sales tax is about 8%, doubling the tax gives a good estimate for a tip.

Some problems require only an **estimate** . Estimates involving percents and fractions can be found by using **compatible numbers** , numbers that go well together because they have common factors.

$\frac{13}{24}$ *13 and 24 are not compatible numbers.*

$\frac{12}{24}$ *12 and 24 are compatible numbers because 12 is a common factor of 12 and 24*

$\frac{12}{24} = \frac{1}{2}$ *Simplify.*

$\frac{13}{24} \approx \frac{1}{2}$ *$\frac{13}{24}$ is nearly equivalent to $\frac{12}{24}$*

When estimating with percents, it helps to know some *benchmarks*. **Benchmarks** are common numbers that serve as points of reference. Some common benchmarks for percents are shown in the table.

Percent	Decimal	Fraction	Percent	Decimal	Fraction
5%	0.05	$\frac{1}{20}$	50%	0.5	$\frac{1}{2}$
10%	0.1	$\frac{1}{10}$	66.$\overline{6}$%	0.$\overline{6}$	$\frac{2}{3}$
25%	0.25	$\frac{1}{4}$	75%	0.75	$\frac{3}{4}$
33.$\overline{3}$%	0.$\overline{3}$	$\frac{1}{3}$	100%	1	1

EXAMPLE 1 **Estimating with Percents**

Estimate.

A 24% of 44

$24\% \approx 25\%$ *Use a benchmark close to 24%.*

$\approx \frac{1}{4}$ *Write 25% as a fraction.*

$\frac{1}{4} \cdot 44 = 11$ *Use mental math: 44 ÷ 4.*

24% of 44 is about 11.

---

1 ## Introduce
Alternate Opener

EXPLORATION

6-2 **Estimate with Percents**

You can use compatible numbers when estimating with percents. For example, to find 24% of 82, use 25% of 80.

0.25 · 80 = 20
So 24% of 82 is approximately 20.

For each problem, estimate using compatible numbers. Then use a calculator to find the actual answer.

		Estimate	Actual
1.	Of 610 students, 34% prefer domestic cars over foreign cars.		
2.	In a survey, 19% of 152 people selected juice as their favorite drink.		
3.	A family wishes to leave a 15% tip on a $32.15 bill at a restaurant.		
4.	In a country with a population of 10,036,724, 48% are males.		

Think and Discuss
5. Discuss your strategies for estimating.
6. Explain how to avoid overestimating or underestimating.

Motivate

Tell students to imagine that a store is celebrating its 19th anniversary, and it is having a sale in which every item is 19% off. Ask students if they know how to estimate the savings on an item priced at $19.99.
About 20% of $20, or $4

Explorations and answers are provided in *Alternate Openers: Explorations Transparencies.*

Estimate.

B **36% of 20**

$$36\% \approx 35\%$$ *Round.*

$$\approx 25\% + 10\%$$ *Break the percent into*
     two benchmarks.

$$35\% \cdot 20 = (25\% + 10\%) \cdot 20$$ *Set up an equation.*

$$= 25\% \cdot 20 + 10\% \cdot 20$$ *Use Distributive Property.*

$$= 5 + 2$$ *25% of 20 is 5, and 10% of 20 is 2.*

36% of 20 is about 7.

EXAMPLE **2**

PROBLEM SOLVING APPLICATION

Angelica ate lunch with a group of friends. The restaurant would not issue separate checks, so each friend had to calculate what she owed. Angelica's entrée, drink, and dessert cost a total of $9.75. If the sales tax rate is 8.25% and Angelica wants to leave a 15% tip, about how much should she pay?

1 **Understand the Problem**

The **answer** is the total amount Angelica should pay for her lunch.

List the important information:
- Angelica's food and drink cost a total of $9.75.
- The sales tax rate is 8.25%.
- Angelica wants to leave a 15% tip.

2 **Make a Plan**

Think: Sales tax and tip together are 23.25% of Angelica's food and drink total (8.25% + 15% = 23.25%). The numbers $9.75 and 23.25% are difficult to work with. Use compatible numbers: $9.75 is close to $10.00; 23.25% is close to 25%.

3 **Solve**

$$\$10.00 \cdot 25\% = \$10.00 \cdot 0.25$$
$$= \$2.50$$
$$\$9.75 + \$2.50 = \$12.25$$

Angelica should pay $12.25.

4 **Look Back**

To determine whether $12.25 is a reasonable estimate of what Angelica should pay, use a calculator to find the tax and the tip for $9.75.

$9.75 \cdot 1.2325 = \$12.02$, so $12.25 is a reasonable estimate.

Power Presentations
with PowerPoint®

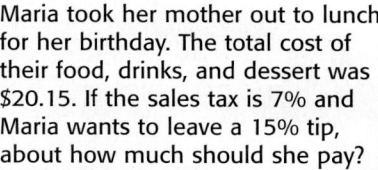

Additional Examples

Example **1**

Estimate.

A. 21% of 66   about 13

B. 36% of 120   about 42

Example **2**

Maria took her mother out to lunch for her birthday. The total cost of their food, drinks, and dessert was $20.15. If the sales tax is 7% and Maria wants to leave a 15% tip, about how much should she pay?

Possible answer: $24.15

Also available on transparency

---

2 **Teach**

Guided Instruction

In this lesson, students learn to estimate with percents by rounding to compatible numbers. Explain how to determine whether numbers are compatible, and if they are not, how to find compatible numbers that are appropriate.

Teaching Tip **Inclusion** After each estimation, have students decide whether their estimate makes sense. Before students work the exercises, remind them that their estimates may vary.

 Reaching All Learners
Through Number Sense

Have each student write the price and sale information for an everyday item. Students should work in groups to estimate each sale price. Then have students exchange papers to find the exact answers. Ask students to compare their answers with their estimates. This activity will give students the opportunity to evaluate their estimates by comparing them with the exact answers.

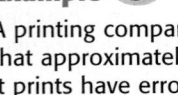

Power Presentations
with PowerPoint®

Additional Examples

Example ③

A printing company has determined that approximately 6% of the books it prints have errors. Out of a printing run of 2050 books, the production manager estimates that 250 books have errors. Estimate to see if the manager's number is reasonable. Explain. **No; Possible answer: About 100 books would have errors. 250 is much greater than 100.**

Also available on transparency

6-2 Exercises

Assignment Guide

If you finished Example ① assign:
Average 1–8, 11–18, 21–30, 47–63
Advanced 11–18, 31–36, 45–63

If you finished Example ② assign:
Average 1–9, 11–19, 21–30, 37–42, 47–63
Advanced 11–19, 31–42, 44–63

If you finished Example ③ assign:
Average 1–30, 37–43, 47–63
Advanced 11–20, 31–63

Homework Quick Check

Quickly check key concepts.
Exercises: 12, 19, 20

State Resources

EXAMPLE ③ *Manufacturing Application*

A company has found that on average 9% of the radios it manufactures are defective. Out of a production run of 1523 radios, the plant manager assumes that 137 are defective. Estimate to see if the plant manager's number is reasonable. Explain.

$$9\% \cdot 1523 \approx 10\% \cdot 1500 \qquad \textit{Use compatible numbers.}$$
$$\approx 0.1 \cdot 1500 \qquad \textit{Write 10\% as a decimal.}$$
$$\approx 150 \qquad \textit{Multiply.}$$

Because 150 is close to 137, the plant manager's number is reasonable.

Think and Discuss

1. **Determine** the ratios that are nearly equivalent to each of the following percents: 23%, 53%, 65%, 12%, and 76%.

2. **Describe** how to find 35% of a number when you know 10% of the number.

6-2 Exercises

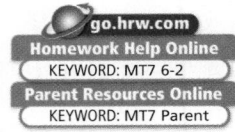

GUIDED PRACTICE

See Example ① **Estimate.**

1. 11% of 507 **50**
2. 26% of 99 **25**
3. 34% of 91 **30**
4. 48% of 124 **62**
5. 20% of 66 **13**
6. $12\frac{1}{2}$% of 87 **11**
7. $66\frac{2}{3}$% of 25 **16**
8. 47% of 80 **36**

See Example ② 9. Arnold ate breakfast at a restaurant. The total cost of his food, juice, and coffee was $6.45. If the sales tax rate is 8% and Arnold wants to leave a 20% tip, about how much should he pay? **Possible answer: $8.55**

See Example ③ 10. Approximately 11% of each batch of yo-yos is defective. Mr. Andersen said that in a batch of 1500 yo-yos, 125 yo-yos would be defective. Estimate to determine if Mr. Andersen's number is reasonable. Explain. **No; Possible answer: 11% of 1500 is a little more than 10% of 1500. 10% of 1500 is 150. 125 is much less then 150.**

INDEPENDENT PRACTICE

See Example ① **Estimate.**

11. 48% of 202 **100**
12. 74% of 39 **30**
13. 101% of 6 **6**
14. 20% of 42 **8**
15. 40% of 81 **32**
16. $62\frac{1}{2}$% of 239 **150**
17. $33\frac{1}{3}$% of 26 **9**
18. 30% of 118 **36**

Possible answers to *Think and Discuss*

1. $\frac{1}{4}, \frac{1}{2}, \frac{2}{3}, \frac{1}{8}, \frac{3}{4}$

2. 35% = 10% + 10% + 10% + 5%
   $= (3 \cdot 10\%) + \frac{1}{2}(10\%)$

---

③ Close

Summarize

Discuss situations in which finding an estimate may be more appropriate than finding an exact calculation. Some examples might include estimating grocery purchases so that the total does not exceed $20, or tipping a waiter. Explain that estimates are not exact answers and that they vary. Ask students to estimate a 15% tip on a check for $39.70.

Possible answer: $6.00

See Example 2

19. Inga wants to buy a new MP3 player that costs $119.99. If the sales tax is 6.35%, about how much should Inga expect to pay? **Possible answer: $126**

See Example 3

20. In a recent election, the leading candidate captured approximately 75% of the 24,082 total votes. The newspaper reported that the winner captured 18,039 votes. Estimate to determine if the newspaper report is reasonable. Explain. **Yes; Possible answer: 75% of 24,000 is about 18,000, which is close to 18,039.**

PRACTICE AND PROBLEM SOLVING

Extra Practice
See page 792.

Choose the best estimate. Write A, B, or C.

21. 5% of 29.4
- Ⓐ 0.15
- Ⓑ 1.5
- Ⓒ 15

22. 50% of 29.85
- Ⓐ 3
- Ⓑ 12
- Ⓒ 15

23. 33.3% of 65
- Ⓐ 2
- Ⓑ 20
- Ⓒ 30

24. 66% of $357.99
- Ⓐ $120
- Ⓑ $240
- Ⓒ $360

25. 75% of $317.99
- Ⓐ $24
- Ⓑ $120
- Ⓒ $240

26. 105% of $776.50
- Ⓐ $80
- Ⓑ $900
- Ⓒ $800

Estimate.

27. 50% of 297 is about what number?
150

28. 75% of 76 is about what number?
60

29. 103% of 40 is about what number?
40

30. 103% of 885 is about what number?
900

31. 50% of 1611 is about what number?
800

32. 50% of 12.42 is about what number?
6

33. $33\frac{1}{3}$% of 87 is about what number?
30

34. 9.6% of 77 is about what number?
8

35. 24% of 402 is about what number?
100

36. 66% of 1.8 is about what number?
1.2

37. On a weekday, 911 cars passed through a city intersection. On Saturday, only 33% of that number passed through the intersection. Approximately how many cars passed through the intersection on the weekend? **≈ 300 cars**

38. A jury wants to give an award of about 9% of $695,531. What is a good estimate of the award? **$70,000**

39. Business The daily circulation for a city newspaper was 498,739. After a six-month period, the circulation dropped 5.1%. Approximately what was the daily circulation at the end of the six-month period? **≈ 475,000**

40. Finance Brooke earns $320 a week. After taxes, her paycheck is only 78% of her earnings. Approximately how much is her paycheck each week? **≈ $240**

41. Physical Science When you snap a light stick, you break a barrier between two chemical compounds. This causes a reaction that releases energy as light. An improvement allows a 9-hour light stick to glow for 50% more time. Approximately how long does the improved light stick glow? **≈ 12 hours**

Physical Science

Freezing a light stick may make it glow longer, but not as brightly.

42. Sports In 2004, Barry Bonds reached base approximately 60% of his 617 plate appearances. Approximately how many times did he reach base? **≈ 360 times**

Math Background

Estimation is an important skill that students should be encouraged to work on continuously. Students should use estimation to check the reasonableness of their answers to problems involving calculations in mathematics, science, and other subjects. Encourage students to estimate problems before they work them and to check answers after they have worked them. Estimation can also be an effective tool for students to use on standardized tests.

RETEACH 6-2

Reteach
6-2 Estimate with Percents

You can estimate the solutions to different types of problems involving percents by rounding numbers.

Type 1: Finding a percent of a number.

Estimate 38% of 470.

First, round the percent to a common percent with an easy fractional equivalent.

$38\% \approx 40\% = \frac{40}{100} = \frac{2}{5}$

Then, round the number to a number divisible by the denominator of the fraction. 500 is divisible by 5.

$470 \approx 500$

Use mental math to multiply.

$\frac{2}{5} \cdot 500$ Think: If $500 \div 5 = 100$, then $100 \cdot 2 = 200$

So, 38% of 470 is about 200.

Complete to estimate each percent. Estimates may vary.

1. 32% of 872

Round to a percent with an easy fractional equivalent: $32\% \approx 33\frac{1}{3}\% = \frac{1}{3}$

Round to hundreds place, divisible by 3: $872 \approx$ __900__

Do mental math to multiply: $\frac{1}{3} \times$ __900__ $=$ __300__

So, 32% of 872 is about __300__.

2. 78% of 495

% to easy fraction:
$78\% \approx$ __80__ $\% = \frac{4}{5}$

divisible by denominator:
$495 \approx$ __500__

Do mental math to multiply.
$\frac{4}{5} \times$ __500__ $=$ __400__

So, 78% of 495 is about __400__.

3. 73% of 1175

% to easy fraction:
$73\% \approx$ __75__ $\% = \frac{3}{4}$

divisible by denominator:
$1175 \approx$ __1200__

Do mental math to multiply.
$\frac{3}{4} \times$ __1200__ $=$ __900__

So, 73% of 1175 is about __900__.

PRACTICE 6-2

Practice B
6-2 Estimate with Percents

Estimate. Estimates may vary.

1. 74% of 99 — about 75
2. 25% of 39 — about 10
3. 52% of 10 — about 5

4. 21% of 50 — about 10
5. 30% of 61 — about 20
6. 24% of 48 — about 12

7. 5% of 41 — about 2
8. 50% of 178 — about 90
9. 33% out of 62 — about 20

Estimate.

10. 48% of 30 is about what number? — about 15

11. 26% of 36 is about what number? — about 9

12. 30% of 22 is about what number? — about 7

13. 21% of 63 is about what number? — about 12

14. Rodney's weekly gross pay is $91. He must pay about 32% in taxes and deductions. Estimate Rodney's weekly take-home pay after deductions. — about $60

15. In the last school election, 492 students voted. Mary received 48% of the votes. About how many votes did she receive? — about 250

16. A restaurant bill for lunch is $14.10. Grace wants to leave a 15% tip and the sales tax rate is 5.5%. About how much will lunch cost Grace in all? — about $17.10

17. A company has found that on average about 6% of the batteries they manufacture are defective. Out of 1,385 batteries, the supervisor assumes that about 83 are defective. Estimate to determine if the manager's number is reasonable? Explain. Yes; 6% of 1,385 is about 5% of 1,400; 10% of 1,400 is 140, and half of 140 is 70. Since 5% of 1,400 is 83 and 70 is close to 70, the estimate is reasonable.

Answers

45. Possible answer: To find 1%, move the decimal point in the number two places left (about 40). To find 10%, move the decimal one place (about 400). 100% is the same as the original number (4027).

TEST PREP DOCTOR For Exercise 49, remind students that to convert from a percent to a decimal, divide the percent by 100 or multiply the percent by 0.01.

Journal

When selling products or services, many businesses give the customer an estimate of the cost of the job before the work is done. Have students write about why businesses provide estimates and about possible problems these estimates could cause.

Power Presentations
with PowerPoint®

6-2 Lesson Quiz

Estimate. Possible answers:

1. 34% of 12   **4**

2. 113% of 80   **90**

3. Ian had dinner with some friends at a restaurant. His food and drink cost $10.25. If the sales tax is 8.25% and he wants to leave a 20% tip, about how much should Ian pay? Possible answer: **$13.23**

4. Approximately 8% of each batch of jeans produced at one factory is defective. Ms. Fleming said that in a batch of 400 jeans, about 35 jeans would be defective. Estimate to determine if her number is reasonable. Explain. **Yes, because 8% of 400 is a little less than 10% of 400. 10% of 400 is 40 and 35 is a little less than 40.**

Also available on transparency

43a. No; Possible answer: 2% of 570,000 is approximately 11,400, which isn't close to 1045. Rhode Island is approximately 0.02% the area of Alaska.

43b. Yes; Possible answer: 60% of 1,000,000 is about 600,000, which is close to 655,435.

43. Social Studies Alaska is the largest state in the United States in total land area, and Rhode Island is the smallest.

a. The area of Rhode Island is approximately 2% the area of Alaska. Determine if this statement is reasonable. Explain.

b. Although Rhode Island is much smaller than Alaska, it has a larger population. Alaska has approximately 60% the population of Rhode Island. Determine if this statement is reasonable. Explain.

c. Estimate the number of people per square mile in Alaska and in Rhode Island. $\approx$ 1 per mi²; $\approx$ 1000 per mi²

Area and Population: 2004		
	Total Land (mi²)	Population
Alaska	571,949	655,435
Rhode Island	1045	1,080,632

Source: U.S. Census Bureau

44. Write a Problem Write a percent estimation problem using the following data: The equatorial circumference of Earth is approximately 40,075 km. The equatorial circumference of the moon is approximately 25% Earth's equatorial circumference. **Possible answer: Estimate the equatorial circumference of the moon. Answer: $\approx$ 10,000 km.**

45. Write About It Explain how you can estimate 1%, 10%, and 100% of 4027.

46. Challenge Explain two ways to estimate 20% of 82.

Possible answer: 20% of 82 is about $\frac{1}{5}$ of 80, or 16. It is also twice 10% of 82, or about $8 + 8 = 16$.

TEST PREP and Spiral Review

47. Multiple Choice 328% of 82 is about what number?
Ⓐ 246   Ⓑ 264   Ⓒ 287   Ⓓ 298

48. Multiple Choice Regina receives a 5% commission on the merchandise she sells. Last week, Regina sold $11,976.57 worth of merchandise. Approximately how much commission does she earn?
Ⓕ $600   Ⓖ $11,400   Ⓗ $550   Ⓙ $10,450

49. Multiple Choice Which is the best estimate for 20% of 703?
Ⓐ 14   Ⓑ 140   Ⓒ 1400   Ⓓ 14,000

Evaluate. (Lesson 4-1)

50. 2^5 **32**   51. $(-3)^2$ **9**   52. $(-7)^3$ **−343**   53. -4^3 **−64**

54. $(-2)^7$ **−128**   55. 5^3 **125**   56. $(-4)^4$ **256**   57. 8^1 **8**

Find the percent, fraction, or decimal equivalent for each of the following.
(Lesson 6-1)

58. $\frac{9}{10}$ as a percent **90%**   59. 46% as a fraction $\frac{23}{50}$ 60. $\frac{3}{8}$ as a decimal **0.375**

61. $\frac{7}{14}$ as a decimal **0.5**   62. 0.78 as a fraction $\frac{39}{50}$ 63. 52.5% as a decimal **0.525**

CHALLENGE 6-2

LESSON 6-2 Challenge
As the Wheel Turns

For each wheel, write a percent problem using estimation. In your problem, use the percent at the center of the wheel and two other numbers on the wheel. The first one in each row is done.

63% of 150 is about 90.

68% of 90 is about 60.

51% of 62 is about 33.

16 is about 23% of 71.

4 is about 11% of 36.

21 is about 38% of 53.

141% of 85 is about 120.

129% of 6 is about 8.

247% of 31 is about 75.

PROBLEM SOLVING 6-2

LESSON 6-2 Problem Solving
Estimate with Percents

Write an estimate.

1. A store requires you to pay 15% up front on special orders. If you plan to special order items worth $74.86, estimate how much you will have to pay up front.
Possible answer: **$11**

2. A store is offering 25% off of everything in the store. Estimate how much you will save on a jacket that is normally $58.99.
Possible answer: **$15**

3. A certain kind of investment requires that you pay a 10% penalty on any money you remove from the investment in the first 7 years. If you take $228 out of the investment, estimate how much of a penalty you will have to pay.
Possible answer: **$25**

4. John notices that about 18% of the earnings from his job go to taxes. If he works 14 hours at $6.25 an hour, about how much of his check will go for taxes?
Possible answer: **$18**

Choose the letter for the best estimate.

5. In its first week, an infant can lose up to 10% of its body weight in the first few days of life. Which is a good estimate of how many ounces a 5 lb 13 oz baby might lose in the first week of life?
A 0.6 oz   C 18 oz
Ⓑ 9 oz   D 22 oz

6. A CD on sale costs $12.89. Sales tax is 4.75%. Which is the best estimate of the total cost of the CD?
F $13.30   H $14.20
Ⓖ $13.55   J $14.50

7. In a class election, Pedro received 52% of the votes. There were 274 students who voted in the election. Which is the best estimate of the number of students who voted for Pedro?
A 70 students   C 125 students
B 100 students   Ⓓ 140 students

8. Mel's family went out for breakfast. The bill was $24.25 plus 5.2% sales tax. Mel wants to leave a 20% tip. Which is the best estimate of the total bill?
F $25.45   Ⓗ $30.25
G $29.25   J $32.25

6-3 Finding Percents

Organizer 6-3

Pacing: Traditional 1 day
Block $\frac{1}{2}$ day

Objective: Students find percents.

Hands-On Lab
In *Hands-On Lab Activities*

Technology Lab
In *Technology Lab Activities*

Online Edition
Tutorial Videos

Countdown to Testing Week 10

Learn to find percents.

The Nielsen Television Ratings monitor the popularity of television shows viewers watch at certain times. Statistics for these shows are reported as a percent of all American homes in which television is being watched at a given time.

© United Feature Syndicate, Inc.

EXAMPLE 1 Finding the Percent One Number Is of Another

What percent of 144 is 64?

Method 1: Set up a proportion to find the percent.

Think: What number is to 100 as 64 is to 144?

$\dfrac{\text{number}}{100} = \dfrac{\text{part}}{\text{whole}}$	*Set up a proportion.*
$\dfrac{n}{100} = \dfrac{64}{144}$	*Substitute.*
$n \cdot 144 = 100 \cdot 64$	*Find the cross products.*
$144n = 6400$	*Simplify.*
$\dfrac{144n}{144} = \dfrac{6400}{144}$	*Divide both sides by 144.*
$n \approx 44.4$	*Simplify.*

64 is approximately 44.4% of 144.

Method 2: Set up an equation to find the percent.

$p \cdot 144 = 64$	*Set up an equation.*
$\dfrac{144p}{144} = \dfrac{64}{144}$	*Divide both sides by 144.*
$p = 0.\overline{4}$, or approximately 0.444.	*Simplify.*

64 is approximately 44.4% of 144. *0.44 is 44%*

Check

$$44.4\% \cdot 144 \overset{?}{=} 64 \qquad \text{Substitute 44.4\% for p.}$$
$$0.444 \cdot 144 \overset{?}{=} 64 \qquad \text{Write a decimal and multiply.}$$
$$63.936 \approx 64 \checkmark \qquad \text{44.4\% of 144 is approximately 64.}$$

Math Humor

Teacher: What is 5% of the power of a 20-watt lightbulb?

Student: A what?

Teacher: Wow, you got that one fast.

State Resources

---

1 Introduce

Alternate Opener

EXPLORATION

6-3 Finding Percents

The circle graph shows results from a mock election in which 40 students were polled.

Percent of Votes Received by Each Candidate

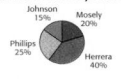
Johnson 15% Mosely 20%
Phillips 25% Herrera 40%

Complete the table to find the number of votes each candidate received.

	Candidate	Percent of Votes	Number of Votes
	Mosely	20%	$0.20 \cdot 40 = 8$
1.	Herrera	40%	
2.	Phillips	25%	
3.	Johnson	15%	

Think and Discuss

4. **Discuss** whether there is a clear winner in the election.
5. **Tell** which two candidates combined received the same total votes as another candidate. Did they also get the same percent of the votes as the other candidate?

Motivate

Ask students percent questions about themselves, such as: "What percent of the students in this class have brown hair?" or "What percent of the students are wearing blue jeans?" Tell students that before class is over, they will be able to answer questions like these.

Explorations and answers are provided in *Alternate Openers: Explorations Transparencies.*

Example 1

A. What percent of 92 is 66? ≈72%

B. What percent of 220 is 88? 40%

Example 2

A. Four friends volunteered to cut the grass around their neighbor's house. Jay cut 23% of the grass, Aimee cut $\frac{1}{5}$ of the grass, Ken cut 0.31 of the grass, and Bryn cut the rest. What percent of the grass did Bryn cut? 26%

B. Jeremy organizes his movie collection by genre. $\frac{2}{5}$ of his collection are dramas, 0.325 are action films, 3% are documentaries, 19.5% are comedies, and the rest of his movies are independent films. What percent of his movie collection are independent films? 5%

Example 3

A. The city of Dallas, Texas has a population of approximately 1,189,000 people. The population of the city of Austin, Texas is 55% of the population of Dallas. To the nearest thousand, what is the population of Austin? 654,000

B. After a drought, a reservoir had only $66\frac{2}{3}$% of the average amount of water. If the average amount of water is 57,000,000 gallons, how much water was in the reservoir after the drought? 38,000,000 gal

Also available on transparency

EXAMPLE 2 *Recreation Application*

A A brother and three sisters built a treehouse in their backyard. Mary did $\frac{1}{4}$ of the work, Joshua did 0.28 of the work, Caroline did 30% of the work, and Laura did the rest. What percent of the work on the treehouse did Laura do?

First, find what percent of the work Mary and Joshua did.

$\frac{1}{4} = 25\%$ and $0.28 = 28\%$

Next, subtract the percents you know from 100% to find the remaining percent.

$100\% - 25\% - 28\% - 30\% = 17\%$

Laura did 17% of the work.

B Emma is planning a vegetable garden for her backyard. She knows that she wants $\frac{3}{8}$ of the garden to have squash, 0.25 to have tomatoes, 12.5% to have carrots, 15% to have cabbage, and the rest to have lettuce. What percent of the garden will have lettuce?

First, find what percent of the garden will have squash and tomatoes.

$\frac{3}{8} = 37.5\%$ and $0.25 = 25\%$

Next, subtract the percents you know from 100% to find the remaining percent.

$100\% - 37.5\% - 25\% - 12.5\% - 15\% = 10\%$

10% of the garden will have lettuce.

EXAMPLE 3 **Finding the Percent of a Number**

A A domestic pig can run about $33\frac{1}{3}$% of the speed of a giraffe. A giraffe can run about 32 mi/h. To the nearest tenth, how fast can a domestic pig run?

Choose a method: Set up an equation.

Think: What speed is $33\frac{1}{3}$% of 32 mi/h?

$s = 33\frac{1}{3}\% \cdot 32$ *Set up an equation.*

$s = \frac{1}{3} \cdot 32$ *$33\frac{1}{3}\%$ is equivalent to $\frac{1}{3}$.*

$s = \frac{32}{3} = 10\frac{2}{3} = 10.\overline{6}$ *Simplify.*

$s \approx 10.7$ *Round to the nearest tenth.*

A domestic pig can run about 10.7 miles per hour.

---

2 Teach

Guided Instruction

In this lesson, students learn to find percents. Explain the relationship among a part, a whole, and a percent (percent × whole = part). Show students that percent problems can be solved by using a proportion (Example 1A) or by setting up and solving an equation (Example 1B). Encourage students to become familiar with both methods.

Reaching All Learners
Through Curriculum Integration

Social Studies Give students the following election results or use election results from a news article.

In an election for mayor, the results were as follows: Garcia, 42%; Jackson, 36%; Shiu, 22%. If 14,000 votes were cast, how many votes did each candidate receive? Garcia: 6006; Jackson: 5148; Shiu: 3146 If a candidate must receive at least 50% of the votes to become mayor, how many votes are needed to become mayor? 7150 How many more votes would the leading candidate have needed to become mayor? 1144

Teaching Tip **Reading Math** In the application problems, you may want to have students identify the part, whole, and percent before solving the problems. Point out that the word *of* can help students identify the whole.

ENGLISH LANGUAGE LEARNERS

Remind students in problems like Examples 3 and 4 to fully answer the question asked by adding the appropriate units to their answers.

B Mt. Churchill, in Alaska, is about 15,638 feet high. The height of Mt. McKinley is approximately 130% of the height of Mt. Churchill. To the nearest foot, find the height of Mt. McKinley.

Choose a method: Set up a proportion.

Think: 130 is to 100 as **what height** is to 15,638 ft?

$$\frac{130}{100} = \frac{h}{15{,}638}$$ Set up a proportion.

$130 \cdot 15{,}638 = 100 \cdot h$ Find the cross products.

$2{,}032{,}940 = 100h$ Simplify.

$\frac{2{,}032{,}940}{100} = \frac{100h}{100}$ Divide both sides by 100.

$20{,}329.4 = h$ Simplify.

$20{,}329 \approx h$ Round to the nearest whole number.

Mt. McKinley is about 20,329 feet high.

Think and Discuss

1. **Show** why 5% of a number is less than $\frac{1}{10}$ of the number.

2. **Demonstrate** two ways to find 70% of a number.

3. **Name** fractions in simplest form that are the same as 40% and as 250%.

6-3 Exercises

GUIDED PRACTICE

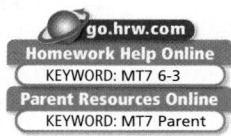
go.hrw.com
Homework Help Online
KEYWORD: MT7 6-3
Parent Resources Online
KEYWORD: MT7 Parent

See Example ① **1.** What percent of 91 is 45? **49.5%**

2. What percent of 1270 is 375? **29.5%**

3. What percent of 240 is 180? **75%**

4. What percent of 186 is 75? **40.3%**

See Example ② **5.** Four friends ordered a pizza. Christopher ate $\frac{1}{5}$, Emma ate 30%, Tanya ate 0.27, and Jamie ate the rest. What percent of the pizza did Jamie eat? **23%**

See Example ③ **6.** Elijah walks 2 miles to school. If Bailey's walk is 80% of the length of Elijah's walk, find the length of Bailey's walk. **1.6 mi**

7. Jay's term paper is 18 pages long. If Madison's paper is 175% of the length of Jay's paper, find the length of Madison's paper. **31.5 pages**

8. Of 109.6 million households, 19,508,800 watched the television show *CSI* during the week of October 3, 2005. What percent of American households watched *CSI* this week? **17.8%**

State Resources

Math Background

Percents are widely used in many disciplines. They are used extensively in business economics to describe many things, including taxes, economic growth, inflation, interest rates, and changes in the stock market. Percents are also useful in consumer economics, including the calculation of sales tax, discounts, withholding tax, and tips. Other applications include sports (e.g., winning percentage, field-goal percentage, and save percentage) and even grading (e.g., 90% or above is an A, etc.). Understanding percents will help students in many areas, including the study of probability (Chapter 10).

INDEPENDENT PRACTICE

See Example 1

9. What percent of 56 is 224? **400%**

10. What percent of 180 is 30? **16.7%**

11. 12.5 is what percent of 1250? **1%**

12. 115 is what percent of 40? **287.5%**

See Example 2

13. The Bishop family bought a case of water containing 24 bottles. During one week, Lydia drank $\frac{1}{8}$ of the bottles, Mitchell drank $33\frac{1}{3}$% of the bottles, Alexa drank 0.25 of the bottles, and Todd drank the rest. What percent of the case did Todd drink? **$29\frac{1}{6}$%**

See Example 3

14. The tallest building in the United States is the Sears Tower in Chicago. The height of the Sears Tower is 1450 feet, which is 240% of the height of the Seattle Space Needle in Washington. Find the height of the Seattle Space Needle to the nearest foot. **604 ft**

15. In Arkansas, the highest elevation is Mount Magazine, and the lowest is the Ouachita River. Mount Magazine is 2753 ft above sea level, which is about 5098% of the elevation of the lowest portion of the state. Find the elevation of the Ouachita River area. **≈ 54 ft above sea level**

PRACTICE AND PROBLEM SOLVING

Extra Practice
See page 792.

Find each number to the nearest tenth.

16. What number is $33\frac{1}{3}$% of 30? **10**

17. What number is $11\frac{1}{3}$% of 215? **24.4**

18. What number is 77% of 9? **6.9**

19. What number is $3\frac{1}{2}$% of 11,400? **399**

20. What number is 166% of 300? **498**

21. What number is $66\frac{2}{3}$% of 750? **500**

Complete each statement.

22. Since 8 is 16% of 50,

   a. 16 is ▓% of 50. **32**

   b. 24 is ▓% of 50. **48**

   c. 80 is ▓% of 50. **160**

23. Since 8 is 5% of 160,

   a. 8 is ▓% of 80. **10**

   b. 8 is ▓% of 40. **20**

   c. 8 is ▓% of 20. **40**

24. Since 15 is 300% of 5,

   a. 15 is ▓% of 10. **150**

   b. 15 is ▓% of 20. **75**

   c. 15 is ▓% of 40. **37.5**

Patterns Describe the patterns shown below.

25. 1% of 1200 = 12
2% of 600 = 12
4% of 300 = 12
8% of 150 = 12
16% of 75 = 12

26. 400% of 320 = 1280
200% of 160 = 320
100% of 80 = 80
50% of 40 = 20
25% of 20 = 5

27. 400% of 5 = 20
200% of 15 = 30
100% of 45 = 45
50% of 135 = 67.5
25% of 405 = 101.25

28. **Social Studies** In 2003, 14% of the 50 largest U.S. cities were located in Texas. How many of the 50 largest U.S. cities were located in Texas in 2003? **7 cities**

29. **Geography** About 600 mi^2 of the 700 mi^2 of the Okefenokee Swamp is located in Georgia. If Georgia is 57,906 mi^2, find the percent of that area that is part of the Okefenokee Swamp. **1.0%**

RETEACH 6-3

LESSON 6-3 Reteach
Finding Percents (continued)

Possibility 2: Find the *is* number.

What is 20% of 80?
$$\frac{symbol\ number}{100} = \frac{is\ number}{of\ number}$$
$$\frac{20}{100} = \frac{x}{80}$$
$$100 \cdot x = 20 \cdot 80$$
$$\frac{100x}{100} = \frac{1600}{100}$$
$$x = 16 \qquad \text{So, 20\% of 80 is 16.}$$

Find the indicated percent of each number.

5. What is 30% of 150?
$$\frac{30}{100} = \frac{x}{150}$$
$$100 \cdot x = \underline{30} \cdot \underline{150}$$
$$\frac{100x}{100} = \frac{4500}{100}$$
$$x = \underline{45}$$
So, 30% of 150 is $\underline{45}$.

6. What is 75% of 205?
$$\frac{75}{100} = \frac{x}{205}$$
$$100 \cdot x = \underline{75} \cdot \underline{205}$$
$$\frac{100x}{100} = \frac{15,375}{100}$$
$$x = \underline{153.75}$$
So, 75% of 205 is $\underline{153.75}$.

7. What is 125% of 300?
$$\frac{125}{100} = \frac{x}{300}$$
$$100 \cdot x = \underline{125} \cdot \underline{300}$$
$$= \frac{37,500}{100}$$
$$100 \cdot x = \frac{200}{3} \cdot 81$$
$$x = \underline{375}$$
So, 125% of 300 is $\underline{375}$.

8. What is $66\frac{2}{3}$% of 81?
$$\frac{66\frac{2}{3}}{100} = \frac{x}{81}$$
$$100 \cdot x = 66\frac{2}{3} \cdot \underline{81}$$
$$\frac{100x}{100}$$
$$100 \cdot x = \underline{5400}$$
$$\frac{100x}{100} = \frac{5400}{100}$$
$$x = \underline{54}$$

PRACTICE 6-3

LESSON 6-3 Practice B
Finding Percents

Find each percent.

1. What percent of 84 is 21? **25%**

2. 24 is what percent of 60? **40%**

3. What percent of 150 is 75? **50%**

4. What percent of 80 is 68? **85%**

5. 36 is what percent of 80? **45%**

6. What percent of 88 is 33? **37.5%**

7. 19 is what percent of 95? **20%**

8. 28.8 is what percent of 120? **24%**

9. What percent of 56 is 49? **87.5%**

10. What percent of 102 is 17? **$16\frac{2}{3}$**

11. What percent of 94 is 42.3? **45%**

12. 90 is what percent of 75? **120%**

13. Daphne bought a used car for $9200. She made a down payment of $1840. Find the percent of the purchase price that is the down payment. **20%**

14. Tricia read $\frac{1}{4}$ of her book on Monday. On Tuesday, she read 36% of the book. On Wednesday, she read 0.27 of the book. She finished the book on Thursday. What percent of the book did she read on Thursday? **12%**

15. An airplane traveled from Boston to Las Vegas making a stop in St. Louis. The plane traveled 2410 miles altogether, which is 230% of the distance from Boston to St. Louis. Find the distance from Boston to St. Louis to the nearest mile. **1048 mi**

16. The first social studies test had 16 questions. The second test had 220% as many questions as the first test. Find the number of questions on the second test. **36 questions**

30. Language Arts The Hawaiian words shown contain all of the letters of the Hawaiian alphabet. The ` is actually a consonant!

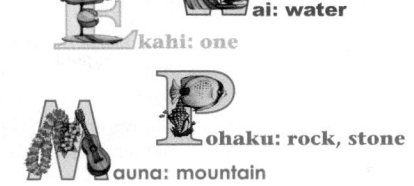
Halakahiki: pineapple

ʻWai: water

ʻEkahi: one

Pohaku: rock, stone

Mauna: mountain

a. What percent of the Hawaiian alphabet are vowels? ≈ **38.5%**

b. To the nearest tenth, what percent of the letters in the English alphabet are also in the Hawaiian alphabet? **46.2%**

31. Multi-Step Joseph, Ana, Lena, and George chipped in money for a friend's gift. The gift cost $45.99 plus $3.45 sales tax. Joseph paid $12.50, Ana paid $\frac{1}{4}$ of the total cost, Lena paid 24% of the total cost, and George paid the rest. Order the people from least amount paid to greatest amount paid. **Lena: $11.87, Ana: $12.36, Joseph: $12.50, George: $12.71**

 32. Choose a Strategy Masco Industries has 285,000 total employees. Of those employees, 85,500 telecommute. What percent of the company's total employees telecommute?

Ⓐ 3%　　Ⓑ 15%　　Ⓒ 30%　　Ⓓ 150%

 33. Write About It A question on a math quiz asks, "What is 175% of 72?" Petra calculates 12.6 as the answer. Is this a reasonable answer? Explain.

34. Challenge Molly cut 10 ft 6 in. from a pipe measuring 8 yd 1 ft. What percent of the pipe's original length did Molly remove, and what is the length of the pipe that remains? **42%; 14 ft 6 in.**

33. Possible answer: This answer is not reasonable because 175% of 72 must be greater than 72. The correct answer is 126.

TEST PREP and Spiral Review

35. Multiple Choice Currently, 96 students are enrolled in the Grove City Dance Center. Of those students, 54 study tap dance. The remaining students study ballet. What percentage of the students study ballet?

Ⓕ 42%　　Ⓖ 43.75%　　Ⓗ 54%　　Ⓙ 56.25%

36. Gridded Response According to the 2003 U.S. Census, approximately 129 million Americans spend 3.4% of a 24-hour day commuting. How many minutes a day does a person in this group spend commuting? ≈ **49 min**

Solve each proportion. (Lesson 5-4)

37. $\frac{x}{3} = \frac{8}{12}$ $x = 2$　　**38.** $\frac{7}{y} = \frac{49}{98}$ $y = 14$　　**39.** $\frac{10}{12} = \frac{b}{6}$ $b = 5$　　**40.** $\frac{12}{36} = \frac{4}{c}$ $c = 12$

41. $\frac{b}{6} = \frac{42}{18}$ **14**　　**42.** $\frac{8}{c} = \frac{64}{24}$ **3**　　**43.** $\frac{11}{33} = \frac{3}{x}$ **9**　　**44.** $\frac{14}{9} = \frac{y}{18}$ **28**

Estimate. (Lesson 6-2)

45. 26% of 398 **100**　　**46.** 48% of 746 **375**　　**47.** 39% of 99 **40**

Objective: Students find a number when the percent is known.

 Online Edition
Tutorial Videos

 Countdown to Testing Week 10

Power Presentations
with PowerPoint®

Warm Up

1. What percent of 20 is 18? 90%
2. What percent of 400 is 50? 12.5%
3. 9 is what percent of 27? $33\frac{1}{3}$%
4. 25 is what percent of 4? 625%

Problem of the Day

The original price of a sweater is $40. The sweater goes on sale for 75% of its original price. Later, the sweater goes on clearance for 50% of its sale price. What is the clearance price of the sweater? $15

Also available on transparency

Math Humor

The store owner offered to order the new football uniforms if the team would pay $33\frac{1}{3}$% of the cost in advance. The players did not accept the offer. They always passed on a third down.

State Resources

 **go.hrw.com**
State Resources Online
KEYWORD: MT7 Resources

6-4 Finding a Number When the Percent Is Known

Learn to find a number when the percent is known.

Carcharocles megalodon, a giant shark that became extinct almost 3 million years ago, had teeth as large as 7.25 inches along an edge. This is 240% bigger than the largest teeth of a modern great white shark.

When one number is known, and its relationship to another number is given by a percent, the other number can be found.

Carcharocles megalodon's jaw may have been 6 feet wide.

EXAMPLE 1 **Finding a Number When the Percent Is Known**

42 is 5% of what number?
Choose a method: Set up an equation to find the number.

$42 = 5\% \cdot n$ *Set up an equation.*
$42 = 0.05n$ *5% = 0.05*
$\dfrac{42}{0.05} = \dfrac{0.05}{0.05}n$ *Divide both sides by 0.05.*
$840 = n$ *Simplify*
42 is 5% of 840.

EXAMPLE 2 **Physical Science Application**

In a science lab, a sample of a compound contains 14.5 grams of magnesium. If 72.5% of the sample is magnesium, find the number of grams the entire sample weighs.
Choose a method: Set up a proportion to find the number.
Think: 72.5 is to 100 as 14.5 g is to what mass?

$\dfrac{72.5}{100} = \dfrac{14.5}{m}$ *Set up a proportion.*
$72.5 \cdot m = 100 \cdot 14.5$ *Find the cross products.*
$72.5m = 1450$ *Simplify.*
$\dfrac{72.5m}{72.5} = \dfrac{1450}{72.5}$ *Divide both sides by 72.5*
$m = 20$ *Simplify.*

The entire sample weighs 20 grams.

---

1 Introduce
Alternate Opener

EXPLORATION

6-4 Finding a Number When the Percent is Known

A CD player is on sale for $15 off the original price. According to the advertisement, this is a 25% discount. You can use what you know about percents to figure out the original price of the CD player.

Think: 25% is $\frac{1}{4}$, so $15 must be $\frac{1}{4}$ of the original price.
You can model the situation as shown.

The original price is $60.
Draw a model to find the original price for each of the following.

1. Amount of discount: $8; percent of discount: 20%
2. Amount of discount: $12; percent of discount: $33\frac{1}{3}$%
3. Amount of discount: $17; percent of discount: 50%

Think and Discuss

4. **Explain** how you could find the value of a number given that 7 is 10% of the number.
5. **Describe** what must be true about a number if you know that 45 is 100% of the number.

Motivate

Make a pair of related statements like "Today is the 90th school day of the year. This school year is 50% over." Ask the students if they can tell from those statements how many days there are in a normal school year. about 180 Have them explain how they arrived at their answers.

Explorations and answers are provided in *Alternate Openers: Explorations Transparencies.*

EXAMPLE 3 *Life Science Application*

Life Science LINK

Reticulated means "net-like" or "forming a network." The reticulated python is named for the pattern on its skin.

A The king cobra can reach a length of 18 feet. This is only about 60% of the length of the largest reticulated python. Find the length of the largest reticulated python.

Choose a method: Set up a proportion.

Think: 60 is to 100 as 18 ft is to what length?

$$\frac{60}{100} = \frac{18}{\ell}$$ *Set up a proportion.*

$$60 \cdot \ell = 100 \cdot 18$$ *Find the cross products.*

$$\frac{60\ell}{60} = \frac{1800}{60}$$ *Divide both sides by 60.*

$$\ell = 30$$ *Simplify.*

The largest reticulated python is 30 feet long.

B *Carcharocles megalodon* had teeth as large as 7.25 inches along an edge. This is 240% of the maximum size of the teeth of a modern great white shark. To the nearest inch, find the maximum size of the teeth of a great white shark.

Choose a method: Set up an equation.

Think: 7.25 in. is 240% of what length?

$$7.25 = 2/40\% \cdot \ell$$ *Set up an equation.*

$$7.25 = 2.40 \cdot \ell$$ *240% = 2.40*

$$\frac{7.25}{2.40} = \frac{\ell}{2.40}$$ *Divide both sides by 2.40.*

$$3 \approx \ell$$ *Simplify.*

The maximum size is about 3 inches along an edge.

You have now seen all three types of percent problems.

Percent Problem	Equation	Proportion
Finding the percent of a number	15% of 120 = n	$\frac{15}{100} = \frac{n}{120}$
Finding the percent one number is of another	p% of 120 = 18	$\frac{p}{100} = \frac{18}{120}$
Finding a number when the percent is known	15% of n = 18	$\frac{15}{100} = \frac{18}{n}$

Possible answers to *Think and Discuss*

1. In the first case, divide the known number by the decimal equivalent of the percent. In the second case, divide the first number by the second and write the answer as a percent.

2. The number is greater than 36 because 36 is a small part (22%) of a larger whole (the number).

Think and Discuss

1. Compare finding a number when a percent is known to finding the percent one number is of another number.

2. Explain whether a number is greater than or less than 36 if 22% of the number is 36.

Power Presentations
with PowerPoint®

Additional Examples

Example 1

60 is 12% of what number? 500

Example 2

Anna earned 85% on a test by answering 17 questions correctly. If each question was worth the same amount, how many questions were on the test? 20

Example 3

A. When a giraffe is born, it is approximately 55% as tall as it will be as an adult. If a baby giraffe is 5.2 feet tall when it is born, how tall will it be when it is full grown, to the nearest tenth of a foot? **9.5 ft**

B. A fisherman caught a lobster that weighed 11.5 lb. This was 70% of the weight of the largest lobster that fisherman had ever caught. What was the weight, to the nearest tenth of a pound, of the largest lobster the fisherman had ever caught? **16.4 lb**

Also available on transparency

2 Teach

Guided Instruction

In this lesson, students learn to find a number when the percent is known. Explain that in the last lesson, students found the percent and the part (of the whole amount) that the percent represents. In this lesson, they will find the whole amount. Explain that they will use equations and proportions similar to those from the last lesson. For each example, you may want to have students identify the part, the percent, and the whole.

Teaching Tip **Multiple Representations** You may want to solve each example using both methods so that students can see that they give the same result.

Reaching All Learners
Through Critical Thinking

Give each student the following set of related percent problems:

1. What percent of 30 is 18? **60%**

2. 18 is 60% of what number? **30**

3. A jacket is on sale for 60% of its original price. The original price was $30. What is the sale price? **$18**

Have students solve the first problem mathematically and then solve the related problems by inspection.

3 Close

Summarize

Review the chart at the end of the lesson. Review both methods for solving percent problems—using equations and proportions. Ask students how they can identify the part, the whole, and the percent in a word problem.

Possible answers: The percent is always labeled with the word "percent" or the % symbol. The whole often follows the phrase "percent of" or "% of" and is the total amount. The part is the portion of the total represented by the percent; it is often less than the whole but can be greater.

Assignment Guide

If you finished Example **1** assign:
Average 1–4, 7–10, 23–44
Advanced 7–10, 13–15, 23–44

If you finished Example **2** assign:
Average 1–5, 7–11, 17–21, 23–44
Advanced 7–11, 13–44

If you finished Example **3** assign:
Average 1–12, 17–21, 23–44
Advanced 7–44

Homework Quick Check

Quickly check key concepts.
Exercises: 8, 11, 12

Math Background

As indicated at the end of the lesson, there are three basic types of percent problems. Equations for all three types can be written using a direct translation approach. If a question is stated using the word "what," then an equation can be written with "what" replaced by a variable, "of" by a multiplication symbol, and "is" by an equal sign. Some examples are shown below:

36 is 4% of what number?
$\rightarrow 36 = 0.04 \cdot x$

What is 82.5% of 250?
$\rightarrow x = 0.825 \cdot 250$

What percent of 162 is 90?
$\rightarrow x \cdot 162 = 90$

State Resources

go.hrw.com
State Resources Online
KEYWORD: MT7 Resources

6-4 **Exercises**

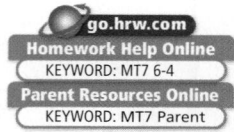
go.hrw.com
Homework Help Online
KEYWORD: MT7 6-4
Parent Resources Online
KEYWORD: MT7 Parent

GUIDED PRACTICE

See Example **1** Find each number to the nearest tenth.

1. 6.9 is $11\frac{1}{2}$% of what number? **60** 2. 92 is $66\frac{2}{3}$% of what number? **138**

3. 12% of what number is 20? **166.7** 4. 30% of what number is 96? **320**

See Example **2** 5. How much water can a 7.4 oz piece of chalk absorb if it can absorb 32% of its weight? **≈ 2.4 oz**

See Example **3** 6. At 2 P.M., a flag pole casts a shadow that is 155% of its actual height. If the shadow is 23.25 ft, what is the actual height of the pole? **15 ft**

INDEPENDENT PRACTICE

See Example **1** Find each number to the nearest tenth.

7. 90 is $66\frac{2}{3}$% of what number? **135** 8. 63 is 15% of what number? **420**

9. 0.75% of what number is 10? **1333.3** 10. 44% of what number is 37.4? **85**

See Example **2** 11. Isaac sold 58 of his baseball cards at a collectors' show. If this represented $14\frac{1}{2}$% of his total collection, how many baseball cards did Isaac have before he sold his cards? **400 cards**

See Example **3** 12. When a tire is labeled "185/70/14," that means it is 185 mm wide, the sidewall height (from the rim to the road) is 70% of its width, and the wheel has a diameter of 14 in. What is the tire's sidewall height? **129.5 mm**

PRACTICE AND PROBLEM SOLVING

Extra Practice
See page 792.

Complete each statement.

13. Since 2% of 500 is 10,   14. Since 100% of 8 is 8,   15. Since 15% of 60 is 9,

a. 4% of ▨ is 10. **250**   a. 50% of ▨ is 8. **16**   a. 30% of ▨ is 9. **30**

b. 8% of ▨ is 10. **125**   b. 25% of ▨ is 8. **32**   b. 45% of ▨ is 9. **20**

c. 16% of ▨ is 10. **62.5** c. 10% of ▨ is 8. **80**   c. 60% of ▨ is 9. **15**

16. In a survey of 175 students, 42 said that their favorite cookout food was hamburgers, and 61 said that their favorite was hot dogs. Give these numbers as percents. **24% hamburgers; ≈ 34.9% hot dogs**

17. **Life Science** The Congress Avenue bridge in Austin, Texas, is home to the largest urban bat colony in the world. Nearly 1.5 million Mexican free-tailed bats live under the bridge. This bat population is approximately 228.3% the population of Austin. What is the population of Austin to the nearest thousand people? **658,000**

RETEACH 6-4

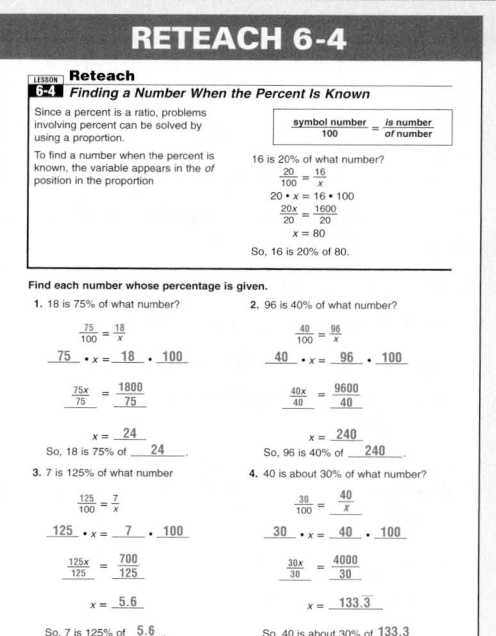

PRACTICE 6-4

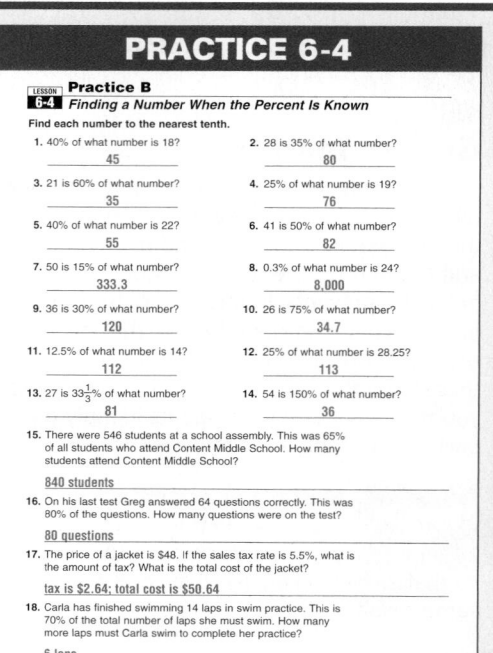

The U.S. census collects information about state populations, economics, income and poverty levels, births and deaths, and so on. This information can be used to study trends and patterns. For Exercises 18–20, round answers to the nearest tenth.

2000 U.S. Census Data			
	Population	Male	Female
Alaska	626,932	324,112	302,820
New York	18,976,457	9,146,748	9,829,709
Age 34 and Under	139,328,990	71,053,554	68,275,436
Age 35 and Over	142,092,916	67,000,009	75,092,907
Total U.S.	281,421,906	138,053,563	143,368,343

18. What percent of New York's population is male? **48%**

19. What percent of the entire country's population, to the nearest tenth of a percent, is made up of people in New York? **6.7%**

20. Tell what percent of the U.S. population each represents.

    a. people 34 and under   **b.** people 35 and over   **c.** male   **d.** female
        49.5%   **50.5%**   **49.1%**   **50.9%**

21. American Indians and Native Alaskans make up about 15.6% of Alaska's population. What is their population, to the nearest thousand? **98,000**

22. ⭐ **Challenge** About 71% of the U.S. population age 85 and over is female. Of the fractions that round to 71% when rounded to the nearest percent, which has the least denominator? $\frac{5}{7}$

go.hrw.com
Web Extra!
KEYWORD: MT7 Census

ONGOING ASSESSMENT and **INTERVENTION**

Diagnose Before the Lesson
6-4 Warm Up, TE p. 288

Monitor During the Lesson
6-4 Know-It Notebook
6-4 Questioning Strategies

Assess After the Lesson
6-4 Lesson Quiz, TE p. 291

Interdisciplinary

Social Studies

Exercises 18–22 involve using U.S. Census data in percent problems. Students study census data from countries around the world in middle school social studies programs, such as Holt, Rinehart & Winston's *People, Places, and Change.*

📝 **TEST PREP and Spiral Review**

23. Multiple Choice There are 72 boys in the eighth-grade class at Lincoln Middle School. The other 55% of the class are girls. How many girls are there?

  Ⓐ 55   Ⓑ 72   Ⓒ 88   Ⓓ 127

24. Gridded Response 25% of what number is 9.6? **38.4**

Each square root is between two integers. Name the integers. (Lesson 4-6)

25. $\sqrt{35}$ **5, 6**   **26.** $\sqrt{45}$ **6, 7**   **27.** $\sqrt{55}$ **7, 8**   **28.** $\sqrt{65}$ **8, 9**   **29.** $\sqrt{140}$ **11, 12**

30. $\sqrt{27}$ **5 and 6**   **31.** $\sqrt{101}$ **10 and 11**   **32.** $\sqrt{42}$ **6 and 7**   **33.** $\sqrt{222}$ **11 and 12**   **34.** $\sqrt{1011}$ **31 and 32**

Find the decimal equivalent of each. (Lesson 6-1)

35. $\frac{5}{8}$ **0.625**   **36.** 212% **2.12**   **37.** 71% **0.71**   **38.** $4\frac{1}{12}$ **4.083**   **39.** $-\frac{3}{4}$ **−0.75**

40. $\frac{4}{5}$ **0.8**   **41.** 123% **1.23**   **42.** 26% **0.26**   **43.** $3\frac{1}{2}$ **3.5**   **44.** $27\frac{1}{5}$ **27.2**

TEST PREP DOCTOR ✚ Point out to students that Exercise 23 is a two-step problem. They must first find the total number of students in the class before calculating the number of girls in the class.

📓 **Journal**

Ask students to describe the process they would use to solve each of the three types of percent problems.

CHALLENGE 6-4

LESSON 6-4 Challenge
In the Chemistry Laboratory

When a chemist dilutes pure acid with another substance, the resulting mixture is no longer pure acid.

Consistent with the words, *pure acid* is 100% acid. So, there are 20 grams of pure acid in 20 grams of a pure-acid solution.

Laura, a chemist, has 20 grams of a solution that is only 40% acid.

1. How many grams of pure acid are there in Laura's acid solution?

    40% of 20 grams = 8 grams

Suppose, now, Laura wants to increase the acid content of the 40% acid solution to make it a 50%-acid solution.

2. What do you think Laura has to do to increase the acid content of the solution? **Possible answer:**

    Add some pure acid; also possible to evaporate.

Laura decides to add *n* ounces of pure acid to increase the acid content of the original 20 grams of 40%-acid solution to make it a 50%-acid solution.

3. Represent in terms of *n* the total number of grams in the new solution.   20 + *n*

4. Represent in terms of *n* the number of grams of pure acid in the new solution.   0.50 (20 + *n*)

Then, the amount of pure acid in the original solution plus the amount of pure acid added equals the amount of pure acid in the new solution.

5. Use the results of Exercises 1 and 4 to write an equation that will find the number *n* of grams of pure acid that will be added to the original solution to increase its acid content from 40% to 50%. Solve the equation.

    8 + n = 0.50(20 + n)
    8 + n = 10 + 0.50n
    n − 0.50n = 10 − 8
    0.50n = 2
    n = 4

6. Explain how to check your result. **Possible answer:**

    There are 24 g in all in the new solution; 50%, or 12 g, are pure acid.
    This is consistent with adding 4 g of pure acid to the original solution
    that had 8 g of pure acid.

PROBLEM SOLVING 6-4

LESSON 6-4 Problem Solving
Finding a Number When the Percent is Known

Write the correct answer.

1. The two longest running Broadway shows are *Cats* and *A Chorus Line.* *A Chorus Line* had 6137, or about 82% of the number of performances that *Cats* had. How many performances of *Cats* were there?

    7484

2. *Titanic* and *Star Wars* have made the most money at the box office. *Star Wars* made about 76.7% of the money that *Titanic* made at the box office. If *Star Wars* made about $461 million, how much did *Titanic* make? Round to the nearest million dollars.

    $601 million

Use the table below. Round to the nearest tenth of a percent.

Public Elementary and Secondary School Enrollment, 2001	
Grades	Population (in thousands)
Pre-K through grade 8	33,952
Grades 9–12	13,736
Total	47,688

3. What percent of students are in Pre-K through 8th grade?

    71.2%

4. What percent of students are in grades 9–12?

    28.8%

Choose the letter for the best answer.

5. In 2000, women earned about 72.2% of what men did. If the average woman's weekly earnings was $491 in 2000, what was the average man's weekly earnings? Round to the nearest dollar.

  A $355   Ⓒ $680
  B $542   D $725

6. The highest elevation in North America is Mt. McKinley at 20,320 ft. The highest elevation in Australia is Mt. Kosciusko, which is about 36% of the height of Mt. McKinley. What is the highest elevation in Australia? Round to the nearest foot.

  F 5480 ft   H 12,825 ft
  Ⓖ 7315 ft   J 56,444 ft

7. The Gulf of Mexico has an average depth of 4,874 ft. This is about 36.2% of the average depth of the Pacific Ocean. What is the average depth of the Pacific Ocean? Round to the nearest foot.

  A 1764 ft   C 10,280 ft
  B 5843 ft   Ⓓ 13,464 ft

8. Karl Malone is the NBA lifetime leader in free throws. He attempted 11,703 and made 8,636. What percent did he make? Round to the nearest tenth of a percent.

  F 1.4%   Ⓗ 73.8%
  G 58.6%   J 135.6%

Power Presentations with PowerPoint®

✓ **6-4 Lesson Quiz**

1. 10 is $12\frac{1}{2}$% of what number? **80**

2. 326 is 25% of what number? **1304**

3. 44% of what number is 11? **25**

4. 290% of what number is 145? **50**

5. Larry has 9 novels about the American Revolutionary War. This represents 15% of his total book collection. How many books does Larry have in all? **60**

Also available on transparency

READY TO GO ON?

Organizer

Objective: Assess students' mastery of concepts and skills in Lessons 6-1 through 6-4.

Resources

 Assessment Resources
Section 6A Quiz

 Test & Practice Generator
 One-Stop Planner®

INTERVENTION ⬅ ➡

Resources

 Ready to Go On?
Intervention and
Enrichment Worksheets

💿 **Ready to Go On? CD-ROM**

🪐 **Ready to Go On? Online**

my.hrw.com

Ready to Go On?

Quiz for Lessons 6-1 Through 6-4

✓ **6-1** **Relating Decimals, Fractions, and Percents**

Compare. Write $<$, $>$, or $=$.

1. $\frac{5}{6}$ ▨ 83% $>$ **2.** $\frac{4}{9}$ ▨ 45% $<$ **3.** 0.03 ▨ 3% $=$ **4.** 6.5 ▨ 65% $>$

Order the numbers from least to greatest.

5. $\frac{1}{4}$, 0.1, 3%, 28% **6.** 130%, $\frac{3}{2}$, 1.25, 10% **7.** $\frac{2}{3}$, 72%, 0.6, $\frac{3}{4}$

10%, 1.25, 130%, $\frac{3}{2}$

3%, 0.1, $\frac{1}{4}$, 28%

0.6, $\frac{2}{3}$, 72%, $\frac{3}{4}$

8. A molecule of ferric oxide is made up of 2 atoms of iron and 3 atoms of oxygen. What percent of the atoms of a ferric oxide molecule is oxygen? **60%**

✓ **6-2** **Estimate with Percents**

Estimate.

9. 48% of 52 **25** **10.** 33% of 613 **200** **11.** $12\frac{1}{2}$% of 57 **7** **12.** 60% of 26 **15**

Estimate the tip for each bill.

13. tip: 10% bill: $28.20 **$3** **14.** tip: 15% bill: $41.80 **$6**

15. Approximately 9.6% of all daily shipments are returned. Ms. Kui said that in a daily shipment of 12,034 packages, approximately 120 would be returned. Estimate to determine if Ms. Kui's number is reasonable. Explain. **No; Possible answer: 10% of 12,000 is about 1200, which is much greater than 120.**

✓ **6-3** **Finding Percents**

16. What number is 32% of 8? **2.56**

17. Of Canada's total area of 9,976,140 km^2, 755,170 km^2 is water. To the nearest tenth of a percent, what part of Canada is water? **≈ 7.6%**

✓ **6-4** **Finding a Number When the Percent Is Known**

18. 27 is 7.5% of what number? **360**

19. 336 is 375% of what number? **89.6**

20. The speed of sound in air at sea level at 32°F is 1088 ft/s. If that represents only 22.04% of the speed of sound in ice-cold water, what is the speed of sound in ice-cold water, to the nearest whole number? **4936 ft/s**

READY TO GO ON?

NO INTERVENE **YES ENRICH**

Diagnose and Prescribe

READY TO GO ON? Intervention, Section 6A			
Ready to Go On? Intervention	🗒 **Worksheets**	💿 **CD-ROM**	🪐 **Online**
✓ Lesson 6-1	6-1 Intervention	Activity 6-1	
✓ Lesson 6-2	6-2 Intervention	Activity 6-2	Diagnose and Prescribe Online
✓ Lesson 6-3	6-3 Intervention	Activity 6-3	
✓ Lesson 6-4	6-4 Intervention	Activity 6-4	

READY TO GO ON?
Enrichment, Section 6A

🗒 **Worksheets**
💿 **CD-ROM**
🪐 **Online**

Ready to Go On?

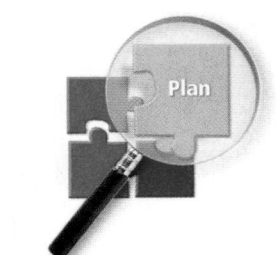

Focus on Problem Solving

Make a Plan

• **Do you need an estimate or an exact answer?**

When you are solving a word problem, ask yourself whether you need an exact answer or whether an estimate is sufficient. For example, if the amounts given in the problem are approximate, only an approximate answer can be given. If an estimate is sufficient, you may wish to use estimation techniques to save time in your calculations.

For each problem below, explain whether an exact answer is needed or whether an estimate is sufficient. Then find the answer.

1. In a poll of 5000 registered voters in a certain district, 2800 favored a proposed new library. What percent favored the new library?

2. Albert needs to score 78% on his final exam to get a B in his math class. If the final is worth 300 points, how many points does he need?

3. Mai is trying to save about $500 for a trip to Hawaii. If she has $125 in an account that earns 7% interest and puts $10 per month in the account, will she have enough in 3 years?

4. Esteban makes $8.30 per hour at his job. If he receives a 3% raise, how much will he be making per hour?

5. Carmen is planning to tile her kitchen floor. The room is 215 square feet. It is recommended that she buy enough tiles for an area 25% greater than the actual kitchen floor space to account for breakage. How many square feet of tile should she buy?

6. There are about 1,032,000 known species of animals on Earth. Of these, about 751,000 are insects. What percent of known species are insects?

Answers

1. 56%
2. 234 points
3. yes
4. $8.55
5. about 265 ft² of tile
6. about 75%

3. An estimation is sufficient because of the word *about*. Even without interest, Mai will have $125 + 36($10) = $485. It is likely that interest will be enough to make her balance over $500.

4. An exact answer is needed. 3% of $8.00 is $0.24, so Esteban's new pay rate should be around $8.50.

5. An estimate is sufficient because the 25% extra is an approximation of how many tiles may be broken. Round 215 to 200; 25% of 200 is 50, so she should buy about 215 + 50 = 265 tiles.

6. An estimation is sufficient because of the word *about*. Round each number: $\frac{750,000}{1,000,000} = \frac{3}{4}$. About 75% of the known species are insects.

Focus on Problem Solving

Organizer

Objective: Focus on making a plan to solve a problem by deciding whether an exact answer or an estimate is needed.

PREMIER Online Edition

Resources

Chapter 6 Resource Book
Reading Strategies

Problem Solving Process

This page focuses on the second step of the problem-solving process:
Make a Plan

Discuss

For each problem, have students tell whether an exact answer is needed and then use estimation to check the reasonableness of their answers. If estimation was all that was required, have them explain how they estimated.

Possible answers:

1. An exact answer is needed. 2800 out of 5000 is a little more than half. The answer should be a little more than 50%.

2. An exact answer is needed. 70% of 300 is 210. 80% of 300 is 240. Albert's score should be between 210 and 240.

State Resources

go.hrw.com
State Resources Online
KEYWORD: MT7 Resources

Applying Percents

Lesson	Materials	MiC and Lab Resources
Lesson 6-5 Percent Increase and Decrease ● Find percent increase and decrease. ☐ SAT-10　☑ ITBS　☑ CTBS　☑ NAEP		
Lesson 6-6 Applications of Percents ● Find commission, sales tax, and withholding tax. ☐ SAT-10　☑ ITBS　☑ CTBS　☑ NAEP	Calculators	**MiC: _It's All the Same_** pp. 9–17 **MiC: _Ups and Downs_** p. 43 **_Technology Lab Activities_** 6-6
Lesson 6-7 Simple Interest ● Compute simple interest. **6-7 Technology Lab** Compute Compound Interest ● Use a calculator to compute compound interest. ☐ SAT-10　☑ ITBS　☑ CTBS　☑ NAEP	Number cubes (MK), calculators	**_Technology Lab Activities_** 6-7

MK = *Manipulatives Kit*

Mathematics in Context

The units ***It's All the Same*** and ***Ups and Downs*** from the
Mathematics in Context © 2006 series can be used with Section 6B.
See Section Planner above for suggestions for integrating *MiC* with
Holt Mathematics.

Section Overview

Percent Increase and Decrease

Lesson 6-5

Why? Percents are often used to describe changes.

> **Percent change** is the ratio of the *amount of change* to the *original amount*.
> $$\text{percent change} = \frac{\text{amount of change}}{\text{original amount}}$$

Find the percent change on a $24 shirt that is on sale for $20.

First, find the **amount of change.**

$24 − $20 = **$4**

Next, find the **percent change.**

$$\frac{\text{amount of change}}{\text{original amount}} = \frac{\$4}{\$24} = \frac{1}{6} = 16\frac{2}{3}\%$$

There was a $16\frac{2}{3}\%$ decrease in the price.

Applications of Percents

Lessons 6-6, 6-7

Why? Percents are used in banking and in sales.

Commission

Last month, a real estate agent sold one house for $90,000, earning a 3% commission on the sale. The agent is paid a monthly salary of $1200 plus commission. What was her total pay last month?

$$\text{commission} = \text{commission rate} \cdot \text{sales}$$
$$= 0.03 \cdot 90{,}000$$
$$= \mathbf{\$2700}$$

$$\text{total pay} = \text{commission} + \text{salary}$$
$$= \$2700 + \$1200$$
$$= \$3900$$

The agent's total pay for last month was $3900.

Simple Interest

Find the amount repaid on a 4-year $13,500 loan at an annual simple interest rate of 6%.

Find the simple interest:

$$\text{simple interest} = \text{principal} \cdot \text{rate} \cdot \text{time}$$
$$I = Prt$$
$$= 13{,}500 \cdot 0.06 \cdot 4$$
$$= \mathbf{\$3240}$$

Find the amount repaid:

$$\text{amount} = \text{principal} + \text{simple interest}$$
$$A = P + I$$
$$= \$13{,}500 + \mathbf{\$3240}$$
$$= \$16{,}740$$

The amount repaid is $16,740.

Pacing: Traditional 1 day
Block $\frac{1}{2}$ day

Objective: Students find percent increase and decrease.

PREMIER Online Edition
Tutorial Videos

Countdown to Testing Week 11

Power Presentations
with PowerPoint®

Warm Up
1. 14,000 is $2\frac{1}{2}$% of what number?
   560,000
2. 39 is 13% of what number? **300**
3. $37\frac{1}{2}$% of what number is 12? **32**
4. 150% of what number is 189? **126**

Problem of the Day
In a school survey, 45% of the students said orange juice was their favorite juice, 25% preferred apple, and 10% preferred grapefruit. The remaining 32 students preferred grape juice. How many students participated in the survey?
160 students

Also available on transparency

Math Humor

Salesperson: I had zero sales this week, but next week I'm going after a 100% increase.

Manager: You should be going after a new job instead.

State Resources

go.hrw.com
State Resources Online
KEYWORD: MT7 Resources

6-5 Percent Increase and Decrease

Learn to find percent increase and decrease.

Vocabulary
percent change
percent increase
percent decrease

Many animals hibernate during the winter to survive harsh conditions and food shortages. While they sleep, their body temperatures drop, their breathing rates decrease, and their heart rates slow. They may even appear to be dead.

"He hums in his sleep."

Percents can be used to describe a change. **Percent change** is the ratio of the *amount of change* to the *original amount*.

$$\text{percent change} = \frac{\text{amount of change}}{\text{original amount}}$$

Percent increase describes how much the original amount increases.
Percent decrease describes how much the original amount decreases.

EXAMPLE 1 Finding Percent Increase or Decrease

Find the percent increase or decrease from 36 to 45.

This is a percent increase.

$45 - 36 = 9$ *First find the amount of change.*

Think: 9 is what percent of 36?

$\dfrac{\text{amount of increase}}{\text{original amount}} \rightarrow \dfrac{9}{36}$ *Set up the ratio.*

$\dfrac{9}{36} = 0.25 = 25\%$ *Find the decimal form. Write as a percent.*

From 36 to 45 is a 25% increase.

EXAMPLE 2 Life Science Application

A The heart rate of a grizzly bear slows from 50 to 8 beats per minute during hibernation. What is the percent decrease?

$50 - 8 = 42$ *First find the amount of change.*

Think: 42 is what percent of 50?

$\dfrac{\text{amount of decrease}}{\text{original amount}} \rightarrow \dfrac{42}{50}$ *Set up the ratio.*

$\dfrac{42}{50} = 0.84 = 84\%$ *Find the decimal form. Write as a percent.*

The grizzly bear's heart rate decreases by 84% during hibernation.

---

1 Introduce
Alternate Opener

EXPLORATION

6-5 Percent Increase and Decrease

1. After his first year at a job, Andrew's original hourly wage of $7.95 increased to $9.54.

   a. Subtract the old hourly wage from the new hourly wage to find the amount by which Andrew's hourly wage increased.

   b. Divide the amount in 1a by Andrew's original hourly wage to compare the amount of increase to the original hourly wage.

   c. Write the decimal in 1b as a percent to find the percent increase in Andrew's hourly wage.

2. An electronics store offers a $100 discount on everything in the store that is priced between $500 and $900. Complete the table to determine the percent of decrease for each price.

Price	$500	$600	$700	$800	$900
Percent of Decrease	$\frac{100}{500} =$ ___%	$\frac{100}{600} =$	$\frac{100}{700} =$	$\frac{100}{800} =$	$\frac{100}{900} =$

Think and Discuss

3. **Explain** how you wrote the decimal in Problem 1c as a percent.

4. **Compare** the percents of decrease in the table in Problem 2.

Motivate

Ask students to name a salary they would like to earn if they had a job (perhaps a student has a part-time job and can name an actual amount earned). Tell students to imagine that they received a 12% increase. Ask if anyone can compute the new salary. Point out to students that this lesson is about percent increase and percent decrease. You may want to discuss other situations involving various increases or decreases.

Explorations and answers are provided in *Alternate Openers: Explorations Transparencies.*

B According to the U.S. Census Bureau, 72.3 million children (aged 17 years and younger) lived in the United States in 2004. It is estimated that there will be 80.3 million children in 2020. What is the percent increase, to the nearest percent?

$80.3 - 72.3 = 8$ *First find the amount of change.*

Think: 8 is what percent of 72.3?

$\dfrac{\text{amount of increase}}{\text{original amount}} = \dfrac{8}{72.3}$ *Set up the ratio.*

$\dfrac{8}{72.3} \approx 0.1107 \approx 11.07\%$ *Find the decimal form. Write as a percent.*

From 2004 to 2020, the number of children in the United States is estimated to increase 11%.

EXAMPLE 3   Using Percent Increase or Decrease to Find Prices

A Anthony bought an LCD monitor originally priced at $750 that was reduced in price by 35%. What was the reduced price?

$\$750 \cdot 35\%$ *First find 35% of $750.*

$\$750 \cdot 0.35 = \$262.50$ *35% = 0.35*

The amount of decrease is $262.50.

Think: The reduced price is $262.50 *less than* $750.

$\$750 - \$262.50 = \$487.50$ *Subtract the amount of decrease.*

The reduced price of the monitor was $487.50.

B Mr. Anzivino received a shipment of refrigerators that cost $966 each. To set the retail price, he marks the price of each refrigerator up $66\frac{2}{3}\%$. What is the retail price of each refrigerator?

$\$966 \cdot 66\frac{2}{3}\%$ *First find $66\frac{2}{3}\%$ of $966.*

$\$966 \cdot \frac{2}{3} = \$644$ $66\frac{2}{3}\% = \frac{2}{3}$

The amount of increase is $644.

Think: The retail price is $644 *more than* $966.

$\$966 + \$644 = \$1610$ *Add the amount of increase.*

The retail price of each refrigerator is $1610.

Think and Discuss

1. **Explain** whether a 150% increase or a 150% decrease is possible.

2. **Compare** finding a 20% increase to finding 120% of a number.

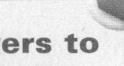
Possible answers to Think and Discuss

1. It is possible to have a 150% increase (e.g., from 10 to 25). It is usually not possible to have a 150% decrease, because a 100% decrease would result in 0, and any decrease beyond that would require negative numbers.

---

2 Teach

Guided Instruction

In this lesson, students learn to find percent increase and decrease. Explain to students that the actual amount of increase or decrease is not the same as the percent of increase or decrease. Emphasize that when calculating the percent, they must compare the amount of increase or decrease with the original amount. Explain that percent increase or decrease problems often involve two steps: solving a percent problem and addition or subtraction. In Example 2, the addition or subtraction is the first step. In Example 3, solving the percent problem is the first step.

 Reaching All Learners
Through Diversity

Ask students to find a fact in another subject area that involves a percent increase or decrease (e.g., social studies: population increase, economics: cost of living increase, health: increase in life expectancy, physical education: decrease in winning times for track events).

Have students prepare a brief report on the topic and include the percent of increase or decrease.

3 Close   ENGLISH LANGUAGE LEARNERS

Summarize

Remind students that when solving percent increase or decrease problems, the original amount is always used as the denominator. Ask students to name as many words as possible that indicate an increase or a decrease. Ask students what a 100% increase means and a 100% decrease means.

Possible answers: Increase: *go up, raise, rise, was higher, inflation, marked up, growth;* decrease: *went down, lowered, discount, savings, reduced, decline;* a 100% increase doubles the original amount; a 100% decrease reduces the original amount to zero.

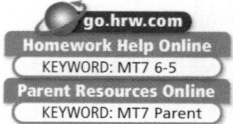

go.hrw.com
Homework Help Online
KEYWORD: MT7 6-5
Parent Resources Online
KEYWORD: MT7 Parent

Assignment Guide

If you finished Example 1 assign:
Average 1–3, 6–8, 11–13, 21, 22, 32–37
Advanced 6–8, 14–16, 21, 22, 28, 30, 32–37

If you finished Example 2 assign:
Average 1–4, 6–9, 11–13, 21, 22, 25, 27, 32–37
Advanced 6–9, 14–16, 21, 22, 27, 28, 30, 32–37

If you finished Example 3 assign:
Average 1–13, 17–22, 24, 25, 27, 32–37
Advanced 6–37

Homework Quick Check

Quickly check key concepts.
Exercises: 8, 9, 10, 18

Math Background

If an amount of increase is followed by an equal amount of decrease, the percent increase and the percent decrease are not equal. Consider the example:

Find the percent of increase from 40 to 50: $\frac{increase}{original\ amount} = \frac{10}{40} = 25\%$.

Find the percent of decrease from 50 to 40: $\frac{decrease}{original\ amount} = \frac{10}{50} = 20\%$.

The explanation for this is that a percent change is based on a comparison to an original amount. When the same amount of change (10) is compared with two different original amounts (40 and 50), you get different percents of change.

State Resources

go.hrw.com
State Resources Online
KEYWORD: MT7 Resources

GUIDED PRACTICE

See Example 1 — Find each percent increase or decrease to the nearest percent.

1. from 40 to 59
48% increase

2. from 85 to 30
65% decrease

3. from 85 to 170
100% increase

See Example 2 — **4.** A population of squirrels rose from 338 to 520 over a period of 3 years. What is the percent increase, to the nearest tenth of a percent? **53.8%**

See Example 3 — **5.** An automobile dealer agrees to reduce the $10,288 sticker price of a new car by 5% for a customer. What is the price of the car for the customer? **$9773.60**

INDEPENDENT PRACTICE

See Example 1 — Find each percent increase or decrease to the nearest percent.

6. from 800 to 1500
88% increase

7. from 0.76 to 0.59
22% decrease

8. from 35 to 19
46% decrease

See Example 2 — **9.** The boiling point of water is lower at higher altitudes. Water boils at 212°F at sea level and 193.7°F at 10,000 ft. What is the percent decrease in the temperatures, to the nearest tenth of a percent? ≈ **8.6%**

See Example 3 — **10.** Mr. Woodruff owns an automobile parts store and typically marks up merchandise 32% over warehouse cost. How much would he charge customers for a rotor that costs him $62.25? **$82.17**

PRACTICE AND PROBLEM SOLVING

Extra Practice
See page 793.

Find each percent increase or decrease to the nearest percent.

11. from $34.70 to $23.20
33% decrease

12. from $72 to $119
65% increase

13. from $320 to $195
39% decrease

14. from $644 to $588
9% decrease

15. from $0.37 to $0.28
24% decrease

16. from $12.50 to $14.75
18% increase

Find each missing number.

17. originally: $400 **$500**
new price: ▨
25% increase

18. originally: 140 **210**
new amount ▨
50% increase

19. originally: ▨ **120**
new amount: 210
75% increase

20. originally: ▨ **$4.47**
new price: $3.80
15% decrease

21. originally: 28 **50**
new amount: 42
▨% increase

22. originally: $45 **40**
new price: $27
▨% decrease

23. Multi-Step A pair of $195 boots are discounted 40%.

a. How much is the price decrease? **$78**

b. What is the sale price of the boots? **$117**

c. If the boots are reduced in price by an additional $66\frac{2}{3}\%$, what will be the new sale price? **$39**

d. What percent decrease does this final sale price represent? **80%**

RETEACH 6-5

LESSON 6-5 **Reteach**
Percent Increase and Decrease (continued)

To find the percent decrease:
• Find the amount of decrease by subtracting the lesser number from the greater.
• Write a fraction: percent decrease = $\frac{amount\ of\ decrease}{original\ amount}$
• If possible, simplify the fraction.
• Rewrite the fraction as a percent.

Carl's weight decreased from 175 lb to 150 lb.
Find the percent of decrease.
percent of decrease = $\frac{175-150}{175} = \frac{25}{175} = \frac{1}{7} = 7\overline{)1.000}^{0.143}$ = 14.3%

Complete to find each percent decrease.

4. Enrollment decreased from 1000 to 950.
$1000 - 950$
= **50**
$\frac{50}{1000} = \frac{5}{100}$
= **5** %

5. Temperature decreased from 75°F to 60°F.
$75 - 60$
= **15**
$\frac{15}{75} = \frac{3}{15} = \frac{20}{100}$
= **20** %

Find the amount of decrease.

percent decrease = $\frac{amount\ of\ decrease}{original\ amount}$

Change the fraction to a percent.

6. Sale price decreased from $22 to $17.
$22 - 17 = 5$
$\frac{5}{22}$
$\frac{5}{22} = 22\overline{)5.000}^{0.227}$ = **22.7** %

Find the amount of decrease.

percent decrease = $\frac{amount\ of\ decrease}{original\ amount}$

Change the fraction to a percent.

PRACTICE 6-5

LESSON 6-5 **Practice B**
Percent Increase and Decrease

Find each percent increase or decrease to the nearest percent.

1. from 16 to 20   **2.** from 30 to 24   **3.** from 15 to 30
increase 25%   decrease 20%   increase 100%

4. from 35 to 21   **5.** from 40 to 46   **6.** from 45 to 63
decrease 40%   increase 15%   increase 40%

7. from 18 to 26.1   **8.** from 24.5 to 21.56   **9.** from 90 to 72
increase 45%   decrease 12%   decrease 20%

10. from 29 to 54   **11.** from 42 to 92.4   **12.** from 38 to 33
increase 86%   increase 120%   decrease 13%

13. from 64 to 36.4   **14.** from 78 to 136.5   **15.** from 89 to 32.9
decrease 43%   increase 75%   decrease 63%

16. Mr. Havel bought a car for $2400 and sold it for $2700. What was the percent of profit for Mr. Havel in selling the car? **12.5%**

17. A computer store buys a computer program for $24 and sells it for $91.20. What is the percent of increase in the price? **280%**

18. A manufacturing company with 450 employees begins a new product line and must add 81 more employees. What is the percent of increase in the number of employees? **18%**

19. Richard earns $2700 a month. He received a 3% raise. What is Richard's new annual salary? **$33,372**

20. Marlis has 765 cards in her baseball card collection. She sells 153 of the cards. What is the percent of decrease in the number of cards in the collection? **20%**

24. Earth Science After the Mount St. Helens volcano erupted in 1980, the elevation of the mountain decreased by about 13.6%. Its elevation had been 9677 ft. What was its elevation after the eruption? **about 8361 ft**

25. Literature A signed hard-cover edition of Harper Lee's *To Kill a Mockingbird* is worth $1500. A paperback version of the novel sells for $6. What is the percent increase in price between the paperback version and the signed hard-cover version? **24,900%**

Harper Lee's *To Kill a Mockingbird* has sold over 10,000,000 copies worldwide and has been translated into more than 25 languages.

26. Multi-Step A video game console that is normally priced at $269.99 has been marked down to 70% of its original price. If sales tax is 8%, how much will Marcus pay for the discounted game console, to the nearest cent? **$204.11**

27. Last year, 12,932 people attended an annual convention. This year, 11,245 people are planning to attend. Does this represent a percent increase or a percent decrease? Find the percent change, to the nearest percent. **Percent decrease; 13%**

28. Critical Thinking Is the percent change the same when a DVD is marked up from $10 to $15 as when it is reduced from $15 to $10? Explain.

29. Choose a Strategy A digital camera originally sold for $249. Two months later, the price was reduced 40%. During a sale, the camera was discounted an additional 15% off the reduced price. What was the final price of the camera?

   Ⓐ $14.94   Ⓑ $22.41   Ⓒ $126.99   Ⓓ $136.95

30. Write About It Describe how you can use mental math to find the percent increase from 75 to 100 and the percent decrease from 100 to 75.

31. Challenge During a sale, the price of a cell phone was decreased by 20%. By what percent must the sale price be increased to restore the original price? **25%**

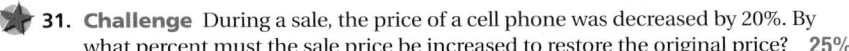

Test Prep and Spiral Review

32. Multiple Choice A washing machine that usually sells for $459 is on sale for $379. What is the percent decrease, to the nearest tenth of a percent?

   Ⓕ 17.4%   Ⓖ 21.1%   Ⓗ 32.8%   Ⓙ 82.6%

33. Extended Response Puzzle Place has discounted its puzzles 20%. A puzzle of a giraffe is priced at $20.95, and a puzzle of a mountain is priced at $16.50. How much will Thomas save on both puzzles? If the sales tax rate is 6%, what is the final cost of the puzzles? **$7.49; $31.76**

34. A square has a perimeter of 56 cm. If the square is dilated by a scale factor of 0.2, what is the length of each side of the new square? (Lesson 5-6) **2.8 cm**

Find each percent or number. (Lesson 6-3)

35. What percent of 122 is 61? **50%**   **36.** What is 35% of 2340? **819**   **37.** What is 145% of 215? **311.75**

CHALLENGE 6-5

 LESSON 6-5 Challenge
The Ups and Downs of the Marketplace

Prices change. The price of a stock can change every few minutes. The price of a house changes over a longer period of time.

The *selling price* of an item is what someone is willing to pay for it. It is a good measure of market value.

Find the current value of each item. Round your answer to the nearest cent

1. a. Amy bought a baseball card for $12. To date, the value of the card increased by 30%, then decreased by 15%, and finally increased by 40%.

Joe bought a baseball card for $12. To date, the value of the card decreased by 10%, then increased by 70%, and finally decreased by 5%.

Whose card is currently worth more? by how much? Explain.

Amy's, by $1.12
$18.56 − $17.44 = $1.12

b. By about what percent must the currently lesser-valued card increase to be of equal value with the greater-valued card? Round your answer to the nearest tenth of a percent.

6.4%

2. a. Jorge's family bought a house for $125,000. To date, the value of the house increased by 5%, then decreased by 25%, and finally increased by 10%.

Gene's family bought a house for $125,000. To date, the value of the house decreased by 5%, then increased by 15%, and finally decreased by 20%.

Whose house is currently worth more? by how much? Explain.

Gene's, by $968.75
$109,250 − $108,281.25
= $968.75

b. By about what percent must the currently lesser-valued house increase to be of equal value with the greater-valued house? Round your answer to the nearest tenth of a percent.

0.9%

PROBLEM SOLVING 6-5

LESSON 6-5 Problem Solving
Percent Increase and Decrease

Use the table below. Write the correct answer.

1. What is the percent increase in the population of Las Vegas, NV from 1990 to 2000? Round to the nearest tenth of a percent.

83.3%

2. What is the percent increase in the population of Naples, FL from 1990 to 2000? Round to the nearest tenth of a percent.

65.3%

Fastest Growing Metropolitan Areas, 1990–2000		
Metropolitan Area	Population 1990	2000	Percent Increase
Las Vegas, NV	852,737	1,563,282	
Naples, FL	152,099	251,377	
Yuma, AZ	106,895		49.7%
McAllen-Edinburg-Mission, TX	383,545		48.5%

3. What was the 2000 population of Yuma, AZ to the nearest whole number?

160,022

4. What was the 2000 population of McAllen-Edinburg-Mission, TX metropolitan area to the nearest whole number?

569,564

For exercises 5–7, round to the nearest tenth. Choose the letter for the best answer.

5. The amount of money spent on automotive advertising in 2000 was 4.4% lower than in 1999. If the 1999 spending was $1812.3 million, what was the 2000 spending?
  A $79.7 million C $1892 million
  Ⓑ$1732.6 million D $1923.5 million

6. In 1967, a 30-second Super Bowl commercial cost $42,000. In 2000, a 30-second commercial cost $1,900,000. What was the percent increase in the cost?
  F 1.7% H 442.4%
  G 44.2% Ⓙ4423.8%

7. In 1896 Thomas Burke of the U.S. won the 100-meter dash with a time of 12.00 seconds. In 2004, Justin Gatlin of the U.S. won a time of 9.85 seconds. What was the percent decrease in the winning time?
  A 2.15% C 21.8%
  Ⓑ17.9% D 45.1%

8. In 1928 Elizabeth Robinson won the 100-meter dash with a time of 12.20 seconds. In 2004, Yuliya Nesterenko won with a time that was about 10.4% less than Robinson's winning time. What was Nesterenko's time, rounded to the nearest hundredth?
  F 9.83 seconds H 12.16 seconds
  Ⓖ10.93 seconds J 13.47 seconds

Answers

28. Possible answer: No, the amount of change is the same, but the original amounts are different. So the resulting percents are different. The percent increase is $\frac{5}{10} = 50\%$, but the percent decrease is $\frac{5}{15} = 33\frac{1}{3}\%$.

30. Possible answer: In both cases, the amount of change is 25. The percent increase is $\frac{25}{75}$, which reduces to $\frac{1}{3}$, or $33\frac{1}{3}\%$. The percent decrease is $\frac{25}{100}$, or 25%.

TEST PREP DOCTOR ✚ For Exercise 30, remind students that they must first find the amount of change by subtracting $379 from $459. Then, they can calculate the percent increase. Students who chose answer **H** found what percent $379 is of $459.

✏️ Journal

Ask students to describe how they would calculate the percent increase in their height over the last year.

Power Presentations with PowerPoint®

✓ 6-5 Lesson Quiz

Find each percent increase or decrease to the nearest percent.

1. from 12 to 15 **25% increase**

2. from 1625 to 1400 **14% decrease**

3. from 37 to 125 **238% increase**

4. from 1.25 to 0.85 **32% decrease**

5. A computer game originally sold for $40 but is now on sale for 30% off. What is the sale price of the computer game? **$28**

Also available on transparency

Pacing: Traditional $1\frac{1}{2}$ days
Block $\frac{3}{4}$ day

Objective: Students find commission, sales tax, and percent of earnings.

Technology Lab
In *Technology Lab Activities*

Online Edition
Tutorial Videos

Countdown to Testing Week 11

Power Presentations
with PowerPoint®

Warm Up

Estimate. Possible answers:
1. 20% of 602   120
2. 133 out of 264   50%
3. 151% of 78   120
4. 0.28 out of 0.95   30%

Problem of the Day

A clothing outlet has a storewide clearance of 10% off all items. In addition, there is a "buy two, get one free" sale on a set of shirts of equal price. What is the total percent price reduction if you buy 3 shirts? 40 %

Also available on transparency

Math Humor

Student: Would you ever punish me for something that I didn't do?
Teacher: Of course not.
Student: Good...I didn't do my homework!

State Resources

go.hrw.com
State Resources Online
KEYWORD: MT7 Resources

6-6 Applications of Percents

Learn to find commission, sales tax, and percent of earnings.

Vocabulary
commission
commission rate
sales tax

Car salespeople often work for *commission*. A **commission** is a fee paid to a person who makes a sale. It is usually a percent of the selling price. This percent is called the **commission rate**.

commission rate • sales = commission

Often salespeople are paid a commission plus a regular salary. The total pay is a percent of the sales they make plus a salary.

EXAMPLE 1 Multiplying by Percents to Find Commission Amounts

Julie is paid a monthly salary of $2100 plus commissions. Last month she sold one car for $39,500, earning a 4% commission on the sale. How much was her commission? What was her total pay for the month?

First find her commission.

$4\% \cdot \$39,500 = c$	commission rate · sales = commission
$0.04 \cdot 39,500 = c$	Change the percent to a decimal.
$1580 = c$	Solve for c.

She earned a commission of $1580 on the sale.

Now find her total pay for last month.

$\$1580 + \$2100 = \$3680$ commission + salary = total pay

Her total pay for last month was $3680.

Sales tax is the tax on the sale of an item or service. It is a percent of the purchase price and is collected by the seller.

EXAMPLE 2 Multiplying by Percents to Find Sales Tax Amounts

If the sales tax rate is 7.75%, how much tax would Meka pay if she bought a portable CD player for $45.80 and two CDs for $15.99 each?

CD player: 1 at $45.80 → $45.80
CDs: 2 at $15.99   → $31.98
                          $77.78   *Total price*

$0.0775 \cdot 77.78 = 6.02795$ *Write the tax rate as a decimal and multiply by the total price.*

Meka would pay $6.03 in sales tax.

---

1 Introduce
Alternate Opener

EXPLORATION

6-6 **Applications of Percents**

You often need to calculate percents when making a purchase.

Use a calculator to find the tax on each item and the total cost of the item including the tax.

	Item	Cost	Tax Rate	Tax	Total Cost = Cost + Tax
1.	CD	$13.95	8%		
2.	DVD	$24.99	8%		
3.	Headphones	$29.95	8%		

Use a calculator to find the total cost of each item.

	Item	Cost	Tax Rate	Total Cost = 1.08 · Cost
4.	CD	$13.95	8%	
5.	DVD	$24.99	8%	
6.	Headphones	$29.95	8%	

Think and Discuss

7. Explain how you calculated the tax on each item in Problems 1–3.
8. Explain why the total cost is the same whether you use the formula *total cost = cost + tax* or the formula *total cost = 1.08 · cost*.

Motivate

Ask students if they've ever shopped in a store where the salesperson seemed especially helpful. Explain that in some stores, the amount an employee earns is based on how much merchandise he or she sells. Tell students that an amount earned based on sales is called a *commission*.

Explorations and answers are provided in *Alternate Openers: Explorations Transparencies*.

EXAMPLE 3 **Using Proportions to Find the Percent of Earnings**

Jorge earns $36,000 yearly. Of that, he pays $12,240 for rent. What percent of Jorge's earnings goes to rent?

Think: What percent of $36,000 is $12,240?

$$\frac{n}{100} = \frac{12,240}{36,000}$$ *Set up a proportion.*

$n \cdot 36,000 = 100 \cdot 12,240$ *Find the cross products.*

$36,000n = 1,224,000$ *Simplify.*

$$\frac{36,000n}{36,000} = \frac{1,224,000}{36,000}$$ *Divide both sides by 36,000.*

$n = 34$ *Simplify.*

So 34% of Jorges's earnings goes to rent.

EXAMPLE 4 **Dividing by Percents to Find Total Sales**

Students in Salim's class sell gift wrap to raise funds for class trips. The class earns 11% on all sales. If the class earned $647.35 this year, how much were the total sales?

Think: 647.35 is 11% of what number?

Let s = total sales

$647.35 = 0.11 \cdot s$ *Set up an equation.*

$$\frac{647.35}{0.11} = \frac{0.11s}{0.11}$$ *Divide each side by 11.*

$5885 = s$ *Simplify.*

The total sales of gift wrap for Salim's class were $5885.

Possible answers to
Think and Discuss

1. Both are based on percents of the price.

2. Yes. The price plus 6% is the same as 106% of the price.

3. Solve $x + 0.05x =$ total cost.

4. Usually, the sales tax would be double. If the tax rate is 8%, the tax on $10 would be $0.80 and the tax on $20 would be $1.60. However, if the tax rate is 8.25%, the tax on $10 would be $0.83 after rounding to the nearest cent, and the tax on $20 would be $1.65.

Think and Discuss

1. **Tell** how finding commission is similar to finding sales tax.

2. **Explain** whether adding 6% sales tax to a total gives the same result as finding 106% of the total.

3. **Explain** how to find the price of an item if you know the total cost after 5% sales tax.

4. **Explain** whether the sales tax on a $20 item would be double the sales tax on a $10 item. Justify your answer.

COMMON ERROR ALERT

When a percent contains a decimal point, students may interpret it as an amount of money. Students may interpret 8.25% as $8.25. Emphasize the difference between a percent and an amount of money.

Power Presentations with PowerPoint®

Additional Examples

Example 1
A real-estate agent is paid a monthly salary of $900 plus commission. Last month he sold one condominium for $65,000, earning a 4% commission on the sale. How much was his commission? What was his total pay last month? $2600; $3500

Example 2
If the sales tax rate is 6.75%, how much tax would Adrian pay if he bought two CDs at $16.99 each and one DVD for $36.29? $4.74

Example 3
Anna earns $1500 monthly. Of that, $114.75 is withheld for Social Security and Medicare. What percent of Anna's earnings are withheld for Social Security and Medicare? 7.65%

Example 4
A furniture sales associate earned $960 in commission in May. If his commission is 12% of sales, how much were his sales in May? $8000

Also available on transparency

---

 2 Teach

Guided Instruction

In this lesson, students learn to find commission, sales tax, and percent of earnings. Explain the meanings of *commission* and *sales tax*. Explain that each is a percent of some amount of money. Students use given percents to find these amounts in Examples 1 and 2. In Example 3, students find what percent of earnings a given amount of rent is. In Example 4, students use a given percent and a given amount of earnings to find an amount sold.

Reaching All Learners
Through Critical Thinking

Have students work in pairs. Tell students that they have been hired to sell cars. They can choose between three salary packages: A) $2500 per month with no commission, B) $1000 per month with 2% commission, or C) no monthly salary and 4% commission. If an average car sells for $20,000, have students calculate the salary they would receive if they sold 1, 3, or 5 cars in a month. Then have them discuss which salary package they would choose.

A) $2500; B) $1400, $2200, or $3000; C) $800, $2400, or $4000

3 Close

Summarize

Ask for volunteers to define each of the vocabulary terms. Remind students that commissions and sales taxes are based on the price of an item. Explain that many taxes are calculated as a percent of earnings, and that they are generally taken before you get a paycheck.

go.hrw.com
Homework Help Online
KEYWORD: MT7 6-6
Parent Resources Online
KEYWORD: MT7 Parent

Assignment Guide

If you finished Example ❶ assign:
Average 1, 5, 19–26
Advanced 5, 15, 19–26

If you finished Example ❷ assign:
Average 1, 2, 5, 6, 9–11, 19–26
Advanced 5, 6, 9–11, 15, 19–26

If you finished Example ❸ assign:
Average 1–3, 5–7, 14, 16, 19–26
Advanced 5–7, 9–11, 14–26

If you finished Example ❹ assign:
Average 1–14, 16, 19–26
Advanced 5–26

Homework Quick Check

Quickly check key concepts.
Exercises: 5, 6, 7, 8

Answers

15. Deborah should choose the salary option that pays $2100 plus 4% of sales. She would make $2300 to $2500 a month. The other salary option of $1800 plus 6.5% of sales would pay less. For sales totals of $10,000, she would make only $2451 a month.

16. $6.77; $16.25; $12.43; $133.82

go.hrw.com
State Resources Online
KEYWORD: MT7 Resources

State Resources

GUIDED PRACTICE

See Example ❶ **1.** Aaron earns a weekly salary of $350 plus a 7% commission on sales. Last week, his sales totaled $3200. What was his total pay? **$574**

See Example ❷ **2.** In a state with a sales tax rate of 7%, Hernando buys a radio for $59.99 and a CD for $13.99. How much is the sales tax? **$5.18**

See Example ❸ **3.** Last year, Nadia earned $31,025. Of that amount, she spent $3612.59 on food. What percent of her income went to food, to the nearest tenth of a percent? **11.6%**

See Example ❹ **4.** Shane works at a computer store. If he earns $20.93 from a 7% commission on the sale of a printer, what is the price of the printer? **$299**

INDEPENDENT PRACTICE

See Example ❶ **5.** Kayla earns a weekly salary of $290 plus a 5.5% commission on sales at a gift shop. How much would she make in a week if she sold $5700 worth of merchandise? **$603.50**

See Example ❷ **6.** The sales tax rate in Brad's town is 4.25%. If he buys 3 lamps for $22.49 each and a sofa for $829.99, how much sales tax does he owe? **$38.14**

See Example ❸ **7.** Jada typically earns $1545 each month, of which $47.20 is spent on electricity. What percent of Jada's earnings are spent on electricity each month, to the nearest tenth of a percent? **3.1%**

See Example ❹ **8.** Heather works in a clothes shop, where she earns a commission of 5% and no weekly salary. What will Heather's weekly sales have to be for her to earn $375 in one week? **$7500**

PRACTICE AND PROBLEM SOLVING

Extra Practice
See page 793.

Find each sales tax to the nearest cent.

9. total sales: $210.13
sales tax rate: 7.25%
$15.23

10. total sales: $42.99
sales tax rate: 9%
$3.87

11. total sales: $895.75
sales tax rate: 4.25%
$38.07

Find the total sales to the nearest cent.

12. commission: $63.06
commission rate: 5% **$1261.20**

13. commission: $2842
commission rate: 3.5% **$81,200**

14. **Consumer Economics** Roz takes home $1600 each month. She budgets 30% of her paycheck for rent, 20% for food, and 10% for utilities. The remainder is divided evenly among entertainment, clothes, transportation, savings, and charity. How much money does Roz budget each month for each category? **rent: $480, food: $320, utilities: $160; entertainment, clothes, transportation, savings, and charity: $128 each**

15. **Critical Thinking** Deborah can choose between a monthly salary of $1800 plus 6.5% of sales or $2100 plus 4% of sales. She expects sales between $5,000 and $10,000 a month. Which salary option should she choose? Explain.

RETEACH 6-6

Reteach
6-6 *Applications of Percents*

Salespeople often earn a **commission**, a percent of their total sales.

Find the commission on a real-estate sale of $125,000 if the commission rate is 4%.

Write the percent as a decimal and multiply.

commission rate × amount of sale = amount of commission
0.04 × $125,000 = $5000

If, in addition to the commission, the salesperson earns a salary of $1000, what is the total pay?

commission + salary = total pay
$5000 + $1000 = $6000

Complete to find each total monthly pay.

1. total monthly sales = $170,000; commission rate = 3%; salary = $1500

amount of commission = 0.03 × $ __170,000__ = $ __5100__

total pay = $ __5100__ + $1500 = $ __6600__

2. total monthly sales = $16,000; commission rate = 5.5%; salary = $1750

amount of commission = __0.055__ × $ __16,000__ = $ __880__

total pay = $ __880__ + $ __1750__ = $ __2630__

A **tax** is a charge, usually a percentage, generally imposed by a government.
Sales tax is the tax on the sale of an item or service.

If the sales tax rate is 7%, find the tax on a sale of $9.49.

Write the tax rate as a decimal and multiply.

tax rate × amount of sale = amount of tax
0.07 × $9.49 = $0.6643 ≈ $0.66

Complete to find each amount of sales tax.

3. item price = $5.19; sales tax rate = 6%

amount of sales tax = 0.06 × $ __5.19__ = $ __0.3114__ ≈ $ __0.31__

4. item price = $250; sales tax rate = 6.75%

amount of sales tax = __0.0675__ × $ __250__ = $ __16.875__ ≈ $ __16.88__

PRACTICE 6-6

Practice B
6-6 *Applications of Percents*

Complete the table to find the amount of sales tax for each sale amount to the nearest cent.

1.
Sale amount	5% sales tax	8% sales tax	6.5% sales tax
$67.50	$3.38	$5.40	$4.39
$98.75	$4.94	$7.90	$6.42
$399.79	$19.99	$31.98	$25.99
$1250.00	$62.50	$100.00	$81.25

Complete the table to find the commission for each sale amount to the nearest cent.

2.
Sale amount	6% commission	9% commission	8.5% commission
$475.00	$28.50	$42.75	$40.38
$2450.00	$147.00	$220.50	$208.25
$12,500.00	$750.00	$1125.00	$1062.50
$98,900.00	$5934.00	$8901.00	$8406.50

3. Alice earns a monthly salary of $315 plus a commission on her total sales. Last month her total sales were $9640, and she earned a total of $1182.60. What is her commission rate? __9%__

4. Phillipe works for a computer store that pays a 12% commission and no salary. What will Phillipe's weekly sales have to be for him to earn $360? __$3000__

5. The purchase price of a book is $35.85. The sales tax rate is 6.5%. How much is the sales tax to the nearest cent? What is the total cost of the book?

__sales tax is $2.33; total cost is $38.18__

6. Who made more commission this month? How much did she make? Salesperson A made 11% of $67,530. Salesperson B made 8% of $85,740.

__Salesperson A $7428.30__

7. Jon earned $38,000 last year. He paid $6,840 towards entertainment. What percent of his earnings did Jon pay in entertainment expenses? __18%__

8. The Cougars won 62% of their games. They won 93 games. How many games did they lose? __57 games__

Economics LINK

Tax brackets are used to determine how much income tax people pay. Depending upon a person's taxable income, tax is given by the formula base tax + tax rate (amount over). "Amount over" refers only to the income above the amount listed. Refer to the table for Exercises 16–18.

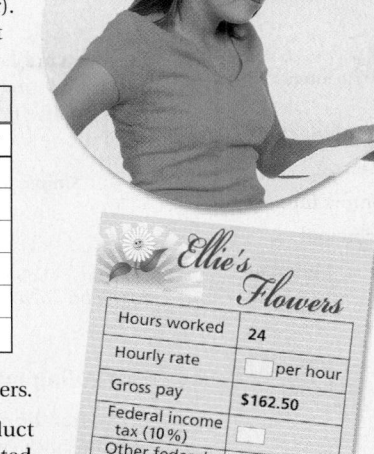

2005 IRS Income Tax Brackets (Single)			
Taxable Income Range	Base Tax	Tax Rate	Amount Over
$0–$7,300	$0	10%	$0
$7,300–$29,700	$730	15%	$7,300
$29,700–$71,950	$4,090	25%	$29,700
$71,950–$150,150	$14,652.50	28%	$71,950
$150,150–$326,450	$36,548.50	33%	$150,150
$326,450 and up	$94,727.50	35%	$326,450

16. Tina's pay stub is shown at right. Find the missing numbers.

Ellie's Flowers

Hours worked	24
Hourly rate	☐ per hour
Gross pay	$162.50
Federal income tax (10%)	☐
Other federal taxes (7.65%)	☐
NET PAY	☐

17. Anna earned $71,458 total in 2005. She was able to deduct $7250 for job-related expenses. This amount is subtracted from her total income to determine her taxable income.
   a. What was Anna's taxable income in 2005? **$64,208**
   b. How much income tax did she owe? **$12,717**
   c. What percent of Anna's total income did the tax represent? **≈ 17.8%**
   d. What percent of her taxable income did the tax represent? **≈ 19.8%**

18. ⭐ **Challenge** Charlena paid $10,050 in taxes in 2005. How much taxable income did she earn that year? **$53,540**

TEST PREP and Spiral Review

19. **Short Answer** Gabrielle earned a weekly salary of $235 plus 8% commission on sales over $500. What was her weekly pay if she had $6,250 in sales? **$695**

20. **Gridded Response** Rafael buys a video game for $49.95. The sales tax rate is 6.5%. What is the total cost, including tax, to the nearest dollar? **$53.20**

Simplify to tell whether the ratios form a proportion. (Lesson 5-1)

21. $\frac{3}{7}$ and $\frac{6}{14}$ **yes**
22. $\frac{5}{8}$ and $\frac{10}{4}$ **no**
23. $\frac{13}{4}$ and $\frac{52}{16}$ **yes**
24. $\frac{22}{7}$ and $\frac{11}{3}$ **no**

Find each percent increase or decrease to the nearest percent. (Lesson 6-5)

25. from 600 to 300 **50% decrease**
26. from $109.99 to $94.99 **14% decrease**

Interdisciplinary LINK

Economics

Exercises 16–18 involve using data from pay stubs and tax tables to solve percent problems. Understanding these types of problems is important in the study of economics.

TEST PREP DOCTOR + For Exercise 19, encourage students to read the problem carefully. Point out that the commission is added to the salary only when the weekly sales exceed $500. That means students must first subtract $500 from $6,250 before calculating the commission.

🖊 Journal

Ask students to write and explain whether they would prefer to have a job that pays commission or one that pays a straight salary.

Power Presentations with PowerPoint®

✓ 6-6 Lesson Quiz

1. Every month, Gillian makes $1600 plus an 8.9% commission on sales. If her sales last month totaled $18,400, what was her total pay? **$3237.60**

2. The sales tax is 5.75%, and the shirt costs $20. What is the total cost of the shirt? **$21.15**

3. Sheridan has a yearly income of $39,650, and he is advised to invest $4500 every year. What percent of his income should he invest, to the nearest tenth of a percent? **11.3%**

4. If you earn a 4% commission, how much would your total sales have to be to make a commission of $115? **$2875**

Also available on transparency

CHALLENGE 6-6

LESSON 6-6 Challenge
Shoppers' Delight

Shoppers save money by buying items on sale.
The amount by which the regular price is reduced is called a **discount**.

amount of discount = discount rate × regular price
sale price = regular price − amount of discount

Find the sale price after each discount.

1. regular price = $899;
   discount rate = 20%
   amount of discount = **$179.80**
   sale price = **$719.20**

2. regular price = $14.99;
   discount rate = 15%
   amount of discount = **$2.25**
   sale price = **$12.74**

Stores may offer discounts in a variety of ways.
Use $100 as the regular price for the item to write your explanations. Possible answers are given:

3. Buy one at regular price. Get a second one for half price. Explain how this is different from getting a 50% discount.
   50% discount: $50 for 1 item and $100 for 2 items
   2nd item half price: $100 for first item and $150 for 2 items

4. Buy two. Get one free. Explain how this is different from getting a 33⅓% discount.
   Buy 2, get 1 free: $200 for 3 items
   33⅓% discount: $200 for 3 items

5. This item is marked down by 10%. Use a coupon and get an additional 10% off. Explain how this is different from getting a 20% discount.
   20% discount on $100 item: pay $80
   After first 10% discount, item price is $90.
   Now, take 10% off $90 and final price is $81.

6. An item is marked "50% off — Today Only Get Another 50% off". Explain why the item is not free.
   The additional 50% is off 50% of the reduced price.
   The item is 25% of the original price.

PROBLEM SOLVING 6-6

LESSON 6-6 Problem Solving
Applications of Percents

Write the correct answer.

1. The sales tax rate for a community is 6.75%. If you purchase an item for $500, how much will you pay in sales tax?
   $33.75

2. A community is considering increasing the sales tax rate 0.5% to fund a new sports arena. If the tax rate is raised, how much more will you pay in sales tax on $500?
   $2.50

3. Trent earned $28,500 last year. He paid $8,265 for rent. What percent of his earnings did Trent pay for rent?
   29%

4. Julie has been offered two jobs. The first pays $400 per week. The second job pays $175 per week plus 15% commission on her sales. How much will she have to sell in order for the second job to pay as much as the first?
   $1500

Choose the letter for the best answer. Round to the nearest cent.

5. Clay earned $2,600 last month. He paid $234 for entertainment. What percent of his earnings did Clay pay in entertainment expenses?
   Ⓐ 9%
   B 11%
   C 30%
   D 90%

6. Susan's parents have offered to help her pay for a new computer. They will pay 30% and Susan will pay 70% of the cost of a new computer. Susan has saved $550 for a new computer. With her parents' help, how expensive of a computer can she afford?
   F $165.00   H $1650.00
   Ⓖ $785.71   J $1833.33

7. Kellen's bill at a restaurant before tax and tip is $22.00. If tax is 5.25% and he wants to leave 15% of the bill including the tax for a tip, how much will he spend in total?
   A $22.17   Ⓒ $26.63
   B $26.46   D $27.82

8. The 8th grade class is trying to raise money for a field trip. They need to raise $600 and the fundraiser they have chosen will give them 20% of the amount that they sell. How much do they need to sell to raise the money for the field trip?
   F $120.00   Ⓗ $3000.00
   G $857.14   J $3200.00

Objective: Students compute simple interest.

Online Edition
Tutorial Videos

Countdown to Testing Week 11

Power Presentations
with PowerPoint®

Warm Up

1. What is 35 increased by 8%? **37.8**

2. What is the percent of decrease from 144 to 120? **$16\frac{2}{3}\%$**

3. What is 1500 decreased by 75%? **375**

4. What is the percent of increase from 0.32 to 0.64? **100%**

Problem of the Day

Maggie is running for class president. A poll revealed that 40% of her classmates have decided to vote for her, 32% have decided to vote for her opponent, and 7 voters are undecided. If she needs 50% of the vote to win, how many of the undecided voters must vote for Maggie for her to win the election? **3**

Also available on transparency

Math Humor

Old bankers never die. They just lose their interest.

State Resources

go.hrw.com
State Resources Online
KEYWORD: MT7 Resources

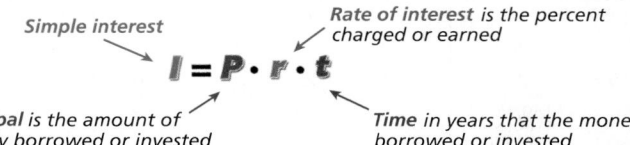
6-7 **Simple Interest**

Learn to compute simple interest.

Vocabulary
interest
simple interest
principal
rate of interest

When you borrow money from a bank, you pay **interest** for the use of the bank's money. When you deposit money into a savings account, you are paid interest. **Simple interest** is one type of fee paid for the use of money.

Simple interest → *Rate of interest is the percent charged or earned*

$$I = P \cdot r \cdot t$$

Principal is the amount of money borrowed or invested

Time in years that the money is borrowed or invested

EXAMPLE 1 **Finding Interest and Total Payment on a Loan**

Tristan borrowed $14,500 from his brother and promised to pay him back over 5 years at an annual simple interest rate of 7%. How much interest will he pay if he pays off the entire loan at the end of the fifth year? What is the total amount he will repay?

First, find the interest he will pay.

$I = P \cdot r \cdot t$	*Use the formula.*
$I = 14{,}500 \cdot 0.07 \cdot 5$	*Substitute. Use 0.07 for 7%.*
$I = 5075$	*Solve for I.*

Tristan will pay $5075 in interest.

You can find the total amount A to be repaid on a loan by adding the principal P to the interest I.

$P + I = A$	*principal + interest = amount*
$14{,}500 + 5075 = A$	*Substitute.*
$19{,}575 = A$	*Solve for A.*

Tristan will repay a total of $19,575 on his loan.

EXAMPLE 2 **Determining the Amount of Investment Time**

Isaiah invested $3500 in a mutual fund at a yearly rate of 6%. He earned $945 in interest. For how long was the money invested?

$I = P \cdot r \cdot t$	*Use the formula.*
$945 = 3500 \cdot 0.06 \cdot t$	*Substitute.*
$945 = 210t$	*Simplify.*
$4.5 = t$	*Solve for t.*

The money was invested for 4.5 years, or 4 years and 6 months.

---

① Introduce

Alternate Opener

EXPLORATION

6-7 **Simple Interest**

Simple interest is the amount earned on money deposited in some savings accounts.

The interest your account earns is calculated using the formula $I = Prt$. For example, if you start a savings account with $100.00 (*principal P*) and your savings account pays 5% (*interest rate r*), the interest (*I*) you will have earned at the end of 1 year (*time t*) will be $0.05 \cdot 100 = \$5$. Your total balance at the end of 1 year will be $100.00 + \$5.00 = \$105.00$.

Complete the table.

	Savings	Interest Rate	Interest	Total Balance
	$100	5%	$0.05 \cdot 100 = \$5$	$100 + 5 = \$105$
1.	$200	6%		
2.	$300		$24	
3.	$500			$550

Think and Discuss
4. **Describe** your strategies for completing the table.
5. **Explain** how to use the formula $I = Prt$ when you need to find an interest rate.

Motivate

Show students some bank advertisements or credit card applications that offer different interest rates. Explain that it is important to understand interest if you want to avoid paying more than necessary for something.

Explorations and answers are provided in *Alternate Openers: Explorations Transparencies.*

EXAMPLE **3** **Computing Total Savings**

Nadia's aunt deposited $3000 into a savings account as a college fund for Nadia. How much will be in this account after 5 years if the account earns a yearly simple interest rate of 3.5%?

$I = P \cdot r \cdot t$	*Use the formula.*
$I = 3000 \cdot 0.035 \cdot 5$	*Substitute. Use 0.035 for 3.5%.*
$I = 525$	*Solve for I.*

Now you can find the total.

$P + I = A$	*Use the formula.*
$3000 + 525 = A$	*Substitute.*
$3525 = A$	*Solve for A.*

Nadia will have $3525 in her savings account after 5 years.

EXAMPLE **4** **Finding the Rate of Interest**

To pay for her college expenses, Hannah borrows $7000. She plans to repay the loan in 5 years at simple interest. If Hannah repays a total of $9187.50, what is the interest rate?

$P + I = A$	*Use the formula.*
$7000 + I = \;\; 9187.5$	*Substitute.*
$\underline{-7000 \qquad\quad -7000}$	*Subtract 7000 from both sides.*
$I = \;\; 2187.5$	*Simplify.*

She paid $2187.50 in interest. Use the amount of interest to find the interest rate.

$I = P \cdot r \cdot t$	*Use the formula.*
$2187.5 = 7000 \cdot r \cdot 5$	*Substitute.*
$2187.5 = 35{,}000r$	*Simplify.*
$\dfrac{2187.5}{35{,}000} = \dfrac{35{,}000r}{35{,}000}$	*Divide both sides by 35,000.*
$0.0625 = r$	*Simplify.*

The simple annual rate is 6.25%, or $6\frac{1}{4}\%$.

Think and Discuss

1. Explain the meaning of each variable in the interest formula.

2. Tell what value should be used for t when referring to 6 months.

3. Name the variables in the simple interest formula that represent dollar amounts.

4. Demonstrate that doubling the time while halving the interest rate results in the same amount of simple interest.

Possible answers to *Think and Discuss*

1. I: simple interest earned, P: amount of money invested or borrowed, r: percent earned or charged, t: number of years the money is borrowed or invested.

2. Since t is always written in years, $t = 0.5$ or $\frac{1}{2}$.

3. I and P

4. interest on $500 at 8% for 1 year is $500 \cdot 0.08 \cdot 1 = \$40$; interest on the same amount at 4% for 2 years is $500 \cdot 0.04 \cdot 2 = \$40$.

Power Presentations with PowerPoint®

Additional Examples

Example **1**

To buy a car, Jessica borrowed $15,000 for 3 years at an annual simple interest rate of 9%. How much interest will she pay if she pays the entire loan off at the end of the third year? What is the total amount that she will repay? $4050; $19,050

Example **2**

Nancy invested $6000 in a bond at a yearly rate of 3%. She earned $450 in interest. How long was the money invested? 2.5 yr, or 2 yr 6 mo

Example **3**

John's parents deposited $1000 into a savings account as a college fund when he was born. How much will John have in this account after 18 years at a yearly simple interest rate of 3.25%? $1585

Example **4**

Mr. Johnson borrowed $8000 for 4 years to make home improvements. If he repaid a total of $10,320, at what interest rate did he borrow the money? 7.25%, or $7\frac{1}{4}\%$

Also available on transparency

---

2 Teach

Guided Instruction

In this lesson, students learn to compute simple interest. Begin by discussing *interest*. Explain to students that there are different kinds of interest, but that the principle of simple interest provides the basis for all types of interest. (Compound interest is addressed in Technology Lab 6-7.) Show them the formula $I = Prt$, and discuss what each of the four variables represents (Teaching Transparency). Emphasize the fact that the time is generally in years and that the rate should be changed to a decimal before using it in the formula. Point out that the formula can be used to solve for any of the four variables.

 Reaching All Learners
Through Cooperative Learning

Have the students work in pairs. Give each pair a store circular with an advertised interest rate for credit purchases and a number cube. Have students "buy" items on the store circular. Tell students to roll the number cube to determine the number of years they will take to pay for the item charged on their credit cards. Using the interest rate on the circular and the number of years rolled on the number cube, students are to calculate the interest they will owe on that item.

3 Close

Summarize

Remind students that they can earn interest on money that they deposit in the bank or invest in some other way. If they borrow money, they must pay interest as a fee to the lender. As the amount of time that the money is deposited or borrowed increases, so does the amount of interest that is paid.

go.hrw.com
Homework Help Online
KEYWORD: MT7 6-7
Parent Resources Online
KEYWORD: MT7 Parent

Assignment Guide

If you finished Example ① assign:
Average 1, 5, 9–12, 17, 22, 24–30
Advanced 5, 13–17, 20, 22–30

If you finished Example ② assign:
Average 1, 2, 5, 6, 9–12, 17, 18, 22, 24–30
Advanced 5, 6, 13–18, 20, 22–30

If you finished Example ③ assign:
Average 1–3, 5–7, 9–12, 17, 18, 22, 24–30
Advanced 5–7, 13–18, 20, 22–30

If you finished Example ④ assign:
Average 1–12, 17, 18, 22, 24–30
Advanced 5–30

Homework Quick Check

Quickly check key concepts.
Exercises: 5, 6, 7, 8

Math Background

While the principle of simple interest is mathematically important, compound interest is used for most applications in the real world. Students may benefit from studying compound interest (Technology Lab 6–7) as it will give them a better understanding of how interest works in the real world.

GUIDED PRACTICE

See Example ① **1.** Nick borrowed $7150, to be repaid after 5 years at an annual simple interest rate of 6.25%. How much interest will be due after 5 years? How much will Nick have to repay? **$2234.38; $9384.38**

See Example ② **2.** Mr. Williams invested $4000 in a bond with a yearly interest rate of 4%. His total interest on the investment was $800. What was the length of the investment? **5 years**

See Example ③ **3.** Paige deposited $1277 in a savings account. How much would she have in the account after 3 years at an annual simple interest rate of 4%? **$1430.24**

See Example ④ **4.** Tom borrowed $35,000 to remodel his house. At the end of the 5-year loan, he had repaid a total of $46,375. At what simple interest rate did he borrow the money? **6.5%**

INDEPENDENT PRACTICE

See Example ① **5.** A bank offers an annual simple interest rate of 7% on home improvement loans. How much would Billy owe if he borrowed $18,500 over a period of 3.5 years? **$23,032.50**

See Example ② **6.** Eliza deposits $8500 in a college fund. If the fund earns an annual simple interest rate of 6.5%, how long must the money be in the fund to earn $9392.50 in interest? **17 years**

See Example ③ **7.** Jessika gave a security deposit of $1200 to her landlord, Mr. Arce, 8 years ago. Mr. Arce now intends to give her the deposit back with simple interest of 2.85%. How much will he return to her? **$1473.60**

See Example ④ **8.** Premier Bank loaned a construction company $275,000 at an annual simple interest rate. After 5 years, the company repaid the bank $350,625. What was the interest rate on the loan? **5.5%**

PRACTICE AND PROBLEM SOLVING

Extra Practice
See page 793.

Find the interest and the total amount to the nearest cent.

9. $315 at 6% per year for 5 years
$94.50, $409.50

10. $800 at 9% per year for 1 year
$72, $872

11. $4250 at 7% per year for 1.5 years
$446.25, $4696.25

12. $550 at 5.5% per year for 3 years
$90.75, $640.75

13. $617 at 6% per year for 3 months
$9.26, $626.26

14. $2975 at 6% per year for 5 years
$892.50, $3867.50

15. $900 at 7.25% per year for 3 years
$195.75, $1,095.75

16. $200 at 7% per year for 9 months
$10.50, $210.50

17. Jabari borrowed $1700 for 15 months at 16% annual simple interest rate. How much interest will he have to pay? What is the total amount he will repay?
$340, $2040

18. Selena borrowed $9500 to buy a used car. The credit union charged 7% simple interest per year. She paid $3325 in interest. For what period of time did she borrow money? **5 years**

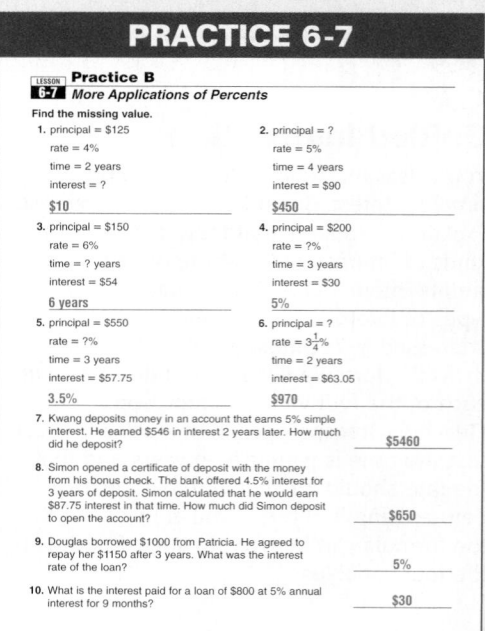

RETEACH 6-7

LESSON **6-7** Reteach
More Applications of Percents (continued)

Situation 3: Find r given I, P, and t.
$2500 was invested for 3 years $I = P \cdot r \cdot t$
and earned $450 in interest. $450 = 2500 \cdot r \cdot 3$
Find the rate of interest. $450 = 7500r$
$\frac{450}{7500} = \frac{7500r}{7500}$
The interest rate was 6%. $0.06 = r$

Find the interest rate in each case.

5. I = $1200; P = $6000; t = 4 years
$I = P \cdot r \cdot t$
$1200 = \underline{6000} \cdot r \cdot 4$
$1200 = \underline{24,000} \, r$
$\frac{1200}{24,000} = \frac{24,000 r}{24,000}$
$\underline{0.05} = r$
The interest rate was **5** %.

6. I = $325; P = $2000; t = 2.5 years
$I = P \cdot r \cdot t$
$325 = \underline{2000} \cdot r \cdot 2.5$
$325 = \underline{5000} \, r$
$\frac{325}{5000} = \frac{5000 r}{5000}$
$\underline{0.065} = r$
The interest rate was **6.5** %.

The total amount A of money in an account after interest has been earned, is the sum of the principal P and the interest I.

Amount = Principal + Interest
A = P + I

Find the amount of money in the account after $3500 has been invested for 3 years at a yearly rate of 6%.
First, find the interest earned.
$I = P \cdot r \cdot t$
$I = 3500 \cdot 0.06 \cdot 3 = $630 \longleftarrow$ interest earned
Then, add the interest to the principal. 3500 + 630 = 4130
So, the total amount in the account after 3 years is $4130.

Find the total amount in the account.

7. principal P = $4500; time t = 2.5 years; interest rate r = 5.5%
$I = P \cdot r \cdot t = \underline{4500} \cdot \underline{0.055} \cdot \underline{2.5} = $ \underline{618.75}$
Total Amount $= P + I = 4500 + \underline{618.75} = \underline{5118.75}$
So, after 2.5 years, the total amount in the account was $ \underline{5118.75}$

PRACTICE 6-7

LESSON **6-7** Practice B
More Applications of Percents

Find the missing value.

1. principal = $125
rate = 4%
time = 2 years
interest = ?
$10

2. principal = ?
rate = 5%
time = 4 years
interest = $90
$450

3. principal = $150
rate = 6%
time = ? years
interest = $54
6 years

4. principal = $200
rate = ?%
time = 3 years
interest = $30
5%

5. principal = $550
rate = 7%
time = 3 years
interest = $57.75
3.5%

6. principal = ?
rate = $3\frac{1}{4}$%
time = 2 years
interest = $63.05
$970

7. Kwang deposits money in an account that earns 5% simple interest. He earned $546 in interest 2 years later. How much did he deposit?
$5460

8. Simon opened a certificate of deposit with the money from his bonus check. The bank offered 4.5% interest for 3 years of deposit. Simon calculated he would earn $87.75 interest in that time. How much did Simon deposit to open the account?
$650

9. Douglas borrowed $1000 from Patricia. He agreed to repay her $1150 after 3 years. What was the interest rate of the loan?
5%

10. What is the interest paid for a loan of $800 at 5% annual interest for 9 months?
$30

Money
LINK

Many bank ATMs in Bangkok, Thailand, are located in sculptures to attract customers.

19. Critical Thinking Meghan and Sabrina compared the amount of interest they each earned on their savings accounts. Each had deposited $1000, but Meghan earned $140 interest and Sabrina earned $157.50. Whose savings account had a higher interest rate? Explain.

20. Money The Smiths will borrow $35,500 from a bank to start a business. They have two loan options. Option A is a 5-year loan; option B is a 4-year loan. Use the graph to answer the following questions.

a. What is the total amount the Smiths would pay under each loan option?

b. What would be the interest rate under each loan option?

c. What would be the monthly payment under each loan option?

d. How much interest will the Smiths save by choosing loan option B?

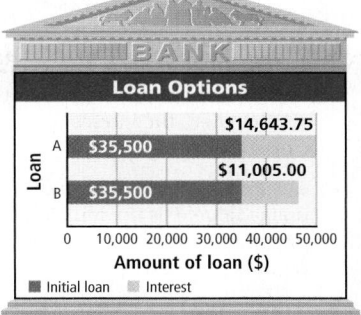

Loan Options

A $35,500 $14,643.75
B $35,500 $11,005.00

0 10,000 20,000 30,000 40,000 50,000
Amount of loan ($)
■ Initial loan ■ Interest

 21. What's the Question? Alice places $700 in a savings account with a simple annual interest rate of 4%. When Alice withdraws the money, she has $840. What is the question?

22. Write About It Which loan would cost a borrower less: $3000 at 6% for 4 years or $3000 at 7.5 for 3 years? How much interest would the borrower save by taking the cheaper loan?

23. Challenge How would the total payment on a 5-year loan at 3% annual simple interest compare with the total payment on a 5-year loan where one-twelfth of that simple interest, 0.25%, is calculated monthly? Give an example.

TEST PREP and Spiral Review

24. Multiple Choice Sam invested $2500 for 2 years in a savings account. The savings account paid an annual simple interest rate of 2.5% How much interest did Sam earn during the 2 years?

Ⓐ $62.50 Ⓑ $125 Ⓒ $1250 Ⓓ $2625

25. Multiple Choice Toni invested $250 in a savings account for 4 years. The total interest earned on the investment was $125. What was the interest rate on the account?

Ⓕ 3.125% Ⓖ 12.5% Ⓗ 125% Ⓙ 1125%

Find the appropriate factor for each conversion. (Lesson 5-3)

26. meters to millimeters
1000 mm/1 m

27. quarts to gallons
1 gal/4 qt

28. gallons to pints
8 pt/1 gal

Find each number. (Lesson 6-4)

29. 19 is 20% of what number? **95**

30. 74% of what number is 481? **650**

Answers

19–23. See p. A6.

 **TEST PREP DOCTOR +** Remind students that to convert the interest rate from a decimal to a percent, they must multiply the decimal by 100. For Exercise 25, students who answered **H** multiplied the decimal by 1000.

 Journal

Ask students to write about why they think that interest rates on savings accounts are low and interest rates on credit cards are high.

Power Presentations
with PowerPoint®

✓ **6-7 Lesson Quiz**

1. A bank is offering 2.5% simple interest on a savings account. If you deposit $5000, how much interest will you earn in one year? **$125**

2. Joshua borrowed $1000 from his friend and paid him back $1050 in six months. What simple annual interest did Joshua pay his friend? **10%**

3. The Hemmings borrowed $3000 for home improvements. They repaid the loan and $600 in simple interest four years later. What simple annual interest rate did they pay? **5%**

4. Mr. Berry had $120,000 in a retirement account. The account paid 4.25% simple interest. How much money was in the account at the end of 10 years? **$171,000**

Also available on transparency

Pacing:
Traditional $\frac{1}{2}$ day
Block $\frac{1}{4}$ day

Objective: Use a calculator to compute compound interest.

Materials: Graphing calculator

 Online Edition
TechKeys, Scientific Calculator

 Countdown to Testing Week 11

Resources

Technology Lab Activities
Lab 6-7 Recording Sheet

Teach

Discuss

Work through *Think and Discuss* item 1 with students, comparing the total compound interest earned with the total simple interest earned. Explain to students that when the same operations are repeated in mathematics, there is often a formula that incorporates these operations.

State Resources

Compute Compound Interest

Use with Lesson 6-7

Compound interest is interest paid not only on the principal but also on any interest that has already been earned. Every time interest is calculated, the interest is added to the principal for future interest calculations.

The formula for compound interest is $A = P\left(1 + \frac{r}{k}\right)^{nk}$, where A is the final dollar value, P is the initial dollar investment, r is the annual interest rate, n is the number of years, and k is the number of compounding periods per year.

Activity 1

❶ Use a calculator to find the value after 9 years of $1500 invested in a savings bank that pays 3% interest compounded annually.

The initial investment P is $1500. The rate r is 3% = 0.03. The interest period is one year. The number of interest periods n is 9, and $k = 1$.

$$A = 1500\left(1 + \frac{0.03}{1}\right)^{9 \cdot 1} = 1500(1.03)^9$$

On your graphing calculator, press

1500 ✕ 1.03 ^ 9 ENTER .

After 9 years, the initial investment of $1500 will be worth $1957.16 (rounded to the nearest cent).

```
1500*1.03^9
         1957.159776
```

❷ Use a calculator to find the value after 9 years of $1500 invested in a savings bank that pays 6% interest compounded semi-annually (twice a year).

The initial investment P is $1500. Since $n = 9$ years and interest is compounded twice a year ($k = 2$), there are $9 \cdot 2 = 18$ interest periods in 9 years. The interest rate for each period r is 6% divided by 2, or 3% = 0.03.

$$A = 1500 \times \left(1 + \frac{0.06}{2}\right)^{9 \cdot 2} = 1500 \times (1.03)^{18}$$

On your calculator, press 1500 ✕ 1.03 ^ 18 ENTER .
You should find that $A = \$2553.65$.

Think and Discuss

1. Compare the value of an initial deposit of $1000 at 6% simple interest for 10 years with the same initial deposit at 6% annual compound interest for 10 years. Which is greater? Why?

Close

Key Concept

You can use a calculator to apply the compound interest formula in various situations.

Assessment

Use a calculator and the compound interest formula to find the value of each investment.

1. $12,500 at 4% annual interest, compounded annually, for 5 years
$15,208.16

2. $800 at $5\frac{1}{2}$ % annual interest, compounded semi-annually for 7 years
$1169.60

Activity 1

Possible answer to *Think and Discuss*

1. Simple interest: $1600; compound interest $1790.85; the compound interest value is greater. With simple interest you earn interest only on the initial deposit. With compound interest you also earn interest on any interest you've already earned.

Answers to *Try This*

1. $3693.64

2. $6781.60

1. Find the value of an initial investment of $2500 for the specified term and interest rate.

   a. 8 years, 5% compounded annually

   b. 20 years, 5% compounded monthly

Activity 2

① Use a calculator to find the initial investment on an account that contains $3693.64 after earning 5% interest compounded annually for 8 years.

Using the formula for compound interest, you have
$3693.64 = P\left(1 + \frac{0.05}{1}\right)^{8 \cdot 1} = P(1.05)^8$. To isolate P, divide both sides of the equation by $(1.05)^8$. This results in $P = 3693.64 \div (1.05)^8$.

On your graphing calculator, press

3693.64 [÷] 1.05 [∧] 8 [ENTER].

The initial investment was $2500.00 (rounded to the nearest cent).

② Use a calculator to check the answer from ①.

If the initial investment was $2500, then
$A = 2500\left(1 + \frac{0.05}{1}\right)^{8 \cdot 1} = 2500(1.05)^8$.

On your graphing calculator, press 2500 [×] 1.05 [∧] 8 [ENTER].
You should find that $A = \$3693.638609$, which rounds to $3693.64.

Think and Discuss

1. Can you think of a time when earning compound interest would be more advantageous than earning simple interest? When would simple interest be better?

Try This

1. Danielle's parents are investing in a college fund for her. They hope to have $10,000 when Danielle starts college in 18 years. If the money in the account earns 6.25% interest compounded semiannually, how much should their initial investment be? Check your answer.

2. Rodney put some money in an account that earned 8% interest compounded quarterly (four times per year) 4 years ago in order to save for a car. If the account now has $2247.58, what was Rodney's initial investment? Check your answer.

Activity 2

Possible answer to *Think and Discuss*

1. Compound interest would be better than simple interest for a savings account that gathers interest for more than one year.

   Simple interest would be better when calculating the amount of interest owned on a loan.

Answers to *Try This*

1. $3302.91

2. $3085.45

Organizer

Objective: Assess students' mastery of concepts and skills in Lessons 6-5 through 6-7.

Resources

 Assessment Resources
Section 6B Quiz

 Test & Practice Generator
One-Stop Planner®

INTERVENTION

Resources

 Ready to Go On?
Intervention and
Enrichment Worksheets

Ready to Go On? CD-ROM

Ready to Go On? Online

 **my.hrw.com**

Ready to Go On?

Quiz for Lessons 6-5 Through 6-7

6-5 Percent Increase and Decrease

Find each percent increase or decrease to the nearest percent.

1. from 40 to 55
37.5% increase

2. from 75 to 150
100% increase

3. from 110 to 82
25% decrease

4. from 87 to 25
71% decrease

5. A population of geese rose from 234 to 460 over a period of two years. What is the percent increase, to the nearest tenth of a percent? **96.6%**

6. Mr. Simmons owns a hardware store and typically marks up merchandise by 28% over warehouse cost. How much would he charge a customer for a hammer that costs him $13.50? **$17.28**

7. A blouse and skirt that normally sell for $39.55 are on sale for 30% off the normal price. What is the sales price? **$27.69**

6-6 Applications of Percents

Find each commission or sales tax to the nearest cent.
$687.50

8. total sales: $12,500 **$406.25**
commission rate: 3.25%

9. total sales: $14.23
sales tax rate: 8.25% **$1.17**

10. total sales: $25,000
commission rate: 2.75%

11. total sales: $251.50
sales tax rate: 7.5% **$18.86**

12. total sales: $10,500
commission rate: 4%
$420

13. total sales: $75.99
sales tax rate: 6.125%
$4.65

14. Josh earns a weekly salary of $300 plus a 6% commission on sales. Last week, his sales totaled $3500. What was his total pay? **$5.10**

6-7 Simple Interest

Find the interest and the total amount to the nearest cent.

15. $225 at 5% per year for 3 years
$33.75; $258.75

16. $775 at 8% per year for 1 year
$62; $837

17. Leroy borrowed $8250 to be repaid after 3 years at an annual simple interest rate of 7.25%. How much interest will be due after 3 years? How much will Leroy have to repay? **$1,794.38; $10,044.38**

18. Kim deposited $1422 in a savings account. How much would she have in the account after 5 years at an annual simple interest rate of 3%? **$1,635.30**

19. Hank borrowed $25,000 to remodel his house. At the end of 3 years, he had repaid a total of $29,125. At what simple interest rate did he borrow the money? **5.5%**

20. Akule borrowed $1500 at an annual simple interest rate of 12%. He paid $270 in interest. For what period of time did Akule borrow the money?
1.5 years or 18 months

READY TO GO ON?

Diagnose and Prescribe

 **NO**
INTERVENE

	READY TO GO ON? Intervention, Section 6B		
Ready to Go On? Intervention	Worksheets	CD-ROM	Online
✓ Lesson 6-5	6-5 Intervention	Activity 6-5	
✓ Lesson 6-6	6-6 Intervention	Activity 6-6	Diagnose and Prescribe Online
✓ Lesson 6-7	6-7 Intervention	Activity 6-7	

 **YES**
ENRICH

READY TO GO ON?
Enrichment, Section 6B
Worksheets
CD-ROM
Online

Get in Gear Mrs. Okendo's class is planning a camping trip. The students need to buy some camping gear. They use the advertisement from Mitchell's Sporting Goods to help them plan their purchases.

1. What is the discount on the lantern as a percent? How much do you save by buying the lantern during the sale?

2. Jake is looking for a tent for under $100. Explain how he can estimate the dollar amount of the discount on the tent at Mitchell's. Will Jake be able to buy his tent there?

3. Mitchell's advertises that all backpacks are discounted at least 25% during the spring sale. Is the statement true? Why or why not?

4. Li Ming needs to buy a sleeping bag, tent, and lantern. How much will these items cost if she buys them at Mitchell's? How much money will she save altogether?

5. Mrs. Okendo buys a set of 8 compasses for the class at Mitchell's. If the sales tax rate is 8.25%, what is the final cost for the compasses?

MITCHELL'S SPORTING GOODS

SPRING SALE!

 18% OFF
COMPASS
REG. PRICE $6

$13.75 OFF THE REGULAR PRICE

BACKPACK REG. PRICE $62.50

14% OFF

TENT REG. PRICE $119

10% OFF

$\frac{2}{5}$ OFF

SLEEPING BAG REG. PRICE $42

LANTERN REG. PRICE $15

Multi-Step Test Prep

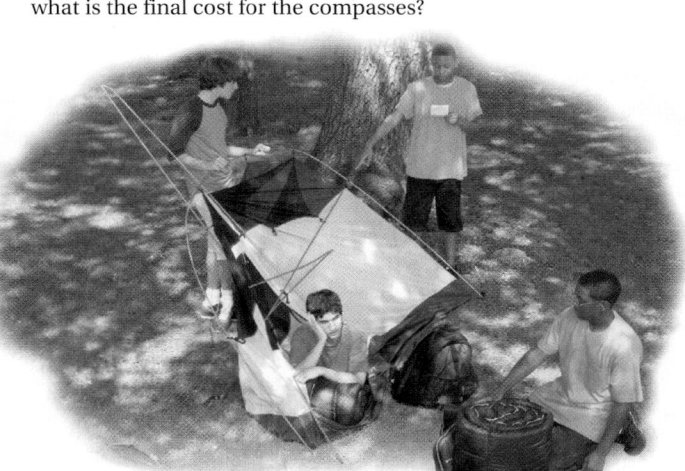

Organizer

Objective: Assess students' ability to apply concepts and skills in Chapter 6 in a real-world format.

🪐 **Online Edition**

Resources

🪐 **Middle School Assessments**
www.mathtekstoolkit.org

Problem	Text reference
1	Lesson 6-1
2	Lesson 6-2
3	Lesson 6-3
4	Lesson 6-4
5	Lesson 6-6

Answers

1. 40%, $6.00

2. Possible estimate: $18. Use compatible numbers to estimate the discount as 15% of $120, which is (10% + 5%) · 120 = 12 + 6 = $18. Jake will not be able to buy the tent at Mitchell's.

3. The statement is not true. The discount on the backpack in the table is 22%.

4. $37.80, $102.34, $9.00; total saved is $26.86

5. $42.61

INTERVENTION ⬅ ➡

Scaffolding Questions

1.  How do you convert a fraction to a percent? Divide the numerator by the denominator, then multiply by 100.

2. When estimating the cost of an item, is it better to estimate a little higher or a little lower than the actual cost? Why? It's better to estimate a little higher, because that way you can usually tell whether you'll have enough money to make the purchase.

3. What information do you need to answer this question? The percent discount of the backpack shown in the ad.

4. Can you add up the percent discounts to find the percent Li Ming will save? No

What is one way to find the approximate percent of Li Ming's savings? Find the average percent discount of the items she plans to buy.

5. To solve this problem, what should you do first, add the sales tax or reduce the price of the item by the percent discount? Why? Reduce the price by the percent discount first, because the sales tax is taken from the final sale amount.

Extension

1. Bill's Sporting Goods advertises lanterns at a regular price of $14 each. During their spring sale, if you buy two lanterns at the regular price, you can buy a third at 50% off. Which store offers the better price for three lanterns? Mitchell's

State Resources

🪐 **go.hrw.com**
State Resources Online
KEYWORD: MT7 Resources

Organizer

Objective: Participate in games to practice and apply skills learned in Chapter 6.

  Online Edition

Resources

📖 **Chapter 6 Resource Book**
Puzzles, Twisters & Teasers

Percent Puzzlers

Purpose: To apply the skill of solving percent problems to perplexing puzzles

Discuss Instruct students that it is often helpful to express percents as decimals or fractions in order to solve a problem. In problem 1, what fraction of his sheep did the farmer put in each pen? $\frac{1}{5}$ in the first pen, $\frac{3}{10}$ in the second pen, $\frac{3}{8}$ in the third pen, and $1 - (\frac{1}{5} + \frac{3}{10} + \frac{3}{8}) = \frac{5}{40} = \frac{1}{8}$ in the fourth pen

Extend Have students search the Internet for more tricky percent problems. Have them prepare their own percent puzzlers to test on a parent or classmate. Check students' work.

Percent Tiles

Purpose: To practice finding percents in a game format

Discuss When a student collects a card, have him or her write an equation to show that the card has been correctly completed.

Extend Have students play again using tiles containing numbers from 1 to 25.

Game Time

Percent Puzzlers

Prove your precision with these perplexing percent puzzlers!

❶ A farmer is dividing his sheep among four pens. He puts 20% of the sheep in the first pen, 30% in the second pen, 37.5% in the third pen, and the rest in the fourth pen. What is the smallest number of sheep he could have? **40**

❷ Karen and Tina are on the same baseball team. Karen has hit in 35% of her 200 times at bat. Tina has hit in 30% of her 20 times at bat. If Karen hits in 100% of her next five times at bat and Tina hits in 80% of her next five times at bat, who will have the higher percentage of hits? **Tina**

❸ Joe was doing such a great job at work that his boss gave him a 10% raise! Then he made such a huge mistake that his boss gave him a 10% pay cut. What percent of his original salary does Joe make now? **99%**

❹ Suppose you have 100 pounds of saltwater that is 99% water (by weight) and 1% salt. Some of the water evaporates so that the remaining liquid is 98% water and 2% salt. How much does the remaining liquid weigh? **50 lb**

Percent Tiles

Use cardboard or heavy paper to make 100 tiles with a digit from 0 through 9 (10 of each) on each tile, and print out a set of cards. Each player draws seven tiles. Lay four cards out on the table as shown. The object of the game is to collect as many cards as possible. To collect a card, use numbered tiles to correctly complete the statement on the card.

A complete set of the rules and game cards are available online.

go.hrw.com
Game Time Extra
KEYWORD: MT7 Games

Materials
• 4-8 in. colored squares of paper
• 2-4$\frac{1}{2}$ in. squares of card stock
• about 12 in. of ribbon
• tape
• glue
• markers

PROJECT **Origami Percents**

Make this spectacular fold-and-hold origami notebook to record facts about percents.

Directions

❶ Fold one of the colored squares of paper in half vertically and then horizontally. Unfold the paper. Then fold the square diagonally and unfold the paper. **Figure A**

❷ Fold the diagonal crease back and forth so that it is easy to work with. Then bring the two ends of the diagonal together as shown in the figure. **Figure B**

❸ Repeat steps 1 and 2 for all of the squares of paper, and set them aside.

❹ Lay the squares of card stock in front of you so that they are about $\frac{1}{4}$ inch apart. Lay the ribbon across the squares as shown, and tape it down. **Figure C**

❺ Glue one of the folded squares onto the piece of card stock on the left. Glue the next folded square onto the first one so that their sides match up and they open in the same direction. Continue with the remaining squares, gluing the last one onto the piece of card stock on the right.

Taking Note of the Math

Write notes from the chapter on the various faces of the folded squares.

A
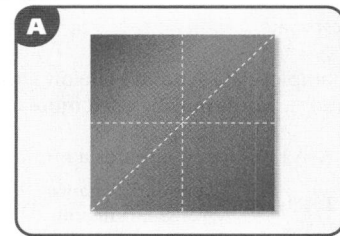

B
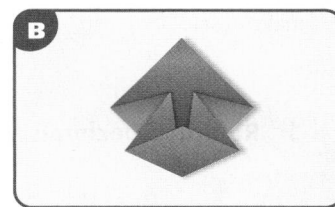

C
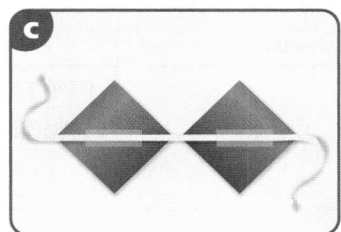

Organizer

Objective: Make a folding origami notebook on which to record notes about percents.

Materials: 4 colored squares of paper (8 in. by 8 in.), 2 squares of card stock (4$\frac{1}{2}$ in. by 4$\frac{1}{2}$ in.), about 12 in. of ribbon, tape, glue, markers

PREMIER **Online Edition**

Using the Page

Preparing the Materials
You can use paper squares that are specifically designed for origami or you can cut squares out of construction paper or copy paper.

Making the Project
To make the project flow more smoothly, demonstrate how to fold the paper squares before students begin folding them on their own.

Extending the Project
Students can make additional folded squares to make a longer chain. Have them use the extra space to write their own practice quiz on percents.

Tips from the Bag Ladies!

This project looks more complicated than it is. If your students are familiar with origami, they may recognize that the paper squares are folded into one of the most basic origami shapes.

As students are gluing the folded squares to each other, emphasize that the squares should all open in the same direction. This will make it much easier to use the resulting booklet.

Organizer

Objective: Help students organize and review key concepts and skills presented in Chapter 6.

 Online Edition
Multilingual Glossary

Resources

 PuzzlePro®
One-Stop Planner®

 Multilingual Glossary Online

go.hrw.com
KEYWORD: MT7 Glossary

 Lesson Tutorial Videos
CD-ROM

 Test & Practice Generator
One-Stop Planner®

Answers

1. percent
2. percent change
3. commission
4. 0.4375
5. 43.75%
6. $1\frac{1}{8}$
7. 112.5%
8. $\frac{7}{10}$
9. 0.7
10. 30
11. 62
12. 3.3
13. 18
14. $7.50
15. $16.00

Study Guide: Review

Vocabulary

benchmark 278
commission 298
commission rate 298
compatible numbers .. 278
estimate 278
interest 302
percent 274
percent change 294
percent decrease 294
percent increase 294
principal 302
rate of interest 302
sales tax 298
simple interest 302

Complete the sentences below with vocabulary words from the list above. Words may be used more than once.

1. A ratio that compares a number to 100 is called a(n) __?__.

2. The ratio $\frac{\text{amount of change}}{\text{original amount}}$ is called the __?__.

3. Percent is used to calculate __?__, a fee paid to a person who makes a sale.

6-1 Relating Decimals, Fractions, and Percents (pp. 274–277)

EXAMPLE

■ Complete the table.

Fraction	Decimal	Percent
$\frac{3}{4}$	0.75	0.75(100) = 75%
$\frac{625}{1000} = \frac{5}{8}$	0.625	0.625(100) = 62.5%
$\frac{80}{100} = \frac{4}{5}$	0.80	80%

EXERCISES

Complete the table.

Fraction	Decimal	Percent
$\frac{7}{16}$	**4.**	**5.**
6.	1.125	**7.**
8.	**9.**	70%

6-2 Estimate with Percents (pp. 278–282)

EXAMPLE

■ Estimate 6% of 17.

6% · 17 ≈ 5% · 20   *Use compatible numbers.*
≈ 0.05 · 20   *Write 5% as a decimal.*
≈ 1   *Multiply.*
6% of 17 is about 1.

EXERCISES

Estimate.

10. 11% of 303
11. 102% of 62
12. $33\frac{1}{3}$% of 10
13. 60% of 34
14. a 15% tip for $48.90
15. a 20% tip for $82.75

EXAMPLE

■ A raw apple weighing 5.3 oz contains about 4.45 oz of water. What percent of an apple is water?

$\dfrac{number}{100} = \dfrac{part}{whole}$ *Set up a proportion.*

$\dfrac{n}{100} = \dfrac{4.45}{5.3}$ *Substitute.*

$5.3n = 445$ *Cross multiply.*

$n = \dfrac{445}{5.3} \approx 83.96 \approx 84\%$

An apple is about 84% water.

EXERCISES

16. The length of a year on Mars is about 687 Earth days. The length of a year on Venus is about 225 Earth days. About what percent of the length of Mars's year is Venus's year?

17. The main span of the Brooklyn Bridge is 1595 feet long. The Golden Gate Bridge is about 263% the length of the Brooklyn Bridge. To the nearest hundred feet, how long is the Golden Gate Bridge?

Answers

16. 33%

17. 4200 ft

18. 7930 mi

19. 5 lb 7 oz

20. 16%

21. 472,750%

22. 34.4%

6-4 **Finding a Number When the Percent Is Known** (pp. 288–291)

EXAMPLE

■ In 2003 the population of Fairbanks, Alaska, was 30,970. This was about 491% of the population of Kodiak, Alaska. To the nearest ten people, find the population of Kodiak in 2003.

$\dfrac{491}{100} = \dfrac{30{,}970}{n}$ *Set up a proportion.*

$491n = 3{,}097{,}000$ *Cross multiply.*

$n = \dfrac{3{,}097{,}000}{491} \approx 6307.5356 \approx 6310$

The population of Kodiak was about 6310.

EXERCISES

18. The diameter at the equator of Saturn is 74,897 miles. This is about 945% of the diameter of Earth at its equator. To the nearest ten miles, find the diameter of Earth at its equator.

19. At the age of 20 weeks, Zoe weighed 16 lb 4 oz. Her birth weight was about $33\frac{1}{3}\%$ of her 20-week weight. To the nearest ounce, what was her birth weight?

6-5 **Percent Increase and Decrease** (pp. 294–297)

EXAMPLE

■ In 1990 there were 639,270 robberies reported in the United States. This number decreased in 2002 to 420,637. What was the percent decrease?

$639{,}270 - 420{,}637 = 218{,}633$ *Amount of decrease*

$\dfrac{amount\ of\ decrease}{original\ amount} = \dfrac{218{,}633}{639{,}270}$

$\approx 0.3420 \approx 34.2\%$

The number of reported robberies decreased by 34.2%.

EXERCISES

20. On sale, a skirt was reduced from $25 to $21. Find the percent decrease.

21. In 1900 the U.S. public debt was $1.2 billion dollars. This number increased to $5674.2 billion dollars in 2000. Find the percent increase.

22. At the beginning of a 40-week medically supervised diet, Arnie weighed 276 lb. After the diet, Arnie weighed 181 lb. Find the percent decrease.

Study Guide: Review

6-6 **Applications of Percents** (pp. 298–301)

EXAMPLE

- As an appliance salesman, Gavin earns a base pay of $525 per week plus a 6% commission on his weekly sales. Last week, his sales totaled $3250. How much did he earn for the week?

  Find the amount of commission.

  6% · $3250 = 0.06 · $3250 = $195

  Add the commission amount to his base pay.

  $195 + $525 = $720

  Last week Gavin earned $720.

EXERCISES

23. As a real estate agent, Kensho earns $4\frac{1}{2}\%$ commission on the houses he sells. In the first quarter of this year, he sold two houses, one for $175,000 and the other for $199,000. How much was Kensho's commission for this quarter?

24. If the sales tax is $8\frac{1}{4}\%$, how much tax would Luisa pay for a picture frame that costs $17.99 and a desk calendar that costs $24.99?

6-7 **Simple Interest** (pp. 302–305)

EXAMPLE

- For home improvements, the Walters borrowed $10,000 for 3 years at simple interest. They repaid a total of $11,050. What was the interest rate of the loan?

  Find the amount of interest.

  $$P + I = A \qquad \text{Use the formula.}$$
  $$10,000 + I = 11,050 \qquad \text{Substitute.}$$
  $$\underline{-10,000 \qquad\quad -10,000} \qquad \text{Subtract 10,000 from both sides.}$$
  $$I = 1050 \qquad \text{Simplify.}$$

  Substitute into the simple interest formula.

  $$I = P \cdot r \cdot t \qquad \text{Use the formula.}$$
  $$1050 = 10,000 \cdot r \cdot 3 \qquad \text{Substitute.}$$
  $$1050 = 30,000r \qquad \text{Simplify.}$$
  $$\frac{1050}{30,000} = \frac{30,000r}{30,000} \qquad \text{Divide both sides by 30,000.}$$
  $$0.035 = r \qquad \text{Simplify.}$$

  The interest rate of the loan was 3.5%.

EXERCISES

Using the simple interest formula, find the missing number.

25. interest = ▓; principal = $14,500; rate = $6\frac{1}{4}\%$ per year; time = $3\frac{1}{2}$ years

26. interest = $32; principal = ▓; rate = 2% per year; time = 4 years

27. interest = $367.50; principal = $1500; rate per year = ▓; time = $3\frac{1}{2}$ years

28. interest = $1787.50; principal = $55,000; rate = $6\frac{1}{2}\%$ per year; time = ▓

Which simple-interest loan would cost the borrower less? How much less?

29. $1000 at 3% for 4 years or $1000 at 3.75% for 3 years

Order the numbers from least to greatest.

1. $\frac{4}{5}$, 75%, 0.82, $\frac{17}{20}$
75%, $\frac{4}{5}$, 0.82, $\frac{17}{20}$

2. $\frac{8}{20}$, 0.35, 15%, 0.2
15%, 0.2, 0.35, $\frac{8}{20}$

75%, $\frac{7}{9}$, 0.08, $\frac{5}{6}$

3. 75%, $\frac{7}{9}$, 0.8, $\frac{5}{6}$

0.45, 49%, $\frac{33}{60}$, 58%

4. 58%, $\frac{33}{60}$, 0.45, 49%

Estimate.

5. 17% of 42 **6**
6. 79% of 122 **96**
7. 32% of 511 **170**
8. 83% of 197 **170**
9. 4% of 1900 **95**
10. 27% of 80 **20**
11. a 15% tip on a $37 bill **$6**
12. a 19% tip on a $53 bill **$10**
13. a 17% tip on a $23 bill **$3**

14. Of the 50 states in the Union, 32% have names that begin with either *M* or *N*. How many states have names beginning with either *M* or *N*? **16**

15. 30 is 12.5% of what number? **240**
16. 244 is 250% of what number? **97.5**
17. $7\frac{1}{2}$ is 5% of what number? **150**
18. 5.6 is 56% of what number **10**

19. At 3 P.M., a chimney casts a shadow that is 135% its actual height. If the shadow is 37.8 ft, what is the actual height of the chimney? **28 ft**

Find each percent increase or decrease to the nearest percent.

20. from 125 to 75
21. from 20 to 62
22. from 236 to 125
23. from 11 to 98
24. from 0.5 to 2
25. from 12.2 to 6.1
26. from 18.4 to 3.2
27. from 0.2 to 6

28. The price for a share of XYZ stock went from $32 to $37 in one month. What was the percent increase to the nearest tenth of a percent? **15.6%**

Find each commission or sales tax to the nearest cent.

$789.75

29. total sales: $13,600 **$374**
commission rate: 2.75%

30. total sales: $135.50 **$11.18**
sales tax rate: 8.25%

31. total sales: $20,250
commission rate: 3.9%

32. Ms. Tan earns $350 per week plus an 8% commission on her shoe sales. She sold $560 last week. What was her total pay for the week? **$394.80**

33. George earns an annual salary of $36,000. In addition to this, he earns a 3% commission on all sales he makes. If George had $264,000 in sales last year, what was his total pay? **$43,920**

34. Dena borrowed $7500 to buy a used car. The credit union charged 9% simple interest per year. She paid $2025 in interest. For what period of time did she borrow the money? **3 years**

35. At Thrift Bank, if you keep $675 in a savings account for 12 years, your money will earn $486 in interest. What annual simple interest rate doesthe bank offer? **6%**

20. **40% decrease**
21. **21% increase**
22. **47% decrease**
23. **791% increase**
24. **300% increase**
25. **50% decrease**
26. **83% decrease**
27. **2900% increase**

Chapter Test

Organizer

Objective: Provide review and practice for Chapters 1–6 and standardized tests.

Online Edition

Resources

 Assessment Resources
Chapter 6 Cumulative Test

 State Test Prep Workbook

 State Test Prep CD-ROM

 State Test Practice Online

go.hrw.com
KEYWORD: MT7 TestPrep

Standardized Test Prep

Cumulative Assessment, Chapters 1–6

Multiple Choice

1. If the figures are similar, what is the scale factor?

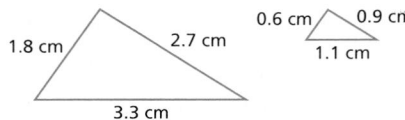

0.6 cm 0.9 cm
1.8 cm 2.7 cm 1.1 cm
3.3 cm

Ⓐ 1:3   Ⓒ 2:9
Ⓑ 2:3   Ⓓ 1:9

2. If the base of a right triangle is 24 centimeters and the hypotenuse is 40 centimeters, what is the area of the triangle?

Ⓕ 384 cm²   Ⓗ 768 cm²
Ⓖ 480 cm²   Ⓙ 960 cm²

3. Which situation corresponds to the graph?

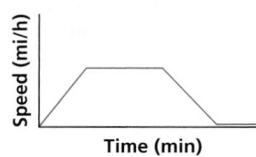

Speed (mi/h)
Time (min)

Ⓐ Jill's dog chases a cat, stops and waits, and then runs down a hill.

Ⓑ Joe's dog sits at his feet, sees a cat and darts off, and then comes back.

Ⓒ Abe's dog chases a squirrel to a tree, runs circles around the tree, and then runs back to Abe and sits down.

Ⓓ Amy's dog walks around the block, then runs to the house, and then sits.

4. Which equation is equivalent to the equation $\frac{1}{2}x + 8 = -10$?

Ⓕ $\frac{1}{2}x = -2$ Ⓗ $x + 8 = -20$

Ⓖ $x + 8 = -5$ Ⓙ $\frac{1}{2}x = -18$

5. Which situation corresponds to the inequality $x < 90$?

Ⓐ Jerry has at least $90 in his bank account.

Ⓑ Jerry owes his mom no more than $90 for his car insurance.

Ⓒ Jerry rented more than 90 videos last year.

Ⓓ Jerry works fewer than 90 hours each month at the newspaper.

6. A refrigerator that usually sells for $879 goes on sale for $649. What is the percent decrease, to the nearest tenth of a percent?

Ⓕ 12.2%   Ⓗ 35.4%
Ⓖ 26.2%   Ⓙ 173.8%

7. The human body is 65% water. Which is NOT an equivalent number?

Ⓐ 0.65   Ⓒ 6.5×10^{-1}

Ⓑ $\frac{13}{20}$ Ⓓ 6.50

8. One in every 3 girls plays a varsity sport in high school. In 1970, 1 in every 27 girls played a varsity sport. What is the percent increase, rounded to the nearest percent?

Ⓕ 8%   Ⓗ 800%
Ⓖ 88%   Ⓙ 888%

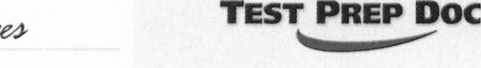
TEST PREP DOCTOR +

For item 4, remind students that in order to simplify the equation, they must subtract 8 from both sides. Students who answer   added 8 to the right side of the equation.

For item 7, remind students that in order to convert a percent to a decimal, they must divide by 100. Students who answered   divided by 10 instead.

Answers

15. 40%; $\frac{p}{100} = \frac{10}{25}$; $p = 40$

16. 40%; Every time Jim fills a jar he puts 1 L of excess into the 10 L jar. After he has filled the 4 L, 3 L, 2 L, and 1 L jars, there are 4 L in the 10 L jar.

$p \cdot 10 = 4$; $p = 0.4$

17–18. See p. A6.

19. See 4-Point Response work sample.

9. Gloria invests $158 in a simple interest account for 4 years at 2% interest. How many dollars did she earn in interest?

Ⓐ $170.64   Ⓒ $12.64

Ⓑ $126.40   Ⓓ $1.26

 HOT TIP! Underline key words, such as *at least*, *rounded to*, and *equivalent*, to help you focus on what is being asked.

Gridded Response

10. Heidi, Mike, Brenda, and Luis won 120 tokens in all at a fair. Heidi won $\frac{1}{5}$ of the tokens, Mike won 0.4 of the tokens, Brenda won 25% of the tokens, and Luis won the rest. How many tokens did Luis win?   **18**

11. Yesenia, a real estate agent, has 32 houses on the market. If she sells 5 of the houses this month, what percent of the houses on the market will she sell? Grid your response as a decimal rounded to the nearest thousandth. **15.625**

12. A recipe calls for 4 cups of strawberries for every 6 cups of whipped topping. If Gino uses 54 cups of whipped topping, how many cups of strawberries does he need?   **36**

13. Six more than $\frac{1}{4}$ of a number is $\frac{1}{3}$ of the number. What is the number?   **72**

14. What is the length of the hypotenuse after a dilation with a scale factor of $\frac{1}{2}$? Round your answer to the nearest hundredth.   **5.66**

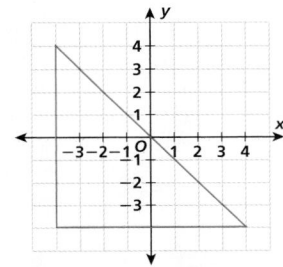

Short Response

15. If 10 kg of acid is added to 15 kg of water, what percent of the resulting solution is acid? Show your work.

16. In the chemistry laboratory, Jim is working with six large jars of capacities 5 L, 4 L, 3 L, 2 L, 1 L, and 10 L. The 5 L jar is filled with an acid mix, and the rest of the jars are empty. Jim uses the 5 L jar to fill the 4 L jar and pours the excess into the 10 L jar. Then he uses the 4 L jar to fill the 3 L jar and pours the excess into the 10 L jar. He repeats the process until all but the 1 L and 10 L jars are empty. What percent of the 10 L jar is now filled? Show your work.

17. Mr. Coluzzi bought a 5-pound bag of Granny Smith apples for $3.99. Individual apples cost $0.82 per pound. Justify whether Mr. Coluzzi made the better buy.

18. Four friends equally shared the cost of a $48.80 gift. They got a 20% discount and paid 7.25% sales tax. How much money did each person pay? Explain.

Extended Response

19. Amanda and Sergio each have $3000 to invest. Amanda invests with her local banker, while Sergio invests his money using an online service. They both invest at a 3% interest rate.

   a. Amanda's banker invests the money using a simple interest plan. If Amanda keeps her money in this plan for 5 years, how much interest will she earn?

   b. What is the value of Sergio's investment if he invests for 5 years compounded annually?

   c. What is the difference in the amount of money earned? Explain your reasoning.

   d. Who earns more money after 5 years?

Short Response Rubric

Items 15–18

2 Points = The student's answer is an accurate and complete execution of the task or tasks.

1 Point = The student's answer contains attributes of an appropriate response but is flawed.

0 Points = The student's answer contains no attributes of an appropriate response.

Extended Response Rubric

Item 19

4 Points = The student demonstrates a thorough understanding of all concepts and shows all work correctly.

3 Points = The student demonstrates a basic understanding of all concepts, but the work shows some flaws reflecting inattentive execution of mathematical procedures or some misunderstanding of the underlying mathematics.

2 Points = The student demonstrates only a partial understanding of the concepts or procedures embodied in the tasks. The approach may be correct but the work shows a misunderstanding of one or more important concepts.

1 Point = The student demonstrates a very limited understanding of the concepts or procedures embodied in the tasks. The response may show some understanding but exhibits many flaws or is incomplete.

0 Points = The student provides no response at all, or a completely incorrect or uninterpretable response.

Student Work Samples for Item 19

4-Point Response

> a. $I = Prt$
> $I = (3000)(0.03)(5)$
> $I = \$450$
> b. $A = P\left(1 + \frac{r}{k}\right)^{nk}$
> $A = (3000)\left(1 + \frac{0.03}{1}\right)^{5 \cdot 1}$
> $A = \$3477.82$
> c. $\$3477.82 - \$3450 = \$27.82$
> Subtract the amount Amanda earned from the amount Sergio earned.
> d. Sergio

The student correctly applied the simple interest and compound interest equations, correctly calculated the amounts, and offered an adequate explanation.

3-Point Response

> a. $I = Prt$
> $I = (3000)(0.30)(5)$
> $I = \$4500$
> b. $A = P\left(1 + \frac{r}{k}\right)^{nk}$
> $A = (3000)\left(1 + \frac{0.30}{k}\right)^{5 \cdot 1}$
> $A = \$11,138.79$
> c. $\$11,138.79 - \$4500 = \$6638.79$
> Subtract Amanda's total from Sergio's total.
> d. Sergio

The student correctly applied the simple interest and compound interest equations, but made a mistake in applying a percent, which caused errors in all calculations.

2-Point Response

> a. $I = Prt$
> $I = 3000 (3)(5)$
> $I = \$45,000$
> b. $A = (Prt)t$
> $A = (3000 \cdot 3 \cdot 5)5$
> $A = \$225,000$
> c. $\$225,000 - \$45,000 = \$180,000$
> Subtract one total from the other.
> d. Sergio

The student made a mistake in applying a percent, which caused errors in all calculations. The student also incorrectly applied the compound interest formula.

Objective: Choose appropriate problem-solving strategies and use them with skills from Chapters 5 and 6 to solve real-world problems.

 Online Edition

⭐ **Punxsutawney Phil**

Reading Strategies

Remind students to think about the strategies they have learned to use to solve percent problems. In problem 1, they can set up an equation to solve for the number of times Phil has seen his shadow during the 15-year period.

Using Data Help students become familiar with the table by making a list of the years Phil has seen his shadow, and another list of the years he has not seen his shadow.

 **Problem Solving on Location**

P E N N S Y L V A N I A

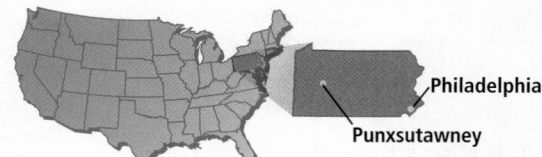

Philadelphia

Punxsutawney

⭐ **Punxsutawney Phil**

Punxsutawney Phil is our country's most famous groundhog. Each year on Groundhog Day (February 2), thousands of visitors trek to Punxsutawney, Pennsylvania, to await his appearance. According to tradition, if Phil comes out of his hole and sees his shadow, there will be six more weeks of winter. If he doesn't see his shadow, there will be an early spring.

Choose one or more strategies to solve each problem.

1. During the 15-year period from 1970 to 1984, the number of times Phil did not see his shadow was 25% of the number of times he did see his shadow. How many times did he see his shadow during this period? **12**

2. Groundhogs hibernate during the winter. While hibernating, their hearts beat at just 4% of their normal rate. A groundhog's normal heart rate is 139% that of a human's. Given that a typical human heart rate is 72 beats per minute, what is a groundhog's hibernating heart rate? **4 beats per minute**

For 3, use the table.

3. The table shows some Groundhog Day results from past years. Assume that the percent of time Phil sees his shadow will remain the same in the future.

   a. Predict the number of times Phil will *not* see his shadow from 2011 to 2018. **3**

   b. How many different ways are there to choose the years in which Phil does not see his shadow during this period? **2**

Phil's Shadow sightings			
1980	yes	1990	no
1981	yes	1991	yes
1982	yes	1992	yes
1983	no	1993	yes
1984	yes	1994	yes
1985	yes	1995	no
1986	no	1996	yes
1987	yes	1997	no
1988	no	1998	yes
1989	yes		

🔍 **Problem Solving Focus**

Encourage students to use the four-step problem-solving process for the problems. Focus on the first step: **Understand the Problem**.

Discuss with students what information is given in problem 2. Ask which type of percent problem that it is. Finding a number when the percent is known

State Resources

 **go.hrw.com**
State Resources Online
KEYWORD: MT7 Resources

Problem Solving Strategies

Draw a Diagram
Make a Model
Guess and Test
Work Backward
Find a Pattern
Make a Table
Solve a Simpler Problem
Use Logical Reasoning
Act It Out
Make an Organized List

✪ The Mural Arts Program

Reading Strategies
ENGLISH LANGUAGE LEARNERS

Discuss with students the importance of identifying all the pertinent information in a problem. In problem 3, extra information is given.

Using Data Ask students to suggest a reasonable scale factor for each of the murals in the table.

Problem Solving Focus

Ask students what strategies they used to solve each problem. Have them compare the different strategies they used to solve problem 1. Two reasonable strategies for solving problem 1 would be the guess and test strategy and solve a simpler problem.

✪ The Mural Arts Program

With more murals than any other U.S. city, Philadelphia is undoubtedly the Mural Capital of the United States. The city's mural arts program was founded in 1984 as a way to combat graffiti. Since then, the walls of more than 2400 buildings have been painted with murals.

Choose one or more strategies to solve each problem.

Philadelphia Murals		
Title	Height (ft)	Width (ft)
Camilla's Dream	28	33
Common Threads	120	62.5
Philadelphia Muses	60	115
Jackie Robinson	30	24

1. For the average mural, the ratio of the height to the width is 3:2. The sum of the height and width is 75 feet. What is the height of the average mural? **45 ft**

2. To create one of the city's murals, artist Don Gensler made a design on his computer and then projected sections of the image onto 5 ft by 5 ft pieces of cloth. The entire mural measured 35 ft by 125 ft. How many pieces of cloth were needed? **175**

For 3 and 4, use the table.

3. An artist makes a $\frac{1}{2}$ in. scale drawing of the Jackie Robinson mural. To help make a grid on the drawing, she makes a small mark every 3 in. around its perimeter. How many marks does he make? **431**

4. One of the murals in the table was created by students from McKinley Elementary School. Their mural has a height-to-width ratio that is less than 1. A scale drawing of their mural using a scale of 1:10 would be around 3 ft tall. Which mural was made by the students? **Jackie Robinson**

CHAPTER
7

Foundations of Geometry

Section 7A
Two-Dimensional Geometry
7-1 **Points, Lines, Planes, and Angles**
7-1 **Hands-On Lab** Bisect Figures
7-2 **Parallel and Perpendicular Lines**
7-2 **Hands-On Lab** Constructions
7-3 **Angles in Triangles**
7-4 **Classifying Polygons**
7-4 **Technology Lab** Exterior Angles of a Polygon
7-5 **Coordinate Geometry**

Section 7B
Patterns in Geometry
7-6 **Congruence**
7-7 **Transformations**
7-7 **Hands-On Lab** Combine Transformations
7-8 **Symmetry**
7-9 **Tessellations**

Pacing Guide for 45-Minute Classes

Calendar Planner
One-Stop Planner®

Chapter 7			**Countdown to Testing Weeks** ⑫, ⑬, ⑭	
DAY 1	**DAY 2**	**DAY 3**	**DAY 4**	**DAY 5**
7-1 Lesson	7-1 Hands-On Lab 7-2 Lesson	7-2 Lesson 7-2 Hands-On Lab	7-3 Lesson	7-4 Lesson
DAY 6	**DAY 7**	**DAY 8**	**DAY 9**	**DAY 10**
7-4 Technology Lab 7-5 Lesson	7-5 Lesson Ready to Go On? Focus on Problem Solving	7-6 Lesson	7-7 Lesson	7-7 Hands-On Lab 7-8 Lesson
DAY 11	**DAY 12**	**DAY 13**	**DAY 14**	
7-8 Lesson 7-9 Lesson	7-9 Lesson Ready to Go On? Multi-Step Test Prep	Chapter 7 Review	Chapter 7 Test	

Pacing Guide for 90-Minute Classes

Calendar Planner
One-Stop Planner®

Chapter 7				
DAY 1	**DAY 2**	**DAY 3**	**DAY 4**	**DAY 5**
7-1 Lesson 7-1 Hands-On Lab 7-2 Lesson	7-2 Lesson 7-2 Hands-On Lab 7-3 Lesson	7-4 Lesson 7-4 Technology Lab 7-5 Lesson	7-5 Lesson Ready to Go On? Focus on Problem Solving 7-6 Lesson	7-7 Lesson 7-7 Hands-On Lab 7-8 Lesson
DAY 6	**DAY 7**			
7-8 Lesson 7-9 Lesson Ready to Go On? Multi-Step Test Prep	Chapter 7 Review Chapter 7 Test			

ONGOING ASSESSMENT and INTERVENTION

DIAGNOSE	PRESCRIBE

Assess Prior Knowledge

Before Chapter 7

Diagnose readiness for the chapter.
Are You Ready? SE p. 321

Prescribe intervention.
Are You Ready? Intervention Skills 60, 68, 82

Formative Assessment

Before Every Lesson

Diagnose readiness for the lesson.
Warm Up TE, every lesson

Prescribe intervention.
Skills Bank SE pp. 820–834
Reteach CRB, Chapters 1–7

During Every Lesson

Diagnose understanding of lesson concepts.
Think and Discuss SE, every lesson
Write About It SE, lesson exercises
Journal TE, lesson exercises

Prescribe intervention.
Questioning Strategies Chapter 7
Reading Strategies CRB, every lesson
Success for ELL pp. 93–110

After Every Lesson

Diagnose mastery of lesson concepts.
Lesson Quiz TE, every lesson
Test Prep SE, every lesson
Test and Practice Generator

Prescribe intervention.
Reteach CRB, every lesson
Problem Solving CRB, every lesson
Test Prep Doctor TE, lesson exercises
Homework Help Online

Before Chapter 7 Testing

Diagnose mastery of concepts in the chapter.
Ready to Go On? SE pp. 352, 372
Focus on Problem Solving SE p. 353
Multi-Step Test Prep SE p. 373
Section Quizzes AR pp. 125–126
Test and Practice Generator

Prescribe intervention.
Ready to Go On? Intervention Chapter 7
Scaffolding Questions TE p. 373

Before High Stakes Testing

Diagnose mastery of benchmark concepts.
Test Tackler SE pp. 380–381
Standardized Test Prep SE pp. 382–383
State Test Prep CD-ROM

Prescribe intervention.
State Test Prep Workbook

Summative Assessment

After Chapter 7

Check mastery of chapter concepts.
Multiple-Choice Tests (Forms A, B, C)
Free-Response Tests (Forms A, B, C)
Performance Assessment AR pp. 127–140
Test and Practice Generator
Check mastery of benchmark concepts.
AYP State Tests

Prescribe intervention.
Reteach CRB, every lesson
Lesson Tutorial Videos Chapter 7

Prescribe intervention.
State Test Prep Workbook

KEY: **SE** = *Student Edition* **TE** = *Teacher's Edition* **CRB** = *Chapter Resource Book* **AR** = *Assessment Resources* Available on CD-ROM  Available online **320B**

CHAPTER
7

Supporting the Teacher

Chapter 7 Resource Book

Practice A, B, C
pp. 3–5, 12–14, 20–22, 28–30, 37–39, 46–48, 55–57, 64–66, 72–74

Reading Strategies ELL
pp. 10, 18, 26, 35, 44, 53, 62, 70, 79

Puzzles, Twisters, and Teasers
pp. 11, 19, 27, 36, 45, 54, 63, 71, 80

Reteach
pp. 6–7, 15, 23, 31–32, 40–41, 49–50, 58–59, 67, 75–76

Problem Solving
pp. 9, 17, 25, 34, 43, 52, 61, 69, 78

Challenge
pp. 8, 16, 24, 33, 42, 51, 60, 68, 77

Parent Letter   pp. 1–2

Transparencies

Lesson Transparencies, Volume 2 .... Chapter 7
• Warm Ups
• Problem of the Day
• Teaching Transparencies
• Lesson Quizzes

Know-It Notebook .... Chapter 7
• Additional Examples   • Chapter Review
• Vocabulary   • Big Ideas

Alternate Openers: Explorations .... pp. 47–55

Countdown to Testing .... pp. 23–28

Teacher Tools

Power Presentations®
Complete PowerPoint® presentations for Chapter 7 lessons

Lesson Tutorial Videos® SPANISH
Holt authors Ed Burger and Freddie Renfro present tutorials to support the Chapter 7 lessons.

One-Stop Planner® SPANISH
Easy access to all Chapter 7 resources and assessments, as well as software for lesson planning, test generation, and puzzle creation

IDEA Works!®
Key Chapter 7 resources and assessments modified to address special learning needs

Lesson Plans .... pp. 47–55

Questioning Strategies .... Chapter 7

Solutions Key .... Chapter 7

Interdisciplinary Posters and Worksheets .... Chapter 7

TechKeys   **Lab Resources**

Project Teacher Support   **Parent Resources**

Workbooks

Homework and Practice Workbook SPANISH
Teacher's Guide .... pp. 24–28

Know-It Notebook
Teacher's Guide .... Chapter 7

Problem Solving Workbook SPANISH
Teacher's Guide .... pp. 24–28

State Test Prep Workbook
Teacher's Guide

Technology Highlights for the Teacher

Power Presentations
Dynamic presentations to engage students. Complete PowerPoint® presentations for every lesson in Chapter 7.

2-1 Solving One-Step Equations

Isolate a variable by using inverse operations which "undo" operations on the variable.

An equation is like a balanced scale. To keep the balance, perform the same operation on both sides.

Inverse Operations	
Operation	**Inverse Operation**
Addition	Subtraction
Subtraction	Addition

One-Stop Planner SPANISH
Easy access to Chapter 7 resources and assessments. Includes lesson-planning, test-generation, and puzzle-creation software.

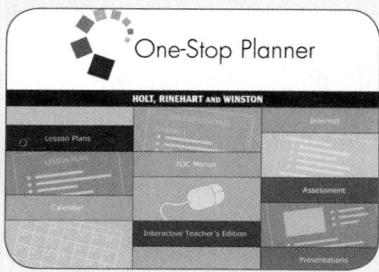

Premier Online Edition SPANISH
Chapter 7 includes Tutorial Videos, Lesson Activities, Lesson Quizzes, Homework Help, and Chapter Project.

Classifying Triangles

KEY: SE = *Student Edition*   **TE** = *Teacher's Edition*   ELL English Language Learners   SPANISH Spanish version available   Available on CD-ROM    Available online

Reaching All Learners

Resources for All Learners

Hands-On Lab Activities...................................... Chapter 7

Technology Lab Activities................................... Chapter 7

Homework and Practice Workbook SPANISH ....pp. 47–55

Know-It Notebook... Chapter 7

Problem Solving Workbook SPANISH ....pp. 47–55

DEVELOPING LEARNERS

Practice A..CRB, every lesson

Reteach..CRB, every lesson

Inclusion..TE pp. 337, 355

Questioning Strategies................................... Chapter 7

Modified Chapter 7 Resources .... *IDEA Works!*

Homework Help **Online** 🪐

ON-LEVEL LEARNERS

Practice B..CRB, every lesson

Puzzles, Twisters, and Teasers.................CRB, every lesson

Modeling..TE p. 369

Cooperative Learning..................................TE p. 348

ADVANCED LEARNERS

Practice C..CRB, every lesson

Challenge..CRB, every lesson

Extension.........................TE pp. 323, 373, 374, 375

Critical Thinking...TE p. 337

English Language Learners

Are You Ready? Vocabulary ....SE p. 321

Vocabulary Connections ....SE p. 322

Lesson Vocabulary ....SE, every lesson

Vocabulary Review...SE p. 376

English Language Learners............TE pp. 323, 325, 326, 341

Reading Strategies ....CRB, every lesson

Success for English Language Learners.................pp. 93–110

Multilingual Glossary 🪐

Reaching All Learners Through...

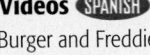

Inclusion ....TE pp. 337, 355

Diversity...TE p. 342

Auditory Cues ....TE p. 331

Kinesthetic Experience ....TE p. 325

Concrete Manipulatives.....................TE pp. 355, 359, 365

Cooperative Learning ....TE p. 348

Modeling..TE p. 369

Critical Thinking ....TE p. 337

Test Prep Doctor..................TE pp. 328, 333, 340, 345, 351, 357, 361, 367, 380, 382

Common Error Alerts ....TE p. 343

Scaffolding Questions..................................TE p. 373

Technology Highlights for Reaching All Learners

📀 Lesson Tutorial Videos SPANISH

Starring Holt authors Ed Burger and Freddie Renfro! Live tutorials to support every lesson in Chapter 7.

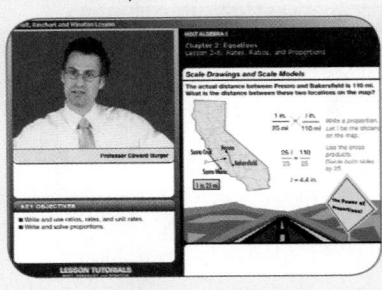

🪐 Multilingual Glossary

Searchable glossary includes definitions in English, Spanish, Vietnamese, Chinese, Hmong, Korean, and 4 other languages.

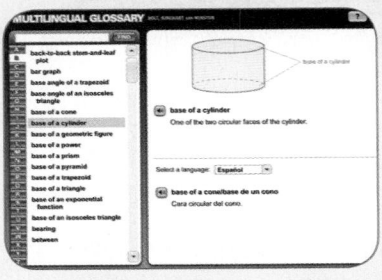

🪐 Online Interactivities

Interactive tutorials provide visually engaging alternative opportunities to learn concepts and master skills.

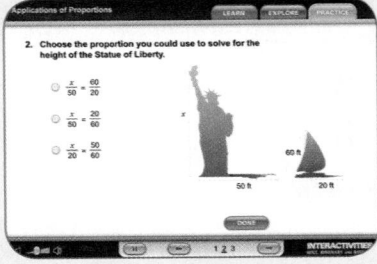

KEY: **SE** = *Student Edition*   **TE** = *Teacher's Edition*   **CRB** = *Chapter Resource Book*   SPANISH Spanish version available   Available on CD-ROM    Available online

CHAPTER 7

Ongoing Assessment

Assessing Prior Knowledge

Determine whether students have the prerequisite concepts and skills for success in Chapter 7.

Are You Ready? SPANISH .... SE p. 321
Warm Up .... TE, every lesson

Test Preparation

Provide review and practice for Chapter 7 and standardized tests.

Multi-Step Test Prep .... SE p. 373
Study Guide: Review .... SE pp. 376–378
Test Tackler .... SE pp. 380–381
Standardized Test Prep .... SE pp. 382–383
Countdown to Testing Transparencies ....pp. 23–28
State Test Prep Workbook
State Test Prep CD-ROM
IDEA Works!

Alternative Assessment

Assess students' understanding of Chapter 7 concepts and combined problem-solving skills.

Chapter 7 Project .... SE p. 320
Performance Assessment SPANISH .... AR pp. 139–140
Portfolio Assessment SPANISH .... AR p. xxxiv

Daily Assessment

Provide formative assessment for each day of Chapter 7.

Questioning Strategies .... Chapter 7
Think and Discuss .... SE, every lesson
Write About It .... SE, lesson exercises
Journal .... TE, lesson exercises
Lesson Quiz .... TE, every lesson
Modified Lesson Quizzes .... IDEA Works!

Weekly Assessment

Provide formative assessment for each week of Chapter 7.

Focus on Problem Solving .... SE p. 353
Multi-Step Test Prep .... SE p. 373
Ready to Go On? SPANISH .... SE pp. 352, 372
Cumulative Assessment .... SE pp. 382–383
Test and Practice Generator SPANISH ...One-Stop Planner

Formal Assessment

Provide summative assessment of Chapter 7 mastery.

Section Quizzes SPANISH .... AR pp. 125–126
Chapter 7 Test .... SE p. 379
Chapter Test (Levels A, B, C) SPANISH .... AR pp. 127–138
    • Multiple-Choice • Free-Response
Cumulative Test SPANISH .... AR pp. 141–144
Test and Practice Generator SPANISH ...One-Stop Planner
Modified Chapter 7 Test .... IDEA Works!

Technology Highlights for the Teacher

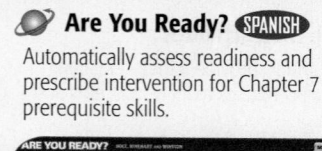 **Are You Ready?** SPANISH
Automatically assess readiness and prescribe intervention for Chapter 7 prerequisite skills.

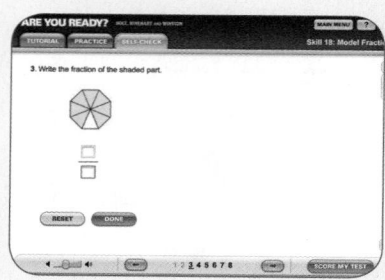

 **Ready to Go On?** SPANISH
Automatically assess understanding of and prescribe intervention for Sections 7A and 7B.

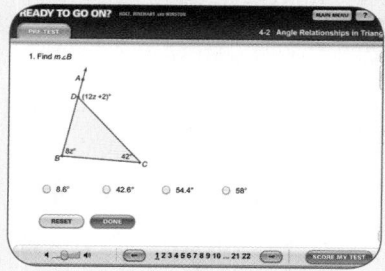

Test and Practice Generator SPANISH
Use Chapter 7 problem banks to create assessments and worksheets to print out or deliver online. Includes dynamic problems.

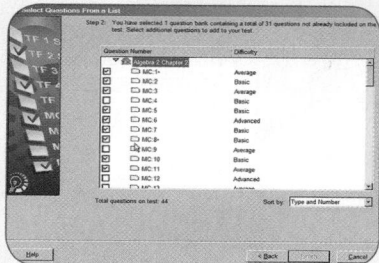

KEY: **SE** = *Student Edition*   **TE** = *Teacher's Edition*   **AR** = *Assessment Resources*   SPANISH Spanish version available   Available on CD-ROM   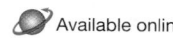 Available online

Formal Assessment

Three levels (A, B, C) of multiple-choice and free-response chapter tests are available in the *Assessment Resources.*

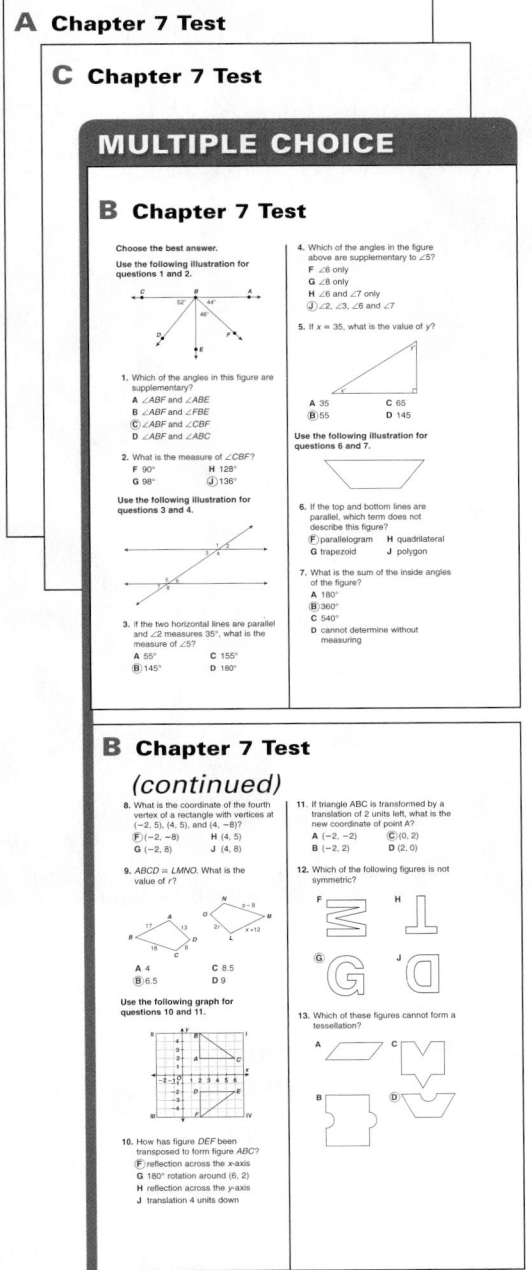

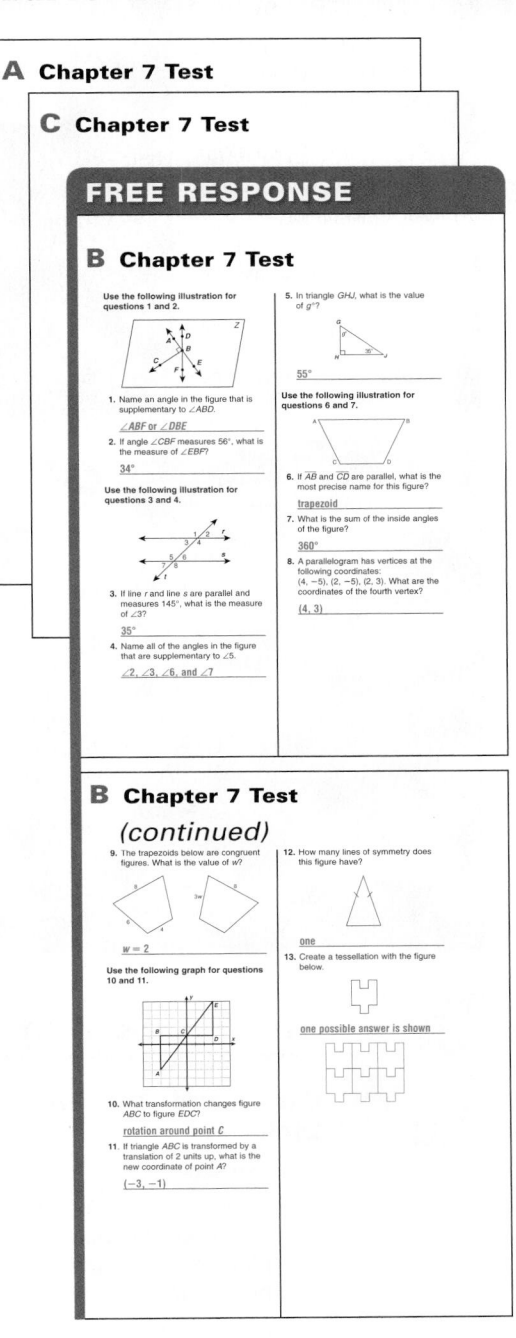

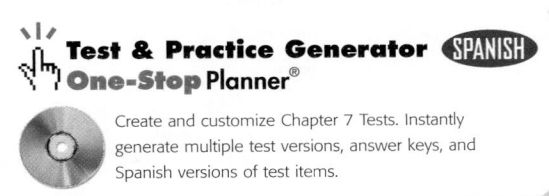

Test & Practice Generator SPANISH
One-Stop Planner®

Create and customize Chapter 7 Tests. Instantly
generate multiple test versions, answer keys, and
Spanish versions of test items.

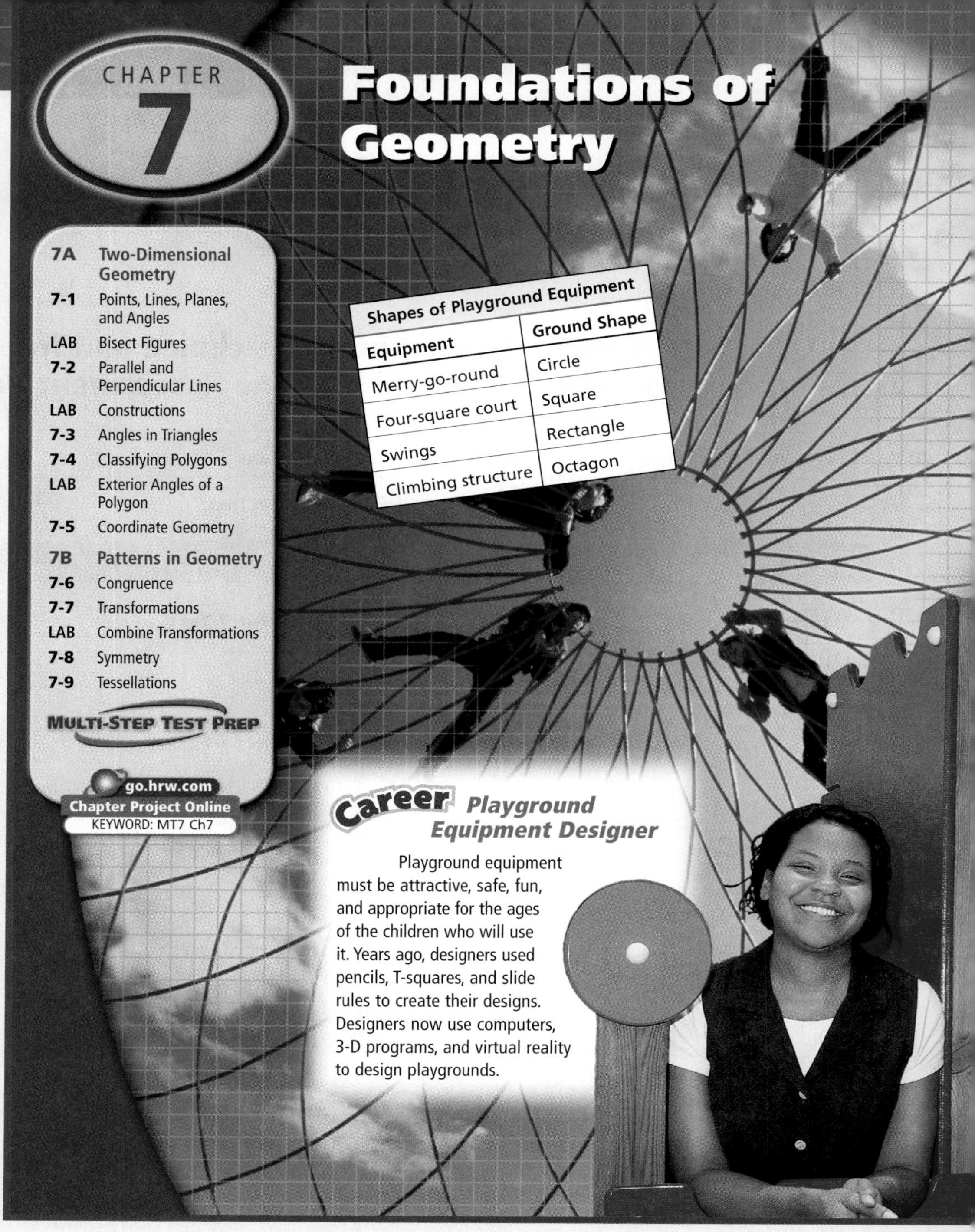

CHAPTER 7

Foundations of Geometry

Why Learn This?

Tell students that the word *geometry* comes from a Greek word meaning "to measure the earth." Learning geometry vocabulary terms can help you describe many shapes and designs that occur in nature as well as in man-made objects. For example, most playground equipment can be described and designed using lines, polygons, and circles.

Using Data

To begin the study of this chapter, have students:

- Sketch the ground shape for each piece of equipment listed. Possible answers:

- Make a sketch of a swing set using only lines. Have them identify any pairs of lines that have the same length. Possible answers:

each side of a swing, each end support, two of the swing seats

MULTI-STEP TEST PREP

On page 373, students use coordinate geometry, transformations, tessellations, and their knowledge of triangles to understand how geometric patterns can be woven into textiles.

7A	**Two-Dimensional Geometry**
7-1	Points, Lines, Planes, and Angles
LAB	Bisect Figures
7-2	Parallel and Perpendicular Lines
LAB	Constructions
7-3	Angles in Triangles
7-4	Classifying Polygons
LAB	Exterior Angles of a Polygon
7-5	Coordinate Geometry
7B	**Patterns in Geometry**
7-6	Congruence
7-7	Transformations
LAB	Combine Transformations
7-8	Symmetry
7-9	Tessellations

MULTI-STEP TEST PREP

go.hrw.com
Chapter Project Online
KEYWORD: MT7 Ch7

Shapes of Playground Equipment

Equipment	Ground Shape
Merry-go-round	Circle
Four-square court	Square
Swings	Rectangle
Climbing structure	Octagon

Career *Playground Equipment Designer*

Playground equipment must be attractive, safe, fun, and appropriate for the ages of the children who will use it. Years ago, designers used pencils, T-squares, and slide rules to create their designs. Designers now use computers, 3-D programs, and virtual reality to design playgrounds.

Problem Solving Project

Understand, Plan, Solve, and Look Back

Have students:

- Complete The Ultimate Playground worksheet to analyze and create playground equipment using points, lines, planes, and angles.
- Make a chart listing playground equipment and the lines and angles that they see.

Physical Science and Social Studies Connection

Project Resources

All project resources for teachers and students are provided online.

Materials:

- The Ultimate Playground worksheet
- construction materials (straws, toothpicks, pipe cleaners, tape, glue)

go.hrw.com
Project Teacher Support
KEYWORD: MT7 PSProject7

ARE YOU READY?

✓ Vocabulary

Choose the best term from the list to complete each sentence.

coordinate axes
coordinate plane
ordered pair
origin
x-axis
x-coordinate
y-axis
y-coordinate

1. In the ___?___ (4, −3), 4 is the ___?___, and −3 is the ___?___. **ordered pair; x-coordinate; y-coordinate**

2. The ___?___ divide the ___?___ into four sections. **coordinate axes; coordinate plane**

3. The point (0, 0) is called the ___?___. **origin**

4. The point (0, −3) lies on the ___?___, while the point (−2, 0) lies on the ___?___. **y-axis; x-axis**

Complete these exercises to review skills you will need for this chapter.

✓ Ordered Pairs

Write the coordinates of the indicated points.

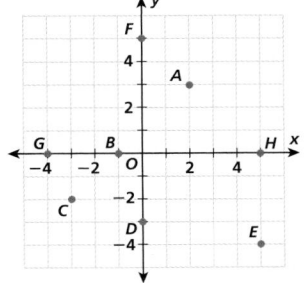

5. point A **(2, 3)**
6. point B **(−1, 0)**
7. point C **(−3, −2)**
8. point D **(0, −3)**
9. point E **(5, −4)**
10. point F **(0, 5)**
11. point G **(−4, 0)**
12. point H **(5, 0)**

✓ Similar Figures

Tell whether the figures in each pair appear to be similar.

13. 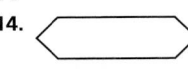 **yes**

14.  **no**

✓ Equations

Solve each equation.

15. $2p = 18$ **p = 9**
16. $7 + h = 21$ **h = 14**
17. $\frac{x}{3} = 9$ **x = 27**
18. $y − 6 = 16$ **y = 22**
19. $4d + 1 = 13$ **d = 3**
20. $−2q − 3 = 3$ **q = −3**
21. $4(z − 1) = 16$ **z = 5**
22. $x + 3 + 4x = 23$ **x = 4**

Determine whether the given values are solutions of the given equations.

23. $\frac{2}{3}x + 1 = 7$ $x = 9$ **yes**
24. $2x − 4 = 6$ $x = −1$ **no**
25. $8 − 2x = −4$ $x = 5$ **no**
26. $\frac{1}{2}x + 5 = −2$ $x = −14$ **yes**

ARE YOU READY?
Diagnose and Prescribe

 **NO INTERVENE**

 **YES ENRICH**

✓ Prerequisite Skill	📜 Worksheets	💿 CD-ROM	🪐 Online
✓ Ordered Pairs	Skill 68	Activity 68	Diagnose and Prescribe Online
✓ Similar Figures	Skill 82	Activity 82	
✓ Equations	Skill 60	Activity 60	

ARE YOU READY? Enrichment, Chapter 7
📜 Worksheets
💿 CD-ROM
🪐 Online

Organizer

Objective: Help students organize the new concepts they will learn in Chapter 7.

 **Online Edition**
Multilingual Glossary

Resources

PuzzlePro®
One-Stop Planner®

 Multilingual Glossary Online

go.hrw.com
KEYWORD: MT7 Glossary

Possible answers to *Vocabulary Connections*

1. An equilateral triangle has three sides of equal length.

2. A polygon is a shape that has many angles.

3. The slope of a line represents the steepness—whether rise or fall—of the line.

Study Guide: Preview

Where You've Been

Previously, you

- located and named points on a coordinate plane.

- recognized geometric concepts and properties in fields such as art and architecture.

- used critical attributes to define similarity.

In This Chapter

You will study

- graphing translations and reflections on a coordinate plane.

- using geometric concepts and properties of geometry to solve problems in fields such as art and architecture.

- using critical attributes to define congruency.

Where You're Going

You can use the skills learned in this chapter

- to find angle measures by using relationships within figures.

- to create tessellations.

- to identify properties of geometry in art and architecture.

Key Vocabulary/Vocabulario

equilateral triangle	triángulo equilátero
line	línea
parallel lines	líneas paralelas
perpendicular lines	rectas perpendiculars
plane	plano
point	punto
polygon	polígono
reflection	reflexión
slope	pendiente
transformation	transformación
translation	translación
transversal	transversal

Vocabulary Connections

To become familiar with some of the vocabulary terms in the chapter, consider the following. You may refer to the chapter, the glossary, or a dictionary if you like.

1. The word *equilateral* contains the roots *equi*, which means "equal," and lateral, which means "of the side." What do you suppose an **equilateral triangle** is?

2. The Greek prefix *poly* means "many," and the root *gon* means "angle." What do you suppose a **polygon** is?

3. Think of what **slope** means when you are talking about a hill. How do you think this applies to lines on a coordinate plane?

Writing Strategy: Keep a Math Journal

By keeping a math journal, you can improve your writing and thinking skills. Use your journal to summarize key ideas and vocabulary from each lesson and to analyze any questions you may have about a concept or your homework.

Journal Entry: Read the entry a student made in her journal.

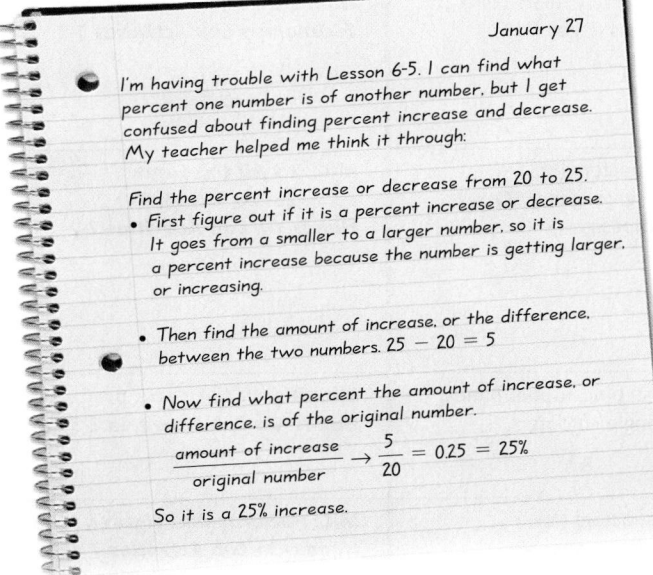

January 27

I'm having trouble with Lesson 6-5. I can find what percent one number is of another number, but I get confused about finding percent increase and decrease. My teacher helped me think it through:

Find the percent increase or decrease from 20 to 25.
- First figure out if it is a percent increase or decrease. It goes from a smaller to a larger number, so it is a percent increase because the number is getting larger, or increasing.

- Then find the amount of increase, or the difference, between the two numbers. 25 − 20 = 5

- Now find what percent the amount of increase, or difference, is of the original number.

$$\frac{\text{amount of increase}}{\text{original number}} \rightarrow \frac{5}{20} = 0.25 = 25\%$$

So it is a 25% increase.

Try This

Begin a math journal. Write in it each day this week, using these ideas as starters. Be sure to date and number each page.

- In this lesson, I already know . . .
- In this lesson, I am unsure about . . .
- The skills I need to complete this lesson are . . .
- The challenges I encountered were . . .
- I handled these challenges by . . .
- In this lesson, I enjoyed/did not enjoy . . .

Reading and Writing Math

Organizer

Objective: Help students apply strategies to understand and retain key concepts.

 Online Edition

Resources

 Chapter 7 Resource Book
Reading Strategies

Writing Strategy: Keep a Math Journal

ENGLISH LANGUAGE LEARNERS

Discuss Students will be able to better understand and retain mathematical concepts if they summarize the key ideas they learn in their own words.

Encourage students to make a journal entry after each lesson.

Extend As students work through Chapter 7, select a few each day to read their journal entries to the class.

Encourage students to share with the rest of the class ideas they found challenging and things they enjoyed or did not enjoy about each lesson.

Possible answers to *Try This*

In this lesson, I already know how to identify perpendicular lines. I'm unsure about corresponding angles. I handled this challenge by asking my teacher for further explanation and working extra examples.

SECTION 7A

Two-Dimensional Geometry

One-Minute Section Planner

Lesson	Materials	MiC and Lab Resources
Lesson 7-1 Points, Lines, Planes, and Angles • Classify and name figures. **7-1 Hands-On Lab** Bisect Figures • Use a compass and straightedge to bisect line segments and angles. ☑ SAT-10　☐ ITBS　☑ CTBS　☑ NAEP	Compasses (MK), customary rulers (MK), straightedges (MK)	**MiC:** *It's All the Same* pp. 2–5 *Hands-On Lab Activities* 7-1 *Technology Lab Activities* 7-1
Lesson 7-2 Parallel and Perpendicular Lines • Identify parallel and perpendicular lines and the angles formed by a transversal. **7-2 Hands-On Lab** Constructions • Use a compass and straightedge to copy angles and construct parallel and perpendicular lines. ☐ SAT-10　☑ ITBS　☑ CTBS　☑ NAEP	Protractors (MK), straightedges (MK), compasses (MK)	**MiC:** *It's All the Same* pp. 3, 23–26, 29–33, 47 *Hands-On Lab Activities* 7-2
Lesson 7-3 Angles in Triangles • Find unknown angles in triangles. ☑ SAT-10　☑ ITBS　☑ CTBS　☑ NAEP	Push pins, rubber bands, triangle cutouts	**MiC:** *It's All the Same* pp. 29–33 *Hands-On Lab Activities* 7-3
Lesson 7-4 Classifying Polygons • Classify and find angles in polygons. **7-4 Technology Lab** Exterior Angles of a Polygon • Use geometry software to study the exterior angles of a polygon. ☑ SAT-10　☑ ITBS　☑ CTBS　☑ NAEP	Protractors (MK), straightedges (MK), graph paper, geometry software	**MiC:** *Patterns and Figures* p. 35 *Hands-On Lab Activities* 7-4 *Technology Lab Activities* 7-4
Lesson 7-5 Coordinate Geometry • Identify polygons in the coordinate plane. ☑ SAT-10　☑ ITBS　☑ CTBS　☑ NAEP	Graph paper	**MiC:** *It's All the Same* pp. 45–49 **MiC:** *Graphing Equations* pp. 3–7 *Technology Lab Activities* 7-5

MK = *Manipulatives Kit*

Mathematics in Context

The units *It's All the Same, Patterns and Figures,* and *Graphing Equations* from the *Mathematics in Context* © 2006 series can be used with Section 7A. See Section Planner above for suggestions for integrating *MiC* with *Holt Mathematics*.

Section Overview

Professional Development

Basic Geometric Figures

Lessons 7-1, 7-2

Why? Points, lines, and planes are the building blocks of geometry.

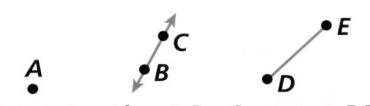

Point A   Line *BC*   Segment *DE*

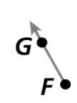 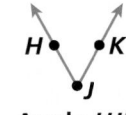

Ray *FG*   Angle *HJK*   Plane ℳ

Perpendicular lines form 90° angles.

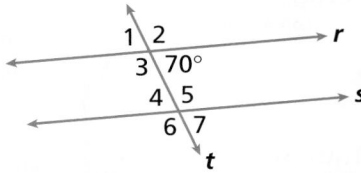

Parallel lines *r* and *s* are intersected by transversal *t*.
m ∠ 1 = m ∠ 4 = m ∠ 7 = 70°
m ∠ 2 = m ∠ 3 = m ∠ 5 = m ∠ 6 = 110°

Polygons

Lessons 7-3, 7-4

Why? Polygons are all around us.

A **polygon** is a closed plane figure formed by three or more segments.

Polygon	Number of Sides	Sum of Angle Measures
	n	180° (*n* − 2)
Triangle	3	180° (3 − 2) = 180°
Quadrilateral	4	180° (4 − 2) = 360°
Pentagon	5	180° (5 − 2) = 540°
Hexagon	6	180° (6 − 2) = 720°
Heptagon	7	180° (7 − 2) = 900°
Octagon	8	180° (8 − 2) = 1080°

Triangles

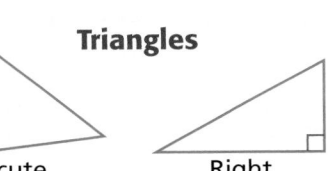

Acute   Right

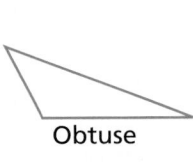 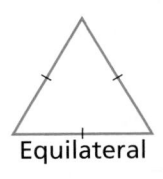

Obtuse   Equilateral

Isosceles   Scalene

Special Quadrilaterals

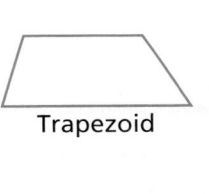 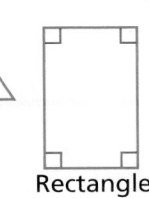 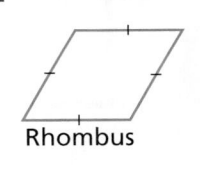 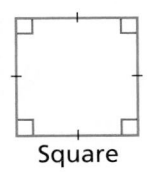 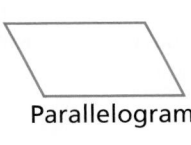

Trapezoid   Rectangle   Rhombus   Square   Parallelogram

Coordinate Geometry

Lesson 7-5

Why? Coordinate geometry is the application of geometry and algebra together on a coordinate plane.

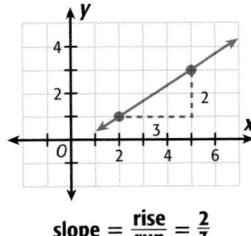

slope = $\frac{\text{rise}}{\text{run}} = \frac{2}{3}$

Parallel Lines
equal slopes

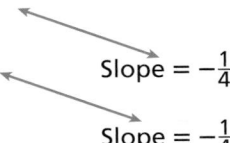

Slope = $-\frac{1}{4}$

Slope = $-\frac{1}{4}$

Perpendicular Lines
product of slopes = −1

Slope = $-\frac{3}{2}$

Slope = $\frac{2}{3}$

$\left(-\frac{3}{2}\right)\left(\frac{2}{3}\right) = -1$

Hands-On Lab
In *Hands-On Lab Activities*

 Technology Lab
In *Technology Lab Activities*

 Online Edition
Tutorial Videos

 Countdown to Testing Week 12

Power Presentations
with PowerPoint®

Warm Up
Solve.
1. $x + 30 = 90$ $x = 60$
2. $103 + x = 180$ $x = 77$
3. $32 + x = 180$ $x = 148$
4. $90 = 61 + x$ $x = 29$
5. $x + 20 = 90$ $x = 70$

Problem of the Day
Mrs. Meyer's class is having a pizza party. Half the class wants pepperoni on the pizza, $\frac{1}{3}$ of the class wants sausage on the pizza, and the rest want only cheese on the pizza. What fraction of Mrs. Meyer's class wants just cheese on the pizza? $\frac{1}{6}$

Also available on transparency

State Resources

go.hrw.com
State Resources Online
KEYWORD: MT7 Resources

7-1 Points, Lines, Planes, and Angles

Learn to classify and name figures.

Points, lines, and planes are the building blocks of geometry. Segments, rays, and angles are defined in terms of these basic figures.

Vocabulary
point   line
plane   segment
ray   angle
right angle
acute angle
obtuse angle
complementary angles
supplementary angles
congruent
vertical angles

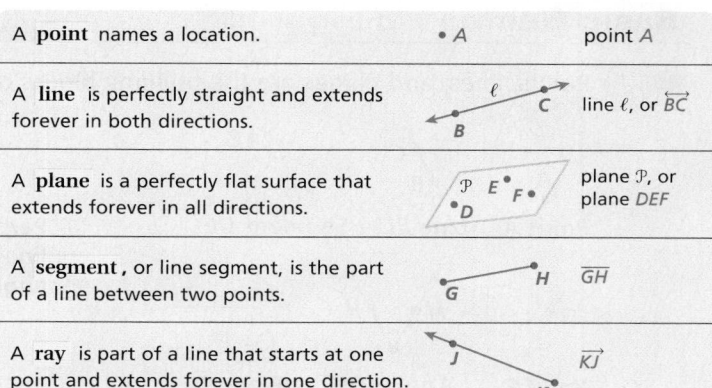

A **point** names a location.	• A point A
A **line** is perfectly straight and extends forever in both directions.	line ℓ, or $\overleftrightarrow{BC}$
A **plane** is a perfectly flat surface that extends forever in all directions.	plane $\mathcal{P}$, or plane DEF
A **segment**, or line segment, is the part of a line between two points.	$\overline{GH}$
A **ray** is part of a line that starts at one point and extends forever in one direction.	$\overrightarrow{KJ}$

$\overleftrightarrow{BC}$ is read "line BC." $\overline{GH}$ is read "segment GH." $\overrightarrow{KJ}$ is read "ray KJ." To name a ray, always write the endpoint first.

EXAMPLE 1   Naming Points, Lines, Planes, Segments, and Rays

Use the diagram to name each figure.

A four points
   Q, R, S, T

B a line
   Possible answers: $\overleftrightarrow{QS}$, $\overleftrightarrow{QR}$ or $\overleftrightarrow{RS}$ *Any 2 points on the line can be used.*

C a plane
   Possible answers: plane $\mathcal{Z}$ or plane QRT   *Any 3 points in the plane that form a triangle can name a plane.*

D four segments
   Possible answers: $\overline{QR}$, $\overline{RS}$, $\overline{RT}$, $\overline{QS}$ *Write the 2 points in any order, for example, $\overline{QR}$ or $\overline{RQ}$.*

E five rays
   $\overrightarrow{RQ}$, $\overrightarrow{RS}$, $\overrightarrow{RT}$, $\overrightarrow{SQ}$, $\overrightarrow{QS}$ *Write the endpoint first.*

---

1 Introduce
Alternate Opener

EXPLORATION

7-1 Points, Lines, Planes, and Angles

In each group, one picture is different from the others. Identify the picture that is different and explain why it is different.

1.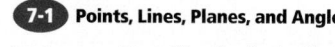

2.

3. Look at the picture for each geometry term and write a real-world example for each term.

Term	Picture	Example
Point	•	
Segment	•—•	
Ray	•—→	
Line	←—→	
Angle	∧	

Think and Discuss
4. **Explain** the difference between a *segment* and a *ray*.

Motivate
On the board, draw a square, a triangle, and a rectangle. Ask the students to identify each figure. Explain to them that they are geometric figures comprised of points, line segments, and angles.

Explorations and answers are provided in *Alternate Openers: Explorations Transparencies.*

An **angle** (∠) is formed by two rays with a common endpoint called the *vertex* (plural, *vertices*). Angles can be measured in degrees. m∠1 means the measure of ∠1. The angle can be named ∠XYZ, ∠ZYX, ∠1, or ∠Y. The vertex must be the middle letter.

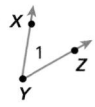

The measures of angles that fit together to form a straight line, such as ∠FKG, ∠GKH, and ∠HKJ, add to 180°.

The measures of angles that fit together to form a complete circle, such as ∠MRN, ∠NRP, ∠PRQ, and ∠QRM, add to 360°.

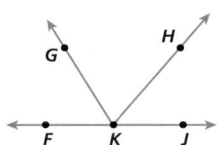

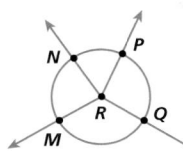

A **right angle** measures 90°. An **acute angle** measures greater than 0° and less than 90°. An **obtuse angle** measures greater than 90° and less than 180°. **Complementary angles** are two angles whose measures add to 90°. **Supplementary angles** are two angles whose measures add to 180°.

EXAMPLE 2 **Classifying Angles**

Use the diagram to name each figure.

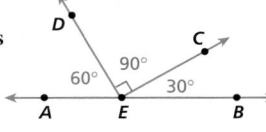

A a right angle
∠DEC

B two acute angles
∠AED, ∠CEB

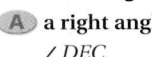
C two obtuse angles
∠AEC, ∠DEB   m∠AEC = 150°; m∠DEB = 120°

D a pair of complementary angles
∠AED, ∠CEB   m∠AED + m∠CEB = 60° + 30° = 90°

E two pairs of supplementary angles
∠AED, ∠DEB   m∠AED + m∠DEB = 60° + 120° = 180°
∠AEC, ∠CEB   m∠AEC + m∠CEB = 150° + 30° = 180°

Congruent figures have the same size and shape.

• Segments that have the same length are congruent.

• Angles that have the same measure are congruent.

• The symbol for congruence is ≅, which is read "is congruent to."

Intersecting lines form two pairs of **vertical angles**. Vertical angles are always congruent, as shown in the next example.

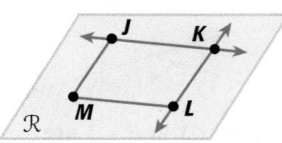
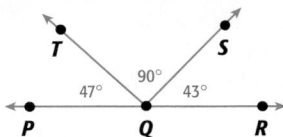
2 Teach

Guided Instruction

In this lesson, students learn to classify and name figures. Discuss the concepts of points, lines, and planes as the building blocks of geometry (Teaching Transparency). Segments and rays are parts of lines, and angles consist of rays. Show students how to classify an angle by using the corner of a piece of paper to represent a right angle.

Teaching Tip
Communicating Math Emphasize the difference between congruence and equality. Remind students that only numerical measures (such as the measure of an angle or the length of a segment) are called equal; figures that are the same shape and size are congruent.

ENGLISH LANGUAGE LEARNERS

Reaching All Learners
Through Kinesthetic Experience

Give each student a straightedge and have them draw the figure below as follows: Draw line *AC* through point *B*. Then draw ray *BE* perpendicular to line *AC* (using the corner of the straightedge). Draw ray *BD*. Draw line *DF* through point *B*. Then have them classify each angle and identify any special angle pairs.

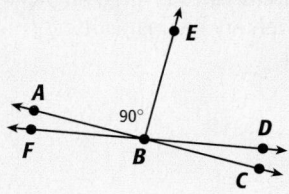

acute: ∠ABF, ∠DBC, ∠EBD; right: ∠ABE, ∠EBC; obtuse: ∠EBF, ∠FBC; complementary: ∠EBD and ∠DBC; supplementary: ∠ABE and ∠EBC, ∠FBE and ∠EBD; vertical angles: ∠ABF and ∠DBC

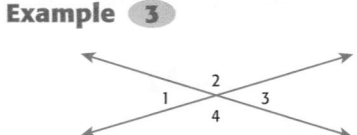

7-1 Exercises

State Resources

EXAMPLE 3 Finding the Measures of Vertical Angles

In the figure, ∠1 and ∠3 are vertical angles, and ∠2 and ∠4 are vertical angles.

A If m∠2 = 75°, find m∠4.

m∠1 = 180° − 75°	∠2 and ∠1 are supplementary.
= 105°	
m∠4 = 180° − 105°	∠1 and ∠4 are supplementary.
= 75°	

So m∠2 = m∠4, or ∠2 ≅ ∠4

B If m∠3 = x°, find m∠1.

m∠1 = 180° − m∠4	∠3 and ∠4 are supplementary.
m∠1 = 180° − (180° − x°)	Substitute 180° − x° for m∠4.
= 180° − 180° + x°	Distributive Property
= x°	Simplify.

So m∠1 = m∠3, or ∠1 ≅ ∠3.

Think and Discuss

1. **Tell** which statements are correct if ∠X and ∠Y are congruent.
   a. ∠X = ∠Y   b. m∠X = m∠Y   c. ∠X ≅ ∠Y   d. m∠X ≅ m∠Y
2. **Explain** why vertical angles must always be congruent.

7-1 Exercises

GUIDED PRACTICE

See Example **1**   Use the diagram to name each figure.

1. three points points X, Y, Z
2. a line $\overleftrightarrow{XY}$
3. a plane plane A or plane XYZ
4. three segments $\overline{XY}, \overline{YZ}, \overline{ZX}$
5. three rays $\overrightarrow{XY}, \overrightarrow{YZ}, \overrightarrow{YX}$

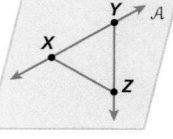

See Example **2**   Use the diagram to name each figure.

6. a right angle ∠AEB or ∠DEB
7. two acute angles ∠BEC, ∠CED
8. an obtuse angle ∠AEC
9. a pair of complementary angles ∠BEC and ∠CED
10. two pairs of supplementary angles ∠AEB and ∠BED, ∠AEC and ∠CED

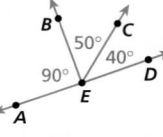

3 Close

ENGLISH LANGUAGE LEARNERS

Summarize

Review the vocabulary terms in the lesson. Ask volunteers to define each term and point out an example in the book. This will reinforce the vocabulary and encourage students to correctly name geometric figures. Discuss ways to remember the names of the different types of angles (e.g., an angle with a small measure is "a cute" little angle, and supplementary begins with s for *straight line*).

Answers to Think and Discuss

1. **b** and **c**; the = sign is used for numerical values, and the ≅ symbol is used for geometric figures.

2. Possible answer: They are always supplementary to the same angle, so they must have the same measure.

In the figure, ∠1 and ∠3 are vertical angles, and ∠2 and ∠4 are vertical angles.

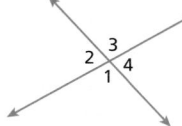

11. If m∠3 = 105°, find m∠1. **105°**

12. If m∠2 = x°, find m∠4. **x°**

INDEPENDENT PRACTICE

See Example ① **Use the diagram to name each figure.**

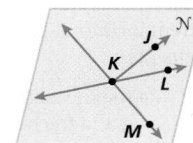

13. four points **14.** two lines $\overleftrightarrow{KL}$, $\overleftrightarrow{KM}$
   points J, K, L, M

15. a plane **16.** three segments
   plane N or plane JKL $\overline{KJ}$, $\overline{KL}$, $\overline{KM}$

17. five rays
   $\overrightarrow{KJ}$, $\overrightarrow{KL}$, $\overrightarrow{KM}$, $\overrightarrow{LK}$, $\overrightarrow{MK}$

See Example ② **Use the diagram to name each figure.**

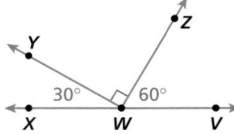

18. a right angle ∠YWZ

19. two acute angles ∠VWZ, ∠YWX

20. two obtuse angles ∠VWY, ∠ZWX

21. a pair of complementary angles
   ∠VWZ, ∠YWX

22. two pairs of supplementary angles
   ∠VWZ and ∠ZWX, ∠VWY and ∠YWX

See Example ③ In the figure, ∠1 and ∠3 are vertical angles, and ∠2 and ∠4 are vertical angles.

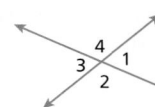

23. If m∠2 = 126°, find m∠4. **126°**

24. If m∠1 = b°, find m∠3. **b°**

PRACTICE AND PROBLEM SOLVING

Extra Practice
See page 794.

Use the figure for Exercises 25–34. Write *true* or *false*. If a statement is false, rewrite it so it is true.

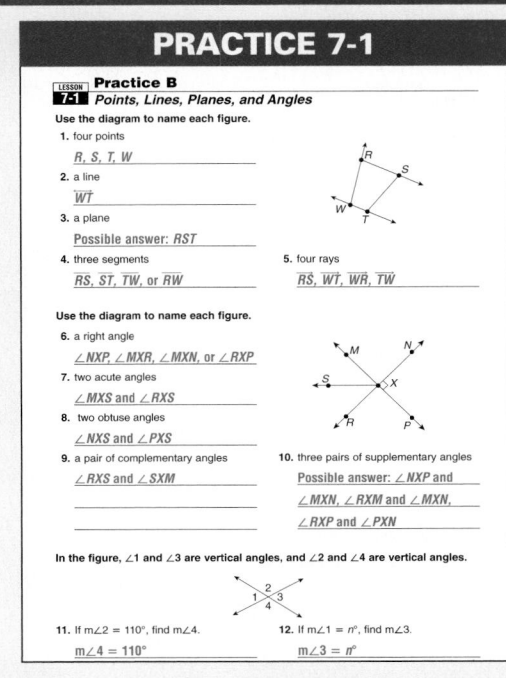

25. $\overleftrightarrow{NQ}$ is a line in the figure. **False; $\overleftrightarrow{NR}$ is a line in the figure.**

26. Rays $\overrightarrow{UQ}$ and $\overrightarrow{UT}$ make up line $\overleftrightarrow{TQ}$. **true**

27. ∠QUR is an obtuse angle. **False; ∠QUR is a right angle.**

28. ∠4 and ∠2 are supplementary. **true**

29. ∠1 and ∠6 are supplementary. **False; ∠1 and ∠6 are complementary.**

30. ∠3 and ∠1 are complementary. **true**

31. If m∠1 = 35°, then m∠6 = 40°. **False; if m∠1 = 35°, then m∠6 = 55°.**

32. If m∠SUN = 150°, then m∠SUR = 150°. **False; if m∠SUN = 150°, then m∠SUR = 30°.**

33. If m∠1 = x°, then m∠PUQ = 180° − x°. **False; if m∠1 = x°, then m∠PUQ = 90° − x°.**

34. m∠1 + m∠3 + m∠5 + m∠6 = 180°. **true**

35. Critical Thinking Two complementary angles have a ratio of 1:2. What is the measure of each angle? **30°, 60°**

Math Background

Points, lines, and planes are mathematical ideas rather than real objects. A point has no size, a line has no width, and a plane has no thickness. The drawings we use to represent points, lines, and planes are real objects; for example, they are composed of chalk dust or ink on paper. Such idealizations of actual objects are called *mathematical abstractions*.

RETEACH 7-1

Reteach
7-1 Points, Lines, Planes, and Angles

Figure	Description	Diagram	Notation Write	Read
Line	an infinite collection of points with no beginning and no end		$\overleftrightarrow{AB}$, or $\overleftrightarrow{BA}$ or ℓ	line AB, line BA, line ℓ
Line Segment	part of a line, with two endpoints		$\overline{AB}$ or $\overline{BA}$	line segement AB, line segment BA
Ray	part of a line, with one endpoint		$\overrightarrow{AB}$	ray AB

Use the diagram, to name each type of figure.

1. $\overline{MP}$ _____ ray
2. k _____ line
3. $\overline{MN}$ _____ line segment
4. $\overline{LJ}$ _____ line segment 5. $\overleftrightarrow{JL}$ _____ line

Acute Angle	Right Angle	Obtuse Angle	Straight Angle
Measures between 0° and 90°	Measures exactly 90°	Measures between 90° and 180°	Measures exactly 180°.

Use the diagram to name each type of angle.

6. ∠BCD _____ right angle
7. ∠BAD _____ acute angle
8. ∠BDA _____ obtuse angle
9. ∠CDA _____ straight angle
10. ∠BDC _____ acute angle 11. ∠ABC _____ acute angle

PRACTICE 7-1

Practice B
7-1 Points, Lines, Planes, and Angles

Use the diagram to name each figure.

1. four points
   R, S, T, W

2. a line
   $\overleftrightarrow{WT}$

3. a plane
   Possible answer: RST

4. three segments
   $\overline{RS}$, $\overline{ST}$, $\overline{TW}$, or $\overline{RW}$

5. four rays
   $\overrightarrow{RS}$, $\overrightarrow{WT}$, $\overrightarrow{WR}$, $\overrightarrow{TW}$

Use the diagram to name each figure.

6. a right angle
   ∠NXP, ∠MXR, ∠MXN, or ∠RXP

7. two acute angles
   ∠MXS and ∠RXS

8. two obtuse angles
   ∠NXS and ∠PXS

9. a pair of complementary angles
   ∠RXS and ∠SXM

10. three pairs of supplementary angles
    Possible answer: ∠NXP and ∠MXN, ∠RXM and ∠MXN, ∠RXP and ∠PXN

In the figure, ∠1 and ∠3 are vertical angles, and ∠2 and ∠4 are vertical angles.

11. If m∠2 = 110°, find m∠4.
    m∠4 = 110°

12. If m∠1 = n°, find m∠3.
    m∠3 = n°

Interdisciplinary LINK

Physical Science

Exercises 36–39 focus on the refraction of light caused by water. The many interactions of light waves are studied in middle school physical science programs, such as *Holt Science & Technology*.

Answers

38–39. See p. A7.

TEST PREP DOCTOR + Students may need help remembering the difference between complementary and supplementary angles in Exercise 40.

Journal

Have students find angles created by objects in the classroom, and then classify the angles as acute, right, or obtuse.

Power Presentations
with PowerPoint®

7-1 Lesson Quiz

In the figure, ∠1 and ∠3 are vertical angles.

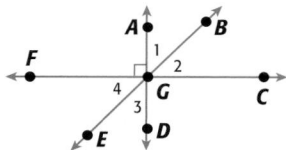

1. Name three points in the figure.
   Possible answer: *A, B,* and *C*

2. Name two lines in the figure.
   Possible answer: $\overleftrightarrow{AD}$ and $\overleftrightarrow{BE}$

3. Name a right angle in the figure.
   Possible answer: ∠AGF

4. Name a pair of complementary angles. Possible answer: ∠1 and ∠2

5. If m∠1 = 47°, then find m∠3. 47°

Also available on transparency

Physical Science LINK

The archerfish can spit a stream of water up to 3 meters in the air to knock its prey into the water. This job is made more difficult by *refraction*, the bending of light waves as they pass from one substance to another. When you look at an object through water, the light between you and the object is refracted. Refraction makes the object appear to be in a different location. Despite refraction, the archerfish still catches its prey.

36. Suppose that the measure of the angle between the bug's actual location and the bug's apparent location is 35°.
   a. Refer to the diagram. Along the fish's line of vision, what is the measure of the angle between the fish and the bug's apparent location? **145°**
   b. What is the relationship of the angles in the diagram? **They are supplementary angles.**

37. In the image, the underwater part of the net appears to be 40° to the right of where it actually is. What is the measure of the angle formed by the image of the underwater part of the net and the part of the net above the water? **140°**

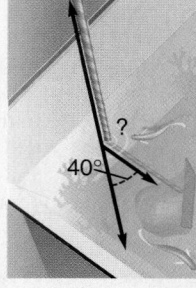

38. ✍ **Write About It** Suppose an archerfish is directly below its prey. Explain why there would be little or no distortion.

39. ★ **Challenge** A person on the shore is looking at a fish in the water. At the same time, the fish is looking at the person from below the surface. Describe what each observer sees, and where the person and the fish actually are in relation to where they appear to be.

TEST PREP and Spiral Review

40. **Multiple Choice** When two angles are complementary, what is the sum of their measures?
    Ⓐ 90° Ⓑ 180° Ⓒ 270° Ⓓ 360°

41. **Gridded Response** ∠1 and ∠3 are supplementary angles. If m∠1 = 63°, find m∠3. **117°**

Multiply. Write the product as one power. *(Lesson 4-3)*

42. $m^3 \cdot m^2$ m^5 43. $w \cdot w^6$ w^7 44. $7^8 \cdot 7^3$ 7^{11} 45. $11^6 \cdot 11^9$ 11^{15}

46. Callie made a 5 in. tall by 7 in. wide postcard. A company would like to sell a poster based on the postcard. The poster will be 2 ft tall. How wide will the poster be? *(Lesson 5-5)* **2.8 ft.**

CHALLENGE 7-1

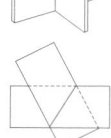

LESSON 7-1 Challenge
Let's Meet!

Materials needed: paper strips, index cards, and scissors

1. Use a flat surface such as the top of your desk to represent a plane. Use strips of paper to represent lines. Move the lines around in the plane (**coplanar lines**) to determine the number of intersections that are possible. Summarize your results in a table.

Number of Coplanar Lines	Possible Number of Points of Intersection
2	0 or 1
3	0, 1, 2, or 3
4	0, 1, 3, 4, 5, or 6
5	0, 1, 4, 5, 6, 7, 8, 9, or 10

2. Slit one index card and connect two cards to model two intersecting planes.
   a. What is the intersection of two planes? a line
   b. Mark the diagram to illustrate the intersection of the two planes.

3. Using index cards to represent planes, determine the number of intersections that are possible. Summarize your results in a table.

Number of Planes	Possible Number of Lines of Intersection
2	0 or 1
3	0, 1, 2, or 3
4	0, 1, 3, 4, 5, or 6
5	0, 1, 4, 5, 6, 7, 8, 9, or 10

PROBLEM SOLVING 7-1

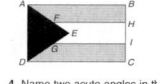

LESSON 7-1 Problem Solving
Points, Lines, Planes, and Angles

Use the flag of the Bahamas to solve the problems.

1. Name four points in the flag.
   Possible answers: *A, B, C, D*

2. Name four segments in the flag.
   Possible answers: $\overline{AB}, \overline{BH}, \overline{HI}, \overline{IC}$

3. Name a right angle in the flag.
   Possible answer: ∠DAB

4. Name two acute angles in the flag.
   Possible answers: ∠AED, ∠DAE

5. Name a pair of complementary angles in the flag.
   Possible answer: ∠DAE, ∠EAB

6. Name a pair of supplementary angles in the flag.
   Possible answer: ∠DGI, ∠IGE

The diagram illustrates a ray of light being reflected off a mirror. The angle of incidence is congruent to the angle of reflection. Choose the letter for the best answer.

7. Name two rays in the diagram.
   A $\overrightarrow{AM}, \overrightarrow{MB}$ C $\overrightarrow{MA}, \overrightarrow{MB}$
   B $\overrightarrow{MA}, \overrightarrow{BM}$ D $\overrightarrow{MA}, \overrightarrow{MB}$

8. Name a pair of complementary angles.
   Ⓕ ∠NMB, ∠BMD   H ∠CMA, ∠AMD
   G ∠AMN, ∠NMB   J ∠CMA, ∠DMB

9. Which angle is congruent to ∠2?
   A ∠1   C ∠3
   B ∠4   D none

10. Find the measure of ∠4.
    F 65°   Ⓗ 25°
    G 35°   J 90°

11. Find the measure of ∠1.
    A 65°   C 25°
    B 35°   D 90°

12. Find the measure of ∠3.
    F 90°   H 35°
    G 45°   Ⓙ 65°

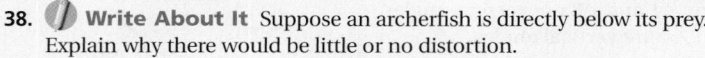
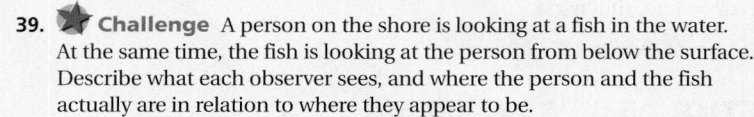

Hands-On LAB 7-1

Bisect Figures

Use with Lesson 7-1

When you *bisect* a figure, you divide it into two congruent parts.

go.hrw.com
Lab Resources Online
KEYWORD: MT7 Lab7

Activity

1 Follow the steps below to bisect a segment.

a. Draw $\overline{JK}$ on your paper. Place your compass point on J and draw an arc. Without changing your compass opening, place your compass point on K and draw an arc.

b. Connect the intersections of the arcs with a line. Measure $\overline{JM}$ and $\overline{KM}$. What do you notice? $\overline{JM} \cong \overline{KM}$

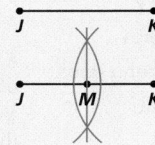

2 Follow the steps below to bisect an angle.

a. Draw acute $\angle H$ on your paper.

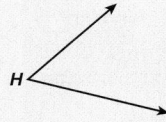

b. Place your compass point on H and draw an arc through both sides of the angle.

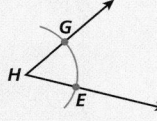

c. Without changing your compass opening, draw intersecting arcs from G and E. Label the intersection D.

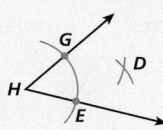

d. Draw $\overrightarrow{HD}$. Measure $\angle GHD$ and $\angle DHE$. What do you notice?

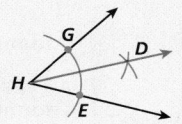

$\angle GHD \cong \angle DHE$

Think and Discuss

1. Explain how to use a compass and a straightedge to divide a segment into four congruent segments. Prove that the segments are congruent.

Try This

Draw each figure, and then use a compass and a straightedge to bisect it. Verify by measuring. **Check students' work.**

1. a 2-inch segment **2.** a 0.5-inch segment **3.** a 6-inch segment

4. a 48° angle **5.** a 90° angle **6.** a 110° angle

Possible answers to *Think and Discuss*

1. Begin by constructing a segment. Use the procedure to bisect the segment. Then bisect each half. The four segments are congruent because each one represents an equal part of the length of the original segment.

Hands-On LAB

Organizer

Use with Lesson 7-1

Pacing:
Traditional $\frac{1}{2}$ day
Block $\frac{1}{4}$ day

Objective: Use a compass and straightedge to bisect line segments and angles.

Materials: Compass, ruler with straightedge, protractor

 Online Edition

 Countdown to Testing Week 12

Resources

 Hands-On Lab Activities
Lab 7-1 Recording Sheet

Teach

Discuss

Students sometimes confuse protractors with compasses. Review the proper use of both tools and remind students that compasses are for drawing and protractors are for measuring angles. Have them practice creating their own angles with a straightedge and measuring them with a protractor.

Close

Key Concept

You can use a compass and straightedge to bisect figures.

Assessment

1. Use a compass and straightedge to construct a right angle.

Check students' constructions.

State Resources

go.hrw.com
State Resources Online
KEYWORD: MT7 Resources

7-1 Hands-On Lab   **329**

Objective: Students identify parallel and perpendicular lines and the angles formed by a transversal.

 Online Edition
Tutorial Videos, Interactivities

 Hands-On Lab
In *Hands-On Lab Activities*

 Countdown to Testing Week 12

Power Presentations
with PowerPoint®

Warm Up

Complete each sentence.

1. Angles whose measures have a sum of 90° are ___?___.
   complementary

2. Vertical angles have equal measures, so they are ___?___.
   congruent

3. Angles whose measures have a sum of 180° are ___?___.
   supplementary

4. A part of a line between two points is called a ___?___.
   segment

Problem of the Day

The square root of 1,813,141,561 is a whole number. Is it odd or even? How do you know?
Odd; An odd number can only be the product of two odd numbers.

Also available on transparency

State Resources

go.hrw.com
State Resources Online
KEYWORD: MT7 Resources

7-2 Parallel and Perpendicular Lines

Learn to identify parallel and perpendicular lines and the angles formed by a transversal.

Vocabulary
parallel lines
perpendicular lines
transversal

Parallel lines are lines in a plane that never meet, such as the opposite sides of a skyscraper's windows. The sides appear to get closer to each other because of *perspective*.

A side and the bottom of a window are like **perpendicular lines**; that is, they intersect at 90° angles.

The sides of the windows are transversals to the top and bottom.

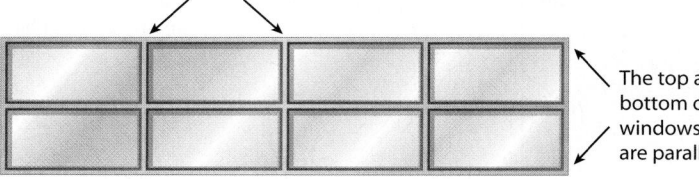

The top and bottom of the windows are parallel.

A **transversal** is a line that intersects two or more lines that lie in the same plane. Transversals to parallel lines form angles with special properties.

EXAMPLE 1 Identifying Congruent Angles Formed by a Transversal

Caution!
You cannot tell if angles are congruent by measuring because measurement is not exact.

Copy and measure the angles formed by the transversal and the parallel lines. Which angles seem to be congruent?

∠1, ∠4, ∠5, and ∠8 all measure 60°.
∠2, ∠3, ∠6, and ∠7 all measure 120°.

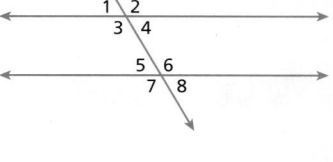

Angles marked in blue appear congruent to each other, and angles marked in red appear congruent to each other.
∠1 ≅ ∠4 ≅ ∠5 ≅ ∠8
∠2 ≅ ∠3 ≅ ∠6 ≅ ∠7

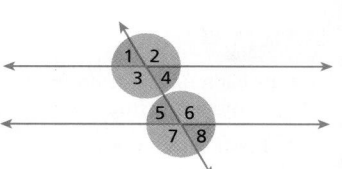

---

1 Introduce
Alternate Opener

EXPLORATION

7-2 Parallel and Perpendicular Lines

A carpenter cuts boards at different angles.
The board below is cut at a 45° angle.

1. Label the angles formed by the cut.
2. Which angles are *congruent*, or have the same measure?
3. Which angles are *supplementary*, or have measures that add to 180°?

The board below is cut at a 30° angle.

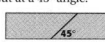

4. Label the angles formed by the cut.
5. Which angles are congruent?
6. Which angles are supplementary?

Think and Discuss

7. **Describe** the top and bottom edges of the boards above. What kinds of lines do they form?
8. **Describe** the angles formed after cutting the board at a 90° angle.

Motivate

To introduce students to the concept of parallel and perpendicular lines, ask them to describe the lines that separate the panes in a window or the lines between tiles on a floor or wall. Ask a volunteer to draw a tic-tac-toe game on the board, and then ask students to describe the lines.

Explorations and answers are provided in *Alternate Openers: Explorations Transparencies.*

Some pairs of the eight angles formed by two parallel lines and a transversal have special names.

| Alternate interior | Alternate exterior | Corresponding |

PROPERTIES OF TRANSVERSALS TO PARALLEL LINES

If two parallel lines are intersected by a transversal,
- corresponding angles are congruent,
- alternate interior angles are congruent,
- and alternate exterior angles are congruent.

If the transversal is perpendicular to the parallel lines, all of the angles formed are congruent 90° angles.

EXAMPLE 2 Finding Angle Measures of Parallel Lines Cut by Transversals

In the figure, line $a \parallel$ line b. Find the measure of each angle.

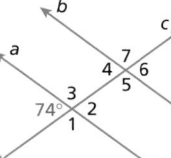

A ∠4
  m∠4 = 74°   *Corresponding angles are congruent.*

B ∠3
  m∠3 + 74° = 180°   *∠3 is supplementary to the 74° angle.*
  $\underline{\;\;-74°\quad\;\;-74°\;\;}$ *Subtract 74° from both sides.*
  m∠3 = 106°   *Simplify.*

C ∠5
  m∠5 = 106°   *∠3 and ∠5 are alternate interior angles, so they are congruent.*

Think and Discuss

1. **Tell** how many different angles would be formed by a transversal intersecting three parallel lines. How many different angle measures would there be?

2. **Explain** how a transversal could intersect two other lines so that corresponding angles are *not* congruent.

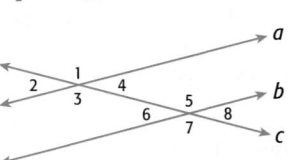

Power Presentations
with PowerPoint®

Additional Examples

Example 1

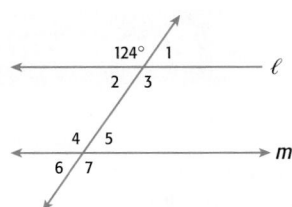

Measure the angles formed by the transversal and the parallel lines. Which angles seem to be congruent?

Angles 1, 3, 5, and 7 all measure 150° and appear to be congruent.

Angles 2, 4, 6, and 8 all measure 30° and appear to be congruent.

Example 2

In the figure, line $\ell \parallel$ line m. Find the measure of each angle.

A. ∠4   124°

B. ∠2   56°

C. ∠6   56°

Also available on transparency

Possible answers to
Think and Discuss

1. 12 angles; at most, two different angle measures (one, if the transversal is perpendicular)

2. when the two other lines are not parallel

---

2 Teach

ENGLISH LANGUAGE LEARNERS

Guided Instruction

In this lesson, students learn to identify parallel and perpendicular lines and the angles formed by a transversal. Before reviewing Example 1, have students look at the diagram and try to identify which angles are congruent. Encourage students to use their knowledge of vertical angles. After students have measured the angles, encourage them to state a hypothesis about the angles formed by parallel lines and a transversal. Before presenting Example 2, review the definitions of complementary and supplementary angles. You may want to use a Teaching Transparency to introduce alternate interior, alternate exterior, and corresponding angles.

Reaching All Learners
Through Auditory Cues

Have students write a set of instructions that describe how to create a pair of parallel lines cut by a transversal. Have students read their instructions aloud to a partner and have the partner follow the instructions to ensure that they are accurate.

Possible answer: Draw two intersecting lines. Measure one of the angles formed by the two intersecting lines. Draw a third line intersecting one of the original lines to form an angle congruent to the angle you measured. This line should be parallel to one of the original lines. Measure all angles in the diagram.

---

3 Close

Summarize

Show the following diagram. Note that $a \parallel b$. Ask students to find the measure of each numbered angle, and ask them to explain how they found each answer.

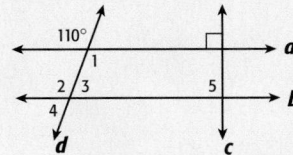

Possible answers: m∠1 and m∠2 = 110° because all obtuse angles formed by the transversal are congruent. m∠3 and m∠4 = 70° because all acute angles are supplementary to any obtuse angle. m∠5 = 90° because the transversal is perpendicular.

7-2 Exercises

go.hrw.com
Homework Help Online
KEYWORD: MT7 7-2
Parent Resources Online
KEYWORD: MT7 Parent

Assignment Guide

If you finished Example **1** assign:
Average 1, 6, 26–33
Advanced 6, 18–20, 26–33

If you finished Example **2** assign:
Average 1–18, 22, 26–33
Advanced 6–33

Homework Quick Check

Quickly check key concepts.
Exercises: 6, 8, 18, 22

Answers

18–20. See p. A7.

Math Background

There are various ways to prove that two lines are parallel. If two lines are cut by a transversal and any of the following is true, then those two lines are parallel:

- A pair of corresponding angles are congruent.
- A pair of alternate interior angles are congruent.
- A pair of alternate exterior angles are congruent.
- A pair of same-side interior angles are supplementary.
- The transversal is perpendicular to both lines.

GUIDED PRACTICE

See Example **1** 1. Measure the angles formed by the transversal and the parallel lines. Which angles seem to be congruent? $\angle 1 \cong \angle 4 \cong \angle 5 \cong \angle 8$ (45°); $\angle 2 \cong \angle 3 \cong \angle 6 \cong \angle 7$ (135°).

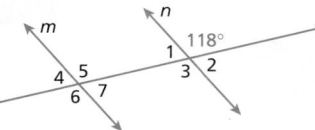

See Example **2** In the figure, line m ∥ line n. Find the measure of each angle.

2. $\angle 1$ 62°   3. $\angle 4$ 62°

4. $\angle 6$ 118°   5. $\angle 7$ 62°

INDEPENDENT PRACTICE

See Example **1** 6. Measure the angles formed by the transversal and the parallel lines. Which angles seem to be congruent? $\angle 1 \cong \angle 4 \cong \angle 5 \cong \angle 8$ (70°); $\angle 2 \cong \angle 3 \cong \angle 6 \cong \angle 7$ (110°)

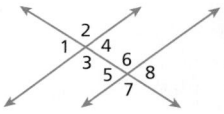

See Example **2** In the figure, line p ∥ line q. Find the measure of each angle.

7. $\angle 1$ 70°

8. $\angle 4$ 70°

9. $\angle 6$ 110°

10. $\angle 7$ 70°

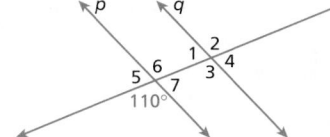

PRACTICE AND PROBLEM SOLVING

Extra Practice
See page 794.

In the figure, line t ∥ line s.

11. Name all angles congruent to $\angle 1$.
$\angle 4, \angle 5$, and $\angle 8$

12. Name all angles congruent to $\angle 2$.
$\angle 3, \angle 6$, and $\angle 7$

13. Possible answers: $\angle 1$ and $\angle 2$, $\angle 1$ and $\angle 3$, $\angle 3$ and $\angle 4$.

13. Name three pairs of supplementary angles.

14. Which line is the transversal? line r

15. If m$\angle 4$ is 51°, what is m$\angle 2$? 129°

16. If m$\angle 7$ is 116°, what is m$\angle 3$? 116°

17. If m$\angle 5$ is 91°, what is m$\angle 2$? 89°

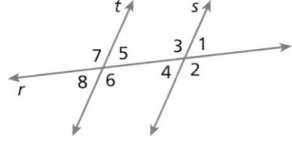

Draw a diagram to illustrate each of the following.

18. line p ∥ line q ∥ line r and line s transversal to lines p, q, and r

19. line m ∥ line n and transversal h with congruent angles $\angle 1$ and $\angle 3$

20. line h ∥ line j and transversal k with eight congruent angles

go.hrw.com
State Resources Online
KEYWORD: MT7 Resources

State Resources

RETEACH 7-2

PRACTICE 7-2

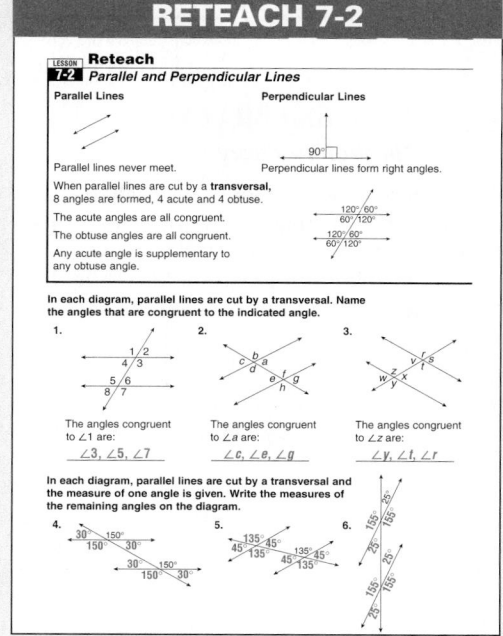

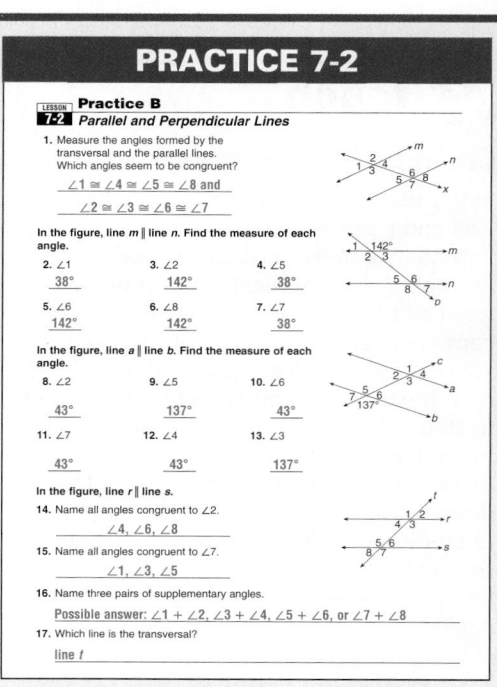

21. Critical Thinking Two parallel lines are cut by a transversal. Can you determine the measures of all the angles formed if given only one angle measure? Explain.

22. Physical Science A periscope contains two parallel mirrors that face each other. With a periscope, a person in a submerged submarine can see above the surface of the water.

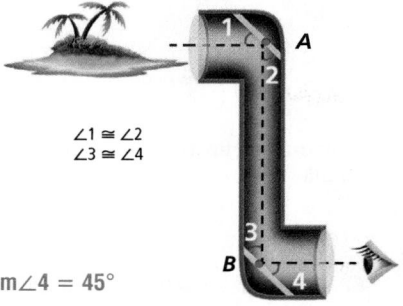

$\angle 1 \cong \angle 2$
$\angle 3 \cong \angle 4$

  a. Name the transversal in the diagram. $\overline{AB}$

  b. If m$\angle 1 = 45°$, find m$\angle 2$, m$\angle 3$, and m$\angle 4$. m$\angle 2 =$ m$\angle 3 =$ m$\angle 4 = 45°$

23. What's the Error? Line a is parallel to line b. Line c is perpendicular to line b. Line c forms a 60° angle with line a. Why is this figure impossible to draw?

24. Write About It Choose an example of abstract art or architecture with parallel lines. Explain how parallel lines, transversals, or perpendicular lines are used in the composition.

25. Challenge In the figure, $\angle 1$, $\angle 4$, $\angle 6$, and $\angle 7$ are all congruent, and $\angle 2$, $\angle 3$, $\angle 5$, and $\angle 8$ are all congruent. Does this mean that line s is parallel to line t? Explain.

TEST PREP and Spiral Review

26. Multiple Choice Two parallel lines are intersected by a transversal. The measures of two corresponding angles that are formed are each 54°. What are the measures of each of the angles supplementary to the corresponding angles?

  Ⓐ 36°   Ⓑ 72°   Ⓒ 108°   Ⓓ 126°

27. Extended Response Suppose a transversal intersects two parallel lines. One angle that is formed is a right angle. What are the measures of the remaining angles? What is the relationship between the transversal and the parallel lines? The measures of the remaining angles are 90°. The transversal is perpendicular to the parallel lines.

Find each number. (Lesson 6-3)

28. What is 15% of 96? 14.4   **29.** What is 146% of 12,500? 18,250

30. What is 0.5% of 1000? 5   **31.** What is 99.9% of 1500? 1498.5

$\angle 1$ and $\angle 3$ are vertical angles, and $\angle 2$ and $\angle 4$ are vertical angles. $\angle 1$ and $\angle 2$ are supplementary angles. (Lesson 7-1)

32. If m$\angle 1 = 25°$, find m$\angle 3$. 25°   **33.** If m$\angle 2 = 95°$, find m$\angle 3$. 85°

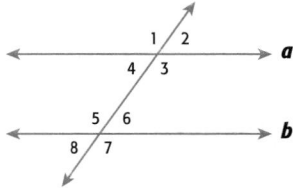

Pacing:
Traditional $\frac{1}{2}$ day
Block $\frac{1}{4}$ day

Objective: Use a compass and straightedge to copy angles and construct parallel and perpendicular lines.

Materials: Compass, ruler with straightedge, protractor

Online Edition

Countdown to Testing Week 12

Resources

Hands-On Lab Activities
Lab 7-2 Recording Sheet

Teach
Discuss

Suggest that students check each mark they make with the compass. This will quickly identify any errors made if they have let the compass slip during any step of the construction. Also, make sure students use their protractors when the lab instructs them to measure angles. Students sometimes confuse protractors with compasses, so remind them that protractors are used for measuring, whereas compasses are used for drawing and constructing.

State Resources

Constructions

Use with Lesson 7-2

Constructing an angle is an important step in the construction of parallel lines.

Activity

❶ Follow the steps below to construct an angle congruent to ∠B.

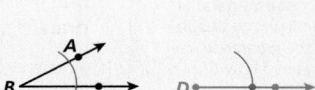

  a. Draw acute ∠ABC on your paper. Draw $\overline{DE}$.

  b. With your compass point on B, draw an arc through ∠ABC. With the same compass opening, place your compass point on D and draw an arc through $\overline{DE}$. Label the intersection point F.

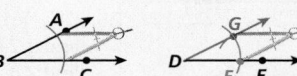

  c. Adjust your compass to the width of the arc intersecting ∠ABC. Place your compass point on F and draw an arc that intersects the arc through $\overline{DE}$ at G. Draw $\overrightarrow{DG}$. Measure ∠ABC and ∠GDF.

❷ Follow the steps below to construct parallel line segments.

  1. Construct $\overline{QR}$ on your paper by placing the point of your compass on Q and the pencil on R below. Draw point Q on your paper and place the point of your compass on it. Make a short arc and draw a line from Q to the arc. The intersection of the point and the arc is R. Draw point S above or below $\overline{QR}$. Draw a line through point S that intersects $\overline{QR}$. Label the intersection T.

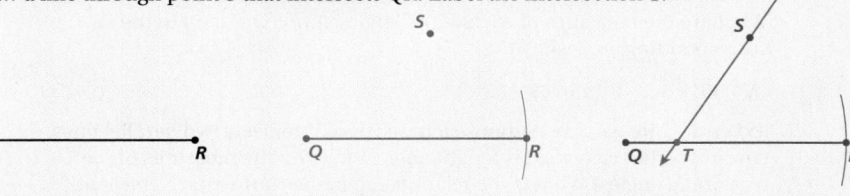

  2. Construct an angle with its vertex at S congruent to ∠STR. Use the method described in ❶. How do you know the lines are parallel? **Corresponding angles are congruent.**

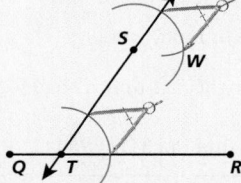

Close
Key Concept

You can use a compass and straightedge to copy angles, and construct parallel and perpendicular lines.

Assessment

1. Construct segment $\overrightarrow{RT}$ and bisect it.

  Check students' constructions.

❸ Follow the steps below to construct perpendicular lines.

a. Draw $\overleftrightarrow{MN}$ on your paper. Draw point P above or below $\overleftrightarrow{MN}$.

b. With your compass point at P, draw an arc intersecting $\overleftrightarrow{MN}$ at points Q and R.

c. Draw arcs from points Q and R, using the same compass opening, that intersect at point S.

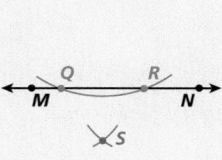

d. Draw $\overleftrightarrow{PS}$. What do you think is true about $\overleftrightarrow{MN}$ and $\overleftrightarrow{PS}$? Check your guess.
$$\overleftrightarrow{MN} \perp \overleftrightarrow{PS}$$

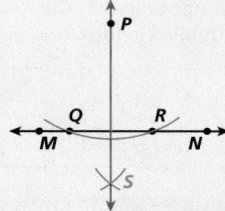

Think and Discuss

1. How many lines can be drawn that are perpendicular to a given line? Explain your answer.

2. Name three ways that you can determine if two lines are parallel.

Try This

Use a compass and a straightedge to construct each figure.

1. an angle congruent to $\angle LMN$

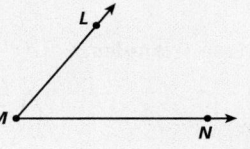

2. a line parallel to $\overleftrightarrow{ST}$

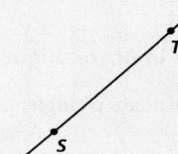

3. a line perpendicular to $\overleftrightarrow{GH}$

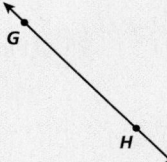

4. an angle congruent to $\angle DEF$

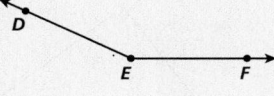

5. a line parallel to $\overleftrightarrow{AB}$

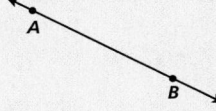

6. a line perpendicular to $\overleftrightarrow{CD}$

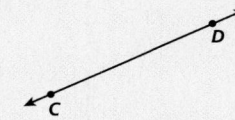

Possible answers to *Think and Discuss*

1. There are an infinite number of lines that can be drawn perpendicular to a given line. Since a line contains an infinite number of points, there are an infinite number of points at which a perpendicular line can intersect the line.

2. 1) Construct a line perpendicular to one of the lines. If it is perpendicular to the other line, the two lines are parallel.

   2) The given information tells you that the lines are parallel.

   3) Draw a third line that intersects both lines, and measure alternate interior angles to see if they have the same measure.

Answers to *Try This*

1–6. Check students' constructions.

7-3 Organizer

Pacing: Traditional 2 days
Block 1 day
Objective: Students find unknown angles in triangles.

 **Online Edition**
Tutorial Videos, Interactivities

Hands-On Lab
In *Hands-On Lab Activities*

Countdown to Testing Week 13

Power Presentations
with PowerPoint®

Warm Up
Solve each equation.
1. $62 + x + 37 = 180$ $x = 81$
2. $x + 90 + 11 = 180$ $x = 79$
3. $2x + 18 = 180$ $x = 81$
4. $180 = 3x + 72$ $x = 36$

Problem of the Day
What is the one hundred fiftieth day of a non-leap year?   May 30

Also available on transparency

 **Math Humor**

The obtuse angle was always complaining about the heat, "I can't take this heat anymore. It must be over 90° in here!"

7-3 Angles in Triangles

Learn to find unknown angles in triangles.

Vocabulary
Triangle Sum Theorem
acute triangle
right triangle
obtuse triangle
equilateral triangle
isosceles triangle
scalene triangle

If you tear off two corners of a triangle and place them next to the third corner, the three angles seem to form a straight angle.

Draw a triangle and extend one side. Then draw a line parallel to the extended side, as shown.

The three angles in the triangle can be arranged to form a straight angle, or 180°.

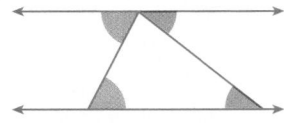

This torn triangle demonstrates an important geometry theorem called the Triangle Sum Theorem.

The sides of the triangle are transversals to the parallel lines.

TRIANGLE SUM THEOREM		
Words	**Numbers**	**Algebra**
The angle measures of a triangle add to 180°.	58° 43° 79°	r° t° s°
	$43° + 58° + 79° = 180°$	$r° + s° + t° = 180°$

An **acute triangle** has 3 acute angles. A **right triangle** has 1 right angle. An **obtuse triangle** has 1 obtuse angle.

EXAMPLE 1   **Finding Angles in Acute, Right, and Obtuse Triangles**

A Find $x°$ in the acute triangle.
$$63° + 42° + x° = 180° \quad \text{Triangle Sum Theorem}$$
$$105° + x° = 180°$$
$$\underline{-105° \qquad -105°} \quad \text{Subtract 105° from}$$
$$x° = 75° \quad \text{both sides.}$$

B Find $y°$ in the right triangle.
$$37° + 90° + y° = 180° \quad \text{Triangle Sum Theorem}$$
$$127° + y° = 180°$$
$$\underline{-127° \qquad -127°} \quad \text{Subtract 127°}$$
$$y° = 53° \quad \text{from both sides.}$$

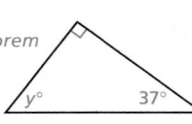

---

1 Introduce

Alternate Opener

7-3 Angles in Triangles

The figure below shows two parallel lines *m* and *n*, and a triangle.

1. What is the sum of the measures of ∠4, ∠1, and ∠5?
2. Name an angle with the same measure as ∠4.
3. Name an angle with the same measure as ∠5.
4. What is the sum of the measures of ∠1, ∠2, and ∠3?

Think and Discuss
5. **Discuss** what would happen to the sum of the measures of ∠1, ∠2, and ∠3 if the triangle above were bigger.
6. **Explain** why each angle measure in an *equilateral triangle* is 60°. (In an equilateral triangle, the three sides are equal.)

Motivate

Use a rubber band to form triangles with different shapes. (Use a push pin and two pencils at a bulletin board, or use three pencils at the chalkboard with a student volunteer.) Show students that if one of the angles gets larger, another angle gets smaller. This fact supports the Triangle Sum Theorem, which states that the sum of the angle measures in any triangle is 180°.

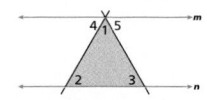
Explorations and answers are provided in *Alternate Openers: Explorations Transparencies.*

C Find $z°$ in the obtuse triangle.

$$13° + 62° + z° = 180°$$ *Triangle Sum Theorem*
$$75° + z° = 180°$$
$$\underline{- 75° \qquad - 75°}$$ *Subtract 75° from*
$$z° = 105°$$ *both sides.*

An **equilateral triangle** has 3 congruent sides and 3 congruent angles. An **isosceles triangle** has at least 2 congruent sides and 2 congruent angles. A **scalene triangle** has no congruent sides and no congruent angles.

E X A M P L E ❷ **Finding Angles in Equilateral, Isosceles, and Scalene Triangles**

A Find the angle measures in the equilateral triangle.

$$3m° = 180°$$ *Triangle Sum Theorem*
$$\frac{3m°}{3} = \frac{180°}{3}$$ *Divide both sides by 3.*
$$m° = 60°$$

All three angles measure 60°.

B Find the angle measures in the isosceles triangle.

$$55° + n° + n° = 180°$$ *Triangle Sum Theorem*
$$55° + 2n° = 180°$$ *Simplify.*
$$\underline{- 55° \qquad\qquad - 55°}$$ *Subtract 55° from both sides.*
$$2n° = 125°$$
$$\frac{2n°}{2} = \frac{125°}{2}$$ *Divide both sides by 2.*
$$n° = 62.5°$$

The angles labeled $n°$ measure 62.5°.

C Find the angle measures in the scalene triangle.

$$2p° + 3p° + 4p° = 180°$$ *Triangle Sum Theorem*
$$9p° = 180°$$ *Simplify.*
$$\frac{9p°}{9} = \frac{180°}{9}$$ *Divide both sides by 9.*
$$p° = 20°$$

The angle labeled $2p°$ measures $2(20°) = 40°$, the angle labeled $3p°$ measures $3(20°) = 60°$, and the angle labeled $4p°$ measures $4(20°) = 80°$.

Additional Examples

Example ❶

A. Find $p°$ in the acute triangle.   63°

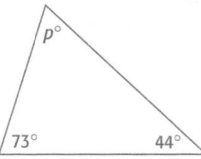

B. Find $c°$ in the right triangle.   48°

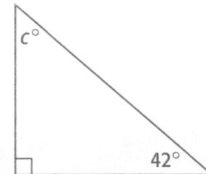

C. Find $m°$ in the obtuse triangle. 95°

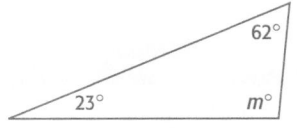

Example ❷

A. Find the angle measures in the equilateral triangle.   60°

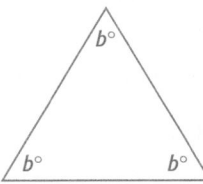

B. Find the angle measures in the isosceles triangle.   59°

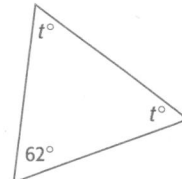

C. Find the angle measures in the scalene triangle.   36°, 54°, 90°

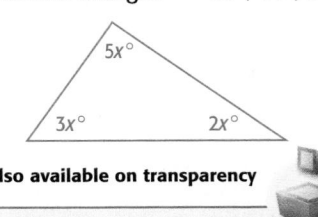

Also available on transparency

---

② Teach

Guided Instruction

In this lesson, students learn to find unknown angles in triangles. The lesson is based on the Triangle Sum Theorem, one of the most important theorems in geometry (Teaching Transparency). Illustrate the Triangle Sum Theorem by tearing off two corners of a paper triangle and placing them next to the third corner to form a straight line, which measures 180°. Explain that a triangle can have at most one right angle or one obtuse angle because of the Triangle Sum Theorem.

Teaching Tip   **Inclusion** For Example 2, explain that in a triangle, angles opposite congruent sides are congruent.

 Reaching All Learners
Through Critical Thinking

Show drawings of a square, a rectangle, and a parallelogram (Teaching Transparency).

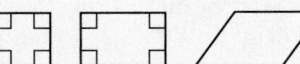

Ask the students, "If a diagonal is drawn in each figure, what types of triangles will be created?"

square: isosceles right triangles

rectangle: scalene right triangles

parallelogram: scalene acute triangles

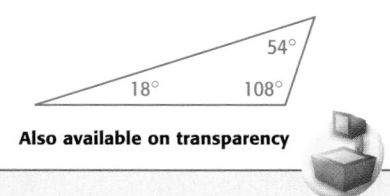

Additional Examples

Example 3

The second angle in a triangle is six times as large as the first. The third angle is half large as the second. Find the angle measures and draw a possible picture.   18°, 108°, 54°

[Triangle diagram: 54°, 18°, 108°]

Also available on transparency

7-3 Exercises

Assignment Guide

If you finished Example ① assign:
Average   1–3, 8–10, 15–17, 34–43
Advanced   8–10, 15–17, 34–43

If you finished Example ② assign:
Average   1–6, 8–13, 15–26, 30, 34–43
Advanced   8–13, 15–26, 30–43

If you finished Example ③ assign:
Average   1–27, 30, 34–43
Advanced   8–43

Homework Quick Check

Quickly check key concepts.
Exercises: 8, 12, 14, 26

State Resources

Answers to *Think and Discuss*

1. A right triangle cannot be equilateral because 90° + 90° + 90° = 270°. A right triangle can be isosceles (as in Example 3) or scalene (e.g., 90°, 60°, and 30°).

2. No; Either would make the sum of the three angles in the triangle greater than 180°.

EXAMPLE 3   Finding Angles in a Triangle That Meets Given Conditions

The second angle in a triangle is twice as large as the first. The third angle is half as large as the second. Find the angle measures and draw a possible figure.

Let $x°$ = first angle measure. Then $2x°$ = second angle measure, and $\frac{1}{2}(2x)° = x°$ = third angle measure.

$x° + 2x° + x° = 180°$ *Triangle Sum Theorem*

$\frac{4x°}{4} = \frac{180°}{4}$ *Simplify, then divide both sides by 4.*

$x° = 45°$

[Triangle diagram: 45°, 45°]

Two angles measure 45° and one angle measures 90°. The triangle has two congruent angles. The triangle is an isosceles right triangle.

Think and Discuss

1. Explain whether a right triangle can be equilateral. Can it be isosceles? scalene?

2. Explain whether a triangle can have 2 right angles. Can it have 2 obtuse angles?

7-3 Exercises

GUIDED PRACTICE

See Example ①   **1.** Find $q°$ in the acute triangle.
   $q° = 77°$
2. Find $r°$ in the right triangle.
   $r° = 59°$
3. Find $s°$ in the obtuse triangle.
   $s° = 120°$

See Example ②   **4.** Find the angle measures in the equilateral triangle. $a° = 60°$

6. $d° = 18°$,
   $4d° = 72°$,
   $5d° = 90°$

5. Find the angle measures in the isosceles triangle. $c° = 56°$

6. Find the angle measures in the scalene triangle.

See Example ③   **7.** The second angle in a triangle is half as large as the first. The third angle is three times as large as the second. Find the angle measures and draw a possible picture.   60°, 30°, 90°

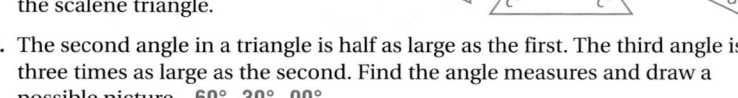

[Triangle diagrams with angles: q°, 70°, 33°; 45° s°, 31° r°, 15°; a°, a°, a°; 68°, c°, c°; 5d°, 4d°, d°]

---

3 Close

Summarize

Review the vocabulary terms. Show the following triangles and ask students to write the equations that are needed to solve for *x* and *r*. Remind students to check their work by making sure their answers add up to 180°.

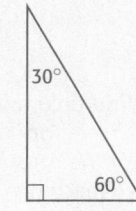

[Triangle diagrams: 30°, x°, 45°; 2r°, r°]

Possible answers:

1. $x° + 30° + 45° = 180°$

2. $r° + 2r° + 90° = 180°$

Answers

7.

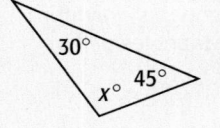

[Triangle diagram: 30°, 60°]

INDEPENDENT PRACTICE

See Example 1

8. Find $r°$ in the acute triangle. $r° = 86°$

9. Find $s°$ in the right triangle. $s° = 58°$

10. Find $t°$ in the obtuse triangle. $t° = 115°$

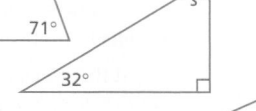

See Example 2

11. Find the angle measures in the equilateral triangle. $w° = 60°$

12. Find the angle measures in the isosceles triangle. $m° = 72°$

13. Find the angle measures in the scalene triangle. $2g° = 20°, 7g° = 70°, 9g° = 90°$

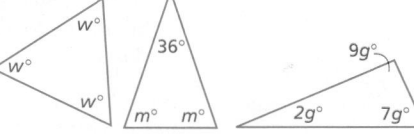

See Example 3

14. The second angle in a triangle is five times as large as the first. The third angle is two-thirds as large as the first. Find the angle measures and draw a possible picture. $27°, 135°, 18°$

PRACTICE AND PROBLEM SOLVING

Extra Practice
See page 794.

Find the value of each variable.

15. 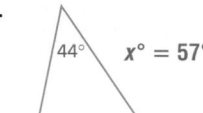 $x° = 57°$

16. 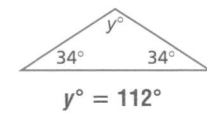 $y° = 112°$

17. 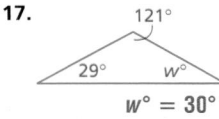 $w° = 30°$

18. 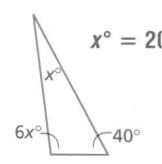 $x° = 20°$

19. 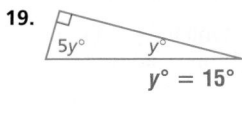 $y° = 15°$

20. 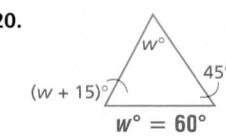 $w° = 60°$

28. Possible answer: No, if two angles measure 40°, the third angle would have to be 100°. It would be an obtuse triangle, not an acute triangle.

Sketch a triangle to fit each description. If no triangle can be drawn, write *not possible.*

21. acute scalene

22. obtuse equilateral
not possible

23. right scalene

24. right equilateral
not possible

25. obtuse scalene

26. acute isosceles

27. Triangle *ABC* is a right triangle and m∠A = 38°. What does the third angle measure? **52°**

28. Can an acute isosceles triangle have two angles that measure 40°? Explain.

29. Triangle *LMN* is an obtuse triangle and m∠L = 25°. ∠M is the obtuse angle. What is the largest m∠N can be to the nearest whole degree? **64°**

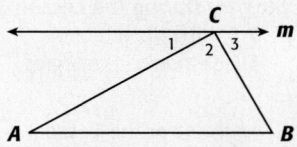
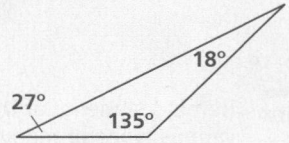
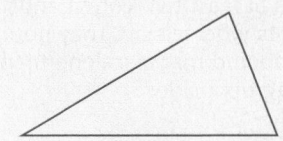
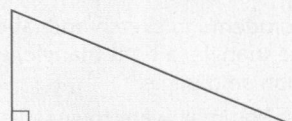
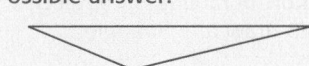
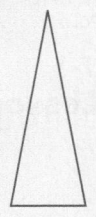
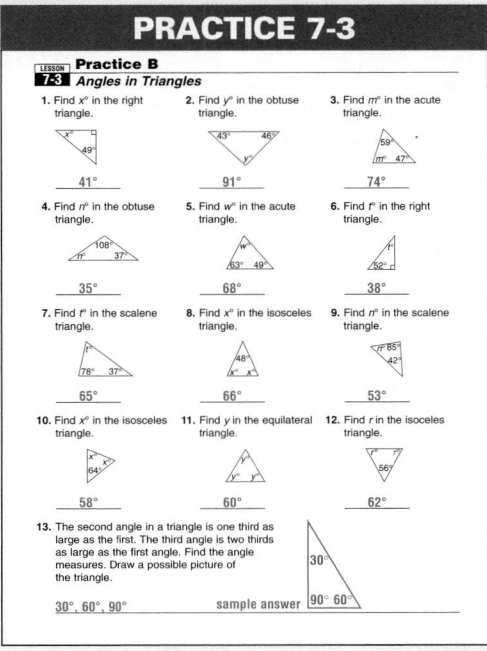

Answers

30, 32. See p. A7.

 Journal

Ask students to sketch and label an acute triangle, a right triangle, and an obtuse triangle.

Note: You may want to suggest that students use the vertical margin line and a horizontal line on notebook paper to draw a right angle.

Power Presentations
with PowerPoint®

7-3 Lesson Quiz

1. Find the missing angle measure in the acute triangle shown. **38°**

2. Find the missing angle measure in the right triangle shown. **55°**

3. Find the missing angle measure in an acute triangle with angle measures of 67° and 63°. **50°**

4. Find the missing angle measure in an obtuse triangle with angle measures of 10° and 15°. **155°**

Also available on transparency

Social Studies American Samoa is a territory of the United States made up of a group of islands in the Pacific Ocean, about halfway between Hawaii and New Zealand. The flag of American Samoa is shown.

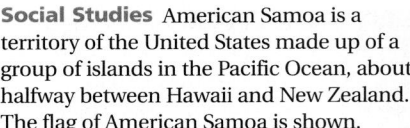

Find the measure of each angle in the blue triangles.

Use your answers to part **a** to find the angle measures in the white triangle.

Classify the triangles in the flag by their sides and angles.

 Choose a Strategy Which of the following sets of angle measures can be used to create an isosceles triangle?

○ 45°, 45°, 95°　　○ 49°, 51°, 80°　　◉ 27°, 27°, 126°　　○ 35°, 55°, 100°

 Write About It Explain how to cut a square or an equilateral triangle in half to form two identical triangles. What are the angle measures in the resulting triangles in each case?

 Challenge Find *x*, *y*, and *z*.
x = 30, *y* = 100, *z* = 50

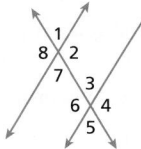 **TEST PREP and Spiral Review**

Multiple Choice Which type of triangle can be constructed with a 50° angle between two 8-inch sides?

○ Equilateral　　◉ Isosceles　　○ Scalene　　○ Obtuse

Short Response Two angles of a triangle are 45° and 30°. What is the measure of the third angle? Is the triangle acute, right, or obtuse? **105°, obtuse**

Each square root s between two ntegers Name the ntegers (Lesson 4-6)

$\sqrt{42}$ **6 and 7**　　$\sqrt{71}$ **8 and 9**　　$\sqrt{35}$ **5 and 6**　　$\sqrt{296}$ **17 and 18**

In the f gure, l ne ‖ l ne (Lesson 7-2)

If m∠1 = 34°, what is m∠7? **34°**

If m∠6 = 125°, what is m∠5? **55°**

If m∠1 = 34°, what is m∠4? **146°**

If m∠5 = 34°, what is m∠2? **146°**

CHALLENGE 7-3

LESSON 7-3 Challenge
Change a This into a That

A **geometric dissection** involves cutting a figure into pieces that can then be rearranged to form another figure.

Trace each figure. Cut up the figure you have traced and rearrange the numbered pieces to form the indicated figure. Sketch your solution.

1. Rearrange the pieces of the equilateral triangle to form a square.

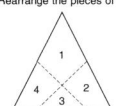 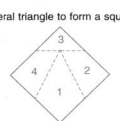

2. Rearrange the pieces of the star to form an equilateral triangle.

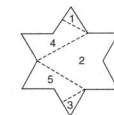 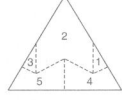

3. Rearrange the pieces of the cross to form an equilateral triangle.

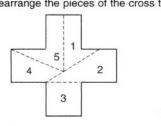 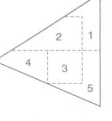

PROBLEM SOLVING 7-3

LESSON 7-3 Problem Solving
Angles in Triangles

The American flag must be folded according to certain rules that result in the flag being folded into the shape of a triangle. The figure shows a frame designed to hold an American flag.

1. Is the triangle acute, right, or obtuse?

　right

2. Is the triangle equilateral, isosceles, or scalene?

　isosceles

3. Find *x*°.
　x = 45°

4. Find *y*°.
　y = 45°

The figure shows a map of three streets. Choose the letter for the best answer.

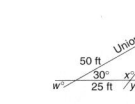

5. Find *x*°.
　A 22°　　C 30°
　Ⓑ 128°　　D 68°

6. Find *w*°.
　F 22°　　Ⓗ 30°
　G 128°　　J 52°

7. Find *y*°.
　A 22°
　B 30°
　Ⓒ 128°
　D 143°

8. Find *z*°.
　Ⓕ 22°
　G 30°
　H 128°
　J 143°

9. Which word best describes the triangle formed by the streets?
　A acute
　B right
　Ⓒ obtuse
　D equilateral

10. Which word best describes the triangle formed by the streets?
　F equilateral
　G isosceles
　Ⓗ scalene
　J acute

7-4 Classifying Polygons

Learn to classify and find angles in polygons.

Vocabulary
polygon
regular polygon
trapezoid
parallelogram
rectangle
rhombus
square

Kites have been around for over 3000 years, when the Chinese made them from bamboo and silk. The most common flat kite is in the shape of a diamond, a type of *quadrilateral* called a *kite*.

A **polygon** is a closed plane figure formed by three or more segments. A polygon is named by the number of its sides.

Polygon	Number of Sides
Triangle	3
Quadrilateral	4
Pentagon	5
Hexagon	6
Heptagon	7
Octagon	8
n-gon	*n*

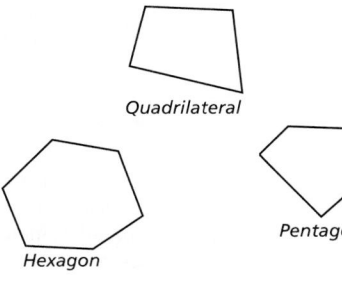

Quadrilateral

Hexagon

Pentagon

EXAMPLE 1 **Finding Sums of the Angle Measures in Polygons**

Find the sum of the angle measures in each figure.

A Find the sum of the angle measures in a quadrilateral.
Divide the figure into triangles.
$2 \cdot 180° = 360°$ *2 triangles*
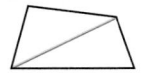

B Find the sum of the angle measures in a pentagon.
Divide the figure into triangles.
$3 \cdot 180° = 540°$ *3 triangles*
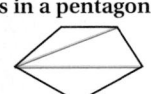

Look for a pattern between the number of sides and the number of triangles.

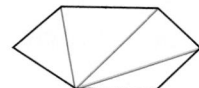
Hexagon:
6 sides
4 triangles

Heptagon:
7 sides
5 triangles

---

1 Introduce

Alternate Opener

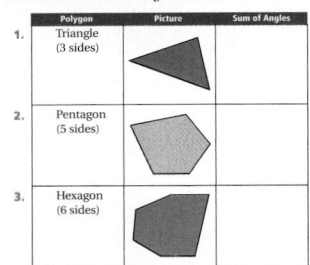

EXPLORATION

7-4 Classifying Polygons

Use a protractor to measure each angle in each figure. Then find the sum of the angle measures.

	Polygon	Picture	Sum of Angles
1.	Triangle (3 sides)		
2.	Pentagon (5 sides)		
3.	Hexagon (6 sides)		

Think and Discuss
4. **Explain** how you know the sum of the angle measures in a square.
5. **Discuss** how you can use the two triangles to show that the sum of the angle measures in a four-sided figure

Explorations and answers are provided in *Alternate Openers: Explorations Transparencies.*

Organizer 7-4

Pacing: Traditional 2 days
Block 1 day
Objective: Students classify and find angles in polygons.

 Hands-On Lab
In *Hands-On Lab Activities*

 Technology Lab
In *Technology Lab Activities*

 Online Edition
Tutorial Videos

 Countdown to Testing Week 13

Power Presentations
with PowerPoint®

Warm Up
1. How many sides does a hexagon have?   6
2. How many sides does a pentagon have?   5
3. How many angles does an octagon have?   8
4. Evaluate $(n - 2)180$ for $n = 7$.   900

Problem of the Day
Jeffrey planted four carnations, three dahlias, seven marigolds, five cornflowers, one geranium, and four mums. He forgot to water them and on each of the two following days, half the remaining flowers died. How many flowers were still living at the end of the second day?   6

Also available on transparency

ENGLISH LANGUAGE LEARNERS

Motivate
Show students the following prefixes: *tri-, quad-, penta-, hexa-, hepta-,* and *octa-*. Ask them to think of words that begin with these prefixes, such as tricycle, quadruple, and octopus. Discuss with students what each prefix means. Tell them that they will be using these prefixes to classify polygons.

State Resources

go.hrw.com
State Resources Online
KEYWORD: MT7 Resources

7-4 Classifying Polygons   **341**

Additional Examples

Example 1

Find the sum of the angle measures in each figure.

A. Find the sum of the angle measures in a hexagon. 720°

B. Find the sum of the angle measures in an octagon. 1080°

Example 2

Find the angle measures in each regular polygon.

A. 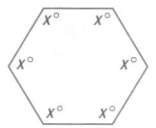 $x° = 120°$

B. 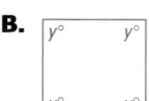 $y° = 90°$

Example 3

Give all of the names that apply to each figure.

A.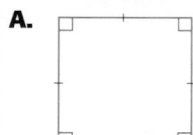
quadrilateral, parallelogram, rectangle, rhombus, square

B.
quadrilateral, parallelogram, rhombus

Also available on transparency

The pattern is that the number of triangles is always 2 less than the number of sides. So an n-gon can be divided into $n - 2$ triangles. The sum of the angle measures of any n-gon is $180°(n - 2)$.

All the sides and angles of a **regular polygon** have equal measures.

EXAMPLE 2 **Finding the Measure of Each Angle in a Regular Polygon**

Find the angle measures in each regular polygon.

Ⓐ 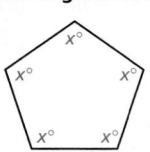   Ⓑ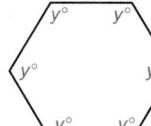

5 congruent angles
$5x° = 180°(5 - 2)$
$5x° = 180°(3)$
$5x° = 540°$
$\frac{5x°}{5} = \frac{540°}{5}$
$x° = 108°$

6 congruent angles
$6y° = 180°(6 - 2)$
$6y° = 180°(4)$
$6y° = 720°$
$\frac{6y°}{6} = \frac{720°}{6}$
$y° = 120°$

Quadrilaterals with certain properties are given additional names. A **trapezoid** has exactly 1 pair of parallel sides. A **parallelogram** has 2 pairs of parallel sides. A **rectangle** has 4 right angles. A **rhombus** has 4 congruent sides. A **square** has 4 congruent sides and 4 right angles.

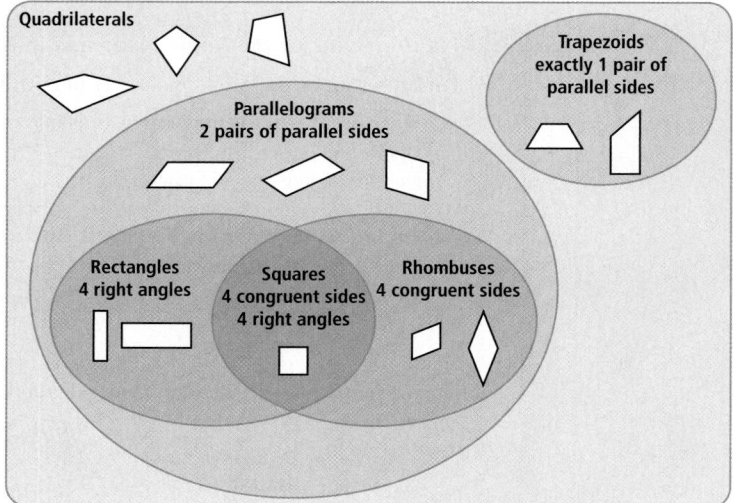

---

2 Teach

Guided Instruction

In this lesson, students learn to classify and find angles in polygons. Discuss how to name (classify) polygons based on the number of sides (Teaching Transparency). Show students how to draw diagonals of an n-sided polygon to form $n - 2$ triangles. Be sure to draw diagonals from one vertex only. Explain that the expression $(n - 2)180°$ gives the sum of the angles of a polygon because the sum of the angles of each triangle is $180°$. Share with students the names and properties of the special quadrilaterals in the lesson (Teaching Transparency).

Reaching All Learners
Through Diversity

Have students find at least 5 quadrilaterals in their everyday lives. They should draw each quadrilateral, state its properties, and write all the names that apply.

Possible answer: A baseball "diamond" is a square, because it has four congruent sides and four right angles. It is a square, a rhombus, a rectangle, a parallelogram, and a quadrilateral.

EXAMPLE 3 Classifying Quadrilaterals

Give all of the names that apply to each figure.

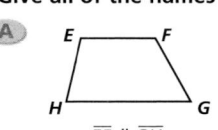 **A**

quadrilateral — *Four-sided polygon*
trapezoid — *1 pair of parallel sides*

$\overline{EF} \parallel \overline{GH}$

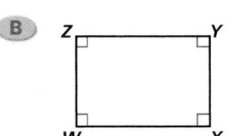 **B**

quadrilateral — *Four-sided polygon*
parallelogram — *2 pairs of parallel sides*
rectangle — *4 right angles*

Think and Discuss

1. **Choose** which is larger, an angle in a regular heptagon or an angle in a regular octagon. Justify your answer.

2. **Explain** why all rectangles are parallelograms and why all squares are rectangles.

 **7-4** **Exercises**

go.hrw.com
Homework Help Online
KEYWORD: MT7 7-4
Parent Resources Online
KEYWORD: MT7 Parent

GUIDED PRACTICE

See Example **1** Find the sum of the angle measures in each figure.

1. 360°

2. 720°

3.  900°

See Example **2** Find the angle measures in each regular polygon.

4. 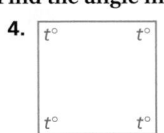 $t° = 90°$

5.  $v° \approx 128.6°$

6. 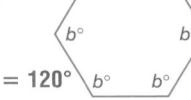 $b° = 120°$

---

3 Close

Summarize

Review the prefixes for classifying polygons and the expression $(n - 2)180°$ for the angle sum of an n-sided polygon. Ask for volunteers to find the angle sum and the measure of an individual angle in a regular polygon with ten sides (decagon).

Possible answers: The angle sum is $(10 - 2)180° = 1440°$. Each angle measures 144°.

COMMON ERROR ALERT

Some students may not understand the reasoning for finding the sums of angle measures in various polygons. Help them to see that the sum of the interior angles of the polygon is the same as the sum of all the angles in all the triangles in the polygon's interior.

Answers to Think and Discuss

1. An angle in a regular octagon (135°) is larger than an angle in a regular heptagon $\left(128\frac{4}{7}°\right)$.

2. Possible answer: All rectangles have two pairs of parallel sides because they have four right angles. This makes them parallelograms. All squares have four right angles, which makes them rectangles.

7-4 **Exercises**

Assignment Guide

If you finished Example **1** assign:
Average 1–3, 10–12, 43–49
Advanced 10–12, 43–49

If you finished Example **2** assign:
Average 1–6, 10–15, 19–32, 43–49
Advanced 10–15, 21–33, 38, 41, 43–49

If you finished Example **3** assign:
Average 1–32, 36, 37, 43–49
Advanced 10–20, 24–49

Homework Quick Check

Quickly check key concepts.
Exercises: 12, 14, 16, 26, 30

State Resources

go.hrw.com
State Resources Online
KEYWORD: MT7 Resources

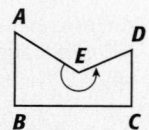 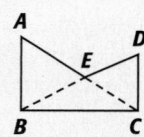
See Example **3**   Give all of the names that apply to each figure.

7.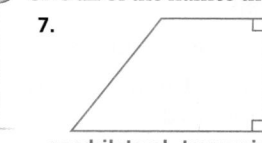
quadrilateral, trapezoid

8.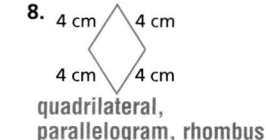
quadrilateral, parallelogram, rhombus

9.
quadrilateral, parallelogram, rectangle

INDEPENDENT PRACTICE

See Example **1**   Find the sum of the angle measures in each figure.

10. 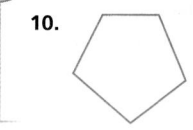 540°

11. 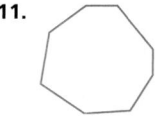 1080°

12. 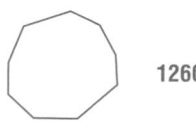 1260°

See Example **2**   Find the angle measures in each regular polygon.

16.
quadrilateral, parallelogram, rhombus, rectangle, square

13. 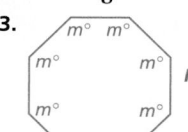 $m° = 135°$

14. 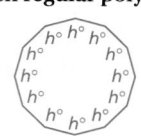 $h° = 150°$

15. 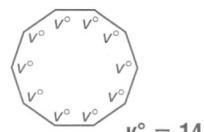 $v° = 144°$

See Example **3**   Give all of the names that apply to each figure.

17.
quadrilateral, parallelogram

18.
quadrilateral, trapezoid

16.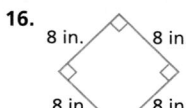

17. 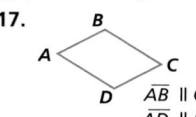 $\overline{AB} \parallel \overline{CD}$ $\overline{AD} \parallel \overline{BC}$

18. 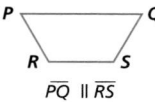 $\overline{PQ} \parallel \overline{RS}$

PRACTICE AND PROBLEM SOLVING

Extra Practice
See page 794.

Find the sum of the angle measures in each regular polygon. Then find the measure of each angle.

19. 20-gon
3240°; 162°

20. 13-gon
1980°; 152.3°

21. 60-gon
10,440°; 174°

22. pentagon
540°; 108°

23. 16-gon
2520°; 157.5°

Find the value of each variable.

24. 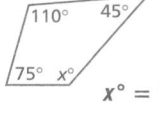 $x° = 130°$

25. 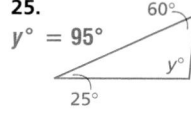 $y° = 95°$

26.  $w° = 137°$

27. 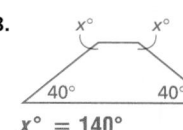 $z° = 97°$

28. 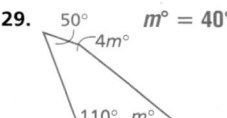 $x° = 140°$

29. 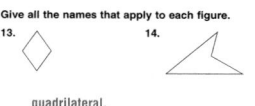 $m° = 40°$

The sum of the angle measures of a polygon is given. Name the polygon.

30. 1080° **31.** 540° **32.** 360° **33.** 1620°
octagon   pentagon   quadrilateral   11-gon

Graph the given vertices on a coordinate plane. Connect the points to draw a polygon and classify it by the number of its sides.

34. $A(0, 3)$, $B(1, 1)$, $C(4, 1)$, $D(5, 3)$, $E(4, 5)$, $F(1, 5)$

35. $A(-3, 2)$, $B(-3, -1)$, $C(1, -3)$, $D(4, 0)$, $E(1, 4)$

Sketch a quadrilateral to fit each description. If no quadrilateral can be drawn, write *not possible*.

36. a parallelogram that is not a rhombus

37. a square that is not a rectangle not possible

38. **Earth Science** Precious stones are often cut in a *brilliant cut* to maximize the light they reflect. The best angles for a cut depend on the type of stone. The best angles for a diamond are shown.
  a. If the pavilion main angle is 41°, find x. $x° = 98°$
  b. If the crown angle is 35°, find y. $y° = 145°$

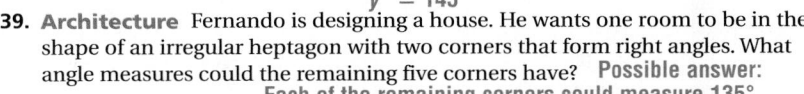
Crown angle
Pavilion main angle

39. **Architecture** Fernando is designing a house. He wants one room to be in the shape of an irregular heptagon with two corners that form right angles. What angle measures could the remaining five corners have? Possible answer: Each of the remaining corners could measure 135°.

40. **What's the Error?** A student said that all squares are rectangles, but not all squares are rhombuses. What was the error?

41. **Write About It** Why is it possible to find the sum of the angle measures of an n-gon using the formula $(180n - 360)°$?

42. **Challenge** Use a diagram and the properties of parallel lines to explain which angles in a parallelogram must be congruent.

TEST PREP and Spiral Review

43. **Multiple Choice** What is the measure of each angle of a regular 15-sided polygon?
  Ⓐ 146°   Ⓑ 148°   Ⓒ 150°   Ⓓ 156°

44. **Short Response** The sum of the angle measures of a regular polygon is 720°. Name the regular polygon. What is the measure of each angle?
regular hexagon; each angle is 120°

Subtract. (Lesson 1-5)

45. $-5 - 12$ −17   **46.** $-25 - 25$ −50   **47.** $34 - (-17)$ 51   **48.** $-30 - 41$ −71

49. The first angle in a triangle is less than 90°. The second angle is $\frac{3}{4}$ as large as the first angle. The third angle is $\frac{2}{3}$ as large as the second angle. Find the angle measures and draw a possible figure. (Lesson 7-3) 80°, 60°, 40°

ONGOING ASSESSMENT
and INTERVENTION

Diagnose Before the Lesson
7-4 Warm Up, TE p. 341

Monitor During the Lesson
7-4 Know-It Notebook
7-4 Questioning Strategies

Assess After the Lesson
7-4 Lesson Quiz, TE p. 345

Answers
34–36, 40–42, 49. See p. A7.

TEST PREP DOCTOR Students may wish to review the pattern between the number of sides of a polygon and the number of triangles into which it can be divided before attempting to solve Exercise 44. In this case, 720 ÷ 180 = 4. The number of sides of this polygon is (4 + 2), or 6, which makes it a regular hexagon. Suggest that students use the equation $6x = 180°(6 - 2)$ to find the measure of each angle in a regular hexagon.

Journal
Have students write about how the expression $(n - 2)180°$ is related to the number of triangles formed by the diagonals of a polygon.

Power Presentations with PowerPoint®

CHALLENGE 7-4

Challenge
7-4 *Slanted View*

1. Refer to parallelogram *ABCD*. Use a ruler.
  a. Is diagonal $\overline{AC} \cong$ diagonal $\overline{BD}$? no
  b. Is $\overline{AM} \cong \overline{MC}$? Is $\overline{DM} \cong \overline{MB}$? yes, yes
  Make a statement about how the diagonals of a parallelogram relate to each other.
  The diagonals of a parallelogram are not congruent but they do bisect each other.

2. Refer to rectangle *ABCD* and your observations in Question 1.
  a. Since a rectangle is a parallelogram, what property should the diagonals have? Use a ruler to verify your conjecture.
  Diagonals bisect each other.
  b. What additional property do the diagonals of a rectangle have?
  Diagonals are congruent.

3. Refer to rhombus *ABCD*.
  a. Since a rhombus is a parallelogram, what property should the diagonals have? Use a ruler to verify your conjecture.
  Diagonals bisect each other.
  b. Are the diagonals congruent? no
  c. Measure the angles with vertex *M*. What additional property do the diagonals of a rhombus have?
  Diagonals are perpendicular to each other.
  d. Measure the angles at each vertex of the rhombus. What additional property do the diagonals of a rhombus have?
  Diagonals bisect the opposite angles.

4. Make a conjecture about the properties of the diagonals of a square. Draw a square and verify your conjectures with a ruler and protractor.
  congruent; perpendicular bisectors of each other; bisect opposite angles

---

PROBLEM SOLVING 7-4

Problem Solving
7-4 *Classifying Polygons*

The figure shows how the glass for a window will be cut from a square piece. Cuts will be made along $\overline{CE}$, $\overline{FH}$, $\overline{IK}$, and $\overline{LB}$.

1. What shape is the window?
  octagon
2. What is the sum of the angle measures of the window?
  1080°
3. What is the measure of each angle of the window?
  135°
4. Based on the angles, what kind of triangle is △*CDE*?
  right triangle
5. Based on the sides, what kind of triangle is △*CDE*?
  isosceles triangle

The figure shows how parallel cuts will be made along $\overline{AD}$ and $\overline{BC}$. $\overline{AB}$ and $\overline{CD}$ are parallel. Choose the letter for the best answer.

6. Which word correctly describes figure *ABCD* after the cuts are made?
  A triangle
  B quadrilateral
  C pentagon
  D hexagon
7. Which word correctly describes figure *ABCD* after the cuts are made?
  F parallelogram
  G trapezoid
  H rectangle
  J rhombus
8. Find the measure of ∠1.
  A 45°
  B 65°
  C 90°
  D 115°
9. Find the measure of ∠2.
  F 45°   **H** 65°
  G 90°   **J** 115°
10. Find the measure of ∠3.
  A 45°   **C** 65°
  B 90°   **D** 115°

7-4 Lesson Quiz

1. Find the sum of the angle measures in a quadrilateral. 360°
2. Find the sum of the angle measures in a hexagon. 720°
3. Find the measure of each angle in a regular octagon. 135°
4. Write all of the names that apply to the figure below. quadrilateral, rhombus, parallelogram

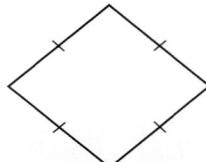

Also available on transparency

Technology LAB Organizer

Use with Lesson 7-4

Pacing:
Traditional $\frac{1}{2}$ day
Block $\frac{1}{4}$ day

Objective: Use a geometry program to study the exterior angles of a polygon.

Materials: Computer with geometry software

Online Edition
TechKeys

Countdown to Testing Week 13

Resources

Technology Lab Activities
Lab 7-4 Recording Sheet

Teach
Discuss

Before proceeding with the computer activity, ask students to draw a square using a protractor and a ruler with a straightedge. Then, have them extend the sides, measure the exterior angles, and calculate the sum of the exterior angle measures.

Technology LAB 7-4
Exterior Angles of a Polygon

Use with Lesson 7-4

go.hrw.com
Lab Resources Online
KEYWORD: MT7 Lab7

The *exterior angles* of a polygon are formed by extending the polygon's sides. Every exterior angle is supplementary to the angle next to it inside the polygon.

Exterior angle

Activity

① Follow the steps to find the sum of the exterior angle measures for a polygon.

a. Use geometry software to make a pentagon. Label the vertices *A* through *E*.

b. Use the **LINE-RAY** tool to extend the sides of the pentagon. Add points *F* through *J* as shown.

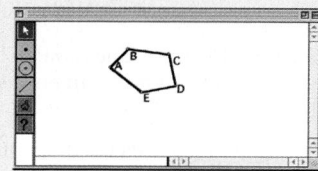

c. Use the **ANGLE MEASURE** tool to measure each exterior angle and the **CALCULATOR** tool to add the measures. Notice the sum.

d. Drag vertices *A* through *E* and watch the sum. Notice that the sum of the angle measures is *always* 360°.

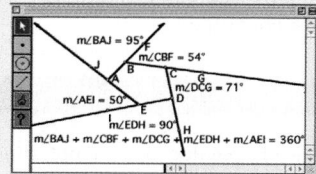
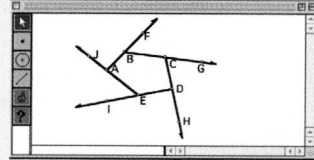
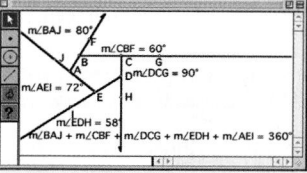

Think and Discuss

1. Suppose you were to drag the vertices of a polygon so that the polygon almost vanishes. How would this show that the sum of the exterior angle measures is 360°? **The sum of the measures of the exterior angles of a regular pentagon is always 360°.**

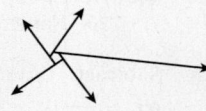

Try This

1. Use geometry software to draw any polygon. Find the sum of its exterior angle measures. Drag its vertices to check that the sum is always the same. **360°; the sum is always 360°.**

Close
Key Concept

The sum of the measures of the exterior angles of a regular polygon is always 360°.

Assessment

1. Use the software to draw a triangle and to measure its exterior angles. What is the sum of the measures of the exterior angles of a triangle? **360°**

2. What general statement can you make about the sum of the measures of the exterior angles of any polygon? **The sum of the measures of the exterior angles of any polygon is 360°.**

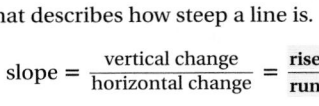
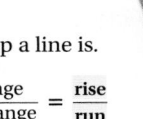

7-5 Coordinate Geometry

Learn to identify polygons in the coordinate plane.

Vocabulary
slope
rise
run

In computer graphics, a coordinate system is used to create images, from simple geometric figures to realistic figures used in movies.

Properties of the coordinate plane can be used to find information about figures in the plane, such as whether lines in the plane are parallel.

Slope is a number that describes how steep a line is.

$$\text{slope} = \frac{\text{vertical change}}{\text{horizontal change}} = \frac{\text{rise}}{\text{run}}$$

Positive slope

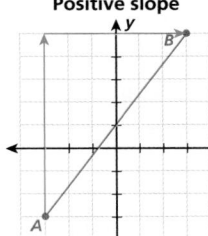

Negative slope

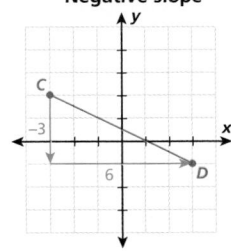

$$\text{slope of } \overline{AB} = \frac{8}{6} = \frac{4}{3}$$

$$\text{slope of } \overline{CD} = \frac{-3}{6} = \frac{-1}{2}$$

The slope of a horizontal line is 0. The slope of a vertical line is undefined.

EXAMPLE 1 Finding the Slope of a Line

Determine if the slope of each line is positive, negative, 0, or undefined. Then find the slope of each line.

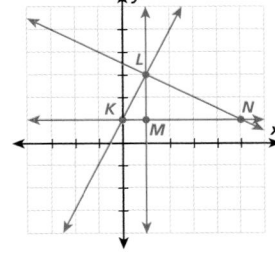

Remember!
When a number is divided by zero, the quotient is undefined. There is no answer.

A $\overleftrightarrow{KL}$
positive; slope of $\overleftrightarrow{KL} = \frac{2}{1} = 2$

B $\overleftrightarrow{LM}$
undefined; slope of $\overleftrightarrow{LM} = \frac{1}{0}$

C $\overleftrightarrow{LN}$
negative; slope of $\overleftrightarrow{LN} = \frac{-2}{4} = -\frac{1}{2}$

D $\overleftrightarrow{KM}$
0; slope of $\overleftrightarrow{KM} = \frac{0}{1}$

---

1 Introduce

Alternate Opener

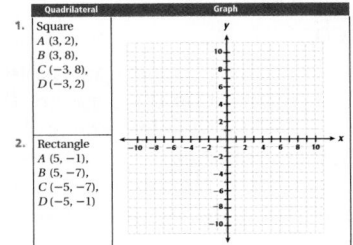

EXPLORATION

7-5 Coordinate Geometry

Quadrilaterals are figures with four sides. Use the coordinate grid to draw each of the following quadrilaterals. Label vertices with A, B, C, and D.

	Quadrilateral	Graph
1.	Square A (3, 2), B (3, 8), C (−3, 8), D (−3, 2)	
2.	Rectangle A (5, −1), B (5, −7), C (−5, −7), D (−5, −1)	

Think and Discuss

3. **Describe** the relationship between the number of sides and the number of vertices of quadrilaterals.

4. **Discuss** whether the relationship you described in Problem 3 is also true for other polygons.

Motivate

Show students two lines that *appear* to be parallel, and ask them if they really are. Suggest that although they appear to be parallel, the appearance is not proof. Explain that by plotting the lines on a coordinate plane, you can find a measure of the "steepness" of each line, called *slope*. Slope can be used to determine if the two lines are truly parallel.

Explorations and answers are provided in *Alternate Openers: Explorations Transparencies*.

Additional Examples

Example 1

Determine if the slope of each line is positive, negative, 0, or undefined. Then find the slope of each line.

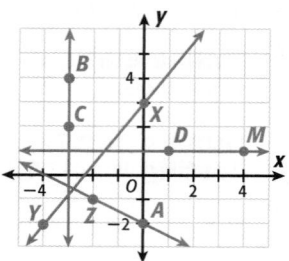

A. $\overleftrightarrow{XY}$ positive; $\frac{5}{4}$ **B.** $\overleftrightarrow{ZA}$ negative; $-\frac{1}{2}$

C. $\overleftrightarrow{BC}$ undefined **D.** $\overleftrightarrow{DM}$ 0

Example 2

Which lines are parallel?
Which lines are perpendicular?

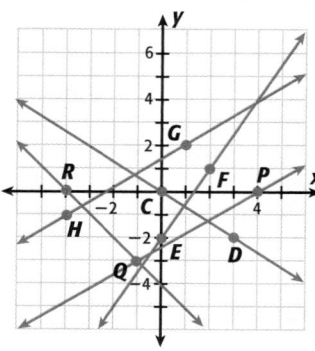

$\overleftrightarrow{GH} \parallel \overleftrightarrow{PQ}, \ \overleftrightarrow{EF} \perp \overleftrightarrow{CD}$

Example 3

Graph the quadrilateral with the given vertices. Give all of the names that apply to the quadrilateral.

$A(3, -2), B(2, -1), C(4, 3), D(5, 2)$

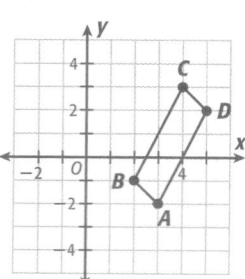

parallelogram

Also available on transparency

Slopes of Parallel and Perpendicular Lines

Two lines with equal slopes are parallel.

Two lines whose slopes have a product of -1 are perpendicular.

EXAMPLE 2 **Finding Perpendicular and Parallel Lines**

Which lines are parallel?
Which lines are perpendicular?

Helpful Hint

If a line has slope $\frac{a}{b}$, then a line perpendicular to it has slope $-\frac{b}{a}$.

slope of $\overleftrightarrow{PQ} = \frac{3}{2}$

slope of $\overleftrightarrow{RS} = \frac{4}{3}$

slope of $\overleftrightarrow{AB} = \frac{3}{2}$

slope of $\overleftrightarrow{PA} = \frac{-2}{2}$ or -1

slope of $\overleftrightarrow{GH} = \frac{-3}{4}$

slope of $\overleftrightarrow{XY} = \frac{-7}{8}$

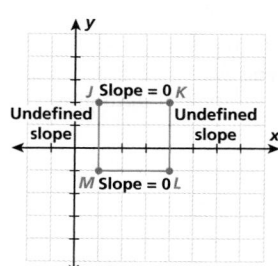

$\overleftrightarrow{PQ} \parallel \overleftrightarrow{AB}$ *The slopes are equal:* $\frac{3}{2} = \frac{3}{2}$

$\overleftrightarrow{RS} \perp \overleftrightarrow{GH}$ *The slopes have a product of* -1: $\frac{4}{3} \cdot \frac{-3}{4} = -1$

EXAMPLE 3 **Using Coordinates to Classify Quadrilaterals**

Graph the quadrilaterals with the given vertices. Give all of the names that apply to each quadrilateral.

A $J(1, 2), K(4, 2),$
$L(4, -1), M(1, -1)$

B $P(-1, 2), Q(2, 1),$
$R(-1, -2), S(-3, 0)$

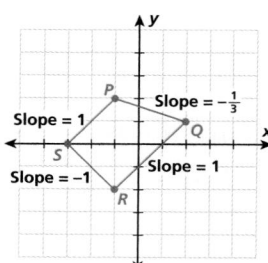

$\overline{JK} \parallel \overline{ML}$ and $\overline{MJ} \parallel \overline{LK}$
$\overline{JK} \perp \overline{LK}, \overline{JK} \perp \overline{MJ},$
$\overline{ML} \perp \overline{LK}$ and $\overline{ML} \perp \overline{MJ}$
parallelogram, rectangle, square, rhombus

$\overline{SP} \parallel \overline{RQ}$
trapezoid

---

2 Teach

Guided Instruction

In this lesson, students learn to identify polygons on the coordinate plane. To begin, you may want to review plotting points and lines on a coordinate plane. Show students how to find the slope of a line by using rise and run (Teaching Transparency). Explain that slope indicates how steep a line is and whether it slants up to the right (positive slope) or down to the right (negative slope). Discuss how to use slope to determine whether a pair of lines are parallel or perpendicular. Then show students how to apply these concepts to classify quadrilaterals.

Reaching All Learners
Through Cooperative Learning

Have students work in pairs. Ask each student to create a quadrilateral *ABCD* on a coordinate plane that satisfies all of the following conditions:

$\overline{AB} \parallel \overline{CD}, \overline{AB} \perp \overline{CB},$ and $\overline{AD}$ not $\parallel \overline{CB}$.

Have partners exchange papers and write the slope of each segment on the diagram. Then have them classify the quadrilateral and decide whether it satisfies the conditions. Finally, have the partners return papers to each other for comparison and discussion.

Possible answers: slopes of zero, undefined, zero, and $\frac{2}{3}$; trapezoid; yes

---

EXAMPLE 4 Finding the Coordinates of a Missing Vertex

Find the coordinates of the missing vertex of square ABCD.

Square ABCD with A(4, 0), B(0, 4), and C(−4, 0)

Step 1 Graph and connect the given points.

Step 2 Complete the figure to find the missing vertex. $\overline{AB}$ has a slope of −1, so $\overline{CD}$ has a slope of −1. $\overline{BC}$ has a slope of 1, so $\overline{AD}$ has a slope of 1.

The coordinates of D are (0, −4).

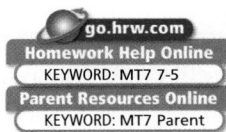

Remember!

In a square opposite sides are parallel.

1. Possible answer: You can use slopes to determine if sides are parallel or perpendicular. If sides have the same slope, they are parallel. If sides have slopes with a product of −1, they are perpendicular.

Think and Discuss

1. Explain how you can use slopes to classify a quadrilateral.

7-5 Exercises

GUIDED PRACTICE

See Example **1** Determine if the slope of each line is positive, negative, 0, or undefined. Then find the slope of each line.

1. $\overleftrightarrow{AD}$ 0

2. $\overleftrightarrow{BE}$ Slope is undefined.

3. $\overleftrightarrow{MN}$ positive slope; 1

4. $\overleftrightarrow{EF}$ negative slope; $-\frac{1}{2}$

See Example **2** **5.** Which lines are parallel? $\overleftrightarrow{AN} \parallel \overleftrightarrow{CD}$

6. Which lines are perpendicular?
$\overleftrightarrow{MN} \perp \overleftrightarrow{AN}, \overleftrightarrow{MN} \perp \overleftrightarrow{CD}$, and $\overleftrightarrow{AD} \perp \overleftrightarrow{BE}$

See Example **3** Graph the quadrilaterals with the given vertices. Give all of the names that apply to each quadrilateral.

7. D(−3, −2), E(−3, 3), F(2, 3), G(2, −2)

8. R(−4, −1), S(−2, 2), T(4, 2), V(5, −1)

See Example **4** Find the coordinates of the missing vertex.

9. rhombus ABCD with A(2, 3), B(3, 1), and D(1, 1) C(2, −1)

10. square JKLM with J(−3, 1), K(0, 1), and L(0, −2) M(−3, −2)

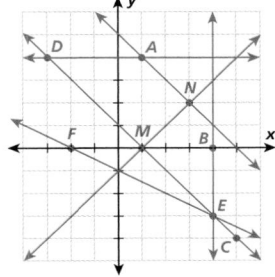

Additional Examples

Example 4

Find the coordinates of the missing vertex of rectangle WXYZ.

Rectangle WXYZ with W(−2, 2), X(3, 2), and Y(3, −4) Z(−2, −4)

Also available on transparency

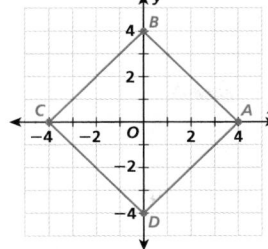

7-5 Exercises

Assignment Guide

If you finished Example **1** assign:
Average 1–4, 11–14, 21–24, 44–53
Advanced 11–14, 21–24, 27–28, 42, 44–53

If you finished Example **2** assign:
Average 1–6, 11–16, 21–24, 26, 44–53
Advanced 11–16, 21–28, 42, 44–53

If you finished Example **3** assign:
Average 1–8, 11–18, 21–24, 26, 31–36, 44–53
Advanced 11–18, 21–28, 30–53

If you finished Example **4** assign:
Average 1–18, 21–24, 26, 31–36, 44–53
Advanced 11–53

Homework Quick Check

Quickly check key concepts.
Exercises: 12, 16, 18, 20

---

3 Close

Summarize

Discuss with students how slope can be used to determine whether lines in a coordinate plane are parallel or perpendicular. Discuss the slopes of horizontal and vertical lines. Remind students that they can use this information to classify quadrilaterals.

Possible answers: If two lines have the same slope, they are parallel. If the product of the slopes of two lines equals −1, the lines are perpendicular. Also, if one line is horizontal and another is vertical, the lines are perpendicular. Horizontal lines have a slope of zero. Vertical lines have undefined slope.

Answers

7. parallelogram, rhombus, rectangle, square

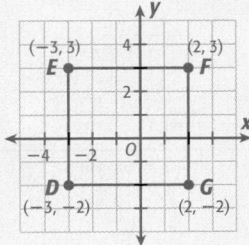

8.

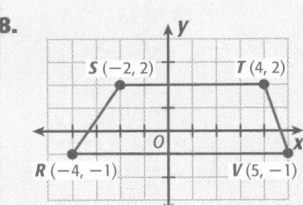

trapezoid

State Resources

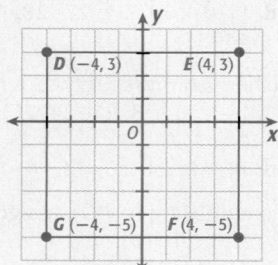
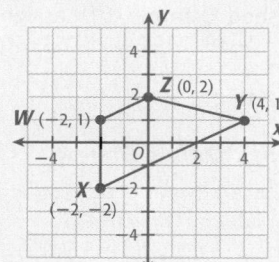
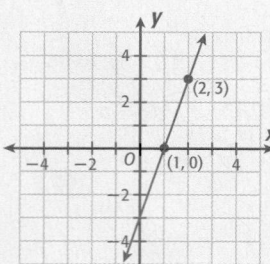
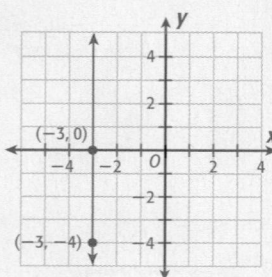
INDEPENDENT PRACTICE

See Example 1   Determine if the slope of each line is positive, negative, 0, or undefined. Then find the slope of each line.

11. $\overrightarrow{AB}$ positive slope, 1   12. $\overrightarrow{EG}$ negative slope, $-\frac{5}{3}$

13. $\overrightarrow{HG}$ 0   14. $\overrightarrow{CH}$ Slope is undefined.

See Example 2   15. Which lines are parallel? $\overleftrightarrow{CD} \parallel \overleftrightarrow{AB}$

16. Which lines are perpendicular?
$\overleftrightarrow{HG} \perp \overleftrightarrow{CH}$, $\overleftrightarrow{FE} \perp \overleftrightarrow{CD}$, and $\overleftrightarrow{FE} \perp \overleftrightarrow{AB}$

See Example 3   Graph the quadrilaterals with the given vertices. Give all of the names that apply to each quadrilateral.

17. $D(-4, 3)$, $E(4, 3)$, $F(4, -5)$, $G(-4, -5)$

18. $W(-2, 1)$, $X(-2, -2)$, $Y(4, 1)$, $Z(0, 2)$

See Example 4   Find the coordinates of the missing vertex.

19. rectangle $ABCD$ with $A(-3, 3)$, $B(4, 3)$, and $D(-3, -1)$ $C(4, -1)$

20. trapezoid $JKLM$ with $J(-1, 5)$, $K(2, 3)$, and $L(2, 1)$ $M(-1, -1)$

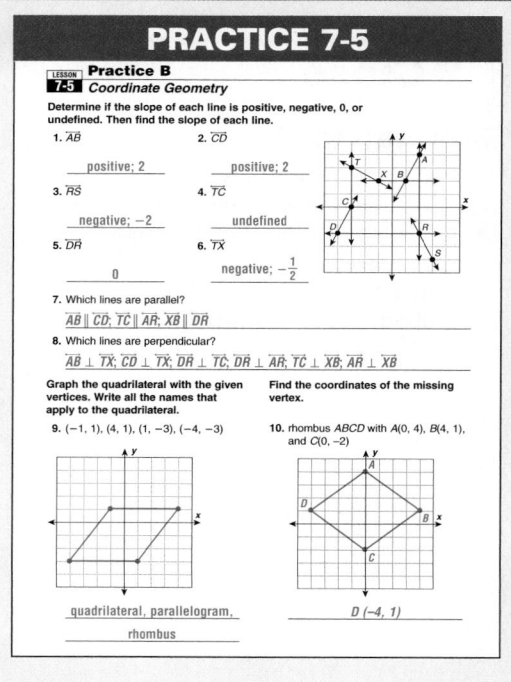

PRACTICE AND PROBLEM SOLVING

Extra Practice
See page 794.

Draw the line through the given points and find its slope.

21. $A(1, 0)$, $B(2, 3)$ 3   22. $C(-3, 0)$, $D(-3, -4)$ undefined

23. $G(4, -2)$, $H(-1, -2)$ 0   24. $E(-2, 1)$, $F(3, -2)$ $-\frac{3}{5}$

25. A line passes through the coordinates $P(1, 3)$ and $Q(-2, -3)$. Identify the slope of $\overrightarrow{PQ}$. Then name two coordinates and the slope of a line perpendicular to $\overrightarrow{PQ}$.   2; Possible answer: $(0, 0)$, $(-2, 1)$; $-\frac{1}{2}$

26. $\overrightarrow{AB} \parallel \overrightarrow{CD}$ and the slope of $\overrightarrow{AB}$ is undefined. What can you tell about the slope of $\overrightarrow{CD}$? Explain.

27. On a coordinate grid draw a line s with slope 0 and a line t with slope 1. Then draw three lines through the intersection of lines s and t that have slopes between 0 and 1.

28. On a coordinate grid draw a line m with slope 0 and a line n with slope -1. Then draw three lines through the intersection of lines m and n that have slopes between 0 and -1.

29. **Critical Thinking** Square $ABCD$ has vertices at $(1, 2)$ and $(1, -2)$. Find the possible coordinates of the two missing vertices to create the square with the least area. Justify your solution.

30. **Critical Thinking** Triangle LMN has vertices at $L(-2, 2)$, $M(0, 0)$, and $N(-5, -1)$. What kind of triangle is it? Explain.

RETEACH 7-5

Reteach
7-5 Coordinate Geometry

Possible Values for Slope

Slope is Positive	Slope is Negative	Slope = 0	Slope is Undefined
Line slants up. Forms acute angle with the positive direction of x-axis.	Line slants down. Forms obtuse angle with positive direction of x-axis.	Horizonal Line Parallel to x-axis.	Vertical Line Perpendicular to x-axis

Plot the given points. Describe the slope of the line that joins them.

1. $(-2, 2)$ and $(2, 5)$

slope is: positive

2. $(-2, -5)$ and $(-2, 2)$

slope is: undefined

3. $(1, 2)$ and $(5, -2)$

slope is: negative

4. $(-2, -2)$ and $(4, -2)$

slope is: 0

PRACTICE 7-5

Practice B
7-5 Coordinate Geometry

Determine if the slope of each line is positive, negative, 0, or undefined. Then find the slope of each line.

1. $\overline{AB}$ positive; 2   2. $\overline{CD}$ positive; 2

3. $\overline{RS}$ negative; -2 4. $\overline{TC}$ undefined

5. $\overline{DR}$ 0   6. $\overline{TX}$ negative; $-\frac{1}{2}$

7. Which lines are parallel?
$\overline{AB} \parallel \overline{CD}$; $\overline{TC} \parallel \overline{AR}$; $\overline{XB} \parallel \overline{DR}$

8. Which lines are perpendicular?
$\overline{AB} \perp \overline{TX}$; $\overline{CD} \perp \overline{TX}$; $\overline{DR} \perp \overline{TC}$; $\overline{DR} \perp \overline{AR}$; $\overline{TC} \perp \overline{XB}$; $\overline{AR} \perp \overline{XB}$

Graph the quadrilateral with the given vertices. Write all the names that apply to the quadrilateral.

9. $(-1, 1)$, $(4, 1)$, $(1, -3)$, $(-4, -3)$

quadrilateral, parallelogram, rhombus

Find the coordinates of the missing vertex.

10. rhombus $ABCD$ with $A(0, 4)$, $B(4, 1)$, and $C(0, -2)$

$D(-4, 1)$

Opposite sides of a rhombus have the same slope. **true**

All of the adjacent sides of quadrilaterals have slopes with a product of -1.

All parallelograms have two pairs of lines with the same slope and adjacent sides that have slopes with a product of -1.

A trapezoid has two pairs of sides that have the same slope.

The slope of a horizontal line is always 0. **true**

The slope of a line through the origin is always defined.
False; possible answer: the slope of the y-axis is undefined.

This figure has two sides with undefined slopes.   **D; rectangle**

This figure has a side with a slope of -1.
C; square

This figure has a side with a slope of 3.
B; right triangle

This figure has a side with a slope of $\frac{1}{3}$.
A; quadrilateral

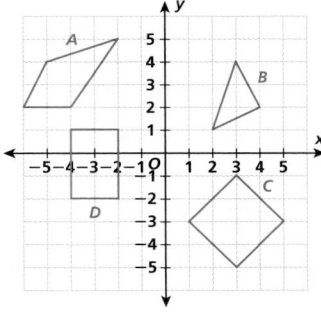

What's the Question? Points $(3, 7)$, $(5, 2)$, $(3, -3)$, and $(1, 2)$ form the vertices of a polygon. The answer is that the segments are not perpendicular. What is the question?

Write About It Explain how using different points on a line to find the slope affects the answer.

Challenge Use a square in a coordinate plane to explain why a line with slope 1 makes a 45° angle with the -axis.

TEST PREP and Spiral Review

Multiple Choice A right triangle has vertices at $(0, 0)$, $(0, 4)$, and $(10, 4)$. What is the slope of the hypotenuse?

- ○ 2.5
- ○ 2
- ○ 1.8
- ○ 0.4

Gridded Response Find the slope of the line that crosses through the points $(2, 4)$ and $(-1, 5)$. $-\frac{1}{3}$

(Lesson 6-4)

60% of what number is 12? **20**

30 is 2% of what number? **1500**

112 is 80% of what number? **140**

90% of what number is 18? **20**

(Lesson 7-4)

15-gon **2,340°**   hexagon **720°**   -gon **180° (n − 2)**   decagon **1440°**

Diagnose Before the Lesson
7-5 Warm Up, TE p. 347

Monitor During the Lesson
7-5 Know-It Notebook
7-5 Questioning Strategies

Assess After the Lesson
7-5 Lesson Quiz, TE p. 351

Answers
32–34, 41–43. See p. A8.

TEST PREP DOCTOR Have students plot the vertices given in Exercise 44 on a coordinate grid. Students will be better able to determine the endpoints of the hypotenuse with the help of a visual aid. Students who chose answer **D** incorrectly found the slope by calculating the run divided by the rise, instead of rise over run.

Journal

Have students give real-world examples of things with very steep slopes, gentle slopes, zero slopes, and undefined slopes. Have them estimate the mathematical value for the slope of each example.

Power Presentations
with PowerPoint®

CHALLENGE 7-5

Challenge
7-5 Are They Lined Up?

You can find the slope of a line by using the coordinates of two points on the line.

slope = $\frac{\text{difference of } y\text{-values}}{\text{difference of } x\text{-values}}$

Be sure to take the differences in the same order.

To find the slope of $\overline{AB}$ with $A(-2, 5)$ and $B(6, 7)$:

slope of $\overline{AB} = \frac{7 - 5}{6 - (-2)} = \frac{2}{8} = \frac{1}{4}$, or

slope of $\overline{AB} = \frac{5 - 7}{-2 - 6} = \frac{-2}{-8} = \frac{1}{4}$

Find the slope of the line joining each pair of points. Verify your result on a graph.

1. (5, 5) and (2, 1) $\frac{4}{3}$

2. (4, 1) and (6, −2) $-\frac{3}{2}$

3. Find the value of k so that the slope of the line joining the points $(k, -3)$ and $(4, 2)$ is $\frac{1}{2}$. $k = -6$

The slope between any two points on a line is the same everywhere on that line; that is, the slope of a given line is *constant*.

Without a graph, determine if each set of points is collinear (lie on the same line). Explain your method.

4. A(0, −4), B(1, −2), and C(3, 2)
slope $\overline{AB}$ = 2; slope $\overline{BC}$ = 2; yes

5. P(−7, −1), Q(1, 7), and R(7, 1)
slope $\overline{PQ}$ = 1; slope $\overline{QR}$ = −1; no

6. Find the value of k so that the points L(−1, 5), M(0, k) and N(1, −1) are collinear. $k = 2$

PROBLEM SOLVING 7-5

Problem Solving
7-5 Coordinate Geometry

The Uniform Federal Accessibility Standards describes the standards for making buildings accessible for the handicapped. The standards say that the least possible slope should be used for a ramp and that the maximum slope of a ramp should be $\frac{1}{12}$.

1. What is the slope of the pictured ramp? Does the ramp meet the standard?

   ramp 12 in. 12 ft
   $\frac{1}{12}$; yes

2. What is the slope of the pictured ramp? Does the ramp meet the standard?

   ramp 12 in. 10 ft
   $\frac{1}{10}$; no

Write the correct answer.

3. Find the slope of the roof.

   8 ft 24 ft
   Slope = $\frac{2}{3}$ or $-\frac{2}{3}$

Choose the letter that represents the slope.

4. Many building codes require that a staircase be built with a maximum rise of 8.25 inches for a minimum tread width (run) of 9 inches.

   A $\frac{8}{9}$ C $\frac{9}{8.25}$
   B $\frac{11}{12}$ D $\frac{12}{11}$

5. Hills that have a rise of about 10 feet for every 17 feet horizontally are too steep for most cars.

   F $\frac{10}{17}$ H $\frac{17}{10}$
   G $\frac{2}{5}$ J $\frac{3}{5}$

6. At its steepest part, an intermediate ski run has a rise of about 4 feet for 10 feet horizontally.

   A $\frac{2}{5}$ C $\frac{5}{2}$
   B $\frac{4}{5}$ D $\frac{5}{4}$

7. Black diamond, or expert, ski slopes often have a rise of 10 feet for every 14 feet horizontally.

   F $\frac{7}{5}$ H $\frac{5}{7}$
   G $\frac{2}{7}$ J $\frac{7}{2}$

7-5 Lesson Quiz
Determine the slope of each line.

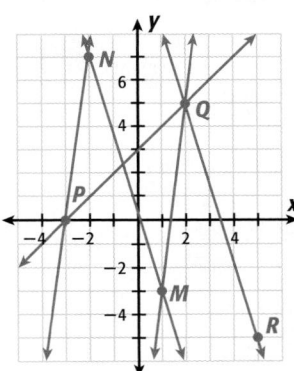

1. $\overleftrightarrow{PQ}$ 1
2. $\overleftrightarrow{MN}$ $-\frac{10}{3}$
3. $\overleftrightarrow{MQ}$ 8
4. $\overleftrightarrow{NP}$ 7
5. Which pairs of lines are parallel?
   $\overleftrightarrow{MN}$, $\overleftrightarrow{RQ}$

Also available on transparency

7-5 Coordinate Geometry **351**

Organizer

Objective: Assess students' mastery of concepts and skills in Lessons 7-1 through 7-5.

Resources

Assessment Resources
Section 7A Quiz

Test & Practice Generator
One-Stop Planner®

INTERVENTION ◀▮▶

Resources

Ready to Go On?
Intervention and
Enrichment Worksheets

⊙ **Ready to Go On? CD-ROM**

🪐 **Ready to Go On? Online**

> **my.hrw.com**

Answers

12–13. See p. A8.

Ready to Go On?

Quiz for Lessons 7-1 Through 7-5

☑ **7-1** **Points, Lines, Planes, and Angles**

Use the diagram to name each figure.

1. two pairs of complementary angles
2. three pairs of supplementary angles
3. two right angles ∠ABE, ∠EBC

1. ∠ABD and ∠DBE,
   ∠EBF and ∠FBC
2. ∠ABD and ∠DBC,
   ∠ABE and ∠EBC,
   ∠ABF and ∠FBC

☑ **7-2** **Parallel and Perpendicular Lines**

In the figure, line *m* ∥ line *n*. Find the measure of each angle.

4. ∠1 55°   5. ∠2 125°   6. ∠3 125°

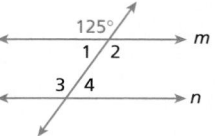

☑ **7-3** **Angles in Triangles**

Find *x*° in each triangle.

7. $x° = 37°$ (83°, 60°, x°)

8. $x° = 53°$ (74°, x°, x°)

9. In △ABC, m∠A = 57°, and ∠B is a right angle. What is m∠C?   33°

☑ **7-4** **Classifying Polygons**

Give all of the names that apply to each figure.

10.   D ——— C
       $\overline{AB} \parallel \overline{CD}$
       A ——— B
       quadrilateral, trapezoid

11.   P
    3 in. / \ 3 in.
    M <   > O   quadrilateral,
    3 in. \ / 3 in.   parallelogram,
       N   rhombus

☑ **7-5** **Coordinate Geometry**

Graph the quadrilaterals with the given vertices. Give all of the names that apply to each quadrilateral. parallelogram   parallelogram, rhombus, rectangle, square

12. A(−2, 1), B(3, 2), C(2, 0), D(−3, −1)   13. P(−3, 4), Q(2, 4), R(2, −1), S(−3, −1)

Find the coordinates of the missing vertex.

14. square ABCD with A(−1, 1), B(2, 1), and C(2, −2)   D(−1, −2)
15. parallelogram PQRS with P(3, 3), Q(4, 2), and R(2, −2) S(1, −1)

READY TO GO ON?
Diagnose and Prescribe

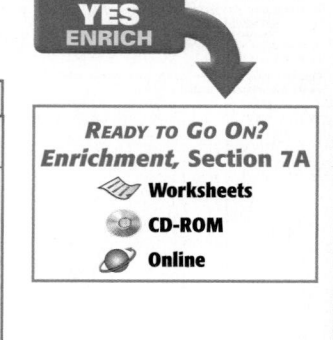

NO INTERVENE	READY TO GO ON? Intervention, Section 7A			YES ENRICH
Ready to Go On? Intervention	▨ **Worksheets**	⊙ **CD-ROM**	🪐 **Online**	**READY TO GO ON?** Enrichment, Section 7A
☑ Lesson 7-1	7-1 Intervention	Activity 7-1		▨ **Worksheets**
☑ Lesson 7-2	7-2 Intervention	Activity 7-2	Diagnose and Prescribe Online	⊙ **CD-ROM**
☑ Lesson 7-3	7-3 Intervention	Activity 7-3		🪐 **Online**
☑ Lesson 7-4	7-4 Intervention	Activity 7-4		
☑ Lesson 7-5	7-5 Intervention	Activity 7-5		

Focus on Problem Solving

Understand the Problem

• **Restate the problem in your own words**

If you write a problem in your own words, you may understand it better. Before writing a problem in your own words, you may need to read it over several times—perhaps aloud, so you can hear yourself say the words.

Once you have written the problem in your own words, you may want to make sure you included all of the necessary information to solve the problem.

Write each problem in your own words. Check to make sure you have included all of the information needed to solve the problem.

1 In the figure, ∠1 and ∠2 are complementary, and ∠1 and ∠5 are supplementary. If m∠1 = 60°, find m∠3 + m∠4.

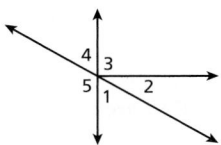

2 In triangle *ABC*, m∠*A* = 35° and m∠*B* = 55°. Use the Triangle Sum Theorem to determine whether triangle *ABC* is a right triangle.

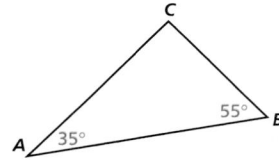

3 The second angle in a quadrilateral is eight times as large as the first angle. The third angle is half as large as the second. The fourth angle is as large as the first angle and the second angle combined. Find the angle measures in the quadrilateral.

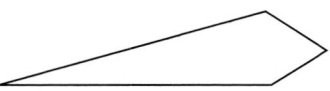

4 Parallel lines *m* and *n* are intersected by a transversal, line *p*. The acute angles formed by line *m* and line *p* measure 45°. Find the measure of the obtuse angles formed by the intersection of line *n* and line *p*.

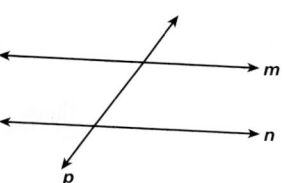

Answers

1. 150°

2. Triangle *ABC* is a right triangle.

3. ≈ 16.4°, ≈ 131.2°, ≈ 65.6°, and ≈ 147.6°

4. 135°

Focus on Problem Solving

Organizer

Objective: Focus on understanding the problem by restating it in your own words.

 Online Edition

Resources

 Chapter 7 Resource Book
Reading Strategies

Problem Solving Process

This page focuses on the first step of the problem-solving process:
Understand the Problem

Discuss

Have students discuss which facts are necessary to solve each problem, and then write each problem in their own words.

Possible answers:

1. m∠1 and m∠2 add up to 90°.
m∠1 and m∠5 add up to 180°.
If m∠1 = 60°, find m∠3 + m∠4.

2. Find out if m∠*C* = 90° when m∠*A* = 35° and m∠*B* = 55°

3. First angle = *x*; second angle = 8*x*; third angle = 4*x*; fourth angle = 9*x*; the angles add up to 360°; find the measure of each angle.

4. Find the supplement of 45°.

State Resources

go.hrw.com
State Resources Online
KEYWORD: MT7 Resources

Patterns in Geometry

One-Minute Section Planner

Lesson	Materials	MiC and Lab Resources
Lesson 7-6 Congruence • Use properties of congruent figures to solve problems. ☐ SAT-10　☑ ITBS　☑ CTBS　☑ NAEP	Triangle cutouts, protractors (MK), rulers (MK), scissors	**MiC:** *It's All the Same* pp. 1–2 *Hands-On Lab Activities* 7-6
Lesson 7-7 Transformations • Transform plane figures using translations, rotations, and reflections. **7-7 Hands-On Lab** Combine Transformations • Use pattern blocks and a coordinate plane to explore compound transformations. ☑ SAT-10　☑ ITBS　☑ CTBS　☑ NAEP	Pattern blocks (MK), protractors (MK), straightedges (MK), graph paper	*Hands-On Lab Activities* 7-7
Lesson 7-8 Symmetry • Identify symmetry in figures. ☐ SAT-10　☑ ITBS　☑ CTBS　☑ NAEP	Cutout figures, construction paper, scissors	*Technology Lab Activities* 7-8
Lesson 7-9 Tessellations • Predict and verify patterns involving tessellations. ☐ SAT-10　☐ ITBS　☐ CTBS　☑ NAEP	Pattern blocks (MK), protractors (MK), cutout figures, scissors	**MiC:** *It's All the Same* pp. 2–3, 35–36 **MiC:** *Patterns and Figures* pp. 28–31

MK = *Manipulatives Kit*

Mathematics in Context

The units *It's All the Same* and *Patterns and Figures* from the *Mathematics in Context* © 2006 series can be used with Section 7B. See Section Planner above for suggestions for integrating *MiC* with *Holt Mathematics*.

Section Overview

Congruence

Lesson 7-6

Why? Congruence is used in many applications, such as replacement parts in machines must be congruent.

> **Congruent polygons** are the same shape and size. Their corresponding sides and angles have equal measures.

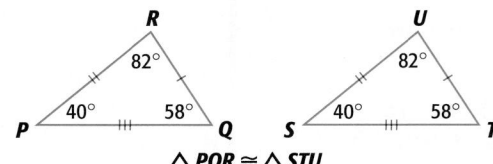

$\triangle PQR \cong \triangle STU$

You can find unknown values in congruent polygons.

If $RQ = x + 8$ and $UT = 20$, then $RQ = UT$.

$$RQ = UT$$
$$x + 8 = 20$$
$$x = 12$$

Transformations

Lesson 7-7

Why? Transformations are useful for creating patterns and designs.

Translation   **Rotation**   **Reflection**

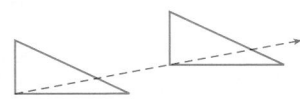   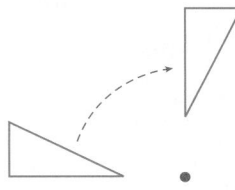   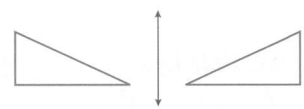

A **translation** slides a figure along a line without turning.

A **rotation** turns the figure around a point, called the **center of rotation**.

A **reflection** flips the figure across a line to create a mirror image.

Symmetry and Tessellations

Lessons 7-8, 7-9

Why? Symmetry occurs in our natural environment. Tessellations are often used to create patterns in art, architecture, and home furnishings.

> The repeating pattern of red and white stripes forms a tessellation.

Line Symmetry   **Rotational Symmetry**   **Tessellation**

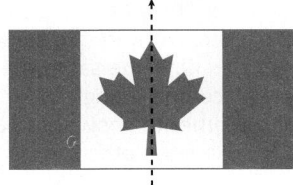   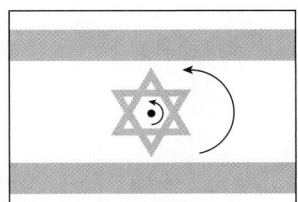   

A figure has **line symmetry** if you can draw a line through it so that the two sides are mirror images of each other.

A figure has **rotational symmetry** if you can rotate the figure less than one full turn around some point so that it coincides with itself.

A **tessellation** is a repeating pattern of plane figures that completely covers a plane with no gaps or overlaps.

Objective: Students use properties of congruent figures to solve problems.

Online Edition
Tutorial Videos

Hands-On Lab
In *Hands-On Lab Activities*

Countdown to Testing Week 13

Power Presentations
with PowerPoint®

Warm Up
Find the measure of the indicated angle.

1. the fourth angle in a quadrilateral containing angles of 100°, 130°, and 75° **55°**

2. the third angle of a right triangle with an angle of 60° **30°**

3. the supplement of a 35° angle **145°**

Problem of the Day
The measure of ∠ABC is 14° less than the measure of its complement, ∠CBD. What is the measure of each angle? m∠ABC = 38°; m∠CBD = 52°

Also available on transparency

State Resources

go.hrw.com
State Resources Online
KEYWORD: MT7 Resources

7-6 Congruence

Learn to use properties of congruent figures to solve problems.

Vocabulary
correspondence

Below are the DNA profiles of two pairs of twins. Twins A and B are identical twins. Twins C and D are fraternal twins.

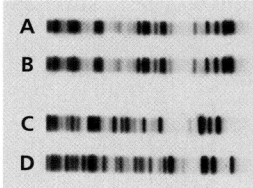

A **correspondence** is a way of matching up two sets of objects. The bands of DNA that are next to each other in each pair match up, or *correspond*. In the DNA of the identical twins, the corresponding bands are the same.

If two polygons are congruent, all of their corresponding sides and angles are congruent.

CONGRUENT TRIANGLES			
Diagram	Statement	Corresponding Angles	Corresponding Sides
(triangles ABC and DEF)	△ABC ≅ △DEF	∠A ≅ ∠D ∠B ≅ ∠E ∠C ≅ ∠F	$\overline{AB} \cong \overline{DE}$ $\overline{BC} \cong \overline{EF}$ $\overline{AC} \cong \overline{DF}$

EXAMPLE 1 Writing Congruence Statements

Write a congruence statement for each pair of congruent polygons.

Helpful Hint
Marks on the sides of a figure can be used to show congruence.
$\overline{KM} \cong \overline{RS}$ (1 mark)
$\overline{KL} \cong \overline{RQ}$ (2 marks)
$\overline{ML} \cong \overline{SQ}$ (3 marks)

A

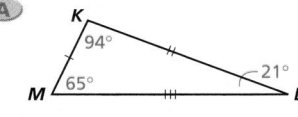

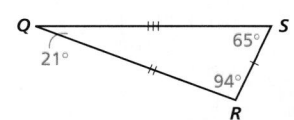

In a congruence statement, the vertices in the second triangle have to be written in order of correspondence with the first triangle.

∠K corresponds to ∠R. ∠K ≅ ∠R
∠L corresponds to ∠Q. ∠L ≅ ∠Q
∠M corresponds to ∠S. ∠M ≅ ∠S

The congruence statement is triangle KLM ≅ triangle RQS.

---

1 Introduce
Alternate Opener

EXPLORATION

7-6 Congruence

Congruent figures have the same size and shape.

Determine whether the figures in each pair are congruent.

1.
2.
3.
4.

Think and Discuss
5. **Explain** how you decided whether the figures in Problems 1–4 were congruent or not.
6. **Find** two examples of objects that are congruent. What makes the two objects congruent?

Motivate
Show the students two triangles that are congruent. Ask them what they notice about the triangles. Help students respond with answers such as "they have the same size and shape," "the sides are the same length," and "the angles have the same measure." Alternately place one triangle on top of the other to show that each completely covers the other.

Explorations and answers are provided in *Alternate Openers: Explorations Transparencies*.

Write a congruence statement for each pair of congruent polygons.

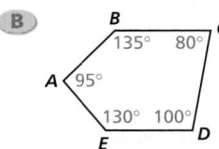

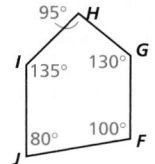

The vertices in the first pentagon are written in order around the pentagon starting at any vertex.

$\angle A$ corresponds to $\angle H$. $\angle A \cong \angle H$

$\angle B$ corresponds to $\angle I$. $\angle B \cong \angle I$

$\angle C$ corresponds to $\angle J$. $\angle C \cong \angle J$

$\angle D$ corresponds to $\angle F$. $\angle D \cong \angle F$

$\angle E$ corresponds to $\angle G$. $\angle E \cong \angle G$

The congruence statement is pentagon $ABCDE \cong$ pentagon $HIJFG$.

EXAMPLE 2 Using Congruence Relationships to Find Unknown Values

In the figure, quadrilateral $PQSR \cong$ quadrilateral $WTUV$.

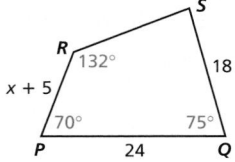

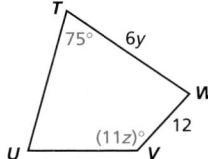

A Find x.

$$x + 5 = 12 \qquad \overline{PR} \cong \overline{WV}$$
$$\underline{\;\;-5 = -5\;\;} \quad \text{Subtract 5 from}$$
$$x \;\;= \;\;7 \qquad \text{both sides.}$$

B Find y.

$$6y = 24 \qquad \overline{WT} \cong \overline{PQ}$$
$$\frac{6y}{6} = \frac{24}{6} \qquad \text{Divide both}$$
$$\qquad\qquad\qquad \text{sides by 6.}$$
$$y = 4$$

C Find z.

$$132 = 11z \qquad \angle R \cong \angle V$$
$$\frac{132}{11} = \frac{11z}{11} \qquad \text{Divide both sides by 11.}$$
$$12 = z$$

Answers to *Think and Discuss*

2. Name one of the polygons by listing its vertices in either clockwise or counter-clockwise order. Write the congruence symbol ($\cong$), then name the other polygon by listing its vertices in corresponding order.

Think and Discuss

1. **Explain** what it means for two polygons to be congruent.

2. **Tell** how to write a congruence statement for two polygons.

Example 1

Write a congruence statement for each pair of congruent polygons.

A.

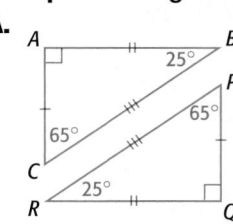

triangle $ABC \cong$ triangle QRP

B.

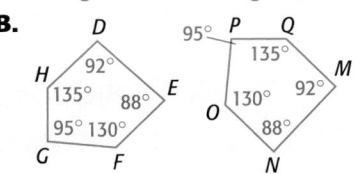

pentagon $DEFGH \cong$ pentagon $MNOPQ$

Example 2

In the figure, quadrilateral $VWXY \cong$ quadrilateral $JKLM$.

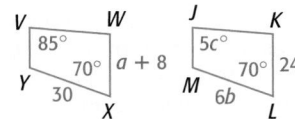

A. Find a. 16 **B.** Find b. 5

C. Find c. 17

Also available on transparency

Possible answers to
Think and Discuss

1. They have the same size and shape.

---

2 Teach

Guided Instruction

In this lesson, students learn to use properties of congruent figures to solve problems. Begin by showing students how to write a congruence statement for a pair of congruent polygons. Make sure students understand the concepts of corresponding angles and corresponding sides. Discuss with students how to use a congruence statement to find an unknown measure of a side or angle and then to solve for a variable.

Communicating Math Students can use a congruence statement to identify a pair of corresponding sides or angles. For example, if $\triangle ABC$ $\cong \triangle DEF$, then side $AC \cong$ side DF.

Reaching All Learners
Through Concrete Manipulatives

Have students work in pairs. Have each student draw a polygon and hand it to their partner. The partner is responsible for drawing a polygon that appears to be congruent to the polygon they were given. Give each student a protractor, a ruler, and a pair of scissors. Students should measure and label all sides and all angles and then determine which pairs are congruent. You may want to set some rules for what is considered congruent (e.g., angle measures within 1° or side lengths within 1 mm). They can then cut out the polygons to check their work.

3 Close

Summarize

Remind students that when polygons are congruent, they have the same size and shape. Make sure students understand the importance of identifying corresponding parts of congruent figures. Show the students a pair of congruent polygons and name one of them. Ask the students to name the other polygon in the correct order and to name congruent parts.

Possible answers: triangles ABC and XYZ; $\angle A \cong \angle X$; $\angle B \cong \angle Y$; $\angle C \cong \angle Z$; $\overline{AB} \cong \overline{XY}$; $\overline{BC} \cong \overline{YZ}$; $\overline{AC} \cong \overline{XZ}$

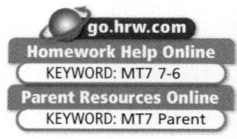

go.hrw.com
Homework Help Online
KEYWORD: MT7 7-6
Parent Resources Online
KEYWORD: MT7 Parent

Assignment Guide

If you finished Example **1** assign:
Average 1, 2, 6, 7, 19–29
Advanced 6, 7, 16, 19–29

If you finished Example **2** assign:
Average 1–14, 19–29
Advanced 6–29

Homework Quick Check

Quickly check key concepts.
Exercises: 6, 8, 12

Math Background

The use of congruent figures is a dominant aspect in geometric patterns and designs. Fabric and wallpaper designs in particular make use of congruent figures by repeating a given figure throughout the material. A repeating pattern of congruent figures that completely covers a surface is a *tessellation* (Lesson 7-9). Sometimes the figures are rotated or reflected throughout the design. Rotations and reflections are types of *transformations* (Lesson 7-7).

GUIDED PRACTICE

See Example **1** Write a congruence statement for each pair of congruent polygons.

1.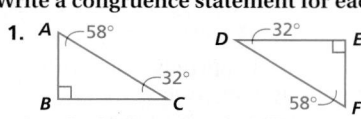

triangle *ABC* ≅ triangle *FED*

2.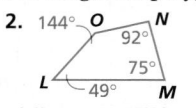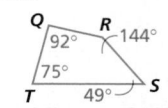

quadrilateral *LMNO* ≅ quadrilateral *STQR*

See Example **2** In the figure, triangle *ABC* ≅ triangle *LMN*.

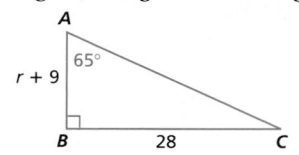 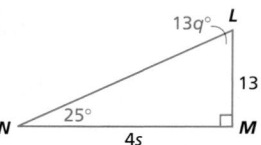

3. Find *q*.   *q* = 5   **4.** Find *r*.   *r* = 4   **5.** Find *s*.   *s* = 7

INDEPENDENT PRACTICE

See Example **1** Write a congruence statement for each pair of congruent polygons.

6.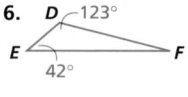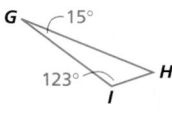

triangle *DEF* ≅ triangle *IHG*

7.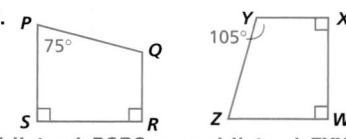

quadrilateral *PQRS* ≅ quadrilateral *ZYXW*

See Example **2** In the figure, quadrilateral *ABCD* ≅ quadrilateral *LMNO*.

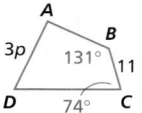 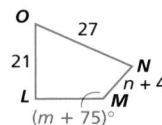

8. Find *m*.   *m* = 56   **9.** Find *n*.   *n* = 7   **10.** Find *p*.   *p* = 7

PRACTICE AND PROBLEM SOLVING

Extra Practice
See page 795.

Find the value of each variable.   *m* = 14, *n* = 32, *p* = 64

11. pentagon *ABCDE* ≅   *x* = 19, *y* = 27,   **12.** hexagon *ABCDEF* ≅
pentagon *PQRST*   *z* = 18.1   hexagon *LMNOPQ*

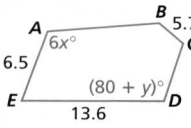 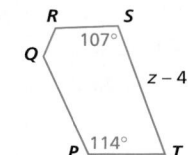 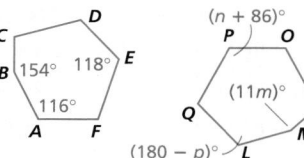

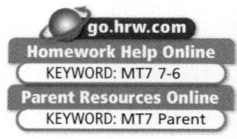
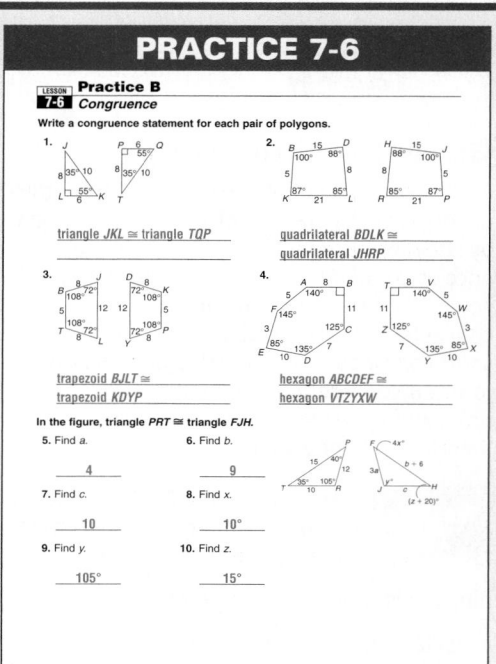

RETEACH 7-6

LESSON 7-6 Reteach
Congruence (continued)

Congruence relations can be used to find unknown values.

∠A ≅ ∠Q
3x = 90
3x/3 = 90/3
x = 30

△ABC ≅ △QPR

Using the congruence relationship, complete to find each unknown value.

4. GF ≅ RA
y − 3 = 10
+3   +3
y = 13

5. ∠C ≅ ∠S
120/120 = 2t
120/2 = 2t/2
60 = t

6. ∠A ≅ ∠F
z/2 = 150
2 × z/2 = 150 × 2
z = 300

7. AZ ≅ FE
3x + 2 = 14
−2   −2
3x = 12
3x/3 = 12/3
x = 4

PRACTICE 7-6

LESSON 7-6 Practice B
Congruence

Write a congruence statement for each pair of polygons.

1.   **2.**

triangle *JKL* ≅ triangle *TQP*   quadrilateral *BDLK* ≅
                                     quadrilateral *JHRP*

3.   **4.**

trapezoid *BJLT* ≅   hexagon *ABCDEF* ≅
trapezoid *KDYP*   hexagon *VTZYXW*

In the figure, triangle *PRT* ≅ triangle *FJH*.

5. Find *a*.   **6.** Find *b*.
     4   9

7. Find *c*.   **8.** Find *x*.
     10   10°

9. Find *y*.   **10.** Find *z*.
     105°   15°

Find the value of each variable.

16. Possible answer: Write a congruence statement for the pair of triangles. Answer: triangle $ABC \cong$ triangle FED

13. quadrilateral $ABCD \cong$ quadrilateral $EFGH$

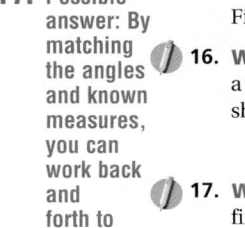

$r = 24$, $s = 120$, $t = 48$

14. heptagon $ABCDEFG \cong$ heptagon $JKLMNOP$

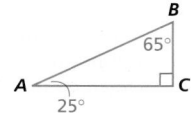 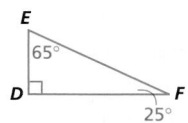

$w = 216$, $x = 408$, $y = 381$

17. Possible answer: By matching the angles and known measures, you can work back and forth to calculate unknown angles.

15. Right triangle $PQR \cong$ right triangle STU. m$\angle P = 28°$ and m$\angle U = 90°$. Find m$\angle Q$. **62°**

16. **Write a Problem** Write and solve a problem about the right triangles shown.

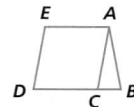 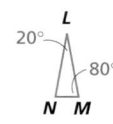

17. **Write About It** How can knowing two polygons are congruent help you find angle measures of the polygons?

18. **Challenge** Triangle $ABC \cong$ triangle LMN and $\overline{AE} \parallel \overline{BD}$. Find m$\angle ACD$.
m$\angle ACD = 100°$

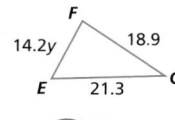 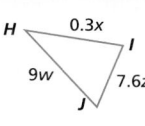

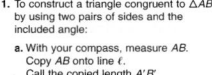 **TEST PREP and Spiral Review**

19. **Multiple Choice** Triangle $EFG \cong$ triangle JIH. Find the value of x.

- (A) 5.67
- (B) 30
- (C) 63
- (D) 71

20. **Multiple Choice** Triangle $ABC \cong$ triangle JKL. m$\angle A = 30°$ and m$\angle B = 50°$. Find the m$\angle K$.

- (F) 30°
- (G) 50°
- (H) 80°
- (J) 100°

21. **Gridded Response** Quadrilateral $ABCD \cong$ quadrilateral $WXYZ$. The length of $\overline{AB} = 21$ and the length of $\overline{WX} = 7m$. Find m. **3**

Find the missing y-coordinate of each ordered pair that is a solution to $y = 4x - 2$. (Lesson 3-2)

22. $(0, y)$ **−2**
23. $(1, y)$ **2**
24. $(3, y)$ **10**
25. $(7, y)$ **26**

The measures of two angles of a triangle are given. Find the measure of the third angle. (Lesson 7-3)

26. 45°, 45° **90°**
27. 30°, 60° **90°**
28. 21°, 82° **77°**
29. 105°, 42° **33°**

CHALLENGE 7-6

LESSON 7-6 Challenge
Cloning

In the following exercises, you will construct a triangle congruent to △ABC by copying three strategic parts.

1. To construct a triangle congruent to △ABC by using two pairs of sides and the included angle:

  a. With your compass, measure AB. Copy AB onto line ℓ. Call the copied length A'B' (read A prime B prime).

  b. With your compass, measure ∠A. Copy ∠A at vertex A' with one side as A'B'.

  c. With your compass, measure AC. Copy AC onto the other side of ∠A', beginning at A' and ending at C'.

  d. Draw C'B'. Use a ruler and protractor to verify that △A'B'C' ≅ △ABC.

2. To construct a triangle congruent to △ABC by using two pairs of angles and the included side:

  a. With your compass, measure AB. Copy AB onto line m. Call the copied length A"B" (read A double prime B double prime).

  b. With your compass, measure ∠A. Copy ∠A at vertex A", with one side as A"B".

  c. With your compass, measure ∠B. Copy ∠B at vertex B", with one side as A"B".

  d. Use C" to label the point where the sides of ∠A" and ∠B" intersect. Use a ruler and protractor to verify that △A"B"C" ≅ △ABC.

PROBLEM SOLVING 7-6

LESSON 7-6 Problem Solving
Congruence

Use the American patchwork quilt block design called Carnival to answer the questions. Triangle AIH ≅ Triangle AIB, Triangle ACJ ≅ Triangle AGJ, Triangle GFJ ≅ Triangle CDJ.

1. What is the measure of ∠IAB?
  45°

2. What is the measure of $\overline{AH}$?
  4 inches

3. What is the measure of $\overline{AG}$?
  6 inches

4. What is the measure of ∠JDC?
  90°

5. What is the measure of $\overline{FG}$?
  4 inches

The sketch is part of a bridge. Trapezoid ABEF ≅ Trapezoid DEBC. Choose the letter for the best answer.

6. What is the measure of $\overline{DE}$?
- A 4 feet
- B 8 feet
- C 16 feet
- D Cannot be determined

7. What is the measure of $\overline{FE}$?
- F 4 feet
- G 16 feet
- H 8 feet
- J 24 feet

8. What is the measure of ∠FAB?
- A 45°
- B 90°
- C 60°
- D 120°

9. What is the measure of ∠ABE?
- F 45°
- G 90°
- H 60°
- J 120°

10. What is the measure of ∠EBC?
- A 45°
- B 90°
- C 60°
- D 120°

11. What is the measure of ∠BED?
- F 45°
- G 90°
- H 60°
- J 120°

12. What is the measure of ∠BCD?
- A 45°
- B 90°
- C 60°
- D 120°

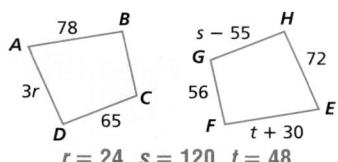 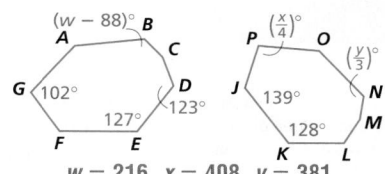

ONGOING ASSESSMENT and INTERVENTION

Diagnose Before the Lesson
7-6 Warm Up, TE p. 354

Monitor During the Lesson
7-6 Know-It Notebook
7-6 Questioning Strategies

Assess After the Lesson
7-6 Lesson Quiz, TE p. 357

TEST PREP DOCTOR For Exercise 20, students who chose answer **J** found the measure of ∠C and ∠L. Remind students that in a congruence statement, the vertices of the second polygon are written in order of correspondence, so ∠K corresponds to ∠B.

Journal

Ask students to find sets of congruent figures in the classroom, around the school, or at home. Suggest that they look at floor patterns, wall decorations, clothing, art, and books. Ask students to record several examples in their journals.

Power Presentations with PowerPoint®

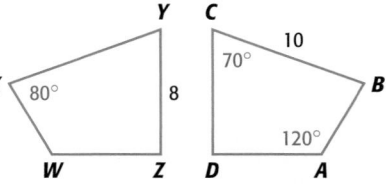

7-6 Lesson Quiz
In the figure, $WXYZ \cong ABCD$.

1. Find XY. **10**
2. Find m$\angle B$. **80°**
3. Find CD. **8**
4. Find m$\angle Z$. **90°**

Also available on transparency

Objective: Students transform plane figures using translations, rotations, and reflections.

 Online Edition
Tutorial Videos

 Countdown to Testing Week 14

Power Presentations
with PowerPoint®

Warm Up

Determine if the following sets of points form a parallelogram.

1. $(-3, 0)$, $(1, 4)$, $(6, 0)$, $(2, -4)$
yes

2. $(1, 2)$, $(-2, 2)$, $(-2, 1)$, $(1, -2)$
no

3. $(2, 3)$, $(-3, 1)$, $(1, -4)$, $(6, -2)$
yes

Problem of the Day

How can you move just one number to a different triangle to make the sum of the numbers in each triangle equal? (*Hint:* There do not have to be exactly 3 numbers in each triangle.)

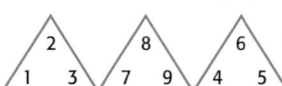

Move 9 into the first triangle.

Also available on transparency

State Resources

 **go.hrw.com**
State Resources Online
KEYWORD: MT7 Resources

7-7 Transformations

Learn to transform plane figures using translations, rotations, and reflections.

Vocabulary
transformation
translation
rotation
center of rotation
reflection
image

When you are on an amusement park ride, you are undergoing a *transformation*. A **transformation** is a change in a figure's position or size. Ferris wheels and merry-go-rounds are *rotations*. Free-fall rides and water slides are *translations*. Translations, rotations, and reflections are types of transformations.

Translation	Rotation	Reflection

A **translation** slides a figure along a line without turning.	A **rotation** turns a figure around a point, called the **center of rotation**.	A **reflection** flips a figure across a line to create a mirror image.

The resulting figure, or **image**, of a translation, rotation, or reflection is congruent to the original figure.

EXAMPLE 1 Identifying Transformations

Identify each as a translation, rotation, reflection, or none of these.

Reading Math
A′ is read "*A* prime." The point *A′* is the image of point *A*.

A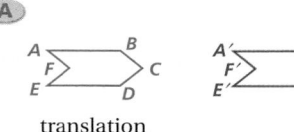
translation

B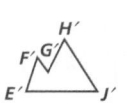
none of these

C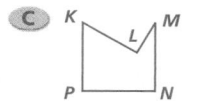
rotation

D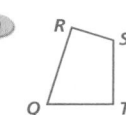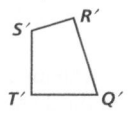
reflection

---

1 Introduce
Alternate Opener

EXPLORATION

7-7 Transformations

1. Draw arrows from all the vertices (corners) of each original figure (blue) to the corresponding vertices of its *image* (red).

Think and Discuss

2. **Explain** whether the transformations in Problem 1 are congruent, which means that the image is the same shape and size as the original figure.

3. **Compare** the transformation of the triangle with the transformations of the other figures. How is it different? Find a name for this transformation.

Motivate

Discuss with students some real-world examples of transformations. You may mention that a pinwheel illustrates the concept of a rotation. You may also point out that the image of trees on a lake represents a reflection. Translations can often be found in tile or clothing patterns. Ask students if they can translate (yes), rotate (yes), or reflect (no) themselves.

Explorations and answers are provided in *Alternate Openers: Explorations Transparencies.*

EXAMPLE 2 Graphing Transformations

Draw the image of a triangle with vertices A(1, 1), B(1, 4), and C(3, 4) after each transformation.

A translation 5 units down

B reflection across the y-axis

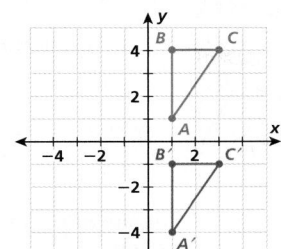

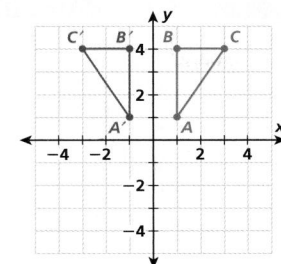

EXAMPLE 3 Describing Graphs of Transformations

Parallelogram EFGH has vertices E(−2, 1), F(3, 1), G(4, 4), and H(−1, 4). Find the coordinates of the image of the indicated point after each transformation.

A translation 2 units down, point E

B 180° rotation around (0, 0), point G

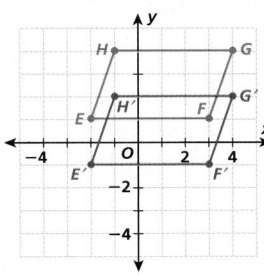

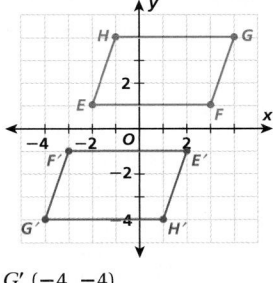

E′ (−2, −1)

G′ (−4, −4)

Answers to *Think and Discuss*

1. always; sometimes (if the line of reflection is vertical or horizontal); sometimes (if the angle of rotation is a multiple of 180°).

2. the x-coordinate remains the same, while the y-coordinate changes sign.

Think and Discuss

1. **Tell** whether the image of a vertical line is sometimes, always, or never vertical after a translation, a reflection, or a rotation.

2. **Describe** what happens to the x-coordinate and the y-coordinate after a point is reflected across the x-axis.

2 Teach

Guided Instruction

In this lesson, students learn to transform plane figures using translations, rotations, and reflections. Illustrate each of the three types of transformations with simple polygons (Teaching Transparency). Explain that when each of these transformations is performed, the resulting polygon (the image) is congruent to the original polygon. Each vertex in the original polygon corresponds to a vertex in the image. The correspondence is indicated by pairing a given point A with its image point A′, a given point B with its image point B′, and so on. Show how to draw transformation images on a coordinate system.

Reaching All Learners
Through Concrete Manipulatives

Have students each create one pattern block of a geometric figure. Give each student three copies of a coordinate plane. On the first plane, ask students to trace the figure and then to translate the figure according to a given rule (e.g., two inches left and one inch down). On the second plane, ask students to trace each figure and reflect it across a line. On the third plane, ask students to rotate each figure according to a given rule (e.g., rotation of 180°). Students should perform the transformations by tracing their pattern blocks in the appropriate places on the coordinate planes.

3 Close

Summarize

Ask students to describe the steps they would take to perform each of the following transformations on a simple figure on a coordinate plane:

1. translation two units to the left

2. reflection across the y-axis

3. rotation of 180° around the origin

Possible answers: **1.** Subtract 2 from the x-coordinate of each point, plot the points, and connect them. **2.** Change each x-coordinate to its opposite, plot the points, and connect them. **3.** Change both coordinates to their opposites, plot the points, and connect them.

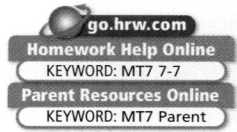

Assignment Guide

If you finished Example **1** assign:
Average 1, 2, 11, 12, 36–43
Advanced 11, 12, 34, 36–43

If you finished Example **2** assign:
Average 1–6, 11–16, 21–23, 36–43
Advanced 11–16, 21–23, 33–43

If you finished Example **3** assign:
Average 1–26, 30–32, 36–43
Advanced 11–43

Homework Quick Check

Quickly check key concepts.
Exercises: 12, 14, 20, 22

Math Background

The three types of transformations discussed in this section are *rigid transformations;* that is, all result in images that maintain the shape and size of the original figures.

A *dilation* is a nonrigid transformation that preserves the shape of the figure but not the size. In a dilation, the figure is contracted or expanded by a constant called the *scale factor.* An example of this type of transformation is an enlargement or reduction of a photograph.

Answers

3–6, 13–16. See p. A8.

State Resources

GUIDED PRACTICE

See Example **1**   Identify each as a translation, rotation, reflection, or none of these.

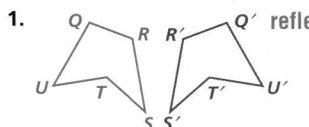

1. reflection

2. rotation

See Example **2**   Draw the image of the parallelogram *ABCD* with vertices (−3, 0), (−4, 3), (1, 4), and (2, 1) after each transformation.

3. translation 1 unit up

4. reflection across the *x*-axis

5. reflection across the *y*-axis

6. 180° rotation around (0, 0)

See Example **3**   Triangle *ABC* has vertices *A*(2, 1), *B*(3, 3), and *C*(1, 2). Find the coordinates of the image of the indicated point after each transformation.

7. translation 4 units down, point *C* (1, −2)

8. reflection across the *x*-axis, point *B* (3, −3)

9. reflection across the *y*-axis, point *C* (−1, 2)

10. 180° rotation around (0,0), point *A* (−2, −1)

INDEPENDENT PRACTICE

See Example **1**   Identify each as a translation, rotation, reflection, or none of these.

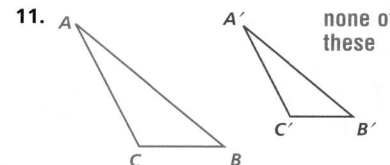

11. none of these

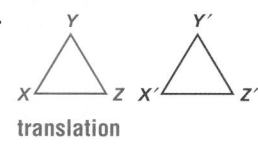

12. translation

See Example **2**   Draw the image of the quadrilateral *ABCD* with vertices (1, 1), (2, 4), (4, 5), and (5, 3) after each transformation.

13. translation 5 units down

14. reflection across the *x*-axis

15. reflection across the *y*-axis

16. 180° rotation around (0, 0)

See Example **3**   Square *ABCD* has vertices *A*(−2, 2), *B*(2, 2), *C*(2, −2), and *D*(−2, −2). Find the coordinates of the image of the indicated point after each transformation.

17. translation 3 units to the left, point *A*   (−5, 2)

18. translation 4 units to the right, point *B*   (6, 2)

19. reflection across the *x*-axis, point *C*   (2, 2)

20. 180° rotation around (0, 0), point *A*   (2, −2)

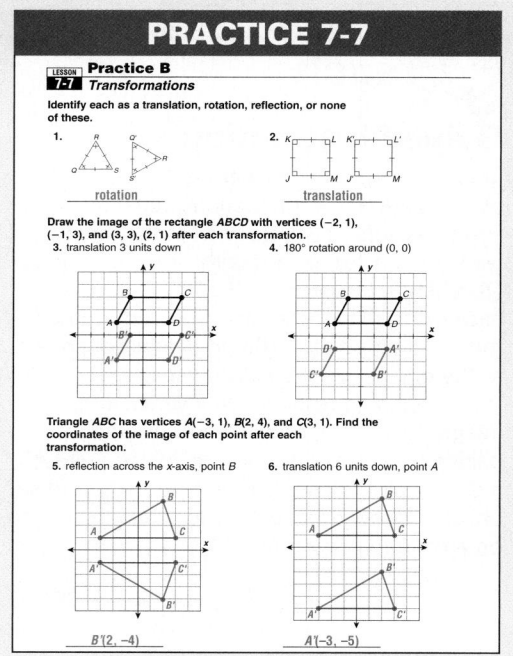

RETEACH 7-7

LESSON **7-7** **Reteach**
Transformations (continued)

When reflecting a point about a horizontal or vertical line, only one of the coordinates changes.

reflection across *y*-axis
x-coordinate goes to its opposite

reflection across *x*-axis
y-coordinate goes to its opposite

When translating a point, add the indicated number of units to each coordinate.

For a translation left or right, add units to the *x*-coordinate. For a translation up or down, add units to the *y*-coordinate.

P(1, 4) is translated 3 units down.

$P(1, 4) \rightarrow P'(1, 4 + (−3))$, or *P*′(1, 1)

Draw and label the image after the reflection.

7. *P*(−1, 2) over the *y*-axis

Draw and label the image after the translation.

8. Translate *A*(−3, 5) 4 units to the right.

PRACTICE 7-7

LESSON **7-7** **Practice B**
Transformations

Identify each as a translation, rotation, reflection, or none of these.

1. rotation

2. translation

Draw the image of the rectangle *ABCD* with vertices (−2, 1), (−1, 3), and (3, 3), (2, 1) after each transformation.

3. translation 3 units down

4. 180° rotation around (0, 0)

Triangle *ABC* has vertices *A*(−3, 1), *B*(2, 4), and *C*(3, 1). Find the coordinates of the image of each point after each transformation.

5. reflection across the *x*-axis, point *B*

6. translation 6 units down, point *A*

B′(2, −4)

A′(−3, −5)

PRACTICE AND PROBLEM SOLVING

Extra Practice
See page 795.

Copy each figure and perform the given transformations.

21. Reflect across line *m*.　**22.** Reflect across line *n*.　**23.** Rotate clockwise 90°.

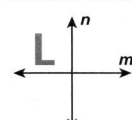　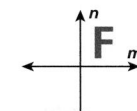　

Give the coordinates of each point after a reflection across the given axis.

24. $(1, 4)$; *x*-axis $(1, -4)$　**25.** $(-3, 2)$; *x*-axis $(-3, -2)$　**26.** (m, n); *x*-axis $(m, -n)$

27. $(5, -2)$; *y*-axis $(-5, -2)$　**28.** $(-2, 4)$; *y*-axis $(2, 4)$　**29.** (m, n); *y*-axis $(-m, n)$

Give the coordinates of each point after a 180° rotation around $(0, 0)$.

30. $(1, 2)$ $(-1, -2)$　**31.** $(-4, 5)$ $(4, -5)$　**32.** (m, n) $(-m, -n)$

 33. Write a Problem Write a problem involving transformations on a coordinate grid that result in a pattern.

 34. Write About It Explain how each type of transformation performed on the arrow would affect the direction the arrow is pointing.

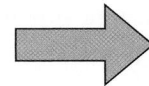

 35. Challenge A triangle has vertices $(2, 5)$, $(3, 7)$, and $(7, 5)$. After a reflection and a translation, the coordinates of the image are $(7, -2)$, $(8, -4)$, and $(12, -2)$. Describe the transformations. **Possible answer: a reflection across the *x*-axis followed by a translation 3 units up and 5 units right**

TEST PREP and Spiral Review

36. Multiple Choice Which best represents the transformation at right?

Ⓐ Translation

Ⓑ Rotation

Ⓒ Reflection

Ⓓ None of these

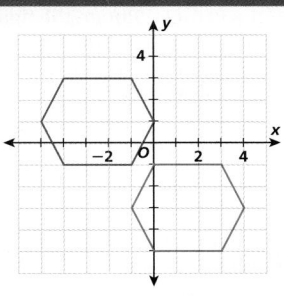

37. Short Response Draw the image of a triangle with vertices $(-1, 2)$, $(3, 3)$, and $(1, -3)$ after a translation 2 units up and 2 units to the right.
The vertices of the image are $(1, 4)$, $(5, 5)$, and $(3, -1)$.

Find each percent increase or decrease to the nearest percent. (Lesson 6-5)

38. from 75 to 90 **20% increase**　**39.** from 1200 to 1400 **17% increase**　**40.** from 44 to 21 **52% decrease**

Draw the line through the given points and find its slope. (Lesson 7-5)

41. $A(5, 2)$, $B(3, 2)$ **0**　**42.** $G(6, -3)$, $H(-4, -9)$ $\frac{3}{5}$　**43.** $C(3, 4)$, $D(0, 0)$ $-\frac{4}{3}$

CHALLENGE 7-7

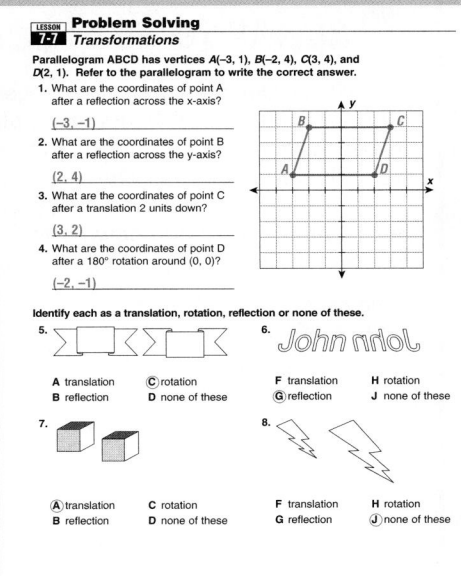

PROBLEM SOLVING 7-7

Answers
21–23, 33–34. See pp. A8–A9.

TEST PREP DOCTOR ✚ Encourage students to look carefully at the original figure and its transformation in Exercise 36. Suggest that students ask themselves if the transformation was created by sliding the original figure along a line without turning, by turning the original figure around a point, by flipping it across a line to create a mirror image, or none of these. Some students may need to draw each transformation on the grid in order to determine the correct answer.

 **Journal**

Have students think about a career that might involve transformations. Have them write how they might use transformations if they had a job in that field. Examples might include art, architecture, sewing, computer graphics, construction, and design.

Power Presentations
with PowerPoint®

7-7 Lesson Quiz

Given the coordinates for the vertices of each pair of quadrilaterals, determine whether each pair represents a translation, rotation, reflection, or none of these.

1. $(2, 2)$, $(4, 0)$, $(3, 5)$, $(6, 4)$ and $(3, -1)$, $(5, -3)$, $(4, 2)$, $(7, 1)$
translation

2. $(2, 3)$, $(5, 5)$, $(1, -2)$, $(5, -4)$ and $(-2, 3)$, $(-5, 5)$, $(-1, -2)$, $(-5, -4)$　reflection

3. $(1, 3)$, $(-1, 2)$, $(2, -3)$, $(4, 0)$ and $(1, -3)$, $(-1, 2)$, $(-2, 3)$, $(-4, 0)$　none

4. $(4, 1)$, $(1, 2)$, $(4, 5)$, $(1, 5)$ and $(-4, -1)$, $(-1, -2)$, $(-4, -5)$, $(-1, -5)$　rotation

Also available on transparency

Combine Transformations

Use with Lesson 7-7

KEY

Pattern blocks =

triangle   rhombus   trapezoid

You can use a coordinate plane when transforming a geometric figure.

Activity 1

❶ Follow the steps below to transform a figure.

a. Place a red pattern block on a coordinate plane. Trace the block, and label the vertices.

b. Translate the figure 3 units down and 5 units right, and then reflect the resulting figure across the *x*-axis. Draw the image and label the vertices.

c. Now place a green pattern block on the same coordinate plane. Trace the block and label the vertices. Rotate the figure 180° around the point (0, 0), and then translate it 4 units up and 3 units right. Draw the image and label the vertices.

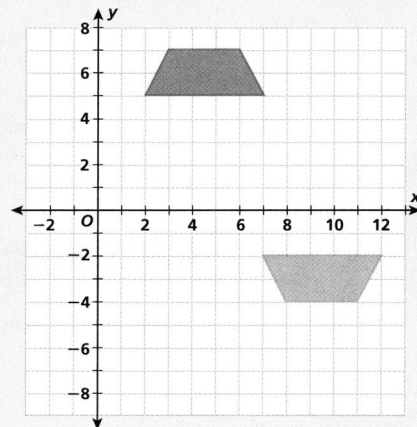

Think and Discuss

1. When you perform two or more transformations on a figure, does it matter in which order the transformations are performed? Explain.

Try This

1. Place a blue pattern block on a coordinate plane. Trace the block, and label the vertices. Perform two different transformations on the figure. Draw the image and label the vertices. Trade with a classmate. Describe the transformations your classmate used.

Teacher to Teacher

I teach coordinate plane concepts using a set of "integer ropes." We take the ropes outside and lay out the coordinate plane using one rope as the *x*-axis and one as the *y*-axis. For this activity, the students were given pieces of red yarn so that they could form the red trapezoids. One group of students was the original, a second group was the translated image, and a third group was the reflected image. The second group walked to the right and down from the original group. The third group helped the class see that the reflected image really is a mirror image of the original.

Lynn Bodet
San Antonio, TX

① Follow the steps below to transform a figure.

a. Place a rhombus on a coordinate plane. Trace the rhombus, and label the vertices.

b. Rotate the figure 90° clockwise about the origin.

c. Reflect the resulting figure across the x-axis. Draw the image and label the vertices.

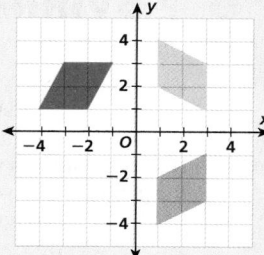

d. Now place a rhombus in the same position as the original figure. Reflect the figure across the line y = x.

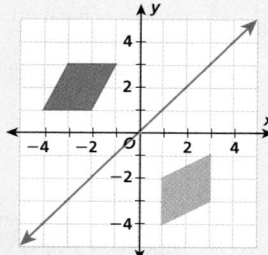

Think and Discuss

1. What do you notice about the images that result from the two transformations in parts **b** and **c** above and the image that results from the single transformation in part **d** above?

Try This

1. Place a pattern block on a coordinate plane. Trace the block and label the vertices. Perform two different transformations on the figure. Draw the image and label the vertices. Explain what single transformation of the original figure would result in the same image.

Describe two different ways to transform each figure from position A to position B.

2.
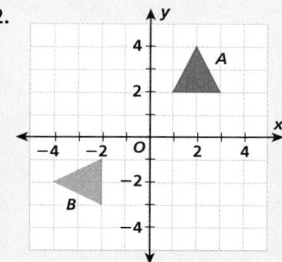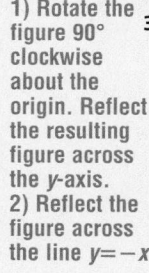

2. Possible answer:
1) Rotate the figure 90° clockwise about the origin. Reflect the resulting figure across the y-axis.
2) Reflect the figure across the line y = −x.

3.
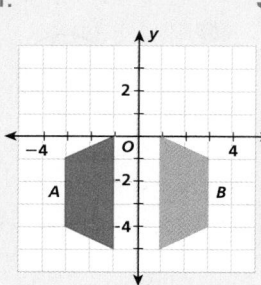

3. Possible answer:
1) Rotate the figure 180° clockwise about the origin. Reflect the resulting figure across the x-axis.
2) Reflect the figure across the y-axis.

Possible answers to
Think and Discuss

1. Yes; the result of doing multiple transformations will not be the same if the order is switched. For example, in the Activity, the vertex at (2, 5) would end up at (7, −8) instead of at (7, −2).

Answers to *Try This*

1. Check students' work.

Answers to
Think and Discuss

1. The two images are the same.

Answers to *Try This*

1. Check students' work.

Objective: Students identify symmetry in figures.

 Technology Lab
In *Technology Lab Activities*

 Online Edition
Tutorial Videos, Interactivities

 Countdown to Testing Week 14

Power Presentations
with **PowerPoint®**

Warm Up
Multiply.

1. $\frac{1}{4} \times 360$ 90   2. $\frac{1}{2} \times 360$ 180

3. $\frac{1}{8} \times 360$ 45   4. $\frac{3}{5} \times 360$ 216

5. $\frac{2}{3} \times 360$ 240

Problem of the Day
Name four plane figures that can be rotated 180° around a center point and look the same after the rotation as they did before.
Possible answer: rectangle, square, parallelogram, regular hexagon

Also available on transparency

State Resources

_____
_____
_____
_____
_____
_____
_____
_____
_____
_____
_____
_____
_____

go.hrw.com
State Resources Online
KEYWORD: MT7 Resources

7-8 **Symmetry**

Learn to identify symmetry in figures.

Vocabulary
line symmetry
line of symmetry
rotational symmetry

Nature provides many beautiful examples of *symmetry*, such as the wings of a butterfly or the petals of a flower. Symmetric objects have parts that are congruent.

A figure has **line symmetry** if you can draw a line through it so that the two sides are mirror images of each other. The line is called the **line of symmetry**.

EXAMPLE 1 **Drawing Figures with Line Symmetry**

Complete each figure. The dashed line is the line of symmetry.

Helpful Hint
If you fold a figure on the line of symmetry, the halves match exactly.

Ⓐ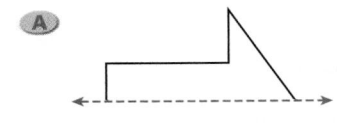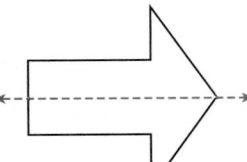

Ⓑ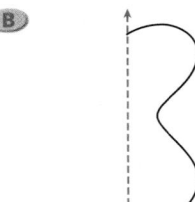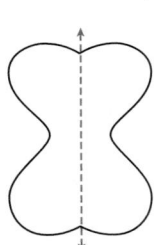

---

1 **Introduce**

Alternate Opener

EXPLORATION

7-8 **Symmetry**

1. Draw one line through each hexagon to form two congruent figures. Use a different line for each hexagon.

2. Draw one line through each figure to form two congruent figures.

Think and Discuss

3. **Draw** a figure that cannot be cut into two congruent figures with one line.

4. **Describe** the characteristics of a figure that can be cut into two congruent figures.

Motivate
Fold a sheet of red construction paper in half. Cut half of a heart shape along the folded edge. Open the folded piece of paper to reveal a complete heart shape. Ask students whether they think there is a benefit to folding the paper before cutting it. The benefit is that both halves of the heart are symmetrical.

Explorations and answers are provided in *Alternate Openers: Explorations Transparencies.*

A figure has **rotational symmetry** if you can rotate the figure around some point so that it coincides with itself. The point is the center of rotation, and the amount of rotation must be less than one full turn, or 360°.

7-fold and 6-fold rotational symmetry mean that the figures coincide with themselves 7 times and 6 times respectively, within one full turn.

7-fold rotational symmetry   6-fold rotational symmetry

EXAMPLE 2 Drawing Figures with Rotational Symmetry

Complete each figure. The point is the center of rotation.

A 2-fold

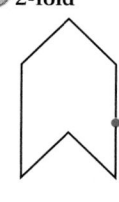 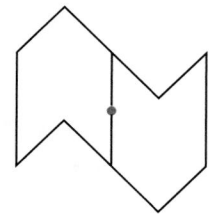

Figure coincides with itself twice every full turn.

B 8-fold

Figure coincides with itself 8 times every full turn.

Answers to *Think and Discuss*

1. The figure coincides with itself after certain transformations, such as reflections or rotations.

2. capitals: A, B, C, D, E, H, I, K, M, O, T, U, V, W, X, and Y; lower case: c, i, l, o, t, u, v, w, and x

3. capitals: H, I, N, O, S, X, Z; lower case: l, o, s, x, and z

Think and Discuss

1. Explain what it means for a figure to be symmetric.

2. Tell which letters of the alphabet have line symmetry.

3. Tell which letters of the alphabet have rotational symmetry.

Example 1

Complete each figure. The dashed line is the line of symmetry.

A.

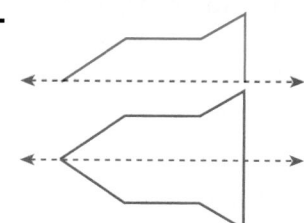

B.

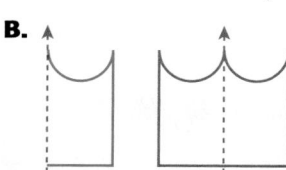

Example 2

Complete each figure. The point is the center of rotation.

A. 2-fold

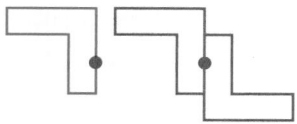

B. 5–fold

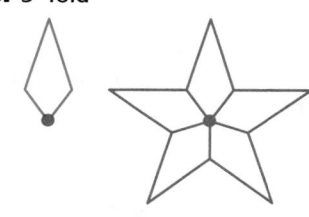 

Also available on transparency

---

2 Teach

Guided Instruction

In this lesson, students learn to identify symmetry in figures. Explain to students that a figure has line symmetry if there is a line that divides the figure into two congruent parts that are reflected images of each other. Point out to students that some figures have more than one line of symmetry. Show an example of rotational symmetry. You may want to use a Teaching Transparency.

Reaching All Learners
Through Concrete Manipulatives

Provide students with some construction paper, scissors, and two cut-out plane figures. One of the cutouts should be half of an image, such as half of a heart or half of a butterfly. Have students fold the paper in half, trace the figure, and cut it out to see what shape it reveals. The second cutout should be a piece of a figure with rotational symmetry, such as a petal from a flower or the point of a star. Instruct students to trace the figure, rotate it, and trace it again until they have completed a circle. Then have them cut out the figure.

3 Close

Summarize

Remind the students that they have been examining two different kinds of symmetry. Both types of symmetry are related to the transformations studied in Lesson 7-7. Line symmetry is related to reflection, and rotational symmetry is related to rotation. Ask students to point out examples of symmetry in the classroom.

Assignment Guide

If you finished Example **1** assign:
Average 1–4, 8–10, 19–22, 27–35
Advanced 8–10, 19–22, 27–35

If you finished Example **2** assign:
Average 1–16, 19–23, 27–35
Advanced 8–35

Homework Quick Check

Quickly check key concepts.
Exercises: 10, 14, 20, 23

Math Background

A special type of symmetry, called *point symmetry,* occurs when a figure has two-fold rotational symmetry. From any point on a figure with point symmetry, a line segment can be drawn through the center of rotation to a corresponding point on the figure. The center of rotation is the midpoint of that line segment.

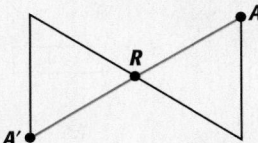

The letter *N* has point symmetry with center of rotation *R. R* is the midpoint of segment *AA'.*

Answers

1–16. See p. A9.

State Resources

go.hrw.com
State Resources Online
KEYWORD: MT7 Resources

7-8 Exercises

GUIDED PRACTICE

See Example **1** Complete each figure. The dashed line is the line of symmetry.

1. 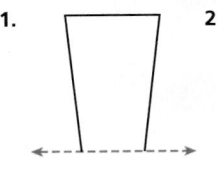 **2.** **3.** 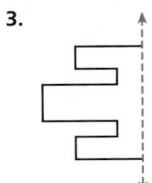 **4.**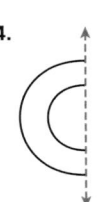

See Example **2** Complete each figure. The point is the center of rotation.

5. 4-fold 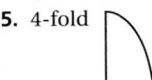 **6.** 6-fold 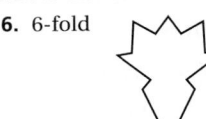 **7.** 3-fold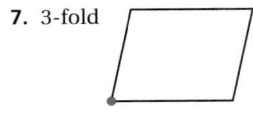

INDEPENDENT PRACTICE

See Example **1** Complete each figure. The dashed line is the line of symmetry.

8. 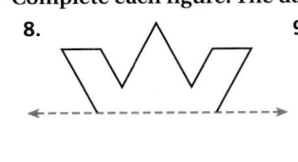 **9.** 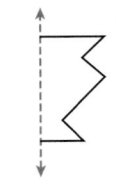 **10.**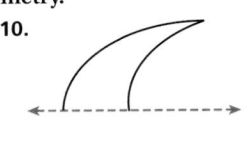

11. 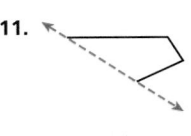 **12.** 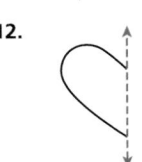 **13.**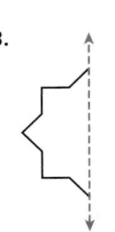

See Example **2** Complete each figure. The point is the center of rotation.

14. 4-fold 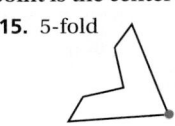 **15.** 5-fold **16.** 2-fold

RETEACH 7-8

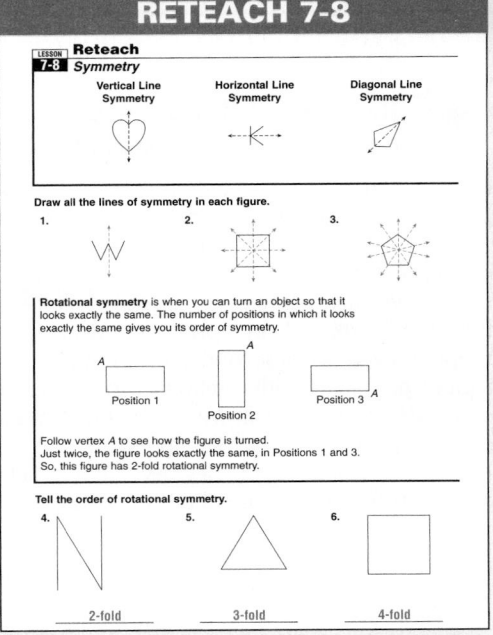

PRACTICE 7-8

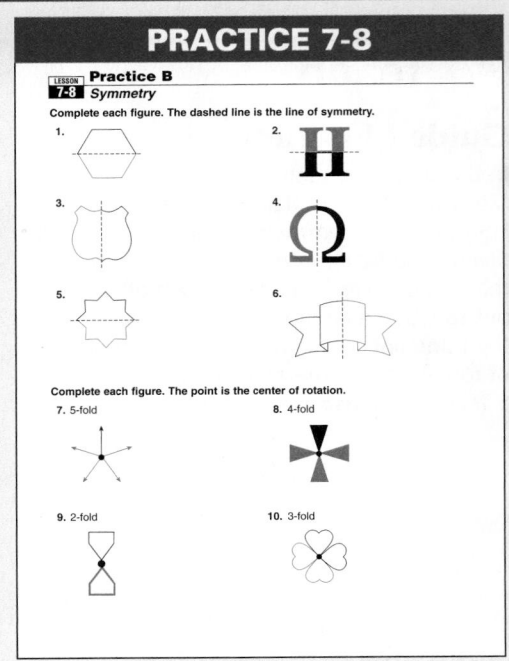

PRACTICE AND PROBLEM SOLVING

Social Studies

In Japan, a kimono that displays the wearer's family crest is worn for ceremonial occasions.

Extra Practice
See page 795.

Draw an example of a figure with each type of symmetry.

17. line and rotational symmetry

18. no symmetry

How many lines of symmetry do the following figures have?

19. square **4**

20. rectangle **2**

21. equilateral triangle **3**

22. isosceles triangle **1**

23. Social Studies Family crests called *ka-mon* have been in use in Japan for many centuries. Copy each crest below. Describe the symmetry, and draw any lines of symmetry or the center of rotation.

a.

Kage Asa no ha

b.
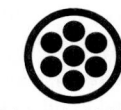
Maru ni shichiyo

c.

Nito Nami

24. Write a Problem Signal flags are hung from lines of rigging on ships. Write a problem about the types of symmetry in the flags. **Check students' work.**

25. Write About It To complete a figure with *n*-fold rotational symmetry, explain how much you rotate each part.

26. Challenge The flag of Switzerland has 180° rotational symmetry. Identify at least three other countries that have flags with 180° rotational symmetry.
Possible answers: Israel, Macedonia, Micronesia, and United Kingdom

TEST PREP and Spiral Review

27. Short Answer Draw a figure that has line symmetry and rotational symmetry.

28. Multiple Choice Which figure has 90° rotational symmetry?

Ⓐ regular pentagon

Ⓒ regular hexagon

Ⓑ square

Ⓓ regular heptagon

Find each unit rate. (Lesson 5-2)

29. 20 bananas for $4.40
$0.22 per banana

30. 496 miles in 16 hours
31 mi/h

31. 20 oz for $3.20
$0.16 per oz

In the figure, *ABCDE ≅ PQRST.* (Lesson 7-6)

32. Find *j.*
j = 5

33. Find *k.* **k = 4**

34. Find *m.*
m = 4

35. Find *n.* **n = 7**

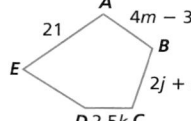
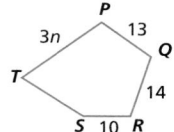

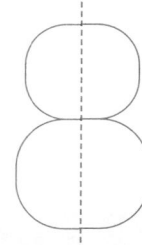

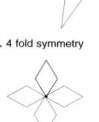

Online Edition
Tutorial Videos

Countdown to Testing Week 14

Power Presentations with PowerPoint®

Warm Up

Identify each polygon.

1. polygon with 10 sides   decagon

2. polygon with 3 congruent sides
   equilateral triangle

3. polygon with 4 congruent sides and no right angles   rhombus

Problem of the Day

If each of the capital letters of the alphabet is rotated 180° around its center, which of them will look the same?   H, I, N, O, S, X, Z

Also available on transparency

Math Fact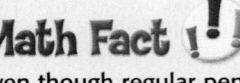

Even though regular pentagons cannot tessellate a plane (see Think and Discuss 1), there are irregular pentagons that can tessellate a plane.

State Resources

_____
_____
_____
_____
_____
_____
_____
_____
_____
_____

go.hrw.com
State Resources Online
KEYWORD: MT7 Resources

7-9 Tessellations

Learn to create tessellations.

Vocabulary
tessellation
regular tessellation

Fascinating designs can be made by repeating a figure or group of figures. These designs are often used in art and architecture.

A repeating pattern of plane figures that completely covers a plane with no gaps or overlaps is a **tessellation**.

In a **regular tessellation**, a regular polygon is repeated to fill a plane. The angle measures at each vertex must add to 360°, so only three regular tessellations exist.

Alcazar Palace in Seville, Spain

Equilateral triangles   **Squares**   **Regular hexagons**

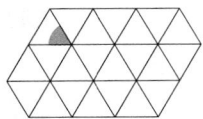   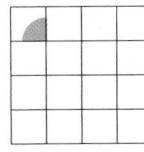   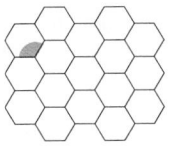

$6 \cdot 60° = 360°$ $4 \cdot 90° = 360°$ $3 \cdot 120° = 360°$

It is also possible to tessellate with polygons that are not regular. Since the angle measures of a triangle add to 180°, six triangles meeting at each vertex will tessellate. The angle measures of a quadrilateral add to 360°, so four quadrilaterals meeting at a vertex will tessellate.

EXAMPLE 1   Creating a Tessellation

Create a tessellation with quadrilateral *ABCD*.

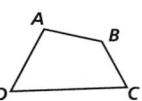

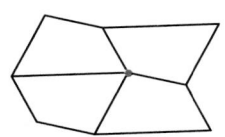

There must be a copy of each angle of quadrilateral ABCD at every vertex.

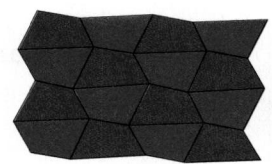

---

1 Introduce
Alternate Opener

EXPLORATION

7-9 Tessellations

Tile floors come in many different designs. For each figure, determine whether or not it could be used as a floor tile. Draw a model to show a possible tiling pattern.

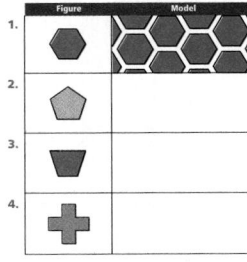

Think and Discuss
5. Draw a figure that cannot be used as a tile for a floor.
6. Describe the common characteristics that make some of the figures above suitable for floor tiles.

Motivate

Show the students an image of the inside of a beehive (Teaching Transparency). Explain that when the bees construct their homes, they don't want the "rooms" to overlap, and they don't want any space between the "rooms." Bees are able to do this by building "rooms" out of hexagons. The inside of a beehive is an example of a tessellation.

Explorations and answers are provided in *Alternate Openers: Explorations Transparencies.*

EXAMPLE 2 Creating a Tessellation by Transforming a Polygon

Use rotations to create a variation of the tessellation in Example 1.

Step 1: Find the midpoint of a side.

Step 2: Make a new edge for half of the side.

Step 3: Rotate the new edge around the midpoint to form the edge of the other half of the side.

Step 4: Repeat with the other sides.

Step 5: Use the figure to make a tessellation.

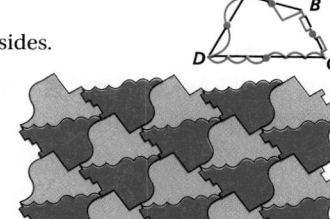

Answers to Think and Discuss

1. The angles in a regular pentagon all measure 108°, and 108 does not divide evenly into 360.

2. Possible answer: Quadrilateral *ABCD* was rotated 180°, then translated up. Quadrilateral *ABCD* was rotated 180° and then translated to the left. Quadrilateral *ABCD* was also translated up and to the left without a rotation.

Think and Discuss

1. Explain why a regular pentagon cannot be used to create a regular tessellation.

2. Describe the transformations used to make the tessellation in Example 2.

go.hrw.com
Homework Help Online
KEYWORD: MT7 7-9
Parent Resources Online
KEYWORD: MT7 Parent

7-9 Exercises

GUIDED PRACTICE

See Example ① **1.** Create a tessellation with quadrilateral *QRST*.

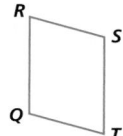

See Example ② **2.** Use rotations to create a variation of the tessellation in Exercise 1.

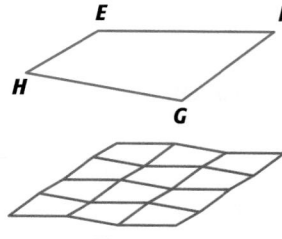

7-9 Exercises

Answers

1–2. See p. A9.

---

2 Teach

Guided Instruction

In this lesson, students learn to predict and verify patterns involving tessellations. Begin by showing the students tessellating designs such as a picture of a honeycomb, a reproduction of an artwork by M. C. Escher, or a piece of clothing or fabric. Emphasize that in any tessellation, there are no gaps or overlaps. Show students the three regular tessellations (Teaching Transparency). Explain that for a regular polygon to tessellate, the measure of an interior angle must be a factor of 360°.

Reaching All Learners
Through Modeling

Have students work in small groups. Give each group a set of pattern blocks (in Manipulatives Kit) containing equilateral triangles, regular hexagons, squares, rhombuses, trapezoids, and parallelograms. Ask each group to create as many different tessellations as they can with the pattern blocks and to draw each tessellation they find on a sheet of paper. If you want to provide an additional challenge, ask students to use a protractor to show that the sum of the measures of the angles around each vertex is 360°.

3 Close

Summarize

Review the requirements for a design to be a tessellation. The design must be a repeating pattern of plane figures that completely covers a plane with no gaps or overlaps.

Remind students that tessellations are found in nature, art, and manufactured structures. The lesson focused mainly on tessellations formed by polygons, but there are many tessellations formed by figures other than polygons.

3–10, 13. See p. A10.

Math Background

Allowing students to learn mathematics through its application in art is a powerful motivator for some students. Other students, however, find the creative side of this work quite challenging. Computer programs can help these students create designs that tessellate. These programs allow a student to experiment with various designs and to see many more possibilities than would be practical with paper and pencil.

It might be useful to investigate the work of M. C. Escher, the artist most often associated with tessellations.

INDEPENDENT PRACTICE

See Example 1

3. Create a tessellation with triangle *PQR*.

See Example 2

4. Use rotations to create a variation of the tessellation in Exercise 3.

PRACTICE AND PROBLEM SOLVING

Extra Practice
See page 795.

Use each shape to create a tessellation.

5.

6.

7.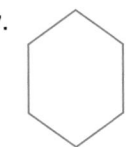

8.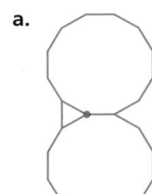

9.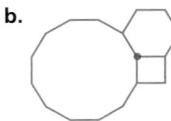

10.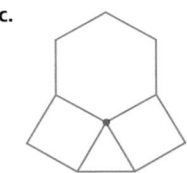

11. A piece is removed from one side of a rectangle and translated to the opposite side. Will this shape tessellate? **Yes, the shape will tessellate.**

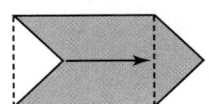

12. A piece is removed from one side of a trapezoid and translated to the opposite side. Will this shape tessellate? **Yes, the shape will tessellate.**

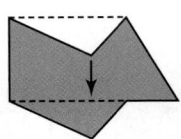

13. In a *semiregular tessellation*, two or more regular polygons are repeated to fill the plane and the vertices are all identical. Use each arrangement of regular polygons to create a semiregular tessellation.

a. **b.** **c.**

RETEACH 7-9

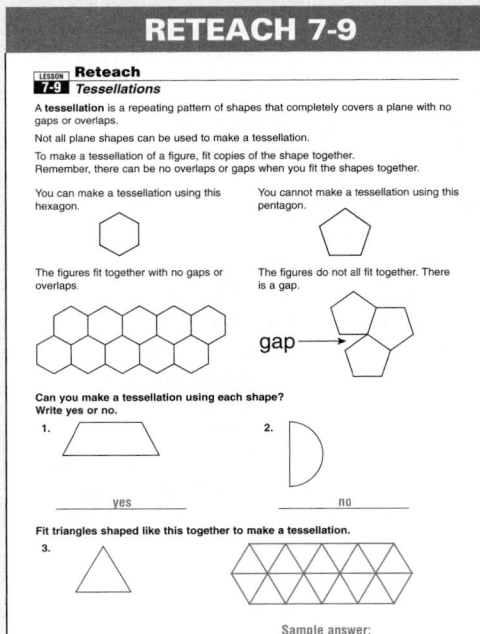

PRACTICE 7-9

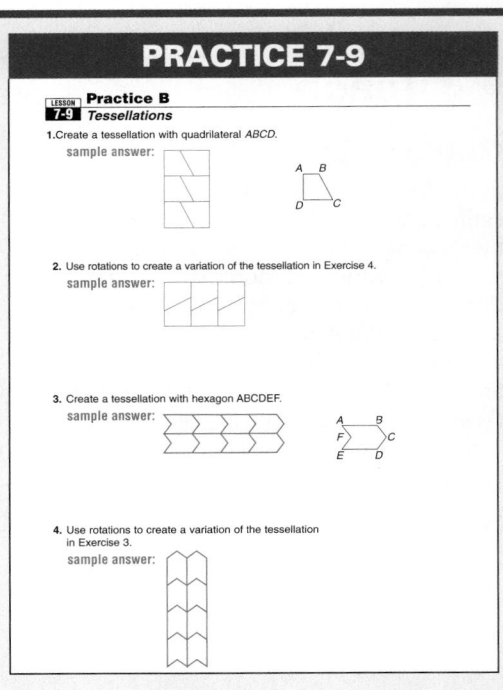

M. C. Escher created works of art by repeating interlocking shapes. He used both regular and nonregular tessellations. He often used what he called *metamorphoses*, in which shapes change into other shapes. Escher used his reptile pattern in many hexagonal tessellations. One of the most famous is entitled simply *Reptiles*.

14. The steps below show the method Escher used to make a bird out of a triangle. Use the bird to create a tessellation.

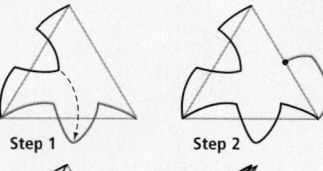

Step 1   Step 2

Step 3   Step 4

15. **Critical Thinking** What regular polygon do you think Escher used to begin *Reptiles*? **hexagon**

16. ⭐ **Challenge** Create an Escher-like tessellation of your own design. **Check students' work.**

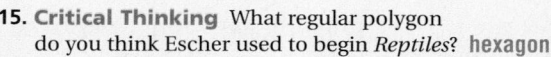 **TEST PREP and Spiral Review**

17. **Multiple Choice** Which of the following shapes will NOT form a regular tessellation?

Ⓐ    Ⓑ    Ⓒ 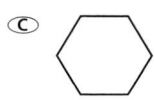   Ⓓ

18. **Short Answer** Which set of polygons will create a tessellation? Explain.
Possible answer: A set of right triangles can tessellate to form a large rectangle or
Write each number in scientific notation. (Lesson 4-4)   **parallelogram.**

19. 3,400,000,000 3.4×10^9 20. 0.00000045 4.5×10^{-7} 21. 28,000 2.8×10^4

Tell whether the two lines described in each exercise are parallel, perpendicular, or neither. (Lesson 7-5) **perpendicular**   **neither**
22. $\overrightarrow{PQ}$ has slope $\frac{3}{2}$. $\overrightarrow{EF}$ has slope $-\frac{2}{3}$.   23. $\overrightarrow{AB}$ has slope $\frac{9}{11}$. $\overrightarrow{CD}$ has slope $-\frac{3}{4}$.

CHALLENGE 7-9

Challenge
7-9 Shapely

A **fractal** is a shape that repeats itself in a pattern. As more stages are generated, the shape becomes more complex.

Starting with a + sign and generating the pattern by adding a half-size + sign in each of the four corners, the first two stages of a fractal are shown.

Level 0   Level 1

1. Generate the next two stages of the fractal.

Level 2   Level 3

Use paper folding to generate a fractal.
Level 0: Begin with a long strip of paper.

2. **Level 1:** Fold the strip right end to left; crease it. Open the strip so that it forms a right angle. Stand the strip on edge on your desk. Look down and sketch this view.

3. **Level 2:** Start at Level 0. Do Level 1 (the pattern) twice. Open the strip so that it forms right angles. Stand the strip on edge on your desk. Look down and sketch this view.

Each side of the right ∠ has been replaced by a right ∠, with sides half the previous.

4. **Level 3:** Start at Level 0. Do the pattern three times.

5. **Level 4:** Start at Level 0. Do the pattern four times.

PROBLEM SOLVING 7-9

Problem Solving
7-9 Tessellations

Create a tessellation using the given figure.
1.   2.

Choose the letter for the best answer.

3. Which figure will NOT make a tessellation?

A   C

B   Ⓓ

4. Which nonregular polygon can always be used to tile a floor?
F pentagon
G triangle
H octagon
J hexagon

5. For a combination of regular polygons to tessellate, the angles that meet at each vertex must add to what?
A 90°
B 180°
Ⓒ 360°
D 720°

Answers
14.

TEST PREP DOCTOR ➕ For Exercise 17, students who did not choose **D** may wish to review how to find the angle measures in a regular polygon. Remind them to apply the formula $nx° = 180°(n - 2)$.

📓 **Journal**

Have each student choose a favorite tessellation from the examples shown in class today. Ask students to write about their choices.

Power Presentations
with PowerPoint®

 7-9
Lesson Quiz

1. Explain why a regular tessellation with regular octagons is impossible.
Each angle measure in a regular octagon is 135° and 135 is not a factor of 360.

2. Can a semiregular tessellation be formed using a regular 12-sided polygon and a regular hexagon? Explain. No; a regular 12-sided polygon has angles that measure 150° and a regular hexagon has angles that measure 120°. No combinations of 120° and 150° add to 360°.

Also available on transparency

Organizer

Objective: Assess students' mastery of concepts and skills in Lessons 7-6 through 7-9.

Resources

 Assessment Resources
Section 7B Quiz

 Test & Practice Generator
One-Stop Planner®

INTERVENTION ◄══►

Resources

 Ready to Go On?
Intervention and
Enrichment Worksheets

💿 **Ready to Go On? CD-ROM**

🪐 **Ready to Go On? Online**

my.hrw.com

Answers

8–9. See p. A10.

Ready to Go On?

Quiz for Lessons 7-6 Through 7-9

☑ **7-6** **Congruence**

In the figure, triangle $ABC \cong$ triangle LMN.

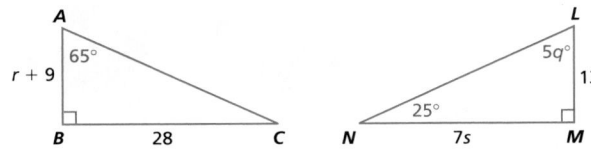

1. Find q. 13   **2.** Find r. 4   **3.** Find s. 4

☑ **7-7** **Transformations**

Identify each as a translation, rotation, reflection, or none of these.

4. 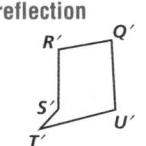 reflection   **5.** 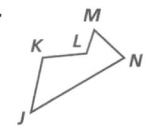 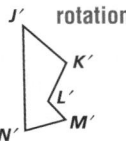 rotation

Quadrilateral $ABCD$ has vertices $A(-7, 5)$, $B(-4, 5)$, $C(-2, 3)$, and $D(-6, 2)$.
Find the coordinates of the image of each point after each transformation.

6. translation 4 units down, point C
$(-2, -1)$

7. reflection across the y-axis, point A
$(7, 5)$

☑ **7-8** **Symmetry**

8. Complete the figure. The dashed line is the line of symmetry.

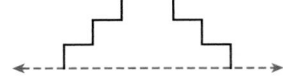

9. Complete the figure with 4-fold rotational symmetry. The point is the center of rotation.

10.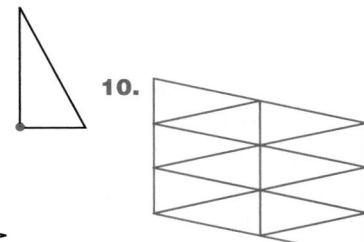

☑ **7-9** **Tessellations**

10. Copy the given figure and use it to create a tessellation.

READY TO GO ON?

NO
INTERVENE

Diagnose and Prescribe

YES
ENRICH

READY TO GO ON? Intervention, Section 7B				**READY TO GO ON? Enrichment, Section 7B**
Ready to Go On? Intervention	📝 **Worksheets**	💿 **CD-ROM**	🪐 **Online**	
☑ Lesson 7-6	7-6 Intervention	Activity 7-6		📝 **Worksheets**
☑ Lesson 7-7	7-7 Intervention	Activity 7-7	Diagnose and Prescribe Online	💿 **CD-ROM**
☑ Lesson 7-8	7-8 Intervention	Activity 7-8		🪐 **Online**
☑ Lesson 7-9	7-9 Intervention	Activity 7-9		

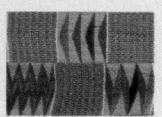

Cloth Creations The Asante people of Ghana are known for weaving Kente cloth, a colorful textile based on repeating geometric patterns. Susan is using a coordinate plane to design her own Kente cloth pattern.

1. Susan starts with triangle *ABC* as shown. Explain how she can use slopes to make sure the triangle is a right triangle.

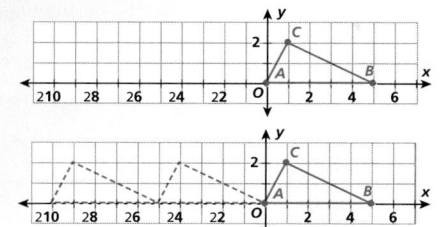

2. To begin the pattern, Susan uses transformations to make a row of triangles that are all congruent to triangle *ABC*. Describe the transformations she should use to make these triangles.

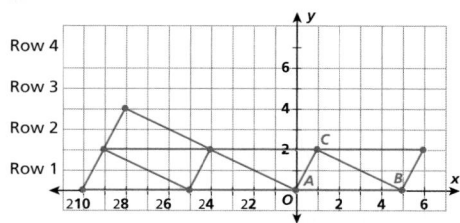

3. Next, she extends the pattern by making additional rows of triangles. The first triangle in Row 2 is shown. Complete the table by writing the coordinates of the top vertex of each triangle in the pattern.

4. What patterns do you notice in the table?

5. Susan's Kente cloth pattern is a tessellation of what types of figures?

Row	Top Vertex of Triangles in Row			
Row 1	(−9, 2)	(−4, 2)	(1, 2)	(6, 2)
Row 2	(−8, 4)	(−3, 4)	(2, 4)	(7, 4)
Row 3	(−7, 6)	(−2, 6)	(3, 6)	(8, 6)
Row 4	(−6, 8)	(−1, 8)	(4, 8)	(9, 8)

Multi-Step Test Prep

Organizer

Objective: Assess students' ability to apply concepts and skills in Chapter 7 in a real-world format.

PREMIER **Online Edition**

Resources

Middle School Assessments
www.mathtekstoolkit.org

Problem	Text reference
1	Lesson 7-5
2	Lesson 7-7
3	Lesson 7-7
4	Lesson 7-5
5	Lesson 7-9

Answers

1. Slope of $\overline{AC}$ = 2; slope of $\overline{CB} = -\frac{1}{2}$. The product of the slopes is −1, so the sides of the triangle are perpendicular. Therefore, the triangle is a right triangle.

2. Translate triangle *ABC* along the *x*-axis: 5 units to the right, 5 units to the left, and 10 units to the left.

4. Possible answer: To go from one row to the next, the *y*-coordinate increases by 2. The *x*-coordinates repeat every 5 rows.

5. Triangles, parallelograms, rectangles, and trapezoids

INTERVENTION

Scaffolding Questions

1. What is true about the two sides of a triangle that make up the right angle? The sides are perpendicular.

2. Is the row of three triangles shown at the right a tessellation? Explain your answer. No. A tessellation completely covers a plane. These three triangles do not.

3. What does the top vertex of each triangle in Row 2 have in common? They all have the same *y*-coordinate.

4. Let the *x*-coordinate of the top vertex of the first triangle in Row 1 be represented by the variable *x*. Write an expression that would represent the *x*-coordinate of the top vertex of the first triangle in Row 2. *x* + 1

5. Is the tessellation in Susan's cloth pattern a regular tessellation? Why or why not? The pattern is not a regular tessellation because the polygon used is not a regular polygon.

Extension

1. The first row of triangles in Susan's pattern begins along the *x*-axis. What pattern in the coordinates of the vertices would you notice if the first row of triangles began along the *y*-axis? The *x*-coordinates of the vertices in each row would be the same. The *y*-coordinates of the vertices would differ by 1 unit from one row to the next.

go.hrw.com
State Resources Online
KEYWORD: MT7 Resources

Organizer

Objective: Participate in games to practice and apply skills learned in Chapter 7.

 Online Edition

Resources

Chapter 7 Resource Book
Puzzles, Twisters & Teasers

Coloring Tessellations

Purpose: To extend the study of tessellations to a coloring problem

Discuss Ask students to explain the rule for coloring the tessellations. No two figures that share an edge can be colored with the same color. Explain why the tessellation of hexagons requires 3 colors. Choose any hexagon and color it with color 1. Color 1 cannot be used to color any of the surrounding hexagons because the surrounding hexagons all share an edge with the center hexagon. So you must color the 6 surrounding hexagons in order with colors 2, 3, 2, 3, 2, and 3.

Extend Give students a map of the United States. Ask them to color the map with as few colors as possible, using a different color for each state so that no states that share a border are the same color. The map can be colored with 4 colors.

Polygon Rummy

Purpose: To practice using the properties of polygons in a card game

Discuss Ask: Is there any set of 3 cards for which there is no polygon that has the properties on all 3 cards? Give an example. yes; triangle, quadrilateral, all angles obtuse What figure satisfies all the properties "pentagon," "all sides congruent," and "all angles congruent"? regular pentagon

Extend Ask students to name the cards that describe a square and those that describe a regular hexagon. Which figure meets the requirements of more cards? 8 cards describe a square; 6 cards describe a regular hexagon; square.

Game Time

Coloring Tessellations

Two of the three regular tessellations—triangles and squares—can be colored with two colors so that no two polygons that share an edge are the same color. The third—hexagons—requires three colors.

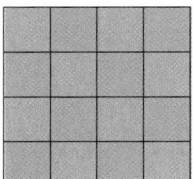 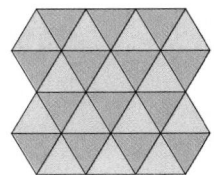 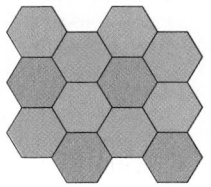

1. Determine if each semiregular tessellation can be colored with two colors. If not, tell the minimum number of colors needed.

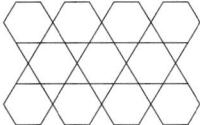 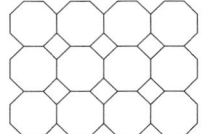 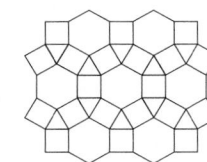

yes   no (3)   yes

2. Try to write a rule about which tessellations can be colored with two colors. A tessellation can be colored with two colors if each figure borders other figures that do not border each other.

Polygon Rummy

The object of this game is to create geometric figures. Each card in the deck shows a property of a geometric figure. To create a figure, you must draw a polygon that matches at least three cards in your hand. For example, if you have the cards "quadrilateral," "a pair of parallel sides," and "a right angle," you could draw a rectangle.

A complete set of rules and playing cards is available online.

go.hrw.com
Game Time Extra
KEYWORD: MT7 Games

Materials
- 3 sheets of white paper
- CD or CD-ROM
- scissors
- tape
- markers
- empty CD case

FOLDNOTES

It's in the Bag!

PROJECT **Project CD Geometry**

Make your own CD to record important facts about plane geometry.

1 Fold a sheet of paper in half. Place a CD on top of the paper so that it touches the folded edge. Trace around the CD. **Figure A**

2 Cut out the CD shape, being careful to leave the folded edge attached. This will create two paper CDs that are joined together. Cut a hole in the center of each paper CD. **Figure B**

3 Repeat steps 1 and 2 with the other two sheets of paper.

4 Tape the ends of the paper CDs together to make a string of six CDs. **Figure C**

5 Accordion fold the CDs to make a booklet. Write the number and name of the chapter on the top CD. Store the CD booklet in an empty CD case.

Taking Note of the Math

Use the blank pages in the CD booklet to take notes on the chapter. Be sure to include definitions and sample problems that will help you review essential concepts about plane geometry.

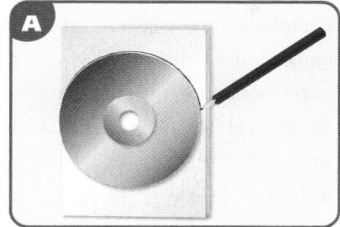

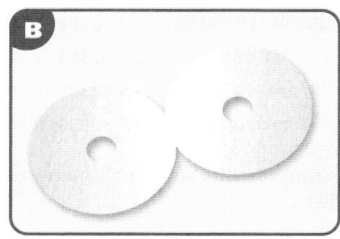

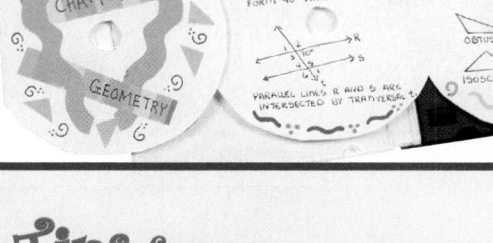

Organizer

Objective: Make a booklet in which to record important facts about plane geometry.

Materials: 3 sheets of white paper, CD or CD-ROM, scissors, tape, markers, empty CD case

PREMIER **Online Edition**

Using the Page

Preparing the Materials
Stores that sell used CDs often have empty CD cases that they will sell at a reasonable price or donate to the school. You might also ask students to save cases from old CD-ROMs.

Making the Project
Remind students to be careful when they cut out the CD shapes so that the two paper CDs remain attached to each other along the folded edge.

Extending the Project
Have students use additional sheets of paper to make longer booklets. Students can use the extra space to record sample geometric figures or homework problems that they need to review.

Tips from the Bag Ladies!

We always get lots of CD-ROMs in the mail from Internet service providers. We never throw those CDs away. This project is just one of the many uses we've found for them!

Students can make two booklets and store them in a double CD case. You can also have students make a square booklet that slides into the cover of the CD case. Note that regular cases or "slim" cases will work equally well for this project.

Organizer

Objective: Help students organize and review key concepts and skills presented in Chapter 7.

 Online Edition
Multilingual Glossary

Resources

 PuzzlePro®
One-Stop Planner®

Multilingual Glossary Online

go.hrw.com
KEYWORD: MT7 Glossary

Lesson Tutorial Videos
CD-ROM

Test & Practice Generator
One-Stop Planner®

Answers

1. parallel lines; perpendicular lines
2. rectangle; rhombus
3. 112°
4. 68°
5. 112°

Study Guide: Review

Vocabulary

acute angle 325	parallel lines 330	rotation 358
acute triangle 336	parallelogram 342	rotational symmetry ...365
angle 325	perpendicular lines 330	run 347
center of rotation 358	plane 324	scalene triangle 337
complementary angles ..325	point 324	segment 324
congruent 325	polygon 341	slope 347
correspondence 354	ray 324	square 342
equilateral triangle 337	rectangle 342	supplementary angles ..325
image 358	reflection 358	tessellation 368
isosceles triangle 337	regular polygon 342	transformation 358
line 324	regular tessellation 368	translation 358
line of symmetry 364	rhombus 342	transversal 330
line symmetry 364	right angle 325	trapezoid 342
obtuse angle 325	right triangle 336	Triangle Sum Theorem .336
obtuse triangle 336	rise 347	vertical angles 325

Complete the sentences below with vocabulary words from the list above.

1. Lines in the same plane that never meet are called __?__.
Lines that intersect at 90° angles are called __?__.

2. A quadrilateral with 4 congruent angles is called a __?__.
A quadrilateral with 4 congruent sides is called a __?__.

7-1 **Points, Lines, Planes, and Angles** (pp. 324–328)

EXAMPLE

■ Find the angle measure.

$m\angle 1$

$m\angle 1 + 122° = 180°$
$\underline{\quad - 122° \quad - 122°}$
$m\angle 1 \quad = \quad 58°$

EXERCISES

Find each angle measure.

3. $m\angle 1$
4. $m\angle 2$
5. $m\angle 3$

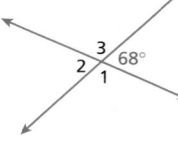

7-2 Parallel and Perpendicular Lines (pp. 330–333)

EXAMPLE

Line $j \parallel$ line k. Find each angle measure.

- m∠1

  m∠1 = 143°

- m∠2

  $$m\angle 2 + 143° = \quad 180°$$
  $$\underline{\quad - 143° \quad - 143°}$$
  $$m\angle 2 \quad = \quad 37°$$

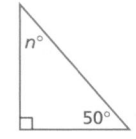

EXERCISES

Line $p \parallel$ line q. Find each angle measure.

6. m∠1
7. m∠2
8. m∠3
9. m∠4
10. m∠5

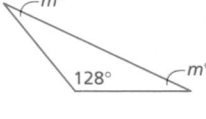

7-3 Angles in Triangles (pp. 336–340)

EXAMPLE

- Find $n°$.

  $$n° + 50° + 90° = \quad 180°$$
  $$n° + 140° = \quad 180°$$
  $$\underline{\quad - 140° \quad - 140°}$$
  $$n° \quad = \quad 40°$$

EXERCISES

11. Find $m°$.

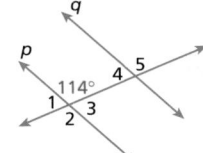

7-4 Classifying Polygons (pp. 341–345)

EXAMPLE

- Find the angle measures in a regular 12-gon.

  $$12x° = 180°(12 - 2)$$
  $$12x° = 180°(10)$$
  $$12x° = 1800°$$
  $$x° = 150°$$

EXERCISES

Find the angle measures in each regular polygon.

12. a regular octagon
13. a regular 11-gon

7-5 Coordinate Geometry (pp. 347–351)

EXAMPLE

- Graph the quadrilateral with the given vertices. Give all the names that apply.

  $D(-2, 1), E(2, 3), F(3, 1), G(-1, -1)$

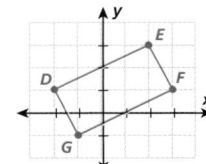

$\overline{DE} \parallel \overline{FG}$
$\overline{EF} \parallel \overline{GD}$
$\overline{DE} \perp \overline{EF}$
parallelogram, rectangle

EXERCISES

Graph the quadrilaterals with the given vertices. Give all the names that apply.

14. $Q(2, 0), R(-1, 1), S(3, 3), T(8, 3)$
15. $K(2, 3), L(3, 0), M(2, -3), N(1, 0)$
16. $W(2, 2), X(2, -2), Y(-1, -3), Z(-1, 1)$

Answers

6. 66°
7. 114°
8. 66°
9. 66°
10. 114°
11. $m° = 26°$
12. 135°
13. 147.3°
14.

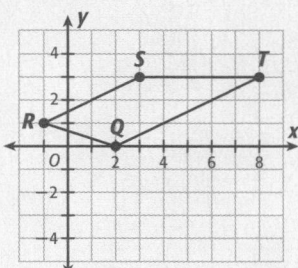

trapezoid

15.

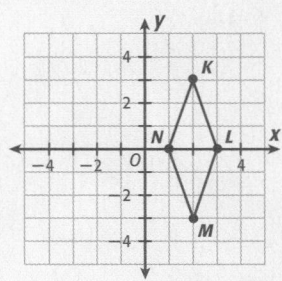

parallelogram, rhombus

16.

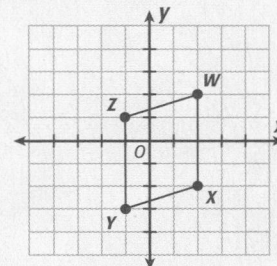

parallelogram

Answers

17. $x = 19$

18. $t = 2.4$

19. $q = 7$

20.

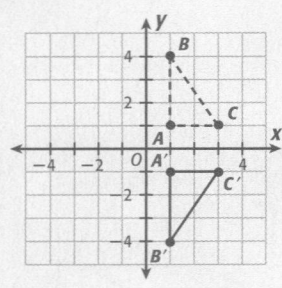

21.

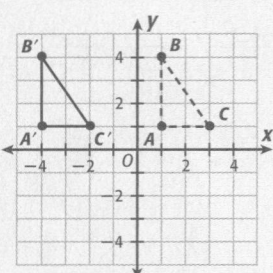

22.

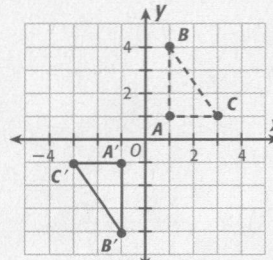

23.

24.

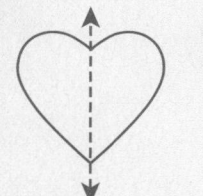

25.

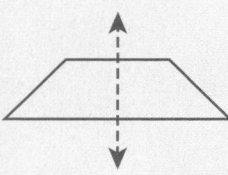

7-6 Congruence (pp. 354–357)

EXAMPLE

■ Triangle $ABC \cong$ triangle FDE. Find x.

$$\begin{aligned} x - 4 &= 4 \\ +4 \quad &\quad +4 \\ x &= 8 \end{aligned}$$

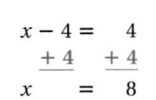

EXERCISES

Triangle $JQZ \cong$ triangle VTZ.

17. Find x.

18. Find t.

19. Find q.

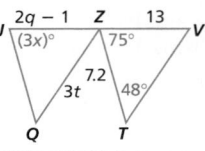

7-7 Transformations (pp. 358–361)

EXAMPLE

■ Draw the image of a triangle with vertices $(-2, 2)$, $(1, 1)$, and $(-3, -2)$ after a 180° rotation around $(0, 0)$.

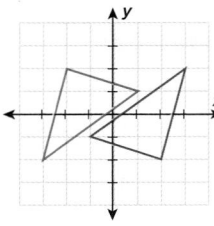

EXERCISES

Draw the image of a triangle ABC with vertices $(1, 1)$, $(1, 4)$, and $(3, 1)$ after each transformation.

20. reflection across the x-axis

21. translation 5 units left

22. 180° rotation around $(0, 0)$

7-8 Symmetry (pp. 364–367)

EXAMPLE

■ Complete the figure. The dashed line is the line of symmetry.

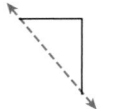 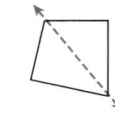

EXERCISES

Complete each figure.

23. 6-fold   **24.**   **25.**

7-9 Tessellations (pp. 368–371)

EXAMPLE

■ Create a tessellation with the figure.

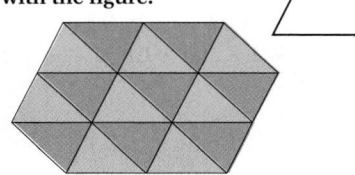 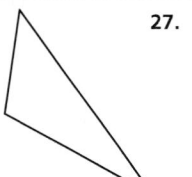

EXERCISES

Create a tessellation with each figure.

26.   **27.**

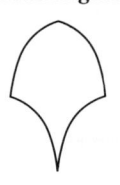

26. Possible answer:

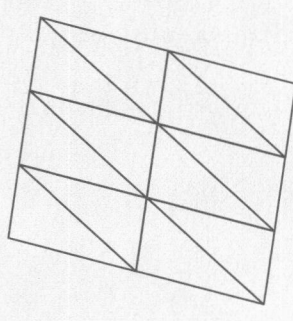

27. Possible answer:

In the figure, line $m \parallel$ line n.

Possible answer: $\angle 1$ and $\angle 2$

1. Name two pairs of supplementary angles.
2. Find the $m\angle 1$. **135°**
3. Find the $m\angle 2$. **45°**
4. Find the $m\angle 3$. **45°**
5. Find the $m\angle 4$. **135°**

6. Two angles in a triangle have measures of 44° and 57°. What is the measure of the third angle? **79°**

7. What are the measures of the congruent angles in an isosceles triangle if the measure of the third angle is 102°? **39°**

Give all of the names that apply to each figure.

8.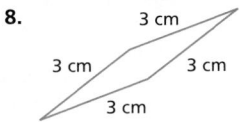
polygon, quadrilateral, parallelogram, rhombus

9.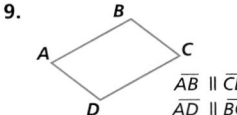
polygon, quadrilateral, parallelogram
$\overline{AB} \parallel \overline{CD}$
$\overline{AD} \parallel \overline{BC}$

Graph the quadrilateral with the given vertices. Give all of the names that apply to each quadrilateral.

10. $A(3,4)$, $B(8,4)$, $C(5,0)$, $D(0,0)$

11. $K(-4,0)$, $L(-2,5)$, $M(2,5)$, $N(4,0)$

Find the coordinates of the missing vertex.

12. rectangle $PQRS$ with $P(0,0)$, $Q(0,4)$, $R(4,4)$ **$S(4, 0)$**

In the figure, quadrilateral $ABCD \cong$ quadrilateral $LMNO$.

13. Find m. **86°**
14. Find n. **5**
15. Find p. **7**

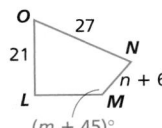

Pentagon $ABCDE$ has vertices $A(1, -2)$, $B(3, -1)$, $C(7, -2)$, $D(6, -4)$, and $E(2, -5)$. Find the coordinates of the image of each point after each transformation.

16. rotation 90° around the origin, point E **$(-5, -2)$**
17. reflection across the x-axis, point C **$(7, 2)$**
18. translation 6 units up, point B **$(3, 5)$**
19. reflection across the y-axis, point A **$(-1, -2)$**
20. Complete the figure. The dashed line is the line of symmetry.

11. trapezoid

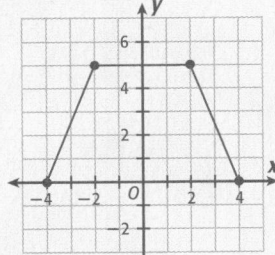

20.

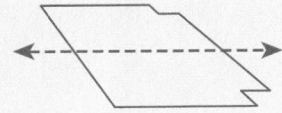

Organizer

Objective: Assess students' mastery of concepts and skills in Chapter 7.

 **Online Edition**

Resources

Assessment Resources

Chapter 7 Tests
• Free Response
  (Levels A, B, C)
• Multiple Choice
  (Levels A, B, C)
• Performance Assessment

IDEA Works! CD-ROM
Modified Chapter 7 Test

Test & Practice Generator
One-Stop Planner®

Answers

10. rhombus; parallelogram

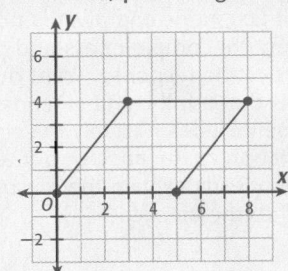

State Resources

 go.hrw.com
State Resources Online
KEYWORD: MT7 Resources

Chapter 7 Test **379**

Organizer

Objective: Provide opportunities to learn and practice common test-taking strategies.

 Online Edition

Resources

 State Test Prep Workbook

 State Test Prep CD-ROM

 State Test Practice Online

 **go.hrw.com**
KEYWORD: MT7 TestPrep

TEST PREP DOCTOR + This Test Tackler focuses on how extended response test items are scored and demonstrates how to write a response worth full credit. Explain that a grader scores responses to these types of test items and awards points based on the completeness and correctness of the response. Point out to students that a full-credit extended response includes not only the correct computation of the answer, but also the ability to clearly explain the reasoning that led to the answer.

Extended Response: Write Extended Responses

Extended response test items often consist of multi-step problems to evaluate your understanding of a math concept. Extended response questions are scored using a 4-point scoring rubric.

EXAMPLE **1**

Extended Response Julianna bought a shirt marked down 20%. She had a coupon for an additional 20% off the sale price. Is this the same as getting 40% off the regular price? Explain your reasoning.

4-point response:

> No, the prices are not the same. Suppose the shirt originally cost $40.
> 20% off a 20% markdown: $40 × 20% = $8; $40 − $8 = $32;
> $32 × 20% = $6.40; $32 − $6.40 = $25.60
> 40% off: $40 × 40% = $16; $40 − $16 = $24

The student answers the question correctly and shows all work.

3-point response:

> Yes, it is the same. If the shirt originally cost $25, it would cost $15
> after taking 20% off of a 20% discount. A 40% discount off $20 is $15.
>
> Shirt original price = $25
> Shirt at 20% off = $20 $25 × 20% = $5; $25 − $5 = $20
> Shirt at 20% off sales price = $15 $20 × 20% = $4; $20 − $4 = $15
> Shirt at 40% off = $15 $25 × 40% = $10; $25 − $10 = $15

The student makes a minor computation error that results in an incorrect answer.

2-point response:

> No, it is not the same. A $30 shirt with 20% off and then an additional
> 20% off is $6. A $30 shirt at 40% off is $12.

The student makes major computation errors and does not show all work.

1-point response:

> It is the same.

The student shows no work and has the wrong answer.

Scoring Rubric

4 points: The student answers all parts of the question correctly, shows all work, and provides a complete and correct explanation.

3 points: The student answers all parts of the question, shows all work, and provides a complete explanation that demonstrates understanding, but the student makes minor errors in computation.

2 points: The student does not answer all parts of the question but shows all work and provides a complete and correct explanation for the parts answered, or the student correctly answers all parts of the question but does not show all work or does not provide an explanation.

1 point: The student gives incorrect answers and shows little or no work or explanation, or the student does not follow directions.

0 points: The student gives no response.

To receive full credit, make sure all parts of the problem are answered. Be sure to show all of your work and to write a neat and clear explanation.

Read each test item and answer the questions that follow.

Item A
Janell has two job offers. Job A pays $500 per week. Job B pays $200 per week plus 15% commission on her sales. She expects to make $7500 in sales per month. Which job pays better? Explain your reasoning.

1. A student wrote this response:

> Job A pays better.

What score should the student's response receive? Explain your reasoning.

2. What additional information, if any, should the student's response include in order to receive full credit?

3. Add to the response so that it receives a score of 4-points.

4. How much would Janell have to make in sales per month for job A and job B to pay the same amount?

Item B
A new MP3 player normally costs $97.99. This week, it is on sale for 15% off its regular price. In addition to this, Jasmine receives an employee discount of 20% off the sale price. Excluding sales tax, what percent of the original price will Jasmine pay for the MP3 player?

5. What information needs to be included in a response to receive full credit?

6. Write a response that would receive full credit.

Item C
Three houses were originally purchased for $125,000. After each year, the value of each house either increased or decreased. Which house had the least value after the third year? What was the value of that house? Explain your reasoning.

| | | Percent Change in Value | | |
House	Original Cost ($)	Year 1	Year 2	Year 3
A	125,000	1%	1%	1%
B	125,000	4%	−2%	−1%
C	125,000	3%	−2%	2%

7. A student wrote this response:

> House A increased 3% over three years. House B increased 1% over three years. House C increased 3% over three years. So, House B had the least value after the third year. Its value increased 1% of $125,000, or $1250, for a total value of $126,250.

What score should the student's response receive? Explain your reasoning.

8. What additional information, if any, should the student's response include in order to receive full credit?

Item D
Kara is trying to save $4500 to buy a used car. She has $3000 in an account that earns a yearly simple interest of 5%. Will she have enough money in her account after 3 years to buy a car? If not, how much more money will she need? Explain your reasoning.

9. What information needs to be included in a response to receive full credit?

10. Write a response that would receive full credit.

Test Tackler

9. The student needs to apply the simple interest formula with a rate of 5%, and then point out that the final amount after 3 years is less than $4500. The student should also include the amount of money Kara still needs to buy the car.

10. $A = P + Prt$
$= 3000 + 3000(0.05)(3)$
$= 3450$
$4500 − 3450 = 1050$

No, she will need $1050 more to buy the car.

Answers

Possible answers:

1. The student should receive 1 point because the student provides a correct answer without giving any explanation.

2. In order to receive full credit, the student needs to show and explain that Job A pays better than Job B. Job A pays $26,000 a year and Job B pays $24,800 a year. Job A pays better.

Job A: $500 × 52 weeks = $26,000 per year

Job B: $200 × 52 weeks = $10,400 per year salary

$8000 × 12 = $96,000 × 15% = $14,400 in expected commission

$10,400 + $14,400 = $24,800 total per year (salary plus commission)

3. Job A pays better: $500 × 4 = $2000. Job B pays ($2000 × 4) + (0.15 × $7500): $800 + 1125 = $1925.

4. $8000

5. The students should display calculations for finding the percent amounts of the sales and the final price after the original amount has been reduced by both sales.

6. $97.99 − 0.15($97.99) = $83.29, $83.29 − 0.2($83.29) = $66.63; After both sales it costs $66.63.

7. The student should receive 2 points because the student makes major computation errors resulting in an incorrect response.

8. The student needs to actually calculate the value of houses after each year and then compare the value of each house after 3 years. They will find House B has a total value of $126,126.

State Resources

Organizer

Objective: Provide review and practice for Chapters 1–7 and standardized tests.

PREMIER **Online Edition**

Resources

 Assessment Resources
Chapter 7 Cumulative Test

 State Test Prep Workbook

 State Test Prep CD-ROM

 State Test Practice Online

go.hrw.com
KEYWORD: MT7 TestPrep

Cumulative Assessment, Chapters 1–7
Multiple Choice

Standardized Test Prep

1. Which angle is a right angle?

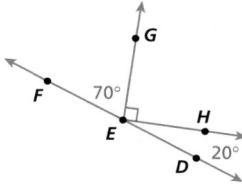

   Ⓐ ∠FED   Ⓒ ∠GEH
   Ⓑ ∠FEG   Ⓓ ∠GED

2. A jeweler buys a diamond for $68 and resells it for $298. What is the percent increase to the nearest percent?

   Ⓕ 3%   Ⓗ 138%
   Ⓖ 33%   Ⓙ 338%

3. A grocery store sells one dozen ears of white corn for $2.40. What is the unit price for one ear of corn?

   Ⓐ 0.05/ear of corn
   Ⓑ $0.20/ear of corn
   Ⓒ $1.30/ear of corn
   Ⓓ $2.40/ear of corn

4. The people of Ireland drink the most milk in the world. All together, they drink more than 602,000,000 quarts each year. What is this number written in scientific notation?

   Ⓕ 60.2×10^5
   Ⓖ 602×10^6
   Ⓗ 6.02×10^8
   Ⓙ 6.02×10^9

5. Cara is making a model of a car that is 14 feet long. What other information is needed to find the length of the model?

   Ⓐ Car's width   Ⓒ Scale factor
   Ⓑ Car's speed   Ⓓ Car's height

6. For which equation is the point a solution to the equation?

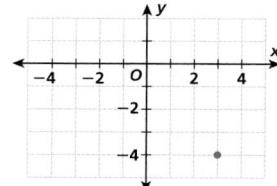

   Ⓕ $y = 2x + 1$ Ⓗ $y = -x + 1$
   Ⓖ $y = 2x - 2$ Ⓙ $y = -2x + 2$

7. What is q in the acute triangle?

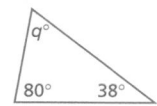

   Ⓐ 62   Ⓒ 118
   Ⓑ 72   Ⓓ 128

8. Which expression represents "twice the difference of a number and 5"?

   Ⓕ $2(x + 5)$ Ⓗ $2(x - 5)$
   Ⓖ $2x - 5$ Ⓙ $2x + 5$

9. For which equation is $x = -1$ the solution?

   Ⓐ $3x + 8 = 11$ Ⓒ $-3x + 8 = 5$
   Ⓑ $8 - x = 9$ Ⓓ $8 + x = 9$

State Resources

TEST PREP DOCTOR ✚

Remind students who chose answer **F** or **G** in item 4 that the first factor of a number written in scientific notation is a number greater than or equal to 1 and less than 10.

Point out to students that **C** and **D** in item 7 can be eliminated because they are not acute angles.

Answers

17. See p. A10.

18.

Number of sides	Number of Diagonals
3	0
4	2
5	6
6	9
7	14
n	$\dfrac{n(n-3)}{2}$

19. See 4-Point Response work sample.

State Resources

go.hrw.com
State Resources Online
KEYWORD: MT7 Resources

10. Marcus bought a shirt that was on sale for 20% off its regular price. If Marcus paid $20 for the shirt, what what its regular price?

   Ⓕ $25   Ⓗ $16

   Ⓖ $40   Ⓙ $30

 HOT TIP! Use logic to eliminate answer choices that are incorrect. This will help you to make an educated guess if you are having trouble with the question.

Gridded Response

Use the following figure for items 11 and 12. Line p is parallel to line q.

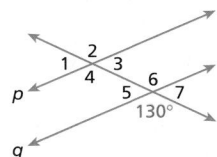

11. What is the measure of ∠4, in degrees?   **130**

12. What is the sum of the measures of ∠2 and ∠6, in degrees?   **260**

13. Maryann bought a purse on sale for 25% off. She paid $36 for the purse before tax. How much did the purse cost originally?   **48**

14. What is the value of the expression $-2xy + y^2$, when $x = -1$ and $y = 4$?   **24**

15. A parallelogram has vertices at $A(-2, 4)$, $B(-1, -1)$, $C(1, 0)$, and $D(0, 5)$. What is the x-coordinate of B after the parallelogram is reflected over the y-axis?   **1**

16. Guillermo invests $180 at a 4% simple interest rate for 6 months. How much money will Guillermo earn in interest? Write your answer as a decimal to the nearest tenth.   **3.60**

Short Response

17. Triangle ABC, with vertices $A(2, 3)$, $B(4, -5)$, $C(6, 8)$, is reflected across the x-axis to form triangle $A'B'C'$.

   a. On a coordinate grid, draw and label triangle ABC and triangle $A'B'C'$.

   b. Give the new coordinates for triangle $A'B'C'$.

18. Complete the table to show the number of diagonals for the polygons with the numbers of sides listed.

Number of Sides	Number of Diagonals
3	0
4	▨
5	▨
6	▨
7	▨
n	▨

Extended Response

19. Four people are introduced to each other at a party, and they all shake hands.

   a. Explain in words how the diagram can be used to determine the number of handshakes exchanged at the party.

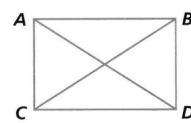

   b. How many handshakes are exchanged?

   c. Suppose that six people were introduced to each other at a party. Draw a diagram similar to the one shown that could be used to determine the number of handshakes exchanged.

Short Response Rubric

Items 17–18

2 Points = The student's answer is an accurate and complete execution of the task or tasks.

1 Point = The student's answer contains attributes of an appropriate response but is flawed.

0 Points = The student's answer contains no attributes of an appropriate response.

Extended Response Rubric

Item 19

4 points = The student demonstrates a thorough understanding of all concepts and shows all work correctly.

3 points = The student demonstrates a basic understanding of all concepts, but the work shows some flaws reflecting inattentive execution of mathematical procedures or some misunderstanding of the underlying mathematics.

2 points = The student demonstrates only a partial understanding of the concepts or procedures embodied in the tasks. The approach may be correct, but the work shows a misunderstanding of one or more important concepts.

1 point = The student demonstrates a very limited understanding of the concepts or procedures embodied in the tasks. The response may show some understanding but exhibits many flaws or is incomplete.

0 points = The student provides no response at all or a completely incorrect or uninterpretable response.

Student Work Samples for Item 19

4-Point Response

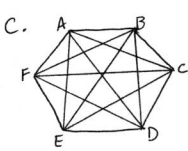

> 19. a. Each vertex is a different person at the party. The lines connecting the vertices are handshakes.
> b. 6 handshakes
> c.

The student correctly explained the diagram in part **a,** calculated the number of handshakes in part **b,** and drew a correct diagram for part **c.**

3-Point Response

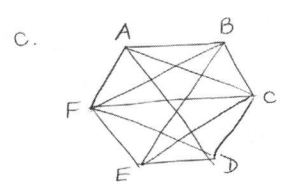

> 19. a. The letters represent the people and the diagonals represent their handshakes.
> b. 6 diagonals ⇒ 6 handshakes
> c.

The student correctly interpreted and applied the given diagram, but failed to draw two of the diagonals in the diagram for part **c.**

2-Point Response

> 19. a. Each letter is a person.
> b. 6
> c.

The student correctly explained part of the diagram in part **a,** and correctly calculated the number of handshakes in part **b.** The explanation is insufficient.

Cumulative Assessment, Chapters 1–7   **383**

CHAPTER 8

Perimeter, Area, and Volume

Section 8A
Perimeter and Area

8-1 **Perimeter and Area of Rectangles and Parallelograms**
8-2 **Hands-On Lab** Explore the Effects of Changing Dimensions
8-2 **Perimeter and Area of Triangles and Trapezoids**
8-3 **Hands-On Lab** Approximate *Pi* by Measuring
8-3 **Circles**

Section 8B
Three-Dimensional Geometry

8-4 **Hands-On Lab** Construct Nets
8-4 **Drawing Three-Dimensional Figures**
8-5 **Hands-On Lab** Find Volume of Prisms and Cylinders
8-5 **Volume of Prisms and Cylinders**
8-6 **Hands-On Lab** Find Volume of Pyramids and Cones
8-6 **Volume of Pyramids and Cones**
8-7 **Hands-On Lab** Find Surface Area of Prisms and Cylinders
8-7 **Surface Area of Prisms and Cylinders**
8-8 **Hands-On Lab** Find Surface Area of Pyramids
8-8 **Surface Area of Pyramids and Cones**
8-9 **Spheres**
8-10 **Scaling Three-Dimensional Figures**
EXTENSION **Symmetry in Three Dimensions**

Pacing Guide for 45-Minute Classes

Chapter 8

Countdown to Testing Weeks **15**, **16**, **17**, **18**

DAY 1	DAY 2	DAY 3	DAY 4	DAY 5
8-1 Lesson	8-1 Hands-On Lab 8-2 Lesson	8-2 Lesson 8-3 Hands-On Lab	8-3 Lesson	Ready to Go On? Focus on Problem Solving 8-4 Hands-On Lab
DAY 6	**DAY 7**	**DAY 8**	**DAY 9**	**DAY 10**
8-4 Hands-On Lab 8-4 Lesson	8-4 Lesson 8-5 Hands-On Lab	8-5 Hands-On Lab 8-5 Lesson	8-5 Lesson 8-6 Hands-On Lab	8-6 Hands-On Lab 8-6 Lesson
DAY 11	**DAY 12**	**DAY 13**	**DAY 14**	**DAY 15**
8-6 Lesson 8-7 Hands-On Lab	8-7 Hands-On Lab 8-7 Lesson	8-7 Lesson 8-8 Hands-On Lab	8-8 Lesson	8-9 Lesson
DAY 16	**DAY 17**	**DAY 18**	**DAY 19**	
8-10 Lesson	Ready to Go On? Multi-Step Test Prep **EXTENSION**	**CHAPTER 8 REVIEW**	**CHAPTER 8 TEST**	

Pacing Guide for 90-Minute Classes

Chapter 8

DAY 1	DAY 2	DAY 3	DAY 4	DAY 5
8-1 Lesson 8-1 Hands-On Lab 8-2 Lesson	8-2 Lesson 8-3 Technology Lab 8-3 Lesson	Ready to Go On? Focus on Problem Solving 8-4 Hands-On Lab 8-4 Lesson	8-4 Lesson 8-5 Hands-On Lab 8-5 Lesson	8-5 Lesson 8-6 Hands-On Lab 8-6 Lesson
DAY 6	**DAY 7**	**DAY 8**	**DAY 9**	**DAY 10**
8-6 Lesson 8-7 Hands-On Lab 8-7 Lesson	8-7 Lesson 8-8 Hands-On Lab 8-8 Lesson	8-9 Lesson 8-10 Lesson	Ready to Go On? Multi-Step Test Prep **EXTENSION** Chapter 8 Review	Chapter 8 Test

ONGOING ASSESSMENT and INTERVENTION

DIAGNOSE	PRESCRIBE

Assess Prior Knowledge

Before Chapter 8

Diagnose readiness for the chapter.	Prescribe intervention.
Are You Ready? SE p. 385	**Are You Ready? Intervention** Skills 11, 40, 44, 45

Formative Assessment

Before Every Lesson

Diagnose readiness for the lesson.	Prescribe intervention.
Warm Up TE, every lesson	**Skills Bank** SE pp. 820–834
	Reteach CRB, Chapters 1–8

During Every Lesson

Diagnose understanding of lesson concepts.	Prescribe intervention.
Think and Discuss SE, every lesson	**Questioning Strategies** Chapter 8
Write About It SE, lesson exercises	**Reading Strategies** CRB, every lesson
Journal TE, lesson exercises	**Success for ELL** pp. 111–130

After Every Lesson

Diagnose mastery of lesson concepts.	Prescribe intervention.
Lesson Quiz TE, every lesson	**Reteach** CRB, every lesson
Test Prep SE, every lesson	**Problem Solving** CRB, every lesson
Test and Practice Generator	**Test Prep Doctor** TE, lesson exercises
	Homework Help Online

Before Chapter 8 Testing

Diagnose mastery of concepts in the chapter.	Prescribe intervention.
Ready to Go On? SE pp. 404, 444	**Ready to Go On? Intervention** Chapter 8
Focus on Problem Solving SE p. 405	**Scaffolding Questions** TE p. 445
Multi-Step Test Prep SE p. 445	
Section Quizzes AR pp. 145–146	
Test and Practice Generator	

Before High Stakes Testing

Diagnose mastery of benchmark concepts.	Prescribe intervention.
Test Tackler SE pp. 380–381	**State Test Prep Workbook**
Standardized Test Prep SE pp. 382–383	
State Test Prep CD-ROM	

Summative Assessment

After Chapter 8

Check mastery of chapter concepts.	Prescribe intervention.
Multiple-Choice Tests (Forms A, B, C)	**Reteach** CRB, every lesson
Free-Response Tests (Forms A, B, C)	**Lesson Tutorial Videos** Chapter 8
Performance Assessment AR pp. 147–160	
Test and Practice Generator	
Check mastery of benchmark concepts.	Prescribe intervention.
AYP State Tests	**State Test Prep Workbook**

KEY: **SE** = *Student Edition* **TE** = *Teacher's Edition* **CRB** = *Chapter Resource Book* **AR** = *Assessment Resources* 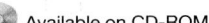 Available on CD-ROM  Available online **384B**

CHAPTER 8

Supporting the Teacher

Chapter 8 Resource Book

Practice A, B, C
pp. 3–5, 12–14, 21–23, 29–31, 38–40, 47–49, 56–58, 65–67, 74–76, 82–84

Reading Strategies ELL
pp. 10, 19, 27, 36, 45, 54, 63, 72, 80, 89

Puzzles, Twisters, and Teasers
pp. 11, 20, 28, 37, 46, 55, 64, 73, 81, 90

Reteach
pp. 6–7, 15–16, 24, 32–33, 41–42, 50–51, 59–60, 68–69, 77, 85–86

Problem Solving
pp. 9, 18, 26, 35, 44, 53, 62, 71, 79, 88

Challenge
pp. 8, 17, 25, 34, 43, 52, 61, 70, 78, 87

Parent Letter   pp. 1–2

Transparencies

Lesson Transparencies, Volume 2 .... Chapter 8
• Warm Ups
• Problem of the Day
• Teaching Transparencies
• Lesson Quizzes

Know-It Notebook .... Chapter 8
• Additional Examples   • Chapter Review
• Vocabulary   • Big Ideas

Alternate Openers: Explorations .... pp. 56–65

Countdown to Testing .... pp. 29–36

Teacher Tools

Power Presentations®
Complete PowerPoint® presentations for Chapter 8 lessons

Lesson Tutorial Videos® SPANISH
Holt authors Ed Burger and Freddie Renfro present tutorials to support the Chapter 8 lessons.

One-Stop Planner® SPANISH
Easy access to all Chapter 8 resources and assessments, as well as software for lesson planning, test generation, and puzzle creation

IDEA Works!®
Key Chapter 8 resources and assessments modified to address special learning needs

Lesson Plans .... pp. 56–65

Questioning Strategies .... Chapter 8

Solutions Key .... Chapter 8

Interdisciplinary Posters and Worksheets .... Chapter 8

TechKeys   **Lab Resources**

Project Teacher Support   **Parent Resources**

Workbooks

Homework and Practice Workbook SPANISH
Teacher's Guide .... pp. 28–33

Know-It Notebook
Teacher's Guide .... Chapter 8

Problem Solving Workbook SPANISH
Teacher's Guide .... pp. 28–33

State Test Prep Workbook
Teacher's Guide

Technology Highlights for the Teacher

 Power Presentations
Dynamic presentations to engage students. Complete PowerPoint® presentations for every lesson in Chapter 8.

2-1 Solving One-Step Equations

Isolate a variable by using inverse operations which "undo" operations on the variable.

An equation is like a balanced scale. To keep the balance, perform the same operation on both sides.

Inverse Operations	
Operation	**Inverse Operation**
Addition	Subtraction
Subtraction	Addition

 One-Stop Planner SPANISH
Easy access to Chapter 8 resources and assessments. Includes lesson-planning, test-generation, and puzzle-creation software.

 Premier Online Edition SPANISH
Chapter 8 includes Tutorial Videos, Lesson Activities, Lesson Quizzes, Homework Help, and Chapter Project.

KEY: **SE** = *Student Edition*   **TE** = *Teacher's Edition*   ELL English Language Learners   SPANISH Spanish version available   Available on CD-ROM    Available online

CHAPTER 8

Reaching All Learners

Resources for All Learners

Hands-On Lab Activities.................................... Chapter 8

Technology Lab Activities.................................... Chapter 8

Homework and Practice Workbook SPANISH ....pp. 56–65

Know-It Notebook.. Chapter 8

Problem Solving Workbook SPANISH ....pp. 56–65

DEVELOPING LEARNERS

Practice A..CRB, every lesson

Reteach..CRB, every lesson

Inclusion..............................TE pp. 428, 433, 446

Questioning Strategies.................................... Chapter 8

Modified Chapter 8 Resources .... *IDEA Works!*

Homework Help **Online**

ON-LEVEL LEARNERS

Practice B..CRB, every lesson

Puzzles, Twisters, and Teasers................CRB, every lesson

Multiple Representations.........................TE p. 389, 409

Cognitive Strategies....................................TE p. 428

ADVANCED LEARNERS

Practice C..CRB, every lesson

Challenge...CRB, every lesson

Extension...............................TE pp. 323, 373, 374, 375

Critical Thinking....................................TE pp. 395, 421

English Language Learners

ENGLISH LANGUAGE LEARNERS

Are You Ready? Vocabulary .... SE p. 385

Vocabulary Connections.................................... SE p. 386

Lesson Vocabulary ....SE, every lesson

Vocabulary Review... SE p. 450

English Language Learners.............TE pp. 387, 401, 446, 457

Reading Strategies ....CRB, every lesson

Success for English Language Learners..............pp. 111–130

Multilingual Glossary

Reaching All Learners Through...

Inclusion...............................TE pp. 428, 433, 446

Visual Cues.....................................TE pp. 409, 447

Kinesthetic Experience ....TE pp. 401, 421

Concrete Manipulatives...........................TE pp. 437, 441

Multiple Representations.........................TE pp. 389, 409

Cognitive Strategies ....TE p. 428

Modeling...TE pp. 414, 433

Critical Thinking...............................TE pp. 395, 421

Test Prep Doctor...................TE pp. 392, 398, 403, 411, 417, 424, 435, 439, 443, 454

Common Error Alerts ....TE pp. 409, 447

Scaffolding Questions................................TE p. 445

Technology Highlights for Reaching All Learners

Lesson Tutorial Videos SPANISH

Starring Holt authors Ed Burger and Freddie Renfro! Live tutorials to support every lesson in Chapter 8.

Multilingual Glossary

Searchable glossary includes definitions in English, Spanish, Vietnamese, Chinese, Hmong, Korean, and 4 other languages.

Online Interactivities

Interactive tutorials provide visually engaging alternative opportunities to learn concepts and master skills.

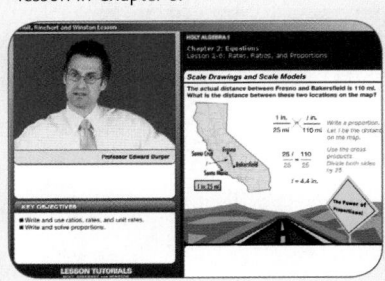
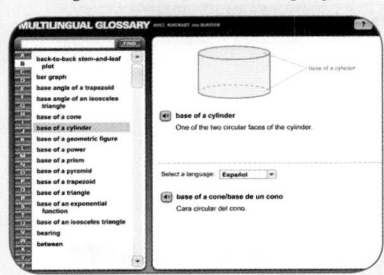
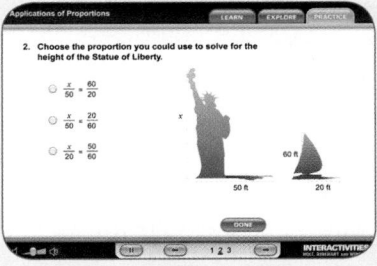

KEY: **SE** = *Student Edition* **TE** = *Teacher's Edition* **CRB** = *Chapter Resource Book* SPANISH Spanish version available Available on CD-ROM Available online

CHAPTER
8

Ongoing Assessment

Assessing Prior Knowledge

Determine whether students have the prerequisite concepts and skills for success in Chapter 8.

Are You Ready? SPANISH .... SE p. 385

Warm Up .... TE, every lesson

Test Preparation

Provide review and practice for Chapter 8 and standardized tests.

Multi-Step Test Prep .... SE p. 445

Study Guide: Review .... SE pp. 450–452

Standardized Test Prep .... SE pp. 454–455

Countdown to Testing Transparencies ....pp. 29–36

State Test Prep Workbook

State Test Prep CD-ROM

IDEA Works!

Alternative Assessment

Assess students' understanding of Chapter 8 concepts and combined problem-solving skills.

Chapter 8 Project .... SE p. 384

Performance Assessment SPANISH ......AR pp. 159–160

Portfolio Assessment SPANISH ....AR p. xxxiv

Daily Assessment

Provide formative assessment for each day of Chapter 8.

Questioning Strategies .... Chapter 8

Think and Discuss .... SE, every lesson

Write About It .... SE, lesson exercises

Journal .... TE, lesson exercises

Lesson Quiz .... TE, every lesson

Modified Lesson Quizzes .... IDEA Works!

Weekly Assessment

Provide formative assessment for each week of Chapter 8.

Focus on Problem Solving .... SE p. 405

Multi-Step Test Prep .... SE p. 445

Ready to Go On? SPANISH .... SE pp. 404, 444

Cumulative Assessment .... SE pp. 454–455

Test and Practice Generator SPANISH ...One-Stop Planner

Formal Assessment

Provide summative assessment of Chapter 8 mastery.

Section Quizzes SPANISH ....AR pp. 145–146

Chapter 8 Test .... SE p. 453

Chapter Test (Levels A, B, C) SPANISH ....AR pp. 147–158
        • Multiple-Choice   • Free-Response

Cumulative Test SPANISH ....AR pp. 161–164

Test and Practice Generator SPANISH ...One-Stop Planner

Modified Chapter 8 Test .... IDEA Works!

Technology Highlights for the Teacher

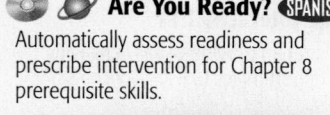 **Are You Ready?** SPANISH
Automatically assess readiness and prescribe intervention for Chapter 8 prerequisite skills.

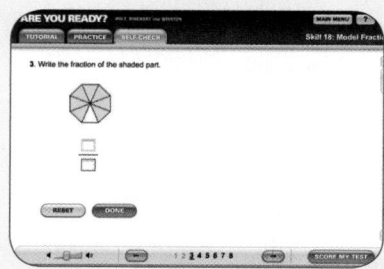

 **Ready to Go On?** SPANISH
Automatically assess understanding of and prescribe intervention for Sections 8A and 8B.

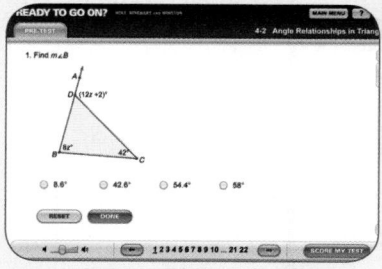

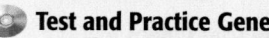 **Test and Practice Generator** SPANISH
Use Chapter 8 problem banks to create assessments and worksheets to print out or deliver online. Includes dynamic problems.

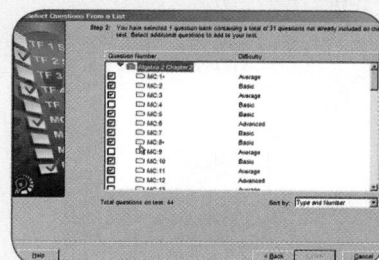

KEY: **SE** = *Student Edition*   **TE** = *Teacher's Edition*   **AR** = *Assessment Resources*   SPANISH Spanish version available   Available on CD-ROM    Available online

Formal Assessment

Three levels (A, B, C) of multiple-choice and free-response chapter tests are available in the *Assessment Resources.*

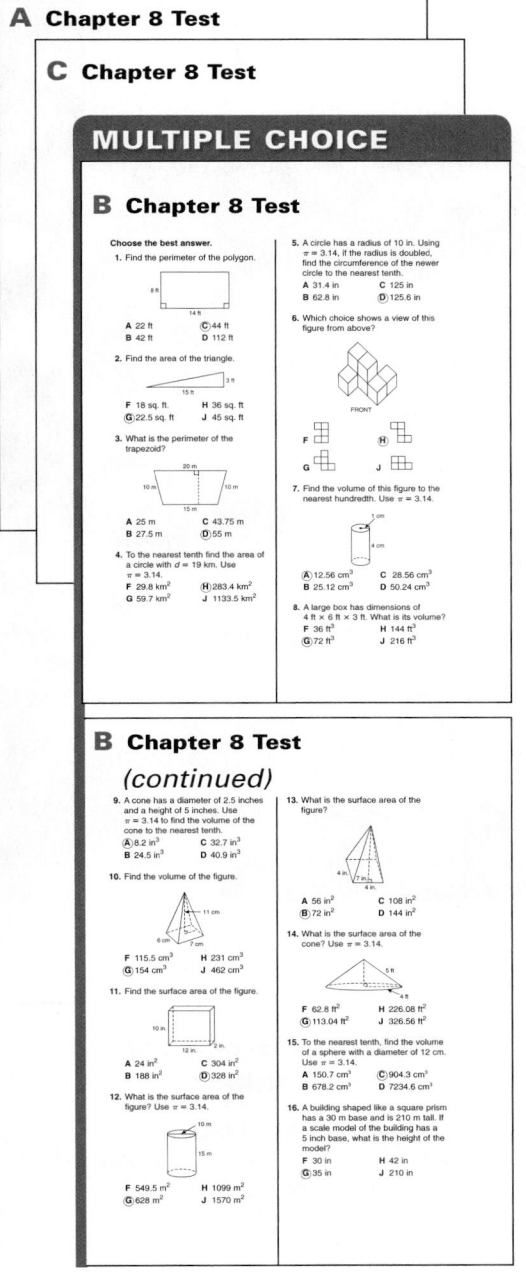

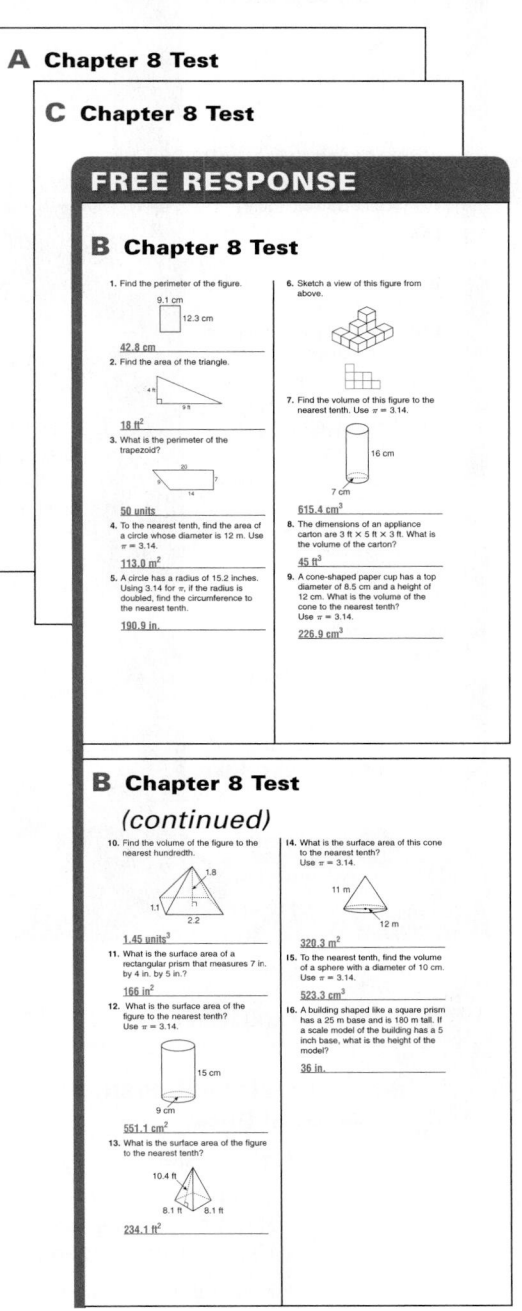

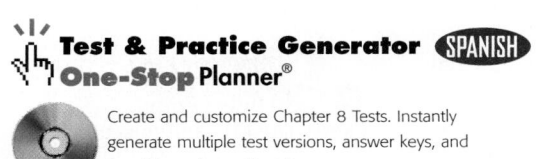

Test & Practice Generator SPANISH
One-Stop Planner®

Create and customize Chapter 8 Tests. Instantly generate multiple test versions, answer keys, and Spanish versions of test items.

384F

Why Learn This?

Tell students that in many careers it is essential to have the ability to recognize two-dimensional (flat) images as three-dimensional objects. Surgeons use flat on-screen images to determine the shapes of masses before operating on them. Also, builders use two-dimensional plans consisting of front and side views of buildings.

Using Data

To begin the study of this chapter, have students:

- Identify each shape in the table.
  A: cone; B: cylinder; C: rectangular prism (box)
- Draw the front, top, and side views of their pencil. Possible answers:

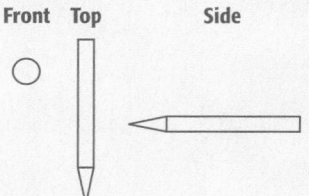

Front   Top   Side

MULTI-STEP TEST PREP On page 445, students use perimeter, area, and volume formulas to calculate data about a family farm.

Perimeter, Area, and Volume

8A	Perimeter and Area
8-1	Perimeter and Area of Rectangles and Parallelograms
LAB	Explore the Effects of Changing Dimensions
8-2	Perimeter and Area of Triangles and Trapezoids
LAB	Approximate *Pi* by Measuring
8-3	Circles
8B	Three-Dimensional Geometry
LAB	Construct Nets
8-4	Drawing Three-Dimensional Figures
LAB	Find Volume of Prisms and Cylinders
8-5	Volume of Prisms and Cylinders
LAB	Find Volume of Pyramids and Cones
8-6	Volume of Pyramids and Cones
LAB	Find Surface Area of Prisms and Cylinders
8-7	Surface Area of Prisms and Cylinders
LAB	Find Surface Area of Pyramids
8-8	Surface Area of Pyramids and Cones
8-9	Spheres
8-10	Scaling Three-Dimensional Figures
Ext	Symmetry in Three Dimensions

MULTI-STEP TEST PREP

go.hrw.com
Chapter Project Online
KEYWORD: MT7 Ch8

Mystery Solid	Front View	Side View	Top View
A	△	△	○
B	▢	▢	○
C	▢	▢	▢

Career *Surgeon*

Today, some surgeons perform specialized operations known as laser surgery. With many laser surgeries, surgeons cannot actually see the three-dimensional area where they are operating; instead, they must rely on what they can see in two-dimensional images projected onto a screen to guide them. See if you can identify each three-dimensional "mystery solid" based on the two-dimensional views in the table.

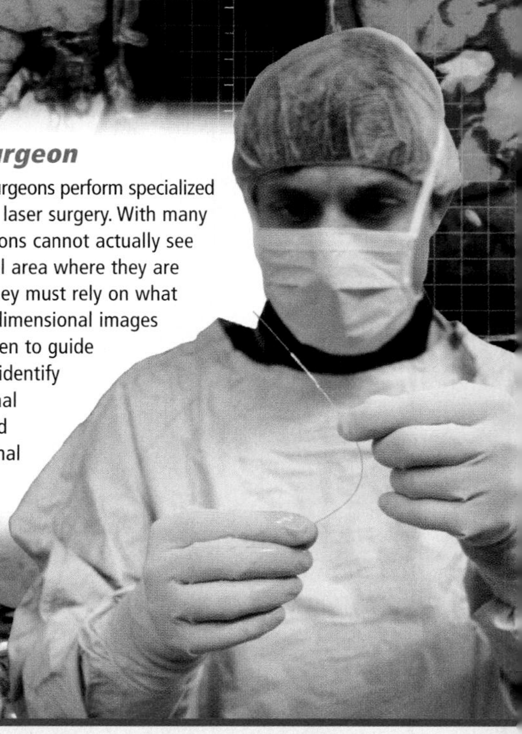

Problem Solving Project

Understand, Plan, Solve, and Look Back

Have students:

- Complete the Mystery Solids worksheet to become familiar with the characteristics of geometric solids.
- Play a game by taking turns showing parts of a three-dimensional object on the overhead and having classmates see how much of the object must be revealed before they can identify the object.
- Do research to discover information on laparoscopic surgery. Interview people who have had laparoscopic surgery or a surgeon who performs the surgery.

Physical Science and Life Science Connection

Project Resources

All project resources for teachers and students are provided online.

Materials:

- The Mystery Solids worksheet
- geometrical and common-item mystery solids
- overhead projector

go.hrw.com
Project Teacher Support
KEYWORD: MT7 PSProject8

ARE YOU READY?

✓ Vocabulary

Choose the best term from the list to complete each sentence.

1. A(n) __?__ is a number that represents a part of a whole. **fraction**

2. A(n) __?__ is another way of writing a fraction. **decimal**

3. To multiply 7 by the fraction $\frac{2}{3}$, multiply 7 by the __?__ of the fraction and then divide the result by the __?__ of the fraction. **numerator; denominator**

4. To round 7.836 to the nearest tenth, look at the digit in the __?__ place. **hundredths**

decimal

denominator

fraction

tenths

hundredths

numerator

Complete these exercises to review skills you will need for this chapter.

✓ Square and Cube Numbers

Evaluate.

5. 16^2 **256**
6. 9^3 **729**
7. $(4.1)^2$ **16.81**
8. $(0.5)^3$ **0.125**

9. $\left(\frac{1}{4}\right)^2$ **$\frac{1}{16}$**
10. $\left(\frac{2}{5}\right)^2$ **$\frac{4}{25}$**
11. $\left(\frac{1}{2}\right)^3$ **$\frac{1}{8}$**
12. $\left(\frac{2}{3}\right)^3$ **$\frac{8}{27}$**

✓ Multiply with Fractions

Multiply.

13. $\frac{1}{2}(8)(10)$ **40**
14. $\frac{1}{2}(3)(5)$ **$7\frac{1}{2}$**
15. $\frac{1}{3}(9)(12)$ **36**
16. $\frac{1}{3}(4)(11)$ **$14\frac{2}{3}$**

17. $\frac{1}{2}(8^2)16$ **512**
18. $\frac{1}{2}(5^2)24$ **300**
19. $\frac{1}{2}(6)(3+9)$ **36**
20. $\frac{1}{2}(5)(7+4)$ **$27\frac{1}{2}$**

✓ Multiply with Decimals

Multiply. Write each answer to the nearest tenth.

21. $2(3.14)(12)$ **75.4**
22. $3.14(5^2)$ **78.5**
23. $3.14(4^2)(7)$ **351.7**
24. $3.14(2.3)^2(5)$ **83.1**

✓ Multiply with Fractions and Decimals

Multiply. Write each answer to the nearest tenth.

25. $\frac{1}{3}(3.14)(5^2)(7)$ **183.2**
26. $\frac{1}{3}(3.14)(5^3)$ **130.8**

27. $\frac{1}{3}(3.14)(3.2)^2(2)$ **21.4**
28. $\frac{4}{3}(3.14)(2.7)^3$ **82.4**

29. $\frac{1}{5}\left(\frac{22}{7}\right)(4^2)(5)$ **50.3**
30. $\frac{4}{11}\left(\frac{22}{7}\right)(3.2^3)$ **37.4**

31. $\frac{1}{2}\left(\frac{22}{7}\right)(1.7)^2(4)$ **18.2**
32. $\frac{7}{11}\left(\frac{22}{7}\right)(9.5)^3$ **1714.8**

Organizer

Objective: Assess students' understanding of prerequisite skills.

Prerequisite Skills

Square and Cube Numbers

Multiply with Fractions

Multiply with Decimals

Multiply with Fractions and Decimals

Assessing Prior Knowledge

INTERVENTION

Diagnose and Prescribe

Use this page to determine whether intervention is necessary or whether enrichment is appropriate.

Resources

 Are You Ready? Intervention and Enrichment Worksheets

 Are You Ready? CD-ROM

Are You Ready? Online

my.hrw.com

ARE YOU READY?
Diagnose and Prescribe

 **NO INTERVENE**

 **YES ENRICH**

✓ Prerequisite Skill	〰 Worksheets	💿 CD-ROM	🪐 Online
	ARE YOU READY? Intervention, Chapter 8		
✓ Square and Cube Numbers	Skill 11	Activity 11	Diagnose and Prescribe Online
✓ Multiply with Fractions	Skill 44	Activity 44	
✓ Multiply with Decimals	Skill 40	Activity 40	
✓ Multiply with Fractions and Decimals	Skill 45	Activity 45	

ARE YOU READY? Enrichment, Chapter 8

〰 **Worksheets**

💿 **CD-ROM**

🪐 **Online**

Organizer

Objective: Help students organize the new concepts they will learn in Chapter 8.

 Online Edition
Multilingual Glossary

Resources

PuzzlePro®
One-Stop Planner®

 Multilingual Glossary Online

go.hrw.com
KEYWORD: MT7 Glossary

Possible answers to *Vocabulary Connections*

1. The circumference of a circle is the distance around the circle.
2. Perimeter is the distance around the outside of a figure.
3. The diameter of a circle is the distance across the circle.

Study Guide: Preview

Where You've Been

Previously, you

- found the perimeter and area of polygons.
- sketched a three-dimensional figure when given the top, side, and front views.
- found the volume of prisms and cylinders.

In This Chapter

You will study

- describing the effects on perimeter and area when the dimensions of a figure change proportionally.
- drawing three-dimensional figures from different perspectives.
- describing the effect on volume when the dimensions of a solid change proportionally.
- finding the surface area and volume of various solids.

Where You're Going

You can use the skills learned in this chapter

- to determine the amount of materials needed to build a fence.
- to determine the amount of paint needed to paint a wall.

Key Vocabulary/Vocabulario

circle	círculo
circumference	circunferincia
cone	cono
cylinder	cilindro
diameter	diámetro
perimeter	perímetro
prism	prisma
pyramid	pirámide
sphere	esfera
surface area	área total

Vocabulary Connections

To become familiar with some of the vocabulary terms in the chapter, consider the following. You may refer to the chapter, the glossary, or a dictionary if you like.

1. The word **circumference** contains the prefix *circum-*, which means "around." What do you suppose the circumference of a circle is?
2. The Greek prefix *peri-* means "around," and the root *meter* means "means of measuring." What do you suppose **perimeter** means?
3. The Greek prefix *dia-* means "across." What do you suppose the **diameter** of a circle is?

Study Strategy: Concept Map

Concept maps are visual tools for organizing information. A concept map shows how key concepts are related and can help you summarize and analyze information in lessons or chapters.

Create a Concept Map

1. Give your concept map a title.

2. Identify the main idea of your concept map.

3. List the key concepts.

4. Link the concepts to show the relationships between the concepts and the main idea.

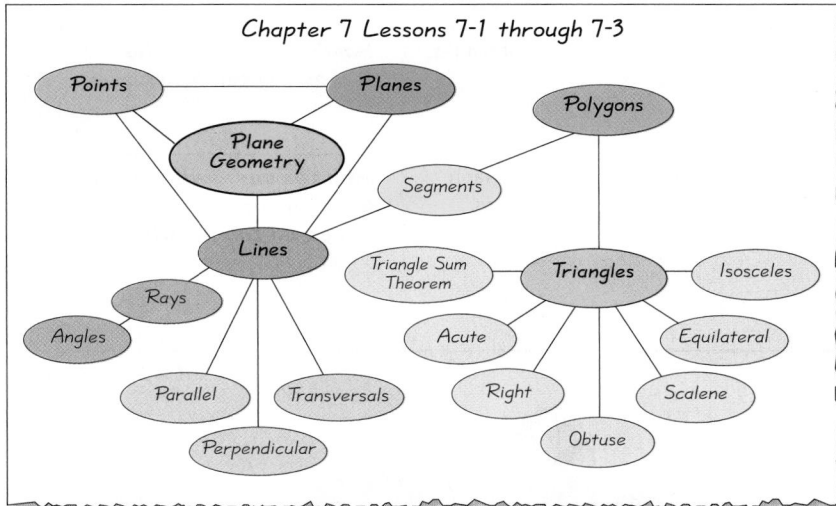

Chapter 7 Lessons 7-1 through 7-3

Try This

1. Complete the concept map above to include Lessons 7-4 and 7-5.

2. Create your own concept map for the concept of transformations.

Reading and Writing Math

Organizer

Objective: Help students apply strategies to understand and retain key concepts.

 Online Edition

Resources

 **Chapter 8 Resource Book**
Reading Strategies

Study Strategy: Concept Map

 ENGLISH LANGUAGE LEARNERS

Discuss Students will retain information longer when they organize it in a way that makes sense to them. A concept map is especially helpful to visual learners. Be sure students realize that there is more than one way to organize information within a concept map.

Extend As students work through Chapter 8, ask them to make a concept map of any lessons they found particularly difficult. Encourage them to exchange their maps with others. This may give them added insight into particular concepts covered in the chapter.

Possible answers to *Try This*

1–2. See p. A10.

One-Minute Section Planner

Lesson	Materials	MiC and Lab Resources
Lesson 8-1 Perimeter and Area of Rectangles and Parallelograms • Find the perimeter and area of rectangles and parallelograms. **8-1 Hands-On Lab** Explore the Effects of Changing Dimensions • Use grid paper to explore how changing dimensions of a figure affects the figure's perimeter and area. ☑ SAT-10 ☑ ITBS ☑ CTBS ☑ NAEP	Grid paper	**MiC:** *Algebra Rules* pp. 42–46 **MiC:** *Ups and Downs* pp. 23–27 ***Hands-On Lab Activities*** 8-1
Lesson 8-2 Perimeter and Area of Triangles and Trapezoids • Find the area of triangles and trapezoids. ☑ SAT-10 ☑ ITBS ☑ CTBS ☑ NAEP	Graph paper, cutout figures, scissors	***Hands-On Lab Activities*** 8-2 ***Technology Lab Activities*** 8-2
8-3 Hands-On Lab Approximate *Pi* by Measuring • Use a ruler and string to measure circles. **Lesson 8-3** Circles • Find the area and circumference of circles. ☑ SAT-10 ☑ ITBS ☑ CTBS ☑ NAEP	Rulers (MK), string, graph paper, calculators, cans, measuring tape (MK)	**MiC:** *Ups and Downs* pp. 27–28 **MiC:** *Algebra Rules* p. 15 ***Hands-On Lab Activities*** 8-3

MK = *Manipulatives Kit*

Mathematics in Context

The units **Ups and Downs** and **Algebra Rules** from the *Mathematics in Context* © 2006 series can be used with Section 8A. See Section Planner above for suggestions for integrating *MiC* with *Holt Mathematics*.

Section Overview

Perimeter and Area of Polygons

Lessons 8-1, 8-2

Why? It is necessary to understand perimeter and area for many real-world applications.

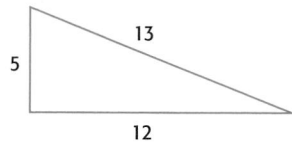

Perimeter is the distance around a figure.

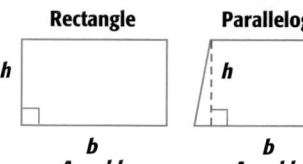

Area is the number of square units inside a figure.

$P = 5 + 12 + 13 = 30$ units

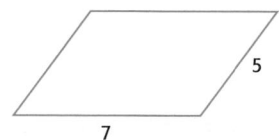

$P = 5 + 5 + 7 + 7 = 24$ units

Rectangle

$A = bh$

Parallelogram

$A = bh$

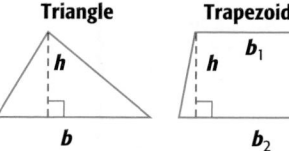

Triangle

$A = \frac{1}{2}bh$

Trapezoid

$A = \frac{1}{2}h(b_1 + b_2)$

Area and Circumference of Circles

Lesson 8-3

Why? You can find the area and circumference of a circle if you know its radius or diameter.

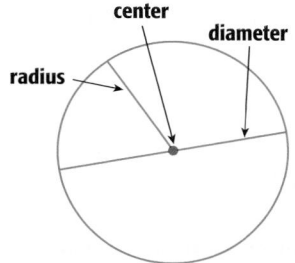

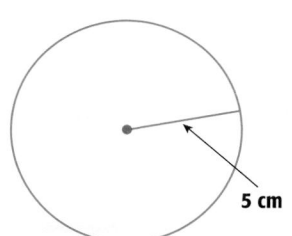

Circumference	Area
$C = \pi d$, or $2\pi r$	$A = \pi r^2$
$= \pi(10)$	$= \pi(5)^2$
$\approx 3.14(10)$	$\approx 3.14(25)$
≈ 31.4 cm	≈ 78.5 cm^2

Use 3.14 or $\frac{22}{7}$ to approximate π.

Objective: Students find perimeter and area of rectangles and parallelograms.

Hands-On Lab
In *Hands-On Lab Activities*

Online Edition
Tutorial Videos

Countdown to Testing Week 15

Power Presentations
with PowerPoint®

Warm Up

Graph the line segment for each set of ordered pairs. Then find the length of the line segment.

1. (−7, 0), (0, 0)   7 units

2. (0, 3), (0, 6)   3 units

3. (−4, −2), (1, −2)   5 units

4. (−5, 4), (−5, −2)   6 units

Problem of the Day

Six pennies are placed around a seventh so that there are no gaps. What figure is formed by connecting the centers of the six outer pennies? a regular hexagon

Also available on transparency

State Resources

go.hrw.com
State Resources Online
KEYWORD: MT7 Resources

8-1 Perimeter & Area of Rectangles & Parallelograms

Learn to find the perimeter and area of rectangles and parallelograms.

Vocabulary
perimeter
area

The NAMES Project Foundation's AIDS Memorial Quilt is a tribute to those who have died of AIDS. The quilt contains more than 82,800 names on more than 44,000 rectangular panels that measure 3 ft by 6 ft. To find the size of the entire quilt, you need to be able to find the perimeter and area of a rectangle.

Any side of a rectangle or parallelogram can be chosen as the base. The height is measured along a line perpendicular to the base.

Rectangle

Base

Parallelogram

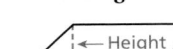
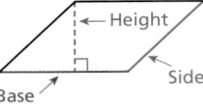

Base   Side

Perimeter is the distance around the outside of a figure. To find the perimeter of a figure, add the lengths of all its sides.

EXAMPLE 1 **Finding the Perimeter of Rectangles and Parallelograms**

Find the perimeter of each figure.

Caution!

When referring to the measurements of a rectangle, the terms *length* (ℓ) and *width* (w) are sometimes used in place of *base* (b) and *height* (h). So the formula for the perimeter of a rectangle can be written as
$P = 2b + 2h = 2ℓ + 2w = 2(ℓ + w)$.

A

4 cm
6 cm

$P = 6 + 6 + 4 + 4$ *Add all side lengths.*
$= 20$ cm

or $P = 2b + 2h$ *Perimeter of rectangle*
$= 2(6) + 2(4)$ *Substitute 6 for b and 4 for h.*
$= 12 + 8 = 20$ cm

B

5 ft
7 ft

$P = 5 + 5 + 7 + 7 = 24$ ft   *Add all side lengths.*

---

1 Introduce

Alternate Opener

EXPLORATION

8-1 Perimeter and Area of Rectangles and Parallelograms

Recall that the area of a rectangle is the product of its length times its width, or the product of its base times its height, *bh*. You can use this fact to develop the formula for the area of a parallelogram.

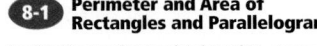

1. Draw a parallelogram on a sheet of graph paper. Label the base and height as shown.

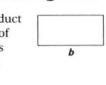

2. Cut out the parallelogram.

3. Now cut a right triangle off the end of the parallelogram as shown.

4. Arrange the two pieces to form a rectangle.

5. What are the base and height of the rectangle you made? What is the rectangle's area?

6. How is the area of the parallelogram related to the area of the rectangle?

Think and Discuss

7. **Explain** how to write a formula for the area of a parallelogram with base *b* and height *h*.

8. **Describe** how you can use your formula to find the area of this parallelogram.

4 cm
6 cm

Motivate

Ask students how many measurements it would take to find the length of a wall in the classroom. one Explain that length is a *one-dimensional* measure because it requires only one measurement. Then ask them how many measurements it would take to find the size (area) of the floor. two Explain that area is *two-dimensional* because it requires two different measurements.

Explorations and answers are provided in *Alternate Openers: Explorations Transparencies.*

Area is the number of square units in a figure. A parallelogram can be cut and the cut piece shifted to form a rectangle with the same base length and height as the original parallelogram. So a parallelogram has the same area as a rectangle with the same base length and height.

Example 1

Find the perimeter of each figure.

A.

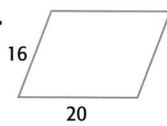
5
14

$P = 38$ units

B.

16
20

$P = 72$ units

Example 2

Graph and find the area of each figure with the given vertices.

A. $(-1, -2), (2, -2), (2, 3), (-1, 3)$

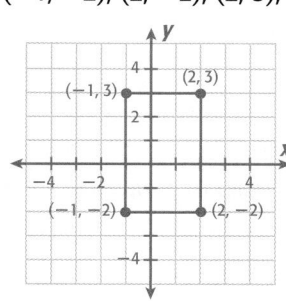
$(-1, 3)$ $(2, 3)$
$(-1, -2)$ $(2, -2)$

$A = 15$ units^2

AREA OF RECTANGLES AND PARALLELOGRAMS			
Words	**Numbers**		**Formula**
The area A of a rectangle or parallelogram is the base length b times the height h.	5 3 $5 \cdot 3 = 15$ units^2 **Rectangle**	5 3 $5 \cdot 3 = 15$ units^2 **Parallelogram**	$A = bh$

Helpful Hint

The formula for the area of a rectangle can also be written as $A = \ell w$.

EXAMPLE 2 Using a Graph to Find Area

Graph and find the area of each figure with the given vertices.

A $(-3, -2), (3, -2), (3, 1), (-3, 1)$

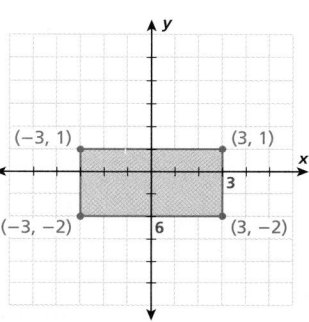
$(-3, 1)$ $(3, 1)$
3
$(-3, -2)$ 6 $(3, -2)$

$A = bh$ *Area of rectangle*
$ = 6 \cdot 3$ *Substitute 6 for b and 3 for h.*
$ = 18$ units^2

---

2 Teach

Guided Instruction

In this lesson, students learn to find perimeter and area of rectangles and parallelograms. Explain to students that *perimeter* is the distance around the outside of a figure. Explain that the perimeter of a figure can be found by adding up all of its side lengths, or for some special figures, by using a formula. Emphasize that perimeter is measured in linear units. Explain that area is a measure of the space inside a two-dimensional figure. Show students how the area of a rectangle can be found by counting the number of unit squares in the figure (Teaching Transparency). For this reason, area is measured in square units.

Reaching All Learners
Through Multiple Representations

Have students use graph paper to find as many different rectangles as possible that have a perimeter of 16 units and then calculate the area of each. Then have them find as many different rectangles as possible that have an area of 24 units^2 and calculate the perimeter of each. Finally, have them describe any patterns they notice in the tables.

Additional Examples

Example 2

Graph and find the area of each figure with the given vertices.

B. (0, 0), (5, 0), (6, 4), (1, 4)

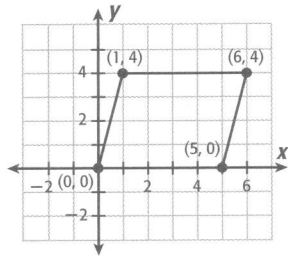

$A = 20$ units^2

Example 3

Find the perimeter and area of the figure.

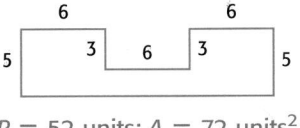

$P = 52$ units; $A = 72$ units^2

Also available on transparency

Answers to Think and Discuss

1. Possible answer: The area of the rectangle with base $2b$ and height $2h$ is four times the area of the rectangle with base b and height h.

2. Because the side lengths of a square are equal, both the base and the height can be represented by the same variable, s. Substituting s into both formulas for b and h gives $A = s^2$ and $P = 4s$.

Caution!

The height of a parallelogram is not the length of its slanted side. The height of a figure is always perpendicular to the base.

Graph and find the area of each figure with the given vertices.

B $(-4, -4), (1, -4), (3, 0), (-2, 0)$

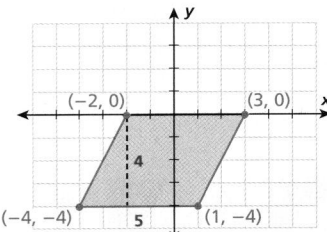

$A = bh$ *Area of rectangle*

$ = 5 \cdot 4$ *Substitute 5 for b and 4 for h.*

$ = 20$ units^2

EXAMPLE 3   **Finding Area and Perimeter of a Composite Figure**

Find the perimeter and area of the figure.

The length of the side that is not labeled is the same as the length of the opposite side, 2 m.

$P = 3 + 2 + 2 + 2 + 3 + 4 + 3 + 1 + 3$
$\ + 5 + 2 + 2$

$ = 32$ m

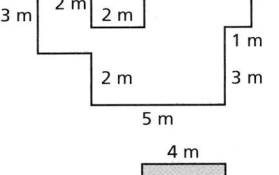

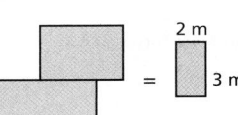

$A = (3 \cdot 2) + (5 \cdot 3) + (4 \cdot 3)$ *Add the areas together.*

$ = 6 + 15 + 12$

$ = 33$ m^2

Think and Discuss

1. **Compare** the area of a rectangle with base b and height h with the area of a rectangle with base $2b$ and height $2h$.

2. **Express** the formulas for the area and perimeter of a square using s for the length of a side.

3 Close

Summarize

Review the important differences between perimeter and area. Remind students that perimeter is the distance around a figure and is measured in linear units. Remind them that area is the space inside a figure and is measured in square units. Show students some concrete examples, such as a photograph. Ask students which measure would help you find how much wood you would need to frame the photograph. perimeter Then ask which would tell you how much glass you would need. area As a challenge, you may want to ask them to estimate both measures.

8-1 **Exercises**

go.hrw.com
Homework Help Online
KEYWORD: MT7 8-1
Parent Resources Online
KEYWORD: MT7 Parent

GUIDED PRACTICE

See Example **1**   Find the perimeter of each figure.

1.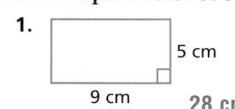
5 cm
9 cm
28 cm

2.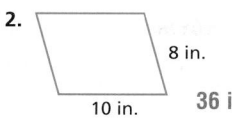
8 in.
10 in.
36 in.

3.
1.5x ft
4.6x ft
12.2x ft

See Example **2**   Graph and find the area of each figure with the given vertices.

4. $(-4, 3), (0, 3), (4, -1), (0, -1)$
16 units²

5. $(-2, -3), (-2, 0), (4, 0), (4, -3)$
18 units²

6. $(-6, -1), (-5, 2), (2, 2), (1, -1)$
21 units²

7. $(-2, 3), (0, 3), (0, -4), (-2, -4)$
14 units²

See Example **3**   **8.** Find the perimeter and area of the figure.
36 m; 29 m²

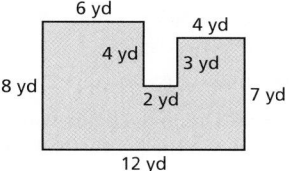
2 m   3 m   1 m
2 m
5 m   3 m
7 m
2 m

INDEPENDENT PRACTICE

See Example **1**   Find the perimeter of each figure.

9.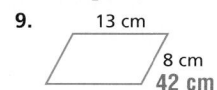
13 cm
8 cm
42 cm

10.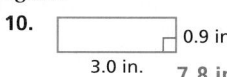
0.9 in.
3.0 in.
7.8 in.

11.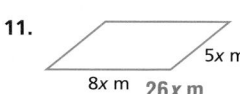
5x m
8x m   **26x m**

See Example **2**   Graph and find the area of each figure with the given vertices.

12. $(-1, -1), (-1, -6), (2, -6), (2, -1)$
15 units²

13. $(0, 3), (6, 3), (3, -1), (-3, -1)$
24 units²

14. $(-1, -2), (-1, 4), (1, 5), (1, -1)$
12 units²

15. $(3, -2), (6, -2), (6, 2), (3, 2)$
12 units²

See Example **3**   **16.** Find the perimeter and area of the figure.
46 yd; 84 yd²

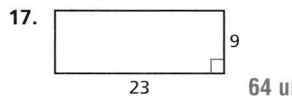
6 yd
4 yd
4 yd   3 yd
8 yd   2 yd   7 yd
12 yd

PRACTICE AND PROBLEM SOLVING

Extra Practice
See page 796.

Find the perimeter of each figure.

17.
9
23
64 units

18.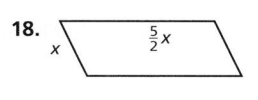
x $\frac{5}{2}x$
7x units

Assignment Guide

If you finished Example 1 assign:
Average   1–3, 9–11, 17, 18, 27–37
Advanced   9–11, 17, 18, 27–37

If you finished Example 2 assign:
Average   1–7, 9–15, 17, 18, 23, 27–37
Advanced   9–15, 17, 18, 21–24, 27–37

If you finished Example 3 assign:
Average   1–20, 23, 27–37
Advanced   9–37

Homework Quick Check

Quickly check key concepts.
Exercises: 10, 14, 16

Answers

4–7, 12–15. See p. A10.

Math Background

The concepts in this lesson are important for more advanced studies in geometry. Students should begin to develop an understanding of dimensions and appropriate units. An object that has one directional measure (e.g., length) is one-dimensional, and its length is measured in linear units. Similarly, an object with two different directional measures (e.g., length and width) is two-dimensional, and its area is measured in square units. It is also important that students be able to apply basic formulas, such as those presented in this lesson.

RETEACH 8-1

PRACTICE 8-1

State Resources

go.hrw.com
State Resources Online
KEYWORD: MT7 Resources

Answers

24. Possible answer: What is the area of the rectangle?

25. Possible answer: The figures have the same area, but the figure with the cutout has a larger perimeter because it has additional sides.

28. See p. A10.

 TEST PREP DOCTOR Encourage students to draw a diagram of the rectangle in Exercise 27 and to label each side with its possible measurements. This will help students identify the incorrect area answer choice.

 Journal

Ask students to write about a real-world situation in which they would need to find the perimeter and area of an object. Have them estimate the measures of the object they have chosen. Examples might include framing a picture or decorating a wall or floor.

Power Presentations
with PowerPoint®

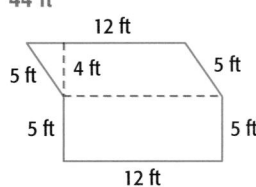

8-1 Lesson Quiz

1. Find the perimeter of the figure.
44 ft

12 ft
5 ft | 4 ft | 5 ft
5 ft | | 5 ft
12 ft

2. Find the area of the figure.
108 ft²

Graph the figure with the given vertices and find its area.
Complete answers on p. A10

3. $(-4, 2), (6, 2), (6, -3), (-4, -3)$
50 units²

4. $(4, -2), (-2, -2), (-3, 5), (3, 5)$
42 units²

Also available on transparency

Find the perimeter and area of each figure.

19.
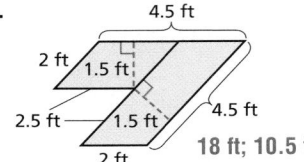
4.5 ft
2 ft 1.5 ft
2.5 ft 1.5 ft 4.5 ft
2 ft
18 ft; 10.5 ft²

20.
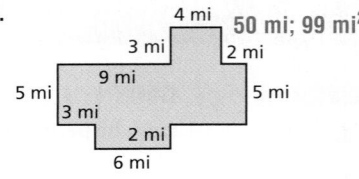
4 mi
50 mi; 99 mi²
3 mi 2 mi
5 mi 9 mi 5 mi
3 mi
2 mi
6 mi

Multi-Step A rectangular ice-skating rink measures 50 ft by 75 ft.

21. It costs $13.50 per foot to install sheets of clear protective plastic around the rink. How much does it cost to enclose the rink with plastic sheets? **$3375**

22. A machine can clear 750 ft² of ice per minute. How long will it take the machine to clear the entire rink? **5 min**

23. **Social Studies** The state of Tennessee is shaped approximately like a parallelogram. Estimate the area of the state. **42,000 mi²**
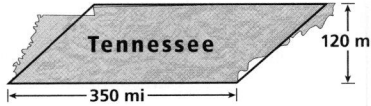
Tennessee | 120 mi
350 mi

24. **What's the Question?** A rectangle has a base 6 mm and height 5.2 mm. If the answer is 31.2 mm², what is the question?

25. **Write About It** A rectangle and an identical rectangle with a smaller rectangle cut from the bottom and placed on top are shown. Do the two figures have the same area? Do they have the same perimeter? Explain.
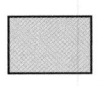
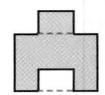

26. **Challenge** A ruler is 30 cm long by 5 cm wide. How many rulers this size can be cut from a 544 cm² rectangular piece of wood with base length 32 cm? **3 rulers**

27. **Multiple Choice** The lengths of the sides of a rectangle are whole numbers. If the rectangle's perimeter is 24 units, which of the following could NOT be the rectangle's area?

(A) 27 square units (B) 24 square units (C) 20 square units (D) 11 square units

28. **Short Response** Graph the figure with vertices (2, 5), (−3, 5), (−5, 1), and (0, 1). Find the area of the figure. Explain how you found the area.

Solve. Check your answer. (Lesson 2-8)

29. $5x + 2 = -18$ $x = -4$

30. $\frac{b}{-6} + 12 = 5$ $b = 42$

31. $\frac{a + 4}{11} = -3$ $a = -37$

32. $\frac{1}{3}x - \frac{1}{4} = \frac{5}{12}$ $x = 2$

State whether each number is rational, irrational, or not a real number. (Lesson 4-7)

33. -14 rational

34. $\sqrt{13}$ irrational

35. $\frac{127}{46,191}$ rational

36. $\sqrt{-\frac{5}{6}}$ not real

37. $\frac{21}{0}$ not a real number

Hands-On LAB 8-1

Explore the Effects of Changing Dimensions

Use with Lesson 8-1

go.hrw.com
Lab Resources Online
KEYWORD: MT7 Lab8

REMEMBER
For polygons to be similar,
• Corresponding angles must be congruent.
• Corresponding sides must have lengths that form equivalent ratios.

You can use grid paper to explore how changing the dimensions of a figure affects the figure's perimeter and area.

Activity

❶ Make the following similar rectangles on grid paper.

Rectangle A: 1 × 2 units   Rectangle B: 2 × 4 units

Rectangle C: 4 × 8 units

Copy the table shown.

Fill in the missing information.

❷ Make two more rectangles that are similar to the rectangles in Part 1. Call them *Rectangles E and F*.

a. Find the base, height, perimeter, and area of each rectangle.

b. Add this information to your table.

Rectangle	Base	Height	Perimeter	Area
A				
B				
C				

Think and Discuss

1. Look at rectangles B and C. How do the bases and heights compare? How do the perimeters and areas compare?

2. How does changing the width and length of the rectangle affect the perimeter? the area? Make a conjecture about the perimeters and areas of similar figures.

Try This

Use grid paper to make four similar figures to each figure given. Make a table of the bases, heights, perimeters, and areas of each. Does your conjecture hold true?

1. rectangle: 2 × 6 units   2. square: 3 × 3 units   3. rectangle: 2 × 8 units

Answers to Think and Discuss

1. The length and width of rectangle C are twice the length and width of rectangle B. The perimeter of rectangle C is twice the perimeter of rectangle B. The area of rectangle C is four times the area of rectangle B.

2. Possible answer: If the ratio that compares the perimeter of a larger rectangle to that of a smaller similar rectangle is x, the ratio that compares the areas of the two rectangles will be x^2.

Answers to *Try This*

1. Check students' work.
2. Check students' work.
3. Check students' work.

Organizer
Use with Lesson 8-1

Pacing:
Traditional 1 day
Block $\frac{1}{2}$ day

Objective: Use grid paper to explore how changing the dimensions of a figure affects the figure's perimeter and area.
Materials: Grid paper

Online Edition

Countdown to Testing Week 15

Resources

Hands-On Lab Activities
Lab 8-1 Recording Sheet

Teach
Discuss

Have students identify the common factors of the widths, lengths, perimeters, and areas listed in their tables.

Close
Key Concept

Changing the dimensions of a figure affects the figure's perimeter and area.

Assessment

1. What is the ratio formed by the perimeters of rectangles A and B? 1:2 of rectangles B and C? 1:2

2. What is the ratio formed by the areas of rectangles A and B? 1:4

State Resources

go.hrw.com
State Resources Online
KEYWORD: MT7 Resources

Objective: Students find the perimeter and area of triangles and trapezoids.

 Hands-On Lab
In *Hands-On Lab Activities*

 Technology Lab
In *Technology Lab Activities*

 Online Edition
Tutorial Videos, Interactivities

 Countdown to Testing Week 15

Power Presentations
with PowerPoint®

Warm Up

A rectangle has sides lengths of 12 ft and 20 ft.

1. find the perimeter. **64 ft**

2. Find the area. **240 ft²** (240 ft^2)

Problem of the Day

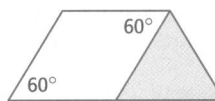

The area of a rhombus with two 60° angles is 24 in². An equilateral triangle is drawn so that one side is a side of the rhombus. What is the area of the triangle? (*Hint:* You don't need a formula.) **12 in²** (12 in^2)

Also available on transparency

State Resources

go.hrw.com
State Resources Online
KEYWORD: MT7 Resources

8-2 Perimeter and Area of Triangles and Trapezoids

Learn to find the perimeter and area of triangles and trapezoids.

The figures show a *fractal* called the Koch snowflake. It is constructed by first drawing an equilateral triangle. Then triangles with sides one-third the length of the original sides are added to the middle of each side. The second step is then repeated over and over again.

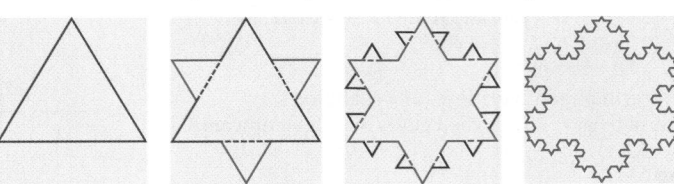

The area and perimeter of each figure is larger than that of the one before it. However, the area of any figure is never greater than the area of the shaded box, while the perimeters increase without bound. To find the area and perimeter of each figure, you must be able to find the area of a triangle..

EXAMPLE 1 Finding the Perimeter of Triangles and Trapezoids

Find the perimeter of each figure.

A 6 cm, 8 cm, 12 cm

$P = 6 + 8 + 12$ *Add all sides.*
$= 26 \text{ cm}$

B 4 in., 6 in., 5 in., 7 in.

$P = 4 + 5 + 6 + 7$ *Add all sides.*
$= 22 \text{ in.}$

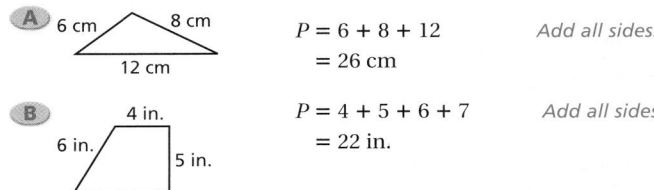

EXAMPLE 2 Finding a Missing Measurement

Find the missing measurement for the trapezoid with perimeter 92 cm.

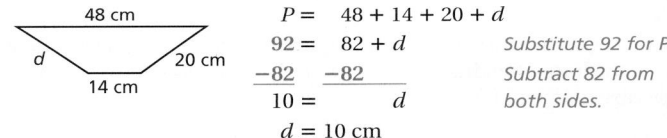

48 cm, d, 20 cm, 14 cm

$P = 48 + 14 + 20 + d$
$92 = 82 + d$ *Substitute 92 for P.*
$\underline{-82 \quad -82}$ *Subtract 82 from*
$10 = d$ *both sides.*
$d = 10 \text{ cm}$

---

1 Introduce

Alternate Opener

EXPLORATION

8-2 Perimeter and Area of Triangles and Trapezoids

You can use what you know about the area of a parallelogram to develop the formula for the area of a triangle.

1. Fold a sheet of paper in half.

2. Draw a triangle on the folded paper. Label the base, b, and height, h, as shown.

3. Cut out the triangle through both layers of paper. This will create a pair of congruent triangles.

4. Arrange the two triangles to form a parallelogram.

5. What are the base and height of the parallelogram you made? What is the parallelogram's area?

6. How is the area of one of the triangles related to the area of the parallelogram?

Think and Discuss

7. **Explain** how to write a formula for the area of a triangle with base b and height h.

8. **Describe** how you can use your formula to find the area of this triangle.   8 ft, 12 ft

Motivate

Cut a parallelogram along a diagonal to form a pair of congruent triangles. Ask students how the area of each triangle compares to the area of the parallelogram. Help them see that each triangle is half of the original figure. Then place two congruent trapezoids side by side to form a parallelogram. Explain that the area of one of the trapezoids is half the area of the parallelogram.

Explorations and answers are provided in *Alternate Openers: Explorations Transparencies.*

EXAMPLE **3** *Multi-Step Application*

A farmer wants to fence a field that is in the shape of a right triangle. He knows that the two shorter sides of the field are 20 yards and 35 yards long. How long will the fence be to the nearest hundredth of a yard?

Find the length of the third side of the field using the Pythagorean Theorem.

$$a^2 + b^2 = c^2$$
$$20^2 + 35^2 = c^2 \qquad \text{Substitute 20 for } a \text{ and 35 for } b.$$
$$400 + 1225 = c^2$$
$$1625 = c^2$$
$$40.31 \approx c \qquad \sqrt{1625} = \sqrt{c^2}$$

Find the perimeter of the field.

$$P = a + b + c$$
$$= 20 + 35 + 40.31 \qquad \text{Add all sides.}$$
$$= 95.31$$

The fence will be 95.31 yards long.

A triangle or a trapezoid can be thought of as half of a parallelogram.

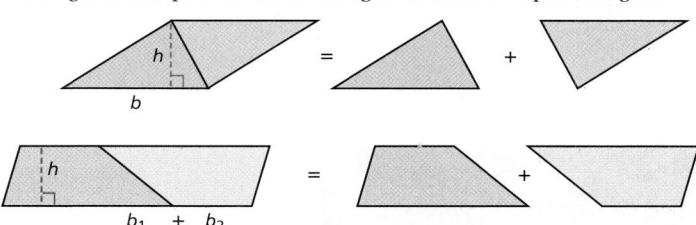

AREA OF TRIANGLES AND TRAPEZOIDS

Words	Numbers	Formula
Triangle: The area A of a triangle is one-half of the base length b times the height h.	$A = \frac{1}{2}(8)(4)$ $= 16$ units^2	$A = \frac{1}{2}bh$
Trapezoid: The area of a trapezoid is one-half the height h times the sum of the base lengths b_1 and b_2.	$A = \frac{1}{2}(2)(3+7)$ $= 10$ units^2	$A = \frac{1}{2}h(b_1 + b_2)$

Reading Math

In the term b_1, the number 1 is called a *subscript*. It is read as "b one" or "b sub-one."

Example 1

Find the perimeter of each figure.

A.

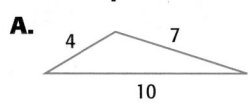

$P = 21$ units

B.

$P = 42$ units

Example 2

Find the missing measurement for the trapezoid with perimeter 71 in.

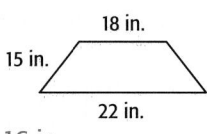

16 in.

Example 3

A homeowner wants to plant a border of shrubs around her yard that is in the shape of a right triangle. She knows that the length of the shortest side of the yard is 12 feet and the length of the longest side is 20 feet. How long will the border be? 48 ft

Also available on transparency

---

2 Teach

Guided Instruction

In this lesson, students learn to find the area of triangles and trapezoids. Remind students that the perimeter of any polygon can be found by adding up all its side lengths. Review the formula for the area of a parallelogram. Use the diagrams in the lesson to show how a triangle or trapezoid can be thought of as half of a parallelogram (Teaching Transparency). Finally, introduce the formulas for area of triangles and trapezoids (Teaching Transparency). Point out that to find the area of a trapezoid, students must find the sum of the lengths of its bases.

Reaching All Learners
Through Critical Thinking

Have students plot the geometric figure with vertices (3, 5), (2, 4), (4, 4), (5, 2), and (−1, 2) on a coordinate grid. Then have them divide the shape into any combination of rectangles, trapezoids, and triangles to find the area of the figure. 9 units^2

Additional Examples

Example 4

Graph and find the area of the figure with vertices (−2, 2), (4, 2), (0, 5).

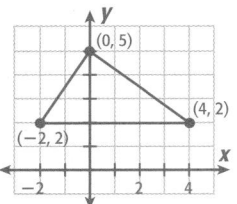

$A = 9 \text{ units}^2$

Also available on transparency

Answers to
Think and Discuss

1. The area doubles.

2. The area doubles.

8-2 **Exercises**

Assignment Guide

If you finished Example **1** assign:
Average 1–3, 12–14, 31, 33, 37–43
Advanced 12–14, 31, 33, 37–43

If you finished Example **2** assign:
Average 1–6, 12–17, 31, 33, 37–43
Advanced 12–17, 27, 31, 33, 37–43

If you finished Example **3** assign:
Average 1–7, 12–18, 31, 33, 37–43
Advanced 12–18, 27, 31, 33, 37–43

If you finished Example **4** assign:
Average 1–24, 29–33, 37–43
Advanced 12–43

Homework Quick Check

Quickly check key concepts.
Exercises: 12, 16, 18, 22

E X A M P L E 4 **Finding the Area of Triangles and Trapezoids**

Graph and find the area of the figure with vertices (−2, 2), (6, 2), (3, 7).

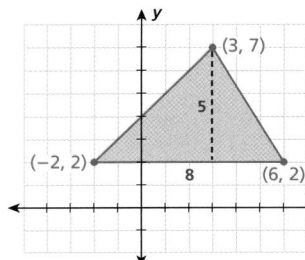

$A = \frac{1}{2}bh$ *Area of a triangle*

$= \frac{1}{2} \cdot 8 \cdot 5$ *Substitute for b and h.*

$= 20 \text{ units}^2$

Think and Discuss

1. Describe what happens to the area of a triangle when the base is doubled and the height remains the same.

2. Describe what happens to the area of a trapezoid when the length of both bases are doubled but the height remains the same.

8-2 **Exercises**

go.hrw.com
Homework Help Online
KEYWORD: MT7 8-2
Parent Resources Online
KEYWORD: MT7 Parent

GUIDED PRACTICE

See Example 1 **Find the perimeter of each figure.**

1.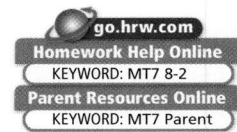
20 ft
18 ft   26 ft
38 ft **102 ft**

2. $5\frac{1}{2}$ yd $4\frac{1}{4}$ yd
5 yd $14\frac{3}{4}$ yd

3.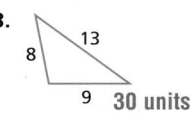
8   13
9 **30 units**

See Example 2 **Find the missing measurement for each figure with the given perimeter.**

4. trapezoid with perimeter 34.5 units
7.7
6.3   a
11.5 **9**

5. trapezoid with perimeter 84 units
27
17   d
21 **19**

6. triangle with perimeter 18 units
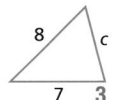
8   c
7 **3**

3 Close

Summarize

Show students a trapezoid that is divided into a rectangle and two triangles, such as the one below.

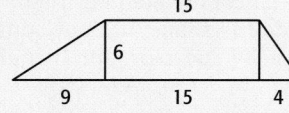
15
6
9   15   4

Have volunteers find the area of the trapezoid and of each individual section. Show them that the area of the trapezoid is equal to the sum of the areas of the sections.

trapezoid: 129 units²; large triangle: 27 units²; rectangle: 90 units²; small triangle: 12 units²; 27 + 90 + 12 = 129 units²

See Example 3   **7.** Jolene is putting trim around the edge of a triangle head scarf. The scarf forms a right triangle with legs that measure 15 inches each. Find how much trim Jolene needs to the nearest tenth of an inch. **51.2 in.**

See Example 4   **Graph and find the area of each figure with the given vertices.**

    8. $(-4, -2)$, $(0, 5)$, $(2, -2)$ **21 units²**   **9.** $(-6, 2)$, $(4, 2)$, $(-2, 4)$, $(-2, -4)$ **42 units²**

    10. $(-5, -4)$, $(0, -4)$, $(-3, 2)$ **15 units²**   **11.** $(0, -1)$, $(-7, -1)$, $(-5, 4)$, $(-2, 4)$ **25 units²**

INDEPENDENT PRACTICE

See Example 1   **Find the perimeter of each figure.**

12. 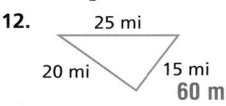 **60 mi**   **13.** 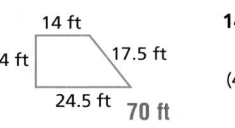 **70 ft**   **14.**

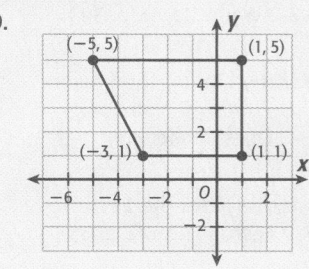

See Example 2   **Find the missing measurement for each figure with the given perimeter.**

15. triangle with perimeter 27 units

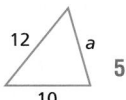

16. triangle with perimeter 34 units

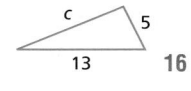

17. trapezoid with perimeter 71 units

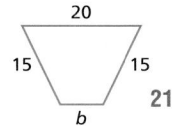

See Example 3   **18.** Miguel is making a stained glass window. He cuts a 12 cm square along the diagonal to create two right triangles. Find the perimeter of each triangle to the nearest tenth of a centimeter. **41 cm**

See Example 4   **Graph and find the area of each figure with the given vertices.**

    19. $(1, 5)$, $(1, 1)$, $(-3, 1)$, $(-5, 5)$ **20 units²**   **20.** $(-4, -1)$, $(3, 5)$, $(1, -1)$ **15 units²**

    21. $(-1, 2)$, $(0, -4)$, $(3, 2)$ **12 units²**   **22.** $(-4, 3)$, $(2, 1)$, $(2, -3)$, $(-4, 25)$ **36 units²**

PRACTICE AND PROBLEM SOLVING

Extra Practice
See page 796.

Find the area of each figure with the given dimensions.

23. triangle: $b = 10$, $h = 12$ **60 units²**   **24.** trapezoid: $b_1 = 8$, $b_2 = 14$, $h = 7$ **77 units²**

25. triangle: $b = 5x$, $h = 10$ **25x units²**   **26.** trapezoid: $b_1 = 4.5$, $b_2 = 8$, $h = 6.7$ **41.875 units²**

27. The perimeter of a triangle is 37.4 ft. Two of its sides measure 16.4 ft and 11.9 ft, respectively. What is the length of its third side? **9.1 ft**

28. The area of a triangle is 126 mm². Its height is 21 mm. What is the length of its base? **12 mm**

29. Multi-Step A right triangle has one leg that is 13 cm long. The hypotenuse is 27 cm long. Find the area of the triangle to the nearest tenth. **153.8 cm²**

Answers

19.

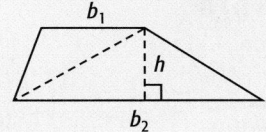

8–11, 20–22. See pp. A10–A11.

Math Background

The formula for the area of a trapezoid is explained in the lesson by forming a parallelogram with two congruent trapezoids. An alternate method is to use a diagonal of a trapezoid to form two triangles.

The area of the trapezoid is the sum of the areas of two triangles that share the same height:

$$A = \tfrac{1}{2}b_1h + \tfrac{1}{2}b_2h = \tfrac{1}{2}h(b_1 + b_2)$$

RETEACH 8-2

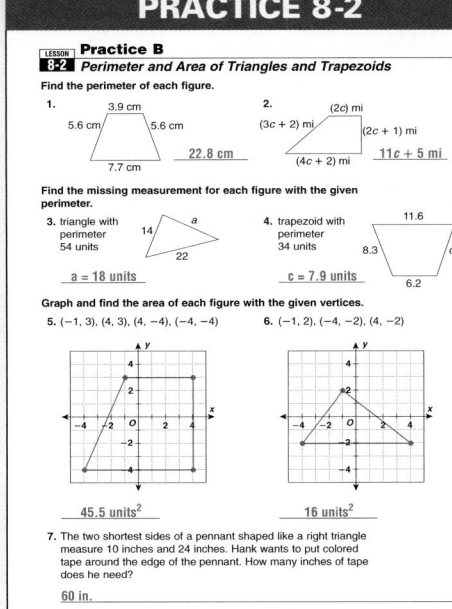

PRACTICE 8-2

State Resources

go.hrw.com
State Resources Online
KEYWORD: MT7 Resources

ONGOING ASSESSMENT
and INTERVENTION

Diagnose *Before* the Lesson
8-2 Warm Up, TE p. 394

Monitor *During* the Lesson
8-2 Know-It Notebook
8-2 Questioning Strategies

Assess *After* the Lesson
8-2 Lesson Quiz, TE p. 398

Interdisciplinary LINK

Physical Science

Exercises 30–36 involve using diagrams to solve problems about the perimeters and areas of wings. Wing shape and lift are studied in middle school science programs, such as *Holt Science and Technology*.

Answers

36. See p. A11.

TEST PREP DOCTOR + For Exercise 37, students who answered **D** did not divide the height by 2 before multiplying it by the sum of the bases. Remind students that the formula for the area of a trapezoid includes a factor of $\frac{1}{2}$.

Journal

Have students write about why it is not always possible to find areas by counting the square units inside a figure.

Power Presentations
with PowerPoint®

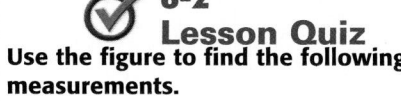

8-2 Lesson Quiz
Use the figure to find the following measurements.

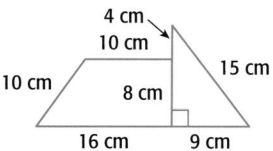

1. the perimeter of the triangle **36 cm**
2. the perimeter of the trapezoid **44 cm**
3. the perimeter of the combined figure **64 cm**
4. the area of the triangle **54 cm²**
5. the area of the trapezoid **104 cm²**

Also available on transparency

Physical Science LINK

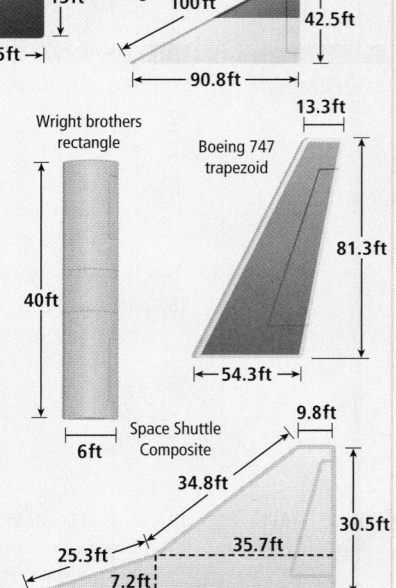

To fly, a plane must overcome gravity and achieve *lift*, the force that allows a flying object to have upward motion. The shape and size of a plane's wings affect the amount of lift that is created. The wings of high-speed airplanes are thin and usually angled back to give the plane more lift.

30. Find the area of a Concorde wing to the nearest tenth of a square foot. **1929.5 ft²**

31. Find the total perimeter of the two wings of a Concorde to the nearest tenth of a foot. **466.6 ft**

32. What is the area of a Boeing 747 wing to the nearest tenth of a square foot? **2747.9 ft²**

33. What is the perimeter of an F-18 wing to the nearest tenth of a foot? **49.8 ft**

34. What is the total area of the two wings of an F-18? **273 ft²**

35. Find the area and perimeter of the wing of a space shuttle rounded to the nearest tenth. **874.6 ft²; 160.4 ft**

36. ⭐ **Challenge** The wing of the Wright brothers' plane is about half the length of a Boeing 747 wing. Compare the area of the Wright brothers' wing with the area of a Boeing 747 wing. Is the area of the Wright brothers' wing half the area of the 747 wing? Explain.

go.hrw.com
Web Extra!
KEYWORD: MT7 Lift

TEST PREP and Spiral Review

37. **Multiple Choice** Find the area of a trapezoid with the dimensions $b_1 = 4$, $b_2 = 6$, and $h = 4.6$.

Ⓐ 16.1 square units Ⓑ 18.4 square units Ⓒ 23 square units Ⓓ 46 square units

38. **Gridded Response** The perimeter of a triangle is 24.9 feet. The length of one side is 9.6 feet. Another side is 8.2 feet. Find the length, in feet, of the third side. **7.1**

Find the appropriate factor for each conversion. (Lesson 5-3)

39. feet to inches $\frac{12 \text{ in.}}{1 \text{ ft}}$ **40.** pints to quarts $\frac{1 \text{ quart}}{2 \text{ pints}}$ **41.** grams to milligrams $\frac{1{,}000 \text{ mg}}{1 \text{ g}}$

Find the area of the quadrilateral with the given vertices. (Lesson 8-1)

42. (0, 0), (0, 9), (5, 9), (5, 0) **45 units²**   **43.** (−3, 1), (4, 1), (6, 3), (−1, 3) **14 units²**

CHALLENGE 8-2

LESSON 8-2 **Challenge**
Fence Me In!

You can find the area of a triangle in the coordinate plane that has no horizontal or vertical side.

Consider △ABC with vertices A(−3, 2), B(8, −3), and C(5, 6).

By drawing horizontal and vertical lines, △ABC is enclosed in rectangle PQBR.

Write the coordinates of the remaining vertices of the rectangle.

1. P __(−3, 6)__
   Q __(8, 6)__
   R __(−3, −3)__

Count boxes or subtract coordinates to find the indicated dimensions. Then find the indicated areas.

2. For rectangle PQBR:
   base RB = __11__ units   height RP = __9__ units   area = __99__ units²

3. For right triangle APC:
   base PC = __8__ units   height AP = __4__ units   area = __16__ units²

4. For right triangle CQB:
   base CQ = __3__ units   height BQ = __9__ units   area = __13.5__ units²

5. For right triangle ARB:
   base RB = __11__ units   height AR = __5__ units   area = __27.5__ units²

6. Explain how to combine the areas of the rectangle and the three right triangles to find the area of △ABC. Then find the area of △ABC.

   △ABC = rectangle PQBR − (△APC + △CQB + △ARB)
   △ABC = 99 − (16 + 13.5 + 27.5) = 42 units²

PROBLEM SOLVING 8-2

LESSON 8-2 **Problem Solving**
Perimeter and Area of Triangles and Trapezoids

Write the correct answer.

1. Find the area of the material required to cover the kite pictured below.
   5 ft²

2. Find the area of the material required to cover the kite pictured below.
   9 ft²

3. Find the approximate area of the state of Nevada.
   109,275 mi²

4. Find the area of the hexagonal gazebo floor.
   30 m²

Choose the letter for the best answer.

5. Find the amount of flooring needed to cover the stage pictured below.
   A 4500 ft²
   B 750 ft²
   C 525 ft²
   Ⓓ 375 ft²

6. Find the combined area of the congruent triangular gables.
   F 7.5 ft²
   Ⓖ 15 ft²
   J 60 ft²
   H 30 ft²

Hands-On LAB 8-3

Approximate *Pi* by Measuring

Use with Lesson 8-3

go.hrw.com
Lab Resources Online
KEYWORD: MT7 Lab8

You can use a ruler and string to measure circles.

Activity

a. Find the distance around three different circular objects by wrapping a piece of string around each of them and using a marker to mark the string where it meets. Be sure that your mark shows on both overlapping parts of the string. Lay the string out straight and use a ruler to measure between the marks. Record the measurements for each object.

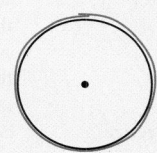

b. Measure the distance across each object. Be sure that you measure each circle at its widest point. Record the measurements for each object. **Check students' work.**

Object	Distance Around	Distance Across	Distance Around / Distance Across

c. Divide the distance around by the distance across for each object. Round each answer to the nearest hundredth and record it.   **Check students' work.**

Think and Discuss

1. What do you notice about the ratios of the distance around each object to the distance across each object?

2. How could you estimate the distance around a circular object without measuring it if you know the distance across?

Try This

1. Choose three circular objects different from the objects you used in the activity.   **Check students' work.**

   a. Measure the distance across each object.

   b. Estimate the distance around each object without measuring.

   c. Measure the distance around each object and compare each measurement with the estimate from **b**.

Possible answers to *Think and Discuss*

1. The ratio is approximately equal to 3.14.

2. Multiply the distance across the circular object by 3.14

Hands-On LAB Organizer

Use with Lesson 8-3

Pacing:
Traditional 1 day
Block $\frac{1}{2}$ day

Objective: Use a ruler and string to measure circles.

Materials: Ruler, string

 Online Edition

 Countdown to Testing Week 15

Resources

 Hands-On Lab Activities
Lab 8-3 Recording Sheet

Teach
Discuss

Ask students what vocabulary terms describe the distance around a circle and the distance across a circle.
circumference; diameter

Close
Key Concept

You can approximate the value of *pi* by dividing the distance around a circle by the distance across the circle.

Assessment

1. What is the meaning of the word *pi*? You may use a dictionary.
   the ratio of the circumference of a circle to its diameter

State Resources

go.hrw.com
State Resources Online
KEYWORD: MT7 Resources

Objective: Students find the circumference and area of circles.

 Hands-On Lab
In *Hands-On Lab Activities*

 Online Edition
Tutorial Videos

 Countdown to Testing Week 16

Power Presentations
with PowerPoint®

Warm Up

1. Find the length of the hypotenuse of a right triangle that has legs 3 in. and 4 in. long. **5 in.**

2. The hypotenuse of a right triangle measures 17 in., and one leg measures 8 in. How long is the other leg? **15 in.**

3. To the nearest centimeter, what is the height of an equilateral triangle with sides 9 cm long? **8 cm**

Problem of the Day

A rectangular box is 3 ft by 4 ft by 12 ft. What is the distance from a top corner to the opposite bottom corner? **13 ft**

Also available on transparency

State Resources

 **go.hrw.com**
State Resources Online
KEYWORD: MT7 Resources

8-3 Circles

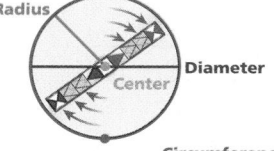

"I love a good G-force face!"

Learn to find the circumference and area of circles.

Vocabulary
circle
radius
diameter
circumference

The 20-G Centrifuge at NASA's Ames Research Center is used to study the effects of hypergravity on human and nonhuman subjects, as well as to evaluate flight hardware. Subjects or equipment are placed in one of the three cabs located on the rotating arm. Each time a cab returns to its starting position, it completes one *circumference* of the centrifuge.

A **circle** is the set of points in a plane that are a fixed distance from a given point, called the *center*. A **radius** connects the center to any point on the circle, and a **diameter** connects two points on the circle and passes through the center.

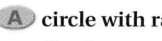

The diameter d is twice the radius r.

$$d = 2r$$

The **circumference** of a circle is the distance around the circle.

Remember!
Pi (π) is an irrational number that is often approximated by the rational numbers 3.14 and $\frac{22}{7}$.

CIRCUMFERENCE OF A CIRCLE		
Words	**Numbers**	**Formula**
The circumference C of a circle is π times the diameter d, or 2π times the radius r.	$C = \pi(6)$ $= 2\pi(3)$ ≈ 18.8 units	$C = \pi d$ or $C = 2\pi r$

EXAMPLE 1 Finding the Circumference of a Circle

Find the circumference of each circle, both in terms of π and to the nearest tenth. Use 3.14 for π.

A circle with radius 4 cm
$C = 2\pi r$
$= 2\pi(4)$
$= 8\pi \text{ cm} \approx 25.1 \text{ cm}$

B circle with diameter 4.5 in.
$C = \pi d$
$= \pi(4.5)$
$= 4.5\pi \text{ in.} \approx 14.1 \text{ in.}$

---

1 Introduce

Alternate Opener

EXPLORATION

8-3 Circles

First estimate the area of each circle by counting squares. Then square each circle's radius. Then compare each estimated area with the square of the radius by computing $\frac{A}{r^2}$.

	Radius	Estimated Area	r^2	$\frac{A}{r^2}$
1.	$r = 1$			
2.	$r = 2$			
3.	$r = 3$			
4.	$r = 4$			

Think and Discuss

5. Discuss how you can make a generalization about how to estimate the area of a circle if you know the radius.

Motivate

Ask students if they like pie. Ask them to describe the shape of a pie. **circle** Then explain that this will help them remember an important number called *pi*. Tell them pi is a special number that they will use to solve problems involving circles.

Explorations and answers are provided in *Alternate Openers: Explorations Transparencies.*

AREA OF A CIRCLE		
Words	Numbers	Formula
The area A of a circle is π times the square of the radius r.	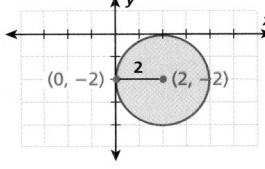 $A = \pi(3^2)$ $= 9\pi$ $\approx 28.3 \text{ units}^2$	$A = \pi r^2$

EXAMPLE 2 **Finding the Area of a Circle**

Find the area of each circle, both in terms of π and to the nearest tenth. Use 3.14 for π.

A circle with radius 5 cm

$A = \pi r^2 = \pi(5^2)$
$= 25\pi \text{ cm}^2 \approx 78.5 \text{ cm}^2$

B circle with diameter 5.6 in.

$A = \pi r^2 = \pi(2.8^2)$ $\frac{d}{2} = 2.8$
$= 7.84\pi \text{ in}^2 \approx 24.6 \text{ in}^2$

EXAMPLE 3 **Finding Area and Circumference on a Coordinate Plane**

Graph the circle with center $(2, -2)$ that passes through $(0, -2)$. Find the area and circumference, both in terms of π and to the nearest tenth. Use 3.14 for π.

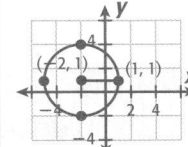

$A = \pi r^2$
$= \pi(2^2)$
$= 4\pi \text{ units}^2$
$\approx 12.6 \text{ units}^2$

$C = \pi d$
$= \pi(4)$
$= 4\pi \text{ units}$
$\approx 12.6 \text{ units}$

EXAMPLE 4 **Physical Science Application**

The radius of the 20-G Centrifuge at NASA's Ames Research Center is 29 ft. If a subject in one of the cabs at the end of the rotating arm remains in the centrifuge for 12 complete revolutions, how far does the subject travel? Use $\frac{22}{7}$ for π.

$C = 2\pi r = 2\pi(29) = \pi(58) \approx \frac{22}{7}\left(\frac{58}{1}\right) = \frac{1276}{7}$ *Find the circumference.*

The distance traveled is the circumference of the centrifuge times the number of revolutions, or about $\frac{1276}{7} \cdot 12 = \frac{15,312}{7} \approx 2187.4$ ft.

1. $A = \pi\left(\frac{d}{2}\right)2$ or

$A = \frac{\pi d^2}{4}$

Think and Discuss

1. Give the formula for the area of a circle in terms of the diameter d.

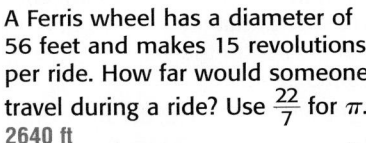
2 Teach

Guided Instruction

In this lesson, students learn to find the area and circumference of circles. Review the diagram of the circular wheel and the vocabulary terms. Point out the important relationship between radius and diameter ($d = 2r$). Explain that circumference, a measure of the distance around the outside of a circle, is like perimeter. Show them how to find circumference using the formula (Teaching Transparency). Explain that a formula is used to find circumference because unlike the perimeter of a polygon, it is not easy to measure. Then show students how to find the area of a circle. Point out that the radius must be squared when finding area.

 Reaching All Learners

Through Kinesthetic Experience

Provide each pair or group of students with cans of various sizes and a tape measure. Have students measure the diameter and circumference of the top of each can and enter the data in a table like the one shown.

Can	C	d	$\frac{C}{d}$

After the measurements are complete, have students use calculators to divide the circumference by the diameter for each circle and enter these results in the last column. Results should be close to pi.

3 Close

ENGLISH LANGUAGE LEARNERS

Summarize

Review the vocabulary terms and the formulas from the lesson. Stress the importance of the difference between radius and diameter. Remind students that pi is the value of the circumference of a circle divided by its diameter. Show them that they can see that the equations $\pi = \frac{C}{d}$ and $C = \pi d$ are equivalent based on their knowledge of solving algebraic equations.

go.hrw.com
Homework Help Online
KEYWORD: MT7 8-3
Parent Resources Online
KEYWORD: MT7 Parent

Assignment Guide

If you finished Example **1** assign:
Average   1, 2, 7, 8, 30–37
Advanced   7, 8, 16–18, 30–37

If you finished Example **2** assign:
Average   1–4, 7–10, 13–15, 30–37
Advanced   7–10, 13–21, 27, 30–37

If you finished Example **3** assign:
Average   1–5, 7–11, 13–15, 30–37
Advanced   7–11, 13–23, 27–37

If you finished Example **4** assign:
Average   1–15, 24–26, 30–37
Advanced   7–16, 21–37

Homework Quick Check

Quickly check key concepts.
Exercises: 8, 10, 11, 12, 14

Answers

5, 11. See p. A11.

Math Background

Although pi is often approximated as 3.14, it is actually an irrational number with an infinite number of nonrepeating decimal digits. Mathematicians have been interested in the value of π for thousands of years.

From 2000 to 1600 B.C.E., the Babylonians approximated π as 3. Modern computers have calculated π to more than 68 billion decimal places.

State Resources

go.hrw.com
State Resources Online
KEYWORD: MT7 Resources

GUIDED PRACTICE

See Example **1**   Find the circumference of each circle, both in terms of π and to the nearest tenth. Use 3.14 for π.

1. circle with diameter 6 cm
   6π cm; 18.8 cm

2. circle with radius 3.2 in.
   6.4π in.; 20.1 in.

See Example **2**   Find the area of each circle, both in terms of π and to the nearest tenth. Use 3.14 for π. 16.8π ft^2; 52.8 ft^2 56.25π cm^2; 176.6 cm^2

3. circle with radius 4.1 ft

4. circle with diameter 15 cm

See Example **3**   **5.** Graph a circle with center $(-2, 1)$ that passes through $(-4, 1)$. Find the area and circumference, both in terms of π and to the nearest tenth. Use 3.14 for π. $A = 4\pi$ units^2; 12.6 units^2 $C = 4\pi$ units; 12.6 units

See Example **4**   **6.** A wheel has a diameter of 3.5 ft. Approximately how far does it travel if it makes 20 complete revolutions? Use $\frac{22}{7}$ for π.   220 ft

INDEPENDENT PRACTICE

See Example **1**   Find the circumference of each circle, both in terms of π and to the nearest tenth. Use 3.14 for π.

7. circle with radius 9 in.
   18π in.; 56.5 in.

8. circle with diameter 6.3 m
   6.3π m; 19.8 m

See Example **2**   Find the area of each circle, both in terms of π and to the nearest tenth. Use 3.14 for π. 256π cm^2; 803.8 cm^2 6.3π yd^2; 19.6 yd^2

9. circle with diameter 32 cm

10. circle with radius 2.5 yd

See Example **3**   **11.** Graph a circle with center $(1, 0)$ that passes through $(-3, 0)$. Find the area and circumference, both in terms of π and to the nearest tenth. Use 3.14 for π.
   $A = 16\pi$ units^2; 50.2 units^2 $C = 8\pi$ units; 25.1 units

See Example **4**   **12.** If the diameter of a wheel is 5 ft, about how many miles does the wheel travel if it makes 134 revolutions? Use $\frac{22}{7}$ for π. (*Hint:* 1 mi = 5280 ft.)   1.7 mi

PRACTICE AND PROBLEM SOLVING

Extra Practice
See page 796.

Find the circumference and area of each circle to the nearest tenth. Use 3.14 for π.

13.   1.7 m
   $C \approx 10.7$ m;
   $A \approx 9.1$ m^2

14.   14 ft
   $C \approx 44.0$ ft;
   $A \approx 153.9$ ft^2

15.   9 in.
   $C \approx 56.5$ in.;
   $A \approx 254.3$ in^2

Find the radius of each circle with the given measurement.

16. $C = 26\pi$ in.   13 in.

17. $C = 12.8\pi$ cm   6.4 cm

18. $C = 15\pi$ ft   7.5 ft

19. $A = 36\pi$ cm^2 6 cm

20. $A = 289\pi$ in^2 17 in.

21. $A = 136.89\pi$ m^2
   11.7 m

RETEACH 8-3

CHAPTER 8-3 Reteach
Circles

A **radius** connects the **center** of a **circle** to any point on the circle.

A **diameter** passes through the center and connects two points on the circle.

diameter d = twice radius r
   $d = 2r$

Circumference is the distance around a circle.

(The symbol $\approx$ means *is approximately equal to*.)

Circumference $C \approx 3$(diameter d)
   $C = \pi d$

Circumference $C \approx 6$(radius r)
   $C = 2\pi r$

For a circle with diameter = 8 in.
   $C = \pi d$
   $C = \pi(8)$
   $C = 8\pi$ in.
   $\pi \approx 3.14$ $C \approx 8(3.14) \approx 25.12$ in.

For a circle with radius = 8 in.
   $C = 2\pi r$
   $C = 2\pi(8)$
   $C = 16\pi$ in.
   $\pi \approx 3.14$ $C \approx 16(3.14) \approx 50.24$ in.

Find the circumference of each circle, exactly in terms of π and approximately when $\pi = 3.14$.

1. diameter = 15 ft
   $C = \pi d$
   $C = \pi(\underline{15}) = \underline{15\pi}$ ft
   $C \approx \pi(\underline{15}) = \underline{47.1}$ ft

2. radius = 4 m
   $C = 2\pi r$
   $C = 2\pi(\underline{4}) = \underline{8\pi}$ m
   $C \approx \underline{8}(3.14) = \underline{25.12}$ m

Area $A \approx 3$(the square of radius r)
   $A = \pi r^2$
   For a circle with radius = 5 in.: $A = \pi r^2 = \pi(5^2) = 25\pi$ in^2
   $A \approx 25(3.14) \approx 78.5$ in^2

Find the area of each circle, exactly in terms of π and approximately when $\pi = 3.14$.

3. radius = 9 ft
   $A = \pi r^2$
   $A = \pi(\underline{9^2}) = \underline{81\pi}$ ft^2
   $A \approx \underline{81}(3.14) \approx \underline{254.34}$ ft^2

4. diameter = 10 m, radius = $\underline{5}$ m
   $A = \pi r^2$
   $A = \pi(\underline{5^2}) = \underline{25\pi}$ m^2
   $A \approx \underline{25}(3.14) \approx \underline{78.5}$ m^2

PRACTICE 8-3

LESSON 8-3 Practice B
Circles

Find the circumference of each circle, both in terms of π and to the nearest tenth. Use 3.14 for π.

1. circle with radius 10 in.
   20π in. or 62.8 in.

2. circle with diameter 13 cm
   13π cm or 40.8 cm

3. circle with diameter 18 m
   18π m or 56.5 m

4. circle with radius 15 ft
   30π ft or 94.2 ft

5. circle with radius 11.5 in.
   23π in. or 72.2 in.

6. circle with diameter 16.4 cm
   16.4π cm or 51.5 cm

Find the area of each circle, both in terms of π and to the nearest tenth. Use 3.14 for π.

7. circle with radius 9 in.
   81π in^2 or 254.3 in^2

8. circle with diameter 14 cm
   49π cm^2 or 153.9 cm^2

9. circle with radius 20 ft
   400π ft^2 or 1256 ft^2

10. circle with diameter 17 m
   72.3π m^2 or 226.9 m^2

11. circle with diameter 15.4 m
   59.3π m^2 or 186.2 m^2

12. circle with radius 22 yd
   484π yd^2 or 1519.8 yd^2

13. Graph a circle with center $(0, 0)$ that passes through $(0, -3)$. Find the area and circumference, both in terms of π and to the nearest tenth. Use 3.14 for π.
   $A = 9\pi$ units^2 or 28.3 units^2;
   $C = 6\pi$ units or 18.8 units

14. A wheel has a radius of 2 1\3 feet. About how far does it travel if it makes 60 complete revolutions? Use $\frac{22}{7}$ for π.
   880 ft

Find the shaded area to the nearest tenth. Use 3.14 for π.

22.

4 yd

4 yd · · 4 yd

4 yd

12.6 yd²

23.
3 m 10 m

5 m

248.1 m²

424 m < C < 440 m

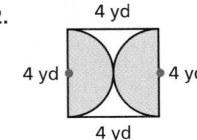
Entertainment

24. Entertainment The London Eye is an observation wheel with a diameter greater than 135 meters and less than 140 meters. Describe the range of the possible circumferences of the wheel to the nearest meter.

25. Sports The radius of a face-off circle on an NHL hockey rink is 15 ft. What are its circumference and area to the nearest tenth? Use 3.14 for π.

26. Food A pancake restaurant serves small silver dollar pancakes and regular-size pancakes.

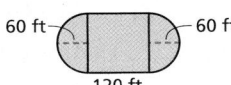
3.5 in.   6 in.

a. What is the area of a silver dollar pancake to the nearest tenth? **9.6 in²**

b. What is the area of a regular pancake to the nearest tenth? **28.3 in²**

c. If 6 silver dollar pancakes are the same price as 3 regular pancakes, which is a better deal?

three regular pancakes

The London Eye takes its passengers on a 30-minute flight that reaches a height of 450 feet above the River Thames.

25.
$C = 30\pi$ ft
≈ 94.2 ft;
$A = 225\pi$ ft²
≈ 706.5 ft²

27. What's the Error? The area of a circle is 121π cm². A student says this means the diameter is 11 in. What is the error?

28. Write About It Explain how you would find the area of the composite figure shown. Then find the area.

60 ft ⌐ 60 ft

120 ft

29. Challenge Graph the circle with center (1, 2) that passes through the point (4, 6). Find its area and circumference, both in terms of π and to the nearest tenth.

$A = 25\pi$ units² ≈ 78.5 units²; $C = 10\pi$ units ≈ 31.4 units

---

TEST PREP and Spiral Review

30. Multiple Choice A circular flower bed has radius 22 inches. What is the circumference of the bed to the nearest tenth of an inch?

Ⓐ 69.1 inches   Ⓑ 103.7 inches   Ⓒ 138.2 inches   Ⓓ 1519.8 inches

31. Gridded Response The first Ferris wheel was constructed for the 1893 World's Fair. It had a diameter of 250 feet. Find the circumference, to the nearest foot, of the Ferris wheel. Use 3.14 for π. **785**

Find the missing angle measure for each triangle. (Lesson 7-3)

32. 70°, 80°, $x°$ **30°**   **33.** 120°, 10°, $x°$ **50°**   **34.** 50°, 20°, $x°$ **110°**   **35.** 100°, 15°, $x°$
65°

Graph and find the area of each figure with the given vertices. (Lesson 8-2)

36. (1, 0), (10, 0), (1, −6) **27 units²**   **37.** (5, 5), (2, 1), (11, 1), (8, 5) **24 units²**

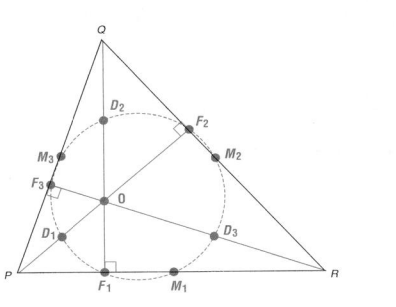

CHALLENGE 8-3

Challenge
8-3 Circles

Work in △PQR at the bottom of this page.

1. Use a ruler to find the midpoints of the three sides of the triangle. Label these midpoints M_1, M_2, M_3.

2. An **altitude** of a triangle is a segment drawn from a vertex perpendicular to the opposite side. Draw the altitude to each side of the triangle. Use F_1, F_2, F_3 to label the foot of each altitude (where the altitude meets the side of the triangle at right angles).

3. The point at which the altitudes meet is the **orthocenter** of the triangle. Label the orthocenter O. Locate the midpoints of $\overline{OP}$, $\overline{OQ}$, $\overline{OR}$, the segments that connect orthocenter O to each vertex. Labels these midpoints D_1, D_2, D_3.

4. If you have been accurate in your measurements, the nine points — M_1, M_2, M_3, F_1, F_2, F_3, D_1, D_2, D_3 — lie on a circle. Draw the **nine-point circle** for △PQR.

PROBLEM SOLVING 8-3

Problem Solving
8-3 Circles

Round to the nearest tenth. Use 3.14 for π. Write the correct answer.

1. The world's tallest Ferris wheel is in Osaka, Japan, and stands 369 feet tall. Its wheel has a diameter of 328 feet. Find the circumference of the Ferris wheel.

1029.9 ft

2. A dog is on a 15-foot chain that is anchored to the ground. How much area can the dog cover while he is on the chain?

706.5 ft²

3. A small pizza has a diameter of 10 inches, and a medium has a diameter of 12 inches. How much more pizza do you get with the medium pizza?

34.5 in²

4. How much more crust do you get with a medium pizza with a diameter of 12 inches than a small pizza with a 10 inch diameter?

6.3 in.

Round to the nearest tenth. Use 3.14 for π. Choose the letter for the best answer.

5. The wrestling mat for college NCAA competition has a wrestling circle with a diameter of 32 feet, while a high school mat has a diameter of 28 feet. How much more area is there in a college wrestling mat than a high school mat?
A 12.6 ft²
Ⓑ 188.4 ft²
C 234.8 ft²
D 753.6 ft²

6. Many tire manufacturers guarantee their tires for 50,000 miles. If a tire has a 16-inch radius, how many revolutions of the tire are guaranteed? There are 63,360 inches in a mile. Round to the nearest revolution.
F 630.6 revolutions
G 3125 revolutions
Ⓗ 31,528,662 revolutions
J 500,000,000 revolutions

7. In men's Olympic discus throwing competition, an athlete throws a discus with a diameter of 8.625 inches. What is the circumference of the discus?
A 13.5 in.
Ⓑ 27.1 in.
C 58.4 in.
D 233.6 in.

8. An athlete in a discus competition throws from a circle that is approximately 8.2 feet in diameter. What is the area of the discus throwing circle?
Ⓕ 52.8 ft²
G 25.7 ft²
H 12.9 ft²
J 211.1 ft²

ONGOING ASSESSMENT
and INTERVENTION

Diagnose Before the Lesson
8-3 Warm Up, TE p. 400

Monitor During the Lesson
8-3 Know-It Notebook
8-3 Questioning Strategies

Assess After the Lesson
8-3 Lesson Quiz, TE p. 403

Answers

27. Possible answer: The student confused diameter with radius. The radius of the circle is 11 in.

28. Possible answer: First find the area of the square with a side length of 120 ft. Then find the area of the two semicircles. The two semi-circles can be put together to form a circle with radius 60 ft. Finally, find the sum of the two areas. $A = 14,400 + 3600\pi \approx 25,704$ ft².

29, 36–37. See p. A11.

TEST PREP DOCTOR Students who chose **A** for Exercise 30 did not correctly apply the circumference formula. Remind students that to find the circumference of a circle when given the radius, they must multiply the product of the radius and *pi* by 2.

Journal
Ask students to write about any ideas they have for remembering the vocabulary terms and formulas from the lesson.

Power Presentations
with PowerPoint®

8-3 Lesson Quiz
Find the circumference of each circle, both in terms of π and to the nearest tenth. Use 3.14 for π.

1. radius 5.6 m **11.2π m; 35.2 m**

2. diameter 113 mm
113π mm; 354.8 mm

Find the area of each circle, both in terms of π and to the nearest tenth. Use 3.14 for π.

3. radius 3 in. **9π in²; 28.3 in²**

4. diameter 1 ft **0.25π ft²; 0.8 ft²**

Also available on transparency

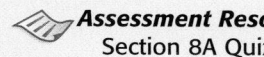

Organizer

Objective: Assess students' mastery of concepts and skills in Lessons 8-1 through 8-3.

Resources

**Assessment Resources**
Section 8A Quiz

Test & Practice Generator
One-Stop Planner®

INTERVENTION

Resources

**Ready to Go On?
Intervention and
Enrichment Worksheets**

💿 **Ready to Go On? CD-ROM**

🪐 **Ready to Go On? Online**

my.hrw.com

Answers

3–6, 11–14, 18. See p. A11.

READY TO GO ON?

Quiz for Lessons 8-1 Through 8-3

✓ 8-1 Perimeter and Area of Rectangles and Parallelograms

Find the perimeter of each figure.

1. 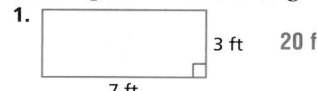 3 ft 7 ft **20 ft**

2.  6.6 cm 3.5 cm **20.2 cm**

Graph and find the area of each figure with the given vertices.

3. $(-4, 4), (2, 4), (2, -3), (-4, -3)$ **42 units²** 4. $(-2, 3), (-2, -1), (2, -1), (2, 4)$ **20 units²**

5. $(-5, 0), (-1, 0), (-6, -3), (-2, -3)$ **12 units²** 6. $(-3, 4), (1, 4), (-4, -3), (0, -3)$

7. Find the perimeter and area of the figure. **28 units²**

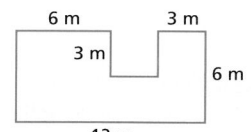 6 m 3 m 3 m 6 m 12 m **42 m; 63 m²**

✓ 8-2 Perimeter and Area of Triangles and Trapezoids

Find the perimeter of each figure.

8. 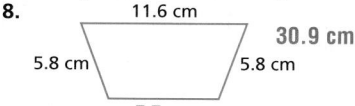 11.6 cm 5.8 cm 5.8 cm 7.7 cm **30.9 cm**

9. 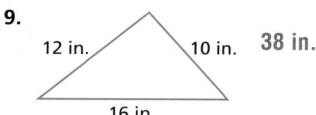 12 in. 10 in. 16 in. **38 in.**

10. Kumiko wants to put a border around a flower garden shaped like a right triangle. The legs of the triangle measure 10 ft and 12 ft. Find how long the border will be to the nearest tenth of a foot. **37.6 ft**

Graph and find the area of each figure with the given vertices.

11. $(-6, -2), (4, -2), (-3, 3)$ **25 units²** 12. $(-4, 0), (0, 0), (3, 3)$ **6 units²**

13. $(2, -2), (3, 3), (-4, 3), (-3, -2)$ **30 units²** 14. $(0, 3), (3, 4), (3, -2), (0, -2)$

16.5 units²

✓ 8-3 Circles

16. $A = 4.6\pi \text{ ft}^2 \approx 14.5 \text{ ft}; C = 4.3\pi \text{ ft} \approx 13.5 \text{ ft}$

17. $A = 56.3\pi \text{ ft}^2 \approx 176.8 \text{ ft}^2; C = 15\pi \text{ ft} \approx 47.1 \text{ ft}$

Find the area and circumference of each circle, both in terms of π and to the nearest tenth. Use 3.14 for π.

15. radius = 19 cm   16. diameter = 4.3 ft   17. radius = $7\frac{1}{2}$ ft

15. $A = 361\pi \text{ cm}^2 \approx 1133.5 \text{ cm}^2; C = 38\pi \text{ cm} \approx 119.3 \text{ cm}$

18. Graph a circle with center $(-3, 1)$ that passes through $(-1, 1)$. Find the area and circumference, both in terms of π and to the nearest tenth. Use 3.14 for π. $A = 4\pi \text{ units}^2 \approx 12.6 \text{ units}^2; C = 4\pi \text{ units} \approx 12.6 \text{ units}$

READY TO GO ON?

Diagnose and Prescribe

**NO
INTERVENE**

**YES
ENRICH**

READY TO GO ON? Intervention, Section 8A			
Ready to Go On? Intervention	〰 **Worksheets**	💿 **CD-ROM**	🪐 **Online**
✓ Lesson 8-1	8-1 Intervention	Activity 8-1	Diagnose and Prescribe Online
✓ Lesson 8-2	8-2 Intervention	Activity 8-2	
✓ Lesson 8-3	8-3 Intervention	Activity 8-3	

READY TO GO ON?
Enrichment, Section 8A

〰 **Worksheets**

💿 **CD-ROM**

🪐 **Online**

Focus on Problem Solving

 Look Back

• Does your solution answer the question?

When you think you have solved a problem, think again. Your answer may not really be the solution to the problem. For example, you may solve an equation to find the value of a variable, but to find the answer the problem is asking for, the value of the variable may need to be substituted into an expression.

Write and solve an equation for each problem. Check to see whether the value of the variable is the answer to the question. If not, give the answer to the question.

① Triangle *ABC* is an isosceles triangle. Find its perimeter.

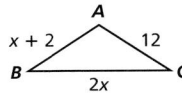

② Find the measure of the smallest angle in triangle *DEF*.

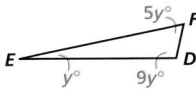

③ Find the measure of the largest angle in triangle *DEF*.

④ Find the area of right triangle *GHI*.

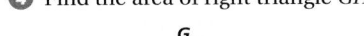
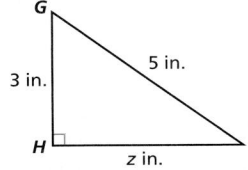

⑤ A *pediment* is a triangular space filled with statuary on the front of a building. The approximate measurements of an isosceles triangular pediment are shown below. Find the area of the pediment.

Answers

1. $x + 2 = 12$; $x = 10$; $12 + 20 + 12 = 34$

2. $15y = 180$; $y = 12°$

3. $9y = 9(12) = 108°$

4. $3^2 + z^2 = 5^2$; $z = 4$; $\frac{1}{2}(4)(3) = 6$ in^2

5. $48^2 + h^2 = 50^2$; $h = 14$; $\frac{1}{2}(96)(14) = 672$ ft^2

One-Minute Section Planner

Lesson	Materials	MiC and Lab Resources
8-4 Hands-On Lab Construct Nets ● Use paper models to explore nets of three-dimensional figures. **Lesson 8-4** Drawing Three-Dimensional Figures ● Draw and identify parts of three-dimensional figures. ☑ SAT-10　☑ ITBS　☑ CTBS　☑ NAEP	Rulers (MK), protractors (MK), tape, dot paper, boxes	**MiC:** *Patterns and Figures* pp. 15–17 *Hands-On Lab Activities* 8-4
8-5 Hands-On Lab Find Volume of Prisms and Cylinders ● Use empty cartons and cans to explore volume of prisms and cylinders. **Lesson 8-5** Volume of Prisms and Cylinders ● Find the volume of prisms and cylinders. ☑ SAT-10　☑ ITBS　☑ CTBS　☑ NAEP	Prism and cylinder models, popcorn, measuring cup, centimeter cubes (MK)	*Hands-On Lab Activities* 8-5 *Technology Lab Activities* 8-5
8-6 Hands-On Lab Find Volume of Pyramids and Cones ● Use models to explore the relationship between volume of prisms and pyramids and between cylinders and cones. **Lesson 8-6** Volume of Pyramids and Cones ● Find the volume of pyramids and cones. ☑ SAT-10　☑ ITBS　☑ CTBS　☐ NAEP	Prism, pyramid, cylinder, and cone models, popcorn, measuring cup, cubes (MK), rulers (MK), scissors, tape	*Hands-On Lab Activities* 8-6 *Technology Lab Activities* 8-6
8-7 Hands-On Lab Find Surface Area of Prisms and Cylinders ● Use models and nets to explore the surface area of prisms and cylinders. **Lesson 8-7** Surface Area of Prisms and Cylinders ● Find the surface area of prisms and cylinders. ☑ SAT-10　☐ ITBS　☑ CTBS　☑ NAEP	Rectangular and triangular prism models, boxes, grid paper	*Hands-On Lab Activities* 8-7
8-8 Hands-On Lab Find Surface Area of Pyramids ● Use models and nets to explore the surface area of regular pyramids. **Lesson 8-8** Surface Area of Pyramids and Cones ● Find the surface area of pyramids and cones. ☑ SAT-10　☐ ITBS　☑ CTBS　☐ NAEP	Rulers (MK), pyramid and cone nets	*Hands-On Lab Activities* 8-8
Lesson 8-9 Spheres ● Find the volume and surface area of spheres. ☑ SAT-10　☑ ITBS　☑ CTBS　☐ NAEP	Sphere models	*Hands-On Lab Activities* 8-9 *Technology Lab Activities* 8-9
Lesson 8-10 Scaling Three-Dimensional Figures ● Make scale models of three-dimensional figures. ☐ SAT-10　☐ ITBS　☐ CTBS　☑ NAEP	Centimeter cubes (MK), cubes (MK), rectangular and triangular prisms	
Extension Symmetry in Three Dimensions ● Identify types of symmetry in three dimensions. ☐ SAT-10　☑ ITBS　☑ CTBS　☐ NAEP	Cheese cubes, loaf of bread	

MK = *Manipulatives Kit*

Mathematics in Context

The unit *Patterns and Figures* from the *Mathematics in Context* © 2006 series can be used with Section 8B. See Section Planner above for suggestions for integrating *MiC* with *Holt Mathematics.*

Section Overview

Three-Dimensional Figures

Lesson 8-4

 Visualizing and drawing three-dimensional figures helps you understand the mathematical concepts and relationships in three-dimensional space.

Three-Dimensional Figures

Vertex

Edge

Face

Drawing Three-Dimensional Figures

Front   Top   Side

Volume and Surface Area

Lessons 8-5 through 8-10

 Prisms, cylinders, pyramids, cones, and spheres are used in art, architecture, and manufacturing.

| **Volume** is the number of **cubic units** needed to **fill** a three-dimensional figure. | **Surface area** is the number of **square units** needed to **cover** all surfaces of a three-dimensional figure. |

Volume and Surface Area Formulas

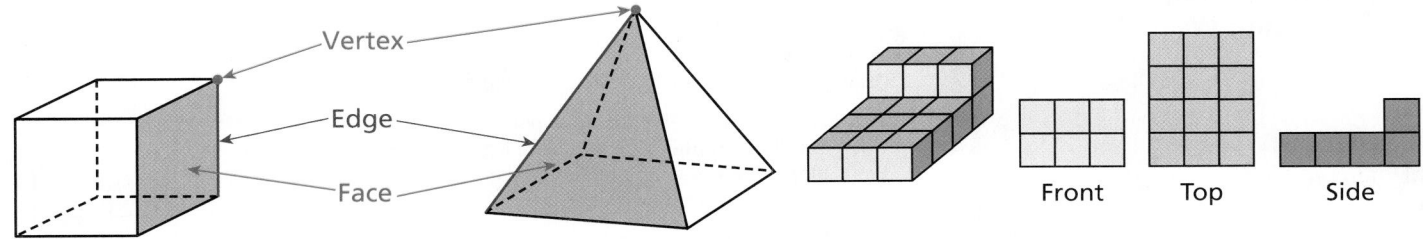

	Prism	**Cylinder**	**Pyramid**	**Cone**	**Sphere**
Volume	$V = Bh$	$V = Bh = (\pi r^2)h$	$V = \frac{1}{3}Bh$	$V = \frac{1}{3}Bh$ $= \frac{1}{3}(\pi r^2)h$	$V = \frac{4}{3}\pi r^3$
Surface area	$S = 2B + F$ $= 2B + Ph$	$S = 2B + L$ $= 2\pi r^2 + 2\pi rh$	$S = B + F$ $= B + \frac{1}{2}p\ell$	$S = B + L$ $= \pi r^2 + \pi r\ell$	$S = 4\pi r^2$

Key for Variables:

B area of base (circle or polygon)
F lateral area of polygon surfaces

h height (always perpendicular to base)
r radius of circular base

P perimeter of base
ℓ slant height

$$S_A = S_B \cdot \left(\frac{1}{2}\right)^2$$

$$V_A = V_B \cdot \left(\frac{1}{2}\right)^3$$

| For any pair of similar figures, the *surface area* of the model figure equals the surface area of the original figure times the scale factor squared. |

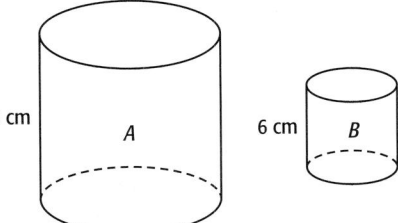

12 cm A 6 cm B

The **scale factor** of cylinder A to cylinder B is $\frac{1}{2}$.

| For any pair of similar three-dimensional figures, the *volume* of the model figure equals the volume of the original figure times the scale factor cubed. |

Hands-On LAB 8-4

Construct Nets

Use with Lesson 8-4

go.hrw.com
Lab Resources Online
KEYWORD: MT7 Lab8

REMEMBER
- A polygon is a closed plane figure formed by three or more line segments.
- Congruent polygons are the same size and shape.

You can explore the faces of a three-dimensional figure by making a *net*, an arrangement of two-dimensional figures that can be folded to form a three-dimensional figure.

Activity 1

Make a net of a box, such as a small cereal box.

  a. Lay one side of the box on paper and trace around it. Flip it on another side and trace around it. Continue flipping and tracing until you have traced around the top, bottom, and each side.

  b. List the polygons you drew.   Check students' answers

  c. Identify any congruent polygons.   Check students' answers

  d. Cut out, fold, and tape your net to make a three-dimensional figure.

Think and Discuss

  1. How many polygons make up a box?   6

  2. What types of polygons are they?   rectangles

  3. Were any polygons congruent? If so, which ones?

Try This

  1. Use your box from Activity 1 to make a different net by flipping it a different way. Are the polygons you drew the same? Cut out, fold, and tape your net. Does it still form the same three-dimensional figure?   Yes; yes

  2. Use what you have learned in this activity to describe a box. Use math terminology in your description.   Check students' work

  3. Make a net of a cube. How many different nets can you make? Draw them. Then list the polygons you drew. Identify any congruent polygons. Use math terminology to describe a cube.

Activity 1
Answers to *Think and Discuss*

3. Yes, the four larger rectangles were congruent and the two smaller rectangles were congruent.

Answers to *Try This*

2. Possible answer: A box is a three-dimensional figure made of six connecting rectangles. The four larger rectangles are congruent and form the lateral faces. The two smaller rectangles are congruent and form the two parallel bases. If the box is a cube, then it is made of six congruent squares.

Activity 2

Make a net of a can.

a. Lay the bottom of the can on paper and trace around it.

b. Tip the can onto its side. Mark the paper where the top and bottom of the can touches the paper.

c. Make a mark on the edge of the can where it touches the paper. Roll the can until the mark comes back to the original position.

d. Make a mark where the can touches the paper at the top and bottom, as you did in part **b.**   Check students' answers

e. Connect the four marks you made in parts **b** and **c.**   Check students' answers

f. Tip the can over to its top, and trace around it.

g. Cut out and tape your net to make a three-dimensional figure.

Think and Discuss

2. one rectangle and two circles

1. How many figures make up a can?   3   **2.** What types of figures are they?

3. Are any of the figures congruent? If so, which ones?   **3.** Yes, the two circles are congruent

Try This

1. Use what you have learned in this activity to describe a can. Use math terminology in your description.

Activity 3

Make a figure like the one shown at right.

a. Use a compass to draw part of a circle.

b. Mark the point where you placed the compass, and connect this point with straight lines to the endpoints of the arc you drew in part **a.**

c. Cut out the figure and bend it so that the two straight edges are touching. Tape the two edges together.

Think and Discuss

1. What kind of figure did you make?   a cone

2. Is there a surface missing from the cone? What is the shape of the missing part?
There is no bottom. It should be a circle.

Try This

1. Make a net of a pyramid. Cut out and tape the net to form a three-dimensional figure. Use math terminology to describe a pyramid.

Activity 2
Answers to *Try This*

1. Possible answer: A can is a three-dimensional figure made of two parallel, congruent circular bases and a rectangle that forms the lateral surface.

Activity 3
Answers to *Try This*

1. Possible answer: A pyramid is a three-dimensional figure with a polygon for a base and lateral faces that are congruent triangles.

Pacing: Traditional 1 day
Block $\frac{1}{2}$ day

Objective: Students draw and identify parts of three-dimensional figures.

Hands-On Lab
In *Hands-On Lab Activities*

Online Edition
Tutorial Videos, Interactivities

Countdown to Testing Week 16

Power Presentations
with PowerPoint®

Warm Up

Find the circumference of each circle, both in terms of π and to the nearest tenth. Use 3.14 for π.

1. radius 2.5 m $\quad$ 5π m; 15.7 m

2. diameter 8.8 cm $\quad$ 8.8π cm; 27.6 cm

Find the area of each circle, both in terms of π and to the nearest tenth. Use 3.14 for π.

3. radius 14 ft $\quad$ 196π ft^2; 615.4 ft^2

4. diameter 14 ft $\quad$ 49π ft^2; 153.9 ft^2

Problem of the Day

What is the least number of lines needed to draw 5 squares? 6

Also available on transparency

Math Humor

Teacher: Why is your perspective drawing a blank sheet of paper?

Student: You told me to draw it with a vanishing point!

State Resources

Learn to draw and identify parts of three-dimensional figures.

Vocabulary
face
edge
vertex
orthogonal views

Drawings of three-dimensional objects are two-dimensional representations. Techniques such as shading and perspective are used to give the appearance of depth to these drawings.

Like the objects they represent, drawings of three-dimensional figures have *faces, edges,* and *vertices.* A **face** is a flat surface, an **edge** is where two faces meet, and a **vertex** is where three or more edges meet.

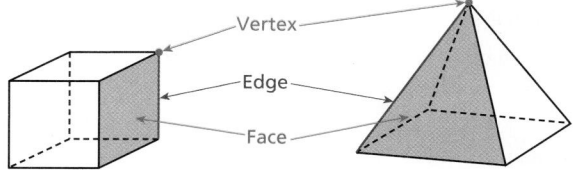

Since in a drawing of a three-dimensional object, you can only see up to three sides of a figure, you have to visualize how the figure looks from other angles. One way to do this is by drawing the *orthogonal views* of the figure. **Orthogonal views** show how the figure looks from different perspectives, such as the front, side, and top views. For figures constructed with cubes, the orthogonal views will be groups of squares.

EXAMPLE **1** **Identifying Vertices, Edges, and Faces**

Name the vertices, edges, and faces of the three-dimensional figure shown.

The vertices are *A, B, C, D, E,* and *F.*

The edges are $\overline{AB}$, $\overline{BC}$, $\overline{CA}$, $\overline{DE}$, $\overline{EF}$, $\overline{FD}$, $\overline{AD}$, $\overline{BE}$, and $\overline{CF}$.

The faces are triangles *ABC* and *DEF* and quadrilaterals *ADFC, ADEB,* and *BEFC.*

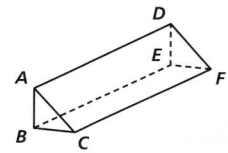

---

1 Introduce

Alternate Opener

8-4 **Drawing Three-Dimensional Figures**

The figure shows an *isometric drawing* of a three-dimensional figure. Given this drawing, you can build the three-dimensional figure using two cubes.

Use cubes to build each of the three-dimensional figures. Then tell how many cubes it takes to build each figure.

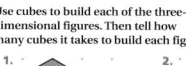

1.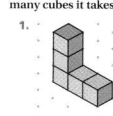

2.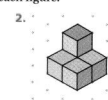

3.

4.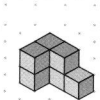

Think and Discuss

5. **Discuss** which of the three-dimensional figures in Problems 1–4 would look exactly the same when viewed from the front, top, and side.

6. **Describe** the top view of the figure in Problem 2.

Motivate

Show students a simple drawing of a square. Draw another square of the same size with a corner at the center of the first square. Then connect the corners of each square to create a cube. Erase the lines that would be hidden if the cube were solid. Explain to students that the technique of making a flat drawing look three-dimensional is called *perspective.*

Explorations and answers are provided in *Alternate Openers: Explorations Transparencies.*

EXAMPLE 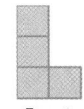 **Drawing a Figure When Given Different Perspectives**

Draw the figure shown in the front, top, and side views.

Front   Top   Side

From the front and side views, there appears to be one cube on the top level, in the back left corner. The top view shows that the bottom layer has three cubes.

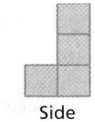

EXAMPLE 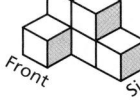 **Drawing Different Perspectives of a Figure**

Draw the front, top, and side views of the figure.

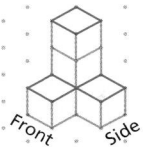

Front: The figure looks like 2 squares on top of three squares.

Front

Top: The figure looks like a row of 3 squares with 1 square below the left square.

Top

Side: The figure looks like 1 square on top of two squares.

Side

When looking at a figure made of cubes, the bottom view is a mirror image of the top view, the back view is a mirror image of the front view, and the side views are mirror images of each other.

Answers to *Think and Discuss*:

1. If the figure were a rectangular prism.

2. If the figure were a cube.

3. It is only possible if the congruent rectangles are squares.

Think and Discuss

1. **Give** a situation in which the front and side views of a figure would be the same.

2. **Give** a situation in which all three views of a figure would be the same.

3. **Explain** whether it is possible for all of the views of a figure to be congruent rectangles.

Example **1**

Name the vertices, edges, and faces of the three-dimensional figure shown.

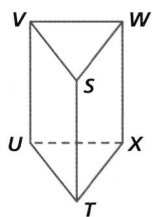

vertices: *S, T, U, V, W, X*

edges: $\overline{VS}$, $\overline{SW}$, $\overline{WV}$, $\overline{UT}$, $\overline{TX}$, $\overline{XU}$, $\overline{VU}$, $\overline{ST}$, $\overline{WX}$

faces: triangles *UTX* and *VSW*, rectangles *VSTU, SWXT, VWXU*

Example **2**

Draw the figure shown in the front, top, and side views.

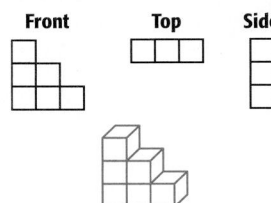

Front   Top   Side

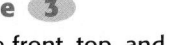

Example **3**

Draw the front, top, and side views of the figure.

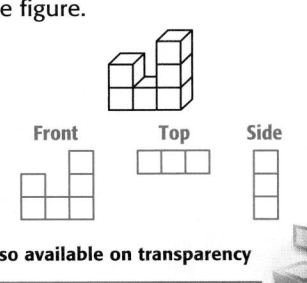

Front   Top   Side

Also available on transparency

---

2 Teach

Guided Instruction

In this lesson, students learn to draw and identify parts of three-dimensional figures. Show students a rectangular box and define the terms *face*, *edge*, and *vertex*. Lead students through the steps in Example 2, using isometric dot paper to create sketches of three-dimensional figures. Then guide them through the examples for drawing sketches of orthogonal views of a figure (Teaching Transparency).

Teaching Tip

Visual Show students pieces of art in which perspective is used (and if possible, some in which it is not used).

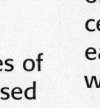 **Reaching All Learners**
Through Multiple Representations

Have boxes of different sizes and shapes available for students to measure (e.g., cereal boxes, paper clip boxes, etc.). Have students work in pairs. Have each student choose a box and measure its dimensions. Ask the students to sketch the box using isometric dot paper (Teacher Tools), letting each space on the paper represent one inch (or one centimeter). When sketches are done, have each student's partner try to determine which box he or she sketched.

3 Close

Summarize

Review how to draw a figure from orthogonal views and how to draw orthogonal views from a three-dimensional figure. Use figures made from cubes to help students see the three-dimensional figure and its orthogonal views.

8-4 Exercises

8-4 Exercises

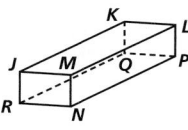
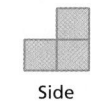

go.hrw.com
Homework Help Online
KEYWORD: MT7 8-4
Parent Resources Online
KEYWORD: MT7 Parent

Assignment Guide

If you finished Example **1** assign:
Average 1, 4, 17–23
Advanced 4, 17–23

If you finished Example **2** assign:
Average 1, 2, 4, 5, 10–12, 17–23
Advanced 4, 5, 10–13, 15–23

If you finished Example **3** assign:
Average 1–12, 14, 17–23
Advanced 4–23

Homework Quick Check

Quickly check key concepts.
Exercises: 4, 5, 6, 12

Answers

2.

3. Front   Top   Side

5.

6. Front   Top   Side

7–9. See p. A11.

GUIDED PRACTICE

See Example **1** 1. Name the vertices, edges, and faces of the three-dimensional figure shown.

faces: quadrilaterals *JKLM, PQRN, JMNR, KLPQ, JKQR,* and *LMNP*

See Example **2** 2. Draw the figure that has the following front, top, and side views.

Front   Top   Side

1. vertices: *J, K, L, M, N, P, Q, R*
edges: $\overline{JK}$, $\overline{KL}$, $\overline{LM}$, $\overline{MJ}$, $\overline{RQ}$, $\overline{QP}$, $\overline{PN}$, $\overline{NR}$, $\overline{JR}$, $\overline{KQ}$, $\overline{LP}$, $\overline{MR}$

See Example **3** 3. Draw the front, top, and side views of the figure.

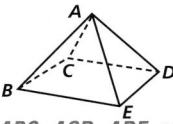

INDEPENDENT PRACTICE

See Example **1** 4. Name the vertices, edges, and faces of the three-dimensional figure shown.
vertices: *A, B, C, D, E*
edges: $\overline{AB}$, $\overline{AC}$, $\overline{AD}$, $\overline{AE}$, $\overline{BC}$, $\overline{CD}$, $\overline{DE}$, $\overline{EB}$
faces: quadrilateral *BCDE* and triangles *ABC, ACD, ADE,* and *AEB*

See Example **2** 5. Draw the figure shown in the front, top, and side views.

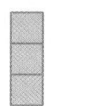      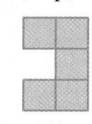
Front   Top   Side

See Example **3** 6. Draw the front, top, and side views of the figure.

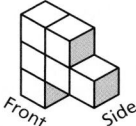

PRACTICE AND PROBLEM SOLVING

Extra Practice
See page 796.

Draw the front, top, and side views of each figure shown.

7. 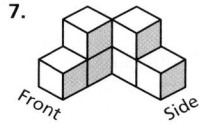   8. 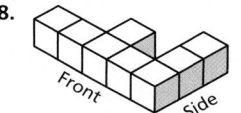   9.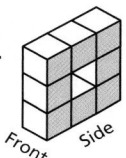

RETEACH 8-4

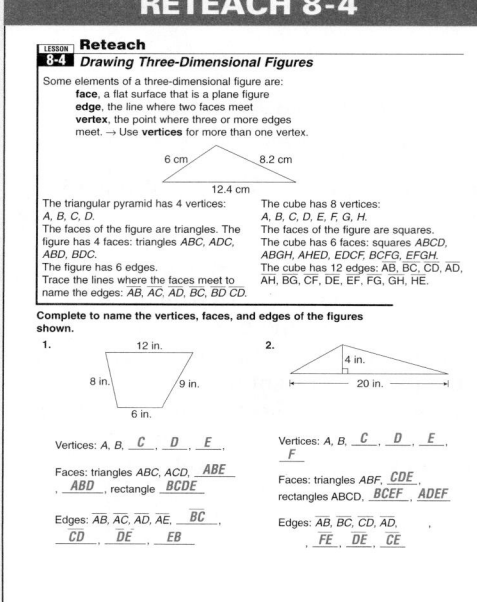

PRACTICE 8-4

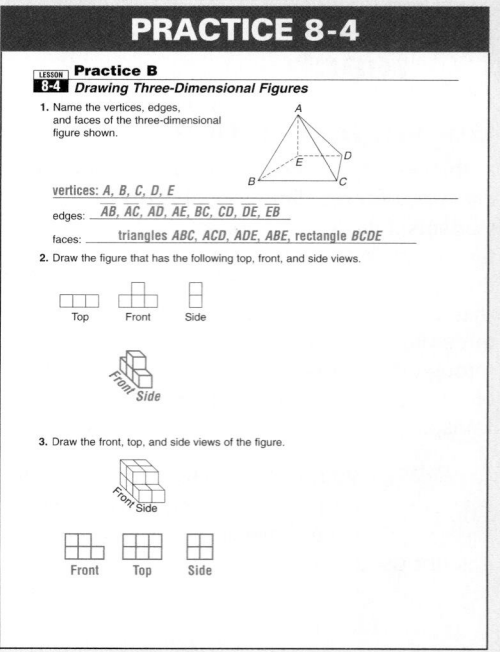

Draw the figure shown in the orthogonal views.

10.

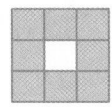 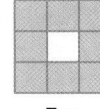 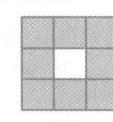

Front   Top   Side

Use isometric dot paper to sketch each figure.

11. a cube 4 units on each side   12. a triangular box 5 units high

13. a rectangular box 2 units high, with a base 5 units by 7 units

14. **Art** The sculpture *123454321* by Sol LeWitt consists of 9 cubes of different sizes. Draw the front, top, and side views of the sculpture.

15. **Write About It** Describe a figure for which the top and front views would be the same.

 16. **Challenge** The video game Tetris is played by stacking seven different configurations of four squares. Choose three different Tetris shapes and draw a figure made of cubes as if the Tetris shapes were the front, top, and side views of the figure. Do not use a single Tetris shape more than twice. **Check students' work.**

15.
Possible answer: The only shape for which all six orthogonal views would be the same is a cube.

TEST PREP and Spiral Review

17. **Multiple Choice** Which is the top view of the figure?

Ⓐ   Ⓑ   Ⓒ   Ⓓ

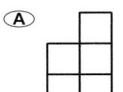 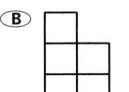 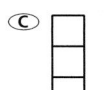 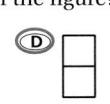

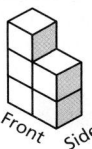

18. **Short Response** Draw the orthogonal views of the figure.

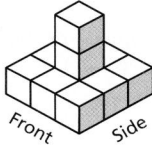

Find each commission to the nearest cent. (Lesson 6-6)

19. total sales: $39.68   20. total sales: $475 **$17.81**   21. total sales: $2,143
commission rate: 4.5% **$1.79**   commission rate: 3.75%   commission rate: 6%
                                                                 $128.58

Find the area of each circle to the nearest tenth. Use 3.14 for π. (Lesson 8-3)

22. circle with radius 7 ft **153.9 ft²**   23. circle with diameter 17 in. **226.9 in.²**

Answers
10–14, 18. See pp. A11–A12.

TEST PREP DOCTOR + Encourage students to make a one-dimensional sketch of the cubes they would see if they looked directly down onto the top of the figure in Exercise 17. This may help them visualize the figure.

Journal

Have students look at some photographs or paintings and describe what they see that pertains to this lesson. They may describe the type of perspective, identify some vertices, faces, and edges, or identify an area of the picture that serves as a vanishing point.

Power Presentations
with PowerPoint®

8-4 Lesson Quiz

1. Draw the figure shown in the front, top, and side views.

Front   Top   Side

2. Draw the front and back views of the figure.

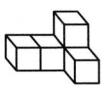

Front   Back

Also available on transparency

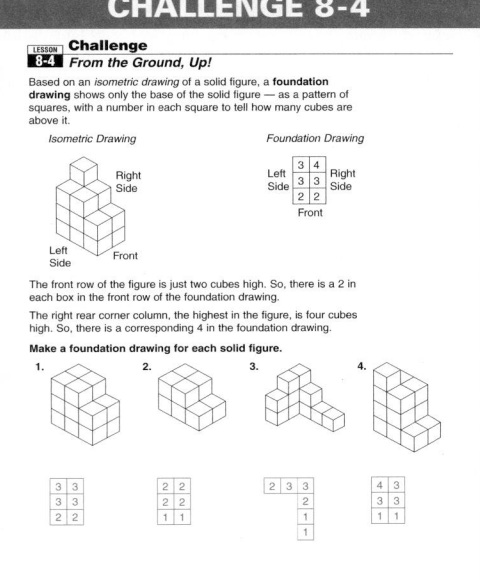

CHALLENGE 8-4

Challenge
8-4 *From the Ground, Up!*

Based on an *isometric drawing* of a solid figure, a **foundation drawing** shows only the base of the solid figure — as a pattern of squares, with a number in each square to tell how many cubes are above it.

Isometric Drawing   *Foundation Drawing*

The front row of the figure is just two cubes high. So, there is a 2 in each box in the front row of the foundation drawing.

The right rear corner column, the highest in the figure, is four cubes high. So, there is a corresponding 4 in the foundation drawing.

Make a foundation drawing for each solid figure.

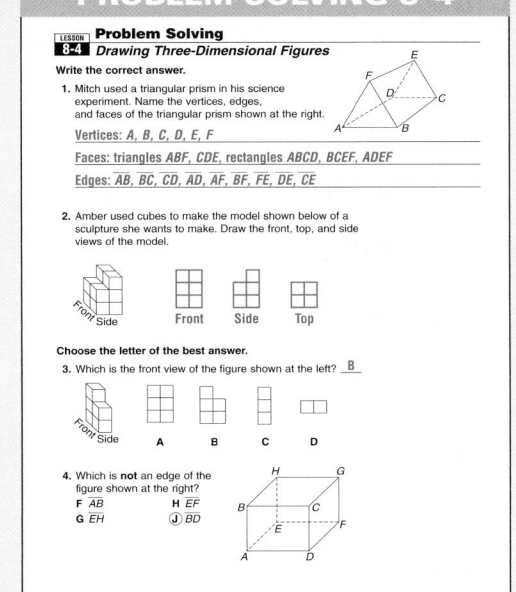

PROBLEM SOLVING 8-4

Problem Solving
8-4 *Drawing Three-Dimensional Figures*

Write the correct answer.

1. Mitch used a triangular prism in his science experiment. Name the vertices, edges, and faces of the triangular prism shown at the right.

Vertices: *A, B, C, D, E, F*

Faces: triangles *ABF, CDE*, rectangles *ABCD, BCEF, ADEF*

Edges: *AB, BC, CD, AD, AF, BF, FE, DE, CE*

2. Amber used cubes to make the model shown below of a sculpture she wants to make. Draw the front, top, and side views of the model.

Choose the letter of the best answer.

3. Which is the front view of the figure shown at the left? **B**

4. Which is **not** an edge of the figure shown at the right?
F *AB*   H *EF*
G *EH*   J *BD*

8-4 Drawing Three-Dimensional Figures **411**

Hands-On LAB

Organizer

Pacing:
Traditional 1 day
Block $\frac{1}{2}$ day

Objective: Use empty cartons and cans to explore the volume of prisms and cylinders.

Materials: Different-sized rectangular prisms, different-sized cylinders, ruler, popcorn, measuring cup, identical-sized cubes

 Online Edition

 Countdown to Testing Week 16

Resources

 Hands-On Lab Activities
Lab 8-5 Recording Sheet

Teach

Discuss

Discuss with students how to use a ruler to precisely measure the dimensions of each figure. Explain that there is more than one way to find the volume of a solid figure.

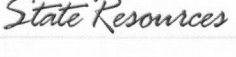
State Resources

go.hrw.com
State Resources Online
KEYWORD: MT7 Resources

Hands-On LAB 8-5

Find Volume of Prisms and Cylinders

Use with Lesson 8-5

go.hrw.com
Lab Resources Online
KEYWORD: MT7 Lab8

You can use models to explore the volume of rectangular prisms and cylinders.

Activity

1 Use five different-sized rectangular prisms, such as empty cartons. **Check students' work.**

a. Cover the bottom of each prism with cubes to find the area of the prism's base. Record the information in a table.

b. Fill the prism with cubes. Find the height. Then count the cubes to find the prism's volume. Record the information in a table.

Object	
Area of Base	
Height	
Volume	

2 Use five different-sized cylinders, such as empty cans. **Check students' work.**

a. Measure the radius of each circular base and calculate its area. Record the information in a table.

b. Measure the height of each cylinder. Record the information in a table.

c. Fill each cylinder with popcorn kernels.

d. Use a measuring cup to find how much popcorn filled the cylinder.

e. Find the approximate volume of each cylinder. 1 cup = 14.4 in³. Record the information in a table.

Think and Discuss   Check students' work.

1. What do you notice about the relationship between the base, the height, and the volume of the rectangular prisms? of the cylinders?

2. Make a conjecture about how to find the volume of any rectangular prism or cylinder.

Try This

1. Use your conjecture to find the volume of a new rectangular prism. Check your conjecture by following the steps in Activity 1. Revise your conjecture as needed.

2. Use your conjecture to find the volume of a new cylinder. Check your conjecture by following the steps in Activity 2. Revise your conjecture as needed.

Close

Key Concept

You can find the volume of a rectangular prism by counting the number of cubes that it takes to fill the prism. You can find the volume of a cylinder by measuring the volume of popcorn it takes to fill the cylinder.

Assessment

1. How could you find the volume of an irregular solid?

Possible answer: Fill the solid with water, then measure the volume of water used with a measuring cup.

Possible answers to *Think and Discuss*

1. The volume of each rectangular prism is the product of the area of the base and the height. The volume of each cylinder is the product of the area of the base and the height.

2. You can find the volume of any rectangular prism or cylinder by multiplying the area of the base times the height of the figure.

Learn to find the volume of prisms and cylinders.

Vocabulary
cylinder
prism

The largest drum ever built measures 4.8 meters in diameter and is 4.95 meters deep. It was built by Asano Taiko Company in Japan. You can use these measurements to find the approximate volume of the drum, which is roughly a *cylinder*.

A **cylinder** is a three-dimensional figure that has two congruent circular bases. A **prism** is a three-dimensional figure named for the shape of its bases. The two bases are congruent polygons. All of the other faces are parallelograms.

The circumference of the Taiko drum pictured is about half that of the largest drum ever made.

Triangular prism   **Rectangular prism**   **Cylinder**

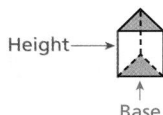   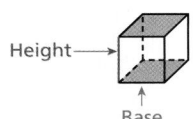   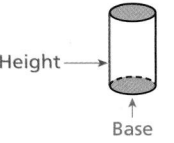

VOLUME OF PRISMS AND CYLINDERS		
Words	**Numbers**	**Formula**
Prism: The volume V of a prism is the area of the base B times the height h.	$B = 2(5)$ $= 10$ units^2 $V = (10)(3)$ $= 30$ units^3	$V = Bh$
Cylinder: The volume of a cylinder is the area of the base B times the height h.	$B = \pi(2^2)$ $= 4\pi$ units^2 $V = (4\pi)(6) = 24\pi$ ≈ 75.4 units^3	$V = Bh$ $= (\pi r^2)h$

EXAMPLE 1 **Finding the Volume of Prisms and Cylinders**

Find the volume of each figure to the nearest tenth. Use 3.14 for π.

A A rectangular prism with base 2 m by 5 m and height 7 m.

$B = 2 \cdot 5 = 10$ m^2 *Area of base*
$V = Bh$ *Volume of prism*
$= 10 \cdot 7 = 70$ m^3

Remember!
Area is measured in *square units.* Volume is measured in *cubic units.*

---

1 Introduce

Alternate Opener

Motivate

Show students prisms and cylinders of different shapes and sizes. Include prisms other than rectangular prisms. Point out that all of the solids you show have at least two congruent surfaces, which are called *bases.* Explain that to find the volume of one of these solids, you would multiply the area of the base by the height.

Explorations and answers are provided in *Alternate Openers: Explorations Transparencies.*

Additional Examples

Example ①

Find the volume of each figure to the nearest tenth. Use 3.14 for π.

A. a rectangular prism with base 2 cm by 5 cm and a height 3 cm

$V = 30$ cm^3

B.

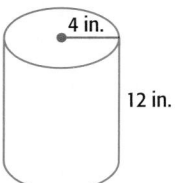

$V = 192\pi \approx 602.9$ in^3

C.

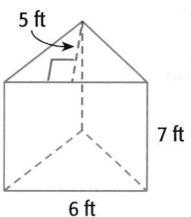

$V = 105$ ft^3

Example ②

A. A juice box measures 3 in. by 2 in. by 4 in. Explain whether tripling the length, width, or height of the box would triple the amount of juice the box holds.
The original box has a volume of 24 in^3. You could triple the volume to 72 in^3 by tripling any one of the dimensions. So tripling the length, width, or height would triple the amount of juice the box would hold.

Also available on transparency

Find the volume of each figure to the nearest tenth. Use 3.14 for π.

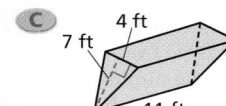

B

$B = \pi(6^2) = 36\pi$ m^2 *Area of base*
$V = Bh$ *Volume of a cylinder*
$= 36\pi \cdot 15$
$= 540\pi \approx 1695.6$ m^3

C

4 ft

$B = \frac{1}{2} \cdot 4 \cdot 7 = 14$ ft^2 *Area of base*
$V = Bh$ *Volume of a prism*
$= 14 \cdot 11$
$= 154$ ft^3

The volume of a rectangular prism can be written as $V = \ell wh$, where ℓ is the length, w is the width, and h is the height.

EXAMPLE ② Exploring the Effects of Changing Dimensions

A A cereal box measures 6 in. by 2 in. by 9 in. Explain whether doubling the length, width, or height of the box would double the amount of cereal the box holds.

Original Dimensions	Double the Length	Double the Width	Double the Height
$V = \ell wh$	$V = (2\ell)wh$	$V = \ell(2w)h$	$V = \ell w(2h)$
$= 6 \cdot 2 \cdot 9$	$= 12 \cdot 2 \cdot 9$	$= 6 \cdot 4 \cdot 9$	$= 6 \cdot 2 \cdot 18$
$= 108$ in^3	$= 216$ in^3	$= 216$ in^3	$= 216$ in^3

The original box has a volume of 108 in^3. You could double the volume to 216 in^3 by doubling any one of the dimensions. So doubling the length, width, or height would double the amount of cereal the box holds.

B A can of corn has a radius of 2.5 in. and a height of 4 in. Explain whether doubling the height of the can would have the same effect on the volume as doubling the radius.

Original Dimensions	Double the Height	Double the Radius
$V = \pi r^2 h$	$V = \pi r^2(2h)$	$V = \pi(2r)^2 h$
$= 2.5^2\pi \cdot 4$	$= 2.5^2\pi \cdot 8$	$= 5^2\pi \cdot 4$
$= 25\pi$ in^3	$= 50\pi$ in^3	$= 100\pi$ in^3

By doubling the height, you would double the volume. By doubling the radius, you would increase the volume four times the original.

---

② Teach

Guided Instruction

In this lesson, students learn to find the volume of prisms and cylinders. Point out that the congruent bases of a prism are polygons (such as rectangles and triangles) and that the bases of a cylinder are circles (Teaching Transparency). Review the area formulas for these figures. Explain that the volume of any prism or cylinder is found by multiplying the area of its base by its height. Explain that because these figures are three-dimensional, volume is measured in cubic units.

Reaching All Learners
Through Modeling

Have students build a variety of prisms using centimeter cubes. Ask students to count the cubes to find the height, area of the base, and volume of each prism and to record the data in a table as shown.

Area of base	Height	Volume

Ask students to find a relationship between the area of the base, the height, and the volume. Possible answer: The volume is the product of the area of the base and the height, or $V = Bh$.

EXAMPLE 3 *Music Application*

The Asano Taiko Company of Japan built the world's largest drum in 2000. The drum's diameter is 4.8 meters, and its height is 4.95 meters. Estimate the volume of the drum.

$d = 4.8 \approx 5, h = 4.95 \approx 5$

$r = \frac{d}{2} = \frac{5}{2} = 2.5$

$V = (\pi r^2)h$ *Volume of a cylinder.*

$\quad = (3.14)(2.5)^2 \cdot 5$ *Use 3.14 for π.*

$\quad = (3.14)(6.25)(5)$

$\quad = 19.625 \cdot 5$

$\quad = 98.125 \approx 98$

The volume of the drum is approximately 98 m³.

To find the volume of a composite three-dimensional figure, find the volume of each part and add the volumes together.

EXAMPLE 4 **Finding the Volume of Composite Figures**

Find the volume of the figure.

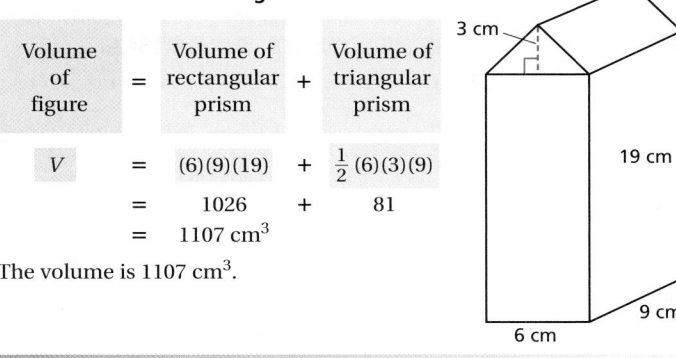

Volume of figure		Volume of rectangular prism		Volume of triangular prism
V	=	$(6)(9)(19)$	+	$\frac{1}{2}(6)(3)(9)$
	=	1026	+	81
	=	1107 cm³		

The volume is 1107 cm³.

Think and Discuss

1. **Use models** to show that two rectangular prisms can have different heights but the same volume.

2. **Apply** your results from Example 2 to make a conjecture about changing dimensions in a triangular prism.

3. **Use a model** to describe what happens to the volume of a cylinder when the diameter of the base is tripled.

 **Close**

Summarize

Review the definitions of *prism* and *cylinder*. Review the formula for finding the volume of each. Discuss the differences between area and volume. You may want to show some examples of two-dimensional and three-dimensional figures and ask students which measure applies to each one. As a challenge, you may want them to estimate the value of each measure.

Possible answer: Area applies to two-dimensional figures and is measured in square units. Volume applies to three-dimensional figures and is measured in cubic units.

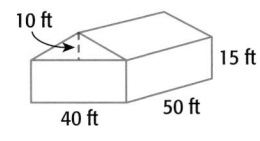
Possible answers to Think and Discuss

1. A prism with a 2 × 3 unit base and a height of 2 units has the same volume (12 units³) as a prism with a 6 × 2 unit base and a height of 1 unit.

2. If you double one dimension of a triangular prism, the prism's volume doubles. If you double two dimensions, the volume becomes 4 times the original volume. If you double three dimensions, the volume becomes 8 times the original volume.

3. The volume will increase by a factor of 3², or 9.

Assignment Guide

If you finished Example **1** assign:
Average 1–3, 7–9, 20–25
Advanced 7–9, 17, 20–25

If you finished Example **2** assign:
Average 1–4, 7–10, 20–25
Advanced 7–10, 17, 20–25

If you finished Example **3** assign:
Average 1–5, 7–11, 13, 20–25
Advanced 7–11, 13–18, 20–25

If you finished Example **4** assign:
Average 1–13, 20–25
Advanced 7–25

Homework Quick Check

Quickly check key concepts.
Exercises: 8, 10, 11, 12

Answers

13b. See p. A12.

Math Background

The volume formula, $V = Bh$, applies to *right* cylinders and prisms, as studied in the lesson, and also to *oblique* cylinders and prisms, in which the axis is not perpendicular to the base.

 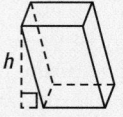

Oblique cylinder   Oblique prism

State Resources

go.hrw.com
State Resources Online
KEYWORD: MT7 Resources

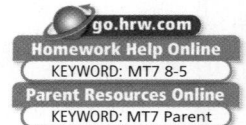
go.hrw.com
Homework Help Online
KEYWORD: MT7 8-5
Parent Resources Online
KEYWORD: MT7 Parent

GUIDED PRACTICE

See Example **1** Find the volume of each figure to the nearest tenth. Use 3.14 for π.

1.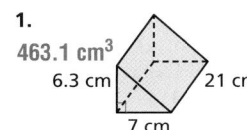
463.1 cm³
6.3 cm   21 cm
7 cm

2.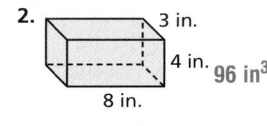
3 in.
4 in.   **96 in³**
8 in.

3.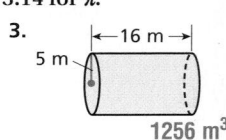
16 m
5 m
1256 m³

See Example **2** **4.** A can of juice has a radius 3 in. and a height 6 in. Explain whether tripling the radius would triple the volume of the can.

See Example **3** **5.** Grain is stored in cylindrical structures called *silos*. Estimate the volume of a silo with diameter 11.1 feet and height 20 feet. **≈ 1500 ft³**

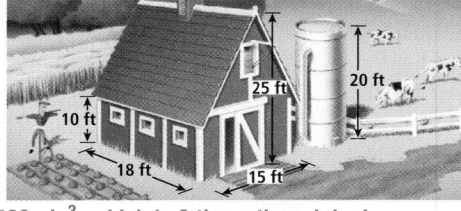
25 ft   20 ft
10 ft
18 ft   15 ft

See Example **4** **6.** Find the volume of the barn. **4725 ft³**

4. No; the volume of the can is 54π in³.
Tripling the radius gives a volume of 486π in³, which is 9 times the original.

INDEPENDENT PRACTICE

See Example **1** Find the volume of each figure to the nearest tenth. Use 3.14 for π.

7.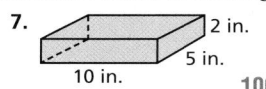
2 in.
5 in.
10 in.   **100 in³**

8.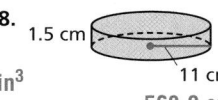
1.5 cm
11 cm
569.9 cm³

9.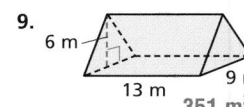
6 m
13 m   9 m
351 m³

See Example **2** **10.** A jewelry box measures 7 in. by 5 in. by 8 in. Explain whether increasing the height 4 times, from 8 in. to 32 in., would increase the volume 4 times.

See Example **3** **11.** A toy box is 5.1 cm by 3.2 cm by 4.2 cm. Estimate the volume of the toy box.

See Example **4** **12.** Find the volume of the treehouse. **168 ft³**

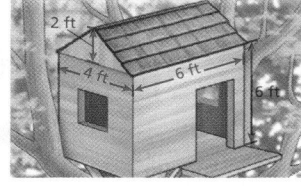
2 ft
4 ft   6 ft
6 ft

10. Yes; the volume of the box is 280 in³. Increasing the height by 4 times gives a volume of 1120 in³, which is 4 times the original.

11. ≈ 60 cm³

PRACTICE AND PROBLEM SOLVING

Extra Practice
See page 797.

13. While Karim was at camp, his father sent him a care package. The box measured 10.2 in. by 19.9 in. by 4.2 in.

a. Estimate the volume of the box. **800 in³**

b. What might be the measurements of a box with twice its volume?

RETEACH 8-5

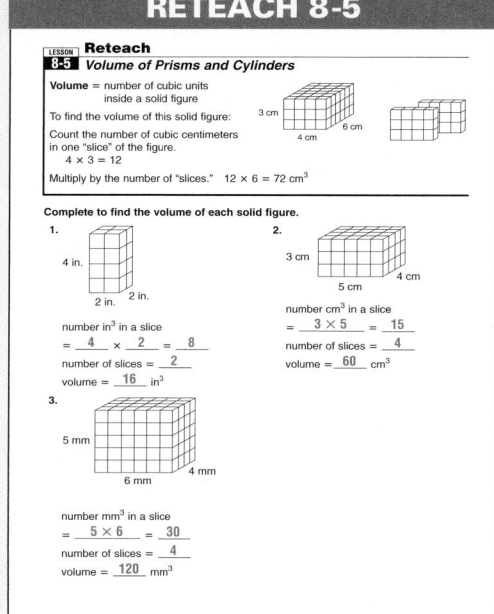

LESSON **8-5** **Reteach**
Volume of Prisms and Cylinders

Volume = number of cubic units inside a solid figure
To find the volume of this solid figure:
Count the number of cubic centimeters in one "slice" of the figure.
$4 \times 3 = 12$
Multiply by the number of "slices." $12 \times 6 = 72$ cm³

3 cm
4 cm   6 cm

Complete to find the volume of each solid figure.

1.
4 in.
2 in.   2 in.
number in³ in a slice
$= \underline{4} \times \underline{2} = \underline{8}$
number of slices $= \underline{2}$
volume $= \underline{16}$ in³

2.
3 cm
5 cm   4 cm
number cm³ in a slice
$= \underline{3 \times 5} = \underline{15}$
number of slices $= \underline{4}$
volume $= \underline{60}$ cm³

3.
5 mm
6 mm   4 mm
number mm³ in a slice
$= \underline{5 \times 6} = \underline{30}$
number of slices $= \underline{4}$
volume $= \underline{120}$ mm³

PRACTICE 8-5

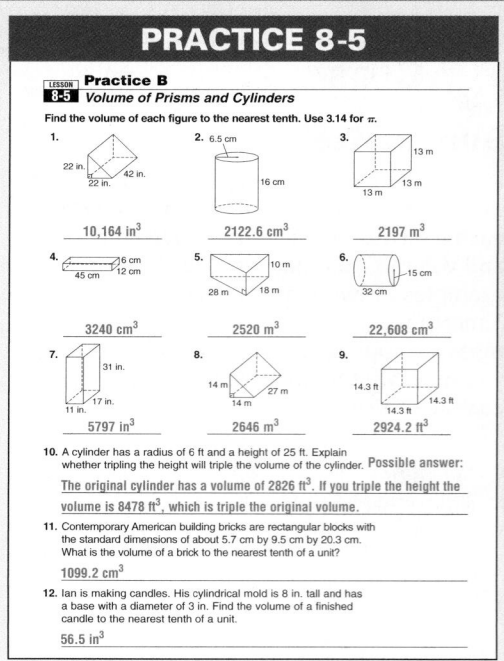

LESSON **8-5** **Practice B**
Volume of Prisms and Cylinders

Find the volume of each figure to the nearest tenth. Use 3.14 for π.

1.
22 in.
22 in.   42 in.
10,164 in³

2.
6.5 cm
16 cm
2122.6 cm³

3.
13 m
13 m   13 m
2197 m³

4.
45 cm   6 cm   12 cm
3240 cm³

5.
10 m
28 m   18 m
2520 m³

6.
15 cm
32 cm
22,608 cm³

7.
31 in.
11 in.   17 in.
5797 in³

8.
14 m   27 m
14 m
2646 m³

9.
14.3 ft
14.3 ft   14.3 ft
2924.2 ft³

10. A cylinder has a radius of 6 ft and a height of 25 ft. Explain whether tripling the height will triple the volume of the cylinder. **Possible answer:**
The original cylinder has a volume of 2826 ft³. If you triple the height the volume is 8478 ft³, which is triple the original volume.

11. Contemporary American building bricks are rectangular blocks with the standard dimensions of about 5.7 cm by 9.5 cm by 20.3 cm. What is the volume of a brick to the nearest tenth of a unit?
1099.2 cm³

12. Ian is making candles. His cylindrical mold is 8 in. tall and has a base with a diameter of 3 in. Find the volume of a finished candle to the nearest tenth of a unit.
56.5 in³

Life Science

Through the 52 large windows of the Giant Ocean Tank, visitors can see 3000 corals and sponges as well as large sharks, sea turtles, barracudas, moray eels, and hundreds of tropical fishes.

14. **Social Studies** The tablet held by the Statue of Liberty is approximately a rectangular prism with volume 1,107,096 in³. Estimate the thickness of the tablet. **about 20.5 in.**

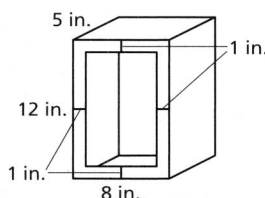

15. **Life Science** The cylindrical Giant Ocean Tank at the New England Aquarium in Boston has a volume of 200,000 gallons.
    a. One gallon of water equals 231 cubic inches. How many cubic inches of water are in the Giant Ocean Tank? **46,200,000 in³**
    b. Use your answer from part **a** as the volume. The tank is 24 ft deep. Find the radius in feet of the Giant Ocean Tank. **about 18.8 ft**

16. **Life Science** As many as 60,000 bees can live in 3 cubic feet of space. There are about 360,000 bees in a rectangular observation beehive that is 2 ft long by 3 ft high. What is the minimum possible width of the observation hive? **3 ft**

17. **What's the Error?** A student read this statement in a book: "The volume of a triangular prism with height 15 in. and base area 20 in. is 300 in³." Correct the error in the statement.

18. **Write About It** Explain why 1 cubic yard equals 27 cubic feet.

19. **Challenge** A 5-inch section of a hollow brick measures 12 inches tall and 8 inches wide on the outside. The brick is 1 inch thick. Find the volume of the brick, not the hollow interior. **180 in³**

TEST PREP and Spiral Review

20. **Multiple Choice** Cylinder A has radius 6 centimeters and height 14 centimeters. Cylinder B has radius half as long as cylinder A. What is the volume of cylinder B? Use 3.14 for π and round to the nearest tenth.

    Ⓐ 393.5 cm³   Ⓑ 395.6 cm³   Ⓒ 422.3 cm³   Ⓓ 791.3 cm³

21. **Multiple Choice** A tractor trailer has dimensions of 13 feet by 53 feet by 8 feet. What is the volume of the trailer?

    Ⓕ 424 ft³   Ⓖ 689 ft³   Ⓗ 2756 ft³   Ⓙ 5512 ft³

Give the coordinates of each point after a reflection across the given axis.
(Lesson 7-7)

22. (−3, 4); y-axis **(3, 4)**   23. (5, 9); x-axis **(5, −9)**   24. (6, −3); y-axis **(−6, −3)**

25. Find the height of a rectangle with perimeter 14 inches and length 3 inches. What is the area of the rectangle? (Lesson 8-1) **4 in.; 12 in²**

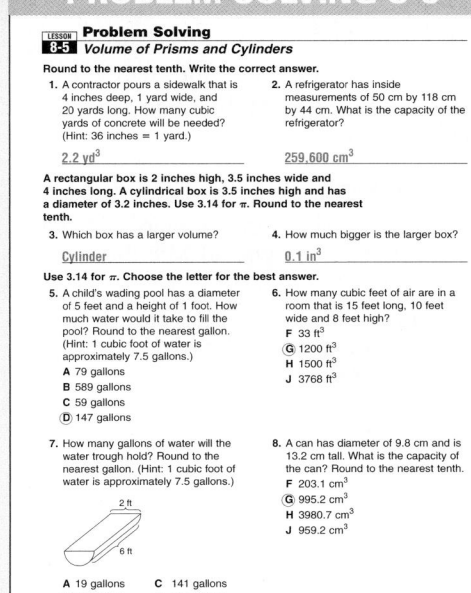

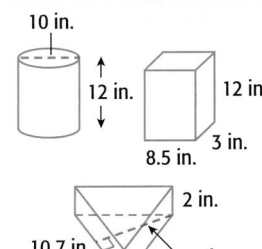

Hands-On LAB 8-6

Find Volume of Pyramids and Cones

Use with Lesson 8-6

go.hrw.com
Lab Resources Online
KEYWORD: MT7 Lab8

You can use containers to explore the relationship between the volumes of pyramids and prisms and the relationship between the volumes of cones and cylinders.

Activity 1

Find or make a hollow prism and a hollow pyramid that have congruent bases and heights.

a. Fill the pyramid with popcorn kernels. Make sure that the popcorn kernels are level with the opening of the pyramid, and then pour the kernels into the prism.

b. Repeat step **a** until the prism is full and the popcorn kernels are level with the top of the prism. Keep track of the number of full pyramids it takes to fill the prism.

Think and Discuss

1. How many full pyramids did it take to fill a prism with a congruent base and height?   3

2. Use a fraction to express the relationship between the volume of a pyramid and the volume of a prism with a congruent base and height. $\frac{1}{3}$

3. If the volume of a prism is Bh, write a rule for the volume of a pyramid.

Try This

1. Use your rule from Think and Discuss 3 to find the volume of another pyramid. Check your rule by following the steps in Activity 1. Revise your rule as needed.   **Check students' work.**

2. The volume of a pyramid is 31 in³. What is the volume of a prism with the same base and height? Explain your reasoning.

3. The volume of a prism is 27 cm³. What is the volume of a pyramid with the same base and height? Explain your reasoning.

4. A glass lantern filled with oil is shaped like a square pyramid. Each side of the base is 5 centimeters long, and the lantern is 11 centimeters tall. What is the volume of the lantern?   **91.7 cm³**

Close
Key Concept

Pyramids and cones are $\frac{1}{3}$ the volume of prisms and cylinders of the same base and height.

Assessment

1. The volume of a prism is 48 in³. What is the volume of a pyramid with the same base and height?   16 in³

2. The volume of a cone is 33 cm³. What is the volume of a cylinder with the same base and height?   99 cm³

Activity 1

Answers to *Try This*

2. 93 in³; The volume of a prism is three times the volume of a pyramid with a congruent base and height.

3. 9 cm³; The volume of a pyramid is $\frac{1}{3}$ the volume of a prism with a congruent base and height.

Find or make a hollow cylinder and a hollow cone that have congruent bases and heights.

   a. Fill the cone with popcorn kernels. Make sure that the popcorn kernels are level with the opening of the cone, and then pour the kernels into the cylinder.

   b. Repeat step **a** until the cylinder is full and the popcorn kernels are level with the top of the cylinder. Keep track of the number of full cones it takes.

Think and Discuss

1. How many full cones did it take to fill a cylinder with a congruent base and height?   **3**

2. Use a fraction to express the relationship between the volume of a cone and the volume of a cylinder with a congruent base and height. $\frac{1}{3}$

3. If the volume of a cylinder is Bh or $\pi r^2 h$, write a rule for the volume of a cone. $\frac{1}{3}Bh$ **or** $\frac{1}{3}\pi r^2 h$

Try This

1. Use your rule from Think and Discuss 3 to find the volume of another cone. Check your rule by following the steps in Activity 2. Revise your rule as needed.   **Check students' work.**

2. The volume of a cone is 3.7 m³. What is the volume of a cylinder with the same base and height? Explain your reasoning.

3. The volume of a cylinder is 228 ft³. What is the volume of a cone with the same base and height? Explain your reasoning.

4. Evan is using a plastic cone to build a sand castle. The cone has a diameter of 10 inches and is 18 inches tall. What is the volume of the cone?   **471 in³**

5. Aneesha has two paper cones. The first cone has a radius of 2 inches and a height of 3 inches. The second cone has the same base but is twice the height. Aneesha says that the second cone has twice the volume of the first cone. Is she correct? Explain your reasoning. **Possible answer: Yes, Aneesha is correct. The volume of the first cone is $\frac{1}{3}\pi(2)^2(3)$, or 4π in³. The volume of the second cone is $\frac{1}{3}\pi(2)^2(6)$, or $2 \cdot 4\pi$ in³. It has twice the volume of the first cone.**

Activity 2

Answers to *Try This*

2. 11.1 m³; The volume of a cylinder is three times the volume of a cone with a congruent base and height.

3. 76 ft³; The volume of a cone is $\frac{1}{3}$ the volume of a cylinder with a congruent base and height.

Teacher to Teacher

These are great labs and students enjoy using colored candies to fill the containers. Then students can eat the colored candies after the lab.

First I would demonstrate the activity for the class. Then students can complete the lab activities at their desks in pairs.

Sharron Ingram
Austin, Texas

Hands-On Lab
In *Hands-On Lab Activities*

Technology Lab
In *Technology Lab Activities*

Online Edition
Tutorial Videos

Countdown to Testing Week 17

Power Presentations
with PowerPoint®

Warm Up

1. Find the volume of a rectangular prism that is 4 in. tall, 16 in. wide, and 48 in. deep. **3072 in³**

2. A cylinder has a height of 4.2 m and a diameter of 0.6 m. To the nearest tenth of a cubic meter, what is the volume of the cylinder? Use 3.14 for π. **1.2 m³**

3. A triangular prism's base is an equilateral triangle. The sides of the triangle are 4 ft, and the height of the prism is 8 ft. To the nearest cubic foot, what is the volume of the prism? **55.4 ft³**

Problem of the Day

A ream of paper (500 sheets) forms a rectangular prism 11 in. by 8.5 in. by 2 in. What is the volume of one sheet of paper? **0.374 in³**

Also available on transparency

State Resources

go.hrw.com
State Resources Online
KEYWORD: MT7 Resources

8-6 Volume of Pyramids and Cones

Learn to find the volume of pyramids and cones.

Vocabulary
pyramid
cone

Also 8.1.C, 8.2.B, 8.7.B, 8.8.B, 8.10.B, 8.14.A, 8.15.a

Part of the Rock and Roll Hall of Fame building in Cleveland, Ohio, is a glass pyramid. The entire building was designed by architect I. M. Pei and has approximately 150,000 ft² of floor space.

A **pyramid** is a three-dimensional figure whose base is a polygon, and all of the other faces are triangles. It is named for the shape of its base. A **cone** has a circular base. The height of a pyramid or cone is measured from the highest point to the base along a line perpendicular to the base.

The Discovery Pyramid at Moody Gardens

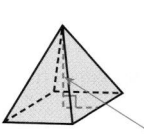
Rectangular pyramid

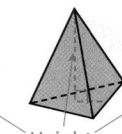
Triangular pyramid

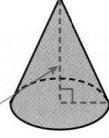
Cone

Height

VOLUME OF PYRAMIDS AND CONES		
Words	**Numbers**	**Formula**
Pyramid: The volume V of a pyramid is one-third of the area of the base B times the height h.	$B = 3(3)$ $= 9$ units² $V = \frac{1}{3}(9)(4)$ $= 12$ units³	$V = \frac{1}{3}Bh$
Cone: The volume of a cone is one-third of the area of the circular base B times the height h.	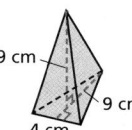 $B = \pi(2^2)$ $= 4\pi$ units² $V = \frac{1}{3}(4\pi)(3)$ $= 4\pi$ ≈ 12.6 units³	$V = \frac{1}{3}Bh$ or $V = \frac{1}{3}\pi r^2 h$

EXAMPLE 1 Finding the Volume of Pyramids and Cones

Find the volume of each figure. Use 3.14 for π.

A

9 cm
9 cm
4 cm

$B = \frac{1}{2}(4 \cdot 9) = 18$ cm²

$V = \frac{1}{3} \cdot 18 \cdot 9$ $V = \frac{1}{3}Bh$

$V = 54$ cm³

---

1 Introduce
Alternate Opener

EXPLORATION

8-6 Volume of Pyramids and Cones

The tip of a sharpened pencil is shaped like a cone. How much of the pencil is lost after the tip is formed? To answer this question, you should know that the volume of a cone is $\frac{1}{3}$ the volume of the cylinder from which it was formed.

The tip of this pencil was formed out of a cylinder with a height of 0.8 cm and a diameter of 1cm. The cylinder had a volume of approximately 0.63 cm³.

0.8 cm
1 cm

volume of cone = $\frac{1}{3}$ · volume of cylinder

volume of cone = $\frac{1}{3}$ · 0.63 = 0.21

Since the tip of the pencil has a volume of 0.21 cm³, 0.42 cm³ was lost when the tip of the pencil was formed.

Find the volume of each cone.

	Volume of Cylinder	Volume of Cone = $\frac{1}{3}$ · Volume of Cylinder
1.	66.9 in³	
2.	99 cm³	
3.	108 in³	

Think and Discuss
4. **Name** familiar objects that are shaped like a cone.
5. **Explain** how to estimate the volume of one of the cone-shaped objects you named in Problem 4.

Motivate

Show students an empty cylinder and an empty cone that have congruent circular bases and equal heights. Have students guess how many cones it will take to fill the cylinder. Fill the cone and pour it into the cylinder. (You can use water or uncooked rice or beans.) Repeat until the cylinder is full. Students will see that the volume of the cylinder is three times the volume of the cone.

Explorations and answers are provided in *Alternate Openers: Explorations Transparencies.*

Find the volume of each figure. Use 3.14 for π.

B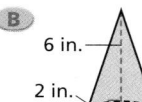
6 in.
2 in.

$B = \pi(2^2) = 4\pi \text{ in}^2$
$V = \frac{1}{3} \cdot 4\pi \cdot 6$ $V = \frac{1}{3}Bh$
$V = 8\pi \approx 25 \text{ in}^3$ *Use 3.14 for π.*

C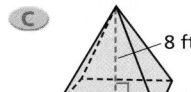
8 ft
7 ft
9 ft

$B = 9 \cdot 7 = 63 \text{ ft}^2$
$V = \frac{1}{3} \cdot 63 \cdot 8$ $V = \frac{1}{3}Bh$
$V = 168 \text{ ft}^3$

D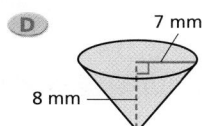
7 mm
8 mm

$B = \pi(7^2) = 49\pi \text{ mm}^2$
$V = \frac{1}{3} \cdot 49\pi \cdot 8$ $V = \frac{1}{3}Bh$
$V = \frac{392}{3}\pi \approx 410.5 \text{ mm}^2$ *Use 3.14 for π.*

EXAMPLE 2   Exploring the Effects of Changing Dimensions

A cone has radius 3 m and height 10 m. Explain whether doubling the height would have the same effect on the volume of the cone as doubling the radius.

Original Dimensions	Double the Height	Double the Radius
$V = \frac{1}{3}\pi r^2 h$	$V = \frac{1}{3}\pi r^2(2h)$	$V = \frac{1}{3}\pi(2r)^2 h$
$= \frac{1}{3}\pi(3^2)(10)$	$= \frac{1}{3}\pi(3^2)(2 \cdot 10)$	$= \frac{1}{3}\pi(2 \cdot 3)^2(10)$
$\approx 94.2 \text{ m}^3$	$\approx 188.4 \text{ m}^3$	$\approx 376.8 \text{ m}^3$

When the height of the cone is doubled, the volume is doubled. When the radius is doubled, the volume becomes 4 times the original volume.

EXAMPLE 3   *Social Studies Application*

Caution!

A lowercase *b* is used to represent the length of the base of a two-dimensional figure. A capital *B* is used to represent the area of the base of a solid figure.

The Great Pyramid of Giza is a square pyramid. Its height is 481 ft, and its base has 756 ft sides. Find the volume of the pyramid.

$B = 756^2 = 571,536 \text{ ft}^2$ *A = bh*
$V = \frac{1}{3}(571,536)(481)$ $V = \frac{1}{3}Bh$
$V = 91,636,272 \text{ ft}^3$

Example 1

Find the volume of each figure. Use 3.14 for π.

A.

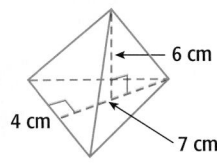
6 cm
4 cm
7 cm

$V = 28 \text{ cm}^3$

B.

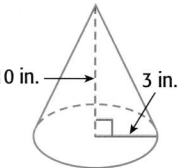
10 in.
3 in.

$V = 30\pi \approx 94.2 \text{ in}^3$

Example 2

A cone has radius 3 ft and height 4 ft. Explain whether tripling the height would have the same effect on the volume of the cone as tripling the radius.

When the height of the cone is tripled, the volume is tripled. When the radius is tripled, the volume becomes 9 times the original volume.

Example 3

The Pyramid of Kukulcán in Mexico is a square pyramid. Its height is 24 m and its base has 55 m sides. Find the volume of the pyramid.
$V = 24,200 \text{ m}^3$

Also available on transparency

---

② Teach

Guided Instruction

In this lesson, students learn to find the volume of pyramids and cones. Remind students how they found the volumes of prisms and cylinders. Illustrate that the volume of a pyramid is $\frac{1}{3}$ the volume of a prism with an equal height and a congruent base (Teaching Transparency). Show that the volume of a cone is $\frac{1}{3}$ the volume of a cylinder with an equal height and a congruent base.

Teaching Tip   **Critical Thinking** Explain to students that the activity in Motivate is not a mathematical proof of the volume formula. The formula will, however, be proven in future math classes.

 **Reaching All Learners**
Through Kinesthetic Experience

Give each group of students a model of a pyramid and a cone, as well as a ruler (nets are provided in Teaching Tools). Have students find the approximate volume of the pyramid and the cone by taking the appropriate measurements. Have students compare the volume of the pyramid and the cone.

Possible answers to Think and Discuss

1. You can double the height of the pyramid. You can double either dimension of the rectangular base. (In fact, you can multiply one dimension by a, the second by b, and the third by c, as long as $abc = 2$. For example, $a = 3$, $b = 2$, and $c = \frac{1}{3}$.)

2. The volume of the pyramid is one-third the volume of the cube. The volume of the cube is $1 \times 1 \times 1 = 1$ in³. The volume of the square pyramid is $\frac{1}{3} \times (1 \times 1)(1) = \frac{1}{3}$ in³.

8-6 Exercises

EXAMPLE 4 Using a Calculator to Find Volume

Some traffic pylons are shaped like cones. Use a calculator to find the volume of a traffic pylon to the nearest hundredth if the radius of the base is 5 inches and the height is 24 inches.

Use the *pi* button on your calculator to find the area of the base.

2nd | π ^ | × | 5 | x^2 | ENTER $B = \pi r^2$

Next, with the area of the base still displayed, find the volume of the cone.

× | 24 | × | (| 1 | ÷ | 3 |) | ENTER $V = \frac{1}{3}Bh$

The volume of the traffic pylon is approximately 628.32 in³.

Think and Discuss

1. **Describe** two or more ways that you can change the dimensions of a rectangular pyramid to double its volume.

2. **Use a model** to compare the volume of a cube with 1 in. sides with a pyramid that is 1 in. high and has a 1 in. square base.

8-6 Exercises

GUIDED PRACTICE

See Example **1**   Find the volume of each figure to the nearest tenth. Use 3.14 for π.

7. Yes, the volume is doubled. The volume of the pyramid is 8 m³. Doubling the height gives a volume of 16 m³.

1.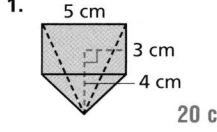
5 cm, 3 cm, 4 cm
20 cm³

2.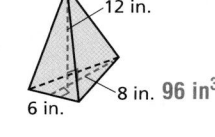
12 in., 6 in., 8 in. 96 in³

3.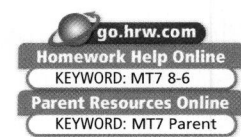
9.3 ft, 3.2 ft
99.7 ft³

4.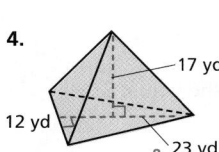
17 yd, 12 yd, 23 yd
782 yd³

5.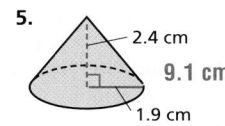
2.4 cm, 1.9 cm
9.1 cm³

6.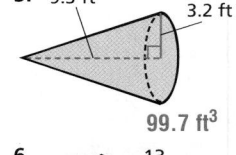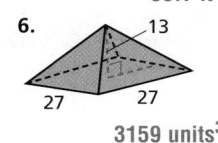
13, 27, 27
3159 units³

See Example **2**   7. A square pyramid has height 6 m and a base that measures 2 m on each side. Explain whether doubling the height would double the volume of the pyramid.

---

③ Close

Summarize

Remind students that the volumes of pyramids and cones are related to the volumes of prisms and cylinders. Show them the table below to emphasize the connection.

Prisms	Pyramids
$V = Bh$	$V = \frac{1}{3}Bh$
Cylinders	**Cones**
$V = Bh$ or $V = \pi r^2 h$	$V = \frac{1}{3}Bh$ or $V = \frac{1}{3}\pi r^2 h$

See Example **3** 8. The Transamerica Pyramid in San Francisco has a base area of 22,000 ft² and a height of 853 ft. What is the volume of the building? **6,255,333⅓ ft³**

See Example **4** 9. Gretchen made a paper cone to hold a gift for a friend. The paper cone was 17 inches high and had a diameter of 6 inches. Use a calculator to find the volume of the paper cone to the nearest hundredth. **160.29 in³**

INDEPENDENT PRACTICE

See Example **1** Find the volume of each figure to the nearest tenth. Use 3.14 for π.

16. Yes, the volume is doubled. The volume of the pyramid is 288 in³. Doubling the height of the base gives a volume of 576 in³.

10. 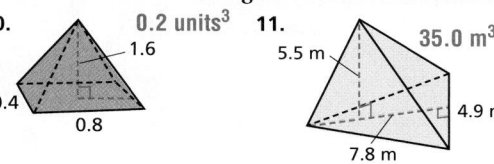 **0.2 units³** 1.6 0.4 0.8

11. 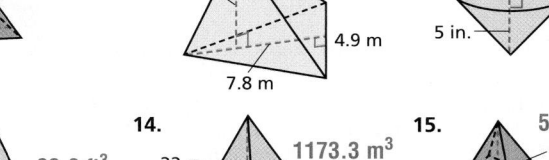 **35.0 m³** 5.5 m 4.9 m 7.8 m

12. 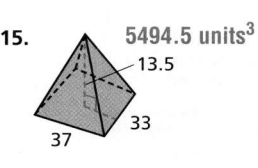 5 in. 5 in. **130.8 in³**

13. 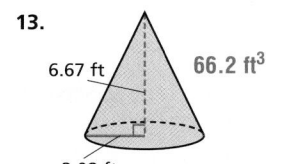 6.67 ft **66.2 ft³** 3.08 ft

14. 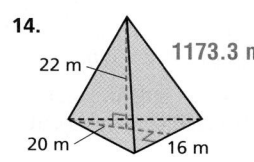 **1173.3 m³** 22 m 20 m 16 m

15. **5494.5 units³** 13.5 37 33

See Example **2** 16. A triangular pyramid has a height of 12 in. The triangular base has a height of 12 in. and a width of 12 in. Explain whether doubling the height of the base would double the volume of the pyramid.

See Example **3** 17. A cone-shaped building is commonly used to store sand. What would be the volume of a cone-shaped building with diameter 50 m and height 20 m to the nearest hundredth? **13,083.33 m³**

See Example **4** 18. Antonio made mini waffle cones for a birthday party. Each waffle cone was 3 inches high and had a radius of ¾ inch. Use a calculator to find the volume of the waffle cone to the nearest hundredth. **1.77 in³**

PRACTICE AND PROBLEM SOLVING

Extra Practice
See page 797.

Find the missing measure to the nearest tenth. Use 3.14 for π.

19. cone:
   radius = 4 in.
   height = ▓ **6 in.**
   volume = 100.5 in³

20. cylinder:
   radius = ▓ **3 m**
   height = 2.5 m
   volume = 70.65 m³

21. triangular pyramid:
   base height = ▓ **11 ft**
   base width = 8 ft
   height = 6 ft
   volume = 88 ft³

22. rectangular pyramid:
   base length = 3 ft
   base width = ▓ **6 ft**
   height = 7 ft
   volume = 42 ft³

23. **Estimation** Orange traffic cones come in a variety of sizes. Approximate the volume in cubic inches of a traffic cone with height 2 feet and diameter 10 inches by using 3 in place of π. **600 in³**

RETEACH 8-6

Reteach
8-6 Volume of Pyramids and Cones

Pyramid: solid figure named for the shape of its base, which is a polygon; all other faces are triangles

Pentagonal Pyramid

This rectangular pyramid and rectangular prism have congruent bases and congruent heights.

Volume of Pyramid = ⅓ Volume of Prism

$V = \frac{1}{3} Bh$

Complete to find the volume of each pyramid.

1. square pyramid
   7 cm
   9 cm
   9 cm

   base is a ___square___

   $V = \frac{1}{3} Bh$

   $V = \frac{1}{3}$ (area of square) × h

   $V = \frac{1}{3}$ (_9_ × _9_) × _7_

   $V = \frac{1}{3}$ × (_81_) × _7_

   $V = $ _189_ cm³

2. rectangular pyramid
   5 in.
   6 in.
   8 in.

   base is a ___rectangle___

   $V = \frac{1}{3} Bh$

   $V = \frac{1}{3}$ (area of rectangle) × h

   $V = \frac{1}{3}$ (_8_ × _6_) × _5_

   $V = \frac{1}{3}$ (_48_) × _5_

   $V = $ _80_ in³

PRACTICE 8-6

Practice B
8-6 Volume of Pyramids and Cones

Find the volume of each figure to the nearest tenth. Use 3.14 for π.

1. 12 ft 9 ft 9 ft **324 ft³**

2. 15 in. 27 in. **6358.5 in³**

3. 20.5 m 12.4 m **3299.2 m³**

4. 23 cm 19 cm 20 cm **2913.3 cm³**

5. 16 ft 18 ft 18 ft **1728 ft³**

6. 17 cm 16 cm **1138.8 cm³**

7. The base of a regular pyramid has an area of 28 in². The height of the pyramid is 15 in. Find the volume. **140 in³**

8. The radius of a cone is 19.4 cm and its height is 24 cm. Find the volume of the cone to the nearest tenth. **9454.2 cm³**

9. Find the volume of a rectangular pyramid if the height is 13 m and the base sides are 12 m and 15 m. **780 m³**

10. A funnel has a diameter of 9 in. and is 16 in. deep. Use a calculator to find the volume of the funnel to the nearest hundredth. **339.29 in³**

11. A square pyramid has a height 18 cm and a base that measures 12 cm on each side. Explain whether tripling the height would triple the volume of the pyramid. **Possible answer:**
   The volume of the original pyramid is 864 cm³. The volume of the new pyramid is 2592 cm³. Therefore, if the height of the pyramid were tripled, its volume would be tripled.

State Resources

go.hrw.com
State Resources Online
KEYWORD: MT7 Resources

Answers

26–27, 36. See p. A12.

24. Architecture The Pyramid of the Sun, in Teotihuacán, Mexico, is about 65 m tall and has a square base with side length 225 m.

   a. What is the volume in cubic meters of the pyramid? **1,096,875 m³**

   b. How many cubic meters are in a cubic kilometer? **1,000,000,000 m³**

   c. What is the volume in cubic kilometers of the pyramid to the nearest thousandth? **0.001 km³**

Architecture

I. M. Pei, designer of the Louvre Pyramid, has designed more than 50 buildings around the world and has won many major awards.

go.hrw.com
Web Extra!
KEYWORD: MT7 Pei

25. Architecture The pyramid at the entrance to the Louvre in Paris has a height of 72 feet and a square base that is 112 feet long on each side. What is the volume of this pyramid? **301,056 ft³**

26. What's the Error? A student says that the formula for the volume of a cylinder is the same as the formula for the volume of a pyramid, $\frac{1}{3}Bh$. What error did this student make?

27. Write About It How would a cone's volume be affected if you doubled the height? the radius? Use a model to help explain.

28. Challenge The diameter of a cone is x cm, the height is 18 cm, and the volume is 96π cm³. What is x? **8**

TEST PREP and Spiral Review

29. Multiple Choice A pyramid has a rectangular base measuring 12 centimeters by 9 centimeters. Its height is 15 centimeters. What is the volume of the pyramid?

  Ⓐ 540 cm³   Ⓑ 405 cm³   Ⓒ 315 cm³   Ⓓ 270 cm³

30. Multiple Choice A cone has diameter 12 centimeters and height 9 centimeters. Using 3.14 for π, find the volume of the cone to the nearest tenth.

  Ⓕ 1,356.5 cm³   Ⓖ 339.1 cm³   Ⓗ 118.3 cm³   Ⓙ 56.5 cm³

31. Gridded Response Suppose a cone has a volume of 104.7 cubic centimeters and a radius of 5 centimeters. Find the height of the cone to the nearest whole centimeter. Use 3.14 for π. **4 cm**

Solve. (Lesson 1-7)

32. $9 + t = 18$ $t = 9$ **33.** $t - 2 = 6$ $t = 8$ **34.** $10 + t = 32$ $t = 22$ **35.** $t + 7 = 7$ $t = 0$

36. Draw the front, top, and side views of the figure. (Lesson 8-4)

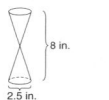

Front   Side

CHALLENGE 8-6

PROBLEM SOLVING 8-6

Hands-On LAB 8-7

Find Surface Areas of Prisms and Cylinders

Use with Lesson 8-7

go.hrw.com
Lab Resources Online
KEYWORD: MT7 Lab8

REMEMBER
• A net is an arrangement of two-dimensional figures that can fold to form a three-dimensional figure.

You can explore the surface area of prisms and cylinders using models and nets.

Activity 1   Check students' work.

① Find six different-sized rectangular and triangular prisms.

   a. Make a net of the prism by tracing around each face on grid paper.

   b. Label the bases A and B. Continue labeling the lateral faces.

   c. Copy the tables shown. Fill in the information for each prism.

Rectangular Prism	
Face	**Area**
Base A	
Base B	
Lateral face C	
Lateral face D	
Lateral face E	
Lateral face F	
Total Surface Area	

Triangular Prism	
Face	**Area**
Base A	
Base B	
Lateral face C	
Lateral face D	
Lateral face E	
Total Surface Area	

② For each prism from ①, find the perimeter of a base. Then multiply the base's perimeter by the prism's height. Finally, find the total area of the lateral faces.

Think and Discuss

1. In ②, how did the product of the base's perimeter and the prism's height compare with the sum of the areas of the lateral faces?   **They are equal**

2. Write a rule for finding the surface area of any prism.   **2(area of base) + (perimeter)(height)**

Try This

1. Use your rule from Think and Discuss 2 to find the surface area of two new prisms. Check your rule by following the steps in ①. Revise your rule as needed.

Answers to
Think and Discuss

1. Possible answer: The area found by counting squares is slightly different due to estimating the area of the bases.

Activity 2 Check students' work.

➊ Find six different-sized cylinders. Follow these steps to make a net for each cylinder.

a. Trace around the top of the cylinder on grid paper.

b. Lay the cylinder on the grid paper so that it touches the circle, and mark its height. Then roll the cylinder one complete revolution, marking where the cylinder begins and ends. Draw a rectangle that has the same height as the cylinder and a width equal to one revolution of the cylinder.

c. Trace the bottom of the cylinder so that it touches the bottom of the rectangle.

d. Find the approximate area of each piece by counting squares.

e. Add the areas to find the total surface area of the cylinder.

f. Copy the table shown. Record the information in the table.

Cylinder		
Face	Area by Counting Squares	Area by Using Formula
Circular base A		
Circular base B		
Lateral face C		
Total Surface Area		

➋ Follow these steps for each cylinder from ➊.

a. Tape your pieces together to make a cylinder.

b. Use area formulas to find the area of each base and the lateral face.

c. Add the areas to find the total surface area of your net.

d. Record the information in the table.

Think and Discuss

1. How did the area found by counting squares compare with the area found by using a formula?

2. How does the circumference of the base compare with the length of the lateral face?   They are the same

3. Make a rule for finding the surface area of any cylinder.   2(area of base) + circumference or $2\pi r^2 + 2\pi rh$

Try This

1. Use your rule from Think and Discuss 3 to find the surface area of a new cylinder. Check your rule by following the steps in the activity. Revise your rule as needed.

8-7 Surface Area of Prisms and Cylinders

Learn to find the surface area of prisms and cylinders.

Vocabulary
surface area
lateral face
lateral surface

An *anamorphic image* is a distorted picture that becomes recognizable when reflected onto a cylindrical mirror.

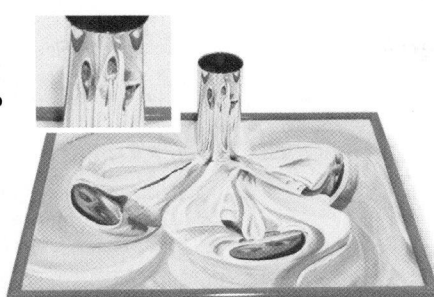

Surface area is the sum of the areas of all surfaces of a figure. The **lateral faces** of a prism are parallelograms that connect the bases. The **lateral surface** of a cylinder is the curved surface.

SURFACE AREA OF PRISMS AND CYLINDERS

Words	Numbers	Formula
Prism: The surface area S of a prism is twice the base area B plus the lateral area F. The lateral area is the base perimeter P times the height h.	$S = 2(3 \cdot 2) + (10)(5) = 62$ units^2	$S = 2B + F$ or $S = 2B + Ph$
Cylinder: The surface area S of a cylinder is twice the base area B plus the lateral area L. The lateral area is the base circumference $2\pi r$ times the height h.	$S = 2\pi(5^2) + 2\pi(5)(6) \approx 345.4$ units^2	$S = 2B + L$ or $S = 2\pi r^2 + 2\pi rh$

EXAMPLE 1 Finding Surface Area

Find the surface area of each figure to the nearest tenth. Use 3.14 for π.

Ⓐ

$$S = 2\pi r^2 + 2\pi rh$$
$$= 2\pi(2^2) + 2\pi(2)(8)$$
$$= 40\pi \text{ m}^2$$
$$\approx 125.6 \text{ m}^2$$

---

1 Introduce

Alternate Opener

EXPLORATION

8-7 Surface Area of Prisms and Cylinders

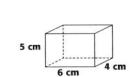

The *surface area* of a three-dimensional figure is the sum of the areas of all the surfaces of the figure. Follow these steps to find the surface area of the prism.

1. Find the area of the bottom face of the prism.
2. What is the total area of the top and bottom faces of the prism?
3. Find the area of the front face of the prism.
4. What is the total area of the front and back faces of the prism?
5. Find the area of one of the side faces of the prism.
6. What is the total area of both side faces of the prism?
7. Add the areas in Steps 2, 4, and 6 to find the surface area.

Think and Discuss

8. **Explain** how you can find the surface area of a rectangular prism.
9. **Describe** a shortcut you can use to find the surface area of a cube.

Motivate

Show students an empty cereal box. Point out that if they find the volume, they will find the amount of cereal the box can hold. Rip the seams so the box will lie flat. Tell the students that now they will find the surface area of shapes like the box. The surface area determines how much cardboard is needed to make the box.

Explorations and answers are provided in *Alternate Openers: Explorations Transparencies.*

Organizer 8-7

Pacing: Traditional 1 day
Block $\frac{1}{2}$ day

Objective: Students find the surface area of prisms and cylinders.

LAB **Hands-On Lab**
In *Hands-On Lab Activities*

Online Edition
Tutorial Videos, Interactivities

Countdown to Testing Week 17

Power Presentations
with PowerPoint®

Warm Up

1. A triangular pyramid has a base area of 1.2 m^2 and a height of 7.5 m. What is the volume of the pyramid?   3 m^3

2. A cone has a radius of 4 cm and a height of 10 cm. What is the volume of the cone to the nearest cubic centimeter? Use 3.14 for π.   167 cm^3

Problem of the Day

An ice cream cone is filled halfway to the top. The radius of the filled part is half the radius at the top. What fraction of the cone's volume is filled? $\frac{1}{8}$

Also available on transparency

State Resources

go.hrw.com
State Resources Online
KEYWORD: MT7 Resources

Additional Examples

Example 1

Find the surface area of each figure to the nearest tenth. Use 3.14 for π.

A.

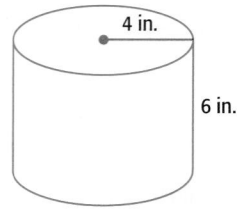

4 in.

6 in.

$S = 80\pi \approx 251.2 \text{ in}^2$

B.

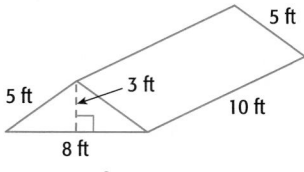

5 ft

5 ft

3 ft

10 ft

8 ft

$S = 204 \text{ ft}^2$

Example 2

A cylinder has diameter 8 in. and height 3 in. Explain whether tripling the height would have the same effect on the surface area as tripling the radius.

They would not have the same effect. Tripling the radius would increase the surface area more than tripling the height.

Example 3

A cylindrical soup can is 7.6 cm in diameter and 11.2 cm tall. What is the area of the label that covers the side of the can?

$L = 85.12\pi \approx 267.3 \text{ cm}^2$

Also available on transparency

Find the surface area of each figure to the nearest tenth. Use 3.14 for π.

B

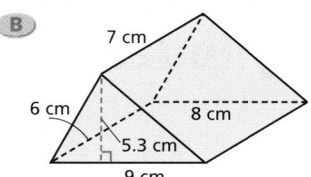

7 cm

6 cm

8 cm

5.3 cm

9 cm

$$S = 2B + Ph$$
$$= 2\left(\frac{1}{2} \cdot 9 \cdot 5.3\right) + (23)(7)$$
$$= 208.7 \text{ cm}^2$$

EXAMPLE 2 Exploring the Effects of Changing Dimensions

A cylinder has diameter 10 in. and height 4 in. Explain whether doubling the height would have the same effect on the surface area as doubling the radius.

Original Dimensions	Double the Height	Double the Radius
$S = 2\pi r^2 + 2\pi rh$	$S = 2\pi r^2 + 2\pi rh$	$S = 2\pi r^2 + 2\pi rh$
$= 2\pi(5)^2 + 2\pi(5)(4)$	$= 2\pi(5)^2 + 2\pi(5)(8)$	$= 2\pi(10)^2 + 2\pi(10)(4)$
$= 90\pi \text{ in}^2 \approx 282.6 \text{ in}^2$	$= 130\pi \text{ in}^2 \approx 408.2 \text{ in}^2$	$= 280\pi \text{ in}^2 \approx 879.2 \text{ in}^2$

They would not have the same effect. Doubling the radius would increase the surface area more than doubling the height.

EXAMPLE 3 Art Application

A Web site advertises that it can turn your photo into an anamorphic image. To reflect the picture, you need to cover a cylinder that is 49 mm in diameter and 107 mm tall with reflective material. Estimate the amount of reflective material you would need.

The diameter of the cylinder is about 50 mm, and the height is about 100 mm.

$L = 2\pi rh$ *Only the lateral surface needs to be covered.*

$= 2\pi(25)(100)$ *diameter $\approx$ 50 mm, so $r \approx$ 25 mm*

$\approx 15,700 \text{ mm}^2$

Answers to *Think and Discuss*

1. The drinking glass only has one base, but a cylinder has two bases. So the surface area of the glass would be $\pi r^2 + 2\pi rh$ instead of $2\pi r^2 + 2\pi rh$.

2. The smaller cube has a surface area of 6 ft² and the larger cube has a surface area of 24 ft², so the larger cube requires 4 times as much paint.

Think and Discuss

1. **Explain** how finding the surface area of a cylindrical drinking glass would be different from finding the surface area of a cylinder.

2. **Compare** the amount of paint needed to cover a cube with 1 ft sides to the amount needed to cover a cube with 2 ft sides.

---

2 Teach

Guided Instruction

In this lesson, students learn to find the surface area of prisms and cylinders. Have students open samples of prisms and cylinders so they can see the two-dimensional surfaces that form the three-dimensional figures (Teaching Transparency). Explain that the surface area is the sum of all the areas of these two-dimensional surfaces.

Teaching Tip **Inclusion** Use the flattened-out diagrams (nets) in the lesson to explain the surface area formulas. Discuss how *F*, the lateral surface area of a prism, corresponds to *L*, the lateral surface area of a cylinder.

Reaching All Learners
Through Cognitive Strategies

Discuss with students descriptions of real-world examples of area and volume, such as the amount of soup in a can, the amount of paper needed to make a label around a can, or the amount of wallpaper needed to cover the walls of a room. Have students identify the measure that applies to each situation and the appropriate formula.

Possible answers: volume of a cylinder: $V = Bh$; lateral surface area of a cylinder: $L = 2\pi rh$; area of lateral faces of a prism: $F = Ph$

3 Close

Summarize

Point out that the formulas for surface area of prisms and cylinders are based on area formulas for rectangles and circles. Discuss the difference between surface area and volume.

Possible answer: Surface area is the sum of the areas of all surfaces of a figure and is measured in square units. Volume is the space that a figure occupies and is measured in cubic units.

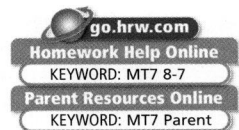

GUIDED PRACTICE

See Example **1** Find the surface area of each figure to the nearest tenth. Use 3.14 for π.

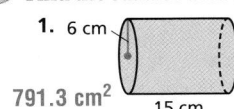

1. 6 cm

791.3 cm² — 15 cm

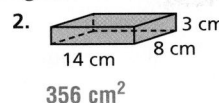

2. 3 cm, 14 cm, 8 cm

356 cm²

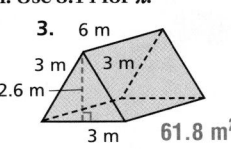

3. 6 m, 3 m, 3 m, 2.6 m, 3 m

61.8 m²

See Example **2** **4.** A rectangular prism is 3 ft by 4 ft by 7 ft. Explain whether doubling all of the dimensions would double the surface area.

See Example **3** **5.** Tilly is covering a can with contact paper, not including its top and bottom. The can measures 8 inches high and has a radius of 2 inches. Estimate the amount of contact paper she needs. **Possible answer: ≈ 96 in²**

INDEPENDENT PRACTICE

See Example **1** Find the surface area of each figure to the nearest tenth. Use 3.14 for π.

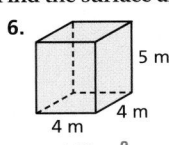

6. 5 m, 4 m, 4 m

112 m²

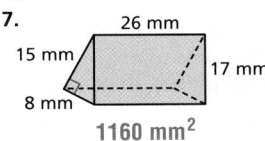

7. 26 mm, 15 mm, 17 mm, 8 mm

1160 mm²

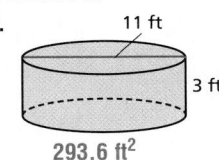

8. 11 ft, 3 ft

293.6 ft²

See Example **2** **9.** A cylinder has diameter 4 ft and height 9 ft. Explain whether halving the diameter has the same effect on the surface area as halving the height.

See Example **3** **10.** Frank is wrapping a present. The box measures 6.2 cm by 9.9 cm by 5.1 cm. Estimate the amount of wrapping paper, not counting overlap, that Frank needs. **≈ 280 cm²**

PRACTICE AND PROBLEM SOLVING

Extra Practice
See page 797.

Find the surface area of each figure with the given dimensions to the nearest tenth. Use 3.14 for π.

11. cylinder: $d = 30$ mm, $h = 49$ mm **1920π ≈ 6028.8 mm²**

12. rectangular prism: $5\frac{1}{4}$ in. by 8 in. by 12 in. **402 in²**

Find the missing dimension in each figure with the given surface area.

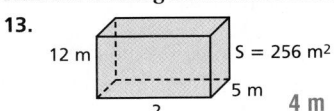

13. 12 m, $S = 256$ m², 5 m, ? **4 m**

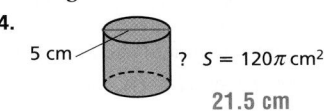

14. 5 cm, ? $S = 120\pi$ cm² **21.5 cm**

Assignment Guide

If you finished Example **1** assign:
Average 1–3, 6–8, 11, 12, 21–29
Advanced 6–8, 11–14, 18, 21–29

If you finished Example **2** assign:
Average 1–4, 6–9, 11, 12, 19, 21–29
Advanced 6–9, 11–14, 18, 19, 21–29

If you finished Example **3** assign:
Average 1–12, 15, 16, 19, 21–29
Advanced 6–29

Homework Quick Check

Quickly check key concepts.
Exercises: 6, 9, 10

Answers

4, 9. See p. A12.

Math Background

Research has found that children who play with blocks and other building toys have a better-developed spatial sense than those who do not. Even older students can benefit from hands-on activities in their study of three-dimensional figures. Many students in high school geometry classes are at a disadvantage that can be partially attributed to a lack of hands-on experience in prior grades. Students should, however, be familiar with basic concepts and have a clear understanding of the objectives of hands-on activities.

RETEACH 8-7

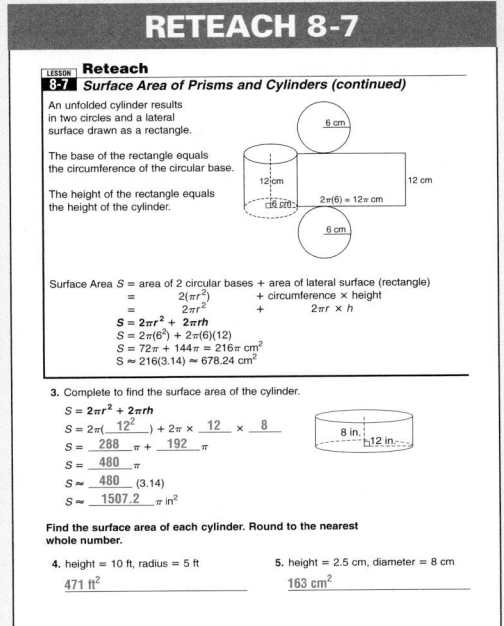

PRACTICE 8-7

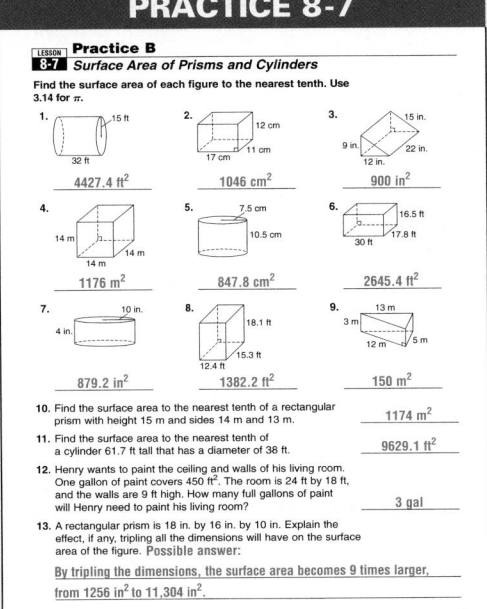

State Resources

go.hrw.com
State Resources Online
KEYWORD: MT7 Resources

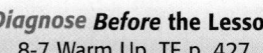

TEST PREP DOCTOR + Students who chose answer **A** for Exercise 21 did not square the radius when finding the area of the cylinder's base. Remind students to write down the formula before calculating the answer.

Journal

Have students consider the question, "Is it possible for two rectangular prisms to have the same volume and different surface areas?" Have them answer the question and include examples to support their answers.

Power Presentations
with PowerPoint®

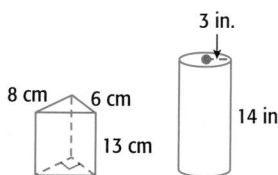

8-7 Lesson Quiz

Find the surface area of each figure to the nearest tenth. Use 3.14 for π.

8 cm 6 cm 13 cm 3 in. 14 in.

1. the triangular prism   360 cm²
2. the cylinder   320.3 in²
3. All outer surfaces of a box are covered with gold foil, except the bottom. The box measures 6 in. long, 4 in. wide, and 3 in. high. How much gold foil was used?   84 in²

Also available on transparency

---

15. Multi-Step Jesse makes rectangular glass aquariums measuring 12 in. by 6 in. by 8 in. Glass costs $0.08 per square inch. How much will the glass for one aquarium cost?   **$34.56**

16. Sports In the snowboard half-pipe, competitors ride back and forth on a course shaped like a cylinder cut in half lengthwise. What is the surface area of this half-pipe course?   **4500π ≈ 14,137 ft²**

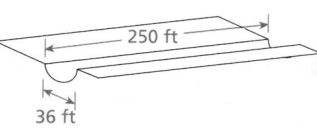
250 ft
36 ft

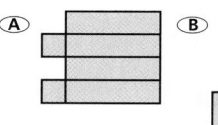 One machine used to shape the inside of a half-pipe is called the Pipe Dragon. Others are the Pipe Master, Turbo Grinder, Scorpion, and Pipe Magician.

17. Multi-Step Olivia is painting the four sides and top of a large trunk. The trunk measures 5 ft long by 3.5 ft deep by 3 ft high. A gallon of paint covers approximately 300 square feet. She wants at least 15% extra paint for waste and overage. How many quarts of paint does she need?   **at least 2 quarts**

18. Choose a Strategy Which of the following nets can be folded into the given three-dimensional figure?

Ⓐ   Ⓑ 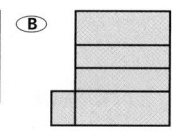   Ⓒ 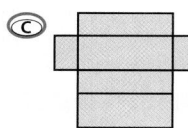   Ⓓ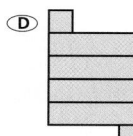

19. Possible answer: Doubling the length of one side of a square prism gives a surface area 1⅔ times the original.

19. Write About It Describe the effect on the surface area of a square prism when you double the length of one of its sides.

20. Challenge A rectangular wood block that is 12 cm by 9 cm by 5 cm has a hole drilled through the center with diameter 4 cm. What is the total surface area of the wood block?   **426 + 12π ≈ 463.7 cm²**

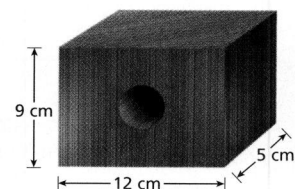
9 cm   12 cm   5 cm

TEST PREP and Spiral Review

21. Multiple Choice Find the surface area of a cylinder with radius 5 feet and height 3 feet. Use 3.14 for π.

Ⓐ 125.6 ft²   Ⓑ 150.72 ft²   Ⓒ 172.7 ft²   Ⓓ 251.2 ft²

22. Gridded Response A rectangular prism has dimensions 2 meters by 4 meters by 18 meters. Find the surface area, in square meters, of the prism.   **232**

Add or subtract. (Lesson 2-3)

23. $-0.4 + 0.7$
0.3

24. $1.35 - 5.6$
-4.25

25. $-0.01 - 0.25$
-0.26

26. $-0.65 + (-1.12)$
-1.77

Find the area of each figure with the given dimensions. (Lesson 8-2)

27. triangle: $b = 4$, $h = 6$
12 units²

28. triangle: $b = 3$, $h = 14$
21 units²

29. trapezoid: $b_1 = 3.4$, $b_2 = 6.6$, $h = 1.8$
9 units²

CHALLENGE 8-7

LESSON 8-7 Challenge
Eight Snips

A **cube** is a prism with six congruent square faces and eight vertices.

By cutting off the corners of the cube ⅓ of the way into each edge, a **truncated cube** is created.

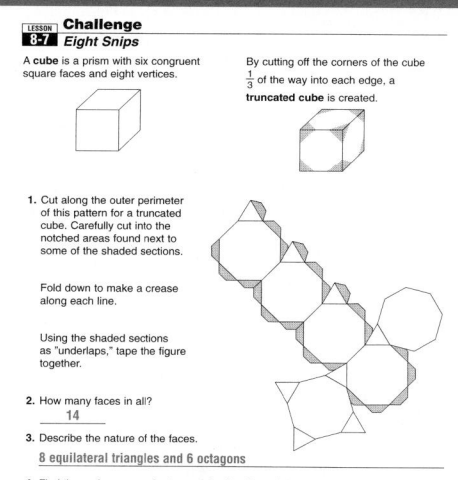

1. Cut along the outer perimeter of this pattern for a truncated cube. Carefully cut into the notched areas found next to some of the shaded sections.

Fold down to make a crease along each line.

Using the shaded sections as "underlaps," tape the figure together.

2. How many faces in all?
   14

3. Describe the nature of the faces.
   8 equilateral triangles and 6 octagons

4. Find the surface area of a truncated cube. The original cube had edge length = 24 in. Use √3 ≈ 1.73. Answer to the nearest tenth of a square inch.
   3130.88 in²

PROBLEM SOLVING 8-7

LESSON 8-7 Problem Solving
Surface Area of Prisms and Cylinders

An important factor in designing packaging for a product is the amount of material required to make the package. Consider the three figures described in the table below. Use 3.14 for π. Round to the nearest tenth. Write the correct answer.

1. Find the surface area of each package given in the table.

2. Which package has the lowest materials cost? Assume all of the packages are made from the same material.
   cylinder

Package	Dimensions	Volume	Surface Area
Prism	Base: 2" × 16" Height = 2"	64 in³	136 in²
Prism	Base: 4" × 4" Height = 4"	64 in³	96 in²
Cylinder	Radius = 2" Height = 5.1"	64.06 in³	89.2 in²

Use 3.14 for π. Round to the nearest hundredth.

3. How much cardboard material is required to make a cylindrical oatmeal container that has a diameter of 12.5 cm and a height of 24 cm, assuming there is no overlap? The container will have a plastic lid.
   1064.66 cm²

4. What is the surface area of a rectangular prism that is 5 feet by 6 feet by 10 feet?
   280 ft²

Use 3.14 for π. Round to the nearest tenth. Choose the letter for the best answer.

5. How much metal is required to make the trough pictured below?
   2 ft   6 ft
   Ⓐ 22.0 ft²   C 44.0 ft²
   B 34.0 ft²   D 56.7 ft²

6. A can of vegetables has a diameter of 9.8 cm and is 13.2 cm tall. How much paper is required to make the label, assuming there is no overlap? Round to the nearest tenth.
   F 203.1 cm²
   Ⓖ 406.2 cm²
   H 557.0 cm²
   J 812.4 cm²

Hands-On LAB 8-8

Find Surface Area of Pyramids

Use with Lesson 8-8

go.hrw.com
Lab Resources Online
KEYWORD: MT7 Lab8

You can explore the surface area of pyramids using models and nets.

Activity   Check students' work.

1. Find six different pyramids. Follow these steps for each one.

   a. Trace around each face on grid paper to make a net. Cut out the net.

   b. Find the approximate area of each face by counting the squares, and add them to find the surface area of the pyramid.

   c. Copy the table shown. Record your observations in the table.

2. Follow these steps for each pyramid from Activity 1.

   a. Fold and tape your net to make a pyramid.

   b. Use area formulas to find the area of the base and each lateral face, and add them to find the surface area of your net.

   c. Record your observations in the table.

Pyramid		
Face	Area by Counting Squares	Area by Using Formula
Base A		
Lateral face B		
Lateral face C		
Lateral face D		
Lateral face E		
Total Surface Area		

Think and Discuss

1. How did the area found by counting compare with the area found by using a formula? **Possible answer: There is a slight difference due to estimating the number of squares in the lateral faces.**

2. Find the product of a base's perimeter and the height of a triangular face, known as the slant height, ℓ. How does this compare with the total area of the triangular faces?   **It is twice the total area.**

3. Make a rule for finding the surface area of any pyramid.

   $$\text{area of base} + \frac{1}{2}(\text{perimeter})(\text{slant height})$$

Try This

1. Use your rule from Think and Discuss 3 to find the surface area of a new pyramid. Check your rule by following the steps in the activity. Revise your rule as needed.

Hands-On LAB   Organizer

Use with Lesson 8-8

Pacing:
Traditional $\frac{1}{2}$ day
Block $\frac{1}{4}$ day

Objective: Use models and nets to explore the surface area of pyramids.

Materials: Rectangular pyramids, grid paper

PREMIER **Online Edition**

Countdown to Testing Week 17

Resources

LAB ***Hands-On Lab Activities***
Lab 8-8 Recording Sheet

Teach

Discuss

Show students a net of a pyramid. Lead students in a discussion of whether you could find $\frac{1}{4}$ or $\frac{1}{2}$ the surface area of the net, then multiply that area by 4 or by 2 to find the total area.

Close

Key Concept

You can find the surface area of a regular pyramid by finding the total area of the net of the figure.

Assessment

Give an example of when it would not be practical to use the method shown in this lab to find the surface area of a regular pyramid. Possible answer: When the net of the pyramid is too big to fit on a piece of grid paper.

State Resources

go.hrw.com
State Resources Online
KEYWORD: MT7 Resources

8-8 Organizer

Pacing: Traditional 1 day
Block $\frac{1}{2}$ day

Objective: Students find the surface area of pyramids and cones.

Hands-On Lab
In *Hands-On Lab Activities*

Online Edition
Tutorial Videos

Countdown to Testing Week 18

Power Presentations
with PowerPoint®

Warm Up

1. A rectangular prism is 0.6 m by 0.4 m by 1.0 m. What is the surface area? **2.48 m²**

2. A cylindrical can has a diameter of 14 cm and a height of 20 cm. What is the surface area to the nearest tenth? Use 3.14 for π. **1186.9 cm²**

Problem of the Day

Sandy is building a model of a pyramid with a hexagonal base. If she uses a toothpick for each edge, how many toothpicks will she need? **12**

Also available on transparency

Math Humor

Pharaoh (to Architect): I want the burial chamber to be built in the center of my tomb.

Architect: You mean in the *pyramiddle*?

8-8 Surface Area of Pyramids and Cones

Learn to find the surface area of pyramids and cones.

Vocabulary
slant height
regular pyramid
right cone

The **slant height** of a pyramid or cone is measured along its lateral surface.

The base of a **regular pyramid** is a regular polygon, and the lateral faces are all congruent.

In a **right cone**, a line perpendicular to the base through the tip of the cone passes through the center of the base.

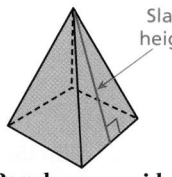 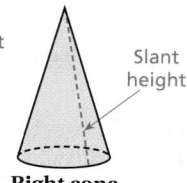

Regular pyramid   **Right cone**

SURFACE AREA OF PYRAMIDS AND CONES

Words	Numbers	Formula
Pyramid: The surface area S of a regular pyramid is the base area B plus the lateral area F. The lateral area is one-half the base perimeter P times the slant height ℓ.	$S = (12 \cdot 12) + \frac{1}{2}(48)(8) = 336$ units²	$S = B + F$ or $S = B + \frac{1}{2}P\ell$
Cone: The surface area S of a right cone is the base area B plus the lateral area L. The lateral area is one-half the base circumference $2\pi r$ times the slant height ℓ.	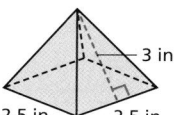 $S = \pi(2^2) + \pi(2)(5) = 14\pi \approx 43.98$ units²	$S = B + L$ or $S = \pi r^2 + \pi r\ell$

EXAMPLE 1 Finding Surface Area

Find the surface area of each figure to the nearest tenth. Use 3.14 for π.

A

$S = B + \frac{1}{2}P\ell$
$= (2.5 \cdot 2.5) + \frac{1}{2}(10)(3)$
$= 21.25$ in²

1 Introduce

Alternate Opener

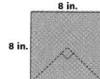
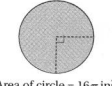
Motivate

Show students an ice cream cone wrapped in paper, or a cone-shaped paper cup. Ask students for the word that describes how much the cone holds. volume Ask students for the term that describes the amount of paper. lateral surface area Tell students that they will find surface area of cones and pyramids.

Explorations and answers are provided in *Alternate Openers: Explorations Transparencies*.

Find the surface area of each figure to the nearest tenth. Use 3.14 for π.

B

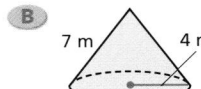
7 m   4 m

$S = \pi r^2 + \pi r \ell$
$= \pi(4)^2 + \pi(4)(7)$
$= 44\pi \approx 138.2 \text{ m}^2$

EXAMPLE 2 Exploring the Effects of Changing Dimensions

A cone has diameter 6 in. and slant height 4 in. Explain whether doubling the slant height would have the same effect on the surface area as doubling the radius. Use 3.14 for π.

Original Dimensions	Double the Slant Height	Double the Radius
$S = \pi r^2 + \pi r \ell$	$S = \pi r^2 + \pi r(2\ell)$	$S = \pi(2r)^2 + \pi(2r)\ell$
$= \pi(3)^2 + \pi(3)(4)$	$= \pi(3)^2 + \pi(3)(8)$	$= \pi(6)^2 + \pi(6)(4)$
$= 21\pi \text{ in}^2 \approx 66.0 \text{ in}^2$	$= 33\pi \text{ in}^2 \approx 103.6 \text{ in}^2$	$= 60\pi \text{ in}^2 \approx 188.4 \text{ in}^2$

They would not have the same effect. Doubling the radius would increase the surface area more than doubling the slant height.

EXAMPLE 3 *Life Science Application*

Life Science

Ant lions are the larvae of an insect similar to a dragonfly. They dig cone-shaped pits in the sand to trap ants and other crawling insects.

An ant lion pit is an inverted cone with the dimensions shown. What is the lateral surface area of the pit?

The slant height, radius, and depth of the pit form a right triangle.

$a^2 + b^2 = \ell^2$ *Pythagorean Theorem*

$(2.5)^2 + 2^2 = \ell^2$

$10.25 = \ell^2$

$\ell \approx 3.2$

$L = \pi r \ell$ *Lateral surface area*

$= \pi(2.5)(3.2) \approx 25.1 \text{ cm}^2$

2.5 cm
2 cm ℓ

Think and Discuss

1. **Compare** the formula for surface area of a pyramid to the formula for surface area of a cone.

2. **Explain** how you would find the slant height of a square pyramid with base edge length 6 cm and height 4 cm.

Example 1

Find the surface area of the figure to the nearest tenth. Use 3.14 for π.

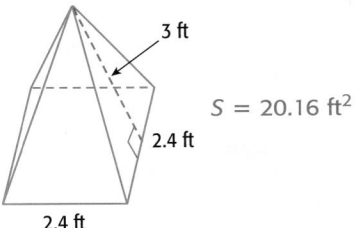
3 ft
2.4 ft
2.4 ft
$S = 20.16 \text{ ft}^2$

Example 2

A cone has diameter 8 in. and slant height 3 in. Explain whether tripling the slant height would have the same effect on the surface area as tripling the radius.

They would not have the same effect. Tripling the radius would increase the surface area more than tripling the slant height.

Example 3

The upper portion of an hourglass is approximately an inverted cone with the given dimensions. What is the lateral surface area of the upper portion of the hourglass?

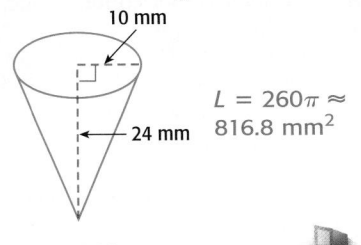
10 mm
24 mm
$L = 260\pi \approx$ 816.8 mm²

Also available on transparency

---

2 Teach

Guided Instruction

In this lesson, students learn to find the surface area of pyramids and cones. Show students nets for a pyramid and a cone. Remind students that they found the total surface area of prisms and cylinders by adding the lateral area and *two* base areas. Note that for pyramids and cones, students will add the lateral area and *one* base area. You may want to display the Teaching Transparency.

Teaching Tip **Inclusion** As you discuss the lesson examples, point out that the same variables are used as in the previous lesson: *B* for area of a base, *F* for lateral area of polygon surfaces, and *L* for lateral area of a curved surface.

Reaching All Learners
Through Modeling

Create a few models of pyramids and cones. (Nets are provided in Teaching Tools.) Give students a list of the surface areas. Ask students to use estimation to match the surface areas and the models. Then allow the students to use rulers to measure one of the models and calculate its surface area. Based on this result, allow students to revise their estimates. Then ask students to measure the remaining models, calculate the surface areas, and compare the actual surface areas with their estimates.

3 Close

Summarize

Suggest to students that being able to visualize how a three-dimensional figure can be formed from a two-dimensional figure will help them understand surface area. Draw the two-dimensional patterns for a prism, a cylinder, a pyramid, and a cone, but do not label them. Ask students to identify each.

Possible answers to Think and Discuss

2. Make a right triangle with its hypotenuse as the slant height of the pyramid, one leg as the height (4), and the other leg as half the base (3). Use the Pythagorean Theorem to find that the slant height is 5.

Assignment Guide

If you finished Example **1** assign:
Average 1–3, 6–8, 11, 12, 19–26
Advanced 6–8, 11, 12, 17, 19–26

If you finished Example **2** assign:
Average 1–4, 6–9, 11, 12, 19–26
Advanced 6–9, 11, 12, 17, 19–26

If you finished Example **3** assign:
Average 1–14, 19–26
Advanced 6–26

Homework Quick Check

Quickly check key concepts.
Exercises: 6, 9, 10, 12

Answers

4, 9. See p. A12.

See p. A12.

Math Background

When you are working with problems involving irrational numbers, such as *pi* and some square roots, different methods of rounding can result in different answers. This is especially true for problems that contain large numbers. For example, the answer to Exercise 14 is ≈ 527,237 ft² if calculated on a calculator and rounded at the last step. However, the answer is 526,800 ft² if the values are rounded to the nearest square foot at each step. Unless otherwise indicated, given answers have been calculated on a calculator and rounded at the last step.

State Resources

go.hrw.com
State Resources Online
KEYWORD: MT7 Resources

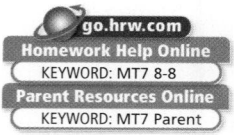
go.hrw.com
Homework Help Online
KEYWORD: MT7 8-8
Parent Resources Online
KEYWORD: MT7 Parent

GUIDED PRACTICE

See Example **1** Find the surface area of each figure to the nearest tenth. Use 3.14 for π.

1. 105 m²
8 m
5 m   5 m

2. 30.6 ft²
5 ft
1.5 ft

3. 9 m 144 m²
6 m   6 m

See Example **2** **4.** A cone has diameter 12 in. and slant height 9 in. Tell whether doubling both dimensions would double the surface area.

See Example **3** **5.** The rooms at the Wigwam Village Motel in Cave City, Kentucky, are cones about 20 ft high and have a diameter of about 20 ft. Estimate the lateral surface area of a room.   ≈ 702.5 ft²

INDEPENDENT PRACTICE

See Example **1** Find the surface area of each figure to the nearest tenth. Use 3.14 for π.

6. 5.5 in.
4 in.
39.9 in²
4 in.   4 in.

7. 6 mm
4 mm
125.6 mm²

8. 4.5 in.   3 in.
24.1 in²
3 in.   3 in.

See Example **2** **9.** A regular square pyramid has a base with 12 yd sides and slant height 5 yd. Tell whether doubling both dimensions would double the surface area.

See Example **3** **10.** In the late 1400s, Leonardo da Vinci designed a parachute shaped like a pyramid. His design called for a tent-like structure made of linen, measuring 21 feet on each side and 12 feet high. Estimate how much material would be needed to make the parachute?   ≈ 669.7 ft²

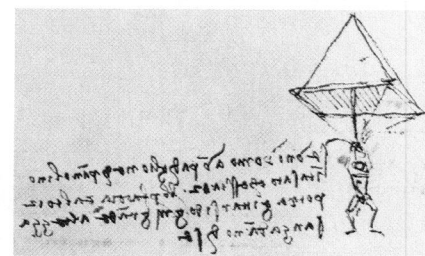

PRACTICE AND PROBLEM SOLVING

Extra Practice
See page 797.

Find the surface area of each figure with the given dimensions. Use 3.14 for π.

0.18 km²

11. regular triangular pyramid:
base area = 0.06 km²
base perimeter = 0.8 km
slant height = 0.3 km

12. cone: $r = 12\frac{1}{2}$ mi
slant height = $44\frac{1}{4}$ mi
$709\frac{3}{8}\pi ≈ 2227.4$ mi²

Extra Practice See page 797.

RETEACH 8-8

Reteach
8-8 *Surface Area of Pyramids and Cones (continued)*

An unfolded cone results in a circle and a lateral surface drawn as a sector of a circle.
5 cm   5 cm
11 cm
11 cm

The slant height of the cone is the radius of the circle sector.

Surface Area S = area of circular base + area of lateral surface (circle sector)

$= \pi r^2 + \frac{1}{2}$ circumference of base × slant height

$= \pi r^2 + \frac{1}{2}(2\pi r) \times \ell$

$S = \pi r^2 + \pi r\ell$
$S = \pi(5^2) + \pi(5)(11)$
$S = 25\pi + 55\pi = 80\pi$ cm²
$S ≈ 80(3.14) ≈ 251.2$ cm²

Complete to find the surface area of the cone.

3. $S = \pi r^2 + \pi\ell$
$S = \pi(\underline{4}^2) + \pi \times \underline{4} \times \underline{7}$
$S = \underline{16}\pi + \underline{28}\pi = \underline{44}\pi$
$S ≈ \underline{44}$ (3.14)
$S ≈ \underline{138.16}$ in²

7 in.
4 in.

Find the surface area of each cone. Round to the nearest whole number.

4. radius = 3 ft, slant height = 5 ft
75 ft²

5. diameter = 8.6 cm, slant height = 10 cm
193 cm²

PRACTICE 8-8

Practice B
8-8 *Surface Area of Pyramids and Cones*

Find the surface area of each figure to the nearest tenth. Use 3.14 for π.

1. 12 ft
15 ft
1017.4 ft²

2. 24 ft
18 ft   18 ft
1188 ft²

3. 15 cm
12 cm
9 cm
423 cm²

4. 13.5 in.
13 in.
1081.7 in²

5. 16 cm
13 cm
11 cm
527 cm²

6. 22.5 in.
19.6 in.   19.6 in.
1266.2 in²

7. 18 m
22 m
2260.8 m²

8. 15 ft
17.9 ft   16.2 ft
801.5 ft²

9. 15.8 m
17.6 m
1657.0 m²

10. Find the surface area of a regular square pyramid with a slant height of 17 m and a base perimeter of 44 m.   495 m²

11. Find the length of the slant height of a square pyramid if one side of the base is 15 ft and the surface area is 765 ft².   18 ft

12. Find the length of the slant height of a cone with a radius of 15 cm and a surface area of 1884 cm².   25 cm

13. A cone has a diameter of 12 ft and a slant height of 20 ft. Explain whether tripling both dimensions would triple the surface area.   Possible answer:
The surface area of the first cone is 489.84 ft². The surface area of the cone with the new dimensions is 4408.56 ft². It increases the surface area by a factor of 9.

16. Possible answer: What is the lateral area of the ice cream cone? Solution: $\pi(2)(11) = 69.08$ in^2

17. Possible answer: Create a right triangle using the slant height as the hypotenuse, the radius of the base as one leg, and the height as the other leg. Then use the Pythagorean Theorem to find the slant height.

13. Earth Science When the Moon is between the Sun and Earth, it casts a conical shadow called the *umbra*. If the shadow is 2140 mi in diameter and 260,955 mi along the edge, what is the lateral surface area of the umbra? $\approx 877{,}201{,}312$ mi^2

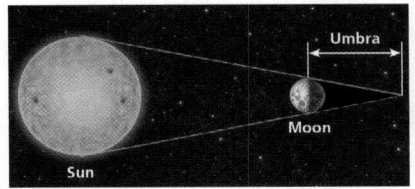

14. Social Studies The Pyramid Arena in Memphis, Tennessee, is 321 feet tall and has a square base with side length 200 yards. What is the lateral surface area of the pyramid in feet? $\approx 527{,}237$ ft^2

15. The table shows the dimensions of three square pyramids.

a. Complete the table. $\approx 481; \approx 277$

b. Which pyramid has the least lateral surface area? What is its lateral surface area? Menkaure; $\approx 191{,}684$ ft^2

c. Which pyramid has the greatest volume? What is its volume? Khufu; $91{,}636{,}272$ ft^3

Dimensions of Giza Pyramids (ft)			
Pyramid	Height	Slant Height	Side of Base
Khufu		612	756
Khafre	471	588	704
Menkaure	216		346

16. Write a Problem An ice cream cone has a diameter of 4 in. and a slant height of 11 in. Write and solve a problem about the ice cream cone.

17. Write About It The height and base dimensions of a cone are known. Explain how to find the slant height.

18. Challenge The oldest pyramid is said to be the Step Pyramid of King Zoser, built around 2650 B.C. in Saqqara, Egypt. The base is a rectangle that measures 358 ft by 411 ft, and the height of the pyramid is 204 ft. Find the lateral surface area of the pyramid. $\approx 215{,}208$ ft^2; answers may vary due to rounding.

TEST PREP and Spiral Review

19. Multiple Choice Find the surface area of a triangular pyramid with base area 12 square meters, base perimeter 24 meters, and slant height 8 meters.

(A) 72 m^2 (B) 108 m^2 (C) 204 m^2 (D) 2304 m^2

20. Gridded Response What is the lateral surface area of a cone with diameter 12 centimeters and slant height 6 centimeters? Use 3.14 for π. 113.04 cm^2

Simplify. (Lesson 1-6)

21. $-4(6 - 8)$ **8**   **22.** $3(-5 - 4)$ **−27**   **23.** $-2(4 - 9)$ **10**   **24.** $-6(8 - 9)$ **6**

Find the volume of each rectangular prism. (Lesson 8-5)

25. length 5 ft, width 3 ft, height 8 ft **120 ft^3**   **26.** length 2.5 m, width 3.5 m, height 7 m **61.25 m^3**

8-8 Lesson Quiz

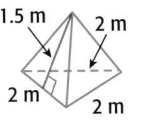

1.5 m, 2 m, 2 m, 2 m

10 in., 4 in.

Find the surface area of each figure to the nearest tenth. Use 3.14 for π.

1. the triangular pyramid 6.2 m^2

2. the cone 175.8 in^2

3. Tell whether doubling the dimensions of the cone will double the surface area. It will more than double the area because you square the radius to find the area of the base.

Also available on transparency

CHALLENGE 8-8

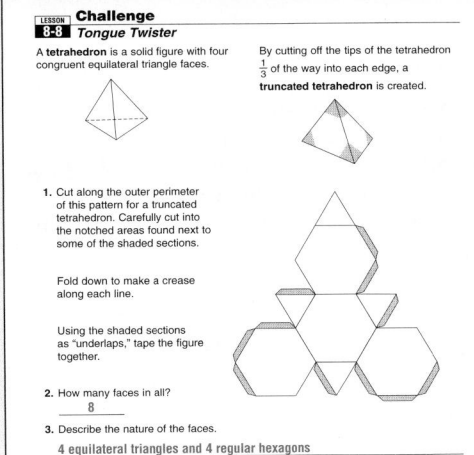

LESSON 8-8 Challenge
Tongue Twister

A **tetrahedron** is a solid figure with four congruent equilateral triangle faces.

By cutting off the tips of the tetrahedron $\frac{1}{3}$ of the way into each edge, a **truncated tetrahedron** is created.

1. Cut along the outer perimeter of this pattern for a truncated tetrahedron. Carefully cut into the notched areas found next to some of the shaded sections.

Fold down to make a crease along each line.

Using the shaded sections as "underlaps," tape the figure together.

2. How many faces in all? 8

3. Describe the nature of the faces. 4 equilateral triangles and 4 regular hexagons

4. Area of Equilateral Triangle $= \frac{s^2}{4}\sqrt{3}$ Area of Regular Hexagon $= \frac{3s^2}{2}\sqrt{3}$

Find the surface area of a truncated tetrahedron with $s = 2$ in. Answer in terms of $\sqrt{3}$. (*Hint:* Add terms, such as $5\sqrt{3} + 2\sqrt{3} = 7\sqrt{3}$)

$4\left(\frac{2^2}{4}\right)\sqrt{3} + 4\left(\frac{3(2^2)}{2}\right)\sqrt{3} = 4\sqrt{3} + 24\sqrt{3} = 28\sqrt{3}$ in^2

PROBLEM SOLVING 8-8

LESSON 8-8 Problem Solving
Surface Area of Pyramids and Cones

Round to the nearest tenth. Use 3.14 for π. Write the correct answer.

1. The Feathered Serpent Pyramid in Teotihuacan, Mexico, is the third largest in the city. Its base is a square that measures 65 m on each side. The pyramid is 19.4 m high and has a slant height of 37.8 m. The lateral faces of the pyramid are decorated with paintings. What is the surface area of the painted faces? 4914 m^2

2. The Sun Pyramid in Teotihuacan, Mexico, is larger than the Feathered Serpent Pyramid. The sides of the square base and the slant height are each about 3.3 times larger than the Feathered Serpent Pyramid. How many times larger is the surface area of the lateral faces of the Sun Pyramid than the Feathered Serpent Pyramid? 10.9 times larger

3. An oil funnel is in the shape of a cone. It has a diameter of 4 inches and a slant height of 6 inches. How much material does it take to make a funnel with these dimensions? 37.7 in^2

4. If the diameter of the funnel in Exercise 6 is doubled, by how much does it increase the surface area of the funnel? 2 times

Round to the nearest tenth. Use 3.14 for π. Choose the letter for the best answer.

5. An ice cream cone has a diameter of 4.2 cm and a slant height of 11.5 cm. What is the surface area of the ice cream cone?
A 4.7 cm^2 (C) 75.83 cm^2
B 19.9 cm^2 D 159.2 cm^2

6. A marker has a conical tip. The diameter of the tip is 1 cm and the slant height is 0.7 cm. What is the area of the writing surface of the marker tip?
(F) 1.1 cm^2 H 2.2 cm^2
G 1.9 cm^2 J 5.3 cm^2

7. A skylight is shaped like a square pyramid. Each panel has a 4 m base. The slant height is 2 m, and the base is open. The installation cost is $5.25 per square meter. What is the cost to install 4 skylights?
A $64   C $218
B $159   (D) $336

8. A paper drinking cup shaped like a cone has a 10 cm slant height and an 8 cm diameter. What is the surface area of the cone?
F 88.9 cm^2 H 251.2 cm^2
(G) 125.6 cm^2 J 301.2 cm^2

Pacing: Traditional 1 day
Block $\frac{1}{2}$ day

Objective: Students find the volume and surface area of spheres.

Hands-On Lab
In *Hands-On Lab Activities*

Technology Lab
In *Technology Lab Activities*

Online Edition
Tutorial Videos

Countdown to Testing Week 18

Power Presentations
with PowerPoint®

Warm Up

1. Find the surface area of a square pyramid whose base is 3 m on a side and whose slant height is 5 m.   **39 m²**

2. Find the surface area of a cone whose base has a radius of 10 in. and whose slant height is 14 in. Use 3.14 for π.   **753.6 in²**

Problem of the Day

Find the slant height of the cone with the following measurements:

The area of its base is one-third of its total surface area. The radius is 4 cm.   **8 cm**

Also available on transparency

State Resources

go.hrw.com
State Resources Online
KEYWORD: MT7 Resources

8-9 Spheres

Learn to find the volume and surface area of spheres.

Vocabulary
sphere
hemisphere
great circle

Earth is not a perfect *sphere*, but it has been molded by gravitational forces into a spherical shape. Earth has a diameter of about 7926 miles and a surface area of about 197 million square miles.

A **sphere** is the set of points in three dimensions that are a fixed distance from a given point, the center. A plane that intersects a sphere through its center divides the sphere into two halves, or **hemispheres**. The edge of a hemisphere is a **great circle**.

Sphere
Radius
Center

Hemisphere
Great circle

The volume of a hemisphere is exactly halfway between the volume of a cone and the volume of a cylinder with the same radius r and height equal to r.

VOLUME OF A SPHERE		
Words	**Numbers**	**Formula**
The volume V of a sphere is $\frac{4}{3}\pi$ times the cube of the radius r.	$V = \frac{4}{3}\pi(3^3)$ $= \frac{108}{3}\pi$ $= 36\pi$ $\approx 113.1 \text{ units}^3$	$V = \frac{4}{3}\pi r^3$

EXAMPLE 1 **Finding the Volume of a Sphere**

Find the volume of a sphere with radius 9 ft, both in terms of π and to the nearest tenth. Use 3.14 for π.

$V = \frac{4}{3}\pi r^3$ *Volume of a sphere*

$= \frac{4}{3}\pi(9)^3$ *Substitute 9 for r.*

$= 972\pi \text{ ft}^3 \approx 3052.1 \text{ ft}^3$

---

1 Introduce

Alternate Opener

Motivate

Ask students to name some sports or games that involve a ball. Ask them if they know the mathematical name for the shape of a ball. **sphere** Tell students that they will learn to find the volume and surface area of spheres.

Explorations and answers are provided in *Alternate Openers: Explorations Transparencies*.

The surface area of a sphere is four times the area of a great circle.

SURFACE AREA OF A SPHERE		
Words	**Numbers**	**Formula**
The surface area S of a sphere is 4π times the square of the radius r.	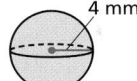 $S = 4\pi(2^2)$ $= 16\pi$ $\approx 50.3 \text{ units}^2$	$S = 4\pi r^2$

 E X A M P L E 2 **Finding Surface Area of a Sphere**

4 mm

Find the surface area, both in terms of π and to the nearest tenth. Use 3.14 for π.

$S = 4\pi r^2$ *Surface area of a sphere*
$\quad = 4\pi(4^2)$ *Substitute 4 for r.*
$\quad = 64\pi \text{ mm}^2 \approx 201.1 \text{ mm}^2$

E X A M P L E 3 **Comparing Volumes and Surface Areas**

Compare the volume and surface area of a sphere with radius 42 cm with that of a rectangular prism measuring $56 \times 63 \times 88$ cm.

Sphere:

$V = \frac{4}{3}\pi r^3 = \frac{4}{3}\pi(42)^3$

$\quad \approx \left(\frac{4}{3}\right)\left(\frac{22}{7}\right)(74,088)$

$\quad \approx 310,464 \text{ cm}^3$

$S = 4\pi r^2 = 4\pi(42)^2$

$\quad = 7056\pi$

$\quad \approx 7056\left(\frac{22}{7}\right) \approx 22,176 \text{ cm}^2$

Rectangular prism:

$V = \ell wh$

$\quad = (56)(63)(88)$

$\quad = 310,464 \text{ cm}^3$

$S = 2\ell w + 2\ell h + 2wh$

$\quad = 2(56)(63) + 2(56)(88) + 2(63)(88)$

$\quad = 28,000 \text{ cm}^2$

The sphere and the prism have approximately the same volume, but the prism has a larger surface area.

 **Think and Discuss**

1. Compare the area of a great circle with the surface area of a sphere.

2. Explain which would hold the most water: a bowl in the shape of a hemisphere with radius r, a cylindrical glass with radius r and height r, or a conical drinking cup with radius r and height r.

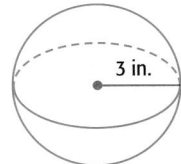
Possible answers to Think and Discuss

1. The area of one great circle would cover $\frac{1}{4}$ of its corresponding sphere because the surface area of a sphere is 4 times the area of one of its great circles.

2 Teach

Guided Instruction

In this lesson, students learn to find the volume and surface area of spheres. Explain that the volume of a hemisphere is the average of the volumes of a cone and a cylinder that each have radius and height equal to the radius of the hemisphere. Share with students that this fact leads to the formula for the volume of a sphere (Teaching Transparency). Explain that the surface area of a sphere is four times the area of one of its great circles. Discuss the conclusion of Example 3: A sphere and a prism that contain the same quantity when filled do not necessarily have the same surface area.

Reaching All Learners
Through Concrete Manipulatives

Have students gather five spheres of different sizes (balls, beads, etc.), measure their diameters, and calculate their volumes and surface areas. Have them record their data in a table like the one below.

Object	Volume	Surface Area

You may want to have students compare findings to see if they used some of the same objects and came up with similar results.

3 Close

Summarize

Remind students that both the volume formula and the surface area formula for spheres involve the radius. Ask students if there seems to be a relationship between the exponent on the radius and the units used for each formula.

Possible answer: Yes; because the radius is cubed in the volume formula, the answer is expressed in cubic units. Because the radius is squared in the surface area formula, the answer is expressed in square units.

Assignment Guide

If you finished Example **1** assign:
Average 1–4, 10–13, 25, 28–36
Advanced 10–13, 24, 25, 27–36

If you finished Example **2** assign:
Average 1–8, 10–17, 19–22, 25, 26, 28–36
Advanced 10–17, 19–22, 24–36

If you finished Example **3** assign:
Average 1–22, 25, 26, 28–36
Advanced 10–36

Homework Quick Check

Quickly check key concepts.
Exercises: 10, 16, 18, 26

Answers

23. See p. A12.

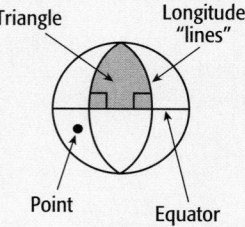

Math Background

Traditional (Euclidean) geometry is based on points, straight lines, and flat planes. In spherical geometry, a point has the traditional meaning, but flat planes are replaced by spherical surfaces, and straight lines are replaced by great circles of the sphere. There are no parallel lines, and there are "triangles" with two right angles.

Triangle   Longitude "lines"

Point   Equator

State Resources

GUIDED PRACTICE

See Example **1**
Find the volume of each sphere, both in terms of π and to the nearest tenth. Use 3.14 for π.
36π cm³; 113.0 cm³ 2304π ft³; 7234.6 ft³   6.6π m³; 20.7 m³   166.7π mi³; 523.3 mi³
1. $r = 3$ cm   **2.** $r = 12$ ft   **3.** $d = 3.4$ m   **4.** $d = 10$ mi

See Example **2**
Find the surface area of each sphere, both in terms of π and to the nearest tenth. Use 3.14 for π.
256π cm²; 803.8 cm²

5. 1 in.   **6.** 7.7 mm   **7.** 8 cm   **8.** 17 yd
4π in²; 12.6 in²   237.2π mm²; 744.7 mm²   289π yd²; 907.5 yd²

See Example **3**
9. Compare the volume and surface area of a sphere with radius 4 in. with that of a cube with sides measuring 6.45 in. **The volume of the sphere and the cube are about equal (≈268 in³). The surface area of the sphere is about 201 in², and the surface area of the cube is about 250 in².**

INDEPENDENT PRACTICE

See Example **1**
Find the volume of each sphere, both in terms of π and to the nearest tenth. Use 3.14 for π.
1.3π in³; 4.2 in³
10. $r = 14$ ft   **11.** $r = 5.7$ cm   **12.** $d = 26$ mm   **13.** $d = 2$ in.

See Example **2**
Find the surface area of each sphere, both in terms of π and to the nearest tenth. Use 3.14 for π.
400π cm²; 1256 cm²

14. 4 ft   **15.** 7.2 m   **16.** 7 km   **17.** 20 cm
64π ft²; 201 ft²   207.4π m²; 651.2 m²   49π km²; 153.9 km²

See Example **3**
18. Compare the volume and surface area of a sphere with diameter 5 ft with that of a cylinder with height 2 ft and a base with radius 3 ft.

10. 3658π ft³; 11,488.3 ft³   **11.** 246.9π cm³; 775.3 cm³   **12.** 2929.3π mm³; 9198.1 mm³

PRACTICE AND PROBLEM SOLVING

Extra Practice
See page 797.

Find the missing measurements of each sphere, both in terms of π and to the nearest hundredth. Use 3.14 for π.

18. The volume of the sphere is 20.8π ft³, and its surface area is 25π ft². The volume of the cylinder is 18π ft³, and its surface area is 30π ft².

19. radius = 6.5 in.
volume = ■   366.17π in³; 1149.76 in³
surface area = 169π in²

20. radius = 11.2 m
volume = 1873.24π m³   501.76π m²; 1575.53 m²
surface area = ■

21. diameter = 6.8 yd
volume = ■ $V = 52.41\pi \approx$ 164.55 yd³;
surface area = ■ $S = 46.24\pi \approx$ 145.19 yd²

22. radius = ■
diameter = 22 in.   11 in.; 484π ≈ 1519.76 in²
surface area = ■

23. See page A13.

23. Use models of a sphere, cylinder, and two cones. The sphere and cylinder have the same diameter and height. The cones have the same diameter and half the height of the sphere. Describe the relationship between the volumes of these shapes.

RETEACH 8-9

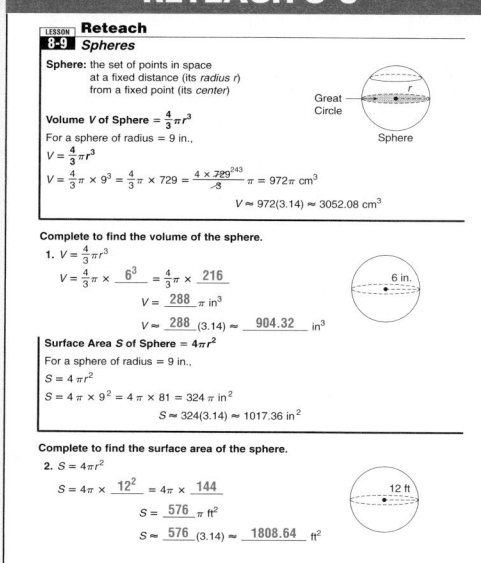

LESSON 8-9 Reteach
Spheres

Sphere: the set of points in space at a fixed distance (its *radius r*) from a fixed point (its *center*)

Volume V of Sphere = $\frac{4}{3}\pi r^3$
For a sphere of radius = 9 in.,
$V = \frac{4}{3}\pi r^3$
$V = \frac{4}{3}\pi \times 9^3 = \frac{4}{3}\pi \times 729 = \frac{4 \times 729^{243}}{3}\pi = 972\pi$ cm³
$V = 972(3.14) \approx 3052.08$ cm³

Complete to find the volume of the sphere.
1. $V = \frac{4}{3}\pi r^3$
$V = \frac{4}{3}\pi \times \underline{6^3} = \frac{4}{3}\pi \times \underline{216}$ 6 in.
$V = \underline{288}\ \pi$ in³
$V \approx \underline{288}\ (3.14) \approx \underline{904.32}$ in³

Surface Area S of Sphere = $4\pi r^2$
For a sphere of radius = 9 in.,
$S = 4\pi r^2$
$S = 4\pi \times 9^2 = 4\pi \times 81 = 324\pi$ in²
$S \approx 324(3.14) \approx 1017.36$ in²

Complete to find the surface area of the sphere.
2. $S = 4\pi r^2$
$S = 4\pi \times \underline{12^2} = 4\pi \times \underline{144}$ 12 ft
$S = \underline{576}\ \pi$ ft²
$S \approx \underline{576}\ (3.14) \approx \underline{1808.64}$ ft²

PRACTICE 8-9

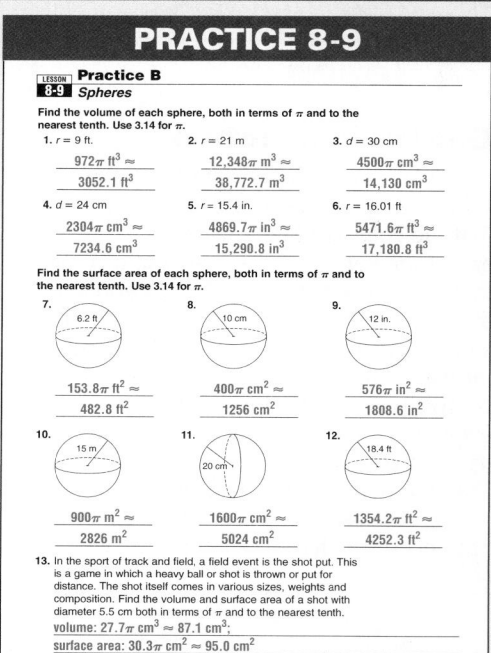

LESSON 8-9 Practice B
Spheres

Find the volume of each sphere, both in terms of π and to the nearest tenth. Use 3.14 for π.
1. $r = 9$ ft.   **2.** $r = 21$ m   **3.** $d = 30$ cm
972π ft³ ≈   12,348π m³ ≈   4500π cm³ ≈
3052.1 ft³   38,772.7 m³   14,130 cm³

4. $d = 24$ cm   **5.** $r = 15.4$ in.   **6.** $r = 16.01$ ft
2304π cm³ ≈   4869.7π in³ ≈   5471.6π ft³ ≈
7234.6 cm³   15,290.8 in³   17,180.8 ft³

Find the surface area of each sphere, both in terms of π and to the nearest tenth. Use 3.14 for π.
7. 6.2 ft   **8.** 10 cm   **9.** 12 in.
153.8π ft² ≈   400π cm² ≈   576π in² ≈
482.8 ft²   1256 cm²   1808.6 in²

10. 15 m   **11.** 20 cm   **12.** 18.4 ft
900π m² ≈   1600π cm² ≈   1354.2π ft² ≈
2826 m²   5024 cm²   4252.3 ft²

13. In the sport of track and field, a field event is the shot put. This is a game in which a heavy ball or shot is thrown or put for distance. The shot itself comes in various sizes, weights and composition. Find the volume and surface area of a shot with diameter 5.5 cm both in terms of π and to the nearest tenth.
volume: 27.7π cm³ ≈ 87.1 cm³;
surface area: 30.3π cm² ≈ 95.0 cm²

Eggs come in many different shapes. The eggs of birds that live on cliffs are often extremely pointed to keep the eggs from rolling. Other birds, such as great horned owls, have eggs that are nearly spherical. Turtles and crocodiles also have nearly spherical eggs, and the eggs of many dinosaurs were spherical.

24. To lay their eggs, green turtles travel hundreds of miles to the beach where they were born. The eggs are buried on the beach in a hole about 40 cm deep. The eggs are approximately spherical, with an average diameter of 4.5 cm, and each turtle lays an average of 113 eggs at a time. Estimate the total volume of eggs laid by a green turtle at one time. ≈ 5392 cm^3

25. Fossilized embryos of dinosaurs called titanosaurid sauropods have recently been found in spherical eggs in Patagonia. The eggs were 15 cm in diameter, and the adult dinosaurs were more than 12 m in length. Find the volume of an egg. ≈ 1767.15 cm^3

26. Hummingbirds lay eggs that are nearly spherical and about 1 cm in diameter. Find the surface area of an egg. ≈ 3.14 cm^2

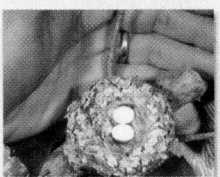

27. ⭐ **Challenge** An ostrich egg has about the same volume as a sphere with a diameter of 5 inches. If the shell is about $\frac{1}{12}$ inch thick, estimate the volume of just the shell, not including the interior of the egg. ≈ 6.33 in^3

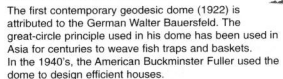

TEST PREP and Spiral Review

28. Multiple Choice The surface area of a sphere is 50.24 square centimeters. What is its diameter? Use 3.14 for π.

(A) 1 cm   (B) 2 cm   (C) 2.5 cm   (D) 4 cm

29. Gridded Response Find the surface area, in square feet, of a sphere with radius 3 feet. Use 3.14 for π. 113.04

Simplify. (Lesson 4-5)

30. $\sqrt{144}$ **12**   **31.** $\sqrt{64}$ **8**   **32.** $\sqrt{169}$ **13**   **33.** $\sqrt{225}$ **15**   **34.** $\sqrt{1}$ **1**

Find the surface area of each figure to the nearest tenth. Use 3.14 for π.
(Lesson 8-8)

35. a square pyramid with base 13 m by 13 m and slant height 7.5 m **364 m^2**

36. a cone with a diameter 90 cm and slant height 125 cm **24,021 cm^2**

Interdisciplinary LINK

Life Science

Exercises 24–27 involve using formulas to find the surface area and volume of eggs. Bird, reptile, and insect eggs are studied in middle school science programs, such as *Holt Science and Technology.*

TEST PREP DOCTOR ✚ Remind students that for Exercise 28, they must solve the equation $S = 4\pi r^2$ for r, then double the value of r to find the diameter of the sphere. Students who chose answer choice **B** found the radius.

🖊 Journal

Remind students that scientific notation is a way to express very large or very small numbers (Lesson 4-4). Ask them to write about some spherical or hemispherical objects with volumes or surface areas that could be expressed in scientific notation. Examples might include the moon or a plant cell.

CHALLENGE 8-9

LESSON 8-9 Challenge
Useful and Intriguing

A **geodesic dome** is a structure made of a complex network of triangles that form a roughly spherical surface. The dome gets its efficiency from the characteristics of a sphere.

The first contemporary geodesic dome (1922) is attributed to the German Walter Bauersfeld. The great-circle principle used in his dome has been used in Asia for centuries to weave fish traps and baskets. In the 1940's, the American Buckminster Fuller used the dome to design efficient houses.

The classic geodesic dome takes its form from the **icosahedron**, a regular solid with 20 equilateral triangles as faces, 30 congruent edges, and 12 vertices.

Consider an icosahedron with edge $s = 12$ ft.

1. Find the surface area with the formula Area of Equilateral Triangle $= \frac{s^2}{4}\sqrt{3}$. Use $\sqrt{3} \approx 1.73$ to answer to the nearest tenth of a square foot.
$20\left(\frac{12^2}{4}\sqrt{3}\right) = 720\sqrt{3} \approx 720(1.73) \approx 1245.6$ ft^2

2. Find the volume with the formula Volume of Icosahedron $= \frac{5}{12}(3 + \sqrt{5})s^2$. Use $\sqrt{5} \approx 2.24$ to answer to the nearest tenth of a cubic foot.
$\frac{5}{12}(3 + \sqrt{5})12^2 = 60(3 + \sqrt{5}) \approx 60(3 + 2.24) \approx 314.4$ ft^3

3. Find an approximate value for the radius r of the sphere that has approximately the same volume as the icosahedron.
$\frac{4}{3}\pi r^3 \approx 314.4 \to \frac{4}{3}(3.14)r^3 \approx 314.4 \to 4.19r^3 \approx 314.4 \to r^3 \approx$
$75 \to r \approx 4.2$

4. Using your value of r, find the surface area of that sphere.
$4(3.14)(4.2^2) \approx 221.6$ ft^3

5. Use your results to make an observation about why a sphere is more efficient than an icosahedron. Possible answer:
For a given volume, a sphere exposes less surface area than an icosahedron.

PROBLEM SOLVING 8-9

LESSON 8-9 Problem Solving
Spheres

Early golf balls were smooth spheres. Later it was discovered that golf balls flew better when they were dimpled. On January 1, 1932, the United States Golf Association set standards for the weight and size of a golf ball. The minimum diameter of a regulation golf ball is 1.680 inches. Use 3.14 for π. Round to the nearest hundredth.

1. Find the volume of a smooth golf ball with the minimum diameter allowed by the United States Golf Association.
2.48 in^3

2. Find the surface area of a smooth golf ball with the minimum diameter allowed by the United States Golf Association.
8.86 in^2

3. Would the dimples on a golf ball increase or decrease the volume of the ball?
decrease

4. Would the dimples on a golf ball increase or decrease the surface area of the ball?
increase

Use 3.14 for π. Use the following information for Exercises 5–6. A track and field expert recommends changes to the size of a shot put. One recommendation is that a shot put should have a diameter between 90 and 110 mm. Choose the letter for the best answer.

5. Find the surface area of a shot put with a diameter of 90 mm.
(A) 25,434 mm^2
B 101,736 mm^2
C 381,520 mm^2
D 3,052,080 mm^2

6. Find the surface area of a shot put with a diameter 110 mm.
F 9,499 mm^2
G 22,834 mm^2
(H) 37,994 mm^2
J 151,976 mm^2

7. Find the volume of the earth if the average diameter of the earth is 7926 miles.
A 2.0 × 10^8 mi^3
(B) 2.6 × 10^{11} mi^3
C 7.9 × 10^8 mi^3
D 2.1 × 10^{12} mi^3

8. An ice cream cone has a diameter of 4.2 cm and a height of 11.5 cm. One spherical scoop of ice cream is put on the cone that has a diameter of 5.6 cm. If the ice cream were to melt in the cone, by how much of it would overflow the cone? Round to the nearest tenth.
F 0 cm^3 (H) 38.8 cm^3
G 12.3 cm^3 J 54.3 cm^3

Power Presentations
with PowerPoint®

✓ **8-9**
Lesson Quiz
Find the volume of each sphere, both in terms of π and to the nearest tenth. Use 3.14 for π.

1. $r = 4$ ft   85.3π ft^3, 267.8 ft^3

2. $d = 6$ m   36π m^3, 113.0 m^3

Find the surface area of each sphere, both in terms of π and to the nearest tenth. Use 3.14 for π.

3. $r = 22$ in.   1936π in^2, 6079.0 in^2

4. $d = 1.5$ mi   2.25π mi^2, 7.1 mi^2

5. A basketball has a circumference of 29 in. To the nearest cubic inch, what is its volume? 412 in^3

Also available on transparency

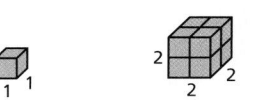 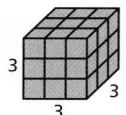
Pacing: Traditional 1 day
Block $\frac{1}{2}$ day

Objective: Students make scale models of solid figures.

Online Edition
Tutorial Videos

Countdown to Testing Week 18

Power Presentations
with PowerPoint®

Warm Up

Find the surface area of each rectangular prism.

1. length 14 cm, width 7 cm, height 7 cm **490 cm²**

2. length 30 in., width 6 in., height 21 in. **1872 in²**

3. length 3 mm, width 6 mm, height 4 mm **108 mm²**

4. length 37 in., width 9 in., height 18 in. **2322 in²**

Problem of the Day

A model of a solid-steel machine tool is built to a scale of 1 cm = 10 cm. The real object will weigh 2500 grams. How much does the model, also made of solid steel, weigh? **2.5 g**

Also available on transparency

Math Humor

When the student was caught climbing the statues in the city park, she explained that she was just doing her math homework—she was *scaling three-dimensional figures*.

State Resources

go.hrw.com
State Resources Online
KEYWORD: MT7 Resources

Learn to make scale models of solid figures.

Vocabulary
capacity

A packaging company sells boxes in a variety of sizes. It offers a supply of cube boxes that measure 1 ft × 1 ft × 1 ft, 2 ft × 2 ft × 2 ft, and 3 ft × 3 ft × 3 ft. What is the volume and surface area of each of these boxes?

Edge Length	1 ft	2 ft	3 ft
Volume	$1 \times 1 \times 1 = 1$ ft³	$2 \times 2 \times 2 = 8$ ft³	$3 \times 3 \times 3 = 27$ ft³
Surface Area	$6 \cdot 1 \times 1 = 6$ ft²	$6 \cdot 2 \times 2 = 24$ ft²	$6 \cdot 3 \times 3 = 54$ ft²

Helpful Hint

Multiplying the linear dimensions of a solid by n creates n^2 as much surface area and n^3 as much volume.

Corresponding edge lengths of any two cubes are in proportion to each other because the cubes are similar. However, volumes and surface areas do not have the same scale factor as edge lengths.

Each edge of the 2 ft cube is 2 times as long as each edge of the 1 ft cube. However, the cube's volume, or **capacity**, is $2^3 = 8$ times as large, and its surface area is $2^2 = 4$ times as large as the 1 ft cube's.

EXAMPLE 1 **Scaling Models That Are Cubes**

A 6 cm cube is built from small cubes, each 2 cm on an edge. Compare the following values.

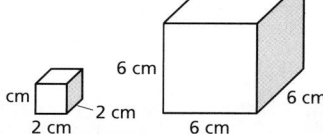

A the edge lengths of the large and small cubes

$$\frac{6 \text{ cm cube}}{2 \text{ cm cube}} \longrightarrow \frac{6 \text{ cm}}{2 \text{ cm}} = 3 \qquad \textit{Ratio of corresponding edges}$$

The edges of the large cube are 3 times as long as those of the small cube.

B the surface areas of the two cubes

$$\frac{6 \text{ cm cube}}{2 \text{ cm cube}} \longrightarrow \frac{216 \text{ cm}^2}{24 \text{ cm}^2} = 9 \qquad \textit{Ratio of corresponding areas}$$

The surface area of the large cube is $3^2 = 9$ times that of the small cube.

C the volumes of the two cubes

$$\frac{6 \text{ cm cube}}{2 \text{ cm cube}} \longrightarrow \frac{216 \text{ cm}^3}{8 \text{ cm}^3} = 27 \qquad \textit{Ratio of corresponding volumes}$$

The volume of the large cube is $3^2 = 27$ times that of the small cube.

---

1 Introduce
Alternate Opener

EXPLORATION

8-10 Scaling Three-Dimensional Figures

A rectangular box has a volume of 2 cubic units. If one of its dimensions is doubled, the volume of the box is doubled. If all three dimensions are doubled, the volume is 8 times the volume of the original box.

Length: 2 Width: 1 Height: 1 Volume: $2 \cdot 1 \cdot 1 = 2$	Length: 2 · 2 = 4 Width: 1 Height: 1 Volume: $4 \cdot 1 \cdot 1 = 4$	Length: 4 Width: 1 · 2 = 2 Height: 1 Volume: $4 \cdot 2 \cdot 1 = 8$	Length: 4 Width: 2 Height: 1 · 2 = 2 Volume: $4 \cdot 2 \cdot 2 = 16$

A box has a length of 3 in., a width of 2 in., and a height of 1 in. Multiply the dimensions of the box by each scale factor. Then find the volume.

	Scale Factor	Length (ℓ)	Width (w)	Height (h)	Volume $\ell \cdot w \cdot h$
	2	3 · 2 = 6 in.	2 · 2 = 4 in.	1 · 2 = 2 in.	6 · 4 · 2 = 48 in³
1.	3				
2.	4				
3.	5				

Think and Discuss

4. **Discuss** how each scale factor affects the volume of the rectangular box.

5. **Predict** what would happen to the volume if you were to multiply each dimension of the box by a scale factor of 0.5.

Motivate

Show students a cube, a rectangular prism that is not a cube, and a triangular prism. Remind students that a cube is a rectangular prism with six congruent square faces. Remind students that a triangular prism is a prism with two parallel congruent triangular bases. Review the formulas for surface area and volume.

Explorations and answers are provided in *Alternate Openers: Explorations Transparencies.*

EXAMPLE 2 Scaling Models That Are Other Solid Figures

The Fuller Building in New York, also known as the Flatiron Building, can be modeled as a trapezoidal prism with the approximate dimensions shown. For a 10 cm tall model of the Fuller Building, find the following.

A What is the scale factor of the model?

$$\frac{10 \text{ cm}}{93 \text{ m}} = \frac{10 \text{ cm}}{9300 \text{ cm}} = \frac{1}{930}$$ *Convert and simplify.*

The scale factor of the model is 1:930.

B What are the other dimensions of the model?

left side: $\frac{1}{930} \cdot 65 \text{ m} = \frac{6500}{930} \text{ cm} \approx 6.99 \text{ cm}$

back: $\frac{1}{930} \cdot 30 \text{ m} = \frac{3000}{930} \text{ cm} \approx 3.23 \text{ cm}$

right side: $\frac{1}{930} \cdot 60 \text{ m} = \frac{6000}{930} \text{ cm} \approx 6.45 \text{ cm}$

front: $\frac{1}{930} \cdot 2 \text{ m} = \frac{200}{930} \text{ cm} \approx 0.22 \text{ cm}$

The trapezoidal base has side lengths 6.99 cm, 3.23 cm, 6.45 cm, and 0.22 cm.

EXAMPLE 3 *Business Application*

A machine fills a cube box that has edge lengths of 1 ft with shampoo samples in 3 seconds. How long does it take the machine to fill a cube box that has edge lengths of 4 ft?

$V = 4 \text{ ft} \cdot 4 \text{ ft} \cdot 4 \text{ ft} = 64 \text{ ft}^3$ *Find the volume of the larger box.*

$\frac{3}{1 \text{ ft}^3} = \frac{x}{64 \text{ ft}^3}$ *Set up a proportion and solve.*

$3 \cdot 64 = x$ *Cross multiply.*

$192 = x$ *Calculate the fill time.*

It takes 192 seconds to fill the larger box.

Possible answers to *Think and Discuss*

1. The volume of the model is $\frac{1}{8}$ the volume of the original object.

2. Possible answer: Multiply each of the dimensions of the prism by the square root of 2.

Think and Discuss

1. **Describe** how the volume of a model compares to the original object if the linear scale factor of the model is 1:2.

2. **Explain** one possible way to double the surface area of a rectangular prism.

2 Teach

Guided Instruction

In this lesson, students learn to make scale models of solid figures. Review with students how to find the volume and surface area of a 1 ft cube, a 2 ft cube, and a 3 ft cube. Share with students that capacity is the same as volume. In Example 1, compare the ratios of corresponding edges, surface areas, and volumes for a 2 ft cube and a 6 ft cube. Point out that the ratio of surface areas is the *square* of the ratio of corresponding edges, and the ratio of volumes is the *cube* of the ratio of corresponding edges. Use Example 2 and Additional Example 2 to teach students how to scale a trapezoidal prism and a rectangular prism. Lastly, demonstrate how proportions and scaling are related such as in Example 3.

Reaching All Learners
Through Concrete Manipulatives

Have students work in pairs. Provide each pair with a set of 8 to 125 centimeter cubes (provided in the Manipulatives Kit). Ask students to build larger cubes from the centimeter cubes. For each larger cube, students should find the length of the edge, the surface area (by counting the visible square centimeters on the faces of the cube), and the volume (by counting the number of centimeter cubes needed to build the larger cube). Have them record their data and compare with another group's data.

3 Close

Summarize

Show students models or drawings of a 1 in. cube and a 1 ft cube. Ask students to find the surface area of each figure in square inches and the volume of each figure in cubic inches. Have them also identify the scale factor if the small cube is a model of the larger cube.

surface areas: 6 in^2 and 864 in^2; volumes: 1 in^3 and 1728 in^3; scale factor: $\frac{1}{12}$

8-10 Exercises

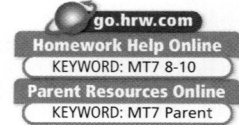

go.hrw.com
Homework Help Online
KEYWORD: MT7 8-10
Parent Resources Online
KEYWORD: MT7 Parent

Assignment Guide

If you finished Example **1** assign:
Average 1–3, 6–8, 11–13, 22, 23, 25–34
Advanced 6–8, 11–18, 22–34

If you finished Example **2** assign:
Average 1–4, 6–9, 11–13, 22, 23, 25–34
Advanced 6–9, 11–20, 22–34

If you finished Example **3** assign:
Average 1–13, 22, 23, 25–34
Advanced 6–10, 14–34

Homework Quick Check

Quickly check key concepts.
Exercises: 8, 9, 10, 12

Math Background

Capacity and volume are both measures of the amount of space inside a three-dimensional object. Capacity is normally used to indicate the amount a container will hold. The tables show some common units.

Volume

U. S. Customary	Metric
$1728 \text{ in}^3 = 1 \text{ ft}^3$	$1000 \text{ mm}^3 = 1 \text{ cm}^3$
$27 \text{ ft}^3 = 1 \text{ yd}^3$	$1{,}000{,}000 \text{ cm}^3 = 1 \text{ m}^3$

Capacity

U. S. Customary	Metric
32 oz = 1 qt	1000 mL = 1 L
4 qt = 1 gal	1000 L = 1 kL

State Resources

go.hrw.com
State Resources Online
KEYWORD: MT7 Resources

GUIDED PRACTICE

See Example **1** An 8 in. cube is built from small cubes, each 2 in. on a side. Compare the following values.

1. the side lengths of the large and small cubes **4:1**

2. the surface areas of the two cubes **16:1** **3.** the volumes of the two cubes **64:1**

See Example **2** **4.** The dimensions of a basketball arena are 500 ft long, 375 ft wide, and 125 ft high. The scale model used to build the arena is 40 in. long. Find the width and height of the model. **width: 30 in.; height: 10 in.**

See Example **3** **5.** A 3 ft by 1 ft by 1 ft fish tank in the shape of a rectangular prism drains in 3 min. How long would it take a 7 ft by 4 ft by 4 ft fish tank to drain at the same rate? **112 min**

INDEPENDENT PRACTICE

See Example **1** A 6 m cube is built from small cubes, each 3 m on a side. Compare the following values.

6. the side lengths of the large and small cubes **2:1**

7. the surface areas of the two cubes **4:1** **8.** the volumes of the two cubes **8:1**

See Example **2** **9.** The Great Pyramid of Giza has a square base measuring 230 m on each side and a height of about 147 m. Nathan is building a model of the pyramid with a 50 cm square base. What is the height to the nearest centimeter of Nathan's model? **32 cm**

See Example **3** **10.** An aboveground pool 5 ft tall with a diameter of 40 ft is filled with water in 50 minutes. How long will it take to fill an aboveground pool that is 6 ft tall with a diameter of 36 ft? **48.6 min**

PRACTICE AND PROBLEM SOLVING

Extra Practice
See page 797.

For each cube, a reduced scale model is built using a scale factor of $\frac{1}{2}$. Find the length of the model and the number of 1 cm cubes used to build it.

11. a 2 cm cube **1 cm; 1 cube**

12. a 6 cm cube **3 cm; 27 cubes**

13. an 18 cm cube **9 cm; 729 cubes**

14. a 4 cm cube **2 cm; 8 cubes**

15. a 14 cm cube **7 cm; 343 cubes**

16. a 16 cm cube **8 cm; 512 cubes**

17. What is the volume in cubic centimeters of a 1 m cube? **1,000,000 cm³**

18. An insulated lunch box measures 7 in. by 9.5 in. by 5 in. A larger version of the lunch box is available. Its dimensions are greater by a linear factor of 1.1. How much greater is the volume of the larger lunch box than the smaller one? What is the volume of the larger lunch box?

18. 1.331 times greater; ≈ 442.6 in³

19. Art A sand castle requires 3 pounds of sand. How much sand would be required to double all the dimensions of the sand castle? **24 lb**

RETEACH 8-10

LESSON 8-10 Reteach
Scaling Three-Dimensional Figures (continued)

The ratio of the volumes V of two cubes is the cube of the scale factor.

The scale factor for these two cubes is 3.

$$\frac{\text{side of larger cube}}{\text{side of smaller cube}} = \frac{9 \text{ in.}}{3 \text{ in.}} = \frac{3}{1} = 3$$

$$\frac{V \text{ larger}}{V \text{ smaller}} = \frac{\ell \times w \times h}{\ell \times w \times h} = \frac{9 \times 9 \times 9}{3 \times 3 \times 3} = \left(\frac{3}{1}\right)^3 = 27$$

Find the scale factor for each pair of cubes. Then find the ratio of the volumes.

5. side of larger cube = 100 in.
side of smaller cube = 25 in.

$$\frac{\text{larger}}{\text{smaller}} = \frac{100 \text{ in.}}{25 \text{ in.}} = \frac{4}{1} = 4$$

scale factor = __4__

ratio of volumes
= (scale factor)³ = (__4__)³ = __64__

6. side of smaller cube = 6 m
side of larger cube = 36 m

$$\frac{\text{smaller}}{\text{larger}} = \frac{6 \text{ m}}{36 \text{ m}} = \frac{1}{6}$$

scale factor = __$\frac{1}{6}$__

ratio of volumes
= (scale factor)³ = $\left(\frac{1}{6}\right)^3 = \frac{1}{216}$

As with the cube, the measures of other similar solids are related in the same ways to their scale factors.

Find the indicated ratios for these similar cylinders.

7. $\frac{\text{height of larger cylinder}}{\text{height of smaller cylinder}} = \frac{16 \text{ in.}}{4 \text{ in.}} = \frac{4}{1}$

8. $\frac{\text{radius of larger cylinder}}{\text{radius of smaller cylinder}} = \frac{8 \text{ in.}}{2 \text{ in.}} = \frac{4}{1}$

9. scale factor = __4__

10. $\frac{\text{area of circular base of larger cylinder}}{\text{area of circular base of smaller cylinder}} = \frac{\pi \cdot (\text{larger radius})^2}{\pi \cdot (\text{smaller radius})^2} = \frac{\pi \cdot (8)^2}{\pi \cdot (2)^2}$

$$= \frac{64\pi}{4\pi} = \frac{16}{1} = 16 = (\text{scale factor})^2$$

PRACTICE 8-10

LESSON 8-10 Practice B
Scaling Three-Dimensional Figures

A 10 in. cube is built from small cubes, each 2 in. on a side. Compare the following values.

1. The side lengths of the two cubes

The sides of the 10 in. cube are 5 times as long as the sides of the 2 in. cube.

2. The surface area of the two cubes

The surface area of the 10 in. cube is 25 times that of the 2 in. cube.

3. The volumes of the two cubes

The volume of the 10 in. cube is 125 times that of the 2 in. cube.

A 9 cm cube is built from small cubes, each 3 cm on a side. Compare the following values.

4. The side lengths of the two cubes

The sides of the 9 cm cube are 3 times as long as the sides of the 3 cm cube.

5. The surface area of the two cubes

The surface area of the 9 cm cube is 9 times that of the 3 cm cube.

6. The volumes of the two cubes

The volume of the 9 cm cube is 27 times that of the 3 cm cube.

7. The dimensions of a warehouse are 120 ft long, 180 ft wide, and 60 ft high. The scale model used to build the warehouse is 20 in. long. Find the width and height of the model of the warehouse.

30 in. wide and 10 in. high

8. It takes a machine 40 seconds to fill a cubic box with sides measuring 10 in. How long will it take the same machine to fill a cubic box with sides measuring 15 in.?

135 seconds

20. Recreation If it took 100,000 Lego® blocks to build a cylindrical monument with a 5 m diameter, about how many Legos would be needed to build a monument with an 8 m diameter and the same height? **256,000**

21. A kitchen sink measures 21 in. by 16 in. by 8 in. It takes 4 minutes 30 seconds to fill with water. A smaller kitchen sink takes 4 min 12 seconds to fill with water.

  a. What is the volume of the smaller kitchen sink? **2508.8 in³; ≈ 10.9 gal**

  b. About how many gallons of water does the smaller kitchen sink hold? (*Hint:* 1 gal = 231 in³) **about 10.9 gal**

 22. Choose a Strategy Six 1 cm cubes are used to build a solid. How many cubes are used to build a scale model of the solid with a linear scale factor of 2 to 1? Describe the tools and techniques you used.

  (A) 12 cubes   (B) 24 cubes   (C) 48 cubes   (D) 144 cubes

 23. Write About It If the linear scale factor of a model is $\frac{1}{5}$, what is the relationship between the volume of the original object and the volume of the model? **Possible answer: The volume of the original object is 125 times the volume of the model.**

 24. Challenge To double the volume of a rectangular prism, what number is multiplied by each of the prism's linear dimensions? Give your answer to the nearest hundredth. **the cube root of 2, or about 1.26**

Test Prep and Spiral Review

25. Multiple Choice A 9-inch cube is created from small cubes, each 1 inch on a side. What is the ratio of the volume of the larger cube to the volume of the smaller cube?

  (A) 1:9   (B) 9:1   (C) 81:1   (D) 729:1

26. Extended Response A 5-inch cube is created from small cubes, each 1 inch on a side. Compare the side lengths, surface area, and volume of the larger to the smaller cube. **ratio of side lengths 5:1, ratio of surface area 25:1, ratio of volume 125:1**

Solve. (Lesson 1-7)

27. $3 + x = 11$ **28.** $y - 6 = 8$ **29.** $13 = w + 11$ **30.** $5.6 = b - 4$
    $x = 8$ $y = 14$ $w = 2$ $b = 9.6$

Find the surface area of each sphere to the nearest tenth. Use $\pi = 3.14$.
(Lesson 8-9)

31. radius 5 mm   **32.** radius 12.2 ft   **33.** diameter 4 in.   **34.** diameter 20 cm
    314 mm²   **1869.4 ft²**   **50.2 in²**   **1256 cm²**

Legoland, in Billund, Denmark, contains Lego models of the Taj Mahal, Mount Rushmore, other monuments, and visitors, too.

Answers
22. Possible answer: I sketched a rectangular prism made of six small cubes and multiplied its dimensions by 2 to create a scaled up rectangular prism. I multiplied the new dimensions together and found that it consisted of 48 smaller cubes.

 **TEST PREP DOCTOR** For Example 25, it is important for students to remember that "a 9-inch cube" describes the length of one side of the cube and not the volume of the cube. They can then calculate the volume of both cubes in order to find the ratio of the two volumes.

Journal
Ask students to write about any model they have built or seen.

Power Presentations
with PowerPoint®

8-10 Lesson Quiz
A 10 cm cube is built from small cubes, each 1 cm on an edge. Compare the following values.

1. the edge lengths of the two cubes **10:1**

2. the surface areas of the two cubes **100:1**

3. the volumes of the two cubes **1000:1**

4. A pyramid has a square base measuring 185 m on each side and a height of 115 m. A model of it has a base 37 cm on each side. What is the height of the model? **23 cm**

5. A cement truck is pouring cement for a new 4 in. thick driveway. The driveway is 90 ft long and 20 ft wide. How long will it take the truck to pour the cement if it releases 10 ft³ of cement per minute? **60 min**

Also available on transparency

CHALLENGE 8-10

LESSON 8-10 Challenge
Cubed and Diced

A 2 × 2 × 2 cube is painted on all six sides. The cube is cut into eight 1 × 1 × 1 cubes. So, the small cubes are painted on just some of the sides.

1. How many of the small cubes are painted:

  a. on all six sides? **0**   **b.** on five sides? **0**

  c. on four sides? **0**   **d.** on three sides? **8**

  e. on two sides? **0**   **f.** on one side? **0**

A 3 × 3 × 3 cube is painted on all six sides. The cube is cut into twenty-seven 1 × 1 × 1 cubes.

2. How many of the small cubes are painted:

  a. on all six sides? **0**

  b. on five sides? **0**   **c.** on four sides? **0**

  d. on three sides? **8**   **e.** on two sides? **12**

  f. on one side? **6**   **g.** on no sides? **1**

A 4 × 2 × 1 rectangular prism is painted on all six sides. The prism is cut into eight 1 × 1 × 1 cubes.

3. Draw the figure.

4. How many of the small cubes are painted:

  a. on four sides? **4**

  b. on three sides? **4**

  c. on two sides? **0**

  d. on one side? **0**

PROBLEM SOLVING 8-10

LESSON 8-10 Problem Solving
Scaling Three-Dimensional Figures

Round to the nearest hundredth. Write the correct answer.

1. The smallest regulation golf ball has a volume of 2.48 cubic inches. If the diameter of the ball were increased by 10%, or a factor of 1.1, what will the volume of the golf ball be?

3.30 cubic inches

2. The smallest regulation golf ball has a surface area of 8.86 square inches. If the diameter of the ball were increased by 10%, what will the surface area of the golf ball be?

10.72 square inches

3. The Feathered Serpent Pyramid in Teotihuacan, Mexico, is the third largest in the city. The dimensions of the Sun Pyramid in Teotihuacan, Mexico, are about 3.3 times larger than the Feathered Serpent Pyramid. How many times larger is the volume of the Sun Pyramid than the Feathered Serpent Pyramid?

35.94

4. The faces of the Feathered Serpent Pyramid and the Sun Pyramid described in Exercise 3 have ancient paintings on them. How many times larger is the surface are of the faces of the Sun Pyramid than the faces of the Feathered Serpent Pyramid?

10.89

Choose the letter for the best answer.

5. John is designing a shipping container that boxes will be packed into. The container he designed will hold 24 boxes. If he doubles the sides of his container, how many times more boxes will the shipping container hold?

  A 2   (C) 8
  B 4   D 192

6. If John doubles the sides of his container from exercise 5, how many times more material will be required to make the container?

  F 2   H 8
  (G) 4   J 192

7. A child's sandbox is shaped like a rectangular prism and holds 2 cubic feet of sand. The dimensions of the next size sandbox are double the smaller sandbox. How much sand will the larger sandbox hold?

  A 4 ft³   (C) 16 ft³
  B 8 ft³   D 32 ft³

8. Maria used two boxes of sugar cubes to create a solid building for a class project. She decides that the building is too small and she will rebuild it 3 times larger. How many more boxes of sugar cubes will she need?

  F 4   H 27
  G 25   (J) 52

READY TO GO ON?

Organizer

Objective: Assess students' mastery of concepts and skills in Lessons 8-4 through 8-10.

Resources

 Assessment Resources
Section 8B Quiz

 Test & Practice Generator
One-Stop Planner®

INTERVENTION ◀═▶

Resources

 Ready to Go On?
Intervention and
Enrichment Worksheets

💿 **Ready to Go On? CD-ROM**

🪐 **Ready to Go On? Online**

my.hrw.com

Answers

1.

Front   Top   Side

Ready to Go On? (sidebar)

READY TO GO ON?

Quiz for Lessons 8-4 Through 8-10

✓ **8-4** **Drawing Three-Dimensional Figures**

1. Draw the front, top, and side views of the figure.

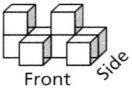
Front   Side

✓ **8-5** **Volume of Prisms and Cylinders**

Find the volume of each figure to the nearest tenth. Use 3.14 for π.

2.
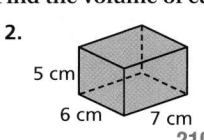
5 cm
6 cm   7 cm
210 cm³

3. 4 in. ←— 24 in. —→
1205.8 in³

4. 2 ft
8 ft   12 ft
96 ft³

✓ **8-6** **Volume of Pyramids and Cones**

Find the volume of each figure to the nearest tenth. Use 3.14 for π.

5.
7
6   5
70 units³

6.
6.5   5
7   9
52.5 units³

7.
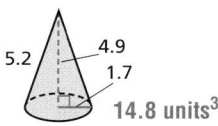
5.2   4.9
1.7
14.8 units³

✓ **8-7** **Surface Area of Prisms and Cylinders**

Find the surface area of the indicated figure to the nearest tenth. Use 3.14 for π.

8. the prism from Exercise 2   **214 cm²**   9. the cylinder from Exercise 3   **703.4 in²**

✓ **8-8** **Surface Area of Pyramids and Cones**

Find the surface area of the indicated figure to the nearest tenth. Use 3.14 for π.

10. the pyramid from Exercise 6   11. the cone from Exercise 7
118.3 units²   **54.7 units²**

✓ **8-9** **Spheres**

Find the surface area and volume of each sphere with the given measurements, both in terms of π and to the nearest tenth. Use 3.14 for π.

12. radius 6.6 mm   13. radius 9 cm   14. diameter 15 yd
1203.6 mm³; 547.1 mm²   **3052.1 cm³; 1017.4 cm²**   **1766.3 yd³; 706.5 yd²**

✓ **8-10** **Scaling Three-Dimensional Figures**

15. The dimensions of a skating arena are 400 ft long, 280 ft wide, and 100 ft high. The scale model used to build the arena is 20 in. long. Find the width and height of the model.   **14 in. wide; 5 in. tall**

NO INTERVENE	**READY TO GO ON?**		YES ENRICH
	Diagnose and Prescribe		

READY TO GO ON? Intervention, Section 8B			
Ready to Go On? Intervention	〰 **Worksheets**	💿 **CD-ROM**	🪐 **Online**
✓ Lesson 8-4	8-4 Intervention	Activity 8-4	
✓ Lesson 8-5	8-5 Intervention	Activity 8-5	
✓ Lesson 8-6	8-6 Intervention	Activity 8-6	Diagnose and Prescribe Online
✓ Lesson 8-7	8-7 Intervention	Activity 8-7	
✓ Lesson 8-8	8-8 Intervention	Activity 8-8	
✓ Lesson 8-9	8-9 Intervension	Activity 8-9	
✓ Lesson 8-10	8-10 Intervention	Activity 8-10	

READY TO GO ON? **Enrichment,** Section 8B
〰 **Worksheets**
💿 **CD-ROM**
🪐 **Online**

Home on the Range Many rural areas in the United States are configured in sections. A section is one square mile, which is equal to 640 acres. A family owns the 4-section farm shown in the diagram. They are preparing information about the farm for their tax return.

1. What is the area in square miles for each of the five crops on the farm?

2. What is the area in acres for each of the crops?

3. A road goes around the perimeter of the field that is planted with barley. What is the length of the road to the nearest tenth of a mile? Explain how you made your calculation.

4. The farm includes a circular reservoir. What is the area of the reservoir to the nearest tenth of a square mile? Use 3.14 for π.

5. How many acres of unused land are there in the square plot that surrounds the reservoir?

6. The reservoir is a cylinder 15 feet deep. How many cubic feet of water does the reservoir hold? Use 3.14 for π. (*Hint:* 1 mile = 5280 feet)

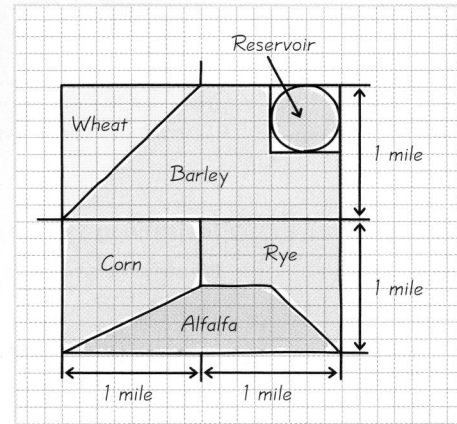

INTERVENTION ⬅◆➡

Scaffolding Questions

1. How can you divide up the barley field into familiar shapes? Possible answer: a triangle, a square, and a rectangle What shape is the corn field? Trapezoid What are the lengths of the bases of this trapezoid? 1 mi and $\frac{1}{2}$ mi

2. What should you do to convert the areas into acres? Multiply the number of square miles by 640

3. How can you find the length of the diagonal portion of the road? Pythagorean Theorem

4. What is the diameter of the reservoir? $\frac{1}{2}$ mi What is the radius of the reservoir? $\frac{1}{4}$ What formula can you use to find the reservoir's area? $A = \pi r^2$

5. How many acres are in the square plot including the reservoir? Why? 160; it is $\frac{1}{4}$ of a section What is the area of the reservoir in acres? 128 acres How can you find the area of the unused land? Subtract: $160 - 128 = 32$ acres

6. What is the radius of the reservoir in feet? 1320 ft What formula should you use to find its volume? $V = \pi r^2 h$

Extension

Which road is longer, the road surrounding the rye field or the road surrounding the alfalfa field? How much longer? Alfalfa; 0.6 mi

---

Organizer

Objective: Assess students' ability to apply concepts and skills in Chapter 8 in a real-world format.

 **Online Edition**

Resources

 Middle School Assessments www.mathtekstoolkit.org

Problem	Text reference
1	Lesson 8-1
2	Lesson 8-2
3	Lesson 8-3
4	Lesson 8-4
5	Lesson 8-5
6	Lesson 8-6

Possible answers:

1. Wheat: $\frac{1}{2}$ mi^2; barley: $1\frac{1}{4}$ mi^2; corn: $\frac{3}{4}$ mi^2; rye: $\frac{5}{6}$ mi^2; alfalfa: $\frac{5}{8}$ mi^2

2. Wheat: 320 acres; barley: 800 acres; corn: 480 acres; rye: 400 acres; alfalfa: 400 acres

3. 5.4 mi; By the Pythagorean Theorem, the diagonal portion of the road has length $\sqrt{1^2 + 1^2} = \sqrt{2} \approx 1.4$ mi. There is also a 2-mile portion of the road and four 0.5-mile portions, so the total length is 5.4 mi.

4. 0.2 mi^2

5. 32 acres

6. 82,067,040 ft^2

State Resources

go.hrw.com
State Resources Online
KEYWORD: MT7 Resources

Pacing: Traditional $\frac{1}{2}$ day
Block $\frac{1}{4}$ day

Objective: Students identify types of symmetry in three dimensions.

 Online Edition

 Countdown to Testing Week 18

Using the Extension

In Lesson 7-8, students identified line symmetry and rotational symmetry and drew figures in two dimensions. In Lesson 8-4, students drew figures in three dimensions. In this extension, students will identify rotational symmetry and bilateral symmetry in three-dimensional figures, and draw cross sections of three-dimensional figures.

EXTENSION

Symmetry in Three Dimensions

Learn to identify types of symmetry in three dimensions.

Vocabulary
bilateral symmetry
cross section

Solid figures can have different kinds of symmetry.

A solid figure with *rotational symmetry* is unchanged in appearance when it is turned a specific number of degrees about a line.

A solid figure with **bilateral symmetry** has two-sided symmetry, or *reflection symmetry*, across a plane.

EXAMPLE 1 Identifying Symmetry in a Solid Figure

Identify all types of symmetry in each figure.

A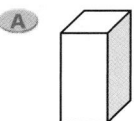

This rectangular prism has both rotational symmetry and bilateral symmetry.

B

This chair has only bilateral symmetry.

When a solid and a plane intersect, the intersection is called a **cross section** .

EXAMPLE 2 Drawing a Cross Section

Draw the cross section and describe its symmetry.

The cross-section is a square, which has four-fold rotational symmetry and line symmetry. There are four lines of symmetry, two from the midpoints of each side to the midpoints of the opposite side and two from the vertices to the corresponding opposite vertices.

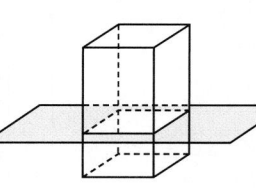

State Resources

go.hrw.com
State Resources Online
KEYWORD: MT7 Resources

---

1 Introduce

Motivate

Use a block of cheese in the shape of a rectangular prism to illustrate rotational symmetry. Use a loaf of bread with a flat bottom to illustrate bilateral symmetry. Slice through each item (or have them presliced) to illustrate a cross section.

2 Teach

Guided Instruction

In this lesson, students learn to identify types of symmetry in three dimensions. Discuss the types of symmetry presented in the introduction (Teaching Transparency), and review Example 1.

Teaching Tip

Inclusion You may want to point out that *bilateral* means "two sided." Point out some objects in the classroom and discuss the types of symmetry that each one has. Show students an example of a cross section after reviewing Example 2.

ENGLISH LANGUAGE LEARNERS

Identify all types of symmetry in each figure.

1.
rotational and bilateral

2.
rotational
and bilateral

3.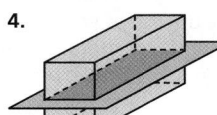
rotational and bilateral

Draw the cross section and describe its symmetry. **Possible answers:**

4.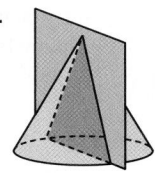
line and rotational

5.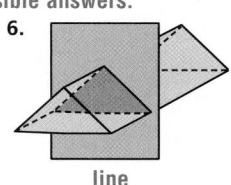
line

6.
line

Identify all types of symmetry in each figure.

7.
rotational

8.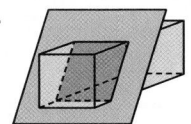
rotational and bilateral

9.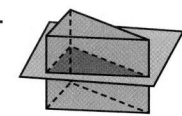
rotational and bilateral

Draw the cross section and describe its symmetry.

10.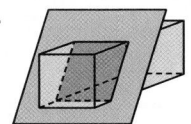
line and rotational

11.
none

13. Possible answer: Yes; the plane must make a vertical intersection through the base of the cone.

15. Possible answer: Yes; the cylinder's height and diameter must be the same length and the plane must intersect vertically.

12. The Transamerica Pyramid in San Francisco is a square pyramid. Each floor is a horizontal cross section of the pyramid. What is the shape of such a cross section? How is the size of each floor related to the size of the floor below it?   **square; smaller**

13. When a plane and a cone intersect, is it possible for the cross-section to be a three-sided figure? Explain.

14. Describe the possible cross sections of a sphere.
circles

15. When a plane and a cylinder intersect, is it possible for the cross-section to be a square? Explain.

Additional Examples

Example 1

Identify all types of symmetry in each figure.

A.

bilateral symmetry

B.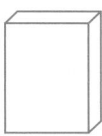

rotational and bilateral symmetry

Example 2

Draw the cross section and describe its symmetry.

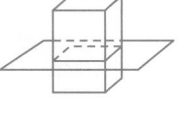

The cross section is a rectangle that has two-fold rotational symmetry and two lines of symmetry.

Also available on transparency

3 Close

Teaching Tip

Visual A cross section does not always have the same symmetry as the solid figure it comes from. The symmetry of the cross section depends partially on the angle of the intersecting plane.

Remind students that the sides and angles of cross sections are not necessarily congruent although they may appear to be.

Summarize

Have students match terms from the lesson with the descriptions below.

1. A figure can be separated into two congruent parts by a plane.

2. A figure can be turned a certain amount less than one full turn to coincide with its original position.

3. the intersection of a solid figure and a plane

1. bilateral symmetry

2. rotational symmetry

3. cross section

Answers

10.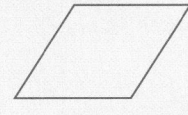

11.

Organizer

Objective: Participate in games to practice and apply skills learned in Chapter 8.

 Online Edition

Resources

Chapter 8 Resource Book
Puzzles, Twisters & Teasers

Planes in Space

Purpose: To apply knowledge of three-dimensional figures to visualizing solids of revolution

Discuss Ask students to describe the technique used to create the figures in the examples.
Possible answer: Begin with a two-dimensional figure (circle, polygon, etc.). Rotate the figure around a line, or translate it along a line to form a three-dimensional figure. What kind of figure is formed when the figure below is rotated around the line shown? cup shape shown below

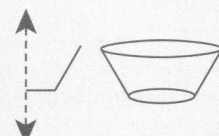

Extend Challenge students to identify objects in the real world that can be described as having been generated by rotating a two-dimensional figure around a line. Have them sketch the figures and lines.
Possible answer:

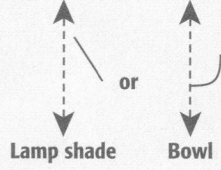

Lamp shade   Bowl

Planes in Space

Some three-dimensional figures can be generated by plane figures.

Experiment with a circle first. Move the circle around. See if you recognize any three-dimensional shapes.

If you rotate a circle around a diameter, you get a sphere.

If you translate a circle up along a line perpendicular to the plane that the circle is in, you get a cylinder.

If you rotate a circle around a line outside the circle but in the same plane as the circle, you get a donut shape called a *torus*.

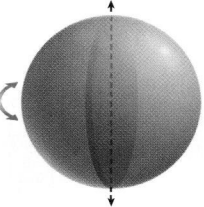   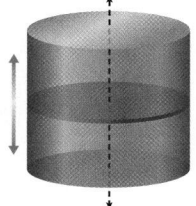   

Draw or describe the three-dimensional figure generated by each plane figure.

1. a square translated along a line perpendicular to the plane it is in   rectangular prism
2. a rectangle rotated around one of its edges   cylinder
3. a right triangle rotated around one of its legs   cone

Triple Concentration

The goal of this game is to form Pythagorean triples, which are sets of three whole numbers a, b, and c such that $a^2 + b^2 = c^2$. A set of cards with numbers on them are arranged face down. A turn consists of drawing 3 cards to try to form a Pythagorean triple. If the cards do not form a Pythagorean triple, they are replaced in their original positions.

A complete set of rules and cards are available online.

go.hrw.com
Game Time Extra
KEYWORD: MT7 Games

Triple Concentration

Purpose: To use the Pythagorean Theorem to test sets of numbers

Discuss When a student draws three cards, ask: How do you know which numbers to substitute for the variables *a, b,* and *c* in the theorem?
Possible answer: The greatest length is always *c*, the hypotenuse. The lengths of *a* and *b*, the legs, are interchangeable.

Extend Have students create and post a table of Pythagorean Triples. Have them do research to find as many triples as they can.
Check students' tables.

Materials
- white paper
- scissors
- decorative paper
- stapler
- hole punch
- twine or yarn
- cardboard tube
- glue
- markers

It's in the Bag!

FOLDNOTES

PROJECT **The Tube Journal**

Use this journal to take notes on perimeter, area, and volume. Then roll up the journal and store it in a tube for safekeeping!

Directions

1 Start with several sheets of paper that measure $8\frac{1}{2}$ inches by 11 inches. Cut an inch off the end of each sheet so they measure $8\frac{1}{2}$ inches by 10 inches.

2 Stack the sheets and fold them in half lengthwise to form a journal that is approximately $4\frac{1}{4}$ inches by 10 inches. Cover the outside of the journal with decorative paper, trim it as needed, and staple everything together along the edge. **Figure A**

3 Punch a hole through the journal in the top left corner. Tie a 6-inch piece of twine or yarn through the hole. **Figure B**

4 Use glue to cover a cardboard tube with decorative paper. Then write the name and number of the chapter on the tube.

Taking Note of the Math

Use your journal to take notes on perimeter, area, and volume. Then roll up the journal and store it in the cardboard tube. Be sure the twine hangs out of the tube so that the journal can be pulled out easily.

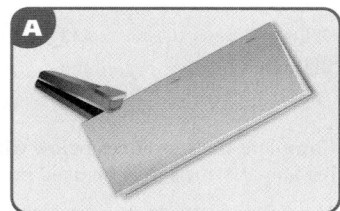

A

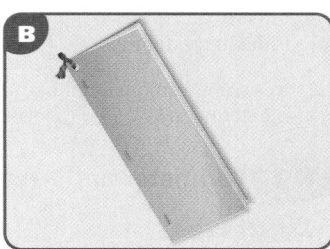

B

It's in the Bag!

Organizer

Objective: Make a journal in which to take notes on perimeter, area, and volume.

Materials: plain white paper, scissors, decorative paper, stapler, hole punch, twine or yarn, cardboard tube, glue, markers

Online Edition

Using the Page

Preparing the Materials

Students should use at least three sheets of paper to make their journals. When the sheets are folded, they will have a 12-page journal.

Making the Project

After students have trimmed the sheets that will form the journal, suggest that they check to be sure the sheets will fit inside the cardboard tube when they are rolled up. If the sheets are still too long, have students cut off another inch or two.

Extending the Project

Have students look through magazines to find photographs of real-world examples of the two- and three-dimensional figures in the chapter. Students can cut out the pictures and add them to the appropriate pages of the journal.

Tips from the Bag Ladies!

Cardboard tubes from rolls of paper towels work best for this project, but students can use any type of cardboard tube. Long tubes from gift wrap can be cut into three tubes that are just the right size. Students can also tape together two small tubes from bathroom tissue to make a single tube that is the correct length.

To make the journals even more useful, consider having students tie a small pen or pencil to the end of the twine.

Organizer

Objective: Help students organize and review key concepts and skills presented in Chapter 8.

Online Edition
Multilingual Glossary

Resources

PuzzlePro®
One-Stop Planner®

Multilingual Glossary Online

go.hrw.com
KEYWORD: MT7 Glossary

Lesson Tutorial Videos
CD-ROM

Test & Practice Generator
One-Stop Planner®

Answers

1. perimeter; area
2. edge; vertex
3. $7\frac{2}{9}$ in²; 12 in.
4. 198 m²; 80 m
5. 9 cm²; 14.2 cm
6. 16 in²; 26.3 in.

Study Guide: Review

Vocabulary

area 389	face 408	pyramid 420
capacity 440	great circle 436	radius 400
circle 400	hemisphere 436	regular pyramid 432
circumference 400	lateral face 427	right cone 432
cone 420	lateral surface 427	slant height 432
cylinder 413	orthogonal views 408	sphere 436
diameter 400	perimeter 388	surface area 427
edge 408	prism 413	vertex 408

Complete the sentences below with vocabulary words from the list above. Words may be used more than once.

1. In a two-dimensional figure, ___?___ is the distance around the outside of the figure, while ___?___ is the number of square units in the figure.

2. In a three-dimensional figure, a(n) ___?___ is where two faces meet, and a(n) ___?___ is where three or more edges meet.

8-1 Perimeter and Area of Rectangles and Parallelograms (pp. 388–392)

EXAMPLE

■ Find the area and perimeter of a rectangle with base 2 ft and height 5 ft.

$A = bh$ $P = 2l + 2w$
$ = 5(2)$ $ = 2(5) + 2(2)$
$ = 10$ ft² $ = 10 + 4 = 14$ ft

EXERCISES

Find the area and perimeter of each figure.

3. a rectangle with base $1\frac{2}{3}$ in. and height $4\frac{1}{3}$ in.

4. a parallelogram with base 18 m, side length 22 m, and height 11 m.

8-2 Perimeter and Area of Triangles and Trapezoids (pp. 394–398)

EXAMPLE

■ Find the area and perimeter of a right triangle with base 6 cm and height 3 cm.

$A = \frac{1}{2}bh = \frac{1}{2}(6)(3) = 9$ cm²
$6^2 + 3^2 = c^2$
$6.71 \approx c$
$P = 6 + 3 + 6.71 = 15.71$ cm

EXERCISES

Find the area and perimeter of each figure.

5. a triangle with base 6 cm, sides 2.1 cm and 6.1 cm, and height 3 cm

6. trapezoid $ABCD$ with $AB = 3.5$ in., $BC = 8.1$ in., $CD = 12.5$ in., and $AD = 2.2$ in., where $\overline{AB} \parallel \overline{CD}$ and $h = 2.0$ in.

8-3 Circles (pp. 400–403)

EXAMPLE

■ Find the area and circumference of a circle with radius 3.1 cm. Use 3.14 for π.

$A = \pi r^2$ $C = 2\pi r$
$= \pi(3.1)^2$ $= 2\pi(3.1)$
$= 9.61\pi \approx 30.2 \text{ cm}^2$ $= 6.2\pi \approx 19.5 \text{ cm}$

EXERCISES

Find the area and circumference of each circle, both in terms of π and to the nearest tenth. Use 3.14 for π.

7. $r = 12$ in. **8.** $r = 4.2$ cm
9. $d = 6$ m **10.** $d = 1.2$ ft

8-4 Drawing Three-Dimensional Figures (pp. 408–411)

EXAMPLE

■ Draw the top view of the figure.

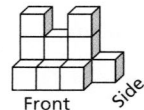 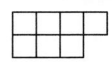

Front Side

EXERCISES

Draw the top view of each figure.

11.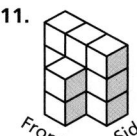
Front Side

12.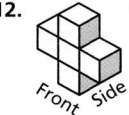
Front Side

13.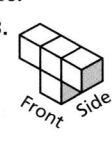
Front Side

8-5 Volume of Prisms and Cylinders (pp. 413–417)

EXAMPLE

■ Find the volume.
$V = Bh = (\pi r^2)h$
$= \pi(4^2)(6)$
$= (16\pi)(6) = 96\pi \text{ cm}^3$
$\approx 301.6 \text{ cm}^3$

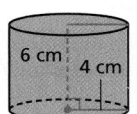
6 cm 4 cm

EXERCISES

Find the volume of each figure.

14.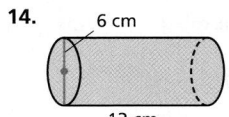
6 cm
12 cm

15.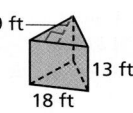
9 ft
13 ft
18 ft

8-6 Volume of Pyramids and Cones (pp. 420–424)

EXAMPLE

■ Find the volume.
$V = \frac{1}{3}Bh = \frac{1}{3}(6)(4)(8)$
$= \frac{1}{3}(24)(8) = 64 \text{ in}^3$

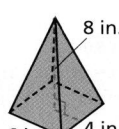
8 in.
6 in. 4 in.

EXERCISES

Find the volume of each figure. Use 3.14 for π.

16.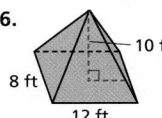
10 ft
8 ft
12 ft

17.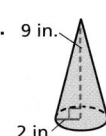
9 in.
2 in.

Answers

7. $A = 144\pi \approx 452.2 \text{ in}^2$;
$C = 24\pi \approx 75.4$ in.

8. $A = 17.6\pi \approx 55.3 \text{ cm}^2$;
$C = 8.4\pi \approx 26.4$ cm

9. $A = 9\pi \approx 28.3 \text{ m}^2$;
$C = 6\pi \approx 18.8$ m

10. $A = 0.4\pi \approx 1.3 \text{ ft}^2$;
$C = 1.2\pi \approx 3.8$ ft

11.

12. ▢▢▢

13. ▢▢▢

14. $432\pi \approx 1357.2 \text{ cm}^2$

15. 1053 ft^3

16. 320 ft^3

17. $12\pi \approx 37.7 \text{ in}^3$

8-7 Surface Area of Prisms and Cylinders (pp. 427–430)

EXAMPLE

■ Find the surface area.
$S = 2B + Ph$
$= 2(6) + (10)(4)$
$= 52$ in^2

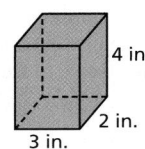

EXERCISES

Find the surface area of the figure.

18.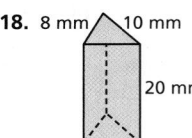

8-8 Surface Area of Pyramids and Cones (pp. 432–435)

EXAMPLE

■ Find the surface area.
$S = B + \frac{1}{2}P\ell$
$= 16 + \frac{1}{2}(16)(5)$
$= 56$ in^2

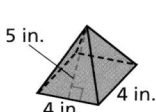

EXERCISES

Find the surface area of each figure.

19. **20.**

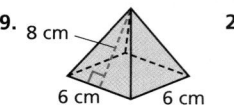

8-9 Spheres (pp. 436–439)

EXAMPLE

■ Find the volume of a sphere of radius 12 cm.
$V = \frac{4}{3}\pi r^3 = \frac{4}{3}\pi(12^3)$
$= 2304\pi$ cm$^3 \approx 7234.6$ cm^3

EXERCISES

Find the volume of each sphere, both in terms of π and to the nearest tenth. Use 3.14 for π.

21. $r = 6$ in.   **22.** $d = 36$ m

8-10 Scaling Three-Dimensional Figures (pp. 440–443)

EXAMPLE

■ A 4 in. cube is built from small cubes, each 2 in. on a side. Compare the volumes of the large cube and the small cube.

$\dfrac{\text{vol. of large cube}}{\text{vol. of small cube}} = \dfrac{4^3 \text{ in}^3}{2^3 \text{ in}^3} = \dfrac{64 \text{ in}^3}{8 \text{ in}^3} = 8$

The volume of the large cube is 8 times that of the small cube.

EXERCISES

A 9 ft cube is built from small cubes, each 3 ft on a side. Compare the indicated measures of the large cube and the small cube.

23. side lengths

24. surface areas

25. volumes

Find the perimeter of each figure.

1.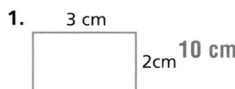
3 cm
2cm **10 cm**

2.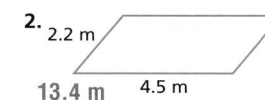
2.2 m
13.4 m   4.5 m

3.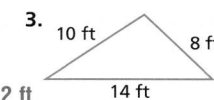
10 ft   8 ft
32 ft   14 ft

Graph and find the area of each figure with the given vertices.

4. $(-3, 2)$, $(-3, -2)$, $(5, -2)$, $(5, 2)$ **32 units²**   **5.** $(2, 4)$, $(7, 4)$, $(5, 0)$, $(0, 0)$ **20 units²**

6. $(-5, 0)$, $(0, 0)$, $(4, 4)$ **10 units²**   **7.** $(0, 4)$, $(3, 6)$, $(3, -3)$, $(0, -3)$ **24 units²**

Find the area and circumference of each circle, both in terms of π and to the nearest tenth. Use 3.14 for π.

8. radius = 15 cm   **9.** diameter = 6.5 ft   **10.** radius = 2.2 m

11. Draw the front, top, and side views of the figure.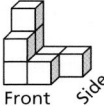
Front   Side

Find the volume of each figure to the nearest tenth. Use 3.14 for π.

12. a cube of side length 8 ft **512 ft³**   **13.** a cylinder of height 5 cm and radius 2 cm   **62.8 cm³**

14. a cone of diameter 12 in. and height 18 in.   **15.** a sphere of radius 9 cm **3052.1 cm³**

16. a rectangular prism with base 5 m by 3 m and height 6 m **90 m³**

17. a pyramid with a 3 ft by 3 ft square base and height 4 ft **12 ft³**   **14. 678.2 in³**

Find the surface area of each figure to the nearest tenth. Use 3.14 for π.

18.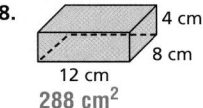
4 cm
8 cm
12 cm
288 cm²

19.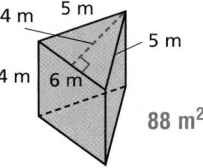
4 m   5 m
5 m
4 m   6 m
88 m²

20.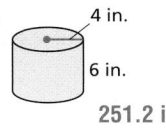
4 in.
6 in.
251.2 in²

21.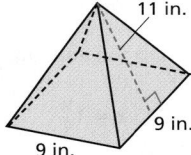
11 in.
9 in.
9 in.
279 in²

22.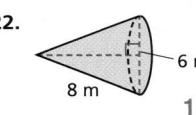
6 m
8 m
103.6 m²

23.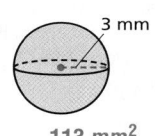
3 mm
113 mm²

24. The dimensions of a history museum are 400 ft long, 200 ft wide, and 75 ft tall. The scale model used to build the museum is 40 in. long. Find the width and height of the model. **width = 20 in., height = 7.5 in.**

Answers

4.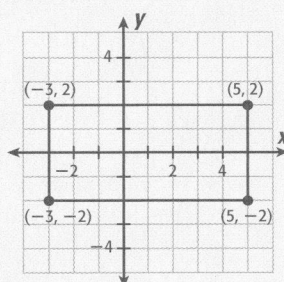
y
4
$(-3, 2)$ $(5, 2)$
x
-2   2   4
$(-3, -2)$ $(5, -2)$
-4

5.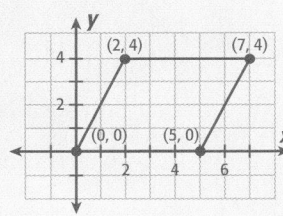
y
4   $(2, 4)$ $(7, 4)$
2
$(0, 0)$ $(5, 0)$ x
2   4   6

6.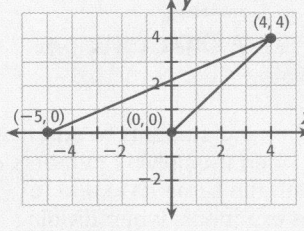
y
4   $(4, 4)$
2
$(-5, 0)$ $(0, 0)$ x
-4   -2   2   4
-2

7.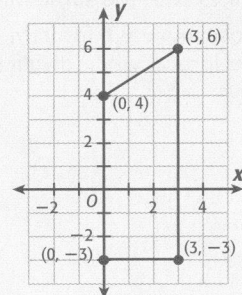
y
6   $(3, 6)$
4   $(0, 4)$
2
x
-2   O   2   4
-2
$(0, -3)$ $(3, -3)$

8–11. See p. A12.

 **CHAPTER TEST**  CHAPTER 8

Organizer

Objective: Assess students' mastery of concepts and skills in Chapter 8.

 Online Edition

Resources

 Assessment Resources

Chapter 8 Tests
• Free Response
 (Levels A, B, C)
• Multiple Choice
 (Levels A, B, C)
• Performance Assessment

 IDEA Works! CD-ROM
Modified Chapter 8 Test

Test & Practice Generator
One-Stop Planner®

State Resources

go.hrw.com
State Resources Online
KEYWORD: MT7 Resources

Organizer

Objective: Provide review and practice for Chapters 1–8 and standardized tests.

 Online Edition

Resources

 Assessment Resources
Chapter 8 Cumulative Test

 State Test Prep Workbook

 State Test Prep CD-ROM

 State Test Practice Online

go.hrw.com
KEYWORD: MT7 TestPrep

Cumulative Assessment, Chapters 1–8
Multiple Choice

1. Which addition equation represents the number line diagram below?

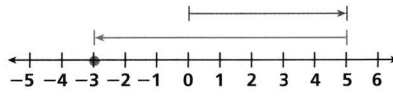

    A $5 + (-8)$ **C** $-5 + 8$

    B $5 + 8$ **D** $-5 + (-8)$

2. Jerome has to replace the tile in his bathroom. Which of the following shapes would NOT cover his bathroom walls with a tessellation?

   F    **H**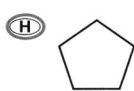

   G    **J**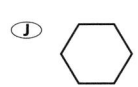

3. If $\frac{g^x}{g^5} = g^{-8}$ and $g^{-3} \cdot g^y = g^{12}$, what is the value of $x + y$?

    A -9 **C** 12

    B -3 **D** 15

4. Eduardo invests his savings at 3% simple interest for 5 years and earns $150 in interest. How much money did Eduardo invest?

    F $10   **H** $1000

    G $22.50   **J** $2250

5. A triangle has angle measures of 78°, $m°$, and $m°$. What is the value of m?

    A 12 **C** 102

    B 51 **D** 141

6. Which word does NOT describe the number $\sqrt{16}$?

    F rational   **H** whole

    G integer   **J** irrational

7. For which positive radius, r, is the circumference of a circle the same as the area of a circle?

    A $r = 1$ **C** $r = 3$

    B $r = 2$ **D** $r = 4$

8. Which equation describes the graph?

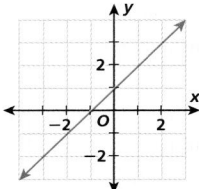

    F $y = x - 1$ **H** $y = 2x + 1$

    G $y = x + 1$ **J** $y = x + 2$

9. Armen rollerblades at a rate of 12 km/h. What is Armen's rate in meters per second?

    A 200 m/s   **C** $\frac{1}{3}$ m/s

    B $3\frac{1}{3}$ m/s   **D** $\frac{3}{10}$ m/s

10. What is the solution to the equation $\frac{2}{3}x + \frac{1}{6} = 1$?

    F $x = \frac{5}{9}$ **H** $x = 1\frac{1}{4}$

    G $x = \frac{4}{5}$ **J** $x = 3\frac{2}{3}$

TEST PREP DOCTOR ✚

For item 3, remind students to add the exponents when multiplying numbers or variables with the same base and to subtract the exponents when dividing numbers or variables with the same base.

Students who chose answer **F** for item 10, did not use the reciprocal when dividing by the coefficient $\frac{2}{3}$.

Answers

17–19. See p A12.

20. See 4-Point Response work sample.

State Resources

go.hrw.com
State Resources Online
KEYWORD: MT7 Resources

11. Suzanne plans to install a fence around the perimeter of her land. How much fencing does she need?

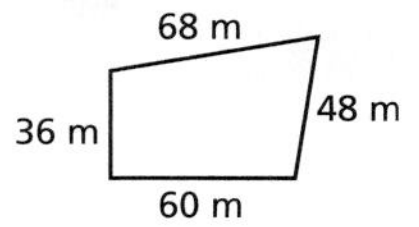

Ⓐ 212 m Ⓒ 2448 m
Ⓑ 368 m Ⓓ 2800 m

HOT TIP! When a variable is used more than one time in an expression or an equation, it always has the same value.

12. The Cougars, the Wildcats, and the Broncos won a total of 18 games during the football season. The Cougars won 2 more games than the Wildcats. The Broncos won $\frac{2}{3}$ as many games as the Wildcats. How many games did the Wildcats win?

Ⓕ 2 Ⓗ 6
Ⓖ 4 Ⓙ 8

Gridded Response

13. A cone-shaped cup has a height of 3 in. and a volume of 9 in^3. What is the length in inches of the diameter of the cone? Round your answer to the nearest hundredth. **3.39**

14. Shaunda measures the diameter of a ball as 12 in. How many cubic inches of air does this ball hold? Round your answer to the nearest tenth. **904.8**

15. What is the *y*-coordinate of the point (−3, 6) that has been translated down 4 units? **2**

16. Given the obtuse triangle, what is the measure of angle *x*, in degrees? **100**

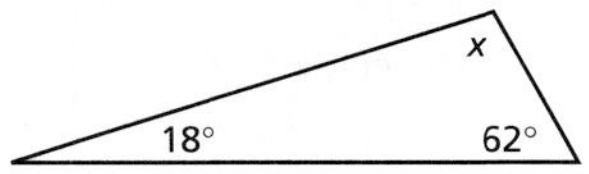

Short Response

17. Draw a rectangle with base length 7 cm and height 4 cm. Then draw a rectangle with base length 14 cm and height 1 cm. Which rectangle has the larger area? Which rectangle has the larger perimeter? Show your work or explain in words how you determined your answers.

18. A cylinder with a height of 6 in. and a diameter of 4 in. is filled with water. A cone with height 6 in. and diameter 2 in. is placed in the cylinder, point down, with its base even with the top of the cylinder. Draw a diagram to illustrate the situation described, and then determine how much water is left in the cylinder. Show your work.

19. An airplane propeller is 37 inches from its tip to the center axis of its rotation. Suppose the propeller spins at a rate of 2500 revolutions per minute. How far will a point on the tip of the propeller travel in one minute? How far will the point on the tip travel in one hour? Show your work or explain in words how you determined your answers.

Extended Response

20. A *geodesic dome* is constructed of triangles. The surface is approximately spherical.
   a. A pattern for a geodesic dome that approximates a hemisphere uses 30 triangles with base 8 ft and height 5.63 ft and 75 triangles with base 8 ft and height 7.13 ft. Find the surface area of the dome.
   b. The base of the dome is approximately a circle with diameter 41 ft. Use a hemisphere with this diameter to estimate the surface area of the dome.
   c. Compare your answer from part **a** with your estimate from part **b**. Explain the difference.

Short Response Rubric

Items 17–19

2 Points = The student's answer is an accurate and complete execution of the task or tasks.

1 Point = The student's answer contains attributes of an appropriate response but is flawed.

0 Points = The student's answer contains no attributes of an appropriate response.

Extended Response Rubric

Item 20

4 points = The student demonstrates a thorough understanding of all concepts and shows all work correctly.

3 points = The student demonstrates a basic understanding of all concepts, but the work shows some flaws reflecting inattentive execution of mathematical procedures or some misunderstanding of the underlying mathematics.

2 points = The student demonstrates only a partial understanding of the concepts or procedures embodied in the tasks. The approach may be correct, but the work shows a misunderstanding of one or more important concepts.

1 point = The student demonstrates a very limited understanding of the concepts or procedures embodied in the tasks. The response may show some understanding but exhibits many flaws or is incomplete.

0 points = The student provides no response at all or a completely incorrect or uninterpretable response.

Student Work Samples for Item 20

4-Point Response

a. area of triangles = surface area
$30 \cdot \frac{1}{2}(8) \cdot 5.63 = 675.6$
$+\ 75 \cdot \frac{1}{2}(8) \cdot 7.13 = 2139$
2814.6ft^2

b. hemisphere surface area = $2\pi r^2$
$r = \frac{1}{2}(41) = 20.5$
$2\pi r^2 = 840.5\pi \approx 2640.5\text{ft}^2$

c. $2814.6 - 2640.5 = 174.1$
The surface area of the dome is 174.1ft² greater. A sphere is smooth and the dome is not.

The student accurately found the surface areas and gave a plausible reason for their differences.

3-Point Response

a. area of triangles equals S.A.
$30 \cdot 0.5 \cdot 8 \cdot 5.63 \approx 676\ \text{ft}^2$
$75 \cdot 0.5 \cdot 8 \cdot 7.13 = 2139\ \text{ft}^2$
$\Rightarrow 676 + 2139 = 2815\ \text{ft}^2$

b. surface area of hemisphere = $2\pi r^2$
$r = 0.5 \cdot 41 \approx 20\ \text{ft}$
$2\pi r^2 = 2 \cdot \pi \cdot 20^2 \approx 2512\ \text{ft}^2$

c. $2815 - 2512 = 303\ \text{ft}^2$
The S.A. of the dome is about 303 ft² larger.

The student correctly applies formulas and concepts in parts **a, b,** and **c,** but applies a rounding strategy that yields numerical values that are far from correct.

2-Point Response

a. $30 \times 8 \times 5.63 = 1351.2$
$75 \times 8 \times 7.13 = 4278$
Surface Area 5629.2

b. $4\pi r^2$ Surface Area
$= 4\pi\left(\frac{d}{2}\right)^2$
$= 4\pi \times (20.5)^2 = 1681\pi = 5281.0$

c. The hemisphere is slightly smaller.

The student left key information out of a formula and calculated correctly but did not give a plausible reason for differences.

Problem Solving on Location

Organizer

Objective: Choose appropriate problem-solving strategies and use them with skills from Chapters 7 and 8 to solve real-world problems.

 Online Edition

⭐ The Nevada State Capitol

Reading Strategies

For problems 1 and 2, encourage students to read each problem carefully and identify all of the important information. It may help students to underline any information they think they will need to solve a problem. Some necessary information is not provided in problems 3 and 4. Ask students what other information they will need to solve these problems, and where will they find it?

Using Data Review the information in the table with students. Challenge them to make sure they understand all concepts, such as the meaning of "Area (per story)."

Problem Solving on Location

NEVADA

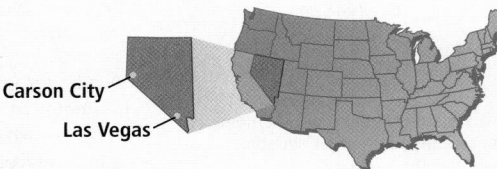

Carson City
Las Vegas

⭐ The Nevada State Capitol

In 1864 Carson City became the capital of Nevada, then the newest state in the union. Six years later, construction was completed on the State Capitol. To this day the building remains the only state capitol with a silver-colored dome. It is only fitting, given that Nevada mines supply more than 40% of the nation's silver.

Choose one or more strategies to solve each problem.

1. The Nevada State Capitol's library is in the shape of a regular octagon. For an upcoming banquet, a string of lights will be hung from each corner of the library's ceiling to each of the other non-adjacent corners. How many strings of lights will be needed? **28**

2. The State Capitol's dome is approximately a hemisphere with a radius of 15 feet. Silver paint for the dome comes in large containers that hold enough paint to cover 600 ft^2 and in small containers that hold enough paint to cover 250 ft^2. How many of each type of 7container should be purchased in order to repaint the outside of the dome? **Two large containers and one small container**

For 3 and 4, use the table.

3. The length of the original State Capitol was 3 times its width. What were the length and width of the original building? **150 ft; 50 ft**

4. In 1914, two rectangular wings were added to the building. The length of each wing is 10 feet more than the width. What is the length and width of each wing? **60 ft; 50 ft**

Nevada State Capitol	
Structure	**Area (per story)**
Original building (1870)	7500 ft^2
North wing (1914)	3000 ft^2
South wing (1914)	3000 ft^2

◩ Problem Solving Focus

Students may find it helpful to use the Guess and Test Strategy to solve problem 4.

Discuss It may be helpful for some students to draw a diagram of the library's ceiling discussed in problem 1. Students may also need to find definitions of terms, such as "regular octagon" and "non-adjacent corners."

State Resources

go.hrw.com
State Resources Online
KEYWORD: MT7 Resources

★ The Luxor Hotel

With more than 4,400 rooms, the Luxor is the second-largest hotel in the United States. The pyramid-shaped building is an unmistakable part of the Las Vegas skyline. Inside, the hotel features nine restaurants, an IMAX theater, a shopping bazaar, and a full-size replica of an Egyptian temple.

Choose one or more strategies to solve each problem.

1. The base of the hotel is a square with a perimeter of 2,600 feet. Along one side, the hotel is lit with lighting fixtures at each corner and every 50 feet in between. How many fixtures are there? **14**

2. Each side of the pyramid is a triangle. The two angles at the base of the triangle have the same measure. The angle at the top of the triangle is 12° greater than the angles at the base. What are the measures of the angles in each triangle? **56°, 56°, 68°**

For 3 and 4, use the diagram.

3. The hotel's Egyptian Ballroom can be subdivided into several smaller rooms, as shown. Rooms A, B, C, E, F, and G are all congruent. What is the length and width of Room G? **38 feet, 32 feet**

4. If the area of the Egyptian Ballroom is 15,680 ft², what are the dimensions of Room D? Round your answer to the nearest tenth of a foot. **96 ft × 47.3 ft**

Egyptian Ballroom

A 1216 ft²	E 1216 ft²	
B 1216 ft²	D	F 1216 ft²	H 3840 ft²
C 1216 ft²	G 1216 ft²	

40 ft

CHAPTER 9

Data and Statistics

Section 9A
Collecting and Describing Data

9-1 **Samples and Surveys**

9-1 **Hands-On Lab** Explore Samples

9-2 **Organizing Data**

9-3 **Measures of Central Tendency**

9-4 **Variability**

9-4 **Technology Lab** Create Box-and-Whisker Plots

Section 9B
Displaying Data

9-5 **Hands-On Lab** Make a Circle Graph

9-5 **Displaying Data**

9-5 **Technology Lab** Create Histograms

9-6 **Misleading Graphs and Statistics**

9-7 **Scatter Plots**

9-7 **Technology Lab** Create a Scatter Plot

9-8 **Choosing the Best Representation of Data**

9-8 **Technology Lab** Use a Spreadsheet to Create Graphs

Pacing Guide for 45-Minute Classes

Chapter 9

Countdown to Testing Weeks ⑲, ⑳, ㉑

DAY 1	DAY 2	DAY 3	DAY 4	DAY 5
9-1 Lesson	9-1 Hands-On Lab 9-2 Lesson	9-2 Lesson	9-3 Lesson	9-4 Lesson
DAY 6	**DAY 7**	**DAY 8**	**DAY 9**	**DAY 10**
9-4 Technology Lab	Ready to Go On? Focus on Problem Solving 9-5 Hands-On Lab	9-5 Lesson	9-5 Technology Lab 9-6 Lesson	9-6 Lesson 9-7 Lesson
DAY 11	**DAY 12**	**DAY 13**	**DAY 14**	**DAY 15**
9-7 Lesson 9-7 Technology Lab	9-8 Lesson	9-8 Technology Lab Ready to Go On? Multi-Step Test Prep	Chapter 9 Review	Chapter 9 Test

Pacing Guide for 90-Minute Classes

Chapter 9

DAY 1	DAY 2	DAY 3	DAY 4	DAY 5
9-1 Lesson 9-1 Hands-On Lab 9-2 Lesson	9-2 Lesson 9-3 Lesson	9-4 Lesson 9-4 Technology Lab	Ready to Go On? Focus on Problem Solving 9-5 Hands-On Lab 9-5 Lesson	9-5 Technology Lab 9-6 Lesson 9-7 Lesson
DAY 6	**DAY 7**	**DAY 8**		
9-7 Lesson 9-7 Technology Lab 9-8 Lesson	9-8 Technology Lab Ready to Go On? Multi-Step Test Prep Chapter 9 Review	Chapter 9 Test		

ONGOING ASSESSMENT and INTERVENTION

DIAGNOSE	PRESCRIBE

Assess Prior Knowledge

Before Chapter 9

Diagnose readiness for the chapter.
Are You Ready? SE p. 459

Prescribe intervention.
Are You Ready? Intervention Skills 1, 16, 17, 90

Formative Assessment

Before Every Lesson

Diagnose readiness for the lesson.
Warm Up TE, every lesson

Prescribe intervention.
Skills Bank SE pp. 820–834
Reteach CRB, Chapters 1–9

During Every Lesson

Diagnose understanding of lesson concepts.
Think and Discuss SE, every lesson
Write About It SE, lesson exercises
Journal TE, lesson exercises

Prescribe intervention.
Questioning Strategies Chapter 9
Reading Strategies CRB, every lesson
Success for ELL pp. 131–146

After Every Lesson

Diagnose mastery of lesson concepts.
Lesson Quiz TE, every lesson
Test Prep SE, every lesson
Test and Practice Generator

Prescribe intervention.
Reteach CRB, every lesson
Problem Solving CRB, every lesson
Test Prep Doctor TE, lesson exercises
Homework Help Online

Before Chapter 9 Testing

Diagnose mastery of concepts in the chapter.
Ready to Go On? SE pp. 482, 506
Focus on Problem Solving SE p. 483
Multi-Step Test Prep SE p. 507
Section Quizzes AR pp. 165–166
Test and Practice Generator

Prescribe intervention.
Ready to Go On? Intervention Chapter 9
Scaffolding Questions TE p. 507

Before High Stakes Testing

Diagnose mastery of benchmark concepts.
Test Tackler SE pp. 514–515
Standardized Test Prep SE pp. 516–517
State Test Prep CD-ROM

Prescribe intervention.
State Test Prep Workbook

Summative Assessment

After Chapter 9

Check mastery of chapter concepts.
Multiple-Choice Tests (Forms A, B, C)
Free-Response Tests (Forms A, B, C)
Performance Assessment AR pp. 167–180
Test and Practice Generator

Prescribe intervention.
Reteach CRB, every lesson
Lesson Tutorial Videos Chapter 9

Check mastery of benchmark concepts.
AYP State Tests

Prescribe intervention.
State Test Prep Workbook

Supporting the Teacher

Chapter 9 Resource Book

Practice A, B, C
pp. 3–5, 11–13, 20–22, 28–30, 36–38, 45–47, 53–55, 61–63

Reading Strategies ELL
pp. 9, 18, 26, 34, 43, 51, 59, 67

Puzzles, Twisters, and Teasers
pp. 10, 19, 27, 35, 44, 52, 60, 68

Reteach
pp. 6, 14–15, 23, 31, 39–40, 48, 56, 64

Problem Solving
pp. 8, 17, 25, 33, 42, 50, 58, 66

Challenge
pp. 7, 16, 24, 32, 41, 49, 57, 65

Parent Letter   pp. 1–2

Transparencies

Lesson Transparencies, Volume 2............................ Chapter 9
• Warm Ups
• Problem of the Day
• Teaching Transparencies
• Lesson Quizzes

Know-It Notebook.. Chapter 9
• Additional Examples   • Chapter Review
• Vocabulary   • Big Ideas

Alternate Openers: Explorations.......................... pp. 66–73

Countdown to Testing.. pp. 37–42

Teacher Tools

Power Presentations®
Complete PowerPoint® presentations for Chapter 9 lessons

Lesson Tutorial Videos® SPANISH
Holt authors Ed Burger and Freddie Renfro present tutorials to support the Chapter 9 lessons.

One-Stop Planner® SPANISH
Easy access to all Chapter 9 resources and assessments, as well as software for lesson planning, test generation, and puzzle creation

IDEA Works!®
Key Chapter 9 resources and assessments modified to address special learning needs

Lesson Plans..pp. 66–73

Questioning Strategies.. Chapter 9

Solutions Key.. Chapter 9

Interdisciplinary Posters and Worksheets.............. Chapter 9

TechKeys   ***Lab Resources***

Project Teacher Support   ***Parent Resources***

Workbooks

Homework and Practice Workbook SPANISH
Teacher's Guide...pp. 33–37

Know-It Notebook
Teacher's Guide.. Chapter 9

Problem Solving Workbook SPANISH
Teacher's Guide...pp. 33–37

State Test Prep Workbook
Teacher's Guide

Technology Highlights for the Teacher

Power Presentations
Dynamic presentations to engage students. Complete PowerPoint® presentations for every lesson in Chapter 9.

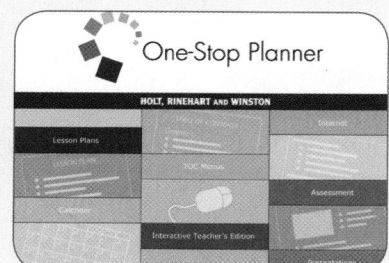

One-Stop Planner SPANISH
Easy access to Chapter 9 resources and assessments. Includes lesson-planning, test-generation, and puzzle-creation software.

Premier Online Edition SPANISH
Chapter 9 includes Tutorial Videos, Lesson Activities, Lesson Quizzes, Homework Help, and Chapter Project.

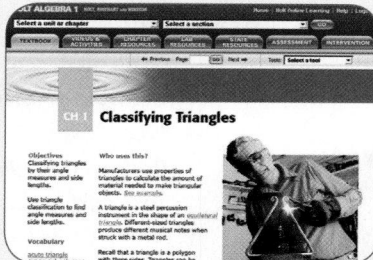

KEY: **SE** = *Student Edition*   **TE** = *Teacher's Edition*   English Language Learners   Spanish version available   Available on CD-ROM    Available online

Reaching All Learners

Resources for All Learners

Hands-On Lab Activities.. Chapter 9

Technology Lab Activities.. Chapter 9

Homework and Practice Workbook **SPANISH** ....pp. 66–73

Know-It Notebook.. Chapter 9

Problem Solving Workbook **SPANISH** ....pp. 66–73

DEVELOPING LEARNERS

Practice A ....CRB, every lesson

Reteach ....CRB, every lesson

Inclusion ....TE pp. 463, 473

Questioning Strategies....................................... Chapter 9

Modified Chapter 9 Resources .... *IDEA Works!*

Homework Help **Online**

ON-LEVEL LEARNERS

Practice B ....CRB, every lesson

Puzzles, Twisters, and Teasers.................CRB, every lesson

Multiple Representations ....TE p. 486

Cooperative Learning ....TE pp. 463, 501

ADVANCED LEARNERS

Practice C ....CRB, every lesson

Challenge ....CRB, every lesson

Extension ....TE pp. 461, 507, 508, 509

Critical Thinking ....TE p. 491

English Language Learners

ENGLISH LANGUAGE LEARNERS

Are You Ready? Vocabulary ....SE p. 459

Vocabulary Connections ....SE p. 460

Lesson Vocabulary ....SE, every lesson

Vocabulary Review...SE p. 510

English Language Learners............TE pp. 461, 463, 473, 490

Reading Strategies ....CRB, every lesson

Success for English Language Learners...............pp. 131–146

Multilingual Glossary

Reaching All Learners Through...

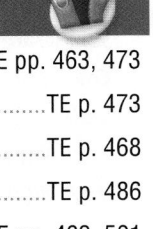

Inclusion ....TE pp. 463, 473

Diversity..TE p. 473

Kinesthetic Experience ....TE p. 468

Multiple Representations ....TE p. 486

Cooperative Learning ....TE pp. 463, 501

Modeling..TE p. 486

Critical Thinking ....TE p. 491

Test Prep Doctor..................TE pp. 465, 471, 475, 480, 488,
                                        493, 497, 503, 514, 515, 516

Common Error Alerts ....TE p. 477

Scaffolding Questions..TE p. 507

Technology Highlights for Reaching All Learners

 Lesson Tutorial Videos **SPANISH**

Starring Holt authors Ed Burger and Freddie Renfro! Live tutorials to support every lesson in Chapter 9.

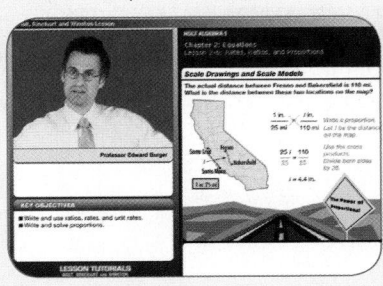

Multilingual Glossary

Searchable glossary includes definitions in English, Spanish, Vietnamese, Chinese, Hmong, Korean, and 4 other languages.

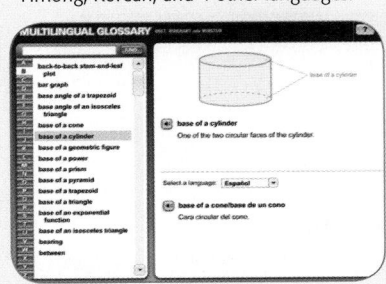

Online Interactivities

Interactive tutorials provide visually engaging alternative opportunities to learn concepts and master skills.

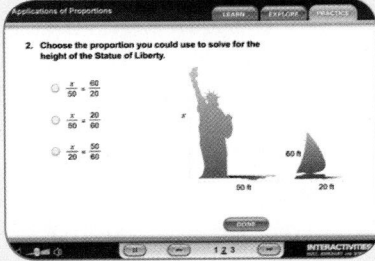

KEY: **SE** = *Student Edition* **TE** = *Teacher's Edition* **CRB** = *Chapter Resource Book* **SPANISH** Spanish version available  Available on CD-ROM 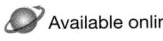 Available online

Ongoing Assessment

Assessing Prior Knowledge

Determine whether students have the prerequisite concepts and skills for success in Chapter 9.

Are You Ready? (SPANISH) .... SE p. 459
Warm Up .... TE, every lesson

Test Preparation

Provide review and practice for Chapter 9 and standardized tests.

Multi-Step Test Prep .... SE p. 507
Study Guide: Review .... SE pp. 510–512
Test Tackler .... SE pp. 514–515
Standardized Test Prep .... SE pp. 516–517
Countdown to Testing Transparencies ....pp. 37–42
State Test Prep Workbook
State Test Prep **CD-ROM**
IDEA Works!

Alternative Assessment

Assess students' understanding of Chapter 9 concepts and combined problem-solving skills.

Chapter 9 Project .... SE p. 458
Performance Assessment (SPANISH) .... AR pp. 179–180
Portfolio Assessment (SPANISH) .... AR p. xxxiv

Daily Assessment

Provide formative assessment for each day of Chapter 9.

Questioning Strategies .... Chapter 9
Think and Discuss .... SE, every lesson
Write About It .... SE, lesson exercises
Journal .... TE, lesson exercises
Lesson Quiz .... TE, every lesson
Modified Lesson Quizzes .... *IDEA Works!*

Weekly Assessment

Provide formative assessment for each week of Chapter 9.

Focus on Problem Solving .... SE p. 483
Multi-Step Test Prep .... SE p. 507
Ready to Go On? (SPANISH) .... SE pp. 482, 506
Cumulative Assessment .... SE pp. 516–517
Test and Practice Generator (SPANISH) ...*One-Stop Planner*

Formal Assessment

Provide summative assessment of Chapter 9 mastery.

Section Quizzes (SPANISH) .... AR pp. 165–166
Chapter 9 Test .... SE p. 513
Chapter Test (Levels A, B, C) (SPANISH) .... AR pp. 167–178
      • Multiple-Choice   • Free-Response
Cumulative Test (SPANISH) .... AR pp. 181–184
Test and Practice Generator (SPANISH) ...*One-Stop Planner*
Modified Chapter 9 Test .... *IDEA Works!*

Technology Highlights for the Teacher

 **Are You Ready?** (SPANISH)
Automatically assess readiness and prescribe intervention for Chapter 9 prerequisite skills.

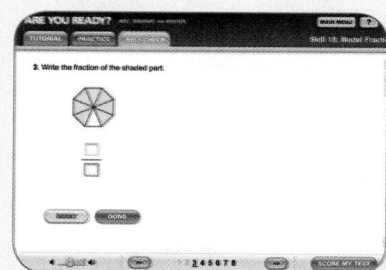

 **Ready to Go On?** (SPANISH)
Automatically assess understanding of and prescribe intervention for Sections 9A and 9B.

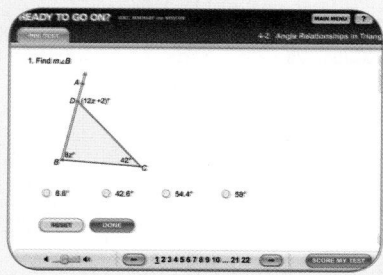

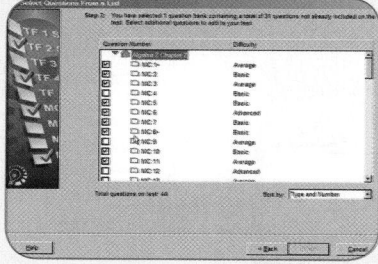 **Test and Practice Generator** (SPANISH)
Use Chapter 9 problem banks to create assessments and worksheets to print out or deliver online. Includes dynamic problems.

KEY: **SE** = *Student Edition*   **TE** = *Teacher's Edition*   **AR** = *Assessment Resources*   (SPANISH) Spanish version available   Available on CD-ROM    Available online

Formal Assessment

Three levels (A, B, C) of multiple-choice and free-response chapter tests are available in the *Assessment Resources.*

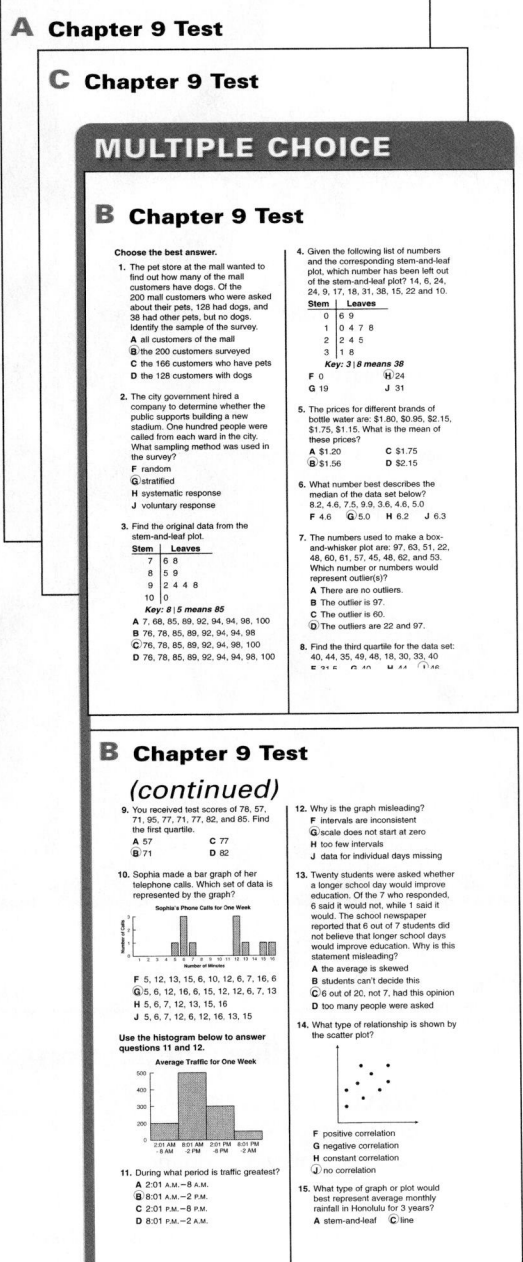

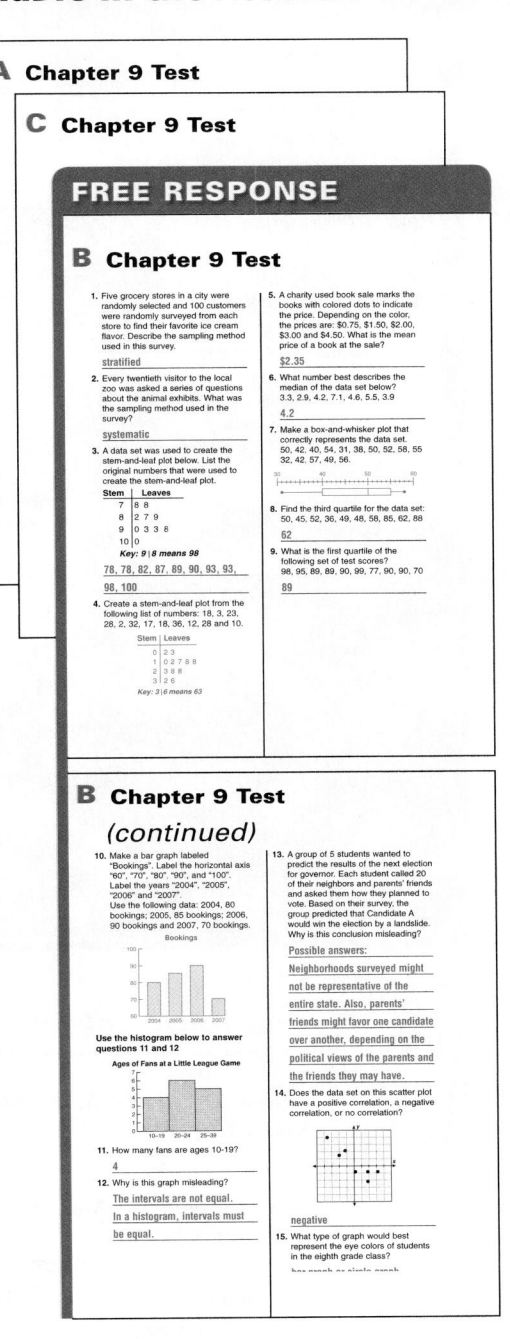

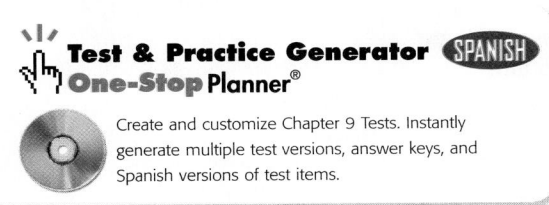

Test & Practice Generator SPANISH
One-Stop Planner®

Create and customize Chapter 9 Tests. Instantly generate multiple test versions, answer keys, and Spanish versions of test items.

Why Learn This?

Tell students that quality assurance is just one of many fields in which information from a small sample can be used to derive information about a large population. For example, a quality assurance specialist can use the information in the table to predict the number of errors in an entire month's production of software.

Using Data

To begin the study of this chapter, have students:

- Identify the company type with the largest number of items sampled.
  stoneworks

- Identify the company type with the fewest number of errors found.
  software

- Predict the number of errors that would be found if 100 items were sampled at a tool company. 8

MULTI-STEP TEST PREP On page 507, students use measures of central tendency, stem-and-leaf plots, misleading graphs, and scatter plots to analyze and organize bowling scores.

9A   **Collecting and Describing Data**

9-1   Samples and Surveys
LAB   Explore Samples
9-2   Organizing Data
9-3   Measures of Central Tendency
9-4   Variability
LAB   Create Box-and-Whisker Plots

9B   **Displaying Data**

LAB   Make a Circle Graph
9-5   Displaying Data
LAB   Create Histograms
9-6   Misleading Graphs and Statistics
9-7   Scatter Plots
LAB   Create a Scatter Plot
9-8   Choosing the Best Representation of Data
LAB   Use a Spreadsheet to Create Graphs

MULTI-STEP TEST PREP

go.hrw.com
Chapter Project Online
KEYWORD: MT7 Ch9

Errors in Samples		
Company Type	Sample Size	Errors
Software	25	2
Stoneworks	100	7
Tools	50	4
Pizza	75	3

Career   *Quality Assurance Specialist*

How do manufacturers know that their products are well made? It is the job of the quality assurance specialist. QA specialists design tests and procedures that allow the companies to determine how good their products are. Because checking every product or procedure may not be possible, QA specialists use sampling to predict the margin of error.

Problem Solving Project

Understand, Plan, Solve, and Look Back

Have students:

- Complete the Making Quality Products worksheet to practice organizing data to describe results.

- Select a company and create a graph. Have them compare their company to the companies of other students.

- Discuss the role of quality assurance in companies. Why do they think this work is important?

- Research companies that have gotten into trouble because of their errors. What did they do to correct their problem?

Social Studies Connection

Project Resources

All project resources for teachers and students are provided online.

Materials:

- Making Quality Products worksheet

go.hrw.com
Project Teacher Support
KEYWORD: MT7 PSProject9

ARE YOU READY?

✓ Vocabulary

Choose the best term from the list to complete each sentence.

1. A __?__ is a uniform measure where equal distances are marked to represent equal amounts.   scale

2. __?__ is the process of approximating to a given __?__.   Rounding; place value

3. Ordered pairs of numbers are graphed on a __?__.   coordinate grid

coordinate grid
place value
rounding
scale

Complete these exercises to review skills you will need for this chapter.

✓ Round Decimals

Round each number to the indicated place value.

4. 34.7826; nearest tenth **34.8**   5. 137.5842; nearest whole number **138**

6. 287.2872; nearest thousandth **287.287**   7. 362.6238; nearest hundred **400**

✓ Compare and Order Decimals

Order each sequence of numbers from greatest to least.

8. 3.005, 3.05, 0.35, 3.5
   3.5; 3.05; 3.005; 0.35
9. 0.048, 0.408, 0.0408, 0.48
   0.48; 0.408; 0.048; 0.0408
10. 5.01, 5.1, 5.011, 5.11
    5.11; 5.1; 5.011; 5.01
11. 1.007, 0.017, 1.7, 0.107
    1.7; 1.007; 0.107; 0.017

✓ Place Value of Whole Numbers

Write each number in standard form.

12. 1.3 million   13. 7.59 million   14. 4.6 billion   15. 2.83 billion
    1,300,000   **7,590,000**   **4,600,000,000**   **2,830,000,000**

✓ Read a Table

Use the table for problems 16–18.

16. Which activity experienced the greatest change in participation from 2000 to 2001? **basketball**

17. Which activity experienced the greatest positive change in participation from 2000 to 2001? **soccer**

18. Which activity experienced the least change in participation from 2000 to 2001? **softball**

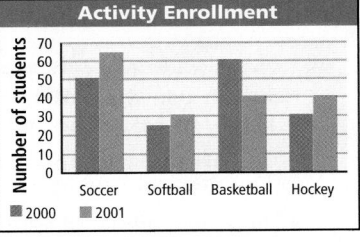

Activity Enrollment

Number of students — Soccer, Softball, Basketball, Hockey
■ 2000   ■ 2001

ARE YOU READY? CHAPTER 9

Organizer

Objective: Assess students' understanding of prerequisite skills.

Prerequisite Skills

Round Decimals

Compare and Order Decimals

Place Value of Whole Numbers

Read a Table

Assessing Prior Knowledge

INTERVENTION

Diagnose and Prescribe

Use this page to determine whether intervention is necessary or whether enrichment is appropriate.

Resources

 Are You Ready? Intervention and Enrichment Worksheets

 Are You Ready? CD-ROM

 Are You Ready? Online

my.hrw.com

ARE YOU READY?

Diagnose and Prescribe

NO INTERVENE

✓ Prerequisite Skill	〰 Worksheets	💿 CD-ROM	🪐 Online
ARE YOU READY? Intervention, Chapter 9			
✓ Round Decimals	Skill 16	Activity 16	Diagnose and Prescribe Online
✓ Compare and Order Decimals	Skill 17	Activity 17	
✓ Place Value of Whole Numbers	Skill 1	Activity 1	
✓ Read a Table	Skill 90	Activity 90	

YES ENRICH

ARE YOU READY? Enrichment, Chapter 9
〰 **Worksheets**
💿 **CD-ROM**
🪐 **Online**

Organizer

Objective: Help students organize the new concepts they will learn in Chapter 9.

Online Edition
Multilingual Glossary

Resources

PuzzlePro®
One-Stop Planner®

Multilingual Glossary Online
go.hrw.com
KEYWORD: MT7 Glossary

Possible answers to Vocabulary Connections

1. The population is the entire group being studied.
2. The median is the middle value of a set of data.
3. A sample is the part of the population being surveyed.

Study Guide: Preview

Where You've Been

Previously, you

- used an appropriate representation for displaying relationships among collected data.
- described a set of data using mean, median, mode, and range.
- made inferences based on analysis of data.

In This Chapter

You will study

- selecting an appropriate representation for displaying relationships among collected data.
- selecting the appropriate measure of central tendency to describe data.
- making predictions and analyzing trends in scatter plots.
- recognizing misuses of graphical information.

Where You're Going

You can use the skills learned in this chapter

- to make predictions based on survey results.
- to conduct advanced research studies in science and social studies courses.

Key Vocabulary/Vocabulario

histogram	histograma
line plot	diagrama de acumulación
mean	media
median	mediana
mode	moda
population	población
sample	muestra
scatter plot	diagrama de dispersión

Vocabulary Connections

To become familiar with some of the vocabulary terms in the chapter, consider the following. You may refer to the chapter, the glossary, or a dictionary if you like.

1. The *population* of an area is the total number of people living in that area. What might **population** mean in the process of gathering data?

2. The word *median* is derived from the Latin word *medius*, meaning "middle." What might the **median** value in a set of data be?

3. When you *sample* a food, you taste a small portion. What might a **sample** be in data collection?

Reading Strategy: Interpret Graphics

Knowing how to interpret figures, diagrams, charts, and graphs will help you gather the information you need to solve the problem.

What You See

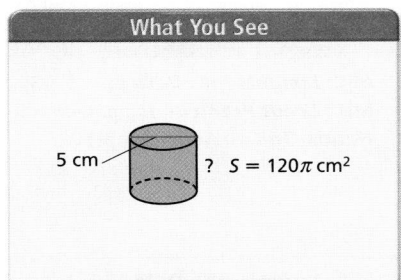

5 cm   ? $S = 120\pi \text{ cm}^2$

How to Interpret

✔ **Read all labels.**

Diameter = 5 cm
Surface Area = 120π cm^2
The height of the cylinder is unknown.

✗ **Do not assume anything**

The height of the cylinder appears to be about the same as the diameter, but you can't know this without calculating the height.

What You See

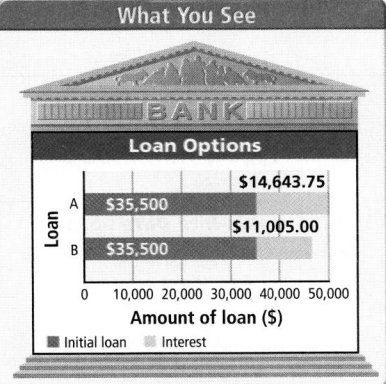

Loan Options

A	$35,500	$14,643.75
B	$35,500	$11,005.00

0   10,000   20,000   30,000   40,000   50,000
Amount of loan ($)

■ Initial loan   ▨ Interest

How to Interpret

✔ **Read the title.**

"Loan Options"

✔ **Read each axis label.**

horizontal Indicates the amounts of the loans measured in dollars

Vertical Indicates the loan options

✔ **Determine what information is represented.**

The amounts of principal and interest for two loans are shown.

Try This

Look up each exercise in the text and answer the corresponding questions.

1. Lesson 1-6 Exercise 36: What is the title of the graph? How deep is the deepest trench?

2. Lesson 2-3 Exercises 38 and 39: What does each number in the graph represent? What source provided the most energy?

3. Lesson 8-8 Exercise 2: What is the slant height of the cone? What is the radius of the base of the cone?

Reading and Writing Math (side tab)

Organizer

Objective: Help students apply strategies to understand and retain key concepts.

 Online Edition

Resources

 Chapter 9 Resource Book
Reading Strategies

Reading Strategy: Interpret Graphics

ENGLISH LANGUAGE LEARNERS

Discuss Encourage students to take time to carefully examine any graphic included in a problem. Suggest they list the information provided in the graphic, the information they are being asked to solve, and any formulas or relationships they know might be helpful.

Extend Students will need to be able to interpret graphic information in subjects other than math. Ask them to bring in an example of a graphic containing information that they ran across in another subject, newspaper, or magazine. Discuss these graphics with the class.

Possible answers to *Try This*

1. Depths of Ocean Trenches; −35,840 feet

2. Each number represents the amount, in quadrillion Btu, of renewable energy used by the United States; hydroelectric

3. 5 ft; 1.5 ft

Collecting and Describing Data

One-Minute Section Planner

Lesson	Materials	MiC and Lab Resources
Lesson 9-1 Samples and Surveys • Recognize biased samples and identify sampling methods. **9-1 Hands-On Lab** Explore Samples • Choose a sampling method, collect data, and summarize the results. ☑ SAT-10 ☐ ITBS ☑ CTBS ☑ NAEP		**MiC:** *Insights Into Data* pp. 11–13 **MiC:** *Great Predictions* pp. 4–9 *Hands-On Lab Activities* 9-1
Lesson 9-2 Organizing Data • Organize data in tables and stem-and-leaf plots. ☑ SAT-10 ☐ ITBS ☐ CTBS ☐ NAEP	Measuring tape	**MiC:** *Insights Into Data* All Sections *Technology Lab Activities* 9-2
Lesson 9-3 Measures of Central Tendency • Find appropriate measures of central tendency. ☑ SAT-10 ☑ ITBS ☑ CTBS ☑ NAEP	Newspapers or magazines	**MiC:** *Insights Into Data* pp. 32–33 **MiC:** *Great Predictions* pp. 28–29 *Technology Lab Activities* 9-3
Lesson 9-4 Variability • Find measures of variability. **9-4 Technology Lab** Create Box-and-Whisker Plots • Use a graphing calculator to produce box-and-whisker plots. ☑ SAT-10 ☑ ITBS ☑ CTBS ☐ NAEP	Graphing calculators	**MiC:** *Insights Into Data* pp. 34–39 *Technology Lab Activities* 9-4

MK = *Manipulatives Kit*

Mathematics in Context

The units **Insights Into Data** and **Great Predictions**
from the *Mathematics in Context* © 2006 series can be used with
Section 9A. See Section Planner above for suggestions for integrating
MiC with *Holt Mathematics*.

Section Overview

Sampling Methods and Biases

Lesson 9-1

 The value and usefulness of data depend on how it is obtained.

For most surveys, a sample of a population is polled to get the data.
For the data to have as little bias as possible, appropriate sampling
methods are required.

Sampling Method	How Members Are Chosen
Random	By chance
Systematic	According to a rule or formula
Stratified	At random from randomly chosen subgroups

Organizing Data

Lesson 9-2

 To be able to analyze data, it is necessary to organize it. Tables and
stem-and-leaf plots provide two methods of organizing data.

| 7 | 5 | 6 | 5 | 5 | 10 | 9 | 9 | 9 | 3 | 3 | 10 | 1 | 0 | 8 |
| 6 | 8 | 2 | 3 | 1 | 5 | 0 | 4 | 6 | 4 | 8 | 9 | 3 | 4 | 4 |

```
        x x x           x
        x x x x       x x
x x     x x x x       x x x
x x x x x x x x x x x x
+--+--+--+--+--+--+--+--+--+--+--+
0  1  2  3  4  5  6  7  8  9  10
```

Stem-and-Leaf Plot

Quiz Scores

Stems	Leaves
7	0 0
8	1 2 5 8 8
9	0 3 5
10	0 *Key: 8|1 means 81*

The 11 scores in this stem-and-leaf plot are
70, 70, 81, 82, 85, 88, 88, 90, 93, 95, and 100.

Central Tendency and Variability

Lessons 9-3, 9-4

 To analyze a set of numerical data, we need ways to describe it. Central tendency
is a way to describe a data set using one number. Variability (variation) of a data
set can be described by several methods.

Measures of Central Tendency

Quiz Scores:

70	70	81	82
85	88	88	90
93	95	100	

Mean $= \dfrac{70 + 70 + 81 + 82 + 85 + 88 + 88 + 90 + 93 + 95 + 100}{11} \approx 85.6$

Median (the middle value, or average of two middle values): 88

Mode (the value or values that occur most often): 70 and 88

Measures of variability can be shown
using a **box-and-whisker plot.**

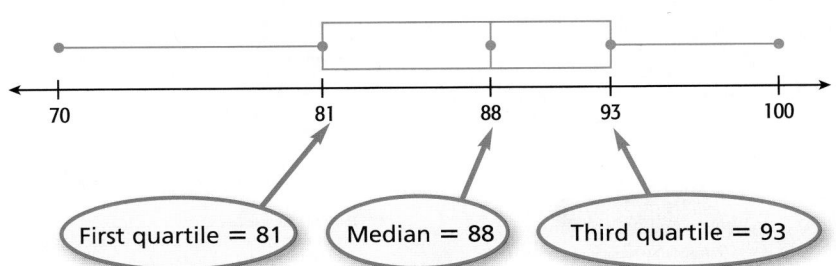

Range = largest value − smallest value
   = 100 − 70 = 30

462B

Objective: Students identify sampling methods and recognize biased samples.

Online Edition
Tutorial Videos

Countdown to Testing Week 19

Power Presentations
with PowerPoint®

Warm Up
Evaluate.
1. $t + 15$ for $t = -5$ — 10
2. $n + (-13)$ for $n = 7$ — -6

Solve for x.
3. $\frac{x}{-3} = -21$ — $x = 63$
4. $7x = -98$ — $x = -14$

Problem of the Day
Mr. Gray's 29 students will be sitting in the gym to watch a play. There are two rows of five chairs, three rows of four chairs, and four rows of two chairs. Is there enough room for all of the students to sit? yes

Also available on transparency

Math Humor
Did you hear the news that everyone in the world now has a telephone? In a recent survey, 100% of the people who were called said that they had one.

State Resources

go.hrw.com
State Resources Online
KEYWORD: MT7 Resources

Learn to identify sampling methods and to recognize biased samples.

Vocabulary
population
sample
random sample
systematic sample
stratified sample
convenience sample
voluntary-response sample
biased sample

A fitness magazine printed a readers' survey. Statements 1, 2, and 3 are interpretations of the results. Which do you think the magazine would use?

1. **The average American exercises 3 times a week.**
2. **The average reader of this magazine exercises 3 times a week.**
3. **The average reader who responded to the survey exercises 3 times a week.**

The **population** is the entire group being considered for a survey. The **sample** is the part of the population being surveyed.

To get accurate information, it is important to use a good sampling method. In a **random sample**, each member of the population has an equal chance of being selected. A random sample is best, but other methods can also be used.

People who read fitness magazines are likely to be interested in exercise. This could make the sample biased in favor of people who exercise more times per week.

Sampling Method	How Members are Chosen
Random	By chance
Systematic	According to a rule or formula
Stratified	At random from randomly chosen subgroups
Convenience	Easiest to reach
Voluntary-response	Members choose to be in the sample

EXAMPLE 1 **Identifying Sampling Methods**

Identify the sampling method used.

A An exit poll taken of every tenth voter.

Systematic   *The rule is to question every tenth voter.*

B Listeners are invited to call in to a radio show to voice their opinions.

Voluntary-response   *Callers choose to participate.*

**1 Introduce**
Alternate Opener

EXPLORATION

9-1 **Samples and Surveys**

A survey is being conducted to determine what items should be offered at the school snack bar. Instead of including every student in the survey, a method of selecting a fair representation of all students must be used.

1. Determine which method of selecting students might provide a sample that fairly represents all of the students in the school.
   Method 1: selecting students whose last names begin with A or B
   Method 2: selecting students who purchased snack bar items in the past week
   Method 3: selecting all eighth-grade students
   Method 4: selecting one-fourth of all students at random
   Method 5: selecting the first 100 students to come to the office to take the survey

2. Explain one way to make the method you chose in Problem 1 even more likely to give a representative sample.

Think and Discuss
3. **Explain** your reasons for selecting the method you chose in Problem 1.

Motivate
Introduce students to the concept of sampling by asking them to think of a question they would like to ask people at school. Discuss how long it would take them to pose the question to everyone in the school. Have students hypothesize different ways that they could conduct a fair survey that would not include every student at the school.

Explorations and answers are provided in *Alternate Openers: Explorations Transparencies.*

Identify the sampling method used.

C In a statewide survey, five counties are randomly chosen, and 100 people are randomly chosen from each county.

Stratified

The five counties are the random subgroups. People are chosen randomly from within the counties.

Sometimes, these sampling methods result in *biased samples*. A **biased sample** does not accurately represent the population. The data collected from biased samples is not reliable.

EXAMPLE 2 Identifying Biased Samples

Identify the population and sample. Give a reason the sample could be biased.

A A radio station manager chooses 1500 names from the local phone book to survey people about their listening habits.

Population	Sample	Possible Bias
People in the local area	Up to 1500 people who take the survey	Not all people are in the phone book.

B An advice columnist asks her readers to write in with their opinions about how to hang the toilet paper on the roller.

Population	Sample	Possible Bias
Readers of the column	Readers who write in	Only readers with strong opinions write in.

C Surveyors in a mall choose shoppers to ask about product preferences.

Population	Sample	Possible Bias
All shoppers in the mall	The people who are polled	Not all of the shoppers in the mall will be near the surveyors.

Possible answers to *Think and Discuss*

1. Use the systematic method and poll every tenth person who walks by.

2. stratified; randomly choose 10 classes and survey 10 randomly-chosen people from each class.

Think and Discuss

1. **Describe** ways to eliminate the possible bias in Example 2C.

2. **Decide** which sampling method would be best to find the number of times a week the average student in your school exercises.

2 Teach

Guided Instruction

In this lesson, students learn to recognize biased samples and identify sampling methods. Discuss the definitions of *population* and *sample* with them. While reviewing the examples (Teaching Transparency), discuss bias with the students. For Example 1B, ask students which groups of people will choose not to call (people who are shy, people who don't have access to a phone, etc.), and how this might influence the results of the survey.

 **Inclusion** Students might have difficulty understanding the different sampling methods. Use the class as the population and create different samples using each of the methods given.

Reaching All Learners
Through Cooperative Learning

Have students work in groups and ask a family member or neighbor to help them develop a survey. The survey can be about the neighborhood, something at school, or anything of interest to the student. Have students get the family member or neighbor to help them develop a survey question, determine a population, and decide on a sampling method that will be unbiased.

Possible answer: Question: What is your favorite type of music?; population: the entire school; method: systematic; survey every third person who walks into school at the beginning of the day.

3 Close

ENGLISH LANGUAGE LEARNERS

Summarize

Review the vocabulary words from the lesson. Discuss biased samples and ask students why someone might intentionally use a biased sample. Have students give an example of each of the sampling methods discussed in the lesson.

Possible answers: Advertisers might use biased samples to help sell their products. Random: Five students' names are drawn out of hat. Systematic: A store owner surveys every third person who enters the store. Stratified: A phone surveyor chooses 5 random letters and then calls 20 random people whose last names begin with each of the letters.

Assignment Guide

If you finished Example **1** assign:
Average 1, 2, 4, 5, 8–12, 18, 21–29
Advanced 4, 5, 8–12, 18, 20–29

If you finished Example **2** assign:
Average 1–16, 18, 21–29
Advanced 4–29

Homework Quick Check
Quickly check key concepts.
Exercises: 4, 6, 16, 18

Answers

7, 13–15. See pp. A12–A13.

Math Background

The United States Census Bureau conducts a survey every ten years to determine the population of the United States. The first U.S. census taken was in 1790. Two hundred men rode on horseback to count the number of people in each household, and data was recorded on small scraps of paper. This census cost the government just $45,000!

Until 1960, the population survey was conducted mostly door to door. At that time, bureau officials realized that this method was inefficient because the population was growing rapidly and becoming more mobile and diverse. By 1980, 90% of the census was taken by mail.

State Resources

go.hrw.com
State Resources Online
KEYWORD: MT7 Resources

9-1 Exercises

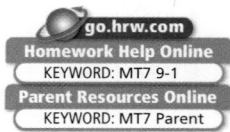
GUIDED PRACTICE

See Example **1** **Identify the sampling method used.**

1. People whose house number ends with a 1 are polled. **systematic**

2. Students sitting at the same lunch table are polled. **convenience**

See Example **2** **Identify the population and sample. Give a reason the sample could be biased.**

3. A pet store owner surveys 100 customers to find out which brand of dog food is most frequently purchased. **Population: pet store customers; sample: 100 customers; possible bias: not all customers have dogs.**

INDEPENDENT PRACTICE

See Example **1** **Identify the sampling method used.**

4. A surveyor flips through the phone book and selects 30 names. **random**

5. A newspaper columnist asks readers to write in with their 10 favorite restaurants. **voluntary response**

See Example **2** **Identify the population and sample. Give a reason the sample could be biased.**

6. A deli owner asks Sunday's customers to choose their favorite mustard.

7. A baseball team asks season ticket holders their preference of concession stands.

PRACTICE AND PROBLEM SOLVING

Extra Practice
See page 798.

Identify the sampling method used.

8. Every fifth name is called from a list of voters. **systematic**

9. The customers in a hair salon are surveyed. **convenience**

10. Each student writes a question on a slip of paper and puts it in a box. The teacher draws one question to discuss. **random**

6. Population: deli customers; sample: Sunday's customers; possible bias: the sample does not include weekday customers.

11. A Web site asks visitors to fill out a survey. **voluntary response**

12. Fifteen classes are randomly chosen. Ten students are randomly chosen from each class. **stratified**

Identify the population and sample. Give a reason the sample could be biased.

13. A teacher asks students who buy lunch if they like the cafeteria food.

14. An architecture firm asks people attending a city council meeting which design for a new city hall they prefer.

15. A biologist studying trees samples blossoms of trees along the river.

RETEACH 9-1

LESSON 9-1 Reteach
Samples and Surveys

A *survey* uses a *small sample* to represent a *large population*.

Sampling Method	How Members of the Sample Are Chosen
Random	By chance; members have an equal chance of selection
Systematic	According to a rule or pattern
Stratified	At random from randomly-chosen subgroups

A senator's office sends workers to ask constituents at a local mall how they feel about floating a bond to acquire land around a reservoir to be preserved as open space.
The population in this survey are all the eligible voters of the state. The shoppers at the mall are the sample of that population.

Identify the sampling method used.

1. A survey calls every 10th name listed in a local phone book.
   systematic

Identify the population and the sample.

2. Kennedy HS seniors planning to attend the prom were asked if senior dues should include a photo taken at the prom.
   Population ___all seniors at Kennedy HS___
   Sample ___Kennedy seniors planning to attend the prom___

A *biased sample* is not a good representative of the population.

A school principal asks parents attending an art workshop if funding for a theater arts program should be included in the school budget. This is a biased sample since the parents attending an art workshop are likely to be in favor of additional art programs.

Identify the population and the sample. Give a reason why the sample could be biased.

3. Homeowners within a 10-mile radius of a nuclear power plant were asked if they think the plant should be closed.
   Population ___NY homeowners___
   Sample ___homeowners in a 10-mi radius of the plant___
   Possible Bias: ___Homeowners close to the plant are more likely to want it closed.___

PRACTICE 9-1

LESSON 9-1 Practice B
Samples and Surveys

Identify the sampling method used.

1. People in the security line at the airport are asked to step out of the line for a more detailed search. The people pulled out of the line have not necessarily done anything wrong, and they are not chosen according to any particular rule.
   random

2. At the 1-mile marker of a marathon, a timekeeper shouts out the time elapsed to every 10th runner that passes by. A statistician records the times shouted.
   systematic

3. A geologist visits 10 randomly-selected lakes in the region and collects soil samples in randomly-selected areas along each shoreline.
   stratified

Identify the population and sample. Give a reason the sample could be biased.

4. At a convention of science teachers, various attendees are asked to name their favorite subject in high school.
   population ___teachers at the convention___
   sample ___teachers surveyed___
   possible bias ___most will say science___

5. Donors participating in a blood drive are given a small amount of money for their blood donation. Before they can give blood, each person is surveyed to find out if they are eligible to give blood.
   population ___blood donors___
   sample ___blood donors (entire population)___
   possible bias ___people may lie to get money___

6. Interviewers at the mall are surveying girls with red hair to find out if a correlation exists between personality and red hair.
   population ___girls with red hair___
   sample ___girls surveyed___
   possible bias ___some girls color their hair___

16. Recreation Marvin looked through the baseball cards he collected 20 years ago. Most of the baseball players began their careers in the 1980s.

a. What is the population of this survey?   professional baseball players

b. Give a reason why the sample could be biased.

17. Business For an advertising campaign, Jared needs to survey people to find out why they like to visit the Gladys Porter Zoo.

a. How can he select an unbiased sample for the survey?

b. How can he make the sampling method systematic?

c. Why would surveying only families with children be biased?

18. What's the Error? Kyla wanted to use a stratified sample to find out the most ordered food product at restaurants. She surveyed every tenth customer from five randomly chosen restaurants. Why is this not a stratified sample?

19. Write About It To plan your class picnic, you survey students about where they want to have the picnic. Choose a sampling method. Explain your choice.

20. Challenge The diagrams show the locations where soil samples will be taken to test for pollution. Identify the sampling method used for each diagram.

18. Possible answer: To be a stratified sample, the customers at each restaurant should have been chosen at random. Instead, they were chosen systematically.

random
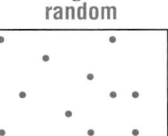

systematic
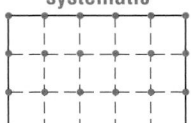

stratified
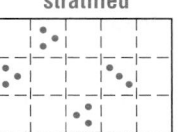

TEST PREP and Spiral Review

21. Multiple Choice Every fifth person standing in line is asked a question. Identify the sampling method used.

(A) Convenience   (B) Random   (C) Stratified   (D) Systematic

22. Short Response At a baseball game, a market researcher randomly asks 100 people to name their favorite sport. Identify the population and sample. Give a reason why the sample could be biased.

Use a number line to find each sum. (Lesson 1-4)

23. $-6 + 11$ 5   **24.** $-31 + (-31)$ -62 **25.** $-8 + 14$ 6

Multiply. Write the product as one power. (Lesson 4-3)

26. $3^6 \cdot 3^7$ 3^{13} **27.** $7^2 \cdot 7^4$ 7^6 **28.** $12^4 \cdot 14^5$ cannot combine   **29.** $x^3 \cdot x^5$ x^8

Answers

16. b. Possible answer: Many baseball players have retired and many more have started playing in the past 20 years.

17, 19, 22. See p. A13.

TEST PREP DOCTOR If students have trouble choosing between **A** and **D** for Exercise 21, point out that choosing every fifth person is formulaic. An example of convenience would be if only the people next in line to the surveyor were asked the question.

Journal

Ask students to write about a survey that they have read about or seen on television. Encourage them to identify the population and sample and to tell whether they think the sample was biased.

Power Presentations with PowerPoint®

✓ **9-1 Lesson Quiz**

Identify the population and sample. Give a reason why the sample could be biased.

1. A high school principal asks the first three people who leave the school play whether they liked it. Population: people who attended the play; sample: the first three people; possible bias: they may have left early because they didn't like it.

Identify the sampling method used.

2. At a baseball game, 10 sections are chosen at random and 10 random people from each section are polled.   stratified

3. A telemarketer calls the people that have a last name beginning with *H*.   systematic

Also available on transparency

Organizer

Pacing:
Traditional $\frac{1}{2}$ day
Block $\frac{1}{4}$ day

Objective: Use a sampling method, collect data, and summarize results.

Materials: Pencil and paper

 Online Edition

 Countdown to Testing Week 19

Resources

 Hands-On Lab Activities
Lab 9-1 Recording Sheet

Teach
Discuss

Discuss with students how the population choices, sampling-method choices, and uniform choices might affect the survey results differently.

Close
Key Concept

Population and sample choices might affect survey results.

Assessment

1. How might a voluntary response sample result in different survey results than a random sample?

   Possible answer: Students opposed to wearing uniforms might volunteer more to answer the survey. This would result in more opposing views than in a random sample.

State Resources

go.hrw.com
State Resources Online
KEYWORD: MT7 Resources

Explore Samples

go.hrw.com
Lab Resources Online
KEYWORD: MT7 Lab9

REMEMBER
- Be organized before starting.
- Be sure that your sample reflects your population.

You can predict data about a population by collecting data from a representative sample.

Activity

Your school district has been discussing the possibility of school uniforms. Each school will get to choose its uniform and colors. Your class has been chosen to make the selection for your school. To be fair, you want the other students in the school to have some input. You conduct a survey to see what the majority of students in your school want.

1. Model the survey by following the steps below.

   a. Choose your population.
   - every student in the school
   - only your class
   - all 8th grade students
   - all girls
   - all boys
   - teachers

   b. Choose two different sampling methods. Discuss the pros and cons of each method listed.
   - random
   - systematic
   - stratified
   - convenience
   - voluntary response

   c. Decide what colors and what uniform choices to present to your sample.
   - pants
   - sweaters
   - school colors
   - shorts
   - jackets
   - navy blue
   - skirts
   - vests
   - forest green

Think and Discuss

1. Explain why choosing the teachers as your population might not be the best choice.

2. How did you decide which colors to present to your sample?

Try This

1. Create forms for your survey listing the different options. Then survey your sample. Make a table of your results. Explain what your table tells you about the population.

Possible answers to *Activity*

1. **a.** every student in the school

   b. A random sample takes the least planning, but could be unintentionally biased. A systematic sample is a little more difficult to execute, but could give more reliable results. A stratified sample requires a great deal of planning, but will ensure that all groups (e.g., grade levels) are represented fairly in the sample.

   c. school colors (maroon and gray) and navy blue; pants, skirts, and vests

Possible answers to *Think and Discuss*

1. The teachers will not be wearing the uniforms and their clothing preferences may be different from the students'.

2. by selecting colors that seem the most popular when students choose their own school clothes

Answers to *Try This*

1. Check students' forms and tables.

Organizing Data

Learn to organize data in tables and stem-and-leaf plots.

Vocabulary
line plot
stem-and-leaf plot

back-to-back
stem-and-leaf plot

Venn diagram

An eighth-grade class participated in a month-long fitness challenge. Below are the numbers of miles each student ran, walked, or biked during the first week.

7 5 6 5 5 10 9 9 9 3 3 10 1 0 8
6 8 2 3 1 5 0 4 6 4 8 9 3 4 4

Organizing raw data can help you see patterns and trends. One way to organize data is to use a *line plot*. A **line plot** uses a number line to show how often a value occurs in a data set.

EXAMPLE 1 Organizing Data in Line Plots

Use a line plot to organize the data for the eighth-grade fitness challenge.

Find the least value, 0, and the greatest value, 10, in the data set. Then draw a number line from 0 to 10. Place an "**x**" above each number on the number line for each time it appears in the data set

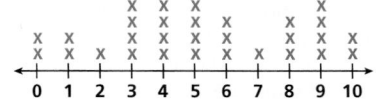

There are 30 numbers in the data set and 30 x's above the number line.

A **stem-and-leaf plot** is a graph used to organize and display data to compare frequencies. Each leaf on the plot represents the right-hand digit in a data value. Each stem represents the remaining left-hand digits.

Stem = first digit(s)

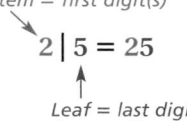

$2 \mid 5 = 25$

Leaf = last digit

EXAMPLE 2 Reading Stem-and-Leaf Plots

List the data values in the stem-and-leaf plot.

```
0 | 2 5
1 | 3 3 7 8
2 | 0 2 6
3 | 1 7        Key: 3|1 means 31
```

The data values are 2, 5, 13, 13, 17, 18, 20, 22, 26, 31, and 37.

Organizer 9-2

Pacing: Traditional $1\frac{1}{2}$ days
Block $\frac{3}{4}$ day

Objective: Students organize data in tables and stem-and-leaf plots.

Technology Lab
In *Technology Lab Activities*

Online Edition
Tutorial Videos

Countdown to Testing Week 19

Power Presentations
with PowerPoint®

Warm Up
Compare. Write < or >.

1. 3(6) ▨ 15   2. 53 − 37 ▨ 19

3. 27 ▨ 2(14)   4. 49 − (−4) ▨ 51

Problem of the Day
If today is Wednesday, what day of the week will it be in 100 days?
Friday

Also available on transparency

Math Humor

First the stem and the leaf conspired to steal water from the tree. Then they decided to take over the whole garden. It was a case of back-to-back stem-and-leaf plots.

---

1 Introduce
Alternate Opener

EXPLORATION

9-2 Organizing Data

1. Students in a class completed a survey in which they were asked how many hours they watched TV during one month. Their responses are shown below.

15	33	10	25	8
72	21	2	30	21
10	20	36	6	16
27	14	47	25	14
33	14	30	15	25

a. Write the numbers in order from least to greatest.

b. Describe how the numbers are spread out.

c. One student from the class was absent on the day of the survey. If the student were asked the same question, what number of hours would you guess might be close to the student's answer?

Think and Discuss

2. **Explain** how writing the numbers in order from least to greatest helps to organize data.

3. **Describe** another way to organize the data using a table.

Motivate

To introduce students to the opening scenario of the lesson, ask some of them whether they prefer walking, running, biking, or participating in another activity to help them stay fit. Point out to students that a plot makes it easy to compare data.

Explorations and answers are provided in *Alternate Openers: Explorations Transparencies.*

State Resources

go.hrw.com
State Resources Online
KEYWORD: MT7 Resources

Additional Examples

Example 1

Use a line plot to organize the math exam scores.

Student Test Scores			
100	95	75	80
60	100	60	75
90	85	80	100
50	90	65	80

```
                    x          x
        x       x   x   x      x
 x     x x      x   x   x x  x x
 +--+--+--+--+--+--+--+--+--+--+--+
50 55 60 65 70 75 80 85 90 95 100
```

Example 2

List the data values in the stem-and-leaf plot.

```
1 | 2 5
4 | 0 1 1
5 | 2 7 9    Key: 1|2 means 12
```

12, 15, 40, 41, 41, 52, 57, 59

Example 3

Use the given data to make a back-to-back stem-and-leaf plot.

U.S. Representatives for Selected States, 1950 and 2000					
	IL	MA	MI	NY	PA
1950	25	14	18	43	31
2000	19	10	15	29	19

```
1950  |   | 2000
 4 8  | 1 | 0 5 9 9
   5  | 2 | 9
   1  | 3 |   Key: |2|9  means 29
   3  | 4 |        8|1|  means 18
```

Example 4

Make a Venn diagram to show how many 8th grade students play soccer.

Survey Results			
Grade	Sport	Grade	Sport
6	baseball	8	tennis
6	tennis	7	soccer
8	soccer	7	baseball
8	baseball	6	soccer
7	soccer	8	soccer

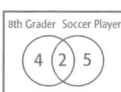
8th Grader Soccer Player
4 (2) 5

Also available on transparency

A **back-to-back stem-and-leaf plot** can be used to compare two sets of data. The stems are in the center, and the left leaves are read in reverse.

EXAMPLE 3 Organizing Data in Back-to-Back Stem-and-Leaf Plots

Use the given data to make a back-to-back stem-and-leaf plot.

Super Bowl Scores, 1995–2005											
	1995	1996	1997	1998	1999	2000	2001	2002	2003	2004	2005
Winning	49	27	35	31	34	23	34	20	48	32	24
Losing	26	17	21	24	19	16	7	17	21	29	21

```
   Losses  |   | Wins
        7  | 0 |
     9 7 7 6| 1 |
  9 6 4 1 1 1| 2 | 0 3 4 7
           | 3 | 1 2 4 4 5    Key:  |3|1 means 31 points
           | 4 | 8 9               1|2 means 21 points
```

Venn diagrams are used to show relationships between sets.

EXAMPLE 4 Organizing Data in Venn Diagrams

In a survey, the genders and ages of people who completed the questions is shown at right. Make a Venn diagram to show the number of people who are female and over age 30.

Draw two circles. Label one circle "Female" and the other circle "Over 30." The region that overlaps represents the characteristics that are shared by both sets of data.

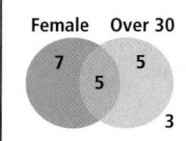
Female   Over 30
7   5
   5
          3

Survey Results			
Gender	Age	Gender	Age
M	18	M	16
F	30	M	35
F	25	F	28
M	50	F	45
M	60	F	35
F	17	M	38
F	42	F	29
F	30	F	46
M	27	M	32
F	48	F	25

Possible answers to
Think and Discuss

1. the set of data that is common to both groups

Think and Discuss

1. **Explain** what the overlapping region represents in a Venn diagram.

---

2 Teach

Guided Instruction

In this lesson, students learn to organize data in line plots, stem-and-leaf plots, and Venn diagrams. Discuss the roles of geometric figures in Venn diagrams.

Stem-and-leaf plots are effective for organizing a data set in which all the values represent the same characteristic. Show students how to order the data first. Then they can determine the stems and the leaves, create a key, and draw the plot. You may want to have students create a stem-and-leaf plot from data that include 3-digit values (e.g., 104, 95, 87, 98, 108, and 100).

Reaching All Learners

Through Kinesthetic Experience

Create groups of four or five students. Have them use the tape measures provided in the Manipulatives Kit to measure one another's height in inches and record the data. Then have each group create a stem-and-leaf plot to display the data. You may also want to combine the data and create a stem-and-leaf plot for the whole class.

go.hrw.com
Homework Help Online
KEYWORD: MT7 9-2
Parent Resources Online
KEYWORD: MT7 Parent

GUIDED PRACTICE

See Example ① 1. Use a line plot to organize the data of ages of children visiting a park.

| 5 | 7 | 8 | 2 | 3 | 3 | 4 | 5 | 8 | 2 |
| 9 | 10 | 9 | 10 | 8 | 8 | 7 | 6 | 6 | 5 |

See Example ② **List the data values in the stem-and-leaf plot.**

2.
```
0 | 2 3 3 7
1 | 1 3 7 7 8
2 | 0 0 7
3 | 4 4 5 5   Key: 3|5 means 35
```
2, 3, 3, 7, 11, 13, 17, 17, 18, 20, 20, 27, 34, 34, 35, 35

3.
```
6 | 3 6 8
7 | 3 3 5 7
8 | 0 0 1 1
9 | 0 4 5 9   Key: 9|9 means 99
```
63, 66, 68, 73, 73, 75, 77, 80, 80, 81, 81, 90, 94, 95, 99

See Example ③ 4. Use the given data to make a back-to-back stem-and-leaf plot.

Political Divisions of the U.S. Senate

Congress	89th	90th	91st	92nd	93rd	94th	95th	96th	97th	98th
Democrats	68	64	57	54	56	61	61	58	46	46
Republicans	32	36	43	44	42	37	38	41	53	54

See Example ④ 5. Make a Venn diagram to show how many eighth-grade female students responded to a recent survey.

Survey Results

Grade	6th	5th	8th	6th	7th	8th	7th	8th	6th	5th
Gender	M	F	M	F	M	F	M	F	F	M

INDEPENDENT PRACTICE

See Example ① 6. Use a line plot to organize the data of the number of books read by students over the summer.

| 3 | 0 | 3 | 6 | 0 | 1 | 2 | 5 | 5 | 5 | 2 |
| 3 | 0 | 0 | 1 | 6 | 0 | 7 | 8 | 6 | 5 | 6 |

See Example ② **List the data values in the stem-and-leaf plot.**

7.
```
5 | 0 1 4 8
6 | 2 6 7
7 | 1 4 5 6 6
8 | 2        Key: 6|2 means 62
```
50, 51, 54, 58, 62, 66, 67, 71, 74, 75, 76, 76, 82

8.
```
0 | 1 5 7
1 | 2 4 6 8
2 | 0 1 7 9
3 | 3 3 4 6   Key: 2|1 means 21
```
1, 5, 7, 12, 14, 16, 18, 20, 21, 27, 29, 33, 33, 34, 36

See Example ③ 9. Use the data given in the map to make a back-to-back stem-and-leaf plot.

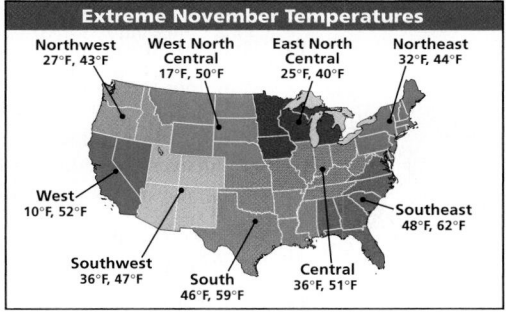

Extreme November Temperatures

Northwest 27°F, 43°F
West North Central 17°F, 50°F
East North Central 25°F, 40°F
Northeast 32°F, 44°F
West 10°F, 52°F
Southeast 48°F, 62°F
Southwest 36°F, 47°F
South 46°F, 59°F
Central 36°F, 51°F

Assignment Guide

If you finished Example ① assign:
Average 1, 6, 12, 20, 22–29
Advanced 6, 12, 20, 22–29

If you finished Example ② assign:
Average 1–3, 6–8, 12, 20, 22–29
Advanced 6–8, 12, 20, 22–29

If you finished Example ③ assign:
Average 1–4, 6–9, 11, 12, 17–20, 22–29
Advanced 6–9, 11, 12, 17–29

If you finished Example ④ assign:
Average 1–20, 22–29
Advanced 6–29

Homework Quick Check

Quickly check key concepts.
Exercises: 6, 8, 9, 10, 16

Answers

1.
```
              x
      x   x x x x
  x x x x x x x x x x
  +-+-+-+-+-+-+-+-+-+-
  2 3 4 5 6 7 8 9 10
```

4.
Democrats		Republicans
	3	2 6 7 8
6 6	4	1 2 3 4
8 7 6 4	5	3 4
8 4 1 1	6	

Key: |4|1 means 41
6|4| means 46

5.
8th Grade — Female
1 | 2 | 3
4

---

3 Close

Summarize

Remind students that line plots, stem-and-leaf plots and Venn diagrams are good ways to organize data and make it easy to understand. Review the three types of data displays in the lesson. Ask students to give an example of a situation that could be represented by each type of display.

Possible answer: A line plot could represent the number of hours students watch TV in one week. A stem-and-leaf plot could show the number of people attending school functions. A Venn diagram could be used to show the relationship between students playing a spring sport and those playing a fall sport.

6.
```
  x
  x             x x
  x       x     x x
  x x x x       x x
  x x x x       x x x x
  +-+-+-+-+-+-+-+-+-
  0 1 2 3 4 5 6 7 8
```
9. See p. A13.

State Resources

go.hrw.com
State Resources Online
KEYWORD: MT7 Resources

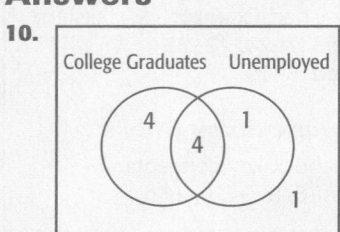
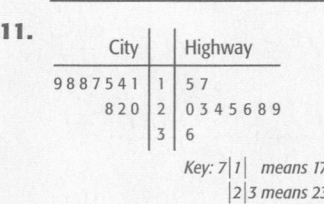
See Example 4

10. Make a Venn diagram to show how many unemployed college graduates responded to a recent survey.

Survey Results												
College Graduate	yes	no	yes	yes	yes	yes	no	yes	no	yes	yes	no
Employed	yes	yes	no	no	yes	no	yes	yes	yes	no	yes	no

PRACTICE AND PROBLEM SOLVING

Extra Practice
See page 798.

11. Use the given data to make a back-to-back stem-and-leaf plot.

Miles per Gallon Ratings of a Car Company's Models										
Model	A	B	C	D	E	F	G	H	I	J
City Miles	11	17	28	19	18	15	18	22	14	20
Highway Miles	15	24	36	28	26	20	23	25	17	29

12. The ages of 20 middle school students are shown in the line plot. List the ages in order from the most frequent to the least frequent.

13, 12, 11, 14, 10, 8, 9, 15

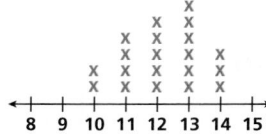

```
                    x
            x   x
    x   x   x
    x   x   x   x   x
    x   x   x   x   x
+---+---+---+---+---+---+---+---
    8   9  10  11  12  13  14  15
```

Use the Venn diagram to answer questions 13–16.

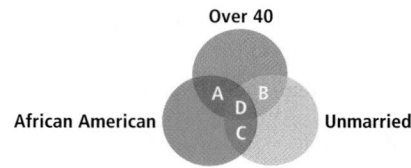

Over 40

African American   Unmarried

13. What does the portion of the Venn diagram labeled "A" represent?
African Americans older than 40 years

14. What does the portion of the Venn diagram labeled "B" represent?
unmarried people older than 40 years

15. What does the portion of the Venn diagram labeled "C" represent?
African Americans who are not married

16. What does the portion of the Venn diagram labeled "D" represent?
unmarried African Americans older than 40 years

The stem-and-leaf plot shows the scores for a recent math test. Use it to answer questions 17–19.

17. How many students took the test? **27**

18. What was the highest score received? How many students received the highest score? **99; 2**

19. What was the lowest score received? **61**

Boys		Girls
1 5	6	9
6 8 8 9	7	1 5 5 5
1 1 1 5 9	8	2 2 8
1 8 9	9	1 2 2 7 9

An author's writing style is as unique as a fingerprint. Punctuation, spelling, and word usage can be used to determine authorship.

Don Foster's methods have also been used to analyze ransom notes and evidence in court cases.

Don Foster used this fact to analyze the 350-year-old poem "A Funeral Elegy." The analysis confirmed that the poem of previously unknown authorship was actually written by William Shakespeare.

20. Act 5 of Shakespeare's *A Midsummer Night's Dream* has the following references to numbers: 1 nine times, 2 three times, 3 six times, 10 two times, 12 one time, and 14 one time. Use the data to make a line plot.

21. ⭐ **Challenge** Select two paragraphs from a work by your favorite author and a third paragraph by a different author. Compare word choices or punctuation use in the three paragraphs. Explain the similarities and differences. Use a line plot or back-to-back stem-and-leaf plot to support your argument.

Check students' work.

Verse	1	2	3	4	5	6	7	8	9	10	11	12	13	14
,	4	8	6	8	10	12	15	10	7	3	5	5	5	11
—	1	1	3	0	1	2	2	0	0	0	1	1	2	2
!	0	0	1	0	0	1	3	1	0	0	0	0	0	1
.	1	1	1	1	1	1	2	1	1	2	2	3	2	1

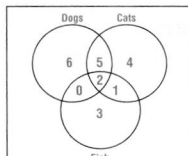

TEST PREP and Spiral Review

22. Multiple Choice For which set of data would it NOT be appropriate to make a stem-and-leaf plot?

Ⓐ Scores of a baseball league's games
Ⓒ Prices of fruit at a local market
Ⓑ Average high temperatures
Ⓓ Instruments played in the band

23. Short Response Use the data to make a back-to-back stem-and-leaf plot of the ages of people who visited an art exhibit. Men: 32, 45, 61, 33, 41, 61; women: 31, 44, 55, 32, 55, 64

Solve each proportion. (Lesson 5-4)

24. $\frac{9}{10} = \frac{x}{15}$ **13.5** **25.** $\frac{2}{w} = \frac{8}{12}$ **3** **26.** $\frac{6}{1} = \frac{d}{3}$ **18** **27.** $\frac{r}{4} = \frac{36}{3}$ **48**

Identify the sampling method used. (Lesson 9-1)

28. Shoppers at a store grand opening place their names in a box. One shopper is chosen at random. **random**

29. Every fourth customer at the grand opening receives a gift certificate. **systematic**

CHALLENGE 9-2

LESSON 9-2 Challenge
Pet Sets

A Venn diagram can show the relationships among three sets of data. Use the survey results shown in the table to complete the Venn diagram.

Number of Students in Mr. Phillips' Math Class Whose Families Have Pets

Dogs	Dogs and Cats	Dogs and Fish	Dogs, Cats, and Fish	Cats	Cats and Fish	Fish
13	7	2	2	12	3	6

Use your Venn diagram to answer the questions.

1. How many of the families have dogs only? _____ 6
2. How many of the families have cats only? _____ 4
3. How many of the families have fish only? _____ 3
4. How many of the families have dogs and fish but no cats? _____ 0
5. How many of the families have cats and fish but no dogs? _____ 1

PROBLEM SOLVING 9-2

LESSON 9-2 Problem Solving
Organizing Data

A consumer survey gathered the following data about what teens do while online.

1. Make a stem-and-leaf plot of the data.

Teens' Activities Online

```
7 | 3 3
8 | 2 6
9 | 5
```
Key: 7 | 3 means 73%

Teens' Activities Online	
Activity	**Percent**
E-mail	95
Use search engines	86
Instant Messaging	82
Visit music sites	73
Enter contests	73

The stem-and-leaf plot that shows the total number of medals won by different countries in the 2000 Summer Olympics. Choose the letter for the best answer.

2. List all the data values in the stem-and-leaf plot.
A 2, 4, 5, 6, 7, 8, 9
B 23, 25, 26, 28, 28, 29, 34, 38, 40, 57, 58, 59, 60, 70, 88, 97
C 23, 25, 26, 28, 29, 34, 38, 57, 58, 59, 88, 97
Ⓓ 23, 25, 26, 28, 29, 34, 38, 57, 58, 59, 88, 97

2000 Olympic Medals
```
2 | 3 5 6 8 8 9
3 | 4 8
4 |
5 | 7 8 9
6 |
7 |
8 | 8
9 | 7
```

3. What is the least number of medals won by a country represented in the stem-and-leaf plot?
F 3
G 4
Ⓗ 23
J 97

4. What is the greatest number of medals won by a country represented in the stem-and-leaf plot?
A 9
B 70
C 79
Ⓓ 97

ONGOING ASSESSMENT and INTERVENTION

Diagnose Before the Lesson
9-2 Warm Up, TE p. 467

Monitor During the Lesson
9-2 Know-It Notebook
9-2 Questioning Strategies

Assess After the Lesson
9-2 Lesson Quiz, TE p. 471

Answers

20, 23. See p. A13.

TEST PREP DOCTOR  In Exercise 22, remind students that stem-and-leaf plots are for numeric data.

✐ Journal

Ask students to write why a back-to-back stem-and-leaf plot is a good way to show the data in Example 4.

Power Presentations with PowerPoint®

✓ 9-2 Lesson Quiz

1. Use a line plot to organize the data of daily rainfall during the month of June.

Inches of Rainfall During June

0	3	4	1	0	0	0	1	0	5	
2	1	0	0	0	0	3	3	0	1	
1	1	0	0	4	4	5	2	1	1	

See p. A13.

2. List the data values in the stem-and-leaf plot. **6, 9, 14, 17, 22, 25**

```
0 | 6 9
1 | 4 7
2 | 2 5    Key: 1 | 5 means 15
```

3. Make a Venn diagram to show how many voters under age 30 responded to the survey.

Survey Results			
Age	**Registered to Vote**	**Age**	**Registered to Vote**
18	yes	55	yes
20	no	31	no
47	no	43	no
62	yes	25	yes
29	yes	19	no

See p. A13.

Also available on transparency

Objective: Students find appropriate measures of central tendency.

Technology Lab
In *Technology Lab Activities*

Online Edition
Tutorial Videos, Interactivities

Countdown to Testing Week 19

Power Presentations
with PowerPoint®

Warm Up
Order the values from least to greatest.

1. 9, 4, 8, 7, 6, 8, 5, 3, 7
3, 4, 5, 6, 7, 7, 8, 8, 9

2. 36, 22, 35, 46, 37, 47, 30
22, 30, 35, 36, 37, 46, 47

Divide.

3. $\frac{198}{3}$ 66   **4.** $\frac{576}{4}$ 144

Problem of the Day
A mom buys a white, a green, a blue, and a yellow sweater for her 4 children. Bill and Bob refuse to wear yellow. Barb doesn't like green. Beth hates green and white. Mom will not put the boys in white, and Bob won't wear blue. Which sweater will each child wear? Barb: white, Beth: yellow, Bob: green, Bill: blue

Also available on transparency

State Resources

go.hrw.com
State Resources Online
KEYWORD: MT7 Resources

9-3 Measures of Central Tendency

Learn to find appropriate measures of central tendency.

Vocabulary
mean
median
mode
range
outlier

Measures of central tendency are used to describe the middle of a data set. Mean, median, and mode are measures of central tendency.

	Measures of Central Tendency and Range
	Description
Mean	To find the mean (average), add the values in the data set. Then divide by the number of values in the set. Use when the data does not have any outliers.
Median	The middle value, or the mean of the two middle values, in an ordered set of data. Use when the data does have outliers.
Mode	The value(s) that occur most frequently. A data set may have no mode, one mode, or several modes. Use when you want to show which value(s) occur most often.
Range	The difference between the least and the greatest values in a data set. Use when you want to show the spread of the data.

An **outlier** is a value that is either far less than or far greater than the rest of the values in the data.

EXAMPLE 1 Finding Measures of Central Tendency and Range

Find the mean, median, mode, and range of the data set.

9, 6, 91, 5, 7, 6, 8, 8, 7, 9

mean: $9 + 6 + 91 + 5 + 7 + 6 + 8 + 8 + 7 + 9 = 156$

$\frac{156}{10} = 15.6$ *Divide by 10.*

median: 5 6 6 7 (7 8) 8 9 9 91   *Order the values.*

5 values   5 values

$\frac{7 + 8}{2} = 7.5$ *Average the two middle values.*

mode: 6, 7, 8, 9   *Four values occur twice each.*

range: $91 - 5 = 86$

---

1 Introduce
Alternate Opener

EXPLORATION

9-3 Measures of Central Tendency

1. Students in a class completed a survey in which they were asked what their heights in inches are. Their responses are shown below.

49	53	60	55	48
72	65	66	58	68
75	65	64	57	59
61	67	64	58	62
63	59	61	55	65

a. Write the numbers in order from least to greatest.
b. What number appears most often?
c. What number is in the middle of the data set?
d. Add the numbers and divide the total by 25 to find the mean.

Think and Discuss

2. **Discuss** which number from Problems 1b, 1c, and 1d best represents the entire set of numbers. Why?
3. **Describe** a set of numbers arranged from least to greatest in which the middle number is not close to the value of the mean.

Motivate
Ask students how teachers decide what grade to give each student at the end of a course. Explain that final grades are often based on the average of the grades earned during a grading period. Discuss the meaning of average and ask students for some other situations in which averages might be used.

Explorations and answers are provided in *Alternate Openers: Explorations Transparencies*.

EXAMPLE 2 Choosing the Best Measure of Central Tendency

Determine and find the most appropriate measure of central tendency or range for each situation. Justify your answer.

A The students in an 8th grade math class received the following scores on a test: 98, 79, 75, 90, 85, 90, 79, 88, 99, 100, 90, 72, 83, 90, 95, 98, 85, 69, 90, 82, 97, and 90. What score occurred most often?

Find the mode.

69, 72, 75, <u>79</u>, <u>79</u>, 82, 83, <u>85</u>, <u>85</u>, 88, <u>90</u>, <u>90</u>, <u>90</u>, <u>90</u>, <u>90</u>, <u>90</u>, 95, 97, <u>98</u>, <u>98</u>, 99, 100

List the scores in order. Underline the scores that appear more than once.

Ninety appears most frequently. The mode is 90.

B For the 2004 NFL season, the top four player salaries were $35,037,700, $19,004,000, $16,536,500, and $16,000,000. What number best describes these salaries?

$35,037,700 is an outlier because it is much greater than the other salaries. Find the median.

$16,000,000, $16,536,500, $19,004,000, $35,037,700

$$\frac{16,536,500 + 19,004,000}{2} = 17,770,250$$

The median of the top four NFL salaries is $17,770,250.

Sometimes you may want to choose a measure of central tendency or range in order to give a certain message about a group of data.

EXAMPLE 3 *Business Application*

A store had sales of $1025, $974, $993, $1001, $1027, $1657, and $1471 during one week. Which measure of data would make the store's sales for the week look the best?

Find each measure of central tendency and the range of the data.

mean: $\frac{1025 + 974 + 993 + 1001 + 1027 + 1657 + 1471}{7} = 1164$

median: 974, 996, 1001, 1025, 1027, 1471, 1657; 1025

mode: There is no mode.

range: 1471 − 974 = 497

The mean makes the sales for the week appear the greatest.

Possible answers to Think and Discuss

1. The range is based on the least and greatest values. If there is an outlier, the range may be very great, even if most of the data are grouped close together.

2. {1, 1, 2, 2, 2, 3, 3}

Think and Discuss

1. Explain how the range is affected by outliers.

2. Give a data set with the same mean, median, and mode.

2 Teach

Guided Instruction

In this lesson, students learn to find appropriate measures of central tendency. Explain that the purpose of a measure of central tendency is to represent a data set with a single value. Point out that there are four different values that can generally be used to represent a set: *mean* (also called *average*), *median, mode,* and *range*. Discuss the definitions of these four terms (Teaching Transparency).

Teaching Tip **Inclusion** Emphasize that students must order data values before finding the median. This will also help them to identify the mode. Remind students that some data sets have more than one mode and others have none.

Reaching All Learners
Through Home Connection

Have students search through a newspaper or magazine at home with a family member or neighbor to find a set of data, such as prices of houses, high temperatures, or points scored by the players on a sports team. Students can then find the mean, median, mode, and range for the data set. Have students identify any outliers. You may want to provide a magazine or newspaper section for students to take home.

3 Close

ENGLISH LANGUAGE LEARNERS

Summarize

Ask students to define *mean, median,* and *mode* in their own words. Discuss which measure of central tendency would be the best indicator of a student's grade in a class.

Possible answers: The mean is the sum of the values divided by the number of values. The median is the number in the middle or the average of the two numbers in the middle. The mode is the number or numbers that appear most often. The mean is most often used for a grade because it is based on all grades earned. The median is based on the number of grades but does not reflect the range, and there might not be a mode for the grades.

Assignment Guide

If you finished Example **1** assign:
Average 1–4, 8–11, 24–29
Advanced 8–11, 21, 23–29

If you finished Example **2** assign:
Average 1–6, 8–13, 15–18, 24–29
Advanced 8–13, 15–18, 21, 23–29

If you finished Example **3** assign:
Average 1–19, 24–29
Advanced 8–29

Homework Quick Check

Quickly check key concepts.
Exercises: 10, 12, 14, 16

Math Background

Using different measures of central tendency can significantly change the way a data set is perceived. For example, suppose the bowling scores for the members of a bowling team are 50, 50, 52, 62, and 101. The mean of the scores is 63, which is higher than four of the five scores. The mode is 50, which is the lowest score. The median is 52, which is the middle value in the set but is substantially below the mean. In cases like this, one number may not be enough to accurately describe the data set.

State Resources

go.hrw.com
State Resources Online
KEYWORD: MT7 Resources

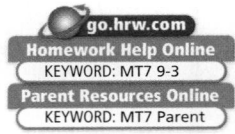

go.hrw.com
Homework Help Online
KEYWORD: MT7 9-3
Parent Resources Online
KEYWORD: MT7 Parent

GUIDED PRACTICE

See Example **1** Find the mean, median, mode, and range of each data set.

1. 35, 21, 34, 44, 36, 42, 29
   ≈ **34.43; 35; no mode; 23**

2. 2.0, 4.4, 6.2, 3.2, 4.4, 6.2
   4.4; 4.4; 4.4 and 6.2; 4.2

3. 7, 5, 4, 6, 8, 3, 5, 2, 5
   5; 5; 5; 6

4. 23, 13, 45, 56, 72, 44, 89, 92, 67
   ≈ **55.67; 56; no mode; 79**

See Example **2** Determine and find the most appropriate measure of central tendency or range for each situation.

5. The ages of the people attending the Harris family reunion are shown in the table. What was the spread in ages? **range; 60**

63	60	38	35	59	57	40	38	9	4	35
35	15	12	10	30	59	59	3	12	4	31

6. The scores on a math test were 80, 79, 90, 95, 85, 82, 96, 94, 81, 49, 92, and 87. What number best describes these scores? **median; 86**

See Example **3** 7. The weekly salaries of the employees of a hair salon are $1025, $975, $823, $750, $1400, $1000, and $823. Which measure of data would make the salaries seem the highest? **mean**

INDEPENDENT PRACTICE

See Example **1** Find the mean, median, mode, and range of each data set.

8. 5, 2, 12, 7, 13, 9, 8 **8; 8; no mode; 11**

9. 92, 88, 84, 86, 88 **87.6; 88; 88; 8**

10. 6, 8, 6, 7, 9, 2, 4, 22 **8; 6.5; 6; 20**

11. 4.3, 1.3, 4.5, 8.6, 9, 3, 2.1, 14 **5.85; 4.4; no mode; 12.7**

See Example **2** Determine and find the most appropriate measure of central tendency or range for each situation.

12. The ages of the students in a middle school choir are 10, 11, 12, 11, 12, 11, 10, 11, 13, 12, 13, 12, 11, 13, 14, 12, 14, 12, 11, and 12. What age appears most often in the list? **mode; 12**

13. The number of customers each day at a deli was 62, 50, 63, 58, 61, 122, and 70. What number best describes this data? **median; 63**

See Example **3** 14. The students in one middle school homeroom received the following scores on their achievement test: 32, 87, 89, 96, 96, 85, 79, 96, 90, 85, 78, 72, 96, 99, 91, 82, 77, 82, and 81. Which measure of data would make the scores appear the highest? **mode**

PRACTICE AND PROBLEM SOLVING

Extra Practice
See page 798.

Which measure of central tendency gives the lowest value for each data set?

15. 20, 17, 42, 26, 27, 12, 31 **mean**

16. 8, 5, 3, 75, 7, 3, 4, 7, 9, 8, 2, 8, 5, 7, 8 **median**

17. 3.3, 4.0, 3.3, 5.6, 4.6, 3.3, 5.6 **mode**

18. 15, 10, 12, 10, 13, 13, 13, 10, 3, 13 **mean**

RETEACH 9-3

LESSON 9-3 Reteach
Measures of Central Tendency

The **mode** of a data set is the value (or values) that occur(s) most often.

2, 4, 10, **3**, 6, **3**, 7
The value 3 occurs most often. So, 3 is the mode.

The **median** of a data set is the middle value—after the values have been ordered.

2, 4, 10, 3, 6, 3, 7 ⟶ 2, 3, 3, **4**, 6, 7, 10
The middle value is 4. So, 4 is the median.

The **mean** of a data set is the average value. Add the values and divide the sum by the number of values in the set.

2, 4, 10, 3, 6, 3, 7 ⟶ $\frac{2+4+10+3+6+3+7}{7} = \frac{35}{7}$, or 5
So, the mean is 5.

The **range** of a data set is the difference between the greatest value and the least value.

2, 4, **10**, 3, 6, 3, 7 ⟶ 10 − 2 = 8
So, the range is 8.

Determine and find the most appropriate measure of central tendency or range for each situation. Refer to the table at the right.

1. Which age was most frequent at the reunion?
   mode; 62 years

2. Which age was the average at the reunion?
   mean; 35 years

3. How spread out are the ages?
   range; 56 years

4. What was the middle age?
   median; 40 years

Smith Family Reunion 2006

Family Member	Age
Aunt Beth	36
Uncle Steve	40
Louise	9
Travis	6
Grandma	62
Grandpa	62
Mom	44
Dad	43
Me	13

PRACTICE 9-3

LESSON 9-3 Practice B
Measures of Central Tendency

Find the mean, median, mode, and range of each data set.

1. 7, 7, 4, 9, 6, 4, 5, 8, 4
   mean: **6**
   median: **6**
   mode: **4**
   range: **5**

2. 1.2, 5.8, 3.7, 9.7, 5.5, 0.3, 8.1
   mean: **4.9**
   median: **5.5**
   mode: **none**
   range: **9.4**

3. 31, 28, 31, 30, 31, 30, 31, 31, 30, 31, 31
   mean: **30.416**
   median: **31**
   mode: **31**
   range: **3**

4. 65, 46, 78, 3, 87, 12, 99, 38, 71, 38
   mean: **53.7**
   median: **55.5**
   mode: **38**
   range: **96**

Determine and find the most appropriate measure of central tendency or range for each situation. Refer to the table at the right for Exercises 3–5.

5. Which measure best describes the middle of the data?
   mean; 8.09

6. Which earthquake magnitude occurred most frequently?
   mode; 7.9

7. How spread out are the data?
   range; 1.9

8. Nicole purchased gasoline 8 times in the last two months. The prices that she paid per gallon each time were $2.19, $2.14, $2.28, $2.09, $2.01, $1.99, $2.19, and $2.39. Which measure makes the prices appear lowest?
   mean; $2.16

Some Major Earthquakes in United States History

Year	Location	Magnitude
1812	Missouri	7.9
1872	California	7.8
1906	California	7.7
1957	Alaska	8.8
1964	Alaska	9.2
1965	Alaska	8.7
1983	Idaho	7.3
1986	Alaska	8.0
1987	Alaska	7.9
1992	California	7.6

19. Astronomy The table shows the approximate distance each planet is from the Sun.

Distance from the Sun									
Planet	Mercury	Venus	Earth	Mars	Jupiter	Saturn	Uranus	Neptune	Pluto
Miles (million)	36	67	93	141	484	887	1784	2796	3661

a. Find the range of the data. **3,625,000,000 miles**

b. Which measure of central tendency makes the planets appear to be closer to the Sun? **median**

20. School Teresa has taken three tests worth 100 points each. Her scores are 85, 93, and 88. She has one test left to take. What score must she get on her last test to get an average of 90? **94**

21. Write a Problem Use your test scores from one course to write a problem about central tendency.

22. Write About It If six friends went to dinner and split the check equally, what measure of central tendency would describe the amount each person paid? Explain.

23. Challenge If $4\left(\dfrac{x + y + z}{3}\right) = 8$, what is the mean of x, y, and z? **2**

TEST PREP and Spiral Review

24. Multiple Choice Which measure of central tendency has the smallest value for the data set: 11, 11, 4, 15, 18, 22, 24, 7?

Ⓐ Mean Ⓑ Median Ⓒ Mode Ⓓ They are all equal.

25. Gridded Response Kelly recorded the number of sit-ups she did each day in the table below. Find the mean number of sit-ups Kelly did per day. **60.4**

Mon	Tue	Wed	Thur	Fri
34	45	66	75	82

Find each number to the nearest tenth. (Lesson 6-3)

26. What number is 55% of 240? **132**

27. What number is $66\frac{2}{3}$% of 847? **564.7**

Identify the population and sample. Give a reason why the sample could be biased. (Lesson 9-1)

28. In December, a store owner asks every third shopper whether they are buying items for themselves or as gifts. **Population: shoppers; sample: every third shopper; possible bias: December is during the gift-buying season.**

29. A market researcher pays a group of shoppers at a mall to fill out a questionnaire about products they are shown.

ONGOING ASSESSMENT and INTERVENTION

Diagnose Before the Lesson
9-3 Warm Up, TE p. 472

Monitor During the Lesson
9-3 Know-It Notebook
9-3 Questioning Strategies

Assess After the Lesson
9-3 Lesson Quiz, TE p. 475

Answers

21. Possible answer: Find the mean, median, and mode for these test grades: 87, 92, 81, and 86.

22. Possible answer: The mean would describe the amount each person paid because it is calculated by finding the total and dividing by the number of people.

29. See p. A13.

TEST PREP DOCTOR For item 24, encourage students to rewrite the data set from least to greatest value. This will make it easier to correctly find the measures of central tendency.

Journal

In five different basketball games, Michael Jordan scored 12, 26, 28, 6, and 51 points. Ask students to explain which measure of central tendency they think best describes this data set.

Power Presentations with PowerPoint®

CHALLENGE 9-3

Challenge
9-3 The Groupie Effect

A class of 29 students reported the number of books read so far this school year.

Number of Books Read
5, 5, 6, 3, 6, 3, 2, 7, 5, 3,
7, 4, 2, 5, 6, 7, 6, 4, 1, 4,
9, 5, 6, 7, 7, 6, 6, 7, 5

This frequency table shows the same data.

Value	1	2	3	4	5	6	7	8	9
Frequency	1	2	3	3	6	7	6	0	1

1. Explain how to find the mode using the ungrouped data. What is the mode?
Look for the score with the highest frequency; mode = 6

2. Explain how to find the mode using the frequency table.
Verify that you obtain the same result as before.
Look for the interval with the highest frequency; mode = 6

3. Explain how to find the median using the ungrouped data. What is the median?
Arrange the data in order. The median is the middle, or 15th score.
median = 5

4. Explain how to find the median using the frequency table. Verify that you obtain the same result as before. Which method do you prefer? Why?
From either end of the frequency row of the table, add frequencies until you get to 15. median = 5. Preferences vary.

5. Explain how to find the mean using the ungrouped data. What is the mean?
Add the 29 scores and divide the sum by 29. mean = 5.14

6. Explain how to find the mean using the frequency table. Verify that you obtain the same result as before. Which method do you prefer? Why?
Multiply each interval by its frequency. Add the products. Divide the sum by 29. mean = 5.14 Preferences will vary.

PROBLEM SOLVING 9-3

Problem Solving
9-3 Measures of Central Tendency

Use the data to each answer.

1. Find the average number of passengers in the world's five busiest airports.
69.22 million

2. Find the median number of passengers in the world's five busiest airports.
68.5 million

Airport	Total Passengers (in millions)
Atlanta, Hartsfield	80.2
Chicago, O'Hare	72.1
Los Angeles	68.5
London, Heathrow	64.6
Dallas/Ft. Worth	60.7

World's Busiest Airports

3. Find the mode of the airport data.
There is no mode.

4. Find the range of the airport data.
19.5 million

Choose the letter for the best answer.

5. What was the mean production of motor vehicles in 1998?
A 8,651,500 vehicles
Ⓑ 10,249,250 vehicles
C 11,264,250 vehicles
D 12,000,000 vehicles

Country	1998	1999
United States	12,047	13,063
Canada	2,568	3,026
Europe	16,332	16,546
Japan	10,050	9904

World Motor Vehicle Production (in thousands) 1998–1999

6. What was the range of production in 1999?
F 9,800,000 vehicles
G 11,480,000 vehicles
H 12,520,000 vehicles
Ⓙ 13,520,000 vehicles

7. What was the median number of vehicles produced in 1999?
A 3,026,000 vehicles
B 3,069,000 vehicles
Ⓒ 3,159,000 vehicles
D 4,559,000 vehicles

8. Which value is largest?
F Mean of 1998 data
G Mean of 1999 data
H Median of 1998 data
Ⓙ Median of 1999 data

9-3 Lesson Quiz
Use the data to find each answer.

Bowler	Game 1	Game 2	Game 3
Tom	205	162	173
Brad	200	172	186
Bill	185	211	184
Casey	184	220	162

1. What is the mean of Brad's scores? **186**

2. What is the mean of all the scores? **187**

3. What is the mode? **184 and 162**

4. What is the median of all the scores? **184.5**

5. What is the range of the scores in Game 2? **58**

Also available on transparency

Online Edition
Tutorial Videos, Interactivities

Countdown to
Testing Week 19

Power Presentations
with PowerPoint®

Warm Up

1. Order the test scores from least to greatest: 89, 93, 79, 87, 91, 88, 92.   79, 87, 88, 89, 91, 92, 93

2. Find the median of the test scores.   89

Find the difference.

3. $17 - 0.9$ 16.1

4. $8.4 - 7.6$ 0.8

5. $9.1 - 5.7$ 3.4

6. $190.3 - 23.4$ 166.9

Problem of the Day

What are the possible values for x in the data set 22, 12, 33, 25, and x if the median is 25?   any number greater than or equal to 25

Also available on transparency

Math Humor

Why did the student shave after reviewing his homework? The teacher took off points because his whiskers were too long.

State Resources

go.hrw.com
State Resources Online
KEYWORD: MT7 Resources

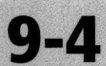

9-4 Variability

Learn to find measures of variability.

Vocabulary
variability
quartile
box-and-whisker plot

The table below summarizes a veterinarian's records for kitten litters born in a given year.

Litter Size	2	3	4	5	6
Number of Litters	1	6	8	11	1

While central tendency describes the middle of a data set, **variability** describes how spread out the data is.

Quartiles divide a data set into four equal parts. The third quartile minus the first quartile is the range for the middle half of the data.

The term *box-and-whisker plot* may remind you of a box of kittens. But it is a way to display data.

Kitten Data

Lower half   *Upper half*

2 3 3 3 3 3 (3) 4 4 4 4 4 4 (4) 4 5 5 5 5 5 (5) 5 5 5 5 6

First quartile: 3   *Median: 4*   *Third quartile: 5*
median of lower half   (second quartile)   median of upper half

EXAMPLE 1 **Finding Measures of Variability**

Find the first and third quartiles for each data set.

A 85, 92, 78, 88, 90, 88, 89

78 (85) 88 88 (89 90) 92   *Order the values.*

first quartile: 85
third quartile: 90

B 13, 14, 16, 18, 18, 21, 12, 21, 11, 19, 15, 13

11, 12, (13, 13,) 14, 15 (16, 18, (18, 19,) 21, 21)   *Order the values.*

first quartile: $\frac{13 + 13}{2} = 13$

third quartile: $\frac{18 + 19}{2} = 18.5$

---

1 Introduce
Alternate Opener

EXPLORATION

9-4 **Variability**

When placed on a number line, values in a data set can be spread out or clustered together.

1. Order the data sets from the ones you think are the least spread out to the most spread out.

Set 1: |45 50 55 60 65 70 75|

Set 2: |45 50 55 60 65 70 75|

Set 3: |45 50 55 60 65 70 75|

Set 4: |45 50 55 60 65 70 75|

Think and Discuss

2. Discuss the strategies you used to order the sets according to the spread of the data.

3. Explain how the spread of set 1 would change if the value 72 were added.

Motivate

To introduce students to variability, review the three measures of central tendency with them: mean, median, and mode. Remind students that a measure of central tendency tells where the data is centered. Ask students if mean, median, or mode gives any indication of how a set of data is spread out. no Tell students that the topic of the new lesson will address how a data set is spread out.

Explorations and answers are provided in *Alternate Openers: Explorations Transparencies*.

A **box-and-whisker plot** shows the distribution of data. The middle half of the data is represented by a "box" with a vertical line at the median. The lower fourth and upper fourth are represented by "whiskers" that extend to the smallest and largest values.

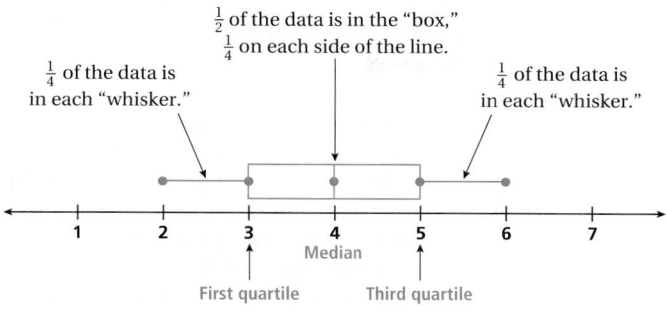

$\frac{1}{2}$ of the data is in the "box," $\frac{1}{4}$ on each side of the line.

$\frac{1}{4}$ of the data is in each "whisker."

$\frac{1}{4}$ of the data is in each "whisker."

Median

First quartile   Third quartile

EXAMPLE 2   **Making a Box-and-Whisker Plot**

Use the given data to make a box-and-whisker plot.

23 16 51 23 56 22 63 51 22 15 19 42 44 50 38 31 47

Step 1: Order the data and find the smallest value, first quartile, median, third quartile, and largest value.

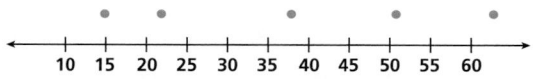

15, 16, 19, 22, 22, 23, 23, 31, 38, 42, 44, 47, 50, 51, 51, 56, 63

smallest value:	15
first quartile:	$\frac{22 + 22}{2} = 22$
median:	38
third quartile:	$\frac{50 + 51}{2} = 50.5$
largest value:	63

Step 2: Draw a number line and plot a point above each value from Step 1.

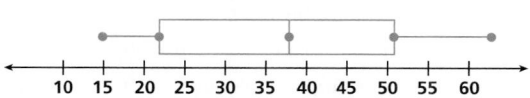

10 15 20 25 30 35 40 45 50 55 60

Step 3: Draw the box and whiskers.

10 15 20 25 30 35 40 45 50 55 60

Power Presentations with PowerPoint®

Additional Examples

Example 1

Find the first and third quartiles for each data set.

A. 15, 83, 75, 12, 19, 74, 21
   first quartile: 15; third quartile: 75

B. 75, 61, 88, 79, 79, 99, 63, 77
   first quartile: 69; third quartile: 83.5

Example 2

Use the given data to make a box-and-whisker plot.

21, 25, 15, 13, 17, 19, 19, 21

12 14 16 18 20 22 24 26 28

Also available on transparency

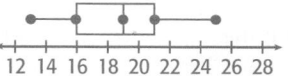

---

2 Teach

Guided Instruction

In this lesson, students learn to find measures of variability. Begin by defining *variability*.

Review with students how to order a set of data and find the median. Have students identify the smallest value and the largest value. The range is the difference between these values.

To find the quartiles, use the median to divide the data set into two equal groups. Find the first quartile (Q1) and the third quartile (Q3) by finding the median of each of the equal groups. A box-and-whisker plot can then be drawn, using the values (Teaching Transparency).

Reaching All Learners
Through Cognitive Strategies

Provide each student with his or her quiz or homework scores so far in the class, or show them a set of example quiz scores. Have students make a box-and-whisker plot of the scores, and then ask what insight the shape of the plot reveals about the student's performance. Point out that boxes with long ranges suggest inconsistent performance, while boxes with small ranges represent consistent performances. Also, explain that low outliers could represent a particular math topic the student has trouble understanding.

Additional Examples

Example 3

These box-and-whisker plots compare the ages of the first ten U.S. presidents with the ages of the last ten presidents (through George W. Bush) when they took office.

Age of First Ten Presidents at Inauguration

51 57 61 68

Age of Last Ten Presidents at Inauguration

43   52 55.5 62   69

```
40      50      60      70
```

A. Compare the medians and ranges.

The median for the first ten presidents is slightly greater.

The range for the last ten presidents is greater.

B. Compare the differences between the third quartile and first quartile for each.

The difference between the third quartile and first quartile is greater for the last ten presidents.

Also available on transparency

9-4 Exercises

Assignment Guide

If you finished Example **1** assign:
Average 1, 2, 7, 8, 13–16, 27–35
Advanced 7, 8, 13–16, 27–35

If you finished Example **2** assign:
Average 1–4, 7–10, 13–19, 27–35
Advanced 7–10, 14–20, 22, 25–35

If you finished Example **3** assign:
Average 1–19, 21, 27–35
Advanced 7–12, 15–35

Homework Quick Check

Quickly check key concepts.
Exercises: 8, 10, 12, 21

EXAMPLE 3 Comparing Data Sets Using Box-and-Whisker Plots

The number of touchdown passes that Brett Favre and Dan Marino threw during the first 14 years of their careers is shown in the box-and-whisker plots at right.

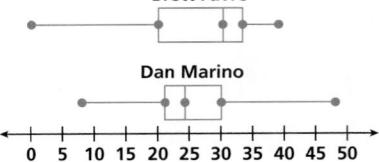

A. Compare the medians and ranges.

Brett Favre's median is greater than Dan Marino's.
Dan Marino's range is greater than Brett Favre's.

B. Compare the ranges of the middle half of the data for each.

The range of the middle of each data set is the length of the "box". So, the range of the middle half of the data is greater for Brett Favre.

5. The medians are equal, but data set B has a much greater range.

6. The range of the middle half of the data is greater for data set B.

Think and Discuss

1. **Explain** why the data must first be ordered from smallest to largest before making a box-and-whisker plot.

2. **Compare** the number of data values in the box with the number of data values in the whiskers.

9-4 Exercises

go.hrw.com
Homework Help Online
KEYWORD: MT7 9-4
Parent Resources Online
KEYWORD: MT7 Parent

GUIDED PRACTICE

See Example **1** Find the first and third quartiles for each data set.

1. 52, 75, 55, 30, 70, 56, 66   **52; 70**   2. 4, 1, 3, 0, 6, 3, 5, 4, 3, 2, 6, 2   **2; 4.5**

See Example **2** Use the given data to make a box-and-whisker plot.

3. 32, 47, 42, 33, 23, 59, 29, 19, 34   4. 41, 11, 26, 58, 54, 32, 38, 56, 21

See Example **3** Use the box-and-whisker plots to compare the data sets.

5. Compare the medians and ranges.

6. Compare the ranges of the middle half of the data for each set.

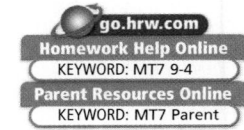

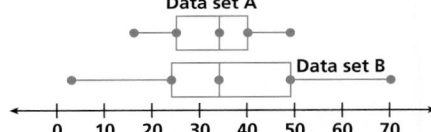

---

3 Close

Summarize

Show students an example of a box-and-whisker plot and ask them to point out the location of the smallest value, the first quartile, the median, the third quartile, and the largest value. Ask them which part of the plot represents the range. Have students describe the change to the plot when a very large outlier is added to the data set.

Possible answers: The smallest and largest values are the ends of the line. The first and third quartiles are the ends of the box. The median is the line in the middle of the box. The range is the length of the line. An outlier would make the line extend far beyond the box to the right.

Possible answers to *Think and Discuss*

1. When the data is ordered, it is easier to find the smallest value, first quartile, median, third quartile, and largest value, all of which are needed to make a box-and-whisker plot.

2. The box contains about the same number of data values as the two whiskers combined.

INDEPENDENT PRACTICE

See Example ① **Find the first and third quartiles for each data set.**

7. 48, 72, 43, 42, 69, 50, 56, 48, 52
    45.5; 62.5

8. 18, 17, 13, 7, 6, 25, 55, 3, 6 **6; 21.5**

See Example ② **Use the given data to make a box-and-whisker plot.**

9. 50, 68, 85, 54, 80, 75, 68

10. 7, 4, 5.7, 1.4, 6.8, 6.3, 11, 3.2

See Example ③ **Use the box-and-whisker plots to compare the data sets.**

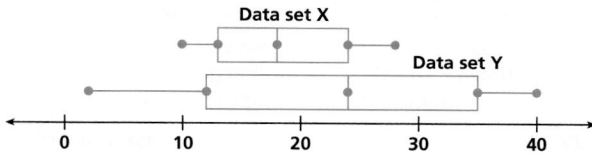

11. Compare the medians and ranges.

12. Compare the ranges of the middle half of the data for each set.

PRACTICE AND PROBLEM SOLVING

Extra Practice
See page 798.

Find the first and third quartiles for each data set.

13. 88, 78, 85, 74, 66, 82, 68 **68; 85**

14. 9, 2, 8, 6, 1, 7, 3, 11 **2.5; 8.5**

15. 46, 53, 67, 29, 35, 54, 49, 61, 35
    35; 57.5

16. 3.5, 3.4, 3.7, 3.5, 3.4, 3.3, 3.4, 3.4
    3.4; 3.5

Use the given data to make a box-and-whisker plot.

17. 87, 79, 95, 99, 67, 71, 83, 91

18. 16, 3, 9.3, 11.3, 14, 7, 7, 4.2, 4.5

19. 0, 2, 5, 2, 1, 3, 5, 2, 4, 3, 5, 4

20. 6.4, 8.0, 6.5, 3.0, 5.4, 2.2, 5.3

21. Earth Science Hurricanes and tropical storms form in all seven ocean basins. Use a box-and-whisker plot to compare the number of tropical storms in every ocean basin per year with the number of hurricanes in every ocean basin per year.

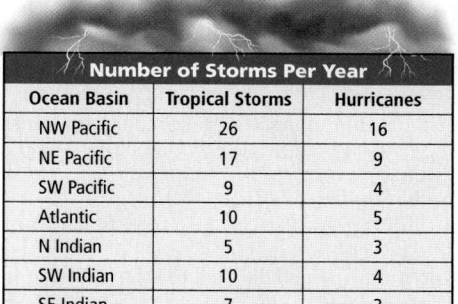

Number of Storms Per Year		
Ocean Basin	Tropical Storms	Hurricanes
NW Pacific	26	16
NE Pacific	17	9
SW Pacific	9	4
Atlantic	10	5
N Indian	5	3
SW Indian	10	4
SE Indian	7	3

11. Data set X has a greater median. Data set Y has a greater range.

12. Data set X has a greater range of the middle half of the data.

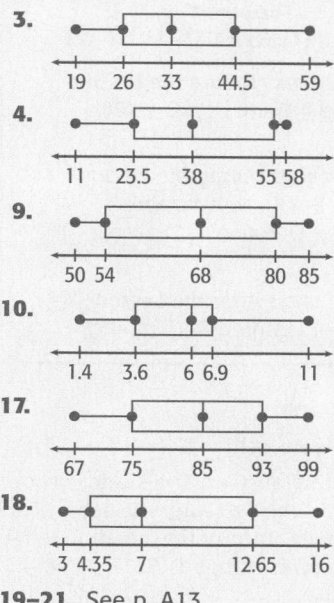
Math Background

A box-and-whisker plot shows the variability of a data set, or how the data set is distributed. One important measure of this is the interquartile range (IQR). The IQR is the difference between the third quartile (Q3) and the first quartile (Q1). The IQR is represented on the plot by the length of the box. If a whisker appears very long compared to the length of the box, then there may be one or more outliers on that whisker. Outliers can be mathematically identified as follows: Subtract 1.5 times the IQR from the first quartile. Any value less than that difference is an outlier. Add 1.5 times the IQR to the third quartile. Any value greater than that sum is an outlier.

State Resources

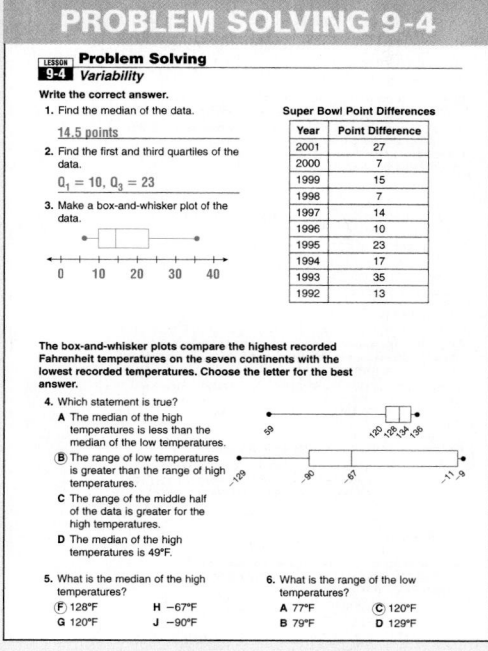

Answers

23, 28. See p. A13.

24. Possible answer: The student subtracted the first and last data values without ordering them first. The correct range is $65 - 25 = 40$.

25. Possible answer: Box-and-whisker plots show how the data are spread out from the median. They also show the range and quartiles.

TEST PREP DOCTOR Students may not recall that the first quartile on a box-and-whisker plot is on the leftmost side of the box. Students who chose **C** or **D** may need to review the five points used to construct box-and-whisker plots.

Journal

Refer students to Example 3 in the lesson. Ask students to write about whether they think Brett Favre or Dan Marino was the better touchdown passer and why.

Power Presentations
with PowerPoint®

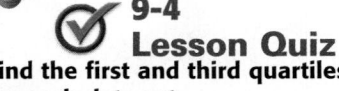

9-4 Lesson Quiz

Find the first and third quartiles for each data set.

1. 48, 52, 68, 32, 53, 47, 51
Q1 = 47; Q3 = 53

2. 3, 18, 11, 2, 7, 5, 9, 6, 13, 1, 17, 8, 0
Q1 = 2.5; Q3 = 12

Use the following data for problems 3 and 4.

91, 87, 98, 93, 89, 78, 94

3. Make a box-and-whisker plot.

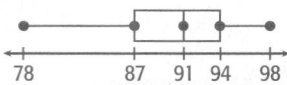
78   87 91 94   98

4. What is the mean?   90

Also available on transparency

---

22. Match each set of data with a box-and-whisker plot.

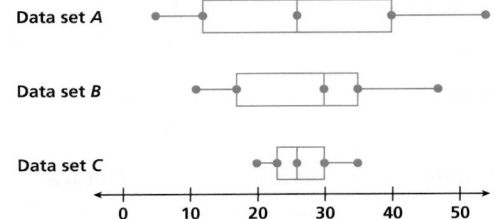

Data set A
Data set B
Data set C

```
   0   10   20   30   40   50
```

a. range: 49	**b.** range: 15	**c.** range: 36
first quartile: 7	first quartile: 18	first quartile: 12
third quartile: 35	third quartile: 25	third quartile: 30
Data set A	Data set B	Data set C

23. Critical Thinking Make a box-and-whisker plot of the following data: 18, 16, 21, 10, 15, 25, 13, 22, 25, 13, 15, 10. Add 50 to the list of data and make a new box-and-whisker plot. How did the addition of an outlier affect the box-and-whisker plot?

 24. What's the Error? A student wrote that the data set 33, 28, 29, 56, 27, 43, 33, 25, 40, 65 has a range of 32. What's the error?

25. Write About It What do box-and-whisker plots tell you about data that measures of central tendency do not?

26. Challenge What would an exceptionally short box with extremely long whiskers tell you about a data set? **Possible answer: The minimum and maximum values are outliers.**

TEST PREP and Spiral Review

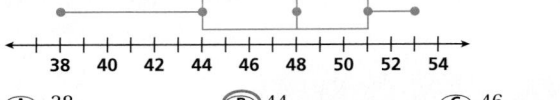

27. Multiple Choice Find the first quartile for the data set shown in the box-and-whisker plot.

```
   38  40  42  44  46  48  50  52  54
```

(A) 38   (B) 44   (C) 46   (D) 48

28. Extended Response Ken recorded his golf scores during a three week period. His scores were: 85, 76, 83, 99, 83, 74, 75, 81, and 87. Find the range, median, and first and third quartiles. Make a box-and-whisker plot of the data. **Range: 25; median: 83; first quartile: 75.5; third quartile: 86**

Find the square roots of each number. (Lesson 4-5)

29. 16   4 and −4   **30.** 81   9 and −9   **31.** 100   10 and −10   **32.** 1   1 and −1

Find the mean, median, and mode of each data set to the nearest tenth. (Lesson 9-3)

33. 3, 5, 5, 6, 9, 3, 5, 2, 5   **34.** 17, 15, 14, 16, 18, 13   **35.** 100, 75, 48, 75, 48, 63, 45
4.8; 5; 5   15.5; 15.5; no mode   64.9; 63; 48 and 75

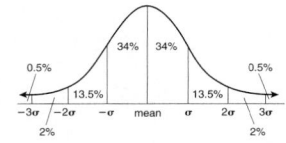

CHALLENGE 9-4

Challenge
9-4 *What's Normal?*

Standard deviation (symbol σ, *sigma*) is a measure of variability that tells how far data are spread out from the mean of a data set.

In many situations, such as scores on the SAT or other standardized tests, the data cluster around the mean in such a way that if they are graphed to show the frequency of measures, the graph appears as a **bell-shaped curve**, also called the **normal curve**.

```
        34%   34%
0.5%                    0.5%
      13.5%      13.5%
  −3σ  −2σ   −σ   mean  σ   2σ   3σ
  2%                              2%
```

If the mean math score for males on the 2001 SAT I was 533 and the standard deviation was 115, determine the scores achieved by about 68% of the male participants.

According to the normal curve, 68% of scores fall between − σ and σ.
mean − σ = 533 − 115 = 418   mean + σ = 533 + 115 = 648
So, the scores for about 68% of the males fell between 418 and 648.

Assume a normal distribution for each situation.

1. A survey of 16-year-olds showed that they watched an average (mean) of 9.4 hours of TV per week, with a standard deviation of 1.2 hours. Determine how many hours of TV were watched by about:

a. 68% of the participants. _between 8.2 and 10.6 hours_

b. 95% of the participants. _between 7 and 11.8 hours_

2. On a certain standardized test, the mean score was 50 and the standard deviation 3. About what percent of the participants scored:

a. between 50 and 56? _47.5%_

b. 44 and 47? _13.5%_

PROBLEM SOLVING 9-4

Problem Solving
9-4 *Variability*

Write the correct answer.

1. Find the median of the data.
14.5 points

2. Find the first and third quartiles of the data.
$Q_1 = 10, Q_3 = 23$

3. Make a box-and-whisker plot of the data.

```
0   10   20   30   40
```

| Super Bowl Point Differences | |
Year	Point Difference
2001	27
2000	7
1999	15
1998	7
1997	14
1996	10
1995	23
1994	17
1993	35
1992	13

The box-and-whisker plots compare the highest recorded Fahrenheit temperatures on the seven continents with the lowest recorded temperatures. Choose the letter for the best answer.

4. Which statement is true?
A The median of the high temperatures is less than the median of the low temperatures.
B The range of low temperatures is greater than the range of high temperatures.
C The range of the middle half of the data is greater for the high temperatures.
D The median of the high temperatures is 49°F.

5. What is the median of the high temperatures?
F 128°F   H −67°F
G 120°F   J −90°F

6. What is the range of the low temperatures?
A 77°F   C 120°F
B 79°F   D 129°F

Technology LAB 9-4

Create Box-and-Whisker Plots

Use with Lesson 9-4

The data below are the heights in inches of the 15 girls in Mrs. Lopez's 8th-grade class.

57, 62, 68, 52, 53, 56, 58, 56, 57, 50, 56, 59, 50, 63, 52

go.hrw.com
Lab Resources Online
KEYWORD: MT7 Lab9

Activity

Graph the heights of the 15 girls in Mrs. Lopez's class on a box-and-whisker plot.

Press **STAT** **Edit** to enter the values into List 1 (**L1**). If necessary, press the up arrow and then **CLEAR** **ENTER** to clear old data. Enter the data from the class into **L1**. Press **ENTER** after each value.

Use the **STAT PLOT** editor to obtain the plot setup menu.

Press **2nd** **Y=** **ENTER**. Use the arrow keys and **ENTER** to select **On** and then the fifth type. **Xlist** should be **L1** and **Freq** should be 1, as shown. Press **ZOOM** **9:ZoomStat**.

Use the **TRACE** key and the ◄ and ► keys to see all five summary statistical values (minimum: **MinX**, first quartile: **Q1**, median: **MED**, third quartile: **Q3**, and maximum: **MaxX**). The minimum value in the data set is 50 in., the first quartile is 52 in., the median is 56 in., the third quartile is 59 in., and the maximum is 68 in.

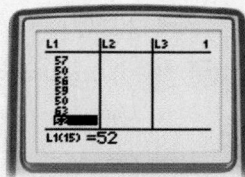

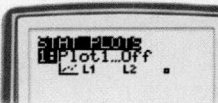

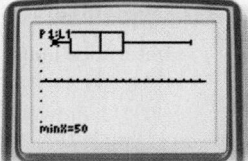

Think and Discuss

1. Explain how the box-and-whisker plot gives information that is hard to see by just looking at the numbers.

Try This

1. The data below shows the number of hours slept one night for ach of the 11 boys from Mrs. Lopez's 8th-grade class.

7.5, 6.5, 5, 6, 8, 7.25, 6.5, 7, 7, 8, 6.75

Make a box-and-whisker plot of this data. What are the minimum, first quartile, median, third quartile, and maximum values of the data set?

minimum: 5;
first quartile: 6.5;
median: 7;
third quartile: 7.5;
maximum: 8

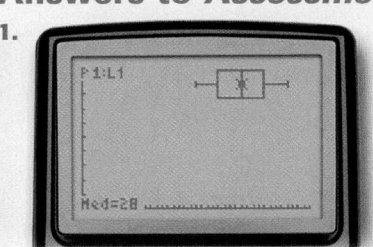
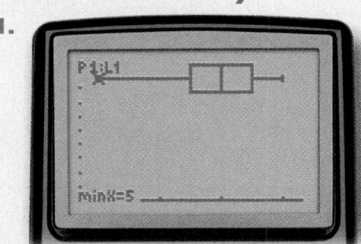

Quiz for Lessons 9-1 Through 9-4

☑ **9-1** **Samples and Surveys**

Identify the sampling method used.

1. Every third student is called from a class roster. **systematic**
2. Fifty customers are chosen by chance from five random grocery stores. **stratified**

Identify the population and sample. Give a reason the sample could be biased.

3. A restaurant owner asks Friday's customers to choose a favorite salsa.
4. A DVD rental manager asks people who rent dramas what their favorite movie is.

☑ **9-2** **Organizing Data**

5. Use a line plot to organize the data of the ages of people playing bridge.

72	78	76	75	79	70	74	80	72	78
71	69	70	72	68	70	69	75	75	74

6. Use the given data to make a back-to-back stem-and-leaf plot.

Greatest Number of Home Runs by a Player, 2000–2004					
	2000	**2001**	**2002**	**2003**	**2004**
American League	47	52	57	47	43
National League	50	73	49	47	48

7. Make a Venn diagram to show how many 2-year-old, male cats were adopted.

Gender	F	M	M	F	M	M	M	F	F	M
Age (y)	1	1	2	3	1	1	2	3	2	2

☑ **9-3** **Measures of Central Tendency**

Determine and find the most appropriate measure of central tendency or range for each situation.

range; 4.9 min

8. The finishing times in minutes for a 5-kilometer run by a group of friends were 21.1, 20.6, 19.7, 20.3, 17.7, and 22.6. What was the spread of the times?

9. The week's average high temperatures in degrees Fahrenheit were 70, 72, 72, 74, 76, 75, and 74. What number best describes the temperatures? **mean; ≈ 73.3°F**

☑ **9-4** **Variability**

Use the given data to make a box-and-whisker plot.

10. 43, 36, 25, 22, 34, 40, 18, 32, 43   11. 21, 51, 36, 38, 45, 52, 28, 16, 41

READY TO GO ON?
Diagnose and Prescribe

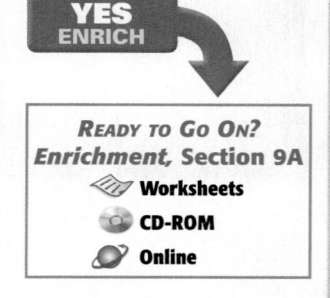

NO
INTERVENE

	READY TO GO ON? Intervention, Section 9A		
Ready to Go On? Intervention	📖 **Worksheets**	⦿ **CD-ROM**	🪐 **Online**
☑ Lesson 9-1	9-1 Intervention	Activity 9-1	
☑ Lesson 9-2	9-2 Intervention	Activity 9-2	Diagnose and Prescribe Online
☑ Lesson 9-3	9-3 Intervention	Activity 9-3	
☑ Lesson 9-4	9-4 Intervention	Activity 9-4	

YES
ENRICH

READY TO GO ON?
Enrichment, Section 9A

📖 **Worksheets**
⦿ **CD-ROM**
🪐 **Online**

Focus on Problem Solving

Make a Plan

• **Identify too much/too little information**

When you read a problem, you must decide if the problem has too much or too little information. If the problem has too much information, you must decide what information to use to solve the problem. If the problem has too little information, then you should determine what additional information you need to solve the problem.

Read the problems below and decide if there is too much or too little information in each problem. If there is too much information, tell what information you would use to solve the problem. If there is too little information, tell what additional information you would need to solve the problem.

1. On Monday, 20 students took an exam. There were 10 students who scored above 85 and 10 students who scored below 85. What was the average score?

2. The average elevation in California is about 2900 ft above sea level. The highest point, Mt. Whitney, has an elevation of 14,494 ft above sea level. The lowest point, Death Valley, has an elevation of 282 ft below sea level. What is the range of elevations in California?

3. Use the table to find the median number of marriages per year in the United States for the years between 1940 and 2000.

4. Aishya is cross-training for a marathon. She ran for 50 minutes on Monday, 70 minutes on Wednesday, and 45 minutes on Friday. On Tuesday and Thursday, she lifted weights at the gym for 45 minutes each day. She swam for 45 minutes over the weekend. What was the average amount of time per day Aishya spent running last week?

Number of Marriages in the United States							
Year	1940	1950	1960	1970	1980	1990	2000
Number (thousands)	1596	1667	1523	2159	2390	2443	2329

Source: National Center for Health Statistics

Answers
1. too little information
2. 14,776 ft
3. too little information
4. 23.6 min/day

Focus on Problem Solving

Organizer

Objective: Focus on identifying too much or too little information.

PREMIER **Online Edition**

Resources

Chapter 9 Resource Book
Reading Strategies

Problem Solving Process

This page focuses on the second step of the problem-solving process:
Make a Plan

Discuss

Have students identify whether the problem gives too little, too much, or just the right amount of information. Then ask them to explain what information is needed.

Possible answers:

1. too little information; need to know each individual score

2. too much information; use the lowest elevation and the highest elevation

3. too little information; need the number of marriages each year from 1941 to 1989

4. too much information; use the number of minutes spent running each day

State Resources

go.hrw.com
State Resources Online
KEYWORD: MT7 Resources

One-Minute Section Planner

Lesson	Materials	MiC and Lab Resources
9-5 Hands-On Lab Make a Circle Graph • Use a compass, ruler, protractor, and paper to make circle graphs. **Lesson 9-5** Displaying Data • Display data in bar graphs, histograms, and line graphs. **9-5 Technology Lab** Create Histograms • Use a graphing calculator to make a histogram. ☐ SAT-10　☐ ITBS　☐ CTBS　☑ NAEP	Compasses (MK), rulers (MK), protractors (MK), social studies books, graphing calculators	**MiC: *Insights Into Data*** pp. 14–15, 23–28, 32–36 **MiC: *Great Predictions*** pp. 24–29 **MiC: *Ups and Downs*** pp. 4–9 ***Hands-On Lab Activities*** 9-5 ***Technology Lab Activities*** 9-5
Lesson 9-6 Misleading Graphs and Statistics • Recognize misleading graphs and statistics. ☑ SAT-10　☐ ITBS　☑ CTBS　☑ NAEP	Newspapers and magazines	**MiC: *Insights Into Data*** pp. 22–29
Lesson 9-7 Scatter Plots • Create and interpret scatter plots. **9-7 Technology Lab** Create a Scatter Plot • Use a graphing calculator to make a scatter plot. ☑ SAT-10　☑ ITBS　☐ CTBS　☑ NAEP	Science books, graphing calculators	**MiC: *Insights Into Data*** pp. 3–5, 44–49, 53–60 ***Hands-On Lab Activities*** 9-7 ***Technology Lab Activities*** 9-7
Lesson 9-8 Choosing the Best Representation of Data • Select the best representation for a set of data. **9-8 Technology Lab** Use a Spreadsheet to Create Graphs • Use a spreadsheet to make circle graphs, line graphs, and bar graphs. ☑ SAT-10　☐ ITBS　☑ CTBS　☑ NAEP	Spreadsheet software	**MiC: *Insights Into Data*** All sections ***Hands-On Lab Activities*** 9-8 ***Technology Lab Activities*** 9-8

MK = *Manipulatives Kit*

Mathematics in Context

The units ***Insights Into Data, Great Predictions,*** and ***Ups and Downs*** from the *Mathematics in Context* © 2006 series can be used with Section 9B. See Section Planner above for suggestions for integrating *MiC* with *Holt Mathematics*.

Section Overview

Types of Graphs, Misleading Graphs and Statistics

Lessons 9-5, 9-6

 To analyze and interpret data, it is useful to have various types of graphs for displaying the data. Some graphs and some statements about data are misleading. Students should learn to recognize misleading graphs and statements.

Types of Graphs

Misleading Graphs and Statistics

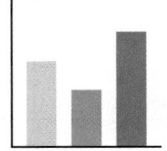 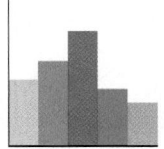 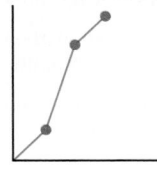 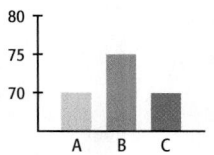

Bar Graph

For data that can be grouped in categories

Histogram

For data that can be grouped in intervals

Line Graph

To show trends or to make estimates

Example

The vertical scale does not begin at zero.

Example

"According to a recent survey, two out of three people preferred our brand over brand *x*."

The survey may have included only a few people.

Scatter Plots, Correlations, Lines of Best Fit

Lesson 9-7

 A scatter plot is one of the best ways to show a correlation between two sets of data. A correlation is a description of a relationship. A line of best fit through a scatter plot is useful for making predictions.

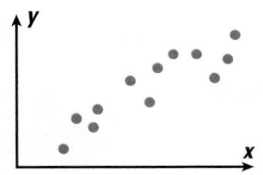  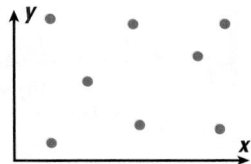 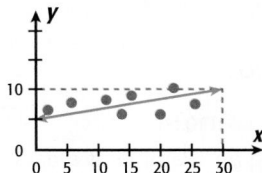

Positive correlation; both data sets increase together.

Negative correlation; as one data set increases, the other decreases.

No correlation; changes in one data set do not affect the other data set.

Predict the value of *y* when *x* = 30. (Using a line of best fit, you can predict that when *x* = 30, *y* will be approximately 10.)

Choosing the Best Representation of Data

Lesson 9-8

 Choosing an appropriate data display depends on the purpose and the data.

	You can use a **bar graph** to display and compare data.		You can use a **line graph** to show how data change over a period of time.
	You can use a **line plot** to show the frequency of values.		You can use a **Venn diagram** to show relationships between two or more data sets.
	You can use a **circle graph** to show how a set of data is divided into parts.	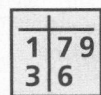	You can use a **stem-and-leaf plot** to show how often data values occur and how they are distributed.

Hands-On LAB 9-5
Make a Circle Graph

Use with Lesson 9-5

go.hrw.com
Lab Resources Online
KEYWORD: MT7 Lab9

WHAT YOU NEED:	REMEMBER
• Compass • Protractor	• A circle measures 360°.
• Ruler • Paper	• Percent compares a number to 100.

Activity

Skunks are legal pets in some states but not in most. Use the information from the table to make a circle graph showing the percents for each category.

a. Use a compass to draw a large circle. Use a ruler to draw a vertical radius.

b. Extend the table to show the percent of states with each category of legality.

c. Use the percents to determine the angle measure of each sector of the graph.

d. Use a protractor to draw each angle clockwise from the radius.

e. Label the graph and each sector. Color the sectors.

Skunks as Pets by State

Legality	Number of States
Legal (no restrictions)	6
Legal with permit	12
Legal in some areas	2
Illegal	27
Other conditions	3

Legality	Number of States	Percent of States	Angle of Section
Legal (no restrictions)	6	$\frac{6}{50} = 12\%$	$\frac{12}{100} \cdot 360 = 43.2°$
Legal with permit	12	$\frac{12}{50} = 24\%$	$\frac{24}{100} \cdot 360 = 86.4°$
Legal in some areas	2	$\frac{2}{50} = 4\%$	$\frac{4}{100} \cdot 360 = 14.4°$
Illegal	27	$\frac{27}{50} = 54\%$	$\frac{54}{100} \cdot 360 = 194.4°$
Other conditions	3	$\frac{3}{50} = 6\%$	$\frac{6}{100} \cdot 360 = 21.6°$

Think and Discuss

1. How many states would need to legalize skunks for the largest sector to be 180°? **2**

Try This

1. Make a circle graph to show only the states where skunks are not illegal.

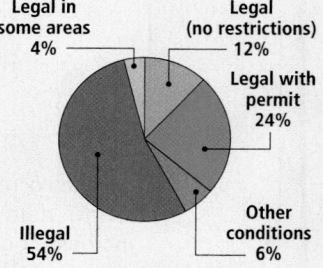

Teacher to Teacher

I use a budgeting project to help students learn about fractions, decimals, and percents. The students are divided into pairs and I distribute job descriptions with monthly incomes, family sizes, and monthly expense lists. The students have to calculate how much (what fraction, decimal, and percent) of their income is used for each expense (mortgage, food, gas & electric, telephone, car payment, car insurance, clothes, savings, entertainment, etc.). Then I have students create a circle graph to display their findings. In some cases, the students find that they do not make enough to cover all expenses, so they must decide which expenses in their budget can be reduced.

Kimberly Johnson-Green
Baltimore, Maryland

Displaying Data

Learn to display data in bar graphs, histograms, and line graphs.

Vocabulary
double-bar graph
frequency table
histogram
double-line graph

In 1990, the United States qualified for the soccer World Cup for the first time in 40 years. Since then, popularity in youth soccer in the United States has grown tremendously.

A **double-bar graph** is used to display and compare two sets of data. You can organize data using a **frequency table** by listing items according to the number of times that the items occur.

Pacing: Traditional 1 day
Block $\frac{1}{2}$ day

Objective: Students display data in bar graphs, histograms, and line graphs.

 Hands-On Lab
In *Hands-On Lab Activities*

 Online Edition
Tutorial Videos

 Countdown to Testing Week 20

EXAMPLE 1 Displaying Data in a Double-Bar Graph

Make a double-bar graph.

The following are the ages when a randomly chosen soccer group of 20 boys and 20 girls began playing in a local youth soccer league.

Age	4	5	6	7	8
Boys	5	10	3	2	0
Girls	2	11	5	1	1

The frequencies are the heights of the bars in the bar graph. Use a different color to represent each gender.

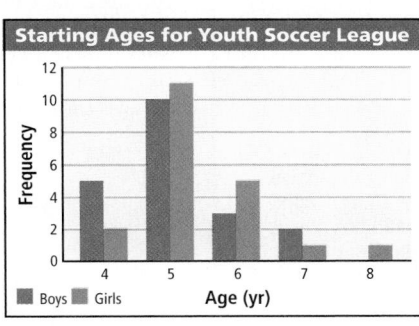

A **histogram** is a bar graph that shows the frequency of data within equal intervals.

Power Presentations
with PowerPoint®

Warm Up
Write each fraction as a decimal.
1. $\frac{2}{5}$ 0.4   2. $\frac{49}{50}$ 0.98
3. $\frac{3}{50}$ 0.06   4. $\frac{7}{10}$ 0.7

Problem of the Day
Your job at the local library is to shelve the returned books. To correctly put the books on the shelves, you need to arrange them in order according to their numbers. Which order is correct?

A. 342.3, 342.5, 342.48, 342.52
B. 342.21, 342.47, 342.4, 342.59
C. 342.1, 342.17, 342.56, 342.76
D. 342.34, 342.43, 342.567, 342.56   C

Also available on transparency

1 Introduce

Alternate Opener

EXPLORATION

9-5 Displaying Data

The bar graph shows the results of a survey about students' lunch beverage preferences.

1. Do at least half the students prefer sports drink? Why?

Students' Beverage Preferences
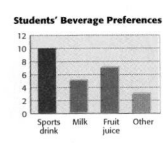

The histogram shows the results of a survey about the amount of time in hours per week that adults spend on the Internet.

2. Did at least half say they spend 20 hours or less? How do you know?

Time Spent on the Internet
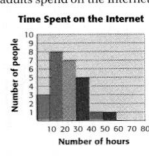

Think and Discuss
3. **Compare** the types of data displayed by the bar graph with the types of data displayed by the histogram.

Motivate

Ask students whether they are familiar with graphs. Ask students to give some examples of where they have seen graphs (e.g., newspapers, magazines, and science or social studies textbooks). Discuss the benefits of presenting information in a graph. You may want to ask students to name some types of graphs (e.g., bar graphs, line graphs, histograms, or circle graphs).

Explorations and answers are provided in *Alternate Openers: Explorations Transparencies.*

State Resources

go.hrw.com
State Resources Online
KEYWORD: MT7 Resources

Additional Examples

Example 1

Make a double-bar graph.

The following are the number of books read in one month by some boys and girls in Grade 8.

Books read	0	1	2	3	4	5
Boys	2	3	3	1	0	1
Girls	2	1	2	4	1	0

See p. A13.

Example 2

Jimmy asked 12 children how much money they received from the tooth fairy. Use the data to make a histogram.

0.35 2.00 0.75 2.50 1.50 3.00 0.25
1.00 1.00 3.50 0.50 3.00

See p. A13.

Example 3

Make a double-line graph of the given data. Use the graph to esti-mate the number of CDs and DVDs sold in 2003.

The Music Shop CD and DVD Sales

Year	CDs sold	DVDs sold
1998	3002	735
2000	3098	1057
2002	4685	3010
2004	5804	4047

See p. A13.

Also available on transparency

EXAMPLE 2 Displaying Data in a Histogram

Edwina asked 10 classmates how many minutes of sleep they had the previous night. Use the data to make a histogram.

460 400 425 440 490 365 435 500 380 505

Make a frequency table with 30-minute intervals. Then make a histogram.

Helpful Hint

Histograms do not have spaces between the bars.

Minutes	Frequency
360–389	2
390–419	1
420–449	3
450–479	1
480–509	3

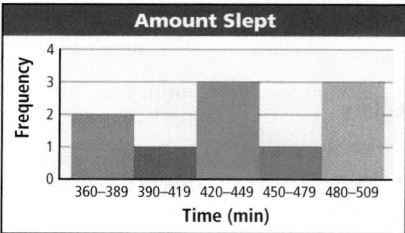

A **double-line graph** is used to show how two related sets of data change over time.

EXAMPLE 3 Displaying Data in a Line Graph

Make a double-line graph of the given data. Use the graph to estimate the number of measles cases and whooping cough cases in 2002.

Plot the data. The graph shows about 200,000 whooping cough cases and about 650,000 measles cases in 2002.

Number of Worldwide Cases		
Year	Measles	Whooping Cough
1992	1,481,971	255,475
1996	870,989	141,445
2000	836,407	186,198
2004	504,742	235,740

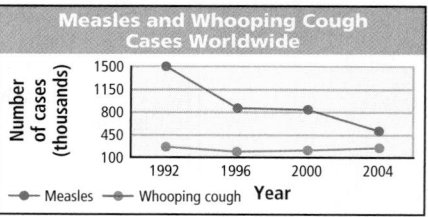

1. Possible answer: In a bar graph, each bar shows the frequency of data items in a specific category. In a histogram, each bar shows the frequency of data items within a range of values.

Think and Discuss

1. Describe the difference between a bar graph and a histogram.

---

2 Teach

Guided Instruction

In this lesson, students learn to display data in bar graphs, histograms, and line graphs. Point out that graphs allow you to visually compare data with ease. Review the examples with students. Discuss the similarities and differences among the types of graphs. Some important points are that each bar in a histogram represents an interval and that line graphs are a good way to show changes over time.

Teaching Tip **Modeling** Remind students that in any given histogram, all intervals must be equal.

Reaching All Learners
Through Multiple Representations

Social Studies Have students look through their social studies book to find a table of values. The table could involve data such as population or precipitation rates. Ask students to work in pairs to create a bar or line graph to show the data. Then have the students explain their graphs to the class.

3 Close

Summarize

Create a table on the board to compare and contrast the three types of graphs studied in the lesson. Ask students to complete the table by listing characteristics for each type of graph.

Possible answers:

Bar graph: Data are grouped; data are displayed in separate bars.

Histogram: Data are grouped into equal intervals; there are no spaces between data bars; it is a type of bar graph.

Line graph: Specific data points are represented; trends are shown; points are drawn directly on vertical lines extending up from the horizontal axis.

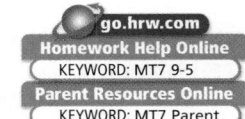

9-5 **Exercises**

GUIDED PRACTICE

See Example ① 1. Make a double-bar graph.
Data Set 1: 11 10 13 11 12 13 13 9 10 11 12 10
Data Set 2: 13 11 12 12 11 9 10 11 12 10 9 11

See Example ② 2. The Freshman National Merit Scholars and their schools are listed for
2004. Use the data to make a histogram with intervals of 50.

3. male:
approximately
73.5 yr;
female:
approximately
79.5 yr

Vanderbilt, 144; Princeton, 192; Duke, 90; Stanford, 217; Yale, 224;
Northwestern, 152; Rice University, 173; Cal Tech, 51; University of
Chicago, 198; M.I.T., 134; University of Texas-Austin, 242; Washington
University, 197

See Example ③ 3. Make a double-line graph
of the given data. Use the
graph to estimate the life
expectancies of a male and
a female born in 1997.

Life Expectancy by Birth Year (U.S.)					
Year	1980	1985	1990	1995	2000
Age Male	70.0	71.1	71.8	72.5	74.3
Age Female	77.4	78.2	78.8	78.9	79.7

Source: National Center for Health Statistics

INDEPENDENT PRACTICE

See Example ① 4. Make a double-bar graph.

Temperature °F	10	15	20	25	30	35	40
Data Set 1	2	6	9	7	4	2	1
Data Set 2	5	7	8	5	4	2	0

See Example ② 5. Restaurants sometimes organize their menus by the number of items in
each price range. Use the entrée prices to make a histogram with intervals
of $10.
$9 $11 $22 $22 $30 $24 $13 $16 $17 $21 $18 $25 $17 $25
$17 $21 $19 $21 $14 $19 $15 $15 $10 $16 $12 $21 $19 $17

See Example ③ 6. Make a double-line graph of the given data. Use the graph to estimate the
populations of Philadelphia and San Francisco in 1995.

6. Philadelphia:
approximately
1,550,000;
San Francisco:
approximately
750,000

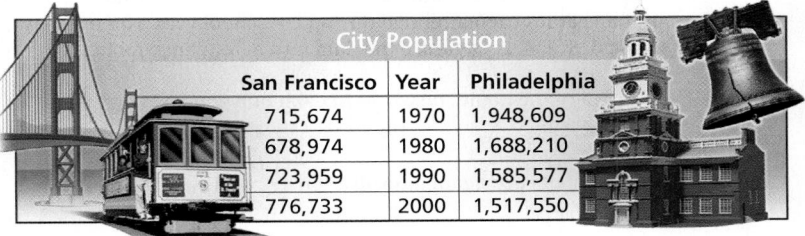

City Population		
San Francisco	**Year**	**Philadelphia**
715,674	1970	1,948,609
678,974	1980	1,688,210
723,959	1990	1,585,577
776,733	2000	1,517,550

Assignment Guide

If you finished Example ① assign:
Average 1, 4, 7, 12–19
Advanced 4, 7, 12–19

If you finished Example ② assign:
Average 1, 2, 4, 5, 7, 8, 12–19
Advanced 4, 5, 7–9, 11–19

If you finished Example ③ assign:
Average 1–8, 12–19
Advanced 4–19

Homework Quick Check
Quickly check key concepts.
Exercises: 4, 5, 6

Answers
1–6. See pp. A13–A14.

Math Background

A graph may be described as a diagram
that shows relationships among
numbers. Graphing is invaluable to the
study of mathematics as it allows
people to visualize trends, patterns,
similarities, and differences.

These concepts will be further explored
through graphing linear equations and
inequalities (Chapter 12) and graphing
functions (Chapter 13). Teachers should
take this opportunity to make sure
students understand the basic concepts
of graphing.

RETEACH 9-5

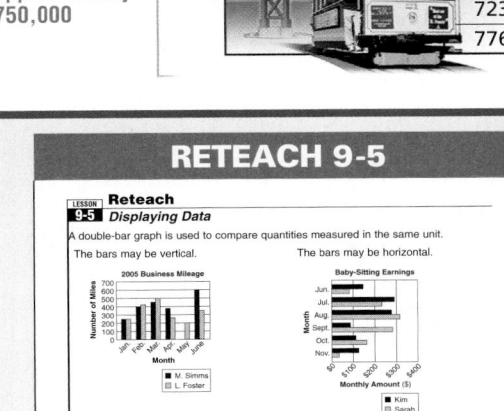

PRACTICE 9-5

LESSON 9-5 Practice B
Displaying Data

1. Make a double-bar graph.

2. Use the data to make a histogram
with intervals of 5.

3. Make a double-line graph of the given data. Use the graph to estimate
the number of radio stations and cable TV systems in 2002.

State Resources

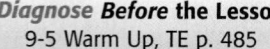
Answers

7–10. See p. A14.

TEST PREP DOCTOR + For Exercise 12, students may want to review the most appropriate uses for bar graphs, frequency tables, line graphs, and stem-and-leaf plots.

Journal

Have students write examples of when it would be appropriate to use a bar graph, a histogram, and a line graph.

Power Presentations
with PowerPoint®

9-5 Lesson Quiz

1. Make a histogram with intervals of 5 using the following data set:
7, 12, 8, 4, 4, 3, 6, 1, 14, 19, 8, 9
See p. A14.

2. Estimate the temperature on January 6 in 2004 and 2005 using the graph below.

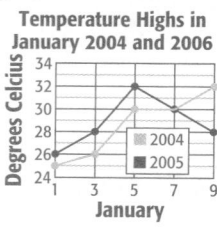

2005: 31°F; 2004: 30°F

Use the graph for problems 3–4.

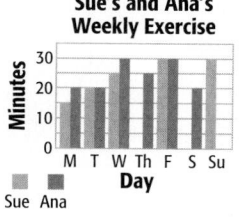

3. On what day did both girls exercise for 30 minutes? Friday

4. On what day(s) did Ana exercise longer than Sue? Monday, Wednesday, Thursday, and Saturday

Also available on transparency

PRACTICE AND PROBLEM SOLVING

Extra Practice
See page 799.

7. Organize the data into a frequency table and make a double-bar graph.
Data set 1: 1 6 3 1 4 6 4 5 6 1 2 5 5 4 2 3 1 6 2 2
Data set 2: 3 1 3 4 2 1 5 6 1 2 6 5 1 6 4 3 3 2 1 5

8. Make a histogram of honey yield per colony with intervals of 4.

Honey-Producing Colonies						
Year	1999	2000	2001	2002	2003	2004
Yield per Colony (pounds)	76.3	83.9	74.0	67.8	70.0	71.8

Source: USDA

9. **Write a Problem** You are given the heights of the players on a soccer team. Determine the number of four different-size jerseys to order. Write a problem using a histogram that would help you find this information.

10. **Write About It** Which kind of graph would you use to compare the average salaries of professional basketball players and professional hockey players from 1995 to 2005?

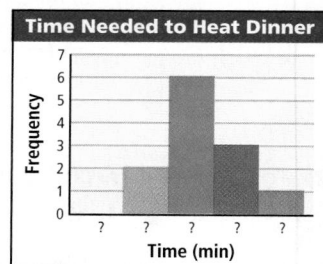

11. **Challenge** Determine the size of the interval used in the histogram using the data below. **every 2 min**

Time needed to heat a frozen dinner in the microwave (min)
4:30 5:30 7:00 4:45 5:20 8:00
3:45 2:30 6:40 6:00 4:30 5:25

13.
Number of games	1	2	3	4	5
Frequency	1	3	2	4	2

TEST PREP and Spiral Review

12. **Multiple Choice** Which data display is most appropriate to show the change in sales over a four-month period?

Ⓐ Bar graph   Ⓑ Frequency table   Ⓒ Line graph   Ⓓ Stem-and-leaf plot

13. **Short Response** A middle school principal asked 12 students the number of football games each attended during the school year. The results were 1, 3, 5, 2, 4, 4, 4, 3, 5, 2, 4, 2. Organize the data into a frequency table.

Find the sum of the angle measures in each polygon. (Lesson 7-4)
14. 18-gon **2,880**   15. 24-gon **3,960**   16. heptagon **900**

Find the range of each set of data. (Lesson 9-4)
17. 16, 32, 1, 54, 30, 28 **53**   18. 105, 969, 350, 87, 410 **882**   19. 0.2, 0.8, 0.65, 0.7, 1.6, 1.1 **1.4**

CHALLENGE 9-5

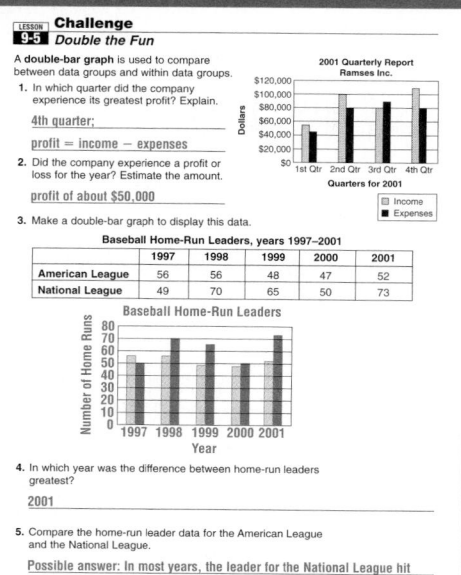

PROBLEM SOLVING 9-5

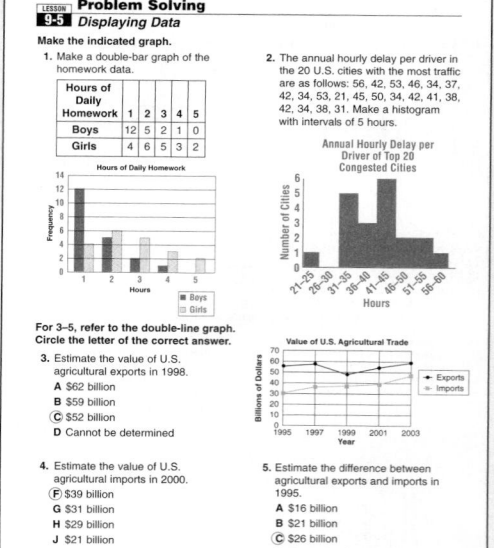

Technology LAB 9-5

Create Histograms

Use with Lesson 9-5

You can use a graphing calculator to make a histogram.

go.hrw.com
Lab Resources Online
KEYWORD: MT7 Lab9

Activity

The frequency table shows the length of the feet of students in Mrs. Alvarez's math class. Use a graphing calculator to make a histogram of the data.

Foot Length (in.)	Number of Students
Less than 5	0
5 to less than 6	1
6 to less than 7	4
7 to less than 8	11
8 to less than 9	7
9 to less than 10	4
10 or greater	1

To enter the data, press [STAT].
Then press [ENTER] to select 1:Edit.

Under L1, enter 1, 2, 3, 4, 5, 6, and 7 to represent the seven intervals. Interval 1 corresponds to "Less than 5," while interval 7 corresponds to "10 or greater."

In L2, enter the number of students for each interval.

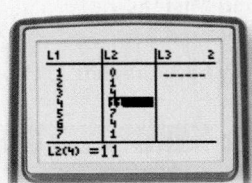

To see a histogram of the data, press [2nd] [Y=] [ENTER] to select "STAT PLOTS 1:"

Scroll and press [ENTER] to select "On" and the histogram icon.
Then scroll to "Freq:" and press [2nd] 2 to paste the data from L2. Press [ZOOM] 9 to view the histogram. Press [TRACE] and the arrow keys to read the histogram.

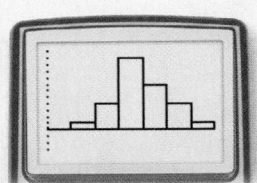

Think and Discuss

1. How would the histogram change if the first interval is left out? Draw the histogram.

2. Explain how you can use the histogram to find the total number of students who have feet that are at least 7 inches long.

Try This

1. Measure the lengths of the right arms of everyone in your classroom. Divide the data into 5 equal intervals. Use a graphing calculator to make a histogram of the data.

Answers to *Think and Discuss*

1. It would look the same.

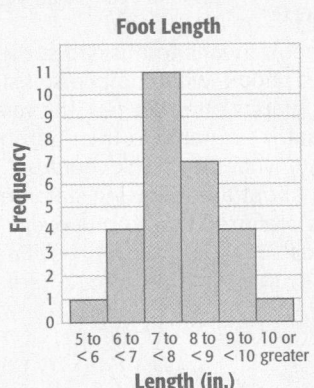

Foot Length

2. Add up the frequency of foot lengths for 7 to less than 8 in., 8 to less than 9 in., 9 to less than 10 in., and 10 in. or greater.

Answers to *Try This*

1. Check students' work.

9-6 Organizer

Pacing: Traditional 1 day
Block $\frac{1}{2}$ day

Objective: Students recognize misleading graphs and statistics.

 Online Edition
Tutorial Videos

 Countdown to Testing Week 20

 **Power Presentations**
with PowerPoint®

Warm Up

Use the graph for problems 1–3.

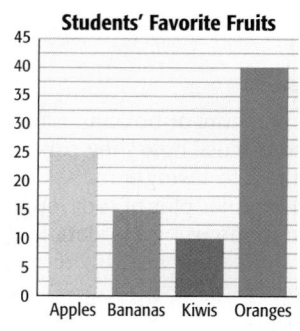

Students' Favorite Fruits

1. How many students like oranges?
   40

2. Which is the least-liked fruit? Kiwi

3. How many students answered the survey? 90

Problem of the Day

Create a data set with five values that will have a mean of 20, a median of 18, and a mode of 15.
Possible answer: 15, 15, 18, 19, 33

Also available on transparency

State Resources

go.hrw.com
State Resources Online
KEYWORD: MT7 Resources

9-6 Misleading Graphs and Statistics

Learn to recognize misleading graphs and statistics.

Graphs and statistics are often used to make advertisements visually appealing. Some advertisements, however, use art to mislead consumers.

EXAMPLE 1 Identifying Misleading Graphs

Explain why each graph is misleading.

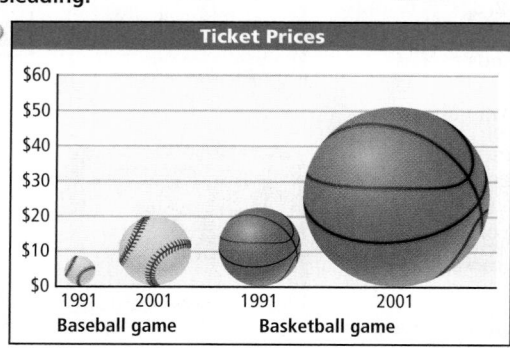

A The heights of the balls are used to represent the ticket prices. However, the areas of the circles and volumes of the balls distort the comparison. The basketball prices are only about $2\frac{1}{2}$ times greater than the baseball prices, but they look like much more.

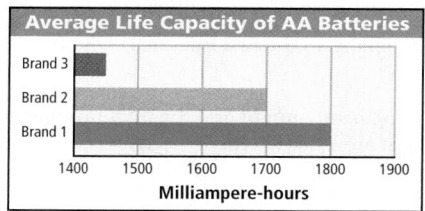

B Since the horizontal scale does not start at 0, the bar for Brand 1 appears to be four times as long as the bar for Brand 3. In fact, the capacity of Brand 1 is only 20% more than Brand 3.

1 Introduce

Alternate Opener

EXPLORATION

9-6 Misleading Graphs and Statistics

The bar graph shows the percent of flavored water drinkers in a survey who prefer each brand of flavored water.

Flavored Water Preference

1. According to the survey, which brand is preferred the most?
2. How would the graph look if the percent scale started at 0% instead of 30%?
3. Why might someone want to display a graph like this?

Think and Discuss

4. **Explain** how the graph's appearance can be misleading.
5. **Discuss** situations that might be likely to involve misleading graphs or statistics.

Motivate

Discuss what it means to mislead someone. Explain that people who compile statistics and create graphs often present the results in a way that is favorable to their purpose. Ask students what they think could be misleading about the following statement: "Brand A is preferred two to one over other brands!" Sample size not specified; perhaps only three people were asked.

ENGLISH LANGUAGE LEARNERS

Explorations and answers are provided in *Alternate Openers: Explorations Transparencies*.

Explain why the graph is misleading.

 **C**

Registered Vehicles

= 9 million cars

= 9 million light trucks

= 9 million heavy trucks

Different-sized icons represent the same number of vehicles. The number of light trucks looks like it is close to the number of cars, but it is really less than half. The number of heavy trucks is less than 5% of the total, but it appears much greater.

EXAMPLE 2 Identifying Misleading Statistics

Explain why each statistic is misleading.

A A housing development features 5 home models with the starting prices of $475,000, $500,000, $225,000, $480,000, and $510,000. The developer places an ad that reads:
"New homes—average price $438,000"

Although $438,000 is the average price, only one model sells below that price. It is likely that a new home owner will pay more than the advertised price of $438,000.

B A movie previews for 12 selected viewers. Eight viewers rate the movie highly. The producer tells the production studio:
"The movie will be a hit because test audiences rate the movie favorably at a rate of 2 to 1."

The sample size is too small. Twice as many people liked the movie, but the difference between 4 and 8 people is not meaningful.

C The revenue for Ski Resort A for November and December was $6,600,000. The revenue for Ski Resort B for January and February was $8,300,000.

The revenues are measured at different times of the year. Weather conditions can change dramatically from month to month, affecting revenue.

Possible answers to *Think and Discuss*

1. a graph starting at zero, but with part of the scale missing.

2. the sample may be randomly chosen, but the sample size may be too small to give a meaningful result.

Think and Discuss

1. **Give an example** of a graph that starts at zero but is still misleading.

2. **Explain** how a statistic can be accurate but still misleading.

Example 1

Explain why each graph is misleading.

A.

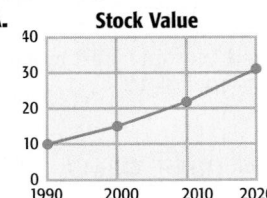

Stock Value

The graph suggests that the stock value will continue to increase through 2020, but there is no way to foresee the future.

B.

Food Donated

 = 100 cans   = 50 boxes   = 20 cases

The icons represent different quantities of food and are different sizes.

Example 2

Explain why each statistic is misleading. See p. A14.

A. Four out of five dentists surveyed preferred UltraClean toothpaste.

B. Shopping at Save-a-Lot can save you up to $100 a month!

C. Sam scored 43 goals for his soccer team during the season, and Jacob scored only 2.

Also available on transparency

2 Teach

Guided Instruction

In this lesson, students learn to recognize misleading graphs and statistics. Refer students to Example 1. Ask them why the graphs are misleading before they read the statements that accompany the graphs.

Allow students to work in pairs to complete Example 2. After reviewing why each statistic is misleading, ask them to rewrite the ad in Example 2A so that it is less misleading.

 Reaching All Learners
Through Critical Thinking

Work with students to find graphs and statistical statements in newspapers or magazines. Ask students to analyze the graphs and statements to decide if any of them seem to be misleading, and why. Ask students to suggest ways to present the information in ways that are more honest.

3 Close

Summarize

Work with students to create a list of ways that graphs or statistics can be misleading. Encourage them to suggest examples.

Possible answers: Symbols in graphs can be distorted in size or shape, or the scale of a graph might not begin at zero. A statistic might be misleading because of an outlier, a sample size for a survey might be too small, or comparison categories might not be equivalent.

9-6 Exercises

go.hrw.com
Homework Help Online
KEYWORD: MT7 9-6
Parent Resources Online
KEYWORD: MT7 Parent

Assignment Guide

If you finished Example **1** assign:
Average 1, 2, 5, 6, 9, 10, 13–17
Advanced 5, 6, 9–17

If you finished Example **2** assign:
Average 1–10, 13–17
Advanced 5–17

Homework Quick Check

Quickly check key concepts.
Exercises: 6, 8, 10

Answers

1–8. See p. A14.

Math Background

Companies and politicians often use statistics to support their own goals. Companies use surveys to make comparisons between their products and competitors' products. When making these comparisons, survey results are often presented as facts, although the details of the survey are usually not included.

In addition, interested parties will use statistics to imply a cause-and-effect relationship when there may not be one. For example, a politician may claim that the economy improved during his or her term when an improvement in the global economy may have actually been the cause.

State Resources

go.hrw.com
State Resources Online
KEYWORD: MT7 Resources

GUIDED PRACTICE

See Example **1** Explain why each graph is misleading.

1.
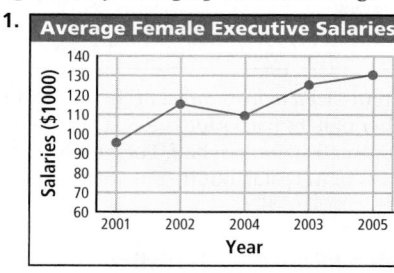

2.
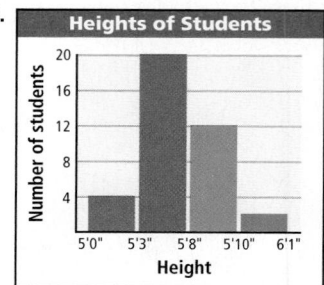

See Example **2** Explain why each statistic is misleading.

3. A stalk of broccoli has 477 mg of potassium. A large carrot has 230 mg of potassium. A small head of cauliflower has 803 mg of potassium.

4. The total number of life jackets sold by Water Sports World from April 1 to September 1 was 619. The total number of life jackets sold by Boats and More from July 1 to September 1 was 153.

INDEPENDENT PRACTICE

See Example **1** Explain why each graph is misleading.

5.
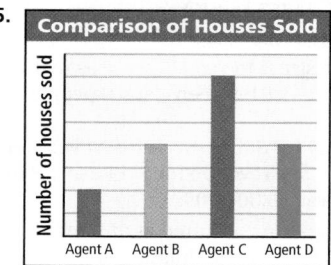

6.

See Example **2** Explain why each statistic is misleading.

7. A survey of 1000 college students found that 110 majored in engineering and 112 majored in the social sciences. A magazine article reports that students prefer the social sciences over engineering.

8. A reporter asked 90 students if they participate in organized athletics. Of the 50 who responded "yes," 26 played on school teams, 14 played in community leagues, and 10 competed in individual competitions. The reporter said, "Half of all students play on school teams."

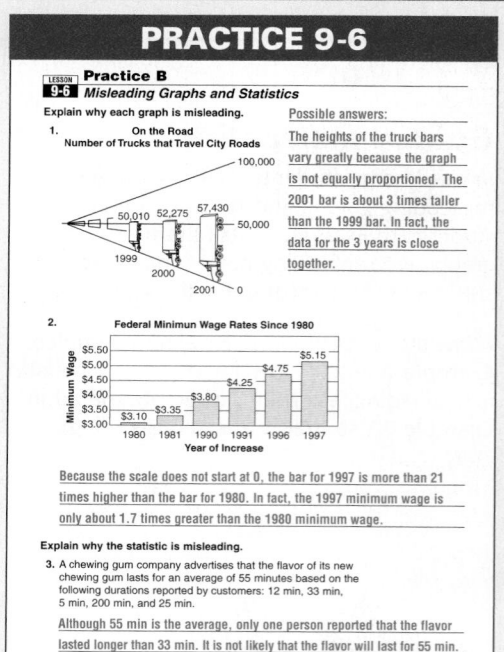

PRACTICE AND PROBLEM SOLVING

Extra Practice
See page 799.

Explain why each graph is misleading.

9.

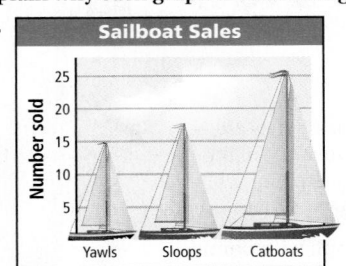

Sailboat Sales

10.

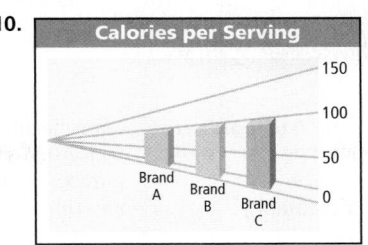

Calories per Serving

12.
Possible answer: Although both graphs show that the stock for company A is performing better than company B, Graph 2 makes it appear that company A is performing much better than company B.

11. Write About It When might you want to use a scale on a graph that does not start at 0? Possible answer: when your scale involves large numbers, such as annual salaries or a country's annual wheat production

12. Challenge The two graphs show the recent performance of two companies' stocks, A and B. Which graph should be shown to the stockholders of company A?

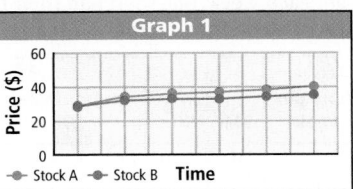

Graph 1

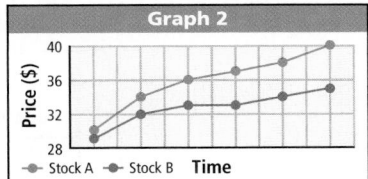

Graph 2

TEST PREP and Spiral Review

13. Multiple Choice Six dentists are surveyed regarding toothpaste. Four dentists recommended Brand X. An ad for Brand X states: "Recommended by 2 out of 3 dentists." Explain why the statement is misleading.

Ⓐ The sample was too large.

Ⓑ The sample was too small.

Ⓒ The sample should have included construction workers.

Ⓓ The statement should say "Recommended by 1 out of 2 dentists."

14. Short Response A salesman earns the following commissions: December $965; January $125; February $170; March $100; April $110; May $120. He tells his friends that he averages $265 per month in commission. Explain why the statistic is misleading. December sales inflated the average. He earned more than $200 during only one month.

Find the area of each figure with the given dimensions. (Lesson 8-2)

15. trapezoid: $b_1 = 3$, $b_2 = 5$, $h = 8$ 32 units^2

16. triangle: $b = 16$, $h = 9$ 72 units^2

17. People responding to a survey had the following ages: 30, 21, 20, 26, 23, 30, 23, 23, 21, 20, 27, 20, 24, 23, and 30. Use the data to make a line plot. (Lesson 9-2)

CHALLENGE 9-6

PROBLEM SOLVING 9-6

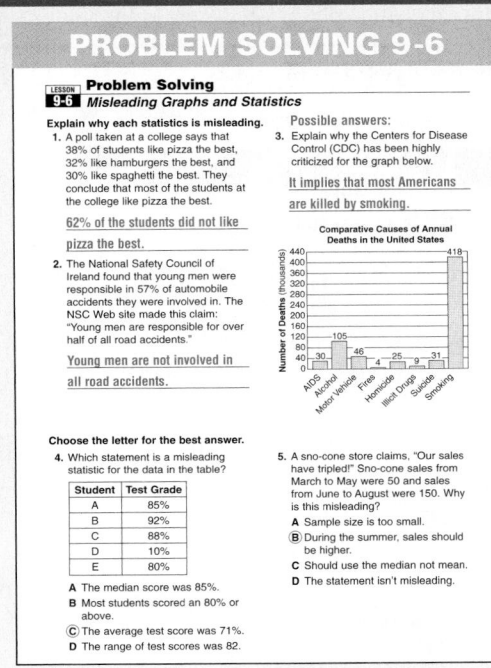

Answers

9. Possible answer: The areas of the sails distort the comparison.

10. Possible answer: The bars are different lengths but represent the same values.

17. See p. A14.

 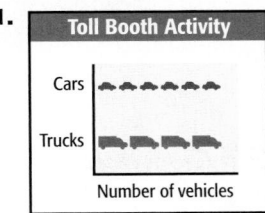
Journal

Have students write a paragraph about why someone might want to mislead the public using statistics or graphs.

9-6 Lesson Quiz

Explain why each graph or statistic is misleading.

1.

Toll Booth Activity

Cars

Trucks

Number of vehicles

The difference in size between the car and the truck symbols distorts the comparison.

2. A budget area of a used-car lot has five cars on it, with prices of $4200, $4700, $4900, $5200, and $900 (a wrecked one). The car ad in the local paper reads "Average priced car on budget lot is $3980."

A low outlier was included in order to bring down the average cost.

Also available on transparency

Hands-On Lab
In *Hands-On Lab Activities*

Technology Lab
In *Technology Lab Activities*

Online Edition
Tutorial Videos

Countdown to Testing Week 21

Power Presentations
with PowerPoint®

Warm Up

Graph each point on the same coordinate plane.

1. $A(5, 20)$ **2.** $B(20, 15)$
3. $C(10, 40)$ **4.** $D(30, 35)$

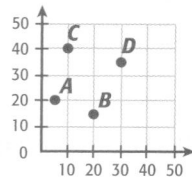

Problem of the Day

What is the least number that can be divided evenly by each of the numbers 1 through 12?   27,720

Also available on transparency

State Resources

go.hrw.com
State Resources Online
KEYWORD: MT7 Resources

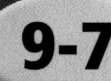

9-7 Scatter Plots

Learn to create and interpret scatter plots.

Vocabulary
scatter plot
correlation
line of best fit

Many health care professionals are concerned about the increase in the number of overweight children. Children are strongly encouraged to be more active.

A **scatter plot** is a graph with points plotted to show a relationship between two sets of data.

EXAMPLE 1   Making a Scatter Plot of a Data Set

A teacher surveyed her students about the amount of physical activity they get each week. She then had their body mass index (BMI) measured. Use her data to make a scatter plot.

Student	Active Hours per Week	BMI	Student	Active Hours per Week	BMI
A	10	16	F	8	18
B	3	25	G	7	21
C	6	24	H	2	28
D	8	20	I	19	9
E	10	16	J	14	12

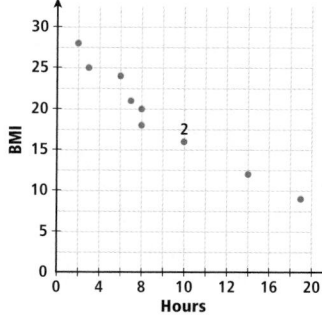

*The points on the scatter plot are (10, 16), (3, 25), (6, 24), (8, 20), (10, 16), (8, 18), (7, 21), (2, 28), (19, 9), and (14, 12). The **2** at (10, 16) indicates that the point occurs twice.*

Correlation describes the relationship between two data sets.
A **line of best fit** is a straight line that comes closest to the points on a scatter plot. One way to estimate a line of best fit is to lay a ruler's edge over the graph and adjust it until it looks closest to all the points.

---

1 Introduce
Alternate Opener

EXPLORATION

9-7 Scatter Plots

1. The table shows the numbers of pages in some paperback books and the books' prices. Plot the data on the graph provided.

Pages	Price ($)
300	2.25
200	1.75
130	1.65
450	3.00
180	1.75
75	1.25
250	2.50

2. The table shows the number of hours some people spent outside and spent watching TV in one day. Plot the data on the graph provided.

TV hours	Outside hours
2.0	1.5
0.5	3.5
1.5	1.5
1.0	2.5
2.5	0.5
1.5	2.0
2.0	0.5

Think and Discuss

3. **Explain** what the shape of a graph tells you about the data being displayed.

Motivate

Discuss cause and effect with the students. Ask them to provide examples of cause-and-effect relationships. Some possible examples follow: The more I practice baseball, the more hits I will get. The more I study, the higher my grades will be. Explain that the term *correlation* describes the relationship between two data sets, but point out that correlation is not the same thing as cause and effect.

Explorations and answers are provided in *Alternate Openers: Explorations Transparencies.*

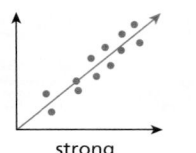 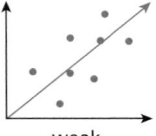 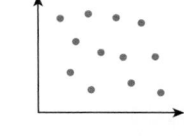 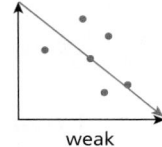 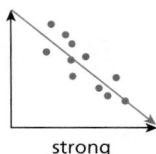

strong   weak   weak   strong

Positive correlation: both data sets increase together.

No correlation: changes in one data set do not affect the other data set.

Negative correlation: as one data set increases, the other decreases.

EXAMPLE 2 Identifying the Correlation of Data

Do the data sets have a positive, a negative, or no correlation?

A The number of hours a plane is in flight and the number of miles flown

Positive correlation: The longer a plane is in flight, the more miles it flies.

B The number of hours in flight and the number of passengers

No correlation: The number of hours in flight does not affect the number of passengers on the plane.

C The number of hours in flight and the gallons of fuel remaining

Negative correlation: The longer a plane is in flight, the less fuel it has.

> **Helpful Hint**
>
> A strong correlation does not mean there is a cause-and-effect relationship. For example, your age and the price of a regular movie ticket are both increasing, so they are positively correlated.

EXAMPLE 3 Using a Scatter Plot to Make Predictions

Use the data to predict the exam grade for a student who studies 10 hours per week.

Hours Studied	5	9	3	12	1
Exam Grade	80	95	75	98	70

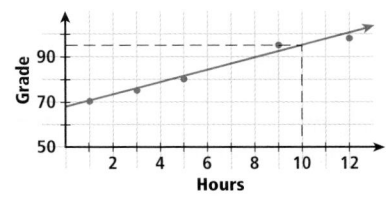

According to the graph, a student who studies 10 hours per week should earn a score of about 95.

Possible answers to
Think and Discuss

1. In a line graph, all of the points are connected. In a scatter plot, the points are not connected.

2. Answers will vary.

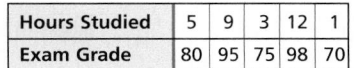

Think and Discuss

1. **Compare** a scatter plot to a line graph.

2. **Give an example** of each type of correlation.

Example 1

Use the given data to make a scatter plot of the weight and height of each member of a basketball team.

Height (in.)	71	68	70	73	74
Weight (lb)	170	160	175	180	190

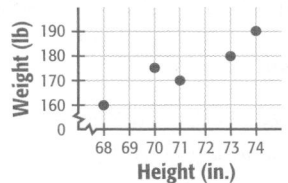

Example 2

Do the data sets have a positive, a negative, or no correlation?

A. the size of a jar of baby food and the number of jars a baby will eat
negative correlation

B. the speed of a runner and the number of races she wins
positive correlation

C. the size of a person and the number of fingers he has
no correlation

Example 3

Use the data to predict how much a worker will earn in tips in 10 hours.

Hours	4	8	3	2	11
Tips ($)	12	20	7	7	26

approximately $24

Also available on transparency

---

2 Teach

Guided Instruction

In this lesson, students learn to create and interpret scatter plots. Review the data in Example 1. Make certain that students understand that BMI is a number that shows weight adjusted for height. Explain that this study shows negative correlation. You may want to display the Teaching Transparency while you discuss correlation. Emphasize the difference between correlation and a cause-and-effect relationship. For example, a low BMI and the number of active hours per week may have a positive correlation, but it does not prove that activity alone lowers BMI.

Reaching All Learners
Through Curriculum Integration

Science Ask students to identify statements or ideas in their science books that represent the three types of correlations. Have them exchange statements and identify each other's statements as having positive, negative, or no correlation.

Possible answers: positive correlation: the size of an animal and its weight; no correlation: the size of an animal and the number of legs it has; negative correlation: the size of an animal and the number of offspring produced

3 Close

Summarize

Review the vocabulary words from the lesson. Then have students explain the differences among positive correlation, negative correlation, and no correlation. Ask students to give examples of each.

Possible answers: Positive means both data sets increase or decrease together (e.g., size of a soda bottle and its price). Negative means one increases and the other decreases (e.g., speed of a runner and the time it takes to run a lap). No correlation means there is no discernable pattern between the two (e.g., size of a soda bottle and its flavor).

9-7 Exercises

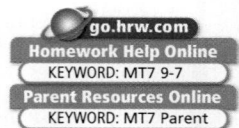

go.hrw.com
Homework Help Online
KEYWORD: MT7 9-7
Parent Resources Online
KEYWORD: MT7 Parent

Assignment Guide

If you finished Example ❶ assign:
Average 1, 5, 14–19
Advanced 5, 14–19

If you finished Example ❷ assign:
Average 1–3, 5–7, 11, 12, 14–19
Advanced 5–7, 9–19

If you finished Example ❸ assign:
Average 1–8, 11, 12, 14–19
Advanced 5–19

Homework Quick Check

Quickly check key concepts.
Exercises: 5, 6, 8, 12

Answers

1, 5. See p. A14.

Math Background

A scatter plot shows a relationship between two sets of data. As in the graph of a line, points are plotted using *x*- and *y*-coordinates. Unlike the graph of a line, the points are not automatically connected.

A line of best fit can be drawn through a scatter plot to show a linear trend in the data. If there is a positive correlation between the data sets, a line of best fit will have a positive slope. If there is a negative correlation between the data sets, a line of best fit will have a negative slope. If there is no correlation between the data sets, there is no line of best fit.

State Resources

go.hrw.com
State Resources Online
KEYWORD: MT7 Resources

GUIDED PRACTICE

See Example ① 1. Use the given data to make a scatter plot.

Country	Area (mi²)	Population
Guatemala	42,467	12,335,580
Honduras	43,715	5,997,327
El Salvador	8,206	5,839,079
Nicaragua	50,503	4,717,132
Costa Rica	19,929	3,674,490
Panama	30,498	2,778,526

See Example ② **Do the data sets have a positive, a negative, or no correlation?**

2. The square footage of a house in a given neighborhood and its price **positive**

3. The age of a house and the number of people living in the house **no correlation**

See Example ③ 4. Use the data to predict the wind chill at 35 mi/h. **approximately −6.7°F**

Apparent Temperature Due to Wind at 15°F						
Wind speed (mi/h)	10	20	30	40	50	60
Wind Chill (°F)	2.7	−2.3	−5.5	−7.9	−9.8	−11.4

INDEPENDENT PRACTICE

See Example ① 5. Use the given data to make a scatter plot.

Car Brand	Cost ($1000)	Fuel Economy (mi/gal)
A	25	19
B	19	31
C	34	15
D	28	23
E	22	33

See Example ② **Do the data sets have a positive, a negative, or no correlation?**

6. The number of weeks a CD has been out and weekly sales **negative**

7. The number of weeks a CD has been out and total sales **positive**

See Example ③ 8. Use the data to predict the apparent temperature at 70% humidity. **73°F**

Temperature Due to Humidity at a Room Temperature of 72°F						
Humidity (%)	0	20	40	60	80	100
Apparent Temperature (°F)	64	67	70	72	74	76

RETEACH 9-7

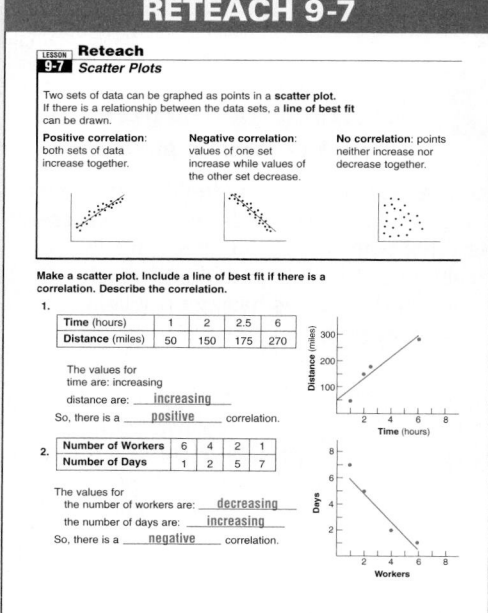

PRACTICE 9-7

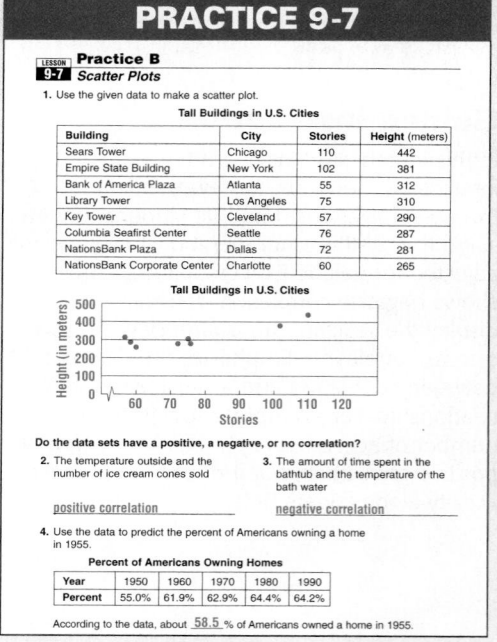

About 50 million Americans suffer from allergies. Airborne pollen generated by trees, grasses, plants, and weeds is a major cause of illness and disability. Because pollen grains are small and light, they can travel through the air for hundreds of miles. Pollen levels are measured in grains per cubic meter.

Some common substances that cause allergies include pollens, dust mites, and mold spores.

9. Use the given data to make a scatter plot. Describe the correlation.

Pollen Levels

Day	Weed Pollen	Grass Pollen
1	350	16
2	51	1
3	49	9
4	309	3
5	488	29
6	30	3
7	65	12

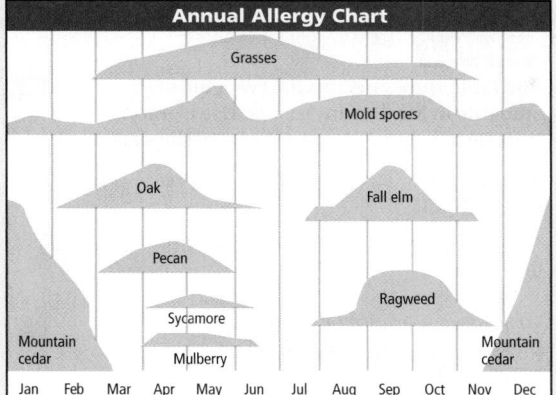

Annual Allergy Chart

Source: Central Texas Allergy and Asthma Center

10. Explain how the pollens are compared in the chart at right.

Use the chart at right to determine if the pollens have a positive, a negative, or no correlation.

11. mountain cedar, grass negative

12. fall elm, ragweed positive

13. ⭐ **Challenge** Use the allergy chart to explain the difference between correlation and a cause-and-effect relationship.

 **go.hrw.com**
Web Extra!
KEYWORD: MT7 Pollen

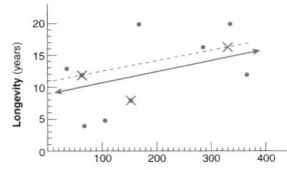

TEST PREP and Spiral Review

14. **Multiple Choice** Does the size of a box of cereal and the price of the cereal have a positive, negative, or no correlation?

Ⓐ Positive   Ⓑ Negative   Ⓒ Scatterplot   Ⓓ No

15. **Short Response** What type of correlation exists between a person's birthday and his or her height? Explain. no correlation; there are people of all heights and there are birthdays on each day of the year

Determine the number of lines of symmetry for each polygon. (Lesson 7-8)

16. square 4   17. equilateral triangle 3   18. regular pentagon 5

19. A bookstore sells 2 copies of *Sail Away* and 4 copies of *Race Car Mania*. The bookstore owner concludes that his customers are twice as likely to buy racing books than sailing books. Identify why this statistic is misleading. (Lesson 9-6)
The sample size is too small.

CHALLENGE 9-7

LESSON 9-7 Challenge
This Fits Nicely!

When two sets of data show a correlation, you can draw a **line of best fit** that approximates a trend.

Here are some data relating the gestation periods of selected animals to their average life spans. The data are separated into 3 equal sets.

	Set I			Set II			Set III		
Gestation (days)	31	61	68	105	151	167	285	330	365
Longevity (years)	13	12	4	5	8	20	15	20	12

1. Determine the **median-median point** for each set of points by getting the median value for the gestation values and the median value for the longevity values.

The median-median point for
Set I is: (61, 12)   Set II is: (151, 8)   Set III is: (330, 15)

2. Make a scatter plot for the given data. Describe the correlation. positive

3. Using an X for each, plot the three median-median points on your graph.
Using a ruler, draw a dotted line through the median-median points for Sets I and III. See graph
Keeping the ruler at the level of the dotted line, estimate the vertical distance between the dotted line and the median-median point for Set II. Then slide the ruler down about one-third this distance. Draw a solid line parallel to the dotted line. This solid line is called the median-median line and it is a line of best fit for the given data. See graph

---

PROBLEM SOLVING 9-7

LESSON 9-7 Problem Solving
Scatter Plots

Use the data given at the right.
1. Make a scatter plot of the data.

Percent of Americans Who Have Completed High School

Year	Percent
1910	13.5
1920	16.4
1930	19.1
1940	24.5
1950	34.3
1960	41.1
1970	55.2
1980	68.6
1990	77.6
1999	83.4

2. Does the data show a positive, negative or no correlation?
Positive

3. Use the scatter plot to predict the percent of Americans who will complete high school in 2010.
About 90%

Choose the letter for the best answer.

4. Which data sets have a positive correlation?
A The length of the lines at amusement park rides and the number of rides you can ride in a day
B The temperature on a summer day and the number of visitors at a swimming pool
C The square miles of a state and the population of the state in the 2000 census
D The length of time spent studying and doing homework and the length of time spent doing other activities

5. Which data sets have a negative correlation?
F The number of visitors at an amusement park and the length of the lines for the rides
G The amount of speed over the speed limit when you get a speeding ticket and the amount of the fine for speeding
H The temperature and the number of people wearing coats
J The distance you live from school and the amount of time it takes to get to school

---

Answers
9–10, 13. See p. A14.

TEST PREP DOCTOR ➕ For Exercise 14, students may find it helpful to consider whether it is generally a better buy to purchase cereal in a larger box than in a smaller box. Also, answer **C** can be eliminated because "scatterplot" is not a choice mentioned in the question.

✏️ Journal

Have students consider the question "Will more people or fewer people buy an item if the price goes up?" Have them explain the relationship and describe the correlation.

Power Presentations
with PowerPoint®

9-7 Lesson Quiz

1. Use the given data to make a scatter plot.

Grading Period	1	2	3	4
Number of A's	5	6	8	10

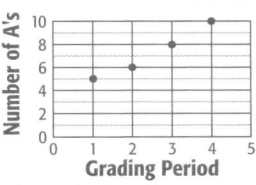

Do the data sets have a positive, a negative, or no correlation?

2. the minimum wage and the year positive

3. amount of precipitation and the day of the week no correlation

4. the number of germs on your hands and the number of times you wash your hands in a day negative

Also available on transparency

Technology LAB 9-7 Create a Scatter Plot

Use with Lesson 9-7

Georgia Performance Standards
M8D4.a, M8D4.b, M8P1.c, M8P1.d

go.hrw.com
Lab Resources Online
KEYWORD: MT7 Lab9

You can use a graphing calculator to make a scatter plot.

Activity 1

The table shows heights and weights of students in Mr. Devany's class. Use a graphing calculator to create a scatter plot of the data.

To enter the data, press STAT ENTER to select "1:Edit"

In L1, enter the heights. In L2, enter the weights.

To see a scatter plot of the data, press 2nd Y= ENTER to select "STAT PLOTS 1:"

Scroll and press ENTER to select "On" and the scatter plot icon. Scroll to "Xlist=" and press 2nd 1.

Scroll to "Ylist=" and press 2nd 2. Finally, scroll to "Mark:" and choose the box.

To view the scatter plot, press ZOOM 9. Press TRACE and the arrow keys to read the histogram.

Height (in.)	Weight (lb)
41	92
43	111
46	105
50	120
51	110
55	107
60	125
62	125
62	125
66	152
69	175
70	210

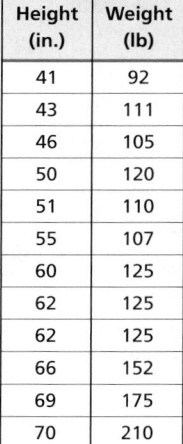
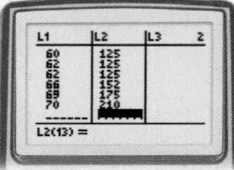
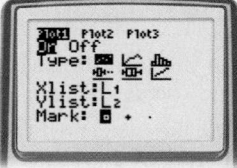
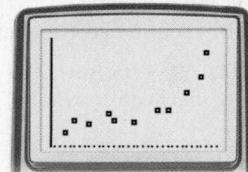

2. Possible answer: The heights and weights of boys could be displayed in one color, and the heights and weights of girls could be displayed in another color.

Think and Discuss

1. Explain what happens when you change the window to [0, 100] by [0, 500]. The data points become more spread out.

2. Suppose you added a third category: boy or girl. How could the height, weight, and gender data be displayed?

Try This

Use a graphing calculator to create a scatter plot of the data.

1.

x	41	43	46	50	51	55	60	62	66	69	70
y	92	111	105	120	110	107	125	142	152	175	210

Activity 1

Answers to *Try This*

1.

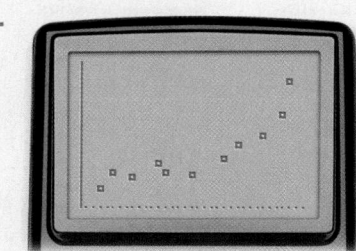

Activity 2

You can use a graphing calculator to find a line of best fit on a scatter plot.

Create a scatter plot of the data shown. Use a line of best fit to predict the value of *y* when *x* = 11.

Follow the steps in Activity 1 to make a scatter plot of the data.

x	y
2	26.1
4	21.5
6	17.4
8	13.2
10	11.7
12	8.5
14	4.2
16	1.9

To find a line of best fit, press **STAT** ▶ 4 to choose "LinReg(ax+b)."

Press **2nd** 1 **,** **2nd** 2 **,** **VARS** ▶ **ENTER** **ENTER** **ENTER** .

Your calculator will display the *y*-intercept and slope of the line of best fit.

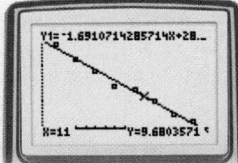

Press **ZOOM** 9 to see the scatter plot and the line of best fit.

You can press **Y=** to see an equation of the line.

To find *y* when *x* = 11, press **2nd** **TRACE** **ENTER** 11 **ENTER** . The screen shows that *y* = 9.68 when *x* = 11.

Think and Discuss

1. What uses might a line of best fit have in the real world?

2. What type of correlation does the data have in Activity 2? How do you know?

Try This

Collect at least 6 pieces of string with different lengths. Measure the length of each piece of string and record the values in L1. Form a square with each piece of string. Measure the length of one side of each square and record the values in L2. Make a scatter plot of the data and find the line of best fit.

1. What should the slope be? (*Hint:* What is the relationship between the perimeter of a square and the length of one side?) $\frac{1}{4}$

2. What is the slope of the line of best fit you found on your calculator? **Check students' work.**

3. Explain why the slope of your line might not match the slope you predicted.

Activity 2

Answers to Think and Discuss

1. Possible answer: A line of best fit can be used to make predictions of future behavior.

2. a negative correlation; The line slants downward from left to right.

Answers to Try This

3. Possible answer: Errors in measurement of the string length and side length of the squares could make the slope of the line of best fit different from the predicted slope.

Pacing: Traditional 1 day
　　　　Block $\frac{1}{2}$ day

Objective: Students will select
the best representation for a set
of data.

Hands-On Lab
In *Hands-On Lab Activities*

Technology Lab
In *Technology Lab Activities*

Online Edition
Tutorial Videos

Countdown to
Testing Week 21

Power Presentations
with PowerPoint®

Warm Up

Solve.

1. $6n - 10 = 44$　　$n = 9$
2. $27 = 3 - 8n$　　$n = -3$
3. $41 + 7x = -8$　　$n = -7$
4. $14 = -6n - 16$　　$n = -5$

Problem of the Day

A data set has a range of 24 and
a mean of 104. If the data set
contains three numbers and the
highest number is 118, then what
are the other two numbers in the
data set? 94 and 100

Also available on transparency

State Resources

go.hrw.com
State Resources Online
KEYWORD: MT7 Resources

Learn to select the best
representation for a set
of data.

In a survey, students were asked, "About
how many hours a year do you volunteer?"
The responses are shown in the table.

Hours Spent Volunteering	
Fewer than 20	15%
20–39	35%
40–59	13%
60–79	7%
80 or more	30%

Data can be represented in several different ways, depending both on
the type of data and the message to be conveyed.

Type of Graph	Common Use
Line graph	Shows change in data over time.
Bar graph	Shows relationships or comparisons between groups.
Circle graph	Compares parts to a whole.
Histogram	Shows the frequency of data divided into equal groups.
Box-and-whisker plot	Shows the distribution and spread of data.
Line plot	Shows the distribution of data.
Scatter plot	Shows the relationship of two data sets.

EXAMPLE **Selecting a Data Display**

A Which graph is a better display of the data on students
volunteering?

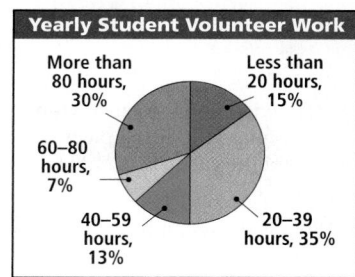
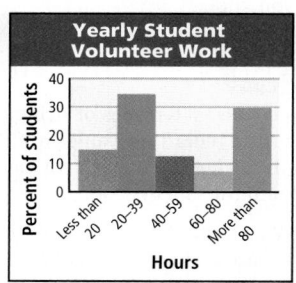

The data shows how groups of people who responded to the survey
compare to the whole. The circle graph is the better representation.

---

1 **Introduce**
Alternate Opener

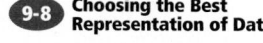
Motivate

Take a class survey to determine how many
students have a cat, a dog, a bird, a fish, or
another pet. Discuss that there are different
ways to display data, such as bar graphs,
line graphs, circle graphs, histograms, scatter
plots, box-and-whisker plots, stem-and-leaf
plots, and line plots. Ask students which type
of representation they would use for the
survey data. Possible answer: bar graph

Explorations and answers are provided in
Alternate Openers: Explorations Transparencies.

B Which graph shows the distribution of test scores better?

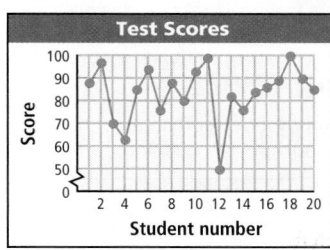

Test Scores

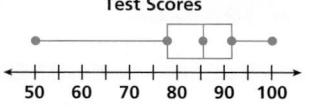

Since the question asks about the distribution of the data, the box-and-whisker plot is the better representation.

EXAMPLE ② **PROBLEM SOLVING APPLICATION**

José spent a week camping and hiking. The data of each hike is recorded in the table. Choose an appropriate data display. Draw the graph. About how long would it have taken José to hike 12 km?

Time (h)	1	1.5	2	3	4.5	6	7
Distance (km)	3.2	4.8	8	10.5	11.2	13.7	15.6

 Understand the Problem

You are looking for the best data display and the estimated time for a 12 km hike.

 Make a Plan

You need to find the relationship between time and distance. Since the data can be written as ordered pairs, plot them in a scatter plot.

3 Solve

Plot the data points on the scatter plot. To estimate the time needed for a 12 km hike, draw the line of best fit. Then find t when $d = 12$. The line of best fit indicates that a 12 km hike would take about 5 hours.

4 Look Back

Look at the table. An 11.2 km hike took 5.5 h and a 13.7 km hike took 6 h, so 5 h for a 12 km hike is reasonable.

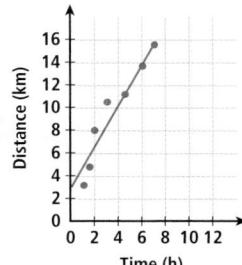

Possible answers to *Think and Discuss*

1. data taken from two or more groups that you want to compare.

2. the height of a child from birth to 5 years old.

Think and Discuss

1. **Describe** the kind of data that is best represented by a bar graph.

2. **Give** a situation in which you would use a line graph to display data.

Additional Examples

Example ①

A. Which graph is a better display of the data on temperature? line graph

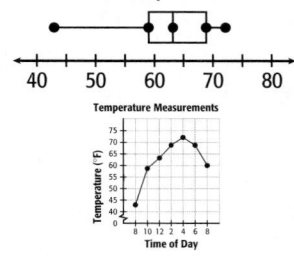

B. Which graph better shows the relationship between the two data sets? scatter plot

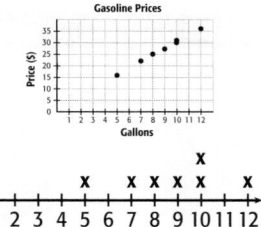

Example ②

The Singer family keeps the budget shown below for their monthly expenses. Choose an appropriate data display and draw the graph. Which two categories account for one-fifth of their budget?

Groceries	$400
Utilities	$330
Mortgage	$850
Clothing	$200
Entertainment	$100
Auto	$500
Savings	$500
Misc.	$120

See p. A14.

Also available on transparency

---

2 Teach

Guided Instruction

In this lesson, students learn to select the best representation for a set of data. Review different types of representations and their characteristics. Discuss which types of graphs are most appropriate for the data in Example 1. Then ask students to look at the data in Example 2. Since there are two sets of data, time needed and distance, discuss how a scatter plot would be the best type of representation for solving the problem.

Reaching All Learners
Through Cooperative Learning

Have small groups look through newspapers and magazines to find three examples of line graphs, bar graphs, circle graphs, scatter plots, line plots, and histograms. Have each group discuss why each display is appropriate to represent the particular data.

3 Close

Summarize

Review characteristics of the five types of data displays in the lesson: the line graph, the bar graph, the circle graph, the box-and-whisker plot, and the scatter plot. Also review the characteristics of the histogram and the line plot. Ask students to give examples of situations that could be represented by each type of display.

go.hrw.com
Homework Help Online
KEYWORD: MT7 9-8
Parent Resources Online
KEYWORD: MT7 Parent

Assignment Guide

If you finished Example **1** assign:
Average 1, 3, 14–18
Advanced 3, 12, 14–18

If you finished Example **2** assign:
Average 1–10, 14–18
Advanced 3–18

Homework Quick Check

Quickly check key concepts.
Exercises: 3, 4, 8, 10

Answers

2.

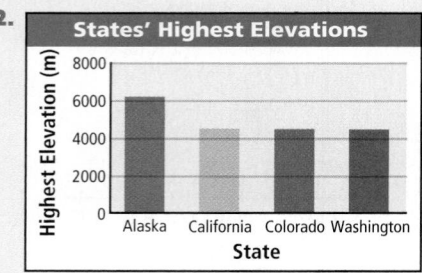

States' Highest Elevations

4.

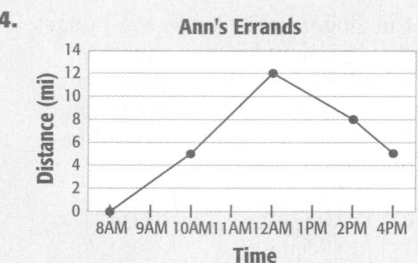

Ann's Errands

5. A line graph would be best because it shows changes over time.

6. A bar graph would be best because it shows the relationships between groups.

7–8. See p. A14.

GUIDED PRACTICE

See Example **1**
1. Which graph is a better display of the numbers of students participating in high school sports? **the bar graph**

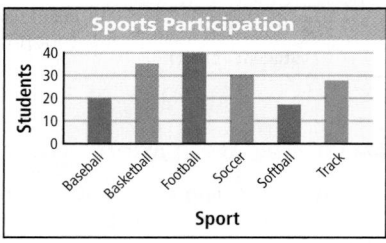
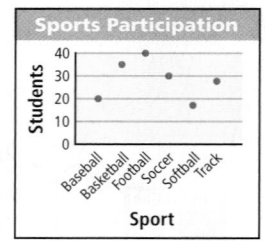

See Example **2**
2. The highest elevations for several states are listed in the table. Choose an appropriate data display and draw the graph. Which of the states shown in the graph has the third highest elevation? **Colorado**

State	Highest Elevation
Alaska	6194 m
California	4421 m
Colorado	4399 m
Washington	4392 m

INDEPENDENT PRACTICE

See Example **1**
3. Which graph is a better display of the percent of times a coin comes up heads and tails in 80 tosses? **the circle graph**

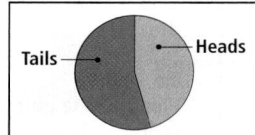
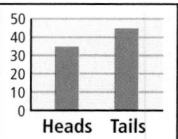

See Example **2**
4. Ann spent the day shopping and running errands. The table shows her distance from home at various times during the day. Choose an appropriate data display and draw the graph. Approximately how far was Ann from home at 11:00 AM? **8.5 mi**

Time	Distance (mi)
8:00 AM	0
10:00 AM	5
12:00 noon	12
2:00 PM	8
4:00 PM	3

PRACTICE AND PROBLEM SOLVING

Extra Practice
See page 799.

Choose the best data display for each situation. Explain.

5. height of a child over time

6. class sizes at a middle school

7. amount of time spent on different tasks during a day

8. comparison of people's shoe sizes to their ages

RETEACH 9-8

PRACTICE 9-8

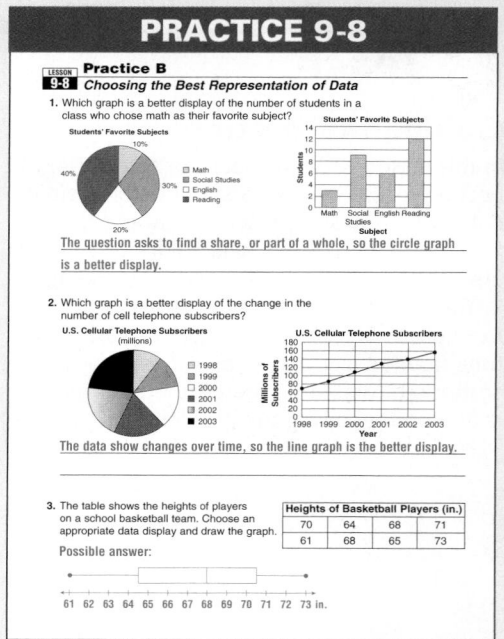

Sports

In 2003, 7000 athletes from 150 countries competed in the Special Olympics World Summer Games.

9. Fitness A survey of exercise habits was conducted. The ages of respondents and the number of minutes they reported exercising weekly are shown. Choose and construct a better display for the data.

Age	Time (min)
13	120
17	120
18	100
19	90
22	150
28	135
32	100
35	180
40	160

(bar graph: Time (min) vs Age (yr), ages 13, 17, 18, 19, 22, 28, 32, 35, 40)

10. Sports What kind of graph would best show the increase in the number of participants in the Special Olympics World Summer Games since it was founded in 1968? **line graph**

11. Write a Problem Write a survey question for which a circle graph would best represent the data. Then collect the data and make the circle graph. **Check students' work**

12. Write About It Explain how you would decide if a line graph or a scatter plot were a better representation of data.

13. Challenge An appliance store sells four brands of televisions. The table shows how many of each brand were sold last month. Which two kinds of graphs could be used to display this data? What message would each kind of graph give about the data?

Brand	Number Sold
A	120
B	130
C	100
D	95

TEST PREP and Spiral Review

14. Multiple Choice What type of display would you least likely construct from data of test scores for a class?

  Ⓐ circle graph   Ⓑ line graph   Ⓒ histogram   Ⓓ bar graph

15. Short Answer Find the mean, median, mode, and range of the data in the stem-and-leaf plot. If any of the measures cannot be found, give the reason.

```
0 | 1 4 9
1 | 3 3 4 7
2 | 1 2 2 2 3 3
```

Find the area of each circle. Round to the nearest tenth, if necessary. Use 3.14 for π. (Lesson 8-3)

16. circle with diameter 10 cm **78.5 cm²**   **17.** circle with radius 5.2 yd **84.9 yd²**

18. A 9 cm cube is built from 1 cm cubes. Compare the ratio of the length of an edge of the large cube to the length of an edge of a small cube. (Lesson 8-10) **9 to 1**

Answers

9, 12–13. See p. A14.

15. mean: ≈ 15.7; median: 17; mode: 22; range: 22

 **TEST PREP DOCTOR** Students may find it helpful to review the most appropriate uses for circle graphs, line graphs, histograms, and bar graphs when solving Exercise 14.

 Journal

Give students a graph from a current magazine or newspaper. Have them critique the graph by writing a short paragraph explaining if the graph was the best choice to represent the data, and why.

Power Presentations with PowerPoint®

9-8 Lesson Quiz ✓

1. Which is a better display of the number of miles ran by members of the track team during one week: a box-and-whisker plot or a scatter plot? box-and-whisker plot

2. The number of boys and girls enrolled in a middle school is shown in the table. Choose an appropriate display for this data and draw the graph. What percent of the students at the middle school are boys? 48.3%

Grade	Girls	Boys
6	140	117
7	133	145
8	130	115

See p. A14.

Also available on transparency

CHALLENGE 9-8

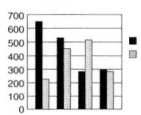

Challenge
9-8 What's Going On?

Invent a situation for the graph. Label the parts of the graph and describe the data it displays.

(coordinate graph)

Labels and answers will vary, but should describe two sets of data with a negative correlation.

(bar graph)

Labels and answers will vary, but should describe two series of data being compared.

(circle graph: 20%, 15%, 10%, 55%)

Labels and answers will vary, but should describe data set with four parts.

PROBLEM SOLVING 9-8

Problem Solving
9-8 Choosing the Best Representation of Data

Write what kind of graph would be best to display the described data.

1. Numbers of times that members of track team ran a mile in the following intervals: 4 min 31 s to 4 min 40 s, 4 min 41 s to 4 min 50 s, 4 min 51 s to 5 min, 5 min 1 s to 5 min 10 s

histogram

2. Distribution and range of students' scores on a history exam

stem-and-wisker-plot

3. Relationship between the amounts of time a student spent on her math homework and the numbers of homework problems she solved

scatter plot

4. Total numbers of victories of eight teams in an intramural volleyball league

bar graph

5. Part of calories in a meal that come from protein

circle graph

6. Numbers of books that a student reads each month over a year

line graph

Choose the letter for the best answer.

7. A bar graph is a good way to display
A data that changes over time.
B parts of a whole.
C distribution of data.
D comparison of different groups of data.

8. A circle graph is a good way to display
F range and distribution of data.
G distribution of data.
H parts of a whole.
J changes in data over time.

9. A scatter plot is a good way to display
A a comparison of different groups of data.
B distribution and range of data.
C the relationship between two sets of data.
D parts of a whole.

10. A box-and-whisker plot is a good way to display
F range and distribution of data.
G the relationship between two sets of data.
H data that changes over time.
J parts of a whole.

9-8 Choosing the Best Representation of Data   **503**

Use a Spreadsheet to Create Graphs

Use with Lesson 9-8

You can use a spreadsheet to make circle graphs, line graphs, and bar graphs. A spreadsheet allows you to model different situations easily.

Activity

1. Suppose a farmer has 22 pigs, 2 milk cows, 4 goats, 3 sheep, and 6 chickens. You can use a spreadsheet to make a circle graph of the data.

	A	B	C	D	E	F	G
1							
2		pig	cow	goat	sheep	chicken	
3		22	2	4	3	6	
4							

In row 2, enter the type of animal.

In row 3, enter the number of each type of animal.

Select the data by clicking in cell B2 and dragging over to cell F3.

Click the Chart Wizard icon in the top toolbar.

Click "Pie" under Chart Type in the Chart Wizard window. (*Pie chart* is another name for a circle graph.)

Click the top left circle graph under the Chart Sub-Type.

Click "Next" until the Finish button appears. Click "Finish."

Chart Wizard icon

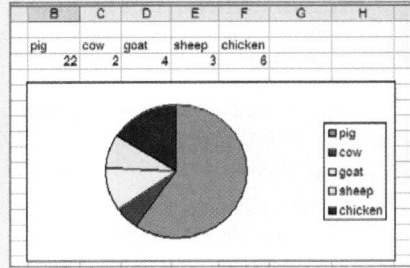

Now change the number of pigs to 12 and the number of goats to 11. Notice how the circle graph changes to reflect the new data.

2 Use the spreadsheet to draw a line graph of the data.

Right click on the graph and select "Chart Type . . ."

Click "Line" and make sure that the top left graph is selected.

Click "OK."

Now change the number of animals. Notice how the line graph changes to reflect the new data.

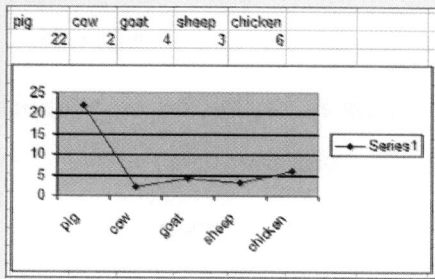

3 Use the spreadsheet to make a bar graph of the data.

Right click on the graph and select "Chart Type . . ."

Click "Column" and make sure that the top left graph is selected.

Click "OK."

Now change the number of animals. Notice how the line graph changes to reflect the new data.

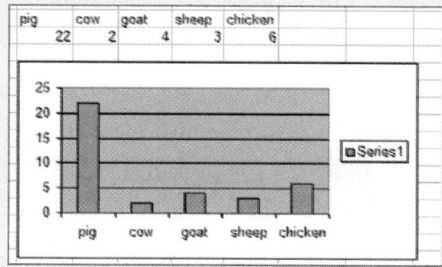

Think and Discuss

1. Compare the three types of graphs. When might you prefer using one type over the others? Which is the best representation of the animal data? Explain.

2. Explain the value of spreadsheets for modeling different situations.

3. Describe a situation when you would want to use a spreadsheet to make a circle graph.

Try This

1. Take a walk in your neighborhood and record the color of the first 30 cars you see. Use a spreadsheet to make a circle graph, a line graph, and a bar graph of your data. Which represents the data best? Explain. **Check students' work**

2. Now record the color of the next 30 cars you see. Modify your data from Try This 1. How did each graph change? **Check students' work**

Possible answers to *Think and Discuss*

1. A circle graph is best to compare percentages of a whole. A line graph is best to show how data change over time. A bar graph is best to compare data from different groups.

2. Spreadsheets allow you to create data displays quickly, without having to draw the displays yourself.

3. A spreadsheet could be used to keep track of the money you spend each week, then to create a circle graph to display how you spend your money in a way that's easy to understand.

Organizer

Objective: Assess students' mastery of concepts and skills in Lessons 9-5 through 9-8.

Resources

Assessment Resources
Section 9B Quiz

Test & Practice Generator
One-Stop Planner®

INTERVENTION ⬅➡

Resources

Ready to Go On?
Intervention and
Enrichment Worksheets

Ready to Go On? CD-ROM

Ready to Go On? Online

my.hrw.com

Answers

1–2, 6, 8. See p. A14.

Quiz for Lessons 9-5 Through 9-8

9-5 Displaying Data

1. Organize the data into a frequency table and make a double-bar graph.

   Data set 1: 3, 5, 4, 2, 5, 2, 3, 3, 6, 5, 3, 3, 4, 2, 1
   Data set 2: 2, 5, 4, 3, 2, 5, 4, 6, 3, 4, 3, 2, 2, 4, 5

Value	1	2	3	4	5	6
Data Set 1	1	3	5	2	3	1
Data Set 2	0	4	3	4	3	1

2. A fitness group calculated the average number of minutes they exercised each day. Use the data to make a histogram with intervals of 10.

   29 31 42 42 50 44 33 36 37 41 38 45 37 45
   37 41 39 41 34 39 35 35 30 36 32 41 39 37

   Possible answers:

   3. The icons represent different quantities of food.

   4. The graph has no scale, so it is impossible to compare the games.

9-6 Misleading Graphs and Statistics

Explain why each graph is misleading.

3.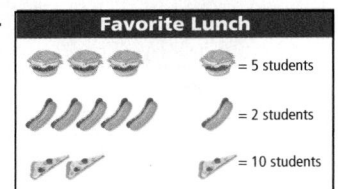
   Favorite Lunch
   = 5 students
   = 2 students
   = 10 students

4.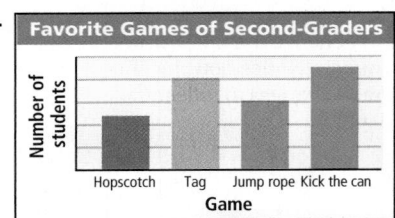
   Favorite Games of Second-Graders
   Number of students
   Hopscotch   Tag   Jump rope   Kick the can
   Game

5. A survey found 39% of students like tacos best, 32% like pizza best, and 29% like hamburgers best. The survey concludes that most students at the middle school like tacos the best. Explain why the statistic is misleading.
   Possible answer: students were only given 3 choices of food.

9-7 Scatter Plots

6. Use the given data of the estimated U.S. population to make a scatter plot.

Year	1998	1999	2000	2001	2002	2003	2004
Population (in millions)	270.2	272.7	282.2	285.1	287.9	290.8	293.7

Does the data set have a positive, a negative, or no correlation?

7. The number of miles on a used car and the price of the used car   negative

9-8 Choosing the Best Representation of Data

8. The eighth-grade chorus had 10 altos, 16 sopranos, 4 bass vocalists, and 10 tenors. Choose an appropriate data display and draw the graph. What percent of the chorus were the altos and tenors?

READY TO GO ON?

Diagnose and Prescribe

NO INTERVENE

Ready to Go On? Intervention	**Worksheets**	**CD-ROM**	**Online**
Lesson 9-5	9-5 Intervention	Activity 9-5	
Lesson 9-6	9-6 Intervention	Activity 9-6	Diagnose and Prescribe Online
Lesson 9-7	9-7 Intervention	Activity 9-7	
Lesson 9-8	9-8 Intervention	Activity 9-8	

READY TO GO ON? Intervention, Section 9B

YES ENRICH

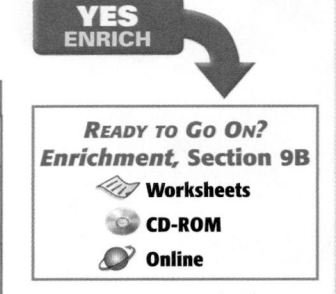
READY TO GO ON?
Enrichment, Section 9B
Worksheets
CD-ROM
Online

Bowled Over A group of middle school students forms a bowling club. The table shows the number of years each student has been bowling and the scores from the group's first trip to the bowling alley.

1. The club's president prepares a newsletter describing the "typical" student in the club. Choose a measure of central tendency to describe the typical number of years that the club members have been bowling. Choose a measure of central tendency to describe their typical score. Justify your choices.

2. Make a stem-and-leaf plot of the scores. What can you say about the scores based on the stem-and-leaf plot?

3. Brian is making a graph showing his score and those of his friends Jessica and Kendall. He wants to make it seem like his score was much greater than those of his friends. Show how he can make a misleading graph.

4. Make a scatter plot of the data.

5. A new student joins the club. She has been bowling for 5 years. Use your scatter plot to predict her score the next time the group goes bowling. **120**

Student	Years Bowling	Score
Jessica	3	90
Brian	3	100
Chandra	2	81
Roberto	7	128
Lee	1	84
Flora	3	92
Mike	4	102
Hisako	3	90
Isabel	6	135
Warren	1	65
Kendall	2	90
Mei	1	77

Multi-Step Test Prep

MULTI-STEP TEST PREP   CHAPTER 9

Organizer

Objective: Assess students' ability to apply concepts and skills in Chapter 9 in a real-world format.

 Online Edition

Resources

 Middle School Assessments
www.mathtekstoolkit.org

Problem	Text reference
1	Lesson 9-3
2	Lesson 9-2
3	Lesson 9-6
4	Lesson 9-7
5	Lesson 9-7

Answers

1. Possible answers: The mean, median, and mode are all 3; The median, 90, since there are high scores that may be outliers

2. Possible answer: Scores cluster around 90; the scores of 128 and 135 are outliers.

```
 6 | 5
 7 | 7
 8 | 1 4
 9 | 0 0 0 2
10 | 0 2
11 |            Key: 6|5 means 65
12 | 8
13 | 5
```

3–4. See p. A14.

State Resources

INTERVENTION

Scaffolding Questions

1. What are the measures of central tendency that can be used to describe data?
mean, median, mode, and range

2. Can you use a back-to-back stem-and-leaf plot to display this data? no Why or why not? A back-to-back stem-and-leaf plot is used to compare two sets of data. This question asks to display one data set, the bowling scores.

3. What are some things you can do to display data in a misleading manner?
Possible answer: You can use a break in the scale, change the scale, or begin the scale at a number other than zero.

4. What information should go along the x-axis? the number of years bowling

What information should go along the y-axis? the scores

5. What must you do to make a prediction from data displayed in a scatter plot?
Draw a line of best fit and extend it to include the data point you're interested in.

Extension

1. Which type of graph would you use if you wanted to show how Roberto's score changed with the number of years he bowled? a line graph

2. Describe the type of data from the bowling club that could be displayed in a circle graph. Possible answer: the number of hours that members bowled each week.

go.hrw.com
State Resources Online
KEYWORD: MT7 Resources

Organizer

Objective: Participate in games to practice and apply skills learned in Chapter 9.

 Online Edition

Resources

Chapter 9 Resource Book
Puzzles, Twisters & Teasers

Distribution of Primes

Purpose: To apply the skill of creating and interpreting scatter plots to the study of prime numbers

Discuss Ask students to explain how the sieve works. Possible answer: Start at 1. Circle 2, and then cross out all its multiples. Circle 3, and then cross out all its multiples. Continue until all the numbers are either circled or crossed out. Ask students why the entire second column is able to be crossed out. All of the numbers in the second column are multiples of 2.

Extend Have students use their scatter plots and lines of best fit to guess the number of primes under 200. Have them use the Internet to check their guesses. There are 46 prime numbers under 200.

Math in the Middle

Purpose: To practice finding the mean, median, and mode in a game format

Discuss Ask students how they will determine which measure (mean, median, or mode) to use. Possible answer: Choose the measure that will allow your game piece to land in the most favorable position.

Extend Have students play the game again, using 8 number cubes instead of 5. Have students round the mean and the median to the nearest whole number.

Game Time

Distribution of Primes

Remember that a prime number is only divisible by 1 and itself. There are infinitely many prime numbers, but there is no algebraic formula to find them. The largest known prime number, discovered on November 14, 2001, is $2^{13,466,917} - 1$. In standard form, this number would have 4,053,946 digits.

Sieve of Eratosthenes

One way to find prime numbers is called the sieve of Eratosthenes. Use a list of whole numbers in order. Cross off 1. The next number, 2, is prime. Circle it. Then cross off all multiples of 2, because they are not prime. Circle the next number on the list. Cross off all of its multiples. Repeat this step until all of the numbers are circled or crossed off. The circled numbers will all be primes.

1̸	②	3	4̸	5	6̸	7	8̸	9	1̸0̸
11	1̸2̸	13	1̸4̸	15	1̸6̸	17	1̸8̸	19	2̸0̸
21	2̸2̸	23	2̸4̸	25	2̸6̸	27	2̸8̸	29	3̸0̸
31	3̸2̸	33	3̸4̸	35	3̸6̸	37	3̸8̸	39	4̸0̸
41	4̸2̸	43	4̸4̸	45	4̸6̸	47	4̸8̸	49	5̸0̸

❶ Use the sieve of Eratosthenes to find all prime numbers less than 50.

❷ Create a scatter plot of the first 15 prime numbers. Use the prime numbers as the *x*-coordinates and their positions in the sequence as the *y*-coordinates; 2 is the 1st prime, 3 is the 2nd prime, and so on.

Prime Number	2	3	5	7	11	13	17	19	23	29	31	37	41	43	47
Position in Sequence	1	2	3	4	5	6	7	8	9	10	11	12	13	14	15

❸ Estimate the line of best fit and use it to estimate the number of primes under 100. Use the sieve of Eratosthenes to check your estimate.

Math in the Middle

This game can be played by two or more players. On your turn, roll 5 number cubes. The number of spaces you move is your choice of the mean, rounded to the nearest whole number; the median; or the mode, if it exists. The winner is the first player to land on the Finish square by exact count.

A complete set of rules and a game board are available online.

go.hrw.com
Game Time Extra
KEYWORD: MT7 Games

Answers

2.

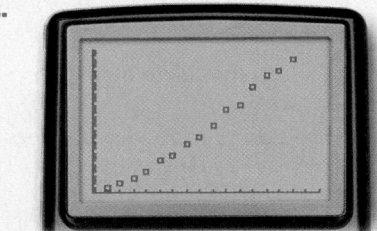

3. There are 25 prime numbers under 100.

Materials
• 5 paper plates
• scissors
• glue
• decorative paper
• markers

It's in the Bag!

PROJECT Data Pop-Ups

Here is a way to take notes on collecting, displaying, and analyzing data that is guaranteed to pop out!

❶ Cut one paper plate in half. You will use the two halves later to make covers for your pop-up book.

❷ Fold each of the remaining paper plates in half. Cut two 1-inch slits in the middle of the folded edge of each plate. The slits should be about 1 inch apart. **Figure A**

❸ Bend the paper between the slits back and forth, and then push it inward as you unfold the plate. This will create a pop-up tab. **Figure B**

❹ Fold the paper plates shut. Glue the bottom of one paper plate to the top of the next paper plate to form a book. Make covers by gluing one of the paper-plate halves onto the front of the book and the other onto the back of the book.

❺ Cut out four small rectangles of decorative paper. After taking notes on these rectangles, you will glue them onto the pop-up tabs in your book. **Figure C**

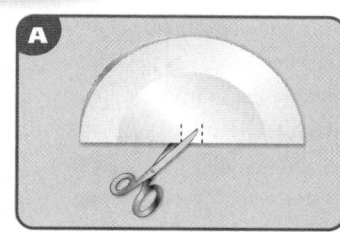
A

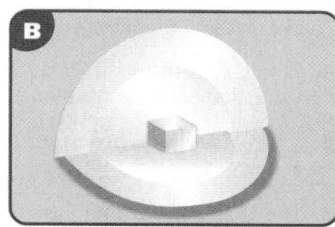
B

C

Taking Note of the Math

Use the rectangles of decorative paper to take notes on collecting, displaying, and analyzing data. Then glue the rectangles to the pop-up tabs inside the book. You can also take notes by writing directly on the paper plates.

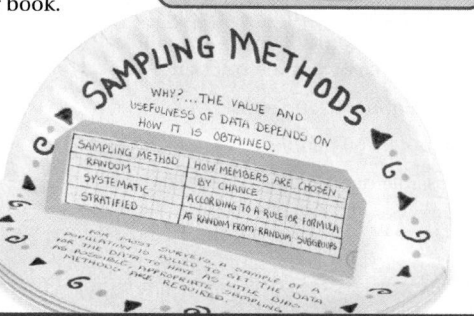

Organizer

Objective: Make a pop-up book in which to take notes on collecting, displaying, and analyzing data.

Materials: 5 paper plates, scissors, glue, decorative paper, markers

Online Edition

Using the Page

Preparing the Materials
For this project, the least-expensive paper plates tend to work best because they can be folded easily.

Making the Project
If possible, prepare a sample paper-plate book ahead of time and have it available as students work on the project. Seeing the finished product will help students understand the steps in creating it.

Extending the Project
Have students make scatter plots on graph paper. Then students can cut out the graphs and glue them to the paper plates.

Tips from the Bag Ladies!

You can make similar pop-up books by starting with rectangular sheets of construction paper. The basic steps remain the same: Fold a sheet of paper in half, cut two slits into the folded edge, bend the paper between the slits back and forth, and then push this piece of paper inward as the sheet is unfolded.

This project works well as an activity for small groups. Each student in the group can make one of the paper plates and use it to take notes on a lesson of the chapter. Then students can glue their plates together to make one pop-up book.

Organizer

Objective: Help students organize and review key concepts and skills presented in Chapter 9.

 Online Edition
Multilingual Glossary

Resources

 PuzzlePro®
One-Stop Planner®

Multilingual Glossary Online

go.hrw.com
KEYWORD: MT7 Glossary

Lesson Tutorial Videos
CD-ROM

Test & Practice Generator
One-Stop Planner®

Answers

1. median; mode

2. variability; variability; range

3. line of best fit; scatter plot; correlation

4. Population: moviegoers; sample: 25 people in line for *Star Wars;* possible bias: people in line for *Star Wars* might have a preference for science fiction movies.

5. Population: cell phone owners; sample: 100 cell phone owners; possible bias: cell phone users might feel that it is okay to use a cell phone at any time.

6. Population: parents of preschoolers; sample: 50 parents of preschoolers; possible bias: parents of preschoolers will probably like and use another playground.

Vocabulary

back-to-back stem-and-leaf plot 467	line of best fit 494	sample 462
biased sample 463	line plot 467	scatter plot 494
box-and-whisker plot ..477	mean 472	stem-and-leaf plot 467
convenience sample ..462	median 472	stratified sample 462
correlation 494	mode 472	systematic sample 462
double-bar graph 485	outlier 472	variability 476
double-line graph 486	population 462	Venn diagram 468
frequency table 485	quartile 476	voluntary-response sample ...462
histogram 485	random sample 462	
	range 472	

Complete the sentences below with vocabulary words from the list above.

1. The ___?___ of a data set is the middle value, while the ___?___ is the value that occurs most often.

2. ___?___ describes how spread out a data set is. One measure of ___?___ is the ___?___.

3. The ___?___ is the line that comes closest to all the points on a(n) ___?___. ___?___ describes the type of relationship between two data sets.

9-1 Samples and Surveys (pp. 462–465)

EXAMPLE

■ **Identify the population and sample. Give a reason the sample could be biased.**

In a community of 1250 people, a pollster asks 250 people living near a railroad track if they want the tracks moved.

Population: 1250 people

Sample: 250 people

Possible bias: People living near tracks are annoyed by the noise and want tracks moved.

EXERCISES

Identify the population and sample. Give a reason the sample could be biased.

4. Out of the 125 people in line for a *Star Wars* movie, 25 are asked to name their favorite type of movie.

5. A pollster surveyed 100 people who owned cell phones about whether they felt it was safe to use cell phones while driving.

6. Fifty parents of children attending local preschools are asked if the community should build a new playground.

9-2 Organizing Data (pp. 467–471)

EXAMPLE

■ Use a line plot to organize the data.

7 10 6 9 7 4 8 9
3 8 2 10 5 9 7

```
                    x   x
            x   x   x   x   x
    x   x   x   x   x   x   x   x
+---+---+---+---+---+---+---+---+---+---+
0   1   2   3   4   5   6   7   8   9   10
```

EXERCISE

Use a line plot to organize the data.

7.

Ages of People at a Skate Park					
12	13	13	14	12	11
14	15	13	13	12	13

9-3 Measures of Central Tendency (pp. 472–475)

EXAMPLE

■ The numbers of people to swim in a public pool each day one week were 50, 65, 72, 3, 85, 105, and 120. Explain which measure of central tendency best describes the middle of these numbers and find it.

Because there is an outlier, the median is the best measure of central tendency.
5, 50, 65, (72), 85, 105, 120

EXERCISE

Explain which measure of central tendency is the most appropriate for the situation and find it.

8. The prices of the cars sold in one month were $17,500; $15,300; $16,800; $65,900; $12,800; $16,300. What number best describes the middle of these numbers?

9-4 Variability (pp. 476–480)

EXAMPLE

■ Use the given data to make a box-and-whisker plot.

7, 10, 14, 16, 17, 17, 18, 20, 20

7 (10 14) 16 (17) (17 18 20) 20

smallest value: 7

first quartile: $\frac{10 + 14}{2} = 12$

median: 17

third quartile: $\frac{18 + 20}{2} = 19$

largest value: 20

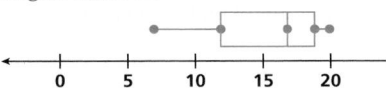

```
+---+---+---+---+---+
0   5   10  15  20
```

EXERCISES

Use the given data to make a box-and-whisker plot.

9. 56, 56, 56, 59, 63, 68, 68, 73, 73, 73

10. 87, 87, 80, 72, 85, 82, 53, 65, 65

11. 80, 80, 80, 82, 85, 87, 87, 90, 90, 90

Study Guide: Review

Answers

7.

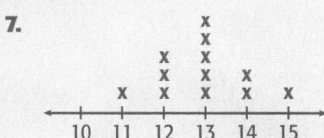

```
                x
                x
            x   x
            x   x   x
    x   x   x   x   x
+---+---+---+---+---+---+
10  11  12  13  14  15
```

8. The median—$16,550—because it is less affected by the outlier, $65,900, than the mean.

9.

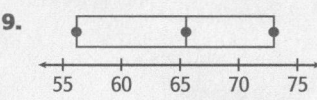

```
+---+---+---+---+---+
55  60  65  70  75
```

10.

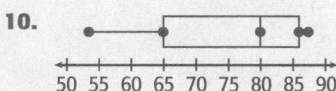

```
+--+--+--+--+--+--+--+--+--+
50 55 60 65 70 75 80 85 90
```

11.

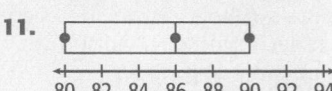

```
+---+---+---+---+---+---+---+
80  82  84  86  88  90  92  94
```

Answers

12.

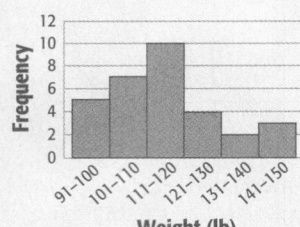

13.

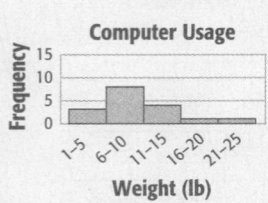

14. The pizza symbols vary in size even though each symbol is worth the same quantity of pizzas.

15. no correlation; The size of a gas tank is not related to the amount the person has driven it.

16. A circle graph, because it best represents percents of a whole.

Study Guide: Review

9-5 Displaying Data (pp. 485–488)

EXAMPLE

■ Make a histogram of the data set.

72, 64, 56, 60, 66, 72, 48, 66, 58, 60, 60, 50, 68, 72, 68, 62, 72, 58, 60, 68

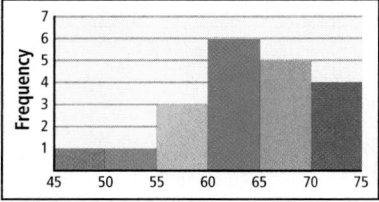

EXERCISES

Make a histogram of each data set.

12.

Weight (lb)	Frequency
91–100	5
101–110	7
111–120	10
121–130	4
131–140	2
141–150	3

13. Computer usage (h/week): 8, 3, 5, 10, 11, 12, 10, 7, 8, 7, 7, 22, 13, 15, 18, 6, 3

9-6 Misleading Graphs and Statistics (pp. 490–493)

EXAMPLE

■ Explain why the graph is misleading.

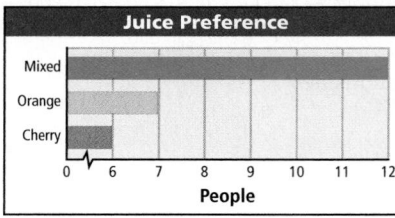

The bar for mixed juice is 7 times longer than the bar for cherry juice, but it is only preferred by 2 times as many people.

EXERCISE

14. Explain why the graph is misleading.

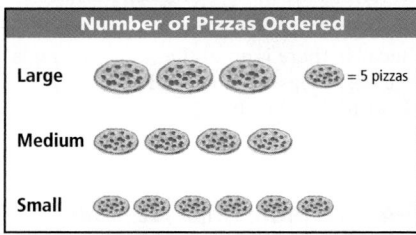

9-7 Scatter Plots (pp. 494–497)

EXAMPLE

■ Does the age of a battery in a flashlight and the intensity of the flashlight beam have a positive, a negative, or no correlation? Explain.

Negative: The older the battery is, the less intense the flashlight beam will be.

■ Choose the best display to compare children's shoe sizes to their heights.

A scatter plot would be the best display because you are comparing two sets of data.

EXERCISES

Does the data set have a positive, a negative, or no correlation? Explain.

15. the number of miles on a car's odometer and the size of the gas tank

Choose the best data display for the situation below. Explain your answer.

16. the amount of money spent in each category of a budget

Identify the sampling method used.

1. Twenty U.S. cities are randomly chosen and 100 people are randomly chosen from each city. **stratified**

2. A telemarketer flips through the phone book and selects 30 names. **systematic**

3. A chef asks the first five customers who order the new dessert if they like it. Identify the population and the sample. Why might the sample be biased?

4. The scores on a history test were 79, 82, 85, 100, 82, 83, 78, 84, 80, 82, and 77. What number best describes the middle of these scores? **mean; 83**

Use the given data to make a box-and-whisker plot.

5. 62, 60, 77, 66, 92, 87, 62, 60, 64

6. 2.2, 6.8, 6.4, 8, 6.5, 4.2, 6.5, 5, 8

3. Population: restaurant customers; sample: 5 customers; Possible bias: only customers who think they will like the dessert will order it.

7. A middle school class calculated the average number of minutes they spent on the phone each day. Use the data to make a histogram with intervals of 10.

| 18 | 31 | 32 | 42 | 50 | 34 | 33 | 36 | 27 | 41 | 5 | 35 | 27 | 15 |
| 37 | 12 | 9 | 31 | 24 | 29 | 10 | 25 | 20 | 66 | 22 | 31 | 9 | 3 |

Explain why each graph is misleading.

8.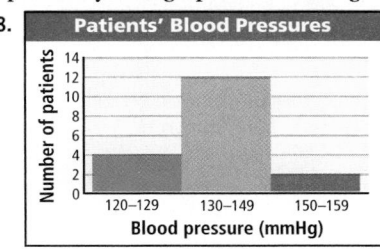

9.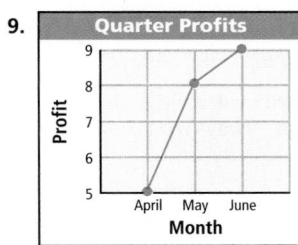

10. Use the given data to make a scatter plot.

Food	Pizza	Hamburger	Taco	Hot Dog	Caesar Salad	Taco Salad
Fat (g)	11	13	14	12	4	21
Calories	374	310	220	270	90	410

11. In a randomly chosen group of 100 people, 38 have type O positive blood, 7 have O negative, 34 have A positive, 6 have A negative, 9 have B positive, 2 have B negative, 3 have AB positive, and 1 has AB negative. Choose an appropriate data display and draw the graph. About what fraction of the population has type O blood?

11. $\frac{45}{100} = \frac{9}{20}$

8. Possible answer: The intervals used in the histogram are not equal.

9. Possible answer: scale does not start at 0, so the changes appear exaggerated.

10.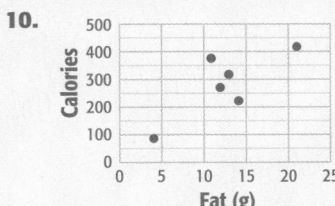

11.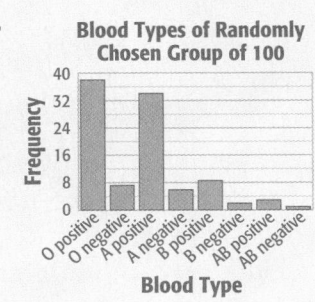

 CHAPTER TEST CHAPTER 9

Organizer

Objective: Assess students' mastery of concepts and skills in Chapter 9.

 Online Edition

Resources

 Assessment Resources

Chapter 9 Tests
• Free Response (Levels A, B, C)
• Multiple Choice (Levels A, B, C)
• Performance Assessment

 IDEA Works! CD-ROM
Modified Chapter 9 Test

Test & Practice Generator
One-Stop Planner®

Answers

5.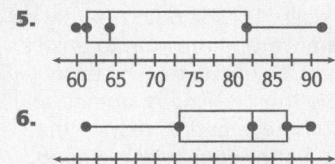

6.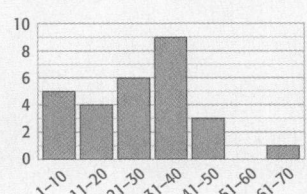

7.

State Resources

Organizer

Objective: Provide opportunities to learn and practice common test-taking strategies.

 Online Edition

Resources

 State Test Prep Workbook

 State Test Prep CD-ROM

 State Test Practice Online

go.hrw.com
KEYWORD: MT7 TestPrep

TEST PREP DOCTOR + This Test Tackler focuses on test items with graphics that may inadvertently mislead students. Advise students that diagrams are not always drawn to scale. They should not rely on the appearance of a drawing to answer the question. Students may need to look at how the drawing is labeled and determine if they need to redraw the diagram to better depict the scenario.

Test Tackler

All Types: Using a Graphic

Sometimes a graph or a picture is given with a test item. Look carefully at any drawings on a test. Keep in mind that figures are not always drawn to scale and can be misleading.

EXAMPLE 1

Multiple Choice The box-and-whisker plot shows the number of sales for the year. What is the range?

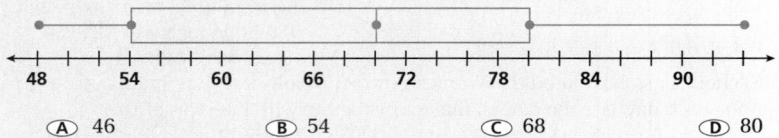

(A) 46   (B) 54   (C) 68   (D) 80

- Look at the box-and-whisker plot. The whiskers extend to the smallest and largest values. The range is the difference between these values.

$$94 - 48 = 46 \qquad \textit{Find the difference.}$$

- The range is 46, so the correct answer is choice A.

- Sometimes you will need to draw a diagram based on the information given in a test item. Always read the question carefully to make sure that your diagram is properly labeled.

EXAMPLE 2

Short Answer An ice rink has an area of 3750 ft^2 and length of 75 ft. What is the perimeter of the ice rink? Explain your reasoning and show your work.

Draw a diagram to help you visualize the problem.

```
┌──────────────┐
│              │
│  3750 ft²    │ h
│              │
└──────────────┘
    75 ft
```

$A = bh$ *You know the area and base. You*
$3750 = 75h$ *need to find the height.*
$50 = h$

$P = 2(b + h)$ *Use the formula for perimeter.*
$P = 2(75 + 50)$ *Substitute the known values.*

The perimeter of the ice rink $P = 2(125)$
is 250 ft. $P = 250$

HOT TIP! Draw a diagram if one is not provided to help you visualize the problem.

Read each test problem and answer the questions that follow.

Item A
A pizza restaurant sells a 12-inch small pizza, a 14-inch medium pizza, and a 16-inch large pizza. How much more pizza do you get for a large pizza than a small pizza? Explain your reasoning and show your work.

1. Draw a diagram to help you visualize the problem.

2. Use information from your diagram to solve the problem.

Item B
A middle school has 1000 students. According to the circle graph, how many students are in track?

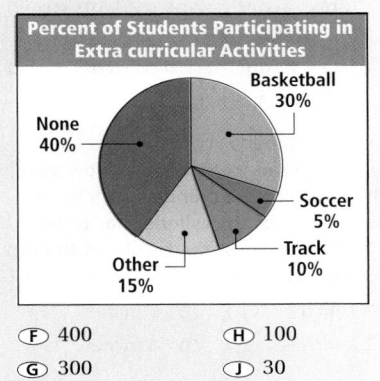

Percent of Students Participating in Extra curricular Activities

- Basketball 30%
- None 40%
- Soccer 5%
- Track 10%
- Other 15%

Ⓕ 400   Ⓗ 100
Ⓖ 300   Ⓙ 30

3. What percent of the students are in track? How do you know?

4. How do you find the number of students who are in track?

Item C
When a rectangle is divided into thirds, three squares are formed, each with a perimeter of 9.6 cm. What is the perimeter of the original rectangle?

5. Draw a diagram to visualize the problem.

6. What information from your diagram do you need to solve the problem?

7. If your answer is a decimal, what do you need to remember to do on the grid?

8. Show how you would grid your response below.

Item D
A 10 cm section of plastic pipe has an inner diameter 12 cm and an outer diameter 16 cm. What is the volume of the solid plastic pipe to the nearest tenth?

Ⓐ 879.2 cm³   Ⓒ 2009.6 cm³
Ⓑ 1130.4 cm³   Ⓓ 3140 cm³

9. Draw a diagram to help you visualize the problem.

10. Use information from your diagram to solve the problem.

Test Tackler

 **TEST PREP DOCTOR** Let students know that just because a test item may not include a diagram, that it may still be beneficial for them to make a quick sketch. Show students the importance of labeling their sketch with the information provided in the test item.

Answers

1. Possible answer: Students should draw three circles to represent the different pizzas. Each pizza should be labeled with its diameter in inches.

2. Possible answer: Find the difference between the area of the large pizza and the small pizza.
   You get 87.92 in² more.
   $A = \pi r^2$

Small 12 in.	Large 16 in.
$A = \pi 6^2$	$A = \pi 8^2$
$A = 36\pi$	$A = 64\pi$
$A = 113.04$	$A = 200.96$

3. 10%; The label on the circle graph for the light red section gives the percent.

4. Change 10% to a decimal and multiply by the total number of students in the school. $0.1 \times 1000 = 100$

5.
   2.4 cm
   2.4 cm   2.4 cm
   2.4 cm [| |] 2.4 cm
   2.4 cm   2.4 cm
   2.4 cm

6. the distance of each side of a square.

7. shade the decimal point in the grid.

8.
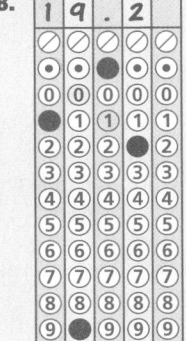
1 9 . 2

9.
16 cm
10 cm
12 cm

10. 879.2 cm³

State Resources

go.hrw.com
State Resources Online
KEYWORD: MT7 Resources

Organizer

Objective: Provide review and practice for Chapters 1–9 and standardized tests.

 Online Edition

Resources

 Assessment Resources
Chapter 9 Cumulative Test

 State Test Prep Workbook

 State Test Prep CD-ROM

 State Test Practice Online

go.hrw.com
KEYWORD: MT7 TestPrep

Standardized Test Prep

Cumulative Assessment, Chapters 1–9

Multiple Choice

1. Which is NOT true for this data set?
10, 10, 10.5, 9, 9.5

- Ⓐ mean < mode
- Ⓑ median > mean
- Ⓒ median = mean
- Ⓓ median = mode

2. In order to participate in after-school activities, a student needs to have a grade point average, *g*, of 2.0 or better. Which inequality represents this requirement?

- Ⓕ $g \geq 2.0$
- Ⓗ $g > 2.0$
- Ⓖ $g \leq 2.0$
- Ⓙ $g < 2.0$

3. Which ordered pair is a solution to the equation $2x + 4y = -18$?

- Ⓐ $(0, -9)$
- Ⓒ $(-11, 1)$
- Ⓑ $(6, 0)$
- Ⓓ $(-3, -4)$

4. Which expression is **NOT** equivalent to $4 \cdot 4 \cdot 4 \cdot 4 \cdot 4$?

- Ⓕ $\frac{1}{4^{-5}}$
- Ⓗ $4^2 \cdot 4^3$
- Ⓖ 20
- Ⓙ 1024

5. A 6-inch model is made to represent a 30-foot plane. What is the scale?

- Ⓐ 1 in. = 5 ft
- Ⓒ 6 in. = 5 ft
- Ⓑ 5 in. = 1 ft
- Ⓓ 30 in. = 5 ft

6. The stem-and-leaf plot shows test scores for a teacher's first and second periods. What can you conclude?

1st period		2nd period
7	6	5 8
6 4 2	7	5 6 9
9 8 6 4 2 0	8	1 3 5 7 7 8 8
9 7 7 2 1	9	0 6 7 8 9

Key: | 9 | 0 means 90
7 | 6 | means 67

- Ⓕ More first period students scored in the 90's.
- Ⓖ Fewer first period students scored 80 or below.
- Ⓗ More second period students scored in the 70's.
- Ⓙ More second period students scored in the 80's.

7. A soup company is producing a cylindrical can to package its new soup. The radius of the cylinder is 1.5 in. and the volume of the cylinder has to be 14 in³. What must the height of the can be, rounded to the nearest whole inch?

- Ⓐ 1 inch
- Ⓒ 3 inches
- Ⓑ 2 inches
- Ⓓ 4 inches

8. Emma buys a refrigerator on sale for $665. This is 30% off the original price. What is the original price of the refrigerator?

- Ⓕ $200
- Ⓗ $1995
- Ⓖ $950
- Ⓙ $2217

 **TEST PREP DOCTOR** ✚

For item 4, be sure students realize that $4 \cdot 4 \cdot 4 \cdot 4 \cdot 4$ is equivalent to 4^5 and not to 4×5.

Answers

15. $n = 5$; There are many ordered pairs that will meet these qualifications. In general, the ordered pairs will be of the form $(x, 5x)$. Two possible ordered pairs are $(1, 5)$ and $(2, 10)$.

16. The bar for apple is 7 times longer than the bar for strawberries, but it is only preferred by 2 times as many people.

17. See 4-Point Response work sample.

State Resources

go.hrw.com
State Resources Online
KEYWORD: MT7 Resources

9. Which is a solution to the equation $-10 + 5x = -25$?

(A) $x = -15$ (C) $x = -3$

(B) $x = -7$ (D) $x = -1$

10. If triangle $JQZ \cong$ triangle VTZ, what is the value of r?

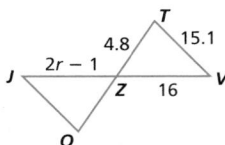

(F) 7.5   (H) 9

(G) 8.5   (J) 33

 Read a graph or diagram as closely as you do the actual question. These visual aids contain important information.

Gridded Response

11. The function $f(t) = -16t^2 + 180$ models the distance an object falls when it is dropped from the top of a building 180 ft tall in t seconds. How many feet does the stone fall after 2 seconds? **116**

Use the box-and-whisker plot to answers questions 12 and 13.

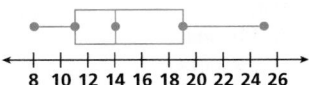

12. What is the range of the data? **17**

13. What is the first quartile of the data? **12**

14. Monica scored 85, 83, 81, 80, and 81 on her last five assignments. What would Monica need to earn on her next assignment to bring her average to an 85? **100**

Short Response

15. Name two ordered pairs (x, y) that satisfy these conditions: The mean of 0, x, and y is twice the median; $0 < x < y$; and $y = nx$ (y is a multiple of x). What is the value of n? Show your work or explain in words how you determined your answer.

16. Explain why the graph is misleading and then redraw it so that it better represents the data.

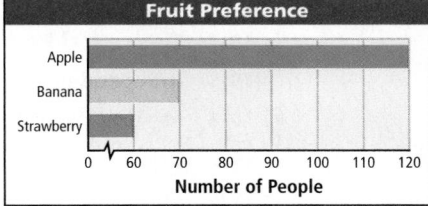

Extended Response

17. Twenty students in a gym class kept a record of their jogging. The results are shown in the scatter plot.

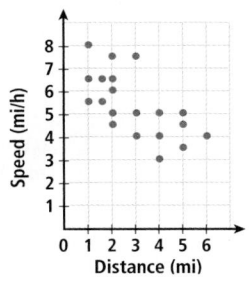

a. Describe the correlation of the data in the scatter plot.

b. Find the average speeds of joggers who run 1, 2, 3, 4, 5, and 6 miles.

c. Explain the relationship between your answer from part **a** and your answers from part **b**.

Short Response Rubric

Items 15–16

2 Points = The student's answer is an accurate and complete execution of the task or tasks.

1 Point = The student's answer contains attributes of an appropriate response but is flawed.

0 Points = The student's answer contains no attributes of an appropriate response.

Extended Response Rubric

Item 17

4 points = The student demonstrates a thorough understanding of all concepts and shows all work correctly.

3 points = The student demonstrates a basic understanding of all concepts, but the work shows some flaws reflecting inattentive execution of mathematical procedures or some misunderstanding of the underlying mathematics.

2 points = The student demonstrates only a partial understanding of the concepts or procedures embodied in the tasks. The approach may be correct, but the work shows a misunderstanding of one or more important concepts.

1 point = The student demonstrates a very limited understanding of the concepts or procedures embodied in the tasks. The response may show some understanding but exhibits many flaws or is incomplete.

0 points = The student provides no response at all or a completely incorrect or uninterpretable response.

Student Work Samples for Item 17

4-Point Response

a. There is a weak negative correlation.

b. $\frac{5.5 + 6.5 + 8}{3} \approx 6.7$

$\frac{4.5 + 5 + 6 + 6.5 + 7.5}{5} = 5.9$

$\frac{4 + 5 + 7.5}{3} = 5.5$

$\frac{3 + 4 + 5}{3} = 4$

$\frac{3.5 + 4.5 + 5}{3} \approx 4.3$

c. A negative correlation is shown on the graph, and the averages decreased as the number of miles increased.

The student understood differences in types of correlations, correctly identified the weak negative correlation, found average speeds, and understood relationships.

3-Point Response

a. A weak negative correlation

b. $\frac{5.5 + 6.5 + 8}{3} \approx 6.7$

$\frac{4 + 5 + 5 + 6 + 6.5 + 7.5}{5} = 5.9$

$\frac{4 + 5 + 7.5}{3} = 5.5$

$\frac{3 + 4 + 5}{3} = 4$

$\frac{3.5 + 4.5 + 5}{3} \approx 4.3$

c. There is a correlation among the average speeds.

The student answers correctly, but does not give a thorough enough explanation for why the averages reflect a negative correlation.

2-Point Response

a. There is a weak negative correlation

b. $5.5 + 6.5 + 8 + 4.5 + 5 + 6 + 6.5 + 7.5 + 4 + 5 + 7.5 + 3 + 4 + 5 + 3.5 + 4.5 + 5 + 4 = 95$

$95 \div 18 \approx 5.28$

c. As the number of joggers went from 1 to 6, the average was 5.28.

The student correctly identified the weak negative correlation, but used wrong data and showed limited understanding of relationships.

CHAPTER

10

Probability

Section 10A
Experimental Probability

10-1 **Probability**

10-2 **Experimental Probability**

10-3 **Technology Lab** Generate Random Numbers

10-3 **Use a Simulation**

10-3 **Hands-On Lab** Use Different Models for Simulations

Section 10B
Theoretical Probability and Counting

10-4 **Theoretical Probability**

10-5 **Independent and Dependent Events**

10-6 **Making Decisions and Predictions**

10-7 **Odds**

10-8 **Counting Principles**

10-9 **Permutations and Combinations**

Pacing Guide for 45-Minute Classes

Chapter 10

Countdown to Testing Weeks ㉒, ㉓

DAY 1	DAY 2	DAY 3	DAY 4	DAY 5
10-1 Lesson	10-2 Lesson	10-3 Technology Lab	10-3 Lesson	10-3 Lesson 10-3 Hands-On Lab
DAY 6	**DAY 7**	**DAY 8**	**DAY 9**	**DAY 10**
Ready to Go On? Focus on Problem Solving 10-4 Lesson	10-4 Lesson	10-5 Lesson	10-6 Lesson	10-7 Lesson
DAY 11	**DAY 12**	**DAY 13**	**DAY 14**	**DAY 15**
10-8 Lesson	10-8 Lesson 10-9 Lesson	10-9 Lesson Ready to Go On? Multi-Step Test Prep	Chapter 10 Review	Chapter 10 Test

Pacing Guide for 90-Minute Classes

Chapter 10

DAY 1	DAY 2	DAY 3	DAY 4	DAY 5
10-1 Lesson 10-2 Lesson	10-3 Technology Lab 10-3 Lesson	10-3 Lesson 10-3 Hands-On Lab Ready to Go On? Focus on Problem Solving 10-4 Lesson	10-4 Lesson 10-5 Lesson	10-6 Lesson 10-7 Lesson
DAY 6	**DAY 7**	**DAY 8**		
10-8 Lesson 10-9 Lesson	10-9 Lesson Ready to Go On? Multi-Step Test Prep Chapter 10 Review	Chapter 10 Test		

ONGOING ASSESSMENT and INTERVENTION

DIAGNOSE	PRESCRIBE

Assess Prior Knowledge

Before Chapter 10

Diagnose readiness for the chapter.
Are You Ready? SE p. 519

Prescribe intervention.
Are You Ready? Intervention Skills 26, 28, 31, 42

Formative Assessment

Before Every Lesson

Diagnose readiness for the lesson.
Warm Up TE, every lesson

Prescribe intervention.
Skills Bank SE pp. 820–834
Reteach CRB, Chapters 1–10

During Every Lesson

Diagnose understanding of lesson concepts.
Think and Discuss SE, every lesson
Write About It SE, lesson exercises
Journal TE, lesson exercises

Prescribe intervention.
Questioning Strategies Chapter 10
Reading Strategies CRB, every lesson
Success for ELL pp. 147–164

After Every Lesson

Diagnose mastery of lesson concepts.
Lesson Quiz TE, every lesson
Test Prep SE, every lesson
Test and Practice Generator

Prescribe intervention.
Reteach CRB, every lesson
Problem Solving CRB, every lesson
Test Prep Doctor TE, lesson exercises
Homework Help Online

Before Chapter 10 Testing

Diagnose mastery of concepts in the chapter.
Ready to Go On? SE pp. 538, 568
Focus on Problem Solving SE p. 539
Multi-Step Test Prep SE p. 569
Section Quizzes AR pp. 185–186
Test and Practice Generator

Prescribe intervention.
Ready to Go On? Intervention Chapter 10
Scaffolding Questions TE p. 569

Before High Stakes Testing

Diagnose mastery of benchmark concepts.
Standardized Test Prep SE pp. 576–577
State Test Prep CD-ROM

Prescribe intervention.
State Test Prep Workbook

Summative Assessment

After Chapter 10

Check mastery of chapter concepts.
Multiple-Choice Tests (Forms A, B, C)
Free-Response Tests (Forms A, B, C)
Performance Assessment AR pp. 187–200
Test and Practice Generator

Check mastery of benchmark concepts.
AYP State Tests

Prescribe intervention.
Reteach CRB, every lesson
Lesson Tutorial Videos Chapter 10

Prescribe intervention.
State Test Prep Workbook

CHAPTER
10

Supporting the Teacher

Chapter 10 Resource Book

Practice A, B, C
pp. 3–5, 12–14, 20–22, 28–30, 37–39, 46–48, 55–57, 63–65, 71–73

Reading Strategies ELL
pp. 10, 18, 26, 35, 44, 53, 61, 69, 78

Puzzles, Twisters, and Teasers
pp. 11, 19, 27, 36, 45, 54, 62, 70, 79

Reteach
pp. 6–7, 15, 23, 31–32, 40–41, 49–50, 58, 66, 74–75

Problem Solving
pp. 9, 17, 25, 34, 43, 52, 60, 68, 77

Challenge
pp. 8, 16, 24, 33, 42, 51, 59, 67, 76

Parent Letter   pp. 1–2

Transparencies

Lesson Transparencies, Volume 2 .... Chapter 10
• Warm Ups
• Problem of the Day
• Teaching Transparencies
• Lesson Quizzes

Know-It Notebook .... Chapter 10
• Additional Examples   • Chapter Review
• Vocabulary   • Big Ideas

Alternate Openers: Explorations .... pp. 74–82

Countdown to Testing .... pp. 43–46

Teacher Tools

Power Presentations®
Complete PowerPoint® presentations for Chapter 10 lessons

Lesson Tutorial Videos® SPANISH
Holt authors Ed Burger and Freddie Renfro present tutorials to support the Chapter 10 lessons.

One-Stop Planner® SPANISH
Easy access to all Chapter 10 resources and assessments, as well as software for lesson planning, test generation, and puzzle creation

IDEA Works!®
Key Chapter 10 resources and assessments modified to address special learning needs

Lesson Plans ....pp. 74–82

Questioning Strategies .... Chapter 10

Solutions Key .... Chapter 10

Interdisciplinary Posters and Worksheets .... Chapter 10

TechKeys   **Lab Resources**

Project Teacher Support   **Parent Resources**

Workbooks

Homework and Practice Workbook SPANISH
Teacher's Guide .... pp. 37–41

Know-It Notebook
Teacher's Guide .... Chapter 10

Problem Solving Workbook SPANISH
Teacher's Guide .... pp. 37–41

State Test Prep Workbook
Teacher's Guide

Technology Highlights for the Teacher

 Power Presentations
Dynamic presentations to engage students. Complete PowerPoint® presentations for every lesson in Chapter 10.

 One-Stop Planner SPANISH
Easy access to Chapter 10 resources and assessments. Includes lesson-planning, test-generation, and puzzle-creation software.

 Premier Online Edition SPANISH
Chapter 10 includes Tutorial Videos, Lesson Activities, Lesson Quizzes, Homework Help, and Chapter Project.

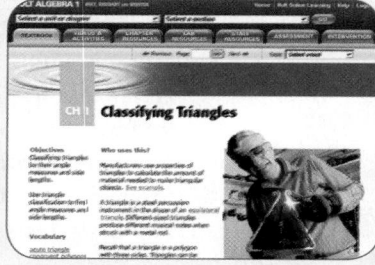

KEY: **SE** = *Student Edition*   **TE** = *Teacher's Edition*   **ELL** English Language Learners   **SPANISH** Spanish version available   Available on CD-ROM    Available online

Reaching All Learners

Resources for All Learners

Hands-On Lab Activities	Chapter 10
Technology Lab Activities	Chapter 10
Homework and Practice Workbook **SPANISH**	pp. 74–82
Know-It Notebook	Chapter 10
Problem Solving Workbook **SPANISH**	pp. 74–82

DEVELOPING LEARNERS

Practice A	CRB, every lesson
Reteach	CRB, every lesson
Inclusion	TE p. 546
Questioning Strategies	Chapter 10
Modified Chapter 10 Resources	IDEA Works!
Homework Help Online	

ON-LEVEL LEARNERS

Practice B	CRB, every lesson
Puzzles, Twisters, and Teasers	CRB, every lesson
Cognitive Strategies	TE pp. 523, 555
Cooperative Learning	TE p. 541

ADVANCED LEARNERS

Practice C	CRB, every lesson
Challenge	CRB, every lesson
Extension	TE pp. 521, 569, 570, 571
Critical Thinking	TE pp. 533, 546, 559, 564

English Language Learners

ENGLISH LANGUAGE LEARNERS

Are You Ready? Vocabulary	SE p. 519
Vocabulary Connections	SE p. 520
Lesson Vocabulary	SE, every lesson
Vocabulary Review	SE p. 572
English Language Learners	TE pp. 521, 533, 542, 546, 579
Reading Strategies	CRB, every lesson
Success for English Language Learners	pp. 147–164
Multilingual Glossary	

Reaching All Learners Through...

Inclusion	TE p. 546
Kinesthetic Experience	TE p. 551
Concrete Manipulatives	TE p. 528
Cognitive Strategies	TE pp. 523, 555
Cooperative Learning	TE p. 541
Graphic Organizers	TE p. 555
Critical Thinking	TE pp. 533, 546, 559, 564
Test Prep Doctor	TE pp. 526, 530, 535, 544, 549, 553, 557, 562, 567, 576
Common Error Alerts	TE pp. 547, 551, 565
Scaffolding Questions	TE p. 569

Technology Highlights for Reaching All Learners

 Lesson Tutorial Videos **SPANISH**

Starring Holt authors Ed Burger and Freddie Renfro! Live tutorials to support every lesson in Chapter 10.

Multilingual Glossary

Searchable glossary includes definitions in English, Spanish, Vietnamese, Chinese, Hmong, Korean, and 4 other languages.

Online Interactivities

Interactive tutorials provide visually engaging alternative opportunities to learn concepts and master skills.

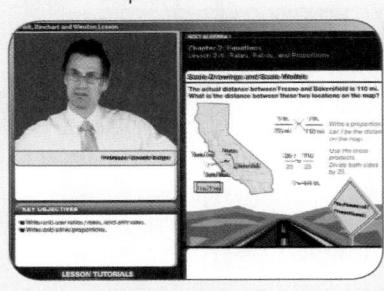
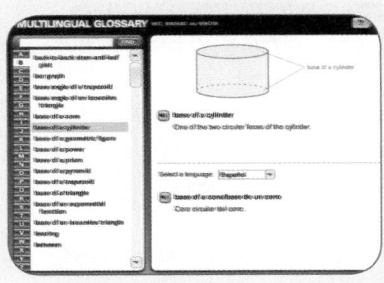
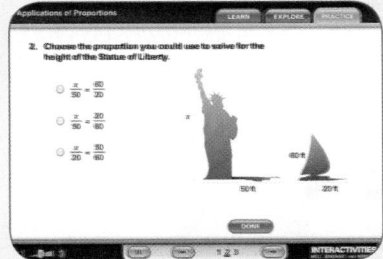

KEY: **SE** = *Student Edition* **TE** = *Teacher's Edition* **CRB** = *Chapter Resource Book* **SPANISH** Spanish version available  Available on CD-ROM  Available online

CHAPTER
10

Ongoing Assessment

Assessing Prior Knowledge

Determine whether students have the prerequisite concepts and skills for success in Chapter 10.

Are You Ready? SPANISH .... SE p. 519
Warm Up .... TE, every lesson

Test Preparation

Provide review and practice for Chapter 10 and standardized tests.

Multi-Step Test Prep................................... SE p. 569
Study Guide: Review .... SE pp. 572–574
Standardized Test Prep........................ SE pp. 576–577
Countdown to Testing Transparencies ....pp. 43–46
State Test Prep Workbook
State Test Prep CD-ROM
IDEA Works!

Alternative Assessment

Assess students' understanding of Chapter 10 concepts and combined problem-solving skills.

Chapter 10 Project............................... SE p. 518
Performance Assessment SPANISH .... AR pp. 199–200
Portfolio Assessment SPANISH .... AR p. xxxiv

Daily Assessment

Provide formative assessment for each day of Chapter 10.

Questioning Strategies............................. Chapter 10
Think and Discuss .... SE, every lesson
Write About It........................... SE, lesson exercises
Journal .... TE, lesson exercises
Lesson Quiz .... TE, every lesson
Modified Lesson Quizzes .... IDEA Works!

Weekly Assessment

Provide formative assessment for each week of Chapter 10.

Focus on Problem Solving .... SE p. 539
Multi-Step Test Prep............................. SE p. 569
Ready to Go On? SPANISH .... SE pp. 538, 568
Cumulative Assessment................... SE pp. 576–577
Test and Practice Generator SPANISH ...One-Stop Planner

Formal Assessment

Provide summative assessment of Chapter 10 mastery.

Section Quizzes SPANISH ....AR pp. 185–186
Chapter 10 Test............................... SE p. 575
Chapter Test (Levels A, B, C) SPANISH ....AR pp. 187–198
    • Multiple-Choice • Free-Response
Cumulative Test SPANISH ....AR pp. 201–204
Test and Practice Generator SPANISH ...One-Stop Planner
Modified Chapter 10 Test .... IDEA Works!

Technology Highlights for the Teacher

Are You Ready? SPANISH
Automatically assess readiness and prescribe intervention for Chapter 10 prerequisite skills.

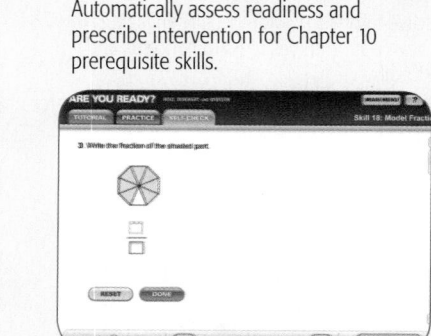

Ready to Go On? SPANISH
Automatically assess understanding of and prescribe intervention for Sections 10A and 10B.

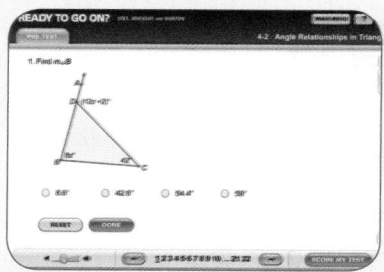

Test and Practice Generator SPANISH
Use Chapter 10 problem banks to create assessments and worksheets to print out or deliver online. Includes dynamic problems.

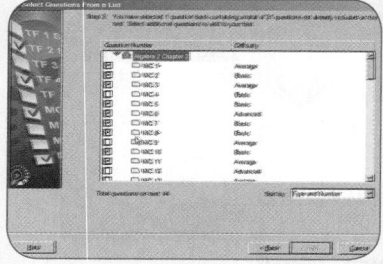

KEY: **SE** = *Student Edition*   **TE** = *Teacher's Edition*   **AR** = *Assessment Resources*   SPANISH Spanish version available   Available on CD-ROM   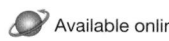 Available online

Formal Assessment

Three levels (A, B, C) of multiple-choice and free-response chapter tests are available in the *Assessment Resources*.

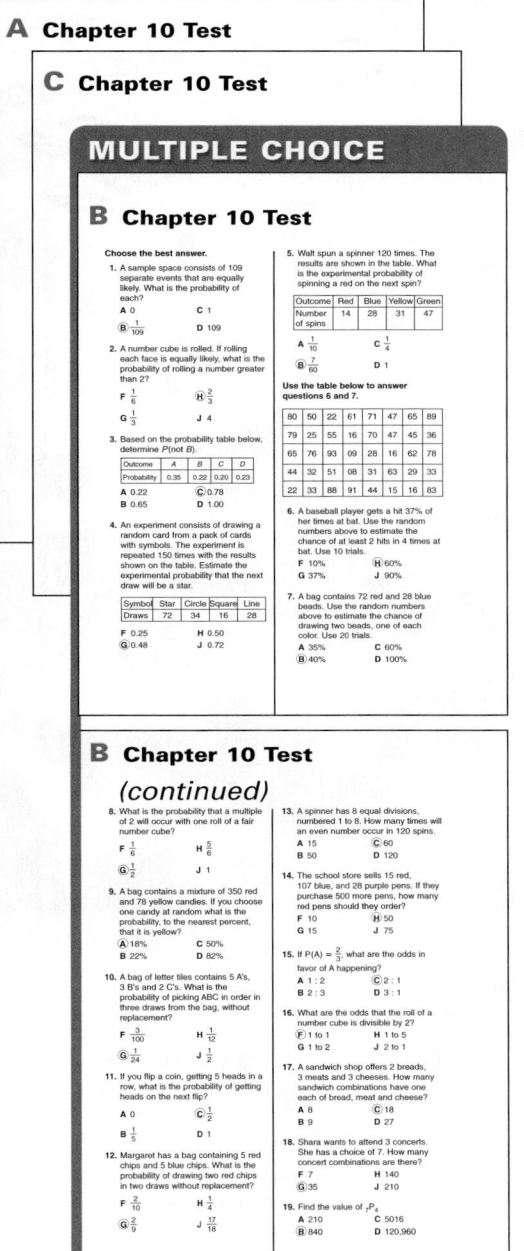

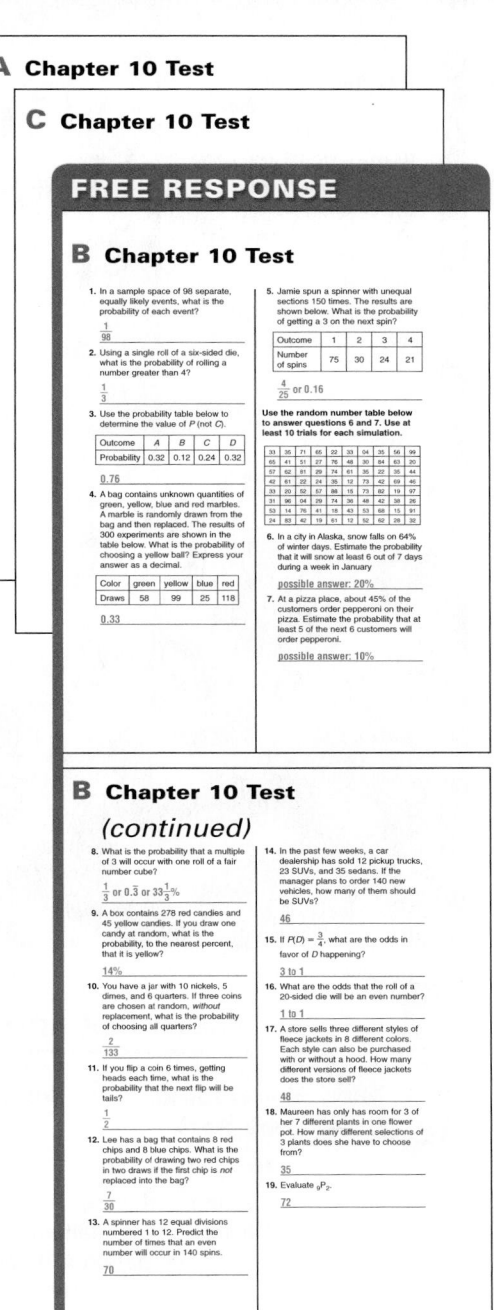

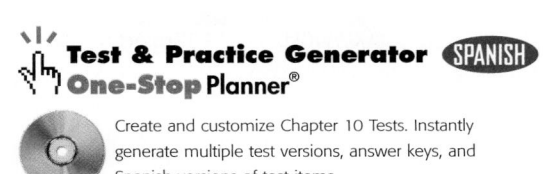

Test & Practice Generator SPANISH
One-Stop Planner®

Create and customize Chapter 10 Tests. Instantly generate multiple test versions, answer keys, and Spanish versions of test items.

518F

Probability

Letter	Code
A	1000001
E	1000101
H	1001000
I	1001001
L	1001100
M	1001101
O	1001111
T	1010100
V	1010110

Why Learn This?

Tell students that cryptography is an important field, especially for military intelligence and information technology. Cryptographers create and crack codes. Using the code shown here, a simple message can be encoded as a complicated-looking string of numbers. A cryptographer's job is to study the message to try to identify recurring patterns as specific letters.

Using Data

To begin the study of this chapter, have students:

- Use the codes from the table to encrypt the word *movie*. 1001101 1001111101011010010011000101

- Determine another word that can be spelled with the given letters, encrypt it, and pass it to another student to decode.

  Possible answer:
  heal: 1001000100010110000001
  1001100

  Puzzle answer:
  I LOVE MATH

MULTI-STEP TEST PREP On page 569, students analyze the probability of pulling geometric shapes out of paper bags.

10A Experimental Probability

10-1 Probability

10-2 Experimental Probability

LAB Generate Random Numbers

10-3 Use a Simulation

LAB Use Different Models for Simulations

10B Theoretical Probability and Counting

10-4 Theoretical Probability

10-5 Independent and Dependent Events

10-6 Making Decisions and Predictions

10-7 Odds

10-8 Counting Principles

10-9 Permutations and Combinations

MULTI-STEP TEST PREP

go.hrw.com
Chapter Project Online
KEYWORD: MT7 Ch10

Career *Cryptographer*

1001001100110010011111010110
1000101100110110000011010101001001000

Is this pattern of zeros and ones some kind of message or secret code? A cryptographer could find out. Cryptographers create and break codes by assigning number values to letters of the alphabet.

Almost all text sent over the Internet is encrypted to ensure security for the sender. Codes made up of zeros and ones, or *binary codes*, are frequently used in computer applications.

Use the table to break the code above.

Problem Solving Project

Understand, Plan, Solve, and Look Back

Have students:

- Examine the string of 1's and 0's. It's a code containing a message. Tell what patterns, if any, they see. Can they break the code?

- Complete the Code Breaking worksheet.

- Create a possible code for the rest of the alphabet, or a new code for the entire alphabet. Use the codes to create messages for their classmates to break.

- Research the history of cryptography.

Social Studies and Technology Connection

Project Resources

All project resources for teachers and students are provided online.

Materials:

- Code Breaking worksheet

go.hrw.com
Project Teacher Support
KEYWORD: MT7 PSProject10

ARE YOU READY?

✓ Vocabulary

Choose the best term from the list to complete each sentence.

1. The term __?__ means "per hundred."   **percent**

2. A __?__ is a comparison of two numbers.   **ratio**

3. In a set of data, the __?__ is the greatest value minus the least value. **range**

4. A __?__ is in simplest form when its numerator and denominator have no common factors other than 1.   **fraction**

fraction

percent

range

ratio

Complete these exercises to review skills you will need for this chapter.

✓ Simplify Ratios

Write each ratio in simplest form.

5. 5:50   **1:10**   6. 95 to 19 **5 to 1**   7. $\frac{20}{100}$ $\frac{1}{5}$ 8. $\frac{192}{80}$ $\frac{12}{5}$

✓ Write Fractions as Decimals

Write each fraction as a decimal.

9. $\frac{52}{100}$ **0.52**   10. $\frac{7}{1000}$ **0.007**   11. $\frac{3}{5}$ **0.6**   12. $\frac{2}{9}$ $0.\overline{2}$

✓ Write Fractions as Percents

Write each fraction as a percent.

13. $\frac{19}{100}$ **19%**   14. $\frac{1}{8}$ **12.5%**   15. $\frac{5}{2}$ **250%**   16. $\frac{2}{3}$ $66\frac{2}{3}\%$, or $66.\overline{6}\%$

17. $\frac{3}{4}$ **75%**   18. $\frac{9}{20}$ **45%**   19. $\frac{7}{10}$ **70%**   20. $\frac{2}{5}$ **40%**

✓ Operations with Fractions

Add. Write each answer in simplest form.

21. $\frac{3}{8} + \frac{1}{4} + \frac{1}{6}$ $\frac{19}{24}$ 22. $\frac{1}{6} + \frac{2}{3} + \frac{1}{9}$ $\frac{17}{18}$ 23. $\frac{1}{8} + \frac{1}{4} + \frac{1}{8} + \frac{1}{2}$ **1**   24. $\frac{1}{3} + \frac{1}{4} + \frac{2}{5}$ $\frac{59}{60}$

Multiply. Write each answer in simplest form.

25. $\frac{3}{8} \cdot \frac{1}{5}$ $\frac{3}{40}$ 26. $\frac{2}{3} \cdot \frac{6}{7}$ $\frac{4}{7}$ 27. $\frac{3}{7} \cdot \frac{14}{27}$ $\frac{2}{9}$ 28. $\frac{13}{52} \cdot \frac{3}{51}$ $\frac{1}{68}$

29. $\frac{4}{5} \cdot \frac{11}{4}$ $2\frac{1}{5}$ 30. $\frac{5}{2} \cdot \frac{3}{4}$ $1\frac{7}{8}$ 31. $\frac{27}{8} \cdot \frac{4}{9}$ $1\frac{1}{2}$ 32. $\frac{1}{15} \cdot \frac{30}{9}$ $\frac{2}{9}$

Organizer

Objective: Assess students' understanding of prerequisite skills.

Prerequisite Skills

Simplify Ratios

Write Fractions as Decimals

Write Fractions as Percents

Operations with Fractions

Assessing Prior Knowledge
INTERVENTION

Diagnose and Prescribe

Use this page to determine whether intervention is necessary or whether enrichment is appropriate.

Resources

 ***Are You Ready? Intervention and Enrichment* Worksheets**

 ***Are You Ready?* CD-ROM**

***Are You Ready?* Online**

my.hrw.com

ARE YOU READY?
Diagnose and Prescribe

NO INTERVENE

YES ENRICH

✓ Prerequisite Skill	*ARE YOU READY?* Intervention, Chapter 10		
	Worksheets	CD-ROM	Online
✓ Simplify Ratios	Skill 28	Activity 28	Diagnose and Prescribe Online
✓ Write Fractions as Decimals	Skill 26	Activity 26	
✓ Write Fractions as Percents	Skill 31	Activity 31	
✓ Operations with Fractions	Skill 42	Activity 42	

ARE YOU READY? Enrichment, Chapter 10

 Worksheets

CD-ROM

Online

Organizer

Objective: Help students organize the new concepts they will learn in Chapter 10.

 Online Edition
Multilingual Glossary

Resources

PuzzlePro®
One-Stop Planner®

Multilingual Glossary Online
go.hrw.com
KEYWORD: MT7 Glossary

Possible answers to *Vocabulary Connections*

1. Dependent events are those that are determined by other events.

2. Independent events are those that are not determined by other events.

3. A simulation in probability is a representation of events that would otherwise be difficult to observe.

CHAPTER 10 Study Guide: Preview

Where You've Been

Previously, you

- found the probability of independent events.

- constructed sample spaces for simple or composite experiments.

- made inferences based on analysis of given or collected data.

In This Chapter

You will study

- finding the probabilities of independent and dependent events.

- selecting and using different models to simulate an event.

- using theoretical probabilities and experimental results to make predictions.

Where You're Going

You can use the skills learned in this chapter

- to make predictions based on theoretical and experimental probabilities in science courses like biology.

- to learn how to create more advanced simulations for use in fields like computer science and meteorology.

Key Vocabulary/Vocabulario

combination	combinación
dependent events	sucesos dependientes
experimental probability	probabilidad experimental
independent events	sucesos independientes
mutually exclusive	mutuamente excluyentes
outcome	resultado
permutation	permutación
probability	probabilidad
simulation	simulación
theoretical probability	probabilidad teórica

Vocabulary Connections

To become familiar with some of the vocabulary terms in the chapter, consider the following. You may refer to the chapter, the glossary, or a dictionary if you like.

1. The word *dependent* means "determined by another." What do you think **dependent events** are?

2. The prefix *in-* means "not." What do you suppose **independent events** are?

3. The word *simulation* comes from the Latin root *simulare*, which means "to represent." What do you think a **simulation** is in probability?

 **Reading** and **Writing Math**

Reading Strategy: Learn Math Vocabulary

Mathematics has a vocabulary all its own. To learn and remember new vocabulary words, use the following study strategies.

- Try to figure out the meanings of new words based on their context.
- Use a dictionary to look up root words or prefixes.
- Relate the new word to familiar everyday words.
- Use mnemonics or memory tricks to remember the definition.

Once you know what a word means, write its definition in your own words.

quartile = four

outlier = out

variability = variable

Term	Study Notes	Definition
Quartile	The root word quart- means "four."	Three values that divide a data set into fourths
Outlier	Relate it to the word out, which means "away from a place."	A value much greater or much less than the others in a data set
Variability	Relate it to the word variable, which is a value that can change.	The spread, or amount of change, of values in a set of data

 **Try This**

Complete the table below.

	Term	Study Notes	Definition
1.	Systematic sample		
2.	Median		
3.	Quartile		
4.	Frequency table		

Reading and Writing Math (side tab)

 **Reading** and **Writing Math**

Organizer

Objective: Help students apply strategies to understand and retain key concepts.

 Online Edition

Resources

Chapter 10 Resource Book
Reading Strategies

ENGLISH LANGUAGE LEARNERS

Reading Strategy: Learn Math Vocabulary

Discuss Let students explain to the class some of the mnemonics they thought up for the *Try This* exercises. Encourage students to share ideas.

Extend Have students read future lessons for homework and have them write definitions and study tips for each new vocabulary term. After you teach a lesson, have students write their own quiz questions using each new term at least once.

Answers to *Try This*

1. *systematic sample:* a sample of a population that has been selected using a pattern; Possible Study Note: Relate it to the word *system,* which means "a method or a procedure for doing something."

2. *median:* the middle number, or the mean (average) of the two middle numbers, in an ordered set of data; Possible Study Note: Visualize a *median strip,* which is a strip of land down the middle of a road that divides lanes of traffic.

3. *quartile:* three values, one of which is the median, that divide a data set into fourths; Possible Study Note: Relate it to the word *quart,* which is one fourth of a gallon, or *quarter,* which is one fourth of a dollar.

4. *frequency table:* a table that lists items together according to the number of times, or frequency, that the items occur; Possible Study Note: Relate it to the word *frequency,* which means "how often" or "the number of times something happens."

Experimental Probability

One-Minute Section Planner

Lesson	Materials	MiC and Lab Resources
Lesson 10-1 Probability • Find the probability of an event by using the definition of probability. ☑ SAT-10 ☑ ITBS ☑ CTBS ☑ NAEP		**MiC: *Great Predictions*** pp. 1–4 ***Hands-On Lab Activities*** 10-1
Lesson 10-2 Experimental Probability • Estimate probability using experimental methods. ☐ SAT-10 ☑ ITBS ☑ CTBS ☑ NAEP	Number cubes (MK), coins (MK), paper clips, plastic lids	**MiC: *Great Predictions*** pp. 24–27, 36–37
10-3 Technology Lab Generate Random Numbers • Use spreadsheet software to generate random numbers. **Lesson 10-3** Problem Solving Skill: Use a Simulation • Use a simulation to estimate probability. **10-3 Hands-On Lab** Use Different Models for Simulations • Use a simulation to model an experiment. ☐ SAT-10 ☐ ITBS ☐ CTBS ☑ NAEP	Spreadsheet software, graphing calculators	**MiC: *Insights Into Data*** pp. 18–19 **MiC: *Great Predictions*** pp. 41–42 ***Hands-On Lab Activities*** 10-3 ***Technology Lab Activities*** 10-3

MK = *Manipulatives Kit*

Mathematics in Context

The units *Great Predictions* and *Insights Into Data* from the *Mathematics in Context* © 2006 series can be used with Section 10A. See Section Planner above for suggestions for integrating *MiC* with *Holt Mathematics*.

Section Overview

Probability

 Probability is used to make plans and predictions. If a weather forecast gives a 30% chance of rain, then there is a 30% probability of rain, based on the study of meteorology and mathematical modeling.

Vocabulary	Definition	Example
Experiment	An activity in which results are observed	Spin a fair spinner that has 5 equal areas.
Outcome	A result of one trial of an experiment	4
Sample space	The set of all possible outcomes of an experiment	1, 2, 3, 4, 5
Event	Any set of one or more outcomes	Spinning a number greater than 2 1, 2, **3**, **4**, **5**
Probability	A number from 0 (0%) to 1 (100%) that tells how likely an event is to happen	P(spinning a number greater than 2) $= \frac{3}{5} = 60\%$

The sum of the probabilities of all possible outcomes in an experiment is 1.

Experimental Probability

 Insurance companies use experimental probability to compare the probabilities that drivers in various categories will be involved in accidents.

> **Experimental probability:**
> $$\frac{\text{number of times event occurs}}{\text{total number of trials}}$$

Example

If you roll a number cube 100 times and you roll a 3 on 18 of those trials, then the experimental probability of rolling a 3, based on this experiment is as follows: probability $= \frac{18}{100} = \frac{9}{50} = 0.18 = 18\%$.

Random Numbers and Simulations

 Random numbers can be used to simulate (model) a real situation.

A basketball player has a free-throw rate of 43%. Estimate the probability that he will make at least 4 of his next 5 free-throw attempts.

Plan	Trials		Results
Use a set of random digits. Group them in pairs.	87 20 41 16 32	4 successes *	In this simulation, 8 trials were used. There were 2 trials in which the player made at least 4 of 5 attempts.
	85 81 56 17 66	1 success	
	19 57 92 81 86	1 success	
Let the numbers 01–43 represent successes and 44–00 represent misses.	18 53 34 26 07	4 successes *	
	74 68 16 56 33	2 successes	Based on this simulation, the probability that the player will make at least 4 of his next 5 free throws is about $\frac{2}{8}$, or 25%.
	54 23 83 28 48	2 successes	
	87 64 98 59 76	0 successes	
	13 05 54 64 98	2 successes	

Pacing: Traditional 2 days
           Block 1 day

Objective: Students find the probability of an event by using the definition of probability.

 Hands-On Lab
In *Hands-On Lab Activities*

 Online Edition
Tutorial Videos

 Countdown to Testing Week 22

Power Presentations
with PowerPoint®

Warm Up

Write each fraction in simplest form.

1. $\frac{16}{20}$ $\frac{4}{5}$ 2. $\frac{12}{36}$ $\frac{1}{3}$

3. $\frac{8}{64}$ $\frac{1}{8}$ 4. $\frac{39}{195}$ $\frac{1}{5}$

Problem of the Day

A careless reader mixed up some encyclopedia volumes on a library shelf. The *Q* volume is to the right of the *X* volume, and the *C* is between the *X* and *D* volumes. The *Q* is to the left of the *G*. *X* is to the right of *C*. From left to right, in what order are the five volumes? *D, C, X, Q, G*

Also available on transparency

Math Humor

Did you hear about the man who wore half a raincoat to work? The weather report said there was a 50% chance of rain.

 *State Resources*

 **go.hrw.com**
State Resources Online
KEYWORD: MT7 Resources

10-1 Probability

Learn to find the probability of an event by using the definition of probability.

Vocabulary
experiment
trial
outcome
sample space
event
probability
impossible
certain

Writing Math
The probability of an event can be written as *P*(event).

An **experiment** is an activity in which results are observed. Each observation is called a **trial** , and each result is called an **outcome**. The **sample space** is the set of all possible outcomes of an experiment.

Experiment	Sample space
• flipping a coin	• heads, tails
• rolling a number cube	• 1, 2, 3, 4, 5, 6
• guessing the number of marbles in a jar	• whole numbers

An **event** is any set of one or more outcomes. The **probability** of an event is a number from 0 (or 0%) to 1 (or 100%) that tells you how likely the event is to happen.

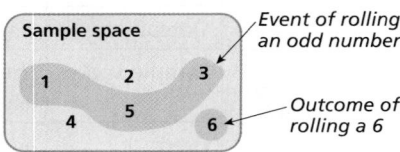

Event of rolling an odd number

Outcome of rolling a 6

• A probability of 0 means the event is **impossible** , or can never happen.

• A probability of 1 means the event is **certain** , or has to happen.

• The probabilities of all the outcomes in the sample space add up to 1.

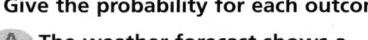

Never happens		Happens about half the time		Always happens
0	$\frac{1}{4}$	$\frac{1}{2}$	$\frac{3}{4}$	1
0	0.25	0.5	0.75	1
0%	25%	50%	75%	100%

EXAMPLE 1 **Finding Probabilities of Outcomes in a Sample Space**

Give the probability for each outcome.

A The weather forecast shows a 30% chance of snow.

Outcome	Snow	No snow
Probability		

The probability of snow is
$P(\text{snow}) = 30\% = 0.3$. The probabilities must add to 1, so the probability of no snow is $P(\text{no snow}) = 1 - 0.3 = 0.7$, or 70%.

---

1 Introduce
Alternate Opener

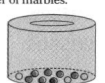
Motivate

Ask students to count the number of students in the room. Ask them if you put all of their names in a hat and pulled one out, how likely it would be for each one to be chosen. Ask how likely it would be for the name of someone from the first row to be chosen. Explain that *probability* is a branch of mathematics that predicts the likelihood of events like these.

Explorations and answers are provided in *Alternate Openers: Explorations Transparencies.*

Give the probability for each outcome.

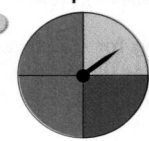

Outcome	Red	Yellow	Blue
Probability			

One-half of the spinner is red, so a reasonable estimate of the probability that the spinner lands on red is $P(\text{red}) = \frac{1}{2}$.

One-fourth of the spinner is yellow, so a reasonable estimate of the probability that the spinner lands on yellow is $P(\text{yellow}) = \frac{1}{4}$.

One-fourth of the spinner is blue, so a reasonable estimate of the probability that the spinner lands on blue is $P(\text{blue}) = \frac{1}{4}$.

Check The probabilities of all the outcomes must add to 1.

$$\frac{1}{2} + \frac{1}{4} + \frac{1}{4} = 1 \checkmark$$

To find the probability of an event, add the probabilities of all the outcomes included in the event.

EXAMPLE 2 Finding Probabilities of Events

A quiz contains 3 multiple-choice questions and 2 true-false questions. Suppose you guess randomly on every question. The table below gives the probability of each score.

Score	0	1	2	3	4	5
Probability	0.105	0.316	0.352	0.180	0.043	0.004

A What is the probability of guessing 4 or more correct?

The event "4 or more correct" consists of the outcomes 4 and 5.
$P(\text{four or more correct}) = 0.043 + 0.004$
$= 0.047$, or 4.7%

B What is the probability of guessing fewer than 3 correct?

The event "fewer than 3 correct" consists of the outcomes 0, 1, and 2.
$P(\text{fewer than 3 correct}) = 0.105 + 0.316 + 0.352$
$= 0.773$, or 77.3%

C What is the probability of failing the quiz (getting 0, 1, 2, or 3 correct) by guessing?

The event "failing the quiz" consists of the outcomes 0, 1, 2, and 3.
$P(\text{failing the quiz}) = 0.105 + 0.316 + 0.352 + 0.18$
$= 0.953$, or 95.3%

2 Teach

Guided Instruction

In this lesson, students learn to find the probability of an event by using the definition of probability. Discuss the new vocabulary. Explain that if an event has a probability of 0, that event *can never* happen (e.g., rolling a 7 on a number cube), and if an event has a probability of 1, that event *will certainly* happen (e.g., rolling a number less than 10 on a number cube). All other possible events have a probability greater than 0 and less than 1 (Teaching Transparency). Emphasize that the sum of the probabilities of all the possible outcomes in the sample space equals 1.

Reaching All Learners
Through Cognitive Strategies

Have students write the complete sample space for the experiments described in some of the exercises in this lesson. An example is given below.

1. Choose two coins from a jar that contains a penny, a nickel, and a dime. penny and nickel, penny and dime, nickel and dime

Example 3

Six students are in a race. Ken's probability of winning is 0.2. Lee is twice as likely to win as Ken. Roy is $\frac{1}{4}$ as likely to win as Lee. Tracy, James, and Kadeem all have the same chance of winning. Create a table of probabilities for the sample space.

Outcome	Probability
Ken	0.2
Lee	0.4
Roy	0.1
Tracy	0.1
James	0.1
Kadeem	0.1

Also available on transparency

EXAMPLE 3 **PROBLEM SOLVING APPLICATION**

Six students are running for class president. Jin's probability of winning is $\frac{1}{8}$. Jin is half as likely to win as Monica. Petra has the same chance to win as Monica. Lila, Juan, and Marc all have the same chance of winning. Create a table of probabilities for the sample space.

1 Understand the Problem

The **answer** will be a table of probabilities. Each probability will be a number from 0 to 1. The probabilities of all outcomes add to 1. List the **important information:**

- $P(\text{Jin}) = \frac{1}{8}$
- $P(\text{Petra}) = P(\text{Monica}) = \frac{1}{4}$
- $P(\text{Monica}) = 2P(\text{Jin}) = 2 \cdot \frac{1}{8} = \frac{1}{4}$
- $P(\text{Lila}) = P(\text{Juan}) = P(\text{Marc})$

2 Make a Plan

You know the probabilities add to 1, so use the strategy **write an equation**. Let p represent the probability for Lila, Juan, and Marc.

$P(\text{Jin}) + P(\text{Monica}) + P(\text{Petra}) + P(\text{Lila}) + P(\text{Juan}) + P(\text{Marc}) = 1$

$$\frac{1}{8} + \frac{1}{4} + \frac{1}{4} + p + p + p = \frac{5}{8} + 3p = 1$$

3 Solve

$$\frac{5}{8} + 3p = 1$$

$$\underline{-\frac{5}{8} \qquad -\frac{5}{8}} \qquad \textit{Subtract } \frac{5}{8} \textit{ from both sides.}$$

$$3p = \frac{3}{8}$$

$$\frac{1}{3} \cdot 3p = \frac{1}{3} \cdot \frac{3}{8} \qquad \textit{Multiply both sides by } \frac{1}{3}.$$

$$p = \frac{1}{8}$$

Outcome	Jin	Monica	Petra	Lila	Juan	Marc
Probability	$\frac{1}{8}$	$\frac{1}{4}$	$\frac{1}{4}$	$\frac{1}{8}$	$\frac{1}{8}$	$\frac{1}{8}$

4 Look Back

Check that the probabilities add to 1.

$$\frac{1}{8} + \frac{1}{4} + \frac{1}{4} + \frac{1}{8} + \frac{1}{8} + \frac{1}{8} = 1 ✔$$

Possible answers to
Think and Discuss

1. usually: 0.8; sometimes: 0.4; always: 1 (only acceptable answer); never: 0 (only acceptable answer)

2. An outcome is any possible result of a *single* trial. An event consists of one or *more* outcomes.

Think and Discuss

1. **Give** a probability for each of the following: usually, sometimes, always, never. Compare your values with the rest of your class.

2. **Explain** the difference between an outcome and an event.

---

3 Close

Summarize

Tell students that Jim is ready to roll a number cube numbered 1 through 6. Ask students to complete each statement with a vocabulary word.

1. Jim rolling the number cube is a(n) __?__.

2. Rolling a 4 is a possible __?__.

3. Rolling a number less than 3 is an example of a(n) __?__.

4. The probability that Jim will roll a 9 is __?__.

5. The probability that Jim will roll a number less than 7 is __?__.

1. experiment; 2. outcome or event;

3. event; 4. zero; 5. one

GUIDED PRACTICE

See Example 1

1. The weather forecast calls for a 60% chance of rain. Give the probability for each outcome. **0.6; 0.4**

Outcome	Rain	No rain
Probability		

See Example 2

2. A game consists of randomly selecting 4 colored ducks from a pond and counting the number of green ducks. The table gives the probability of each outcome.

Number of Green Ducks	0	1	2	3	4
Probability	0.043	0.248	0.418	0.248	0.043

2. What is the probability of selecting at most 1 green duck? **0.291**

3. What is the probability of selecting more than 1 green duck? **0.709**

See Example 3

4. There are 4 teams in a school tournament. Team A has a 25% chance of winning. Team B has the same chance as Team D. Team C has half the chance of winning as Team B. Create a table of probabilities for the sample space.

INDEPENDENT PRACTICE

See Example 1

5. Give the probability for each outcome. $\frac{1}{3}, \frac{1}{3}, \frac{1}{6}, \frac{1}{6}$

Outcome	Red	Blue	Yellow	Green
Probability				

See Example 2

Customers at Pizza Palace can order up to 5 toppings on a pizza. The table gives the probabilities for the number of toppings ordered on a pizza.

Number of Toppings	0	1	2	3	4	5
Probability	0.205	0.305	0.210	0.155	0.123	0.002

6. What is the probability that at least 2 toppings are ordered? **0.49**

7. What is the probability that fewer than 3 toppings are ordered? **0.72**

See Example 3

8. Five students are trying out for the lead role in a school play. Kim and Sasha have the same chance of being chosen. Kris has a 30% chance of being chosen, and Lei and Denali are both half as likely to be chosen as Kris. Create a table of probabilities for the sample space.

Assignment Guide

If you finished Example **1** assign:
Average   1, 5, 19–28
Advanced   5, 15–28

If you finished Example **2** assign:
Average   1–3, 5–7, 9–12, 19–28
Advanced   5–7, 11, 12, 15–28

If you finished Example **3** assign:
Average   1–13, 19–28
Advanced   5–8, 11–28

Homework Quick Check

Quickly check key concepts.
Exercises: 5, 6, 8, 13

Answers
4, 8. See p. A14.

Math Background

Probability plays an important role in many aspects of daily life. Predictions about the weather, results of elections, and winners of sporting events are based on probabilities. When an insurance company determines a rate to charge for a policy, it uses probability theory. When doctors choose a method of treatment for an injury and when people decide which investments to make, they often use probability theory.

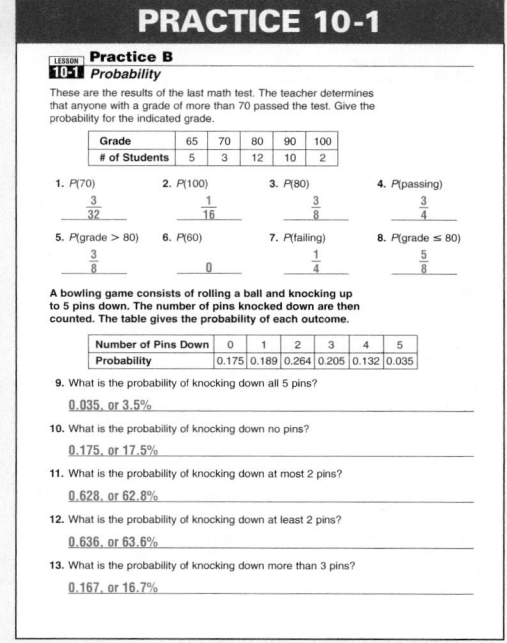

RETEACH 10-1

Reteach
10-1 Probability

The **probability** that something will happen is how often you can expect that **event** to occur. This depends upon how many outcomes are possible, the **sample space.**

In the spinner shown, the circle is divided into four equal parts. There are 4 possible outcomes.

So, in a single spin:

$P(A) = P(B) = P(C) = P(D) = 25\% = \frac{1}{4}$

Complete to give the probability for each event.

	1. A fair coin is tossed.	**2.** A number cube is rolled.
List all the possible outcomes.	heads, tails	1, 2, 3, 4, 5, 6
How many outcomes in sample space?	2	6
Find the probability of the event shown.	$P(\text{heads}) = \frac{1}{2}$	$P(5) = \frac{1}{6}$

• A probability of 0 means the event is **impossible**, or can never happen.
On the spinner above, $P(F) = 0$.
• A probability of 1 means the event is **certain**, or has to happen.
In one roll of a number cube, $P(\text{a whole number from 1 through 6}) = 1$.

Give the probability for each event.

3. selecting a rectangle from the set of squares

$P(\text{rectangle}) = \underline{1}$

4. selecting a negative number from the set of whole numbers

$P(\text{negative number}) = \underline{0}$

• The sum of the probabilities of all the possible outcomes in a sample space is 1.
If the probability of *snow* is 30%, then the probability of *no snow* is 70%.
$P(\text{snow}) + P(\text{no snow}) = 1$

5. If the probability of selecting a senior for a committee is 60%, then the probability of not selecting a senior is:

40%

6. If the probability of choosing a red ball from a certain box is 0.35, then the probability of not choosing a red ball is:

0.65

PRACTICE 10-1

Practice B
10-1 Probability

These are the results of the last math test. The teacher determines that anyone with a grade of more than 70 passed the test. Give the probability for the indicated grade.

Grade	65	70	80	90	100
# of Students	5	3	12	10	2

1. $P(70)$ $\frac{3}{32}$

2. $P(100)$ $\frac{1}{16}$

3. $P(80)$ $\frac{3}{8}$

4. $P(\text{passing})$ $\frac{3}{4}$

5. $P(\text{grade} > 80)$ $\frac{3}{8}$

6. $P(60)$ 0

7. $P(\text{failing})$ $\frac{1}{4}$

8. $P(\text{grade} \leq 80)$ $\frac{5}{8}$

A bowling game consists of rolling a ball and knocking up to 5 pins down. The number of pins knocked down are then counted. The table gives the probability of each outcome.

Number of Pins Down	0	1	2	3	4	5
Probability	0.175	0.189	0.264	0.205	0.132	0.035

9. What is the probability of knocking down all 5 pins?

0.035, or 3.5%

10. What is the probability of knocking down no pins?

0.175, or 17.5%

11. What is the probability of knocking down at most 2 pins?

0.628, or 62.8%

12. What is the probability of knocking down at least 2 pins?

0.636, or 63.6%

13. What is the probability of knocking down more than 3 pins?

0.167, or 16.7%

State Resources

go.hrw.com
State Resources Online
KEYWORD: MT7 Resources

Answers

14. Possible answer: Find the probabilities of A and B in decimal form, and then subtract their sum from 1. Divide the difference by 2.

15. Possible answer: rolling an 8 on a number cube labeled 1 to 6

16. Possible answer: The probabilities must have a sum of 1, but they do not have to be equal. For example, one could be 0.4 and the other could be 0.6.

17–18. See p. A14.

TEST PREP DOCTOR + Students frequently confuse percent chance with probability. Point out that both Exercise 19 and 20 ask for a probability, even though a percent chance is given in the problem statement. Remind students that a percent chance is a percent between 0% and 100% and a probability is a number between 0 and 1.

Journal

Ask students to identify some examples of probability in their everyday lives. Examples may include weather forecasts, sports, or board games.

Power Presentations
with PowerPoint®

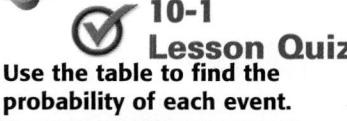

10-1 Lesson Quiz

Use the table to find the probability of each event.

Outcome	Probability
1	0.024
2	0.327
3	0.126
4	0.341
5	0.182

1. 1 or 2 occurring   0.351
2. 3 not occurring   0.874
3. 2, 3, or 4 occurring   0.794

Also available on transparency

PRACTICE AND PROBLEM SOLVING

Extra Practice See page 800.

Use the table to find the probability of each event.

Outcome	A	B	C	D	E
Probability	0.306	0	0.216	0.115	0.363

9. A, C, or E occurring   **0.885**
10. B or D occurring   **0.115**
11. A, B, D, or E occurring   **0.784**
12. A not occurring   **0.694**

13. Consumer A cereal company puts "prizes" in some of its boxes to attract shoppers. There is a 0.005 probability of getting two tickets to a movie theater, $\frac{1}{8}$ probability of finding a watch, 12.5% probability of getting an action figure, and 0.2 probability of getting a sticker. What is the probability of not getting any prize? **0.545**

14. Critical Thinking You are told there are 4 possible events that may occur. Event A has a 25% chance of occurring, event B has a probability of $\frac{1}{5}$ and events C and D have an equal likelihood of occurring. What steps would you take in order to find the probabilities of events C and D?

15. Give an example of an event that has 0 probability of occurring.

 16. What's the Error? Two people are playing a game. One of them says, "Either I will win or you will. The sample space contains two outcomes, so we each have a probability of one-half." What is the error?

 17. Write About It Suppose an event has a probability of *p*. What can you say about the value of *p*? What is the probability that the event will not occur? Explain.

 18. Challenge List all possible events in the sample space with outcomes A, B, and C.

TEST PREP and Spiral Review

19. Multiple Choice The local weather forecaster said there is a 30% chance of rain tomorrow. What is the probability that it will NOT rain tomorrow?

(A) 0.7   (B) 0.3   (C) 70   (D) 30

20. Gridded Response A sports announcer states that a runner has an 84% chance of winning a race. Give the probability, as a fraction in lowest terms, that the runner will NOT win the race. $\frac{4}{25}$

Evaluate the powers of 10. (Lesson 4-2)
21. 10^{-4} 0.0001   **22.** 10^{-1} 0.1   **23.** 10^{-5} 0.00001   **24.** 10^{-7} 0.0000001

Find the slope of the line through the given points. (Lesson 7-5)
25. $A(-2, 5), B(-2, 4)$ undefined   **26.** $G(4, -3), H(5, 2)$ 5   **27.** $R(8, 4), S(10, 1)$ $-\frac{3}{2}$ **28.** $J(3, 2), K(-1, 2)$ 0

CHALLENGE 10-1

LESSON 10-1 Challenge
Why We Look Like Our Parents

Each parent carries two genes with respect to a specific trait and each passes one of these genes on to an offspring who then also has two genes for that trait.

In pea plants, a tall gene is dominant over a short gene. So, if a pea plant has at least one tall gene, the plant is tall. If T represents *tall* and t represents *short*, one way to represent the gene makeup with respect to height of a tall pea plant would be Tt.

1. What is another way to represent the gene makeup with respect to height of a tall pea plant?   TT

An early 20th-century English geneticist, Reginald Punnett, invented a method to display the gene makeup of parents and their offspring.

2. The **Punnett square** at the right shows the gene makeup of one tall parent plant as the labels for the columns. Insert your result from Question 1 for the other tall parent plant as the row labels.

3. a. The label for each column has been inserted in each box of its column, as the first gene of the offspring plant. Insert your labels for each row as the second gene of each offspring plant.

b. According to the two genes now in each of the boxes for the new offspring plants, tell if the new plant will be tall or short.

c. What is the probability that an offspring of these tall parent plants will be tall? $\frac{4}{4}$ or 1 or 100%

4. Suppose the gene makeup for both tall parent pea plants is Tt.
a. Complete a Punnett square to display the gene makeup of the offspring.
b. What is the probability that an offspring of these tall parent plants will be tall? $\frac{3}{4}$ or 75%

PROBLEM SOLVING 10-1

LESSON 10-1 Problem Solving
Probability

Write the correct answer.

1. To get people to buy more of their product, a company advertises that in selected boxes of their popsicles is a super hero trading card. There is a $\frac{1}{4}$ chance of getting a trading card in a box. What is the probability that there will not be a trading card in the box of popsicles that you buy? $\frac{3}{4}$

2. The probability of winning a lucky wheel television game show in which 6 preselected numbers are spun on a wheel numbered 1–49 is $\frac{1}{13,983,816}$ or 0.000007151%. What is the probability that you will not win the game show? $\frac{13,983,815}{13,983,816}$

Based on world statistics, the probability of identical twins is 0.004, while the probability of fraternal twins is 0.023.

3. What is the probability that a person chosen at random from the world will be a twin?   0.027, or 2.7%

4. What is the probability that a person chosen at random from the world will not be a twin?   0.973, or 97.3%

Use the table below that shows the probability of multiple births by country. Choose the letter for the best answer.

5. In which country is it most likely to have multiple births?
A Japan   C Sweden
(B) United States   D Switzerland

6. In which country is it least likely to have multiple births?
(F) Japan   H Sweden
G United States   J Switzerland

7. In which two countries are multiple births equally likely?
A United Kingdom, Canada
B Canada, Switzerland
(C) Sweden, United Kingdom
D Japan, United States

Probability of Multiple Births

Country	Probability
Canada	0.012
Japan	0.008
United Kingdom	0.014
United States	0.029
Sweden	0.014
Switzerland	0.013

10-2 Experimental Probability

Learn to estimate probability using experimental methods.

Vocabulary
experimental probability

Despite the rising price of gasoline, sports utility vehicles (SUV's) remain popular. The public perception of the safety of SUV's varies widely. The accident rate of SUV's is about the same as with other vehicles, but SUV's tend to have a higher rate among accidents involving fatalities. Insurance companies estimate the probability of accidents by studying accident rates for different types of vehicles.

In **experimental probability**, the likelihood of an event is estimated by repeating an experiment many times and observing the number of times the event happens. That number is divided by the total number of trials. The more the experiment is repeated, the more accurate the estimate is likely to be.

$$\text{probability} \approx \frac{\text{number of times the event occurs}}{\text{total number of trials}}$$

EXAMPLE 1 Estimating the Probability of an Event

A After 1000 spins of the spinner, the following information was recorded. Estimate the probability of the spinner landing on red.

Outcome	Blue	Red	Yellow
Spins	448	267	285

$$\text{probability} \approx \frac{\text{number of spins that landed on red}}{\text{total number of spins}} = \frac{267}{1000} = 0.267$$

The probability of landing on red is about 0.267, or 26.7%.

B A marble is randomly drawn out of a bag and then replaced. The table shows the results after 100 draws. Estimate the probability of drawing a yellow marble.

Outcome	Green	Red	Yellow	Blue	White
Draws	12	35	21	18	14

$$\text{probability} \approx \frac{\text{number of yellow marbles drawn}}{\text{total number of draws}} = \frac{21}{100} = 0.21$$

The probability of drawing a yellow marble is about 0.21, or 21%.

Motivate

Flip a coin two times and note the results. Ask students to predict how many heads and how many tails you would get if you flipped the coin 100 times. Tell students that if you actually performed the experiment, the results would provide a way to estimate the probability of getting heads or of getting tails on a flip of a coin.

Explorations and answers are provided in *Alternate Openers: Explorations Transparencies.*

Additional Examples

Example 1

A marble is randomly drawn out of a bag and then replaced. The table shows the results after fifty draws.

Outcome	Green	Red	Yellow
Draw	12	15	23

A. Estimate the probability of drawing a red marble.
$P(red) = 0.3$

B. Estimate the probability of drawing a green marble.
$P(green) = 0.24$

C. Estimate the probability of drawing a yellow marble.
$P(yellow) = 0.46$

Example 2

Use the table to compare the probability that the Huskies will win their next game with the probability that the Knights will win their next game.

Team	Wins	Games
Huskies	79	138
Cougars	85	150
Knights	90	146

The Knights are more likely to win.

Also available on transparency

C A researcher has been observing the types of vehicles passing through an intersection. Of the last 50 cars, 29 were sedans, 9 were trucks, and 12 were SUV's. Estimate the probability that the next vehicle through the intersection will be an SUV.

Outcome	Sedan	Truck	SUV
Observations	29	9	12

probability $\approx \dfrac{\text{number of SUV's}}{\text{total number of vehicles}} = \dfrac{12}{50} = 0.24 = 24\%$

The probability that the next vehicle through the intersection will be an SUV is about 0.24, or 24%.

EXAMPLE 2 *Safety Application*

Use the table to compare the probability of being involved in a fatal traffic crash in an SUV with being in a fatal traffic crash in a mid-size car.

Traffic Crashes in Ohio, 2004		
Vehicle Class	Number of Fatal Crashes	Total Number of Crashes
Sub-compact cars	23	7, 962
Compact cars	266	110,598
Mid-size cars	464	200,433
Full-size cars	161	76,570
Minivan	97	45,043
SUV	172	75,593

Source: Ohio Department of Public Safety

probability $\approx \dfrac{\text{number of fatal crashes}}{\text{total number of crashes}}$

probability of SUV $\approx \dfrac{172}{75,593} \approx 0.0023$

probability of mid-size car $\approx \dfrac{464}{200,433} \approx 0.0023$

In 2004, an SUV was just as likely to be involved in a fatal traffic crash as a mid-size car.

Possible answers to *Think and Discuss*

1. The red section appears to be about 25% of the spinner, so the probability should be close to 25%. That estimate is close to the experimental probability of 26.7%.

2. 15 green, 10 red, 10 yellow, 10 blue, and 6 white

Think and Discuss

1. Compare the probability in Example 1A of the spinner landing on red to what you think the probability should be.

2. Give a possible number of marbles of each color in the bag in Example 1B. Explain your reasoning.

---

2 Teach

Guided Instruction

In this lesson, students learn to estimate probability using experimental methods. Explain that *experimental probability* is a ratio that compares the number of times a particular event occurs to the total number of trials. Point out that experimental probability is based on actual results, so the experimental probability for an event may differ from one experiment to the next. However, as the number of trials in each experiment increases, the difference in the probabilities is likely to decrease.

Reaching All Learners
Through Concrete Manipulatives

Have students work in pairs. Give each pair of students one number cube. Have one student toss the number cube 15 times while the other student records the number of times each of the outcomes, 1 through 6, occurs. Then have them switch roles and repeat the experiment. Finally, have them compare the results of the two experiments. Discuss the different results with students. If time permits, you may want to add up all of the data to find the cumulative experimental probability.

3 Close

Summarize

Remind students that experimental probability is based on actual results, so the experimental probability for an event from one experiment may be different than the experimental probability for the same event from a different experiment. Discuss with students why experimental probability is more reliable with a greater number of trials.

Possible answer: Sometimes you can have runs of outcomes (like getting four tails in a row on coin flips) that make the experimental probability seem much different than it usually is.

GUIDED PRACTICE

See Example 1

1. A game spinner was spun 500 times. It was found that A was spun 170 times, B was spun 244 times, and C was spun 86 times. Estimate the probability that the spinner will land on A. **0.34**

2. A coin was randomly drawn from a bag and then replaced. After 300 draws, it was found that 45 pennies, 76 nickels, 92 dimes, and 87 quarters had been drawn. Estimate the probability of drawing a quarter. **0.29**

See Example 2

3. Use the table to compare the probability that a student walks to school to the probability that a student bikes to school. **≈ 0.136; ≈ 0.113; more likely to walk**

4. Use the table to compare the probability that a student takes the bus to school to the probability that a student rides in a car to school. **≈ 0.34; ≈ 0.41**

Mode of Transportation	Number of Students
Bus	265
Car	313
Walk	105
Bike	87

INDEPENDENT PRACTICE

See Example 1

5. A researcher polled 260 students at a university and found that 83 of them owned a laptop computer. Estimate the probability that a randomly selected college student owns a laptop computer. **≈ 0.319**

6. Keisha made 12 out of her last 58 shots on goal. Estimate the probability that she will make her next shot on goal. **≈ 0.207**

See Example 2

7. Stefan polled 113 students about the number of siblings they have. Use the table to compare the probability that a student has one sibling to the probability that a student has two siblings. **≈ 0.398; ≈ 0.239; more likely to have one sibling**

8. Use the table to compare the probability that a student has no siblings to the probability that a student has three siblings. **≈ 0.12; ≈ 0.13**

Number of Siblings	Number of Students
0	14
1	45
2	27
3	15
4+	12

PRACTICE AND PROBLEM SOLVING

Extra Practice
See page 800.

Use the table for Exercises 7–11.
Estimate the probability of each event.

9. A batter hits a single. **0.25**

10. A batter hits a double. **0.15**

11. A batter hits a triple. **0.025**

12. A batter hits a home run. **0.1**

13. A batter makes an out. **0.35**

Result	Number
Single	20
Double	12
Triple	2
Home run	8
Walk	10
Out	28
Total	80

10-2 Exercises

Assignment Guide

If you finished Example 1 assign:
Average 1, 2, 5, 6, 18–25
Advanced 5, 6, 18–25

If you finished Example 2 assign:
Average 1–16, 18–25
Advanced 5–25

Homework Quick Check

Quickly check key concepts.
Exercises: 6, 8, 16

Math Background

Students will probably be familiar with the idea that the probability of getting heads on a flip of a coin is 50/50, which means 50% or $\frac{1}{2}$. Explain that such a probability is called a *theoretical probability* (Lesson 10-4). *Experimental probability* is a ratio that uses *actual results* of an experiment. We expect the experimental probability to get closer to the theoretical probability as the number of trials increases. Experimental probability has numerous real-world applications, including insurance, sports, and weather forecasts.

State Resources

go.hrw.com
State Resources Online
KEYWORD: MT7 Resources

RETEACH 10-2

LESSON 10-2 Reteach
Experimental Probability

A machine is filling boxes of apples by choosing 50 apples at random from a selection of six types of apples. An inspector records the results for one filled box in the table below.

Type	Pink Lady	Red Delicious	Granny Smith	Golden Delicious	Fuji	MacIntosh
Number	8	12	6	4	15	5

The inspector then expands the table to find the experimental probability.

$$probability = \frac{number\ of\ type\ of\ apple}{total\ number\ of\ apples}$$

Type	Pink Lady	Red Delicious	Granny Smith	Golden Delicious	Fuji	MacIntosh
Experimental Probability (ratio)	$\frac{8}{50}$, or $\frac{4}{25}$	$\frac{12}{50}$, or $\frac{6}{25}$	$\frac{6}{50}$, or $\frac{3}{25}$	$\frac{4}{50}$, or $\frac{2}{25}$	$\frac{15}{50}$, or $\frac{3}{10}$	$\frac{5}{50}$, or $\frac{1}{10}$
Experimental Probability (percent)	16%	24%	12%	8%	30%	10%

Find each sum for the apple experiment.

1. The sum of the experimental probability ratios.

$$probability = \frac{8}{50} + \frac{12}{50} + \frac{6}{50} + \frac{4}{50} + \frac{15}{50} + \frac{5}{50} = \frac{50}{50}\ or\ \underline{1}$$

2. The sum of the experimental probability percents.

$$probability = 16\% + 24\% + 12\% + 8\% + 30\% + 10\% = \underline{100}\%\ or\ \underline{1}$$

Complete the table to find the experimental probability.

3. Five types of seed are inserted at random in a pre-seeded strip ready for planting.

Type	Marigold	Impatiens	Snapdragon	Daisy	Petunia
Number	40	100	80	60	120
Experimental Probability (ratio)	$\frac{40}{400}$, or $\frac{1}{10}$	$\frac{100}{400}$, or $\frac{1}{4}$	$\frac{80}{400}$, or $\frac{1}{5}$	$\frac{60}{400}$, or $\frac{3}{20}$	$\frac{120}{400}$, or $\frac{3}{10}$
Experimental Probability (percent)	10%	25%	20%	15%	30%

PRACTICE 10-2

LESSON 10-2 Practice B
Experimental Probability

1. A number cube was thrown 150 times. The results are shown in the table below. Estimate the probability for each outcome.

Outcome	1	2	3	4	5	6
Frequency	33	21	15	36	27	18
Probability	22%	14%	10%	24%	18%	12%

A movie theater sells popcorn in small, medium, large and jumbo sizes. The customers of the first show purchase 4 small, 20 medium, 40 large, and 16 jumbo containers of popcorn. Estimate the probability of the purchase of each of the different size containers of popcorn.

2. P(small container)

$\frac{1}{20}$ or 5%

3. P(medium container)

$\frac{1}{4}$ or 25%

4. P(large container)

$\frac{1}{2}$ or 50%

5. P(jumbo container)

$\frac{1}{5}$ or 20%

Janessa polled 154 students about their favorite winter sport.

Outcome	Frequency
Skiing	46
Sledding	21
Snowboarding	64
Ice Skating	14
Other	9

6. Use the table to compare the probability that a student chose snowboarding to the probability that a student chose skiing.

≈0.415; ≈0.299; more likely

7. Use the table to compare the probability that a student chose ice skating to the probability that a student chose sledding.

≈0.091; ≈0.136; less likely

8. The class president made 75 copies of the flyer advertising the school play. It was found that 8 of the copies were defective. Estimate the probability that a flyer will be printed properly. ≈0.893

Interdisciplinary LINK

Earth Science

Exercises 14–17 involve calculating probabilities using data about earthquakes. Students study earthquakes in middle school earth science programs, such as *Holt Science & Technology*.

 **TEST PREP DOCTOR** If students have trouble making a plan for Exercise 19, ask them to estimate how many students will buy a banana if only 50 more students come to lunch ... 17 100 more students ... 17 × 2 = 34 150 more students ... 17 × 3 = 51 Then, show them how to set up a proportion to solve the problem more rapidly.

 Journal

Ask students to write how the data in Example 2 helps explain why insurance rates differ for different age groups.

Power Presentations
with PowerPoint®

 10-2 Lesson Quiz

1. Of 425, 234 seniors were enrolled in a math course. Estimate the probability that a randomly selected senior is enrolled in a math course. **0.55, or 55%**

2. Mason made a hit 34 out of his last 125 times at bat. Estimate the probability that he will make a hit his next time at bat. **0.27, or 27%**

3. Christina polled 176 students about their favorite ice cream flavor. 63 students' favorite flavor is vanilla and 40 students' favorite flavor is strawberry. Compare the probability of a student's liking vanilla to a student's liking strawberry. **about 36% to about 23%**

Also available on transparency

Earth Science LINK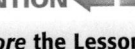

The strength of an earthquake is measured on the Richter scale. A *major* earthquake measures between 7 and 7.9 on the Richter scale, and a *great* earthquake measures 8 or higher. The table shows the number of major and great earthquakes per year worldwide from 1985 to 2004.

14. Estimate the probability that there will be more than 15 major earthquakes next year. **0.2**

15. Estimate the probability that there will be fewer than 12 major earthquakes next year. **0.3**

16. Estimate the probability that there will be no great earthquakes next year. **0.4**

17. ⭐ **Challenge** Estimate the probability that there will be more than one major earthquake in the next month.
Possible answer: 0.7

go.hrw.com
Web Extra!
KEYWORD: MT7 Quake

Number of Earthquakes Worldwide					
Year	Major	Great	Year	Major	Great
1985	13	1	1995	22	3
1986	5	1	1996	14	1
1987	11	0	1997	16	0
1988	8	0	1998	11	1
1989	6	1	1999	18	0
1990	12	0	2000	14	1
1991	11	0	2001	15	1
1992	23	0	2002	13	0
1993	15	1	2003	14	1
1994	13	2	2004	14	2

TEST PREP and Spiral Review

18. **Multiple Choice** A spinner was spun 220 times. The outcome was red 58 times. Estimate the probability of the spinner landing on red.

Ⓐ about 0.126　　Ⓑ about 0.225　　Ⓒ about 0.264　　Ⓓ about 0.32

19. **Short Response** A researcher observed students buying lunch in a cafeteria. Of the last 50 students, 22 bought an apple, 17 bought a banana, and 11 bought a pear. If 150 more students buy lunch, estimate the number of students who will buy a banana. Explain. **51; The probability is $\frac{17}{50}$. Solve the proportion $\frac{17}{50} = \frac{x}{150}$; $x = 51$**

Evaluate each expression for the given value of the variable. (Lesson 2-3)

20. $45.6 + x$ for $x = -11.1$ **34.5**　21. $17.9 - b$ for $b = 22.3$ **−4.4**　22. $r + (-4.9)$ for $r = 31.8$ **26.9**

A spinner is divided into 8 equal sections. There are 3 red sections, 4 blue, and 1 green. Give the probability of each outcome. (Lesson 10-1)

23. red $\frac{3}{8}$　　　24. blue $\frac{1}{2}$　　　25. green $\frac{1}{8}$

Technology LAB 10-3

Generate Random Numbers

Use with Lesson 10-3

go.hrw.com
Lab Resources Online
KEYWORD: MT7 Lab10

A spreadsheet can be used to generate random decimal numbers that are greater than or equal to 0 but less than 1. By using formulas, you can shift these numbers into a useful range.

Activity

1 Use a spreadsheet to generate five random decimal numbers that are between 0 and 1. Then convert these numbers to integers from 1 to 10.

a. Type **=RAND()** into cell A1 and press **ENTER**. A random decimal number appears.

	A
1	0.063515
2	

b. Click to highlight cell A1. Go to the **Edit** menu and **Copy** the contents of A1. Then click and drag to highlight cells A2 through A5. Go to the **Edit** menu and use **Paste** to fill cells A2 through A5.

	A
1	0.20589
2	0.837083
3	0.445334
4	0.939134
5	0.993354
6	

Notice that the random number in cell A1 changed when you filled the other cells.

RAND() gives a decimal number greater than or equal to 0, but less than 1. To generate random integers from 1 to 10, you need to do the following:

- Multiply **RAND()** by 10 (to give a number greater than or equal to 0 but less than 10).

- Use the **INT** function to drop the decimal part of the result (to give an integer from 0 to 9).

- Add 1 (to give an integer from 1 to 10).

c. Change the formula in A1 to **=INT(10*RAND()) + 1** and press **ENTER**. Repeat the process in part **b** to fill cells A2 through A5.

A2	▼	= =INT(10*RAND()) + 1

	A	B	C	D
1	9			
2	1			
3	7			
4	7			
5	6			
6				

The formula **=INT(10*RAND()) + 1** generates random integers from 1 to 10.

Think and Discuss

1. Explain how **INT(10*RAND()) + 1** generates random integers from 1 to 10.

Try This

1. Use a spreadsheet to simulate 3 spins of a spinner with 4 equal regions.

Teacher to Teacher

Using a spreadsheet to generate random numbers is much better than using a graphing calculator to penetrate random numbers. Because students are able to view all of the data at one time, they see that the numbers generated are indeed random, even if they do not appear to be random with just a few trials. Being able to view all of the data helps students to understand the nature of random numbers and how they are used in simulations better.

Brenda Lynch
Montgomery, TX

Technology LAB

Organizer
Use with Lesson 10-3

Pacing:
Traditional 1 day
Block $\frac{1}{2}$ day

Objective: Use spreadsheet software to generate random numbers.
Materials: Spreadsheet software

PREMIER Online Edition

Resources

Technology Lab Activities
Lab 10-3 Recording Sheet

Teach
Discuss

Explain to students that accurate ways of creating randomness is crucial in statistics. Have them warm up by experimenting with spreadsheet functions.

Close
Key Concept

You can use spreadsheet software to generate random numbers, which can be used to simulate experiments.

Assessment

1. What command creates a random number? **RAND()**

2. Describe the random numbers generated by the command RAND(). They are decimal values between 0 and 1.

3. What command creates a random whole number between 1 and 7? **INT(7*RAND()) + 1**

Answers
Think and Discuss, Try This. See p. A14.

State Resources

go.hrw.com
State Resources Online
KEYWORD: MT7 Resources

Hands-On Lab
In *Hands-On Lab Activities*

Online Edition
Tutorial Videos

Countdown to Testing Week 22

Power Presentations
with PowerPoint®

Warm Up

1. There are 25 out of 216 sophomores enrolled in a physical-education course. Estimate the probability that a randomly selected sophomore is enrolled in a physical-education course. **0.12**

2. A spinner was spun 230 times. It landed on red 120 times, green 65 times, and yellow 45 times. Estimate the probability of its landing on red. **0.52**

Problem of the Day

If a triangle is worth 7 and a rectangle is worth 8, how much is a hexagon worth? **10**

Also available on transparency

Math Humor

Teacher: Why are you tickling your math homework?

Student: Aren't we supposed to *stimulate* the problem?

State Resources

go.hrw.com
State Resources Online
KEYWORD: MT7 Resources

10-3 **Use a Simulation**
 Problem Solving Strategy

Learn to use a simulation to estimate probability.

Vocabulary
simulation
random numbers

In football, many factors are used to evaluate how good a quarterback is. One important factor is the quarterback's ability to complete passes.

If a quarterback has a completion percentage of 64%, he completes about 64 of every 100 passes he throws. What is the probability that he will complete at least 6 of 10 passes thrown? A simulation can help you estimate this probability.

A **simulation** is a model of a real situation. In a set of **random numbers**, each number has the same probability of occurring, and no pattern can be used to predict the next number. Random numbers can be used to simulate random events in real situations. The table is a set of 280 random digits.

During the 2004 season, Indianapolis's Peyton Manning had a completion percentage of 67.6%.

87244	11632	85815	61766	19579	28186	18533	42633
74681	65633	54238	32848	87649	85976	13355	46498
53736	21616	86318	77291	24794	31119	48193	44869
86585	27919	65264	93557	94425	13325	16635	28584
18394	73266	67899	38783	94228	23426	76679	41256
39917	16373	59733	18588	22545	61378	33563	65161
96916	46278	78210	13906	82794	01136	60848	98713

EXAMPLE **1** **PROBLEM SOLVING APPLICATION**

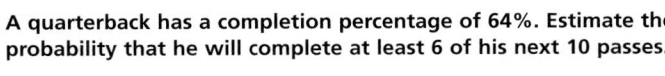

A quarterback has a completion percentage of 64%. Estimate the probability that he will complete at least 6 of his next 10 passes.

1 **Understand the Problem**

The **answer** will be the probability that he will complete at least 6 of his next 10 passes. It must be a number between 0 and 1. List the **important information:**

• The probability that the quarterback will complete a pass is 0.64.

---

1 **Introduce**
Alternate Opener

EXPLORATION

10-3 **Use a Simulation**

You can use a calculator to simulate flipping a coin 30 times.

• Press the ▬ key.
• Select **PRB**.
• Select **5:randInt(**.
• Key in 0, 1, 6.
• Press the ▬ key five times.

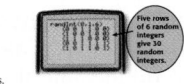

Five rows of 6 random integers give 30 random integers.

Assume that 1 means heads and 0 means tails to answer each question.

1. How many heads did you get in the 30 simulated flips?
2. How many tails did you get in the 30 simulated flips?
3. What is the experimental probability of flipping heads? (*Hint:* Write a fraction that compares the number of heads to 30 flips.)
4. What is the experimental probability of flipping tails? (*Hint:* Write a fraction that compares the number of tails to 30 flips.)
5. Use a calculator to simulate 100 flips, and compute the experimental probability of flipping heads.

Think and Discuss

6. **Explain** how to perform simulations on a calculator.
7. **Discuss** what you think would happen to the experimental probability as you increase the number of simulated flips.

Motivate

Ask every student to write any single digit on a piece of paper. Make a list on the chalkboard of all the students' digits. Tell the class that this list of numbers is like a list of random digits. Explain that there are computer programs that will generate lists of random numbers and that such lists can be used to simulate random events.

Explorations and answers are provided in *Alternate Openers: Explorations Transparencies.*

2 Make a Plan

Use a simulation to model the situation. Use digits from the table, grouped in pairs. The numbers 01–64 represent completed passes, and the numbers 65–00 represent incomplete passes. Each group of 20 digits represents one trial. You can start anywhere on the table.

3 Solve

The first 20 digits in the table are shown below.
87244 11632 85815 61766

The digits can be grouped in ten pairs, as shown below.
87 **24** **41** **16** **32** 85 81 **56** **17** 66
This represents 6 of 10 completed passes.

If you continue using the table, the next nine trials are as follows.

19 **57** 92 81 86 **18** **53** **34** **26** **33**   *7 completed passes*
74 68 **16** **56** **33** **54** **23** 83 **28** **48**   *7 completed passes*
87 **64** 98 **59** 76 **13** **35** **54** **64** 98   *6 completed passes*
53 73 **62** **16** **16** 86 **31** 87 72 91   *5 completed passes*
24 79 **43** **11** **19** **48** **19** **34** **48** 69   *8 completed passes*
86 **58** **52** 79 **19** 65 **26** **49** **35** **57**   *7 completed passes*
94 **42** **51** **33** **25** **16** **63** **52** 85 84   *7 completed passes*
18 **39** **47** **32** 66 67 89 93 87 83   *4 completed passes*
94 **22** 82 **34** **26** 76 67 94 **12** **56**   *5 completed passes*

Out of the 10 trials, 7 represented 6 or more completed passes. Based on this simulation, the probability of completing at least 6 of 10 passes is about 0.70, or 70%.

4 Look Back

A completion percentage of 64% means the quarterback completes about 64 of every 100 passes. This ratio is equivalent to 6.4 out of 10 passes, so he should make at least 6 passes most of the time. The answer is reasonable.

Helpful Hint

Calculators and computers can generate sets of approximately random numbers. A formula is used to generate the numbers, so they are not truly random, but they work for most simulations.

Think and Discuss

1. **Explain** why a random number generator on a computer or calculator is useful for estimating probability by simulation.

2. **Tell** how you could use a simulation to estimate the probability that a quarterback who has a completion percentage of 50% will make at least 7 of 10 passes.

**Possible answers to
Think and Discuss**

1. Computers or calculators can generate random numbers quickly, and they can generate multiple-digit numbers. In addition, they can generate as many numbers as you need.

2. Use a coin. You could let heads represent a completed pass. Flip a coin 10 times (or 10 coins at once) for each trial. Then find in how many trials at least 7 of the outcomes were heads.

---

2 Teach

Guided Instruction

In this lesson, students learn to use a simulation to estimate probability. Discuss the meaning of *simulation*. Explain that the number of random digits in the list in the lesson (280) is arbitrary and that the way they are grouped on the page is only for ease of reading. Also explain that they could choose any number on the list as a starting point. Work carefully through the example, as this subject may be new for many students. You may want to use the table of random numbers on the Teaching Transparency.

ENGLISH LANGUAGE LEARNERS

 **Reaching All Learners**
Through Critical Thinking

Have students use the data from Example 1 to perform another simulation. Instruct them to start at a different place in the table of random digits or, if possible, have them use a calculator or computer to generate different random digits. When they have completed their simulations, discuss the different results with the class. If some results are different, ask students to explain why.

Possible answer: Probability is only an estimate. It never guarantees that a specific event will happen.

---

3 Close

Summarize

Review the steps for creating and using a simulation. Remind students that to use a simulation to estimate a probability, they need a given probability, such as a quarterback's having already made 64% of his passes. Emphasize that simulations are only estimates and that they cannot be used to predict exactly what will happen.

10-3 Exercises

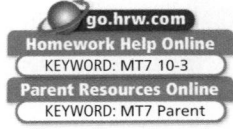

Assignment Guide

If you finished Example **1** assign:
Average 1–10, 13–20
Advanced 5–20

Quickly check key concepts.
Exercises: 8, 10

Math Background

Example 1 in the lesson refers to a 64% pass completion rate. This percent is similar to an experimental probability because it is based on the ratio

$$\frac{\text{completed passes}}{\text{attempted passes}}$$

A batting average in baseball is also similar to an experimental probability. If a player gets 24 hits in 50 at bats, his batting average is $\frac{\text{number of hits}}{\text{number of at bats}} = \frac{24}{50} = .480$. As with experimental probability, sports statistics such as these can be used to estimate the probability of an event, whether that event is completing a pass or getting a hit.

State Resources

GUIDED PRACTICE

See Example **1** Use the table of random numbers to simulate each situation. Use at least 10 trials for each simulation.

49064	12830	66783	14965	81537	24935	69675	32681
42893	42668	70963	58827	17354	42190	36165	29827
21705	89446	38703	21274	90049	19036	37971	05322
52737	40117	54132	11152	02985	82873	28197	89796

1. Liza makes free throws at a rate of 81%. If she takes 8 free throws during a game, estimate the probability that she will make at least 6 free throws. **Possible answer: 90%**

2. During the summer, a city has a 15% chance of a day with a temperature over 90°F. Estimate the probability that at least 3 days have a temperature over 90°F during the last week in August. **Possible answer: 10%**

3. Customers at a carnival game win about 25% of the time. Estimate the probability that no more than 1 of the next 6 customers will win the game. **Possible answer: 60%**

4. Marcelo completes a sale with approximately 32% of the customers he meets. If he has 6 customer appointments tomorrow, estimate the probability that he will complete at least 3 sales. **Possible answer: 20%**

INDEPENDENT PRACTICE

See Example **1** Use the table of random numbers to simulate each situation. Use at least 10 trials for each simulation.

63415	12776	31960	42974	36444	23826	46320	48308
41591	43536	64118	53147	23544	61352	12954	57628
26446	12734	22435	42612	24834	21961	12526	22832
16522	33043	21997	15738	25788	33205	55699	33357
53040	39923	29591	64384	58166	39164	54474	38970

5. Veronica gets a hit 32% of the time she bats. Estimate the probability that she will get at least 5 hits in her next 10 at bats. **Possible answer: 30%**

6. At a local fast-food restaurant, about 83% of the customers order their food to go. Estimate the probability that 6 of the next 7 customers will order their food to go. **Possible answer: 100%**

7. A local radio station is having a contest. Each time you call in, your chances of winning are 6%. If you call in 10 times, estimate the probability that you will win more than once. **Possible answer: 10%**

8. Kyle works at a juice bar. He knows about 45% of the customers by name. Estimate the probability that he will know the names of at least 7 of the next 9 customers. **Possible answer: 20%**

RETEACH 10-3

Reteach
10-3 Use a Simulation

Situation: Strout's Market is having a contest. They give a puzzle piece to each customer at the checkout. A customer who collects all 10 different puzzle pieces gets $100 in store credit.

Using a table of random numbers, you can model the situation to estimate how many times a customer would have to shop to collect all 10 puzzle pieces.

3	1	9	4	1	1	8	8
5	7	4	5	7	7	9	0
7	0	3	0	1	3	5	0
0	4	3	8	9	5	3	8
2	6	1	7	6	7	6	9
0	8	2	6	5	5	9	2

• Start anywhere in the table. Count the numbers you pass as you "collect" the digits 0-9.

Suppose you start at the top of Column 3 and move to the right. List each number until you have collected all the numbers 0–9.

9 4 1 1 8 8 5 7 4 5 7 7 9 0 7 0 3 0 1 3 5 0 0 4 3 8 9 5 3 8 2 6

You had to go through 32 numbers to get each number at least once (underscored).

• Do the experiment again.

Suppose you start at the bottom of Column 4 and move to the right. When you reach the end of the row, go to the beginning of the table.

6 5 5 9 2 3 1 9 4 1 1 8 8 5 7 4 5 7 7 9 0

You had to go through 21 numbers to get each number at least once (underscored).

• Find the average of your results. $\frac{32 + 21}{2} = \frac{53}{2} = 26.5$

So, on average, you need to shop 27 times to get all 10 pieces to win $100 credit.

Model each situation. Use the list of random numbers shown above. Do two trials. Tell where you start for each trial. Possible answers shown.

1. A box of Whammos contains a toy dinosaur. If there are 10 different model dinosaurs in the collection, estimate how many boxes of Whammos you would have to buy to get all 10 dinosaurs.

top Col. 2, go right, 33; bottom Col. 5, go right, 38; on average, about 36 boxes

2. For this spinner, estimate how many times you would have to spin the pointer to get the numbers 1–10.

top Col.8, next row, 27; bottom Col. 1, right, 18; about 23 times

---

PRACTICE 10-3

Practice B
10-3 Use a Simulation

Use the table of random numbers for the problems below.

8125	4764	7693	3675	1642	7988	7048	9135	3138	3256
9566	4413	7215	7992	4320	7438	3805	5413	8847	2397
7336	5393	8623	8570	5095	5685	6695	3570	3605	4656
6470	6065	8239	2953	5942	6496	8899	0701	5368	2106
5210	2570	8137	3587	3578	6657	6636	7188	5717	1770
4329	4110	2655	8258	9928	3873	5609	3695	7091	0368
5315	2654	0484	4601	4336	6624	5403	5870	8545	3905
2361	9097	3753	2498	0544	0923	6099	1737	4025	1221
2677	7741	5342	9844	3722	5120	8742	1382	2842	7386
3292	5084	1130	2747	0664	9718	6072	9432	7008	2024

Mr. Domino gave the same math test to all three of his math classes. In the first two classes, 80% of the students passed the test. If the third class has 20 students, estimate the number of students who will pass the test.

1. Using the first row as the first trial, count the successful outcomes and name the unsuccessful outcomes.

16 out of 20 successful; 81, 93, 88, 91

2. Count and name the successful outcomes in the second row as the second trial.

16 out of 20 successful; 95, 92, 88, 97

Determine the successful outcomes in the remaining rows of the random number table.

3. third row	4. fourth row	5. fifth row	6. sixth row
14	16	17	16

7. seventh row	8. eighth row	9. ninth row	10. tenth row
18	16	16	16

11. Based on the simulation, estimate the probability that 80% of the class will pass the math test. **90%**

PRACTICE AND PROBLEM SOLVING

Extra Practice
See page 800.

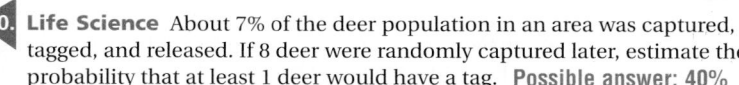

Life Science

The capture-release-recapture method uses ratios to estimate the size of wild populations.

Use the table of random numbers for Exercises 9 and 10. Use at least 10 trials to simulate each situation.

19067	26149	88557	80696	88246	56652	73023	56838
98048	26387	65953	94163	66233	57325	65618	76782
32958	47253	24960	32052	16921	54925	44766	33115
89164	06342	98577	44523	72304	38221	33506	63923

9. **Entertainment** A radio station plays a song from the 1980s about 60% of the time. What is the probability that at least 4 of the next 5 songs are from the 1980s? **Possible answer: 10%**

10. **Life Science** About 7% of the deer population in an area was captured, tagged, and released. If 8 deer were randomly captured later, estimate the probability that at least 1 deer would have a tag. **Possible answer: 40%**

11. **Write About It** A silk screener checks the prints on T-shirts. If 2% of the T-shirts were defective, how could you estimate the probability that no more than 1 T-shirt in each case of 144 would be defective?

12. **Challenge** A box of tulip bulbs has bulbs in 5 colors. The probabilities for each color are given below. Vijay likes red and yellow best. Rosa likes blue and red best. If each chooses 6 bulbs randomly, estimate the probability that they will each get at least one of their favorites. **Possible answer: 50%**

Color	Red	Yellow	Blue	Orange	Pink
Probability	0.3	0.1	0.3	0.2	0.1

TEST PREP and Spiral Review

13. **Multiple Choice** Diego hit a home run 25% of his times at bat. He wants to estimate his probability of hitting at least 3 home runs during his next 10 at bats. Using a random number table, he performs 10 trials. Of the 10 trials, 2 represented 3 or more home runs. What is the probability that Diego will hit 3 home runs during his next 10 at bats?

    (A) 2%   (B) 20%   (C) 25%   (D) 30%

14. **Short Response** In a certain area, 11% of the wolf population is tagged and released. Describe how to use a random number table to determine the probability that at least 2 out of the next 10 wolves caught will be tagged.

Find the appropriate factor for each conversion. (Lesson 5-3)

15. quarts to pints $\frac{2 \text{ pints}}{1 \text{ quart}}$ 16. inches to yards $\frac{1 \text{ yard}}{36 \text{ inches}}$ 17. millimeters to meters $\frac{1 \text{ m}}{1000 \text{ mm}}$

A spinner was spun 400 times. It landed on red 192 times, blue 144 times, and green 64 times. Estimate the probability of each event. (Lesson 10-2)

18. spinner landing on red **0.48**   19. spinner landing on green **0.16**   20. spinner landing on blue **0.36**

Answers

11. Possible answer: Use a simulation with each trial using 144 two-digit numbers from a random number table. Let the numbers 01 and 02 represent defective items and the numbers 03–00 represent items that are not defective.

14. See p. A14.

TEST PREP DOCTOR + Remind students to pay close attention to the data in the simulation in Exercise 13, since the results will not always be intuitive.

Journal

Ask students to describe a way to generate random numbers without using a computer or a calculator.

Power Presentations with PowerPoint®

10-3 Lesson Quiz

1. Use the table of random numbers to simulate the situation.

38094	76211	43659	29272
76005	93391	19587	47380
33442	40809	27904	95412
69632	48461	25654	55889
42231	39983	13802	24483
52730	15604	80949	46351
10580	59765	76431	38586
62987	40440	93594	30198
64926	17672	68735	35168
19085	35497	30798	21966

Lydia gets a hit 34% of the time she bats. Estimate the probability that she will get **at least** 4 hits in her next 10 at bats. **Possible answer: 30%**

Also available on transparency

CHALLENGE 10-3

LESSON 10-3 Challenge
Rolling and Tossing

To design a simulation, you may use different devices, such as number cubes or coins.

Situation: At Sonia's Spa, two-thirds of the female clients come to lose weight. For an article about spas, a female client at Sonia's was interviewed. What is the probability that this woman is at the spa to lose weight?

Simulation: To model a ratio of $\frac{2}{3}$, you can use a number cube so that

4 of the outcomes—1, 2, 3, 4—represent *came to lose weight* and 2 of the outcomes—5, 6—represent *did not come to lose weight.*

Then, P(came to lose weight) $= \frac{4}{6}$, or $\frac{2}{3}$.

To carry out this simulation, Kim rolled a number cube 10 times, with the following results: 4 5 2 6 6 6 1 2 4 3

1. How many of the 10 trials resulted in a woman who came to the spa to lose weight? _____ 6

2. Find P(came to lose weight). Answer as a ratio and as a percent. _____ $\frac{3}{5}$ or 60%

Situation: A study shows that a new medication has a 50% chance of curing the condition for which it is prescribed. Keith's doctor prescribes the medication for him. What is the probability that the medication will cure Keith's condition?

3. Using a cube numbered 1–6, describe a simulation.
Possible answer: 1, 2, 3 represent *cures*;
4, 5, 6 represent *does not cure.*

4. Carry out your simulation for 10 trials. Calculate P(cures). Answer as a ratio and as a percent.
Answers will vary.

5. Using a coin, describe a simulation.
Possible answer: heads represents *cures*;
tails represents *does not cure.*

6. Carry out your simulation for 10 trials. Calculate P(cures). Answer as a ratio and as a percent.
Answers will vary.

PROBLEM SOLVING 10-3

LESSON 10-3 Problem Solving
Use a Simulation

Use the table of random numbers below. Use at least 10 trials to simulate each situation. Write the correct answer.

1. Of people 18–24 years of age, 49% do volunteer work. If 10 people ages 18–24 were chosen at random, estimate the probability that at least 4 of them do volunteer work.

87244	11632	85815	61766	
19579	28186	18533	24633	
74581	65633	54238	32848	
87549	85976	13355	46498	
53736	21616	86318	77291	
24794	31119	48193	44869	
86585	27919	65264	93557	
94425	13325	16635	25840	
18394	73266	67899	38783	
94228	23426	76679	41256	

Possible answer: 80%

2. In the 2000 Presidential election, 56% of the population of North Carolina voted for George W. Bush. If 10 people were chosen at random from North Carolina, estimate the probability that at least 8 of them voted for Bush.
Possible answer: 10%

3. Forty percent of households with televisions watched the 2001 Super Bowl game. If 10 households with televisions are chosen at random, estimate the probability that at least 3 watched the 2001 Super Bowl.
Possible answer: 90%

Use the table above and at least 10 trials to simulate each situation. Choose the letter for the best estimate.

4. As of August 2000, 42% of U.S. households had Internet access. If 10 households are chosen at random, estimate the probability that at least 5 of them will have Internet access.
A 0%   C 60%
B 30%   D 90%

5. On average, there is rain 20% of the days in April in Orlando, FL. Estimate the probability that it will rain at least once during your 7-day vacation in Orlando in April.
F 20%   H 70%
G 50%   J 40%

6. Kareem Abdul-Jabaar is the NBA lifetime leader in field goals. During his career, he made 56% of the field goals he attempted. In a given game, estimate the probability that he would make at least 6 out of 10 field goals.
A 40%   C 80%
B 60%   D 100%

7. At the University of Virginia 39% of the applicants are accepted. If 10 applicants to the University of Virginia are chosen at random, estimate the probability that at least 4 of them are accepted to the University of Virginia.
F 10%   H 80%
G 40%   J 70%

Organizer

Use with Lesson 10-3

Hands-On LAB

Pacing:
Traditional $\frac{1}{2}$ day
Block $\frac{1}{4}$ day

Objective: Use a simulation to model an experiment that would be difficult to perform.

Materials: Number cube, coin, 10 x 10 grid paper

Online Edition

Countdown to Testing Week 22

Resources

Hands-On Lab Activities
Lab 10-3 Recording Sheet

Teach

Discuss

Let students explain to the class some of their simulations for a *Try This* exercise. Emphasize that the simplest methods are often best.

Close

Key Concept

Using different types of simulations for different situations will make them more effective.

Assessment

1. How can a deck of cards be used to simulate an experiment?

Possible answer: Let different cards represent different events. For every trial, shuffle all the cards and deal one from the top.

State Resources

---

go.hrw.com
State Resources Online
KEYWORD: MT7 Resources

Hands-On LAB 10-3

Use Different Models for Simulations

Use with Lesson 10-3

go.hrw.com
Lab Resources Online
KEYWORD: MT7 Lab10

You can use a simulation to model an experiment that would be difficult to perform.

Activity 1

A cereal company discovered that 1 out of 6 boxes did not contain a prize. Suppose you buy 10 boxes of the cereal. What is the probability that you will buy a cereal box without a prize?

Use a number cube to simulate buying a box of cereal. Let 6 represent a box without a prize and 1–5 represent a box with a prize.

a. Copy the table. Then roll the number cube 10 times to represent buying 10 boxes of cereal. Tally your results.

b. Find the experimental probability of buying a box without a prize.

Number Rolled	Frequency
1 (prize)	
2 (prize)	
3 (prize)	
4 (prize)	
5 (prize)	
6 (no prize)	

Think and Discuss

1. What other methods could you use to simulate this situation? Which methods are best? Explain. **Check students' work.**

Try This

1. Roll the number cube 100 times. What is the experimental probability of buying a box without a prize? How does this probability compare with your earlier result? **Check students' work.**

Activity 2

Each Thursday, a radio station randomly plays new releases 50% of the time. What is the probability that 6 of the next 10 songs will be new releases on any given Thursday?

You can use a coin to simulate playing a new release. Let heads represent a new release and tails represent a song that is not a new release.

a. Copy the table. For each trial, toss the coin 10 times to represent playing 10 songs. Tally your results. Complete 5 trials.

b. In how many trials did heads appear 6 or more times?

c. Find the experimental probability that 6 of the next 10 songs on any given Thursday will be new releases.

Trial	Heads (new)	Tails (not new)
1		
2		
3		
4		
5		

1. Why is tossing a coin a good way to simulate this situation?

2. What other methods could you use to simulate this situation? Which methods are best? Explain. **Check students' work.**

Try This

1. Toss the coin 100 times. What is the experimental probability that 6 of the next 10 songs are new releases? How does this probability compare with your earlier result? **Check students' work.**

Activity 3

Belinda makes 80% of her free throws. What is the probability that she will make 8 out of her next 10 free throws?

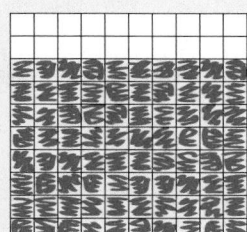

1. You can use an area model to simulate Belinda's shooting a free throw. Color 80 squares on a sheet of 10-by-10 grid paper to represent free throws made. The remaining 20 blank squares will represent free throws missed.

   a. For each trial, flip a dime 10 times onto the grid paper. Do not count a result if the dime does not land completely within the grid. Flip the dime again. If the dime lands completely within the shaded area, count it as a free throw made. If the dime lands in the unshaded area or partly in both the shaded and unshaded areas, count it as a free throw missed. Tally your results. Complete 10 trials.

   b. Find the experimental probability of Belinda's making 8 out of the next 10 free throws.

Think and Discuss

1. What other methods could you use to simulate this situation? **Check students' work.**

2. Why are 80 squares filled in and 20 squares left blank? Does it matter which 80 squares are filled in? Explain.

Try This

Select and conduct a simulation to find the experimental probability. Explain which method you chose and why.

1. Raul works for a pet groomer. He knows about 70% of the pets from previous visits. Estimate the probability that he will know at least 6 of the next 8 pets that arrive. **Possible answer: 52.5%**

2. At a local restaurant, about 50% of the customers order dessert. Estimate the probability that 4 out of the next 10 customers will order dessert. **Possible answer: 20%**

Activity 2

Possible answers to
Think and Discuss

1. There are two possible outcomes for the situation and two possible outcomes for tossing a coin.

Activity 3

Answers to
Think and Discuss

2. The 80 squares that are filled in represent the number of free throws that Belinda makes, and the 20 blank squares represent the number of free throws that she misses; Check students' work.

READY TO
GO ON?

Organizer

Objective: Assess students' mastery of concepts and skills in Lessons 10-1 through 10-3.

Resources

 Assessment Resources
Section 10A Quiz

 Test & Practice Generator
One-Stop Planner®

INTERVENTION

Resources

 Ready to Go On?
Intervention and
Enrichment Worksheets

 **Ready to Go On? CD-ROM**

Ready to Go On? Online

my.hrw.com

Answers

5.

Student	Jennifer	Anjelica	Debra	Yolanda
Prob.	0.3	0.3	0.2	0.2

Ready to Go On?

READY TO GO ON?

Quiz for Lessons 10-1 Through 10-3

✓ **10-1** **Probability**

Use the table to find the probability of each event.

Outcome	A	B	C	D
Probability	0.3	0.1	0.4	0.2

1. $P(C)$ **0.4**   **2.** $P(\text{not } B)$ **0.9**   **3.** $P(A \text{ or } D)$ **0.5**   **4.** $P(A, B, \text{ or } C)$ **0.8**

5. There are 4 students in a race. Jennifer has a 30% chance of winning. Anjelica has the same chance as Jennifer. Debra and Yolanda have equal chances. Create a table of probabilities for the sample space.

✓ **10-2** **Experimental Probability**

A colored chip is randomly drawn from a box and then replaced. The table shows the results after 400 draws.

Outcome	Red	Green	Blue	Yellow
Draws	76	172	84	68

6. Estimate the probability of drawing a red chip. **0.19**

7. Estimate the probability of drawing a green chip. **0.43**

8. Use the table to compare the probability of drawing a blue chip to the probability of drawing a yellow chip. **0.21; 0.17; more likely to draw blue**

✓ **10-3** **Use a Simulation**

Use the table of random numbers to simulate each situation. Use at least 10 trials for each simulation.

```
93840   03363   31168   57602   19464   52245   98744   61040
68395   76832   56386   45060   57512   38816   51623   23252
16805   92120   74443   49176   49898   62042   65847   15380
85178   78842   16598   28335   84837   76406   53436   45043
```

9. At a local school, 58% of the tenth-grade students play a musical instrument. Estimate the probability that at least 6 out of 8 randomly selected tenth-grade students play a musical instrument. **Possible answer: 30%**

10. Kayla has a package of 100 multicolored beads that contains 15 purple beads. If she randomly selects 8 beads to make a friendship bracelet, estimate the probability that she will get more than 1 purple bead. **Possible answer: 0%**

READY TO GO ON?

Diagnose and Prescribe

NO INTERVENE

YES ENRICH

READY TO GO ON? Intervention, Section 10A			
Ready to Go On? Intervention	Worksheets	CD-ROM	Online
✓ Lesson 10-1	10-1 Intervention	Activity 10-1	
✓ Lesson 10-2	10-2 Intervention	Activity 10-2	Diagnose and Prescribe Online
✓ Lesson 10-3	10-3 Intervention	Activity 10-3	

READY TO GO ON?
Enrichment, Section 10A
Worksheets
CD-ROM
Online

Focus on Problem Solving

Focus on
Problem Solving

 Understand

Understand the Problem
• Understand the words in the problem

Words that you don't understand can make a simple problem seem difficult. Before you try to solve a problem, you will need to know the meaning of the words in it.

If a problem gives a name of a person, place, or thing that is difficult to understand, such as *Eulalia*, you can use another name or a pronoun in its place. You could replace *Eulalia* with *she*.

Read the problems so that you can hear yourself saying the words.

Copy each problem, and circle any words that you do not understand. Look up each word and write its definition, or use context clues to replace the word with a similar word that is easier to understand.

1 A point in the circumscribed triangle is chosen randomly. What is the probability that the point is in the circle?

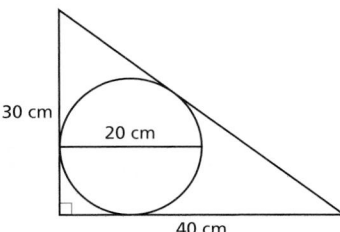

30 cm
20 cm
40 cm

2 A chef observed the number of people ordering each antipasto from the evening's specials. Estimate the probability that the next customer will order gnocchi al veneta.

Antipasto	Saltimbocca Alla Romana	Gnocchi Al Veneta	Galleto Alla Griglia
Number Ordered	16	21	13

3 Evelina and Ilario play chess 3 times a week. They have had 6 stalemates in the last 10 weeks. Estimate the probability that Evelina and Ilario will have a stalemate the next time they play chess.

4 A pula has a coat of arms on the obverse and a running zebra on the reverse. If a pula is tossed 150 times and lands with the coat of arms facing up 70 times, estimate the probability of its landing with the zebra facing up.

Answers
1. 52%
2. 42%
3. 20%
4. $53\frac{1}{3}$%

3. Replace *Evelina* with *Evelyn*. Replace *Ilario* with *Ellery*. Replace *stalemate* with *game with no winner*. Evelyn and Ellery play chess 3 times a week. They have had 6 games with no winner in the last 10 weeks. Estimate the probability that Evelyn and Ellery will have a game with no winner the next time they play chess.

4. Replace *pula* with *coin*. Replace *obverse* with *one side*. Replace *reverse* with *other side*. A coin has a coat of arms on one side and a running zebra on the other side. If the coin is tossed 150 times and lands with the coat of arms facing up 70 times, estimate the probability of its landing with the zebra facing up.

 Focus on Problem Solving

Organizer

Objective: Focus on understanding the words in a problem.

 **Online Edition**

Resources
Chapter 10 Resource Book
Reading Strategies

Problem Solving Process
This page focuses on the first step of the problem-solving process:
Understand the Problem

Discuss
Have students rewrite each problem, replacing unknown words with alternative words or phrases or with the definition of the word.

Possible answers:

1. A *circumscribed triangle* is a triangle whose segments are tangent to a circle. A point in the triangle shown is chosen randomly. What is the probability that the point is in the circle?

2. Replace *antipasto* with *appetizer*. Replace *Gnocchi Al Veneta* with *pasta*. A chef observed the number of people ordering each appetizer from the evening's specials. Estimate the probability that the next customer will order pasta.

State Resources

go.hrw.com
State Resources Online
KEYWORD: MT7 Resources

One-Minute Section Planner

Lesson	Materials	MiC and Lab Resources
Lesson 10-4 Theoretical Probability • Estimate probability using theoretical methods. ☑ SAT-10 ☑ ITBS ☑ CTBS ☑ NAEP	Index cards, deck of cards	**MiC: *Great Predictions*** pp. 32–34
Lesson 10-5 Independent and Dependent Events • Find the probabilities of independent and dependent events. ☑ SAT-10 ☑ ITBS ☑ CTBS ☑ NAEP	Two-color counters (MK)	**MiC: *Great Predictions*** pp. 12–19, 34–35, 40–44 ***Hands-On Lab Activities*** 10-5 ***Technology Lab Activities*** 10-5
Lesson 10-6 Making Decisions and Predictions • Use probability to make decisions and predictions. ☑ SAT-10 ☑ ITBS ☐ CTBS ☑ NAEP		**MiC: *Great Predictions*** pp. 24–29 ***Technology Lab Activities*** 10-6
Lesson 10-7 Odds • Convert between probabilities and odds. ☐ SAT-10 ☐ ITBS ☐ CTBS ☐ NAEP		
Lesson 10-8 Counting Principles • Find the number of possible outcomes in an experiment. ☑ SAT-10 ☐ ITBS ☐ CTBS ☑ NAEP		**MiC: *Great Predictions*** pp. 18–19
Lesson 10-9 Permutations and Combinations • Find permutations and combinations. ☑ SAT-10 ☐ ITBS ☐ CTBS ☐ NAEP		***Hands-On Lab Activities*** 10-9

MK = *Manipulatives Kit*

Mathematics in Context

The unit ***Great Predictions*** from the *Mathematics in Context*
© 2006 series can be used with Section 10B. See Section Planner
above for suggestions for integrating *MiC* with *Holt Mathematics*.

Section Overview

Probability and Odds

Lessons 10-4, 10-7

 Why? Understanding probability and odds will help you to make informed choices.

Theoretical probability	Odds in Favor	Odds Against
number of favorable outcomes / number of possible outcomes Because a number cube has six equally likely outcomes, the probability of rolling a 6 is $\frac{1}{6}$.	**a:b** a = number of favorable outcomes b = number of unfavorable outcomes If the probability of an event is $\frac{1}{6}$, then the odds in favor of the event are 1:5.	**b:a** a = number of favorable outcomes b = number of unfavorable outcomes If the probability of an event is $\frac{1}{6}$, then the the odds against the event are 5:1.

Independent and Dependent Events

Lessons 10-5, 10-6

 Why? Understanding how one event affects another will help you plan.

Independent Events

The occurrence of one event **does not** affect the probability of the other.

Example:

Roll a number cube and toss a coin. Find the probability of rolling a number less than 3 and getting heads.

$$P(3, \text{heads}) = \frac{2}{6} \cdot \frac{1}{2} = \frac{1}{6} = 16\frac{2}{3}\%$$

Dependent Events

The occurrence of one event **does** affect the probability of the other.

Example:

Pick two marbles from a bag containing 4 red marbles and 1 blue marble without replacing the first. Find the probability of picking two red marbles.

$$P(\text{red, red}) = \frac{4}{5} \cdot \frac{3}{4} = \frac{12}{20} = 60\%$$

You can use probabilities to help make decisions and predictions in future events.

Counting Methods

Lessons 10-8, 10-9

 Why? Understanding counting methods will help you to handle large numbers.

> The **Fundamental Counting Principle** If there are m ways to choose a first item and n ways to choose a second, then there are $m \cdot n$ ways to choose both items.

Combinations are ways to choose things from a group if **order does not matter.**

> The number of **combinations** of n things taken r at a time is given by the formula
> $$_nC_r = \frac{n!}{r!(n-r)!}.$$

The number of combinations of 5 things taken 3 at a time

$$_5C_3 = \frac{5!}{3!2!} = \frac{5 \cdot 4 \cdot 3 \cdot 2 \cdot 1}{(3 \cdot 2 \cdot 1)(2 \cdot 1)} = 10$$

Permutations are ways to choose things from a group if **order does matter.**

> The number of **permutations** of n things taken r at a time is given by the formula
> $$_nP_r = \frac{n!}{(n-r)!}.$$

The number of permutations of 5 things taken 3 at a time

$$_5P_3 = \frac{5!}{2!} = \frac{5 \cdot 4 \cdot 3 \cdot 2 \cdot 1}{2 \cdot 1} = 60$$

Pacing: Traditional $1\frac{1}{2}$ days
Block $\frac{3}{4}$ day

Objective: Students estimate probability using theoretical methods.

Online Edition
Tutorial Videos, Interactivities

Countdown to Testing Week 22

Power Presentations
with PowerPoint®

Math Humor

If you want to win the flip of a coin, call, "Heads, I win. Tails, you lose."

State Resources

Learn to estimate probability using theoretical methods.

Vocabulary
theoretical probability
equally likely
fair
mutually exclusive
disjoint events

In the game of Monopoly®, you can get out of jail if you roll doubles, but if you roll doubles three times in a row, you have to go to jail. Your turn is decided by the probability that both dice will be the same number.

Theoretical probability is used to estimate probabilities by making certain assumptions about an experiment. Suppose a sample space has 5 outcomes that are **equally likely**, that is, they all have the same probability, x. The probabilities must add to 1.

$$x + x + x + x + x = 1$$
$$5x = 1$$
$$x = \frac{1}{5}$$

THEORETICAL PROBABILITY FOR EQUALLY LIKELY OUTCOMES

Suppose there are n equally likely outcomes in the sample space of an experiment.

- The probability of each outcome is $\frac{1}{n}$.
- The probability of an event is $\frac{\text{number of outcomes in the event}}{n}$.

A coin, die, or other object is called **fair** if all outcomes are equally likely.

EXAMPLE 1 Calculating Theoretical Probability

An experiment consists of rolling a fair number cube. Find the probability of each event.

A $P(5)$

The number cube is fair, so all 6 outcomes in the sample space are equally likely: 1, 2, 3, 4, 5, and 6.

$$P(5) = \frac{\text{number of outcomes for 5}}{6} = \frac{1}{6}$$

B $P(\text{even number})$

There are 3 possible even numbers: 2, 4, and 6.

$$P(\text{even number}) = \frac{\text{number of possible even numbers}}{6} = \frac{3}{6} = \frac{1}{2}$$

1 Introduce
Alternate Opener

Motivate

Show the students five index cards, numbered 1, 2, 3, 3, and 3. Put the five cards in a bag and ask the students which number they think you will most likely pull out. Now show three cards numbered 1, 2, and 3. Put the three cards in a bag and ask the students which number they think you will most likely pull out.

Explorations and answers are provided in *Alternate Openers: Explorations Transparencies*.

Suppose you roll two fair number cubes. Are all outcomes equally likely? It depends on how you consider the outcomes. You could look at the number on each number cube or at the total shown on the number cubes.

If you look at the total, all outcomes are not equally likely. For example, there is only one way to get a total of 2, 1 + 1, but a total of 5 can be 1 + 4, 2 + 3, 3 + 2, or 4 + 1.

EXAMPLE 2 · Calculating Probability for Two Fair Number Cubes

An experiment consists of rolling two fair number cubes. Find the probability of each event.

A $P(\text{total shown} = 1)$

First find the sample space that has all outcomes equally likely.

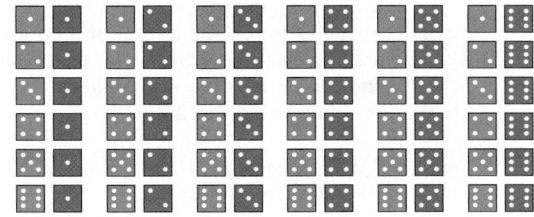

There are 36 possible outcomes in the sample space. Then find the number of outcomes in the event "total shown = 1." There is no way to get a total of 1, so $P(\text{total shown} = 1) = \frac{0}{36} = 0$.

B $P(\text{at least one 6})$

There are 11 outcomes in the event rolling "at least one 6":

$P(\text{at least one 6}) = \frac{11}{36}$

EXAMPLE 3 · Altering Probability

A bag contains 5 blue chips and 8 green chips. How many yellow chips should be added so that the probability of drawing a green chip is $\frac{2}{5}$?

Adding chips to the bag will increase the number of possible outcomes. Let x equal the number of yellow chips.

$\frac{8}{13 + x} = \frac{2}{5}$	*Set up a proportion.*
$2(13 + x) = 8(5)$	*Find the cross products.*
$26 + 2x = 40$	*Multiply.*
$-26 \qquad -26$	*Subtract 26 from both sides.*
$\frac{2x}{2} = \frac{14}{2}$	*Divide both sides by 2.*
$x = 7$	

Seven yellow chips should be added to the bag.

2 Teach

Guided Instruction

In this lesson, students learn to calculate probability using theoretical methods. Remind the students that an experimental probability ratio compares the number of times an event *actually* occurs to the total number of *actual* trials. In theoretical probability, there are no actual trials or actual results. If you can identify all possible outcomes and assume that all those possible outcomes are *equally likely,* you can create a theoretical probability ratio (Teaching Transparency).

 **Reaching All Learners**
Through Cooperative Learning

Provide each group of students with a deck of playing cards. Have each group write five probability problems for another group to solve. Examples include finding the probability of drawing an eight, a diamond, or a red jack. After each group has written five questions, have them exchange lists with another group. Students can then solve the problems by identifying the outcomes that make each event occur. You may want each group to return the solved problems to the original group for review.

Additional Examples

Example 4

Suppose you are playing a game in which you roll two fair dice. If you roll a total of five you will win. If you roll a total of two, you will lose. If you roll anything else, the game continues. What is the probability that the game will end on your next roll? $\frac{1}{36}$

Also available on transparency

Possible answers to *Think and Discuss*

1. There are four outcomes in the sample space: (H, H), (H, T), (T, H), and (T, T).

2. Choosing letters in Scrabble®, which has different numbers of tiles for different letters

---

Two events are **mutually exclusive**, or **disjoint events**, if they cannot both occur in the same trial of an experiment. For example, rolling a 5 and an even number on a number cube are mutually exclusive events because they cannot both happen at the same time. Suppose A and B are two mutually exclusive events.

- $P(\text{both } A \text{ and } B \text{ will occur}) = 0$
- $P(\text{either } A \text{ or } B \text{ will occur}) = P(A) + P(B)$

EXAMPLE 4 Finding the Probability of Mutually Exclusive Events

Suppose you are playing a game of Monopoly and have just rolled doubles two times in a row. If you roll doubles again, you will go to jail. You will also go to jail if you roll a total of 3 because you are 3 spaces away from the "Go to Jail" square. What is the probability that you will go to jail?

It is impossible to roll doubles and a total of 3 at the same time, so the events are mutually exclusive. Add the probabilities to find the probability of going to jail on the next roll.

The event "doubles" consists of six outcomes—(1, 1), (2, 2), (3, 3), (4, 4), (5, 5), and (6, 6)—so $P(\text{doubles}) = \frac{6}{36}$.

The event "total = 3" consists of two outcomes, (1, 2) and (2, 1), so $P(\text{total of 3}) = \frac{2}{36}$.

$$P(\text{going to jail}) = P(\text{doubles}) + P(\text{total} = 3)$$
$$= \frac{6}{36} + \frac{2}{36}$$
$$= \frac{8}{36}$$

The probability of going to jail is $\frac{8}{36} = \frac{2}{9}$, or about 22.2%.

Think and Discuss

1. **Describe** a sample space for tossing two coins that has all outcomes equally likely.

2. **Give an example** of an experiment in which it would not be reasonable to assume that all outcomes are equally likely.

③ Close

ENGLISH LANGUAGE LEARNERS

Summarize

Review the concepts of theoretical probability. Ask students to define *mutually exclusive.* Ask them to provide examples of events that are mutually exclusive and events that are not mutually exclusive.

Possible answers: Mutually exclusive events cannot occur in the same trial of an experiment (e.g., rolling a 5 and a 6 on one roll of a number cube). Events that are not mutually exclusive include rolling an odd number or a number greater than 4 on a number cube and drawing a queen or a heart from a deck of cards.

10-4 Exercises

go.hrw.com
Homework Help Online
KEYWORD: MT7 10-4
Parent Resources Online
KEYWORD: MT7 Parent

GUIDED PRACTICE

See Example ① An experiment consists of rolling a fair number cube. Find the probability of each event.

1. P(odd number) $\frac{1}{2}$

2. P(2 or 4) $\frac{1}{3}$

See Example ② An experiment consists of rolling two fair number cubes. Find the probability of each event.

3. P(total shown = 10) $\frac{1}{12}$

4. P(rolling two 2's) $\frac{1}{36}$

5. P(rolling two odd numbers) $\frac{1}{4}$

6. P(total shown > 8) $\frac{5}{18}$

See Example ③ **7.** What color should you shade the blank region so that the probability of the spinner landing on that color is $\frac{1}{2}$? **red**

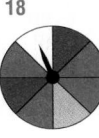

See Example ④ **8.** Suppose you are playing a game in which two fair dice are rolled. To make the first move, you need to roll doubles or a sum of 3 or 11. What is the probability that you will be able to make the first move? $\frac{5}{18}$

INDEPENDENT PRACTICE

See Example ① An experiment consists of rolling a fair number cube. Find the probability of each event.

9. P(9) **0**

10. P(not 6) $\frac{5}{6}$

11. P(< 5) $\frac{2}{3}$

12. P(> 3) $\frac{1}{2}$

See Example ② An experiment consists of rolling two fair number cubes. Find the probability of each event.

13. P(total shown = 3) $\frac{1}{18}$

14. P(at least one even number) $\frac{3}{4}$

15. P(total shown > 0) **1**

16. P(total shown < 9) $\frac{13}{18}$

See Example ③ **17.** A bag contains 20 pennies, 25 nickels, and 15 quarters. How many dimes should be added so that the probability of drawing a quarter is $\frac{1}{6}$? **30**

See Example ④ **18.** Suppose you are playing a game in which two fair dice are rolled. You need 9 to land on the finish by an exact count or 3 to land on a "roll again" space. What is the probability of landing on the finish or rolling again? $\frac{1}{6}$

PRACTICE AND PROBLEM SOLVING

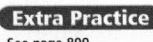
Extra Practice
See page 800.

Three fair coins are tossed: a penny, a dime, and a quarter. Find the sample space with all outcomes equally likely. Then find each probability.

19. P(TTH) $\frac{1}{8}$

20. P(THH) $\frac{1}{8}$

21. P(dime heads) $\frac{1}{2}$

22. P(exactly 2 tails) $\frac{3}{8}$

23. P(0 tails) $\frac{1}{8}$

24. P(at most 1 tail) $\frac{1}{2}$

Assignment Guide

If you finished Example ① assign:
Average 1, 2, 9–12, 28–34
Advanced 9–12, 28–34

If you finished Example ② assign:
Average 1–6, 9–16, 19–23, 28–34
Advanced 9–16, 19–23, 28–34

If you finished Example ③ assign:
Average 1–7, 9–17, 19–23, 28–34
Advanced 9–17, 19–23, 28–34

If you finished Example ④ assign:
Average 1–26, 28–34
Advanced 9–34

Homework Quick Check
Quickly check key concepts.
Exercises: 12, 14, 17, 18, 22

Answers
19–24. See p. A14.

Math Background

In probability study, the words *outcome* and *event* have very precise meanings. An outcome is a particular result of one trial of an experiment. An event is either a single outcome or a set of outcomes. Suppose an experiment is to roll two fair number cubes, and we are interested in the probabilities of the sums that could occur. We call rolling a sum of 5 an event, and it consists of the following possible outcomes: (1, 4), (2, 3), (3, 2), and (4, 1).

RETEACH 10-4

LESSON Reteach
10-4 Theoretical Probability (continued)

For this spinner:
$P(\text{odd}) = \frac{3}{6}$, or $\frac{1}{2}$ $P(\text{even}) = \frac{1}{6}$
You cannot get an odd number
and an even number $P(\text{odd and even}) = 0$
in the same spin.

Events that cannot occur in the same trial are called **mutually exclusive**.

A number is drawn from {−6, −4, 0, 2, 4, 7, 9}.
List the possible favorable results for each event. Tell if the events are mutually exclusive.

6. *Event A*: get an odd number
_7, 9_
Event B: get a negative number
_−6, −4_
Are *A* and *B* mutually exclusive? Explain.
yes; no number in both

7. *Event C*: get a multiple of 3
_−6, 9_
Event D: get an even number
_−6, −4, 0, 2, 4_
Are *C* and *D* mutually exclusive? Explain.
no; −6 in both events

For the spinner at the top of this page:
$P(\text{odd}) = \frac{3}{6}$, or $\frac{1}{2}$ $P(\text{even}) = \frac{1}{6}$ $P(\text{odd or even}) = \frac{3}{6} + \frac{1}{6} = \frac{4}{6}$, or $\frac{2}{3}$

A number is drawn from {−6, −4, 0, 5, 6, 7, 9}.
Find the indicated probabilities.

7. odd numbers are: 5, 7, 9   **8.** numbers > 6 are: _7, 9_
numbers < 0 are: _−6, −4_   even numbers: _−6, −4, 0, 6_
$P(\text{odd}) = \frac{3}{7}$ $P(\text{number} > 6) = \frac{2}{7}$
$P(\text{number} < 0) = \frac{2}{7}$ $P(\text{even number}) = \frac{4}{7}$
$P(\text{odd number or number} < 0) =$ $P(\text{number} > 6 \text{ or even number}) =$
$\frac{3}{7} + \frac{2}{7} = \frac{5}{7}$ $\frac{2}{7} + \frac{4}{7} = \frac{6}{7}$

PRACTICE 10-4

LESSON Practice B
10-4 Theoretical Probability

An experiment consists of rolling two fair number cubes.
Find the probability of each event.

1. P(3)   **2.** P(7)
$\frac{1}{6}$ 0

3. P(1 or 4)   **4.** P(not 5)
$\frac{1}{3}$ $\frac{5}{6}$

5. P(< 5)   **6.** P(> 4)
$\frac{2}{3}$ $\frac{1}{3}$

7. P(2 or odd)   **8.** P(≤ 3)
$\frac{2}{3}$ $\frac{1}{2}$

An experiment consists of rolling two fair number cubes.
Find the probability of each event.

9. P(total shown = 3)   **10.** P(total shown = 7)   **11.** P(total shown = 9)
$\frac{1}{18}$ $\frac{1}{6}$ $\frac{1}{9}$

12. P(total shown = 2) **13.** P(total shown = 4) **14.** P(total shown = 13)
$\frac{1}{36}$ $\frac{1}{12}$ 0

15. P(total shown > 8) **16.** P(total shown ≤ 12) **17.** P(total shown < 7)
$\frac{5}{18}$ 1 $\frac{5}{12}$

18. A bag contains 9 pennies, 8 nickels, and 5 dimes. How many quarters should be added to the bag so the probability of drawing a dime is $\frac{1}{6}$? _8 quarters_

19. In a game two fair number cubes are rolled. To make the first move, you need to roll a total of 6, 7, or 8. What is the probability that you will be able to make the first move? $\frac{4}{9}$

State Resources

go.hrw.com
State Resources Online
KEYWORD: MT7 Resources

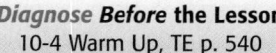
Interdisciplinary

Life Science

Exercises 25–27 involve using a Punnett square to determine probabilities of genetic traits. Students study Punnett squares and genetic combinations in middle school life science programs, such as *Holt Science & Technology*.

Answers

27. See p. A14.

 If students answer $\frac{1}{6}$ for Exercise 29, they may have calculated the probability of rolling a 2 instead of rolling a 2 or higher. Suggest that they carefully write out all of the different successful events before they calculate the probability.

 Journal

Ask students to write about how probability has affected a game they have played.

Power Presentations
with PowerPoint®

 10-4
Lesson Quiz

An experiment consists of rolling a fair number cube. Find each probability.

1. P(rolling an odd number) $\frac{1}{2}$

2. P(rolling a prime number) $\frac{1}{2}$

An experiment consists of rolling two fair number cubes. Find each probability.

3. P(rolling two 3's) $\frac{1}{36}$

4. P(total shown > 10) $\frac{1}{12}$

Also available on transparency

Life Science LINK

What color are your eyes? Can you roll your tongue? These traits are determined by the genes you inherited from your parents. A *Punnett square* shows all possible gene combinations for two parents whose genes are known.

To make a Punnett square, draw a two-by-two grid. Write the genes of one parent above the top row and the other parent along the side. Then fill in the grid as shown.

	B	b
b	Bb	bb
b	Bb	bb

25. In the Punnett square above, one parent has the gene combination *Bb*, which represents one gene for brown eyes and one gene for blue eyes. The other parent has the gene combination *bb*, which represents two genes for blue eyes. If all outcomes in the Punnett square are equally likely, what is the probability of a child with the gene combination *bb*? $\frac{1}{2}$

26. Make a Punnett square for two parents who both have the gene combination *Bb*.

  a. If all outcomes in the Punnett square are equally likely, what is the probability of a child with the gene combination *BB*? $\frac{1}{4}$

  b. The gene combinations *BB* and *Bb* will result in brown eyes, and the gene combination *bb* will result in blue eyes. What is the probability that the couple will have a child with brown eyes? $\frac{3}{4}$

27. ⭐ **Challenge** The combinations *Tt* and *TT* represent the ability to roll your tongue, while *tt* means you cannot roll your tongue. Draw a Punnett square that results in a probability of $\frac{1}{2}$ that the child can roll his or her tongue. Explain whether the parents can roll their tongues.

TEST PREP and Spiral Review

28. Multiple Choice A bag has 3 red marbles and 6 blue marbles in it. What is the probability of drawing a red marble?

  Ⓐ 1   Ⓑ $\frac{2}{3}$ Ⓒ $\frac{1}{3}$ Ⓓ $\frac{1}{2}$

29. Gridded Response On a fair number cube, what is the probability, written as a fraction, of rolling a 2 or higher? $\frac{5}{6}$

Determine whether each ordered pair is a solution of $y = 3x - 2$. (Lesson 3-1)

30. (3, 11)   no   **31.** (0, −2)   yes   **32.** (−1, −5)   yes   **33.** (−4, 10)   no

34. Wallace completed 27 of his last 38 passes. Estimate the probability that he will complete his next pass. (Lesson 10-2)   ≈ 0.71

CHALLENGE 10-4

Challenge
10-4 *Picture This*

Venn diagrams can be used to illustrate and solve problem situations involving probability.

Consider a cube numbered 1–6.

Let *Event A* = rolling an even number on the cube.
  favorable outcomes = 2, 4, 6

Let *Event B* = rolling a number less than 5 on the cube.
  favorable outcomes = 1, 2, 3, 4

Note that the numbers 2 and 4 are in both events and, thus, lie in the intersection of the two circles that represent Events A and B.

So, to determine the probability of getting an even number that is also less than 5, the favorable outcomes are in the intersection of the circles.

$P(A \text{ and } B) = \frac{\text{number of favorable outcomes}}{\text{total number of possible outcomes}} = \frac{2}{6}, \text{ or } \frac{1}{3}$

Then, to determine the probability of getting an even number *or* a number that is less than 5, count the elements in the intersection only once.

$P(A \text{ or } B) = \frac{\text{number of favorable outcomes}}{\text{total number of possible outcomes}} = \frac{5}{6}$

Draw a Venn diagram to solve each problem. A cube numbered 1–6 is rolled once.

1. Find the probability of getting an odd number that is greater than 2.

  Event A = a number that is __odd__

  Event B = a number that is __>2__

2. Find the probability of getting an even number or a number less than 3.

  Event A = a number that is __even__

  Event B = a number that is __<3__

$P(A \text{ and } B) = \underline{\frac{2}{6}, \text{ or } \frac{1}{3}}$ $P(A \text{ or } B) = \underline{\frac{4}{6}, \text{ or } \frac{2}{3}}$

PROBLEM SOLVING 10-4

Problem Solving
10-4 *Theoretical Probability*

A company that sells frozen pizzas is running a promotional special. Out of the next 100,000 boxes of pizza produced, randomly chosen boxes will be prize winners. There will be one grand prize winner who will receive $100,000. Five hundred first prize winners will get $1000, and 3,000 second prize winners will get a free pizza. Write the correct answer in fraction and percent form.

1. What is the probability that the box of pizza you just bought will be a grand prize winner?

  $\frac{1}{100,000}$; 0.001%

2. What is the probability that the box of pizza you just bought will be a first prize winner?

  $\frac{1}{200}$; 0.5%

3. What is the probability that the box of pizza you just bought will be a second prize winner?

  $\frac{3}{100}$; 3%

4. What is the probability that you will win anything with the box of pizza you just bought?

  $\frac{3,501}{100,000}$; 3.501%

Researchers at the National Institutes of Health are recommending that instead of screening all people for certain diseases, they can use a Punnett square to identify the people who are most likely to have the disease. By only screening these people, the cost of screening will be less. Fill in the Punnett square below and use them to choose the letter for the best answer.

5. What is the probability of DD?

  A 0%   C 50%
  Ⓑ 25%   D 75%

	D	d
D	DD	Dd
d	Dd	dd

6. What is the probability of Dd?

  F 25%   H 75%
  Ⓖ 50%   J 100%

7. What is the probability of dd?

  A 0%   C 50%
  Ⓑ 25%   D 75%

8. DD or Dd indicates that the patient will have the disease. What is the probability that the patient will have the disease?

  F 25%   Ⓗ 75%
  G 50%   J 100%

10-5 **Independent and Dependent Events**

Learn to find the probabilities of independent and dependent events.

Vocabulary
compound event
independent events
dependent events

Skydivers carry two *independent* parachutes. One parachute is the primary parachute, and the other is for emergencies.

A compound **event** is made up of two or more separate events. To find the probability of a compound event, you need to know if the events are independent or dependent.

Events are **independent events** if the occurrence of one event does not affect the probability of the other. Events are **dependent events** if the occurrence of one does affect the probability of the other.

EXAMPLE 1 Classifying Events as Independent or Dependent

Determine if the events are dependent or independent.

A a coin landing heads on one toss and tails on another toss
The result of one toss does not affect the result of the other, so the events are independent.

B drawing a 6 and then a 7 from a deck of cards
Once one card is drawn, the sample space changes. The events are dependent.

FINDING THE PROBABILITY OF INDEPENDENT EVENTS

If A and B are independent events, then $P(A \text{ and } B) = P(A) \cdot P(B)$.

EXAMPLE 2 Finding the Probability of Independent Events

An experiment consists of spinning the spinner 3 times.

A What is the probability of spinning a 2 all 3 times?
The result of each spin does not affect the results of the other spins, so the spin results are independent.
For each spin, $P(2) = \frac{1}{5}$.
$P(2, 2, 2) = \frac{1}{5} \cdot \frac{1}{5} \cdot \frac{1}{5} = \frac{1}{125} = 0.008$ *Multiply.*

Organizer 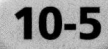 **10-5**

Pacing: Traditional 1 day
Block $\frac{1}{2}$ day
Objective: Students find the probabilities of independent and dependent events.

LAB **Hands-On Lab**
In *Hands-On Lab Activities*

Technology Lab
In *Technology Lab Activities*

PREMIER **Online Edition**
Tutorial Videos, Interactivities

Countdown to Testing Week 23

Power Presentations
with PowerPoint®

Warm Up
Multiply. Write each fraction in simplest form.
1. $\frac{2}{5} \times \frac{3}{5}$ $\frac{6}{25}$ **2.** $\frac{1}{6} \times \frac{3}{4}$ $\frac{1}{8}$
Write each fraction as a decimal.
3. $\frac{2}{5}$ 0.4   **4.** $\frac{32}{125}$ 0.256

Problem of the Day
The area of a spinner is 75% red and 25% blue. However, the probability of its landing on red is only 50%. Sketch a spinner to show how this can be.
Possible answer:

Also available on transparency

---

1 Introduce
Alternate Opener

EXPLORATION

10-5 **Independent and Dependent Events**

When the occurrence of one event affects the probability of a second event, the events are *dependent*. Otherwise, they are *independent*.
Classify each pair of events as dependent or independent.

	Events	Independent	Dependent
1.	**Event A:** Drawing a 3 from a deck without replacing it **Event B:** Drawing another 3 from the same deck.		
2.	**Event A:** Tossing heads on a flip of a coin **Event B:** Tossing heads on a second flip of the same coin		
3.	**Event A:** Running between 5:00 P.M. and 5:30 P.M. **Event B:** Drinking water between 5:30 P.M. and 6:00 P.M.		
4.	**Event A:** Drawing a blue marble and putting it back in a bag that contains 6 blue marbles and 4 red marbles **Event B:** Drawing another blue marble from the same bag		

Think and Discuss
5. Discuss real-world examples of dependent events and independent events.

Motivate
Put two pairs of identical items in a container (e.g., two pennies and two nickels). Ask students to find the probability of choosing one of the items. 50% Choose one item and, without replacing it, repeat the same question. 33% or 67% depending on the first event Help students understand that the probability has changed because the sample space has changed.

Explorations and answers are provided in *Alternate Openers: Explorations Transparencies.*

State Resources

go.hrw.com
State Resources Online
KEYWORD: MT7 Resources

10-5 Independent and Dependent Events **545**

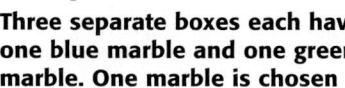
Additional Examples

Example 1

Determine if the events are dependent or independent.

A. getting tails on a coin toss and rolling a 6 on a number cube
independent

B. getting 2 red gumballs out of a gumball machine   dependent

Example 2

Three separate boxes each have one blue marble and one green marble. One marble is chosen from each box.

A. What is the probability of choosing a blue marble from each box?
0.125

B. What is the probability of choosing a blue marble, then a green marble, and then a blue marble? 0.125

C. What is the probability of choosing at least one blue marble? 0.875

Also available on transparency

An experiment consists of spinning the spinner 3 times. For each spin, all outcomes are equally likely.

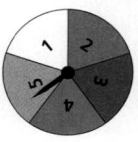

B **What is the probability of spinning an even number all 3 times?**

For each spin, $P(\text{even}) = \frac{2}{5}$.

$P(\text{even, even, even}) = \frac{2}{5} \cdot \frac{2}{5} \cdot \frac{2}{5} = \frac{8}{125} = 0.064$ *Multiply.*

C **What is the probability of spinning a 2 at least once?**

Think: $P(\text{at least one 2}) + P(\text{not 2, not 2, not 2}) = 1$.

For each spin, $P(\text{not 2}) = \frac{4}{5}$.

$P(\text{not 2, not 2, not 2}) = \frac{4}{5} \cdot \frac{4}{5} \cdot \frac{4}{5} = \frac{64}{125} = 0.512$ *Multiply.*

Subtract from 1 to find the probability of spinning at least one 2.

$1 - 0.512 = 0.488$

To calculate the probability of two dependent events occurring, do the following:

1. Calculate the probability of the first event.

2. Calculate the probability that the second event would occur if the first event had already occurred.

3. Multiply the probabilities.

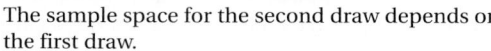

FINDING THE PROBABILITY OF DEPENDENT EVENTS

If A and B are dependent events, then $P(A \text{ and } B) = P(A) \cdot P(B \text{ after } A)$.

Suppose you draw 2 marbles without replacement from a bag that contains 3 purple and 3 orange marbles. On the first draw,

$P(\text{purple}) = \frac{3}{6} = \frac{1}{2}$.

The sample space for the second draw depends on the first draw.

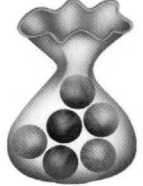

Before first draw

Outcome of first draw	Purple	Orange
Sample space for second draw	2 purple 3 orange	3 purple 2 orange

If the first draw was purple, then the probability of the second draw being purple is

$P(\text{purple}) = \frac{2}{5}$.

So the probability of drawing two purple marbles is

$P(\text{purple, purple}) = \frac{1}{2} \cdot \frac{2}{5} = \frac{1}{5}$.

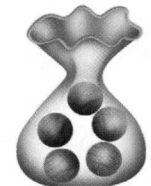

After first draw

---

2 **Teach**

ENGLISH LANGUAGE LEARNERS

Guided Instruction

In this lesson, students learn to find the probabilities of independent and dependent events. Define *independent* and *dependent events*. Explain that the probability of two or more events is the product of the individual probabilities (Teaching Transparency). Emphasize that dependent events have different sample spaces.

Teaching Tip   **Inclusion** You may want to review multiplication of fractions with the students.

Reaching All Learners
Through Critical Thinking

Have students work in small groups. Give each group a bag containing 4 red counters and 2 yellow counters. Ask the students to calculate the probabilities $P(\text{red, red})$ and $P(\text{yellow, yellow})$ with and without replacement. Have students compare the results and explain how the probabilities change between independent and dependent events.

Possible answers: $\frac{4}{9}$; $\frac{1}{9}$; $\frac{2}{5}$; $\frac{1}{15}$; The probabilities for the dependent events are lower because drawing the first counter reduces the number of the same colored counters in the sample space.

EXAMPLE 3 Finding the Probability of Dependent Events

A jar contains 16 quarters and 10 nickels.

A If 2 coins are chosen at random, what is the probability of getting 2 quarters?

Because the first coin is not replaced, the sample space is different for the second coin, so the events are dependent. Find the probability that the first coin chosen is a quarter.

$$P(\text{quarter}) = \frac{16}{26} = \frac{8}{13}$$

If the first coin chosen is a quarter, then there would be 15 quarters and a total of 25 coins left in the jar. Find the probability that the second coin chosen is a quarter.

$$P(\text{quarter}) = \frac{15}{25} = \frac{3}{5}$$

$\frac{8}{13} \cdot \frac{3}{5} = \frac{24}{65}$ *Multiply.*

The probability of getting two quarters is $\frac{24}{65}$.

B If 2 coins are chosen at random, what is the probability of getting 2 coins that are the same?

There are two possibilities: 2 quarters or 2 nickels. The probability of 2 quarters was calculated in Example 3A. Now find the probability of getting 2 nickels.

$$P(\text{nickel}) = \frac{10}{26} = \frac{5}{13}$$ *Find the probability that the second coin chosen is a nickel.*

If the first coin chosen is a nickel, there are now only 9 nickels and 25 total coins in the jar.

$$P(\text{nickel}) = \frac{9}{25}$$ *Find the probability that the second coin chosen is a nickel.*

$\frac{5}{13} \cdot \frac{9}{25} = \frac{9}{65}$ *Multiply.*

The events of 2 quarters and 2 nickels are mutually exclusive, so you can add their probabilities.

$\frac{24}{65} + \frac{9}{65} = \frac{33}{65}$ *P(quarters) + P(nickels)*

The probability of getting 2 coins the same is $\frac{33}{65}$.

> **Remember!**
> Two mutually exclusive events cannot both happen at the same time.

Think and Discuss

1. **Give an example** of a pair of independent events and a pair of dependent events.

2. **Tell** how you could make the events in Example 1B independent events.

Power Presentations
with PowerPoint®

Additional Examples

Example 3

The letters in the word *dependent* are placed in a box.

A. If two letters are chosen at random, what is the probability that they will both be consonants? $\frac{5}{12}$

B. If two letters are chosen at random, what is the probability that they will both be consonants or both be vowels? $\frac{1}{2}$

Also available on transparency

Possible answers to Think and Discuss

1. independent: rolling a pair of 3's on two number cubes; dependent: choosing the letter *Q* and the letter *U* in the game Scrabble®

2. Replace the first card in the deck before drawing the second card.

---

3 Close

Summarize

Discuss the difference between dependent and independent events. Have students identify each of the following as dependent or independent events:

1. a football team winning two games in a row   independent

2. drawing the names of two brothers out of a hat   dependent

3. drawing a red and then a green piece of candy from the same bag   dependent

4. rolling a pair of 6's on two number cubes and flipping two coins on heads independent

10-5 Exercises

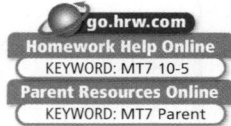

go.hrw.com
Homework Help Online
KEYWORD: MT7 10-5
Parent Resources Online
KEYWORD: MT7 Parent

Assignment Guide

If you finished Example **1** assign:
Average   1, 2, 6, 7, 20–24
Advanced 6, 7, 20–24

If you finished Example **2** assign:
Average   1–3, 6–9, 13, 15, 20–24
Advanced 6–9, 13–15, 20–24

If you finished Example **3** assign:
Average   1–13, 15, 16, 20–24
Advanced 6–24

Homework Quick Check

Quickly check key concepts.
Exercises: 6, 8, 10, 16

Math Background

Some students may want to know how to calculate probabilities for games. A simple example is finding the probability that two cards drawn from a standard deck of 52 cards will match. Drawing a pair of matching cards consists of two dependent events. Drawing a pair of aces is equivalent to drawing an ace and then drawing another ace from the remaining 51 cards.

$$P(\text{ace, ace}) = \frac{4}{52} \cdot \frac{3}{51} = \frac{1}{221}$$

There are 13 cards in each suit, and the probability of drawing a pair of any of those 13 cards is calculated the same way, so $P(\text{any pair}) = \frac{1}{221} \cdot 13 = \frac{1}{17}$, or about 6%.

GUIDED PRACTICE

See Example **1**   Determine if the events are dependent or independent.

1. drawing a red and a blue marble at the same time from a bag containing 6 red and 4 blue marbles   **dependent**

2. drawing a heart from a deck of cards and a coin landing on tails   **independent**

See Example **2**   An experiment consists of spinning each spinner once.

3. Find the probability that the first spinner lands on yellow and the second spinner lands on 8. $\frac{1}{32}$

See Example **3**   A sock drawer contains 10 white socks, 6 black socks, and 8 blue socks.

4. If 2 socks are chosen at random, what is the probability of getting a pair of white socks? $\frac{15}{92}$

5. If 3 socks are chosen at random, what is the probability of getting first a black sock, then a white sock, and then a blue sock? $\frac{10}{253}$

INDEPENDENT PRACTICE

See Example **1**   Determine if the events are dependent or independent.

6. drawing the name Roberto from a hat without replacing it and then drawing the name Paulo from the hat   **dependent**

7. rolling 2 fair number cubes and getting both a 1 and a 6   **independent**

See Example **2**   An experiment consists of tossing 2 fair coins, a penny and a nickel.

8. Find the probability of heads on the penny and tails on the nickel. $\frac{1}{4}$

9. Find the probability that both coins will land the same way. $\frac{1}{2}$

See Example **3**   A box contains 4 berry, 3 cinnamon, 4 apple, and 5 carob granola bars.

10. If Dawn randomly selects 2 bars, what is the probability that they will both be cinnamon? $\frac{1}{40}$

11. If two bars are selected randomly, what is the probability that they will be the same kind? $\frac{5}{24}$

PRACTICE AND PROBLEM SOLVING

Extra Practice
See page 801.

A box contains 6 red marbles, 4 blue marbles, and 8 yellow marbles.

12. Find $P(\text{yellow then red})$ if a marble is selected, and then a second marble is selected without replacing the first marble. $\frac{8}{51}$

13. Find $P(\text{yellow then red})$ if a marble is selected, and replaced, and then a second marble is selected. $\frac{4}{27}$

State Resources

go.hrw.com
State Resources Online
KEYWORD: MT7 Resources

RETEACH 10-5

Reteach
10-5 Independent and Dependent Events

Carlos is to draw 2 straws at random from a box of straws that contains 4 red, 4 white, and 4 striped straws.

$P(\text{1st straw is striped}) = \frac{4}{12}$ ← number of striped straws
                                          ← total number of straws

If Carlos *returns* the 1st straw to the box before drawing the 2nd straw, the probability that the 2nd straw is striped remains the same.

$P(\text{2nd straw is striped})$

$= \frac{4}{12}$ ← same number of striped straws
        ← same total number of straws

When the 1st straw is returned before the 2nd draw, the 2nd draw occurs as though the 1st draw never happened, **independent events**.

$P(\text{striped and striped}) = \frac{4}{12} \times \frac{4}{12}$
$= \frac{1}{3} \times \frac{1}{3} = \frac{1}{9}$

If Carlos *does not return* the first straw to the box before drawing the second straw, the probability that the second straw is striped changes.

$P(\text{2nd straw is striped})$

$= \frac{3}{11}$ ← one striped straw has been taken
        ← one less straw in total number

When the 1st straw is not returned before the 2nd draw, the number of straws remaining is changed, **dependent events**.

$P(\text{striped and striped}) = \frac{4}{12} \times \frac{3}{11}$
$= \frac{1}{3} \times \frac{3}{11} = \frac{1}{11}$

Describe the events as independent or dependent.

1. Josh tosses a coin and spins a spinner.   independent

2. Ana draws a colored toothpick from a jar. Without replacing it, she draws a second toothpick.   dependent

3. Sue draws a card from a deck of cards and replaces it. Then she draws a second card from the deck.   independent

Each situation begins with a box of marbles that contains 2 red, 3 blue, 4 green, and 3 yellow marbles. Complete to find each probability.

4. A 1st marble is drawn and replaced. Then a 2nd marble is drawn.
$P(\text{red and blue}) = \frac{2}{12} \times \frac{3}{12} = \frac{1}{24}$

5. A 1st marble is drawn and not replaced. A 2nd marble is drawn.
$P(\text{red and blue}) = \frac{2}{12} \times \frac{3}{11} = \frac{1}{22}$

6. A 1st marble is drawn and replaced. Then a 2nd marble is drawn.
$P(\text{red and red}) = \frac{2}{12} \times \frac{2}{12} = \frac{1}{36}$

7. A 1st marble is drawn and not replaced. A 2nd marble is drawn.
$P(\text{red and red}) = \frac{2}{12} \times \frac{1}{11} = \frac{1}{66}$

PRACTICE 10-5

Practice B
10-5 Independent and Dependent Events

Determine if the events are dependent or independent.

1. choosing a tie and shirt from the closet   independent

2. choosing a month and tossing a coin   independent

3. rolling two fair number cubes once, then rolling them again if you received the same number on both number cubes on the first roll   dependent

An experiment consists of rolling a fair number cube and tossing a fair coin.

4. Find the probability of getting a 5 on the number cube and tails on the dime. $\frac{1}{12}$

5. Find the probability of getting an even number on the number cube and heads on the dime. $\frac{1}{4}$

6. Find the probability of getting a 2 or 3 on the number cube and heads on the dime. $\frac{1}{6}$

A box contains 3 red marbles, 6 blue marbles, and 1 white marble. The marbles are selected at random, one at a time, and are not replaced. Find the probability.

7. $P(\text{blue and red})$
$\frac{1}{5} = 0.2$

8. $P(\text{white and blue})$
$\frac{1}{15} \approx 0.06\overline{6}$

9. $P(\text{red and white})$
$\frac{1}{30} \approx 0.03\overline{3}$

10. $P(\text{red and white and blue})$
$\frac{1}{40} = 0.025$

11. $P(\text{red and red and blue})$
$\frac{1}{20} = 0.05$

12. $P(\text{red and blue and blue})$
$\frac{1}{8} = 0.125$

13. $P(\text{red and red and red})$
$\frac{1}{120} = 0.0083\overline{3}$

14. $P(\text{white and blue and blue})$
$\frac{1}{24} = 0.041\overline{6}$

15. $P(\text{white and red and white})$
0

Games

This giant Scrabble game was held on the 50th anniversary of Scrabble. Each tile was 100 times the size of a standard tile, and the board was nearly 100 ft by 100 ft.

14. You roll a fair number cube twice. What is the probability of rolling two 3's if the first roll is a 5? Explain.   **Possible answer: The probability of rolling two 3's is 0 if the first roll is a 5 because it will be impossible to get two 3's.**

15. **School** On a quiz, there are 5 true-false questions. A student guesses on all 5 questions. What is the probability that the student gets all 5 questions right? $\frac{1}{32} = 0.03125$

16. **Games** The table shows the Scrabble® tiles available at the start of a game. There are 100 tiles: 42 vowels, 56 consonants, and 2 blanks. To begin play, each player draws a tile. The player with the tile closest to the beginning of the alphabet goes first. A blank tile beats any letter.

Scrabble Letter Distribution		
A-9	B-2	C-2
D-4	E-12	F-2
G-3	H-2	I-9
J-1	K-1	L-4
M-2	N-6	O-8
P-2	Q-1	R-6
S-4	T-6	U-4
V-2	W-2	X-1
Y-2	Z-1	blank-2

  a. If you draw first, what is the probability that you will select an *A*? $\frac{9}{100} = 0.09$

  b. If you draw first and do not replace the tile, what is the probability that you will select an *E* and your opponent will select an *I*? $\frac{3}{275} \approx 0.01$

  c. If you draw first and do not replace the tile, what is the probability that you will select an *E* and your opponent will win the first turn? $\frac{19}{825} \approx 0.02$

 17. **Write a Problem** Write a problem about the probability of an event in a board game, and then solve it.   **Check students' work.**

 18. **Write About It** In an experiment, two cards are drawn from a deck. How is the probability different if the first card is replaced before the second card is drawn than if the first card is not replaced?

 19. **Challenge** Suppose you deal yourself 7 cards from a standard 52-card deck. What is the probability that you will deal all red cards? ≈ 0.0049

TEST PREP and Spiral Review

20. **Multiple Choice** If *A* and *B* are independent events such that $P(A) = 0.14$ and $P(B) = 0.28$, what is the probability that both *A* and *B* will occur?

  (A) 0.0392   (B) 0.0784   (C) 0.24   (D) 0.42

21. **Gridded Response** A bag contains 8 red marbles and 2 blue marbles. What is the probability, written as a fraction, of choosing a red marble and a blue marble from the bag at the same time? $\frac{8}{45}$

Find the first and third quartiles for each data set. (Lesson 9-4)

22. 19, 24, 13, 18, 21, 8, 11   **11; 21**   **23.** 56, 71, 84, 66, 52, 11, 80   **52; 80**

24. An experiment consists of rolling two fair number cubes. Find the probability of rolling a total of 14. (Lesson 10-4)   **0**

ONGOING ASSESSMENT and INTERVENTION

Diagnose *Before* the Lesson
10-5 Warm Up, TE p. 545

Monitor *During* the Lesson
10-5 Know-It Notebook
10-5 Questioning Strategies

Assess *After* the Lesson
10-5 Lesson Quiz, TE p. 549

Answers

18. Possible answer: If the first card is replaced, then the number of cards to choose from is the same for each draw. If the card is not replaced, there will be one fewer card to choose from when the second card is drawn.

TEST PREP DOCTOR + For Exercise 20, students who answered **D** attempted to calculate the probability of *both* events by *adding* the probabilities of each event. Remind students that the probability of both events occurring is found by multiplying the given probabilities.

 Journal

Ask students to write in their own words the difference between dependent events and independent events.

Power Presentations with PowerPoint®

✓ **10-5 Lesson Quiz**

Determine if each event is dependent or independent.

1. drawing a red ball from a bucket and then drawing a green ball without replacing the first   dependent

2. spinning a 7 on a spinner three times in a row   independent

3. A bucket contains 5 yellow and 7 red balls. If 2 balls are selected randomly without replacement, what is the probability that they will both be yellow? $\frac{5}{33}$

Also available on transparency

Objective: Students use probability to make decisions and predictions.

 Technology Lab
In *Technology Lab Activities*

 Online Edition
Tutorial Videos

 Countdown to Testing Week 23

 **Power Presentations**
with PowerPoint®

Warm Up

Solve each proportion.
1. $\frac{x}{5.1} = \frac{6}{1.7}$ 18   **2.** $\frac{24}{108} = \frac{n}{9}$ 2
3. $\frac{65}{0.1} = \frac{13}{x}$ 0.02   **4.** $\frac{46}{n} = \frac{200}{46}$ 10.58

Problem of the Day

Aidan is playing a board game using two six-sided number cubes. He wins if he doesn't roll a six or a seven. What is the probability that Aidan will win on his next turn? $\frac{25}{36}$

Also available on transparency

Math Humor

Doctor: I have good news and bad news. The bad news is that you only have a 20% chance of living.

Patient: That's awful! What's the good news?

Doctor: There is only a 10% chance that I'm right.

State Resources

 **go.hrw.com**
State Resources Online
KEYWORD: MT7 Resources

10-6 Making Decisions and Predictions

Learn to use probability to make decisions and predictions.

Aliza works for a store that sells socks. She conducted a survey to learn about color preferences. She recorded the colors of the last 100 pairs of socks sold. Aliza can use the results of her survey to decide how many pairs of socks of each color to order from the maker.

Probability can be used to make decisions or predictions. Use the probability of an event's occurring to set up a proportion to find the number of times an event is likely to occur.

EXAMPLE 1 Using Probability to Make Decisions and Predictions

A The table shows the colors of the last 100 pairs of socks sold. Aliza plans to place an order for 1200 pairs of socks. How many blue pairs of socks should she order?

Pairs of Socks Sold	
Color	**Number**
Black	9
Blue	20
Gold	6
Green	22
Purple	25
Red	18

$\dfrac{\text{number of blue pairs of socks sold}}{\text{total number of pairs of socks sold}} = \dfrac{20}{100}$, or $\dfrac{1}{5}$ *Find the probability of selling a blue pair of socks.*

$\dfrac{1}{5} = \dfrac{n}{1200}$ *Set up a proportion.*

$1 \cdot 1200 = 5n$ *Find the cross products.*

$\dfrac{1200}{5} = \dfrac{5n}{5}$ *Divide both sides by n.*

$240 = n$

Aliza should order 240 blue pairs of socks.

---

1 Introduce

Alternate Opener

EXPLORATION

10-6 **Making Decisions and Predictions**

Kate sells shirts and caps that have a school logo on them. Both the shirts and the caps are available in red or black. The table shows the number of shirts and caps that Kate sold during her first week of business.

	Red	Black
Shirts	125	75
Caps	60	40

1. What was the total number of shirts sold during the first week?

2. What fraction of the shirts that were sold were red shirts?

3. Kate assumes that future sales will be similar to the first week's sales. She plans to order 2000 more shirts. How many of these should be red shirts?

4. In general, when Kate sells a shirt, what is the probability that it is a red shirt?

5. What was the total number of caps sold during the first week?

6. What fraction of the caps that were sold were black caps?

7. Kate places an order for 5000 more caps. How many of these should be black caps?

Think and Discuss

8. Explain how you determined the number of red shirts that Kate should order in Problem 3.

9. Explain how you determined the number of black caps that Kate should order in Problem 6.

Motivate

Explain to students that we use probability to make decisions and predictions all the time in everyday life. If a weatherperson forecasts a high chance of rain, we may carry an umbrella to work or school. People diagnosed with a high probability of heart disease may alter their diet and exercise habits. Coaches and sports managers use experimental probabilities such as batting averages to determine the skills of their athletes.

Explorations and answers are provided in *Alternate Openers: Explorations Transparencies.*

B At a carnival, a spinner is used to determine a player's prize. If the spinner lands on red, the player gets a stuffed animal. Suppose the spinner is spun 160 times. What is the best prediction of the number of stuffed animals that will be given away?

$$\frac{\text{number of possible red outcomes}}{\text{total possible outcomes}} = \frac{1}{8}$$
Find the theoretical probability of spinning red.

$$\frac{1}{8} = \frac{n}{160}$$
Set up a proportion.

$$1 \cdot 160 = 8n$$
Find the cross products.

$$\frac{160}{8} = \frac{8n}{8}$$
Divide both sides by 8.

$$20 = n$$

Approximately 20 stuffed animals will be given away.

Probability is often used to determine whether a game is fair. A game involving chance is fair if each player is equally likely to win.

EXAMPLE 2 Deciding Whether a Game Is Fair

In a game, two players each roll two fair dice and add the two numbers. Player A wins with a sum of 6 or less. Otherwise player B wins. Decide whether the game is fair.

List all possible outcomes.

$1 + 1 = 2$ $2 + 1 = 3$ $3 + 1 = 4$ $4 + 1 = 5$ $5 + 1 = 6$ $6 + 1 = 7$
$1 + 2 = 3$ $2 + 2 = 4$ $3 + 2 = 5$ $4 + 2 = 6$ $5 + 2 = 7$ $6 + 2 = 8$
$1 + 3 = 4$ $2 + 3 = 5$ $3 + 3 = 6$ $4 + 3 = 7$ $5 + 3 = 8$ $6 + 3 = 9$
$1 + 4 = 5$ $2 + 4 = 6$ $3 + 4 = 7$ $4 + 4 = 8$ $5 + 4 = 9$ $6 + 4 = 10$
$1 + 5 = 6$ $2 + 5 = 7$ $3 + 5 = 8$ $4 + 5 = 9$ $5 + 5 = 10$ $6 + 5 = 11$
$1 + 6 = 7$ $2 + 6 = 8$ $3 + 6 = 9$ $4 + 6 = 10$ $5 + 6 = 11$ $6 + 6 = 12$

Find the theoretical probability of each player's winning.

$$P(\text{player A winning}) = \frac{15}{36}$$
There are 15 combinations with a sum of 6 or less

$$P(\text{player B winning}) = \frac{21}{36}$$
There are 21 combinations with a sum greater than 6.

Since $\frac{15}{36} \neq \frac{21}{36}$, the game is not fair.

1. Possible answer: Two players take turns rolling a 6-sided number cube. If the cube lands on a number from 1 to 3, the first player wins. Otherwise, the other player wins. Each player has a 0.5 probability of winning.

Think and Discuss

1. Give an example of a game that is fair. Explain how you know.

Power Presentations
with PowerPoint®

Additional Examples

Example 1

A. The table shows the satisfaction rating in a business's survey of 500 customers. Of their 240,000 customers, how many should the business expect to be unsatisfied? **16,800**

Pleased	Satisfied	Unsatisfied
126	339	35

B. Jared randomly draws a card from a 52-card deck and tries to guess what it is. If he tries this trick 1040 times over the course of his life, what is the best prediction for the amount of times it works? **20**

Example 2

In a game, two players each flip a coin. Player A wins if exactly one of the two coins is heads. Otherwise, player B wins. Determine whether the game is fair. **fair**

Also available on transparency

---

2 Teach

Guided Instruction

Confirm that students understand the difference between experimental and theoretical probability. Discuss with them how to use probability to make decisions and predictions. Emphasize that, in the long run, these predictions are much more useful. For example, if you roll a 6-sided number cube six times, it is unlikely that 50% of those rolls will land on an even-numbered face. However, if you roll it 10,000 times, it will be very close to 50%. Define "fair game," and discuss how to determine whether a game is fair.

Reaching All Learners
Through Kinesthetic Experience

Simulate lesson Example 1B by splitting up the 160 spins as evenly as possible amongst the class. The spins themselves can be simulated by flipping a coin three times. If it lands on heads all three times, it should be counted as a spin that landed on silver. Count up the spins and see how close the result is to 20. Remind students that even though 20 was the best guess, it is still unlikely that there would end up being exactly 20 silver spins.

3 Close

Summarize

Explain that to common observers, many events seem random. Knowing probability allows one to make educated decisions and predictions that are more accurate than random guessing.

10-6 Exercises

go.hrw.com
Homework Help Online
KEYWORD: MT7 10-6
Parent Resources Online
KEYWORD: MT7 Parent

Assignment Guide

If you finished Example **1** assign:
Average 1–3, 6, 7, 10–14, 16, 17, 21–27
Advanced 6, 7, 10–14, 16–27

If you finished Example **2** assign:
Average 1–14, 16, 17, 21–27
Advanced 6–27

Homework Quick Check

Quickly check key concepts.
Exercises: 6, 8, 12

GUIDED PRACTICE

See Example **1**   A store sells cases to hold CDs. The table shows the capacities of the last 200 cases sold. The store is going to order 1500 more CD cases. Use probability to decide how many of each type of case to order.

CD Cases Sold	
Capacity	Number
24 CDs	70
32 CDs	13
64 CDs	24
96 CDs	52
160 CDs	41

   1. 24-CD case **525**   **2.** 96-CD case **390**

   3. Players use a spinner to move around a game board. Suppose the spinner is spun 40 times. Predict how many times the spinner will land on "Get a Clue!" **8**

See Example **2**   **Decide whether each game is fair.**

   4. Roll two fair number cubes labeled 1–6. Add the two numbers. Player A wins if the sum is odd. Player B wins if the sum is even. **fair; $\frac{1}{2} = \frac{1}{2}$**

   5. Toss three fair coins. Player A wins if exactly 2 heads land up. Otherwise Player B wins. **not fair; $\frac{3}{8} \neq \frac{5}{8}$**

INDEPENDENT PRACTICE

See Example **1**   **6.** In her last ten 10K runs, Celia had the following times in minutes: 50:30, 50:37, 48:29, 50:46, 51:12, 49:19, 49:50, 51:19, 53:39, and 53:54. Based on these results, what is the best prediction of the number of times Celia will run faster than 50 minutes in her next 30 runs? **9**

   7. Football games begin with a coin toss to decide who kicks off and who receives. The Cougars won the coin toss in their first 2 games. Predict how many coin tosses the Cougars will win in their next 10 games. **5**

See Example **2**   **Decide whether each game is fair.**

   8. Roll two fair number cubes labeled 1–6. Add the two numbers. Player A wins if the sum is a multiple of 3. Otherwise Player B wins. **not fair; $\frac{1}{3} \neq \frac{2}{3}$**

   9. A spinner is divided evenly into 8 sections. There are 4 blue sections, 2 red, 1 green, and 1 yellow. Player A wins if the spinner lands on blue. Otherwise Player B wins. **fair; $\frac{1}{2} = \frac{1}{2}$**

PRACTICE AND PROBLEM SOLVING

Extra Practice
See page 801.

A fair number cube is labeled 1–6. Predict the number of outcomes for the given number of rolls.

10. outcome: 3
number of rolls: 36 **6**

11. outcome: even number
number of rolls: 50 **25**

12. outcome: not 2
number of rolls: 72 **60**

13. outcome: greater than 6
number of rolls: 100 **0**

RETEACH 10-6

Reteach
10-6 *Making Decisions and Predictions*

Probability can be used to make predictions about data.

The spinner has 5 equal sections. To predict how many times you will land on the number 1 in 30 spins, first find the probability of landing on 1 in one spin. Then multiply 30 spins by that probability.

Step 1 Find the probability.

$$P(1) = \frac{\text{number of 1s}}{\text{number of equal sections}} = \frac{2}{5}$$

Step 2 Multiply the number of spins by the probability. There are 30 spins and $P(1) = \frac{2}{5}$.

$$30 \times \frac{2}{5} = 6 \times 2 = 12$$

You will spin about 12 1s in 30 spins.

Each situation begins with a box of marbles that contains 2 red, 3 blue, 4 green, and 3 yellow marbles. Complete to find each probability.

1. Predict how many times you will land on C in 32 spins?

  a. $P(C) = \frac{1}{4}$

  b. $32 \times P(C) = 32 \times \frac{1}{4} = 8$

  c. about __8__ times

2. Predict how many times you will land on B in 48 spins?

  a. $P(B) = \frac{1}{4}$

  b. $48 \times P(B) = \frac{48 \times \frac{1}{4}}{} = 12$

  c. about __12__ times

3. Predict how many times you will land on A in 50 spins?

  a. $P(A) = \frac{1}{2}$

  b. $50 \times \frac{1}{2} = 25$

  c. about __25__ times

PRACTICE 10-6

Practice B
10-6 *Making Decisions and Predictions*

A sports store sells water bottles in different colors. The table shows the colors of the last 200 water bottles sold. The manager plans to order 1800 new water bottles.

Water Bottles Sold	
Color	Number
Red	30
Blue	50
Green	25
Yellow	10
Purple	10
Clear	75

1. How many red water bottles should the manager order? __270__

2. How many green water bottles should the manager order? __225__

3. How many clear water bottles should the manager order? __675__

4. If the carnival spinner lands on 10, the player gets a large stuffed animal. Suppose the spinner is spun 30 times. Predict how many large stuffed animals will be given away. __5__

Decide whether the game is fair.

5. Roll two fair number cubes labeled 1–6. Player A wins if both numbers are the same. Player B wins if both numbers are different.

not fair: $\frac{1}{6} \neq \frac{5}{6}$

6. Roll two fair number cubes labeled 1–6. Add the numbers. Player A wins if the sum is 5 or less. Player B wins if the sum is 9 or more.

fair: $\frac{5}{18} = \frac{5}{18}$

7. Toss three fair coins. Player A wins if exactly one tail lands up. Otherwise Player B wins.

not fair: $\frac{3}{8} \neq \frac{5}{8}$

---

14. School Before a school election, a sample of voters gave Karim 28 votes, Marisol 41, and Richard 11. Based on these results, predict the number of votes for each candidate if 1600 students vote.
Karim:560; Marisol: 820; Richard: 220

15. Critical Thinking Jack suggested the following game to Charlie: "Let's roll two dice. We'll subtract the smaller number from the larger. If the difference is 0, 1, or 2, I get a point. If the difference is 3, 4, or 5, you get a point." Charlie thought the game sounded fair. Decide whether Charlie was correct. If he was not, describe a way to make the game fair.

16. Estimation An ice-skating rink inspects 23 pairs of skates and finds 2 pairs to be defective. Estimate the probability that a pair of skates chosen at random will be defective. The rink has 121 pairs of ice skates. Estimate the number of pairs that are likely to be defective. $\frac{1}{12}$; **10**

17. School There are 540 students in Marla's school. In her classroom, there are 2 left-handed students and 18 right-handed students. Predict the number of left-handed students in the whole school. **54**

18. Write a Problem Use sports statistics from the newspaper or Internet to write a prediction problem using probability. **Check students' work.**

19. Write About It If you make a prediction based on experimental probability, how accurate will your prediction be?

20. Challenge A bag contains 10 number tiles labeled 1–10. Which 2 number tiles would you remove from the bag to increase the chances of the following events: drawing an even tile, drawing a multiple of 3, and drawing a number less than 5? Explain. **5 and 7 because they are not desired outcomes**

TEST PREP and Spiral Review

21. Multiple Choice In a survey of 500 potential voters, Susan Wilson was picked by 182 people, Anthony Altimuro by 96, Laura Carson by 128, and Paul Johannson by 94. In the actual election, which is the best estimate of the percent of votes Anthony Altimuro can expect to receive?

(A) 19% (B) 24% (C) 48% (D) 96%

22. Short Answer A game consists of spinning the spinner twice and adding the results. Player A wins if the sum is 4. Otherwise Player B wins. Decide whether the game is fair. **not fair; $\frac{1}{3} \neq \frac{2}{3}$**

Find the area of each figure with the given dimensions. (Lesson 8-2)

23. triangle: $b = 26$, $h = 16$ **208 units^2**

24. trapezoid: $b_1 = 14$, $b_2 = 18$, $h = 9$ **144 units^2**

25. triangle: $b = 10m$, $h = 8$ **40m units^2**

26. trapezoid: $b_1 = 6.2$, $b_2 = 11$, $h = 5.4$ **46.44 units^2**

27. A company manufactures a toy cube that is 4 in. on each edge. If the length of each edge is doubled, what will be the effect on the volume of the cube? (Lesson 8-5) **The volume is 8 times as large.**

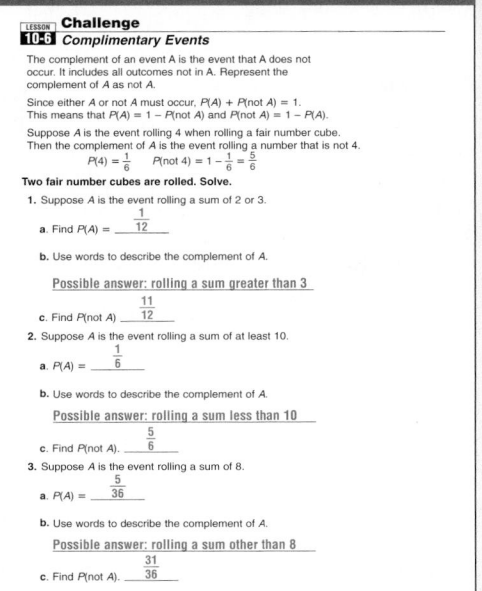
Answers

15. The game is not fair. There are many more losing events for Charlie than winning events. A possible way to make it fair would be to let Charlie win if the difference is 0 in addition to when the difference is 3, 4, or 5.

19. See p. A14.

Journal

Have students explain a scenario in which probability is present in their daily lives. Ask them to make at least two predictions or decisions based on that probability.

10-6 Lesson Quiz

1. Out of the 35 products a salesperson sold last week, 8 of them were products worth over $200. About how many of these products should the salesperson expect to sell if he has 140 customers next month? **32**

2. A student answers all 12 multiple choice questions on a quiz at random. Each multiple choice question has 4 choices. What is the best guess for the amount of multiple choice questions the student will answer correctly? **3**

3. In a game, two players each roll a 6-sided number cube and add the two numbers. If the roll is a 6 or less, player A wins. If the roll is 8 or more, player B wins. If the roll is a 7, the players tie and roll again. Is this a fair game? **Yes**

Also available on transparency

Online Edition
Tutorial Videos

 Countdown to Testing Week 23

Power Presentations
with PowerPoint®

Warm Up

A bag contains 15 nickels, 10 dimes, and 5 quarters. Two coins are drawn without replacement.

1. Find the probability that the first is a dime and the second is a quarter. $\frac{5}{87}$

2. Find the probability that they are both nickels. $\frac{7}{29}$

Problem of the Day

Larissa was born in August. What is the probability that she was born on an odd-numbered day? ≈ 0.52

Also available on transparency

Math Humor

At the ice cream shop, the worker climbed a ladder to change the prices on the sign. When the numbers 3, 5, 7, and 9 slipped and fell into his favorite ice cream, he thought it was his lucky day. After all, the odds were in his flavor.

State Resources

go.hrw.com
State Resources Online
KEYWORD: MT7 Resources

10-7 Odds

Learn to convert between probabilities and odds.

Vocabulary
odds in favor
odds against

Schools often sell raffle tickets as a way to raise money. Family and friends buy the tickets and have a chance to win a prize. The odds of winning depend on the number of tickets sold and the number of prizes raffled.

The **odds in favor** of an event is the ratio of favorable outcomes to unfavorable outcomes. The **odds against** an event is the ratio of unfavorable outcomes to favorable outcomes.

odds in favor **a:b** a = number of favorable outcomes
odds against **b:a** b = number of unfavorable outcomes
                           $a + b$ = total number of outcomes

EXAMPLE 1 Finding Odds

Jordan Middle School sold 552 raffle tickets for the chance to be a teacher for the day. Minnie bought 6 raffle tickets.

A What are the odds in favor of Minnie's winning the raffle?

The number of favorable outcomes is 6, and the number of unfavorable outcomes is $552 - 6 = 546$. Minnie's odds in favor of winning the raffle are 6 to 546, or 1 to 91.

B What are the odds against Minnie's winning the raffle?

The odds in favor of Minnie's winning are 1 to 91, so the odds against her winning are 91 to 1.

Probability and odds are related. The odds in favor of rolling a two on a fair number cube are 1:5. There is 1 way to get a two and 5 ways not to get a two. The sum of the numbers in the ratio is the denominator of the probability, $\frac{1}{6}$.

CONVERTING ODDS TO PROBABILITIES

If the odds in favor of an event are $a:b$, then the probability of the event's occurring is $\frac{a}{a+b}$.

---

1 Introduce
Alternate Opener

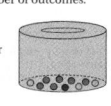

EXPLORATION

10-7 Odds

When you find the *odds in favor* of an event, you compare the number of favorable outcomes to the number of unfavorable outcomes. With *probability*, you compare the number of favorable outcomes to the total number of outcomes.

The plastic container at right contains 10 marbles: 4 red, 3 yellow, 2 green, and 1 blue. The odds in favor of drawing a green marble are 2 to 8, because 2 marbles are green and 8 marbles are not green.

Use the definitions of *odds in favor* and *probability* to complete the table.

		Probability	Odds in Favor
	Drawing a green marble	$\frac{2}{10} = \frac{1}{5}$	2:8
1.	Drawing a red marble		
2.	Drawing a yellow marble		
3.	Drawing a blue marble		

Think and Discuss
4. **Explain** the difference between odds and probability.

Motivate

Ask students if they have ever won anything in a contest that involved a game piece. Examples of game pieces may include restaurant soda cups, tops of soda bottles, or cereal boxes. Explain that some games and/or prizes are easier to win than others because games have different odds.

Explorations and answers are provided in *Alternate Openers: Explorations Transparencies.*

EXAMPLE 2 Converting Odds to Probabilities

A If the odds in favor of winning movie passes are 1:10, what is the probability of winning movie passes?

$$P(\text{movie passes}) = \frac{1}{1 + 10} = \frac{1}{11}$$

On average, there is 1 win for every 10 losses, so someone wins 1 out of every 11 times.

B If the odds against winning a flat-screen television are 39,999:1, what is the probability of winning a flat-screen television?

If the odds against winning the television are 39,999:1, then the odds in favor of winning the television are 1:39,999.

$$P(\text{television}) = \frac{1}{1 + 39,999} = \frac{1}{40,000} = 0.000025$$

Suppose that the probability of an event is $\frac{1}{3}$. This means that, on average, it will happen in 1 out of every 3 trials, and it will not happen in 2 out of every 3 trials. The odds in favor of the event are 1:2, and the odds against the event are 2:1.

CONVERTING PROBABILITIES TO ODDS

If the probability of an event is $\frac{m}{n}$, then the odds in favor of the event are $m:(n - m)$ and the odds against the event are $(n - m):m$.

EXAMPLE 3 Converting Probabilities to Odds

A The probability of winning a CD player is $\frac{1}{75}$. What are the odds in favor of winning a CD player?

On average, 1 out of every 75 people wins, and the other 74 people lose. The odds in favor of winning the CD player are 1:(75 − 1), or 1:74.

B The probability of winning an electric scooter is $\frac{1}{125,000}$. What are the odds against winning a scooter?

On average, 1 out of every 125,000 people wins, and the other 124,999 people lose. The odds against winning the scooter are (125,000 − 1):1, or 124,999:1.

Think and Discuss

1. **Explain** the difference between probability and odds.

2. **Compare** the odds in favor of an event with the odds against it.

---

1. Possible answer: Odds are either ratios of favorable outcomes to unfavorable outcomes or ratios of unfavorable outcomes to favorable outcomes. Probabilities are ratios of favorable outcomes to total possible outcomes.

Possible answers to *Think and Discuss*

2. The ratio of favorable to unfavorable outcomes represents the odds in favor of an event, and the ratio of unfavorable to favorable outcomes represents the odds against an event.

---

2 Teach

Guided Instruction

In this lesson, students learn to convert between probabilities and odds. Explain that odds are a different way to look at probability. Odds compare the favorable and unfavorable outcomes, instead of comparing one of those to the total number of outcomes (Teaching Transparency).

Teaching Tip **Cognitive Strategies** Emphasize that the sum of the numbers in a ratio of odds is the denominator of the related probability ratio. If the probability of an event is $\frac{3}{8}$, then the odds in favor of the event are 3:5 and the odds against the event are 5:3. In either case, 3 + 5 = 8.

Reaching All Learners
Through Graphic Organizers

Have students create graphic organizers to compare and contrast probability and odds, and have them include examples. When they have completed their organizers, have them share them with each other.

Example:

Experiment: rolling double 6's on a pair of number cubes

Probability and Odds	
P(double 6's)	**Odds in Favor**
$\frac{1}{36}$	1:35
P(not double 6's)	**Odds Against**
$\frac{35}{36}$	35:1

3 Close

Summarize

Review the connection between probability and odds. Ask students if the phrase "50/50" refers to probability or odds, and ask them to explain the answer.

Possible answer: The statement "50/50" refers to odds. It represents equal chances of an event occurring or not occurring. The corresponding probability statement would be $\frac{50}{100}$, or $\frac{1}{2}$.

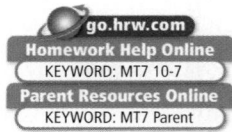

go.hrw.com
Homework Help Online
KEYWORD: MT7 10-7
Parent Resources Online
KEYWORD: MT7 Parent

Assignment Guide

If you finished Example **1** assign:
Average 1, 2, 7, 8, 13–18, 27–31
Advanced 7, 8, 13–18, 21, 24–31

If you finished Example **2** assign:
Average 1–4, 7–10, 13–18, 22, 27–31
Advanced 7–10, 13–18, 21–31

If you finished Example **3** assign:
Average 1–20, 22, 27–31
Advanced 7–31

Homework Quick Check

Quickly check key concepts.
Exercises: 8, 10, 12, 16, 22

Math Background

In state-run lotteries, the higher the odds against an event occurring, the higher the payoff. However, the payoff is never exactly proportional to the odds that are used for any particular event because the sponsor of the activity generally takes a portion of the revenue. For example, the probability of randomly picking a particular three-digit number is $\frac{1}{1000}$ because there are 1000 three-digit numbers (from 000 through 999). A proportionate payoff for a $1 winning number would be $1000. However, a likely payoff amount by a typical state-run lottery would be only $500.

State Resources

go.hrw.com
State Resources Online
KEYWORD: MT7 Resources

GUIDED PRACTICE

See Example **1** — Monroe Middle School is holding a raffle for a new bicycle. Jonathan bought 7 of the 945 tickets that were sold.

1. What are the odds in favor of Jonathan's winning the raffle? **1:135**

2. What are the odds against Jonathan's winning the raffle? **135:1**

See Example **2**
3. If the odds in favor of winning a trip for two to Hawaii are 1:141,999, what is the probability of winning the trip? $\frac{1}{142,000}$

4. If the odds against winning a digital camera are 25,999:1, what is the probability of winning the camera? $\frac{1}{26,000}$

See Example **3**
5. The probability of winning a CD is $\frac{1}{80}$. What are the odds in favor of winning the CD? **1:79**

6. The probability of winning a vacation is $\frac{1}{22,750}$. What are the odds against winning the vacation? **22,749:1**

INDEPENDENT PRACTICE

See Example **1** — A teachers' convention is giving away a new computer as a door prize. Each of the 2240 attendees is given 5 tickets for chances to win the computer.

7. What are the odds in favor of winning the computer? **1:2240**

8. What are the odds against winning the computer? **2240:1**

See Example **2**
9. If the odds in favor of winning a new portable music player are 1:8999, what is the probability of winning the player? $\frac{1}{9000}$

10. If the odds against being randomly selected for a committee are 19:1, what is the probability of being selected? $\frac{1}{20}$

See Example **3**
11. The probability of winning a gift certificate is $\frac{1}{620}$. What are the odds in favor of winning the gift certificate? **1:619**

12. The probability of winning a portable DVD player is $\frac{1}{12,000}$. What are the odds against winning the player? **11,999:1**

PRACTICE AND PROBLEM SOLVING

Extra Practice
See page 801.

You roll two fair number cubes. Find the odds in favor of and against each event.

13. rolling two 1's **1:35; 35:1**

14. rolling a total of 6 **5:31; 31:5**

15. rolling a total of 4 **1:11; 11:1**

16. rolling doubles **1:5; 5:1**

17. rolling an odd and an even number **1:1; 1:1**

18. rolling a 5 and a 3 **1:17; 17:1**

19. The probability of choosing a black card from a standard deck is 50%. What are the odds in favor of choosing a black card? **1:1**

RETEACH 10-7

Reteach
10-7 Odds

Baseball fans do not usually ask "What is the probability that the New York Yankees will win the World Series this year?"

Fans who want to know the chances of a team winning usually ask "What are the *odds* that the Yankees will win?"

Odds that an event *E* will or will not occur can be defined as a ratio of probabilities.

$$\text{odds in favor} = \frac{P(E)}{P(\text{not } E)} \qquad \text{odds against} = \frac{P(\text{not } E)}{P(E)}$$

What are the odds in favor of getting a 4 in one roll of a numbered cube?

$$P(4) = \frac{1}{6} \quad P(\text{not } 4) = \frac{5}{6} \quad \text{odds}(4) = \frac{P(4)}{P(\text{not } 4)} = \frac{\frac{1}{6}}{\frac{5}{6}} = \frac{1}{5}$$

So, the odds in favor of getting a 4 are 1 to 5.

Complete to find the indicated odds. In each case, a cube numbered 1–6 is rolled once.

1. Find the odds in favor of getting a number greater than 4.

$$P(>4) = \frac{2}{6} \quad P(\text{not} >4) = \frac{4}{6} \quad \text{odds }(>4) = \frac{P(>4)}{P(\text{not} >4)} = \frac{\frac{2}{6}}{\frac{4}{6}} = \frac{2}{4}, \text{ or } \frac{1}{2}$$

So, the odds in favor of getting a number greater than 4 are 1 to 2 .

2. Find the odds against getting a 3.

$$P(3) = \frac{1}{6} \quad P(\text{not } 3) = \frac{5}{6} \quad \text{odds}(\text{not } 3) = \frac{P(\text{not } 3)}{P(3)} = \frac{\frac{5}{6}}{\frac{1}{6}} = \frac{5}{1}$$

So, the odds against getting a 3 are 5 to 1 .

3. Find the odds in favor of getting an even number.

$$P(\text{even}) = \frac{3}{6} \quad P(\text{not even}) = \frac{3}{6} \quad \text{odds}(\text{even}) = \frac{P(\text{even})}{P(\text{not even})} = \frac{\frac{3}{6}}{\frac{3}{6}} = \frac{3}{3}, \text{ or } \frac{1}{1}$$

So, the odds in favor of getting an even number are 1 to 1 .

PRACTICE 10-7

Practice B
10-7 Odds

A bag contains 9 red marbles, 5 green marbles, and 6 purple marbles.

1. Find P(red marble)
$\frac{9}{20} = 0.45$

2. Find P(green marble)
$\frac{1}{4} = 0.25$

3. Find P(purple marble)
$\frac{3}{10} = 0.3$

4. Find the odds in favor of choosing a red marble.
9:11

5. Find the odds against choosing a red marble.
11:9

6. Find the odds in favor of choosing a green marble.
5:15 = 1:3

7. Find the odds against choosing a green marble.
15:5 = 3:1

8. Find the odds in favor of choosing a purple marble.
6:14 = 3:7

9. Find the odds against choosing a purple marble.
14:6 = 7:3

10. Find the odds in favor of not choosing a green marble.
15:5 = 3:1

11. Find the odds in favor of choosing a red or purple marble.
14:6 = 7:3

12. If the probability of Helena winning the contest is $\frac{2}{5}$, what are the odds in favor of Helena winning the contest?
2:3

13. The odds in favor of the Bruins winning the Stanley Cup are 5 to 4. What is the probability that the Bruins will win the Stanley Cup?
$\frac{5}{9} \approx 0.555$

---

20. Earth Science A newspaper reports that there is a 70% probability of an earthquake of magnitude 6.7 or greater striking the San Francisco Bay Area by 2030. What are the odds in favor of the earthquake's happening? **7:3**

21. Ruben and Manuel play dominoes twice a week. Over the last 12 weeks, Ruben has won 16 times. Estimate the odds in favor of Manuel's winning the next match. **1:2**

22. Business To promote sales, a cereal company is putting game pieces inside 2,000,000 of its cereal boxes. Of these pieces, 50 win a DVD player, and 10 win a trip to New York City.

a. What are the odds in favor of winning a DVD player? **1:39,999**

b. What is the probability of winning a prize in the contest? $\frac{3}{100,000}$

c. What are the odds against winning a prize in the contest? **99,997:3**

23. Critical Thinking Suppose you are in two contests that are independent of each other. You are given the odds of winning one at 1:4 and the odds of winning the other at 3:20. How would you find the odds of winning both?

24. What's the Error? A company receives 6 applications for one job. All of the candidates are equally likely to be selected for the job. One of the candidates figures that the odds in favor of her being selected are 1:6. What error has the candidate made?

25. Write About It A computer randomly selects a digit from 0 to 9. Describe how to determine the odds that the number selected will be greater than 6.

26. Challenge A spinner has three outcomes, regions A, B, or C. Region A is twice as large as regions B or C. Regions B and C have the same size. Find the odds in favor of the spinner landing on A. **1:1**

TEST PREP and Spiral Review

27. Multiple Choice The probability of winning a raffle is $\frac{1}{1200}$. What are the odds in favor of winning the raffle?

Ⓐ 1:1200 Ⓑ 1:1199 Ⓒ 1199:1 Ⓓ 1200:1

28. Gridded Response The odds of winning a bicycle is 1:149. What is the probability, written as a fraction, of winning a bicycle? $\frac{1}{150}$

Find the interest and the total amount to the nearest cent. (Lesson 6-7)

29. $300 at 5% per year for 2 years **$30, $330** **30.** $750 at 4.5% per year for 4 years **$135, $885**

31. Toss two fair coins. Player A wins if the coins land with two heads or two tails facing up. Otherwise, Player B wins. Decide whether the game is fair. **fair;** $\frac{1}{2} = \frac{1}{2}$

Answers

23. Possible answer: Find the probability for winning each contest and then add to find the probability for both contests. Convert the probability into odds.

24–25. See p. A14.

TEST PREP DOCTOR For Exercise 27, students who answered **C** found the odds against—instead of the odds in favor of—winning the raffle. Ask them to check their answer by reading it to themselves and comparing it to the given probability. Odds that are 1199 to 1 mean that the event is very likely to occur, but the probability of the event is $\frac{1}{1200}$, which means it is extremely unlikely. Thus, the student should know that the odds are incorrect.

Journal

Ask students to write about a common phrase that refers to odds, such as "What are the odds?" or "against all odds."

Power Presentations with PowerPoint®

10-7 Lesson Quiz

Of 200 people at the grand opening of a store, 10 will win door prizes.

1. Estimate the odds of winning a door prize. **1:19**

2. Estimate the odds against winning a door prize. **19:1**

3. If the odds of winning a new computer are 1:899, what is the probability of winning the computer? $\frac{1}{900}$

4. The probability of winning a new truck is $\frac{1}{600,000}$. What are the odds against winning the truck? **599,999:1**

Also available on transparency

CHALLENGE 10-7

LESSON 10-7 Challenge
All Sizes and Shapes

The most common shaped die is a cube numbered 1 through 6. However, dice come in a variety of shapes. The illustrations show a cube and five other polyhedral dice. All but one of these six dice are regular polyhedrons.

The table below shows the probability of rolling a 1 and the odds in favor of rolling a 1, not a 1, an even number, and a number that is a multiple of 5.

	A	B	C	D	E	F	G
1	Number of sides	Name of shape	P(1)	Odds(1)	Odds (not 1)	Odds (even)	Odds (multiple of 5)
2	4	tetrahedron	0.25	1:3	3:1	1:1	0:4
3	6	cube	0.16	1:5	5:1	1:1	1:5
4	8	octahedron	0.125	1:7	7:1	1:1	1:7
5	10	decahedron	0.1	1:9	9:1	1:1	2:8
6	12	dodecahedron	0.083	1:11	11:1	1:1	1:5

Answer each question.

1. The formula for cell C2 is $\frac{1}{A2}$. What does the A2 represent in the probability formula?

total number of outcomes

2. The first number in the ratio in cell F5 is $\frac{A5}{2}$. What does this number represent?

How many even sides there are on the die

3. Complete the rest of the table. See chart above.

PROBLEM SOLVING 10-7

LESSON 10-7 Problem Solving
Odds

In the last 25 Summer Olympics since 1900, an American man has won the gold medal in the 400-meter dash 18 times. Write the correct answer.

1. Find the probability that an American man will win the gold medal in the 400-meter dash in the next Summer Olympics. $\frac{18}{25}$

2. Find the probability that an American man will not win the gold medal in the 400-meter dash in the next Summer Olympics. $\frac{7}{25}$

3. Find the odds that an American man will win the gold medal in the 400-meter dash in the next Summer Olympics. **18:7**

4. Find the odds that an American man will not win the gold medal in the 400-meter dash in the next Summer Olympics. **7:18**

Use the table below that shows the probability that a player will end up on a certain square after a single roll in a game of Monopoly.

Square	Probability	Rank
In Jail	$\frac{39}{1000}$	1
Illinois Ave.	$\frac{32}{1000}$	2
Go	$\frac{31}{1000}$	3
Boardwalk	$\frac{26}{1000}$	18
Park Place	$\frac{22}{1000}$	33

Probability of Ending Up on a Monopoly Square

5. What are the odds that you will end up in jail on your next roll in a game of Monopoly?
A 39:1000 B 39:961 C 1000:961 D 961:39

6. What are the odds that you will end up on Boardwalk on your next roll in a game of Monopoly?
A 13:500 B 500:13 C 13:487 D 487:13

7. What are the odds that you will not end up on Boardwalk on your next roll in a game of Monopoly?
F 487:500 G 500:487 H 13:487 J 487:13

8. What are the odds that you will end up on Go on your next roll in a game of Monopoly?
A 31:969 B 969:31 C 31:1000 D 1000:31

9. What are the odds that you will not end up on Park Place on your next roll in a game of Monopoly?
F 11:489 G 489:11 H 489:500 J 500:489

Objective: Students find the number of possible outcomes in an experiment.

 Online Edition
Tutorial Videos, Interactivities

Countdown to Testing Week 23

Power Presentations
with PowerPoint®

Warm Up

An experiment consists of rolling a fair number cube with faces numbered 2, 4, 6, 8, 10, and 12. Find each probability.

1. P(rolling an even number)   1
2. P(rolling a prime number) $\frac{1}{6}$
3. P(rolling a number > 7) $\frac{1}{2}$

Problem of the Day

There are 10 players in a chess tournament. How many games are needed for each player to play every other player one time? 45

Also available on transparency

State Resources

 **go.hrw.com**
State Resources Online
KEYWORD: MT7 Resources

10-8 Counting Principles

Learn to find the number of possible outcomes in an experiment.

Vocabulary

Fundamental Counting Principle

tree diagram

Addition Counting Principle

The demand for new telephone numbers is exploding as people are using extra phone lines, cellular phones, pagers, computer modems, and fax machines. To meet the demand, state regulators are adding new area codes.

Phone numbers have ten digits beginning with the three-digit area code. This results in over a billion possible phone numbers!

THE FUNDAMENTAL COUNTING PRINCIPLE

If there are m ways to choose a first item and n ways to choose a second item after the first item has been chosen, then there are $m \cdot n$ ways to choose all the items.

EXAMPLE **1** **Using the Fundamental Counting Principle**

A telephone company is assigned a new area code and can issue new 7-digit phone numbers. All phone numbers are equally likely.

A Find the number of possible 7-digit phone numbers.
Use the Fundamental Counting Principle.

first digit	second digit	third digit	fourth digit	fifth digit	sixth digit	seventh digit
?	?	?	?	?	?	?
10 choices	10 choices	10 choices	10 choices	10 choices	10 choices	10 choices

$10 \cdot 10 \cdot 10 \cdot 10 \cdot 10 \cdot 10 \cdot 10 = 10{,}000{,}000$

The number of possible 7-digit phone numbers is 10,000,000.

B Find the probability of being assigned the phone number 555-1234.

$$P(\text{555-1234}) = \frac{1}{\text{number of possible phone numbers}}$$
$$= \frac{1}{10{,}000{,}000}$$
$$= 0.0000001$$

---

1 Introduce

Alternate Opener

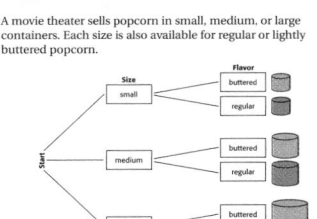

EXPLORATION

10-8 Counting Principles

A movie theater sells popcorn in small, medium, or large containers. Each size is also available for regular or lightly buttered popcorn.

1. How many possible options are there for buying popcorn at the movie theater?
2. How many options are there if the theater adds two new flavors—cheddar cheese and caramel?

Think and Discuss
3. **Explain** how you counted the number of options in Problem 2.
4. **Discuss** whether the number of options in Problem 1 would be different if you were to start with flavor followed by size.

Motivate

Tell the students that you would like a sandwich with 1 kind of lunch meat and 1 kind of cheese. Ask them how many different kinds of sandwiches could be made by choosing from 3 kinds of lunch meat and 2 kinds of cheese. 6 List the different possibilities, and show students that the number of possible sandwiches is equal to 2 × 3.

Explorations and answers are provided in *Alternate Openers: Explorations Transparencies.*

A telephone company is assigned a new area code and can issue new 7-digit phone numbers. All phone numbers are equally likely.

C Find the probability of a phone number that does not contain an 8.

First use the Fundamental Counting Principle to find the number of phone numbers that do not contain an 8.

$9 \cdot 9 \cdot 9 \cdot 9 \cdot 9 \cdot 9 \cdot 9 = 4{,}782{,}969$ possible phone numbers without an 8

There are 9 choices for any digit except 8.

$P(\text{no } 8) = \frac{4{,}782{,}969}{10{,}000{,}000} \approx 0.478$

The Fundamental Counting Principle tells you only the *number* of outcomes in some experiments, not what the outcomes are. A **tree diagram** is a way to show all of the possible outcomes.

EXAMPLE 2 Using a Tree Diagram

You pack 2 pairs of pants, 3 shirts, and 2 sweaters for your vacation. Describe all of the outfits you can make if each outfit consists of a pair of pants, a shirt, and a sweater.

You can find all of the possible outcomes by making a tree diagram. There should be $2 \cdot 3 \cdot 2 = 12$ different outfits.

Each "branch" of the tree diagram represents a different outfit. The outfit shown in the circled branch could be written as (black, red, gray). The other outfits are as follows:
(black, red, tan), (black, green, gray), (black, green, tan),
(black, yellow, gray), (black, yellow, tan),
(blue, red, gray), (blue, red, tan), (blue, green, gray),
(blue, green, tan), (blue, yellow, gray), (blue, yellow, tan).

THE ADDITION COUNTING PRINCIPLE

If one group contains m objects and a second group contains n objects, and the groups have no objects in common, then there are $m + n$ total objects to choose from.

---

2 Teach

Guided Instruction

In this lesson, students learn to find the number of possible outcomes in an experiment. Introduce students to the Fundamental Counting Principle (Teaching Transparency). Show students how a diagram can be helpful. If they are to put numbers, letters, or other objects in order, they can draw a diagram of blanks to help them think about how many items can be placed in each position. If the number of items is small, a tree diagram can be used to organize objects.

Teach

Reaching All Learners
Through Critical Thinking

Show students the following letters and digits: *A, E, B, G, T,* 1, 2, 3, 4.

Have students draw a tree diagram to show all the possible ways to use these symbols to write a three-symbol code in the form *vowel-consonant-digit.*

Then have students discuss how many ways there are to create three symbol codes in the forms *consonant-vowel-digit, vowel-consonant-digit,* and *digit-consonant-vowel.* Students should see that the order does not affect the number of possible outcomes. **24; 24; 24; 24**

Possible answers to
Think and Discuss

1. Another shirt would give you $2 \cdot 4 \cdot 2 = 16$ outfits. Another pair of pants would give you $3 \cdot 3 \cdot 2 = 18$ outfits. If you want to have as many outfits as possible, it would be better to bring another pair of pants.

EXAMPLE 3 Using the Addition Counting Principle

How many items can you choose from Bergen's Deli menu?

Bergen's Deli Menu		
Sandwiches	**Salads**	**Soups**
Turkey	Cobb Salad	Tomato
Ham	Taco Salad	Chicken Noodle
Roast Beef	Grilled Chicken Salad	Split Pea
Rueben		

None of the lists contains identical items, so use the Addition Counting Principle.

Total Choices	=	Sandwiches	+	Salads	+	Soups
T	=	4	+	3	+	3	= 10

There are 10 items to choose from.

Think and Discuss

1. **Suppose** in Example 2 you could pack one more item. Which would you bring, another shirt or another pair of pants? Explain.

10-8 Exercises

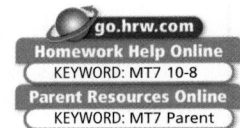
GUIDED PRACTICE

See Example **1** Employee identification codes at a company contain 2 letters followed by 3 digits. All codes are equally likely.

1. Find the number of possible identification codes. **676,000**

2. Find the probability of being assigned the ID *AB*123. **≈ 0.00000148**

3. Find the probability that an ID code does not contain the number 5. **0.729**

See Example **2** 4. The soup choices at a restaurant are clam chowder, baked potato, and split pea. The sandwich choices are egg salad, roast beef, and pastrami. Describe all of the different soup and sandwich options available.

See Example **3** 5. Fahti checked out 3 mysteries, 3 historical fiction books, and 2 biographies from the library. How many choices of books does she have to read? **8**

3 Close

Summarize

Remind students that to calculate a probability, it is necessary to know the number of possible outcomes in an experiment. They can find this by using tree diagrams or by using counting principles.

Answers

4. 9 options: (clam chowder, egg salad), (clam chowder, roast beet), (clam chowder, pastrami), (baked potato, egg salad), (baked potato, roast beef), (baked potato, pastrami), (split pea, egg salad), (split pea, roast beef), (split pea, pastrami)

See Example 1 License plates in a certain state contain 3 letters followed by 4 digits. Assume that all combinations are equally likely.

6. Find the number of possible license plates. 175,760,000

7. Find the probability of not being assigned a plate containing *C* or *D*. ≈ 0.7865

8. Find the probability of receiving a plate containing no vowels (*A, E, I, O, U*).
≈ 0.5269

See Example 2 **9.** A clothing catalog offers a shirt in red, blue, yellow, or green, with a choice of petite or regular, and in small, medium, or large sizes. Describe all of the different shirts that are available.

10. 6 ways:
(car, plane),
(car, boat),
(train, plane),
(train, boat),
(plane, plane),
(plane, boat)

10. There are 3 ways to travel from Los Angeles to San Francisco (car, train, or plane) and 2 ways to travel from San Francisco to Honolulu (plane or boat). Describe all the ways a person can travel from Los Angeles to Honolulu with a stopover in San Francisco.

See Example 3 **11.** A company makes cell phone face plates. It offers 6 solid colors, 6 prints, and 6 transparent colors. How many different face plates does the company offer? 18

PRACTICE AND PROBLEM SOLVING

Extra Practice
See page 801.

Find the number of possible outcomes.

12. dogs: terrier, retriever, hound, poodle
toys: bone, ball 8

13. sausage: Polish, bratwurst, chicken apple
condiment: ketchup, mustard, relish 9

14. car: sedan, coupe, minivan
color: red, blue, white, black 12

15. destinations: Paris, London, Rome
months: May, June, July, August 12

16. An airline confirmation code is 6 letters that can repeat. How many confirmation codes are possible? 308,915,766

17. A personal code for an online account must be 6 characters, either letters or numbers, which can repeat. How many codes are possible? 2,176,782,336

18. A car model is sold in 6 colors, with or without air conditioning, with or without a moon roof, and with either automatic or standard transmission. In how many different ways can this car model be sold? 48 ways

19. Sarah needs to register for one course in each of the six subject areas. The school offers 5 math courses, 4 foreign language courses, 3 science courses, 3 English courses, 5 social studies courses, and 6 elective courses. In how many ways can she register? 5400

20. A computer password consists of 4 letters. The password is case sensitive, which means upper-case and lower-case letters are different characters. $\frac{1}{26,873,856}$ What is the probability of randomly being assigned the password YarN?

Math Background

There are often different ways to find a probability. One method involves *complementary events*. Complementary events are events that are mutually exclusive and together contain all the outcomes in the sample space. The sum of the probabilities of complementary events is 1. In Example 1C, the events, "a phone number does not contain an 8" and "a phone number contains at least one 8" are complementary. To find the probability that a phone number contains at least one 8, subtract the probability that a phone number does not contain an 8 from 1.

$$P \text{ (at least one 8)} = 1 - P \text{ (no 8)}$$
$$\approx 1 - 0.478$$
$$\approx 0.522$$

Answers

9. 24 shirts: (red, petite, small), (red, petite, medium), (red, petite, large), (red, regular, small), (red, regular, medium), (red, regular, large), (blue, petite, small), (blue, petite, medium), (blue, petite, large), (blue, regular, small), (blue, regular, medium), (blue, regular, large), (yellow, petite, small), (yellow, petite, medium), (yellow, petite, large), (yellow, regular, small), (yellow, regular, medium), (yellow, regular, large), (green, petite, small), (green, petite, medium), (green, petite, large), (green, regular, small), (green, regular, medium), (green, regular, large)

RETEACH 10-8

LESSON 10-8 Reteach
Counting Principles

The Fundamental Counting Principle can help you solve some problems about situations that involve more than one activity.

the number of ways in which one activity can be performed	×	the number of ways in which a second activity can be performed	=	the total number of ways in which both activities can be performed

Apply the Fundamental Counting Principle to find the total number of possibilities in each situation.

1. Kelly has 6 shirts and 4 coordinating pants. The number of possible shirt-pants outfits is: 6×4 , or 24

2. The menu for dinner lists 2 soups, 4 meats, and 3 desserts. How many different meals that have one soup, one meat, and one dessert are possible? $2 \times 4 \times 3$, or 24

A **tree diagram** helps you see all the possibilities in a sample space.

If three coins are tossed at the same time, list all the possible outcomes.

List, in a column, the 2 possibilities for the 1st coin.

For each possibility for the 1st coin, list the 2 possibilities for the 2nd coin.

For each possibility for the 2nd coin, list the 2 possibilities for the 3rd coin.

Read the diagram across to write the list of all possible outcomes.

In this situation, there are $2 \times 2 \times 2 = 8$ possible outcomes.

	Outcomes
H—H—H	HHH
H—H—T	HHT
H—T—H	HTH
H—T—T	HTT
T—H—H	THH
T—H—T	THT
T—T—H	TTH
T—T—T	TTT
1st coin 2nd coin 3rd coin	

Draw a tree diagram and list the outcomes.

3. A vendor is selling cups of ice cream. There are 2 different sizes of cups: small (S), or large (L). There are 2 different flavors of ice cream: vanilla (V) or chocolate (C). There are 2 different toppings: fudge (F) or pineapple (P).

	Outcomes
S—V—F	SVF
S—V—P	SVP
S—C—F	SCF
S—C—P	SCP
L—V—F	LVF
L—V—P	LVP
L—C—F	LCF
L—C—P	LCP
cup ice cream topping	

PRACTICE 10-8

LESSON 10-8 Practice B
Counting Principles

Employee identification codes at a company contain 2 letters followed by 2 numbers. All codes are equally likely.

1. Find the number of possible identification codes. 67,600

2. Find the probability of being assigned the code MT49. $\frac{1}{67,600} \approx 0.000015$

3. Find the probability that an ID code of the company does not contain the letter A as the second letter of the code. $\frac{65,000}{67,600} = \frac{25}{26} \approx 0.962$

4. Find the probability that an ID code of the company does not contain the number 2. $\frac{54,756}{67,600} = \frac{81}{100} = 0.81$

5. Mrs. Sharpe is planning her dinners for next week. The choices for the entree are roast beef, turkey, or pork. The choices of carbohydrates are mashed potatoes, baked potatoes, or noodles. The vegetable choices are broccoli, spinach, or carrots. Make a tree diagram indicating the possible outcomes for each entree.

6. How many different meals could Mrs. Sharpe prepare? 27

Find the probability for each of the following.

7. *P*(dinner with baked potato) $\frac{1}{3} = 0.333$

8. *P*(dinner with noodles and carrots) $\frac{1}{9} = 0.111$

9. Mitch bought 2 sports magazines, 3 guitar magazines, and 3 news magazines. How many choices of magazines does he have to read? 8

State Resources

go.hrw.com
State Resources Online
KEYWORD: MT7 Resources

Answers
21b–22. See p. A14.

TEST PREP DOCTOR ✚ Students may be confused at the phrase "B or D" in Exercise 25. To get them started, ask leading questions such as, "If the first character of the password cannot be a B or a D, how many letters can it be?" Once the student knows all the possible ways for each character, remind them to use the Fundamental Counting Principle.

Journal
Remind students of the examples of creating outfits of clothing or making a sandwich. Ask students to write about another situation in their lives in which they may want to consider all the possible outcomes of an event.

Power Presentations
with PowerPoint®

✓ 10-8 Lesson Quiz
Personal identification numbers (PINs) contain 2 letters followed by 4 digits. Assume that all codes are equally likely.

1. Find the number of possible PINs. **6,760,000**

2. Find the probability that a PIN will not contain a 6. **0.6561**

A lunch menu consists of 3 types of sandwiches, 2 types of soup, and 3 types of fruit.

3. What is the total number of lunch items on the menu? **8**

4. A student wants to order one sandwich, one bowl of soup, and one piece of fruit. How many different lunches are possible? **18**

Also available on transparency

Technology

In the process of spin-coating a CD-ROM, the disc is rotated at high speeds. This process is used to apply layers as thin as $\frac{1}{8}$ of a micron, which is 640 times thinner than a human hair.

21. **Technology** Tim is buying a new computer from an online store. His options are shown at right. He can choose a color, one software package, and one hardware option.

   a. How many computer choices are available? **36**

   b. Tim decides he wants a red computer. Describe all of the choices available to him.

22. **Write About It** Describe when you would want to use the Fundamental Counting Principle instead of a tree diagram. Describe when a tree diagram would be more useful than the Fundamental Counting Principle.

23. **Challenge** A password can have letters, numerals, or 32 other special symbols in each of its 6-character spaces. There are two restrictions. The password cannot begin with a special symbol or 0, and it cannot end with a vowel (A, E, I, O, U). Find the total number of passwords. **47,145,934,080**

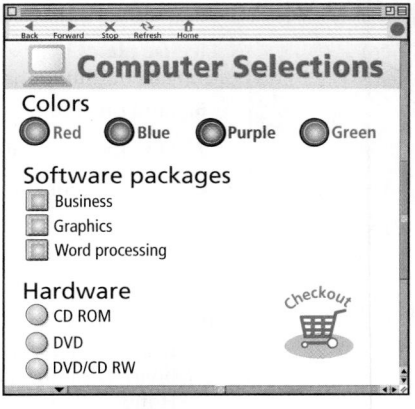

TEST PREP and Spiral Review

24. **Multiple Choice** Lynnwood High School requires all staff members to have a 6-character computer password that contains 2 letters and 4 numbers. Find the number of possible passwords.

   Ⓐ 2,600,000　　　Ⓑ 6,760,000　　　Ⓒ 17,576,000　　　Ⓓ 45,697,600

25. **Gridded Response** A password contains 3 letters from the alphabet and 2 digits (0–9). Find the probability, written as a decimal, of NOT having a password with a B or D. **0.852**

Evaluate each expression. (Lesson 4-5)

26. $\sqrt{121} + \sqrt{25}$ **16**　　　27. $(4+3)^2$ **49**　　　28. $\frac{\sqrt{441}}{\sqrt{144}}$ **$\frac{7}{4}$**　　　29. $\sqrt{5^2 + 12^2}$ **13**

Use the table of random numbers to answer the following question. Use at least 10 trials to simulate the situation. (Lesson 10-3)　　**Possible answer is given.**

82	78	3	56	86	14	96	96	46	23	62	28	75	61	64	6	30
4	12	62	54	98	30	94	11	46	22	24	55	89	92	41	79	15
58	69	73	19	73	95	45	26	39	37	91	57	90	19	7	38	44

30. At a local restaurant, 45% of the customers order spaghetti. Estimate the probability that 6 of the next 10 customers will order spaghetti. **10%**

CHALLENGE 10-8

LESSON 10-8 Challenge
Answer the Phone

The world is divided into 9 telephone numbering zones. The North American Numbering Plan (NANP) was developed in 1947 to enable direct dialing without the need for an operator.

NANP numbers are 10 digits in length, of the form

N X X - N X X - X X X X
area code　prefix　line number

Originally, the plan created 86 areas and allowed for expansion to 144 areas. In 1995, NANP expanded to 792 area codes.

1. For the 3-digit area code NXX, the plan allows N to be any digit 2–9. Currently, there are no restrictions on the other 2 digits of the area code. How many area codes are possible?

   $8 \times 10 \times 10$, or 800

2. For the 3-digit prefix, the plan allows N to be any digit 2–9. How many line numbers are possible for a given prefix?

   $10 \times 10 \times 10 \times 10$, or 10,000

3. How many telephone numbers are possible for a given area code?

   $800 \times 10,000$, or 8,000,000

Some of the prefixes are reserved for services. They are of the form N11 where N is any digit 2–9.

The most familiar service code is 911, reserved for emergency calls. Other commonly assigned service codes are 411 (local directory assistance), 611 (repairs), 711 (teletypewriter [hearing/speech impaired]), 811 (business office).

4. If all the service code prefixes are removed, how many telephone numbers are possible for a given area code?

   $8,000,000 - 8 \times 10 \times 10 \times 10 \times 10$, or 7,920,000

Some other prefixes are not available for general use, such as:

   555 (information), 800 and 888 (usually, but not always, toll free), 900 (pay per call).

5. For each prefix that is not available for general use, how many fewer telephone numbers are available for general use?

   10,000

PROBLEM SOLVING 10-8

LESSON 10-8 Problem Solving
Counting Principles

Write the correct answer.

1. The 5-digit zip code system for United States mail was implemented in 1963. How many different possibilities of zip codes are there with a 5-digit zip code where each digit can be 0 through 9?

   100,000

2. In 1983, the ZIP +4 zip code system was introduced so mail could be more easily sorted by the 5-digit zip code plus an additional 4 digits. How many different possibilities of zip codes are there with the ZIP +4 system?

   1,000,000,000

3. In Canada, each postal code has 6 symbols. The first, third and fifth symbols are letters of the alphabet and the second, fourth and sixth symbols are digits from 0 through 9. How many possible postal codes are there in Canada?

   17,576,000

4. In the United Kingdom the postal code has 6 symbols. The first, second, fifth and sixth are letters of the alphabet and the third and fourth are digits from 0 through 9. How many possible postal codes are there in the United Kingdom?

   45,697,600

Choose the letter for the best answer.

5. In Sharon Springs, Kansas, all of the phone numbers begin 852–4. The only differences in the phone numbers are the last 3 digits. How many possible phone numbers can be assigned using this system?

   A 729　　　C 6561
   Ⓑ 1000　　　D 10,000

6. Many large cities have run out of phone numbers and so a new area code must be introduced. How many different phone numbers are there in a single area code if the first digit can't be zero?

   F 90,000　　　Ⓗ 9,000,000
   G 4,782,969　　　J 10,000,000

7. How many different phone numbers are possible using a 3-digit area code and a 7-digit phone number if the first digit of the area code and phone number cannot be zero?

   A 3,486,784,401　　　C 9,500,000,000
   Ⓑ 8,100,000,000　　　D 10,000,000,000

8. A shipping service offers to send packages by ground delivery using 2 different companies, by next day air using 3 different companies, and by 2-day air using 3 different companies. How many different shipping options does the service offer?

   F 3　　　H 10
   Ⓖ 8　　　J 18

Learn to find permutations and combinations.

Vocabulary
factorial
permutation
combination

Most MP3 players have a shuffle feature that allows you to play songs in a random order. You can use *factorials* to find out how many song orders are possible.

The **factorial** of a number is the product of all the whole numbers from the number down to 1. The factorial of 0 is defined to be 1.

$$5! = 5 \cdot 4 \cdot 3 \cdot 2 \cdot 1 = 120$$

EXAMPLE 1 **Evaluating Expressions Containing Factorials**

Evaluate each expression.

Reading Math
Read 8! as "eight factorial."

Ⓐ 8!
$$8 \cdot 7 \cdot 6 \cdot 5 \cdot 4 \cdot 3 \cdot 2 \cdot 1 = 40,320$$

Ⓑ $\dfrac{7!}{4!}$

$$\dfrac{7 \cdot 6 \cdot 5 \cdot \cancel{4} \cdot \cancel{3} \cdot \cancel{2} \cdot \cancel{1}}{\cancel{4} \cdot \cancel{3} \cdot \cancel{2} \cdot \cancel{1}}$$ *Write out each factorial and simplify.*

$$7 \cdot 6 \cdot 5 = 210$$ *Multiply remaining factors.*

Ⓒ $\dfrac{14!}{(11 - 4)!}$ *Subtract within parentheses.*

$$\dfrac{14!}{7!}$$

$$\dfrac{14 \cdot 13 \cdot 12 \cdot 11 \cdot 10 \cdot 9 \cdot 8 \cdot \cancel{7} \cdot \cancel{6} \cdot \cancel{5} \cdot \cancel{4} \cdot \cancel{3} \cdot \cancel{2} \cdot \cancel{1}}{\cancel{7} \cdot \cancel{6} \cdot \cancel{5} \cdot \cancel{4} \cdot \cancel{3} \cdot \cancel{2} \cdot \cancel{1}}$$

$$14 \cdot 13 \cdot 12 \cdot 11 \cdot 10 \cdot 9 \cdot 8 = 17,297,280$$

A **permutation** is an arrangement of things in a certain order.

If no letter can be used more than once, there are 6 permutations of the first 3 letters of the alphabet: *ABC, ACB, BAC, BCA, CAB,* and *CBA.*

first letter		second letter		third letter
？		？		？
3 choices	·	2 choices	·	1 choice

The product can be written as a factorial.

$$3 \cdot 2 \cdot 1 = 3! = 6$$

Organizer 10-9

Pacing: Traditional 2 days
Block 1 day
Objective: Students find permutations and combinations.

 Hands-On Lab
In *Hands-On Lab Activities*

 Online Edition
Tutorial Videos, Interactivities

 Countdown to Testing Week 23

Power Presentations
with PowerPoint®

Warm Up

Find the number of possible outcomes.

1. bagels: plain, egg, wheat, onion
   meat: turkey, ham, roast beef, tuna 16

2. eggs: scrambled, over easy, hard boiled
   meat: sausage patty, sausage link, bacon, ham 12

3. How many different 4-digit phone extensions are possible? 10,000

Problem of the Day

What is the probability that a 2-digit whole number will contain exactly one 1? $\frac{17}{90}$

Also available on transparency

1 Introduce
Alternate Opener

EXPLORATION

10-9 **Permutations and Combinations**

Alfonso and Barb race against each other in a 5K race. There are two ways they can finish.

First Place	Second Place
Alfonso	Barb
Barb	Alfonso

1. Carl joins Alfonso and Barb. Complete the table to show all of the different ways they can finish.

	First Place	Second Place	Third Place
a.	Alfonso	Barb	Carl
b.			
c.			
d.			
e.			

2. Complete the table to show all of the different ways 2 of the 3 runners can finish in a tie for first place.

	First Place (tie)	Second Place
	Alfonso and Barb	Carl
a.		
b.		

Think and Discuss

3. **Explain** how you could find the number of ways 5 runners could finish.

Motivate

Tell students to imagine that they own a pizza restaurant and that they offer 4 different toppings for the pizzas. Ask students how many choices there are for a one-topping, a two-topping, and a three-topping pizza without repeating any topping twice. Ask students what kinds of combinations of toppings they might like. Help them see that there are many possible choices that involve combinations.

State Resources

go.hrw.com
State Resources Online
KEYWORD: MT7 Resources

Explorations and answers are provided in *Alternate Openers: Explorations Transparencies.*

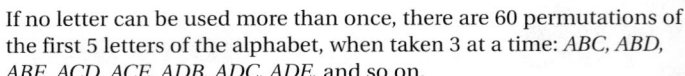

Example 1

Evaluate each expression.

A. 9!   362,880

B. $\frac{8!}{6!}$ 56

C. $\frac{10!}{(9-2)!}$ 720

Example 2

Jim has 6 different books.

A. Find the number of orders in which the 6 books can be arranged on a shelf.   720

B. If the shelf has room for only 3 of the books, find the number of ways 3 of the 6 books can be arranged.   120

Also available on transparency

If no letter can be used more than once, there are 60 permutations of the first 5 letters of the alphabet, when taken 3 at a time: *ABC, ABD, ABE, ACD, ACE, ADB, ADC, ADE,* and so on.

first letter		second letter		third letter
?		?		?
5 choices	·	4 choices	·	3 choices = 60 permutations

Notice that the product can be written as a quotient of factorials.

$$60 = 5 \cdot 4 \cdot 3 = \frac{5 \cdot 4 \cdot 3 \cdot 2 \cdot 1}{2 \cdot 1} = \frac{5!}{2!}$$

PERMUTATIONS

The number of permutations of n things taken r at a time is

$$_nP_r = \frac{n!}{(n-r)!}.$$

EXAMPLE 2 Finding Permutations

There are 7 swimmers in a race.

A Find the number of orders in which all 7 swimmers can finish.

The number of swimmers is 7.

$$_7P_7 = \frac{7!}{(7-7)!} = \frac{7!}{0!} = \frac{7 \cdot 6 \cdot 5 \cdot 4 \cdot 3 \cdot 2 \cdot 1}{1} = 5040$$

All 7 swimmers are taken at a time.

There are 5040 permutations. This means there are 5040 orders in which 7 swimmers can finish.

B Find the number of ways the 7 swimmers can finish first, second, and third.

The number of swimmers is 7.

$$_7P_3 = \frac{7!}{(7-3)!} = \frac{7!}{4!} = \frac{7 \cdot 6 \cdot 5 \cdot \cancel{4} \cdot \cancel{3} \cdot \cancel{2} \cdot \cancel{1}}{\cancel{4} \cdot \cancel{3} \cdot \cancel{2} \cdot \cancel{1}} = 210$$

The top 3 places are taken at a time.

There are 210 permutations. This means that the 7 swimmers can finish in first, second, and third in 210 ways.

A **combination** is a selection of things in any order.

If no letter can be used more than once, there is only 1 combination of the first 3 letters of the alphabet. *ABC, ACB, BAC, BCA, CAB,* and *CBA* are considered to be the same combination of *A, B,* and *C* because the order does not matter.

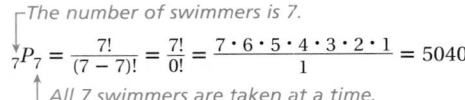

Remember!

By definition, 0! = 1.

---

2 Teach

Guided Instruction

In this lesson, students learn to find permutations and combinations. Begin by explaining how to find the *factorial* of a number. Define *permutation* and emphasize that order is important. Show students how to use the formula to find the number of permutations of n things taken r at a time (Teaching Transparency). When explaining combinations, emphasize that order is not important. Show students how to use the formula to find the number of combinations of n things taken r at a time.

Reaching All Learners
Through Critical Thinking

Give students a sheet that contains several factorial expressions that are applications of the permutations and combinations formulas (e.g., $\frac{9!}{3!}$, $\frac{8!}{5!3!}$, $\frac{5!}{3!2!}$, and $\frac{6!}{3!}$). Have students write a situation involving permutations or combinations that could be represented by each factorial expression. Then have students evaluate the expressions to find the answer to the situations they have written.
$\frac{9!}{3!} = 60{,}480$; $\frac{8!}{5!3!} = 56$; $\frac{5!}{3!2!} = 10$; $\frac{6!}{3!} = 120$

If no letter is used more than once, there are 10 combinations of the first 5 letters of the alphabet, when taken 3 at a time. To see this, look at the list of permutations below.

These 6 permutations are all the same combination.

ABC	ABD	ABE	ACD	ACE	ADE	BCD	BCE	BDE	CDE
ACB	ADB	AEB	ADC	AEC	AED	BDC	BEC	BED	CED
BAC	BAD	BAE	CAD	CAE	DAE	CBD	CBE	DBE	DCE
BCA	BDA	BEA	CDA	CEA	DEA	CDB	CEB	DEB	DEC
CAB	DAB	EAB	DAC	EAC	EAD	DCB	EBC	EBD	ECD
CBA	DBA	EBA	DCA	ECA	EDA	DBC	ECB	EDB	EDC

In the list of 60 permutations, each combination is repeated 6 times. The number of combinations is $\frac{60}{6} = 10$.

COMBINATIONS

The number of combinations of n things taken r at a time is

$$_nC_r = \frac{_nP_r}{r!} = \frac{n!}{r!(n-r)!}.$$

EXAMPLE 3 **Finding Combinations**

A gourmet pizza restaurant offers 10 topping choices.

A Find the number of 3-topping pizzas that can be ordered.

10 possible toppings

$$_{10}C_3 = \frac{10!}{3!(10-3)!} = \frac{10!}{3!7!} = \frac{10 \cdot 9 \cdot 8 \cdot \cancel{7} \cdot \cancel{6} \cdot \cancel{5} \cdot \cancel{4} \cdot \cancel{3} \cdot \cancel{2} \cdot \cancel{1}}{(3 \cdot 2 \cdot 1)(\cancel{7} \cdot \cancel{6} \cdot \cancel{5} \cdot \cancel{4} \cdot \cancel{3} \cdot \cancel{2} \cdot \cancel{1})} = 120$$

3 toppings chosen at a time

There are 120 combinations. This means that there are 120 different 3-topping pizzas that can be ordered.

B Find the number of 6-topping pizzas that can be ordered.

10 possible toppings

$$_{10}C_6 = \frac{10!}{6!(10-6)!} = \frac{10!}{6!4!} = \frac{10 \cdot 9 \cdot 8 \cdot 7 \cdot \cancel{6} \cdot \cancel{5} \cdot \cancel{4} \cdot \cancel{3} \cdot \cancel{2} \cdot \cancel{1}}{(\cancel{6} \cdot \cancel{5} \cdot \cancel{4} \cdot \cancel{3} \cdot \cancel{2} \cdot \cancel{1})(4 \cdot 3 \cdot 2 \cdot 1)} = 210$$

6 toppings chosen at a time

There are 210 combinations. This means that there are 210 different 6-topping pizzas.

Think and Discuss

1. Explain the difference between a combination and a permutation.

2. Give an example of an experiment where order is important and one where order is not important.

Power Presentations with PowerPoint®

Additional Examples

Example 3

Mary wants to join a book club that offers a choice of 10 new books each month.

A. If Mary wants to buy 2 books, find the number of different pairs she can buy. **45**

B. If Mary wants to buy 7 books, find the number of different sets of 7 books she can buy. **120**

Also available on transparency

Possible answers to *Think and Discuss*

1. The order of the things does not matter in a combination—all possible groupings of the same things make one combination. But the order of the things does matter in a permutation—changing the order results in different permutations.

2. Order is important if you are choosing 3 different officers from a club with 20 members, but it is not important if you are choosing 3 committee members from the same group.

---

3 Close

Summarize

Discuss the difference between permutations and combinations. Ask students to determine which would apply to each situation below.

1. toppings on a pizza combinations

2. letters in a password permutations

3. members on a committee combinations

4. first, second, and third place finishers in a race permutations

Possible answers: Permutations are arrangements of things in a specific order. Combinations are selections of things in any order.

10-9 Exercises

go.hrw.com
Homework Help Online
KEYWORD: MT7 10-9
Parent Resources Online
KEYWORD: MT7 Parent

Assignment Guide

If you finished Example **1** assign:
Average 1–4, 9–12, 17, 18, 23, 41–45
Advanced 9–12, 17, 18, 23, 26, 41–45

If you finished Example **2** assign:
Average 1–6, 9–14, 17–19, 23, 24, 33, 36, 41–45
Advanced 9–14, 17–19, 24, 29, 30, 32, 33, 36, 41–45

If you finished Example **3** assign:
Average 1–24, 33–37, 41–45
Advanced 9–16, 22–45

Homework Quick Check

Quickly check key concepts.
Exercises: 12, 14, 16, 36

Math Background

A type of permutation not considered in the lesson is a *circular permutation*, in which the objects are arranged in a circle. The number of circular permutations of n objects is $(n - 1)!$. For example, the number of ways to seat 8 people around a circular table is $(8 - 1)!$, or 5040. Another type of permutation involves repeated objects. The number of permutations of n objects with n_1 of the same type is given by the formula $_nP_r = \frac{n!}{n_1!}$. For example, the word *ladder* contains 6 letters with d used 2 times. The number of permutations of the letters is $\frac{6!}{2!} = 360$.

GUIDED PRACTICE

See Example **1** Evaluate each expression.

1. $6!$ **720**
2. $\frac{7!}{3!}$ **840**
3. $\frac{9!}{(7-3)!}$ **15,120**
4. $\frac{5!}{(4-1)!}$ **20**

See Example **2** There are 11 runners in a race.

5. In how many possible orders can all 11 runners finish the race? **39,916,800**

6. How many ways can the 11 runners finish first, second, and third? **990**

See Example **3** A group of 8 people are forming several committees.

7. Find the number of different 3-person committees that can be formed. **56**

8. Find the number of different 6-person committees that can be formed. **28**

INDEPENDENT PRACTICE

See Example **1** Evaluate each expression.

9. $4!$ **24**
10. $\frac{8!}{2!}$ **20,160**
11. $\frac{4!}{(3-2)!}$ **24**
12. $\frac{9!}{(8-5)!}$ **60,480**

See Example **2** Ann has 7 books she wants to put on her bookshelf.

13. How many possible arrangements of books are there? **5040**

14. Suppose Ann has room on the shelf for only 4 of the 7 books. In how many ways can she arrange the books now? **840**

See Example **3** If Dena joins a CD club, she gets 8 free CDs.

15. If Dena can select from a list of 32 CDs, how many groups of 8 different CDs are possible? **10,518,300**

16. If Dena can select from a list of 48 CDs, how many groups of 8 different CDs are possible? **377,348,994**

PRACTICE AND PROBLEM SOLVING

Extra Practice
See page 801.

Evaluate each expression.

17. $\frac{8!}{(8-3)!}$ **336**
18. $\frac{11!}{6!(11-6)!}$ **462**
19. $_{10}P_{10}$ **3,628,800**
20. $_8C_3$ **56**

21. $_{15}C_{15}$ **1**
22. $_{10}C_7$ **120**
23. $\frac{12!}{10!}$ **132**
24. $_8P_4$ **1680**

Simplify each expression.

25. $_nC_n$ **1**
26. $\frac{n!}{(n-1)!}$ **n**
27. $_nC_0$ **1**
28. $_nC_{n-1}$ **n**

29. $_nP_0$ **1**
30. $_nP_n$ **$n!$**
31. $_nC_1$ **n**
32. $_nP_1$ **n**

33. **Sports** How many ways can a coach choose the first, second, third, and fourth runners in a relay race from a team of 10 runners? **5040**

RETEACH 10-9

Reteach
10-9 Permutations and Combinations

Factorial: a string of factors that counts down to 1
$6! = 6 \cdot 5 \cdot 4 \cdot 3 \cdot 2 \cdot 1$
To evaluate an expression with factorials, cancel common factors.
$\frac{5!}{3!} = \frac{5 \cdot 4 \cdot 3 \cdot 2 \cdot 1}{3 \cdot 2 \cdot 1} = 5 \cdot 4 = 20$

Complete to evaluate each expression.

1. $\frac{7!}{4!} = \frac{7 \cdot 6 \cdot 5 \cdot 4 \cdot 3 \cdot 2 \cdot 1}{4!} =$
   $= 7 \cdot \underline{6 \cdot 5} = \underline{210}$

2. $\frac{6!}{(5-2)!} = \frac{6!}{3!} = \frac{6 \cdot 5 \cdot 4 \cdot 3 \cdot 2 \cdot 1}{3 \cdot 2 \cdot 1}$
   $= 6 \cdot 5 \cdot 4 = \underline{120}$

Permutation: an arrangement in which order is important
$wxyz$ is not the same as $yxzw$

Apply the Fundamental Counting Principle to find how many permutations are possible using all 4 letters w, x, y, z with no repetition.
$\frac{4}{\text{1st letter}} \times \frac{3}{\text{2nd letter}} \times \frac{2}{\text{3rd letter}} \times \frac{1}{\text{4th letter}} = 4! = 24$ possible arrangements

When you arrange n things, $n!$ permutations are possible.

Complete to find the number of permutations.

3. In how many ways can 6 people be seated on a bench that seats 6?
   $6! = \frac{6 \cdot 5 \cdot 4 \cdot 3 \cdot 2 \cdot 1}{}$
   $= \underline{720}$ possibilities

4. How many 5-digit numbers can be made using the digits 7, 4, 2, 1, 8 without repetitions?
   $5! = \frac{5 \cdot 4 \cdot 3 \cdot 2 \cdot 1}{}$
   $= \underline{120}$ possibilities

Apply the Fundamental Counting Principle to find how many permutations are possible using 4 letters 2 at a time, with no repetitions.
$\frac{4}{\text{1st letter}} \times \frac{3}{\text{2nd letter}} = 12$ possible 2-letter arrangements

Apply the Fundamental Counting Principle.

5. In how many ways can 6 people be seated on a bench that seats 4?
   $\frac{6}{\text{1st seat}} \times \frac{5}{\text{2nd seat}} \times \frac{4}{\text{3rd seat}} \times \frac{3}{\text{4th seat}} = \underline{360}$ possibilities

6. How many 3-digit numbers can be made using the digits 7, 4, 2, 1, 8 without repetitions?
   $\frac{5}{\text{1st digit}} \times \frac{4}{\text{2nd digit}} \times \frac{3}{\text{3rd digit}} = \underline{60}$ possibilities

---

PRACTICE 10-9

Practice B
10-9 Permutations and Combinations

Evaluate each expression.

1. $10!$ — **3,628,800**
2. $13!$ — **6,227,020,800**
3. $11! - 8!$ — **39,876,480**

4. $12! - 9!$ — **478,638,720**
5. $\frac{15!}{8!}$ — **32,432,400**
6. $\frac{18!}{12!}$ — **13,366,080**

7. $\frac{13!}{(17-12)!}$ — **51,891,840**
8. $\frac{19!}{(15-2)!}$ — **19,535,040**
9. $\frac{15!}{(18-10)!}$ — **32,432,400**

10. Signaling is a means of communication through signals or objects. During the time of the American Revolution, the colonists used combinations of a barrel, basket, and a flag placed in different positions atop a pole. How many different signals could be sent by using 3 flags, one above the other on a pole, if 8 different flags were available?
    336

11. From a class of 25 students, how many different ways can 4 students be selected to serve in a mock trial as the judge, defending attorney, prosecuting attorney, and the defendant?
    303,600

12. How many different 4 people committees can be formed from a group of 15 people?
    1365

13. The girls' basketball team has 12 players. If the coach chooses 5 girls to play at a time, how many different teams can be formed?
    792

14. A photographer has 50 pictures to be placed in an album. How many combinations will the photographer have to choose from if there will be 6 pictures placed on the first page?
    15,890,700

34. Cooking Cole is making a fruit salad. He can choose from the following fruits: oranges, apples, pears, peaches, grapes, strawberries, cantaloupe, and honeydew melon. If he wants to have 4 different fruits, how many possible fruit salads can he make? **70**

35. Art An artist is making a painting of three squares, one inside the other. He has 12 different colors to choose from. How many different paintings could he make if the squares are all different colors? **1320**

36. Sports At a track meet, there are 5 athletes competing in the decathlon.
   a. Find the number of orders in which all 5 athletes can finish. **120**
   b. Find the number of orders in which the 5 athletes can finish in first, second, and third places. **60**

37. Life Science There are 11 different species of birds in a forest. In how many ways can researchers capture, tag, and release birds of 6 different species? **462**

38. What's the Question? There are 12 different items available at a buffet. Customers can choose up to 4 of these items. If the answer is 495, what is the question? **Possible answer: How many possible combinations of 4 items are there?**

39. Write About It Explain how you could use combinations and permutations to find the probability of an event.

40. Challenge How many ways can a local chapter of the Mathematical Association of America schedule 4 speakers for 4 different meetings in one day if all of the speakers are available on any of 3 dates? **72**

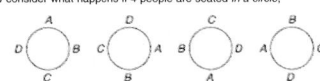

TEST PREP and Spiral Review

41. Multiple Choice In how many ways can 8 students form a single-file line if each student's place in line must be considered?
   (A) 40,320   (B) 5040   (C) 8   (D) 1

42. Short Response A group of 15 people are forming committees. Find the number of different 4-person committees that can be formed. Then find the number of different 5-person committees that can be formed. Show your work. **4-person committee: 1365; 5-person committee: 3003**

43. Draw the front, top, and side views of the figure at right. (Lesson 8-4)

Describe the number of different combinations that can be made using one item from each category. (Lesson 10-8)

44. 3 shirts **84**
   4 pairs of shorts
   7 pairs of socks

45. 4 kinds of bread
   5 kinds of meat
   3 kinds of chips **60**

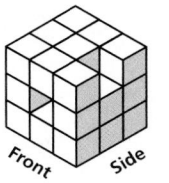
Front   Side

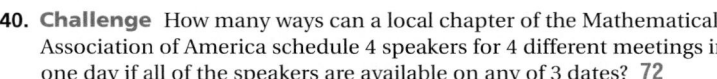

Organizer

Objective: Assess students' mastery of concepts and skills in Lessons 10-4 through 10-9.

Resources

Assessment Resources
Section 10B Quiz

Test & Practice Generator
One-Stop Planner®

INTERVENTION

Resources

Ready to Go On?
Intervention and
Enrichment Worksheets

Ready to Go On? CD-ROM

Ready to Go On? Online

my.hrw.com

Ready to Go On?

Quiz for Lessons 10-4 Through 10-9

10-4 **Theoretical Probability**

An experiment consists of rolling two fair number cubes. Find the probability of each event.

1. P(total shown = 7) $\frac{1}{6}$ 2. P(two 5's) $\frac{1}{36}$ 3. P(two even numbers) $\frac{1}{4}$

10-5 **Independent and Dependent Events**

4. An experiment consists of tossing 2 fair coins, a penny and a nickel. Find the probability of tails on the penny and heads on the nickel. $\frac{1}{4}$

5. A jar contains 5 red marbles, 2 blue marbles, 4 yellow marbles, and 4 green marbles. If two marbles are chosen at random, what is the probability that they will be the same color? $\frac{23}{105}$

10-6 **Making Decisions and Predictions**

6. Players use the spinner shown to move around a game board. Suppose the spinner is spun 50 times. Predict how many times it will land on "Lose your turn." ≈ 13

7. A spinner is divided evenly into 6 sections. There are 3 blue sections, 2 red, and 1 white. Player A wins if the spinner lands on blue. Otherwise Player B wins. Decide whether the game is fair. fair; $\frac{1}{2} = \frac{1}{2}$

10-7 **Odds**

8. If the odds in favor of winning a trip for two to New York City are 1:259,999, what is the probability of winning the trip? $\frac{1}{260,000}$

10-8 **Counting Principles**

Family identification codes at a preschool contain 3 letters followed by 3 digits. All codes are equally likely.

9. Find the probability of being assigned the ID BCD352. 0.000000568

10. A catalog company offers backpacks in 5 solid colors, 4 prints, and 4 cartoon characters. How many choices of backpacks are there? 13

10-9 **Permutations and Combinations**

Evaluate each expression.

11. 7! **5040**   12. 5! **120**   13. $\frac{6!}{2!}$ **360**   14. $\frac{8!}{(6-3)!}$ **6720**

15. There are 10 cross-country skiers in a race. In how many possible orders can all 10 skiers finish the race? 3,628,800

READY TO GO ON?
Diagnose and Prescribe

NO
INTERVENE

YES
ENRICH

READY TO GO ON? Intervention, Section 10B			
Ready to Go On? Intervention	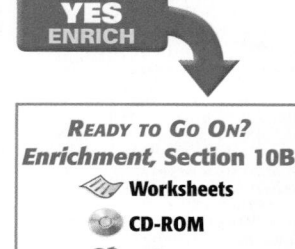Worksheets	CD-ROM	Online
Lesson 10-4	10-4 Intervention	Activity 10-4	
Lesson 10-5	10-5 Intervention	Activity 10-5	
Lesson 10-6	10-6 Intervention	Activity 10-6	Diagnose and Prescribe Online
Lesson 10-7	10-7 Intervention	Activity 10-7	
Lesson 10-8	10-8 Intervention	Activity 10-8	
Lesson 10-9	10-9 Intervention	Activity 10-9	

READY TO GO ON?
Enrichment, Section 10B

Worksheets
CD-ROM
Online

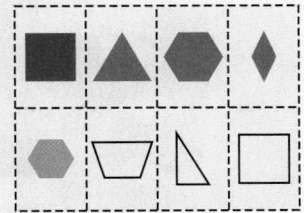

Perplexing Polygons In Mrs. Mac's class, each student is given a set of polygon cards to cut out along the dotted lines. Each student places the cards in his or her own brown paper bag.

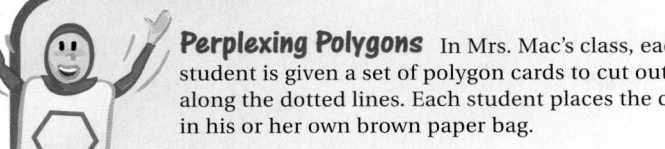

1. Juan draws a polygon from his bag at the same time that Monica draws a polygon from her bag. They do this experiment 50 times and replace the polygons each time before drawing again. How many times would Juan be expected to draw a shaded polygon at the same time that Monica draws a triangle?

2. Kyle draws twice from his bag of polygons. After the first draw, he does not put the polygon back in the bag. Predict the number of times he might draw a square and then a triangle if he conducts this experiment 24 times.

3. Eight students place all of their polygons into a hat. What is the probability of drawing a hexagon?

4. The students are asked to remove 16 polygons from the hat. How can they do this so that the probability of drawing a hexagon remains the same?

5. Eight of the students place all of their polygons into a single bag. Describe how to remove polygons from this bag so that the probability of drawing a hexagon is $\frac{1}{5}$.

Multi-Step Test Prep

Organizer

Objective: Assess students' ability to apply concepts and skills in Chapter 10 in a real-world format.

PREMIER **Online Edition**

Resources

 Middle School Assessments
www.mathtekstoolkit.org

Problem	Text reference
1	Lessons 10-5, 10-6
2	Lessons 10-5, 10-6
3	Lesson 10-4
4	Lesson 10-4
5	Lesson 10-4

Answers

1. 8 times
2. 2 times
3. $\frac{1}{4}$
4. Remove any 16 polygons as long as exactly 4 of them are hexagons.
5. Possible answer: Remove 4 hexagons

INTERVENTION

Scaffolding Questions

1. Are the events in this experiment dependent or independent? Independent What is the probability that Juan draws a shaded polygon? $\frac{5}{8}$ What is the probability Monica draws a triangle? $\frac{1}{4}$

2. Are the events in this experiment dependent or independent? Dependent What is the probability of drawing a square on the first pick? $\frac{1}{4}$ What is the probability of drawing a triangle on the second pick? $\frac{2}{7}$

3. How many polygons are in the hat altogether? 64 How many of the polygons are hexagons? 16

4. How many polygons will remain in the hat when the 16 polygons are removed?

48 How many of those need to be hexagons so that the probability of drawing a hexagon is still $\frac{1}{4}$? 12

5. Suppose you remove all but one hexagon from the bag. What else must you do to make the probability of drawing a hexagon $\frac{1}{5}$? Remove all but 4 of the other polygons

Extension

1. Construct a bag in which the probability of drawing a shaded square is $\frac{1}{4}$ and the probability of drawing a right triangle is $\frac{1}{10}$. You must have at least one of each of the eight shapes in the bag. Possible answer: 10 shaded squares, 4 right triangles, 26 other shapes

Organizer

Objective: Participate in games to practice and apply skills learned in Chapter 10.

Online Edition

Resources

Chapter 10 Resource Book
Puzzles, Twisters & Teasers

The Paper Chase

Purpose: To apply the skill of finding probability to a brainteaser

Discuss Ask students to explain how to determine the answer to problem 1. (Hint: You should treat the $\frac{2}{10}$ chance that the paper gets lost as if there were 2 more drawers that you will never be able to check, for a total of 10 drawers.)

The probability that the paper is in any searchable drawer is $\frac{8}{10}$. If it is not in the first drawer, then there are only 9 possibilities left for where it might be, and 7 of those are the remaining searchable drawers. So the probability that the paper is in one of the remaining searchable drawers is $\frac{7}{9}$.

Extend Challenge students to write a similar problem, changing the probability that a paper gets lost and the number of drawers. Have them use their information to determine a formula for the probability of finding a paper.

Possible answer: Let n be the number of drawers that have already been checked. The probability of finding the paper in a specific unchecked drawer is $\frac{(8-n)}{(10-n)}$, a decreasing function, and the probability of finding the paper in the next drawer is $\frac{1}{(10-n)}$, an increasing function.

Permutations

Purpose: To practice finding permutations in a game format

Discuss Have students practice making English words using permutations of the letters *A, I, M, R,* and *N.*

Possible answers: *MAN, RAIN, RAN, RAM, RIM,* and *AIR.*

Extend Have students repeat the game, using 2 vowels and 5 consonants. The first player to reach 150 points wins.

Game Time

The Paper Chase

Stephen's desk has 8 drawers. When he receives a paper, he usually chooses a drawer at random to put it in. However, 2 out of 10 times he forgets to put the paper away, and it gets lost.

The probability that a paper will get lost is $\frac{2}{10}$, or $\frac{1}{5}$.

• What is the probability that a paper will get put into a drawer? $\frac{4}{5}$

• If all drawers are equally likely to be chosen, what is the probability that a paper will get put in drawer 3? $\frac{1}{10}$

When Stephen needs a document, he looks first in drawer 1 and then checks each drawer in order until the paper is found or until he has looked in all the drawers.

❶ If Stephen checked drawer 1 and didn't find the paper he was looking for, what is the probability that the paper will be found in one of the remaining 7 drawers? $\frac{7}{9}$

❷ If Stephen checked drawers 1, 2, and 3, and didn't find the paper he was looking for, what is the probability that the paper will be found in one of the remaining 5 drawers? $\frac{5}{7}$

❸ If Stephen checked drawers 1–7 and didn't find the paper he was looking for, what is the probability that the paper will be found in the last drawer? $\frac{1}{3}$

Try to write a formula for the probability of finding a paper.

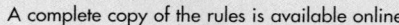

Permutations

Use a set of Scrabble™ tiles, or make a similar set of lettered cards. Draw 2 vowels and 3 consonants, and place them face up in the center of the table. Each player tries to write as many permutations as possible in 60 seconds. Score 1 point per permutation, with a bonus point for each permutation that forms an English word.

A complete copy of the rules is available online.

go.hrw.com
Game Time Extra
KEYWORD: MT7 Games

It's in the Bag!

Materials
- 7 large sticky notes
- glue
- markers

PROJECT **Probability Post-Up**

Fold sticky notes into an accordion booklet. Then use the booklet to record notes about probability.

Directions

❶ Make a chain of seven overlapping sticky notes by placing the sticky portion of one note on the bottom portion of the previous note. **Figure A**

❷ Glue the notes together to make sure they stay attached.

❸ Accordion-fold the sticky notes. The folds should occur at the bottom edge of each note in the chain. **Figure B**

❹ Write the name and number of the chapter on the first sticky note.

Taking Note of the Math

Use the sticky-note booklet to record key information from the chapter. Be sure to include definitions, examples of probability experiments, and anything else that will help you review the material in the chapter.

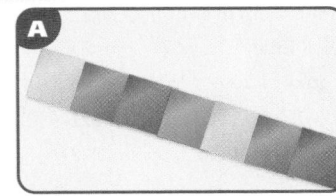

A

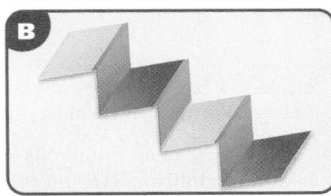

B

Organizer

Objective: Make a sticky-note booklet in which to record notes on probability.

Materials: 7 large sticky notes, glue, markers

 PREMIER **Online Edition**

Using the Page

Preparing the Materials
Four-inch square sticky notes work especially well for this project. A pad of sticky notes typically contains 90 or 100 notes, which is enough for 12 to 14 students.

Making the Project
When students accordion-fold the booklet, they should fold back the first sticky note so that it forms a cover for the booklet.

Extending the Project
Students can make longer booklets by adding additional sticky notes. Have students use the extra space to draw sample outcomes of probability experiments involving coins, spinners, or number cubes.

Tips from the Bag Ladies!

It's nice to use sticky notes of several different colors in each booklet so that the individual pages really stand out.

Health-care professionals often get pads of sticky notes from pharmaceutical companies. Check with physicians or pharmacists in your area. They may be able to donate pads of sticky notes to your class.

Organizer

Objective: Help students organize and review key concepts and skills presented in Chapter 10.

Online Edition
Multilingual Glossary

Resources

Multilingual Glossary Online

go.hrw.com
KEYWORD: MT7 Glossary

Lesson Tutorial Videos
CD-ROM

Answers

1. probability; impossible; certain

2. sample space

3. permutation; combination

4. 0.85; 0.15

Study Guide: Review

Vocabulary

Addition Counting Principle 559
certain 522
combination 564
dependent events 545
disjoint events 542
equally likely 540
event 522
experiment 522

experimental probability 527
factorial 563
fair 540
Fundamental Counting Principle 558
impossible 522
independent events ... 545
mutually exclusive 542
odds against 554

odds in favor 554
outcome 522
permutation 563
probability 522
random numbers 532
sample space 522
simulation 532
theoretical probability . 540
tree diagram 559
trial 522

Complete the sentences below with vocabulary words from the list above. Words may be used more than once.

1. The ___?___ of an event tells you how likely the event is to happen.
   • A probability of 0 means it is ___?___ for the event to occur.
   • A probability of 1 means it is ___?___ that the event will occur.

2. The set of all possible outcomes of an experiment is called the ___?___.

3. A(n) ___?___ is an arrangement where order is important.
   A(n) ___?___ is an arrangement where order is not important.

10-1 Probability (pp. 522–526)

EXAMPLE

■ Of the garbage collected in a city, it is expected that about $\frac{1}{5}$ of the garbage will be recycled.

Outcome	Recycled	Not Recycled
Probability		

$P(\text{recycled}) = \frac{1}{5} = 0.2 = 20\%$

$P(\text{not recycled}) = 1 - \frac{1}{5} = \frac{4}{5} = 0.8 = 80\%$

EXERCISES

Give the probability for each outcome.

4. About 85% of the people attending a band's CD signing have already heard the CD.

Outcome	Heard	Not Heard
Probability		

Study Guide: Review

10-2 Experimental Probability (pp. 527–530)

EXAMPLE

■ The table shows the results of spinning a spinner 72 times. Estimate the probability of the spinner landing on red.

Outcome	White	Red	Blue	Black
Spins	18	28	12	14

probability $\approx \frac{28}{72} = \frac{7}{18} \approx 0.389 = 38.9\%$

EXERCISES

5. The table shows the result of rolling a number cube 80 times. Estimate the probability of rolling a 4.

Outcome	1	2	3	4	5	6
Rolls	13	15	10	12	5	25

10-3 Use a Simulation (pp. 532–535)

EXAMPLE

■ At a local school, 75% of the students study a foreign language. If 5 students are chosen randomly, estimate the probability that at least 4 study a foreign language. Use the random number table to make a simulation with at least 4 trials.

08 57 09 92 75   27 37 87 52 36
16 73 29 39 73   78 65 88 02 42

The probability is about $\frac{3}{4}$, or 75%.

EXERCISES

08570 99275 27378 75236 16732
93973 78658 80242 53191 86579

6. On an assembly line, 20% of the items are rejected. Estimate the probability that at least 3 of the next 6 items are rejected. Use the random number table to make a simulation with at least 4 trials.

10-4 Theoretical Probability (pp. 540–544)

EXAMPLE

■ A fair number cube is rolled once. Find the probability of getting a 4.

$P(4) = \frac{1}{6}$

EXERCISES

7. A marble is drawn at random from a box that contains 8 red, 15 blue, and 7 white marbles. What is the probability of getting a red marble?

10-5 Independent and Dependent Events (pp. 545–549)

EXAMPLE

■ Two marbles are drawn from a jar containing 5 blue marbles and 4 green. What is P(blue, green) if the first marble is not replaced?

	P(blue)	P(green)	P(blue, green)
Not replaced	$\frac{5}{9}$	$\frac{4}{8}$	$\frac{20}{72} \approx 0.28$

EXERCISES

8. A fair number cube is rolled four times. What is the probability of getting a 6 all four times?

9. Two cards are drawn at random from a deck that has 26 red and 26 black cards. What is the probability that the first card is red and the second card is black?

Answers

5. 0.15, or 15%
6. Possible answer: 10%
7. $\frac{4}{15}$
8. $\frac{1}{1296}$
9. $\frac{13}{51}$

Answers

10. 20 laps

11. 3:10

12. 2,600,000

13. ≈0.59

14. 120

15. 210

10-6 **Making Decisions and Predictions** (pp. 550–553)

EXAMPLE

■ A director needs to order 600 T-shirts. Last summer she gave out 210 blue and 150 red T-shirts. Approximately how many red T-shirts should she order?

$\frac{150}{360} = \frac{5}{12}$ *Find the probability of red.*

$\frac{5}{12} = \frac{n}{600}$ *Set up a proportion.*

$12n = 3000$ *Solve for n.*

$n = 250$

She should order 250 red T-shirts.

EXERCISES

10. The speeds of each of 10 laps by a NASCAR racer were measured. The approximate speeds in miles per hour were 188.2, 188.8, 191.2, 191.4, 189.1, 187.6, 186.3, 191.1, 190.3, and 189.5. If the driver goes 50 more laps, what is the best prediction of the number of laps that will be at a speed greater than 190 miles per hour?

10-7 **Odds** (pp. 554–557)

EXAMPLE

■ A digit from 1 to 9 is selected at random. What are the odds in favor of selecting an even number?

favorable ⟶ 4:5 ⟵ *unfavorable*

EXERCISES

11. A letter is selected at random from the alphabet. What are the odds in favor of getting a letter in the word *RANDOM*?

10-8 **Counting Principles** (pp. 558–562)

EXAMPLE

■ A code contains 4 letters. How many possible codes are there?

26 · 26 · 26 · 26 = 456,976 codes

EXERCISES

ID codes contain 1 letter followed by 5 digits. All codes are equally likely.

12. Find the number of possible ID codes.

13. Find the probability that a code does not contain the digit 0.

10-9 **Permutations and Combinations** (pp. 563–567)

EXAMPLE

■ Blaire has 5 plants to arrange on a shelf that will hold 3 plants. How many ways are there to arrange the plants if the order is important? if the order is not important?

important: $_5P_3 = \frac{5!}{(5-3)!} = \frac{5!}{2!} = 60$ ways

not important: $_5C_3 = \frac{5!}{3!\,(5-3)!} = 10$ ways

EXERCISES

14. Five children are arranged in a row of swings. How many different arrangements are possible?

15. A school's mock trial team has 10 members. A team of 6 students will be chosen to represent the school at a competition. How many different teams are possible?

Use the table to find the probability of each event.

1. $P(D)$ **0.5**
2. $P(\text{not } A)$ **0.8**
3. $P(B \text{ or } C)$ **0.3**

Outcome	A	B	C	D
Probability	0.2	0.2	0.1	0.5

4. There are 4 cyclists in a race. Kyle has a 50% chance of winning. Lance has the same chance as Miguel. Eddie has a $\frac{1}{5}$ chance of winning. Create a table of probabilities for the sample space.

A coin is randomly drawn from a box and then replaced. The table shows the results.

5. Estimate the probability of each outcome. **0.26; 0.35; 0.19; 0.2**

Outcome	Penny	Nickel	Dime	Quarter
Probability	26	35	19	20

6. Estimate $P(\text{penny or nickel})$. **0.61**
7. Estimate $P(\text{not dime})$. **0.81**
8. In Eastwood neighborhood, 37% of the families have a cat. Each block has 16 families, 8 on each side. Estimate the probability that 3 or more families on one side of a given block have a cat. Use the random number table to make a simulation with at least 10 trials. **Possible answer: 70%**

97120	08320	17871	21826	74838	37240	36810	20423
12562	45677	88983	94930	31599	76585	61429	05379
34628	46304	66531	96270	21309	31567	30762	47240
30883	71946	25948	97988	26267	21350	59356	43952

An experiment consists of rolling two fair number cubes. Find the probability of each event.

9. $P(\text{total shown} = 3)$ $\frac{1}{18}$
10. $P(\text{rolling two 6's})$ $\frac{1}{36}$
11. $P(\text{total} < 2)$ **0**

12. A jar contains 6 red tiles, 2 blue, 3 yellow, and 5 green. If two tiles are chosen at random, what is the probability that they both will be green? $\frac{1}{12}$

13. A spinner is divided evenly into 9 sections. They are numbered 1 to 9. Player A wins if the spinner lands on odd. Otherwise Player B wins. Decide whether the game is fair. **not fair;** $\frac{5}{9} \neq \frac{4}{9}$

14. The probability of winning a new widescreen TV is $\frac{1}{1,000,000}$. What are the odds against winning the TV? **999,999:1**

15. A code contains 4 letters and 2 numbers. How many possible codes are there? **45,697,600**

16. There are 8 swimmers in a race. In how many possible orders can all 8 swimmers finish the race? **40,320**

Chapter Test

 **CHAPTER TEST**

CHAPTER 10

Organizer

Objective: Assess students' mastery of concepts and skills in Chapter 10.

 **Online Edition**

Resources

Assessment Resources

Chapter 10 Tests
- Free Response
  (Levels A, B, C)
- Multiple Choice
  (Levels A, B, C)
- Performance Assessment

IDEA Works! CD-ROM
Modified Chapter 10 Test

Test & Practice Generator
One-Stop Planner®

Answers

4.

Winner	Kyle	Lance	Miguel	Eddie
Probability	0.5	0.15	0.15	0.2

State Resources

 **go.hrw.com**
State Resources Online
KEYWORD: MT7 Resources

Organizer

Objective: Provide review and practice for Chapters 1–10 and standardized tests.

 Online Edition

Resources

 Assessment Resources
Chapter 10 Cumulative Test

 State Test Prep Workbook

 State Test Prep CD-ROM

 State Test Practice Online

go.hrw.com
KEYWORD: MT7 TestPrep

CHAPTER
10

STANDARDIZED
TEST PREP

go.hrw.com
State Test Practice Online
KEYWORD: MT7 TestPrep

Standardized Test Prep

Cumulative Assessment, Chapters 1–10

Multiple Choice

1. In a box containing marbles, 78 are blue, 24 are orange, and the rest are green. If the probability of selecting a green marble is $\frac{2}{5}$, how many green marbles are in the box?

  Ⓐ 30   Ⓒ 102
  Ⓑ 68   Ⓓ 150

2. In the chart below, the amount represented by each shaded square is twice that represented by each unshaded square. What is the ratio of gold to silver?

Precious Metals Company Supply of Gold and Silver

Silver

Gold

  Ⓕ $\frac{19}{22}$ Ⓗ $\frac{22}{19}$
  Ⓖ $\frac{13}{19}$ Ⓙ $\frac{19}{11}$

3. For which set of data are the mean, median, and mode all the same?

  Ⓐ 3, 1, 3, 3, 5   Ⓒ 2, 1, 1, 1, 5
  Ⓑ 1, 1, 2, 5, 6   Ⓓ 10, 1, 3, 5, 1

4. What is the value of $(-2 - 4)^3 + 3^0$?

  Ⓕ −215   Ⓗ 217
  Ⓖ −8   Ⓙ 219

5. About what percent of 75 is 55?

  Ⓐ 25%   Ⓒ 75%
  Ⓑ 66%   Ⓓ 135%

6. Which does NOT describe $\frac{\sqrt{25}}{-5}$?

  Ⓕ real   Ⓗ integer
  Ⓖ rational   Ⓙ median

7. The figure formed by the vertices $(-2, 5)$, $(2, 5)$, $(4, -1)$, and $(0, -1)$ can be best described by which type of quadrilateral?

  Ⓐ square   Ⓒ parallelogram
  Ⓑ rectangle   Ⓓ trapezoid

8. How many vertices are in the prism below?

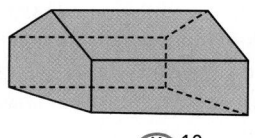

  Ⓕ 7   Ⓗ 10
  Ⓖ 8   Ⓙ 12

9. The triangular reflecting pool has an area of 350 ft². If the height of the triangle is 25 ft, what is the length of the hypotenuse to the nearest tenth?

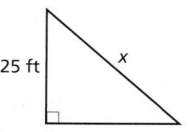

25 ft   x

  Ⓐ 28.7 ft   Ⓒ 38.9 ft
  Ⓑ 37.5 ft   Ⓓ 42.3 ft

10. If the probability of selecting a red marble is $\frac{1}{14}$, what are the odds in favor of selecting a red marble?

  Ⓕ $\frac{13}{14}$ Ⓖ $\frac{2}{13}$ Ⓗ $\frac{1}{13}$ Ⓙ $\frac{1}{15}$

State Resources

go.hrw.com
State Resources Online
KEYWORD: MT7 Resources

TEST PREP DOCTOR ✚

Probability word problems such as item 1 are often too abstract for students to remember an effective solution strategy. Remind them that proportions are often used in these situations. Show them how to set up a proportion, such as $\frac{2}{5} = \frac{x}{102 + x}$, which uses the variable x for the unknown amount of green marbles. Remind them how to solve proportions using cross products. Try to keep students from using trial and error, except as a last resort.

Answers

17. $\frac{1}{2}$

18. 98.4%

19. See 4-Point Response work sample.

11. If the diameter of the dartboard is 10 in., what is the area of the 50-point portion, to the nearest tenth of a square inch?

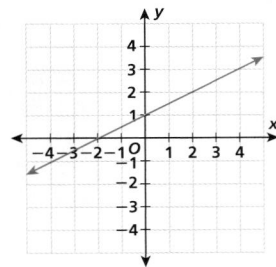

25 points — 50 points
100 points — 2 in.
2 in.

(A) 3.1 in²   (C) 9.4 in²
(B) 6.3 in²   (D) 25.1 in²

Draw a picture to help you see if your answer is reasonable.

Gridded Response

Use the following graph for items 12 and 13.

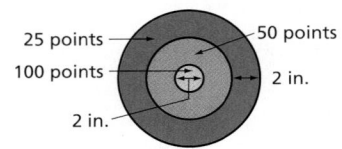

12. Find the x-coordinate of the ordered pair whose y-coordinate is 1. **0**

13. Determine the value of y when x = 6. **4**

14. What is the probability of rolling an even number on a number cube and tossing a heads on a coin? $\frac{1}{4}$ or 0.25

15. Teresa has to create a password that contains 1 digit and 2 letters. Find the number of possible passwords. **6760**

16. What is the value of x for the equation $7 = \frac{2}{3}x - 3$? **15**

Short Response

17. A dart thrown at the square board shown lands in a random spot. What is the probability that it lands in the blue square? Show your work.

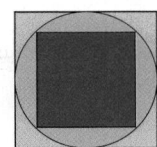

18. The pilot of a hot-air balloon is trying to land in a 2 km square field. There is a large tree in each corner. The ropes will tangle in a tree if the balloon lands within $\frac{1}{7}$ km of the tree's trunk. What is the probability the balloon will land without getting caught in a tree? Express your answer to the nearest tenth of a percent. Show your work.

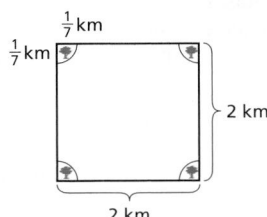

$\frac{1}{7}$ km
$\frac{1}{7}$ km
2 km
2 km

Extended Response

19. Students are choosing a new mascot and color. The mascot choices are a bear, a lion, a jaguar, or a tiger. The color choices are red, orange, or blue.

   a. How many different combinations do the students have to choose from? Show your work.

   b. If a second school color is added, either gold or silver, how many different combinations do the students have to choose from? Show your work.

   c. How would adding a choice from among n names change the number of combinations to choose from?

Short Response Rubric

Items 17–18

2 Points = The student's answer is an accurate and complete execution of the task or tasks.

1 Point = The student's answer contains attributes of an appropriate response but is flawed.

0 Points = The student's answer contains no attributes of an appropriate response.

Extended Response Rubric

Item 19

4 points = The student demonstrates a thorough understanding of all concepts and shows all work correctly.

3 points = The student demonstrates a basic understanding of all concepts, but the work shows some flaws reflecting inattentive execution of mathematical procedures or some misunderstanding of the underlying mathematics.

2 points = The student demonstrates only a partial understanding of the concepts or procedures embodied in the tasks. The approach may be correct, but the work shows a misunderstanding of one or more important concepts.

1 point = The student demonstrates a very limited understanding of the concepts or procedures embodied in the tasks. The response may show some understanding but exhibits many flaws or is incomplete.

0 points = The student provides no response at all or a completely incorrect or uninterpretable response.

Student Work Samples for Item 19

4 Point Response

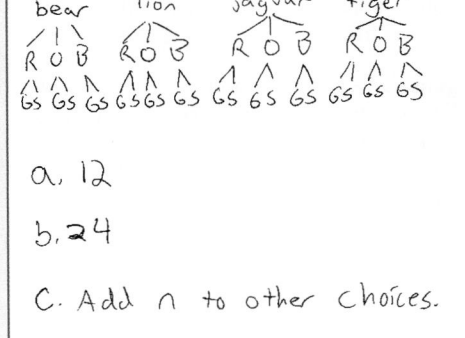

The student correctly applies the Fundamental Counting Principle for all three parts.

3 Point Response

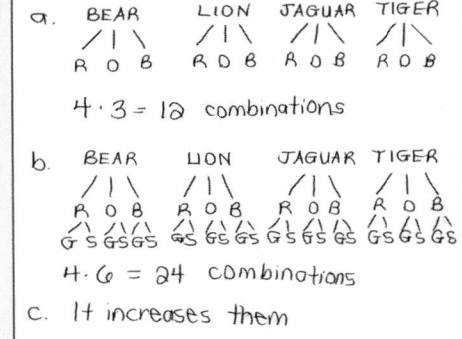

The student correctly uses a tree for parts **a** and **b**, but the answer to part **c** is ambiguous and poorly explained.

2 Point Response

a. BEAR   LION   JAGUAR   TIGER
   R O B   R O B   R O B   R O B
   4·3 = 12 combinations

b. BEAR   LION   JAGUAR   TIGER
   R O B   R O B   R O B   R O B
   GS GS GS GS GS GS GS GS GS GS GS GS
   4·6 = 24 combinations

c. It increases them

The student applied a useful counting strategy to reach the correct answers in parts **a** and **b**. However, by the students' incorrect answer to part **c**, it is clear that the student does not grasp the concepts being evaluated.

Problem Solving on Location

Organizer

Objective: Choose appropriate problem-solving strategies and use them with skills from Chapters 9 and 10 to solve real-world problems.

 Online Edition

✪ Clemson Tigers Football

Reading Strategies

Students are accustomed to reading sentences in order from top to bottom, but this restriction can be crippling in math problems, where information is not always presented in a useful order. Have students read through problems 2 and 3 and then rewrite each problem in their own words. Discuss whether or not these changes make the problem easier to understand.

Using Data Have students locate a year on the bar graph and tell how many total points were scored that season. Ask them to predict the total points scored in the 2005 season.

State Resources

go.hrw.com
State Resources Online
KEYWORD: MT7 Resources

Problem Solving on Location

SOUTH CAROLINA

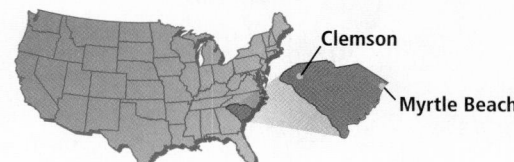

Clemson

Myrtle Beach

✪ Clemson Tigers Football

For the past two decades, Clemson University's football team has been one of the sport's greatest success stories. Since 1985, the Clemson Tigers have appeared in 16 bowl games, placing them among the nation's most consistently winning teams during that period.

Choose one or more strategies to solve each problem.

1. The Clemson Tigers' team colors are orange, purple, and white. The players' jerseys and pants are available in all three colors. How many different uniforms can the team make by choosing a color for the jersey and a color for the pants? **9**

2. The entrance to the team's locker room has an enormous photo of the university's stadium. The perimeter of the photo is 78 feet. The length is 21 feet greater than the width. What are the length and width of the photo? **9 ft × 30 ft**

For 3, use the graph.

3. During the 1998 season, the Tigers scored 104 fewer points than during the 1999 season. During the 1999 season, they scored 43 fewer points than the median of the seasons shown in the graph. How many points did the Tigers score during the 1998 season? **218**

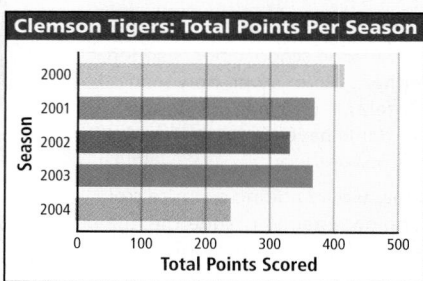

Clemson Tigers: Total Points Per Season

Season (vertical axis): 2000, 2001, 2002, 2003, 2004

Total Points Scored (horizontal axis): 0, 100, 200, 300, 400, 500

Problem Solving Focus

Encourage students to use the four-step problem-solving process for the problems. Focus on the second step: **(2) Plan.**

Discuss the given data in problem 2, and ask students what two pieces of information they will need to solve for before they can find the length and width of the photo. First set up an equation that represents the perimeter of the photo, and then use the given information to write an equation representing the relationship between the length and the width.

SOUTH CAROLINA HALL OF FAME

Problem Solving Strategies

Draw a Diagram
Make a Model
Guess and Test
Work Backward
Find a Pattern
Make a Table
Solve a Simpler Problem
Use Logical Reasoning
Act It Out
Make an Organized List

★ The South Carolina Hall of Fame

What do President Andrew Jackson, jazz musician Dizzy Gillespie, and athlete Lucile Godbold have in common? All of them were born in South Carolina, and all have been inducted into the South Carolina Hall of Fame. Located in Myrtle Beach, the hall honors citizens of the state who have made lasting contributions in a wide range of fields.

Choose one or more strategies to solve each problem.

1. Each year, 10 living nominees and 10 deceased nominees are selected for induction into the hall. The judges pick one from each group. How many different pairs of possible inductees are there? **100**

2. The hall includes five inductees from the field of medicine. Their portraits are to be lined up next to each other. In how many different ways can the portraits be arranged? **120**

For 3 and 4, use the graph.

3. The graph shows the total number of inductees in the South Carolina Hall of Fame. Assume that new inductees continue to be added to the hall at the same rate. Predict the total number of inductees in 2020. **103**

4. In what year will there be more than 100 inductees for the first time? **2019**

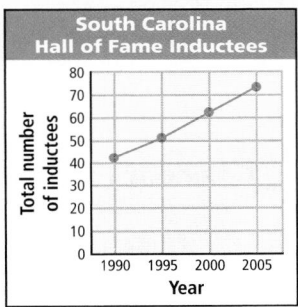

South Carolina Hall of Fame Inductees

★ The South Carolina Hall of Fame

Reading Strategies

While students are reading, ask them to be aware of words and phrases that may give solution strategies. For example, problem 1 asks for the number of different pairs of inductees, and problem 2 asks how many different ways portraits can be arranged. When problems ask for the number of "possibilities" or "ways," it is usually an indication that the solution will require counting strategies.

Using Data Remind students that, according to the information given in problem 1, two people are usually inducted every year. Is the graph consistent with this information? Explain. Yes; The graph increases at about two inductees per year.

Problem Solving Focus

Discuss strategies for the first two problems with students. For problem 1, compare making a tree diagram with using the Fundamental Counting Principle. Explain that applying counting principles is much faster than drawing diagrams. For problem 2, point out the word "arrange" and ask students what math vocabulary term deals with rearranging the elements of a set. Permutations

CHAPTER 11

Multi-Step Equations and Inequalities

Section 11A	Section 11B
Solving Linear Equations	**Solving Equations and Inequalities**
11-1 Simplifying Algebraic Expressions	11-4 Solving Inequalities by Multiplying and Dividing
11-2 Solving Multi-Step Equations	11-5 Solving Two-Step Inequalities
11-3 **Hands-On Lab** Model Equations with Variables on Both Sides	11-6 Systems of Equations
11-3 Solving Equations with Variables on Both Sides	

Pacing Guide for 45-Minute Classes

Calendar Planner
One-Stop Planner®

Chapter 11

Countdown to Testing Week 24

DAY 1	DAY 2	DAY 3	DAY 4	DAY 5
11-1 Lesson	11-2 Lesson	11-3 Hands-On Lab 11-3 Lesson	11-3 Lesson	Ready to Go On? Focus on Problem Solving 11-4 Lesson
DAY 6	**DAY 7**	**DAY 8**	**DAY 9**	**DAY 10**
11-4 Lesson 11-5 Lesson	11-5 Lesson 11-6 Lesson	11-6 Lesson Ready to Go On? Multi-Step Test Prep	Chapter 11 Review	Chapter 11 Test

Pacing Guide for 90-Minute Classes

Calendar Planner
One-Stop Planner®

Chapter 11

DAY 1	DAY 2	DAY 3	DAY 4	DAY 5
11-1 Lesson 11-2 Lesson	11-3 Hands-On Lab 11-3 Lesson	Ready to Go On? Focus on Problem Solving 11-4 Lesson 11-5 Lesson	11-5 Lesson 11-6 Lesson Ready to Go On? Multi-Step Test Prep	Chapter 11 Review Chapter 11 Test

ONGOING ASSESSMENT and INTERVENTION

DIAGNOSE	PRESCRIBE

Assess Prior Knowledge

Before Chapter 11

Diagnose readiness for the chapter.

Are You Ready? SE p. 581

Prescribe intervention.

Are You Ready? Intervention Skills 49, 53, 55

Formative Assessment

Before Every Lesson

Diagnose readiness for the lesson.

Warm Up TE, every lesson

Prescribe intervention.

Skills Bank SE pp. 820–834

Reteach CRB, Chapters 1–11

During Every Lesson

Diagnose understanding of lesson concepts.

Think and Discuss SE, every lesson

Write About It SE, lesson exercises

Journal TE, lesson exercises

Prescribe intervention.

Questioning Strategies Chapter 11

Reading Strategies CRB, every lesson

Success for ELL pp. 165–176

After Every Lesson

Diagnose mastery of lesson concepts.

Lesson Quiz TE, every lesson

Test Prep SE, every lesson

Test and Practice Generator

Prescribe intervention.

Reteach CRB, every lesson

Problem Solving CRB, every lesson

Test Prep Doctor TE, lesson exercises

Homework Help Online

Before Chapter 11 Testing

Diagnose mastery of concepts in the chapter.

Ready to Go On? SE pp. 598, 612

Focus on Problem Solving SE p. 599

Multi-Step Test Prep SE p. 613

Section Quizzes AR pp. 205–206

Test and Practice Generator

Prescribe intervention.

Ready to Go On? Intervention Chapter 11

Scaffolding Questions TE p. 613

Before High Stakes Testing

Diagnose mastery of benchmark concepts.

Test Tackler SE pp. 620–621

Standardized Test Prep SE pp. 622–623

State Test Prep CD-ROM

Prescribe intervention.

State Test Prep Workbook

Summative Assessment

After Chapter 11

Check mastery of chapter concepts.

Multiple-Choice Tests (Forms A, B, C)

Free-Response Tests (Forms A, B, C)

Performance Assessment AR pp. 207–220

Test and Practice Generator

Check mastery of benchmark concepts.

AYP State Tests

Prescribe intervention.

Reteach CRB, every lesson

Lesson Tutorial Videos Chapter 11

Prescribe intervention.

State Test Prep Workbook

CHAPTER 11

Supporting the Teacher

Chapter 11 Resource Book

Practice A, B, C
pp. 3–5, 11–13, 20–22, 29–31, 37–39, 46–48

Reading Strategies ELL
pp. 9, 18, 27, 35, 44, 53

Puzzles, Twisters, and Teasers
pp. 10, 19, 28, 36, 45, 54

Reteach
pp. 6, 14–15, 23–24, 32, 40–41, 49–50

Problem Solving
pp. 8, 17, 26, 34, 43, 52

Challenge
pp. 7, 16, 25, 33, 42, 51

Parent Letter   pp. 1–2

Transparencies

Lesson Transparencies, Volume 2........................... Chapter 11
• Warm Ups
• Problem of the Day
• Teaching Transparencies
• Lesson Quizzes

Know-It Notebook... Chapter 11
• Additional Examples   • Chapter Review
• Vocabulary   • Big Ideas

Alternate Openers: Explorations...........................pp. 83–88

Countdown to Testing..pp. 47–48

Teacher Tools

Power Presentations®
Complete PowerPoint® presentations for Chapter 11 lessons

Lesson Tutorial Videos® SPANISH
Holt authors Ed Burger and Freddie Renfro present tutorials to support the Chapter 11 lessons.

One-Stop Planner® SPANISH
Easy access to all Chapter 11 resources and assessments, as well as software for lesson planning, test generation, and puzzle creation

IDEA Works!®
Key Chapter 11 resources and assessments modified to address special learning needs

Lesson Plans ....pp. 83–88

Questioning Strategies....................................... Chapter 11

Solutions Key .... Chapter 11

Interdisciplinary Posters and Worksheets............. Chapter 11

TechKeys   **Lab Resources**

Project Teacher Support   **Parent Resources**

Workbooks

Homework and Practice Workbook SPANISH
Teacher's Guide...pp. 42–44

Know-It Notebook
Teacher's Guide... Chapter 11

Problem Solving Workbook SPANISH
Teacher's Guide...pp. 42–44

State Test Prep Workbook
Teacher's Guide

Technology Highlights for the Teacher

Power Presentations
Dynamic presentations to engage students. Complete PowerPoint® presentations for every lesson in Chapter 11.

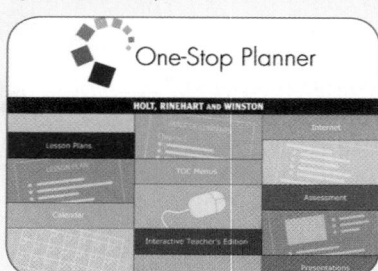

One-Stop Planner SPANISH
Easy access to Chapter 11 resources and assessments. Includes lesson-planning, test-generation, and puzzle-creation software.

Premier Online Edition SPANISH
Chapter 11 includes Tutorial Videos, Lesson Activities, Lesson Quizzes, Homework Help, and Chapter Project.

KEY: **SE** = *Student Edition*   **TE** = *Teacher's Edition*   ELL English Language Learners   SPANISH Spanish version available   Available on CD-ROM   Available online

Reaching All Learners

Resources for All Learners

Hands-On Lab Activities..............................Chapter 11

Technology Lab Activities...........................Chapter 11

Homework and Practice Workbook SPANISH ....pp. 83–88

Know-It Notebook..Chapter 11

Problem Solving Workbook SPANISH ....pp. 83–88

DEVELOPING LEARNERS

Practice A ....CRB, every lesson

Reteach ....CRB, every lesson

Inclusion ....TE p. 589

Questioning Strategies................................Chapter 11

Modified Chapter 11 Resources .... *IDEA Works!*

Homework Help Online

ON-LEVEL LEARNERS

Practice B ....CRB, every lesson

Puzzles, Twisters, and Teasers ....CRB, every lesson

Multiple Representations ....TE p. 605

Cooperative Learning ....TE p. 589

ADVANCED LEARNERS

Practice C ....CRB, every lesson

Challenge ....CRB, every lesson

Extension ....TE pp. 583, 613, 614, 615

Critical Thinking ....TE p. 609

English Language Learners

ENGLISH
LANGUAGE
LEARNERS

Are You Ready? Vocabulary ....SE p. 581

Vocabulary Connections ....SE p. 582

Lesson Vocabulary ....SE, every lesson

Vocabulary Review...SE p. 616

English Language Learners ....TE pp. 583, 584, 600

Reading Strategies ....CRB, every lesson

Success for English Language Learners...............pp. 165–176

Multilingual Glossary

Reaching All Learners Through...

Inclusion ....TE p. 589

Visual Cues...TE pp. 585, 601

Kinesthetic Experience ....TE p. 594

Concrete Manipulatives...............................TE p. 585

Multiple Representations ....TE p. 605

Cooperative Learning ....TE p. 589

Critical Thinking..TE p. 609

Test Prep Doctor...................TE pp. 587, 591, 597, 603, 607,
611, 620, 622

Common Error Alerts ....TE pp. 585, 589,
594, 601, 605

Scaffolding Questions..................................TE p. 613

Technology Highlights for Reaching All Learners

 Lesson Tutorial Videos SPANISH

Starring Holt authors Ed Burger and Freddie Renfro! Live tutorials to support every lesson in Chapter 11.

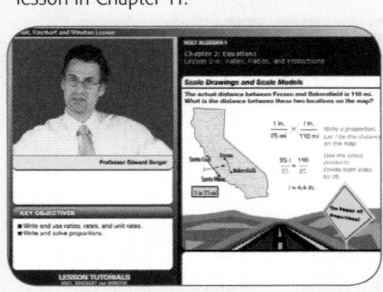

Multilingual Glossary

Searchable glossary includes definitions in English, Spanish, Vietnamese, Chinese, Hmong, Korean, and 4 other languages.

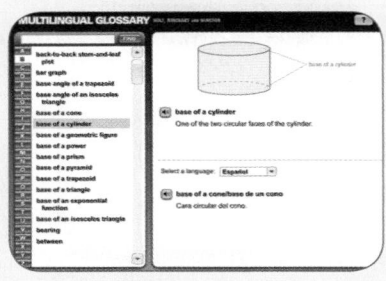

Online Interactivities

Interactive tutorials provide visually engaging alternative opportunities to learn concepts and master skills.

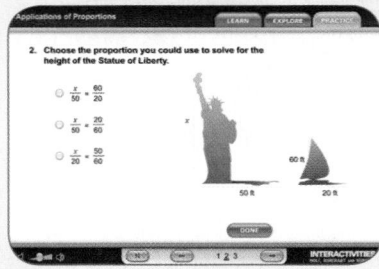

KEY: **SE** = *Student Edition*   **TE** = *Teacher's Edition*   **CRB** = *Chapter Resource Book*   SPANISH Spanish version available    Available on CD-ROM    Available online

Ongoing Assessment

Assessing Prior Knowledge

Determine whether students have the prerequisite concepts and skills for success in Chapter 11.

Are You Ready? SPANISH .... SE p. 581
Warm Up .... TE, every lesson

Test Preparation

Provide review and practice for Chapter 11 and standardized tests.

Multi-Step Test Prep .... SE p. 613
Study Guide: Review .... SE pp. 616–618
Test Tackler .... SE pp. 620–621
Standardized Test Prep .... SE pp. 622–623
Countdown to Testing Transparencies ....pp. 47–48
State Test Prep Workbook
State Test Prep CD-ROM
IDEA Works!

Alternative Assessment

Assess students' understanding of Chapter 11 concepts and combined problem-solving skills.

Chapter 11 Project .... SE p. 580
Performance Assessment SPANISH .... AR pp. 219–220
Portfolio Assessment SPANISH .... AR p. xxxiv

Daily Assessment

Provide formative assessment for each day of Chapter 11.

Questioning Strategies .... Chapter 11
Think and Discuss .... SE, every lesson
Write About It .... SE, lesson exercises
Journal .... TE, lesson exercises
Lesson Quiz .... TE, every lesson
Modified Lesson Quizzes .... *IDEA Works!*

Weekly Assessment

Provide formative assessment for each week of Chapter 11.

Focus on Problem Solving .... SE p. 599
Multi-Step Test Prep .... SE p. 613
Ready to Go On? SPANISH .... SE pp. 598, 612
Cumulative Assessment .... SE pp. 622–623
Test and Practice Generator SPANISH ...*One-Stop Planner*

Formal Assessment

Provide summative assessment of Chapter 11 mastery.

Section Quizzes SPANISH .... AR pp. 205–206
Chapter 11 Test .... SE p. 619
Chapter Test (Levels A, B, C) SPANISH ...... AR pp. 207–218
    • Multiple-Choice   • Free-Response
Cumulative Test SPANISH .... AR pp. 221–224
Test and Practice Generator SPANISH ...*One-Stop Planner*
Modified Chapter 11 Test .... *IDEA Works!*

Technology Highlights for the Teacher

Are You Ready? SPANISH
Automatically assess readiness and prescribe intervention for Chapter 11 prerequisite skills.

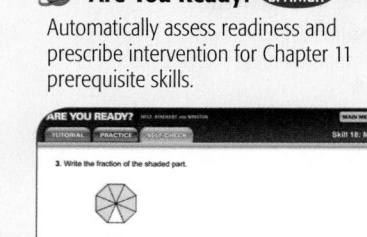

Ready to Go On? SPANISH
Automatically assess understanding of and prescribe intervention for Sections 11A and 11B.

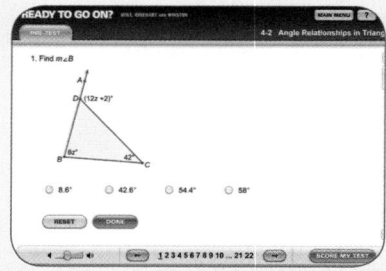

Test and Practice Generator SPANISH
Use Chapter 11 problem banks to create assessments and worksheets to print out or deliver online. Includes dynamic problems.

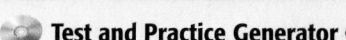
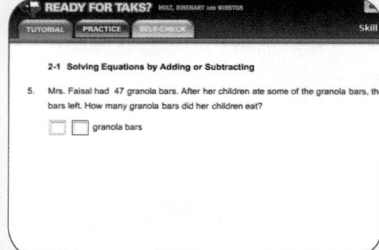

KEY: **SE** = *Student Edition*   **TE** = *Teacher's Edition*   **AR** = *Assessment Resources*   SPANISH Spanish version available   Available on CD-ROM    Available online

Formal Assessment

Three levels (A, B, C) of multiple-choice and free-response chapter tests are available in the *Assessment Resources.*

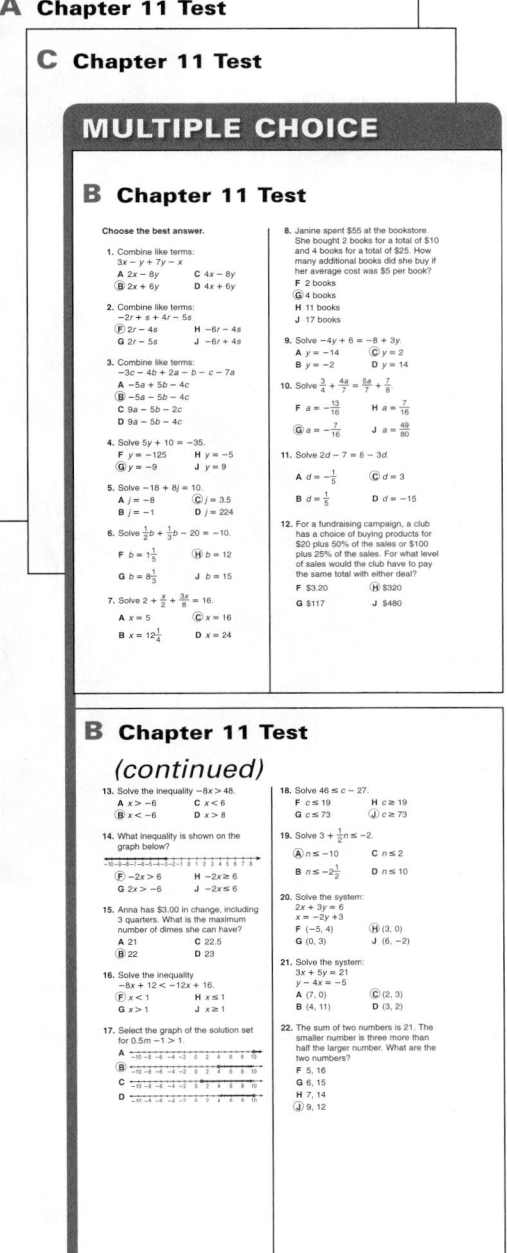

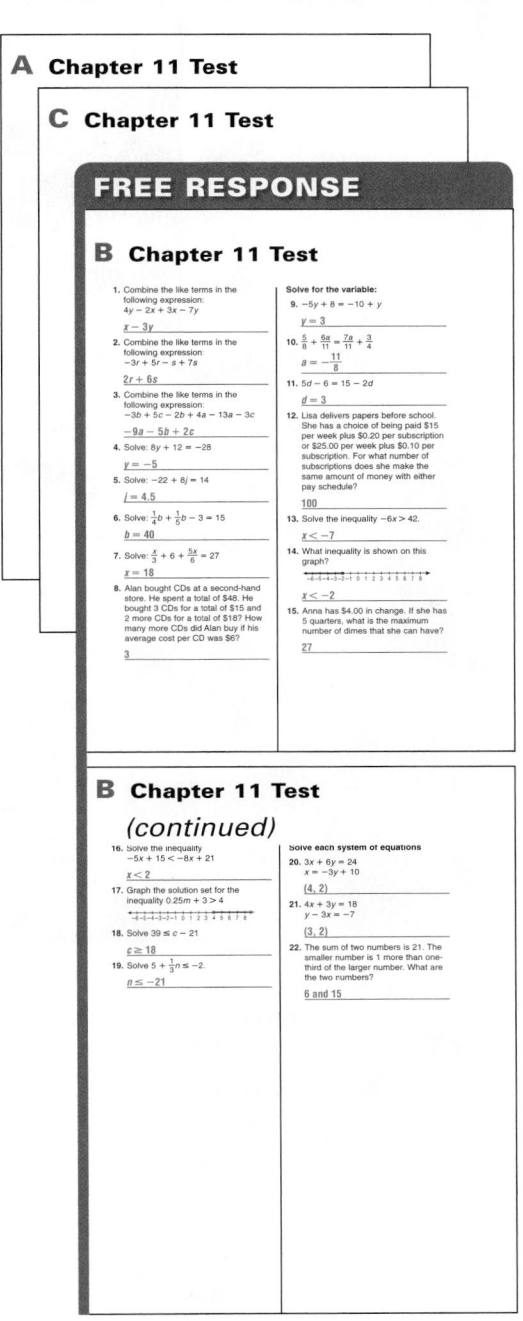

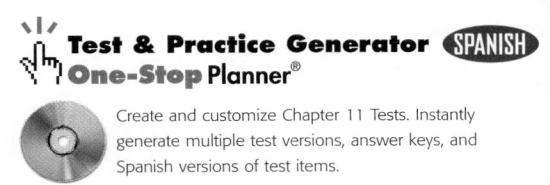

Test & Practice Generator SPANISH
One-Stop Planner®

Create and customize Chapter 11 Tests. Instantly generate multiple test versions, answer keys, and Spanish versions of test items.

Multi-Step Equations and Inequalities

Why Learn This?

Tell students that equations and inequalities can be used in many real-world applications. For example, a hydrologist might use an equation to determine the difference between two rivers' discharge rates. The discharge rate of each river is known. The difference is unknown and might be represented with the variable d. To find the difference between the discharge rates of the Colorado and Snake Rivers, the equation $726.04 = d + 314.6$ can be used.

Using Data

To begin the study of this chapter, have students:

- Write the rivers in order from greatest discharge rate to least discharge rate. Columbia, Missouri, Snake, Colorado
- Find the discharge rate in m^3/h of the Snake River. 2,613,744 m^3/h
- Determine which of the rivers' discharge rates is a solution to the inequality $d \geq 726$. Snake, Missouri, and Columbia Rivers

MULTI-STEP TEST PREP On page 613, students write inequalities to model different scenarios for the cost of renting an ice rink.

11A	Solving Linear Equations
11-1	Simplifying Algebraic Expressions
11-2	Solving Multi-Step Equations
LAB	Model Equations with Variables on Both Sides
11-3	Solving Equations with Variables on Both Sides
11B	Solving Equations and Inequalities
11-4	Solving Inequalities by Multiplying or Dividing
11-5	Solving Two-Step Inequalities
11-6	Systems of Equations

MULTI-STEP TEST PREP

go.hrw.com
Chapter Project Online
KEYWORD: MT7 Ch11

River	Location	Discharge (m^3/s)
Colorado	Glen Canyon Dam, CO	314.6
Snake	Hells Canyon Dam, ID	726.04
Missouri	St. Joseph, MO	1751.4
Columbia	The Dalles, OR	6331.65

Career *Hydrologist*

Hydrologists measure water flow between rivers, streams, lakes, and oceans. They map their results to record locations and movement of water above and below the earth's surface.

Hydrologists are involved in projects such as water-resource studies, field irrigation, flood management, soil-erosion prevention, and the study of water discharge from creeks, streams, and rivers. The table shows the rate of water discharge for four U.S. rivers.

Problem Solving Project

Understand, Plan, Solve, and Look Back

Have students:

- Complete the Water Flows Downhill worksheet.
- Create an equation for calculating river discharge by relating water velocity (m/s) and stream cross section (m^2).
- Draw a picture to visualize the equation, showing river discharge, water velocity, and stream cross section.
- Research to discover facts about a local river.

Earth Science Connection

Project Resources
All project resources for teachers and students are provided online.

Materials:
- Water Flows Downhill worksheet

go.hrw.com
Project Teacher Support
KEYWORD: MT7 PSProject11

ARE YOU READY?

✓ Vocabulary

Choose the best term from the list to complete each sentence.

1. A letter that represents a value that can change is called a(n) __?__. **variable**

2. A(n) __?__ has one or more variables. **algebraic expression**

3. The algebraic expression $5x^2 - 3y + 4x^2 + 7$ has four __?__. Because they have the same variable raised to the same power, $5x^2$ and $4x^2$ are __?__. **terms; like terms**

4. When you individually multiply the numbers inside the parentheses by the factor outside the parentheses, you are applying the __?__. **Distributive Property**

algebraic expression
Distributive Property
like terms
terms
variable

Complete these exercises to review skills you will need for this chapter.

✓ Distribute Multiplication

Replace each ▪ with a number so that each equation illustrates the Distributive Property.

5. $6 \cdot (11 + 8) = 6 \cdot 11 + 6 \cdot$ ▪   **8**   6. $7 \cdot (14 + 12) =$ ▪ $\cdot 14 +$ ▪ $\cdot 12$ **7**

7. $9 \cdot (6 -$ ▪$) = 9 \cdot 6 - 9 \cdot 2$ **2**   8. $14 \cdot ($▪$ - 7) = 14 \cdot 20 - 14 \cdot 7$ **20**

✓ Simplify Algebraic Expressions

Simplify each expression by applying the Distributive Property and combining like terms.

9. $3(x + 2) + 7x$ **10x + 6**   10. $4(y - 3) + 8y$ **12y − 12**   11. $2(z - 1) - 3z$ **−z − 2**

12. $-4(t - 6) - t$ **−5t + 24**   13. $-(r - 3) - 8r$ **−9r + 3**   14. $-5(4 - 2m) + 7$ **10m − 13**

✓ Connect Words and Equations

Write an equation to represent each situation.

15. The perimeter P of a rectangle is the sum of twice the length ℓ and twice the width w.   **$P = 2\ell + 2w$**

16. The volume V of a rectangular prism is the product of its three dimensions: length ℓ, width w, and height h.   **$V = \ell wh$**

17. The surface area S of a sphere is the product of 4π and the square of the radius r.   **$S = 4\pi r^2$**

18. The cost c of a telegram of 18 words is the cost f of the first 10 words plus the cost a of each additional word.   **$c = f + 8a$**

Organizer

Objective: Help students organize the new concepts they will learn in Chapter 11.

Online Edition
Multilingual Glossary

Resources

PuzzlePro®
One-Stop Planner®

***Multilingual Glossary* Online**

go.hrw.com
KEYWORD: MT7 Glossary

Possible answers to *Vocabulary Connections*

1. Equivalent expressions are expressions that are equal.

2. To simplify an expression is to make it less complicated.

3. Like terms are terms that are alike or similar.

4. A system of equations is a group of related equations.

Study Guide: Preview

Where You've Been

Previously, you

- used models to solve equations.

- solved inequalities by adding or subtracting.

- determined if an ordered pair is a solution to an equation.

In This Chapter

You will study

- finding solutions to application problems using algebraic equations.

- solving multi-step equations.

- solving inequalities by multiplying or dividing.

- determining if an ordered pair is a solution to a system of equations.

- solving a system of equations.

Where You're Going

You can use the skills learned in this chapter

- to calculate profits or losses generated by the number of items a business produces.

- to solve complex application problems involving systems of equations and systems of inequalities in higher-level math courses.

Key Vocabulary/Vocabulario

equivalent expression	expresiónes equivalents
like term	términos semejantes
simplify	simplificar
solution of a system of equations	soluciones de un sistema de ecuaciones
system of equations	sistema de ecuaciones
term	término

Vocabulary Connections

To become familiar with some of the vocabulary terms in the chapter, consider the following. You may refer to the chapter, the glossary, or a dictionary if you like.

1. The word *equivalent* contains the same root as the word *equal*. What do you think **equivalent expressions** are?

2. The word *simplify* means "make less complicated." What do you think it means to **simplify** an expression?

3. The adjective *like* means "alike." What do you suppose **like terms** are?

4. A *system* is a group of related objects. What do you think a **system of equations** is?

Reading and Writing Math

Writing Strategy: Write to Justify

The icon appears throughout the book. This icon identifies questions that require you to write a problem or an explanation. Being able to justify your answer is proof that you have an understanding of the concept. You can use a four-step method to write a justification for your solution.

> **From Lesson 10-4**
>
>  **8. Write About It** Suppose you are playing a game in which two fair dice are rolled. To make the first move, you need to roll doubles or a sum of 3 or 11. What is the probability that you will be able to make the first move? $\frac{5}{18}$

Step 1 Rewrite the problem statement in your own words.

Find the probability of rolling a double or a sum of 3 or 11.

Step 2 Make a table or other graphic to help explain your thinking.

1,1	1,2	1,3	1,4	1,5	1,6
2,1	2,2	2,3	2,4	2,5	2,6
3,1	3,2	3,3	3,4	3,5	3,6
4,1	4,2	4,3	4,4	4,5	4,6
5,1	5,2	5,3	5,4	5,5	5,6
6,1	6,2	6,3	6,4	6,5	6,6

Highlight the number of ways you can roll a double or a sum of 11 or 3.

Step 3 Give evidence that you have answered the question.

The probability of rolling a double is $\frac{6}{36}$.

The probability of rolling a sum of 3 is $\frac{2}{36}$.

The probability of rolling a sum of 11 is $\frac{2}{36}$.

Step 4 Write a complete response.

The events are mutually exclusive, so you add the probabilities. The probability that you will roll a double or a sum of 11 or 3 is $\frac{6}{36} + \frac{2}{36} + \frac{2}{36} = \frac{10}{36} = \frac{5}{18}$ or approximately 28%.

Try This

Describe a situation using two fair number cubes where the probability that two mutually exclusive events will occur is $\frac{1}{4}$. Justify your answer.

Organizer

Objective: Help students apply strategies to understand and retain key concepts.

PREMIER Online Edition

Resources

Chapter 11 Resource Book
Reading Strategies

Writing Strategy: Write to Justify

ENGLISH LANGUAGE LEARNERS

Discuss Students will be able to justify their responses if they understand the problem. Ask students to rewrite the problem in their own words.

Reinforce to students that they gather evidence as they solve a problem. Presenting their evidence in a logical way is part of their justification.

Extend As students work through Chapter 11, ask them to justify their responses and answers.

Have students relate the new math concepts in the exercises to what they already know.

Possible answers to *Try This*

Suppose you were to roll a number cube twice. The probability of getting an odd number on the first roll is $\frac{1}{2}$ and the probability of rolling an even number on the second roll is $\frac{1}{2}$. These are mutually exclusive events.

Solving Linear Equations

One-Minute Section Planner

Lesson	Materials	MiC and Lab Resources
Lesson 11-1 Simplifying Algebraic Expressions • Combine like terms in an expression. ☑ SAT-10　☑ ITBS　☑ CTBS　☑ NAEP	Cutout shapes	**MiC:** *Algebra Rules* pp. 3–6, 8–9, 47 *Hands-On Lab Activities* 11-1
Lesson 11-2 Solving Multi-Step Equations • Solve multi-step equations. ☑ SAT-10　☐ ITBS　☑ CTBS　☑ NAEP	Algebra tiles (MK)	**MiC:** *Graphing Equations* pp. 28–31 **MiC:** *Algebra Rules* pp. 37–38 *Technology Lab Activities* 11-2
11-3 Hands-On Lab Model Equations with Variables on Both Sides • Use algebra tiles to model equations with variables on both sides. **Lesson 11-3** Solving Equations with Variables on Both Sides • Solve equations with variables on both sides of the equal sign. ☑ SAT-10　☐ ITBS　☑ CTBS　☑ NAEP	Algebra tiles (MK), index cards	**MiC:** *Algebra Rules* pp. 37–38 **MiC:** *Graphing Equations* pp. 31–35 *Hands-On Lab Activities* 11-3 *Technology Lab Activities* 11-3

MK = *Manipulatives Kit*

Mathematics in Context

The units **Algebra Rules** and **Graphing Equations** from the *Mathematics in Context* © 2006 series can be used with Section 11A. See Section Planner above for suggestions for integrating *MiC* with *Holt Mathematics*.

Section Overview

Simplifying Algebraic Expressions

Lesson 11-1

Why? Combining like terms helps to simplify algebraic expressions.

> **Like terms** can be grouped together because they have the same variable raised to the same power.

Simplify: $7(a + b) - 4a + 6 - 5b + 8$

$7a + 7b - 4a + 6 - 5b + 8$

$7a + 7b - 4a + 6 - 5b + 8$

$3a + 2b + 14$

> Combine Coefficients:
> $7 - 4 = 3$
> $7 - 5 = 2$
> $6 + 8 = 14$

> Identify like terms.

> The Distributive Property states that $a(b + c) = ab + ac$ for all a, b, and c.

Multi-Step Equations

Lesson 11-2

Why? Some problems require equations that have more than two steps.

Jack had a $5 gift certificate for a restaurant. After a 15% tip was added to the bill, the $5 was deducted. Jack actually paid $18. What was the original bill before the tip was added?

Solve

$$b + 0.15b - 5 = 18$$
$$1.15b - 5 = 18$$
$$\underline{+\ 5 \qquad\quad +\ 5}$$
$$1.15b = 23$$
$$\frac{1.15b}{1.15b} = \frac{23}{1.15}$$
$$b = 20$$

The original bill was $20.

Check

$$b + 0.15b - 5 = 18$$
$$20 + 0.15(20) - 5 \stackrel{?}{=} 18$$
$$20 + \quad 3 \quad - 5 \stackrel{?}{=} 18$$
$$18 \stackrel{?}{=} 18 \checkmark$$

Equations with Variables on Both Sides

Lesson 11-3

Why? A problem may require an equation that has a variable on both sides of the equal sign.

The members of a book club spend the same amount for refreshments at each meeting. At one meeting they bought 6 bagels and spent $9.90 on beverages. At the next meeting they bought 8 bagels and spent $8.20 on beverages. What was the cost of each bagel?

Solve

$$6x + 9.90 = 8x + 8.20$$
$$\underline{-\ 6x \qquad\quad -\ 6x}$$
$$9.90 = 2x + 8.20$$
$$\underline{-\ 8.20 \qquad -\ 8.20}$$
$$1.70 = 2x$$
$$\frac{1.70}{2} = \frac{2x}{2}$$
$$0.85 = x$$

The cost of each bagel was $0.85.

Check

$$6x + 9.90 = 8x + 8.20$$
$$6(0.85) + 9.90 \stackrel{?}{=} 8(0.85) + 8.20$$
$$5.10 + 9.90 \stackrel{?}{=} 6.80 + 8.20$$
$$15 \stackrel{?}{=} 15 \checkmark$$

Pacing: Traditional 1 day
Block $\frac{1}{2}$ day

Objective: Students combine like terms in an expression.

 Hands-On Lab
In *Hands-On Lab Activities*

 Online Edition
Tutorial Videos

 Countdown to Testing Week 24

Power Presentations
with PowerPoint®

Warm Up
Simplify.
1. $9 + 13 - 5 + 3$ 20
2. $16 - 8 + 4 - 1$ 11
3. $6 + 9 - 10 + 3$ 8
4. $17 + 8 - 20 - 2$ 3

Problem of the Day
Ray and Katrina are wandering through the wildlife preserve. They observe and count a total of 15 wild turkeys and deer and a total of 46 legs. How many of each did they see? **7 turkeys, 8 deer**

Also available on transparency

 **Math Fact**

From 1939 to 1970, there were more than 30 volumes of mathematics published under the name Nicolas Bourbaki. In fact, there was no such person. The name was used by a group of mathematicians.

State Resources

 **go.hrw.com**
State Resources Online
KEYWORD: MT7 Resources

11-1 Simplifying Algebraic Expressions

Learn to combine like terms in an expression.

Vocabulary
term
like term
equivalent expression
simplify

Roosevelt High School holds an Academic Challenge each year. Local high school teams compete in four subject areas: math, English, history, and science. Students from each grade level have rated their strongest subject.

3 M	3 E	2 H	1 S
5 M	1 E	4 H	2 S
2 M	3 E	1 H	2 S
1 M	2 E	1 H	3 S
11 Math	9 English	8 History	8 Science

9 Freshmen
12 Sophomores
8 Juniors
7 Seniors

Students from different grades who chose the same subject are similar to *like terms* in an expression. **Terms** in an expression are separated by plus or minus signs.

$$7x + 5 - 3y + 2x$$

Helpful Hint
Constants such as 4, 0.75, and 11 are like terms because none of them have a variable.

Like terms, such as $7x$ and $2x$ in the expression above, can be grouped together because they have the same variable raised to the same power. Often, like terms have different coefficients. When you combine like terms, you change the way an expression looks but not the value of the expression. **Equivalent expressions** have the same value for all values of the variables.

EXAMPLE 1 Combining Like Terms to Simplify

Combine like terms.

A $(7x) + (2x)$ *Identify like terms.*
   $9x$ *Combine coefficients: $7 + 2 = 9$.*

B $(5m) - (2m) + 8 - (3m) + 6$ *Identify like terms.*
   $0m + 14$ *Combine coefficients.*
   14 *Simplify.*

---

1 Introduce
Alternate Opener

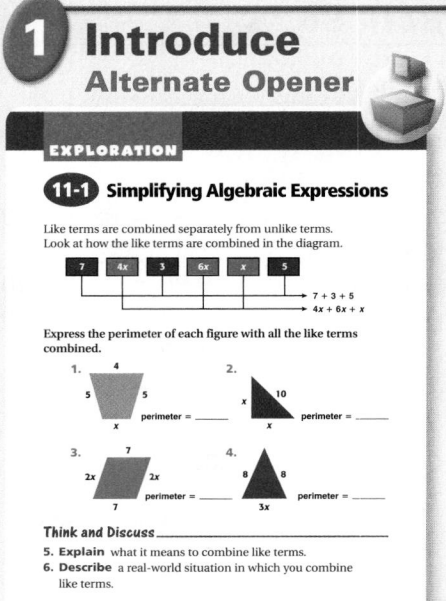

EXPLORATION

11-1 Simplifying Algebraic Expressions

Like terms are combined separately from unlike terms. Look at how the like terms are combined in the diagram.

| 7 | 4x | 3 | 6x | x | 5 |

7 + 3 + 5
4x + 6x + x

Express the perimeter of each figure with all the like terms combined.

Think and Discuss
5. **Explain** what it means to combine like terms.
6. **Describe** a real-world situation in which you combine like terms.

Motivate
Ask students if they have ever heard the phrase, "You are trying to compare apples to oranges." Have them tell you what they think it means. Explain that apples and oranges cannot be compared because they are unlike objects.

ENGLISH LANGUAGE LEARNERS

Explorations and answers are provided in *Alternate Openers: Explorations Transparencies.*

EXAMPLE 2 Combining Like Terms in Two-Variable Expressions

Combine like terms.

A $7a + 4a + 3b + 5$

$\boxed{7a} + \boxed{4a} + \bigcirc{3b} + \bigcirc{5}$ *Identify like terms.*

$11a + 3b + 5$ *Combine coefficients: $7 + 4 = 11$.*

B $k + 3n - 2n + 4k$

$\boxed{1k} + \bigcirc{3n} - \bigcirc{2n} + \boxed{4k}$ *Identify like terms; the coefficient of k is 1 because $1k = k$.*

$5k + n$ *Combine coefficients.*

C $3f - 9g + 15$

$\boxed{3f} - \bigcirc{9g} + \bigcirc{15}$ *No like terms*

To **simplify** an expression, perform all possible operations, including combining like terms.

EXAMPLE 3 Using the Distributive Property to Simplify

Remember!

The Distributive Property states that $a(b + c) = ab + ac$ for all real numbers a, b, and c. For example, $2(3 + 5) = 2(3) + 2(5)$.

Simplify $6(y + 8) - 5y$.

$6(y + 8) - 5y$

$6(y) + 6(8) - 5y$ *Distributive Property*

$6y + 48 - 5y$ *Multiply.*

$1y + 48$ *Combine coefficients: $6 - 5 = 1$.*

$y + 48$ *$1y = y$*

EXAMPLE 4 Combining Like Terms to Solve Algebraic Equations

Solve $9x - x = 136$.

$9x - x = 136$ *Identify like terms. The coefficient of x is 1.*

$8x = 136$ *Combine coefficients: $9 - 1 = 8$.*

$\dfrac{8x}{8} = \dfrac{136}{8}$ *Divide both sides by 8.*

$x = 17$ *Simplify.*

Think and Discuss

1. **Describe** the first step in simplifying the expression $2 + 8(3y + 5) - y$.

2. **Tell** how many sets of like terms are in the expression in Example 1B. What are they?

Power Presentations with PowerPoint®

 Additional Examples

Example 1
Combine like terms.
A. $14a - 5a$ $9a$
B. $7y + 8 - 3y - 1 + y$ $5y + 7$

Example 2
Combine like terms.
A. $9x + 3y - 2x + 5$ $7x + 3y + 5$
B. $5t + 7p - 3p - 2t$ $3t + 4p$
C. $4m + 9n - 2$ no like terms

Example 3
Simplify $6(5 + n) - 2n$. $30 + 4n$

Example 4
Solve $x + 3x = 48$. $x = 12$

Also available on transparency

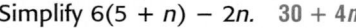

Possible Answers to Think and Discuss

1. Use the Distributive Property to simplify $8(3y + 5)$ to $24y + 40$.

2. There are two sets of like terms: $5m$, $2m$, and $3m$; and 8 and 6.

---

2 Teach

Guided Instruction

In this lesson, students learn to combine like terms in an expression. Make sure students understand that all constants are like terms and that terms with variables are like terms only if they have the same variable raised to the same power. Point out that unlike terms remain separate in a simplified expression.

Teaching Tip

Visual Students may use one of the following methods to be sure they have included all terms:

• color-coded underlining
• drawing circles, squares, or triangles
• lightly crossing out terms

Reaching All Learners
Through Concrete Manipulatives

Provide students with cut-out shapes like the following: squares labeled with x's, circles labeled with y's, and triangles labeled with 1's. Use the same shapes but different colors for subtracted expressions (e.g., "minus x"). Have students use the cut-outs to simplify expressions, such as $2x + 1 + 3y + 5 + 4x$ $(6x + 3y + 6)$ and $5x + 6y - 3 - 2x - 3y$ $(3x + 3y - 3)$. Remind students that a pair of cut-outs having the same shape but different colors equals zero.

3 Close

Summarize

Show students the expression $2a + 5b + 5 - a + 3$. Ask students how many terms are in the expression, and to identify the like terms. Ask them to simplify the expression by combining the like terms. Remind students that simplifying like terms is another important step in simplifying expressions and solving equations.

5; $2a$ and a, 5 and 3; $a + 5b + 8$

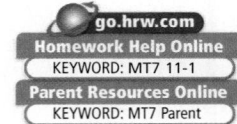

go.hrw.com
Homework Help Online
KEYWORD: MT7 11-1
Parent Resources Online
KEYWORD: MT7 Parent

Assignment Guide

If you finished Example **1** assign:
Average 1–6, 19–27, 52, 58–65
Advanced 19–27, 52, 55, 56, 58–65

If you finished Example **2** assign:
Average 1–12, 19–33, 52, 58–65
Advanced 19–33, 52, 53, 55, 56, 58–65

If you finished Example **3** assign:
Average 1–15, 19–39, 47–49, 52, 58–65
Advanced 19–39, 46–49, 52, 53, 55, 56, 58–65

If you finished Example **4** assign:
Average 1–45, 47–52, 58–65
Advanced 19–65

Homework Quick Check

Quickly check key concepts.
Exercises: 24, 30, 38, 44, 50, 52

Math Background

When you combine like terms that have a variable, you are using the Distributive Property.

$5x + 3x = (5 + 3)x = 8x$

$ba + ca = (b + c)a$

So when you simplify expressions like $2(y + 9) + 3y$, you are actually using the Distributive Property twice.

$$2(y + 9) + 3y = 2(y) + 2(9) + 3y$$
$$= 2y + 18 + 3y$$
$$= 2y + 3y + 18$$
$$= (2 + 3)y + 18$$
$$= 5y + 18$$

State Resources

go.hrw.com
State Resources Online
KEYWORD: MT7 Resources

GUIDED PRACTICE

See Example **1** Combine like terms.

1. $9x - 4x$ $5x$
2. $2z + 5 + 3z$ $5z + 5$
3. $6f + 3 - 4f + 5 + 10f$ $12f + 8$
4. $9g + 8g$ $17g$
5. $7p - 9 - p$ $6p - 9$
6. $3x + 5 - x + 3 + 4x$ $6x + 8$

See Example **2**
7. $6x + 4y - x + 4y$ $5x + 8y$
8. $4x + 5y - y + 3x$ $7x + 4y$
9. $5x + 3y + 4x - 2y$ $9x + y$
10. $6p + 3p + 7z - 3z$ $9p + 4z$
11. $7g + 5h - 12$ $7g + 5h - 12$
12. $3h + 4m + 7h - 4m$ $10h$

See Example **3** Simplify.
13. $4(r + 3) - 3r$ $r + 12$
14. $7(3 + x) + 2x$ $9x + 21$
15. $7(t + 8) - 5t$ $2t + 56$

See Example **4** Solve.
16. $6n - 4n = 68$ $n = 34$
17. $y + 5y = 90$ $y = 85$
18. $5p - 2p = 51$ $p = 17$

INDEPENDENT PRACTICE

See Example **1** Combine like terms.
19. $7y + 6y$ $13y$
20. $4z - 5 - 2z$ $2z - 5$
21. $3a + 6 - 2a + 9 + 5a$ $6a + 15$
22. $5z - z$ $4z$
23. $9x + 3 - 4x$ $5x + 3$
24. $9b + 6 - 3b - 3$ $6b + 3$
25. $14p - 5p$ $9p$
26. $7a + 8 - 3a$ $4a + 8$
27. $3x + 9 + 3x - 4 + 7x$ $13x + 5$

See Example **2**
28. $3z + 4z + b - 5$ $7z + b - 5$
29. $5a + a + 4z - 3z$ $6a + z$
30. $9x + 8y + 2x - 8 - 4y$ $11x + 4y - 8$
31. $6x + 2 + 3x + 6q$ $9x + 6q + 2$
32. $7d - d + 3e + 12$ $6d + 3e + 12$
33. $16a + 7c + 5 - 7a + c$ $9a + 8c + 5$

See Example **3** Simplify.
34. $5(y + 2) - y$ $4y + 10$
35. $2(3y - 7) + 6y$ $12y - 14$
36. $3(x + 6) + 8x$ $11x + 18$
37. $3(4y + 5) + 8$ $12y + 23$
38. $6(2x - 8) - 9x$ $3x + 48$
39. $4(4x - 4) + 3x$ $19x - 16$

See Example **4** Solve.
40. $7x - x = 72$ $x = 12$
41. $9p - 4p = 30$ $p = 6$
42. $p + 3p = 16$ $p = 4$
43. $3y + 5y = 64$ $y = 8$
44. $a + 6a = 98$ $a = 14$
45. $8x - 3x = 60$ $x = 12$

PRACTICE AND PROBLEM SOLVING

Extra Practice
See page 802.

46. **Hobbies** Charlie has x state quarters. Ty has 3 more quarters than Charlie has. Vinnie has 2 times as many quarters as Ty has. Write and simplify an expression to show how many state quarters they have in all. $4x + 9$

47. **Geometry** A rectangle has length $5x$ and width x. Write and simplify an expression for the perimeter of the rectangle. $2(5x + x); 12x$

Simplify. $42k + 8\ell + 14$
48. $6(4\ell + 7k) - 16\ell + 14$
49. $5d + 7 + 4d - 2d - 6$ $7d + 1$

Solve.

50. $13(g + 2) = 78$ $g = 4$

51. $2(3x - 7) = 76$ $x = 15$

Write and simplify an expression for each situation.

52. Business A promoter charges \$7 for each adult ticket, plus an additional \$2 per ticket for tax and handling. What is the total cost of x tickets?
$7x + 2x = 9x$

53. Sports Use the information below to find how many medals of each kind were won by the four countries in the 2004 Summer Olympics.
$49g + 53s + 44b$

United States	Great Britain	Brazil	Lithuania
35 Gold	9 Gold	4 Gold	1 Gold
39 Silver	9 Silver	3 Silver	2 Silver
29 Bronze	12 Bronze	3 Bronze	0 Bronze

54. Business A homeowner ordered 14 square yards of carpet for part of the first floor of a new house and 12 square yards of carpet for the basement. The total cost of the order was \$832 before taxes. Write and solve an equation to find the price of each square yard of carpet before taxes.
$14x + 12x = 832$; $x = 32$; \$32

55. What's the Error? A student said that $3x + 4y$ can be simplified to $7xy$ by combining like terms. What error did the student make?

56. Write About It Write an expression that can be simplified by combining like terms. Then write an expression that cannot be simplified, and explain why it is already in simplest form.

57. Challenge Simplify and solve $3(5x + 4 - 2x) + 5(3x - 3) = 45$.
$24x - 3 = 45$; $x = 2$

55. Possible answer: The expression $3x + 4y$ does not have any like terms and cannot be simplified further.

56. Possible answer: The expression $4x + 2x$ can be simplified to $6x$ by combining like terms. The expression $4x + 2y$ cannot be simplified because there are no like terms.

TEST PREP and Spiral Review

58. Multiple Choice Terrance bought 3 markers. His sister bought 5 markers. Terrance and his sister spent a total of \$16 on the markers. What was the price of each marker?

(A) \$16   (B) \$8   (C) \$4   (D) \$2

59. Gridded Response Simplify $3(2x + 7) + 10x$. What is the coefficient of x?   16

Give the quadrant of each point. (Lesson 3-2)

60. (6, 8) Quadrant I   **61.** (4, −3) Quadrant IV   **62.** (−9, 2) Quadrant II

Find each percent increase or decrease to the nearest percent. (Lesson 6-5)

63. from \$125 to \$160
28% increase

64. from \$241 to \$190
21% decrease

65. from \$21.95 to \$34.50
57% increase

ONGOING ASSESSMENT
and INTERVENTION

Diagnose *Before* the Lesson
11-1 Warm Up, TE p. 584

Monitor *During* the Lesson
11-1 Know-It Notebook
11-1 Questioning Strategies

Assess *After* the Lesson
11-1 Lesson Quiz, TE p. 587

TEST PREP DOCTOR + For Exercise 58, encourage students to read the problem and examine the answers carefully. If students select **A**, they did not realize that they need to divide the total by the number of markers. If they add to find the total number of markers and divide the cost by the number of markers, they will choose **D** as the correct answer.

Journal

Refer students to the Academic Challenge example at the start of the lesson. Have students write about other real-world examples that can be modeled by like terms. Other examples may include pitchers on different baseball teams or coins that a group of friends have.

Power Presentations
with PowerPoint®

11-1 Lesson Quiz

Combine like terms.

1. $3x + 4 + 2x$ $5x + 4$

2. $13k + 6 - 8m + 9 + k$
$14k - 8m + 15$

Simplify.

3. $4(3x + 6) - 7x$ $5x + 24$

4. $6(x + 5) + 3x$ $9x + 30$

Solve.

5. $6y + y = 42$ $y = 6$

6. The Accounting Department ordered 15 boxes of pens. The Marketing Department ordered 9 boxes of pens. If the total cost of the combined order was \$72, what is the price of each box?   \$3

Also available on transparency

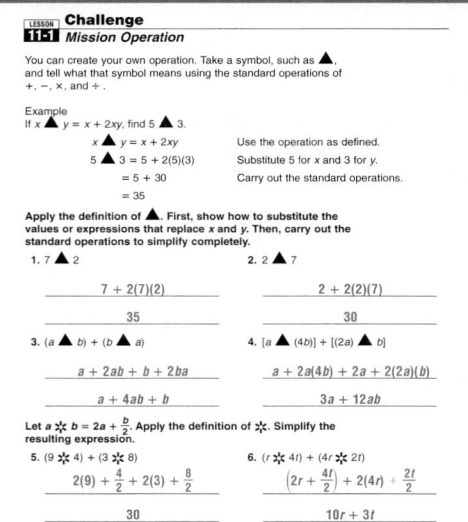

CHALLENGE 11-1

LESSON 11-1 Challenge
Mission Operation

You can create your own operation. Take a symbol, such as ▲, and tell what that symbol means using the standard operations of $+$, $-$, $\times$, and $\div$.

Example
If $x \blacktriangle y = x + 2xy$, find $5 \blacktriangle 3$.

$x \blacktriangle y = x + 2xy$ Use the operation as defined.
$5 \blacktriangle 3 = 5 + 2(5)(3)$ Substitute 5 for x and 3 for y.
$= 5 + 30$ Carry out the standard operations.
$= 35$

Apply the definition of ▲. First, show how to substitute the values or expressions that replace x and y. Then, carry out the standard operations to simplify completely.

1. $7 \blacktriangle 2$
$7 + 2(7)(2)$
35

2. $2 \blacktriangle 7$
$2 + 2(2)(7)$
30

3. $(a \blacktriangle b) + (b \blacktriangle a)$
$a + 2ab + b + 2ba$
$a + 4ab + b$

4. $[a \blacktriangle (4b)] + [(2a) \blacktriangle b]$
$a + 2a(4b) + 2a + 2(2a)(b)$
$3a + 12ab$

Let $a \mathbin{\text{✼}} b = 2a + \frac{b}{2}$. Apply the definition of ✼. Simplify the resulting expression.

5. $(9 \mathbin{\text{✼}} 4) + (3 \mathbin{\text{✼}} 8)$
$2(9) + \frac{4}{2} + 2(3) + \frac{8}{2}$
30

6. $(r \mathbin{\text{✼}} 4t) + (4r \mathbin{\text{✼}} 2t)$
$\left(2r + \frac{4t}{2}\right) + 2(4r) + \frac{2t}{2}$
$10r + 3t$

PROBLEM SOLVING 11-1

LESSON 11-1 Problem Solving
Simplifying Algebraic Expressions

Write the correct answer.

1. An item costs x dollars. The tax rate is 5% of the cost of the item, or $0.05x$. Write and simplify an expression to find the total cost of the item with tax.
$x + 0.05x$; $1.05x$

2. A sweater costs d dollars at regular price. The sweater is reduced by 20%, or $0.2d$. Write and simplify an expression to find the cost of the sweater before tax.
$d - 0.2d$; $0.8d$

3. Consecutive integers are integers that differ by one. You can represent consecutive integers as x, $x + 1$, $x + 2$ and so on. Write an equation and solve to find three consecutive integers whose sum is 33.
10, 11, 12

4. Consecutive even integers can be represented by x, $x + 2$, $x + 4$ and so on. Write an equation and solve to find three consecutive even integers whose sum is 54.
16, 18, 20

Choose the letter for the best answer.

5. In Super Bowl XXXV, the total number of points scored was 41. The winning team outscored the losing team by 27 points. What was the final score of the game?
A 33 to 8
(B) 34 to 7
C 22 to 2
D 18 to 6

6. A high school basketball court is 34 feet longer than it is wide. If the perimeter of the court is 268, what are the dimensions of the court?
F 234 ft by 34 ft
G 67 ft by 67 ft
H 70 ft by 36 ft
(J) 84 ft by 50 ft

7. Julia ordered 2 hamburgers and Steven ordered 3 hamburgers. If their total bill before tax was \$7.50, how much did each hamburger cost?
(A) \$1.50
B \$1.25
C \$1.15
D \$1.02

8. On three tests, a student scored a total of 258 points. If the student improved his performance on each test by 5 points, what was the score on each test?
(F) 81, 86, 91
G 80, 85, 90
H 75, 80, 85
J 70, 75, 80

Objective: Students solve multi-step equations.

 Technology Lab
In Technology Lab Activities

 Online Edition
Tutorial Videos

 Countdown to Testing Week 24

Power Presentations
with PowerPoint®

Warm Up
Solve.
1. $3x = 102$ $x = 34$
2. $\frac{y}{15} = 15$ $y = 225$
3. $z - 100 = 21$ $z = 121$
4. $1.1 + 5w = 98.6$ $w = 19.5$

Problem of the Day
Ana has twice as much money as Ben, and Ben has three times as much as Clio. Together they have $160. How much does each person have? Ana, $96; Ben, $48; Clio, $16

Also available on transparency

Math Humor
What did one math book say to the other? Leave me alone—I've got my own problems!

State Resources

 **go.hrw.com**
State Resources Online
KEYWORD: MT7 Resources

11-2 Solving Multi-Step Equations

Learn to solve multi-step equations.

To solve a multi-step equation, you may have to simplify the equation first by combining like terms.

EXAMPLE 1   **Solving Equations That Contain Like Terms**

Solve.

$$3x + 5 + 6x - 7 = 25$$

$3x + 5 + 6x - 7 =$	25	
$9x - 2 =$	25	*Combine like terms.*
$\underline{+2 \qquad +2}$		*Add 2 to both sides.*
$9x =$	27	
$\dfrac{9x}{9} = \dfrac{27}{9}$		*Divide both sides by 9.*
$x =$	3	

Check

$$3x + 5 + 6x - 7 = 25$$
$$3(3) + 5 + 6(3) - 7 \stackrel{?}{=} 25 \qquad \textit{Substitute 3 for x.}$$
$$9 + 5 + 18 - 7 \stackrel{?}{=} 25 \qquad \textit{Multiply.}$$
$$25 \stackrel{?}{=} 25 ✔$$

If an equation contains fractions, it may help to multiply both sides of the equation by the least common denominator (LCD) to clear the fractions before you isolate the variable.

EXAMPLE 2   **Solving Equations That Contain Fractions**

Solve.

A $\dfrac{3y}{7} + \dfrac{5}{7} = -\dfrac{1}{7}$

$$7\left(\frac{3y}{7} + \frac{5}{7}\right) = 7\left(-\frac{1}{7}\right) \qquad \textit{Multiply both sides by 7.}$$

$$\overset{1}{7}\left(\frac{3y}{\overset{}{7}}\right) + \overset{1}{7}\left(\frac{5}{\overset{}{7}}\right) = \overset{1}{7}\left(-\frac{1}{\overset{}{7}}\right) \qquad \textit{Distributive Property}$$

$$3y + 5 = -1$$
$$\underline{\qquad -5 \quad -5} \qquad \textit{Subtract 5 from both sides.}$$
$$3y = -6$$
$$\frac{3y}{3} = \frac{-6}{3} \qquad \textit{Divide both sides by 3.}$$
$$y = -2$$

---

1 Introduce

Alternate Opener

EXPLORATION

11-2 Solving Multi-Step Equations

José and Rebecca want to rent sports equipment at the city park. José wants to rent inline skates, and Rebecca wants to rent a motor scooter.

| Inline skates
$3.00, plus $1.50 per hour | Motor scooter
$10.00, plus $2.75 per hour |

Individual costs (c) $c = 3 + 1.50x$ and $c = 10 + 2.75x$

Combined cost (C) $C = 3 + 1.50x + 10 + 2.75x$

Use the equation $C = 3 + 1.50x + 10 + 2.75x$ to answer each question.
1. How much would José and Rebecca pay for 2 hours' rental?
2. How much would José and Rebecca pay for 3 hours' rental?
3. If their total rental cost is $38.50, for how many hours did they use the equipment?

Think and Discuss
4. **Explain** how to combine like terms in the equation $C = 3 + 1.50x + 10 + 2.75x$.
5. **Discuss** whether it makes sense to combine like terms when each item of sports equipment is rented for a different number of hours.

Motivate

Show students an equation, such as $2x + 1 = 7$, and represent the equation using algebra tiles. You may want to use the overhead algebra tiles provided in the Teacher's Manipulatives Kit.

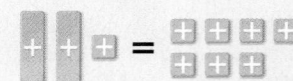

Ask students to solve the equation, always keeping it balanced. $x = 3$

Explorations and answers are provided in *Alternate Openers: Explorations Transparencies.*

Remember!

The least common denominator (LCD) is the smallest number that each of the denominators will divide into.

Solve.

B $\frac{4p}{9} + \frac{p}{3} - \frac{1}{2} = \frac{11}{6}$

The LCD is 18.

$$18\left(\frac{4p}{9} + \frac{p}{3} - \frac{1}{2}\right) = 18\left(\frac{11}{6}\right)$$ *Multiply both sides by 18.*

$$\overset{2}{18}\left(\frac{4p}{\overset{}{9}}\right) + \overset{6}{18}\left(\frac{p}{\overset{}{3}}\right) - \overset{9}{18}\left(\frac{1}{\overset{}{2}}\right) = \overset{3}{18}\left(\frac{11}{\overset{}{6}}\right)$$ *Distributive Property*

$$8p + 6p - 9 = 33$$

$$14p - 9 = 33$$ *Combine like terms.*

$$\underline{+\,9 \quad +\,9}$$ *Add 9 to both sides.*

$$14p \quad = 42$$

$$\frac{14p}{14} = \frac{42}{14}$$ *Divide both sides by 14.*

$$p = 3$$

EXAMPLE 3   *Travel Application*

On the first day of her vacation, Carly rode her motorcycle m miles in 4 hours. On the second day, she rode twice as far in 7 hours. If her average speed for the two days was 62.18 mi/h, how far did she ride on the first day? Round your answer to the nearest tenth of a mile.

Carly's average speed is her combined speeds for the two days divided by 2.

$$\frac{\text{Day 1 speed} \; + \; \text{Day 2 speed}}{2} = \text{average speed}$$

$$\frac{\frac{m}{4} + \frac{2m}{7}}{2} = 62.18$$ *Substitute $\frac{m}{4}$ for Day 1 speed and $\frac{2m}{7}$ for Day 2 speed.*

$$\overset{1}{\cancel{2}}\left(\frac{\frac{m}{4} + \frac{2m}{7}}{\cancel{2}^{\,1}}\right) = 2(62.18)$$ *Multiply both sides by 2.*

$$28\left(\frac{m}{4} + \frac{2m}{7}\right) = 28(124.36)$$ *Multiply both sides by the LCD 28.*

$$7m + 8m = 3482.08$$ *Simplify.*

$$\frac{15m}{15} = \frac{3482.08}{15}$$ *Combine like terms. Divide both sides by 15.*

$$m \approx 232.14$$

Carly rode approximately 232.1 miles on the first day.

Think and Discuss

1. List the steps required to solve $3x - 4 + 2x = 7$.

2. Tell how you would clear the fractions in $\frac{3x}{4} - \frac{2x}{3} + \frac{5}{8} = 1$.

Possible answers to Think and Discuss

1. Combine like terms ($3x$ and $2x$). Add 4 to both sides. Divide both sides by 5. The answer is $x = \frac{11}{5}$.

2. Multiply both sides by 24.

---

2 Teach

Guided Instruction

In this lesson, students learn to solve multi-step equations. Remind students that they can use the Commutative Property of Addition to rearrange terms; this will be helpful for combining like terms. Before discussing the equations that have fractions, review how to find the LCD of a set of fractions.

Teaching Tip   **Inclusion** Remind students to check each solution by substituting it into the *original equation*. This will help them catch mistakes that were made early in the solution process.

 Reaching All Learners
Through Cooperative Learning

Have students work in pairs to play equation tic-tac-toe (Teaching Tool). Have students cut out the equations and mix them up. Then have each student randomly draw one equation and solve it. Repeat until one student in each group gets three across, down, or diagonally.

3 Close

Summarize

Ask students to write a reasonable first step to solve each of the following equations.

1. $\frac{2a}{5} - \frac{4a}{5} = 3$

2. $\frac{x}{6} - \frac{4x}{3} = \frac{x}{9}$

3. $3t - 1 + t - 5t = 1$

Possible answers:

1. Multiply both sides of the equation by 5.

2. Multiply both sides of the equation by 18.

3. Combine like terms.

Assignment Guide

If you finished Example **1** assign:
Average 1–6, 12–17, 26, 27, 41–47
Advanced 12–17, 26, 27, 29, 31, 32, 35, 39, 41–47

If you finished Example **2** assign:
Average 1–10, 12–23, 25–28, 41–47
Advanced 12–23, 28–32, 35, 38–47

If you finished Example **3** assign:
Average 1–28, 33, 34, 41–47
Advanced 12–24, 28–47

Homework Quick Check

Quickly check key concepts.
Exercises: 12, 18, 24, 28

Math Background

Multi-step equations can often be solved using different methods. Clearing fractions is one method of solving equations that contain fractions, but multiplying by the LCD is not the required first step for solving these types of equations. For example, the equation in Example 2A can be solved as follows:

$$\frac{3y}{7} + \frac{5}{7} = -\frac{1}{7}$$
$$\frac{3y}{7} + \frac{5}{7} - \frac{5}{7} = -\frac{1}{7} - \frac{5}{7}$$
$$(7)\frac{3y}{7} = -\frac{6}{7}(7)$$
$$3y = -6$$
$$y = -2$$

State Resources

go.hrw.com
State Resources Online
KEYWORD: MT7 Resources

11-2 Exercises

go.hrw.com
Homework Help Online
KEYWORD: MT7 11-2
Parent Resources Online
KEYWORD: MT7 Parent

GUIDED PRACTICE

See Example **1**   Solve.

1. $7d - 12 + 2d + 3 = 18$ $d = 3$

2. $3y + 4y + 6 = 20$ $y = 2$

3. $10e - 2e - 9 = 39$ $e = 6$

4. $4c - 5 + 14c = 67$ $c = 4$

5. $5h + 6 + 8h - 3h = 76$ $h = 7$

6. $7x - 2x + 3 = -32$ $x = -7$

See Example **2**   7. $\frac{4x}{13} + \frac{3}{13} = -\frac{1}{13}$ $x = -1$

8. $\frac{y}{2} - \frac{5y}{6} + \frac{1}{3} = \frac{1}{2}$ $y = -\frac{1}{2}$

9. $\frac{4}{5} - \frac{2p}{5} = \frac{6}{5}$ $p = -1$

10. $\frac{15}{8}z + \frac{1}{4} = 4$ $z = 2$

See Example **3**   11. **Travel** Barry's family drove 843 mi to see his grandparents. On the first day, they drove 483 mi. On the second day, how long did it take to reach Barry's grandparents' house if they averaged 60 mi/h?   **6 hours**

INDEPENDENT PRACTICE

See Example **1**   Solve.

12. $5n + 3n - n + 5 = 26$ $n = 3$

13. $-81 = 7k + 19 + 3k$ $k = -10$

14. $36 - 4c - 3c = 22$ $c = 2$

15. $12 + 5w - 4w = 15$ $w = 3$

16. $37 = 15a - 5a - 3$ $a = 4$

17. $30 = 7y - 35 + 6y$ $y = 5$

See Example **2**   18. $\frac{3}{8} + \frac{p}{8} = 3\frac{1}{8}$ $p = 22$

19. $\frac{7h}{12} - \frac{4h}{12} = \frac{18}{12}$ $h = 6$

20. $\frac{4g}{16} - \frac{3}{8} - \frac{g}{16} = \frac{3}{16}$ $g = 3$

21. $\frac{7}{12} = \frac{3m}{6} - \frac{m}{3} + \frac{1}{4}$ $m = 2$

22. $\frac{4}{13} = -\frac{2b}{13} + \frac{6b}{26}$ $b = 4$

23. $\frac{3x}{4} - \frac{21x}{32} = -1\frac{1}{8}$ $x = -12$

See Example **3**   24. **Recreation** Lydia rode 243 miles in a three-day bike trip. On the first day, Lydia rode 67 miles. On the second day, she rode 92 miles. How many miles per hour did she average on the third day if she rode for 7 hours?   **12 mi/h**

PRACTICE AND PROBLEM SOLVING

Extra Practice
See page 802.

Solve and check.

25. $\frac{5n}{8} - \frac{1}{2} = \frac{3}{4}$ $n = 2$

26. $4n + 11 - 7n = -13$ $n = 8$

27. $7b - 2 - 12b = 63$ $b = -13$

28. $\frac{x}{2} + \frac{2}{3} = \frac{5}{6}$ $x = \frac{1}{3}$

29. $-2x - 7 + 3x = 10$ $x = 17$

30. $\frac{3r}{4} - \frac{4}{5} = \frac{7}{10}$ $r = 2$

31. $4y - 3 - 9y = 32$ $y = -7$

32. $7n - 10 - 9n = -13$ $n = \frac{3}{2}$

33. **Finance** Alessia is paid 1.4 times her normal hourly rate for each hour she works over 30 hours in a week. Last week she worked 35 hours and earned $436.60. What is her normal hourly rate?   **$11.80 per hour**

RETEACH 11-2

Reteach
11-2 Solving Multi-Step Equations

To combine like terms, add (or subtract) coefficients.

$2m + 3m = (2 + 3)m = 5m$ $x - 3x = (1 - 3)x = -2x$

To solve an equation that contains like terms, first combine the like terms.

$2m + 3m = 35 - 25$ **Check:** Substitute into the original.

$5m = 10$ Combine like terms. $2m + 3m = 35 - 25$
$\frac{5m}{5} = \frac{10}{5}$ Divide by 5. $2(2) + 3(2) \stackrel{?}{=} 35 - 25$
$m = 2$ $4 + 6 \stackrel{?}{=} 10$
$10 = 10$ ✔

$x + 6 - 3x + 5 = 13$ **Check:** $x + 6 - 3x + 5 = 13$
$-2x + 11 = 13$ Combine like terms. $-1 + 6 - 3(-1) + 5 \stackrel{?}{=} 13$
$\underline{-11 \quad -11}$ Subtract 11. $-1 + 6 + 3 + 5 \stackrel{?}{=} 13$
$-2x = 2$ $-1 + 14 \stackrel{?}{=} 13$
$\frac{-2x}{-2} = \frac{2}{-2}$ Divide by -2. $13 = 13$ ✔
$x = -1$

Complete to solve and check each equation.

1. $4z - 7z = -20 - 1$ **Check:** $4z - 7z = -20 - 1$
$\underline{-3}z = \underline{-21}$ Combine like terms. $4(\underline{7}) - 7(\underline{7}) \stackrel{?}{=} -20 - 1$
$\frac{-3z}{-3} = \frac{-21}{-3}$ Divide. $\underline{28} - \underline{49} \stackrel{?}{=} -21$
$z = \underline{7}$ $-21 = -21$ ✔

2. $t + 1 - 4t + 8 = 21$ **Check:** $t + 1 - 4t + 8 = 21$
$\underline{-3}t + \underline{9} = \underline{21}$ Combine like terms. $\underline{-4} + 1 - 4(\underline{-4}) + 8 \stackrel{?}{=} \underline{21}$
$\underline{-9 \quad -9}$ Subtract. $\underline{-4} + 1 + \underline{16} + 8 \stackrel{?}{=} 21$
$\underline{-3}t = \underline{12}$ $\underline{-4} + \underline{25} \stackrel{?}{=} 21$
$\frac{-3t}{-3} = \frac{12}{-3}$ Divide. $21 = 21$ ✔
$t = \underline{-4}$

PRACTICE 11-2

Practice B
11-2 Solving Multi-Step Equations

Solve.

1. $2x + 5x + 4 = 25$ $x = 3$

2. $9 + 3y - 2y = 14$ $y = 5$

3. $16 = 4w + 2w - 2$ $w = 3$

4. $26 = 3b - 2 - 7b$ $b = -7$

5. $31 + 4t - t = 40$ $t = 3$

6. $14 - 2x + 4x = 20$ $x = 3$

7. $\frac{5m}{8} - \frac{6}{8} + \frac{3m}{8} = \frac{2}{8}$ $m = 1$

8. $-4\frac{2}{3} = \frac{2n}{3} + \frac{1}{3} + \frac{n}{3}$ $n = -5$

9. $7a + 16 - 3a = -4$ $a = -5$

10. $\frac{x}{2} + 1 + \frac{3x}{4} = -9$ $x = -8$

11. $7m + 3 - 4m = -9$ $m = -4$

12. $\frac{2x}{5} + 3 - \frac{4x}{5} = \frac{1}{5}$ $x = 7$

13. $\frac{7k}{8} - \frac{3}{4} - \frac{5k}{16} = \frac{3}{8}$ $k = 2$

14. $6y + 9 - 4y = -3$ $y = -6$

15. $\frac{5a}{6} - \frac{7}{12} + \frac{3a}{4} = -2\frac{1}{6}$ $a = -1$

16. The measure of an angle is 28° greater than its complement. Find the measure of each angle.

   angle = 59°; complement = 31°

17. The measure of an angle is 21° more than twice its supplement. Find the measure of each angle.

   angle = 127°; supplement = 53°

18. The perimeter of the triangle is 126 units. Find the measure of each side.

   $AC = 25$ units; $BC = 50$ units;
   $AB = 51$ units

19. The base angles of an isosceles triangle are congruent. If the measure of each of the base angles is twice the measure of the third angle, find the measure of all three angles.

   36°; 72°; 72°

Sports

You can estimate the weight in pounds of a fish that is L inches long and G inches around at the thickest part by using the formula $W \approx \frac{LG^2}{800}$.

34. Geometry The obtuse angle of an isosceles triangle measures 120°. Write and solve an equation to find the measure of the base angles.
$180 = 120 + 2x; \ x = 30°$

35. Critical Thinking The sum of two consecutive numbers is 63. What are the two numbers? Explain your solution.

36. Sports The average weight of the top 5 fish at a fishing tournament was 12.3 pounds. The weights of the second-, third-, fourth-, and fifth-place fish are shown in the table. What was the weight of the heaviest fish?
14.6 lb

Winning Entries	
Caught by	**Weight (lb)**
Wayne S.	
Carla P.	12.8
Deb N.	12.6
Virgil W.	11.8
Brian B.	9.7

37. Physical Science The formula $K = \frac{F - 32}{1.8} + 273$ is used to convert a temperature from degrees Fahrenheit to kelvins. Water boils at 373 kelvins. Use the formula to find the boiling point of water in degrees Fahrenheit. **212°F**

38. What's the Error? A student's work in solving an equation is shown. What error has the student made, and what is the correct answer?

$$\frac{1}{5}x + 5x = 13$$
$$x + 5x = 65$$
$$6x = 65$$
$$x = \frac{65}{6}$$

Possible answer: The student forgot to multiply $5x$ times 5 to get $25x$. The correct answer is $x = 2.5$.

39. Write About It Compare the steps used to solve the following.

$$4x - 8 = 16 \qquad \qquad 4(x - 2) = 16$$

40. Challenge List the steps you would use to solve the following equation.

$$\frac{4\left(\frac{1}{3}x - \frac{1}{4}\right) + \frac{4}{3}x}{3} + 1 = 6$$

TEST PREP and Spiral Review

41. Multiple Choice Solve $4k - 7 + 3 + 5k = 59$.

Ⓐ $k = 6$ Ⓑ $k = 6.6$ Ⓒ $k = 7$ Ⓓ $k = 11.8$

42. Gridded Response Antonio's first four test grades were 85, 92, 91, and 80. What must he score on the next test to have an 88 test average? **92**

Find the volume of each figure to the nearest tenth. Use 3.14 for π. (Lesson 8-5) **1200.1 ft³**

43. cube with side length 3 in. **27 in³** **44.** cylinder with $d = 14$ ft and $h = 7.8$ ft

Combine like terms. (Lesson 11-1)

45. $9m + 8 - 4m + 7 - 5m$ **46.** $6t + 3k - 15$ **47.** $5a + 3 - b + 1$
15 **$6t + 3k - 15$** **$5a - b + 4$**

CHALLENGE 11-2

Challenge
11-2 Use the Power of Algebra!

An equation may be used to solve a problem involving angle measure in a triangle.

In isosceles triangle ABC, the measure of vertex angle C is 30° more than the measure of each base angle. Find the measure of each angle of the triangle.

Let x = the number of degrees in m∠A.
Then x = the number of degrees in m∠B.
And $x + 30$ = the number of degrees in m∠C.

The sum of the measures of the angles of a triangle is 180°.

$x + x + x + 30 = 180$
$3x + 30 = 180$ Combine like terms.
$\underline{-30 \quad -30}$ Subtract 30.
$3x = 150$
$\frac{3x}{3} = \frac{150}{3}$ Divide by 3.
$x = 50$ ← m base ∠
$x + 30 = 80$ ← m vertex ∠

Check:
m base ∠ = 50°
m base ∠ = 50°
m vertex ∠ = 80°
180° ✓

So, the measure of each base angle is 50° and the measure of the vertex angle is 80°.

Write and solve an equation to find the measures of the angles of each triangle.

1. The measure of each of the base angles of an isosceles triangle is 9° less than 4 times the measure of the vertex angle.
$x + 4x - 9 + 4x - 9 = 180$
$9x - 18 = 180$
$\underline{+ 18 \quad + 18}$
$9x = 198$
$\frac{9x}{9} = \frac{198}{9}$
$x = 22$
$4x - 9 = 79$
measure of each base angle = $\underline{79°}$
measure of vertex angle = $\underline{22°}$

2. The measure of the vertex angle of an isosceles triangle is one-fourth that of a base angle.
$x + x + \frac{x}{4} = 180$
$4 \cdot x + 4 \cdot x + 4 \cdot \frac{x}{4} = 4 \cdot 180$
$9x = 720$
$\frac{9x}{9} = \frac{720}{9}$
$x = 80$
$\frac{x}{4} = 20$
measure of each base angle = $\underline{80°}$
measure of vertex angle = $\underline{20°}$

PROBLEM SOLVING 11-2

Problem Solving
11-2 Solving Multi-Step Equations

A taxi company charges $2.25 for the first mile and then $0.20 per mile for each mile after the first, or $F = \$2.25 + \$0.20(m - 1)$ where F is the fare and m is the number of miles.

1. If Juan's taxi fare was $6.05, how many miles did he travel in the taxi?
20 miles

2. If Juan's taxi fare was $7.65, how many miles did he travel in the taxi?
28 miles

A new car loses 20% of its original value when you buy it and then 8% of its original value per year, or $D = 0.8V - 0.08Vy$ where D is the value after y years with an original value V.

3. If a vehicle that was valued at $20,000 new is now worth $9,600, how old is the car?
4 years

4. A 6-year old vehicle is worth $12,000. What was the original value of the car?
$37,500

The equation used to estimate typing speed is $S = \frac{1}{5}(w - 10e)$, where S is the accurate typing speed, w is the number of words typed in 5 minutes and e is the number of errors. Choose the letter of the best answer.

5. Jane can type 55 words per minute (wpm). In 5 minutes, she types 285 words. How many errors would you expect her to make?
Ⓐ 0 Ⓒ 2
Ⓑ 1 Ⓓ 5

6. If Alex types 300 words in 5 minutes with 5 errors, what is his typing speed?
Ⓕ 48 wpm Ⓗ 59 wpm
Ⓖ 50 wpm Ⓙ 60 wpm

7. Johanna receives a report that says her typing speed is 65 words per minute. She knows that she made 4 errors in the 5-minute test. How many words did she type in 5 minutes?
Ⓐ 285 Ⓒ 365
Ⓑ 329 Ⓓ 1825

8. Cecil can type 35 words per minute. In 5 minutes, she types 255 words. How many errors would you expect her to make?
Ⓕ 2 Ⓗ 6
Ⓖ 4 Ⓙ 8

ONGOING ASSESSMENT and INTERVENTION

Diagnose Before the Lesson
11-2 Warm Up, TE p. 588

Monitor During the Lesson
11-2 Know-It Notebook
11-2 Questioning Strategies

Assess After the Lesson
11-2 Lesson Quiz, TE p. 591

Answers

35. 31 and 32; Possible answer: Let n equal one number and $n + 1$ be the next consecutive number. Then $n + (n + 1) = 63$, so $2n + 1 = 63$, or $n = 31$.

39. Possible answer: To solve the first equation, I would add 8 to both sides and then divide both sides by 4 to find that $x = 6$. To solve the second equation, I would divide both sides by 4 and then add 2 to both sides to find that $x = 6$. Alternately, I could distribute the 4 in the second equation and follow the steps for solving the first equation.

40. See p. A15.

TEST PREP DOCTOR For Exercise 41, have students identify the constants and terms with k as like terms. If students select **D** as the answer, they did not combine like terms correctly.

Journal

Ask students to compare the process of solving a multi-step equation with the process of checking the solution.

Power Presentations with PowerPoint®

11-2 Lesson Quiz

Solve.
1. $6x + 3x - x + 9 = 33$ $x = 3$
2. $29 = 5x + 21 + 3x$ $x = -3.75$
3. $\frac{5}{8} + \frac{x}{8} = \frac{33}{8}$ $x = 28$
4. $\frac{6x}{7} - \frac{2x}{21} = \frac{25}{21}$ $x = 1\frac{9}{16}$
5. Linda is paid double her normal hourly rate for each hour she works over 40 hours in a week. Last week she worked 52 hours and earned $544. What is her hourly rate? **$8.50**

Also available on transparency

Organizer
Use with Lesson 11-3

Pacing:
Traditional $\frac{1}{2}$ day
Block $\frac{1}{4}$ day

Objective: Use algebra tiles to model equations with variables on both sides.

Materials: Algebra tiles

Online Edition
Algebra Tiles

Resources

Hands-On Lab Activities
Lab 11-3 Recording Sheet

Teach
Discuss
Have students use guess-and-check to solve $2x - 4 = -6 + 3x$. **2** Then have them use algebra tiles to model and solve the equation.

Close
Key Concept
Using algebra tiles to model an equation helps you to see how the terms can be grouped.

Assessment
1. Model and solve the equation
$x - 5 = -x + 3$.

  $x = 4$

Answers to *Think and Discuss*
See p. A15.

Hands-On LAB 11-3
Model Equations with Variables on Both Sides
Use with Lesson 11-3

KEY
Algebra tiles
$\blacksquare = x$ $\blacksquare = -x$
$\blacksquare = 1$ $\blacksquare = -1$

REMEMBER
It will not change the value of an expression if you add or remove zero.
$\blacksquare + \blacksquare = 0$ $\blacksquare + \blacksquare = 0$

To solve an equation with the same variable on both sides of the equal sign, you must first add or subtract to eliminate the variable term from one side of the equation.

Activity
1 Model and solve the equation $-x + 2 = 2x - 4$.

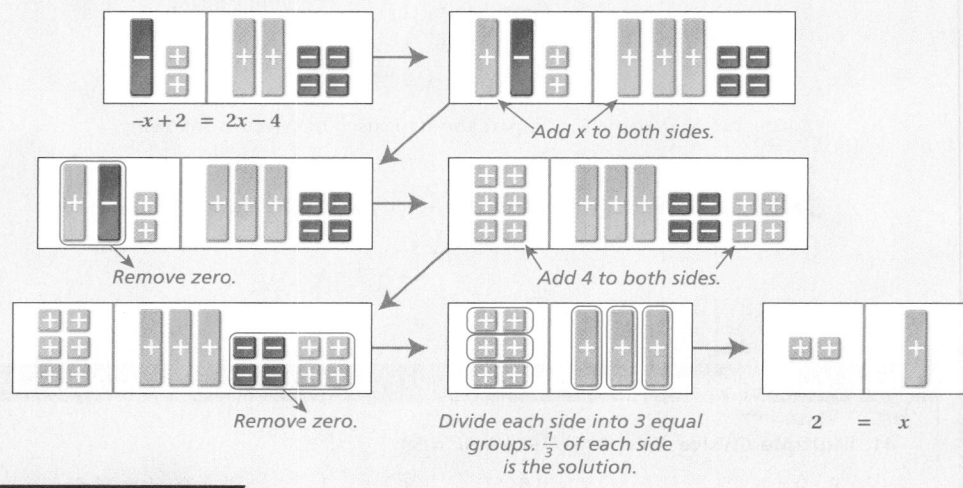

$-x + 2 = 2x - 4$
Add x to both sides.
Remove zero.
Add 4 to both sides.
Remove zero.
Divide each side into 3 equal groups. $\frac{1}{3}$ of each side is the solution.
$2 = x$

Think and Discuss
1. How would you check the solution to $-x + 2 = 2x - 4$ using algebra tiles?

2. Why must you isolate the variable terms by having them on only one side of the equation?

Try This
Model and solve each equation. Check students' models.
1. $x + 3 = -x - 3$ $x = -3$
2. $3x = -3x + 18$ $x = 3$
3. $6 - 3x = -4x + 8$ $x = 2$
4. $3x + 3x + 2 = x + 17$ $x = 3$

Kathy Henry
El Paso, Texas

Teacher to Teacher
Students can work in pairs to do this lab. After working through the lab in pairs, each pair can create their own problems and exchange with other pairs. Have students describe their steps using the words "zero pairs" and "inverse operations."

11-3 Solving Equations with Variables on Both Sides

Some problems produce equations that have variables on both sides of the equal sign. For example, Happy Paws, a dog-sitting service, charges a flat fee of $19.00 plus $1.50 per hour. A rival service, Woof Watchers, charges a flat fee of $15.00 plus $2.75 per hour. Find the number of hours for which the cost will be the same for both dog-sitting services.

Expression for Happy Paws **$19.00 + 1.5h$**   **$15.00 + 2.75h$** *Expression for Woof Watchers*

$$19.00 + 1.5h = 15.00 + 2.75h$$

The variable h in these expressions represents the number of hours. The two expressions are equal when the cost is the same.

Solving an equation with variables on both sides is similar to solving an equation with a variable on only one side. You can add or subtract a term containing a variable on both sides of an equation.

EXAMPLE 1 Solving Equations with Variables on Both Sides

Solve.

Helpful Hint

Check your solution by substituting the value back into the original equation. For example,
$2(3) + 3 = 3(3)$
or $9 = 9$.

A $2a + 3 = 3a$

$$
\begin{array}{rl}
2a + 3 = & 3a \\
\underline{-2a \qquad -2a} & \quad \text{Subtract 2a from both sides.} \\
3 = & a
\end{array}
$$

B $3v - 8 = 7 + 8v$

$$
\begin{array}{rl}
3v - 8 = & 7 + 8v \\
\underline{-3v \qquad\quad -3v} & \quad \text{Subtract 3v from both sides.} \\
-8 = & 7 + 5v \\
\underline{-7 \quad -7} & \quad \text{Subtract 7 from both sides.} \\
-15 = 5v \\
\dfrac{-15}{5} = \dfrac{5v}{5} & \quad \text{Divide both sides by 5.} \\
-3 = v
\end{array}
$$

---

1 Introduce

Alternate Opener

Motivate

Show students the following algebra tiles modeling an equation.

Ask them to write the equation that is represented by the tiles. $3x + 1 = 2x + 5$ Tell them that they will learn how to solve this kind of equation in the new lesson.

Explorations and answers are provided in *Alternate Openers: Explorations Transparencies.*

Power Presentations
with PowerPoint®

Additional Examples

Example 1
Solve.
A. $4x + 6 = x$ $x = -2$
B. $9b - 6 = 5b + 18$ $b = 6$
C. $9w + 3 = 9w + 7$ no solution

Example 2
Solve.
A. $10z - 15 - 4z = 8 - 2z - 15$
$z = 1$
B. $\frac{y}{5} + \frac{3y}{5} - \frac{3}{4} = y - \frac{7}{10}$
$y = -\frac{1}{4}$

Also available on transparency

Helpful Hint
If the variables in an equation are eliminated and the resulting statement is false, the equation has no solution.

Solve.

C $g + 7 = g - 3$
$g + 7 = g - 3$
$\underline{-g -g}$ *Subtract g from both sides.*
$7 \neq -3$

There is no solution. There is no number that can be substituted for the variable g to make the equation true.

To solve multi-step equations with variables on both sides, first combine like terms and clear fractions. Then add or subtract variable terms to both sides so that the variable occurs on only one side of the equation. Then use properties of equality to isolate the variable.

EXAMPLE 2   Solving Multi-Step Equations with Variables on Both Sides

Solve.

A $2c + 4 - 3c = -9 + c + 5$
$2c + 4 - 3c = -9 + c + 5$
$-c + 4 = -4 + c$ *Combine like terms.*
$\underline{+c +c}$ *Add c to both sides.*
$4 = -4 + 2c$
$\underline{+4 +4}$ *Add 4 to both sides.*
$8 = 2c$
$\frac{8}{2} = \frac{2c}{2}$ *Divide both sides by 2.*
$4 = c$

B $\frac{2w}{3} - \frac{5w}{6} + \frac{1}{4} = w + \frac{11}{9}$
$\frac{2w}{3} - \frac{5w}{6} + \frac{1}{4} = w + \frac{11}{9}$
$36\left(\frac{2w}{3} - \frac{5w}{6} + \frac{1}{4}\right) = 36\left(w + \frac{11}{9}\right)$ *Multiply by LCD, 36.*
$^{12}\cancel{36}\left(\frac{2w}{\cancel{3}^1}\right) - {}^6\cancel{36}\left(\frac{5w}{\cancel{6}^1}\right) + {}^9\cancel{36}\left(\frac{1}{\cancel{4}}\right) = 36(w) + {}^4\cancel{36}\left(\frac{11}{\cancel{9}^1}\right)$ *Distributive Property*
$24w - 30w + 9 = 36w + 44$
$-6w + 9 = 36w + 44$ *Combine like terms.*
$\underline{+6w +6w }$ *Add 6w to both sides.*
$9 = 42w + 44$
$\underline{-44 -44 }$ *Subtract 44 from both sides.*
$-35 = 42w$
$\frac{-35}{42} = \frac{42w}{42}$ *Divide both sides by 42.*
$-\frac{5}{6} = w$

---

2 Teach

Guided Instruction

In this lesson, students solve equations with variables on both sides of the equal sign. In Example 1, explain that the variable appears on both sides of the equal sign. They want to add or subtract a variable term so that the variable appears on one side only. The paragraph just before Example 2 is an excellent summary of the process of solving multi-step equations. (See also Summarize.) Note that in Example 2A, there are like terms to combine, and in Example 2B, there are fractions to clear.

Reaching All Learners
Through Kinesthetic Experience

Give each student a card containing an expression like $2x + 4$ or $3x - 7$ (Teaching Tool). Have the students form two concentric circles, each with an equal number of students, so that they are facing each other. Have each pair of students facing each other form an equation by setting their expressions equal to each other, and then have them solve that equation. After each pair agrees on their solution, have the circles rotate two students to the right and continue the process.

EXAMPLE 3 *Business Application*

Happy Paws charges a flat fee of $19.00 plus $1.50 per hour to keep a dog during the day. A rival service, Woof Watchers, charges a flat fee of $15.00 plus $2.75 per hour. Find the number of hours for which you would pay the same total fee to both services.

$$19.00 + 1.5h = \quad 15.00 + 2.75h \quad \text{\textit{Let h represent the number of hours.}}$$
$$\underline{\quad -1.5h =} \quad \underline{\quad -1.5h} \quad \text{\textit{Subtract 1.5h from both sides.}}$$
$$19.00 \quad = \quad 15.00 + 1.25h$$
$$\underline{-15.00} \quad \underline{\quad -15.00} \quad \text{\textit{Subtract 15.00 from both sides.}}$$
$$4.00 \quad = \quad 1.25h$$
$$\frac{4.00}{1.25} = \frac{1.25h}{1.25} \quad \text{\textit{Divide both sides by 1.25}}$$
$$3.2 = h$$

The two services cost the same when used for 3.2 hours.

EXAMPLE 4 *Multi-Step Application*

Elaine runs the same distance every day. On Mondays, Fridays, and Saturdays, she runs 3 laps on the track and then runs 5 more miles. On Tuesdays and Thursdays, she runs 4 laps on the track and then runs 2.5 more miles. On Wednesdays, she just runs laps. How many laps does she run on Wednesdays?

First solve for the distance around the track.

$$3x + 5 = \quad 4x + 2.5 \quad \text{\textit{Let x represent the distance around the track.}}$$
$$\underline{-3x} \quad = \underline{-3x} \quad \text{\textit{Subtract 3x from both sides.}}$$
$$5 = \quad x + 2.5$$
$$\underline{-2.5} \quad \underline{-2.5} \quad \text{\textit{Subtract 2.5 from both sides.}}$$
$$2.5 = \quad x \quad \text{\textit{The track is 2.5 miles around.}}$$

Now find the total distance Elaine runs each day.

$$3x + 5 \quad \text{\textit{Choose one of the original expressions.}}$$
$$3(2.5) + 5 = 12.5 \quad \text{\textit{Elaine runs 12.5 miles each day.}}$$

Find the number of laps Elaine runs on Wednesdays.

$$2.5n = 12.5 \quad \text{\textit{Let n represent the number of 2.5-mile laps.}}$$
$$\frac{2.5n}{2.5} = \frac{12.5}{2.5} \quad \text{\textit{Divide both sides by 2.5.}}$$
$$n = 5$$

Elaine runs 5 laps on Wednesdays.

> **Caution!** //////
> The value of the variable is not necessarily the answer to the question.

1. Possible answer: $3x + 4 = 3x - 2$; if the variables in an equation are eliminated and the resulting statement is false, then the equation has no solution.

Think and Discuss

1. Explain how you would solve the equation $3x + 4 - 2x = 6x + 2 - 5x + 2$. What do you think the solution means?

Possible answers to Think and Discuss

1. Combine like terms: $x + 4 = x + 4$, subtract x from both sides: $4 = 4$; since this statement is always true, any number you substitute for x is a solution.

③ Close

Summarize

Review the process for solving multi-step equations to this point:

- Clear fractions.
- Combine like terms.
- Get the variable on only one side of the equation.
- Undo addition and subtraction.
- Undo multiplication and division.

You may want to create a poster of these steps to display in the classroom.

11-3 Exercises

go.hrw.com
Homework Help Online
KEYWORD: MT7 11-3
Parent Resources Online
KEYWORD: MT7 Parent

Assignment Guide

If you finished Example **1** assign:
Average 1–6, 13–18, 25, 26, 39–47
Advanced 13–18, 25, 26, 39–47

If you finished Example **2** assign:
Average 1–10, 13–22, 25–28, 39–47
Advanced 13–22, 27–32, 36, 38–47

If you finished Example **3** assign:
Average 1–11, 13–23, 25–28, 35, 39–47
Advanced 13–23, 27–33, 35, 36, 38–47

If you finished Example **4** assign:
Average 1–28, 34, 35, 39–47
Advanced 13–47

Homework Quick Check

Quickly check key concepts.
Exercises: 18, 22, 23, 24, 28

Math Background

Solving an equation is a process of writing equivalent equations.

$$x + 2 = x + 3$$
$$\underline{-x \qquad -x}$$
$$2 = \qquad 3$$

← Equivalent equations

The first and third lines are equivalent equations, so if $2 = 3$ is false, then $x + 2 = x + 3$ is also false. This means that $x + 2 = x + 3$ has no solutions.

GUIDED PRACTICE

See Example **1** Solve.

1. $6x + 3 = x + 8$ $x = 1$
2. $5a - 5 = 7 + 2a$ $a = 4$
3. $2x + 7 = 10x - 9$ $x = 2$
4. $4y - 2 = 6y + 6$ $y = -4$
5. $13x + 15 = 11x - 25$ $x = -20$
6. $5t - 5 = 5t + 7$ no solution

See Example **2**
7. $5x - 2 + 3x = 17 + 12x - 23$ $x = 1$
8. $\frac{3n}{4} + \frac{n}{12} - 6 = 5 + 2n - 18$ $n = 6$
9. $\frac{5}{12} + \frac{11d}{12} - 3 = 3d + 7 - 4d$ $d = 5$
10. $4(x - 5) + 2 = x + 3$ $x = 7$

See Example **3**
11. A long-distance phone company charges $0.027 per minute and a $2 monthly fee. Another long-distance phone company charges $0.035 per minute with no monthly fee. Find the number of minutes for which the charges for both companies would be the same. **2.5 min**

See Example **4**
12. June has a set of folding chairs. If she arranges the chairs in 5 rows, she has 2 chairs left over. If she arranges them in 3 rows of the same length, she has 14 left over. How many chairs does she have? **32 chairs**

INDEPENDENT PRACTICE

See Example **1** Solve.

13. $3n + 16 = 7n$ $n = 4$
14. $8x - 3 = 11 - 6x$ $x = 1$
15. $5n + 3 = 14 - 6n$ $n = 1$
16. $3(2x + 11) = 6x + 33$ all real numbers
17. $6x + 3 = x + 8$ $x = 1$
18. $7y - 8 = 5y + 4$ $y = 6$

See Example **2**
19. $\frac{3p}{8} + \frac{7p}{16} - \frac{3}{4} = \frac{1}{4} + \frac{p}{16} + \frac{1}{2}$ $p = 2$
20. $4(x - 5) - 5 = 6x + 7.4 - 4x$ $x = 16.2$
21. $\frac{1}{2}(2n + 6) = 5n - 12 - n$ $n = 5$
22. $\frac{a}{26} - 5.5 + 2a = \frac{9}{13} + \frac{20a}{13} + \frac{4}{13}$ $a = 13$

See Example **3**
23. Al's Rentals charges $25 per hour to rent a Windsurfer™ and a wet suit. Wendy's charges $20 per hour plus $15 extra for a wet suit. Find the number of hours for which the total charges for both would be the same. **3 h**

See Example **4**
24. Sean and Laura have the same number of action figures in their collections. Sean has 6 complete sets plus 2 individual figures, and Laura has 3 complete sets plus 20 individual figures. How many figures are in a complete set? **6 figures**

PRACTICE AND PROBLEM SOLVING

Extra Practice
See page 802.

Solve and check.
25. $3y - 1 = 13 - 4y$ $y = 2$
26. $4n + 8 = 9n - 7$ $n = 3$
27. $5n + 20n = 5(n + 20)$ $n = 5$
28. $3(4x - 2) = 12x$ no solution
29. $100(x - 3) = 450 - 50x$ $x = 5$
30. $2p - 12 = 12 - 2p$ $p = 6$

RETEACH 11-3

Reteach
11-3 Solving Equations with Variables on Both Sides

If there are variable terms on both sides of an equation, first collect them on one side. Do this by adding or subtracting.

If possible, collect the variable terms on the side where the on coefficient will be positive.

$$\begin{array}{l} 5x = 2x + 12 \\ \underline{-2x \; -2x} \end{array}$$ To collect on left side, subtract 2x.

Check: Substitute into the original equation.
$5x = 2x + 12$
$5(4) \stackrel{?}{=} 2(4) + 12$
$20 \stackrel{?}{=} 8 + 12$
$20 = 20$ ✓

$3x = 12$
$\frac{3x}{3} = \frac{12}{3}$ Divide by 3.
$x = 4$

$$\begin{array}{l} -6z + 28 = 9z - 2 \\ \underline{+6z \qquad +6z} \end{array}$$ To collect on right side, add 6z.

$28 = 15z - 2$
$\underline{+2 \qquad +2}$ Add 2.
$30 = 15z$
$\frac{30}{15} = \frac{15z}{15}$ Divide by 15.
$2 = z$

Check: $-6z + 28 = 9z - 2$
$-6(2) + 28 \stackrel{?}{=} 9(2) - 2$
$-12 + 28 \stackrel{?}{=} 18 - 2$
$16 = 16$ ✓

Complete to solve and check each equation.

1. $9m = 4m - 25$ To collect on left, subtract.
$\underline{-4m \; -4m}$
$5m = -25$
$\frac{5m}{5} = \frac{-25}{5}$ Divide.
$m = \underline{-5}$

Check: $9m = 4m - 25$
$9(\underline{-5}) \stackrel{?}{=} 4(\underline{-5}) - 25$
$\underline{-45} \stackrel{?}{=} \underline{-20} - 25$
$-45 = -45$ ✓

2. $3h - 7 = 5h + 1$ To collect on right, subtract.
$\underline{-3h \quad -3h}$
$-7 = \underline{2}h + 1$
$\underline{-1 \qquad -1}$ Subtract.
$\underline{-8} = \underline{2}h$
$\frac{-8}{2} = \frac{2h}{2}$ Divide.
$-4 = h$

Check: $3h - 7 = 5h + 1$
$3(\underline{-4}) - 7 \stackrel{?}{=} 5(\underline{-4}) + 1$
$\underline{-12} - 7 \stackrel{?}{=} \underline{-20} + 1$
$-19 = -19$ ✓

PRACTICE 11-3

Practice B
11-3 Solving Equations with Variables on Both Sides

Solve.

1. $7x - 11 = -19 + 3x$ $x = -2$
2. $11a + 9 = 4a + 30$ $a = 3$
3. $4t + 14 = \frac{6t}{5} + 7$ $t = -2.5$
4. $19c + 31 = 26c - 74$ $c = 15$
5. $\frac{3y}{8} - 9 = 13 + \frac{y}{8}$ $y = 88$
6. $\frac{3k}{5} + 44 = \frac{12k}{25} + 8$ $k = -300$
7. $10a - 37 = 6a + 51$ $a = 22$
8. $5w + 9.9 = 4.8 + 8w$ $w = 1.7$
9. $15 - x = 2(x + 3)$ $x = 3$
10. $15y + 14 = 2(5y + 6)$ $y = -0.4$
11. $14 - \frac{w}{8} = \frac{3w}{4} - 21$ $w = 40$
12. $\frac{1}{2}(6x - 4) = 4x - 9$ $x = 7$
13. $4(3d - 2) = 8d - 5$ $d = \frac{3}{4}$
14. $\frac{x}{3} + 11 = \frac{x}{2} - 3$ $y = 84$
15. $\frac{2x - 9}{3} = 8 - 3x$ $x = 3$

16. Forty-eight decreased by a number is the same as the difference of four times the number and seven. Find the number. **11**

17. The square and the equilateral triangle at the right have the same perimeter. Find the length of the sides of the triangle. **12 units**

Physical Science

Sodium and chlorine bond together to form sodium chloride, or salt. The atomic structure of sodium chloride causes it to form cubes.

Both figures have the same perimeter. Find each perimeter.

31.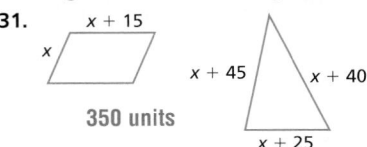

350 units

32.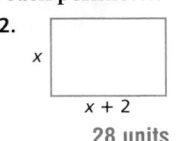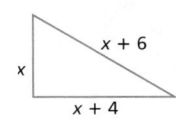

28 units

33. Find two consecutive whole numbers such that $\frac{3}{4}$ of the first number is 5 more than $\frac{1}{2}$ the second number. (*Hint:* Let n represent the first number. Then $n + 1$ represents the next consecutive whole number.) **22, 23**

34. **Physical Science** An atom of chlorine (Cl) has 6 more protons than an atom of sodium (Na). The atomic number of chlorine is 5 less than twice the atomic number of sodium. The atomic number of an element is equal to the number of protons per atom.

   a. How many protons are in an atom of chlorine? **17**

   b. What is the atomic number of sodium? **11**

36. Possible answer: Substitute different values for t. The equation is true for any value of t that is a real number, so the solution is all real numbers.

35. **Business** George and Aaron work for different car dealerships. George earns a monthly salary of $2500 plus a 5% commission on his sales. Aaron earns a monthly salary of $3000 plus a 3% commission on his sales. How much must both sell to earn the same amount in a month? **$25,000**

36. **Choose a Strategy** Solve the following equation for t. How can you determine the solution once you have combined like terms?

$$3(t - 24) = 7t - 4(t + 18)$$

37. **Write About It** Two cars are traveling in the same direction. The first car is going 45 mi/h, and the second car is going 60 mi/h. The first car left 2 hours before the second car. Explain how you could solve an equation to find how long it will take the second car to catch up to the first car.

38. **Challenge** Solve the equation $\frac{x+2}{8} = \frac{6}{7} + \frac{x-1}{2}$. $x = -\frac{2}{7}$

TEST PREP and Spiral Review

39. **Multiple Choice** Find three consecutive integers so that the sum of the first two integers is 10 more than the third integer.

  Ⓐ $-7, -6, -5$ Ⓑ $4, 5, 6$ Ⓒ $11, 12, 13$ Ⓓ $35, 36, 37$

40. **Multiple Choice** Solve $6w - 15 = 9w$.

  Ⓕ $w = 3$ Ⓖ $w = 0$ Ⓗ $w = -1$ Ⓙ $w = -5$

Write each number in scientific notation. (Lesson 4-4)

41. 0.00000064 42. $7,390,000,000$ 43. -0.0000016 44. $-4,100,000$
  6.4×10^{-7} 7.39×10^{9} -1.6×10^{-6} -4.1×10^{6}

Solve. (Lesson 11-2)

45. $6x - 3 + x = 4$ $x = 1$ 46. $32 = 13 - 4x + 21$ $x = 0.5$ 47. $5x + 14 - 2x = 23$ $x = 3$

CHALLENGE 11-3

LESSON 11-3 Challenge
A Handy Tool!

A **lever** is a bar that can turn about a fixed point called the **fulcrum**.

The ancient Greek mathematician Archimedes knew the power of the *lever principle*. He has been quoted as saying "Give me a place to stand and I will move the Earth."

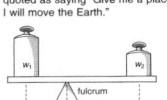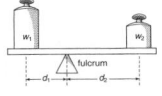

The Lever Principle

A weight w_1 is placed on one arm of a lever at a distance d_1 from the fulcrum. A second weight w_2 is placed on the other arm at a distance d_2 from the fulcrum.

$$w_1 \cdot d_1 = w_2 \cdot d_2$$

This equation may be used to solve a problem involving the lever principle.

A 14-foot plank is used as a lever with a 120-lb box on one end and a 90-lb box on the other end. If the boxes balance one another, how far from the fulcrum is each box?

Let $x = $ 120-lb box's distance from fulcrum.
Then $14 - x = $ 90-lb box's distance from fulcrum.

$w_1 \cdot d_1 = w_2 \cdot d_2$
$120 \cdot x = 90 \cdot (14 - x)$
$120x = 1260 - 90x$
$\underline{+90x \qquad\quad +90x}$
$210x = 1260$
$\frac{210x}{210} = \frac{1260}{210}$
$x = 6$ ft ← 120-lb box's distance from the fulcrum.
$14 - x = 8$ ft ← 90-lb box's distance from the fulcrum.

Write and solve an equation.

A 21-ft plank is used as a lever with a 108-lb barrel on one end and an 81-lb barrel on the other end. If the barrels balance one another, how far from the fulcrum is the 108-lb barrel?

The 108-lb barrel is ___9 ft___ from the fulcrum.

Let $x = $ 108-lb barrel's distance from fulcrum.
Then $21 - x = $ 81-lb barrel's distance.

$108x = 81(21 - x)$
$108x = 1701 - 81x$
$189x = 1701$
$x = 9$

PROBLEM SOLVING 11-3

LESSON 11-3 Problem Solving
Solving Equations with Variables on Both Sides

The chart below describes three long-distance calling plans. Round to the nearest minute. Write the correct answer.

1. For what number of minutes will plan A and plan B cost the same?

   250 minutes

Long-Distance Plans		
Plan	Monthly Access Fee	Charge per minute
A	$3.95	$0.08
B	$8.95	$0.06
C	$0	$0.10

2. For what number of minutes per month will plan B and plan C cost the same?

   224 minutes

3. For what number of minutes will plan A and plan C cost the same?

   198 minutes

Choose the letter for the best answer.

4. Carpet Plus installs carpet for $100 plus $8 per square yard of carpet. Carpet World charges $75 for installation and $10 per square yard of carpet. Find the number of square yards of carpet for which the cost including carpet and installation is the same.

  A 1.4 yd²   Ⓒ 12.5 yd²
  B 9.7 yd²   D 87.5 yd²

5. One shuttle service charges $10 for pickup and $0.10 per mile. The other shuttle service has no pickup fee but charges $0.35 per mile. Find the number of miles for which the cost of the shuttle services is the same.

  F 2.5 miles
  G 22 miles
  Ⓗ 40 miles
  J 48 miles

6. Joshua can purchase tile at one store for $0.99 per tile, but he will have to rent a tile saw for $25. At another store he can buy tile for $1.50 per tile and borrow a tile saw for free. Find the number of tiles for which the cost is the same. Round to the nearest tile.

  A 10 tiles   C 25 tiles
  B 13 tiles   Ⓓ 49 tiles

7. One plumber charges a fee of $75 per service call plus $15 per hour. Another plumber has no flat fee, but charges $25 per hour. Find the number of hours for which the cost of the two plumbers is the same.

  F 2.1 hours   Ⓗ 7.5 hours
  G 7 hours   J 7.8 hours

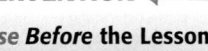
Answers

37. Possible answer: When the second car catches the first, the cars will have traveled an equal distance. Since distance can be calculated by multiplying rate and time, the situation can be represented by the equation $45(t + 2) = 60t$. Solving for t gives $t = 6$. The second car will catch the first car after 6 hours.

 **TEST PREP DOCTOR** Students may need to be reminded how to represent consecutive integers algebraically for Exercise 39. Show them that if they let x be the first integer, then the next two integers are $x + 1$ and $x + 2$. After they set up an equation and solve, encourage them to check their answer. Ask them to make sure the first two integers add up to ten more than the third.

 Journal

Have students describe the kind of equation that has no solution.

Power Presentations
with PowerPoint®

✓ **11-3 Lesson Quiz**

Solve.

1. $4x + 16 = 2x$ $x = -8$
2. $8x - 3 = 15 + 5x$ $x = 6$
3. $2(3x + 11) = 6x + 4$ no solution
4. $\frac{1}{4}x = \frac{1}{2}x - 9$ $x = 36$
5. An apple has about 30 more calories than an orange. Five oranges have about as many calories as 3 apples. How many calories are in each? An orange has 45, an apple has 75

Also available on transparency

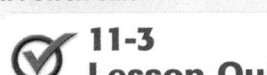

Organizer

Objective: Assess students' mastery of concepts and skills in Lessons 11-1 through 11-3.

Resources

 Assessment Resources
Section 11A Quiz

 Test & Practice Generator
 One-Stop Planner®

INTERVENTION

Resources

 Ready to Go On?
Intervention and
Enrichment Worksheets

🔘 **Ready to Go On? CD-ROM**

🪐 **Ready to Go On? Online**

my.hrw.com

Ready to Go On?

Quiz for Lessons 11-1 Through 11-3

☑ **11-1 Simplifying Algebraic Expressions**

Simplify.

1. $5x + 3x$ **8x**
2. $6p - 6 - p$ **5p − 6**
3. $2t + 3 - t + 4 + 5t$ **6t + 7**
4. $3x + 4y - x + 2y$ **2x + 6y**
5. $4n + 2m + 8n - 2m$ **12n**
6. $5b + 5c - 10$ **5b + 5c − 10**
7. $2(r + 1) - r$ **r + 2**

Solve.

8. $9y - 5y = 8$ **y = 2**
9. $7x + 2x = 45$ **x = 5**

☑ **11-2 Solving Multi-Step Equations**

Solve.

10. $2c + 6c + 8 = 32$ **c = 3**
11. $\frac{3x}{7} - \frac{2}{7} = \frac{10}{7}$ **x = 4**
12. $\frac{t}{4} + \frac{t}{3} = \frac{7}{12}$ **t = 1**
13. $\frac{4m}{3} - \frac{m}{6} = \frac{7}{2}$ **m = 3**
14. $\frac{3}{4}b - \frac{1}{5}b = 11$ **b = 20**
15. $\frac{r}{3} + 7 - \frac{r}{5} = -3$ **r = −75**
16. $30k + 88 = 163$ **k = 2.5**

17. Marlene drove 540 miles to visit a friend. She drove 3 hours and stopped for gas. She then drove 4 hours and stopped for lunch. How many more hours did she drive if her average speed for the trip was 60 miles per hour?   **2 h**

☑ **11-3 Solving Equations with Variables on Both Sides**

Solve.

18. $4x + 11 = x + 2$ **x = −3**
19. $q + 5 = 2q + 7$ **q = −2**
20. $6n + 21 = 4n + 57$ **n = 18**
21. $2m + 6 = 2m - 1$ **no solution**
22. $9w - 2w + 8 = 4w + 38$ **w = 10**
23. $-4a - 2a + 11 = 6a - 13$ **a = 2**
24. $\frac{7}{12}y - \frac{1}{4} = 2y - \frac{5}{3}$ **y = 1**

25. The rectangle and the triangle have the same perimeter. Find the perimeter of each figure.   **58 units**

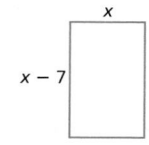
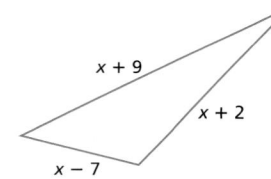

READY TO GO ON?
Diagnose and Prescribe

 **NO INTERVENE**

READY TO GO ON? Intervention, Section 11A			
Ready to Go On? Intervention	📝 **Worksheets**	💿 **CD-ROM**	🪐 **Online**
☑ Lesson 11-1	11-1 Intervention	Activity 11-1	Diagnose and Prescribe Online
☑ Lesson 11-2	11-2 Intervention	Activity 11-2	
☑ Lesson 11-3	11-3 Intervention	Activity 11-3	

 **YES ENRICH**

READY TO GO ON?
Enrichment, Section 11A

📝 **Worksheets**

 💿 **CD-ROM**

 🪐 **Online**

Focus on Problem Solving

Make a Plan
• **Write an equation**

Several steps may be needed to solve a problem. It often helps to write an equation that represents the steps.

Example:

Juan's first 3 exam scores are 85, 93, and 87. What does he need to score on his next exam to average 90 for the 4 exams?

Let x be the score on his next exam. The average of the exam scores is the sum of the 4 scores, divided by 4. This amount must equal 90.

Average of exam scores = 90

$$\frac{85 + 93 + 87 + x}{4} = 90$$

$$\frac{265 + x}{4} = 90$$

$$4\left(\frac{265 + x}{4}\right) = 4(90)$$

$$265 + x = 360$$

$$\underline{-265 \qquad -265}$$

$$x = 95$$

Juan needs a 95 on his next exam.

Read each problem and write an equation that could be used to solve it.

1. The average of two numbers is 34. The first number is three times the second number. What are the two numbers? **51 and 17**

2. Nancy spends $\frac{1}{3}$ of her monthly salary on rent, 0.1 on her car payment, $\frac{1}{12}$ on food, and 20% on other bills. She has $680 left for other expenses. What is Nancy's monthly salary? **$2400**

3. A vendor at a concert sells new and used CDs. The new CDs cost 2.5 times as much as the old CDs. If 4 used CDs and 9 new CDs cost $159, what is the price of each item? **Used CDs cost $6; new CDs cost $15.**

4. Amanda and Rick have the same amount to spend on school supplies. Amanda buys 4 notebooks and has $8.60 left. Rick buys 7 notebooks and has $7.55 left. How much does each notebook cost? **$0.35**

Solving Equations and Inequalities

One-Minute Section Planner

Lesson	Materials	MiC and Lab Resources
Lesson 11-4 Solving Inequalities by Multiplying and Dividing • Solve and graph inequalities by using multiplication and division. ☑ SAT-10 ☑ ITBS ☑ CTBS ☑ NAEP		
Lesson 11-5 Solving Two-Step Inequalities • Solve two-step inequalities and graph the solutions of an inequality on a number line. ☐ SAT-10 ☑ ITBS ☑ CTBS ☑ NAEP		***Hands-On Lab Activities*** 11-5
Lesson 11-6 Systems of Equations • Solve systems of equations. ☐ SAT-10 ☐ ITBS ☐ CTBS ☐ NAEP	Calculators	**MiC:** *Graphing Equations* pp. 38–41 **MiC:** *Algebra Rules* pp. 38–39

MK = *Manipulatives Kit*

Mathematics in Context

The units *Graphing Equations* and *Algebra Rules* from the *Mathematics in Context* © 2006 series can be used with Section 11B. See Section Planner above for suggestions for integrating *MiC* with *Holt Mathematics.*

Section Overview

Multiplication and Division Inequalities

Lesson 11-4

Why? Solving one-step inequalities prepares students for solving multi-step inequalities.

$$5x < 4$$

$$\frac{5x}{5} < \frac{4}{5}$$

$$x < \frac{4}{5}$$

$$\frac{x}{-2} \le -9$$

$$-2 \cdot \frac{x}{-2} \ge -9(-2)$$

$$x \ge 18$$

> Multipliction or division by a **negative** number reverses the inequality symbol.

Solving and Graphing Two-Step Inequalities

Lesson 11-5

Why? To solve some problems, you need to write and solve inequalities.

A T-shirt retailer must pay $120 for a design and $4 per shirt. How many T-shirts would he have to sell at $9 per shirt to make a profit?

$$R > C$$

$$9x > 120 + 4x$$

$$\underline{-4x \qquad\quad -4x}$$

$$5x > 120$$

$$\frac{5x}{5} > \frac{120}{5}$$

$$x > 24$$

> He will make a profit if his revenue R is greater than his cost C.

> The retailer would have to sell more than 24 T-shirts to make a profit.

Systems of Equations

Lesson 11-6

Why? If a problem has more than one condition to be satisfied, it may require a system of equations.

Is $(3, -2)$ a solution of the system of equations?

$$2x + y = 4$$
$$x - y = 8$$

$$
\begin{array}{cc}
2x + y = 4 & x - y = 8 \\
2(3) + (-2) \overset{?}{=} 4 & 3 - (-2) \overset{?}{=} 8 \\
6 + (-2) \overset{?}{=} 4 & 5 \ne 8\ \text{✗} \\
4 \overset{?}{=} 4\ \text{✔} &
\end{array}
$$

$(3, -2)$ is *not* a solution because it does *not* satisfy *both* equations.

Is $(4, -4)$ a solution of the system of equations?

$$2x + y = 4$$
$$x - y = 8$$

$$
\begin{array}{cc}
2x + y = 4 & x - y = 8 \\
2(4) + (-4) \overset{?}{=} 4 & 4 - (-4) \overset{?}{=} 8 \\
8 + (-4) \overset{?}{=} 4 & 8 = 8\ \text{✔} \\
4 \overset{?}{=} 4\ \text{✔} &
\end{array}
$$

$(4, -4)$ *is* a solution because it satisfies *both* equations.

Solve the system.

$$y = 2x + 3$$
$$y = x - 5$$

$$2x + 3 = x - 5$$
$$\underline{-x \qquad\quad -x}$$
$$x + 3 = -5$$
$$\underline{-3 \quad -3}$$
$$x = -8$$

Now substitute -8 for x into either original equation, and solve for y.

$$y = x - 5$$
$$y = -8 - 5$$
$$y = -13$$

The solution is $(-8, -13)$.

11-4 Organizer

Pacing: Traditional 1 day
Block $\frac{1}{2}$ day

Objective: Students solve and graph inequalities by using multiplication or division.

 Online Edition
Tutorial Videos

 Countdown to Testing Week 24

Power Presentations
with PowerPoint®

Warm Up

Solve.

1. $2x + 8 = x - 7$ $x = -15$

2. $-4(x + 3) = -5x - 2$ $x = 10$

3. $5x + x + (-11) = 25 - 3x$
$x = 4$

4. $6n + 9 - 4n = 3n$ $n = 9$

Problem of the Day

Find an integer x that makes the following three inequalities true:
$9 < x < 14$, $2x > 22$, and $2x > -13$
$x = 12$

Also available on transparency

Math Humor

What time is it when a father gives his daughter 15 cents and his son 10 cents? A quarter to two.

State Resources

_____
_____
_____
_____
_____
_____
_____
_____
_____
_____

go.hrw.com
State Resources Online
KEYWORD: MT7 Resources

11-4 Solving Inequalities by Multiplying or Dividing

Learn to solve and graph inequalities by using multiplication or division.

Laid end to end, the paper used by personal computer printers each year would circle the earth more than 800 times. To find out how many sheets of paper this is, you can solve an inequality by dividing.

The steps for solving inequalities by multiplying or dividing are the same as for solving equations, with one exception. If both sides of an inequality are multiplied or divided by a negative number, the inequality symbol must be reversed.

EXAMPLE 1 **Solving Inequalities by Multiplying or Dividing**

Solve and graph.

Ⓐ $24 > \dfrac{h}{5}$

$5 \cdot 24 > 5 \cdot \dfrac{h}{5}$ *Multiply both sides by 5.*

$120 > h$, or $h < 120$

115 116 117 118 119 120 121 122

Remember!

When graphing an inequality on a number line, an open circle means that the point is not part of the solution and a closed circle means that the point is part of the solution.

Check

According to the graph, 119 should be a solution because $119 < 120$, and 121 should not be a solution because $121 > 120$.

$24 > \dfrac{h}{5}$ $24 > \dfrac{h}{5}$

$24 \overset{?}{>} \dfrac{119}{5}$ *Substitute* $24 \overset{?}{>} \dfrac{121}{5}$ *Substitute*

$24 \overset{?}{>} 23.8$ ✔ *119 for h.* $24 \overset{?}{>} 24.2$ ✘ *121 for h.*

So 119 is a solution.   So 121 is not a solution.

Ⓑ $-7x \geq 42$

$\dfrac{-7x}{-7} \leq \dfrac{42}{-7}$ *Divide both sides by -7; $\geq$ changes to $\leq$.*

$x \leq -6$

-12 -11 -10 -9 -8 -7 -6 -5 -4

---

1 Introduce

Alternate Opener

EXPLORATION

11-4 Solving Inequalities by Multiplying or Dividing

You can discover an important property of inequalities by looking for patterns.

1. Multiply both sides of each inequality by 2. Write the resulting numbers under the original inequality as shown in **1a**. Then insert the correct inequality symbol, < or >, to make the new inequality true.

   a. $\dfrac{3}{6} > \dfrac{2}{4}$ **b.** $-4 < -1$ **c.** $2 > -3$

2. Multiply both sides of each inequality by -2. Write the resulting numbers under the original inequality as shown in **2a**. Then insert the correct inequality symbol, < or >, to make the new inequality true.

   a. $\dfrac{3}{-6} > \dfrac{2}{-4}$ **b.** $-4 < -1$ **c.** $2 > -3$

Think and Discuss

6. **Describe** any patterns you notice.
7. **Explain** what happens when you multiply both sides of an inequality by a negative number.

Motivate

ENGLISH LANGUAGE LEARNERS

Explain to students that inequalities are often used in real life to calculate the least amount or the greatest amount of a quantity. Teach students that the phrases, "more than," "less than," least," and "greatest," are often clues that they are dealing with an inequality. Remind them that to find how many sheets of paper circle the earth more than 800 times, they will use an inequality.

Explorations and answers are provided in *Alternate Openers: Explorations Transparencies.*

EXAMPLE 2 **PROBLEM SOLVING APPLICATION**

If all the sheets of paper used by personal computer printers each year were laid end to end, they would circle the earth more than 800 times. The earth's circumference is about 25,120 mi (1,591,603,200 in.), and one letter-size sheet of paper is 11 in. long. How many sheets of paper are used each year?

1 Understand the Problem

The **answer** is the number of sheets of paper used by personal computer printers in one year. **List the important information:**
- The amount of paper would circle the earth *more than* 800 times.
- Once around the earth is 1,591,603,200 in.
- One sheet of paper is 11 in. long.

Show the relationship of the information:

| the number of sheets of paper | · | the length of one sheet | > | 800 | · | the distance around the earth |

2 Make a Plan

Use the relationship to *write an inequality*. Let x represent the number of sheets of paper.

| x | · | 11 in. | > | 800 | · | 1,591,603,200 in. |

3 Solve

$11x > 800 \cdot 1,591,603,200$

$11x > 1,273,282,560,000$ *Simplify.*

$\dfrac{11x}{11} > \dfrac{1,273,282,560,000}{11}$ *Divide both sides by 11.*

$x > 115,752,960,000$

More than 115,752,960,000 sheets of paper are used by personal computer printers in one year.

4 Look Back

To circle the earth once takes $\frac{1,591,603,200}{11} = 144,691,200$ sheets of paper; to circle it 800 times would take $800 \cdot 144,691,200 = 115,752,960,000$ sheets.

Possible answers to *Think and Discuss:*

1. $<, \leq$; Since -15 is less than 15, it can be either sign that includes less than.

2. Divide both sides by -4. Reverse the inequality symbol since you are dividing by a negative number. $x \geq -6$

Think and Discuss

1. **Give** all the symbols that make $5 \cdot -3 \quad 15$ true. Explain.

2. **Explain** how you would solve the inequality $-4x \leq 24$.

Power Presentations
with PowerPoint®

Additional Examples

Example 1

Solve and graph.

A. $12 < \frac{a}{4}$ $a > 48$

43 44 45 46 47 48 49 50 51 52

B. $-9b \leq 45$ $b \geq -5$

-10 -8 -6 -4 -2 0

Example 2

A rock-collecting club needs to make at least $500. They are buying rocks for $2.50 and selling them for $4.00. What is the least number of rocks the club must sell to make their goal? 334

Also available on transparency

Possible answers to Think and Discuss

1. $<, \leq$; Since -15 is less than 15, it can be either sign that includes less than.

2. Divide both sides by -4. Reverse the inequality symbol, since you are dividing by a negative number; $x \geq 6$

---

2 Teach

Guided Instruction

In this lesson, students solve and graph inequalities by using multiplication and division. It is helpful to point out to students that solving inequalities is often similar to solving equations. Point out that if you multiply or divide by a negative number on both sides you must reverse the inequality sign.

Reaching All Learners
Through Visual Cues

Have students identify when they multiply or divide by a negative number with a highlighter in their notebook. By making a special effort to identify these instances, they will pay careful attention to when they need to reverse the inequality sign.

3 Close

Summarize

Remind students that to solve and graph inequalities using multiplication and division, they should do the following:

- Reverse the inequality when multiplying both sides of an inequality by a negative number.
- Use closed endpoints for $\leq$, $\geq$ and open endpoints for $<$ or $>$.
- Check graphs by choosing a number in the solution set of the inequality and make sure it is highlighted in the graph.

11-4 Exercises

go.hrw.com
Homework Help Online
KEYWORD: MT7 11-4
Parent Resources Online
KEYWORD: MT7 Parent

Assignment Guide

If you finished Example **1** assign:
Average   1–8, 10–17, 19–22,
             33–34, 38–43
Advanced 10–17, 22–30, 33–35,
             38–43

If you finished Example **2** assign:
Average   1–22, 31–34, 38–43
Advanced 10–18, 22–43

Homework Quick Check

Quickly check key concepts.
Exercises: 10, 18, 22, 34

Answers

1. (number line) 15 16 17 18 19 20 21 22 23
2. (number line) −7 −5 −3 −1 1 3
3. (number line) 100 110 120 130 140
4. (number line) 1 2 3 4 5 6 7 8 9 10
5. (number line) −44 −43 −42 −41 −40 −39 −38 −37

6–8, 10–17, 19–26. See pp. A15–A16.

31. Possible answer: The total weight of the cartons cannot exceed 2,200 pounds, so $42w \le 2{,}200 \to w \le 52.38$. This means that no more than 52 cartons can be carried on the elevator at one time if no people ride with them.

32. Possible answer: Since Marisol spends twice as much time reading as she spends doing homework, $\frac{r}{2} \ge 40 \to r \ge 80$. That means Marisol can spend at least 80 min, or 1 hr 20 min, reading.

State Resources

go.hrw.com
State Resources Online
KEYWORD: MT7 Resources

GUIDED PRACTICE

See Example **1** **Solve and graph.**

1. $\frac{r}{3} > 6$ $r > 18$
2. $-4w > 12$ $w < -3$
3. $20 \ge \frac{j}{6}$ $120 \ge j$
4. $6r \le 30$ $r \le 5$
5. $10 \le \frac{a}{-4}$ $a \ge -40$
6. $-36 < -2m$ $18 > m$
7. $\frac{r}{-3} < 21$ $r > -63$
8. $-20 \ge 5x$ $-4 \ge x$

See Example **2** 9. The owner of a sandwich shop is selling the special of the week for $5.90. At this price, he makes a profit of $3.85 on each sandwich sold. To make a total profit of at least $400 from the special, what is the least number of sandwiches he must sell?   104 sandwiches: $\frac{\$400}{\$3.85}$

INDEPENDENT PRACTICE

See Example **1** **Solve and graph.**
10. $-8 < r$

10. $-16 < 2r$
11. $15 < \frac{x}{5}$ $75 < x$
12. $-18w \ge -54$ $w \le 3$
13. $11 \le \frac{p}{-7}$ $-77 \ge p$
14. $\frac{t}{9} > 4$ $t > 36$
15. $9h > 108$ $h > 12$
16. $\frac{a}{-7} < 14$ $a > -98$
17. $-16q \le 64$ $q \ge -4$

See Example **2** 18. **Social Studies** A bill in the U.S. House of Representatives passed because at least $\frac{2}{3}$ of the members present voted in favor of it. If the bill received 284 votes, at least how many members of the House of Representatives were present for the vote?   426 members

PRACTICE AND PROBLEM SOLVING

Extra Practice
See page 803.

19. 6 > r

Solve and graph.
19. $-18 < -3r$ $6 > r$
20. $27 < \frac{x}{-3}$ $-51 > x$
21. $17w \ge -51$ $w \ge 3$
22. $101 \le \frac{p}{-7}$ $-\frac{101}{7} \ge p$... (shown as $-\frac{101}{7} \ge p$)
23. $\frac{t}{-19} > -5$ $t < 95$
24. $3h > 108$ $h > 36$
25. $\frac{a}{10} < 12$ $a < 120$
26. $-6q \le -72$ $q \ge 12$

Write and solve an algebraic inequality.

27. Nine times a number is less than 99.   Possible answer: $9x < 99$, $x < 11$
28. The quotient of a number and 6 is at least 8.   Possible answer: $\frac{n}{6} \ge 8$, $n \ge 48$
29. The product of −7 and a number is no more than −63.   Possible answer: $-7x \le -63$, $n \ge 9$
30. The quotient of some number and 3 is greater than 18.   Possible answer: $\frac{n}{3} > 18$, $n > 54$

Write and solve an algebraic inequality. Then explain the solution.

31. A school receives a shipment of books. There are 60 cartons, and each carton weighs 42 pounds. The school's elevator can hold 2200 pounds. What is the greatest number of cartons that can be carried on the elevator at one time if no people ride with them?

32. Each evening, Marisol spends at least twice as much time reading as she spends doing homework. If Marisol works on her homework for 40 minutes, how much time can she spend reading?

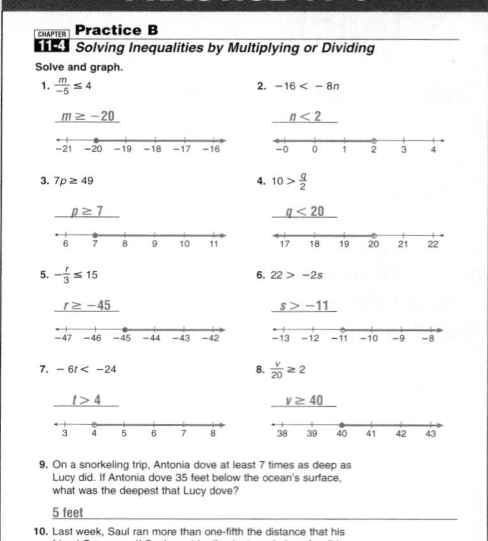

RETEACH 11-4

Reteach
11-4 *Solving Inequalities by Multiplying or Dividing*

To solve an inequality, multiply and divide the same way you would solve an equation. But, if you multiply or divide by a negative number, you must reverse the inequality sign.

Divide by a Positive Number
$2x < 14$
$\frac{2x}{2} < \frac{14}{2}$
$x < 7$

Divide by a Negative Number
$-2x < 14$
$\frac{-2x}{-2} > \frac{14}{-2}$ Reverse the inequality sign.
$x > -7$

To check your solution, choose two numbers from the graph and substitute them into the original equation. Choose a number that should be a solution and a number that should not be a solution.

Check
According to the graph, −6 should be a solution, but −8 should not be.
$-2x < 14$ $-2x < 14$
$-2 \cdot -8 \overset{?}{>} 14$ $-2 \cdot -6 \overset{?}{>} 14$
$-8 > -7 x$ $-6 > -7$ ✔

Complete to solve. Then graph the equation and check.
1. $-3y \ge 24$
$\frac{-3y}{-3} \le \frac{24}{-3}$
$y \le -8$
(number line) −12 −11 −10 −9 −8 −7
Values used to check solution will vary, but should include one number ≤ −8 and one number > −8.

2. $\frac{s}{-9} < 4$
$-9 \cdot \frac{s}{-9} > -9 \cdot 4$
$s > -36$
(number line) −38 −37 −36 −35 −34 −33
Values used to check solution will vary, but should include one number ≤ −36 and one number > −36.

PRACTICE 11-4

Practice B
11-4 *Solving Inequalities by Multiplying or Dividing*

Solve and graph.
1. $\frac{m}{-5} \le 4$
$m \ge -20$
(number line) −21 −20 −19 −18 −17 −16

2. $-16 < -8n$
$n < 2$
(number line) −0 0 1 2 3 4

3. $7p \ge 49$
$p \ge 7$
(number line) 6 7 8 9 10 11

4. $10 > \frac{q}{2}$
$q < 20$
(number line) 17 18 19 20 21 22

5. $-\frac{r}{3} \le 15$
$r \ge -45$
(number line) −47 −46 −45 −44 −43 −42

6. $22 > -2s$
$s > -11$
(number line) −13 −12 −11 −10 −9 −8

7. $-6t < -24$
$t > 4$
(number line) 3 4 5 6 7 8

8. $\frac{v}{20} \ge 2$
$v \ge 40$
(number line) 38 39 40 41 42 43

9. On a snorkeling trip, Antonia dove at least 7 times as deep as Lucy did. If Antonia dove 35 feet below the ocean's surface, what was the deepest that Lucy dove?
5 feet

10. Last week, Saul ran more than one-fifth the distance that his friend Omar ran. If Saul ran 14 miles last week, how far did Omar run?
less than 70 miles

Choose the graph that represents each inequality.

33. $-2y < 14$

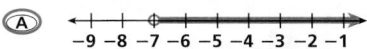

Ⓐ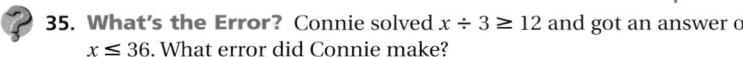

Ⓑ

Ⓒ

34. $6 \geq \frac{h}{5}$

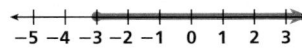

Ⓐ

Ⓑ

Ⓒ

35. What's the Error? Connie solved $x \div 3 \geq 12$ and got an answer of $x \leq 36$. What error did Connie make?

36. Write About It The expressions *no more than, at most,* and *less than or equal to* all indicate the same relationship between values. Write a problem that uses this relationship. Write the problem using each of the three expressions.

37. Challenge Angel weighs 5 times as much as his dog. When they stand on a scale together, it gives a reading of less than 163 pounds. If both their weights are whole numbers, what is the most each can weigh? **27 lb, 135 lb**

35. Possible answer: Connie reversed the direction of the inequality sign that should be reversed only when multiplying or dividing by a negative number.

36. Possible answer: The product of 3 and some number is no more than 21; the product of 3 and some number is at most 21; the product of 3 and some number is less than or equal to 21.

TEST PREP and Spiral Review

38. Multiple Choice Which inequality is shown by the graph?

Ⓐ $w \leq -3$ Ⓑ $w > -3$ Ⓒ $w \geq -3$ Ⓓ $-3 < w$

39. Gridded Response In order to have the $200 he needs for a bike, Kevin plans to put money away each week for the next 15 weeks. What is the minimum amount in dollars that Kevin will need to average each week in order to reach his goal? **at least $13.34 per week**

41. $\frac{9}{36}$, or $\frac{1}{4}$

An experiment consists of rolling two fair number cubes. Find each probability. (Lesson 10-4)

40. $P(\text{total shown} > 10)$ $\frac{3}{36}$, or $\frac{1}{12}$ **41.** $P(\text{two odd numbers})$ **42.** $P(\text{two 6's})$ $\frac{1}{36}$

43. In a chess tournament, 8 students will play against each other once. How many games will there be in all? (Lesson 10-6) **28 games**

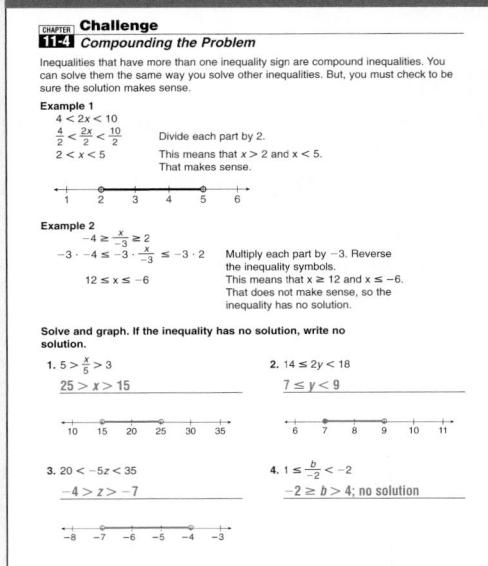

CHALLENGE 11-4

CHAPTER 11-4 Challenge
Compounding the Problem

Inequalities that have more than one inequality sign are compound inequalities. You can solve them the same way you solve other inequalities. But, you must check to be sure the solution makes sense.

Example 1
$4 < 2x < 10$
$\frac{4}{2} < \frac{2x}{2} < \frac{10}{2}$ Divide each part by 2.
$2 < x < 5$ This means that $x > 2$ and $x < 5$. That makes sense.

Example 2
$-4 \geq \frac{x}{-3} \geq 2$
$-3 \cdot -4 \leq -3 \cdot \frac{x}{-3} \leq -3 \cdot 2$ Multiply each part by -3. Reverse the inequality symbols.
$12 \leq x \leq -6$ This means that $x \geq 12$ and $x \leq -6$. That does not make sense, so the inequality has no solution.

Solve and graph. If the inequality has no solution, write no solution.

1. $5 > \frac{x}{5} > 3$ $25 > x > 15$

2. $14 \leq 2y < 18$ $7 \leq y < 9$

3. $20 < -5z < 35$ $-4 > z > -7$

4. $1 \leq \frac{b}{-2} < -2$ $-2 \geq b > 4$; no solution

PROBLEM SOLVING 11-4

CHAPTER 11-4 Problem Solving
Solving Inequalities by Multiplying or Dividing

Write the correct answer

1. A bottle contains at least 4 times as much juice as a glass contains. The bottle contains 32 fluid ounces. Write an inequality that shows this relationship. $4x \leq 32$

2. Solve the inequality in Exercise 1. What is the greatest amount the glass could contain? $x \leq 8$; 8 fluid ounces

3. In the triple jump, Katrina jumped less than one-third the distance that Paula jumped. Katrina jumped 5 ft 6 in. Write an inequality that shows this relationship. $\frac{x}{3} > 66$

4. Solve the inequality in Exercise 3. How far could Paula could have jumped? $x > 198$; more than 198 in., or 16 ft 6 in.

Choose the letter for the best answer.

5. Melinda earned at least 3 times as much money this month as last month. She earned $567 this month. Which inequality shows this relationship?
A $567 < x$ C $567 > 3x$
B $567 < 3x$ D $567 \geq 3x$

6. The shallow end of a pool is less than one-quarter as deep as the deep end. The shallow end is 3 feet deep. Which inequality shows this relationship?
F $4 > 3x$ H $\frac{x}{4} > 3$
G $4x < 3$ J $\frac{x}{4} < 3$

7. Arthur worked in the garden more than half as long as his brother. Arthur worked 6 hours in the garden. How long did his brother work in the garden?
A less than 3 hours
B 3 hours
C less than 12 hours
D more than 12 hours

8. The distance from Bill's house to the library is no more than 5 times the distance from his house to the park. If Bill's house is 10 miles from the library, what is the greatest distance his house could be from the park?
F 2 miles
G more than 2 miles
H 20 miles
J less than 20 miles

ONGOING ASSESSMENT and INTERVENTION

Diagnose Before the Lesson
11-4 Warm Up, TE p. 600

Monitor During the Lesson
11-4 Know-It Notebook
11-4 Questioning Strategies

Assess After the Lesson
11-4 Lesson Quiz, TE p. 603

TEST PREP DOCTOR If students have difficulty with Exercise 39, have them write an inequality to represent the amount Kevin needs to save each week. They should begin with the inequality $200 \leq 15d$, such that d is the amount in dollars saved each week. They should simplify this to $13.33 \leq d$ or $d \geq 13.33$. Kevin should save at least $13.34 per week to make his goal of $200.

Journal

Ask students to describe some real-world situations in which they might use an inequality.

Power Presentations with PowerPoint®

11-4 Lesson Quiz
Solve and graph.

1. $-14x > 28$ $x < -2$

2. $\frac{x}{3} < 15$ $x < 45$

3. $18 < -6x$ $-3 > x$

4. $\frac{q}{8} \leq 5$ $q \geq 40$

5. Jared isn't supposed to carry more than 35 pounds in his backpack. He has 8 textbooks and each book weighs 5 pounds. What is the greatest amount of textbooks he can carry in his backpack at one time?
No more than 4

Also available on transparency

Pacing: Traditional 1 day
Block $\frac{1}{2}$ day

Objective: Students solve two-step inequalities and graph the solutions of an inequality on a number line.

 Hands-On Lab
In *Hands-on Lab Activities*

 Online Edition
Tutorial Videos, Interactivities

 Countdown to Testing Week 24

Power Presentations
with PowerPoint®

Warm Up
Solve.

1. $6x + 36 = 2x$ $x = -9$

2. $4x - 13 = 15 + 5x$ $x = -28$

3. $5(x - 3) = 2x + 3$ $x = 6$

4. $\frac{7}{8} + x = \frac{13}{16}$ $x = -\frac{1}{16}$

Problem of the Day
Find an integer x that makes the following two inequalities true:

$4 < x^2 < 16$ *and* $x < 2.5$ $x = -3$

Also available on transparency

Math Humor
What did the marine biologist call an algebraic expression consisting of 8 terms added together? An *octo-plus*

State Resources

 **go.hrw.com**
State Resources Online
KEYWORD: MT7 Resources

11-5 Solving Two-Step Inequalities

Learn to solve two-step inequalities and graph the solutions of an inequality on a number line.

The drama club at Deer Run High School is planning its annual spring musical. They have $610.75 left from fund-raising earlier in the year, but they estimate that the costumes and sets will cost $1100.00. In order to raise the extra money they will need and at least break even on the production, the drama club is planning to sell tickets to the musical for $4.75 each. You can set up and solve a two-step inequality to find the least number of tickets the drama club will need to sell.

EXAMPLE 1 Solving Two-Step Inequalities

Solve and graph.

A $7y - 4 > 24$

$$\begin{aligned} 7y - 4 &> 24 \\ \underline{+4 \quad +4} \quad & \quad \text{Add 4 to both sides.} \\ 7y &> 28 \\ \frac{7y}{7} &> \frac{28}{7} \quad \text{Divide both sides by 7.} \\ y &> 4 \end{aligned}$$

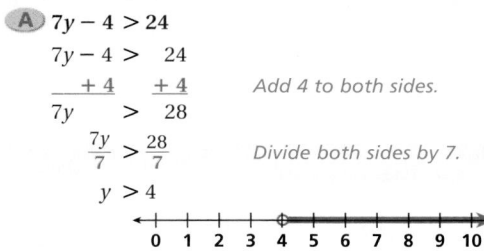

Remember!
If both sides of an inequality are multiplied or divided by a negative number, the inequality symbol must be reversed.

B $-2x + 4 \leq 3$

$$\begin{aligned} -2x + 4 &\leq 3 \\ \underline{-4 \quad -4} \quad & \quad \text{Subtract 4 from both sides.} \\ -2x &\leq -1 \\ \frac{-2x}{-2} &\geq \frac{-1}{-2} \quad \text{Divide both sides by } -2; \text{ change } \leq \text{ to } \geq. \\ x &\geq \frac{1}{2} \end{aligned}$$

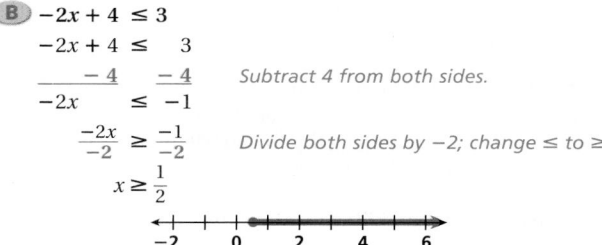

Recall that when an equation or an inequality contains fractions, it is often easier to multiply both sides by the LCD to clear the fractions.

---

1 Introduce
Alternate Opener

 **EXPLORATION**

11-5 Solving Two-Step Inequalities

Rosa is offered two telephone service options when she buys her new cell phone.

Cell phone option A	Cell phone option B
$25, plus 12.5¢ per minute	$90, plus unlimited minutes

1. Complete the table to compare the costs under each option for the given number of minutes.

Minutes	Cost Under Option A	Cost Under Option B
220	$25 + 0.125 \cdot 220 = \$52.50$	$90
320		
420		
520		
620		

2. Solve the inequality $25 + 0.125x < 90$. What does the solution tell you about option A and option B?

3. Solve the inequality $25 + 0.125x > 90$. What does the solution tell you about option A and option B?

Think and Discuss

4. Explain how you solved the inequalities in Problems 2 and 3.

Motivate
Tell students that a goal in a fund-raiser is to take in more money than is spent. To accomplish that, you may need to determine the *least number* of items that must be sold to make a profit. One way to determine the least number of items is to write and solve an inequality.

Explorations and answers are provided in *Alternate Openers: Explorations Transparencies*.

EXAMPLE **2** | **Solving Inequalities That Contain Fractions**

Solve $\frac{-3x}{8} + \frac{5}{6} \leq \frac{7}{12}$ and graph the solution.

$$24\left(\frac{-3x}{8} + \frac{5}{6}\right) \leq 24\left(\frac{7}{12}\right)$$ *Multiply by the LCD, 24.*

$$24\left(\frac{-3x}{8}\right) + 24\left(\frac{5}{6}\right) \leq 24\left(\frac{7}{12}\right)$$ *Distributive Property*

$$-9x + 20 \leq 14$$

$$\underline{\quad -20 \quad\quad -20\quad}$$ *Subtract 20 from both sides.*

$$-9x \leq -6$$

$$\frac{-9x}{-9} \geq \frac{-6}{-9}$$ *Divide both sides by −9; change ≤ to ≥.*

$$x \geq \frac{6}{9}$$

$$x \geq \frac{2}{3}$$ *Simplify.*

[number line from $-1\frac{2}{3}$ to $1\frac{2}{3}$ with arrow starting at $\frac{2}{3}$]

EXAMPLE  **3** | *School Application*

Possible answers to *Think and Discuss*

1. Use the same steps for both, but if you multiply or divide an inequality by a negative number, you must reverse the inequality symbol.

2. To solve the inequality $-2x + 1 > 7$, subtract 1 from both sides, divide both sides by -2, and reverse the inequality symbol. To solve the inequality $2 - \frac{x}{5} < 3$, subtract 2 from both sides, multiply both sides by -5, and reverse the inequality symbol.

The drama club plans to present its annual spring musical. They have $610.75 left from fund-raising, but they estimate that the entire production will cost $1100.00. If they sell tickets for $4.75 each, how many must they sell to at least break even?

In order to at least break even, ticket sales plus the money in the budget must be greater than or equal to the cost of the production.

$$4.75t + 610.75 \geq 1100.00$$

$$\underline{\quad -610.75 \quad\quad -610.75\quad}$$ *Subtract 610.75 from both sides.*

$$4.75t \geq 489.25$$

$$\frac{4.75t}{4.75} \geq \frac{489.25}{4.75}$$ *Divide both sides by 4.75.*

$$t \geq 103$$

The drama club must sell at least 103 tickets in order to break even.

Think and Discuss

1. Compare solving a multi-step equation with solving a multi-step inequality.

2. Describe two situations in which you would have to reverse the inequality symbol when solving a multi-step inequality.

Power Presentations
with PowerPoint®

Additional Examples

Example **1**

Solve and graph.

A. $4x + 1 > 13$ $x > 3$

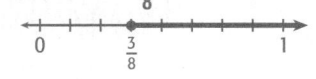

B. $-9x + 7 \geq 25$ $x \leq -2$

Example **2**

Solve $\frac{2x}{5} + \frac{3}{4} \geq \frac{9}{10}$ and graph the solution. $x \geq \frac{3}{8}$

[number line from 0 to 1 with arrow starting at $\frac{3}{8}$]

Example **3**

A school's Spanish club is selling bumper stickers. They bought 100 for $55, and have to give the company 15 cents for every sticker sold. If they plan to sell each bumper sticker for $1.25, how many do they have to sell to make a profit?   more than 50

Also available on transparency

---

2 **Teach**

Guided Instruction

In this lesson, students solve two-step inequalities and graph the solutions of an inequality on a number line. Remind students that the process of solving inequalities is the same as the process of solving equations, with one exception. The exception is that if you multiply or divide both sides of an inequality by a negative number, you must reverse the inequality symbol. (See Math Background.) Remind students how to graph inequalities on a number line.

 Reaching All Learners
Through Critical Thinking

Give students inequalities and possible solution sets, such as those given below. Have students graph each solution set and check it by choosing a number from the solution set and substituting it into the inequality. If the solution set is incorrect, have students provide the correct answer.

1. $2x + 17 > 5; x < -6$

2. $\frac{2t}{3} + \frac{1}{2} < \frac{1}{6}; t < -\frac{1}{2}$

3. $\frac{x}{2} + \frac{x}{4} < \frac{15}{8}; x > \frac{5}{2}$

1. incorrect; $x > -6$

2. correct

3. incorrect; $x < \frac{5}{2}$

---

3 **Close**

Summarize

Remind students that to solve a multi-step inequality, they should do the following:

- Clear fractions.

- Combine like terms.

- Get the variable on one side of the inequality only.

- Undo addition and subtraction.

- Undo multiplication and division, remembering to reverse the inequality symbol if they multiply or divide both sides of an inequality by a negative number.

11-5 Exercises

go.hrw.com
Homework Help Online
KEYWORD: MT7 11-5
Parent Resources Online
KEYWORD: MT7 Parent

Assignment Guide

If you finished Example **1** assign:
Average 1–6, 14–19, 30–32, 47–54
Advanced 14–19, 27–30, 45, 47–54

If you finished Example **2** assign:
Average 1–12, 14–25, 30–35, 47–54
Advanced 14–25, 33–39, 45–54

If you finished Example **3** assign:
Average 1–26, 30–35, 40–42, 47–54
Advanced 14–26, 33–54

Homework Quick Check

Quickly check key concepts.
Exercises: 16, 22, 26, 30

Answers

1–12, 14–25, 27–38. See p. A16.

Math Background

To better understand why an inequality symbol must be reversed when multiplying or dividing by a negative number, use an inequality such as $10 > 8$ to examine the following four possibilities.

- Multiply each side by 2: $20 > 16$ (true)
- Divide each side by 2: $5 > 4$ (true)
- Multiply each side by -2: $-20 < -16$ (The inequality sign must be reversed to make it true.)
- Divide each side by -2: $-5 < -4$ (The inequality sign must be reversed to make it true.)

State Resources

go.hrw.com
State Resources Online
KEYWORD: MT7 Resources

GUIDED PRACTICE

See Example **1** Solve and graph.

1. $3k + 5 > 11$ $k > 2$
2. $2z - 29.5 \le 10.5$ $z \le 20$
3. $6y + 12 < -36$ $y < -8$
4. $-4x + 6 \ge 14$ $x \le -2$
5. $2y + 2.5 \ge 16.5$ $y \ge 7$
6. $3k - 2 > 13$ $k > 5$

See Example **2** **7.** $\frac{x}{15} + \frac{1}{5} < \frac{2}{5}$ $x < 3$
8. $\frac{b}{10} - \frac{3}{5} \ge -\frac{1}{2}$ $b \ge 1$
9. $\frac{h}{3} - 2 \le -\frac{5}{3}$ $h \le 1$
10. $\frac{c}{8} + \frac{1}{2} > \frac{3}{4}$ $c > 2$
11. $\frac{1}{2} + \frac{d}{6} < \frac{1}{3}$ $d < -1$
12. $\frac{2}{3} \ge \frac{6m}{9}$ $m \le 1$

See Example **3** **13.** The chess club is selling caps to raise $425 for a trip. They have $175 already. If the club members sell caps for $12 each, at least how many caps do they need to sell to make enough money for their trip? **at least 21 caps**

INDEPENDENT PRACTICE

See Example **1** Solve and graph.

14. $8k - 6 > 18$ $k > 3$
15. $5x + 3 > 23$ $x > 4$
16. $3p + 3 \ge -36$ $p \ge -13$
17. $13 \ge 11q - 9$ $q \le 2$
18. $3.6 + 7.2n < 25.2$ $n < 3$
19. $-7x - 15 \ge 34$ $x \le -7$

See Example **2** **20.** $\frac{p}{15} + \frac{4}{5} < \frac{1}{3}$ $p < -7$
21. $\frac{a}{9} + \frac{2}{3} \ge \frac{1}{3}$ $a \ge -3$
22. $-\frac{1}{3} + \frac{n}{12} > -\frac{1}{4}$ $n > 1$
23. $-\frac{2}{3} \le \frac{1}{18}k - \frac{5}{6}$ $k \ge 3$
24. $\frac{4}{7} + \frac{n}{14} \le -\frac{3}{7}$ $n \le -14$
25. $\frac{1}{3} + \frac{r}{18} < \frac{1}{2}$ $r < 3$

See Example **3** **26.** Josef is on the planning committee for the eighth-grade party. The food, decoration, and entertainment costs a total of $350. The committee has $75 already. If the committee sells the tickets for $5 each, at least how many tickets must be sold to cover the remaining cost of the party? **at least 55 tickets**

PRACTICE AND PROBLEM SOLVING

Extra Practice
See page 803.

Solve and graph.

27. $3p - 11 \le 11$ $p \le \frac{22}{3}$
28. $9n + 10 > -17$ $n > -3$
29. $3 - 5w < 8$ $w > -1$
30. $-6x - 18 \ge 6$ $x \le -4$
31. $12a + 4 > 10$ $a > \frac{1}{2}$
32. $-4y + 3 \ge 17$ $y \le -\frac{7}{2}$
33. $3q - 5q > -12$ $q < 6$
34. $\frac{3m}{4} > \frac{5}{8}$ $m > \frac{5}{6}$
35. $4b - 3.2 < 7.6$ $b < 2.7$
36. $3k + 6 \ge 4$ $k \ge -\frac{2}{3}$
37. $\frac{90}{4} \le -\frac{5}{6}f$ $f \le -27$
38. $-\frac{5}{9}v \ge -\frac{1}{3}$ $v \le \frac{3}{5}$

39. **Critical Thinking** What is the least whole number that is a solution of $2r - 4.4 > 8.6$? **7**

40. **Entertainment** A speech is being given in a gymnasium that can hold no more than 650 people. A permanent bleacher will seat 136 people. The event organizers are setting up 25 rows of chairs. At most, how many chairs can be in each row? **at most 20 chairs**

RETEACH 11-5

Reteach
11-5 *Solving Two-Step Inequalities*

To solve an inequality, undo operations the same way you would with an equation. But, when multiplying or dividing by a negative number, reverse the inequality symbol.

$3x + 2 > 11$ To undo addition,
$\quad -2 \quad -2$ subtract 2.
$3x \quad > 9$ To undo multiplication,
$\frac{3x}{3} \quad > \frac{9}{3}$ divide by 3.
$x \quad > 3$
The solution set contains all real numbers greater than 3.

$-3x + 2 > 11$ To undo addition,
$\quad -2 \quad -2$ subtract 2.
$-3x \quad > 9$ To undo multiplication,
$\frac{-3x}{-3} \quad < \frac{9}{-3}$ divide by -3 and
$x \quad < -3$ change $>$ to $<$.
The solution set contains all real numbers less than -3.

Complete to solve and graph.

1. $2t + 1 \le 9$ To undo addition,
$\quad -1 \quad -1$ subtract.
$2t \quad \le 8$ To undo multiplication,
$\frac{2t}{2} \quad \le \frac{8}{2}$ divide.
$t \quad \le 4$

2. $-2t + 1 \le 9$ To undo addition,
$\quad -1 \quad -1$ subtract.
$-2t \quad \le 8$ To undo multiplication,
$\frac{-2t}{-2} \quad \ge \frac{8}{-2}$ divide by -2 and
$t \quad \ge -4$ change $\le$ to $\ge$.

3. $-3z - 2 > 1$
$\quad +2 \quad +2$
$-3z \quad > 3$
$\frac{-3z}{-3} \quad \frac{3}{-3}$
$z \quad < -1$

4. $3z - 2 > 1$
$\quad +2 \quad +2$
$3z \quad > 3$
$\frac{3z}{3} \quad \frac{3}{3}$
$z \quad > 1$

PRACTICE 11-5

Practice B
11-5 *Solving Two-Step Inequalities*

Solve and graph.

1. $4x - 2 < 26$
$x < 7$

2. $6 - \frac{1}{5}y \le 7$
$y \ge -5$

3. $2x + 27 \ge 15$
$x \ge -6$

4. $10x > 14x + 8$
$x < -2$

5. $7 - 4w \le 19$
$w \ge -3$

6. $\frac{k}{5} + \frac{3}{20} < \frac{3}{10}$
$k < \frac{3}{4}$

7. $4.8 - 9.6x \le 12$
$x \ge -1$

8. $\frac{2}{9} + \frac{y}{3} > \frac{1}{3}$
$y > \frac{1}{3}$

9. One-third of a number, decreased by thirty-six, is at most twenty-two. Find the number.
$n \le 174$

10. Jack wants to run at least 275 miles before the baseball season begins. He has already run 25 miles. He plans to run 2.5 miles each day. At this rate, what is the fewest number of days he will need to reach his goal?
100 weeks

41. Katie and April are making a string of beads for *pi* day (March 14). The string already has 70 beads. If there are only 30 more days until *pi* day, and they want to string 1000 beads by then, at least how many beads do they have to string each day? **at least 31 beads**

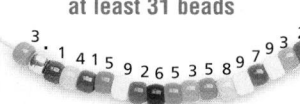

42. Sports The Astros have won 35 and lost 52 baseball games. They have 75 games remaining. At least how many of the remaining 75 games must the Astros win to have a winning season? (*Hint:* A winning season means they win more than 50% of their games.) **at least 47 games**

43. Economics Satellite TV customers can either purchase a dish and receiver for $249 or pay a $50 fee and rent the equipment for $12 a month.

  a. How much would it cost to rent the equipment for 9 months? **$158**

  b. How many months would it take for the rental charges to exceed the purchase price? **17 mo**

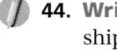 **44. Write a Problem** Write and solve an inequality using the following shipping rates for orders from a mail-order catalog.

Mail-Order Shipping Rates

Merchandise Amount	$0.01–$25.00	$25.01–50.00	$50.01–75.00	$75.01–125.00	$125.01 and over
Shipping Cost	$3.95	$5.95	$7.95	$9.95	$11.95

 45. Write About It Describe two ways to solve the inequality $-3x - 4 < x$.

46. Challenge Solve the inequality $\frac{x}{5} - \frac{x}{6} \geq \frac{1}{15}$. $x \geq 2$

TEST PREP and Spiral Review

47. Multiple Choice Solve $3g - 6 > 18$.

  (A) $g > 21$ (B) $g > 8$ (C) $g > 6$ (D) $g > 4$

48. Short Response Solve and graph $\frac{5x}{6} + \frac{1}{2} < \frac{2}{3}$. $x < \frac{1}{5}$

Complete each figure. The dashed line is the line of symmetry. (Lesson 7-8)

49. 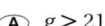   **50.**    **51.**

Solve. (Lesson 11-3)

52. $4w + 3 = w$ $w = -1$ **53.** $13a + 10 = 70 - 2a$ $a = 4$ **54.** $2x - 5 = 9x + 9$ $x = -2$

CHALLENGE 11-5

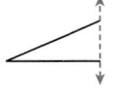 **Challenge**
11-5 *Updated Pony Express*

Pat wants to send some copies of her newly published book to friends.

According to the U.S. Postal Service:

Rates are based on the weight of the piece and the zone (distance from origin to destination ZIP code).

 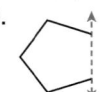

The combined length and girth (perimeter of an end) of a package may not exceed 108 inches.

1. Pat wants the box that contains books to be 6 inches high, and twice as long as it is wide.

Let *x* represent the width of a box that Pat might use.

Write and solve an inequality to find all possible widths for a box that will satisfy the postal requirements and Pat's conditions.

$2(x) + 2(6) + 2x \leq 108$
$4x + 12 \leq 108$
$4x \leq 96$
$x \leq 24$

possible width: ≤ 24 inches

2. Pat's husband, Mike, suggests that the box be 8 inches high and that the length be 3 times the width.

Let *z* represent the length of a box that Mike suggests.

Write and solve an inequality to find, to the nearest inch, the maximum length for a box that will satisfy.

$2\left(\frac{z}{3}\right) + 2(8) + z \leq 108$
$2z + 48 + 3z \leq 324$
$5z + 48 \leq 324$
$5z \leq 276$
$z \leq 55.2$

maximum length: 55 inches

3. On May 1, 2002, Pat shipped a book containing a book to a friend who lives in Zone 4. Pat paid $2.08 to ship this package.

According to the table below, write an inequality to show the weight of this package. $2.5 < x \leq 3$

Bound Printed Matter Rates

Weight Not Over (pounds)	Local, Zones 1&2	Zone 3	Zone 4	Zone 5	Zone 6	Zone 7	Zone 8
1.0	$1.80	$1.83	$1.87	$1.93	$1.99	$2.06	$2.21
1.5	1.80	1.83	1.87	1.93	1.99	2.06	2.21
2.0	1.84	1.88	1.94	2.02	2.10	2.19	2.38
2.5	1.90	1.95	2.00	2.11	2.21	2.33	2.57
3.0	1.94	2.00	2.08	2.20	2.32	2.46	2.75
3.5	1.99	2.06	2.15	2.29	2.43	2.60	2.93
4.0							

PROBLEM SOLVING 11-5

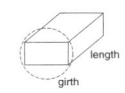 **Problem Solving**
11-5 *Solving Two-Step Inequalities*

A school club is selling printed T-shirts to raise $650 for a trip. The table shows the profit they will make on each shirt after they pay the cost of production.

Shirt	Profit
50/50	$5.50
100% cotton	$7.82

1. Suppose the club already has $150, at least how many 50/50 shirts must they sell to make enough money for the trip?

  91 shirts

2. Suppose the club already has $100, but it plans to spend $50 on advertising. At least how many 100% cotton shirts must they sell to make enough money for the trip?

  77 shirts

3. Suppose the club sold thirty 50/50 shirts on the first day of sales. At least how many more 50/50 shirts must they sell to make enough money for the trip?

  89 shirts

For Exercises 4–5, use this equation to estimate typing speed, $S = \frac{w}{5} - 2e$, where *S* is the accurate typing speed, *w* is the number of words typed in 5 minutes, and *e* is the number of errors. Choose the letter for the best answer.

4. One of the qualifications for a job is a typing speed of at least 65 words per minute. If Jordan knows that she will be able to type 350 words in five minutes, what is the maximum number of errors she can make?

  A 0   C 3
  (B) 2   D 4

5. Tanner usually makes 3 errors every 5 minutes when he is typing. If his goal is an accurate typing speed of at least 55 words per minute, how many words does he have to be able to type in 5 minutes?

  F 61 words   (H) 305 words
  G 300 words   J 325 words

6. A taxi charges $2.05 per ride and $0.20 for each mile, which can be written as $F = \$2.05 + \$0.20m$. How many miles can you travel in the cab and have the fare be less than $10?

  A 15   (C) 39
  B 25   D 43

7. Celia's long distance company charges $5.95 per month plus $0.06 per minute. If Celia has budgeted $30 for long distance, what is the maximum number of minutes she can call long distance per month?

  F 375 minutes   H 405 minutes
  (G) 400 minutes   J 420 minutes

Answers
44–45, 48–51. See p. A16.

 **TEST PREP DOCTOR** Many students are intimidated by fractions in inequalities, such as in Exercise 48. Help them find the LCD by pointing out that 2 and 3 are both factors of 6. Emphasize that fractions can be eliminated from most equations and inequalities in just one step by multiplying every term by the LCD.

 Journal
Ask students to describe some real-world situations in which an inequality might be more useful than an equation.

Power Presentations with PowerPoint®

 11-5 Lesson Quiz
Solve and graph.

1. $4x - 6 > 10$ $x > 4$

2. $7x + 9 < 3x - 15$ $x < -6$

3. $w - 3w < 32$ $w > -16$

4. $\frac{2}{3}w + \frac{1}{4} \leq \frac{1}{2}$ $w \leq \frac{3}{8}$

5. Antonio has budgeted an average of $45 a month for entertainment. For the first five months of the year he has spent $48, $39, $60, $48, and $33. How much can Antonio spend in the sixth month without exceeding his average budget?   no more than $42

Also available on transparency

Pacing: Traditional 1 day
Block $\frac{1}{2}$ day
Objective: Students solve
systems of equations.

 Online Edition
Tutorial Videos, Interactivities

 **Countdown to
Testing Week 25**

Power Presentations
with PowerPoint®

Warm Up

Solve for the indicated variable.

1. $P = R - C$ for R $\quad R = P + C$
2. $V = \frac{1}{3}Ah$ for A $\quad \frac{3V}{h} = A$
3. $R = \frac{C - S}{t}$ for C $\quad Rt + S = C$

Problem of the Day

At an audio store, stereos have 2
speakers and home-theater systems
have 5 speakers. There are 30
sound systems with a total of 99
speakers. How many systems are
stereo systems and how many are
home-theater systems? **17 stereo
systems, 13 home-theater systems**

Also available on transparency

Math Humor

Teacher: If billions come after millions,
what comes after billions?

Student: The IRS.

State Resources

go.hrw.com
State Resources Online
KEYWORD: MT7 Resources

11-6 Systems of Equations

Learn to solve
systems of equations.

Vocabulary
system of equations
solution of a system
of equations

Tickets for a concert are $40 for
main-floor seats and $25 for upper-level
seats. A total of 2000 concert tickets were
sold. The total ticket sales were $62,000.
How many main-floor tickets were sold
and how many upper-level tickets were
sold? You can solve this problem using
two equations.

A **system of equations** is a set
of two or more equations that
contain two or more variables.
A **solution of a system of equations** is
a set of values that are solutions of all of the equations. If the system
has two variables, the solutions can be written as ordered pairs.

EXAMPLE 1 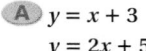 **Solving Systems of Equations**

Solve each system of equations.

A $y = x + 3$
$y = 2x + 5$

The expressions $x + 3$ and $2x + 5$ both equal y. So by the
Transitive Property they equal each other.

$$y = x + 3 \qquad\qquad y = 2x + 5$$
$$x + 3 = 2x + 5$$

Caution!

When solving systems
of equations,
remember to find
values for all of the
variables.

Solve the equation to find x.

$$\begin{array}{rcl} x + 3 &=& 2x + 5 \\ -x && -x \\ \hline 3 &=& x + 5 \\ -5 && -5 \\ \hline -2 &=& x \end{array}$$

Subtract x from both sides.

Subtract 5 from both sides.

To find y, substitute -2 for x in one of the original equations.
$y = x + 3 = -2 + 3 = 1$
The solution is $(-2, 1)$.

B $y = 3x + 8$
$y = -7 + 3x$

$$\begin{array}{rcl} 3x + 8 &=& -7 + 3x \\ -3x && -3x \\ \hline 8 &\ne& -7 \end{array}$$

Transitive Property

Subtract $3x$ from both sides.

The system of equations has no solution.

---

1 Introduce
Alternate Opener

EXPLORATION

11-6 Systems of Equations

You can compare Celsius temperatures with Fahrenheit
temperatures by graphing each formula as an equation
using the variables x and y.

To convert °C to °F   To convert °F to °C

$F = \frac{9}{5} \cdot C + 32$ $C = \frac{5}{9} \cdot (F - 32)$

$y = \frac{9}{5} \cdot x + 32$ $y = \frac{5}{9} \cdot (x - 32)$

The calculator screens below show how to graph the two
equations.

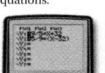 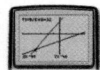

1. Which temperature is the same in both degrees Celsius
and degrees Fahrenheit?
2. Substitute the temperature you found in Problem 1 for x in
each equation above.

Think and Discuss
3. **Discuss** what happened when you substituted the
temperature found in Problem 1 in each equation.
4. **Explain** what the point of intersection of the two
graphs represents.

Motivate

Draw a line through the points (4, 0) and
(7, −2) and another line through the points
(−1, −4) and (7, −2) on the same coordinate system (Teaching Transparency). Note
that the lines intersect at the point (7, −2).
Tell students that the point (7, −2) is a
solution of both of the linear equations on
the graph.

Explorations and answers are provided in
Alternate Openers: Explorations Transparencies.

To solve a general system of two equations with two variables, you can solve both equations for *x* or both for *y*.

EXAMPLE 2 Solving Systems of Equations by Solving for a Variable

Solve the system of equations.

A $x - y = 3$
$x + 5y = 39$

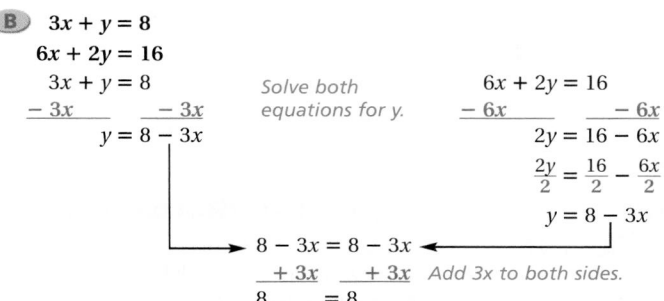

$$x - y = 3$$
$$\underline{+\ y \qquad +\ y}$$
$$x \qquad = 3 + y$$

Solve both equations for x.

$$x + 5y = 39$$
$$\underline{-\ 5y \qquad -\ 5y}$$
$$x \qquad = 39 - 5y$$

$$3 + y = 39 - 5y$$
$$\underline{+\ 5y \qquad +\ 5y} \quad \text{Add 5y to both sides.}$$
$$3 + 6y = 39$$
$$\underline{-\ 3 \qquad -\ 3} \quad \text{Subtract 3 from both sides.}$$
$$6y = 36$$
$$\frac{6y}{6} = \frac{36}{6} \quad \text{Divide both sides by 6.}$$
$$y = 6$$

$$x = 3 + y$$
$$= 3 + 6 = 9 \quad \text{Substitute 6 for y.}$$

The solution is (9, 6).

Helpful Hint

You can solve for either variable. It is usually easiest to solve for a variable that has a coefficient of 1.

B $3x + y = 8$
$6x + 2y = 16$

$$3x + y = 8$$
$$\underline{-\ 3x \qquad -\ 3x}$$
$$y = 8 - 3x$$

Solve both equations for y.

$$6x + 2y = 16$$
$$\underline{-\ 6x \qquad -\ 6x}$$
$$2y = 16 - 6x$$
$$\frac{2y}{2} = \frac{16}{2} - \frac{6x}{2}$$
$$y = 8 - 3x$$

$$8 - 3x = 8 - 3x$$
$$\underline{+\ 3x \qquad +\ 3x} \quad \text{Add 3x to both sides.}$$
$$8 = 8$$

Since 8 = 8 is always true, the system of equations has an infinite number of solutions.

Think and Discuss

1. **Compare** an equation to a system of equations.

2. **Describe** how you would know whether (−1, 0) is a solution of the system of equations below.

$$x + 2y = -1$$
$$-3x + 4y = 3$$

Possible answers to Think and Discuss

1. An equation is a statement that says that two quantities are equal. A system of equations is more than one equation.

2. Substitute −1 for *x* and 0 for *y* in both equations. If the pair is a solution to both equations, it is a solution to the system. The ordered pair (−1, 0) is a solution to the system.

---

2 Teach

Guided Instruction

In this lesson, students learn to solve systems of equations. Remind students that in Lesson 3-1 they learned to test an ordered pair to see whether it is a solution to an equation. Discuss the definition of a *system of equations.* Explain that for an ordered pair to be the solution to a system of equations, the ordered pair must be a solution to *both* equations. You may want to point out that on a graph, the ordered pair gives the coordinates of the point of intersection (Chapter 12 Extension).

 Reaching All Learners
Through Critical Thinking

Give students several sets of two systems of equations, such as those given below. Have students complete tables to find ordered pair solutions for the equations. Ask them to find the solutions to each system of two equations by identifying the ordered pair that appears in both tables for that system.

1. $2x + y = 7$
   $x - 3y = 0$ (3, 1)

2. $2x - 5y = 1$
   $-3x + 4y = 2$ (−2, −1)

3. $2x + y = 1$
   $x - 2y = 8$ (2, −3)

3 Close

Summarize

Remind students that an ordered pair is a solution to a system of equations only if it satisfies *both* equations in the system. Also remind them that to solve a system, they can solve each equation for the same variable and then set the results equal to each other.

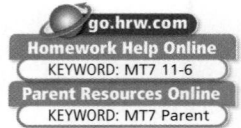

go.hrw.com
Homework Help Online
KEYWORD: MT7 11-6
Parent Resources Online
KEYWORD: MT7 Parent

Assignment Guide

If you finished Example ① assign:
Average 1–6, 13–18, 26, 27, 41–49
Advanced 13–18, 26–28, 38, 41–49

If you finished Example ② assign:
Average 1–30, 35, 41–49
Advanced 13–25, 29–49

Homework Quick Check

Quickly check key concepts.
Exercises: 14, 20, 35

Math Background

Most of the systems of equations in the lesson are linear equations with one solution. The graphs of these equations are lines that intersect at one point with the coordinates given by the solution. Some systems of linear equations, however, have no solution, and some have an infinite number of solutions. If the equations can be graphed as two different parallel lines, then the lines never intersect, and there is no solution to the system. If the equations can be graphed as the same line, then there are an infinite number of solutions.

GUIDED PRACTICE

See Example ① Solve each system of equations.

1. $y = x + 1$
   $y = 2x - 1$ (2, 3)

2. $y = -2x + 3$
   $y = 5x - 4$ (1, 1)

3. $y = 3x - 5$
   $y = 6x + 7$ (−4, −17)

4. $y = 6x - 12$
   $y = -9x + 3$ (1, −6)

5. $y = 5x + 7$
   $y = -3x + 7$ (0, 7)

6. $y = 3x + 5$
   $y = 3x - 10$ no solution

See Example ②

7. $2x + 2y = 16$
   $2x + 6y = 28$ (5, 3)

8. $x + y = 20$
   $x = y - 4$ (8, 12)

9. $x + 2y = 21$
   $-x + 3y = 29$ (1, 10)

10. $5x - 2y = 4$
    $11x + 4y = -8$ (0, −2)

11. $x = -3y$
    $7x - 2y = -69$ (−9, 3)

12. $-4x - 5y = -7$
    $11y = 2x + 37$ (−2, 3)

INDEPENDENT PRACTICE

See Example ① Solve each system of equations.

13. $y = -2x - 1$
    $y = 2x + 3$ (−1, 1)

14. $y = 3x + 6$
    $y = x + 2$ (−2, 0)

15. $y = 5x - 3$
    $y = -3x + 13$ (2, 7)

16. $y = x + 6$
    $y = -2x - 12$ (−6, 0)

17. $y = 3x - 1$
    $y = -2x + 9$ (2, 5)

18. $y = -2x - 6$
    $y = 3x + 29$ (−7, 8)

See Example ②

19. $3x + 3y = 15$
    $3x - 6y = -12$ (2, 3)

20. $2x + y = 11$
    $-x + 2y = 2$ (4, 3)

21. $y = 5x - 2$
    $4x + 3y = 13$ (1, 3)

22. $5x - 9y = 11$
    $3x + 7y = 19$ (4, 1)

23. $12x + 18y = 30$
    $4x - 13y = 67$ (7, −3)

24. $-14x - 11y = 97$
    $-12y + 11x = 27$ (−3, −5)

PRACTICE AND PROBLEM SOLVING

Extra Practice
See page 803.

25. **Crafts** Robin cross-stitches bookmarks and wall hangings. A bookmark takes her $1\frac{1}{2}$ days, and a wall hanging takes her 4 days. Robin recently spent 18 days cross-stitching 7 items. Solve the system of equations to find the number of bookmarks and the number of wall hangings that Robin cross-stitched.

$$1\frac{1}{2}b + 4w = 18$$
$$b + w = 7$$

4 bookmarks and 3 wall hangings

Solve each system of equations.

26. $y = 3x - 2$
    $y = x + 2$ (2, 4)

27. $y = -11x + 5$
    $y = 10x - 37$ (2, −17)

28. $5x + 5y = -5$
    $5x - 5y = 25$ (2, −3)

29. $3x - y = 5$
    $x - 4y = -2$ (2, 1)

30. $2x + 6y = 1$
    $4x - 3y = 0$ $\left(\frac{1}{10}, \frac{2}{15}\right)$

31. $x + 1.5y = 7.4$
    $3x - 0.5y = -6.8$ (−1.3, 5.8)

32. $\frac{1}{5}x + \frac{3}{8}y = \frac{1}{2}$
    $2x + 3.75y = 5$ There are an infinite number of solutions.

33. $0.25x + 0.6y = 2.5$
    $\frac{1}{4}x - \frac{3}{5}y = 3\frac{3}{7}$ no solution

34. $3x + 2y = -44$
    $-3x + 4y = 2$ (−10, −7)

State Resources

go.hrw.com
State Resources Online
KEYWORD: MT7 Resources

RETEACH 11-6

Reteach
11-6 Systems of Equations (continued)

Sometimes, you first have to solve one equation for a variable.
Solve the system: $y + 3x = 7$
$x + 2y = 4$

Solve the first equation for y.
$$y + 3x = 7$$
$$\underline{-3x \quad -3x}$$ Subtract 3x.
$$y = 7 - 3x$$

Substitute for y in the second equation.
$$x + 2y = 4$$ second equation
$$x + 2(7 - 3x) = 4$$ Replace y with 7 − 3x.

Solve for x.
$$x + 14 - 6x = 4$$ Distributive property
$$-5x + 14 = 4$$ Combine like terms.
$$\underline{-14 \quad -14}$$ Subtract 14.
$$\frac{-5x}{-5} = \frac{-10}{-5}$$ Divide by −5.
$$x = 2$$

Substitute the x-value into the first equation to get the corresponding y-value.
$$y + 3x = 7$$
$$y + 3(2) = 7$$
$$y + 6 = 7$$
$$y + 6 - 6 = 7 - 6$$
$$y = 1$$

Check: Substitute both values in each of the original equations.
$y + 3x = 7$ $x + 2y = 4$ $x = 2$ and $y = 1$
$1 + 3(2) \stackrel{?}{=} 7$ $2 + 2(1) \stackrel{?}{=} 4$ The solution of the
$7 = 7$✔ $4 = 4$✔   system is (2, 1).

Solve and check this system.

4. $y - 2x = 0$
   $x - 2y = 6$

Solve the first equation for y.
$$y - 2x = 0$$
$$y = 2x$$

Use the result to substitute for y in the second equation.
$$x - 2y = 6$$
$$x - 2(\underline{2x}) = 6$$

Solve the resulting equation for x.

$$x = \underline{-2}$$

Substitute the x-value to get the corresponding y-value.
$$\underline{y = 2x}$$
$$\underline{y = 2(-2)}$$
$$y = \underline{-4}$$

Check:
$$y - 2x = 0 \qquad x - 2y = 6$$

So, the ordered pair $\underline{(-3, -4)}$ is the solution of the system.

PRACTICE 11-6

Practice B
11-6 Systems of Equations

Solve each system of equations.

1. $y = 2x - 4$
   $g = x - 1$
   (3,2)

2. $y = -x + 10$
   $y = x + 2$
   (4,6)

3. $y = 2x - 1$
   $y = -3x - 6$
   (−1, −3)

4. $y = 2x$
   $y = 12 - x$
   (4,8)

5. $y = 2x - 3$
   $y = 2x + 1$
   no solution

6. $y = 3x - 1$
   $y = x + 1$
   (1,2)

7. $x + y = 0$
   $5x + 2y = -3$
   (−1,1)

8. $2x - 3y = 0$
   $2x + y = 8$
   (3,2)

9. $2x + 3y = 6$
   $4x + 6y = 12$
   infinite number

10. $6x - y = -14$
    $2x - 3y = 6$
    (−3, −4)

11. The sum of two numbers is 24. The second number is 6 less than the first. Write a system of equations and solve it find the number.

$\underline{x + y = 24; y = x - 6; (15, \ 9)}$

15. Kerry and Luke biked a total of 18 miles in one weekend. Kerry biked 4 miles more than Luke. Write a system of equations and solve it to find how far each boy biked.

$\underline{x + y = 18; x + 4 = y; (7, \ 11); \text{Luke biked 7 miles, and}}$
$\underline{\text{Kerry biked 11 miles}}$

35. Gustav has 35 dimes and quarters that total $5.00. Solve the system of equations to find how many dimes and how many quarters he has.

$$d + q = 35$$ **25 dimes and 10 quarters**
$$0.1d + 0.25q = 5$$

36. Entertainment Tickets for a concert are $40 for main-floor seats and $25 for upper-level seats. A total of 2000 concert tickets were sold. The ticket sales were $62,000. Let m represent the number of main-floor tickets and u represent the number of upper-level tickets.

  a. Write an equation about the total number of tickets sold. $m + u = 2000$

  b. Write an equation about the total ticket sales. $40m + 25u = 62,000$

  c. Solve the system of equations to find how many main-floor tickets were sold and how many upper-level tickets were sold. **800 main-floor and 1200 upper-level**

37. Geometry The perimeter of the rectangle is 114 units. The perimeter of the triangle is 63 units. Find x and y. $x = 11$ and $y = 6$

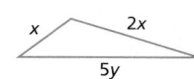

38. Possible answer:
Lucy has $20.40
in dimes and
quarters. If
she has 110
coins total,
how many
dimes and how
many quarters
does she have?
**64 dimes and
56 quarters**

38. Write a Problem Write a word problem that requires using a system of equations to solve. Solve the problem.

39. Write About It List the steps you would use to solve the system of equations. Explain which variable you would solve for and why.

$$x + 2y = 7$$
$$2x + y = 8$$

40. Challenge Solve the system of equations $5x - y - 12z = 61$
$$-2x + 11y + 8z = 4$$
$$-12x - 8y + 12z = -24$$
$$(-13, 6, -11)$$

TEST PREP and Spiral Review

41. Multiple Choice Carlos has $3.35 in dimes and quarters. If he has a total of 23 coins, how many dimes does he have?

(A) 9   (B) 11   (C) 16   (D) 18

42. Gridded Response Solve the system of equations. What is the y-value? **6**

$$2x + 3y = 10$$
$$x + 5y = 26$$

Solve each proportion. (Lesson 5-4)

43. $\frac{2}{3} = \frac{x}{6}$ $x = 4$ **44.** $\frac{3}{4} = \frac{d}{28}$ $d = 21$ **45.** $\frac{5}{1} = \frac{r}{7}$ $r = 35$ **46.** $\frac{10}{3} = \frac{40}{w}$ $w = 12$

Solve. (Lesson 11-2)

47. $4z - 2z = 23 + 17$ $z = 20$ **48.** $3p + 5p + 15 = 39$ $p = 3$ **49.** $20y - 7 + 11y = 2$ $y = \frac{9}{31}$

Answers

39. Possible answer: Solve $x + 2y = 7$ for x, and then solve $2x + y = 8$ for x. Then set the resulting expressions equal to each other, and solve that equation for y. Then substitute the value of y into the equation $2x + y = 8$, and solve that equation for x. Then write the solution as an ordered pair (3, 2).

Organizer

Objective: Assess students' mastery of concepts and skills in Lessons 11-4 through 11-6.

Resources

 Assessment Resources
Section 11B Quiz

 Test & Practice Generator
One-Stop Planner®

INTERVENTION ⬅️➡️

Resources

 Ready to Go On?
Intervention and
Enrichment Worksheets

💿 *Ready to Go On?* CD-ROM

🪐 *Ready to Go On?* Online

my.hrw.com

Answers

1–12, 14–22. See p. A16.

Quiz for Lessons 11-4 Through 11-6

Ready to Go On?

☑ **11-4** Solving Inequalities by Multiplying or Dividing

Solve and graph.

1. $-5x > 15$ $x < -3$ **2.** $\frac{t}{4} > 8$ $t > 32$ **3.** $9 \geq \frac{k}{3}$ $k \leq 27$ **4.** $7r \leq 49$ $r \leq 7$

5. $8 \leq \frac{b}{-2}$ $b \leq -16$ **6.** $-32 < -4n$ $n < 8$ **7.** $\frac{y}{-4} < 4$ $y > -16$ **8.** $-24 \geq 6m$ $m \leq -4$

9. $8 < -2a$ $a < -4$ **10.** $-n > -10$ $n < 10$ **11.** $\frac{h}{2} \leq -42$ $h \leq -84$ **12.** $3d \geq -15$ $d \geq -5$

13. Rachael is serving lemonade from a pitcher that holds 60 ounces. What are the possible numbers of 7-ounce juice glasses she can fill from one pitcher? $g \leq 8$; 8 glasses or less

☑ **11-5** Solving Two-Step Inequalities

Solve and graph.

14. $2k + 4 > 10$ $k > 3$ **15.** $0.5z - 5.5 \leq 4.5$ $z \leq 20$ **16.** $5y + 10 < -25$ $y < -7$

17. $\frac{3x}{5} - \frac{9}{15} \leq \frac{3}{5}$ $x \leq 2$ **18.** $\frac{2h}{3} + \frac{7}{6} \geq -\frac{1}{6}$ $y \geq -2$ **19.** $\frac{1}{2} + \frac{3c}{8} > \frac{1}{4}$ $c > -\frac{2}{3}$

20. $\frac{1}{3} + \frac{t}{9} < -2$ $t \leq -21$ **21.** $\frac{1}{3} - \frac{3x}{4} \geq \frac{5}{6}$ $x \leq -\frac{2}{3}$ **22.** $\frac{3}{7} + \frac{m}{14} \leq -\frac{2}{7}$ $m \leq -10$

23. Jillian must average at least 90 on two quiz scores before she can move to the next skill level. Jillian got a 92 on her first quiz. What scores could Jillian get on her second quiz in order to move to the next skill level? $t \geq 88$; a score of 88 or better

☑ **11-6** Systems of Equations

Solve each system of equations.

24. $y = -3x + 2$ $(1, -1)$ **25.** $y = 5x - 3$ $(3, 12)$ **26.** $y = -2x + 6$ $(3, 0)$
$y = 4x - 5$ $y = 2x + 6$ $y = 3x - 9$

27. $x + y = 8$ $(5, 3)$ **28.** $2x + y = 12$ $(5, 2)$ **29.** $4x - 3y = 33$ $(3, -7)$
$x + 3y = 14$ $3x - y = 13$ $x = -4y - 25$

30. The sum of two numbers is 18. Their difference is 8.

  a. If the numbers are x and y, write a system of equations to describe their sum and their difference. $x + y = 18$; $x - y = 8$

  b. Solve the system to find the numbers   5 and 13

READY TO GO ON?
Diagnose and Prescribe

NO
INTERVENE

	READY TO GO ON? Intervention, Section 11B		
Ready to Go On? Intervention	📄 **Worksheets**	💿 **CD-ROM**	🪐 **Online**
☑ Lesson 11-4	11-4 Intervention	Activity 11-4	Diagnose and Prescribe Online
☑ Lesson 11-5	11-5 Intervention	Activity 11-5	
☑ Lesson 11-6	11-6 Intervention	Activity 11-6	

YES
ENRICH

READY TO GO ON?
Enrichment, Section 11B
📄 **Worksheets**
💿 **CD-ROM**
🪐 **Online**

Skate Away Ms. Lucinda wants to treat her class of 30 students to a skating party to celebrate the end of the school year.

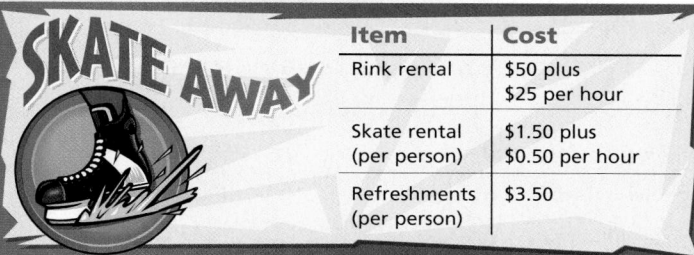

Item	Cost
Rink rental	$50 plus $25 per hour
Skate rental (per person)	$1.50 plus $0.50 per hour
Refreshments (per person)	$3.50

1. Ms. Lucinda considers renting the rink at Skate Away. How much would it cost to rent the rink for x hours?

2. Another rink, Skate Palace, charges $100 plus $15 per hour to rent the rink. Write and solve an equation to find the number of hours for which the cost of renting the rink at Skate Palace is the same as the cost of renting the rink at Skate Away.

3. Ms. Lucinda decides to take the class to Skate Away. How much will it cost to rent skates for 30 students for x hours? How much will it cost to buy refreshments for 30 students?

4. Ms. Lucinda has budgeted $400 for the party. Write and solve an inequality to find the maximum number of hours the class can have its party at Skate Away. Be sure to include the cost of the rink, the skates, and the refreshments.

5. The final bill for the party was $380. How long did the party last?

Multi-Step Test Prep

MULTI-STEP TEST PREP

CHAPTER 11

Organizer

Objective: Assess students' ability to apply concepts and skills in Chapter 11 in a real-world format.

 Online Edition

Resources

 Middle School Assessments
www.mathtekstoolkit.org

Problem	Text reference
1	Lesson 11-1
2	Lesson 11-2
3	Lesson 11-3
4	Lesson 11-4
5	Lesson 11-5

Answers

1. $50 + 25x$ if x = number of hours

2. $100 + 15x = 50 + 25x$; when the number of hours is 5

3. $30(1.50 + 0.50x)$; $30(3.50) = 105$

4. $50 + 25x + 30(1.50 + 0.50x) + 105 < 400$ so $x < 5$

5. 4.5 hours

INTERVENTION

Scaffolding Questions

1. What does it cost to rent the rink for 3 hours? **$125** for 4 hours? **$150** What should you do to figure out the cost for any given number of hours? **Multiply the number of hours by $25 and then add $50**

2. What does it cost to rent the rink at Skate Palace for x hours? **$100 + 15x$** What equation should you solve to find out when the costs are equal? **$50 + 25x = 100 + 15x$**

3. How much does it cost to rent skates for one student for x hours? **$1.5 + 0.5x$** How can you use this to write an expression to find the cost for 30 students? **Multiply by 30 and simplify**

4. What expression gives the total cost of the party for x hours? **$50 + 25x + 45 + 15x + 105$** How can you simply the expression? **Combine like terms to write it as $200 + 40x$** What inequality should you solve? **$200 + 40x \leq 400$**

5. What equation should you solve? **$200 + 40x = 380$** What is the first step in solving the equation? **Subtract 200 from both sides**

Extension

1. Assume cost of renting skates and buying refreshments is the same at Skate Palace. How much did Ms. Lucinda save by having the party at Skate Away? **$5**

State Resources

 **go.hrw.com**
State Resources Online
KEYWORD: MT7 Resources

Organizer

Objective: Participate in games to practice and apply skills learned in Chapter 11.

 Online Edition

Resources

📄 **Chapter 11 Resource Book**
Puzzles, Twisters & Teasers

Trans-Plants

Purpose: To apply the skill of solving equations to solving a riddle

Discuss Be sure students understand how to decode the message. Work through the first equation with them. Because the solution is $a = -14$, they will place an a above each place where -14 appears in the message.

Extend Have students work in teams of 4 to write new equations for the letters of the alphabet. Have each group write a message in code and trade equations and messages with another group to solve.

Check students' work.

24 Points

Purpose: To practice writing expressions in a game format

Discuss When students get "24," have them write the expression for their teammates to see. Have each team member evaluate the expression to verify that it has a value of 24.

Extend Have students play the game with the target number -24.

Game Time

Trans-Plants

Solve each equation below. Then use the values of the variables to decode the answer to the question.

$3a + 17 = -25$ $\quad a = -14$ $\qquad 24 - 6n = 54$ $\quad n = -5$

$2b - 25 + 5b = 7 - 32$ $\quad b = 0$ $\qquad 8.4o - 6.8 = 14.2 + 6.3o$ $\quad o = 10$

$2.7c - 4.5 = 3.6c - 9$ $\quad c = 5$ $\qquad 4p - p + 8 = 2p + 5$ $\quad p = -3$

$\frac{5}{12}d + \frac{1}{6}d + \frac{1}{3}d + \frac{1}{12}d = 6$ $\quad d = 6$ $\qquad 16 - 3q = 3q + 40$ $\quad q = -4$

$4e - 6e - 5 = 15$ $\quad e = -10$ $\qquad 4 + \frac{1}{3}r = r - 8$ $\quad r = 18$

$420 = 29f - 73$ $\quad f = 17$ $\qquad \frac{2}{3}s - \frac{5}{6}s + \frac{1}{2} = -\frac{3}{2}$ $\quad s = 12$

$2(g + 6) = -20$ $\quad g = -16$ $\qquad 4 - 15 = 4t + 17$ $\quad t = -7$

$2h + 7 = -3h + 52$ $\quad h = 9$ $\qquad 45 + 36u = 66 + 23u + 31$ $\quad u = 4$

$96i + 245 = 53$ $\quad i = 2$ $\qquad 6v + 8 = -4 - 6v$ $\quad v = -1$

$3j + 7 = 46$ $\quad j = 13$ $\qquad 4w + 3w - 6w = w + 15 + 2w - 3w$ $\quad w = 15$

$\frac{1}{2}k = \frac{3}{4}k - \frac{1}{2}$ $\quad k = 2$ $\qquad x + 2x + 3x + 4x + 5 = 75$ $\quad x = 7$

$30l + 240 = 50l - 160$ $\quad l = 20$ $\qquad \frac{4 - y}{5} = \frac{2 - 2y}{8}$ $\quad y = -11$

$4m + \frac{3}{8} = \frac{67}{8}$ $\quad m = 2$ $\qquad -11 = 25 - 4.5z$ $\quad z = 8$

What happens to plants that live in a math classroom?

$-7, 9, -10, -11$	$-16, 18, 10, 15$	$12, -4, 4, -14, 18, -10$	$18, 10, 10, -7, 12$
T H E Y	G R O W	S Q U A R E	R O O T S

24 Points

This traditional Chinese game is played using a deck of 52 cards numbered 1–13, with four of each number. The cards are shuffled, and four cards are placed face up in the center. The winner is the first player who comes up with an expression that equals 24, using each of the numbers on the four cards once.

Complete rules and a set of game cards are available online.

go.hrw.com
Game Time Extra
KEYWORD: MT7 Games

It's in the Bag!

Materials
- magazine
- glue
- scissors
- index cards

It's in the Bag!

PROJECT Picture Envelopes

Make these picture-perfect envelopes in which to store your notes on the lessons of this chapter.

Directions

1 Flip through a magazine and carefully tear out six pages with full-page pictures that you like.

2 Lay one of the pages in front of you with the picture face down. Fold the page into thirds as shown, and then unfold the page. **Figure A**

3 Fold the sides in, about 1 inch, and then unfold. Cut away the four rectangles at the corners of the page. **Figure B**

4 Fold in the two middle flaps. Then fold up the bottom and glue it onto the flaps. **Figure C**

5 Cut the corners of the top section at an angle to make a flap. **Figure D**

6 Repeat the steps to make five more envelopes. Label them so that there is one for each lesson of the chapter.

Taking Note of the Math

Use index cards to take notes on the lessons of the chapter. Store the cards in the appropriate envelopes.

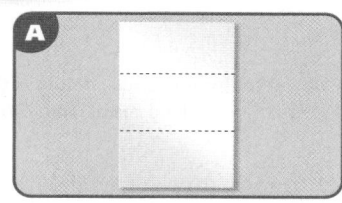
A

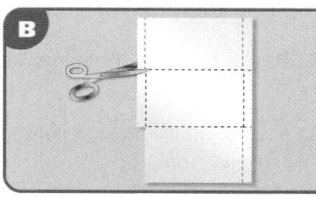
B

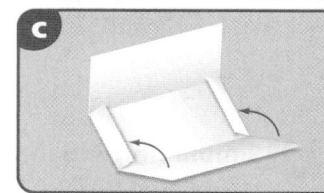
C

D

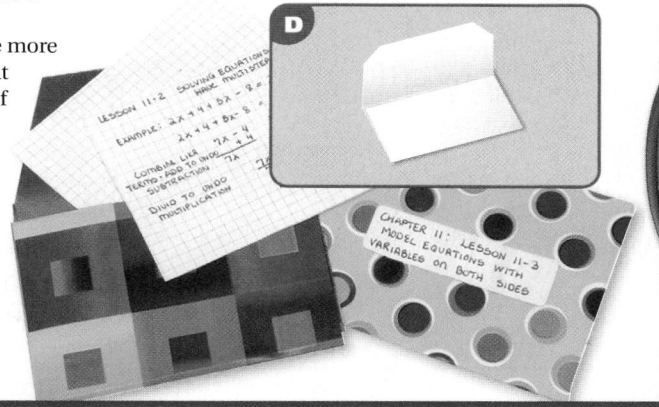

Organizer

Objective: Make envelopes in which to store index cards with notes on the chapter.

Materials: magazine, glue, scissors, index cards

PREMIER Online Edition

Using the Page

Preparing the Materials
If time is limited, have students select pages from magazines at home and ask them to bring in the detached pages.

Making the Project
Before students glue the bottom flap to the side flaps, have them check that an index card will fit inside the envelope.

Extending the Project
Ask students to use several index cards to write the steps in solving a multi-step equation. Each card should contain one step. Then have students shuffle the cards and put them in an envelope. Students can trade envelopes with a partner and try to order the steps in solving their partner's equation.

Tips from the Bag Ladies!

The envelopes tend to turn out best if students choose magazine pages that do not contain a lot of text. Also, there's no reason to limit the pages to magazines. Our students have done the project with catalogs, calendars, old maps, and posters.

Once students have made their envelopes and filled them with index cards, they can store everything in a small plastic zipper bag.

Organizer

Objective: Help students organize and review key concepts and skills presented in Chapter 11.

Online Edition
Multilingual Glossary

Resources

PuzzlePro®
One-Stop Planner®

Multilingual Glossary Online

go.hrw.com
KEYWORD: MT7 Glossary

Lesson Tutorial Videos
CD-ROM

Test & Practice Generator
One-Stop Planner®

Answers

1. systems of equations
2. like terms
3. solution of a system of equations
4. terms
5. $19m - 10$
6. $14w + 6$
7. $2x + 3y$
8. $2t^2 - 4t + 3t^3$
9. $y = 6$
10. $z = 7$
11. $y = 5$
12. $z = 8$

Study Guide: Review

Vocabulary

equivalent expression 584

like term 584

simplify 585

solution of a system of equations 608

system of equations 608

term 584

Complete the sentences below with vocabulary words from the list above. Words may be used more than once.

1. A group of two or more equations that contain two or more variables is called a(n) __?__.

2. Terms that have the same variable raised to the same power are __?__.

3. A set of values that are solutions of all the equations of a system is the __?__.

4. __?__ in an expression are set apart by plus or minus signs.

11-1 Simplifying Algebraic Expressions (pp. 584–587)

EXAMPLE

■ Simplify.
$3(z - 6) + 2z$
$3z - 3(6) + 2z$ *Distributive Property*
$3z - 18 + 2z$ *3z and 2z are like terms.*
$5z - 18$ *Combine coefficients.*

■ Solve.
$14p - 8p = 54$
$6p = 54$ *Combine like terms.*
$\dfrac{6p}{6} = \dfrac{54}{6}$ *Divide both sides by 6.*
$p = 9$

EXERCISES

Simplify.

5. $5(3m - 2) + 4m$

6. $12w + 2(w + 3)$

7. $4x + 3y - 2x$

8. $2t^2 - 4t + 3t^3$

Solve.

9. $7y + y = 48$

10. $8z - 2z = 42$

11. $6y + y = 35$

12. $9z - 3z = 48$

11-2 Solving Multi-Step Equations (pp. 588–591)

EXAMPLE

■ Solve.

$$\frac{5x}{9} - \frac{x}{6} + \frac{1}{3} = \frac{3}{2}$$

$18\left(\frac{5x}{9} - \frac{x}{6} + \frac{1}{3}\right) = 18\left(\frac{3}{2}\right)$ *Multiply both sides by 18.*

$18\left(\frac{5x}{9}\right) - 18\left(\frac{x}{6}\right) + 18\left(\frac{1}{3}\right) = 18\left(\frac{3}{2}\right)$ *Distributive Property*

$10x - 3x + 6 = 27$ *Simplify.*

$7x + 6 = 27$ *Combine like terms.*

$\underline{\quad -6 \quad -6\quad}$ *Subtract 6 from*

$7x \quad = \quad 21$ *both sides.*

$\frac{7x}{7} = \frac{21}{7}$ *Divide both sides by 7.*

$x = 3$

EXERCISES

Solve.

13. $3y + 6 + 4y - 7 = -8$

14. $5h - 6 - h + 10 = 12$

15. $\frac{2t}{3} + \frac{1}{3} = -\frac{1}{3}$

16. $\frac{2r}{5} - \frac{4}{5} = \frac{2}{5}$

17. $\frac{z}{3} - \frac{3z}{4} + \frac{1}{2} = -\frac{1}{3}$

18. $\frac{3a}{8} - \frac{a}{12} + \frac{7}{2} = 7$

11-3 Solving Equations with Variables on Both Sides (pp. 593–597)

EXAMPLE

■ Solve.

$3x + 5 - 5x = -12 + x + 2$

$-2x + 5 = -10 + x$ *Combine like terms.*

$\underline{+2x \qquad\quad +2x}$ *Add 2x to both sides.*

$5 = -10 + 3x$

$\underline{+10 \quad +10}$ *Add 10 to both sides.*

$15 = \qquad 3x$

$\frac{15}{3} = \frac{3x}{3}$ *Divide both sides by 3.*

$5 = x$

EXERCISES

Solve.

19. $12s = 8 + 2(5s + 3)$

20. $\frac{5c}{8} - \frac{c}{3} = \frac{5c}{6} - 13$

21. $4 - 5x = 3 + x$

22. $4 - 2y = 4y$

23. $2n + 8 = 2n - 5$

24. $\frac{2z}{3} - \frac{3}{2} = \frac{3z}{2} - \frac{17}{3}$

11-4 Solving Inequalities by Multiplying or Dividing (pp. 600–603)

EXAMPLE

■ Solve and graph.

$\frac{z}{-13} \le -10$

$(-13)\frac{z}{-13} \ge (-13)-10$ *Multiply both sides by -13. Change ≤ to ≥.*

$z \ge 130$

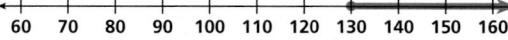

EXERCISES

Solve and graph.

25. $\frac{m}{6} \ge 3$

26. $4n \le -12$

27. $-8 < \frac{t}{2}$

28. $-5p > 15$

29. $9 \ge -\frac{b}{3}$

30. $-6a < -48$

Answers

13. $y = -1$
14. $h = 2$
15. $t = -1$
16. $r = 3$
17. $z = 2$
18. $a = 12$
19. $s = 7$
20. $c = 24$
21. $x = \frac{1}{6}$
22. $y = \frac{2}{3}$
23. no solution
24. $z = 5$
25. $m \ge 18$

14 15 16 17 18 19 20 21 22

26. $n \le -3$

−6 −5 −4 −3 −2 −1 0 1 2

27. $t > -16$

−20 −18 −16 −14 −12

28. $p < -3$

−6 −4 −2 0 2 4

29. $b \ge -27$

−32 −30 −28 −26 −24

30. $a > 8$

3 4 5 6 7 8 9 10 11 12 13

31. $z > 1$

32. $h \geq 16$

33. $a < 24$

34. $x \geq -6$

35. $k > 3$

36. $y > \frac{1}{8}$

37. $(-2, 1)$

38. $(2, 6)$

39. $(3, 5)$

40. $(3, -2)$

41. no solution

42. infinite solutions

43. a. $x + y = 32; 2x = 6y$

   b. $x = 24; y = 8$

   c. $24 + 8 = 32; 2(24) = 6(8)$
   or $48 = 48$

Study Guide: Review

11-5 Solving Two-Step Inequalities (pp. 604–607)

EXAMPLE

■ Solve and graph.

$$-3x - 3 < 9$$

$$\begin{array}{r} -3x - 3 < 9 \\ +3 \quad +3 \\ \hline -3x \quad < 12 \end{array}$$ *Add 3 to both sides.*

$$\frac{-3x}{-3} > \frac{12}{-3}$$ *Divide both sides by −3. Change < to >.*

$$x > -4$$

EXERCISES

Solve and graph.

31. $5z - 12 > -7$

32. $2h - 7 \geq 5$

33. $10 > \frac{a}{3} + 2$

34. $\frac{x}{3} - 8 \geq -10$

35. $5 - 3k < -4$

36. $2y + \frac{3}{4} > 1$

11-6 Systems of Equations (pp. 608–611)

EXAMPLE

■ Solve the system of equations.

$$4x + y = 3$$
$$x + y = 12$$

Solve both equations for y.

$$\begin{array}{r} 4x + y = 3 \\ -4x \quad -4x \\ \hline y = -4x + 3 \end{array} \qquad \begin{array}{r} x + y = 12 \\ -x \quad -x \\ \hline y = -x + 12 \end{array}$$

$$-4x + 3 = -x + 12$$

$$\begin{array}{r} +4x \quad +4x \\ \hline 3 = 3x + 12 \end{array}$$ *Add 4x to both sides.*

$$\begin{array}{r} -12 \quad -12 \\ \hline -9 = 3x \end{array}$$ *Subtract 12 from both sides.*

$$\frac{-9}{3} = \frac{3x}{3}$$ *Divide both sides by 3.*

$$-3 = x$$

$$y = -4x + 3$$
$$= -4(-3) + 3$$ *Substitute −3 for x.*
$$= 12 + 3$$
$$= 15$$

The solution is $(-3, 15)$.

EXERCISES

Solve each system of equations.

37. $y = x + 3$
   $y = 2x + 5$

38. $2x - y = -2$
   $x + y = 8$

39. $4x + 3y = 27$
   $2x - y = 1$

40. $4x + y = 10$
   $x - 2y = 7$

41. $y = x - 2$
   $-x + y = 2$

42. $y = 3x + 1$
   $3x - y = -1$

43. The sum of two numbers is 32. Twice the first number is equal to six times the second number. Find each number.

   a. Use a different variable to represent each number and write an equation for each of the first two sentences.

   b. Solve the system of equations.

   c. Check your answer.

Simplify.

1. $7x + 5x$ **12x**

2. $m + 3m - 3$ **4m − 3**

3. $6n + 1 - n + 5n$ **10n + 1**

4. $2y + 2z + 2$ **2y + 2z + 2**

5. $3(s + 2) - s$ **2s + 6**

6. $10b + 8(b - 1)$ **18b − 8**

Solve.

7. $10x - 2x = 16$ **x = 2**

8. $\frac{3y + 5y}{3} = 8$ **y = 3**

9. $6t + 4t = 120$ **t = 12**

10. $4c + 6 + 2c = 24$ **c = 3**

11. $\frac{2x}{5} - \frac{3}{5} = \frac{11}{5}$ **x = 7**

12. $\frac{2}{5}b - \frac{1}{4}b = 3$ **b = 20**

13. $15 - 6g + 8 = 19$ **g = $\frac{2}{3}$**

14. $93 + 50k = 218$ **k = 2.5**

15. $\frac{w}{4} - \frac{w}{5} - \frac{1}{3} = \frac{16}{15}$ **w = 28**

16. On her last three quizzes, Elise scored 84, 96, and 88. What grade must she get on her next quiz to have an average of 90 for all four quizzes? **92**

Solve.

17. $3x + 13 = x + 1$ **x = −6**

18. $q + 7 = 2q + 5$ **q = 2**

19. $8n + 24 = 3n + 59$ **n = 7**

20. $m + 5 = m - 3$ **no solution**

21. $-3a + 9 = 3a - 9$ **a = 3**

22. $\frac{3z}{2} - \frac{17}{3} = \frac{2z}{3} - \frac{3}{2}$ **z = 5**

23. The square and the equilateral triangle have the same perimeter. Find the perimeter of each figure. **24 units**

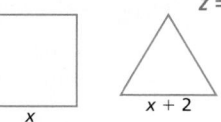

Solve and graph.

24. $\frac{t}{3} > 8$ **t > 24**

25. $-5w > 30$ **w < −150**

26. $12 \geq \frac{h}{4}$ **h ≤ 48**

27. $-36 \leq 6y$ **y ≤ −6**

28. $-56 < -7m$ **m < 8**

29. $\frac{b}{-4} < 8$ **b > −32**

30. $-12q \geq 48$ **q ≤ −4**

31. $\frac{g}{4} \leq -5$ **g ≤ −20**

32. Glenda has a $40 gift certificate to a café that sells her favorite tuna sandwich for $3.75 after tax. What are the possible numbers of tuna sandwiches that Glenda can buy with her gift certificate? **10 sandwiches or fewer**

Solve and graph.

33. $6m + 4 > 2$ **m > −$\frac{1}{3}$**

34. $8 - 3p > 14$ **p < −2**

35. $4z + 4 \geq -8$ **z ≥ −3**

36. $\frac{x}{10} + \frac{1}{2} \geq \frac{2}{5}$ **x ≥ −1**

37. $\frac{3}{4} - \frac{c}{8} < \frac{1}{2}$ **c > 2**

38. $\frac{2}{3} > \frac{1}{2} - \frac{d}{6}$ **d > −1**

Solve each system of equations.

39. $x - 2y = 16$
    $x - y = 8$ **(0, −8)**

40. $y = 2x + 6$
    $y = 2x - 3$ **no solution**

41. $x + 5y = 11$
    $4x - y = 2$ **(1, 2)**

42. $2y + x = 6$
    $3y + 4x = 4$ **(−2, 4)**

43. $y = 5x + 10$
    $y = x - 2$ **(−3, −5)**

44. $x - 5y = 4$
    $-2x + 10y = -8$ **infinite number of solutions**

31.
```
  ←+——+——+——●——+——+——→
 −25  −23  −21  −19  −17
```

33.
```
  ←+——+——+——+——○——+——+——+——+——→
  −4 −3 −2 −1  0  1  2  3  4
```

34.
```
  ←——————————————⊕——+——+——+——→
  −6 −5 −4 −3 −2 −1  0  1  2
```

35.
```
  ←+——+——+——●————————————→
  −6 −5 −4 −3 −2 −1  0  1  2
```

36.
```
  ←+——+——+——+——+——●——+——+——→
  −6 −5 −4 −3 −2 −1  0  1  2
```

37.
```
  ←+——+——+——●——————————→
  −2     0     2     4     6     8
```

38.
```
  ←+——+——+——+——○——+——+——+——+——→
  −5 −4 −3 −2 −1  0  1  2  3
```

 CHAPTER **11**

Organizer

Objective: Assess students' mastery of concepts and skills in Chapter 11.

 Online Edition

Resources

 Assessment Resources

Chapter 11 Tests
- Free Response
  (Levels A, B, C)
- Multiple Choice
  (Levels A, B, C)
- Performance Assessment

 IDEA Works! CD-ROM
Modified Chapter 11 Test

Test & Practice Generator
 **One-Stop** Planner®

Answers

24.
```
  ←+——+——+——+——⊕——+——+——+——+——→
 20 21 22 23 24 25 26 27 28 29
```

25.
```
  ←————————————————————————→
  −3 −4 −5 −6 −7 −8 −9
```

26.
```
  ←+——+——+——+——+——●——+——+——+——+——→
 43 44 45 46 47 48 49 50 51 52 53
```

27.
```
  ←————————————●——+——+——+——→
 −11  −9  −7  −5  −3  −1
```

28.
```
  ←————————●——+——+——+——→
  100  110  120  130  140
```

29.
```
  ←+——+——+——+——⊕——+——+——+——→
 −37  −35  −33  −31  −29
```

30.
```
  ←+——+——+——●—————————————→
  −9  −7  −5  −3  −1   1
```

State Resources

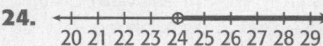

Organizer

Objective: Provide opportunities to learn and practice common test-taking strategies.

 Online Edition

Resources

 State Test Prep Workbook

 State Test Prep CD-ROM

 State Test Practice Online

go.hrw.com
KEYWORD: MT7 TestPrep

TEST PREP DOCTOR The Test Tackler focuses on reading each option thoroughly before making a choice. Students should be reminded to eliminate each choice that is false. Sometimes they will be left with only one response that is possibly correct. Once they have eliminated the false responses, they should compare the responses that are left in order to find the correct one.

Read each problem aloud and then each option. Review with students how to find probability and odds. Students may also need to review how to solve multi-step equations and two-step inequalities.

Multiple Choice:
Answering Context-Based Test Items

For some test items, you cannot answer just by reading the problem statement. You will need to read each option carefully to determine the correct response. Review each option and eliminate those that are false.

EXAMPLE 1

Multiple Choice

Which statement is true for the given spinner?

Ⓐ The probability of spinning green is $\frac{1}{3}$.

Ⓑ The probability of spinning blue is $\frac{1}{6}$.

Ⓒ The probability of spinning white is the same as the probability of spinning green.

Ⓓ The probability of spinning green is the same as the probability of spinning yellow or white.

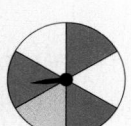

Read each option carefully. Eliminate options that are false.

Option A: Find the probability of spinning green.

$$P(\text{green}) = \frac{3}{6}, \text{ or } \frac{1}{2} \qquad \text{Option A is false.}$$

Option B: Find the probability of spinning blue.

$$P(\text{blue}) = \frac{0}{6}, \text{ or } 0 \qquad \text{Option B is false.}$$

Option C: Find the probabilities and compare.

$$P(\text{white}) = \frac{2}{6}, \text{ or } \frac{1}{3} \qquad P(\text{green}) = \frac{3}{6}, \text{ or } \frac{1}{2}$$

$\frac{1}{3} \neq \frac{1}{2}$, so $P(\text{white}) \neq P(\text{green})$

Option C is false.

Option D: Find the probabilities and compare.

$$P(\text{green}) = \frac{3}{6}, \text{ or } \frac{1}{2} \qquad P(\text{white or yellow}) = \frac{2}{6} + \frac{1}{6} = \frac{3}{6}, \text{ or } \frac{1}{2}$$

$\frac{1}{2} = \frac{1}{2}$, $P(\text{green}) = P(\text{white or yellow})$

Option D is true. It is the correct response.

Read each test item and answer the questions that follow.

Item A

Which equation has a solution of $x = 3$?

Ⓐ $2x - 6 = 3(x - 1)$

Ⓑ $-2x - 6 = \frac{3}{2}(-2x - 2)$

Ⓒ $2(x - 6) = 3x - 1$

Ⓓ $-2(x - 6) = x - 3$

1. What property do you have to use to solve each equation?

2. What two methods could you use to determine if $x = 3$ is a solution of one of the equations?

3. Which is the correct option? Explain.

Item B

An experiment consists of rolling a fair number cube labeled 1 to 6. Which statement is true?

Ⓕ $P(\text{odd}) = P(\text{even})$

Ⓖ $P(\text{multiple of } 3) > P(\text{multiple of } 2)$

Ⓗ $P(7) = 1$

Ⓙ $P(\text{less than } 4) = P(\text{greater than } 5)$

4. What does *multiple* mean? What are multiples of 3? What are multiples of 2?

5. How many numbers are less than 4 on the number cube? How many numbers are greater than 5?

6. Which is the correct option? Explain.

Item C

Which inequality has 0 as a part of its solution set?

Ⓐ $-3y < -6$

Ⓒ $4 - 9y < 13$

Ⓑ $8a + 3 > 7$

Ⓓ $-\frac{5t}{6} > 5$

7. What must you remember to do if you multiply or divide both sides of an inequality by a negative number?

8. Which is the correct option? Explain.

Item D

A poll was taken at Jefferson Middle School. Which statement is true for the given data?

Favorite Type of Movie	Number of Students
Drama	25
Comedy	40
Science fiction	28
Action	32

Ⓕ The probability that a student at Jefferson Middle School does *not* like dramas best is $\frac{4}{5}$.

Ⓖ The odds in favor of a student liking comedies best are 8:25.

Ⓗ Out of a population of 1200 students, you can predict that 280 students will like science fiction movies best.

Ⓙ The odds against a student liking action movies best are 125:32.

9. How can you find the probability of an event not occurring?

10. How can you use probability to make a prediction?

11. Which is the correct option? Explain.

Test Tackler

Answers

1. You have to use the Distributive Property in each equation in order to solve for *x*.

2. Method 1: You could solve each equation and find which one has 3 as a solution.

   Method 2: You could substitute 3 for *x* into each equation and see which equation is true.

3. Option B is correct:
   $$-2x - 6 = \frac{3}{2}(-2x - 2)$$
   $$-2x - 6 = -3x - 3$$
   $$-6 = -x - 3$$
   $$-3 = -x$$
   $$3 = x$$
   or
   $$-2x - 6 = \frac{3}{2}(-2x - 2)$$
   $$-2(3) - 6 = \frac{3}{2}(-2(3) - 2)$$
   $$-6 - 6 = \frac{3}{2}(-6 - 2)$$
   $$-12 = \frac{3}{2}(-8)$$
   $$-12 = -12$$

4. The product of any number and a whole number is a multiple of that number. The multiples of 3 include 3, 6, 9, 12, 15, ... The multiples of 2 include 2, 4, 6, 8, 10, ...

5. There are 3 numbers less than 4: 1, 2, and 3. There is 1 number greater than 5: 6.

6. The correct response is F. There are 3 possible outcomes for odd: 1, 3, and 5. There are 3 possible outcomes for even: 2, 4, and 6.
   $$P(\text{odd}) = \frac{3}{6}, \text{ or } \frac{1}{2}$$
   $$P(\text{even}) = \frac{3}{6}, \text{ or } \frac{1}{2}$$
   $$P(\text{odd}) = P(\text{even})$$

7. If you multiply or divide both sides of an inequality by a negative number, you must reverse the inequality symbol.

State Resources

8. The correct response is C.
   $$4 - 9y < 13$$
   $$\frac{-4 \quad -4}{-9y < 9}$$ Subtract 4 from both sides.

   $$\frac{-9y}{-9} > \frac{9}{-9}$$ Divide each side by -9; change $<$ to $>$.
   $$y > -1$$
   $0 > -1$, so it is part of the solution set.

9. To find the probability of an event not occurring, find the probability of the event occurring and subtract it from 1.

10. Write the known probability as one ratio. Write another ratio of the number of favorable outcomes to the total number of possible outcomes. Then write a proportion by having the two ratios equal each other. Solve the proportion.

11. The correct response is F. Find the total number of students who voted:
    $25 + 40 + 28 + 32 = 125$. Estimate the probability of voting for drama.

    $$P \approx \frac{\text{number of students who voted for drama}}{\text{total number of students who voted}}$$
    $$\approx \frac{25}{125}, \text{ or } \frac{1}{5}$$

    Subtract this probability from 1 to estimate the probability of not voting for drama.
    $$1 - \frac{1}{5} = \frac{4}{5}$$
    $$P(\text{not voting for drama}) = \frac{4}{5}$$

go.hrw.com
State Resources Online
KEYWORD: MT7 Resources

CHAPTER
11
STANDARDIZED
TEST PREP

CHAPTER
11

STANDARDIZED
TEST PREP

go.hrw.com
State Test Practice Online
KEYWORD: MT7 TestPrep

Organizer

Objective: Provide review and practice for Chapters 1–11 and standardized tests.

 Online Edition

Resources

 Assessment Resources
Chapter 11 Cumulative Test

 State Test Prep Workbook

 State Test Prep CD-ROM

 State Test Practice Online

go.hrw.com
KEYWORD: MT7 TestPrep

Cumulative Assessment, Chapters 1–11
Multiple Choice

1. Clarissa has 6 red socks, 4 black socks, 10 white socks, and 2 blue socks in a drawer. If Clarissa chooses one sock at a time, what is the probability that she will choose 2 black socks?

- (A) $\frac{7}{22}$
- (C) $\frac{3}{121}$
- (B) $\frac{2}{11}$
- (D) $\frac{7}{22}$

2. Which situation describes the graph?

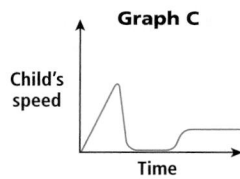
Graph C
Child's speed

Time

- (F) Linda sits on her bike.
  Linda runs to see the neighbor's dog.
  Linda sits and pets the dog.
- (G) Jim climbs on the jungle gym.
  Jim slides down the pole.
  Jim lies in the sand and rests.
- (H) Carlos runs to answer the phone.
  Carlos sits and talks on the phone.
  Carlos walks into another room.
- (J) Juan walks to his friend's house.
  Juan knocks on the door.
  Juan leaves his friend's house.

3. Which ordered pair is the solution of the following system of equations?
$$y = 2x + 6$$
$$x + y = 27$$

- (A) (3, 12)
- (C) (7, 20)
- (B) (10, 26)
- (D) (20, 7)

4. At lunch, each student writes his or her name on a piece of paper and puts the paper in a barrel. The principal draws five names for a free lunch. What type of sampling method is this?

- (F) stratified
- (H) random
- (G) systematic
- (J) biased

5. A trapezoid has two bases b_1 and b_2 and height h. For which values of b_1, b_2, and h is the area of a trapezoid equal to 32 in^2?

- (A) $b_1 = 9$ in., $b_2 = 7$ in., $h = 2$ in.
- (B) $b_1 = 5$ in., $b_2 = 3$ in., $h = 4$ in.
- (C) $b_1 = 2$ in., $b_2 = 8$ in., $h = 4$ in.
- (D) $b_1 = 9$ in., $b_2 = 7$ in., $h = 4$ in.

6. Between which two integers does $-\sqrt{67}$ lie?

- (F) -7 and -6
- (H) -10 and -11
- (G) -9 and -8
- (J) -8 and -7

7. What is the sum of the angle measures of this polygon?

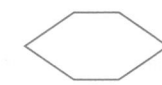

- (A) 180°
- (C) 720°
- (B) 360°
- (D) 1080°

8. If Serena buys a $96 bracelet for 20% off, how much money does Serena save?

- (F) $1.92
- (H) $19.20
- (G) $9.60
- (J) $76.80

Standardized Test Prep

State Resources

go.hrw.com
State Resources Online
KEYWORD: MT7 Resources

 **TEST PREP DOCTOR** +

For item 6, students may have trouble finding the answer in the right range of numbers. For example, if students choose **J**, they may have correctly identified that the square root is close to -8. However, they have not chosen the correct range of two numbers. Suggest that students choose a number that is above and below $-\sqrt{67}$ in order to find the correct answer of **G**.

Answers

15. a. $a + b = 58$ and
$2a = b + 8$

b. $a = 22, b = 36$

16. $4c + 30 = 62$ and
$2c + 46 = 62$; $c = 8$

17. See 4-Point Response work sample.

9. Which value of x is the solution of the equation $\frac{3x}{8} - \frac{3}{4} = \frac{1}{6}$?

Ⓐ $x = \frac{9}{22}$ Ⓒ $x = 1\frac{5}{9}$

Ⓑ $x = \frac{5}{9}$ Ⓓ $x = 2\frac{4}{9}$

HOT TIP! When finding the solution to an equation on a multiple-choice test, work backward by substituting the answer choices provided into the equation.

Gridded Response

10. To prepare for her final exam, Sheyla studied 4 hours on Monday, 3 hours on Tuesday, 1 hour on Wednesday, and 3 hours on Thursday. What is the difference between the median and the mean of the number of hours Sheyla studied? **0.25, or $\frac{1}{4}$**

11. Zina has 10 coins consisting of nickels and dimes in her pocket. She calculates that she has $0.70 altogether. If Zina has two more nickels than dimes, how many nickels does she have? **6**

12. In a school of 1575 students, there are 870 females. What is the ratio of females to males in simplest form? **58/47**

13. An $8\frac{1}{2}$ in. × 11 in. photograph is being cropped to fit into a special frame. One-fourth of an inch will be cropped from all sides of the photo. What is the area, in square inches, of the photograph that will be seen in the frame? **84**

14. The perimeters of the two figures have the same measure. What is the perimeter of either figure? **360**

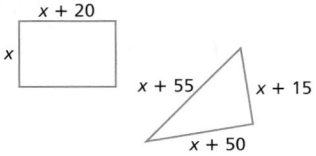

Short Response

15. Two numbers have a sum of 58. Twice the first number is 8 more than the second number.

　a. Write a system of equations that can be used to find the two numbers.

　b. What are the two numbers? Show your work.

16. Alfred and Eugene each spent $62 on campsite and gasoline expenses during their camping trip. Each campsite they used had the same per-night charge. Alfred paid for 4 nights of campsites and $30 of gasoline. Eugene paid for 2 nights of campsites and $46 of gasoline. Write an equation that could be used to determine the cost of one night's stay at a campsite. What was the cost of one night's stay at a campsite?

Extended Response

17. You are designing a house to fit on a rectangular lot that has 90 feet of lake frontage and is 162 feet deep. The building codes require that the house not be built closer than 10 feet to the lot boundary lines.

　a. Write an inequality and solve it to find how long the front of the house facing the lake can be.

　b. If you want the house to cover no more than 20% of the lot, what would be the maximum square footage of the house?

　c. If you want to spend a maximum of $100,000 building the house, to the nearest whole dollar, what would be the maximum you could spend per square foot for a 1988-square-foot house?

Standardized Test Prep

Student Work Samples for Item 17

4-Point Response

a. x = length of front of house
$\quad x < 90 - 2(10)$
$\quad x < 70$

b. A = area, l = length of lot, w = width of lot
$\quad A = lw = (162)(90) = 14,580$
$\quad (0.20) = 20\%$
$\quad (0.20)(14,580) = 2916 \, ft^2$

c. $\quad \dfrac{100,000}{1988} > \dfrac{1988x}{1988}$ if x = cost/ft^2
$\quad 50.3 > x$
$\quad$ cost must be less than $50/$ft^2$

The student wrote the correct inequality and found both the maximum square footage and maximum amount per square foot given the conditions.

3-Point Response

a. let l = length of front of house
$\quad l < 70$

b. let A = area, l = length of lot,
$\quad$ w = width of lot
$\quad (.20)(14,580) = 2916 \, ft^2$

c. $100,000 > 1988x$ if x = cost/ft^2
$\quad$ cost must be less than $50/$ft^2$

The student wrote and solved the correct inequality. However, the explanations are insufficient.

2-Point Response

a. X = 90

b. $20 \cdot 90 \cdot 162$
$\quad = 291,600$

c. $x(100,000) > \left(\dfrac{1988}{x}\right)x$
$\quad 100,000x > 1988$

The student exhibits a very limited understanding of the concepts involved. Very little work is shown. Explanations are lacking.

CHAPTER
12

Graphing Lines

Section 12A	Section 12B
Linear Equations	**Linear Relationships**
12-1 **Graphing Linear Equations**	12-5 **Direct Variation**
12-2 **Slope of a Line**	12-6 **Graphing Inequalities in Two Variables**
12-3 **Using Slopes and Intercepts**	12-7 **Lines of Best Fit**
12-3 **Technology Lab** Graph Equations in Slope-Intercept Form	**EXTENSION** Solving Systems of Equations by Graphing
12-4 **Point-Slope Form**	

Pacing Guide for 45-Minute Classes

Calendar Planner
One-Stop Planner®

Chapter 12

DAY 1	DAY 2	DAY 3	DAY 4	DAY 5
12-1 Lesson	12-2 Lesson	12-3 Lesson	12-3 Technology Lab 12-4 Lesson	12-4 Lesson Ready to Go On? Focus on Problem Solving
DAY 6	**DAY 7**	**DAY 8**	**DAY 9**	**DAY 10**
12-5 Lesson	12-5 Lesson 12-6 Lesson	12-6 Lesson 12-7 Lesson	12-7 Lesson Ready to Go On? Multi-Step Test Prep	**EXTENSION**
DAY 11	**DAY 12**			
Chapter 12 Review	Chapter 12 Test			

Pacing Guide for 90-Minute Classes

Calendar Planner
One-Stop Planner®

Chapter 12

DAY 1	DAY 2	DAY 3	DAY 4	DAY 5
12-1 Lesson 12-2 Lesson	12-3 Lesson 12-3 Technology Lab 12-4 Lesson	12-4 Lesson Ready to Go On? Focus on Problem Solving 12-5 Lesson	12-5 Lesson 12-6 Lesson 12-7 Lesson	12-7 Lesson Ready to Go On? Multi-Step Test Prep **EXTENSION**
DAY 6				
Chapter 12 Review Chapter 12 Test				

ONGOING ASSESSMENT and INTERVENTION

	DIAGNOSE	PRESCRIBE

Assess Prior Knowledge

Before Chapter 12

Diagnose readiness for the chapter.
Are You Ready? SE p. 625

Prescribe intervention.
Are You Ready? Intervention Skills 47, 54, 60, 62

Formative Assessment

Before Every Lesson

Diagnose readiness for the lesson.
Warm Up TE, every lesson

Prescribe intervention.
Skills Bank SE pp. 820–834
Reteach CRB, Chapters 1–12

During Every Lesson

Diagnose understanding of lesson concepts.
Think and Discuss SE, every lesson
Write About It SE, lesson exercises
Journal TE, lesson exercises

Prescribe intervention.
Questioning Strategies Chapter 12
Reading Strategies CRB, every lesson
Success for ELL pp. 177–190

After Every Lesson

Diagnose mastery of lesson concepts.
Lesson Quiz TE, every lesson
Test Prep SE, every lesson
Test and Practice Generator

Prescribe intervention.
Reteach CRB, every lesson
Problem Solving CRB, every lesson
Test Prep Doctor TE, lesson exercises
Homework Help Online

Before Chapter 12 Testing

Diagnose mastery of concepts in the chapter.
Ready to Go On? SE pp. 648, 664
Focus on Problem Solving SE p. 649
Multi-Step Test Prep SE p. 665
Section Quizzes AR pp. 225–226
Test and Practice Generator

Prescribe intervention.
Ready to Go On? Intervention Chapter 12
Scaffolding Questions TE p. 665

Before High Stakes Testing

Diagnose mastery of benchmark concepts.
Standardized Test Prep SE pp. 674–675
State Test Prep CD-ROM

Prescribe intervention.
State Test Prep Workbook

Summative Assessment

After Chapter 12

Check mastery of chapter concepts.
Multiple-Choice Tests (Forms A, B, C)
Free-Response Tests (Forms A, B, C)
Performance Assessment AR pp. 227–240
Test and Practice Generator

Prescribe intervention.
Reteach CRB, every lesson
Lesson Tutorial Videos Chapter 12

Check mastery of benchmark concepts.
AYP State Tests

Prescribe intervention.
State Test Prep Workbook

KEY: **SE** = *Student Edition* **TE** = *Teacher's Edition* **CRB** = *Chapter Resource Book* **AR** = *Assessment Resources* Available on CD-ROM Available online **624B**

CHAPTER 12

Supporting the Teacher

Chapter 12 Resource Book

Practice A, B, C
pp. 3–5, 12–14, 21–23, 30–32, 38–40, 46–48, 55–57

Reading Strategies ELL
pp. 10, 19, 28, 36, 44, 53, 62

Puzzles, Twisters, and Teasers
pp. 11, 20, 29, 37, 45, 54, 63

Reteach
pp. 6–7, 15–16, 24–25, 33, 41, 49–50, 58–59

Problem Solving
pp. 9, 18, 27, 35, 43, 52, 61

Challenge
pp. 8, 17, 26, 34, 42, 51, 60

Parent Letter pp. 1–2

Transparencies

Lesson Transparencies, Volume 2..........................Chapter 12
• Warm Ups
• Problem of the Day
• Teaching Transparencies
• Lesson Quizzes

Know-It Notebook.................................Chapter 12
• Additional Examples   • Chapter Review
• Vocabulary   • Big Ideas

Alternate Openers: Explorations.............................pp. 89–95

Teacher Tools

Power Presentations®
Complete PowerPoint® presentations for Chapter 12 lessons

Lesson Tutorial Videos® SPANISH
Holt authors Ed Burger and Freddie Renfro present tutorials to
support the Chapter 12 lessons.

One-Stop Planner® SPANISH
Easy access to all Chapter 12 resources and assessments,
as well as software for lesson planning, test generation,
and puzzle creation

IDEA Works!®
Key Chapter 12 resources and assessments modified to address
special learning needs

Lesson Plans ....pp. 89–95

Questioning Strategies...............................Chapter 12

Solutions Key ....Chapter 12

Interdisciplinary Posters and Worksheets.............Chapter 12

TechKeys   **Lab Resources**

Project Teacher Support   **Parent Resources**

Workbooks

Homework and Practice Workbook SPANISH
Teacher's Guide...pp. 45–48

Know-It Notebook
Teacher's Guide...Chapter 12

Problem Solving Workbook SPANISH
Teacher's Guide...pp. 45–48

State Test Prep Workbook
Teacher's Guide

Technology Highlights for the Teacher

 Power Presentations
Dynamic presentations to engage students.
Complete PowerPoint® presentations for
every lesson in Chapter 12.

2-1 Solving One-Step Equations

Isolate a variable by using inverse operations which
"undo" operations on the variable.

An equation is like a balanced scale. To keep the
balance, perform the same operation on both sides.

Inverse Operations	
Operation	**Inverse Operation**
Addition	Subtraction
Subtraction	Addition

 One-Stop Planner SPANISH
Easy access to Chapter 12 resources and
assessments. Includes lesson-planning, test-
generation, and puzzle-creation software.

 **Premier Online Edition** SPANISH
Chapter 12 includes Tutorial Videos,
Lesson Activities, Lesson Quizzes,
Homework Help, and Chapter Project.

KEY: **SE** = *Student Edition*   **TE** = *Teacher's Edition*   English Language Learners   Spanish version available    Available on CD-ROM   Available online

Reaching All Learners

Resources for All Learners

Hands-On Lab Activities................................ Chapter 12

Technology Lab Activities........................... Chapter 12

Homework and Practice Workbook **SPANISH**...........pp. 89–95

Know-It Notebook..................................... Chapter 12

Problem Solving Workbook **SPANISH** ....pp. 89–95

DEVELOPING LEARNERS

Practice A.....................................CRB, every lesson

Reteach.......................................CRB, every lesson

Inclusion...TE p. 634

Questioning Strategies........................... Chapter 12

Modified Chapter 12 Resources ................. *IDEA Works!*

Homework Help **Online**

ON-LEVEL LEARNERS

Practice B.....................................CRB, every lesson

Puzzles, Twisters, and Teasers.................CRB, every lesson

Multiple Representations..................TE pp. 634, 645

Cognitive Strategies...............................TE p. 656

ADVANCED LEARNERS

Practice C.....................................CRB, every lesson

Challenge......................................CRB, every lesson

Extension............................TE pp. 627, 665, 668, 669

Critical Thinking................................TE p. 629

English Language Learners

Are You Ready? Vocabulary.......................... SE p. 625

Vocabulary Connections............................ SE p. 626

Lesson Vocabulary.........................SE, every lesson

Vocabulary Review................................ SE p. 670

English Language Learners.................TE pp. 627, 652, 677

Reading Strategies.........................CRB, every lesson

Success for English Language Learners..............pp. 177–190

Multilingual Glossary

Reaching All Learners Through...

Inclusion...TE p. 634

Visual Cues.......................................TE p. 666

Kinesthetic Experience ....TE p. 651

Multiple Representations ....TE pp. 634, 645

Cognitive Strategies ....TE p. 656

Cooperative Learning ....TE p. 661

Modeling...TE p. 639

Critical Thinking ....TE p. 629

Test Prep Doctor..................TE pp. 632, 637, 642, 647, 654, 659, 663, 674

Common Error Alerts ....TE pp. 629, 635, 657, 667

Scaffolding Questions..............................TE p. 665

Technology Highlights for Reaching All Learners

 Lesson Tutorial Videos **SPANISH**

Starring Holt authors Ed Burger and Freddie Renfro! Live tutorials to support every lesson in Chapter 12.

 Multilingual Glossary

Searchable glossary includes definitions in English, Spanish, Vietnamese, Chinese, Hmong, Korean, and 4 other languages.

Online Interactivities

Interactive tutorials provide visually engaging alternative opportunities to learn concepts and master skills.

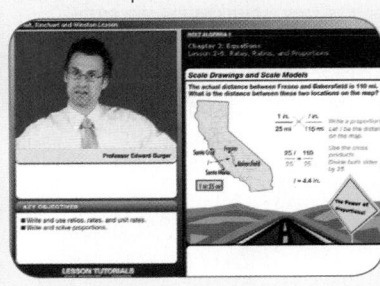

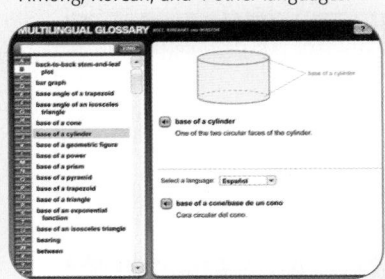

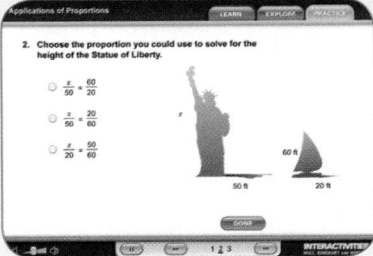

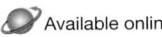

KEY: **SE** = *Student Edition*   **TE** = *Teacher's Edition*   **CRB** = *Chapter Resource Book*   **SPANISH** Spanish version available   Available on CD-ROM   Available online

Ongoing Assessment

Assessing Prior Knowledge

Determine whether students have the prerequisite concepts and skills for success in Chapter 12.

Are You Ready? SPANISH .... SE p. 625
Warm Up .... TE, every lesson

Test Preparation

Provide review and practice for Chapter 12 and standardized tests.

Multi-Step Test Prep .... SE p. 665
Study Guide: Review .... SE pp. 670–672
Standardized Test Prep .... SE pp. 674–675
State Test Prep Workbook
***State Test Prep* CD-ROM**
IDEA Works!

Alternative Assessment

Assess students' understanding of Chapter 12 concepts and combined problem-solving skills.

Chapter 12 Project .... SE p. 624
Performance Assessment SPANISH .... AR pp. 239–240
Portfolio Assessment SPANISH .... AR p. xxxiv

Daily Assessment

Provide formative assessment for each day of Chapter 12.

Questioning Strategies .... Chapter 12
Think and Discuss .... SE, every lesson
Write About It .... SE, lesson exercises
Journal .... TE, lesson exercises
Lesson Quiz .... TE, every lesson
Modified Lesson Quizzes .... *IDEA Works!*

Weekly Assessment

Provide formative assessment for each week of Chapter 12.

Focus on Problem Solving .... SE p. 649
Multi-Step Test Prep .... SE p. 665
Ready to Go On? SPANISH .... SE pp. 648, 664
Cumulative Assessment .... SE pp. 674–675
Test and Practice Generator SPANISH ...One-Stop Planner

Formal Assessment

Provide summative assessment of Chapter 12 mastery.

Section Quizzes SPANISH .... AR pp. 225–226
Chapter 12 Test .... SE p. 673
Chapter Test (Levels A, B, C) SPANISH .... AR pp. 227–238
• Multiple-Choice • Free-Response
Cumulative Test SPANISH .... AR pp. 241–244
Test and Practice Generator SPANISH ...One-Stop Planner
Modified Chapter 12 Test .... *IDEA Works!*

Technology Highlights for the Teacher

Are You Ready? SPANISH
Automatically assess readiness and prescribe intervention for Chapter 12 prerequisite skills.

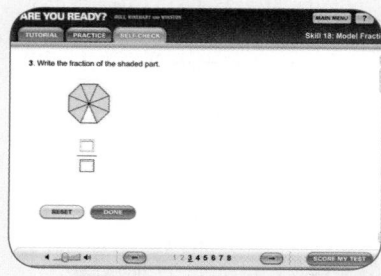

Ready to Go On? SPANISH
Automatically assess understanding of and prescribe intervention for Sections 12A and 12B.

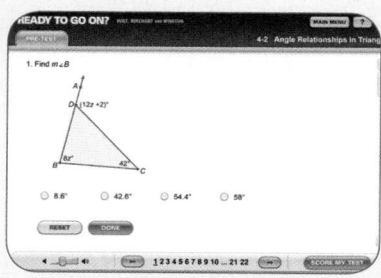

Test and Practice Generator SPANISH
Use Chapter 12 problem banks to create assessments and worksheets to print out or deliver online. Includes dynamic problems.

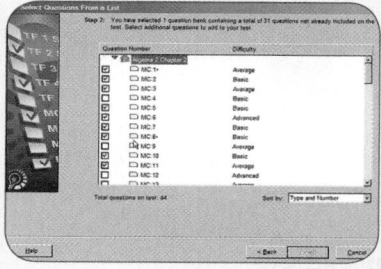

KEY: **SE** = *Student Edition* **TE** = *Teacher's Edition* **AR** = *Assessment Resources* SPANISH Spanish version available ⊙ Available on CD-ROM 🪐 Available online

Formal Assessment

Three levels (A, B, C) of multiple-choice and free-response chapter tests are available in the *Assessment Resources.*

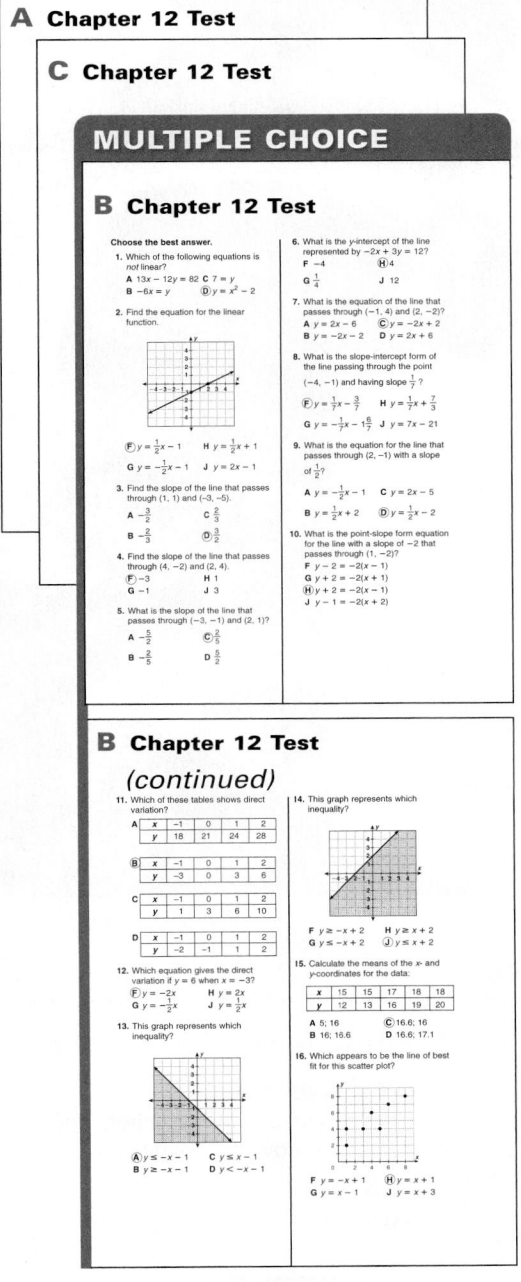

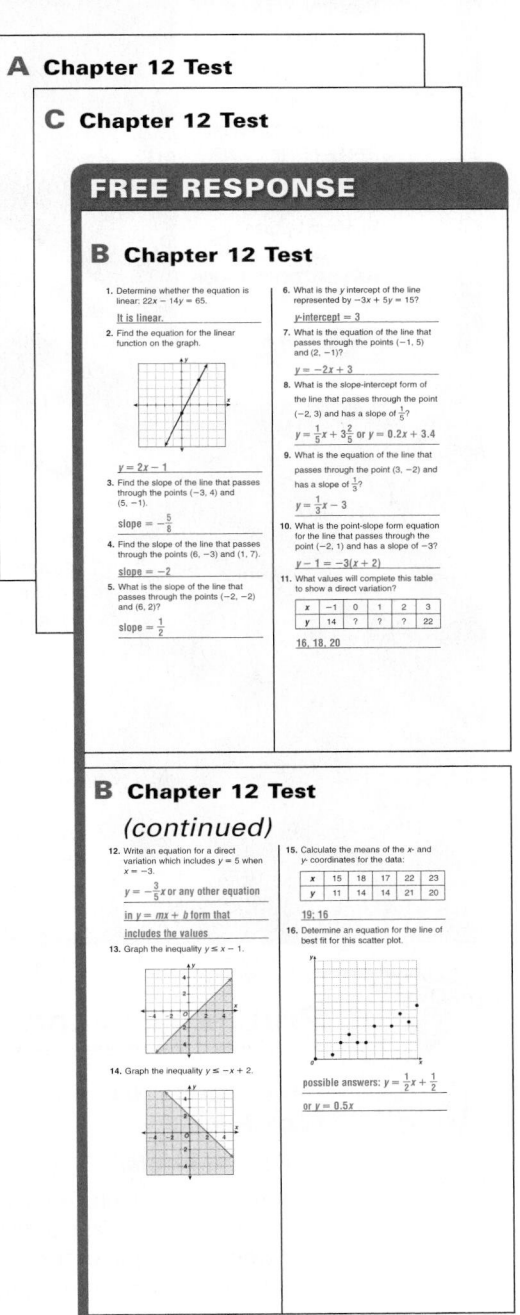

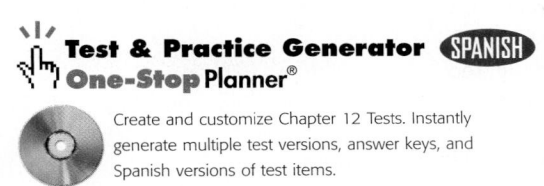

Graphing Lines

Why Learn This?

Remind students that line graphs are used to track the change in a quantity over time. A line graph would be useful to a wildlife ecologist studying data about the whooping crane population because a linear graph would make it easy to see what is happening to the population at a glance. The wildlife ecologist can use the line graph to show whether the population is increasing or decreasing and whether the rate of increase or decrease is fast or slow.

Using Data

To begin the study of this chapter, have students:

- Make a line graph to show the whooping crane population from 1940 to 2000.

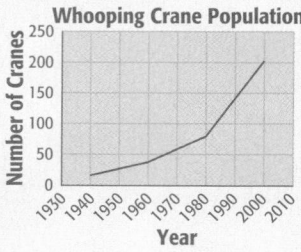

Whooping Crane Population

- Use their line graph to determine the time period in which the whooping crane population increased the most. 1980 to 2000

MULTI-STEP TEST PREP On page 665, students evaluate the cost of two different cell phone plans using linear equations.

12A Linear Equations
12-1 Graphing Linear Equations
12-2 Slope of a Line
12-3 Using Slopes and Intercepts
LAB Graph Equations in Slope-Intercept Form
12-4 Point-Slope Form
12B Linear Relationships
12-5 Direct Variation
12-6 Graphing Inequalities in Two Variables
12-7 Lines of Best Fit
Ext Solving Systems of Equations by Graphing

MULTI-STEP TEST PREP

go.hrw.com
Chapter Project Online
KEYWORD: MT7 Ch12

Whooping Crane Population				
Year	1940	1960	1980	2000
Cranes	15	36	79	202

Career Wildlife Ecologist

Whatever happened to the Carolina parakeet and the passenger pigeon, two species of birds that once inhabited the United States? They are now as extinct as *Tyrannosaurus rex*. The primary focus of wildlife ecologists is to keep other animals from becoming extinct.

They have been successful with the whooping crane, the largest wild bird in North America. The table shows how the whooping crane has come back from the brink of extinction.

Problem Solving Project

Understand, Plan, Solve, and Look Back

Have students:

- Examine the table. Ask them what seems to have happened to the whooping crane over the last 60 years. Why did those changes occur?

- Complete the Whooping it Up worksheet.

- Estimate what the whooping crane population will be in 2050. Describe how they reached the conclusion.

- Do research on an endangered species. What environmental issues face the population? What is the prediction of population change in the future?

Earth Science Connection

Project Resources

All project resources for teachers and students are provided online.

Materials:

- Whooping it Up worksheet

go.hrw.com
Project Teacher Support
KEYWORD: MT7 PSProject12

ARE YOU READY?

✓ Vocabulary

Choose the best term from the list to complete each sentence.

1. The expression $4 - 3$ is an example of a(n) __?__ expression. **subtraction**

2. When you divide both sides of the equation $2x = 20$ by 2, you are __?__. **solving for the variable**

3. An example of a(n) __?__ is $3x > 12$. **inequality in one variable**

4. The expression $7 - 6$ can be rewritten as the __?__ expression $7 + (-6)$. **addition**

addition

equation

inequality in one variable

solving for the variable

subtraction

Complete these exercises to review skills you will need for this chapter.

✓ Operations with Integers

Simplify.

5. $\frac{7-5}{-2}$ **−1** 6. $\frac{-3-5}{-2-3}$ **$\frac{8}{5}$** 7. $\frac{-8+2}{-2+8}$ **−1** 8. $\frac{-16}{-2}$ **8** 9. $\frac{-22}{2}$ **−11** 10. $-12 + 9$ **−3**

✓ Evaluate Expressions

Evaluate each expression for the given value of the variable.

11. $3x - 2$ for $x = -2$ **−8**   12. $4y - 8 + \frac{1}{2}y$ for $y = 2$ **1**

13. $3(x + 1)$ for $x = -2$ **−3**   14. $-3(y + 2) - y$ for $y = -1$ **−2**

✓ Equations

Solve.

15. $3p - 4 = 8$ **$p = 4$**   16. $2(a + 3) = 4$ **$a = -1$** 17. $9 = -2k + 27$ **$k = 9$**

18. $3s - 4 = 1 - 3s$ **$s = \frac{5}{6}$** 19. $7x + 1 = x$ **$x = -\frac{1}{6}$** 20. $4m - 5(m + 2) = 1$ **$m = -11$**

Determine whether each ordered pair is a solution to $-\frac{1}{2}x + 3 = y$.

21. $(4, 1)$ **yes**   22. $\left(-\frac{8}{2}, 2\right)$ **no**   23. $(0, 5)$ **no**   24. $(-4, 5)$ **yes**

25. $(8, 1)$ **no**   26. $(2, 2)$ **yes**   27. $(-2, 4)$ **yes**   28. $(0, 1)$ **no**

✓ Solve Inequalities in One Variable

Solve and graph each inequality.

29. $x + 4 > 2$ **$x > -2$**   30. $-3x < 9$ **$x > -3$**   31. $x - 1 \le -5$ **$x \le -4$**

Organizer

Objective: Help students organize the new concepts they will learn in Chapter 12.

 Online Edition
Multilingual Glossary

Resources

 PuzzlePro®
One-Stop Planner®

 **Multilingual Glossary Online**
go.hrw.com
KEYWORD: MT7 Glossary

Possible answers to Vocabulary Connections

1. The graph of a linear equation would look like a line.

2. The *y*-intercept is where the line crosses the *y*-axis.

3. Direct variation has a graph that is a straight line.

4. The boundary line represents the limit of the linear inequality.

CHAPTER 12 Study Guide: Preview

Where You've Been

Previously, you

- located and named points on a coordinate plane using ordered pairs of integers.

- graphed data to demonstrate relationships between sets of data.

In This Chapter

You will study

- locating and naming points on a coordinate plane using ordered pairs of rational numbers.

- generating different representations of data using tables, graphs, and equations.

- graphing linear equations using slope and *y*-intercept.

- graphing inequalities involving two variables on a coordinate plane.

Where You're Going

You can use the skills learned in this chapter

- to predict the distance a car needs to come to a complete stop, given its speed.

- to estimate the maximum distance a robotic vehicle can travel during a given period of time.

Key Vocabulary/Vocabulario

boundary line	línea de límite
constant of proportionality	constante de proporcionalidad
direct variation	variación directa
linear equation	ecuación lineal
linear inequality	desigualdad lineal
point-slope form	forma punto-pendiente
slope-intercept form	forma pendiente-intersección
x-intercept	intersección con el eje de las *x*
y-intercept	intersección con el eje de las *y*

Vocabulary Connections

To become familiar with some of the vocabulary terms in the chapter, consider the following. You may refer to the chapter, the glossary, or a dictionary if you like.

1. The word *linear* means "relating to a line." What do you think the graph of a **linear equation** looks like?

2. The word *intercept* can mean "to interrupt a course or path." Where on a graph do you think you should look to find the **y-intercept** of a line?

3. The adjective *direct* can mean "passing in a straight line." What do you suppose the graph of an equation with **direct variation** looks like?

4. A *boundary* is a limit. What do you think the **boundary line** represents in a graph of a linear inequality?

Reading and Writing Math

Writing Strategy: Use Your Own Words

Explaining a concept in your own words will help you better understand it. For example, learning to solve two-step inequalities might seem difficult if the textbook does not use the same words that you would use.

As you work through each lesson, do the following:

- Identify the important concepts.
- Use your own words to explain the concepts.
- Use examples to help clarify your thoughts.

What Miguel Reads

Solving a two-step inequality uses the same inverse operations as solving a two-step equation.

Multiplying or dividing an inequality by a negative number reverses the inequality symbol.

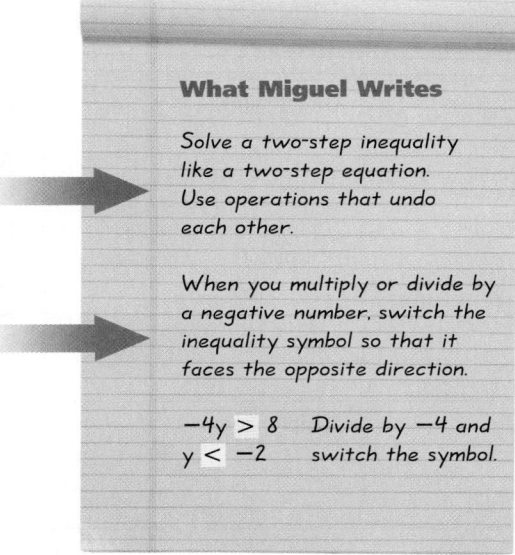

What Miguel Writes

Solve a two-step inequality like a two-step equation. Use operations that undo each other.

When you multiply or divide by a negative number, switch the inequality symbol so that it faces the opposite direction.

$-4y > 8$ Divide by -4 and
$y < -2$ switch the symbol.

 **Try This**

Rewrite each statement in your own words.

1. Like terms can be grouped together because they have the same variable raised to the same power.

2. If an equation contains fractions, consider multiplying both sides of the equation by the least common denominator (LCD) to clear the fractions before you isolate the variable.

3. To solve multi-step equations with variables on both sides, first combine like terms and then clear fractions. Then add or subtract variable terms on both sides so that the variable occurs on only one side of the equation. Then use properties of equality to isolate the variable.

Organizer

Objective: Help students apply strategies to understand and retain key concepts.

 Online Edition

Resources

 Chapter 12 Resource Book
Reading Strategies

ENGLISH LANGUAGE LEARNERS

Writing Strategy: Use Your Own Words

Discuss Students may understand a concept better if they can explain it in their own words.

Emphasize that students should practice using their own words to explain math concepts and problems aloud and in writing.

Extend As students work through Chapter 12, ask them to explain concepts, processes, and problems in their own words. Encourage them to use examples to further demonstrate their understanding.

Possible answers to *Try This*

1. Like terms are similar with the same variable to the same power.

2. Multiply an equation with fractions by the LCD to remove the fractions.

3. Combine like terms and clear fractions in a multi-step equation. Then isolate the variable by adding and subtracting terms and using the properties of equality to isolate the variable.

Linear Equations

One-Minute Section Planner

Lesson	Materials	MiC and Lab Resources
Lesson 12-1 Graphing Linear Equations • Identify and graph linear equations. ☑ SAT-10 ☐ ITBS ☐ CTBS ☑ NAEP	Graph paper, graphing calculators	**MiC:** *Graphing Equations* pp. 11–14, 21–23 **MiC:** *Algebra Rules* pp. 16–17 *Hands-On Lab Activities* 12-1 *Technology Lab Activities* 12-1
Lesson 12-2 Slope of a Line • Find the slope of a line and use slope to understand and draw graphs. ☐ SAT-10 ☑ ITBS ☐ CTBS ☑ NAEP	Graph paper	**MiC:** *Graphing Equations* pp. 15–17 **MiC:** *Algebra Rules* pp. 18–19 *Technology Lab Activities* 12-2
Lesson 12-3 Using Slopes and Intercepts • Use slopes and intercepts to graph linear equations. **12-3 Technology Lab** Graph Equations in Slope-Intercept Form • Use a graphing calculator to graph equations in slope-intercept form. ☐ SAT-10 ☑ ITBS ☐ CTBS ☑ NAEP	Graph paper, graphing calculators	**MiC:** *Graphing Equations* pp. 21–23 **MiC:** *Algebra Rules* pp. 20–21 *Hands-On Lab Activities* 12-3 *Technology Lab Activities* 12-3
Lesson 12-4 Point-Slope Form • Find the equation of a line given one point and the slope. ☐ SAT-10 ☐ ITBS ☐ CTBS ☑ NAEP	Graph paper	

MK = *Manipulatives Kit*

Mathematics in Context

The units **Graphing Equations** and **Algebra Rules** from the *Mathematics in Context* © 2006 series can be used with Section 12A. See Section Planner above for suggestions for integrating *MiC* with *Holt Mathematics.*

Section Overview

Graphing Linear Equations and Using Slope

Lessons 12-1, 12-2

Why? Many relationships can be represented by linear equations. The slope of a linear graph is a measure of the rate of change of one variable with respect to the other variable.

Graph linear equation $y = 2x + 1$.

x	y
−1	−1
0	1
2	5

$$\text{Slope} = \frac{\text{rise}}{\text{run}} = \frac{y_2 - y_1}{x_2 - x_1}$$

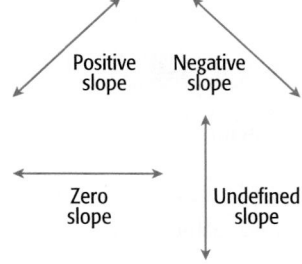

Positive slope   Negative slope

Zero slope   Undefined slope

Slopes and Intercepts

Lesson 12-3

Why? The slope-intercept form of an equation of a line is often used to express a relationship.

Intercepts of a Line

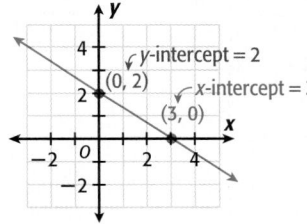

y-intercept = 2
(0, 2)
x-intercept = 3
(3, 0)

Slope-Intercept Form of a Linear Equation

Slope   y-intercept

$$y = mx + b$$

To graph a linear equation in this form, plot the y-intercept, b, at (0, b). Then use the slope to find a second point.

Standard Form of a Linear Equation

$$Ax + By = C,$$

where A, B, and C are real numbers.

To graph a linear equation in this form, find the x-intercept and the y-intercept. Then plot and connect the two points.

Point-Slope Form

Lesson 12-4

Why? The point-slope form of a linear equation is convenient for some purposes.

Point-Slope Form of a Linear Equation

$$y - y_1 = m(x - x_1)$$

(x_1, y_1) is a point on the line. m is the slope of the line.

Write an equation of the line with slope $\frac{1}{2}$ that passes through point $(-3, 5)$.

$$y - y_1 = m(x - x_1)$$
$$y - 5 = \frac{1}{2}(x - (-3))$$
$$y - 5 = \frac{1}{2}(x + 3)$$

Objective: Students identify and graph linear equations.

Hands-On Lab
In *Hands-On Lab Activities*

Technology Lab
In *Technology Lab Activities*

Online Edition
Tutorial Videos

Power Presentations
with PowerPoint®

Warm Up

Solve each equation for *y*.

1. $6y - 12x = 24$ $\qquad y = 2x + 4$
2. $-2y - 4x = 20$ $\qquad y = -2x - 10$
3. $2y - 5x = 16$ $\qquad y = \frac{5}{2}x + 8$
4. $3y + 6x = 18$ $\qquad y = -2x + 6$

Problem of the Day

The same photo book of Niagara Falls costs $5.95 in the United States and $8.25 in Canada. If the exchange rate is $1.49 in Canadian dollars for each U.S. dollar, in which country is the book a better deal? Canada

Also available on transparency

Math Humor

Even though the graph maker didn't shave for a week, everyone still liked to hear him tell his tales. It was another example of the popularity of the *hairy plotter* stories.

State Resources

go.hrw.com
State Resources Online
KEYWORD: MT7 Resources

12-1 Graphing Linear Equations

Learn to identify and graph linear equations.

Vocabulary
linear equation

Light travels faster than sound. That's why you see lightning before you hear thunder. The *linear equation* $d = 0.2s$ expresses the approximate distance, *d*, in miles of a thunderstorm for a given number of seconds, *s*, between the lightning flash and the thunder rumble.

A **linear equation** is an equation whose solutions fall on a line on the coordinate plane. All solutions of a particular linear equation fall on the line, and all the points on the line are solutions of the equation. To find a solution that lies between two points (x_1, y_1) and (x_2, y_2), choose an *x*-value between x_1 and x_2 and find the corresponding *y*-value.

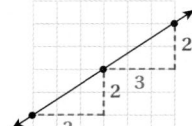

Reading Math

Read x_1 as "x sub one" or "x one."

If an equation is linear, a constant change in the *x*-value corresponds to a constant change in the *y*-value. The graph shows an example where each time the *x*-value increases by 3, the *y*-value increases by 2.

 EXAMPLE 1 **Graphing Equations**

Graph each equation and tell whether it is linear.

A $y = 3x - 4$

x	3x − 4	y	(x, y)
0	3(0) − 4	−4	(0, −4)
1	3(1) − 4	−1	(1, −1)
2	3(2) − 4	2	(2, 2)
3	3(3) − 4	5	(3, 5)

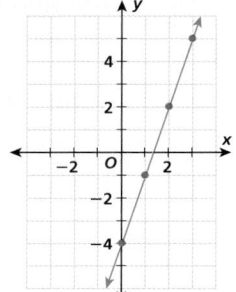

The equation $y = 3x - 4$ is a linear equation because it is the graph of a straight line, and each time *x* increases by 1 unit, *y* increases by 3 units.

---

1 Introduce

Alternate Opener

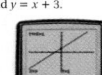
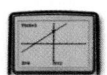

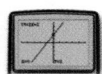
Motivate

Show students the three equations $y = x^2$, $y = 2x$, and $y = \frac{2}{x}$ (Teaching Transparency). Show them the three related graphs without telling them which graph belongs to which equation. Tell the students that one of the graphs is a line and one of the equations is a linear equation and that today they will learn how to graph an equation and determine whether it is linear.

Explorations and answers are provided in *Alternate Openers: Explorations Transparencies.*

Graph each equation and tell whether it is linear.

B $y = -x^2$

x	$-x^2$	y	(x, y)
-2	$-(-2)^2$	-4	(-2, -4)
-1	$-(-1)^2$	-1	(-1, -1)
0	$-(0)^2$	0	(0, 0)
1	$-(1)^2$	-1	(1, -1)
2	$-(2)^2$	-4	(2, -4)

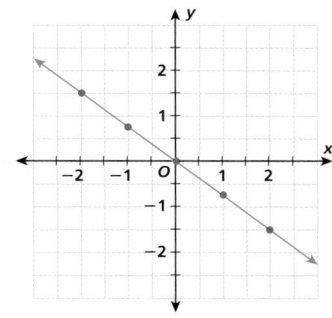

The equation $y = -x^2$ is not a linear equation because its graph is not a straight line. Also notice that as x increases by a constant of 1, the change in y is not constant.

x	-2	-1	0	1	2
y	-4	-1	0	-1	-4

+3   +1   -1   -3

C $y = -\dfrac{3x}{4}$

x	$-\dfrac{3x}{4}$	y	(x, y)
-2	$-\dfrac{3(-2)}{4}$	$\dfrac{3}{2}$	$\left(-2, \dfrac{3}{2}\right)$
-1	$-\dfrac{3(-1)}{4}$	$\dfrac{3}{4}$	$\left(-1, \dfrac{3}{4}\right)$
0	$-\dfrac{3(0)}{4}$	0	(0, 0)
1	$-\dfrac{3(1)}{4}$	$-\dfrac{3}{4}$	$\left(1, -\dfrac{3}{4}\right)$
2	$-\dfrac{3(2)}{4}$	$-\dfrac{3}{2}$	$\left(2, -\dfrac{3}{2}\right)$

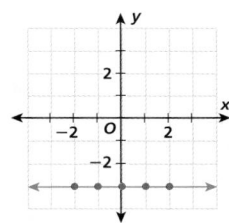

The equation $y = -\frac{3x}{4}$ is a linear equation because the points form a straight line. Each time the value of x increases by 1, the value of y decreases by $\frac{3}{4}$, or y decreases by 3 each time x increases by 4.

D $y = -3$

x	-3	y	(x, y)
-2	-3	-3	(-2, -3)
-1	-3	-3	(-1, -3)
0	-3	-3	(0, -3)
1	-3	-3	(1, -3)
2	-3	-3	(2, -3)

For any value of x, y = -3.

The equation $y = -3$ is a linear equation because the points form a straight line. As the value of x increases, the value of y has a constant change of 0.

---

② Teach

Guided Instruction

In this lesson, students identify and graph linear equations. Demonstrate how to find a solution to a linear equation by selecting any x-value and finding the corresponding y-value. Use the diagram to point out that a constant change in x-values corresponds to a constant change in y-values (3 right and 2 up). Show students some tips for choosing x-values.

Teaching Tip **Number Sense** For example, if x has a fractional coefficient with a denominator of 4 (as in Example 1C), convenient values for x would be multiples of 4.

Reaching All Learners
Through Critical Thinking

Give students the following tables of values.

1.

x	-3	-2	-1	0	1	2	3
y	4	3	2	1	2	3	4

2.

x	-3	-2	-1	0	1	2	3
y	8	6	4	2	0	-2	-4

Have them use the method of differences to determine which sets of values could show linear relationships.

1. differences: -1, -1, -1, 1, 1, 1; not linear

2. differences: -2, -2, -2, -2, -2, -2; linear

Power Presentations
with PowerPoint®

Additional Examples

Example ①

Graph each equation and tell whether it is linear.

A. $y = 3x - 1$

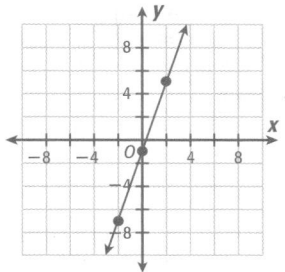

linear

B. $y = x^3$

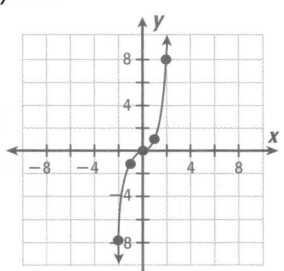

not linear

C. $y = \dfrac{2x}{3}$

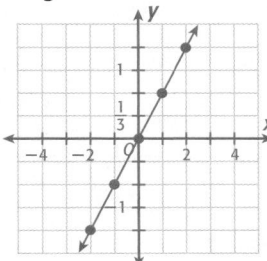

linear

D. $y = 2$

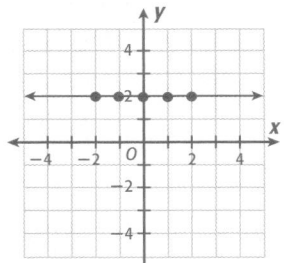

linear

Also available on transparency

Additional Examples

Example 2

A lift on a ski slope rises according to the equation $a = 130t + 6250$, where a is the altitude in feet and t is the number of minutes that a skier has been on the lift. Five friends are on the lift. What is the altitude of each person if they have been on the ski lift for the times listed in the table? Draw a graph that represents the relationship between the time on the lift and the altitude.

Skier	Time on Lift	
Anna	4 minutes	6770 ft
Tracy	3 minutes	6640 ft
Kwani	2 minutes	6510 ft
Tony	1.5 minutes	6445 ft
George	1 minute	6380 ft

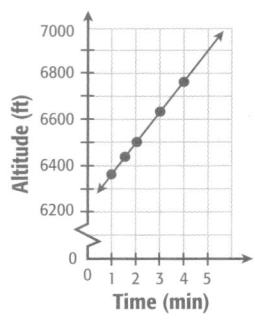

Also available on transparency

Possible answers to *Think and Discuss*

1. The equation is not linear because by the definition of a linear equation, *all* solutions must lie on a straight line when graphed on a coordinate plane.

2. The equation $y = 3x^2$ is not linear because constant changes in x do not produce constant changes in y.

3. It does not make sense to have the lightning strike a negative distance away from the listener, nor does it make sense to have negative seconds pass before thunder was heard. This would imply that the thunder is heard before the lightning even strikes.

EXAMPLE 2 *Physical Science Application*

Physical Science

In a typical year Georgia will experience between 50–70 thunderstorm days. On average, lightning strikes every square mile in Georgia about 16 times every year.

The equation $d = 0.2s$ represents the approximate distance, d, in miles of a thunderstorm when s seconds pass between a flash of lightning and the sound of thunder. About how far is the thunderstorm from each student listed in the table? Draw a graph that represents the relationship between the time between lightning and thunder and the distance of the storm from the student.

Student	Time Between Flash and Thunder (s)
Sandy	5
Diego	9
Ted	4
Cecilia	11
Massoud	8

s	$d = 0.2s$	d	(s, d)
5	$d = 0.2(5)$	1.0	$(5, 1)$
9	$d = 0.2(9)$	1.8	$(9, 1.8)$
4	$d = 0.2(4)$	0.8	$(4, 0.8)$
11	$d = 0.2(11)$	2.2	$(11, 2.2)$
8	$d = 0.2(8)$	1.6	$(8, 1.6)$

The approximate distances are Sandy, 1 mile; Diego, 1.8 miles; Ted, 0.8 mile; Cecilia, 2.2 miles; and Massoud, 1.6 miles. This is a linear equation because when s increases by 10 seconds, d increases by 2 miles.

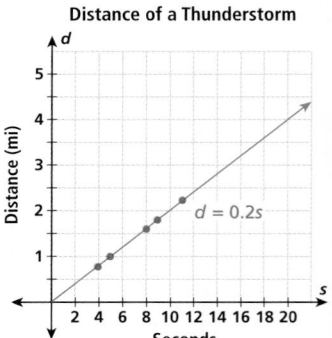

Think and Discuss

1. **Explain** whether an equation is linear if three ordered-pair solutions lie on a straight line but a fourth does not.

2. **Compare** the equations $y = 3x + 2$ and $y = 3x^2$. Without graphing, explain why one of the equations is not linear.

3. **Describe** why neither number in the ordered pair can be negative in Example 2.

---

3 Close

Summarize

Review the steps for graphing an equation.

- Choose a value for x.
- Substitute the x-value into the equation, and find the corresponding y-value.
- Form an ordered pair with the x-value and y-value.
- Graph the ordered pair.
- Repeat the process until you have at least 3 points to sketch the graph.

You may want to point out that this method is useful—not only for linear equations, but for many other equations, as well.

12-1 Exercises

go.hrw.com
Homework Help Online
KEYWORD: MT7 12-1
Parent Resources Online
KEYWORD: MT7 Parent

GUIDED PRACTICE

See Example **1** Graph each equation and tell whether it is linear.

1. $y = x + 1$ linear

2. $y = -3x$ linear

3. $y = x^3$ not linear

See Example **2** **4. Life Science** *Tyrannosaurus rex* was one of the largest meat-eaters that ever lived. By 14 years of age, a *T. rex* was growing about 4 pounds every day. If you found a *T. rex* that was 14 years old, the equation $w = 4d + 5110$ would represent the weight w of the animal d days later. How much would it weigh after 2 days? after 3.5 days? after 5 days? Graph the equation and tell whether it is linear? **5118 lb; 5124 lb; 5130 lb; linear**

INDEPENDENT PRACTICE

See Example **1** Graph each equation and tell whether it is linear.

5. $y = \frac{1}{4}x - 1$ linear

6. $y = -5$ linear

7. $y = \frac{1}{3}x^2$ not linear

8. $x = 4$ linear

9. $y = x^2 - 12$ not linear

10. $y = 3x + 2$ linear

See Example **2** **11. Business** A charter bus service charges a \$125 transportation fee plus \$8.50 for each passenger. This is represented by the equation $C = 8.5p + 125$, where C is the total cost based on p passengers. What is the total cost of transportation for the following numbers of passengers: 50, 100, 150, 200, and 250? Graph the equation and tell whether it is linear. **\$550, \$975, \$1400, \$1825, \$2250; linear**

PRACTICE AND PROBLEM SOLVING

Extra Practice
See page 804.

12. The minute hand of a clock moves $\frac{1}{10}$ degree every second. If you look at the clock when the minute hand is 10 degrees past the 12, you can use the equation $y = \frac{1}{10}x + 10$ to find how many degrees past the 12 the minute hand is after x seconds. Graph the equation and tell whether it is linear. **linear**

13. Physical Science The force exerted on an object by Earth's gravity is given by the formula $F = 9.8m$, where F is the force in newtons and m is the mass of the object in kilograms. How many newtons of gravitational force are exerted on a student with mass 52 kg? **509.6 N**

14. Consumer Math At a rate of \$0.08 per kilowatt-hour, the equation $C = 0.08t$ gives the cost of a customer's electric bill for using t kilowatt-hours of energy. Complete the table of values and graph the energy cost equation for t ranging from 0 to 1000. **\$43.20, \$46.40, \$49.60, \$52.80, \$56.00, \$59.20**

Kilowatt-hours (t)	540	580	620	660	700	740
Cost in Dollars (C)						

12-1 Exercises

Assignment Guide

If you finished Example **1** assign:
Average 1–3, 5–10, 15–20, 30–37
Advanced 5–10, 18–23, 28–37

If you finished Example **2** assign:
Average 1–13, 15–20, 30–37
Advanced 5–14, 20–37

Homework Quick Check
Quickly check key concepts.
Exercises: 8, 9, 11, 20

Answers

1–12, 14. See pp. A16–A17.

Math Background

Linear equations fit into the general category of *polynomial equations*. Linear equations (e.g., $y = x$ and $y = \frac{3}{2}x - 4$) are called *first* degree because the greatest power of x is 1.

Quadratic equations (e.g., $y = x^2$ and $y = 3x^2 + 2x - 7$) are second degree because the greatest power of x is 2.

Cubic equations (e.g., $y = x^3$ and $y = x^3 - 2x^2 + 7x + 3$) are third degree, and so on.

RETEACH 12-1

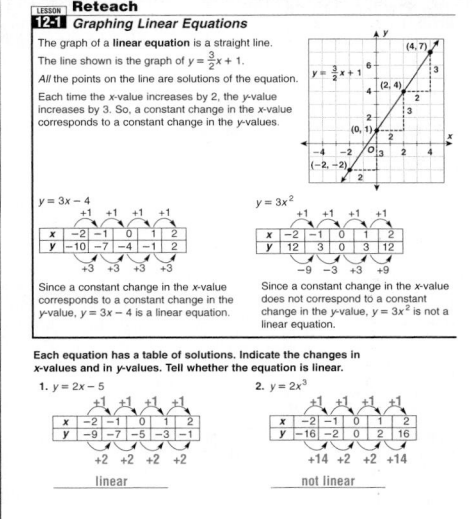

PRACTICE 12-1

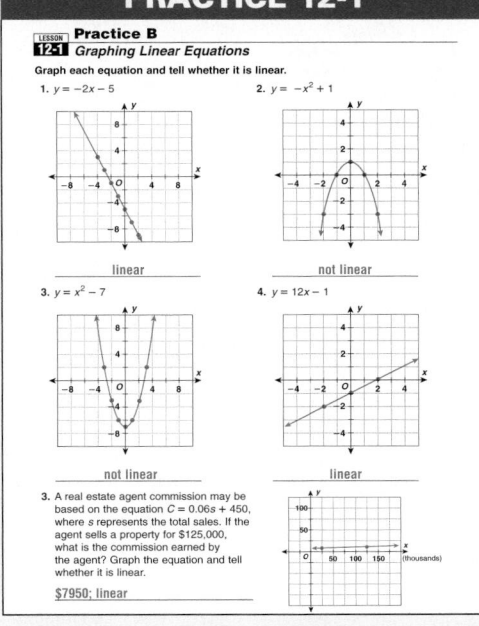

State Resources

go.hrw.com
State Resources Online
KEYWORD: MT7 Resources

Answers

15–23. See p. A17.

24. $d = 254h$; linear; Possible answer: If you choose several values for h, solve the equation for d, and plot the points on a coordinate grid, they will form a straight line.

25–26, 28–29, 32. See p. A17.

 TEST PREP DOCTOR Ask students to read Exercise 31 and summarize the key pieces of information in their own words. If students select **G**, they multiplied 15 by 8 to find the cost of 8 pizzas, but did not add the delivery charge of $4.50. If they choose **H** or **I**, they did not multiply 15 by 8 to get the cost for 8 pizzas.

 Journal

Ask students to write about how to tell whether a graph shows a linear equation.

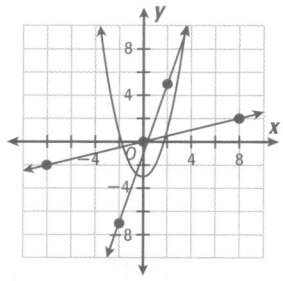

12-1 Lesson Quiz

Graph each equation and tell whether it is linear.

1. $y = 3x - 1$ yes

2. $y = \frac{1}{4}x$ yes

3. $y = x^2 - 3$ no

Also available on transparency

Evaluate each equation for $x = -1, 0,$ and 1. Then graph the equation.

15. $y = 2x$ $(-1, -2),$ $(0, 0), (1, 2)$

16. $y = 3x + 4$ $(-1, 1),$ $(0, 4), (1, 7)$

17. $y = 5x - 1$ $(-1, -6),$ $(0, -1), (1, 4)$

18. $y = x - 8$ $(-1, -9),$ $(0, -8), (1, -7)$

19. $y = 2x - 3$ $(-1, -5),$ $(0, -3), (1, -1)$

20. $y = 2x + 4$ $(-1, 2),$ $(0, 4), (1, 6)$

21. $y = 2x - 4$ $(-1, -6), (0, -4), (1, -2)$

22. $y = x + 6$ $(-1, 5), (0, 6), (1, 7)$

23. $y = 2x + 3.5$ $(-1, 1.5), (0, 3.5), (1, 5.5)$

Transportation

France's *Train à Grande Vitesse* has served over 1,000,000,000 passengers since it began service in 1981.

24. **Transportation** France's high-speed train, *Train à Grande Vitesse* (TGV), has a best-average speed of 254 kilometers per hour. Write an equation that gives the distance the train travels in h hours. Is this a linear equation? Explain.

25. **Entertainment** A driving range charges $3 to rent a golf club plus $2.25 for every bucket of golf balls you drive. Write an equation that shows the total cost of driving b buckets of golf balls. Graph the equation. Is it linear?
$C = 2.25b + 3$; linear

26. **Critical Thinking** A movie theater charges $6.50 per ticket. For groups of 20 or more, tickets are reduced to $4.50 each. Graph the total cost for groups consisting of between 5 and 30 people. Is the relationship linear? Explain your reasoning. **No, the relationship is not linear. The overall graph is not a straight line. The line bends at $x = 20$ people**

27. **What's the Question?** The equation $C = 7.5n + 1275$ gives the total cost of producing n engines. If the answer is $16,275, what is the question? **Possible answer: How much does it cost to produce 2000 engines?**

28. **Write About It** Explain how you could show that $y = 6x + 2$ is a linear equation.

29. **Challenge** Three solutions of an equation are (2, 2), (4, 4), and (6, 6). Draw one possible graph that would show that the equation is not a linear equation.

30. **Multiple Choice** A landscaping company charges $35 for a consultation fee, plus $50 per hour. How much would it cost to hire the company for 3 hours?

   Ⓐ $225   Ⓑ $185   Ⓒ $150   Ⓓ $135

31. **Multiple Choice** Perfect Pizza charges $15 per pizza, plus a $4.50 delivery charge per order. How much would it cost to have 8 pizzas delivered in one order?

   Ⓕ $124.50   Ⓖ $120   Ⓗ $51   Ⓙ $36

32. **Short Response** Evaluate the equation $y = 3x - 5$ for $x = -1, 0, 1$. Then graph the equation. **−8, −5, −2**

Simplify. Write the product or quotient as one power. (Lesson 4-3)

33. $3^4 \cdot 3^{-2}$ **9**   34. $\frac{2^5}{2^9}$ **$\frac{1}{16}$**   35. $10^5 \cdot 10^2$ **10,000,000**   36. $\frac{10^{-3}}{5^3}$ **cannot combine**

37. The scores on a spelling test were 80, 90, 85, 95, 85, 80, 95, 100, 90, 80, 80, 80, and 85. What number best describes the middle of these scores? (Lesson 9-3) **mean; 86.5**

CHALLENGE 12-1

Challenge
12-1 A Recognition Factor

Different kinds of equations have different kinds of graphs. By studying the graphs of different kinds of equations, you can learn to recognize characteristics of the equations.

1. Complete the table of values to graph each equation. Draw all the graphs on the given grid. Write each equation near its graph.

a. $y = 2x + 1$

x	y
−4	−7
−3	−5
−2	−3
−1	−1

b. $y = x^2 + 1$

x	y
−1	2
0	1
1	2
2	5

c. $xy = 6$

x	y
1	6
2	3
3	2
6	1

d. $x + y = -1$

x	y
−5	4
−4	3
−3	2
−2	1

2. Analyze the equations in Exercise 1 and your graphs of the equations. Make a conjecture about how you might recognize a linear equation without graphing it.

Possible answer: In a linear equation, both variables are raised to the first power. Also the variable terms are separated by + or −, not x or ÷.

PROBLEM SOLVING 12-1

Problem Solving
12-1 Graphing Linear Equations

Write the correct answer.

1. The distance in feet traveled by a falling object is found by the formula $d = 16t^2$ where d is the distance in feet and t is the time in seconds. Graph the equation. Is the equation linear?

The equation is not linear.

2. The formula that relates Celsius to Fahrenheit is $F = \frac{9}{5}C + 32$. Graph the equation. Is the equation linear?

The equation is linear.

Wind chill is the temperature that the air feels like with the effect of the wind. The graph below shows the wind chill equation for a wind speed of 25 mph. For Exercises 3–6, refer to the graph.

3. If the temperature is 40° with a 25 mph wind, what is the wind chill?
   A 6°   Ⓒ 29°
   B 20°   D 40°

4. If the temperature is 20° with a 25 mph wind, what is the wind chill?
   Ⓕ 3°   H 13°
   G 10°   J 20°

5. If the temperature is 0° with a 25 mph wind, what is the wind chill?
   A −30°   C −15°
   Ⓑ −24°   D 0°

6. If the wind chill is 10° and there is a 25 mph wind, what is the actual temperature?
   F −11°   H 15°
   G 0°   Ⓙ 25°

12-2 Slope of a Line

Learn to find the slope of a line and use slope to understand and draw graphs.

Remember!
You looked at slope on the coordinate plane in Lesson 7-5 (p. 347).

In skiing, *slope* refers to a slanted mountainside. The steeper a slope is, the higher its difficulty rating will be. In math, slope defines the "slant" of a line. The larger the absolute value of the slope is, the "steeper," or more vertical, the line will be.

Linear equations have constant slope. For a line on the coordinate plane, slope is the following ratio:

$$\text{slope} = \frac{\text{vertical change}}{\text{horizontal change}} = \frac{\text{change in } y}{\text{change in } x}$$

This ratio is often called $\frac{\text{rise}}{\text{run}}$, or "rise over run," where *rise* is the number of units moved up or down and *run* is the number of units moved left or right. Slope can be positive, negative, zero, or undefined.

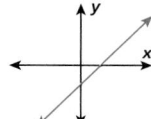 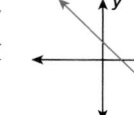 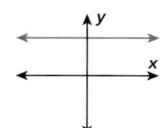 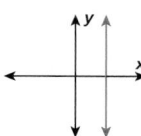

Positive slope   Negative slope   Zero slope   Undefined slope

If you know any two points on a line, or two solutions of a linear equation, you can find the slope of the line without graphing. The slope of a line through the points (x_1, y_1) and (x_2, y_2) is as follows:

$$\frac{y_2 - y_1}{x_2 - x_1}$$

EXAMPLE 1   **Finding Slope, Given Two Points**

Find the slope of the line that passes through (1, 7) and (9, 1).

Let (x_1, y_1) be (1, 7) and (x_2, y_2) be (9, 1).

$$\frac{y_2 - y_1}{x_2 - x_1} = \frac{1 - 7}{9 - 1}$$ *Substitute 1 for y_2, 7 for y_1, 9 for x_2, and 1 for x_1.*

$$= \frac{-6}{8} = -\frac{3}{4}$$

The slope of the line that passes through (1, 7) and (9, 1) is $-\frac{3}{4}$.

Slope measures the rate of change in an algebraic relationship. Linear equations have constant rates of change. This means that the rate of change is always the same. This is shown in a graph by a straight line.

1 Introduce

Alternate Opener

12-2 Slope of a Line

Joseph plots a graph of his 300-mile trip to the coast.

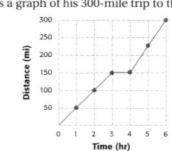

1. Calculate his average speed for the first 3 hours. (*Hint:* Divide the distance traveled during the first three hours by 3.)

2. What happens between hours 3 and 4?

3. Calculate his average speed for the last 2 hours. (*Hint:* Divide the distance traveled during the last two hours by 2.)

Think and Discuss

4. **Discuss** how you could find Joseph's average speed between hours 3 and 4.

5. **Discuss** how average speed is related to the shape of the graph.

Motivate

Ask students if they have ever been skiing or seen it on television. Discuss the difference between the beginner's trail, often called the *bunny slope,* and the expert's trail, often called the *black diamond slope.* Generally the black diamond slope will be much steeper than the bunny slope.

Explorations and answers are provided in *Alternate Openers: Explorations Transparencies.*

Power Presentations
with PowerPoint®

Additional Examples

Example 1

Find the slope of the line that passes through $(-2, -3)$ and $(4, 6)$. $\frac{3}{2}$

Example 2

Determine whether each graph shows a constant or variable rate of change. Explain your reasoning.

A.

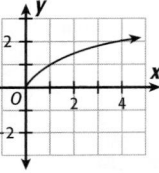

Constant; the slope between any two points is always the same

B.

variable; the slope between any two sets of points in Quadrant I is different

Example 3

The table shows the total cost of fruit per pound purchased at the grocery store. Use the data to make a graph. Find the slope of the line and explain what it shows.

Cost of Fruit	
Pounds	Cost
0	0
5	15
10	30
15	45

3; For every pound of fruit, you will pay another $3.

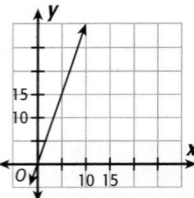

Also available on transparency

Nonlinear equations have variable rates of change. This means that the rate of change is different between different values. This is shown in a graph by a curved line.

EXAMPLE 2 **Identifying Constant and Variable Rates of Change in Graphs**

Determine whether each graph shows a constant or variable rate of change. Explain your reasoning.

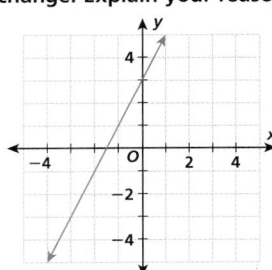

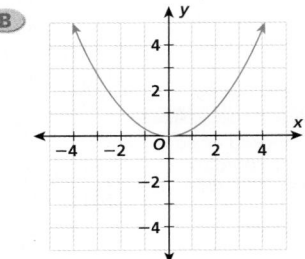

The graph shows a constant rate of change. The slope between any two points is always the same.

The graph shows a variable rate of change. The slope is negative in Quadrant II and positive in Quadrant I.

EXAMPLE 3 *Physical Science Application*

The table shows the volume of water released by Hoover Dam over a certain period of time. Use the data to make a graph. Find the slope of the line and explain what it shows.

Graph the data.

Water Released from Hoover Dam	
Time (s)	Volume of Water (m³)
5	75,000
10	150,000
15	225,000
20	300,000

Helpful Hint

You can use any two points to find the slope of the line.

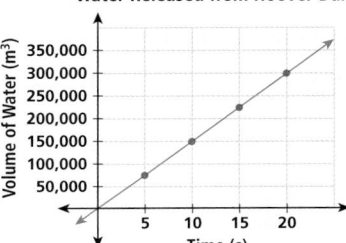

Find the slope of the line.

$$\frac{y_2 - y_1}{x_2 - x_1} = \frac{150,000 - 75,000}{10 - 5}$$

$$= \frac{75,000}{5} = 15,000$$

The slope of the line is 15,000. This means that for every second that passed, 15,000 m³ of water was released from Hoover Dam.

---

2 Teach

Guided Instruction

In this lesson, students find the slope of a line and use it to understand and draw graphs. Remind students that in linear equations, a constant change in *x*-values corresponds to a constant change in *y*-values. Explain that this relationship is called *slope* (Teaching Transparency). Remind students that they have worked with slope before as $\frac{\text{rise}}{\text{run}}$ (Lesson 3-2).

Teaching Tip **Inclusion** Emphasize that any two points on a line will yield the same slope and that the points can be used in the slope formula in either order, but the order must be the same for *y*'s and *x*'s.

Reaching All Learners
Through Multiple Representations

Give students graphs of four lines (one with positive slope, one with negative slope, one with zero slope, and one with undefined slope) and five pairs of points (one for each line and one extraneous pair). Have students use the slope formula to determine the slope between each pair of points and to match the points with the appropriate graph.

Think and Discuss

1. Explain why it does not matter which point you choose as (x_1, y_1) and which point you choose as (x_2, y_2) when finding slope.

2. Give an example of two pairs of points from each of two parallel lines.

12-2 Exercises

go.hrw.com
Homework Help Online
KEYWORD: MT7 12-2
Parent Resources Online
KEYWORD: MT7 Parent

GUIDED PRACTICE

See Example **1**   Find the slope of the line that passes through each pair of points.

1. $(2, 5)$ and $(3, 6)$ **1**   **2.** $(2, 6)$ and $(0, 2)$ **2**   **3.** $(-2, 4)$ and $(6, 6)$ $\frac{1}{4}$

See Example **2**   Determine whether each graph shows a constant or variable rate of change. Explain your reasoning.

4. 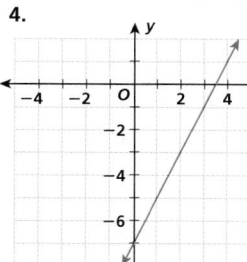   **5.**   **6.**

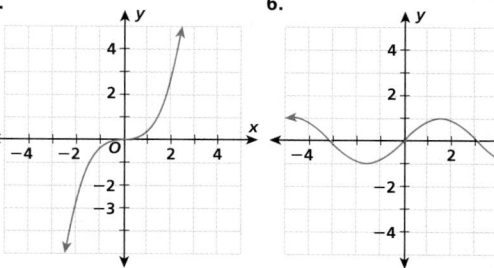

7. The slope of the line is 5. This means that Marvin earned $5 for each hour he worked.

See Example **3**   **7.** The table shows how much money Marvin earned while helping his mother with yard work one weekend. Use the data to make a graph. Find the slope of the line and explain what it shows.

Time (h)	Money Earned
3	$15
5	$25
7	$35
9	$45

INDEPENDENT PRACTICE

See Example **1**   Find the slope of the line that passes through each pair of points.

8. $(-2, -2)$ and $(-4, 1)$ $-\frac{3}{2}$ **9.** $(0, 0)$ and $(4, -2)$ $-\frac{1}{2}$ **10.** $(3, -6)$ and $(2, -1)$ -5

11. $(4, 2)$ and $(0, 5)$ $-\frac{3}{4}$ **12.** $(-2, -3)$ and $(2, 4)$ $\frac{7}{4}$ **13.** $(0, -4)$ and $(-7, 2)$ $-\frac{6}{7}$

3 Close

Summarize

Remind students that slope describes the steepness of the line and is defined as the ratio of vertical change to horizontal change (rise over run). Show students a coordinate grid, and ask them to describe a line with each type of slope (positive, negative, zero, and undefined). As they describe each line, draw an example on the coordinate grid.

Answers

4. constant; The slope between any two points is always the same.

5. variable; The slope is steeper at the ends than in the middle.

6. variable; Some parts of the graph have positive slopes and other parts have negative slopes.

7.

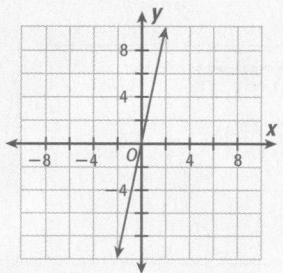

Answers

14. variable; The slope is positive in Quadrant III and negative in Quadrant IV. Also, the slope is less steep in the middle of the graph and steeper on the edges.

15. constant; The slope between any two points is always the same.

16. constant; The slope between any two points is always the same.

17.

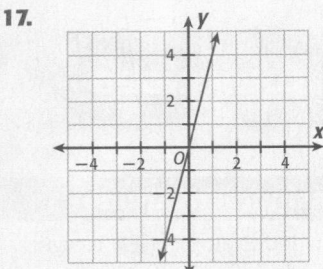

Math Background

Some important points about slope:

• The slope of a line is constant regardless of which points are used to calculate it.

• The order in which the points are used in the slope formula will not affect the slope.

• Vertical lines have an undefined slope. For any two points on the line, the run is zero, so
$$\frac{\text{rise}}{\text{run}} = \frac{\text{(any value)}}{0} = \text{undefined}.$$

• Horizontal lines have a slope of zero. For any two points on the line, the rise is zero, so
$$\frac{\text{rise}}{\text{run}} = \frac{0}{\text{(any nonzero value)}} = 0.$$

See Example **2** **Determine whether each graph shows a constant or variable rate of change. Explain your reasoning.**

14.   **15.**   **16.**

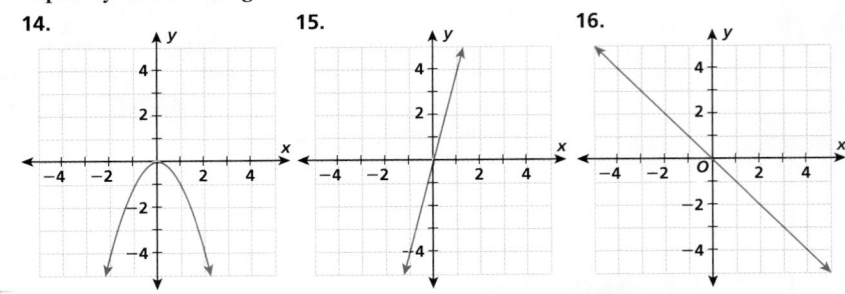

See Example **3**

17. The table shows how much water was in a swimming pool as it was being filled. Use the data to make a graph. Find the slope of the line and explain what it shows.

Time (min)	Amount of Water (gal)
10	40
13	52
16	64
19	76

The slope of the line is 4. This means that the amount of water increased by 4 gallons every minute.

PRACTICE AND PROBLEM SOLVING

Extra Practice
See page 804.

For Exercises 18–21, match each graph with the situation described. Tell whether the rate of change is positive, negative, zero, or undefined.

Ⓐ 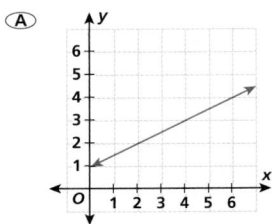   Ⓑ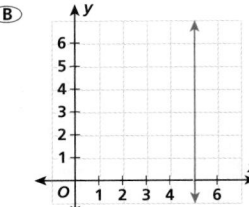

Ⓒ 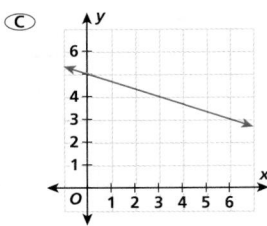   Ⓓ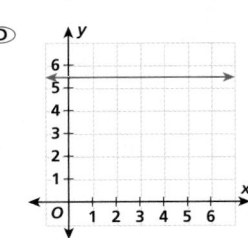

18. A car travels at a constant speed for a number of hours.   **Graph D; zero**

19. A bicyclist pedals up a hill over time.   **Graph A; positive**

20. The descent of an airplane as it lands at the airport.   **Graph C; negative**

21. The path of a rocket as it takes off from the ground.   **Graph B; undefined**

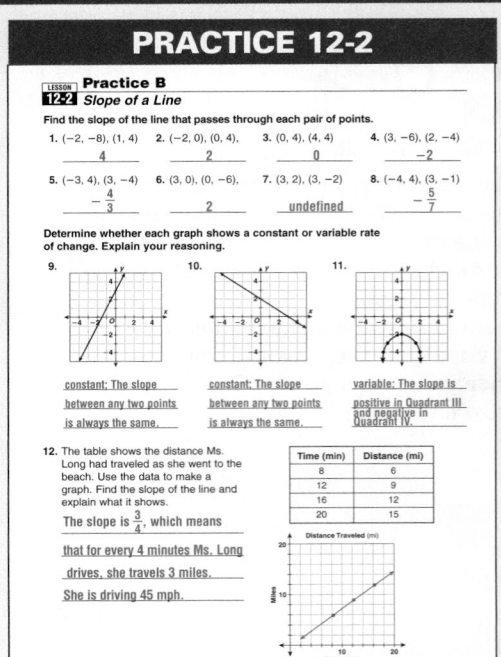

22. Safety A wheelchair ramp rises 1.5 feet for every 18 feet of horizontal distance it covers. Find the rate of change of the ramp. $\frac{1}{12}$

23. Architecture The Luxor Hotel in Las Vegas, Nevada, has a 350-foot-tall glass pyramid. The elevator of the pyramid moves at an incline such that its rate of change is -4 feet in the vertical direction for every 5 feet in the horizontal direction. Graph the line that describes the path it travels. (*Hint:* The point (0, 350) is the top of the pyramid.) $y = -\frac{4}{5}x + 350$

24. A large container holds 5 gallons of water. It begins leaking at a constant rate. After 10 minutes, the container has 3 gallons of water left. At what rate is the water leaking? After how many minutes will the container be empty? **1 gal every 5 min; 25 min**

25. Construction The angle, or pitch, of a roof is the number of inches it rises vertically for every 12 inches it extends horizontally. Morgan's roof has a pitch of 0. What does this mean?

26. Manufacturing A factory produces widgets at a constant rate. After 3 hours, 2520 widgets have been produced. After 8 hours, 6720 widgets have been produced. At what rate are the widgets being produced? How long will it take to produce 10,080 widgets? **840 widgets per hour; 12 hours**

 27. What's the Error? The slope of the line through the points (2, 5) and $(-2, -5)$ is $\frac{2-(-2)}{5-(-5)} = \frac{2}{5}$. What is the error in this statement?

 28. Write About It The equation of a vertical line is $x = a$, where a is any number. Explain why the slope of a vertical line is undefined, using a specific vertical line.

29. Challenge Graph the equations $y = 3x - 4$, $y = -\frac{1}{3}x$, and $y = 3x + 2$ on one coordinate plane. Identify the rate of change of each line. Explain how to tell whether a graph has a constant or variable rate of change.

TEST PREP and Spiral Review

30. Multiple Choice Which best describes the slope of the line that passes through points (4, −4) and (9, −4)?

   Ⓐ positive   Ⓑ negative   Ⓗ zero   Ⓓ undefined

31. Gridded Response What is the slope of the line that passes through points $(-5, 4)$ and $(-7, -2)$? **3**

Do the data sets have a positive, a negative, or no correlation? (Lesson 9-7)

32. The number of weeks a book has been published and weekly sales   **negative**

33. The number of weeks a book has been published and total sales   **positive**

Graph each equation and tell whether it is linear. (Lesson 12-1)

34. $y = 2x + 3$ **35.** $y = 3x^2$ **36.** $y = -6$
    linear   **not linear**   **linear**

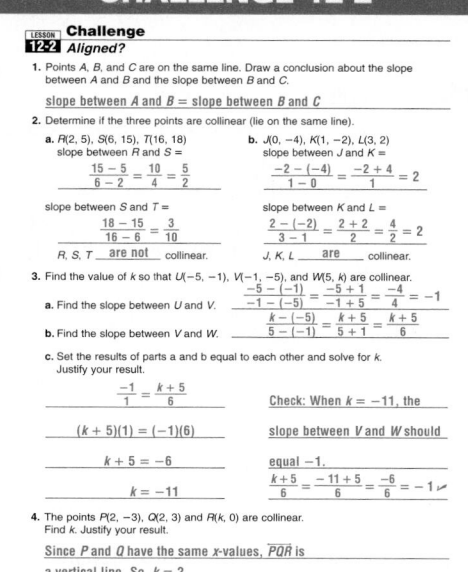

ONGOING ASSESSMENT
and INTERVENTION ◀⬤▶

Diagnose Before the Lesson
12-2 Warm Up, TE p. 633

Monitor During the Lesson
12-2 Know-It Notebook
12-2 Questioning Strategies

Assess After the Lesson
12-2 Lesson Quiz, TE p. 637

Answers
23, 25, 27–29, 34–36.
See pp. A17–A18.

 **TEST PREP DOCTOR ➕** Encourage students to write out the expression in Exercise 30 for slope $\frac{y_2 - y_1}{x_2 - x_1}$ and to identify where the ordered pair values belong in the slope expression. If students choose **A** or **B**, they have placed the numbers in the wrong places. If students select **D**, they have placed the x-values in the numerator and y-values in the denominator.

 Journal

Have students write about the difference between a line that has zero slope and a line that has an undefined slope.

Power Presentations
with PowerPoint®

☑ **12-2**
Lesson Quiz
Find the slope of the line passing through each pair of points.

1. (4, 3) and $(-1, 1)$ $\frac{2}{5}$

2. $(-1, 5)$ and (4, 2) $-\frac{3}{5}$

3. The table shows how much money Susan earned as a house painter for one afternoon. Use the data to make a graph. Find the slope of the line and explain what it shows.

Time (h)	Money Earned
2	$14
5	$35
8	$56
11	$77

See p. A18.

Also available on transparency

CHALLENGE 12-2

LESSON 12-2 Challenge
Aligned?

1. Points A, B, and C are on the same line. Draw a conclusion about the slope between A and B and the slope between B and C.

slope between A and B = slope between B and C

2. Determine if the three points are collinear (lie on the same line).

a. $R(2, 5)$, $S(6, 15)$, $T(16, 18)$
slope between R and S =
$$\frac{15 - 5}{6 - 2} = \frac{10}{4} = \frac{5}{2}$$

slope between S and T =
$$\frac{18 - 15}{16 - 6} = \frac{3}{10}$$

R, S, T __are not__ collinear.

b. $J(0, -4)$, $K(1, -2)$, $L(3, 2)$
slope between J and K =
$$\frac{-2 - (-4)}{1 - 0} = \frac{-2 + 4}{1} = 2$$

slope between K and L =
$$\frac{2 - (-2)}{3 - 1} = \frac{2 + 2}{2} = \frac{4}{2} = 2$$

J, K, L __are__ collinear.

3. Find the value of k so that $U(-5, -1)$, $V(-1, -5)$, and $W(5, k)$ are collinear.

a. Find the slope between U and V. $\frac{-5 - (-1)}{-1 - (-5)} = \frac{-5 + 1}{-1 + 5} = \frac{-4}{4} = -1$

b. Find the slope between V and W. $\frac{k - (-5)}{5 - (-1)} = \frac{k + 5}{5 + 1} = \frac{k + 5}{6}$

c. Set the results of parts a and b equal to each other and solve for k. Justify your result.

$\frac{-1}{1} = \frac{k + 5}{6}$ Check: When $k = -11$, the

$(k + 5)(1) = (-1)(6)$ slope between V and W should

$k + 5 = -6$ equal -1.

$k = -11$ $\frac{k + 5}{6} = \frac{-11 + 5}{6} = \frac{-6}{6} = -1$ ✓

4. The points $P(2, -3)$, $Q(2, 3)$ and $R(k, 0)$ are collinear. Find k. Justify your result.

Since P and Q have the same x-values, $\overline{PQR}$ is a vertical line. So, $k = 2$.

PROBLEM SOLVING 12-2

LESSON 12-2 Problem Solving
Slope of a Line

Write the correct answer.

1. The state of Kansas has a fairly steady slope from the east to the west. At the eastern side, the elevation is 771 ft. At the western edge, 413 miles across the state, the elevation is 4039 ft. What is the approximate slope of Kansas?

-0.0015

2. The Feathered Serpent Pyramid in Teotihuacan, Mexico, has a square base. From the center of the base to the center of an edge of the pyramid is 32.5 m. The pyramid is 19.4 m high. What is the slope of each face of the pyramid?

$\frac{19.4}{32.5}$

3. On a highway, a 6% grade means a slope of 0.06. If a highway covers a horizontal distance of 0.5 miles and the elevation change is 184.8 feet, what is the grade of the road? (Hint: 5280 feet = 1 mile.)

7%

4. The roof of a house rises vertically 3 feet for every 12 feet of horizontal distance. What is the slope, or pitch of the roof?

$\frac{1}{4}$

Use the graph for Exercises 5–8.

5. Find the slope of the line between 1990 and 1992.
   A $\frac{2}{11}$ C $\frac{11}{2}$
   B $\frac{35}{3982}$ D $\frac{11}{1992}$

6. Find the slope of the line between 1994 and 1996.
   F $\frac{7}{2}$ H $\frac{2}{7}$
   G $\frac{37}{3990}$ J $\frac{7}{1996}$

7. Find the slope of the line between 1998 and 2000.
   Ⓐ 1
   B $\frac{1}{999}$
   C $\frac{1}{1000}$
   D 2

Number of Earthquakes Worldwide with a Magnitude of 7.0 or Greater
1990 1992 1994 1996 1998 2000

8. What does it mean when the slope is negative?
   F The number of earthquakes stayed the same.
   G The number of earthquakes increased.
   Ⓗ The number of earthquakes decreased.
   J It means nothing.

Objective: Students use slopes and intercepts to graph linear equations.

Hands-On Lab
In *Hands-On Lab Activities*

Online Edition
Tutorial Videos, Interactivities

Power Presentations
with PowerPoint®

Warm Up
Find the slope of the line that passes through each pair of points.

1. (3, 6) and (−1, 4) $\frac{1}{2}$

2. (1, 2) and (6, 1) $-\frac{1}{5}$

3. (4, 6) and (2, −1) $\frac{7}{2}$

4. (−3, 0) and (−1, 1) $\frac{1}{2}$

Problem of the Day
Write the equation of a straight line that passes through fewer than two quadrants on a coordinate plane.
$x = 0$ or $y = 0$

Also available on transparency

Math Humor

How do you clean the graph of a linear equation? With *slope suds.*

State Resources

go.hrw.com
State Resources Online
KEYWORD: MT7 Resources

12-3 Using Slopes and Intercepts

Learn to use slopes and intercepts to graph linear equations.

Vocabulary
x-intercept
y-intercept
slope-intercept form

The Java Cafe sells $25 gift cards. A medium coffee costs $2.50. The linear equation $y = -2.50x + 25$ relates the number of dollars y remaining on the card to the number of medium coffees x that a customer buys.

You can graph a linear equation easily by finding the *x-intercept* and the *y-intercept*. The **x-intercept** of a line is the value of x where the line crosses the *x*-axis (where $y = 0$). The **y-intercept** of a line is the value of y where the line crosses the *y*-axis (where $x = 0$).

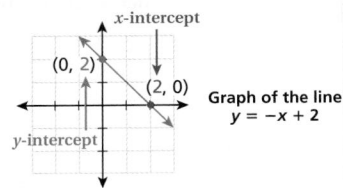

Graph of the line $y = -x + 2$

EXAMPLE 1 Finding *x*-intercepts and *y*-intercepts to Graph Linear Equations

Find the *x*-intercept and *y*-intercept of the line $3x + 4y = 12$. Use the intercepts to graph the equation.

Helpful Hint
The form $Ax + By = C$, where A, B, and C are real numbers, is called the Standard Form of a Linear Equation.

Find the *x*-intercept ($y = 0$).
$$3x + 4y = 12$$
$$3x + 4(0) = 12$$
$$3x = 12$$
$$\frac{3x}{3} = \frac{12}{3}$$
$$x = 4$$
The *x*-intercept is 4.

Find the *y*-intercept ($x = 0$).
$$3x + 4y = 12$$
$$3(0) + 4y = 12$$
$$4y = 12$$
$$\frac{4y}{4} = \frac{12}{4}$$
$$y = 3$$
The *y*-intercept is 3.

The graph of $3x + 4y = 12$ is the line that crosses the *x*-axis at the point (4, 0) and the *y*-axis at the point (0, 3).

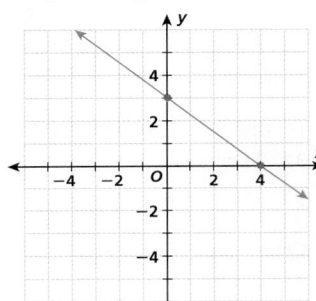

---

1 Introduce
Alternate Opener

EXPLORATION

12-3 Using Slopes and Intercepts

On the graph below, 40 is called the *y-intercept* and 8 is called the *x-intercept.*

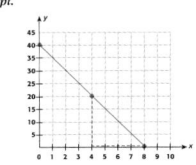

1. How do the rise and run compare to the intercepts?

2. Find the slope of the line by dividing the *y*-intercept by the *x*-intercept and then changing the sign of the quotient. Express the slope as a fraction in simplest form.

3. Consider the triangle drawn along the dashed lines below the line. Divide the vertical distance (20) by the horizontal distance (4), change the sign, and then compare this fraction with the fraction you found in Problem 2.

Think and Discuss
4. **Explain** how to calculate the slope of a line using the *x*- and *y*-intercepts.
5. **Explain** how to calculate the slope of a line using any two points on the line.

Motivate
Ask students, "What do all the points on the *y*-axis have in common?" The *x*-coordinate is zero. "What do all the points on the *x*-axis have in common?" The *y*-coordinate is zero. Tell students that those two facts will help them graph lines a new way.

Explorations and answers are provided in *Alternate Openers: Explorations Transparencies.*

In an equation written in **slope-intercept form** , $y = mx + b$, m is the slope and b is the y-intercept.

$$y = mx + b$$

Slope ↗ y-intercept ↗

E X A M P L E ② **Using Slope-Intercept Form to Find Slopes and y-intercepts**

Write each equation in slope-intercept form, and then find the slope and y-intercept.

Helpful Hint

For an equation such as $y = x - 6$, write it as $y = x + (-6)$ to read the y-intercept, -6.

Ⓐ $y = x$

$$y = x$$
$$y = 1x + 0$$ *Rewrite the equation to show each part.*

$m = 1$ $b = 0$

The slope of the line $y = x$ is 1, and the y-intercept is 0.

Ⓑ $8x = 5y$

$$8x = 5y$$
$$5y = 8x$$ *Reflexive Property*
$$\frac{5y}{5} = \frac{8x}{5}$$ *Divide both sides by 5 to solve for y.*
$$y = \frac{8}{5}x + 0$$ *The equation is in slope-intercept form.*

$m = \frac{8}{5}$ $b = 0$

The slope of the line $8x = 5y$ is $\frac{8}{5}$, and the y-intercept is 0.

Ⓒ $3x + 7y = 9$

$$3x + 7y = 9$$
$$\underline{-3x \qquad\qquad -3x}$$ *Subtract 3x from both sides.*
$$7y = 9 - 3x$$
$$7y = -3x + 9$$ *Rewrite to match slope-intercept form.*
$$\frac{7y}{7} = \frac{-3x}{7} + \frac{9}{7}$$ *Divide both sides by 7.*
$$y = -\frac{3}{7}x + \frac{9}{7}$$ *The equation is in slope-intercept form.*

$m = -\frac{3}{7}$ $b = \frac{9}{7}$

The slope of the line $3x + 7y = 9$ is $-\frac{3}{7}$, and the y-intercept is $\frac{9}{7}$.

Example ①

Find the x-intercept and y-intercept of the line $4x - 3y = 12$. Use the intercepts to graph the equation.
x-intercept: 3; y-intercept: -4

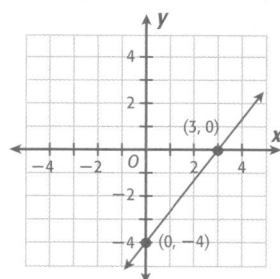

Example ②

Write each equation in slope-intercept form, and then find the slope and y-intercept.

A. $2x + y = 3$ $y = -2x + 3$; $m = -2; b = 3$

B. $5y = 3x$ $y = \frac{3}{5}x + 0$; $m = \frac{3}{5}; b = 0$

C. $4x + 3y = 9$ $y = -\frac{4}{3}x + 3$; $m = -\frac{4}{3}; b = 3$

Also available on transparency

---

② **Teach**

Guided Instruction

In this lesson, students learn to use slopes and intercepts to graph linear equations. Review the definitions of *x-intercept* and *y-intercept*. Ask students to find the x-intercept and y-intercept of a line and to use the intercepts to graph the line. Have students use the slope-intercept form of a linear equation to find slopes and y-intercepts. Then show students how to write the equation of a line, given two points on the line.

Reaching All Learners
Through Modeling

Give each student two related sets of linear equations, one with the same slopes and different y-intercepts (e.g., $y = 2x + 3$, $y = 2x - 2$, and $y = 2x$) and one with different slopes and the same y-intercepts (e.g., $y = 3x + 2$, $y = -\frac{1}{2}x + 2$, and $y = x + 2$). Have students graph each set of lines on the same coordinate plane. When students have completed the graphs, discuss the results with the class.

Additional Examples

Example 3

A video club charges $8 to join, and $1.25 for each DVD that is rented. The linear equation $y = 1.25x + 8$ represents the amount of money y spent after renting x DVDs. Graph the equation using the slope and y-intercept. $\quad m = 1.25;\ b = 8$

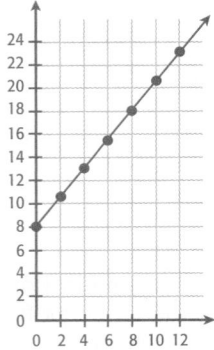

Example 4

Write the equation of the line that passes through $(3, -4)$ and $(-1, 4)$ in slope-intercept form.
$y = -2x + 2$

Also available on transparency

Possible answers to Think and Discuss

1. The line has a y-intercept of 3 and a slope of -5. It crosses the y-axis at $(0, 3)$ and slants down 5 units for every 1 unit right.

2. A student has $30 in a savings account. He plans to add $5 every week. The total amount A in the account can be represented by $A = 5w + 30$, where w is the number of weeks.

EXAMPLE **3** *Consumer Application*

Helpful Hint

The y-intercept represents the initial amount on the card ($25). The slope represents the rate of change ($-\$2.50$ per medium coffee).

The cash register deducts $2.50 from a $25 Java Cafe gift card for every medium coffee the customer buys. The linear equation $y = -2.50x + 25$ represents the number of dollars y on the card after x medium coffees. Graph the equation using the slope and y-intercept.

$y = -2.50x + 25$ — *The equation is in slope-intercept form.*

$m = -2.50 \qquad b = 25$

The slope of the line is -2.50, and the y-intercept is 25. The line crosses the y-axis at $(0, 25)$ and moves down 2.5 units for every 1 unit it moves right.

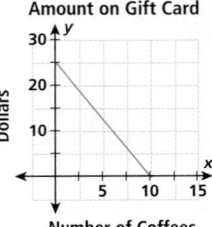

EXAMPLE **4** **Writing Slope-Intercept Form**

Write the equation of the line that passes through $(-3, 1)$ and $(2, -1)$ in slope-intercept form.

Find the slope.

$$\frac{y_2 - y_1}{x_2 - x_1} = \frac{-1 - 1}{2 - (-3)}$$

$$= \frac{-2}{5} = -\frac{2}{5} \qquad \text{The slope is } -\frac{2}{5}.$$

Substitute either point and the slope into the slope-intercept form and solve for b.

$$y = mx + b$$

$$-1 = -\frac{2}{5}(2) + b \qquad \text{Substitute 2 for } x, -1 \text{ for } y, \text{ and } -\frac{2}{5} \text{ for } m.$$

$$-1 = -\frac{4}{5} + b \qquad \text{Simplify.}$$

$$\underline{+\frac{4}{5} \qquad +\frac{4}{5}} \qquad \text{Add } \frac{4}{5} \text{ to both sides.}$$

$$-\frac{1}{5} = b$$

Write the equation of the line, using $-\frac{2}{5}$ for m and $-\frac{1}{5}$ for b.

$$y = -\frac{2}{5}x + \left(-\frac{1}{5}\right), \text{ or } y = -\frac{2}{5}x - \frac{1}{5}$$

Think and Discuss

1. **Describe** the line represented by the equation $y = -5x + 3$.

2. **Give** a real-life example with a graph that has a slope of 5 and a y-intercept of 30.

---

3 Close

Summarize

Review the different methods for graphing lines:

- using a table of values to plot points

- plotting a point and using $\frac{\text{rise}}{\text{run}}$ to plot other points

- plotting the x- and y-intercepts

- using the slope-intercept form of a line to determine the slope and to plot the y-intercept

Remind students that for a single equation, any of these methods will result in the same graph.

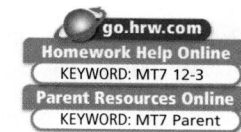

go.hrw.com
Homework Help Online
KEYWORD: MT7 12-3
Parent Resources Online
KEYWORD: MT7 Parent

GUIDED PRACTICE

See Example **1** Find the *x*-intercept and *y*-intercept of each line. Use the intercepts to graph the equation.

1. $x - y = 4$ **2.** $3x + 5y = 15$ **3.** $2x + 3y = -12$ **4.** $-5x + 2y = 10$
$(4, 0), (0, -4)$ $(5, 0), (0, 3)$ $(-6, 0), (0, -4)$ $(2, 0), (0, -5)$

See Example **2** Write each equation in slope-intercept form, and then find the slope and *y*-intercept.

5. $3x = 9y$ **6.** $3x - y = 14$ **7.** $2x - 8y = 32$ **8.** $x + 4y = 12$

See Example **3** **9.** A freight company charges $25 plus $4.50 per pound to ship an item that weighs *n* pounds. The total shipping charges are given by the equation $C = 4.5n + 25$. Identify the slope and *y*-intercept, and use them to graph the equation for *n* between 0 and 50 pounds. $m = 4.5; b = 25$

See Example **4** Write the equation of the line that passes through each pair of points in slope-intercept form.

10. $(-2, -7)$ and $(3, 8)$ **11.** $(0, 3)$ and $(2, -5)$ **12.** $(3, 5)$ and $(6, 6)$
$y = 3x - 1$ $y = -4x + 3$ $y = \frac{1}{3}x + 4$

INDEPENDENT PRACTICE

See Example **1** Find the *x*-intercept and *y*-intercept of each line. Use the intercepts to graph the equation. $\left(\frac{7}{2}, 0\right), (0, 7)$

13. $4y = 24 - 12x$ **14.** $5x = 15 + 3y$ **15.** $-y = 12 - 4x$ **16.** $2x + y = 7$
$(2, 0), (0, 6)$ $(3, 0), (0, -5)$ $(3, 0), (0, -12)$

See Example **2** Write each equation in slope-intercept form, and then find the slope and *y*-intercept.

17. $-y = 3x$ **18.** $5y + 3x = 10$ **19.** $-4y - 8x = 8$ **20.** $3y + 6x = -15$

See Example **3** **21.** A computer salesperson receives a weekly salary of $250 plus a commission of $12 for each computer sold. Total weekly pay is given by the equation $P = 12n + 250$, where *n* is the number of computers he sells. Identify the slope and *y*-intercept, and use them to graph the equation for *n* between 0 and 50 computers. $m = 12; b = 250$

See Example **4** Write the equation of the line that passes through each pair of points in slope-intercept form. $y = \frac{1}{5}x - 3$

22. $(0, -6)$ and $(3, 15)$ **23.** $(-1, 1)$ and $(3, -3)$ **24.** $(-5, -4)$ and $(15, 0)$
$y = 7x - 6$ $y = -x$

PRACTICE AND PROBLEM SOLVING

Extra Practice
See page 804.

Use the *x*-intercept and *y*-intercept of each line to graph the equation.

25. $y = 2x - 10$ **26.** $y = \frac{1}{2}x + 3$ **27.** $y = 5x - 1.5$ **28.** $y = -\frac{3}{4}x + 10$

Possible answer: $y = x + 4$

29. Write an equation that has the same *y*-intercept as $y = 2x + 4$.

12-3 Exercises

Assignment Guide

If you finished Example **1** assign:
Average 1–4, 13–16, 28, 33–41
Advanced 13–16, 25–28, 33–41

If you finished Example **2** assign:
Average 1–8, 13–20, 28, 33–41
Advanced 13–20, 26–29, 33–41

If you finished Example **3** assign:
Average 1–9, 13–21, 28, 31, 33–41
Advanced 13–21, 27–31, 33–41

If you finished Example **4** assign:
Average 1–24, 28, 31, 33–41
Advanced 13–24, 27–41

Homework Quick Check

Quickly check key concepts.
Exercises: 14, 20, 21, 22

Answers

1–9, 13–21, 25–28. See p. A18.

Math Background

The methods for graphing lines used in this section are mainly used for graphing lines that are not horizontal or vertical. For horizontal lines, there is a *y*-intercept, but no *x*-intercept (unless the horizontal line is the *x*-axis), and the slope is zero. For vertical lines, there is an *x*-intercept, but no *y*-intercept (unless the vertical line is the *y*-axis), and the slope is undefined.

State Resources

go.hrw.com
State Resources Online
KEYWORD: MT7 Resources

RETEACH 12-3

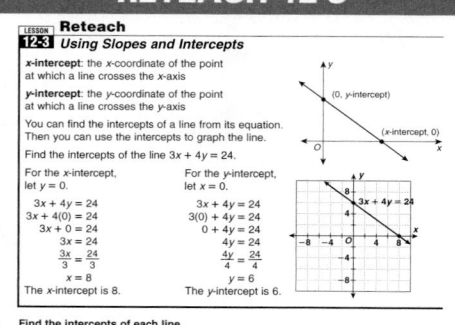

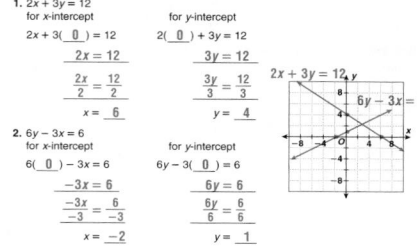

PRACTICE 12-3

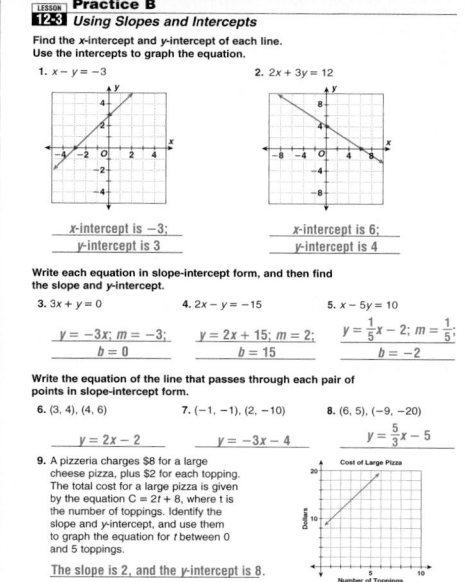

Interdisciplinary

Life Science

Exercises 30–32 involve using linear equations to solve problems involving climbing rates and altitude sickness. The effects of altitude on respiration are studied in middle school life science programs, such as *Holt Science & Technology*.

Answers

30–32, 34. See pp. A18–A19.

Journal

Ask students to describe situations in which one method of graphing lines might be more useful than another.

Power Presentations
with PowerPoint®

12-3 Lesson Quiz

Write each equation in slope-intercept form, and then find the slope and *y*-intercept.

1. $2y - 6x = -10$ $y = 3x - 5$; $m = 3$; $b = -5$

2. $-5y - 15x = 30$ $y = -3x - 6$; $m = -3$; $b = -6$

Write the equation of the line that passes through each pair of points in slope-intercept form.

3. $(0, 2)$ and $(4, -1)$ $y = -\frac{3}{4}x + 2$

4. $(-2, 2)$ and $(4, -4)$ $y = -x$

Also available on transparency

Often people will get sick at high altitudes because there is less oxygen and lower atmospheric pressure.

Acute Mountain Sickness (AMS) occurs if you ascend in altitude too quickly without giving your body time to adjust. It usually occurs at altitudes over 10,000 feet above sea level. To prevent AMS you should not ascend more than 1,000 feet per day. And every time you climb a total of 3,000 feet, your body needs two nights to adjust.

30. The map shows a team's plan for climbing Long's Peak in Rocky Mountain National Park.

   a. Make a graph of the team's plan of ascent and find the slope of the line. (Day number should be your *x*-value, and altitude should be your *y*-value.)

   b. Find the *y*-intercept and explain what it means.

   c. Write the equation of the line in slope-intercept form.

   d. Does the team run a high risk of getting AMS?

31. The equation that describes a mountain climber's ascent up Mount McKinley in Alaska is $y = 955x + 16{,}500$, where *x* is the day number and *y* is the altitude at the end of the day. What are the slope and *y*-intercept? What do they mean in terms of the climb?

32. ⭐ **Challenge** Make a graph of the ascent of a team that follows the rules to avoid AMS exactly and spends the minimum number of days climbing from base camp (17,600 ft) to the summit of Mount Everest (29,035 ft). Can you write a linear equation describing this trip? Explain your answer.

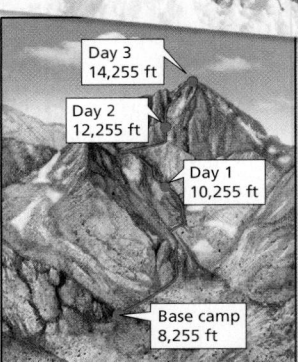

Day 3
14,255 ft

Day 2
12,255 ft

Day 1
10,255 ft

Base camp
8,255 ft

TEST PREP and Spiral Review

33. Multiple Choice What is the equation in slope-intercept form of the line that passes through points $(1, 6)$ and $(-1, -2)$?

  Ⓐ $y = 2x + 4$ Ⓑ $y = -3x + 6$ Ⓒ $y = 4x - 2$ Ⓓ $y = 4x + 2$

34. Extended Response Write the equation $9x + 7y = 63$ in slope-intercept form. Then identify *m* and *b*. Graph the line. $y = -\frac{9}{7}x + 9$; $m = -\frac{9}{7}$; $b = 9$

Find each unit rate. (Lesson 5-2)

35. \$31.75 for 5 hours
\$6.35 per hour

36. 24 carts for 12 classrooms
2 carts per classroom

37. \$44 for 8 beef burritos
\$5.50 per burrito

Find the slope of the line that passes through each pair of points. (Lesson 12-2)

38. $(2, 3), (4, 8)$ $\frac{5}{2}$ **39.** $(3, -1), (7, 4)$ $\frac{5}{4}$ **40.** $(-6, 1), (-7, 7)$ -6 **41.** $(5, 4), (-11, 0)$ $\frac{1}{4}$

Technology LAB 12-3

Graph Equations in Slope-Intercept Form

Use with Lesson 12-3

go.hrw.com
Lab Resources Online
KEYWORD: MT7 Lab12

To graph $y = x + 1$, a linear equation in slope-intercept form, in the standard graphing calculator window, press [Y=] ; enter the right side of the equation, [X,T,θ,n] [+] 1; and press [ZOOM] **6:ZStandard.**

From the slope-intercept equation, you know that the slope of the line is 1. Notice that the standard window distorts the screen, and the line does not appear to have a great enough slope.

Press [ZOOM] **5:ZSquare.** This changes the scale for x from -10 to 10 to -15.16 to 15.16. The graph is shown at right. Or press [ZOOM] **8:ZInteger** [ENTER] . This changes the scale for x to -47 to 47 and the scale for y to -31 to 31.

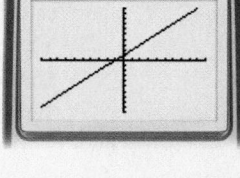

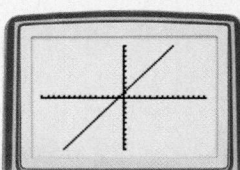

Activity

1 Graph $2x + 3y = 36$ in the integer window. Find the x- and y-intercepts of the graph.

First solve $3y = -2x + 36$ for y.

$y = \frac{-2x + 36}{3}$, so $y = -\frac{2}{3}x + 12$.

Press [Y=] ; enter the right side of the equation,
[(] [(−)] 2 [÷] 3 [)] [X,T,θ,n] [+] 12; and press
[ZOOM] **8:ZInteger** [ENTER] .

Press [TRACE] to see the equation of the line and the y-intercept. The graph in the **ZInteger** window is shown.

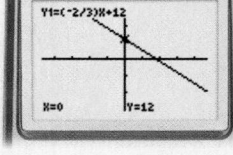

Think and Discuss

1. How do the ratios of the range of y to the range of x in the **ZSquare** and **ZInteger** windows compare?
Possible answers to *Think and Discuss*
The ratios 15.16 to 10 and 47 to 31 are roughly equal.

Try This

Graph each equation in a square window.

1. $y = 3x$ 2. $3y = x$ 3. $3y - 6x = 15$ 4. $2x + 5y = 40$

Answers to *Try This*

1.
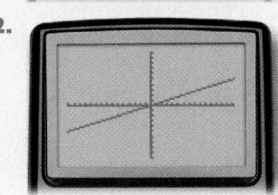

2.
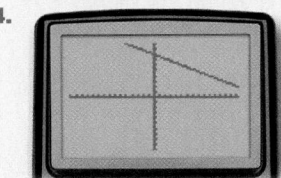

3.
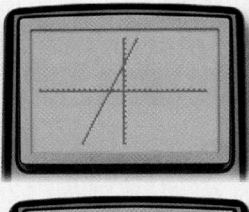

4.

Technology LAB

Organizer

Use with Lesson 12-3

Pacing:
Traditional $\frac{1}{2}$ day
Block $\frac{1}{4}$ day

Objective: Use a graphing calculator to graph equations in slope-intercept form.

Materials: Graphing calculator

PREMIER Online Edition
Graphing Calculator, TechKeys

Resources

LAB *Technology Lab Activities*
Lab 12-3 Recording Sheet

Teach

Discuss

Students should observe the effects of adjusting the viewing window on the shape of the graph. They should compare and contrast the view of the line when the window is square to a standard viewing window.

Close

Key Concept

A square viewing window allows students to observe the true slope of a line.

Assessment

1. Use the graphing calculator to find the y-value of the equation $y = \frac{3}{4}x + 5$ when $x = 2$.
$y = 6\frac{1}{2}$, or $\frac{13}{2}$

2. Use the graphing calculator to find the x-intercept of the graph of the equation $y = -\frac{1}{3}x - 2$. $(-6, 0)$

State Resources

go.hrw.com
State Resources Online
KEYWORD: MT7 Resources

Pacing: Traditional 1 day
Block $\frac{1}{2}$ day

Objective: Students find the equation of a line given one point and the slope.

Online Edition
Tutorial Videos

Power Presentations
with PowerPoint®

Warm Up

Write the equation of the line that passes through each pair of points in slope-intercept form.

1. $(0, -3)$ and $(2, -3)$ $y = -3$

2. $(5, -3)$ and $(5, 1)$ $x = 5$

3. $(-6, 0)$ and $(0, -2)$
$y = -\frac{1}{3}x - 2$

4. $(4, 6)$ and $(-2, 0)$ $y = x + 2$

Problem of the Day

Without using equations for horizontal or vertical lines, write the equations of four lines that form a square.
Possible answer: $y = x + 2$, $y = x - 2$, $y = -x + 2$, $y = -x - 2$

Also available on transparency

Math Humor

When the student tried to stretch out the horizontal axis of his graph, the paper ripped—too much *x-tension.*

State Resources

go.hrw.com
State Resources Online
KEYWORD: MT7 Resources

12-4 Point-Slope Form

Learn to find the equation of a line given one point and the slope.

Vocabulary
point-slope form

Lasers aim light along a straight path. If you know the destination of the light beam (a point on the line) and the slant of the beam (the slope), you can write an equation in *point-slope form* to calculate the height at which the laser is positioned.

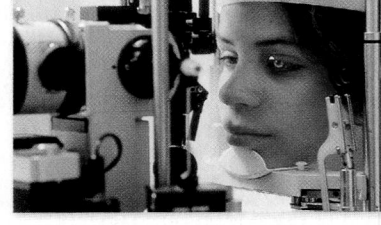

The **point-slope form** of an equation of a line with slope m passing through (x_1, y_1) is $y - y_1 = m(x - x_1)$.

Point on the line	Point-slope form
(x_1, y_1)	$y - y_1 = m(x - x_1)$
	Slope

EXAMPLE 1 Using Point-Slope Form to Identify Information About a Line

Use the point-slope form of each equation to identify a point the line passes through and the slope of the line.

A $y - 9 = -\frac{2}{3}(x - 21)$

$y - y_1 = m(x - x_1)$

$y - 9 = -\frac{2}{3}(x - 21)$ *The equation is in point-slope form.*

$m = -\frac{2}{3}$ *Read the value of m from the equation.*

$(x_1, y_1) = (21, 9)$ *Read the point from the equation.*

The line defined by $y - 9 = -\frac{2}{3}(x - 21)$ has slope $-\frac{2}{3}$, and passes through the point $(21, 9)$.

B $y - 2 = 3(x + 8)$

$y - y_1 = m(x - x_1)$

$y - 2 = 3(x + 8)$

$y - 2 = 3[x - (-8)]$ *Rewrite using subtraction instead*

$m = 3$ *of addition.*

$(x_1, y_1) = (-8, 2)$

The line defined by $y - 2 = 3(x + 8)$ has slope 3, and passes through the point $(-8, 2)$.

---

1 Introduce

Alternate Opener

EXPLORATION

12-4 Point-Slope Form

The graph shows the point $(2, 4)$.

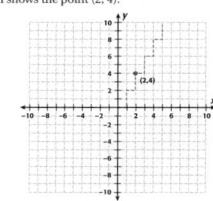

1. Draw a line that rests on the "stairs" drawn with a dashed line and that passes through the point $(2, 4)$.

2. Calculate the slope of the line by dividing the vertical distance of each step by the horizontal distance of each step of the stairs.

3. Use the *point-slope form* $y - y_1 = m(x - x_1)$ to find the equation for the line. (*Hint:* $y_1 = 4$, $x_1 = 2$, and $m =$ the slope you found in Problem 2.)

Think and Discuss

4. **Explain** why the equation $y - y_1 = m(x - x_1)$ is called the point-slope form of a line.

Motivate

Remind students that in the last lesson, they used the slope-intercept method to graph lines. They started at the *y*-intercept and then used the slope to find another point to determine the line. Ask students if the same general method would work if the graph were started at a point other than the *y*-intercept.
yes

Explorations and answers are provided in *Alternate Openers: Explorations Transparencies.*

EXAMPLE 2 **Writing the Point-Slope Form of an Equation**

Write the point-slope form of the equation with the given slope that passes through the indicated point.

A the line with slope −2 passing through (4, 1)

$y - y_1 = m(x - x_1)$

$y - 1 = -2(x - 4)$ *Substitute 4 for x_1, 1 for y_1, and −2 for m.*

The equation of the line with slope −2 that passes through (4, 1) in point-slope form is $y - 1 = -2(x - 4)$.

B the line with slope 5 passing through (−2, 4)

$y - y_1 = m(x - x_1)$

$y - 4 = 5[x - (-2)]$ *Substitute −2 for x_1, 4 for y_1, and 5 for m.*

$y - 4 = 5(x + 2)$

The equation of the line with slope 5 that passes through (−2, 4) in point-slope form is $y - 4 = 5(x + 2)$.

EXAMPLE 3 *Medical Application*

Suppose that laser eye surgery is modeled on a coordinate grid. The laser is positioned at the *y*-intercept so that the light shifts down 1 mm for each 40 mm it shifts to the right. The light reaches the center of the cornea of the eye at (125, 0). Write the equation of the light beam in point-slope form, and find the height of the laser.

As *x* increases by 40, *y* decreases by 1, so the slope of the line is $-\frac{1}{40}$. The line must pass through the point (125, 0).

$y - y_1 = m(x - x_1)$

$y - 0 = -\frac{1}{40}(x - 125)$ *Substitute 125 for x_1, 0 for y_1, and $-\frac{1}{40}$ for m.*

The equation of the line the laser beam travels along, in point-slope form, is $y = -\frac{1}{40}(x - 125)$. Substitute 0 for *x* to find the *y*-intercept.

$y = -\frac{1}{40}(0 - 125)$

$y = -\frac{1}{40}(-125)$

$y = 3.125$

The *y*-intercept is 3.125, so the laser is at a height of 3.125 mm.

2. Possible answer: Find the slope by dividing the difference of the *y*-coordinates by the difference of the *x*-coordinates. Substitute the slope and one of the given points into the equation $y - y_1 = m(x - x_1)$.

Think and Discuss

1. Describe the line, using the point-slope equation, that has a slope of 2 and passes through (−3, 4).

2. Tell how you find the point-slope form of the line when you know the coordinates of two points.

2 Teach

Guided Instruction

In this lesson, students learn to find the equation of a line, given one point and the slope. Introduce students to the *point-slope form* of a line, $y - y_1 = m(x - x_1)$. You may want to use the Teaching Transparency. As the name suggests, the equation requires one point and the slope. Show students how to identify the slope and a point, given the equation of a line. Then show them how to write an equation, given the slope and a point.

Reaching All Learners
Through Multiple Representations

Give students four different equations for the same line. Have students graph each equation using a different method (standard form using intercepts: $4x - 2y = 8$; slope-intercept form using slope and *y*-intercept: $y = 2x - 4$; point-slope form using slope and one point: $y + 2 = 2(x - 1)$; and using a table of values created from a non-standard form: $4x = 2y + 8$). Students should discover that there are many possible forms of the equation of a line.

3 Close

Summarize

Discuss with students which method they would use to write an equation for each line described below. You may want to point out that any acceptable method will work, but some may be easier in certain cases.

1. line with a *y*-intercept at (0, −2) and a slope of 1

2. line with a slope of 4 through the point (2, 1)

3. line through the points (0, 3) and (4, 1)

Possible answers:

1. slope-intercept form

2. point-slope form

3. either form

Assignment Guide

If you finished Example **1** assign:
Average 1–6, 10–15, 29–36
Advanced 10–15, 29–36

If you finished Example **2** assign:
Average 1–8, 10–17, 20, 29–36
Advanced 10–17, 19–23, 27–36

If you finished Example **3** assign:
Average 1–18, 20, 24, 25, 29–36
Advanced 10–36

Homework Quick Check

Quickly check key concepts.
Exercises: 12, 16, 18, 20

Answers

23. See p. A19.

Math Background

The many formulas associated with linear equations can lead to some confusion. It may help to see the relation of the equations to the slope formula, $m = \frac{y_2 - y_1}{x_2 - x_1}$.

Multiplying both sides of this formula by $(x_2 - x_1)$ and replacing the point (x_2, y_2) with the variables x and y yields the point-slope form of a line, $y - y_1 = m(x - x_1)$.

Substituting a point on the line with coordinates $(0, b)$ into this equation yields $y - b = mx$, which is easily changed to the slope-intercept form of a line, $y = mx + b$.

---

go.hrw.com
Homework Help Online
KEYWORD: MT7 12-4
Parent Resources Online
KEYWORD: MT7 Parent

GUIDED PRACTICE

See Example **1** Use the point-slope form of each equation to identify a point the line passes through and the slope of the line. **Possible answers are given.**

1. $y - 2 = -3(x + 6)$
$(-6, 2), -3$

2. $y - 8 = 7(x - 14)$
$(14, 8), 7$

3. $y + 3.7 = 3.2(x - 1.7)$
$(1.7, -3.7), 3.2$

4. $y + 1 = 11(x - 1)$
$(1, -1), 11$

5. $y + 6 = -4(x - 8)$
$(8, -6), -4$

6. $y - 7 = 4(x + 3)$
$(-3, 7), 4$

See Example **2** Write the point-slope form of the equation with the given slope that passes through the indicated point.

7. the line with slope 5 passing
through $(0, 6)$ $y - 6 = 5x$

8. the line with slope -8 passing
through $(-11, 7)$
$y - 7 = -8(x + 11)$

See Example **3** **9.** A basement filled with water from a rainstorm is drained at a rate of 10.5 liters per minute. After 40 minutes, there are 840 liters of water remaining. Write the equation of a line in point-slope form that models the situation. How long does it take to drain the basement?
$y - 840 = -10.5(x - 40)$;
$(120, 0)$ or 120 min.

INDEPENDENT PRACTICE

See Example **1** Use the point-slope form of each equation to identify a point the line passes through and the slope of the line. **Possible answers are given.**

10. $y - 2 = \frac{3}{4}(x + 9)$

11. $y + 9 = 4(x + 5)$

12. $y - 2 = -\frac{1}{6}(x - 11)$

13. $y - 13 = 16(x - 4)$
$(4, 13), 16$

14. $y - 5 = -1.4(x - 6.7)$
$(6.7, 5), -1.4$

15. $y + 9 = 1(x - 3)$
$(3, -9), 1$

See Example **2** Write the point-slope form of the equation with the given slope that passes through the indicated point.

16. the line with slope -5 passing
through $(-3, -5)$ $y + 5 = -5(x + 3)$

17. the line with slope 6 passing
through $(-3, 0)$ $y = 6(x + 3)$

See Example **3** **18.** A stretch of highway has a 5% grade, so the road rises 1 ft for each 20 ft of horizontal distance. The beginning of the highway $(x = 0)$ has an elevation of 2344 ft. Write an equation in point-slope form, and find the highway's elevation 7500 ft from the beginning. $y - 2344 = 0.05x$;
2719 ft above sea level

PRACTICE AND PROBLEM SOLVING

Extra Practice
See page 805.

10. $(-9, 2), \frac{3}{4}$

11. $(-5, -9), 4$

12. $(11, 2), -\frac{1}{6}$

Write the point-slope form of each line described below.

19. the line parallel to $y = 4x - 5$ that passes through $(-2, 3)$ $y - 3 = 4(x + 2)$

20. the line perpendicular to $y = -3x$ that passes through $(8, -2)$ $y + 2 = \frac{1}{3}(x - 8)$

21. the line perpendicular to $y = x + 2$ that passes through $(-5, -7)$
$y + 7 = -1(x + 5)$

22. the line parallel to $y = -10x - 5$ that passes through $(-3, 0)$ $y = -10(x + 3)$

23. **Critical Thinking** Compare finding the equation of a line using two known points to finding it using one known point and the slope of the line.

RETEACH 12-4

LESSON 12-4 Reteach
Point-Slope Form

$y - y_1 = m(x - x_1)$
slope
(x_1, y_1) are the coordinates of a known point on the line.

If a minus sign precedes a coordinate value, use that value.

If a plus sign, precedes a coordinate value, use the opposite of that value.

$y - 3 = 7(x - 1)$
$(1, 3)$ is on the line; slope $m = 7$

$y + 3 = 7(x + 1)$
$(-1, -3)$ is on the line; slope $m = 7$

Identify the slope of each line and a point it passes through.

1. $y + 2 = 5(x - 3)$
$m = \underline{5}$

2. $y - 4 = -3(x + 5)$
$m = \underline{-3}$

Which sign for each coordinate? (same or opposite)
opposite; same   same; opposite

Coordinates of a point on the line: $(-3, 2)$ $(5, -4)$

To write an equation for the line with slope -4 that passes through $(6, -2)$, substitute $m = -4$, $x_1 = 6$, $y_1 = -2$ into the point-slope form.

$y - y_1 = m(x - x_1)$
$y - (-2) = -4(x - 6)$
$y + 2 = -4(x - 6)$

Write the point-slope form of the equation with the given slope that passes through the given point.

3. $m = 3$; $(x_1, y_1) = (7, 2)$
$y - y_1 = m(x - x_1)$
$y - \underline{2} = \underline{3}(x - \underline{7})$

4. $m = -5$; $(x_1, y_1) = (2, 6)$
$y - y_1 = m(x - x_1)$
$y - \underline{6} = \underline{-5}(x - \underline{2})$

5. $m = \frac{1}{2}$; $(x_1, y_1) = (-8, 1)$
$y - y_1 = m(x - x_1)$
$y - \underline{1} = \underline{\frac{1}{2}}(x + \underline{8})$

6. $m = -\frac{3}{4}$; $(x_1, y_1) = (0, -1)$
$y - y_1 = m(x - x_1)$
$y + \underline{1} = \underline{-\frac{3}{4}}(x - \underline{0})$

PRACTICE 12-4

LESSON 12-4 Practice B
Point-Slope Form

Use the point-slope form of each equation to identify a point the line passes through and the slope of the line.

1. $y - 2 = 4(x - 1)$
$m = 4$;
$(x_1, y_1) = (1, 2)$

2. $y + 1 = 2(x - 3)$
$m = 2$;
$(x_1, y_1) = (3, -1)$

3. $y - 4 = -3(x + 1)$
$m = -3$;
$(x_1, y_1) = (-1, 4)$

4. $y + 5 = -2(x + 6)$
$m = -2$;
$(x_1, y_1) = (-6, -5)$

5. $y + 4 = -9(x + 3)$
$m = -9$;
$(x_1, y_1) = (-3, -4)$

6. $y - 7 = -7(x - 7)$
$m = -7$;
$(x_1, y_1) = (7, 7)$

7. $y - 10 = 6(x - 8)$
$m = 6$;
$(x_1, y_1) = (8, 10)$

8. $y + 12 = 2.5(x + 4)$
$m = 2.5$;
$(x_1, y_1) = (-4, -12)$

9. $y + 8 = \frac{1}{2}(x - 3)$
$m = \frac{1}{2}$;
$(x_1, y_1) = (3, -8)$

Write the point-slope form of the equation with the given slope that passes through the indicated point.

10. the line with slope -1 passing through $(2, 5)$
$y - 5 = -1(x - 2)$

11. the line with slope 2 passing through $(-1, 4)$
$y - 4 = 2(x + 1)$

12. the line with slope 4 passing through $(-3, -2)$
$y + 2 = 4(x + 3)$

13. the line with slope 3 passing through $(7, -6)$
$y + 6 = 3(x - 7)$

14. the line with slope -3 passing through $(-6, 4)$
$y - 4 = -3(x + 6)$

15. the line with slope -2 passing through $(5, 1)$
$y - 1 = -2(x - 5)$

16. Michael was driving at a constant speed of 60 mph when he crossed the Sandy River. After 1 hour, he passed a highway marker for mile 84. Write an equation in point-slope form, and find which highway marker he will pass 90 minutes after crossing the Sandy River.
$y - 84 = 60(x - 1)$; highway marker for 114 miles

Earth Science

Mount Etna, a volcano in Sicily, Italy, has been erupting for over half a million years. It is one of the world's most active volcanoes. When it erupted in 1669 it almost completely destroyed the city of Catania.

go.hrw.com
Web Extra!
KEYWORD: MT7 Etna

24. Life Science An elephant's tusks grow throughout its life. Each month, an elephant tusk grows about 1 cm. Suppose you started observing an elephant when its tusks were 12 cm long. Write an equation in point-slope form that describes the length of the elephant's tusks after m months of observation. $\ell - 12 = m$

25. Earth Science Jorullo is a cinder cone volcano in Mexico. Suppose Jorullo is 315 m tall, 50 m from the center of its base. Use the slope of a cinder cone to write a possible equation in point-slope form that approximately models the height of the volcano, x meters from the center of its base. **Possible answer:** $y - 315 = -0.6(x - 50)$

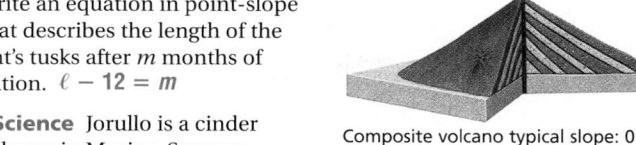

Shield volcano typical slope: 0.03–0.17

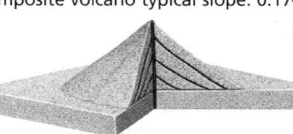

Composite volcano typical slope: 0.17–0.5

Cinder cone volcano typical slope: 0.5–0.65

26. Write a Problem Write a problem about the point-slope form of an equation using the data on a car's fuel economy.

Fuel Economy		
Gas Tank Capacity	City Efficiency	Highway Efficiency
14 gal	26 mi/gal	34 mi/gal

27. Write About It Explain how you could convert an equation in point-slope form to slope-intercept form. **Possible answer: Solve the equation for y, and simplify.**

28. Challenge The value of one line's x-intercept is the opposite of the value of its y-intercept. The line contains the point $(9, -3)$. Find the point-slope form of the equation.

📝 **TEST PREP and Spiral Review**

29. Multiple Choice What is the point-slope form of a line that is parallel to $y = \frac{3}{4}x - 5$ and passes through the point $(-16, 5)$?

Ⓐ $y - 5 = \frac{3}{4}(x - 16)$

Ⓑ $y - 5 = -\frac{4}{3}(x + 16)$

Ⓒ $y - 5 = \frac{3}{4}(x + 16)$

Ⓓ $y - 5 = -\frac{4}{3}(x - 16)$

30. Gridded Response Use the point-slope form of the equation $y - 6 = 8(x + 1)$. What is the y-value of the y-intercept? **14**

Combine like terms. (Lesson 11-1)

31. $7x - 5y + 18$
$7x - 5y + 18$

32. $3x + y + 5y - 2x$
$x + 6y$

33. $8y - 2x - 8y - 2x$
$-4x$

Write each equation in slope-intercept form, and then find the slope and y-intercept. (Lesson 12-3)

34. $2x = 8y$
$y = \frac{1}{4}x; m = \frac{1}{4}; b = 0$

35. $x - y = 5$
$y = x - 5; m = 1; b = -5$

36. $4x + 4y = 4$
$y = -x + 1; m = -1; b = 1$

CHALLENGE 12-4

Challenge
12-4 So Everyone Gets the Same Answer

The **standard form** of a line is $Ax + By = C$ where A, B, and C are real numbers.

To write an equation of a line, you need to know two pieces of information.

When the slope and the y-intercept are known, use $y = mx + b$.
When the slope and a point on the line are known, use $y - y_1 = m(x - x_1)$.

You can use either the slope-intercept form or the point-slope form to write an equation in standard form.

Write an equation in standard form for the line that contains side $\overline{AB}$ of triangle ABC.

Use $A(1, 0)$ and $B(4, 5)$ to find the slope of $\overline{AB}$. $m = \frac{5 - 0}{4 - 1} = \frac{5}{3}$

Substitute $m = \frac{5}{3}$ and $(x_1, y_1) = (1, 0)$ into point-slope form. $y - 0 = \frac{5}{3}(x - 1)$

Write the equation in standard form.

clear fractions	$3y = 5(x - 1)$
distribute	$3y = 5x - 5$
add and subtract	$5x - 3y = 5$

Write the standard form of the equation for each indicated line.

1. $\overline{MN}$ of right triangle MNO
$3x + 4y = 12$

2. $\overline{JL}$ of parallelogram $JKLM$
$4x - y = 18$

PROBLEM SOLVING 12-4

Problem Solving
12-4 Point-Slope Form

Write the correct answer.

1. A 1600 square foot home in Houston will sell for about $102,000. The price increases about $43.41 per square foot. Write an equation that describes the price y of a house in Houston, based on the square footage x.
$y - 102,000 = 43.41(x - 1600)$

2. Write the equation in Exercise 1 in slope-intercept form.
$y = 43.41x + 32,544$

3. Wind chill is a measure of what temperature feels like with the wind. With a 25 mph wind, 40°F will feel like 29°F. Write an equation in point-slope form that describes the wind chill y based on the temperature x, if the slope of the line is 1.337.
$y - 29 = 1.337(x - 40)$

4. With a 25 mph wind, what does a temperature of 0°F feel like?
-24.48°F

From 2 to 13 years, the growth rate for children is generally linear. Choose the letter of the correct answer.

5. The average height of a 2-year old boy is 36 inches, and the average growth rate per year is 2.2 inches. Write an equation in point-slope form that describes the height of a boy y based on his age x.
A $y - 36 = 2(x - 2.2)$
B $y - 2 = 2.2(x - 36)$
Ⓒ $y - 36 = 2.2(x - 2)$
D $y - 2.2 = 2(x - 36)$

6. The average height of a 5-year old girl is 44 inches, and the average growth rate per year is 2.4 inches. Write an equation in point-slope form that describes the height of a girl y based on her age x.
F $y - 2.4 = 44(x - 5)$
Ⓖ $y - 44 = 2.4(x - 5)$
H $y - 44 = 5(x - 2.4)$
J $y - 5 = 2.4(x - 44)$

7. Write the equation from Exercise 6 in slope-intercept form.
A $y = 2.4x - 100.6$
B $y = 44x - 217.6$
C $y = 5x + 32$
Ⓓ $y = 2.4x + 32$

8. Use the equation in Exercise 6 to find the average height of a 13-year old girl.
F 56.3 in.
Ⓖ 63.2 in.
H 69.4 in.
J 97 in.

Answers

26. Possible answer: Write an equation in point-slope form for the number of highway miles y that a car can travel after using x gallons of gas. Answer: $y = -34(x - 14)$

28. Possible answer: $y + 3 = x - 9$

TEST PREP DOCTOR ➕ For Exercise 29, ask students to identify the slope of a parallel line. They should identify the slope as $\frac{3}{4}$. If students choose **B** or **D**, they did not identify the slope correctly. Ask students to substitute one of the points into point-slope form to find the correct answer, **C**.

Journal

Ask students to write about why they think there are so many different ways to write equations of lines. Ask students whether they think all of the forms are useful.

Power Presentations with PowerPoint®

12-4 Lesson Quiz

Use the point-slope form of each equation to identify a point the line passes through and the slope of the line.

1. $y + 6 = 2(x + 5)$
$(-5, -6)$, 2

2. $y - 4 = -\frac{2}{5}(x - 6)$
$(6, 4)$, $-\frac{2}{5}$

Write the point-slope form of the equation with the given slope that passes through the indicated point.

3. the line with slope 4 passing through $(3, 5)$
$y - 5 = 4(x - 3)$

4. the line with slope -2 passing through $(-2, 4)$
$y - 4 = -2(x + 2)$

Also available on transparency

Organizer

Objective: Assess students' mastery of concepts and skills in Lessons 12-1 through 12-4.

Resources

 Assessment Resources
Section 12A Quiz

 Test & Practice Generator
One-Stop Planner®

INTERVENTION

Resources

 Ready to Go On?
Intervention and
Enrichment Worksheets

🔘 **Ready to Go On? CD-ROM**

🪐 **Ready to Go On? Online**

my.hrw.com

Answers

1–4, 9. See p. A19.

Ready to Go On?

Quiz for Lessons 12-1 Through 12-4

✓ 12-1 Graphing Linear Equations

Graph each equation and tell whether it is linear.

1. $y = 2 - 4x$ **linear**
2. $x = 2$ **linear**
3. $y = 3x^2$ **not linear**

4. At Maggi's Music, the equation $u = \frac{3}{4}n + 1$ represents the price for a used CD u with a selling price n when the CD was new. How much will a used CD cost for each of the listed new prices? Graph the equation and tell whether it is linear. **$7, $10, $11.50, $16; linear**

New Price	Used Price
$8	
$12	
$14	
$20	

✓ 12-2 Slope of a Line

Find the slope of the line that passes through each pair of points.

5. $(6, 3)$ and $(2, 4)$ $\ -\frac{1}{4}$
6. $(1, 4)$ and $(-1, -3)$ $\ \frac{7}{2}$
7. $(0, -3)$ and $(-4, 0)$ $\ -\frac{3}{4}$

8. Determine whether the graph shows a constant or variable rate of change. **variable**

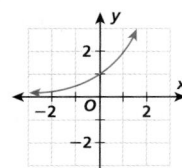

✓ 12-3 Using Slopes and Intercepts

9. A camp charges families $625 per month for one child and then $225 per month for each additional child. The linear equation $y = 225x + 625$ represents the amount a family would pay for x additional children. Identify the slope and y-intercept, and use them to graph the equation.
$m = 225;\ b = 625$

Write the equation of the line that passes through each pair of points in slope-intercept form.

10. $(-4, 3)$ and $(-2, 1)$
$y = -x - 1$
11. $(2, 7)$ and $(5, 2)$
$y = -\frac{5}{3}x + \frac{31}{3}$
12. $(4, 2)$ and $(2, -5)$
$y = \frac{7}{2}x - 12$

✓ 12-4 Point-Slope Form

Use the point-slope form of each equation to identify a point the line passes through and the slope of the line. Possible points are given.

13. $y + 5 = -3(x - 2)$
$(2, -5); 3$
14. $y = -(x + 3)$ $(-3, 0); -1$
15. $y - 7 = -3x$ $(0, 7); -3$

Write the point-slope form of the equation with the given slope that passes through the indicated point.
$y - 2 = -3(x - 7)$
16. slope -3, passing through $(7, 2)$
$y - 3 = 2(x + 5)$
17. slope 2, passing through $(-5, 3)$

READY TO GO ON?
Diagnose and Prescribe

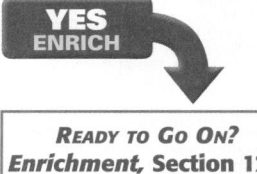
NO
INTERVENE

YES
ENRICH

READY TO GO ON? Intervention, Section 12A			
Ready to Go On? Intervention	🖎 **Worksheets**	🔘 **CD-ROM**	🪐 **Online**
✓ Lesson 12-1	12-1 Intervention	Activity 12-1	
✓ Lesson 12-2	12-2 Intervention	Activity 12-2	Diagnose and Prescribe Online
✓ Lesson 12-3	12-3 Intervention	Activity 12-3	
✓ Lesson 12-4	12-4 Intervention	Activity 12-4	

READY TO GO ON?
Enrichment, Section 12A
🖎 **Worksheets**
🔘 **CD-ROM**
🪐 **Online**

Focus on Problem Solving

Understand the Problem

• Identify important details in the problem

When you are solving word problems, you need to find the information that is important to the problem.

You can write the equation of a line if you know the slope and one point on the line or if you know two points on the line.

Example:

A school bus carrying 40 students is traveling toward the school at **30 mi/hr**. After **15 minutes**, it has **20 miles to go**. How far away from the school was the bus when it started?

You can write the equation of the line in point-slope form.

$$y - y_1 = m(x - x_1)$$
$$y - (-20) = 30(x - 0.25) \quad \text{The slope is the rate of change, or 30.}$$
$$y + 20 = 30x - 7.5 \quad \text{15 minutes = 0.25 hours}$$
$$\underline{-20 \qquad \qquad -20} \quad \text{(0.25, -20) is a point on the line.}$$
$$y = 30x - 27.5$$

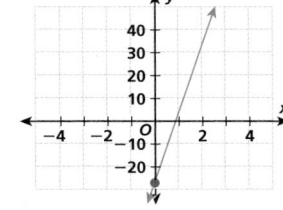

The y-intercept of the line is -27.5. At 0 minutes, the bus had 27.5 miles to go.

 Read each problem, and identify the information needed to write the equation of a line. Give the slope and one point on the line, or give two points on the line.

1 At sea level, water boils at 100°C. At an altitude of 600 m, water boils at 95°C. If the relationship is linear, estimate the temperature that water would boil at an altitude of 1800 m.

2 Omar earns a weekly salary of $560, plus a commission of 8% of his total sales. How many dollars in merchandise does he have to sell to make $600 in one week?

3 A community activities group has a goal of passing out 5000 fliers advertising a charity run. On Saturday, the group passed out 2000 fliers. If the group can pass out 600 fliers per week, how long will it take them to pass out the remaining fliers to the community?

4 Kayla rents a booth at a craft fair. If she sells 50 bracelets, her profit is $25. If she sells 80 bracelets, her profit is $85. What would her profit be if she sold 100 bracelets?

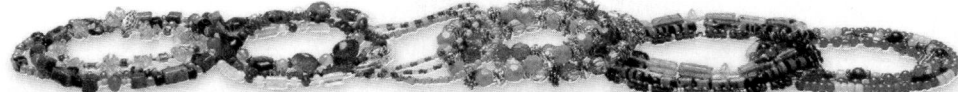

Answers

1. 85°C
2. $500
3. 5 weeks
4. $125

Organizer

Objective: Focus on better understanding the problem by identifying the important details

 Online Edition

Resources

Chapter 12 Resource Book
Reading Strategies

Problem Solving Process

This page focuses on the first step of the problem-solving process:

Understand the Problem

Discuss

Have students discuss what information in the problem is necessary to write the equation. Have them give the slope and one point on the line, or have them give two points on the line.

Possible answers:

1. At sea level, water boils at 100°C. At an altitude of 600 M, water boils at 95°C. (0, 100); (600, 95)

2. He earns a weekly salary of $560, plus a commission of 8% of his sales. $m = 8\%$, or 0.08, or $\frac{8}{10}$; (0, 560)

3. The group passed out 2000 fliers and can pass out 600 fliers per week. $m = 600$; (0, 2000)

4. If she sells 50 bracelets, her profit is $25. If she sells 80 bracelets, her profit is $85. (50, 25); (80, 85)

State Resources

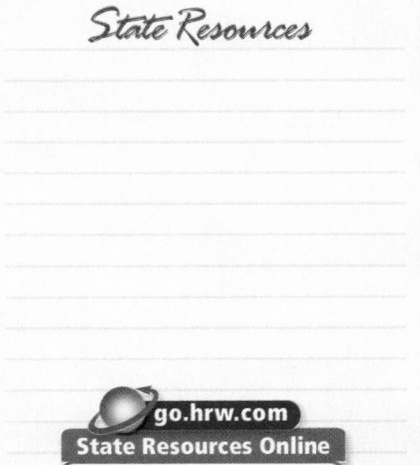

go.hrw.com
State Resources Online
KEYWORD: MT7 Resources

Linear Relationships

One-Minute Section Planner

Lesson	Materials	MiC and Lab Resources
Lesson 12-5 Direct Variation • Recognize direct variation by graphing tables of data and checking for constant ratios. ☐ SAT-10 ☐ ITBS ☐ CTBS ☐ NAEP	Graph paper, scales, paper cups, coins (MK)	**Hands-On Lab Activities** 12-5
Lesson 12-6 Graphing Inequalities in Two Variables • Graph inequalities on the coordinate plane. ☐ SAT-10 ☐ ITBS ☐ CTBS ☐ NAEP	Graph paper	**Hands-On Lab Activities** 12-6 **Technology Lab Activities** 12-6
Lesson 12-7 Lines of Best Fit • Recognize relationships in data and find the equation of a line of best fit. ☐ SAT-10 ☐ ITBS ☐ CTBS ☑ NAEP	Graph paper, straightedges (MK)	**MiC: Insights Into Data** pp. 53–59 **Hands-On Lab Activities** 12-7
Extension Solving Systems of Equations by Graphing • Solve a system of equations by graphing. ☐ SAT-10 ☐ ITBS ☐ CTBS ☐ NAEP	Graph paper	

MK = *Manipulatives Kit*

Mathematics in Context

The unit **Insights into Data** from the *Mathematics in Context* © 2006 series can be used with Section 12B. See Section Planner above for suggestions for integrating *MiC* with *Holt Mathematics*.

Section Overview

Direct Variation

 Why? Data sets may be related by direct variation.

> *y* **varies directly** with *x* if there is some constant *k* such that $y = kx$.
> *k* is called the **constant of proportionality.**

Distance on map (in.)	*x*	3	5	8
Actual distance (mi)	*y*	36	60	96

There is direct variation. The constant of proportionality is 12.

$$y = k \cdot x$$
$$36 = 12 \cdot 3$$
$$60 = 12 \cdot 5$$
$$96 = 12 \cdot 8$$

What actual distance corresponds to a distance of 4 inches on the map?

$$y = k \cdot x$$
$$y = 12 \cdot 4$$
$$y = 48 \text{ miles}$$

Graphing Inequalities in Two Variables

 Why? An inequality in two variables has an infinite number of ordered pair solutions. The only way to indicate the solutions is to graph them.

> Draw a dashed boundary line for < and > symbols. Draw a solid boundary line for ≤ and ≥ symbols.

To graph $y < \frac{1}{3}x - 2$, graph the equation $y = \frac{1}{3}x - 2$ with a dashed line for the boundary line. Shade the side of the boundary line containing solutions.

Test point *A*(3, 2).
$$y < \frac{1}{3}x - 2$$
$$2 \overset{?}{<} \frac{1}{3}(3) - 2$$
$$2 \overset{?}{<} -1 \; ✗$$

(3, 2) *is not* a solution.

Test point *B*(3, −4).
$$y < \frac{1}{3}x - 2$$
$$-4 \overset{?}{<} \frac{1}{3}(3) - 2$$
$$-4 \overset{?}{<} -1 \; ✔$$

(3, −4) *is a* solution.

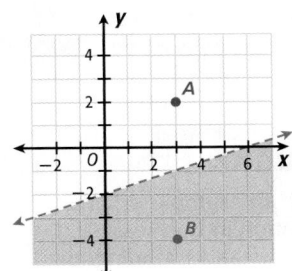

Lines of Best Fit

Why? When there is a correlation in a data set, you can use a line of best fit to approximate the trend in the data and to make predictions.

The line of best fit is the line that comes closest to all the points on a scatter plot. There are about the same number of points on both sides of the line.

Step 1 Find the coordinates of point *A* by finding the mean of all the *x*-coordinates and the mean of all the *y*-coordinates.

Step 2 Draw a line of best fit through *A*.

Step 3 Estimate the coordinates of some other point *B* on the line.

Step 4 Use points *A* and *B* to find the equation of the line of best fit.

$$m = \frac{5 - 3}{9 - 4} = \frac{2}{5} = 0.4$$
$$y - y_1 = m(x - x_1)$$
$$y - 3 = 0.4(x - 4)$$
$$y - 3 = 0.4x - 1.6$$
$$y = 0.4x + 1.4$$

Data

x	1	3	3	5	6	6
y	1	1	4	2	4	6

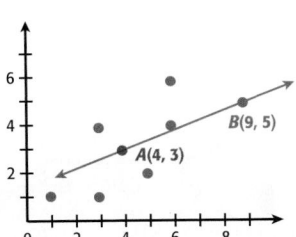

Objective: Students recognize direct variation by graphing tables of data and checking for constant ratios.

Hands-On Lab
In *Hands-On Lab Activities*

Online Edition
Tutorial Videos

Power Presentations
with PowerPoint®

Warm Up

Use the point-slope form of each equation to identify a point the line passes through and the slope of the line.

1. $y - 3 = -\frac{1}{7}(x - 9)$ $(9, 3), -\frac{1}{7}$
2. $y + 2 = \frac{2}{3}(x - 5)$ $(5, -2), \frac{2}{3}$
3. $y - 9 = -2(x + 4)$ $(-4, 9), -2$
4. $y - 5 = -\frac{1}{4}(x + 7)$ $(-7, 5), -\frac{1}{4}$

Problem of the Day

Where do the lines defined by the equations $y = -5x + 20$ and $y = 5x - 20$ intersect? **(4, 0)**

Also available on transparency

Math Humor

Teacher: Give an example of direct variation in business.
Student: Volume and spending: the *louder* I yell, the more time my mom makes me *spend* in my room.

State Resources

go.hrw.com
State Resources Online
KEYWORD: MT7 Resources

12-5 Direct Variation

Learn to recognize direct variation by graphing tables of data and checking for constant ratios.

Vocabulary
direct variation
constant of proportionality

An amplifier can create 125 watts of sound from an input signal with 1 watt of power. The same amplifier, with the same settings, will create 625 watts of sound with a 5-watt input, 5000 watts of sound with a 40-watt input, and so on.

The ratio of watts of sound to watts of power is constant. The amplifier creates 125 watts of sound for every 1 watt of power.

$$\frac{\text{watts of sound}}{\text{watts of power}} = \frac{125}{1} = \frac{625}{5} = \frac{5000}{40}$$

DIRECT VARIATION

Words	Numbers	Algebra
For **direct variation**, two variable quantities are related proportionally by a constant positive ratio. The ratio is called the **constant of proportionality**.	$8 = k$ $16 = 2k$ $24 = 3k$	$y = kx$ $k = \frac{y}{x}$

The number of watts of sound the amplifier puts out *varies directly* with the watts of power and is represented by the equation $y = kx$. The constant ratio k is 125.

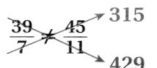 **EXAMPLE 1** **Determining Whether a Data Set Varies Directly**

Determine whether the data sets show direct variation.

Helpful Hint

The graph of a direct-variation equation is always linear *and* always contains the point (0, 0). The variables x and y either increase together or decrease together.

A

Shoe Sizes					
U.S. Size	7	8	9	10	11
European Size	39	41	43	44	45

Make a graph that shows the relationship between the U.S. sizes and the European sizes. The graph is not linear.

You can also compare ratios to see if a direct variation occurs.

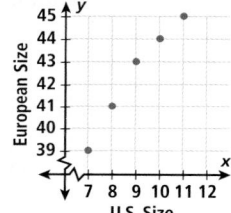

$\frac{39}{7} \times \frac{45}{11}$ $\begin{array}{c}315\\429\end{array}$ $315 \neq 429$
The ratios are not proportional.

The relationship of the data is not a direct variation.

1 Introduce
Alternate Opener

EXPLORATION

12-5 Direct Variation

In a **direct variation**, when one quantity increases or decreases, the other quantity does the same. The table below shows the number of stamps x and the price y for each number.

Notice that when the number of stamps is doubled, the price is also doubled.

Stamps x	1	2	3	4	5	6
Price y	$0.37	$0.74	$1.11	$1.48	$1.85	$2.22

1. Use each pair of values (x, y) in the table to complete the graph.

2. To find the *constant of proportionality*, divide each price in the table by each number of stamps.

3. What feature of the graph tells you that the graph is of a direct variation?

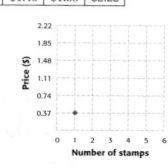

Think and Discuss
4. **Explain** the relationship between a constant of proportionality and the slope of the line.
5. **Give** a real-world example of a direct variation.

Motivate

Give students a few examples of direct variation, for example, "The more groceries I buy, the more money I spend," or "The less sleep I get, the less energy I have." Tell students that if two variables are in direct variation, as one gets larger, the other gets proportionally larger, *or* as one gets smaller, the other gets proportionally smaller.

Explorations and answers are provided in *Alternate Openers: Explorations Transparencies*.

Determine whether the data sets show direct variation.

B

Number of Watts of Sound for Watts of Power					
Input Signal Power (W)	6	8	12	20	28
Output Sound Intensity $\left(\frac{W}{m^2}\right)$	4.5	6	9	15	21

Make a graph that shows the relationship between the input power and the output intensity.

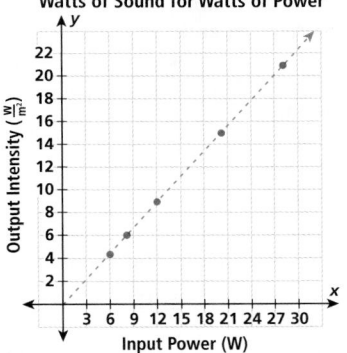

Watts of Sound for Watts of Power

Plot the points.
The points lie in a straight line.
(0, 0) is on the line.

You can also compare ratios to see if direct variation occurs.

$$\frac{6}{4.5} = \frac{8}{6} = \frac{12}{9} = \frac{20}{15} = \frac{28}{21}$$ *Compare ratios. The ratio is constant.*

The ratios are proportional. The relationship is a direct variation.

EXAMPLE 2 **Finding Equations of Direct Variation**

Find each equation of direct variation, given that *y* varies directly with *x*.

A *y* is 48 when *x* is 3

$y = kx$	*y varies directly with x.*
$48 = k \cdot 3$	*Substitute for x and y.*
$16 = k$	*Solve for k.*
$y = 16x$	*Substitute 16 for k in the original equation.*

B *y* is 15 when *x* is 10

$y = kx$	*y varies directly with x.*
$15 = k \cdot 10$	*Substitute for x and y.*
$\frac{3}{2} = k$	*Solve for k.*
$y = \frac{3}{2}x$	*Substitute $\frac{3}{2}$ for k in the original equation.*

---

2 Teach

Guided Instruction

In this lesson, students learn to recognize direct variation by graphing tables of data and checking for constant ratios. Explain that direct variation is very similar to linear equations. In direct variation, the constant of proportionality *k* replaces slope, and the *y*-intercept is always 0 (Teaching Transparency). Show students how to check for constant ratios to identify direct variation. Then show students how to find the constant of variation, given two values.

Reaching All Learners
Through Kinesthetic Experience

Have students work in small groups. Give each group of students a scale, a paper cup, and 30 pennies. Have students adjust the scale so that the weight of the cup registers as zero. Have students weigh five pennies and record the number of pennies and the weight. Then have them repeat the procedure for 10, 15, 20, 25, and 30 pennies. Using the data recorded in this experiment, have students explain whether they believe the variables are in direct variation and explain why. You may want to allow for slight variations in the weights of individual pennies.

Example 3

Mrs. Perez has $4000 in a CD and $4000 in a money market account. The amount of interest she has earned since the beginning of the year is organized in the following table. Determine whether there is a direct variation between either data set and time. If so, find the equation of direct variation.

Time (mo)	Interest from CD ($)	Interest from Money Market ($)
0	0	0
1	17	19
2	34	37
3	51	55
4	68	73

A. interest from CD and time
direct variation; $y = 17x$

B. interest from money market and time no direct variation

Also available on transparency

Answers to Think and Discuss

1. The slope is the constant of proportionality, k. The y-intercept is always 0.

2. Possible answer: A proportional linear relationship is a direct variation between the variables. However, a non-proportional relationship is not a direct variation and thus will have a y-intercept other than 0.

EXAMPLE 3   *Physical Science Application*

When a driver applies the brakes, a car's total stopping distance is the sum of the reaction distance and the braking distance. The reaction distance is the distance the car travels before the driver presses the brake pedal. The braking distance is the distance the car travels after the brakes have been applied.

Determine whether there is a direct variation between either data set and speed. If so, find the equation of direct variation.

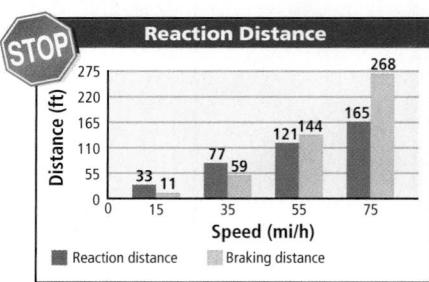

A reaction distance and speed

$$\frac{\text{reaction distance}}{\text{speed}} = \frac{33}{15} = 2.2 \qquad \frac{\text{reaction distance}}{\text{speed}} = \frac{77}{35} = 2.2$$

The first two pairs of data result in a common ratio. In fact, all of the reaction distance to speed ratios are equivalent to 2.2.

$$\frac{\text{reaction distance}}{\text{speed}} = \frac{33}{15} = \frac{77}{35} = \frac{121}{55} = \frac{165}{75} = 2.2$$

The variables are related by a constant ratio of 2.2 to 1, and (0, 0) is included. The equation of direct variation is $y = 2.2x$, where x is the speed, y is the reaction distance, and 2.2 is the constant of proportionality.

B braking distance and speed

$$\frac{\text{braking distance}}{\text{speed}} = \frac{11}{15} = 0.7\overline{3} \qquad \frac{\text{braking distance}}{\text{speed}} = \frac{59}{35} = 1.69$$

$$0.7\overline{3} \neq 1.69$$

If any of the ratios are not equal, then there is no direct variation. It is not necessary to compute additional ratios.

Think and Discuss

1. **Describe** the slope and the y-intercept of a direct variation equation.

2. **Compare** and contrast proportional and non-proportional linear relationships.

---

3 Close

Summarize

ENGLISH LANGUAGE LEARNERS

Remind students that direct variation can be determined by checking for constant ratios or by graphing and seeing whether the graph is a straight line that passes through the origin. Point out that the phrase *direct variation* suggests that there is a direct relationship between the changes in the variables (i.e., as one variable increases, the other increases proportionally).

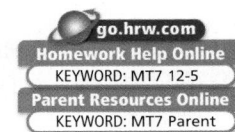

12-5 Exercises

go.hrw.com
Homework Help Online
KEYWORD: MT7 12-5
Parent Resources Online
KEYWORD: MT7 Parent

GUIDED PRACTICE

See Example **1** Make a graph to determine whether the data sets show direct variation.

1. The table shows an employee's pay per number of hours worked. **yes**

Hours Worked	0	1	2	3	4	5	6
Pay ($)	0	9.50	19.00	28.50	38.00	47.50	57.00

See Example **2** Find each equation of direct variation, given that y varies directly with x.

2. y is 12 when x is 3 $y = 4x$

3. y is 18 when x is 6 $y = 3x$

4. y is 10 when x is 12 $y = \frac{5}{6}x$

5. y is 5 when x is 10 $y = \frac{1}{2}x$

6. y is 360 when x is 3 $y = 120x$

7. y is 4 when x is 36 $y = \frac{1}{9}x$

See Example **3** **8.** The table shows how many hours it takes to travel 600 miles, depending on your speed in miles per hour. Determine whether there is direct variation between the two data sets. If so, find the equation of direct variation. **no direct variation**

Speed (mi/h)	5	6	7.5	10	15	30	60
Time (h)	120	100	80	60	40	20	10

INDEPENDENT PRACTICE

See Example **1** Make a graph to determine whether the data sets show direct variation.

9. The table shows the amount of current flowing through a 12-volt circuit with various resistances. **no**

Resistance (ohms)	48	24	12	6	4	3	2
Current (amps)	0.25	0.5	1	2	3	4	6

See Example **2** Find each equation of direct variation, given that y varies with x.

10. y is 3.5 when x is 3.5 $y = x$

11. y is 3 when x is 9 $y = \frac{1}{3}x$

12. y is 96 when x is 4 $y = 24x$

13. y is 4 when x is 26 $y = \frac{2}{13}x$

14. y is 48 when x is 3 $y = 16x$

15. y is 5 when x is 50 $y = \frac{1}{10}x$

See Example **3** **16.** The table shows how many hours it takes to drive certain distances at a speed of 30 miles per hour. Determine whether there is direct variation between the two data sets. If so, find the equation of direct variation.

Distance (mi)	15	30	60	90	120	150	180
Time (h)	0.5	1	2	3	4	5	6

Assignment Guide

If you finished Example **1** assign:
Average 1, 9, 17–20, 26–32
Advanced 9, 17–21, 24, 26–32

If you finished Example **2** assign:
Average 1–7, 9–15, 17–20, 26–32
Advanced 9–15, 17–21, 24, 26–32

If you finished Example **3** assign:
Average 1–20, 26–32
Advanced 9–32

Homework Quick Check

Quickly check key concepts.
Exercises: 9, 14, 16, 18

Answers

1.

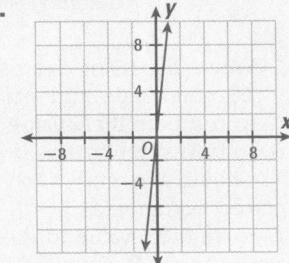

9.

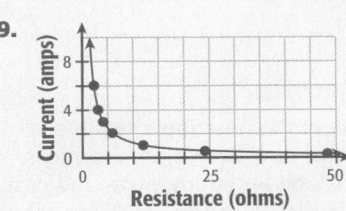

16. direct variation; $t = \frac{1}{30}d$

RETEACH 12-5

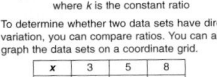

Reteach
12-5 Direct Variation

Two data sets have **direct variation** if they are related by a constant ratio, the **constant of proportionality**. A graph of the data sets is linear and passes through (0, 0).

$y = kx$ equation of direct variation, where k is the constant ratio

To determine whether two data sets have direct variation, you can compare ratios. You can also graph the data sets on a coordinate grid.

x	3	5	8
y	15	25	40

$\frac{y}{x} = \frac{15}{3} = \frac{25}{5} = \frac{40}{8} = \frac{5}{1}$ ← constant ratio

$k = 5 \rightarrow y = 5x$

The graph of the data sets is linear and passes through (0, 0).
So, the data sets show direct variation.

Determine whether the data sets show direct variation. If there is a constant ratio, identify it and write the equation of direct variation. Plot the points and tell whether the graph is linear.

1.
x	1	2	4	8
y	8	4	2	1

constant ratio? **no**
If yes, equation. _____
Is the graph linear? **no**

2.
x	0	2	3	5
y	0	20	30	50

constant ratio? **yes, 10**
If yes, equation. **$y = 10x$**
Is the graph linear? **yes**

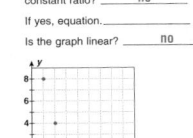

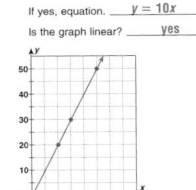

PRACTICE 12-5

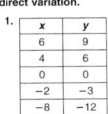

Practice B
12-5 Direct Variation

Make a graph to determine whether the data sets show direct variation.

1.
x	y
6	9
4	6
0	0
−2	−3
−8	−12

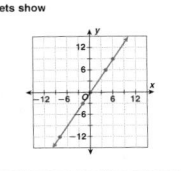

The data sets show direct variation.

2. Write the equation of direct variation for Exercise 1.
$y = 1.5x$ or $y = \frac{3}{2}x$

Find each equation of direct variation, given that y varies with x.

3. y is 32 when x is 4
$y = 8x$

4. y is −10 when x is −20
$y = \frac{1}{2}x$

5. y is 63 when x is −7
$y = −9x$

6. y is 40 when x is 50
$y = \frac{4}{5}x$

7. y is 87.5 when x is 25
$y = 3.5x$

8. y is 90 when x is 270
$y = \frac{1}{3}x$

9. The table shows the length and width of various U.S. flags. Determine whether there is direct variation between the two data sets. If so, find the equation of direct variation.

Length (ft)	2.85	5.7	7.6	9.88	11.4
Width (ft)	1.5	3	4	5.2	6

There is direct variation between the lengths and widths of the flags.
$y = 1.9x$, where y is the length, x is the width, and 1.9 is the constant of proportionality

State Resources

go.hrw.com
State Resources Online
KEYWORD: MT7 Resources

Answers

24. Possible answer: The constant of proportionality represents the slope of the line graphed by a direct variation equation. The greater the constant, the steeper the slope of the line.

TEST PREP DOCTOR ✦ When discussing Exercise 26, encourage students to compare the *y*-value to the *x*-value. In lowest terms, this is the slope. This should allow them to identify the correct equation as **C**. If students compare the *x*-value to the *y*-value, they will choose **B**.

🖊 Journal

Ask students to describe a real-world example of direct variation. Examples might include an hourly wage, the cost of renting a video game, or the number of cookies made with various amounts of flour.

Power Presentations
with PowerPoint®

✓ 12-5 Lesson Quiz

Find each equation of direct variation, given that *y* varies directly with *x*.

1. *y* is 78 when *x* is 3. $y = 26x$

2. *x* is 45 when *y* is 5. $y = \frac{1}{9}x$

3. *y* is 6 when *x* is 5. $y = \frac{6}{5}x$

4. The table shows the amount of money Bob makes for different amounts of time he works. Determine whether there is a direct variation between the two sets of data. If so, find the equation of direct variation.

Hours	4	5	6	7	8
Pay	$48	$60	$72	$84	$96

direct variation; $y = 12x$

Also available on transparency

PRACTICE AND PROBLEM SOLVING

Extra Practice
See page 805.

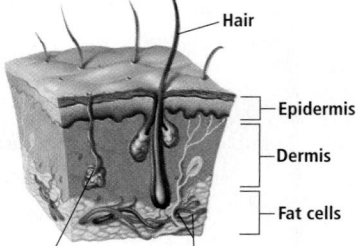
Life Science

Although snakes shed their skins all in one piece, most reptiles shed their skins in much smaller pieces.

Tell whether each equation represents direct variation between *x* and *y*.

17. $y = 217x$ yes **18.** $y = -3x^2$ no **19.** $y = \frac{k}{x}$ no **20.** $y = 4\pi x$ yes

21. Critical Thinking Is every linear relationship a direct variation? Is every direct variation a linear relation? Explain. **No; yes; a direct variation is a linear relationship in which the y-intercept is always 0.**

22. Life Science The weight of a person's skin is related to body weight by the equation $s = \frac{1}{16}w$, where *s* is skin weight and *w* is body weight.

a. Does this equation show direction variation between body weight and skin weight? **yes**

b. If a person calculates skin weight as $9\frac{3}{4}$ lb, what is the person's body weight? **156 lb**

Hair — Epidermis — Dermis — Fat cells — Sweat gland — Blood vessels

 23. Write a Problem The perimeter *P* of a square varies directly with the length *l* of a side. Write a direct variation problem about the perimeter of a square. **Check students' work.**

 24. Write About It Describe how the constant of proportionality *k* affects the appearance of the graph of a direct variation equation.

 25. Challenge Watermelons are being sold at 79¢ a pound. What condition would have to exist for the price paid and the number of watermelons sold to represent a direct variation? **Each watermelon would need to be exactly the same weight.**

TEST PREP and Spiral Review

26. Multiple Choice Given that *y* varies directly with *x*, what is the equation of direct variation if *y* is 16 when *x* is 20?

Ⓐ $y = 1\frac{1}{5}x$ Ⓑ $y = \frac{5}{4}x$ Ⓒ $y = \frac{4}{5}x$ Ⓓ $y = 0.6x$

27. Gridded Response If *y* varies directly with *x*, what is the value of *x* when $y = 14$ and $k = \frac{1}{2}$? **28**

Explain why the statistic is misleading. (Lesson 9-6) **Possible answers**

28. A market researcher surveyed 100 people. Of the 100 people surveyed, 60 own a car. Of the 60 people who own a car, 20 own a white car. The market researcher proclaimed: "One-third of all people own a white car." **The statement does not include the 40 people who do not own a car.**

Find the slope and y-intercept of each equation. (Lesson 12-3)

29. $y = 4x - 2$ $m = 4, b = -2$ **30.** $y = -2x + 12$ $m = -2, b = 12$ **31.** $y = -0.25x$ $m = -0.25, b = 0$ **32.** $y = -x - 4$ $m = -1, b = -4$

CHALLENGE 12-5

LESSON 12-5 Challenge
Different Paths, Same Result

Problems of direct variation can be solved with two methods.
If *r* varies directly with *h*, and *r* = 13.5 when *h* = 3, find *r* when *h* = 7.

Method 1: Find the constant of variation.

$\frac{r}{h} = k$

$\frac{13.5}{3} = k$ Use a pair of known values.

$4.5 = k$ constant of variation

$r = 4.5h$ equation of variation

$r = 4.5(7) = 31.5$

So, when *h* = 7, *r* = 31.5.

Method 2: Write a proportion.

$\frac{r_1}{h_1} = \frac{r_2}{h_2}$

$\frac{13.5}{3} = \frac{r_2}{7}$ Use all known values.

$3r_2 = 13.5(7)$ Cross multiply.

$\frac{3r_2}{3} = \frac{94.5}{3}$

$r_2 = 31.5$

So, when *h* = 7, *r* = 31.5.

Use both methods to solve each problem.

1. *y* varies directly as *x*. If *y* = 16 when *x* = 5, find *y* when *x* = 9.

$\frac{y}{x} = k$

$\frac{16}{5} = k$

$3.2 = k$

$y = 3.2x$

$y = 3.2(9) = 28.8$

So, when *x* = 9, *y* = ___28.8___.

$\frac{y_1}{x_1} = \frac{y_2}{x_2}$

$\frac{16}{5} = \frac{y_2}{9}$

$5y_2 = 16(9)$

$\frac{y_2}{5} = \frac{144}{5}$

$y_2 = 28.8$

2. *A* varies directly as s^2. If *A* = 75 when *s* = 5, find *A* when *s* = 7.

$\frac{A}{s^2} = k$

$\frac{75}{5^2} = k; k = 3$

$A = 3s^2$

$A = 3(7^2) = 147$

So, when *s* = 7, *A* = ___147___.

$\frac{A_1}{(s_1)^2} = \frac{A_2}{(s_2)^2}$

$\frac{75}{5^2} = \frac{A_2}{7^2}; 25A_2 = 75(49)$

$\frac{25A_2}{25} = \frac{3675}{25}$

$A_2 = 147$

PROBLEM SOLVING 12-5

LESSON 12-5 Problem Solving
Direct Variation

Determine whether the data sets show direct variation. If so, find the equation of direct variation.

1. The table shows the distance in feet traveled by a falling object in certain times.

Time (s)	0	0.5	1	1.5	2	2.5	3
Distance (ft)	0	4	16	36	64	100	144

No direct variation

2. The R-value of insulation gives the material's resistance to heat flow. The table shows the R-value for different thicknesses of fiberglass insulation.

Thickness (in)	1	2	3	4	5	6
R-value	3.14	6.28	9.42	12.56	15.7	18.84

Direct variation; R = 3.14t

3. The table shows the lifting power of hot air.

Hot Air (ft³)	50	100	500	1000	2000	3000
Lift (lb)	1	2	10	20	40	60

Direct variation; $L = \left(\frac{1}{50}\right)H$

4. The table shows the relationship between degrees Celsius and degrees Fahrenheit.

°Celsius	−10	−5	0	5	10	20	30
°Fahrenheit	14	23	32	41	50	68	86

No direct variation

The relationship between your weight on Earth and your weight on other planets is direct variation. The table below shows how much a person who weights 100 lb on Earth would weigh on the moon and different planets.

Solar System Objects	Weight (lb)
Moon	16.6
Jupiter	236.4
Pluto	6.7

5. Find the equation of direct variation for the weight on earth *e* and on the moon *m*.

Ⓐ *m* = 0.166*e* Ⓒ *m* = 6.02*e*
Ⓑ *m* = 16.6*e* Ⓓ *m* = 1660*e*

6. How much would a 150 lb person weigh on Jupiter?

Ⓕ 63.5 lb Ⓗ 354.6 lb
Ⓖ 286.4 lb Ⓙ 483.7 lb

7. How much would a 150 lb person weigh on Pluto?

Ⓐ 5.8 lb Ⓒ 12.3 lb
Ⓑ 10.05 lb Ⓓ 2238.8 lb

Graphing Inequalities in Two Variables

Learn to graph inequalities on the coordinate plane.

Vocabulary
boundary line
linear inequality

Graphing can help you visualize the relationship between a summer camp's growing capacity and the number of years that have passed.

A graph of a linear equation separates the coordinate plane into three parts: the points on one side of the line, the points on the **boundary line**, and the points on the other side of the line.

Each point in the coordinate plane makes one of these three statements true:

Equality ————► $y = x + 2$

Inequality ⟨ $y > x + 2$
⟨ $y < x + 2$

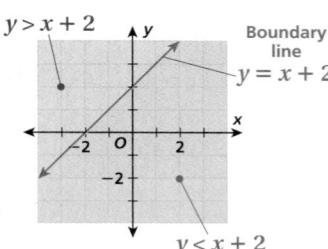

When the equality symbol is replaced in a linear equation by an inequality symbol, the statement is a **linear inequality**. Any ordered pair that makes the linear inequality true is a solution.

EXAMPLE 1 — Graphing Inequalities

Graph each inequality.

A $y > x + 3$

First graph the boundary line $y = x + 3$. Since no points that are on the line are solutions of $y > x + 3$, make the line *dashed*. Then determine on which side of the line the solutions lie.

$(0, 0)$	*Test a point not on the line.*
$y > x + 3$	
$0 \overset{?}{>} 0 + 3$	*Substitute 0 for x*
$0 \overset{?}{>} 3$	*and 0 for y.*

Since $0 > 3$ is not true, $(0, 0)$ is not a solution of $y > x + 3$. Shade the side of the line that does not include $(0, 0)$.

Helpful Hint
Any point on the line $y = x + 3$ is not a solution of $y > x + 3$ because the inequality symbol > means only "greater than" and does not include "equal to."

Organizer — 12-6

Pacing: Traditional 1 day
Block $\frac{1}{2}$ day
Objective: Students graph inequalities on the coordinate plane.

LAB **Hands-On Lab**
In *Hands-On Lab Activities*

Technology Lab
In *Technology Lab Activities*

PREMIER **Online Edition**
Tutorial Videos

Power Presentations with PowerPoint®

Warm Up

Find each equation of direct variation, given that y varies directly with x.

1. y is 18 when x is 3. $y = 6x$

2. x is 60 when y is 12. $y = \frac{1}{5}x$

3. y is 126 when x is 18. $y = 7x$

4. x is 4 when y is 20. $y = 5x$

Problem of the Day

The circumference of a pizza varies directly with its diameter. If you graph that direct variation, what will the slope be? π

Also available on transparency

Math Humor

Teacher: Define *inequality*.
Student: When one motel is as good as another

---

1 Introduce

Alternate Opener

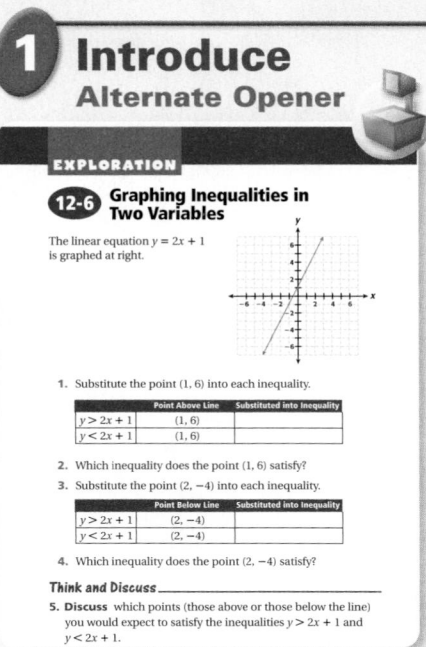

12-6 Graphing Inequalities in Two Variables

The linear equation $y = 2x + 1$ is graphed at right.

1. Substitute the point (1, 6) into each inequality.

	Point Above Line	Substituted into Inequality
$y > 2x + 1$	(1, 6)	
$y < 2x + 1$	(1, 6)	

2. Which inequality does the point (1, 6) satisfy?
3. Substitute the point (2, −4) into each inequality.

	Point Below Line	Substituted into Inequality
$y > 2x + 1$	(2, −4)	
$y < 2x + 1$	(2, −4)	

4. Which inequality does the point (2, −4) satisfy?

Think and Discuss
5. **Discuss** which points (those above or those below the line) you would expect to satisfy the inequalities $y > 2x + 1$ and $y < 2x + 1$.

Motivate

Remind students of the inequalities they studied in earlier lessons (Lessons 1-9, 11-4, and 11-5). Remind them that the difference between a simple equation (e.g., $x + 4 = 6$) and a simple inequality (e.g., $x + 4 \geq 6$) is that the equation has a single solution but the inequality has many solutions.

Explorations and answers are provided in *Alternate Openers: Explorations Transparencies.*

State Resources

go.hrw.com
State Resources Online
KEYWORD: MT7 Resources

Example 1

Graph each inequality.

A. $y < x - 1$

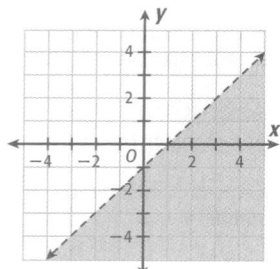

B. $y \geq 2x + 1$

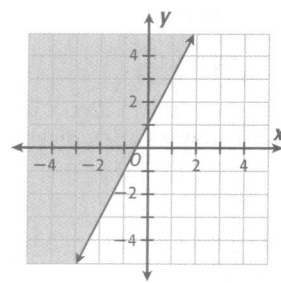

C. $2y + 5x < 6$

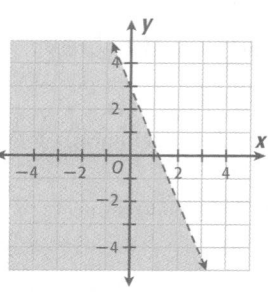

Also available on transparency

Graph each inequality.

B $y \leq x + 1$

First graph the boundary line $y = x + 1$. Since points that are on the line are solutions of $y \leq x + 1$, make the line *solid.* Then shade the part of the coordinate plane in which the rest of the solutions of $y \leq x + 1$ lie.

$(2, 1)$ *Choose any point not on the line.*

$y \leq x + 1$

$1 \overset{?}{\leq} 2 + 1$ *Substitute 2 for x and 1 for y.*

$1 \overset{?}{\leq} 3$ ✔

Since $1 \leq 3$ is true, $(2, 1)$ is a solution of $y \leq x + 1$. Shade the side of the line that includes the point $(2, 1)$.

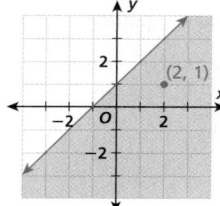

C $6y + 3x \leq 12$

First write the inequality in slope-intercept form.

$6y + 3x \leq 12$

$6y \leq -3x + 12$ *Subtract 3x from both sides.*

$y \leq -\frac{1}{2}x + 2$ *Divide both sides by 6.*

Then graph the line $y = -\frac{1}{2}x + 2$. Since points that are on the line are solutions of $y \leq -\frac{1}{2}x + 2$, make the line *solid.* Then shade the part of the coordinate plane in which the rest of the solutions of $y \leq -\frac{1}{2}x + 2$ lie.

$(0, 0)$ *Choose any point not on the line.*

$6y + 3x \leq 12$

$6(0) + 3(0) \overset{?}{\leq} 12$ *Substitute 0 for x and 0 for y.*

$0 \overset{?}{\leq} 12$ ✔

Since $0 \leq 2$ is true, $(0, 0)$ is a solution of $y \leq -\frac{1}{2}x + 2$. Shade the side of the line that includes the point $(0, 0)$.

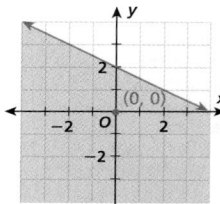

---

2 Teach

Guided Instruction

In this lesson, students learn to graph inequalities on the coordinate plane. Remind students how to graph linear equations. Explain that a graph of a linear equation separates the coordinate plane into three parts: the points on one side of the line, the points on the *boundary line,* and the points on the other side of the line (Teaching Transparency). Show students how to graph a linear inequality. Explain that if the inequality contains "equal to," the boundary line is drawn solid. Otherwise, the boundary line is drawn dashed.

Reaching All Learners
Through Cognitive Strategies

Give students a coordinate grid and the following four linear inequalities:

$y < -2$
$y > 4$
$y > 3x + 1$
$y > -2x + 10$

Have students graph the inequalities and identify the geometric shape that remains unshaded on the coordinate grid. trapezoid You may want to have students check each other's work after graphing each inequality.

EXAMPLE 2 · *Social Studies Application*

Helpful Hint

The phrase "up to 300" can be translated as "less than or equal to 300."

Camp Wakatobi opened in 2000 with room for up to 300 middle school students. Since then, the camp has increased its capacity by 60 students every 2 years. Graph the relationship between the years elapsed and the camp's capacity. If Camp Wakatobi continues to grow at the same rate, will it have enough room for 750 students in the year 2012?

First find the equation of the line that corresponds to the inequality. The year 2000 is year 0, 2001 is year 1, and so on.

In year 0, the camp capacity was 300. ⟶ point (0, 300)

In year 2, the camp capacity was 360. ⟶ point (2, 360)

$m = \frac{360 - 300}{2 - 0} = \frac{60}{2} = 30$ *With two known points, find the slope.*

$y = 30x + 300$ *The y-intercept is 300.*

Graph the boundary line $y = 30x + 300$. Since points on the line are solutions of $y \le 30x + 300$, make the line *solid*.

Shade the part of the coordinate plane in which the rest of the solutions of $y \le 30x + 300$ lie.

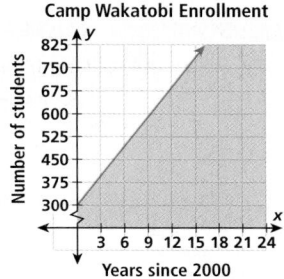

Camp Wakatobi Enrollment

(5, 0)   *Choose any point not on the line.*

$y \le 30x + 300$

$0 \overset{?}{\le} 30(5) + 300$ *Substitute 5*

$0 \overset{?}{\le} 450$ ✔   *for x and 0 for y.*

Since $0 \le 450$ is true, (5, 0) is a solution of $y \le 30x + 300$. Shade the part on the side of the line that includes point (5, 0).

The point (12, 750) is not included in the shaded area, so the camp would not have room for 750 students in the year 2012.

Think and Discuss

1. **Describe** the graph of $5x + y < 15$. Tell how it would change if < were changed to ≥.

2. **Compare and contrast** the use of an open circle, a closed circle, a dashed line, and a solid line when graphing inequalities.

3. **Explain** how you can tell if a point on the line is a solution of the inequality.

4. **Name** a linear inequality for which the graph is a horizontal dashed line and all points below it.

---

3 Close

Summarize

Remind students that inequality graphs will have solid boundary lines if the inequality symbols are ≤ or ≥ and dashed boundary lines if the inequality symbols are < or >. They can determine which side of the boundary line to shade by testing points.

Students will often forget to draw the boundary line dashed when it is appropriate to do so. To help prevent this, ask students to write whether they plan to draw the line solid or dashed before they begin to graph the inequality.

Power Presentations with PowerPoint®

Additional Examples

Example 2

A successful screenwriter can write no more than seven and a half pages of dialogue each day. Graph the relationship between the number of pages the writer can write and the number of days. At this rate, would the writer be able to write a 200-page screenplay in 30 days?

$y \le 7.5x$; yes

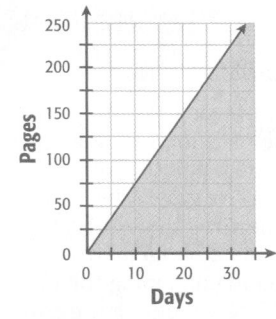

Days

Also available on transparency

Possible answers to Think and Discuss

1. The graph includes the dashed line $y = -5x + 15$ with shading below and left of the line. If the symbol were changed to ≥, the line would be solid and the shading would be on the opposite side of the line.

2. A closed circle and a solid line both mean that the points are included in the solution set. An open circle and a dashed line both mean that the points are not included in the solution set.

3. If the line is solid, the point is a solution.

4. $y < 2$

12-6 Exercises

go.hrw.com
Homework Help Online
KEYWORD: MT7 12-6
Parent Resources Online
KEYWORD: MT7 Parent

Assignment Guide

If you finished Example ① assign:
Average 1–6, 8–13, 15, 18–23, 28–34
Advanced 8–13, 15, 18–23, 25–34

If you finished Example ② assign:
Average 1–23, 28–34
Advanced 8–34

Homework Quick Check

Quickly check key concepts.
Exercises: 10, 14, 20

Answers

1–17. See p. A19.

Math Background

The process of using test points to check solutions is important in graphing inequalities. Test points can often clarify which side of the graph should be shaded. If the coordinates of a test point make the original inequality true, then the region containing the test point should be shaded. If the coordinates make the original inequality false, the opposite region should be shaded. The process of checking solutions and solution regions by using substitution is an invaluable algebraic skill.

State Resources

go.hrw.com
State Resources Online
KEYWORD: MT7 Resources

GUIDED PRACTICE

See Example ① Graph each inequality.

1. $y < x + 3$
2. $y \geq 3x - 2$
3. $y > -2x + 1$
4. $5x + y \leq 2$
5. $y \leq \frac{3}{4}x + 4$
6. $\frac{1}{3}x - \frac{1}{6}y < -1$

See Example ②
7. **a.** The organizers of a bicycle trip have a budget of $450 to buy spare tires and tire repair kits. They can buy spare tires for $18 each and repair kits for $15 each. Write and graph an inequality showing the different ways the organizers can spend their budget. $18t + 15r \leq 450$
   b. Can the organizers of the bicycle trip buy 15 spare tires and 10 tire repair kits and still be within their budget? **yes**

INDEPENDENT PRACTICE

See Example ① Graph each inequality.

8. $y \leq -\frac{1}{2}x - 4$
9. $y < -2.5x + 1.5$
10. $-3(4x + y) \geq -6$
11. $2x - \frac{2}{3}y > -3$
12. $3x - 5y > 7$
13. $4\left(\frac{3}{4}x + \frac{1}{4}y\right) \leq -4$

See Example ②
14. **a.** To avoid the bends, a diver should ascend no faster than 30 feet per minute. Write and graph an inequality showing the relationship between the depth of a diver and the time required to ascend to the surface. $d \leq 30t$
    b. If a diver who begins at a depth of 77 ft ascends to the surface in 2.6 minutes, is the diver in danger of developing the bends? **no**

PRACTICE AND PROBLEM SOLVING

Extra Practice
See page 805.

15. **a.** Graph the inequality $y \geq x + 4$.
    b. Name an ordered pair that is a solution of the inequality. Possible answer: (1, 5)
    c. Is (2, 4) a solution of $y \geq x + 4$? Explain how to check your answer.
    d. Which side of the line $y = x + 4$ is shaded? **the upper side**
    e. Name an ordered pair that is a solution of $y < x + 4$. Possible answer: (0, 3)

15c. No; you can check by substituting (2, 4) into the inequality and evaluating.

16. **Food** The school cafeteria needs to buy no more than 28 pounds of apples. A supermarket sells 4-pound and 7-pound bags of apples. Write and graph an inequality showing the number of 4-pound and 7-pound bags of apples the cafeteria can buy. $4x + 7y \leq 28$

17. **Estimation** The amount of money Natasha spends for her birthday party is a function of the number of people who attend the party. This can be expressed by the inequality $y \geq \frac{14}{3}x + 20$ for x people. Graph an inequality showing the possible numbers of people x for a party that costs y dollars. If Natasha wants to invite 10 people, approximately how much money will she spend? **about $70**

RETEACH 12-6

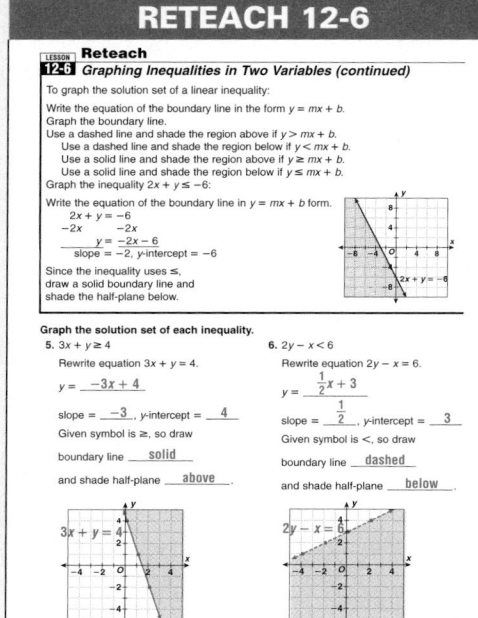

PRACTICE 12-6

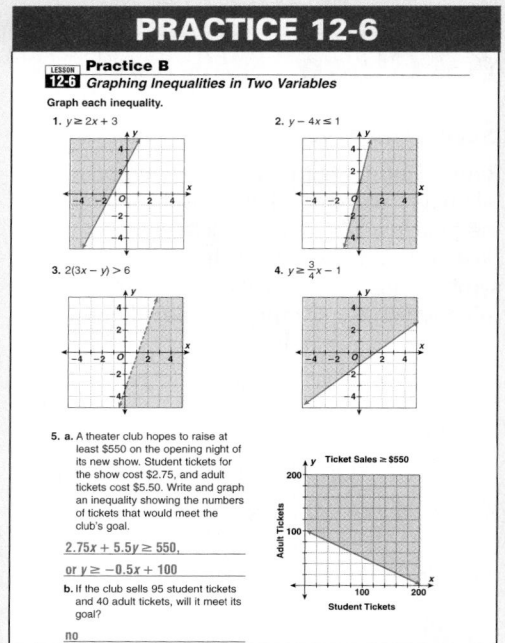

Tell whether the given ordered pair is a solution of each inequality shown.

18. $y \leq 2x + 4$, (2, 1) **yes**

19. $y > -5x + 2$, (−2, 12) **no**

20. $y \geq 4x - 4$, (4, 15) **yes**

21. $y > -x + 12$, (0, 14) **yes**

22. $y \geq 3.2x + 1.8$, (6, 23) **yes**

23. $y \leq 5(x - 2)$, (2, 2) **no**

 24. Earth Science A weather balloon can ascend at a rate of up to 800 feet per minute.

Sunny Day Weather Balloons

Rise up to 800 ft/min!

   a. Write an inequality showing the relationship between the distance the balloon can ascend and the number of minutes. $d \leq 800t$

   b. Graph the inequality for time between 0 and 30 minutes.

   c. Can the balloon ascend to a height of 2 miles within 15 minutes? (*Hint:* 1 mile is equal to 5280 feet.) **yes**

 25. Choose a Strategy Which of the following ordered pairs is NOT a solution of the inequality $3x + 8y \leq 111$? Describe the tools and techniques you used.

   Ⓐ (0, 0)   Ⓑ (−5, 16)   Ⓒ (−3, −14)   Ⓓ (6, 9)

 26. Write About It When you graph a linear inequality that is solved for *y*, when do you shade above the boundary line and when do you shade below it? When do you use a dashed line?

27. Challenge Graph the region that satisfies all three inequalities: $x \geq -3$, $y \geq 2$, and $y < -\frac{1}{3}x + 3$.

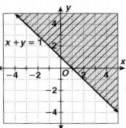 **TEST PREP and Spiral Review**

28. Multiple Choice On a local highway, a car can travel no faster than 55 miles per hour. Which of the following is an inequality showing the relationship between the distance driven by the car and the number of hours?

   Ⓕ $d \leq \frac{t}{55}$ Ⓖ $d \leq \frac{55}{t}$ Ⓗ $d \leq 55t$ Ⓙ $d \geq 55t$

29. Short Response Graph the inequality $y > 3x - 1$. Is the ordered pair (4, −2) a solution of the inequality? **no**

Solve. (Lesson 11-2)

30. $4n - 3 + 5n + 2 = 8$
   $n = 1$

31. $6m + 2 - m = -28$
   $m = -6$

32. $1.4p + 7 - 3.9p = -2$
   $p = 3.6$

Write the point-slope form of each equation with the given slope that passes through the indicated point. (Lesson 12-4)

33. slope 5, passing through (4, 1)
   $y - 1 = 5(x - 4)$

34. slope −2, passing through (6, −6)
   $y + 6 = -2(x - 6)$

Answers
24b, 25–27, 29. See p. A20.

 **TEST PREP DOCTOR ✚** Help students become familiar with useful phrases in inequality word problems. Ask students which inequality is implied by the phrase "no faster than" in Exercise 28.

 Journal

Ask students to explain which inequality symbol they would use to describe each of the following word phrases: *as low as, not more than, at least,* and *as much as.*

Power Presentations
   with PowerPoint®

 12-6 Lesson Quiz

Graph each inequality.

1. $y < -\frac{1}{3}x + 4$

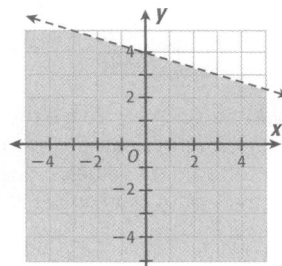

2. $4y + 2x > 12$

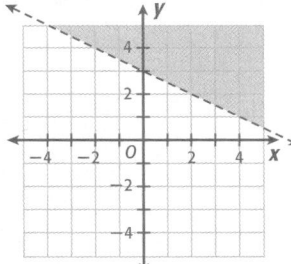

Tell whether the given ordered pair is a solution of each inequality.

3. $y < x + 15$ (−2, 8) **yes**

4. $y \geq 3x - 1$ (7, −1) **no**

Also available on transparency

CHALLENGE 12-6

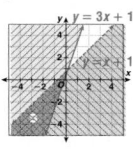

LESSON 12-6 Challenge
Two at a Time

To solve a system of two linear inequalities graphically find the solution set for each linear inequality and mark off the part that overlaps.

Graph the solution set of the system: $\begin{array}{l} x + y \geq 1 \\ y < x - 3 \end{array}$

Work with the first inequality.
Rewrite $x + y = 1$ as $y = -x + 1$. Since line is now in $y = mx + b$ form and given symbol is ≥, draw solid boundary line and shade half-plane above line.

Work with the second inequality.
Since boundary line $y = x - 3$ is in $y = mx + b$ form and given symbol is <, draw dashed boundary line and shade half-plane below the line.

Use a shading opposite to the first shading so that the overlap is visible.

So, the solution set to the system is the cross-hatched region labeled *S*.

Graph the solution set *S* for each system.

1. $\begin{array}{l} y \geq 3x + 1 \\ y < x + 1 \end{array}$

2. $\begin{array}{l} 2x - y \leq 4 \\ 3x + y < 6 \end{array}$

PROBLEM SOLVING 12-6

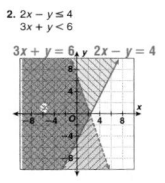

LESSON 12-6 Problem Solving
Graphing Inequalities in Two Variables

The senior class is raising money by selling popcorn and soft drinks. They make \$0.25 profit on each soft drink sold, and \$0.50 on each bag of popcorn. Their goal is to make at least \$500.

1. Write an inequality showing the relationship between the sales of *x* soft drinks and *y* bags of popcorn and the profit goal.

   $0.25x + 0.5y \geq 500$

2. Graph the inequality from exercise 1.

3. List three ordered pairs that represent a profit of exactly \$500.

   Possible answers: (800, 600), (400, 800), (1600, 200).

4. List three ordered pairs that represent a profit of more than \$500.

   Possible answers: (400, 900), (800, 700), (1600, 300).

5. List three ordered pairs that represent a profit of less than \$500.

   Possible answers: (400, 200), (800, 400), (1200, 100).

A vehicle is rated to get 19 mpg in the city and 25 mpg on the highway. The vehicle has a 15-gallon gas tank. The graph below shows the number of miles you can drive using no more than 15 gallons.

6. Write the inequality represented by the graph.

   A $\frac{x}{19} + \frac{y}{25} < 15$
   B $\frac{x}{19} + \frac{y}{25} \leq 15$
   C $\frac{x}{19} + \frac{y}{25} \geq 15$
   D $\frac{x}{19} + \frac{y}{25} > 15$

7. Which ordered pair represents city and highway miles that you can drive on one tank of gas?

   F (200, 150)   H (250, 75)
   G (50, 350)   Ⓙ (100, 175)

8. Which ordered pair represents city and highway miles that you cannot drive on one tank of gas?

   A (100, 200)   C (50, 275)
   B (150, 200)   D (250, 25)

Pacing: Traditional 1 day
Block $\frac{1}{2}$ day

Objective: Students recognize relationships in data and find the equation of a line of best fit.

Hands-On Lab
In *Hands-On Lab Activities*

Online Edition
Tutorial Videos

Power Presentations
with PowerPoint®

Warm Up

Answer the questions about the inequality $5x + 10y > 30$.

1. Would you use a solid or dashed boundary line?   *dashed*

2. Would you shade above or below the boundary line?   *above*

Problem of the Day

Write an inequality whose positive solutions form a triangular region with an area of 8 square units. (*Hint:* Sketch such a region on a coordinate plane.)
Possible answer: $y < -x + 4$

Also available on transparency

Math Humor

The line wanted so much to be the line of best fit, but it didn't come close to any of the plotted data values. I guess you could say it was *dis-a-pointed*.

State Resources

go.hrw.com
State Resources Online
KEYWORD: MT7 Resources

Learn to recognize relationships in data and find the equation of a line of best fit.

The graph shows the winning times for the women's 3000 meter Olympic speed skating event. As is the case with many Olympic sports, the athletes keep improving and setting new records, so there is a correlation between the year and the winning time.

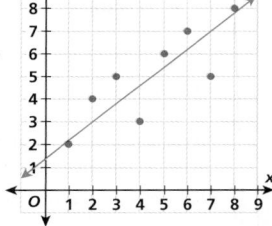

Winning Times for Women's 3000-Meter Olympic Speed Skating

When data show a correlation, you can estimate and draw a *line of best fit* that approximates a trend for a set of data and use it to make predictions.

To estimate the equation of a line of best fit:
- calculate the means of the x-coordinates and y-coordinates: (x_m, y_m).
- draw the line through (x_m, y_m) that appears to best fit the data.
- estimate the coordinates of another point on the line.
- find the equation of the line.

EXAMPLE 1 **Finding a Line of Best Fit**

Plot the data and find a line of best fit.

x	2	4	5	1	3	8	6	7
y	4	3	6	2	5	8	7	5

Plot the data points and find the mean of the x- and y-coordinates.

$$x_m = \frac{2+4+5+1+3+8+6+7}{8} = 4.5 \qquad y_m = \frac{4+3+6+2+5+8+7+5}{8} = 5$$

$$(x_m, y_m) = (4.5, 5)$$

Remember!

A line of best fit is a line that comes close to all the points on a scatter plot. Try to draw the line so that about the same number of points are above the line as below the line.

Draw a line through (4.5, 5) that best represents the data.

Estimate and plot the coordinates of another point on that line, such as (2, 3). Find the equation of the line.

$m = \frac{5-3}{4.5-2} = \frac{2}{2.5} = 0.8$ *Find the slope.*

$y - y_1 = m(x - x_1)$ *Use point-slope form.*

$y - 5 = 0.8(x - 4.5)$ *Substitute.*

$y - 5 = 0.8x - 3.6$

$y = 0.8x + 1.4$

The equation of a line of best fit is $y = 0.8x + 1.4$.

1 Introduce

Alternate Opener

EXPLORATION

12-7 **Lines of Best Fit**

The table shows student enrollment at a college by year. The enrollment numbers are graphed below.

Year	2001	2002	2003	2004	2005	2006	2007	2008
Enrollment	950	995	1011	1020	1035			

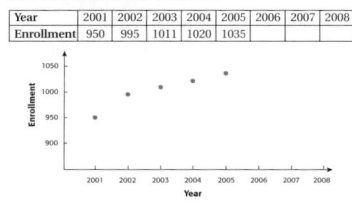

1. Find x_m, the mean of the x-values of the points on the graph.
2. Find y_m, the mean of the y-values of the points on the graph.
3. Plot (x_m, y_m). Lay the edge of a ruler on the graph through (x_m, y_m). Pivot the ruler around (x_m, y_m) and draw the line that you think is closest to the line of best fit.

Think and Discuss
4. **Predict** the enrollment for 2006, 2007, and 2008 by using the line of best fit.

Motivate

Show students a scatter plot that approximates a line. Place a ruler or yardstick at different positions on the scatter plot, and ask students which position they think best approximates the data. When the class has agreed on a good position, explain that the line is a possible *line of best fit*. This is a line that has a minimal amount of distance between each of the data points and itself.

Explorations and answers are provided in *Alternate Openers: Explorations Transparencies*.

EXAMPLE 2 *Sports Application*

Find a line of best fit for the women's 3000-meter speed skating. Use the equation of the line to predict when the winning time will be 0 minutes. Is it reasonable to make this prediction? Explain.

Year	1964	1968	1972	1976	1980	1984	1988	1992	1994	1998	2002
Winning Time (min)	5.25	4.94	4.87	4.75	4.54	4.41	4.20	4.33	4.29	4.12	3.96

Let 1960 represent year 0. The first point is then (4, 5.25), and the last point is (42, 3.96). Plot the data points and find the mean of the x- and y-coordinates.

$$x_m = \frac{4 + 8 + 12 + 16 + 20 + 24 + 28 + 32 + 34 + 38 + 42}{11} \approx 23.5$$

$$y_m = \frac{5.25 + 4.94 + 4.87 + 4.75 + 4.54 + 4.41 + 4.20 + 4.33 + 4.29 + 4.12 + 3.96}{11} \approx 4.5$$

$$(x_m, y_m) = (23.5, 4.5)$$

Draw a line through (23.5, 4.5) that best represents the data.

Estimate and plot the coordinates of another point on that line, (8, 5).

Find the equation of that line.

Winning Times for Women's 3000-Meter Speed Skating

$$m = \frac{5 - 4.5}{8 - 23.5} = \frac{0.5}{-15.5} \approx -0.03$$

$y - y_1 = m(x - x_1)$

$y - 4.5 = -0.03(x - 23.5)$

$y - 4.5 = -0.03x + 0.7$ Round 0.705 to 0.7.

$y = -0.03x + 5.2$

The equation of a line of best fit is $y = -0.03x + 5.2$.

The winning time is 0 minutes at the x-intercept, when $y = 0$.

$0 = -0.03x + 5.2$ *Substitute.*

$-5.2 = -0.03x$ *Solve for x, which represents the*

$173.\overline{3} = x$ *number of years since 1960.*

$1960 + 173 = 2133$ *Add to find the year.*

The winning time will be 0 in 2133. It is not reasonable to make this prediction because it is impossible for the winning time to be 0.

Caution!

Remember that x represents the number of years since 1960. It does not represent the year 173, which would be unreasonable.

Possible answers to Think and Discuss

1. A line of best fit shows the trend of the data and can be used to make predictions.

2. A line of best fit does not have to include any of the points in the data.

Think and Discuss

1. **Describe** what a line of best fit can tell you.

2. **Tell** whether a line of best fit must include one or more points in the data.

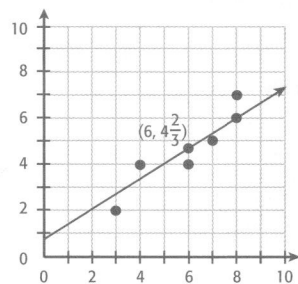

2 Teach

Guided Instruction

In this lesson, students recognize relationships in data and find the equation of a line of best fit. Lead students through the steps for finding the equation of a line of best fit. Remind students that the equation is an approximation and that a line of best fit only approximates the data.

 **Teaching Tip**

Communicating Math Encourage students to understand that, depending on their choice of a second point, their line of best fit equation may be different from others' equations.

Reaching All Learners
Through Cooperative Learning

Have students work in pairs. Give each pair of students a set of data with which to draw a scatter plot. Then have them find a line of best fit by placing a straightedge in different positions on the scatter plot until they believe they have found the best position for the line. Have students trace the line and write the equation of their line of best fit. To make the activity more interesting, you may want to give the groups a piece of dry spaghetti to use in place of a straightedge.

3 Close

Summarize

Remind students that to find the line of best fit, they begin by finding the average values of the x- and y-coordinates. Then, using this point and an estimate of the coordinates of another point on the line, they can write an equation for a line.

12-7 Exercises

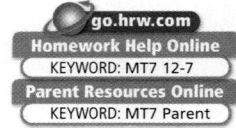

go.hrw.com
Homework Help Online
KEYWORD: MT7 12-7
Parent Resources Online
KEYWORD: MT7 Parent

Assignment Guide

If you finished Example **1** assign:
Average 1, 2, 4, 5, 7–10, 15–24
Advanced 4, 5, 7–10, 14–24

If you finished Example **2** assign:
Average 1–10, 15–24
Advanced 4–24

Homework Quick Check

Quickly check key concepts.
Exercises: 4, 6, 8

Answers

1–6. See p. A20.

Math Background

The statistical process of finding a line of best fit is often called a *linear regression*. The name regression suggests that instead of using an equation to find data values, specific data values are used to create an equation. The line of best fit in a linear regression is obtained by minimizing the sum of the squares of the distances from the line to the data points. Graphing calculators and statistics software packages can easily calculate and draw a line of best fit.

GUIDED PRACTICE

See Example **1** Plot the data and find a line of best fit.

1. Possible answer: $y = 1.6x + 2.57$

x	2	3	5	1	7	4	6
y	6	8	11	4	14	8	12

2. Possible answer: $y = x - 8$

x	20	80	30	50	110	60	90
y	13	75	20	40	100	54	82

See Example **2** **3. Life Science** Find a line of best fit for the life expectancy data. Use the equation of the line to predict when the life expectancy will be 200 years of age. Is it reasonable to make this prediction? Explain.

Year	1993	1994	1995	1996	1997	1998	1999	2000	2001	2002
Life Expectancy: Age (y)	75.5	75.7	75.8	76.1	76.5	76.7	76.7	77.0	77.2	77.3

INDEPENDENT PRACTICE

See Example **1** Plot the data and find a line of best fit.

4. Possible answer: $y = 3.5x$

x	10	25	5	30	20	15	35
y	35	87	17	105	70	52	122

5. Possible answer: $y = -10x + 9$

x	0.1	0.5	0.2	0.4	0.6	0.3	0.7
y	8	5	7	4	3	5	3

See Example **2** **6. Consumer Math** Find a line of best fit for the used-car data. Use the equation of the line to predict what the car's value will be when it is 15 years old. Is it reasonable to make this prediction? Explain.

Age of Car (y)	1	2	3	4	5	6	7	8	9
Value ($)	$12,500	$10,500	$9,200	$8,200	$5,800	$5,000	$4,200	$3,500	$3,000

PRACTICE AND PROBLEM SOLVING

Extra Practice
See page 805.

Tell whether a line of best fit for each scatter plot would have a positive or negative slope. If a line of best fit would not be appropriate for the data, write *neither*.

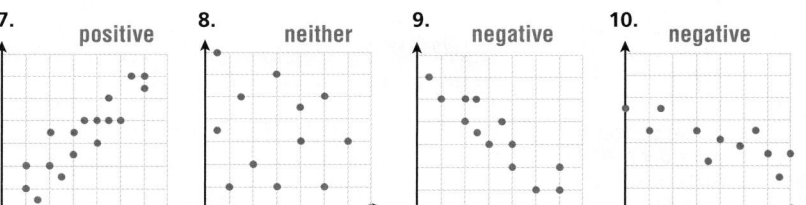

7.   positive   8.   neither   9.   negative   10.   negative

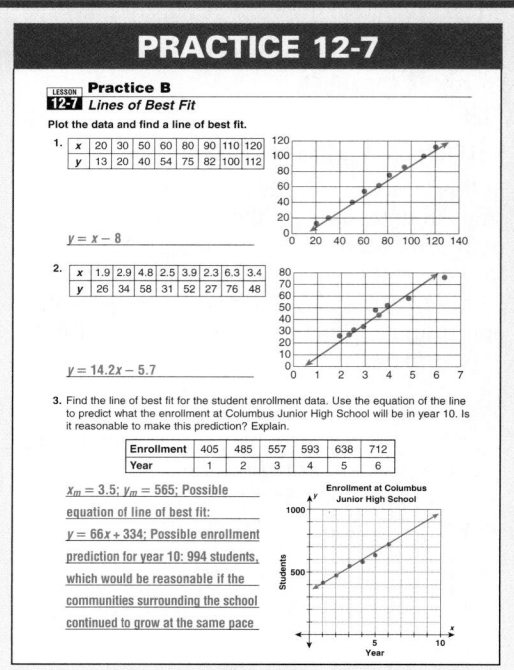

RETEACH 12-7

PRACTICE 12-7

go.hrw.com
State Resources Online
KEYWORD: MT7 Resources

Economics LINK

Economic analysts study trends in data dealing with how and what people buy. They often make predictions about future markets based on these economic trends. The table shows data on how many American households owned a computer.

Computer Ownership in the U.S.				
Year	1993	1997	2000	2001
Total U.S. Households (millions)	99.1	102.2	105.2	109.1
U.S. Households Owning a Computer (millions)	22.6	37.4	53.7	61.5

Source: U.S. Census

11. Let 1989 represent year 0 along the *x*-axis.

   a. What is the mean number of years for the data shown? **7**

   b. Find the percent of U.S. households owning a computer for each year shown in the table, to the nearest tenth. Then find the mean. **22.8%, 36.6%, 51.0%, 56.4%; mean = 36.28%**

12. Let *y* represent the percent of U.S. households that owned a computer between 1989 and 2001. Find a line of best fit, and plot it on the same graph as the data points. Use the point (7, 36) to write the equation of the line of best fit. $y = 3x + 15$

13. Predict the percent of U.S. households owning a computer in the year 2010. Justify your prediction.

14. ⭐ **Challenge** What information does the slope of the line of best fit give you? What would a negative slope mean?

go.hrw.com
Web Extra!
KEYWORD: MT7 Economy

TEST PREP and Spiral Review

15. **Multiple Choice** What type of slope would a line of best fit for the scatter plot at right have? If a line of best fit would not be appropriate, choose neither.

  Ⓐ positive   Ⓑ negative   Ⓒ zero   Ⓓ neither

16. **Short Response** Plot the data and find a line of best fit.

x	0	0.5	1	1.5	1.75	2	2.5
y	4	3.5	1	1.5	1	0	0

$y = -2x + 4$

Solve each inequality. (Lesson 11-5)

17. $4x + 3 - x > 15$ **18.** $3 - 7x \le 24$ **19.** $3x + 9 < -3$ **20.** $1 - x \ge 11$
   $x > 4$ $x \ge -3$ $x < -4$ $x \le -10$

Find the *x*-intercept and *y*-intercept of each line. (Lesson 12-3)

21. $3x - 8y = 48$ **22.** $5y - 15x = -45$ **23.** $13x + 2y = 26$ **24.** $9x + 27y = 81$
   (16, 0), (0, −6)   (3, 0), (0, −9)   (2, 0), (0, 13)   (9, 0), (0, 3)

CHALLENGE 12-7

Challenge
12-7 *Use the Power of Technology*

You can use a calculator to write an equation for the line of best fit. The following instructions are for the TI-83.

x	2	4	5	1	3	8	6	7
y	4	8	7	3	4	8	5	9

To enter the data in the calculator:
Display the Statistics menu.   Press STAT
Choose the EDIT option.   Press ENTER
Enter the *x*-values into list L1.   Press 2 ENTER Press 4 ENTER
Move to list L2.   Press ▶ Clear if necessary.
Enter the *y*-values into list L2.   Press 4 ENTER Press 8 ENTER
To get the slope and *y*-intercept for the line of best fit for this data set:
Display the Y = editor.   Press Y =
Display the Statistics menu.   Press STAT
Select the 4th option from CALC.   Press ▶ 4
Your screen reads **LinReg(ax + b)**.
Attach L1 and L2 to your screen.   Press 2nd L1 , 2nd L2 ,
Attach Y1 to your screen.   Press VARS ▶ ENTER 1
Get the slope and *y*-intercept.   Press ENTER
The top part of your screen reads **LinReg**
$y = ax + b$
$a = .7380952381$ This is the slope.
$b = 2.678571429$ This is the *y*-intercept.

Use the information to write an equation for the line of best fit. $y = 0.74x + 2.68$
Compare these values to those in your text for Example 1.

Use a calculator to write an equation for the line of best fit for this data set.

x	3	8	4	4	5	7	1	6
y	5	14	8	9	12	3	2	11

$y = 1.13x + 2.65$

PROBLEM SOLVING 12-7

Problem Solving
12-7 *Lines of Best Fit*

Write the correct answer. Round to the nearest hundredth.

1. The table shows in what year different average speed barriers were broken at the Indianapolis 500. If *x* is the year, with *x* = 0 representing 1900, and *y* is the average speed, find the mean of the *x*- and *y*-coordinates.

Barrier (mi/h)	Year	Average Speed (mi/h)
80	1914	82.5
100	1925	101.1
120	1949	121.3
140	1962	140.9
160	1972	163.0
180	1990	186.0

$x_m = 52; y_m = 132.47$

2. Graph the data from exercise 1 and find the equation of the line of best fit.
Possible answer:
$y = 1.34x + 62.79$

3. Use your equation to predict the year the 210 mph barrier will be broken.
Possible answer: **2010**

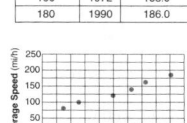

The percent of the U.S. population who smokes can be represented by the line of best fit with the equation $y = -0.57x + 44.51$ where *x* is the year, *x* = 0 represents 1960, and *y* is the percent of the population who smokes. Circle the letter of the correct answer.

4. Which term describes the percent of the population that smokes?
  A Increasing   C No change
  Ⓑ Decreasing   D Cannot tell

5. Use the equation to predict the percent of smokers in 2005.
  F 13.16%   H 24.56%
  Ⓖ 18.86%   J 41.66%

6. Use the equation to predict when the percent of smokers will be less than 15%.
  A 1996   Ⓒ 2012
  B 2010   D 2023

7. Use the equation to predict the percent of smokers in 2010.
  F 10.31%   Ⓗ 16.01%
  G 11.01%   J 12.71%

Answers

12.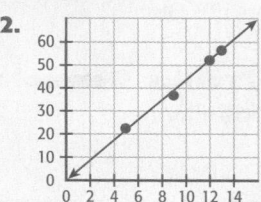

13. Possible answer: 78%; This is an estimation determined by substituting the value for 2010 into the line of best fit.

14. The slope of 3 indicates that the percent of U.S. households owning a computer increases by 3 each year. A negative slope would mean the percent would decrease over time.

16. See p. A20.

TEST PREP DOCTOR ➕ Encourage students to draw a line in their notebooks that would reflect the direction and slope of a line of best fit for Exercise 15. Ask students to describe the slope. They should describe the slope as positive, **A**.

Journal

Ask students to write about how they estimate the coordinates of a point on a line of best fit.

Power Presentations with PowerPoint®

✓ **12-7 Lesson Quiz**

Plot the data to find the line of best fit. See p. A20.

1.

x	2	3	5	1	7	4	6
y	6	8	11	4	14	8	12

Possible answer: $y = 2x + 1$

2.

x	0.1	0.5	0.2	0.4	0.6	0.3	0.7
y	8	5	7	4	3	5	3

Possible answer: $y = -10x + 9$

Also available on transparency

Organizer

Objective: Assess students' mastery of concepts and skills in Lessons 12-5 through 12-7.

Resources

 Assessment Resources
Section 12B Quiz

 **Test & Practice Generator**
One-Stop Planner®

Answers

1, 6–15. See pp. A20–21.

Quiz for Lessons 12-5 Through 12-7

12-5 Direct Variation

1. The table shows an employee's pay per number of hours worked. Make a graph to determine whether the data sets show direct variation. **yes**

Hours Worked	0	1	2	3	4	5	6
Pay ($)	0	8.50	17.00	25.50	34.00	42.50	51.00

Find each equation of direct variation, given that y varies directly with x.

2. y is 10 when x is 2 $y = 5x$

3. y is 16 when x is 4 $y = 4x$

4. y is 2.5 when x is 2.5 $y = x$

5. y is 2 when x is 8 $y = \frac{1}{4}x$

12-6 Graphing Inequalities in Two Variables

Graph each inequality.

6. $y > -3x + 2$

7. $4x + y \le 1$

8. $y \le \frac{2}{3}x + 3$

9. $\frac{1}{2}x - \frac{1}{4}y < -1$

10. $y < -1.5x + 2.5$

11. $-4(2x + y) \ge -8$

12. **a.** The organizers of a fishing outing have a prize budget of $150 to buy shirts and hats for the participants. They can buy shirts for $10 each and hats for $12 each. Write and graph an inequality showing the different ways the organizers can spend their prize budget. $10s + 12h \le 150$

   b. Can the organizers of the fishing outing purchase 7 hats and 6 shirts and still be within their prize budget? **yes**

12-7 Lines of Best Fit

15. Possible answer: $y = 0.3x + 10.4$ (1995 represents year 0); $14.30; yes, the answer seems reasonable.

Plot the data and find a line of best fit. Possible answer: $y = 1.9x - 0.26$

13.

x	2	7	3	4	6	1	9	5
y	4	13	7	8	11	2	17	10

14.

x	0.4	0.5	0.3	0.7	0.2	0.8	0.1	0.6
y	5	5	6	2	8	1	8	3

Possible answer: $y = -10.7x + 9.6$

15. Find a line of best fit for the price of a retailer's stock. Use the equation of the line to predict the stock price in 2008. Is it reasonable to make this prediction? Explain.

Year	1999	2000	2001	2002	2003	2004	2005
Stock Price ($)	11.70	11.95	12.28	12.54	12.77	13.00	13.26

READY TO GO ON?
Diagnose and Prescribe

NO
INTERVENE

YES
ENRICH

	READY TO GO ON? Intervention, Section 12B		
Ready to Go On? Intervention	**Worksheets**	**CD-ROM**	**Online**
Lesson 12-5	12-5 Intervention	Activity 12-5	Diagnose and Prescribe Online
Lesson 12-6	12-6 Intervention	Activity 12-6	
Lesson 12-7	12-7 Intervention	Activity 12-7	

READY TO GO ON? Enrichment, Section 12B

 Worksheets

CD-ROM

Online

Talk, Talk, Talk Mrs. Kim decides to buy a cell phone for her son, Jason. As shown in the table, Mrs. Kim found two companies that offer special rates for students. Unlike many of their competitors, these companies do not round the time to the nearest minute; they charge only for the exact amount of time each customer uses.

Cell Phone Plans	
Talk Cheap	No monthly fee; $0.55 per minute
Talk Easy	$35 monthly fee; $0.15 per minute

1. Build a table, make a graph, and write an equation to represent the cost of cellular service for each company.

2. If price is the only factor, which plan is better? Explain.

3. Which company should Mrs. Kim choose if Jason never uses more than 30 minutes of phone time in a month?

4. If Jason knows the cost of each plan for 30 minutes, can he double this cost to find the cost for 60 minutes? Explain your answer.

2. Talk Cheap offers the better deal if Jason talks less than 88 minutes per month. Otherwise, Talk Easy offers the better deal.

3. Talk Cheap.

4. No, because the cost of Talk Easy involves a flat fee.

Multi-Step Test Prep

Organizer

Objective: Assess students' ability to apply concepts and skills in Chapter 12 in a real-world format.

 Online Edition

Resources

Middle School Assessments
www.mathtekstoolkit.org

Problem	Text reference
1	Lesson 12-1
2	Lesson 12-1
3	Lesson 12-1
4	Lesson 12-1

Answers

1. See p. A21.

INTERVENTION

Scaffolding Questions

1. What values should you use in the table? The cost of each plan with different numbers of minutes

2. Which plan is cheaper under 80 minutes? Talk Cheap Which plan is cheaper over 90 minutes? Talk Easy

3. What plan is automatically more than $35 a month? Talk Easy

4. What is the cost of each plan for 30 minutes? $16.50 and $39.50 What is the cost of both plans for 60 minutes? $33 and $44

Extension

1. What is the point at which both plans cost the same? At 87.5 minutes, both plans cost $48.125

State Resources

go.hrw.com
State Resources Online
KEYWORD: MT7 Resources

Solving Systems of Equations by Graphing

Pacing: Traditional 1 day
Block $\frac{1}{2}$ day

Objective: Students solve a system of equations by graphing.

Online Edition

Using the Extension

In Lesson 11–6, students solved systems of equations algebraically. In Lesson 12-1, students identified and graphed linear equations. In this extension, students solve a system of equations by graphing.

Learn to solve a system of equations by graphing.

Recall that two or more equations considered together form a system of equations. You've solved systems of equations using substitution. You can also use graphing to help you solve a system.

When you graph a system of linear equations in the same coordinate plane, their point of intersection is the solution of the system.

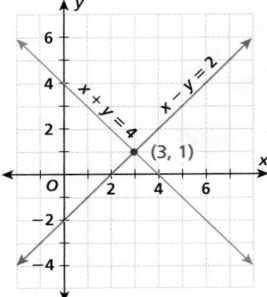

EXAMPLE 1 **Using a Graph to Solve a System of Linear Equations**

Solve the system graphically, and check your answer algebraically.

$$3x + y = 5$$
$$y - x = 1$$

Write each equation in slope-intercept form.

$3x + y = 5$ $y - x = 1$
$y = -3x + 5$ $y = x + 1$

slope = -3, y-intercept = 5   slope = 1, y-intercept = 1

Use each slope and y-intercept to graph the equations. The point of intersection of the graphs appears to be (1, 2), which is the solution of the system.

Check by substituting $x = 1$ and $y = 2$ into each of the *original* equations in the system.

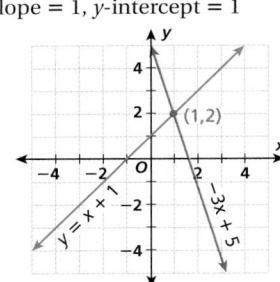

Check

$3x + y = 5$ $y - x = 1$
$3(1) + 2 \stackrel{?}{=} 5$ $2 - 1 \stackrel{?}{=} 1$
$3 + 2 \stackrel{?}{=} 5$ $1 \stackrel{?}{=} 1$ ✔
$5 \stackrel{?}{=} 5$ ✔

The ordered pair (1, 2) checks in the original system of equations, so (**1, 2**) is the solution.

---

1 Introduce

Motivate

Have students recall solving systems of equations by substitution (Lesson 11-6). Remind students that the solution to the system was an ordered pair. Point out that graphing the system of equations will yield a visual solution to the system. Emphasize that visual solutions must be checked algebraically to prove that they are actual solutions.

2 Teach

Guided Instruction

Show students how to solve a system of equations by graphing. Point out that graphing will not always yield a solution that is easy to identify because the solution of a system of equations does not necessarily contain integers. Stress that graphing does not provide a proven solution and that solutions obtained by graphing should always be checked algebraically. Show students how to approximate the solution to an application problem by graphing a system of equations.

Visual For Example 2, have students make each unit on the x-axis 2 and each unit on the y-axis 1000.

EXAMPLE 2 Graphing a System of Linear Equations to Solve a Problem

A plane left Tokyo traveling at 500 mi/h. After the plane had traveled 3000 miles, a second plane started along the same route, flying at 700 mi/h. How many hours after leaving Tokyo will the second plane catch up with the first plane?

Let t = the number of hours and d = the distance in miles.

For plane 1, $d = 500t + 3000$.
For plane 2, $d = 700t$.

Graph each equation. The point of intersection appears to be (15, 10,500).

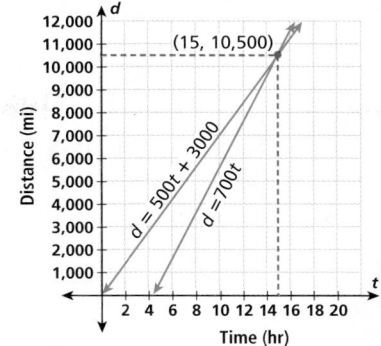

Check

$10,500 \stackrel{?}{=} 500(15) + 3000$ $10,500 \stackrel{?}{=} 700(15)$
$10,500 \stackrel{?}{=} 10,500$ ✔ $10,500 \stackrel{?}{=} 10,500$ ✔

Plane 2 will catch up with plane 1 after 15 hours in flight, 10,500 miles from Tokyo.

EXTENSION Exercises

7. Yes; let t = the number of minutes and d = the distance in meters; second bicyclist: $d = 150t$; first bicyclist: $d = 120t + 105$.

8. First plan; let t = the number of minutes used and c = the cost in dollars; first plan: $c = 4.95 + 0.07t$; second plan: $c = 0.009t$.

Tell whether the ordered pair is the solution of each given system.

1. (5, 11) $y = 3x - 4$
   $y = 2x + 1$
   yes
2. (0, 2) $y = 3x + 2$
   $y = 4x$
   no
3. (4, −7) $2x + y = 1$
   $-3x + y = -9$
   no

Solve each system graphically, and check your answer algebraically.

4. $y = 2x$
   $y = 3x - 3$ (3, 6)
5. $y = -3x + 2$
   $y = \frac{1}{3}x + 2$ (0, 2)
6. $y - x = -3$
   $x - 3y = 9$ (0, −3)

7. A bicyclist is racing toward the finish line. The finish line is 550 meters from a second bicyclist. The first bicyclist is pedaling at 120 meters per minute, and the second bicyclist races behind him at 150 meters per minute. If the first bicyclist had a 105-meter head start, will the second bicyclist catch him in time to tie the race?

8. Melissa has a choice of two phone plans. The first plan has a monthly fee of $4.95 and charges 7 cents per minute. The second plan has no monthly fee, but charges 9 cents per minute. If Melissa averages about 260 minutes of calls per month, which plan is better for her?

COMMON ERROR ALERT

In Exercises 2 and 3, some students may think that because the point is a solution to the first equation in the system, the point is a solution to the system. Remind students that the point must be a solution to both equations.

Additional Examples

Example 1

Solve the system graphically, and check your answer algebraically.

$4x + y = 8$
$y - x = 3$

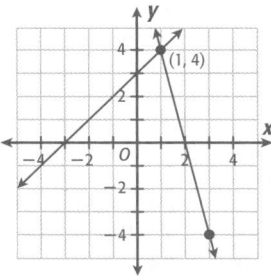

(1, 4)

Example 2

A fishing boat leaves Boston traveling east at 16 knots (nautical miles per hour). After the fishing boat has traveled 40 nautical miles, a Coast Guard cutter follows the boat, traveling at 26 knots. After how many hours will the Coast Guard cutter catch up with the fishing boat?
4 hours

Also available on transparency

3 Close

Summarize

Review the two methods that students have learned to solve systems of equations. They can solve systems algebraically, or they can solve by graphing and check the answer algebraically. Emphasize that it is important to check solutions when either method is used.

Have the students solve the system graphically and check their work by substituting.

$x + y = 9$
$x - y = 1$
(5, 4)

Answers

4

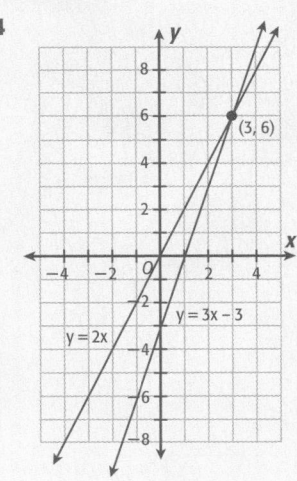

5–8. See p. A21.

State Resources

go.hrw.com
State Resources Online
KEYWORD: MT7 Resources

Chapter 12 Extension   **667**

Game Time

Organizer

Objective: Participate in games to practice and apply skills learned in Chapter 12.

 Online Edition

Resources

 Chapter 12 Resource Book
Puzzles, Twisters & Teasers

Graphing in Space

Purpose: To extend graphing skills into three dimensions

Discuss After graphing the point (3, 4, 1), have students explain how the point's actual location is different from where it appears to be on the graph. Discuss the difficulties in drawing three-dimensional graphs on two-dimensional paper.

Possible answer: The point seems to be in the plane formed by the *y*- and *z*-axes (the plane of the paper). Think of the *x*- and *y*-axes as being on the floor, and the *z*-axis as being a pole extending up from the floor. The point (3, 4, 1) is located above the floor, because the *z*-coordinate is 1.

Extend Challenge students to create a model of the three coordinate axes in a three-dimensional coordinate system using dowels or straws held together with string or tape. Have students plot and show the locations of the points (−2, 3, 1) and (4, −1, −2) and the planes *y* = 2 and *x* = −4.

Check students' work.

Line Solitaire

Purpose: To practice writing linear equations in a game format

Discuss Before playing, have students practice drawing 7 points on paper and drawing 3 lines so that each point lies in a different region.

Extend Have students repeat the game, using only 4 plotted points and 2 dividing lines.

Game Time

Graphing in Space

You can graph a point in two dimensions using a coordinate plane with an *x*- and a *y*-axis. Each point is located using an ordered pair (*x*, *y*). In three dimensions, you need three coordinate axes, and each point is located using an ordered triple (*x*, *y*, *z*).

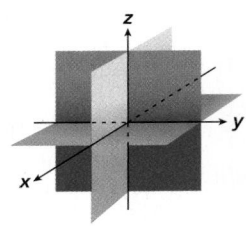

To graph a point, move along the *x*-axis the number of units of the *x*-coordinate. Then move left or right the number of units of the *y*-coordinate. Then move up or down the number of units of the *z*-coordinate.

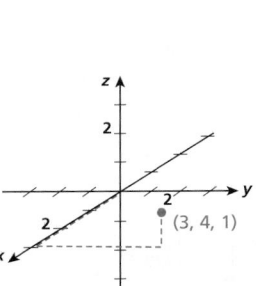

Plot each point in three dimensions.

1 (1, 2, 5)   **2** (−2, 3, −2)

3 (4, 0, 2)

The graph of the equation *y* = 2 in three dimensions is a plane that is perpendicular to the *y*-axis and is two units to the right of the origin.

Describe the graph of each plane in three dimensions.

4 *x* = 3   **5** *z* = 1   **6** *y* = −1

Line Solitaire

Roll a red and a blue number cube to generate the coordinates of points on a coordinate plane. The *x*-coordinate of each point is the number on the red cube, and the *y*-coordinate is the number on the blue cube. Generate seven ordered pairs and plot the points on the coordinate plane. Then try to write the equations of three lines that divide the plane into seven regions so that each point is in a different region.

A complete copy of the rules is available online.

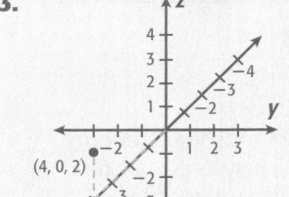
go.hrw.com
Game Time Extra
KEYWORD: MT7 Games

Answers

1.

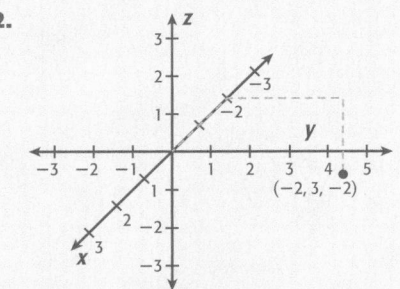

2.

3.

4. vertical plane parallel to the *y*-*z* plane that crosses through *x* = 3

5. horizontal plane parallel to the *x*-*y* plane that crosses through *z* = 1

6. vertical plane parallel to the *x*-*z* plane that crosses through *y* = −1

Materials
- small paper bag
- scissors
- tape
- graph paper
- stapler

It's in the Bag!

FOLDNOTES

PROJECT ## Graphing Tri-Fold

Use this organizer to hold notes, vocabulary, and practice problems related to graphing.

Directions

1 Hold the bag flat with the flap facing you at the bottom. Fold up the flap. Cut off the part of the bag above the flap. **Figure A**

2 Unfold the bag. Cut down the middle of the top layer of the bag until you get to the flap. Then cut across the bag just above the flap, again cutting only the top layer of the bag. **Figure B**

3 Open the bag. Cut away the sides at the bottom of the bag. These sections are shaded in the figure. **Figure C**

4 Unfold the bag. There will be three equal sections at the bottom of the bag. Fold up the bottom section and tape the sides to create a pocket. **Figure D**

5 Trim several pieces of graph paper to fit in the middle section of the bag. Staple them to the bag to make a booklet.

Taking Note of the Math

Write definitions of vocabulary words behind the "doors" at the top of your organizer. Graph sample linear equations on the graph paper. Use the pocket at the bottom of the organizer to store notes on the chapter.

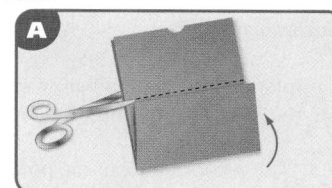
A

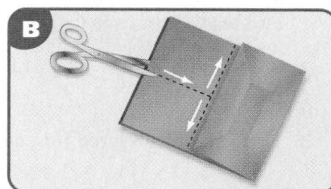
B

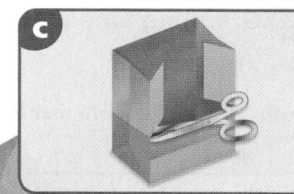
C

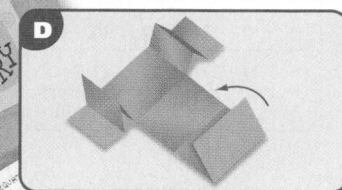
D

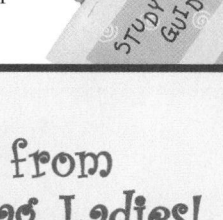

Organizer

Objective: Make an organizer to store notes about graphs of lines.

Materials: small paper bag, scissors, tape, graph paper, stapler

PREMIER **Online Edition**

Using the Page

Preparing the Materials

The project works best when students begin with folded, unused paper bags. If students use recycled bags, have them begin by flattening them into their original shape.

Making the Project

You may want to demonstrate each step of the project in front of the class while students make their organizers. In particular, be sure students understand that in step 2 they must cut only the top layer of the bag.

Extending the Project

Have students use index cards to make flash cards for the chapter. Students can store the flash cards in the pocket of their organizer.

Tips from the Bag Ladies!

We usually make one of the organizers along with the class. The demonstration helps answer any questions that students may have as they follow the directions. You might even make your organizer out of a large grocery bag so that it's easy for all students to see the demonstration.

This project is infinitely adaptable. Once students have made their organizers, they can add library pockets, plastic zipper bags, and/or small stacks of sticky notes.

Organizer

Objective: Help students organize and review key concepts and skills presented in Chapter 12.

 Online Edition
Multilingual Glossary

Resources

 **PuzzlePro®**
One-Stop Planner®

 Multilingual Glossary Online

go.hrw.com
KEYWORD: MT7 Glossary

 Lesson Tutorial Videos
CD-ROM

Test & Practice Generator
One-Stop Planner®

Answers

1. *x*-intercept; *y*-intercept
2. slope-intercept form; point-slope form
3. direct variation
4. linear

5. linear

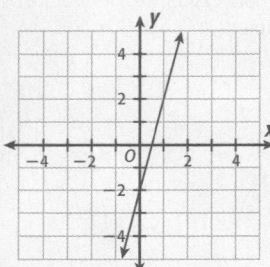

6. not linear

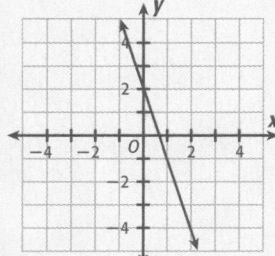

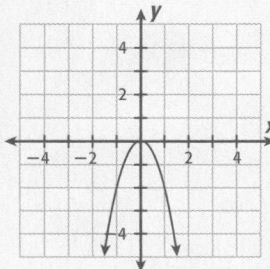

Study Guide: Review

Vocabulary

boundary line 655
constant of proportionality 650
direct variation 650
linear equation 628
linear inequality 655
point-slope form 644
slope-intercept form 639
x-intercept 638
y-intercept 638

Complete the sentences below with vocabulary words from the list above. Words may be used more than once.

1. The *x*-coordinate of the point where a line crosses the *x*-axis is its ___?___, and the *y*-coordinate of the point where the line crosses the *y*-axis is its ___?___.

2. $y = mx + b$ is the ___?___ of a line, and $y - y_1 = m(x - x_1)$ is the ___?___ .

3. Two variables related by a constant ratio are in ___?___.

12-1 Graphing Linear Equations (pp. 628–632)

EXAMPLE

■ Graph $y = x - 2$. Tell whether it is linear.

x	x − 2	y	(x, y)
−1	−1 − 2	−3	(−1, −3)
0	0 − 2	−2	(0, −2)
1	1 − 2	−1	(1, −1)
2	2 − 2	0	(2, 0)

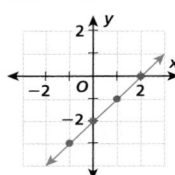

$y = x - 2$ is linear; its graph is a straight line.

EXERCISES

Graph each equation and tell whether it is linear.

4. $y = 4x - 2$
5. $y = 2 - 3x$
6. $y = -2x^2$
7. $y = 2x^3$
8. $y = -x^3$
9. $y = 2x$
10. $y = \frac{12}{x}$ for $x \neq 0$
11. $y = -\frac{10}{x}$ for $x \neq 0$

---

7. not linear

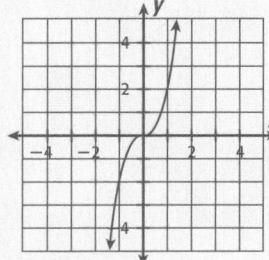

8. not linear

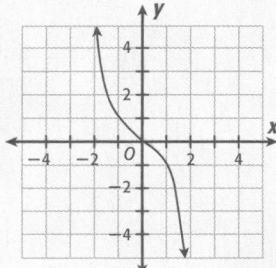

9. linear

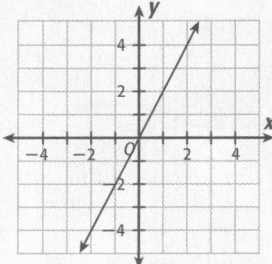

10. not linear

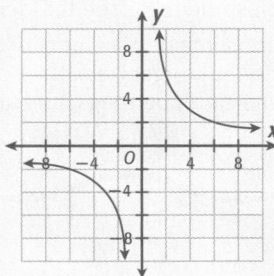

12-2 Slope of a Line (pp. 633–637)

EXAMPLE

- Find the slope of the line that passes through $(-1, 2)$ and $(1, 3)$.

  Let (x_1, y_1) be $(-1, 2)$ and (x_2, y_2) be $(1, 3)$.

  $$\frac{y_2 - y_1}{x_2 - x_1} = \frac{3 - 2}{1 - (-1)}$$
  $$= \frac{1}{2}$$

  The slope of the line that passes through $(-1, 2)$ and $(1, 3)$ is $\frac{1}{2}$.

EXERCISES

Find the slope of the line that passes through each pair of points.

12. $(4, 2)$ and $(8, 5)$

13. $(4, 3)$ and $(5, -1)$

14. $(3, 3)$ and $(-2, -3)$

15. $(-1, 2)$ and $(5, -4)$

16. $(-3, -3)$ and $(-4, -2)$

17. $(-2, -3)$ and $(0, 0)$

18. $(-5, 7)$ and $(-1, -2)$

12-3 Using Slopes and Intercepts (pp. 638–642)

EXAMPLE

- Write $3x + 4y = 12$ in slope-intercept form. Identify the slope and y-intercept.

  $3x + 4y = 12$
  $4y = -3x + 12$ *Subtract 3x from both sides.*
  $\frac{4y}{4} = \frac{-3x}{4} + \frac{12}{4}$ *Divide both sides by 4.*
  $y = -\frac{3}{4}x + 3$ *slope-intercept form*
  $m = -\frac{3}{4}$ and $b = 3$

EXERCISES

Write each equation in slope-intercept form. Identify the slope and y-intercept.

19. $3y = 4x + 15$ 20. $5y = 6x - 10$

21. $2x + 3y = 12$ 22. $4y - 7x = 12$

Write the equation of the line that passes through each pair of points in slope-intercept form.

23. $(0, 4)$ and $(-1, 1)$

24. $(-1, 5)$ and $(2, -4)$

25. $(6, 5)$ and $(-3, 8)$

26. $(3, -1)$ and $(-1, -3)$

12-4 Point-Slope Form (pp. 644–647)

EXAMPLE

- Write the point-slope form of the line with slope -4 that passes through $(3, -2)$.

  $y - y_1 = m(x - x_1)$
  $y - (-2) = -4(x - 3)$ *Substitute 3 for x_1,*
  $y + 2 = -4(x - 3)$ *-2 for y_1, -4 for m.*

  In point-slope form, the equation of the line with slope -4 that passes through $(3, -2)$ is $y + 2 = -4(x - 3)$.

EXERCISES

Write the point-slope form of each line with the given conditions.

27. slope 2, passes through $(3, 4)$

28. slope -4, passes through $(-2, 3)$

29. slope $-\frac{5}{6}$, passes through $(0, -3)$

30. slope $\frac{2}{7}$, passes through $(0, 0)$

Answers

11. not linear

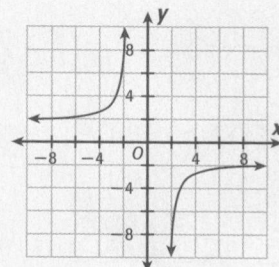

12. $\frac{3}{4}$

13. -4

14. $\frac{6}{5}$

15. -1

16. -1

17. $\frac{3}{2}$

18. $-\frac{9}{4}$

19. $y = \frac{4}{3}x + 5$; $m = \frac{4}{3}$; $b = 5$

20. $y = \frac{6}{5}x - 2$; $m = \frac{6}{5}$; $b = -2$

21. $y = -\frac{2}{3}x + 4$; $m = -\frac{2}{3}$; $b = 4$

22. $y = \frac{7}{4}x + 3$; $m = \frac{7}{4}$; $b = 3$

23. $y = 3x + 4$

24. $y = -3x + 2$

25. $y = -\frac{1}{3}x + 7$

26. $y = \frac{1}{2}x - \frac{5}{2}$

27. $y - 4 = 2(x - 3)$

28. $y - 3 = -4(x + 2)$

29. $y + 3 = -\frac{5}{6}x$

30. $y = \frac{2}{7}x$

Answers

31. $y = 6x$

32. $y = 13x$

33. $y = \frac{1}{7}x$

34.

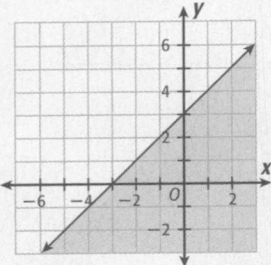

35.

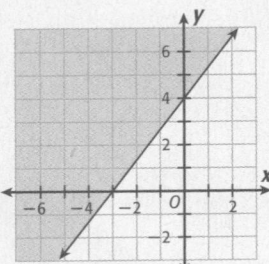

36.

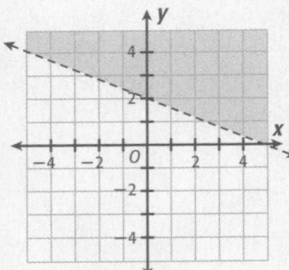

37.

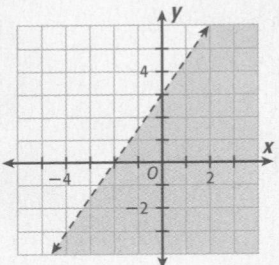

38.

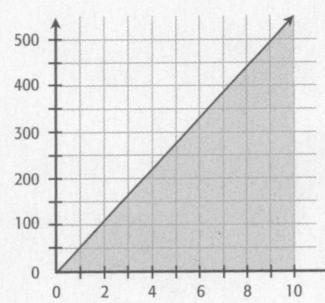

Study Guide: Review

12-5 Direct Variation (pp. 650–654)

EXAMPLE

■ y varies directly with x, and y is 32 when x is 4. Write the equation of direct variation.

$y = kx$ y varies directly with x.

$32 = k \cdot 4$ Substitute 4 for x and 32 for y.

$8 = k$ Solve for k.

$y = 8x$ Substitute 8 for k in the original equation.

EXERCISES

y varies directly with x. Write the equation of direct variation for each set of conditions.

31. y is 42 when x is 7

32. y is 78 when x is 6

33. y is 8 when x is 56

12-6 Graphing Inequalities in Two Variables (pp. 655–659)

EXAMPLE

■ Graph the inequality $y > x - 4$.

Graph $y = x - 4$ as a dashed line. Test $(0, 0)$ in the inequality; $0 > -4$ is true, so shade the side of the line that contains $(0, 0)$.

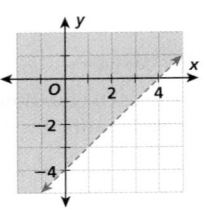

EXERCISES

Graph each inequality.

34. $y \le x + 3$

35. $3y \ge 4x + 12$

36. $2x + 5y > 10$

37. $2y - 3x < 6$

38. Jon can input up to 55 data items per minute. Graph the relationship between the number of minutes and the number of data items he inputs.

12-7 Lines of Best Fit (pp. 660–663)

EXAMPLE

■ Plot the data and find a line of best fit.

x	3	4	5	5	6	7
y	4	2	4	5	7	5

Calculate the means of x and y.

$x_m = \frac{30}{6} = 5$ $y_m = \frac{27}{6} = 4.5$

Draw a line through $(5, 4.5)$ to fit the data. Estimate another point on the line, $(3, 3)$. Find the slope, 0.75, and use point-slope form to write an equation of the line.

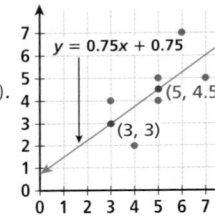

$y - 3 = 0.75(x - 3)$

$y = 0.75x + 0.75$ is a line of best fit.

EXERCISES

Plot the data and find a line of best fit.

39.

x	2	3	3	5	5	6
y	2	5	7	5	8	6

40.

x	1	3	4	4	6	7
y	2	1	4	7	6	7

41.

x	10	20	30	40	50	60
y	7	18	32	38	54	61

42.

x	10	25	40	55	70	85
y	67	58	41	29	28	20

39. Possible answer: $y = 1.5x - 0.5$

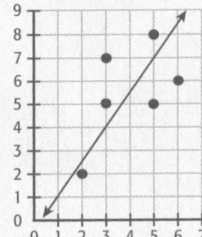

40. Possible answer: $y = 1.25x - 0.7$

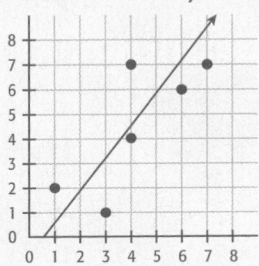

41. Possible answer: $y = 1.1x - 3.5$

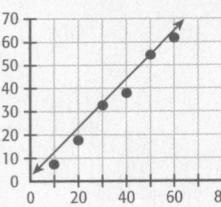

42. Possible answer: $y = -0.6x + 70$

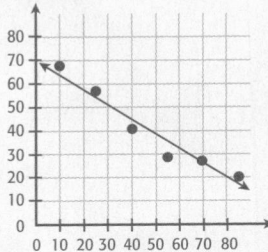

Graph each equation and tell whether it is linear.

1. $y = x + 2$ **linear** **2.** $y = -2x$ **linear** **3.** $y = -2x^2$ **not linear** **4.** $y = 0.5x + 1$ **linear**

Find the slope of the line that passes through each pair of points.

5. $(0, -8)$ and $(-1, -10)$ **2** **6.** $(0, -2)$ and $(-5, 0)$ $-\frac{2}{5}$ **7.** $(3, 1)$ and $(0, 3)$ $-\frac{2}{3}$

8. Determine whether the graph shows a constant or variable rate of change. **constant**

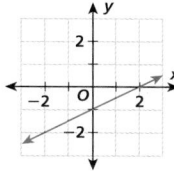

Write the equation of the line that passes through each pair of points in slope-intercept form.

9. $(-1, -6)$ and $(2, 6)$
$y = 4x - 2$
10. $(0, 5)$ and $(3, -1)$
$y = -2x + 5$
11. $(-6, -3)$ and $(12, 0)$
$y = \frac{1}{6}x - 2$

Use the point-slope form of each equation to identify a point the line passes through and the slope of the line.

12. $y - 4 = -2(x + 7)$
$(-7, 4); -2$
13. $y + 2.4 = 2.1(x - 1.8)$
$(1.8, -2.4); 2.1$
14. $y + 8 = -6(x - 9)$
$(9, -8); -6$

Write the point-slope form of the equation with the given slope that passes through the indicated point.

15. slope -2, passing through $(-4, 1)$
$y - 1 = -2(x + 4)$
16. slope 3, passing through $(2, 0)$
$y = 3(x - 2)$

Find each equation of direct variation, given that y varies directly with x.

17. y is 225 when x is 25
$y = 9x$
18. y is 0.1875 when x is 0.25
$y = 0.75x$
19. x is 13 when y is 91
$y = 7x$

Graph each inequality.

20. $y > x + 3$ **21.** $3y \le x - 6$ **22.** $2y + 3x \ge 12$ **23.** $y < 4x + \frac{1}{2}$

24. a. A dragonfly beats its wings up to 30 times per second. Write and graph an inequality showing the relationship between flying time and the number of times the dragonfly beats its wings. $w \le 30s$

b. Is it possible for a dragonfly to beat its wings 1000 times in half a minute? **yes**

Plot the data and find a line of best fit.

25.

x	10	25	5	40	30	20	15	35
y	25	62	13	100	75	48	39	88

26.

x	0	2	2	3	4	7
y	6	6	5	2	1	1

2.
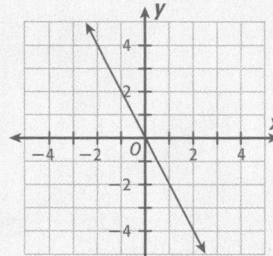

4.
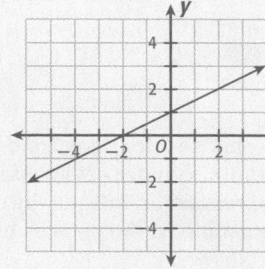

3.
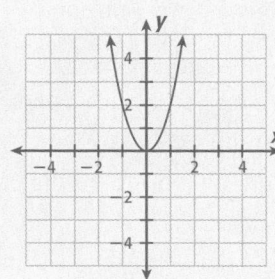

20.
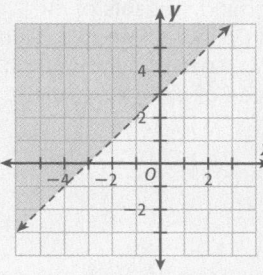

21–26. See p. A21.

Organizer

Objective: Assess students' mastery of concepts and skills in Chapter 12.

 Online Edition

Resources

 Assessment Resources

    Chapter 12 Tests
    • Free Response
      (Levels A, B, C)
    • Multiple Choice
      (Levels A, B, C)
    • Performance Assessment

    IDEA Works! CD-ROM
    Modified Chapter 12 Test

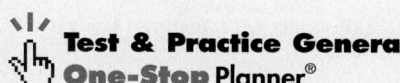 **Test & Practice Generator**
One-Stop Planner®

Answers

1.
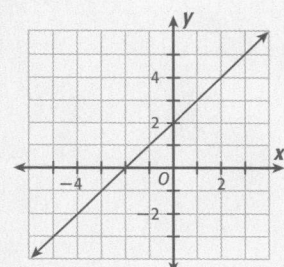

State Resources

Organizer

Objective: Provide review and practice for Chapters 1–12 and standardized tests.

 Online Edition

Resources

 Assessment Resources
Chapter 12 Cumulative Test

 State Test Prep Workbook

 State Test Prep CD-ROM

 State Test Practice Online

go.hrw.com
KEYWORD: MT7 TestPrep

CHAPTER
12

STANDARDIZED
TEST PREP

go.hrw.com
State Test Practice Online
KEYWORD: MT7 TestPrep

Cumulative Assessment, Chapters 1–12
Multiple Choice

Standardized Test Prep

1.

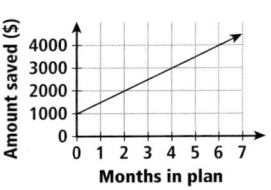

The line graph shows the activity of a savings account. What does the *y*-intercept represent?

Ⓐ Every month $1000 is deposited.

Ⓑ The initial deposit is $1000.

Ⓒ There is no initial deposit.

Ⓓ After the second month, there is $2000 in the savings account.

2. Which of the following is NOT a rational number?

Ⓕ $-\sqrt{196}$ Ⓗ $-\sqrt{10}$

Ⓖ $-5.8\overline{3}$ Ⓙ $-\frac{2}{3}$

3. What is the volume of a sphere whose surface area is 200.96 cm²? Use 3.14 for π.

Ⓐ 50.24 cm³   Ⓒ 267.95 cm³

Ⓑ 133.98 cm³   Ⓓ 803.84 cm³

4. Which inequality describes the graph?

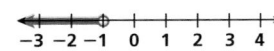

Ⓕ $x < -1$ Ⓗ $x \le -1$

Ⓖ $x > -1$ Ⓙ $x \ge -1$

5. The rectangle and the triangle have the same area. What is the perimeter of the rectangle?

Ⓐ 192 in.   Ⓒ 56 in.

Ⓑ 64 in.   Ⓓ 32 in.

6. There are 36 dogs in an animal shelter that houses 144 animals. Which percent represents the portion of the animals that are dogs?

Ⓕ 10%   Ⓗ 75%

Ⓖ 25%   Ⓙ 400%

7. In the box-and-whisker plot below, what is the difference between the first and third quartiles?

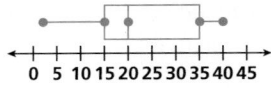

Ⓐ 5   Ⓒ 20

Ⓑ 12.5   Ⓓ 28.5

8. A cell phone store offers 10 different colors, 4 different face plates, and 6 different ring tones. How many different phones does a customer have to choose from?

Ⓕ 240   Ⓗ 64

Ⓖ 120   Ⓙ 20

TEST PREP DOCTOR ✚

Students who choose **F** for item 2 did not realize that 196 is a perfect square, making the expression an integer. Encourage them to examine all the choices before choosing their answer.

For item 8, remind students of the Fundamental Counting Principle. Students who choose **J** added the given numbers together instead of multiplying them.

Answers

16. about 68°.

17. parallelogram; *AB* and *CD* are parallel and *BC* and *DA* are parallel.

18. $y = -2x$; It is a direct variation because it is in the form $y - kx$ where -2 is the constant of variation.

19. See 4-Point Response work sample.

9. Which figure has line symmetry, but not rotational symmetry?

Ⓐ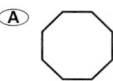

Ⓒ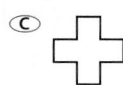

Ⓑ

Ⓓ

 Remember that you can write both fractions and terminating decimals as answers for gridded-response test questions.

Gridded Response

10. What is the value of x so that the slope of the line passing through the points $(-1, 4)$ and $(x, 1)$ is $-\frac{3}{4}$? **3**

11. If $\triangle JKL$ and $\triangle MNP$ are similar, what is the perimeter of $\triangle JKL$? **54**

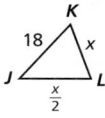   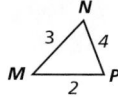

12. What is the slope of a line perpendicular to the line $y - 6 = -4(x + 8)$? **1/4 or 0.25**

13. What is $f(-2)$ for the function $f(x) = -\frac{2}{3}x - \frac{7}{8}$? **11/24**

14. In a school with 1248 students, there are 24 students whose last name is Perez. What is the probability that a student whose last name is Perez will be chosen at random? Write your answer as a fraction in simplest form. **1/52**

15. Maya ran every day for a week. She ran 3 miles on Sunday and increased her distance $\frac{1}{2}$ mile each day. What was the mean distance, in miles, that Maya ran for the week? **4.5**

Short Response

16. Scientists have found that a linear equation can be used to model the relation between the outdoor temperature and the number of chirps per minute crickets make. If a snowy tree cricket makes 100 chirps/min at 63°F and 178 chirps/min at 77°F, at what approximate temperature does the cricket make 126 chirps/min? Show your work.

17. Plot the points $A(-5, -4)$, $B(1, -2)$, $C(2, 3)$, and $D(-4, 1)$. Use straight segments to connect the four points in order. Then find the slope of each line segment. What special kind of quadrilateral is $ABCD$? Explain.

18. Write an equation in slope-intercept form that has the same slope as $-6x - 3y = 3$ and the same y-intercept as $-3y + 5 = 9x + 5$. Tell whether your equation is a direct variation. Explain.

Extended Response

19. Paul Revere had to travel 3.5 miles to Charlestown from Boston by boat. Assume that from Charlestown to Lexington, he was able to ride a horse that traveled at a rate of $\frac{1}{8}$ mile per minute. His total distance traveled y is the sum of the distance to Charlestown and the distance from Charlestown to Lexington.

  a. Write a linear equation that could be used to find the distance y Paul Revere traveled in x minutes.

  b. What does the slope of the line represent?

  c. What does the y-intercept of the line represent?

  d. Graph your equation from part **a** on a coordinate plane.

Student Work Samples for Item 19

4-Point Response

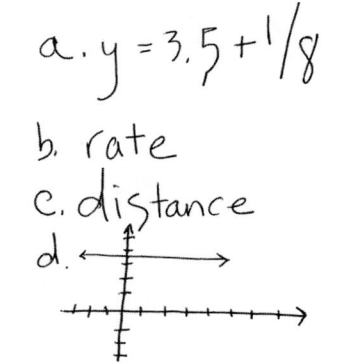

The student applied the variables correctly, wrote a correct equation, and correctly interpreted the slope and y-intercept.

3-Point Response

The student wrote the correct equation, made an adequate graph, but shows an incorrect understanding of the slope and y-intercept.

2-Point Response

The student needs a more detailed explanation for parts **b** and **c**, and their graph needs more detail. The equation in part **a** is missing the x-variable.

Problem Solving on Location

Organizer

Objective: Choose appropriate problem-solving strategies and use them with skills from Chapters 11 and 12 to solve real-world problems.

Online Edition

⭐ The Chesapeake Bay Bridge

Reading Strategies

Ask students to identify important pieces of information in each problem. In problem 1, the important information is the toll for each vehicle and the extra charges. In problem 2, the year and the number of vehicles are important to solving the problem. In problem 3, important information is given in the graph.

Using Data Ask students to figure out the number of westbound and eastbound cars at 0 hour and 1 hour using the graph. At 0 hour, there are 0 westbound and eastbound cars. At 1 hour, there are 3000 eastbound cars and 4500 westbound cars.

Problem Solving on Location

MARYLAND

Baltimore

⭐ The Chesapeake Bay Bridge

The Chesapeake Bay Bridge is actually two bridges in one. The original two-lane structure opened to traffic in 1952. In 1973, construction was completed on a second span alongside the first. Today, the side-by-side bridges carry more than 25 million vehicles per year, and the 4.3-mile crossing has become world famous for its spectacular views.

Choose one or more strategies to solve each problem.

1. When the bridge opened in 1952, the toll for each vehicle was $1.40, plus $0.25 per passenger other than the driver. On opening day, the driver of a bus paid a toll of $3.15. How many people were in the bus? **8 people**

2. In 2001, about 24 million vehicles crossed the Chesapeake Bay Bridge. In 2004, about 26 million vehicles crossed the bridge. Suppose the number of crossings continues to increase by 2 million vehicles every 3 years. In what year will the number of crossings reach 34 million? **2016**

For 3, use the graph.

3. The bridge's westbound span has three lanes, while the eastbound span has only two. This means the westbound span can carry more vehicles per hour, as shown in the graph. In a 24-hour period, how many more vehicles can cross the westbound span than the eastbound span? **36,000 vehicles**

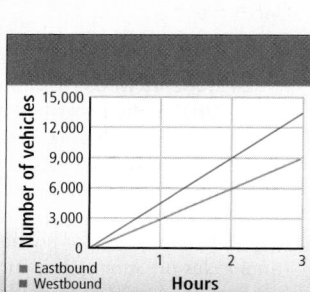

Problem Solving Focus

Encourage students to use the problem solving strategy: **Find a Pattern.**

Discuss with students how they might find a pattern in problem 3. Ask them to find the number of westbound and eastbound cars after one hour has passed. Then, ask students to find the number of westbound and eastbound cars after two hours have passed. What pattern do they notice? 4500 and 3000; 9000 and 6000; the number of cars has doubled after an hour.

State Resources

go.hrw.com
State Resources Online
KEYWORD: MT7 Resources

Problem Solving Strategies

Draw a Diagram
Make a Model
Guess and Test
Work Backward
Find a Pattern
Make a Table
Solve a Simpler Problem
Use Logical Reasoning
Act It Out
Make an Organized List

⭐ Baltimore Kinetic Sculpture Race

Reading Strategies

Encourage students to identify important information in each problem. Remind them that they may need to refer to key information in the initial problem, as well as in each numbered problem. In problem 1, it is important to know the fees per pilot and pit crew and the total amount paid. In problem 2, it is important to know the rate and the total length of the race. In problem 3, it is important to know which combination of 5 violations will total 6 hours and 30 minutes.

Using Data Discuss the information given on the table with students. information about types of violations and penalties. Have students use the information in the table to make different combinations of penalties to total 6 hours and 30 minutes.

⭐ The Baltimore Kinetic Sculpture Race

The annual Baltimore Kinetic Sculpture Race is a 15-mile race over land and sea that involves sculptures powered by humans. In recent years, entries in the madcap race have included a nine-seat platypus, a floating teapot, and a giant sea turtle built from old bicycle parts.

Choose one or more strategies to solve each problem.

1. Each team in the race consists of pilots and a pit crew. The entry fee for pilots is $25 and the entry fee for pit-crew members is $15. A team of seven paid an entry fee of $135. How many pilots were on the team? **3 pilots**

2. A team completes the first 2 miles of the race in 1 hour. They complete the first 4 miles of the race in 2 hours. If they continue at this rate, how long will it take the team to complete the entire course? **7.5 h**

For 3, use the table.

3. If a team breaks one of the rules of the race, a penalty is added to their total time. The table shows the penalties for various violations of the rules. A team had five different violations, for a total penalty of 6 hours and 30 minutes. Which rules did the team break? **A, B, C, E, and F**

Baltimore Kinetic Sculpture Race: Penalties	
Violation	**Penalty**
A. Lost safety equipment	1 hour
B. Pilot gets wet	30 minutes
C. Sculpture is pushed or pulled	3 hours
D. Sculpture goes off course	2 hours
E. Sculpture drifts out of bounds in harbor	1 hour
F. Team gets help from a motor vehicle	1 hour

 Problem Solving Focus

Ask students what strategies they used to solve each problem. Have them compare the different strategies they each used to solve problem 3. One student might use guess-and-check to find a combination of violations that would total 6 hours and 30 minutes with only 5 separate violations. Another student might use logical reasoning to conclude that because the overall time of 6 hours and 30 minutes is so long, the team must have incurred one of the longer violations such as **C** or **D**, as well as a number of smaller violations like **A**, **E**, and **F**.

CHAPTER 13

Sequences and Functions

Section 13A		Section 13B	
Sequences		**Functions**	
13-1	Terms of Arithmetic Sequences	13-4	Linear Functions
13-2	Terms of Geometric Sequences	13-5	Exponential Functions
13-3	Hands-On Lab Explore the Fibonacci Sequence	13-6	Quadratic Functions
13-3	Other Sequences	13-6	Technology Lab Explore Cubic Functions
		13-7	Inverse Variation

Pacing Guide for 45-Minute Classes

Chapter 13

DAY 1	DAY 2	DAY 3	DAY 4	DAY 5
13-1 Lesson	13-2 Lesson	13-3 Hands-On Lab 13-3 Lesson	13-3 Lesson Ready to Go On? Focus on Problem Solving	13-4 Lesson
DAY 6	**DAY 7**	**DAY 8**	**DAY 9**	**DAY 10**
13-5 Lesson	13-6 Lesson	13-6 Hands-On Lab 13-7 Lesson	13-7 Lesson Ready to Go On? Multi-Step Test Prep	Chapter 13 Review
DAY 11				
Chapter 13 Test				

Pacing Guide for 90-Minute Classes

Chapter 13

DAY 1	DAY 2	DAY 3	DAY 4	DAY 5
13-1 Lesson 13-2 Lesson	13-3 Hands-On Lab 13-3 Lesson Ready to Go On? Focus on Problem Solving	13-4 Lesson 13-5 Lesson	13-6 Lesson 13-6 Hands-On Lab 13-7 Lesson	13-7 Lesson Ready to Go On? Multi-Step Test Prep Chapter 13 Review
DAY 6				
Chapter 13 Test				

ONGOING ASSESSMENT and INTERVENTION

	DIAGNOSE	PRESCRIBE

Assess Prior Knowledge

Before Chapter 13

Diagnose readiness for the chapter.

Are You Ready? SE p. 679

Prescribe intervention.

Are You Ready? Intervention Skills 13, 28, 54, 64

Formative Assessment

Before Every Lesson

Diagnose readiness for the lesson.

Warm Up TE, every lesson

Prescribe intervention.

Skills Bank SE pp. 820–834
Reteach CRB, Chapter 1–13

During Every Lesson

Diagnose understanding of lesson concepts.

Think and Discuss SE, every lesson
Write About It SE, lesson exercises
Journal TE, lesson exercises

Prescribe intervention.

Questioning Strategies Chapter 13
Reading Strategies CRB, every lesson
Success for ELL pp. 191–204

After Every Lesson

Diagnose mastery of lesson concepts.

Lesson Quiz TE, every lesson
Test Prep SE, every lesson
Test and Practice Generator

Prescribe intervention.

Reteach CRB, every lesson
Problem Solving CRB, every lesson
Test Prep Doctor TE, lesson excercises
Homework Help Online

Before Chapter 13 Testing

Diagnose mastery of concepts in the chapter.

Ready to Go On? SE pp. 698, 718
Focus on Problem Solving SE p. 699
Multi-Step Test Prep SE p. 719
Section Quizzes AR pp. 245–246
Test and Practice Generator

Prescribe intervention.

Ready to Go On? Intervention Chapter 13
Scaffolding Questions TE p. 719

Before High Stakes Testing

Diagnose mastery of benchmark concepts.

Test Tackler SE pp. 726–727
Standardized Test Prep SE pp. 728–729
State Test Prep CD-ROM

Prescribe intervention.

State Test Prep Workbook

Summative Assessment

After Chapter 13

Check mastery of chapter concepts.

Multiple-Choice Tests (Forms A, B, C)
Free-Response Tests (Forms A, B, C)
Performance Assessment AR pp. 247–260
Test and Practice Generator

Check mastery of benchmark concepts.

AYP State Tests

Prescribe intervention.

Reteach CRB, every lesson
Lesson Tutorial Videos Chapter 13

Prescribe intervention.

State Test Prep Workbook

KEY: **SE** = *Student Edition*   **TE** = *Teacher's Edition*   **CRB** = *Chapter Resource Book*   **AR** = *Assessment Resources*   Available on CD-ROM   Available online   **678B**

Supporting the Teacher

Chapter 13 Resource Book

Practice A, B, C
pp. 3–5, 12–14, 21–23, 29–31, 38–40, 47–49, 56–58

Reading Strategies ELL
pp. 10, 19, 27, 36, 45, 54, 62

Puzzles, Twisters, and Teasers
pp. 11, 20, 28, 37, 46, 55, 63

Reteach
pp. 6–7, 15–16, 24, 32–33, 41–42, 50–51, 59

Problem Solving
pp. 9, 18, 26, 35, 44, 53, 61

Challenge
pp. 8, 17, 25, 34, 43, 52, 60

Parent Letter   pp. 1–2

Transparencies

Lesson Transparencies, Volume 2.......................Chapter 13
 • Warm Ups
 • Problem of the Day
 • Teaching Transparencies
 • Lesson Quizzes

Know-It Notebook...Chapter 13
 • Additional Examples   • Chapter Review
 • Vocabulary   • Big Ideas

Alternate Openers: Explorations.................pp. 96–102

Teacher Tools

Power Presentations®
Complete PowerPoint® presentations for Chapter 13 lessons

Lesson Tutorial Videos® SPANISH
Holt authors Ed Burger and Freddie Renfro present tutorials to support the Chapter 13 lessons.

One-Stop Planner® SPANISH
Easy access to all Chapter 13 resources and assessments, as well as software for lesson planning, test generation, and puzzle creation

IDEA Works!®
Key Chapter 13 resources and assessments modified to address special learning needs

Lesson Plans ....pp. 96–102

Questioning Strategies.................................Chapter 13

Solutions Key ....Chapter 13

Interdisciplinary Posters and Worksheets..........Chapter 13

TechKeys 🪐   **Lab Resources** 🪐

Project Teacher Support 🪐   **Parent Resources** 🪐

Workbooks

Homework and Practice Workbook SPANISH
 Teacher's Guide...pp. 48–51

Know-It Notebook
 Teacher's Guide..Chapter 13

Problem Solving Workbook SPANISH
 Teacher's Guide...pp. 48–51

State Test Prep Workbook
 Teacher's Guide

Technology Highlights for the Teacher

 Power Presentations
Dynamic presentations to engage students. Complete PowerPoint® presentations for every lesson in Chapter 13.

2-1 Solving One-Step Equations

Isolate a variable by using inverse operations which "undo" operations on the variable.

An equation is like a balanced scale. To keep the balance, perform the same operation on both sides.

Inverse Operations	
Operation	**Inverse Operation**
Addition	Subtraction
Subtraction	Addition

 One-Stop Planner SPANISH
Easy access to Chapter 13 resources and assessments. Includes lesson-planning, test-generation, and puzzle-creation software.

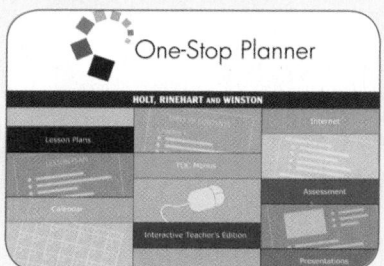

 Premier Online Edition SPANISH
Chapter 13 includes Tutorial Videos, Lesson Activities, Lesson Quizzes, Homework Help, and Chapter Project.

KEY: **SE** = *Student Edition*   **TE** = *Teacher's Edition*   ELL English Language Learners   SPANISH Spanish version available   Available on CD-ROM    Available online

Reaching All Learners

Resources for All Learners

Hands-On Lab Activities................................ Chapter 13

Technology Lab Activities............................ Chapter 13

Homework and Practice Workbook **SPANISH** ....pp. 96–102

Know-It Notebook..................................... Chapter 13

Problem Solving Workbook **SPANISH** ....pp. 96–102

DEVELOPING LEARNERS

Practice A ....CRB, every lesson

Reteach ....CRB, every lesson

Inclusion ....TE p. 715

Questioning Strategies............................. Chapter 13

Modified Chapter 13 Resources .... *IDEA Works!*

Homework Help Online

ON-LEVEL LEARNERS

Practice B ....CRB, every lesson

Puzzles, Twisters, and Teasers.................CRB, every lesson

Multiple Representations ....TE p. 701

Cognitive Strategies ....TE p. 705

ADVANCED LEARNERS

Practice C ....CRB, every lesson

Challenge ....CRB, every lesson

Extension ....TE pp. 681, 719, 720, 721

Critical Thinking ....TE pp. 683, 688

English Language Learners

ENGLISH LANGUAGE LEARNERS

Are You Ready? Vocabulary .... SE p. 679

Vocabulary Connections ....SE p. 680

Lesson Vocabulary ....SE, every lesson

Vocabulary Review..................................SE p. 722

English Language Learners............TE pp. 681, 689, 709, 714

Reading Strategies ....CRB, every lesson

Success for English Language Learners..............pp. 191–204

Multilingual Glossary

Reaching All Learners Through...

Inclusion ....TE p. 715

Visual Cues ....TE p. 709

Concrete Manipulatives...........................TE p. 694

Multiple Representations ....TE p. 701

Cognitive Strategies ....TE p. 705

Modeling ....TE p. 701

Critical Thinking ....TE pp. 683, 688

Test Prep Doctor ....TE pp. 686, 691, 697, 703, 711, 717, 726, 728

Common Error Alerts ....TE pp. 683, 689

Scaffolding Questions...............................TE p. 719

Technology Highlights for Reaching All Learners

 Lesson Tutorial Videos **SPANISH**

Starring Holt authors Ed Burger and Freddie Renfro! Live tutorials to support every lesson in Chapter 13.

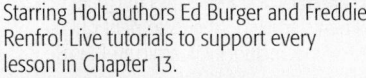

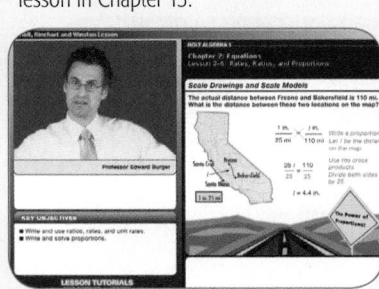

Multilingual Glossary

Searchable glossary includes definitions in English, Spanish, Vietnamese, Chinese, Hmong, Korean, and 4 other languages.

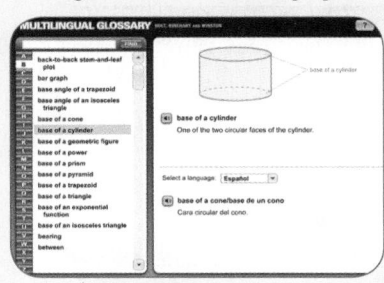

Online Interactivities

Interactive tutorials provide visually engaging alternative opportunities to learn concepts and master skills.

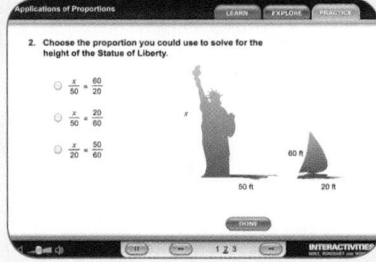

KEY: **SE** = *Student Edition*   **TE** = *Teacher's Edition*   **CRB** = *Chapter Resource Book*   **SPANISH** Spanish version available   Available on CD-ROM   Available online

678D

Ongoing Assessment

Assessing Prior Knowledge

Determine whether students have the prerequisite concepts and skills for success in Chapter 13.

Are You Ready? SPANISH .... SE p. 679
Warm Up .... TE, every lesson

Test Preparation

Provide review and practice for Chapter 13 and standardized tests.

Multi-Step Test Prep .... SE p. 719
Study Guide: Review .... SE pp. 722–724
Test Tackler .... SE pp. 726–727
Standardized Test Prep .... SE pp. 728–729
State Test Prep Workbook
State Test Prep CD-ROM
IDEA Works!

Alternative Assessment

Assess students' understanding of Chapter 13 concepts and combined problem-solving skills.

Chapter 13 Project .... SE p. 678
Performance Assessment SPANISH .... AR pp. 259–260
Portfolio Assessment SPANISH .... AR p. xxxiv

Daily Assessment

Provide formative assessment for each day of Chapter 13.

Questioning Strategies .... Chapter 13
Think and Discuss .... SE, every lesson
Write About It .... SE, lesson exercises
Journal .... TE, lesson exercises
Lesson Quiz .... TE, every lesson
Modified Lesson Quizzes .... *IDEA Works!*

Weekly Assessment

Provide formative assessment for each week of Chapter 13.

Focus on Problem Solving .... SE p. 699
Multi-Step Test Prep .... SE p. 719
Ready to Go On? SPANISH .... SE pp. 698, 718
Cumulative Assessment .... SE pp. 728–729
Test and Practice Generator SPANISH ...One-Stop Planner

Formal Assessment

Provide summative assessment of Chapter 13 mastery.

Section Quizzes SPANISH .... AR pp. 245–246
Chapter 13 Test .... SE p. 725
Chapter Test (Levels A, B, C) SPANISH .... AR pp. 247–258
     • Multiple-Choice   • Free-Response
Cumulative Test SPANISH .... AR pp. 261–264
Test and Practice Generator SPANISH ...One-Stop Planner
Modified Chapter 13 Test .... *IDEA Works!*

Technology Highlights for the Teacher

Are You Ready? SPANISH
Automatically assess readiness and prescribe intervention for Chapter 13 prerequisite skills.

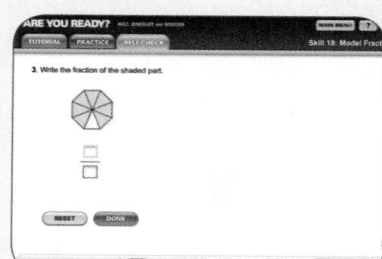

Ready to Go On? SPANISH
Automatically assess understanding of and prescribe intervention for Sections 13A and 13B.

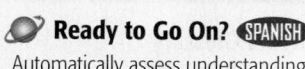
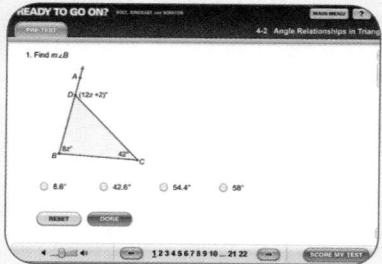

Test and Practice Generator SPANISH
Use Chapter 13 problem banks to create assessments and worksheets to print out or deliver online. Includes dynamic problems.

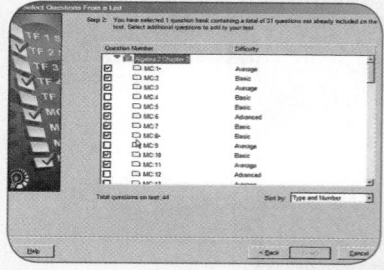

KEY: **SE** = *Student Edition*   **TE** = *Teacher's Edition*   **AR** = *Assessment Resources*   SPANISH Spanish version available   Available on CD-ROM   Available online

Formal Assessment

Three levels (A, B, C) of multiple-choice and free-response chapter tests are available in the *Assessment Resources.*

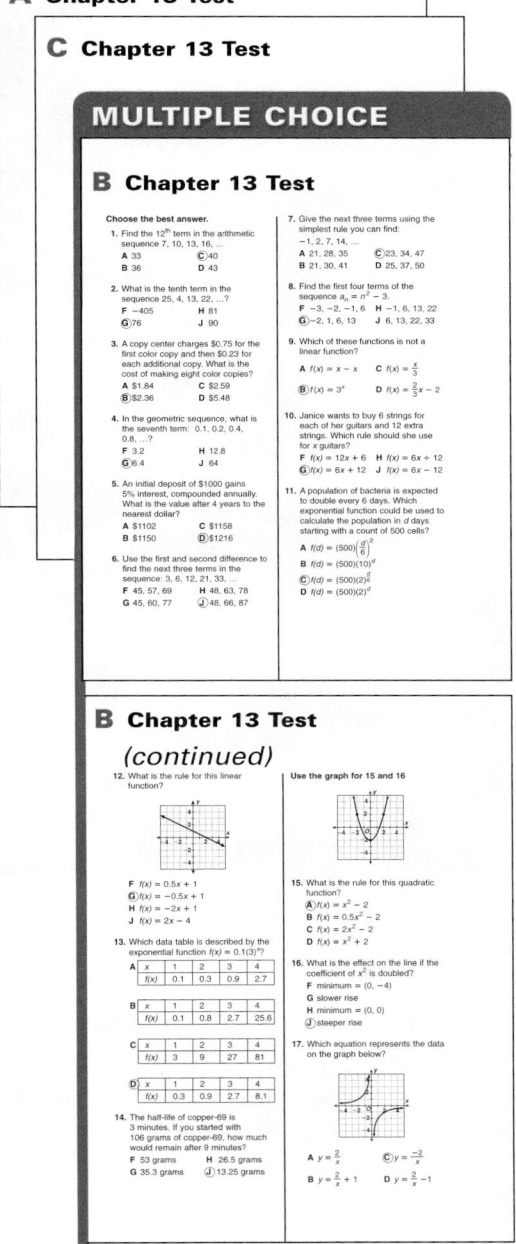

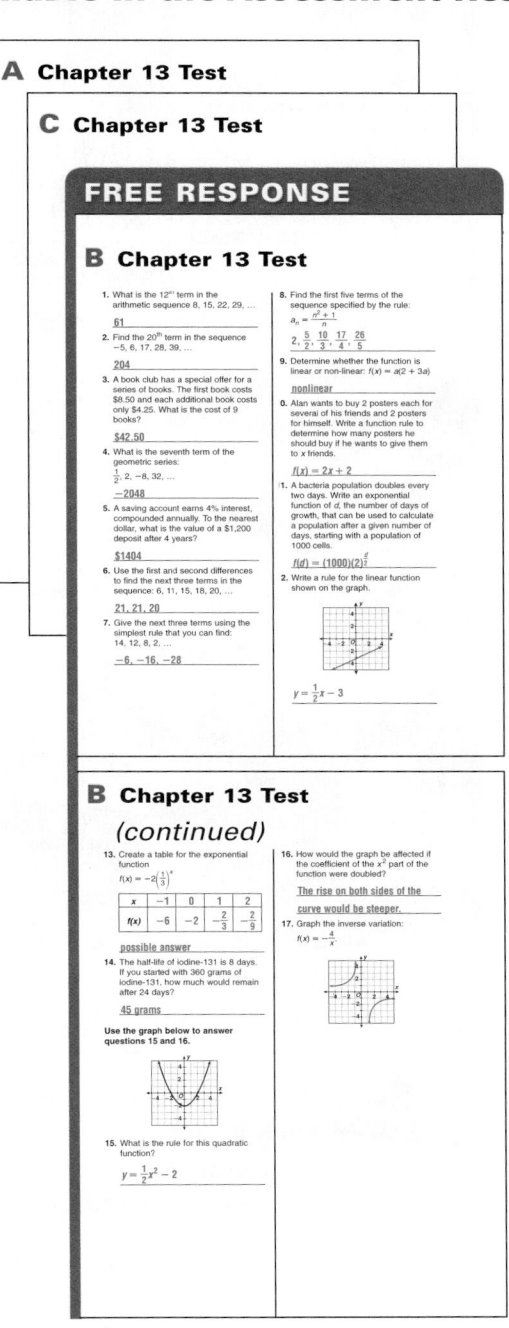

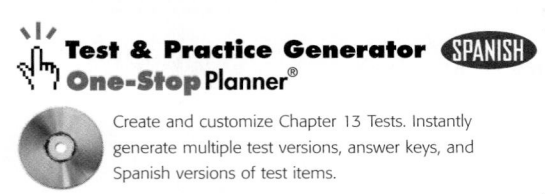

Why Learn This?

Tell students that many professions require people to study change and record data. A bacteriologist studies doubling time (the amount of time necessary for a bacteria population to double) under different conditions by recording the population at fixed intervals. The increasing populations are written in a list called a *sequence*. The bacteriologist studies the sequence and determines how long it took the population to double in size. Each set of conditions produces a different sequence and a different doubling time.

Using Data

To begin the study of this chapter, have students:

- Identify the doubling time for *E. coli* bacteria under low-growth-medium conditions. 60 minutes

- Think about the relationship between doubling time and temperature. What is one way to control the population of *E. coli* bacteria? The lower the temperature, the longer the doubling time. To control the population growth, maintain a low temperature.

MULTI-STEP TEST PREP On page 719, students write the rule for a function, then use the function to predict beaver population trends.

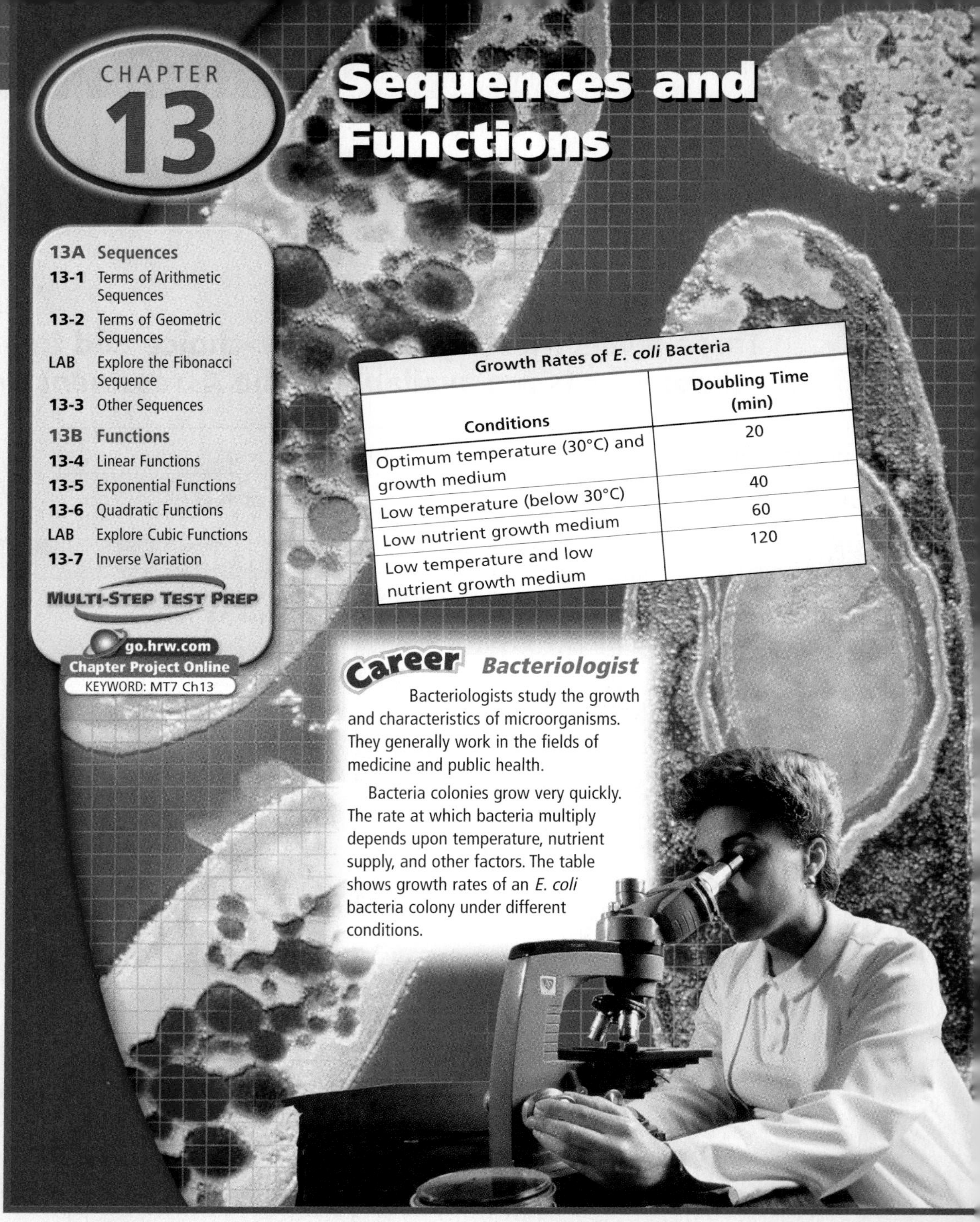

CHAPTER
13

13A Sequences
13-1 Terms of Arithmetic Sequences
13-2 Terms of Geometric Sequences
LAB Explore the Fibonacci Sequence
13-3 Other Sequences

13B Functions
13-4 Linear Functions
13-5 Exponential Functions
13-6 Quadratic Functions
LAB Explore Cubic Functions
13-7 Inverse Variation

MULTI-STEP TEST PREP

go.hrw.com
Chapter Project Online
KEYWORD: MT7 Ch13

Sequences and Functions

Growth Rates of *E. coli* Bacteria	
Conditions	Doubling Time (min)
Optimum temperature (30°C) and growth medium	20
Low temperature (below 30°C)	40
Low nutrient growth medium	60
Low temperature and low nutrient growth medium	120

Career *Bacteriologist*

Bacteriologists study the growth and characteristics of microorganisms. They generally work in the fields of medicine and public health.

Bacteria colonies grow very quickly. The rate at which bacteria multiply depends upon temperature, nutrient supply, and other factors. The table shows growth rates of an *E. coli* bacteria colony under different conditions.

Problem Solving Project

Understand, Plan, Solve, and Look Back

Have students:

- Complete the Addition by Division worksheet.

- Make a table showing the doubling of bacteria 20 times. Use the table to plot a growth curve.

- Plot curves to demonstrate the growth of an *E. coli* population under the conditions listed in the table. At what point would the population exceed that of people living in the United States? Estimate at what point the population would exceed the population of humans on Earth.

Life Science Connection

Project Resources

All project resources for teachers and students are provided online.

Materials:

- The Addition by Division worksheet

go.hrw.com
Project Teacher Support
KEYWORD: MT7 PSProject13

ARE YOU READY?

✓ Vocabulary

Choose the best term from the list to complete each sentence.

1. An equation whose solutions fall on a line on a coordinate plane is called a(n) __?__. **linear equation**

2. When the equation of a line is written in the form $y = mx + b$, m represents the __?__ and b represents the __?__. **slope; y-intercept**

3. To write an equation of the line that passes through (1, 3) and has slope 2, you might use the __?__ of the equation of a line. **point-slope form**

linear equation

point-slope form

slope

x-intercept

y-intercept

Complete these exercises to review skills you will need for this chapter.

✓ Number Patterns

Find the next three numbers. Then describe the pattern.

4. $\frac{1}{-3}, \frac{3}{-4}, \frac{5}{-5}, \ldots$

5. $2, 3, 6, 11, 18, \ldots$ **27, 38, 51; increase by next larger odd integer**

6. $-11, -8, -5, \ldots$ **−2, 1, 4; add 3**

7. $4, 2\frac{1}{2}, 1, \ldots$
$-\frac{1}{2}, -2, -3\frac{1}{2}$; **decrease by** $1\frac{1}{2}$

✓ Evaluate Expressions

Evaluate each expression for the given values of the variables.

8. $a + (b - 1)c$ for $a = 6, b = 3, c = -4$ **−2**

9. $a \cdot b^c$ for $a = -2, b = 4, c = 2$ **−32**

10. $(ab)^c$ for $a = 3, b = -2, c = 2$ **36**

11. $-(a + b) + c$ for $a = -1, b = -4, c = -10$ **−5**

✓ Graph Linear Equations

Use the slope and the y-intercept to graph each line.

12. $y = \frac{2}{3}x + 4$ 13. $y = -\frac{1}{2}x - 2$ 14. $y = 3x + 1$

15. $2y = 3x - 8$ 16. $3y + 2x = 6$ 17. $x - 5y = 5$

✓ Simplify Ratios

Write each ratio in simplest form.

18. $\frac{3}{9}$ $\frac{1}{3}$ 19. $\frac{21}{5}$ 20. $\frac{-12}{4}$ **−3**   21. $\frac{27}{45}$ $\frac{3}{5}$ 22. $\frac{3}{-45}$ **−$\frac{1}{15}$**   23. $\frac{20}{-8}$ **−$\frac{5}{2}$**

already in simplest terms

ARE YOU READY?

Organizer

Objective: Assess students' understanding of prerequisite skills.

Prerequisite Skills

Number Patterns

Evaluate Expressions

Graph Linear Equations

Simplify Ratios

Assessing Prior Knowledge

INTERVENTION

Diagnose and Prescribe

Use this page to determine whether intervention is necessary or whether enrichment is appropriate.

Resources

 **Are You Ready? Intervention and Enrichment Worksheets**

💿 **Are You Ready? CD-ROM**

🪐 **Are You Ready? Online**

my.hrw.com

Answers

4. $\frac{7}{-6}, \frac{9}{-7}, \frac{11}{-8}, \ldots$; increase the numerator by 2 and decrease the denominator 1.

12–17. See p. A21.

ARE YOU READY?

Diagnose and Prescribe

 **NO INTERVENE**

 **YES ENRICH**

✓ Prerequisite Skill	📝 Worksheets	💿 CD-ROM	🪐 Online
ARE YOU READY? Intervention, Chapter 13			
✓ Number Patterns	Skill 13	Activity 13	
✓ Evaluate Expressions	Skill 54	Activity 54	Diagnose and Prescribe Online
✓ Graph Linear Equations	Skill 64	Activity 64	
✓ Simplify Ratios	Skill 28	Activity 28	

ARE YOU READY? Enrichment, Chapter 13

📝 **Worksheets**

💿 **CD-ROM**

🪐 **Online**

Organizer

Objective: Help students organize the new concepts they will learn in Chapter 13.

 Online Edition
Multilingual Glossary

Resources

PuzzlePro®
One-Stop Planner®

 Multilingual Glossary Online

go.hrw.com
KEYWORD: MT7 Glossary

Possible answers to *Vocabulary Connections*

1. An exponential function is a function that has an exponent in its function rule.

2. Because inverse means "opposite," as the first variable increases, the second one decreases.

Study Guide: Preview

CHAPTER
13 **Study Guide: Preview**

Where You've Been

Previously, you

- described the relationship between the terms in a sequence and their positions in the sequence.

- graphed data to demonstrate relationships in familiar concepts.

In This Chapter

You will study

- finding and evaluating an algebraic expression to determine any term in an arithmetic sequence.

- using function rules to describe patterns in sequences.

- determining if a sequence can be arithmetic, geometric, or neither.

Where You're Going

You can use the skills learned in this chapter

- to use interest rates to predict the interest earned on money invested in a savings account.

- to understand and explore topics in physics, such as waves, cycles, and frequencies.

Key Vocabulary/Vocabulario

common ratio	razón común
exponential function	función exponencial
geometric sequence	sucesión geométrica
inverse variation	variación inversa
linear function	función lineal
parabola	parábola
quadratic function	función cuadrática

Vocabulary Connections

To become familiar with some of the vocabulary terms in the chapter, consider the following. You may refer to the chapter, the glossary, or a dictionary if you like.

1. The word *exponential* means "relating to an exponent." What do you think makes a function an **exponential function**?

2. The word *inverse* means "opposite." If two variables are related by an **inverse variation**, what do you think happens to the value of the second variable as the value of the first variable increases?

Reading and Writing Math

Study Strategy: Use Multiple Representations

By using multiple representations to introduce a math concept, you can understand the concept more clearly. As you study, take note of the use of the tables, lists, graphs, diagrams, symbols, and words to help clarify concepts.

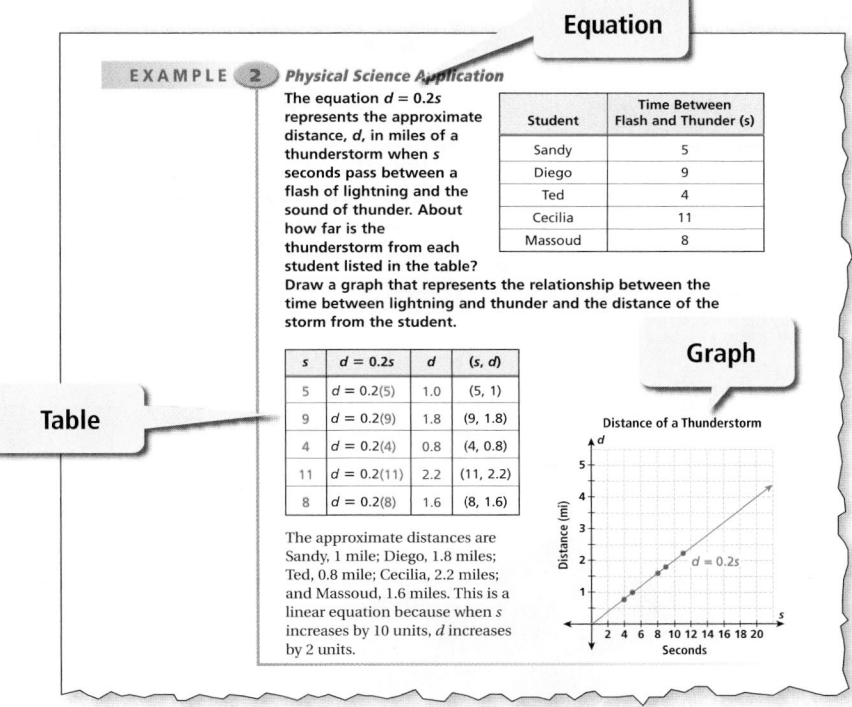

Equation

E X A M P L E 2 Physical Science Application

The equation $d = 0.2s$ represents the approximate distance, d, in miles of a thunderstorm when s seconds pass between a flash of lightning and the sound of thunder. About how far is the thunderstorm from each student listed in the table?

Student	Time Between Flash and Thunder (s)
Sandy	5
Diego	9
Ted	4
Cecilia	11
Massoud	8

Draw a graph that represents the relationship between the time between lightning and thunder and the distance of the storm from the student.

Table

Graph

s	$d = 0.2s$	d	(s, d)
5	$d = 0.2(5)$	1.0	(5, 1)
9	$d = 0.2(9)$	1.8	(9, 1.8)
4	$d = 0.2(4)$	0.8	(4, 0.8)
11	$d = 0.2(11)$	2.2	(11, 2.2)
8	$d = 0.2(8)$	1.6	(8, 1.6)

The approximate distances are Sandy, 1 mile; Diego, 1.8 miles; Ted, 0.8 mile; Cecilia, 2.2 miles; and Massoud, 1.6 miles. This is a linear equation because when s increases by 10 units, d increases by 2 units.

Distance of a Thunderstorm

Try This

Find a different representation for each relationship.

1. The area A of a certain rectangle is 48 cm^2. The base is 3 times longer than the height. What are the dimensions of the rectangle?

2.
x	-2	-1	0
y	0	1	2

3. $x = -2$

Organizer

Objective: Help students apply strategies to understand and retain key concepts.

PREMIER Online Edition

Resources

Chapter 13 Resource Book
Reading Strategies

Study Strategy: Use Multiple Representations

ENGLISH LANGUAGE LEARNERS

Discuss Students may be hesitant to learn new concepts in a different way. Reinforce that learning multiple representations of the concepts in Chapter 13 will lead to a deeper understanding of the material.

Extend Functions are covered extensively in Chapter 13. This is a good opportunity to have students represent a function in various ways, including equations, tables, and graphs. This approach will be especially helpful in Lessons 13-4 through 13-6.

Possible answers to *Try This*

1. Write and solve an equation to represent the problem.

   $48 = 3h \cdot h$

   $48 = 3h^2$

   $16 = h^2$

   $\sqrt{16} = h$

   $4 = h; 12 = b$

2.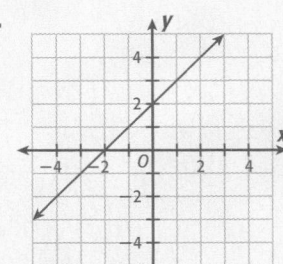

3.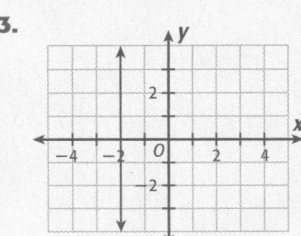

SECTION 13A

Sequences

One-Minute Section Planner

Lesson	Materials	MiC and Lab Resources
Lesson 13-1 Terms of Arithmetic Sequences • Find terms in an arithmetic sequence. ☐ SAT-10 ☑ ITBS ☐ CTBS ☑ NAEP		**MiC:** *Algebra Rules* pp. 1–3
Lesson 13-2 Terms of Geometric Sequences • Find terms in a geometric sequence. ☐ SAT-10 ☐ ITBS ☐ CTBS ☑ NAEP		**MiC:** *Ups and Downs* pp. 29–31, 43 *Hands-On Lab Activities* 13-2 *Technology Lab Activities* 13-2
13-3 Hands-On Lab Explore the Fibonacci Sequence • Use square tiles to explore the Fibonacci sequence. **Lesson 13-3** Other Sequences • Find patterns in sequences. ☐ SAT-10 ☑ ITBS ☐ CTBS ☑ NAEP	Square tiles (MK), toothpicks	*Hands-On Lab Activities* 13-3

MK = *Manipulatives Kit*

Mathematics in Context

The units **Algebra Rules** and **Ups and Downs** from the *Mathematics in Context* © 2006 series can be used with Section 13A. See Section Planner above for suggestions for integrating *MiC* with *Holt Mathematics.*

Section Overview

Terms of Arithmetic Sequences

Lesson 13-1

 A **sequence** is a list of numbers or objects, called **terms,** in a certain order. Many relationships can be represented by arithmetic sequences.

> In an **arithmetic sequence,** the difference between consecutive terms is constant. This difference is called the **common difference.**

> nth Term of an Arithmetic Sequence
> The nth term, a_n, of an arithmetic sequence with common difference d is
> $$a_n = a_1 + (n - 1)d.$$

Example: 5, 7, 9, 11, . . .
The **common difference** is $9 - 7 = 2.$

Find the 15th term of the sequence: 5, 7, 9, 11, ...
$$a_n = a_1 + (n - 1)d$$
$$a_{15} = 5 + (15 - 1)2$$
$$a_{15} = 33$$

Terms of Geometric Sequences

Lesson 13-2

 Exponential growth and decay can be represented by geometric sequences.

> In a **geometric sequence,** the ratio of consecutive terms is constant. This ratio is called the **common ratio.**

> nth Term of a Geometric Sequence
> The nth term, a_n, of a geometric sequence with common ratio r is
> $$a_n = a_1 r^{n-1}.$$

Example: 6, 18, 54, 162, . . .

The **common ratio** is $\frac{18}{6} = 3.$

Find the 12th term of the sequence: 6, 18, 54, 162, ...
$$a_n = a_1 \cdot r^{n-1}$$
$$a_{12} = 6 \cdot 3^{12-1}$$
$$a_{12} = 6 \cdot 3^{11}$$
$$a_{12} = 1{,}062{,}882$$

Other Sequences

Lesson 13-3

 Many patterns in nature, such as spirals in the centers of sunflowers, can be represented by the numbers of the Fibonacci sequence.

> If you subtract consecutive terms of a sequence, you get the **first differences.** If you subtract consecutive terms of the first differences, you get the **second differences.**

Term, n	1	2	3	4	5	6	7
Triangular Number	1	3	6	10	15	21	28

First differences   2   3   4   5   6   7

Second differences   1   1   1   1   1

$1 + 2$ $3 + 5$ $8 + 13$

1, 1, 2, 3, 5, 8, 13, 21, . . .

> In the **Fibonacci sequence,** the first two terms are 1, 1. After this, every term is the sum of the two previous terms.

$1 + 1$ $2 + 3$ $5 + 8$

682B

Online Edition
Tutorial Videos, Interactivities

Power Presentations
with PowerPoint®

Warm Up

Find the next two numbers in the pattern, using the simplest rule you can find.

1. 1, 5, 9, 13, . . .   **17, 21**

2. 100, 50, 25, 12.5, . . .   **6.25, 3.125**

3. 80, 87, 94, 101, . . .   **108, 115**

4. 3, 9, 7, 13, 11, . . .   **17, 15**

Problem of the Day

Write the last part of this set of equations so that its graph is the letter W.

$y = -2x + 4$ for $0 \le x \le 2$

$y = 2x - 4$ for $2 < x \le 4$

$y = -2x + 12$ for $4 < x \le 6$

Possible answer: $y = 2x - 12$ for $6 < x \le 8$

Also available on transparency

Math Humor

In a sequence of bus stops, the most appropriate name for the last item would be the *term*-inal.

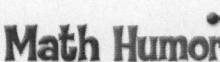 *State Resources*

 go.hrw.com
State Resources Online
KEYWORD: MT7 Resources

13-1 Terms of Arithmetic Sequences

Learn to find terms in an arithmetic sequence.

Ruben recently joined a preferred-customer club at a local bookstore. He received 200 points for joining and gets an additional 50 points each time he buys a book. The points can then be used to get free merchandise.

The number of points Ruben has in his account is 250 after buying 1 book, 300 after buying 2 books, 350 after buying 3 books, and so on.

After 1 book	After 2 books	After 3 books	After 4 books
250	300	350	400

Difference $300 - 250 = 50$

Difference $350 - 300 = 50$

Difference $400 - 350 = 50$

In Chapter 3, you learned that in an arithmetic sequence, the difference between one term and the next is always the same and is called the *common difference*. The number of points in Ruben's account after each book purchased forms an arithmetic sequence with a common difference of 50.

EXAMPLE 1 Identifying Arithmetic Sequences

Determine if each sequence could be arithmetic. If so, give the common difference.

Caution!

You cannot tell if a sequence is arithmetic by looking at a finite number of terms because the next term might not fit the pattern. This is why we say a sequence *could be* arithmetic.

A 7, 11, 15, 19, 23, . . .

7   11   15   19   23, . . .   *The terms increase by 4.*
   4   4   4   4

The sequence could be arithmetic with a common difference of 4.

B 1, 3, 9, 27, 81, . . .

1   3   9   27   81, . . .   *Find the difference of each term and the term before it.*
   2   6   18   54

The sequence is not arithmetic since it does not have a common difference.

---

1 Introduce

Alternate Opener

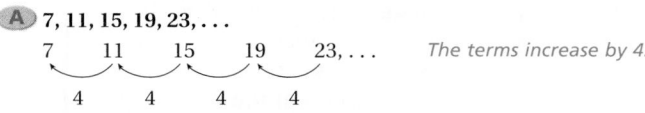

EXPLORATION

13-1 Terms of Arithmetic Sequences

In an *arithmetic sequence*, the difference between one term and the next is always the same.

The table shows the first four terms of an arithmetic sequence.

Term 1	Term 2	Term 3	Term 4	Term 5	Term 6	Term 7
10	16	22	28			

1. Find the difference between two consecutive terms.

2. Find the next three terms.

3. Find a short way to find the 20th term.

The table shows an arithmetic sequence with the first three terms missing.

Term 1	Term 2	Term 3	Term 4	Term 5	Term 6	Term 7
			88	84	80	76

4. Find the difference between two consecutive terms.

5. Find the first three terms.

Think and Discuss

6. Discuss the similarities and differences between the two sequences.

7. Explain your strategy for finding the 20th term in the first sequence.

Motivate

Tell students that you want to buy some bottled water that costs $1.50 per bottle. Ask them how much it would cost to buy 1 bottle. Write the answer on the board. Then ask them how much it would cost to buy 2, 3, 4, and 5 bottles. Explain that the list of numbers (1.50, 3.00, 4.50, 6.00, 7.50 . . .) is an arithmetic sequence. Ask students how they would determine the next number in the sequence. Add 1.50 to the previous term.

Explorations and answers are provided in *Alternate Openers: Explorations Transparencies.*

Determine if each sequence could be arithmetic. If so, give the common difference.

C 200, 191, 182, 173, 164, . . .

200　191　182　173　164, . . .　*The terms decrease by 9.*
　　−9　−9　−9　−9

The sequence could be arithmetic with a common difference of −9.

D $1, \frac{5}{4}, \frac{3}{2}, \frac{7}{4}, 2, \ldots$

1　$\frac{5}{4}$　$\frac{3}{2}$　$\frac{7}{4}$　2, . . .　*The terms increase by $\frac{1}{4}$.*
　$\frac{1}{4}$　$\frac{1}{4}$　$\frac{1}{4}$　$\frac{1}{4}$

The sequence could be arithmetic with a common difference of $\frac{1}{4}$.

E 6, 1, −4, −9, −14, . . .

6　1　−4　−9　−14, . . .　*The terms decrease by 5.*
　−5　−5　−5　−5

The sequence could be arithmetic with a common difference of −5.

Suppose you wanted to know the 100th term of the arithmetic sequence 5, 7, 9, 11, 13, ... If you do not want to find the first 99 terms, look for a pattern in the terms of the sequence.

Helpful Hint

Subscripts are used to show the positions of terms in the sequence. The first term is a_1, read "a sub one," the second is a_2, and so on.

Term Number	a_1	a_2	a_3	a_4	a_5
Term	5	7	9	11	13
Pattern	5 + 0(2)	5 + 1(2)	5 + 2(2)	5 + 3(2)	5 + 4(2)

The common difference d is 2. For the 2nd term, **one** 2 is added to a_1, which is 5. For the 3rd term, **two** 2's are added to 5. The pattern shows that for each term, the **number of 2's added** is one less than the **term number**, or $(n − 1)$.

The 100th term is the first term, 5, plus 99 times the common difference, 2.

$$a_{100} = 5 + 99(2) = 5 + 198 = 203$$

FINDING THE *n*th TERM OF AN ARITHMETIC SEQUENCE

The *n*th term a_n of an arithmetic sequence with common difference d and first term a_1 is

$$a_n = a_1 + (n − 1)d.$$

Power Presentations
with PowerPoint®

Additional Examples

Example 1

Determine if each sequence could be arithmetic. If so, give the common difference.

A. 5, 8, 11, 14, 17, . . .
yes; 3

B. 1, 3, 6, 10, 15, . . .
no

C. 65, 60, 55, 50, 45, . . .
yes; −5

D. 5.7, 5.8, 5.9, 6, 6.1, . . .
yes; 0.1

E. 1, 0, −1, 0, 1, . . .
no

Also available on transparency

---

2 Teach

Guided Instruction

In this lesson, students learn to find terms in an arithmetic sequence. Define the vocabulary terms in the lesson opener. Show students how to find differences by subtracting each term from the next term; explain that arithmetic sequences must have a common difference between terms. Use the table following Example 1 to derive the formula for the *n*th term of an arithmetic sequence. For Example 2A, you may want to use the formula to find the 16th term and then verify it by extending the sequence.

Reaching All Learners
Through Critical Thinking

Give each student the following arithmetic sequences that have various missing terms. For each sequence, ask students to identify the common difference and to fill in any missing terms.

1. 3, __, __, 15, __, 23 . . .
$d = 4$; 7, 11, 19

2. 52, __, 46, __, 40, __, . . .
$d = −3$; 49, 43, 37

3. 7, __, 31, __, __, 67, . . .
$d = 12$; 19, 43, 55

4. __, 4, __, __, __, −16, . . .
$d = −5$; 9, −1, −6, −11

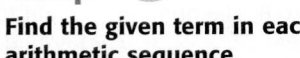
Example 2

Find the given term in each arithmetic sequence.

A. 10th term: 1, 3, 5, 7, ...   19

B. 18th term: 100, 93, 86, 79, ...
−19

C. 21st term: 25, 25.5, 26, 26.5, ...
35

D. 14th term: $a_1 = 13$, $d = 5$ 78

Example 3

The senior class held a bake sale. At the beginning of the sale, there was $20 in the cash box. Each item in the sale cost 50 cents. At the end of the sale, there was $63.50 in the cash box. How many items were sold during the bake sale?   87

Also available on transparency

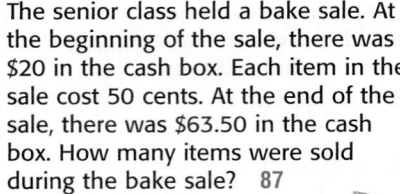

Possible answers to *Think and Discuss*

1. Find the differences between the successive terms to see if there is a common difference.

2. By finding the first ten terms, the tenth term is 23 (5, 7, 9, 11, 13, 15, 17, 19, 21, 23). By using the formula, the tenth term is also 23: 5 + (10 − 1)(2) = 5 + 18 = 23.

EXAMPLE 2 **Finding a Given Term of an Arithmetic Sequence**

Find the given term in each arithmetic sequence.

A 16th term: 4, 7, 10, 13, ...
$$a_n = a_1 + (n - 1)d$$
$$a_{16} = 4 + (16 - 1)3$$
$$a_{16} = 49$$

B 22nd term: 28, 23, 18, 13, ...
$$a_n = a_1 + (n - 1)d$$
$$a_{22} = 28 + (22 - 1)(-5)$$
$$a_{22} = -77$$

C 11th term: −7, −2, 3, 8, ...
$$a_n = a_1 + (n - 1)d$$
$$a_{11} = -7 + (11 - 1)5$$
$$a_{11} = 43$$

D 30th term: $a_1 = 4$, $d = 12$
$$a_n = a_1 + (n - 1)d$$
$$a_{30} = 4 + (30 - 1)12$$
$$a_{30} = 352$$

You can use the formula for the nth term of an arithmetic sequence to solve for other variables.

EXAMPLE 3 *Consumer Application*

Ruben recently joined a preferred-customer club at a bookstore. He received 200 points for signing up and he will get 50 points for every book he buys. How many books does he have to buy to collect 1000 points?

Identify the arithmetic sequence: 250, 300, 350, ...

$a_1 = 250$	$a_1 = 250$ = number of points after the first book
$d = 50$	$d = 50$ = common difference
$a_n = 1000$	$a_n = 1000$ = number of points needed

Let n represent the number of books that will earn him a total of 1000 points. Use the formula for arithmetic sequences.

$a_n = a_1 + (n - 1)d$	Solve for n.
$1000 = 250 + (n - 1)50$	Substitute the given values.
$1000 = 250 + 50n - 50$	Distributive Property
$1000 = 200 + 50n$	Combine like terms.
$800 = 50n$	Subtract 200 from both sides.
$16 = n$	Divide both sides by 50.

After buying 16 books, Ruben will have collected 1000 points.

Think and Discuss

1. **Explain** how to determine if a sequence might be an arithmetic sequence.

2. **Compare** your answers for the 10th term of the arithmetic sequence 5, 7, 9, 11, 13, ... by finding all of the first 10 terms and by using the formula.

---

3 Close

Summarize

Remind students that there are many different types of number patterns. Emphasize that arithmetic sequences must have common differences between terms. Review the formula for finding the nth term of an arithmetic sequence. Ask students to explain when the formula might be more useful than extending a sequence.

Possible answer: The formula is easier when you are trying to find a term far from the start of the sequence (the nth term, where n is very large).

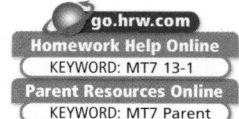

go.hrw.com
Homework Help Online
KEYWORD: MT7 13-1
Parent Resources Online
KEYWORD: MT7 Parent

13-1 Exercises

GUIDED PRACTICE

See Example 1 Determine if each sequence could be arithmetic. If so, give the common difference.

1. 4, 6, 8, 10, 12, . . . **yes; 2**
2. 16, 14, 13, 11, 10, . . . **no**
3. $\frac{2}{9}, \frac{1}{3}, \frac{4}{9}, \frac{5}{9}, \frac{2}{3}, \ldots$ **yes;** $\frac{1}{9}$

4. 87, 78, 69, 60, 51, . . . **yes; −9**
5. $\frac{1}{3}, \frac{1}{9}, \frac{1}{27}, \frac{1}{81}, \frac{1}{243}, \ldots$ **no**
6. 6, 4, 2, 0, −2, . . . **yes; −2**

See Example 2 Find the given term in each arithmetic sequence.

7. 17th term: 5, 7, 9, 11, . . . **37**
8. 26th term: 3, 8, 13, 18, . . . **128**

9. 31st term: −2, −5, −8, −11, . . . **−92**
10. 40th term: $a_1 = 13$, $d = 4$ **169**

See Example 3 **11.** Postage for a first-class letter costs $0.39 for the first ounce and $0.24 for each additional ounce. If a letter costs $1.59 to mail, how many ounces is it? **6 oz**

INDEPENDENT PRACTICE

See Example 1 Determine if each sequence could be arithmetic. If so, give the common difference.

12. $\frac{1}{3}, \frac{2}{3}, 1, 1\frac{1}{3}, 1\frac{2}{3}, \ldots$ **yes;** $\frac{1}{3}$
13. 5, 3, 1, −1, −3, . . . **yes; −2**
14. $\frac{1}{5}, \frac{3}{5}, \frac{4}{5}, 1\frac{1}{5}, 1\frac{2}{5}, \ldots$ **no**

15. 6, 29, 52, 75, 98, . . . **yes; 23**
16. $\frac{4}{7}, 1\frac{2}{7}, 2, 2\frac{5}{7}, 3\frac{2}{7}, \ldots$ **no**
17. 0.1, 0.4, 0.7, 1, 1.3, . . . **yes; 0.3**

See Example 2 Find the given term in each arithmetic sequence.

18. 12th term: 4, 2, 0, −2, . . . **−18**
19. 23rd term: 0.1, 0.15, 0.2, 0.25 **1.2**

20. 25th term: $a_1 = 1$, $d = 5$ **121**
21. 16th term: $a_1 = 38.5$, $d = -2.5$ **1**

See Example 3 **22.** Oscar received 50 tokens for entering a race, plus 7 tokens each hour. If his total number of tokens was 113, for how many hours did he race? **9 hr**

PRACTICE AND PROBLEM SOLVING

Extra Practice
See page 806.

Find the next three terms of each arithmetic sequence.

23. 11, 14, 17, 20, . . . **23, 26, 29**
24. −16, −9, −2, 5, . . . **12, 19, 26**
25. 103, 90, 77, 64, . . . **51, 38, 25**

26. The 6th term of an arithmetic sequence is 142. The common difference is 12. What are the first four terms of the arithmetic sequence? **82, 94, 106, 118**

Find the first five terms of each arithmetic sequence.

27. $a_1 = 1$, $d = 2$ **1, 3, 5, 7, 9**
28. $a_1 = 2$, $d = 8$ **2, 10, 18, 26, 34**
29. $a_1 = 0$, $d = 0.25$ **0, 0.25, 0.5, 0.75, 1**

30. The 1st term of an arithmetic sequence is 7. The common difference is 9. What position in the sequence is the term 160? **18th**

Assignment Guide

If you finished Example 1 assign:
Average 1–6, 12–17, 23–25, 37–44
Advanced 12–17, 23–25, 35, 37–44

If you finished Example 2 assign:
Average 1–10, 12–21, 23–25, 27–29, 37–44
Advanced 12–21, 23–30, 34–44

If you finished Example 3 assign:
Average 1–25, 27–29, 31, 32, 37–44
Advanced 12–44

Homework Quick Check
Quickly check key concepts.
Exercises: 12, 18, 22, 24, 28

Math Background

Noted math educator Lynn Arthur Steen once said, "Mathematics is the science of patterns." The study of sequences introduces students to the concept that the relationships among numbers are perhaps more important than the numbers themselves. By recognizing patterns in numbers, students will better understand more complicated mathematical relationships, such as linear, quadratic, and exponential functions. In addition, recognizing patterns can be a very useful problem-solving skill.

RETEACH 13-1

Reteach
13-1 Terms of Arithmetic Sequences

In an **arithmetic sequence**, the difference between terms is constant. The difference is called the **common difference**.

This is an arithmetic sequence with a common difference of 3.
2, 5, 8, 11, 14, . . .
3 3 3 3

This is not an arithmetic sequence since there is no common difference.
2, 5, 9, 14, 20, . . .
3 4 5 6

Complete to determine if each sequence is arithmetic.

1. 20, 16, 12, 8, 4, . . .
−4 −4 −4 −4
arithmetic? **yes**

2. 1, 2, 4, 8, 16, . . .
1 2 4 8
arithmetic? **no**

3. 0.1, 0.2, 0.3, 0.4, . . .
0.1 0.1 0.1
arithmetic? **yes**

4. $\frac{1}{2}$, 1, $\frac{3}{2}$, 2, $\frac{5}{2}$, . . .
$\frac{1}{2}$ $\frac{1}{2}$ $\frac{1}{2}$ $\frac{1}{2}$
arithmetic? **yes**

5. 2, $\frac{3}{2}$, 1, $\frac{1}{2}$, 0, . . .
$-\frac{1}{2}$ $-\frac{1}{2}$ $-\frac{1}{2}$ $-\frac{1}{2}$
arithmetic? **yes**

6. 3, 1, 0, $-\frac{1}{2}$, $-\frac{1}{4}$, . . .
−2 −1 $-\frac{1}{2}$ $\frac{1}{4}$
arithmetic? **no**

You can use the common difference to find any term in an arithmetic sequence.
4, 6, 8, 10, 12, . . . This arithmetic sequence has a common difference of 2.
2 2 2 2

This is the 1st term of the sequence.   4
For the 2nd term, add the common difference × 1   4 + 2 × 1 = 6
For the 3rd term, add the common difference × 2   4 + 2 × 2 = 8
For the 4th term, add the common difference × 3   4 + 2 × 3 = 10
For the 5th term, add the common difference × 4   4 + 2 × 4 = 12
For the nth term, add the common difference × (n − 1)   4 + 2 × (n − 1)

Complete to find the given term of the arithmetic sequence
4, 6, 8, 10, 12, . . .

7. the 9th term
4 + 2 × **8** = **20**

8. the 20th term
4 + 2 × **19** = **42**

9. the 100th term
4 + 2 × **99** = **202**

PRACTICE 13-1

Practice B
13-1 Terms of Arithmetic Sequences

Determine if each sequence could be arithmetic. If so, give the common difference.

1. 18, 20, 22, 24, 26, . . . **2**
2. 48, 42, 36, 30, 24, . . . **−6**
3. 15, 30, 60, 120, 240, . . . **no**

4. 10.4, 8.3, 6.2, 4.1, 2, . . . **−2.1**
5. $\frac{1}{3}, \frac{1}{9}, \frac{1}{27}, \frac{1}{81}, \frac{1}{243}, \ldots$ **no**
6. 83, 66, 49, 32, 15, . . . **−17**

7. 8.1, 2.7, 0.9, 0.3, 0.1, . . . **no**
8. $\frac{2}{3}, \frac{4}{3}, 2, \frac{8}{3}, \frac{10}{3}, \ldots$ $\frac{2}{3}$
9. −58, −35, −12, 11, 34, . . . **23**

Find the given term in each arithmetic sequence.

10. 14th term: 60, 68, 76, 84, 92, . . . **164**
11. 35th term: 3.5, 3.8, 4.1, 4.4, 4.7, . . . **13.7**

12. 21st term: 103, 84, 65, 46, 27, . . . **−277**
13. 22nd term: −2, −5, −8, −11, −14, . . . **−65**

14. 16th term: 73, 44, 15, −14, −43, . . . **−362**
15. 50th term: −9, 2, 13, 24, 35, . . . **530**

16. 19th term: −87, −78, −69, −60, −51, . . . **75**
17. 25th term: $3\frac{1}{4}, 3\frac{1}{2}, 3\frac{3}{4}, 4, 4\frac{1}{4}, \ldots$ $9\frac{1}{4}$

18. A cook started with 26 ounces of special sauce. She used 1.4 ounces of the sauce in each of a number of dishes and had 2.2 ounces left over. How many dishes did she make with the sauce? **18 dishes**

19. Kuang started the basketball season with 54 points in his career. He scores 3 points more each game he plays. How many games will it take for him to have scored a total of 132 points in his basketball career? **26 games**

State Resources

go.hrw.com
State Resources Online
KEYWORD: MT7 Resources

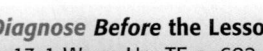
Answers

32. a. 7, 9, 11, 13, 15

33. first: $127.50, $180, $232.50, $285;
second: $115.50, $181, $246.50, $312; the first law firm

35. Possible answer: Subtract each term from the next term to find the common difference. If the common difference is positive, the terms of the sequence are increasing. If it is negative, they are decreasing.

Journal

Ask students to write the formula $a_n = a_1 + (n - 1)d$, to explain what each variable represents, and to create an arithmetic sequence to use as an example.

Power Presentations
with PowerPoint®

13-1 Lesson Quiz

Determine if each sequence could be arithmetic. If so, give the common difference.

1. 42, 49, 56, 63, 70, . . .   yes; 7

2. 1, 2, 4, 8, 16, 32, . . .   no

Find the given term in each arithmetic sequence.

3. 15th term: $a_1 = 7$, $d = 5$ 77

4. 24th term: 1, $\frac{5}{4}$, $\frac{3}{2}$, $\frac{7}{4}$; 2 $\frac{27}{4}$, or 6.75

5. 52nd term: $a_1 = 14.2$; $d = -1.2$ -47

Also available on transparency

---

31. Fitness Marissa cuts 7 seconds off her time for every lap she runs around the track. At noon, the stopwatch read 11:53. Write the first four terms of an arithmetic sequence modeling the situation. ($a_1 = 11:53$)
11:53, 11:46, 11:39, 11:32

32. Recreation The rates for a mini grand-prix course are shown in the flyer.

   a. What are the first 5 terms of the arithmetic sequence that represents the fees for the course?

   b. What would the rate be for 9 laps? **$23**

   c. If the cost of a license plus n laps is $11, find n. **3**

33. Critical Thinking One law firm charges an administrative fee of $75, plus a $52.50 fee for each half hour of consultation. A second law firm charges an administrative fee of $50, plus a $65.50 fee for each half hour of consultation. What are the first 4 terms of the arithmetic sequences that represent the rates of the law firms? Which law firm charges less for 4 half-hour consultations?

 34. Write a Problem Write an arithmetic sequence problem using $a_5 = -25$ and $d = 5.5$.   Possible answer: What are the first two terms of the arithmetic sequence with $a_5 = -25$ and $d = 5.5$? Answer: -47 and -41.5

35. Write About It Explain how to find the common difference of an arithmetic sequence. What can you say about the terms of a sequence if the common difference is positive? if the common difference is negative?

 36. Challenge The 1st term of an arithmetic sequence is 3, and the common difference is 6. Find two consecutive terms of the sequence that have a sum of 108. What positions are the terms in the sequence?
51 and 57; 9th and 10th

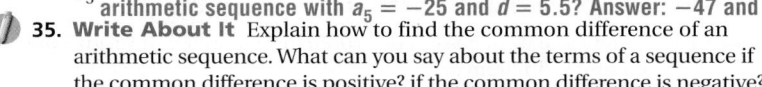
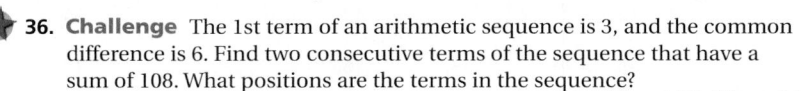

TEST PREP and Spiral Review

37. Multiple Choice Use of an Internet service at a hotel costs $2.50 plus $0.25 per minute. Rebecca was charged $14.25 for one usage. For how many minutes did she use the Internet service?

   Ⓐ 5.7   Ⓑ 46   Ⓒ 47   Ⓓ 57

38. Gridded Response What is the 20th term in the arithmetic sequence 2, 6, 10, 14, . . .? **78**

Solve. (Lesson 2-7) $k = -9.4$ $c = -\frac{2}{7}$

39. $x + \frac{1}{6} = -\frac{5}{6}$ $x = -1$ **40.** $\frac{y}{2.4} = -3$ $y = -7.2$ **41.** $k - 11.6 = -21$ **42.** $23\frac{5}{7} = c + 24$

population: the cable company's customers; sample: the cable company's customers

Identify the population and sample. (Lesson 9-1)

43. A cable company surveys customers whose last names begin with an "s." whose last names begin with an "s."

44. The principal asks every other busload of students if their ride was comfortable.
population: students who rode the bus; sample: students on every other bus

---

CHALLENGE 13-1

Challenge
13-1 *Learn from "The Prince of Mathematics"*

When the German mathematician Karl Gauss was a schoolboy, his teacher gave the problem of summing the integers from 1 through 100, hoping it would keep the class quiet. But young Karl wrote the correct answer after only a few seconds. How did he do it?

This is the sum.	$S = 1 + 2 + 3 + ... + 98 + 99 + 100$
Reverse the numbers.	$S = 100 + 99 + 98 + ... + 3 + 2 + 1$
Add vertically.	$2S = 101 + 101 + 101 + ... + 101 + 101 + 101$

This sum contains one hundred addends of 101.

$2S = 100(101)$

$\frac{2S}{2} = \frac{100(101)}{2}$

$S = \frac{100}{2}(101) = 50(101) = 5050$

Gauss had come upon a method for finding the sum $S_n = \frac{n}{2}(a_1 + a_n)$ of any number of terms in an arithmetic sequence.

Applying the formula to the original problem:

Substitute $n = 100$, $a_1 = 1$, $a_n = 100$ $S_{100} = \frac{100}{2}(1 + 100) = 50(101) = 5050$

1. Now that you know how to find the sum of the first 100 integers, and you know what the sum is, can you just divide by 2 to find the sum of the first 50 even integers? of the first 50 odd integers? Explain.

No; $5050 \div 2 = 2525$

sum of first 50 even: $S_{50} = \frac{50}{2}(2 + 100) = 25(102) = 2550$

sum of first 50 odd: $S_{50} = \frac{50}{2}(1 + 99) = 25(100) = 2500$

2. Find the sum of the first 750 integers.
$S_{750} = \frac{750}{2}(1 + 750) = 375(751) = 281,625$

3. Find the sum of the first 100 terms of this arithmetic sequence: 3, 6, 9, 12, ...
(Hint: First find the 100th term.)
$a_{100} = 3 + (100 - 1)3 = 300$

$S_{100} = \frac{100}{2}(3 + 300) = 50(303) = 15,150$

PROBLEM SOLVING 13-1

Problem Solving
13-1 *Terms of Arithmetic Sequences*

A section of seats in an auditorium has 18 seats in the first row. Each row has two more seats than the previous row. There are 25 rows in the section. Write the correct answer.

1. List the number of seats in the second, third and fourth rows of the section.

20, 22, 24

2. How many seats are in the 10th row?

36

3. How many seats are in the 15th row?

46

4. In which row are there 32 seats?

8th row

For 5–10, refer to the table below, which shows the boiling temperature of water at different altitudes. Choose the letter of the correct answer.

5. What is the common difference?
  Ⓐ $-1.8°F$ C $-2.8°F$
  B $1.8°F$ D $6°F$

6. According to the table, what would be the boiling point of water at an altitude of 10,000 feet?
  F $192.2°F$ H $226.4°F$
  Ⓖ $194°F$ J $228.2°F$

7. According to the table, what would be the boiling point of water at an altitude of 15,000 feet?
  A $181.4°F$ Ⓒ $185°F$
  B $183.2°F$ D $235.4°F$

8. Estimate the boiling point of water in Jacksonville, Florida, which has an elevation of 0 feet.
  F $0°F$ Ⓗ $212°F$
  G $208.4°F$ J $213.8°F$

9. The highest point in the United States is Mt. McKinley, Alaska, with an elevation of 20,320 feet. Estimate the boiling point of water at the top of Mt. McKinley.
  A $172.4°F$ C $244.4°F$
  Ⓑ $176°F$ D $246.2°F$

10. At which elevation will the boiling point of water be less than 150°F?
  F $28,000$ ft   H $32,000$ ft
  G $30,000$ ft   Ⓙ $35,000$ ft

Altitude (thousands of feet)	Boiling point of water (°F)
1	210.2
2	208.4
3	206.6
4	204.8
5	203

Learn to find terms in a geometric sequence.

Vocabulary
geometric sequence
common ratio

Joey mows his family's yard every week. His mother offers him a choice of $10 per week, or 1¢ the first week, 2¢ the second week, 4¢ the third week, and so on.

Week 1	Week 2	Week 3	Week 4
1¢	2¢	4¢	8¢

Ratio $\frac{2}{1} = 2$ Ratio $\frac{4}{2} = 2$ Ratio $\frac{8}{4} = 2$

The weekly amounts Joey would get paid in this plan form a geometric sequence.

In a **geometric sequence**, the ratio of one term to the next is always the same. This ratio is called the **common ratio**. The common ratio is multiplied by each term to get the next term.

EXAMPLE 1 Identifying Geometric Sequences

Determine if each sequence could be geometric. If so, give the common ratio.

A 162, 54, 18, 6, 2, . . .

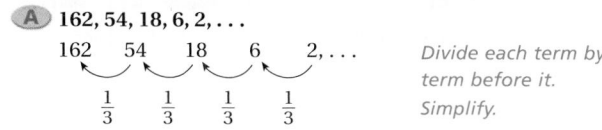

162   54   18   6   2, . . .   *Divide each term by the term before it.*
$\frac{1}{3}$ $\frac{1}{3}$ $\frac{1}{3}$ $\frac{1}{3}$ *Simplify.*

The sequence could be geometric with a common ratio of $\frac{1}{3}$.

B 7, −7, 7, −7, 7, . . .

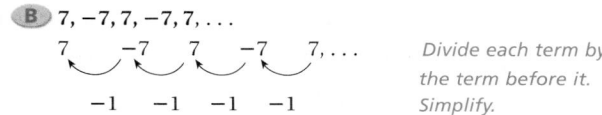

7   −7   7   −7   7, . . .   *Divide each term by the term before it.*
−1   −1   −1   −1   *Simplify.*

The sequence could be geometric with a common ratio of −1.

C 2, 5, 8, 11, 14, . . .

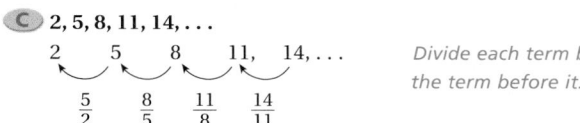

2   5   8   11   14, . . .   *Divide each term by the term before it.*
$\frac{5}{2}$ $\frac{8}{5}$ $\frac{11}{8}$ $\frac{14}{11}$

The sequence is not geometric since it does not have a common ratio.

Organizer 13-2

Pacing: Traditional 1 day
Block $\frac{1}{2}$ day

Objective: Students find terms in a geometric sequence.

 Technology Lab
In *Technology Lab* Activities

 Hands-On Lab
In *Hands-On Lab* Activities

 Online Edition
Tutorial Videos

Power Presentations
with PowerPoint®

Warm Up

1. Determine if the sequence could be arithmetic. If so, give the common difference.
   100, 50, 25, 12.5, . . . no

Find the given term in each arithmetic sequence.

2. 12th term; $a_1 = 30$, $d = 0.5$ 35.5

3. 55th term: 4, 28, 52, 76 1300

Problem of the Day

Two students begin counting by 3's at the same time. One counts up from 0, and the other counts down from 120. If each says one number every second, will both students ever say the same number at the same time? yes (60)

Also available on transparency

---

1 Introduce

Alternate Opener

EXPLORATION

13-2 Terms of Geometric Sequences

In a *geometric sequence*, the ratio of one term to the next is always the same.

The table shows the first four terms of a geometric sequence.

Term 1	Term 2	Term 3	Term 4	Term 5	Term 6	Term 7
10	20	40	80			

1. Find the ratio between two consecutive terms.
2. Find the next three terms.
3. Find a short way to find the 20th term.

The table shows a geometric sequence with the first three terms missing.

Term 1	Term 2	Term 3	Term 4	Term 5	Term 6	Term 7
			150	75	37.5	18.75

4. Find the ratio between two consecutive terms.
5. Find the first three terms.

Think and Discuss

6. **Discuss** the similarities and differences between the two sequences.
7. **Explain** your strategy for finding the 20th term in the first sequence.

Motivate

Ask students to suppose that on Monday you tell two students a secret. On Tuesday, each of them tells two more students. On Wednesday, each of those students tells two more. If this pattern continues, how many people will be told on Friday? 32 How many people in all will know the secret? 63, including the teacher

Explorations and answers are provided in *Alternate Openers: Explorations Transparencies.*

State Resources

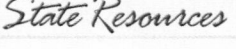 go.hrw.com
State Resources Online
KEYWORD: MT7 Resources

Example 1

Determine if each sequence could be geometric. If so, give the common ratio.

A. 1, 5, 25, 125, 625, . . . yes; 5

B. 1, 3, 9, 12, 15, . . . no

C. 81, 27, 9, 3, 1, . . . yes; $\frac{1}{3}$

D. −3, 6, −12, 24, −48, . . . yes; −2

Example 2

Find the given term in each geometric sequence.

A. 11th term: −2, 4, −8, 16, . . .
−2048

B. 9th term: 100, 70, 49, 34.3, . . .
5.764801

C. 10th term: 0.01, 0.1, 1, 10, . . .
10,000,000

D. 7th term: 1000, 200, 40, 8, . . .
$\frac{8}{125}$, or 0.064

Example 3

Tara sells computers. She has the option of earning (1) $50 per sale or (2) $1 for the first sale, $2 for the second sale, $4 for the third sale, and so on, where each sale is worth twice as much as the previous sale. If Tara estimates that she can sell 10 computers a week, which option should she choose? option 2

Also available on transparency

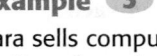

Determine if each sequence could be geometric. If so, give the common ratio.

D 2, −5, 12.5, −31.52, 78.125, . . .

$$2 \quad -5 \quad 12.5 \quad -31.25 \quad 78.125, \ldots \quad \text{Divide each term by the term before it.}$$
$$-2.5 \quad -2.5 \quad -2.5 \quad -2.5 \qquad \text{Simplify.}$$

The sequence could be geometric with a common ratio of −2.5.

Suppose you wanted to find the 15th term of the geometric sequence 2, 6, 18, 54, 162, ... If you do not want to find the first 14 terms, look for a pattern in the terms of the sequence.

Term Number	a_1	a_2	a_3	a_4	a_5
Term	2	6	18	54	162
Pattern	$2(3)^0$	$2(3)^1$	$2(3)^2$	$2(3)^3$	$2(3)^4$

The common ratio r is 3. For the 2nd term, a_1, or 2, is multiplied by 3 once. For the 3rd term, 2 is multiplied by 3 twice. The pattern shows that for each term, the **number of times 3 is multiplied** is one less than the **term number**, or $(n - 1)$.

The 15th term is the first term, 2, times the common ratio, 3, raised to the 14th power.

$$a_{15} = 2(3)^{14} = 2(4{,}782{,}969) = 9{,}565{,}938$$

FINDING THE nth TERM OF A GEOMETRIC SEQUENCE

The nth term a_n of a geometric sequence with common ratio r is
$$a_n = a_1 r^{n-1}.$$

EXAMPLE 2 **Finding a Given Term of a Geometric Sequence**

Find the given term in each geometric sequence.

A 14th term: 3, 12, 48, 192, . . .
$r = \frac{12}{3} = 4$
$a_{14} = 3(4)^{13} = 201{,}326{,}592$

B 49th term: 2, −2, 2, −2, 2, . . .
$r = \frac{-2}{2} = -1$
$a_{49} = 2(-1)^{48} = 2$

C 7th term: 7, $\frac{7}{3}$, $\frac{7}{9}$, $\frac{7}{27}$, $\frac{7}{81}$, . . .
$r = \frac{\frac{7}{3}}{7} = \frac{1}{3}$
$a_7 = 7\left(\frac{1}{3}\right)^6 = \frac{7}{129}$

D 20th term: 500, 300, 180, 208, . . .
$r = \frac{300}{500} = 0.6$
$a_{20} = 500(0.6)^{19} \approx 0.03$

---

2 Teach

Guided Instruction

In this lesson, students learn to find terms in a geometric sequence. Show students that they can find the *common ratio* of a geometric sequence by taking each term and dividing it by the preceding term. Point out that, in geometric sequences, successive terms are found by multiplying by the common ratio. Show students how to derive the formula for finding the nth term of a geometric sequence. Review the sequences in Example 2 and emphasize that geometric sequences can get very large or very small quickly.

Reaching All Learners
Through Critical Thinking

Give students two numbers to begin a sequence, such as 2 and 4. Have students continue the sequence in two different ways, one to make it an arithmetic sequence (e.g., 2, 4, 6, 8, 10 . . .) and the other to make it a geometric sequence (e.g., 2, 4, 8, 16, 32 . . .). Ask students to evaluate each sequence to the tenth term and to identify the common difference or common ratio for each sequence.

EXAMPLE 3 *Money Application*

For mowing his family's yard every week, Joey has two options for payment: (1) $10 per week or (2) 1¢ the first week, 2¢ the second week, 4¢ the third week, and so on, where he makes twice as much each week as he made the week before. If Joey will mow the yard for 15 weeks, which option should he choose?

If Joey chooses $10 per week, he will get a total of 15($10) = $150.

If Joey chooses the second option, his payment for just the 15th week will be more than the total of all the payments in option 1.

$$a_{15} = (\$0.01)(2)^{14} = (\$0.01)(16,384) = \$163.84$$

Option 1 gives Joey more money in the beginning, but option 2 gives him a larger total amount.

Think and Discuss

1. **Compare** arithmetic sequences with geometric sequences.

2. **Describe** how you find the common ratio in a geometric sequence.

13-2 Exercises

go.hrw.com
Homework Help Online
KEYWORD: MT7 13-2
Parent Resources Online
KEYWORD: MT7 Parent

GUIDED PRACTICE

See Example 1 Determine if each sequence could be geometric. If so, give the common ratio.

1. $-6, -3, 0, 3, 6, \ldots$ **no** 2. $3, 6, 12, 24, 48, \ldots$ **yes; 2** 3. $\frac{2}{3}, -\frac{2}{3}, \frac{2}{3}, -\frac{2}{3}, \frac{2}{3}, \ldots$ **yes; −1**

4. $1, 2.5, 6.25, 15.625, \ldots$ **yes; 2.5** 5. $\frac{4}{81}, \frac{4}{27}, \frac{4}{9}, \frac{4}{3}, \ldots$ **yes; 3** 6. $-2, -4, -8, -16, \ldots$ **yes; 2**

See Example 2 Find the given term in each geometric sequence.

7. 12th term: $3, 6, 12, 24, 48, \ldots$ **6144** 8. 91st term: $\frac{1}{5}, -\frac{1}{5}, \frac{1}{5}, -\frac{1}{5}, \frac{1}{5}, \ldots$ $\frac{1}{5}$

9. 15th term: $531,441; 177,147; 59,049;$ $19,683; 6561$ $\frac{1}{9}$ 10. 7th term: $1, 5, 25, 125, 625, \ldots$ **15,625**

See Example 3 11. Heather makes $5.50 per hour. Every 4 months, she is eligible for a 3% raise. How much will she make after 3 years if she gets a raise every 4 months? **$7.18 per hour**

13-2 Exercises

Assignment Guide

If you finished Example **1** assign:
Average 1–6, 12–17, 25–28, 48–55
Advanced 12–17, 25–28, 48–55

If you finished Example **2** assign:
Average 1–10, 12–23, 25–34, 48–55
Advanced 1–23, 25–39, 45–55

If you finished Example **3** assign:
Average 1–34, 40–42, 48–55
Advanced 12–28, 32–55

Homework Quick Check

Quickly check key concepts.
Exercises: 12, 18, 24, 28, 32

---

3 Close

Summarize
ENGLISH LANGUAGE LEARNERS

Review the vocabulary and the formula from the lesson. Ask students to describe what happens to a geometric sequence with a first term of 3 and each of the common ratios below.

a. 5 **b.** −2 **c.** $\frac{1}{4}$

Possible answers: **a.** The terms get very large very quickly. **b.** The terms alternate between positive and negative values and get farther from zero. **c.** The terms get very small very quickly.

Possible answers to *Think and Discuss*

1. In an arithmetic sequence, a certain number (the common difference) is added to each term to find the next term. In a geometric sequence, a certain number (the common ratio) is multiplied by each term to get the next term.

2. Divide each term by the term before it.

State Resources

go.hrw.com
State Resources Online
KEYWORD: MT7 Resources

Math Background

In arithmetic sequences, the terms increase toward positive infinity or decrease toward negative infinity. This is also true of geometric sequences with a common ratio that is greater than 1. However, if the common ratio is greater than zero and less than 1, the terms of the sequence will get closer and closer to zero. Mathematicians refer to this by saying that the sequence has zero as its limit. The concept of limits is important in more advanced math courses, such as calculus.

INDEPENDENT PRACTICE

See Example 1 **Determine if each sequence could be geometric. If so, give the common ratio.**

12. $81, 27, 9, 3, 1, \ldots$ yes; $\frac{1}{3}$

13. $\frac{1}{3}, \frac{1}{27}, \frac{1}{9}, \frac{1}{81}, \ldots$ no

14. $2, 5, 8, 11, \ldots$ no

15. $784, 392, 196, 98, \ldots$ yes; $\frac{1}{2}$

16. $1, -2, 4, -8, 16, \ldots$ yes; -2

17. $6, 2, \frac{2}{3}, \frac{2}{9}, \ldots$ yes; $\frac{1}{3}$

See Example 2 **Find the given term in each geometric sequence.**

18. 6th term: $\frac{1}{2}, 1, 2, 4, \ldots$ 16

19. 7th term: $2401, 2058, 1764, 1512, \ldots$ $952\frac{8}{49}$

20. 6th term: $16, -4, 1, -\frac{1}{4}, \ldots$ $-\frac{1}{64}$

21. 8th term: $2, 6, 18, 54, \ldots$ 4374

22. 21st term: $\frac{1}{28}, \frac{1}{14}, \frac{1}{7}, \frac{2}{7}, \ldots$ $37,449\frac{1}{7}$

23. 5th term: $1, 2.5, 6.25, 15.625, \ldots$ 39.0625

See Example 3 **24.** A video game displays 55,000 points after the first level is completed. One fifth of the total points are added at the end of each level. How many points are there at the end of the fifth level? **114,048 points**

PRACTICE AND PROBLEM SOLVING

Extra Practice
See page 806.

Find the next three terms of each geometric sequence.

25. $a_1 = 54$, common ratio $= \frac{1}{3}$ 18, 6, 2

26. $a_1 = 5$, common ratio $= 3$ 15, 45, 135

27. $a_1 = \frac{1}{81}$, common ratio $= -3$ $-\frac{1}{27}, \frac{1}{9}, -\frac{1}{3}$

28. $a_1 = 6$, common ratio $= 1.5$ 9, 13.5, 20.25

Find the first five terms of each geometric sequence.

29. $a_1 = 2, r = 1$ 2, 2, 2, 2, 2

30. $a_1 = 5, r = -1$ 5, -5, 5, -5, 5

31. $a_1 = 30, r = 2.1$ 30, 63, 132.3, 277.83, 583.443

32. $a_1 = 32, r = \frac{5}{2}$ 32, 80, 200, 500, 1250

33. $a_1 = 10, r = 0.25$ 10, 2.5, 0.625, 0.15625, 0.0390625

34. $a_1 = 56, r = -5$ 56, -280, 1400, -7000, 35,000

35. Find the 1st term of a geometric sequence with 5th term $\frac{81}{5}$ and common ratio 3. $\frac{1}{5}$

36. Find the 4th term of a geometric sequence with 10th term 64 and common ratio -2. 1

37. Find the 1st term of a geometric sequence with 3rd term $\frac{32}{147}$ and common ratio $\frac{4}{7}$. $\frac{2}{3}$

38. Find the 1st term of a geometric sequence if $a_4 = 28$ and $r = 2$. 3.5

39. Find the 6th term of a geometric sequence with 4th term 12 and 5th term 18. 27

40. **Sports** In the women's NCAA volleyball tournament, 64 teams compete in the first round. There are 32 teams remaining in the second round, 16 teams remaining in the third round, and so on. How many teams are remaining in the sixth round? **2 teams**

41. **Life Science** Under controlled conditions, a culture of bacteria triples in size every 3 days. How many cells of the bacteria are in the culture after 3 weeks if there were originally 28 cells? **61,236 cells**

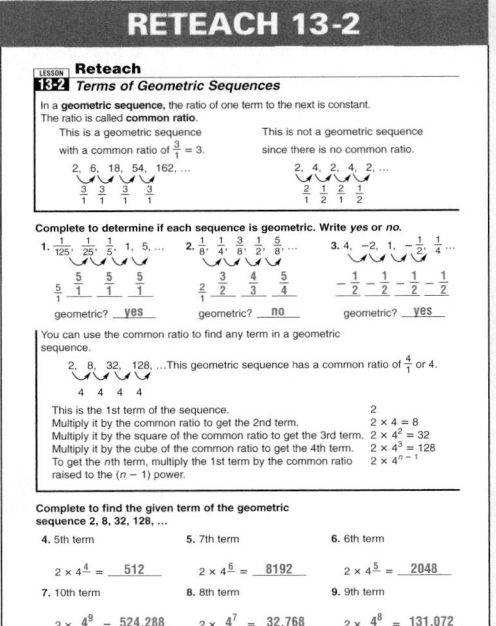

RETEACH 13-2

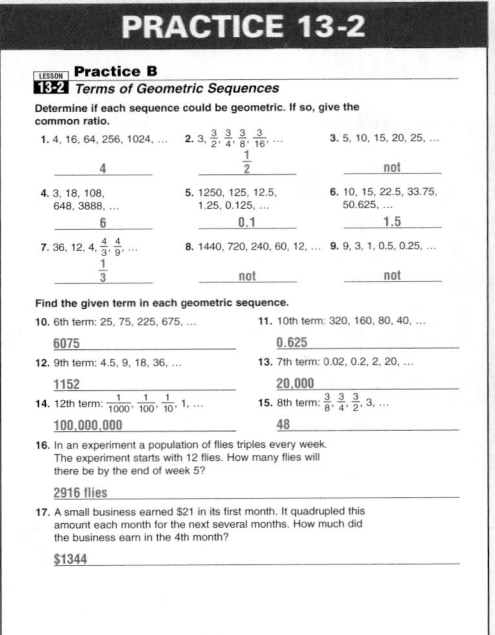

PRACTICE 13-2

42. Economics A car that was originally valued at $14,000 depreciates at the rate of 20% per year. This means that after each year, the car is worth 80% of its worth the previous year. What is the value of the car after 7 years? Round to the nearest dollar.   **$2936**

43. Physical Science A rubber ball is dropped from a height of 256 ft. After each bounce, the height of the ball is recorded.

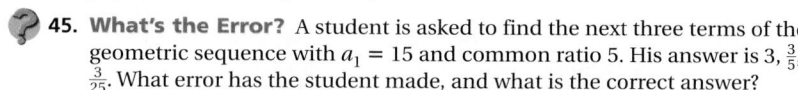

Height of Bouncing Ball					
Number of Bounces	1	2	3	4	5
Height (ft)	192	144	108	81	60.75

a. Could the heights in the table form a geometric sequence? If so, what is the common ratio?   yes; $\frac{3}{4}$

b. Estimate the height of the ball after the 8th bounce. Round your answer to the nearest foot.   **26 ft**

44. Multi-Step Town A has a population of 600 and is growing at a rate of 2% per year. Town B has a population of 500 and is growing at a rate of 4% per year. If these rates continue, which town will have the greater population after 10 years? Explain.

45. What's the Error? A student is asked to find the next three terms of the geometric sequence with $a_1 = 15$ and common ratio 5. His answer is 3, $\frac{3}{5}$, $\frac{3}{25}$. What error has the student made, and what is the correct answer?

46. Write About It Compare a geometric sequence with $a_1 = 3$ and $r = 4$ with a geometric sequence with $a_1 = 4$ and $r = 3$.

47. Challenge The 4th term in a geometric sequence is 923. The 9th term is 224,289. Find the 6th term.   **8307**

TEST PREP and Spiral Review

48. Multiple Choice A tank holds 40,800 gallons of gasoline. One-half of the gasoline remaining in the tank is sold each day. How many gallons of gasoline are left in the tank after the 6th day?

Ⓐ 12   Ⓑ 127   Ⓒ 1,275   Ⓓ 12,750

49. Short Response Determine if the sequence 10, 5, $\frac{5}{2}$, $\frac{5}{4}$, $\frac{5}{8}$, ... could be geometric. If so, give the common ratio. If not, explain why not.   yes; common ratio = $\frac{1}{2}$

Solve. (Lesson 1-8)

50. $\frac{m}{-3} = 4$ $m = -12$ **51.** $64 = 4x$ $x = 16$ **52.** $\frac{x}{-6} = -2$ $x = 12$

Simplify. (Lesson 11-1)

53. $3(p + 7) - 5p$ $-2p + 21$ **54.** $4x + 5(2x - 9)$ $14x - 45$ **55.** $8 + 7(y + 5) - 3$ $40 + 7y$

CHALLENGE 13-2

LESSON 13-2 Challenge
What's That Sum?

You can use a formula to find the sum of n terms of a geometric sequence with common ratio r. $S_n = \frac{a_1 - a_1 r^n}{1 - r}$

Find the sum of the first 5 terms of the geometric sequence 5, 15, 45, ...

$S_n = \frac{a_1 - a_1 r^n}{1 - r}$ Find r. $r = \frac{15}{5} = 3$

$S_5 = \frac{5 - 5 \cdot 3^5}{1 - 3}$ Substitute $n = 5$, $a_1 = 5$, $r = 3$.

$S_5 = \frac{5 - 5 \cdot 243}{1 - 3} = \frac{5 - 1215}{-2} = \frac{-1210}{-2} = 605$

So, the sum of the first 5 terms of the sequence is 605.

Check: 5 + 15 + 45 + 135 + 405 = 605

Use the formula to find each sum. Check your work by adding the terms with a calculator.

1. 32, 16, 8, ...
Find the sum of the first 6 terms.

$S_n = \frac{a_1 - a_1 r^n}{1 - r}$

$S_6 = \frac{32 - 32\left(\frac{1}{2}\right)^6}{1 - \frac{1}{2}}$

$S_6 = \frac{32 - 32\left(\frac{1}{64}\right)}{1 - \frac{1}{2}}$

$S_6 = \frac{32 - \frac{1}{2}}{1 - \frac{1}{2}} = \frac{31\frac{1}{2}}{\frac{1}{2}}$

$S_6 =$ _____ **63**

Check:

32 + 16 + 8 + 4 + 2
+ 1 = 63

2. −3, 15, −75, ...
Find the sum of the first 5 terms.

$S_n = \frac{a_1 - a_1 r^n}{1 - r}$

$S_5 = \frac{-3 - (-3)(-5)^5}{1 - (-5)}$

$S_5 = \frac{-3 + 3(-3125)}{1 + 5}$

$S_5 = \frac{-3 - 9375}{6} = \frac{-9378}{6}$

$S_5 =$ _____ **−1563**

Check:

−3 + 15 + (−75) + 375 +
(−1875) = −1563

PROBLEM SOLVING 13-2

LESSON 13-2 Problem Solving
Terms of Geometric Sequences

For Exercises 1–2, determine if the sequence could be geometric. If so, find the common ratio. Write the correct answer.

1. A computer that was worth $1000 when purchased was worth $800 after six months, $640 after a year, $512 after 18 months, and $409.60 after two years.

Could be geometric; 0.8

2. A student works for a starting wage of $6.00 per hour. She is told that she can expect a $0.25 raise every six months.

Not geometric

3. A piece of paper that is 0.01 inches thick is folded in half repeatedly. If the paper were folded 6 times, how thick would the result be?

0.64 inches

4. A vacuum pump removes one-half of the air in a container with each stroke. How much of the original air is left in the container after 8 strokes?

$\frac{1}{256}$

For exercises 5–8, assume that the cost of a college education increases an average of 5% per year. Choose the letter of the correct answer.

5. If the in-state tuition at the University of Florida is $2256 per year, what will the tuition be in 10 years?
A $3174.24
B $3333.14
C $3499.80
Ⓓ $3674.79

6. If it costs $3046 per year for tuition for a Virginia resident at the University of Virginia now, how much will tuition be in 8 years?
F $4183.26
G $4286.03
Ⓗ $4500.33
J $4725.35

7. If it costs $25,839 per year in tuition to attend Northwestern University now, how much will tuition be in 5 years?
A $31,407.47
Ⓑ $32,977.84
C $37,965.97
D $42,483.72

8. If you start attending Northwestern University in 5 years and attend for 4 years, how much will you spend in total for tuition?
Ⓕ $142,138.61
G $135,370.12
H $131,911.36
J $169,934.88

Answers

44. Town B; town A will have an estimated population of 731 and Town B will have an estimated population of 740.

45. Possible answer: The student divided by the common ratio instead of multiplying by it. The correct answer is 75, 375, 1875.

46. Possible answer: Even though both sequences have 12 as their second terms, the sequence with the greater common ratio grows much faster than the sequence with the lesser common ratio.

TEST PREP DOCTOR + Encourage students to write a geometric sequence with a common ratio of $\frac{1}{2}$ for Exercise 48. Be sure they understand that the first day begins with 40,800 gallons.

Journal

Ask students to write about whether they could determine if a sequence is arithmetic or geometric when given only the first two terms.

Power Presentations
with PowerPoint®

13-2 Lesson Quiz

Determine if each sequence could be geometric. If so, give the common ratio.

1. 200, 100, 50, 25, 12.5, ...   yes; $\frac{1}{2}$

2. 4, 8, 12, 16, ...   no

Find the given term in each geometric sequence.

3. 7th term: $\frac{1}{3}$, 1, 3, 9, ...   243

4. 20th term: $a_1 = 800$, $r = 0.8$ ≈11.53

Also available on transparency

Organizer

Use with Lesson 13-3

Pacing:
Traditional $\frac{1}{2}$ day
Block $\frac{1}{4}$ day

Objective: Use square tiles to explore the Fibonacci sequence.

Materials: Square tiles

 Online Edition

Resources

 **Hands-On Lab Activities**
Lab 13-3 Recording Sheet

Teach

Discuss

Explain how to form successive stacks of tiles. Using the rule from the Fibonacci sequence, how many tiles will be in the third stack? the fourth stack? **2; 3**

Close

Key Concept

Square tiles can be used to help students visualize and conceptualize the Fibonacci sequence.

Assessment

1. Find the 11th term of the Fibonacci sequence. **89**

2. What sequence is formed by taking the difference of consecutive terms in the Fibonacci sequence?
0, 1, 1, 2, 3, 5, 8,...; the same as the Fibonacci sequence, but the terms begin at 0

 **Explore the Fibonacci Sequence**

Use with Lesson 13-3

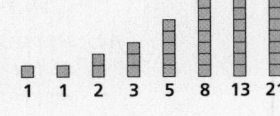
go.hrw.com
Lab Resources Online
KEYWORD: MT7 Lab13

Activity

Use square tiles to model the following numbers:

1   1   2   3   5   8   13   21

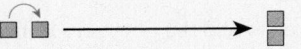

Place the first stack of tiles on top of the second stack of tiles. What do you notice?

The first two stacks added together are equal in height to the third stack.

Place the second stack of tiles on top of the third stack of tiles. What do you notice?

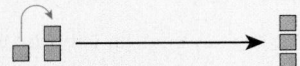

The second stack and the third stack added together are equal in height to the fourth stack.

This sequence is called the **Fibonacci sequence.** By adding two successive numbers, you get the next number in the sequence. The sequence will go on forever.

Think and Discuss

1. If there were a term before the 1 in the sequence, what would it be? Explain your answer. **0; 0 + 1 = 1, so it would be the only way for the pattern to work.**

2. Could the numbers 377, 610, and 987 be part of the Fibonacci sequence? Explain. **Yes, because 377 + 610 = 987.**

Try This

1. Use your square tiles to find the next two numbers in the sequence. What are they? **34, 55**

2. The 20th and 21st terms of the Fibonacci sequence are 6765 and 10,946. What is the 22nd term? **17,711**

Sue McMillen
North Tonawanda, New York

Teacher to Teacher

This is an extension to the study of the Fibonacci sequence that my students enjoy. While their tiles are showing the Fibonacci sequence, I have them identify which numbers are odd and which are even. They quickly notice the pattern for their tiles as OOEOOEOO. I ask them if they think the pattern continues. They generate the next few Fibonacci numbers and decide that it does. Then I ask them to show why the pattern works. If they get stuck, I remind them to consider how they found each number in the sequence (by adding the tiles from the two previous stacks), and this usually helps them get started. By using the properties of sums of odd and even numbers, they are able to show why the pattern works and verify that it will always continue.

13-3 Other Sequences

Learn to find patterns in sequences.

Vocabulary
first differences
second differences
Fibonacci sequence

The first five *triangular numbers* are shown below.

 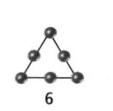 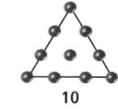 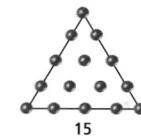

1   3   6   10   15

To continue the sequence, you can draw the triangles, or you can look for a pattern. If you subtract every term from the one after it, the **first differences** create a new sequence. If you do not see a pattern, you can repeat the process and find the **second differences**.

Term	1	2	3	4	5	6	7
Triangular Number	1	3	6	10	15	21	28

First differences   2   3   4   5   6   7
Second differences   1   1   1   1   1

EXAMPLE 1 Using First and Second Differences

Use first and second differences to find the next three terms in each sequence.

A 1, 7, 22, 46, 79, 121, 172, . . .

Sequence	1	7	22	46	79	121	172	232	301	379
1st Differences	6	15	24	33	42	51	60	69	78	
2nd Differences	9	9	9	9	9	9	9	9		

Remember!
The second difference is the difference between the first differences.

The next 1st difference in the table is going to be **9** more than the one before it, or **60**. This means that the next number in the sequence is **60** more than 172. So the next three terms are 232, 301, and 379.

B 5, 5, 7, 13, 25, 45, 75, . . .

Sequence	5	5	7	13	25	45	75	117	173	245
1st Differences	0	2	6	12	20	30	42	56	72	
2nd Differences	2	4	6	8	10	12	14	16		

The next three terms are 117, 173, and 245.

Motivate

Show students the sequence 1, 1, 2, 3, 5, 8, ... Ask them if this is an arithmetic sequence. no Ask them if it is a geometric sequence. no Ask them if they can find a rule to determine the next terms in the sequence. add the previous two terms together Explain that many different types of sequences are neither arithmetic nor geometric.

Explorations and answers are provided in *Alternate Openers: Explorations Transparencies.*

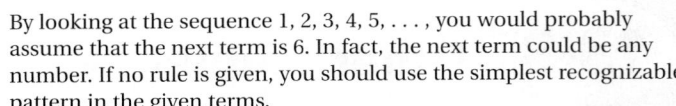
Additional Examples

Example 1

Use first and second differences to find the next three terms in each sequence.

A. 1, 8, 19, 34, 53, . . . 76, 103, 134

B. 12, 15, 21, 32, 50, . . . 77, 115, 166

Example 2

Give the next three terms in each sequence, using the simplest rule you can find.

A. 1, 2, 1, 1, 2, 1, 1, 1, 2, . . . 1, 1, 1

B. $\frac{2}{5}, \frac{3}{7}, \frac{4}{9}, \frac{5}{11}, \frac{6}{13} \cdots$ $\frac{7}{15}, \frac{8}{17}, \frac{9}{19}$

C. 1, 11, 6, 16, 11, 21, . . . 16, 26, 21

D. 1, −2, 3, −4, 5, −6, . . . 7, −8, 9

Example 3

Find the first five terms of the sequence defined by $a_n = n(n - 2)$.
−1, 0, 3, 8, 15

Example 4

Suppose a, b, c, and d are four consecutive numbers in the Fibonacci sequence. Complete the following table and guess the pattern.

a, b, c, d	$\frac{b}{a}$	$\frac{d}{c}$
3, 5, 8, 13	$\frac{5}{3} \approx 1.6667$	$\frac{13}{8} = 1.625$
13, 21, 34, 55	$\frac{21}{13} \approx 1.615$	$\frac{55}{34} \approx 1.618$
55, 89, 144, 233	$\frac{89}{55} \approx 1.618$	$\frac{233}{144} \approx 1.618$

The ratios are approximately equal to 1.618 (the golden ratio).

Also available on transparency

By looking at the sequence 1, 2, 3, 4, 5, . . . , you would probably assume that the next term is 6. In fact, the next term could be any number. If no rule is given, you should use the simplest recognizable pattern in the given terms.

EXAMPLE 2 Finding a Rule Given Terms of a Sequence

Give the next three terms in each sequence using the simplest rule you can find.

A $\frac{1}{2}, \frac{1}{3}, \frac{1}{4}, \frac{1}{5}, \frac{1}{6}, \cdots$ 4

The next three terms are $\frac{1}{7}, \frac{1}{8},$ and $\frac{1}{9}.$

Add 1 to the denominator of the previous term. This could be written as the algebraic rule $a_n = \frac{1}{n + 1}.$

B 1, −1, 3, −3, 5, −5, . . .

The next three terms are 7, −7, and 9.

Each positive term is followed by its opposite, and the next term is 2 more than the previous positive term.

C 2, 4, 8, 16, 32, 64, . . .

The next three terms are 128, 256, and 512.

Multiply the previous term by 2. This could be written as the algebraic rule $a_n = 2^n.$

D 1, 4, 9, 16, 25, 36, . . .

The next three terms are 49, 64, and 81.

The terms could be perfect squares. This could be written as the algebraic rule $a_n = n^2.$

Sometimes an algebraic rule is used to define a sequence.

EXAMPLE 3 Finding Terms of a Sequence Given a Rule

Find the first five terms of the sequence defined by $a_n = \frac{n + 1}{n + 2}.$

$a_1 = \frac{1 + 1}{1 + 2} = \frac{2}{3}$

$a_2 = \frac{2 + 1}{2 + 2} = \frac{3}{4}$

$a_3 = \frac{3 + 1}{3 + 2} = \frac{4}{5}$

$a_4 = \frac{4 + 1}{4 + 2} = \frac{5}{6}$

$a_5 = \frac{5 + 1}{5 + 2} = \frac{6}{7}$

The first five terms are $\frac{2}{3}, \frac{3}{4}, \frac{4}{5}, \frac{5}{6},$ and $\frac{6}{7}.$

---

2 Teach

Guided Instruction

In this lesson, students learn to find patterns in sequences. Use the lesson opener to show students how to use the method of differences to determine a pattern. As you review Example 2, remind students that more than one rule may apply to a given sequence. Review how to use algebraic rules to define sequences and determine terms. Introduce students to the *Fibonacci sequence.*

Reaching All Learners
Through Concrete Manipulatives

Let students work in pairs or small groups, and give each group at least 30 toothpicks. Ask them to make a 1-by-1 square with toothpicks and to record the number of toothpicks needed. Then have them do the same for larger squares, as shown in the diagram on the recording sheet. The number of toothpicks represents a sequence with common second differences. Students can use their results to determine how many toothpicks they would need for larger squares.

A famous sequence called the **Fibonacci sequence** is defined by the following rule: Add the two previous terms to find the next term.

$$1 + 1 = 2 \quad 1 + 2 = 3 \quad 2 + 3 = 5 \quad 3 + 5 = 8 \quad 5 + 8 = 13 \quad 8 + 13 = 21$$

EXAMPLE **4** **Using the Fibonacci Sequence**

Suppose a, b, c, and d are four consecutive numbers in the Fibonacci sequence. Complete the following table and guess the pattern.

a, b, c, d	bc	ad
1, 1, 2, 3	1(2) = 2	1(3) = 3
3, 5, 8, 13	5(8) = 40	3(13) = 39
13, 21, 34, 55	21(34) = 714	13(55) = 715
55, 89, 144, 233	89(144) = 12,816	55(233) = 12,815

The product of the two middle terms is either one more or one less than the product of the two outer terms.

Think and Discuss

1. **Find** the first and second differences for the sequence of pentagonal numbers: 1, 5, 12, 22, 35, 51, 70, ...

go.hrw.com
Homework Help Online
KEYWORD: MT7 13-3
Parent Resources Online
KEYWORD: MT7 Parent

13-3 **Exercises**

GUIDED PRACTICE

See Example **1** Use first and second differences to find the next three terms in each sequence.

1. 1, 6, 20, 43, 75, 116, 166, . . .
225, 293, 370

2. 5, 10, 30, 65, 115, 180, . . .
260, 355, 465

3. 10, 10, 13, 22, 40, 70, 115, . . .
178, 262, 370

4. 4, 6, 16, 42, 92, 174, 296, . . .
466, 692, 982

See Example **2** Give the next three terms in each sequence using the simplest rule you can find.

5. $\frac{1}{3}, \frac{3}{5}, \frac{5}{7}, \frac{7}{9}, \frac{9}{11}, \frac{11}{13}, \ldots$ $\frac{13}{15}, \frac{15}{17}, \frac{17}{19}$

6. 3, −4, 5, −6, 7, −8, 9, . . .   −10, 11, −12

7. 2, 3, 4, 2, 3, 4, 2, . . .   3, 4, 2

8. 1, 4, 9, 16, 25, . . .   36, 49, 64

3 Close

Summarize

Review the different methods for identifying possible rules for sequences. When given a sequence, students can first determine if it is arithmetic or geometric. If it is neither, they should look for any identifiable patterns or use second differences to find a rule. You may want to point out that these methods will not always lead to a rule for a given sequence.

Answers to Think and Discuss

1. first differences: 4, 7, 10, 13, 16, 19; second differences: 3, 3, 3, 3

Assignment Guide

If you finished Example **1** assign:
Average 1–4, 13–16, 27, 32–39
Advanced 13–16, 27, 32–39

If you finished Example **2** assign:
Average 1–8, 13–20, 27, 32–39
Advanced 13–20, 27–39

If you finished Example **3** assign:
Average 1–11, 13–23, 27, 32–39
Advanced 13–23, 27–39

If you finished Example **4** assign:
Average 1–27, 32–39
Advanced 13–39

Homework Quick Check

Quickly check key concepts.
Exercises: 14, 18, 22, 24

State Resources

go.hrw.com
State Resources Online
KEYWORD: MT7 Resources

Math Background

Linear equations have a common first difference for successive integer x-values.

Linear equation $y = 2x - 3$

x	0	1	2	3	4
y	−3	−1	1	3	5
diff.		2	2	2	2

Quadratic equations have a common second difference for successive integer x-values.

Quadratic equation $y = 2x^2 - 3$

x	0	1	2	3	4	5
y	−3	−1	5	15	29	47
1st diff.		2	6	10	14	18
2nd diff.			4	4	4	4

See Example 3 **Find the first five terms of each sequence defined by the given rule.**

9. $a_n = \dfrac{2n}{n+4}$ $\dfrac{2}{5}, \dfrac{2}{3}, \dfrac{6}{7}, 1, \dfrac{10}{9}$

10. $a_n = (n+1)(n+2)$ 6, 12, 20, 30, 42

11. $a_n = \dfrac{2-n}{n} + 1$ $2, 1, \dfrac{2}{3}, \dfrac{1}{2}, \dfrac{2}{5}$

See Example 4 12. Suppose a, b, and c are three consecutive numbers in the Fibonacci sequence. Complete the following table and guess the pattern.

a, b, c	ac	b^2
1, 1, 2	2	1
3, 5, 8	24	25
13, 21, 34	442	441
55, 89, 144	7920	7921

The product ac is either one more or one less than b^2.

INDEPENDENT PRACTICE

See Example 1 **Use first and second differences to find the next three terms in each sequence.**

13. 12, 24, 37, 51, 66, 82, 99, . . .
   117, 136, 156

14. −13, −9, 0, 14, 33, 57, 86, . . .
   120, 159, 203

15. 22, 23, 26, 32, 42, 57, 78, . . .
   106, 142, 187

16. 0.01, 0.02, 0.08, 0.24, 0.55, . . .
   1.06, 1.82, 2.88

See Example 2 **Give the next three terms in each sequence using the simplest rule you can find.**

17. 1, −1, 2, −2, 3, −3, . . .
   4, −4, 5

18. 1, 4, 3, 6, 5, 8, 7, . . . 10, 9, 12

19. 2.2, 2.02, 2.002, 2.0002, . . .
   2.00002, 2.000002, 2.0000002

20. $1, \dfrac{1}{8}, \dfrac{1}{27}, \dfrac{1}{64}, \dfrac{1}{125}, \dfrac{1}{216}, \cdots$
   $\dfrac{1}{343}, \dfrac{1}{512}, \dfrac{1}{729}$

See Example 3 **Find the first five terms of each sequence defined by the given rule.**

21. $a_n = \dfrac{n-2}{n+2}$ $-\dfrac{1}{3}, 0, \dfrac{1}{5}, \dfrac{1}{3}, \dfrac{3}{7}$

22. $a_n = n(n-1) - 2n$ −2, −2, 0, 4, 10

23. $a_n = \dfrac{3n}{n+1}$ $\dfrac{3}{2}, 2, \dfrac{9}{4}, \dfrac{12}{5}, \dfrac{5}{2}$

See Example 4 24. Suppose a, b, c, d, and e are five consecutive numbers in the Fibonacci sequence. Complete the following table and guess the pattern.

a, b, c, d, e	ae	bd	c^2
1, 1, 2, 3, 5	5	3	4
3, 5, 8, 13, 21	63	65	64
13, 21, 34, 55, 89	1157	1155	1156

c^2 is either one more or one less than ae and bd.

PRACTICE AND PROBLEM SOLVING

Extra Practice
See page 806.

The first 14 terms of the Fibonacci sequence are 1, 1, 2, 3, 5, 8, 13, 21, 34, 55, 89, 144, 233, and 377.

25. Where in this part of the sequence are the even numbers? Where do you think the next four even numbers will occur? 3rd, 6th, 9th, 12th terms; 15th, 18th, 21st, 24th terms

26. Where in this part of the sequence are the multiples of 3? Where do you think the next four multiples of 3 will occur? 4th, 8th, 12th terms; 16th, 20th, 24th, 28th terms

27. **Geometry** What are the next three numbers in the sequence of rectangular numbers: 2, 6, 12, 20, 30, . . . ? 42, 56, 72

RETEACH 13-3

LESSON **Reteach**
13-3 *Other Sequences*

Differences can help you find patterns in some sequences.

Find the next number in the sequence: 1, 6, 15, 28, 45, . . .

Find the **first differences**.   1, 6, 15, 28, 45, **66**
   5 9 13 17 **21**

Find the **second differences**.   4 4 4 4

Use the second and first diffences to calculate the next term.

Complete to find the next term in each sequence.

1. 1, 4, 9, 16, 25, . . .
   3 5 7 9
   2 2 2

   The next term in the sequence is:
   25 + __11__ = __36__

2. 1, 8, 21, 40, 65, . . .
   7 13 19 25
   6 6 6

   The next term in the sequence is:
   65 + __31__ = __96__

A rule is used to define a sequence.

Write a rule for this sequence: $\dfrac{1}{2}, \dfrac{2}{3}, \dfrac{3}{4}, \dfrac{4}{5}, \dfrac{5}{6}, \cdots$

A possible rule is that the numerator of a term is the number of that terms position, and the denominator is 1 more than the numerator.

This can be written algebraically as $a_n = \dfrac{n}{n+1}$.

Using this rule, the 10th term of the sequence is $a_{10} = \dfrac{10}{10+1} = \dfrac{10}{11}$.

Use the given rule to write the 5th and 10th terms.

3. 1, 8, 27, 64, . . .
   $a_n = n^3$
   $a_5 = (\underline{5})^3 = \underline{125}$
   $a_{10} = (\underline{10})^3 = \underline{1000}$

4. 1, 3, 6, 10, . . .
   $a_n = \dfrac{n(n+1)}{2}$
   $a_5 = \dfrac{(5)(5+1)}{2} = \underline{15}$
   $a_{10} = \dfrac{(10)(10+1)}{2} = \underline{55}$

5. 1, −3, 1, −3, . . .
   $a_n = 2(-1)^{n+1} - 1$
   $a_5 = 2(-1)^{5+1} - 1$
   $= \underline{1}$
   $a_{10} = 2(-1)^{10+1} - 1$
   $= \underline{-3}$

PRACTICE 13-3

LESSON **Practice B**
13-3 *Other Sequences*

Use first and second differences to find the next three terms in each sequence.

1. 3, 6, 10, 15, 21, . . .
   28, 36, 45

2. 11, 14, 18, 25, 37, . . .
   56, 84, 123

3. 10, 16, $22\dfrac{1}{3}$, 29, 36, . . .
   $43\dfrac{1}{3}$, 51, 59

4. 14.5, 22.5, 31, 40, 49.5, . . .
   59.5, 70, 81

Give the next three terms in each sequence using the simplest rule you can find.

5. 6, 7, 10, 19, 38, . . .
   71, 122, 195

6. 0.5, 2, 4.5, 8, 12.5, . . .
   18, 24.5, 32

7. 36, 55, 80, 111, 148, . . .
   191, 240, 295

8. 3, 10, 21, 36, 55, . . .
   78, 105, 136

9. 1, 6, 15, 28, 45, . . .
   66, 91, 120

10. 0, 11, 30, 57, 92, . . .
   135, 186, 245

Find the first five terms of each sequence defined by the given rule.

11. $a_n = \dfrac{n^2 + 2}{n}$
   3, 3, $3\dfrac{2}{3}$, $4\dfrac{1}{2}$, $5\dfrac{2}{5}$

12. $a_n = \dfrac{5n - 2}{n + 1}$
   $1\dfrac{1}{2}$, $2\dfrac{2}{3}$, $3\dfrac{1}{4}$, $3\dfrac{3}{5}$, $3\dfrac{5}{6}$

13. $a_n = \dfrac{3n^2}{n + 2}$
   1, 3, $5\dfrac{2}{5}$, 8, $10\dfrac{5}{7}$

14. Suppose a, b, and c are three consecutive numbers in the Fibonacci sequence. Complete the following table and guess the pattern.

a, b, c	ab	bc
1, 1, 2	1	2
2, 3, 5	6	15
5, 8, 13	40	104
13, 21, 34	273	714
34, 55, 89	1870	4895

The difference of bc and ab is the square of b.

Pitch is the frequency of a musical note, measured in units called *hertz* (Hz). A pitch is named by its octave. A_4 is in the 4th octave on the piano keyboard and is often called middle A.

55 Hz 110 Hz 165 Hz 220 Hz ? Hz 440 Hz ? Hz
275 Hz

28. What kind of sequence is represented by the frequencies of $A_1, A_2, A_3, A_4, \ldots$? Write a rule to calculate these frequencies. **geometric; $a_n = 55 \cdot 2^{(n-1)}$**

When a string of an instrument is played, its vibrations create many different frequencies. These varying frequencies are called *harmonics*.

Frequencies of Harmonics on A_1					
Harmonic	Fundamental (1st)	2nd	3rd	4th	5th
Note	A_1	A_2	E_2	A_3	$C_3^{\#}$

29. What is the frequency of the note E_3 if it is the 6th harmonic on A_1? **330 Hz**

30. ✍ **Write About It** Describe the sequence represented by the frequencies of different harmonics. Write a rule to calculate these frequencies. **arithmetic; $a_n = 55n$**

31. ⭐ **Challenge** In music, an important interval is a *fifth*. As you progress around the circle of fifths, the pitch frequencies are approximately as shown (rounded to the nearest tenth). What type of sequence do the frequencies form in clockwise order from C? Write the rule for the sequence. If the rule holds all the way around the circle, what would the frequency of the note F be?

go.hrw.com
Web Extra!
KEYWORD: MT7 Pitch

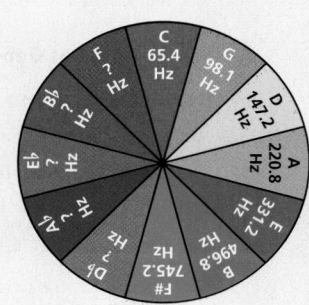

TEST PREP and Spiral Review

32. Multiple Choice What is the 11th term of a sequence defined by $a_n = \frac{n-1}{n}$?

Ⓐ $\frac{1}{11}$ Ⓑ $-\frac{10}{11}$ Ⓒ $\frac{10}{11}$ Ⓓ $\frac{11}{12}$

33. Gridded Response What is the 4th term of a sequence defined by $a_n = \frac{n+1}{n+2}$? **$\frac{2}{3}, \frac{3}{4}, \frac{4}{5}, \frac{5}{6}$**

Write each number in standard notation. (Lesson 4-4)

34. 8.21×10^5 **821,000**   **35.** 2.07×10^{-7} **0.000000207**   **36.** -1.4×10^3 **−1400**

Determine if each sequence could be geometric. If so, give the common ratio. (Lesson 13-2)

37. $5, 10, 15, 20, 25, \ldots$ **no**   **38.** $3, 6, 12, 24, 48, \ldots$ **yes; 2**   **39.** $1, -3, 9, -27, 81, \ldots$ **yes; −3**

CHALLENGE 13-3

LESSON 13-3 Challenge
Follow the Short-Cut

The Greek capital letter *sigma*, Σ, is used to mean "take the sum of what follows."

What follows Σ is a general term that is a rule for each term of a *summation*.

The general term is written with an *index*, shown by one letter (often, *n*).

The *limits* for the index are written above Σ (upper limit) and below Σ (lower limit).

The first term of the summation is formed by substituting the lower limit for the index into the general term.

Each succeeding term of the summation is formed by using successive integral values of the index, until the upper limit is reached.

$\sum_{n=1}^{5} 2^n$ This notation means take the sum of terms of the form 2^n for consecutive integral values of n beginning with $n = 1$ and ending with $n = 5$.

$\sum_{n=1}^{5} 2^n = 2^1 + 2^2 + 2^3 + 2^4 + 2^5$
$\sum_{n=1}^{5} 2^n = 2 + 4 + 8 + 16 + 32 = 62$

Evaluate each summation.

1. $\sum_{n=1}^{5} 4n$

$= 4(1) + 4(2) + 4(3) + 4(4) + 4(5)$
$= \underline{4 + 8 + 12 + 16 + 20}$
$= \underline{60}$

2. $\sum_{n=1}^{3} (n^2 + 1)$

$= \underline{(1^2 + 1) + (2^2 + 1) + (3^2 + 1)}$
$= \underline{(2) + (5) + (10)}$
$= \underline{17}$

3. $\sum_{n=1}^{4} \frac{6}{n}$

$= \underline{\frac{6}{1} + \frac{6}{2} + \frac{6}{3} + \frac{6}{4}}$
$= \underline{6 + 3 + 2 + 1.5}$
$= \underline{12.5}$

4. $\sum_{n=1}^{4} \frac{n}{n+1}$

$= \underline{\frac{1}{1+1} + \frac{2}{2+1} + \frac{3}{3+1} + \frac{4}{4+1}}$
$= \underline{\frac{1}{2} + \frac{2}{3} + \frac{3}{4} + \frac{4}{5}}$
$= \underline{\frac{30}{60} + \frac{40}{60} + \frac{45}{60} + \frac{48}{60} = 2\frac{43}{60}}$

PROBLEM SOLVING 13-3

LESSON 13-3 Problem Solving
Other Sequences

A toy rocket is launched and the height of the rocket during its first four seconds is recorded. Write the correct answer.

1. Find the first differences for the rocket's heights.

$\underline{176, 144, 112, 80}$

2. Find the second differences.

$\underline{-32, -32, -32}$

3. Use the first and second differences to predict the height of the rocket at 5, 6, and 7 seconds.

Time (sec)	Height (ft)
0	0
1	176
2	320
3	432
4	512
5	560
6	576
7	560

4. What is the maximum height of the rocket?

$\underline{576 \text{ ft}}$

5. When will the rocket hit the ground?

$\underline{12 \text{ seconds after takeoff}}$

For exercises 6–9, refer to the table below, which shows the number of diagonals for different polygons. Choose the letter for the correct answer.

6. What are the first differences for the diagonals?

A 1, 1, 1, 1   Ⓒ 2, 3, 4, 5
B 3, 2, 0, 3, 7   D 2, 7, 14, 23

Polygon	Sides	Diagonals
Triangle	3	0
Quadrilateral	4	2
Pentagon	5	5
Hexagon	6	9
Heptagon	7	14

7. What are the second differences?

Ⓕ 1, 1, 1   H 5, 7, 8
G 1, 2, 3, 4   J 7, 9, 11, 13

8. How many diagonals does a nonagon (9 sides) have?

A 21
B 24
Ⓒ 27
D 32

9. Which rule will give the number of diagonals d for s sides?

F $d = \frac{s(s+1)}{2}$
G $d = s(s-3)(s-2) - 1$
Ⓗ $d = \frac{s(s-3)}{2}$
J $d = (s-3)(s-2)$

Answers

31. Geometric sequence; $a_n = 65.4 \cdot 1.5^{(n-1)}$; the note F would have a frequency of about 5656.9 Hz.

TEST PREP DOCTOR ➕ Mental math can be used to replace n with 11 in Exercise 32. Choice **B** can be eliminated because it is negative, and **D** can be eliminated because it has a denominator of 12.

 Journal

Ask students to write about the steps they would take to identify a rule for a given sequence.

Power Presentations
with PowerPoint®

✔ **13-3 Lesson Quiz**

1. Use first and second differences to find the next three terms in the following sequence: 2, 18, 48, 92, 150, 222, 308, . . . **408, 522, 650**

2. Give the next three terms in the sequence, using the simplest rule you can find. 2, 5, 10, 17, 26 . . . **37, 50, 65**

3. Find the first five terms of the sequence defined by $a_n = n(n+1)$. **2, 6, 12, 20, 30**

Also available on transparency

READY TO GO ON?

Organizer

Objective: Assess students' mastery of concepts and skills in Lessons 13-1 through 13-3.

Resources

 Assessment Resources
Section 13A Quiz

 Test & Practice Generator
One-Stop Planner®

INTERVENTION ⬅➡

Resources

 Ready to Go On?
Intervention and
Enrichment Worksheets

💿 **Ready to Go On? CD-ROM**

🪐 **Ready to Go On? Online**

my.hrw.com

Ready to Go On? (sidebar tab)

Quiz for Lessons 13-1 Through 13-3

✓ **13-1** **Terms of Arithmetic Sequences**

Determine if each sequence could be arithmetic. If so, give the common difference.

1. 12, 13, 15, 17, . . . **no** **2.** 13, 26, 39, 52, . . . **yes; 13** **3.** 19, 60, 101, 174, . . . **no**

Find the given term in each arithmetic sequence.

4. 8th term: 5, 8, 11, 14, . . . **26** **5.** 16th term: 9, 8.8, 8.6, . . . **6**

6. 14th term: $7, 7\frac{1}{3}, \frac{2}{3}, \ldots$ $11\frac{1}{3}$ **7.** 7th term: $a_1 = 26, d = 11$, **−40**

8. Carmen makes 20 bracelets during the first week to sell at next year's fair. Each week, she makes 4 more than the previous week. In which week will she make 100 bracelets? **21st week**

✓ **13-2** **Terms of Geometric Sequences**

Determine if each sequence could be geometric. If so, give the common ratio.

9. 1, −4, 16, −64, . . . **yes; −4** **10.** 3, −3, −9, −15, . . . **no** **11.** 50, 10, 2, 0.4, . . . **yes; 0.2**

Find the given term in each geometric sequence.

12. 5th term: 11, 44, 176, . . . **2816** **13.** 9th term: 36, 12, 4, . . . $\frac{4}{729} \approx 0.005487$

14. 12th term: $-\frac{4}{3}, 4, -12, \ldots$ **236, 196** **15.** 17th term: 10,000; 1000; 100; . . . **0.000000000001**

16. The purchase price of a machine at a factory was $500,000. Each year, the value of the machine depreciates by 5%. To the nearest dollar, what is the value of the machine after 6 years? **$367,546**

✓ **13-3** **Other Sequences**

Use first and second differences to find the next three terms in each sequence.

17. 7, 7, 9, 13, 19, . . . **27, 37, 49** **18.** 2, 10, 22, 38, 58, . . . **82, 110, 142**

19. −5, −9, −10, −8, −3, . . . **5, 16, 30**

Give the next three terms in each sequence using the simplest rule you can find.

20. $\frac{1}{2}, \frac{4}{5}, \frac{7}{8}, \frac{10}{11}, \ldots$ $\frac{13}{14}, \frac{16}{17}, \frac{19}{20}$ **21.** 1, 16, 81, 256, . . . **625, 1296, 2401**

Find the first five terms of each sequence defined by the given rule.

22. $a_n = 4n - 7$ **−3, 1, 5, 9, 13** **23.** $a_n = 2^{n-1}$ **1, 2, 4, 8, 16**

24. $a_n = (-1)^n \cdot 2n$ **−2, 4, −6, 8, −10** **25.** $a_n = (n+2)^2 - 2$ **7, 14, 23, 34, 47**

READY TO GO ON?
Diagnose and Prescribe

NO
INTERVENE

YES
ENRICH

READY TO GO ON? **Intervention**	*READY TO GO ON? Intervention, Section 13A*		
	📝 **Worksheets**	💿 **CD-ROM**	🪐 **Online**
✓ Lesson 13-1	13-1 Intervention	Activity 13-1	Diagnose and Prescribe Online
✓ Lesson 13-2	13-2 Intervention	Activity 13-2	
✓ Lesson 13-3	13-3 Intervention	Activity 13-3	

READY TO GO ON?
Enrichment, Section 13A

📝 **Worksheets**
💿 **CD-ROM**
🪐 **Online**

Focus on Problem Solving

Solve

Make a Plan
• Choose a method of computation

When solving problems, you must decide which calculation method is best: paper and pencil, calculator, or mental math. Your decision will be based on many factors, such as the problem context, the numbers involved, and your own number sense. Use the following table as a guideline.

Paper and Pencil	Calculator	Mental Math
Use when solving multi-step problems so you can see how the steps relate.	Use when working complex operations.	Use when performing basic operations or generating simple estimates.

For each problem, tell whether you would use a calculator, mental math, or pencil and paper. Justify your choice, and then solve the problem.

1 The local high school radio station has 500 CDs. Each week, the music manager gets 25 new CDs. How many CDs will the station have in 8 weeks?

2 There are 360 deer in a forest. The population each year is 10% more than the previous year. How many deer will there be after 3 years?

3 Heidi works 8-hour shifts frosting cakes. She has frosted 12 cakes so far, and she thinks she can frost 4 cakes an hour during the rest of her shift. How many more hours will it take for her to frost a total of 32 cakes?

4 Kai has $170 in a savings account that earns 3% simple interest each year. How much interest will he have earned in 14 years?

5 A company's logo is in the shape of an isosceles triangle. When appearing on the company's stationery, the logo has a base of 5.1 cm and legs measuring 6.9 cm each. When appearing on a company poster, the similar logo has a base of 14.79 cm. Estimate the length of each leg of the logo on the poster.

6 Margo and her friends decided to hike the Wildcat Rock trail. After hiking $\frac{1}{4}$ of the way, they turned back because it began to rain. How far did they hike in all?

Trail	Distance (mi)
Meadowlark	$5\frac{3}{8}$
Key Lake	$4\frac{1}{2}$
Wildcat Rock	$6\frac{1}{4}$
Eagle Lookout	8

the length of each leg of the logo must be about $7 \cdot 3 = 21$ cm.

6. Paper and pencil; First, identify the distance being used, $6\frac{1}{4}$ or $\frac{25}{4}$ miles. $\frac{1}{4}$ of $\frac{25}{4}$ is $\frac{1}{4} \cdot \frac{25}{4} = \frac{25}{16}$. Since they hiked $\frac{1}{4}$ out of the way and then had to hike the same distance back to where they started, they hiked $2 \cdot \frac{25}{16} = \frac{25}{8} = 3\frac{1}{8}$ miles in all.

Focus on Problem Solving

Organizer

Objective: Focus on choosing a method of computation.

 Online Edition

Resources

 Chapter 13 Resource Book
Reading Strategies

Problem Solving Process

This page focuses on the second step of the problem-solving process:
Make a Plan

Discuss

Have students discuss how they decided to use a calculator, mental math, or pencil and paper to solve each problem.

Possible answers:

1. Mental math; 8 multiples of 25 is a total of 200 CDs in 8 weeks, so the total will be 200 + 500 = 700.

2. Calculator; Use a calculator to find 110% of each of the previous years' populations.

3. Paper and pencil; First, Heidi has already frosted 12 cakes, so there are 32 − 12 = 20 cakes left to frost. At 4 cakes an hour, it will take her $\frac{20}{4} = 5$ more hours to frost a total of 32 cakes.

4. Calculator; Use the formula $I = Prt$ to find that Kai will earn $I = (\$170)(0.03)(14) = \$71.40$

5. Mental math; The ratio of the bases is about 15 cm to 5 cm, or 3. Therefore,

State Resources

 **go.hrw.com**
State Resources Online
KEYWORD: MT7 Resources

Functions

One-Minute Section Planner

Lesson	Materials	MiC and Lab Resources
Lesson 13-4 Linear Functions ● Identify linear functions. ☑ SAT-10 ☑ ITBS ☑ CTBS ☑ NAEP		**MiC:** *Graphing Equations* pp. 21–23 **MiC:** *Algebra Rules* pp. 16–17
Lesson 13-5 Exponential Functions ● Identify and graph exponential functions. ☐ SAT-10 ☐ ITBS ☐ CTBS ☑ NAEP	Graph paper	**MiC:** *Ups and Downs* pp. 29–31, 44–45 **Technology Lab Activities** 13-5
Lesson 13-6 Quadratic Functions ● Identify and graph quadratic functions. **13-6 Technology Lab** Explore Cubic Functions ● Use a graphing calculator to explore cubic functions. ☐ SAT-10 ☐ ITBS ☐ CTBS ☑ NAEP	Graph paper, graphing calculators	**MiC:** *Ups and Downs* pp. 43–45 **Hands-On Lab Activities** 13-6 **Technology Lab Activities** 13-6
Lesson 13-7 Inverse Variation ● Recognize inverse variation by graphing tables of data. ☐ SAT-10 ☐ ITBS ☐ CTBS ☐ NAEP		

MK = *Manipulatives Kit*

Mathematics in Context

The units **Graphing Equations** and **Ups and Downs** from the *Mathematics in Context* © 2006 series can be used with Section 13B. See Section Planner above for suggestions for integrating *MiC* with *Holt Mathematics*.

Section Overview

Types of Functions

Lessons 13-4, 13-5, 13-6

Why? Different types of functions are used to model a variety of real-world relationships. The speed of a car can be modeled by a linear function. The cross section of a satellite dish can be modeled by a quadratic function. Population growth can be modeled by an exponential function.

Linear function

$f(x) = mx + b$

The slope is m.
The y-intercept is b.
The graph is a line.

Exponential function

$f(x) = p \cdot a^x$

The y-intercept is p.

Quadratic function

$f(x) = ax^2 + bx + c$

The y-intercept is c.
The graph is a parabola.

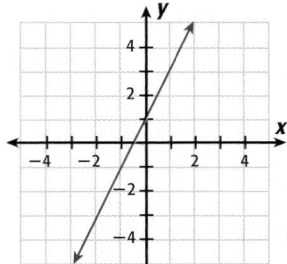

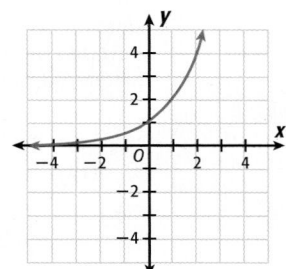

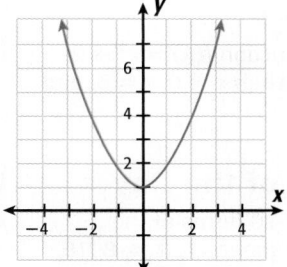

Inverse Variation

Lesson 13-8

Why? One example of an inverse-variation relationship is the frequency of a piano string and the string's length. The shorter the string is, the higher the frequency.

Words	Numbers	Algebra
An **inverse variation** is a function in which the product of the variables is a constant.	$y = \dfrac{120}{x}$ $xy = 120$	$y = \dfrac{k}{x}$ $xy = k$

Warm Up

Determine if each relationship represents a function.

1.

x	1	2	3	4
y	1	8	27	64

yes

2. $y = 3x^2 - 1$ yes

3. For the function $f(x) = x^2 + 2$, find $f(x)$ when $x = 0$, $x = 3$, and $x = -2$. 2, 11, 6

Problem of the Day

Take the first 20 terms of the geometric sequence 1, 2, 4, 8, 16, 32, ... Why can't you put those 20 numbers into two groups such that each group has the same sum?

All the numbers except 1 are even, so the sum of the 20 numbers is odd and cannot be divided into two equal integer sums.

Also available on transparency

Math Fact

The only straight line that is not a function is a vertical line.

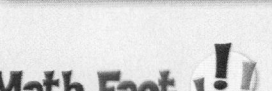

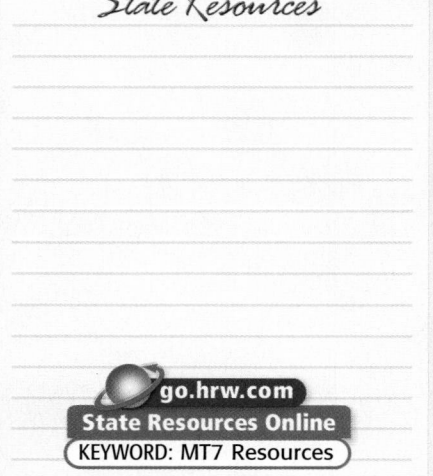

State Resources

go.hrw.com
State Resources Online
KEYWORD: MT7 Resources

13-4 Linear Functions

Learn to identify linear functions.

Vocabulary
linear function
function notation

When filled, a space shuttle's main fuel tank holds about 529,000 gallons of liquid hydrogen and liquid oxygen. During lift-off, this fuel flows to the engines at a rate of 1035 gallons per second.

Fuel Remaining in Tank					
Time (s)	0	1	2	3	4
Fuel (gal)	529,000	527,965	526,930	525,895	524,860

Notice that the fuel amounts form an arithmetic sequence with common difference of −1035. Also, the data can be plotted on a coordinate plane as a line with slope −1035 and y-intercept 529,000.

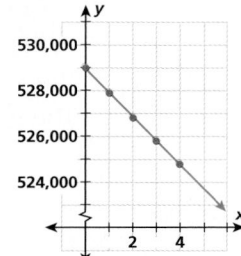

A **linear function** can be described by a linear equation. You can use **function notation** to show that the output value of the function f, written $f(x)$, corresponds to the input value x.

Reading Math

$f(x)$ is read "f of x."
$f(1)$ is read "f of 1."

$f(x) = 2x$ The output y is the rule of f applied to x.
$f(1) = 2(1)$ f(1) means evaluate f(x) for x = 1.

The graph of a linear function is a line. The linear function $f(x) = mx + b$ has a **slope** of m and a y-intercept of b.

EXAMPLE 1 Identifying Linear Functions

Determine whether $f(x) = 2x - 2$ is linear.

$f(x) = 2x - 2$
Graph the function.
$f(x) = 2x - 2$ does represent a linear function because its graph is a straight line. It has a slope of 2 and a y-intercept of −2.

---

1 Introduce

Alternate Opener

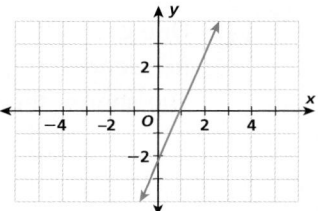

Motivate

Ask the students if they remember what m and b represent in the equation $y = mx + b$. Help students identify m as the slope and b as the y-intercept of a line. Now that students are familiar with the notation $f(x)$, ask them to write $y = mx + b$ in function notation.
$f(x) = mx + b$

EXPLORATION

13-4 Linear Functions

Many everyday situations can be represented with *linear functions*.

For each situation, write a rule and complete the table.

1. A car beginning at time = 0 hours travels 60 miles per hour.

Input x (hr)	Rule y = ___	Output y (mi)
0	60 · 0	0
1	60 · 1	60
2		120
3		
4		

2. A club that has $2000.00 in its treasury plans to spend $150.00 per week.

Input x (weeks)	Rule y = ___	Output y ($)
0		2000
1		1850
2		1700
3		
4		

Think and Discuss

3. **Explain** how you determined the rules in Problems 1 and 2.

Explorations and answers are provided in *Alternate Openers: Explorations Transparencies.*

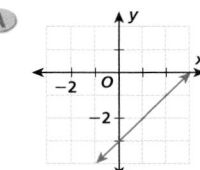

EXAMPLE 2 **Writing the Equation for a Linear Function**

Write a rule for each linear function.

A

B

x	y
−2	−16
−1	−13
1	−7
2	−4

Step 1 Identify the y-intercept b from the graph.

$b = -3$

Step 2 Locate another point (x, y).

$(1, -2)$

Step 3 Substitute the x- and y-values into the equation $f(x) = mx + b$, and solve for m.

$-2 = m(1) + -3$

$1 = m$

The rule is $f(x) = 1x + (-3)$ or $f(x) = x - 3$.

Step 1 Locate two points. $(1, -7)$ and $(2, -4)$

Step 2 Find the slope m.

$m = \dfrac{y_2 - y_1}{x_2 - x_1} = \dfrac{-4 - (-7)}{2 - 1} = 3$

Step 3 Substitute the x- and y-values into the equation $f(x) = mx + b$, and solve for m.

$-7 = 3(1) + b$

$-10 = b$

The rule is $f(x) = 3x + (-10)$ or $f(x) = 3x - 10$.

EXAMPLE 3 **Physical Science Application**

At lift-off, the space shuttle's main fuel tank contains about 529,000 gallons of liquid hydrogen and liquid oxygen. This fuel flows to the engines at a rate of 1035 gallons per second. Find a rule for the linear function that describes the amount remaining in the tank. Use it to find out how much fuel is left after 8 minutes.

$$f(x) = mx + 529,000$$

The y-intercept is the volume of fuel at lift-off, 529,000 gal.

$$527,965 = m(1) + 529,000$$

At 1 s after lift-off, there are 529,000 − 1035, or 527,965, gal remaining.

$527,965 = m + 529,000$

$\underline{- \; 529,000 \qquad - \; 529,000}$

$-1035 = m$

The rule for the function is $f(x) = -1035x + 529,000$.

After 8 minutes, or 480 seconds, there will be $f(480) = -1035(480) + 529,000 = 32,200$ gal.

Possible answer to Think and Discuss

1. Substitute the y-intercept and the coordinates of a point on the graph into the equation $y = mx + b$, and solve for m. Write the equation using the values from m and b that you found.

Think and Discuss

1. **Describe** how to use a graph to find the equation of a linear function.

Power Presentations with PowerPoint®

Additional Examples

Example ①

Determine whether the function $f(x) = 2x^3$ is linear. not linear

Example ②

Write a rule for each linear function.

A.

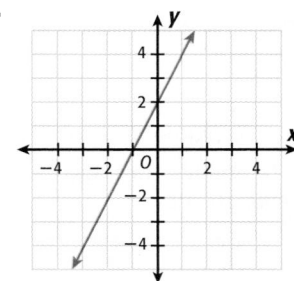

$f(x) = 2x + 2$

B.

x	−3	−1	1	3
y	−8	−2	4	10

$f(x) = 3x + 1$

Example ③

A video club costs \$15 to join. Each video that is rented costs \$1.50. Find a rule for the linear function that describes the total cost of renting videos as a member of the club, and find the total cost of renting 12 videos. $f(x) = 1.5x + 15$; \$33

Also available on transparency

---

2 Teach

Guided Instruction

In this lesson, students learn to identify linear functions. Review with students how to find the y-intercept from a graph or table. Review the slope formula $m = \dfrac{y_2 - y_1}{x_2 - x_1}$. Show students how to substitute values into the equation $f(x) = mx + b$ to solve for m or b.

Multiple Representations Point out that all non-vertical straight lines are functions because they have exactly one y-value for each x-value. This means linear equations can be written using function notation.

Reaching All Learners
Through Modeling

Physical Science Show students the table below (Teaching Transparencies) and explain that the relationship between the two temperatures is linear. Then have students write a rule for Fahrenheit temperature as a function of Celsius temperature.

Temperature (°C)	Temperature (°F)
−10	14
0	32
25	77
50	122
100	212

$F = 1.8C + 32$

3 Close

Summarize

Review the connection between the equations $y = mx + b$ and $f(x) = mx + b$. Remind students that when asked to write a rule for a linear function, they must replace the m with the value for slope and the b with the value of the y-intercept.

13-4 **Exercises**

go.hrw.com
Homework Help Online
KEYWORD: MT7 13-4
Parent Resources Online
KEYWORD: MT7 Parent

Assignment Guide

If you finished Example **1** assign:
Average 1–3, 7–9, 20–29
Advanced 7–9, 17–29

If you finished Example **2** assign:
Average 1–5, 7–11, 20–29
Advanced 7–11, 17–29

If you finished Example **3** assign:
Average 1–12, 14, 15, 20–29
Advanced 7–29

Homework Quick Check

Quickly check key concepts.
Exercises: 8, 10, 12

Math Background

Function notation makes it simpler to ask common questions in mathematics. For example, without function notation, the following question can be asked:

If $y = 3x - 4$, find the value of y when $x = 2$.

Using function notation, the same question can be stated more simply:

If $f(x) = 3x - 4$, find $f(2)$.

GUIDED PRACTICE

See Example **1** Determine whether each function is linear.

1. $f(x) = x + 3$ linear   **2.** $f(x) = x^3 + 1$ not linear   **3.** $f(x) = 6x - 3$ linear

See Example **2** Write a rule for each linear function.

4.

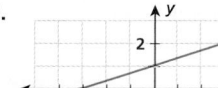

$f(x) = 2x + 2$

5.

x	y
−1	6
0	4
1	2
2	0

$f(x) = -2x + 4$

See Example **3** **6.** Liza earns \$480 per week for 40 hours of work. If she works overtime, she makes \$18 per overtime hour. Find a rule for the linear function that describes her weekly salary if she works x hours of overtime. Use it to find how much Liza earns if she works 6 hours of overtime. $f(x) = 18x + 480$; \$588

INDEPENDENT PRACTICE

See Example **1** Determine whether each function is linear.

7. $f(x) = -4x + 8$
linear

8. $f(x) = -\frac{3}{4}x - 5$
linear

9. $f(x) = \frac{7}{x}$
not linear

See Example **2** Write a rule for each linear function.

10.

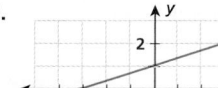

$f(x) = \frac{1}{3}x + 1$

11.

x	y
−1	−11
0	−5
1	1
2	7

$f(x) = 6x - 5$

See Example **3** **12.** A swimming pool contains 1500 gallons of water. The pool is being drained for the season at a rate of 35 gallons per minute. Find a rule for the linear function that describes the amount of water in the tank. Use it to determine how much will be in the tank after 25 minutes.
$f(t) = 1500 - 35t$; 625 gal

PRACTICE AND PROBLEM SOLVING

Extra Practice
See page 807.

13. Estimation Suppose a baby weighed 8 pounds at birth, and gained about 1.2 pounds each month during the first year of life. To the nearest pound, approximately what was the weight of the baby during the seventh month? 16 lb

State Resources

go.hrw.com
State Resources Online
KEYWORD: MT7 Resources

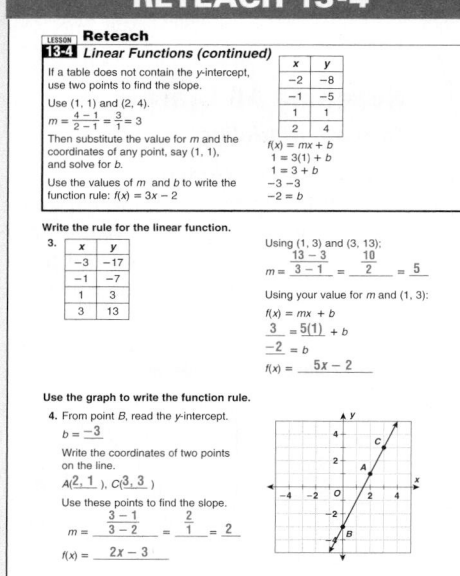

RETEACH 13-4

PRACTICE 13-4

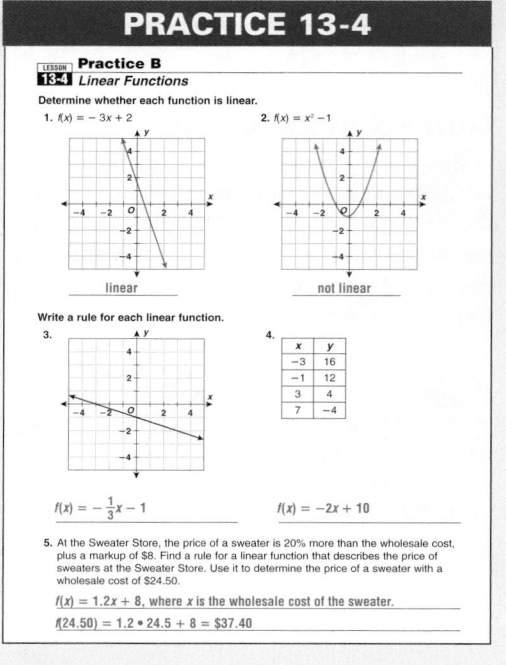

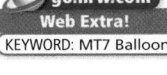
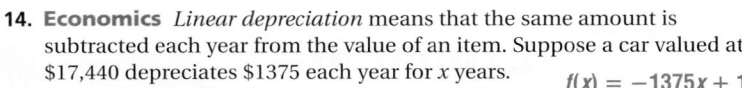

14. Economics *Linear depreciation* means that the same amount is subtracted each year from the value of an item. Suppose a car valued at $17,440 depreciates $1375 each year for x years. $f(x) = -1375x + 17,440$

  a. Write a linear function for the car's value after x years.

  b. What will the car's value be in 7 years? **$7815**

15. Recreation A hot air balloon at a height of 1245 feet above sea level is ascending at a rate of 5 feet per second. $f(x) = 5x + 1245$

  a. Write a linear function that describes the balloon's height after x seconds.

  b. What will the balloon's height be in 5 minutes? How high will it have climbed from its original starting point? **2745 ft; 1500 ft**

16. Business The table shows a carpenter's cost for wood and the price the carpenter charges the customer for the wood.

Carpenter Cost	$45	$52	$60.50	$80
Selling Price	$54	$62.40	$72.60	$96

  a. Write a linear function for the selling price of wood that costs the carpenter x dollars. $f(x) = 1.2x$

  b. If the cost to the carpenter is $340, what is the customer's cost? **$408**

17. What's the Question? Consider the function $f(x) = -2x + 6$. If the answer is -4, what is the question? **What is $f(5)$?**

18. Possible answer: If the exponent for x is 1, then the function is linear.

 **18. Write About It** Explain how you can determine whether a function is linear without graphing it or making a table of values.

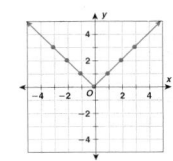 **19. Challenge** What is the only kind of line on a coordinate plane that is not a linear function? Give an example of such a line.
  a vertical line; possible answer: $x = 5$

TEST PREP and Spiral Review

20. Multiple Choice The function $f(x) = 12,800 - 1100x$ gives the value of a car x years after it was purchased. What will the car's value be in 8 years?

  (A) $4000 (B) $5100 (C) $6200 (D) $7300

21. Extended Response A swimming pool contains 1800 gallons of water. It is being drained at a rate of 50 gallons per minute. Find a rule for the linear function that describes the amount of water in the pool. Use the rule to determine the amount of water in the pool after 30 minutes. After how many minutes will the pool be empty? $f(t) = -50t + 1800$; 300 gal; 36 min

Multiply. Write each answer in simplest form. (Lesson 2-4)

22. $-8\left(3\frac{3}{4}\right)$ **−30** **23.** $\frac{6}{7}\left(\frac{7}{19}\right)$ **$\frac{6}{19}$** **24.** $-\frac{5}{8}\left(-\frac{6}{15}\right)$ **$\frac{1}{4}$** **25.** $-\frac{9}{10}\left(\frac{7}{12}\right)$ **$-\frac{21}{40}$**

Use a calculator to find each value. Round to the nearest tenth. (Lesson 4-6)

26. $\sqrt{35}$ **5.9** **27.** $\sqrt{45}$ **6.7** **28.** $\sqrt{55}$ **7.4** **29.** $\sqrt{65}$ **8.1**

TEST PREP DOCTOR In Exercise 20, make sure students follow the order of operations by multiplying 1100 times 8 before subtracting from 12,800. If students chose **B, C,** or **D,** they found the car's value after 7, 6, and 5 years.

 **Journal**

Have students write about why they think it might be helpful to write a rule for a function to represent a real-world situation, such as the one presented in Example 3.

Power Presentations
with PowerPoint®

13-4 Lesson Quiz

Determine whether each function is linear.

1. $f(x) = 4x^2$ not linear

2. $f(x) = 3x + 1$ linear

Write the rule for each linear function.

3.
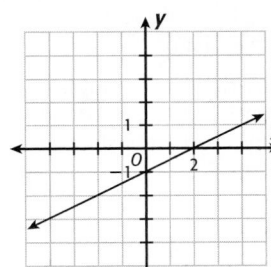

$f(x) = \frac{1}{2}x - 1$

4.
x	-3	0	3	5	7
y	-10	-1	8	14	20

$f(x) = 3x - 1$

5. Andre sells toys at the craft fair. He pays $60 to rent the booth. Materials for his toys are $4.50 per toy. Find a rule for the linear function that describes Andre's expenses for the day. Determine his expenses if he sold 25 toys.
$f(x) = 4.50x + 60$; $172.50

Also available on transparency

Objective: Students identify and graph exponential functions.

Technology Lab
In *Technology Lab Activities*

Online Edition
Tutorial Videos

Power Presentations
with PowerPoint®

Warm Up

Write the rule for each linear function.

1.

x	−2	−1	0	1	2
y	8	3	−2	−7	−12

$f(x) = -5x - 2$

2.

x	−3	0	3	5	7
y	0	6	12	16	20

$f(x) = 2x + 6$

Problem of the Day

One point on the graph of the mystery linear function is (4, 4). No value of *x* gives a *y*-value of 3. What is the mystery function? $y = 4$

Also available on transparency

Math Humor

The math student had trouble graphing the exponential function. No matter how hard he tried, he just couldn't get it straight.

State Resources

go.hrw.com

State Resources Online

KEYWORD: MT7 Resources

13-5 Exponential Functions

Learn to identify and graph exponential functions.

Vocabulary
exponential function
exponential growth
exponential decay

Many computer viruses spread automatically by sending copies of themselves to all of the contacts in a computer user's e-mail address book. Suppose a certain computer virus is sent to 15 computers and infects 60 computers in 2 hours, 240 computers in 4 hours, 960 computers in 6 hours, and so on. The number of computers infected would form a geometric sequence.

A function rule that describes the pattern is $f(x) = 15(4)^x$, where 15 is a_1, the starting number, and 4 is *r* the common ratio. This type of function is an **exponential function** .

FORM OF AN EXPONENTIAL FUNCTION

An exponential function has the form $f(x) = a_1 \cdot r^x$, where $a_1 \neq 0$, $r > 0$, and $r \neq 1$.

In an exponential function, the **y-intercept is $f(0) = a_1$.** The expression r^x is defined for all values of *x*, so the domain of $f(x) = a_1 \cdot r^x$ is all real numbers.

EXAMPLE 1 **Graphing Exponential Functions**

Create a table for each exponential function, and use it to graph the function.

A $f(x) = \frac{1}{2} \cdot 2^x$

x	y	
−2	$\frac{1}{8}$	$\frac{1}{2} \cdot 2^{-2} = \frac{1}{2} \cdot \frac{1}{4}$
−1	$\frac{1}{4}$	$\frac{1}{2} \cdot 2^{-1} = \frac{1}{2} \cdot \frac{1}{2}$
0	$\frac{1}{2}$	$\frac{1}{2} \cdot 2^0 = \frac{1}{2} \cdot 1$
1	1	$\frac{1}{2} \cdot 2^v = \frac{1}{2} \cdot 2$
2	2	$\frac{1}{2} \cdot 2^2 = \frac{1}{2} \cdot 4$

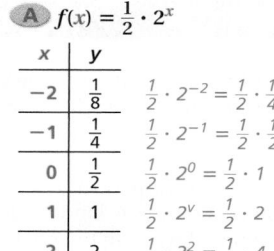
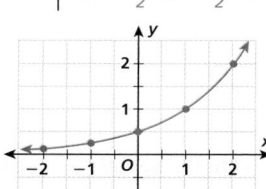

B $f(x) = 2 \cdot \left(\frac{1}{2}\right)^x$

x	y	
−2	8	$2 \cdot \left(\frac{1}{2}\right)^{-2} = 2 \cdot 4$
−1	4	$2 \cdot \left(\frac{1}{2}\right)^{-1} = 2 \cdot 2$
0	2	$2 \cdot \left(\frac{1}{2}\right)^0 = 2 \cdot 1$
1	1	$2 \cdot \left(\frac{1}{2}\right)^1 = 2 \cdot \frac{1}{2}$
2	$\frac{1}{2}$	$2 \cdot \left(\frac{1}{2}\right)^2 = 2 \cdot \frac{1}{4}$

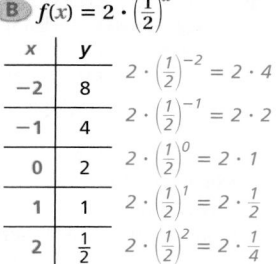
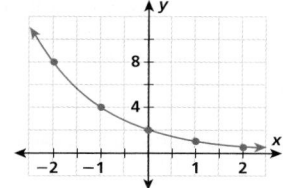

---

1 Introduce
Alternate Opener

EXPLORATION

 13-5 **Exponential Functions**

Scientists use *exponential functions* to make predictions about populations. Consider the model for a deer population, which begins with 1000 deer in year 0.

1. Use a calculator to complete the table.

Input x (year)	Rule 1000(1.1)^x	Output y (number of deer)
0	$1000(1.1)^0$	1000
1	$1000(1.1)^1$	1100
2	$1000(1.1)^2$	
3		
4		
10		

2. Determine the year in which the deer population will be greater than 3000 for the first time.

Think and Discuss

3. **Discuss** the difference between a linear function and an exponential function.

4. **Explain** what percent increase per year in the deer population the exponential model shows.

Motivate

Remind students that the terms in a geometric sequence can increase very quickly. Give them the example 2, 4, 8, 16, 32 . . . . Tell them that these terms could be generated by an exponential function of the form $y = 2^x$. Show students how the ordered pairs (1, 2), (2, 4), (3, 8), (4, 16), and (5, 32) satisfy this function.

Explorations and answers are provided in *Alternate Openers: Explorations Transparencies.*

In the exponential function $f(x) = a_1 \cdot r^x$ if $r > 1$, the output gets larger as the input gets larger. In this case, f is called an **exponential growth** function.

EXAMPLE 2 Using an Exponential Growth Function

An e-mail computer virus was initially sent to 15 different computers. After 2 hours, it had infected 60 computers, after 4 hours, 240 computers, and after 6 hours, 960 computers. If this trend continues, how many computers will be infected after 24 hours?

Hours Elapsed	0	2	4	6
Number of Two-Hour Intervals	0	1	2	3
Computers Infected	15	60	240	960

$f(x) = a_1 \cdot r^x$ *Write the function.*
$f(x) = 15 \cdot r^x$ *$f(0) = a_1$*
$f(x) = 15 \cdot 4^x$ *The common ratio is 4.*
24 hours is 12 two-hour intervals, so let $x = 12$.
$f(12) = 15 \cdot 4^{12} = 251{,}658{,}240$ *Substitute 12 for x.*
251,658,240 computers will be infected in 24 hours.

In the exponential function $f(x) = a_1 \cdot r^x$, if $r < 1$, the output gets smaller as x gets larger. In this case, f is called an **exponential decay** function.

EXAMPLE 3 Using an Exponential Decay Function

Technetium-99m has a *half-life* of 6 hours, which means it takes 6 hours for half of the substance to decompose. Find the amount of technetium-99m remaining from a 100 mg sample after 90 hours.

Hours	0	6	12	18	24
Number of Half-lives x	0	1	2	3	4
Technetium-99m $f(x)$ (mg)	100	50	25	12.5	6.25

$f(x) = a_1 \cdot r^x$ *Write the function.*
$f(x) = 100 \cdot r^x$ *$f(0) = a_1$*
$f(x) = 100 \cdot \left(\frac{1}{2}\right)^x$ *The common ratio is $\frac{1}{2}$.*
Divide 90 hours by 6 hours to find the number of half-lives: $x = 15$.
$f(15) = 100 \cdot \left(\frac{1}{2}\right)^{15} \approx 0.003$ *Substitute 15 for x.*
There is approximately 0.003 mg left after 90 hours.

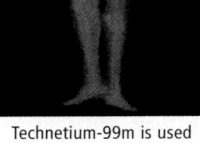

Physical Science

Technetium-99m is used to diagnose diseases in humans and animals.

Think and Discuss

1. Compare the graphs of exponential growth and decay functions.

Possible answers to Think and Discuss

1. The curves have the same basic shape, but they are reflections of each other over the y-axis. The curve in an exponential growth graph goes up and to the right, but the curve in an exponential decay graph goes down and to the right.

---

2 Teach

Guided Instruction

In this lesson, students learn to identify and graph exponential functions. Review positive and negative exponents with students. Although noninteger values of x are not covered in the lesson, you may want students to be aware that exponential functions are defined for these x-values and that calculators can demonstrate this. When students prepare their coordinate planes to graph the functions, suggest that they consider the ordered pairs they need to graph before they begin to number the axes.

Reaching All Learners

Through Cognitive Strategies

Have students work in groups of three. Give each group a piece of graph paper. Have each student in a group create a table of values for a different one of the three functions $f(x) = 2^x$, $f(x) = 3^x$, and $f(x) = 5^x$. When the three tables are completed, have the students graph their functions on the same graph. Then discuss the similarities and differences among the three graphs.

Possible answer: All graphs contain the point (0, 1) and have similar shapes, but larger a-values cause the graph to curve upward more sharply.

3 Close

Summarize

Remind students that exponential functions will either increase if the base is greater than one or decrease if the base is less than one. You may want to point out that exponential functions are used to model real-world situations that occur over relatively short periods of time. For example, the exponential model in Example 2 would break down at some point due to real-world limitations.

13-5 Exercises

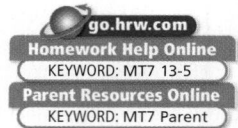

go.hrw.com
Homework Help Online
KEYWORD: MT7 13-5
Parent Resources Online
KEYWORD: MT7 Parent

Assignment Guide

If you finished Example **1** assign:
Average   1–6, 9–14, 17–20, 24, 33–38
Advanced   9–14, 17–26, 33–38

If you finished Example **2** assign:
Average   1–7, 9–15, 17–20, 24, 33–38
Advanced   9–15, 17–26, 33–38

If you finished Example **3** assign:
Average   1–20, 24, 28–30, 33–38
Advanced   9–38

Homework Quick Check

Quickly check key concepts.
Exercises: 12, 15, 16, 18, 24

Answers

1–6, 9–14, 24–26. See pp. A22–A23.

Math Background

The addition and subtraction operations are inverse functions, as are the multiplication and division operations. Another pair of inverse functions is $f(x) = x^2$ and $f(x) = \sqrt{x}$.

This section introduced one-half of another pair of inverse functions. The exponential function $f(x) = 10^x$ is the inverse function of $f(x) = \log_{10} x$. This pair of inverse functions will be explored in high school mathematics courses.

State Resources

go.hrw.com
State Resources Online
KEYWORD: MT7 Resources

GUIDED PRACTICE

See Example **1**   Create a table for each exponential function, and use it to graph the function.

1. $f(x) = 2^x$ **2.** $f(x) = 50 \cdot \left(\frac{1}{3}\right)^x$ **3.** $f(x) = 2 \cdot 3^x$

4. $f(x) = 0.02 \cdot 4^x$ **5.** $f(x) = 5 \cdot -(2^x)$ **6.** $f(x) = \frac{1}{2} \cdot 3^x$

See Example **2**   **7.** At the beginning of an experiment, a bacteria colony has a mass of 3×10^{-7} grams. If the mass of the colony triples every 10 hours, predict what the mass of the colony will be after 50 hours. **7.29 × 10⁻⁵ g**

See Example **3**   **8.** Radioactive glucose is used in cancer detection. It has a half-life of 100 minutes. Predict how much of a 100 mg sample remains after 24 hours.
≈ 0.0046 mg

INDEPENDENT PRACTICE

See Example **1**   Create a table for each exponential function, and use it to graph the function.

9. $f(x) = 2 \cdot 3^x$ **10.** $f(x) = -4(0.4)^x$ **11.** $f(x) = \left(\frac{3}{4}\right)^x$

12. $f(x) = 12\left(\frac{1}{6}\right)^x$ **13.** $f(x) = 1 \cdot 7^x$ **14.** $f(x) = 2.3 \cdot 5.1^x$

See Example **2**   **15.** A group of environmentalists preserved 300 exotic birds at a wildlife sanctuary. The population will triple every 6 years. Write an exponential function to calculate the number of birds that will be at the sanctuary at the end of each 6-year period. What will the predicted population be in 18 years?

15. $f(x) = 300 \cdot 3^x$; 8100 birds

See Example **3**   **16.** Cesium-137 is a radioactive element with a half-life of 30 years. It is used to study soil erosion. Predict how much of a 60 mg sample of cesium-137 would remain after 210 years. **0.46875 mg**

PRACTICE AND PROBLEM SOLVING

Extra Practice
See page 807.

For each exponential function, find $f(-3)$, $f(0)$, and $f(3)$.

17. $f(x) = 2^x$ **18.** $f(x) = 0.3^x$ **19.** $f(x) = 10^x$ **20.** $f(x) = 200 \cdot \left(\frac{1}{2}\right)^x$
$\frac{1}{8}$, 1, 8   **1600, 200, 25**

17. $\frac{1}{8}$, 1, 8

18. $\frac{1000}{27}$, 1, $\frac{27}{1000}$

19. $\frac{1}{1000}$, 1, 1000

Write the equation of the exponential function that passes through the given points. Use the form $f(x) = p \cdot a^x$.

21. (0, 3) and (1, 6)   **22.** (0, 6) and (1, 2)   **23.** (0, 1) and (2, 16)
$f(x) = 3 \cdot 2^x$ $f(x) = 6\left(\frac{1}{3}\right)^x$ $f(x) = 1 \cdot 4^x$

Graph the exponential function of the form $f(x) = p \cdot a^x$.

24. $p = 5, a = 3$ **25.** $p = -1, a = \frac{1}{4}$ **26.** $p = 100, a = 0.01$

27. Physical Science The current in a circuit dies off exponentially, losing half its strength every 2.5 milliseconds. Predict what percent of the original current remains after 15 milliseconds. **1.5625%**

RETEACH 13-5

A function that has the input value x in the exponent is called an **exponential function**. The base number a is positive. $f(x) = a^x$

<u>Situation 1</u> $a > 1$, say $a = 3$ <u>Situation 2</u> $a < 1$, say $a = \frac{1}{3}$

$f(x) = 3^x$ $f(x) = \left(\frac{1}{3}\right)^x$

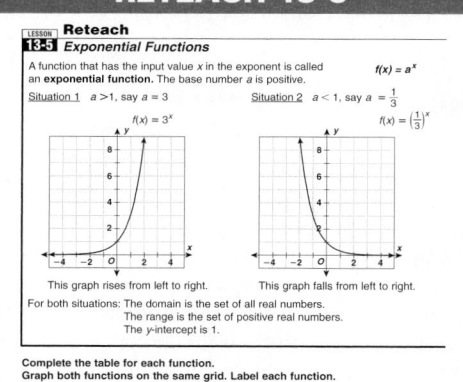

This graph rises from left to right.   This graph falls from left to right.

For both situations: The domain is the set of all real numbers.
The range is the set of positive real numbers.
The y-intercept is 1.

Complete the table for each function.
Graph both functions on the same grid. Label each function.

1. $f(x) = 2^x$

x	y
−2	$2^{-2} = \frac{1}{2^2}$ $= \frac{1}{4}$
−1	$2^{-1} = \frac{1}{2^1}$ $= \frac{1}{2}$
0	$2^0 = \frac{1}{2^0}$ $= 1$
1	$2^1 = 2$
2	$2^2 = 4$

2. $f(x) = \left(\frac{1}{2}\right)^x$

x	y
−2	$\left(\frac{1}{2}\right)^{-2} = \left(\frac{2}{1}\right)^2$ $= 4$
−1	$\left(\frac{1}{2}\right)^{-1} = \left(\frac{2}{1}\right)$ $= 2$
0	$\left(\frac{1}{2}\right)^0 = 1$
1	$\left(\frac{1}{2}\right)^1 = \frac{1}{2}$
2	$\left(\frac{1}{2}\right)^2 = \frac{1}{4}$

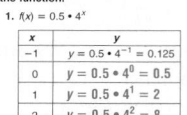

$y = \left(\frac{1}{2}\right)^x$ $y = 2^x$

PRACTICE 13-5

Create a table for each exponential function, and use it to graph the function.

1. $f(x) = 0.5 \cdot 4^x$

x	y
−1	$y = 0.5 \cdot 4^{-1} = 0.125$
0	$y = 0.5 \cdot 4^0 = 0.5$
1	$y = 0.5 \cdot 4^1 = 2$
2	$y = 0.5 \cdot 4^2 = 8$

2. $f(x) = \frac{1}{3} \cdot 3^x$

x	y
−1	$y = \frac{1}{3} \cdot 3^{-1} = \frac{1}{9}$
0	$y = \frac{1}{3} \cdot 3^0 = \frac{1}{3}$
1	$y = \frac{1}{3} \cdot 3^1 = 1$
2	$y = \frac{1}{3} \cdot 3^2 = 3$

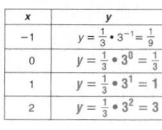

3. A forestry department introduce 500 fish to a lake. The fish are expected to increase at a rate of 35% each year. Write an exponential function to calculate the number of fish in the lake at the end of each year. Predict how many fish will be in the lake at the end of 5 years. $f(x) = 500 (1.35)^x$; 2242 fish

4. A stock valued at $756 has been declining steadily at the rate of 4% a year for the last few years. If this decline continues, predict what the value of the stock will be at the end of 3 years. $668.86

5. Todd's starting salary at his new job is $400 a week. He is promised a 3% increase in salary every year. Predict to the nearest dollar what Todd's expected yearly salary will be after working for 4 years. $23,411

Health LINK

The half-life of a substance in the body is the amount of time it takes for your body to metabolize half of the substance. An exponential decay function can be used to model the amount of the substance in the body.

Acetaminophen is the active ingredient in many pain and fever medications. Use the table for Exercises 28–30.

Acetaminophen Levels in the Body				
Elapsed Time (hr)	0	3	5	6
Substance Remaining (mg)	160	80	50.4	40

Vitamin deficiencies can cause serious diseases, such as scurvy, rickets, and beriberi.

28. How much acetaminophen was present initially? **160 mg**

29. Find the half-life of acetaminophen. Write an exponential function that describes the level of acetaminophen in the body.

30. If you take 500 mg of acetaminophen, what percent of that amount will be in your system after 9 hours? **12.5%**

31. ✏️ **Write About It** The half-life of vitamin C is about 6 hours. If you take a 60 mg vitamin C tablet at 9:00 A.M., how much of the vitamin will still be present in your system at 9:00 P.M.? Explain.

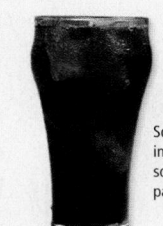

Sources of caffeine include coffee, sodas, and some pain medications.

32. ⭐ **Challenge** In children, the half-life of caffeine is about 3 hours. If a child has a 12 oz soft drink containing 40 mg caffeine at noon and another at 6:00 P.M., about how much caffeine will be present at 10:00 P.M.? **≈ 19.8 mg**

TEST PREP and Spiral Review

33. **Multiple Choice** The half-life of a particular radioactive isotope of thorium is 8 minutes. If 160 grams of the isotope are initially present, how many grams will remain after 40 minutes?

Ⓐ 1.25 grams Ⓑ 2.5 grams Ⓒ 5 grams Ⓓ 10 grams

34. **Gridded Response** Use the exponential function $f(x) = 5^x$. What is the value of $f(4)$? **625**

Find the volume of each cone to the nearest cubic unit. (Lesson 8-6)

35. radius 10 mm; height 12 mm **1257 mm³**   36. diameter 4 ft; height 5.7 ft **24 ft³**

Two fair number cubes are rolled. Find the probability of each event. (Lesson 10-4)

37. P(two odd numbers) $\frac{1}{4}$ 38. P(a two and a prime number) $\frac{1}{12}$

CHALLENGE 13-5

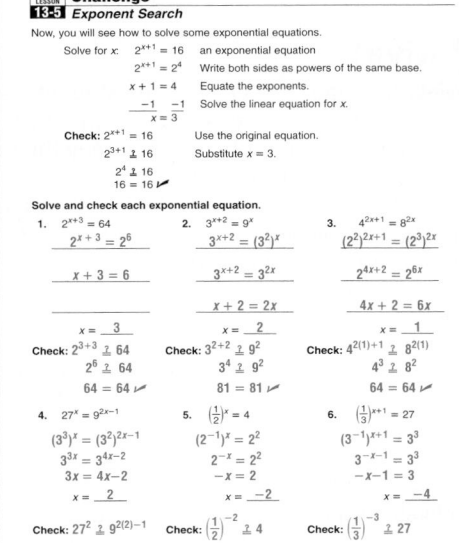

ONGOING ASSESSMENT and INTERVENTION ⬅️➡️

Diagnose Before the Lesson
13-5 Warm Up, TE p. 704

Monitor During the Lesson
13-5 Know-It Notebook
13-5 Questioning Strategies

Assess After the Lesson
13-5 Lesson Quiz, TE p. 707

Interdisciplinary LINK

Health

Exercises 28–32 involve using exponential functions to solve problems related to drug levels in the human body. Students learn about acetaminophen and other drugs in middle school health programs such as Holt, Rinehart & Winston's *Decisions for Health*.

Answers

29. 3 hr; $f(x) = 160 \cdot \left(\frac{1}{2}\right)^x$, where x is the number of 3-hour intervals.

31. See p. A23.

TEST PREP DOCTOR ➕ Students can use the exponential function $f(x) = 160\left(\frac{1}{2}\right)^5$ to solve Exercise 33. Remind them that they will need to divide 40 minutes by 8 minutes to get the number of half-lives, 5, for the function.

✏️ Journal

Tell students to imagine that they are archaeologists and that they have just discovered a mummy in an Egyptian tomb. Have them write about how they could find out how old the mummy is.

Power Presentations with PowerPoint®

✓ 13-5 Lesson Quiz

1. Create a table for the exponential function $f(x) = 3 \cdot \left(\frac{1}{2}\right)^x$, and use it to graph the function. See p. A23.

2. Linda invested $200 in an account that will double her balance every 3 years. Write an exponential function to calculate her account balance. What will her balance be in 12 years? $f(x) = 200 \cdot 2^x$, where x is the number of 3-year periods; $3200

Also available on transparency

PROBLEM SOLVING 13-5

Objective: Students identify and graph quadratic functions.

Hands-On Lab
In *Hands-On Lab Activities*

Technology Lab
In *Technology Lab Activities*

Online Edition
Tutorial Videos

Power Presentations
with PowerPoint®

Warm Up

Sandra is studying a bacteria colony that has a mass of 300 grams. If the mass of the colony doubles every 2 hours, what will its mass be after 20 hours? **307,200 grams**

Problem of the Day

The time t in seconds that it takes a penny to fall a certain distance d in feet can be modeled using the equation $t = \sqrt{\frac{2d}{32}}$. How much time will it take for a penny to fall 64 ft?
2 s

Also available on transparency

Math Humor

The baseball player understood linear functions but had trouble with quadratic functions. He never knew what to do when someone threw him a *curve*.

State Resources

go.hrw.com
State Resources Online
KEYWORD: MT7 Resources

13-6 Quadratic Functions

Learn to identify and graph quadratic functions.

Vocabulary
quadratic function
parabola

A **quadratic function** contains a variable that is squared. In the quadratic function
$$f(x) = ax^2 + bx + c$$
the y-intercept is c. The graphs of all quadratic functions have the same basic shape, called a **parabola** . The cross section of the large mirror in a telescope is a parabola. Because of a property of parabolas, starlight that hits the mirror is reflected toward a single point, called the *focus*.

The mirror of this telescope is made of liquid mercury that is rotated to form a parabolic shape.

EXAMPLE 1 **Graphing Quadratic Functions**

Create a table for each quadratic function, and use it to graph the function.

A $f(x) = x^2 - 3$

x	$f(x) = x^2 - 3$
-3	$(-3)^2 - 3 = 6$
-2	$(-2)^2 - 3 = 1$
-1	$(-1)^2 - 3 = -2$
0	$(0)^2 - 3 = -3$
1	$(1)^2 - 3 = -2$
2	$(2)^2 - 3 = 1$
3	$(3)^2 - 3 = 6$

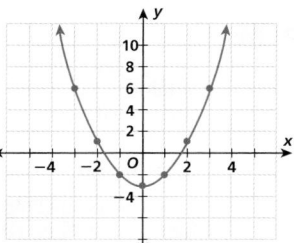

Plot the points and connect them with a smooth curve.

B $f(x) = x^2 + x - 2$

x	$f(x) = x^2 + x - 2$
-3	$(-3)^2 + (-3) - 2 = 4$
-2	$(-2)^2 + (-2) - 2 = 0$
-1	$(-1)^2 + (-1) - 2 = -2$
0	$(0)^2 + 0 - 2 = -2$
1	$(1)^2 + 1 - 2 = 0$
2	$(2)^2 + 2 - 2 = 4$
3	$(3)^2 + 3 - 2 = 10$

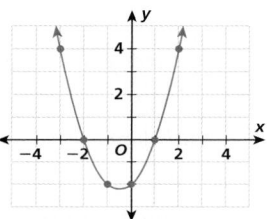

Plot the points and connect them with a smooth curve.

---

1 Introduce

Alternate Opener

EXPLORATION

13-6 Quadratic Functions

The variable in a *quadratic function* is squared. The graph of $y = (x - 2)(x + 3)$ shows that the function has two x-intercepts, $x = -3$ and $x = 2$, and one y-intercept, $y = -6$.

Graph each quadratic function on a graphing calculator. Use the given window settings to find the x- and y-intercepts.
1. $y = (x + 5)(x + 1)$ **2.** $y = (x - 4)(x - 2)$

 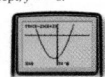

Think and Discuss
3. Discuss the relationship between the function rule and the intercepts, the points where the graph crosses the x- and y-axes.

Motivate

Review the types of functions the students have studied so far (linear and exponential). Ask students what happens when they throw a ball into the air. Does the ball travel in a straight line like a linear function? no Does it curve up and away forever like an exponential function? no Explain that the ball travels in a path that can be described by a new type of function.

Explorations and answers are provided in *Alternate Openers: Explorations Transparencies.*

EXAMPLE 2 *Astronomy Application*

In a *liquid mirror,* a container of liquid mercury is rotated around an axis. Gravity and centrifugal force cause the liquid to form a parabolic shape. The cross section of a liquid mirror that rotates at 10 revolutions per minute is approximated by the graph of $f(x) = 0.027x^2$. If the diameter of the mirror is 3 m, about how much higher are the sides than the center?

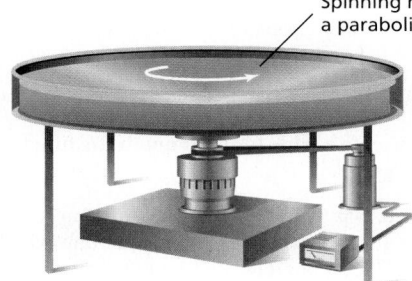

Spinning mercury forms a parabolic surface.

First create a table of values. Then graph the cross section.

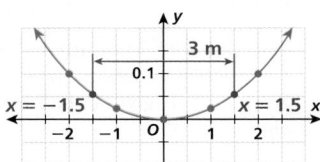

x	f(x)
−2	$0.027(−2)^2 = 0.108$
−1	$0.027(−1)^2 = 0.027$
0	$0.027(0)^2 = 0$
1	$0.027(1)^2 = 0.027$
2	$0.027(2)^2 = 0.108$

The center of the mirror is at $x = 0$, and the height is 0 m. If the diameter of the mirror is 3 m, the highest point on the sides is at $x = 1.5$. The height is $f(1.5) = 0.027(1.5)^2 \approx 0.06$ m. The sides are about 0.06 m higher than the center.

Possible answers to Think and Discuss

1. The graphs have the same shape, but the graph for $f(x) = x^2 + 1$ is translated up one unit.

2. a smooth line with line symmetry that is narrower at the bottom and continues to get wider as the x-values get farther away from 0.

Think and Discuss

1. **Compare** the graphs of $f(x) = x^2$ and $f(x) = x^2 + 1$.

2. **Describe** the shape of a parabola.

Example 1

Create a table for each quadratic function, and use it to graph the function.

A. $f(x) = x^2 + 1$

x	−2	−1	0	1	2
f(x)	5	2	1	2	5

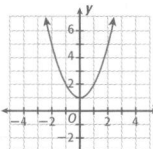

B. $f(x) = x^2 − x + 1$

x	−2	−1	0	1	2
f(x)	7	3	1	1	3

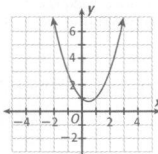

Example 2

A reflecting surface of a television antenna was formed by rotating the parabola $f(x) = 0.1x^2$ about its axis of symmetry. If the antenna has a diameter of 4 feet, about how much higher are the sides than the center? **0.4 ft**

Also available on transparency

---

② Teach

ENGLISH LANGUAGE LEARNERS

Guided Instruction

In this lesson, students learn to identify and graph quadratic functions. Explain that a *quadratic function* has a squared variable, such as x^2. Show the students that graphs of these functions are in a shape similar to the letter U and are called *parabolas.* Explain that in order to graph the quadratic functions, students will find ordered pairs in the same way they have done with previous functions. Help students recognize that vertical line symmetry exists in each of the parabolas.

Reaching All Learners
Through Visual Cues

Have students graph the following set of parabolas on the same coordinate plane: $f(x) = x^2$, $f(x) = x^2 + 2$, and $f(x) = x^2 + 4$. Ask them to identify any relationship between changes in the equations of the functions and changes in the graphs of the functions. Then ask them to test their hypotheses by guessing how the graphs $f(x) = x^2 − 2$ and $f(x) = x^2 − 4$ will look. Have students discuss their hypotheses and findings.

③ Close

Summarize

Remind students that the graph of a quadratic equation is a parabola with vertical line symmetry. Ask students to classify each function below as linear, exponential, or quadratic.

a. $f(x) = 2x^2 − 8x$ **b.** $f(x) = 4 − x$

c. $f(x) = 3 \cdot 3^x$ **d.** $f(x) = 3x + 8$

e. $f(x) = 2^x$ **f.** $f(x) = x^2 − 7$

a. quadratic; **b.** linear; **c.** exponential; **d.** linear; **e.** exponential; **f.** quadratic

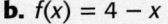

13-6 Exercises

go.hrw.com
Homework Help Online
KEYWORD: MT7 13-6
Parent Resources Online
KEYWORD: MT7 Parent

Assignment Guide

If you finished Example **1** assign:
Average 1–3, 5–7, 9–18, 28–35
Advanced 5–7, 9–19, 22, 26–35

If you finished Example **2** assign:
Average 1–18, 20, 21, 28–35
Advanced 5–12, 17–35

Homework Quick Check
Quickly check key concepts.
Exercises: 6, 8, 12, 18

Answers

1–3, 5–7, 15–19, 21. See p. A23.

Math Background

Some quadratic functions are given in what is called *factored form.* The benefit of presenting the functions in this way is that the *x*-intercepts can be quickly determined. The property involved is called the *Zero Product Property,* and it states that if the product of two factors is zero, then one or both of the factors must be zero. (If $ab = 0$, then $a = 0$ or $b = 0$.) Applying this property to a quadratic function in factored form yields the *x*-intercept(s). For example:

$$f(x) = (x - 4)(x + 6)$$
$$0 = (x - 4)(x + 6)$$
$$(x - 4) = 0 \text{ or } (x + 6) = 0$$
$$x = 4 \text{ or } \qquad x = -6$$

State Resources

go.hrw.com
State Resources Online
KEYWORD: MT7 Resources

GUIDED PRACTICE

See Example **1** Create a table for each quadratic function, and use it to graph the function.

1. $f(x) = x^2 + 5$ **2.** $f(x) = x^2 - 3$ **3.** $f(x) = x^2 + 1.5x$

See Example **2**   **4. Sports** The function $f(t) = -0.15t^2 + 2.4t + 5.1$ gives the height in feet of a baseball t seconds after it was thrown. What was the height of the baseball when it was initially thrown ($t = 0$)? **5.1 ft**

INDEPENDENT PRACTICE

See Example **1** Create a table for each quadratic function, and use it to graph the function.

5. $f(x) = x^2 + x + 2$ **6.** $f(x) = -x^2 + 2$ **7.** $f(x) = 3x^2 - 2$

See Example **2**   **8. Manufacturing** The function $f(x) = 2x^2 - 300x + 14{,}450$ gives the cost of manufacturing x items per day. Which number of items will give the lowest cost per day: 40, 75, or 90? What will the cost be? **75; \$3200**

PRACTICE AND PROBLEM SOLVING

Extra Practice
See page 807.

Find $f(-3)$, $f(0)$, and $f(3)$ for each quadratic function.

9. $f(x) = x^2 + 6$ **15, 6, 15**   **10.** $f(x) = \frac{1}{2}x^2$ **4.5, 0, 4.5**   **11.** $f(x) = x^2 + 3x$ **0, 0, 18**

12. $f(x) = x^2 + 9$ **0, −9, 0**   **13.** $f(x) = 3x^2 - x + 7$ **37, 7, 31**   **14.** $f(x) = \frac{x^2}{3} - 1$ **2, −1, 2**

Create a table for each quadratic function, and use it to find the *x*-intercepts.

15. $f(x) = (x - 4)(x + 12)$ **$x = 4$, $x = -12$**   **16.** $f(x) = (x - 2)(x - 5)$ **$x = 2$, $x = 5$**

17. $f(x) = (x - 1)(x + 3)$ **$x = 1$, $x = -3$**   **18.** $f(x) = x(x - 9)$ **$x = 0$, $x = 9$**

19. The sum of two numbers is 12. The sum of their squares is given by the function $f(x) = x^2 + (12 - x)^2$. Create a table of values using $x = 4, 5, 6, 7,$ and 8. Which pair of numbers gives the least sum of squares? What is the sum of their squares? **6 and 6; 72**

20. Hobbies The height of a model airplane launched from the top of a 24 ft hill is given by the function $f(t) = -0.08t^2 + 2.6t + 24$. Find the height of the airplane after 4, 8, and 16 seconds. Round to the nearest tenth of a foot. What can you tell about the direction of the airplane? **33.1 ft, 40 ft, 45 ft; the airplane is flying up.**

21. Physical Science The height of a toy rocket launched straight up with an initial velocity of 48 feet per second is given by the function $f(t) = 48t - 16t^2$. The time t is in seconds.

   a. Graph the function for $t = 0, 0.5, 1, 1.5, 2, 2.5,$ and 3.

   b. When is the rocket at its highest point? What is its height? **$t = 1.5$ s; 36 ft**

   c. How many seconds does it take for the rocket to land? **3 s**

RETEACH 13-6

LESSON 13-6 Reteach
Quadratic Functions

A **quadratic function** has a variable that is squared.

general quadratic function $f(x) = ax^2 + bx + c$
        square term   y-intercept
        $f(x) = x^2 - 4x + 3$

The graph of a quadratic function is a **parabola**, a curve that falls on one side of a turning point and rises on the other. You can make a table of a function's values and use them to graph the function.

x	$f(x) = x^2 - 4x + 3$
−1	$f(-1) = (-1)^2 - 4(-1) + 3 = 8$
0	$f(0) = 0^2 - 4(0) + 3 = 3$
1	$f(1) = 1^2 - 4(1) + 3 = 0$
2	$f(2) = 2^2 - 4(2) + 3 = -1$
3	$f(3) = 3^2 - 4(3) + 3 = 0$
4	$f(4) = 4^2 - 4(4) + 3 = 3$
5	$f(5) = 5^2 - 4(5) + 3 = 8$

Complete the table for the quadratic function and use it to graph the function.

1. $f(x) = x^2 - 2x - 3$

x	$f(x) = x^2 - 2x - 3$
−2	$f(-2) = (-2)^2 - 2(-2) - 3 = 5$
−1	$f(-1) = (-1)^2 - 2(-1) - 3 = 0$
0	$f(0) = (0)^2 - 2(0) - 3 = -3$
1	$f(1) = (1)^2 - 2(1) - 3 = -4$
2	$f(2) = (2)^2 - 2(2) - 3 = -3$
3	$f(3) = (3)^2 - 2(3) - 3 = 0$
4	$f(4) = (4)^2 - 2(4) - 3 = 5$

PRACTICE 13-6

LESSON 13-6 Practice B
Quadratic Functions

Create a table for each quadratic function, and use it to make a graph.

1. $f(x) = x^2 - 5$

x	$f(x) = x^2 - 5$
−3	$f(-3) = (-3)^2 - 5 = 4$
−1	$f(-1) = (-1)^2 - 5 = -4$
0	$f(0) = (0)^2 - 5 = -5$
2	$f(2) = (2)^2 - 5 = -1$
3	$f(3) = (3)^2 - 5 = 4$

2. $f(x) = x^2 - 2x + 3$

x	$f(x) = x^2 - 2x + 3$
3	$f(3) = (3)^2 - 2(3) + 3 = 6$
2	$f(2) = (2)^2 - 2(2) + 3 = 3$
1	$f(1) = (1)^2 - 2(1) + 3 = 2$
0	$f(0) = (0)^2 - 2(0) + 3 = 3$
−1	$f(-1) = (-1)^2 - 2(-1) + 3 = 6$

3. Find $f(-3)$, $f(0)$, $f(3)$ for each quadratic function.

	$f(-3)$	$f(0)$	$f(3)$
$f(x) = x^2 - 2x + 1$	16	1	4
$f(x) = x^2 - 6$	3	−6	3
$f(x) = x^2 - x + 3$	15	3	9

4. The function $f(t) = -4.9t^2$ gives the distance in meters that an object will fall toward Earth in t seconds. Find the distance an object will fall in 1, 2, 3, 4, and 5 seconds. (Note that the distance traveled by a falling object is shown by a negative number.)

4.9 m, 19.6 m, 44.1 m, 78.4 m, and 122.5 m

22. The graph of a linear function is a straight line. The graph of a quadratic function is a parabola. The linear function equation contains a variable to the first power. The quadratic function equation contains a variable squared.

22. Describe the difference between a linear function and a quadratic function in terms of their graphs and their function equations.

23. Business A store owner can sell 30 digital cameras a week at a price of $150 each. For every $5 drop in price, she can sell 2 more cameras a week. If x is the number of $5 price reductions, the weekly sales function is $f(x) = (30 + 2x)(150 - 5x)$.

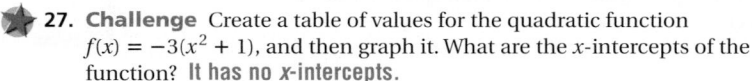

Predicted Sales			
Price	$150	$145	$140
Number Sold	30	32	34
Weekly Sales	$4500	$4640	$4760

a. Find $f(x)$ for $x = 3, 4, 5, 6,$ and 7.

b. How many $5 price reductions will result in the highest weekly sales? **7**

23a.
$4860, $4940, $5000, $5040, $5060

24. Critical Thinking The height of an object dropped from the top of a 16 ft ladder is given by the function $f(t) = -t^2 + 16$. Find $f(4)$. What does this tell you about $t = 4$ seconds? Does this equation seem more realistic for dropping a rock or a feather? Explain.

25. Choose a Strategy Suppose the function $f(x) = -5x^2 + 300x + 1250$ gives a company's profit for producing x items. How many items should be produced to maximize profit?

Ⓐ 25   Ⓑ 30   Ⓒ 35   Ⓓ 40

26. Write About It Which will grow faster as x gets larger, $f(x) = x^2$ or $f(x) = 2^x$? Check by testing each function for several values of x.

27. Challenge Create a table of values for the quadratic function $f(x) = -3(x^2 + 1)$, and then graph it. What are the x-intercepts of the function? **It has no x-intercepts.**

TEST PREP and Spiral Review

28. Multiple Choice The height of a tennis ball thrown straight up with an initial velocity of 64 meters per second is given by the function $f(t) = 64t - 16t^2$. The time t is in seconds. How many seconds does it take for the tennis ball to land?

Ⓕ 0 s   Ⓖ 4 s   Ⓗ 16 s   Ⓙ 64 s

29. Gridded Response What is the positive x-intercept of the quadratic function $f(x) = x^2 + 2x - 36$?   **7**

The scale of a drawing is 2 in. = 3 ft. Find the actual measurement for each length in the drawing. (Lesson 5-8)

30. 1 in. **1.5 ft**   **31.** 5 in. **7.5 ft**   **32.** 12 in. **18 ft**   **33.** 8.5 in. **12.75 ft**

Find the first and third quartiles for each data set. (Lesson 9-4)

34. 55, 60, 40, 45, 70, 65, 35, 40, 75, 50, 60, 80   **35.** 52, 22, 18, 30, 41, 23, 31, 23, 39, 37
23, 39   **45, 65**

CHALLENGE 13-6

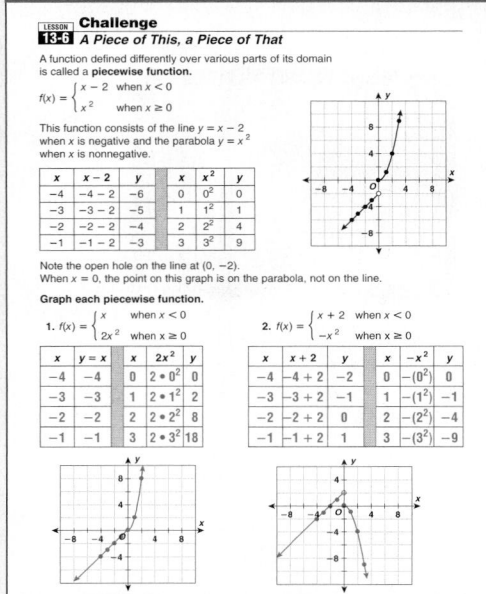

Challenge
13-6 *A Piece of This, a Piece of That*

A function defined differently over various parts of its domain is called a *piecewise function*.

$f(x) = \begin{cases} x - 2 & \text{when } x < 0 \\ x^2 & \text{when } x \geq 0 \end{cases}$

This function consists of the line $y = x - 2$ when x is negative and the parabola $y = x^2$ when x is nonnegative.

x	$x-2$	y		x	x^2	y
−4	−4−2	−6		0	0^2	0
−3	−3−2	−5		1	1^2	1
−2	−2−2	−4		2	2^2	4
−1	−1−2	−3		3	3^2	9

Note the open hole on the line at (0, −2). When $x = 0$, the point on this graph is on the parabola, not on the line.

Graph each piecewise function.

1. $f(x) = \begin{cases} x & \text{when } x < 0 \\ 2x^2 & \text{when } x \geq 0 \end{cases}$

x	$y=x$		x	$2x^2$	y
−4	−4		0	$2 \cdot 0^2$	0
−3	−3		1	$2 \cdot 1^2$	2
−2	−2		2	$2 \cdot 2^2$	8
−1	−1		3	$2 \cdot 3^2$	18

2. $f(x) = \begin{cases} x + 2 & \text{when } x < 0 \\ -x^2 & \text{when } x \geq 0 \end{cases}$

x	$x+2$	y		x	$-x^2$	y
−4	−4+2	−2		0	$-(0^2)$	0
−3	−3+2	−1		1	$-(1^2)$	−1
−2	−2+2	0		2	$-(2^2)$	−4
−1	−1+2	1		3	$-(3^2)$	−9

PROBLEM SOLVING 13-6

Problem Solving
13-6 *Quadratic Functions*

To find the time it takes an object to fall, you can use the equation $h = -16t^2 - vt + s$ where h is the height in feet, t is the time in seconds, v is the initial velocity, and s is the starting height in feet. Write the correct answer.

1. If a construction worker drops a tool from 240 feet above the ground, how many feet above the ground will it be in 2 seconds? Hint: $v = 0$, $s = 240$.

176 feet

2. How long will it take the tool in Exercise 1 to hit the ground? Round to the nearest hundredth.

3.87 seconds

3. The Gateway Arch in St. Louis, Missouri is the tallest manmade memorial. The arch rises to a height of 630 feet. If you throw a rock down from the top of the arch with a velocity of 20 ft/s, how many feet above the ground will the rock be in 2 seconds?

526 feet

4. Will the rock in exercise 3 hit the ground within 6 seconds of throwing it?

yes

The average monthly rainfall for Seattle, Washington can be approximated by the equation $f(x) = 0.147x^2 - 1.890x + 7.139$ where x is the month (January: $x = 1$, February, $x = 2$, etc.) and $f(x)$ is the monthly rainfall in inches. Choose the letter for the best answer.

5. What is the average monthly rainfall in Seattle for the month of January?
A 3.7 in   C 7.6 in
Ⓑ 5.4 in   D 9.2 in

6. What is the average monthly rainfall in Seattle for the month of April?
F 0.2 in   Ⓗ 1.9 in
G 1.4 in   J 2.8 in

7. What is the average monthly rainfall in Seattle for the month of August?
A 1.1 in   C 5.6 in
Ⓑ 1.4 in   D 6.8 in

8. In what month does it rain the least in Seattle, Washington?
F May   H July
Ⓖ June   J August

Answers
24, 26–27. See pp. A23–A24.

TEST PREP DOCTOR ➕ For Exercise 28, students can eliminate choice **F** because 0 seconds is not feasible. Choices **H** and **J** can also be quickly eliminated because they will result in a negative height.

Journal
Ask students to write about why a negative x-value will often produce a positive y-value in a quadratic function.

Power Presentations with PowerPoint®

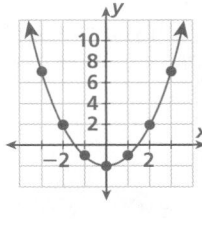

13-6 Lesson Quiz
Create a table for each quadratic function, and use it to graph the function.

1. $f(x) = x^2 - 2$

x	$f(x)$
−3	7
−2	2
−1	−1
0	−2
1	−1
2	2
3	7

2. $f(x) = x^2 + x - 6$

x	$f(x)$
−3	0
−2	−4
−1	−6
0	−6
1	−4
2	0
3	6

3. The function $f(t) = 40t - 5t^2$ gives the height of an arrow in meters t seconds after it is shot upward. What is the height of the arrow after 5 seconds? **75 m**

Also available on transparency

Pacing:
Traditional $\frac{1}{2}$ day
Block $\frac{1}{4}$ day

Objective: Use a graphing calculator to explore cubic functions.

Materials: Graphing calculator

 Online Edition
Graphing Calculator, TechKeys

Resources

 Technology Lab Activities
Lab 13-6 Recording Sheet

Teach
Discuss

Have students use the Table feature to make a table of values for $y = 3x - 4$. Then find the value of x when $y = 5$. 3 Discuss how this solution method relates to solving by graphing.

Close
Key Concept

You can use a calculator to analyze how geometric and algebraic properties of functions are related.

Assessment

1. What sequence of keystrokes is needed to graph the cubic function $y = x^3 - 2x^2 + 3x - 4$?

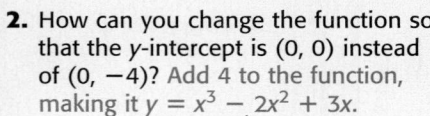

2. How can you change the function so that the y-intercept is (0, 0) instead of (0, −4)? Add 4 to the function, making it $y = x^3 - 2x^2 + 3x$.

State Resources

 **go.hrw.com**
State Resources Online
KEYWORD: MT7 Resources

Technology

 **LAB** **Explore Cubic Functions**
13-6

Use with Lesson 13-6

 **go.hrw.com**
Lab Resources Online
KEYWORD: MT7 Lab13

You can use your graphing calculator to explore cubic functions. To graph the cubic equation $y = x^3$ in the standard graphing calculator window, press [Y=] ; enter the right side of the equation, [X,T,θ,n] [∧] 3; and press [ZOOM] **6:ZStandard**. Notice that the graph goes from the lower left to the upper right and crosses the x-axis once, at $x = 0$.

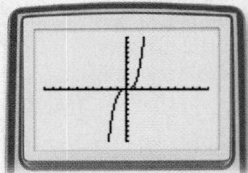

Activity 1

① Graph $y = -x^3$. Describe the graph.

Press [Y=] , and enter the right side of the equation,
[(−)] [X,T,θ,n] [∧] 3.

The graph goes from the upper left to the lower right and crosses the x-axis once.

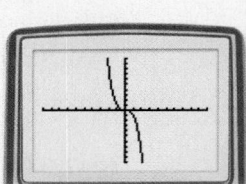

② Graph $y = x^3 + 3x^2 - 2$. Describe the graph.

Press [Y=] ; enter the right side of the equation,
[X,T,θ,n] [∧] 3 [+] 3 [X,T,θ,n] [x²] [−] 2;
and press [ZOOM] **6:ZStandard**.

The graph goes from the lower left to the upper right and crosses the x-axis three times.

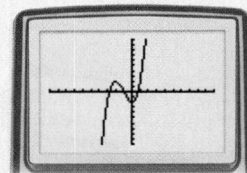

The sign determines whether the cubic curve rises or falls from left to right.

Think and Discuss

1. How does the sign of the x^3-term affect the graph of a cubic function?

2. How could you find the value of 8^3 from the graph of $y = x^3$?
Use the TRACE feature to trace until $x = 8$. The y-value gives 8^3.

Try This

Graph each function and describe the graph.

1. $y = x^3 - 3$ **2.** $y = x^3 + 4x^2 - 3$ **3.** $y = (x - 3)^3$ **4.** $y = 6 - x^3$

Activity 1
Answers to *Try This*

1.

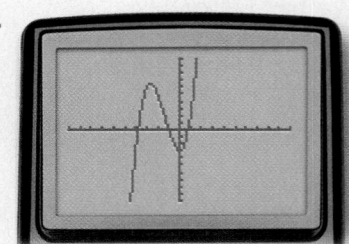

The graph goes from the lower left to the upper right, crosses the y-axis at $y = -3$, and crosses the x-axis once.

2.

The graph goes from the lower left to the upper right, crosses the y-axis at $y = -3$, and crosses the x-axis three times.

1 Compare the graphs of $y = x^3$ and $y = x^3 + 3$.

Graph **Y₁=X^3** and **Y₂=X^3+3** on the same screen, as shown. Use the **TRACE** button and the ◀ and ▶ buttons to trace to any integer value of x. Then use the ▲ and ▼ keys to move from one function to the other to compare the values of y for both functions for the value of x. You can also press **2nd** **GRAPH** (TABLE) to see a table of values for both functions.

The graph of $y = x^3 + 3$ is translated up 3 units from the graph of $y = x^3$.

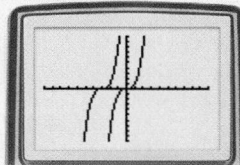

2 Compare the graphs of $y = x^3$ and $y = (x + 3)^3$.

Graph **Y₁=X^3** and **Y₂=(X+3)^3** on the same screen. Notice that the graph of $y = (x + 3)^3$ is the graph of $y = x^3$ moved left 3 units. Press **2nd** **GRAPH** (TABLE) to see a table of values. The graph of $y = (x + 3)^3$ is translated left 3 units from the graph of $y = x^3$.

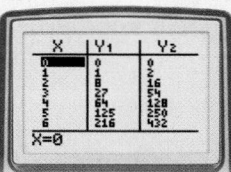

3 Compare the graphs of $y = x^3$ and $y = 2x^3$.

Graph **Y₁=X^3** and **Y₂=2X^3** on the same screen. Use the **TRACE** button and the arrow keys to see the values of y for any value of x. Press **2nd** **GRAPH** (TABLE) to see a table of values.

The graph of $y = 2x^3$ is stretched upward from the graph of $y = x^3$. The y-value for $y = 2x^3$ increases twice as fast as it does for $y = x^3$. The table of values is shown.

Think and Discuss

1. What function would translate $y = x^3$ right 5 units? $y = (x - 5)^3$

2. Do you think that the methods shown of translating a cubic function would have the same result on a quadratic function? Explain.
Yes; adding and subtracting numbers from a function will always have the same effect because the y-value will be changed in the same way.

Try This

Compare the graph of $y = x^3$ to the graph of each function.

1. $y = x^3 - 3$	**2.** $y = (x - 8)^3$	**3.** $y = \left(\frac{1}{3}\right)x^3$	**4.** $y = 7 - x^3$
The graph is translated 3 units down.	The graph is translated 8 units right.	The graph is flattened.	The graph is reflected over the x-axis and moved 7 units up.

Activity 1

Answers to *Try This*

3.

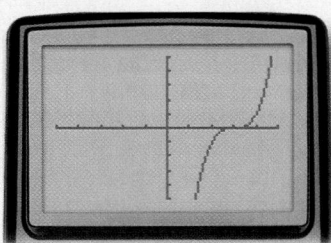

The graph goes from the lower left to the upper right, it is translated three units to the right, and crosses the x-axis once.

4.

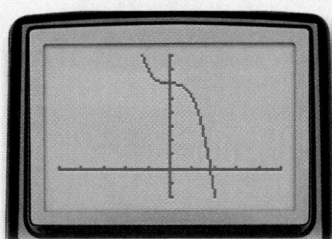

The graph goes from the upper left to the lower right, crosses the y-axis at $y = 6$, and crosses the x-axis once.

Objective: Students recognize inverse variation by graphing tables of data.

 **Online Edition**
  Tutorial Videos

Power Presentations
  with PowerPoint®

Warm Up

Find $f(-4)$, $f(0)$, and $f(3)$ for each quadratic function.

1. $f(x) = x^2 + 4$ 20, 4, 13

2. $f(x) = \frac{1}{4}x^2$ 4, 0, $\frac{9}{4}$

3. $f(x) = 2x^2 - x + 3$ 39, 3, 18

Problem of the Day

Use the digits 1–8 to fill in 3 pairs of values in the table of a direct variation function. Use each digit exactly once. The 2 and 3 have already been used.

x	8	32	56
y	1	4	7

Also available on transparency

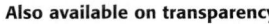 **Math Humor**

Teacher: Why did you turn in this poem?

Student: You said you wanted an example of *in verse* variation!

 *State Resources*

go.hrw.com
State Resources Online
KEYWORD: MT7 Resources

13-7 Inverse Variation

41.2Hz

82.4Hz

164.8Hz

Learn to recognize inverse variation by graphing tables of data.

Vocabulary
  inverse variation

The frequency of a string on a double bass is related to its length. You can double a string's frequency by placing your finger at the halfway point of the string. The lowest note on a standard double bass is E_1. As you place your fingers at various fractions of the string's length, the frequency will *vary inversely.*

Full length: **41.2 Hz**
$\frac{1}{2}$ the length: **82.4 Hz**
$\frac{1}{4}$ the length: **164.8 Hz**

The fraction of the string length times the frequency is always 41.2.

INVERSE VARIATION		
Words	**Numbers**	**Algebra**
An **inverse variation** is a relationship in which one variable quantity increases as another variable quantity decreases. The product of the variables is a **constant**.	$y = \frac{120}{x}$ $xy = 120$	$y = \frac{k}{x}$ $xy = k$ $(k \neq 0)$

EXAMPLE 1 **Identifying Inverse Variation**

Determine whether each relationship is an inverse variation.

A The table shows the number of days needed to build a house based on the size of the work crew.

Crew Size	3	4	6	12	24
Days of Construction	56	42	28	14	7

Helpful Hint

To determine if a relationship is an inverse variation, check if the product of x and y is always the same number.

$3(56) = 168; 4(42) = 168; 6(28) = 168; 12(14) = 168; 24(7) = 168$
$xy = 168$ *The product is always the same.*
The relationship shows an inverse variation: $y = \frac{168}{x}$.

B The table shows the number of CDs produced in a given time.

CDs Produced	52	78	104	130	143	169
Time (min)	4	6	8	10	11	13

$52(4) = 208; 78(6) = 468$ *The product is not always the same.*
The relationship is not an inverse variation.

---

1 Introduce

Alternate Opener

EXPLORATION

13-7 **Inverse Variation**

In an *inverse variation*, when one quantity increases, the other decreases.

Water pressure is measured in pounds per square inch (psi). Water pressure decreases as the height at which each home is located increases.

C

Height: 60 ft
Pressure: ?

B

Height: 30 ft
Pressure: 30 psi

A

Height: 15 ft
Pressure: 60 psi

Water pump

1. For house A and house B, multiply the water pressure by the height at which each house is located.

2. What do you notice about the products in Problem 1?

3. Predict the water pressure for house C.

Think and Discuss

4. Explain how you predicted the water pressure for house C.

5. Give another example of an inverse variation.

Motivate

ENGLISH LANGUAGE LEARNERS

Remind students of the formula for direct variation, $y = kx$ (Lesson 12-5). Point out that direct variation means that the quantities change *directly* with each other. That means if one increases, the other increases, and vice-versa. Ask students if they know the meaning of the word *inverse.* opposite or reverse Ask students to guess what happens in *inverse variation.* As one quantity increases, the other decreases.

Explorations and answers are provided in *Alternate Openers: Explorations Transparencies.*

In the inverse variation relationship $y = \frac{k}{x}$, where $k \neq 0$, y is a function of x. The function is not defined for $x = 0$, so the domain is all real numbers except 0.

EXAMPLE 2 Graphing Inverse Variations

Create a table. Then graph each inverse variation function.

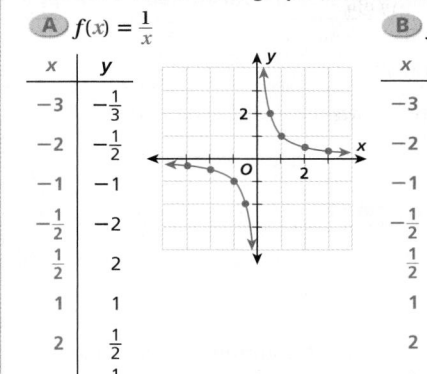

A $f(x) = \frac{1}{x}$

x	y
−3	$-\frac{1}{3}$
−2	$-\frac{1}{2}$
−1	−1
$-\frac{1}{2}$	−2
$\frac{1}{2}$	2
1	1
2	$\frac{1}{2}$
3	$\frac{1}{3}$

B $f(x) = \frac{-2}{x}$

x	y
−3	$\frac{2}{3}$
−2	1
−1	2
$-\frac{1}{2}$	4
$\frac{1}{2}$	−4
1	−2
2	−1
3	$-\frac{2}{3}$

EXAMPLE 3 *Music Application*

The frequency of a double bass string changes according to the fraction of its length that is allowed to vibrate. Find the inverse variation function, and use it to find the resulting frequency when $\frac{1}{16}$ of the string E_1 is allowed to vibrate.

Frequency of E_1 by Fraction of the Original String Length				
Frequency (Hz)	41.2	82.4	164.8	329.6
Fraction of the Length	1	$\frac{1}{2}$	$\frac{1}{4}$	$\frac{1}{8}$

You can see from the table that $xy = 41.2(1) = 41.2$. So $y = \frac{41.2}{x}$. If the string is reduced to $\frac{1}{16}$ of its length, then its frequency will be $y = 41.2 \div \left(\frac{1}{16}\right) = 41.2 \cdot 16 = 659.2$ Hz. This note is called E_5.

Answers to *Think and Discuss*

1. $k = 3$

2. Possible answer: one quantity increases as the other decreases, and the product of the x- and y-values is a constant number

Think and Discuss

1. Identify k in the inverse variation $y = \frac{3}{x}$.

2. Describe how you know if a relationship is an inverse variation.

---

2 Teach

Guided Instruction

In this lesson, students learn to recognize inverse variation by graphing tables of data. Introduce students to the concept of *inverse variation* and its formula. As you work through the examples, point out that one quantity increases as the other decreases, but emphasize that this alone does not make inverse variation. In inverse variation, the product of the x- and y-values must be constant.

Reaching All Learners
Through Inclusion

Display three cylinders with the same height but increasing diameter. Tell students that the first cylinder is full of water. Discuss where they think the water height on the other cylinders would be if the water from the first cylinder is poured into them. Explain that the amount of water remains constant, and as the diameter of the cylinders increase, the height of the water decreases. Allow students to experiment and record data if desired. Discuss how this illustrates an inverse variation relationship. The diameter and height vary inversely.

3 Close

Summarize

Remind students that in an inverse variation, the product of the x-value and the y-value in each ordered pair is a constant. When graphing an inverse variation, the graph is a pair of curves.

13-7 Exercises

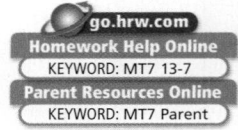

go.hrw.com
Homework Help Online
KEYWORD: MT7 13-7
Parent Resources Online
KEYWORD: MT7 Parent

Assignment Guide

If you finished Example **1** assign:
Average 1, 2, 8, 9, 25–32
Advanced 8, 9, 15–17, 23, 25–32

If you finished Example **2** assign:
Average 1–6, 8–13, 25–32
Advanced 8–13, 15–17, 23, 25–32

If you finished Example **3** assign:
Average 1–18, 20, 23, 25–32
Advanced 8–32

Homework Quick Check

Quickly check key concepts.
Exercises: 8, 10, 14, 16

Answers

3–6, 10–13. See p. A24.

Math Background

When a function of the form $y = \frac{k}{x}$ ($k \neq 0$) is graphed, it does not intersect the x-axis or the y-axis but continues to get closer and closer to each axis. When a curve gets and stays arbitrarily close to a line, the line is called an *asymptote.* The reason that the x-axis is an asymptote is that as the x-values increase, the y-values continue to decrease but never reach zero. The y-axis is an asymptote because as x-values decrease, the y-values continue to increase toward infinity but never reach infinity.

State Resources

go.hrw.com
State Resources Online
KEYWORD: MT7 Resources

GUIDED PRACTICE

See Example **1** Determine whether each relationship is an inverse variation.

1. The table shows the number of soccer balls produced in a given time. no

Soccer Balls Produced	56	98	122	168	210
Time (min)	4	7	8	12	15

2. The table shows the painting time of a new house based on the number of workers. yes

Painting Time (hr)	6	7	10.5	21	42
Number of Workers	7	6	4	2	1

See Example **2** Create a table. Then graph each inverse variation function.

3. $f(x) = \frac{4}{x}$ **4.** $f(x) = \frac{3}{x}$ **5.** $f(x) = \frac{1}{3x}$ **6.** $f(x) = \frac{2}{3x}$

See Example **3** **7.** Ohm's law relates the current in a circuit to the resistance. Find the inverse variation function, and use it to find the current in a 12-volt circuit with 16 ohms of resistance.

Current (amps)	0.15	0.2	1	3	6
Resistance (ohms)	80	60	12	4	2

$y = \frac{12}{x}$; $\frac{3}{4}$ amps

INDEPENDENT PRACTICE

See Example **1** Determine whether each relationship is an inverse variation.

8. The table shows the time it takes a model car to travel a certain distance, depending on the speed of the car. yes

Speed of Car (ft/s)	40	48	60	80	120
Time (s)	3	2.5	2	1.5	1

9. The table shows the number of miles bicycled in a given time. no

Miles Bicycled	1	2	2.5	5	6
Time (min)	6	12	15	30	36

See Example **2** Create a table. Then graph each inverse variation function.

10. $f(x) = -\frac{2}{x}$ **11.** $f(x) = \frac{1}{4x}$ **12.** $f(x) = -\frac{1}{3x}$ **13.** $f(x) = -\frac{4}{5x}$

See Example **3** **14.** According to Boyle's law, when the volume of a gas decreases, the pressure increases. Find the inverse variation function, and use it to find the pressure of the gas if the volume is decreased to 8 liters.

Volume (L)	2	4	25	40	50
Pressure (atm)	20	10	1.6	1	0.8

$y = \frac{40}{x}$; 5 atm

RETEACH 13-7

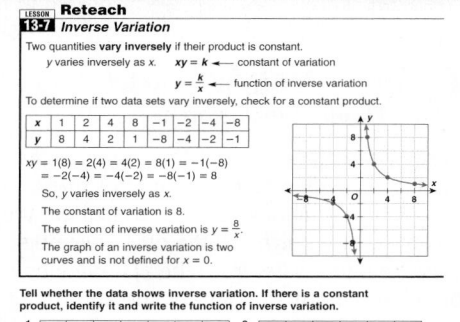

PRACTICE 13-7

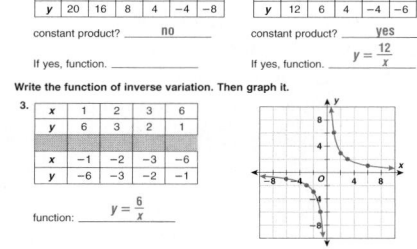

PRACTICE AND PROBLEM SOLVING

Extra Practice
See page 807.

Find the inverse variation equation, given that x and y vary inversely.

15. $y = 3$ when $x = 3$ $y = \dfrac{9}{x}$ 16. $y = 10$ when $x = 2$ $y = \dfrac{20}{x}$ 17. $y = 13$ when $x = 2$ $y = \dfrac{26}{x}$

18. If y varies inversely with x and $y = 24$ when $x = 4$, find k.   **96**

19. The height of a triangle with area 72 cm^2 varies inversely with the length of its base. If $b = 48$ cm when $h = 3$ cm, find b when $h = 12$ cm.   **12 cm**

20. **Physical Science** If a constant force of 20 newtons (N) is applied to an object, the mass of the object varies inversely with its acceleration. The table contains data for several objects of different sizes.

Mass (kg)	2	5	20	10	4
Acceleration (m/s²)	10	4	1	2	5

a. Use the table to write an inverse variation function. $y = \dfrac{20}{x}$

b. What is the mass of an object if its acceleration is 8 m/s^2?   **2.5 kg**

21. **Finance** Mr. Anderson wants to earn $50 in interest over a 1-year period from a savings account. The principal he must deposit varies inversely with the interest rate of the account. If the interest rate is 5%, he must deposit $1000. If the interest rate is 3.125%, how much must he deposit?   **$1600**

 22. **Write a Problem** Write a problem that can be solved using inverse variation. Use facts and formulas from your science book. **Check students' work.**

 23. **Write About It** Explain the difference between direct variation and inverse variation.

24. **Challenge** The resistance of a 100 ft piece of wire varies inversely with the square of its diameter. If the diameter of the wire is 3 in., it has a resistance of 3 ohms. What is the resistance of a wire with a diameter of 1 in.?   **27 ohms**

23.
Possible answer:
In direct
variation,
the variables
increase or
decrease
together. It
is of the form
$y = kx$.
In inverse
variation,
one variable
increases
as the
other decreases.
It is of the form
$y = \dfrac{k}{x}$.

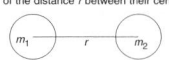

TEST PREP and Spiral Review

25. **Multiple Choice** If y varies inversely with x and $y = 16$ when $x = 8$, what is k?

Ⓐ 2   Ⓑ 4   Ⓒ 64   Ⓓ 128

26. **Gridded Response** If y varies inversely with x and $y = 24$ when $x = 3$, what is the value of x when $y = 18$?   **4**

Solve. (Lesson 2-7)

27. $x - \dfrac{3}{2} = \dfrac{7}{2}$ $x = 5$

28. $-\dfrac{3}{4}x + 6 = 8$ $x = -\dfrac{8}{3}$

29. $\dfrac{1}{2}x - \dfrac{2}{3} = 6$ $x = \dfrac{40}{3}$

Solve each inequality. (Lesson 11-5)

30. $12x - 4 > 3x + 14$ $x > 2$

31. $6p + 11 < 10 + 5p$ $p < -1$

32. $5 + 4k \geq 18 + 2k$ $k \geq \dfrac{13}{2}$

CHALLENGE 13-7

LESSON 13-7 Challenge
When an Apple Fell on His Head!

The English physicist Sir Isaac Newton is said to have recognized the force of gravity as a result of having an apple fall from a tree under which he was seated. He later reasoned that any two objects attract one another gravitationally.

Newton's Law of Gravitation

The force of attraction F between two particles varies directly with the product of their masses, m_1 and m_2, and inversely as the square of the distance r between their centers.

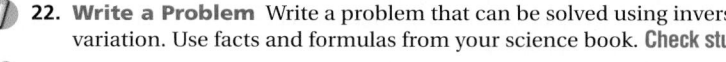

$F = \dfrac{G m_1 m_2}{r^2}$ G is the universal gravitational constant.

If the masses are expressed in kilograms, kg, the distance in meters, m, and the force in newtons, N, the value of the universal gravitational constant $G = 6.67 \times 10^{-11}$ N • m^2/kg^2.

Find the gravitational force exerted by the Earth on a 1-kg mass on its surface.

mass of object, m_1 = 1.0 kg
mass of Earth, m_2 = 6.0 × 10^{24} kg
distance = radius of Earth = 6.4 × 10^6 m

$F = \dfrac{G m_1 m_2}{r^2} = \dfrac{6.67 \times 10^{-11}(1.0)(6.0 \times 10^{24})}{(6.4 \times 10^6)^2}$

$= \dfrac{(6.67)(1.0)(6.0) \times 10^{-11+24}}{(6.4)^2 \times 10^{12}}$

$= \dfrac{40.02 \times 10^{13}}{40.96 \times 10^{12}} = 0.977 \times 10 = 9.8$ N

1. Find the gravitational force exerted by the moon on the Earth.
   mass of moon = 7.3 × 10^{22} kg, Earth-moon distance = 3.8 × 10^7 m

$F = \dfrac{G m_1 m_2}{r^2} = \dfrac{6.67 \times 10^{-11}(7.3 \times 10^{22})(6.0 \times 10^{24})}{(3.8 \times 10^7)^2}$

$= \dfrac{(6.67)(7.3)(6.0) \times 10^{-11+22+24}}{(3.8)^2 \times 10^{7 \times 2}}$

$F = \underline{2.0 \times 10^{22} \text{ N}}$

2. Find the gravitational force exerted by the Earth on the moon.

$F = \underline{2.0 \times 10^{22} \text{ N, same as that of moon on Earth}}$

PROBLEM SOLVING 13-7

LESSON 13-7 Problem Solving
Inverse Variation

For a given focal length of a camera, the f-stop varies inversely with the diameter of the lens. The table below gives the f-stop and diameter data for a focal length of 400 mm. Round to the nearest hundredth.

1. Use the table to write an inverse variation function.

$f(d) = \dfrac{400}{d}$

f-stop	diameter (mm)
1	400
2	200
4	100
8	50
16	25
32	12.5

2. What is the diameter of a lens with an f-stop of 1.4?

$\underline{285.71 \text{ mm}}$

3. What is the diameter of a lens with an f-stop of 11?

$\underline{36.36 \text{ mm}}$

4. What is the diameter of a lens with an f-stop of 22?

$\underline{18.18 \text{ mm}}$

The inverse square law of radiation says that the intensity of illumination varies inversely with the square of the distance to the light source.

5. Using the inverse square law of radiation, if you halve the distance between yourself and a fire, by how much will you increase the heat you feel?

A 2
Ⓑ 4
C 8
D 16

6. Using the inverse square law of radiation, if you double the distance between a radio and the transmitter, how will it affect the signal intensity?

Ⓕ $\dfrac{1}{4}$ as strong
G $\dfrac{1}{2}$ as strong
H twice as strong
J 4 times stronger

7. Using the inverse square law of radiation, if you increase the distance between yourself and a light by 4 times, how will it affect the light's intensity?

Ⓐ $\dfrac{1}{16}$ as strong
B $\dfrac{1}{4}$ as strong
C $\dfrac{1}{2}$ as strong
D twice as strong

8. Using the inverse square law of radiation if you move 3 times closer to a fire, how much more intense will the fire feel?

F $\dfrac{1}{3}$ as strong
G 3 times stronger
Ⓗ 9 times stronger
J 27 times stronger

ONGOING ASSESSMENT
and **INTERVENTION** ◀◀▶▶

Diagnose *Before* the Lesson
13-7 Warm Up, TE p. 714

Monitor *During* the Lesson
13-7 Know-It Notebook
13-7 Questioning Strategies

Assess *After* the Lesson
13-7 Lesson Quiz, TE p. 717

TEST PREP DOCTOR ✚ Some students may be able to solve Exercise 25 mentally. Others may find it helpful to write out the equation. Students who choose **A** divided 16 by 8 rather than multiplying them to find the constant.

 Journal

Ask students to explain the difference between direct variation and inverse variation and to give an example of each.

Power Presentations
with PowerPoint®

13-7 Lesson Quiz

Tell whether each relationship is an inverse variation.

1.

x	5	15	25	75
y	45	15	9	3

yes

2.

x	10	25	40	50
y	40	25	10	10

no

3. Graph the inverse variation function $f(x) = \dfrac{1}{4x}$.

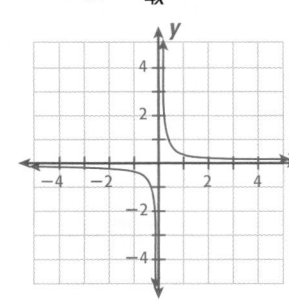

Also available on transparency

Organizer

Objective: Assess students' mastery of concepts and skills in Lessons 13-4 through 13-7.

Resources

Assessment Resources
Section 13B Quiz

Test & Practice Generator
One-Stop Planner®

INTERVENTION ⬅➡

Resources

Ready to Go On?
Intervention and
Enrichment Worksheets

Ready to Go On? CD-ROM

Ready to Go On? Online

my.hrw.com

Answers

6–8, 10–11, 13–15. See pp. A24–A25.

Quiz for Lessons 13-4 Through 13-7

✓ 13-4 Linear Functions

Determine whether each function is linear.

1. $f(x) = 2x^3$ not linear　　**2.** $f(x) = 3x + 1$ linear　　**3.** $f(x) = \frac{2}{3}x - 2$ linear

4. Write a rule for the linear function. $f(x) = -2x + 4$

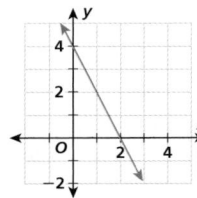

5. Kayo earns $560 per week. If she works overtime, she makes $21 per overtime hour. Find a rule for the linear function that describes her weekly salary if she works x hours of overtime. Use the rule to find how much Kayo earns if she works 8 hours of overtime. $f(x) = 21x + 560$; $728

✓ 13-5 Exponential Functions

Create a table for each exponential function, and use it to graph the function.

6. $f(x) = 3^x$　　　　**7.** $f(x) = 0.01 \cdot 5^x$　　　　**8.** $f(x) = \left(\frac{2}{3}\right)^x$

9. Ernio invested $500 in an account where his balance will double every 8 years. Write an exponential function to calculate his account balance. What will his balance be in 32 years? $f(x) = 500 \cdot 2^x$; $8000

✓ 13-6 Quadratic Functions

Create a table for each quadratic function, and use it to graph the function.

10. $f(x) = x^2 + 4$　　　　　　**11.** $f(x) = x^2 + 2.5x$

12. The function $f(x) = 2x^2 - 300x + 14{,}450$ gives the cost of manufacturing x items per day. Which number of items will give the lowest cost per day: 50, 70, or 85? What will the cost be? 70; $3250

✓ 13-7 Inverse Variation

Create a table. Then graph each inverse variation function.

13. $f(x) = \frac{2}{x}$　　　　**14.** $f(x) = \frac{1}{2x}$　　　　**15.** $f(x) = \frac{1}{x}$

READY TO GO ON?
Diagnose and Prescribe

NO
INTERVENE

YES
ENRICH

READY TO GO ON? Intervention, Section 13B			
Ready to Go On? Intervention	Worksheets	CD-ROM	Online
✓ Lesson 13-4	13-4 Intervention	Activity 13-4	
✓ Lesson 13-5	13-5 Intervention	Activity 13-5	Diagnose and Prescribe Online
✓ Lesson 13-6	13-6 Intervention	Activity 13-6	
✓ Lesson 13-7	13-7 Intervention	Activity 13-7	

READY TO GO ON?
Enrichment, Section 13B

Worksheets
CD-ROM
Online

Beset by Beavers Greg and Maria are wildlife biologists. They are studying beaver population trends in a national forest. There are currently 200 beavers in the forest. The table shows Greg's and Maria's predictions for the beaver population in future years.

1. Write a rule based on Greg's prediction that gives the beaver population in year n. Then use the rule to find the population in year 8.

2. According to Greg's predictions, in what year will the beaver population be 500? Explain.

3. Write a rule based on Maria's prediction that gives the beaver population in year n. Then use the rule to find the population in year 8.

4. A third biologist, Amir, makes his predictions using the function $f(x) = 5x^2 + 195$, where x is the year. Use the function to find the beaver population that Amir predicts in year 8. **5150**

5. Which of the three biologists predicts the greatest beaver population in year 12? **Amir; 9150** What is this population?

Beaver Population Predictions		
Year	Greg's Predictions	Maria's Predictions
1	200	200
2	230	220
3	260	242
4	290	266

Multi-Step Test Prep

Organizer

Objective: Assess students' ability to apply concepts and skills in Chapter 13 in a real-world format.

PREMIER **Online Edition**

Resources

 Middle School Assessments
www.mathtekstoolkit.org

Problem	Text reference
1	Lesson 13-4
2	Lesson 13-4
3	Lesson 13-4
4	Lesson 13-6
5	Lesson 13-6

Answers

1. $a_n = 200 + (n-1)30$; 410

2. Year 11. Solve $500 = 200 + (n-1)30$ to find that $n = 11$.

3. $a_n = 200(1.1)^{n-1}$; 389.7

INTERVENTION ⬅⬛➡

Scaffolding Questions

1. What type of sequence is formed by Greg's population predictions? Arithmetic Why? The difference between one term and the next is always the same What is the general rule for finding the nth term of an arithmetic sequence?
$a_n = a_1 + (n-1)d$

2. What equation can you write as a first step in solving this problem?
$500 = 200 + (n-1)30$

3. What type of sequence is formed by Maria's population predictions? Geometric Why? The ratio of one term to the next is always the same What is the general rule for finding the nth term of a geometric sequence? $a_n = a_1 r^{n-1}$ What is the common ratio? 1.1

4. What is the population when $x = 1$? 200 How can you use the function to find the beaver population in year 8? Find $f(8)$

5. What population does Greg predict in year 12? 530 What population does Maria predict in year 12? 570.6 What population does Amir predict in year 12? 915

Extension

1. According to Greg's predictions, in what year will the beaver population be greater than 10,000 for the first time? Year 28

State Resources

go.hrw.com
State Resources Online
KEYWORD: MT7 Resources

Organizer

Objective: Participate in games to practice and apply skills learned in Chapter 13.

 Online Edition

Resources

📖 *Chapter 13 Resource Book*
Puzzles, Twisters & Teasers

Squared Away

Purpose: To apply the problem-solving skill of writing sequences to solve a puzzle

Discuss Ask students to explain how to determine the number of different squares in a square of side length *n*.

The number of $n \times n$ squares is 1^2, or 1. The number of $(n - 1) \times (n - 1)$ squares is 2^2, or 4. The number of $(n - 2) \times (n - 2)$ squares is 3^2, or 9. The number of $(n - a) \times (n - a)$ squares is $(a + 1)^2$. Add the number of squares of each size to find the total number.

Extend Challenge students to notice other patterns in the tables used to record *Size of Square* and *Number of Squares*. Have them test hypotheses by testing their rule on the tables for $4 \times 4, 5 \times 5, 6 \times 6$, and 7×7 squares.

Possible answer: Find the area of each size square and multiply it by the number of squares of that size. The products are square numbers that form a palindrome pattern when listed in order. For example, for a 4×4 square, the products are as follows:

1   4×4 square = 16 square units
4   3×3 squares = 36 square units
9   2×2 squares = 36 square units
16 1×1 squares = 16 square units

What's Your Function?

Purpose: To practice identifying functions in a game format

Discuss When a team guesses a function correctly, have them demonstrate that each input/output pair used is a solution to the function.

Extend Have students create new function cards, including linear, quadratic, and cubic functions. Use the new equation cards to play again.

Game Time

Squared Away

How many squares can you find in the figure at right?

Did you find 30 squares?

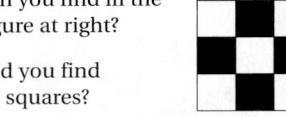

There are four different-sized squares in the figure.

Size of Square	Number of Squares
4 × 4	1
3 × 3	4
2 × 2	9
1 × 1	16
Total	**30**

3 × 3 squares

2 × 2 squares

The total number of squares is $1 + 4 + 9 + 16 = 1^2 + 2^2 + 3^2 + 4^2$.

Draw a 5 × 5 grid and count the number of squares of each size. Can you see a pattern?

What is the total number of squares on a 6 × 6 grid? a 7 × 7 grid? Can you come up with a general formula for the sum of squares on an $n \times n$ grid?

What's Your Function?

One member from the first of two teams draws a function card from the deck, and the other team tries to guess the rule of the function. The guessing team gives a function input, and the card holder must give the corresponding output. Points are awarded based on the type of function and number of inputs required.

Complete rules and function cards are available online.

go.hrw.com
Game Time Extra
KEYWORD: MT7 Games

Answers

$5 \times 5 \rightarrow 55$ squares
$6 \times 6 \rightarrow 91$ squares
$7 \times 7 \rightarrow 140$ squares
$8 \times 8 \rightarrow 204$ squares

Possible answer:

$n \times n \rightarrow 1^2 + 2^2 + 3^2 + \cdots + n^2 = \dfrac{n(n + 1)(2n + 1)}{6}$

Materials
• decorative paper
• glue
• markers

PROJECT **Springboard to Sequences**

Make this springy organizer to record notes on sequences and functions.

Directions

❶ Cut out four squares of decorative paper that are 6 inches by 6 inches.

❷ Fold one of the squares of paper in half vertically and then horizontally. Unfold the paper. Then fold the square diagonally and unfold the paper. **Figure A**

❸ Fold the diagonal crease back and forth so that it is easy to work with. Then bring the two ends of the diagonal together as shown. **Figure B**

❹ Fold the other squares of paper in the same way.

❺ Insert one folded square into another—one facing up, the next facing down—so that a pair of inner faces match up. Glue the matching faces together. **Figure C**

❻ Do the same with the remaining squares to complete the springboard.

Taking Note of the Math

Write notes about sequences and functions on the various sections of the springboard.

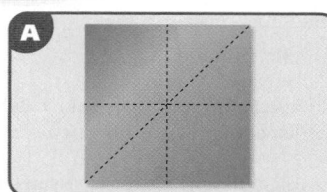
A

B

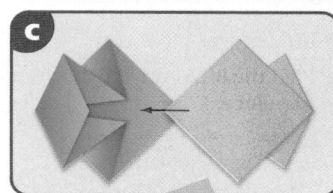
C

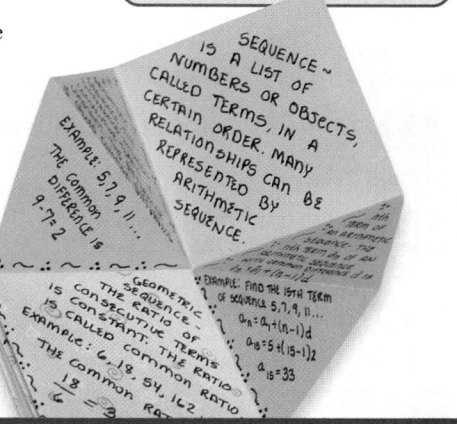

Organizer

Objective: Make a "springboard" on which students can take notes about sequences and functions.
Materials: decorative paper, glue, markers

Online Edition

Using the Page

Preparing the Materials

You may want to cut out the squares of paper for students before beginning the project. In this case, use a paper cutter to trim sheets of decorative paper to the correct size.

Making the Project

Show students how to fold one of the squares of paper. Once students know this basic folding technique, the rest of the project should flow smoothly.

Extending the Project

Students can add extra folded squares to make longer springboards. Have students use the additional space to draw sample graphs of each type of function in the chapter.

Tips from the Bag Ladies!

Students can make larger springboards by starting with larger squares of paper. This will give them more room for notes. Students can also make longer versions of the springboard by simply attaching additional folded squares. No matter which version of the project you use with your class, you might have students attach a string to the end of their springboards so that they can hang them like mobiles.

Organizer

Objective: Help students organize and review key concepts and skills presented in Chapter 13.

 Online Edition
Multilingual Glossary

Resources

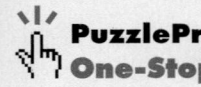 **PuzzlePro®**
One-Stop Planner®

 Multilingual Glossary Online
go.hrw.com
KEYWORD: MT7 Glossary

 Lesson Tutorial Videos
CD-ROM

 Test & Practice Generator
One-Stop Planner®

Answers

1. sequence

2. arithmetic sequence; geometric sequence

3. Fibonacci sequence

4. 29

5. 0.85

6. $\frac{10}{3}$

7. −3072

8. $\frac{64}{625}$, or ≈ 0.1024

9. −2

Study Guide: Review

Vocabulary

common ratio 687
exponential decay 705
exponential function 704
exponential growth 705
Fibonacci sequence 695
first differences 693
function notation 700

geometric sequence 687
inverse variation 714
linear function 700
parabola 708
quadratic function 708
second differences 693

Complete the sentences below with vocabulary words from the list above. Words may be used more than once.

1. A list of numbers or terms in a certain order is called a(n) ___?___.

2. A sequence in which there is a common difference is a(n) ___?___; a sequence in which there is a common ratio is a(n) ___?___.

3. A famous sequence in which you add the two previous terms to find the next term is the ___?___.

13-1 Terms of Arithmetic Sequences (pp. 682–686)

EXAMPLE

■ Find the 8th term of the arithmetic sequence: 17, 14, 11, 8, ...

$d = 14 − 17 = −3$
$a_n = a_1 + (n − 1)d$
$a_8 = 17 + (8 − 1)(−3)$
$a_8 = 17 − 21$
$a_8 = −4$

EXERCISES

Find the given term in each arithmetic sequence.

4. 6th term: 4, 9, 14, . . .

5. 5th term: 0.05, 0.25, 0.45, . . .

6. 7th term: $\frac{1}{3}, \frac{5}{6}, \frac{4}{3}, \ldots$

13-2 Terms of Geometric Sequences (pp. 687–691)

EXAMPLE

■ Find the 8th term of the geometric sequence: 9, 18, 36, 72, ...

$r = \frac{18}{9} = 2$

$a_n = a_1 r^{n−1}$

$a_8 = 9(2)^{8−1} = 1152$

EXERCISES

Find the given term in each geometric sequence.

7. 6th term: 3, −12, 48, −192, . . .

8. 5th term: $\frac{1}{4}, \frac{1}{5}, \frac{4}{25}, \ldots$

9. 40th term: 2, −2, 2, −2, . . .

13-3 Other Sequences (pp. 693–697)

EXAMPLE

■ Find the first four terms of the sequence defined by $a_n = -3(-1)^{n-1} - 2$.

$a_1 = -3(-1)^{1-1} - 2 = -5$
$a_2 = -3(-1)^{2-1} - 2 = 1$
$a_3 = -3(-1)^{3-1} - 2 = -5$
$a_4 = -3(-1)^{4-1} - 2 = 1$

The first four terms are -5, 1, -5, and 1.

EXERCISES

Find the first four terms of each sequence defined by the given rule.

10. $a_n = 5n + 2$

11. $a_n = n^2 + 3$

12. $a_n = 6(-1)^n + 3n$

13. $a_n = n! + 1$

13-4 Linear Functions (pp. 700–703)

EXAMPLE

Write the rule for each linear function.

■
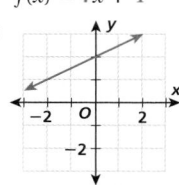

x	y
−2	−10
−1	−3
0	4
1	11

The y-intercept is $f(0) = 4$.

$f(x) = mx + 4$ $f(x) = mx + b$

Substitute and solve for m.

$11 = m(1) + 4$ $(x, y) = (1, 11)$
$7 = m$
$f(x) = 7x + 4$

■
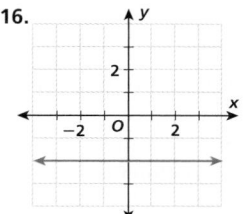

From the graph, $b = 2$.

$f(x) = mx + 2$

For point $(2, 3)$:

$3 = m \cdot 2 + 2$
$\underline{-2 \qquad\qquad -2}$
$\dfrac{1}{2} = \dfrac{m \cdot 2}{2}$
$\dfrac{1}{2} = m$
$f(x) = \dfrac{1}{2}m + 2$

EXERCISES

Write the equation for each linear function.

14.

x	y
−2	−3
−1	−2
0	−1
1	0

15.

x	y
−4	2
−2	3
0	4
2	5

16.

Answers

10. 7, 12, 17, 22

11. 4, 7, 12, 19

12. −3, 12, 3, 18

13. 2, 3, 7, 25

14. $f(x) = x - 1$

15. $f(x) = \frac{1}{2}x + 4$

16. $f(x) = -2$

Answers

17.

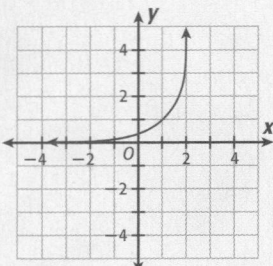

18.

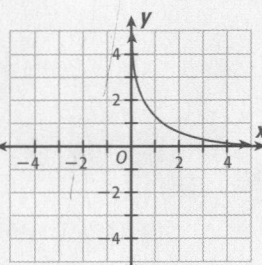

19.

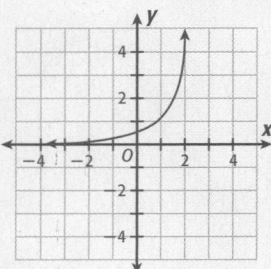

20.

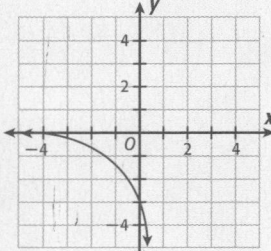

21.

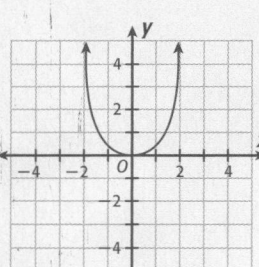

22.

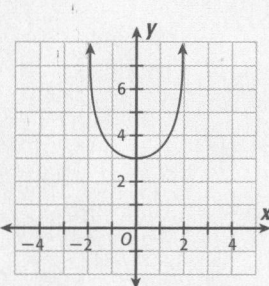

Study Guide: Review

13-5 Exponential Functions (pp. 704–707)

EXAMPLE

■ Graph the exponential function.
$f(x) = 0.1 \cdot 4^x$

x	f(x)
−2	0.00625
−1	0.025
0	0.1
1	0.4
2	1.6

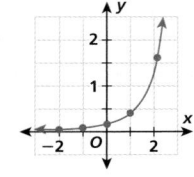

EXERCISES

Graph each exponential function.

17. $f(x) = 0.3 \cdot 4^x$

18. $f(x) = 6 \cdot \left(\frac{1}{3}\right)^x$

19. $f(x) = 3^x$

20. $f(x) = -3 \cdot 12^x$

13-6 Quadratic Functions (pp. 708–711)

EXAMPLE

■ Graph the quadratic function.
$f(x) = x^2 + 2x - 1$

x	f(x)
−3	2
−2	−1
−1	−2
0	−1
1	2
2	7
3	14

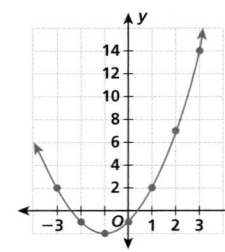

EXERCISES

Graph each quadratic function.

21. $f(x) = 2x^2$

22. $f(x) = x^2 + 3$

23. $f(x) = 2x^2 - x$

24. $f(x) = x^2 + 5x + 6$

13-7 Inverse Variation (pp. 714–717)

EXAMPLE

■ Graph the inverse variation function.
$f(x) = \frac{6}{x}$

x	y
−3	−2
−2	−3
−1	−6
1	6
2	3
3	2

EXERCISES

Graph each inverse variation function.

25. $f(x) = \frac{10}{x}$

26. $f(x) = \frac{14}{x}$

27. $f(x) = -\frac{6}{x}$

28. $f(x) = -\frac{2}{x}$

23.

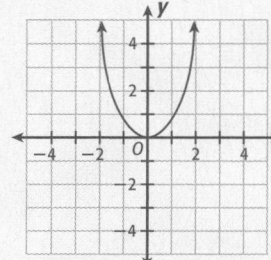

24.

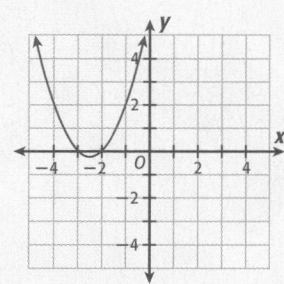

25.

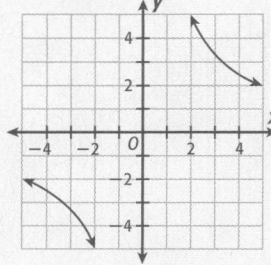

26.

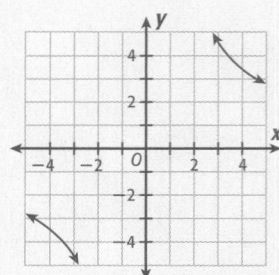

27–28. See p. A25.

Find the given term in each arithmetic sequence.

1. 21st term: $-4, -8, -12, -16, \ldots$ **-84**

2. 13th term: $7, 7\frac{1}{5}, 7\frac{2}{5}, \ldots$ **$9\frac{2}{5}$**

3. 24th term: $2, 6, 10, 14, \ldots$ **94**

4. 30th term: $a_1 = 11, d = 5$ **156**

Find the given term in each geometric sequence.

5. 7th term: $8, 32, 128, \ldots$ **32,768**

6. 101st term: $\frac{1}{3}, -\frac{1}{3}, \frac{1}{3}, -\frac{1}{3}, \ldots$ **$\frac{1}{3}$**

7. A tank contains 54,000 gallons of water. One-third of the water remaining in the tank is removed each day. How much water is left in the tank on the 15th day? **$\approx$ 184.98 gal**

Find the first five terms of each sequence, defined by the given rule.

8. $a_n = 6n - 2$
4, 10, 16, 22, 28

9. $a_n = \frac{4n}{n+2}$ **$\frac{4}{3}, 2, \frac{12}{5}, \frac{8}{3}, \frac{20}{7}$**

10. $a_n = (n+2)(n+3)$
12, 20, 30, 42, 56

Write a rule for each linear function.

11.

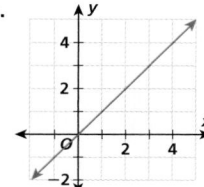

$f(x) = x$

12.

x	y
-8	-7
-4	-4
0	-1
4	2

$f(x) = 0.75x - 1$

13. A small pool contains 1200 gallons of water. The pool is being drained at a rate of 45 gallons per minute. Find a rule for the linear function that describes the amount of water in the pool, and use the rule to determine how much water will be in the pool after 15 minutes. **$f(t) = -45t + 1200$; 525 gal**

Create a table for each exponential function, and use it to graph the function.

14. $f(x) = -2 \cdot (0.2)^x$

15. $f(x) = 10 \cdot \left(\frac{1}{5}\right)^x$

16. $f(x) = 4^x$

Create a table for each quadratic function, and use it to graph the function.

17. $f(x) = x^2 + x + 3$

18. $f(x) = 2x^2 - 1$

19. $f(x) = x^2 - x + 1$

Create a table. Then graph each inverse variation function.

20. $f(x) = \frac{6}{x}$

21. $f(x) = \frac{10}{x}$

22. $f(x) = -\frac{1}{2x}$

15.

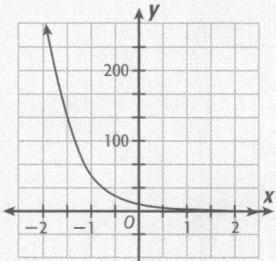

x	f(x)
-2	250
-1	50
0	10
1	2
2	0.4

16.

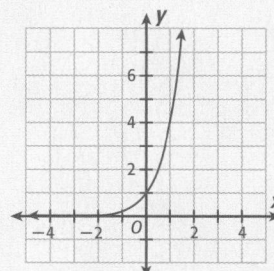

x	f(x)
-2	$\frac{1}{16}$
-1	$\frac{1}{4}$
0	1
1	4
2	16

17–22. See p. A25.

CHAPTER TEST

CHAPTER
13

Organizer

Objective: Assess students' mastery of concepts and skills in Chapter 13.

PREMIER
 Online Edition

Resources

 Assessment Resources
Chapter 13 Tests
• Free Response
(Levels A, B, C)
• Multiple Choice
(Levels A, B, C)
• Performance Assessment

 IDEA Works! CD-ROM
Modified Chapter 13 Test

Test & Practice Generator
One-Stop Planner®

Answers

14.

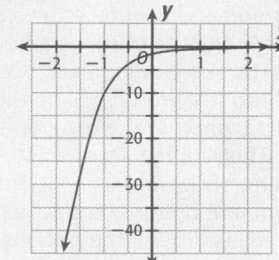

x	f(x)
-2	-50
-1	-10
0	-2
1	-0.4
2	-0.08

State Resources

 go.hrw.com
State Resources Online
KEYWORD: MT7 Resources

Organizer

Objective: Provide opportunities to learn and practice common test-taking strategies.

 Online Edition

Resources

 State Test Prep **Workbook**

 State Test Prep **CD-ROM**

 State Test Practice **Online**

go.hrw.com
KEYWORD: MT7 TestPrep

TEST PREP DOCTOR + This Test Tackler focuses on how to work backwards to obtain the correct response to a multiple-choice test item. If students do not know how to solve a problem, encourage them to use the choice options to make an educated guess. By substituting each possible answer into the problem, students can determine whether the answer is reasonable. This strategy involves students' working backward, using mental math to eliminate options, and watching for distracters among the options.

Multiple Choice: Work Backward

When you do not know how to solve a multiple-choice test item, use the answer choices and work backward to make a guess. Try each option in the test item to see if it is correct and reasonable.

EXAMPLE 1

If $a_n = 2 + 6(n - 1)$, which term n results in $a_n = 26$?

　(A) -5　　　(B) 4　　　(C) 5　　　(D) 6

Use the answer choices to work backward to find the value of n that makes the equation true.

Option A: If $n = -5$, then $26 = 2 + 6(-5 - 1)$ would be true.
$2 + 6(-5 - 1) = 2 + 6(-6) = 2 + (-36) = -34$. $-34 \neq 26$, so $n \neq -5$.

Option B: If $n = 4$, then $26 = 2 + 6(4 - 1)$ would be true.
$2 + 6(4 - 1) = 2 + 6(3) = 2 + 18 = 20$. $20 \neq 26$, so $n \neq 4$.

Option C: If $n = 5$, then $26 = 2 + 6(5 - 1)$ would be true.
$2 + 6(5 - 1) = 2 + 6(4) = 2 + 24 = 26$. $26 = 26$, so $n = 5$.

Option C is the correct response.

EXAMPLE 2

What is the equation of the line that passes through the points $(-1, -1)$ and $(1, 3)$?

　(F) $y = 2x$　　(G) $y = x$　　(H) $y = x + 1$　　(J) $y = 2x + 1$

Substitute for x and y to find a true equation.

Option F: Try $(-1, -1)$. $y = 2x$; $-1 \stackrel{?}{=} 2(-1)$; $-1 \neq -2$
Option F is not the correct response.

Option G: Try $(-1, -1)$. $y = x$; $-1 = -1$; The first point is true.
Now try $(1, 3)$: $1 \neq 3$. Option G is not the correct response.

Option H: Try $(-1, -1)$. $y = x + 1$; $-1 \stackrel{?}{=} -1 + 1$; $-1 \neq 0$
Option H is not the correct response.

Option J: The other three options are false.

Try $(-1, -1)$. $y = 2x + 1$; $-1 \stackrel{?}{=} 2(-1) + 1$; $-1 = -1$

Try $(1, 3)$. $y = 2x + 1$; $3 \stackrel{?}{=} 2(1) + 1$; $3 = 3$

Test Tackler

Read each test item and answer the questions that follow.

ITEM A
What are the next three terms in the sequence 3, 8, 18, 38, . . . ?

(A) 48, 58, 68   (C) 58, 78, 98

(B) 76, 156, 316   (D) 78, 158, 318

1. Explain which option you can eliminate because it is not reasonable.

2. Explain how to work backward to find the correct response.

ITEM B
The 6th term of an arithmetic sequence is 18. The common difference is 3. What is the 1st term of the sequence?

(F) 1   (H) 3

(G) 2   (J) 4

3. Describe how to use mental math to eliminate at least one option.

4. Describe how you know by working backward that options F and G are incorrect.

ITEM C
The 3rd term of a geometric sequence is 12. The common ratio is 2. What is the 1st term of the sequence?

(A) $\frac{1}{3}$ (C) 3

(B) 1   (D) 8

5. Options A and D are distracters. Explain how these options were generated.

6. Explain how to work backward to find the correct response.

ITEM D
Which equation best describes the graph of the quadratic equation?

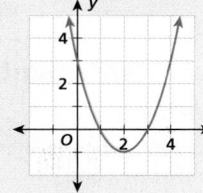

(F) $f(x) = x^2 + 4x - 3$

(G) $f(x) = x^2 - 4x + 3$

(H) $f(x) = x^2 - 3$

(J) $f(x) = x^2 + 4x + 3$

7. Can any of the options be eliminated immediately? Explain.

8. Explain how to work backward to find the correct response.

ITEM E
Which graph represents the equation $y = \frac{3}{x}$?

(A) 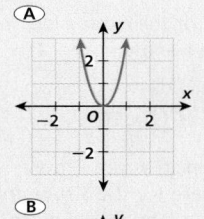   (C)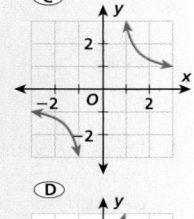

(B) 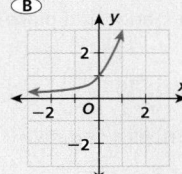   (D)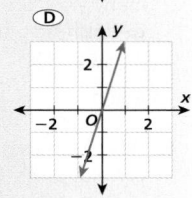

9. Explain which options you can eliminate because they are not reasonable.

10. Describe how to work backward to find the correct response.

Test Tackler

Answers
Possible answers:

1. Choice A is unreasonable because the difference between 48 and 38 is not great enough to be the next term.

2. Determine the common difference for each sequence and see which option has the same common difference as the sequence given in the problem.

3. Choice J can be eliminated. If the 6th term is 18, then 4 is too great to be the first number in the sequence.

4. Choice F is incorrect because if 1 was the first term and the common difference is 3, then the sequence would be 1, 4, 7, 10, 13, 16, 19, . . . and the 6th term would be 16, not 18. Similarly, Choice G is incorrect because if 2 was the 1st term and the common difference is 3, then the sequence would be 2, 5, 8, 11, 14, 17, 20, . . . and the 6th term would be 17, not 18.

5. Choice A is the reciprocal of the correct response, and Choice D is the common ratio cubed.

6. Work backwards by taking each option and multiplying it by the square of the common ratio, 2. If the number 3 is multiplied by the square of the common ratio, 2, then the result would be 12.

7. Yes, Choices F and H can be eliminated immediately. If $x = 0$, then $f(x)$ would equal -3. This does not correspond with the graph.

8. Substitute the point $(2, -1)$ into each equation and see for which equation it makes the equation true.

9. Choice D can be eliminated immediately. It is a straight line, and the equation $y = \frac{3}{x}$ is not linear because it is not in the form $y = mx + b$.

10. You can tell by looking at the equation that $x \neq 0$ because it would be undefined. Every option except for option B has a solution for $x = 0$. Therefore, option B must be the correct response.

State Resources

Organizer

Objective: Provide review and practice for Chapters 1–13 and standardized tests.

 Online Edition

Resources

 Assessment Resources
Chapter 13 Cumulative Test

 State Test Prep Workbook

 State Test Prep CD-ROM

 State Test Practice Online

go.hrw.com
KEYWORD: MT7 Testprep

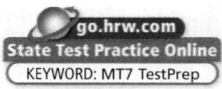
Standardized Test Prep

Cumulative Assessment, Chapters 1–13

Multiple Choice

1. Which equation represents a direct variation between x and y?

 A $y = x + 2$ **C** $y = 2x$

 B $y = \frac{2}{x}$ **D** $y = 2 - x$

2. The sum of two numbers is 304 and their difference is 112. What is the greater of the two numbers?

 F 96   **H** 208

 G 192   **J** 416

3. What is the 1st term of the geometric sequence with 8th term $\frac{1}{16}$ and common ratio $\frac{1}{2}$?

 A $\frac{1}{2048}$ **C** 4

 B $\frac{1}{56}$ **D** 8

4. What is the value of the expression $3xy - 2y^2$ if $x = -1$ and $y = 2$?

 F 14   **H** -2

 G 2   **J** -14

5. There are 5 runners in a race. How many ways are there for the 5 runners to finish first, second, and third place?

 A 30   **C** 120

 B 60   **D** 180

6. Which data set describes a negative correlation?

 F a person's eye color and height

 G a person's height and weight

 H the distance traveled and the time it takes to travel

 J the age of a light bulb and the intensity of the light beam

7. Which expression represents the perimeter of the figure?

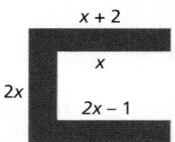

 A $10x$ **C** $6x + 1$

 B $10x + 2$ **D** $10x^2 + 4$

8. In the histogram below, which interval contains the median score?

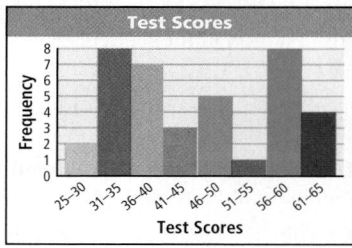

 F 31–35   **H** 41–45

 G 36–40   **J** 46–50

9. A triangle has two angles whose measures are 70° each. Which description fits this triangle?

 A acute   **C** scalene

 B obtuse   **D** equilateral

10. The rotational speed of a gear varies inversely as the number of teeth on the gear. A gear with 15 teeth has a rotational speed of 48 rpm. How many teeth are on a gear that has a rotational speed of 40 rpm?

 F 13 teeth   **H** 58 teeth

 G 18 teeth   **J** 128 teeth

State Resources

TEST PREP DOCTOR ✚

Remind students of the definition of median for item 8. Suggest that they add up all the frequencies to find the total number of elements in the data set, and then use that information to locate the median. Make sure students understand the difference between direct and indirect variation. Students who choose **B** for item 1 or **F** for item 10 may be confusing the two.

Answers

18–19. See p. A25.

20. 126.4 in.; $a_n = 112.5(1.06)^{n-1}$

21. See 4-Point Response work sample.

go.hrw.com
State Resources Online
KEYWORD: MT7 Resources

11. An animal shelter needs to find homes for 40 dogs and 60 cats. If 15% of the dogs are female and 25% of the cats are female, what percent of the animals are female?

   (A) 21%   (C) 40%

   (B) 22%   (D) 42%

 HOT TIP! When trying to find the pattern in a sequence, find the first and second differences to see if there is a common difference.

Gridded Response

Use the graph for items 12 and 13.

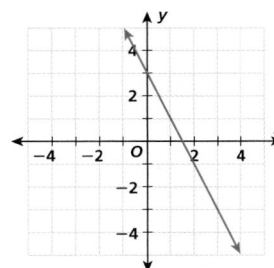

12. What is the slope of a line perpendicular to the line graphed? $\frac{1}{2}$ or 0.5

13. What is the y-intercept of the line perpendicular to the line graphed that passes through the point (2, 2)? **1**

14. If $3^{3x-2} = 81$, what is the value of x? **2**

15. If y varies inversely with x and $y = \frac{2}{9}$ when $x = \frac{1}{3}$, what is the constant of variation? $\frac{2}{27}$

16. What is the x-intercept of the function $f(x) = 4x^2 - 20x + 25$? $\frac{5}{2}$ or 2.5

17. The length of a rectangle is one-third the width. If the perimeter of the rectangle is 56 units, what is the area in square units? **147**

Short Response

18. Write out the next three terms of the sequence.

$$\sqrt{2},\ \sqrt{2+\sqrt{2}},\ \sqrt{2+\sqrt{2+\sqrt{2}}},$$

$$\sqrt{2+\sqrt{2+\sqrt{2+\sqrt{2}}}},\ldots$$

Use your calculator to evaluate each term of the sequence. Describe what seems to be happening to the terms of the sequence.

19. A basketball player throws a basketball in a path defined by the function $f(x) = -16x^2 + 20x + 7$, where x is the time in seconds and $f(x)$ is the height in feet. Graph the function, and estimate how long it would take the basketball to reach its maximum height.

20. When playing the trombone, a musician produces different notes by changing the effective length of the tube by moving it in and out. This movement produces a sequence of lengths that form a geometric sequence. If the length is 119.3 inches in the 2nd position and 134.0 inches in the 4th position, what is the length in the 3rd position? Write a rule that would describe this relationship.

Extended Response

21. Consider the sequence 3, 4, 6, 9, 13, . . .

  a. Determine whether the sequence is arithmetic, geometric, or neither. Explain your answer.

  b. Find the difference between each pair of consecutive terms. What pattern do you notice?

  c. How many differences do you have to find before there is a common difference? Use your pattern to find the next three terms.

Standardized Test Prep

Short Response Rubric

Items 18–20

2 Points = The student's answer is an accurate and complete execution of the task or tasks.

1 Point = The student's answer contains attributes of an appropriate response but is flawed.

0 Points = The student's answer contains no attributes of an appropriate response.

Extended Response Rubric

Item 21

4 points = The student demonstrates a thorough understanding of all concepts and shows all work correctly.

3 points = The student demonstrates a basic understanding of all concepts, but the work shows some flaws reflecting inattentive execution of mathematical procedures or some misunderstanding of the underlying mathematics.

2 points = The student demonstrates only a partial understanding of the concepts or procedures embodied in the tasks. The approach may be correct, but the work shows a misunderstanding of one or more important concepts.

1 point = The student demonstrates a very limited understanding of the concepts or procedures embodied in the tasks. The response may show some understanding but exhibits many flaws or is incomplete.

0 points = The student provides no response at all, or a completely incorrect or uninterpretable response.

Student Work Samples for Item 21

4-Point Response

a. 3, 4, 6, 9, 13
   1 2 3 4
Neither; there is no common difference, so it's not arithmetic. There is no common ratio, so it's not geometric.

b. 1, 2, 3, 4; the difference increases by 1 each time.

c. 3, 4, 6, 9, 13, 18, 24, 31
   1 2 3 4 5 6 7
   Common difference of 1 after 2nd difference; 18, 24, 31

The student offered adequate explanations to each part and correctly identified the next three terms in the sequence.

3-Point Response

a. neither

b. 1, 2, 3, 4; the numbers are going up by 1.

c. 3, 4, 6, 9, 13, 18, 24, 31
   1 2 3 4 5 6 7
   1 1 1 1 1

The student offered correct answers to all three parts, but failed to offer an explanation in part **a,** and did not mention the second difference in **c.**

2-Point Response

a. neither

b. 1, 2, 3, 4 are the differences.

c. 3, 4, 6, 9, 13, 18, 24, 31
            next 3 terms

The student showed little understanding of first, second, and common differences, or the difference between arithmetic and geometric sequences.

CHAPTER
14

Polynomials

Section 14A	Section 14B
Introduction to Polynomials	**Polynomial Operations**
14-1 **Polynomials**	14-3 **Hands-On Lab** Model Polynomial Addition
14-1 **Hands-On Lab** Model Polynomials	14-3 **Adding Polynomials**
14-2 **Simplifying Polynomials**	14-4 **Hands-On Lab** Model Polynomial Subtraction
	14-4 **Subtracting Polynomials**
	14-5 **Multiplying Polynomials by Monomials**
	14-6 **Hands-On Lab** Multiply Binomials
	14-6 **Multiplying Binomials**
	EXTENSION Dividing Polynomials by Monomials

Pacing Guide for 45-Minute Classes

Chapter 14

DAY 1	DAY 2	DAY 3	DAY 4	DAY 5
14-1 Lesson	14-1 Hands-On Lab 14-2 Lesson	14-2 Lesson Ready to Go On? Focus on Problem Solving	14-3 Hands-On Lab 14-3 Lesson	14-3 Lesson 14-4 Hands-On Lab
DAY 6	**DAY 7**	**DAY 8**	**DAY 9**	**DAY 10**
14-4 Lesson	14-5 Lesson	14-6 Hands-On Lab 14-6 Lesson	14-6 Lesson Ready to Go On? Multi-Step Test Prep	**EXTENSION**
DAY 11	**DAY 12**			
Chapter 14 Review	Chapter 14 Test			

Pacing Guide for 90-Minute Classes

Chapter 14

DAY 1	DAY 2	DAY 3	DAY 4	DAY 5
14-1 Lesson 14-1 Hands-On Lab 14-2 Lesson	14-2 Lesson Ready to Go On? Focus on Problem Solving 14-3 Hands-On Lab 14-3 Lesson	14-3 Lesson 14-4 Hands-On Lab 14-4 Lesson	14-5 Lesson 14-6 Hands-On Lab 14-6 Lesson	14-6 Lesson Ready to Go On? Multi-Step Test Prep **EXTENSION**
DAY 6				
Chapter 14 Review Chapter 14 Test				

ONGOING ASSESSMENT and INTERVENTION

DIAGNOSE	PRESCRIBE

Assess Prior Knowledge

Before Chapter 14

Diagnose readiness for the chapter.
Are You Ready? SE p. 731

Prescribe intervention.
Are You Ready? Intervention Skills 12, 47, 49, 85

Formative Assessment

Before Every Lesson

Diagnose readiness for the lesson.
Warm Up TE, every lesson

Prescribe intervention.
Skills Bank SE pp. 820–834
Reteach CRB, Chapters 1–14

During Every Lesson

Diagnose understanding of lesson concepts.
Think and Discuss SE, every lesson
Write About It SE, lesson exercises
Journal TE, lesson exercises

Prescribe intervention.
Questioning Strategies Chapter 14
Reading Strategies CRB, every lesson
Success for ELL pp. 205–216

After Every Lesson

Diagnose mastery of lesson concepts.
Lesson Quiz TE, every lesson
Test Prep SE, every lesson
Test and Practice Generator

Prescribe intervention.
Reteach CRB, every lesson
Problem Solving CRB, every lesson
Test Prep Doctor TE, lesson exercises
Homework Help Online

Before Chapter 14 Testing

Diagnose mastery of concepts in the chapter.
Ready to Go On? SE pp. 744, 766
Focus on Problem Solving SE p. 745
Multi-Step Test Prep SE p. 767
Section Quizzes AR pp. 265–266
Test and Practice Generator

Prescribe intervention.
Ready to Go On? Intervention Chapter 14
Scaffolding Questions TE p. 767

Before High Stakes Testing

Diagnose mastery of benchmark concepts.
Standardized Test Prep SE pp. 776–777
State Test Prep CD-ROM

Prescribe intervention.
State Test Prep Workbook

Summative Assessment

After Chapter 14

Check mastery of chapter concepts.
Multiple-Choice Tests (Forms A, B, C)
Free-Response Tests (Forms A, B, C)
Performance Assessment AR pp. 267–280
Test and Practice Generator

Check mastery of benchmark concepts.
AYP State Tests

Prescribe intervention.
Reteach CRB, every lesson
Lesson Tutorial Videos Chapter 14

Prescribe intervention.
State Test Prep Workbook

CHAPTER
14

Supporting the Teacher

Chapter 14 Resource Book

Practice A, B, C
pp. 3–5, 11–13, 20–22, 28–30, 36–38, 44–46

Reading Strategies ELL
pp. 9, 18, 26, 34, 42, 50

Puzzles, Twisters, and Teasers
pp. 10, 19, 27, 35, 43, 51

Reteach
pp. 6, 14–15, 23, 31, 39, 47

Problem Solving
pp. 8, 17, 25, 33, 41, 49

Challenge
pp. 7, 16, 24, 32, 40, 48

Parent Letter   pp. 1–2

Transparencies

Lesson Transparencies, Volume 2 .... Chapter 14
• Warm Ups
• Problem of the Day
• Teaching Transparencies
• Lesson Quizzes

Know-It Notebook .... Chapter 14
• Additional Examples   • Chapter Review
• Vocabulary   • Big Ideas

Alternate Openers: Explorations .... pp. 103–108

Teacher Tools

Power Presentations®
Complete PowerPoint® presentations for Chapter 14 lessons

Lesson Tutorial Videos® SPANISH
Holt authors Ed Burger and Freddie Renfro present tutorials to support the Chapter 14 lessons.

One-Stop Planner® SPANISH
Easy access to all Chapter 14 resources and assessments, as well as software for lesson planning, test generation, and puzzle creation

IDEA Works!®
Key Chapter 14 resources and assessments modified to address special learning needs

Lesson Plans .... pp. 103–108

Questioning Strategies .... Chapter 14

Solutions Key .... Chapter 14

Interdisciplinary Posters and Worksheets .... Chapter 14

TechKeys 🌐   *Lab Resources* 🌐

Project Teacher Support 🌐   *Parent Resources* 🌐

Workbooks

Homework and Practice Workbook SPANISH
Teacher's Guide .... pp. 52–54

Know-It Notebook
Teacher's Guide .... Chapter 14

Problem Solving Workbook SPANISH
Teacher's Guide .... pp. 52–54

State Test Prep Workbook
Teacher's Guide

Technology Highlights for the Teacher

Power Presentations
Dynamic presentations to engage students. Complete PowerPoint® presentations for every lesson in Chapter 14.

2-1 Solving One-Step Equations

Isolate a variable by using inverse operations which "undo" operations on the variable.

An equation is like a balanced scale. To keep the balance, perform the same operation on both sides.

Inverse Operations	
Operation	**Inverse Operation**
Addition	Subtraction
Subtraction	Addition

One-Stop Planner SPANISH
Easy access to Chapter 14 resources and assessments. Includes lesson-planning, test-generation, and puzzle-creation software.

Premier Online Edition SPANISH
Chapter 14 includes Tutorial Videos, Lesson Activities, Lesson Quizzes, Homework Help, and Chapter Project.

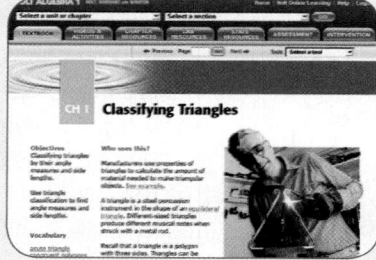

Classifying Triangles

Reaching All Learners

Resources for All Learners

Hands-On Lab Activities	Chapter 14
Technology Lab Activities	Chapter 14
Homework and Practice Workbook SPANISH	pp. 103–108
Know-It Notebook	Chapter 14
Problem Solving Workbook SPANISH	pp. 103–108

DEVELOPING LEARNERS

Practice A	CRB, every lesson
Reteach	CRB, every lesson
Inclusion	TE pp. 748, 753, 757
Questioning Strategies	Chapter 14
Modified Chapter 14 Resources 💿	*IDEA Works!*
Homework Help Online 🪐	

ON-LEVEL LEARNERS

Practice B	CRB, every lesson
Puzzles, Twisters, and Teasers	CRB, every lesson
Cognitive Strategies	TE p. 769
Cooperative Learning	TE p. 757

ADVANCED LEARNERS

Practice C	CRB, every lesson
Challenge	CRB, every lesson
Extension	TE pp. 733, 767, 770, 771
Critical Thinking	TE p. 735

English Language Learners

Are You Ready? Vocabulary	SE p. 731
Vocabulary Connections	SE p. 732
Lesson Vocabulary	SE, every lesson
Vocabulary Review	SE p. 772
English Language Learners	TE p. 734, 741
Reading Strategies	CRB, every lesson
Success for English Language Learners	pp. 205–216
Multilingual Glossary 🪐	

Reaching All Learners Through...

Inclusion	TE pp. 748, 753, 757
Kinesthetic Experience	TE p. 741
Concrete Manipulatives	TE pp. 748, 753
Cognitive Strategies	TE p. 769
Cooperative Learning	TE p. 757
Modeling	TE p. 763
Critical Thinking	TE p. 735
Test Prep Doctor	TE pp. 737, 743, 750, 755, 759, 765, 776
Common Error Alerts	TE pp. 757, 763, 769
Scaffolding Questions	TE p. 767

Technology Highlights for Reaching All Learners

 Lesson Tutorial Videos SPANISH

Starring Holt authors Ed Burger and Freddie Renfro! Live tutorials to support every lesson in Chapter 14.

 Multilingual Glossary

Searchable glossary includes definitions in English, Spanish, Vietnamese, Chinese, Hmong, Korean, and 4 other languages.

🪐 **Online Interactivities**

Interactive tutorials provide visually engaging alternative opportunities to learn concepts and master skills.

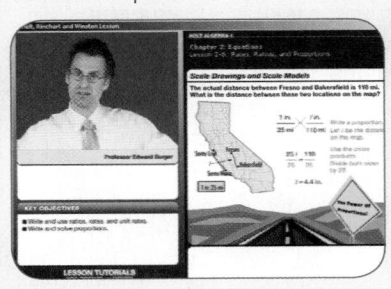

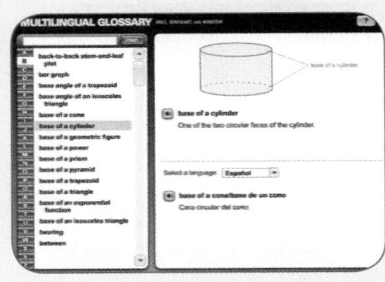

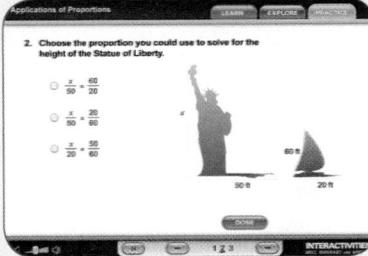

KEY: **SE** = *Student Edition* **TE** = *Teacher's Edition* **CRB** = *Chapter Resource Book*  Spanish version available  Available on CD-ROM  Available online

CHAPTER
14

Ongoing Assessment

Assessing Prior Knowledge

Determine whether students have the prerequisite concepts and skills for success in Chapter 14.

Are You Ready? SPANISH 🪐 💿 .... SE p. 731
Warm Up ✋ 💿 .... TE, every lesson

Test Preparation

Provide review and practice for Chapter 14 and standardized tests.

Multi-Step Test Prep .... SE p. 767
Study Guide: Review .... SE pp. 772–774
Standardized Test Prep .... SE pp. 776–777
State Test Prep Workbook
State Test Prep CD-ROM 💿
IDEA Works! 💿

Alternative Assessment

Assess students' understanding of Chapter 14 concepts and combined problem-solving skills.

Chapter 14 Project .... SE p. 730
Performance Assessment SPANISH .... AR pp. 279–280
Portfolio Assessment SPANISH .... AR p. xxxiv

Daily Assessment

Provide formative assessment for each day of Chapter 14.

Questioning Strategies .... Chapter 14
Think and Discuss .... SE, every lesson
Write About It .... SE, lesson exercises
Journal .... TE, lesson exercises
Lesson Quiz ✋ 💿 .... TE, every lesson
Modified Lesson Quizzes 💿 .... *IDEA Works!*

Weekly Assessment

Provide formative assessment for each week of Chapter 14.

Focus on Problem Solving .... SE p. 745
Multi-Step Test Prep .... SE p. 767
Ready to Go On? SPANISH 🪐 💿 .... SE pp. 744, 766
Cumulative Assessment .... SE pp. 776–777
Test and Practice Generator SPANISH 💿 ...*One-Stop Planner*

Formal Assessment

Provide summative assessment of Chapter 14 mastery.

Section Quizzes SPANISH .... AR pp. 265–266
Chapter 14 Test .... SE p. 775
Chapter Test (Levels A, B, C) SPANISH .... AR pp. 267–278
    • Multiple-Choice   • Free-Response
Cumulative Test SPANISH .... AR pp. 281–284
Test and Practice Generator SPANISH 💿 ...*One-Stop Planner*
Modified Chapter 14 Test 💿 .... *IDEA Works!*

Technology Highlights for the Teacher

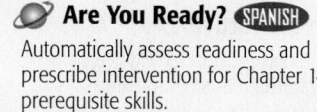 **Are You Ready?** SPANISH

Automatically assess readiness and prescribe intervention for Chapter 14 prerequisite skills.

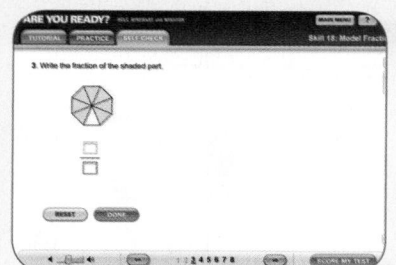

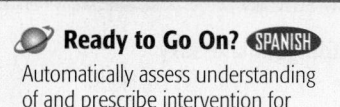 **Ready to Go On?** SPANISH

Automatically assess understanding of and prescribe intervention for Sections 14A and 14B.

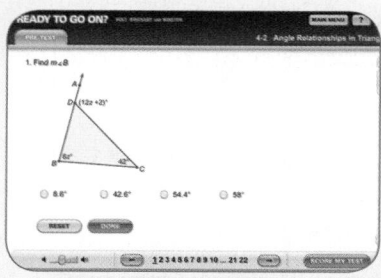

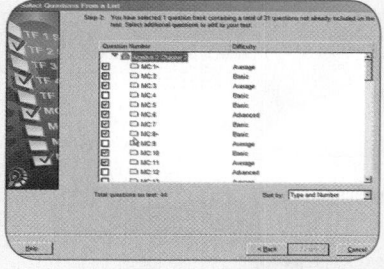 **Test and Practice Generator** SPANISH

Use Chapter 14 problem banks to create assessments and worksheets to print out or deliver online. Includes dynamic problems.

KEY: **SE** = *Student Edition*   **TE** = *Teacher's Edition*   **AR** = *Assessment Resources*   SPANISH Spanish version available   💿 Available on CD-ROM   🪐 Available online

CHAPTER
14

Formal Assessment

Three levels (A, B, C) of multiple-choice and free-response chapter tests are available in the *Assessment Resources*.

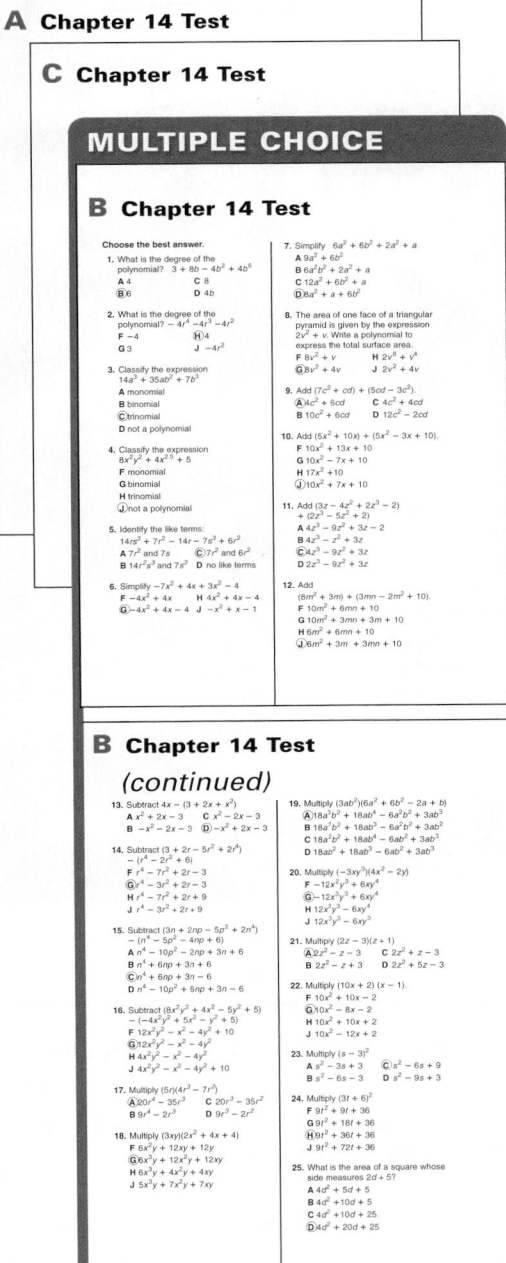

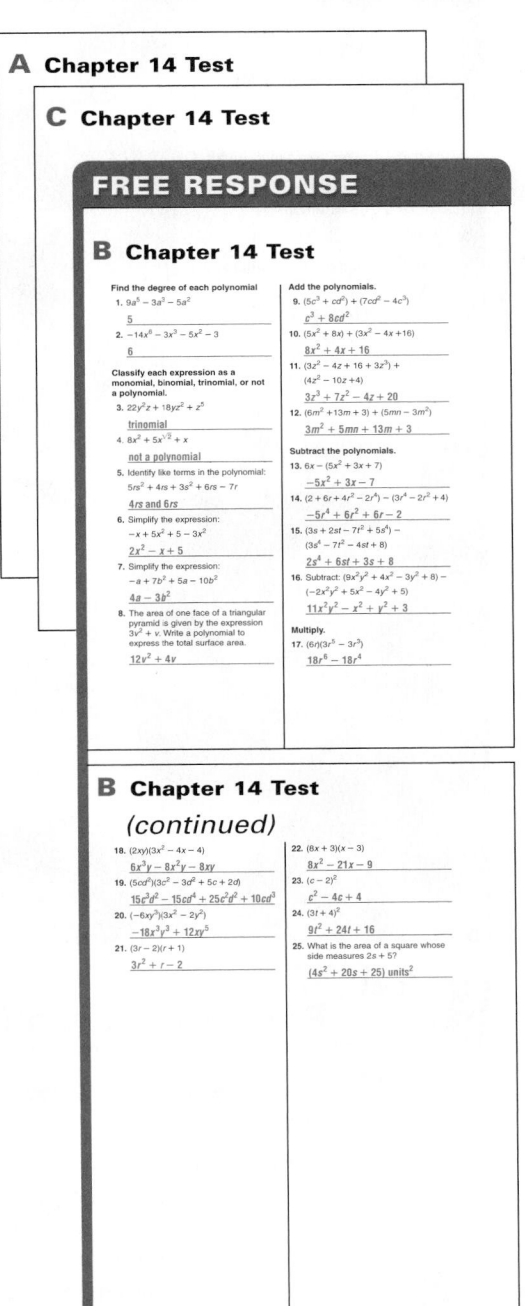

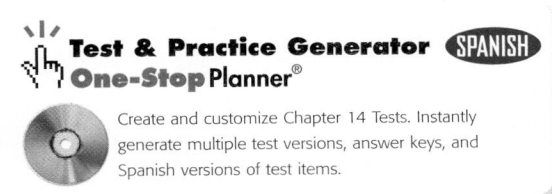

Test & Practice Generator SPANISH
One-Stop Planner®

Create and customize Chapter 14 Tests. Instantly generate multiple test versions, answer keys, and Spanish versions of test items.

CHAPTER
14 **Polynomials**

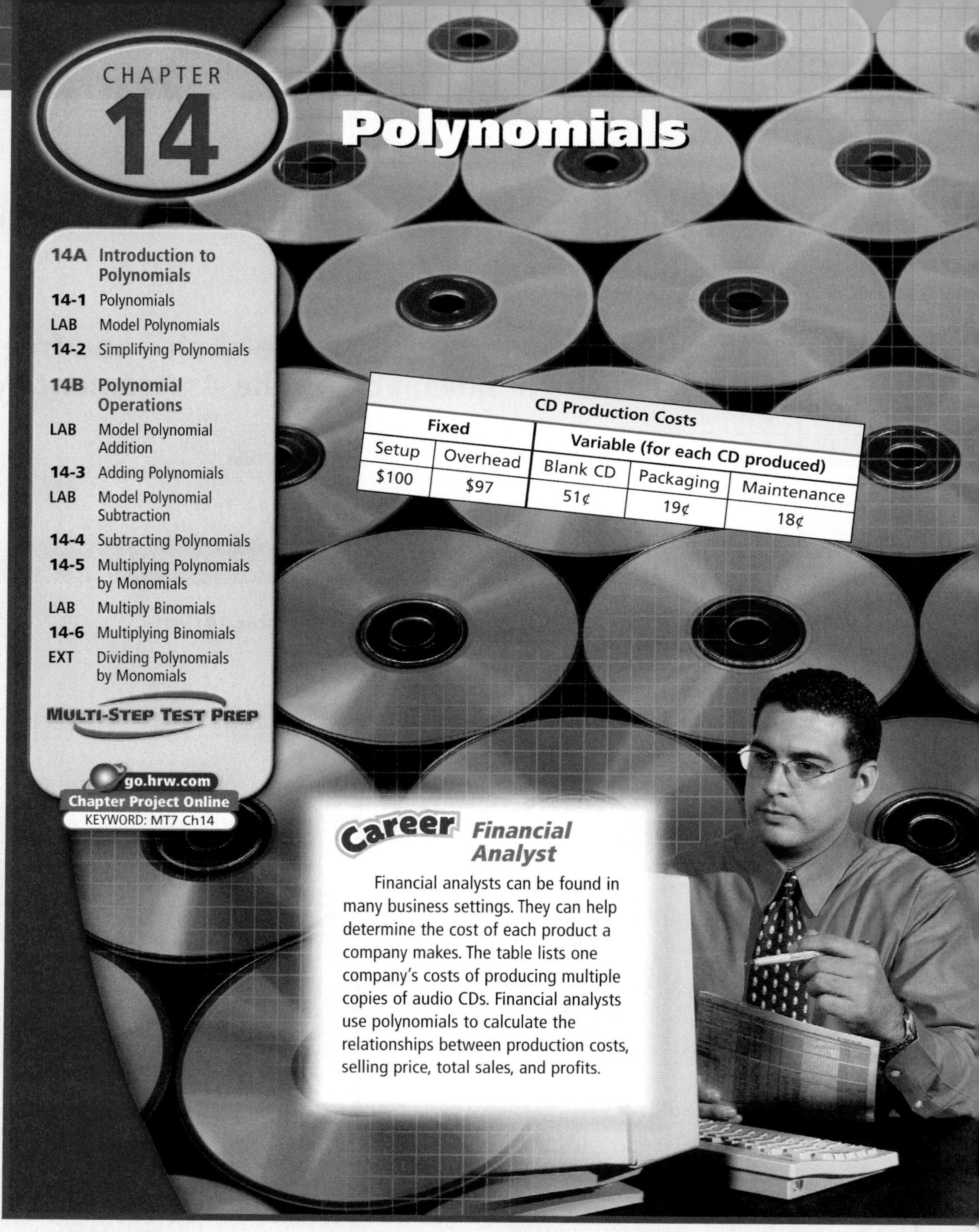

Why Learn This?

Tell students that polynomial expressions are used in many real-world applications. The total production cost of a CD depends on the cost of the materials needed to produce it, the cost of labor, the payment made to the artist, and many other factors. These fixed and variable costs might be written into an expression that a record company could use to determine the selling price of the CD. The expression might take the form of a polynomial.

Using Data

To begin the study of this chapter, have students:

- Discuss the difference between fixed and variable costs. Fixed costs do not change with the number of CDs produced; variable costs do.

- Write an expression to show the cost of producing n CDs.
  $197 + 0.88n$

- Use the expression to find the cost of producing 1000 CDs.
  $197 + 0.88(1000) = \$1077$

MULTI-STEP TEST PREP On page 767, students use polynomials to find dimensions for a kitchen remodeling project.

14A Introduction to Polynomials
14-1 Polynomials
LAB Model Polynomials
14-2 Simplifying Polynomials

14B Polynomial Operations
LAB Model Polynomial Addition
14-3 Adding Polynomials
LAB Model Polynomial Subtraction
14-4 Subtracting Polynomials
14-5 Multiplying Polynomials by Monomials
LAB Multiply Binomials
14-6 Multiplying Binomials
EXT Dividing Polynomials by Monomials

MULTI-STEP TEST PREP

go.hrw.com
Chapter Project Online
KEYWORD: MT7 Ch14

CD Production Costs				
Fixed		Variable (for each CD produced)		
Setup	Overhead	Blank CD	Packaging	Maintenance
$100	$97	51¢	19¢	18¢

Career *Financial Analyst*

Financial analysts can be found in many business settings. They can help determine the cost of each product a company makes. The table lists one company's costs of producing multiple copies of audio CDs. Financial analysts use polynomials to calculate the relationships between production costs, selling price, total sales, and profits.

Problem Solving Project

Understand, Plan, Solve, and Look Back

Have students:

- Complete the What Did We Make? worksheet to learn more about algebra and polynomials.

- Write this statement as an algebraic equation: Total cost equals fixed costs plus variable costs times the number of units. Does this equation contain any polynomials? Why or why not?

- Explain which variables affect the fixed costs of a company.

- Explain which aspects are affected by the number of CDs that are produced at one time.

Social Studies Connection

Project Resources

All project resources for teachers and students are provided online.

Materials:

- What Did We Make? worksheet

go.hrw.com
Project Teacher Support
KEYWORD: MT7 PSProject14

ARE YOU READY?

✓ Vocabulary

Choose the best term from the list to complete each sentence.

1. __?__ have the same variables raised to the same powers. **like terms**
2. In the expression $4x^2$, 4 is the __?__. **coefficient**
3. $5 + (4 + 3) = (5 + 4) + 3$ by the __?__. **Associative Property**
4. $3 \cdot 2 + 3 \cdot 4 = 3(2 + 4)$ by the __?__. **Distributive Property**

Associative Property

coefficient

Distributive Property

like terms

Complete these exercises to review skills you will need for this chapter.

✓ Subtract Integers

Subtract.

5. $12 - 4$ **8**
6. $8 - 10$ **−2**
7. $14 - (-4)$ **18**
8. $-9 - 5$ **−14**
9. $-9 - (-5)$ **−4**
10. $9 - (-5)$ **14**

✓ Exponents

Multiply. Write each product as one power.

11. $3^4 \cdot 3^6$ 3^{10}
12. $10^2 \cdot 10^3$ 10^5
13. $x \cdot x^5$ x^6
14. $5^5 \cdot 5^5$ 5^{10}
15. $y^2 \cdot y^6$ y^8
16. $z^3 \cdot z^3$ z^6
17. $a^2 \cdot a$ a^3
18. $b \cdot b$ b^2

✓ Distributive Property

Rewrite using the Distributive Property.

19. $5(7 + 8)$
$5 \cdot 7 + 5 \cdot 8$
20. $3(x + y)$
$3x + 3y$
21. $(a + b)6$
$6a + 6b$
22. $(r + s)4$
$4r + 4s$

✓ Area

Find the area of the shaded portion in each figure.

23.  15 cm, 36 cm
540 cm³

24. 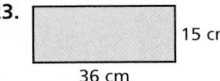 3 in., 9 in.
13.5 in²

25. 36 m, 24 m, 42 m, 84 m
2664 m²

26. 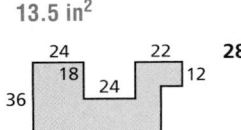 6 ft, 13 ft
39 ft²

27. 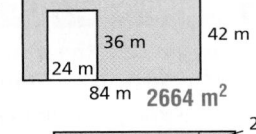 24, 22, 18, 24, 12, 36, 60
1848 units²

28. 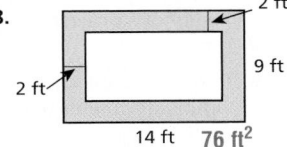 2 ft, 9 ft, 2 ft, 14 ft
76 ft²

Organizer

Objective: Help students organize the new concepts they will learn in Chapter 14.

 Online Edition
Multilingual Glossary

Resources

 **PuzzlePro®**
One-Stop Planner®

 Multilingual Glossary Online

go.hrw.com
KEYWORD: MT7 Glossary

Possible answers to *Vocabulary Connections*

1. A monomial has one term, a binomial has two terms, and a trinomial has three terms.
2. Monomials, binomials, and trinomials are all examples of polynomials.

Study Guide: Preview

Where You've Been

Previously, you

- classified figures by their characteristics.
- simplified numerical expressions.
- added, subtracted, and multiplied rational numbers.
- found the GCF of two or more numbers.

In This Chapter

You will study

- classifying polynomials by the number of terms.
- simplifying polynomial expressions by combining like terms.
- adding, subtracting, and multiplying monomials and binomials.
- using GCF to factor and divide polynomials.

Where You're Going

You can use the skills learned in this chapter

- to use polynomials to find the height of a projectile given its time in flight.
- to solve complex area and volume problems in higher math courses.

Key Vocabulary/Vocabulario

binomial	binomio
degree of a polynomial	grado de un polinomio
monomial	monomio
polynomial	polinomio
trinomial	trinomio

Vocabulary Connections

To become familiar with some of the vocabulary terms in the chapter, consider the following. You may refer to the chapter, the glossary, or a dictionary if you like.

1. The root of the words *monomial*, *binomial*, and *trinomial* is *-nomial*, which tells you how many different terms with exponents are in an algebraic expression. How many terms with exponents do you think there are in a **monomial**? in a **binomial**? in a **trinomial**?

2. The prefix *poly-* means "many." Knowing what you do about how the word *polygon* relates to the words *pentagon*, *hexagon*, and *octagon*, how do you think the word **polynomial** relates to the words *monomial*, *binomial*, and *trinomial*?

Study Strategy: Study for a Final Exam

A cumulative final exam will cover material you have learned over the course of the year. You must be prepared if you want to be successful. It may help you to make a study timeline like the one below.

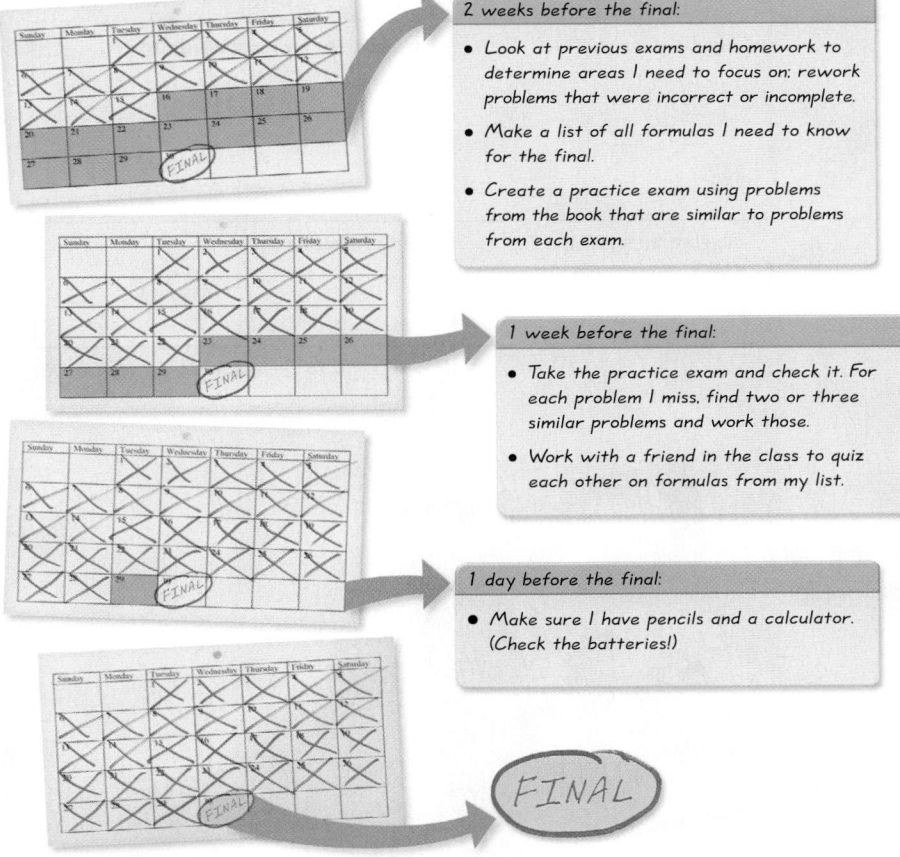

2 weeks before the final:

- Look at previous exams and homework to determine areas I need to focus on; rework problems that were incorrect or incomplete.
- Make a list of all formulas I need to know for the final.
- Create a practice exam using problems from the book that are similar to problems from each exam.

1 week before the final:

- Take the practice exam and check it. For each problem I miss, find two or three similar problems and work those.
- Work with a friend in the class to quiz each other on formulas from my list.

1 day before the final:

- Make sure I have pencils and a calculator. (Check the batteries!)

FINAL

Try This

Complete the following to help you prepare for your cumulative test.

1. Create a timeline that you will use to study for your final exam.

Reading and Writing Math

 Reading and **Writing Math**

CHAPTER **14**

Organizer

Objective: Help students apply strategies to understand and retain key concepts.

 Online Edition

Resources

Chapter 14 Resource Book
Reading Strategies

Study Strategy:
Study for a Final Exam

Discuss Explain to students that a final exam is a cumulative test of the knowledge from a course, and is different from a chapter test. Give examples of topics that may be covered on a final exam. Suggest that students take more time to study for the final exam, since it covers more material than a chapter test. Discourage cramming for any test.

Extend Ask students to use the strategy presented here to create a timeline they can use to study for the Chapter 14 Chapter Test.

Possible answers to *Try This*

1. 2 weeks before the final:

1. Look at previous tests.
2. Make sure I remember how to solve all the problems.
3. Rework problems I missed.
4. Make flash cards of all the formulas I will need to know.
5. Create a practice exam.

1 week before the final:

1. Take the practice exam.
2. Review the lessons that covered topics I missed on the exam.
3. Have someone quiz me using my formula flash cards.

1 day before the final:

1. Get a good night's sleep.
2. Make sure I have pencils and a calculator with fresh batteries.

Introduction to Polynomials

One-Minute Section Planner

Lesson	Materials	MiC and Lab Resources
Lesson 14-1 Polynomials ● Classify polynomials by degree and by the number of terms. **14-1 Hands-On Lab** Model Polynomials ● Use algebra tiles to model polynomials. ☐ SAT-10 ☑ ITBS ☐ CTBS ☐ NAEP	Algebra tiles (MK)	*Hands-On Lab Activities* 14-1
Lesson 14-2 Simplifying Polynomials ● Simplify polynomials. ☐ SAT-10 ☑ ITBS ☐ CTBS ☐ NAEP	Algebra tiles (MK), coins (MK), index cards	**MiC:** *Algebra Rules* pp. 44–47

MK = *Manipulatives Kit*

Mathematics in Context

The unit **Algebra Rules** from the *Mathematics in Context* © 2006 series can be used with Section 14A. See Section Planner above for suggestions for integrating *MiC* with *Holt Mathematics*.

Section Overview

Professional Development

Polynomials

Lesson 14-1

Why? **Polynomial** expressions are the building blocks of polynomial functions, which are used to model, represent, and analyze many real-world situations.

> A **monomial** is a number or a product of numbers and variables with exponents that are whole numbers.

Examples	
Monomials	$2n$, x^3, $4a^4b^3$, 7
Not Monomials	$p^{2.4}$, 2^x, $\sqrt{x}$, $\dfrac{5}{g^2}$

> A **polynomial** is one monomial or the sum or difference of monomials.

Polynomials	
Monomial (1 term)	$10ab^2$
Binomial (2 terms)	$9x^2 + 2$
Trinomial (3 terms)	$2a^2 + 3a - 5$

The **degree** of a polynomial is the degree of the term with the greatest degree.

$$4x^2 \quad + \quad 2x^5 \quad + \quad x \quad + \quad 5$$

Degree 2   Degree 5   Degree 1   Degree 0

Degree 5

Simplifying Polynomials

Lesson 14-2

Why? In order to solve polynomial equations, you need to know how to simplify polynomials.

> Like terms have the same variables raised to the same powers.

Example: $5x^2y + 2xy^2 + 6x^2y + 7y$

Like terms

> To simplify a polynomial, add or subtract like terms. You may need to use the Distributive Property to simplify a polynomial.

$$2(3ab^2 - 6b) + 2ab^2 + 5$$

$$2 \cdot 3ab^2 - 2 \cdot 6b + 2ab^2 + 5 \qquad \textit{Distributive Property}$$

$$6ab^2 - 12b + 2ab^2 + 5$$

$$8ab^2 - 12b + 5 \qquad \textit{Combine like terms.}$$

Pacing: Traditional 1 day
Block $\frac{1}{2}$ day

Objective: Students classify polynomials by degree and by the number of terms.

 **Online Edition**
Tutorial Videos

Power Presentations
with PowerPoint®

Warm Up

Identify the base and exponent of each power.

1. 3^4 3; 4   **2.** 2^a 2; a   **3.** x^5 x; 5

Determine whether each number is a whole number.

4. 0 yes   **5.** −3 no   **6.** 5 yes

Problem of the Day

If you take a whole number *n*, raise it to the third power, and then divide the result by *n*, what is the resulting expression? n^2

Also available on transparency

Math Fact

There are different mathematical meanings of the word *degree*. It is used as a unit of measure for temperature, as a unit of measure for angles, and as a means to classify polynomials.

State Resources

_____
_____
_____
_____
_____
_____
_____
_____
_____
_____
_____
_____

 **go.hrw.com**
State Resources Online
KEYWORD: MT7 Resources

Learn to classify polynomials by degree and by the number of terms.

Vocabulary
monomial
polynomial
binomial
trinomial
degree of a polynomial

Some fireworks shows are synchronized to music for dramatic effect. *Polynomials* are used to compute the exact height of each firework when it explodes.

The simplest type of polynomial is called a *monomial*. A **monomial** is a number or a product of numbers and variables with exponents that are whole numbers.

Monomials	$2n$, x^3, $4a^4b^3$, 7
Not monomials	$p^{2.4}$, 2^x, $\sqrt{x}$, $\frac{5}{g^2}$

EXAMPLE 1 Identifying Monomials

Determine whether each expression is a monomial.

A $\frac{1}{3}x^4y^7$

monomial

4 and 7 are whole numbers.

B $10xy^{0.3}$

not a monomial

0.3 is not a whole number.

A **polynomial** is one monomial or the sum or difference of monomials. Polynomials can be classified by the number of terms. A monomial has 1 term, a **binomial** has 2 terms, and a **trinomial** has 3 terms.

EXAMPLE 2 Classifying Polynomials by the Number of Terms

Classify each expression as a monomial, a binomial, a trinomial, or not a polynomial.

A $35.55h + 19.55g$

binomial   *Polynomial with 2 terms*

B $-2x^3y$

monomial   *Polynomial with 1 term*

C $6x^2 - 4xy + \frac{2}{x}$

not a polynomial   *A variable is in the denominator.*

D $7mn + 4m - 5n$

trinomial   *Polynomial with 3 terms*

---

1 Introduce

Alternate Opener

EXPLORATION

14-1 Polynomials

An object is dropped from an initial height of 144 feet. The graph shows its height versus time.

Height of Falling Object

Time (s) x	Equation y = 144 − 16x²	Height (ft) y
0	y = 144 − 16(0)² = 144	144
1		
2		
3		

1. What does the point (0, 144) represent?

2. When does the object reach the ground?

3. You can use the equation y = 144 − 16x² to model the object's fall. Complete the table and label the points on the graph.

Think and Discuss
_____

4. Explain why the graph of a falling object is not a straight line.

ENGLISH LANGUAGE LEARNERS

Motivate

Give students a group of words like *monolingual, bilingual,* and *trilingual.* Discuss the meaning of each word and its prefix. able to speak one, two, or three languages, respectively Then introduce the new vocabulary terms *monomial, binomial,* and *trinomial.* Ask students to think about the meaning of each word.

Explorations and answers are provided in *Alternate Openers: Explorations Transparencies.*

The *degree of a term* is the sum of the exponents of the variables in the term. A polynomial can be classified by its degree. The **degree of a polynomial** is the same as the term with the greatest degree.

$$\underbrace{\underset{\text{Degree 2}}{4x^2} + \underset{\text{Degree 5}}{2x^5} + \underset{\text{Degree 2}}{xy} + \underset{\text{Degree 0}}{5}}_{\text{Degree 5}}$$

EXAMPLE 3 Classifying Polynomials by Their Degrees

Find the degree of each polynomial.

A $6x^2 + 3x + 4$

$$\underset{\text{Degree 2}}{6x^2} + \underset{\text{Degree 1}}{3x} + \underset{\text{Degree 0}}{4}$$

The greatest degree is 2, so the degree of $6x^2 + 3x + 4$ is 2.

B $6 + 3m^2 + 4m^5$

$$\underset{\text{Degree 0}}{6} + \underset{\text{Degree 2}}{3m^2} + \underset{\text{Degree 5}}{4m^5}$$

The greatest degree is 5, so the degree of $6 + 3m^2 + 4m^5$ is 5.

EXAMPLE 4 Physics Application

The height in feet of a firework launched straight up into the air from *s* feet off the ground at velocity *v* after *t* seconds is given by the polynomial $-16t^2 + vt + s$. Find the height of a firework launched from a 10 ft platform at 200 ft/s after 5 seconds.

$-16t^2 + vt + s$	*Write the polynomial expression for height.*
$-16(5)^2 + 200(5) + 10$	*Substitute 5 for t, 200 for v, and 10 for s.*
$-400 + 1000 + 10$	*Simplify.*
610	

The firework is 610 ft high 5 seconds after launching.

Social Studies LINK

These colorfully decorated fireworks are part of a traditional Chinese New Year celebration.

Think and Discuss

1. Describe two ways you can classify a polynomial. Give a polynomial with three terms, and classify it two ways.

2. Explain why $-5x^2 - 3$ is a polynomial but $-5x^{-2} - 3$ is not.

Possible answers to Think and Discuss

1. You can classify a polynomial by the number of terms and by the degree. The polynomial $5x^3 + 3x + 1$ is a trinomial with a degree of 3.

2. $-5x^2 - 3$ is a difference of monomials; The exponent of $-5x^{-2} - 3$ is not a whole number.

---

2 Teach

Guided Instruction

In this lesson, students learn to classify polynomials by degree and the number of terms. After discussing the meanings of *monomial*, *binomial*, and *trinomial*, review Examples 1 and 2. You may want to give some additional examples of expressions that are not polynomials, such as $(3x^2 + 2\sqrt{x})$ and $(4x^3 + 5x^{-2})$. Explain why these are not polynomials. Explain that the degree of a monomial with one variable is the exponent of the variable. Point out that the degree of a constant is zero.

Reaching All Learners
Through Critical Thinking

Give each student some related polynomials, such as $3xy$ and $3 + x - y$. Have students classify each polynomial by its number of terms. Then have them identify the operations $(+, -, \text{or} \times)$ used in each polynomial. Finally, have students draw a conclusion about how operations are related to types of polynomials.

3 Close

Summarize

Remind students that a polynomial is a monomial or the sum or difference of monomials. A binomial has two monomial terms, and a trinomial has three monomial terms. The degree of a monomial with one variable is the exponent of the variable. The degree of a polynomial is the degree of the monomial with the greatest degree.

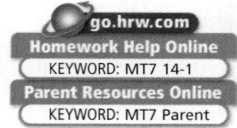

go.hrw.com
Homework Help Online
KEYWORD: MT7 14-1
Parent Resources Online
KEYWORD: MT7 Parent

Assignment Guide

If you finished Example **1** assign:
Average 1–4, 13–18, 50–57
Advanced 13–18, 48, 50–57

If you finished Example **2** assign:
Average 1–8, 13–24, 50–57
Advanced 13–24, 48, 50–57

If you finished Example **3** assign:
Average 1–11, 13–30, 33–44, 50–57
Advanced 13–30, 33–44, 46–48, 50–57

If you finished Example **4** assign:
Average 1–45, 50–57
Advanced 13–57

Homework Quick Check
Quickly check key concepts.
Exercises: 16, 20, 26, 31, 37

Math Background

The lesson addresses degree only for polynomials containing one variable. The degree of a monomial is the sum of the exponents of each variable. For example, $5x^2yz^4$ has a degree of 7, because $2 + 1 + 4 = 7$.

The degree of a polynomial is the greatest degree of its terms. For example, $3ab^5 + a^2b^2$ has a degree of 6, because the degree of $3ab^5$ is 6, and the degree of a^2b^2 is 4.

GUIDED PRACTICE

See Example **1** Determine whether each expression is a monomial.
1. $-2x^2y$ **yes** 2. $\frac{4}{3x}$ **no** 3. $\sqrt{3x}$ **no** 4. 9 **yes**

See Example **2** Classify each expression as a monomial, a binomial, a trinomial, or not a polynomial.
5. $\frac{3}{4}x + y$ **binomial** 6. $5r - 3r^2 + 6$ **trinomial** 7. $\frac{3}{x^2} + 2x$ **not a polynomial** 8. 2 **monomial**

See Example **3** Find the degree of each polynomial.
9. $-7m^5 + 3m^8$ **8** 10. $x^4 - 4$ **4** 11. 52 **0**

See Example **4** 12. The trinomial $-16t^2 + 24t + 72$ describes the height in feet of a ball thrown straight up from a 72 ft platform with a velocity of 24 ft/s after t seconds. What is the ball's height after 2 seconds? **56 feet**

INDEPENDENT PRACTICE

See Example **1** Determine whether each expression is a monomial.
13. $5.2x^3$ **yes** 14. $-3x^{-4}$ **no** 15. $\frac{5y^4}{6x}$ **no**
16. $\frac{4}{7}x^4y^2$ **yes** 17. 210 **yes** 18. 3^x **no**

See Example **2** Classify each expression as a monomial, a binomial, a trinomial, or not a polynomial.
19. $-9m^2n^6$ **monomial** 20. $6g^{\frac{1}{3}}h^2$ **not a polynomial** 21. $4x^3 + 2x^5 + 3$ **trinomial**
22. $-a + 3$ **binomial** 23. $2\sqrt{x}$ **not a polynomial** 24. $5v^3s$ **monomial**

See Example **3** Find the degree of each polynomial.
25. $2x^2 - 7x + 1$ **2** 26. $-3m^2 + 4m^3 - 2$ **3** 27. $-2 + 3x + 4x^4$ **4**
28. $6p^4 + 7p^2$ **4** 29. $n + 2$ **1** 30. $3y^8$ **8**

See Example **4** 31. The volume of a box with height x, length $x + 2$, and width $3x - 5$ is given by the trinomial $3x^3 - x^2 - 10x$. What is the volume of the box if its height is 2 inches? **8 in³**

PRACTICE AND PROBLEM SOLVING

Extra Practice
See page 808.

32. **Transportation** The distance in feet required for a car traveling at r mi/h to come to a stop can be approximated by the binomial $\frac{r^2}{20} + r$. About how many feet will be required for a car to stop if it is traveling at 70 mi/h? **about 315 ft**

RETEACH 14-1

LESSON **Reteach**
14-1 *Polynomials*

Expressions such as $2x$ and $4y^2$ are called **monomials**. A monomial has only one term. Monomials do <u>not</u> have fractional exponents, negative exponents, variable exponents, roots of variables, or variables in a denominator.

Determine whether each expression is a monomial.
1. $3x - 5$ **no** 2. $-9a^4$ **yes** 3. $21m^{0.5}$ **no** 4. $7m^3n^2$ **yes**

A monomial or a sum or difference of monomials is called a **polynomial**. Polynomials can be classified by the number of terms. A monomial has 1 term, a **binomial** has 2 terms, and a **trinomial** has 3 terms.

Classify each expression as a monomial, a binomial, a trinomial, or not a polynomial.
5. $7y + 3x^2 + 5$ **trinomial** 6. $6y + \sqrt{x}$ **not a polynomial**
7. m^2n **monomial** 8. $-6a + 2b^4$ **binomial**

The degree of a polynomial is the degree of the term with the greatest degree. The **degree** of a term is the greatest value of a variable's exponent.

terms
$3x^5 + 5x^3 + 6$
5th degree 3rd degree 0 degree
The above polynomial is a 5th degree trinomial.

Find the degree of each polynomial.
9. $5x + 3x^3 + 2x^2$ **3** 10. $-3m^4 + m^2 + 2$ **4** 11. $4y + 2y^3 + y^5$ **5** 12. $7a^2 + 8a$ **2**

PRACTICE 14-1

LESSON **Practice B**
14-1 *Polynomials*

Determine whether each expression is a monomial.
1. $-135x^5$ **yes** 2. $2.4x^3y$ **19 yes** 3. $\frac{2p^2}{q^2}$ **no**
4. $3r^{\frac{1}{2}}$ **no** 5. $43a^2b^{6.1}$ **no** 6. $\frac{7}{9}x^2yz^5$ **yes**

Classify each expression as a monomial, a binomial, a trinomial, or not a polynomial.
7. $-8.9xy + \frac{6}{y^5}$ **not a polynomial** 8. $\frac{9}{8}ab^8c^2d$ **monomial** 9. $x^8 + x + 1$ **trinomial**
10. $-7pq^{-2}r^4$ **not a polynomial** 11. $5n^{15} - 9n + \frac{1}{3}$ **trinomial** 12. $r^8 - 5.5r^{75}$ **binomial**

Find the degree of each polynomial.
13. $7 - 14x$ **1** 14. $5a + a^2 + \frac{6}{7}a^3$ **3** 15. $7w - 16u + 3v$ **1**
16. $9p - 9q - 9p^3 - 9q^2$ **3** 17. $z^9 + 10y^8 - x$ **9** 18. $100,050 + \frac{4}{5}k - k^4$ **4**

19. The volume of a box with height x, length $x - 1$, and width $2x + 2$ is given by the trinomial $2x^3 - 2x$. What is the volume of the box if its height is 4 feet? **120 ft³**

20. The trinomial $-16t^2 + 32t + 32$ describes the height in feet of a ball thrown upward after t seconds. What is the height of the ball $\frac{5}{8}$ seconds after it was thrown? **45.75 feet**

Classify each expression as a monomial, a binomial, a trinomial, or not a polynomial. If it is a polynomial, give its degree.

33. $4x^3$ monomial; 3   **34.** $7x^{0.7} + 3x$ **35.** $-\frac{5}{6}x + \frac{3}{5}x^2$ binomial; 2   **36.** $7y^2 - 6y$
        not a polynomial   binomial; 2

37. $2f^3 + 5f^5 - f$ **38.** $3 - \frac{2}{x}$ **39.** $6x + 4\sqrt{x}$ **40.** $6x^{-4}$
   trinomial; 5   not a polynomial   not a polynomial   not a polynomial

41. $3b^2 - 9b - 8b^3$ **42.** $4 + 5x$ **43.** $2x^{\frac{1}{2}} - 3x^4 + 5$ **44.** 5 monomial; 0
   trinomial; 3   binomial; 1   not a polynomial

45. Transportation Gas mileage at speed s can be estimated using the given polynomials. Evaluate the polynomials to complete the table.

		Gas Mileage (mi/gal)		
		40 mi/h	50 mi/h	60 mi/h
Compact	$-0.025s^2 + 2.45s - 30$	28	30	27
Midsize	$-0.015s^2 + 1.45s - 13$	21	22	20
Van	$-0.03s^2 + 2.9s - 53$	15	17	13

46. Possible answer: I looked for the polynomial with the highest degree.

46. Critical Thinking Without solving, tell which of the following binomials has the greatest value when $x = 10$. Explain what method you used.

(A) $3x^5 + 8$ (B) $3x^8 + 8$ (C) $3x^2 + 8$ (D) $3x^6 + 8$

47. What's the Error? A student says that the degree of the polynomial $4b^5 - 7b^9 + 6b$ is 5. What is the error?

48. Write About It Give some examples of words that start with *mono-*, *bi-*, *tri-*, and *poly-*, and relate the meaning of each to polynomials.

49. Challenge The base of a triangle is described by the binomial $x + 2$, and its height is described by the trinomial $2x^2 + 3x - 7$. What is the area of the triangle if $x = 5$?   203 units^2

TEST PREP and Spiral Review

50. Multiple Choice The height in feet of a soccer ball kicked straight up into the air from s feet off the ground at velocity v after t seconds is given by the trinomial $-16t^2 + vt + s$. What is the height of the soccer ball kicked from 2 feet off the ground at 90 ft/s after 3 seconds?

(F) 3 ft   (G) 15 ft   (H) 90 ft   (J) 128 ft

51. Gridded Response What is the degree of the polynomial $6 + 7k^4 - 8k^9$?   9

Write each number in scientific notation. (Lesson 4-4)

52. 4,080,000 4.08×10^6 **53.** -0.000035 -3.5×10^{-5} **54.** 5,910,000,000 5.91×10^9

Solve. (Lesson 11-1)

55. $15x - 8x = 91$ $x = 13$ **56.** $3j + 14 = 5j$ $j = 7$ **57.** $4m - 1000 = -6m$ $m = 100$

Answers

47. Possible answer: The student needs to look at all three terms of the polynomial to determine the degree, not just the degree of the first term. The degree is 9.

48. Possible answer: *Monorail, bicycle, tripod, polygon;* a monorail has one rail for a track, and a monomial has one term. A bicycle has two wheels, and a binomial has two terms. A tripod has three legs, and a trinomial has three terms. A polygon can have many sides, and a polynomial can have many terms.

TEST PREP DOCTOR For Exercise 50, students may find it helpful to rewrite the trinomial, substituting the given values for s, v, and t. In the first term of the trinomial, students may mistakenly square the product of -16 and 3, rather than squaring 3 and *then* multiplying by -16.

 Journal

Ask students to write an algebraic expression that is not a polynomial and to explain why it is not a polynomial.

Power Presentations with PowerPoint®

14-1 Lesson Quiz

Determine whether each expression is a monomial.

1. $5a^2z^4$ yes   **2.** $3\sqrt{x}$ no

Classify each expression as a monomial, a binomial, a trinomial, or not a polynomial.

3. $2x^2 - 3x - 6$ trinomial

4. $3m^3 + 4m$ binomial

Find the degree of each polynomial.

5. $3a^2 + a^5 + 26$ 5

6. $2c^3 - c^2$ 3

Also available on transparency

Hands-On LAB Organizer

Use with Lesson 14-1

Pacing:
Traditional $\frac{1}{2}$ day
Block $\frac{1}{4}$ day

Objective: Use algebra tiles to model polynomials

Materials: Algebra tiles

 Online Edition
Algebra Tiles

Resources

 Hands-On Lab Activities
Lab 14-1 Recording Sheet

Teach

Discuss

Be sure students understand what each algebra tile represents.

Close

Key Concept

You can use algebra tiles to represent monomials and polynomials.

Assessment

1. Represent the polynomial $2x + 1$ with algebra tiles.

2. Write the polynomial modeled by the tiles below.

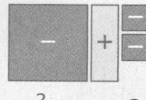

$-x^2 + x - 2$

Hands-On LAB 14-1 Model Polynomials

Use with Lesson 14-1

go.hrw.com
Lab Resources Online
KEYWORD: MT7 Lab14

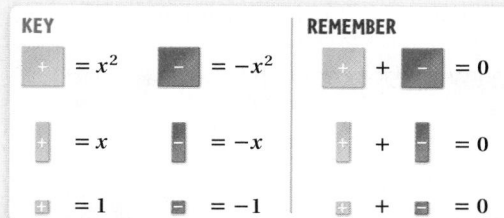

You can use algebra tiles to model polynomials. To model the polynomial $4x^2 + x - 3$, you need four x^2-tiles, one x-tile, and three -1-tiles.

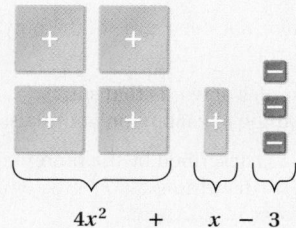

$$4x^2 \quad + \quad x \; - \; 3$$

Activity 1

1 Use algebra tiles to model the polynomial $2x^2 + 4x + 6$.

All signs are positive, so use all yellow tiles.

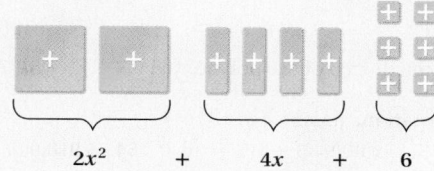

$$2x^2 \quad + \quad 4x \quad + \quad 6$$

State Resources

go.hrw.com
State Resources Online
KEYWORD: MT7 Resources

Miguel Carrizales
San Antonio, Texas

Teacher to Teacher

As students progress from the concrete to the abstract, it is important for them to be able to visualize abstract concepts such as polynomials. I like to have students create large models of polynomials that can be displayed in the classroom. Students work in pairs to create the models on poster board. After the posters are displayed, each team can identify the different polynomials that are modeled. The students enjoy moving around and seeing other students' work.

② Use algebra tiles to model the polynomial $-x^2 + 6x - 4$.

Modeling $-x^2 + 6x - 4$ is similar to modeling $2x^2 + 4x + 6$. Remember to use red tiles for negative values.

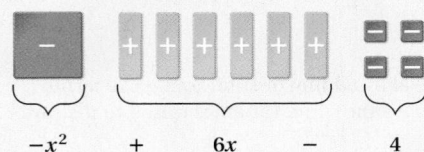

$$-x^2 \qquad + \qquad 6x \qquad - \qquad 4$$

Think and Discuss

1. How do you know when to use red tiles?   Possible answer: Red tiles represent terms that have negative coefficients.

Try This

Use algebra tiles to model each polynomial.

1. $2x^2 + 3x - 5$ **2.** $-4x^2 + 5x - 1$ **3.** $5x^2 - x + 9$

Activity 2

① Write the polynomial modeled by the tiles below.

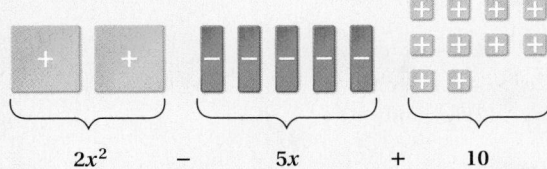

$$2x^2 \qquad - \qquad 5x \qquad + \qquad 10$$

The polynomial modeled by the tiles is $2x^2 - 5x + 10$.

Think and Discuss

1. How do you know the coefficient of the x^2 term in Activity 2?   There are two large, square, yellow tiles, so the coefficient is 2.

Try This

Write a polynomial modeled by each group of algebra tiles.

1.

$2x^2 - 2x$

2.

$x^2 - 2x + 1$

3.
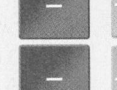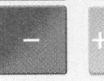

$-2x^2 + 3x - 2$

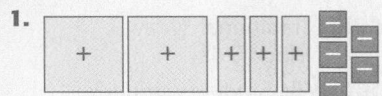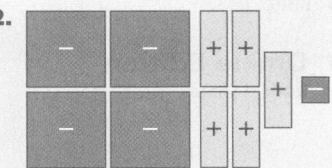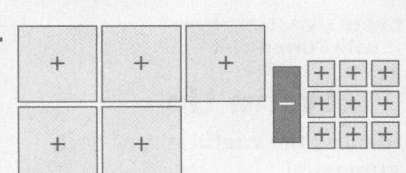

Pacing: Traditional 1 day
Block $\frac{1}{2}$ day
Objective: Students simplify polynomials.

Online Edition
Tutorial Videos

Warm Up

Identify the coefficient of each monomial.

1. $3x^4$ 3   **2.** ab 1
3. $\frac{x}{2}$ $\frac{1}{2}$ **4.** $-cb^3$ −1

Use the Distributive Property to simplify each expression.

5. $9(6 + 7)$ 117   **6.** $4(10 − 2)$ 32

Problem of the Day

Warren drank 3.5 gallons of water in one week. Find the average number of *ounces* of water Warren drank each day that week. 64 oz

Also available on transparency

Math Humor

How do you know when your parrot is a mathematician? It says, "Polly wants a nomial."

Learn to simplify polynomials.

You can simplify a polynomial by adding or subtracting like terms. Remember that like terms have the same variables raised to the same powers.

Like terms   *The variables have the same powers.*

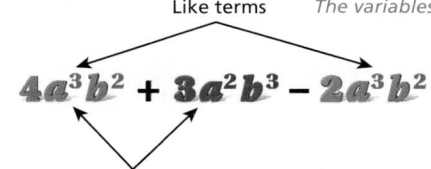

Not like terms   *The variables have different powers.*

EXAMPLE 1   **Identifying Like Terms**

Identify the like terms in each polynomial.

A $2a + 4a^2 − 3 + 5a − 6a^2$
$(2a) + \boxed{4a^2} − 3 + (5a) − \boxed{6a^2}$ *Identify like terms.*
Like terms: $2a$ and $5a$, $4a^2$ and $−6a^2$

B $−4x^5y^3 + 12x^5y^3 − 4x^3 − 6x^5y^3$
$(−4x^5y^3) + (12x^5y^3) − 4x^3 − (6x^5y^3)$ *Identify like terms.*
Like terms: $−4x^5y^3$, $12x^5y^3$, and $−6x^5y^3$

C $5m^2 − 3mn + 4m$
$5m^2 − 3mn + 4m$ *Identify like terms.*
There are no like terms.

To simplify a polynomial, combine like terms. It may be easier to arrange the terms in *descending* order (highest degree to lowest degree) before combining like terms.

EXAMPLE 2   **Simplifying Polynomials by Combining Like Terms**

Simplify.

A $x^2 + 5x^4 − 6 + 7x^2 + 3x^4 − 4x^2$
$5x^4 + 3x^4 + x^2 + 7x^2 − 4x^2 − 6$ *Arrange in descending order.*
$(5x^4) + (3x^4) + \boxed{x^2} + \boxed{7x^2} − \boxed{4x^2} − 6$ *Identify like terms.*
$8x^4 + 4x^2 − 6$ *Combine coefficients:*
$5 + 3 = 8$ and $1 + 7 − 4 = 4$

1 Introduce

Alternate Opener

EXPLORATION

14-2 Simplifying Polynomials

You can use algebra tiles to model polynomials. The polynomial $2x^2 + 2x + 2 + x^2 − x − 3$ is modeled below.

1. Use tiles to show that $2x^2 + 2x + 2 + x^2 − x − 3 = 3x^2 + x − 1$.

Use algebra tiles to simplify each expression.

2. $4x^2 − 2x − 5 − 3x^2 + x − 4$
3. $3x^2 − x + 1 − x^2 − x + 3$

Think and Discuss

4. Explain how you can use tiles to simplify polynomials.
5. Explain why you cannot simplify the polynomial $3x^2 + 4x − 9$.

Motivate

Show students a small pile of various coins. You may want to use the play money provided in the Manipulatives Kit. Ask students how they would sort the money. Group like coins together. Explain that like terms in polynomials can be grouped in the same way. You may want to remind students that they have worked with like terms before.

Explorations and answers are provided in *Alternate Openers: Explorations Transparencies.*

Simplify.

B $-5a^2b + 12ab^2 - 4a^2b - ab^2 + 3ab$

$\underbrace{-5a^2b} + \boxed{12ab^2} - \underbrace{4a^2b} - \boxed{ab^2} + 3ab$ *Identify like terms.*

$-9a^2b + 11ab^2 + 3ab$ *Combine coefficients:*
     $-5 - 4 = -9$ and $12 - 1 = 11$

Sometimes you may need to use the Distributive Property to simplify a polynomial.

EXAMPLE 3   **Simplifying Polynomials by Using the Distributive Property**

Simplify.

A $4(3x^2 + 5x)$

$4(3x^2 + 5x)$ *Distributive Property*

$4 \cdot 3x^2 + 4 \cdot 5x$

$12x^2 + 20x$

B $2(4ab^2 - 5b) + 3ab^2 + 6$

$2(4ab^2 - 5b) + 3ab^2 + 6$ *Distributive Property*

$2 \cdot 4ab^2 - 2 \cdot 5b + 3ab^2 + 6$

$8ab^2 - 10b + 3ab^2 + 6$

$11ab^2 - 10b + 6$ *Combine like terms.*

EXAMPLE 4   **Business Application**

A *board foot* is 1 ft by 1 ft by 1 in. of lumber. The amount of lumber that can be harvested from a tree with diameter d in. is approximately $20 + 0.005(d^3 - 30d^2 + 300d - 1000)$ board feet. Use the Distributive Property to write an equivalent expression.

$20 + 0.005(d^3 - 30d^2 + 300d - 1000) = 20 + 0.005d^3 - 0.15d^2 + 1.5d - 5$
$= 15 + 0.005d^3 - 0.15d^2 + 1.5d$

Possible answers to
Think and Discuss

1. The terms are either numbers or terms with the same variables raised to the same powers, and they are separated by plus or minus signs.

2. $8(3x + 2) = 24x + 16;$
$8x + 3x = 11x$

Think and Discuss

1. **Tell** how you know when you can combine like terms.

2. **Give** an example of an expression that you could simplify by using the Distributive Property and an expression that you could simplify by combining like terms.

2 Teach

Guided Instruction

In this lesson, students learn to simplify polynomials. First, be sure that students know how to identify like terms. You may want to use the Teaching Transparency. Explain that like terms are either constants or terms with the same variables raised to the same powers. After students are able to identify like terms, discuss how to simplify polynomials by combining like terms. Then discuss how to use the Distributive Property to simplify expressions.

 Reaching All Learners
Through Kinesthetic Experience

Have students work in groups. Each group should write one of the following monomials on a piece of paper:

$3x^2$, 3, $\frac{1}{2}x^4$, x, $-5x$, $-2x^3$, $5x^2$, 0, x^3, $\frac{1}{2}x^4$

Have each group find the other group whose card contains a like term; then, have them combine all of the like terms into one term.

3 and 0, $-5x$ and x, $3x^2$ and $5x^2$, $-2x^3$ and x^3, $\frac{1}{2}x^4$ and $\frac{1}{2}x^4$ Then you may want to have the class write all of the terms as one polynomial.

$x^4 - x^3 + 8x^2 - 4x + 3$

3 Close

ENGLISH LANGUAGE LEARNERS

Summarize

Ask students to define *like terms*. Remind them that like terms can be combined by addition or subtraction. Make sure students understand how to apply the Distributive Property to polynomials.

Possible answer: Like terms are terms that have the same variable(s) raised to the same powers. Constants are also considered like terms.

go.hrw.com
Homework Help Online
KEYWORD: MT7 14-2
Parent Resources Online
KEYWORD: MT7 Parent

Assignment Guide

If you finished Example **1** assign:
Average 1, 2, 9, 10, 29–34,
Advanced 9, 10, 29–34

If you finished Example **2** assign:
Average 1–4, 9–12, 17, 18, 29–34
Advanced 9–12, 17, 18, 28–34

If you finished Example **3** assign:
Average 1–7, 9–15, 17–22, 29–34
Advanced 9–15, 19–24, 28–34

If you finished Example **4** assign:
Average 1–22, 25, 26, 29–34
Advanced 9–34

Homework Quick Check

Quickly check key concepts.
Exercises: 10, 12, 14, 16

Math Background

In the lesson, Example 3 addresses using the Distributive Property to simplify expressions. The process of combining like terms used in Example 2 is also an application of the Distributive Property (e.g., $3x + 2x = (3 + 2)x = 5x$).

The Distributive Property may be used several times in the simplification of a polynomial. For example:

$4(3x + 2z) + 5x - 6z$
$\quad 12x + 8z + 5x - 6z$
$\quad 12x + 5x + 8z - 6z$
$\quad (12 + 5)x + (8 - 6)z$
$\qquad 17x + 2z$

go.hrw.com
State Resources Online
KEYWORD: MT7 Resources

State Resources

GUIDED PRACTICE

See Example **1** Identify the like terms in each polynomial.

1. $-3b^2 + 5b + 4b^2 - b + 6$ $-3b^2$ and $4b^2$, $5b$ and $-b$

2. $7mn - 5m^2n^2 + 8m^2n + 4m^2n^2$ $-5m^2n^2$ and $4m^2n^2$

See Example **2** Simplify.

3. $2x^2 - 3x + 5x^2 + 7x - 5$ $7x^2 + 4x - 5$

4. $6 - 3b + 2b^4 - 7b^2 + 9 + 4b - 3b^2$ $2b^4 - 10b^2 + b + 15$

See Example **3** **5.** $4(3x - 8)$ $12x - 32$ **6.** $7(2x^2 + 4x)$ $14x^2 + 28x$ **7.** $5(3a^2 - 5a) + 2a^2 + 4a$ $17a^2 - 21a$

See Example **4** **8.** The level of nitric oxide emissions, in parts per million, from a car engine is approximated by the polynomial $-40,000 + 5x(800 - x^2)$, where x is the air-fuel ratio. Use the Distributive Property to write an equivalent expression. $-40,000 + 4000x - 5x^3$

INDEPENDENT PRACTICE

See Example **1** Identify the like terms in each polynomial.

9. $-t + 4t^2 - 5t^2 + 5t - 2$ $-t$ and $5t$, $4t^2$ and $-5t^2$

10. $8rs - 3r^2s^2 + 5r^2s^2 + 2rs - 5$ $8rs$ and $2rs$, $-3r^2s^2$ and $5r^2s^2$

See Example **2** Simplify.

11. $2p - 3p^2 + 5p + 12p^2$ $9p^2 + 7p$

12. $3fg + f^2g - fg^2 - 3fg + 4f^2g + 6fg^2$ $5f^2g + 5fg^2$

See Example **3** **13.** $5(x^2 - 5x) + 4x^2 - 7x$ $9x^2 - 32x$ **14.** $2(b - 3) + 5b - 3b^2$ $7b - 6 - 3b^2$ **15.** $\frac{1}{2}(6y^3 - 8) + 3y^3$ $6y^3 - 4$

See Example **4** **16.** The concentration of a certain medication in an average person's bloodstream h hours after injection can be estimated using the expression $6(0.03h - 0.002h^2 - 0.01h^3)$. Use the Distributive Property to write an equivalent expression. $-0.06h^3 - 0.012h^2 + 0.18h$

PRACTICE AND PROBLEM SOLVING

Extra Practice
See page 808.

Simplify.

17. $2s^2 - 3s + 10s^2 + 5s - 3$ $12s^2 + 2s - 3$

18. $5gh^2 + 4g^2h + 2g^2h - g^2h$ $5gh^2 + 5g^2h$

19. $2(x^2 - 5x + 4) - 3x + 7$ $2x^2 - 13x + 15$

20. $5(x - x^5 + x^3) - 3x$ $-5x^5 + 5x^3 + 2x$

21. $4(2m - 3m^2) + 7(3m^2 - 4m)$ $9m^2 - 20m$

22. $6b^4 + 2b^2 + 3(b^2 - 6)$ $6b^4 + 5b^2 - 18$

23. $5mn - 3m^3n^2 + 3(m^3n^2 + 4mn)$ $17mn$

24. $3(4x + y) + 2(3x - 2y)$ $18x - y$

25. **Life Science** The rate of flow in cm/s of blood in an artery at d cm from the center is given by the polynomial $1000(0.04 - d^2)$. Use the Distributive Property to write an equivalent expression. $40 - 1000d^2$

RETEACH 14-2

LESSON 14-2 Reteach
Simplifying Polynomials

You can simplify a polynomial by combining like terms. Like terms have the same variables raised to the same powers. All constants are like terms.

$9 + 6y^3 - 8 + 7x^2y^3 + 3x^2y^3$
like terms   like terms

$7x^2y^3$ and $3x^2y^3$ both have the variable x raised to the 2nd power and the variable y raised to the 3rd power. Therefore, they are like terms.

Identify the like terms in each polynomial

1. $m + 3m^2 - 2m + 6 + 2m^2$
m and $-2m$; $3m^2$ and $2m^2$

2. $b - a^2b^2 - 2 + a^2 + 2a^2b^2$
$2a^2b^2$ and $-a^2b^2$

3. $x^3 + 2 + 4x^3 - 9 + x$
x^3 and $4x^3$; 2 and -9

4. $9 + 4dg^2 + 4 + 6dg^2 + d^2$
$4dg^2$ and $6dg^2$, 4 and 9

To simplify a polynomial, combine like terms. To combine like terms, add or subtract the coefficients. The variables and the exponents do not change.

$7x^2y^3 - 6y^3 + 3x^2y^3$
$7x^2y^3 + 6y^3 + 3x^2y^3$ Identify like terms.
$10x^2y^3 + 6y^3$ Combine coefficients of like terms.
$7 + 3 = 10$

Simplify.

5. $8a + 3ab^2 + 3a + 2ab^2$
$5ab^2 + 11a$

6. $x^3 + 1 + 2x^3 + 3xy^2 - 3$
$3x^3 + 3xy^2 - 2$

7. $y^4 + 2x^2y^3 - 3x^2 + 2y^4$
$3y^4 + 2x^2y^3 - 3x^2$

PRACTICE 14-2

LESSON 14-2 Practice B
Simplifying Polynomials

Identify the like terms in each polynomial.

1. $x^2 - 8x + 3x^2 + 6x - 1$
x^2 and $3x^2$, $-8x$ and $6x$

2. $2c^2 + d^3 + 3d^3 - 2c^2 + 6$
$2c^2$ and $-2c^2$, d^3 and $3d^3$

3. $2x^2 - 2xy - 2y^2 + 3xy + 3x^2$
$2x^2$ and $3x^2$, $-2xy$ and $3xy$

4. $2 - 9x + x^2 - 3 + x$
$-9x$ and x, 2 and -3

5. $xy - 5x + y - x + 10y - 3y^2$
$-5x$ and $-x$, y and $10y$

6. $6p + 2p^2 + pq + 2q^3 - 2p$
$6p$ and $-2p$

7. $3a + 2b + a^2 - 5b + 7a$
$3a$ and $7a$, $2b$ and $-5b$

8. $10m - 3m^2 + 9m^2 - 3m - m^3$
$10m$ and $-3m$,
$-3m^2$ and $9m^2$

Simplify.

9. $2h - 9hk + 6h - 6k$
$8h - 9hk - 6k$

10. $9(x^2 + 2xy - y^2) - 2(x^2 + xy)$
$7x^2 + 16xy - 9y^2$

11. $7qr - q^2r^3 + 2q^2r^3 - 6qr$
$q^2r^3 + qr$

12. $8v^4 + 3v^2 + 2v^2 - 16$
$8v^4 + 5v^2 - 16$

13. $3(x + 2y) + 2(2x - 3y)$
$7x$

14. $7(1 - x) + 3x^2y + 7x - 7$
$3x^2y$

15. $6(9y + 1) + 8(2 - 3y)$
$30y + 22$

16. $a^2b - a^2 + ab^2 - 3a^2b + ab$
$-2a^2b - a^2 + ab^2 + ab$

17. A student in Tracey's class created the following expression:
$y^3 - 3y + 4(y^2 - y^3)$. Use the Distributive Property to write an equivalent expression.
$-3y^3 + 4y^2 - 3y$

Art

Abstract artists often use geometric shapes, such as cubes, prisms, pyramids, and spheres, to create sculptures.

26. Suppose the volume of a sculpture is approximately $s^3 + 0.52s^3 + 0.18s^3 + 0.33s^3$ cm^3 and the surface area is approximately $6s^2 + 3.14s^2 + 7.62s^2 + 3.24s^2$ cm^2.

    a. Simplify the polynomial expression for the volume of the sculpture, and find the volume of the sculpture for $s = 5$. **$2.03s^3$; 253.75 cm^3**

    b. Simplify the polynomial expression for the surface area of the sculpture, and find the surface area of the sculpture for $s = 5$. **$20s^2$; 500 cm^2**

Balanced/Unbalanced O by Fletcher Benton

27. A sculpture features a large ring with an outer lateral surface area of about $44xy$ in^2, an inner lateral surface area of about $38xy$ in^2, and 2 bases, each with an area of about $41y$ in^2. Write and simplify a polynomial that expresses the surface area of the ring. **$82xy + 82y$ in^2**

28. ⭐ **Challenge** The volume of the ring on the sculpture from Exercise 27 is $49\pi xy^2 - 36\pi xy^2$ in^3. Simplify the polynomial, and find the volume for $x = 12$ and $y = 7.5$. Give your answer both in terms of π and to the nearest tenth. **$13\pi xy^2$; $8775\pi \approx 27{,}567.5$ in^3**

Pyramid Balancing Cube and Sphere, artist unknown

go.hrw.com
Web Extra!
KEYWORD: MT7 Art

TEST PREP and Spiral Review

29. **Multiple Choice** Simplify the expression $4x^2 + 8x^3 - 9x^2 + 2x$.

    Ⓐ $8x^3 - 5x^4 + 2x$ Ⓑ $8x^3 + 13x^2 + 2x$ Ⓒ $8x^3 - 5x^2 + 2x$ Ⓓ $5x^3$

30. **Short Response** Identify the like terms in the polynomial $3x^4 + 5x^2 - x^4 + 4x^2$. Then simplify the polynomial. **The like terms are: "$3x^4$ and $-x^4$" and "$5x^2$ and $4x^2$"; $2x^4 + 9x^2$**

Find each percent to the nearest tenth. (Lesson 6-3)

31. What percent of 82 is 42? **51.2%**   32. What percent of 195 is 126? **64.6%**

Create a table for each quadratic function, and use it to make a graph. (Lesson 13-6)

33. $f(x) = -x^2 + 1$ 34. $f(x) = x^2 + 2x - 1$

CHALLENGE 14-2

LESSON 14-2 Challenge
Coming To Terms

For each polynomial, use the simplified polynomial to find the missing term.

	Polynomial	Simplified Polynomial	Missing Term
1.	$7x^2 - 4x + \_ + 3x - 5$	$5x^2 - x - 5$	$-2x^2$
2.	$6(9x + \_)$	$54x + 18$	3
3.	$12 + 2m + 3m^4 - 8m^2 + 5 + \_ - 7m^2$	$3m^4 - 15m^2 + 6m + 17$	$4m$
4.	$\_ (2b^2 - 9b) + 4b^2 + 11b$	$14b^2 - 34b$	5
5.	$7(x^3 + 3x) - 5x^3 + \_$	$2x^3 + 11x$	$-10x$
6.	$4ab + \_ + 3a^2b^2 + 2ab - 8$	$2a^2b^2 + 6ab - 8$	$-a^2b^2$
7.	$\_ + 7 + 10w^2 - 4w^2 + 5w - 2$	$6w^2 + 4w + 5$	$-w$
8.	$2(t - 7) + \_ - 2t^2$	$-2t^2 + 14t - 14$	$12t$
9.	$3hk - h^2k + hk^2 + 4hk + \_ + 3hk^2$	$4hk^2 - 3h^2k + 7hk$	$-2h^2k$
10.	$4y^3 + 6y - 7y^2 + 2y^3 + \_$	$6y^3 - 6y^2 + 6y$	y^2
11.	$\_ - n^3 - \frac{1}{4}n^4 + \frac{1}{2}n^3 - \frac{1}{3}n^3$	$\frac{1}{4}n^4 - \frac{5}{6}n^3$	$\frac{1}{2}n^4$
12.	$3(12v^3 + \_ + 2v^3) + v^3$	$46v^3$	v^3
13.	$1.5pq^3 + 0.7p^2q + \_ + 2.4p^2q$	$1.5pq^3 + 3.1p^2q - 3.8pq$	$-3.8pq$
14.	$-9(\_ + 8w) + 4(-2w^2 + 18w)$	w^2	$-w^2$

PROBLEM SOLVING 14-2

LESSON 14-2 Problem Solving
Simplifying Polynomials

Write the correct answer.

1. The area of a trapezoid can be found using the expression $\frac{h}{2}(b_1 + b_2)$ where h is height, b_1 is the length of base$_1$, and b_2 is the length of base$_2$. Use the Distributive Property to write an equivalent expression.

   $\frac{hb_1}{2} + \frac{hb_2}{2}$

2. The sum of the measures of the interior angles of a polygon with n sides is $180(n - 2)$ degrees. Use the Distributive Property to write an equivalent expression, and use the expression to find the sum of the measures of the interior angles of an octagon.

   $180n - 360$; 1,080 degrees

3. The volume of a box of height h is $2h^4 + h^3 + h^2 + h$ cubic inches. Simplify the polynomial and then find the volume if the height of the box is 3 inches.

   $2h^4 + h^3 + 2h^2 + h$; 210 cubic inches

4. The height, in feet, of a rocket launched upward from the ground with an initial velocity of 64 feet per second after t seconds is given by $16(4t - t^2)$. Write an equivalent expression for the rocket's height after t seconds. What is the height of the rocket after 4 seconds?

   $64t - 16t^2$; 0 ft

Circle the letter of the correct answer.

5. The surface area of a square pyramid with base b and slant height l is given by the expression $b(b + 2l)$. What is the surface area of a square pyramid with base 3 inches and slant height 5 inches?

   A 13 square inches
   B 19 square inches
   Ⓒ 39 square inches
   D 55 square inches

6. The volume of a box with a width of $3x$, a height of $4x - 2$, and a length of $3x + 5$ can be found using the expression $3x(12x^2 + 14x - 10)$. Which is this expression, simplified by using the Distributive Property?

   F $36x^2 + 42x - 30$
   G $15x^3 + 17x^2 - 7x$
   H $36x^3 + 14x - 10$
   Ⓙ $36x^3 + 42x^2 - 30x$

Interdisciplinary

Art

Exercises 26–28 involve applying polynomial concepts to finding the volume and surface area of sculptures. Knowing these measurements can help artists determine the amount of materials they need to complete a project.

Answers

33–34. See p. A25.

TEST PREP DOCTOR ➕ Students who chose answer **D** in Exercise 29 mistakenly combined the coefficients of unlike terms. Recommend that students review the definition of like terms.

🖊 Journal

Explain that you want to evaluate $3x^2 + 5x + 2x^2 - 4x$ for $x = 3$. Ask students to explain whether you should evaluate or simplify the polynomial first. Have them justify their opinions.

Power Presentations
with PowerPoint®

☑ **14-2 Lesson Quiz**

Identify the like terms in each polynomial.

1. $2x^2 - 3z + 5x^2 + z + 8z^2$
   $2x^2$ and $5x^2$, z and $-3z$

2. $2ab^2 + 4a^2b - 5ab^2 - 4 + a^2b$
   $2ab^2$ and $-5ab^2$, $4a^2b$ and a^2b

Simplify.

3. $5(3x^2 + 2)$ $15x^2 + 10$

4. $-2k^2 + 10 + 8k^2 + 8k - 2$
   $6k^2 + 8k + 8$

5. $3(2mn^2 + 3n) + 6mn^2$
   $12mn^2 + 9n$

Also available on transparency

READY TO GO ON?

Organizer

Objective: Assess students' mastery of concepts and skills in Lessons 14-1 through 14-2.

Resources

 Assessment Resources
Section 14A Quiz

 Test & Practice Generator
One-Stop Planner®

Ready to Go On? (vertical tab)

INTERVENTION

Resources

 Ready to Go On?
Intervention and
Enrichment Worksheets

 Ready to Go On? CD-ROM

 Ready to Go On? Online

my.hrw.com

Quiz for Lessons 14-1 Through 14-2

✓ 14-1 Polynomials

Determine whether each expression is a monomial.

1. $\frac{1}{5x^2}$ no
2. $\frac{1}{3}x^2 - x^3$ no
3. $7c^2d^8$ yes

Classify each expression as a monomial, a binomial, a trinomial, or not a polynomial.

4. $\frac{1}{x} + x^2$ not a polynomial
5. $a^3 + 2a - 17$ trinomial
6. $y + 2$ binomial

Find the degree of each polynomial.

7. $u^6 + 7$ 6
8. $3c^2 + c^5 + c + 1$ 5
9. 43 0

10. The depth, in feet below the ocean surface, of a submerging exploration submarine after y minutes can be approximated by the polynomial $0.001y^4 - 0.12y^3 + 3.6y^2$. Estimate the depth after 45 minutes. **456 ft**

✓ 14-2 Simplifying Polynomials

Identify the like terms in each polynomial.
$-z^2$ and $4z^2$, $7z$ and $-z$
11. $-5x^2y^2 + 4xy + x^2y^2$ $-5x^2y^2$ and x^2y^2
12. $-z^2 + 7z + 4z^2 - z + 9$
13. $t + 8 - 2t - 6$ t and $-2t$, -6 and 8
14. $8ab + 3ac + 5bc - 4ac + 6ab$
$8ab$ and $6ab$, $3ac$ and $-4ac$

Simplify.
15. $6 + 3b^5 - 2b^3 + 7 - 5b^3$ $3b^5 - 7b^3 + 13$
16. $6y^2 + y + 7y^2 - 4y - 5$ $13y^2 - 3y - 5$
17. $6(x^2 - 7x) + 2x^2 + 7x$ $8x^2 - 35x$
18. $y + 5 - 5y - 4(5y + 2)$ $-24y - 3$

Solve.

19. The area of one face of a cube is given by the expression $3s^2 + 5s$. Write a polynomial to represent the total surface area of the cube. **$18s^2 + 30s$**

20. The area of each lateral face of a regular square pyramid is given by the expression $\frac{1}{2}b^2 + 2b$. Write a polynomial to represent the lateral surface area of the pyramid. **$2b^2 + 8b$**

READY TO GO ON?
Diagnose and Prescribe

NO
INTERVENE

READY TO GO ON? Intervention, Section 14A			
Ready to Go On? Intervention	Worksheets	CD-ROM	Online
✓ Lesson 14-1	14-1 Intervention	Activity 14-1	Diagnose and Prescribe Online
✓ Lesson 14-2	14-2 Intervention	Activity 14-2	

YES
ENRICH

READY TO GO ON?
Enrichment, Section 14A
Worksheets
CD-ROM
Online

Focus on Problem Solving

 Look Back

• Estimate to check that your answer is reasonable

Before you solve a word problem, you can often read through the problem and make an estimate of the correct answer. Make sure your answer is reasonable for the situation in the problem. After you have solved the problem, compare your answer with the original estimate. If your answer is not close to your estimate, check your work again.

Each problem below has an incorrect answer given. Explain why the answer is not reasonable, and give your own estimate of the correct answer.

1 The perimeter of rectangle *ABCD* is 48 cm. What is the value of *x*?

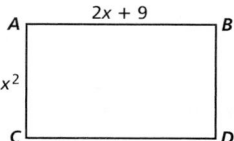

Answer: x = −5

2 A patio layer can use $4x + 6y$ ft of accent edging to divide a patio into three sections measuring *x* ft long by *y* ft wide. If each section must be at least 15 ft long and have an area of at least 165 ft^2, what is the minimum amount of edging needed for the patio?

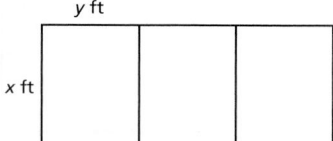

Answer: 52 ft

3 A baseball is thrown straight up from a height of 3 ft at 30 mi/h. The height of the baseball in feet after *t* seconds is $-16t^2 + 44t + 3$. How long will it take the baseball to reach its maximum height?

Answer: 5 minutes

4 Jacob deposited $2000 in a savings account that earns 6% simple interest. The amount of money he has in his account after *t* years is $P + Prt$, where *P* is the initial amount of money in the account and *r* is the interest rate expressed as a decimal. How much money will he have in the account after 7 years?

Answer: $1925

Answers

1. 3 cm

2. 126 ft

3. 1.375 s

4. $2840

3. It's impossible for a person to throw a baseball that continues to go up for 5 minutes. A more realistic answer would be 1 or 2 seconds.

4. The amount in the account after 7 years cannot be less than the original deposit. The amount of interest earned in 1 year is 6% of $2000, which is $120. Earning about $100 each year for 7 years gives interest of about $700 and a total balance of about $2700.

 **Focus on Problem Solving**

Organizer

Objective: Focus on estimating to check that your answer is reasonable.

 Online Edition

Resources

Chapter 14 Resource Book
Reading Strategies

Problem Solving Process

This page focuses on the last step of the problem-solving process:
Look Back

Discuss

Have students discuss why the answer given for each problem is unreasonable. Then have them explain how to estimate a more reasonable answer.

Possible answers:

1. Distance cannot be a negative number, so the length $2x + 9$ must be positive. Because of the two x^2 terms that are part of the perimeter, the value of *x* must be less than 5. A more reasonable estimate would be 3.

2. If the length *x* is at least 15 ft, then $4x$ is at least 60 ft. So, 52 ft of fencing is not nearly enough. If the length is 15 ft and the area is at least 165 ft^2, the width must be at least 11 ft. So, a reasonable estimate of the amount of fencing needed is about $4(15) + 6(11) = 126$.

State Resources

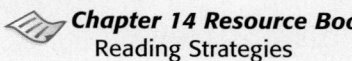
go.hrw.com
State Resources Online
KEYWORD: MT7 Resources

Polynomial Operations

One-Minute Section Planner

Lesson	Materials	MiC and Lab Resources
14-3 Hands-On Lab Model Polynomial Addition • Use algebra tiles to model polynomial addition. **Lesson 14-3** Adding Polynomials • Add polynomials. ☐ SAT-10 ☐ ITBS ☐ CTBS ☐ NAEP	Algebra tiles (MK), graphing calculators	**MiC:** *Algebra Rules* pp. 3–8 *Hands-On Lab Activities* 14-3
14-4 Hands-On Lab Model Polynomial Subtraction • Use algebra tiles to model polynomial subtraction. **Lesson 14-4** Subtracting Polynomials • Subtract polynomials. ☐ SAT-10 ☐ ITBS ☐ CTBS ☐ NAEP	Algebra tiles (MK)	**MiC:** *Algebra Rules* pp. 3–8 *Hands-On Lab Activities* 14-4
Lesson 14-5 Multiplying Polynomials by Monomials • Multiply polynomials by monomials. ☐ SAT-10 ☐ ITBS ☐ CTBS ☐ NAEP	Algebra tiles (MK), index cards	**MiC:** *Algebra Rules* pp. 8–9
14-6 Hands-On Lab Multiply Binomials • Use algebra tiles to model multiplying binomials. **Lesson 14-6** Multiplying Binomials • Multiply binomials. ☐ SAT-10 ☐ ITBS ☐ CTBS ☐ NAEP	Algebra tiles (MK), graphing calculators	**MiC:** *Algebra Rules* pp. 48–50 *Hands-On Lab Activities* 14-6 *Technology Lab Activities* 14-6
Extension Dividing Polynomials by Monomials • Divide polynomials by monomials. ☐ SAT-10 ☐ ITBS ☐ CTBS ☐ NAEP		

MK = *Manipulatives Kit*

Mathematics in Context

The unit *Algebra Rules* from the *Mathematics in Context* © 2006 series can be used with Section 14B. See Section Planner above for suggestions for integrating *MiC* with *Holt Mathematics.*

Section Overview

Polynomials

Lessons 14-3, 14-4

Why? Sums and differences of polynomials can be used to represent real-world measurements such as perimeters.

Adding Polynomials	Subtracting Polynomials
To add polynomials, combine like terms.	**To subtract polynomials,** add the opposite.
$\begin{aligned} 3a^2b^2 + 2a^2 - 5ab \\ a^2 - 3ab - 2 \\ + 6ab + 1 \\ \hline 3a^2b^2 + 3a^2 - 2ab - 1 \end{aligned}$	$\begin{aligned} (3x^2y^2 + xy - 5x) \\ - (6x + 4xy - 5) \end{aligned} \longrightarrow \begin{aligned} 3x^2y^2 + xy - 5x \\ - 4xy - 6x + 5 \\ \hline 3x^2y^2 - 3xy - 11x + 5 \end{aligned}$

Multiplying and Dividing Polynomials

Lessons 14-5, 14-6, Extension

Why? Products of polynomials can be used to represent real-world measurements such as areas.

Multiplying Polynomials

To **multiply two monomials,** multiply the coefficients and add the exponents of the variables that are the same.	To **multiply a polynomial by a monomial,** use the Distributive Property.	To **multiply two binomials,** use the FOIL method.
$(5m^2n^3)(6m^3n^6)$ $5 \cdot 6 \cdot m^{(2+3)}n^{(3+6)}$ $30m^5n^9$	$-4a^2b(2a^4b^3 + 5a^2b^3)$ $-8a^6b^4 - 20a^4b^4$	$(x + y)(x + z)$ $x^2 + xz + yx + yz$ First Outer Inner Last terms terms terms terms

Dividing Polynomials

To **divide a monomial by a monomial,** divide the coefficients and subtract the exponents of like variables in the denominator from those in the numerator.	To **divide a polynomial by a monomial,** divide each term of the polynomial by the monomial.
$\dfrac{6x^9y^3}{4x^6y^2} = \dfrac{3}{2}x^{(9-6)}y^{(3-2)}$ $= \dfrac{3}{2}x^3y^1$ $= \dfrac{3}{2}x^3y$	$\dfrac{x^4 + 5x^3 - 7x^2}{x^2} = \dfrac{x^4}{x^2} + \dfrac{5x^3}{x^2} - \dfrac{7x^2}{x^2}$ $= x^{(4-2)} + 5x^{(3-2)} - 7x^{(2-2)}$ $= x^2 + 5x^1 - 7x^0$ $= x^2 + 5x - 7$

Organizer

Use with Lesson 14-3

Pacing:
Traditional $\frac{1}{2}$ day
Block $\frac{1}{4}$ day

Objective: Use algebra tiles to model polynomial addition.

Materials: Algebra tiles

Online Edition
Algebra Tiles

Resources

Hands-On Lab Activities
Lab 14-3 Recording Sheet

Teach

Discuss

Remind students what a zero pair means. Ask them to give examples of zero pairs.

Close

Key Concept

You can use algebra tiles to model polynomial addition.

Assessment

Use algebra tiles to find each sum.

1. $(x^2 + 3x - 1) + (x^2 - x + 1)$
$2x^2 + 2x$

2. $(3y^2 - 2y) + (2y^2 + 2y + 4)$
$5y^2 + 4$

Model Polynomial Addition

Use with Lesson 14-3

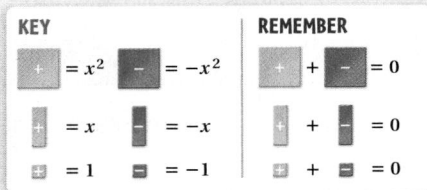

You can use algebra tiles to model polynomial addition.

Activity

1 Use algebra tiles to find the sum $(2x^2 - 2x + 3) + (x^2 + x - 5)$.

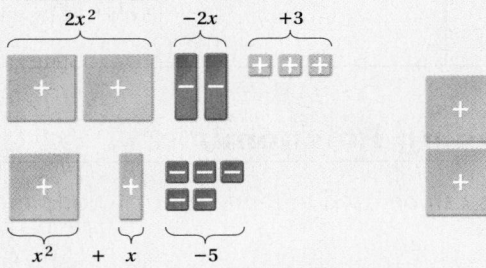

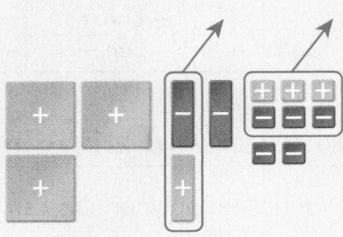

Use tiles to represent all terms from both expressions.

Remove any zero pairs.

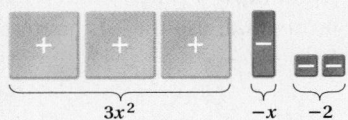

The remaining tiles represent the sum $3x^2 - x - 2$.

Think and Discuss Possible answers to *Think and Discuss*

1. Explain what happens when you add the x-terms in $(-2x + 5) + (2x - 4)$.
$-2x + 2x$ represents a zero pair, so the sum of the x-terms is 0.

Try This

Use algebra tiles to find each sum.

1. $(3m^2 + 2m + 6) + (4m^2 + m + 3)$ $7m^2 + 3m + 9$ **2.** $(-5b^2 + 4b - 1) + (b - 1)$ $-5b^2 + 5b - 2$

State Resources

14-3 Adding Polynomials

Learn to add polynomials.

Mina wants to put a mat and a frame around a picture that is 11 inches by 14 inches. If m is the width of the mat and f is the width of the frame, you can add polynomials to find an expression for the amount of framing material Mina needs.

Remember, the Associative Property of Addition states that for any values of a, b, and c, $a + b + c = (a + b) + c = a + (b + c)$. You can use this property to add polynomials.

EXAMPLE 1 Adding Polynomials Horizontally

Add.

A $(6x^2 - 3x + 4) + (7x - 6)$

$(6x^2 - 3x + 4) + (7x - 6)$

$6x^2 - 3x + 4 + 7x - 6$ *Associative Property*

$6x^2 + 4x - 2$ *Combine like terms.*

B $(-4cd^2 - 3cd + 6) + (7cd - 6cd^2 - 6)$

$(-4cd^2 - 3cd + 6) + (7cd - 6cd^2 - 6)$

$-4cd^2 - 3cd + 6 + 7cd - 6cd^2 - 6$ *Associative Property*

$-10cd^2 + 4cd$ *Combine like terms.*

C $(ab^2 + 4a) + (3ab^2 + 4a - 3) + (a + 5)$

$(ab^2 + 4a) + (3ab^2 + 4a - 3) + (a + 5)$

$ab^2 + 4a + 3ab^2 + 4a - 3 + a + 5$ *Associative Property*

$4ab^2 + 9a + 2$ *Combine like terms.*

You can also add polynomials in a vertical format. Write the second polynomial below the first one, lining up the like terms. If the terms are rearranged, remember to keep the correct sign with each term.

---

1 Introduce

Alternate Opener

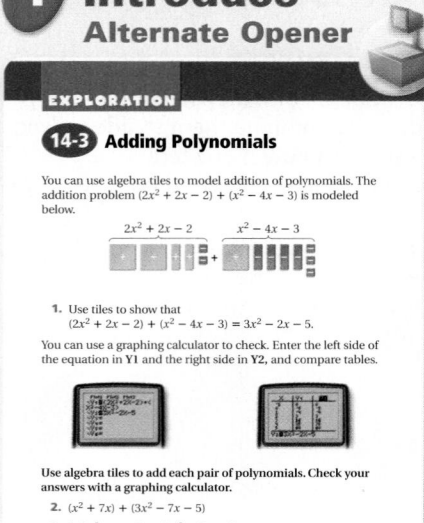

EXPLORATION

14-3 Adding Polynomials

You can use algebra tiles to model addition of polynomials. The addition problem $(2x^2 + 2x - 2) + (x^2 - 4x - 3)$ is modeled below.

$2x^2 + 2x - 2$ $x^2 - 4x - 3$

1. Use tiles to show that $(2x^2 + 2x - 2) + (x^2 - 4x - 3) = 3x^2 - 2x - 5$.

You can use a graphing calculator to check. Enter the left side of the equation in **Y1** and the right side in **Y2**, and compare tables.

Use algebra tiles to add each pair of polynomials. Check your answers with a graphing calculator.

2. $(x^2 + 7x) + (3x^2 - 7x - 5)$
3. $(-3x^2 - x - 1) + (4x^2 - 3x - 2)$

Think and Discuss
4. **Explain** how you can use tiles to add polynomials.

Motivate

Ask students to imagine that two students collected coins to donate to a local charity. Louis collected 3 rolls of quarters, 3 rolls of dimes, and 2 rolls of nickels. Lisa collected 2 rolls of quarters, 4 rolls of dimes, and 3 rolls of nickels. Ask students how they could determine the total amount of money collected. Possible answer: Add the number of each type of roll together, and multiply by the value of each roll. Point out that this example models addition of polynomials.

Explorations and answers are provided in *Alternate Openers: Explorations Transparencies.*

Additional Examples

Example 1

Add.

A. $(5x^3 + x^2 + 2) + (4x^3 + 6x^2)$
$9x^3 + 7x^2 + 2$

B. $(6x^3 + 8y^2 + 5xy) + (4xy - 2y^2)$
$6x^3 + 6y^2 + 9xy$

C. $(3x^2y - 5x) + (4x + 7) + 6x^2y$
$9x^2y - x + 7$

Example 2

Add.

A. $(4x^2 + 2x + 11) + (2x^2 + 6x + 9)$
$6x^2 + 8x + 20$

B. $(3mn^2 - 6m + 6n) + (5mn^2 + 2m - n)$
$8mn^2 - 4m + 5n$

C. $(-x^2y^2 + 5x^2) + (-2y^2 + 2) + (x^2 + 8)$
$-x^2y^2 + 6x^2 - 2y^2 + 10$

Example 3

Rachel wants to frame two photographs. The first photograph has dimensions b inches and h inches, and each dimension of the other photograph is twice the corresponding dimension of the first. She needs enough wood for the frames to cover both perimeters, and the width of the wood is $1\frac{1}{2}$ inches. Find an expression for the length of wood she needs to frame both photographs. $6b + 6h + 24$ in.

Also available on transparency

EXAMPLE **2** **Adding Polynomials Vertically**

Add.

Ⓐ $(5a^2 + 4a + 2) + (4a^2 + 3a + 1)$

$$\begin{array}{l} 5a^2 + 4a + 2 \\ \underline{+\ 4a^2 + 3a + 1} \\ 9a^2 + 7a + 3 \end{array}$$

Place like terms in columns.
Combine like terms.

Ⓑ $(2xy^2 + 3x - 4y) + (8xy^2 - 2x + 3)$

$$\begin{array}{l} 2xy^2 + 3x - 4y \\ \underline{+\ 8xy^2 - 2x\quad\ \ + 3} \\ 10xy^2 +\ \ x - 4y + 3 \end{array}$$

Place like terms in columns.
Combine like terms.

Ⓒ $(4a^2b^2 + 3a^2 - 6ab) + (-4ab + a^2 - 5) + (3 + 7ab)$

$$\begin{array}{l} 4a^2b^2 + 3a^2 - 6ab \\ \qquad\quad a^2 - 4ab - 5 \\ \underline{+\qquad\qquad\qquad 7ab + 3} \\ 4a^2b^2 + 4a^2 - 3ab - 2 \end{array}$$

Place like terms in columns.
Combine like terms.

EXAMPLE **3** **Art Application**

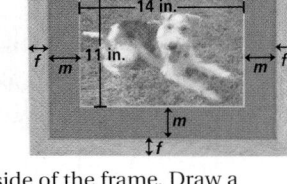

Mina is putting a mat of width m and a frame of width f around an 11-inch by 14-inch picture. Find an expression for the amount of framing material she needs.

The amount of material Mina needs equals the perimeter of the outside of the frame. Draw a diagram to help you determine the outer dimensions of the frame.

Base $= 14 + m + m + f + f$ Height $= 11 + m + m + f + f$
$\quad\ \ = 14 + 2m + 2f$ $\quad\quad\ = 11 + 2m + 2f$

$P = (11 + 2m + 2f) + (14 + 2m + 2f) + (11 + 2m + 2f) + (14 + 2m + 2f)$
$\quad = 11 + 2m + 2f + 14 + 2m + 2f + 11 + 2m + 2f + 14 + 2m + 2f$
$\quad = 50 + 8m + 8f$ *Combine like terms.*

She will need $50 + 8m + 8f$ inches of framing material.

Possible answers to Think and Discuss

1. To add horizontally, you apply the Commutative and Associative Properties to reorder and regroup the terms. To add vertically, you line up the like terms in columns.

2. It is an application for the Associative Property of addition.

Think and Discuss

1. **Compare** adding $(5x^2 + 2x) + (3x^2 - 2x)$ vertically with adding it horizontally.

2. **Explain** why you can remove parentheses from polynomials to add the polynomials.

---

② Teach

Guided Instruction

In this lesson, students learn to add polynomials. Explain that adding polynomials is very similar to the process of simplifying polynomials studied in the previous lesson. Show students the horizontal and vertical methods of adding polynomials.

Teaching Tip   **Inclusion** Encourage students to be sure to keep the correct sign with each term as they move or reorder the terms in a problem.

Reaching All Learners
Through Concrete Manipulatives

Give each student or group of students a set of algebra tiles (provided in the Manipulatives Kit). Have students use the algebra tiles to add polynomials, such as $(2x^2 + 3x + 1)$ and $(x^2 - 2x - 3)$. $3x^2 + x - 2$ Remind students that a pair of tiles having the same shape but different colors equals zero and can be removed from the expression.

③ Close

Summarize

Remind students that they need to identify like terms and combine them to add polynomials. Ask them how many terms they will end up with if they add two trinomials.

Possible answer: It will depend on the number of like terms in the trinomials. If each trinomial is already simplified, the number of terms in the sum will be between 3 and 6.

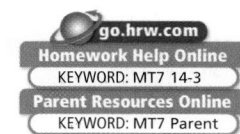
go.hrw.com
Homework Help Online
KEYWORD: MT7 14-3
Parent Resources Online
KEYWORD: MT7 Parent

GUIDED PRACTICE

See Example **1** Add.

1. $(5x^3 + 6x - 1) + (-3x + 7)$ $5x^3 + 3x + 6$

2. $(22x - 6) + (14x - 3)$ $36x - 9$

3. $(r^2s + 3rs) + (4r^2s - 8rs) + (6r^2s + 14rs)$ $11r^2s + 9rs$

See Example **2** 4. $(4b^2 - 5b + 10) + (6b^2 + 7b - 8)$ $10b^2 + 2b + 2$

5. $(9ab^2 - 5ab + 6a^2b) + (8ab - 12a^2b + 6) + (6ab^2 + 5a^2b - 14)$ $15ab^2 + 3ab - a^2b - 8$

6. $(h^4j - hj^3 + hj - 6) + (5hj^3 + 5) + (6h^4j - 7hj)$ $7h^4j + 4hj^3 - 6hj - 1$

See Example **3** 7. Colette is putting a mat of width $3w$ and a frame of width w around a 16-inch by 48-inch poster. Find an expression for the amount of frame material she needs. $128 + 32w$ in.

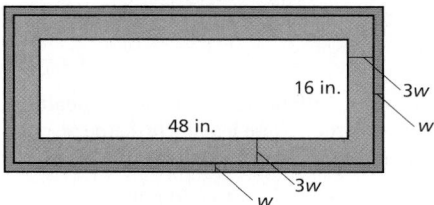

INDEPENDENT PRACTICE

See Example **1** Add.

8. $(5x^2y - 4xy + 3) + (7xy - 3x^2y)$ $2x^2y + 3xy + 3$

9. $(5g - 9) + (7g^2 - 4g + 8)$ $7g^2 + g - 1$

10. $(6bc - 2b^2c^2 + 8bc^2) + (6bc - 3bc^2)$ $12bc - 2b^2c^2 + 5bc^2$

11. $(9h^4 + 5h - 4h^6) + (h^6 - 6h + 3h^4)$ $-3h^6 + 12h^4 - h$

12. $(4pq - 5p^2q + 9pq^2) + (6p^2q - 11pq^2) + (2pq^2 - 7pq + 6p^2q)$ $-3pq + 7p^2q$

See Example **2** 13. $(8t^2 + 4t + 3) + (5t^2 - 8t + 9)$ $13t^2 - 4t + 12$

14. $(5b^3c^2 - 3b^2c + 2bc) + (8b^3c^2 - 3bc + 14) + (b^2c - 5bc - 9)$ $13b^3c^2 - 2b^2c - 6bc + 5$

15. $(w^2 - 3w + 5) + (-2w - 3w^2 - 1) + (w^2 + w - 6)$ $-w^2 - 4w - 2$

See Example **3** 16. Each side of an equilateral triangle has length $w + 3$. Each side of a square has length $4w - 2$. Write an expression for the sum of the perimeter of the equilateral triangle and the perimeter of the square. $19w + 1$

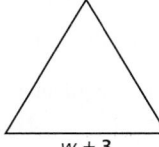 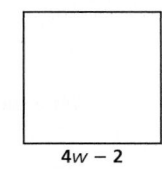

$w + 3$ $4w - 2$

Assignment Guide

If you finished Example **1** assign:
Average 1–3, 8–12, 17, 18, 25, 27–36
Advanced 8–12, 17, 18, 22, 23, 25–36

If you finished Example **2** assign:
Average 1–6, 8–15, 17, 18, 25, 27–36
Advanced 8–15, 17, 18, 22, 23, 25–36

If you finished Example **3** assign:
Average 1–21, 25, 27–36,
Advanced 8–36

Homework Quick Check

Quickly check key concepts.
Exercises: 12, 14, 16

Math Background

Adding polynomials vertically demonstrates the same principle as using place value to add numbers. Consider the examples below.

$$\begin{array}{r} 3x^2 + 4x + 1 \\ + \quad x^2 + 5x + 6 \\ \hline 4x^2 + 9x + 7 \end{array}$$

$$\begin{array}{rcl} 341 & \longrightarrow & 3(10^2) + 4(10) + 1 \\ + \ 156 & \longrightarrow & 1(10^2) + 5(10) + 6 \\ \hline & & 4(10^2) + 9(10) + 7 \end{array}$$

RETEACH 14-3

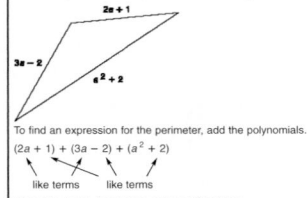

LESSON 14-3 Reteach
Adding Polynomials

Adding polynomials is like simplifying polynomials.
You can regroup the terms and then combine like terms. Or you cn place the polynomials in columns and then combine like terms.

Find an expression for the perimeter of the triangle below.

To find an expression for the perimeter, add the polynomials.

$(2a + 1) + (3a - 2) + (a^2 + 2)$

like terms   like terms

Place like terms in columns and combine them.

$$\begin{array}{r} 2a + 1 \\ 3a - 2 \\ + \ a^2 \qquad + 2 \\ \hline a^2 + 5a + 1 \end{array}$$

So, an expression for the perimeter of the triangle is $a^2 + 5a + 1$.

Add.

1. $(3x^2 + 3xy^3 + 5y + 2) + (4xy^3 - 3y)$
$$\begin{array}{r} 3x^2 + 3xy^3 + 5y + 2 \\ + \qquad 4xy^3 - 3y \\ \hline 3x^2 + 7xy^3 + 2y + 2 \end{array}$$

2. $(4a^2b - 3a^2 + 3b) + (6a^2b + 4ab - 2b)$
$$\begin{array}{r} 4a^2b - 3a^2 \qquad + 3b \\ + \ 6a^2b \qquad + 4ab - 2b \\ \hline 10a^2b - 3a^2 + 4ab + b \end{array}$$

3. $(4mn + 5n^3 + 3n) + (3m^2 + 5n)$
$\underline{4mn + 3m^2 + 5n^3 + 8n}$

4. $(-5r^3 + 2r + 7) + (2r^3 + 4r^2 - 6r + 1)$
$\underline{-3r^3 + 4r^2 - 4r + 8}$

PRACTICE 14-3

LESSON 14-3 Practice B
Adding Polynomials

Add.

1. $(a^2 + a + 3) + (15a^2 + 2a + 9)$
$\underline{16a^2 + 3a + 12}$

2. $(5x + 2x^2) + (3x - 2x^2)$
$\underline{8x}$

3. $(mn - 10 + mn^2) + (5 + 3mn - 4mn^2)$
$\underline{-3mn^2 + 4mn - 5}$

4. $(7y^2z + 9 + yz^2) + (y^2z - 2yz^2)$
$\underline{8y^2z - yz^2 + 9}$

5. $(s^3 + 3s - 3) + (2s^3 + 9s - 2) + (s - s^3)$
$\underline{2s^3 + 13s - 5}$

6. $(6wv - 4w^2v + 7wv^2) + (5w^2v - 7wv^2) + (wv^2 - 5wv + 6w^2v)$
$\underline{7w^2v + wv^2 + wv}$

7. $(6b^2c^2 - 4b^2c + 3bc) + (9b^2c^2 - 4bc + 12) + (2b^2c - 3bc - 8)$
$\underline{15b^2c^2 - 2b^2c - 4bc + 4}$

8. $(7e^2 + 3e + 2) + (9 - 6e + 4e^2) + (9e + 2 - 6e^2) + (4e^2 - 7e + 8)$
$\underline{9e^2 - e + 21}$

9. $(f^4g - fg^3 + 2fg - 4) + (3fg^3 + 3) + (4f^4g - 5fg) + (3 - 12fg^3 + f^4g)$
$\underline{6f^4g - 10fg^3 - 3fg + 2}$

10. Six blocks of height $4h + 4$ each and 3 blocks of height $8 - 2h$ each are stacked on top of each other to form one big tower. Find an expression for the overall height of the tower.
$\underline{18h + 48}$

go.hrw.com
State Resources Online
KEYWORD: MT7 Resources

State Resources

ONGOING ASSESSMENT
and INTERVENTION

Diagnose *Before* the Lesson
14-3 Warm Up, TE p. 747

Monitor *During* the Lesson
14-3 Know-It Notebook
14-3 Questioning Strategies

Assess *After* the Lesson
14-3 Lesson Quiz, TE p. 750

Answers

21. Possible answer: Add the expression representing the distance from the airport to the first plane to the expression representing the distance from the airport to the second plane. The planes are $4x^2 - 48x + 500$ miles apart after 2 hours.

TEST PREP DOCTOR For Exercise 27, students who chose answer **F** found only half the combined perimeter. They may want to review the formula for finding the perimeter of a rectangle.

Journal

Show students the following polynomial addition problem:
$(2x^2 + 3x + 4) + (3x^2 + 5x + 3)$.
Have them compare this problem to the addition problem $234 + 353$.

Power Presentations
with PowerPoint®

14-3 Lesson Quiz

Add.

1. $(2m^2 - 3m + 7) + (7m^2 - 1)$
$9m^2 - 3m + 6$

2. $(yz^2 + 5yz + 7) + (2yz^2 - yz)$
$3yz^2 + 4yz + 7$

3. $(2xy^2 + 2x - 6) + (5xy^2 + 3y + 8)$
$7xy^2 + 2x + 3y + 2$

4. $(3np^3 + 4n) + (5np^3 - n - 6) + (2n - 3)$
$8np^3 + 5n - 9$

5. The base of an isosceles triangle has length $x + 4$. The two legs of the triangle have lengths $3x + y$. Write an expression for the perimeter of the triangle.
$7x + 2y + 4$

Also available on transparency

PRACTICE AND PROBLEM SOLVING

Extra Practice
See page 808.

Business

According to the Toy Industry Association, $24.6 billion was spent on toys worldwide in 2000.

go.hrw.com
Web Extra!
KEYWORD: MT7 Toys

25. Possible answer: First identify like terms. Then add like terms by adding their coefficients.

Add.

17. $(3w^2y + 3wy^2 - 4wy) + (5wy - 2wy^2 + 7w^2y) + (wy^2 - 5wy - 3w^2y)$
$7w^2y + 2wy^2 + 4wy$

18. $(2p^2t - 3pt + 5) + (p^2t + 2pt^2 - 3pt) + (1 - 5pt^2 + p^2t)$
$4p^2t - 6pt + 6 - 3pt^2$

19. Geometry Write and simplify an expression for the combined volumes of a sphere with volume $\frac{4}{3}\pi r^3$, a cube with volume r^3, and a prism with volume $r^3 + 4r^2 + 5r + 2$. Use 3.14 for π. $\approx 6.19r^3 + 4r^2 + 5r + 2$

20. Business The cost of producing n toys at a factory is given by the polynomial $0.5n^2 + 3n + 12$. The cost of packaging is $0.25n^2 + 5n + 4$. Write and simplify an expression for the total cost of producing and packaging n toys.
$0.75n^2 + 8n + 16$

21. Critical Thinking Two airplanes depart from the same airport, traveling in opposite directions. After 2 hours, one airplane is $x^2 + 2x + 400$ miles from the airport, and the other airplane is $3x^2 - 50x + 100$ miles from the airport. How could you determine the distance between the two planes? Explain.

22. Write two polynomials whose sum is $3m^2 + 4m + 6$.
Possible answer: $(2m^2 + 2m + 3) + (m^2 + 2m + 3)$

23. Choose a Strategy What is the missing term?
$(-6x^2 + 4x - 3) + (3x^2 + \blacksquare - 5) = -3x^2 - 6x - 8$

Ⓐ $2x$ Ⓑ $-2x$ Ⓒ $-10x$ Ⓓ $10x$

24. Write a Problem A plane leaves an airport heading north at $x + 3$ mi/h. At the same time, another plane leaves the same airport, heading south at $x + 4$ mi/h. Write a problem using the speeds of both planes.
Possible answer: How far apart will the planes be after 3 hours?
Answer: $6x + 21$ mi

25. Write About It Explain how to add polynomials.

26. Challenge What polynomial would have to be added to $6x^2 - 4x + 5$ so that the sum is $3x^2 + 4x - 7$?
$-3x^2 + 8x - 12$

TEST PREP and Spiral Review

27. Multiple Choice Debbie is putting a deck of width $5w$ around her 20 foot by 80 foot pool. Which is the expression for the perimeter of the pool and deck combined?

Ⓕ $100 + 10w$ Ⓖ $150 + 15w$ Ⓗ $200 + 20w$ Ⓙ $250 + 25w$

28. Gridded Response What is the sum of $(-10x^3 + 4x^4 - 3x^5 - 10)$, $(9x^3 - 8x^4 + 20x^5 + 15)$, and $(x^3 + 4x^2 - 17x^5 + 2)$? 7

Using the scale 1 in. = 6 ft, find the height or length of each object. (Lesson 5-8)

29. a 14 in. tall model of an office building 84 ft

30. a 2.5 in. long model of a train 15 ft

31. a 7 in. tall model of a billboard 42 ft

32. a 4.5 in. long model of an airplane 27 ft

Find the fraction equivalent of each decimal or percent. (Lesson 6-1)

33. 1.1 $\frac{11}{10}$ or $1\frac{1}{10}$ **34.** 58% $\frac{29}{50}$ **35.** 0.24 $\frac{6}{25}$ **36.** 300% 3

CHALLENGE 14-3

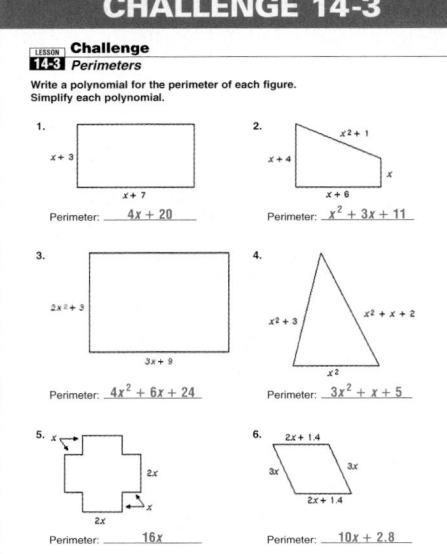

LESSON 14-3 **Challenge** Perimeters

Write a polynomial for the perimeter of each figure. Simplify each polynomial.

1. [rectangle] $x + 3$, $x + 7$
Perimeter: $4x + 20$

2. [figure] $x^2 + 1$, $x + 4$, x, $x + 6$
Perimeter: $x^2 + 3x + 11$

3. [square] $2x^2 + 3$, $3x + 9$
Perimeter: $4x^2 + 6x + 24$

4. [triangle] $x^2 + 3$, $x^2 + x + 2$, x^2
Perimeter: $3x^2 + x + 5$

5. [figure] x, $2x$, $2x$, x, $2x$
Perimeter: $16x$

6. [parallelogram] $2x + 1.4$, $3x$, $3x$, $2x + 1.4$
Perimeter: $10x + 2.8$

PROBLEM SOLVING 14-3

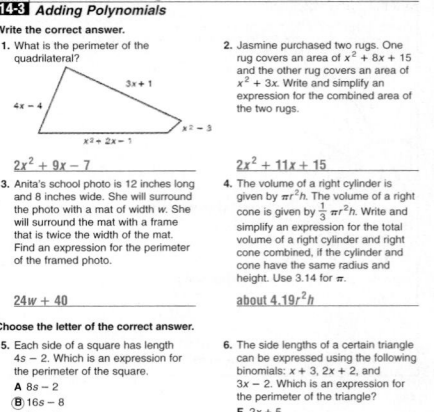

LESSON 14-3 **Problem Solving** Adding Polynomials

Write the correct answer.

1. What is the perimeter of the quadrilateral? $4x - 4$, $3x + 1$, $x^2 + 2x - 1$
$2x^2 + 9x - 7$

2. Jasmine purchased two rugs. One rug covers an area of $x^2 + 8x + 15$ and the other rug covers an area of $x^2 + 3x$. Write and simplify an expression for the combined area of the two rugs.
$2x^2 + 11x + 15$

3. Anita's school photo is 12 inches long and 8 inches wide. She will surround the photo with a mat of width w. She will surround the mat with a frame that is twice the width of the mat. Find an expression for the perimeter of the framed photo.
$24w + 40$

4. The volume of a right cylinder is given by $\pi r^2 h$. The volume of a right cone is given by $\frac{1}{3}\pi r^2 h$. Write and simplify an expression for the total volume of a right cylinder and right cone combined, if the cylinder and cone have the same radius and height. Use 3.14 for π.
about $4.19r^2 h$

Choose the letter of the correct answer.

5. Each side of a square has length $4s - 2$. Which is an expression for the perimeter of the square?
A $8s - 2$
Ⓑ $16s - 8$
C $8s - 4$
D $16s - 4$

6. The side lengths of a certain triangle can be expressed using the following binomials: $x + 3$, $2x + 2$, and $3x - 2$. Which is an expression for the perimeter of the triangle?
F $2x + 5$
G $2x - 1$
H $3x + 5$
Ⓙ $6x + 3$

7. What polynomial can be added to $2x^2 + 3x + 1$ to get $2x^2 + 8x$?
A $5x$
B $5x + 1$
C $5x^2 - 1$
Ⓓ $5x - 1$

8. Which of the following sums is NOT a binomial when simplified?
Ⓕ $(b^2 + 5b + 1) + (b^2 - 5b + 1)$
G $(b^2 + 5b + 1) + (b^2 - 5b - 1)$
H $(b^2 + 5b + 1) + (b^2 - 5b + 1)$
J $(b^2 + 5b + 1) + (-b^2 + 5b + 1)$

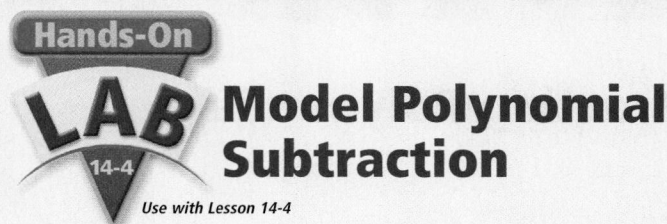

go.hrw.com
Lab Resources Online
KEYWORD: MT7 Lab14

KEY **REMEMBER**

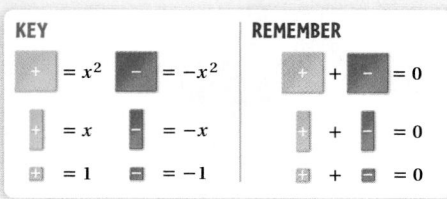

You can use algebra tiles to model polynomial subtraction.

Activity

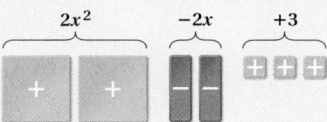

1 Use algebra tiles to find the difference $(2x^2 - 2x + 3) - (x^2 + x - 3)$.

$2x^2 \qquad -2x \qquad +3$

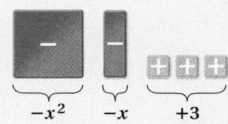

$-x^2 \quad -x \quad +3$

Remember, subtracting is the same as adding the opposite. Use the opposite of each term in $x^2 + x - 3$.

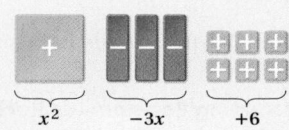

$x^2 \qquad -3x \qquad +6$

Remove any zero pairs.

The remaining tiles represent the difference $x^2 - 3x + 6$.

Think and Discuss

1. Why do you have to add the opposite when subtracting?
   Subtraction is the same as addition of the opposite.

Try This

Use algebra tiles to find each difference.

1. $(6m^2 + 2m) - (4m^2)$ $2m^2 + 2m$

2. $(-5b^2 - 9) - (b - 9)$ $-5b^2 - b$

Hands-On

LAB
Organizer
Use with Lesson 14-4

Pacing:
Traditional $\frac{1}{2}$ day
Block $\frac{1}{4}$ day

Objective: Use algebra tiles to model polynomial subtraction.

Materials: Algebra tiles

PREMIER **Online Edition**
Algebra Tiles

Resources

Hands-On Lab Activities
Lab 14-4 Recording Sheet

Teach

Discuss

Review the rules for subtracting integers. Remind students that only like terms can be combined.

Close

Key Concept

You can use algebra tiles to model polynomial subtraction.

Assessment

Use algebra tiles to find each difference.

1. $(6y^2 + 3y + 1) - (y^2 + y - 1)$
   $5y^2 + 2y + 2$

2. $(-4x^2 - 4) - (-x^2 + 2x)$
   $-3x^2 - 2x - 4$

State Resources

go.hrw.com
State Resources Online
KEYWORD: MT7 Resources

Objective: Students subtract polynomials.

Online Edition
Tutorial Videos

Power Presentations
with PowerPoint®

Warm Up

Write the opposite of each integer.

1. 10 -10 **2.** -7 7

Subtract.

3. $19 - (-12)$ **4.** $-16 - 21$
31   -37

Add.

5. $(3x^2 + 7) + (x^2 - 3x)$
$4x^2 - 3x + 7$

6. $(2m^2 - 3m) + (-5m^2 + 2)$
$-3m^2 - 3m + 2$

Problem of the Day

Tara has 4 pairs of shorts, 3 tops, and 2 pairs of sandals. If she wants to wear a completely different outfit than she wore yesterday, how many combinations does she have to choose from? 6

Also available on transparency

Math Humor

Why was the expression $\frac{0}{3x^5}$ always cold? It was 5 degrees below zero.

State Resources

go.hrw.com
State Resources Online
KEYWORD: MT7 Resources

14-4 Subtracting Polynomials

Learn to subtract polynomials.

Manufacturers can use polynomials to estimate the cost of making a product and the revenue from sales. To estimate profits, they would subtract these polynomials.

Subtraction is the opposite of addition. To subtract a polynomial, you need to find its opposite.

EXAMPLE 1 **Finding the Opposite of a Polynomial**

Find the opposite of each polynomial.

A $8x^3y^6z$
$-(8x^3y^6z)$
$-8x^3y^6z$

B $12x^2 - 5x$
$-(12x^2 - 5x)$
$-12x^2 + 5x$ *Distributive Property*

C $-3ab^2 - 4ab + 3$
$-(-3ab^2 - 4ab + 3)$
$3ab^2 + 4ab - 3$ *Distributive Property*

To subtract a polynomial, add its opposite.

EXAMPLE 2 **Subtracting Polynomials Horizontally**

Subtract.

A $(n^3 - n + 5n^2) - (7n - 4n^2 + 9)$
$= (n^3 - n + 5n^2) + (-7n + 4n^2 - 9)$ *Add the opposite.*
$= n^3 - n + 5n^2 - 7n + 4n^2 - 9$ *Associative Property*
$= n^3 + 9n^2 - 8n - 9$ *Combine like terms.*

B $(-2cd^2 + cd + 4) - (-7cd^2 + 2 - 5cd)$
$= (-2cd^2 + cd + 4) + (7cd^2 - 2 + 5cd)$ *Add the opposite.*
$= -2cd^2 + cd + 4 + 7cd^2 - 2 + 5cd$ *Associative Property*
$= 5cd^2 + 6cd + 2$ *Combine like terms.*

---

1 Introduce

Alternate Opener

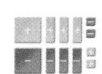

EXPLORATION

14-4 **Subtracting Polynomials**

You can use algebra tiles to find the opposite of a polynomial. To do this, replace each tile with its opposite.

The opposite of
$x^2 + 3x - 2$
is
$-x^2 - 3x + 2$.

Use algebra tiles to find the opposite of each polynomial.

1. $4x^2 - 2x - 5$
2. $-x^2 - 7x + 3$
3. $2x^2 + 3x - 3$

Think and Discuss

4. **Explain** how you can use tiles to find opposites.
5. **Discuss** how opposites of polynomials might be useful if you were subtracting polynomials.

Motivate

Ask students what steps they would take to solve the subtraction problem 8 − (−8). Possible answer: Change subtraction to addition of the opposite. Remind students that they have learned this concept before (Lesson 1-5). Explain that the same principle applies to subtraction of polynomials.

Explorations and answers are provided in *Alternate Openers: Explorations Transparencies.*

You can also subtract polynomials in a vertical format. Write the second polynomial below the first one, lining up the like terms.

EXAMPLE **3** **Subtracting Polynomials Vertically**

Subtract.

A $(x^3 + 4x + 1) - (6x^3 + 3x + 5)$

$$\begin{array}{r} (x^3 + 4x + 1) \\ - (6x^3 + 3x + 5) \end{array} \longrightarrow \begin{array}{r} x^3 + 4x + 1 \\ + -6x^3 - 3x - 5 \\ \hline -5x^3 + x - 5 \end{array}$$ *Add the opposite.*

B $(4m^2n - 3mn - 4m) - (-8m^2n - 6mn + 3)$

$$\begin{array}{r} (4m^2n - 3mn - 4m) \\ - (-8m^2n - 6mn + 3) \end{array} \longrightarrow \begin{array}{r} 4m^2n - 3mn - 4m \\ + 8m^2n + 6mn \quad\quad - 3 \\ \hline 12m^2n + 3mn - 4m - 3 \end{array}$$ *Add the opposite.*

C $(4x^2y^2 + xy - 6x) - (7x + 5xy - 6)$

$$\begin{array}{r} (4x^2y^2 + xy - 6x) \\ - (7x + 5xy - 6) \end{array} \longrightarrow \begin{array}{r} 4x^2y^2 + xy - 6x \\ + \quad\quad -5xy - 7x + 6 \\ \hline 4x^2y^2 - 4xy - 13x + 6 \end{array}$$ *Rearrange terms as needed.*

EXAMPLE **4** *Business Application*

Suppose the cost in dollars of producing x model kits is given by the polynomial $400{,}000 + 3x$ and the revenue generated from sales is given by the polynomial $20x - 0.00004x^2$. Find a polynomial expression for the profit from making and selling x model kits, and evaluate the expression for $x = 200{,}000$.

$20x - 0.00004x^2 - (400{,}000 + 3x)$ *revenue − cost*

$20x - 0.00004x^2 + (-400{,}000 - 3x)$ *Add the opposite.*

$20x - 0.00004x^2 - 400{,}000 - 3x$ *Associative Property*

$17x - 0.00004x^2 - 400{,}000$ *Combine like terms.*

The profit is given by the polynomial $17x - 0.00004x^2 - 400{,}000$. For $x = 200{,}000$,

$17(200{,}000) - 0.00004(200{,}000)^2 - 400{,}000 = 1{,}400{,}000$

The profit is \$1,400,000, or \$1.4 million.

Think and Discuss

1. Explain how to find the opposite of a polynomial.

2. Compare subtracting polynomials with adding polynomials.

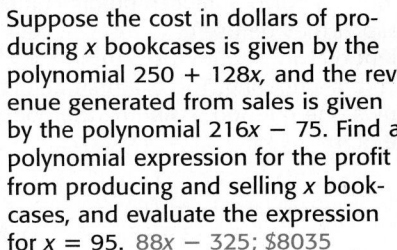
---

2 **Teach**

Guided Instruction

In this lesson, students learn to subtract polynomials. First review how to find and express the opposite of a polynomial. Emphasize the importance of distributing the opposite sign to every term in the polynomial that is being subtracted. Students can do this operation horizontally or vertically.

Teaching Tip   **Inclusion** Discuss how distributing a negative sign results in changing the sign of every term of a polynomial.

Reaching All Learners

Through Concrete Manipulatives

Group students in pairs, and provide each pair with a set of algebra tiles (provided in the Manipulatives Kit). Have one student in each group create a polynomial, and have the other create its opposite. Then have them exchange roles and repeat the activity.

3 **Close**

Summarize

Remind students that to subtract a polynomial, they must add its opposite. Remind them that the opposite of a polynomial contains the opposite of every monomial in the polynomial.

Possible answers to *Think and Discuss*

1. Change the sign of every term in the polynomial to its opposite.

2. To subtract a polynomial, you first change the polynomial that is being subtracted to its opposite, and then you add.

Assignment Guide

If you finished Example ① assign:
Average 1–6, 14–19, 36–44
Advanced 14–19, 33, 36–44

If you finished Example ② assign:
Average 1–9, 14–22, 27, 28, 34, 36–44
Advanced 14–22, 27–29, 33–44

If you finished Example ③ assign:
Average 1–12, 14–25, 27–29, 34, 36–44
Advanced 14–25, 27–29, 33–44

If you finished Example ④ assign:
Average 1–29, 32, 34, 36–44
Advanced 14–44

Homework Quick Check

Quickly check key concepts.
Exercises: 18, 22, 24, 26

Math Background

The concept of distributing a minus sign through a polynomial can be difficult to grasp. It may be useful to insert a coefficient of 1 in front of the parentheses before distributing. The example below shows one method of finding the opposite of $4x^2 - 2x + 7$.

$$-(4x^2 - 2x + 7)$$
$$-1(4x^2 - 2x + 7)$$
$$(-1)(4x^2) + (-1)(-2x) + (-1)(7)$$
$$-4x^2 + 2x - 7$$

GUIDED PRACTICE

See Example ① **Find the opposite of each polynomial.**

1. $4x^2y$ $-4x^2y$
2. $-5x + 4xy^5$ $5x - 4xy^5$
3. $3x^2 - 8x + 5$ $-3x^2 + 8x - 5$
4. $-5y^2 - 2y + 4$ $5y^2 + 2y - 4$
5. $-8x^3 + 5x - 6$ $8x^3 - 5x + 6$
6. $6xy^2 + 4y + 2$ $-6xy^2 - 4y - 2$

See Example ② **Subtract.**

7. $(2b^3 + 5b^2 - 8) - (4b^3 + b - 12)$ $-2b^3 + 5b^2 - b + 4$
8. $7b - (4b^2 + 3b - 12)$ $-4b^2 + 4b + 12$
9. $(4m^2n - 7mn + 3mn^2) - (-5mn - 4m^2n)$ $8m^2n + 3mn^2 - 2mn$

See Example ③ 10. $(8x^2 - 4x + 1) - (5x^2 + 2x + 3)$ $3x^2 - 6x - 2$
11. $(-2x^2y - xy + 3x - 4) - (4xy - 7x + 4)$ $-2x^2y - 5xy + 10x - 8$
12. $(-5ab^2 + 4ab - 3a^2b) - (7 - 5ab + 3ab^2 + 4a^2b)$ $-8ab^2 - 7a^2b + 9ab - 7$

See Example ④ 13. The volume of a rectangular prism, in cubic inches, is given by the expression $x^3 + 3x^2 - 5x + 7$. The volume of a smaller rectangular prism is given by the expression $5x^3 - 6x^2 + 7x - 14$. How much greater is the volume of the larger rectangular prism? $-4x^3 + 9x^2 - 12x + 21$ in^3

INDEPENDENT PRACTICE

26. $t^3 - 3t^2 - 3t + 100$

See Example ① **Find the opposite of each polynomial.**

14. $-4rn^2$ $4rn^2$
15. $3v - 5v^2$ $-3v + 5v^2$
16. $4m^2 - 6m + 2$ $-4m^2 + 6m - 2$
17. $4xy^2 + 2xy$ $-4xy^2 - 2xy$
18. $-8n^6 + 5n^3 - n$ $8n^6 - 5n^3 + n$
19. $-9b^2 - 2b - 9$ $9b^2 + 2b + 9$

See Example ② **Subtract.**

20. $(6w^2 + 3w + 6) - (3w^2 + 4w - 5)$ $3w^2 - w + 11$
21. $(14a + a^2) - (8 + a^2 + 9a)$ $5a - 8$
22. $(7r^2s^2 - 5rs^2 + 6r^2s + 7rs) - (3rs^2 - 3r^2s + 8rs)$ $7r^2s^2 - 8rs^2 + 9r^2s - rs$

See Example ③ 23. $(4x^2 + 6x - 1) - (3x^2 + 9x - 5)$ $x^2 - 3x + 4$
24. $(3a^2b^2 - 4ab - 2a - 4) - (4a^2b^2 + 5a - 3b + 6)$ $-a^2b^2 - 4ab - 7a + 3b - 10$
25. $(4pt^2 - 6p^3 + 5p^2t^2) - (5p^2 - 6pt^2 + 7p^2t^2)$ $-6p^3 - 5p^2 - 2p^2t^2 + 10pt^2$

See Example ④ 26. The current in an electrical circuit at t seconds is $4t^3 - 5t^2 + 2t + 200$ amperes. The current in another electrical circuit is $3t^3 - 2t^2 + 5t + 100$ amperes. Write an expression to show the difference in the two currents.

State Resources

RETEACH 14-4

Reteach
14-4 Subtracting Polynomials

When subtracting polynomials, you can distribute a factor of −1.

Subtract. $(5x^2 + 7x + 3) - (4x^2 + 3x - 5)$.

Rewrite the expression. $(5x^2 + 7x + 3) + (-1)(4x^2 + 3x - 5)$.

Apply the Distributive Property.

$-1(4x^2 + 3x - 5) = (-1 \cdot 4x^2) + (-1 \cdot 3x) + (-1 \cdot -5) = -4x^2 - 3x + 5$

Distributing the −1 changes the sign of each term.
$(5x^2 + 7x + 3) + (-4x^2 - 3x + 5)$

Use the Associative Property to remove parentheses and combine like terms.

$5x^2 + 7x + 3 - 4x^2 - 3x + 5 = x^2 + 4x + 8$

Subtract.

1. $(3b^3 + 4b^2 + 6) - (b^3 - 5b - 3)$

$3b^3 + 4b^2 + 6 + -1(b^3 - 5b - 3)$ Rewrite the expression.
$3b^3 + 4b^2 + 6 + (-b^3 + 5b + 3)$ Apply the Distributive Property.
$3b^3 + 4b^2 + 6 - b^3 + 5b + 3$ Remove the parentheses.

$\underline{2b^3 + 4b^2 + 5b + 9}$

2. $(3m^2n^2 - 4m^2n + m^2) - (m^2n^2 + 5m^2n - 5)$

$\underline{2m^2n^2 - 9m^2n + m^2 + 5}$

3. $(2x^3y^2 + x^2y - 4) - (x^2y - 8x + 3)$

$\underline{2x^3y^2 + 8x - 7}$

4. $(6y^2 + 3xy - 9x^2) - (-4y^2 + 8xy + x^2)$

$\underline{10y^2 - 5xy - 10x^2}$

PRACTICE 14-4

Reteach
14-4 Subtracting Polynomials

When subtracting polynomials, you can distribute a factor of −1.

Subtract. $(5x^2 + 7x + 3) - (4x^2 + 3x - 5)$.

Rewrite the expression. $(5x^2 + 7x + 3) + (-1)(4x^2 + 3x - 5)$.

Apply the Distributive Property.

$-1(4x^2 + 3x - 5) = (-1 \cdot 4x^2) + (-1 \cdot 3x) + (-1 \cdot -5) = -4x^2 - 3x + 5$

Distributing the −1 changes the sign of each term.
$(5x^2 + 7x + 3) + (-4x^2 - 3x + 5)$

Use the Associative Property to remove parentheses and combine like terms.

$5x^2 + 7x + 3 - 4x^2 - 3x + 5 = x^2 + 4x + 8$

Subtract.

1. $(3b^3 + 4b^2 + 6) - (b^3 - 5b - 3)$

$3b^3 + 4b^2 + 6 + -1(b^3 - 5b - 3)$ Rewrite the expression.
$3b^3 + 4b^2 + 6 + (-b^3 + 5b + 3)$ Apply the Distributive Property.
$3b^3 + 4b^2 + 6 - b^3 + 5b + 3$ Remove the parentheses.

$\underline{2b^3 + 4b^2 + 5b + 9}$

2. $(3m^2n^2 - 4m^2n + m^2) - (m^2n^2 + 5m^2n - 5)$

$\underline{2m^2n^2 - 9m^2n + m^2 + 5}$

3. $(2x^3y^2 + x^2y - 4) - (x^2y - 8x + 3)$

$\underline{2x^3y^2 + 8x - 7}$

4. $(6y^2 + 3xy - 9x^2) - (-4y^2 + 8xy + x^2)$

$\underline{10y^2 - 5xy - 10x^2}$

PRACTICE AND PROBLEM SOLVING

Extra Practice
See page 809.

Subtract.

27. $(6a + 3b - 5ab) - (6a + 5b - 7ab)$ $-2b + 2ab$

28. $(4pq^2 - 6p^2q + 3pq) - (7pq^2 + 7p^2q - 3pq)$ $-3pq^2 - 13p^2q + 6pq$

29. $(9y^2 - 5x^2y + x^2) - (3y^2 + 7x^2y - 4x^2)$
    $6y^2 - 12x^2y + 5x^2$

30. The area of the rectangle is $2a^2 - 4a + 5$ cm^2.
    The area of the square is $a^2 - 2a - 6$ cm^2.
    What is the area of the shaded region?
    $a^2 - 2a + 11$ cm^2

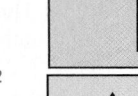

34.
Possible answer:
Find the opposite
of $5x^3 - 3x - 6$,
and add it to
$4x^3 + 7x + 1$.
The result is
$-x^3 + 10x + 7$.

31. The area of the square is $4x^2 - 2x - 6$ in^2. The
    area of the triangle is $2x^2 + 4x - 5$ in^2. What is
    the area of the shaded region?
    $2x^2 - 6x - 1$ in^2

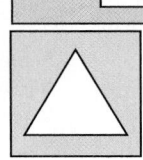

32. **Business** The price in dollars of one share of stock after y years is
    modeled by the expression $3y^3 - 6y + 4.25$. The price of one share of
    another stock is modeled by $3y^3 + 24y + 25.5$. What expression shows the
    difference in price of the two stocks after y years? $30y + 21.25$ **dollars**

33. **Choose a Strategy** Which polynomial has the greatest value when $x = 6$?

    (A) $x^2 - 3x + 8$ (C) $-x^3 - 30x - 200$

    (B) $2x^4 + 7x + 14$ (D) $x^5 - 100x^4 + 10$

34. **Write About It** Explain how to subtract the polynomial
    $5x^3 - 3x - 6$ from $4x^3 + 7x + 1$.

35. **Challenge** Find the values of a, b, c, and d that make the equation true.
    $(2t^3 - at^2 - 4bt - 6) - (ct^3 + 4t^2 + 7t + 1) = 4t^3 - 5t^2 - 15t + d$
    $a = 1; b = 2; c = -2; d = -7$

TEST PREP and Spiral Review

36. **Multiple Choice** What is the opposite of the polynomial
    $-4a^2b - 3ab^2 + 5ab$?

    (F) $4a^2b + 3ab^2 + 5ab$ (H) $-4a^2b - 3ab^2 - 5ab$

    (G) $4a^2b - 3ab^2 + 5ab$ (J) $4a^2b + 3ab^2 - 5ab$

37. **Extended Response** A square has an area of $x^2 + 10x + 25$. A triangle
    inside the square has an area of $x^2 - 4$. Create an expression for the area of
    the square minus the area of the triangle. Evaluate the expression for $x = 8$.
    $10x + 29; 109$

Find the two square roots of each number. (Lesson 4-5)

38. 49 ± 7 39. 9 ± 3 40. 81 ± 9 41. 169 ± 13

Simplify. (Lesson 14-2) $-3x^3y^2 - 2x^2y$ $-zy^3 - 5zy$ $18x^2 - 36x - 6$
42. $x^3y^2 - 2x^2y - 4x^3y^2$ 43. $4(zy^3 - 2zy) + 3zy - 5zy^3$ 44. $6(3x^2 - 6x - 1)$

Objective: Students multiply polynomials by monomials.

 Online Edition
Tutorial Videos

Power Presentations
with PowerPoint®

Warm Up

Multiply. Write each product as one power.

1. $x \cdot x$ x^2 2. $6^2 \cdot 6^3$ 6^5
3. $k^2 \cdot k^8$ k^{10} 4. $19^5 \cdot 19^2$ 19^7
5. $m \cdot m^5$ m^6 6. $26^6 \cdot 26^5$ 26^{11}

7. Find the volume of a rectangular prism that measures 5 cm by 2 cm by 6 cm. **60 cm³**

Problem of the Day

Charlie added 3 binomials, 2 trinomials, and 1 monomial. What is the greatest possible number of terms in the sum? 13

Also available on transparency

 **Math Humor**

Why did the binomial get mad when the mathematician added the term $4x^3$? He didn't like being given the third degree.

State Resources

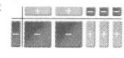 **go.hrw.com**
State Resources Online
KEYWORD: MT7 Resources

 **14-5** **Multiplying Polynomials by Monomials**

Learn to multiply polynomials by monomials.

Chrystelle is making a square planter box in her woodworking class. The box's height is to be 3 inches more than the side length of its base. The volume of the box is found by multiplying a polynomial by a monomial.

Remember that when you multiply two powers with the same bases, you add the exponents. To multiply two monomials, multiply the coefficients and add the exponents of the variables that are the same.

$$(5m^2n^3)(6m^3n^6) = 5 \cdot 6 \cdot m^{2+3}n^{3+6} = 30m^5n^9$$

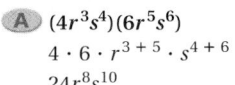

EXAMPLE 1 **Multiplying Monomials**

Multiply.

Ⓐ $(4r^3s^4)(6r^5s^6)$

$4 \cdot 6 \cdot r^{3+5} \cdot s^{4+6}$ *Multiply coefficients and add exponents.*
$24r^8s^{10}$

Ⓑ $(9x^2y)(-2x^3yz^6)$

$9 \cdot -2 \cdot x^{2+3} \cdot y^{1+1} \cdot z^6$ *Multiply coefficients and add exponents.*
$-18x^5y^2z^6$

To multiply a polynomial by a monomial, use the Distributive Property. Multiply every term of the polynomial by the monomial.

EXAMPLE 2 **Multiplying a Polynomial by a Monomial**

Multiply.

Ⓐ $\frac{1}{4}x(y + z)$

Helpful Hint

When multiplying a polynomial by a negative monomial, be sure to distribute the negative sign.

$\frac{1}{4}x(y + z)$ *Multiply each term in the parentheses by $\frac{1}{4}x$.*
$\frac{1}{4}xy + \frac{1}{4}xz$

Ⓑ $-5a^2b(3a^4b^3 + 6a^2b^3)$

$-5a^2b(3a^4b^3 + 6a^2b^3)$ *Multiply each term in the parentheses*
$-15a^6b^4 - 30a^4b^4$ *by $-5a^2b$.*

---

1 **Introduce**

Alternate Opener

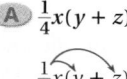

EXPLORATION

14-5 **Multiplying Polynomials by Monomials**

You can use algebra tiles to model multiplication. The model shows that $2(-3) = -6$.

Find each product.

1. $2(2x - 3)$ 2. $x(2x - 3)$

Use algebra tiles to model and find each product.

3. $2(3x + 2)$ 4. $2x(3x - 1)$

Think and Discuss

5. **Explain** how area applies to modeling multiplication.
6. **Write** the factors and product modeled by the tiles shown.

Motivate

Ask students to add the following polynomials:

$$\begin{aligned} 2x^2 + 3x - 6 \\ 2x^2 + 3x - 6 \\ 2x^2 + 3x - 6 \\ + 2x^2 + 3x - 6 \end{aligned}$$

The sum is $8x^2 + 12x - 24$. Ask students whether they can tell you another way to find the answer. Multiply $4(2x^2 + 3x - 6)$.

Explorations and answers are provided in *Alternate Openers: Explorations Transparencies.*

Multiply.

C $5rs^2(r^2s^4 + 3rs^3 - 4rst)$

$5rs^2(r^2s^4 + 3rs^3 - 4rst)$
$5r^3s^6 + 15r^2s^5 - 20r^2s^3t$

Multiply each term in the parentheses by $5rs^2$.

 **EXAMPLE** **PROBLEM SOLVING APPLICATION**

Chrystelle is making a planter box with a square base. She wants the height of the box to be 3 inches more than the side length of the base. If she wants the volume of the box to be 6804 in³, what should the side length of the base be?

1 Understand the Problem

If the side length of the base is s, then the height is $s + 3$. The volume is $s \cdot s \cdot (s + 3) = s^2(s + 3)$. The **answer** will be a value of s that makes the volume of the box equal to 6804 in³.

2 Make a Plan

You can make a table of values for the polynomial to try to find the value of s. Use the Distributive Property to write the expression $s^2(s + 3)$ another way. Use substitution to complete the table.

3 Solve

$s^2(s + 3) = s^3 - 3s^2$ *Distributive Property*

s	15	16	17	18
$s^3 + 3s^2$	$15^3 + 3(15)^2$ = 4050	$16^3 + 3(16)^2$ = 4864	$17^3 + 3(17)^2$ = 5780	$18^3 + 3(18)^2$ = 6804

The side length of the base should be 18 inches.

4 Look Back

If the side length of the base were 18 inches and the height were 3 inches more, or 21 inches, then the volume would be $18 \cdot 18 \cdot 21 = 6804$ in³. The answer is reasonable.

Think and Discuss

1. Compare multiplying two monomials with multiplying a polynomial by a monomial.

Possible answers to Think and Discuss

1. To multiply two monomials, multiply the coefficients and add exponents of powers with the same bases. To multiply a polynomial by a monomial, apply the Distributive Property and multiply the resulting monomials.

---

2 Teach

Guided Instruction

In this lesson, students learn to multiply polynomials by monomials. Review the rules for multiplying powers (Lesson 4-3). Show students how to multiply monomials by multiplying coefficients and adding the exponents of powers with the same bases. Then show them how to use the Distributive Property to multiply a polynomial by a monomial.

 **Inclusion** Remind students to pay attention to the sign of each term when they multiply.

 Reaching All Learners
Through Cooperative Learning

Divide students into groups of three and have them each write a monomial. Have two students in each group add their expressions to create a binomial. (If they happen to have like terms, they can create a monomial.) Then have the group multiply the binomial (or monomial) by the remaining monomial. Repeat with each of the other two pairs in each group.

3 Close

Summarize

Remind students that the Distributive Property can be used to multiply a polynomial by a monomial. Explain that the Distributive Property works for numbers, expressions, and polynomials. Ask students how many terms result from multiplying a polynomial by a monomial.

Possible answer: The number of terms in the resulting polynomial is the same as in the original polynomial.

14-5 Exercises

go.hrw.com
Homework Help Online
KEYWORD: MT7 14-5
Parent Resources Online
KEYWORD: MT7 Parent

Assignment Guide

If you finished Example **1** assign:
Average 1–6, 12–17, 25–27, 42–48
Advanced 12–17, 25–27, 42–48

If you finished Example **2** assign:
Average 1–10, 12–23, 25–34, 42–48
Advanced 12–23, 25–36, 40–48

If you finished Example **3** assign:
Average 1–34, 38, 42–48
Advanced 12–24, 29–48

Homework Quick Check
Quickly check key concepts.
Exercises: 16, 20, 24

Math Background

Factoring the greatest common factor from a polynomial is an important algebraic skill that is essentially the opposite of multiplying a polynomial by a monomial. (See Chapter 14 Extension.) Understanding how to multiply polynomials is a prerequisite for factoring. When you factor the GCF from a polynomial, you divide out the greatest monomial factor that is common to all terms. Then you write the new expression as a monomial times a polynomial. For example, the greatest common factor of the polynomial $4x^4 + 6x^3 + 8x^2$ is $2x^2$. Factoring the polynomial yields $2x^2(2x^2 + 3x + 4)$.

GUIDED PRACTICE

See Example **1** Multiply.
6. $130g^{10}h^5$

1. $(-5s^2t^2)(3st^3)$ $-15s^3t^5$
2. $(x^2y^3)(6x^4y^3)$ $6x^6y^6$
3. $(5h^2j^4)(-7h^4j^6)$ $-35h^6j^{10}$
4. $6m(4m^5)$ $24m^6$
5. $7p^3r(5pr^4)$ $35p^4r^5$
6. $13g^5h^3(10g^5h^2)$

See Example **2**
7. $2h(3m - 4h)$ $6hm - 8h^2$
8. $4ab(a^2b - ab^2)$ $4a^3b^2 - 4a^2b^3$
9. $-3x(x^2 - 5x + 10)$ $-3x^3 + 15x^2 - 30x$
10. $6c^2d(3cd^3 - 5c^3d^2 + 4cd)$ $18c^3d^4 - 30c^5d^3 + 24c^3d^2$

See Example **3**
11. The formula for the area of a trapezoid is $A = \frac{1}{2}h(b_1 + b_2)$, where h is the trapezoid's height and b_1 and b_2 are the lengths of its bases. Use the Distributive Property to simplify the expression. Then use the expression to find the area of a trapezoid with height 12 in. and base lengths 9 in. and 7 in.
$A = \frac{1}{2}b_1h + \frac{1}{2}b_2h$; 96 in²

INDEPENDENT PRACTICE

See Example **1** Multiply.
21. $-6c^4d^3 + 12c^2d^3$
12. $(6x^2y^5)(-3xy^4)$ $-18x^3y^9$
13. $(-gh^3)(-2g^2h^5)$ $2g^3h^8$
14. $(4a^2b)(2b^3)$ $8a^2b^4$
15. $(-s^4t^3)(2st)$ $-2s^5t^4$
16. $12x^9y^7\left(\frac{1}{2}x^3y\right)$ $6x^{12}y^8$
17. $2.5j^3(3h^5j^7)$ $7.5h^3j^{10}$

See Example **2**
18. $(3m^3n^4)(1 - 5mn^5)$ $3m^3n^4 - 15m^4n^9$
19. $3z(5z^2 - 4z)$ $15z^3 - 12z^2$
20. $-3h^2(6h + 3h^3)$ $-18h^3 - 9h^5$
21. $-3cd(2c^3d^2 - 4cd^2)$
22. $-2b(4b^4 - 7b + 10)$ $-8b^5 + 14b^2 - 20b$
23. $-3s^2t^2(4s^2t + 5st - 2s^2t^2)$ $-12s^4t^3 - 15s^3t^3 + 6s^4t^4$

See Example **3**
24. A rectangle has a base of length $3x^2y$ and a height of $2x^3 - 4xy - 3$. Write and simplify an expression for the area of the rectangle. Then find the area of the rectangle if $x = 2$ and $y = 1$.
$6x^5y - 12x^3y^2 - 9x^2y$; 60 units²

PRACTICE AND PROBLEM SOLVING

Extra Practice
See page 809.

Multiply.
25. $(-3b^2)(8b^4)$ $-24b^6$
26. $(4m^2n)(2mn^4)$ $8m^3n^5$
27. $(-2a^2b^2)(-3ab^4)$ $6a^3b^6$
28. $7g(g - 5)$ $7g^2 - 35g$
29. $-3m^2(m^3 - 5m)$ $-3m^5 + 15m^3$
30. $2ab(3a^2b + 3ab^2)$ $6a^3b^2 + 6a^2b^3$
31. $x^4(x - x^3y^5)$ $x^5 - x^7y^5$
32. $m(x + 3)$ $mx - 3m$
33. $f^2g^2(3 + f - g^3)$ $3f^2g^2 + f^3g^2 - f^2g^5$
34. $x^2(x^2 - 4x + 9)$ $x^4 - 4x^3 + 9x^2$
35. $(4m^2p^4)(5m^2p^4 - 3mp^3 + 6m^2p)$ $20m^4p^8 - 12m^3p^7 + 24m^4p^5$
36. $-3wz(5w^4z^2 + 4wz^2 - 6w^2z^2)$ $-15w^5z^3 - 12w^2z^3 + 18w^3z^3$
37. Felix is building a cylindrical-shaped storage container. The height of the container is $x^3 - y^3$. Write and simplify an expression for the volume using the formula $V = \pi r^2h$. Then find the volume with $r = 1\frac{1}{2}$ feet, $x = 3$, and $y = -1$. 63π

State Resources

go.hrw.com
State Resources Online
KEYWORD: MT7 Resources

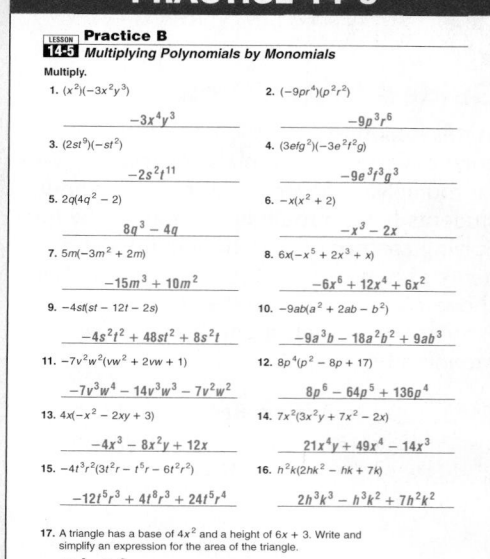

RETEACH 14-5

LESSON **14-5** Reteach
Multiplying Polynomials by Monomials

To multiply a monomial by a monomial, follow the steps used in the example below.
$(7x^2y^3)(3xy^4)$

1. Multiply the coefficients.
$(7)(3) = 21$

2. Multiply the variables.
To multiply two powers with the same base, you keep the base and **add** the exponents.
$(x^2)(x) = (x^2)(x^1) = x^3$ $(y^3)(y^4) = y^7$

Remember: If a variable has no exponent, the exponent is 1.
$x = x^1$

3. Write the monomial product.
$21x^3y^7$

Multiply.
1. $(3x^2)(4x^3y^2)$ $12x^5y^2$
2. $(6a^3b)(2a^3b^4)$ $12a^6b^5$
3. $(2m^4n^2)(-5m^2n^2)$ $-10m^6n^4$

To multiply a polynomial by a monomial, multiply each term of the polynomial by the monomial.
$4a^2 + 2ab + 6b^2$
$\times \qquad 3a$
$12a^5 + 6a^4b + 18a^3b^2$

Multiply.
4. $3r^2s^3 - 2r^2 + 10$
$\times \qquad 2s$
$6r^2s^4 - 4r^2s + 20s$
5. $5x^5 + x^2 - 3x$
$\times \qquad 4x^3$
$20x^8 + 4x^5 - 12x^4$
6. $m^2n - 3mn^2 - 8n^3$
$\times \qquad -3mn$
$-3m^3n^2 + 9m^2n^3 + 24mn^4$

PRACTICE 14-5

LESSON **14-5** Practice B
Multiplying Polynomials by Monomials

Multiply.
1. $(x^2)(-3x^2y^3)$
$-3x^4y^3$
2. $(-9pr^4)(p^2r^2)$
$-9p^3r^6$
3. $(2st^9)(-st^2)$
$-2s^2t^{11}$
4. $(3efg^2)(-3e^2f^2g)$
$-9e^3f^3g^3$
5. $2q(4q^2 - 2)$
$8q^3 - 4q$
6. $-x(x^2 + 2)$
$-x^3 - 2x$
7. $5m(-3m^2 + 2m)$
$-15m^3 + 10m^2$
8. $6x(-x^5 + 2x^3 + x)$
$-6x^6 + 12x^4 + 6x^2$
9. $-4st(st - 12t - 2s)$
$-4s^2t^2 + 48st^2 + 8s^2t$
10. $-9ab(a^2 + 2ab - b^2)$
$-9a^3b - 18a^2b^2 + 9ab^3$
11. $-7v^2w^2(vw^2 + 2vw + 1)$
$-7v^3w^4 - 14v^3w^3 - 7v^2w^2$
12. $8p^4(p^2 - 8p + 17)$
$8p^6 - 64p^5 + 136p^4$
13. $4x(-x^2 - 2xy + 3)$
$-4x^3 - 8x^2y + 12x$
14. $7x^2(3x^2y + 7x^2 - 2x)$
$21x^4y + 49x^4 - 14x^3$
15. $-4t^3r^2(3t^2r - t^5r - 6t^2r^2)$
$-12t^5r^3 + 4t^8r^3 + 24t^5r^4$
16. $h^2k(2hk^2 - hk + 7k)$
$2h^3k^3 - h^3k^2 + 7h^2k^2$
17. A triangle has a base of $4x^2$ and a height of $6x + 3$. Write and simplify an expression for the area of the triangle.
$12x^3 + 6x^2$

38. Health The table gives some formulas for finding the target heart rate for a person of age a exercising at p percent of his or her maximum heart rate.

Target Heart Rate		
	Male	**Female**
Nonathletic	$p(220 - a)$	$p(226 - a)$
Fit	$\frac{1}{2}p(410 - a)$	$\frac{1}{2}p(422 - a)$

   a. Use the Distributive Property to simplify each expression.

   b. Use your answer from part **a** to write an expression for the difference between the target heart rate for a fit male and for a fit female. Both people are age a and are exercising at p percent of their maximum heart rates. $-6p$

40. The number of terms in the answer is the same as the number of terms in the polynomial. The degree of the answer is the degree of the polynomial plus the degree of the monomial.

 39. What's the Question? A square prism has a base area of x^2 and a height of $3x + 4$. If the answer is $3x^3 + 4x^2$, what is the question? If the answer is $14x^2 + 16x$, what is the question?   **Possible answers: What is the volume of the prism? What is the surface area of the prism?**

 40. Write About It If a polynomial is multiplied by a monomial, what can you say about the number of terms in the answer? What can you say about the degree of the answer?

41. Challenge On a multiple-choice test, if the probability of guessing each question correctly is p, then the probability of guessing two or more correctly out of four is $6p^2(1 - 2p - p^2) + 4p^3(1 - p) + p^4$. Simplify the expression. Then write an expression for the probability of guessing fewer than two out of four correctly. $6p^2 - 8p^3 - 9p^4$; $-1 - 6p^2 + 8p^3 + 9p^4$

TEST PREP and Spiral Review

42. Multiple Choice The width of a rectangle is 13 feet less than twice its length. What is the width of the rectangle if the area is 24 ft^2?

   (A) 3 ft   (B) 8 ft   (C) 9 ft   (D) 13 ft

43. Short Response A triangle has base $10cd^2$ and height $3c^2d^2 - 4cd^2$. Write and simplify an expression for the area of the triangle. Then evaluate the expression for $c = 2$ and $d = 3$. $15c^3d^4 - 20c^2d^4$; 3,240 square units

Find the surface area of each figure to the nearest tenth. Use 3.14 for π. (Lesson 8-7)

44. a rectangular prism with base 4 in. by 3 in. and height 2.5 in.   59 in.^{2}

45. a cylinder with radius 10 cm and height 7 cm   1,067.6 cm^2

Find the inverse variation equation, given that x and y vary inversely. (Lesson 13-7)

46. $y = 4$ when $x = 12$ $y = \frac{48}{x}$ **47.** $y = 16$ when $x = 4$ $y = \frac{64}{x}$ **48.** $y = 9$ when $x = 5$ $y = \frac{45}{x}$

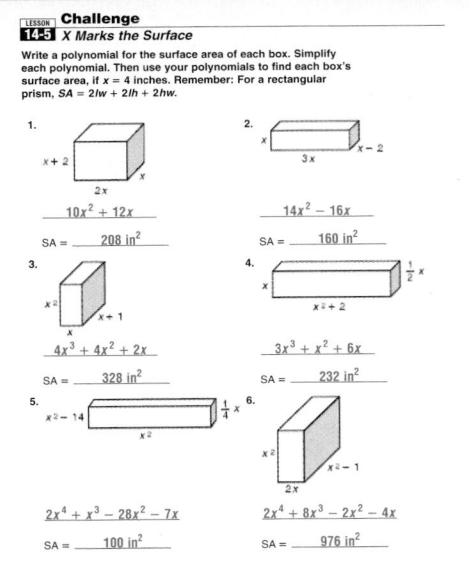

CHALLENGE 14-5

Challenge
14-5 X Marks the Surface

Write a polynomial for the surface area of each box. Simplify each polynomial. Then use your polynomials to find each box's surface area, if $x = 4$ inches. Remember: For a rectangular prism, $SA = 2\ell w + 2\ell h + 2hw$.

1.
$x + 2$
$2x$
$10x^2 + 12x$
$SA = \underline{208}$ in^2

2.
$3x$, $x - 2$, x
$14x^2 - 16x$
$SA = \underline{160}$ in^2

3.
x^2, $x + 1$, x
$4x^3 + 4x^2 + 2x$
$SA = \underline{328}$ in^2

4.
$x^2 + 2$, $\frac{1}{2}x$
$3x^3 + x^2 + 6x$
$SA = \underline{232}$ in^2

5.
$x^2 - 14$, x^2
$2x^4 + x^3 - 28x^2 - 7x$
$SA = \underline{100}$ in^2

6.
$\frac{1}{4}x$, x^2, $2x$, $x^2 - 1$
$2x^4 + 8x^3 - 2x^2 - 4x$
$SA = \underline{976}$ in^2

PROBLEM SOLVING 14-5

Problem Solving
14-5 Multiplying Polynomials by Monomials

Write the correct answer.

1. A rectangle has a width of $5n^2$ inches and a length of $3n^2 + 2n + 1$ inches. Write and simplify an expression for the area of the rectangle. Then find the area of the rectangle if $n = 2$ inches.
$15n^4 + 10n^3 - 5n^2$;
300 square inches

2. The area of a parallelogram is found by multiplying the base and the height. Write and simplify an expression for the area of the parallelogram below.

$3mn$, $5n - 7$
$15mn^3 - 21mn^2$

3. A parallelogram has a base of $2x^2$ inches and a height of $x^2 + 2x - 1$ inches. Write an expression for the area of the parallelogram. What is the area of the parallelogram if $x = 2$ inches?
$2x^4 + 4x^3 - 2x^2$;
88 square inches

4. A rectangle has a length of $x^2 + 2x - 1$ meters and a width of x^2 meters. Write an expression for the area of the rectangle. What is the area of the rectangle if $x = 3$ meters?
$x^4 + 2x^3 - x^2$; 126 m^2

Circle the letter of the correct answer.

5. A rectangle has a width of $3x$ feet. Its length is $2x + \frac{1}{6}$ feet. Which expression shows the area of the rectangle?
A $5x + \frac{1}{6}$
B $6x^2 + \frac{1}{6}x^2$
C $6x^2 + \frac{1}{6}$
(D) $6x^2 + \frac{1}{2}x$

6. Which expression shows the area of the shaded region of the drawing?

$h^2 + 4h - 7$, $2h$, h, $h + 6$
F $2h^3 + 8h - 14h$
G $2h^3 + 9h^2 - 8h$
(H) $2h^3 + 7h^2 - 20h$
J $2h^3 + 7h^2 - 8h$

ONGOING ASSESSMENT
and INTERVENTION

Diagnose Before the Lesson
14-5 Warm Up, TE p. 756

Monitor During the Lesson
14-5 Know-It Notebook
14-5 Questioning Strategies

Assess After the Lesson
14-5 Lesson Quiz, TE p. 759

Answers

38. a.

	Male	Female
Nonathletic	$220p - pa$	$226p - pa$
Fit	$205p - \frac{1}{2}pa$	$211p - \frac{1}{2}pa$

TEST PREP DOCTOR Students can eliminate answer choice **D** for Exercise 42, since a width of 13 ft is too large for the rectangle described in the problem.

Journal
Ask students to explain how multiplying 321 by 3 is similar to multiplying a polynomial by a monomial.

Power Presentations with PowerPoint®

✓ 14-5 Lesson Quiz

Multiply.

1. $(3a^2b)(2ab^2)$ $6a^3b^3$

2. $(4x^2y^2z)(-5xy^3z^2)$ $-20x^3y^5z^3$

3. $3n(2n^3 - 3n)$ $6n^4 - 9n^2$

4. $-5p^2(3q - 6p)$ $-15p^2q + 30p^3$

5. $-2xy(2x^2 + 2y^2 - 2)$ $-4x^3y - 4xy^3 + 4xy$

6. The width of a garden is 5 feet less than 2 times its length. Find the garden's length and width if its area is 63 ft^2. $\ell = 7$ ft, $w = 9$ ft

Also available on transparency

Organizer

Use with Lesson 14-6

Pacing:
Traditional $\frac{1}{2}$ day
Block $\frac{1}{4}$ day

Objective: Use algebra tiles to model multiplying binomials.
Materials: Algebra tiles

 Online Edition
Algebra Tiles

Resources

 Hands-On Lab Activities
Lab 14-6 Recording Sheet

Teach
Discuss

Discuss with students what each algebra tile represents and how to model the product of two binomials.

Close
Key Concept

You can use algebra tiles to model multiplying binomials.

Assessment

Use algebra tiles to model each product.

1. $(x + 2)(x - 4)$

2. $(2x - 1)(x + 3)$

Multiply Binomials

14-6

Use with Lesson 14-6

go.hrw.com
Lab Resources Online
KEYWORD: MT7 Lab14

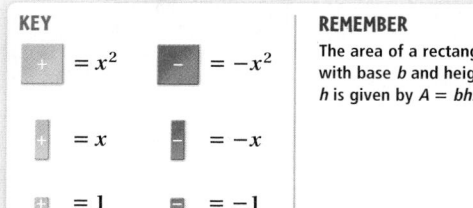

KEY		REMEMBER
$\boxed{+} = x^2$ $\boxed{-} = -x^2$		The area of a rectangle with base b and height h is given by $A = bh$.
$\boxed{+} = x$ $\boxed{-} = -x$		
$\boxed{+} = 1$ $\boxed{-} = -1$		

You can use algebra tiles to find the product of two binomials.

Activity 1

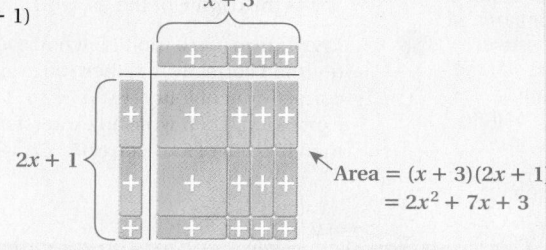

1 To model the product of $(x + 3)(2x + 1)$ with algebra tiles, make a rectangle with base $x + 3$ and height $2x + 1$.

Area $= (x + 3)(2x + 1)$
$= 2x^2 + 7x + 3$

2 Use algebra tiles to find the product of $(x - 2)(-x + 1)$.

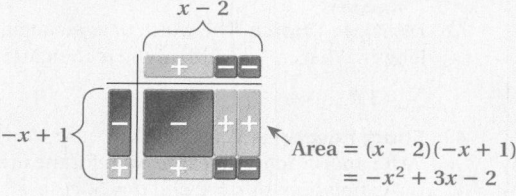

2. Make a rectangle with base $x + 3$ and height $x - 3$. The product has one yellow x^2-tile, 3 red x-tiles, 3 yellow x-tiles, and 9 red unit tiles. The 3 red and 3 yellow x-tiles form 2 zero pairs. The product is $x^2 - 9$.

Area $= (x - 2)(-x + 1)$
$= -x^2 + 3x - 2$

Think and Discuss

1. Explain how to determine the signs of each term in the product when you are multiplying $(x - 3)(x - 2)$.

2. How can you use algebra tiles to find $(x + 3)(x - 3)$?

The product of two negatives or two positives is positive, so the x^2 and constant terms are positive. The product of a positive and a negative is negative, so the x-terms are negative.

Answers to Assessment

1.

x + 2

x − 4

$x^2 - 2x - 8$

2.

2x − 1

x + 3

$2x^2 + 5x - 3$

go.hrw.com
State Resources Online
KEYWORD: MT7 Resources

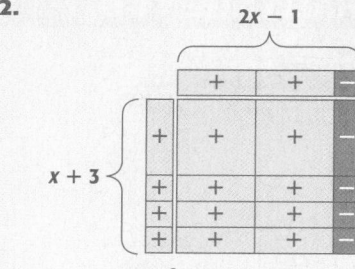

Use algebra tiles to find each product.

1. $(x + 4)(x - 4)$ **2.** $(x - 3)(x + 2)$ **3.** $(x - 5)(-x + 3)$

Activity 2

Write two binomials whose product is modeled by the algebra tiles below, and then write the product as a polynomial expression.

The base of the rectangle is $x - 5$ and the height is $x - 2$, so the binomial product is $(x - 5)(x - 2)$.

The model shows one x^2-tile, seven $-x$-tiles, and ten 1-tiles, so the polynomial expression is $x^2 - 7x + 10$.

Think and Discuss

1. Write an expression modeled by the algebra tiles below. How many zero pairs are modeled? Describe them.

$x^2 + x - 2$; one zero pair is modeled; the pair is one yellow x-tile and one red x-tile.

Try This

Write two binomials whose product is modeled by each set of algebra tiles below, and then write the product as a polynomial expression.

1.

$(x + 2)(x + 2)$;
$x^2 + 4x + 4$

2.

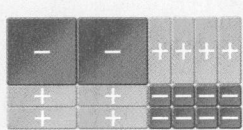

$(x + 2)(x - 3)$;
$x^2 - x - 6$

3.

$(-2x + 4)(x - 2)$;
$-2x^2 + 8x - 8$

Activity 1

Answers to *Try This*

1.

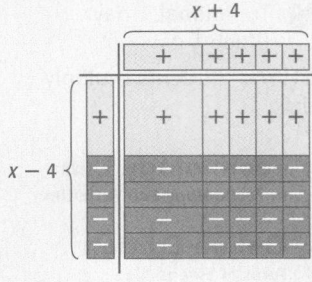

$(x + 4)(x - 4) = x^2 - 16$

2.

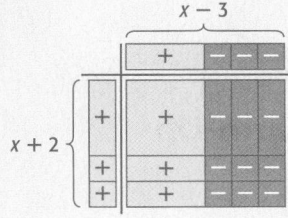

$(x - 3)(x + 2) = x^2 - x - 6$

3.

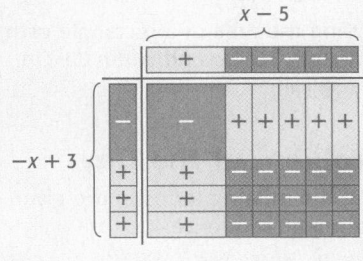

$(x - 5)(-x + 3) =$
$x^2 + 8x - 5$

Pacing: Traditional 1 day
Block $\frac{1}{2}$ day

Objective: Students multiply binomials.

Technology Lab
In *Technology Lab* Activities

Online Edition
Tutorial Videos

Power Presentations
with PowerPoint®

Warm Up

Multiply.

1. $x(x + 2)$ $x^2 + 2x$

2. $-3(p - 4)$ $-3p + 12$

3. $2x(3x - 7)$ $6x^2 - 14x$

4. Find the area of a rectangle with length 16 cm and width 21 cm.
336 cm^2

Problem of the Day

Find the missing terms in the given arithmetic sequence.

170, ■, ■, ■, 140, . . .
162.5, 155, 147.5

Also available on transparency

Math Humor

Two binomials wanted to go their separate ways. What did they say when they were multiplied together? "Drats! Foiled again!"

State Resources

go.hrw.com
State Resources Online
KEYWORD: MT7 Resources

14-6 Multiplying Binomials

Learn to multiply binomials.

Vocabulary
FOIL

Jordan Middle School is designing a cactus garden. One raised bed will measure 12 ft by 5 ft. There will be a bark covered walkway of width x feet around the raised flower bed. To find the area of the bark walkway, you need to multiply two binomials.

You can use the Distributive Property to multiply two binomials.

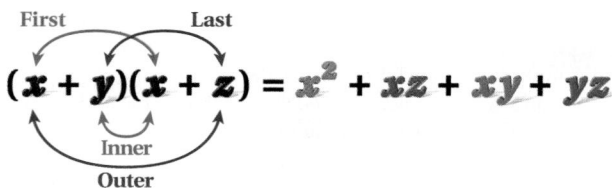
$$(x + y)(x + z) = x(x + z) + y(x + z) = x^2 + xz + xy + yz$$

The product can be simplified using the **FOIL** method: the First terms, the Outer terms, the Inner terms, and the Last terms of the binomials.

First   Last

$$(\boldsymbol{x} + \boldsymbol{y})(\boldsymbol{x} + \boldsymbol{z}) = \boldsymbol{x}^2 + \boldsymbol{xz} + \boldsymbol{xy} + \boldsymbol{yz}$$

Inner
Outer

EXAMPLE 1   **Multiplying Two Binomials**

Multiply.

Helpful Hint

When you multiply two binomials, you will get four products. Then combine like terms.

A $(p + 2)(3 - q)$

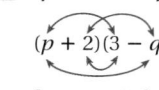
$(p + 2)(3 - q)$ *FOIL*

$3p - pq + 6 - 2q$

B $(m + n)(p + q)$

$(m + n)(p + q)$

$mp + mq + np + nq$

C $(x + 2)(x + 5)$

$(x + 2)(x + 5)$ *FOIL*

$x^2 + 5x + 2x + 10$
$x^2 + 7x + 10$ *Combine like terms.*

D $(3m + n)(m - 2n)$

$(3m + n)(m - 2n)$

$3m^2 - 6mn + mn - 2n^2$
$3m^2 - 5mn - 2n^2$

---

1 Introduce

Alternate Opener

Motivate

Ask students to multiply 42 by 25. 1050 Show them that the numbers can also be multiplied by using the Distributive Property as shown below.

$$(42)(25)$$
$$(40 + 2)(20 + 5)$$
$$(40)(20 + 5) + (2)(20 + 5)$$
$$(40)(20) + (40)(5) + (2)(20) + (2)(5)$$
$$800 + 200 + 40 + 10$$
$$1050$$

Explorations and answers are provided in *Alternate Openers: Explorations Transparencies*.

EXAMPLE 2 Multi-Step

Find the area of a bark walkway of width x ft around a 12 ft by 5 ft raised flower bed.

Area of
Walkway =   Total Area   − Flower Bed

$= (5 + 2x)(12 + 2x) \quad - (5)(12)$

$= 60 + 10x + 24x + 4x^2 \; - 60$

$\qquad\qquad 4x^2 + 34x$

The walkway area is $34x + 4x^2$ ft^2.

12 ft

5 ft

Binomial products of the form $(a + b)^2$, $(a − b)^2$, and $(a + b)(a − b)$ are often called *special products*.

EXAMPLE 3 Special Products of Binomials

Multiply.

A $(x − 3)^2$

$(x − 3)(x − 3)$

$x^2 − 3x − 3x + 3^2$

$x^2 − 6x + 9$

B $(a + b)^2$

$(a + b)(a + b)$

$a^2 + ab + ab + b^2$

$a^2 + 2ab + b^2$

C $(n + 3)(n − 3)$

$(n + 3)(n − 3)$

$n^2 − 3n + 3n − 3^2$

$n^2 − 9$ $−3n + 3n = 0$

Special Products of Binomials

$(a + b)^2 = a^2 + ab + ab + b^2 = a^2 + 2ab + b^2$

$(a − b)^2 = a^2 − ab − ab + b^2 = a^2 − 2ab + b^2$

$(a + b)(a − b) = a^2 − ab + ab − b^2 = a^2 − b^2$

Possible answers to
Think and Discuss

1. 4 terms:
$(a + b)(c + d) = ac + ad + bc + bd;$

3 terms:
$(x + 1)(x + 2) = x^2 + 3x + 2;$

2 terms:
$(x + 1)(x − 1) = x^2 − 1$

Think and Discuss

1. Give an example of a product of two binomials that has 4 terms, one that has 3 terms, and one that has 2 terms.

Power Presentations with PowerPoint®

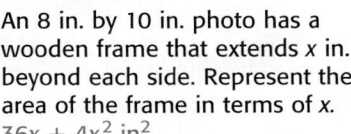

Additional Examples

Example 1

Multiply.

A. $(n − 2)(m − 8)$
$nm − 8n − 2m + 16$

B. $(x + 3)(x + z)$
$x^2 + xz + 3x + 3z$

C. $(a + 3)(a + 5)$
$a^2 + 8a + 15$

D. $(x − 4y)(x + 7y)$
$x^2 + 3xy − 28y^2$

Example 2

An 8 in. by 10 in. photo has a wooden frame that extends x in. beyond each side. Represent the area of the frame in terms of x.
$36x + 4x^2$ in^2

Example 3

Multiply.

A. $(x + 6)^2$ $x^2 + 12x + 36$

B. $(n − m)^2$ $n^2 − 2nm + m^2$

C. $(x − 7)(x + 7)$ $x^2 − 49$

Also available on transparency

2 Teach

Guided Instruction

In this lesson, students learn to multiply binomials. Explain that the Distributive Property is used to multiply binomials. Demonstrate how the mnemonic device FOIL can help students remember the necessary steps (Teaching Transparency). As you work the examples, take care to show the four products separately before simplifying. Introduce students to the special binomial products: $(a + b)^2$, $(a − b)^2$, and $(a + b)(a − b)$. Encourage students to write the perfect square binomials as the product of two binomials before they multiply.

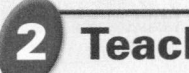

Reaching All Learners
Through Modeling

Show students a rectangle that has side lengths $(x + 4)$ and $(x + 2)$ and is divided into four smaller rectangles. Have students write expressions for the areas of the smaller rectangles and add them to find an expression for the area of the largest rectangle. Then have them find the area of the largest rectangle by using the FOIL method. Finally, have them compare their results. You may want to have students work in pairs or small groups. Since the area of each of the small rectangles are x^2, $4x$, $2x$, and 8, the area of the largest rectangle is $x^2 + 4x + 2x + 8 = x^2 + 6x + 8$. By FOIL, the area of the largest rectangle is $(x + 4)(x + 2) = x^2 + 6x + 8$. The results are the same.

3 Close

Summarize

Remind students that the FOIL method is an application of the Distributive Property. Ask students to explain why the expressions in Example 3 are called *special products*.

Possible answer: The expressions in Examples 3A and 3B are binomials raised to the second power (perfect square binomials). The expression in Example 3C is a binomial multiplied by a similar binomial with a different sign in the middle.

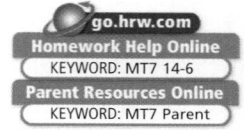
Assignment Guide

If you finished Example **1** assign:
Average   1–6, 12–20, 29–31,
45–53
Advanced 12–20, 33–35, 39,
45–53

If you finished Example **2** assign:
Average   1–7, 12–21, 29–31, 41,
45–53
Advanced 12–21, 33–35, 39,
41–53

If you finished Example **3** assign:
Average   1–33, 36, 38, 40, 41,
45–53
Advanced 12–53

Homework Quick Check

Quickly check key concepts.
Exercises: 20, 21, 24, 36, 38

Math Background

To multiply binomials vertically, you can use a method similar to the traditional method of multiplying two-digit numbers. For example, the product of $(x + 2)(x + 3)$ may be found as shown below.

$$\begin{array}{r} x + 2 \\ \times\quad x + 3 \\ \hline 3x + 6 \\ x^2 + 2x \\ \hline x^2 + 5x + 6 \end{array}$$

This method can also be useful when you are multiplying polynomials with more than two terms.

State Resources

go.hrw.com
State Resources Online
KEYWORD: MT7 Resources

GUIDED PRACTICE

See Example **1** Multiply.

1. $(x - 5)(y + 4)$
$xy + 4x - 5y - 20$

2. $(x - 3)(x + 7)$
$x^2 + 4x - 21$

3. $(3m - 5)(4m + 9)$
$12m^2 + 7m - 45$

4. $(h + 2)(3h + 4)$
$3h^2 + 10h + 8$

5. $(m - 2)(m - 7)$
$m^2 - 9m + 14$

6. $(b + 3c)(4b + c)$
$4b^2 + 13bc + 3c^2$

See Example **2** **7.** A courtyard is constructed in a 20 ft by 30 ft space. There is a walkway of width x all the way around the courtyard. Find the area of the walkway.
$600 - 200x + 4x^2$ ft^2

See Example **3** Multiply.

8. $(x + 2)^2$
$x^2 + 4x + 4$

9. $(b - 3)(b + 3)$
$b^2 - 9$

10. $(x - 4)^2$
$x^2 - 8x + 16$

11. $(3x + 5)^2$
$9x^2 + 30x + 25$

INDEPENDENT PRACTICE

See Example **1** Multiply.

12. $(x + 4)(x - 3)$
$x^2 + x - 12$

13. $(v - 1)(v + 5)$
$v^2 + 4v - 5$

14. $(w + 6)(w + 2)$
$w^2 + 8w + 12$

15. $(3x - 5)(x + 6)$
$3x^2 + 13x - 30$

16. $(4m - 1)(3m + 2)$
$12m^2 + 5m - 2$

17. $(3b - c)(4b + 5c)$
$12b^2 + 11bc - 5c^2$

18. $(3t - 1)(t + 1)$
$3t^2 + 2t - 1$

19. $(3r + s)(4r - 5s)$
$12r^2 - 11rs - 5s^2$

20. $(5n - 3b)(n + 2b)$
$5n^2 + 7bn - 6b^2$

See Example **2** **21. Construction** The Gonzalez family is having a pool to swim laps built in their backyard. The pool will be 25 yards long by 5 yards wide. There will be a cement deck of width x yards around the pool. Find the total area of the pool and the deck. $100 + 50x + 4x^2$ yd^2

See Example **3** Multiply.

22. $(x - 5)^2$
$x^2 - 10x + 25$

23. $(b + 3)^2$
$b^2 + 6b + 9$

24. $(x - 4)(x + 4)$
$x^2 - 16$

25. $(2x + 3)(2x - 3)$
$4x^2 - 9$

26. $(4x - 1)^2$
$16x^2 - 8x + 1$

27. $(a + 7)^2$
$a^2 + 14a + 49$

PRACTICE AND PROBLEM SOLVING

Extra Practice
See page 809.

Multiply.

28. $(m - 6)(m + 6)$
$m^2 - 36$

29. $(b - 5)(b + 12)$
$b^2 + 7b - 60$

30. $(q + 6)(q + 5)$
$q^2 + 11q + 30$

31. $(t - 9)(t - 4)$
$t^2 - 13t + 36$

32. $(g + 3)(g - 3)$
$g^2 - 9$

33. $(3b + 7)(b - 4)$
$3b^2 - 5b - 28$

34. $(3t - 1)(6t + 7)$
$18t^2 + 15t - 7$

35. $(4m - n)(m + 3n)$
$4m^2 + 11mn - 3n^2$

36. $(3a + 6b)^2$
$9a^2 + 36ab + 36b^2$

37. $(r + 5)(r - 5)$
$r^2 - 25$

38. $(5q - 2)^2$
$25q^2 - 20q + 4$

39. $(3r - 2s)(5r - 4s)$
$15r^2 - 22rs + 8s^2$

40.
$300 - 70x + 4x^2$ in^2

40. A metalworker makes a box from a 15 in. by 20 in. piece of tin by cutting a square with side length x out of each corner and folding up the sides. Write and simplify an expression for the area of the base of the box.

Life Science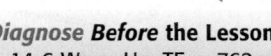

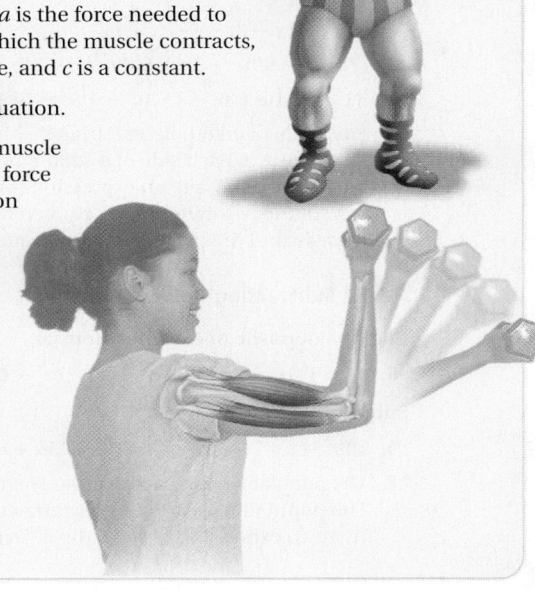

A. V. Hill (1886–1977) was a biophysicist and pioneer in the study of how muscles work. He studied muscle contractions in frogs and came up with an equation relating the force generated by a muscle to the speed at which the muscle contracts. Hill expressed this relationship as

$$(P + a)(V + b) = c,$$

where P is the force generated by the muscle, a is the force needed to make the muscle contract, V is the speed at which the muscle contracts, b is the smallest contraction rate of the muscle, and c is a constant.

41. Use the FOIL method to simplify Hill's equation.
$PV + bP + aV + ab = c$

42. Suppose the force a needed to make the muscle contract is approximately $\frac{1}{4}$ the maximum force the muscle can generate. Use Hill's equation to write an equation for a muscle generating the maximum possible force M. Simplify the equation.

43.  **Write About It** In Hill's equation, what happens to V as P increases? What happens to P as V increases? (*Hint:* You can substitute the value of 1 for a, b, and c to help you see the relationship between P and V.)

44. ⭐ **Challenge** Solve Hill's equation for P. Assume that no variables equal 0.
$P = \frac{c}{V + b} - a$

TEST PREP and Spiral Review

45. Multiple Choice Which polynomial shows the result of using the FOIL method to find $(x - 2)(x + 6)$?

Ⓐ $x^2 - 12$ Ⓑ $x^2 + 6x - 2x - 12$ Ⓒ $2x - 2x - 12$ Ⓓ $x^2 + 4$

46. Gridded Response Multiply $(3a - 2b)$ and $(5a + 8b)$. What is the coefficient of ab?
14

Find the scale factor that relates each model to the actual object. (Lesson 5-8)

47. 14 in. model, 70 in. object   1:5
48. 8 cm model, 16 cm object   1:2
49. 4 in. model, 6 ft 8 in. object   1:20
50. 2 cm model, 50 cm object   1:25

Simplify. (Lesson 14-2)

51. $-4(m^2 - 3m + 6)$
$-4m^2 + 12m - 24$

52. $3(a^2b - 4a + 3ab) - 2ab$
$3a^2b - 12a + 7ab$

53. $x^2y + 4(xy^2 - 3x^2y + 4xy)$
$-11x^2y + 4xy^2 + 16xy$

Interdisciplinary

Life Science

Exercises 41–44 relate polynomial concepts to muscle contraction. Muscles and their contractions are studied in middle school life science programs, such as *Holt Science & Technology*.

Answers

42. $(M + \frac{1}{4}M)(V + b) = c$;
$\frac{5}{4}MV + \frac{5}{4}Mb = c$

43. Possible answer: As P increases, V decreases, and as V increases, P decreases.

TEST PREP DOCTOR ➕ Students who chose answer **A** did not multiply the inner terms of the binomials in Exercise 45. If students pick the wrong answer, they should review the FOIL method.

Journal

Ask students to explain the FOIL method of multiplication.

Organizer

Objective: Assess students' mastery of concepts and skills in Lessons 14-3 through 14-6.

Resources

Assessment Resources
Section 14B Quiz

Test & Practice Generator
One-Stop Planner®

INTERVENTION ◀▬▬▶

Resources

Ready to Go On? Intervention and Enrichment Worksheets

Ready to Go On? CD-ROM

Ready to Go On? Online

my.hrw.com

Ready to Go On?

Quiz for Lessons 14-3 Through 14-6

✓ 14-3 Adding Polynomials

Add.

1. $(8x^3 + 6x - 3) + (-2x + 6)$ $\quad 8x^3 + 4x + 3$

2. $(30x - 7) + (12x - 5)$ $\quad 42x - 12$

3. $(7b^3c^2 - 6b^2c + 3bc) + (8b^3c^2 - 5bc + 13) + (4b^2c - 5bc - 9)$ $\quad 3. 15b^3c^2 - 2b^2c - 7bc + 4$

4. $(2w^2 - 4w + 6) + (-3w - 4w^2 - 5) + (w^2 + 4 - 4)$ $-w^2 - 7w + 1$

5. Each side of an equilateral triangle has length $w + 2$. Each side of a square has length $3w - 4$. Write an expression for the sum of the perimeter of the equilateral triangle and the perimeter of the square. $15w - 10$

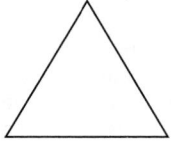 

$w + 2$ $\qquad$ $3w - 4$

✓ 14-4 Subtracting Polynomials

Find the opposite of each polynomial.

6. $-3x + 4xy^3$ $\quad 3x - 4xy^3$

7. $2m^2 - 6m + 3$ $\quad -2m^2 + 6m - 3$

8. $5v - 7v^2$ $\quad -5v + 7v^2$

Subtract.

9. $10b^2 - (3b^2 + 6b - 8)$ $\quad 7b^2 - 6b + 8$

10. $(13a + a^2) - (9 + a + 7a)$ $\quad a^2 + 5a - 9$

11. $(6x^2 + 6x) - (3x^2 + 7x)$ $\quad 3x^2 - x$

12. The population of a bacteria colony after h hours is $4h^3 - 5h^2 + 2h + 200$. The population of another bacteria colony is $3h^3 - 2h^2 + 5h + 200$. Write an expression to show the difference between the two populations. $h^3 - 3h^2 - 3h$

✓ 14-5 Multiplying Polynomials and Monomials

Multiply.

13. $(4x^3y^3)(-3xy^6)$ $\quad -12x^4y^9$

14. $(-s^2t^3)(st)$ $\quad -s^3t^4$

15. $(3hj^5)(-6h^4j^5)$ $\quad -18h^5j^{10}$

16. $5c^2d(3cd^3 - 2c^3d^2 + 4cd)$ $\quad 16. 15c^3d^4 - 10c^5d^3 + 20c^3d^2$

17. $-4s^2t^2(4s^2t + 3st - s^2t^2)$ $\quad 17. -16s^4t^3 - 12s^3t^3 + 4s^4t^4$

18. A triangle has a base of length $2x^2y$ and a height of $x^3 - xy - 2$. Write and simplify an expression for the area of the triangle. Then find the area of the triangle if $x = 2$ and $y = 1$. $x^5y - x^3y^2 - 4x^2y$; 8

✓ 14-6 Multiplying Binomials

Multiply.

19. $(x - 2)(x + 6)$ $\quad x^2 + 4x - 12$

20. $(3m - 4)(2m + 8)$ $\quad 6m^2 + 16m - 32$

21. $(n - 5)(n - 3)$ $\quad n^2 - 8n + 15$

22. $(x - 6)^2$ $\quad x^2 - 12x + 36$

23. $(x - 5)(x + 5)$ $\quad x^2 - 25$

24. $(3x + 2)(3x - 2)$ $\quad 9x^2 - 4$

25. A rug is placed in a 10 ft × 20 ft room so that there is an uncovered strip of width x all the way around the rug. Find the area of the rug. $4x^2 - 72x + 320$

READY TO GO ON?
Diagnose and Prescribe

NO INTERVENE ⬇

READY TO GO ON? Intervention, Section 14B			
Ready to Go On? Intervention	 **Worksheets**	 **CD-ROM**	 **Online**
✓ Lesson 14-3	14-3 Intervention	Activity 14-3	
✓ Lesson 14-4	14-4 Intervention	Activity 14-4	Diagnose and Prescribe Online
✓ Lesson 14-5	14-5 Intervention	Activity 14-5	
✓ Lesson 14-6	14-6 Intervention	Activity 14-6	

YES ENRICH ⬇

READY TO GO ON? Enrichment, Section 14B

 **Worksheets**

CD-ROM

Online

Cooking Up a New Kitchen

Javier is a contractor who remodels kitchens. He drew the figure to help calculate the dimensions of a countertop surrounding a sink that is x inches long and y inches wide.

1. Write a polynomial that Javier can use to find the perimeter of the outer edge of the countertop. $2x + 2y + 40$

2. Someone orders a countertop for a sink that is 18 inches long and 12 inches wide. Javier puts tape around the outer edge of the countertop to protect it while it is being moved. Use the polynomial to determine how many inches of tape are needed. **100 in.**

3. Write a polynomial that Javier can use to find the area of the countertop for any size sink. $8x + 12y + 96$

4. The marble for the countertop costs $1.25 per square inch. Write a polynomial that gives the cost of the countertop. $10x + 15y + 120$

5. Find the cost of the countertop for the 18-inch by 12-inch sink. Explain your answer.

Multi-Step Test Prep

Organizer

Objective: Assess students' ability to apply concepts and skills in Chapter 14 in a real-world format.

 Online Edition

Resources

 Middle School Assessments
www.mathtekstoolkit.org

Problem	Text reference
1	Lesson 14-1
2	Lesson 14-2
3	Lesson 14-3
4	Lesson 14-4
5	Lesson 14-5

Answers

5. $480; To find the cost, evaluate $10x + 15y + 120$ for $x = 18$ and $y = 12$;
$(10 \times 18) + (15 \times 12) + 120 = \$480$

INTERVENTION

Scaffolding Questions

1. What is the formula used to find the perimeter of a rectangle? $2(l + w)$

2. How long is the countertop? **30 in.** How wide is the countertop? **20 in.**

3. Does the area of the countertop also include the area of the sink? **No**

4. What are the units for the area of the countertop? in^2

5. Why can't you find the cost of the countertop by multiplying $1.25(6 + 6 + 4 + 4)$? Possible answer: Because that expression does not take into account the length and width of the sink.

Extension

1. What if someone wanted a sink half the size of the 18-inch by 12-inch sink Javier is installing. Can you still use the same polynomial you found in item 3 to calculate the area of the countertop? Explain.

Possible answer: You can use the polynomial from item 3 to find the area of the countertop for any size sink, because the length and width of the sink are represented by variables that can change.

State Resources

 **go.hrw.com**
State Resources Online
KEYWORD: MT7 Resources

Pacing: Traditional 1 day
Block $\frac{1}{2}$ day
Objective: Students divide poly-
nomials by monomials.

Online Edition

Using the Extension

In Lesson 14-5, students multiplied polynomials by monomials. In this extension, students will divide polynomials by monomials. Teaching these concepts will reinforce the properties of exponents, and these skills will be useful in more-advanced applications, such as factoring polynomials.

State Resources

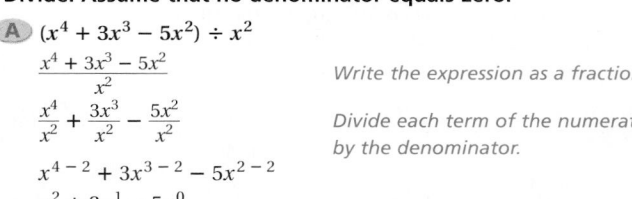

go.hrw.com
State Resources Online
KEYWORD: MT7 Resources

EXTENSION | # Dividing Polynomials by Monomials

Learn to divide polynomials by monomials.

Remember that when you divide a monomial by a monomial, you subtract the exponents of variables that are in the denominator from the exponents of the like variables that are in the numerator.

EXAMPLE 1 Dividing Monomials by Monomials

Divide. Assume that no denominator equals zero.

A $\dfrac{12x^7}{2x^3}$

$6x^{7-3}$ *Divide coefficients. Subtract exponents of like variables.*

$6x^4$

B $\dfrac{8x^7y^4}{6x^5y^3}$

$\dfrac{4}{3}x^{7-5}y^{4-3}$ *Divide coefficients. Subtract exponents of like variables.*

$\dfrac{4}{3}x^2y^1 = \dfrac{4}{3}x^2y$

When you divide a polynomial by a monomial, you divide each term of the polynomial by the monomial.

EXAMPLE 2 Dividing Polynomials by Monomials

Divide. Assume that no denominator equals zero.

Remember!
For any nonzero number x, $x^0 = 1$.

A $(x^4 + 3x^3 - 5x^2) \div x^2$

$\dfrac{x^4 + 3x^3 - 5x^2}{x^2}$ *Write the expression as a fraction.*

$\dfrac{x^4}{x^2} + \dfrac{3x^3}{x^2} - \dfrac{5x^2}{x^2}$ *Divide each term of the numerator by the denominator.*

$x^{4-2} + 3x^{3-2} - 5x^{2-2}$

$x^2 + 3x^1 - 5x^0$

$x^2 + 3x - 5$ *Simplify.*

B $(x^6y^2 - x^3y^5 - 3x^2y^7) \div x^2y$

$\dfrac{x^6y^2 - x^3y^5 - 3x^2y^7}{x^2y}$ *Write the expression as a fraction.*

$\dfrac{x^6y^2}{x^2y} - \dfrac{x^3y^5}{x^2y} - \dfrac{3x^2y^7}{x^2y}$ *Divide each term of the numerator by the denominator.*

$x^{6-2}y^{2-1} - x^{3-2}y^{5-1} - 3x^{2-2}y^{7-1}$

$x^4y - xy^4 - 3y^6$ *Simplify.*

---

1 Introduce

Motivate

Have students calculate $\frac{8 + 12}{4}$. 5 Have them calculate $\frac{8}{4} + \frac{12}{4}$. 5 Explain that the answers are the same because the expressions are equal. Point out that in the fractional expression $\frac{8 + 12}{4}$, $(8 + 12)$ is a polynomial, and 4 is a monomial. Explain to students that they have just divided a polynomial by a monomial.

2 Teach

Guided Instruction

In this extension, students learn to divide polynomials by monomials. Review the properties for dividing powers (Lesson 4-3). Remind students that to divide a monomial by a monomial, the exponents of variables that are in the denominator are subtracted from the exponents of the like variables that are in the numerator. Then show students how to divide each term of the numerator by the denominator. Work through Example 3 carefully because this information will be new to many students.

You can sometimes use division to factor a polynomial into a product of a monomial and a polynomial. The monomial is the product of the GCF of the coefficients and the lowest power of each variable in the polynomial.

EXAMPLE 3 Factoring Polynomials

Factor each polynomial.

A $3x^3 + 9x^5 - 6x^2$

The GCF of the coefficients is 3, and the lowest power of the variable is x^2, so factor out $3x^2$.

$$\frac{3x^3 + 9x^5 - 6x^2}{3x^2} = x + 3x^3 - 2$$

Write the polynomial as a product.
$3x^3 + 9x^5 - 6x^2 = 3x^2(x + 3x^3 - 2)$

B $16a^4b + 12a^3b$

The GCF of the coefficients is 4, and the lowest powers of the variables are a^3 and b, so factor out $4a^3b$.

$$\frac{16a^4b + 12a^3b}{4a^3b} = 4a + 3$$

Write the polynomial as a product.
$16a^4b + 12a^3b = 4a^3b(4a + 3)$

 **EXTENSION**

Exercises

8. $5a^5 + 3a^3 + 4a^2$
9. $p^4q^3 - 4p^2q$
13. $2m^2n(2n^2 - 3m)$
16. $5pq^2(p^2q^2 + 3pq + 1)$
19. $4xy(x^3y^7 + 4x^2y - 2)$

Divide. Assume that no denominator equals zero.

1. $\frac{12a^5}{4a^2}$ $3a^3$

2. $\frac{32m^5}{8m^3}$ $4m^2$

3. $\frac{12a^4b^2}{2a^2b}$ $6a^2b$

4. $\frac{-12x^2y}{x^2y}$ -12

5. $\frac{36a^5b^5c^7}{12a^4bc^3}$ $3ab^4c^4$

6. $\frac{30x^7y^8z^6}{14x^7y^7z^3}$ $\frac{15}{7}yz^3$

7. $\frac{6x^5 + 9x^2}{3x}$ $2x^4 + 3x$

8. $\frac{15a^8 + 9a^6 + 12a^5}{3a^3}$

9. $\frac{13p^9q^6 - 52p^7q^4}{13p^5q^3}$

10. $\frac{j^4k^3 - 4j^6k^5}{3j^3k}$ $\frac{1}{3}jk^2 + \frac{4}{3}j^3k^4$

11. $\frac{27a^6b^{13} - 18a^{12}b^8}{9a^3b^8}$ $3a^3b^5 - 2a^9$

12. $\frac{12x^5 + 9x^4 + 15x^2}{x}$ $12x^4 + 9x^3 + 15x$

Factor each polynomial.

13. $4m^2n^3 - 6m^3n$

14. $x^2y^3 + x^3y^2$ $x^2y^2(y + x)$

15. $15z^3 + 25z^6$ $5z^3(3 + 5z^3)$

16. $5p^3q^4 + 15p^2q^3 + 5pq^2$

17. $15a^2 + 10a^3 + 5a^7$ $5a^2(3 + 2a + a^5)$

18. $r^5s^3 + r^7s^4 + r^6s^8$ $r^5s^3(1 + r^2s + rs^5)$

19. $4x^4y^8 + 16x^3y^2 - 8xy$

20. $36d + 12f$ $12(3d + f)$

21. $-3n + 3n^2$ $-3n(1 - n)$

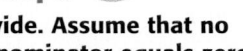
Additional Examples

Example 1

Divide. Assume that no denominator equals zero.

A. $\frac{24z^7}{4z}$ $6z^6$

B. $\frac{10a^3b^7}{6a^2b^7}$ $\frac{5a}{3}$

Example 2

Divide. Assume that no denominator equals zero.

A. $(a^5 + 6a^4 - 8a^2) \div a^2$ $a^3 + 6a^2 - 8$

B. $(r^6s^2 - r^5s - 4r^3s^4) \div r^2s$ $r^4s - r^3 - 4rs^3$

Example 3

Factor each polynomial.

A. $5y^4 - 10y^2 - 20y$ $5y(y^3 - 2y - 4)$

B. $8x^2y^4z^5 + 20x^3y^3z^4$ $4x^2y^3z^4(2yz + 5x)$

Also available on transparency

---

3 Close

Teaching Tip **Math Connection**
Encourage students to check each division by multiplying their answer by the original monomial divisor in the problem. The product should equal the polynomial given in the original problem.

Summarize

Review the process for dividing monomials. Explain that a polynomial with more than one term can be divided by a monomial one term at a time. You may want to point out that the factoring in the Extension is the inverse operation of multiplying a polynomial by a monomial (Lesson 14-5).

Game Time

Organizer

Objective: Participate in games to practice and apply skills learned in Chapter 14.

Online Edition

Resources

📖 ***Chapter 14 Resource Book***
Puzzles, Twisters & Teasers

Short Cuts

Purpose: To apply the skill of multiplying binomials to developing a multiplication trick

Discuss Ask students to explain how the trick works. What general expression can you write to represent a two-digit number that ends in 5? $10n + 5$, where n is the digit in the tens place What is the square of the expression? $100n^2 + 100n + 25$ or $100n(n + 1) + 25$ How does the square of the expression model a numerical answer? The expression $100n(n + 1)$ provides the hundreds (and thousands) place of the answer; the 25 provides the tens and ones places.

Extend Challenge students to create a trick for multiplying two-digit numbers with a first digit of 2, and then with first digits of 3, 4, and 5. Ask them to look for a pattern.

$(20 + n)(20 + b) =$
$400 + 20(n + b) + nb$

$(30 + n)(30 + b) =$
$900 + 30(n + b) + nb$

$(40 + n)(40 + b) =$
$1600 + 40(n + b) + nb$

$(50 + n)(50 + b) =$
$2500 + 50(n + b) + nb$

Rolling for Tiles

Purpose: To practice operations with monomials in a game format

Discuss When a student models an expression that can be added, subtracted, multiplied, or divided to equal a polynomial on the game board, have him or her demonstrate the operation for the class.

Extend Have students create new polynomial expressions for the game board. Use the new expressions to play again.

Short Cuts

You can use properties of algebra to explain many arithmetic shortcuts. For example, to square a two-digit number that ends in 5, multiply the first digit by one more than the first digit, and then place a 25 at the end.

To find 35^2, multiply the first digit, 3, by one more than the first digit, 4. You get $3 \cdot 4 = 12$. Place a 25 at the end, and you get 1225. So $35^2 = 1225$.

Why does this shortcut work? You can use FOIL to multiply 35 by itself:

$35^2 = 35 \cdot 35 = (30 + 5)(30 + 5) = 900 + 150 + 150 + 25$
$\qquad\qquad\qquad\qquad\qquad\qquad = 900 + 300 + 25$
$\qquad\qquad\qquad\qquad\qquad\qquad = 1200 + 25 \qquad 1200 = 30 \cdot 40$
$\qquad\qquad\qquad\qquad\qquad\qquad = 1225$

First use the shortcut to find each square. Then use FOIL to multiply the number by itself.

1. 15^2 **225**   2. 45^2 **2025**   3. 85^2 **7225**   4. 65^2 **4225**   5. 25^2 **625**

6. Can you explain why the shortcut works?

Use FOIL to multiply each pair of numbers.

7. $11 \cdot 14$ **154**   8. $12 \cdot 16$ **192**   9. $13 \cdot 15$ **195**   10. $14 \cdot 17$ **238**   11. $18 \cdot 19$ **342**

12. Write a shortcut for multiplying two-digit numbers with a first digit of 1.

Rolling for Tiles

For this game, you will need a number cube, a set of algebra tiles, and a game board. Roll the number cube, and draw an algebra tile:

$1 = $ ▣ , $2 = $ ▭ , $3 = $ ▮ , $4 = $ ▬ , $5 = $ ▨ , $6 = $ ▬ .

The goal is to model expressions that can be added, subtracted, multiplied, or divided to equal the polynomials on the game board.

A complete set of rules and a game board are available online.

go.hrw.com
Game Time Extra
KEYWORD: MT7 Games

Answers

6. Possible answer: The shortcut is an application of the FOIL method. The expression $(10n + 5)^2$ is equal to $100n^2 + 100n + 25$, or $100n(n + 1) + 25$. The 25 provides the tens and ones places, and $n(n + 1)$ provides the hundreds (and thousands) place(s).

12. Possible answer: The general product can be represented by $(10 + a)(10 + b)$. Applying FOIL yields $100 + 10(a + b) + ab$. So the shortcut is to add 100, 10 times the sum of the last 2 digits, and the product of the last 2 digits together.

FOLDNOTES

It's in the Bag!

Organizer

Objective: Make a "petal" notebook on which to record notes about polynomials.

Materials: 3 sheets of decorative paper, ruler, compass, scissors, glue, markers

Materials
- 3 sheets of decorative paper
- ruler
- compass
- scissors
- glue
- markers

PROJECT **Polynomial Petals**

Pick a petal and find a fact about polynomials!

Directions

❶ Draw a 5-inch square on a sheet of decorative paper. Use a compass to make a semicircle on each side of the square. Cut out the shape. **Figure A**

❷ Draw a $3\frac{1}{2}$-inch square on another sheet of decorative paper. Use a compass to make a semicircle on each side of the square. Cut out the shape.

❸ Draw a $2\frac{1}{2}$-inch square on the last sheet of decorative paper. Use a compass to make a semicircle on each side of the square. Cut out the shape.

❹ Glue the medium square onto the center of the large square so that the squares are at a 45° angle to each other. **Figure B**

❺ Glue the small square onto the center of the medium square in the same way.

Taking Note of the Math

Write examples of different types of polynomials on the petals. Then use the remaining petals to take notes on the key concepts from the chapter. When you're done, fold up the petals.

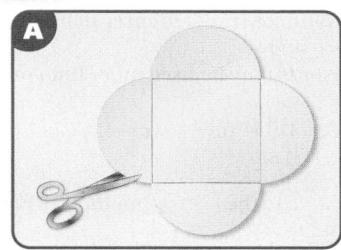

A

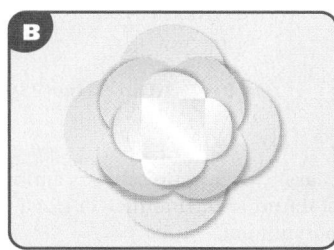

B

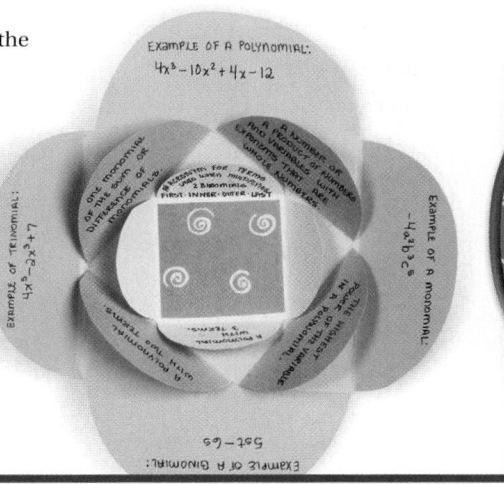

Using the Page

Preparing the materials
You can do this project with any type of decorative paper (construction paper, wallpaper samples, gift wrap, etc.) or you can use card stock.

Making the Project
Encourage students to draw the squares carefully. If students make the squares accurately, they will fit together perfectly in the last steps of the project.

Extending the Project
Have students write on the petals in a question-and-answer format. The top of each petal should contain a question about polynomials. The underside of the petal should contain the answer. Students can then quiz each other by exchanging their projects.

Tips from the Bag Ladies!

Scrapbook paper works really well for this project because it is decorated on both sides, but ordinary construction paper is also fine.

If students make the squares slightly smaller, they can store the project in an empty CD case. In fact, it's an interesting challenge to have students calculate the appropriate sizes for the squares so that one fits correctly on top of the next and the finished product fits in a CD case.

Organizer

Objective: Help students organize and review key concepts and skills presented in Chapter 14.

Online Edition
Multilingual Glossary

Resources

PuzzlePro®
One-Stop Planner®

Multilingual Glossary Online

go.hrw.com
KEYWORD: MT7 Glossary

Lesson Tutorial Videos
CD-ROM

Test & Practice Generator
One-Stop Planner®

Answers

1. polynomial; degree
2. FOIL; binomials
3. binomial; trinomial
4. trinomial
5. not a polynomial
6. not a polynomial
7. monomial
8. not a polynomial
9. binomial
10. 8
11. 4
12. 3
13. 5
14. 6

Vocabulary

binomial 734
degree of a polynomial 735
FOIL 762

monomial 734
polynomial 734
trinomial 734

Complete the sentences below with vocabulary words from the list above.
Words may be used more than once.

1. $4x^3 - 10x^2 + 4x - 12$ is an example of a __?__ whose __?__ is 3.

2. Use the __?__ method to find the product of two __?__.

3. A polynomial with 2 terms is called a __?__. A polynomial with 3 terms is called a __?__.

14-1 Polynomials (pp. 734–737)

EXAMPLE

Classify each expression as a monomial, a binomial, a trinomial, or not a polynomial.

■ $4x^5 - 2x^3 + 7$
  trinomial

■ $4xy - \frac{3}{x^4} + 7x^2y^4$
  not a polynomial

Find the degree of each polynomial.

■ $x^3 - 2x + 1$
  degree 3

■ $n + 3n^4 + 16n^2$
  degree 4

EXERCISES

Classify each expression as a monomial, a binomial, a trinomial, or not a polynomial.

4. $-5t^2 + 7t - 8$

5. $r^{-4} + 3r^{-2} + 5$

6. $12g + 7g^3 - \frac{5}{g^2}$

7. $-4a^2b^3c^5$

8. $\sqrt{x} - 2\sqrt{xy}$

9. $6st - 7s$

Find the degree of each polynomial.

10. $-3x^5 - 6x^8 + 5x$

11. $x^4 - 4x^2 + 3x - 1$

12. $14 + 8r^2 - 9r^3$

13. $\frac{1}{3}m^3 - \frac{1}{6}m^5 + \frac{7}{9}m^2$

14. $-3x^6 + 5x^5 - 9x$

14-2 Simplifying Polynomials (pp. 740–743)

EXAMPLE

Simplify.

■ $5x^2 - 2x + 4 - 5x - 3 + 4x^2$

$\boxed{5x^2} - \boxed{2x} + \boxed{4} - \boxed{5x} - \boxed{3} + \boxed{4x^2}$

$9x^2 - 7x + 1$

■ $4(2x - 7) - 5x + 4$

$\boxed{8x} - \boxed{28} - \boxed{5x} + \boxed{4}$

$3x - 24$

EXERCISES

Simplify.

15. $4t^2 - 6t + 3t - 4t^2 + 7t^2 + 1$

16. $4gh - 5g^2h + 7gh - 4g^2h$

17. $4(5mn - 3m)$

18. $4(2a^2 - 4b) + 6b$

19. $5(4st^2 - 6t) + 16st^2 + 7t$

14-3 Adding Polynomials (pp. 747–750)

EXAMPLE

Add.

■ $(3x^2 - 2x) + (5x^2 + 3x + 2)$

$\boxed{3x^2} - \boxed{2x} + \boxed{5x^2} + \boxed{3x} + 2$ *Identify like terms.*

$8x^2 + x + 2$ *Combine like terms.*

■ $(8t^3 + 4t + 6) + (4t^2 - 7t - 2)$

$\quad 8t^3 \qquad\quad + 4t + 6$ *Place like terms*
$+ \qquad 4t^2 - 7t - 2$ *in columns.*
$\overline{8t^3 + 4t^2 - 3t + 4}$ *Combine like terms.*

EXERCISES

Add.

20. $(4x^2 + 3x - 7) + (2x^2 - 5x + 12)$

21. $(5x^4 - 3x^2 + 4x - 2) + (4x^2 - 5x + 9)$

22. $(5h + 5) + (2h^2 + 3) + (3h - 1)$

23. $(3xy^2 - 5x^2y - 4xy) + (3x^2y + 6xy - xy^2)$

24. $(4n^2 + 6) + (3n^2 - 2) + (8 + 6n^2)$

14-4 Subtracting Polynomials (pp. 752–755)

EXAMPLE

■ Subtract.

$(6x^2 - 4x + 5) - (7x^2 - 8x + 2)$
$6x^2 - 4x + 5 + (-7x^2 + 8x - 2)$ *Add the opposite.*
$6x^2 - 4x + 5 - 7x^2 + 8x - 2$ *Associative Property*
$-x^2 + 4x + 3$ *Combine like terms.*

EXERCISES

Subtract.

25. $(x^2 - 4) - (4 - 5x^2)$

26. $(w^2 - 4w + 6) - (2w^2 + 8w - 8)$

27. $(3x^2 + 8x - 9) - (7x^2 - 8x + 5)$

28. $(4ab^2 - 5ab + 7a^2b) - (3a^2b + 6ab)$

29. $(3p^3q^2 - 4p^2q^2) - (2pq^2 + 4p^3q^2)$

Answers

15. $7t^2 - 3t + 1$

16. $11gh - 9g^2h$

17. $20mn - 12m$

18. $8a^2 - 10b$

19. $36st^2 - 23t$

20. $6x^2 - 2x + 5$

21. $5x^4 + x^2 - x + 7$

22. $2h^2 + 8h + 7$

23. $2xy^2 - 2x^2y + 2xy$

24. $13n^2 + 12$

25. $6x^2 - 8$

26. $-w^2 - 12w + 14$

27. $-4x^2 - 16x - 14$

28. $4ab^2 - 11ab + 4a^2b$

29. $-p^3q^2 - 4p^2q^2 - 2pq^2$

14-5 **Multiplying Polynomials by Monomials** (pp. 756–759)

EXAMPLE

Multiply.

■ $(3x^2y^3)(2xy^2)$

$(3x^2y^3)(2xy^2)$ *Multiply the coefficients and add the exponents.*

$3 \cdot 2 \cdot x^{2+1}y^{3+2}$

$6x^3y^5$

■ $(-2ab^2)(4a^2b^2 - 3ab + 6a - 8)$

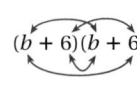

$(-2ab^2)(4a^2b^2 - 3ab + 6a - 8)$

$-8a^3b^4 + 6a^2b^3 - 12a^2b^2 + 16ab^2$

EXERCISES

Multiply.

30. $(4st^3)(s - 3st + 8)$

31. $-6a^2b(-2a^2b^2 - 5ab^2 + 6a - 4b)$

32. $2m(m^2 - 8m + 1)$

33. $-5h(3gh^4 - 2g^3h^2 + 6h - 4g)$

34. $\frac{1}{2}j^3k^2(4j^2k - 3jk^2 + 2j^3k^3)$

35. $3x^2y^5(-5x^4y^7 + 6x^5y^9 - 8xy + 4xy^2)$

14-6 **Multiplying Binomials** (pp. 762–765)

EXAMPLE

Multiply.

■ $(r + 8)(r - 6)$

$(r + 8)(r - 6)$ *FOIL*

$r^2 - 6r + 8r - 48$ *Combine like terms.*

$r^2 + 2r - 48$

■ $(b + 6)^2$

$(b + 6)(b + 6)$ *FOIL*

$b^2 + 6b + 6b + 36$ *Combine like terms.*

$b^2 + 12b + 36$

EXERCISES

Multiply.

36. $(p - 6)(p - 2)$

37. $(b + 4)(b + 6)$

38. $(3r - 1)(r + 4)$

39. $(3a + 4b)(a - 5b)$

40. $(m - 7)^2$

41. $(3t - 6)(3t + 6)$

42. $(3b - 7t)(2b + 4t)$

43. $(10 - 3x)(4 + x)$

44. $(y - 11)^2$

Classify each expression as a monomial, a binomial, a trinomial, or not a polynomial.

1. $t^2 + 2t^{0.5} - 4$ **not a polynomial** **2.** $-\frac{1}{2}a^3b^6$ **monomial**

3. $4m^4 - 5m + 8$ **trinomial**

Find the degree of each polynomial.

4. $6 - 9b + 2m^4$ **4** **5.** 54 **0** **6.** $4 + y$ **1**

7. The volume of a cube with side length $x + 2$ is given by the polynomial $x^3 + 6x^2 + 12x + 8$. What is the volume of the cube if $x = 3$? **125**

Simplify. **10.** $-4x^2y + 3xy^2$ **11.** $27b^2 - 37b$

8. $2a - 4b - 5b + 6a - 2b$ **8a − 11b** **9.** $3(x^2 - 6x + 10)$ **$3x^2 - 18x + 30$**

10. $-2x^2y + 3xy^2 - 4x^2y + 2x^2y$ **11.** $6(4b^2 - 7b) + 3b^2 + 5b$

12. The area of one face of a cube is given by the expression $2s^2 + 9s$. Write a polynomial to represent the total surface area of the cube. **$12s^2 + 54s$**

Add. **15.** $5bc - b^2c^2 + 4bc^2$ **16.** $-h^6 + 6h^5 + 5h^4 + 3h^3 - 2h$

13. $(4x^2 + 2x - 1) + (-2x + 5)$ **$4x^2 + 4$** **14.** $(12x - 5) + (9x - 5)$ **21x − 10**

15. $(3bc - b^2c^2 + 5bc^2) + (2bc - bc^2)$ **16.** $(6h^5 + 3h^3 - 2h^6) + (h^6 - 2h + 5h^4)$

17. $(b^3c^2 - 8b^2c + 5bc) + (6b^3c^2 - 4bc + 3) + (b^2c - 3bc - 11)$ **$7b^3c^2 - 7b^2c - 2bc - 8$**

18. Harold is placing a mat of width $w + 4$ around a 16 in. by 20 in. portrait. Write an expression for the perimeter of the outer edge of the mat. **8w + 104**

19. $-3mn + mn^2$ **20.** $4a - 6$

Subtract. **21.** $10a^2b - 7a^2b^2 + 6ab^2$ **22.** $j^4 - 5j^3 + 9j^2 - 2j - 1$

19. $(4m^2n - 5mn + mn^2) - (-2mn + 4m^2n)$ **20.** $(12a + a^2) - (6 + a^2 + 8a)$

21. $(3a^2b - 5a^2b^2 + 6ab^2) - (2a^2b^2 - 7a^2b)$ **22.** $(j^4 + 7j^2 - 4j) - (5j^3 - 2j^2 - 6j + 1)$

23. A circle whose area is $2x^2 + 3x - 4$ is cut from a rectangular piece of plywood with area $4x^2 + 3x - 1$ and discarded. Write an expression for the area of the remaining plywood. **$2x^2 - 6x + 3$**

27. $a^4 - 4a^2 + 5a$ **29.** $3a^4b^2 - 6a^4b + 24a^4$

28. $6m^6n^8 - 15m^5n^6$ **30.** $x^2 + 14x + 24$

Multiply.

24. $(3x)(5x^4)$ **$15x^5$** **25.** $(4x^2y)(-5xy^3)$ **$-20x^3y^4$** **26.** $(2a^2b^4)(5a^4b^5)$ **$10a^6b^9$**

27. $a(a^3 - 4a + 5)$ **28.** $3m^3n^4(2m^3n^4 - 5m^2n^2)$ **29.** $3a^3(ab^2 - 2ab + 8a)$

30. $(x + 2)(x + 12)$ **31.** $(x + 2)(x - 4)$ **$x^2 - 2x - 8$** **32.** $(a - 3)(a - 7)$ **$a^2 - 10a + 21$**

33. A student forms a box from a 10 in. by 15 in. piece of cardboard by cutting a square with side length x out of each corner and folding up the sides. Write and simplify an expression for the area of the base of the box. **$4x^3 - 50x^2 + 150x$**

Chapter Test

Organizer

Objective: Provide review and practice for Chapters 1–14 and standardized tests.

 Online Edition

Resources

 Assessment Resources
Chapter 14 Cumulative Test

 State Test Prep Workbook

 State Test Prep CD-ROM

 State Test Practice Online

go.hrw.com
KEYWORD: MT7 TestPrep

Cumulative Assessment, Chapters 1–14
Multiple Choice

1. The school's drama club sells tickets for their performance. Student tickets cost $6 and non-student tickets cost $10. If they sold 680 tickets for a total of $5280, how many student tickets did they sell?

(A) 680 tickets   (C) 300 tickets
(B) 380 tickets   (D) 260 tickets

2. What is the measure of $\angle GJH$?

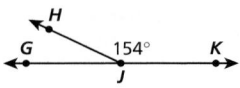

(F) 26°   (H) 64°
(G) 36°   (J) 206°

3. Giancarlo is using a paper cone as a drinking cup. How much water can the cup hold? Use 3.14 for π.

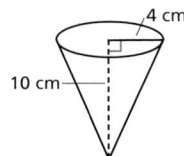

(A) 41.9 cm³   (C) 167.47 cm³
(B) 502.4 cm³   (D) 1507.2 cm³

4. Twenty-two percent of the sales of a general store are due to snack sales. If the store sold $1350 worth of goods, how much of the total was due to snack sales?

(F) $167   (H) $1053
(G) $297   (J) $2970

5. If rectangle *MNQP* is similar to rectangle *ABDC*, then what is the area of rectangle *ABDC*?

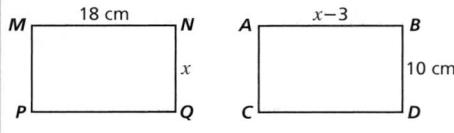

(A) 44 cm²   (C) 120 cm²
(B) 66 cm²   (D) 270 cm²

6. The simplest form of the product of the binomials $(2x - 6)$ and $(2x + 6)$ is which type of polynomial?

(F) Zero   (H) Binomial
(G) Monomial   (J) Trinomial

7. If the area of a circle is 49π and the circumference of the circle is 14π, what is the diameter of the circle?

(A) 7 units   (C) 21 units
(B) 14 units   (D) 49 units

8. Nationally, there were 217.8 million people age 18 and over and 53.3 million children ages 5 to 17 as of July 1, 2003, according to estimates released by the U.S. Census Bureau. How do you write the number of people age 5 and older in scientific notation?

(F) 2.711×10^2 (H) 2.711×10^7
(G) 2.711×10^6 (J) 2.711×10^8

TEST PREP DOCTOR +

Students who choose **J** for item 2 subtracted the measure of $\angle HJK$ from 360°. Encourage students to review common angle measures.

If students solve for item 6 by multiplying the binomials, point out that they could have saved time if they had recognized it as a special product of the form $(a - b)(a + b) = a^2 - b^2$.

Answers

15. a. area of the triangle = $x^2 + 2x$; area of the square = $9x^2 + 24x + 16$
   b. area of blue region = $8x^2 + 22x + 16$

16. $2x^2 + 11x + 15$

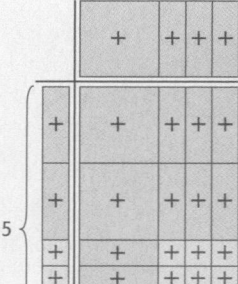
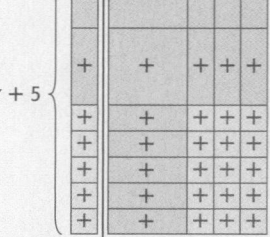

17. See 4-Point Response work sample.

9. What is the *y*-intercept of the line that passes through the points $(-3, 8)$ and $(2, -2)$?

Ⓐ $(0, -2)$ Ⓒ $(0, 2)$

Ⓑ $(0, 0)$ Ⓓ $(0, 6)$

 If a problem involves decimals, you may be able to eliminate answer choices that do not have the correct number of places after the decimal point.

Gridded Response

Use the following data for questions 10 and 11.

In 2003, the state of Virginia broke its record for the number of days in a row that it rained. The table shows the number of days in a row each rain station recorded rain.

Station	May 2003 Rain Days
Charlottesville	22
Bedford	20
Norfolk	17
Bremo Bluff	17
Brookneal	19
Lexington	19
Lynchburg	21
Meadows of Dan	18
Richmond	21
Somerset	20

10. Find the mean number of days in a row that it rained. **19.4**

11. Find the median number of days in a row that it rained. **19.5**

12. A fair number cube is rolled twice. What is the probability that the outcomes of the two rolls will have a sum of 4? **1/12**

13. What is the length, in centimeters, of the diagonal of a square with side length 8 cm? Round your answer to the nearest hundredth. **11.31**

14. If the rule for a geometric sequence is given by $a_n = 4\left(\frac{1}{2}\right)^{n-1}$, what is the 10th term of the sequence? **1/128 or .0078**

Short Response

15. A quilt is made by connecting squares like the one below.

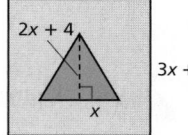

a. Write an expression for the area of the triangle and an expression for the area of the square.

b. Write an expression for the area of the blue region.

16. Draw a model for the product of the two binomials $(x + 3)$ and $(2x + 5)$ with the following tiles. Use the model to determine the product.

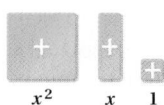

x^2 x 1

Extended Response

17. A cake pan is made by cutting four squares from a 18 cm by 24 cm piece of tin and folding the sides as shown.

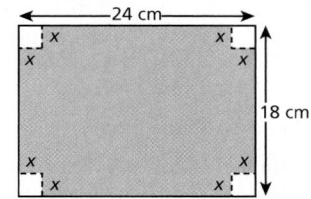

a. Write an expression for the length, width, and height of the cake pan in terms of *x*.

b. Multiply the expressions from part **a** to find a polynomial that gives the volume of the cake pan.

c. Evaluate the polynomial for $x = 1$, $x = 2$, $x = 3$, and $x = 4$. Which value of *x* gives the cake pan with the largest volume? Give the dimensions and the volume of the largest cake pan.

Short Response Rubric

Items 15–16

2 Points = The student's answer is an accurate and complete execution of the task or tasks.

1 Point = The student's answer contains attributes of an appropriate response but is flawed.

0 Points = The student's answer contains no attributes of an appropriate response.

Extended Response Rubric

Item 17

4 points = The student demonstrates a thorough understanding of all concepts and shows all work correctly.

3 points = The student demonstrates a basic understanding of all concepts, but the work shows some flaws reflecting inattentive execution of mathematical procedures or some misunderstanding of the underlying mathematics.

2 points = The student demonstrates only a partial understanding of the concepts or procedures embodied in the tasks. The approach may be correct, but the work shows a misunderstanding of one or more important concepts.

1 point = The student demonstrates a very limited understanding of the concepts or procedures embodied in the tasks. The response may show some understanding but exhibits many flaws or is incomplete.

0 points = The student provides no response at all or a completely incorrect or uninterpretable response.

Student Work Samples for Item 17

4-Point Response

```
17.a. length = 24-2x
      width = 18-2x
      height = x
   b. V = (24-2x)(18-2x)(x)
        = x(432-48x-36x+4x²)
        = 432x-84x²+4x³
   c. when x=1, V=352
      when x=2, V=560
      when x=3, V=648
      when x=4, V=640
   When x=3, the cake pan has the largest
   volume. Height=3cm, Width=12cm,
   Length=18cm, Volume=648 cm³
```

The student correctly created the expressions, multiplied them together, and identified the dimensions of the box that maximized the volume.

3-Point Response

```
   a. length = 24-2x
      width = 18-2x
      height = x
   b. V = (24-2x)(18-2x)·x
        = x(432-48x-36x+4x²)
        = 4x³-84x²+432
   c. When x=1, V=352
      x=2, V=128
      x=3, V=-216
      x=4, V=-656
   When x=1, the cake pan has the
   largest volume (h=1 cm, l=22cm,
   w=16 cm, V=352 cm³)
```

The student understood the concepts, but neglected to distribute *x* to one of the terms in part **b**. This error results in incorrect responses to part **C**.

2-Point Response

```
17. a.  l = 24-x
        w = 18-x
        h = x
    b. volume = (24-x)(18-x)(x)
       volume = (432-24x-18x-x²)x
       volume = 432x-42x²-x³
    c.  x=1, 389     x=2, 688
        x=3, 891     x=4, 992
    Volume is largest when x=4.
    l=20  w=14  h=4  V=992
```

The student correctly applied the proper method at each step, but created two expressions incorrectly. The student also incorrectly multiplied in part **b**.

Problem Solving on Location

Organizer

Objective: Choose appropriate problem-solving strategies and use them with skills from Chapters 13 and 14 to solve real-world problems.

 Online Edition

⭐ Catfish

Reading Strategies

It's helpful for students to rewrite problems in their own words, especially when the problems contain multiple steps and several pieces of information. Have students rewrite problem 2 in their own words. Possible answer: First find how many catfish are on the farm by multiplying 17 acres by 6000 catfish per acre. Divide the result by 153,000 pounds to find the average weight of each catfish.

Using Data Have students identify the labels of the axes in the graph. vertical axis: Millions of pounds; horizontal axis: Year Ask how many pounds of Mississippi catfish were produced in 2000. about 380,000,000 lb

Problem Solving on Location

MISSISSIPPI

Belzoni

Laurel

⭐ Catfish

Catfish is one of the five most popular seafoods in the United States. Mississippi produces about 75% of the nation's supply of catfish. Belzoni hosts the annual World Catfish Festival, an event that draws more than 20,000 catfish lovers each year.

Choose one or more strategies to solve each problem.

1. In 2003, Mississippi had 405 catfish farms. In 2004, the number of farms in the state increased by 1.5%. If the number of catfish farms continues to increase by 1.5% each year, about how many catfish farms will the state have in 2011? **456**

2. On a typical catfish farm, the pond is stocked with 6000 catfish per acre, the pond covers 17 acres, and the total weight of the fish in the pond is 153,000 pounds. On average, how much does each catfish weigh? **1.5 lb**

For 3 and 4, use the graph.

3. Assume that catfish production continues to increase at the rate shown in the graph. How many pounds of catfish will be produced in Mississippi in 2020? **575,000,000 lb**

4. In what year will catfish production in Mississippi hit 630 million pounds? **2026**

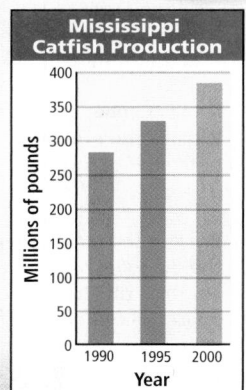

Mississippi Catfish Production

(Millions of pounds vs. Year: 1990 ≈ 280, 1995 ≈ 330, 2000 ≈ 385)

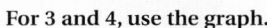

🧩 Problem Solving Focus

Encourage students to use the four-step problem-solving process for the problems. Focus on the second step: **(2) Make a Plan.**

Discuss with students what strategy they used to solve problem 1. Possible methods include graphs, tables, functions, or geometric series. Ask students to explain the advantages and disadvantages of their method and encourage them to try the problem again using a different strategy.

Problem Solving Strategies

Draw a Diagram
Make a Model
Guess and Test
Work Backward
Find a Pattern
Make a Table
Solve a Simpler Problem
Use Logical Reasoning
Act It Out
Make an Organized List

⭐ The Lauren Rogers Museum of Art

Since it opened in 1923, the Lauren Rogers Museum of Art had one of the finest—and most diverse—collections of art in the South. Nestled among the oaks of Laurel, Mississippi, the museum houses hundreds of Japanese prints, American and European paintings, and Native-American baskets.

Choose one or more strategies to solve each problem.

1. The museum's collection includes a painting called *Landscape with Windmill*. The length of the painting is 4 in. greater than its width. The perimeter of the painting is 52 in. What are the dimensions of the painting?   **11 in. × 15 in.**

For 2 and 3, use the table.

2. The frame of *The Message* has an equal width on all sides of the painting. The perimeter of the frame is 132 inches. What is the width of the frame?   **3 in.**

3. Only one painting in the table is by an English artist. The area of the painting is less than 800 in² and the perimeter of the painting is greater than 108 in. Which painting was painted by an English artist?   **Miss Grace Hundley**

| Paintings at the Lauren Rogers Museum of Art ||
Title	Dimensions
Knitting Reveries	55 in. by 37 in.
The Message	30 in. by 24 in.
Mythological Scene	38.5 in. by 51.6 in.
Miss Grace Hundley	30 in. by 25 in.
Young Girl Reading Beneath a Tree	32.9 in. by 27.2 in.

Knitting Reveries by Louis-Edouard Dubufe

☆ The Lauren Rogers Museum of Art

Reading Strategies

Discuss with students how to translate word phrases into algebraic expressions. Remind them that words such as *height* and *length* are often the variables in algebraic expressions, and that perimeter and area can be expressed in terms of height and width. Ask how to express the second sentence of Problem 1 as an algebraic expression. Possible answer: $\ell = 4 + w$

Using Data Discuss with students what information the table gives. the dimensions of several paintings at the Lauren Rogers Museum of Art Ask which painting has the greatest area. Knitting Reveries Which painting has the greatest perimeter? Knitting Reveries

🧩 Problem Solving Focus

Encourage students to use the four-step problem-solving process for the problems. Focus on the last step: **(4) Look Back.**

Ask students what equations and expressions they created to solve each problem. Encourage them to substitute their answers back into their original equations to make sure they're correct.

Student Handbook

 Extra Practice **782**

Problem-Solving Handbook **789**

Draw a Diagram

Make a Model

Guess and Test

Work Backward

Find a Pattern

Make a Table

Solve a Simpler Problem

Use Logical Reasoning

Act It Out

Make an Organized List

Skills Bank **792**

Review Skills **792**

Place Value to the Billions

Round Whole Numbers and Decimals

Long Division and Whole Numbers

Solve for a Variable

Factors and Multiples

Divisibility Rules

Prime and Composite Numbers

Percents Less Than 1% and Greater Than 100%

Greatest Common Factor (GCF)

Least Common Multiple (LCM)

Compatible Numbers

Mixed Numbers and Fractions

Multiply and Divide Decimal by Powers of 10
Multiply Decimals
Divide Decimals
Terminating and Repeating Decimals
Order of Operations
Properties
Cubes and Cube Roots
Skew Lines
Choose Appropriate Units of Measurements
Measure Angles
Informal Geometry Proofs
Iteration

Preview Skills **795**
Relative, Cumulative, and Relative Cumulative Geometry
Frequency Polygons
Parallel Lines and Transversals
Circles
Matrices
Networks

Science **797**
Compare and Order Measurements
Temperature Conversion
Customary and Metric Rulers
Precision and Significant Digits
Greatest Possible Error
pH
Richter Scale

Selected Answers **799**

Additional Answers **A1**

Glossary **A31**

Teacher's Edition Index **A70**

Table of Measures, Symbols, and Formulas . . . . **inside back cover**

Extra Practice

LESSON 1-1

Evaluate each expression for the given value(s) of the variable(s).

1. $3 + x$ for $x = 5$ 8
2. $6m - 2$ for $m = 3$ 16
3. $2(p + 3)$ for $p = 8$ 22
4. $4x + y$ for $x = 1, y = 3$ 7
5. $2y - x$ for $x = 3, y = 6$ 9
6. $5x + 1.5y$ for $x = 2, y = 4$ 16

LESSON 1-2

Write an algebraic expression for each word phrase.

7. seven less than a number b $b - 7$
8. eight more than the product of 7 and a $7a + 8$
9. a quotient of 8 and a number m $8 \div m$
10. five times the sum of c and 18 $5(c + 18)$

Write a word phrase for each algebraic expression.

11. $9 + \frac{x}{4}$ 9 plus the quotient of x and 4
12. $19x - 14$ 14 less than the product of 19 and x
13. $\frac{1}{3}(x + 1)$ $\frac{1}{3}$ of the sum of x and 1
14. $\frac{4}{x} - 100$ 100 less than the quotient of 4 and x
15. Write a word problem that can be evaluated by the algebraic expression $x - 122$, and then evaluate the expression for $x = 225$. Possible answer: There are 122 students on a field trip. If x students went to school this morning, how many students did not go on the field trip? $255 - 122 = 133$

LESSON 1-3

16. In a miniature golf game the scores of four brothers relative to par are Jesse 3, Jack −2, James −5, and Jarod 1. Use <, >, or = to compare Jack's and Jarod's scores, and then list the brothers in order from the lowest score to the highest. $-2 < 1$; James, Jack, Jarod, Jesse

Write the integers in order from least to greatest.

17. −4, 6, −2 −4, −2, 6
18. 1, −16, 9 −16, 1, 9
19. −14, −2, −19 −19, −14, −2

Find the additive inverse of each integer.

20. −10 10
21. 4 −4
22. 1 −1
23. −21 21

Evaluate each expression.

24. $|9| + |-4|$ 13
25. $|-3| + |-19|$ 22
26. $|52 - 12|$ 40

LESSON 1-4

Add.

27. $-4 + 6$ 2
28. $3 + (-8)$ −5
29. $-6 + (-2)$ −8
30. $7 + (-11)$ −4

Evaluate each expression for the given value of the variable.

31. $x + 9$ for $x = -8$
32. $x + 3$ for $x = -3$
33. $x + 5$ for $x = -7$

34. The middle school registrar is checking her records. Use the information at right to find the net change in the number of students for this school for the week. 2 students

	Students Registering	Students Withdrawing
Monday	4	2
Tuesday	6	7
Wednesday	5	5
Thursday	1	4
Friday	4	0

LESSON 1-5

Subtract.

35. $-6 - 4$ −10
36. $8 - (-3)$ 11
37. $-6 - (-3)$ −3
38. $-5 - 8$ −13

Evaluate each expression for the given value of the variable.

39. $7 - x$ for $x = -4$ 11
40. $-8 - s$ for $s = -6$ −2
41. $-8 - b$ for $b = 12$ −20

42. An elevator rises 351 feet above ground level and then drops 415 feet to the basement. What is the position of the elevator relative to ground level? −64 feet

LESSON 1-6

Multiply or divide.

43. $8(-6)$ −48
44. $\frac{-63}{7}$ −9
45. $-7(-3)$ 21
46. $\frac{52}{-4}$ −13

Simplify.

47. $8(4 - 5)$ −8
48. $-5(9 - 11)$ 10
49. $-4(-16 - 4)$ 80
50. $3 + 7(10 - 14)$ −25

51. A golfer plays 18 holes of golf. On 5 holes she is under par by 1. On 6 holes she is over par by 2. She is even on the remaining holes. What is her score? over par by 1

LESSON 1-7

Solve.

52. $4 + x = 13$ $x = 9$
53. $t - 3 = 8$ $t = 11$
54. $17 = m + 11$ $m = 6$
55. $5 + a = 7$ $a = 2$
56. $p - 5 = 23$ $p = 28$
57. $31 + y = 50$ $y = 19$
58. $18 + k = 34$ $k = 16$
59. $g - 16 = 23$ $g = 39$
60. Richard biked 39 miles on Saturday. This is 13 more miles than Trevor biked. How many miles did Trevor bike on Saturday? 26 miles

LESSON 1-8

Solve and check.

61. $\frac{a}{-4} = -2$ $a = 8$
62. $-49 = 7d$ $d = -7$
63. $\frac{c}{-2} = -8$ $c = 16$
64. $-57 = 3p$ $p = -19$
65. $-8b = 64$ $b = -8$
66. $144 = -9y$ $y = -16$
67. $\frac{x}{-78}$ $x = -156$
68. $19c = 152$ $c = 8$
69. Jessica hiked a total of 36 miles on her vacation. This is 4 times as far as she hikes on a typical weekend. How many miles does Jessica hike on a typical weekend? 9 miles

LESSON 1-9

Compare. Write < or >.

70. $15 - 8$ ▨ 6 >
71. $3(7)$ ▨ 23 <
72. $51 - 18$ ▨ 34 <
73. $4(16)$ ▨ 62 >

Solve and graph each inequality.

74. $x - 3.5 \geq 7$ $x \geq 10.5$
75. $5p < 40$ $p < 8$
76. $2 \leq \frac{a}{3}$ $6 \leq a$
77. $h - 5 \leq 13$ $h \leq 18$

74. [number line −2 0 2 4 6 8 10 12 14]
75. [number line −2 0 2 4 6 8 10 12 14]
76. [number line −2 0 2 4 6 8 10 12 14]
77. [number line 10 12 14 16 18 20 22 24]

LESSON 2-1

Simplify.

1. $\frac{12}{96}$ $\frac{1}{8}$
2. $\frac{6}{16}$ $\frac{3}{8}$
3. $\frac{-10}{15}$ $-\frac{2}{3}$
4. $\frac{14}{42}$ $\frac{1}{3}$

Write each decimal as a fraction in simplest form.

5. 0.4 $\frac{2}{5}$
6. 0.05 $\frac{1}{20}$
7. 0.12 $\frac{3}{25}$
8. 0.625 $\frac{5}{8}$

Write each fraction as a decimal.

9. $\frac{3}{8}$ 0.375
10. $\frac{1}{4}$ 0.25
11. $\frac{9}{4}$ 2.25
12. $\frac{3}{5}$ 0.6

LESSON 2-2

Compare. Write <, >, or =.

13. $\frac{6}{7}$ ▨ $\frac{4}{5}$ >
14. $\frac{11}{15}$ ▨ $\frac{9}{10}$ <
15. $\frac{1}{3}$ ▨ $\frac{5}{6}$ <
16. $-\frac{4}{9}$ ▨ $\frac{1}{8}$ <
17. $1\frac{5}{8}$ ▨ $1\frac{2}{3}$ <
18. $-2\frac{1}{8}$ ▨ $-2\frac{1}{5}$ >
19. $\frac{12}{17}$ ▨ 0.75 <
20. $5\frac{7}{8}$ ▨ 5.9 <

LESSON 2-3

21. Hannah and Elizabeth drove to Niagara Falls for vacation. Hannah drove $98\frac{3}{4}$ miles and Elizabeth drove 106.44 miles. How far did they drive together? 205.19 miles

Add or subtract. Write each answer in simplest form.

22. $\frac{3}{4} - \frac{7}{4}$ −1
23. $\frac{19}{8} + \frac{11}{8}$ $\frac{15}{4}$, or $3\frac{3}{4}$
24. $\frac{5}{4} - \frac{15}{4}$ $-\frac{5}{2}$, or $-2\frac{1}{2}$
25. $-\frac{7}{4} + \frac{11}{4}$ 1
26. $\frac{9}{2} - \frac{15}{2}$ −3
27. $\frac{11}{2} + \frac{14}{2}$ $\frac{25}{2}$, or $12\frac{1}{2}$
28. $\frac{9}{3} - \frac{22}{3}$ $-\frac{13}{3}$, or $-4\frac{1}{3}$
29. $-\frac{21}{3} + \frac{16}{3}$ $-\frac{5}{3}$, or $-1\frac{2}{3}$

Evaluate each expression for the given value of the variable.

30. $32.9 + x$ for $x = -15.8$ 17.1
31. $21.3 + a$ for $a = -37.6$ −16.3
32. $-\frac{3}{5} + z$ for $z = 3\frac{1}{5}$ $\frac{13}{5}$, or $2\frac{3}{5}$

LESSON 2-4

Multiply. Write each answer in simplest form.

33. $-\frac{3}{4}\left(-\frac{5}{9}\right)$ $\frac{5}{12}$
34. $\frac{7}{12}\left(-\frac{3}{5}\right)$ $-\frac{7}{20}$
35. $-\frac{4}{5}\left(-\frac{9}{10}\right)$ $\frac{18}{25}$
36. $-\frac{3}{7}\left(\frac{13}{14}\right)$ $-\frac{39}{98}$
37. $-4.7(-8)$ 37.6
38. $-4.1(8.6)$ −35.26
39. $-0.06(5.2)$ −0.312
40. $-0.003(-2.6)$ 0.0078

41. Rosie ate $2\frac{1}{2}$ bananas on Saturday. On Sunday she ate $\frac{1}{2}$ as many bananas as she ate on Saturday. How many bananas did Rosie eat over the weekend? $3\frac{3}{4}$ bananas

LESSON 2-5

Divide. Write each answer in simplest form.

42. $2\frac{3}{4} \div \frac{1}{3}$ $\frac{33}{4}$, or $8\frac{1}{4}$
43. $5\frac{1}{5} \div \frac{7}{8}$ $\frac{208}{35}$, or $5\frac{33}{35}$
44. $3\frac{5}{9} \div \frac{3}{4}$ $\frac{128}{27}$, or $4\frac{20}{27}$
45. $3\frac{1}{8} \div \frac{2}{5}$ $\frac{125}{16}$, or $7\frac{13}{16}$
46. $5.68 \div 0.2$ 28.4
47. $7.65 \div 0.05$ 153
48. $1.76 \div 0.8$ 2.2
49. $0.744 \div 8$ 0.093

Evaluate each expression for the given value of the variable.

50. $\frac{7.4}{x}$ for $x = 0.5$ 14.8
51. $\frac{11.88}{x}$ for $x = 0.08$ 148.5
52. $\frac{15.3}{x}$ for $x = -1.2$ −12.75

53. Yolanda is making bows that take $21\frac{1}{2}$ inches of ribbon to make. She has 344 inches of ribbon. How many bows can she make? 16

LESSON 2-6

Add or Subtract.

54. $\frac{8}{9} + \frac{2}{7}$ $\frac{74}{63}$, or $1\frac{11}{63}$
55. $\frac{3}{8} - \frac{2}{3}$ $-\frac{7}{24}$
56. $\frac{2}{3} + \frac{1}{7}$ $\frac{17}{21}$
57. $\frac{5}{6} - \frac{4}{9}$ $\frac{7}{18}$
58. $4\frac{1}{5} + \left(-2\frac{1}{7}\right)$ $\frac{72}{35}$, or $2\frac{2}{35}$
59. $3\frac{2}{3} + \left(-1\frac{7}{8}\right)$ $\frac{43}{24}$, or $1\frac{19}{24}$
60. $4\frac{1}{8} + \left(-1\frac{3}{5}\right)$ $\frac{101}{40}$, or $2\frac{21}{40}$
61. $8\frac{1}{7} + \left(-4\frac{1}{10}\right)$ $\frac{283}{70}$, or $4\frac{3}{70}$

Evaluate each expression for the given value of the variable.

62. $8\frac{1}{2} + x$ for $x = 4\frac{2}{9}$ $\frac{229}{18}$, or $12\frac{13}{18}$
63. $n - \frac{1}{9}$ for $n = -1\frac{7}{8}$ $-\frac{143}{72}$, or $-1\frac{71}{72}$
64. $1\frac{1}{8} + y$ for $y = -\frac{4}{7}$ $\frac{31}{56}$

65. A container has $10\frac{1}{2}$ gallons of milk. If the children at a preschool drink $7\frac{3}{4}$ gallons of milk, how many gallons of milk are left in the container? $2\frac{3}{4}$ gallons

LESSON 2-7

Solve.

66. $x - 3.2 = 5.1$ $x = 8.3$
67. $-3.1p = 15.5$ $p = -5$
68. $\frac{a}{-2.3} = 7.9$ $a = -18.17$
69. $-4.3x = 34.4$ $x = -8$
70. $m - \frac{1}{3} = \frac{5}{8}$ $m = \frac{23}{24}$
71. $x - \frac{3}{7} = \frac{1}{9}$ $x = \frac{34}{63}$
72. $4\frac{1}{2}w = \frac{25}{4}$ $w = \frac{5}{6}$
73. $\frac{9}{10}z = \frac{5}{8}$ $z = \frac{25}{36}$

74. It is estimated that it will take Peter $9\frac{3}{4}$ hours to paint a room. If he gets two of his friends to help him and they work at the same rate as him, how long should it take them to paint the room? $3\frac{1}{4}$ hours

LESSON 2-8

75. A bill from the plumber was $383. The plumber charged $175 for parts and $52 per hour for labor. How long did the plumber work at this job? 4 hours

76. Alicia bought $116 worth of flowers and some bushes for around her house. The bushes cost $28 each, and the bill totaled $340. How many bushes did she buy? 8 bushes

Solve.

77. $\frac{a}{2} - 3 = 8$ $a = 22$
78. $2.4 = -0.8x + 3.2$ $x = 1$
79. $\frac{6 + z}{4} = 4$ $z = 6$
80. $\frac{c}{6} + 2 = 5$ $c = 18$
81. $0.9m - 1.6 = -5.2$ $m = -4$
82. $\frac{x - 4}{3} = 7$ $x = 25$
83. $\frac{b}{5} + 2 = -3$ $b = -25$
84. $2.1d + 0.7 = 7$ $d = 3$
85. $\frac{p + 5}{3} = 6$ $p = 13$
86. $\frac{c}{6} - 8 = 3$ $c = 66$
87. $\frac{r - 6}{9} = 5$ $r = 51$
88. $-8.6 = 3.4k - 1.8$ $k = -2$

Extra Practice ▪ Chapter 3

LESSON 3-1

Determine whether each ordered pair is a solution of $2x + 3y = 16$.

1. $(1, 5)$ no   2. $(5, 2)$ yes   3. $(2, 4)$ yes   4. $(3, 3)$ no

Use the given values to make a table of solutions. For 5–6, see p. Axx.

5. $y = x - 3$ for $x = -2, -1, 0, 1, 2$ 6. $y = 3x + 2$ for $x = -2, -1, 0, 1, 2$

7. The cost of mailing a letter is $0.23 per ounce plus $0.14. The equation that gives the total cost c of mailing a letter is $c = 0.23w + 0.14$, where w is the weight in ounces. What is the cost of mailing a 5-ounce letter? $1.29

LESSON 3-2

Graph each point on a coordinate plane. For 8–13, see p. Axx.

8. $(4, 3)$ 9. $(3, 0)$ 10. $(-1, 3)$

11. $(0, -5)$ 12. $(-2, -4)$ 13. $(4, -2)$

Complete each table of ordered pairs. Graph each ordered pair on a coordinate plane. For 14–15, see p. Axx.

14. $x + 3 = y$

x	x + 3	y	(x, y)
1	1 + 3	4	(1, 4)
2	2 + 3	5	(2, 5)
3	3 + 3	6	(3, 6)
4	4 + 3	7	(4, 7)

15. $3x = y$

x	3x	y	(x, y)
2	3(2)	6	(2, 6)
4	3(4)	12	(4, 12)
6	3(6)	18	(6, 18)
8	3(8)	24	(8, 24)

LESSON 3-3

Tell which graph corresponds to each situation described below. For 16–18, see p. Axx.

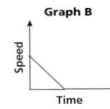

Graph A   Graph B   Graph C

16. A person riding a bike increases speed and then maintains a high speed.

17. A person riding a bike goes up a hill and then accelerates going down the other side of the hill.

18. A person riding a race slows down after he reaches the finish line and then comes to a stop.

Extra Practice ▪ Chapter 3

LESSON 3-4

Make a table and graph of each function. For 19–22, see p. Axx.

19. $y = x + 1$ 20. $y = -x - 2$ 21. $y = 3x + 1$ 22. $y = 4(x - 1)$

Determine if each relationship represents a function.

23.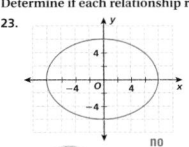
no

24.
x	y
-3	1
-1	-1
0	-2
2	0
4	2
yes

25.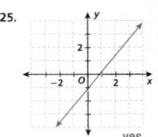
yes

LESSON 3-5

26. The cost a caterer charges for a party is represented by the equation $c = \$13p$, where c is the amount paid to the caterer and p is the number of guests that will be attending the party. Make a table and sketch a graph of the equation. For 26, see p. Axx.

27. Use the table to make a graph and write an equation.
$y = \frac{2}{3}x + 2$

x	0	3	6	9	12
y	2	4	6	8	10

28. Use the graph to make a table and write an equation for each line.
a. $y = -2x$
b. $y = \frac{1}{2}x + 1$
c. $y = \frac{2}{3}x + \frac{1}{3}$
d. $y = -\frac{1}{2}x - 2$

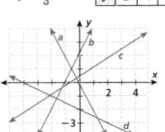

LESSON 3-6

Find the common difference and the next three terms in each arithmetic sequence.

29. $2, 7, 12, 17, \ldots$ 5; 22, 27, 32   30. $16, 19, 22, 25, \ldots$ 3; 28, 31, 34   31. $50, 44, 38, 32, \ldots$ 6; 26, 20, 14

32. $-15, -6, 3, 12, \ldots$ 9; 21, 30, 39   33. $\frac{1}{4}, \frac{3}{4}, 1\frac{1}{4}, 1\frac{3}{4}, \ldots$ $\frac{1}{2}$; $2\frac{1}{4}, 2\frac{3}{4}, 3\frac{1}{4}$ 34. $-6, -10, -14, -18, \ldots$ -4; $-22, -26, -30$

Find a function that describes each arithmetic sequence. Use y to identify each term in the sequence and n to identify each term's position.

35. $1, 5, 9, 13, \ldots$ $y = 4n - 3$ 36. $2, 11, 20, 29, \ldots$ $y = 9n - 7$ 37. $-2, -5, -8, -11, \ldots$ $y = -3n + 1$

38. An air-conditioning repair company charges a $54 service fee per visit, plus $50 per hour for labor. Find a function that describes the arithmetic sequence. Then find the total charges for a service call that lasts $2\frac{1}{2}$ hours. $y = \$50n + \$54; \$179$

Extra Practice ▪ Chapter 4

LESSON 4-1

Write in exponential form.

1. $3 \cdot 3 \cdot 3 \cdot 3$ 3^4 2. $6a \cdot 6a \cdot 6a \cdot 6a \cdot 6a$ $(6a)^5$ 3. $(-9) \cdot (-9)$ $(-9)^2$ 4. b b^1

Evaluate.

5. 2^5 32   6. 3^4 81   7. $(-6)^2$ 36   8. $(-3)^5$ -243

9. 5^3 125   10. 8^5 32,768   11. $(-2)^4$ 16   12. $(-7)^3$ -343

Evaluate each expression for the given values of the variables.

13. x^3 for $x = -3$ -27 14. $k^2 + 3k$ for $k = -2$ -2

15. $s^4 + y(s + 3)$ for $s = 1$ and $y = -2$ -7 16. $10 + x^2 - \frac{x}{2}(y + 4)$ for $x = 3$ and $y = -2$ $\frac{7}{16}$

17. The formula for the area of a circle is $A = \pi r^2$. Use the formula to find the area of a circle with a radius of 7 cm. $153.86\ \text{cm}^2$

LESSON 4-2

Evaluate the powers of 10.

18. 10^{-1} 0.1   19. 10^{-2} 0.01   20. 10^{-3} 0.001   21. 10^{-4} 0.0001

Evaluate.

22. $(-4)^{-2}$ $\frac{1}{16}$ 23. 3^{-3} $\frac{1}{27}$ 24. $(-5)^{-4}$ $\frac{1}{625}$

25. $\frac{3^2}{3^4} + (9 + 3)^0$ $1\frac{1}{9}$ 26. $13 - (-3) + 19(1 + 2)^2$ 187   27. $4^5 \cdot 3^2 \cdot (-3)^{-3}$ $-\frac{1024}{3}$

LESSON 4-3

Multiply or divide. Write the product or the quotient as one power.

28. $2^4 \cdot 2^5$ 2^9 29. $w^7 \cdot w^7$ w^{14} 30. $\frac{4^9}{4^9}$ 4^0 31. $\frac{c^6}{c^2}$ c^4

32. $\frac{x^3}{y^3}$ $\left(\frac{x}{y}\right)^3$ 33. $(3^0)^4$ 3^0 34. $(3^{-2})^3$ 3^{-6} 35. $(-a^3)^4$ a^{12}

LESSON 4-4

Write each number in standard notation.

36. 2.4×10^3 2,400   37. 3.62×10^5 362,000   38. 5.036×10^{-4} 0.0005036   39. 8.93×10^{-2} 0.0893

Write each number in scientific notation.

40. 0.00384 3.84×10^{-3} 41. 1,450,000,000 1.450×10^9 42. 0.654 6.54×10^{-1}

43. In the 2003 regular season, approximately 36,661,000 fans attended National League baseball games. The attendance for American League games was approximately 30,908,000 fans. Approximately how many more fans attended National League games than American League games? Write your answer in scientific notation. 5.753×10^6 more fans

---

Extra Practice ▪ Chapter 4

LESSON 4-5

Find the two square roots of each number.

44. 25 5, -5 45. 49 7, -7 46. 289 17, -17 47. 169 13, -13

Evaluate each expression.

48. $2\sqrt{4}$ 4   49. $3\sqrt{49}$ 21   50. $\sqrt{99 + 45}$ 12   51. $\sqrt{33 - 8}$ 5

52. The area of a square garden is 1,681 square feet. What are the dimensions of the garden? 41 feet × 41 feet

LESSON 4-6   For 53–56, see p. Axx.

Each square root is between two integers. Name the integers. Explain your answer.

53. $\sqrt{30}$ 54. $\sqrt{61}$ 55. $\sqrt{93}$ 56. $-\sqrt{124}$

Use a calculator to find each value. Round to the nearest tenth.

57. $\sqrt{200}$ 14.1   58. $\sqrt{185}$ 13.6   59. $\sqrt{462}$ 21.5   60. $\sqrt{219}$ 14.8

61. Each tile on Michelle's patio is 18 square inches. If her patio is square shaped and consists of 81 tiles, about how big is her patio? 38.2 inches × 38.2 inches

LESSON 4-7

Write all names that apply to each number.

62. $\sqrt{5}$ irrational, real   63. -61.2 rational, real   64. $\frac{\sqrt{16}}{2}$ whole, integer, rational, real   65. -6 integer, rational, real

State if the number is rational, irrational, or not a real number.

66. $\sqrt{\frac{4}{25}}$ rational   67. $\sqrt{-9}$ not real   68. $\sqrt{17}$ irrational   69. $\frac{13}{0}$ not real

Find a real number between each pair of numbers. Possible answers:

70. $5\frac{1}{8}$ and $5\frac{2}{8}$ $5\frac{3}{16}$ 71. $4\frac{1}{3}$ and $4\frac{2}{3}$ $4\frac{1}{2}$ 72. $3\frac{5}{7}$ and $3\frac{6}{7}$ $3\frac{11}{14}$

LESSON 4-8

Solve for the unknown side in each right triangle to the nearest tenth.

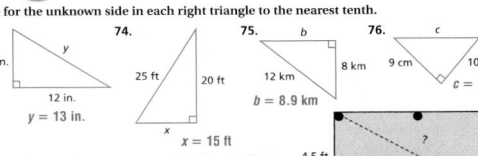

73. 5 in., 12 in., $y = 13$ in.   74. 25 ft, 20 ft, $x = 15$ ft   75. b, 8 km, 12 km, $b = 8.9$ km   76. c, 9 cm, 10 cm, $c = 13.5$ cm

77. A professional tournament pool table typically measures 4.5 ft by 9 ft. How far is it from one corner pocket to the opposite corner pocket? Round to the nearest hundredth of a foot. 10.06 ft

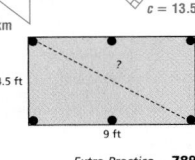

Extra Practice ■ Chapter 5

LESSON 5-1

Find two ratios that are equivalent to each given ratio. Possible answers:
1. $\frac{5}{10}$ $\frac{10}{20}, \frac{1}{2}$ 2. $\frac{9}{12}$ $\frac{18}{24}, \frac{3}{4}$ 3. $\frac{25}{35}$ $\frac{50}{70}, \frac{5}{7}$ 4. $\frac{30}{35}$ $\frac{60}{70}, \frac{6}{7}$

Simplify to tell whether the ratios form a proportion.
5. $\frac{5}{30}$ and $\frac{3}{18}$ yes   6. $\frac{12}{21}$ and $\frac{16}{28}$ yes   7. $\frac{15}{21}$ and $\frac{10}{16}$ no   8. $\frac{52}{64}$ and $\frac{91}{112}$ yes

LESSON 5-2

9. A penny has a mass of 2.5 g and a volume of approximately 0.442 cm³. What is the approximate density of a penny?   5.66 g/cm³

10. Nikko jogs 3 miles in 30 minutes. How many miles does she jog per hour?   6 miles

Estimate the unit rate.   50 mg/oz
11. 384 milligrams calcium for 8 oz of yogurt   12. $57.50 for 5 hours $12/h

13. Find the unit rate for each brand of detergent, and determine which brand is the best buy.
Bubbling detergent, at 2.3¢ per ounce

Product	Size	Price
Pizzazz detergent	128 oz	$3.08
Spring Clean detergent	64 oz	$1.60
Bubbling detergent	196 oz	$4.51

LESSON 5-3

Find the appropriate factor for each conversion.
14. quart to gallon $\frac{1 \text{ gallon}}{4 \text{ quarts}}$ 15. mile to foot $\frac{5280 \text{ feet}}{1 \text{ mile}}$
16. meter to centimeter $\frac{100 \text{ centimeters}}{1 \text{ meter}}$ 17. milligram to gram $\frac{1 \text{ gram}}{1000 \text{ milligrams}}$

18. A three-toed sloth has a top speed of 0.22 feet per second. A giant tortoise has a top speed of 2.992 inches per second. Convert both speeds to miles per hour, and determine which animal is faster.
Sloth: 0.15 mi/h; tortoise: 0.17 mi/h; the tortoise is faster.

LESSON 5-4

Tell whether the ratios are proportional.
19. $\frac{7}{8}$ and $\frac{3}{4}$ no   20. $\frac{3}{4}$ and $\frac{24}{32}$ yes   21. $\frac{32}{48}$ and $\frac{18}{27}$ yes   22. $\frac{12}{20}$ and $\frac{6}{12}$ no

Solve each proportion.
23. $\frac{186 \text{ miles}}{3 \text{ hours}} = \frac{\blacksquare \text{ miles}}{5 \text{ hours}}$ 310 miles   24. $\frac{10 \text{ invitations}}{12 \text{ envelopes}} = \frac{15 \text{ invitations}}{\blacksquare \text{ envelopes}}$ 18 envelopes
25. $\frac{3}{8} = \frac{n}{12}$ $n = 4.5$ 26. $\frac{c}{15} = \frac{3}{45}$ $c = 1$ 27. $\frac{7}{18} = \frac{3}{m}$ $m = 7\frac{5}{7}$ 28. $\frac{5}{f} = \frac{8}{12}$ $f = 7.5$

29. Ricki jogged 4 miles in 36 minutes. At this rate, how long would it take Ricki to jog 12 miles?   108 minutes

30. An 18-pound weight is positioned 6 in. from a fulcrum. At what distance from the fulcrum must a 24-pound weight be positioned to keep the scale balanced?   4.5 in.

790   Extra Practice

Extra Practice ■ Chapter 5

LESSON 5-5

30. Khaled scans a photo that is 5 in. wide by 7 in. long into his computer. If he scales the length down to 3.5 in., how wide should the similar photo be?   2.5 in.

31. Mutsuko drew an 8.5-inch-wide by 11-inch-tall picture that will be turned into a 34-inch-wide poster. How tall will the poster be?   44 in.

32. A right triangle has legs that measure 3 cm and 4 cm. Another right triangle has legs that measure 5 cm and 12 cm. Are the triangles similar?   no

LESSON 5-6

Tell whether each transformation is a dilation.
33.   yes   34.   no   35.   yes

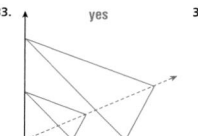 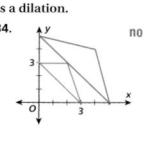 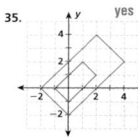

36. A figure has vertices at (2, 3), (3, 6), (6, 7), and (7, 2). The figure is dilated by a scale factor of 1.5 with the origin as the center of dilation. What are the vertices of the image?   (3, 4.5), (4.5, 9), (9, 10.5), (10.5, 3)

LESSON 5-7

37. Brian casts a 9 ft shadow at the same time that Carrie casts an 8 ft shadow. If Brian is 6 ft tall, how tall is Carrie?   about 5.3 feet

38. A telephone pole cast an 80 ft shadow, while a 3.5 ft tall child standing nearby casts a 6 ft shadow. How tall is the pole?   about 46.7 feet

LESSON 5-8

39. What is the scale of a drawing where a 95 ft tall building is 6 in. tall?   1 in:15.83 ft

40. On a scale drawing of a house plan, the master bathroom is $1\frac{1}{2}$ inches wide and $2\frac{5}{8}$ inches long. If the scale of the drawing is $\frac{3}{16}$ inches = 1 foot, what are the actual dimensions of the bathroom?   8 ft × 14 ft

41. Julio uses a scale of $\frac{1}{8}$ inch = 1 foot when he paints landscapes. In one painting, a giant sequoia tree is 34.375 inches tall. How tall is the real tree?   275 ft

42. A model of a skyscraper was made using a scale of 0.5 in:5 ft. If the actual skyscraper is 570 feet tall, how many feet tall is the model?   4.75 ft

Extra Practice   791

Extra Practice ■ Chapter 6

LESSON 6-1

Compare. Write <, >, or =.
1. $\frac{3}{5} \blacksquare 62\%$ <   2. $\frac{2}{3} \blacksquare 66\frac{2}{3}\%$ =   3. 24% $\blacksquare$ 0.25   <   4. 1% $\blacksquare$ 0.11   <

Order the numbers from least to greatest.
5. 0.11, 11.5%, 10%, $\frac{1}{8}$ 10%, 0.11, 11.5%, $\frac{1}{8}$ 6. $\frac{1}{5}$, 100%, $26\frac{2}{3}\%$, 0.3 $\frac{1}{5}$, $26\frac{2}{3}\%$, 0.3, 100%
7. $\frac{7}{6}$, 115%, 83, 83.3%   83.3%, 115%, $\frac{7}{6}$, 83   8. 67.5%, $\frac{7}{3}$, 160%, 2.2   67.5%, 160%, 2.2, $\frac{7}{3}$

9. A molecule of ammonia is made up of 3 atoms of hydrogen and 1 atom of nitrogen. What percent of the atoms of an ammonia molecule are hydrogen?   75%

LESSON 6-2

Estimate.
10. 51% of 1019   510   11. 33% of 60   20   12. 60% of 79   48   13. $66\frac{2}{3}\%$ of 211   140

14. Approximately 23% of each class walks to school. A student said that in a class of 20 students, approximately 2 students walk to school. Estimate to determine if the student's number is reasonable. Explain.
Possible answer: No, 23% is close to 25%. 25% of 20 is 5. 5 is much more than 2.

LESSON 6-3

15. What percent of 364 is 92?   about 25.3%   16. What percent of 48 is 5?   about 10.4%
17. What percent of 164 is 444?   about 270.7%   18. 4 is what percent of 50?   8%

19. Mt. McKinley in Alaska is 20,320 feet tall. The height of Mt. Everest is about 143% of the height of Mt. McKinley. Estimate the height of Mt. Everest. Round to the nearest thousand.   about 29,000 ft

20. A restaurant bill for $64.45 was split among four people. Dona paid 25% of the bill. Sandy paid $\frac{1}{5}$ of the bill. Mara paid $14.25. Greta paid the remainder of the bill. Who paid the most money?   Greta

LESSON 6-4

21. 38 is 42% of what number?   about 90.5   22. 46 is 74% of what number?   about 62.2
23. 23 is 8% of what number?   287.5   24. 93 is 62% of what number?   150
25. 315 is 92% of what number?   about 342.3   26. 52 is 120% of what number?   about 22,727.3

27. A certain rock is a compound of several minerals. Tests show that the sample contains 17.3 grams of quartz. If 27.5% of the rock is quartz, find the mass in grams of the entire rock.   about 62.9 grams

28. The Alabama River is 729 miles in length, or about 31% of the length of the Mississippi River. Estimate the length of the Mississippi River. Round to the nearest mile.   2352 miles

792   Extra Practice

Extra Practice ■ Chapter 6

LESSON 6-5

Find each percent increase or decrease to the nearest percent.
29. from 10 to 17   70% increase   30. from 38 to 65   71% increase   31. from 91 to 44   52% decrease   32. from 3 to 25   733% increase
33. from 86 to 27   69% decrease   34. from 38 to 46   21% increase   35. from 19 to 60   216% increase   36. from 88 to 23   74% decrease

37. A stereo that sells for $895 is on sale for 20% off the regular price. What is the sale price of the stereo? $716

38. Mr. Schultz owns a hardware store and typically marks up merchandise 28% over warehouse cost. How much would he charge for a wrench that costs him $12.45? $15.94

LESSON 6-6

39. An electronics salesperson sold $15,486 worth of computers last month. She makes 3% commission on all sales and earns a monthly salary of $1200. What was her total pay last month? $1664.58

40. Jon bought a printer for $189 and a set of printer cartridges for $129. Sales tax on these items was 6.5%. What is Jon's total bill for these items? $338.67

41. Last year, Wendy earned $36,825. From this amount, $3830.50 was spent on food. What percent of her income went to food, to the nearest tenth of a percent?   10.4%

42. In her shop, Stephanie earns 16% on all the clothes she sells. This month she earned $3920. What were her total sales of clothes? $24,500

43. Eli works in a clothes shop where he earns a commission of 8% and no weekly salary. What will Eli's weekly sales have to be for him to earn $425? $5,312.50

LESSON 6-7

44. Fatin borrowed $6500 to make home repairs and to put in a new skylight. The bank charges $7\frac{1}{2}\%$ simple interest over 5 years. What is the total Fatin will repay the bank? $8,937.50

45. Rebekah invested $15,000 in a mutual fund at a yearly rate of 8%. She earned $7200 in simple interest. How long was the money invested?   6 years

46. Shu earned $1000, which he used to buy a 10-year certificate of deposit (CD). The CD paid simple interest at 8%. What will the CD be worth at the end of 10 years? $1800

47. Rich borrowed $16,000 for 12 years at simple interest to help pay for his schooling. If he repaid a total of $31,360, at what interest rate did he borrow the money?   8%

Extra Practice   793

Extra Practice ▪ Chapter 7

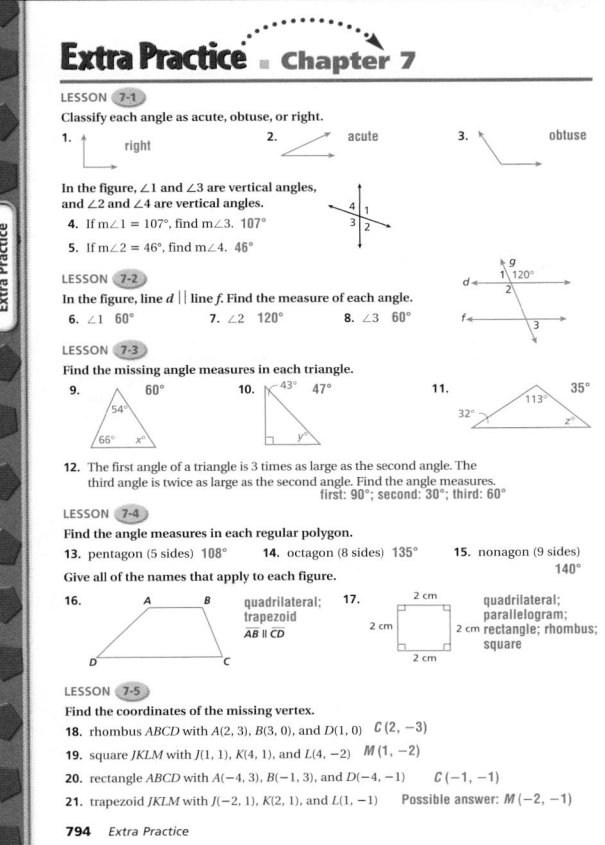

LESSON 7-1

Classify each angle as acute, obtuse, or right.

1. right 2. acute 3. obtuse

In the figure, ∠1 and ∠3 are vertical angles, and ∠2 and ∠4 are vertical angles.

4. If m∠1 = 107°, find m∠3. 107°

5. If m∠2 = 46°, find m∠4. 46°

LESSON 7-2

In the figure, line d ∥ line f. Find the measure of each angle.

6. ∠1 60° 7. ∠2 120° 8. ∠3 60°

LESSON 7-3

Find the missing angle measures in each triangle.

9. 60° 10. 43° 47° 11. 113° 35°

12. The first angle of a triangle is 3 times as large as the second angle. The third angle is twice as large as the second angle. Find the angle measures.
first: 90°; second: 30°; third: 60°

LESSON 7-4

Find the angle measures in each regular polygon.

13. pentagon (5 sides) 108° 14. octagon (8 sides) 135° 15. nonagon (9 sides) 140°

Give all of the names that apply to each figure.

16. quadrilateral; trapezoid $\overline{AB}$ ∥ $\overline{CD}$

17. quadrilateral; parallelogram; rectangle; rhombus; square

LESSON 7-5

Find the coordinates of the missing vertex.

18. rhombus ABCD with A(2, 3), B(3, 0), and D(1, 0) C (2, −3)

19. square JKLM with J(1, 1), K(4, 1), and L(4, −2) M (1, −2)

20. rectangle ABCD with A(−4, 3), B(−1, 3), and D(−4, −1) C (−1, −1)

21. trapezoid JKLM with J(−2, 1), K(2, 1), and L(1, −1) Possible answer: M (−2, −1)

Extra Practice ▪ Chapter 7

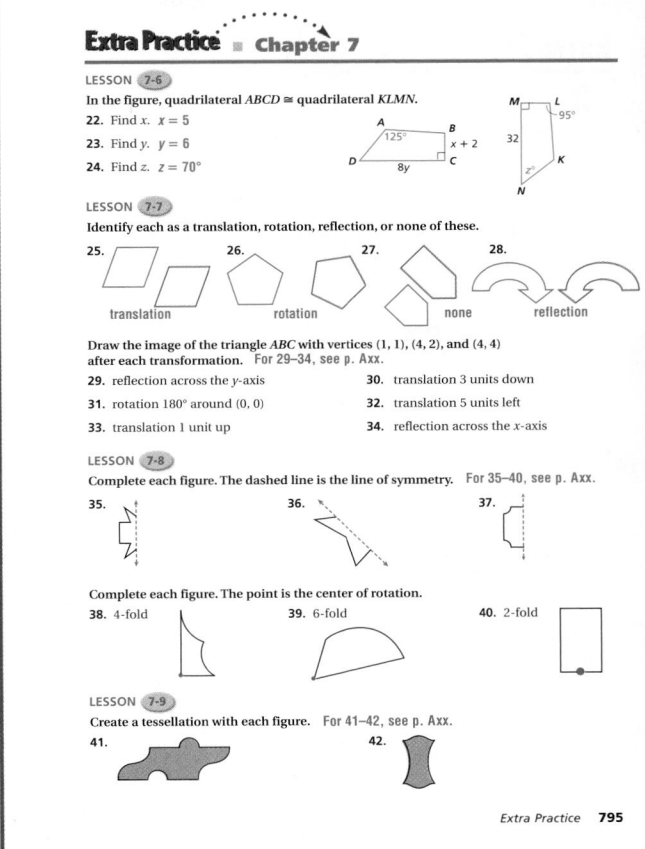

LESSON 7-6

In the figure, quadrilateral ABCD ≅ quadrilateral KLMN.

22. Find x. x = 5

23. Find y. y = 6

24. Find z. z = 70°

LESSON 7-7

Identify each as a translation, rotation, reflection, or none of these.

25. translation 26. rotation 27. none 28. reflection

Draw the image of the triangle ABC with vertices (1, 1), (4, 2), and (4, 4) after each transformation. For 29–34, see p. Axx.

29. reflection across the y-axis 30. translation 3 units down

31. rotation 180° around (0, 0) 32. translation 5 units left

33. translation 1 unit up 34. reflection across the x-axis

LESSON 7-8

Complete each figure. The dashed line is the line of symmetry. For 35–40, see p. Axx.

35. 36. 37.

Complete each figure. The point is the center of rotation.

38. 4-fold 39. 6-fold 40. 2-fold

LESSON 7-9

Create a tessellation with each figure. For 41–42, see p. Axx.

41. 42.

Extra Practice ▪ Chapter 8

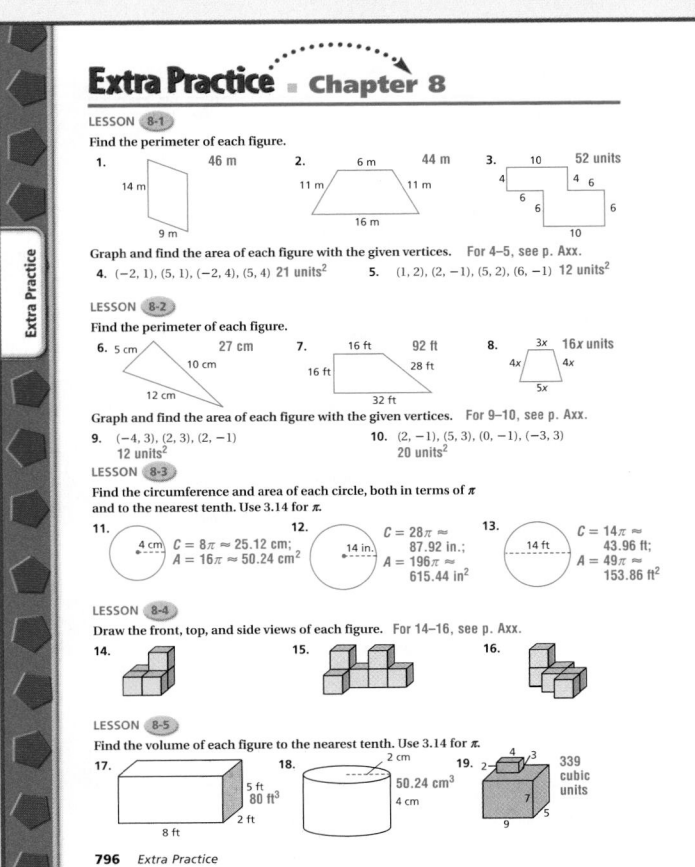

LESSON 8-1

Find the perimeter of each figure.

1. 46 m 2. 44 m 3. 52 units

Graph and find the area of each figure with the given vertices. For 4–5, see p. Axx.

4. (−2, 1), (5, 1), (−2, 4), (5, 4) 21 units² 5. (1, 2), (2, −1), (5, 2), (6, −1) 12 units²

LESSON 8-2

Find the perimeter of each figure.

6. 27 cm 7. 92 ft 8. 16x units

Graph and find the area of each figure with the given vertices. For 9–10, see p. Axx.

9. (−4, 3), (2, 3), (2, −1) 12 units² 10. (2, −1), (5, 3), (0, −1), (−3, 3) 20 units²

LESSON 8-3

Find the circumference and area of each circle, both in terms of π and to the nearest tenth. Use 3.14 for π.

11. $C = 8\pi \approx 25.12$ cm; $A = 16\pi \approx 50.24$ cm²

12. $C = 28\pi \approx 87.92$ in.; $A = 196\pi \approx 615.44$ in²

13. $C = 14\pi \approx 43.96$ ft; $A = 49\pi \approx 153.86$ ft²

LESSON 8-4

Draw the front, top, and side views of each figure. For 14–16, see p. Axx.

14. 15. 16.

LESSON 8-5

Find the volume of each figure to the nearest tenth. Use 3.14 for π.

17. 80 ft³ 18. 50.24 cm³ 19. 339 cubic units

Extra Practice ▪ Chapter 8

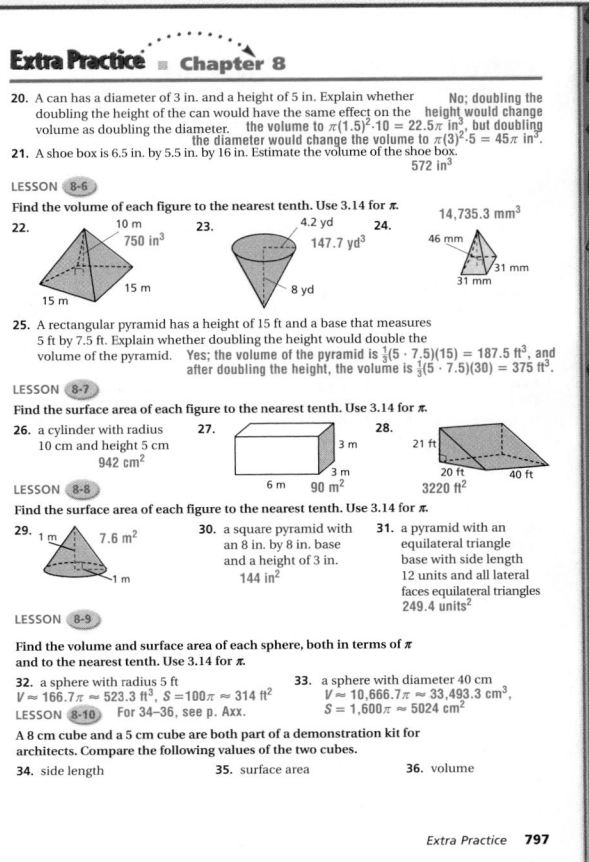

20. A can has a diameter of 3 in. and a height of 5 in. Explain whether doubling the height of the can would have the same effect on the volume as doubling the diameter. No; doubling the height would change the volume to $\pi(1.5)^2 \cdot 10 = 22.5\pi$ in³, but doubling the diameter would change the volume to $\pi(3)^2 \cdot 5 = 45\pi$ in³.

21. A shoe box is 6.5 in. by 5.5 in. by 16 in. Estimate the volume of the shoe box. 572 in³

LESSON 8-6

Find the volume of each figure to the nearest tenth. Use 3.14 for π.

22. 750 in³ 23. 147.7 yd³ 24. 14,735.3 mm³

25. A rectangular pyramid has a height of 15 ft and a base that measures 5 ft by 7.5 ft. Explain whether doubling the height would double the volume of the pyramid. Yes; the volume of the pyramid is $\frac{1}{3}(5 \cdot 7.5)(15) = 187.5$ ft³, and after doubling the height, the volume is $\frac{1}{3}(5 \cdot 7.5)(30) = 375$ ft³.

LESSON 8-7

Find the surface area of each figure to the nearest tenth. Use 3.14 for π.

26. a cylinder with radius 10 cm and height 5 cm 942 cm²

27. 90 m²

28. 3220 ft²

LESSON 8-8

Find the surface area of each figure to the nearest tenth. Use 3.14 for π.

29. 7.6 m²

30. a square pyramid with an 8 in. by 8 in. base and a height of 3 in. 144 in²

31. a pyramid with an equilateral triangle base with side length 12 units and all lateral faces equilateral triangles 249.4 units²

LESSON 8-9

Find the volume and surface area of each sphere, both in terms of π and to the nearest tenth. Use 3.14 for π.

32. a sphere with radius 5 ft $V \approx 166.7\pi \approx 523.3$ ft³, $S = 100\pi \approx 314$ ft²

33. a sphere with diameter 40 cm $V \approx 10,666.7\pi \approx 33,493.3$ cm³, $S = 1,600\pi \approx 5024$ cm²

LESSON 8-10 For 34–36, see p. Axx.

An 8 cm cube and a 5 cm cube are both part of a demonstration kit for architects. Compare the following values of the two cubes.

34. side length 35. surface area 36. volume

LESSON (9-1)

Identify the sampling method used.

1. A questionnaire is distributed to every eighth diner entering a restaurant. **systematic**

2. In a state survey, 10 cities are chosen at random, and 100 people are chosen from each city. **stratified**

Identify the population and sample. Give a reason why the sample could be biased.

3. A company surveys 100 employees who belong to 5 different high tech companies about their opinion on company benefits. **population: people who work for high tech companies; sample: 100 employees; possible bias: not all companies have the same benefits**

LESSON (9-2) For 4–5, see p. Axx.

4. Use a line plot to organize the data of the number of miles biked by students over a weekend.

Number of Miles Biked by Students
12 21 12 8 10 15 15 18 12 11 9 10 9 6 0 5 12 5 14 14 10 8 12 10 9

5. Use the given data to make a back-to-back stem-and-leaf plot.

World Series Win/Loss Records of Selected Teams (through 2001)						
Team	Yankees	Pirates	Giants	Tigers	Cardinals	Dodgers	Orioles
Wins	26	5	5	4	9	6	3
Losses	12	2	11	5	6	12	4

LESSON (9-3)

Determine and find the most appropriate measure of central tendency or range for each situation.

6. The number of animals seen each day of the week at a veterinarian's office was 22, 31, 20, 44, 39, 29. What number best describes the middle of this data? **median: 30**

7. Mr. Lucky sold five houses for the following prices: $125,000; $425,000; $178,000; $155,000; $105,000. What measure of central tendency or range would make the house prices seem the highest? **range: $320,000**

LESSON (9-4)

Find the first and third quartiles for each data set.

8. 27, 31, 26, 24, 33, 31, 24, 28, 31, 24, 22, 27, 31, 28, 26 **first quartile: 24; third quartile: 31**

9. 84, 79, 77, 72, 81, 82, 89, 94, 72, 80, 76, 80, 83, 86, 73 **first quartile: 76; third quartile: 84**

Use the given data to make a box-and-whisker plot. For 11–12, see p. Axx.

10. 11, 4, 9, 17, 16, 12, 5, 16, 9, 11, 13

11. 57, 53, 52, 31, 48, 59, 64, 86, 56, 54, 55

LESSON (9-5) For 12, see p. Axx.

12. Organize the data into a frequency table and make a double-bar graph. The following are the ages of 24 men and women between the ages of 45 and 50 with high cholesterol.

Men: 48, 46, 50, 50, 45, 46, 45, 47, 49, 46, 45, 48

Women: 50, 47, 49, 49, 46, 48, 50, 49, 48, 49, 50, 45

LESSON (9-6)

Explain why each graph or statistic is misleading.

13.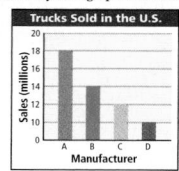

Trucks Sold in the U.S.

Possible answer: The scale used for the *y*-axis is inconsistent, so the differences appear exaggerated.

14. A market researcher randomly selected 12 shoppers to sample 4 brands of cereal labeled *A*, *B*, *C*, and *D*. Of the shoppers, 6 selected *C*, 2 selected *A*, 2 selected *B*, and 2 selected *D*. An ad for brand *C* is heard to say, "Preferred 3 to 1 over other brands."

15. A car lot has five cars for sale at the following prices: $14,000, $13,000, $15,000, $2,000, and $16,000. It has a banner boasting an average price of $12,000 per car. **Possible answer: $2000 is an outlier. All the other cars on the lot cost more than $12,000**

LESSON (9-7)

Use the given data to make a scatter plot.

16. The table shows the relationship between the number of years of post high school education and salary.

Number of Years of Post High School Education and Salary										
Years	1	1	3	4	4	4	5	5	6	8	8
Salary ($1,000's)	18	20.5	28	35	51	43	58	52	64	58	75	73.5

Do the data sets have a positive, a negative, or no correlation?

17. the number of sales and the amount of a salesperson's commission **positive correlation**

18. the height of a dog and its life expectancy **no correlation**

LESSON (9-8)

Choose the best data display for each situation. Explain your choice.

19. how Benetta spent her time one day **circle graph, so that you could compare the parts to the whole**

20. the price of Carlos' stock over one week **line plot, so that you can see how data changed over time**

LESSON (10-1)

Refer to the spinner at right. Give the probability for each outcome.

1. red $\frac{3}{8}$
2. blue $\frac{3}{8}$
3. yellow $\frac{1}{4}$
4. not red $\frac{5}{8}$
5. not blue $\frac{5}{8}$
6. not yellow $\frac{3}{4}$

7. The probability that Kim will win a game is $\frac{1}{4}$. Kelvin and Chelsea have half as much chance of winning as Kim does. Sasha is four times as likely to win the game as Kelvin is. Create a table of probabilities for the sample space.

Outcome	Kim	Kelvin	Chelsea	Sasha
Probability	$\frac{1}{4}$	$\frac{1}{8}$	$\frac{1}{8}$	$\frac{1}{2}$

LESSON (10-2)

A utensil is drawn from a drawer and replaced. The table shows the results after 100 draws.

Outcomes	Draws
Spoon	33
Knife	36
Fork	31

8. Estimate the probability of drawing a spoon. **33%**

9. Estimate the probability of not drawing a spoon. **67%**

A sales assistant tracks the sales of a particular sweater. The table shows the data after 1000 sales.

Outcomes	Sales
White	361
Beige	207
Brown	189
Black	243

10. Estimate the probability that the next customer will buy a brown sweater. **18.9%**

11. Estimate the probability of the next sweater sold not being brown or beige. **60.4%**

LESSON (10-3)

Use the table of random numbers to simulate each situation. Use at least 10 trials for each simulation.

53736 85815 87649 31119 16635 65161 27919 86585 32848 94425 61378 41256
11632 46278 38783 87649 13325 60848 74681 54238 94228 82794 23426 46498

12. A golfer has an 81% chance of making a putt on the first try. Estimate the probability that he will make the putt on the first try at least 9 of his next 10 times. **Possible answer: 30%**

13. A field-goal kicker has a 74% chance of making successful field goals. Estimate the probability that he will make at least 8 of his next 10 field goal attempts. **Possible answer: 20%**

LESSON (10-4)

An experiment consists of rolling a fair number cube. There are 6 possible outcomes: 1, 2, 3, 4, 5, and 6. Find the probability of each event.

14. *P*(rolling an odd number) $\frac{1}{2}$
15. *P*(rolling a 2) $\frac{1}{6}$
16. *P*(rolling a number greater than 3) $\frac{1}{2}$
17. *P*(rolling a 7) **0**

An experiment consists of rolling two fair number cubes. Find each probability.

18. *P*(rolling a total of 4) $\frac{1}{12}$
19. *P*(rolling a total less than 2) **0**
20. *P*(rolling a total greater than 12) **0**
21. *P*(rolling a total of 9) $\frac{1}{9}$

LESSON (10-5)

22. An experiment consists of rolling a fair number cube 3 times. For each toss, all outcomes are equally likely. What is the probability of rolling a 2 three times in a row? $\frac{1}{216}$

23. A jar contains 3 blue marbles and 9 red marbles. What is the probability of drawing 2 red marbles at the same time? $\frac{6}{11}$

LESSON (10-6)

24. Kylie practiced barrel racing around a course 10 times. Her times, in seconds, were 13.849, 13.960, 14.133, 14.186, 13.946, 13.952, 14.054, 14.065, 14.296, and 14.383. If she practices 40 more times, what is the best prediction of the number of times that will be less than 14 seconds? **16 times**

25. Toss four coins. Player A wins if exactly 3 heads land up. Otherwise Player B wins. Is this game fair? **no**

LESSON (10-7)

26. At a wrestling meet, 192 participants competed for 12 trophies. Estimate the odds of winning a trophy. **1:15**

27. If the odds against winning a contest are 9999:1, what is the probability of winning the contest? $\frac{1}{10,000}$

LESSON (10-8) For 30, see p. Axx.

A computer randomly generates a 4-character computer password of 3 digits followed by 1 letter.

28. Find the number of possible passwords. **26,000**

29. Find the probability that an assigned password does not contain a *P*. $\frac{25}{26}$

30. A dancer has a choice of 2 dresses, 4 scarves, and 4 pairs of shoes. Draw a tree diagram to show all the possible outcomes.

LESSON (10-9)

Evaluate each expression.

31. 9! **362,880**
32. $\frac{6!}{3!}$ **120**
33. $\frac{5!}{11!}$ **0.000003**
34. $\frac{7!}{(15-7)!}$ **0.125**

35. There are 10 college football teams in the conference. Find the number of orders in which all 10 teams can finish the season. **3,628,800**

36. Find the number of ways the 10 teams can finish first, second, and third in the conference. **720**

Extra Practice ▪ Chapter 11

LESSON 11-1

Combine like terms.

1. $5x + 4x + 7x$ **16x**
2. $6x - 4x + 9 + 5x + 7$ **7x + 16**
3. $2x + 3 - 2x + 5$ **8**
4. $7a - 2b + 6 + 4b - 5a$ **2a + 2b + 6**
5. $4s + 9t - 9$ **4s + 9t − 9**
6. $6m + 4n - 6m + n$ **5n**

Simplify.

7. $6(y + 4) - y$ **5y + 24**
8. $3(3b - 3) + 3b$ **12b − 9**
9. $4(x + 2) + 3x - 8$ **7x**

Solve.

10. $4x + 7 = 87$ **x = 20**
11. $2a - 3 = 41$ **a = 22**
12. $9b + 4 = 67$ **b = 7**
13. $6h - 12 = 78$ **h = 15**
14. $5y + 3y = 24$ **y = 3**
15. $8d - 3d = 40$ **d = 8**
16. $2m + m = 42$ **m = 14**
17. $9x - x = 48$ **x = 6**
18. $a + 6a = 49$ **a = 7**
19. $2p + 8p = 100$ **p = 10**
20. $12y - 8y = 44$ **y = 11**
21. $5f + 7f + 3f = 30$ **f = 2**

LESSON 11-2

Solve.

22. $4a - 5 + 2a + 9 = 28$ **a = 4**
23. $5 - 8b + 6 - 2b = 61$ **b = −5**
24. $4x - 6 - 8x - 9 = 21$ **x = −9**
25. $g - 9 + 4g + 6 = 12$ **g = 3**
26. $2 - 3f - 5 + 5f = 6$ **f = $\frac{9}{2}$**
27. $4r - 8 + 7 - 6r = -9$ **r = 4**
28. $\frac{4a}{11} - \frac{7}{11} = -\frac{3}{11}$ **a = 1**
29. $\frac{1}{11} - \frac{2b}{11} = \frac{7}{11}$ **b = −3**
30. $\frac{4z}{11} + \frac{3}{11} = -1$ **z = $-\frac{14}{4}$ or $-\frac{7}{2}$**
31. $\frac{8}{5} - \frac{5m}{5} = \frac{23}{5}$ **m = −3**
32. $\frac{9}{11} - \frac{3s}{11} = \frac{3}{11}$ **s = 2**
33. $\frac{4p}{3} - \frac{2}{3} = 6$ **p = 5**
34. $\frac{2f}{4} - 4 = -\frac{24}{4}$ **f = 4**
35. $\frac{10c}{16} - \frac{16}{16} = \frac{56}{16}$ **c = 6**
36. $\frac{9x}{4} - \frac{45}{4} + \frac{36x}{4} = \frac{-126}{4}$ **x = −1**
37. $\frac{42y}{6} - \frac{9}{6} + \frac{16y}{6} = \frac{396}{6}$ **y = 4**
38. $\frac{27a}{12} + \frac{15}{12} - \frac{8a}{12} = \frac{36}{12}$ **a = −1**
39. $\frac{4b}{2} + \frac{6}{2} - \frac{6}{2} = \frac{12}{2}$ **b = 3**

40. A round-trip car ride took 12 hours. The first half of the trip took 7 hours at a rate of 45 miles per hour. What was the average rate of speed on the return trip? **63 miles per hour**

LESSON 11-3

Solve.

41. $5x - 6 = 2x$ **x = 2**
42. $4w + 5 = 20 - w$ **w = 3**
43. $3y + 12 = -3y$ **y = −2**
44. $2b + 6 = -b + 3$ **b = −1**
45. $4z - 2 = z + 1$ **z = 1**
46. $-4a - 4 = a + 11$ **a = −3**
47. $4p - 6 = 3 + 4p$ **no solution**
48. $6 + 5c = 3c - 4$ **c = −5**
49. $7d - 3 + 2d = 5d - 8 + 1$ **d = −1**
50. $3f - 4 - 5f = f + 4 + f$ **f = −2**
51. $5k - 4 = 3k - 6 + 2k$ **x = 6**
52. $\frac{w}{4} + \frac{5}{8} - \frac{2w}{8} = \frac{7}{8}$ **w = 1**
53. $\frac{a}{3} - \frac{1}{6} + \frac{5a}{6} = \frac{a}{6} + \frac{2a}{3} + \frac{a}{3}$ **a = 10**
54. $\frac{2q}{3} + \frac{5}{9} - \frac{q}{6} = \frac{5q}{6} - \frac{2}{9}$ **q = 2**

55. A cafeteria charges a fixed price per ounce for the salad bar. A sandwich costs $3.10, and a large drink costs $1.75. If a 7-ounce salad and a drink cost the same as a 4-ounce salad and a sandwich, how much does the salad cost per ounce? **$0.45**

Extra Practice ▪ Chapter 11

LESSON 11-4

Solve and graph. For 56–71, see p. Axx.

56. $3x > -36$ **x > −12**
57. $5 \leq \frac{v}{2} \leq v$, or **$v \geq 10$**
58. $\frac{2r}{3} < 8$ **r < 12**
59. $6k > 24$ **k > 4**
60. $-40 \geq 4q$ **−10 ≥ q**
61. $\frac{3}{4}m > 18$ **m > 24**
62. $-9x > 72$ **x < −8**
63. $-2 \leq -\frac{s}{3}$ **−6 ≤ s, or s ≥ −6**
64. $5 \geq -b$ **−5 ≤ b, or b ≥ −5**
65. $16 > -4c$ **−4 < c, or c > −4**
66. $\frac{p}{3} > -6$ **p > −18**
67. $-3d < -12$ **d > 4**
68. $3 > -\frac{w}{5} - 15$ **−15 < w, or w > −15**
69. $-3h \geq -2$ **h ≤ $\frac{2}{3}$**
70. $-f \leq 4$ **f ≥ −4**
71. $-5y > -55$ **y < 11**

72. Reese is running for student council president. In order for a student to be elected president, at least $\frac{1}{3}$ of the students must vote for him. If there are 432 students in a class, at least how many students must vote for Reese in order for him to be elected class president? **at least 144 students**

LESSON 11-5

Solve and graph. For 73–88, see p. Axx.

73. $3a + 6 < 12$ **a < 2**
74. $-5 \leq 4x + 7$ **−3 ≤ x, or x ≥ −3**
75. $2b + 8 > 16$ **b > 4**
76. $6c + 8 \geq -4$ **c ≥ −2**
77. $5 > 4d - 3$ **2 > d, or d < 2**
78. $-8f + 6 \leq 14$ **f ≥ −1**
79. $-3g + 2 \geq -4$ **g ≤ 2**
80. $-3 < 7h - 10$ **1 < h, or h > 1**
81. $4z + 8 \leq -4$ **z ≤ −3**
82. $7y + 1 > 8$ **y > 1**
83. $9 < 3z - 9$ **6 < z, or z > 6**
84. $a + \frac{3}{8} > \frac{1}{2}$ **a > 1**
85. $\frac{x}{6} - \frac{1}{3} > -\frac{2}{3}$ **x > −2**
86. $\frac{1}{2}k + 8 \geq 9$ **k ≥ 2**
87. $\frac{d}{4} + \frac{2}{5} < 2$ **d < $\frac{12}{5}$**
88. $\frac{2}{3} + \frac{p}{6} < \frac{7}{6}$ **p < 3**

89. Nikko wants to make flyers promoting a library book sale. The printer charges $40 plus $0.03 per flyer. How many flyers can Nikko have made without spending more than the library's $54 budget? **466 flyers**

LESSON 11-6

Solve each system of equations.

90. $x - 2y = -10$
    $5x + 2y = -2$ **(−2, 4)**
91. $y = 2x$
    $y = x + 6$ **(6, 12)**
92. $3x + 4y = 17$
    $-2x + 4y = 2$ **(3, 2)**
93. $y + 2x = 5$
    $y = x - 4$ **(3, −1)**
94. $y + 2x = -2$
    $2y - 2x = 14$ **(−3, 4)**
95. $y = x + 4$
    $y = 2x + 6$ **(−2, 2)**
96. $y = 3x - 1$
    $y = 2x + 2$ **(3, 8)**
97. $-y = x + 1$
    $y = -2x - 4$ **(−3, 2)**
98. $2x + y = 0$
    $2x + 3y = 8$ **(−2, 4)**
99. $x + y = -5$
    $x - 2y = 7$ **(−1, −4)**
100. $y = x - 1$
     $-3x + 3y = 4$ **no solution**
101. $-x - y = 0$
     $y = x + 8$ **(−4, 4)**
102. $5k - 4 = 3k$
     $x - y - 5 = 0$ **infinite solutions**
103. $2y = x + 6$
     $4y + 2x = -4$ **(−4, 1)**
104. $3y - 2x = -2$
     $y + 2x = -6$ **(−2, −2)**
105. $y = 2x + 1$
     $2x + y = 4$ **no solution**
106. $-3y - x = 2$
     $2y + 2x = 4$ **(−2, 4)**
107. $y = 2x - 5$
     $2x - y - 5 = 0$ **infinite solutions**
108. $y = 3x$
     $2y + 3x = -18$ **(−2, −6)**
109. $y = -x$
     $4y + x = 21$ **(−7, 7)**

Extra Practice ▪ Chapter 12

LESSON 12-1

Graph each equation and tell whether it is linear. For 1–5, see p. Axx.

1. $y = 4x - 2$ **linear**
2. $y = -2x + 1$ **linear**
3. $y = x^2 - 4$ **not linear**
4. $y = -x - 3$ **linear**

5. A home improvement store charges a base fee of $150, plus $25 for each hour of machinery rental. The cost C for h hours is given by $C = 25h + 150$. Find the cost for 1, 2, 3, 4, and 5 hours. Is this a linear equation? Draw a graph that represents the relationship between the cost and the number of hours of rental.
   1 hr = $175; 2 hr = $200; 3 hr = $225; 4 hr = $250; 5 hr = $275; linear

LESSON 12-2

Find the slope of the line that passes through each pair of given points. For 10, see p. Axx.

6. (3, 4) and (−2, 2) **$\frac{2}{5}$**
7. (6, 2) and (−2, −6) **1**
8. (3, 3) and (1, −4) **$\frac{7}{2}$**
9. (−2, 4) and (1, 1) **−1**

10. The table shows how much money Andy and Margie made working at the concession stand at a baseball game one weekend. Use the data to make a graph. Find the slope of the line and explain what it shows.
    The slope of the line is $\frac{15}{2}$ or 7.5. This means that for every hour they work, they earn $7.50.

Time (hr)	Money Earned
2	$15
4	$30
6	$45
8	$60

LESSON 12-3

Find the x-intercept and y-intercept of each line. Use the intercepts to graph the equation. For 11–14, see p. Axx.

11. $5x - 3y = 8$ **$\left(\frac{8}{5}, 0\right)$; $\left(0, -\frac{8}{3}\right)$**
12. $3y - x = 9$ **(−9, 0); (0, 3)**
13. $7x + 1 = 4y$ **$\left(-\frac{1}{7}, 0\right)$; $\left(0, \frac{1}{4}\right)$**
14. $3y + x = 5$ **(5, 0); $\left(0, \frac{5}{3}\right)$**

Write each equation in slope-intercept form, and then find the slope and y-intercept.

15. $3x = y$ **y = 3x; m = 3; b = 0**
16. $3y = 5x$ **$y = \frac{5}{3}x$; $m = \frac{5}{3}$; b = 0**
17. $5x - y = 8$ **y = 5x − 8; m = 5; b = −8**
18. $6y + 7 = 2x$ **$y = \frac{1}{3}x - \frac{7}{6}$; $m = \frac{1}{3}$; $b = -\frac{7}{6}$**

Write the equation of the line that passes through each pair of points in slope-intercept form.

19. (5, −1) and (−7, −4) **$y = \frac{1}{4}x - \frac{9}{4}$**
20. (5, 1) and (−1, −5) **y = x − 4**
21. (4, 9) and (−5, 3) **$y = \frac{2}{3}x + \frac{19}{3}$**

LESSON 12-4

Use the point-slope form of each equation to identify a point the line passes through and the slope of the line. 22–27, possible points given.

22. $y - 2 = \frac{1}{3}(x + 1)$ **(−1, 2); $m = \frac{1}{3}$**
23. $y + 3 = -3(x - 2)$ **(2, −3); m = −3**
24. $y - 4 = -\frac{1}{3}(x - 5)$ **(5, 4); $m = -\frac{1}{3}$**
25. $y + 5 = 2(x - 1)$ **(1, −5); m = 2**
26. $y - 2 = \frac{4}{3}(x + 5)$ **(−5, 2); $m = \frac{4}{3}$**
27. $y = -\frac{3}{4}(x - 4)$ **(4, 0); $m = -\frac{3}{4}$**

Write the point-slope form of the equation with the given slope that passes through the indicated point.

28. the line with slope 2 passing through (1, 4) **y − 4 = 2(x − 1)**
29. the line with slope $\frac{1}{4}$ passing through (−3, 2) **$y - 2 = -\frac{1}{4}(x + 3)$**

Extra Practice ▪ Chapter 12

LESSON 12-5

Determine whether the data sets show direct variation.

30.

Weight of Patient	Medication Prescribed (mg)
100	50
120	60
140	70
160	80

yes

31.

Cost of Item	Shipping and Handling
$10.80	$2
$27.82	$4
$43.20	$5
$55.00	$6

no

Find each equation of direct variation, given that y varies directly with x.

32. y is 24 when x is 8. **y = 3x**
33. y is 18 when x is 12. **$y = \frac{3}{2}x$**
34. y is 96 when x is 3. **y = 32x**
35. y is 8 when x is 4. **y = 2x**
36. y is 102 when x is 17. **y = 6x**
37. y is 17 when x is 6. **$y = \frac{17}{6}x$**

38. Instructions for a chemical concentrate swimming pool cleaner state that 2 ounces of concentrate should be added to every $1\frac{1}{2}$ gallons of water used. How many ounces of concentrate should be added to 18 gallons of water? **$c = \frac{4}{3}w$; 24 ounces**

39. The distance d an object falls varies directly with the square of the time t of the fall. This is expressed by the formula $d = k \cdot t^2$. An object falls 90 feet in 3 seconds. How far will the object fall in 15 seconds? **2250 ft**

LESSON 12-6

Graph each inequality. For 40–48, see p. Axx.

40. $y \leq x - 3$
41. $y > x + 3$
42. $6x - 3y \geq 9$
43. $4y - 12 < 2x$
44. $3y - 9x < 15$
45. $3y + 9 > 5x$
46. $x - 5y < 2$
47. $-2y \geq x - 3$

48. A teacher needs to buy no more than 20 pens. Pens come in packages of 4 or 5. Write and graph an inequality showing the number of 4-pen and 5-pen packages the teacher can buy. **$4x + 5y \leq 20$**

LESSON 12-7

Plot the data and find a line of best fit. For 49–50, see p. Axx.

49.

x	6	4	8	5	1	7	2	3
y	5	3	6	2	2	5	1	4

$y = \frac{5}{7}x + \frac{2}{7}$

50. Find a line of best fit for the men's Olympic winning times in the 50-meter freestyle. Use the equation of the line to predict what the winning time will be in 2068. Is it reasonable to make this prediction? Explain.
    $y = -0.01x + 22.09$; 21.29 s; Possible answer: Yes, it is reasonable that in 2068 the time may have improved by 0.64 seconds since 2004.

Year	1988	1992	1996	2000	2004
Winning Time (s)	22.14	21.94	22.13	21.98	21.93

LESSON 13-1

Determine if each sequence could be arithmetic. If so, give the common difference.

1. 213, 204, 195, 186, 177, 168, . . .   yes; −9   **2.** 13, 24, 36, 49, 63, 78, . . .   no

3. 16.5, 16.9, 17.3, 17.7, 18.1, . . .   yes; 0.4   **4.** 151, 156, 160, 165, 169, 174, . . .   no

Find the given term in each arithmetic sequence.

5. 15th term: 8, 16, 24, 32, . . .   120   **6.** 25th term: 100, 97, 94, 91, . . .   28

7. 17th term: 53, 44, 35, 26, . . .   −91   **8.** 41st term: 841, 828, 815, 802, . . .   321

9. Meka received 2000 frequent flier miles when she applied for a credit card. For every $1000 she spends, she will receive 500 more miles. How much does she have to spend to have 5000 miles? $n = 7$; she will have to spend $(n − 1)\$1000$, or $6 \times \$1000$ ($6000), to reach 5000 miles.

LESSON 13-2

Determine if each sequence could be geometric. If so, give the common ratio.

10. 8192, 4096, 2048, 1024, 512, 256, . . .   yes; $\frac{1}{2}$ **11.** 1, 9, 81, 729, 6561, 59,049, . . .   yes; 9

12. 4, 8, 24, 120, 720, 5040, . . .   no   **13.** 13, 39, 117, 351, 1053, 3159, . . .   yes; 3

Find the given term in each geometric sequence.

14. 11th term: −5, 5, −5, 5, . . .   −5   **15.** 44th term: 2, 4, 8, 16, . . .   17,592,186,044,416

16. 8th term: 236, 118, 59, 29.5, . . .   1.84375   **17.** 20th term: 2, 6, 18, 54, . . .   2,324,522,934

18. The oil from a 12,000-gallon oil tank leaks at a rate of 6% per hour after being cracked in an accident. If the tank is not repaired, how many gallons of oil will be left after 6 hours?   8278 gallons

LESSON 13-3

Use first and second differences to find the next three terms in each sequence.

19. 11, 18, 30, 47, 69, 96, . . .   128, 165, 207   **20.** 15, 22, 32, 45, 61, 80, . . .   102, 127, 155

21. 10.5, 15.25, 20.75, 27, 34, 41.75, . . .   50.25, 59.5, 69.5   **22.** 6, 11, 17, 25, 36, 51, . . .   71, 97, 130

23. 217, 231, 246, 262, 279, 297, . . .   316, 336, 357   **24.** 47, 52, 57.5, 64, 72, 82, . . .   94.5, 110, 129

Give the next three terms in each sequence using the simplest rule you can find.

25. 1, 3, 5, 7, 9, . . .   11, 13, 15   **26.** 1, $\frac{1}{3}$, $\frac{1}{6}$, $\frac{1}{9}$, $\frac{1}{12}$, $\frac{1}{15}$, . . . $\frac{1}{18}$, $\frac{1}{21}$, $\frac{1}{24}$ **27.** 4, 7, 10, 13, 16, . . .   19, 22, 25

Find the first five terms of each sequence defined by the given rule.

28. $a_n = \frac{n}{n+1}$ $\frac{1}{2}, \frac{2}{3}, \frac{3}{4}, \frac{4}{5}, \frac{5}{6}$ **29.** $a_n = n(n+2)$ 3, 8, 15, 24, 35   **30.** $a_n = n(n−1) + 3n$ 3, 8, 15, 24, 35

31. $a_n = 3n\left(\frac{1}{n}\right)$ 3, 3, 3, 3, 3   **32.** $a_n = 6n$ 6, 12, 18, 24, 30   **33.** $a_n = \left(\frac{n}{n+2}\right)n$ $\frac{1}{3}, 1, \frac{9}{5}, \frac{8}{3}, \frac{25}{7}$

LESSON 13-4

Determine whether each function is linear.

34. $f(x) = −\frac{1}{x} + 4$ not linear   **35.** $f(x) = 6^x + 2$ not linear   **36.** $f(x) = \frac{2}{3}x$ linear

37. $f(x) = 3x^{−5}$ not linear   **38.** $f(x) = 0.5x + 8$ linear   **39.** $f(x) = 9$ linear

Write a rule for each linear function.

40.

$f(x) = \frac{x}{2} + 3$

41.

x	y
−2	−5
−1	−3
0	−1
1	1
2	3

$f(x) = 2x − 1$

42.

x	y
−2	4
−1	3
0	2
1	1
2	0

$f(x) = 2 − x$

43. Reo's cell phone company charges a monthly fee of $12, plus $0.10 each minute that he talks on the phone. Find a rule for the linear function that describes the monthly phone charges if Reo uses his phone x hours in a month, and use it to find how much he pays if he talks 72 minutes in a month. $f(x) = \$12 + \$0.10x$; $19.20

LESSON 13-5   For 44–47, see p. Axx.

Create a table for each exponential function, and use it to graph the function.

44. $f(x) = 2 \cdot 3^x$ **45.** $f(x) = \frac{1}{4} \cdot 5^x$ **46.** $f(x) = 0.25 \cdot 3^x$ **47.** $f(x) = 3 \cdot 11^x$

48. The isotope cobalt-60, found in radioactive waste, has a half-life of 5 years. Predict how much of a 275 g sample of cobalt-60 would remain after 40 years.   1.07422 g

LESSON 13-6   For 49–51, see p. Axx.

Create a table for each quadratic function, and use it graph the function.

49. $f(x) = x^2 − 2$ **50.** $f(x) = x^2 − x + 8$ **51.** $f(x) = (x − 2)(x + 3)$

52. The Taipei 101 skyscraper is 508 meters tall. The tallest occupied floor is 438 meters from the ground. The function $f(t) = −16t^2 + h$ gives the time t in seconds for an object to fall from height h. About how long would it take an object to fall from the tallest occupied floor in the Taipei 101 skyscraper?   ≈ 5.23 s

LESSON 13-7   For 54–57, see p. Axx.

Determine whether the relationship is an inverse variation.

53. The table shows the number of trading cards a shop has listed at given prices.

Quantity of Trading Card	24,000	10,000	750	480	150
List Value ($)	0.50	1.20	16.00	25.00	80.00

yes

Create a table. Then graph each inverse variation function.

54. $f(x) = \frac{4}{x}$ **55.** $f(x) = \frac{−1.5}{x}$ **56.** $f(x) = \frac{5}{4x}$ **57.** $f(x) = \frac{1}{2}x$

LESSON 14-1

Determine whether each expression is a monomial.

1. $\frac{1}{4}r^2st^5$ yes   **2.** $−6xy^3$ yes   **3.** 2^yx^4 no   **4.** $\frac{3m^3}{n^5}$ no

Classify each expression as a monomial, a binomial, a trinomial, or not a polynomial.

5. $−4x^3 + x^2 + \frac{1}{4}$ trinomial   **6.** $−9x^5y^2z^4$ monomial   **7.** $\frac{4}{5}m^4n^3 + m^3$ binomial   **8.** $h − 2h^{0.5} + 1$ not a polynomial

9. $xw^7 − 7wz$ binomial   **10.** $−\frac{3}{z^4}$ not a polynomial   **11.** $\frac{2}{3}a^4 + a^3 − 5$ trinomial   **12.** $13st^6$ monomial

Find the degree of each polynomial.

13. $3x^3 + 4x^2 + 8$ 5   **14.** $b^2 − 9b^3 − b^4 − 8$ 4   **15.** $4 − t$ 1   **16.** $z^2 + 5z^6 − 9z^3$ 6

17. The trinomial $−16t^2 + vt + 12$ describes the height in feet of a baseball thrown straight up at a velocity of v ft/s from a 12-foot platform after t seconds. Find the height of the ball after 3 seconds if $v = 55$ ft/s.   33 ft

18. The trinomial $−4x^2 + 270x − 2000$ gives the net profit, in dollars, that a custom bicycle manufacturer earns by selling x bikes in a given month. Find the net profit for a month if $x = 15$ bicycles.

LESSON 14-2

Identify the like terms in each polynomial.

19. $−s − 5r^2 + 7r − 9r^2 + 3s$ −s and 3s, −5r² and −9r²   **20.** $4x^2 − 9 − 7x + x^5 + 10$ −9 and 10

21. $5x^2y − 7x^2z + 7yz^2 − 3x^2y + xz^2$ 5x²y and −3x²y   **22.** $−3mn + 3p^2 + 3p − 5p^2 + 3mn$ −3mn and 3mn, 3p² and −5p²

23. $8s^2 + 6 − 7s + 6s^4 − 13$ 6 and −13   **24.** $25 + 15xy − 10x^2 + 3xy − 5y^2 − 5$ 25 and −5, 15xy and 3xy

Simplify.

25. $5z^2 + 2z − z^2 + 11z − 9$ 4z² + 13z − 9   **26.** $5 − 7(a^2 − 9) + 3a^2 − 7$ −4a² + 61

27. $−y^2z + 8xz − 6xy^2 + 10y^2z + xy^2$ −5xy² + 8xz + 9y²z   **28.** $5c^2 + 11cd − d^2 − 5(c^2 − d^2)$ −2c(c + d)

29. $5(a^2b^2 + 3ab) + 3(ab^2 − 5ab)$ 5a²b² + 3ab²   **30.** $2s^2t^2 + st^2 + 5s^2t^2 − 7s^2t − 3st^2 + s^2t$ 7s²t² − 2st² − 6s²t

31. A rectangle has a width of 12 cm and a length of $(2x^2 + 6)$ cm. The area is given by the expression $12(2x^2 + 6)$ cm². Use the Distributive Property to write an equivalent expression.   24x² + 72

32. A parallelogram has a base of $(3x^2 − 4)$ in. and a height of 4 in. The area is given by the expression $4(3x^2 − 4)$ in². Use the Distributive Property to write an equivalent expression.   12x² − 16

LESSON 14-3

Add. $−5x^3y^2 + 3x^2y^3 + 4xy$ $3a^2 − 3ab^2 + 2b^2$

33. $(2x^2y^3 − 7x^3y^2 + xy) + (x^2y^3 + 2x^3y^2 + 3xy)$ **34.** $(3a^2 + 4ab^2) + (a^2b + 2b^2) + (−a^2b − 7ab^2)$

35. $(m^3 + 3m^2n^2 + 4) + (6m^2n^2 − 9)$ m³ + 9m²n² − 5   **36.** $(10r^3s^2 − 7r^2s + 4r) + (−4r^3s^2 + 3r)$ 6r³s² − 7r²s + 7r

37. A rectangle has a width of $(x − 7)$ cm and a length of $(3x + 5)$ cm. An equilateral triangle has sides of length $x^2 − 2x + 3$. Write an expression for the sum of the perimeters of the rectangle and the triangle.   3x² + 2x + 5

LESSON 14-4

Find the opposite of each polynomial.

38. $−6xy − 2y^3$ 6xy + 2y³   **39.** $4a^3b + 7ab − 8$ −4a³b − 7ab + 8

40. $−2x^6 − 3x + x^3$ 2x⁶ + 3x − x³   **41.** $7g^5 + gh^4$ −7g⁵ − gh⁴

Subtract. $2x^2 + 2xy − 5y^2 + 8$

42. $(5x^2 + 2xy − 3y^2) − (3x^2 + 2y^2 − 8)$ **43.** $14a − (5a^3 − 3a + 6)$ −5a³ + 17a − 6

44. $(5r^2s^2 + 9r^2s + rs) − (−3r^2s − 7rs + 2r^2)$ 5r²s² + 12r²s + 8rs − 2r²   **45.** $(12y^3 − 6xy + 1) − (8xy − 2x + 1)$ 12y³ − 14xy + 2x

46. The area of the larger rectangle is $10x^2 − 2x + 15$ cm². The area of the smaller rectangle is $5x^2 − 3x$ cm². What is the area of the shaded region?   5x² + x + 15 cm²

LESSON 14-5

Multiply.

47. $(5xy^2)(7x^3y^2)$ 35x⁴y⁴   **48.** $(2a^2bc^2)(−5a^3b^2)$ −10a⁵b³c²

49. $(6m^3n^4)(2mn)$ 12m⁴n⁵   **50.** $6r(9s − 5t)$ 54st − 30r²

51. $−p(2p^2 + pq − 5)$ −2p³ − p²q + 5p   **52.** $3xy^2(2x^3y^2 + 4x^2y − xy^6 − 11xy)$ 6x⁴y⁴ + 12x³y³ − 3x²y⁸ − 33x²y³

53. A rectangle has a width of $3x^2y$ ft and a length of $2x^2 + 4xy + 7$ ft. Write and simplify an expression for the area of the rectangle. Then find the area of the rectangle if $x = 2$ and $y = 3$.   6x⁴y + 12x³y² + 21x²y + 24x²y²; 1404 ft²

LESSON 14-6

Multiply. $y^2 + 2y − 15$ $s^2 − 2s − 15$ $12m^2 − m − 6$

54. $(y + 5)(y − 3)$ **55.** $(s + 3)(s − 5)$ **56.** $(3m + 2)(4m − 3)$

57. $(y + 1)^2$ **58.** $(d − 5)^2$ **59.** $(a + 9)(a − 9)$

y² + 2y + 1   d² − 10d + 25   a² − 81

Problem Solving Handbook

Draw a Diagram

When problems involve objects, distances, or places, drawing a diagram can make the problem clearer. You **can draw a diagram** to help understand the problem and to solve the problem.

Problem Solving Strategies

Draw a Diagram | Make a Table
Make a Model | Solve a Simpler Problem
Guess and Test | Use Logical Reasoning
Work Backward | Use a Venn Diagram
Find a Pattern | Make an Organized List

June is moving her cat, dog, and goldfish to her new apartment. She can only take 1 pet with her on each trip. She cannot leave the cat and the dog or the cat and the goldfish alone together. How can she get all of her pets safely to her new apartment?

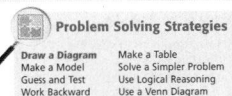

Understand the Problem

The answer will be the description of the trips to her new apartment. At no time can the cat be alone with the dog or the goldfish.

Make a Plan

Draw a diagram to represent each trip to and from the apartment.

Solve

In the beginning, the cat, dog, and goldfish are all at her old apartment.

Old Apartment		New Apartment	
June, Cat, Dog, Fish	June, Cat →	June, Cat	Trip 1: She takes the cat and returns alone.
June, Dog, Fish	← June	Cat	
June, Dog, Fish	June, Dog →	June, Dog, Cat	Trip 2: She takes the dog and returns with the cat.
June, Cat, Fish	← June, Cat	Dog	
June, Cat, Fish	June, Fish →	June, Dog, Fish	Trip 3: She takes the fish and returns alone.
June, Cat	← June	Dog, Fish	
June, Cat	June, Cat →	June, Cat, Dog, Fish	Trip 4: She takes the cat.

Look Back

Check to make sure that the cat is never alone with either the fish or the dog.

PRACTICE

1. There are 8 flags evenly spaced around a circular track. It takes Ling 15 s to run from the first flag to the third flag. At this pace, how long will it take her to run around the track twice? **120 s, or 2 min**

2. A frog is climbing a 22-foot tree. Every 5 minutes, it climbs up 3 feet, but slips back down 1 foot. How long will it take it to climb the tree? **55 min**

810 *Problem Solving Handbook*

Make a Model

A problem that involves objects may be solved by making a model out of similar items. **Make a model** to help you understand the problem and find the solution.

Problem Solving Strategies

Draw a Diagram | Make a Table
Make a Model | Solve a Simpler Problem
Guess and Test | Use Logical Reasoning
Work Backward | Use a Venn Diagram
Find a Pattern | Make an Organized List

The volume of a rectangular prism can be found by using the formula $V = \ell wh$, where ℓ is the length, w is the width, and h is the height of the prism. Find all possible rectangular prisms with a volume of 16 cubic units and dimensions that are all whole numbers.

Understand the Problem

You need to find the different possible prisms. The length, width, and height will be whole numbers whose product is 16.

Make a Plan

You can use unit cubes to make a model of every possible rectangular prism. Work in a systematic way to find all possible answers.

Solve

Begin with a $16 \times 1 \times 1$ prism.

$16 \times 1 \times 1$

Keeping the height of the prism the same, explore what happens to the length as you change the width. Then try a height of 2. Notice that an $8 \times 2 \times 1$ prism is the same as an $8 \times 1 \times 2$ prism turned on its side.

$8 \times 2 \times 1$ Not a rectangular prism $4 \times 4 \times 1$ $4 \times 2 \times 2$

The possible dimensions are $16 \times 1 \times 1$, $8 \times 2 \times 1$, $4 \times 4 \times 1$, and $4 \times 2 \times 2$.

Look Back

The product of the length, width, and height must be 16. Look at the prime factorization of the volume: $16 = 2 \cdot 2 \cdot 2 \cdot 2$. Possible dimensions:

$1 \cdot 1 \cdot (2 \cdot 2 \cdot 2 \cdot 2) = 1 \cdot 1 \cdot 16$ $1 \cdot 2 \cdot (2 \cdot 2 \cdot 2) = 1 \cdot 2 \cdot 8$

$1 \cdot (2 \cdot 2) \cdot (2 \cdot 2) = 1 \cdot 4 \cdot 4$ $2 \cdot 2 \cdot (2 \cdot 2) = 2 \cdot 2 \cdot 4$

PRACTICE

2. Isosceles triangle, parallelogram, rectangle, kite, and other shapes

1. Four unit squares are arranged so that each square shares a side with another square. How many different arrangements are possible? **7**

2. Four triangles are formed by cutting a rectangle along its diagonals. What possible shapes can be formed by arranging these triangles?

Problem Solving Handbook 811

Guess and Test

When you think that guessing may help you solve a problem, you can use **guess and test**. Using clues to make guesses can narrow your choices for the solution. Test whether your guess solves the problem, and continue guessing until you find the solution.

Problem Solving Strategies

Draw a Diagram | Make a Table
Make a Model | Solve a Simpler Problem
Guess and Test | Use Logical Reasoning
Work Backward | Use a Venn Diagram
Find a Pattern | Make an Organized List

North Middle School is planning to raise $1200 by sponsoring a car wash. They are going to charge $4 for each car and $8 for each minivan. How many vehicles would have to be washed to raise $1200 if they plan to wash twice as many cars as minivans?

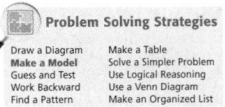

Understand the Problem

You must determine the number of cars and the number of minivans that need to be washed to make $1200. You know the charge for each vehicle.

Make a Plan

You can **guess and test** to find the number of cars and minivans. Guess the number of cars, and then divide it by 2 to find the number of minivans.

Solve

You can organize your guesses in a table.

	Cars	Minivans	Money Raised	
First guess	200	100	$4(200) + $8(100) = $1600	Too high
Second guess	100	50	$4(100) + $8(50) = $800	Too low
Third guess	150	75	$4(150) + $8(75) = $1200	

They should wash 150 cars and 75 minivans, or 225 vehicles.

Look Back

The total raised is $4(150) + $8(75) = $1200, and the number of cars is twice the number of minivans. The answer is reasonable.

PRACTICE

1. At a baseball game, adult tickets cost $15 and children's tickets cost $8. Twice as many children attended as adults, and the total ticket sales were $2480. How many people attended the game? **80 adults and 160 children = 240 people**

2. Angie is making friendship bracelets and pins. It takes her 6 minutes to make a bracelet and 4 minutes to make a pin. If she wants to make three times as many pins as bracelets, how many pins and bracelets can she make in 3 hours? **30 pins and 10 bracelets**

812 *Problem Solving Handbook*

Work Backward

To solve a problem that asks for an initial value that follows a series of steps, you may want to **work backward**.

Problem Solving Strategies

Draw a Diagram | Make a Table
Make a Model | Solve a Simpler Problem
Guess and Test | Use Logical Reasoning
Work Backward | Use a Venn Diagram
Find a Pattern | Make an Organized List

Tyrone has two clocks and a watch. If the power goes off during the day, the following happens:

- Clock A stops and then continues when the power comes back on.
- Clock B stops and then resets to 12:00 A.M. when the power comes back on.

When Tyrone gets home, his watch reads 4:27 P.M., clock B reads 5:21 A.M., and clock A reads 3:39 P.M. What time did the power go off, and for how long was it off?

Understand the Problem

You need to find the time that the power went off and how long it was off. You know how each clock works.

Make a Plan

Work backward to the time that the power went off. Subtract from the correct time of 4:27, the time on Tyrone's watch.

Solve

The difference between the correct time and the time on clock A is the length of time the power was off.

4:27 – 3:39 = 0:48 *The power was off for 48 minutes.*

Clock B reset to 12:00 when the power went on.

5:21 – 12:00 = 5:21 *The power came on 5 hours and 21 minutes ago.*

Subtract 5:21 from the correct time to find when the power came on.

4:27 – 5:21 = 11:06 *The power came on at 11:06 A.M.*

Subtract 48 minutes from 11:06 to find when the power went off.

11:06 – 0:48 = 10:18

The power went off at 10:18 A.M. and was off for 48 minutes.

Look Back

If the power went off at about 10 A.M. for about an hour, it would come on at about 11 A.M., and each clock would run for about $5\frac{1}{2}$ hours.

PRACTICE

1. Jackie is 4 years younger than Roger. Roger is $2\frac{1}{2}$ years older than Jade. Jade is 14 years old. How old is Jackie? **$12\frac{1}{2}$ years old**

2. Becca is directing a play that starts at 8:15 P.M. She wants the cast ready 10 minutes before the play starts. The cast needs 45 minutes to put on make-up, 15 minutes for a director's meeting, and then 35 minutes to get in costume. What time should the cast arrive? **6:30 P.M.**

Problem Solving Handbook 813

Find a Pattern

If a problem involves numbers, shapes, or even codes, noticing a pattern can often help you solve it. To solve a problem that involves patterns, you need to use small steps that will help you **find a pattern**.

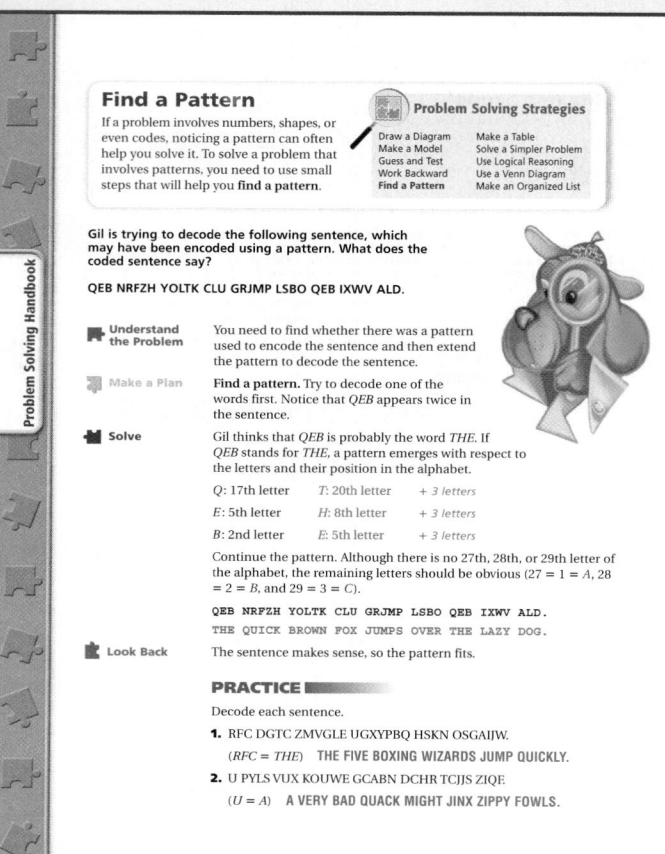

Problem Solving Strategies

Draw a Diagram   Make a Table
Make a Model   Solve a Simpler Problem
Guess and Test   Use Logical Reasoning
Work Backward   Use a Venn Diagram
Find a Pattern   Make an Organized List

Gil is trying to decode the following sentence, which may have been encoded using a pattern. What does the coded sentence say?

QEB NRFZH YOLTK CLU GRJMP LSBO QEB IXWV ALD.

Understand the Problem
You need to find whether there was a pattern used to encode the sentence and then extend the pattern to decode the sentence.

Make a Plan
Find a pattern. Try to decode one of the words first. Notice that *QEB* appears twice in the sentence.

Solve
Gil thinks that *QEB* is probably the word *THE*. If *QEB* stands for *THE*, a pattern emerges with respect to the letters and their position in the alphabet.

Q: 17th letter   T: 20th letter   + 3 letters
E: 5th letter   H: 8th letter   + 3 letters
B: 2nd letter   E: 5th letter   + 3 letters

Continue the pattern. Although there is no 27th, 28th, or 29th letter of the alphabet, the remaining letters should be obvious (27 − 1 = A, 28 − 2 = B, and 29 − 3 = C).

QEB NRFZH YOLTK CLU GRJMP LSBO QEB IXWV ALD.
THE QUICK BROWN FOX JUMPS OVER THE LAZY DOG.

Look Back
The sentence makes sense, so the pattern fits.

PRACTICE

Decode each sentence.

1. RFC DGTC ZMVGLE UGXYPBQ HSKN OSGAIJW.
   (*RFC = THE*)   THE FIVE BOXING WIZARDS JUMP QUICKLY.

2. U PYLS VUX KOUWE GCABN DCHR TCJJS ZIQE
   (*U = A*)   A VERY BAD QUACK MIGHT JINX ZIPPY FOWLS.

814   *Problem Solving Handbook*

Make a Table

To solve a problem that involves a relationship between two sets of numbers, you can **make a table**. A table can be used to organize data so that you can look at relationships and find the solution.

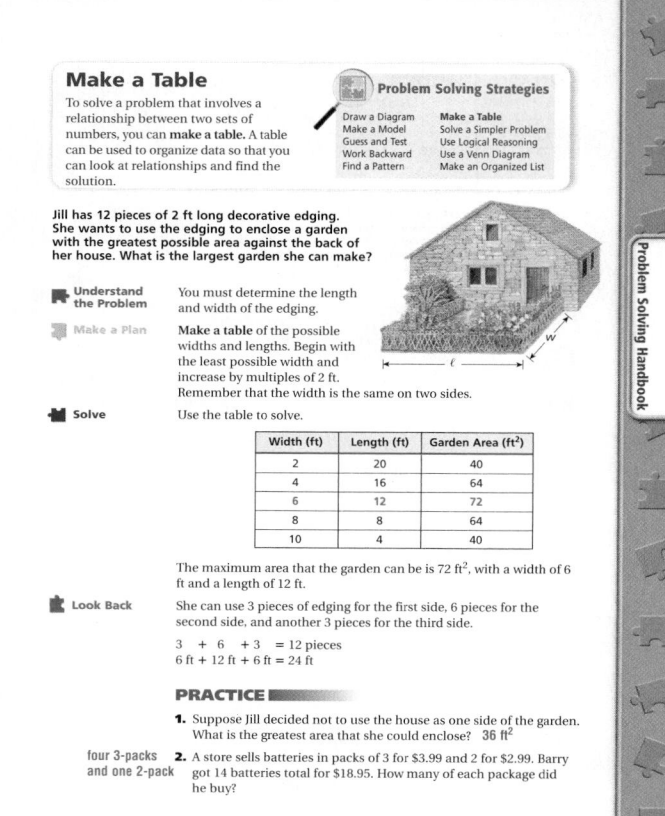

Problem Solving Strategies

Draw a Diagram   **Make a Table**
Make a Model   Solve a Simpler Problem
Guess and Test   Use Logical Reasoning
Work Backward   Use a Venn Diagram
Find a Pattern   Make an Organized List

Jill has 12 pieces of 2 ft long decorative edging. She wants to use the edging to enclose a garden with the greatest possible area against the back of her house. What is the largest garden she can make?

Understand the Problem
You must determine the length and width of the edging.

Make a Plan
Make a table of the possible widths and lengths. Begin with the least possible width and increase by multiples of 2 ft. Remember that the width is the same on two sides.

Solve
Use the table to solve.

Width (ft)	Length (ft)	Garden Area (ft²)
2	20	40
4	16	64
6	12	72
8	8	64
10	4	40

The maximum area that the garden can be is 72 ft², with a width of 6 ft and a length of 12 ft.

Look Back
She can use 3 pieces of edging for the first side, 6 pieces for the second side, and another 3 pieces for the third side.

3 + 6 + 3 = 12 pieces
6 ft + 12 ft + 6 ft = 24 ft

PRACTICE

1. Suppose Jill decided not to use the house as one side of the garden. What is the greatest area that she could enclose?   36 ft²

four 3-packs and one 2-pack
2. A store sells batteries in packs of 3 for $3.99 and 2 for $2.99. Barry got 14 batteries total for $18.95. How many of each package did he buy?

Problem Solving Handbook   815

Solve a Simpler Problem

If a problem contains large numbers or requires many steps, try to **solve a simpler problem** first. Look for similarities between the problems, and use them to solve the original problem.

Problem Solving Strategies

Draw a Diagram   Make a Table
Make a Model   **Solve a Simpler Problem**
Guess and Test   Use Logical Reasoning
Work Backward   Use a Venn Diagram
Find a Pattern   Make an Organized List

Noemi heard that 10 computers in her school would be connected to each other. She thought that there would be a cable connecting each computer to every other computer. How many cables would be needed if this were true?

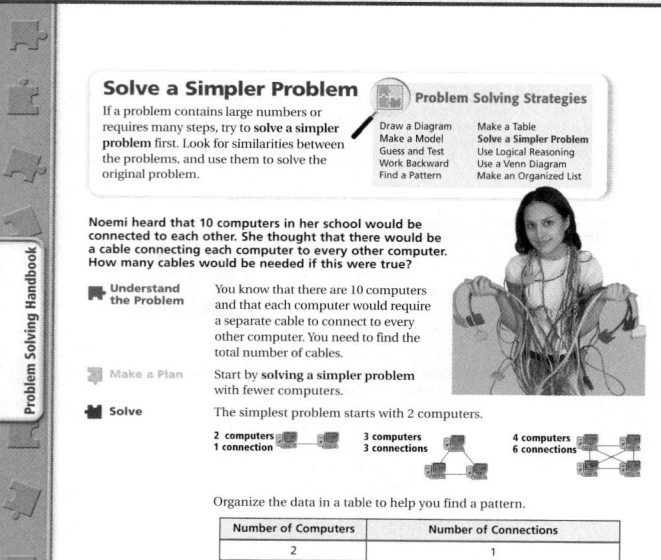

Understand the Problem
You know that there are 10 computers and that each computer would require a separate cable to connect to every other computer. You need to find the total number of cables.

Make a Plan
Start by **solving a simpler problem** with fewer computers.

Solve
The simplest problem starts with 2 computers.

2 computers   3 computers   4 computers
1 connection   3 connections   6 connections

Organize the data in a table to help you find a pattern.

Number of Computers	Number of Connections
2	1
3	1 + 2 = 3
4	1 + 2 + 3 = 6
5	1 + 2 + 3 + 4 = 10
10	1 + 2 + 3 + 4 + 5 + 6 + 7 + 8 + 9 = 45

So if a separate cable were needed to connect each of 10 computers to every other one, 45 cables would be required.

Look Back
Extend the number of computers to check that the pattern continues.

PRACTICE

1. A banquet table seats 2 people on each side and 1 at each end. If 6 tables are placed end to end, how many seats can there be?   26

2. How many diagonals are there in a dodecagon (a 12-sided polygon)?   54

816   *Problem Solving Handbook*

Use Logical Reasoning

Sometimes a problem may provide clues and facts to help you find a solution. You can **use logical reasoning** to help solve this kind of problem.

Problem Solving Strategies

Draw a Diagram   Make a Table
Make a Model   Solve a Simpler Problem
Guess and Test   **Use Logical Reasoning**
Work Backward   Use a Venn Diagram
Find a Pattern   Make an Organized List

Kim, Lily, and Suki take ballet, tap, and jazz classes (but not in that order). Kim is the sister of the person who takes ballet. Lily takes tap.

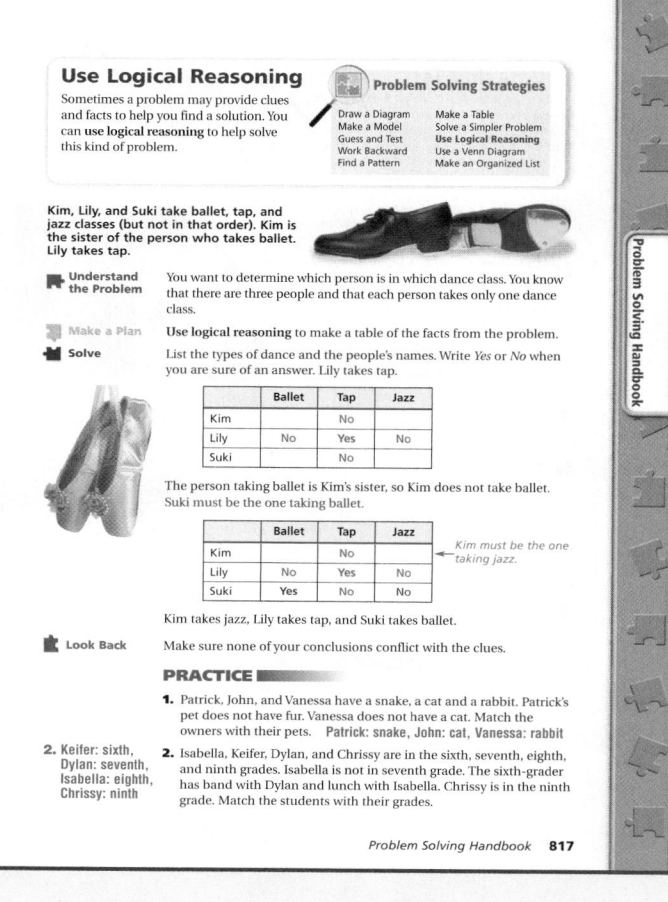

Understand the Problem
You want to determine which person is in which dance class. You know that there are three people and that each person takes only one dance class.

Make a Plan
Use logical reasoning to make a table of the facts from the problem.

Solve
List the types of dance and the people's names. Write *Yes* or *No* when you are sure of an answer. Lily takes tap.

	Ballet	Tap	Jazz
Kim		No	
Lily	No	Yes	No
Suki		No	

The person taking ballet is Kim's sister, so Kim does not take ballet. Suki must be the one taking ballet.

	Ballet	Tap	Jazz
Kim	No	No	
Lily	No	Yes	No
Suki	Yes	No	No

Kim must be the one taking jazz.

Kim takes jazz, Lily takes tap, and Suki takes ballet.

Look Back
Make sure none of your conclusions conflict with the clues.

PRACTICE

1. Patrick, John, and Vanessa have a snake, a cat and a rabbit. Patrick's pet does not have fur. Vanessa does not have a cat. Match the owners with their pets.   Patrick: snake, John: cat, Vanessa: rabbit

2. Keifer: sixth, Dylan: seventh, Isabella: eighth, Chrissy: ninth
2. Isabella, Keifer, Dylan, and Chrissy are in the sixth, seventh, eighth, and ninth grades. Isabella is not in seventh grade. The sixth-grader has band with Dylan and lunch with Isabella. Chrissy is in the ninth grade. Match the students with their grades.

Problem Solving Handbook   817

Act It Out

Some problems involve actions or processes. To solve these problems, you can **act it out**. Actively modeling the problem can help you find the solution.

Problem Solving Strategies

Draw a Diagram
Make a Model
Guess and Test
Work Backward
Find a Pattern

Make a Table
Solve a Simpler Problem
Use Logical Reasoning
Act It Out
Make an Organized List

Kyle and Jared are playing Rock-Paper-Scissors. For each round, the players show either a fist (rock), an open hand (paper), or two fingers (scissors). The friends play many rounds. In what percentage of the rounds should they expect to show matching hands?

Understand the Problem

List the important information.

- The two players can each show one of three things: rock, paper, or scissors.

The answer will be the percentage of rounds in which the players can expect to match.

Make a Plan

Act it out to list all the possible outcomes of a round. Find the fraction of outcomes that involve matching hands and then write the fraction as a percent.

Solve

Work with a partner. Take the roles of the players and work together to show all the possible outcomes for one round. Circle the outcomes in which the players match.

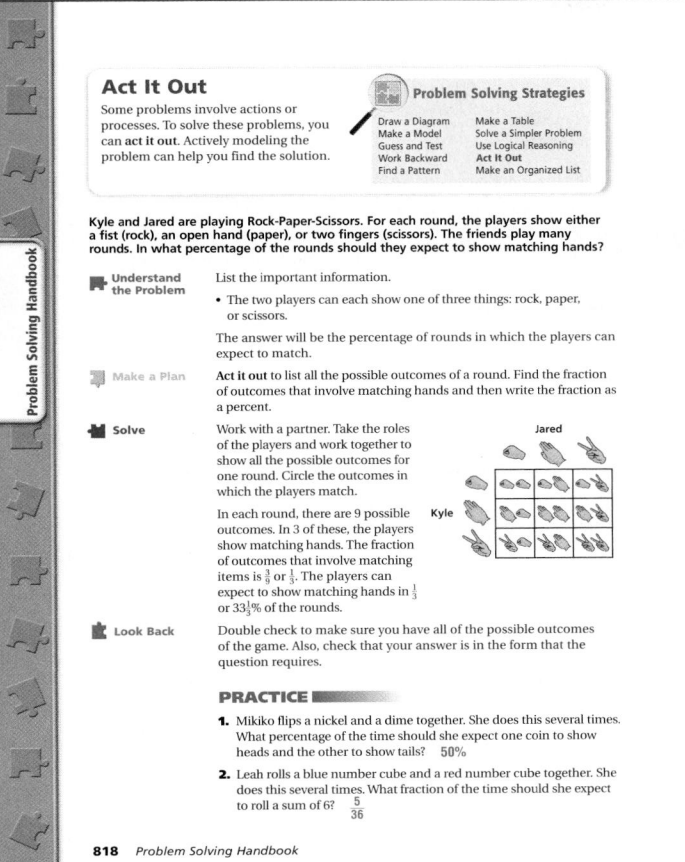

In each round, there are 9 possible outcomes. In 3 of these, the players show matching hands. The fraction of outcomes that involve matching items is $\frac{3}{9}$ or $\frac{1}{3}$. The players can expect to show matching hands in $\frac{1}{3}$ or $33\frac{1}{3}\%$ of the rounds.

Look Back

Double check to make sure you have all of the possible outcomes of the game. Also, check that your answer is in the form that the question requires.

PRACTICE

1. Mikiko flips a nickel and a dime together. She does this several times. What percentage of the time should she expect one coin to show heads and the other to show tails?   50%

2. Leah rolls a blue number cube and a red number cube together. She does this several times. What fraction of the time should she expect to roll a sum of 6? $\frac{5}{36}$

Make an Organized List

In some problems, you will need to find out exactly how many different ways an event can happen. When solving this kind of problem, it is often helpful to **make an organized list**. This will help you count all the possible outcomes.

Problem Solving Strategies

Draw a Diagram
Make a Model
Guess and Test
Work Backward
Find a Pattern

Make a Table
Solve a Simpler Problem
Use Logical Reasoning
Use a Venn Diagram
Make an Organized List

What is the greatest amount of money you can have in coins (quarters, dimes, nickels, and pennies) without being able to make change for a dollar?

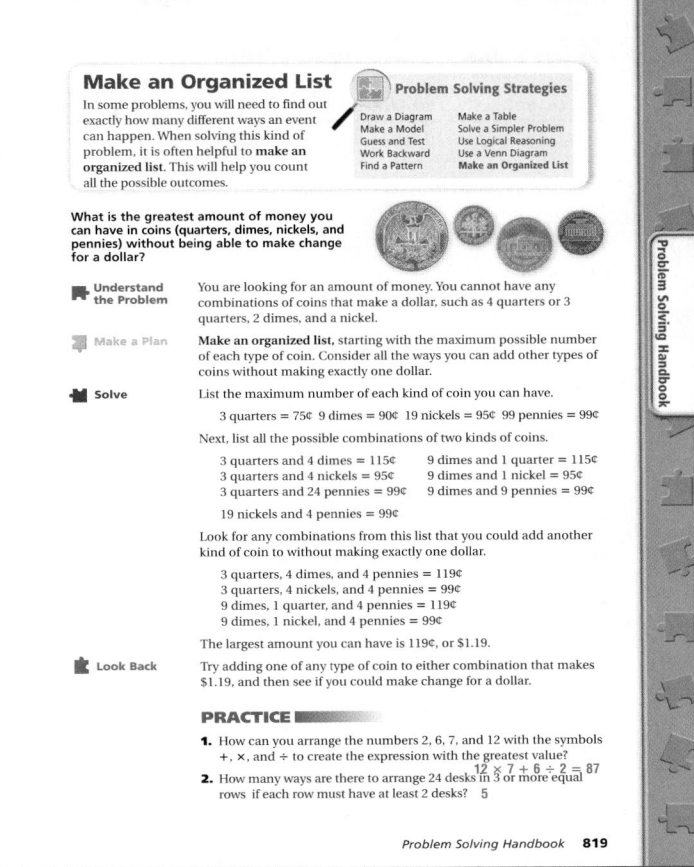

Understand the Problem

You are looking for an amount of money. You cannot have any combinations of coins that make a dollar, such as 4 quarters or 3 quarters, 2 dimes, and a nickel.

Make a Plan

Make an organized list, starting with the maximum possible number of each type of coin. Consider all the ways you can add other types of coins without making exactly one dollar.

Solve

List the maximum number of each kind of coin you can have.

3 quarters = 75¢   9 dimes = 90¢   19 nickels = 95¢   99 pennies = 99¢

Next, list all the possible combinations of two kinds of coins.

3 quarters and 4 dimes = 115¢   9 dimes and 1 quarter = 115¢
3 quarters and 4 nickels = 95¢   9 dimes and 1 nickel = 95¢
3 quarters and 24 pennies = 99¢   9 dimes and 9 pennies = 99¢
19 nickels and 4 pennies = 99¢

Look for any combinations from this list that you could add another kind of coin to without making exactly one dollar.

3 quarters, 4 dimes, and 4 pennies = 119¢
3 quarters, 4 nickels, and 4 pennies = 99¢
9 dimes, 1 quarter, and 4 pennies = 119¢
9 dimes, 1 nickel, and 4 pennies = 99¢

The largest amount you can have is 119¢, or $1.19.

Look Back

Try adding one of any type of coin to either combination that makes $1.19, and then see if you could make change for a dollar.

PRACTICE

1. How can you arrange the numbers 2, 6, 7, and 12 with the symbols +, ×, and ÷ to create the expression with the greatest value?
$12 \times 7 + 6 \div 2 = 87$

2. How many ways are there to arrange 24 desks in 3 or more equal rows if each row must have at least 2 desks?   5

Skills Bank

Skills Bank — Review Skills

Place Value to the Billions

A place-value chart can help you read and write numbers. The number 345,012,678,912.5784 (three hundred forty-five billion, twelve million, six hundred seventy-eight thousand, nine hundred twelve and five thousand seven hundred eighty-four ten-thousandths) is shown.

Billions	Millions	Thousands	Ones	Tenths	Hundredths	Thousandths	Ten-Thousandths
345,	012,	678,	912	5	7	8	4

EXAMPLE

Name the place value of the digit.

A the 7 in the thousands column
7 ⟶ ten thousands place

B the 0 in the millions column
0 ⟶ hundred millions place

C the 5 in the billions column
5 ⟶ one billion, or billions, place

D the 8 to the right of the decimal point
8 ⟶ thousandths

PRACTICE

Name the place value of the underlined digit.

1. 123,456,789,123.0594
2. 123,456,789,123.0594
3. 123,456,789,123.0594
4. 123,456,789,123.0594
5. 123,456,789,123.0594
6. 123,456,789,123.0594

1. hundred millions
2. ten billions
3. thousandths
4. ones
5. tenths
6. millions

Round Whole Numbers and Decimals

To round to a certain place, follow these steps.
1. Locate the digit in that place, and consider the next digit to the right.
2. If the digit to the right is 5 or greater, round up. Otherwise, round down.
3. Change each digit to the right of the rounding place to zero.

EXAMPLE

A Round 125,439.378 to the nearest thousand.
125,439.378 *Locate digit.*
The digit to the right is less than 5, so round down.
125,000.000 = 125,000

B Round 125,439.378 to the nearest tenth.
125,439.378 *Locate digit.*
The digit to the right is greater than 5, so round up.
125,439.400 = 125,539.4

PRACTICE

Round 259,345.278 to the place indicated.

1. hundred thousand
2. ten thousand
3. thousand
4. hundred

1. 300,000
2. 260,000
3. 259,000
4. 259,300

Long Division with Whole Numbers

You can use long division to divide large numbers.

EXAMPLE

Divide 8208 by 72.

```
     114
72)8208
    72↓       Place the first number under the long division symbol.
   ___        Subtract.
   100        Bring down the next digit.
    72↓       Subtract.
   ___        Bring down the next digit.
   288        Subtract.
   288
   ___
     0
```

PRACTICE

Divide.

1. 125)4125 33
2. 158)20,698 131
3. 268)4556 17
4. 39)3471 89
5. 99)4653 47
6. 321)38,841 121
7. 120)5040 42
8. 108)10,476 97
9. 741)107,445 145

Solve for a Variable

In the equation $y = 2x + 3$, the variable y is isolated because it is alone on one side of the equation. You can use inverse operations to rearrange an equation and isolate any variable. This is called **solving for a variable**.

EXAMPLE

Solve $m - t = 6$ for m.

$$m - t = 6$$
$$\underline{+ t \quad + t}$$
$$m = 6 + t$$

Since t is subtracted from m, add t to both sides of the equation to undo the subtraction.

PRACTICE

1. Solve $r + s = 120$ for r. $r = 120 - s$
2. Solve $\frac{x}{k} = 32$ for x. $x = 32k$
3. Solve $y = x + 5$ for x. $x = y - 5$
4. Solve $3m = n + 1$ for m. $m = \frac{n+1}{3}$
5. Solve $3s + 2 = t$ for s. $s = \frac{t-2}{3}$
6. Solve $4p - 2r = 0$ for p. $p = \frac{r}{2}$

Factors and Multiples

When two numbers are multiplied to form a third, the two numbers are said to be **factors** of the third number. **Multiples** of a number can be found by multiplying the number by 1, 2, 3, 4, and so on.

EXAMPLE

A List all the factors of 48.
$1 \cdot 48 = 48$, $2 \cdot 24 = 48$, $3 \cdot 16 = 48$, $4 \cdot 12 = 48$, and $6 \cdot 8 = 48$
So the factors of 48 are 1, 2, 3, 4, 6, 8, 12, 16, 24, and 48.

B Find the first five multiples of 3.
$3 \cdot 1 = 3$, $3 \cdot 2 = 6$, $3 \cdot 3 = 9$, $3 \cdot 4 = 12$, and $3 \cdot 5 = 15$
So the first five multiples of 3 are 3, 6, 9, 12, and 15.

PRACTICE

List all the factors of each number.

1. 8 1, 2, 4, 8
2. 20 1, 2, 4, 5, 10, 20
3. 9 1, 3, 9
4. 51 1, 3, 17, 51
5. 16 1, 2, 4, 8, 16
6. 27 1, 3, 9, 27

Write the first five multiples of each number.

7. 9 9, 18, 27, 36, 45
8. 10 10, 20, 30, 40, 50
9. 20 20, 40, 60, 80, 100
10. 15 15, 30, 45, 60, 75
11. 7 7, 14, 21, 28, 35
12. 18 18, 36, 54, 72, 90

Divisibility Rules

A number is divisible by another number if the division results in a remainder of 0. Some divisibility rules are shown below.

A number is divisible by . . .	Divisible	Not Divisible
2 if the last digit is an even number.	11,994	2,175
3 if the sum of the digits is divisible by 3.	216	79
4 if the last two digits form a number divisible by 4.	1,028	621
5 if the last digit is 0 or 5.	15,195	10,007
6 if the number is even and divisible by 3.	1,332	44
8 if the last three digits form a number divisible by 8.	25,016	14,100
9 if the sum of the digits is divisible by 9.	144	33
10 if the last digit is 0.	2,790	9,325

PRACTICE

Determine which of these numbers each number is divisible by: 2, 3, 4, 5, 6, 8, 9, 10

1. 56 2, 4, 8
2. 200 2, 4, 5, 8, 10
3. 75 3, 5
4. 324 2, 3, 6, 9
5. 42 2, 3, 6
6. 812 2, 4
7. 784 2, 4, 8
8. 501 3
9. 2345 5
10. 555,555 3, 5
11. 3009 3
12. 2001 3

Prime and Composite Numbers

A **prime number** has exactly two factors, 1 and the number itself.

A **composite number** has more than two factors.

2 Factors: 1 and 2; prime
11 Factors: 1 and 11; prime
47 Factors: 1 and 47; prime

4 Factors: 1, 2, and 4; composite
12 Factors: 1, 2, 3, 4, 6, and 12; composite
63 Factors: 1, 3, 7, 9, 21, and 63; composite

EXAMPLE

Determine whether each number is prime or composite.

A 17
Factors
1, 17 ⟶ prime

B 16
Factors
1, 2, 4, 8, 16 ⟶ composite

C 51
Factors
1, 3, 17, 51 ⟶ composite

PRACTICE

Determine whether each number is prime or composite.

1. 5 prime
2. 14 composite
3. 18 composite
4. 2 prime
5. 23 prime
6. 27 composite
7. 13 prime
8. 39 composite
9. 72 composite
10. 49 composite
11. 9 composite
12. 89 prime

Percents Less Than 1% and Greater Than 100%

You can convert a percent to a decimal by deleting the percent sign and moving the decimal point two places to the left. This can help you understand percents less than 1% and greater than 100%.

$0.\overset{\curvearrowright}{0}\overset{\curvearrowright}{0}2\% = 0.002$

$1\overset{\curvearrowright}{3}\overset{\curvearrowright}{5}.\% = 1.35$

EXAMPLE

Find the percent of each number.

A 0.5% of 280
0.5% of 280 = 0.005 · 280   *Write the percent as a decimal.*
= 1.4   *Multiply.*

B 140% of 60
140% of 60 = 1.4 · 60   *Write the percent as a decimal.*
= 84   *Multiply.*

PRACTICE

Find the percent of each number.

1. 0.8% of 90 0.72
2. 0.2% of 6 0.012
3. 150% of 88 132
4. 260% of 40 104

Greatest Common Factor (GCF)

The **greatest common factor (GCF)** of two whole numbers is the greatest factor the numbers have in common.

EXAMPLE

Find the GCF of 24 and 32.

Method 1: List all the factors of both numbers.

Find all the common factors.

24: 1, 2, 3, 4, 6, 8, 12, 24
32: 1, 2, 4, 8, 16, 32

The common factors are 1, 2, 4, and 8.
So the GCF is 8.

Method 2: Find the prime factorizations.

Then find the common prime factors.

24: $2 \cdot 2 \cdot 2 \cdot 3$
32: $2 \cdot 2 \cdot 2 \cdot 2 \cdot 2$

The common prime factors are 2, 2, and 2.
The product of these is the GCF.
So the GCF is $2 \cdot 2 \cdot 2 = 8$.

PRACTICE

Find the GCF of each pair of numbers by either method.

1. 9, 15 3 **2.** 25, 75 25 **3.** 18, 30 6 **4.** 4, 10 2 **5.** 12, 17 1 **6.** 30, 96 6
7. 54, 72 18 **8.** 15, 20 5 **9.** 40, 60 20 **10.** 40, 50 10 **11.** 14, 21 7 **12.** 14, 28 14

Least Common Multiple (LCM)

The **least common multiple (LCM)** of two numbers is the smallest common multiple the numbers share.

EXAMPLE

Find the least common multiple of 8 and 10.

Method 1: List multiples of both numbers.

8: 8, 16, 24, 32, 40, 48, 56, 64, 72, 80
10: 10, 20, 30, 40, 50, 60, 70, 80, 90

The smallest common multiple is 40.

So the LCM is 40.

Method 2: Find the prime factorizations. Then find the most occurrences of each factor.

8: $2 \cdot 2 \cdot 2$
10: $2 \cdot 5$

The LCM is the product of the factors.

$2 \cdot 2 \cdot 2 \cdot 5 = 40$ So the LCM is 40.

PRACTICE

Find the LCM of each pair of numbers by either method.

1. 2, 4 4 **2.** 3, 15 15 **3.** 10, 25 50 **4.** 10, 15 30 **5.** 3, 7 21 **6.** 18, 27 54
7. 12, 21 84 **8.** 9, 21 63 **9.** 24, 30 120 **10.** 9, 18 18 **11.** 16, 24 48 **12.** 8, 36 72

Compatible Numbers

Compatible numbers are close to the numbers in a problem and divide without a remainder. You can use compatible numbers to estimate quotients.

EXAMPLE

Use compatible numbers to estimate each quotient.

A) $6134 \div 32$
$6134 \div 32$
$6000 \div 30 = 200 \longleftarrow$ Estimate
$\uparrow$
Compatible numbers

B) $647 \div 7$
$647 \div 7$
$630 \div 7 = 90 \longleftarrow$ Estimate
$\uparrow$
Compatible numbers

PRACTICE

Estimate the quotient by using compatible numbers.   Possible answers are given.

1. $345 \div 5$ 70 **2.** $5474 \div 23$ 220 **3.** $46,170 \div 18$ 2,500 **4.** $749 \div 7$ 100
5. $861 \div 41$ 20 **6.** $1225 \div 2$ 600 **7.** $968 \div 47$ 20 **8.** $3456 \div 432$ 8
9. $5765 \div 26$ 200 **10.** $25,012 \div 64$ 500 **11.** $99,170 \div 105$ 100 **12.** $868 \div 8$ 100

Mixed Numbers and Fractions

Mixed numbers can be written as fractions greater than 1, and fractions greater than 1 can be written as mixed numbers.

EXAMPLE

A) Write $\frac{23}{5}$ as a mixed number.

$\frac{23}{5}$ Divide the numerator by the denominator.

$\begin{array}{r} 4 \\ 5\overline{)23} \\ \underline{20} \\ 3 \end{array} \longrightarrow 4\frac{3}{5} \longleftarrow$ Write the remainder as the numerator of a fraction.

B) Write $6\frac{2}{7}$ as a fraction.

Multiply the denominator by the whole number.

Add the product to the numerator.

$6\frac{2}{7} \longrightarrow 7 \cdot 6 = 42 \longrightarrow 42 + 2 = 44$

Write the sum over $\longrightarrow \frac{44}{7}$
the denominator.

PRACTICE

Write each mixed number as a fraction. Write each fraction as a mixed number.

1. $\frac{22}{5}$ $4\frac{2}{5}$ **2.** $9\frac{1}{7}$ $\frac{64}{7}$ **3.** $\frac{41}{8}$ $5\frac{1}{8}$ **4.** $5\frac{7}{9}$ $\frac{52}{9}$
5. $\frac{7}{3}$ $2\frac{1}{3}$ **6.** $4\frac{9}{11}$ $\frac{53}{11}$ **7.** $\frac{47}{16}$ $2\frac{15}{16}$ **8.** $3\frac{3}{8}$ $\frac{27}{8}$
9. $\frac{31}{9}$ $3\frac{4}{9}$ **10.** $8\frac{2}{3}$ $\frac{26}{3}$ **11.** $\frac{33}{5}$ $6\frac{3}{5}$ **12.** $12\frac{1}{9}$ $\frac{109}{9}$

Multiply and Divide Decimals by Powers of 10

Notice the pattern below.

$0.24 \cdot 10 = 2.4$	$10 = 10^1$
$0.24 \cdot 100 = 24$	$100 = 10^2$
$0.24 \cdot 1000 = 240$	$1000 = 10^3$
$0.24 \cdot 10,000 = 2400$	$10,000 = 10^4$

*Think: When multiplying decimals by powers of 10, move the decimal point one place to the **right** for each power of 10, or for each zero.*

Notice the pattern below.

$0.24 \div 10 = 0.024$
$0.24 \div 100 = 0.0024$
$0.24 \div 1000 = 0.00024$
$0.24 \div 10,000 = 0.000024$

*Think: When dividing decimals by powers of 10, move the decimal point one place to the **left** for each power of 10, or for each zero.*

PRACTICE

Find each product or quotient.

1. $10 \cdot 9.26$ 92.6 **2.** $0.642 \cdot 100$ 64.2 **3.** $10^3 \cdot 84.2$ 84,200 **4.** $0.44 \cdot 10^4$ 4400
5. $69.7 \cdot 1000$ 69,700 **6.** $11.32 \div 10$ 1.132 **7.** $678 \cdot 10^8$ 67,800,000,000 **8.** $1.276 \div 1000$ 0.001276
9. $536.5 \div 10^2$ 5.365 **10.** $5.92 \div 10^3$ 0.00592 **11.** $25 \div 10,000$ 0.0025 **12.** $6.519 \cdot 10^2$ 651.9

Multiply Decimals

When multiplying decimals, multiply as you would with whole numbers. The sum of the number of decimal places in the factors equals the number of decimal places in the product.

EXAMPLE

Find each product.

A) $81.2 \cdot 6.547$

$\begin{array}{r} 6.547 \longleftarrow 3\ decimal\ places \\ \times\ \ 81.2 \longleftarrow 1\ decimal\ place \\ \hline 1\ 3094 \\ 6\ 5470 \\ 523\ 7600 \\ \hline 531.6164 \longleftarrow 4\ decimal\ places \end{array}$

B) $0.376 \cdot 0.12$

$\begin{array}{r} 0.376 \longleftarrow 3\ decimal\ places \\ \times\ \ 0.12 \longleftarrow 2\ decimal\ places \\ \hline 752 \\ 3760 \\ \hline 0.04512 \longleftarrow 5\ decimal\ places \end{array}$

PRACTICE

Find each product.

1. $6.8 \cdot 3.4$ 23.12 **2.** $2.56 \cdot 4.6$ 11.776 **3.** $6.787 \cdot 7.6$ 51.5812 **4.** $0.98 \cdot 4.6$ 4.508
5. $0.97 \cdot 0.76$ 0.7372 **6.** $0.5 \cdot 3.761$ 1.8805 **7.** $42 \cdot 17.654$ 741.468 **8.** $7.005 \cdot 32.1$ 224.8605
9. $9.76 \cdot 16.254$ 158.63904 **10.** $296.5 \cdot 2.4$ 711.60 or 711.6 **11.** $7.7 \cdot 6.5$ 50.05 **12.** $8.92 \cdot 2.8$ 24.976
13. $3.65 \cdot 4.2$ 15.33 **14.** $0.002 \cdot 8.1$ 0.0162 **15.** $0.03 \cdot 0.204$ 0.00612 **16.** $98.6 \cdot 4.9$ 483.14

Divide Decimals

When dividing with decimals, set up the division as you would with whole numbers. Pay attention to the decimal places, as shown below.

EXAMPLE

Find each quotient.

A) $89.6 \div 16$

$\begin{array}{r} 5.6 \\ 16\overline{)89.6} \\ \underline{80} \\ 96 \\ \underline{96} \\ 0 \end{array}$

B) $3.4 \div 4$

$\begin{array}{r} 0.85 \\ 4\overline{)3.40} \\ \underline{3\ 2} \\ 20 \\ \underline{20} \\ 0 \end{array}$ Place decimal point.
$\longleftarrow$ Insert zeros if necessary.

PRACTICE

Find each quotient.

1. $242.76 \div 68$ 3.57 **2.** $40.5 \div 18$ 2.25 **3.** $121.03 \div 98$ 1.235 **4.** $3.6 \div 4$ 0.9
5. $1.58 \div 5$ 0.316 **6.** $0.2835 \div 2.7$ 0.105 **7.** $8.1 \div 0.09$ 90 **8.** $0.42 \div 0.28$ 1.5
9. $480.48 \div 7.7$ 62.4 **10.** $36.9 \div 0.003$ 12,300 **11.** $0.784 \div 0.04$ 19.6 **12.** $15.12 \div 0.063$ 240

Terminating and Repeating Decimals

You can change a fraction to a decimal by dividing. If the resulting decimal has a finite number of digits, it is **terminating**. Otherwise, it is **repeating**.

EXAMPLE

Write $\frac{4}{5}$ and $\frac{2}{3}$ as decimals. Are the decimals terminating or repeating?

$\frac{4}{5} = 4 \div 5$ $\begin{array}{r} 0.8 \\ 5\overline{)4.0} \\ \underline{4\ 0} \\ 0 \end{array} \longrightarrow \frac{4}{5} = 0.8$

$\frac{2}{3} = 2 \div 3$ $\begin{array}{r} 0.6666 \\ 3\overline{)2.0000} \\ \underline{1\ 8} \\ 20 \end{array} \longrightarrow \frac{2}{3} = 0.6666...$
$\longrightarrow$ This pattern will repeat.

The number 0.8 is a terminating decimal.   The number 0.6666 . . . is a repeating decimal.

PRACTICE
For 1–18, see p. A22

Write as a decimal. Is the decimal terminating or repeating?

1. $\frac{1}{5}$ **2.** $\frac{1}{3}$ **3.** $\frac{3}{11}$ **4.** $\frac{3}{8}$ **5.** $\frac{7}{9}$ **6.** $\frac{7}{15}$
7. $\frac{3}{4}$ **8.** $\frac{5}{6}$ **9.** $\frac{4}{11}$ **10.** $\frac{1}{9}$ **11.** $\frac{1}{12}$ **12.** $\frac{11}{12}$
13. $\frac{5}{9}$ **14.** $\frac{8}{11}$ **15.** $\frac{7}{8}$ **16.** $\frac{23}{25}$ **17.** $\frac{3}{20}$ **18.** $\frac{5}{11}$

Order of Operations

When simplifying expressions, follow the order of operations.

1. Simplify within parentheses.
2. Evaluate exponents and roots.
3. Multiply and divide from left to right.
4. Add and subtract from left to right.

EXAMPLE

A Simplify the expression $3^2 \times (11 - 4)$.

$3^2 \times (11 - 4)$

$3^2 \times 7$ *Simplify within parentheses.*

9×7 *Evaluate the exponent.*

63 *Multiply.*

B Use a calculator to simplify the expression $19 - 100 \div 5^2$.

If your calculator follows the order of operations, enter the following keystrokes:

$19 - 100 \div 5$ [x²] [ENTER] The result is 15.

If your calculator does not follow the order of operations, insert parentheses so that the expression is simplified correctly.

$19 - (100 \div 5$ [x²]) [ENTER] The result is 15.

PRACTICE

Simplify each expression.

1. $45 - 15 \div 3$ **40**
2. $51 + 48 \div 8$ **57**
3. $35 \div (15 - 8)$ **5**
4. $\sqrt{9} \times 5 - 15$ **0**
5. $24 \div 3 - 6 + 12$ **14**
6. $(6 \times 8) \div 2^2$ **12**
7. $20 - 3 \times 4 + 30 \div 6$ **13**
8. $3^2 - 10 \div 2 + 4 \times 2$ **12**
9. $27 \div (3 + 6) + 6^2$ **39**
10. $4 \div 2 + 8 \times 2^3 - 4$ **62**
11. $33 - \sqrt{64} \times 3 - 5$ **4**
12. $(8^2 \times 4) - 12 \times 13 + 5$ **105**

Use a calculator to simplify each expression.

13. $6 + 20 \div 4$ **11**
14. $37 - 21 + 7$ **34**
15. $9^2 - 32 \div 8$ **77**
16. $10 \div 2 + 8 \times 2$ **21**
17. $\sqrt{25} + 4 \times 6$ **29**
18. $4 \times 12 - 4 + 8 \div 2$ **48**
19. $28 - 3^2 + 27 \div 3$ **28**
20. $9 + (50 - 16) \div 2$ **26**
21. $4^2 - (10 \times 8) \div 5$ **0**
22. $30 + 22 \div 11 - 7 - 3^2$ **16**
23. $3 + 7 \times 5 - 1$ **37**
24. $38 \div 2 + \sqrt{81} \times 4 - 31$ **24**

Properties

The following are basic properties of addition and multiplication when a, b, and c are real numbers.

	Addition		**Multiplication**
Closure:	$a + b$ is a real number.	Closure:	$a \cdot b$ is a real number.
Commutative:	$a + b = b + a$	Commutative:	$a \cdot b = b \cdot a$
Associative:	$(a + b) + c = a + (b + c)$	Associative:	$(a \cdot b) \cdot c = a \cdot (b \cdot c)$
Identity Property of Zero:	$a + 0 = a$ and $0 + a = a$	Identity Property of One:	$a \cdot 1 = a$ and $1 \cdot a = a$
		Multiplication Property of Zero:	$a \cdot 0 = 0$ and $0 \cdot a = 0$

The following properties are true when a, b, and c are real numbers.

Distributive: $a \cdot (b + c) = a \cdot b + a \cdot c$ **Transitive:** If $a = b$ and $b = c$, then $a = c$.

EXAMPLE

Name the property shown.

A $4 \cdot (7 \cdot 2) = (4 \cdot 7) \cdot 2$ **B** $4 \cdot (7 + 2) = (4 \cdot 7) + (4 \cdot 2)$
Associative Property of Multiplication   Distributive Property

PRACTICE

Give an example of each of the following properties, using real numbers. **Answers will vary.**

1. Associative Property of Addition
2. Commutative Property of Multiplication
3. Closure Property of Multiplication
4. Distributive Property
5. Multiplication Property of Zero
6. Identity Property of Addition
7. Transitive Property
8. Closure Property of Addition

Name the property shown.

9. $4 + 0 = 4$ Identity of Addition
10. $(6 + 3) + 1 = 6 + (3 + 1)$ Associative of Addition
11. $7 \cdot 51 = 51 \cdot 7$ Commutative of Multiplication
12. $5 \cdot 456 = 456 \cdot 5$ Commutative of Multiplication
13. $17 \cdot (1 + 3) = 17 \cdot 1 + 17 \cdot 3$ Distributive
14. $1 \cdot 5 = 5$ Identity of Multiplication
15. $(8 \cdot 2) \cdot 5 = 8 \cdot (2 \cdot 5)$ Associative of Multiplication
16. $72 + 1234 = 1234 + 72$ Commutative of Addition
17. $0 \cdot 12 = 0$ Zero Property of Multiplication
18. $15.7 \cdot 1.3 = 1.3 \cdot 15.7$ Commutative of Multiplication
19. $8.2 + (9.3 + 7) = (8.2 + 9.3) + 7$ Associative of Addition
20. $85.98 \cdot 0 = 0$ Zero Property of Multiplication
21. If $x = 3.5$ and $3.5 = y$, then $x = y$.   Transitive
22. $12a \cdot 15b = 15b \cdot 12a$ Commutative of Multiplication
23. $(2x + 3y) + 8z = 2x + (3y + 8z)$ Associative of Addition
24. $0 \cdot 6m^2n = 0$ Zero Property of Multiplication
25. $8j + 32k = 32k + 8j$ Commutative of Addition
26. If $3 + 8 = 11$ and $11 = x$, then $3 + 8 = x$.   Transitive

---

Cubes and Cube Roots

The volume of the cube at right is $5 \cdot 5 \cdot 5$ or 125. Because 5 is a factor 3 times, you can use an exponent to write the expression as 5^3, which is read "5 cubed."

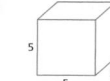

Finding **cube root** is the inverse of cubing a number. The symbol $\sqrt[3]{}$ means "cube root." For example, $\sqrt[3]{125} = 5$.

EXAMPLE

Evaluate each expression.

A 8^3

$8^3 = 8 \cdot 8 \cdot 8$ *Use 8 as a factor 3 times.*

$= 512$ *Multiply.*

B $\sqrt[3]{64}$

$\sqrt[3]{64} = 4$ $4^3 = 4 \cdot 4 \cdot 4 = 64$, so $\sqrt[3]{64} = 4$.

PRACTICE

Evaluate each expression.

1. 2^3 **8**
2. 1^3 **1**
3. 7^3 **343**
4. 10^3 **1000**
5. $\sqrt[3]{8}$ **2**
6. $\sqrt[3]{27}$ **3**
7. $\sqrt[3]{1000}$ **10**
8. $\sqrt[3]{1}$ **1**

Skew Lines

Parallel lines are lines in the same plane that do not intersect. Skew lines also do not intersect. **Skew lines** are lines that are not parallel that lie in two different planes

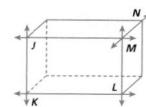

EXAMPLE

Tell whether the lines appear to be parallel, skew, or neither.

A $\overline{JK}$ and $\overline{MN}$

$\overline{JK}$ and $\overline{MN}$ are skew.   *The lines are in different planes and are not parallel.*

B $\overline{JK}$ and $\overline{KL}$

$\overline{JK}$ and $\overline{KL}$ are neither parallel nor skew.   *The lines intersect, so they are neither parallel nor skew*

PRACTICE

Tell whether the lines appear to be parallel, skew, or neither.

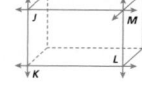

1. $\overline{AB}$ and $\overline{CD}$ **Parallel**
2. $\overline{CD}$ and $\overline{DE}$ **Neither**
3. $\overline{BC}$ and $\overline{DE}$ **Skew**

Choose Appropriate Units of Measurement

You can use the following benchmarks to help you choose appropriate units of measurement.

	Customary Unit	**Benchmark**
Length	Inch (in.)	Length of a small paper clip
	Foot (ft)	Length of a standard sheet of paper
	Mile (mi)	Length of about 18 football fields
Weight	Ounce (oz)	Weight of a slice of bread
	Pound (lb)	Weight of 3 apples
	Ton	Weight of a buffalo
Capacity	Fluid ounce (fl oz)	Amount of water in 2 tablespoons
	Cup (c)	Capacity of a standard measuring cup
	Gallon (gal)	Capacity of a large milk jug

	Metric Unit	**Benchmark**
Length	Millimeter (mm)	Thickness of a dime
	Centimeter (cm)	Width of your little finger
	Meter (m)	Width of a doorway
	Kilometer (km)	Length of 10 football fields
Mass	Milligram (mg)	Mass of a grain of sand
	Gram (g)	Mass of a small paper clip
	Kilogram (kg)	Mass of a textbook
Capacity	Milliliter (mL)	Amount of liquid in an eyedropper
	Liter (L)	Amount of water in a large water bottle
	Kiloliter (kL)	Capacity of 2 large refrigerators

EXAMPLE

1. Pounds; similar to the weight of many apples.
2. Inches; similar to the length of several small paper clips.

A Choose the most appropriate customary unit to measure the length of a sofa. Justify your answer.

feet; the length of a sofa is similar to the length of several sheets of paper.

B Choose the most appropriate metric unit to measure the capacity of a sink. Justify your answer.

liters; the capacity of a sink is similar to the capacity of several large water bottles.
3. Grams; similar to the mass of several small paper clips.

PRACTICE

Choose the most appropriate customary unit for each measurement. Justify your answer.
1. the weight of a laptop computer
2. the height of a sparrow
4. Millimeters; similar to the thickness of a dime.

Choose the most appropriate metric unit for each measurement. Justify your answer.
3. the mass of a walnut
4. the thickness of a piece of cardboard

Measure Angles

You can use a protractor to measure angles. To measure an angle, place the base of the protractor on one of the rays of the angle and center the base on the vertex. Look at the protractor scale that has zero on the first ray. Read the scale where the second ray crosses it. Extend the rays, if necessary.

EXAMPLE

Use a protractor to measure the angles of quadrilateral *ABCD*.

The measure of ∠*A*, or m∠*A*, equals 120°.

The measure of ∠*B*, or m∠*B*, equals 90°.

The measure of ∠*C*, or m∠*C*, equals 90°.

The measure of ∠*D*, or m∠*D*, equals 60°.

PRACTICE

Use a protractor to measure the angles of each polygon.

1.
m∠*X* = 40°,
m∠*Y* = 90°,
m∠*Z* = 50°

2.
m∠*A* = 75°, m∠*B* = 60°,
m∠*C* = 120°, m∠*D* = 105°

3.
m∠*D* = 150°,
m∠*E* = 130°,
m∠*F* = 70°,
m∠*G* = 115°,
m∠*H* = 75°

4.
m∠*J* = 55°,
m∠*K* = 60°,
m∠*L* = 65°

832 *Skills Bank*

Informal Geometry Proofs

Inductive reasoning involves examining a set of data to determine a pattern and then making a conjecture about the data. In **deductive reasoning**, you reach a conclusion by using logical reasoning based on given statements or premises that you assume to be true.

EXAMPLE

A Use inductive reasoning to determine the 30th number of the sequence.
3, 5, 7, 9, 11, . . .
Examine the pattern to determine the relationship between each term in the sequence and its value.

Term	1st	2nd	3rd	4th	5th
Value	3	5	7	9	11

$1 \cdot 2 + 1 = 2 + 1 = 3$ $4 \cdot 2 + 1 = 8 + 1 = 9$
$2 \cdot 2 + 1 = 4 + 1 = 5$ $5 \cdot 2 + 1 = 10 + 1 = 11$
$3 \cdot 2 + 1 = 6 + 1 = 7$

To obtain each value, multiply the term by 2 and add 1. So the 30th term is
$30 \cdot 2 + 1 = 60 + 1 = 61$.

B Use deductive reasoning to make a conclusion from the given premises.
Premise: Makayla needs at least an 89 on her exam to get a B for the quarter in math class.
Premise: Makayla got a B for the quarter in math class.
Conclusion: Makayla got at least an 89 on her exam.

PRACTICE

Use inductive reasoning to determine the 100th number in each pattern.

1. $\frac{1}{2}$, 1, $1\frac{1}{2}$, 2, $2\frac{1}{2}$, . . .   **50**   **2.** 1, 4, 9, 16, 25, . . .   **10,000**

3. 4, 6, 8, 10, 12, . . .   **202**   **4.** 0, 3, 6, 9, 12, 15, . . .   **297**

Use deductive reasoning to make a conclusion from the given premises.

5. Premise: If it is raining, then there must be a cloud in the sky.
Premise: It is raining.   **There is a cloud in the sky.**

6. Premise: A quadrilateral with four congruent sides and four right angles is a square.
Premise: Quadrilateral *ABCD* has four right angles.
Premise: Quadrilateral *ABCD* has four congruent sides.   **Quadrilateral *ABCD* is a square.**

7. Premise: Darnell is 3 years younger than half his father's age.
Premise: Darnell's father is 40 years old.   **Darnell is 17 years old.**

Skills Bank **833**

Iteration

An **iteration** is a step in the process of repeating something over and over again. You can show the steps of the process in an **iteration diagram**.

EXAMPLE

A Use the iteration diagram below, and complete the process three times.

Start with 4. → Add 8.

4 → 12 → 20 → 28
Start Stage 1 Stage 2 Stage 3

B For the pattern below, state the iteration and give the next three numbers in the pattern.
1, 5, 25, 125, . . .
To get from one stage to the next, the iteration is to multiply by 5.
$125 \cdot 5 = 625$ $625 \cdot 5 = 3125$ $3125 \cdot 5 = 15{,}625$
The next three numbers in the pattern are 625, 3125, and 15,625.

PRACTICE

Use the diagram at right. Write the results of the first three iterations.

1. Start with 1.
3, 9, 27
2. Start with 8.
24, 72, 216
3. Start with 2.
6, 18, 54
4. Start with 25.
75, 225, 675
5. Start with −3.
−9, −27, −81
6. Start with −7.
−21, −63, −189

Start with a number. → Multiply by 3.

For each pattern, state the iteration and give the next three numbers in the pattern.

7. 11, 17, 23, 29, . . .
add 6; 35, 41, 47
8. 5, 10, 20, 40, . . .
multiply by 2; 80, 160, 320
9. 345, 323, 301, 279, . . .
subtract 22; 257, 235, 213
10. 30, 75, 120, 165, . . .
add 45; 210, 255, 300
11. 15, 7, −1, −9, . . .
subtract 8; −17, −25, −33
12. 1, $1\frac{2}{3}$, $2\frac{1}{3}$, 3, . . .
add $\frac{2}{3}$; $3\frac{2}{3}$, $4\frac{1}{3}$, 5

A **fractal** is a geometric pattern that is *self similar*, so each stage of the pattern is similar to a portion of another stage of the pattern. For example, the Koch snowflake is a fractal formed by beginning with a triangle and then adding an equilateral triangle to each segment of the triangle.

For 13–14, see p. A22

Draw the next two stages of each fractal.

13.
Stage 0   Stage 1

14.
Stage 0   Stage 1

834 *Skills Bank*

 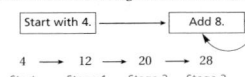

Skills Bank   Preview Skills

Relative, Cumulative, and Relative Cumulative Frequency

A **frequency table** lists each value or range of values of the data set followed by its **frequency**, or number of times it occurs.

Relative frequency is the frequency of a value or range of values divided by the total number of data values.

Cumulative frequency is the frequency of all data values that are less than a given value.

Relative cumulative frequency is the cumulative frequency divided by the total number of values.

Test Score	Frequency
66–70	3
71–75	1
76–80	4
81–85	7
86–90	5
91–95	6
96–100	2

EXAMPLE

The frequency table above shows a range of test scores and the frequency, or the number of students who scored in that range.

A Find the relative frequency of test scores in the range 76–80.
$3 + 1 + 4 + 7 + 5 + 6 + 2 = 28$ *Find the total number of test scores.*
There are 4 test scores in the range 76–80. The relative frequency is $\frac{4}{28} \approx 0.14$.

B Find the cumulative frequency of test scores less than 86.
$7 + 4 + 1 + 3 = 15$ *Add the frequencies of all test scores less than 86.*
The cumulative frequency of test scores less than 86 is 15.

C Find the relative cumulative frequency of test scores less than 86.
$\frac{15}{28} \approx 0.54$ *Divide the cumulative frequency by the total number of values.*
The relative cumulative frequency of test scores less than 86 is 0.54.

PRACTICE

The frequency table shows the frequency of each range of heights among Mrs. Dawkin's students.

Height	Frequency
4 ft–4 ft 5 in.	2
4 ft 6 in–4 ft 11 in.	8
5 ft–5 ft 5 in.	10
5 ft 6 in–5 ft 11 in.	6
6 ft–6 ft 5 in.	1

1. What is the relative frequency of heights in the range 5 ft–5 ft 5 in.?   **0.37**

2. What is the relative frequency of heights in the range 4 ft–4 ft 5 in.?   **0.07**

3. What is the cumulative frequency of heights less than 6 ft?   **26**

4. What is the cumulative frequency of heights less than 5 ft?   **10**

5. What is the relative cumulative frequency of heights less than 5 ft 6 in.?   **0.74**

6. What is the relative cumulative frequency of heights less than 5 ft?   **0.37**

Skills Bank **835**

Frequency Polygons

A **histogram** is a common way to represent frequency tables. A histogram is a bar graph with no space between the bars. Each bar can represent a range of values of a data set.

A **frequency polygon** is made by connecting the midpoints of the tops of all of the bars of a histogram.

EXAMPLE

A The frequency table shows the frequency of the number of push-ups done by the students in a gym class. Draw a histogram and frequency polygon of the data.

Label the horizontal axis with the number of push-ups. Label the vertical axis with the frequency.

Push-ups Done in 1 Minute	
Number of Push-ups	Frequency
0–9	3
10–19	6
20–29	11
30–39	10
40–49	4
50–59	2

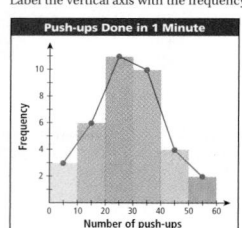

Push-ups Done in 1 Minute

The frequency polygon is made up of the red points and red segments connecting the points.

PRACTICE

For 1–2, see p. A22

Use each frequency table to draw a histogram and frequency polygon of the data.

1.

Books Read over the Summer	
Number of Books	Frequency
0–2	5
3–5	8
6–8	12
9–11	6
12–14	4
15–17	2

2.

Miles Driven One Way to Work	
Number of Miles	Frequency
0–4	6
5–9	5
10–14	13
15–19	9
20–24	4
25–29	1

Parallel Lines and Transversals

Recall that a transversal is a line that intersects two or more other lines. When three parallel lines are intersected by two transversals, the parallel lines divide the transversals proportionally.

In the figure, lines ℓ, m, and n are parallel. Lines r and s are transversals. You can conclude that $\frac{AB}{BC} = \frac{DE}{EF}$.

EXAMPLE

A Line $p \parallel$ line $q \parallel$ line r. Write a proportion based on the figure.

Lines j and k are transversals. The segments on the transversals are proportional.

$$\frac{AC}{CE} = \frac{BD}{DF}$$

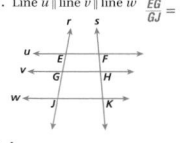

B Line $u \parallel$ line $v \parallel$ line w. Find x.

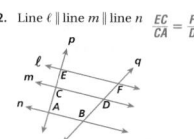

$\dfrac{DE}{EF} = \dfrac{GH}{HJ}$	The segments on the transversals are proportional.
$\dfrac{4}{6} = \dfrac{6}{x}$	$DE = 4$, $EF = 6$, $GH = 6$, $HJ = x$
$4x = 6 \cdot 6$	Find cross products.
$4x = 36$	Multiply.
$x = 9$	Divide both sides by 4.

PRACTICE

Write a proportion based on each figure.

1. Line $u \parallel$ line $v \parallel$ line w $\dfrac{EG}{GJ} = \dfrac{FH}{HK}$

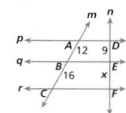

2. Line $\ell \parallel$ line $m \parallel$ line n $\dfrac{EC}{CA} = \dfrac{FD}{DB}$

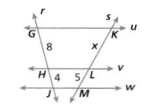

Find x.

3. Line $p \parallel$ line $q \parallel$ line r 12

4. Line $u \parallel$ line $v \parallel$ line w 10

Circles

A circle can be named by its center, using the ⊙ symbol. A circle with a center labeled C would be named ⊙C. An unbroken part of a circle is called an **arc.** There are major arcs and minor arcs.

A **minor arc** of a circle is an arc that is shorter than half the circle and named by its endpoints. A **major arc** of a circle is an arc that is longer than half the circle and named by its endpoints and one other point on the arc.

$\overset{\frown}{AB}$ is a minor arc.

$\overset{\frown}{BAC}$ is a major arc.

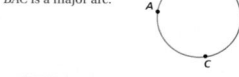

A **radius** connects the center with a point on a circle.

radius $\overline{CD}$

A **secant** is a line that intersects a circle at two points.

secant $\overleftrightarrow{EF}$

A **central angle** has its vertex at the center of the circle.

central angle $\angle JKL$

A **chord** connects two points point on a circle. A **diameter** is a chord that passes through the center of a circle. A **semicircle** is an arc whose endpoints lie on a diameter.

chord $\overline{AB}$
diameter $\overline{CD}$
semicircle $\overset{\frown}{CAD}$

A **tangent** is a line that intersects a circle at one point.

tangent $\overleftrightarrow{GH}$

An **inscribed angle** has its vertex on the circle.

inscribed angle $\angle MNP$

PRACTICE

Use the given diagram of ⊙A for exercises 1–6.

1. Name a radius. $\overline{AB}$ or $\overline{AK}$

2. What two chords make up the inscribed angle?

3. Name a secant. $\overleftrightarrow{FG}$ $\overline{CD}$ and $\overline{CE}$

4. Give the tangent line. $\overleftrightarrow{HJ}$

5. Name the central angle. $\angle BAK$

6. Name the inscribed angle. $\angle DCE$

Matrices

A **matrix** is a rectangular arrangement of data enclosed in brackets. Matrices are used to list, organize, and sort data.

The **dimensions** of a matrix are given by the number of horizontal **rows** and vertical **columns** in the matrix. For example, Matrix A below is an example of a 3×2 ("3-by-2") matrix because it has 3 rows and 2 columns, for a total of 6 **elements**. The number of rows is always given first. So a 3×2 matrix is not the same as a 2×3 matrix.

$$A = \begin{bmatrix} 86 & 137 \\ 103 & 0 \\ 115 & 78 \end{bmatrix} \begin{matrix} \leftarrow \text{Row 1} \\ \leftarrow \text{Row 2} \\ \leftarrow \text{Row 3} \end{matrix}$$

Column 1   Column 2

Each matrix element is identified by its row and column. The element in row 2 column 1 is 103. You can use the notation $a_{21} = 103$ to express this.

EXAMPLE

Use the data shown in the bar graph to create a matrix.

The matrix can be organized with the votes in each year

as the columns: $\begin{bmatrix} 12 & 5 \\ 6 & 11 \\ 2 & 4 \end{bmatrix}$

or with the votes in each year as the rows:

$\begin{bmatrix} 12 & 6 & 2 \\ 5 & 11 & 4 \end{bmatrix}$

Number of Votes

For 4–6, see p. A22

PRACTICE

Use matrix B for Exercises 1–3. $B = \begin{bmatrix} 1 & 0 & 7 & 4 \\ 0 & 1 & 3 & 8 \\ 6 & 5 & 2 & 9 \end{bmatrix}$

1. B is a ▦ × ▦ matrix. 3   4

2. Name the element with a value of 5. b_{32}

3. What is the value of b_{13}? 7

4. A football team scored 24, 13, and 35 points in three playoff games. Use this data to write a 3×1 matrix.

5. The greatest length and average weight of some whale species are as follows: finback whale—50 ft, 82 tons; humpback whale—33 ft, 49 tons; bowhead whale—50 ft, 59 tons; blue whale—84 ft, 98 tons; right whale—50 ft, 56 tons. Organize this data in a matrix.

6. The second matrix in the example is called the *transpose* of the first matrix. Write the transpose of matrix B above. What are its dimensions?

Networks

A **network** is a set of points and line segments or arcs that connect the points. Networks are useful in many real-world situations. The network at right at represents the flight routes of a small airline.

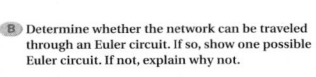

The points of a network are called **vertices**. The line segments or arcs connecting the vertices are called **edges**. The **degree** of a vertex is the number of edges touching the vertex. For example, vertex *D* has degree 3.

A **circuit** is a path along the edges that begins and ends at the same vertex and does not go through any edge more than once. An Euler circuit is a circuit that goes through every edge. An **Euler circuit** exists only when every vertex of a network has an even degree.

EXAMPLE

The map shows the highways that connect the cities on a florist's delivery route.

A Construct a network to represent the situation.

Use vertices to represent the cities and edges to represent the highways.

B Determine whether the network can be traveled through an Euler circuit. If so, show one possible Euler circuit. If not, explain why not.

First find the degree of each vertex.

Vertex	M	R	S	T
Degree	2	2	4	2

Every vertex has an even degree, so the network can be traveled by an Euler circuit, as shown.

PRACTICE

The map shows the roads and the houses of five families on Jake's newspaper route.

1. Construct a network to represent the situation.

2. Determine whether the network you drew in Exercise 1 can be traveled through an Euler circuit. If so, show one possible Euler circuit. If not, explain why not. **2.** No. Vertices *M* and *J* do not have an even degree.

840 *Skills Bank*

Compare and Order Measurements

You can use **conversion factors** to compare and order measurements.

Common Metric to Customary Conversions		
Length	Mass	Capacity
1 cm ≈ 0.394 in.	1 g ≈ 0.035 oz	1 mL ≈ 0.034 fl oz
1 m ≈ 3.281 ft	1 g ≈ 0.002 lb	1 L ≈ 33.814 fl oz
1 m ≈ 1.094 yd	1 kg ≈ 35.274 oz	1 L ≈ 1.057 qt
1 km ≈ 0.621 mi	1 kg ≈ 2.205 lb	1 L ≈ 0.264 gal

Common Customary to Metric Conversions		
Length	Mass	Capacity
1 in. ≈ 2.54 cm	1 oz ≈ 28.35 g	1 fl oz ≈ 29.574 mL
1 ft ≈ 0.305 m	1 oz ≈ 0.028 kg	1 fl oz ≈ 0.03 L
1 yd ≈ 0.914 m	1 lb ≈ 453.592 g	1 qt ≈ 0.946 L
1 mi ≈ 1.609 km	1 lb ≈ 0.454 kg	1 Gal ≈ 3.785 L

EXAMPLE

A Compare 8 cm and 5 in. by writing < or >.

$\quad$ 1 cm ≈ 0.394 in. *Find the conversion factor to convert centimeters to inches.*

$\quad$ 8 cm ≈ 8(0.394) in. *Convert 8 cm to inches.*

$\quad\quad\quad$ ≈ 3.152 in. *Multiply.*

Since 3.152 in. < 5 in., 8 cm < 5 in.

B Write the measurements 700 g, 25 kg, and 50 lb in order from least to greatest.

First convert the metric measurements to pounds.

$\quad$ 700 g ≈ 700(0.002) lb *Use the conversion factor 1g ≈ 0.002 lb.*

$\quad\quad\quad$ ≈ 1.4 lb *Multiply.*

$\quad$ 25 kg ≈ 25(2.205) lb *Use the conversion factor 1kg ≈ 2.205 lb.*

$\quad\quad\quad$ ≈ 55.125 lb *Multiply.*

Since 1.4 lb < 50 lb < 55.125 lb, the correct order is 700 g, 50 lb, 25 kg.

PRACTICE

Compare each set of measurements by writing < or >.

1. 3 gal and 12 L	2. 6 km and 5 mi	3. 20 kg and 40 lb
3 gal < 12 L	6 km < 5 mi	20 kg > 40 lb

Write each set of measurements in order from least to greatest.

4. 60 ft, 4 yd, 12 m	5. 23 oz, 2 lb, 0.5 kg	6. 4 gal, 18.5 qt, 20 L
4 yd, 12 m, 60 ft	0.5 kg, 23 oz, 2 lb	4 gal, 18.5 qt, 20 L

841 *Skills Bank*

Temperature Conversion

In the United States, the Fahrenheit (°F) temperature scale is the common scale used. For example, weather reports and body temperatures are given in degrees Fahrenheit. The metric temperature scale is Celsius (°C) and is commonly used in science applications. Temperatures given in one scale can be converted to the other system using one of the formulas below.

Formulas

Fahrenheit to Celsius (°F to °C) $\quad \frac{5}{9}(F - 32) = C$

Celsius to Fahrenheit (°C to °F) $\quad \frac{9}{5}C + 32 = F$

EXAMPLES

A Convert 77°F to degrees Celsius.

$$\frac{5}{9}(F - 32) = C$$
$$\frac{5}{9}(77 - 32) = C$$
$$\frac{5}{9}(45) = C$$
$$25 = C$$

B Convert 103°C to degrees Fahrenheit.

$$\frac{9}{5}C + 32 = F$$
$$\frac{9}{5}(103) + 32 = F$$
$$185.4 + 32 = F$$
$$217.4 = F$$

PRACTICE

Convert each temperature to degrees Celsius. Give the temperature to the nearest tenth of a degree.

1. 7°F −13.9°C	2. 0°F −17.8°C
3. 12°F −11.1°C	4. 40°F 4.4°C
5. 100°F 37.8°C	6. 32°F 0°C
7. 25°F −3.9°C	8. 212°F 100°C
9. −50°F −45.6°C	10. −8°F −22.2°C

Convert each temperature to degrees Fahrenheit. Give the temperature to the nearest tenth of a degree.

11. 0°C 32°F	12. 10°C 50°F
13. 22°C 71.6°F	14. 55°C 131°F
15. 212°C 413.6°F	16. 1°C 33.8°F
17. 100°C 212°F	18. 80°C 176°F
19. 95°C 203°F	20. 32°C 89.6°F
21. 31°C 87.8°F	22. 42°C 107.6°F
23. −6°C 21.2°F	24. −40°C −40°F

842 *Skills Bank*

Customary and Metric Rulers

A metric ruler is divided into centimeter units, and each centimeter is divided into 10 millimeter units. A metric ruler that is 1 meter long is a *meter stick*.

$\quad$ 1 m = 100 cm

$\quad$ 1 cm = 10 mm

EXAMPLE

What is the length of the segment?

Since the segment is longer than 5 cm and shorter than 6 cm, its length is a decimal value between these measurements. The digit in the ones place is the number of centimeters and the digit in the tenths place is the number of millimeters. The length of the segment is 5.6 cm.

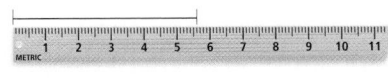

PRACTICE

Use a metric ruler to find the length of each segment.

1. ⊢―――⊣ 2.9 cm $\qquad$ 2. ⊢―――――――――⊣ 8 cm

A customary ruler is usually 12 inches long. The ruler is read in fractional units rather than in decimals. Each inch typically has a long mark at $\frac{1}{2}$ inch, shorter marks at $\frac{1}{4}$ and $\frac{3}{4}$ inch, even shorter marks at $\frac{1}{8}$, $\frac{3}{8}$, $\frac{5}{8}$, and $\frac{7}{8}$ inch, and the shortest marks at the remaining 16ths inches.

EXAMPLE

What is the length of the segment?

Since the segment is longer than 2 inches and shorter than 3 inches, its length is a mixed number with 2 as the whole number part. The fractional part is $\frac{11}{16}$. The length of the segment is $2\frac{11}{16}$ inches.

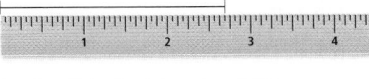

PRACTICE

Use a customary ruler to find the length of each segment.

3. ⊢―――――⊣ $3\frac{3}{4}$ in.  $\qquad$ 4. ⊢――⊣ $1\frac{7}{16}$ in.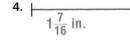

843 *Skills Bank*

Precision and Significant Digits

In a measurement, all digits that are known with certainty are called **significant digits** . The more precise a measurement is, the more significant digits there are in the measurement. The table shows some rules for identifying significant digits.

Rule	Example	Number of Significant Digits
All nonzero digits	15.32	All 4
Zeros beween significant digits	43,001	All 5
Zeros after the last nonzero digit that are to the right of the decimal point	0.0070	2; 0.0070

Zeros at the end of a whole number are assumed to be nonsignificant. (Example: 500)

EXAMPLE

A Which is a more precise measurement, 14 ft or 14.2 ft?

Because 14.2 ft has three significant digits and 14 has only two, 14.2 ft is more precise. In the measurement 14.2 ft, each 0.1 ft is measured.

B Determine the number of significant digits in 20.04 m, 200 m, and 200.0 m.

20.04   All 4 digits are significant.
200   There is 1 significant digit.
200.0   All 4 digits are significant.

When calculating with measurements, the answer can only be as precise as the least precise measurement.

C Multiply 16.3 m by 2.5 m. Use the correct number of significant digits in your answer.

When multiplying or dividing, use the least number of significant digits of the numbers.

$16.3 \text{ m} \cdot 2.5 \text{ m} = 40.75$

Round to 2 significant digits. $\longrightarrow 41 \text{ m}^2$

D Add 4500 in. and 70 in. Use the correct number of significant digits in your answer.

When adding or subtracting, line up the numbers. Round the answer to the last significant digit that is farthest to the left.

4500 in.   *5 is farthest left. Round to*
+ 70 in.   *hundreds.*
4570 Round to the hundreds. $\longrightarrow$ 4600 in.

PRACTICE

Tell which is more precise.

1. 31.8 g or 32 g 31.8 g
2. 496.5 mi or 496.50 mi 496.50 mi
3. 3.0 ft or 3.001 ft 3.001 ft

Determine the number of significant digits in each measurement.

4. 12 lb 2
5. 14.00 mm 4
6. 1.009 yd 4
7. 20.87 s 4

Perform the indicated operation. Use the correct number of significant digits in your answer.

8. 210 m + 43 m 250 m
9. 4.7 ft · 1.04 ft 4.9 ft²
10. 6.7 s − 0.08 s 6.6 s

Greatest Possible Error

The smaller the units used to measure something, the greater the precision of the measurement. The **greatest possible error** of a measurement is half the smallest unit. This is written as ± 0.5 unit, which is read as "plus or minus 0.5 unit."

EXAMPLES

A Which is a more precise measurement, 292 cm or 3 m?

The more precise measurement is 292 cm because its unit of measurement, 1 cm, is smaller than 1 m.

B Find the greatest possible error for a measurement of 2.4 cm.

The smallest unit is 0.1 cm.
$0.5 \times 0.1 = 0.05$
The greatest possible error is ± 0.05 cm.

2.3 cm   2.35 cm   2.4 cm   2.45 cm   2.5 cm

PRACTICE

Tell which is a more precise measurement.

1. 40 cm or 412 mm 412 mm
2. 3.2 ft or 1 yd 3.2 ft
3. 7 ft or 87 in. 87 in.
4. 3116 m or 3 km 3,116 m
5. 1 mi or 5281 ft 5,281 ft
6. 0.04 m or 4.2 cm 4.2 cm

Find the greatest possible error of each measurement.

7. 5 ft ±0.5 ft
8. 22 mm ±0.5 mm
9. 12.5 mi ±0.05 mi
10. 60 km ±0.5 km
11. 2.06 cm ±0.005 cm
12. 0.08 g ±0.005 g

pH (Logarithmic Scale)

pH is a measure of the concentration of hydrogen ions in a solution. pH ranges from 0 to 14. An *acid* has a pH below 7 and a *base* has a pH above 7. A pH of 7 is *neutral* and a hydrogen ion concentration of 1×10^{-7} mol/L. The exponent is the opposite of the pH.

0 Strong acids   Weak acids 7 Weak bases   Strong bases 14

EXAMPLES

A Write the pH of the solution, given the hydrogen ion concentration.

coffee: 1×10^{-5} mol/L
The coffee is acidic, with a pH of 5.

B Write the hydrogen ion concentration of the solution in mol/L.

antacid solution: pH = 10.0
1×10^{-10} mol/L in the antacid solution

PRACTICE

Write the pH of each solution, given the hydrogen ion concentration.

1. seawater: 1×10^{-8} mol/L 8
2. lye: 1×10^{-13} mol/L 13
3. borax: 1×10^{-9} mol/L 9

Write the hydrogen ion concentration in mol/L.

4. drain cleaner: pH = 14.0 1×10^{-14}
5. lemon juice: pH = 2.0 1×10^{-2}
6. milk: pH = 7.0 1×10^{-7}

Richter Scale

An earthquake is classified according to its magnitude. The Richter scale is a mathematical system that compares the sizes and magnitudes of earthquakes.

The magnitude is related to the height, or *amplitude*, of seismic waves as recorded by a seismograph during an earthquake. The higher the number is on the Richter scale, the greater the amplitude of the earthquake's waves.

Earthquakes per Year	Magnitude on the Richter Scale	Severity
1	8.0 and higher	Great
18	7.0–7.9	Major
120	6.0–6.9	Strong
800	5.0–5.9	Moderate
6200	4.0–4.9	Light
49,000	3.0–3.9	Minor
≈ 3,300,000	below 3.0	Very minor

The Richter scale is a *logarithmic scale*, which means that the numbers in the scale measure factors of 10. An earthquake that measures 6.0 on the Richter scale is 10 times as great as one that measures 5.0.

The largest earthquake ever measured registered 8.9 on the Richter scale.

EXAMPLE

How many times greater is an earthquake that measures 5.0 on the Richter scale than one that measures 3.0?

You can divide powers of 10, with the magnitudes as the exponents.

$\frac{10^5}{10^3} = 10^2$

A 5.0 quake is 100 times greater than a 3.0 quake.

PRACTICE

Describe the severity of an earthquake with each given Richter scale reading.

1. 7.6 major
2. 4.2 light
3. 5.0 moderate
4. 2.0 very minor
5. 3.6 minor
6. 8.4 great

Each pair of numbers repesents two earthquake magnitudes on the Richter scale. How many times greater is the first earthquake in each pair? (Use a calculator for 10–12.)

7. 6.0 and 4.0 100
8. 8.0 and 5.0 1000
9. 7.0 and 3.0 10,000
10. 7.5 and 5.5 100
11. 5.7 and 5.3 2.5
12. 8.6 and 7.1 31.6

Selected Answers

4-7 Exercises

1. irrational, real **3.** rational, real **5.** rational **7.** irrational **9.** rational **11.** not real **15.** $\frac{3}{16}$ **17.** rational, real **19.** integer, rational, real **21.** rational **23.** irrational **25.** irrational **27.** no real **31.** whole, integer, rational, real **33.** irrational, real **35.** rational, real **37.** irrational, real **39.** rational, real **41.** rational, real **43.** $-\sqrt{16}$ is the negative of the square root of 1. $\sqrt{-16}$ is undefined and not real. **55.** $x \geq 0$ **57.** $x \geq 2$ **59.** $x \leq 5$ **63.** D **65.** C **67.** 17 **69.** 7 **71.** −27 **73.** 81

4-8 Exercises

1. 15 **3.** 8.5 **5.** 8 **7.** 16 **9.** 13 **11.** 11.7 **13.** 12.4 **15.** 17 mi **17.** $\sqrt{65} \approx 8.1$ **19.** 78 **21.** $\sqrt{1391} \approx 37.3$ **23.** no **25.** yes **27.** yes **29.** no **31.** 22.6 ft **37.** G **39.** 9 **41.** 51 **43.** 6.48 **45.** 8.19

Chapter 4 Study Guide: Review

1. base, exponent **2.** irrational number **3.** scientific notation **4.** Pythagorean theorem; legs; hypotenuse **5.** real numbers **6.** 7^3 **7.** $(-3)^2$ **8.** k^4 **9.** $(-9)^1$ **10.** $(-2)^2d^2$ **11.** $(3n)^3$ **12.** $6x^2$ **13.** 10^4 **14.** 625 **15.** −32 **16.** −1 **17.** 256 **18.** −3 **19.** 64 **20.** −27 **21.** 25 **22.** 15 **23.** 1296 **24.** 100,000 **25.** −128 **26.** $\frac{1}{125}$ **27.** $-\frac{1}{64}$ **28.** $\frac{1}{11}$ **29.** $\frac{1}{10{,}000}$ **30.** 1 **31.** $-\frac{1}{36}$ **32.** $-\frac{1}{81}$ **33.** $\frac{1}{100}$ **34.** $\frac{1}{8}$ **35.** $-\frac{1}{27}$ **36.** $\frac{1}{3}$ **37.** 1 **38.** $\frac{1}{2}$ **39.** $\frac{1}{72}$ **40.** 0 **41.** 4^7 **42.** 9^6 **43.** p^4 **44.** 15^3 **45.** cannot combine **46.** x^{10} **47.** 8^3 **48.** 9^2 **49.** m^5 **50.** 3^7 **51.** 4^0 or 1 **52.** y^9 **53.** 5^3 **54.** y^5 **55.** k^0, or 1 **56.** 1620 **57.** 0.00162 **58.** 910,000 **59.** 0.000091 **60.** 8×10^{-9} **61.** 7.3×10^7 **62.** 9.6×10^{-6} **63.** 5.64×10^{10} **64.** 4 and −4 **65.** 30 and −30 **66.** 26 and −26 **67.** 5 **68.** $\frac{1}{2}$ **69.** 9 **70.** 89.4 in. **71.** 167.1 cm **72.** 9 and 10 **73.** rational **74.** irrational **75.** not a real number **76.** irrational **77.** rational **78.** not a real number **80.** 10 **81.** 10 **82.** 14.1 inches

Chapter 5

5-1 Exercises

1. $\frac{3}{7}, \frac{12}{28}$ **3.** $\frac{3}{1}, \frac{42}{14}$ **5.** $\frac{24}{34}, \frac{60}{85}$ **7.** $\frac{2}{3} \neq \frac{5}{9}$; no **9.** $\frac{2}{3} = \frac{2}{3}$; yes **11.** $\frac{2}{14}, \frac{3}{21}$ **13.** $\frac{7}{6}, \frac{28}{24}$ **15.** $\frac{22}{100}, \frac{44}{200}$ **17.** $\frac{3}{5} = \frac{3}{5}$; yes **19.** $\frac{1}{3} \neq \frac{1}{4}$; no **21.** no; $\frac{1}{3}$ **23.** no; $\frac{8}{14}$ **25.** yes **27.** no; $\frac{3}{14}$ **29.** yes **31.** no **33.** $\frac{2}{4} = \frac{3}{6}; \frac{2}{5} = \frac{4}{10}; \frac{12}{3} = \frac{4}{1}; \frac{12}{8} = \frac{9}{6}$ **37.** C **39.** yes **41.** > **43.** > **45.** −5.44 **47.** 0.642

5-2 Exercises

1. ≈7.26g/cm^3 **3.** about 40 students per bus **5.** about 500 Calories per serving **7.** 38 oz box **9.** 3.52 g/cm^3 **11.** about 30 chairs per row **13.** about \$12 per CD **15.** 1 yard of ribbon **17.** 50.25 mi/h **19.** \$2.35 per taco **21.** approximately \$5 per magazine **23.** approximately 50 words per minute **25.** \$0.16/fl oz; 90 fl oz **27.** 30.9 lb **29a.** Tom: $25\frac{3}{8}$ frames per hour; Cherise: 27 frames per hour; Tina: $28\frac{3}{8}$ frames per hour **b.** Tina **c.** $1\frac{5}{8}$ **d.** 24 **33.** F **35.** $p = 20$ **37.** $w = 15$ **39.** $\frac{6}{10}, \frac{9}{15}$ **41.** $\frac{8}{22}, \frac{12}{33}$

5-3 Exercises

1. $\frac{60\text{ s}}{1\text{ min}}$ **3.** $\frac{1\text{ kg}}{1000\text{ g}}$ **5.** 7.5 mi/h **7.** $\frac{1000\text{ mm}}{1\text{m}}$ **9.** $\frac{1\text{ hr}}{60\text{ min}}$ **11.** 1.8 km/h **13.** 480 cereal boxes **15.** 6 fish **17.** ≈ 5.8 mi **19.** ≈ 1.14 g **21.** 28.75 tons **23.** 10.3 m/s **25.** ≈ 2.85 gal **31.** B **32.** H **33.** 32 **35.** 4096 **37.** 0.00000001 **39.** 128 **41.** m^{13} **43.** ≈ \$0.175 per oz **45.** \$249 per monitor

5-4 Exercises

1. yes **3.** no **5.** no **7.** 330 mi **9.** \$9 **11.** 525 **13.** 10 **15.** $5\frac{1}{3}$ in. **17.** yes **19.** yes **21.** \$103.92 **23.** \$48 **25.** 9 **27.** 24 **29.** \$22.50 **31.** $\frac{8}{4}, \frac{24}{12}$ **33.** $\frac{81}{39}, \frac{27}{13}$ **35.** $\frac{0.5}{6}, \frac{1}{12}$ **37.** 14 molecules **41.** B **43.** 16 **45.** −33 **47.** $293\frac{1}{3}$ feet per second

5-5 Exercises

1. △ABC ~ △FDE **3.** 16.5 cm **5.** ≈ 2.98 in. **7.** similar **9.** similar **13.** $x = 6$ ft **15.** 18 in. **17.** 8 cm **23.** 70 **25.** $y = x + 3$ **27.** $y = 5.4$ **29.** $k = 5$

5-6 Exercises

1. no **3.**

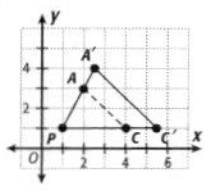

5. A′(2, −1); B′(1, −2); C′(4, −3); D′(3, −1) **7.** no **11.** A′(−9, 5); B′(15, 12); C′(−6, −9) **13.** A′(3, 6); B′(10.5, 6); C′(10.5, 0); D′(3,0) **19.** 19.2 ft; 76.8 ft; 368.64 ft^2 **21.** −15 **23.** 15 yd

5-7 Exercises

1. 128 yd **3.** 100 m **5.** 4 ft **7.** 7.2 m **9.** 85 ft **11.** 65 ft **15.** C **17.** $-\frac{1}{5}$ **19.** $\frac{1}{6}$ **21.** 3^4 **23.** $(-2)^3$

5-8 Exercises

1. 1 in.:1.25 ft **3.** 14 in. **5.** 1 cm = 1.5 m **7.** 7.5 ft **9.** enlarges **11.** reduces **13.** enlarges **15.** $\frac{12}{1}$ **17.** $\frac{1}{45}$ **19.** $\frac{1}{20}$ **21.** 630 ft **23.** 6.25 ft **25.** ≈18 in. **27.** ≈945 in.^{2}; ≈6.6 ft^2 **29.** ≈298 ft^2 **31.** D **33.** rational **35.** irrational **37.** \$11.25 per hour **39.** 12 players per team

850 Selected Answers

Chapter 5 Study Guide: Review

1. ratio; proportion **2.** rate; unit rate **3.** similar; scale factor **4.** dilation; enlargement; reduction **5.** Possible answers: $\frac{1}{2}, \frac{2}{4}$ **6.** Possible answers: $\frac{3}{6}, \frac{4}{8}$ **7.** Possible answers: $\frac{7}{12}, \frac{14}{24}$ **8.** yes **9.** no **10.** yes **11.** no **12.** \$0.30 per disk; \$0.29 per disk; 75 disks **13.** \$3.75 per box; \$3.75 per box; unit prices are the same **14.** \$2.89 per divider; \$4.00 per divider; 8-pack **15.** 90,000 m/h **16.** 4500 ft/min **17.** $583\frac{1}{3}$ m/min **18.** $x = 15$ **19.** $h = 6$ **20.** $w = 21$ **21.** $x = 29\frac{1}{3}$ **22.** 12.5 in. **23.** 3.125 in.

24.

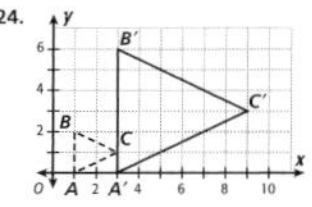

25.

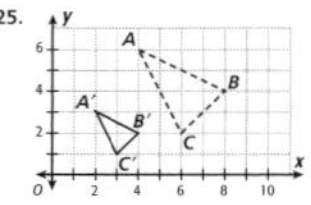

26.

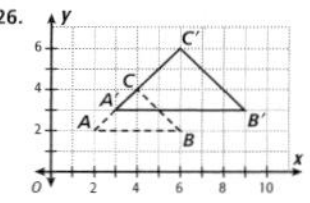

27. 18 ft **28.** 6.2 ft **29.** 64.8 m **30.** 6.6 in. **31.** 1 in:16 ft **32.** 46 mi **33.** 57.5 mi **34.** 153 mi **35.** 72.5 mi

Chapter 6

6-1 Exercises

1. $\frac{1}{4}$ **3.** 87.5% **5.** < **7.** = **9.** 0.3, $33\frac{1}{3}$%, 36%, $\frac{3}{8}$ **11.** $33\frac{1}{3}$% **13.** $\frac{39}{100}$ **15.** 125% **17.** < **19.** = **21.** 0.04, $\frac{2}{5}$, 42%, 70% **23.** 40%, 30%, 20%, 10% **25.** 40%, 30%, 25%, 5% **33.** G **35.** < **37.** = **39.** 4

6-2 Exercises

1. 50 **3.** 30 **5.** 13 **7.** 16 **11.** 100 **13.** 6 **15.** 32 **17.** 9 **21.** B **23.** B **25.** C **27.** 150 **29.** 40 **31.** 800 **33.** 30 **35.** 100 **37.** ≈ 300 cars **39.** ≈ 475,000 **41.** ≈ 12 hours **43a.** No **b.** Yes **47.** B **49.** B **51.** 9 **53.** −64 **55.** 125 **57.** 8 **59.** $\frac{23}{50}$ **61.** 0.5 **63.** 0.525

6-3 Exercises

1. 49.5% **3.** 17.8% **5.** 1.6 mi **7.** 400% **9.** 1% **11.** 1.0% **13.** 604 ft **15.** 10 **17.** 6.9 **19.** 498 **21a.** 32 **b.** 48 **c.** 160 **23a.** 150 **b.** 75 **c.** 37.5 **27.** ≈ 49 min **29.** Lena: \$11.87, Ana: \$12.36, Joseph: \$12.50, George: \$12.71 **33.** G **35.** $x = 2$ **37.** $b = 5$ **39.** 100 **41.** 40

6-4 Exercises

1. 60 **3.** 166 **5.** ≈ 2.4 oz **7.** 135 **9.** 1333.3 **11.** 400 cards **13a.** 250 **b.** 125 **c.** 62.5 **15a.** 30 **b.** 20 **c.** 15 **17.** 658,000 **19.** 6.7% **21.** 98,000 **23.** C **25.** 5, 6 **27.** 7, 8 **29.** 11, 12 **31.** 2.12 **33.** $4.08\overline{3}$

6-5 Exercises

1. 48% increase **3.** 100% increase **5.** \$9773.60 **7.** 22% increase **9.** ≈ 8.6% **11.** 33% decrease **13.** 39% decrease **15.** 24% decrease **17.** \$500 **19.** 120 **21.** 50 **23a.** \$78 **b.** \$117 **c.** \$39 **d.** 80% **25.** 24,900% **31.** \$7.49; \$31.76 **33.** 50% **35.** 311.75

6-6 Exercises

1. \$574 **3.** 11.6% **5.** \$603.50 **7.** 3.1% **9.** \$15.23 **11.** \$38.07 **13.** \$81,200 **17a.** \$64,208 **b.** \$12,717 **c.** ≈ 17.8% **d.** ≈ 19.8% **19.** B **21.** yes **23.** yes **25.** 50% decrease

6-7 Exercises

1. \$2234.38; \$9384.38 **3.** \$1430.24 **5.** \$23,032.50 **7.** \$1473.60 **9.** \$94.50, \$409.50 **11.** \$446.25, \$4696.25 **13.** \$9.26, \$626.26 **15.** \$195.75, \$1,095.75 **17.** \$340, \$2040 **25.** G **27.** 1 gal/4 qt **29.** 95

Chapter 6 Study Guide: Review

1. percent **2.** percent change **3.** commission **4.** 0.4375 **5.** 43.75% **6.** $1\frac{1}{8}$ **7.** 112.5% **8.** $\frac{7}{10}$ **9.** 0.7 **10.** 30 **11.** 62 **12.** 3.3 **13.** 18 **14.** \$7.50 **15.** \$16.00 **16.** 33% **17.** 4200 ft **18.** 7930 mi **19.** 5 lb 7 oz **20.** 16% **21.** 472,750% **22.** 34.4% **23.** \$16,830 **24.** \$3.55 **25.** \$3171.88 **26.** \$400 **27.** 7% **28.** 0.5 yr **29.** \$1000 at 3.75% for 3 years; \$7.50

Chapter 7

7-1 Exercises

1. points X, Y, Z **3.** plane A or plane XYZ **5.** $\overrightarrow{XY}, \overrightarrow{YZ}, \overrightarrow{YX}$ **7.** $\angle BEC, \angle CED$ **9.** $\angle BEC$ and $\angle CED$ **11.** 105° **13.** points J, K, L, M **15.** plane N or plane JKL **17.** $\overrightarrow{KJ}, \overrightarrow{KL}, \overrightarrow{KM}, \overrightarrow{LK}, \overrightarrow{MK}$ **19.** $\angle VWZ, \angle YWX$ **21.** $\angle VWZ, \angle YWX$ **23.** 126° **25.** False **27.** False **29.** False **31.** False **33.** False **35.** 30°, 60° **37.** 140° **41.** 117° **43.** w^7 **45.** 11^{15}

Selected Answers 851

7-2 Exercises

1. $\angle 1 \cong \angle 4 \cong \angle 5 \cong \angle 8 (45°)$; $\angle 2 \cong \angle 3 \cong \angle 6 \cong \angle 7 (135°)$ **3.** 62° **5.** 62° **7.** 70° **9.** 110° **11.** $\angle 4$, $\angle 5$, and $\angle 8$ **13.** Possible answers: $\angle 1$ and $\angle 2$, $\angle 1$ and $\angle 3$, $\angle 3$ and $\angle 4$ **15.** 129° **17.** 89° **27.** The measures of the remaining angles are 90°. The transversal is perpendicular to the parallel lines. **29.** 18,250 **31.** 25°

7-3 Exercises

1. 77° **3.** 120° **5.** 56° **7.** 60°, 30°, 90° **9.** 58° **11.** 60° **13.** $2g° = 20°$, $7g° = 70°$, $9g° = 90°$ **15.** 57° **17.** 30° **19.** 15° **27.** 52° **29.** 64° **31.** C **33.** $x° = 30°$, $y° = 100°$; $z° = 50°$ **35.** 105°, obtuse **37.** 8 and 9 **39.** 17 and 18 **41.** 55° **43.** 146°

7-4 Exercises

1. 360° **3.** 900° **5.** $v° \approx 128.6°$ **7.** quadrilateral, trapezoid **9.** quadrilateral, parallelogram, rectangle **11.** 1080° **13.** $m° = 135°$ **15.** $v° = 144°$ **17.** quadrilateral, parallelogram **19.** 3240°; 162° **21.** 10,440°; 174° **23.** 2520°; 157.5° **25.** $y° = 95°$ **27.** $z° = 97°$ **29.** $m° = 40°$ **31.** pentagon **33.** 11-gon **37.** not possible **43.** regular hexagon **45.** −50 **47.** −71

7-5 Exercises

1. 0 **3.** positive slope; 1 **5.** $\overline{AN} \parallel \overline{CD}$ **7.** parallelogram, rhombus, rectangle, square

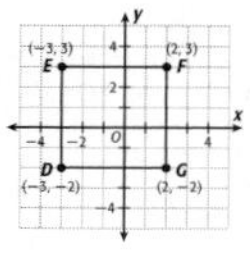

9. $C(2, -1)$ **11.** positive slope, 1 **13.** 0 **15.** $\overline{CD} \parallel \overline{AB}$ **17.**

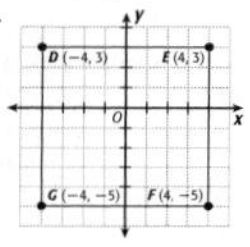

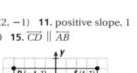

19. $C(4, -1)$ **21.** 3 **23.** 0 **25.** slope $\overline{PE} = 2$ **31.** true **33.** false **35.** true **37.** D; rectangle **39.** B; right triangle **45.** A **47.** 20 **49.** 1500 **51.** 2,340° **53.** $180°(n-2)$

7-6 Exercises

1. triangle $ABC \cong$ triangle FED **3.** $q = 5$ **5.** $s = 7$ **7.** quadrilateral $PQRS \cong$ quadrilateral $ZYXW$ **9.** $n = 7$ **11.** $x = 19$, $y = 27$, $z = 18.1$ **13.** $r = 24$, $s = 120$, $t = 48$ **15.** 62° **19.** C **21.** 3 **23.** 2 **25.** 26 **27.** 90° **29.** 33

7-7 Exercises

1. reflection

3.

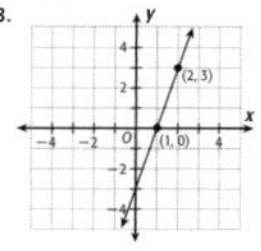

5.

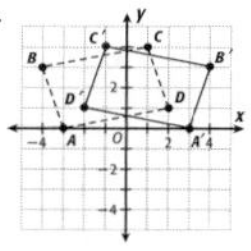

7. (1, −2) **9.** (−2, 1) **11.** none of these

13.

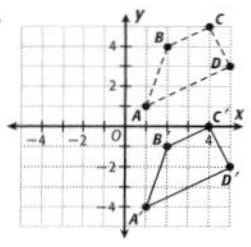

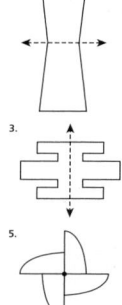

15.

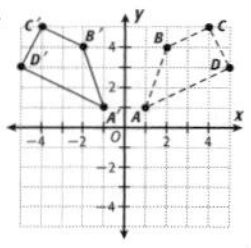

17. (−5, 2) **19.** (2, 2) **25.** (−3, −2) **27.** (−5, −2) **29.** $(-m, n)$ **31.** (4, −5) **37.** The vertices of the image are (1, 4), (5, 5), and (3, −1). **39.** 17% increase **41.** 0

7-8 Exercises

1.

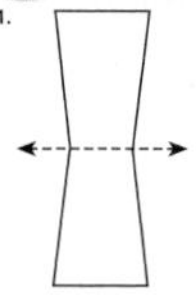

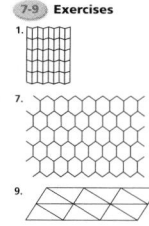

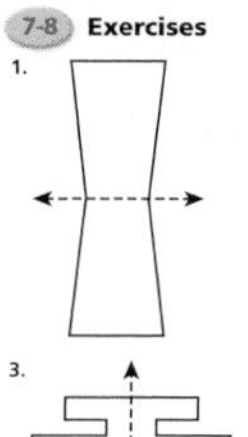

3.

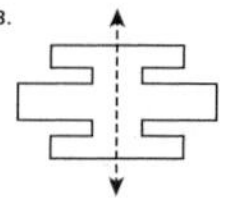

5.

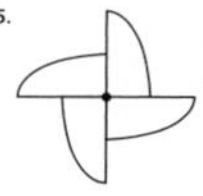

852 Selected Answers

7.

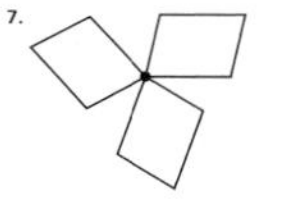

9.

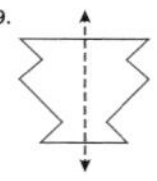

11.

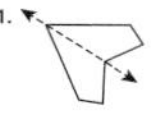

13.

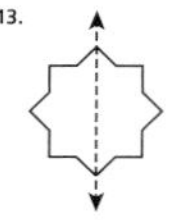

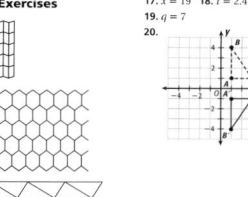

15.

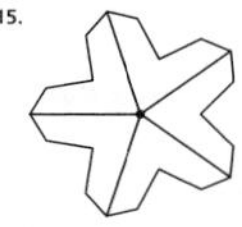

21. 2 lines **23.** 1 line **25.** 2 lines **31.** G **33.** 31 mi/h **35.** $j = 5$ **37.** $m = 4$

7-9 Exercises

1.

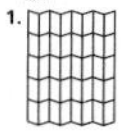

7.

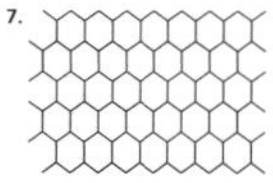

9.

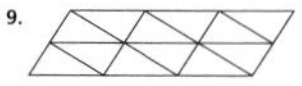

11. yes **15.** hexagon **21.** 4.5×10^{-7} **23.** perpendicular

Chapter 7 Study Guide: Review

1. parallel lines; perpendicular lines **2.** rectangle; rhombus **3.** 112° **4.** 68° **5.** 112° **6.** 66° **7.** 114° **8.** 66° **9.** 66° **10.** 114° **11.** $m^0 = 26°$ **12.** 135° **13.** 147.3°

14.

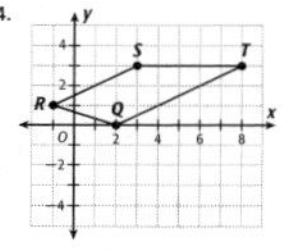

trapezoid

15.

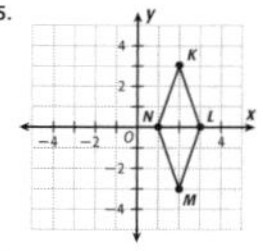

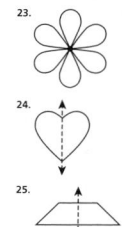

16.

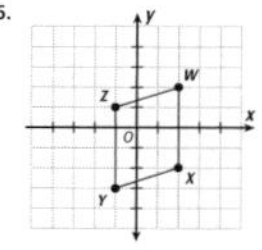

17. $x = 19$ **18.** $t = 2.4$ **19.** $q = 7$

20.

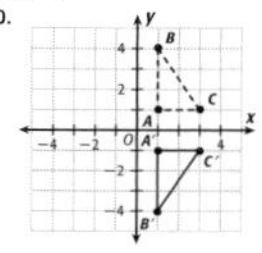

21.

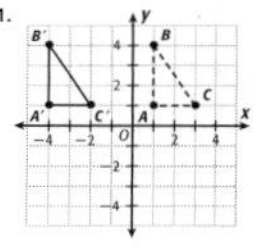

22.

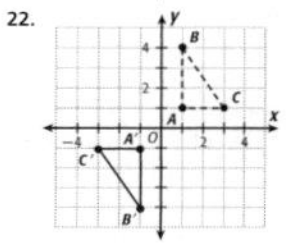

23.

24.

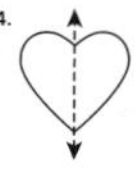

25.

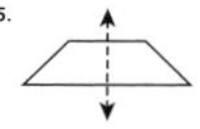

26. Possible answer:

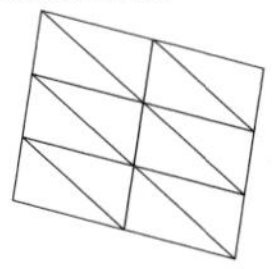

27. Possible answer:

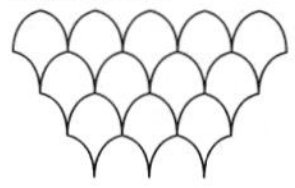

Selected Answers 853

Selected Answers

800 Selected Answers pages 850–853

Chapter 8

8-1 Exercises
1. 28 cm 3. 12.2x ft 5. 18 units²
7. 14 units² 9. 42 cm
11. 26x units 13. 24 units²
15. 12 units² 17. 64 units
19. 18 ft; 10.5 ft² 21. $3375
23. 42,000 mi² 27. B 29. x = −4
31. a = −37 33. rational
35. rational 37. not a real number

8-2 Exercises
1. 102 ft 3. 30 units 5. 19
7. 51.2 in. 9. 42 units²
15. 25 units² 13. 70 ft 15. 15
17. 21 19. 20 units² 21. 12 units²
23. 60 units² 25. 25x units²
27. 9.1 ft 29. 1929.5 ft²
31. 2747.9 ft² 33. 273 ft² 37. 7.1
39. $\frac{1}{2}$ quart 41. 45 units²

8-3 Exercises
1. 6π cm; 18.8 cm 3. 16.8π ft²;
52.8 ft² 5. A = 4π units²;
12.6 units²; C = 4π units; 12.6 units
7. 8π in.; 56.5 in. 9. 256π cm²
803.8 cm² 11. A = 16π units²;
50.2 units²; C = 8π units; 25.1 units
13. C ≈ 10.7 m; A ≈ 9.1 m²
15. C ≈ 56.5 in.; A ≈ 254.3 in.²
17. 6.4 cm 19. 24 in. 11.7 m
23. 248.1 in² 25. C = 30π ft²
94.2; ft; A = 225π ft² 29. ≈ 706.5 ft²
31. 785 33. 50° 35. 65°
37. 24 units²

8-4 Exercises
1. vertices: J, K, L, M, N, P, Q, R
edges: $\overline{JK}, \overline{KL}, \overline{LM}, \overline{MJ}$, etc.; faces:
quadrilaterals JKLM, PQRN, etc.
17. D 19. $1.79 21. $128.58
23. 226.9 in.²

8-5 Exercises
1. 463.1 cm³ 3. 1256 m³
5. ≈ 1500 ft³ 7. 300 in³ 9. 351 m³
11. ≈ 60 cm³ 13a. 800 in³

15a. 46,200,000 in³ b. about 18.8 ft
21. J 23. (5, −9) 25. 4 in.

8-6 Exercises
1. 20 cm³ 3. 99.7 ft³ 5. 9.1 cm³
7. Yes 9. 160.29 in³ 11. 35.0 m³
13. 66.2 ft³ 15. 5494.5 units³
17. 13,083.33 m³ 19. 6 in. 21. 11 ft
23. 600 in³ 25. 301,056 ft³ 29. A
31. 4 cm 33. t = 8 35. t = 0

8-7 Exercises
1. 791.3 cm² 3. 61.8 m²
7. 1160 mm² 9. no 11. 1920² ≈
6028.8 mm² 13. 4 m 15. $34.56
17. at least 2 quarts 21. J 23. 0.3
25. −0.26 27. 12 units²
29. 9 units²

8-8 Exercises
1. 105 m² 3. 144 m² 5. ≈ 702.5 ft²
7. 125.6 mm² 9. no 11. 0.18 km²
13. ≈ 877,201,312 m² 15a. ≈ 481;
≈ 277 b. Menkaure; ≈ 191,684 ft²
c. Khufu; 91,636,272 ft³ 19. B
21. 8 23. 10 25. 120 ft³

8-9 Exercises
1. 36π cm³; 113.0 cm³ 3. 6.6π m³;
207 m³ 5. 4π in²; 12.6 in²
7. 256π cm²; 803.8 cm² 9. The
volume of the sphere and the cube
are about equal 11. 246.9π cm³
13. 1.3 in³ 15. 207.4π m²
17. 400π cm² 19. 366.17π in³
21. V = 52.41π ≈ 164.55 yd³;
S = 46.24π ≈ 145.19 yd² 23. 30 km
25. ≈ 5392 cm³ 27. ≈ 3.14 cm²
29. J 31. 12 33. 13 35. 1
37. 24,021 cm²

8-10 Exercises
1. 4:1 3. 64:1 5. 112 min 7. 4:1
9. 32 cm 11. 1 cm 13. 9 cm
15. 7 cm 17. 1,000,000 cm³
21a. 2508.8 in³; ≈ 10.9 gal
b. about 2541 in³ 25. D 29. w = 2
31. 1869.4 ft² 33. 1256 cm²

Chapter 8 Study Guide: Review
1. perimeter, area 2. edge, vertex
3. about 7.18 in², 12 in. 4. 198 m²,
80 m 5. 9 cm² 6. 16 in²
7. 452.16 in² 8. 55.3896 cm²
9. 28.26 m² 10. 1.1304 ft²
11.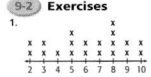
12.
13.
14. 339.12 cm³ 15. 1053 ft³
16. 320 ft³ 17. 37.68 in³
18. 680 mm² 19. 132 cm²
20. 439.6 in² 21. 904.32 in³
22. 24,416.64 m³ 23. 3 times as
small 24. 9 times as small
25. 27 times as small

Chapter 9

9-1 Exercises
1. systematic 3. Population: pet
store customers 5. voluntary
response 7. Population: people
who attend the team's games
9. convenience 11. voluntary
response 13. stratified
15. Population: city residents
21. D 23. 5 25. 6 27. 7^6 29. x^8

9-2 Exercises
1. [box plot]
3. 63, 66, 68, 73, 73, 75, 77, 80, 81,
81, 90, 94, 95, 99 7. 50, 51, 54, 58,
62, 66, 67, 71, 74, 75, 76, 76, 82
9.

Coldest		Warmest
7 0	1	
7 5	2	
6 6 2	3	
8 6	4	0 3 4 7
	5	0 1 2 9
	6	2

Key: 7|1| means 17°
4|0 means 40°

11. 13, 12, 11,14,10, 8, 9, 15
13. African Americans older than

40 years 15. African Americans
who are not married 17. 27 19. 61
25. 3 27. 48 29. systematic

9-3 Exercises
1. ≈ 34, 43, 35, no mode 3. 5
5. range 7. mean 9. 87.6
11. 5.85 13. median 15. mean
17. mode 19a. 3,625,00,000 miles
b. median 25. 60.4 27. 564.7
29. Population: shoppers; sample:
paid shoppers at a mall

9-4 Exercises
1. 52
3. [box plot]
19 26 33 44.5 59
5. The medians are equal, but data
set B has a much greater range.
7. 85.5
9. [box plot]
50 54 68 84 99
11. Data set X has a greater
median. 13. 68; 85 15. 35
17. [box plot] 67 75 85 93 99
19. [box plot]
27. Range: 25 29. 9 and −9
31. 1 and −1 33. 15.5

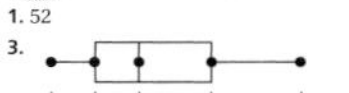

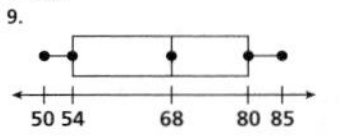

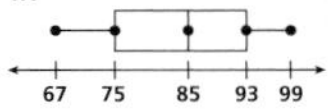

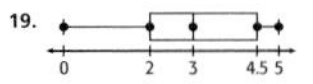

9-5 Exercises
1.

Data	Frequency Data Set 1	Frequency Data Set 2
9	5	2
10	2	5
11	3	4
12	3	1
13	3	1

3. male: approximately 73.5 yr;
female: approximately 79.5 yr

5.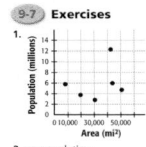
Entrée prices ($)

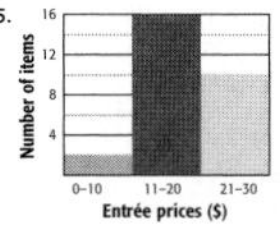

7.

Data	Frequency Data Set 1	Frequency Data Set 2
1	4	5
2	3	4
3	2	4
4	2	2
5	3	3
6	3	3

13. C 15. 2,880 17. 900 19. 882

9-6 Exercises
1. Possible answer: The scale does
not start at zero, so changes appear
exaggerated. 3. Possible answer:
The fruits are all different sizes.
5. Possible answer: The graph has
no scale, so it's impossible to
compare the money earned.
7. Possible answer: The difference
between the two groups' responses
is only 2. 13. B 15. 32 units²

9-7 Exercises
1. [scatter plot]
Population (millions) vs Area (mi²)
3. no correlation
5. [scatter plot]
Miles per gallon vs Price ($1000)
7. positive 9. positive 11. negative
15. no correlation 17. 3 19. The
sample size is too small.

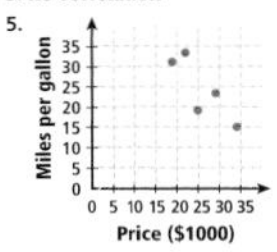

9-8 Exercises
1. bar graph 3. circle graph
5. line graph 7. circle graph
15. mode: 22 17. 84.9 yd²

Chapter 9 Study Guide: Review
1. median 2. variability 3. line of
best fit 4. population: moviegoers
5. sample: 100 people who own
cell phones 6. sample: 50 parents
of middle-school-aged children
7.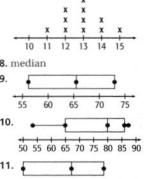
10 11 12 13 14 15
8. median
9.
55 60 65 70
10.
50 55 60 65 70 75 80 85 90
11.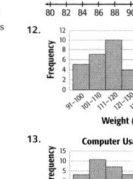
80 82 84 86 88 90 92 94
12. [histogram] Frequency vs Weight (lb)
91-100 ... 141-150
13. [histogram] Computer Usage
Frequency vs Weight (lb)
14. Different sized icons represent
the same number of pizzas
ordered. 15. no correlation
16. circle graph

Chapter 10

10-1 Exercises
1. 0.6; 60.4 3. 0.709 5. $\frac{1}{5}, \frac{1}{5}, \frac{1}{5}, \frac{1}{5}$
7. 0.72 9. 0.885 11. 0.784
13. 0.545 19. A 21. 0.0001
23. 0.00001 25. undefined
27. $-\frac{3}{2}$

10-2 Exercises
1. 0.34 3. more likely to walk
5. ≈ 0.319 7. more likely to have
one sibling 9. 0.25 11. 0.025
13. 0.35 15. 0.3 19. 51 21. −4.4
23. $\frac{3}{8}$ 25. $\frac{1}{8}$

10-3 Exercises
13. B 15. $\frac{2 \text{ pints}}{1 \text{ quart}}$ 17. $\frac{1 \text{ m}}{1000 \text{ mm}}$
19. 0.16

10-4 Exercises
1. $\frac{1}{2}$ 3. $\frac{1}{12}$ 5. $\frac{1}{4}$ 7. red 9. 0 11. $\frac{1}{2}$
13. $\frac{1}{18}$ 15. $\frac{1}{2}$ 17. 30 19. $\frac{1}{2}$ 21. $\frac{1}{2}$
23. $\frac{1}{8}$ 25. $\frac{1}{2}$ 29. $\frac{5}{9}$ 31. yes 33. no

10-5 Exercises
1. dependent 3. $\frac{1}{32}$ 5. $\frac{10}{253}$
7. independent 9. $\frac{9}{2}$ 11. $\frac{1}{24}$ 13. $\frac{4}{27}$
15. $\frac{3}{8}$ ≈ 0.03125 21. $\frac{1}{9}$ 23. 52

10-6 Exercises
1. 525 3. B 5. not fair 7. 5
9. fair 11. 25 13. 0.17 54 21. A
23. 208 units² 25. 40m units²
27. The volume is 8 times as large.

10-7 Exercises
1. 1:135 3. $\frac{1}{142,000}$ 5. 1:79
7. 1:2240 9. $\frac{1}{9000}$ 11. 1:619
13. 1:35; 35:1 15. 1:11; 11:1
17. 1:1; 1:1 19. 1:1 21. 1:2 27. B
29. $30, $330 31. fair

10-8 Exercises
1. 676,000 3. 0.729 5. 8
7. 0.7865 9. 24 shirts 11. 18

13. 9 15. 12 17. 2,176,782,336
19. 5400 23. G 25. 16 27. $\frac{7}{4}$
29. 10%

10-9 Exercises
1. 720 3. 15,120 5. 39,916,800
7. 56 9. 24 11. 24 13. 5040
15. 10,518,300 17. 336
19. 3,628,800 21. 1 23. 132 25. 1
27. 1 29. 1 31. n 33. 5040
35. 1320 37. 462 41. A 45. 60

Chapter 10 Study Guide: Review
1. probability 2. sample space
3. permutation 4. 0.85, 0.15
5. 0.15 7. $\frac{4}{5}$ 8. $\frac{6}{25}$ 9. $\frac{13}{1296}$
10. 20 laps 11. 3:10 12. 2,600,000
14. ≈ 0.59 14. 120 15. 210

Chapter 11

11-1 Exercises
1. 5x 3. 12f + 8 5. 6p − 9
7. 5x + 8y 9. 9x + y
11. 7g + 5h − 12 13. r + 12
15. 2t + 56 17. y = 15 19. 13y
21. 6a + 15 23. 5x + 3 25. 9p
27. 13x + 5 29. 6a + z
31. 9x + 6q + 2 33. 9a + 8c + 5
35. 12y − 14 37. 12y + 23
39. 19x − 16 41. p = 6 43. y = 8
45. x = 12 47. 12x 49. 7d + 1
51. x = 3 53. 49g + 53s + 44b
59. D 63. 28% increase
65. 57% increase

11-2 Exercises
1. d = 3 3. e = 6 5. h = 7
7. x = −1 9. p = −1 11. 6
13. k = −10 15. w = 3 17. y = 5
19. h = 6 21. m = 2 23. x = −12
25. n = 27 27. b = −13 29. x = 17
31. y = −7 33. $11.80 per hour
35. 31 and 32 37. 212°F 41. C
43. 27 in³ 45. 15 47. 5a − b + 4

11-3 Exercises
1. x = 1 3. x = 2 5. x = −20
7. x = 1 9. d = 5 11. 2.5 min
13. n = 4 15. n = 1 17. x = 4
19. p = 2 21. n = 5 23. 3 h
25. y = 2 27. n = 5 29. x = 3
31. 350 units 33. 22, 23 39. J
41. 7.39×10^9 43. -4.1×10^6
45. x = 0.5

11-4 Exercises
1. r > 18 3. 120 ≥ j, or j ≤ 120
5. −40 ≥ a, or a ≤ −40
7. y > −63 9. 104 sandwiches:
$\frac{\$400}{\$3.85}$ 11. 75 < x, or x > 75
13. −77 ≥ p, or p ≤ −77
15. h > 12 17. q ≥ 14 19. 6 > r,
or r < 6 21. w ≥ −3 23. t < 95
25. a < 120 27. x < 110 29. n ≥ 9
31. x ≥ −128 35. C 39. C
41. $\frac{1}{36}$, or $\frac{1}{12}$ 43. $\frac{1}{36}$

11-5 Exercises
1. k > 2 3. y < −8 5. y ≥ 7
7. x < 3 9. h ≤ 1 11. d < −1
13. at least 21 caps 15. x > 4
17. q ≤ 2 19. x ≤ −7 21. a ≥ −3
23. k ≥ 3 25. r < 3 27. p ≥ $\frac{22}{5}$
29. w > −1 31. a > $\frac{1}{3}$ 33. q < 6
35. b < 2.7 37. f ≤ −27 39. 7
41. at least 31 beads 43a. $158
b. 17 mo 47. B 53. a = 4

11-6 Exercises
1. (2, 3) 3. (−4, 7) 5. (0, 7)
7. (5, 3) 9. (1, 10) 11. (−9, 3)
13. (−1, 1) 15. (2, 7) 17. (2, 5)
19. (2, 3) 21. (1, 3) 23. (7, −3)
25. 4 bookmarks and 3 wall
hangings 27. (2, −17) 29. (2, 1)
31. (−1.3, 5.8) 33. no solution
35. 25 dimes and 10 quarters
37. x = 11 and y = 6 41. 6
43. a = 21 45. w = 12 47. p = 3

Chapter 11 Study Guide: Review
1. system of equations 2. like
terms 3. solution of a system of
equations 4. terms 5. 19m − 10
6. 14w + 6 7. 2x + 3y
8. 2t² − 4t + 3t³ 9. j − 6
10. 2 + 1 5. 12 = 8
13. v = −1 14. h = 2 15. t = −1
16. r = 3 17. z = 2 18. x = 12
22. y = $\frac{2}{3}$, no solution
24. z = 5 25. m ≥ 18 26. n ≤ −3
27. t > −16 28. p < −3
29. b ≥ −27 30. a > 8 31. z > 1
32. h ≤ 33 33. a < 24 34. x ≥ −1
35. k > 3 36. y > $\frac{1}{8}$ 37. (−2, 1)
39. (2, 6) 39. (3, 5) 40. (3, −2)
41. no solution 42. infinite
solutions 43a. x + y = 32 b. x = 8

Chapter 12

12-1 Exercises
1. linear 3. not linear 5. linear
7. not linear 9. not linear
11. linear 13. 509.6 N
15. (−1, −2), (0, 0), (1, 2)
17. (−1, −6), (0, −1), (1, 4)
19. (−1, −5), (0, −3), (1, −1)
21. (−1, −6), (0, −4), (1, −2)
23. (−1, 1.5), (0, 3.5), (1, 5.5)
25. C = 2.25b + 3 29. B
31. −8, −5, −2 33. $\frac{1}{16}$
35. cannot combine

12-2 Exercises
1. 3, $\frac{1}{4}$ 5. The graph shows a
variable rate of change. 7. The
slope of the line is 5. 9. $-\frac{1}{2}$
11. $-\frac{3}{4}$ 13. $-\frac{6}{5}$ 15. The graph
shows a constant rate of change.
17. The slope of the line is 4.
19. Graph A 21. Graph B
23. y = $-\frac{4}{5}$x + 350 25. The
roof is flat. 29. H 31. negative

12-3 Exercises
1. (4, 0), (0, −4) 3. (−6, 0), (0, −4)
5. y = $\frac{1}{3}$x 7. y = $\frac{1}{4}$x − 4 9. m =
4.5; b = 25 11. y = −4x + 3

13. (2, 0), (0, 6) 15. (3, 0), (0, −12)
17. y = −3x 19. y = −2x − 2
21. m = 12 23. y = −x
31. slope = 955 33. D 35. $6.35
per hour 37. $5.50 per burrito
39. $\frac{4}{5}$ 41. $\frac{1}{4}$

12-4 Exercises
1. y − 6 = 5x 3. y − 840 =
−10.5(x − 40) 5. y = 6(x + 3)
17. y − 3 = 4(x + 2)
21. y + 7 = −1(x + 5) 29. G
31. 7x − 5y + 18 33. −4x
37. y = x − 5

12-5 Exercises
1. yes 3. y = 3x 5. y = $\frac{1}{2}$x
7. y = $\frac{1}{3}$x 9. no 11. y = $\frac{1}{3}$x
13. y = $\frac{1}{13}$x 15. y = $\frac{1}{10}$x 17. yes
19. no 21. No; 27. 28 29. m = 4
31. m = −0.25

12-6 Exercises
7a. 18r + 15r ≤ 450 b. yes
17. about $70 19. no 21. yes
23. no 25. B 29. no 31. m = −6
33. y − 1 = 5(x − 4)

12-7 Exercises
3. no 7. positive 9. negative
11a. 7 11b. 14.6%, 22.8%, 36.6%,
51.0%, 56.4%; mean = 36.28%

Chapter 12 Study Guide: Review
1. x-intercept; y-intercept
2. slope intercept form; point-
slope form 3. direct variation
4. linear 5. linear 6. not linear
7. not linear 8. linear 9. linear
9. linear 10. not linear 11. not
linear 12. $-\frac{3}{4}$ 13. −4 14. $-\frac{5}{4}$
15. −1 16. −1 17. $\frac{3}{4}$ 18. $-\frac{9}{2}$
19. y = $\frac{4}{3}$x + 3 20. y = $\frac{6}{5}$x − 2
21. y = $-\frac{2}{3}$x + 4 22. y = $\frac{7}{4}$x + 3
23. y = 3x + 4 24. y = −3x + 2
25. y = $-\frac{1}{3}$x + 7 26. y = $\frac{1}{2}$x − 2
27. y = 2x − 2 28. y = −4x − 5
29. y = $-\frac{5}{3}$x − 3 30. y = 2x
31. y = 6x 32. y = 13x 33. y = $\frac{1}{7}$x

Chapter 13

13-1 Exercises
1. yes 3. yes 5. no 7. 37
9. −92 11. 6 oz 13. yes 15. yes
17. yes 19. 1.2 21. 1 23. 25, 26,
29, 25, 51, 38, 25 27. 1, 3, 5, 7, 9
33. 0.25, 0.5, 0.75, 1 31. 11:53,
11:46, 11:32 33. first: $127.50,
$180, $232.50, $285 37. C
39. x = −1 41. k = −9.4
43. sample: the cable companies
customers whose last names
begin with an "s."

13-2 Exercises
1. no 3. yes 5. yes 7. 6144 9. $\frac{1}{9}$
11. $7.18 13. no 15. yes 17. yes
19. 952 $\frac{8}{49}$ 21. 4.1374 23. 39.0625
25. 18.6, 22 27. $-\frac{1}{9}$ 29. 2 31. 30
33. 10 35. $\frac{1}{3}$ 37. $\frac{5}{3}$ 39. 27
41. 61,236 cells 43a. yes; $\frac{3}{4}$
b. 26 ft 49. yes 51. x = 16
53. −2p + 21 55. 40 + 7y

13-3 Exercises
1. 225 3. 178 5. $\frac{13}{15}$ 7. 3 9. $\frac{2}{5}$
11. 22 13. 117 15. 106 17. 4
19. 2.00002 21. $-\frac{1}{3}$ 23. 2
25. 3rd, 6th, 9th, 12th terms
27. 42 29. 880 Hz 33. H
35. 821,000 37. −1400 39. yes

13-4 Exercises
1. linear 3. linear 5. not linear
7. f(x) = 2x + 2 9. f(x) = 18x + 480
11. linear 13. not linear 15. linear
17. f(x) = 6x − 5 19. 16 lb
21a. f(x) = 5x + 1245 21b. 2745 ft
27. f(x) = −50r + 1800 29. $\frac{6}{19}$
40. $-\frac{21}{40}$ 33. 6.7 35. 8.1

13-5 Exercises
7. 7.29×10^{-5} g 15. $f(x) = 300 \cdot 3^t$
17. $\frac{1}{8}$, 1, 8 19. $\frac{1}{1000}$, 1, 1000
21. $f(x) = 3 \cdot 2^x$ 23. $f(x) = 1 \cdot 4^x$
25. 3 hours 27. 1.5625%
29. It has no x-intercepts. 33. C
35. 1.257 mm³ 37. $\frac{1}{4}$

13-6 Exercises
5. 5.1 ft 11. 15 13. 0 15. 37
17. $x = 4$, $x = -12$ 19. $x = 1$,
$x = -3$ 21. 6 and 6 27. B 31. 7
33. 7.5 ft 35. 12.75 ft 37. 45, 65

13-7 Exercises
1. no 7. $y = \frac{12}{9}$ 9. no 15. $y = \frac{9}{x}$
17. $y = \frac{26}{x}$ 19. 12 cm 21. $1600
25. D 27. $x = 5$ 29. $x = \frac{40}{3}$
31. $p < -1$

Chapter 13 Study Guide: Review
1. sequence 2. arithmetic sequence; geometric sequence
3. Fibonacci sequence 4. 29
5. 0.85 6. $\frac{10}{3}$ 7. -3072 8. $\frac{64}{625}$
9. -2 10. $\frac{1}{7}$ 11. 4 12. -3 13. 2
14. $f(x) = x - 1$ 15. $f(x) = \frac{1}{2}x + 4$
16. $f(x) = -2$

Chapter 14

14-1 Exercises
1. yes 3. no 5. binomial 7. not a polynomial 9. 8 11. 0 13. yes
15. no 17. yes 19. monomial
21. trinomial 23. not a polynomial 25. 2 27. 4 29. 1
31. 8 in³ 33. monomial
35. binomial 37. trinomial
39. not a polynomial
41. trinomial 43. not a polynomial 51. 9
53. -3.5×10^{-5} 55. $x = 13$
57. $m = 100$

14-2 Exercises
1. $-3b^2$ and $4b^2$ 3. $7x^2 + 4x - 5$
5. $12x - 32$ 7. $17a^2 - 21a$
9. $-t$ and $5t$ 11. $9p^2 + 7p$
13. $9x^2 - 32x$ 15. $6y^3 - 4$
17. $12s^2 + 2s - 3$
19. $2x^2 - 13x + 15$ 21. $9m^2 - 20m$ 23. $17mn$ 25. $40 - 1000d^2$
27. $82xy + 82y$ in² 29. C
31. 51.2%

14-3 Exercises
1. $5x^3 + 3x + 6$ 3. $11r^2s + 9rs$
5. $15ab^2 + 3ab - a^2b - 8$
7. $128 + 32w$ in. 9. $7g^2 + g - 1$
11. $-3h^6 + 12h^4 - h$
13. $13t^2 - 4t + 12$
15. $-w^2 - 4w - 2$
17. $7w^2y + 2wy^24wy$
19. $\approx 6.19r^3 + 4r^2 + 5r + 2$ 27. C
29. 84 ft 31. 42 ft 33. $\frac{11}{10}$ 35. $\frac{6}{25}$

14-4 Exercises
1. $-4x^2y$ 3. $-3x^2 + 8x - 5$
5. $8x^3 - 5x + 6$ 7. $-2b^3 + 5b^2 - b + 4$ 9. $-4m^2n - 7mn + 3mn^2$
11. $-2x^2y - 5xy + 10x - 8$
13. $-4x^3 + 9x^2 - 12x + 21$ in³
15. $-3r + 5r^2$ 17. $-4xy^2 - 2xy$
19. $9b^2 + 2b + 9$ 21. $5a - 8$
23. $x^2 - 3x + 4$ 25. $-6p^3 - 5p^2 - 2p^2t^2 + 10pt^2$ 27. $-2b + 2ab$
29. $6y^2 - 12x^2y + 5x^2$ 31. $2x^2 - 6x - 1$ in² 33. B 37. $10x + 29$
39. ±3 41. ±13 43. $-zy^3 - 5zy$

14-5 Exercises
1. $-15s^3t^5$ 3. $-35h^6j^{10}$ 5. $35p^4r^5$
7. $6hm - 8h^2$ 9. $-3x^3 + 15x^2 - 30x$ 11. $A = \frac{1}{2}b_1h + \frac{1}{2}b_2h$
13. $2g^3h^8$ 15. $-2s^3t^4$ 17. $7.5h^3j^{10}$
19. $15z^3 - 12z^2$ 21. $-6c^4d^3 + 12c^2d^3$ 23. $-12s^4t^3 - 15s^3t^3 + 6s^4t^4$ 25. $-24b^6$ 27. $6a^3b^6$
29. $-3m^5 + 15m^3$ 31. $x^5 - x^2y^5$
33. $3f^9g^2 + f^3g^2 - f^2g^5$
35. $20m^4p^5 - 12m^3p^7 + 24m^4p^5$
37. $63x$ 43. $15x^3d^4 - 20c^2d^4$
45. 1,067.6 cm² 47. $y = \frac{64}{x}$

14-6 Exercises
1. $xy + 4x - 5y - 20$ 3. $12m^2 + 7m - 45$ 5. $m^2 - 9m + 14$
7. $600 - 200x + 4x^2$ ft² 9. $b^2 - 9$
11. $9x^2 + 30x + 25$ 13. $v^2 + 4v - 5$
15. $3x^2 + 13x - 30$ 17. $12b^2 + 11bc - 5c^2$ 19. $12r^2 - 11rs - 5s^2$
21. $100 + 50x + 4x^2$ yd² 23. $b^2 + 6b + 9$ 25. $4x^2 - 9$ 27. $a^2 + 14a + 49$ 29. $b^2 + 7b + -60$
31. $r^2 - 13r + 36$ 33. $3b^2 - 5b - 28$ 35. $4m^2 + 11mn - 3n^2$
37. $r^2 - 25$ 39. $15r^2 - 22rs + 8s^2$
41. $PV + bP + aV + ab = c$
45. B 47. 1:5 49. 1:20
51. $-4m^2 + 12m - 24$
53. $-11x^2y + 4xy^2 + 16xy$

Chapter 14 Study Guide: Review
1. polynomial: degree of a polynomial 2. FOIL; binomial
3. binomial. trinomial
4. trinomial 5. not a polynomial
6. not a polynomial 7. monomial
8. not a polynomial 9. binomial
10. 8 11. 4 12. 3 13. 5 14. 6
15. $7t^2 - 3t + 1$ 16. $11gh - 9g^2h$
17. $20mn - 12m$ 18. $8a^2 - 10b$
19. $36st^2 - 23st$ 20. $6x^2 - 2x + 5$
21. $5x^4 + x^2 - x + 7$ 22. $2h^2 + 8h + 7$ 23. $2xy^2 - 2x^2y + 2xy$
24. $13n^2 + 12$ 25. $6x^2 - 8$
26. $-w^2 - 12w + 14$ 27. $-4x^2 - 16x - 14$ 28. $4ab^2 - 11ab + 4a^2b$
29. $-p^3q^2 - 4p^2q^2 - 2pq^2$
30. $12s^2t^4 + 4s^2t^3 + 32st^3$
31. $12a^4b^3 + 30a^3b^3 - 36a^3b + 24a^2b^2$ 32. $2m^3 - 16m^2 + 2m$
33. $10g^3h^3 - 15gh^3 + 20gh - 30h^2$
34. $2j^9k^3 - \frac{3}{2}j^4k^4 + j^6k^5$
35. $18x^7y^{14} - 15x^6y^{12} + 12x^3y^7 - 24x^3y^6$ 36. $p^2 - 8p + 72$ 37. $b^2 + 10b + 24$ 38. $3r^2 + 11r - 4$
39. $3a^2 - 11ab - 20b$
40. $m^2 - 14m + 49$ 41. $9t^2 - 36$
42. $6b^2 - 2bt - 28t^2$ 43. $-3x^2 - 2x^2 + 40$ 44. $y^2 - 22y + 121$

Additional Answers

Chapter 1

1-2 Exercises

5. 18 plus the product of 43 and s

6. 37 less than the quotient of 22 and r

7. 10 plus the quotient of y and 31

8. the product of 29 and b minus 93

10. Possible answer: Calvin has 450 less songs on his MP3 player than his friend Brian. How many songs does Calvin have on his MP3 player if Brian has 1325 songs? 875 songs

16. 142 minus the product of 19 and t

17. the product of 16 and g plus 12

18. 14 plus the quotient of 5 and d

19. 15 less than the quotient of w and 182

20. $\frac{1680}{n}$; \$168, \$140, \$120, \$105

21. Possible answer: The total cost of a new radiator is \$372 plus labor. How much is the total cost if the cost of labor is \$137? \$509

1-5 Exercises

33. Cleopatra takes the throne and Napoleon invades Egypt.

34. Possible answer: The number of the year expressed in B.C.E. decreases as time goes forward. This is what happens with the negative part of the number line. As you move to the right and get closer to zero, the absolute value of the numbers decreases.

35. Possible answer: The calculations that involve an C.E. and B.C.E. year would be one less than originally calculated. But any calculations strictly in C.E. or B.C.E. would remain the same.

1-9 Exercises

7.

8.

9.

10.

11.

12.

13.

14.

21.

22.

23.

24.

25.

26.

27.

28.

45.

46.

47.

48.

49.

50.

51.

52.

1B Ready To Go On?

18.

19.

20.

21.

22.

23.

Chapter 2

2-1 Exercises

61b. 3×3; 2×3;
2×2; 3×5;
$2 \times 2 \times 2 \times 2$; 5×5;
$2 \times 2 \times 2$; $2 \times 2 \times 2$

c. $0.\overline{4}$; repeating
$0.1\overline{6}$; repeating
0.25; terminating
$0.4\overline{6}$; repeating
0.5625; terminating
0.48; terminating
0.625; terminating
0.375; terminating

64. Possible answer: The student did not follow the rule for dividing a negative number by a negative number. The simplified fraction should be positive.

65. Possible answer: If the prime factors of the denominators are 2's and 5's, the fraction is equivalent to a terminating decimal. If there are any other prime factors, the fraction is equivalent to a repeating decimal.

2-8 Exercises

45.

46.

47.

48.

Chapter 3

3-1 Exercises

5.

x	y	(x, y)
1	2	(1, 2)
2	4	(2, 4)
3	6	(3, 6)
4	8	(4, 8)

6.

x	y	(x, y)
-4	-17	$(-4, -17)$
-3	-13	$(-3, -13)$
-2	-9	$(-2, -9)$
-1	-5	$(-1, -5)$

12.

x	y	(x, y)
1	1	(1, 1)
2	3	(2, 3)
3	5	(3, 5)
4	7	(4, 7)

13.

x	y	(x, y)
-4	-3	$(-4, -3)$
-3	0	$(-3, 0)$
-2	3	$(-2, 3)$
-1	6	$(-1, 6)$

14.

x	y	(x, y)
2	3	(2, 3)
4	11	(4, 11)
6	19	(6, 19)
8	27	(8, 27)

15.

x	y	(x, y)
2	2	(2, 2)
4	8	(4, 8)
6	14	(6, 14)
8	20	(8, 20)

27.

x	y	(x, y)
1	0	(1, 0)
2	2	(2, 2)
3	4	(3, 4)
4	6	(4, 6)

28.

x	y	(x, y)
−4	−13	(−4, −13)
−3	−10	(−3, −10)
−2	−7	(−2, −7)
−1	−4	(−1, −4)

29.

x	y	(x, y)
1	8	(1, 8)
2	9	(2, 9)
3	10	(3, 10)
4	11	(4, 11)

30.

x	y	(x, y)
2	8	(2, 8)
4	14	(4, 14)
6	20	(6, 20)
8	26	(8, 26)
10	32	(10, 32)

3-2 Exercises

7–14.

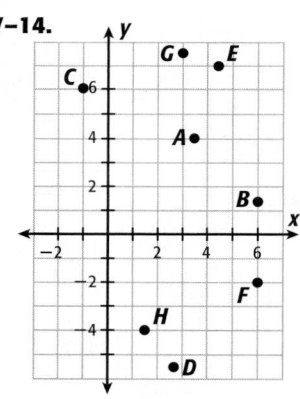

15.

x	x + 0.5	y	(x, y)
0	0 + 0.5	0.5	(0, 0.5)
1	1 + 0.5	1.5	(1, 1.5)
2	2 + 0.5	2.5	(2, 2.5)

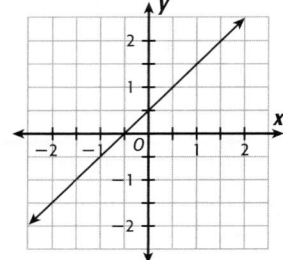

16.

x	$\frac{1}{2}x - 1$	y	(x, y)
0	$\frac{1}{2}(0) - 1$	−1	(0, −1)
1	$\frac{1}{2}(1) - 1$	$-\frac{1}{2}$	$(1, -\frac{1}{2})$
2	$\frac{1}{2}(2) - 1$	0	(2, 0)

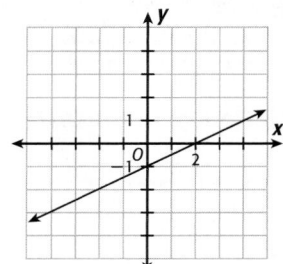

23–30.

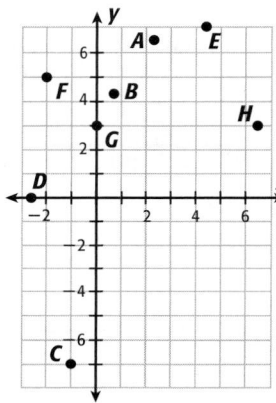

31.

x	$\frac{1}{3}x$	y	(x, y)
0	$\frac{1}{3}(0)$	0	(0, 0)
1	$\frac{1}{3}(1)$	$\frac{1}{3}$	$(1, \frac{1}{3})$
2	$\frac{1}{3}(2)$	$\frac{2}{3}$	$(2, \frac{2}{3})$

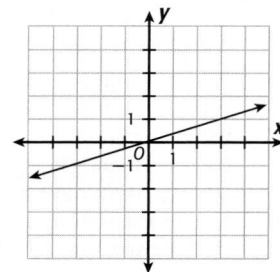

32.

x	2x + 1.5	y	(x, y)
0	2(0) + 1.5	1.5	(0, 1.5)
1	2(1) + 1.5	3.5	(1, 3.5)
2	2(2) + 1.5	5.5	(2, 5.5)

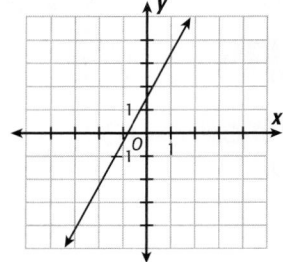

33.

x	55x	y	(x, y)
6.5	55(6.5)	357.5	(6.5, 357.5)
7.5	55(7.5)	412.5	(7.5, 412.5)
8.5	55(8.5)	467.5	(8.5, 467.5)

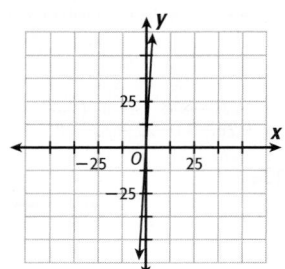

34.

x	$\frac{x}{16} + 1$	y	(x, y)
16	$\frac{16}{16} + 1$	2	(16, 2)
32	$\frac{32}{16} + 1$	3	(32, 3)
48	$\frac{48}{16} + 1$	4	(48, 4)
64	$\frac{64}{16} + 1$	5	(64, 5)
80	$\frac{80}{16} + 1$	6	(80, 6)

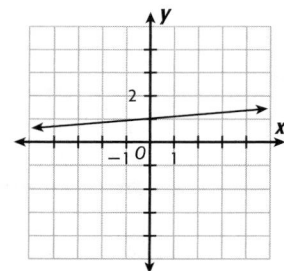

40.

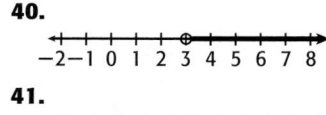

41.

42.

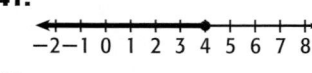

43.

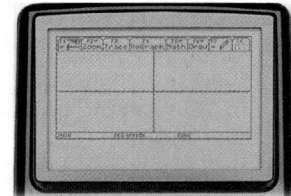
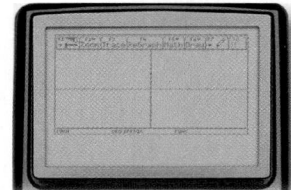
3-3 Exercises

11. 93 min; 70 min; 72 min; Possible graph:

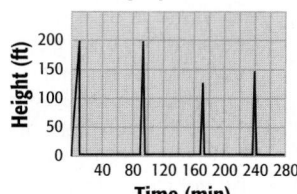

3A Ready To Go On?

15.

x	7x + 3	y	(x, y)
0	7(0) + 3	3	(0, 3)
1	7(1) + 3	10	(1, 10)
2	7(2) + 3	17	(2, 17)

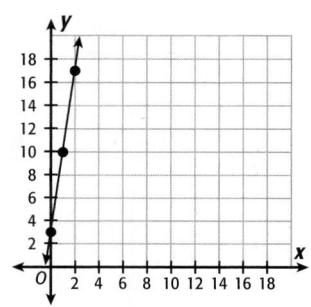

16.

x	−3x + 1	y	(x, y)
0	−3(0) + 1	1	(0, 1)
1	−3(1) + 1	−2	(1, −2)
2	−3(2) + 1	−5	(2, −5)

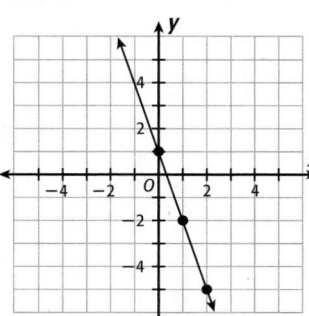

17.

x	$\frac{3}{4}x$	y	(x, y)
0	$\frac{3}{4}(0)$	0	(0, 0)
1	$\frac{3}{4}(1)$	$\frac{3}{4}$	$(1, \frac{3}{4})$
2	$\frac{3}{4}(2)$	$\frac{3}{2}$	$(2, \frac{3}{2})$

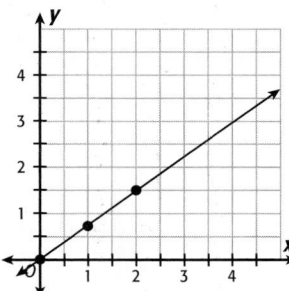

18.

x	1.2x + 3	y	(x, y)
0	1.2(0) + 3	3	(0, 3)
1	1.2(1) + 3	4.2	(1, 4.2)
2	1.2(2) + 3	5.4	(2, 5.4)

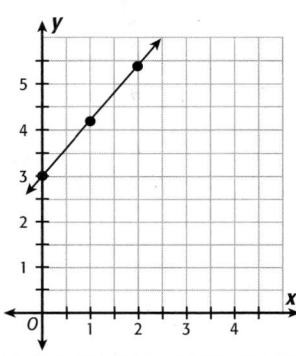

3-4 Exercises

1.

x	2x − 4	y
−2	2(−2) − 4	−8
0	2(0) − 4	−4
2	2(2) − 4	0

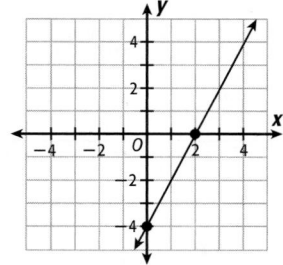

2.

x	3x + 4	y
−2	3(−2) + 4	−2
0	3(0) + 4	4
2	3(2) + 4	10

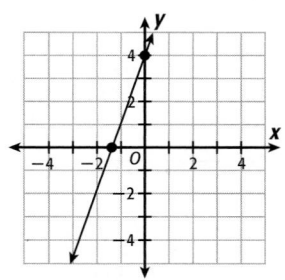

3.

x	4x − 3	y
−2	4(−2) − 3	−11
0	4(0) − 3	−3
2	4(2) − 3	5

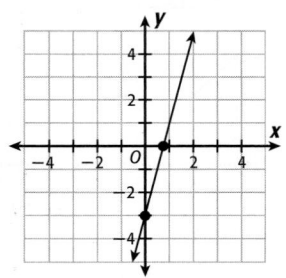

4.

x	−x + 1	y
−2	−(−2) + 1	3
0	−(0) + 1	1
2	−(2) + 1	−1

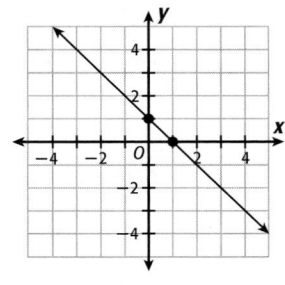

8.

x	2x + 5	y
−2	2(−2) + 5	1
0	2(0) + 5	5
2	2(2) + 5	9

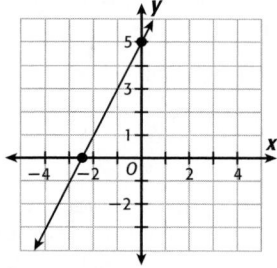

9.

x	3(x + 1)	y
−2	3(−2 + 1)	−3
0	3(0 + 1)	3
2	3(2 + 1)	9

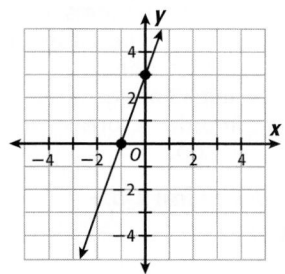

10.

x	−(3 − x)	y
−2	−(3 − (−2))	−5
0	−(3 − 0)	−3
2	−(3 − 2)	−1

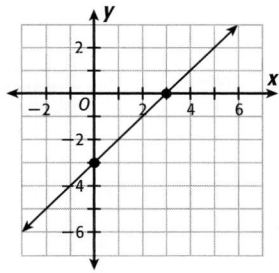

11.

x	2(1 − 2x)	y
−2	2(1 − 2(−2))	10
0	2(1 − 2(0))	2
2	2(1 − 2(2))	−6

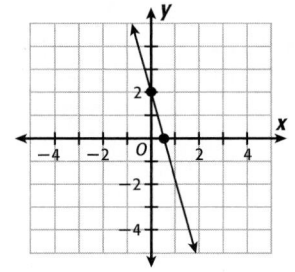

19c.

x	50x − 750	y
5	50(5) − 750	−500
7	50(7) − 750	−400
10	50(10) − 750	−250
12	50(12) − 750	−150

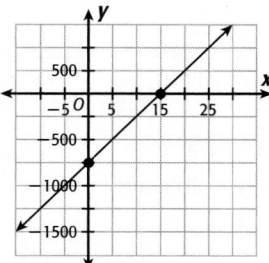

20.

x	50x − 750	y
0	50(0) − 750	−750
7	50(7) − 750	−400
15	50(15) − 750	0

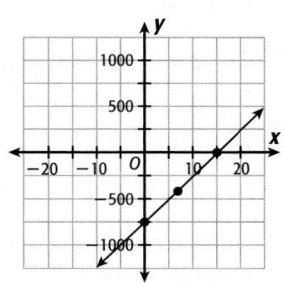

24. When x = 0, the function is not defined.

x	y
−3	$-\frac{1}{3}$
−2	$-\frac{1}{2}$
−1	−1
−0.5	−2
−0.25	−4
0.25	4
0.5	2
1	1
2	$\frac{1}{2}$
3	$\frac{1}{3}$

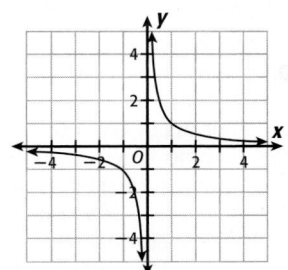

3-5 Exercises

2.

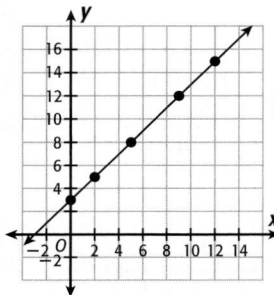

$y = x + 3$

4. Possible answer:

s	0	1	2	3	4
h	0	−0.5	−1.0	−1.5	−2.0

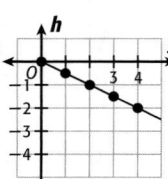

5.

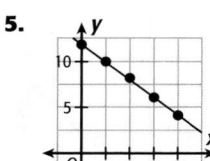

$y = 12 − x$

7. Possible answer:

g	0	1	2	3	4	5
d	0	20	40	60	80	100

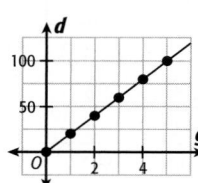

8. The graph does not show the same relationship; the graph shows $y = 4x − 1$

9. Possible answer:

x	0	1	2	3	4	5
y	0	2.5	5	7.5	10	12.5

$y = 2.5x$

10. a. Possible answer: A student gets three hours of computer game time for the first month of school. He gets two additional hours for each month after that during the school year.

b. Every week, a tutor spends 3 hours with each of her students and an additional 3 hours preparing her lesson plans.

11.

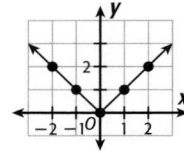

Possible answer: The curve looks like two different lines extending from the origin.

13. Possible Answer

x	200	400	600	800
y	−1500	−1000	−500	0

When 800 items are sold, there will be no profit or loss; so, the number of units that need to be sold in order to break even is 800.

3-5 Lesson Quiz

1.

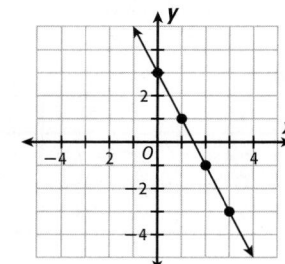

Possible answer:

x	w
0	3
1	1
2	−1
3	−3

2.

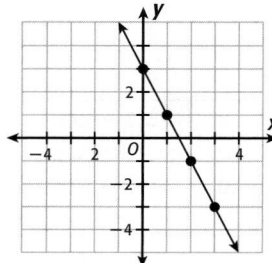

3. Possible answer:

x	y
−1	−3
0	1
1	5
2	9

3-6 Exercises

53.

x	y
−2	−7
0	−1
2	5

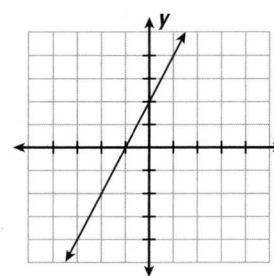

54.

x	y
−2	−2
0	2
2	6

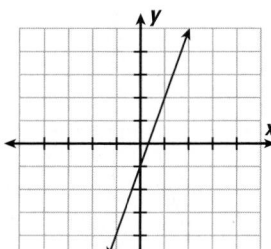

55.

x	y
−2	2
0	0
2	−2

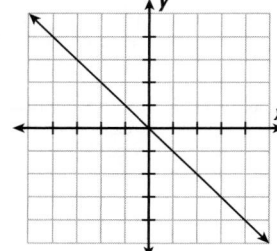

3B Ready To Go On?

1.

x	x + 7	y
−1	−1 + 7	6
0	0 + 7	7
1	1 + 7	8

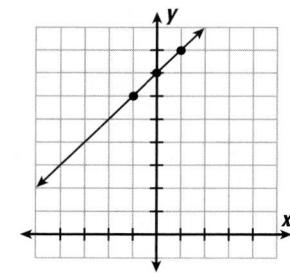

2.

x	4x + 2	y
−1	4(−1) + 2	−2
0	4(0) + 2	2
1	4(1) + 2	6

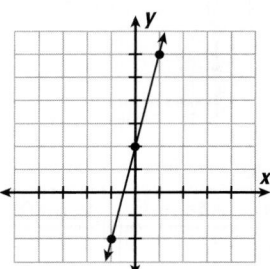

3.

x	$\frac{2}{3}x + \frac{1}{3}$	y
−1	$\frac{2}{3}(−1) + \frac{1}{3}$	$−\frac{1}{3}$
0	$\frac{2}{3}(0) + \frac{1}{3}$	$\frac{1}{3}$
1	$\frac{2}{3}(1) + \frac{1}{3}$	11

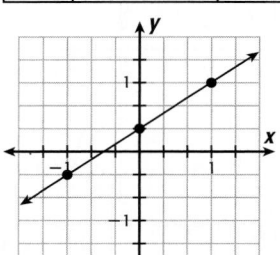

4.

x	5.2x	y
−1	5.2(−1)	−5.2
0	5.2(0)	0
1	5.2(1)	5.2

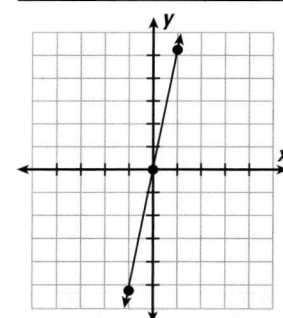

9. $y = 3x + 7$

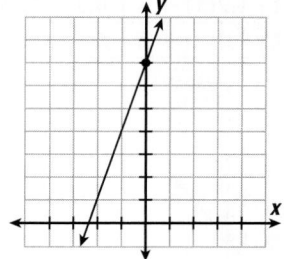

10. $y = \frac{1}{2}x + 2$

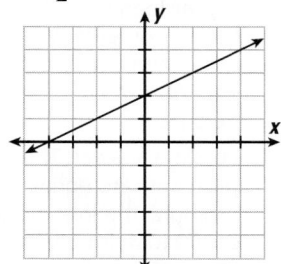

11. $y = \frac{3}{2}x - 2$

x	y
0	-2
1	$-\frac{1}{2}$
2	1

12. $y = 2x$

x	y
0	-2
1	$-\frac{1}{2}$
2	1

13.

d	8d	p
0	8(0)	0
50	8(50)	400
100	8(100)	800

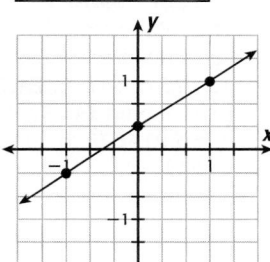

Multi-Step Test Prep

5.

Time (s)	Distance (ft)
0	2
1	5
2	8
3	11
4	11
5	11
6	11

Chapter 3 Test

11. Possible answer:

x	0	1	2	3
y	-5	-7	-9	-11

---

24. 59,049

25. 1

4-2 Exercises

37. $11^{-4} = \frac{1}{11} \cdot \frac{1}{11} \cdot \frac{1}{11} \cdot \frac{1}{11} = \frac{1}{14,641}$

38. $1^{10} = \frac{1}{1} \cdot \frac{1}{1} \cdot \frac{1}{1} \cdot \frac{1}{1} \cdot \frac{1}{1} \cdot \frac{1}{1} \cdot \frac{1}{1} \cdot \frac{1}{1} \cdot \frac{1}{1} \cdot \frac{1}{1} = 1$

39. $-6^{-3} = -1 \cdot \left(\frac{1}{6}\right) \cdot \left(\frac{1}{6}\right) \cdot \left(\frac{1}{6}\right) = -\frac{1}{216}$

40. $(-6)^{-3} \left(\frac{1}{6}\right) \cdot \left(\frac{1}{6}\right) \cdot \left(\frac{1}{6}\right) = -\frac{1}{216}$

41.

n	n^{-2}	$-2n$
-5	$\frac{1}{25}$	10
-4	$\frac{1}{16}$	8
-3	$\frac{1}{9}$	6
-2	$\frac{1}{4}$	4
-1	1	2
0	undefined	0
1	1	-2
2	$\frac{1}{4}$	-4
3	$\frac{1}{9}$	-6
4	$\frac{1}{16}$	-8
5	$\frac{1}{25}$	-10

42. Possible answer: The pattern is $-1, 1, -1, 1, \ldots$. $(-1)^{-100} = 1$. -1 raised to an even power is 1; -1 raised to an odd power is -1.

43. Possible answer: 1, 1, 1; for any value of n, $n^1 \cdot n^{-1} = 1$. Any number multiplied by its reciprocal is equal to 1.

50. 512, 64, 8, 1, $\frac{1}{8}$, $\frac{1}{64}$, each value is the previous value divided by 8; $\frac{1}{512}$

4-4 Exercises

51. Possible answer: The number with the greater power of 10 is greater. If the two numbers have equal powers of 10, then the number with the greater factor is greater.

52. Possible answer: The number would be between 0 and 1. If the power of ten has a negative exponent, the number can be written as a fraction with a denominator that is a positive power of ten. Because

---

the denominator will be larger than the numerator (by the rules of scientific notation), the fraction will be less than one.

53. The decimal needs to move 13 places. The decimal will need to move right to change 2.96 to the original number so the exponent is positive. 2.96×10^{13}

4-5 Exercises

35. Possible answer: No, 68.06 ft^2 is approximately 64 ft^2. $\sqrt{64} = 8$, so a better estimate would be 8 ft.

4-6 Exercises

1. 6 and 7; possible answer: 40 is between 36 and 49

2. -9 and -10; possible answer: 90 is between 81 and 100

3. 12 and 13; possible answer: 156 is between 144 and 169

4. -17 and -18; possible answer: 306 is between 289 and 324

12. -7 and -8; possible answer: 52 is between 49 and 56

13. 1 and 2; possible answer: 3 is between 1 and 4

14. 24 and 25; possible answer: 600 is between 576 and 625

15. -44 and -45; possible answer: 2000 is between 1936 and 2025

36. 800 ft/s

37. a. approximately 610 mi/h
   b. approximately 7.8 hr

38. Possible answer: The student should have multiplied before taking the square root.

39. $\approx 10,753$ ft

4-6 Technology Lab
Think and Discuss

1. No, it's not surprising because negative exponents indicate fractions not negative values.

---

12. Possible answer:

x	0	1	2	3
y	$-\frac{2}{3}$	$-\frac{1}{15}$	$-\frac{8}{15}$	$-1\frac{2}{15}$

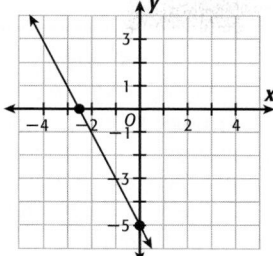

13.

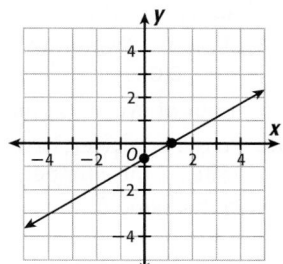

$y = 3x$

14.

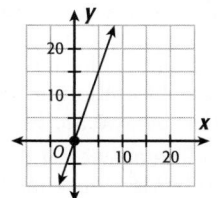

$y = 3x$

17.

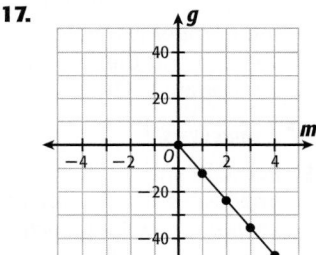

Chapter 4

Are You Ready?

17. 16,807

18. 1728

19. 81

20. 14,641

21. 262,144

22. 8

23. 100,000,000

Additional Answers

Try This

1. $\frac{1}{16} \approx 0.06$

2. 1; 1.4142; 1.7321; 2

3. $\frac{1}{1} = 1$; $\frac{1}{4} = 0.25$; $\frac{1}{25} = 0.04$

Assessment

1. Enter

 3

and then

TblStart = 2

and **ΔTbl** = 1. Enter 2nd

GRAPH and read the values in the table: 0.125, 0.03704, 0.01563.

4-8 Hands-On Lab
Try This

2. Possible answer: using a sheet of $8\frac{1}{2}$ in. by 11 in. paper:

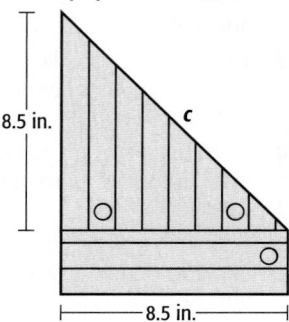

$8.5^2 + 8.5^2 = c^2$

$144.5 = c^2$

$12.02 = c$

The length of the folded edge is about 12.02 inches.

Chapter 5

5-1 Exercises

7. $\frac{2}{3} \neq \frac{5}{9}$; no

8. $\frac{7}{4} = \frac{7}{4}$; yes

9. $\frac{2}{3} = \frac{2}{3}$; yes

16. $\frac{1}{2} \neq \frac{5}{32}$; no

17. $\frac{3}{5} = \frac{3}{5}$; yes

18. $\frac{1}{3} = \frac{1}{3}$; yes

19. $\frac{1}{3} \neq \frac{1}{4}$; no

22. No; February is the only month that is equivalent to 4 weeks (28 days). Other months have 30 or 31 days.

---

23. $\frac{2}{4} = \frac{3}{6}$; $\frac{2}{5} = \frac{4}{10}$; $\frac{12}{3} = \frac{4}{1}$; $\frac{12}{8} = \frac{9}{6}$;

Possible answer: $\frac{3}{9} \neq \frac{2}{10}$

35. Possible answer: Multiply the numerator and denominator by the same number.

36. $\frac{3}{9} = \frac{27}{81}$; $\frac{9}{3} = \frac{81}{27}$; $\frac{27}{81} = \frac{3}{9}$; $\frac{81}{27} = \frac{9}{3}$; $\frac{3}{27} = \frac{9}{81}$; $\frac{9}{81} = \frac{3}{27}$; $\frac{3}{27} = \frac{81}{9}$; $\frac{81}{9} = \frac{27}{3}$

5-5 Exercises

18. Possible answer: A scale drawing of a rectangular-shaped table is 9 cm wide and 12 cm long. If the table is 3 ft wide, how long is the table? Solution: $\frac{9}{3} = \frac{12}{x}$; 4 ft

19. False; Possible answer: Some, not all, similar figures are congruent. Similar figures have pro-portional measurements. If those measurements are also *equal,* then the figures are congruent.

5-6 Exercises

3.

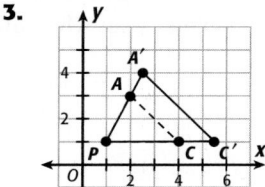

4.

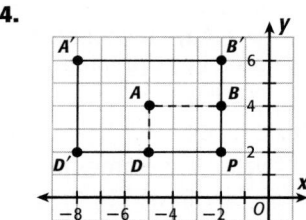

9.

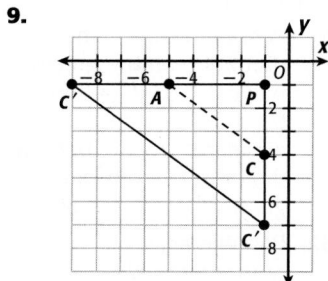

10.

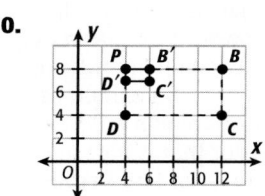

Chapter 6

6-1 Exercises

26. $\frac{7}{8}$, 100%, 1.125; Possible answer: Each number increases by $\frac{1}{8}$, and the numbers are written in the following order: fraction, percent, decimal, . . .

27. Possible answer: finding scores for a test that has a total of 75 points possible

29. Possible answer: The student used 6% instead of 0.06%. Written as a ratio, 0.06% is $\frac{6}{10,000}$, or 6 out of every 10,000.

30. Possible answer: First write all the numbers in the same form: $\frac{1}{3} = 0.3 = 33.3\%$ and $0.33 = 33\%$. Then compare and order the percents: 30%, 33%, 33.3%. Finally, write the numbers in their original form in the same order: 30%, 0.33, $\frac{1}{3}$.

31. Possible answer: If the number is a decimal, you can find the equivalent percent by multiplying by 100, or you can find the equivalent fraction by writing the value over the correct power of 10. If the number is a fraction, you can find the decimal by dividing the numerator by the denominator. If the number is a percent, you can find the decimal by dividing by 100.

6-7 Exercises

19. Possible answer: It is impossible to tell without knowing how long each kept money in her account. Sabrina may have had a lower interest rate but kept her money in the account longer.

20. a. A: $50, 143.75, B: $46,505

b. A: 8.25%, B: 7.75%

c. A: $835.73, B: $968.85

d. 3638.75

21. How long did Alice keep her money in the savings account?

---

22. Possible answer: the 3-year loan would cost the borrower less ($675, compared with $720). The interest saved would be $45.

23. Possible answer: The payments are equal. For example, the interest on a $1000 loan for 5 years at 3% is 1000 · 0.03 · 5 = $150. The interest on the same loan with a monthly rate of 0.25% is 1000 · 0.0025 · 60 = $150.

Cumulative Assessment

17. Possible answer: Mr. Coluzzi made the better buy because 5 pounds of apples for $3.99 is about $0.80 per pound, which is better than $0.82 per pound for individual apples.

18. Possible answer: The discount was $48.80 × 0.2 = $9.76. The dis-counted price was $48.80 − $9.76 = $39.04. The total price plus sales tax was $39.04 × 1.0725 = $41.87. Each person paid $41.87 ÷ 4 = $10.4675, or about $10.47.

Chapter 7

7-1 Exercises

38. Possible answer: When light approaches in a direction perpendicular to the surface, there will be no refraction.

39. Possible answer: The person on the shore sees the fish in a position that is above where the fish actually is; the fish sees the person above where the person actually is.

7-2 Exercises

18. Possible answer:

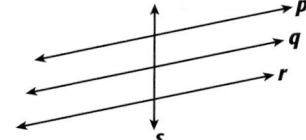

---

19. Possible answer:

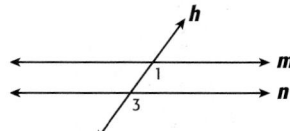

20. Possible answer:

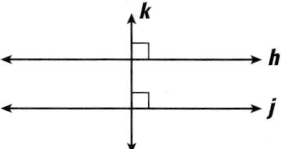

21. Possible answer: Yes, vertical angles are congruent, corresponding angles are congruent, alternate interior angles are congruent, and alternate exterior angles are congruent. Therefore, if you are given one angle measure, you can find three other angles congruent to the original. All other angles will be supplementary to the first four angles you found.

23. Possible answer: If line c is perpendicular to line b, it must also be perpendicular to line a and therefore form a 90° angle with line a.

24. Check students' work.

25. Possible answer: No, unless all of the angles are right angles. The acute angles between line s and line t will be two angles in an isosceles triangle.

7-3 Exercises

30a. $w° = 75°$; $y° = 75°$; two right angles

b. $x° = 30°$; $z° = 75°$; $m° = 75°$

c. The two blue triangles are right scalene triangles, and the white triangle is an acute isosceles triangle.

32. Possible answer: Cut the square in half diagonally. The angle measures are 90°, 45°, and 45°. Cut the triangle from one vertex to the midpoint of the opposite side. The angles are 30°, 60°, and 90°.

7-4 Exercises

34.

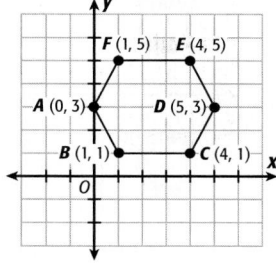

hexagon

35.

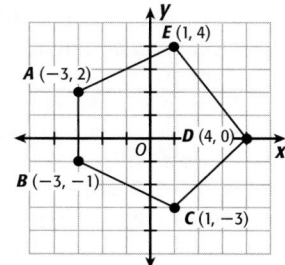

pentagon

36. Possible answer:

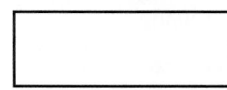

40. Possible answer: A rectangle has four right angles; a rhombus has four congruent sides. A square has four right angles and four congruent sides, so it is a rectangle and a rhombus.

41. Possible answer: The formula for the sum of the angle measures of a polygon, $180(n - 2)$, can be written as $180n - 360$ using the Distributive Property.

42. Possible answer: If you extend the sides of a parallelogram, each side becomes a transversal to a pair of parallel lines, so the corresponding angles 1, 2, 3, and 4 are all congruent. Angles 3 and 6 are vertical angles, so $\angle 6 \cong \angle 3 \cong \angle 1$. Angles 5 and 7 are supplementary to congruent angles, so $\angle 5 \cong \angle 7$. Therefore, the angles in the opposite corners of a parallelogram are congruent.

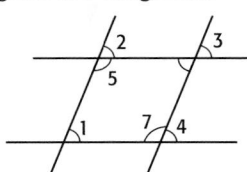

49.

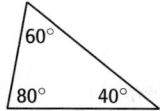

7-5 Exercises

23.

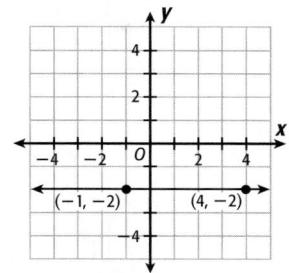

24.

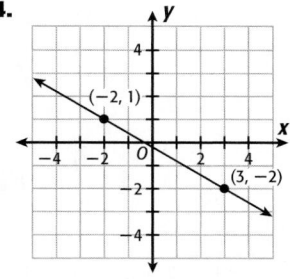

26. The slope of $\overleftrightarrow{CD}$ is also undefined because parallel lines have the same slope.

27. Possible answer:

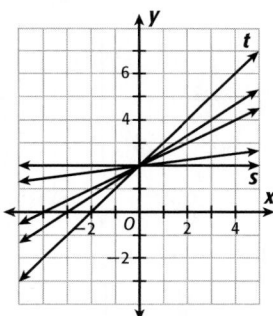

28. Possible answer:

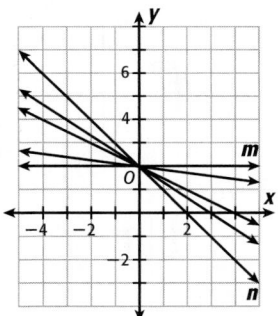

29. Possible answer: The given vertices are the endpoints for the diagonal of the square. The missing vertices are $(-1, 0)$ and $(3, 0)$. This forms a square with an area of 8 square units.

30. Possible answer: It is a right triangle because the slope of $\overleftrightarrow{LM} = -1$ and the slope of $\overleftrightarrow{LN} = 1$. The product of the slope is -1, so the line segments are perpendicular and form a right angle.

32. False: possible answer: all of the adjacent sides of a trapezoid are not perpendicular.

33. False; possible answer: a rhombus that is not a square does not have adjacent sides that are perpendicular.

34. False; possible answer: a trapezoid has only one pair of sides that have the same slope.

41. Possible answer: Are the points the vertices of a square?

42. Possible answer: The slope of a line will have the same value, regardless of which two points on a line you use to determine the slope.

43. Possible answer: Draw a square with vertices $(0, 0)$, $(1, 0)$, $(1, 1)$, and $(0, 1)$. A line through the diagonal has a slope of 1 and cuts the square into two congruent right triangles that have angle measures 45°, 45°, and 90°.

7A Ready To Go On?

12.

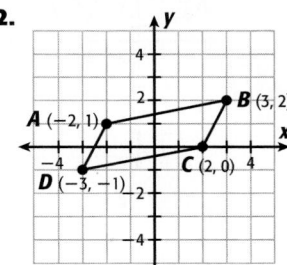

13.

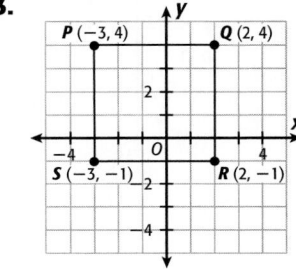

7-7 Additional Examples

2A.

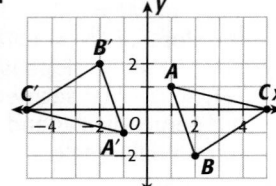

2B.

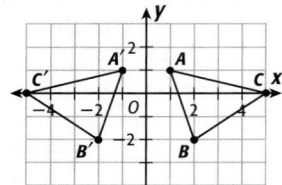

7-7 Exercises

3.

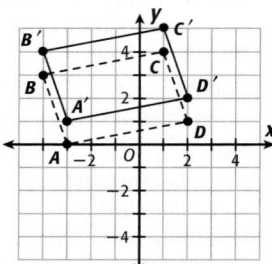

4.

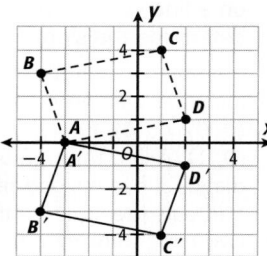

5.

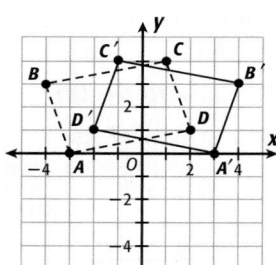

6.

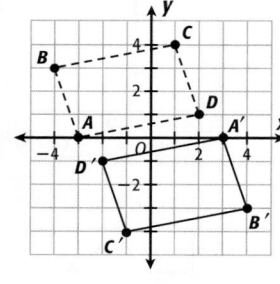

13.

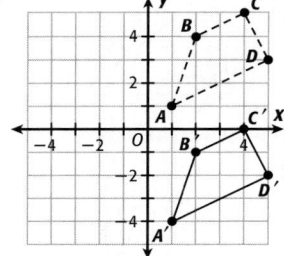

14.

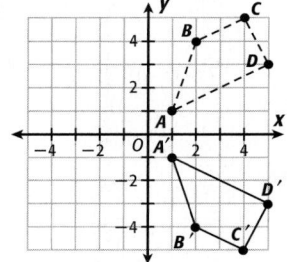

15.

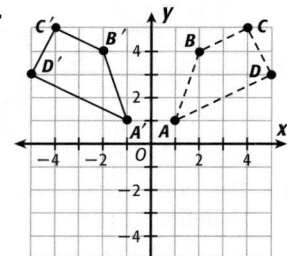

16.

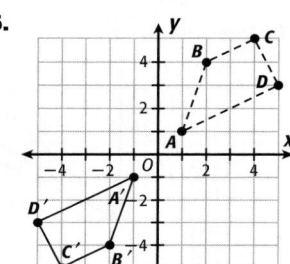

21.

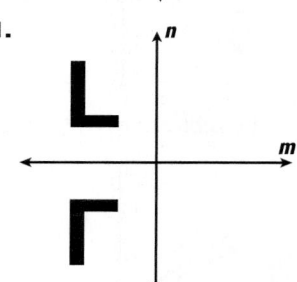

22.

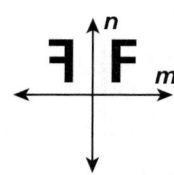

23.

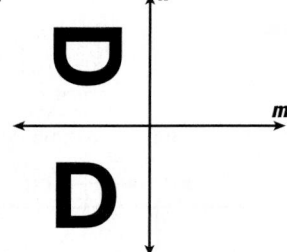

33. Possible answer: Draw a triangle. Translate it down 5 units and up 5 units. Translate all three figures left 5 units and right 5 units.

34. Possible answer: Any translation or a reflection across a horizontal line will not affect the direction. A reflection across a vertical line will reverse the direction. Rotations or reflections over other lines will change the direction by varying amounts.

7-8 Exercises

1.

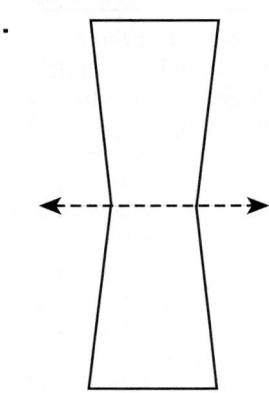

2.

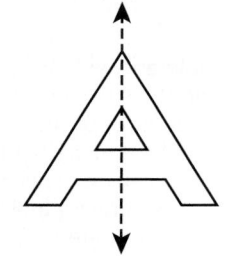

3.

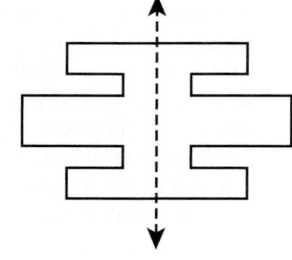

4.

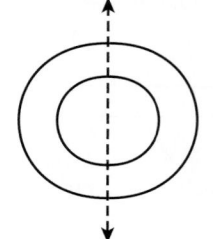

5.

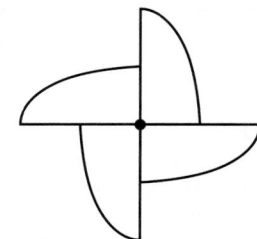

6.

7.

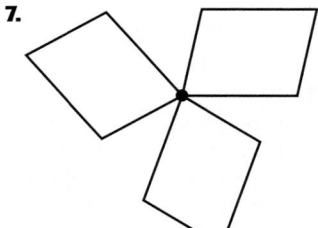

8.

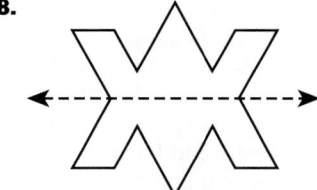

9.

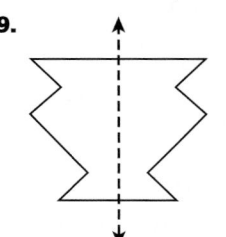

10.

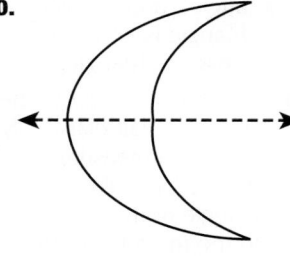

11.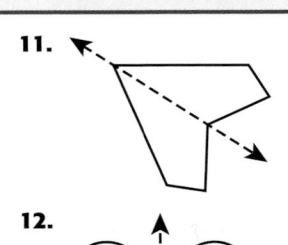

12.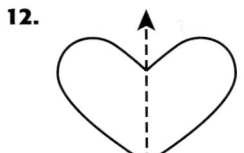

13.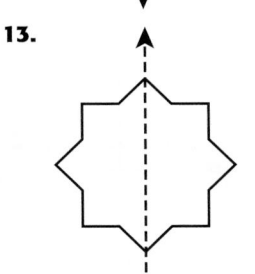

14.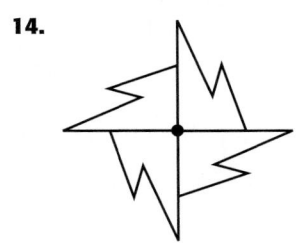

15.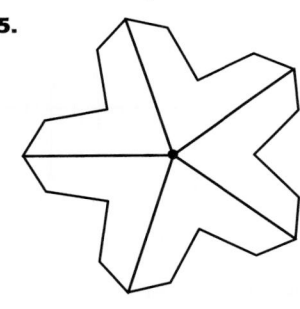

16.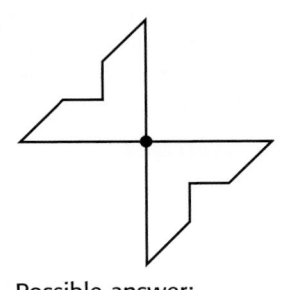

17. Possible answer:

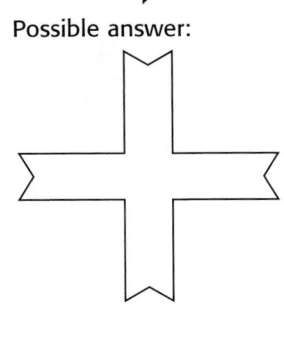

18. Possible answer:

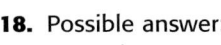

23. a.

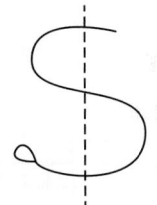

Kage Asa no ha
There are 6 lines of symmetry and 6-fold rotational symmetry around the center.

b.

Maru ni shichiyo
There are 6 lines of symmetry and 6-fold rotational symmetry around the center.

c. There is no line symmetry and no rotational symmetry.

25. Possible answer: Each part should be rotated $\left(\frac{360}{n}\right)$ degrees.

7-9 Exercises

1.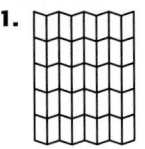

2. Possible answer:

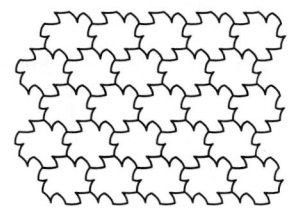

3.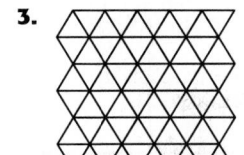

4.

5.

6.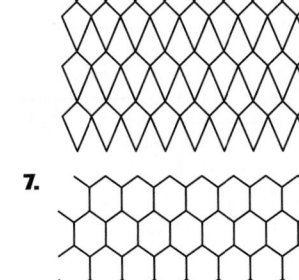

7.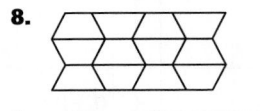

8.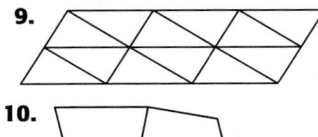

9.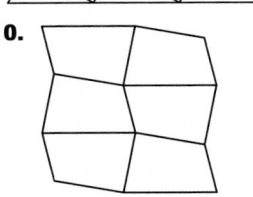

10.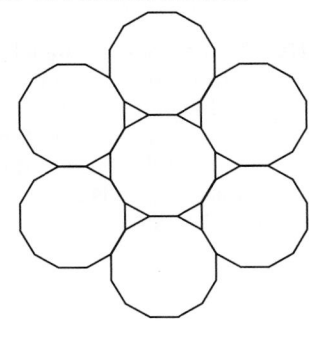

13. a. Possible answer:

b. Possible answer:

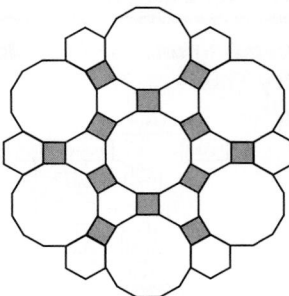

c. Possible answer:

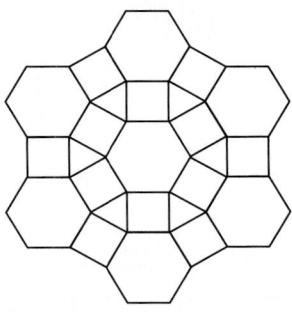

7B Ready To Go On?

8.

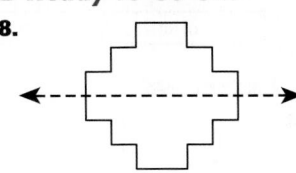

9.

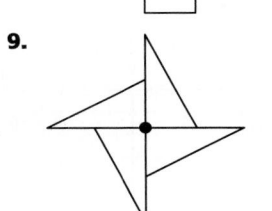

Cumulative Assessment

17. a.

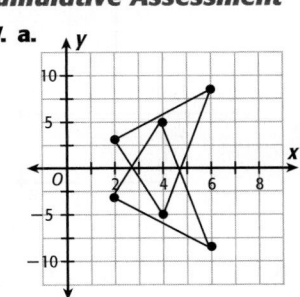

b. $A'(2, -3)$, $B'(4, 5)$, $C'(6, -8)$

Chapter 8

Reading and Writing Math
Try This

1.

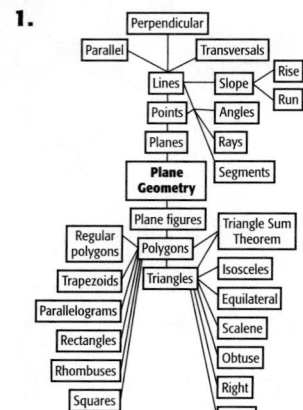

2.

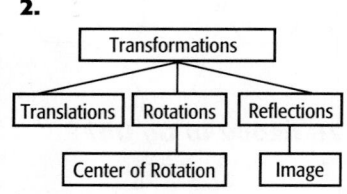

8-1 Exercises

4.

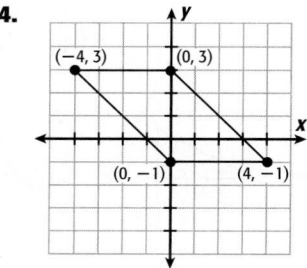

5.

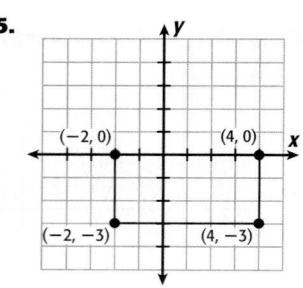

6.

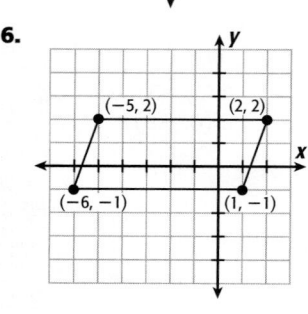

7.

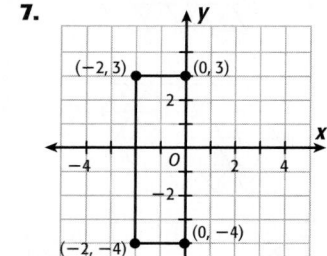

12.

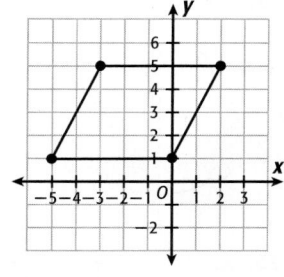

13.

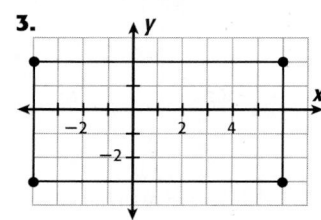

14.

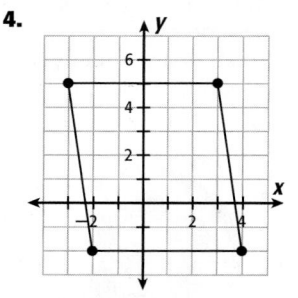

15.

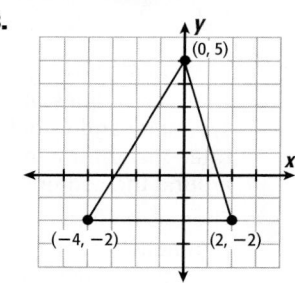

28. The area of the parallelogram is 20 square units. The height of the parallelogram is 4 units and the length of the base of the parallelogram is 5 units. 4 × 5 = 20

11.

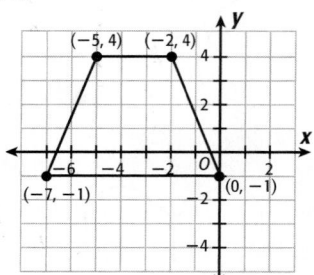

8-1 Lesson Quiz

3.

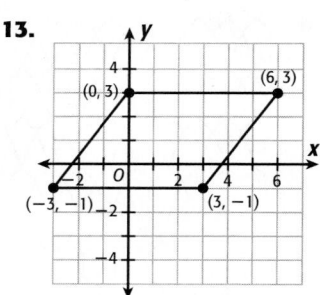

4.

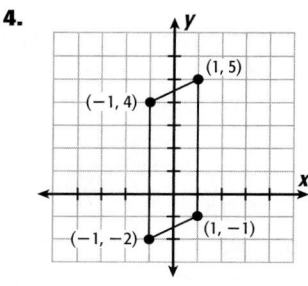

8-2 Exercises

8.

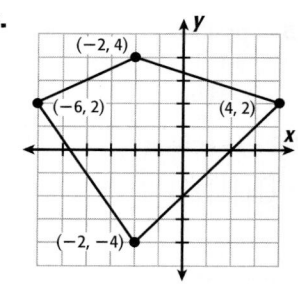

9.

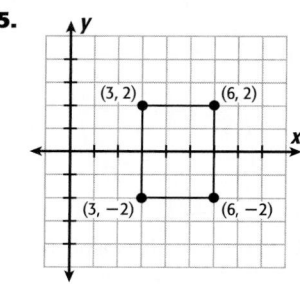

10.

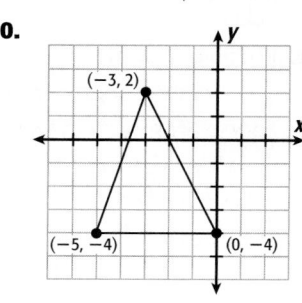

20.

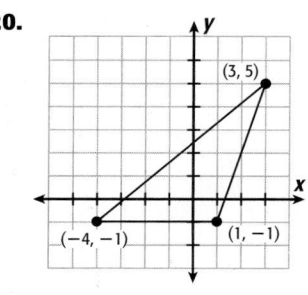

21.

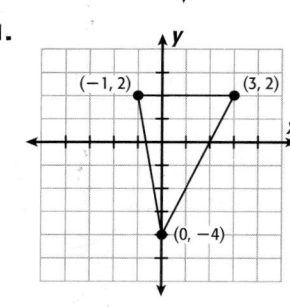

22.

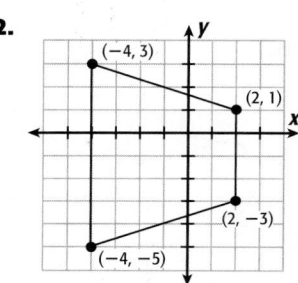

36. Possible answer: No; the area of the Boeing 747 wing is more than 11 times the area of the Wright brothers' wing.

8-3 Exercises

5.

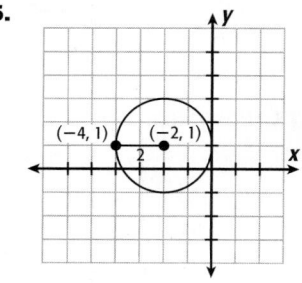

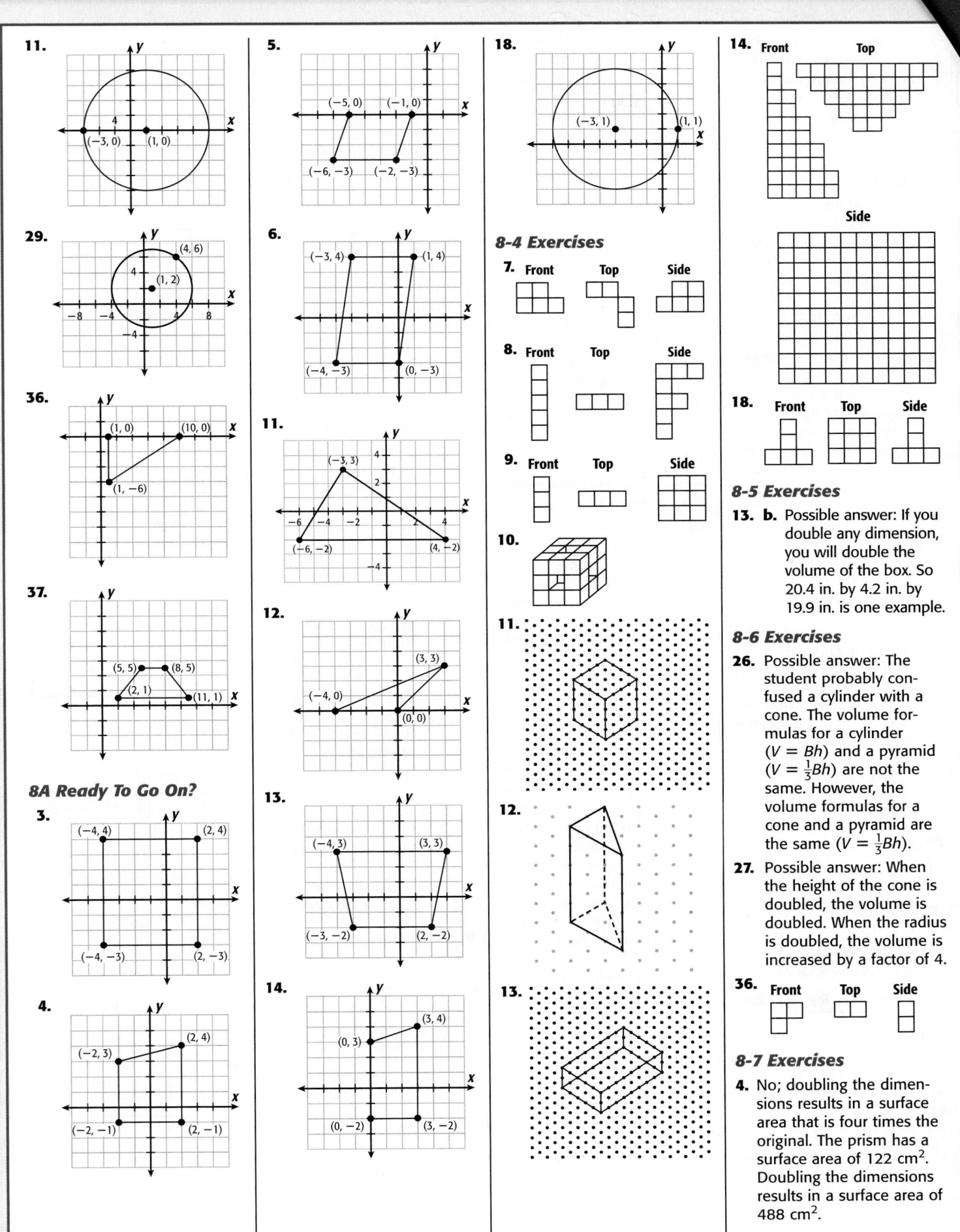

11.

29.

36.

37.

8A Ready To Go On?

3.

4.

5.

6.

11.

12.

13.

14.

18.

8-4 Exercises

7. Front   Top   Side

8. Front   Top   Side

9. Front   Top   Side

10.

11.

12.

13.

14. Front   Top

Side

18. Front   Top   Side

8-5 Exercises

13. b. Possible answer: If you double any dimension, you will double the volume of the box. So 20.4 in. by 4.2 in. by 19.9 in. is one example.

8-6 Exercises

26. Possible answer: The student probably confused a cylinder with a cone. The volume formulas for a cylinder ($V = Bh$) and a pyramid ($V = \frac{1}{3}Bh$) are not the same. However, the volume formulas for a cone and a pyramid are the same ($V = \frac{1}{3}Bh$).

27. Possible answer: When the height of the cone is doubled, the volume is doubled. When the radius is doubled, the volume is increased by a factor of 4.

36. Front   Top   Side

8-7 Exercises

4. No; doubling the dimensions results in a surface area that is four times the original. The prism has a surface area of 122 cm². Doubling the dimensions results in a surface area of 488 cm².

9. No; they do not have the same effect. Halving the diameter would result in a surface area of 76.2392 ft², while halving the height would result in a surface area of 95.9584 ft².

8-8 Exercises

4. No; doubling the dimensions results in a surface area that is 4 times the original. The cone has a surface area of 282.6 in². Doubling the dimensions results in a surface area of 1120.4 in².

9. No; doubling the dimensions results in a surface area that is 4 times the original. The pyramid has a surface area of 264 yd². Doubling the dimensions results in a surface area of 1056 yd².

8-9 Exercises

23. Possible answer: Because the volume of a hemisphere is exactly halfway between the volume of a cone and the volume of a cylinder with the same radius and height, it can be shown that the volume of a sphere is exactly halfway between the volume of a cylinder with the same diameter and height and two cones with the same diameter and half the height.

Chapter 8 Test

8. $A = 225\pi \approx 706.5$ cm²; $C = 30\pi \approx 94.2$ cm

9. $A = 10.6\pi \approx 33.3$ ft²; $C = 6.5\pi \approx 20.4$ ft

10. $A = 4.75\pi \approx 15.2$ m²; $C = 4.4\pi \approx 13.8$ m

11. **Front**   **Top**   **Side**

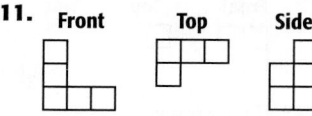

Cumulative Assessment

17.

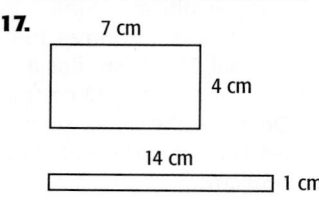

7 cm
4 cm
14 cm
1 cm

Rectangle with dimensions 7 cm × 4 cm has the larger area; rectangle with dimensions 14 cm × 1 cm has the larger perimeter

18.

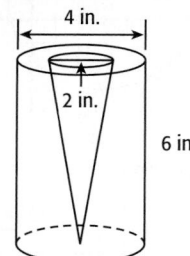

4 in.
2 in.
6 in.

69.11 in.³ of water left in the cylinder

19. 2500 revolutions per minute; 552 miles in one hour

Chapter 9

9-1 Additional Examples

2A. Population: record store customers
Sample: customers who make a purchase
Possible bias: Customers who make a purchase might be more interested in music than others in the store.

2B. Population: students in the school
Sample: classmates
Possible bias: She polls more eighth-graders than students in other grades.

2C. Population: people who listen to the radio show
Sample: people who hear the question and who call in
Possible bias: The radio only receives feedback from people who listen to that station, and therefore who already enjoy the type of music played on the station.

9-1 Exercises

7. Population: people who attend the team's games; sample; people other than season ticket holders attend baseball games

---

13. Population: students; sample: students who buy the entrée; possible bias: the students who buy the entrée may be the people who like the food in the cafeteria.

14. Population: city residents; sample: people attending the city council meeting; possible bias: most citizens don't attend council meetings.

15. Population: trees; sample: trees along the river; possible bias: the trees sampled have a better source of water than the others.

17. **a.** Possible answer: Randomly select visitors leaving the zoo.

   b. Possible answer: Select every tenth visitor leaving the zoo.

   c. Possible answer: People visiting with children might only visit the zoo because they have children.

19. Possible answer: I would choose a systematic sampling method. I would ask every third person on the roster to fill out a form. This way, I would get a good idea of my class's overall preference for location.

22. Population: visitors to a baseball game; sample: 100 visitors at the baseball game; possible bias: visitors to a baseball game may be more inclined to choose baseball as their favorite sport.

9-2 Exercises

9.

Coldest		Warmest
7 0	1	
7 5	2	
6 6 2	3	
8 6	4	0 3 4 7
	5	0 1 2 9
	6	2

Key: 7|1| means 17°
|4|0 means 40°

20.

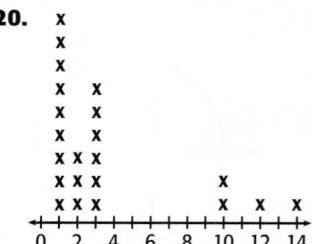

23.

Men		Women
3 2	3	1 2
5 1	4	4
	5	5 5
1 1	6	4

9-2 Lesson Quiz

1.

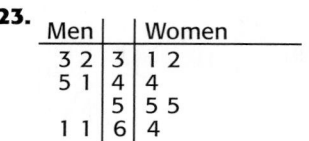

3.

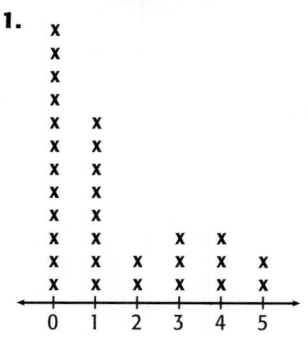

Under 30   Registered Voter
5   3   5

9-3 Exercises

29. Population: shoppers; sample: paid shoppers at a mall; possible bias: The people may answer favorably because they are being paid.

9-4 Exercises

19.

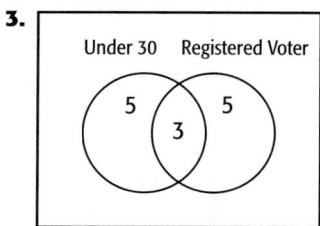

0   2   3   4.5 5

20.

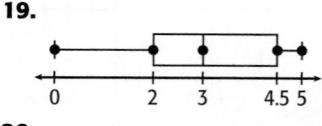

2.2   3   5.4   6.5   8

21.

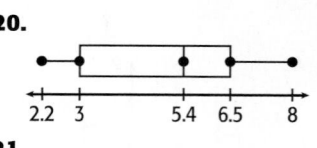

Hurricanes
34   9   16

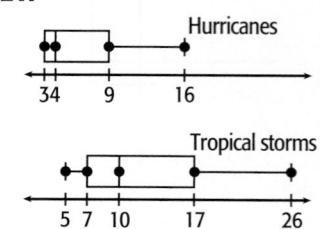

Tropical storms
5 7 10   17   26

Possible answer: The median number of tropical storms is greater than the median number of hurricanes.

23.

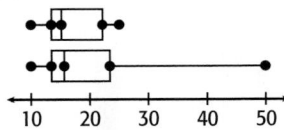

The introduction of an outlier created a disproportionately long whisker.

28.

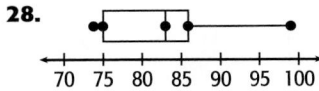

9A Ready To Go On?

3. Population: all customers of the restaurant
Sample: the customers in the restaurant on Friday
Possible bias: Some patrons do not like salsa.

4. Population: all customers of the rental store
Sample: customers who rent dramas
Possible bias: Not all customers who rent dramas also like other types of movies.

5.

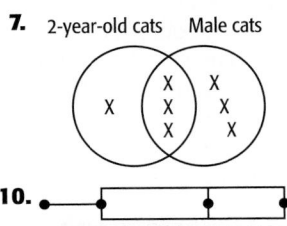

6.

American League		National League
3, 7, 7	4	7, 8, 9
2, 7	5	0
	6	
	7	3

7.

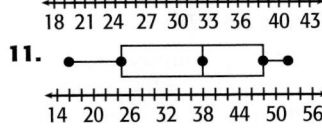

10.

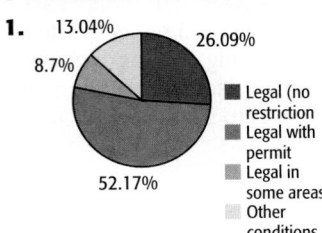

11.

9-5 Hands-On Lab

1.
13.04%
26.09%
8.7%
52.17%

Legal (no restriction)
Legal with permit
Legal in some areas
Other conditions

9-5 Additional Examples

1.

Number of Books Read by 8th-grade Students

Boys Girls

2.

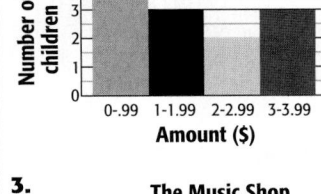

3.

The Music Shop CD and DVD Sales

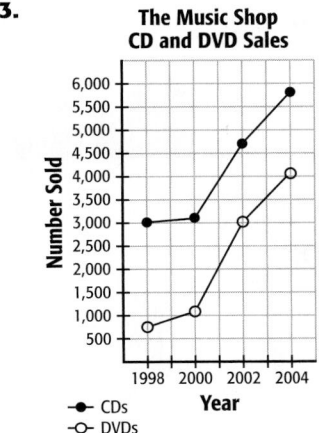

— CDs
—○— DVDs

CDs about 5750;
DVDs about 3500

9-5 Exercises

1.

Data	Frequency Data Set 1	Frequency Data Set 2
9	1	2
10	3	2
11	3	4
12	2	3
13	3	1

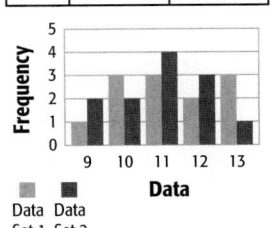

Data Set 1 Data Set 2

2.

Freshman National Merit Scholars (2004)

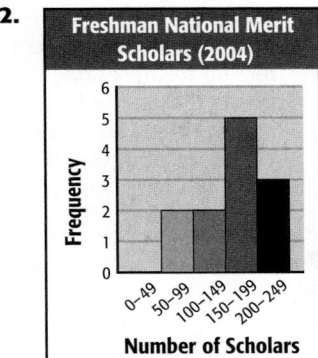

Number of Scholars

3.

Life Expectancy by Birth Year (U.S.)

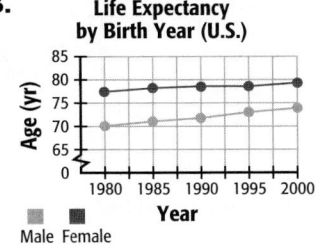

Male Female

4.

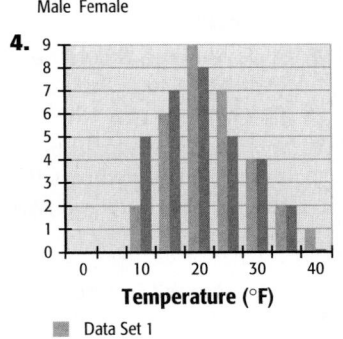

Data Set 1
Data Set 2

5.

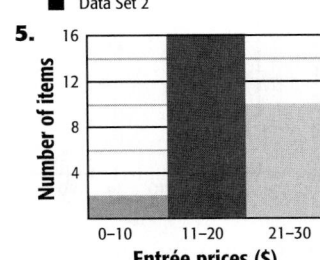

Entrée prices ($)

6.

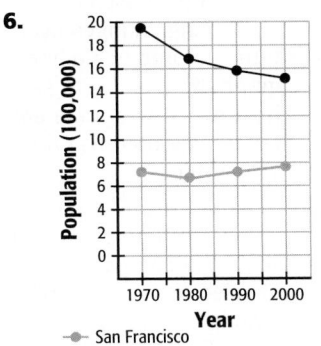

San Francisco
Philadelphia

7.

Data	Frequency Data Set 1	Frequency Data Set 2
1	4	5
2	4	3
3	2	4
4	3	2
5	3	3
6	4	3

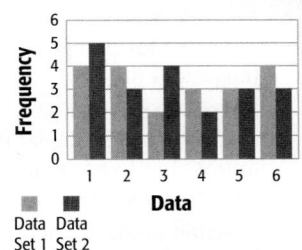

Data Set 1 Data Set 2

8.

Honey-Producing Colonies 1999-2004

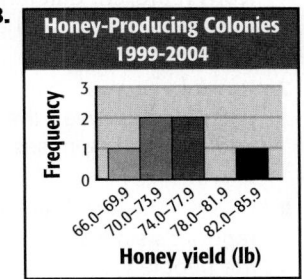

Honey yield (lb)

9. Possible answer: correlate the range of heights with each jersey size. Organize the data into a frequency table and make a histogram.

10. Possible answer: Choose a double-line graph, so you can compare how the salaries change year to year.

9-5 Lesson Quiz

1.

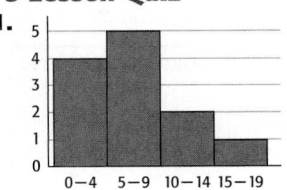

9-6 Additional Examples

2A. This statement does not give the sample size or state what UltraClean was compared with.

2B. The words *up to* mean that is the maximum you can save, but there is no guarantee that you will save that amount.

2C. Jacob may have played most of his time on defense.

9-6 Exercises

1. Possible answer: The scale does not start at zero, so changes appear exaggerated.

2. Possible answer: The intervals used in the histogram are not equal.

3. Possible answer: The fruits are all different sizes.

4. Possible answer: The sales are for different lengths of time.

5. Possible answer: The graph has no scale, so it's impossible to compare the money earned.

6. Possible answer: The icons represent different quantities of food and are different sizes.

7. Possible answer: The difference between the two groups' responses is only 2.

8. Possible answer: The reporter's statistics ignore the people who do not play sports.

17.

```
                x
        x       x               x
  x  x  x                       x
  x  x     x  x      x  x        x
 20 21 22 23 24 25 26 27 28 29 30
```

9-7 Exercises

1.
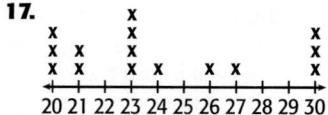

5.
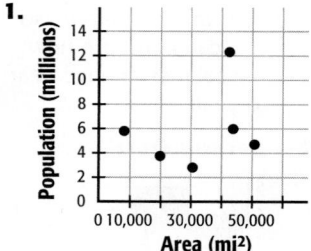

9.
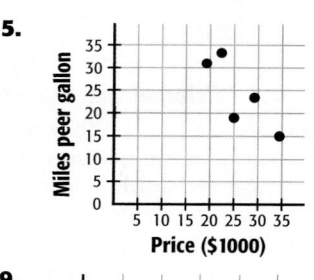
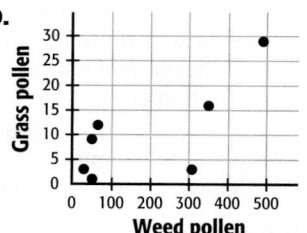

There is a positive correlation between the pollen levels.

10. Possible answer: The pollen irritants are shown during the months in which they occur throughout the year. The height of each shaded area shows the severity of the pollen count.

13. Possible answer: Some pollens are positively correlated because the plants they come from bloom under the same conditions, but one plant does not cause the other plant to bloom.

9-8 Additional Examples

2.
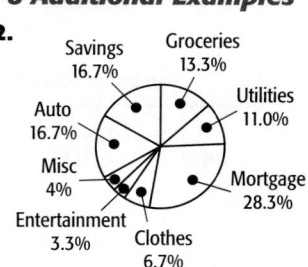

Singer Family Budget

auto and entertainment

9-8 Exercises

7. A circle graph would be best because it shows percentages of a whole.

8. A scatter plot would be best because it shows the relationship between two data sets.

9.
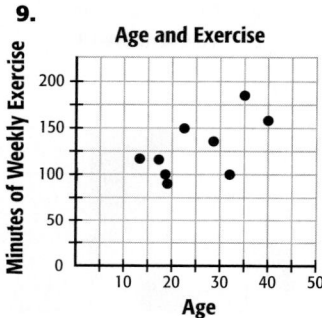

12. Possible answer: If I wanted to show how something changes over time, I would use a line graph. If I wanted to see how two sets of data are related, I would use a scatter plot.

13. a bar graph and a pictograph; Both graphs would show the comparisons of sales of the different brands.

9-8 Lesson Quiz

2.
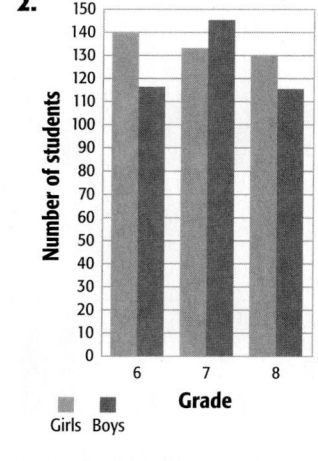

9B Ready To Go On?

1.
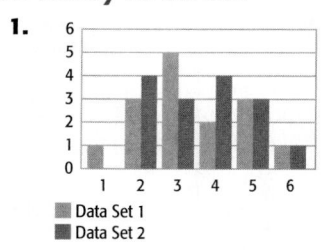

2.
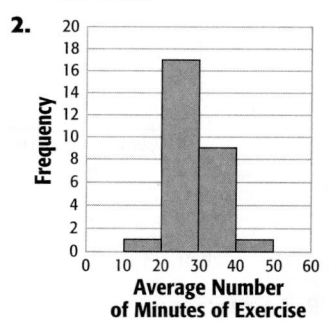

6.
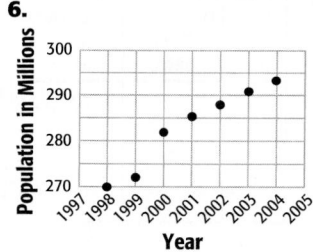

8.
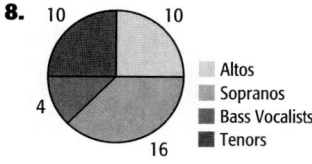

Multi-Step Test Prep

3. Possible answer:
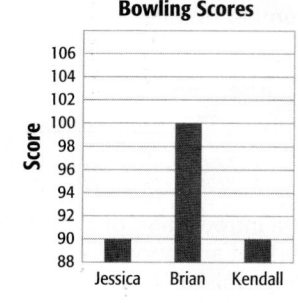

4.
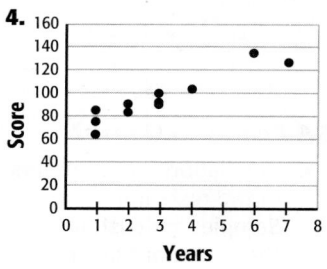

Chapter 10

10-1 Exercises

4.

Team	A	B	C	D
Prob.	0.25	0.3	0.15	0.3

8.

Candidate	Probability
Kim	0.2
Sasha	0.2
Kris	0.3
Lei	0.15
Denali	0.15

17. Possible answer: The value of p is greater than or equal to 0 and less than or equal to 1. The probability that the event will not occur is $1 - p$, because the two probabilities must add to 1.

18. A, B, C, (A and B), (A and C), (B and C), and (A, B, and C)

10-3 Technology Lab
Think and Discuss

1. **RAND()** returns a random decimal number greater than or equal to zero but less than 1. **(10*RAND())** multiplies 10 by the decimal generated, resulting in a random decimal greater than or equal to zero but less than 10.

INT(10*RAND()) tells the spreadsheet to give only integers from zero to 9, meaning only 0, 1, 2, 3, 4, 5, 6, 7, 8, or 9.
INT(10*RAND()) + 1 adds 1 to the random integer from 0 to 9, resulting in a random integer from 1 to 10.

Try This

1. If each region is represented by the integers 1 through 4, then the formula is **INT(4*RAND()) + 1.** The numbers generated will vary.

10-3 Exercises

14. Possible answer: Let the numbers 01–11 represent tagged wolves. Let the numbers 12–00 represent wolves that are not tagged. Use 20 digits grouped in 10 pairs as a trial. Perform 10 trials. Count the number of times 01–11 appear in each trial. Then determine how many trials have those numbers appearing at least 2 times. The probability is how many trials out of 10 represent at least 2 tagged wolves.

10-4 Exercises

19–24.

Penny	Dime	Quarter	Outcome
H	H	H	HHH
H	H	T	HHT
H	T	H	HTH
H	T	T	HTT
T	H	H	THH
T	H	T	THT
T	T	H	TTH
T	T	T	TTT

27. Possible answer:

	T	t
t	Tt	tt
t	Tt	tt

One parent has a *Tt* combination and can roll his or her tongue, and the other has a *tt* combination and cannot roll his or her tongue.

10-6 Exercises

19. The accuracy of the prediction will vary depending on the accuracy of the experiment.

10-7 Exercises

24. Possible answer: The candidate compared her chances with all possible outcomes instead of with only the 5 unfavorable outcomes. The answer should be 1:5.

25. Possible answer: Determine the number of favorable outcomes and compare that number with the number of unfavorable outcomes. There are 3 favorable outcomes and 7 unfavorable outcomes, so the odds of the computer selecting a number less than 3 are 3:7.

10-8 Exercises

21. b. 9 choices: (red, business, CD ROM), (red, business, DVD), (red, business, DVD/CD RW), (red, graphics, CD ROM), (red, graphics, DVD), (red, graphics, DVD/CD RW), (red, word processing, CD ROM), (red, word processing, DVD), (red, word processing, DVD/CD RW)

22. Possible answer: The Fundamental Counting Principle is more useful when the total number of outcomes is desired and when the number of outcomes is large. A tree diagram is more useful when you want to list all of the outcomes in a sample space.

10-9 Exercises

39. Possible answer: You could find the number of outcomes in the sample space of an event by using permutations (if order is important) or combinations (if order is unimportant). Then you could divide the number of desired outcomes by

the number of outcomes in the sample space to find probability.

43.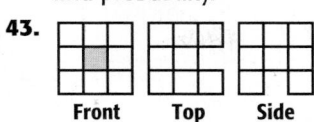
Front Top Side

Chapter 11

11-2 Exercises

40. Possible answer: Subtract 1 from both sides. Multiply both sides by 3 to clear the large fraction. Distribute the 4. Multiply both sides by 3 to clear the fractions. Combine like terms to get $8x - 3 = 45$. Add 3 to both sides, and then divide both sides by 8 to find that $x = 6$.

11-3 Hands-On Lab
Think and Discuss

1. Possible answer: Replace each yellow x bar with 2 yellow unit squares. Replace each red x bar with 2 red unit squares. See whether the equation balances.

2. Possible answer: to be able to see what number of unit tiles one variable tile is equal to

11-4 Exercises

6. (number line 13–22, open circle at 18)

7. (number line −68 to −60, open circle at −62)

8. (number line −8 to 0, closed circle at −4)

10. (number line −12 to −4, open circle at −8)

11. (number line 70–78, open circle at 75)

12. (number line −2 to 8, closed circle at 2)

13. (number line −82 to −74, closed circle at −78)

14. (number line 32–40, open circle at 36)

15. (number line 8–17, open circle at 13)

16. (number line −102 to −94, open circle at −98)

17. (number line −8 to 2, closed circle at −4)

19. (number line 1–11, open circle at 6)

20. (number line −86 to −78, open circle at −82)

21. (number line −1 to 8, closed circle at 3)

22. (number line −711 to −705, closed circle at −707)

23. (number line 90–99, open circle at 94)

24. (number line 31–40, open circle at 35)

25. (number line 116–122, open circle at 119)

26. (number line 7–16, closed circle at 12)

11-5 Exercises

1. (number line −3 to 7, open circle at 2)

2. (number line 15–24, closed circle at 19)

3. (number line −12 to −4, open circle at −8)

4. $x \le -2$ (number line −5 to 0, closed circle at −2)

5. (number line 2–12, closed circle at 7)

6. $k > 5$ (number line 0 to 10, open circle at 5)

7. $x < 3$ (number line 0 to 5, open circle at 3)

8. (number line −4 to 5, closed circle at 2)

9. $h \le 1$ (number line −5 to 5, closed circle at 1)

10. $c > 2$ (number line 0 to 5, open circle at 2)

11. (number line −5 to 4, open circle at 0)

12. (number line −4 to 5, closed circle at 2)

14. (number line −2 to 8)

15. (number line −1 to 9)

16. (number line −18 to −8)

17. (number line −3 to 7)

18. $n < 3$ (number line 0 to 5)

19. (number line −12 to −2)

20. (number line −12 to −2)

21. $a \geq -3$ (number line −5 to 0)

22. (number line 0 to 2)

23. $k \geq 3$ (number line 0 to 5)

24. $n \leq -14$ (number line −16 to −12)

25. $r < 3$ (number line 0 to 5)

27. $p \leq \frac{22}{3}$ (number line 7, $7\frac{1}{3}$, 8)

28. $n > -3$ (number line −5 to 0)

29. $w > -1$ (number line −5 to 0)

30. $x \leq -4$ (number line −8 to 0)

31. $a > \frac{1}{2}$ (number line 0, 1, $\frac{1}{2}$, 2)

32. $y \leq -\frac{7}{2}$ (number line −4, $-3\frac{1}{2}$, −2)

33. $q < 6$ (number line 2, 4, 6, 8)

34. $m > \frac{5}{6}$ (number line 0, $\frac{1}{2}$, $\frac{5}{6}$, 1)

35. $b < 2.7$ (number line 2, 2.5, 2.7, 3)

36. $k \geq -\frac{2}{3}$ (number line −1, $-\frac{2}{3}$, 0)

37. $f \leq -27$ (number line −30, −27, −25)

38. $v \leq \frac{3}{5}$ (number line 0, $\frac{3}{5}$, 1)

44. Possible answer: Sergio paid $5.95 for the shipping on this last purchase, and his total was less than $49.45. Write and solve an inequality to describe the cost of the merchandise he bought. Answer: $x + \$5.95 < \$49.95$; $x < \$43.50$.

45. Possible answer: Method 1: Subtract x from both sides. Add 4 to both sides. Divide both sides by −4, and reverse the inequality symbol. Method 2: Add $3x$ to both sides, and divide both sides by 4.

48. (number line 0, 0.2)

49. (figure)

50. (figure)

51. (figure)

11B Ready To Go On?

1. (number line −8 to 2)

2. (number line 28 to 36)

3. (number line 22 to 30)

4. (number line 2 to 12)

5. (number line −20 to −12)

6. (number line 3 to 13)

7. (number line −20 to −12)

8. (number line −8 to 2)

9. (number line −1 to 8)

10. (number line 16 to 24)

11. (number line −12 to −4)

12. (number line −2 to 6)

14. (number line −1 to 8)

15. (number line 16 to 24)

16. (number line −12 to −4)

17. (number line −2 to 6)

18. (number line −6 to 2)

19. (number line −2 to 1)

20. (number line −25 to −17)

21. (number line −6 to 2)

22. (number line −14 to −6)

Chapter 12

Are You Ready?

29. (number line −4 to 4)

30. (number line −4 to 6)

31. (number line −8 to 0)

12-1 Exercises

1.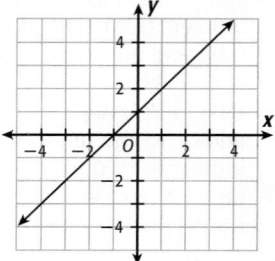

2.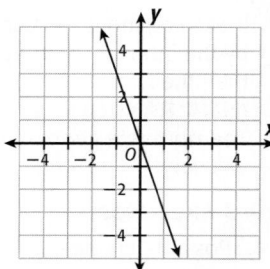

3.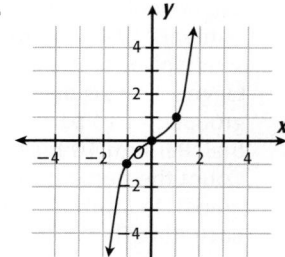

4.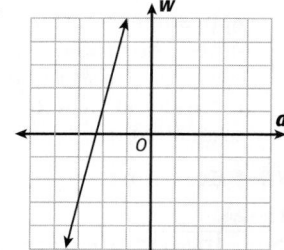

5.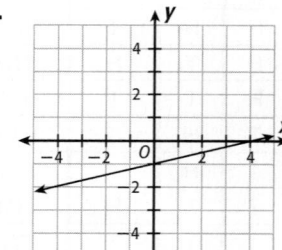

6.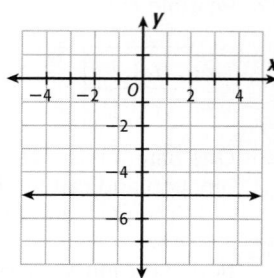

7.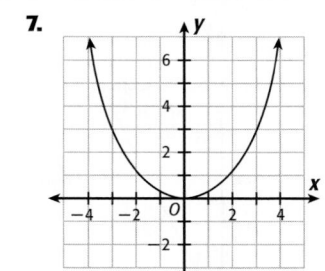

8.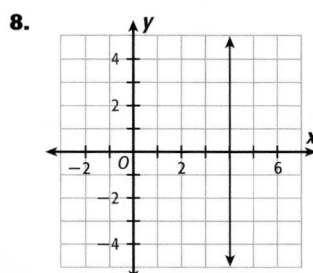

9.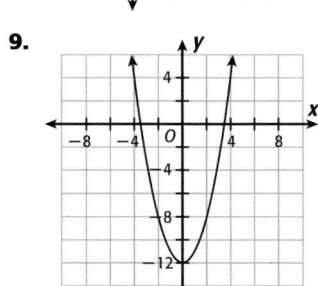

10.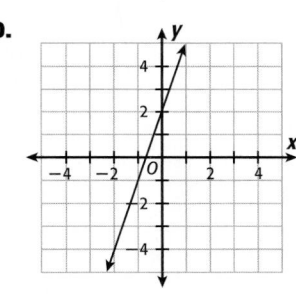

11.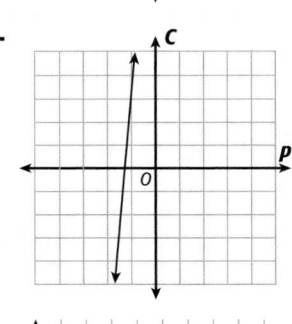

12.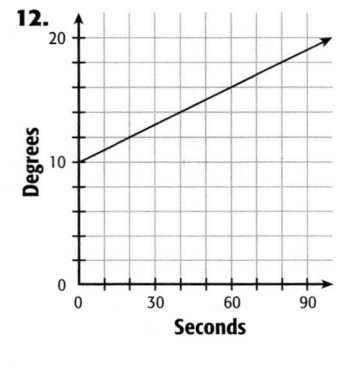

14.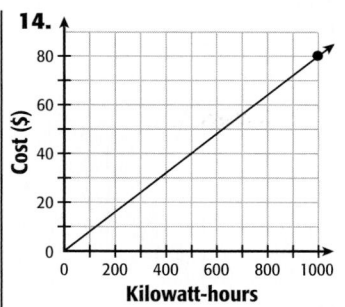

15.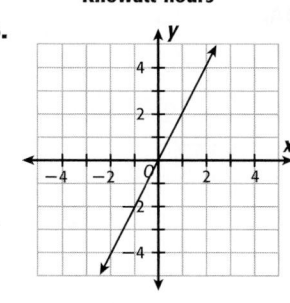

16.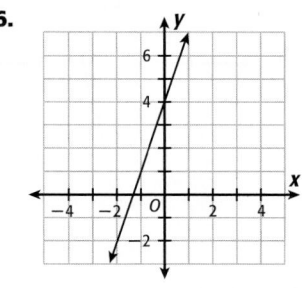

17.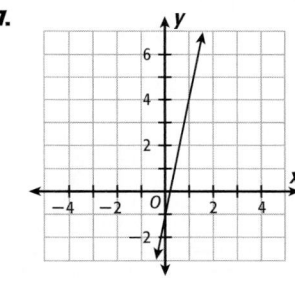

18.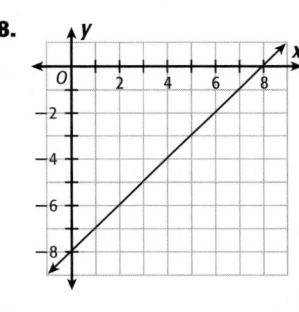

19.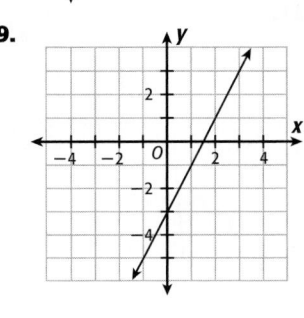

20.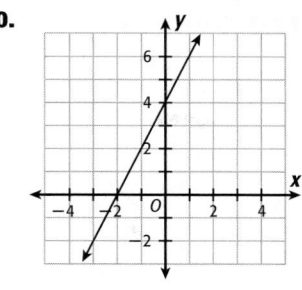

21. $(-1, -6)$, $(0, -4)$, $(1, -2)$

22.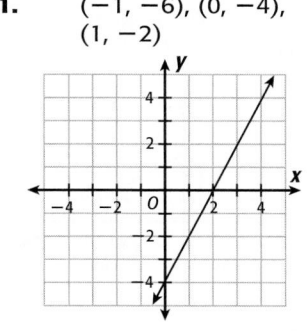

23.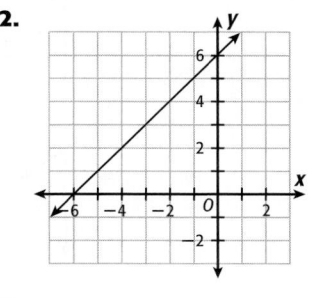

25.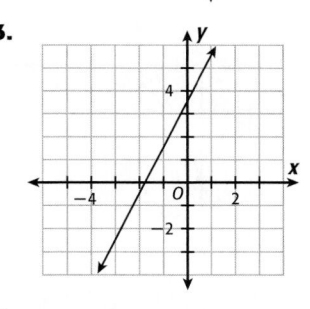

26.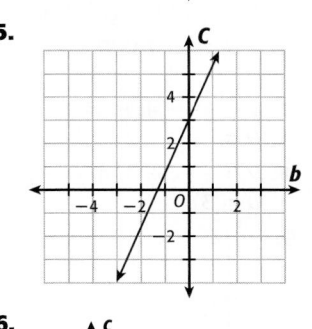

28. Possible answer: Choose several values for *x*, and solve the equation for *y*. Plot the points on the coordinate grid and see whether they form a straight line.

29. Possible answer:

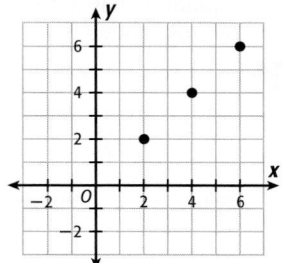

32.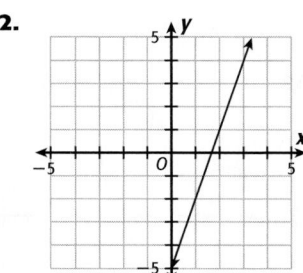

12-2 Exercises

23.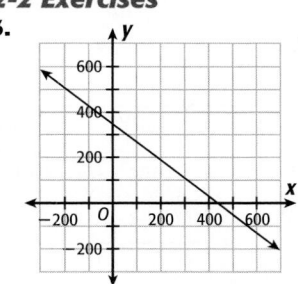

25. The vertical rise must be 0, $\frac{0}{12}$, so the roof extends only horizontally. The roof is flat.

27. Possible answer: The formula for slope is $\frac{y_2 - y_1}{x_2 - x_1}$ so the *y*-values should be in the numerator instead of the *x*-values.

28. Possible answer: For the line $x = 2$, find the slope by using any two points on the line. Using the points $(2, 4)$ and $(2, 6)$, the slope is, $\frac{6 - 4}{2 - 2} = \frac{2}{0}$ which is undefined.

29. Slopes of $y = 3x - 4$ and $y = 3x + 2$ are 3. Slope of $y = -\frac{1}{3}x$ is $-\frac{1}{3}$. If the change in y is constant for every value of x, then the graph has a constant rate of change. Therefore, the graph of each of the three equations has a constant rate of change.

34.
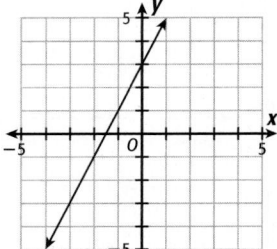

35.
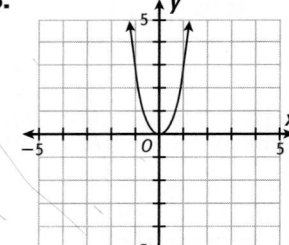

36.
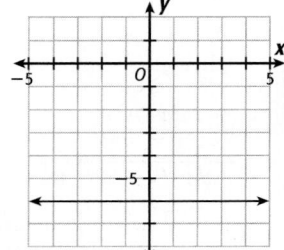

12-2 Lesson Quiz

3.
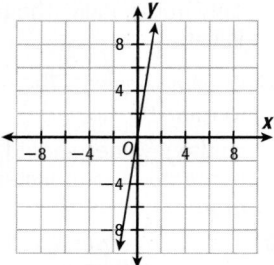

The slope of the line is 7. This means that Susan earned 7 dollars for every hour she worked.

12-3 Exercises

1.
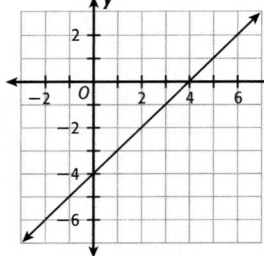

2.
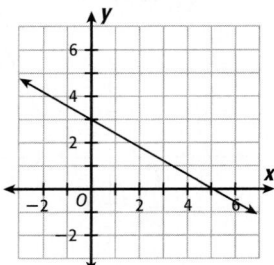

3.
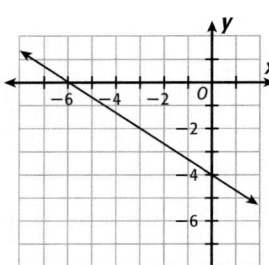

4.
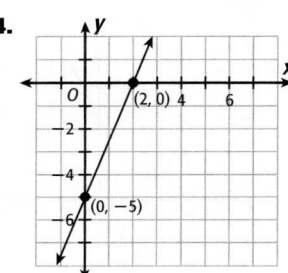

5. $y = \frac{1}{3}x$; $m = \frac{1}{3}$; $b = 0$

6. $y = 3x - 14$; $m = 3$, $b = -14$

7. $y = \frac{1}{4}x - 4$; $m = \frac{1}{4}$; $b = -4$

8. $y = -\frac{1}{4}x + 3$; $m = -\frac{1}{4}$; $b = 3$

9.
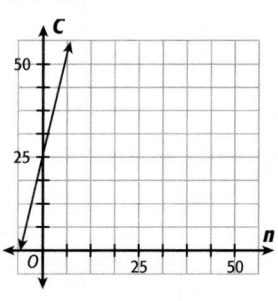

13.
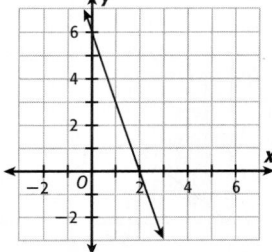

14.
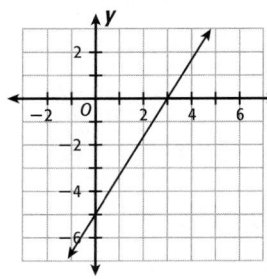

15.
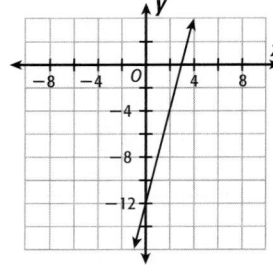

16. x-intercept: 3.5
y-intercept: 7
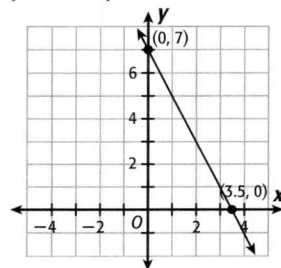

17. $y = -3x$; $m = -3$; $b = 0$

18. $y = -\frac{3}{5}x + 2$; $m = -\frac{3}{5}$; $b = 2$

19. $y = -2x - 2$; $m = -2$; $b = -2$

20. $y = -2x - 5$; $m = -2$; $b = -5$

21.
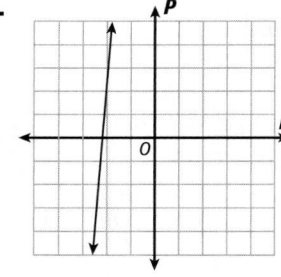

25.
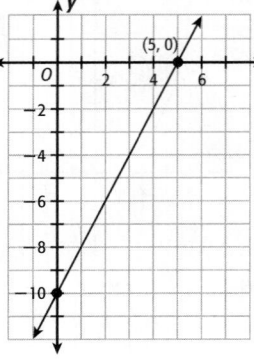

26.
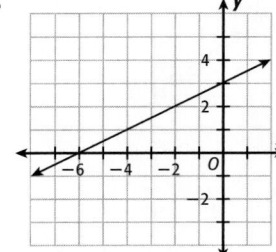

27.
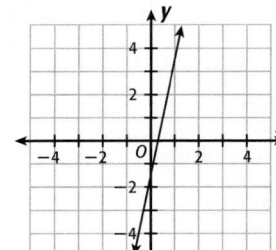

28.
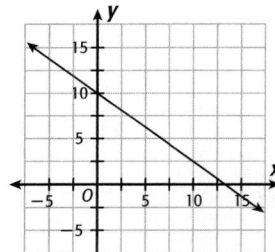

30. a. $m = 2000$
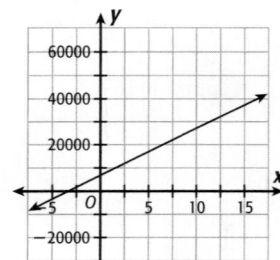

b. 8255 ft, the altitude of the base camp

c. $y = 2000x + 8255$

d. yes

31. Slope: 955 ft per day; y-intercept: 16,500 ft; the slope is the number of feet climbed each day, and the y-intercept is the starting altitude.

32.

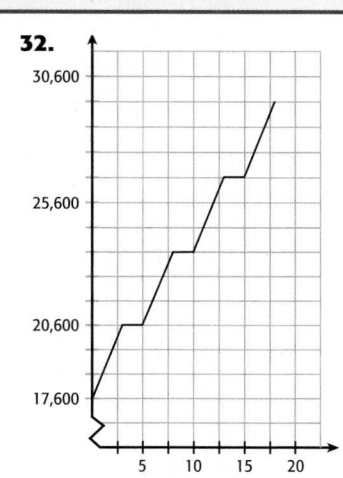

No, the graph is not linear, because on some days the team does not ascend at all.

34.

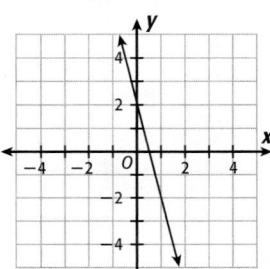

12-4 Exercises

23. If you have only two points on the line, you must first find the slope of the line. When you know the slope and one point on the line, you can write the equation using point-slope or slope-intercept form.

12A Ready To Go On?

1.

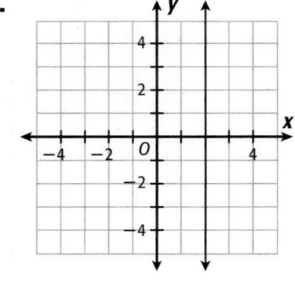

2.

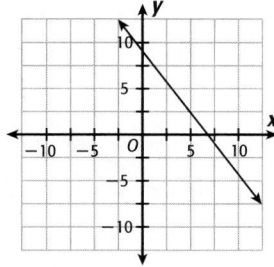

3.

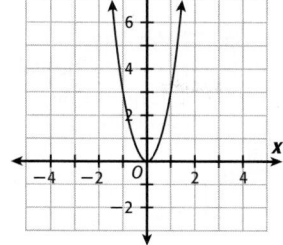

4.

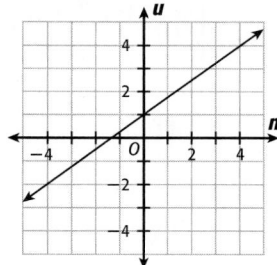

9.

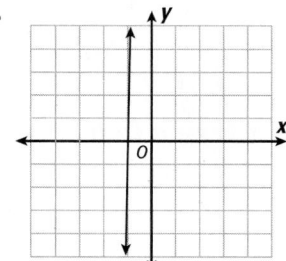

12-6 Exercises

1.

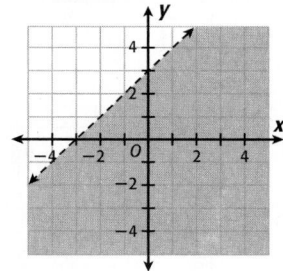

2.

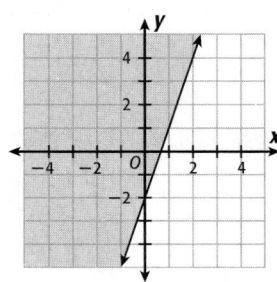

3.

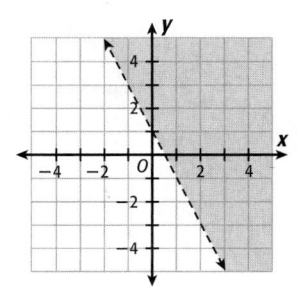

4.

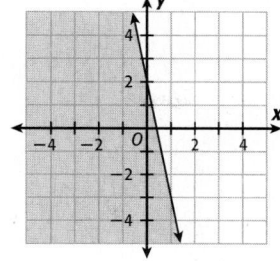

5.

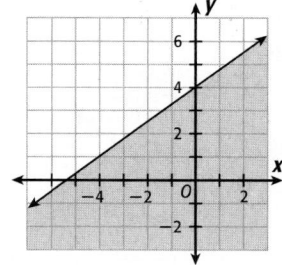

6.

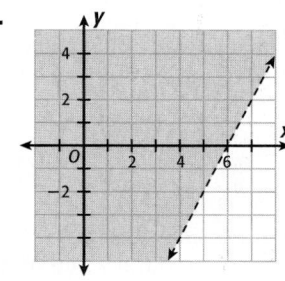

7. a.

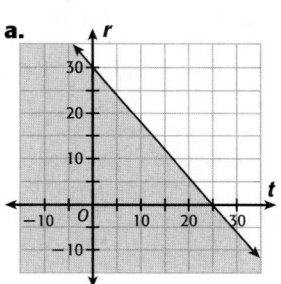

8.

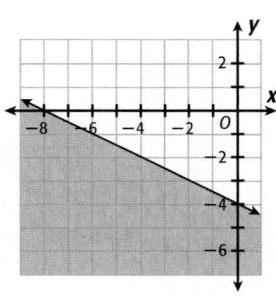

9.

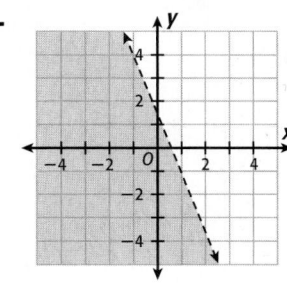

10.

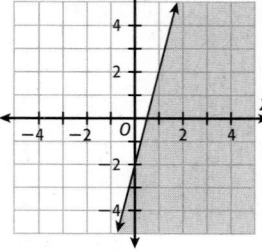

11.

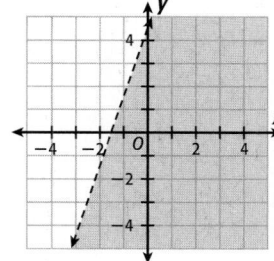

12.

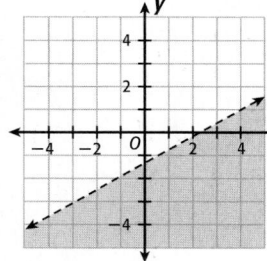

13.

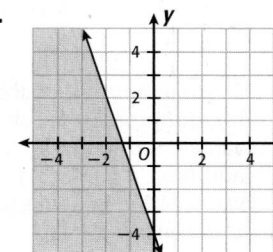

14. a.

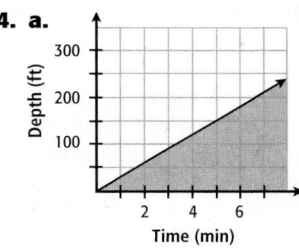

15. a.

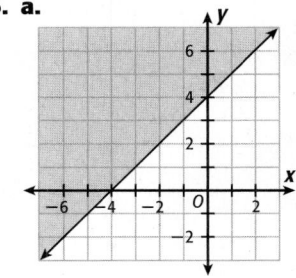

16.

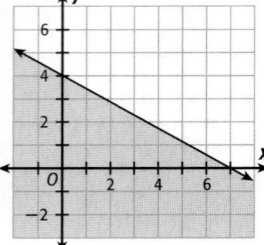

17.

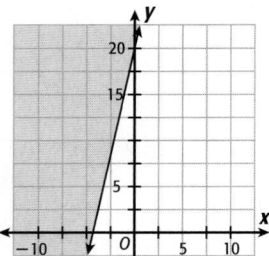

24. b.

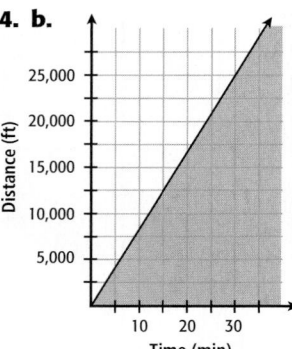

25. Possible answer: I substituted the ordered pair values into the inequality and then calculated the value of the left side to test if the inequality was true.

26. Possible answer: If $y >$ or $\geq$ a quantity, shade above the line. If $y <$ or $\leq$ a quantity, shade below the line. If the inequality is $\leq$ or $\geq$, draw a solid line. If the inequality is $<$ or $>$, draw a dashed line.

27.

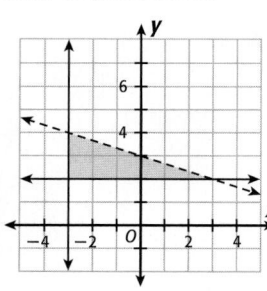

29.

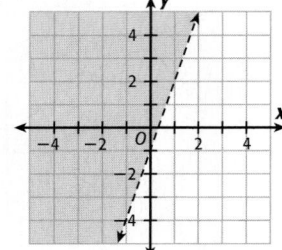

12-7 Exercises

1.

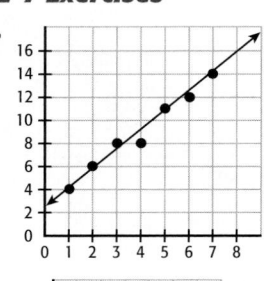

2.

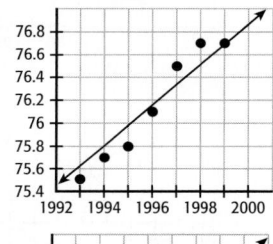

3. Possible answer: $y = 0.22x + 75.46$; in the year 2559; no, the answer is not reasonable unless there are advances in science that will allow bodies to live well beyond 100 years.

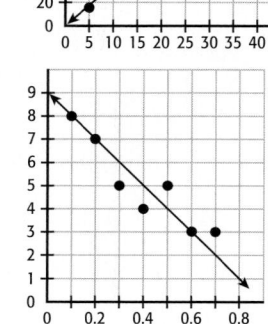

4.

5.

6. Possible answer: $y = -1207x + 12{,}913$; $-\$5192$; no, the answer is not reasonable. The value of the car should be a positive amount.

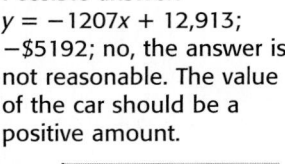

16.

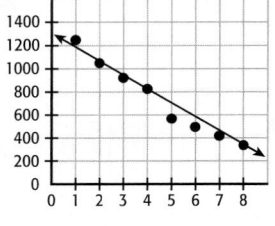

12-7 Lesson Quiz

1.

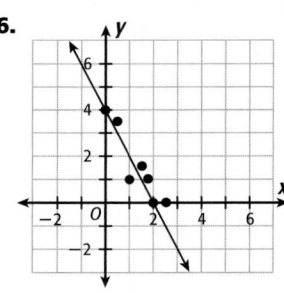

2.

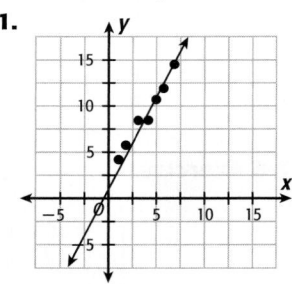

12B Ready To Go On?

1.

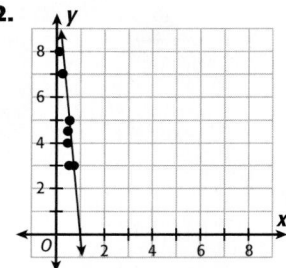

yes

6.

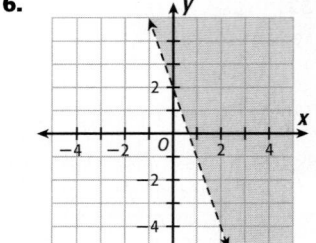

7.

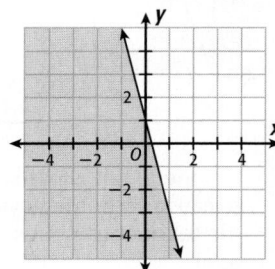

8.

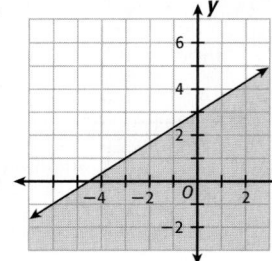

9.

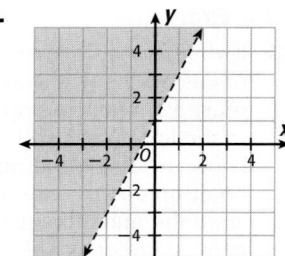

10.

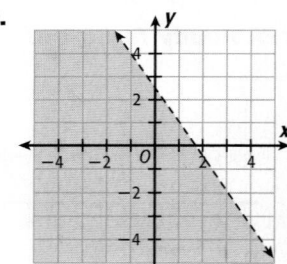

11.

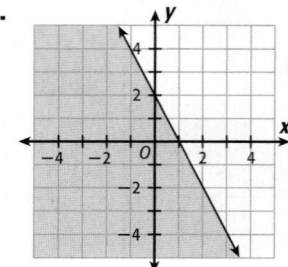

12. a.

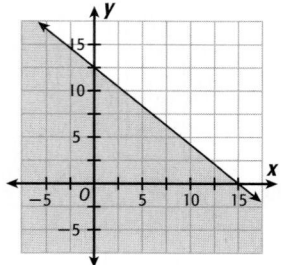

13.

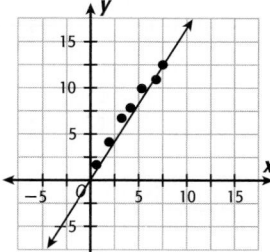

14.

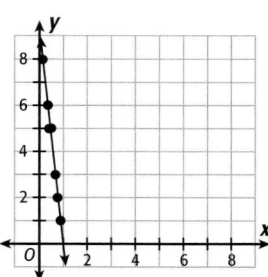

15. Possible answer:
$y = 0.26x + 11.72$ is a line of best fit for when $x = 0$ is the year 1999. Using the equation, in 2009, $x = 8$ and $y = 14.06$; 14.06 is a reasonable stock price.

Multi-Step Test Prep

1.

Time	Talk Cheap	Talk Easy
0	$0	$35.00
10	$550	$36.50
20	$11.00	$38.00
30	$16.50	$39.50
40	$22.00	$41.00
50	$27.50	$42.50
60	$33.00	$44.00
70	$38.50	$45.50
80	$44.00	$47.00
90	$49.50	$48.50

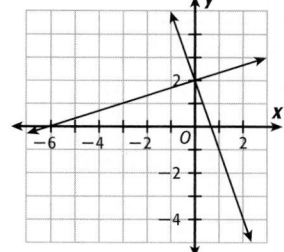

$y = 0.55x$ and
$y = 0.15x + 35$

Chapter 12 Extension

5.

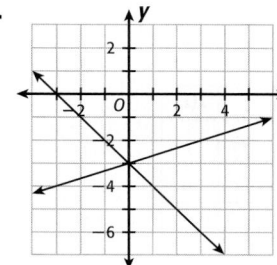

6.

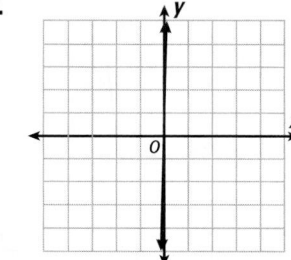

7.

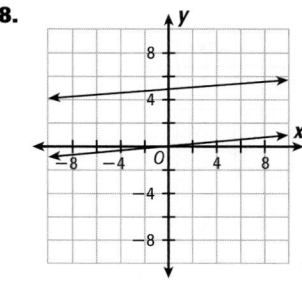

8.

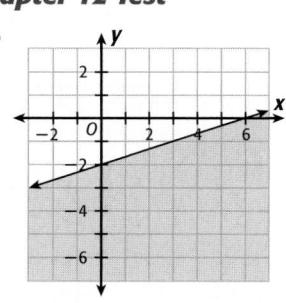

Chapter 12 Test

21.

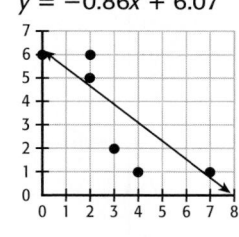

22.

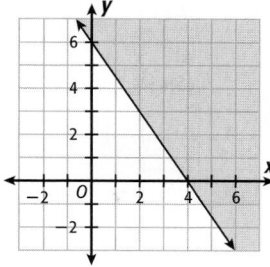

23.

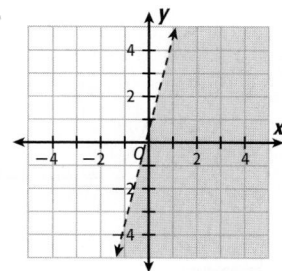

24. a.

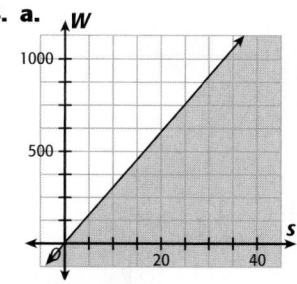

25. Possible answer:
$y = 2.49x + 0.21$

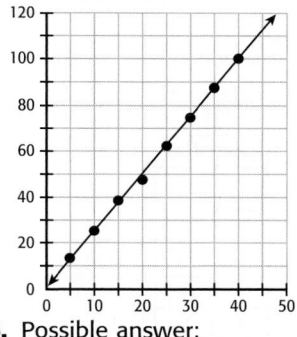

26. Possible answer:
$y = -0.86x + 6.07$

Chapter 13

Are You Ready?

12. $y = \frac{2}{3}x + 4$

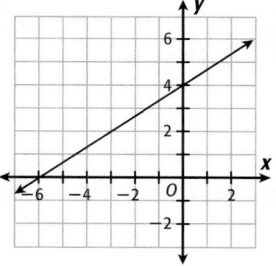

13. $y = -\frac{1}{2}x - 2$

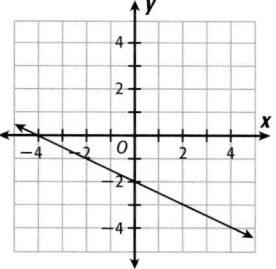

14. $y = 3x + 1$

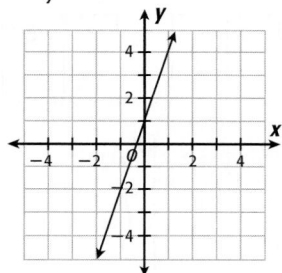

15. $2y = 3x - 8$

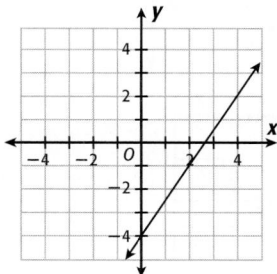

16. $3y + 2x = 6$

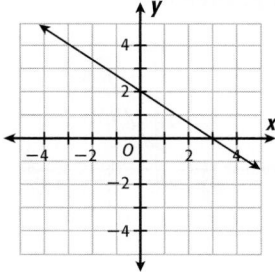

17. $x - 5y = 5$

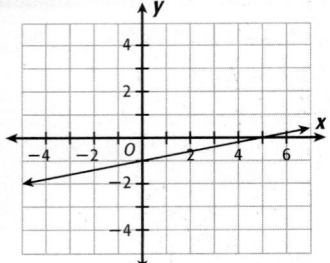

13-5 Additional Examples

1.A.

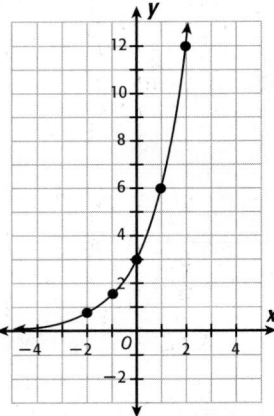

x	−2	−1	0	1	2
y	$\frac{3}{4}$	$\frac{3}{2}$	3	6	12

1.B.

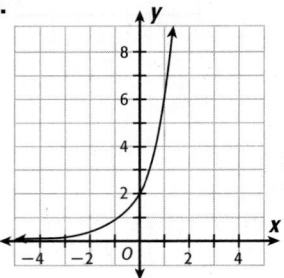

x	f(x)
−2	$\frac{2}{9}$
−1	$\frac{2}{3}$
0	2
1	6
2	18

13-5 Exercises

1.

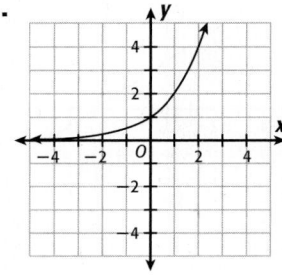

---

x	f(x)
−2	$\frac{1}{4}$
−1	$\frac{1}{2}$
0	1
1	2
2	4

2.

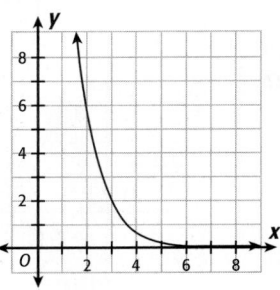

x	f(x)
0	50
1	$\frac{50}{3}$
2	$\frac{50}{9}$
3	$\frac{50}{27}$
4	$\frac{50}{81}$

3.

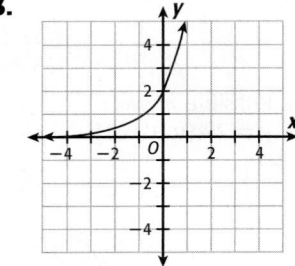

x	f(x)
−2	$\frac{2}{9}$
−1	$\frac{2}{3}$
0	2
1	6
2	18

4.

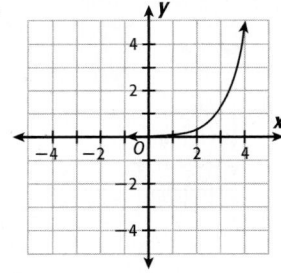

x	f(x)
0	0.02
1	0.08
2	0.32
3	1.28
4	5.12

5.

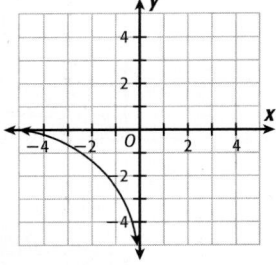

x	f(x)
0	−5
1	−10
2	−20
3	−40
4	−80

6.

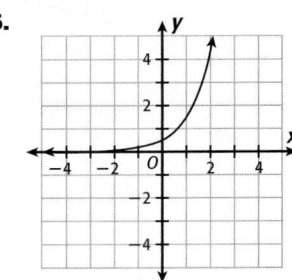

x	f(x)
0	$\frac{1}{2}$
1	$\frac{3}{2}$
2	$\frac{9}{2}$
4	$\frac{27}{2}$

9.

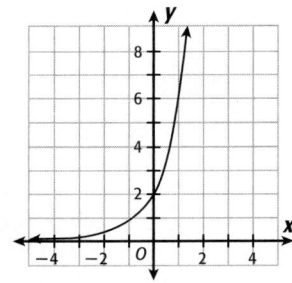

x	f(x)
−2	$\frac{2}{9}$
−1	$\frac{2}{3}$
0	2
1	6
2	18

10.

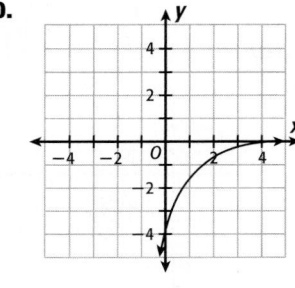

---

x	f(x)
−2	−25
−1	−10
0	−4
1	−1.6
2	−0.64

11.

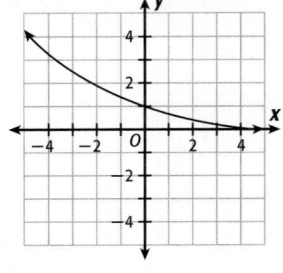

x	f(x)
−2	$\frac{16}{9}$
−1	$\frac{4}{3}$
0	1
1	$\frac{3}{4}$
2	$\frac{9}{16}$

12.

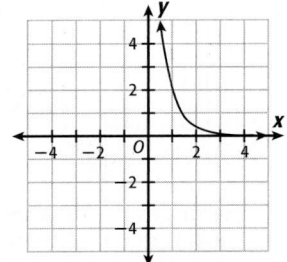

x	f(x)
−2	432
−1	72
0	12
1	2
2	$\frac{1}{3}$

13.

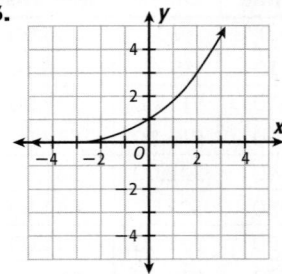

x	f(x)
0	1
1	1.7
2	2.89
3	4.913

14.

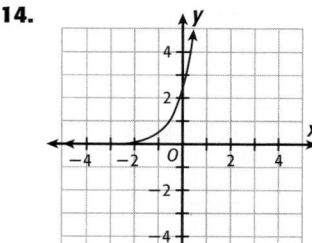

x	f(x)
0	2.3
1	11.73
2	59.823
3	305.0973

24.

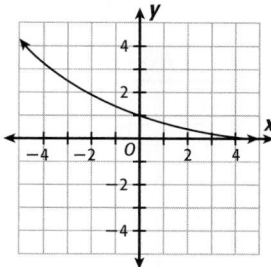

25. $f(c) = -1 \cdot \left(\frac{1}{4}\right)^x$

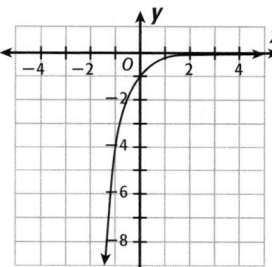

26. $f(x) = 100 \cdot (0.01)^x$

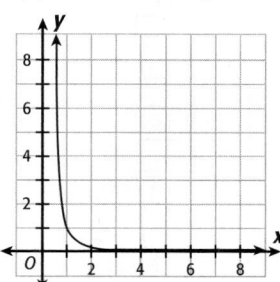

31. Use the function $f(x) = p \cdot a^x$. The common ratio a is $\frac{1}{2}$ and $f(0) = 60$. Divide 12 hours by 6 hours to find the number of half-lives: $x = 2$. Thus $f(2) = 60\left(\frac{1}{2}\right)^2 = 15$ mg.

13-5 Lesson Quiz

1.

x	−2	−1	0	1	2
y	12	6	3	$\frac{3}{2}$	$\frac{3}{4}$

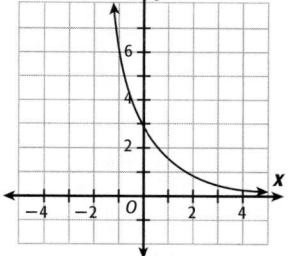

13-6 Exercises

1.

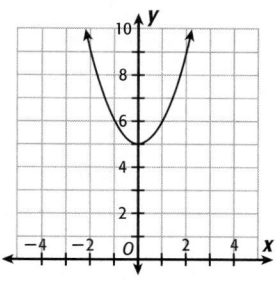

x	f(x)
−3	14
−2	9
−1	6
0	5
1	6
2	9
3	14

2.

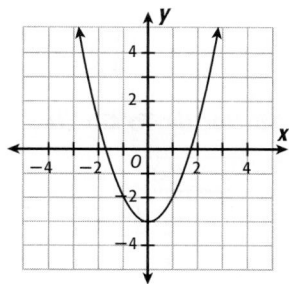

x	f(x)
−3	6
−2	1
−1	−2
0	−3
1	−2
2	1
3	6

3.

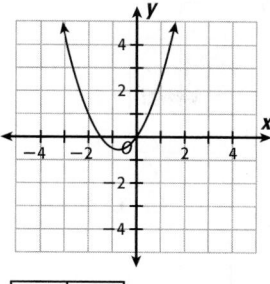

x	f(x)
−3	4.5
−2	1
−1	−0.5
0	0
1	2.5
2	7
3	13.5

5.

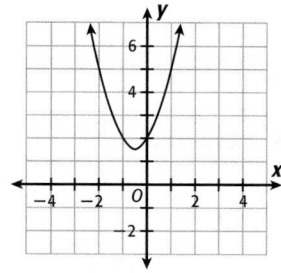

x	f(x)
−3	8
−2	4
−1	2
0	2
1	4
2	8
3	14

6.

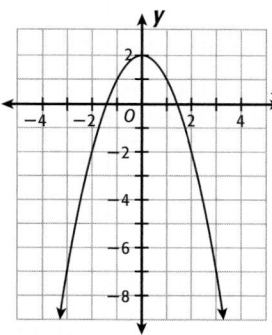

x	f(x)
−3	−7
−2	−2
−1	1
0	2
1	1
2	−2
3	−7

7.

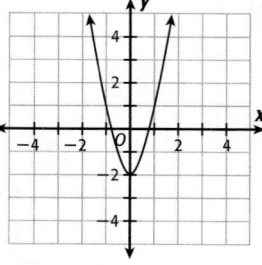

x	f(x)
−3	25
−2	10
−1	1
0	−2
1	1
2	10
3	25

15.

x	f(x)
−12	0
−8	−48
−4	−64
0	−48
4	0
8	80
12	192

16.

x	f(x)
0	10
1	4
2	0
3	−2
4	−2
5	0
6	4

17.

x	f(x)
−4	5
−3	0
−2	−3
−1	−4
0	−3
1	0
2	5

18.

x	f(x)
−3	36
0	0
3	−18
6	−18
9	0
12	36

19.

x	f(x)
4	80
5	74
6	72
7	74
8	80

21. a.

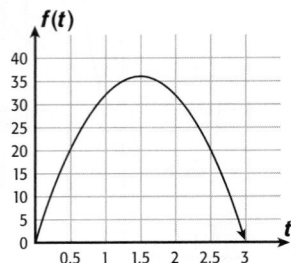

f(t) graph

24. $f(4) = 0$; The object reaches the ground 4 seconds after it was dropped; a feather; a feather would take longer to reach the ground because of air resistance, whereas a rock would probably reach the ground in less than 4 seconds.

26. Possible answer: The function $f(x) = 2^x$ will grow more quickly as x gets larger. For example, when $x = 10$, 2^{10} is 1024, but 10^2 is only 100.

27.

x	−2	−1	0	1	2
f(x)	−15	−6	−3	−6	−15

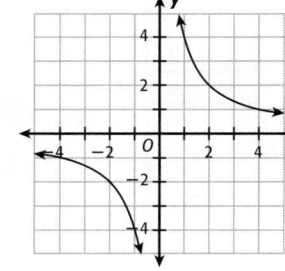

13-7 Additional Examples

2.A.

x	y
−3	$-\frac{4}{3}$
−2	−2
−1	−4
$-\frac{1}{2}$	−8
$\frac{1}{2}$	8
1	4
2	2
3	$\frac{4}{3}$

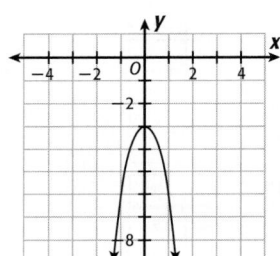

2.B.

x	y
−3	$\frac{1}{6}$
−2	$\frac{1}{4}$
−1	$\frac{1}{2}$
$-\frac{1}{2}$	1
$\frac{1}{2}$	−1
1	$-\frac{1}{2}$
2	$-\frac{1}{4}$
3	$-\frac{1}{6}$

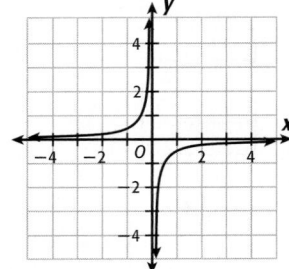

13-7 Exercises

3.

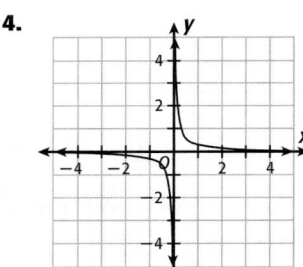

4.

5.

6.

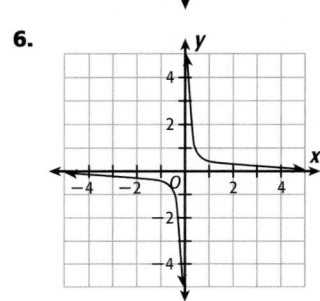

10.

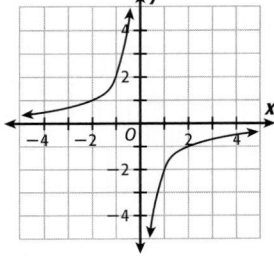

11.

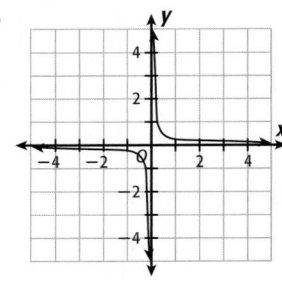

12.

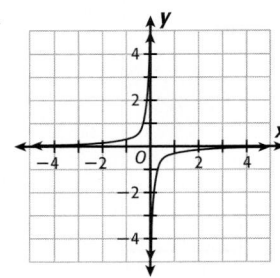

13.

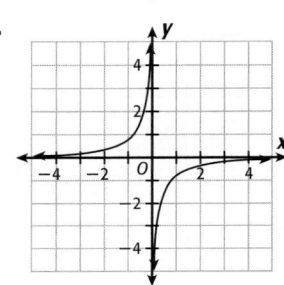

13B Ready To Go On?

6.

x	f(x)
−2	$\frac{1}{9}$
−1	$\frac{1}{3}$
0	1
1	3
2	9

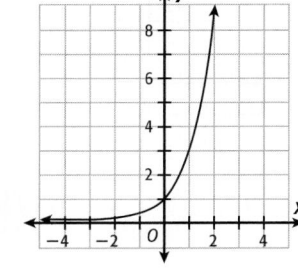

7.

x	f(x)
0	0.01
1	0.05
2	0.25
3	1.25
4	6.25

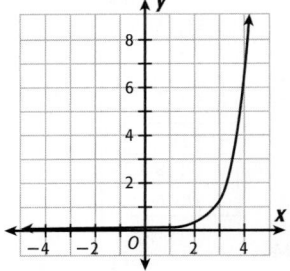

8.

x	f(x)
−2	$\frac{9}{4}$
−1	$\frac{3}{2}$
0	1
1	$\frac{2}{3}$
2	$\frac{4}{9}$

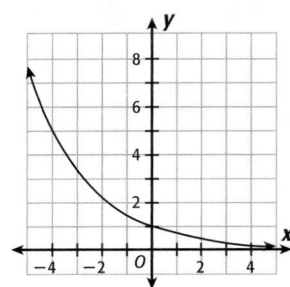

10.

x	f(x)
−3	1.5
−2	−1
−1	−1.5
0	0
1	3.5
2	9
3	16.5

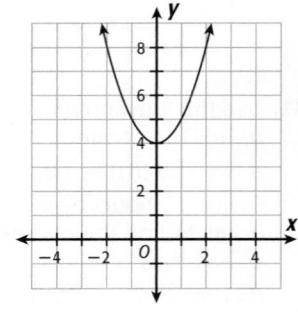

11.

x	f(x)
−3	13
−2	8
−1	5
0	4
1	5
2	8
3	13

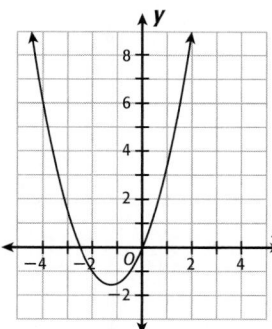

13.

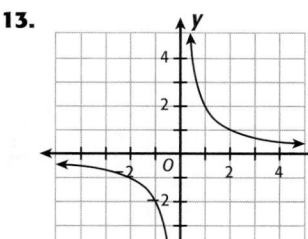

14.

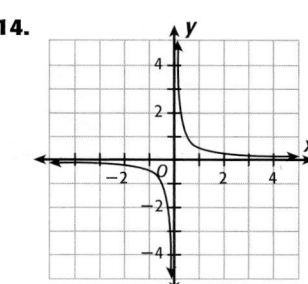

15.

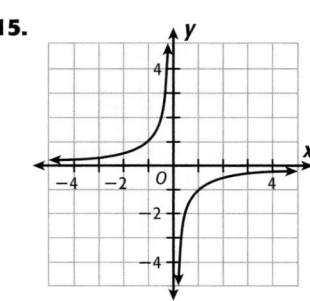

Study Guide: Review

27.

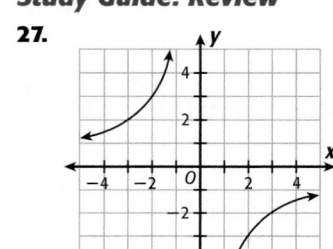

28.

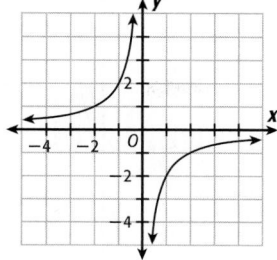

Chapter 13 Test

17.

x	f(x)
−3	9
−2	5
−1	3
0	3
1	5
2	9
3	15

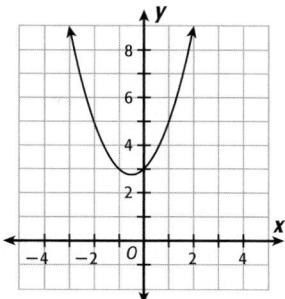

18.

x	f(x)
−3	17
−2	7
−1	1
0	−1
1	1
2	7
3	17

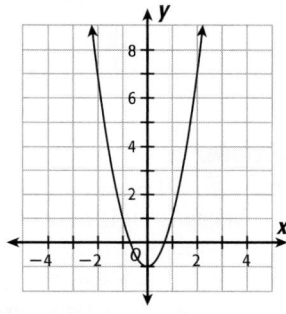

19.

x	f(x)
−3	13
−2	7
−1	3
0	1
1	1
2	3
3	7

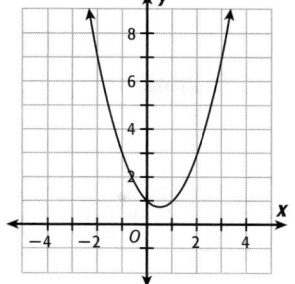

20.

x	f(x)
−4	−1.5
−2	−3
−1	−6
1	6
2	3
4	1.5

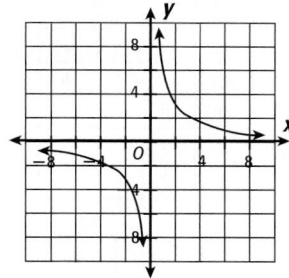

21.

x	f(x)
−4	−2.5
−2	−5
−1	−10
1	10
2	5
4	2.5

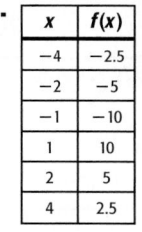

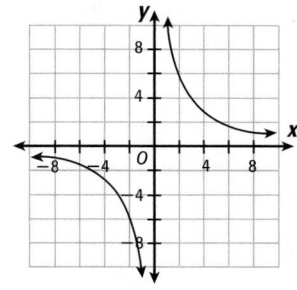

22.

x	y
−4	$\frac{1}{8}$
−2	$\frac{1}{4}$
−1	$\frac{1}{2}$
1	$-\frac{1}{2}$
2	$-\frac{1}{4}$
4	$-\frac{1}{8}$

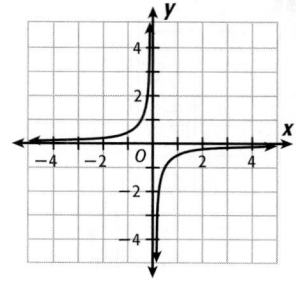

Cumulative Assessment

18.

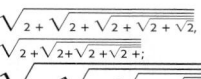

$$\sqrt{2+\sqrt{2+\sqrt{2+\sqrt{2+\sqrt{2}}}}},$$
$$\sqrt{2+\sqrt{2+\sqrt{2+\sqrt{2}+}}};$$
$$\sqrt{2+\sqrt{2+\sqrt{2+\sqrt{2+\sqrt{2+\sqrt{2}}}}}}$$

1.414, 1.84, 1.96, 1.9903, 1.9975, 1.9993, 1.9998, ...

Each term in this sequence is getting closer and closer to 2. It does not appear that any term in the sequence will ever be greater than 2.

19.

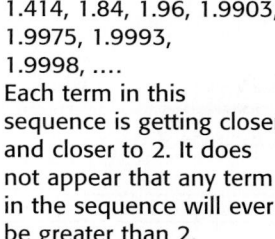

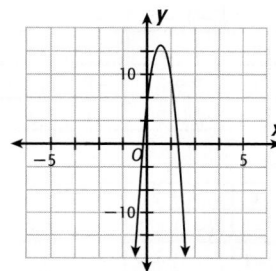

$\frac{2}{3}$ second

Chapter 14

14-2 Exercises

33.

x	f(x)
−2	−3
−1	0
0	1
1	0
1	−3

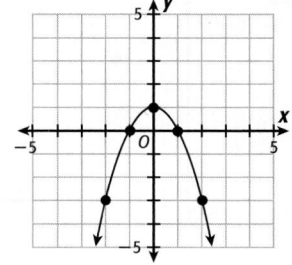

34.

x	f(x)
−2	−1
−1	−3
0	−1
1	2
2	7

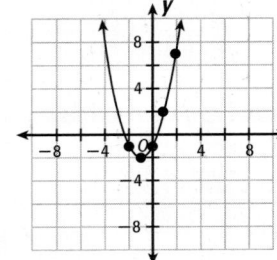

Extra Practice

Chapter 3

5.

x	x − 3	y	(x, y)
−2	−2 − 3	−5	(−2, −5)
−1	−1 − 3	−4	(−1, −4)
0	0 − 3	−3	(0, −3)
1	1 − 3	−2	(1, −2)
2	2 − 3	−1	(2, −1)

6.

x	3x + 2	y	(x, y)
−2	3(−2) + 2	−4	(−2, −4)
−1	3(−1) + 2	−1	(−1, −1)
0	3(0) + 2	2	(0, 2)
1	3(1) + 2	5	(1, 5)
2	3(2) + 2	8	(2, 8)

8–13.

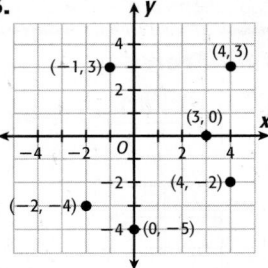

14.

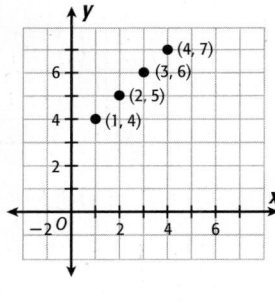

15.

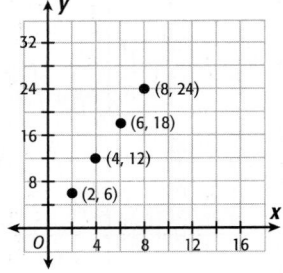

19.

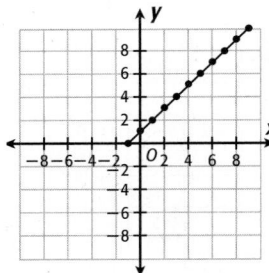

x	x + 1	y
−2	−2 + 1	−1
−1	−1 + 1	0
0	0 + 1	1
1	1 + 1	2
2	2 + 1	3

20.

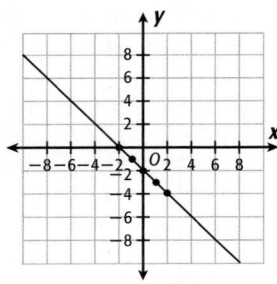

x	−x − 2	y
−2	−(−2) − 2	0
−1	−(−1) − 2	−1
0	−(0) − 2	−2
1	−(1) − 2	−3
2	−(2) − 2	−4

21.

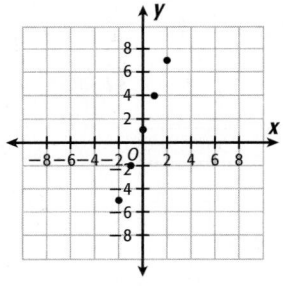

x	3x + 1	y
−2	3(−2) + 1	−5
−1	3(−1) + 1	−2
0	3(0) + 1	1
1	3(1) + 1	4
2	3(2) + 1	7

22.

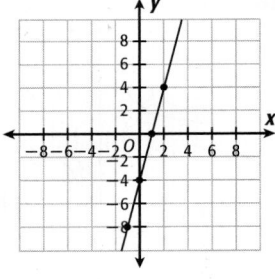

x	4(x − 1)	y
−2	4(−2 − 1)	−12
−1	4(−1 − 1)	−8
0	4(0 − 1)	−4
1	4(1 − 1)	0
2	4(2 − 1)	4

26.

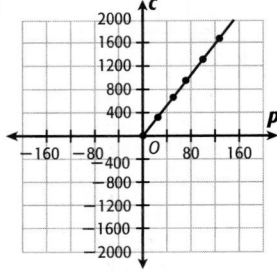

p	13p	c
25	13(25)	$325
50	13(50)	$650
75	13(75)	$975
100	13(100)	$1300
125	13(125)	$1625

27.

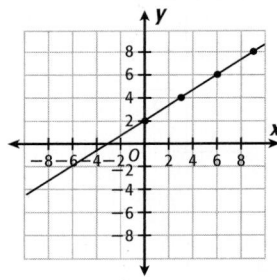

Chapter 4

53. $\sqrt{30}$ is between 5 and 6 because 30 is between 25 and 36.

54. $\sqrt{61}$ is between 7 and 8 because 61 is between 49 and 64.

55. $\sqrt{93}$ is between 9 and 10 because 93 is between 81 and 100.

56. $-\sqrt{124}$ is between 11 and 12 because 124 is between 121 and 144.

Chapter 7

29.

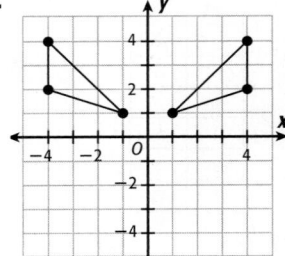

30.

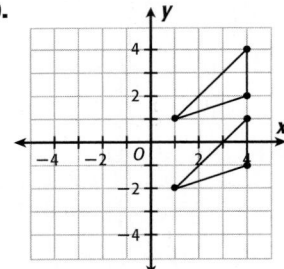

31.

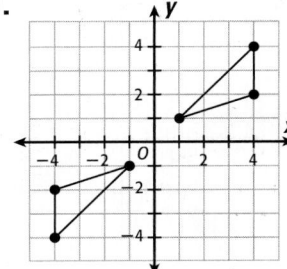

32.

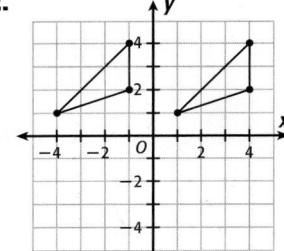

33.

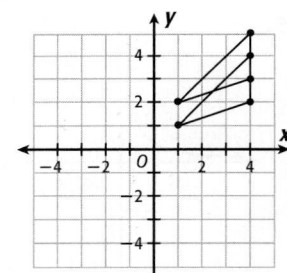

34.

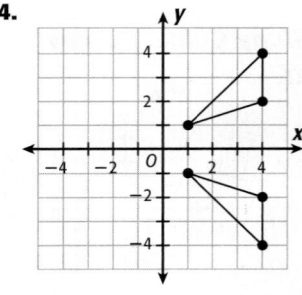

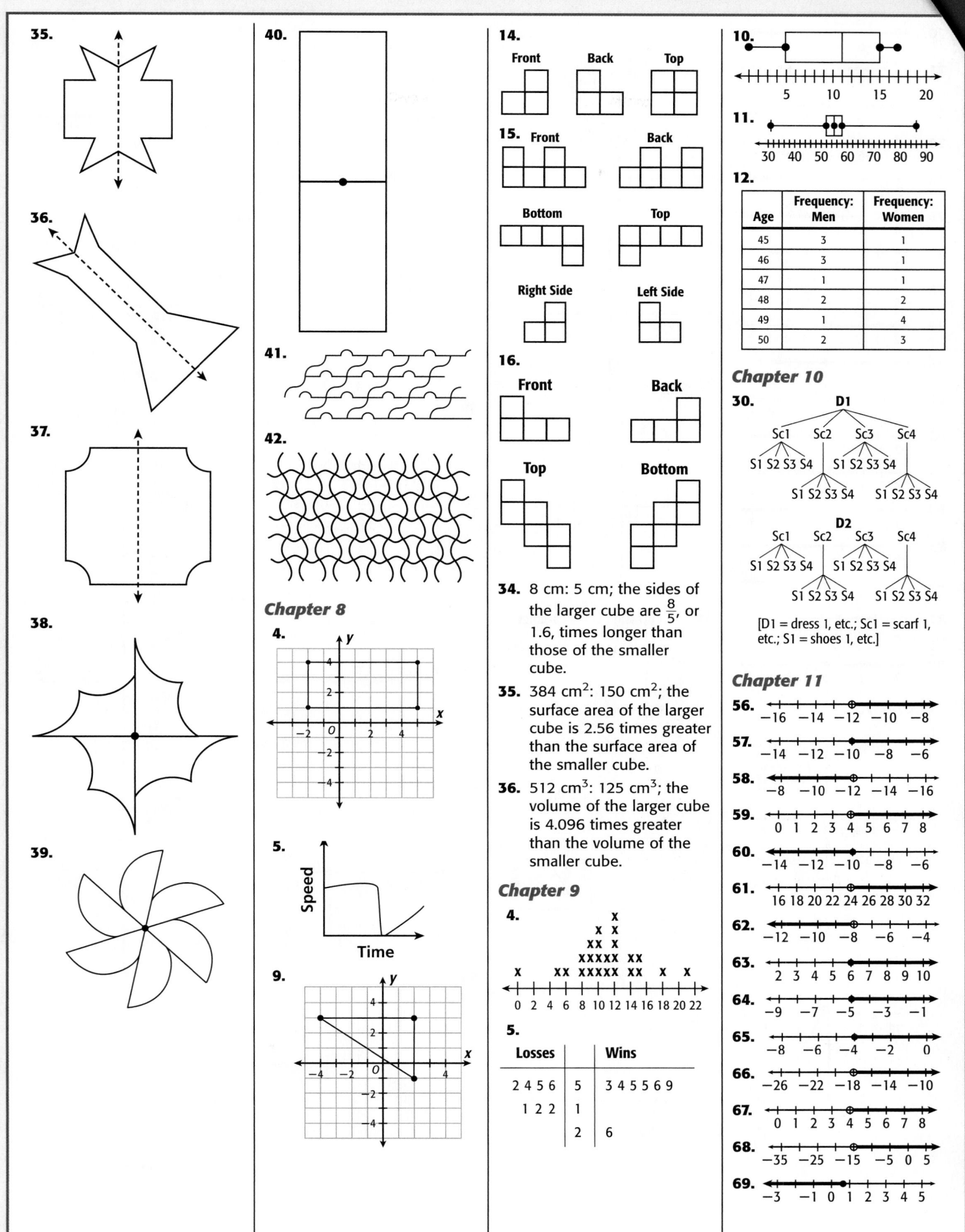

35.

36.

37.

38.

39.

40.

41.

42.

Chapter 8

4.

5.

9.

14.
Front Back Top

15. Front Back
Bottom Top
Right Side Left Side

16.
Front Back
Top Bottom

34. 8 cm: 5 cm; the sides of the larger cube are $\frac{8}{5}$, or 1.6, times longer than those of the smaller cube.

35. 384 cm²: 150 cm²; the surface area of the larger cube is 2.56 times greater than the surface area of the smaller cube.

36. 512 cm³: 125 cm³; the volume of the larger cube is 4.096 times greater than the volume of the smaller cube.

Chapter 9

4.
```
              x
         x    x
         x x  x
         xx   x
         xxxxx  xx
x        xx  xxxxx  xx    x    x
+--+--+--+--+--+--+--+--+--+--+--+
0  2  4  6  8 10 12 14 16 18 20 22
```

5.

Losses		Wins
2 4 5 6	5	3 4 5 5 6 9
1 2 2	1	
	2	6

10.

11.

12.

Age	Frequency: Men	Frequency: Women
45	3	1
46	3	1
47	1	1
48	2	2
49	1	4
50	2	3

Chapter 10

30.
D1
Sc1 Sc2 Sc3 Sc4
S1 S2 S3 S4 S1 S2 S3 S4
S1 S2 S3 S4 S1 S2 S3 S4

D2
Sc1 Sc2 Sc3 Sc4
S1 S2 S3 S4 S1 S2 S3 S4
S1 S2 S3 S4 S1 S2 S3 S4

[D1 = dress 1, etc.; Sc1 = scarf 1, etc.; S1 = shoes 1, etc.]

Chapter 11

56.

57.

58.

59.

60.

61.

62.

63.

64.

65.

66.

67.

68.

69.

70.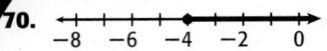

71.

73.

74.

75.

76.

77.

78.

79.

80.

81.

82.

83.

84.

85.

86.

87.

88.

Chapter 12

1.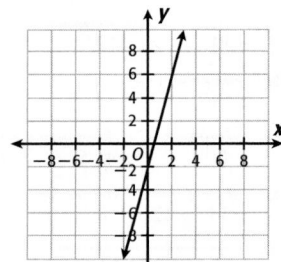

2.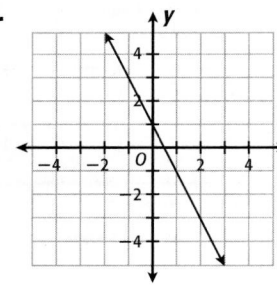

3.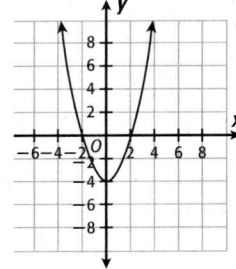

4.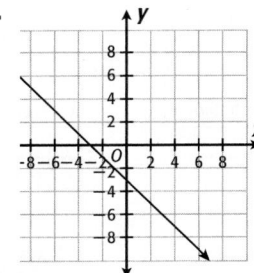

5.

10. Concession Stand Earnings

11.

12.

13.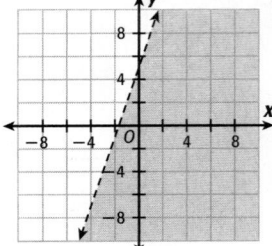

14.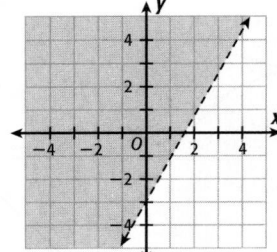

40.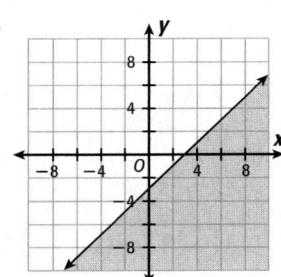

41.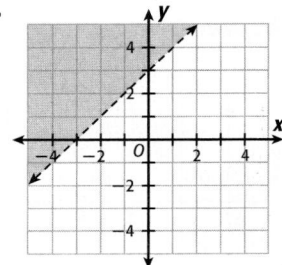

42.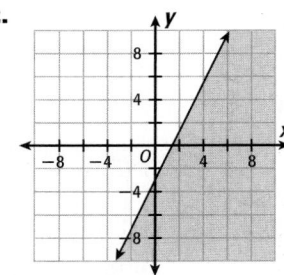

43.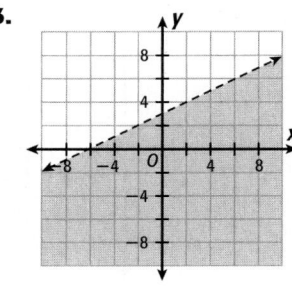

44.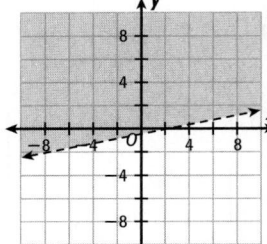

45.

46.

47.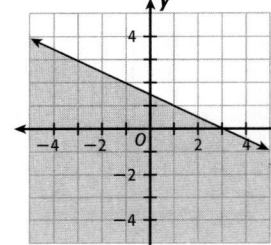

48.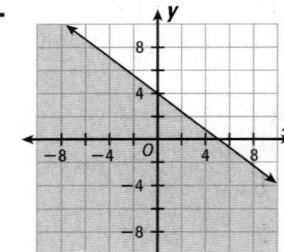

49.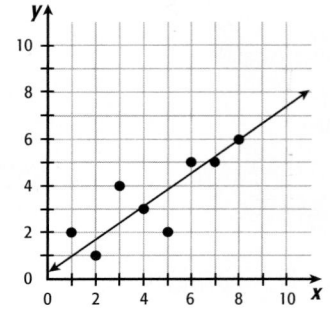

50.

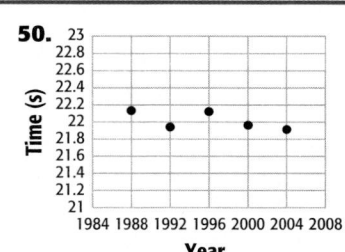

Chapter 13

44.

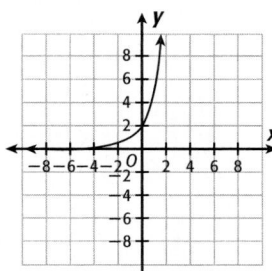

45.

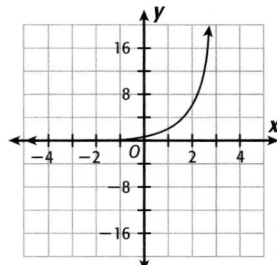

46.

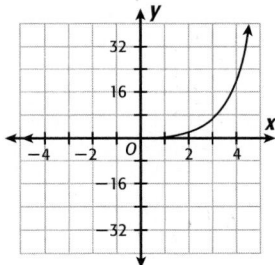

47.

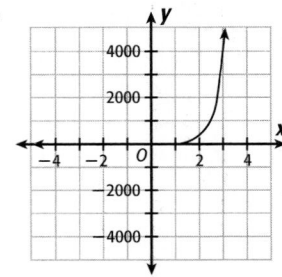

49.

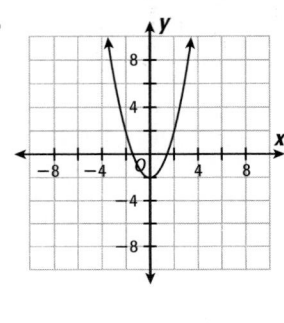

50.

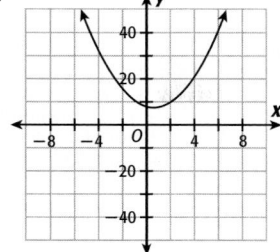

51.

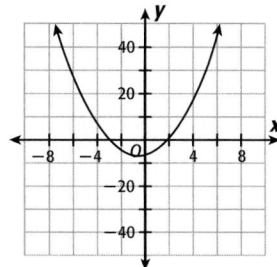

54.

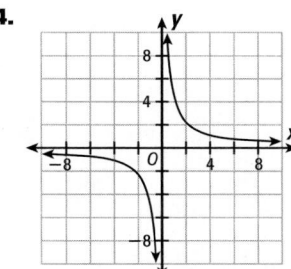

55.

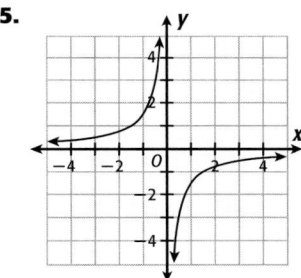

56.

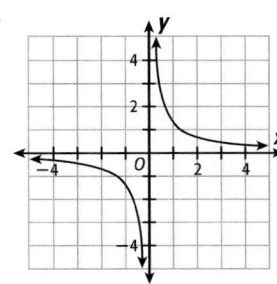

57.

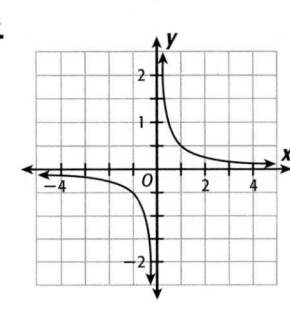

Skills Bank

Terminating and Repeating Decimals

1. 0.2; terminating

2. $0.\overline{3}$; repeating

3. $0.\overline{27}$; repeating

4. 0.375; terminating

5. $0.\overline{7}$; repeating

6. $0.4\overline{6}$; repeating

7. 0.75; terminating

8. $0.8\overline{3}$; repeating

9. $0.3\overline{6}$; repeating

10. 0.5; terminating

11. $0.\overline{1}$; repeating

12. $0.91\overline{6}$; repeating

13. $0.\overline{5}$; repeating

14. $0.\overline{72}$; repeating

15. 0.875; terminating

16. 0.92; terminating

17. 0.15; terminating

18. $0.\overline{45}$; repeating

Iteration

13.

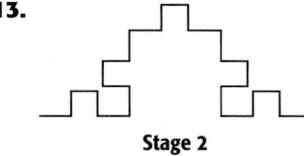

Stage 2

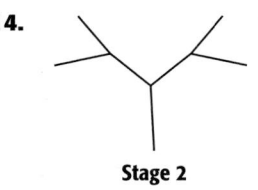

Stage 3

14.

Stage 2

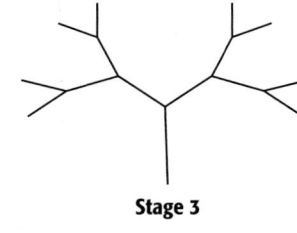

Stage 3

Frequency Polygons

1.

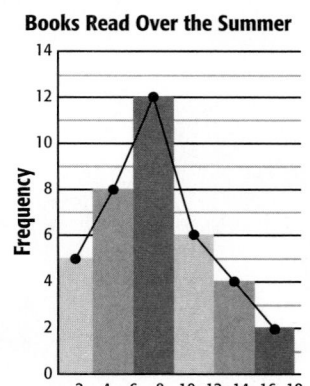

2.

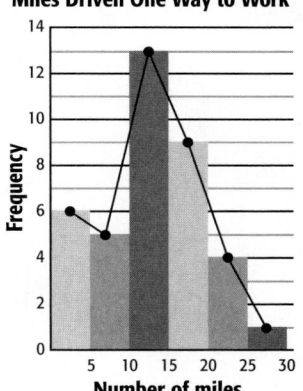

Matrices

4. $\begin{bmatrix} 24 \\ 13 \\ 35 \end{bmatrix}$

5. Possible answer:

$\begin{bmatrix} 50 & 33 & 50 & 84 & 50 \\ 82 & 49 & 59 & 98 & 56 \end{bmatrix}$

6. $\begin{bmatrix} 1 & 0 & 6 \\ 0 & 1 & 5 \\ 7 & 3 & 2 \\ 4 & 8 & 9 \end{bmatrix}$; 4×3

Glossary/Glosario

go.hrw.com
Multilingual Glossary Online
KEYWORD: MT7 Glossary

ENGLISH	SPANISH	EXAMPLES
absolute value The distance of a number from zero on a number line; shown by ||. (p. 15)	**valor absoluto** Distancia a la que está un número de 0 en una recta numérica. El símbolo del valor absoluto es ||.	$\|-5\| = 5$
accuracy The closeness of a given measurement or value to the actual measurement or value.	**exactitud** Cercanía de una medida o valor a la medida o valor real.	
acute angle An angle that measures less than 90°. (p. 325)	**ángulo agudo** Ángulo que mide menos de 90°.	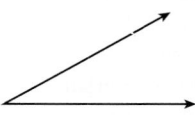
acute triangle A triangle with all angles measuring less than 90°. (p. 336)	**triángulo acutángulo** Triángulo en el que todos los ángulos miden menos de 90°.	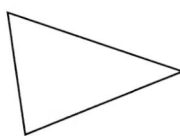
Addition Counting Principle If one group contains m objects and a second group contains n objects, and the groups have no objects in common, then there are $m + n$ total objects to choose from. (p. 559)	**Principio de conteo en suma** Si un grupo tiene m objetos, otro grupo tiene n objetos y los grupos no tienen objetos en común, entonces hay un total de $m + n$ objetos para elegir.	A restaurant offers 3 types of juice and 4 types of iced tea. There are $3 + 4 = 7$ total drinks to choose from.
Addition Property of Equality The property that states that if you add the same number to both sides of an equation, the new equation will have the same solution. (p. 34)	**Propiedad de igualdad de la suma** Propiedad que establece que puedes sumar el mismo número en ambos lados de una ecuación y la ecuación resultante tendrá la misma solución.	$$\begin{array}{rcl} 14 - 6 = & & 8 \\ \underline{+\,6} & & \underline{+\,6} \\ 14 \ \ = & & 14 \end{array}$$
Addition Property of Opposites The property that states that the sum of a number and its opposite equals zero.	**Propiedad de suma de los opuestos** Propiedad que establece que la suma de un número y su opuesto es cero.	$12 + (-12) = 0$
additive inverse The opposite of a number. (p. 14)	**inverso aditivo** El opuesto de un número.	The additive inverse of 5 is -5.
adjacent angles Angles in the same plane that have a common vertex and a common side.	**ángulos adyacentes** Ángulos en el mismo plano que están uno al lado del otro y comparten un vértice y un lado.	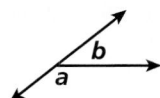

algebraic expression An expression that contains at least one variable. (p. 6)

expresión algebraica Expresión que contiene una o más variables.

$x + 8$
$4(m - b)$

---

algebraic inequality An inequality that contains at least one variable. (p. 44)

desigualdad algebraica Desigualdad que contiene una o más variables.

$x + 3 > 10$
$5a > b + 3$

---

alternate exterior angles A pair of angles on the outer sides of two lines cut by a transversal that are on opposite sides of the transversal. (p. 331)

ángulos alternos externos Par de ángulos en los lados externos de dos líneas intersecadas por una transversal, que están en lados opuestos de la transversal.

∠a and ∠d are alternate exterior angles.

---

alternate interior angles A pair of angles on the inner sides of two lines cut by a transversal that are on opposite sides of the transversal. (p. 331)

ángulos alternos internos Par de ángulos en los lados internos de dos líneas intersecadas por una transversal, que están en lados opuestos de la transversal.

∠r and ∠v are alternate interior angles.

---

angle A figure formed by two rays with a common endpoint called the vertex. (p. 325)

ángulo Figura formada por dos rayos con un extremo común llamado vértice.

---

angle bisector A line, segment, or ray that divides an angle into two congruent angles. (p. 329)

bisectriz de un ángulo Línea, segmento o rayo que divide un ángulo en dos ángulos congruentes.

---

arc An unbroken part of a circle. (p. 838)

arco Parte continua de un círculo.

---

area The number of square units needed to cover a given surface. (p. 389)

área El número de unidades cuadradas que se necesitan para cubrir una superficie.

The area is 10 square units.

---

arithmetic sequence An ordered list of numbers in which the difference between consecutive terms is always the same. (p. 142)

sucesión aritmética Lista ordenada de números en la que la diferencia entre términos consecutivos siempre es la misma.

The sequence 2, 5, 8, 11, 14... is an arithmetic sequence.

ENGLISH	SPANISH	EXAMPLES
Associative Property of Addition The property that states that for all real numbers *a*, *b*, and *c*, the sum is always the same, regardless of their grouping. (p. 829)	**Propiedad asociativa de la suma** Propiedad que establece que para todos los números reales *a*, *b* y *c*, la suma siempre es la misma sin importar cómo se agrupen.	$a + b + c = (a + b) + c = a + (b + c)$
Associative Property of Multiplication: The property that states that for all real numbers *a*, *b*, and *c*, their product is always the same, regardless of their grouping. (p. 829)	**Propiedad asociativa de la multiplicación** Propiedad que establece que para todos los números reales *a*, *b* y *c*, el producto siempre es el mismo, sin importar cómo se agrupen.	$a \cdot b \cdot c = (a \cdot b) \cdot c = a \cdot (b \cdot c)$
average The sum of a set of data divided by the number of items in the data set; also called *mean*. (p. 472)	**media** La suma de todos los elementos, dividida entre el número total de elementos en el conjunto de datos. También se llama *promedio*.	Data set: 4, 6, 7, 8, 10 Average: $\frac{4 + 6 + 7 + 8 + 10}{5}$ $= \frac{35}{5} = 7$

ENGLISH	SPANISH	EXAMPLES
back-to-back stem-and-leaf plot A stem-and-leaf plot that compares two sets of data by displaying one set of data to the left of the stem and the other to the right. (p. 468)	**diagrama doble de tallo y hojas** Diagrama de tallo y hojas que compara dos conjuntos de datos presentando uno de ellos a la izquierda del tallo y el otro a la derecha.	Data set A: 9, 12, 14, 16, 23, 27 Data set B: 6, 8, 10, 13, 15, 16, 21 Set A | | Set B 9 | 0 | 6 8 6 4 2 | 1 | 0 3 5 6 3 7 | 2 | 1 *Key:* |2| 1 means 21 7 |2| means 27
bar graph A graph that uses vertical or horizontal bars to display data. (p. 485)	**gráfica de barras** Gráfica en la que se usan barras verticales u horizontales para presentar datos.	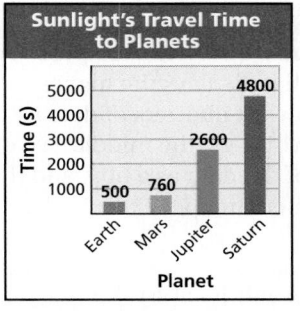
base When a number is raised to a power, the number that is used as a factor is the base. (p. 162)	**base** En un número elevado a una potencia, el número que se usa como factor es la base.	$3^5 = 3 \cdot 3 \cdot 3 \cdot 3 \cdot 3$; 3 is the base.

ENGLISH	SPANISH	EXAMPLES
base (of a polygon or three-dimensional figure) A side of a polygon; a face of a three-dimensional figure by which the figure is measured or classified. (p. 413)	**base (de un polígono o figura tridimensional)** Lado de un polígono; cara de una figura tridimensional según la cual se mide o se clasifica una figura.	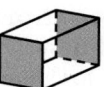 Bases of a cylinder Bases of a prism Base of a cone Base of a pyramid
biased sample A sample that does not fairly represent the population. (p. 463)	**muestra no representativa** Muestra que no representa de forma justa la población.	
binomial A polynomial with two terms. (p. 734)	**binomio** Polinomio con dos términos.	$x + y$ $2a^2 - 3$ $4m^3n^2 + 6mn^4$
bisect To divide into two congruent parts. (p. 329)	**trazar una bisectriz** Dividir en dos partes congruentes.	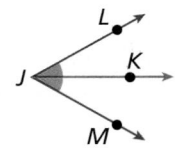 $\overrightarrow{JK}$ bisects $\angle LJM$
boundary line The set of points where the two sides of a two-variable linear inequality are equal. (p. 655)	**línea de límite** Conjunto de puntos donde los dos lados de una desigualdad lineal con dos variables son iguales.	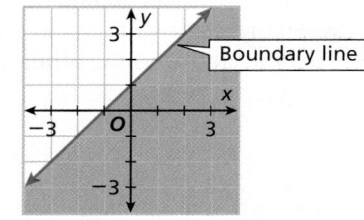 Boundary line
box-and-whisker plot A graph that displays the highest and lowest quarters of data as whiskers, the middle two quarters of the data as a box, and the median. (p. 477)	**gráfica de mediana y rango** También conocida como gráfica de "caja y bigotes" ya que muestra los cuartiles superior e inferior como "bigotes", los dos cuartiles intermedios como una "caja", así como la medana de los datos.	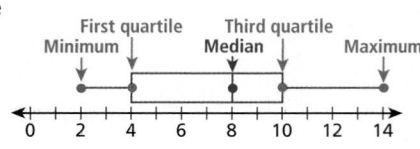
break (graph) A zigzag on a horizontal or vertical scale of a graph that indicates that some of the numbers on the scale have been omitted.	**discontinuidad (gráfica)** Zig-zag en la escala horizontal o vertical de una gráfica que indica la omisión de algunos números de la escala.	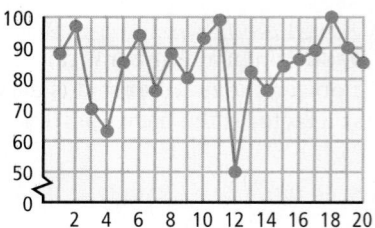

 **C**

capacity The amount a container can hold when filled. (p. 440)	**capacidad** Cantidad que cabe en un recipiente cuando se llena.	A large milk container has a capacity of 1 gallon.

ENGLISH	SPANISH	EXAMPLES
Celsius A metric scale for measuring temperature in which 0°C is the freezing point of water and 100°C is the boiling point of water; also called *centigrade*.	**Celsius** Escala métrica para medir temperatura, en la que 0 °C es el punto de congelación del agua y 100 °C es el punto de ebullición. También se le llama *centígrada*.	
center (of a circle) The point inside a circle that is the same distance from all the points on the circle. (p. 294)	**centro (de un círculo)** Punto interior de un círculo que se encuentra a la misma distancia de todos los puntos de la circunferencia.	
center of dilation The point of intersection of lines through each pair of corresponding vertices in a dilation. (p. 244)	**centro de una dilatación** Punto de intersección de las líneas que pasan a través de cada par de vértices correspondientes.	center
center of rotation The point about which a figure is rotated. (p. 358)	**centro de rotación** Punto alrededor del cual se hace girar una figura.	90° 90° Center 90° 90°
central angle An angle formed by two radii with its vertex at the center of a circle. (p. 838)	**ángulo central** Ángulo formado por dos radios y cuyo vértice se encuentra en el centro de un círculo.	
certain (probability) Sure to happen; an event that is certain has a probability of 1. (p. 522)	**seguro (probabilidad)** Que con seguridad sucederá. Representa una probabilidad de 1.	When rolling a number cube, it is certain that you will roll a number less than 7.
chord A segment with its endpoints on a circle. (p. 838)	**cuerda** Segmento de recta cuyos extremos forman parte de un círculo.	A Chord B
circle The set of all points in a plane that are the same distance from a given point called the center. (p. 400)	**círculo** Conjunto de puntos en un plano que se encuentran a la misma distancia de un punto llamado centro.	
circle graph A graph that uses sectors of a circle to compare parts to the whole and parts to other parts. (p. 484)	**gráfica circular** Gráfica que usa secciones de un círculo para comparar partes con el todo y con otras partes.	**Residents of Mesa, AZ** 65+ Under 18 45–64 13% 27% 19% 11% 30% 18–24 25–44
circuit A path in a graph that begins and ends at the same vertex. (p. 840)	**circuito** Una trayectoria en una gráfica que empieza y termina en el mismo vértice.	

ENGLISH	SPANISH	EXAMPLES
circumference The distance around a circle. (p. 400)	**circunferencia** Distancia alrededor de un círculo.	Circumference
clockwise A circular movement to the right in the direction shown.	**en sentido de las manecillas del reloj** Movimiento circular hacia la derecha en la dirección que se indica.	
coefficient The number that is multiplied by the variable in an algebraic expression. (p. 6)	**coeficiente** Número que se multiplica por la variable en una expresión algebraica.	5 is the coefficient in $5b$.
combination An arrangement of items or events in which order does not matter. (p. 564)	**combinación** Agrupación de objetos o sucesos en la que el orden no es importante.	For objects A, B, C, and D, there are 6 different combinations of 2 objects: AB, AC, AD, BC, BD, CD.
commission A fee paid to a person for making a sale. (p. 298)	**comisión** Pago que recibe una persona por realizar una venta.	
commission rate The fee paid to a person who makes a sale expressed as a percent of the selling price. (p. 298)	**tasa de comisión** Pago que recibe una persona por hacer una venta, expresado como un porcentaje del precio de venta.	A commission rate of 5% and a sale of $10,000 results in a commission of $500.
common denominator A denominator that is the same in two or more fractions.	**común denominador** Denominador que es el mismo en dos o más fracciones.	The common denominator of $\frac{5}{8}$ and $\frac{2}{8}$ is 8.
common difference The difference between any two successive terms in an arithmetic sequence. (p. 142)	**diferencia común** Diferencia entre dos términos consecutivos de una sucesión aritmética.	In the arithmetic sequence 3, 5, 7, 9, 11, ..., the common difference is 2.
common factor A number that is a factor of two or more numbers. (p. 824)	**factor común** Número que es factor de dos o más números.	8 is a common factor of 16 and 40.
common multiple A number that is a multiple of each of two or more numbers. (p. 824)	**común múltiplo** Número que es múltiplo de dos o más números.	15 is a common multiple of 3 and 5.
common ratio The ratio each term is multiplied by to produce the next term in a geometric sequence. (p. 687)	**razón común** Razón por la que se multiplica cada término para obtener el siguiente término de una sucesión geométrica.	In the geometric sequence 32, 16, 8, 4, 2, ..., the common ratio is $\frac{1}{2}$.
Commutative Property of Addition The property that states that two or more numbers can be added in any order without changing the sum. (p. 828)	**Propiedad conmutativa de la suma** Propiedad que establece que dos o más números se pueden sumar en cualquier orden sin alterar la suma.	$8 + 20 = 20 + 8$; $a + b = b + a$

ENGLISH	SPANISH	EXAMPLES
Commutative Property of Multiplication The property that states that two or more numbers can be multiplied in any order without changing the product. (p. 828)	**Propiedad conmutativa de la multiplicación** Propiedad que establece que dos o más números se pueden multiplicar en cualquier orden sin alterar el producto.	$6 \cdot 12 = 12 \cdot 6; a \cdot b = b \cdot a$
compatible numbers Numbers that are close to the given numbers that make estimation or mental calculation easier. (p. 278)	**números compatibles** Números que pueden reemplazar a otros en un problema por ser más fáciles de usar en estimaciones o cálculos mentales.	To estimate $7{,}957 + 5{,}009$, use the compatible numbers 8,000 and 5,000: $8{,}000 + 5{,}000 = 13{,}000$.
complementary angles Two angles whose measures add to 90°. (p. 325)	**ángulos complementarios** Dos ángulos cuyas medidas suman 90°.	The complement of a 53°angle is a 37° angle.
composite number A number greater than 1 that has more than two whole-number factors. (p. 823)	**número compuesto** Número mayor que 1 que tiene más de dos factores que son números cabales.	4, 6, 8, and 9 are composite numbers.
compound event An event made up of two or more simple events.	**suceso compuesto** Suceso formado por dos o más sucesos simples.	Rolling a 3 on a number cube and spinning a 2 on a spinner is a compound event.
compound inequality A combination of more than one inequality.	**desigualdad compuesta** Combinación de dos o más desigualdades.	$x \geq -2$ or $x < 10$ $-2 \leq x < 10$
compound interest Interest earned or paid on principal and previously earned or paid interest. (p. 306)	**interés compuesto** Interés que se gana o se paga sobre el capital y los intereses previamente ganados o pagados.	If $100 is put into an account with an interest rate of 5% compounded monthly, then after 2 years, the account will have $100\left(1 + \frac{0.05}{12}\right)^{12 \cdot 2} = \$110.49$
cone A three-dimensional figure with one vertex and one circular base. (p. 420)	**cono** Figura tridimensional con un vértice y una base circular.	
congruent Having the same size and shape. (p. 325)	**congruentes** Que tiene la misma forma y tamaño.	$\overline{PQ} \cong \overline{RS}$

ENGLISH	SPANISH	EXAMPLES
congruent angles Angles that have the same measure. (p. 238)	**ángulos congruentes** Ángulos que tienen la misma medida.	$\angle ABC = \angle DEF$
congruent segments Segments that have the same length. (p. 238)	**segmentos de recta congruentes** Segmentos que tienen la misma longitud.	$\overline{PQ} \cong \overline{SR}$
constant A value that does not change. (p. 6)	**constante** Valor que no cambia.	$3, 0, \pi$
constant of proportionality A constant ratio of two variables related proportionally. (p. 650)	**constante de proporcionalidad** Razón constante de dos variables que están relacionadas en forma proporcional. *Ejemplo:* $5 = k$, $10 = 2k$, y $15 = 3k$	In $y = 5x$, the constant of proportionality is 5.
convenience sample A sample based on members of the population that are readily available. (p. 462)	**muestra de conveniencia** Una muestra basada en miembros de la población que están fácilmente disponibles.	
conversion factor A fraction whose numerator and denominator represent the same quantity but use different units; the fraction is equal to 1 because the numerator and denominator are equal. (p. 224)	**factor de conversión** Fracción cuyo numerador y denominador representan la misma cantidad pero con unidades distintas; la fracción es igual a 1 porque el numerador y el denominador son iguales.	$\dfrac{24 \text{ hours}}{1 \text{ day}}$ and $\dfrac{1 \text{ day}}{24 \text{ hours}}$
coordinate One of the numbers of an ordered pair that locate a point on a coordinate graph. (p. 122)	**coordenada** Uno de los números de un par ordenado que localizan un punto en un plano cartesiano.	The coordinates of *A* is 2. The coordinates of *B* are $(-2, 3)$
coordinate plane (coordinate grid) A plane formed by the intersection of a horizontal number line called the *x*-axis and a vertical number line called the *y*-axis. (p. 122)	**plano cartesiano (cuadrícula de coordenadas)** Plano formado por la intersección de una recta numérica horizontal llamada eje de las *x* y otra vertical llamada eje de las *y*.	

ENGLISH	SPANISH	EXAMPLES
correlation The description of the relationship between two data sets. (p. 494)	**correlación** Descripción de la relación entre dos conjuntos de datos.	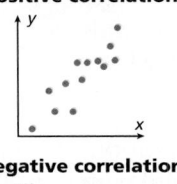 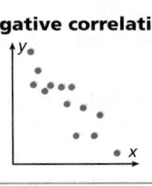 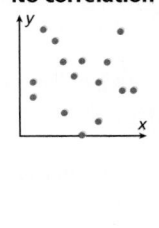
correspondence The relationship between two or more objects that are matched. (p. 354)	**correspondencia** La relación entre dos o más objetos que coinciden.	$\angle A$ and $\angle D$ are corresponding angles. 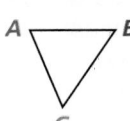 $\overline{AB}$ and $\overline{DE}$ are corresponding sides.
corresponding angles (for lines) Angles formed by a transversal cutting two or more lines and that are in the same relative position. (p. 331)	**ángulos correspondientes (en líneas)** Ángulos formados por una transversal que interseca dos o más líneas y que están en la misma posición relativa.	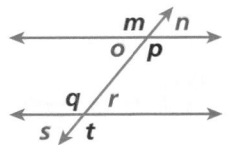 $\angle m$ and $\angle q$ are corresponding angles.
corresponding angles (in polygons) Matching angles of two or more polygons. (p. 238)	**ángulos correspondientes (en polígonos)** Ángulos que están en la misma posición relativa en dos o más polígonos.	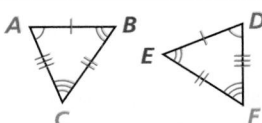 $\angle A$ and $\angle D$ are corresponding angles.
corresponding sides Matching sides of two or more polygons. (p. 238)	**lados correspondientes** Lados que se localizan en la misma posición relativa en dos o más polígonos.	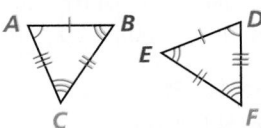 $\overline{AB}$ and $\overline{DE}$ are corresponding sides.
counterclockwise A circular movement to the left in the direction shown.	**en sentido de las manecillas del reloj** Movimiento circular hacia la derecha en la dirección que se indica.	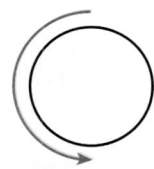
cross product The product of numbers on the diagonal when comparing two ratios. (p. 229)	**producto cruzado** Multiplicación cruzada de los numeradores y denominadores de dos razones.	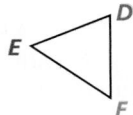 For the proportion $\frac{2}{3} = \frac{4}{6}$, the cross products are $2 \cdot 6 = 12$ and $3 \cdot 4 = 12$

ENGLISH	SPANISH	EXAMPLES
cube (geometric figure) A rectangular prism with six congruent square faces. (pp. 154, 300)	**cubo (figura geométrica)** Prisma rectangular con seis caras cuadradas congruentes.	
cube (in numeration) A number raised to the third power. (p. 830)	**cubo (en numeración)** Número elevado a la tercera potencia.	$2^3 = 2 \cdot 2 \cdot 2 = 8$ 8 is the cube of 2.
cumulative frequency The sum of successive data items. (p. 835)	**frecuencia acumulativa** Muestra el total acumulado de las frecuencias.	
customary system of measurement The measurement system often used in the United States.	**sistema métrico de medición** Sistema decimal de pesos y medidas empleado universalmente en las ciencias y de uso común en todo el mundo.	inches, feet, miles, ounces, pounds, tons, cups, quarts, gallons
cylinder A three-dimensional figure with two parallel, congruent circular bases connected by a curved lateral surface. (p. 413)	**cilindro** Figura tridimensional con dos bases circulares paralelas y congruentes, unidas por una superficie lateral curva.	

D

decagon A polygon with ten sides.	**decágono** Polígono de diez lados.	
degree The unit of measure for angles or temperature. (p. 324)	**grado** Unidad de medida para ángulos y temperaturas.	
degree of a polynomial The highest power of the variable in a polynomial. (p. 735)	**grado de un polinomio** La potencia más alta de la variable en un polinomio.	The polynomial $4x^5 - 6x^2 + 7$ has degree 5
Density Property The property that states that between any two real numbers, there is always another real number. (p. 192)	**Propiedad de densidad** Propiedad según la cual entre dos números reales cualesquiera siempre hay otro número real.	
denominator The bottom number of a fraction that tells how many equal parts are in the whole. (p. 64)	**denominador** Número que está abajo en una fracción y que indica las partes en que se divide el entero.	In the fraction $\frac{2}{5}$, 5 is the denominator.
dependent events Events for which the outcome of one event affects the probability of the other. (p. 545)	**sucesos dependientes** Sucesos en los que el resultado del primero no afecta la probabilidad del segundo.	A bag contains 3 red marbles and 2 blue marbles. Drawing a red marble and then drawing a blue marble without replacing the first marble is an example of dependent events.

ENGLISH	SPANISH	EXAMPLES
diagonal A line segment that connect two non-adjacent vertices of a polygon.	**diagonal** Segmento de recta que une dos vértices no adyacentes de un polígono.	
diameter A line segment that passes through the center of a circle and has endpoints on the circle, or the length of that segment. (p. 400)	**diámetro** Segmento de recta que pasa por el centro de un círculo y tiene sus extremos en la circunferencia, o bien la longitud de ese segmento.	
difference The result when one number is subtracted from another.	**diferencia** El resultado de restar un número de otro.	
dilation A transformation that enlarges or reduces a figure. (p. 244)	**dilatación** Transformación que agranda o reduce una figura.	
dimensions (geometry) The length, width, or height of a figure.	**dimensiones (geometría)** Longitud, anchura o altura de una figura.	
dimensions (of a matrix) The number of horizontal rows and vertical columns in a matrix. (p. 839)	**dimensiones (de una matriz)** Número de filas y columnas que hay en una matriz.	
direct variation A relationship between two variables in which the data increase or decrease together at a constant rate. (p. 650)	**variación directa** Relación entre dos variables en la que los datos aumentan o disminuyen juntos a una tasa constante.	$y = 2x$
discount The amount by which the original price is reduced.	**descuento** Cantidad que se resta al precio original de un artículo.	
Distributive Property The property that states if you multiply a sum by a number, you will get the same result if you multiply each addend by that number and then add the products. (p. 829)	**Propiedad distributiva** Propiedad que establece que si multiplicas una suma por un número, obtienes el mismo resultado que si multiplicas cada sumando por ese número y luego sumas los productos.	$5 \cdot 21 = 5(20 + 1) = (5 \cdot 20) + (5 \cdot 1)$
dividend The number to be divided in a division problem.	**dividendo** Número que se divide en un problema de división.	In $8 \div 4 = 2$, 8 is the dividend.
divisible Can be divided by a number without leaving a remainder. (p. 822)	**divisible** Que se puede dividir entre un número sin dejar residuo.	18 is divisible by 3.

ENGLISH	SPANISH	EXAMPLES
Division Property of Equality The property that states that if you divide both sides of an equation by the same nonzero number, the new equation will have the same solution. (p. 39)	**Propiedad de igualdad de la división** Propiedad que establece que puedes dividir ambos lados de una ecuación entre el mismo número distinto de cero, y la ecuación resultante tendrá la misma solución.	
divisor The number you are dividing by in a division problem.	**divisor** El número entre el que se divide en un problema de división.	In $8 \div 4 = 2$, 4 is the divisor.
dodecahedron A polyhedron with 12 faces.	**dodecaedro** Poliedro de 12 caras.	
domain The set of all possible input values of a function. (p. 134)	**dominio** Conjunto de todos los posibles valores de entrada de una función.	The domain of the function $y = x^2 + 1$ is all real numbers.
double-bar graph A bar graph that compares two related sets of data. (p. 485)	**gráfica de doble barra** Gráfica de barras que compara dos conjuntos de datos relacionados.	
double-line graph A line graph that shows how two related sets of data change over time. (p. 486)	**gráfica de doble línea** Gráfica lineal que muestra cómo cambian con el tiempo dos conjuntos de datos relacionados.	

E

edge The line segment along which two faces of a polyhedron intersect. (p. 408)	**arista** Segmento de recta formado por la intersección de dos caras de un poliedro.	Edge
elements (of a matrix) Individual entries in a matrix. (p. 839)	**elementos (de una matriz)** Entradas individuales de una matriz.	
endpoint A point at the end of a line segment or ray.	**extremo** Punto al final de un segmento de recta o rayo.	A ·————· B ·————→ D

ENGLISH	SPANISH	EXAMPLES
enlargement An increase in size of all dimensions in the same proportions. (p. 253)	**agrandamiento** Aumento de tamaño de todas las dimensiones en las mismas proporciones.	
equally likely Outcomes that have the same probability. (p. 540)	**igualmente probables** Resultados que tienen la misma probabilidad.	When tossing a coin, the outcomes "heads" and "tails" are equally likely.
equation A mathematical sentence that shows that two expressions are equivalent. (p. 34)	**ecuación** Enunciado matemático que indica que dos expresiones son equivalentes.	$x + 4 = 7$ $6 + 1 = 10 - 3$
equilateral triangle A triangle with three congruent sides. (p. 337)	**triángulo equilátero** Triángulo con tres lados congruentes.	
equivalent Having the same value. (p. 584)	**equivalentes** Que tienen el mismo valor. (pág. 28)	
equivalent expression Equivalent expressions have the same value for all values of the variables. (p. 584)	**expresión equivalente** Las expresiones equivalentes tienen el mismo valor para todos los valores de las variables.	$4x + 5x$ and $9x$ are equivalent expressions.
equivalent fractions Fractions that name the same amount or part.	**fracciones equivalentes** Fracciones que representan la misma cantidad o la misma parte de un todo.	$\frac{1}{2}$ and $\frac{2}{4}$ are equivalent fractions.
equivalent ratios Ratios that name the same comparison. (p. 216)	**razones equivalentes** Razones que representan la misma comparación.	$\frac{1}{2}$ and $\frac{2}{4}$ are equivalent ratios.
estimate (n) An answer that is close to the exact answer and is found by rounding or other methods. **(v)** To find such an answer. (p. 278)	**estimación (n)** Una solución aproximada a la respuesta exacta que se halla mediante el redondeo u otros métodos. **estimar (v)** Hallar una solución aproximada a la respuesta exacta.	500 is an estimate for the sum $98 + 287 + 104$.
evaluate To find the value of a numerical or algebraic expression. (p. 6)	**evaluar** Hallar el valor de una expresión numérica o algebraica.	Evaluate $2x + 7$ for $x = 3$ $2x + 7$ $2(3) + 7$ $6 + 7$ 13.
even number A whole number that is divisible by two.	**número par** Número cabal divisible entre 2.	
event An outcome or set of outcomes of an experiment or situation. (p. 522)	**suceso** Resultado o conjunto de resultados posibles de un experimento o situación.	When rolling a number cube, the event "an odd number" consists of the outcomes 1, 3, and 5.

ENGLISH	SPANISH	EXAMPLES
expanded form A number written as the sum of the values of its digits.	**forma desarrollada** Número escrito como suma de los valores de sus dígitos.	236,536 written in expanded form is 200,000 + 30,000 + 6,000 + 500 + 30 + 6.
experiment (probability) In probability, any activity based on chance (such as tossing a coin). (p. 522)	**experimento (probabilidad)** En probabilidad, cualquier actividad basada en la posibilidad, como lanzar una moneda.	Tossing a coin 10 times and noting the number of "heads".
experimental probability The ratio of the number of times an event occurs to the total number of trials, or times that the activity is performed. (p. 527)	**probabilidad experimental** Razón del número de veces que ocurre un suceso al número total de pruebas o a las veces que se realiza el experimento.	Kendra attempted 27 free throws and made 16 of them. Her experimental probability of making a free throw is $\frac{\text{number made}}{\text{number attempted}} = \frac{16}{27} \approx 0.59$.
exponent The number that indicates how many times the base is used as a factor. (p. 162)	**exponente** Número que indica cuántas veces se usa la base como factor.	$2^3 = 2 \times 2 \times 2 = 8$; 3 is the exponent.
exponential form A number is in exponential form when it is written with a base and an exponent. (p. 162)	**forma exponencial** Un número está en forma exponencial cuando se escribe con una base y un exponente.	4^2 is the exponential form for $4 \cdot 4$.
exponential function A nonlinear function in which the variable is in the exponent. (p. 704)	**función exponencial** Función no lineal en la que la variable está en el exponente.	$f(x) = 4^x$
expression A mathematical phrase that contains operations, numbers, and/or variables. (p. 6)	**expresión** Enunciado matemático que contiene operaciones, números y(o) variables.	$6x + 1$

F

ENGLISH	SPANISH	EXAMPLES
face A flat surface of a polyhedron. (p. 408)	**cara** Superficie plana de un poliedro.	
factor A number that is multiplied by another number to get a product. (p. 822)	**factor** Número que se multiplica por otro para hallar un producto.	7 is a factor of 21 since $7 \cdot 3 = 21$.
factorial The product of all whole numbers except zero that are less than or equal to a number. (p. 563)	**factorial** El producto de todos los números cabales menores o iguales a un número, excepto cero.	4 factorial $= 4! = 4 \cdot 3 \cdot 2 \cdot 1$

Fahrenheit A temperature scale in which 32°F is the freezing point of water and 212°F is the boiling point of water.

Fahrenheit Escala de temperatura en la que 32° F es el punto de congelación del agua y 212° F es el punto de ebullición.

---

fair When all outcomes of an experiment are equally likely, the experiment is said to be fair. (p. 540)

justo Un experimento es justo si todos los resultados posibles son igualmente probables.

When tossing a coin, heads and tails are equally likely, so it is a fair experiment.

Fibonacci sequence The infinite sequence of numbers (1, 1, 2, 3, 5, 8, 13,...); starting with the third term, each number is the sum of the two previous numbers; it is named after the thirteenth century mathematician Leonardo Fibonacci. (p. 695)

sucesión de Fibonacci La sucesión infinita de números (1, 1, 2, 3, 5, 8, 13...); a partir del tercer término, cada número es la suma de los dos anteriores. Esta sucesión lleva el nombre de Leonardo Fibonacci, un matemático del siglo XIII.

1, 1, 2, 3, 5, 8, 13, . . .

---

first differences A sequence formed by subtracting each term of a sequence from the next term. (p. 693)

primeras diferencias Sucesión que se forma al restar cada término de una sucesión del término siguiente.

For the sequence 4, 7, 10, 13, 16, . . . , the first differences are all 3.

---

first quartile The median of the lower half of a set of data; also called *lower quartile*. (p. 476)

primer cuartil La mediana de la mitad inferior de un conjunto de datos. También se llama *cuartil inferior*.

FOIL An acronym for the terms used when multiplying two binomials: the First, Inner, Outer, and Last terms. (p. 762)

FOIL Acrónimo en inglés de los términos que se usan al multiplicar dos binomios: Primeros (First), Internos (Inner), Externos (Outer), Últimos (Last).

$$(x + 2)(x - 3) = x^2 - 3x + 2x$$
$$= x^2 - 3x + 2x$$

---

formula A rule showing relationships among quantities.

fórmula Regla que muestra relaciones entre cantidades.

$A = \ell w$ is the formula for the area of a rectangle.

---

fractal A structure with repeating patterns containing shapes that are like the whole but are of different sizes throughout. (p. 834)

fractal Estructura con patrones repetidos que contienen figuras similares al patrón general pero de diferente tamaño.

---

fraction A number in the form $\frac{a}{b}$, where $b \neq 0$.

fracción Número escrito en la forma $\frac{a}{b}$, donde $b \neq 0$.

$\frac{2}{3}$

---

frequency table A table that lists items together according to the number of times, or frequency, that the items occur. (p. 485)

tabla de frecuencia Tabla que organiza los datos de acuerdo al número de veces o frecuencia con que aparece cada valor.

Data set: 1, 1, 2, 2, 3, 4, 5, 5, 5, 6, 6
Frequency table:

Data	Frequency
1	2
2	2
3	1
4	1
5	3
6	2

Glossary/Glosario

function An input-output relationship that has exactly one output for each input. (p. 134)

función Regla que relaciona dos cantidades de forma que a cada valor de entrada corresponde exactamente un valor de salida.

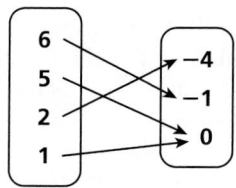

---

function notation The notation used to describe a function. (p. 700)

notación de funciones Notación que se usa para describir una función.

Equation: $y = 2x$
Function notation: $f(x) = 2x$

---

function table A table of ordered pairs that represent solutions of a function.

tabla de función Tabla de pares ordenados que representan soluciones de una función.

x	3	4	5	6
y	7	9	11	13

Fundamental Counting Principle If one event has m possible outcomes and a second event has n possible outcomes after the first event has occurred, then there are $m \cdot n$ total possible outcomes for the two events. (p. 558)

Principio fundamental de conteo Si un suceso tiene m resultados posibles y un segundo suceso tiene n resultados posibles, después de ocurrido el primer suceso, entonces hay $m \cdot n$ posibles resultados en total para los dos sucesos.

There are 4 colors of shirts and 3 colors of pants. There are $4 \cdot 3 = 12$ possible outfits.

---

geometric sequence An ordered list of numbers that has a common ratio between consecutive terms. (p. 687)

sucesión geométrica Lista ordenada de números que tiene una razón común entre términos consecutivos.

The sequence 2, 4, 8, 16. . . is a geometric sequence.

---

graph A set of points and the line segments or arcs that connect the points. Also called a network. (p. 122)

gráfica Conjunto de puntos y los segmentos de recta o arcos que los conectan. También se le llama red.

---

graph of an equation A graph of the set of ordered pairs that are solutions of the equation. (p. 123)

gráfica de una ecuación Gráfica del conjunto de pares ordenados que son soluciones de la ecuación.

$y = x - 1$

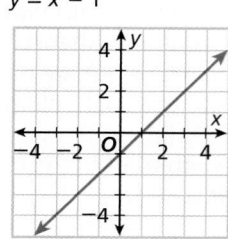

---

great circle A circle on a sphere such that the plane containing the circle passes through the center of the sphere. (p. 436)

círculo máximo Círculo de una esfera tal que el plano que contiene el círculo pasa por el centro de la esfera.

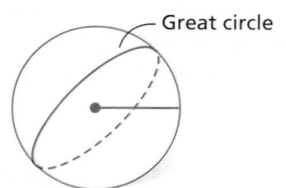
Great circle

---

greatest common factor (GCF) The largest common factor of two or more given numbers. (p. 824)

máximo común divisor (MCD) El mayor de los factores comunes compartidos por dos o más números.

The GCF of 27 and 45 is 9.

height In a pyramid or cone, the perpendicular distance from the base to the opposite vertex. (p. 420)

altura En una pirámide o cono, la distancia perpendicular que va de la base y al vértice opuesto.

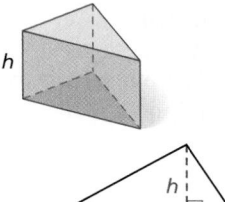

In a triangle or quadrilateral, the perpendicular distance from the base to the opposite vertex or side. (p. 395)

En un triángulo o cuadrilátero, la distancia perpendicular que va de la base de la figura al vértice o lado opuesto.

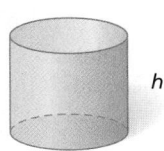

In a prism or cylinder, the perpendicular distance between the bases. (p. 413)

En un prisma o cilindro, la distancia perpendicular entre las bases.

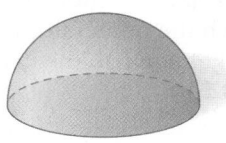

hemisphere A half of a sphere. (p. 436)

hemisferio La mitad de una esfera.

heptagon A seven-sided polygon. (p. 341)

heptágono Polígono de siete lados.

hexagon A six-sided polygon. (p. 341)

hexágono Polígono de seis lados.

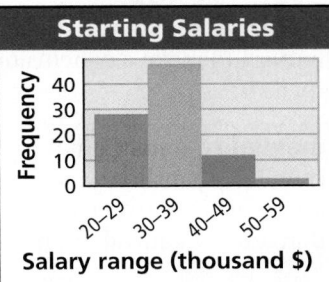

histogram A bar graph that shows the frequency of data within equal intervals. (p. 485)

histograma Gráfica de barras que muestra la frecuencia de los datos en intervalos iguales.

Starting Salaries

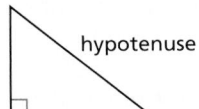

hypotenuse In a right triangle, the side opposite the right angle. (p. 196)

hipotenusa En un triángulo rectángulo, el lado opuesto al ángulo recto.

hypotenuse

Identity Property of One The property that states that the product of 1 and any number is that number. (p. 829)

Propiedad de identidad del uno Propiedad que establece que el producto de 1 y cualquier número es ese número.

$4 \cdot 1 = 4$
$-3 \cdot 1 = -3$

Glossary/Glosario

ENGLISH	SPANISH	EXAMPLES
Identity Property of Zero The property that states the sum of zero and any number is that number. (p. 829)	**Propiedad de identidad del cero** Propiedad que establece que la suma de cero y cualquier número es ese número.	$4 + 0 = 4$ $-3 + 0 = -3$
image A figure resulting from a transformation. (p. 358)	**imagen** Figura que resulta de una transformación.	
impossible (probability) Can never happen; an event that is impossible has a probability of 0. (p. 522)	**imposible (en probabilidad)** Que nunca puede ocurrir. Suceso cuya probabilidad de ocurrir es 0.	When rolling a standard number cube, rolling a 7 is an impossible event.
improper fraction A fraction in which the numerator is greater than or equal to the denominator. (p. 825)	**fracción impropia** Fracción cuyo numerador es mayor o igual que el denominador.	$\frac{17}{5}, \frac{3}{3}$
independent events Events for which the outcome of one event does not affect the probability of the other. (p. 545)	**sucesos independientes** Sucesos en los que el resultado del primero no afecta la probabilidad del segundo.	A bag contains 3 red marbles and 2 blue marbles. Drawing a red marble, replacing it, and then drawing a blue marble is an example of independent events.
indirect measurement The technique of using similar figures and proportions to find a measure. (p. 248)	**medición indirecta** La técnica de usar proporciones y figuras semejantes para hallar una medida.	
inductive reasoning Using a pattern to make a conclusion. (p. 833)	**razonamiento inductivo** Uso de un patrón para sacar una conclusión.	
inequality A mathematical sentence that shows the relationship between quantities that are not equivalent. (p. 44)	**desigualdad** Enunciado matemático que muestra una relación entre cantidades que no son equivalentes.	$5 < 8$ $5x + 2 \geq 12$
input The value substituted into an expression or function. (p. 134)	**valor de entrada** Valor que se usa para sustituir una variable en una expresión o función.	For the function $y = 6x$, the input 4 produces an output of 24.
inscribed angle An angle formed by two chords with its vertex on a circle. (p. 838)	**ángulo inscrito** Ángulo formado por dos cuerdas y cuyo vértice está en un círculo.	
integers The set of whole numbers and their opposites. (p. 14)	**enteros** Conjunto de todos los números cabales y sus opuestos.	... $-3, -2, (1, 0, 1, 2, 3, ...$

ENGLISH	SPANISH	EXAMPLES
interest The amount of money charged for borrowing or using money. (p. 302)	**interés** Cantidad de dinero que se cobra por el préstamo o uso del dinero, o la cantidad que se gana al ahorrar dinero.	
interior angles Angles on the inner sides of two lines cut by a transversal.	**ángulos internos** Ángulos en los lados internos de dos líneas intersecadas por una transversal.	$\angle 1$ is an interior angle.
intersecting lines Lines that cross at exactly one point.	**líneas secantes** Líneas que se cruzan en un solo punto.	
interval The space between marked values on a number line or the scale of a graph.	**intervalo** El espacio entre los valores marcados en una recta numérica o en la escala de una gráfica.	
inverse operations Operations that undo each other: addition and subtraction, or multiplication and division. (p. 34)	**operaciones inversas** Operaciones que se anulan mutuamente: suma y resta, o multiplicación y división.	Addition and subtraction are inverse operations: $5 + 3 + 8; 8 - 3 = 5$ Multiplication and division are inverse operations: $2 \cdot 3 = 6; 6 \div 3 = 2$
inverse variation A relationship in which one variable quantity increases as another variable quantity decreases; the product of the variables is a constant. (p. 714)	**variación inversa** Relación en la que una cantidad variable aumenta a medida que otra cantidad variable disminuye; el producto de las variables es una constante.	$xy = 7, y = \frac{7}{x}$
irrational number A number that cannot be expressed as a ratio of two integers or as a repeating or terminating decimal. (p. 191)	**número irracional** Número que no se puede expresar como una razón de dos enteros ni como decimal periódico o cerrado.	$\sqrt{2}, \pi$
isolate the variable To get a variable alone on one side of an equation or inequality in order to solve the equation or inequality. (p. 34)	**despejar la variable** Dejar sola la variable en un lado de una ecuación o desigualdad para resolverla.	$x + 7 = 22$ $\underline{-7 \quad -7}$ $x \quad = 15$ $\frac{12}{3} = \frac{3x}{3}$ $4 = x$
isometric drawing A representation of a three-dimensional figure that is drawn on a grid of equilateral triangles. (p. 302)	**dibujo isométrico** Representación de una figura tridimensional que se dibuja sobre una cuadrícula de triángulos equiláteros.	
isosceles triangle A triangle with at least two congruent sides. (p. 337)	**triángulo isósceles** Triángulo que tiene al menos dos lados congruentes.	

ENGLISH	SPANISH	EXAMPLES

L

lateral face In a prism or a pyramid, a face that is not a base. (p. 427)

cara lateral En un prisma o pirámide, una cara que no es la base.

Bases
Lateral face
Right prism

lateral surface In a cylinder, the curved surface connecting the circular bases; in a cone, the curved surface that is not a base. (p. 427)

superficie lateral En un cilindro, superficie curva que une las bases circulares y forma los lados del cilindro; en un cono, la superficie curva que no es la base.

Lateral surface
Right cylinder

least common denominator (LCD) The least common multiple of two or more denominators. (p. 68)

mínimo común denominador (mcd) El múltiplo común más pequeño de dos o más denominadores.

The LCD of $\frac{3}{4}$ and $\frac{5}{6}$ is 12.

least common multiple (LCM) The smallest whole number, other than zero, that is a multiple of two or more given numbers. (p. 824)

mínimo común múltiplo (mcm) El menor de los múltiplos de dos o más números que no sea cero.

The LCM of 6 and 10 is 30.

legs In a right triangle, the sides that include the right angle; in an isosceles triangle, the pair of congruent sides. (p. 196)

catetos En un triángulo rectángulo, los lados adyacentes al ángulo recto. En un triángulo isósceles, el par de lados congruentes.

leg
leg

like fractions Fractions that have the same denominator.

fracciones semejantes Fracciones que tienen el mismo denominador.

$\frac{5}{12}$ and $\frac{7}{12}$ are like fractions.

like terms Two or more terms that have the same variable raised to the same power. (p. 584)

términos semejantes Términos que contienen la misma variable elevada a la misma potencia.

In the expression $3a + 5b + 12a$, $3a$ and $12a$ are like terms.

line A straight path that extends without end in opposite directions. (p. 324)

línea Trayectoria recta que se extiende de manera indefinida en direcciones opuestas.

line graph A graph that uses line segments to show how data changes. (p. 486)

gráfica lineal Gráfica que muestra cómo cambian los datos mediante segmentos de recta.

Marlon's Video Game Scores

Score
1200
800
400
0
1 2 3 4 5 6
Game number

line of best fit A straight line that comes closest to the points on a scatter plot. (p. 494)

línea de mejor ajuste La línea recta que más se aproxima a los puntos de un diagrama de dispersión.

160
120
80
40
0
40 80 120 160

ENGLISH	SPANISH	EXAMPLES
line of reflection A line that a figure is flipped across to create a mirror image of the original figure. (p. 358)	**línea de reflexión** Línea sobre la cual se voltea una figura para crear una imagen idéntica de la figura original.	
line of symmetry The imaginary "mirror" in line symmetry. (p. 364)	**eje de simetría** El "espejo" imaginario de una simetría axial.	
line plot A number line with marks or dots that show frequency. (p. 467)	**diagrama de acumulación** Una recta numérica con marcas o puntos que indican la frecuencia.	
line segment A part of a line between two endpoints. (p. 324)	**segmento de recta** Parte de una línea entre dos extremos.	
line symmetry A figure has line symmetry if one half is a mirror-image of the other half. (p. 364)	**eje de simetría** El "espejo" imaginario en la simetría axial.	
linear equation An equation whose solutions form a straight line on a coordinate plane. (p. 628)	**ecuación lineal** Ecuación cuyas soluciones forman una línea recta en un plano cartesiano.	$y = 2x + 1$
linear function A function whose graph is a straight line. (p. 700)	**función lineal** Función cuya gráfica es una línea recta.	$y = x - 1$
linear inequality A mathematical sentence using <, >, ≤, or ≥ whose graph is a region with a straight-line boundary. (p. 655)	**desigualdad lineal** Enunciado matemático que usa los símbolos <, >, ≤, o ≥ y cuya gráfica es una región con una línea de límite recta.	

major arc An arc that is more than half of a circle. (p. 838)	**arco mayor** Arco que es más de la mitad de un círculo.	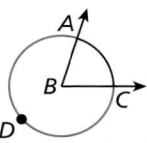

$\overgroup{ADC}$ is a major arc of the circle.

ENGLISH	SPANISH	EXAMPLES
matrix A rectangular arrangement of data enclosed in brackets. (p. 839)	**matriz** Arreglo rectangular de datos encerrado entre corchetes.	$\begin{bmatrix} 1 & 0 & 3 \\ -2 & 2 & -5 \\ 7 & -6 & 3 \end{bmatrix}$
mean The sum of a set of data divided by the number of items in the data set; also called *average*. (p. 472)	**promedio** La suma de un conjunto de datos dividida entre el número de elementos en el conjunto. También se le llama *media*.	Data set: 4, 6, 7, 8, 10 Mean: $\frac{4+6+7+8+10}{5} = \frac{35}{5} = 7$
measure of central tendency A measure used to describe the middle of a data set; the mean, median, and mode are measures of central tendency. (p. 472)	**medida de tendencia dominante** Medida empleada para describir la parte media de un conjunto de datos; la media, la mediana y la moda son medidas de tendencia dominante.	
median The middle number, or the mean (average) of the two middle numbers, in an ordered set of data. (p. 472)	**mediana** El número intermedio, o la media (el promedio), de los dos números intermedios en un conjunto ordenado de datos.	Data set: 4, 6, 7, 8, 10 Median: 7
metric system of measurement A decimal system of weights and measures that is used universally in science and commonly throughout the world.	**sistema métrico de medición** Sistema decimal de pesos y medidas empleado universalmente en las ciencias y de uso común en todo el mundo.	centimeters, meters, kilometers, gram, kilograms, milliliters, liters
midpoint The point that divides a line segment into two congruent line segments.	**punto medio** El punto que divide un segmento de recta en dos segmentos de recta congruentes.	 *B* is the midpoint of $\overline{AC}$.
minor arc An arc that is less than half of a circle. (p. 838)	**arco menor** Arco que es menor que la mitad de un círculo.	 $\overset{\frown}{AC}$ is the minor arc of the circle.
mixed number A number made up of a whole number that is not zero and a fraction. (p. 825)	**número mixto** Número que contiene un número cabal mayor que cero y una fracción. (pág. 765)	$4\frac{1}{8}$
mode The number or numbers that occur most frequently in a set of data; when all numbers occur with the same frequency, we say there is no mode. (p. 472)	**moda** Valor o valores más frecuentes en un conjunto de datos; si todos los números aparecen con la misma frecuencia, no hay moda.	Data set: 3, 5, 8, 8, 10 Mode: 8
monomial A number or a product of numbers and variables with exponents that are whole numbers. (p. 734)	**monomio** Un número o un producto de números y variables con exponentes que son números cabales.	$3x^2y^4$

ENGLISH	SPANISH	EXAMPLES
Multiplication Property of Equality The property that states that if you multiply both sides of an equation by the same number, the new equation will have the same solution. (p. 40)	**Propiedad de igualdad de la multiplicación** Propiedad que establece que puedes multiplicar ambos lados de una ecuación por el mismo número y la ecuación resultante tendrá la misma solución.	$3 \cdot 4 = 12$ $3 \cdot 4 \cdot 2 = 12 \cdot 2$ $24 = 24$
Multiplication Property of Zero The property that states that for all real numbers a, $a \cdot 0 = 0$ and $0 \cdot a = 0$. (p. 829)	**Propiedad de multiplicación del cero** Propiedad que establece que para todos los números reales a, $a \cdot 0 = 0$ y $0 \cdot a = 0$.	
multiplicative inverse A number times its multiplicative inverse is equal to 1; also called *reciprocal*. (p. 80)	**inverso multiplicativo** Un número multiplicado por su inverso multiplicativo es igual a 1. También se le llama *recíproco*.	The multiplicative inverse of $\frac{4}{5}$ is $\frac{5}{4}$.
multiple The product of any number and a non-zero whole number is a multiple of that number. (p. 822)	**múltiplo** El producto de cualquier número y un número cabal es un múltiplo de ese número.	
mutually exclusive Two events are mutually exclusive if they cannot occur in the same trial of an experiment. (p. 542)	**mutuamente excluyentes** Dos sucesos son mutuamente excluyentes cuando no pueden ocurrir en la misma prueba de un experimento.	When rolling a number cube, rolling a 3 and rolling an even number are mutually exclusive events.

N

ENGLISH	SPANISH	EXAMPLES
negative correlation Two data sets have a negative correlation if one set of data values increases while the other decreases. (p. 495)	**correlación negativa** Caso en que los valores de un conjunto de datos aumentan mientras que los valores de otro conjunto de datos disminuyen.	
negative integer An integer less than zero. (p. 15)	**entero negativo** Entero menor que cero.	-2 is a negative integer.
net An arrangement of two-dimensional figures that can be folded to form a polyhedron. (p. 406)	**plantilla** Un arreglo de figuras bidimensionales que se puede plegar o doblar para formar un poliedro.	
no correlation Two data sets have no correlation when there is no relationship between their data values. (p. 495)	**sin correlación** Caso en que los valores de los dos conjuntos no muestran ninguna relación.	

ENGLISH	SPANISH	EXAMPLES
nonlinear function A function whose graph is not a straight line.	**función no lineal** Función cuya gráfica no es una línea recta.	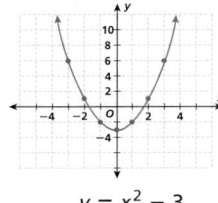 $y = x^2 - 3$
nonterminating decimal A decimal that never ends. (p. 191)	**decimal no cerrado** Decimal que nunca termina.	
numerator The top number of a fraction that tells how many parts of a whole are being considered. (p. 64)	**numerador** El número de arriba de una fracción; indica cuántas partes de un todo se están considerando.	$\frac{4}{5}$ ◄— numerator
numerical expression An expression that contains only numbers and operations.	**expresión numérica** Expresión matemática que incluye sólo números y operaciones matemáticas.	$(2 \cdot 3) + 1$

 0

ENGLISH	SPANISH	EXAMPLES
obtuse angle An angle whose measure is greater than 90° but less than 180°. (p. 325)	**ángulo obtuso** Ángulo cuya medida es mayor de 90° pero menor de 180°.	
obtuse triangle A triangle containing one obtuse angle. (p. 336)	**triángulo obtusángulo** Triángulo que tiene un ángulo obtuso.	
octagon An eight-sided polygon. (p. 239)	**octágono** Polígono de ocho lados.	
odd number A whole number that is not divisible by two.	**número impar** Número cabal que no es divisible entre 2.	
odds A comparison of favorable outcomes and unfavorable outcomes. (p. 554)	**posibilidades** Comparación de resultados favorables y no favorables.	
odds against The ratio of the number of unfavorable outcomes to the number of favorable outcomes. (p. 554)	**posibilidades en contra** Razón del número de resultados posibles no favorables con respecto al número de resultados posibles favorables.	The odds against rolling a 3 on a number cube are 5:1.
odds in favor The ratio of the number of favorable outcomes to the number of unfavorable outcomes. (p. 554)	**posibilidades a favor** Razón del número de resultados posibles favorables con respecto al número de resultados posibles desfavorables.	The odds in favor of rolling a 3 on a number cube are 1:5.

ENGLISH	SPANISH	EXAMPLES
opposites Two numbers that are an equal distance from zero on a number line; also called *additive inverse*. (p. 14)	**opuestos** Dos números que están a la misma distancia de cero en una recta numérica. También se llaman *inversos aditivos*.	5 and −5 are opposites. 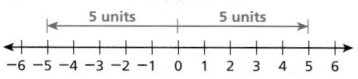
order of operations A rule for evaluating expressions: First perform the operations in parentheses, then compute powers and roots, then perform all multiplication and division from left to right, and then perform all addition and subtraction from left to right. (p. 828)	**orden de las operaciones** Regla para evaluar expresiones: primero se hacen las operaciones entre paréntesis, luego se hallan las potencias y raíces, después todas las multiplicaciones y divisiones de izquierda a derecha ,y por último todas las sumas y restas de izquierda a derecha.	$4^2 + 8 \div 2$ Evaluate the power. $16 + 8 \div 2$ Divide. $16 + 4$ Add. 20
ordered pair A pair of numbers that can be used to locate a point on a coordinate plane. (p. 118)	**par ordenado** Par de números que sirven para localizar un punto en un plano cartesiano.	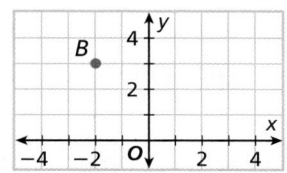 The coordinates of *B* are (−2, 3).
origin The point where the *x*-axis and *y*-axis intersect on the coordinate plane; (0, 0). (p. 122)	**origen** Punto de intersección entre el eje de las *x* y el eje de las *y* se cruzan en el plano cartesiano; (0, 0).	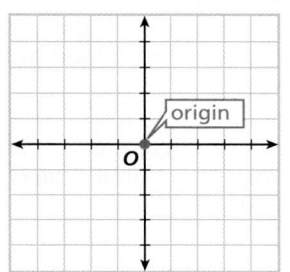
orthogonal views A drawing that shows the top, bottom, front, back, and side views of a three-dimensional object. (p. 408)	**vista ortogonal** Un dibujo que muestra la vista superior, inferior, frontal, posterior y lateral de un objeto de tres dimensiones.	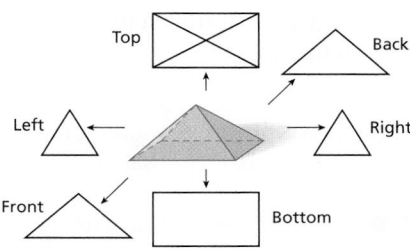
outcome (probability) A possible result of a probability experiment. (p. 522)	**resultado posible (en probabilidad)** Un posible resultado de un experimento de probabilidad.	When rolling a number cube, the possible outcomes are 1, 2, 3, 4, 5, and 6.
outlier A value much greater or much less than the others in a data set. (p. 472)	**valor extremo** Valor mucho mayor o mucho menor que los demás de un conjunto de datos.	
output The value that results from the substitution of a given input into an expression or function. (p. 134)	**valor de salida** Valor que resulta después de sustituir una variable con un valor de entrada en una función o expresión.	For the function $y = 6x$, the input 4 produces an output of 24.

P

parabola The graph of a quadratic function. (p. 708)

parábola Gráfica de una función cuadrática.

parallel lines Lines in a plane that do not intersect. (p. 330)

líneas paralelas Líneas que se encuentran en el mismo plano pero que nunca se intersecan.

parallelogram A quadrilateral with two pairs of parallel sides. (p. 342)

paralelogramo Cuadrilátero con dos pares de lados paralelos.

pentagon A five-sided polygon. (p. 341)

pentágono Polígono de cinco lados.

percent A ratio comparing a number to 100. (p. 274)

porcentaje Razón que compara un número con el número 100.

$45\% = \frac{45}{100}$

percent change The amount stated as a percent that a number increases or decreases. (p. 294)

porcentaje de cambio Cantidad expresada como un porcentaje en que un número aumenta o disminuye.

percent decrease A percent change describing a decrease in a quantity. (p. 294)

porcentaje de disminución Porcentaje en que una cifra disminuye.

An item that costs $8 is marked down to $6. The amount of the decrease is $2 and the percent of decrease is $\frac{2}{8} = 0.25 = 25\%$.

percent increase A percent change describing an increase in a quantity. (p. 294)

porcentaje de incremento Porcentaje en que una cifra aumenta.

The price of an item increases from $8 to $12. The amount of the increase is $4 and the percent of increase is $\frac{4}{8} = 0.5 = 50\%$

perfect square A square of a whole number. (p. 182)

cuadrado perfecto El cuadrado de un número cabal.

$5^2 = 25$, so 25 is a perfect square.

perimeter The distance around a polygon. (p. 388)

perímetro Distancia alrededor de un polígono.

18 ft

6ft

perimeter =
18 + 6 + 18 + 6 = 48 ft

permutation An arrangement of items or events in which order is important. (p. 563)

permutación Arreglo de objetos o sucesos en el que el orden es importante.

For objects *A*, *B*, and *C*, there are 6 different permutations: *ABC*, *ACB*, *BAC*, *BCA*, *CAB*, *CBA*.

perpendicular bisector A line that intersects a segment at its midpoint and is perpendicular to the segment. (p. 227)

mediatriz Línea que cruza un segmento en su punto medio y es perpendicular al segmento.

ℓ

A   *B*

Glossary/Glosario

ENGLISH	SPANISH	EXAMPLES
perpendicular lines Lines that intersect to form right angles. (p. 330)	**líneas perpendiculares** Líneas que al intersecarse forman ángulos rectos.	
perspective A technique used to make three-dimensional objects appear to have depth and distance on a flat surface. (p. 408)	**perspectiva** Técnica que sirve para hacer que los objetos tridimensionales parezcan tener profundidad y distancia en una superficie plana.	
pi (π) The ratio of the circumference of a circle to the length of its diameter; $\pi \approx 3.14$ or $\frac{22}{7}$. (p. 400)	**pi (π)** Razón de la circunferencia de un círculo a la longitud de su diámetro; $\pi \approx 3.14$ ó $\frac{22}{7}$.	
plane A flat surface that extends forever. (p. 324)	**plano** Superficie plana que se extiende de manera indefinida en todas direcciones.	
point An exact location in space. (p. 324)	**punto** Ubicación exacta en el espacio.	$P \bullet$
point-slope form The equation of a line in the form of $y - y_1 = m(x - x_1)$, where m is the slope and (x_1, y_1) is a specific point on the line. (p. 644)	**forma de punto y pendiente** Ecuación lineal en la forma $y - y_1 = m(x - x_1)$, donde m es la pendiente y (x^1, y^1) es un punto específico de la línea.	$y - 3 = 2(x - 3)$
polygon A closed plane figure formed by three or more line segments that intersect only at their endpoints (vertices). (p. 341)	**polígono** Figura cerrada plana, formada por tres o más segmentos de recta que se intersecan sólo en sus extremos (vértices).	
polyhedron A three-dimensional figure in which all the surfaces or faces are polygons.	**poliedro** Figura tridimensional cuyas superficies o caras tiene forma de polígonos.	
polynomial One monomial or the sum or difference of monomials. (p. 734)	**polinomio** Un monomio o la suma o resta de monomios.	$2x^2 + 3xy - 7y^2$
population The entire group of objects or individuals considered for a survey. (p. 462)	**población** Grupo completo de objetos o individuos que se desea estudiar.	In a survey about study habits of middle school students, the population is all middle school students.
positive correlation Two data sets have a positive correlation when their data values increase or decrease together.	**correlación positiva** Caso en el que los valores de ambos conjuntos de datos aumentan o disminuyen al mismo tiempo.	

positive integer An integer greater than zero. (p. 15)

entero positivo Entero mayor que cero.

2 is a positive integer.

---

power A number produced by raising a base to an exponent. (p. 162)

potencia Número que resulta al elevar una base a un exponente.

$2^3 = 8$, so 2 to the 3rd power is 8.

---

prime factorization A number written as the product of its prime factors. (p. 823)

factorización prima Número que se escribe como el producto de sus factores primos.

$10 = 2 \cdot 5$,
$24 = 2^3 \cdot 3$

---

prime number A whole number greater than 1 that has exactly two factors, itself and 1. (p. 823)

número primo Un número cabal mayor que 1 que tiene exactamente dos factores el l y sí mismo.

5 is prime because its only factors are 5 and 1.

---

principal The initial amount of money borrowed or saved. (p. 302)

capital Cantidad inicial de dinero depositada o recibida en préstamo.

---

principal square root The nonnegative square root of a number. (p. 182)

raíz cuadrada principal Raíz cuadrada no negativa de un número.

$\sqrt{25} = 5$; the principal square root of 25 is 5.

---

prism A polyhedron that has two congruent, polygon-shaped bases and other faces that are all parallelograms. (p. 413)

prisma Poliedro con dos bases congruentes con forma de polígono y caras con forma de paralelogramos.

---

probability A number from 0 to 1 (or 0% to 100%) that describes how likely an event is to occur. (p. 522)

probabilidad Un número entre 0 y 1 (ó 0% y 100%) que describe la posibilidad de que un suceso ocurra.

A bag contains 3 red marbles and 4 blue marbles. The probability of randomly choosing a red marble is $\frac{3}{7}$.

---

product The result when two or more numbers are multiplied.

producto Resultado de multiplicar dos o más números.

The product of 4 and 8 is 32.

---

proper fraction A fraction in which the numerator is less than the denominator.

fracción propia Fracción en la que el numerador es menor que el denominador.

$\frac{3}{4}, \frac{1}{12}, \frac{7}{8}$

---

proportion An equation that states that two ratios are equivalent. (p. 216)

proporción Ecuación que establece que dos razones son equivalentes.

$\frac{2}{3} = \frac{4}{6}$

---

protractor A tool for measuring angles. (pp. 330, 832)

transportador Instrumento para medir ángulos.

---

pyramid A polyhedron with a polygon base and triangular sides that all meet at a common vertex. (p. 420)

pirámide Poliedro cuya base es un polígono y tiene caras triangulares que terminan en un vértice común.

ENGLISH	SPANISH	EXAMPLES

Pythagorean Theorem In a right triangle, the square of the length of the hypotenuse is equal to the sum of the squares of the lengths of the legs. (p. 195)

Teorema de Pitágoras En un triángulo rectángulo, la suma de los cuadrados de los catetos es igual al cuadrado de la hipotenusa.

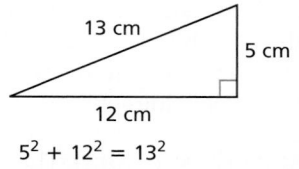

$5^2 + 12^2 = 13^2$
$25 + 144 = 169$

quadrant The x- and y-axes divide the coordinate plane into four regions. Each region is called a quadrant. (p. 122)

cuadrante El eje de las x y el eje de las y dividen el plano cartesiano en cuatro regiones. Cada región recibe el nombre de cuadrante.

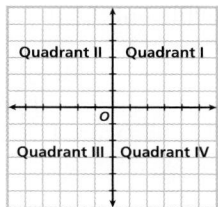

quadratic function A function of the form $y = ax^2 + bx + c$, where $a \neq 0$. (p. 708)

función cuadrática Función de la forma $y = ax^2 + bx + c$, donde $a \neq 0$.

$y = x^2 - 6x + 8$

quadrilateral A four-sided polygon. (p. 341)

cuadrilátero Polígono de cuatro lados.

quarterly Four times a year. (p. 307)

trimestral Cuatro veces al año.

quartile Three values, one of which is the median, that divide a data set into fourths. (p. 476)

cuartil Cada uno de tres valores, uno de los cuales es la mediana, que dividen en cuartos un conjunto de datos.

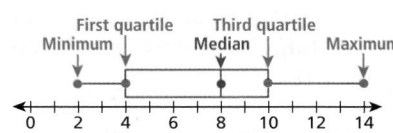

quotient The result when one number is divided by another.

cociente Resultado de dividir un número entre otro.

In $8 \div 4 = 2$, 2 is the quotient.

radical symbol The symbol $\sqrt{\ }$ used to represent the nonnegative square root of a number. (p. 146)

símbolo de radical El símbolo $\sqrt{\ }$ que se usa para representar la raíz cuadrada no negativa de un número.

radius A line segment with one endpoint at the center of the circle and the other endpoint on the circle, or the length of that segment. (p. 400)

radio Segmento de recta con un extremo en el centro de un círculo y el otro en la circunferencia. También se llama radio a la longitud de ese segmento.

random numbers In a set of random numbers, each number has an equal chance of appearing. (p. 532)

muestra aleatoria Muestra que da a cada miembro de una población la misma posibilidad de ser elegido.

ENGLISH	SPANISH	EXAMPLES
random sample A sample in which each individual or object in the entire population has an equal chance of being selected. (p. 462)	**números aleatorios** En un conjunto de números aleatorios, todos los números tienen la misma probabilidad de ser seleccionados.	
range (in statistics) The difference between the greatest and least values in a data set. (p. 472)	**rango (en estadística)** Diferencia entre los valores máximo y mínimo de un conjunto de datos.	Data set: 3, 5, 7, 7, 12 Range: 12 − 3 = 9
range (of a function) The set of all possible output values of a function. (p. 134)	**rango (en una función)** El conjunto de todos los valores posibles de una función.	The range of $y = \|x\|$ is $y \geq 0$.
rate A ratio that compares two quantities measured in different units. (p. 220)	**relación** Comparación de dos cantidades expresadas con unidades diferentes.	The speed limit is 55 miles per hour or 55 mi/h.
rate of interest The percent charged or earned on an amount of money; see *simple interest.* (p. 302)	**tasa de interés** Porcentaje que se cobra por una cantidad de dinero prestada o que se gana por una cantidad de dinero ahorrada; ver *interés simple.*	
ratio A comparison of two quantities by division. (p. 216)	**razón** Comparación de dos cantidades mediante una división.	12 to 25, 12:25, $\frac{12}{25}$
rational number Any number that can be expressed as a ratio of two integers. (p. 64)	**número racional** Número que se puede escribir como una razón de dos enteros.	6 can be expressed as $\frac{6}{1}$. 0.5 can be expressed $\frac{1}{2}$.
ray A part of a line that starts at one endpoint and extends forever. (p. 324)	**rayo** Parte de una línea que inicia en un extremo y se extiende de manera indefinida.	
real number A rational or irrational number. (p. 191)	**número real** Número racional o irracional.	
reciprocal One of two numbers whose product is 1; also called *multiplicative inverse.* (p. 80)	**recíproco** Uno de dos números cuyo producto es igual a 1. También se llama *inverso multiplicativo.*	The reciprocal of $\frac{2}{3}$ is $\frac{3}{2}$.
rectangle A parallelogram with four right angles. (p. 342)	**rectángulo** Paralelogramo con cuatro ángulos rectos.	
rectangular prism A polyhedron whose bases are rectangles and whose other faces are parallelograms. (p. 413)	**prisma rectangular** Poliedro cuyas bases son rectángulos y sus caras tienen forma de paralelogramos.	
reduction A decrease in the size of all dimensions. (p. 253)	**reducción** Disminución de tamaño en todas las dimensiones de una figura.	

ENGLISH	SPANISH	EXAMPLES
reflection A transformation of a figure that flips the figure across a line. (p. 358)	**reflexión** Transformación que ocurre cuando se voltea una figura sobre la línea de reflexión.	
regular polygon A polygon with congruent sides and angles. (p. 342)	**polígono regular** Polígono con lados y ángulos congruentes.	
regular pyramid A pyramid whose base is a regular polygon and whose lateral faces are all congruent. (p. 432)	**pirámide regular** Pirámide que tiene un polígono regular como base y caras laterales congruentes.	
relatively prime Two numbers are relatively prime if their greatest common factor (GCF) is 1. (p. 64)	**primo relativo** Dos números son primos relativos si su máximo común divisor (MCD) es 1.	8 and 15 are relatively prime.
repeating decimal A decimal in which one or more digits repeat infinitely. (pp. 191, 827)	**decimal periódico** Decimal en el que uno o más dígitos se repiten de manera indefinida.	$0.757575\ldots = 0.\overline{75}$
rhombus A parallelogram with all sides congruent. (p. 342)	**rombo** Paralelogramo en el que todos los lados son congruentes.	
right angle An angle that measures 90°. (p. 325)	**ángulo recto** Ángulo que mide exactamente 90°.	
right cone A cone in which a perpendicular line drawn from the base to the tip (vertex) passes through the center of the base. (p. 432)	**cono regular** Cono en el que una línea perpendicular trazada de la base a la punta (vértice) pasa por el centro de la base.	
right triangle A triangle containing a right angle. (p. 336)	**triángulo rectángulo** Triángulo que tiene un ángulo recto.	
rise The vertical change when the slope of a line is expressed as the ratio $\frac{\text{rise}}{\text{run}}$, or "rise over run." (p. 347)	**distancia vertical** El cambio vertical cuando la pendiente de una línea se expresa como la razón $\frac{\text{razón distancia vertical}}{\text{distancia horizontal}}$, o "distancia vertical sobre distancia horizontal".	For the points $(3, -1)$ and $(6, 5)$ the rise is $5 - (-1) = 6$.

ENGLISH	SPANISH	EXAMPLES

rotation A transformation in which a figure is turned around a point. (p. 358)

rotación Transformación que ocurre cuando una figura gira alrededor de un punto.

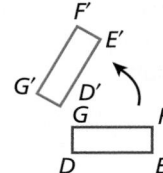

rotational symmetry A figure has rotational symmetry if it can be rotated less than 360° around a central point and coincide with the original figure. (p. 365)

simetría de rotación Ocurre cuando una figura gira menos de 360° alrededor de un punto sin dejar de ser congruente con la figura original.

run The horizontal change when the slope of a line is expressed as the ratio $\frac{\text{rise}}{\text{run}}$, or "rise over run." (p. 347)

distancia horizontal El cambio horizontal cuando la pendiente de una línea se expresa como la $\frac{\text{razón distancia vertical}}{\text{distancia horizontal}}$, o "distancia vertical sobre distancia horizontal".

For the points (3, −1) and (6, 5) the run is 6 − 3 = 3.

sales tax A percent of the cost of an item, which is charged by governments to raise money. (p. 298)

impuesto sobre la venta Porcentaje del costo de un artículo que los gobiernos cobran para recaudar fondos.

sample A part of the population. (p. 462)

muestra Parte del grupo o población que se desea estudiar.

sample space All possible outcomes of an experiment. (p. 522)

espacio muestral Todos los resultados posibles de un experimento.

When rolling a number cube, the sample space is 1, 2, 3, 4, 5, 6.

scale The ratio between two sets of measurements. (p. 252)

escala La razón entre dos conjuntos de medidas.

1 cm: 5 mi

scale drawing A drawing that uses a scale to make an object smaller than (a reduction) or larger than (an enlargement) the real object. (p. 252)

dibujo a escala Dibujo que usa una escala para que un objeto se vea proporcionalmente menor (reducción) o mayor (ampliación) que el objeto real al que representa.

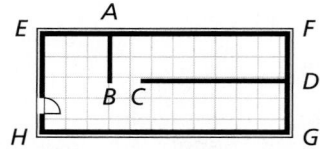

A blueprint is an example of a scale drawing.

scale factor The ratio used to enlarge or reduce similar figures. (p. 239)

factor de escala Razón empleada para agrandar o reducir figuras semejantes.

scale model A proportional model of a three-dimensional object. (p. 253)

modelo a escala Modelo proporcional de un objeto tridimensional.

ENGLISH	SPANISH	EXAMPLES
scalene triangle A triangle with no congruent sides. (p. 337)	**triángulo escaleno** Triángulo que no tiene lados congruentes.	
scatter plot A graph with points plotted to show a possible relationship between two sets of data. (p. 494)	**diagrama de dispersión** Gráfica de pares ordenados que se usa para mostrar una posible relación entre dos conjuntos de datos.	
scientific notation A method of writing very large or very small numbers by using powers of 10. (p. 174)	**notación científica** Método abreviado que se usa para escribir números muy grandes o muy pequeños usando potencias de 10.	$12{,}560{,}000{,}000{,}000 =$ 1.256×10^{13}
second differences A sequence formed from differences of differences between terms of a sequence. (p. 693)	**segundas diferencias** Sucesión formada a partir de las diferencias de diferencias entre términos de una sucesión.	For the sequence 1, 4, 9, 16, 25…, the first differences are 3, 5, 7, 9, …, and the second differences are all 2.
second quartile The median of a set of data. (p. 476)	**segundo cuartil** La mediana de un conjunto de datos.	Data set: 4, 6, 7, 8, 10 Second quartile: 7
segment A part of a line between two endpoints. (p. 324)	**segmento** Parte de una línea entre dos extremos.	
sequence An ordered list of numbers. (p. 142)	**sucesión** Lista ordenada de números.	2, 4, 6, 8, 10, . . .
side A line bounding a geometric figure; one of the faces forming the outside of an object. (p. 388)	**lado** Segmento de recta que delimita las figuras geométricas; una de las caras que forman la parte exterior de un objeto.	
similar Figures with the same shape but not necessarily the same size are similar. (p. 238)	**semejantes** Figuras que tienen la misma forma, pero no necesariamente el mismo tamaño.	
simple interest A fixed percent of the principal. It is found using the formula $I = Prt$, where P represents the principal, r the rate of interest, and t the time. (p. 302)	**interés simple** Un porcentaje fijo del capital. Se calcula con la fórmula $I = Crt$, donde C representa el capital, r, la tasa de interés, y t, el tiempo.	$100 is put into an account with a simple interest rate of 5%. After 2 years, the account will have earned $I = 100 \cdot 0.05 \cdot 2 = \$10.$
simplest form A fraction is in simplest form when the numerator and denominator have no common factors other than 1. (p. 64)	**mínima expresión** Una fracción está en su mínima expresión cuando el numerador y el denominador no tienen más factor común que 1.	Fraction: $\frac{8}{12}$ Simplest form: $\frac{2}{3}$

ENGLISH	SPANISH	EXAMPLES
simplify To write a fraction or expression in simplest form. (p. 585)	**simplificar** Escribir una fracción o expresión en su mínima expresión.	
simulation A model of an experiment, often one that would be too difficult or too time-consuming to actually perform. (p. 532)	**simulación** Representación de un experimento que en muchos casos sería demasiado difícil o tomaría demasiado tiempo realizarlo.	
slant height The distance from the base of a cone to its vertex, measured along the lateral surface. (p. 432)	**altura inclinada** Distancia de la base de un cono a su vértice, medida a lo largo de la superficie lateral.	Slant height
slope A measure of the steepness of a line on a graph; the rise divided by the run. (p. 347)	**pendiente** Medida de la inclinación de una línea en una gráfica. La distancia vertical dividida entre la distancia horizontal.	$\text{Slope} = \frac{\text{rise}}{\text{run}} = \frac{3}{4}$ $(-2, -1)$ $(2, 2)$
slope-intercept form A linear equation written in the form $y = mx + b$, where m represents slope and b represents the y-intercept. (p. 639)	**forma de pendiente-intersección** Ecuación lineal escrita en la forma $y = mx + b$, donde m es la pendiente y b es la intersección con el eje de las y.	$y = 6x - 3$
solution of an equation A value or values that make an equation true. (p. 34)	**solución de una ecuación** Valor o valores que hacen verdadera una ecuación.	Equation: $x + 2 = 6$ Solution: $x = 4$
solution of an inequality A value or values that make an inequality true. (p. 44)	**solución de una desigualdad** Valor o valores que hacen verdadera una desigualdad.	Inequality: $x + 3 \geq 10$ Solution: $x \geq 7$
solution of a system of equations A set of values that make all equations in a system true. (p. 608)	**solución de un sistema de ecuaciones** Conjunto de valores que hacen verdaderas todas las ecuaciones de un sistema.	System: $\begin{cases} x + y = -1 \\ -x + y = -3 \end{cases}$ Solution: $(1, 2)$
solution set The set of values that make a statement true. (p. 44)	**conjunto solución** Conjunto de valores que hacen verdadero un enunciado.	Inequality: $x + 3 \geq 5$ Solution set: $x \geq 2$ $-4\ -3\ -2\ -1\ \ 0\ \ 1\ \ 2\ \ 3\ \ 4\ \ 5\ \ 6$
solve To find an answer or a solution. (p. 34)	**resolver** Hallar una respuesta o solución.	

ENGLISH	SPANISH	EXAMPLES
sphere A three-dimensional figure with all points the same distance from the center. (p. 436)	**esfera** Figura tridimensional en la que todos los puntos están a la misma distancia del centro.	
square A rectangle with four congruent sides. (p. 342)	**cuadrado** Rectángulo con cuatro lados congruentes.	
square (numeration) A number raised to the second power. (p. 182)	**cuadrado (en numeración)** Número elevado a la segunda potencia.	In 5^2, the number 5 is squared.
square root One of the two equal factors of a number. (p. 182)	**raíz cuadrada** Uno de los dos factores iguales de un número.	$16 = 4 \cdot 4$, or $16 = -4 \cdot -4$, so 4 and -4 are square roots of 16.
stem-and-leaf plot A graph used to organize and display data so that the frequencies can be compared. (p. 467)	**diagrama doble de tallo y hojas** Diagrama de tallo y hojas que compara dos conjuntos de datos presentando uno de ellos a la izquierda del tallo y el otro a la derecha.	Stem | Leaves 3 | 2 3 4 4 7 9 4 | 0 1 5 7 7 7 8 5 | 1 2 2 3 *Key: 3|2 means 3.2*
stratified sample A sample of a population that has been divided into subgroups. (p. 462)	**muestra por estratos** Muestra de una población que ha sido dividida en subgrupos.	In a nationwide survey, ten states are randomly chosen and 500 people are randomly chosen from each of these states.
substitute To replace a variable with a number or another expression in an algebraic expression. (p. 6)	**sustituir** Reemplazar una variable por un número u otra expresión en una expresión algebraica.	Substituting 3 for m in the expression $5m - 2$ gives $5(3) - 2 = 15 - 2 = 13$.
Subtraction Property of Equality The property that states that if you subtract the same number from both sides of an equation, the new equation will have the same solution. (p. 35)	**Propiedad de igualdad de la resta** Propiedad que establece que puedes restar el mismo número en ambos lados de una ecuación y la ecuación resultante tendrá la misma solución.	$14 - 6 = 8$ $\underline{ - 6 = -6}$ $14 - 12 = 2$
sum The result when two or more numbers are added.	**suma** Resultado de sumar dos o más números.	
supplementary angles Two angles whose measures have a sum of 180°. (p. 325)	**ángulos suplementarios** Dos ángulos cuyas medidas suman 180°.	30° 150°
surface area The sum of the areas of the faces, or surfaces, of a three-dimensional figure. (p. 427)	**área total** Suma de las áreas de las caras, o superficies, de una figura tridimensional.	12 cm, 6 cm, 8 cm Surface area = $2(8)(12) + 2(8)(6) + 2(12)(6) = 432$ cm^2

system of equations A set of two or more equations that contain two or more variables. (p. 608)

sistema de ecuaciones Conjunto de dos o más ecuaciones que contienen dos o más variables.

$$\begin{cases} x + y = -1 \\ -x + y = -3 \end{cases}$$

---

systematic sample A sample of a population that has been selected using a pattern. (p. 462)

muestra sistemática Muestra de una población, la cual se elije mediante un patrón.

To conduct a phone survey, every tenth name is chosen from the phone book.

T

term (in an expression) The parts of an expression that are added or subtracted. (p. 584)

término (en una expresión) Las partes de una expresión que se suman o se restan.

$3x^2 +$ $6x -$ 8

Term   Term   Term

---

term (in a sequence) An element or number in a sequence. (p. 142)

término (de una sucesión) Elemento o número de una sucesión.

5 is the third term in the sequence 1, 3, 5, 7, 9, ...

---

terminating decimal A decimal number that ends or terminates. (pp. 191, 827)

decimal cerrado Decimal que termina debido a que tiene un número determinado de posiciones decimales.

6.75

---

tessellation A repeating pattern of plane figures that completely cover a plane with no gaps or overlaps. (p. 368)

teselado Patrón repetido de figuras planas que cubren totalmente un plano sin traslaparse ni dejar huecos.

---

theoretical probability The ratio of the number of equally likely outcomes in an event to the total number of possible outcomes. (p. 540)

probabilidad teórica Razón del número de resultados igualmente probales al número de resultados posibles.

When rolling a number cube, the theoretical probability of rolling a 4 is $\frac{1}{6}$.

---

third quartile The median of the upper half of a set of data; also called *upper quartile*. (p. 476)

tercer cuartil La mediana de la mitad superior de un conjunto de datos. También se llama *cuartil superior*.

---

transformation A change in the size or position of a figure. (p. 358)

transformación Cambio en el tamaño o la posición de una figura.

$\triangle ABC \longrightarrow \triangle A'B'C'$

Preimage

Image

$ABC \longrightarrow A'B'C'$

---

translation A movement (slide) of a figure along a straight line. (p. 358)

traslación Desplazamiento de una figura a lo largo de una línea recta.

ENGLISH	SPANISH	EXAMPLES
transversal A line that intersects two or more lines. (p. 330)	**transversal** Línea que cruza dos o más líneas.	
trapezoid A quadrilateral with exactly one pair of parallel sides. (p. 342)	**trapecio** Cuadrilátero que tiene exactamente un par de lados paralelos.	
tree diagram A branching diagram that shows all possible combinations or outcomes of an event. (p. 559)	**diagrama de árbol** Diagrama ramificado que muestra todas las posibles combinaciones o resultados de un suceso.	
trial In probability, a single repetition or observation of an experiment. (p. 522)	**prueba** En probabilidad, una sola repetición u observación de un experimento.	When rolling a number cube, each roll is one trial.
triangle A three-sided polygon.	**triángulo** Polígono de tres lados.	
Triangle Sum Theorem The theorem that states that the measures of the angles in a triangle add up to 180°. (p. 336)	**Teorema de la suma del triángulo** Teorema que establece que las medidas de los ángulos de un triángulo suman 180°.	
triangular prism A polyhedron whose bases are triangles and whose other faces are parallelograms. (p. 413)	**prisma triangular** Poliedro cuyas bases son triángulos y sus demás caras tienen forma de paralelogramos.	
trinomial A polynomial with three terms. (p. 734)	**trinomio** Polinomio con tres términos.	$4x^2 + 3xy = 5y^2$

U

unbiased sample A sample is unbiased if every individual in the population has an equal chance of being selected. (p. 463)	**muestra imparcial** Una muestra es imparcial si cada individuo de la población tiene la misma posibilidad de ser seleccionado.	
unit conversion The process of changing one unit of measure to another.	**conversión de unidades** Proceso que consiste en cambiar una unidad de medición en otra.	
unit conversion factor A fraction used in unit conversion in which the numerator and denominator represent the same amount but are in different units. (p. 224)	**factor de conversión de unidades** Fracción que se usa para la conversión de unidades, donde el numerador y el denominador representan la misma cantidad pero con unidades distintas.	$\frac{60 \text{ min}}{1 \text{ h}}$ or $\frac{1 \text{ h}}{60 \text{ min}}$

ENGLISH	SPANISH	EXAMPLES
unit price A unit rate used to compare prices. (p. 221)	**precio unitario** Relación unitaria que sirve para comparar precios.	Cereal costs $0.23 per ounce.
unit rate A rate in which the second quantity in the comparison is one unit. (p. 220)	**tasa unitaria** Una relación en donde la segunda cantidad de comparación es la unidad.	10 cm per minute

V

ENGLISH	SPANISH	EXAMPLES
variability The spread of values in a set of data. (p. 476)	**variabilidad** Medida en que se extienden los valores de un conjunto de datos.	The data set {1, 5, 7, 10, 25} has greater variability than the data set {8, 8, 9, 9, 9}.
variable A symbol used to represent a quantity that can change. (p. 6)	**variable** Letra o símbolo que representa una cantidad que puede cambiar.	In the expression $2x + 3$, x is the variable.
Venn diagram A diagram that is used to show relationships between sets. (p. 468)	**diagrama de Venn** Diagrama que sirve para mostrar las relaciones entre conjuntos.	Transformations / Rotations
vertex On an angle or polygon, the point where two sides intersect; on a polyhedron, the intersection of three or more faces; on a cone or pyramid, the top point. (p. 408)	**vértice** En un ángulo o polígono, el punto de intersección de dos lados; en un poliedro, el punto de intersección de tres o más caras; en un cono o pirámide, la punta.	A is the vertex of $\angle CAB$.
vertical angles A pair of opposite congruent angles formed by intersecting lines. (p. 325)	**ángulos opuestos por el vértice** Par de ángulos congruentes y opuestos formados por líneas secantes. En el diagrama, $\angle a$ y $\angle c$ son opuestos por el vértice, lo mismo que $\angle b$ y $\angle d$.	$\angle 1$ and $\angle 3$ are vertical angles.
volume The number of cubic units needed to fill a given space. (p. 413)	**volumen** Número de unidades cúbicas que se necesitan para llenar un espacio.	4 ft, 3 ft, 12 ft. Volume = $3 \cdot 4 \cdot 12 = 144$ ft^2
voluntary-response sample A sample in which members choose to be in the sample. (p. 462)	**muestra de respuesta voluntaria** Una muestra en la que los miembros eligen participar.	A store provides survey cards for customers who wish to fill them out.

ENGLISH	SPANISH	EXAMPLES

x-axis The horizontal axis on a coordinate plane. (p. 122)

eje de las x El eje horizontal del plano cartesiano.

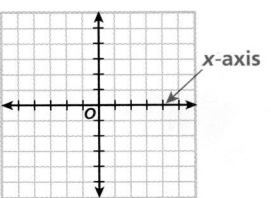

x-coordinate The first number in an ordered pair; it tells the distance to move right or left from the origin (0, 0). (p. 122)

coordenada x El primer número de un par ordenado; indica la distancia que debes moverte hacia la izquierda o la derecha desde el origen, (0, 0).

5 is the x-coordinate in (5, 3).

x-intercept The x-coordinate of the point where the graph of a line crosses the x-axis. (p. 638)

intersección con el eje de las x Coordenada x del punto donde la gráfica de una recta cruza el eje de las x.

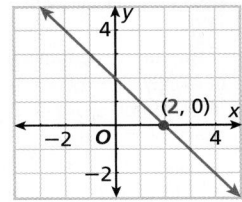

The x-intercept is 2.

y-axis The vertical axis on a coordinate plane. (p. 122)

eje de las y El eje vertical del plano cartesiano.

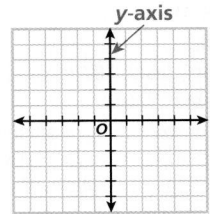

y-coordinate The second number in an ordered pair; it tells the distance to move up or down from the origin (0, 0). (p. 122)

coordenada y El segundo número de un par ordenado; indica la distancia que debes moverte hacia arriba o abajo desde el origen, (0, 0).

3 is the y-coordinate in (5, 3).

y-intercept The y-coordinate of the point where the graph of a line crosses the y-axis. (p. 638)

intersección con el eje de las y Coordenada y del punto donde la gráfica de una recta cruza el eje de las y.

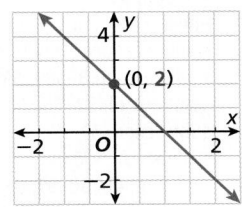

The y-intercept is 2.

Z

zero pair A number and its opposite, which add to 0.

par nulo Un número y su opuesto, cuya suma es 0.

18 and −18

Index

A

Absolute value, 15
Abstract art, 743
Acetaminophen, 707
Act It Out, 818
Acute angles, 325
Acute Mountain Sickness (AMS), 642
Acute triangles, 336
Addition
 Associative Property of, 747
 of fractions, 89
  with unlike denominators, 85–86
 of integers, 18–19
 of polynomials, 747–748
  modeling, 746
 of rational numbers, 72–73
 solving equations by, 34–36
Addition Counting Principle, 559–560
Addition Property of Equality, 34, 37
Additional Examples
*Additional Examples appear in every
lesson. Some examples: 7, 11, 15, 19, 23*
Additive inverses, 14
AIDS Memorial Quilt, 388
Alaska, 282
Albers, Josef, 567
Algebra
*The development of algebra skills and
concepts is a central focus of this course
and is found throughout this book.*
 absolute value, 15
 arithmetic sequences and, 142–143
 equations, 32–33, 34
  addition, 34–35
  checking solutions of, 34, 35,
   39–40
  decimal, solving, 92, 98
  division, 39–40
  linear, 628–630
  multiplication, 39–40
  multi-step, 588–589, 592, 593–595
  solutions of, 32–33, 34
  subtraction, 34–35
  systems of, 608–609
  two-step, 40, 96–97, 98–99
 exponential functions, 704–705
 expressions, 6–7, 10–11, 584–585
  translating between tables and, 6, 11
  variables and, 6–7
 functions, 134–135
  exponential, 704–705
  graphing, 134–135, 138–139
  linear, 700–701
  tables and, 134–135, 138–139
  quadratic, 708–709
 inequalities, 44–45, 600–601, 604–605

 proportions, 216–217
  and indirect measurement, 248–249
  in scale drawings, models, and maps,
   252–253, 256–257
  in similar figures, 236–237, 238–239
  solving, 229–231
  tiles, 32–33, 96–97, 592
Algebra tiles, 32–33, 96–97, 588, 592,
 593, 692, 738–739, 746, 748, 751, 753,
 760–761
Algebraic expressions, 6, 10–11
 simplifying, 584–585
Algebraic inequalities, 44
Allergies, 497
Alternate exterior angles, 331
Alternate interior angles, 331
American Samoa, 340
Amplitude, 846
AMS (Acute Mountain Sickness), 642
Amusement park rides, 358
Analysis
 dimensional, 224–226
 unit, 224
**Analyzing, collecting, and displaying
 data,** 458–517
Anamorphic images, 427
Anatomy, 176
Andromeda Galaxy, 177
Angles, 325
 acute, 325
 alternate exterior, 331
 alternate interior, 331
 bisector, 329
 central, of a circle, 838
 classifying, 325
 complementary, 325
 congruent, 238
 corresponding, 331
 exterior, of polygons, 346
 measuring, 832
 obtuse, 325
 points and lines and planes and,
  324–326
 protractor, measuring with, 832
 right, 325
 supplementary, 325
 in triangles, 336–338
 vertical, 325
Animals, 79
Animals Link, 79
Answering context–based test items,
 620–621
Ant lions, 433
Aperture, 247
Applications
 Anatomy, 176
 Animals, 79
 Architecture, 254, 424, 637
 Art, 241, 411, 428, 442, 567, 748
 Astronomy, 37, 172, 475, 709
 Business, 46, 136, 172, 218, 230, 281,
  441, 465, 473, 557, 587, 595, 703, 711,
  741, 750, 753, 755
 Chemistry, 17, 220

 Computer, 183
 Conservation, 141
 Construction, 125, 637, 764
 Consumer application, 526, 640, 684
 Consumer Economics, 78, 300
 Consumer Math, 100, 119
 Cooking, 567
 Crafts, 610
 Design, 74
 Earth Science, 17, 23, 28, 29, 94, 297,
  345, 435, 480, 557, 647, 659
 Economics, 21, 607, 691, 703
 Energy, 75
 Entertainment, 9, 218, 223, 403, 535,
  606, 611, 632
 Environment, 217
 Finance, 8, 281, 717
 Fitness, 503, 686
 Food, 227, 403, 658
 Games, 185, 549
 Geography, 248, 254, 277, 285, 480
 Geometry, 120, 163, 586, 591, 611, 696,
  750
 Graphic Design, 9
 Health, 19, 79, 759
 History, 121
 Hobbies, 185, 219, 586, 710
 Home Economics, 137
 Language Arts, 184, 287
 Life Science, 71, 165, 177, 227, 228, 252,
  253, 284, 288, 290, 294–295, 417,
  433, 535, 567, 647, 654, 691, 742
 Literature, 297
 Measurement, 87
 Medical, 645
 Meteorology, 71
 Money, 40, 175, 305, 689
 Multi-Step, 395, 595, 763
 Music, 125, 415, 715
 Nutrition, 94
 Patterns, 168, 277, 286
 Photography, 247
 Physical Science, 7, 38, 177, 226, 231,
  232, 241, 275, 281, 288, 333, 401, 591,
  597, 630, 631, 635, 652, 691, 701, 706,
  711, 717
 Physics, 735
 Recreation, 42, 77, 86, 284, 443, 465,
  686, 703
 Safety, 528, 637
 School, 475, 549, 553, 605
 Social Studies, 37, 69, 84, 178, 282, 286,
  340, 367, 392, 417, 421, 435, 602, 657
 Sports, 14, 27, 47, 66, 70, 72, 74, 137,
  145, 184, 227, 281, 403, 430, 503,
  567, 587, 591, 607, 661, 690, 710
 Technology, 562
 Transportation, 227, 228, 632, 737
 Travel, 140, 143, 589
Approximating pi by measuring, 399
Arc, of a circle, 838
Archerfish, 328
Architecture, 254, 424, 637
Architecture Link, 255
Are You Ready?, 3, 61, 115, 159, 213, 271,
 321, 385, 459, 519, 581, 625, 679, 731

Area, 389
  of circles, 401
  of parallelograms, 388–390
  perimeter and volume and, 384–457
  of rectangles, 388–390
  surface, 427
    of cones, 432–433
    of cylinders, 425–428
    of prisms, 425–428
    of pyramids, 431–433
    of spheres, 437
  of trapezoids, 394–396
  of triangles, 394–396

Arguments, writing convincing, 215

Arithmetic sequences, 142–143
  finding nth term of, 683–684
  terms of, 682–684

Art, 241, 411, 428, 442, 567, 748

Art Link, 241, 371, 567, 743

Aspect ratio, 223

Assessment
  Chapter Test, 55, 109, 153, 207, 265, 315, 379, 453, 513, 575, 673, 691, 725, 775
  Cumulative Assessment, 58–59, 110–111, 156–157, 208–209, 268–269, 316–317, 382–383, 454–455, 516–517, 576–577, 622–623, 674–675, 728–729, 776–777
  for labs
  Assessment for labs is given in every lab. Some examples: 32, 89, 96, 126, 179
  Journal
  Journal suggestions are given in lesson exercises. Some examples: 9, 13, 17, 21, 25
  Lesson Quiz
  Lesson Quiz appears in every lesson. Some examples: 9, 13, 17, 21, 25
  Ongoing, *see* Assessment Options
  Ready to Go On?, 39, 48, 90, 102, 132, 146, 180, 200, 234, 258, 292, 308, 352, 372, 404, 444, 482, 506, 538, 568, 598, 612, 648, 664, 698, 718, 744, 766
  Standardized Test Prep, 58–59, 110–111, 156–157, 208–209, 268–269, 316–317, 382–383, 454–455, 516–517, 576–577, 622–623, 674–675, 728–729, 776–777
  Study Guide: Preview, 4, 62, 116, 160, 214, 272, 322, 386, 460, 520, 582, 626, 680, 732
  Study Guide: Review, 52–54, 106–108, 150–152, 204–206, 262–264, 312–314, 376–378, 450–452, 510–512, 572–574, 616–618, 670–672, 722–724, 772–774
  Test Tackler
    All Types: Using a Graphic, 514–515
    Extended Response: Write Extended Responses, 380–381
    Gridded Response: Write Gridded Responses, 154–155

    Multiple Choice
      Answering Context–Based Test Items, 620–621
      Eliminate Answer Choices, 56–57
      Work Backward, 726–727
    Short Response: Write Short Responses, 266–267
  Warm Up
  Warm Up appears in every lesson. Some examples: 6, 10, 14, 18, 22

Assessment Options, 2B, 2E, 60B, 60E, 114B, 114E, 158B, 158E, 212B, 212E, 270B, 270E, 320B, 320E, 384B, 384E, 458B, 458E, 518B, 518E, 580B, 580E, 624B, 624E, 678B, 678E, 730B, 730E

Assignment Guide
An Assignment Guide appears in every lesson. Some examples: 8, 12, 16, 20, 24

Associative Property, 747
  of Addition, 74, 829
  of Multiplication, 829

Astronomy, 37, 172, 475, 709

Atlantic City boardwalk, 113

Atomic mass, 177

Atoms, 158

Auditory Cues, 331

Axes, 122

B

Back-to-back stem-and-leaf plot, 467

Bacteria, 165, 201, 678

Balance of trade, 21

Balance scale, 34, 651

Baltimore Kinetic Sculpture Race, 677

Bar graphs, 500
  histograms, 836

Bases, 162

Beavers, 719

Benchmarks, 278

Best fit, lines of, 494, 660–661

Best representations of data, choosing, 500–501

Biased samples, 463

Bilateral symmetry, 446

Binary codes, 518

Binary fission, 165

Binomials, 734
  multiplication of, 760–761, 762–763
  special products of, 763

Bisecting figures, 329

Blood pressure, 233

Board foot, 741

Boeing 747, 398

Bonds, Barry, 281

Bonsai, 212

Boundary line, 655

Bourbaki, Nicolas, 584

Box-and-whisker plots, 477, 500
  creating, 481

Boyle's Law, 716

Brilliant cut, 345

British thermal units (Btu), 75

Business, 46, 136, 172, 218, 230, 281, 441, 465, 473, 557, 587, 595, 703, 711, 741, 750, 753, 755

Business Link, 465, 750

Butterflies, 71

C

Caffeine, 707

Calculator
  graphing, *see* Graphing calculator
  order of operations on a, 828

Calder, Alexander, 229

Camera lens, 247

Capacity, 440

Career
  Bacteriologist, 678
  Cryptographer, 518
  Financial Analyst, 730
  Firefighter, 2
  Horticulturist, 212
  Hydrologist, 580
  Nuclear Physicist, 158
  Nutritionist, 60
  Pharmacist, 114
  Playground Equipment Designer, 320
  Quality Assurance Specialist, 458
  Sports Statistician, 270
  Surgeon, 384
  Wildlife Ecologist, 624

Career Link, 424

Carlsbad Caverns, 22

Catfish, 778

Caution!, 45, 77, 163, 182, 191, 330, 388, 390, 421

Cavalieri's principle, 416

CD-ROM, 562

Celsius temperature
  converting between Fahrenheit and, 842
  scale, 103

Center
  of a circle, 400
  of dilation, 242–243, 244
  of rotation, 358

Centimeter cubes, 414, 441

Central angle, 838

Central tendency, measures of, 472–473

Certain event, 522

Challenge
Challenge exercises are found in every lesson. Some examples: 9, 13, 17, 21, 25 Reduced Challenge pages appear in every lesson. Some examples: 9, 13, 17, 21, 25

Changing dimensions, exploring effects of, 393

Chapter Project Online, 2, 60, 114, 158, 212, 270, 320, 384, 458, 518, 580, 624, 678, 730

Chapter Test, 55, 109, 153, 207, 265, 315, 379, 453, 513, 575, 673, 691, 725, 775, *see also* Assessment

Chemistry, 17, 220

Chesapeake Bay Bridge, 676

Chess, 185

Chord, of a circle, 838

Choose a Strategy, 9, 29, 84, 165, 228, 247, 287, 297, 340, 430, 443, 562, 597, 659, 711, 750, 755

Choosing best representations of data, 500–501

Chord, 838

Cincinnati Zoo, 465

Circle(s), 400–401, 838
  arcs of, 838
  area of, 401
  central angles of, 838
  chords of, 838
  circumference, 400
  diameter, 400
  great, 436
  graphs, 484, 500
  inscribed angles of, 838
  radius, 400
  secant of, 838

Circle graphs, 500
  making, 484

Circuit, network, 840

Circumference, 400

Classifying
  angles, 325
  polygons, 341–343
  real numbers, 191–192
  three-dimensional figures, 413, 420

Clemson Tigers Football, 578

Closure Property
  of Addition, 829
  of Multiplication, 829

Coefficients, 6

Cognitive Strategies, 45, 81, 163, 221, 342, 428, 523, 555, 656, 705

Coins, 19, 523, 527, 536–537, 545, 551, 651, 740

Collecting, displaying, and analyzing data, 458–517

Combinations, 564–565

Combining like terms, 584–585

Combining transformations, 362–363

Commission, 298

Commission rate, 298

Common denominator, 68

Common difference, 142, 682

Common Error Alert, *see* Intervention

Common factor, 822
  greatest (GCF), 824

Common multiple, 822
  least (LCM), 824

Common ratio, 687

Communicating Math, 27, 99, 163, 167, 221, 337, 355, 463, 555, 661, 753
  apply, 415
  choose, 221, 343

compare, 19, 27, 45, 163, 239, 245, 289, 295, 390, 422, 428, 433, 437, 478, 495, 528, 555, 605, 609, 630, 684, 689, 705, 709, 748, 753, 757

compare and contrast, 657

describe, 19, 23, 36, 69, 99, 119, 128, 135, 176, 183, 217, 231, 245, 253, 280, 359, 369, 396, 415, 422, 441, 463, 486, 501, 542, 585, 605, 609, 630, 640, 645, 652, 657, 661, 689, 701, 709, 715, 735, 748

decide, 183, 463

demonstrate, 285, 303

discuss, 187

determine, 176, 187, 221, 280

explain, 7, 15, 19, 23, 36, 41, 65, 69, 73, 86, 93, 99, 119, 143, 163, 171, 176, 183, 192, 197, 217, 226, 231, 249, 253, 275, 289, 295, 299, 303, 326, 331, 338, 343, 349, 355, 365, 369, 428, 433, 437, 441, 468, 473, 478, 491, 524, 533, 555, 565, 595, 601, 630, 635, 657, 684, 735, 753

express, 11, 167, 390

find, 695

give, 11, 41, 45, 65, 119, 123, 128, 217, 226, 409, 473, 501, 524, 528, 601

give an example, 7, 73, 77, 86, 217, 275, 415, 491, 495, 542, 547, 551, 565, 635, 640, 741, 763

identify, 135, 715

list, 27, 171, 589

model, 82

name, 77, 285, 303, 657

show, 163, 275, 285

suppose, 27, 560

tell, 7, 82, 86, 167, 192, 197, 231, 299, 303, 326, 331, 355, 359, 365, 533, 547, 585, 589, 645, 652, 661, 741

use, 192

Think and Discuss
Think and Discuss is found in every lesson. Some examples: 7, 11, 15, 19, 23

Write About It
Write About It exercises are found in every lesson. Some examples: 9, 13, 17, 21, 25

Commutative Property, 74, 78, 529, 829

Comparing
  customary units and metric units, 841
  rational numbers, 68–69

Compass, 329, 334–335

Compatible numbers, 278, 825

Complementary angles, 325

Composite Figures
  area of, 390
  perimeter of, 390
  volume of, 415

Composite Numbers, 823

Compound Events, 545–547

Compound interest, 306
  computing, 306–307

Computer, 183

Computer graphics, 347

Computer ownership, 663

Computer viruses, 704

Computing compound interest, 306–307

Concept maps, 387

Conclusions, *see* Geometry proofs, informal

Concorde, 398

Concrete Manipulatives, 19, 40, 69, 86, 163, 355, 359, 365, 437, 441, 463, 528, 585, 694, 748, 753, *see also* Manipulatives

Cones, 420
  right, 432
  surface area of, 432–433
  volume of, 420–422
    exploring, 418–419

Congruence, 354–355

Congruent angles, 238

Congruent figures, 325

Congruent triangles, 354

Conjectures, *see* Geometry proofs, informal

Conservation, 141

Constant of proportionality, 650

Constants, 6

Constructing
  graphs, using spreadsheets for, 504–505
  nets, 406–407

Construction, 125, 637, 764

Constructions, 334–335

Consumer application, 526, 640, 684

Consumer Economics, 78, 300

Consumer Math, 100, 119

Context-based test items, answering, 620–621

Convenience samples, 462

Converse of the Pythagorean Theorem, 196, 198, 199

Conversion factors, 224, 841
  units of measure, 224–226

Converting
  customary units to metric units, 841
  metric units to customary units, 841
  odds to probabilities, 554–555
  probabilities to odds, 555

Convincing arguments, writing, 215

Cooking, 567

Coordinate geometry, 347–349

Coordinate plane, 122
  graphing on a, 122–123

Coordinates, 122–123

Cooperative Learning, 7, 35, 45, 93, 99, 139, 183, 217, 303, 348, 501, 541, 589, 661, 757

Cornell system of note taking, 161

Correlation, 494–495

Correspondence, 354

Corresponding angles, 331

Corresponding sides, 238, 354–355

Counters, 163, 546

Counting Principles, 558–560

Index

Crafts, 610
Crazy Horse Memorial, 235
Creating
  box-and-whisker plots, 481
  histograms, 489
  scatter plots, 498–499
Crelle's Journal, 184
Critical Thinking, 13, 17, 23, 27, 29, 42,
  67, 70, 73, 121, 123, 135, 145, 167, 168,
  171, 199, 219, 227, 239, 289, 297, 299,
  305, 327, 333, 350, 351, 371, 395, 421,
  480, 491, 526, 533, 546, 557, 559, 564,
  591, 605, 606, 609, 629, 654, 686, 711,
  737, 750
Cross products, 229
Cross section, 446
Crown of Great Britain, 345
Cube(s), 830
Cube roots, 830
Cubic functions, exploring, 712–713
Cubic units, 413
Cullinan diamond, 94
Cumulative Assessment, 58–59, 110–111,
  156–157, 208–209, 268–269, 316–317,
  382–383, 454–455, 516–517, 576–577,
  622–623, 674–675, 728–729, 776–777,
  see also Assessment
Cumulative frequency, 835
  relative, 835
Cumulative test, studying for a, 733
Customary rulers, 242–243, 256–257, 329,
  355, 399, 406–407, 412, 421, 433, 484
Customary system of measurement,
  224–226, 837
  converting between metric and, 841
  measuring in, 843
Cutout figures, 86, 365, 585
Cylinders, 413
  surface area of, 427–428
    exploring, 425–426
  volume of, 413–415
    exploring, 412

D

da Vinci, Leonardo, 434
Dance rhythms, 125
Dase, Zacharias, 184
Data, *see also* Displaying and organizing
  data
  analyzing, collecting, and displaying,
    458–517
  choosing best representations of,
    500–501
  displaying, 485–486
  organizing, 467–468
Decay, exponential, 705
Decimal grids, 276, 537
Decimals
  addition of, 72, 73, 92
  comparing, 69
  converting between percents and
    fractions and, 274–275

division, 81, 827
  fractions and, 65
  multiplication, 77, 92, 826
    by powers of ten, 826
  ordering, 69
  repeating, 65, 827
  rounding, 821
  subtraction of, 72, 73, 92
  terminating, 65, 827
  writing as percents, 274–275
Decisions, making, 550–551
Deck of cards, 536, 541
Deep Blue, 185
Degrees of polynomials, 735
Denominator(s), 64
  like, adding and subtracting with, 73
  unlike, adding and subtracting with,
    85–86
Density, 220
Density Property of rational numbers,
  192
Dependent events, 545–547
  finding probability of, 546–547
Depreciation, linear, 703
Descartes, René, 162
Design, 74
Degree, of a network vertex, 840
Diagonals, 341
Diagram
  iteration, 834
  tree, 559
Diameter, 400
Diastolic blood pressure, 233
Difference, common, 142, 682
Differences, first, 693
Digits, significant, 844
Dilation, center of, 242–243, 244
Dilations, 244–245
  exploring, 242–243
Dimensional analysis, 224–226
Dimensions
  changing, exploring effects of, 393
  matrix, 839
  three, symmetry in, 446
Direct variation, 650–652
Discounts, 295
Disjoint events, 542
Displaying and organizing data,
  485–486
  bar graphs, 500
  circle graphs, 484, 500
  double-bar graphs, 485
  double-line graphs, 486
  frequency polygons, 836
  frequency tables, 485, 835
  histograms, 485, 489, 500, 836
  line graphs, 500
  misleading graphs, 490–491
  stem-and-leaf plots
    back-to-back, 467
Distracter, 56
Distributive Property, 586, 741, 742, 757,
  762, 763, 829

Divisibility rules, 822
Division
  of decimals, 81, 827
    by powers of ten, 826
  of fractions, 80–81
  of integers, 26–27
  long, 821
  of numbers in scientific notation, 179
  of polynomials by monomials,
    768–769
  of powers, 170
  of rational numbers, 80–82
  solving equations by, 39–41
  solving inequalities by, 600–601
Division Property of Equality, 39, 40
DNA model, 253
Domain, 134
Double-bar graphs, 485
Double-line graphs, 486
Draw a diagram, 810
Drawing three-dimensional figures,
  408–409
Drawings, scale, 252
Duckweed plants, 177

E

Earth, 174, 436
Earth Science, 17, 23, 28, 29, 94, 297, 345,
  435, 480, 557, 647, 659
Earth Science Link, 17, 29, 88, 131, 345,
  530, 647, 659
Earthquakes, 530
  Richter scale, 846
Economics, 21, 607, 691, 703
Economics Link, 21, 301, 663
Edge,
  of a three-dimensional figure, 408
  of a network, 840
Edison, Thomas, 137
Effective notes, taking, 161
Eggs, 439
Energy, 75
English Language Learners, 6, 10, 15, 63,
  65, 81, 135, 163, 192, 197, 211, 215, 220,
  238, 273, 275, 284, 295, 319, 323, 325,
  326, 341, 387, 401, 446, 457, 461, 463,
  473, 490, 521, 533, 542, 546, 579, 583,
  584, 600, 627, 652, 677, 681, 689, 709,
  714, 734, 741
Entries, of a matrix, 838
Enlargement, 253
Entertainment, 9, 218, 223, 403, 535, 606,
  611, 632
Entertainment Link, 403, 611
Environment, 217
Equality
  Addition Property of, 34, 37
  Division Property of, 39, 40
  Multiplication Property of, 40
  Subtraction Property of, 35
Equally likely outcomes, 540

Index

Equations, 34
  graphs of, 123
  linear, *see* Linear equations
  multi-step, *see* Multi-step equations
  in slope-intercept form, graphing, 643
  solving, *see* Solving equations
  Standard Form of, 638
  systems of, *see* Systems of equations
  tables and graphs and, 138–139
  two-step, *see* Two-step equations
  with variables on both sides, modeling, 592
Equilateral triangles, 337
Equivalent expressions, 584
Equivalent ratios, 216
Error, greatest possible, 845
Escher, M. C., 369, 370, 371
Estimate, 278
Estimating
  with percents, 278–280
  quotients, 825
  square roots, 186–187
Estimation, 24, 84, 87, 165, 173, 184, 223, 281, 423, 480, 659, 703
Evaluating algebraic expressions, 6
  powers and roots, 190
Events, 522
  dependent, *see* Dependent events
  disjoint, 542
  independent, *see* Independent events
  mutually exclusive, 542
Experiment, 522
Experimental probability, 527–528
Exploring
  cubic functions, 712–713
  dilations, 242–243
  effects of changing dimensions, 393
  right triangles, 195
  sampling, 466
  similarity, 236–237
Exponent(s), 162–163
  integer, looking for patterns in, 166–167
  negative, 166
  properties of, 170–171
  roots and, 158–211
Exponential decay, 705
Exponential form, 162
Exponential functions, 704–705
Exponential growth, 705
Expressions
  algebraic, 6, 10–11
    simplifying, 584–585
  equivalent, 584
  simplifying numerical, 828
  variables and, 6–7
Extended Response, 88, 141, 169, 223, 297, 333, 380–381, 443, 480, 642, 703, 755
  Write Extended Responses, 380–381
Extension
  Dividing Polynomials by Monomials, 768–769
  Solving Systems of Equations by Graphing, 666–667
  Symmetry in Three Dimensions, 446

Exterior angles of polygons, 346
Extra Practice, 782–809
Euclid, 324
Euclidean geometry, 438
Euler circuit, 840
Euler, Leonhard, 130
Exploration
Reduced Exploration pages appear in every lesson. Some examples: 6, 10, 14, 18, 22
Extension
  Game Time, 50, 104, 148, 202, 260, 310, 374, 448, 508, 570, 614, 668, 720, 770
  It's in the Bag, 51, 105, 149, 203, 261, 311, 375, 449, 509, 571, 615, 669, 721, 771
  Multi-Step Test Prep, 49, 103, 147, 201, 259, 309, 373, 445, 507, 569, 613, 665, 719, 767
  Reading and Writing Math, 5, 63, 117, 161, 215, 273, 323, 387, 461, 521, 583, 627, 681, 733
Eyes, pupils of, 244

F

Faces, 408
  lateral, 427
Factorials, 563
Factor(s), 822
  common, 822, 824
  conversion, 224, 841
  greatest common (GCF), 824
  scale, 239
Fahrenheit temperature
  converting between Celsius and, 842
  scale, 103
Fair objects, 540
Family crests, 367
Ferris wheel, 403
Fibonacci sequence, 692, 694, 695
Fifth, 697
Figures
  bisecting, 329
  composite, 390, 415
  congruent, 325
  dilating, 244–245
  similar, 238–239
  three-dimensional, *see* Three-dimensional figures
Finance, 8, 281, 717
Find a Pattern, 814
Finding
  *n*th term of an arithmetic sequence, 683–684
  *n*th term of a geometric sequence, 688
  numbers when percents are known, 288–289
  percents, 283–285
  probability of dependent events, 546–547
  probability of independent events, 545–546

  surface area of prisms and cylinders, 425–426
  surface area of pyramids, 431
  volume of prisms and cylinders, 412
  volume of pyramids and cones, 418–419
Fireworks, 735
First differences, 693
Fish weight, 591
Fitness, 503, 686
Flatiron Building, 441
Flip, *see* Reflection
Florida, 121
Focus, of a parabola, 708
Focus on Problem Solving
  Look Back, 91, 405, 745
  Make a Plan, 133, 293, 483, 599
  Solve, 31, 181, 235, 699
  Understand the Problem, 353, 539, 649
FOIL mnemonic, 762, 763
Food, 227, 403, 658
Foster, Don, 471
Fountain of Youth, 121
Formulas, *see* inside back cover
Fractals, 394, 834
Fraction(s)
  addition of, 72–73, 89
    with unlike denominators, 85–86
  relating, to decimals and percents, 274–275
  subtraction of, 72–73, 89
    with unlike denominators, 85–86
  unit, 104
  writing as mixed numbers, 825
  writing as terminating and repeating decimals, 827
Fraction form, dividing rational numbers in, 80
Frequency, 835
  cumulative, 835
  polygons, 836
  relative, 835
  relative cumulative, 835
  tables, 485, 835
Fulcrum, 229
Fuller Building, 441
Function notation, 700
Functions, 134–135
  cubic, exploring, 712–713
  exponential, 704–705
  graphs and sequences and, 114–157
  linear, 700–701
  quadratic, 708–709
  sequences and, 678–729
Fundamental Counting Principle, 558–559, 579

G

Game Time
  Coloring Tessellations, 374
  Copy-Cat, 260
  Crazy Cubes, 50
  Distribution of Primes, 508

Egg Fractions, 104
Egyptian Fractions, 104
Equation Bingo, 202
Find the Phony!, 148
Graphing in Space, 668
Line Solitaire, 668
Magic Squares, 202
Math in the Middle, 508
Math Magic, 50
The Paper Chase, 570
Percent Puzzlers, 310
Percent Tiles, 310
Permutations, 570
Planes in Space, 448
Polygon Rummy, 374
Rolling for Tiles, 770
Short Cuts, 770
Sprouts, 148
Squared Away, 720
Tic-Frac-Toe, 260
Trans-Plants, 614
Triple Concentration, 448
24 Points, 614
What's Your Function?, 720
Game Time Extra, 50, 104, 148, 202, 260, 310, 374, 448, 508, 570, 614, 668, 720, 770
Games, 185, 549
Games Link, 185, 549
Garfield, James, 196
Gas mileage, 737
GCF (greatest common factor), 824
Generating random numbers, 531
Geography, 248, 254, 277, 285, 480
Geometric sequences, 687
finding *n*th term of, 688
terms of, 687–689
Geometry, 320–383
The development of geometry skills and concepts is a central focus of this course and is found throughout this book.
angles, 325–326, 330–331, 334–335, 336–338, 341–342, 346, 354–355
building blocks of, 324–326
circles, 400–401
area of, 401
exploring, 399
circumference of, 400
cylinders
volume of, 412, 413–415
surface area of, 425–426, 427–428
cones
volume of, 418–419, 420–422
surface area of, 432–433
coordinate, 347–349
lines, 324–326
parallel, 330–331
perpendicular, 330–331
of reflection, 358–359
skew, 830
of symmetry, 364–365
transversal, 330–331
measurement and, 832, 841, 843
parallel line relationships, 837

parallelograms, 342
area of, 389
perimeter of, 388
polygons, 341–343, 346, 355
diagonals in, 341
finding angle measures in, 341–342
regular, 342
prisms, 412, 413–415
volumes of, 412, 413–415
surface area of, 425–426, 427–428
proofs, informal, 833
pyramids, 418–419, 420–421
volume of, 418–419, 420–421
surface area of, 431, 432–433
rectangles, 388–390
area of, 389–390
exploring area and perimeter of, 393
perimeter of, 388–390
rhombuses, 342
software, 346
sphere, 436–437
three-dimensional figures, 406–407, 408–409, 440–441, 446
drawing views of, 406–407, 408–409
modeling, 256–257, 406–407, 408–409, 440–441,
trapezoids
area of, 395–396
perimeter of, 394
triangles, 195
area of, 395–396
perimeter of, 394
Geometry software, 346
Geysers, 131
Giant Ocean Tank, 417
Giant shark, 288, 289
Gigabyte, 173
Glenn Research Center, 211
go.hrw.com, *see* Online Resources
Global Challenge yacht race, 47
Global temperature, 71
Gold, 220
Gold bullion, 223
Golden Rectangle, 222
Googol, 173
Graphic Design, 9
Graph(s)
bar, 500
circle, *see* Circle graphs
constructing, using spreadsheets for, 504–505
double-bar, 485
double-line, 486
of equations, 123
equations and tables and, 138–139
functions and sequences and, 114–157
interpreting, 127–128
line, 500
misleading, 490–491
Graphic Organizers, 15, 192, 555
Graphics
interpreting, 461
using, 514–515

Graphing
on a coordinate plane, 122–123
equations in slope-intercept form, 643
inequalities, 45
in two variables, 655–657
linear equations, 628–630
lines, 624–677
points, 126
solving systems of equations by, 666–667
transformations, 359
Graphing calculator, 89, 126, 179, 190, 306–307, 481, 489, 498–499, 504, 643, 712–713
adding and subtracting fractions, 89
computing compound interest, 306–307
creating box-and-whisker plots, 481
creating histograms, 489
creating a scatter plot, 498–499
evaluating powers and roots, 190
exploring cubic functions, 712–713
graphing equations in slope-intercept form, 643
graphing points, 126
multiplying and dividing numbers in scientific notation, 179
Great circle, 436, 838
Great Lakes, 31
Great Pyramid of Giza, 421
Greatest common factor (GCF), 824
Greatest possible error, 845
Gridded Response, 9, 21, 25, 38, 43, 67, 75, 84, 101, 137, 154–155, 165, 189, 199, 228, 233, 241, 287, 291, 301, 328, 351, 357, 398, 403, 424, 430, 435, 439, 475, 515, 526, 544, 549, 587, 591, 611, 637, 647, 654, 686, 707, 711, 717, 737, 750, 765
Write Gridded Responses, 154–155
Grids, 276, 537
Groundhogs, 318
Growth, exponential, 705
Guess and Test, 812
Guided Instruction
Guided Instruction appears in every lesson. Some examples: 7, 11, 15, 19, 23
Gulliver's Travels, 239

H

Half-life, 707
Hands-On Lab
Approximate Pi by Measuring, 399
Bisect Figures, 329
Combine Transformations, 362–363
Construct Nets, 406–407
Constructions, 334–335
Explore Dilations, 242–243
Explore the Effects of Changing Dimensions, 393
Explore Right Triangles, 195
Explore Sampling, 466
Explore Similarity, 236–237

Fibonacci Sequence, 692
Find Surface Area of Pyramids, 431
Find Surface Areas of Prisms and
    Cylinders, 425–426
Find Volumes of Prisms and Cylinders,
    412
Find Volumes of Pyramids and Cones,
    418–419
Make a Circle Graph, 484
Make a Scale Model, 256–257
Model Equations with Variables on Both
    Sides, 592
Model Polynomial Addition, 746
Model Polynomial Subtraction, 751
Model Polynomials, 738–739
Model Solving Equations, 32–33
Model Two-Step Equations, 96–97
Multiply Binomials, 760–761
Use Different Models for Simulations,
    536–537
Harmonics, 697
Hawaiian alphabet, 287
Health, 19, 79, 759
Health Link, 233, 707
Heart rate, target, 759
Height
    of parallelograms, 388–390
    slant, 432–433
    using indirect measurement to find,
        248–249
    using scales and scale drawings to find,
        440–441
Helpful Hint, 10, 11, 18, 34, 36, 76, 118,
    119, 122, 138, 174, 175, 229, 239, 245,
    253, 275, 285, 348, 354, 359, 364, 389,
    413, 440, 486, 495, 533, 584, 594, 604,
    608, 609, 638, 639, 640, 650, 655, 656,
    657, 682, 714, 762
Hemispheres, 436
Henry, Jodie, 74
Heptagons, 341
Hertz (Hz), 697
Hexagons, 341
Hill, A. V., 765
Histograms, 485, 500, 836
    creating, 489
History, 121
History Link, 121
Hobbies, 185, 219, 586, 710
Home Economics, 137
Home Economics Link, 137
Homework Help Online
*Homework Help Online is available for
every lesson. Refer to the go.hrw.com
box at the beginning of each exercise
set. Some examples: 8, 12, 16, 20, 24*
Horned lizards, 191
Hot air balloons, 703
Hot Tip!, 57, 59, 111, 155, 157, 209, 267,
    269, 317, 381, 383, 455, 515, 517, 577,
    621, 623, 675, 727, 729, 777
Hurricanes, 480
Hypotenuse, 196
Hz (Hertz), 697

Ice Hotel, 17
Ice House, 112
Identity Property of One, 829
Identity Property of Zero, 829
Images, 358
    anamorphic, 427
Impossible event, 522
Improper fractions, writing as mixed
    numbers, 825
Inclusion, 19, 23, 40, 82, 99, 135, 167, 217,
    279, 337, 428, 433, 446, 463, 473, 546,
    589, 634, 715, 748, 753, 757
Independent events, 545–547
    finding probability of, 545–546
Indirect measurement, 248–249
Inductive reasoning, 833
Industrial supplies, 21
Inequalities, 44
    algebraic, 44
    graphing, 45
    introduction to, 44–45
    linear, 655
    multi-step, 580–623
    solving, 45
        by multiplication or division, 600–601
    two-step, solving, 604–605
    in two variables, graphing, 655–657
Input, 134
Inscribed angle, of a circle, 838
Integer chips, 19
Integer exponents, looking for
    patterns in, 166–167
Integers, 14
    absolute value, 15
    addition of, 18–19
    division of, 26–27
    multiplication of, 26–27
    and order of operations, 27
    ordering, 14–15
    subtraction of, 22–23
Intercepts, using, 638–640
Interdisciplinary Link, 25, 88, 101, 131,
    169, 189, 233, 255, 291, 301, 328, 398,
    439, 530, 544, 642, 707, 765
Interest, 302
    compound, *see* Compound interest
    rate of, 302
    simple, 302–303
Interpreting
    graphics, 461
    graphs and tables, 127–128
Interquartile range (IQR), 479
Interstate highway system, 43
Intervention
    Common Error Alert, 15, 23, 35, 40, 45,
        65, 69, 77, 81, 99, 139, 143, 163, 171,
        175, 183, 192, 217, 225, 249, 279, 289,
        299, 303, 343, 447, 477, 547, 551, 565,
        585, 589, 594, 601, 605, 629, 634,
        657, 667, 683, 689, 757, 763, 769

    Scaffolding Questions, 49, 103, 147, 201,
        259, 309, 373, 445, 507, 569, 613,
        665, 719, 767
    Test Prep Doctor
    *Test Prep Doctor appears in lesson
    exercises. Some examples: 9, 13, 17,
    21, 25*
Inverse operations, 34, 80
Inverse variation, 714–715
Inverses, additive, 14
Investment time, 302
Ions, 38
Irrational numbers, 191
Isosceles triangles, 337
Iteration, 834
It's in the Bag
    Canister Carry-All, 105
    Clipboard Solutions for Graphs,
        Functions, and Sequences, 149
    Data Pop-Ups, 509
    Graphing Tri-Fold, 669
    It's a Wrap, 203
    Note-Taking Taking Shape, 51
    Origami Percents, 311
    Picture Envelopes, 615
    Polynomial Petals, 771
    Probability Post-Up, 571
    Project CD Geometry, 375
    Springboard to Sequences, 721
    The Tube Journal, 449
    A Worthwhile Wallet, 261

Jordan, Michael, 475
Journal
*Journal suggestions appear in lesson
exercises. Some examples: 9, 13, 17, 21, 25*
Journals, math, keeping, 323

Kasparov, Garry, 185
Keeping math journals, 323
Kente cloth, 373
Kilobyte, 173
Kinesthetic Experience, 11, 128, 187, 249,
    275, 325, 401, 421, 468, 551, 594, 651, 741
Kites, 341
Koch snowflake, 394, 834
Königsberg bridge problem, 130
Krill, 169

Lab Resources Online, 32, 89, 96, 126,
    179, 190, 195, 236, 242, 306, 329, 334,
    346, 362, 393, 399, 406, 412, 418, 425,
    431, 466, 471, 481, 484, 489, 498, 504,
    531, 536, 592, 643, 692, 712, 738, 746,
    751, 760

Language, *see* English Language Learners
Language Arts, 184, 287
Language Arts Link, 471
Laser surgery, 384
Lateral faces, 427
Lateral surface, 427
Lauren Rogers Museum of Art, 779
LCD (least common denominator), 68
LCM (least common multiple), 68, 824
Learning math vocabulary, 521
Least common denominator (LCD), 68
Least common multiple (LCM), 68
Lee, Harper, 297
Legoland, 443
Legs, 196
Length
    customary units of, 224–226, 837
    metric units of, 837
Lesson Quiz
A Lesson Quiz appears in every lesson.
Some examples: 9, 13, 17, 21, 25
Lessons, reading, for understanding, 117
LeWitt, Sol, 411
Life Science, 71, 165, 177, 227, 228, 252,
    253, 284, 288, 290, 294–295, 417, 433,
    535, 567, 647, 654, 691, 742
Life Science Link, 101, 165, 177, 417, 433,
    439, 497, 535, 544, 642, 654, 765
Lift, 398
Light bulb filament, 137
Light sticks, 281
Like denominators, adding and
    subtracting with, 72–73
Like terms, 584, 740
Lilliputians, 239
Lincoln, Abraham, 86
Line(s), 324
    of best fit, 494, 660–661
    boundary, 655
    graphing, 624–677
    parallel, 330–331, 830, 837
    perpendicular, 330–331
    points and planes and angles and,
      324–326
    skew, 830
    slope of a, 633–635
    of symmetry, 364
    symmetry, 364
    transversals to, 331, 837
Line graphs, 500
Line plots, 467, 500
Line segments, 324
Line symmetry, 364–365
Linear depreciation, 703
Linear equations, 628
    graphing, 628–630
Linear functions, 700–701
Linear inequalities, 655
Link
    Animals, 79
    Architecture, 255
    Art, 241, 371, 567, 743

    Business, 465, 750
    Career, 424
    Earth Science, 17, 29, 88, 131, 345,
      530, 647, 659
    Economics, 21, 301, 663
    Entertainment, 403, 611
    Games, 185, 549
    Health, 233, 707
    History, 121
    Home Economics, 137
    Language Arts, 471
    Life Science, 101, 165, 177, 289, 417,
      433, 439, 497, 535, 544, 642, 654,
      765
    Literature, 297
    Meteorology, 71
    Money, 305
    Music, 125, 697
    Photography, 247
    Physical Science, 281, 328, 333, 398,
      691, 705
    Recreation, 86, 703
    Science, 169, 189
    Social Studies, 25, 43, 291, 367, 735
    Sports, 47, 430, 503, 591
    Technology, 562
    Transportation, 632
Liquid mirror, 709
Literature, 297
Literature Link, 297
Logarithmic scale, 845–846
London Eye, 403
Long division, 821
Looking for patterns in integer
    exponents, 166–167
Loomis, E. S., 196
Louvre Pyramid, 239, 424
Luxor Hotel, 457, 637

M

Magic squares, 202
Make a Model, 811
Make an Organized List, 819
Make a Table, 815
Making
    circle graphs, 484
    decisions, 550–551
    predictions, 550–551
    scale models, 256–257
Manipulatives
    Algebra tiles, 32–33, 96–97, 588, 592,
      593, 692, 738–739, 746, 748, 751,
      753, 760–761
    Balance scale, 34, 651
    Centimeter cubes, 414, 441
    Coins, 19, 523, 527, 536–537, 545, 551,
      651, 740
    Counters, 163, 546
    Customary rulers, 242–243, 256–257,
      329, 355, 399, 406–407, 412, 421,
      433, 484
    Cutout figures, 86, 365, 585

    Decimal grids, 276, 537
    Deck of cards, 536, 541
    Grids, 276, 537
    Integer chips, 19
    Metric rulers, 236–237, 252
    Nets, 425–426, 428, 431, 433
    Number cubes, 236–237, 528, 536
    Pattern blocks, 362–363, 369
    Play money, 740
    Three-dimensional models, 418–419,
      425–426, 428, 431, 433, 440
Maryland, 676–677
Math, translating between words and,
    63
Math Background, 8, 12, 20, 24, 28, 37, 42,
    46, 66, 74, 78, 83, 87, 94, 100, 120, 124,
    130, 136, 164, 168, 172, 177, 184, 188,
    193, 218, 222, 227, 232, 240, 246, 254,
    276, 281, 286, 290, 296, 300, 304, 327,
    332, 339, 344, 350, 356, 360, 366, 370,
    391, 397, 402, 416, 423, 429, 434, 438,
    442, 464, 470, 474, 479, 487, 492, 496,
    525, 529, 534, 543, 548, 556, 561, 566,
    586, 590, 596, 606, 610, 631, 636, 641,
    646, 658, 662, 685, 690, 696, 702, 706,
    710, 716, 736, 742, 749, 754, 758, 764
Math expressions
    translating, into word phrases, 11
    translating word phrases into, 10
Math Fact, 22, 39, 44, 162, 278, 368, 584,
    700, 734
Math Humor, 10, 14, 18, 26, 34, 64, 68,
    72, 76, 80, 85, 92, 98, 118, 134, 138,
    166, 170, 182, 196, 216, 220, 229, 238,
    244, 248, 252, 274, 283, 288, 294, 298,
    302, 336, 408, 413, 432, 440, 462, 467,
    476, 532, 540, 545, 550, 588, 600, 604,
    608, 628, 633, 638, 644, 650, 655, 660,
    682, 687, 693, 700, 704, 708, 714, 740,
    747, 752, 762
Math journals, keeping, 323
Math vocabulary, learning, 521
Matrix (matrices), 839
Matrushka dolls, 84
McGwire, Mark, 480
Mean, 472
Measurement, 87
The development of measurement skills
and concepts is a central focus of this
course and is found throughout this book.
    angle, 832
    and approximating pi, 399
    customary system of, 224–226, 837,
      843
    indirect, 248–249
    metric system of, 831, 843
Measuring angles, 840
Measures of central tendency and
    range, 472–473
Median, 472
Medical, 645
Mercury (planet), 37
Metamorphoses, 371
Meteorology, 71

Meteorology Link, 71
Meter stick, 843
Metric rulers, 236–237, 252,
Metric system of measurement, 831
  converting between customary and, 841
  measuring in, 843
Metropolitan Opera House, 611
Midpoint, 329
Mirror, liquid, 709
Misleading graphs and statistics,
  490–491
Mississippi, 778–779
Mixed numbers, 825
Mode, 472
Modeling, 197, 253, 369, 414, 433, 486,
  639, 701, 763
  equations with variables on both sides,
    592
  polynomial addition, 746
  polynomial subtraction, 751
  polynomials, 738–739
  solving equations, 32–33
  two-step equations, 96–97
Models
  scale, see Scale models
  using different, for simulations,
    536–537
Mole (mol), 177
Mona Lisa, 241
Money, 40, 175, 305, 689
Money Link, 305
Monomials, 734
  division of polynomials by, 768–769
  multiplication of polynomials by,
    756–757
Monopoly, 540
Motivate
*Motivate appears in every lesson. Some
examples: 6, 10, 14, 18, 22*
Mount Etna, 647
Multi-Step, 42, 70, 87, 95, 120, 125, 188,
  223, 287, 296, 392, 395, 430, 691
Multi-Step Application, 395, 595, 763
Multi-step equations
  and inequalities, 580–623
  solving, 588–589
Multi-Step Test Prep, 49, 103, 147, 201,
  259, 309, 373, 445, 507, 569, 613, 665,
  719, 767
Multiple, 822
  least common (LCM), 824
Multiple Choice
*Multiple Choice test items are found in
every lesson. Some examples: 9, 13, 17,
21, 25*
  Answering Context-Based Test Items,
    620–621
  Eliminate Answer Choices, 56–57
  Work Backward, 726–727
Multiple Representations, 65, 77, 143,
  167, 245, 289, 389, 409, 486, 605, 634,
  645, 701
Multiple representations, using, 681

Multiplication
  of binomials, 760–761, 762–763
  of decimals, 77, 92, 826
    by powers of ten, 826
  of integers, 26–27
  of numbers in scientific notation, 179
  of polynomials, by monomials, 756–757
  of powers, 170
  of rational numbers, 76–77
  solving equations by, 39–41
  solving inequalities by, 600–601
Multiplication Property of Equality, 40
Multiplication Property of Zero, 829
Muscle contractions, 765
Music, 125, 415, 715
Music Link, 125, 697
Mutually exclusive events, 542

n–gons, 341
Nanoguitar, 166
Negative correlation, 495
Negative exponents, 166
Negative slope, 633
Neptune, 177
Nets, 425–426, 428, 431, 433
  constructing, 406–407
Networks, 840
Neutrons, 177
Nevada, 456–457
Nevada State Capitol, 456
Newborns, 274
New Jersey, 112–113
Newtons (N), 36
Niagara Falls, 88
Nickels, 275
Nielsen Television Ratings, 283
No correlation, 495
Notation
  function, 700
  scientific, 174–176, 179
Note Taking Strategies, see Reading and
  Writing Math
Notes, taking effective, 161
*n*th term, finding
  of an arithmetic sequence, 683–684
  of a geometric sequence, 688
Number cubes, 236–237, 528, 536
Number line, 18
Number Sense, 77, 81, 279, 629
Numbers
  compatible, 278, 825
  composite, 823
  division of, in scientific notation, 179
  finding, when percents are known,
    288–289
  irrational, 191
  mixed, 825
  multiplication of, in scientific notation,
    179
  prime, 508, 823

  random, 531–532
  rational, see Rational numbers
  real, 191–192
  relatively prime, 64
  triangular, 693
Numerator, 64
Nutrient requirements, 60
Nutrition, 94

Obtuse angles, 325
Obtuse triangles, 336
Ocean trenches, 29
Octagons, 341
Odds, 554–555
  against, 554
  converting, to probabilities, 554–555
  converting probabilities to, 555
  in favor, 554
Ohio, 210–211
Ohio & Erie Canal, 210
Ohm's Law, 716
Old Faithful, 131
One-Minute Section Planner, 6A, 32A,
  64A, 92A, 118A, 134A, 162A, 182A,
  216A, 236A, 274A, 294A, 324A, 354A,
  388A, 406A, 462A, 484A, 522A, 540A,
  584A, 600A, 628A, 650A, 682A, 700A,
  734A, 746A
Online Resources
  Chapter Project Online, 2, 60, 114, 158,
    212, 270, 320, 384, 458, 518, 580,
    624, 678, 730
  Game Time Extra, 50, 104, 148, 202,
    260, 310, 374, 448, 508, 570, 614,
    668, 720, 770
  Homework Help Online
  *Homework Help Online is available for
  every lesson. Refer to the go.hrw.com
  box at the beginning of each exercise
  set. Some examples: 8, 12, 16, 20, 24*
  Lab Resources Online, 32, 89, 96, 126,
    179, 190, 195, 236, 242, 306, 329,
    334, 346, 362, 393, 399, 406, 412,
    418, 425, 431, 466, 471, 481, 484, 489,
    498, 504, 531, 536, 592, 643, 692,
    712, 738, 746, 751, 760
  Parent Resources Online
  *Parent Resources Online is available
  for every lesson. Refer to the
  go.hrw.com box at the beginning of
  each exercise set. Some examples:
  8, 12, 16, 20, 24*
  Project Teacher Support, 2, 60, 114, 158,
    212, 270, 320, 384, 458, 518, 580,
    624, 678, 730
  State Test Practice Online, 58, 110, 156,
    208, 268, 316, 382, 454, 516, 576,
    622, 674, 728, 776
  Web Extra!, 25, 101, 131, 185, 233, 255,
    291, 333, 371, 398, 424, 497, 530, 611,
    647, 663, 697, 703, 743, 750
Open circle, 45

Operations
    inverse, 34, 80
    order of, 6, 828
Opposites, 14
Order of operations, 6, 828
Ordered pairs, 118–119
Ordering
    measurements, customary and metric,
      224, 841
    rational numbers, 68–69
Organizing data, 467–468
Origami, 311
Origin, 122
Orthogonal views, 408
Outcomes, 522
    equally likely, 540
Outlier, 472
Output, 134

P

Pacing guide, 2A, 60A, 114A, 158A, 212A,
    270A, 320A, 384A, 458A, 518A, 580A,
    624A, 678A, 730A
*A guide for pacing appears in every lesson
and lab. Some examples: 6, 10, 14, 18, 32*
Pairs, ordered, 118–119
Pandas, 6
Parabola, 708
Parallel lines, 330–331, 837
    properties of transversals to, 331, 837
    and skew lines, 830
Parallelograms, 342
    area of, 388–390
    perimeter of, 388–390
Parent Resources Online
*Parent Resources Online are available
for every lesson. Refer to the
go.hrw.com box at the beginning of
each exercise set. Some examples: 8, 12,
16, 20, 24*
Parentheses, 6, 828
Pattern blocks, 362–363, 369
Patterns, 168, 277, 286
    in integer exponents, looking for,
      166–167
    and iterations, 834
Pediment, 405
Pei, I. M., 420, 424
PEMDAS mnemonic, 6
Pennsylvania, 318–319
Pentagons, 341
Percent(s), 270–319
    applications of, 298–299
    defined, 274
    estimating with, 278–280
    finding, 283–285
      using an equation, 284
      using a proportion, 283
    greater than one hundred, 823
    known, finding numbers for, 288–289
    less than one, 823

    relating, to decimals and fractions,
      274–275
Percent change, 294
Percent decrease, 294–295
Percent increase, 294–295
Perfect squares, 182
Perimeter, 186, 388
    area and volume and, 384–457
    of parallelograms, 388–390
    of rectangles, 388–390
    of trapezoids, 394–396
    of triangles, 394–396
Periscopes, 333
Permutations, 563–564
Perpendicular lines, 330–331
Perspective, 330–331
pH, 845
Philadelphia Mural Arts Program, 319
Phone numbers, 558
Photography, 247
Photography Link, 247
Physical Science, 7, 38, 177, 226, 231, 232,
    241, 275, 281, 288, 333, 401, 591, 597,
    630, 631, 635, 652, 691, 701, 706, 711, 717
Physical Science Link, 281, 328, 333, 398,
    691, 705
Physics, 735
Pi (π), 194, 400
    approximating, by measuring, 399
Piersol, Aaron, 72
Pitch, 697
Pixels, 183
Place value, 820
Planes, 324
    points and lines and angles and, 324–326
Play money, 740
Playground equipment, 320
Plimpton 322, 196
Pluto, 177
Point symmetry, *see* Rotational symmetry
Point-slope form, 644–645
Points, 324
    graphing, 126
    lines and planes and angles and,
      324–326
Polygon(s), 341, 569
    classifying, 341–343
    exterior angles of, 346
    frequency, 836
    regular, 342
    similar, 238
Polynomials, 730–779
    addition of, 747–748
      modeling, 746
    defined, 734–735
    degrees of, 735
    division of, by monomials, 768–769
    modeling, 738–739
    multiplication of, by monomials,
      756–757
    simplifying, 740–741
    subtraction of, 752–753
      modeling, 751

Ponce de León, 121
Population, 462
Positive correlation, 495
Positive slope, 633
Power(s), 162
    division of, 170
    evaluating, 190
    multiplication of, 170
    raising powers to, 171
    zero, 167
Power Presentations with PowerPoint
*These appear in every lesson. Some
examples: 6, 7, 8, 10, 11*
Practice
*Reduced Practice pages appear in every
lesson. Some examples: 8, 12, 16, 20, 24*
Precision, 844–845
Predictions, making, 550–551
Price, unit, 221
Prime factorization, 824
Prime numbers, 508, 823
Principal, 302
Principal square root, 182
Prisms, 413
    lateral faces, 427
    rectangular, 413
    surface area of, 427–428
    triangular, 413
      finding, 425–426
    volume of, 413–415
      exploring, 412
Probability, 518–579
    converting, to odds, 555
    converting odds to, 554–555
    defined, 522–524
    of dependent events, finding, 546–547
    experimental, 527–528
    of independent events, finding,
      545–546
    theoretical, 540–542
Problem of the Day
*Problem of the Day appears in every
lesson. Some examples: 6, 10, 14, 18, 22*
Problem Solving
*Problem solving is a central focus of this
course and is found throughout this book.
Reduced Problem Solving pages appear in
every lesson. Some examples: 9, 13, 17,
21, 25*
Problem Solving Application, 36, 82,
    98–99, 186–187, 225, 249, 279, 501,
    524, 532–533, 601, 757
Problem Solving Handbook, 810–819, *see
also* Problem Solving Strategies
Problem Solving on Location
    Maryland, 676–677
    Mississippi, 778–779
    Nevada, 456–457
    New Jersey, 112–113
    Ohio, 210–211
    Pennsylvania, 318–319
    South Carolina, 578–579
Problem Solving Skill
    analyze units, 224–226

Index

estimate with compatible numbers, 278–280
look for patterns, 166–167
Problem Solving Strategies, 532–533
Act It Out, 818
Draw a Diagram, 810
Find a Pattern, 814
Guess and Test, 812
Make a Model, 811
Make an Organized List, 819
Make a Table, 815
Solve a Simpler Problem, 816
Use Logical Reasoning, 817
Work Backward, 813
Problems, reading, for understanding, 273
Production costs, 730
Projects, 2, 60, 114, 158, 212, 270, 320, 384, 458, 518, 580, 624, 678, 730
Proofs, informal geometry, 833
Properties
Associative, 74, 747, 829
Closure, 829
Commutative, 74, 78, 589, 829
Distributive, 586, 741, 742, 757, 762, 763, 829
Division, of Equality, 39, 40
Identity
of Zero, for addition, 829
of One, for multiplication, 829
Subtraction, of Equality, 35, 37
Transitive, 829
Zero Product, 710
Proportionality, constant of, 650
Proportions, 216
and indirect measurement, 248
and percent, 283
ratios and, 216–217
ratios and similarity and, 212–269
solving, 229–231
using, to find scales, 252
Protons, 177
Protractors, 330
Punnett squares, 544
Punxsutawney Phil, 318
Pupils of eyes, 244
Pyramid of the Sun, 424
Pyramids, 420
regular, 432
surface area of, 432–433
exploring, 431
volume of, 420–422
exploring, 418–419
Pythagoras, 196
Pythagorean Theorem, 195, 196–197, 198, 448
and area, 395
converse of the, 196, 198, 199
Pythagorean triples, 199, 448

Quadrants, 122
Quadratic functions, 708–709

Quadrilaterals, 341
classifying, 348
Quartiles, 476
Quilts, 182
Quotients, estimating, 825

Radical symbol, 182
Radius, 400
Raising powers to powers, 171
Random numbers, 532
generating, 531
Random samples, 462
Range, 134, 472
measures of, 472–473
Rate of interest, 302
Rates, 220
commission, 298
ratios and unit rates and, 220–221
unit, *see* Unit rates
Rational numbers, 60–113, 191
addition of, 72–73
comparing, 68–69
defined, 64
Density Property of, 192
division of, 80–82
multiplication of, 76–77
ordering, 68–69
solving equations with, 92–93
subtraction of, 72–73
Ratios, 216
common, 687
equivalent, 216
proportions and, 216–217
proportions and similarity and, 212–269
rates and unit rates and, 220–221
Rays, 324
Reaching All Learners
Through Auditory Cues, 331
Through Cognitive Strategies, 81, 342, 428, 523, 656, 705
Through Concrete Manipulatives, 19, 40, 69, 86, 163, 355, 359, 365, 437, 441, 463, 528, 585, 694, 748, 753
Through Cooperative Learning, 7, 35, 45, 93, 99, 139, 183, 217, 303, 348, 501, 541, 589, 661, 757
Through Critical Thinking, 23, 27, 73, 123, 135, 171, 239, 289, 299, 337, 395, 491, 533, 546, 559, 564, 605, 609, 629, 683, 688, 735, 763
Through Curriculum Integration, 225, 284, 477, 495
Through Diversity, 230, 295, 342,
Through Graphic Organizers, 15, 192, 555
Through Home Connection, 175, 221, 473
Through Inclusion, 715
Through Kinesthetic Experience, 11, 128, 187, 249, 275, 325, 401, 421, 468, 551, 594, 651, 741
Through Modeling, 197, 253, 369, 414, 433, 639, 701, 763

Through Multiple Representations, 65, 77, 143, 167, 245, 389, 409, 486, 605, 634, 645
Through Number Sense, 279
Through Visual Cues, 119, 709, 601
Reading and Writing Math, 5, 63, 117, 161, 215, 273, 323, 387, 461, 521, 583, 627, 681, 733
Reading Math, 7, 162, 171, 216, 238, 252, 274, 275, 284, 325, 358, 395, 563, 628, 700
Reading problems for understanding, 273
Reading Strategies, *see also* Reading and Writing Math
Interpret Graphics, 461
Learn Math Vocabulary, 521
Read a Lesson for Understanding, 117
Read Problems for Understanding, 273
Use Your Book for Success, 5
Ready to Go On?, 39, 48, 90, 102, 132, 146, 180, 200, 234, 258, 292, 308, 352, 372, 404, 444, 482, 506, 538, 568, 598, 612, 648, 664, 698, 718, 744, 766
Real numbers, 191–192
properties of, 829
Reasoning, inductive and deductive, 833
Reciprocals, 80
Recreation, 42, 77, 86, 284, 443, 465, 686, 703
Recreation Link, 86, 703
Rectangles, 342
area of, 388–390
perimeter of, 388–390
Rectangular prism, 413
Rectangular pyramid, 420
Recycling, 217
Reduction, 253
Reflection symmetry, 446
Reflections, 358
Refraction, 328
Regular polygons, 342
Regular pyramids, 432
Regular tessellations, 368
Relating decimals, fractions, and percents, 274–275
Relative cumulative frequency, 835
Relative frequency, 835
Relatively prime numbers, 64
Remember!, 6, 14, 44, 64, 68, 73, 92, 167, 183, 224, 347, 349, 400, 585, 589, 600, 633, 660, 768
Repeating decimals, 65, 827
Representations of data, *see also* Displaying and organizing data
choosing best, 500–501
multiple, using, 681
Reptiles,(M.C. Escher) 371
Reptiles, 654
Reteach
Reduced Reteach pages appear in every lesson. Some examples: 8, 12, 16, 20, 24
Reticulated python, 289

Index

Rhode Island, 282
Rhombuses, 342
Richter scale, 846
Right angles, 325
Right cones, 432
Right triangles, 336
  exploring, 195
  finding angles in, 336
  finding lengths of legs in, 195, 395
Rise, 347, 633
Rock and Roll Hall of Fame, 420
Roddick, Andy, 226
Roots
  cube, 830
  evaluating, 190
  exponents and, 158–211
  square, 182–187
Rotation, 358
  center of, 358
Rotational symmetry, 365, 446
Rounding
  decimals, 820
  whole numbers, 820
Run, 347, 633
Ruth, Babe, 480

Safety, 528, 637
Sales tax, 298
Sample(s), 462
  biased, 463
  convenience, 462
  random, 462
  stratified, 462
  surveys and, 462–463
  systematic, 462
  voluntary-response, 462
Sample space, 522
Sampling, exploring, 466
Scaffolding Questions, 49, 103, 147, 201, 259, 309, 373, 445, 507, 569, 613, 665, 719, 767
Scale, 252
  logarithmic, 845
Scale drawings, 252
Scale factors, 239
Scale models, 253, 259
  making, 256–257
Scalene triangles, 337
Scaling three-dimensional figures, 440–441
Scatter plots, 494–495, 500
  creating, 498–499
School, 475, 549, 553, 605
Science Link, 169, 189
Scientific notation, 174–176
  division of numbers in, 179
  multiplication of numbers in, 179
Scrabble, 549
Secant, of a circle, 838
Second differences, 693

Section Overview, 6B, 32B, 64B, 92B, 118B, 134B, 162B, 182B, 216B, 236B, 274B, 294B, 324B, 354B, 388B, 406B, 462B, 484B, 522B, 540B, 584B, 600B, 628B, 650B, 682B, 700B, 734B, 746B
Sections, 445
Segments, line, 324
Selected Answers, 847–xxx
Self-similar patterns, 834,
Semiregular tessellations, 370
Sequences, 142
  arithmetic, *see* Arithmetic sequences
  Fibonacci, 692, 695
  functions and, 678–729
  geometric, *see* Geometric sequences
  graphs and functions and, 114–157
  other, 693–695
Shakespeare, William, 471
Short Response, 13, 29, 47, 95, 131, 145, 173, 178, 185, 219, 247, 251, 255, 266–267, 340, 345, 361, 371, 392, 411, 465, 471, 488, 493, 497, 503, 514, 515, 530, 553, 567, 607, 632, 659, 663, 691, 697, 743, 759
  Write Short Responses, 266–267
Sieve of Eratosthenes, 508
Significant digits, 844
Silos, 416
Similar figures, 236–239
  and dilations, 244–245
  and indirect measurement, 248–249
  and scale drawings and models, 252–253
Similar polygons, 238
Similarity
  exploring, 236–237
  ratios and proportions and, 212–269
Simple interest, 302–303
Simplify, 585
Simplifying
  numerical expressions using a calculator, 828
  algebraic expressions, 584–585
  polynomials, 740–741
Simulations, 532
  using, 532–533
  using different models for, 536–537
Skew lines, 830
Slant height, 432
Slide, *see* Translation
Slope, 347, 633
  of a line, 633–635
  using, 638–640
Slope-intercept form, 639
  graphing equations in, 643
Snakes, 101
Snowboard half-pipe, 430
Social Studies, 37, 69, 84, 178, 282, 286, 340, 367, 392, 417, 421, 435, 602, 657
Social Studies Link, 25, 43, 367, 735
Solid circle, 45
Solid figures, *see* Three-dimensional figures
Solution set, 44
Solutions of systems of equations, 608

Solve a Simpler Problem, 816
Solving
  equations, *see* Solving equations
  inequalities, *see* Solving inequalities
  multi-step equations, 588–589
  proportions, 229–231
  systems of equations by graphing, 666–667
  two-step equations, 98–99
  two-step inequalities, 604–605
  for a variable, 821
Solving equations
  by addition, 34–36
  using addition and subtraction properties, 34–36
  with decimals, 92, 98
  by division, 39–41
  linear, 628–630
  modeling, 32–33
  multi-step, 588–589, 592–595
  by multiplication, 39–41
  with rational numbers, 92–93
  by subtraction, 34–36
  systems of, 608–609
  two-step, 98–99
  with variables on both sides, 593–595
Solving inequalities, 45, 600–601, 604–605
  by multiplication or division, 600–601
South Carolina, 578–579
South Carolina Hall of Fame, 579
Special Olympics World Summer Games, 503
Special products, 763
Spheres, 436–437
  surface area of, 437
  volume of, 436
Spiral Review
  Spiral Review questions are found in every lesson. Some examples: 9, 13, 17, 21, 25
Sports, 14, 27, 47, 66, 70, 72, 74, 137, 145, 184, 227, 281, 403, 430, 503, 567, 587, 591, 607, 661, 690, 710
Sports Link, 47, 430, 503, 591
Sports utility vehicles (SUV's), 527
Spreadsheets
  generating random numbers, 531
  using, to construct graphs, 504–505
Square(s), 342
  magic, 202
  perfect, 182
  square roots and, 182–183
Square roots
  estimating, 186–187
  principal, 182
  squares and, 182–183
Square units, 413
Standard Form of an Equation, 638
Standardized Test Prep, 58–59, 110–111, 156–157, 208–209, 268–269, 316–317, 382–383, 454–455, 516–517, 576–577, 622–623, 674–675, 728–729, 776–777, *see also Assessment*

Index

Standardized Test Strategies, see Standardized Test Prep

State Test Practice Online, 58, 110, 156, 208, 268, 316, 382, 454, 516, 576, 622, 674, 728, 776

Statisticians, 270

Statistics, misleading, 490–491

Steen, Lynn Arthur, 685

Stem-and-leaf plot, 467
    back-to-back, 468

Step Pyramid of King Zoser, 435

Stratified samples, 462

Strong correlation, 495

Study Guide: Preview, 4, 62, 116, 160, 214, 272, 322, 386, 460, 520, 582, 626, 680, 732, see also Assessment

Study Guide: Review, 52–54, 106–108, 150–152, 204–206, 262–264, 312–314, 376–378, 450–452, 510–512, 572–574, 616–618, 670–672, 722–724, 772–774, see also Assessment

Study Strategies, see also Reading and Writing Math
    Concept Map, 387
    Study for a Cumulative Test, 733
    Take Effective Notes, 161
    Use Multiple Representations, 681

Subscripts, 395

Substitute, 6

Subtraction
    of fractions, 89
        with unlike denominators, 85–86
    of integers, 22–23
    of polynomials, 752–753
        modeling, 751
    of rational numbers, 72–73
    solving equations by, 34–36

Subtraction Property of Equality, 35, 37

Summarize
Summarize appears in every lesson. Some examples: 7, 11, 15, 19, 23

Super Ball, 691

Supplementary angles, 325

Surface, lateral, 427

Surface area, 427
    of cones, 432–433
    of cylinders, 427–428
        exploring, 425–426
    of prisms, 427–428
        exploring, 425–426
    of pyramids, 432–433
        exploring, 431
    of spheres, 437

Surveys, samples and, 462–463

SUV's (sports utility vehicles), 527

Swift, Jonathan, 239

Symmetry, 364–365
    bilateral, 446
    line, 364
    line of, 364
    reflection, 446
    rotational, 365, 446
    in three dimensions, 446

Systematic samples, 462

Systems of equations, 608–609
    solutions of, 608
    solving, by graphing, 666–667

Systolic blood pressure, 233

Tables
    equations and graphs and, 138–139
    frequency, 485, 835
    interpreting, 127–128

Taiwan, 178

Taking effective notes, 161

Target heart rate, 759

Tax, sales, 298

Tax brackets, 301

Teacher to Teacher, 32, 96, 126, 190, 195, 237, 362, 419, 484, 531, 592, 692, 738

Teaching Tip
    Cognitive Strategies, 45, 163, 221, 555
    Communicating Math, 27, 325, 355, 661
    Critical Thinking, 167, 421
    Inclusion, 19, 23, 40, 82, 99, 135, 167, 217, 279, 337, 428, 433, 446, 463, 473, 546, 589, 634, 748, 753, 757
    Math Connection, 769
    Modeling, 486
    Multiple Representations, 289, 701
    Number Sense, 77, 81, 629
    Reading Math, 7, 275, 284
    Visual, 15, 239, 249, 409, 447, 585, 666

Technetium-99m, 705

Technology, 562
    Geometry software, 346
    Graphing calculators, 89, 126, 179, 190, 306–307, 481, 489, 498–499, 504, 643, 712–713
    Spreadsheet software, 504–505, 531

Technology Lab
    Add and Subtract Fractions, 89
    Compute Compound Interest, 306–307
    Create Box-and-Whisker Plots, 481
    Create Histograms, 489
    Create a Scatter Plot, 498–499
    Evaluate Powers and Roots, 190
    Explore Cubic Functions, 712–713
    Exterior Angles of a Polygon, 346
    Generate Random Numbers, 531
    Graph Equations in Slope-Intercept Form, 643
    Graph Points, 126
    Multiply and Divide Numbers in Scientific Notation, 179
    Use a Spreadsheet to Construct Graphs, 504–505

Technology Link, 562

Television Ratings, Nielsen, 283

Temperature,
    conversions, 842
    global, 71
    scales, 103

Terabyte, 173

Term number, 683

Terminating decimals, 65, 827

Terms, 142, 584
    of arithmetic sequences, 682–684
        finding nth, 683–684
    of geometric sequences, 687–689
        finding nth, 688
    like, 584

Tessellations, 368–369
    regular, 368
    semiregular, 370

Test, cumulative, studying for a, 733

Test items, context–based, answering, 620–621

Test Prep
Test Prep questions are found in every lesson. Some examples: 9, 13, 17, 21, 25

Test Prep Doctor,
Test Prep Doctor appears in lesson exercises. Some examples: 9, 13, 17, 21, 25

Test Tackler, see also Assessment
    All Types: Using a Graphic, 514–515
    Extended Response: Write Extended Responses, 380–381
    Gridded Response: Write Gridded Responses, 154–155
    Multiple Choice
        Answering Context–Based Test Items, 620–621
        Eliminate Answer Choices, 56–57
        Work Backward, 726–727
    Short Response: Write Short Responses, 266–267

Test Taking Strategy, see Test Tackler

Test Taking Tips, see Hot Tip!

Tetris, 411

Think and Discuss
Think and Discuss is found in every lesson. Some examples: 7, 11, 15, 19, 23

Theoretical probability, 540–542

Three-dimensional figures
    drawing, 408–409
    scaling, 440–441
    surface area of, 425, 431–433, 437
    volume of, 412–415, 418–422, 436

Three-dimensional models, 418–419, 425–426, 428, 431, 433, 440

Three dimensions, symmetry in, 446

Tides, 28

Time, investment, 302

Timeline, 25

Tips, 278

To Kill a Mockingbird, 297

Torus, 448

Toxic gases, 2

Toys, 750

Train à Grande Vitesse, 632

Transamerica Pyramid, 423, 447

Transformations, 358–359
    combining, 362–363
    graphing, 359

Translating
    math expressions into word phrases, 11
    word phrases into mathexpressions, 10
    between words and math, 63

Translations, 358

Transpose, of a matrix, 839
Transportation, 227, 228, 632, 737
Transportation Link, 632
Transversals, 330
  to parallel lines, properties of, 331
Trapezoids, 342
  area of, 394–396
  perimeter of, 394–396
Travel, 140, 143, 589
Tree diagrams, 559
Trenches, ocean, 29
Trial, 522
Triangle Sum Theorem, 327, 336, 339
Triangles, 341
  acute, 336
  angles in, 336–338
  area of, 394–396
  congruent, 354
  equilateral, 337
  isosceles, 337
  obtuse, 336
  perimeter of, 394–396
  right, *see* Right triangles
  scalene, 337
Triangular numbers, 693
Triangular prism, 413
Triangular pyramid, 420
Trinomials, 734
Trump Tower, 256
Tsunamis, 189
Turns, *see* Rotations
Twins, 354
Two-step equations
  modeling, 96–97
  solving, 98–99
Two-step inequalities, solving, 604–605
Tyrannosaurus rex, 254

Umbra, 435
Unbiased sample, 463
Undefined slope, 633
Understanding
  reading lessons for, 117
  reading problems for, 273
Unit(s)
  choosing appropriate, 831
  conversion factors, 841
  customary, 831
  metric, 831
Unit analysis, 224
Unit fractions, 104
Unit price, 221
Unit rates, 220
  ratios and rates and, 220–221
United States census, 291, 464
Unlike denominators
  addition of fractions with, 85–86
  subtraction of fractions with, 85–86
Use Logical Reasoning, 817
Using
  different models for simulations, 536–537

graphics, 514–515
intercepts, 638–640
multiple representations, 681
simulations, 532–533
slopes, 638–640
spreadsheets to construct graphs, 504–505
your book for success, 5
your own words, 627

Value, absolute, 15
Variability, 476–478
Variable(s)
  on both sides
    modeling equations with, 592
    solving equations with, 593–595
  expressions and, 6–7
  solving for, 821
  two, graphing inequalities in, 655–657
Variation
  direct, 650–652
  inverse, 714–715
Venn diagrams, 468
Vertex
  of an angle, 325
  of a three-dimensional figure, 408
  of a network, 840
Vertical angles, 325
Vertical line test, 135
Views, orthogonal, 408
Viruses, computer, 704
Visual Cues, 15, 119, 239, 249, 409, 447, 585, 601, 666, 709
Vocabulary, math, learning, 521
Vocabulary Connections, 4, 62, 116, 160, 214, 272, 322, 386, 460, 520, 582, 626, 680, 732
Volcanoes, 647
Volume
  of cones, 420–422
    exploring, 418–419
  of cylinders, 413–415
    exploring, 412
  perimeter and area and, 384–457
  of prisms, 413–415
    exploring, 412
  of pyramids, 420–422
    exploring, 418–419
  of spheres, 436
Voluntary-response samples, 462

Warm Up
Warm Up appears in every lesson. Some examples: 6, 10, 14, 18, 22
Water discharge, 580
Weak correlation, 495
Weather balloons, 659
Web Extra!, 25, 101, 131, 185, 233, 255, 291, 333, 371, 398, 424, 497, 530, 611, 647, 663, 697, 703, 743, 750

Whales, 169
What's the Error?, 13, 21, 38, 67, 71, 79, 95, 121, 145, 173, 185, 189, 194, 219, 223, 228, 277, 333, 345, 350, 403, 417, 424, 480, 493, 526, 535, 553, 557, 587, 591, 603, 637, 691, 737
What's the Question?, 136, 305, 351, 392, 567, 632, 703, 759
Whole numbers
  long division, 821
  rounding, 821
Whooping cranes, 624
Word phrases
  translating, into math expressions, 10
  translating math expressions into, 11
Words
  and math, translating between, 63
  using your own, 627
Work Backward, 726–727, 813
Write About It
Write About It exercises are found in every lesson. Some examples: 9, 13, 17, 21, 25
Write a Problem, 47, 75, 125, 141, 178, 199, 241, 251, 282, 357, 361, 367, 435, 475, 488, 503, 549, 553, 607, 647, 654, 686, 717, 750
Writing
  convincing arguments, 215
  extended responses, 380–381
  gridded responses, 154–155
  to justify, 583
  short responses, 266–267
Writing Math, 65, 331, 683
Writing Strategies, *see also* Reading and Writing Math
  Keep a Math Journal, 323
  Translate Between Words and Math, 63
  Use Your Own Words, 627
  Write a Convincing Argument, 215
  Write to Justify, 583

x-axis, 122
x-coordinate, 122
x-intercept, 638

y-axis, 122
y-coordinate, 122
y-intercept, 638
Yosemite National Park, 86

Zero power, 167
Zero Product Property, 710
Zero slope, 633

Credits

■ Staff Credits

Bruce Albrecht, Nancy Behrens, Justin Collins, Lorraine Cooper, Marc Cooper, Jennifer Craycraft, Martize Cross, Nina Degollado, Lydia Doty, Sam Dudgeon, Kelli R. Flanagan, Mary Fraser, Stephanie Friedman, Jeff Galvez, José Garza, Diannia Green, Jennifer Gribble, Liz Huckestein, Jevara Jackson, Kadonna Knape, Cathy Kuhles, Jill M. Lawson, Peter Leighton, Christine MacInnis, Rosalyn K. Mack, Jonathan Martindill, Virginia Messler, Susan Mussey, Kim Nguyen, Matthew Osment, Chris Rankin, Manda Reid, Patrick Ricci, Michael Rinella, Michelle Rumpf-Dike, Beth Sample, Annette Saunders, John Saxe, Kay Selke, Robyn Setzen, Patricia Sinnott, Victoria Smith, Jeannie Taylor, Ken Whiteside, Sherri Whitmarsh, Aimee F. Wiley, Alison Wohlman

■ Photo Credits

Student Handbook TOC: (standing boy), Sam Dudgeon/HRW; (sitting girl), John Langford.

Chapter 1: 2–3 (bkgd), Peter Skinner/Photo Researchers, Inc.; 2 (br), Tom Tracy/Getty Images/FPG International; 6 (tr), Keren Su/Animals Animals; 9 (tr), The Kobal Collection; 10 (t), Robert Landau/CORBIS; 14 (t), Don Couch/HRW; 17 (t), © Layne Kennedy/CORBIS; 18 (t), Victoria Smith/HRW; 21 (t), Peter Van Steen; 22 (t), Chad Ehlers/PictureQuest; 25 (coin), Araldo de Luca/CORBIS; 25 (pyramid), Steve Vidler/SuperStock; 25 (painting), The Art Archive/Napoleonic Museum Rome/Dagli Orti; 25 (Cleopatra), Bettmann/CORBIS; 26 (t), Dennis MacDonald/ PhotoEdit Inc.; 29 (tl), Peter David/Getty Images; 36 (tr), Sam Dudgeon/HRW; 39 (tr), Joseph de Sciose; 47 (l), Fotopress, Ross Setford/AP Photo; 49 (tl), iStock Photo; 49 (b), HRW; 50 (br), Randall Hyman; 51 (4), Sam Dudgeon/HRW. **Chapter 2:** 60-61 (bkgd), Kevin R. Morris/CORBIS; 60 (br), Sam Dudgeon/HRW; 60 (food pyramid), Courtesy Food & Drug Administration; 64, Ann Heisenfelt/AP Photo; 68 (t), Getty Images; 71 (tl), NASA; 72 (tr), © Lucy Nicholson/Reuters/CORBIS; 76 (t), Sam Dudgeon/ HRW; 79 (tl), John Giustina/Bruce Coleman, Inc.; 84 (tr), Mark Tomalty/Masterfile; 85 (tr), Jimmy Chin/National Geographic Image Collection; 86 (l), Library of Congress; 88 (tr), © Lester Lefkowitz/CORBIS; 088 (cr); 91 (b), Dean Conger/CORBIS; 98 (t), Eric Gaillard/Reuters/CORBIS; 101 (tr), AFP/CORBIS; 101 (cr), Karl H. Switak/Photo Researchers, Inc.; 103 (b), AP Photo; 104 (br), Jenny Thomas/HRW; 105 (br), Sam Dudgeon/HRW; 112 (hockey), Courtesy Ice House, Hackensack, NJ; 112 (br), Photodisc/Getty Images; 113 (all), Photos courtesy of the Atlantic City Convention & Visitors Authority. **Chapter 3:** 114–115 (bkgd), © Brooks/Brown/Photo Researchers, Inc.; 114 (b), © Jose Luis Pelaez, Inc./CORBIS; 118 (t), Sam Dudgeon/ HRW; 121 (tl), Bettmann/CORBIS; 125 (r), Laurence Fleury/Photo Researchers, Inc.; 127 (t), David Townsend Images; 131 (t), Alec Pytlowany/Masterfile; 133 (b), Sam Dudgeon/HRW; 137 (l), Schenectady Museum; Hall of Electrical History Foundation/CORBIS; 138 (t), U.S. Navy Photo; 147 (all), Sam Dudgeon/HRW; 148 (b), Victoria Smith/HRW; 149 (b), HRW. **Chapter 4:** 158–159 (bkgd), Science Photo Library/Photo Researchers, Inc.; 158 (b), Dean Conger/CORBIS; 165 (l), S. Lowry/Univ. Ulster/Getty Images/Stone; 166 (t), Lidija Sekaric/Harold G. Craighead, CCMR/CNF, Cornell University; 169 (t), Francois Gohier/Photo Researchers, Inc.; 169 (c), Flip Nicklin/Minden Pictures; 173 (c), PEANUTS © Universal Press Syndicate; 174 (t), Victoria Smith/HRW; 175 (t), Peter Van Steen/HRW; 178 (bl), Joe McDonald/CORBIS; 182 (t), © Victoria & Albert Museum, London/Art Resource; 183 (t), © Roberto Rivera; 185 (l), Uimonen Ilkka/CORBIS/SYGMA; 185, Peter Van Steen/HRW; 186 (t), Sam Dudgeon/HRW; stained glass artist: Leanne Ohlenburg; 189 (t), Chris Butler/Photo Researchers, Inc.; 191 (tr), Joseph T. Collins/Photo Researchers, Inc.; 196 Loukas Hapsis/On Location; 201 (tl), Classic PIO Partners; 201 (b) SciMAT/Photo Researchers, Inc.; 202 (br), Randall Hyman; 203 (b) Sam Dudgeon/HRW; 210 (c), Photo by William C. Bennett, Collection of the Massillon Museum; 210 (b), Bruce S. Ford/City of Akron; 211 (all), NASA John H. Glenn Research Center at Lewis Field. **Chapter 5:** 212–213 (bkgd), Galen Rowell/ CORBIS; 212 (b), Michael S. Yamashita/CORBIS; 216 (tr), Dave Jacobs/Index Stock Imagery, Inc.; 219 Sam Dudgeon/HRW; 220 (tr), Courtesy Jens of Sweden; 224 (tr), Joe Skipper/Reuters/Corbis; 229 (tr), Art on File/CORBIS; 233 (tr), © 2004 EyeWire Collection; 233 (cr), © Andrew Syred/Microscopix Photolibrary; 233 (bc), Ed Reschke/Peter Arnold, Inc.; 235 (bl), Robb deWall/Crazy Horse Memorial; 238 (paper cube), HRW; 238 (t), Rubberball/Alamy; 241 (tl), Layne Kennedy/CORBIS; 244 (eyes), Phil Jude/Science Photo Library/Photo Researchers, Inc.; 247 (cl), Peter Van Steen/HRW; 248 (tl), Courtesy Troop 32, Arlington Heights, IL; 252 (tr), "Iowa Countryside Outside of Cedar Rapids Iowa" by Stan Herd, photo

© Jon Blumb; 253 (cl), Digital Art/CORBIS; 255 (tr), David Young-Wolff/PhotoEdit Inc.; 256 (c), Lee Snider/CORBIS; 257 (tc), Sam Dudgeon/HRW; 259 (br), Richard Meier & Partners Architects LLP; 259 (tl), Sam Dudgeon/HRW; 260 (t), Digital Image © 2004 PhotoDisc; 260 (br), Ken Karp/HRW; 261 (b), Sam Dudgeon/HRW. **Chapter 6:** 270–271 (bkgd), Chuck Solomon/Sports Illustrated; 270 (b), Clive Mason/Allsport/Getty Images; 274 (tr), © Charles Gullung/Getty Images; 278 (tr), John Langford/HRW; 281 (bl), Peter Van Steen/HRW; 283 (c), PEANUTS © Universal Press Syndicate; 288 (tr), Jeff Rotman/Photo Researchers Inc.; 289 (tl), Hans Reinhard/Bruce Coleman, Inc.; 291 (tr), © Katy Winn/CORBIS; 293 (cricket, wasp, ladybugs), Digital Image © 2004 PhotoDisc; 293 (black & white beetles, European mantis), Stockbyte; 293 (ants, earwig, green beetle, mantis with extended wings), Brand X Pictures; 293 (harlequin beetle), Digital Image © 2004 Artville; 294 (tr), © The New Yorker Collection 1992 Danny Shanahan from cartoonbank.com. All Rights Reserved.; 297 (tr), Lyn Topinka/USGS/Cascades Volcano Observatory; 297 (tl), © Katy Winn/CORBIS; 299 (cr), Peter Van Steen/HRW; 301 (tr), Sam Dudgeon/HRW; 305 (tl), AFP/CORBIS; 309 (tl), Stephanie Friedman/HRW; 309 (b), Sam Dudgeon/HRW; 310 (br), Victoria Smith/HRW; 311 (b), Sam Dudgeon/HRW; 318 (c), © Reuters/CORBIS; 319 (t), Bob Krist/CORBIS; 319 (br), © 2004 Conrad Gloos c/o MIRA. **Chapter 7:** 320–321 (bkgd), Richard T. Nowitz/CORBIS; 320 (br), Victoria Smith/HRW; 328 (tr), Stephen Dalton/Photo Researchers, Inc.; 330 (tr), Richard Meier & Partners Architects LLP; 333 (tl), Hulton-Deutsch Collection/CORBIS; 341 (tr), © Stockbyte; 345 (tl), Jonathan Blair/CORBIS; 347 (all), © Lucasfilm, Ltd.; 354 (tr), Seth Kushner/Getty Images/Stone; 354 (tl), Science Photo Library/Photo Researchers, Inc.; 358 (tr), © Carol Leigh/Grant Heilman Photography, Inc.; 364 (tc), Image © /Dmitriy Margolin; 364 (tr), PhotoDisc/Getty Images; 365 (tc), Garry Black/Masterfile; 367 (tl), Grant V. Faint/Getty Images/The Image Bank; 368 (tr), Harry Lentz/Art Resource, NY; 373 (bl), Bob Burch/Jenny Thomas/HRW; Index Stock; 373 (tl), Chris Barton/PhotographersDirect.com; 374 (br), 375 (b), Sam Dudgeon/HRW. **Chapter 8:** 384–385 (bkgd), UHB Trust/Getty Images/Stone; 384 (br), Rob Crandall/Alamy Photos; 388 (tr), Corbis/PictureQuest; 398 (tr), Benelux/ZEFA/H. Armstrong Roberts; 400 (tr), © 2005 David Farley; 403 (tl), © Robert Harding Picture Library Ltd/Alamy; 405 (b), Dave G. Houser/ Houserstock; 411 (cr), (photo) © 2006 Sol LeWitt//Artists Rights Society (ARS), New York. Photography by Mike Kilyon. 413 (tr), Kenneth Hamm/Photo Japan; 417 (tr), Dallas and John Heaton/CORBIS; 417 (tl), G. Leavens/Photo Researchers, Inc.; 420 (tr), Paul Spinelli/Getty Images Sport; 421 (br), Will & Deni McIntyre/Photo Researchers, Inc.; 424 (tl), Owen Franken/CORBIS; 424 (tr), Steve Vidler/SuperStock; 427 (tr), © 2004 Kelly Houle; 428 (c), Peter Van Steen/HRW; 430 (tl), © Todd Patrick; 433 (br), Robert & Linda Mitchell Photography; 434 (br), Baldwin H. Ward & Kathryn C. Ward/CORBIS; 436 (tr), Imtek Imagineering/Masterfile; 439 (tr), Darryl Torckler/Getty Images/Stone; 439 (turtle eggs), Dwight Kuhn Photography; 439 (fossil eggs), Sinclair Stammers/Science Photo Library/Photo Researchers, Inc.; 439 (br), Ron Austing/Frank Lane Picture Agency/CORBIS; 441 (tr), Gail Mooney/ CORBIS; 443 (tr), Chris Lisle/CORBIS; 445 (tl), PhotoDisc/Getty Images; 445 (b), © Grant Heilman/Grant Heilman Photography; 446 (tl), Sam Dudgeon/HRW; 446 (tc), Art Stein/Photo Researchers, Inc.; 446 (tr), Neil Rabinowitz/CORBIS; 447 (br), © John Elk III; 448 (br), HRW; 449 (br), HRW; 456 (cl), Library of Congress; 456 (bl), Joe Cavaretta/AP Photo; 456 (cr), Nevada State Museum; 457 (cr), © D. Hurst/ Alamy; 457 (tc), Bruce Cashin/Index Stock; 457 (bl), © D. Hurst/Alamy. **Chapter 9:** 458–459 (bkgd), David Joel/Stone/Getty Images; 458 (br), Sam Dudgeon/HRW; 465 (tl), © Ron Austing/Frank Lane Picture Agency/CORBIS; 467 (tr), Digital Vision; 471 (tr), © Richard Schultz; 476 (tr), Peter Van Steen/HRW/Kittens courtesy of Austin Humane Society/SPCA; 483 (br), Richard Cummins/CORBIS; 485 (tr), Tracy Frankel/Getty Images; 494 (tr), Rudi Von Briel/PhotoEdit, Inc.; 497 (grass pollen), Dr. Jeremy Burgess/Science Photo Library/Photo Researchers, Inc.; 497 (weed pollen), Ralph C. Eagle, Jr. M.D./Photo Researchers, Inc.; 500 (tr), Michael Newman/PhotoEdit, Inc.; 507 (b), Design Pics; 507 (tl), PhotoDisc/Getty Images; 508 (b), HRW; 509 (b), Sam Dudgeon/HRW. **Chapter 10:** 518–519 (bkgd), Erlendur Berg/SuperStock; 518 (br), Bettmann/ CORBIS; 522 (tr), © Royalty-free/Corbis; 522 (cr), Peter Van Steen/HRW; 527 (tr), AP Photo; 530 (tc), Reuters NewMedia Inc./CORBIS; 530 (tr), David Weintraub/Photo Researchers, Inc.; 532 (tr), Andy Hayt/Sports Illustrated; 535 (tl), Raymond Gehman/CORBIS; 539 (br), Simon Watson/FoodPix/Getty Images; 540 (tr), Sam Dudgeon/HRW; 542 (cr), Peter Van Steen/HRW; 544 (tr), Sam Dudgeon/HRW; 545 (tr), Digital Vision; 549 (tl), Corbis/Sygma; 550 (tr), HRW; 557 (tr), iStock Photo; 558 (tc), © Scott Adams, Inc. All rights reserved. Licensed by United Feature Syndicate; 562 (tr), Steve Kahn/Getty Images/FPG International; 563 (tr), Rubberball/GettyImages; 567 (tl), The Newark Museum/Art Resource, NY; 570 (br), Jenny Thomas/HRW; 571 (b), Sam Dudgeon/HRW; 578 (cr), Craig Jones/Getty Images

Sport; 578 (br), Doug Pensinger/Getty Images Sport; 578 (tr), Clemson University Athletics; 579 (tc), Courtesy Myrtle Beach Convention and Visitors Bureau; 579 (br), AP Photo; 579 (cr), The Granger Collection, New York; 579 (cr), Lucile Godbold Papers, J. Drake Edens Library Archives, Columbia College, Columbia, SC. **Chapter 11:** 580–581 (bkgd), Tom Bean/Getty Images/Stone; 580 (br), David Edwards Photography; 589 (cl), Stuart Dee/The Image Bank/Getty Images; 591 (tl), Buddy Mays/CORBIS; 591 (tr), Peter Van Steen/HRW; 593 (tr), © Margaret Bryant/Bryant Dog Photography; 597 (tl), Andrew Syred/Science Photo Library/Photo Researchers, Inc.; 599 (b), Sam Dudgeon/HRW; 600 (tr), Jeffrey Oh; 604 (tr), © Bill Bachman/Danita Delimont - Agent; 605 (c), Fotopic/Index Stock; 607 (t), Peter Van Steen/HRW; 608 (tr), Corbis; 611 (tl), Rafael Macia/Photo Researchers, Inc.; 613 (tl), © Comstock, Inc.; 613 (b), © Dean Fox/SuperStock; 614 (br), Jenny Thomas; 615 (b), Sam Dudgeon/HRW. **Chapter 12:** 624–625 (bkgd), Tom Stack/Painet; 624 (br), Gary Braasch; 628 (tr), Don Klumpp/Getty Images; 632 (tl), AP Photo; 633 (tr), Diaphor Agency/Index Stock; 642 (tr), Jeff Schultz/AlaskaStock Images; 644 (tr), John Greim/Science Photo Library/Photo Researchers, Inc.; 647 (tl), Art Wolfe/Getty Images/The Image Bank; 649 (b), Sam Dudgeon/HRW; 652 (tr), Patrick Gnan; 654 (tl), E.R. Degginger/Bruce Coleman, Inc.; 655 (tr), Chris Luneski/Alamy; 659 (tl), Nick Caloyianis/National Geographic Image Collection; 660 (tr), Duomo/CORBIS; 665 (tl), iStock Photo; 665 (b), © Michael Wong/Corbis; 668 (br), Jenny Thomas/HRW; 669 (b), Sam Dudgeon/HRW; 676 (cr), AP Photo; 676 (b), Kenneth Garrett/National Geographic Collection/Getty Images; 677 (tl), AP Photo; 677 (cr), Courtesy American Visionary Art Museum; 677 (tc), Courtesy American Visionary Art Museum. **Chapter 13:** 678–679 (bkgd), C.N.R.I./Phototake; 678 (br), Stevie Grand/Science Photo Library/Photo Researchers, Inc.; 682 (tr), Victoria Smith/HRW; 691 (tl), Courtesy Wham-O®; 699 (b), George McCarthy/ CORBIS; 700 (tr), NASA; 703 (tl), Ron Johnson/Index Stock; 705 (bl), GJLP/Science Photo Library/Photo Researchers, Inc.; 707 (all), John Langford/HRW; 708 (tr), Chip Simons Photography; 711 (tr), Sam Dudgeon/HRW; 714 (tr), Louis Turner/Alamy; 719 (tr), Stephanie Friedman/HRW; 719 (cr), Harry Engels/Photo Researchers, Inc.; 719 (b), Alan and Sandy Carey/Photo Researchers, Inc.; 720 (br), Randall Hyman/ HRW; 721 (b), Sam Dudgeon/HRW. **Chapter 14:** 730–731 (bkgd), © W. Cody/CORBIS; 730 (br), HRW; 734 (tr), iStock Photo; 735 (bl), © Dave G. Houser/CORBIS; 743 (cr), © Paul Eekhoff/Masterfile; 743 (tr), Private Collection/ Bridgeman Art Library/ © 2002 Fletcher Benton/Artists Rights Society (ARS), New York; 745 (cr), Steve Gottlieb/Stock Connection/PictureQuest; 747 (tr), HRW; 748 (c), HRW; 750 (tl), Stephen Mallon/The Image Bank/Getty Images; 752 (tr), HRW; 753 (bl), HRW; 756 (tr), HRW; 757 (tr), Victoria Smith/HRW; 759 (tr), HRW; 762 (tr), Mark Gibson/Gibson Stock Photography; 769 (tl), iStock Photo; 769 (bl), © Jeff Greenberg/Photo Edit Inc.; 769 (br), Photodisc/Getty Images; 770 (br), Sam Dudgeon/HRW; 771 (b), Sam Dudgeon/HRW; 778 (all), Julian Toney/Belzoni Banner; 779 (all), Courtesy of the Lauren Rogers Museum of Art, Laurel, Mississippi.

■ Art Credits

Chapter 1: 5, Argosy; 12 (t), Jeffrey Oh; 25 (bkgd), Stephen Durke/Washington Artists; 27 (c), Argosy; 29 (cr), Argosy; 31 (bl), Argosy; 38 (tr), Argosy; 43 (tr), Mark Betcher; 44 (t), Nenad Jakesebic; 44 (c), Greg Geisler; 47 (r), Ortelius Design; 50 (tr), Ted Williams; 51 (all), Leslie Kell. **Chapter 2:** 63 (cards), Argosy; 67 (tr), Argosy; 79 (tr), Argosy; 82 (tr), Fian Arroyo; 92 (t), Cindy Jeftovic; 95 (r), Mark Heine; 103 (tl), Argosy; 104 (tr), Nenad Jakesevic; 105 (tr), Leslie Kell; 105 (cr), Leslie Kell; 112 (tr), Leslie Kell. **Chapter 3:** 122 (t), Mark Heine; 134 (tr), Jeffrey Oh; 134 (cl), Jeffrey Oh; 134 (cr), Jeffrey Oh; 145 (c), Tom Klare; 148 (t), Cindy Jeftovic; 149 (A–C), Leslie Kell; 149 (B), Leslie Kell; 149 (C), Leslie Kell. **Chapter 4:** 161 (c), Leslie Kell; 162 (tr), Greg Geisler; 174 (c), Leslie Kell; 177 (tr), Stephen Durke/ Washington Artists; 178 (t), Argosy; 181 (b), Argosy; 189 (c), Argosy; 199 (t), Argosy; 202 (tr), Jeffrey Oh; 203 (all), Leslie Kell; 210 (tc), Leslie Kell.
Chapter 5: 215 (paper), Leslie Kell; 217 (cl), Leslie Kell; 218 (r), Argosy; 223 (tr), Argosy; 225 (tr), Argosy; 227 (br), Argosy; 248 (c), Karen Minot; 249 (c), Argosy; 250 (all), Argosy; 251 (c), Karen Minot; 255 (cr), © Jeremy Boon, Sam Dudgeon/HRW Photo; 257 (tr), Leslie Kell; 261 (A–C), Leslie Kell.
Chapter 6: 273 (tc), Leslie Kell; 277 (tr), Jane Sanders; 284 (br), Gary Otteson; 287 (tr), Doug Bowles; 301 (cr), Stephen Durke/Washington Artists; 305 (tr), Argosy; 309 (c), Argosy; 310 (tr), Gary Otteson; 311 (A–C) Leslie Kell; 318 (tc), Leslie Kell; 318 (b), Jeffrey Oh. **Chapter 7:** 323 (c), Leslie Kell; 328 (tr-inset), Argosy; 328 (cr), Argosy; 330 (c), Argosy; 333 (tr), Jeffrey Oh; 336 (tr), Argosy; 340 (tr), Argosy; 345 (cr), Argosy; 364 (cl), Argosy; 365 (tl), Argosy; 367 (a–c), Argosy; 367 (cr), Leslie Kell; 371 (cl), Argosy; 375 (A–C) Leslie Kell. **Chapter 8:** 387 (c), Leslie Kell; 389 (tc), Argosy; 392 (cr), Ortelius Design; 398 (c), Argosy; 400 (cl), Argosy; 400 (cr), Argosy; 403 (pancakes), Jeffrey Oh; 408 (tr), Dave Clegg; 411 (c), Argosy; 416 (tc),

Mark Heine; 416 (bc), Karen Minot; 418 (all), Leslie Kell; 430 (cr), Argosy; 433 (br), Argosy; 435 (tr), Dan Stuckenschneider; 445 (cr), Argosy; 446 (cr), Argosy; 447 (1.), Argosy; 447 (2.), Argosy; 447 (3.), Argosy; 447 (7.), Argosy; 447 (8.), Argosy; 448 (cl), Argosy; 448 (c), Argosy; 448 (cr), Argosy; 449 (A–B), Leslie Kell; 456 (tc), Leslie Kell. **Chapter 9:** 461 (l), Leslie Kell; 462 (tr), Gary Otteson; 469 (c), Argosy; 469 (br), Ortelius Design; 475, Argosy; 479 (br), Argosy; 487 (b), Daniel James; 488 (t), Argosy; 490 (tr), Jeffrey Oh; 490 (c), Argosy; 491 (t), Argosy; 492 (tr), Argosy; 492 (br), Argosy; 493 (tl), Argosy; 496 (tr), Ortelius Design; 497 (cr), Argosy; 506 (food), Leslie Kell; 509 (A–C), Leslie Kell; 512 (food), Leslie Kell.
Chapter 10: 521 (cr), Argosy; 529 (br), Argosy; 546 (br), Jeffrey Oh; 554 (tr), Kevin Rechin; 554 (c), Greg Geisler; 559 (c), Argosy; 562 (tr), Jeffrey Oh; 569 (br), Dave Clegg; 569 (tl), Dave Clegg; 570 (tr), Gary Otteson; 571 (A–B), Leslie Kell; 578 (tc), Leslie Kell. **Chapter 11:** 584 (tc), Dave Clegg; 584 (c), Greg Geisler; 587 (t), Argosy; 593 (c), Leslie Kell; 613 (c), Leslie Kell; 614 (tr), John Etheridge; 615 (A–D), Leslie Kell. **Chapter 12:** 627 Leslie Kell; 633 (b), Greg Geisler; 638 (tr), Tom Klare; 639 (tc), Greg Geisler; 642 (cr), Nenad Jakesevic; 647 (all), Patrick Gnan; 650 (tr), Dave Clegg; 654 (tr), Christy Krames; 659 (r), HRW; 663 (tr), Gary Otteson; 668 (tc), Argosy; 668 (tr), Lance Lekander; 669 (A–D), Leslie Kell; 676 (tc), Leslie Kell. **Chapter 13:** 686 (tr), Gary Otteson; 687 (tr), Fian Arroyo; 697 (t), Argosy; 704 (tr), Dave Clegg; 708 (c), Argosy; 720 (tr), Gary Otteson; 721 (A–C), Leslie Kell. **Chapter 14:** 737 (tc), Argosy; 740 (tc), Greg Geisler; 762 (c), Greg Geisler; 763 (tr), Danial Stuckenschneider; 765 (tr), Gary Otteson; 770 (tr), Gary Otteson; 771 (A & B), Leslie Kell; 778 (tc), Leslie Kell.

All Teacher-to-Teacher photos courtesy of the teachers.

Formulas

Perimeter

Square	$P = 4s$
Rectangle	$P = 2\ell + 2w$ or $P = 2(\ell + w)$
Polygon	$P =$ sum of the lengths of the sides

Circumference

Circle	$C = 2\pi r$ or $C = \pi d$

Volume

Prism	$V = Bh$
Rectangular prism	$V = \ell w h$
Cylinder	$V = \pi r^2 h$ or $V = Bh$
Pyramid	$V = \frac{1}{3}Bh$
Cone	$V = \frac{1}{3}\pi r^2 h$ or $V = \frac{1}{3}Bh$
Sphere	$V = \frac{4}{3}\pi r^3$

Area

Square	$A = s^2$
Rectangle	$A = \ell w$ or $A = bh$
Parallelogram	$A = bh$
Triangle	$A = \frac{1}{2}bh$ or $A = \frac{bh}{2}$
Trapezoid	$A = \frac{1}{2}(b_1 + b_2)h$ or $A = \frac{(b_1 + b_2)h}{2}$
Circle	$A = \pi r^2$

Surface Area

Prism	$S = 2B + Ph$
Cylinder	$S = 2\pi r^2 + 2\pi rh$
Regular Pyramid	$S = B + \frac{1}{2}P\ell$
Cone	$S = \pi r^2 + \pi r\ell$
Sphere	$S = 4\pi r^2$

Probability

Experimental	probability $\approx \dfrac{\text{number of times the event occurs}}{\text{total number of trials}}$
Theoretical	probability $= \dfrac{\text{number of outcomes in the event}}{\text{number of outcomes in the sample space}}$
Permutations	$_nP_r = \dfrac{n!}{(n-r)!}$
Combinations	$_nC_r = \dfrac{_nP_r}{r!} = \dfrac{n!}{r!(n-r)!}$
Dependent events	$P(A \text{ and } B) = P(A) \cdot P(B \text{ after } A)$
Independent events	$P(A \text{ and } B) = P(A) \cdot P(B)$